NEW PERSPECTIVE EDITION

HAMMOND
Citation
WORLD ATLAS

HAMMOND INCORPORATED
MAPLEWOOD, NEW JERSEY

New York   Chicago   Boston   Atlanta   Los Angeles   San Francisco

CONTENTS

INTRODUCTION TO A NEW CONCEPT IN ATLASES

An atlas may be defined as "a collection of maps in one volume." The first atlas of this type was prepared by Abraham Ortelius, a Flemish geographer. Ortelius had traveled widely for his time and had an acquaintance with all of the well-known geographers then living. In the year 1570 he literally took individual maps and bound them together by hand to make a volume. He included, in Latin, short descriptions of the various countries. The title of this first atlas was *Theatrum Orbis Terrarum*. The atlas achieved instant popularity as interested persons were quick to see its convenience. For many years the volume of Ortelius was considered a standard geographical authority in Europe.

As time went on new atlases were brought out by later publishers but, for the most part, they followed the basic concept of the original atlas. In these printings maps followed each other, the continuity usually determined by geographical location or by the continent in which the various countries or sections appeared. Later on, atlas publishers added an index section and, still later, other sections which covered statistics, historical data as illustrated by historical maps, information on the economies of various countries, etc. In order to obtain all the facts on one given country it was often necessary to refer to as many as four or five sections.

Here at Hammond we held many round table discussions with our editors to determine if a better way could be found to produce an atlas that would put reference material quickly and conveniently at the command of the reader. We also did extensive research in the library field and marketing research in retail outlets. It seemed plain to us that the only logical way to produce an atlas would be to follow the method used in most encyclopedias, i.e., to present all information on any given country, state, etc. as a unit. Because we felt the index should accompany each map, it meant printing many more forms in color since text material would then have to be printed as part of color forms. It was further apparent that political maps only were no longer enough for our present day world. It was evident also that it would be necessary to include the following information in a quality atlas — topographic data, economic facts, flags, and in some cases, special historical treatments as well as special subject information dealing with an important feature of a given country, state or province. Since it would be impossible to put all this information on **one** map, we soon realized that a series of maps on each country was necessary. Because transportation enters into our life so vitally, it was clear that maps of this subject should be included.

Finally, it was decided to eliminate all "turn" pages — the top of each map would be toward the top of the page.

With our own studies and our marketing analysis before them, the Hammond editors laid out the first roughs of what are now the New Perspective Editions of the Hammond Atlases. The atlas you are now reading makes it possible for a person to realize quickly the interrelationship between the topography of a country, its economics and its political makeup.

There are two types of indexes normally used in atlases. The first is an index of a given map and the second is an overall A to Z world index of all localities on the maps arranged alphabetically. The first, for example, is most convenient when you are interested in planning a trip in one given country. It is much easier to have to refer only to the cities involved on that one map than to look through thousands of names to find the desired city name. Of course, the longer world A to Z index is essential when the name of a city is known but its country, state or province is unknown. Thus, each index has a very vital use and in the New Perspective Atlases it was decided that employing both systems would give the user the method essential for finding needed facts.

A reputable publisher of atlases will have the maps revised to the date of publication. However, census information in most atlases varies widely as far as the number of cities and towns which are listed with populations, as well as the up-to-dateness of the figures given. In our discussions with librarians it became clear that where an atlas is used by a student, for instance, to compare the populations of various countries, cities, etc., no atlas stated the date or authenticity of the figures given. It was thus decided that this information should be readily available and it has been included in the gazetteer section in the front of your New Perspective Edition Atlas. Some populations are from a census taken within a very few months of the date of publication of your atlas. In other instances there may have been no census taken in an underdeveloped area later than, perhaps, the late 30's or early 40's. In such cases, estimates by various accepted authorities have to be used.

All this information is given to the user in a straightforward manner so that in comparing figures of various areas of the world it can be realized that all statistics are not of equal quality or from the same census year. In later editions, of course, as new figures are available, these atlases will reflect the changes.

The initial reception of this new series of atlases has been more than gratifying, and it has confirmed our original premise that present-day living demands more than just an atlas in the original sense of the word. We hope you will get many hours of enjoyment and much valuable information from this easy-to-use atlas.

The preparation of the New Perspective Atlases has truly involved all members of our creative staff. Thus, it is impossible to acknowledge each person's work individually. I would therefore, like to say "Well Done" to all editors, cartographers, artists, and designers as well as cameramen, color separation technicians, and typesetting and printing personnel, for their collective accomplishments that have made this project possible.

Caleb D. Hammond

President
HAMMOND INCORPORATED

GAZETTEER-INDEX OF THE WORLD

This alphabetical list of continents, countries, states, colonial possessions and other major geographical areas provides a quick reference to their area, population, capital or chief town, map page number and index key thereon. The last named indicates the square on the respective page in which the name may be found. An indication of the population sources used is also included, and refers both to the total figures given in this Gazetteer-Index and to the populations appearing in greater detail with the maps throughout the atlas. The population figures used in each case are the latest reliable figures obtainable. A glance at the sources will show that the dates vary considerably throughout the world. In certain areas where no census has ever been taken, we must rely on official estimates. In other areas where censuses have been taken at infrequent intervals, we again rely on estimates. A notable example is that of Argentina, where the latest detailed figures available are from the 1947 census, obviously now outdated. The key to the abbreviations used in the Gazetteer-Index follows:

cap = capital	isl, isls = island, islands	SSR = Soviet Socialist Republic
CE = census (local or undetermined)	OE = official estimate	terr = territories
cit = cities	oth = other populations	TP = total population
dept = departments	PC = preliminary census	UK = United Kingdom
dist = districts	pref = prefectures	UN = United Nations
est = estimate	prov = provinces	USA = United States of America
FC = final census	prov dist = provincial districts	ws = with suburbs
int div = internal divisions	reg = regions	

Country	Area (Square Miles)	Population	Capital or Chief Town	Page and Index Ref.	Sources of Population Data
★Afghanistan	250,000	15,227,000	Kabul	68/A 2	TP—64 OE; cap (& ws) & Kandahar (& ws)—64 OE; Herat, Jalalabad & Mazar-i-Sharif—62 OE; oth—59 OE
Africa	11,850,000	304,000,000	....	102/......	64 UN est
Alabama, U.S.A.	51,609	3,462,000	Montgomery	194/......	TP—65 OE; oth—60 FC & OE
Alaska, U.S.A.	586,400	253,000	Juneau	196/......	TP—65 OE; oth—60 FC & OE
★Albania	11,096	1,867,000	Tiranë	45/E 5	TP—65 OE; oth—63 OE
Alberta, Canada	255,285	1,456,000	Edmonton	182/......	TP—66 OE; cap (ws) & Calgary (ws)—66 OE; oth—61 FC
★Algeria	919,353	12,300,000	Algiers	106/D 3	TP—64 UN est; Saharan dept, cit—63 OE; oth—60 FC
American Samoa	76	26,000	Pago Pago	87/J 7	TP—65 OE; oth—60 FC
Andaman & Nicobar Is., India	3,215	63,548	Port Blair	68/G 6	61 FC
Andorra	175	11,000	Andorra la Vella	33/G 1	TP—62 OE; cap—63 UN est
Angola	481,351	5,119,000	Luanda	115/C 6	TP—65 OE; oth—60 FC
Antarctica	5,500,000	....		5/......	....
Antigua & Dependencies	171	62,000	St. Johns	156/G 3; 161/E11	TP—64 OE; oth—60 FC
★Argentina	1,078,266	22,352,000	Buenos Aires	143/......	TP—65 OE; cap (& ws), prov, cit (part)—60 PC; oth—47 FC
Arizona, U.S.A.	113,909	1,608,000	Phoenix	198/......	TP—65 OE; oth—60 FC & OE
Arkansas, U.S.A.	53,104	1,960,000	Little Rock	202/......	TP—65 OE; oth—60 FC & OE
Armenian S.S.R., U.S.S.R.	11,500	1,958,000	Erivan	52/F 6	TP—62 OE; cit over 100,000—63 OE; oth—59 FC
Ascension Island	34	478	Georgetown	102/A 5	TP—64 OE
Ashmore & Cartier Islands, Australia	....	....	....	88/C 2	....
Asia	16,500,000	1,852,946,000	....	54/......	63 UN est
★Australia	2,974,581	11,002,811	Canberra	88/......	TP & states—64 OE; cap (& A.C.T.)—65 OE; oth—61 FC
Australian Antarctic Territory	2,472,000	....	....	5/C 5	....
Australian Capital Territory	939	85,676	Canberra	97/E 4	TP—65 OE; oth—61 FC
★Austria	32,369	7,193,000	Vienna	41/......	TP—64 OE; cap—62 UN est; oth—61 FC
Azerbaidzhan S.S.R., U.S.S.R.	33,100	4,117,000	Baku	52/G 6	TP—62 OE; cit over 100,000—63 OE; oth—59 FC
Azores Islands, Portugal	890	327,480	Ponta Delgada, Angra do Heroísmo, Horta	32/......	60 FC
Bahama Islands	4,404	133,000	Nassau	156/C 1	TP, cap—64 OE; oth—63 FC
Bahrein	231	182,203	Manama	59/F 4	TP—65 OE; oth—59 FC
Balearic Islands, Spain	1,936	443,327	Palma	33/H 3	60 FC
Barbados	166	244,000	Bridgetown	161/B 8	TP—65 OE; oth—60 FC
Basutoland (Lesotho)	11,716	745,000	Maseru	118/D 5	TP, cap—65 OE; oth—56 FC
Bechuanaland (Botswana)	222,000	559,000	Gaberones	118/C 4	TP—65 OE; oth—64 PC
★Belgium	11,775	9,328,000	Brussels	27/......	TP—64 OE; oth—61 FC
Bermuda	21	49,000	Hamilton	156/H 3	TP—65 OE; oth—60 FC
Bismarck Archipelago, Terr. of New Guinea	19,660	163,634	Rabaul	87/E 6	TP—64 OE; oth—64 OE, 61 CE
★Bolivia	412,777	3,702,000	La Paz, Sucre	136/......	TP—65 OE; dept, caps, cit (part)—62 OE; oth—60 FC
Bonin & Volcano Islands	105	205	Yankee Town	87/E 3	64 FC
Botswana (Bechuanaland)	222,000	559,000	Gaberones	118/C 4	TP—65 OE; oth—64 PC
★Brazil	3,286,170	82,222,000	Brasília	132/......	TP, states—65 OE; cap—61 OE; oth—61 FC
British Columbia, Canada	366,255	1,838,000	Victoria	184/......	TP—66 OE; Vancouver (ws)—66 OE; oth—61 FC
★British Guiana (Guyana)	89,480	628,000	Georgetown	131/B 3	TP, cap (& ws), New Amsterdam—64 OE; oth—60 FC
British Honduras	8,867	106,000	Belize City	154/C 2	TP—65 OE; cap (ws)—62 OE; oth—60 FC
British Solomon Islands Prot.	14,600	139,730	Honiara	87/F 6	TP—64 OE; isls—63 OE; cap—59 OE
Brunei	2,226	97,000	Brunei	85/E 4	TP—64 OE; oth—60 FC
★Bulgaria	42,796	8,211,000	Sofia	45/F 4	TP—65 OE; cap (ws) & cit (part)—63 OE; oth—56 PC
★Burma	261,610	24,229,000	Rangoon	72/B 2	TP—64 OE; cap, Mandalay, Moulmein—58 OE; oth—53 CE
★Burundi	10,747	2,780,000	Bujumbura	115/E 4	TP—64 UN est; cap—60 UN est; oth—59 OE
★Byelorussian S.S.R. (White Russian S.S.R.), U.S.S.R.	80,100	8,316,000	Minsk	52/C 4	TP—64 OE; cit over 100,000—63 OE; oth—59 FC
California, U.S.A.	158,693	18,602,000	Sacramento	204/......	TP—65 OE; oth—60 FC & OE
★Cambodia	69,884	6,200,000	Phnom Penh	72/E 4	TP—64 UN est; oth—62 PC
★Cameroon	178,368	5,150,000	Yaoundé	115/B 2	TP—65 OE; cap—62 CE; cit—64, 62, 61, 57 OE
★Canada	3,851,809	19,785,000	Ottawa	162/......	TP—66 OE; cit (ws) (part)—66 OE; oth—61 FC
Canal Zone	362	53,900	Balboa Heights	154/G 6	TP—64 OE; oth—60 FC
Canary Islands, Spain	2,894	944,448	Las Palmas, Santa Cruz	33/B 4	60 FC
Cape of Good Hope, South Africa	262,875	3,936,306	Cape Town	118/C 6	60 FC
Cape Verde Islands	1,557	220,000	Praia	106/D 8	TP—64 UN est; oth—60 PC
Caroline Islands, Terr. Pacific Is.	525	49,107	....	87/E 5	TP—64 OE; oth—63 OE
Cayman Islands	104	9,000	Georgetown	156/B 3	TP—64 OE; oth—60 FC

★Member of the United Nations.

Gazetteer-Index of the World

Country	Area (Square Miles)	Population	Capital or Chief Town	Page and Index Ref.	Sources of Population Data
Celebes, Indonesia	72,986	6,288,043	Makassar	85/G 6	TP—61 PC; cit—54—57 OE
★Central African Republic	239,382	1,320,000	Bangui	115/C 2	TP—64 OE; cap—64 CE; oth—61, 58, 57 OE
Central America	217,813	13,571,000	....	154/......	64 UN est
★Ceylon	25,332	10,965,000	Colombo	68/E 7	TP—64 OE; oth—63 FC
★Chad	455,598	2,830,000	Fort–Lamy	111/C 4	TP—64 UN est; cap (ws)—63 OE; cap, cit (part)—61 OE; oth—63, 57 OE
Channel Islands	75	112,000	Saint Helier, Saint Peter Port	13/E 7	TP—64 UN est; oth—61 FC & PC
Chatham Islands, N.Z.	372	510	Waitangi	100/D 7	64 OE
★Chile	286,396	8,567,000	Santiago	138/......	TP—65 OE; cap (ws) & cit over 100,000—63 OE; oth—60 FC
China (mainland)	3,745,296	700,000,000	Peking	77/......	TP—62 UN est; prov, cap, cit (part)—58 OE; oth—57 OE, 53 FC
★China (Taiwan)	13,885	12,429,000	Taipei	77/K 7	TP—65 OE; cap & cit (part)—63 OE; oth—59 OE
Christmas Island, Australia	64	3,382	Edinburgh	54/O11	64 OE
Cocos (Keeling Is.), Australia	5	663	Home I.	54/N11	64 OE
★Colombia	439,828	17,787,000	Bogotá	126/......	TP—65 UN est; cap (& ws)—64 PC; int div & cap—64 OE; oth—51 FC
Colorado, U.S.A.	104,247	1,969,000	Denver	208/......	TP—65 OE; oth—60 FC & OE
Comoro Islands	849	212,000	Moroni	118/G 2	TP—65 OE; cap, isls—61 OE; oth—58 FC
★Congo, Democratic Rep. of the	902,274	15,627,000	Léopoldville	115/C 4	TP—65 OE; cap, cit (part)—59 OE; oth—58 OE
★Congo, Republic of	175,676	1,012,800	Brazzaville	115/B 4	TP—62 CE; cap (ws)—61 CE; cap, cit (part)—61 OE; oth—63 OE, 62 CE, 57 OE
Connecticut, U.S.A.	5,009	2,832,000	Hartford	210/......	TP—65 OE; oth—60 FC & OE
Cook Islands	99	20,000	Avarua	87/K 7	TP—64 OE; isls—63 OE; cap—51 FC
Corsica, France	3,367	275,465	Ajaccio	28/B 6	62 FC
★Costa Rica	19,238	1,467,000	San José	154/E 5	TP—65 OE; oth—63 FC
Crete, Greece	3,232	483,075	Iráklion (Candia)	45/G 8	61 FC
★Cuba	42,857	7,631,000	Havana	158/......	TP—65 OE; cap (& ws)—62 OE; oth—61 OE, 53 FC
Curaçao, Neth. Antilles	173	129,676	Willemstad	161/G 8	TP—62 OE; oth—60 FC
★Cyprus	3,572	591,000	Nicosia	63/E 5	TP—65 OE; cap (& ws)—63 OE; oth—60 FC
★Czechoslovakia	49,356	14,058,000	Prague	41/......	TP—64 OE; oth—62 OE
★Dahomey	42,471	2,300,000	Porto–Novo	106/E 7	TP, cap, Cotonou—64 OE; oth—63, 61 OE
Daito Islands, Ryukyu Is.	18	4,396	....	87/D 3	TP—60 FC
Delaware, U.S.A.	2,057	505,000	Dover	245/......	TP—65 OE; oth—60 FC & OE
★Denmark	16,556	4,684,000	Copenhagen	21/......	TP—63 OE; oth—60 FC
District of Columbia, U.S.A.	61	801,000	Washington	245/F 5	TP—65 OE; oth—60 FC
Dominica	305	65,000	Roseau	161/E 7	TP—64 OE; oth—60 FC
★Dominican Republic	19,129	3,573,000	Santo Domingo	158/......	TP—65 OE; oth—60 PC
East Germany (German Democratic Rep.)	41,535	17,135,867	Berlin (East)	22/......	TP, cap, dist, cit over 10,000—63 OE; oth—57 FC
★Ecuador	115,000	5,084,000	Quito	128/......	TP—65 OE; cit over 100,000—63 OE; oth—62 FC
Egypt (United Arab Republic)	386,000	28,900,000	Cairo	111/E 2	TP—64 OE; cap & cit (part)—62 OE; oth—60 FC
★El Salvador	8,060	2,859,000	San Salvador	154/C 4	TP—65 OE; cap—63 OE; oth—61 FC
England, U.K.	50,327	44,724,910	London	13/......	TP, co, cit (part)—64 OE; oth—61 FC
Equatorial Guinea, Spain	10,836	267,000	Santa Isabel	115/A 3	TP, terr—65 OE; oth—60 FC
Estonian S.S.R., U.S.S.R.	17,400	1,235,000	Tallinn	52/C 3; 53/......	TP—62 OE; cit over 100,000—63 OE; oth—59 FC
★Ethiopia	457,148	22,200,000	Addis Ababa	111/G 5	TP, cap, Asmara—64 OE; prov—62 OE; cit—62, 58, 56 OE
Europe	4,129,908	610,818,000	....	7/......	63 UN est
Faerøe Islands, Denmark	540	34,596	Tórshavn	21/B 2	60 FC
Falkland Islands	4,618	2,132	Stanley	120/E 8	TP—64 OE; oth—62 FC
Fernando Po, Equatorial Guinea	785	72,000	Santa Isabel	115/A 3	TP—65 OE; oth—60 FC
Fiji Islands	7,036	464,000	Suva	87/H 8	TP—65 OE; cap & Rotuma—63 OE; oth—56 FC
★Finland	130,500	4,586,000	Helsinki	18/......	TP—64 OE; cap (ws)—62 UN est; oth—63 OE
Florida, U.S.A.	58,560	5,805,000	Tallahassee	212/......	TP—65 OE; oth—60 FC & OE
★France	212,736	46,520,271	Paris	28/......	62 FC
French Guiana	35,135	36,000	Cayenne	131/E 3	TP—64 OE; oth—61 FC
French Polynesia	1,544	86,000	Papeete	87/L 8	TP—64 UN est; cap—65 OE; oth—62 FC
French Somaliland	8,492	80,000	Djibouti	111/H 5	TP—64 OE; cap—63 OE; oth—61 OE
★Gabon	90,733	462,000	Libreville	115/B 4	TP—65 OE; cap—64 OE; oth—61 FC, 61, 57 OE
★Gambia	4,033	330,000	Bathurst	106/A 6	TP—65 OE; cap—64 OE; oth—63 FC
Georgia, U.S.A.	58,876	4,357,000	Atlanta	216/......	TP—65 OE; oth—60 FC & OE
Georgian S.S.R., U.S.S.R.	29,400	4,271,000	Tbilisi	52/F 6	TP—62 OE; cit over 100,000—63`OE; oth—59 FC
Germany, East (German Democratic Rep.)	41,535	17,135,867	Berlin (East)	22/......	TP, cap, dist, cit over 10,000—63 OE; oth—57 FC
Germany, West (Federal Republic)	95,914	57,974,000	Bonn	22/......	TP—64 OE; cap, states, cit over 20,000—63 OE; oth—61 FC
★Ghana	91,844	7,600,000	Accra	106/D 7	TP—64 UN est; oth—60 FC
Gibraltar	2	24,502	Gibraltar	33/D 4	61 FC
Gilbert & Ellice Islands	196	49,879	Bairiki	87/J 6	63 PC
★Great Britain & Northern Ireland (United Kingdom)	94,214	54,065,700	London	10/......	TP—64 OE; (see England, Wales, Scotland & Northern Ireland)
★Greece	51,182	8,550,000	Athens	45/F 6	TP—64 OE; oth—61 FC
Greenland	839,999	37,000	Godthaab	4/B12	TP—64 OE
Grenada	133	93,000	Saint George's	156/G 4; 161/D 9	TP—64 UN est; oth—60 FC
Guadeloupe & Dependencies	688	306,000	Basse–Terre	156/F 4; 161/A 5	TP—64 OE; oth—61 FC
Guam	209	72,000	Agaña	87/E 4	TP—64 OE; oth—60 FC
★Guatemala	45,452	4,343,000	Guatemala	154/B 3	TP—65 UN est; oth—64 PC
Guiana, French	35,135	36,000	Cayenne	131/E 3	TP—64 OE; oth—61 FC
Guiana, Netherlands (Surinam)	54,300	362,000	Paramaribo	131/C 3	TP—64 PC; cap—62 OE; dist—59 OE; cit—50 FC
★Guinea	96,525	3,420,000	Conakry	106/B 6	TP, cap (ws), Kankan, Kindia—64 OE; cap—60 CE; oth—63, 61, 58, 55 OE
Guinea, Portuguese	13,948	525,000	Bissau	106/A 6	TP—64 OE; oth—60 PC
★Guyana	89,480	628,000	Georgetown	131/B 3	TP, cap (& ws), New Amsterdam—64 OE; oth—60 FC
★Haiti	10,714	4,660,000	Port–au–Prince	158/......	TP—65 OE; cap, cit (part)—61 OE; oth—58 OE, 50 FC
Hawaii, U.S.A.	6,424	711,000	Honolulu	218/......	TP—65 OE; oth—60 FC & OE
Heard & McDonald Islands, Australia	....	....	....	3/T 8	....
★Holland (Netherlands)	12,883	12,041,970	The Hague, Amsterdam	27/......	TP, prov—64 OE; oth—60 FC
★Honduras	45,000	2,315,000	Tegucigalpa	154/D 3	TP—65 UN est; oth—61 FC
Honduras, British	8,867	106,000	Belize City	154/C 2	TP—65 OE; cap (ws)—62 OE; oth—60 FC
Hong Kong	391	3,982,100	Victoria	77/H 7	TP—66 OE; oth—61 FC
★Hungary	35,875	10,123,000	Budapest	41/......	TP—64 OE; cit over 10,000—62 OE; oth—60 FC

Gazetteer-Index of the World

Country	Area (Square Miles)	Population	Capital or Chief Town	Page and Index Ref.	Sources of Population Data
★Iceland	39,709	187,000	Reykjavík	21/B 1	TP—63 OE; cap (ws)—62 UN est; oth—61 OE
Idaho, U.S.A.	83,557	692,000	Boise	220/......	TP—65 OE; oth—60 FC & OE
Ifni, Spain	676	61,000	Sidi Ifni	106/B 3	TP—64 UN est; cap—60 FC
Illinois, U.S.A.	56,400	10,644,000	Springfield	222/......	TP—65 OE; oth—60 FC & OE
★India	1,196,995	476,278,000	New Delhi	68/......	TP, cit over 100,000—64 OE; oth—61 FC
Indiana, U.S.A.	36,291	4,885,000	Indianapolis	227/......	TP—65 OE; oth—60 FC & OE
Indonesia	735,268	102,200,000	Djakarta	85/......	TP—64 UN est; cap (& ws), isls (part), cit (part)—61 PC; oth—54—57 OE
Iowa, U.S.A.	56,290	2,760,000	Des Moines	229/......	TP—65 OE; oth—60 FC & OE
★Iran	628,000	22,860,000	Tehran	66/......	TP—64 OE; cap, cit (part)—63 OE; oth—56 FC
★Iraq	116,000	7,004,000	Baghdad	66/......	TP—64 OE; cap (ws)—57 FC; prov—62 OE; cit over 100,000—63 OE; oth—57 FC
★Ireland (Eire)	26,601	2,849,000	Dublin	17/......	TP—64 OE; oth—61 FC
Ireland, Northern, U.K.	5,459	1,458,000	Belfast	17/......	TP, co, cap—64 OE; oth—61 FC
Isle of Man	227	48,000	Douglas	13/C 3	TP—64 UN est; oth—61 FC
★Israel	7,978	2,565,000	Jerusalem	65/......	TP—65 OE; cap, Haifa, Tel Aviv—63 OE; oth—61 FC
★Italy	116,286	50,849,000	Rome	34/......	TP—64 OE; oth—61 FC & PC
★Ivory Coast	183,397	3,750,000	Abidjan	106/C 7	TP, cap (ws)—64 OE; oth—63, 61, 59, 54 OE
★Jamaica	4,411	1,745,000	Kingston	158/......	TP—65 OE; oth—60 FC
★Japan	142,743	98,399,074	Tokyo	81/......	TP, cap—65 PC; pref—64 OE; cap (ws), cit over 120,000—63 OE, oth—60 FC
Java, Indonesia	48,842	60,909,381	Djakarta	85/J 2	TP—61 PC; oth—61 PC, 54-57 OE
★Jordan	34,750	1,900,000	Amman	65/......	TP—64 UN est; oth—61 FC
Kansas, U.S.A.	82,264	2,234,000	Topeka	232/......	TP—65 OE; oth—60 FC & OE.
Kazakh S.S.R., U.S.S.R.	1,061,600	10,934,000	Alma–Ata	48/G 5	TP—62 OE; cit over 100,000—63 OE; oth—59 FC
Kentucky, U.S.A.	40,395	3,179,000	Frankfort	237/......	TP—65 OE; oth—60 FC & OE
★Kenya	219,730	9,376,000	Nairobi	115/G 3	TP—64 OE; oth—62 FC
Kirghiz S.S.R., U.S.S.R.	76,100	2,318,000	Frunze	48/H 5	TP—62 OE; cit over 100,000—63 OE; oth—59 FC
Korea, North	49,096	10,930,000	P'yŏngyang	81/......	TP—64 UN est; cap, Kaesŏng—60 OE
Korea, South	36,152	28,155,000	Seoul	81/......	TP—65 OE; oth—62 OE
★Kuwait	8,000	468,042	Al Kuwait	59/E 4	TP—65 PC; cap (ws)—61 FC; oth—65 PC
★Laos	89,343	1,960,000	Vientiane	72/D 3	TP—64 UN est; cap—59 OE; cap (ws)—62 OE; oth—59 OE
Latvian S.S.R., U.S.S.R.	24,600	2,170,000	Riga	52/B 3; 53/......	TP—62 OE; cit over 100,000—63 OE; oth—59 FC
★Lebanon	3,475	2,500,000	Beirut	63/F 6	TP—64 UN est; cap (ws)—62 OE; oth—61 OE
Lesotho (Basutoland)	11,716	745,000	Maseru	118/D 5	TP, cap—65 OE; oth—56 FC
★Liberia	43,000	1,066,000	Monrovia	106/C 7	TP—64 OE; cap—62 PC; oth—58 CE
★Libya	679,358	1,559,399	Tripoli, Benghazi	111/......	64 PC
Liechtenstein	65	18,000	Vaduz	39/J 2	TP—63 OE; oth—60 FC
Lithuanian S.S.R., U.S.S.R.	25,200	2,852,000	Vilna	52/B 3; 53/......	TP—62 OE; cit over 100,000—63 OE; oth—59 FC
Louisiana, U.S.A.	48,523	3,534,000	Baton Rouge	238/......	TP—65 OE; oth—60 FC & OE
★Luxembourg	999	327,000	Luxembourg	27/J 9	TP—63 OE; cap—62 OE; oth—60 FC
Macao	6	174,000	Macao	77/H 7	TP—64 UN est; oth—60 FC
Madeira Islands, Portugal	308	268,937	Funchal	33/A 2	60 FC
Maine, U.S.A.	33,215	993,000	Augusta	242/......	TP—65 OE; 60 FC & OE
★Malagasy Republic	241,094	6,180,000	Tananarive	118/H 3	TP—64 OE; oth—62 OE
★Malawi	36,829	3,900,000	Zomba	115/F 6	TP—64 UN est; cap (ws)—62 UN est; oth—61 OE, 56 CE
Malaya, Malaysia	50,690	7,810,000	Kuala Lumpur	72/D 6	TP—64 OE; oth—57 FC
★Malaysia, Federation of	129,374	9,148,000	Kuala Lumpur	72/D 6; 85/E 4	TP—64 OE; states—65 OE; oth—60 FC (Sabah, Sarawak); 57 FC (Malaya)
★Maldive Islands	115	94,527	Malé	54/L 9	63 FC
★Mali	584,942	4,430,000	Bamako	106/C 6	TP—64 UN est; cap (ws)—60 OE; oth—63, 61 OE
★Malta	122	329,326	Valletta	34/E 7	63 OE
Man, Isle of	227	48,000	Douglas	13/C 3	TP—64 UN est; oth—61 FC
Manitoba, Canada	251,000	959,000	Winnipeg	179/......	TP—66 OE; cap (ws)—66 OE; oth—61 OE
Mariana Islands, Terr. Pacific Is.	142	10,275	Garapan	87/E 4	TP—64 OE; oth—63 OE
Marquesas Islands, French Polynesia	480	4,837	Atuona	87/N 6	62 FC
Marshall Islands, Terr. Pacific Is.	61	18,205	Majuro	87/G 4	TP—64 OE; oth—63 OE
Martinique	425	310,000	Fort-de-France	161/D 5	TP—64 OE; oth—61 FC
Maryland, U.S.A.	10,577	3,519,000	Annapolis	245/......	TP—65 OE; oth—60 FC & OE
Massachusetts, U.S.A.	8,257	5,348,000	Boston	249/......	TP—65 OE; oth—60 FC & OE
★Mauritania	328,185	1,000,000	Nouakchott	106/B 5	TP, cap—64 OE; Idjil—61 OE; oth—63 OE
Mauritius	720	734,000	Port Louis	118/G 5	TP—65 OE; cap—64 OE; oth—62 FC
★Mexico	760,373	40,913,000	Mexico City	150/......	TP—65 OE; cap, cit (part)—63 OE; oth—60 FC
Michigan, U.S.A.	58,216	8,218,000	Lansing	250/......	TP—65 OE; oth—60 FC & OE
Midway Islands	2	2,355	....	87/J 3	65 OE
Minnesota, U.S.A.	84,068	3,554,000	St. Paul	254/......	TP—65 OE; oth—60 FC & OE
Mississippi, U.S.A.	47,716	2,321,000	Jackson	256/......	TP—65 OE; oth—60 FC & OE
Missouri, U.S.A.	69,686	4,497,000	Jefferson City	261/......	TP—65 OE; oth—60 FC & OE
Moldavian S.S.R., U.S.S.R.	13,100	3,106,000	Kishinev	52/C 5	TP—62 OE; cit over 100,000—63 OE; oth—59 FC
Monaco	370 acres	22,297	Monaco	28/G 6	61 FC
★Mongolia	625,946	1,044,000	Ulan Bator	77/......	TP—64 OE; prov—62 OE; oth—65 OE
Montana, U.S.A.	147,138	706,000	Helena	262/......	TP—65 OE; oth—60 FC & OE
Montserrat	32	13,000	Plymouth	156/F 3	TP—63 OE; cap—60 FC
★Morocco	171,583	12,959,000	Rabat	106/C 2	TP—64 OE; oth—60 FC
Mozambique	297,731	6,914,000	Lourenço Marques	118/E 4	TP—65 OE; cap (& ws)—60 FC; oth—60 PC
Muscat and Oman	82,000	565,000	Muscat	59/G 5	TP—64 UN est; oth—60 OE
Natal, South Africa	33,578	2,979,920	Pietermaritzburg	118/E 5	60 FC
Nauru	8	5,000	Makwa	87/G 6	64 OE
Nebraska, U.S.A.	77,227	1,477,000	Lincoln	264/......	TP—65 OE; oth—60 FC & OE
★Nepal	54,000	9,900,000	Katmandu	68/E 3	TP—64 OE; oth—61 PC
★Netherlands	12,883	12,041,970	The Hague, Amsterdam	27/......	TP, prov—64 OE; oth—60 FC
Netherlands Antilles	383	207,000	Willemstad	156/E 4	TP—65 OE; isls—62 OE; oth—60 FC
Nevada, U.S.A.	110,540	440,000	Carson City	266/......	TP—65 OE; oth—60 FC & OE
New Britain, Terr. of New Guinea	14,600	116,588	Rabaul	87/F 6	TP—64 OE; oth—64 OE, 61 CE
New Brunswick, Canada	28,354	626,000	Fredericton	170/......	TP—66 OE; oth—61 FC
New Caledonia	7,201	73,886	Nouméa	87/G 8	TP—64 OE; Bourail—63 OE; oth—63 FC
Newfoundland, Canada	156,185	501,000	St. John's	166/......	TP—66 OE; oth—61 FC
New Guinea, Territory of	93,000	1,575,966	Port Moresby	85/B 6; 87/F 6	TP—65 OE; oth—64 OE, 61 CE
New Guinea, West (West Irian)	161,514	800,000	Sukarnapura (Hollandia)	85/J 6	TP—64 UN est; cap—62 OE; oth—60 OE

Gazetteer-Index of the World

Country	Area (Square Miles)	Population	Capital or Chief Town	Page and Index Ref.	Sources of Population Data
New Hampshire, U.S.A.	9,304	669,000	Concord	268/	TP—65 OE; oth—60 FC & OE
New Hebrides	5,700	66,000	Vila	87/G 7	TP, cit, Efate I.—64 OE; oth—61 OE
New Jersey, U.S.A.	7,836	6,774,000	Trenton	273/	TP—65 OE; oth—60 FC & OE
New Mexico, U.S.A.	121,666	1,029,000	Santa Fe	274/	TP—65 OE; oth—60 FC & OE
New South Wales, Australia	309,433	4,086,293	Sydney	97/	TP—64 OE; oth—61 FC
New York, U.S.A.	49,576	18,073,000	Albany	276/	TP—65 OE; oth—60 FC & OE
★New Zealand	103,934	2,640,117	Wellington	100/	TP, prov dist, cap, cit (& ws) (part)—64 OE; oth—61 FC
★Nicaragua	57,143	1,754,000	Managua	154/D 4	TP—65 UN est; oth—63 FC
★Niger	501,930	3,193,000	Niamey	106/F 5	TP, cap—64 OE; oth—63 OE
★Nigeria	356,093	56,400,000	Lagos	106/F 6	TP—64 OE; reg, cap, cit (part)—63 FC; oth—53 FC
Niue	100	5,044	Alofi	87/K 7	64 OE
Norfolk Island, Australia	13.5	853	Kingston	88/L 5	63 OE
North America	9,124,000	286,000,000	....	146/	64 UN est
North Borneo (Sabah), Malaysia	29,387	518,000	Jesselton	85/F 4	TP—65 OE; oth—60 FC
North Carolina, U.S.A.	52,712	4,914,000	Raleigh	281/	TP—65 OE; oth—60 FC & OE
North Dakota, U.S.A.	70,665	652,000	Bismarck	282/	TP—65 OE; oth—60 FC & OE
Northern Ireland, U.K.	5,459	1,458,000	Belfast	17/	TP, co, cap, Londonderry—64 OE; oth—61 FC
Northern Territory, Australia	523,620	28,822	Darwin	93/	TP—64 OE; oth—61 FC
North Korea	49,096	10,930,000	P'yŏngyang	81/	TP—64 UN est; cap, Kaesŏng—60 OE
North Vietnam	63,370	17,900,000	Hanoi	72/E 3	TP—64 UN est; oth—60 CE
Northwest Territories, Canada	1,304,903	26,000	Fort Smith	187/	TP—66 OE; oth—61 FC
★Norway	124,560	3,681,000	Oslo	18/	TP—64 OE; oth—60 FC
Nova Scotia, Canada	21,425	759,000	Halifax	168/	TP—66 OE; oth—61 FC
Oceania	....	17,821,000	....	87/	64 OE
Ohio, U.S.A.	41,222	10,245,000	Columbus	284/	TP—65 OE; oth—60 FC & OE
Oklahoma, U.S.A.	69,919	2,482,000	Oklahoma City	288/	TP—65 OE; oth—60 FC & OE
Oman, Muscat and	82,000	565,000	Muscat	59/G 5	TP—64 UN est; oth—60 OE
Ontario, Canada	412,582	6,832,000	Toronto	175, 177/	TP, cit (ws) (part)—66 OE; oth—61 FC
Orange Free State, South Africa	49,866	1,386,547	Bloemfontein	118/D 4	60 FC
Oregon, U.S.A.	96,981	1,899,000	Salem	291/	TP—65 OE; oth—60 FC & OE
Orkney Islands, Scotland	376	18,424	Kirkwall	15/J 1	TP—64 OE; oth—64 OE & 61 FC
Pacific Islands, Territory of the	680	88,215	Garapan	87/F 5	TP, isl groups—64 OE; oth—63 OE
★Pakistan	364,218	100,762,000	Rawalpindi, Dacca	68/	TP—64 OE; oth—61 FC
Palau Islands, Terr. Pacific Is.	189	10,628	Koror	87/D 5	TP—64 OE; oth—63 OE
★Panama	28,575	1,244,000	Panamá	154/G 6	TP—65 OE; cap & Colón—64 OE; oth—60 FC
Papua, Australia	90,600	573,411	Port Moresby	85/C 7	TP—65 OE; oth—64 OE, 61 CE
★Paraguay	150,518	1,996,000	Asunción	144/	TP, cap, cit (part)—65 OE; oth—62 PC
Pennsylvania, U.S.A.	45,333	11,520,000	Harrisburg	294/	TP—65 OE; oth—60 FC & OE
★Persia (Iran)	238,000	22,860,000	Tehran	66/	TP—64 OE; cap, cit (part)—63 OE; oth—56 FC
★Peru	513,000	11,649,600	Lima	128/	TP, dept—65 OE; oth—61 FC
★Philippines, Republic of the	115,600	32,345,000	Quezon City	82/	TP—65 OE; oth—60 FC
Phoenix Islands	16	1,018	Canton I.	87/H 6	63 OE
Pitcairn Islands	2	91	Adamstown	87/O 8	65 OE
★Poland	119,734	31,161,000	Warsaw	47/	64 OE
★Portugal	35,413	9,123,000	Lisbon	33/	TP—64 OE; oth—60 FC
Portuguese Guinea	13,948	525,000	Bissau	106/A 6	TP—64 OE; oth—60 PC
Portuguese Timor	7,332	543,000	Dili	85/H 7	TP—64 OE; oth—60 FC
Prince Edward Island, Canada	2,184	108,000	Charlottetown	168/E 2	TP—66 OE; oth—61 FC
Puerto Rico	3,421	2,650,000	San Juan	161/	TP—65 OE; oth—60 FC
Qatar	5,000	60,000	Doha	59/F 4	TP—64 OE; cap—63 OE; oth—57 OE
Québec, Canada	594,860	5,712,000	Québec	172, 174/	TP, Montréal (ws)—66 OE; oth—61 FC
Queensland, Australia	667,000	1,571,982	Brisbane	95/	TP—64 OE; oth—61 FC
Réunion	970	387,000	Saint–Denis	118/F 5	TP—65 OE; oth—61 FC
Rhode Island, U.S.A.	1,214	920,000	Providence	249/	TP—65 OE; oth—60 FC & OE
Rhodesia	150,333	4,260,000	Salisbury	118/D 3	TP, cit (part)—65 OE; oth—62 FC
Río Muni, Equatorial Guinea	10,045	195,000	Santa Isabel	115/B 3	TP—65 OE; oth—60 FC
★Rumania	91,671	19,092,000	Bucharest	45/F 3	TP—65 OE; reg, cit (& ws) over 20,000—63 OE; oth—56 FC
Russian S.F.S.R., U.S.S.R.	6,501,500	122,084,000	Moscow	48/D 4	TP—62 OE; cit over 100,000—63 OE; oth—59 FC
★Rwanda	10,169	3,018,000	Kigali	115/E 4	TP—64 OE; oth—59 OE
Ryukyu Islands	921	935,000	Naha	81/L 7	TP—64 OE; cap—63 OE; oth—60 FC
Sabah, Malaysia	29,387	518,000	Jesselton	85/F 4	TP—65 OE; oth—60 FC
Saint Christopher–Nevis–Anguilla	138	62,000	Basseterre	156/F 3; 161/D11	TP—64 UN est; oth—60 FC
Saint Helena	47	4,613	Jamestown	102/B 6	64 OE
Saint Lucia	233	94,000	Castries	161/G 6	TP—63 OE; oth—60 FC
Saint Pierre & Miquelon	93	4,990	Saint–Pierre	166/C 4	62 FC
Saint Vincent	150	86,000	Kingstown	161/A 8	TP, cap (ws)—64 OE; oth—60 FC
Sakhalin, U.S.S.R.	35,400	630,000	Yuzhno–Sakhalinsk	48/P 4	TP—61 OE; oth—59 FC
★Salvador, El	8,060	2,859,000	San Salvador	154/C 4	TP—65 OE; cap—63 OE; oth—61 FC
San Marino	38	17,000	San Marino	34/D 3	TP, cap (ws)—64 OE
São Tomé e Príncipe	372	64,406	São Tomé	106/F 8	TP—60 FC; oth—60 PC
Sarawak, Malaysia	47,071	820,000	Kuching	85/E 5	TP—65 OE; oth—60 FC
Sardinia, Italy	9,301	1,419,362	Cagliari	34/B 4	TP—61 FC; oth—61 FC & PC
Saskatchewan, Canada	251,700	953,000	Regina	181/	TP, Regina & Saskatoon (ws)—66 OE; oth—61 FC
★Saudi Arabia	350,000	7,000,000	Riyadh, Mecca	59/D 4	TP—65 OE; caps—62 CE; cit (part)—62 CE; oth—59, 56 OE
Scotland, U.K.	30,411	5,206,400	Edinburgh	15/	TP, co, cit (part), isls (part)—64 OE; oth—61 FC
★Senegal	77,401	3,400,000	Dakar	106/A 5	TP—64 OE; oth—63 OE
Seychelles	157	46,000	Victoria	118/H 5	TP—64 OE; oth—60 FC
Shetland Islands, Scotland	550	17,719	Lerwick	15/M 3	TP—64 OE; oth—64 OE, 61 FC
★Siam (Thailand)	200,148	30,591,000	Bangkok	72/	TP—65 OE; cap & Thonburi (ws)—63 OE; oth—60 FC
Sicily, Italy	9,926	4,721,001	Palermo	34/E 6	TP—61 FC; oth—61 FC & PC
★Sierra Leone	27,925	2,200,000	Freetown	106/B 7	TP—64 OE; oth—63 FC
★Singapore	220	1,844,000	Singapore	72/F 6	TP—65 OE; cap (ws)—64 OE; cap—63 OE; oth—57 FC
Society Islands, French Polynesia	650	68,245	Papeete	87/L 7	TP—62 FC, cap—65 OE; oth—62 FC
Solomon Islands, Terr. of New Guinea	4,070	57,550	Sohano	87/F 6	TP—64 OE; oth—64 OE, 61 CE
Solomon Islands Prot., British	14,600	139,730	Honiara	87/F 6	TP, cap—65 CE; oth—63 OE, 59 CE
★Somali Republic	262,000	2,350,000	Mogadishu	115/H 3	TP—64 OE; prov—53 CE; cap—63 OE; oth—57 OE
Somaliland, French	8,492	80,000	Djibouti	111/H 5	TP—64 OE; cap—63 OE; oth—61 OE
★South Africa	472,733	17,487,000	Cape Town, Pretoria	118/C 5	TP—64 OE; oth—60 FC
South America	6,894,000	162,000,000	....	120/	64 UN est

Gazetteer-Index of the World

Country	Area (Square Miles)	Population	Capital or Chief Town	Page and Index Ref.	Sources of Population Data
South Arabia	110,000	1,613,000	Aden	59/E 7	TP—65 OE; cap—55 FC; oth—60 OE, 55 FC
South Australia, Australia	380,070	1,020,174	Adelaide	94/......	TP—64 OE; oth—61 FC
South Carolina, U.S.A.	31,055	2,542,000	Columbia	296/......	TP—65 OE; oth—60 FC & OE
South Dakota, U.S.A.	77,047	703,000	Pierre	298/......	TP—65 OE; oth—60 FC & OE
South Korea	36,152	28,155,000	Seoul	81/......	TP—65 OE; oth—62 OE
South Vietnam	65,726	15,715,000	Saigon	72/F 4	TP—64 OE; cap—62 CE; oth—60 OE
South-West Africa	317,725	551,000	Windhoek	118/B 3	TP—64 OE; oth—60 FC
★Spain	195,258	31,339,000	Madrid	33/......	TP—64 OE; cap (ws)—63 OE; oth—60 FC
Spanish Sahara, Spain	103,243	42,000	El Aaiúm	106/B 4	TP—64 OE; cap—62 OE; oth—60 FC
★Sudan	967,500	13,540,000	Khartoum	111/E 4	TP—65 OE; cap, Omdurman—64 OE; oth—56 FC
Sumatra, Indonesia	164,148	14,982,910	Medan	85/B 5	TP—61 PC; oth—61 PC, 54-57 FC
Surinam (Netherlands Guiana)	54,300	362,000	Paramaribo	131/C 3	TP—64 PC; cap—62 OE; dist—59 OE; cit—50 FC
Svalbard, Norway	24,294	3,431	Longyearbyen	18/D 2	60 FC
Swaziland	6,704	292,000	Mbabane	118/E 5	TP—64 OE; oth—62 CE
★Sweden	173,394	7,626,978	Stockholm	18/......	TP—64 OE; cap (ws)—62 UN est; oth—64 OE
Switzerland	15,944	6,030,000	Bern	39/......	TP—64 OE; cantons & cit over 10,000—62 OE; oth—60 FC
★Syria	72,587	5,399,000	Damascus	63/G 5	TP—64 OE; cap, cit (part)—63 OE; oth—62 OE
Tadzhik S.S.R., U.S.S.R.	54,900	2,188,000	Dushanbe	48/H 6	TP—62 OE; cit over 100,000—63 OE; oth—59 FC
Tahiti, French Polynesia	600	45,430	Papeete	87/L 7	TP—62 FC; cap—65 OE
★Tanzania	343,726	10,514,000	Dar es Salaam	115/F 5	TP—65 OE; Zanz. prov entries—58 FC; Tang. entries—57 FC
Tasmania, Australia	26,215	373,640	Hobart	99/......	TP—64 OE; oth—61 FC
Tennessee, U.S.A.	42,244	3,845,000	Nashville	237/......	TP—65 OE; oth—60 FC & OE
Texas, U.S.A.	267,339	10,551,000	Austin	302/......	TP—65 OE; oth—60 FC & OE
★Thailand	200,148	30,591,000	Bangkok	72/D 3	TP—65 OE; cap & Thonburi (ws)—63 OE; oth—60 FC
Tibet, China	469,413	1,270,000	Lhasa	77/C 5	TP cit (part)—58 OE; oth—57 OE, 53 FC
Timor, Indonesia	24,450	702,638	Kupang	85/H 7	TP—61 PC; oth—61 PC, 54-57 FC
Timor, Portuguese	7,332	543,000	Dili	85/H 7	TP—64 OE; oth—60 FC
★Togo	20,733	1,642,000	Lomé	106/E 7	TP—65 OE; cap (ws)—62 OE; oth—63 OE
Tokelau Islands	4	2,000	Fakaofo	87/J 6	TP—64 OE; oth—63 OE
Tonga	269	78,000	Nuku'alofa	87/J 8	TP—65 OE; oth—56 FC
Transkei, South Africa	15,590	1,439,195	Umtata	118/D 6	60 FC
Transvaal, South Africa	110,450	6,273,477	Pretoria	118/D 4	60 FC
★Trinidad and Tobago	1,864	950,000	Port-of-Spain	156/G 5; 161/A10	TP—64 UN est; oth—60 FC
Tristan da Cunha	38	250	Edinburgh	3/O7	65 OE
Trucial Oman	12,000	111,000	Dubai	59/F 5	TP—64 OE; cap (ws)—62 OE; oth—57 OE
Tuamotu Archipelago, French Polynesia	332	7,097	Apataki	87/M 7	62 FC
★Tunisia	48,300	4,565,000	Tunis	106/F 2	TP—64 OE; cap (ws)—61 OE; oth—61 OE, 56 FC
★Turkey	296,185	31,118,000	Ankara	63/......	TP—64 OE; oth—60 FC
Turkmen S.S.R., U.S.S.R.	187,200	1,683,000	Ashkhabad	48/F 6	TP—62 OE; cit over 100,000—63 OE; oth—59 FC
Turks and Caicos Islands	202	6,308	Grand Turk	156/D 2	TP cit—63 OE; oth—60 FC
★Uganda	80,301	7,551,000	Kampala	115/F 3	TP—65 OE; oth—59 FC
★Ukrainian S.S.R., U.S.S.R.	220,600	43,091,000	Kiev	52/D 5	TP—64 OE; cit over 100,000—63 OE; oth—59 FC
★Union of Soviet Socialist Republics	8,570,600	226,253,000	Moscow	48/......	TP—64 OE; SSR—62 & 64 OE; int div—61 OE; cap, cit over 100,000—63 OE; oth—59 FC
★United Arab Republic (Egypt)	386,000	28,900,000	Cairo	111/E 2	TP—64 OE; cap & cit (part)—62 OE; oth—60 FC
★United Kingdom	94,214	54,065,700	London	10/......	TP—64 OE; (see England, Wales, Scotland & Northern Ireland)
★United States of America	3,615,211	196,164,000	Washington	188/......	TP—66 OE; states—65 OE; oth—60 FC & OE
★Upper Volta	105,841	4,763,000	Ouagadougou	106/D 6	TP—65 OE; Batié—61 OE; oth—63 OE
★Uruguay	72,172	2,682,000	Montevideo	145/......	TP—64 OE; cap—62 OE; cap (ws)—63 PC; oth—59, 52 OE
Utah, U.S.A.	84,916	990,000	Salt Lake City	304/......	TP—65 OE; oth—60 FC & OE
Uzbek S.S.R., U.S.S.R.	157,400	8,986,000	Tashkent	48/G 5	TP—62 OE; cit over 100,000—63 OE; oth—59 FC
Vatican City	109 acres	904	....	34/B 6	64 OE
★Venezuela	352,143	8,722,000	Caracas	124/......	TP—65 OE; cap (ws), cit over 100,000—64 OE; oth—61 FC & PC
Vermont, U.S.A.	9,609	397,000	Montpelier	268/......	TP—65 OE; oth—60 FC & OE
Victoria, Australia	87,884	3,080,215	Melbourne	97/......	TP—64 OE; oth—61 FC
Vietnam, North	63,370	17,900,000	Hanoi	72/E 3	TP—64 UN est; oth—60 CE
Vietnam, South	65,726	15,715,000	Saigon	72/F 4	TP—64 OE; cap—62 CE; oth—60 OE
Virginia, U.S.A.	40,815	4,457,000	Richmond	307/......	TP—65 OE; oth—60 FC & OE
Virgin Islands (British)	58	8,000	Road Town	156/H 1	TP—64 OE; oth—60 FC
Virgin Islands (U.S.A.)	132	40,600	Charlotte Amalie	161/A-G4	TP—64 OE; oth—60 FC.
Wake Island	3	1,097	....	87/G 4	60 FC
Wales, U.K.	8,017	2,676,390	Cardiff	13/......	TP co, cit (part)—64 OE; oth—61 FC
Wallis and Futuna Islands	106	8,611	Matautu	87/J 7	65 OE
Walvis Bay, Cape of Good Hope, South Africa	374	12,648	Walvis Bay	118/A 4	61 FC
Washington, U.S.A.	68,192	2,990,000	Olympia	310/......	TP—65 OE; oth—60 FC & OE
Western Australia, Australia	975,920	784,107	Perth	92/......	TP—65 OE; oth—61 FC
Western Samoa	1,133	122,000	Apia	87/J7	TP—64 OE; oth—61 FC
West Germany (Federal Republic)	95,914	57,974,000	Bonn	22/......	TP—64 OE; cap, states, cit over 20,000—63 OE; oth—61 FC
West Irian	161,514	800,000	Sukarnapura (Hollandia)	85/J 6	TP—64 UN est; cap—62 OE; oth—60 OE
West Virginia, U.S.A.	24,181	1,812,000	Charleston	312/......	TP—65 OE; oth—60 FC & OE
★White Russian S.S.R. (Byelorussian S.S.R.), U.S.S.R.	80,100	8,316,000	Minsk	52/C 4	TP—64 OE; cit over 100,000—63 OE; oth—59 FC
Wisconsin, U.S.A.	56,154	4,144,000	Madison	317/......	TP—65 OE; oth—60 FC & OE
World	57,510,000	3,218,000,000	....	1, 3/......	63 UN est
Wyoming, U.S.A.	97,914	340,000	Cheyenne	319/......	TP—65 OE; oth—60 FC & OE
Yap, Terr. Pacific Is.	87	3,508	Yap (Yankee Town)	87/D 5	TP—64 OE; oth—63 OE
★Yemen	75,000	5,000,000	San'a, Ta'izz	59/D 7	TP—64 UN est; oth—59 OE
★Yugoslavia	99,079	19,503,000	Belgrade	45/C 3	TP—65 OE; cap, cit over 10,000—63 OE; oth—61 FC
Yukon Territory, Canada	207,076	15,000	Whitehorse	187/E 3	TP—66 OE; oth—61 FC
★Zambia	290,320	3,710,000	Lusaka	115/E 7	TP—65 OE; cap (ws)—65 OE; cap—63 PC; oth—63 FC & PC, 61 OE

INTRODUCTION TO THE MAPS AND INDEXES

The following notes have been added to aid the reader in making the best use of this atlas. Though he may be familiar with maps and map indexes, the publisher believes that a quick review of the material below will add to his enjoyment of this reference work.

Arrangement — The Plan of the Atlas. The atlas has been designed with maximum convenience for the user as its objective. All geographically related information pertaining to a country or region appears on adjacent pages, eliminating the task of searching throughout the entire volume for data on a given area. Thus, the reader will find, conveniently assembled, political, topographic, economic, transportation and special maps of a political area or region, accompanied by detailed map indexes, statistical data, and illustrations of the national flags of the area.

The sequence of country units in this American-designed atlas is international in arrangement. Units on the world as a whole are followed by a section on the polar regions which, in turn, is followed by pages devoted to Europe and its countries. Every continent map is accompanied by special population distribution, climatic and vegetation maps of that continent. Following the maps of the European continent and its countries, the geographic sequence plan proceeds as follows: Asia, the Pacific and Australia, Africa, South America, North America, and ends with detailed coverage on the United States.

Political Maps — The Primary Reference Tool. The most detailed maps in each country unit are the *political maps.* It is our feeling that the reader is likely to refer to these maps more often than to any other in the book when confronted by such questions as — Where? How big? What is it near? Answering these common queries is the function of the political maps. Each political map stresses *political* phenomena — countries, internal political divisions, boundaries, cities and towns. The major political unit or units, shown on the map, are banded in distinctive colors for easy identification and delineation. First-order political subdivisions (states, provinces, counties on the state maps) are shown, scale permitting.

The reader is advised to make use of the *legend* appearing under the title on each political map. Map *symbols,* the special "language" of maps, are explained in the legend. Each variety of dot, circle, star or interrupted line has a special meaning which should be clearly understood by the user so that he may interpret the map data correctly.

Each country has been portrayed at a *scale* commensurate with its political, areal, economic or tourist importance. In certain cases, a whole map unit may be devoted to a single nation if that nation is considered to be of prime interest to most atlas users. In other cases, several nations will be shown on a single map if, as separate entities, they are of lesser relative importance. Areas of dense settlement and important significance within a country have been enlarged and portrayed in inset maps inserted on the margins of the main map. The reader is advised to refer to the linear or "bar" scale appearing on each map or map inset in order to ascertain the basic scale of the map or to determine the distance between points.

The *projection* system used for each map is noted near the title of the map. Map projections are the special graphic systems used by cartographers to render the curved three-dimensional surface of the globe on a flat surface. Optimum map projections determined by the attributes of the area have been used by the publishers for each map in the atlas.

A word here as to the choice of place names on the maps. Throughout the atlas names appear, with a few exceptions, in their local official spellings. However, conventional Anglicized spellings are used for major geographical divisions and for towns and topographic features for which English forms exist; i.e., "Spain" instead of "España" or "Munich" instead of "München." Names of this type are normally followed by the local official spelling in parentheses. As an aid to the user the indexes are cross-referenced for all current and most former spellings of such names.

Names of cities and towns in the United States follow the forms listed in the *Directory of Post Offices* of the United States Post Office Department. Domestic physical names follow the decisions of the Board on Geographic Names, U.S. Department of the Interior, and of various state geographic name boards.

It is the belief of the publishers that the boundaries shown in a general reference atlas should reflect current geographic and political realities. This policy has been followed consistently in the atlas. The presentation of *de facto* boundaries in cases of territorial dispute between various nations does not imply the political endorsement of such boundaries by the publisher, but simply the honest representation of boundaries as they exist at the time of the printing of the atlas maps.

Indexes — Pinpointing a Location. Each political map is accompanied by a comprehensive index of the place names appearing on the map. For quickly locating any city, town, village, river, lake or any other topographic feature within the confines of the subject area of the map, consult the map index as your first step. The name of the feature sought will be found in its proper alphabetical sequence with a key reference letter-number combination corresponding to its location on the map. After noting the key reference letter-number combination for the place name, turn to the map. The place name will be found within the square formed by the two lines of latitude and the two lines of longitude which enclose the co-ordinates — i.e., the marginal letters and numbers. The diagram below illustrates the system of indexing.

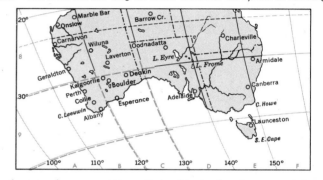

In the case of maps consisting entirely of insets, the place name is found near the intersection point of the imaginary lines connecting the co-ordinates at right angles. See below.

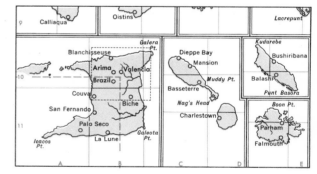

Where space on the map has not permitted giving the complete form of the place name, the complete form is shown in the index. Where a place is known by more than one name or by various spellings of the same name, the different forms have been included in the index. Physical features are listed under their proper names and not according to their generic terms; that is to say, Rio Negro will be found under Negro and not under Rio Negro. On the other hand, Rio Grande will be found under Rio Grande. Accompanying most index entries for cities and towns, and for other political units, are *population figures* for the particular entries. The large number of population figures in the atlas makes this work one of the most comprehensive statistical sources available to the public today. The population figures have been taken from the latest official censuses and estimates of the various nations. Dates and sources for the population figures are listed in the Gazetteer-Index of the World preceding this section.

Population and area figures for countries and major political units are listed in bold type *fact lists* on the margins of the indexes. In addition, the capital, largest city with its population, highest point, monetary unit, principal languages and the prevailing religions of the country concerned are also listed. The Gazetteer-Index of the World on the preceding pages provides a quick reference index for countries and other important areas. Though population and area figures for each major unit are also found in the map section, the Gazetteer-Index provides a conveniently arranged statistical comparison contained in five pages. As mentioned, dates and sources of the population figures appearing in the country indexes are also listed in this section.

Relief Maps. Accompanying each political map is a relief map of the area. The purpose of the relief map is to illustrate the surface configuration (TOPOGRAPHY) of the region. A shading technique in color simulates the relative ruggedness of the terrain — plains, plateaus, valleys, hills and mountains. Graded colors, ranging from greens for lowlands, yellows for intermediate elevations to browns in the highlands, indicate the height above sea level of each part of the land. A vertical scale at the margin of the map shows the approximate height in meters and feet represented by each color.

Economic Maps — Agriculture, Industry and Resources. One of the most interesting features that will be found in each country unit is the economic map. From this map one can determine the basic activities of a nation as expressed through its economy. A perusal of the map yields a full understanding of the area's economic geography and natural resources.

The agricultural economy is manifested in two ways: color bands and commodity names. The color bands express broad categories of *dominant land use*, such as, cereal belts, forest lands, livestock range lands, nonagricultural wastes. The red commodity names, on the other hand, pinpoint the areas of production of *specific* crops; i.e., wheat, cotton, sugar beets, etc.

Major mineral occurrences are denoted by standard letter symbols appearing in blue. The relative size of the letter symbols signifies the relative importance of the deposit.

The manufacturing sector of the economy is presented by means of diagonal line patterns expressing the various *industrial areas* of consequence within a country. The products of each major industrial area are listed in boxes at the margin of the map.

The fishing industry is represented by names of commercial fish species appearing offshore in blue letters. Major waterpower sites are designated by blue symbols.

Transportation and Highway Maps. Appearing throughout the atlas are transportation maps of the continents and major regions. In highly developed areas the highway network is presented on the map (Western Europe, North America, Australia). In less developed regions (Asia, Africa, South America), the railroad network is given priority, supplemented by a representation of connecting roads.

In the portion of the atlas devoted to the United States, individual highway maps of each of the states appear. The major highway network of the state is shown — the new interstate limited access highways, federal roads and important state roads. The series should prove useful to the reader in planning both pleasure and business trips alike.

The publishers have tried to make this work the most comprehensive and useful atlas available, and it is hoped that it will prove a valuable reference work. Any constructive suggestions from the reader will be welcomed.

SOURCES AND ACKNOWLEDGMENTS

A multitude of sources goes into the making of a large-scale reference work such as this. To list them all would take many pages and would consume space better devoted to the maps and reference materials themselves. However, certain general sources were very useful in preparing this work and are listed below.

STATISTICAL OFFICE OF THE UNITED NATIONS.
Demographic Yearbook. New York. Issued annually.

STATISTICAL OFFICE OF THE UNITED NATIONS.
Statistical Yearbook. New York. Issued annually.

THE GEOGRAPHER, U.S. DEPARTMENT OF STATE.
International Boundary Study papers. Washington. Various dates.

UNITED STATES BOARD ON GEOGRAPHIC NAMES.
Decisions on Geographic Names in the United States. Washington. Various dates.

UNITED STATES BOARD ON GEOGRAPHIC NAMES.
Official Standard Names Gazetteers. Washington. Various dates.

CANADIAN PERMANENT COMMITTEE ON GEOGRAPHICAL NAMES.
Gazetteer of Canada series. Ottawa. Various dates.

UNITED STATES POST OFFICE DEPARTMENT.
Directory of Post Offices. Washington. 1965.

UNITED STATES POST OFFICE DEPARTMENT.
Postal Bulletin. Washington. Issued weekly.

UNITED STATES DEPARTMENT OF THE INTERIOR. BUREAU OF MINES.
Minerals Yearbook. 4 vols. Washington. Various dates.

UNITED STATES GEOLOGICAL SURVEY.
Mineral Investigations Resource maps. Washington. Various dates.

UNITED STATES DEPARTMENT OF THE INTERIOR. BUREAU OF COMMERCIAL FISHERIES.
Fishery Statistics of the United States. Washington. 1963.

UNITED STATES DEPARTMENT OF COMMERCE. JOINT PUBLICATIONS RESEARCH SERVICE.
JPRS reports dealing with foreign geography. Washington. Various dates.

CARTACTUAL.
Cartactual — Topical Map Service. Budapest. Issued quarterly.

AMERICAN GEOGRAPHICAL SOCIETY.
Focus. New York. Issued ten times a year.

A sample list of sources used for specific countries follows:

Albania
DREJTORIA E STATISTIKËS.
Vjetari Statistikov i Republika Popullore e Shqipërisë 1964. Tiranë.

Antarctica
AMERICAN GEOGRAPHICAL SOCIETY.
Antarctic Map Folio Series. New York. 1964–.

Australia
COMMONWEALTH BUREAU OF CENSUS AND STATISTICS.
Census of the Commonwealth of Australia, 30th June, 1961. Canberra.
DEPARTMENT OF NATIONAL DEVELOPMENT.
Atlas of Australian Resources. Canberra. 1952–.

Bahrein
FINANCE DEPARTMENT.
4th Census of Population 1965. Bahrein.

Brazil
CONSELHO NACIONAL DE ESTATÍSTICA.
Anuário Estatístico do Brasil 1963. Rio de Janeiro.
CONSELHO NACIONAL DE GEOGRAFICA.
Atlas do Brasil. Rio de Janeiro. 1960.

Canada
DEPARTMENT OF MINES AND TECHNICAL SURVEYS.
Atlas of Canada. Ottawa. 1957.
DOMINION BUREAU OF STATISTICS.
Canada Year Book 1965. Ottawa.

Ceylon
DEPARTMENT OF CENSUS AND STATISTICS.
The Ceylon Government Gazette (July 19, 1963). The Census of Population, July 8, 1963. Colombo.

Germany
STATISTISCHES BUNDESAMT.
Statistisches Jahrbuch für die Bundesrepublik Deutschland 1964. Wiesbaden.

Guatemala
DIRECCIÓN GENERAL DE ESTADÍSTICA.
1964 Trimestre Estadístico: Julio, Agosto, Septiembre. Guatemala.

India
GOVERNMENT OF INDIA PRESS.
Census of India, Paper No. 1 of 1962. 1961 Census, Final Population Totals. Delhi:

Israel
CENTRAL BUREAU OF STATISTICS.
Statistical Abstract of Israel 1963. Jerusalem.

Libya
CENSUS AND STATISTICAL DEPARTMENT.
Preliminary Results of the General Population Census 1964. Tripoli.

Malagasy Republic
INSTITUT NATIONAL DE LA STATISTIQUE ET LA RECHERCHE ECONOMIQUE.
Population de Madagascar au 1er Janvier 1964.

Malta
CENTRAL OFFICE OF STATISTICS.
Demographic Review of the Maltese Islands for the Year 1962. Valletta.

New Zealand
DEPARTMENT OF STATISTICS.
Population at 1 April 1965, Supplement to June 1965 Monthly Abstract of Statistics. Wellington.

South Arabia
GOVERNMENT OF SOUTH ARABIA.
Annual Report on the Federal Health Service 1963.

Sweden
STATISTISKA CENTRALBYRÅN.
Folkmängden i Kommuner och Församlingar 31.12.1964. Stockholm.

U.S.S.R.
MAIN ADMINISTRATION OF GEODESY AND CARTOGRAPHY.
Atlas of the U.S.S.R. Moscow. 1962.

United Kingdom
GENERAL REGISTER OFFICE. HER MAJESTY'S STATIONERY OFFICE.
Census 1961—England and Wales. London.

Western Samoa
BUREAU OF STATISTICS.
Western Samoa Statistical Bulletin—August 1964. Apia.

GLOSSARY OF ABBREVIATIONS

A

A. A. F. — Army Air Field
Acad. — Academy
A. C. T. — Australian Capital Territory
adm. — administration
adm. city-co. — administrative
   city-county
A. F. B. — Air Force Base
Afgh., Afghan. — Afghanistan
Afr. — Africa
Ala. — Alabama
Alb. — Albania
Alg. — Algeria
Alta. — Alberta
Amer. — American
Amer. Samoa — American Samoa
And. — Andorra
Ant. — Antarctica
Ar. — Arabia
arch. — archipelago
Arg. — Argentina
Ariz. — Arizona
Ark. — Arkansas
A. S. S. R. — Autonomous Soviet
   Socialist Republic
Austr., Austral. — Australian, Australia
aut. — autonomous
Aut. Obl. — Autonomous Oblast
aut. prov. — autonomous province

B

B. — Bay
Bah. Is. — Bahama Islands
Barb. — Barbados
Battlef. — Battlefield
Bch. — Beach
Bech. — Bechuanaland
Belg. — Belgium
Berm. — Bermuda
Bol. — Bolivia
Br. — Branch
Br. — British
Braz. — Brazil
Br. Col. — British Columbia
Br. Gui. — British Guiana
Br. Hond. — British Honduras
Br. Sol. Is. — Solomon Islands
   Protectorate, British
Bulg. — Bulgaria

C

c. — cape
Calif. — California
can. — canal
cap. — capital
Centr. Afr. Rep. — Central African
   Republic
Cent. Amer. — Central America
C. G. Sta. — Coast Guard Station
C. H. — Court House
chan. — channel
Chan. Is. — Channel Islands
Chem. Ctr. — Chemical Center
co. — county
C. of G. H. — Cape of Good Hope
Col. — Colombia
Colo. — Colorado
comm. — commissary
Conn. — Connecticut
cont. — continent
cord. — cordillera (mountain range)
C. Rica — Costa Rica
C. S. — County Seat
C. Verde Is. — Cape Verde Islands
Cy. — City
C. Z. — Canal Zone
Czech. — Czechoslovakia

D

D. C. — District of Columbia
Del. — Delaware
Dem. — Democratic
Dem. Rep. of the Congo — Democratic
   Republic of the Congo (Léopoldville)
Den. — Denmark
depr. — depression
dept. — department
des. — desert
dist., dist's — district, districts
div. — division
Dom. Rep. — Dominican Republic
dry riv. — dry river

E

E. — East
Ec., Ecua. — Ecuador
E. Ger. — East Germany

elec. div. — electoral division
El Salv. — El Salvador
Eng. — England
Eq. Guin. — Equatorial Guinea
escarp. — escarpment
est. — estuary
Eth. — Ethiopia

F

Falk. Is. — Falkland Islands
Fern. Po — Fernando Po
Fin. — Finland
Fk., Fks. — Fork, Forks
Fla. — Florida
for. — forest
Fr. — France, French
Fr. Gui. — French Guiana
Fr. Poly. — French Polynesia
Fr. Som. — French Somaliland
Ft. — Fort

G

G. — Gulf
Ga. — Georgia
Game Res. — Game Reserve
Ger. — Germany
geys. — geyser
Gibr. — Gibraltar
Gilb. & Ell. Is. — Gilbert and Ellice
   Islands
glac. — glacier
gov. — governorate
Gr. — Group
Greenl. — Greenland
Gt. Brit. — Great Britain
Guad. — Guadeloupe
Guat. — Guatemala
Gui. — Guiana

H

har., harb., hbr. — harbor
hd. — head
highl. — highland, highlands
hist. — historic, historical
Hond. — Honduras
Hts. — Heights
Hung. — Hungary

I

i., isl., — island, isle
Ice., Icel. — Iceland
Ida. — Idaho
Ill. — Illinois
Ind. — Indiana
ind. city — independent city
Indon. — Indonesia
Ind. Res. — Indian Reservation
int. div. — internal division
inten. — intendency
interm. str. — intermittent stream
Int'l — International
Ire. — Ireland
is., isls. — islands
Isr. — Israel
isth. — isthmus

J

Jam. — Jamaica
Jct. — Junction
jud. div. — judicial division

K

Kans. — Kansas
Ky. — Kentucky

L

L. — Lake, Loch, Lough
La. — Louisiana
Lab. — Laboratory
lag. — lagoon
Ld. — Land
Leb. — Lebanon
Liecht. — Liechtenstein
Lux. — Luxembourg

M

Malag. Rep. — Malagasy Republic
Malaysia — Malaysia, Federation of
Man. — Manitoba
Mart. — Martinique
Mass. — Massachusetts
Maur. — Mauritius
Md. — Maryland
met. area — metropolitan area
Mex. — Mexico
Mich. — Michigan

Minn. — Minnesota
Miss. — Mississippi
Mo. — Missouri
Mon. — Monument
Mong. — Mongolia
Mont. — Montana
Mor. — Morocco
Moz., Mozamb. — Mozambique
mt. — mountain, mount
mts. — mountains

N

N., No. — North, Northern
N. Amer. — North America
N. A. S. — Naval Air Station
Nat'l — National
Nat'l Cem. — National Cemetery
Nat'l Mem. Park — National Memorial
   Park
Nat'l Mil. Park — National Military
   Park
Nat'l Pkwy. — National Parkway
Nav. Base — Naval Base
Nav. Sta. — Naval Station
N. B., N. Br. — New Brunswick
N. C. — North Carolina
N. Dak. — North Dakota
Nebr. — Nebraska
Neth. — Netherlands
Neth. Ant. — Netherlands Antilles
Nev. — Nevada
New Cal. — New Caledonia
Newf. — Newfoundland
New Hebr. — New Hebrides
N. H. — New Hampshire
Nic. — Nicaragua
N. Ire. — Northern Ireland
N. J. — New Jersey
N. Mex. — New Mexico
Nor. — Norway, Norwegian
No. Terr. — Northern Territory
   (Australia)
N. S. — Nova Scotia
N. S. W. — New South Wales
N. W. T. — Northwest Territories
   (Canada)
N. Y. — New York
N. Z. — New Zealand

O

Obl. — Oblast
O. F. S. — Orange Free State
Okla. — Oklahoma
Okr. — Okrug
Ont. — Ontario
Ord. Depot — Ordnance Depot
Oreg. — Oregon

P

Pa. — Pennsylvania
Pac. — Pacific
Pac. Is. — Pacific Islands,
   Territory of the
Pak. — Pakistan
Pan. — Panama
Par. — Paraguay
par. — parish
passg. — passage
P. E. I. — Prince Edward Island
pen. — peninsula
Phil. Is. — Philippines, Republic of the
pk. — peak
plat. — plateau
Port. — Portugal, Portuguese
P. Rico — Puerto Rico
pref. — prefecture
prom. — promontory
prot. — protectorate
prov. — province, provincial
prov. dist. — provincial district
pt. — point

Q

Que. — Quebec
Queens. — Queensland

R

R. — River
ra. — range
Rec., Recr. — Recreation, Recreational
Ref. — Refuge
reg. — region
Rep. — Republic
Rep. of Congo — Congo, Republic of
   (Brazzaville)
res. — reservoir
Res. — Reservation, Reserve

Rhod. — Rhodesia
R. I. — Rhode Island
riv. — river
Rum. — Rumania

S

S. — South
Sa. — Sierra
S. Afr., S. Africa — South Africa
salt dep. — salt deposit
salt des. — salt desert
S. Amer. — South America
São T. & Pr. — São Tomé and Príncipe
Sask. — Saskatchewan
Saudi Ar. — Saudi Arabia
S. Aust., S. Austral. — South Australia
S. C. — South Carolina
Scot. — Scotland
Sd. — Sound
S. Dak. — South Dakota
Sen. — Senegal
sen. dist. — senatorial district
Seych. — Seychelles
S. F. S. R. — Soviet Federated Socialist
   Republic
Sing. — Singapore
S. Leone — Sierra Leone
S. Marino — San Marino
So. Arabia — South Arabia
Sol. Is. Prot. — Solomon Islands
   Protectorate, British
Sp. — Spanish
Spr., Sprs. — Spring, Springs
S. S. R. — Soviet Socialist Republic
St., Ste. — Saint, Sainte
Sta. — Station
St. Chr.-N.-A. — Saint Christopher-
   Nevis-Anguilla
St. P. & M. — Saint Pierre and
   Miquelon
str., strs. — strait, straits
Sur. — Surinam
S. W. Afr. — South-West Africa
Swaz. — Swaziland
Switz. — Switzerland

T

Tanz. — Tanzania
Tas. — Tasmania
Tenn. — Tennessee
terr., terrs. — territory, territories
Terr. N. G. — New Guinea, Territory of
Tex. — Texas
Thai. — Thailand
Trin. & Tob. — Trinidad and Tobago
Tr. Oman — Trucial Oman
Tun. — Tunisia
twp. — township

U

U. A. R. — United Arab Republic
   (Egypt)
U. K. — United Kingdom
Upp. Volta — Upper Volta
urb. area — urban area
Urug. — Uruguay
U. S. — United States
U. S. S. R. — Union of Soviet Socialist
   Republics
Ut. — Utah

V

Va. — Virginia
Vall. — Valley
Ven., Venez. — Venezuela
V. I. (Br.) — Virgin Islands (British)
V. I. (U. S.) — Virgin Islands (U. S.)
Vic. — Victoria
Vill. — Village
vol. — volcano
Vt. — Vermont

W

W. — West, Western
Wash. — Washington
W. Aust., W. Austral. — Western
   Australia
W. Ger. — West Germany
Wis. — Wisconsin
W. Samoa — Western Samoa
W. Va. — West Virginia
Wyo. — Wyoming

Y

Yugo. — Yugoslavia
Yukon — Yukon Territory

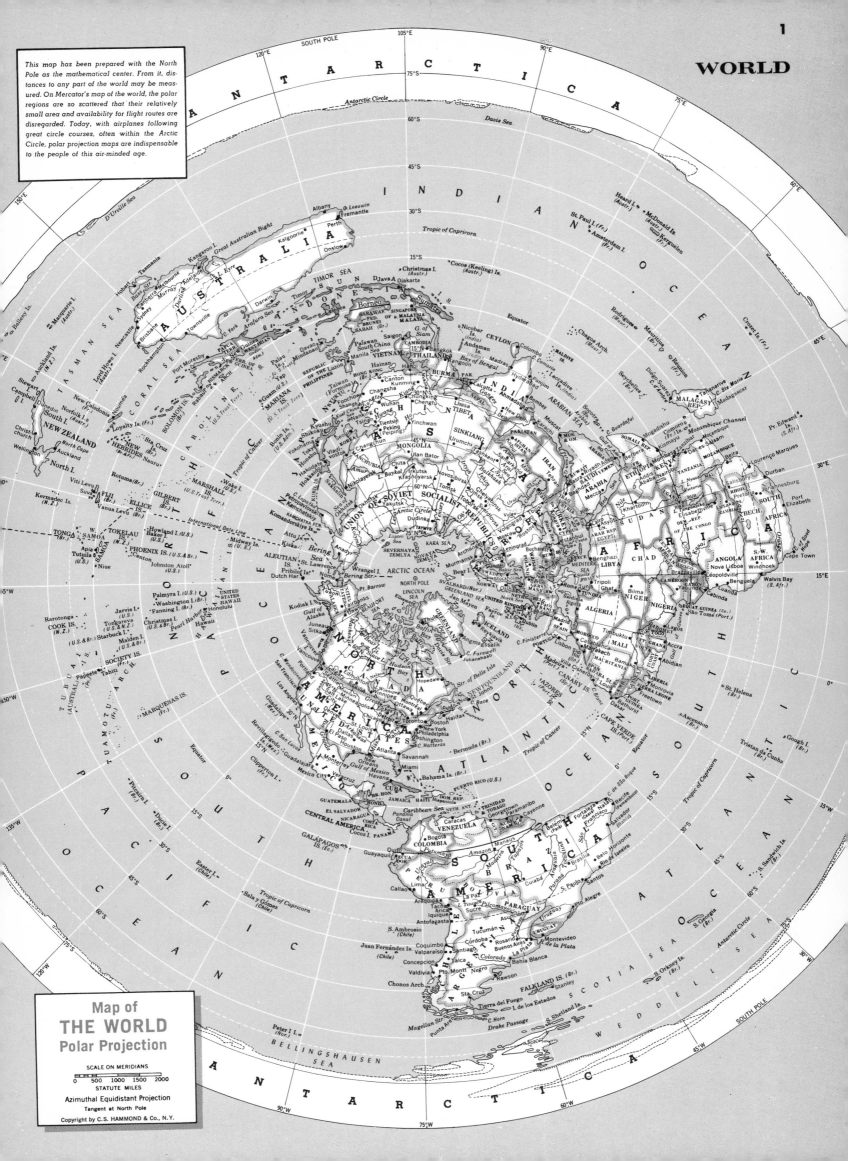

WORLD

1

This map has been prepared with the North Pole as the mathematical center. From it, distances to any part of the world may be measured. On Mercator's map of the world, the polar regions are so scattered that their relatively small area and availability for flight routes are disregarded. Today, with airplanes following great circle courses, often within the Arctic Circle, polar projection maps are indispensable to the people of this air-minded age.

Map of
THE WORLD
Polar Projection

SCALE ON MERIDIANS
0   500 1000 1500 2000
STATUTE MILES

Azimuthal Equidistant Projection
Tangent at North Pole

Copyright by C.S. Hammond & Co., N.Y.

World -Mercator

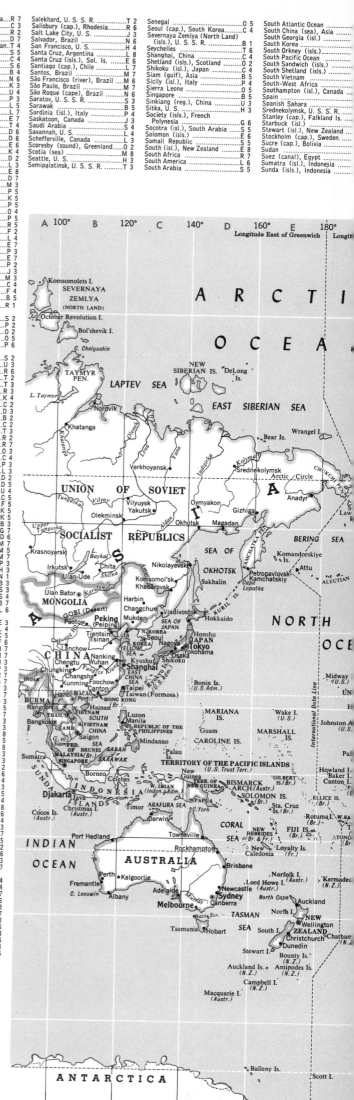

WORLD—Mercator

LAND AREA	57,510,000 sq. mi.
WATER AREA	139,440,000 sq. mi.
TOTAL SURFACE AREA	196,950,000 sq. mi.
POPULATION	3,218,000,000

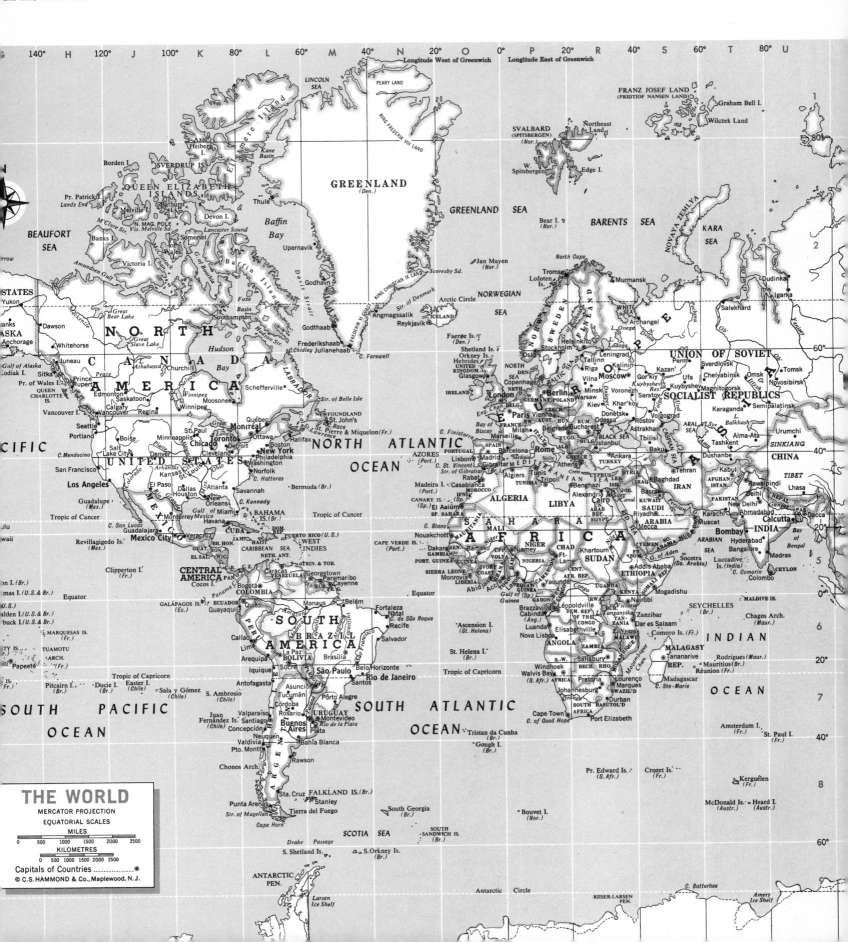

ARCTIC OCEAN

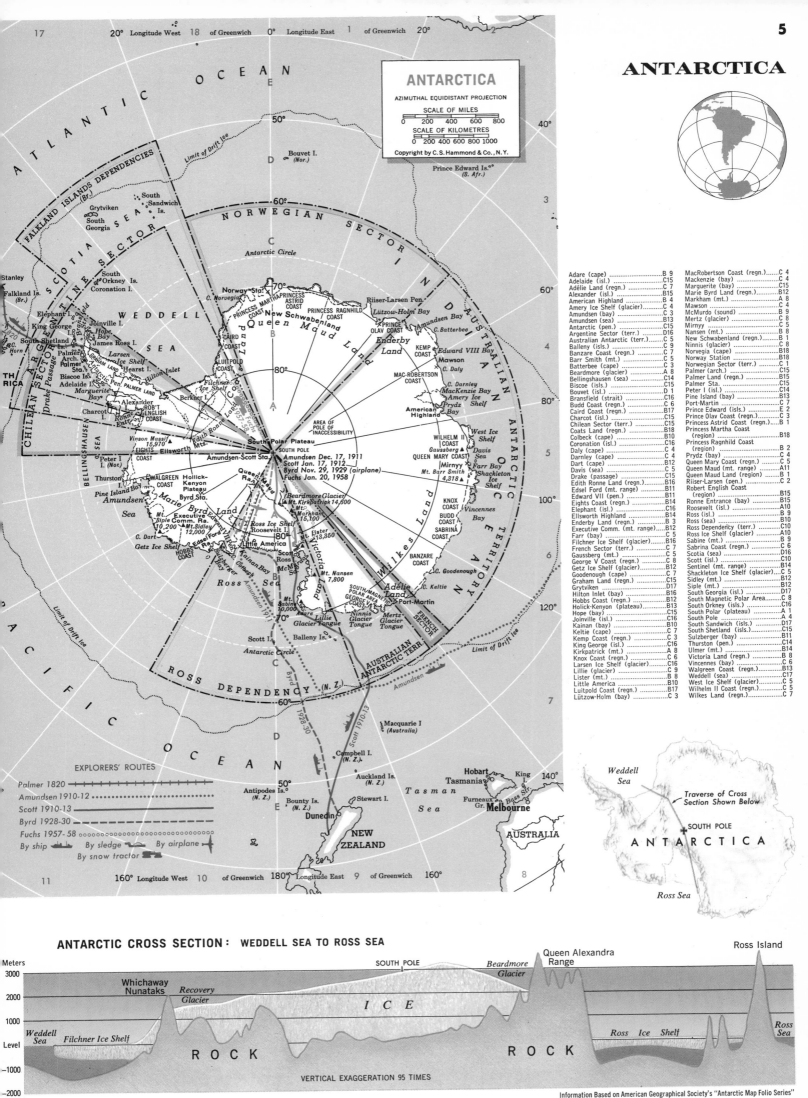

ANTARCTICA

ANTARCTICA
AZIMUTHAL EQUIDISTANT PROJECTION
SCALE OF MILES
0   200   400   600   800
SCALE OF KILOMETRES
0   200 400 600 800 1000
Copyright by C.S. Hammond & Co., N.Y.

EXPLORERS' ROUTES
Palmer 1820
Amundsen 1910-12
Scott 1910-13
Byrd 1928-30
Fuchs 1957-58
By ship   By sledge   By airplane
By snow tractor

Amundsen Dec. 17, 1911
Scott Jan. 17, 1912
Byrd Nov. 29, 1929 (airplane)
Fuchs Jan. 20, 1958

Traverse of Cross
Section Shown Below
SOUTH POLE
ANTARCTICA
Weddell Sea
Ross Sea

ANTARCTIC CROSS SECTION: WEDDELL SEA TO ROSS SEA

SOUTH POLE — Beardmore Glacier — Queen Alexandra Range — Ross Island
Whichaway Nunataks — Recovery Glacier
ICE
Weddell Sea — Filchner Ice Shelf
ROCK   ROCK
Ross Ice Shelf — Ross Sea

Meters: 3000, 2000, 1000, Level, -1000, -2000

VERTICAL EXAGGERATION 95 TIMES

Information Based on American Geographical Society's "Antarctic Map Folio Series"

The government of the United States has not recognized the incorporation of Estonia, Latvia and Lithuania into the Soviet Union, nor does it recognize as final the de facto western limit of Polish administration in Germany (the Oder-Neisse line).

EUROPE

AREA	4,129,908 sq. mi.
POPULATION	610,818,000
LARGEST CITY	Paris (greater) 8,569,238
HIGHEST POINT	El'brus 18,481 ft.
LOWEST POINT	Caspian Sea —92 ft.

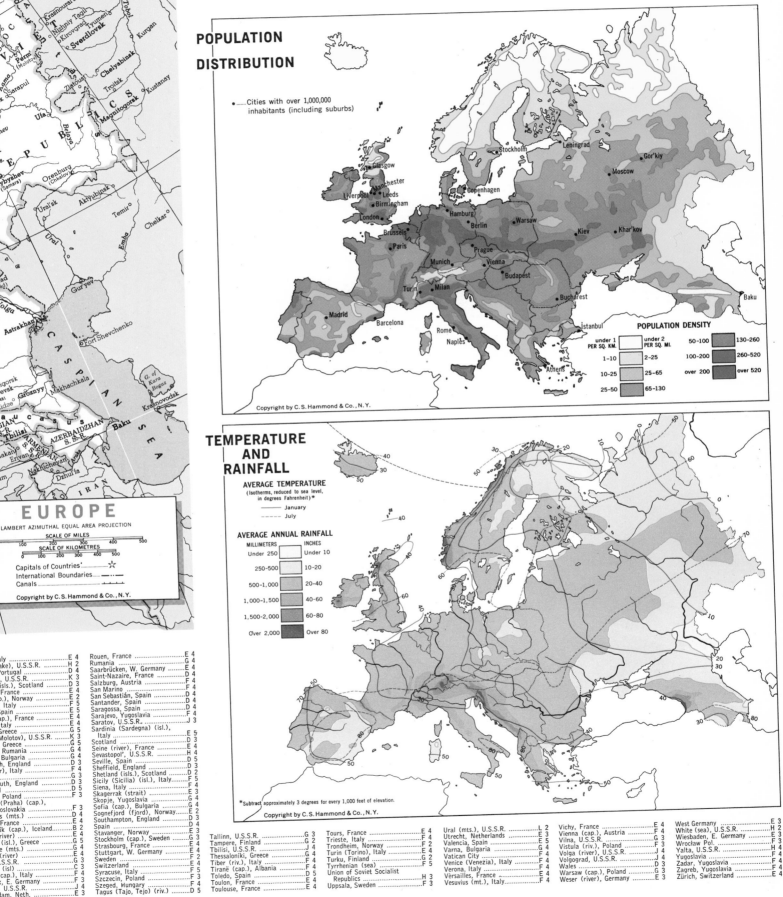

POPULATION DISTRIBUTION

•.... Cities with over 1,000,000 inhabitants (including suburbs)

POPULATION DENSITY

under 1 PER SQ. KM.	under 2 PER SQ. MI.
1-10	2-25
10-25	25-65
25-50	65-130
50-100	130-260
100-200	260-520
over 200	over 520

Copyright by C.S. Hammond & Co., N.Y.

TEMPERATURE AND RAINFALL

AVERAGE TEMPERATURE
(Isotherms, reduced to sea level, in degrees Fahrenheit) *

— January
-- July

AVERAGE ANNUAL RAINFALL

MILLIMETERS	INCHES
Under 250	Under 10
250-500	10-20
500-1,000	20-40
1,000-1,500	40-60
1,500-2,000	60-80
Over 2,000	Over 80

* Subtract approximately 3 degrees for every 1,000 feet of elevation.

Copyright by C.S. Hammond & Co., N.Y.

EUROPE

LAMBERT AZIMUTHAL EQUAL AREA PROJECTION

SCALE OF MILES
0   100   200   300   400   500

SCALE OF KILOMETRES
0   100   200   300   400   500

Capitals of Countries..............☆
International Boundaries......——·——
Canals.........................

Copyright by C.S. Hammond & Co., N.Y.

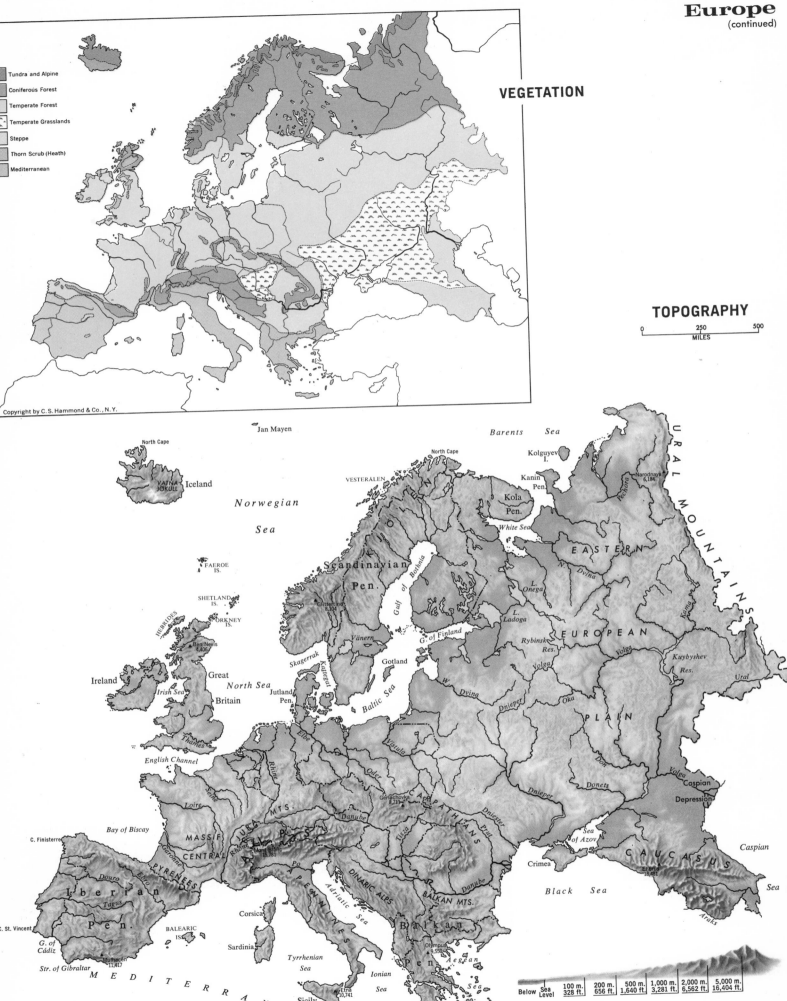

VEGETATION

Tundra and Alpine
Coniferous Forest
Temperate Forest
Temperate Grasslands
Steppe
Thorn Scrub (Heath)
Mediterranean

Copyright by C.S. Hammond & Co., N.Y.

TOPOGRAPHY

0   250   500
MILES

Below | Sea Level | 100 m. 328 ft. | 200 m. 656 ft. | 500 m. 1,640 ft. | 1,000 m. 3,281 ft. | 2,000 m. 6,562 ft. | 5,000 m. 16,404 ft.

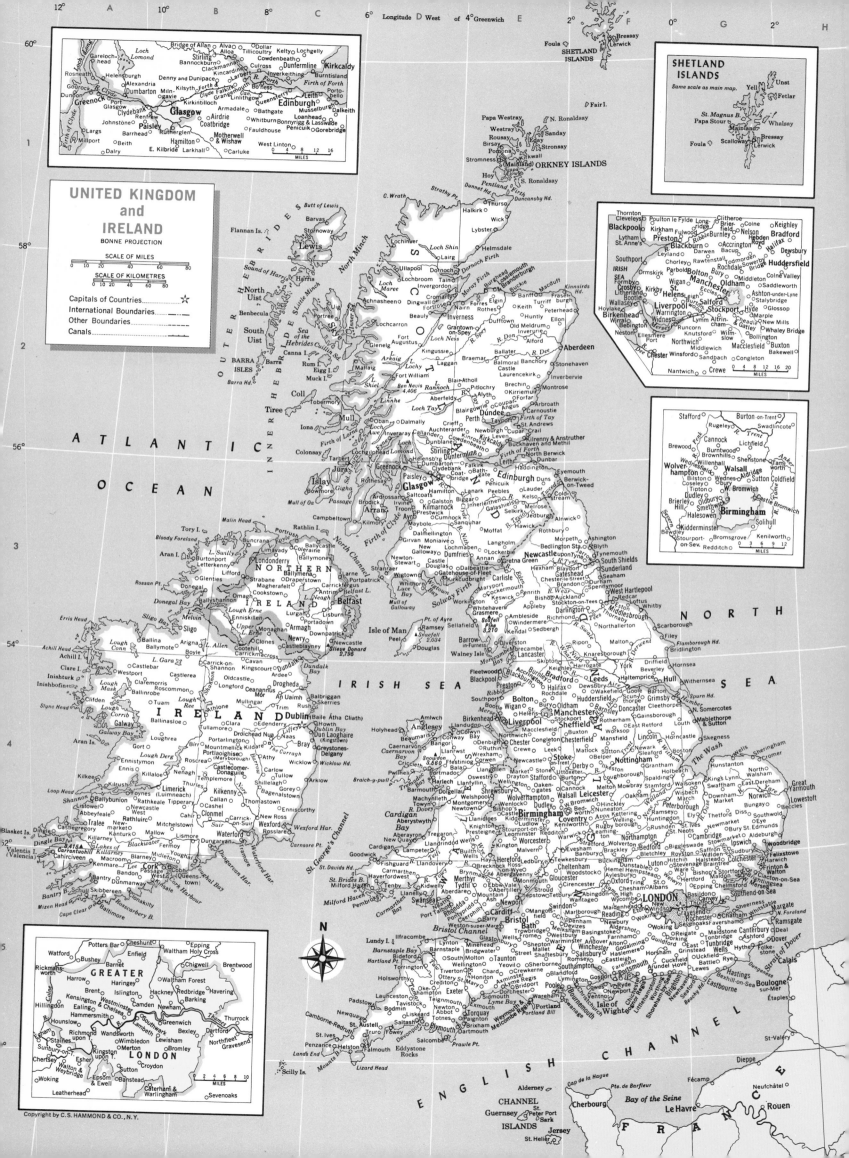

UNITED KINGDOM and IRELAND

UNITED KINGDOM

AREA	94,214 sq. mi.
POPULATION	54,065,700
CAPITAL	London
LARGEST CITY	London (greater) 7,864,500
HIGHEST POINT	Ben Nevis 4,406 ft.
MONETARY UNIT	pound sterling
MAJOR LANGUAGES	English, Gaelic, Welsh
MAJOR RELIGIONS	Protestant, Roman Catholic

IRELAND

26,601 sq. mi.
2,849,000
Dublin
Dublin (greater) 595,288
Carrantuohill 3,414 ft.
Irish pound
English, Gaelic
Roman Catholic

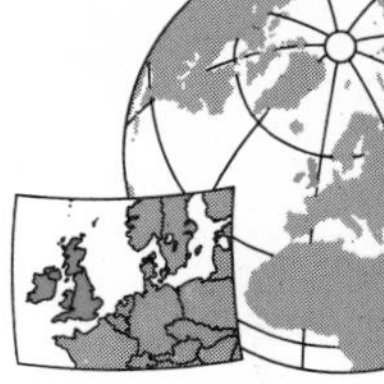

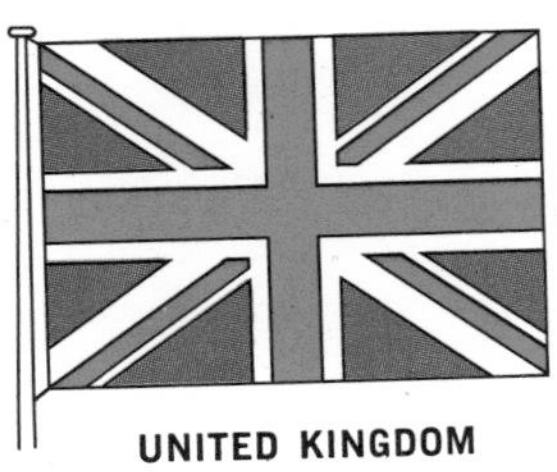

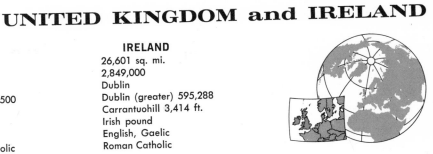

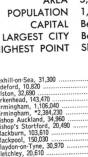

UNITED KINGDOM

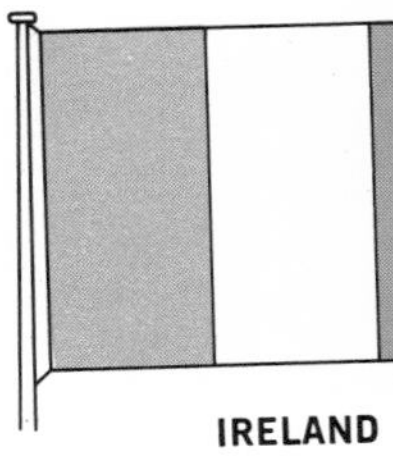

IRELAND

GREATER LONDON

CITIES and TOWNS

stead, 41,870 ....B 6
king, 175,000 ....C 5
net, 317,910 ....B 5
ley, 210,270 ....C 5
nt, 296,030 ....B 5
ntwood, 54,230 ....C 5
mley, 305,640 ....B 5
shey, 23,450 ....B 5
nden, 243,360 ....B 5
erham and Warlingham,
6,350 ....B 6
ertsey, 42,870 ....B 6
eshunt, 39,040 ....B 5
gwell, 52,000 ....C 5
oydon, 328,890 ....B 6
rtford, 46,420 ....C 5
ling, 304,740 ....B 5
ham, 31,470 ....B 5
field, 270,140 ....B 5
ping, 10,370 ....C 5
som and Ewell, 71,700 ....B 6
her, 62,140 ....B 6
avesend, 53,590 ....C 5
eenwich, 231,500 ....C 5
ackney, 254,720 ....B 5
ammersmith, 216,940 ....B 5
aringey, 257,640 ....B 5
arrow, 210,250 ....B 5
avering, 249,750 ....C 5
illingdon, 232,520 ....B 5
ounslow, 208,170 ....B 5
lington, 259,160 ....B 5
ensington and Chelsea,
219,190 ....B 5
ingston-upon-Thames, 146,450...B 6
ambeth, 340,470 ....B 5
eatherhead, 37,270 ....B 6
ewisham, 291,670 ....B 5
ondon (cap.), *7,864,500 ....B 5
lerton, 186,040 ....B 5
ewham, 260,400 ....B 5
orthfleet, 23,780 ....C 5
otters Bar, 24,120 ....B 5
edbridge, 248,000 ....C 5
ichmond-upon-Thames, 182,080..B 5
ickmansworth, 39,130 ....A 5
evenoaks, 18,100 ....C 6
outhwark, 310,910 ....B 5
taines, 53,240 ....B 5
unbury-on-Thames, 37,040 ....B 6
utton, 79,008 ....B 6
Thurrock, 118,390 ....C 5
Waltham Forest, 243,840 ....B 5
Waltham Holy Cross, 12,390 ....B 5
Wandsworth, 333,940 ....B 5
Walton and Weybridge, 48,400...B 6
Watford, 76,340 ....B 5
Westminster, 270,140 ....B 5
Wimbledon, 56,760 ....B 5
Woking, 74,230 ....B 6

PHYSICAL FEATURES

Colne (river) ....A 5
Thames (river) ....C 5

BIRMINGHAM AREA

CITIES and TOWNS

Aldridge, 58,890 ....G 3
Bewdley, 5,190 ....F 3
Bilston, 32,690 ....G 3
Birmingham, 1,106,040 ....G 3
Birmingham, *2,384,230 ....G 3
Brewood, 5,751 ....F 2
Brierley Hill, 59,510 ....G 3
Bromsgrove, 36,790 ....G 3
Brownhills, 28,700 ....G 2
Burntwood, †12,085 ....G 2
Burton-on-Trent, 50,540 ....G 2
Cannock, 45,060 ....G 2
Castle Bromwich, 9,205 ....G 3
Coseley, 41,320 ....G 3
Dudley, 63,890 ....G 3
Halesowen, 45,190 ....G 3
Kenilworth, 17,480 ....G 3
Kidderminster, 43,450 ....G 3
Lichfield, 18,130 ....G 2
Oldbury, 54,180 ....G 3
Redditch, 35,960 ....G 3
Rugeley, 15,140 ....G 2
Shenstone, 5,174 ....G 3
Smethwick, 67,750 ....G 3
Solihull, 99,300 ....G 3
Stafford, 49,480 ....G 2
Stourport-on-Severn, 13,400 ....G 3
Sutton Coldfield, 77,980 ....G 3
Swadlincote, 19,640 ....G 2
Tamworth, 16,120 ....G 3
Tipton, 37,990 ....G 3
Walsall, 119,910 ....G 3
Wednesbury, 34,760 ....G 3
Wednesfield, 35,070 ....G 3
West Bromwich, 97,600 ....G 3
Willenhall, 35,160 ....G 3
Wolverhampton, 150,200 ....G 3

PHYSICAL FEATURES

Anker (river) ....G 3
Penk (river) ....G 2
Severn (river) ....F 3
Tame (river) ....G 3
Trent (river) ....G 2

LIVERPOOL-MANCHESTER AREA

CITIES and TOWNS

Accrington, 38,510 ....G 1
Altrincham, 41,250 ....G 2
Ashton-under-Lyne, 49,380 ....G 2
Bacup, 16,890 ....G 1
Bakewell, 3,980 ....G 2
Bebington, 54,070 ....F 2
Birkenhead, 143,470 ....F 2
Blackburn, 103,610 ....G 1
Blackpool, 150,030 ....F 1
Bollington, 5,700 ....G 2
Bolton, 159,190 ....G 2
Bootle, 83,040 ....F 2
Bradford, 298,220 ....H 1
Brierfield, 7,280 ....G 1
Burnley, 79,250 ....G 1
Burtonwood, †2,766 ....G 2
Bury, 62,080 ....G 2
Buxton, 19,390 ....G 2
Cheadle and Gatley, 51,630 ....G 2
Chester, 59,800 ....F 2
Chorley, 31,060 ....G 2
Clitheroe, 12,550 ....G 1
Colne, 19,030 ....G 1
Colne Valley, 21,140 ....G 2
Congleton, 17,400 ....G 2
Crewe, 52,950 ....G 2
Crosby, 59,930 ....F 2
Darwen, 29,110 ....G 1
Dewsbury, 53,490 ....H 2
Eccles, 42,530 ....G 2
Ellesmere Port, 48,200 ....F 2
Formby, 14,370 ....F 2
Fulwood, 17,640 ....G 1
Glossop, 18,690 ....G 2
Halifax, 95,450 ....G 1
Hebden Royd, 9,140 ....G 1
Hoylake, 32,630 ....F 2
Huddersfield, 132,270 ....G 2
Hyde, 35,380 ....G 2
Keighley, 56,190 ....H 1
Kirkby, 57,360 ....F 2
Kirkham, 6,020 ....F 1
Knutsford, 10,010 ....G 2
Leigh, 46,360 ....G 2
Leyland, 20,670 ....F 1
Litherland, 25,170 ....F 2
Liverpool, 729,140 ....F 2
Liverpool, *1,384,740 ....F 2
Longridge, 5,120 ....G 1
Lymm, 7,960 ....G 2
Lytham Saint Anne's, 36,510 ....F 1
Macclesfield, 38,540 ....G 2
Manchester, 644,500 ....G 2
Manchester, *2,448,960 ....G 2
Marple, 19,920 ....G 2
Middleton, 58,360 ....G 2
Middlewich, 7,480 ....G 2
Nantwich, 10,980 ....G 2
Nelson, 31,540 ....G 1
Neston, 13,980 ....F 2
New Mills, 8,670 ....G 2
Northwich, 19,460 ....G 2
Oldham, 112,670 ....G 2
Ormskirk, 24,350 ....F 2
Parbold, †976 ....G 2
Poulton le Fylde, 14,670 ....F 1
Preston, 110,390 ....F 1
Rawtenstall, 23,510 ....G 2
Rochdale, 86,180 ....G 2
Runcorn, 27,170 ....G 2
Saddleworth, 17,600 ....G 2
Saint Helens, 105,310 ....F 2
Salford, 150,350 ....G 2
Sandbach, 10,350 ....G 2
Southport, 80,080 ....F 2
Sowerby Bridge, 17,150 ....G 2
Stalybridge, 21,660 ....G 2
Stockport, 142,500 ....G 2
Thornton Cleveleys, 22,020 ....F 1
Todmorden, 16,810 ....G 2
Wallasey, 103,320 ....F 2
Warrington, 75,110 ....F 2
Whaley Bridge, 5,290 ....G 2
Widnes, 53,670 ....F 2
Wigan, 77,250 ....G 2
Wilmslow, 26,700 ....G 2
Winsford, 14,120 ....G 2
Wirral, 24,060 ....F 2

PHYSICAL FEATURES

Dee (river) ....F 2
Irish (sea) ....F 2
Mersey (river) ....F 2
Ribble (river) ....G 1

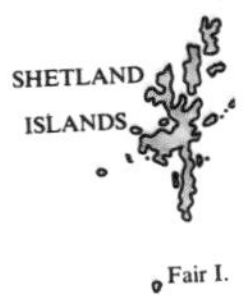

SHETLAND
ISLANDS
Fair I.

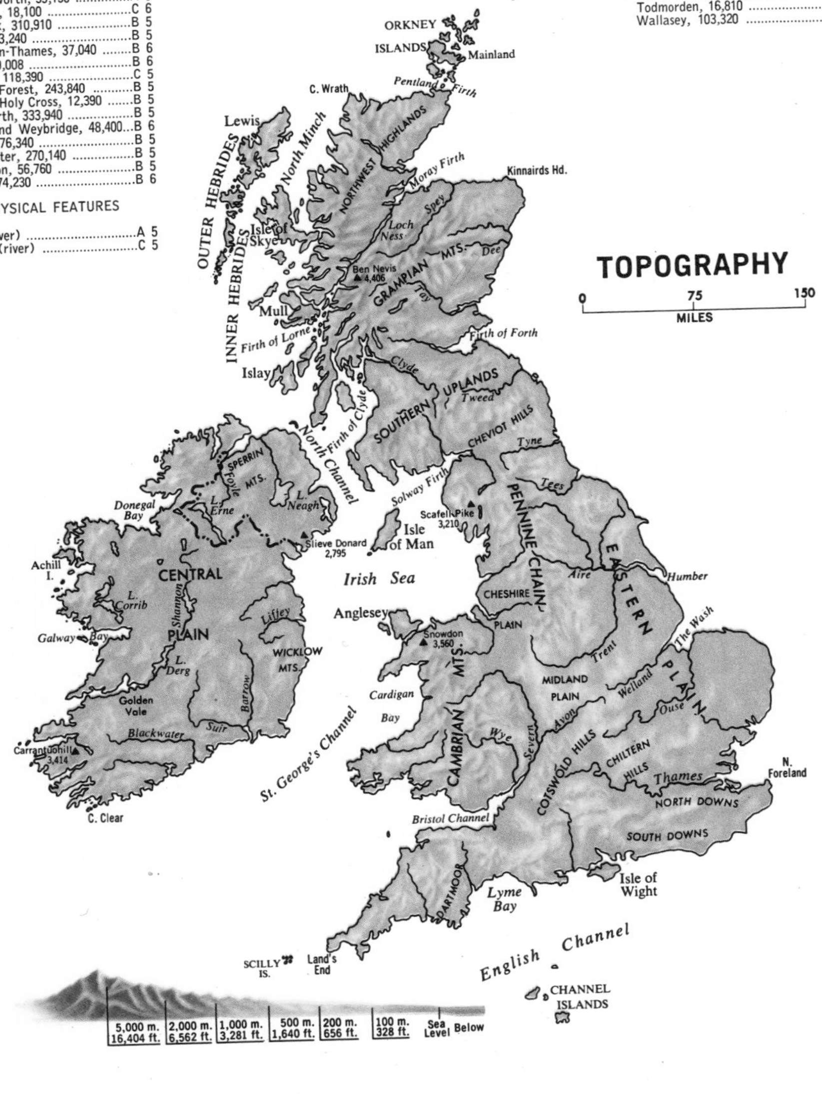

ORKNEY
ISLANDS
Mainland
Pentland Firth
C. Wrath
Lewis
OUTER HEBRIDES
North Minch
NORTHWEST HIGHLANDS
Moray Firth
Kinnairds Hd.
Isle of Skye
INNER HEBRIDES
Loch Ness
Spey
Ben Nevis 4,406
GRAMPIAN MTS.
Dee
Mull
Firth of Lorne
Tay
Firth of Forth
Islay
Clyde
SOUTHERN UPLANDS
Firth of Clyde
Tweed
CHEVIOT HILLS
North Channel
Tyne
SPERRIN MTS.
L. Neagh
Tees
Solway Firth
Scafell Pike 3,210
Donegal Bay
L. Erne
Slieve Donard 2,795
Isle of Man
PENNINE CHAIN
Achill I.
CENTRAL
L. Corrib
Shannon
Irish Sea
Humber
EASTERN
Aire
CHESHIRE PLAIN
Galway Bay
PLAIN
Liffey
Anglesey
Snowdon 3,560
WICKLOW MTS.
The Wash
L. Derg
Barrow
Trent
MIDLAND PLAIN
Welland
Ouse
Golden Vale
Cardigan Bay
CAMBRIAN MTS.
Blackwater
Suir
Wye
Severn
Avon
COTSWOLD HILLS
CHILTERN HILLS
Carrantuohill 3,414
St. George's Channel
Thames
N. Foreland
NORTH DOWNS
C. Clear
Bristol Channel
SOUTH DOWNS
DARTMOOR
Lyme Bay
Isle of Wight
English Channel
SCILLY IS.
Land's End
CHANNEL ISLANDS
5,000 m. 16,404 ft.
2,000 m. 6,562 ft.
1,000 m. 3,281 ft.
500 m. 1,640 ft.
200 m. 656 ft.
100 m. 328 ft.
Sea Level
Below

TOPOGRAPHY

0 75 150
MILES

ENGLAND

AREA	50,327 sq. mi.
POPULATION	44,724,910
CAPITAL	London
LARGEST CITY	London (greater) 7,864,500
HIGHEST POINT	Scafell Pike 3,210 ft.

WALES

AREA	8,017 sq. mi.
POPULATION	2,676,390
LARGEST CITY	Cardiff 260,340
HIGHEST POINT	Snowdon 3,560 ft.

SCOTLAND

AREA	30,411 sq. mi.
POPULATION	5,206,400
CAPITAL	Edinburgh
LARGEST CITY	Glasgow (greater) 1,795,638
HIGHEST POINT	Ben Nevis 4,406 ft.

NORTHERN IRELAND

AREA	5,459 sq. mi.
POPULATION	1,458,000
CAPITAL	Belfast
LARGEST CITY	Belfast (greater) 528,700
HIGHEST POINT	Slieve Donard 2,795 ft.

ENGLAND

(map on page 13)

COUNTIES

Bedfordshire, 410,430 ....G 5
Berkshire, 556,000 ....F 6
Buckinghamshire, 528,010 ....G 6
Cambridgeshire and the Isle of
Ely, 290,390 ....H 5
Cheshire, 1,430,220 ....E 4
Cornwall, 346,770 ....C 7
Cumberland, 296,980 ....D 3
Derbyshire, 901,440 ....F 4
Devonshire, 851,120 ....D 7
Dorsetshire, 327,250 ....E 7
Durham, 1,533,030 ....F 3
Essex, 1,199,040 ....H 6
Gloucestershire, 1,033,670 ....E 6
Hampshire (Hants), 1,436,060 ....F 6
Herefordshire, 136,370 ....E 5
Hertfordshire, 847,620 ....G 6
Huntingdon and Peterborough,
170,180 ....G 5
Isle of Wight, 95,380 ....F 7
Kent, 1,266,610 ....H 6
Lancashire, 5,165,040 ....E 4
Leicestershire, 701,570 ....F 5
Lincolnshire-Holland, 104,530 ....G 5
Lincolnshire-Kesteven, 143,920 ....G 5
Lincolnshire-Lindsey, 520,990 ....G 4
London (greater city), 7,864,500 ..G 6
Norfolk, 572,360 ....H 5
Northamptonshire, 416,960 ....G 5
Northumberland, 827,080 ....E 2
Nottinghamshire, 935,040 ....F 4
Oxfordshire, 332,470 ....F 6
Rutlandshire, 26,000 ....G 5
Shropshire (Salop), 311,880 ....E 5
Somersetshire, 625,740 ....E 6
Southampton (Hampshire),
1,436,060 ....F 6
Staffordshire, 1,798,510 ....E 5
Suffolk, East, 361,410 ....J 5
Suffolk, West, 139,450 ....G 7
Surrey, 955,910 ....G 6
Sussex, East, 692,510 ....H 7
Sussex, West, 436,770 ....G 7
Warwickshire, 2,082,250 ....F 5
Westmorland, 66,600 ....E 3
Wight, Isle of, 95,380 ....F 7
Wiltshire, 457,100 ....F 6
Worcestershire, 596,680 ....E 5
Yorkshire-East Riding, 537,620 ....G 4
Yorkshire-North Riding, 577,280 ..F 3
Yorkshire-West Riding,
3,703,770 ....F 4

CITIES and TOWNS

Abingdon, 15,680 ....F 6
Accrington, 38,510 ....E 4
Aldershot, 33,690 ....G 6
Alfreton, 22,830 ....F 4
Andover, 18,900 ....F 6
Arnold, 29,380 ....G 4
Ashford, 29,470 ....H 6
Ashington, 26,600 ....F 2
Aylesbury, 32,510 ....G 6
Banbury, 23,080 ....F 5
Barnet, 317,910 ....G 6
Barnsley, 75,260 ....F 4
Barnstaple, 16,280 ....D 6
Barrow-in-Furness, 65,180 ....D 3
Basildon, 103,110 ....H 6
Basingstoke, 30,360 ....F 6
Bath, 82,750 ....E 6
Batley, 40,276 ....F 4
Bedford, 66,430 ....G 5
Bedlington Station
(Bedlingtonshire), 30,670 ....F 2
Bedworth, 34,890 ....F 5
Beeston and Stapleford, 58,410 ...F 5
Belper, 15,760 ....F 4
Benfleet, 38,740 ....H 6
Berwick-on-Tweed, 11,840 ....F 2
Beverley, 16,530 ....G 4
Bexhill-on-Sea, 31,300 ....H 7
Bideford, 10,820 ....C 6
Bilston, 32,690 ....E 5
Birkenhead, 143,470 ....D 4
Birmingham, 1,106,040 ....F 5
Birmingham, *2,384,230 ....F 5
Bishop Auckland, 34,960 ....F 3
Bishop's Stortford, 20,490 ....H 6
Blackburn, 103,610 ....E 4
Blackpool, 150,030 ....D 4
Blaydon-on-Tyne, 30,970 ....F 3
Bletchley, 20,610 ....G 5
Blyth, 36,320 ....F 2
Bognor Regis, 29,620 ....G 7
Bolsover, 11,800 ....F 4
Bolton, 159,190 ....E 4
Bootle, 83,040 ....D 4
Boston, 25,060 ....H 5
Bournemouth, 151,090 ....F 7
Bradford, 298,220 ....F 4
Braintree and Bocking, 21,060 ....H 6
Brandon and Byshottles, 19,530 ..F 3
Brentwood, 54,230 ....H 6
Bridgwater, 26,300 ....D 6
Bridlington, 26,250 ....G 3
Brighouse, 31,830 ....F 4
Brighton, 162,650 ....G 7
Bristol, 432,070 ....E 6
Brixham, 11,390 ....D 7
Broadstairs and St. Peter's,
18,970 ....J 6
Bromsgrove, 36,790 ....E 5
Burgess Hill, 15,490 ....G 7
Burnham-on-Sea, 10,480 ....D 6
Burnley, 79,250 ....E 4
Burton-on-Trent, 50,540 ....F 5
Bury, 62,080 ....E 4
Bury Saint Edmunds, 22,270 ....H 5
Buxton, 19,390 ....F 4
Camborne-Redruth, 36,700 ....B 7
Cambridge, 98,390 ....H 5
Cannock, 45,060 ....E 5
Canterbury, 32,020 ....J 6
Carlisle, 71,290 ....D 3
Carlton, 40,240 ....G 5
Castleford, 39,930 ....F 4
Caterham and Warlingham,
36,350 ....G 6
Chatham, 51,220 ....H 6
Cheadle and Gatley, 51,630 ....F 5
Chelmsford, 52,920 ....H 6
Cheltenham, 74,910 ....F 6
Chesham, 19,100 ....G 6
Cheshunt, 39,040 ....G 6
Chester, 59,800 ....E 4
Chester-le-Street, 19,380 ....F 3
Chesterfield, 69,590 ....F 4
Chichester, 20,280 ....G 7
Chippenham, 18,510 ....F 6
Chorley, 31,060 ....E 4
Christchurch, 28,000 ....F 7
Cirencester, 12,640 ....F 6
Clacton-on-Sea, 30,780 ....J 6
Cleethorpes, 33,430 ....H 4
Clevedon, 11,670 ....E 6
Clitheroe, 12,550 ....E 4
Coalville, 27,070 ....F 5
Colchester, 68,290 ....H 6
Colne, 19,030 ....E 4
Congleton, 17,400 ....F 4
Consett, 38,000 ....F 3
Corby, 42,770 ....G 5
Coventry, 315,670 ....F 5
Cowes, 17,590 ....F 7
Crawley, 59,000 ....G 6
Crewe, 52,950 ....E 4
Crook and Willington, 24,450 ....F 3
Croydon, 328,890 ....G 6
Cuckfield, 22,070 ....G 6
Dalton-in-Furness, 10,360 ....D 3
Darlington, 84,320 ....F 3
Deal, 25,740 ....J 6
Derby, 130,030 ....F 5
Dewsbury, 53,490 ....F 4
Doncaster, 87,100 ....G 4
Dorchester, 13,200 ....E 7
Dorking, 23,020 ....G 6
Dover, 36,080 ....J 6
Dunstable, 27,270 ....G 6
Durham, 23,050 ....F 3
Ealing, 304,740 ....G 6
East Grinstead, 16,390 ....G 6
East Retford, 18,290 ....G 4
Eastbourne, 63,530 ....H 7
Eastleigh, 39,970 ....F 7
Ellesmere Port, 48,200 ....E 4
Ely, 10,010 ....H 5
Epping, 10,370 ....H 6
Eston, 38,390 ....F 3
Evesham, 12,980 ....F 5

(continued on following page)

United Kingdom and Ireland
(continued)

ENGLAND (continued)

Exeter, 81,810 .... D 7
Exmouth, 20,810 .... D 7
Falmouth, 17,320 .... C 7
Fareham, 68,690 .... F 7
Farnborough, 37,190 .... G 6
Farnham, 28,970 .... G 6
Faversham, 13,500 .... J 6
Felixstowe, 17,750 .... J 6
Fleet, 16,580 .... G 6
Fleetwood, 28,440 .... D 4
Folkestone, 43,470 .... J 6
Frinton and Walton, 10,770 .... J 6
Frome, 11,700 .... E 6
Gainsborough, 17,210 .... G 4
Gateshead, 101,760 .... F 3
Gillingham, 77,070 .... H 6
Glossop, 18,690 .... F 4
Gloucester, 71,650 .... E 6
Godalming, 17,590 .... G 6
Goole, 18,680 .... G 4
Gosport, 72,240 .... F 7
Grantham, 25,670 .... G 5
Gravesend, 53,590 .... H 6
Great Yarmouth, 52,720 .... J 5
Greenwich, 231,500 .... H 6
Grimsby, 95,300 .... H 4
Guildford, 54,090 .... G 6
Guisborough, 12,990 .... G 3
Halifax, 95,450 .... F 4
Haltemprice, 47,180 .... G 4
Harlow, 63,540 .... H 6
Harrogate, 58,230 .... F 4
Hartlepool, 18,100 .... F 3
Harwich, 14,150 .... J 6
Haslemere, 13,210 .... G 6
Haslingden, 14,210 .... E 4
Hastings, 66,690 .... H 7
Heanor, 24,190 .... F 5
Hemel Hempstead, 61,890 .... G 6
Hereford, 43,950 .... E 5
Herne Bay, 22,930 .... J 6
Hertford, 17,970 .... G 6
Hetton-le-Hole, 17,230 .... F 3
Heysham (Morecambe and Heysham), 40,570 .... D 3
High Wycombe, 54,060 .... G 6
Hinckley, 42,270 .... F 5
Hitchin, 24,990 .... G 5
Horsham, 23,250 .... G 6
Hove, 72,780 .... G 7
Hoylake, 32,630 .... D 4
Hucknall, 24,670 .... F 4
Huddersfield, 132,270 .... F 4
Hull (Kingston-upon-Hull), 300,320 .... G 4
Huntingdon and Godmanchester, 11,400 .... G 5
Hythe, 10,590 .... H 6
Ilkeston, 34,990 .... F 5
Ilkely, 18,960 .... F 4
Ipswich, 120,120 .... J 5
Jarrow, 26,770 .... F 3
Keighley, 56,190 .... F 4
Kendal, 18,730 .... E 3
Kenilworth, 17,480 .... F 5
Kettering, 38,840 .... G 5
Keynsham, 16,460 .... E 6
Kidderminster, 43,450 .... E 5
King's Lynn, 27,830 .... H 5
Kingston-upon-Hull (Hull), 300,320 .... G 4
Kingston-upon-Thames, 146,450 .... G 6
Kingswood, 27,640 .... E 6
Kirkby-in-Ashfield, 22,120 .... F 4
Knottingley, 13,320 .... F 4
Knutsford, 10,010 .... E 4
Lancaster, 47,860 .... E 3
Leamington (Royal Leamington Spa), 44,300 .... F 5
Leatherhead, 37,270 .... G 6
Leeds, 508,790 .... F 4
Leeds, *1,721,360 .... F 4
Leek, 19,100 .... E 4
Leicester, 267,050 .... G 5
Leigh, 46,360 .... E 4
Leighton Buzzard, 12,880 .... G 6
Letchworth, 26,560 .... G 6
Lewes, 13,890 .... H 7
Leyland, 20,670 .... E 4
Lichfield, 18,130 .... F 5
Lincoln, 77,180 .... G 4
Littlehampton, 17,060 .... G 7
Liverpool, 729,140 .... D 4
Liverpool, *1,384,740 .... D 4
London (cap.), 7,864,500 .... G 6
Long Eaton, 31,440 .... F 5
Loughborough, 39,270 .... F 5
Louth, 11,390 .... H 4
Lowestoft, 47,540 .... J 5
Luton, 147,770 .... G 6
Lymington, 30,610 .... F 7
Lytham Saint Anne's, 36,510 .... D 4
Macclesfield, 38,540 .... F 4
Maidenhead, 39,560 .... G 6
Maidstone, 62,300 .... H 6
Maldon, 11,330 .... H 6
Malvern, 28,030 .... E 5
Manchester, 644,500 .... E 4
Manchester, *2,448,960 .... E 4
Mangotsfield, 24,530 .... E 6
Mansfield, 54,670 .... F 4
March, 13,240 .... H 5
Margate, 47,260 .... J 6
Maryport, 12,220 .... D 3
Matlock, 19,390 .... F 4
Melton Mowbray, 16,850 .... G 5
Middlesbrough, 157,740 .... F 3
Morecambe and Heysham, 40,570 .... E 3
Morley, 42,590 .... F 4
Morpeth, 13,630 .... F 2
Nantwich, 10,980 .... E 4
Nelson, 31,540 .... E 4
New Windsor, 29,030 .... G 6
Newark, 24,780 .... G 4
Newbury, 21,380 .... F 6
Newcastle (Newcastle-under-Lyme), 77,000 .... E 5
Newcastle-upon-Tyne, 260,750 .... F 2
Newcastle-upon-Tyne, *853,300 .... F 2
Newham, 260,400 .... H 6
Newmarket, 11,460 .... H 5
Newport, 19,110 .... F 7
Newquay, 11,530 .... B 7
Newton Abbot, 18,650 .... D 7
Northampton, 106,120 .... G 5
Northfleet, 23,780 .... H 6
Northwich, 19,460 .... E 4
Norton-Radstock, 13,180 .... E 6
Norwich, 119,150 .... J 5
Nottingham, 311,850 .... F 5
Nuneaton, 60,010 .... F 5
Oakengates, 13,930 .... E 5
Old Fletton, 12,290 .... G 5
Oldham, 112,670 .... E 4
Ormskirk, 24,350 .... E 4
Oswestry, 11,940 .... E 5
Otley, 11,770 .... F 4
Oxford, 108,880 .... F 6
Paignton, 31,000 .... D 7
Penrith, 10,870 .... E 3
Penzance, 18,950 .... B 7
Peterborough, 64,770 .... G 5
Plymouth, 213,800 .... D 7
Pontefract, 28,320 .... F 4
Poole, 94,770 .... E 7
Portland, 11,800 .... E 7
Portslade, 17,520 .... G 7
Portsmouth, 221,470 .... G 7
Preston, 110,390 .... E 4
Prudhoe, 10,470 .... F 3
Ramsgate, 38,200 .... J 6
Rawmarsh, 19,600 .... F 4
Reading, 123,310 .... F 6
Redcar, 34,340 .... G 3
Redditch, 35,960 .... F 5
Reigate, 55,150 .... G 6
Ripley, 17,720 .... F 4
Ripon, 10,760 .... F 3
Rochdale, 86,180 .... E 4
Rochester, 52,360 .... H 6
Rotherham, 86,510 .... F 4
Rugby, 54,950 .... F 5
Rugeley, 15,140 .... E 5
Runcorn, 27,170 .... E 4
Rushden, 17,490 .... G 5
Ryde, 20,350 .... F 7
Saint Albans, 51,520 .... G 6
Saint Austell, 25,500 .... C 7
Saint Helens, 105,310 .... E 4
Salisbury, 35,800 .... F 6
Saltburn-by-the-Sea, 13,920 .... G 3
Sandbach, 10,350 .... E 4
Sandown-Shanklin, 13,510 .... F 7
Scarborough, 42,190 .... G 3
Scunthorpe, 69,600 .... G 4
Seaford, 14,030 .... H 7
Seaham, 25,470 .... F 3
Selby, 10,670 .... F 4
Sevenoaks, 18,100 .... H 6
Sheerness, 13,770 .... H 6
Sheffield, 490,930 .... F 4
Shildon, 13,940 .... F 3
Shipley, 29,800 .... F 4
Shoreham-by-Sea, 18,050 .... G 7
Shrewsbury, 51,130 .... E 5
Sidmouth, 10,680 .... D 7
Sittingbourne and Milton, 25,480 .... H 6
Skegness, 12,560 .... H 4
Skelton and Brotton, 13,330 .... G 3
Skipton, 13,140 .... E 3
Slough, 84,900 .... G 6
Smethwick, 67,750 .... F 5
South Shields, 108,770 .... F 3
Southampton, 208,710 .... F 7
Southend-on-Sea, 165,780 .... H 6
Southport, 80,080 .... D 4
Southwick, 11,790 .... G 7
Spalding, 15,180 .... G 5
Spennymoor, 18,820 .... F 3
Stafford, 49,480 .... F 5
Stalybridge, 21,660 .... F 4
Stamford, 12,650 .... G 5
Stockport, 142,500 .... E 4
Stockton-on-Tees, 83,330 .... F 3
Stoke-on-Trent, 263,910 .... E 4
Stourbridge, 45,910 .... E 5
Stourport-on-Severn, 13,400 .... E 5
Stratford-on-Avon, 17,400 .... F 5
Stretford, 60,270 .... E 4
Stroud, 18,030 .... E 6
Sunderland, 189,630 .... F 3
Sutton-in-Ashfield, 40,500 .... F 4
Swindon, 97,460 .... F 6
Tamworth, 16,120 .... F 5
Taunton, 36,840 .... D 6
Teignmouth, 11,640 .... D 7
Thornaby-on-Tees, 22,770 .... F 3
Thurrock, 118,390 .... H 6
Tiverton, 13,450 .... D 7
Tonbridge, 26,030 .... H 6
Torquay, 52,220 .... D 7
Trowbridge, 16,490 .... E 6
Truro, 14,240 .... C 7
Tunbridge Wells (Royal Tunbridge Wells), 41,280 .... H 6
Tynemouth, 71,890 .... F 2
Ulverston, 10,370 .... D 3
Wakefield, 60,130 .... F 4
Wallasey, 103,320 .... D 4
Wallsend, 49,320 .... F 2
Walsall, 119,910 .... F 5
Ware, 12,460 .... H 6
Warminster, 10,420 .... E 6
Warrington, 75,110 .... E 4
Warwick, 16,870 .... F 5
Watford, 76,340 .... G 6
Wednesbury, 34,760 .... E 5
Wellingborough, 31,910 .... G 5
Wellington, 15,580 .... E 5
Welwyn (Welwyn Garden City), 39,560 .... G 6
Wenlock, 15,050 .... E 5
West Bromwich, 97,600 .... F 5
West Hartlepool, 78,360 .... G 3
Weston-super-Mare, 43,620 .... E 6
Weymouth and Melcombe Regis, 42,130 .... E 7
Whitby, 12,340 .... G 3
Whitehaven, 27,500 .... D 3
Whitley Bay, 38,140 .... F 2
Whitstable, 20,340 .... J 6
Widnes, 53,670 .... E 4
Wigan, 77,250 .... E 4
Wigston, 24,240 .... G 5
Wilmslow, 26,700 .... E 4
Winchester, 30,310 .... F 6
Windsor (New Windsor), 29,030 .... G 6
Winsford, 14,120 .... E 4
Wisbech, 17,520 .... G 5
Witham, 10,190 .... H 6
Woking, 74,230 .... G 6
Wokingham, 14,620 .... F 6
Wolverhampton, 150,200 .... E 5
Wolverton, 13,040 .... G 5
Wombwell, 19,010 .... F 4
Worcester, 67,580 .... F 5
Workington, 29,770 .... D 3
Worksop, 35,400 .... F 4
Worthing, 80,580 .... G 7
Yeovil, 25,140 .... E 7
York, 105,230 .... F 4

PHYSICAL FEATURES

Aire (river) .... F 4
Avon (river) .... F 5
Avon (river) .... F 6
Axe Edge (mt.) .... F 4
Ayre (point) .... C 3
Beachy (head) .... H 7
Bigbury (bay) .... C 7
Blackwater (river) .... J 6
Bridlington (bay) .... G 3
Bristol (channel) .... C 6
Brown Willy (mt.) .... C 7
Carter Fell (mt.) .... E 2
Cheviot (hills) .... E 2
Cornish Heights (hills) .... B 7
Cotswold (hills) .... E 6
Cross Fell (mt.) .... E 3
Cumbrian (mts.) .... D 3
Dartmoor (forest) .... C 7
Dee (river) .... D 4
Derwent (river) .... G 4
Don (river) .... F 4
Dorset Heights (hills) .... E 7
Dover (strait) .... J 6
Dukeries, The (dist.) .... F 4
Dungeness (prom.) .... J 7
East Anglian Heights (hills) .... H 5
Eddystone (rocks) .... C 7
Eden (river) .... E 3
English (channel) .... D 8
Esk (river) .... D 2
Exmoor (forest) .... D 6
Flamborough (head) .... H 3
Formby (head) .... D 4
Foulness (isl.), 316 .... J 6
Hartland (point) .... C 6
High Will Hays (mt.) .... C 7
Holy (Lindisfarne) (isl.), 190 .... F 2
Humber (river) .... H 4
Land's End (prom.) .... B 7
Liddel Water (river) .... F 2
Lincoln Wolds (hills) .... G 4
Lindisfarne (Holy) (isl.), 190 .... F 2
Little Ouse (river) .... H 5
Lizard (head) .... B 8
Lundy (isl.), 32 .... C 6
Lune (river) .... E 3
Lyme (bay) .... E 7
Manacles, The (rocks) .... C 7
Mendip (hills) .... E 6
Mersea (isl.), 3,416 .... J 6
Morte (point) .... C 6
Mounts (bay) .... B 8
Naze, The (prom.) .... J 6
Nene (river) .... H 5
New Forest (dist.) .... F 7
Nidd (river) .... F 3
North Foreland (prom.) .... J 6
North Tyne (river) .... E 2
Orfordness (prom.) .... J 5
Ouse (river) .... F 3
Ouse (river) .... H 5
Parrett (river) .... E 6
Peak, The (mt.) .... F 4
Peel Fell (mt.) .... E 2
Pennine (range) .... E 3
Portland (pen.) .... E 7
Prawle (point) .... D 7
Ribble (river) .... D 4
Saint Austell (bay) .... C 7
Saint Bees (head) .... D 3
Saint Mary's (isl.), 1,736 .... A 8
Scafell Pike (mt.) .... D 3
Scilly (isls.), 2,288 .... A 8
Selsey Bill (point) .... G 7
Severn (river) .... E 5
Sheppey (isl.), 27,211 .... H 6
Skiddaw (mt.) .... D 3
Sclent (channel) .... F 7
Solway (firth) .... D 3
South Downs (hills) .... G 7
South Tyne (river) .... E 3
Spithead (channel) .... F 7
Spurn (head) .... H 4
Swale (river) .... F 3
Tamar (river) .... C 7
Tees (river) .... F 3
Thames (river) .... H 6
Till (river) .... E 2
Trent (river) .... G 4
Tresco (isl.), 283 .... A 7
Trevose (head) .... B 7
Tweed (river) .... E 2
Tyne (river) .... F 3
Ure (river) .... F 3
Walney (isl.), 9,811 .... D 3
Wash, The (bay) .... H 4
Waveney (river) .... J 5
Wear (river) .... F 3
Wharfe (river) .... F 4
Widemouth (bay) .... C 7
Wight (isl.), 95,752 .... F 7
Witham (river) .... G 4
Wye (river) .... D 5
Yare (river) .... J 5

WALES

COUNTIES

Anglesey, 53,650 .... C 4
Breconshire, 54,320 .... D 6
Caernarvonshire, 119,820 .... C 5
Cardiganshire, 53,250 .... C 5
Carmarthenshire, 166,600 .... C 6
Denbighshire, 176,840 .... D 4
Flintshire, 155,150 .... D 4
Glamorganshire, 1,244,290 .... D 6
Merionethshire, 38,870 .... D 5
Monmouthshire, 456,230 .... E 6
Montgomeryshire, 43,720 .... D 5
Pembrokeshire, 95,350 .... C 6
Radnorshire, 18,300 .... D 5

CITIES and TOWNS

Aberayron, 1,220 .... C 5
Aberdare, 38,910 .... D 6
Abergavenny, 9,770 .... E 6
Abergele, 9,000 .... D 4
Abertillery, 24,760 .... E 6
Aberystwyth, 9,920 .... C 5
Amlwch, 3,270 .... C 4
Ammanford, 6,250 .... C 6
Bala, 1,640 .... D 5
Bangor, 14,200 .... C 4
Barmouth, 2,270 .... C 5
Barry, 42,460 .... D 6
Beaumaris, 1,930 .... C 4
Bethesda, 4,160 .... C 4
Betws-y-Coed, 770 .... C 4
Brecknock, 5,890 .... D 6
Bridgend, 15,180 .... D 6
Brynmawr, 6,410 .... D 6
Builth Wells, 1,600 .... D 5
Burry Port, 5,920 .... C 6
Caerleon, 5,390 .... E 6
Caernarvon, 9,170 .... C 4
Caerphilly, 36,890 .... D 6
Cardiff, 260,340 .... E 6
Cardigan, 3,850 .... C 5
Carmarthen, 12,820 .... C 6
Chepstow, 7,460 .... E 6
Colwyn Bay, 23,490 .... D 4
Conway, 11,430 .... D 4
Cowbridge, 1,140 .... D 6
Criccieth, 1,620 .... C 5
Cwmamman, 4,200 .... D 6
Denbigh, 8,370 .... D 4
Dolgellau, 2,490 .... D 5
Ebbw Vale, 28,100 .... D 6
Ffestiniog, 6,560 .... D 5
Fishguard and Goodwick, 4,940 .... B 6
Flint, 14,040 .... D 4
Goodwick (Fishguard and Goodwick), 4,940 .... B 5
Haverfordwest, 8,870 .... C 6
Hay, 1,320 .... D 5
Holyhead, 10,560 .... C 4
Holywell, 8,560 .... D 4
Kidwelly, 2,910 .... C 6
Knighton, 1,810 .... D 5
Lampeter, 2,080 .... C 5
Llandeilo, 1,930 .... C 6
Llandovery, 2,020 .... D 6
Llandrindod Wells, 3,160 .... D 5
Llandudno, 16,490 .... D 4
Llanelly, 29,270 .... C 6
Llanfairfechan, 3,010 .... C 4
Llanfyllin, 1,230 .... D 5
Llangefni, 3,300 .... C 4
Llangollen, 3,000 .... D 5
Llanidloes, 2,350 .... D 5
Llanrwst, 2,490 .... D 4
Llwchwr, 25,260 .... D 6
Machynlleth, 1,810 .... D 5
Menai Bridge, 2,230 .... C 4
Merthyr Tydfil, 58,310 .... D 6
Milford Haven, 12,960 .... B 6
Mold, 7,350 .... D 4
Monmouth, 5,820 .... E 6
Montgomery, 970 .... D 5
Mountain Ash, 29,510 .... D 6
Narberth, 1,050 .... C 6
Neath, 30,520 .... D 6
New Quay, 950 .... C 5
Newcastle Emlyn, 660 .... C 5
Newport, 107,590 .... E 6
Newtown, 5,490 .... D 5
Neyland, 2,180 .... C 6
Pembroke, 13,410 .... B 6
Penarth, 21,350 .... D 6
Penmaenmawr, 3,840 .... C 4
Pontypool, 39,000 .... E 6
Pontypridd, 35,160 .... D 6
Port Talbot, 51,750 .... D 6
Porthcawl, 11,880 .... D 6
Portmadoc, 3,930 .... C 5
Prestatyn, 12,070 .... D 4
Presteigne, 1,210 .... D 5
Pwllheli, 3,750 .... C 5
Rhondda, 99,130 .... D 6
Rhyl, 21,570 .... D 4
Risca, 15,200 .... D 6
Ruthin, 3,740 .... D 4
Swansea, 170,160 .... C 6
Tenby, 4,470 .... C 6
Towyn, 4,110 .... C 5
Welshpool, 6,460 .... D 5
Wrexham, 36,300 .... E 4

PHYSICAL FEATURES

Bardsey (isl.), 17 .... C 5
Berwyn (mts.) .... D 5
Braich-y-Pwll (prom.) .... C 5
Bristol (channel) .... E 5
Cader Idris (mts.) .... D 5
Caldy (isl.), 61 .... C 6
Cambrian (mts.) .... D 5
Cardigan (bay) .... C 5
Carmel (head) .... C 4
Clwyd (river) .... D 4
Dee (river) .... D 4
Gower (pen.), 12,656 .... C 6
Great Ormes (head) .... C 4
Holyhead (Holy) (isl.), 12,550 .... C 4
Lleyn (pen.), 20,394 .... C 5
Menai (strait) .... C 4
Pencilan (head) .... C 5
Plynlimmon (mt.) .... D 5
Ramsey (isl.) .... B 6
Saint Brides (bay) .... B 6
Saint David's (head) .... B 6
Saint George's (channel) .... B 5
Saint Gowans (head) .... B 6
Severn (river) .... D 5
Skerries (isls.) .... C 4
Skomer (isl.) .... B 6
Snowdon (mt.) .... D 4
Swansea (bay) .... C 6
Teifi (river) .... C 5
Towy (river) .... D 6
Tremadoc (bay) .... C 5
Usk (river) .... D 6
Wye (river) .... D 5

ISLE OF MAN

Total Population 48,000

CITIES and TOWNS

Douglas (cap.), 18,821 .... C 3
Onchan, 3,281 .... C 3
Peel, 2,483 .... C 3
Ramsey, 3,789 .... C 3

PHYSICAL FEATURES

Ayre (point) .... C 3
Calf of Man (isl.) .... B 3
Langness (prom.) .... C 3
Snaefell (mt.) .... C 3
Spanish (head) .... C 4

CHANNEL ISLANDS

Total Population 112,000

CITIES and TOWNS

Saint Anne, Alderney, †1,472 .... E 8
Saint Helier (cap.), Jersey, 26,594 .... E 8
Saint Peter Port (cap.), Guernsey, 15,706 .... E 8
Saint Sampson's, Guernsey, †5,917 .... E 8

PHYSICAL FEATURES

Alderney (isl.), 1,472 .... E 8
Guernsey (isl.), 45,028 .... E 8
Herm (isl.), 9,847 .... E 8
Jersey (isl.), 63,550 .... E 8
Sark (isl.), 560 .... E 8

*City and suburbs.
†Population of parish.

SCOTLAND

(map on page 15)

COUNTIES

Aberdeen, 321,426 .... L 5
Angus, 280,156 .... K 6
Argyll, 59,646 .... F 7
Ayr, 347,389 .... H 9
Banff, 46,041 .... K 5
Berwick, 22,044 .... L 8
Bute, 13,602 .... F 8
Caithness, 28,493 .... J 3
Clackmannan, 42,320 .... J 7
Dumfries, 88,472 .... J 9
Dunbarton, 197,437 .... G 7
East Lothian, 52,637 .... L 8
Fife, 321,110 .... K 7
Forfar (Angus), 280,156 .... K 6
Inverness, 81,165 .... G 5
Kincardine, 25,739 .... M 6
Kinross, 6,525 .... K 7
Kirkcudbright, 28,354 .... H 9
Lanark, 1,606,568 .... J 8
Midlothian, 592,033 .... K 8
Moray, 51,076 .... K 5
Nairn, 8,413 .... J 5
Orkney, 18,424 .... K 1
Peebles, 13,559 .... K 8
Perth, 126,912 .... H 7
Renfrew, 349,809 .... G 8
Ross and Cromarty, 57,568 .... F 4
Roxburgh, 42,946 .... L 9
Selkirk, 20,563 .... K 9
Stirling, 197,434 .... H 7
Sutherland, 13,313 .... G 3
West Lothian, 98,849 .... J 8
Wigtown, 28,658 .... G10
Zetland, 17,719 .... M 3

CITIES and TOWNS

Abbotsford .... L 8
Aberchirder, 797 .... L 4
Aberdeen, 185,034 .... N 5
Aberfeldy, 1,526 .... J 6
Aberfoyle, †1,316 .... H 7
Aberlour, 1,026 .... K 5
Abernethy, 580 .... K 7
Aboyne, ▲1,555 .... L 5
Acharacle, ▲314 .... E 6
Achiltibuie, ▲197 .... F 3
Achnasheen .... F 4
Airdrie, 34,911 .... D 2
Alexandria, ◉3,285 .... B 2
Alford, †1,180 .... L 5
Alloa, 13,989 .... E 1
Alloway .... G 9
Alness, †1,040 .... H 4
Alva, 4,074 .... J 7
Alyth, 1,803 .... K 6
Annan, 5,831 .... K10
Applecross, ▲254 .... E 5
Arbroath, 20,063 .... L 6
Ardgour, ▲179 .... F 6
Ardrishaig .... F 8
Ardrossan .... G 8
Ardvasar .... E 5
Arinagour .... C 6
Arisaig, ▲682 .... E 6
Armadale, 6,457 .... E 2
Arrochar, †740 .... G 7
Auchinleck, ▲5,890 .... H 9
Auchterarder, 2,440 .... J 7
Auchtermuchty, 1,399 .... K 7
Auldearn, ◉556 .... J 4
Aultbea .... E 4
Aviemore .... J 5
Avoch, †1,252 .... H 4
Ayr, 45,697 .... G 9
Ayton, ▲1,053 .... M 8
Badachro .... E 4
Badcall .... F 3
Ballachulish, ▲1,039 .... F 6
Ballantrae, †861 .... F 9
Ballater, 1,125 .... K 5
Balmaha .... C 1
Balmoral Castle, ▲377 .... K 5
Balquhidder, †637 .... H 7
Baltasound .... M 2
Banavie .... F 6
Banchory, 1,972 .... M 5
Banff, 3,318 .... L 4
Bannockburn, ◉3,090 .... D 1
Barr, †469 .... G 9
Barrhead, 16,129 .... C 2
Barvas, ▲3,703 .... D 3
Bathgate, 13,467 .... J 8
Bearsden, 19,902 .... C 2
Beauly, ◉1,387 .... G 5
Beith, †6,712 .... B 2
Bellshill, ▲24,569 .... D 2
Berriedale, ◉322 .... K 3
Bettyhill .... H 3
Biggar, 1,863 .... J 8
Birsay, ▲839 .... K 1
Bishopbriggs, 15,967 .... D 2
Blair-Atholl, ▲1,162 .... J 6
Blairgowrie and Rattray, 5,192 .... J 6
Blantyre, ▲17,506 .... D 2
Boddam .... N 5
Bonar Bridge, ▲927 .... H 4
Bo'ness, 13,262 .... J 7
Bonhill, ◉4,005 .... B 2
Bonnybridge, ◉7,192 .... D 2
Bonnyrigg and Lasswade, 6,737 .... K 8
Bower, †675 .... K 3
Bowmore, ▲1,289 .... D 8
Bracadale, ▲246 .... D 5
Braemar, ▲478 .... K 5
Brechin, 7,065 .... L 6
Bridge of Allan, 3,613 .... D 1
Broadford, ▲1,180 .... E 5
Brodick, ▲1,188 .... F 8
Brora .... J 3
Buckhaven and Methil, 20,600 .... L 7
Buckie, 7,695 .... L 4
Bunessan .... D 7
Burghead, 1,422 .... J 4
Burntisland, 5,945 .... K 7
Burravoe .... N 2
Cairn Ryan G10
Callander, 1,792 .... H 7
Cambuslang, †22,942 .... D 2
Campbeltown, 6,610 .... E 9
Cannich, ▲136 .... G 5
Canonbie, †1,354 .... K 9
Cargill, †1,215 .... K 7
Carloway, ▲628 .... C 3
Carluke, †11,929 .... E 2
Carnoustie, 5,472 .... L 6
Carnwath, 2,562 .... J 8
Carsphairn, †238 .... H 9
Carstairs Jct., †2,656 .... J 8
Castlebay, ◉1,032 .... B 6
Castle Douglas, 3,260 .... H10
Cawdor, ◉249 .... J 5
Ceres, †1,298 .... L 7
Chirnside, †1,111 .... M 8
Clackmannan, †3,030 .... J 7
Closeburn, †1,173 .... J 9
Clydebank, 50,385 .... C 2
Coatbridge, 54,688 .... D 2
Cockburnspath, †635 .... M 8
Cockenzie and Port Seton, 3,534 .... L 8
Coldingham, ▲1,674 .... M 8
Coldstream, 1,231 .... M 8
Colmonell, ▲705 .... G 9
Corpach .... F 6
Coupar Angus, 2,042 .... K 6
Cove and Kilcreggan, 962 .... B 1
Cowdenbeath, 11,438 .... K 7
Coylton, ▲1,617 .... H 9
Craignure .... E 7
Crail, 1,082 .... L 7
Crawford, ▲787 .... J 9
Creetown, ▲269 .... H10
Crieff, 5,661 .... J 7
Crinan .... E 7
Cromarty, 623 .... J 4
Cullen, 1,347 .... L 4
Cults, ◉3,910 .... M 5
Cumbernauld, 11,450 .... D 2
Cumnock and Holmhead, 5,709 .... H 9
Cupar, 5,958 .... K 7
Dalbeattie, 3,103 .... J10
Dalkeith, 9,058 .... K 8
Dalmally .... G 7
Dalmellington, ▲5,595 .... H 9
Dalry, Ayr, †6,507 .... B 2
Dalry, Kirkcudbright, †752 .... H 9
Dalwhinnie .... H 6
Darvel, 3,204 .... H 8
Daviot, †683 .... H 5
Denny and Dunipace, 8,017 .... D 1
Dingwall, 3,912 .... H 4
Dores, †512 .... H 5
Dornoch, 975 .... H 4
Douglas, ▲3,004 .... J 8
Doune, 791 .... H 7
Drummore G10
Dufftown, 1,528 .... K 5
Dumbarton, 26,496 .... B 2
Dumfries, 27,574 .... J 9
Dunbar, 4,292 .... M 8
Dunbeath, ◉402 .... K 3
Dunblane, 3,410 .... D 1
Dundee, 185,228 .... K 7
Dundonald, ▲2,187 .... H 8
Dunfermline, 49,555 .... J 7
Dunkeld, †733 .... J 6
Dunnet, †681 .... K 2
Dunnottar, ▲388 .... M 6
Dunoon, 9,308 .... A 2
Duns, 1,939 .... M 8
Dunscore, †876 .... J 9
Dunvegan .... D 5
Durness, ▲373 .... G 2
Dyce, †1,898 .... M 5
Earlston, †1,831 .... L 8
East Kilbride, 39,150 .... C 2
East Linton, 900 .... L 7
Ecclefechan .... K 9
Edderton, †376 .... H 4
Eddleston, †488 .... K 8
Edinburgh (cap.), 473,270 .... K 8
Edzell, †889 .... L 6
Elderslie, ◉5,476 .... C 2
Elgin, 12,277 .... K 4
Elie and Earlsferry, 930 .... L 7
Ellon, 1,485 .... M 5
Elvanfoot .... J 9
Eriboll .... G 3
Errol, †1,833 .... K 7
Ettrick, ▲218 .... K 9
Evanton .... H 4
Ewes, †183 .... K 9
Eyemouth, 2,197 .... M 8
Falkirk, 38,042 .... E 1
Fearn, †1,261 .... J 4
Fetteresso, ◉757 .... M 6
Findhorn .... K 4
Findochty, 1,300 .... K 4
Findon .... K 4
Fochabers, ◉1,193 .... K 4
Ford .... F 7
Fordoun, †1,377 .... M 6
Forfar, 10,150 .... L 6
Forres, 4,799 .... K 4
Fort Augustus, ▲887 .... G 5
Fort William, 2,775 .... F 6
Fortingall, ▲263 .... H 6
Fortrose, 930 .... H 4
Fraserburgh, 10,729 .... M 4
Gairloch, ◉758 .... E 4
Galashiels, 12,269 .... L 8
Galston, 3,991 .... H 8
Gardenstown, ◉986 .... M 4
Garelochhead, ◉2,276 .... A 1
Gatehouse-of-Fleet, 806 .... H10
Girvan, 6,194 .... G 9
Glamis, †753 .... L 6
Glasgow, 1,018,582 .... D 2
Glasgow, *1,795,638 .... D 2
Glenbarr .... E 8
Glenelg, ▲290 .... E 5
Glenisla, ▲250 .... K 6
Glenluce, †1,778 .... G10
Glenrothes, 16,000 .... K 7
Golspie, ◉1,167 .... H 4
Gourock, 10,169 .... B 2
Grangemouth, 20,425 .... J 8
Grantown-on-Spey, 1,597 .... J 5
Greenlaw, ◉778 .... M 8
Greenock, 74,492 .... A 2
Gretna Green, ◉1,930 .... K 9
Haddington, 5,645 .... L 8
Halkirk, †1,474 .... K 3
Hamilton, 43,967 .... D 2
Harris, ▲1,503 .... C 4
Hawick, 16,178 .... L 9
Helensburgh, 9,882 .... B 1
Helmsdale .... K 3
Hillswick .... M 2
Hobkirk, †568 .... L 9
Hopeman, ◉1,126 .... K 4
Howmore, ▲937 .... A 5
Huntly, 3,841 .... L 5
Hurlford, ▲1,000 .... H 8
Hutton, †469 .... K 9
Innerleithen, 2,261 .... K 8
Insch, †1,348 .... L 5
Insh, ▲1,189 .... J 5
Inveraray, 511 .... F 7
Inverbervie, 931 .... M 6
Invergordon, 1,780 .... H 4
Inverie, ▲128 .... E 5
Inverkeilor, †947 .... M 6
Inverkeithing, 3,978 .... K 7
Inverness, 30,266 .... H 5
Inverurie, 5,277 .... M 5
Irvine, 18,951 .... G 8
Jamestown, ◉5,692 .... C 1
Jedburgh, 3,679 .... M 9
John O'Groat's .... K 2
Johnshaven .... M 6
Johnstone, 19,876 .... B 2
Keiss, ▲553 .... K 2
Keith, 4,227 .... L 4
Kelso, 3,915 .... M 8
Kentallen .... F 6
Kilbarchan, ◉3,910 .... B 2
Kilbirnie, †8,733 .... B 2
Kilbride, ▲1,358 .... F 7
Kildonan, †1,207 .... J 3
Kildrummy, †273 .... L 5
Kilfinan, †1,095 ....
Killin, ▲863 ....
Kilmacolm, †4,528 ....
Kilmarnock, 48,273 ....
Kilmelfort, ▲148 ....
Kilmonivaig, ▲968 ....
Kilmory, ▲482 ....
Kilmuir, ▲365 ....
Kilninian, ▲285 ....
Kilrenny and Anstruther, 2,90
Kilsyth, 9,687 ....
Kilwinning, 7,468 ....
Kincardine, ▲579 ....
Kincardine O'Neil, †1,531 ....
Kingussie, 1,031 ....
Kinloch Rannoch ....
Kinlochbervie, ▲451 ....
Kinlochleven, ◉616 ....
Kinross, 2,345 ....
Kintail, ▲324 ....
Kintore, 794 ....
Kirkcaldy, 51,996 ....
Kirkcolm, †1,017 ....
Kirkcowan, †695 ....
Kirkcudbright, 2,563 ....
Kirkintilloch, 19,587 ....
Kirkoswald, ▲1,836 ....
Kirkpatrick, †934 ....
Kirkwall, 4,293 ....
Kirriemuir, 3,855 ....
Kyle of Lochalsh ....
Laggan, †551 ....
Lairg, †1,049 ....
Lamlash, ◉687 ....
Lanark, 8,369 ....
Langholm, 2,360 ....
Larbert, ◉3,627 ....
Largs, 8,893 ....
Larkhall, ▲16,996 ....
Latheron, ◉409 ....
Lauder, 612 ....
Laurencekirk, 1,436 ....
Leith, 51,378 ....
Lennoxtown, ◉3,161 ....
Lerwick, 5,729 ....
Leslie, 3,301 ....
Lesmahagow, ▲8,322 ....
Leuchars, †3,631 ....
Leven, 8,739 ....
Leverburgh, ▲990 ....
Linlithgow, 4,819 ....
Lochaline ....
Lochboisdale, ▲1,406 ....
Lochbroom, ◉1,400 ....
Lochcarron, †707 ....
Lochgelly, 8,772 ....
Lochgilphead, 1,275 ....
Lochinver ....
Lochmaben, 1,286 ....
Lochmaddy, ◉865 ....
Lochranza, ◉283 ....
Lochwinnoch, †3,885 ....
Lockerbie, 2,890 ....
Logierait, ▲914 ....
Lossiemouth and Branderburgh, 6,109 ....
Loth, †207 ....
Luss, ▲451 ....
Lybster, ◉826 ....
Macduff, 3,520 ....
Mallaig ....
Markinch, 2,444 ....
Marykirk, †1,076 ....
Mauchline, †4,453 ....
Maybole, 4,657 ....
Meigle, †1,001 ....
Melness ....
Melrose, 2,189 ....
Melvaig ....
Melvich ....
Methlick, †1,254 ....
Methven, †1,530 ....
Mid Yell ....
Millport, 1,279 ....
Milngavie, 9,097 ....
Moffat, 2,002 ....
Moniaive ....
Monifieth, 3,665 ....
Montrose, 10,783 ....
Motherwell and Wishaw, 76,249 ....
Moulin, ▲586 ....
Muirkirk, †3,657 ....
Musselburgh, 17,805 ....
Muthill, †1,197 ....
Nairn, 4,985 ....
Neilston, ◉3,340 ....
New Abbey, †773 ....
Newarthill, ◉6,755 ....
Newburgh, Aberdeen .... N
Newburgh, Fife, 2,293 .... K
New Cumnock, †6,927 .... H
New Deer, ▲2,620 .... M
New Galloway, 337 .... H
Newmilns and Greenholm, 3,433 .... H
Newport on Tay, 3,382 L
Newton-Stewart, 1,949 .... G
Nigg, †454 .... J
North Berwick, 3,860 L
Oban, 6,554 .... F
Old Meldrum, 1,087 .... M
Orphir, †507 .... K
Oykell Bridge, ▲120 .... G
Paisley, 96,637 C
Peebles, 5,416 .... K
Penicuik, 6,578 .... K
Perth, 41,497 .... J
Peterhead, 13,097 .... N
Pierowall .... K
Pitlochry, 2,445 .... J
Pittenweem, 1,568 L
Plockton .... E
Poolewe, ◉1,013 .... E
Port Appin .... F
Portaskaig .... D
Port Ellen .... D
Port Erroll .... N
Port Glasgow, 22,524 .... B
Portknockie, 1,189 L
Portlethen, ▲932 .... M
Portmahomack, †608 .... J
Portobello, 27,141 .... K
Port of Ness .... D
Portpatrick, †1,061 .... F
Portree, ▲1,753 .... D
Portsoy, 1,739 L
Port William .... G
Prestonpans, 3,183 L
Prestwick, 12,501 .... G
Queensferry, 3,067 .... K
Quendale .... M
Rackwick .... K
Reay, †865 .... J
Renfrew, 18,234 C
Renton, ◉4,011 .... B
Rhynie, †597 L
Rogart, †463 .... H
Rosehearty, 1,114 .... M
Rosneath, ▲794 .... A
Rothes, 1,087 .... K
Rothesay, 6,934 .... F
Rothiemay, †678 L
Rutherglen, 26,023 C
Ruthwell, †563 .... K
Saddell, ▲638 .... E

(continued on page 14)

United Kingdom and Ireland
(continued)

SCOTLAND (continued)

Saint Andrews, 10,350 ... L 7
Saint Boswells, †1,353 ... L 8
Saint Combs ... N 4
Saint Cyrus, †997 ... M 6
Saint Margaret's Hope ... L 2
Saint Mary's ... L 2
Saint Ninians, △14,774 ... D 1
Salen, △393 ... E 7
Saltcoats, 14,353 ... G 8
Sandness, △180 ... M 3
Sandwick, △1,171 ... N 3
Sanquhar, 2,133 ... J 9
Scalasaig ... D 7
Scalloway ... M 3
Scarinish ... C 7
Scone, ◉2,977 ... K 7
Scourie, △288 ... F 3
Scrabster, ◉503 ... J 2
Selkirk, 5,571 ... L 8
Shieldaig, △304 ... E 5
Shotts, △9,466 ... E 2
Skipness, △163 ... F 8
Snizort, △607 ... D 5
Stevenston, 10,632 ... G 8
Stewarton, 3,411 ... H 8
Stirling, 27,503 ... D 1
Stonehaven, 4,430 ... M 6
Stonehouse, †4,051 ... M 8
Stoneykirk, †1,701 ... G10
Stornoway, 5,248 ... C 3
Stow, †1,099 ... L 8
Strachur, †580 ... F 7
Stranraer, 9,355 ... G10
Strathaven ... H 8
Strathdon, †656 ... L 5
Strichen, △6,577 ... M 4
Stromness, 1,593 ... K 2
Strontian, △227 ... E 6
Tain, 1,721 ... H 4
Talisker ... C 5
Tarbert, △421 ... F 8
Tarbert (Harris), △1,503 ... C 4
Tarland, †638 ... L 5
Tayport, 3,044 ... L 7
Thornhill, ◉1,441 ... J 9
Thurso, 9190 ... K 2
Tillicoultry, 4,039 ... J 7
Tobermory, 634 ... D 6
Tomdoun ... F 5
Tomintoul, △355 ... K 5
Tongue, †707 ... H 3
Torridon ... F 5
Tranent, 6,427 ... L 8
Traquair, †394 ... K 8
Troon, 9,955 ... G 8
Turriff, 2,768 ... M 4
Tweedsmuir, †153 ... J 9
Uig, Inverness ... D 4
Uig, Ross and Cromarty, △907 ... B 3
Ullapool, ◉1,138 ... F 4
Voe ... M 3
Walls, △372 ... M 3
West Calder, ◉1,058 ... K 8
West Kilbride, †4,396 ... G 8
West Linton, †1,618 ... K 8
Whitburn, 7,791 ... E 2
Whithorn, 1,020 ... H10
Wick, 7,545 ... K 3
Wigtown, 1,201 ... H10
Yarrow, †342 ... K 8
Yetholm, †651 ... M 8

PHYSICAL FEATURES

Abbey (head) ... J10
A'Chralaig (mt.) ... F 5
Affric (lake) ... G 5
Ailsa Craig (isl.), 10 ... F 9
Aird (pt.) ... D 4
Almond (riv.) ... J 7
Alness (riv.) ... H 4
Alsh (inlet) ... E 5
Annan (riv.) ... K 9
Appin (dist.), 429 ... F 6
Ardgour (dist.), 299 ... F 6
Ardivachar (pt.) ... A 5
Ardle (riv.) ... K 6
Ardnamurchan (dist.), 772 ... D 6
Ardnamurchan (pt.) ... D 6
Argyll (dist.), 4,900 ... F 7
Arisaig (dist.), 682 ... E 6
Arisaig (sound) ... E 6
Arkaig (lake) ... F 6
Arran (isl.), 3,450 ... F 8
Ascrib (isls.) ... C 4
Askival (mt.) ... D 6
Assynt (dist.), 800 ... F 3
Assynt (lake) ... G 3
Auskerry (isl.), 3 ... M 1
Avon (riv.) ... K 5
Awe (lake) ... F 7
Ayr (riv.) ... H 9
Badenoch (dist.), 6,473 ... H 6
Baleshare (isl.), 59 ... A 4
Barra (head) ... A 6
Barra (isl.), 1,369 ... A 5
Barra (isls.), 1,467 ... B 6
Barra (passg.) ... B 6
Barra (sound) ... A 5
Battock (mt.) ... L 6
Beauly (firth) ... H 5
Beauly (riv.) ... H 5
Beinn Bheigeir (mt.) ... D 8
Bell Rock (isl.), 3 ... M 7
Ben Alder (mt.) ... G 6
Ben Avon (mt.) ... K 5
Benbecula (isl.), 1,358 ... A 5
Benbecula (sound) ... A 5
Ben Dearg (mt.) ... G 4
Benderloch (dist.) ... F 7
Beneveian (lake) ... G 5
Ben Griam More (mt.) ... H 3
Ben Hee (mt.) ... G 3
Ben Hope (mt.) ... G 3
Ben Klibreck (mt.) ... H 3
Ben Lawers (mt.) ... H 6
Ben Macdhui (mt.) ... J 5
Ben Mhor (mt.) ... B 5
Ben More (mt.), Argyll ... E 7
Ben More (mt.), Perth ... G 7
Ben More Assynt (mt.) ... G 3
Ben Nevis (mt.) ... F 6
Ben Vorlich (mt.) ... H 7
Ben Wyvis (mt.) ... G 4
Berneray (isl.), 3 ... A 6
Berneray (isl.), 201 ... B 4
Black Isle (dist.), 5,673 ... H 4
Blackwater (res.) ... G 6
Boisdale (inlet) ... B 5
Boreray (isl.), 5 ... B 4
Boreray (isl.) ... B 8
Bracadale (inlet) ... C 5
Braemar (dist.), 5,091 ... K 5
Bran (falls) ... J 6
Breadalbane (dist.) ... H 7
Bressay (isl.), 300 ... N 3
Brims Ness (prom.) ... J 2
Broad (bay) ... D 3
Broad Law (mt.) ... K 9
Broom (inlet) ... F 4
Brora (riv.) ... H 3
Brough (head) ... K 1
Brough Ness (prom.) ... L 2
Buchan (dist.), 53,172 ... M 4
Buchan Ness (prom.) ... N 5
Buddon Ness (prom.) ... L 7
Burrow (head) ... H10
Bute (isl.), 8,784 ... F 8
Bute (sound) ... F 8
Butt of Lewis (prom.) ... D 3
Cairn Gorm (mt.) ... J 5
Cairngorm (mts.) ... J 5
Cairnsmore (mt.) ... H 9
Cairntoul (mt.) ... J 5
Caledonian (canal) ... G 5
Canna (isl.), 24 ... C 5
Canna (sound) ... C 6
Caolisport (inlet) ... E 8
Carn Eige (mt.) ... F 5
Carn Mor (mt.) ... K 5
Carrick (dist.), 21,867 ... G 9
Carron (inlet) ... E 5
Carron (river) ... G 4
Cellar (head) ... D 3
Cheviot (hills) ... L 9
Clar Nan (lake) ... J 3
Clisham (mt.) ... C 4
Clyde (falls) ... J 8
Clyde (firth) ... F 9
Clyde (river) ... G 8
Cnoc Moy (mt.) ... E 9
Coire (lake) ... H 3
Coll (isl.), 147 ... C 6
Colonsay (isl.), 164 ... C 6
Conon (river) ... H 4
Copinsay (isl.), 3 ... L 2
Corryvreckan (gulf) ... E 7
Corsewall (pt.) ... F 9
Cowal (dist.), 16,808 ... F 7
Creag Meagaidh (mt.) ... G 6
Cree (river) ... G 9
Creran (inlet) ... F 7
Cromarty (firth) ... H 4
Cuillin (hills) ... D 5
Cuillin (sound) ... D 5
Cumbraes (isls.), 1,329 ... A 2
Dee (riv.) ... H 9
Dee (riv.) ... M 5
Dennis (head) ... M 1
Deveron (riv.) ... L 5
Dhuheartach (isl.), 3 ... C 7
Don (riv.) ... L 5
Doon (lake) ... G 9
Doon (riv.) ... G 9
Dornoch (firth) ... J 4
Duich (inlet) ... F 5
Duirinish (dist.), 1,070 ... C 5
Dulnain (riv.) ... J 5
Dun (isl.) ... B 8
Duncansby (head) ... L 2
Dunnet (bay) ... J 2
Dunnet (head) ... J 2
Dunvegan (head) ... C 4
Dunvegan (inlet) ... C 4
Durness, Kyle of (inlet) ... G 2
Earn (lake) ... H 7
Earn (riv.) ... J 7
East Loch Tarbert (inlet) ... C 4
Eck (lake) ... F 7
Eday (isl.), 200 ... L 1
Eddrachillis (bay) ... F 3
Eden (riv.) ... L 7
Egilsay (isl.), 54 ... L 1
Eigg (isl.), 74 ... D 6
Eigg (sound) ... D 6
Eil (inlet) ... F 6
Eishort (inlet) ... D 5
Enard (bay) ... F 3
Eport (inlet) ... B 4
Eriboll (inlet) ... G 2
Ericht (lake) ... H 6
Eriskay (isl.), 231 ... B 5
Erisort (inlet) ... D 3
Esk (riv.) ... L 9
Etive (inlet) ... F 7
Ettrick Pen (mt.) ... K 9
Ewe (inlet) ... E 4
Eye (pen.) ... D 3
Eynhallow (sound) ... K 1
Eynort (inlet) ... B 5
Fair (isl.), 64 ... L 3
Fannich (lake) ... F 4
Farrar (riv.) ... G 5
Fetlar (isl.), 100 ... N 2
Fife Ness (prom.) ... L 7
Findhorn (riv.) ... J 5
Fionn (lake) ... F 4
Fladdachuain (isl.) ... D 4
Flannan (isls.), 3 ... A 3
Fleet (inlet) ... J 4
Foinaven (mt.) ... G 3
Formartine (dist.), 15,010 ... M 5
Forth (firth) ... L 7
Forth (riv.) ... H 7
Forth and Clyde (canal) ... H 8
Foula (isl.), 54 ... L 3
Foyers (falls) ... H 5
Fyne (inlet) ... F 8
Gair (inlet) ... E 4
Gairloch (dist.), 1,750 ... E 4
Gallan (head) ... B 3
Galloway (dist.), 57,012 ... H10
Galloway, Mull of (prom.) ... G10
Garioch (dist.), 7,950 ... L 5
Garry (lake) ... G 5
Garry (riv.) ... J 6
Gasker (isl.) ... B 4
Gigha (isl.), 163 ... E 8
Gigha (passg.) ... E 8
Gigha (sound) ... E 8
Girdle Ness (prom.) ... N 5
Glas Maol (mt.) ... K 6
Glass (lake) ... G 4
Glass (riv.) ... G 5
Glenelg (dist.), 413 ... E 5
Goat Fell (mt.) ... F 8
Grampian (mts.) ... G 6
Great Bernera (isl.), 317 ... C 3
Greenstone (pt.) ... E 4
Grimsay (isl.), 239 ... B 5
Gruinard (bay) ... E 4
Gruinard (dist.) ... F 4
Gruinart (inlet) ... D 8
Gulvain (mt.) ... F 6
Gunna (isl.) ... C 6
Gunna (sound) ... C 6
Halladale (riv.) ... J 3
Handa (isl.) ... F 3
Harris (dist.), 2,493 ... C 4
Harris (sound) ... B 4
Haskeir (isls.) ... A 4
Hebrides (isls.), 49,234 ... A 5
Hebrides, Inner (isls.), 16,625 ... D 5
Hebrides, Outer (isls.), 32,609 ... A 5
Hebrides (sea) ... C 5
Helmsdale (riv.) ... J 3
Herma Ness (prom.) ... M 2
Holm (sound) ... L 2
Holy (isl.), 7 ... F 9
Holy Loch (inlet) ... F 8
Hope (lake) ... G 3
Hourn (inlet) ... F 5
Hoy (isl.), 511 ... K 2
Hoy (sound) ... K 2
Hynish (bay) ... C 7
Inchard (inlet) ... F 3
Inchkeith (isl.), 3 ... K 7
Indaal (inlet) ... D 8
Inner (sound) ... E 5
Inner Hebrides (isls.), 16,625 ... D 5
Inver (inlet) ... F 3
Iona (isl.), 130 ... D 7
Iona (sound) ... D 7
Isla (riv.) ... K 6
Islay (isl.), 3,850 ... D 8
Islay (sound) ... D 8
Jura (isl.), 249 ... E 7
Jura (sound) ... E 7
Katrine (lake) ... G 7
Keal, Na (inlet) ... D 7
Kebock (head) ... D 3
Kilbrennan (sound) ... F 9
Kinnairds (head) ... N 4
Kintyre (dist.), 11,660 ... E 9
Kintyre, Mull of (prom.) ... E 9
Knapdale (dist.), 2,711 ... E 8
Knoydart (dist.), 1,234 ... E 5
Kyle (dist.) ... H 9
Laggan (bay) ... D 8
Lammermuir (hills) ... L 8
Langavat (lake) ... C 3
Laxford (inlet) ... F 3
Lennox (hills) ... C 1
Leven (inlet) ... F 6
Leven (lake) ... K 7
Lewis (dist.), 21,548 ... C 3
Lewis, Butt of (prom.) ... D 3
Liddel Water (riv.) ... L 9
Linnhe (inlet) ... F 6
Lismore (isl.), 155 ... F 7
Little Minch (sound) ... C 4
Lochaber (dist.), 7,591 ... F 6
Lochalsh (dist.), 1,651 ... E 5
Lochnager (mt.) ... K 6
Lochy (lake) ... G 6
Lomond (lake) ... G 7
Long (inlet) ... B 1
Longa (isl.) ... E 4
Lorne (dist.), 12,656 ... F 7
Lorne (firth) ... E 7
Lothians (dist.) ... K 8
Loyal (lake) ... H 3
Lubnaig (lake) ... H 7
Luce (bay) ... G10
Lyon (riv.) ... H 6
Maddy (inlet) ... B 4
Mainland (isl.), 13,282 ... N 3
Mainland (Pomona) (isl.), 13,495 ... K 1
Mam Soul (mt.) ... F 5
Mar (dist.), 16,918 ... E 4
Maree (lake) ... F 4
May (isl.), 7 ... M 7
Merrick (mt.) ... H 9
Mhor (lake) ... H 5
Minginish (dist.), 578 ... D 5
Mingulay (isl.) ... A 6
Moidart (dist.), 247 ... E 6
Monach (isls.) ... A 4
Monach (sound) ... A 4
Monadhliath (mts.) ... H 5
Monar (lake) ... F 5
Morar (dist.), 1,106 ... E 6
Morar (lake) ... E 6
Moray (firth) ... J 4
More (lake) ... G 3
Moriston (riv.) ... G 5
Morven (dist.), 420 ... E 6
Morven (mt.) ... J 3
Muck (isl.), 29 ... D 6
Muirnag (hill) ... D 3
Mull (head) ... L 1
Mull (head) ... L 2
Mull (isl.), 2,234 ... E 7
Mull (sound) ... E 7
Nairn (riv.) ... J 5
Na Keal (inlet) ... D 7
Nan Clar (lake) ... J 3
Naver (lake) ... H 3
Naver (riv.) ... H 3
Neave (isl.) ... H 2
Neist (pt.) ... C 5
Ness (lake) ... H 5
Ness (riv.) ... H 5
Nevis (inlet) ... E 5
Nith (riv.) ... J 9
North (chan.) ... E 9
North (sound) ... L 1
North Esk (riv.) ... L 6
North Minch (sound) ... E 3
North Ronaldsay (firth) ... M 1
North Ronaldsay (isl.), 150 ... M 1
North Uist (isl.), 1,620 ... A 4
Noss (head) ... L 3
Noup (head) ... K 1
Oa, Mull of (prom.) ... D 8
Ochil (hills) ... J 7
Oich (riv.) ... G 5
Oigh Sgeir (isl.), 3 ... C 6
Oldany (isl.) ... F 3
Orchy (riv.) ... G 7
Orkney (isls.), 18,424 ... J 1
Oronsay (isl.), 2 ... D 7
Oronsay (passg.) ... D 7
Orrin (riv.) ... G 5
Outer Hebrides (isls.), 32,609 ... A 5
Oykell (riv.) ... G 4
Pabbay (isl.) ... A 6
Pabbay (isl.), 2 ... B 4
Papa Stour (isl.), 55 ... L 3
Papa Westray (isl.), 139 ... L 1
Paps of Jura (peaks) ... E 8
Park (dist.), 797 ... C 3
Peel Fell (mt.) ... L 9
Pentland (firth) ... K 2
Pladda (isl.), 6 ... F 9
Pomona (isl.), 13,495 ... K 1
Priest (isl.) ... E 4
Queensberry (mt.) ... J 9
Quoich (lake) ... F 5
Raasay (isl.), 211 ... D 5
Raasay (sound) ... D 5
Rannoch (dist.), 832 ... H 6
Rannoch (lake) ... H 6
Rattray (head) ... N 4
Renish (pt.) ... C 4
Resort (inlet) ... B 3
Rhinns (pt.) ... C 8
Rhu Coigach (cape) ... E 3
Roag (inlet) ... C 3
Roan (isl.) ... H 2
Rona (isl.) ... B 7
Rona (isl.), 49 ... D 4
Ronay (isl.) ... B 5
Ross of Mull (pen.), 471 ... D 7
Rousay (isl.), 237 ... K 1
Rudha Hunish (cape) ... D 4
Rudh Re (cape) ... E 4
Rum (isl.), 40 ... D 6
Rum (sound) ... D 6
Ryan (inlet) ... F 9
Saint Abbs (head) ... M 8
Saint Andrews (bay) ... L 7
Saint Kilda (isl.), 65 ... B 8
Saint Magnus (bay) ... M 3
Saint Mary's Loch (lake) ... K 9
Sanda (isl.), 7 ... E 9
Sanday (isl.), Inverness ... D 5
Sanday (isl.), Orkney, 650 ... M 1
Sanday (sound) ... L 1
Sandray (isl.) ... B 6
Scalpay (isl.), 470 ... C 4
Scalpay (isl.), 2 ... E 5
Scapa Flow (chan.) ... K 2
Scarba (isl.), 5 ... E 7
Scarp (isl.), 46 ... B 3
Scavaig (inlet) ... D 5
Scradain (inlet) ... D 7
Scurdie Ness (prom.) ... M 6
Seaforth (inlet) ... C 4
Sgurr a Choir Ghlais (mt.) ... G 5
Sgurr Mor (mt.) ... F 4
Sgurr Na Ciche (mt.) ... F 5
Sgurr Na Lapaich (mt.) ... F 5
Shapinsay (isl.), 400 ... L 1
Shee Water (riv.) ... J 6
Shell (inlet) ... D 4
Shetland (isls.), 17,719 ... M 3
Shiant (isls.) ... D 4
Shiel (lake) ... E 6
Shin (falls) ... H 4
Shin (lake) ... G 3
Shona (isl.), 11 ... E 6
Sidlaw (hills) ... K 6
Sinclair's (bay) ... K 2
Skeir Graitich (isl.) ... D 4
Skerryvore (isl.), 3 ...
Skye (isl.), 7,400 ...
Sleat (dist.), 523 ...
Sleat (pt.) ...
Sleat (sound) ...
Small (isls.), 170 ...
Snizort (inlet) ...
Soa (isl.) ...
Soay (isl.) ...
Soay (isl.), 11 ...
Solway (firth) ...
South Esk (riv.) ...
South Ronaldsay (isl.), 980 ...
South Uist (isl.), 2,376 ...
Spean (riv.) ...
Spey (riv.) ...
Staffa (isl.) ...
Staffin (bay) ...
Start (pt.) ... M
Stinchar (riv.) ... C
Stoer (pt.) ... F
Stornoway (harb.) ... D
Storr, The (mt.) ... D
Strathbogie (dist.), 9,152 ... L
Strathmore (dist.) ...
Strathy (pt.) ... H
Stroma (isl.), 12 ... K
Stronsay (firth) ... L
Stronsay (isl.), 500 ... M
Sulisker (isl.) ... B
Sumburgh (head) ... M
Summer (isls.) ... E
Sunart (inlet) ... E
Swona (isl.), 3 ... K
Taransay (isl.), 5 ... B
Tarbat Ness (prom.) ... J
Tarbert (inlet) ... D
Tay (firth) ... L
Tay (lake) ... H
Tay (riv.) ... K
Teith (riv.) ... H
Teviot (riv.) ... L
Texa (isl.) ... D
Thurso (riv.) ... J
Tilt (riv.) ... J
Tiree (isl.), 993 ... C
Tirry (riv.) ... H
Tiumpan (head) ... D
Toe (head) ... B
Tolsta (head) ... D
Ton Mhor (pt.) ... C
Tongue, Kyle of (inlet) ... G
Tor Ness (prom.) ... K
Torridon (inlet) ... E
Treig (lake) ... G
Treshnish (isls.) ... C
Trodday (isl.) ... D
Trossachs, The (valley) ... H
Trotternish (dist.), 389 ... D
Troup (head) ... M
Tuath (inlet) ... D
Tummel (falls) ... J
Tummel (river) ... J
Turnberry (pt.) ... G
Tweed (riv.) ... M
Tyne (riv.) ... M
Ugie (riv.) ... N
Ulva (isl.), 28 ... D
Unst (isl.), 1,200 ... N
Vallay (isl.) ... A 4
Vaternish (dist.), 198 ... C 4
Vaternish (pt.) ... C 4
Vatersay (isl.), 95 ... A 6
Voil (lake) ... G 7
Watten (lake) ... K 3
West Burra (isl.), 561 ... M 3
West Loch Tarbert (inlet) ... B 4
Westray (firth) ... K 1
Westray (isl.), 872 ... K 1
Whalsay (isl.), 764 ... N 3
Whiten (head) ... G 2
Wiay (isl.) ... B 5
Wide (firth) ... L 1
Wigtown (bay) ... H10
Wrath (cape) ... F 2
Yarrow Water (riv.) ... L 8
Yell (isl.), 1,150 ... M 2
Yell (sound) ... M 2
Ythan (riv.) ... M 5

*City and suburbs.
†Population of parish.
△Population of subdistrict or division.
◉Population of district.

AGRICULTURE, INDUSTRY and RESOURCES

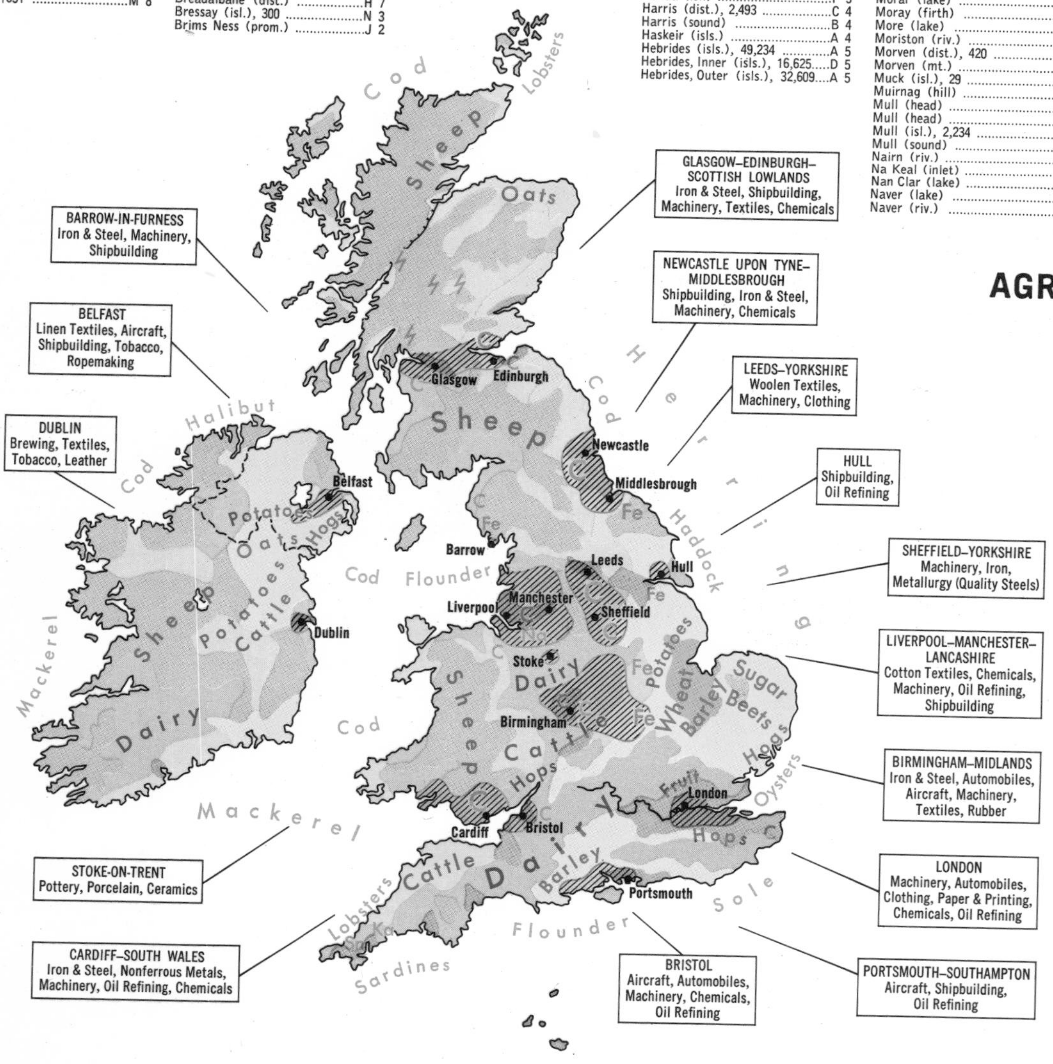

GLASGOW–EDINBURGH–SCOTTISH LOWLANDS
Iron & Steel, Shipbuilding, Machinery, Textiles, Chemicals
BARROW-IN-FURNESS
Iron & Steel, Machinery, Shipbuilding
NEWCASTLE UPON TYNE–MIDDLESBROUGH
Shipbuilding, Iron & Steel, Machinery, Chemicals
BELFAST
Linen Textiles, Aircraft, Shipbuilding, Tobacco, Ropemaking
LEEDS–YORKSHIRE
Woolen Textiles, Machinery, Clothing
DUBLIN
Brewing, Textiles, Tobacco, Leather
HULL
Shipbuilding, Oil Refining
SHEFFIELD–YORKSHIRE
Machinery, Iron, Metallurgy (Quality Steels)
LIVERPOOL–MANCHESTER–LANCASHIRE
Cotton Textiles, Chemicals, Machinery, Oil Refining, Shipbuilding
BIRMINGHAM–MIDLANDS
Iron & Steel, Automobiles, Aircraft, Machinery, Textiles, Rubber
STOKE-ON-TRENT
Pottery, Porcelain, Ceramics
LONDON
Machinery, Automobiles, Clothing, Paper & Printing, Chemicals, Oil Refining
CARDIFF–SOUTH WALES
Iron & Steel, Nonferrous Metals, Machinery, Oil Refining, Chemicals
BRISTOL
Aircraft, Automobiles, Machinery, Chemicals, Oil Refining
PORTSMOUTH–SOUTHAMPTON
Aircraft, Shipbuilding, Oil Refining
Cod
Lobsters
Oats
Sheep
Glasgow
Edinburgh
Halibut
Herring
Haddock
Newcastle
Middlesbrough
Belfast
Potatoes
Hogs
Barrow
Flounder
Leeds
Hull
Manchester
Liverpool
Sheffield
Dublin
Cattle
Mackerel
Dairy
Stoke
Birmingham
Wheat
Barley
Sugar Beets
Fruit
London
Oysters
Cardiff
Bristol
Portsmouth
Sole
Sardines

DOMINANT LAND USE

- Cereals (chiefly oats, barley)
- Truck Farming, Horticulture
- Dairy, Mixed Farming
- Livestock, Mixed Farming
- Pasture Livestock

MAJOR MINERAL OCCURRENCES

- C — Coal
- Fe — Iron Ore
- Ka — Kaolin (china clay)
- Na — Salt
- Sn — Tin
- Water Power
- Major Industrial Areas

SCOTLAND

CONIC PROJECTION

SCALE OF MILES

SCALE OF KILOMETRES

Capital .... ★   County Boundaries ----
County Seats .... ▲   Canals ....

Copyright by C.S. HAMMOND & CO., N.Y.

United Kingdom and Ireland
(continued)

IRELAND

COUNTIES

Carlow, 33,342 ... H 6
Cavan, 56,594 ... G 4
Clare, 73,702 ... D 6
Cork, 330,443 ... D 7
Galway, 149,887 ... D 5
Donegal, 113,842 ... F 2
Dublin, 718,332 ... J 5
Kerry, 116,458 ... B 7
Kildare, 64,402 ... H 5
Kilkenny, 61,668 ... G 6
Laoighis, 45,069 ... G 6
Leitrim, 33,470 ... E 3
Leix (Laoighis), 45,069 ... G 6
Limerick, 133,339 ... D 7
Longford, 30,643 ... F 4
Louth, 67,378 ... J 4
Mayo, 123,330 ... C 4
Meath, 65,122 ... H 4
Monaghan, 47,088 ... H 3
Offaly, 51,533 ... F 5
Roscommon, 59,217 ... E 4
Sligo, 53,561 ... D 3
Tipperary, 123,822 ... F 6
Waterford, 71,439 ... F 7
Westmeath, 52,861 ... G 5
Wexford, 83,308 ... H 7
Wicklow, 58,473 ... J 5

CITIES and TOWNS

Abbeydorney, 164 ... B 7
Abbeyfeale, 1,272 ... C 7
Abbeylara, 113 ... F 4
Abbeyleix, 1,085 ... G 6
Achill Sound, 277 ... B 4
Aclare, 117 ... D 3
Adare, 590 ... D 6
Aghadoe, †371 ... C 7
Aghagower, †558 ... C 4
Ahascragh, 234 ... E 5
Annagassan, 194 ... J 4
Annascaul, 212 ... B 7
An Uaimh, 3,998 ... H 4
Ardagh, Limerick, 122 ... C 7
Ardagh, Longford, 102 ... F 4
Ardara, 547 ... E 2
Ardee, 2,710 ... H 4
Ardfinnan, 428 ... F 7
Ardmore, 290 ... F 8
Ardrahan, †266 ... D 5
Arklow, 5,390 ... J 6
Arthurstown, 136 ... H 7
Arva, 512 ... F 4
Ashford, 309 ... J 5
Askeaton, 706 ... D 6
Athboy, 680 ... H 4
Athea, 299 ... C 7
Athenry, 1,266 ... D 5
Athleague, 132 ... E 4
Athlone, 9,624 ... F 5
Athy, 3,842 ... H 6
Aughrim, 528 ... J 6
Avoca, 248 ... J 6
Bagenalstown (Muinebeag), 2,071 ... H 6
Baile Atha Cliath (Dublin) (cap.), 537,448 ... K 5
Bailieborough, 1,136 ... G 4
Balbriggan, 2,943 ... J 4
Balla, 324 ... C 4
Ballaghaderreen, 1,308 ... E 4
Ballina, 6,027 ... C 3
Ballinagh, 389 ... G 4
Ballinakill, 315 ... G 6
Ballinamore, 793 ... F 3
Ballinasloe, 5,711 ... E 5
Ballincollig, 960 ... D 8
Ballindine, 222 ... C 4
Ballingarry, Limerick, 360 ... D 7
Ballingarry, Tipperary, 209 ... F 6
Ballinlough, 252 ... D 4
Ballinrobe, 1,165 ... C 4
Ballintober, †938 ... E 4
Ballintra, 250 ... E 2
Ballisodare, 529 ... E 3
Ballybay, 716 ... G 3
Ballybofey, 1,030 ... F 2
Ballybunion, 1,163 ... B 7
Ballycanew, 168 ... J 6
Ballycarney, †309 ... J 6
Ballycastle, 191 ... C 3
Ballyconnell, 592 ... F 3
Ballycotton, 412 ... E 8
Ballydehob, 303 ... C 8
Ballydesmond, 178 ... C 7
Ballyduff, 379 ... B 7
Ballygar, 315 ... E 4
Ballyhaunis, 1,174 ... D 4
Ballyheigue, 417 ... B 7
Ballyjamesduff, 581 ... G 4
Ballylanders, 280 ... E 7
Ballylongford, 594 ... B 6
Ballymahon, 830 ... F 4
Ballymakeery-Ballyvourney, 321 ... C 8
Ballymore, 179 ... F 5
Ballymore Eustace, 348 ... J 5
Ballymote, 965 ... D 3
Ballynacargy, 288 ... G 4
Ballyporeen, 270 ... E 7
Ballyragget, 478 ... G 6
Ballyroan, 122 ... G 6
Ballyshannon, 2,322 ... E 3
Ballytore, 269 ... H 5
Ballyvaughn, 152 ... C 5
Balrothery, 102 ... J 4
Baltimore, 188 ... C 9
Baltinglass, 116 ... H 6
Banagher, 1,050 ... F 5
Bandon, 2,308 ... D 8
Bannow, †820 ... H 7
Bantry, 2,234 ... C 8
Barna, 143 ... C 5
Belmullet, 724 ... B 3
Belturbet, 1,093 ... G 3
Birr, 3,221 ... F 5
Blackrock, Cork, †18,721 ... E 8
Blackrock, Dublin, 12,396 ... J 5
Blackwater, 216 ... J 7
Blarney, 995 ... D 8
Blessington, 491 ... J 5
Borris, 413 ... H 6
Borrisokane, 750 ... E 6
Boyle, 1,739 ... E 4
Bray (Brí Chualann), 11,688 ... K 5
Bruff, 545 ... D 7
Bunclody-Carrickduff, 891 ... H 6
Buncrana, 2,960 ... G 1
Bundoran, 1,326 ... E 3
Bunmahon, 265 ... G 7
Burtonport, 224 ... E 2
Buttevant, 981 ... D 7
Cahir, 1,662 ... F 7
Cahirciveen, 1,659 ... A 8
Callan, 1,346 ... G 7
Cappamore, 501 ... E 6
Cappawhite, 318 ... E 6
Cappoquin, 806 ... F 7
Carbury, †926 ... H 5
Carlingford, 471 ... J 3
Carlow, 7,708 ... H 6
Carndonagh, 1,016 ... G 1
Carnew, 551 ... H 6
Carrick, 153 ... D 2
Carrickmacross, 1,940 ... H 4
Carrick-on-Shannon, 1,497 ... F 4
Carrick-on-Suir, 4,672 ... F 7
Carrigaholt, 160 ... B 6
Carrigallen, 202 ... F 4
Carrigart, 196 ... F 1
Carrowkeel, 118 ... G 1
Cashel, 2,679 ... F 7
Castlebar, 5,482 ... C 4
Castlebellingham, 656 ... J 4
Castleblaney, 2,127 ... H 3
Castlebridge, 181 ... J 7
Castlecomer-Donaguile, 1,129 ... G 6
Castledermot, 551 ... H 6
Castlefin, 565 ... F 2
Castlegregory, 235 ... A 7
Castleisland, 1,718 ... B 7
Castlemaine, 171 ... B 7
Castlepollard, 778 ... G 4
Castlerea, 1,568 ... D 4
Castletown, 264 ... F 6
Castletownbere, 721 ... B 8
Castletownroche, 381 ... D 7
Castletownshend, 177 ... C 9
Cavan, 3,208 ... G 4
Ceanannus Mór, 2,193 ... G 4
Celbridge, 1,305 ... H 5
Charlestown-Bellahy, 727 ... D 4
Charleville (Rathluirc), 1,956 ... D 7
Clara, 2,477 ... F 5
Claregalway, 627 ... D 5
Claremorris, 1,519 ... C 4
Clashmore, 175 ... F 8
Clifden, 1,025 ... B 5
Cloghan, 399 ... G 6
Clogh-Chatsworth, 303 ... F 5
Clogheen, 576 ... F 7
Clogherhead, 685 ... J 4
Clonakilty, 2,417 ... D 8
Clonaslee, 275 ... F 5
Clondalkin, 3,434 ... J 5
Clones, 2,107 ... G 3
Clonfert, †465 ... E 5
Clonmacnoise, †411 ... F 5
Clonmany, 238 ... G 1
Clonmel, 10,640 ... F 7
Clonroche, 193 ... H 7
Cloon, 106 ... F 4
Cloughjordan, 479 ... E 6
Cloyne, 612 ... E 8
Coachford, 275 ... D 8
Cóbh, 5,266 ... E 8
Coill Dubh, 645 ... H 5
Collooney, 553 ... E 3
Cong, 178 ... C 4
Convoy, 616 ... F 2
Coolaney, 124 ... D 3
Coole, 344 ... G 4
Coolgreany, 124 ... J 6
Cootehill, 1,296 ... G 3
Cork, 77,980 ... E 8
Corofin, 362 ... C 6
Courtmacsherry, 205 ... D 8
Courtown Harbour-Riverchapel, 396 ... J 6
Crookhaven, 62 ... B 9
Croom, 720 ... D 6
Crosshaven, 858 ... E 8
Crossmolina, 777 ... C 3
Crusheen, †475 ... D 6
Culdaff, 108 ... G 1
Cullen, 113 ... C 7
Daingean, 679 ... G 5
Dalkey, 5,754 ... J 5
Delvin, 165 ... G 4
Dingle, 1,460 ... A 7
Doaghbeg, †795 ... F 1
Donabate, 318 ... J 5
Donegal, 1,458 ... F 2
Doneraile, 725 ... D 7
Dooagh, 387 ... A 4
Douglas, †3,113 ... D 8
Drishane, †1,511 ... C 7
Drogheda, 17,085 ... J 4
Droichead Nua, 3,668 ... H 5
Dromahair, 229 ... E 3
Dromin, †390 ... H 4
Dromore West, 99 ... D 3
Drumcar, †1,205 ... J 4
Drumcliffe, 772 ... E 3
Drumconrath, 195 ... H 4
Drumkeerin, 136 ... E 3
Drumlish, 343 ... F 4
Drumshanbo, 565 ... E 3
Dublin (cap.), 537,448 ... K 5
Dublin, *595,288 ... K 5
Duleek, 379 ... J 4
Dunboyne, 521 ... H 5
Duncannon, 226 ... H 7
Dundalk, 19,790 ... H 3
Dunfanaghy, 324 ... F 1
Dunganstown ... G 7
Dungarvan, 5,188 ... F 7
Dungloe, 793 ... E 2
Dunkineely, 261 ... E 2
Dún Laoghaire, 47,792 ... K 5
Dunlavin, 416 ... H 5
Dunleen, 529 ... J 4
Dunmanway, 1,411 ... C 8
Dunmore, 500 ... D 4
Dunmore East, 547 ... G 7
Dunshaughlin, 231 ... H 5
Durrow, Laoighis, 439 ... G 6
Durrow, Westmeath, 435 ... F 5
Easky, 317 ... D 3
Edenderry, 2,691 ... G 5
Elphin, 494 ... E 4
Emyvale, 255 ... G 3
Ennis, 5,699 ... D 6
Enniscorthy, 5,754 ... J 7
Enniskerry, 652 ... J 5
Ennistymon, 1,145 ... C 6
Eyrecourt, 355 ... E 5
Fahan, 322 ... G 1
Feakle, 129 ... D 6
Fenit, 308 ... B 7
Ferbane, 896 ... F 5
Fermoy, 3,241 ... E 7
Ferns, 557 ... J 6
Fethard, Tipperary, 962 ... F 7
Fethard, Wexford, 218 ... H 7
Fiddown, 152 ... G 7
Foxford, 876 ... C 4
Foynes, 686 ... C 6
Frankford (Kilcormac), 1,018 ... F 5
Frenchpark, 155 ... E 4
Freshford, 656 ... G 6
Galbally, 266 ... E 7
Galway, 22,028 ... C 5
Geashill, 170 ... G 5
Glandore, 151 ... C 8
Glencolumbkille, 95 ... D 2
Glengarriff, 392 ... C 8
Glenties, 828 ... E 2
Glenville, 146 ... E 7
Glin, 763 ... C 6
Golden, 153 ... F 7
Gorey, 2,671 ... J 6
Gort, 1,044 ... D 5
Gowran, 365 ... G 6
Granard, 1,044 ... F 4
Greencastle, 233 ... H 1
Greenore, 142 ... J 4
Greystones-Delgany, 3,551 ... K 5
Hacketstown, 509 ... H 6
Holycross, 921 ... F 6
Hospital, 572 ... E 7
Howth, 5,614 ... K 5
Inchigeela, 157 ... C 8
Inniscrone, 533 ... C 3
Johnstown, 326 ... G 6
Kanturk, 1,985 ... D 7
Keel, 459 ... A 4
Kells, 128 ... G 7
Kells (Ceanannus Mór), 2,193 ... G 4
Kenmare, 1,046 ... B 8
Kilbaha ... B 6
Kilbeggan, 799 ... G 5
Kilbeheny, 86 ... E 7
Kilcar, 229 ... D 2
Kilcock, 739 ... H 5
Kilconnell, 113 ... E 5
Kilcoole, 549 ... K 5
Kilcormac, 1,018 ... F 5
Kilcullen, 637 ... H 5
Kildare, 2,551 ... H 5
Kildysart, 295 ... C 6
Kilfenora, 135 ... C 6
Kilfinane, 565 ... D 7
Kilflynn, 87 ... B 7
Kilgarvan, 183 ... B 8
Kilkee, 1,392 ... B 6
Kilkelly, 257 ... D 4
Kilkenny, 10,159 ... G 6
Killala, 337 ... C 3
Killaloe, 835 ... D 6
Killarney, 6,825 ... C 7
Killavullen, 167 ... D 7
Killenaule, 531 ... F 6
Killeshandra, 397 ... F 3
Killimor, 195 ... E 5
Killinaboy, †303 ... C 6
Killiney, 2,578 ... J 5
Killorglin, 1,100 ... B 7
Killucan-Rathwire, 314 ... G 4
Killybegs, 1,065 ... E 2
Kilmacrennan, 251 ... F 1
Kilmacthomas, 446 ... G 7
Kilmallock, 1,159 ... D 7
Kilmihill, 264 ... C 6
Kilnaleck, 279 ... G 4
Kilronan, 231 ... B 5
Kilrush, 2,861 ... C 6
Kilsheelan, 172 ... F 7
Kiltimagh, 980 ... C 4
Kilworth, 334 ... E 7
Kingscourt, 793 ... H 4
Kingstown (Dún Laoghaire), 47,792 ... K 5
Kinlough, 203 ... E 3
Kinnegad, 351 ... G 5
Kinnitty, 275 ... F 5
Kinsale, 1,587 ... D 8
Kinvara, 338 ... D 5
Knightstown, 337 ... A 8
Knock, 218 ... D 4
Knocklong, 289 ... D 7
Knocktopher, 127 ... G 7
Labasheeda, 142 ... C 6
Laghey, 184 ... E 2
Lahinch, 389 ... C 6
Lanesborough-Ballyleague, 720 ... E 4
Laracor, 386 ... H 4
Laytown-Bettystown, 766 ... J 4
Leenane, 123 ... B 4
Leighlinbridge, 457 ... H 6
Leitrim, 111 ... F 3
Leixlip, 915 ... H 5
Letterkenny, 4,329 ... F 2
Lifford, 864 ... F 2
Limerick, 50,786 ... D 6
Liscarroll, 228 ... D 7
Lisdoonvarna, 625 ... C 5
Lismore, 810 ... F 7
Listowel, 7,859 ... C 7
Littleton, 274 ... F 6
Longford, 3,558 ... F 4
Loughrae, 2,784 ... E 5
Louisburgh, 346 ... B 4
Louth, 207 ... J 4
Lucan-Doddsborough, 1,657 ... J 5
Luimneach (Limerick), 50,786 ... D 6
Lusk, 495 ... J 4
Macroom, 2,169 ... C 8
Malahide, 2,534 ... J 5
Malin, 164 ... G 1
Mallow, 5,545 ... D 7
Manorhamilton, 920 ... E 3
Manulla, †774 ... C 4
Maryborough (Portlaoighise), 3,133 ... G 5
Maynooth, 1,753 ... H 5
Meathas Truim, 624 ... G 4
Midleton, 2,772 ... E 8
Milford, 611 ... F 1
Millstreet, 1,283 ... D 7
Miltown Malbay, 700 ... C 6
Minard, †426 ... A 7
Mitchelstown, 2,655 ... E 7
Moate, 1,261 ... F 5
Mohill, 905 ... F 4
Monaghan, 4,013 ... G 3
Monasterevan, 1,273 ... H 5
Moneygall, 284 ... F 6
Monivea, 222 ... D 5
Mooncoin, 507 ... G 7
Mount Bellew, 306 ... D 5
Mountcharles, 400 ... E 2
Mountmellick, 2,436 ... G 5
Mountrath, 1,051 ... F 5
Moville, 1,097 ... G 1
Moycullen, 127 ... C 5
Moynalty, 128 ... H 4
Muff, 219 ... G 1
Muinebeag, 2,071 ... H 6
Mullagh, 213 ... H 4
Mullaghmore, 137 ... D 3
Mullinahone, 322 ... F 7
Mullinavat, 339 ... G 7
Mullingar, 5,834 ... G 4
Naas, 4,023 ... H 5
Navan (An Uaimh), 3,998 ... H 4
Nenagh, 4,317 ... E 6
Newbliss, 192 ... G 3
Newbridge (Droichead Nua), 3,668 ... H 5
Newcastle West, 2,527 ... C 7
New Inn, 164 ... F 7
Newmarket, 791 ... C 7
Newmarket-on-Fergus, 807 ... D 6
Newport, Mayo, 459 ... C 4
Newport, Tipperary, 581 ... E 6
New Ross, 4,494 ... H 7
Newtownforbes, 318 ... F 4
Newtownmountkennedy-Killadreenan, 935 ... J 5
Newtownsandes, 304 ... C 6
O'Briensbridge-Montpelier, 232 ... D 6
Oldcastle, †358 ... G 4
Oola, 314 ... E 6
Oranmore, 346 ... D 5
Oughterard, 618 ... C 5
Parknasilla, †380 ... B 8
Passage East, 494 ... G 7
Passage West, 2,561 ... E 8
Patrickswell, 305 ... D 6
Pettigo, 313 ... F 2
Portarlington, 2,846 ... G 5
Portlaoighise, 3,133 ... G 5
Portlaw, 1,113 ... G 7
Portmarnock, 669 ... J 5
Portumna, 836 ... E 5
Queenstown (Cóbh), 5,266 ... E 8
Rahan, †635 ... F 5
Ramelton, 759 ... F 1
Raphoe, 818 ... F 2
Rathangan, 569 ... G 5
Rathcormac, 267 ... E 7
Rathdowney, 896 ... F 6
Rathdrum, 1,128 ... J 6
Rathgormack, †288 ... F 7
Rathkeale, 1,459 ... D 7
Rathluirc, 1,956 ... D 7
Rathmore, 417 ... J 5
Rathmullen, 491 ... F 1
Rathnew-Merrymeeting, 861 ... J 6
Rathvilly, 293 ... H 6
Ratoath, 289 ... J 5
Rosapenna, †905 ... F 1
Roscommon, 1,600 ... E 4
Roscrea, 3,372 ... F 6
Rosscarbery, 380 ... C 8
Rosslare, 529 ... J 7
Roundstone, 250 ... A 5
Rush, 2,118 ... J 4
Saggart, 426 ... F 2
Saint Johnstown, 458 ... F 2
Sallybrook-Riverstown, 563 ... E 8
Scariff-Tuamgraney, 600 ... E 6
Schull, 419 ... B 8
Shannon Airport, 234 ... D 6
Shercock, 254 ... G 4
Shillelagh, 202 ... J 6
Shinrone, 402 ... F 5
Sixmilebridge, 448 ... D 6
Skerries, 2,721 ... J 4
Skibbereen, 2,028 ... C 8
Slane, 421 ... H 4
Sligo, 13,145 ... E 3
Sneem, 282 ... B 8
Spiddal, 134 ... C 5
Stradbally, Laoighis, 792 ... G 5
Stradbally, Waterford, 213 ... F 7
Stranorlar, 848 ... F 2
Strokestown, 707 ... E 4
Swanlinbar, 306 ... F 3
Swinford, 1,115 ... C 4
Swords, 1,816 ... J 5
Taghmon, 347 ... H 7
Tallow, 819 ... E 7
Tarbert, 455 ... C 6
Teltown, 684 ... H 4
Templemore, 1,779 ... F 6
Templetouhy, 156 ... F 6
Termonfeckin, 300 ... J 4
Thomastown, 1,209 ... G 7
Thurles, 6,421 ... F 6
Timoleague, 291 ... D 8
Tinahely, 417 ... H 6
Tipperary, 4,684 ... E 7
Toomevara, 231 ... E 6
Tralee, 10,723 ... B 7
Tramore, 2,882 ... G 7
Trim, 1,371 ... H 4
Tuam, 3,500 ... D 4
Tubbercurry, 878 ... D 3
Tulla, 389 ... D 6
Tullamore, 6,243 ... G 5
Tullaroan, 118 ... G 6
Tullow, 1,725 ... H 6
Tynagh, †425 ... E 5
Tyrellspass, 259 ... G 5
Upperchurch, †442 ... E 6
Urlingford, 562 ... F 6
Ventry, †441 ... A 7
Virginia, 515 ... G 4
Waterford, 28,216 ... G 7
Waterville, 702 ... A 8
Westport, 2,882 ... C 4
Wexford, 11,328 ... H 7
Whitegate, 397 ... E 8
Wicklow, 3,125 ... K 6
Woodford, 264 ... E 5
Youghal, 5,043 ... F 8

PHYSICAL FEATURES

Achill (head) ... A 4
Achill (isl.), 4,220 ... A 4
Aherlow (riv.) ... E 7
Allen (lake) ... E 3
Allen, Bog of (marsh) ... H 5
Allow (riv.) ... D 7
Annalee (riv.) ... G 3
Anner (riv.) ... F 7
Aran (isl.), 948 ... D 2
Aran (isls.), 1,651 ... B 5
Arklow (bank) ... K 6
Arrow (lake) ... E 3
Awbeg (riv.) ... D 7
Ballinskelligs (bay) ... A 8
Ballycotton (bay) ... F 8
Ballyheige (bay) ... B 7
Ballyhoura (mts.) ... E 7
Ballynakill (harb.) ... A 4
Ballysadare (bay) ... D 3
Ballyteige (bay) ... H 7
Bandon (riv.) ... D 8
Bann (riv.) ... J 6
Bantry (bay) ... B 8
Barrow (riv.) ... H 7
Baurtregaum (mt.) ... A 7
Bear (isl.), 382 ... C 4
Beltra (lake) ... C 4
Ben Dash (hill) ... C 6
Benwee (head) ... B 3
Bertraghboy (bay) ... A 5
Black (head) ... C 5
Blacksod (bay) ... A 3
Blackstairs (mt.) ... H 6
Blackwater (riv.) ... D 7
Blackwater (riv.) ... H 4
Blasket (isls.) ... A 7
Bloody Foreland (prom.) ... E 1
Blue Stack (mts.) ... E 2
Boderg (lake) ... E 4
Boggeragh (mts.) ... D 7
Bolus (head) ... A 8
Bonet (riv.) ... E 3
Boyne (riv.) ... J 4
Brandon (bay) ... A 7
Brannock (isls.) ... A 5
Bray (head) ... A 8
Bride (riv.) ... E 7
Broad Haven (harb.) ... B 3
Brosna (riv.) ... F 5
Bull, The (isl.) ... A 8
Caha (mts.) ... B 8
Cahore (pt.) ... J 6
Cark (mt.) ... F 2
Carlingford (inlet) ... J 3
Carnsore (pt.) ... J 7
Carra (lake) ... C 4
Carrantuohill (mt.) ... B 7
Carrigan (head) ... D 2
Carrowmore (lake) ... B 3
Clara (hills) ... D 8
Clare (riv.) ... D 5
Clare with Inishturk (isls.), 313 ... A 4
Clear (cape) ... B 9
Clear (isl.) ... C 9
Clew (bay) ... B 4
Clonakilty (bay) ... D 8
Comeragh (mts.) ... F 7
Conn (lake) ... C 3
Connaught (prov.), 419,465 ... C 4
Connemara (dist.), 23,841 ... B 5
Cork (harb.) ... E 8
Corrib (lake) ... C 5
Courtmacsherry (bay) ... D 8
Croagh Patrick (mt.) ... C 4
Crossfarnoge (pt.) ... J 7
Culdaff (bay) ... G 1
Cullin (lake) ... C 4
Curragh, The ... H 5
Cutra (lake) ... D 5
Dee (riv.) ... H 4
Deel (riv.) ... C 3
Deel (riv.) ... D 7
Deel (riv.) ... F 2
Derg (lake) ... E 6
Derg (lake) ... F 2
Derravaragh (lake) ... G 4
Derryveagh (mts.) ... E 2
Devilsbit (mt.) ... F 6
Dingle (bay) ... A 7
Donegal (bay) ... D 3
Donegal (pt.) ... B 6
Doulus (head) ... A 8
Downpatrick (head) ... C 3
Drum (hills) ... F 7
Dublin (bay) ... J 5
Dunaff (head) ... G 1
Dunany (pt.) ... J 4
Dúndalk (bay) ... J 4
Dunkellin (riv.) ... D 5
Dunmanus (bay) ... B 8
Dursey (isl.) ... A 8
Eask (lake) ... E 2
Ennell (lake) ... G 5
Erkina (riv.) ... G 6
Erne (riv.) ... E 3
Erris (head) ... A 3
Fanad (head) ... F 1
Fastnet Rock (isl.) ... B 9
Feale (riv.) ... C 7
Feagh (lake) ... B 4
Fergus (riv.) ... D 6
Finn (riv.) ... F 2
Finn (riv.) ... G 3
Flesk (riv.) ... C 7
Foul (sound) ... B 5
Foyle (inlet) ... G 1
Foyle (riv.) ... G 2
Galley (head) ... D 9
Galty (mts.) ... E 7
Galtymore (mt.) ... E 7
Galway (bay) ... C 5
Gara (lake) ... E 4
Garadice (lake) ... F 3
Gartan (lake) ... F 2
Garvan (isls.) ... G 1
Gill (lake) ... E 3
Glandore (harb.) ... C 9
Glen (lake) ... F 1
Glyde (riv.) ... H 4
Gola (isl.) ... E 1
Golden Vale (plain) ... E 7
Gorumna (isl.), †1,730 ... B 5
Gowna (lake) ... G 4
Grand (canal) ... G 5
Great Blasket (isl.) ... A 7
Greenore (pt.) ... J 7
Gregory's (sound) ... B 5
Gweebarra (bay) ... D 2
Gweebarra (riv.) ... E 2
Hags (head) ... B 6
Helvick (head) ... G 7
High (isl.) ... A 4
Hook (head) ... H 7
Horn (head) ... E 1
Iar Connaught (dist.), 4,051 ... C 5
Inishbofin (isl.), 248 ... A 4
Inishbofin (isl.) ... E 1
Inisheer (isl.), 358 ... B 5
Inishmaan (isl.), 357 ... C 5
Inishmore (isl.), 936 ... B 5
Inishmurray (isl.) ... D 3
Inishowen (head) ... H 1
Inishowen (pen.) ... G 1
Inishshark (isl.) ... A 4
Inishtrahull (isl.) ... G 1
Inishturk with Clare (isls.), 313 ... A 4
Inny (riv.) ... A 8
Inny (riv.) ... F 4
Inver (bay) ... E 2
Ireland's Eye (isl.) ... K 5
Irish (sea) ... K 4
Joyce's Country (dist.), 2,425 ... B 4
Keeper (mt.) ... E 6
Kenmare (riv.) ... A 8
Kerry (head) ... A 7
Key (lake) ... E 3
Kilkieran (bay) ... B 5
Killala (bay) ... C 3
Killary (harb.) ... A 4
Kinsale, Old Head of (head) ... E 8
Kippure (mt.) ... J 5
Knockadoon (head) ... F 8
Knockanefune (mt.) ... C 7
Knockboy (mt.) ... B 8
Knockmealdown (mts.) ... F 7
Lady's Island Lake (inlet) ... J 7
Lambay (isl.) ... K 5
Lamb's (head) ... A 8
Laune (riv.) ... B 7
Leane (lake) ... B 7
Leane (lake) ... G 4
Lee (riv.) ... D 8
Leinster (mt.) ... H 6
Leinster (prov.), 1,332,149 ... G 5
Lettermullen (isl.) ... B 5
Liffey (riv.) ... H 5
Liscannor (bay) ... B 6
Little Brosna (riv.) ... E 5
Long Island (bay) ... B 9
Loop (head) ... B 6
Loughros More (bay) ... D 2
Lugnaquillia (mt.) ... J 6
Lung (riv.) ... D 4
Macgillicuddy's Reeks (mts.) ... B 8
Macnean (lake) ... F 3
Maigue (riv.) ... D 6
Maine (riv.) ... C 7
Malin (head) ... G 1
Mangerton (mt.) ... C 8
Mask (lake) ... C 4
Maumakeogh (mt.) ... C 3
Maumturk (mts.) ... B 5
Melvin (lake) ... E 3
Mine (head) ... F 8
Mizen (head) ... B 9
Mizen (head) ... K 6
Moher (cliffs) ... B 6
Monavullagh (mts.) ... F 7
Moy (riv.) ... C 3
Muckish (mt.) ... E 1
Muckno (lake) ... H 3
Mulkear (riv.) ... E 6
Mullaghareirk (mts.) ... C 7
Mulroy (bay) ... F 1
Munster (prov.), 849,203 ... D 7
Mutton (isl.) ... B 6
Mweelrea (mt.) ... B 4
Mweenish (isl.) ... B 5
Nagles (mts.) ... E 7
Nenagh (riv.) ... E 6
Nephin (mt.) ... C 3
Nephin Beg (mt.) ... B 3
Nore (riv.) ... G 7
North (sound) ... B 5
North Inishkea (isl.) ... A 3
Omey (isl.) ... A 5
Oughter (lake) ... G 3
Ovoca (riv.) ... J 6
Owell (lake) ... G 4
Owenmore (riv.) ... B 3
Owenmore (riv.) ... D 3
Owey (isl.) ... D 1
Ox (Slieve Gamph) (mts.) ... D 3
Paps, The (mt.) ... C 7
Partry (mts.) ... C 4
Pollaphuca (res.) ... J 5
Puffin (isl.) ... A 8
Punchestown ... H 5
Ramor (lake) ... G 4
Rathlin O'Birne (isl.) ... C 2
Ree (lake) ... F 5
Rinn (lake) ... F 4
Roaringwater (bay) ... B 9
Rosscarbery (bay) ... D 9
Rosses (bay) ... D 1
Rosskeeragh (pt.) ... D 3
Rosslare (bay) ... J 7
Royal (canal) ... G 4
Saint Finan's (bay) ... A 8
Saint George's (chan.) ... K 7
Saint John's (pt.) ... D 2
Saltee (isls.) ... H 7
Scarriff (isl.) ... A 8
Seven (heads) ... D 8
Seven Hogs, The (isls.) ... A 7
Shannon (riv.) ... E 6
Shannon, Mouth of the (est.) ... B 6
Sheeffry (hills) ... B 4
Sheep Haven (harb.) ... F 1
Sheeps (head) ... B 8
Shehy (mts.) ... C 8
Sherkin (isl.) ... C 9
Silvermine (mts.) ... E 6
Slaney (riv.) ... H 7
Slieve Anierin (mt.) ... F 3
Slieve Aughty (mts.) ... D 5
Slieve Bernagh (mt.) ... D 6
Slieve Bloom (mts.) ... F 5
Slieveboy (mt.) ... H 6
Slieve Callan (mt.) ... C 6
Slievecar (mt.) ... B 3
Slievecarran (mt.) ... C 5
Slieve Elva (mt.) ... C 5
Slievefelim (mts.) ... E 6
Slieve Gamph (mts.) ... D 3
Slieve League (mt.) ... D 2
Slieve Mishkish (mts.) ... B 8
Slievenaman (mt.) ... F 7
Slieve Rushen (mt.) ... F 3
Slieve Snaght (mt.) ... E 2
Sligo (bay) ... D 3
Slyne (head) ... A 5
Smerwick (harb.) ... A 7
South (sound) ... C 5
Stacks (mts.) ... B 7
Suck (riv.) ... E 5
Sugarloaf (mt.) ... B 8
Suir (riv.) ... G 7
Swilly (inlet) ... F 1
Swilly (riv.) ... F 2
Tara (hill) ... H 4
Tawin (isl.) ... C 5
Toe (head) ... C 9
Tory (isl.) ... E 1
Tory (sound) ... E 1
Tralee (bay) ... B 7
Tramore (bay) ... G 7
Trawbreaga (bay) ... F 1
Truskmore (mt.) ... E 3
Twelve Pins (mt.) ... B 4
Ulster (prov.), 217,524 ... G 2
Valentia (Valencia) (isl.), 926 ... A 8
Veagh (lake) ... F 1
Waterford (harb.) ... G 7
Wexford (bay) ... J 7
Wicklow (mts.) ... J 6
Wicklow (head) ... K 6
Youghal (bay) ... F 8

NORTHERN IRELAND

COUNTIES

Antrim, 289,700 ... J 2
Armagh, 120,500 ... H 3
Belfast (city), 410,300 ... K 2
Down, 277,400 ... J 3
Fermanagh, 51,500 ... F 3
Londonderry, 172,200 ... H 2
Tyrone, 136,400 ... G 2

CITIES and TOWNS

Aghadowey, †679 ... H 1
Ahoghill, 885 ... J 2
Annalong, 553 ... K 3
Antrim, 1,448 ... J 2
Ardglass, 737 ... K 3
Armagh, 10,062 ... H 3
Armoy, 383 ... J 1
Augher, 222 ... G 3
Aughnacloy, 805 ... H 3
Ballycastle, 2,642 ... J 1
Ballyclare, 4,440 ... J 2
Ballygally, 276 ... K 2
Ballygawley, 427 ... G 3
Ballyhalbert, 336 ... K 3
Ballykelly, 367 ... G 1
Ballymena, 14,734 ... J 2
Ballymoney, 3,409 ... J 1
Ballynahinch, 2,042 ... J 3
Ballynure, 291 ... K 2
Ballywalter, 789 ... K 2
Banbridge, 6,114 ... J 3
Bangor, 23,862 ... K 2
Belfast (cap.), 410,300 ... K 2
Belfast, *528,700 ... J 2
Bellaghy, 663 ... H 2
Belleek, 162 ... E 3
Beragh, 349 ... G 2
Bessbrook, 3,199 ... J 3
Brookeborough, 294 ... G 3
Broughshane, 716 ... J 2
Bushmills, 936 ... J 1
Caledon, 350 ... H 3
Carnlough, 586 ...
Carrickfergus, 10,211 ...
Carrowdore, 297 ...
Castlederg, 1,367 ...
Castlewellan, 1,241 ...
Claudy, 286 ...
Clogher, 197 ...
Cloghy, 393 ...
Coalisland, 1,351 ...
Coleraine, 11,901 ...
Comber, 3,987 ...
Cookstown, 4,969 ...
Crossgar, 842 ...
Crossmaglen, 932 ...
Crumlin, 394 ...
Cullybackey, 758 ...
Cushendall, 618 ...
Derrygonnelly, 296 ...
Dervock, 558 ...
Doagh 486 ...
Donaghdee, 3,218 ...
Downpatrick, 4,235 ...
Draperstown, 592 ...
Dromara, 280 ...
Dromore, Down, 2,124 ...
Dromore, Tyrone, 503 ...
Drumquin, 307 ...
Dundrum, 641 ...
Dungannon, 6,511 ...
Dungiven, 1,102 ...
Dunnamanagh, 352 ...
Ederny, 227 ...
Enniskillen, 7,406 ...
Feeny, 206 ...
Fintona, 990 ...
Garvagh, 550 ...
Gilford, 780 ...
Glenarm, 673 ...
Glenavy, 1,306 ...
Glynn, 389 ...
Gortin, 261 ...
Greyabbey, 611 ...
Hillsborough, 806 ...
Hilltown, 309 ...
Holywood, 8,069 ...
Irvinestown, 934 ...
Jonesborough, 274 ...
Keady, 1,637 ...
Kells, 495 ...
Kesh, †689 ...
Kilkeel, 2,497 ...
Killeter, †442 ...
Killough, 504 ...
Killyleagh, 1,876 ...
Kilrea, 952 ...
Kircubbin, 843 ...
Lack, †571 ...
Larne, 16,350 ...
Limavady, 4,325 ...
Lisburn, 17,700 ...
Lisnaskea, 977 ...
Londonderry, 56,300 ...
Loughbrickland, 300 ...
Loughgall, †1,086 ... H
Lurgan, 17,872 ...
Maghera, 1,607 ... H
Magherafelt, 2,459 ... H
Maguire's Bridge, 339 ... G
Markethill, 813 ... H
Middletown, 161 ... H
Millisle, 386 ... K
Moira, 501 ... J
Moneymore, 807 ... H
Moy, 751 ... H
Newcastle, 3,724 ... J
Newry, 12,429 ... J
Newtownabbey, 37,448 ... K
Newtownards, 13,083 ... K
Newtownbutler, 358 ... G
Newtownhamilton, 589 ... H
Newtownstewart, 1,125 ... G
Omagh, 8,109 ... G
Pomeroy, 349 ... H
Portadown, 18,609 ... H
Portaferry, 1,406 ... K
Portglenone, 613 ... H
Portrush, 4,265 ... H
Portstewart, 3,950 ... H
Randalstown, 1,579 ... J
Rasharkin, 799 ... J
Rathfriland, 1,558 ... J
Rostrevor, 1,265 ... J
Saintfield, 702 ... K
Sion Mills, 1,616 ... G
Sixmilecross, 245 ... H
Stewartstown, 621 ... H
Strabane, 7,783 ... G
Strangford, 413 ... K
Tanderagee, 1,281 ... H
Templepatrick, †775 ... J
Tempo, 269 ... G
Trillick, 220 ... G
Tynan, †805 ... H
Warrenpoint, 3,245 ... J
Whitehead, 2,169 ... K

PHYSICAL FEATURES

Arney (riv.) ... F 3
Bann (riv.) ... H 2
Beg (lake) ... J 2
Belfast (inlet) ... K 2
Binevenagh (mt.) ... H 1
Blackwater (riv.) ... H 3
Bush (riv.) ... H 1
Copeland (isl.) ... K 2
Derg (riv.) ... F 2
Divis (mt.) ... J 2
Dundrum (bay) ... K 3
Erne (lake) ... F 3
Fair (head) ... J 1
Foyle (inlet) ... G 1
Foyle (riv.) ... G 2
Garron (pt.) ... K 1
Giant's Causeway ... H 1
Knocklayd (mt.) ... J 1
Lagan (riv.) ... K 2
Larne (inlet) ... K 2
Macnean (lake) ... F 3
Magee, Island (pen.) ... K 2
Magilligan (pt.) ... H 1
Maidens, The (isls.) ... K 2
Main (riv.) ... J 2
Mourne (mts.) ... J 3
Mourne (riv.) ... G 2
Mullaghearn (mt.) ... G 2
Neagh (lake) ... J 2
North (chan.) ... K 1
Owenkillew (riv.) ... G 2
Rathlin (isl.), 159 ... J 1
Red (bay) ... K 1
Roe (riv.) ... H 1
Saint John's (pt.) ... K 3
Slemish (mt.) ... J 2
Slieve Beagh (mt.) ... G 3
Slieve Donard (mt.) ... K 3
Slieve Gullion (mt.) ... J 3
Sperrin (mts). ... G 2
Strangford (inlet) ... K 3
Torr (head) ... K 1
Trostan (mt.) ... J 1
Ulster (prov.), 1,458,000 ... G 2
Upper Lough Erne (lake) ... F 3

*City and suburbs.
†Population of district.

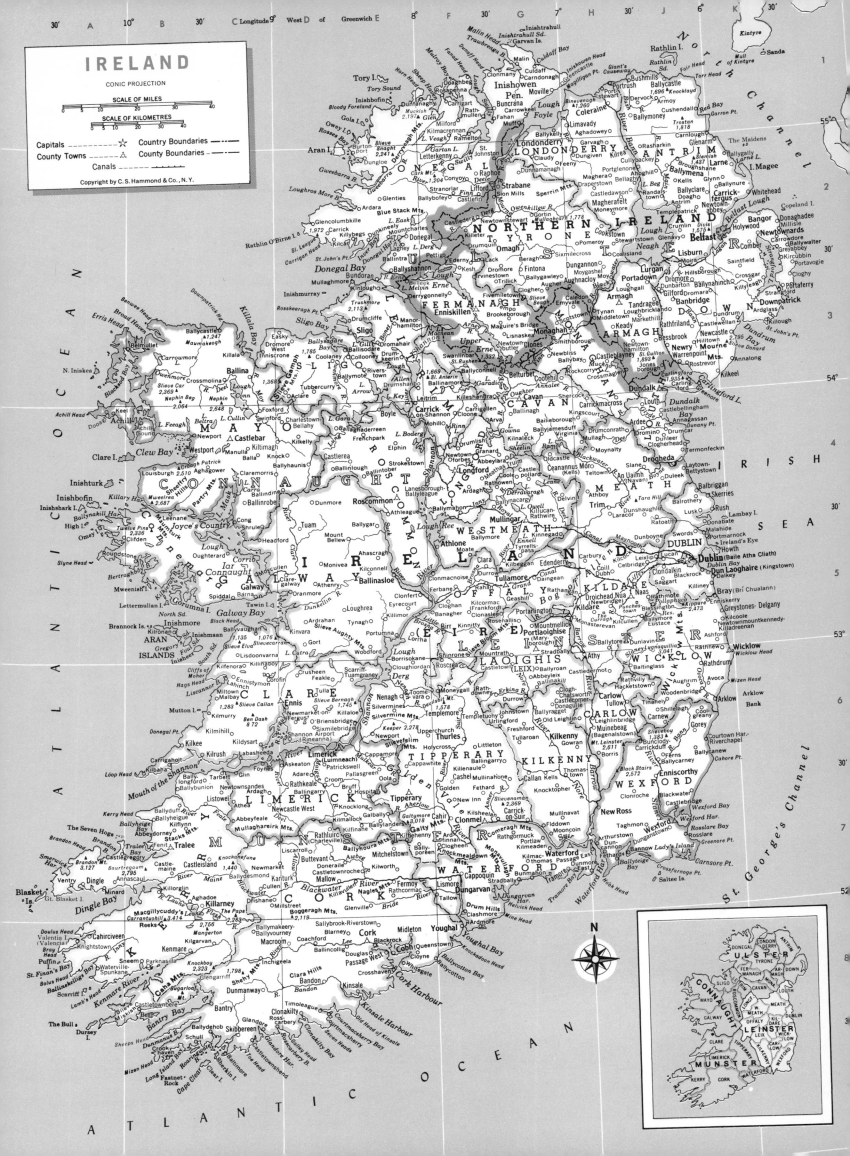

NORWAY, SWEDEN, FINLAND, DENMARK and ICELAND

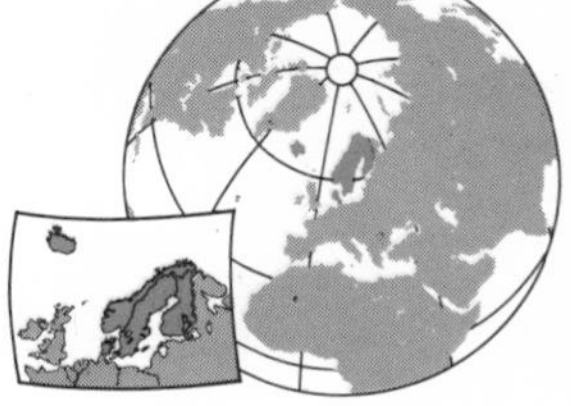

	NORWAY	SWEDEN	FINLAND
AREA	124,560 sq. mi.	173,394 sq. mi.	130,500 sq. mi.
POPULATION	3,681,000	7,626,978	4,586,000
CAPITAL	Oslo	Stockholm	Helsinki
LARGEST CITY	Oslo (greater) 579,498	Stockholm (greater) 1,180,490	Helsinki (greater) 594,248
HIGHEST POINT	Glittertind 8,104 ft.	Kebnekaise 6,965 ft.	Mt. Haltia 4,343 ft.
MONETARY UNIT	krone (crown)	krona (crown)	markka (mark)
MAJOR LANGUAGES	Norwegian	Swedish	Finnish, Swedish
MAJOR RELIGIONS	Protestant	Protestant	Protestant

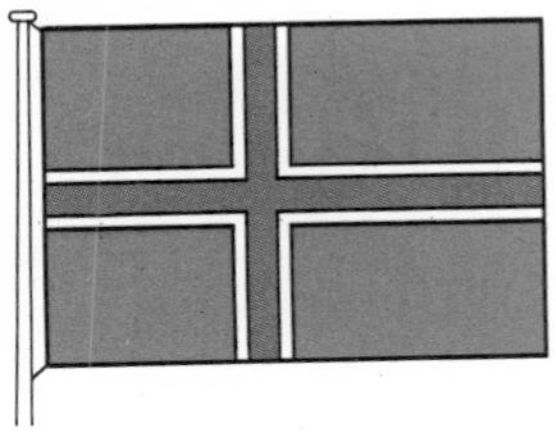

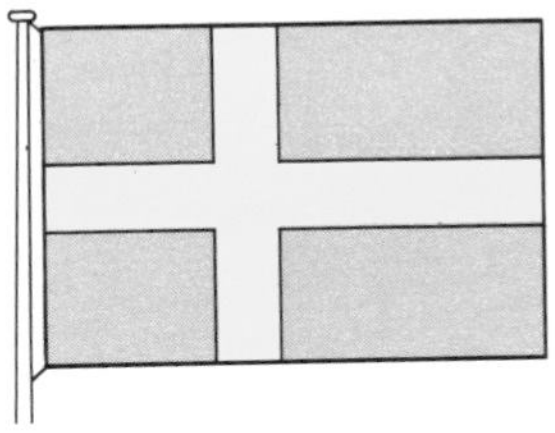

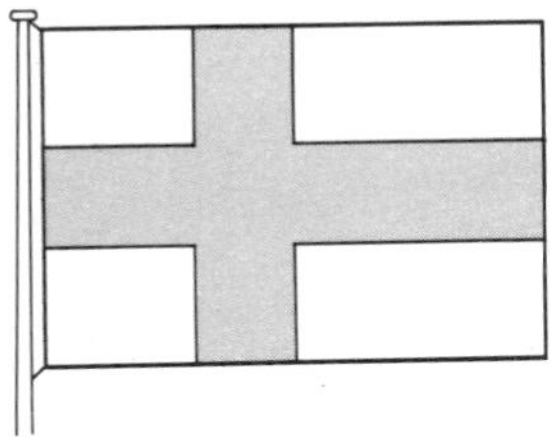

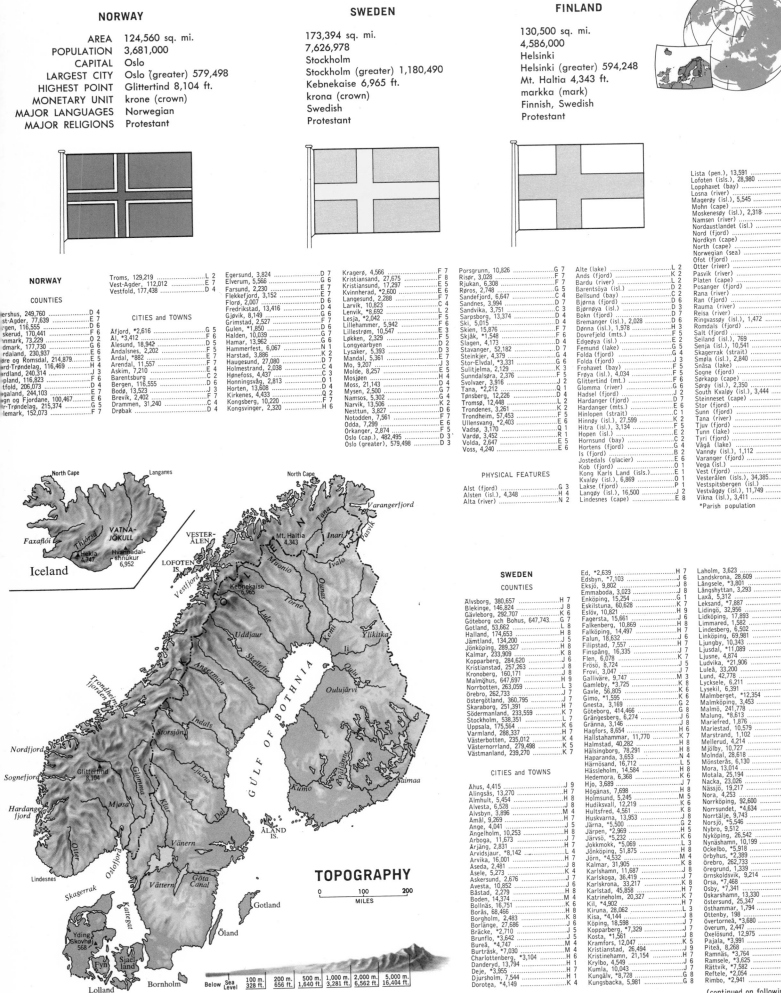

NORWAY

COUNTIES

ershus, 249,760 ... D 4
st-Agder, 77,639 ... E 7
rgen, 116,555 ... D 6
skerud, 170,441 ... F 6
nmark, 73,229 ... O 2
dmark, 177,730 ... G 6
rdaland, 230,937 ... E 6
øre og Romsdal, 214,879 ... E 5
rd-Trøndelag, 116,469 ... H 4
rdland, 240,314 ... J 3
pland, 116,823 ... F 6
tfold, 206,073 ... D 4
galand, 244,103 ... E 7
gn og Fjordane, 100,467 ... E 6
r-Trøndelag, 215,374 ... G 5
lemark, 152,073 ... F 7
Troms, 129,219 ... L 2
Vest-Agder, 112,012 ... E 7
Vestfold, 177,438 ... D 4

CITIES and TOWNS

Åfjord, *2,616 ... G 5
Ål, *3,412 ... F 6
Ålesund, 18,942 ... D 5
Åndalsnes, 2,202 ... F 5
Årdal, *882 ... E 7
Arendal, 11,557 ... F 7
Askim, 7,210 ... E 4
Barentsburg ... C 2
Bergen, 116,555 ... D 6
Bodø, 13,523 ... J 3
Brevik, 2,402 ... F 7
Drammen, 31,240 ... C 4
Drøbak ... D 4
Egersund, 3,824 ... D 7
Elverum, 5,566 ... G 6
Farsund, 2,230 ... E 7
Flekkefjord, 3,152 ... E 7
Florø, 2,007 ... D 6
Fredrikstad, 13,416 ... D 4
Gjøvik, 8,149 ... G 6
Grimstad, 2,527 ... F 7
Gulen, *1,850 ... D 6
Halden, 10,039 ... G 7
Hamar, 13,962 ... G 6
Hammerfest, 6,067 ... N 1
Harstad, 3,886 ... K 2
Haugesund, 27,080 ... D 7
Holmestrand, 2,038 ... C 4
Hønefoss, 4,437 ... C 3
Honningsvåg, 2,813 ... O 1
Horten, 13,608 ... D 4
Kirkenes, 4,433 ... Q 2
Kongsberg, 10,220 ... F 7
Kongsvinger, 2,320 ... H 6
Kragerø, 4,566 ... F 7
Kristiansand, 27,675 ... F 8
Kristiansund, 17,297 ... E 5
Kvinnherad, *2,600 ... E 6
Langesund, 2,288 ... F 7
Larvik, 10,823 ... C 4
Lenvik, *8,692 ... L 2
Lesja, *2,042 ... F 5
Lillehammer, 5,942 ... F 6
Lillestrøm, 10,547 ... E 3
Løkken, 2,329 ... F 5
Longyearbyen ... D 2
Lysaker, 5,393 ... D 3
Mandal, 5,361 ... E 7
Mo, 9,207 ... J 3
Molde, 8,257 ... E 5
Mosjøen ... H 4
Moss, 21,143 ... D 4
Mysen, 2,500 ... G 7
Namsos, 5,302 ... G 4
Narvik, 13,506 ... K 2
Nesttun, 3,827 ... D 6
Notodden, 7,561 ... F 7
Odda, 7,299 ... E 6
Orkanger, 2,874 ... F 5
Oslo (cap.), 482,495 ... D 3
Oslo (greater), 579,498 ... D 3
Porsgrunn, 10,826 ... G 7
Risør, 3,028 ... F 7
Rjukan, 6,308 ... F 7
Røros, 2,748 ... G 5
Sandefjord, 6,647 ... C 4
Sandnes, 3,994 ... D 7
Sandvika, 3,751 ... C 3
Sarpsborg, 13,374 ... D 4
Ski, 5,015 ... D 4
Skien, 15,876 ... F 7
Skjåk, *1,548 ... F 6
Slagen, 4,173 ... D 4
Stavanger, 52,182 ... D 7
Steinkjer, 4,379 ... G 4
Stor-Elvdal, *3,331 ... G 6
Sulitjelma, 2,129 ... K 3
Sunndalsøra, 2,376 ... F 5
Svolvaer, 3,916 ... J 2
Tana, *2,212 ... Q 1
Tønsberg, 12,226 ... D 4
Tromsø, 12,448 ... L 2
Trondenes, 3,261 ... K 2
Trondheim, 57,453 ... F 5
Ullensvang, *2,403 ... E 6
Vadsø, 3,170 ... Q 1
Vardø, 3,452 ... R 1
Volda, 2,647 ... E 5
Voss, 4,240 ... E 6

PHYSICAL FEATURES

Alst (fjord) ... G 3
Alsten (isl.), 4,348 ... H 4
Alta (river) ... N 2
Alte (lake) ... L 2
Ands (fjord) ... K 2
Bardu (river) ... L 2
Barentsöya (isl.) ... D 2
Bellsund (bay) ... C 2
Bjørna (fjord) ... D 6
Bjørnøya (isl.) ... D 3
Bokn (fjord) ... D 7
Bremanger (isl.), 2,028 ... D 6
Dønna (isl.), 1,978 ... H 3
Dovrefjeld (mts.) ... F 5
Edgeøya (isl.) ... E 2
Femund (lake) ... G 5
Folda (fjord) ... G 4
Folda (fjord) ... J 3
Frohavet (bay) ... F 5
Frøya (isl.), 4,034 ... F 5
Glittertind (mt.) ... F 6
Glomma (river) ... G 6
Hadsel (fjord) ... J 2
Hardanger (fjord) ... D 7
Hardanger (mts.) ... E 6
Hinlopen (strait) ... C 1
Hinnøy (isl.), 27,599 ... K 2
Hitra (isl.), 3,134 ... F 5
Hopen (isl.) ... E 2
Hornsund (bay) ... C 2
Hortens (fjord) ... G 4
Is (fjord) ... B 2
Jostedals (glacier) ... E 6
Kob (fjord) ... O 1
Kong Karls Land (isls.) ... E 1
Kvaløy (isl.), 6,869 ... O 1
Lakse (fjord) ... P 1
Langøy (isl.), 16,500 ... J 2
Lindesnes (cape) ... E 8
Lista (pen.), 13,591 ... E 7
Lofoten (isls.), 28,980 ... H 2
Lopphavet (bay) ... M 1
Losna (river) ... G 6
Magerøy (isl.), 5,545 ... P 1
Mohn (cape) ... E 1
Moskenesøy (isl.), 2,318 ... H 3
Namsen (river) ... H 4
Nordaustlandet (isl.) ... D 1
Nord (fjord) ... E 6
Nordkyn (cape) ... Q 1
North (cape) ... P 1
Norwegian (sea) ... F 3
Ofot (fjord) ... K 2
Otter (river) ... E 7
Pasvik (river) ... Q 2
Platen (cape) ... D 1
Posanger (fjord) ... O 1
Rana (river) ... J 3
Ran (fjord) ... H 3
Rauma (river) ... F 5
Reisa (river) ... M 2
Ringvassøy (isl.), 1,472 ... L 2
Romdals (fjord) ... E 5
Salt (fjord) ... J 3
Seiland (isl.), 769 ... N 1
Senja (isl.), 10,541 ... K 2
Skagerrak (strait) ... E 8
Smøla (isl.), 2,840 ... E 5
Snåsa (lake) ... H 4
Sogne (fjord) ... D 6
Sørkapp (cape) ... C 2
Sørøy (isl.), 2,350 ... N 1
South Kvaløy (isl.), 3,444 ... K 2
Steinneset (cape) ... E 2
Stor (fjord) ... D 2
Sunn (fjord) ... D 6
Tana (river) ... P 1
Tjuv (fjord) ... D 2
Tunn (lake) ... H 4
Tyri (fjord) ... C 3
Vågå (lake) ... F 6
Vannøy (isl.), 1,112 ... L 1
Varanger (fjord) ... Q 1
Vega (isl.) ... G 4
Vest (fjord) ... H 3
Vesterålen (isls.), 34,385 ... J 2
Vestspitsbergen (isl.) ... C 2
Vestvågøy (isl.), 11,749 ... H 3
Vikna (isl.), 3,411 ... G 4

*Parish population

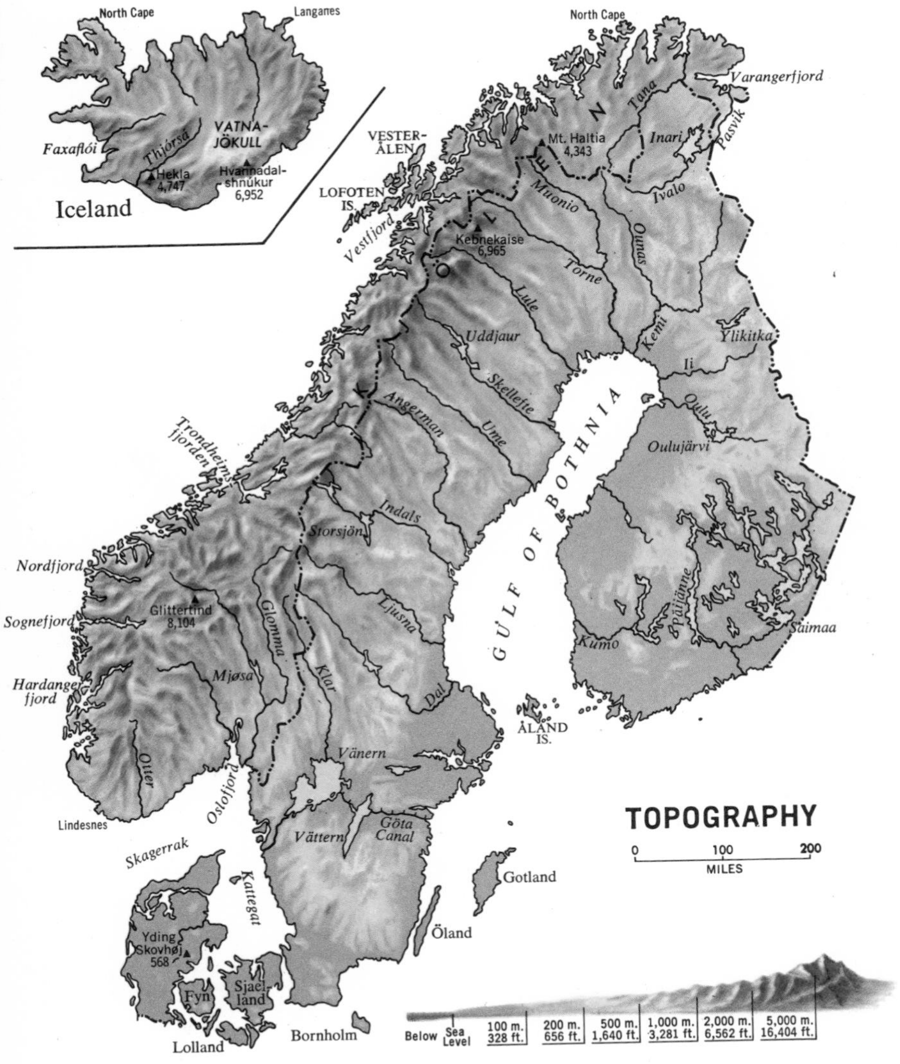
North Cape
Langanes
Faxaflói
Thjórsá
VATNA-JÖKULL
Hekla 4,747
Hvannadal-shnúkur 6,952
Iceland
North Cape
Varangerfjord
Tana
Pasvik
VESTER-ÅLEN
LOFOTEN IS.
Vestfjord
Mt. Haltia 4,343
Inari
Muonio
Ivalo
Ounas
Kebnekaise 6,965
Torne
Lule
Kemi
Ylikitka
Uddjaur
Ii
Skellefte
Ume
Angerman
Oulu
GULF OF BOTHNIA
Trondheimsfjorden
Oulujärvi
Indals
Storsjön
Nordfjord
Glittertind 8,104
Sognefjord
Glomma
Ljusna
Saimaa
Kumo
Hardanger fjord
Mjøsa
Klar
Dal
ÅLAND IS.
Otter
Oslofjord
Vänern
Lindesnes
Skagerrak
Vättern
Göta Canal
Gotland
Kattegat
Öland
Yding Skovhøj 568
Fyn
Sjaelland
Lolland
Bornholm
TOPOGRAPHY
0 100 200
MILES
Below Sea Level
100 m. 328 ft.
200 m. 656 ft.
500 m. 1,640 ft.
1,000 m. 3,281 ft.
2,000 m. 6,562 ft.
5,000 m. 16,404 ft.

SWEDEN

COUNTIES

Älvsborg, 380,657 ... H 7
Blekinge, 146,824 ... J 8
Gävleborg, 292,707 ... K 6
Göteborg och Bohus, 647,743 ... G 7
Gotland, 53,662 ... L 8
Halland, 174,653 ... H 8
Jämtland, 134,200 ... J 5
Jönköping, 289,327 ... H 8
Kalmar, 233,909 ... K 8
Kopparberg, 284,620 ... J 6
Kristianstad, 257,263 ... J 8
Kronoberg, 160,171 ... J 8
Malmöhus, 647,697 ... H 9
Norrbotten, 263,059 ... L 3
örebro, 262,733 ... J 7
östergötland, 360,795 ... J 7
Skaraborg, 251,391 ... H 7
Södermanland, 233,559 ... K 7
Stockholm, 538,351 ... L 7
Uppsala, 175,564 ... K 6
Varmland, 288,337 ... H 7
Västerbotten, 235,012 ... K 4
Västernorrland, 279,498 ... K 5
Västmanland, 239,270 ... K 7

CITIES and TOWNS

Åhus, 4,415 ... J 9
Alingsås, 13,270 ... H 7
Älmhult, 5,454 ... H 8
Alvesta, 6,528 ... J 8
Alvsbyn, 3,896 ... M 4
Åmål, 9,269 ... H 7
Ange, 4,041 ... J 5
Ängelholm, 10,253 ... H 8
Arboga, 11,673 ... J 7
Årjäng, 2,831 ... H 7
Arvidsjaur, *8,142 ... L 4
Arvika, 16,001 ... H 7
Åseda, 2,481 ... J 8
Åsele, 5,273 ... K 4
Askersund, 2,676 ... J 7
Avesta, 10,852 ... J 6
Båstad, 2,279 ... H 8
Boden, 14,374 ... M 4
Bollnäs, 16,751 ... K 6
Borås, 68,466 ... H 8
Borgholm, 2,483 ... K 8
Borlänge, 27,686 ... J 6
Bräcke, *2,710 ... J 5
Brunflo, *3,642 ... J 5
Bureå, *4,747 ... M 4
Burträsk, *7,030 ... M 4
Charlottenberg, *3,104 ... H 6
Danderyd, 13,794 ... H 1
Deje, *3,955 ... H 7
Djursholm, 7,544 ... H 1
Dorotea, *4,149 ... K 4
Ed, *2,639 ... H 7
Edsbyn, *7,103 ... J 6
Eksjö, 9,802 ... J 8
Emmaboda, 3,023 ... J 8
Enköping, 15,254 ... G 1
Eskilstuna, 60,628 ... K 7
Eslöv, 10,821 ... H 9
Fagersta, 15,661 ... J 6
Falkenberg, 10,869 ... H 8
Falköping, 14,497 ... H 7
Falun, 18,632 ... J 6
Filipstad, 7,557 ... H 7
Finspång, 16,335 ... J 7
Flen, 6,078 ... K 7
Frösö, 8,724 ... J 5
Frovi, 3,047 ... J 7
Galliväre, 9,747 ... M 3
Gamleby, *3,725 ... K 8
Gavle, 56,805 ... K 6
Gimo, *1,595 ... K 6
Gnesta, 3,169 ... G 2
Göteborg, 414,466 ... G 8
Grängesberg, 6,274 ... J 6
Gränna, 3,146 ... J 8
Hagfors, 8,654 ... H 6
Hallstahammar, 11,770 ... K 7
Halmstad, 40,282 ... H 8
Hälsingborg, 78,291 ... H 8
Haparanda, 3,653 ... N 4
Härnösand, 16,712 ... L 5
Hässleholm, 14,584 ... H 8
Hedemora, 6,368 ... K 6
Hjo, 3,689 ... J 7
Höganäs, 7,698 ... H 8
Holmsund, 5,245 ... M 5
Hudiksvall, 12,219 ... K 6
Hultsfred, 4,561 ... K 8
Huskvarna, 13,953 ... J 8
Järna, *5,500 ... G 2
Järpen, *2,969 ... H 5
Järvsö, *5,232 ... K 6
Jokkmokk, *5,069 ... L 3
Jönköping, 51,875 ... H 8
Jörn, *4,532 ... M 4
Kalmar, 31,905 ... K 8
Karlshamn, 11,687 ... J 8
Karlskoga, 36,419 ... J 7
Karlskrona, 33,217 ... K 8
Karlstad, 45,858 ... H 7
Katrineholm, 20,327 ... K 7
Kil, *4,902 ... H 7
Kiruna, 28,062 ... L 3
Kisa, *4,144 ... J 8
Köping, 18,598 ... J 7
Kopparberg, *7,329 ... J 7
Kosta, *1,561 ... J 8
Kramfors, 12,047 ... K 5
Kristianstad, 26,494 ... J 9
Kristinehamn, 21,154 ... H 7
Krylbo, 4,549 ... J 6
Kumla, 10,043 ... J 7
Kungälv, *8,728 ... G 8
Kungsbacka, 5,981 ... G 8
Laholm, 3,623 ... H 8
Landskrona, 28,609 ... H 9
Långsele, *3,801 ... K 5
Långshyttan, 3,293 ... K 6
Laxå, 5,312 ... J 7
Leksand, *7,887 ... J 6
Lidingö, 32,956 ... H 1
Lidköping, 17,893 ... H 7
Limmared, 1,582 ... H 8
Lindesberg, 6,502 ... J 7
Linköping, 69,981 ... K 7
Ljungby, 10,343 ... J 8
Ljusdal, *11,089 ... J 6
Ljusne, 4,874 ... K 6
Ludvika, *21,906 ... J 6
Luleå, 33,200 ... N 4
Lund, 42,778 ... H 9
Lycksele, 6,211 ... L 4
Lysekil, 6,391 ... G 7
Malmberget, *12,354 ... M 3
Malmköping, 3,453 ... F 1
Malmö, 241,778 ... H 9
Malung, *8,613 ... H 6
Mariefred, 1,876 ... G 1
Mariestad, 10,579 ... H 7
Marstrand, 1,102 ... G 8
Mellerud, 4,214 ... H 7
Mjölby, 10,727 ... J 7
Molndal, 28,618 ... H 8
Mönsterås, 6,130 ... K 8
Mora, 13,014 ... J 6
Motala, 25,194 ... J 7
Nacka, 23,026 ... H 1
Nässjö, 19,217 ... J 8
Nora, 4,253 ... J 7
Norrköping, 92,600 ... K 7
Norrsundet, *4,634 ... K 6
Norrtälje, 9,743 ... L 7
Norsjö, *5,546 ... L 4
Nybro, 9,512 ... J 8
Nyköping, 26,542 ... K 7
Nynäshamn, 10,199 ... L 7
Ockelbo, *5,918 ... K 6
örbyhus, *2,389 ... K 6
örebro, 262,733 ... J 7
öregrund, 1,339 ... L 6
örnskoldsvik, 9,214 ... L 5
Orsa, *7,468 ... J 6
Osby, *7,341 ... J 8
Oskarshamn, 13,330 ... K 8
östersund, 25,347 ... J 5
östhammar, 1,794 ... L 6
Ottenby, 198 ... K 8
övertorneå, *3,680 ... N 3
överum, 2,447 ... K 7
Oxelösund, 12,975 ... K 7
Pajala, *3,991 ... N 3
Piteå, 8,268 ... M 4
Ramnäs, *3,764 ... J 7
Ramsele, *3,625 ... K 5
Rättvik, *7,582 ... J 6
Reftele, *2,054 ... H 8
Rimbo, *2,941 ... L 7

(continued on following page)

Norway, Sweden, Finland, Denmark and Iceland
(continued)

SWEDEN (continued)

Ronneby, 9,546 ..... J 8
Säffle, 10,713 ..... H 7
Sala, 11,214 ..... K 7
Saltsjöbaden, 5,994 ..... J 1
Sandviken, 23,146 ..... K 6
Särna, *2,131 ..... H 6
Säter, 4,501 ..... J 6
Sävsjö, 5,207 ..... J 8
Sigtuna, 2,656 ..... H 1
Simrishamn, 4,667 ..... J 9
Skänninge, 3,078 ..... J 7
Skara, 9,213 ..... H 7
Skellefteå, 23,669 ..... M 4
Skön, 15,213 ..... K 5
Skövde, 24,402 ..... H 7
Söderhamn, 11,941 ..... K 6
Söderköping, 5,632 ..... K 7
Södertälje, 38,172 ..... G 1
Sollefteå, 9,042 ..... K 5
Sollentuna, 31,060 ..... H 1
Solna, 54,281 ..... H 1
Sölvesborg, 6,188 ..... J 9
Sorsele, *3,760 ..... K 4
Stockholm (cap.), 795,976 ..... G 1
Stockholm (greater), 1,180,490 ..... G 1
Storuman, 2,112 ..... K 4
Storvik, 2,272 ..... K 6
Strängnäs, 8,611 ..... F 1
Strömstad, 4,145 ..... G 7
Strömsund, *6,271 ..... K 5
Sundbyberg, 27,393 ..... G 1
Sundsvall, 30,423 ..... K 5
Sunne, *8,862 ..... H 7
Sveg, 2,272 ..... J 5
Tidaholm, 6,820 ..... J 7
Tierp, 3,942 ..... K 6
Tillberga, 297 ..... K 7
Timra, 11,804 ..... K 5
Torsby, *6,736 ..... H 6
Torshälla, 6,636 ..... K 7
Tranås, 16,188 ..... J 7
Trelleborg, 20,678 ..... H 9
Trollhättan, 33,812 ..... H 7
Trosa, 1,546 ..... K 7
Uddevalla, 35,266 ..... G 7
Ulricehamn, 8,275 ..... H 8
Umeå, 24,736 ..... M 5
Uppsala, 82,361 ..... L 7
Vadstena, 4,307 ..... J 7
Vaggeryd, 4,724 ..... J 8
Valdemarsvik, 3,420 ..... K 7
Vänersborg, 18,906 ..... H 7
Vännäs, 4,052 ..... L 5
Vansbro, 2,951 ..... H 6
Vara, 2,862 ..... H 7
Varberg, 15,298 ..... G 8
Värnamo, 14,283 ..... J 8
Västerås, 82,055 ..... J 7
Västerhäninge, *8,509 ..... H 1
Västervik, 18,765 ..... K 8
Vaxholm, 4,094 ..... J 1
Vaxjö, 26,933 ..... J 8
Vetlanda, 9,601 ..... J 8
Vilhelmina, 3,036 ..... K 4
Vimmerby, 6,707 ..... J 8
Virserum, *3,591 ..... J 8
Visby, 16,345 ..... L 8
Vislanda, *2,496 ..... H 8
Ystad, 13,633 ..... H 9

PHYSICAL FEATURES

Angerman (river) ..... K 5
Asnen (lake) ..... J 8
Bothnia (gulf) ..... M 5
Byske (river) ..... L 4
Fårö (isl.), 842 ..... L 8
Göta (river) ..... H 7
Gotland (isl.), 53,480 ..... L 8
Hornslandet (pen.) ..... K 6
Kalix (river) ..... N 3
Kalmarsund (sound) ..... K 8
Kattegat (strait) ..... G 8
Kebnekaise (mt.) ..... L 3
Lainio (river) ..... N 3
Lapland (dist.) ..... M 2
Lule (river) ..... M 3
Muonio (river) ..... M 2
öland (isl.), 23,265 ..... K 8
Ornö (isl.), 271 ..... J 1
österdal (river) ..... H 6
Pite (river) ..... M 4
Skellefte (river) ..... L 4
Stora Lulevatten (lake) ..... L 3
Storuman (lake) ..... K 4
Sulitjelma (mt.) ..... K 3
Torne (river) ..... M 3
Torneträsk (lake) ..... L 2
Uddjaur (lake) ..... L 4
Ume (river) ..... L 4
Vänern (lake) ..... H 7
Vättern (lake) ..... J 7
Vesterdal (river) ..... H 6
Vindel (river) ..... L 4
Vojmsjön (lakes) ..... J 4
*Parish population

FINLAND

PROVINCES

Ahvenanmaa, 21,274 ..... L 6
Häme, 597,267 ..... O 6
Keski-Suomi, 247,972 ..... O 5
Kuopio, 270,118 ..... P 5
Kymi, 345,571 ..... Q 6
Lappi, 214,383 ..... P 3
Mikkeli, 234,015 ..... P 6
Oulu, 415,110 ..... P 4
Pohjois-Karjala, 204,742 ..... Q 5
Turku-Pori, 667,508 ..... N 6
Uusimaa, 879,029 ..... O 6
Vaasa, 448,627 ..... N 5

CITIES and TOWNS

Äänekoski, 7,388 ..... O 5
Åbo (Turku), 131,992 ..... N 6
Alavus (Alavo), 1,029 ..... N 5
Björneborg (Pori), 57,380 ..... M 6
Borgå (Porvoo), 12,140 ..... O 6
Brahestad (Raahe), 5,667 ..... O 4
Ekenäs (Tammisaari), 5,844 ..... N 6
Forssa, 11,000 ..... N 6
Fredrikshamn (Hamina), 10,343 ..... P 6
Gamlakarleby (Kokkola), 17,381 ..... N 5
Haapajärvi, 2,895 ..... O 5
Haapamäki, 2,200 ..... O 5
Hämeenlinna (Tavastehus), 30,747 ..... O 6
Hamina, 10,343 ..... P 6
Hangö (Hanko), 8,729 ..... N 7
Heinola, 11,993 ..... P 6
Helsinki (Helsingfors) (cap.), 470,410 ..... O 6
Helsinki (greater), 594,248 ..... O 6
Himanka, 1,268 ..... N 5
Hyrynsalmi, 1,283 ..... Q 4
Hyvinkää (Hyvinge), 21,750 ..... O 6
Iisalmi, 6,320 ..... P 5
Ilomantsi, 1,835 ..... R 5
Imatra, 34,782 ..... Q 6
Ivalo, 2,555 ..... P 2
Jakobstad (Pietarsaari), 16,497 ..... N 5
Joensuu, 30,081 ..... R 5
Juuka, 1,545 ..... Q 5
Jyväskylä, 43,959 ..... O 5
Kajaani, 16,558 ..... P 4
Kalajoki, 3,711 ..... N 4
Karis (Karjaa), 4,935 ..... N 6
Karkkila, 5,120 ..... N 6
Kaskö (Kaskinen), 1,446 ..... M 5
Kauttua, 1,970 ..... M 6
Kemi, 29,352 ..... O 4
Kemijärvi, 5,425 ..... P 3
Kerava (Kervo), 10,594 ..... O 6
Kittilä, 1,668 ..... O 3
Kokemäki, *9,711 ..... N 6
Kokkola (Gamlakarleby), 17,381 ..... N 5
Kotka, 31,424 ..... P 6
Kouvola, 19,760 ..... P 6
Kristiinankaupunki (Kristinestad), 2,724 ..... N 5
Kuhmo, 2,709 ..... Q 4
Kuopio, 47,626 ..... Q 5
Kurikka, 1,881 ..... M 5
Kuusamo, 3,216 ..... Q 4
Lahti, 72,676 ..... O 6
Lappeenranta, 22,860 ..... P 6
Lauritsala, 12,216 ..... Q 6
Lieksa, 4,580 ..... R 5
Loimaa, 6,130 ..... N 6
Lovisa (Loviisa), 7,054 ..... P 6
Maarianhamina (Mariehamn), 7,075 ..... M 7
Mänttä, 6,815 ..... O 6
Mariehamn (Maarianhamina), 7,075 ..... M 7
Mikkeli (Sankt Michel), 21,182 ..... P 6
Muonio, 1,041 ..... O 3
Naantali (Nådendal), 2,848 ..... M 6
Nivala, 1,571 ..... O 5
Nokia, 18,362 ..... N 6
Nurmes, 2,341 ..... Q 5
Nykarleby (Uusikaarlepyy), 1,176 ..... N 5
Nyslott (Savonlinna), 15,779 ..... Q 6
Nystad (Uusikaupunki), 4,668 ..... M 6
Oulainen, 3,295 ..... O 4
Oulu (Uleåborg), 63,339 ..... O 4
Parikkala, 1,481 ..... Q 6
Parkano, 1,988 ..... N 6
Pello, 1,865 ..... O 3
Pieksämäki, 11,119 ..... P 5
Pietarsaari (Jakobstad), 16,497 ..... N 5
Pori (Björneborg), 57,380 ..... M 6
Porvoo (Borgå), 12,140 ..... O 6
Posio, *7,235 ..... Q 3
Pudasjärvi, *15,530 ..... P 4
Raahe (Brahestad), 5,667 ..... O 4
Rauma (Raumo), 22,480 ..... M 6
Riihimäki, 21,440 ..... O 6
Rovaniemi, 23,367 ..... O 3
Saarijärvi, 1,907 ..... O 5
Salo, 11,801 ..... N 6
Sankt Michel (Mikkeli), 21,182 ..... P 6
Savonlinna, 15,779 ..... Q 6
Savukoski, 448 ..... Q 3
Seinäjoki, 16,814 ..... N 5
Sodankylä, 2,458 ..... P 3
Sotkamo, 1,719 ..... Q 4
Suolahti, 5,022 ..... O 5
Suomussalmi, 1,006 ..... Q 4
Suonenjoki, 3,191 ..... P 5
Tammerfors (Tampere), 134,202 ..... N 6
Tammisaari (Ekenäs), 5,844 ..... N 6
Tampere (Tammerfors), 134,202 ..... N 6
Tapiola, 8,786 ..... O 6
Tavastehus (Hameenlinnä), 30,747 ..... O 6
Teuva, 1,027 ..... N 5
Toijala, 7,178 ..... N 6
Tornio (Torneå), 6,219 ..... O 4
Turku (Åbo), 131,992 ..... N 6
Uleåborg (Oulu), 63,339 ..... O 4
Ulvila (Ulvsby), *7,544 ..... N 6
Utsjoki, 629 ..... P 2
Uusikaarlepyy (Nykarleby), 1,176 ..... N 5
Uusikaupunki (Nystad), 4,668 ..... M 6
Vaala, 571 ..... P 4
Vaasa (Vasa), 44,629 ..... M 5
Valkeakoski, 14,825 ..... N 6
Vammala, 5,062 ..... N 6
Varkaus, 23,082 ..... Q 5
Vasa (Vaasa), 44,629 ..... M 5

PHYSICAL FEATURES

Åland (isls.) ..... L 6
Finland (gulf) ..... P 7
Haltia (mt.) ..... M 2
Hankö Udd (prom.) ..... N 7
Hauki (lake) ..... Q 5
Ii (river) ..... O 4
Inari (lake) ..... P 2
Juo (lake) ..... Q 5
Kala (river) ..... O 4
Kalla (lake) ..... P 5
Keitele (lake) ..... O 5
Kemi (lake) ..... Q 3
Kemi (river) ..... O 3
Kianta (lake) ..... Q 4
Kilpis (lake) ..... M 2
Kittinen (river) ..... P 3
Kivi (lake) ..... O 5
Koitere (lake) ..... R 5
Kuusamo (lake) ..... Q 4
Langelmä (lake) ..... O 6
Lapland (reg.) ..... O 2
Lapuan (river) ..... N 5
Lesti (lake) ..... O 5
Muo (lake) ..... R 4
Muonio (river) ..... M 2
Nasi (lake) ..... O 6
Onkivesi (lake) ..... P 5
Orihvesi (lake) ..... Q 5
Oulu (river) ..... O 4
Ounas (river) ..... O 3
Päijänne (lake) ..... O 6
Pasvik (river) ..... Q 2
Pielinen (lake) ..... Q 5
Puru (lake) ..... Q 6
Puula (lake) ..... P 5
Pyhä (lake) ..... M 6
Pyhä (lake) ..... O 5
Saimaa (lake) ..... Q 6
Siika (river) ..... O 4
Simo (lake) ..... P 3
Simo (river) ..... O 4
Tana (river) ..... P 2
Tornio (river) ..... O 3
Vallgrund (isl.) ..... M 5
Ylikitka (lake) ..... Q 3
*Population of commune

DENMARK

CITIES and TOWNS

Aabenraa, 14,219 ..... C 7
Aabybro, 1,346 ..... C 3
Aakirkeby, 1,461 ..... F 9
Aalborg, 85,800 ..... D 4
Aalestrup, 1,763 ..... C 4
Aarhus, 119,568 ..... D 5
Aars, 3,206 ..... C 4
Aarup, 1,286 ..... D 7
Ærøskøbing, 1,273 ..... D 8
Allingaabro, 1,312 ..... D 5
Allinge-Sandvig, 2,114 ..... F 8
Andsager, 1,033 ..... B 6
Arden, 1,365 ..... C 4
Asaa, 1,265 ..... D 3
Askov, 575 ..... C 7
Asnæs, 1,120 ..... E 6
Assens, 4,937 ..... D 7
Assens, 1,236 ..... D 4
Augustenborg, 1,926 ..... D 8
Aulum, 1,253 ..... B 5
Auning, 1,314 ..... D 5
Bælum, 638 ..... D 4
Bagenkop, 705 ..... D 8
Ballerup, 9,392 ..... F 6
Ballum, 890 ..... B 7
Bandholm, 712 ..... E 8
Bedsted, 851 ..... B 4
Birkerød, 14,846 ..... F 6
Bjerringbro, 3,582 ..... C 5
Bogense, 2,968 ..... D 6
Bolderslev, 691 ..... C 8
Børkop, 1,051 ..... C 6
Borup, 894 ..... E 7
Brabrand, 5,139 ..... C 5
Brædstrup, 1,619 ..... C 6
Bramminge, 2,900 ..... B 7
Brande, 4,151 ..... C 6
Broager, 1,601 ..... C 8
Brønderslev, 9,454 ..... C 3
Brøns, 865 ..... B 7
Brørup, 2,106 ..... C 7
Brovst, 1,640 ..... C 3
Bryrup, 1,019 ..... C 5
Byrum, 939 ..... E 3
Christiansfeld, 819 ..... C 7
Copenhagen (København) (cap.), 712,950 ..... F 6
Copenhagen (greater), 1,262,159 ..... F 6
Dragør, 4,243 ..... F 6
Dronninglund, 1,647 ..... D 3
Dybvad, 817 ..... D 3
Ebeltoft, 2,227 ..... D 5
Egernsund, 1,230 ..... C 8
Egtved, 1,012 ..... C 6
Ejby, 1,309 ..... D 7
Ejstrupholm, 913 ..... C 6
Elsinore (Helsingør), 26,658 ..... F 6
Esbjerg, 55,171 ..... B 7
Faaborg, 2,170 ..... B 6
Faaborg, 5,135 ..... D 7
Fakse, 2,002 ..... F 7
Fakse Ladeplads, 1,579 ..... F 7
Farsø, 1,581 ..... C 4
Farum, 4,101 ..... F 6
Fjerritslev, 1,925 ..... C 3
Fredensborg, 3,448 ..... F 6
Fredericia, 29,870 ..... C 6
Frederiksberg, 114,285 ..... F 6
Frederikshavn, 22,522 ..... D 3
Frederikssund, 5,722 ..... E 6
Frederiksværk, 4,435 ..... E 5
Fuglebjerg, 967 ..... E 7
Gedser, 1,262 ..... F 8
Gedsted, 965 ..... C 4
Gelsted, 653 ..... C 7
Gentofte, 88,308 ..... F 6
Gilleleje, 2,219 ..... F 5
Give, 1,800 ..... C 6
Gjerlev, 901 ..... D 4
Glamsbjerg, 1,719 ..... D 7
Glostrup, 21,845 ..... F 6
Glumsø, 767 ..... E 7
Gørding, 1,107 ..... B 7
Gørlev, 1,379 ..... E 7
Graasten, 2,414 ..... C 8
Græsted, 1,078 ..... F 5
Gram, 1,801 ..... C 7
Grenaa, 9,088 ..... D 5
Grindsted, 5,289 .....
Gylling, 520 .....
Haarby, 1,225 .....
Haarlev, 1,253 .....
Haderslev, 19,735 .....
Hadsten, 2,525 .....
Hadsund, 3,424 .....
Hals, 1,563 .....
Hammel, 2,462 .....
Hammerum, 1,544 .....
Hansted, 510 .....
Hasle, 1,487 .....
Haslev, 6,155 .....
Havdrup, 1,048 .....
Hedensted, 1,717 .....
Hellebæk, 1,870 .....
Helsingør, 26,658 .....
Henne, 1,159 .....
Herning, 24,790 .....
Hillerød, 11,605 .....
Hinnerup, 937 .....
Hirtshals, 4,177 .....
Hjallerup, 1,241 .....
Hjerm, 532 .....
Hjerting, 996 .....
Hjørring, 15,038 .....
Hobro, 8,208 .....
Højer, 1,400 .....
Højslev, 889 .....
Holbæk, 15,475 .....
Holeby, 1,345 .....
Holstebro, 18,563 .....
Holsted, 1,081 .....
Holte, 6,718 .....
Høng, 1,950 .....
Hornslet, 1,637 .....
Hornum, 834 .....
Horsens, 37,261 .....
Hørsholm, 12,401 ..... F
Hørve, 906 ..... E
Hou, 548 ..... D
Humlum, 1,343 ..... E
Hundested, 3,806 ..... E
Hurup, 2,160 ..... E
Hvidbjerg, 978 ..... E
Hviding, 677 ..... E
Ikast, 5,797 C
Jelling, 1,228 C
Jerslev, 718 ..... D
Juelsminde, 950 ..... D
Jyderup, 2,305 ..... E
Kalundborg, 9,763 ..... E
Karby, 930 ..... B
Karise, 923 ..... F
Karup, 1,137 C
Kastrup, 20,305 ..... F
Kerteminde, 4,024 ..... D
Kjellerup, 2,637 C
Klakksvik, Faerøe Is., 3,894 ..... B
Klitmøller, 550 ..... B
København (Copenhagen), (cap.), 721,381 ..... F
Køge, 12,294 ..... F
Kolding, 35,101 C
Kolind, 814 ..... D
Korsør, 14,276 ..... E
Kværndrup, 776 ..... D
Langaa, 2,119 C
Lem, 837 ..... B
Lemvig, 5,783 ..... B
Løgstør, 3,435 C
Løgumkloster, 1,907 ..... B
Lohals, 640 ..... E
Løjt Kirkeby, 725 C
Løkken, 1,506 C
Løsning, 1,110 C
Lundby, 549 ..... E
Lunderskov, 1,181 C
Lyngby, 63,712 ..... F
Malling, 955 ..... D
Mariager, 1,483 ..... D
Maribo, 5,235 ..... E
Marstal, 1,986 ..... D
Middelfart, 8,801 C
Møgeltønder, 680 ..... B
Næstved (Nastved), 19,617 ..... E
Nakskov, 16,639 ..... E
Neksø, 3,220 ..... F
Nibe, 2,494 C
Nordborg, 2,563 C
Nordby, 1,975 ..... B
Nordby, 313 ..... D
Nørre-Aaby, 1,844 C
Nørre-Alslev, 1,062 ..... E
Nørre-Broby, 715 ..... D
Nørre-Nebel, 753 ..... B
Nørresundby, 10,456 ..... D
Nørrevorupør, 610 ..... B
Nyborg, 11,667 ..... D
Nykøbing, Holbæk, 4,803 ..... E

AGRICULTURE, INDUSTRY and RESOURCES

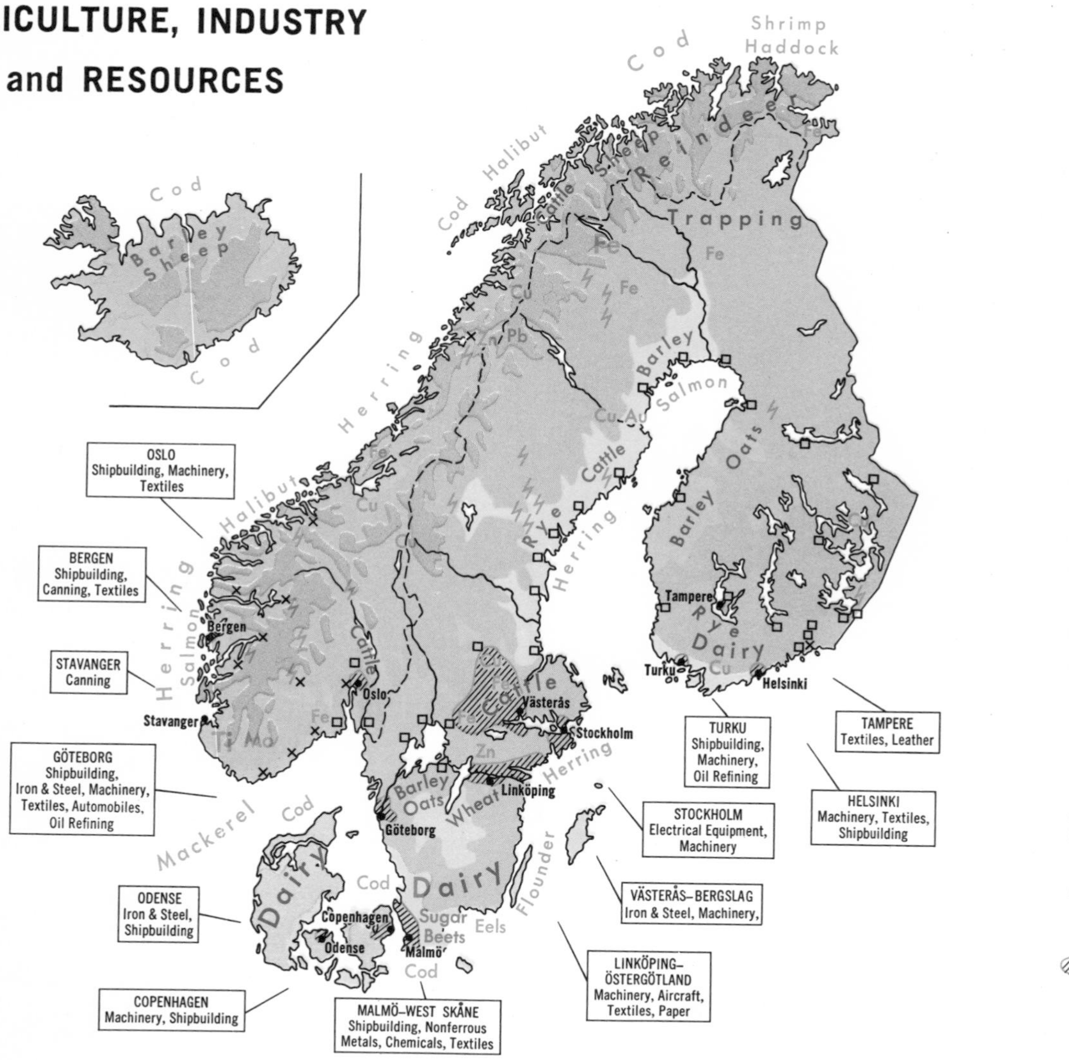
Shrimp
Haddock
Cod
Halibut
Cattle
Sheep
Reindeer
Trapping
Fe
Barley
Sheep
Cod
Cod
Herring
Zn Pb
Cu
Barley
Salmon
Cu Au
Oats
Cattle
Halibut
Rye
Herring
OSLO
Shipbuilding, Machinery, Textiles
BERGEN
Shipbuilding, Canning, Textiles
STAVANGER
Canning
Bergen
Herring
Salmon
Cattle
Oslo
Stavanger
Ti Mo
Cattle
Västerås
Stockholm
Tampere
Rye
Dairy
Turku
Helsinki
GÖTEBORG
Shipbuilding, Iron & Steel, Machinery, Textiles, Automobiles, Oil Refining
Zn
Herring
Barley
Oats
Wheat
Linköping
Göteborg
Mackerel
Cod
Dairy
Cod
Dairy
Flounder
Copenhagen
Odense
Sugar Beets
Eels
Malmö
Cod
ODENSE
Iron & Steel, Shipbuilding
COPENHAGEN
Machinery, Shipbuilding
MALMÖ–WEST SKÅNE
Shipbuilding, Nonferrous Metals, Chemicals, Textiles
LINKÖPING–ÖSTERGÖTLAND
Machinery, Aircraft, Textiles, Paper
VÄSTERÅS–BERGSLAG
Iron & Steel, Machinery,
STOCKHOLM
Electrical Equipment, Machinery
TURKU
Shipbuilding, Machinery, Oil Refining
HELSINKI
Machinery, Textiles, Shipbuilding
TAMPERE
Textiles, Leather

DOMINANT LAND USE

- Cash Cereals, Dairy
- Dairy, Cattle, Hogs
- Dairy, General Farming
- General Farming (chiefly cereals)
- Nomadic Sheep Herding
- Forests, Limited Mixed Farming
- Nonagricultural Land

MAJOR MINERAL OCCURRENCES

Au Gold
Cu Copper
Fe Iron
Mo Molybdenum
Pb Lead
Ti Titanium
Zn Zinc

Water Power
Major Industrial Areas
× Electrochemical & Electrometallurgical Centers
□ Paper, Pulp & Sawmilling Centers

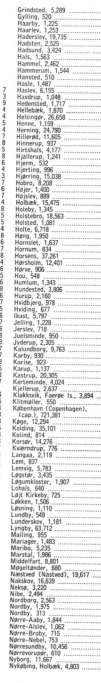

Norway, Sweden, Finland, Denmark and Iceland
(continued)

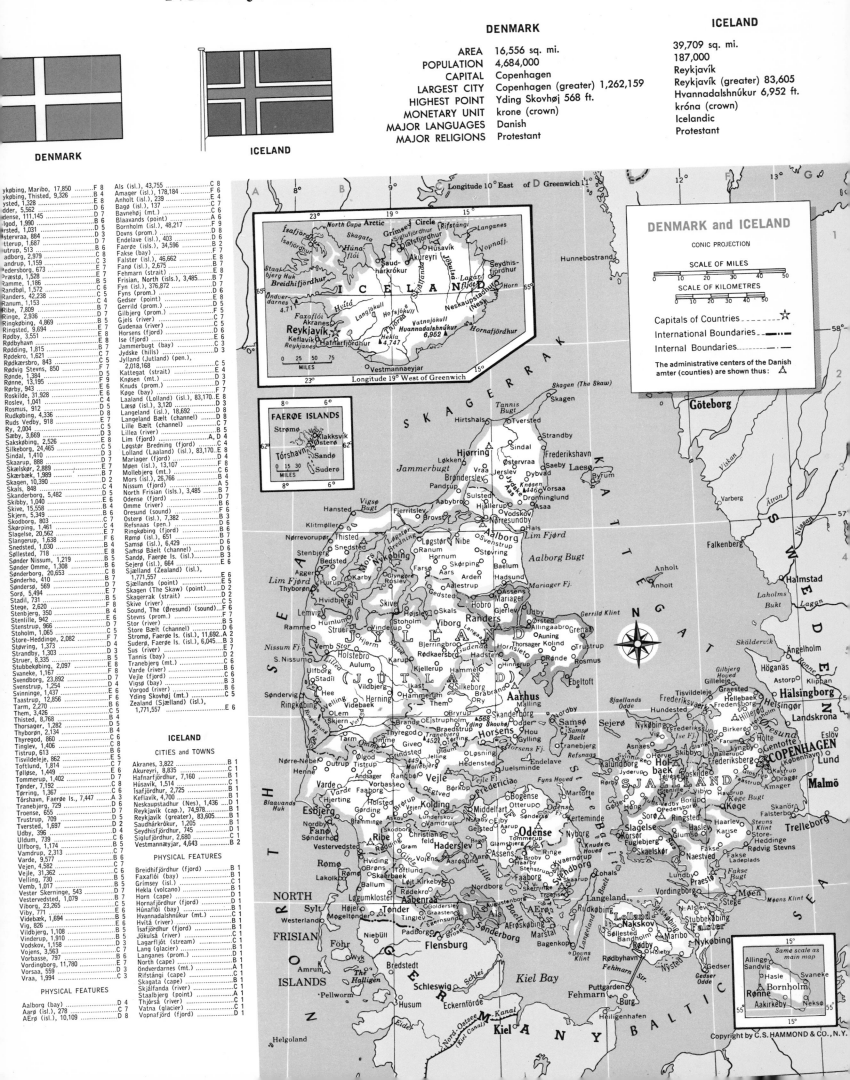

DENMARK

ICELAND

	DENMARK	ICELAND
AREA	16,556 sq. mi.	39,709 sq. mi.
POPULATION	4,684,000	187,000
CAPITAL	Copenhagen	Reykjavík
LARGEST CITY	Copenhagen (greater) 1,262,159	Reykjavík (greater) 83,605
HIGHEST POINT	Yding Skovhøj 568 ft.	Hvannadalshnúkur 6,952 ft.
MONETARY UNIT	krone (crown)	króna (crown)
MAJOR LANGUAGES	Danish	Icelandic
MAJOR RELIGIONS	Protestant	Protestant

ykøbing, Maribo, 17,850 ...F 8
ykøbing, Thisted, 9,326 ...B 4
ysted, 1,328 ...D 6
dder, 5,562 ...D 7
dense, 111,145 ...E 7
lgod, 1,990 ...C 6
rsted, 1,031 ...D 3
stervaa, 884 ...C 4
lterup, 1,687 ...B 7
utrup, 513 ...C 6
adborg, 2,979 ...C 3
andrup, 1,159 ...C 8
edersborg, 673 ...E 7
Præstø, 1,528 ...F 7
Ramme, 1,186 ...C 5
Randbøl, 1,572 ...C 6
Randers, 42,238 ...C 4
Ranum, 1,153 ...C 4
Ribe, 7,809 ...D 7
Ringe, 2,936 ...E 7
Ringkøbing, 4,869 ...E 7
Ringsted, 9,694 ...E 7
Rødby, 3,551 ...E 8
Rødbyhavn ...E 8
Rødding, 1,815 ...C 7
Rødekro, 1,621 ...C 7
Rødkærsbro, 843 ...C 5
Rødvig Stevns, 850 ...F 7
Rønde, 1,384 ...D 5
Rønne, 13,195 ...E 6
Rørby, 943 ...E 6
Roskilde, 31,928 ...C 4
Roslev, 1,041 ...C 4
Rosmus, 912 ...D 5
Rudkøbing, 4,336 ...D 8
Ruds Vedby, 918 ...C 5
Ry, 2,004 ...C 5
Sæby, 3,669 ...D 3
Sakskøbing, 2,526 ...E 8
Silkeborg, 24,465 ...D 5
Sindal, 1,410 ...D 3
Skaarup, 888 ...E 7
Skælskør, 2,889 ...B 7
Skærbæk, 1,989 ...D 2
Skagen, 10,390 ...C 4
Skals, 848 ...C 4
Skanderborg, 5,482 ...D 5
Skibby, 1,040 ...E 6
Skive, 15,558 ...B 4
Skjern, 5,349 ...B 6
Skodsborg, 803 ...C 7
Skørping, 1,461 ...E 7
Slagelse, 20,562 ...F 6
Slangerup, 1,638 ...E 8
Snedsted, 1,030 ...E 8
Søllested, 718 ...B 5
Sønder Nissum, 1,219 ...B 5
Sønder Omme, 1,308 ...B 6
Sønderborg, 20,653 ...C 8
Sønderho, 410 ...B 7
Søndersø, 569 ...D 7
Sorø, 5,494 ...E 7
Stadil, 731 ...B 5
Stege, 2,620 ...F 8
Stenbjerg, 350 ...B 5
Stenlille, 942 ...D 7
Stenstrup, 966 ...C 5
Stoholm, 1,065 ...C 5
Store-Heddinge, 2,082 ...F 7
Støvring, 1,373 ...D 3
Strandby, 1,303 ...D 3
Struer, 8,335 ...B 5
Stubbekøbing, 2,097 ...E 8
Svaneke, 1,167 ...D 7
Svendborg, 23,892 ...D 7
Svenstrup, 1,254 ...E 8
Svinninge, 1,437 ...F 6
Taastrup, 12,856 ...B 5
Tarm, 2,270 ...C 5
Them, 3,768 ...B 4
Thisted, 8,768 ...B 4
Thorsager, 1,282 ...B 4
Thyborøn, 2,134 ...B 4
Thyregod, 860 ...C 6
Tinglev, 1,406 ...C 6
Tistrup, 613 ...B 6
Tisvildeleje, 862 ...E 5
Toftlund, 1,814 ...C 7
Tølløse, 1,449 ...E 6
Tommerup, 1,402 ...D 7
Tønder, 7,192 ...C 8
Tørring, 1,367 ...C 6
Tørshavn, Faerøe Is., 7,447 ...A 3
Tranebjerg, 729 ...D 6
Troense, 655 ...D 5
Trustrup, 709 ...D 5
Tversted, 1,697 ...D 2
Udby, 396 ...D 4
Uldum, 739 ...C 7
Ulfborg, 1,174 ...B 6
Vamdrup, 2,313 ...C 7
Varde, 9,577 ...C 7
Vejen, 4,582 ...B 6
Vejle, 31,362 ...C 7
Velling, 730 ...C 6
Vemb, 1,017 ...B 5
Vester Skerninge, 543 ...B 5
Vestervedsted, 1,079 ...D 7
Viborg, 23,265 ...B 7
Viby, 771 ...C 5
Videbæk, 1,694 ...E 6
Vig, 826 ...B 5
Vildbjerg, 1,108 ...E 6
Vinderup, 1,910 ...B 5
Vodskov, 1,158 ...B 6
Vojens, 3,563 ...D 3
Vorbasse, 797 ...C 7
Vordingborg, 11,780 ...B 6
Vorsaa, 559 ...E 7
Vraa, 1,994 ...D 3
...C 3

PHYSICAL FEATURES

Aalborg (bay) ...D 4
Aarø (isl.), 278 ...C 7
Ærø (isl.), 10,109 ...D 8
Als (isl.), 43,755 ...C 8
Amager (isl.), 178,184 ...F 6
Anholt (isl.), 239 ...C 7
Bagø (isl.), 137 ...C 7
Bavnehøj (mt.) ...C 6
Blaavands (point) ...A 6
Bornholm (isl.), 48,217 ...F 9
Dovns (prom.) ...D 8
Endelave (isl.), 403 ...B 2
Faerøe (isls.), 34,596 ...F 7
Falster (isl.), 46,662 ...E 8
Fanø (isl.), 2,675 ...B 7
Fehmarn (strait) ...E 8
Frisian, North (isls.), 3,485 ...B 7
Fyn (isl.), 376,872 ...D 7
Fyns (prom.) ...D 6
Gedser (point) ...E 8
Gerrild (prom.) ...D 5
Gilbjerg (prom.) ...F 5
Gjels (river) ...C 7
Gudenaa (river) ...D 6
Horsens (fjord) ...E 6
Ise (fjord) ...F 6
Jammerbugt (bay) ...C 3
Jydske (hills) ...D 3
Jylland (Jutland) (pen.), 2,018,168 ...C 5
Kattegat (strait) ...E 4
Knøsen (mt.) ...D 3
Knuds (prom.) ...F 7
Køge (bay) ...F 7
Laaland (Lolland) (isl.), 83,170 ...E 8
Læsø (isl.), 3,120 ...D 3
Langeland (isl.), 18,692 ...D 8
Langeland Bælt (channel) ...C 7
Lille Bælt (channel) ...C 7
Lillea (river) ...A, D 4
Lim (fjord) ...B 4
Løgstør Bredning (fjord) ...C 4
Lolland (Laaland) (isl.), 83,170 ...E 8
Mariager (fjord) ...D 4
Møen (isl.), 13,107 ...F 8
Mollebjerg (mt.) ...C 6
Mors (isl.), 26,766 ...B 4
Nissum (fjord) ...A 5
North Frisian (isls.), 3,485 ...D 7
Odense (fjord) ...B 6
Omme (river) ...F 6
Øresund (sound) ...B 3
Østerø (isl.), 7,382 ...B 3
Ringkøbing (fjord) ...D 6
Refsnaes (prom.) ...B 7
Rømø (isl.), 651 ...B 7
Samsø (isl.), 6,429 ...D 6
Samsø Bælt (channel) ...D 6
Sandø, Faerøe Is. (isl.) ...D 6
Sejerø (isl.), 664 ...E 6
Sjælland (Zealand) (isl.), 1,771,557 ...E 5
Sjællands (point) ...E 5
Skagen (The Skaw) (point) ...D 2
Skagerrak (strait) ...C 2
Skive (river) ...B 5
Sound, The (Øresund) (sound) ...F 6
Stevns (prom.) ...F 7
Stor (river) ...B 5
Store Bælt (channel) ...D 6
Stromø, Faerøe Is. (isl.), 11,692 ...A 2
Suderø, Faerøe Is. (isl.), 6,045 ...E 7
Sus (river) ...D 2
Tannis (bay) ...C 6
Tranebjerg (mt.) ...B 6
Varde (river) ...B 6
Vejle (fjord) ...B 3
Vejrs (bay) ...B 3
Vorgod (river) ...C 5
Yding Skovhøj (mt.) ...C 5
Zealand (Sjælland) (isl.), 1,771,557 ...E 6

ICELAND

CITIES and TOWNS

Akranes, 3,822 ...B 1
Akureyri, 8,835 ...C 1
Hafnarfjördhur, 7,160 ...B 1
Húsavík, 1,514 ...C 1
Ísafjördhur, 2,725 ...B 1
Keflavík, 4,700 ...B 1
Neskaupstadhur (Nes), 1,436 ...D 1
Reykjavík (cap.), 74,978 ...B 1
Reykjavík (greater), 83,605 ...B 1
Saudhárkrókur, 1,205 ...C 1
Seydhisfjördhur, 745 ...D 1
Siglufjördhur, 2,680 ...C 1
Vestmannaeyjar, 4,643 ...B 2

PHYSICAL FEATURES

Breidhifjördhur (fjord) ...B 1
Faxaflói (bay) ...B 1
Grímsey (isl.) ...C 1
Hekla (volcano) ...C 1
Horn (cape) ...D 1
Hornafjördhur (fjord) ...D 1
Húnaflói (bay) ...C 1
Hvannadalshnúkur (mt.) ...C 1
Hvítá (river) ...C 1
Ísafjördhur (fjord) ...B 1
Jökulsá (river) ...C 1
Lagarfljót (stream) ...D 1
Lang (glacier) ...C 1
Langanes (prom.) ...D 1
North (cape) ...C 1
Önderdarnes (mt.) ...A 1
Rifstángi (cape) ...C 1
Skagata (cape) ...B 1
Skjálfanda (river) ...C 1
Staalbjerg (point) ...A 1
Thjórsá (river) ...C 1
Vatna (glacier) ...C 1
Vopnafjörd (fjord) ...D 1

GERMANY

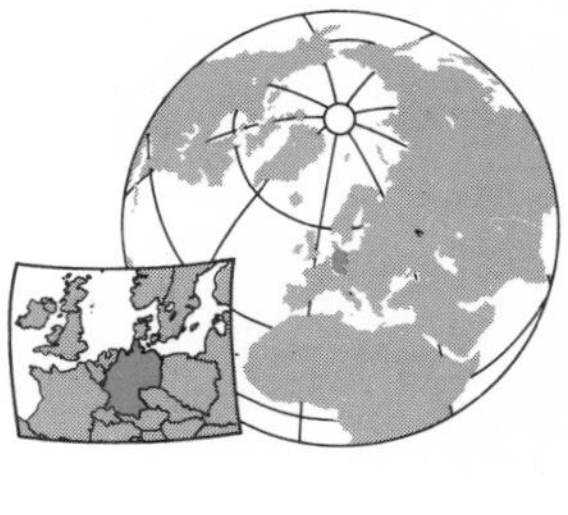

WEST GERMANY

AREA	95,914 sq. mi.
POPULATION	57,974,000
CAPITAL	Bonn
LARGEST CITY	Berlin (West) 2,187,000
HIGHEST POINT	Zugspitze 9,721 ft.
MONETARY UNIT	West German Deutsch mark
MAJOR LANGUAGE	German
MAJOR RELIGIONS	Protestant, Roman Catholic

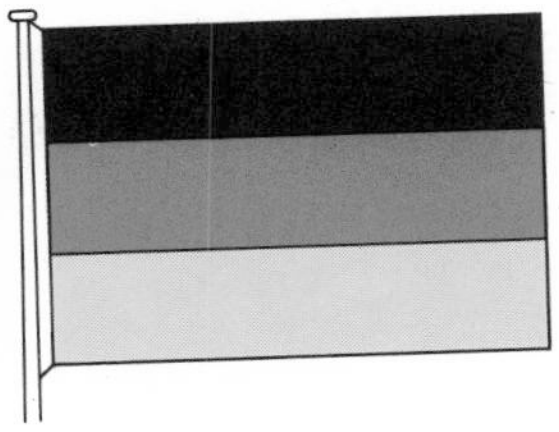

EAST GERMANY

AREA	41,535 sq. mi.
POPULATION	17,135,867
CAPITAL	Berlin (East)
LARGEST CITY	Berlin (East) 1,061,218
HIGHEST POINT	Fichtelberg 3,980 ft.
MONETARY UNIT	East German Deutsch mark
MAJOR LANGUAGE	German
MAJOR RELIGIONS	Protestant, Roman Catholic

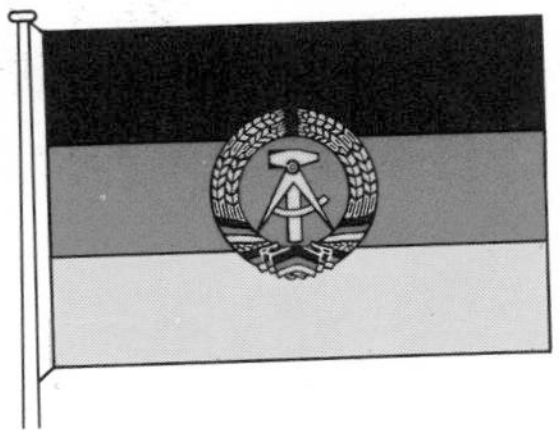

WEST GERMANY

STATES

Baden-Württemberg, 8,081,000....C 4
Bavaria, 9,805,000 ....D 4
Berlin (West) (Free City), 2,187,000 ....E 4
Bremen, 721,084 ....C 2
Hamburg, 1,851,172 ....D 2
Hesse, 4,974,000 ....C 3
Lower Saxony, 6,762,000 ....C 2
North Rhine-Westphalia, 16,276,000 ....B 3
Rhineland-Palatinate, 3,494,000...B 4
Saarland, 1,103,000 ....B 4
Schleswig-Holstein, 2,364,000 ....C 1

CITIES and TOWNS

Aachen, 174,293 ....B 3
Aalen, 31,814 ....D 4
Ahlen, 40,485 ....B 3
Ahrensburg, 21,178 ....D 2
Aix-la-Chapelle (Aachen), 169,769 ....B 3
Alfeld, 13,081 ....C 2
Alsdorf, 30,957 ....B 3
Altena, 24,007 ....B 3
Alzey, 11,927 ....C 4
Amberg, 42,493 ....E 4
Andernach, 20,825 ....B 3
Ansbach, 32,948 ....D 4
Arnsberg, 21,305 ....C 3
Aschaffenburg, 54,131 ....C 4
Augsburg, 210,537 ....D 4
Aurich, 12,982 ....B 2
Backnang, 23,725 ....C 4
Bad Dürkheim, 12,458 ....C 4
Bad Godesberg, 65,119 ....B 3
Bad Harzburg, 11,201 ....D 3
Bad Hersfeld, 23,004 ....C 3
Bad Homburg, 37,340 ....C 3
Bad Honnef, 15,500 ....B 3
Bad Kissingen, 12,865 ....D 3
Bad Kreuznach, 35,101 ....B 4
Bad Lauterberg, 10,118 ....D 3
Bad Mergentheim, 11,608 ....D 4
Bad Nauheim, 13,431 ....C 3
Bad Oeynhausen, 14,121 ....C 2
Bad Oldesloe, 15,988 ....D 2
Bad Pyrmont, 14,343 ....C 2
Bad Reichenhall, 13,147 ....E 5
Bad Salzuflen, 16,575 ....C 2
Bad Schwartau, 15,287 ....D 2
Bad Segeberg, 11,673 ....D 2
Bad Tölz, 12,064 ....D 5
Bad Vilbel, 14,237 ....C 3
Bad Wildungen, 11,210 ....C 3
Baden-Baden, 40,029 ....C 4
Balingen, 11,647 ....C 4
Bamberg, 74,115 ....D 4
Bayreuth, 61,835 ....D 4
Bendorf, 14,018 ....B 3
Bensheim, 24,060 ....C 4
Berchtesgaden, 4,795 ....E 5
Bergisch Gladbach, 41,902 ....B 3
Berlin (West), 2,187,000 ....E 4
Beuel, 31,836 ....B 3
Biberach, 21,524 ....C 4
Bielefeld, 172,843 ....C 2
Bietigheim, 16,649 ....C 4
Bingen, 20,210 ....B 4
Böblingen, 25,366 ....C 4
Bocholt, 45,675 ....B 3
Bochum, 361,096 ....B 3
Bonn (cap.), 143,748 ....B 3
Borghorst, 15,527 ....B 2
Borken, 12,254 ....B 3
Bottrop, 112,150 ....B 3
Brackwede, 25,999 ....C 3
Brake, 15,939 ....C 2
Braunschweig (Brunswick), 241,275 ....D 2
Bremen, 577,931 ....C 2
Bremerhaven, 143,153 ....C 2
Brilon, 11,887 ....C 3
Bruchsal, 22,578 ....C 4
Brühl, 35,302 ....B 3
Brunswick, 241,275 ....D 2
Bückeburg, 11,933 ....C 2
Burghausen, 13,205 ....E 4
Burgsteinfurt, 12,241 ....B 2
Buxtehude, 15,735 ....C 2
Cassel (Kassel), 207,507 ....C 3
Celle, 58,506 ....D 2
Charlottenburg, 224,538 ....F 4
Clausthal-Zellerfeld, 15,300....D 3
Cleves (Kleve), 21,483 ....B 3
Cloppenburg, 15,214 ....B 2
Coblenz (Koblenz), 99,240 ....B 3
Coburg, 44,237 ....D 3
Coesfeld, 20,348 ....B 3
Cologne, 832,392 ....B 3
Constance (Konstanz), 52,651....C 5
Crailsheim, 14,387 ....D 4
Cuxhaven, 44,123 ....C 2
Dachau, 28,998 ....D 4
Darmstadt, 139,612 ....C 4
Deggendorf, 17,082 ....E 4
Delmenhorst, 57,312 ....C 2
Detmold, 31,236 ....C 3
Dillenburg, 10,658 ....C 3
Dillingen, 11,158 ....D 4
Donaueschingen, 10,715 ....C 5
Donauwörth, 10,200 ....D 4
Dorsten, 36,323 ....B 3
Dortmund, 650,942 ....B 3
Duderstadt, 10,709 ....D 3
Dudweiler, 28,854 ....B 4
Duisburg, 501,123 ....B 3
Dülmen, 16,740 ....B 3
Düren, 49,138 ....B 3
Düsseldorf, 703,989 ....B 3
Eberbach, 12,492 ....C 4
Ebingen, 21,092 ....C 4
Eckernförde, 19,540 ....D 1
Ehingen, 10,266 ....C 4
Eichstätt, 10,625 ....D 4
Einbeck, 18,602 ....C 3
Ellwangen, 12,538 ....D 4
Elmshorn, 34,962 ....C 2
Emden, 45,713 ....B 2
Emmendingen, 13,203 ....B 4
Emmerich, 16,822 ....B 3
Erkelenz, 11,729 ....B 3
Erlangen, 69,552 ....D 4
Eschwege, 24,091 ....D 3
Eschweiler, 39,590 ....B 3
Espelkamp, 10,454 ....C 2
Essen, 729,351 ....B 3
Esslingen, 83,236 ....C 4
Ettlingen, 19,390 ....C 4
Euskirchen, 20,287 ....B 3
Eutin, 16,924 ....D 1
Fellbach, 26,040 ....C 4
Flensburg, 98,464 ....C 1
Forchheim, 20,947 ....D 4
Frankenthal, 33,949 ....C 4
Frankfurt-am-Main, 694,245....C 3
Frechen, 26,613 ....B 3
Freiburg, 150,437 ....B 5
Freising, 27,562 ....D 4
Freudenstadt, 14,213 ....C 4
Friedberg, 17,311 ....C 3
Friedrichshafen, 37,148....C 5
Fulda, 45,131 ....C 3
Fürstenfeldbruck, 17,633 ....D 4
Fürth, 98,335 ....D 4
Füssen, 10,700 ....D 5
Gaggenau, 12,537 ....C 4
Garmisch-Partenkirchen, 25,011...D 5
Geesthacht, 20,809 ....D 2
Geislingen, 25,844 ....C 4
Geldern, 10,209 ....B 3
Gelsenkirchen, 380,628 ....B 3
Giessen, 66,291 ....C 3
Gifhorn, 17,677 ....D 2
Glückstadt, 12,331 ....C 2
Goch, 15,195 ....B 3
Göggingen, 14,589 ....D 4
Göppingen, 48,937 ....C 4
Goslar, 41,431 ....D 3
Göttingen, 80,373 ....D 3
Grevenbroich, 21,955 ....B 3
Griesheim, 13,701 ....C 4
Gronau, 25,560 ....B 2
Gummersbach, 32,009 ....B 3
Günzburg, 11,800 ....D 4
Gütersloh, 52,346 ....C 3
Haar, 10,204 ....D 4
Hagen, 198,758 ....B 3
Haltern, 14,712 ....B 3
Hamburg, 1,851,172 ....D 2
Hameln, 50,436 ....C 2
Hamm, 70,641 ....B 3
Hanau, 47,207 ....C 3
Hannover (Hanover), 571,332....C 2
Hassloch, 15,350 ....C 4
Haunstetten, 16,750 ....D 4
Heide, 19,983 ....C 1
Heidelberg, 126,519 ....C 4
Heidenheim, 48,790 ....D 4
Heilbronn, 89,100 ....C 4
Helmstedt, 29,543 ....D 2
Hennef, 13,238 ....B 3
Herford, 55,663 ....C 2
Herne, 111,229 ....B 3
Hildesheim, 96,296 ....D 2
Hockenheim, 13,213 ....C 4
Hof, 57,129 ....D 3
Holzminden, 22,789 ....C 3
Homburg, 29,725 ....B 4
Höxter, 15,156 ....C 3
Hürth, 45,695 ....B 3
Husum, 23,804 ....C 1
Ibbenbüren, 15,676 ....B 2
Idar-Oberstein, 30,182 ....B 4
Immenstadt, 10,049 ....D 5
Ingolstadt, 53,405 ....D 4
Iserlohn, 55,257 ....B 3
Itzehoe, 36,084 ....C 2
Jülich, 14,687 ....B 3
Kaiserslautern, 86,259 ....B 4
Karlsruhe, 249,528 ....C 4
Kassel, 211,773 ....C 3
Kaufbeuren, 34,686 ....D 5
Kehl, 13,121 ....B 4
Kelheim, 11,927 ....D 4
Kempten, 43,116 ....D 5
Kevelaer, 11,878 ....B 3
Kiel, 270,803 ....C 1
Kirchheim, 25,007 ....C 4
Kitzingen, 17,784 ....D 4
Kleve, 21,483 ....B 3
Koblenz, 101,163 ....B 3
Köln (Cologne), 832,392....B 3
Konstanz, 52,651 ....C 5
Korbach, 15,084 ....C 3
Kornwestheim, 26,296 ....C 4
Krefeld, 216,871 ....B 3
Kulmbach, 23,467 ....D 3
Lage, 12,869 ....C 3
Lahr, 22,599 ....B 4
Lampertheim, 19,218 ....C 4
Landau, 28,725 ....C 4
Landsberg, 13,413 ....D 4
Landshut, 49,514 ....E 4
Langen, 20,957 ....C 4
Langenhagen, 26,736 ....C 2
Lauenburg, 10,713 ....D 2
Lauf, 12,863 ....D 4
Leer, 20,524 ....B 2
Lehrte, 21,257 ....D 2
Lemgo, 21,365 ....C 2
Lengerich, 21,020 ....B 2
Leverkusen, 94,641 ....B 3
Lichtenfels, 11,270 ....D 3
Limburg, 15,578 ....C 3
Lindau, 24,187 ....C 5
Lingen, 25,156 ....B 2
Lippstadt, 37,502 ....C 3
Lohr, 11,078 ....C 4
Lörrach, 30,536 ....B 5
Lübeck, 236,601 ....D 2
Lüdenscheid, 58,239 ....B 3
Ludwigsburg, 73,512 ....C 4
Ludwigshafen, 171,510 ....C 4
Lüneburg, 59,563 ....D 2
Lünen, 72,171 ....B 3
Mainz, 139,352 ....C 4
Mannheim, 321,102 ....C 4
Marburg, 44,853 ....C 3
Marktredwitz, 15,523 ....E 3
Marl, 71,508 ....B 3
Mayen, 17,268 ....B 3
Memmingen, 29,801 ....D 5
Meppen, 14,924 ....B 2
Merzig, 12,139 ....B 4
Meschede, 12,625 ....C 3
Metzingen, 11,819 ....C 4
Minden, 48,705 ....C 2
Mittenwald, 8,516 ....D 5
Mölln, 13,774 ....D 2
Mönchengladbach, 153,361 ....B 3
Mosbach, 11,343 ....C 4
Mülheim an der Ruhr, 189,910....B 3
Münden, 20,210 ....C 3
Munich (München), 1,157,306.....D 4
Münster, 189,656 ....B 3
Neckarsulm, 15,299 ....C 4
Neheim-Hüsten, 33,913 ....C 3
Neu-Isenburg, 25,362 ....C 3
Neu-Ulm, 24,305 ....D 4
Neuburg, 16,461 ....D 4
Neumarkt, 15,795 ....D 4
Neumünster, 75,045 ....C 1
Neunkirchen, 45,625 ....B 4
Neuss, 101,388 ....B 3
Neustadt (Rhineland-Palatinate), 31,567 ....B 4
Neustadt (Schleswig-Holstein), 14,466 ....D 1
Neustadt bei Coburg, 12,569 ....D 3
Neuwied, 26,359 ....B 3
Nienburg, 22,055 ....C 2
Norden, 16,144 ....B 2
Nordenham, 26,876 ....C 2
Nordhorn, 39,429 ....B 2
Nördlingen, 14,350 ....D 4
Northeim, 19,263 ....C 3
Nuremberg (Nürnberg), 466,146..D 4
Nürtingen, 20,505 ....C 4
Oberammergau, 4,603 ....D 5
Oberhausen, 259,827 ....B 3
Oberlahnstein, 12,388 ....B 3
Oberursel, 22,207 ....C 3
Ochtrup, 13,207 ....B 2
Offenbach, 118,043 ....C 3
Offenburg, 27,569 ....B 4
Oldenburg, 126,209 ....B 2
Opladen, 34,204 ....B 3
Osnabrück, 140,964 ....C 2
Osterholz-Scharmbeck, 13,856....C 2
Osterode, 16,160 ....D 3
Paderborn, 53,984 ....C 3
Papenburg, 15,014 ....B 2
Passau, 31,791 ....E 4
Peine, 29,879 ....D 2
Pforzheim, 82,524 ....C 4
Pfullingen, 13,598 ....C 4
Pinneberg, 28,397 ....C 2
Pirmasens, 53,164 ....B 4
Plettenberg, 28,380 ....C 3
Plön, 10,818 ....D 1
Porz, 50,906 ....B 3
Preetz, 12,763 ....D 1
Radolfzell, 13,607 ....C 5
Rastatt, 24,067 ....C 4
Rastede, 14,235 ....C 2
Ratingen, 36,020 ....B 3
Ratzeburg, 11,359 ....D 2
Ravensburg, 31,269 ....C 5
Recklinghausen, 130,149 ....B 3
Regensburg, 125,256 ....E 4
Remscheid, 128,619 ....B 3
Rendsburg, 35,721 ....C 1
Reutlingen, 67,407 ....C 4
Rheda, 13,468 ....C 3
Rheine, 44,322 ....B 2
Rheinfelden, 14,642 ....B 5
Rheinhausen, 68,126 ....B 3
Rheydt, 94,004 ....B 3
Rosenheim, 31,611 ....D 5
Rotenburg, 14,464 ....C 2
Rothenburg, 11,134 ....D 4
Rottweil, 17,885 ....C 4
Rüsselsheim, 39,597 ....C 4
Saarbrücken, 133,101 ....B 4
Saarlouis (Saarlautern), 36,807..B 4
Säckingen, 11,326 ....C 5
Salzgitter, 113,178 ....D 2
Sankt Ingbert, 28,352 ....B 4
Schleswig, 33,766 ....C 1
Schöneberg, 193,790 ....E 4
Schöningen, 16,145 ....D 2
Schramberg, 18,114 ....C 4
Schwabach, 23,696 ....D 4
Schwäbisch Gmünd, 41,050 ....C 4
Schwäbisch Hall, 21,866 ....C 4
Schwandorf, 16,062 ....E 4
Schweinfurt, 56,894 ....D 3
Schwelm, 33,986 ....B 3
Schwenningen, 31,743 ....C 4
Schwetzingen, 14,992 ....C 4
Seesen, 12,062 ....D 3
Selb, 19,260 ....E 3
Sennestadt, 26,712 ....C 3
Siegburg, 33,974 ....B 3
Siegen, 49,404 ....C 3
Sindelfingen, 26,127 ....C 4
Singen, 33,267 ....C 5
Soest, 33,304 ....C 3
Solingen, 172,168 ....B 3
Soltau, 14,366 ....C 2
Sonthofen, 12,902 ....D 5
Spandau, 172,663 ....E 3
Speyer, 38,485 ....C 4
Stade, 30,530 ....C 2
Stadthagen, 14,865 ....C 2
Starnberg, 10,497 ....D 4
Stolberg, 37,462 ....B 3
Straubing, 36,348 ....E 4
Stuttgart, 640,465 ....C 4
Sulzbach-Rosenberg, 19,559....D 4
Tailfingen, 15,459 ....C 4
Tempelhof, 142,952 ....F 4
Traunstein, 14,394 ....E 5
Travemünde, 16,355 ....D 2
Trier (Treves), 87,141 ....B 4
Tübingen, 49,631 ....C 4
Tuttlingen, 24,874 ....C 5
Überlingen, 10,501 ....C 5
Uelzen, 25,035 ....D 2
Uetersen, 16,032 ....C 2
Ulm, 92,701 ....C 4
Varel, 12,382 ....C 2
Vechta, 13,460 ....C 2
Verden, 17,449 ....C 2
Viersen, 41,890 ....B 3
Villingen, 31,889 ....C 4
Völklingen, 42,644 ....B 4
Walsrode, 12,996 ....C 2
Wangen, 13,317 ....C 5
Wanne-Eickel, 107,834 ....B 3
Warendorf, 15,833 ....B 3
Wedel, 24,951 ....C 2
Weiden, 41,711 ....D 4
Weidenau, 17,231 ....C 3
Weilheim, 12,329 ....D 5
Weingarten, 14,783 ....C 5
Weinheim, 27,859 ....C 4
Weissenburg, 13,902 ....D 4
Wertheim, 11,329 ....C 4
Wesel, 32,002 ....B 3
Westerstede, 15,372 ....B 2
Wetzlar, 37,277 ....C 3
Wiedenbrück, 14,465 ....C 3
Wiesbaden, 257,975 ....B 3
Wilhelmshaven, 100,354 ....B 2
Witten, 96,462 ....B 3
Wolfenbüttel, 38,030 ....D 2
Wolfsburg, 64,560 ....D 2
Worms, 62,392 ....C 4
Wunstorf, 13,688 ....C 2
Wuppertal, 422,870 ....B 3
Würzburg, 119,745 ....C 4
Zirndorf, 11,984 ....D 4
Zweibrücken, 32,924 ....B 4
Zwischenahn, 16,864 ....B 2

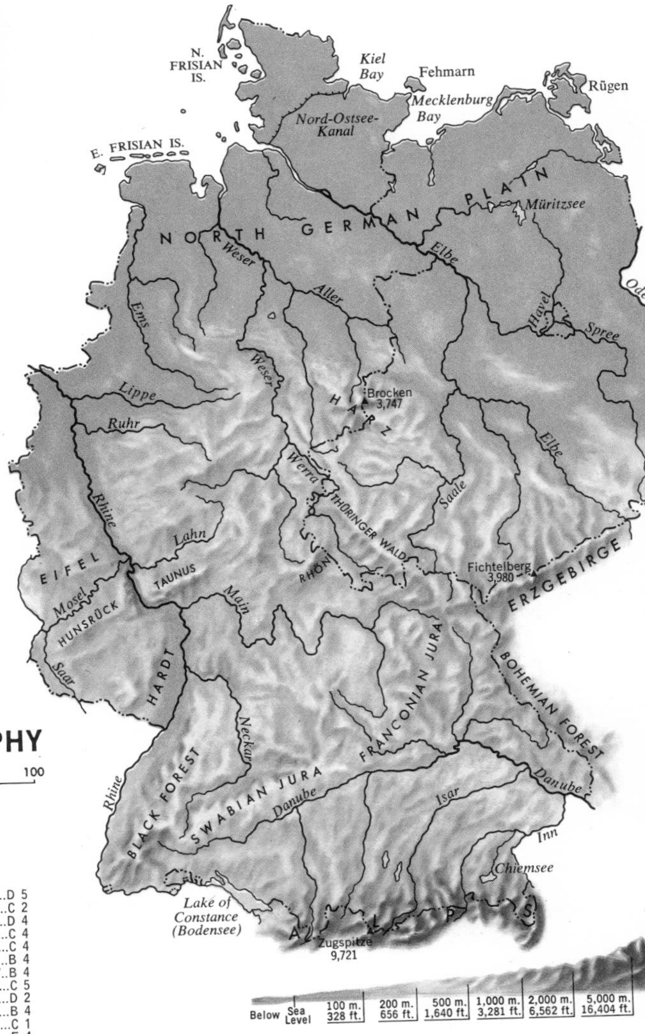

N. FRISIAN IS.
Kiel Bay
Fehmarn
Rügen
Mecklenburg Bay
Nord-Ostsee-Kanal
E. FRISIAN IS.
NORTH GERMAN PLAIN
Müritzsee
Elbe
Oder
Weser
Aller
Ems
Havel
Spree
Lippe
Brocken 3,747
HARZ
Neisse
Ruhr
Werra
Saale
Rhine
THÜRINGER WALD
Lahn
EIFEL
TAUNUS
RHÖN
Fichtelberg 3,980
ERZGEBIRGE
Mosel
HUNSRÜCK
Main
Saar
HARDT
FRANCONIAN JURA
BOHEMIAN FOREST
Neckar
BLACK FOREST
SWABIAN JURA
Danube
Isar
Inn
Chiemsee
Lake of Constance (Bodensee)
ALPS
Zugspitze 9,721
Below Sea Level
100 m. 328 ft.
200 m. 656 ft.
500 m. 1,640 ft.
1,000 m. 3,281 ft.
2,000 m. 6,562 ft.
5,000 m. 16,404 ft.

TOPOGRAPHY

0 50 100
MILES

PHYSICAL FEATURES

Aller (riv.) ....C 2
Allgäu Alps (mts.) ....D 5
Altmühl (riv.) ....D 4
Alz (riv.) ....E 4
Ammersee (lake) ....D 4
Bavarian (forest) ....E 4
Bavarian Alps (mts.) ....D 5
Black (forest) ....C 4
Bodensee (Constance) (lake)....C 5
Bohemian (forest) ....E 4
Breisgau (reg.), 580,848 ....B 5
Chiemsee (lake) ....E 5
Constance (lake) ....C 5
Danube (Donau) (riv.)....C 4
Dollart (estuary) ....B 2
Dümmer (lake) ....C 2
East Friesland (reg.), 553,610....B 2
East Frisian (isls.), 21,003....B 2
Eder (res.) ....C 3
Eider (riv.) ....C 1
Elbe (riv.) ....C 2
Ems (riv.) ....B 2
Fehmarn (isl.), 12,162 ....D 1
Feldberg (mt.) ....B 5
Fichtelgebirge (mts.) ....D 3
Franconian Jura (mts.)....D 4
Frankenwald (forest) ....D 3
Fulda (riv.) ....C 3
Grosser Arber (mt.) ....E 4
Hardt (mts.) ....C 4
Harz (mts.) ....D 3
Hegau (reg.), 150,000 ....C 5
Helgoland (bay) ....C 1
Helgoland (isl.), 1,818 ....B 1
Hunsrück (mts.) ....B 4
Iller (riv.) ....D 4
Inn (riv.) ....E 4
Isar (riv.) ....E 4
Jade (bay) ....C 2
Kaiserstuhl (mt.) ....B 4
Kiel (canal) ....C 1
Königssee (lake) ....E 5
Lahn (riv.) ....C 3
Lech (riv.) ....D 4
Leine (riv.) ....C 2
Lippe (riv.) ....C 3
Lüneburger Heide (dist.) ....C 2
Main (riv.) ....C 4
Mecklenburg (bay) ....D 1
Mosel (riv.) ....B 3
Neckar (riv.) ....C 4
Nord-Ostsee (Kiel) (canal)....C 1
Norderney (isl.), 7,341 ....B 2
North (sea) ....A 1
North Frisian (isls.), 31,992....B 1
Oberpfälzer Wald (for.)....E 4
Odenwald (forest) ....C 4
Oker (riv.) ....D 2
Regen (riv.) ....E 4
Regnitz (riv.) ....D 4
Rhine (Rhein) (riv.)....B 3
Rhön (mts.) ....D 3
Ruhr (riv.) ....B 3
Saar (riv.) ....B 4
Salzach (riv.) ....E 5
Sauer (riv.) ....B 4
Sauerland (reg.) ....B 3
Schlei (inlet) ....C 1
Schneeberg (mt.) ....D 3
Schwarzwald (Black) (forest)...C 4
Spessart (mt. range) ....C 4
Starnbergersee (lake) ....D 5
Steigerwald (forest) ....D 4
Steinhuder (lake) ....C 2
Swabian Jura (mts.) ....C 4
Sylt (isl.), 17,592 ....C 1
Tauber (riv.) ....C 4
Taunus (mt. range) ....C 3
Tegernsee (lake) ....D 5
Teutoburger Wald (for.) ....C 2
Vechte (riv.) ....B 2
Vogelsberg (mt.) ....C 3
Walchensee (lake) ....D 5
Wasserkuppe (mt.) ....C 3
Watzmann (mt.) ....E 5
Werra (riv.) ....D 3
Weser (riv.) ....C 2
Westerwald (forest) ....C 3
Wurmsee (Starnbergersee)(lake) D 5
Zugspitze (mt.) ....D 5

(continued on following page)

Germany
(continued)

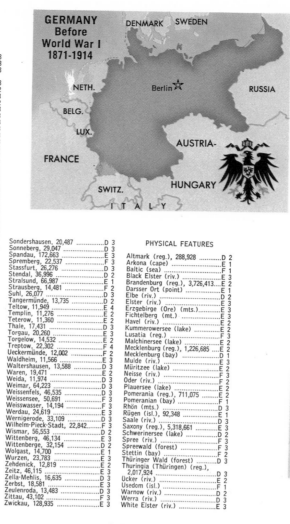

GERMANY Before World War I 1871-1914

GERMANY Between Wars 1919-1937

Occupied GERMANY 1945-1949

AGRICULTURE, INDUSTRY and RESOURCES

DOMINANT LAND USE

- Wheat, Sugar Beets
- Cereals (chiefly rye, oats, barley)
- Potatoes, Rye
- Dairy, Livestock
- Mixed Cereals, Dairy
- Truck Farming
- Grapes, Fruit
- Forests

MAJOR MINERAL OCCURRENCES

Ag	Silver	Lg	Lignite
C	Coal	Mg	Magnesium
Cu	Copper	O	Petroleum
Fe	Iron Ore	Pb	Lead
G	Natural Gas	U	Uranium
Gr	Graphite	Zn	Zinc
K	Potash		

⚡ Water Power

〰 Major Industrial Areas

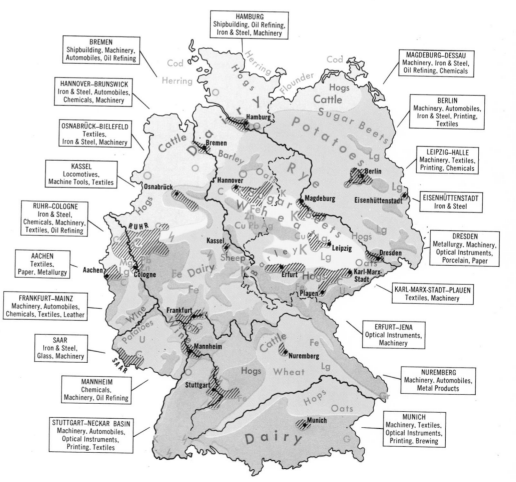

HAMBURG
Shipbuilding, Oil Refining, Iron & Steel, Machinery

BREMEN
Shipbuilding, Machinery, Automobiles, Oil Refining

MAGDEBURG-DESSAU
Machinery, Iron & Steel, Oil Refining, Chemicals

HANNOVER-BRUNSWICK
Iron & Steel, Automobiles, Chemicals, Machinery

BERLIN
Machinery, Automobiles, Iron & Steel, Printing, Textiles

OSNABRÜCK-BIELEFELD
Textiles, Iron & Steel, Machinery

LEIPZIG-HALLE
Machinery, Textiles, Printing, Chemicals

KASSEL
Locomotives, Machine Tools, Textiles

EISENHÜTTENSTADT
Iron & Steel

RUHR-COLOGNE
Iron & Steel, Chemicals, Machinery, Textiles, Oil Refining

DRESDEN
Metallurgy, Machinery, Optical Instruments, Porcelain, Paper

AACHEN
Textiles, Paper, Metallurgy

KARL-MARX-STADT-PLAUEN
Textiles, Machinery

FRANKFURT-MAINZ
Machinery, Automobiles, Chemicals, Textiles, Leather

ERFURT-JENA
Optical Instruments, Machinery

SAAR
Iron & Steel, Glass, Machinery

NUREMBERG
Machinery, Automobiles, Metal Products

MANNHEIM
Chemicals, Machinery, Oil Refining

STUTTGART-NECKAR BASIN
Machinery, Automobiles, Optical Instruments, Printing, Textiles

MUNICH
Machinery, Textiles, Optical Instruments, Printing, Brewing

NETHERLANDS, BELGIUM and LUXEMBOURG

NETHERLANDS

AREA	12,883 sq. mi.
POPULATION	12,041,970
CAPITAL	The Hague, Amsterdam
LARGEST CITY	Amsterdam (greater) 911,248
HIGHEST POINT	Vaalserberg 1,056 ft.
MONETARY UNIT	guilder
MAJOR LANGUAGES	Dutch
MAJOR RELIGIONS	Protestant, Roman Catholic

BELGIUM

11,775 sq. mi.
9,328,000
Brussels
Brussels (greater) 1,439,536
Botrange 2,277 ft.
Belgian franc
French (Walloon), Flemish
Roman Catholic

LUXEMBOURG

999 sq. mi.
327,000
Luxembourg
Luxembourg 73,850
Ardennes Plateau 1,825 ft.
Luxembourg franc
Mosel-frankisch (German dialect)
Roman Catholic

NETHERLANDS

PROVINCES

Drenthe, 312,176	K 3
Friesland, 478,931	H 4
Gelderland, 1,274,042	H 4
Groningen, 475,462	F 5
North Brabant, 1,495,559	F 5
Limburg, 886,026	J 4
North Holland, 2,057,322	F 3
Overijssel, 775,759	J 4
South Holland, 2,706,810	E 5
Utrecht, 680,678	J 4
Zeeland, 283,465	D 6

CITIES and TOWNS

Aalsmeer, 12,763	F 4
Aalst, 4,423	G 6
Aalten, 8,083	K 5
Aardenburg, 1,663	C 6
Akkrum, 2,296	H 2
Alkmaar, 42,765	F 3
Alkmaar (greater), 44,811	F 3
Almelo, 46,195	K 4
Amersfoort, 67,254	H 4
Amstelveen, 37,634	B 5
Amsterdam (cap.), 868,445	B 4
Amsterdam (greater), 911,248	B 4
Andijk, 4,301	G 3
Apeldoorn, 78,961	J 3
Appelscha, 1,622	K 2
Appingedam, 8,505	K 2
Arnhem, 120,091	H 4
Arnhem (greater), 151,824	H 4
Assen, 25,216	K 3
Asten, 5,462	H 6
Axel, 5,873	D 6
Baarle-Nassau, 1,519	F 6
Badhoevedorp, 8,699	B 5
Balkbrug, 2,468	J 3
Barneveld, 7,499	H 4
Beilen, 4,232	K 3
Bergeijk (Hof), 3,533	G 6
Bergen, 9,295	F 3
Bergen op Zoom, 33,190	E 5
Bergum, 2,981	H 2
Berkel, 3,433	F 5
Berkhout, 1,314	F 3
Beverwijk, 32,533	F 4
Blerick, 14,593	J 6
Bloemendaal, 5,492	E 4
Bodegraven, 5,648	F 4
Bolsward, 8,077	H 2
Borculo, 3,607	J 4
Borger, 1,806	K 3
Borne, 10,053	K 4
Boskoop, 9,474	F 4
Boxmeer, 6,024	H 5
Boxtel, 12,436	G 5
Breda, 102,332	F 5
Breezand, 1,962	F 3
Breskens, 3,394	C 6
Brielle, 3,817	E 5
Broek, 1,309	C 4
Brouwershaven, 1,078	D 5
Brummen, 4,244	J 4
Buiksloot, 23,738	B 4
Bussum, 39,642	G 4
Coevorden, 7,212	K 3
Colijnsplaat, 1,477	D 5
Culemborg, 11,083	G 5
Cuyk, 5,443	H 5
Dalen, 1,437	K 3
De Bilt, 12,921	G 4
Dedemsvaart, 6,384	J 3
Delft, 72,291	E 4
Delfzijl, 13,810	K 2
Den Burg, 3,579	F 3
Den Helder, 43,366	F 3
Denekamp, 3,776	L 3
Deurne, 8,331	H 6
Deventer, 54,669	J 4
Dieman, 5,821	C 5
Dieren, 8,612	J 4
Dinxperlo, 3,531	K 5
Dirksland, 2,739	E 5
Doesburg, 7,199	J 4
Doetinchem, 17,692	J 5
Dokkum, 7,323	H 2
Domburg, 1,227	C 5
Dongen, 12,452	F 5
Doorn, 7,148	G 4
Dordrecht, 80,714	F 5
Dordrecht (greater), 100,250	F 5
Drachten, 16,529	J 2
Driebergen, 10,748	G 4
Druten, 4,171	H 5
Duivendrecht, 2,656	C 5
Echt, 4,711	H 6
Edam, 3,928	G 4
Ede, 28,095	H 4
Eefde, 2,396	J 4
Egmond aan Zee, 4,135	E 3
Eindhoven, 161,178	H 4
Elburg, 2,779	H 5
Elst, 6,003	H 5
Emmeloord, 7,251	H 3
Emmen, 16,470	K 3
Enkhuizen, 9,946	G 3
Enschede, 105,481	K 4
Epe, 5,388	J 4
Erica, 3,326	K 3
Ermelo, 7,279	H 4
Etten, 7,125	F 5
Flushing, 29,141	C 6
Franeker, 8,849	H 2
Geertruidenberg, 4,275	F 5
Geldermalsen, 4,449	G 5
Geldrop, 14,183	H 7
Geleen, 20,293	H 5
Gemert, 8,344	H 5
Gendringen, 2,235	J 5
Genemuiden, 4,210	J 3
Gennep, 4,888	H 5
Giessendam, 3,905	F 5
Giethoorn, 1,794	J 3
Goes, 14,896	D 5
Goirle, 8,331	G 5
Goor, 7,445	K 4
Gorinchem, 20,621	G 5
Gorredijk, 3,006	J 2
Gouda, 41,939	F 4
Gouda (greater), 42,471	F 4
Grave, 4,188	H 5
Groenlo, 5,451	K 4
Groesbeek, 6,564	H 5
Groningen, 140,234	K 2
Grouw, 3,191	H 2
Haarlem, 167,673	F 4
Haarlem (greater), 224,053	F 4
Haarlemmermeer (Hoofddorp), 4,949	
Hague, The (cap.), 602,448	E 4
Hague, The (greater), 691,521	E 4
Halfweg, 2,171	B 5
Hallum, 1,424	H 2
Hardenberg, 3,080	J 3
Harderwijk, 14,054	H 4
Hardinxveld, 8,334	G 5
Harlingen, 11,594	G 2
Hasselt, 2,432	J 3
Hattem, 7,142	J 4
Heemstede, 25,027	F 4
Heer, 4,189	H 7
Heerde, 3,821	H 4
Heerenveen, 10,709	H 3
Heerlen, 15,638	J 7
Heiloo, 11,193	F 3
Hellendoorn, 2,606	J 4
Hellevoetsluis, 2,321	E 5
Helmond, 41,742	H 6
Hengelo, Gelderland, 1,939	J 4
Hengelo, Overijssel, 57,936	K 4
Heusden, 1,955	G 5
Hillegom, 13,245	E 4
Hilvarenbeek, 3,585	G 6
Hilversum, 99,386	G 4
Hippolytushoef, 3,035	F 3
Hoek, 1,210	D 6
Hoek van Holland (Hook of Holland), 5,114	D 5
Hoensbroek, 9,442	H 7
Hof, 3,533	G 6
Holwerd, 1,691	H 2
Hoofddorp, 4,949	B 5
Hoogeveen, 14,368	J 3
Hoogezand, 8,493	K 2
Hoogkarspel, 2,330	G 3
Hook of Holland, 5,114	D 5
Hoorn, 15,754	G 3
Horst, 4,955	H 6
Huissen, 5,238	J 5
Huizen, 15,567	G 4
Hulst, 5,093	E 6
IJlst, 1,394	H 2
IJmuiden, 3,587	E 4
IJsselstein, 5,705	G 4
IJzendijke, 1,701	D 6
Joure, 5,509	H 3
Kampen, 25,464	H 3
Katwijk aan Zee, 21,980	J 3
Kerkdriel en Thij), 1,466	G 5
Kerkrade, 10,284	J 7
Kerkrade, 10,284	J 7
Kesteren, 1,225	H 5
Kloosterveen, 3,385	K 3
Kollum, 2,543	J 2
Koog aan de Zaan, 7,384	A 4
Krimpen aan den IJssel, 8,495	F 5
Landsmeer, 6,970	G 4
Laren, 13,334	G 4
Leek, 2,133	F 2
Leerdam, 10,161	G 5
Leeuwarden, 78,247	H 4
Leiden, 95,964	E 4
Leiden (greater), 116,838	H 3
Lemmer, 4,399	H 3
Lent, 2,032	H 5
Lisse, 10,687	F 4
Lith, 1,366	G 5
Lochem, 6,635	J 4
Lonneker, 1,599	L 4
Loon op Zand, 3,032	G 5
Losser, 6,655	L 4
Maarssen, 8,748	H 6
Maasbree, 1,731	H 6
Maassluis, 12,877	E 5
Maastricht, 85,188	H 7
Maastricht (greater), 96,200	H 7
Makkum, 2,416	H 2
Margraten, 1,470	H 7
Medemblik, 4,996	G 3
Meerssen, 5,489	H 7
Meppel, 16,874	J 3
Middelburg, 21,982	D 5
Middelharnis, 4,798	F 3
Middenmeer, 1,775	F 3
Millingen aan den Rijn, 3,577	J 5
Monnikendam, 3,099	C 4
Montfoort, 2,628	G 4
Muiden, 2,508	G 4
Muntendam, 2,987	K 2
Naaldwijk, 8,110	E 4
Naarden, 14,155	G 4
Neede, 5,155	K 4
Nieuw-Buinen, 3,966	K 3
Nieuw-Schoonebeek, 1,602	L 2
Nieuwe Pekela, 4,015	L 2
Nieuwendam, 15,679	C 4
Nieuweschans, 1,689	L 2
Nieuwkoop, 3,447	H 4
Nijkerk, 8,904	H 4
Nijmegen, 127,172	H 5
Nijmegen (greater), 132,880	H 5
Nijverdal, 11,986	J 4
Noordwijk, 7,920	E 4
Norg, 1,395	J 2
Numansdorp, 2,751	E 5
Nunspeet, 7,103	H 4
Oisterwijk, 9,559	G 5
Oldenzaal, 17,713	K 4
Olst, 2,534	J 4
Ommen, 3,372	J 3
Onstwedde, 1,867	K 2
Oostburg, 3,731	C 6
Oosterhout, 18,202	F 5
Oostzaan, 4,420	B 4
Ootmarsum, 2,284	K 4
Oss, 25,184	H 5
Oud-Beijerland, 6,819	D 5
Ouddorp, 3,105	D 5
Oude-Pekela, 6,515	L 2
Oude-Tonge, 2,459	E 5
Oudenbosch, 7,492	E 5
Oudewater, 4,094	F 4
Purmerend, 9,286	F 4
Putten, 6,160	H 4
Raalte, 5,005	J 4
Renkum, 8,032	H 5
Reusel, 3,919	G 6
Rheden, 6,388	J 4
Rhenen, 7,704	H 5
Ridderkerk, 10,007	F 5
Rijnsburg, 6,301	E 4
Rijssen, 13,350	J 4
Rijswijk, 35,581	E 4
Roden, 2,724	J 2
Roermond, 25,728	J 6
Roosendaal, 32,881	F 5
Rotterdam, 683,903	E 5
Rotterdam (greater), 827,326	E 5
Ruurlo, 1,822	J 4
's Gravendeel, 4,531	E 5
's Gravenhage (The Hague) (cap.), 602,435	E 4
's Gravenhage (greater), 691,521	E 4
's Gravenzande, 6,691	E 4
's Heerenberg, 5,196	J 5
's Hertogenbosch, 71,597	G 5
Sappemeer, 5,779	K 2
Schagen, 4,271	F 3
Scheveningen, 80,015	E 4
Schiedam, 75,421	E 5
Schijndel, 9,487	G 5
Schiphol, 3,368	B 5
Schoonebeek, 1,869	L 3
Schoonhoven, 6,156	F 5
Sint Annaland, 2,342	E 5
Sint Jacobiparochie, 1,246	H 2
Sittard, 27,548	H 6
Sliedrecht, 16,572	F 5
Slochteren, 2,003	K 2
Sloterdijk, 1,215	B 5
Sluis, 2,050	C 6
Smilde (Kloosterveen), 3,385	K 3
Sneek, 20,349	H 2
Soest, 14,925	G 4
Soesterberg, 4,627	G 4
Stadskanaal, 8,198	L 3
Staphorst, 3,330	J 3
Steenbergen, 5,654	E 5
Steenwijk, 10,330	J 3
Steenwijkerwold (Kerkbuurt en Thij), 1,466	J 3
Stiens, 2,008	J 2
Tegelen, 16,539	J 6
Ter Apel, 2,508	L 3
Terneuzen, 11,924	D 6
Tholen, 2,937	E 5
Tiel, 16,094	H 5
Tilburg, 130,818	G 6
Twello, 5,935	J 4
Uden, 8,763	H 5
Uitgeest, 4,758	F 4
Uithoorn, 6,966	F 4
Uithuizen, 3,748	K 2
Ulrum, 1,557	H 2
Urk, 5,700	H 3
Utrecht, 251,257	H 6
Vaals, 6,883	J 7
Valkenswaard, 16,252	H 6
Veendam, 12,781	K 2

(continued on following page)

AGRICULTURE, INDUSTRY and RESOURCES

DOMINANT LAND USE

- Dairy, Truck Farming
- Cash Crops, Livestock
- Mixed Cereals, Dairy
- Specialized Horticulture
- Grapes, Wine
- Forests
- Sand Dunes

MAJOR MINERAL OCCURRENCES

C	Coal	Na	Salt
Fe	Iron Ore	O	Petroleum

///// Major Industrial Areas

AMSTERDAM–HAARLEM
Shipbuilding, Machinery

ROTTERDAM
Shipbuilding, Machinery,
Oil Refining

ENSCHEDE
Textiles,
Cotton Industry

EINDHOVEN
Electrical Machinery,
Automobiles

LIÈGE
Iron & Steel, Machinery,
Nonferrous Metals,
Armaments

ANTWERP
Shipbuilding, Heavy Machinery,
Oil Refining

GHENT-FLANDERS
Textiles, Chemicals

VERVIERS
Textiles

BRUSSELS
Metallurgy,
Textiles, Chemicals

LUXEMBOURG
Iron & Steel, Machinery,
Chemicals

MONS–CHARLEROI
Iron & Steel, Metallurgy,
Machinery, Chemicals

Netherlands, Belgium and Luxembourg
(continued)

NETHERLANDS (continued)

Veenendaal, 22,906 ....G 4
Veenhuizen, 1,294 ....J 2
Veghel, 9,279 ....H 5
Velp, 18,488 ....J 5
Velsen, 51,511 ....F 4
Venlo, 33,349 ....J 6
Venraij, 11,047 ....H 6
Vianen, 4,511 ....G 5
Vlaardingen, 68,002 ....E 5
Vlagtwedde, 1,672 ....L 3
Vlijmen, 4,475 ....G 5
Vlissingen (Flushing), 29,141.......C 6
Volendam, 44,059 ....G 4
Voorburg, 3,549 ....E 4
Vorden, 2,812 ....J 4
Vreeswijk, 3,794 ....G 4
Vrieseveen, 6,510 ....K 4
Vught, 17,073 ....G 5
Waalwijk, 17,460 ....F 5
Wageningen, 19,935 ....H 5
Wamel, 1,646 ....H 5
Weert, 19,119 ....H 6
Weesp, 10,512 ....C 5
West-Terschelling, 2,028..................G 2
Westkapelle, 2,306 ....C 5
Westzaan, 3,505 ....A 4
Wierden, 5,604 ....K 4
Wijhe, 3,046 ....J 4
Wijk aan Zee, 2,414 ....E 4
Wiik bij Duurstede, 3,398 ....G 5
Wijk en Aalburg, 1,633 ....G 5
Wildervank, 5,280 ....K 2
Winschoten, 14,430 ....L 2
Winsum, 1,204 ....K 2
Winterswijk, 16,752 ....K 5
Woerden, 12,924 ....F 4
Wolvega, 6,620 ....J 3
Workum, 3,195 ....G 3
Wormerveer, 12,681 ....F 4
Yerseke, 4,799 ....E 6
Zaandam, 47,347 ....B 4
Zaandijk, 4,916 ....B 4
Zaltbommel, 5,613 ....G 5
Zandvoort, 13,163 ....E 4
Zeist, 41,468 ....G 4
Zevenaar, 5,540 ....J 5
Zevenbergen, 5,854 ....E 5
Zierikzee, 6,732 ....D 5
Zundert, 4,132 ....F 6
Zutphen, 24,561 ....J 4
Zwanenburg, 6,999 ....B 4
Zwartsluis, 2,974 ....H 3
Zwijndrecht, 19,536 ....F 5
Zwolle, 52,109 ....J 3

PHYSICAL FEATURES

Alkmaardermeer (lake) ....F 3
Ameland (isl.), 2,544 ....H 2
Bergumeer (lake) ....J 2
Beulaker Wijde (lake) ....H 3
Borndiep (channel) ....H 2
De Fluessen (lake) ....G 3
De Honte (estuary) ....D 6
De Peel (region) ....H 6
De Zaan (river) ....B 4
Dollart (bay) ....L 2
Dommel (river) ....H 6
Duiveland (isl.), 13,317 ....D 5
East Flevoland Polder, 863..........H 4
Eastern Scheldt (estuary) ....D 5
Eijerlandsche Gat (strait) ....F 2
Friesche Gat (channel) ....J 2
Galgenberg (hill) ....H 4
Goeree (isl.) ....D 5
Grevelingen (strait) ....E 5
Griend (isl.) ....G 2
Groninger Wad (sound) ....J 2
Groote IJ Polder, 20 ....B 4
Haarlemmermeer Polder, 43,924..B 5
Haringvliet (strait) ....E 5
Het IJ (estuary) ....C 4
Hoek van Holland (cape) ....D 5
Hondsrug (hills) ....K 3
Houtrak Polder, 339....................A 4
Hunse (river) ....K 3
IJmeer (bay) ....C 4
IJssel (river) ....J 4
IJsselmeer (lake) ....G 3
Lauwers (channel) ....J 1
Lauwers Zee (bay) ....J 2
Lek (river) ....F 5
Lemelerberg (hill) ....J 4
Linde (river) ....J 3
Lower Rhine (river) ....H 5
Maas (river) ....G 5
Mark (river) ....F 6
Marken (isl.), 1,583......................G 4
Markerwaard Polder ....G 3
Marsdiep (channel) ....F 3
Noordergat (channel) ....F 2
North (sea) ....E 3
North Beveland (isl.), 6,777..........D 5
North East Polder, 28,545 ....H 3
North Holland (canal) ....C 4
North Sea (canal) ....F 4
Old Rhine (river) ....E 4
Ooster Eems (channel) ....K 1
Oostzaan Polder, 5,333 ....B 4
Orange (canal) ....K 3
Overflakkee (isl.), 27,814...........E 5
Pinkegat (channel) ....H 2
Regge (river) ....K 4
Roer (river) ....J 6
Rottumeroog (isl.), 3 ....J 1
Schiermonnikoog (isl.), 792 ....J 1
Schouwen (isl.), 9,731 ....D 5
Simonszand (isl.) ....J 1
Slotermeer (lake) ....H 3
Sneekermeer (lake) ....H 2
South Beveland (isl.), 61,968.......D 6
South Flevoland Polder ....G 4
Terschelling (isl.), 3,595 ....G 2
Texel (isl.), 10,674 ....F 2
Tjeukemeer (lake) ....H 3
Vaalserberg (mt.) ....J 7
Vecht (river) ....J 4
Vechte (river) ....J 3
Veeregat (channel) ....D 5
Veluwe (region) ....H 4
Vlie Stroom (strait) ....G 2
Vlieland (isl.), 728 ....F 2
Voorne (isl.), 22,742 ....D 5
Waal (river) ....G 5
Waddenzee (sound) ....G 2
Walcheren (isl.), 82,043 ....C 5
West Frisian (isls.), 18,336 ....F 2
Wester Eems (channel) ....K 1
Western Scheldt (De Honte) (estuary) ....D 6
Westgat (channel) ....F 3
Wieringermeer Polder, 8,467.............G 3
Wilhelmina (canal) ....G 6
Willems (canal) ....G 5

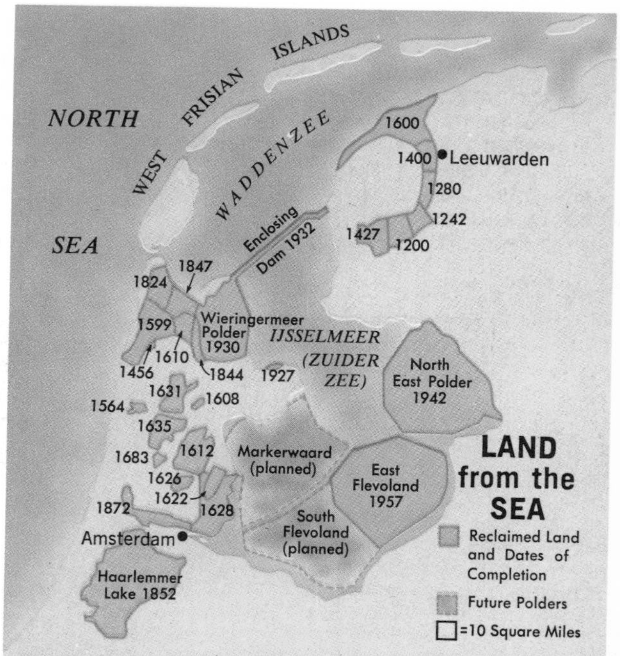

For centuries the Dutch have been renowned for the drainage of marshes and the construction of polders, i.e., arable land reclaimed from the sea. Future projects will convert much of the present IJsselmeer to agricultural land.

BELGIUM

PROVINCES

Antwerp, 1,443,355 ....F 6
Brabant, 1,992,139 ....F 7
East Flanders, 1,272,005 ....D 7
Hainault, 1,248,854 ....D 7
Liège, 1,003,526 ....H 7
Limburg, 574,606 ....G 7
Luxembourg, 216,848 ....G 9
Namur, 369,432 ....F 8
West Flanders, 1,068,976 ....B 7

CITIES and TOWNS

Aalst, 45,092 ....D 7
Aalter, 7,796 ....C 6
Aarlen (Arlon), 13,272 ....H 9
Aarschot, 12,123 ....F 7
Aat (Ath), 10,965 ....D 7
Adinkerke, 2,609 ....A 6
Alken, 7,236 ....G 7
Alost (Aalst), 45,092 ....D 7
Amay, 7,072 ....G 7
Andenne, 7,787 ....G 8
Anderlecht, 94,677 ....B 9
Anderlues, 12,377 ....E 8
Antoing, 3,476 ....C 7
Antwerp (Antwerpen), 253,295...E 6
Ardooie, 7,123 ....C 7
Arendonk, 8,862 ....G 6
Arlon, 13,272 ....H 9
As, 3,769 ....H 6
Asse, 12,158 ....E 7
Assebroek, 14,422 ....C 6
Ath, 10,965 ....D 7
Athus, 7,027 ....H 9
Audenarde (Oudenaarde), 6,923..D 7
Auderghem, 27,600 ....C 9
Autelbas, 1,502 ....H 9
Auvelais, 8,338 ....F 8
Aywaille, 3,645 ....H 8
Baerle-Duc, 2,044 ....F 6
Balen, 13,696 ....G 6
Barvaux, 1,574 ....H 8
Basècles, 4,277 ....D 7
Bastogne (Bastenaken), 6,151....H 9
Beaumont, 1,725 ....E 8
Beauraing, 2,383 ....F 8
Berchem, 48,667 ....E 6
Berchem-Sainte-Agathe, 15,867...B 9
Bergen (Mons), 26,973 ....E 8
Bertrix, 4,466 ....G 9
Beveren, 14,891 ....E 6
Bilzen, 6,426 ....G 7
Binche, 10,279 ....E 8
Blankenberge, 10,199 ....C 6
Bocholt, 5,163 ....H 6
Boom, 17,468 ....E 6
Borgerhout, 51,182 ....E 6
Borgloon, 3,499 ....G 7
Borgworm (Waremme), 6,646....G 7
Bouillon, 3,017 ....G 9
Bourg-Leopold (Leopoldsburg), 9,375 ....G 6
Boussu, 11,473 ....D 8
Braine-l'Alleud, 14,023 ....E 7
Braine-le-Comte, 10,779 ....D 7
Bredene, 8,772 ....B 6
Bree, 7,031 ....H 6
Bruges (Brugge), 52,220 ....C 6
Brussels (Bruxelles) (cap.) (greater), 1,439,536 ....C 9
Charleroi, 26,175 ....E 8
Châtelet, 15,378 ....E 8
Châtelineau, 19,763 ....F 8
Chièvres, 3,295 ....D 7
Chimay, 3,180 ....E 8
Ciney, 7,007 ....G 8
Comblain-au-Pont, 3,464 ....G 8
Comines, 8,373 ....B 7
Couillet, 14,424 ....E 8
Courcelles, 17,275 ....E 8
Courtrai, 43,606 ....C 7
Couvin, 3,840 ....F 8
Deinze, 6,004 ....D 7
Denderleeuw, 9,378 ....E 7
Dendermonde, 9,815 ....E 6
Dessel, 6,491 ....G 6
Deurne, 68,703 ....F 6
Diegem, 4,451 ....C 9
Diest, 9,816 ....F 7
Diksmuide, 3,812 ....B 6
Dilbeek, 10,791 ....B 9
Dinant, 6,851 ....G 8
Dison, 9,049 ....H 7
Dixmude (Diksmuide), 3,812..............B 6
Doel, 1,477 ....E 6
Doornik (Tournai), 33,263..................C 7
Dour, 10,785 ....D 8
Drogenbos, 4,026 ....B 9
Drongen, 7,799 ....D 6
Dudzele, 2,049 ....C 6
Duffel, 13,250 ....F 6
Ecaussinnes d'Enghien, 6,619......E 7
Edingen (Enghien), 4,225..............D 7
Eeklo, 18,510 ....D 6
Eernegem, 5,833 ....B 6
Eigenbrakel (Braine-l'Alleud), 14,023 ....E 7
Ekeren, 21,452 ....E 6
Ellezelles, 4,088 ....D 7
Enghien, 4,225 ....D 7
Ensival, 5,624 ....H 7
Erquelinnes, 4,642 ....E 8
Esneux, 5,394 ....H 7
Essen, 9,850 ....F 6
Etterbeek, 52,837 ....C 9
Eupen, 14,445 ....J 7
Evere, 22,460 ....C 9
Evergem, 11,332 ....D 6
Flémalle-Haute, 7,601 ....G 7
Fleurus, 8,274 ....F 8
Florennes, 3,882 ....F 8
Florenville, 2,378 ....G 9
Forest, 51,503 ....B 9
Fosse, 3,787 ....F 8
Frameries, 11,880 ....D 8
Frasnes-lez-Buissenal, 2,771 ....D 7
Furnes (Veurne), 7,330..................B 6
Ganshoren, 15,346 ....B 9
Gaurain-Ramecroix, 3,532 ....D 7
Geel, 27,007 ....F 6
Geeraardsbergen, 9,582 ....D 7
Geldenaken (Jodoigne), 4,262......F 7
Gembloux, 5,875 ....F 7
Gemmenich, 2,485 ....H 7
Genk, 47,416 ....H 7
Gent (Ghent), 157,811 ....D 6
Gentbrugge, 22,222 ....D 6
Ghent, 157,811 ....D 6
Gilly, 23,858 ....E 8
Gosselies, 11,010 ....E 8
Grammont (Geeraardsbergen), 9,582 ....D 7
Haacht, 4,066 ....F 7
Hal (Halle), 19,339 ....E 7
Halen, 3,427 ....G 7
Halle, 19,339 ....E 7
Hamme, 16,974 ....E 6
Hamont, 6,025 ....H 6
Hannut (Hannuit), 2,884 ....G 7
Harelbeke, 16,778 ....C 7
Hasselt, 36,618 ....G 7
Havelange, 1,535 ....G 8
Heist, 8,677 ....C 6
Heist-op-den-Berg, 12,717 ....F 6
Herentals, 17,451 ....F 6
Herselt, 6,828 ....F 6
Herstal, 29,606 ....H 7
Herve, 4,057 ....H 7
Hoboken, 30,557 ....E 6
Hoei (Huy), 13,447 ....G 8
Hoeselt, 5,101 ....H 7
Hoogstraten, 4,200 ....F 6
Hornu, 10,845 ....D 8
Houffalize, 1,302 ....H 8
Huy 13,447 ....G 8
Ieper, 18,121 ....B 7
Ingelmunster, 9,785 ....C 7
Ixelles, 94,211 ....C 9
Izegem, 17,095 ....C 7
Jambes, 13,106 ....F 8
Jemappes, 13,092 ....D 8
Jemeppe, 12,727 ....G 7
Jette, 34,927 ....B 9
Jodoigne, 4,262 ....F 7
Jumet, 28,713 ....E 8
Kain, 4,728 ....C 7
Kalmthout, 11,006 ....F 6
Kapellen, 11,474 ....F 6
Kessel-Lo, 20,098 ....F 7
Knokke, 13,649 ....C 6
Koekelare, 6,372 ....B 6
Koekelberg, 16,442 ....B 9
Koersel, 9,340 ....G 6
Kontich, 10,923 ....E 6
Kortemark, 5,748 ....C 6
Kortrijk (Courtrai), 43,606...............C 7
Kraainem, 8,226 ....C 9
La Louvière, 23,107 ....E 8
La Roche-en-Ardenne, 1,760...........G 8
Lanaken, 7,444 ....H 7
Landen, 4,970 ....G 7
Langemark, 4,686 ....B 7
Lede, 9,795 ....D 7
Ledeberg, 11,232 ....D 7
Lens, 1,852 ....D 7
Leopoldsburg, 9,375 ....G 6
Lessines (Lessen), 9,242 ....D 7
Leuven (Louvain), 32,524.........................F 7
Leuze, 7,002 ....D 7
Libramont, 2,445 ....G 9
Lichtervelde, 6,914 ....C 6
Liedekerke, 9,602 ....D 7
Liège, 153,240 ....H 7
Lier (Lierre), 28,755 ....F 6
Lierneux, 2,864 ....H 8
Limbourg (Limburg), 3,833.....................J 7
Linkebeek, 3,762 ....C10
Lokeren, 25,819 ....D 6
Lommel, 17,923 ....G 6
Looz (Borgloon), 3,499 ....G 7
Louvain, 32,524 ....F 7
Luik (Liège), 153,240 ....H 7
Maaseik, 8,068 ....H 6
Machelen, 7,004 ....C 9
Maldegem, 13,694 ....C 6
Malines (Mechelen), 64,772 ....F 6
Malmédy, 6,355 ....J 8
Marche-en-Famenne, 4,360 ....G 8
Marchin, 4,429 ....G 8
Marcinelle, 25,090 ....E 8
Marienbourg, 1,654 ....E 8
Martelange, 1,583 ....H 9
Mechelen, 64,772 ....F 6
Meerhout, 7,945 ....G 6
Meerle, 2,666 ....F 6
Melsbroek, 2,013 ....D 9
Menen (Menin), 22,451 ....C 7
Merchtem, 8,189 ....D 7
Merelbeke, 12,759 ....D 7
Merksem, 36,098 ....E 6
Merksplas, 4,912 ....F 6
Messancy, 2,830 ....H 9
Mettet, 3,160 ....F 8
Meulebeke, 10,487 ....C 7
Moeskron (Mouscron), 36,554.................................C 7
Mol, 24,794 ....G 6
Molenbeek-Saint-Jean, 63,528.................................B 9
Mons, 26,973 ....E 8
Montegnée, 11,405 ....G 7
Montignies-sur-Sambre, 24,143...............................F 8
Mortsel, 25,731 ....E 6
Mouscron, 36,554 ....C 7
Namur (Namen), 32,511 ....F 8
Neerlinter, 1,418 ....G 7
Neerpelt, 7,600 ....G 6
Neufchâteau, 2,696 ....G 9
Nieuwpoort (Nieuport), 6,899 ....B 6
Ninove, 11,831 ....D 7
Nivelles (Nijvel), 14,345 ....E 7
Oostende (Ostend), 56,494..B 6
Oostkamp, 8,138 ....C 6
Ophoven, 2,214 ....H 6
Opwijk, 9,225 ....E 7
Ostend, 56,494 ....B 6
Oud-Turnhout, 7,383 ....F 6
Oudenaarde, 6,923 ....D 7
Ougrée, 21,364 ....H 7
Overijse, 12,389 ....F 7
Overpelt, 8,708 ....G 6
Peer, 5,838 ....G 6
Péruwelz, 7,668 ....D 8
Perwez (Perwijs), 2,730 ....F 7
Philippeville, 1,559 ....E 8
Poperinge, 12,350 ....B 7
Poppel, 2,084 ....G 6
Putte, 6,752 ....F 6
Quaregnon, 18,019 ....D 8
Quiévrain, 5,597 ....D 8
Raeren, 3,265 ....J 7
Rance, 1,522 ....E 8
Rebecq Rognon, 3,733 ....E 7
Renaix (Ronse), 25,106 ....D 7
Retie, 5,820 ....G 6
Rochefort, 4,003 ....G 8
Roeselare, 35,645 ....C 7
Roeulx, 2,639 ....E 8
Ronse, 25,106 ....D 7
Roulers (Roeselare), 35,645..............C 7
Ruisbroek, 5,306 ....B 9
's Gravenbrakel (Braine-le-Comte), 10,779 ....D 7
Saint-Georges, 5,854 ....G 7
Saint-Gérard, 1,664 ....F 8
Saint-Gilles, 55,101 ....B 9
Saint-Hubert, 3,108 ....G 8
Saint-Josse-ten-Noode, 24,463...............C 9
Saint-Léger, 1,561 ....H 9
Saint-Vith (Sankt-Vith), 2,708..............J 8
Schaerbeek, 117,180 ....C 9
Schoten, 26,060 ....F 6
Seraing, 41,239 ....G 7
Sint-Amandsberg, 24,359 ....D 6
Sint-Andries, 13,409 ....C 6
Sint-Lenaarts, 4,301 ....F 6
Sint-Niklaas, 47,819 ....E 6
Sint-Pieters-Leeuw, 15,002 ....B 9
Sint-Truiden (Saint-Trond), 20,776 ....G 7
Sivry, 1,464 ....E 8
Soignies, 10,874 ....E 8
Spa, 9,055 ....H 8
Staden, 5,531 ....B 7
Stavelot, 4,500 ....H 8
Steenokkerzeel, 3,277 ....C 9
Stene, 7,113 ....B 6
Stokkem, 3,263 ....H 6
Strombeek-Bever, 8,654 ....C 9
Tamines, 7,886 ....F 8
Tamise (Temse), 14,063 ....E 6
Templeuve, 3,612 ....C 7
Temse, 14,063 ....E 6
Termonde (Dendermonde), 9,815 ....E 6
Tessenderlo, 9,643 ....G 6
Theux, 5,238 ....H 8
Thuin, 5,660 ....E 8
Tielt, Brabant, 3,690 ....F 7
Tielt, West Flanders, 13,455.......................................C 7
Tienen (Tirlemont), 22,736..F 7
Tongeren (Tongres), 16,176 ....G 7
Torhout, 13,465 ....C 6
Tournai, 33,263 ....C 7
Tronchiennes (Drongen), 7,799...................................D 6
Tubize (Tubeke), 9,483 ....E 7
Turnhout, 36,444 ....F 6
Uccle (Ukkel), 71,725 ....B 9
Verviers, 35,453 ....H 7
Veurne, 7,330 ....B 6
Vielsalm, 3,698 ....J 8
Vilvoorde (Vilvorde), 31,441..F 7
Virton, 3,421 ....H 9
Visé, 6,018 ....H 7
Vorst (Forest), 51,503 ....B 9
Waarschoot, 7,870 ....D 6
Waasten (Warneton), 3,002...B 7
Waha, 2,608 ....G 8
Waimes, 2,705 ....J 8
Walcourt, 2,042 ....F 8
Wandre, 6,722 ....H 7
Waregem, 16,014 ....C 7
Waremme, 6,646 ....G 7
Warneton, 3,002 ....B 7
Wasmes, 14,173 ....D 7
Waterloo, 11,846 ....E
Watermael-Boitsfort, 23,488.........C
Watervliet, 1,922 ....D
Wavre (Waver), 9,706 ....F
Weismes (Waimes), 2,705 ....J
Wemmel, 10,040 ....B
Wenduine, 1,800 C
Wervik, 12,442 ....B
Westende, 2,415 ....B
Westerlo, 7,297 ....F
Wetteren, 20,206 ....D
Wezembeek-Oppem, 8,551 C
Wezet (Visé), 6,018 ....H
Willebroek, 15,359 ....E
Wingene, 7,146 C
Woluwe-Saint-Lambert, 38,202...C
Woluwe-Saint-Pierre, 32,749 C
Wolvertem, 4,085 ....E
Ypres (Ieper), 18,121 ....B
Yvoir, 1,881 ....F
Zaventem, 9,179 C
Zeebrugge C
Zele, 17,648 ....E
Zellik, 3,931 ....B
Zelzate, 10,593 ....D
Zinnik (Soignies), 10,874.............................D
Zonhoven, 11,487 ....G
Zottegem, 6,630 ....D 7

PHYSICAL FEATURES

Albert (canal) ....F 6
Ardennes (plateau) ....F 9
Botrange (mt.) ....J 8
Dender (river) ....D 7
Dyle (river) ....F 7
Hohe Venn (plateau) ....H 8
Lesse (river) ....F 8
Mark (river) ....F 6
Meuse (river) ....F 8
Nethe (river) ....F 6
Ourthe (river) ....H 8
Rupel (river) ....F 7
Scheldt (Schelde) (river) ....C 7
Schnee Eifel (plateau) ....J 8
Semois (river) ....G 9
Senne (river) ....E 7
Vesdre (river) ....H 7
Weisserstein (mt.) ....J 8
Yser (river) ....B 7
Zitterwald (plateau) ....J 8

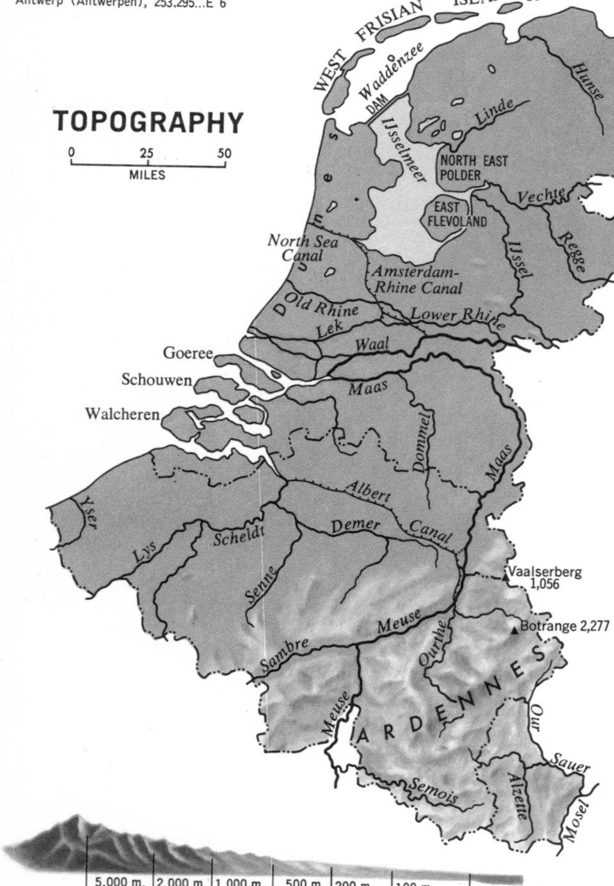

LUXEMBOURG

CITIES and TOWNS

Clervaux, 982 ....J 9
Diekirch, 4,373 ....J 9
Differdange, 17,570 ....H 9
Dudelange, 14,583 ....J10
Echternach, 3,395 ....J 9
Esch-sur-Alzette, 27,842 ....J 9
Esch-sur-Sauer, 318 ....H 9
Ettelbrück, 4,610 ....J 9
Grevenmacher, 2,726 ....J 9
Luxembourg (cap.), 73,850 ....J 9
Mersch, 1,512 ....J 9
Pétange, 5,939 ....H 9
Redange, 868 ....H 9
Remich, 1,792 ....J 9
Troisvierges, 964 ....J 9
Vianden, 1,457 ....J 9
Wasserbillig, 1,925 ....J 9
Wiltz, 3,891 ....H 9

PHYSICAL FEATURES

Alzette (river) ....J 9
Clerf (river) ....J 9
Eisling (mts.) ....H 9
Mosel (river) ....J 9
Our (river) ....J 9
Sauer (river) ....J 9

FRANCE

CONIC PROJECTION

SCALE OF MILES

SCALE OF KILOMETRES

Capitals of Countries .... ☆
Capitals of Departments .... △
International Boundaries .... —·—·—
Department Boundaries .... —··—
Canals .... ———

© C.S. HAMMOND & Co., N.Y.

PARIS and ENVIRONS

CORSICA

Same Scale as Main Map

FRANCE

AREA 212,736 sq. mi.
POPULATION 46,520,271
CAPITAL Paris
LARGEST CITY Paris (greater) 8,569,238
HIGHEST POINT Mont Blanc 15,781 ft.
MONETARY UNIT franc
MAJOR LANGUAGE French
MAJOR RELIGION Roman Catholic

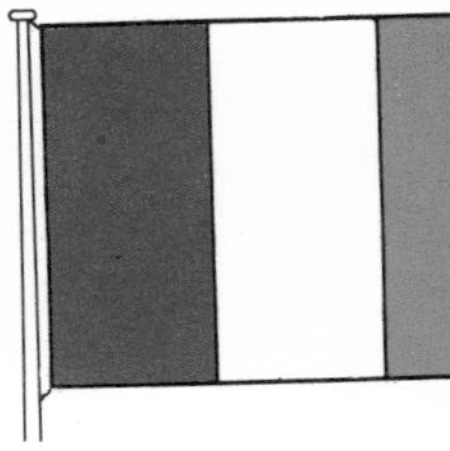

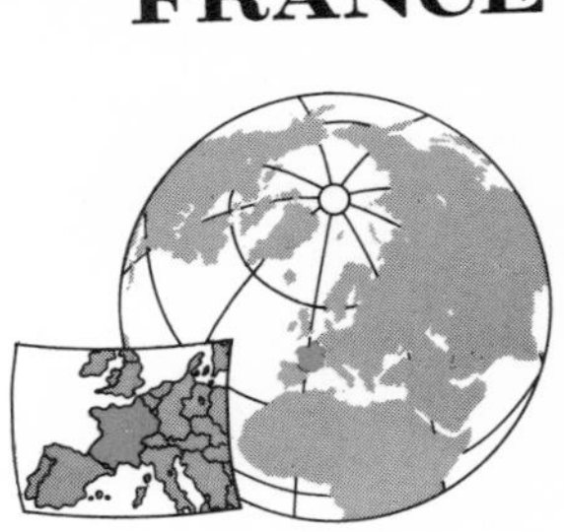

DEPARTMENTS

327,146 ....F 4
e, 512,920 ....E 3
r, 380,221 ....E 4
s-Maritimes, 618,265....G 6
che, 248,516 ....F 5
nnes, 300,247 ....F 3
ge, 137,192 ....D 6
e, 255,099 ....E 3
e, 269,782 ....E 6
ron, 290,442 ....E 5
Rhin, 770,150 ....G 3
es-Alpes, 91,843 ....G 5
ses-Pyrénées, 466,038 ....C 6
ort (terr.), 109,371 ....G 4
ches-du-Rhône, 1,248,355....F 6
ados, 480,686 ....C 3
tal, 172,977 ....E 5
rente, 327,658 ....D 5
rente-Maritime, 470,897....C 5
r, 293,514 ....E 4
rèze, 237,926 ....D 5
sica (Corse), 275,465....B 6
e-d'Or, 387,869 ....F 4
es-du-Nord, 501,923 ....B 3
use, 163,515 ....D 4
ux-Sèvres, 321,118 ....C 4
rdogne, 375,455 ....D 5
ubs, 384,881 ....G 4
ôme, 304,227 ....F 5
re, 361,904 ....D 3
re-et-Loir, 277,546 ....D 3
istère, 749,553 ....A 3
rd, 435,482 ....F 6
rs, 182,264 ....D 6
ronde, 935,448 ....C 5
ut-Rhin, 547,920 ....G 4
ute-Garonne, 594,633 ....D 6
ute-Loire, 211,036 ....E 5
ute-Marne, 208,446 ....F 3
ute-Saône, 208,440 ....G 4
ute-Savoie, 329,230 ....G 5
ute-Vienne, 332,514 ....D 5
utes-Alpes, 87,406 ....G 5
utes-Pyrénées, 211,433 ....D 6
érault, 516,658 ....E 6
e-et-Vilaine, 614,268....C 3
dre, 251,342 ....D 4
dre-et-Loire, 395,210 ....D 4
ère, 729,789 ....F 5
ura, 225,682 ....F 4
andes, 260,495 ....C 5
oir-et-Cher, 250,741 ....D 4
oire, 696,348 ....F 5
oire-Atlantique, 803,372....C 4
oiret, 389,854 ....E 4
ot, 149,929 ....D 5
ot-et-Garonne, 275,028 ....D 5
ozère, 81,868 ....E 5
Maine-et-Loire, 556,272 ....C 4
Manche, 446,878 ....C 3
Marne, 442,195 ....F 3
Mayenne, 250,030 ....C 3
Meurthe-et-Moselle, 678,078....G 3
Meuse, 215,985 ....F 3
Morbihan, 530,833 ....B 4
Moselle, 919,412 ....G 3
Nièvre, 245,921 ....E 4
Nord, 2,293,112 ....E 2
Oise, 481,289 ....E 3
Orne, 280,549 ....C 3
Pas-de-Calais, 1,366,282 ....E 2
Puy-de-Dôme, 508,928 ....E 5
Pyrénées-Orientales, 251,231....E 6
Rhône, 1,116,664 ....F 5
Saône-et-Loire, 535,772 ....F 4
Sarthe, 443,019 ....D 3
Savoie, 266,678 ....G 5
Seine, 5,646,446 ....B 1
Seine-et-Marne, 524,486 ....E 3
Seine-et-Oise, 2,298,931 ....E 3
Seine-Maritime, 1,035,844 ....D 3
Somme, 488,225 ....E 3
Tarn, 319,560 ....E 6
Tarn-et-Garonne, 175,847 ....D 5
Var, 469,557 ....G 6
Vaucluse, 303,536 ....F 6
Vendée, 408,928 ....C 4
Vienne, 331,619 ....D 4
Vosges, 380,676 ....G 3
Yonne, 269,826 ....E 4

CITIES and TOWNS

Abbeville, 21,744 ....D 2
Agde, 7,695 ....E 6
Agen, 30,639 ....D 5
Aix-en-Provence, 553,398....F 6
Aix-les-Bains, 17,324 ....G 5
Ajaccio, 40,829 ....B 7
Albert, 10,203 ....E 2
Albertville, 11,122 ....G 5
Albi, 31,672 ....E 6
Alençon, 24,299 ....D 3
Alès, 23,571 ....E 5
Ambérieu-en-Bugey, 7,498 ....F 5
Ambert, 5,604 ....E 5
Amboise, 7,332 ....D 4
Amiens, 101,677 ....D 3
Angers, 109,614 ....C 4
Angoulême, 46,924 ....D 5
Annecy, 42,304 ....G 5
Annonay, 12,559 ....F 5
Antibes, 24,730 ....G 6
Apt, 6,251 ....F 6
Arcachon, 14,738 ....F 4
Argentan, 11,724 ....D 3
Argenteuil, 82,007 ....A 1
Argenton-sur-Creusot, 5,874 ....D 4
Arles, 29,251 ....F 6
Armentières, 23,168 ....E 2
Arras, 40,969 ....E 2
Asnières, 81,747 ....A 1
Aubagne, 12,610 ....F 6
Aubenas, 5,739 ....F 5
Aubervilliers, 70,592 ....B 1
Aubusson, 5,343 ....E 4
Auch, 16,109 ....D 6
Audincourt, 12,433 ....G 4
Aulnay-sous-Bois, 47,417 ....B 1
Auray, 7,802 ....B 4
Aurignac, 742 ....D 6
Aurillac, 23,179 ....E 5
Autun, 14,003 ....F 4
Auxerre, 28,949 ....E 4
Avallon, 5,656 ....E 4
Avesnes-sur-Helpe, 6,028 ....F 2
Avignon, 64,581 ....F 6
Avion, 20,730 ....E 2
Avranches, 8,828 ....C 3
Bagnères-de-Bigorre, 8,958 ....D 6
Bagnères-de-Luchon, 3,857 ....D 6
Bagnolet, 31,442 ....B 2
Bagnols-sur-Cèze, 11,831 ....F 5
Bar-le-Duc, 17,988 ....F 3
Bar-sur-Seine, 2,408 ....F 3
Barfleur, 847 ....C 3
Bastia, 49,929 ....B 6
Bayeux, 9,335 ....C 3
Bayonne, 30,865 ....C 6
Beaucaire, 8,243 ....F 6
Beaune, 14,695 ....F 4
Beauvais, 33,559 ....E 3
Bédarieux, 6,976 ....E 6
Belfort, 45,576 ....G 4
Belley, 5,080 ....F 5
Berck, 12,684 ....D 2
Bergerac, 20,972 ....D 5
Bernay, 8,049 ....D 3
Besançon, 90,203 ....G 4
Bessèges, 5,047 ....F 5
Béthune, 22,530 ....E 2
Béziers, 57,601 ....E 6
Biarritz, 24,273 ....C 6
Blois, 30,081 ....D 4
Bolbec, 11,922 ....D 3
Bondy, 38,032 ....B 1
Bordeaux, 246,186 ....C 5
Boulogne-Billancourt, 106,559....A 2
Boulogne-sur-Mer, 49,036 ....D 2
Bourg-en-Bresse, 28,813 ....F 4
Bourges, 55,216 ....E 4
Bourgoin, 8,413 ....F 5
Bressuire, 6,500 ....C 4
Brest, 130,867 ....A 3
Briançon, 6,756 ....G 5
Briare, 3,713 ....E 4
Brignoles, 6,432 ....G 6
Brioude, 6,087 ....E 5
Brive-la-Gaillarde, 38,105....D 5
Bruay-en-Artois, 30,876 ....E 2
Caen, 88,449 ....C 3
Cahors, 15,528 ....D 5
Calais, 70,127 ....D 2
Caluire-et-Cuire, 25,718 ....F 5
Calvi, 2,523 ....B 6
Cambrai, 32,601 ....E 2
Cannes, 54,967 ....G 6
Carcassonne, 37,190 ....D 6
Carentan, 4,786 ....C 3
Carmaux, 12,688 ....E 5
Carpentras, 14,169 ....F 5
Casteljaloux, 4,603 ....D 5
Castelnaudary, 7,944 ....E 6
Castelsarrasin, 6,765 ....D 6
Castres, 32,012 ....E 6
Cavaillon, 12,062 ....F 6
Cayeux-sur-Mer, 2,240 ....D 2
Céret, 4,813 ....E 6
Cette (Sète), 35,910 ....E 6
Chalon-sur-Saône, 40,056 ....F 4
Chalonnes-sur-Loire, 2,308 ....C 4
Châlons-sur-Marne, 39,658 ....F 3
Chambéry, 41,011 ....F 5
Chambord, 175 ....D 4
Chamonix-Mont-Blanc, 5,412 ....G 5
Champigny-sur-Marne, 57,807 ....C 2
Chantilly, 8,106 ....E 3
Charenton-le-Pont, 22,203 ....B 2
Charleville, 24,543 ....F 3
Charolles, 2,968 ....F 4
Chartres, 31,085 ....D 3
Château-Chinon, 2,443 ....E 4
Château-du-Loir, 4,481 ....D 4
Château-Gontier, 7,000 ....C 4
Château-Renault, 4,020 ....D 4
Château-Salins, 2,121 ....G 3
Château-Thierry, 9,356 ....E 3
Châteaubriant, 9,985 ....C 4
Châteaudun, 11,107 ....D 3
Châteauneuf-sur-Loire, 4,016 ....E 4
Châteauroux, 44,227 ....D 4
Châtellerault, 25,162 ....D 4
Châtillon, 20,884 ....B 2
Châtillon-sur-Indre, 2,373 ....D 4
Châtillon-sur-Seine, 5,389 ....F 4
Chaumont, 21,642 ....F 3
Chauny, 12,348 ....E 3
Chazelles-sur-Lyon, 4,956 ....F 5
Cherbourg, 37,096 ....C 3
Chinon, 5,122 ....D 4
Choisy-le-Roi, 40,577 ....B 2
Cholet, 34,543 ....C 4
Clamart, 47,929 ....A 2
Clamecy, 4,995 ....E 4
Clermont, 5,942 ....E 3
Clermont-Ferrand, 124,531 ....E 5
Clichy, 56,305 ....B 1
Cluny, 3,293 ....F 4
Cognac, 20,033 ....C 5
Colmar, 51,624 ....G 3
Colombes, 76,849 ....A 1
Commentry, 7,794 ....E 4
Commercy, 7,008 ....F 3
Compiègne, 23,833 ....E 3
Concarneau, 11,691 ....A 4
Condom, 4,577 ....D 6
Corbeil-Essonnes, 26,479 ....E 3
Corte, 5,268 ....B 7
Cosne, 8,032 ....E 4
Coulommiers, 9,302 ....E 3
Courbevoie, 59,437 ....A 2
Coutances, 7,709 ....C 3
Coutras, 4,236 ....C 5
Creil, 18,344 ....E 3
Crépy-en-Valois, 7,271 ....E 3
Crest, 4,819 ....F 5
Cusset, 10,512 ....E 4
Dax, 16,016 ....C 6
Deauville, 5,024 ....C 3
Decazeville, 10,678 ....E 5
Decize, 5,713 ....E 4
Denain, 29,307 ....E 2
Dieppe, 29,853 ....D 3
Digne, 9,788 ....G 5
Digoin, 7,901 ....F 4
Dijon, 133,975 ....F 4
Dinan, 12,730 ....B 3
Dinard, 7,944 ....B 3
Dôle, 20,719 ....F 4
Domrémy-la-Pucelle, 171 ....F 3
Douai, 46,091 ....E 2
Douarnenez, 18,558 ....A 3
Doué-la-Fontaine, 3,819 ....C 4
Doullens, 5,584 ....E 2
Draguignan, 11,526 ....G 6
Drancy, 65,649 ....B 1
Dreux, 20,227 ....D 3
Dunkirk (Dunkerque), 26,197....E 2
Elbeuf, 18,701 ....D 3
Elne, 5,128 ....E 6
Embrun, 3,586 ....G 5
Épernay, 21,365 ....E 3
Épinal, 29,449 ....G 3
Ernée, 3,880 ....C 3
Erstein, 6,115 ....G 3
Étampes, 13,219 ....E 3
Étaples, 8,618 ....D 2
Eu, 6,548 ....D 3
Évreux, 34,398 ....D 3
Falaise, 5,977 ....C 3
Fécamp, 19,308 ....D 3
Figeac, 6,942 ....D 5
Firminy, 25,013 ....F 5
Flers, 12,616 ....C 3
Foix, 7,106 ....D 6
Fontainebleau, 19,677 ....E 3
Fontenay-le-Comte, 8,880....C 4
Fontenay-sous-Bois, 37,458 ....C 2
Forbach, 19,291 ....G 3
Forcalquier, 2,068 ....F 6
Fougères, 23,928 ....C 3
Fourmies, 14,231 ....F 2
Fréjus, 10,459 ....G 6
Gaillac, 6,413 ....D 6
Gannat, 5,061 ....E 4
Gap, 18,116 ....G 5
Gardanne, 5,320 ....F 6
Gennevillers, 42,562 ....B 1
Gentilly, 19,005 ....B 2
Gex, 1,411 ....G 4
Gien, 8,773 ....E 4
Gisors, 5,952 ....D 3
Givet, 7,219 ....F 2
Givors, 17,062 ....F 5
Gourdon, 2,914 ....D 5
Gournay-en-Bray, 3,957 ....D 3
Granville, 9,439 ....C 3
Grasse, 25,161 ....G 6
Graulhet, 7,996 ....E 6
Gray, 6,963 ....F 4
Grenoble, 155,677 ....G 5
Guebwiller, 10,436 ....G 4
Guéret, 10,487 ....D 4
Guingamp, 8,829 ....B 3
Guise, 6,249 ....E 3
Haguenau, 20,357 ....G 3
Ham, 4,193 ....E 3
Harfleur, 3,787 ....D 3
Hautmont, 18,529 ....F 2
Havre (Le Havre), 182,504....C 3
Hayange, 10,987 ....F 3
Hazebrouck, 16,034 ....E 2
Hendaye, 6,674 ....C 6
Hénin-Liétard, 25,527 ....E 2
Hennebont, 7,618 ....B 4
Héricourt, 7,088 ....G 4
Hirson, 11,570 ....F 3
Honfleur, 8,822 ....D 3
Hyères, 18,301 ....G 6
Ille-sur-Têt, 4,305 ....E 6
Issoire, 10,345 ....E 5
Issoudun, 13,198 ....D 4
Issy-les-Moulineaux, 51,440 ....A 2
Ivry-sur-Seine, 53,229 ....B 2
Jarnac, 4,280 ....C 5
Joigny, 7,035 ....E 3
Jonzac, 3,523 ....C 5
La Baule-Escoublac, 314 ....B 4
La Charité-sur-Loire, 4,742 ....E 4
La Châtre, 3,716 ....D 4
La Ciotat, 17,552 ....F 6
La Ferté-Macé, 3,943 ....C 3
La Flèche, 9,257 ....C 4
La Grand-Combe, 10,333 ....E 5
La Pallice ....C 4
La Réole, 3,967 ....C 5
La Roche-sur-Yon, 22,231 ....C 4
La Rochelle, 65,581 ....C 4
La Seyne-sur-Mer, 22,471 ....F 6
La Souterraine, 3,512 ....D 4
La Tour-du-Pin, 4,508 ....F 5
L'Aigle, 6,476 ....D 3
Lamballe, 4,963 ....B 3
Landerneau, 11,278 ....B 3
Langeac, 4,442 ....E 5
Langogne, 3,913 ....E 5
Langon, 4,630 ....C 5
Langres, 7,648 ....F 4
Lannion, 6,469 ....B 3
Laon, 23,528 ....E 3
Lapalisse, 2,687 ....E 4
Laval, 35,835 ....C 3
Lavaur, 4,010 ....D 6
Lavelanet, 7,518 ....E 6
Le Blanc, 5,371 ....D 4
Le Bourget, 10,077 ....B 1
Le Cateau, 8,765 ....E 2
Le Chesnay, 13,223 ....A 2
Le Creusot, 33,002 ....F 4
Le Croisic, 3,821 ....B 4
Le Havre, 182,504 ....C 3
Le Mans, 128,814 ....C 3
Le Puy, 22,396 ....F 5
Le Teil, 7,688 ....F 5
Le Touquet-Paris-Plage, 3,959 ....D 2
Le Tréport, 5,785 ....D 2
Le Vigan, 3,362 ....E 5
Lens, 42,508 ....E 2
Les Andelys, 5,307 ....D 3
Les Sables-d'Olonne, 18,267 ....B 4
Lesparre-Médoc, 2,428 ....C 5
Levallois-Perret, 61,801 ....A 1
Levie, 2,983 ....B 7
Lézignan-Corbières, 6,626 ....E 6
Libourne, 15,050 ....C 5
Liévin, 35,042 ....E 2
L'Île-Rousse, 1,750 ....B 6
Lille, 191,863 ....E 2
Limoges, 113,378 ....D 5
Limoux, 7,876 ....E 6
Lisieux, 20,441 ....D 3
Loches, 4,526 ....D 4
Lodève, 6,320 ....E 6
Longwy, 21,919 ....F 3
Lons-le-Saunier, 15,570 ....F 4
Lorient, 58,504 ....B 4
Loudéac, 3,751 ....B 3
Loudun, 5,243 ....D 4
Lourdes, 15,691 ....C 6
Louviers, 12,554 ....D 3
Luçon, 7,291 ....C 4
Lunel, 7,240 ....E 6
Lunéville, 21,250 ....G 3
Lure, 6,141 ....G 4
Luxeuil-les-Bains, 8,158 ....G 4
Lyon, 524,834 ....F 5
Mâcon, 25,012 ....F 4
Maisons-Alfort, 50,965 ....B 2
Maisons-Laffitte, 19,085 ....A 1
Malakoff, 33,600 ....A 2
Mamers, 4,689 ....D 3
Manosque, 7,429 ....G 6
Mantes-la-Jolie, 18,885 ....D 3
Marennes, 3,797 ....C 5
Marmande, 10,191 ....C 5
Marseille, 767,146 ....F 6
Martigues, 14,655 ....F 6
Marvejols, 3,933 ....E 5
Maubeuge, 27,208 ....F 2
Mauléon-Licharre, 4,400 ....C 6
Mauriac, 2,954 ....E 5
Mayenne, 8,393 ....C 3
Mazamet, 14,843 ....E 6
Meaux, 21,960 ....E 3
Mehun-sur-Yèvre, 5,111 ....E 4
Melun, 26,061 ....E 3
Mende, 7,647 ....E 5
Menton, 17,211 ....G 6
Metz, 101,496 ....G 3
Meudon, 29,004 ....A 2
Mézières, 11,725 ....F 3
Millau, 19,215 ....E 5
Mirecourt, 6,640 ....G 3
Modane, 4,679 ....G 5
Moissac, 6,262 ....D 5
Mont-de-Marsan, 18,059 ....C 6
Mont-Dore, 1,897 ....E 5
Mont-Saint-Michel, 102 ....C 3
Montargis, 15,700 ....E 3
Montauban, 29,716 ....D 5
Montbard, 6,272 ....F 4
Montbéliard, 21,040 ....G 4
Montbrison, 8,327 ....E 5
Montceau-les-Mines, 8,201 ....F 4
Montdidier, 5,405 ....E 3
Montélimar, 15,811 ....F 5
Montfort, 2,182 ....C 3
Montigny-les-Metz, 22,325 ....G 3
Montluçon, 54,947 ....E 4
Montmorillon, 5,094 ....D 4
Montpellier, 109,116 ....E 6
Montreuil, 92,040 ....B 2
Montrouge, 45,224 ....B 2
Morlaix, 15,472 ....B 3
Morteau, 5,179 ....G 4
Moulins, 23,187 ....E 4
Moûtiers, 3,717 ....G 5
Moyeuvre-Grande, 15,146 ....G 3
Mulhouse, 107,946 ....G 4
Murat, 2,315 ....E 5
Muret, 4,742 ....D 6
Nancy, 127,729 ....G 3
Nanterre, 83,155 ....A 1
Nantes, 234,747 ....C 4
Narbonne, 30,388 ....E 6
Nemours, 6,313 ....E 3
Nérac, 4,192 ....D 5
Neufchâteau, 4,452 ....F 3
Neufchâtel-en-Bray, 5,460 ....D 3
Neuilly-sur-Seine, 72,570 ....A 1
Nevers, 38,716 ....E 4
Nice, 278,714 ....G 6
Nîmes, 85,884 ....F 6
Niort, 36,265 ....C 4
Nogent-le-Rotrou, 8,822 ....D 3
Nogent-sur-Seine, 3,690 ....E 3
Noisy-le-Sec, 31,120 ....B 1
Noyon, 9,019 ....E 3
Nyons, 3,599 ....F 5
Oloron-Sainte-Marie, 12,113 ....C 6
Orange, 17,202 ....F 5
Orléans, 82,812 ....D 3
Orly, 18,184 ....B 2
Orthez, 6,735 ....C 6
Oullins, 24,314 ....F 5
Oyonnax, 14,636 ....F 4
Paimpol, 5,362 ....B 3
Pamiers, 12,026 ....D 6
Pantin, 46,276 ....B 1
Paray-le-Monial, 9,005 ....F 4
Paris (cap.), 2,790,091 ....B 2
Paris (greater), 8,569,238 ....B 2
Parthenay, 9,052 ....C 4
Pau, 57,476 ....C 6
Périgueux, 36,585 ....D 5
Péronne, 5,078 ....E 3
Perpignan, 82,626 ....E 6
Pessac, 22,065 ....C 5
Pézenas, 6,792 ....E 6
Pithiviers, 7,213 ....E 3
Ploërmel, 3,454 ....B 4
Poitiers, 59,799 ....D 4
Poligny, 3,717 ....F 4
Pont-à-Mousson, 12,427 ....G 3
Pont-l'Abbé, 5,819 ....A 4
Pont-l'Évêque, 2,787 ....D 3
Pontarlier, 15,191 ....G 4
Pontivy, 8,749 ....B 3
Pontoise, 14,898 ....E 3
Port-Louis, 4,140 ....B 4
Port-Saint-Louis-du-Rhône, 5,289..F 6
Port-Vendres, 4,141 ....E 6
Porto-Vecchio, 3,176 ....B 7
Prades, 5,344 ....E 6
Privas, 6,417 ....F 5
Provins, 7,243 ....E 3
Puteaux, 39,640 ....A 2
Quiberon, 2,393 ....B 4
Quillan, 4,285 ....E 6
Quimper, 40,223 ....A 4
Quimperlé, 9,280 ....B 4
Rambouillet, 10,631 ....D 3
Redon, 7,681 ....C 4
Reims, 133,142 ....E 3
Remiremont, 9,020 ....G 3
Rennes, 145,093 ....C 3
Rethel, 7,352 ....F 3
Revel, 5,264 ....E 6
Rezé, 20,602 ....C 4
Rive-de-Gier, 14,898 ....F 5
Roanne, 51,468 ....E 4
Rochefort, 26,490 ....C 4
Rodez, 20,438 ....E 5
Romans-sur-Isère, 24,167 ....F 5
Romilly-sur-Seine, 15,537 ....F 3
Romorantin-Lanthenay, 10,830....D 4
Roubaix, 112,567 ....E 2
Rouen, 118,775 ....D 3
Royan, 16,144 ....C 5

(continued on following page)

TOPOGRAPHY

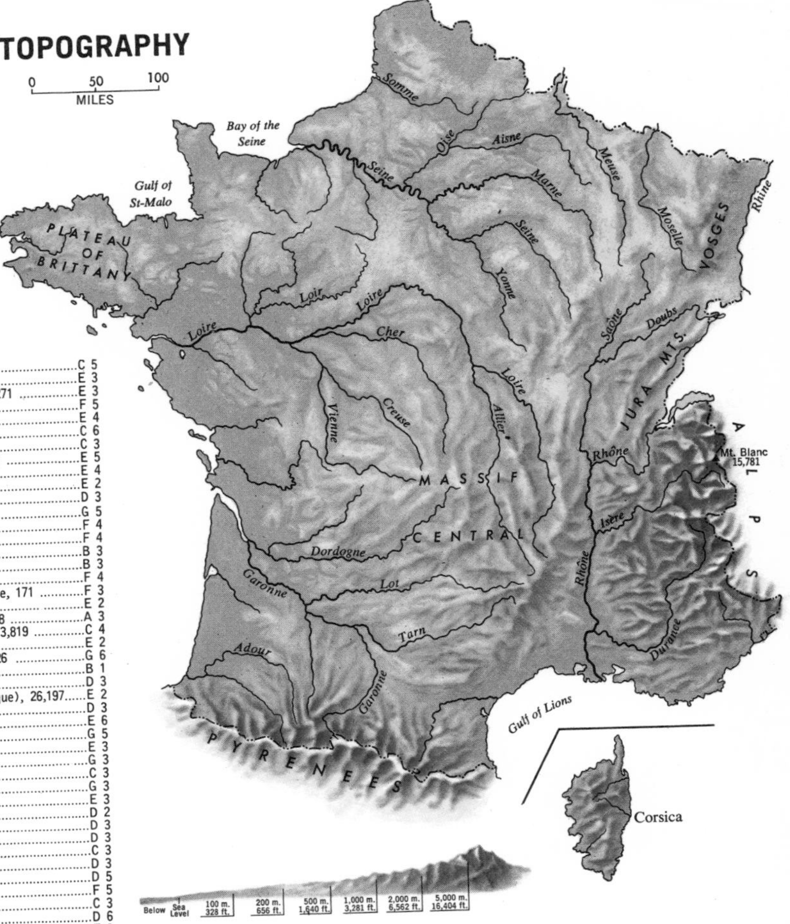
0 50 100
MILES
Bay of the Seine
Gulf of St-Malo
PLATEAU OF BRITTANY
Somme
Oise
Aisne
Seine
Marne
Meuse
Moselle
Rhine
VOSGES
Loir
Loire
Yonne
Cher
Saône
Doubs
JURA MTS.
Creuse
Vienne
Allier
Rhône
MASSIF CENTRAL
Mt. Blanc 15,781
ALPS
Isère
Dordogne
Garonne
Lot
Tarn
Durance
Adour
Gulf of Lions
PYRENEES
Corsica
Below Sea Level
100 m. 328 ft.
200 m. 656 ft.
500 m. 1,640 ft.
1,000 m. 3,281 ft.
2,000 m. 6,562 ft.
5,000 m. 16,404 ft.

HISTORIC PROVINCES

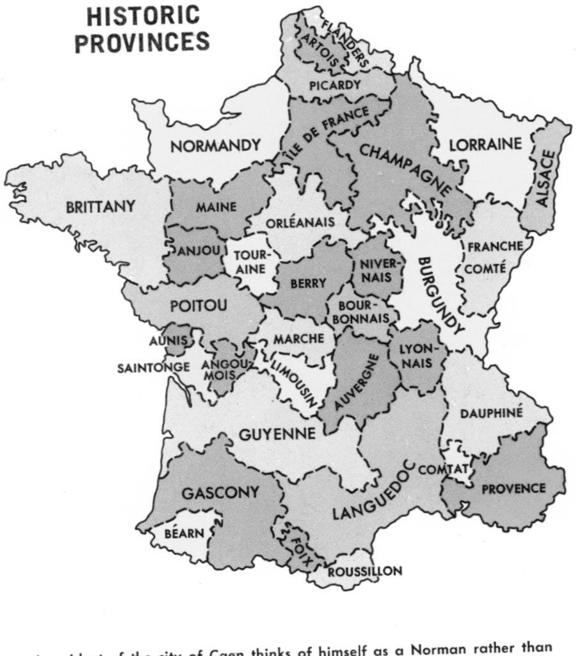
FLANDERS
ARTOIS
PICARDY
NORMANDY
ILE DE FRANCE
CHAMPAGNE
LORRAINE
ALSACE
BRITTANY
MAINE
ORLÉANAIS
ANJOU
TOUR-AINE
BERRY
NIVER-NAIS
BURGUNDY
FRANCHE COMTÉ
POITOU
BOUR-BONNAIS
AUNIS
MARCHE
LYON-NAIS
SAINTONGE
ANGOU-MOIS
LIMOUSIN
AUVERGNE
DAUPHINÉ
GUYENNE
GASCONY
LANGUEDOC
COMTAT
PROVENCE
BÉARN
FOIX
ROUSSILLON

A resident of the city of Caen thinks of himself as a Norman rather than as a citizen of the modern department of Calvados. In spite of the passing of nearly two centuries, the historic provinces which existed before 1790 command the local patriotism of most Frenchmen.

France

(continued)

Rueil-Malmaison, 46,515 ....A 2
Ruffec, 3,808 ....D 5
Sable-sur-Sarthe, 6,383 ....C 4
Saint-Affrique, 5,655 ....E 6
Saint-Amand-Mont-Rond, 10,412 ....E 4
Saint-Brieuc, 42,211 ....B 3
Saint-Céré, 3,283 ....D 5
Saint-Chamond, 17,060 ....F 5
Saint-Claude, 11,526 ....F 4
Saint-Cloud, 26,433 ....A 2
Saint-Denis, 93,783 ....B 1
Saint-Dié, 22,200 ....G 3
Saint-Dizier, 33,511 ....F 3
Saint-Étienne, 200,528 ....F 5
Saint-Florent-sur-Cher, 5,283 ......E 4
Saint-Flour, 5,336 ....E 5
Saint-Gaudens, 7,945 ....D 6
Saint-Germain-en-Laye, 32,916....D 3
Saint-Gilles, 5,347 ....F 6
Saint-Girons, 6,678 ....D 6
Saint-Jean-d'Angély, 7,868 ....C 4
Saint-Jean-de-Luz, 9,056 ....C 6
Saint-Jean-de-Maurienne, 5,231...G 5
Saint-Jean-Pied-de-Port, 1,612.....C 6
Saint-Junien, 8,449 ....D 5
Saint-Lô, 14,884 ....C 3
Saint-Malo, 16,981 ....B 3
Saint-Mandé, 24,279 ....B 2
Saint-Marcellin, 4,946 ....F 5
Saint-Maur-des-Fossés, 70,295.....B 2
Saint-Mihiel, 5,203 ....F 3
Saint-Nazaire, 49,331 ....B 4
Saint-Omer, 18,180 ....E 2
Saint-Ouen, 51,471 ....B 1
Saint-Pol, 6,271 ....A 3
Saint-Pol-sur-Ternoise, 5,124.......E 2
Saint-Quentin, 60,633 ....E 3
Saint-Raphaël, 9,470 ....G 6
Saint-Servan-sur-Mer, 13,479.......C 3
Saint-Tropez, 4,677 ....G 6
Saint-Valéry-sur-Somme, 2,986....D 2
Saint-Vallier, 4,070 ....F 5
Saint-Yrieix-la-Perche, 3,905.......D 5
Sainte-Menehould, 3,703 ....F 3
Sainte-Mère-Église, 768 ....C 3
Sainte-Savine, 11,861 ....E 3
Saintes, 23,594 ....C 4
Salins-les-Bains, 4,061 ....F 4
Salon-de-Provence, 16,930 ....F 6
Sarlat, 5,012 ....D 5
Sarralbe, 3,170 ....G 3
Sarrebourg, 10,728 ....G 3
Sarreguemines, 16,851 ....G 3
Sartène 4,160 ....B 7
Saumur, 20,466 ....D 4
Saverne, 8,855 ....G 3
Sceaux, 18,936 ....A 2
Schiltigheim, 25,019 ....G 3
Sedan, 20,261 ....F 3
Segré, 4,760 ....C 4
Sélestat, 13,568 ....G 3
Semur-en-Auxois, 3,168 ....F 4
Senlis, 8,717 ....E 3
Sens, 19,692 ....E 3
Sète, 35,910 ....E 6
Sèvres, 20,119 ....A 2
Sézanne, 5,216 ....E 3
Sisteron, 4,651 ....G 5
Soissons, 22,890 ....E 3
Sotteville-lès-Rouen, 32,998.........D 3
Stiring-Wendel, 15,028 ....G 3
Strasbourg, 225,964 ....H 3
Suresnes, 38,980 ....A 2
Tarare, 11,926 ....F 5
Tarascon, 6,475 ....F 6
Tarbes, 46,162 ....D 6
Thann, 7,538 ....G 4
Thiers, 12,396 ....E 5
Thionville, 31,636 ....G 3
Thonon-les-Bains, 14,478 ....G 4
Thouars, 11,016 ....C 4
Tonneins, 5,204 ....D 5
Tonnerre, 5,359 ....E 4
Toul, 13,353 ....F 3
Toulon, 160,142 ....F 6
Toulouse, 254,791 ....D 6
Tourcoing, 89,187 ....E 2
Tournon, 5,883 ....F 5
Tournus, 5,966 ....F 4
Tours, 91,374 ....D 4
Trouville, 5,965 ....C 3
Troyes, 67,074 ....F 3
Tulle, 16,477 ....D 5
Ussel, 6,796 ....E 5
Uzès, 4,825 ....F 5
Valence, 49,840 ....F 5
Valenciennes, 45,019 ....E 2
Valognes, 4,545 ....C 3
Vannes, 26,846 ....B 4
Vence, 5,630 ....G 6
Vendôme, 12,847 ....D 4
Vénissieux, 28,705 ....F 5
Verdun, 21,406 ....F 3
Verneuil-sur-Avre, 4,865 ....D 3
Vernon, 15,872 ....D 3
Versailles, 84,860 ....A 2
Vesoul, 10,794 ....F 4
Vichy, 30,610 ....E 4
Vienne, 24,277 ....F 5
Vierzon, 30,395 ....D 4
Villefranche, 5,236 ....G 6
Villefranche-de-Rouergue, 7,914...E 5
Villefranche-sur-Saône, 24,102 ....F 4
Villejuif, 43,714 ....B 2
Villemomble, 24,533 ....C 1
Villeneuve, 28,110 ....E 3
Villeneuve-sur-Lot, 14,862...........D 5
Villeurbanne, 105,156 ....F 5
Vincennes, 50,425 ....B 2
Vire, 8,889 ....C 3
Vitré, 9,335 ....C 3
Vitry-le-François, 14,487.............F 3
Vitry-sur-Seine, 65,607 ....B 2
Vittel, 4,975 ....F 3
Vizille, 6,130 ....F 5
Voiron, 11,105 ....F 5
Wassy, 2,812 ....F 3
Wissembourg, 4,917 ....G 3
Yvetot, 7,503 ....D 3

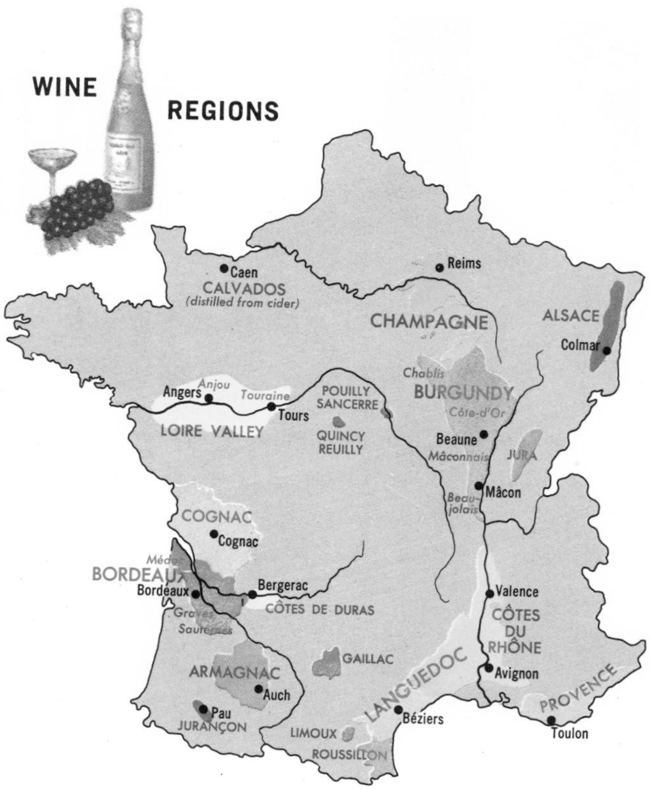

WINE
REGIONS
Caen
CALVADOS
(distilled from cider)
Reims
CHAMPAGNE
ALSACE
Colmar
Chablis
BURGUNDY
Côte-d'Or
Anjou
Touraine
Angers
Tours
POUILLY
SANCERRE
LOIRE VALLEY
QUINCY
REUILLY
Beaune
Mâconnais
JURA
Beaujolais
Mâcon
COGNAC
Cognac
Médoc
BORDEAUX
Bordeaux
Bergerac
CÔTES DE DURAS
Graves
Sauternes
Valence
CÔTES
DU
RHÔNE
GAILLAC
ARMAGNAC
Auch
LANGUEDOC
Avignon
PROVENCE
Pau
JURANÇON
Béziers
LIMOUX
ROUSSILLON
Toulon

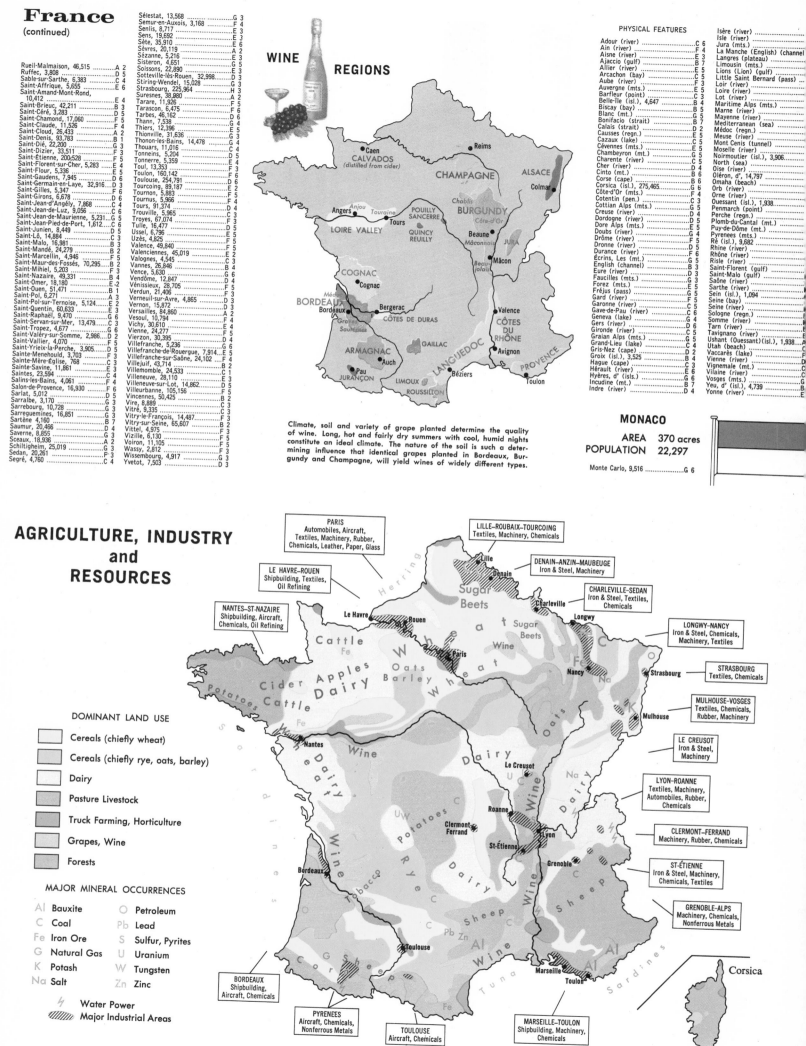

Climate, soil and variety of grape planted determine the quality of wine. Long, hot and fairly dry summers with cool, humid nights constitute an ideal climate. The nature of the soil is such a determining influence that identical grapes planted in Bordeaux, Burgundy and Champagne, will yield wines of widely different types.

PHYSICAL FEATURES

Adour (river) ....C 6
Ain (river) ....F 4
Aisne (river) ....E 3
Ajaccio (gulf) ....B 7
Allier (river) ....E 5
Arcachon (bay) ....C 5
Aube (river) ....F 3
Auvergne (mts.) ....E 5
Barfleur (point) ....C 3
Belle-Île (isl.), 4,647 ....B 4
Biscay (bay) ....B 5
Blanc (mt.) ....G 5
Bonifacio (strait) ....B 7
Calais (strait) ....D 2
Causses (regn.) ....E 5
Cazaux (lake) ....C 5
Cévennes (mts.) ....E 5
Chambeyron (mt.) ....G 5
Charente (river) ....C 5
Cher (river) ....D 4
Cinto (mt.) ....B 6
Corse (cape) ....B 6
Corsica (isl.), 275,465............G 6
Côte-d'Or (mts.) ....F 4
Cotentin (pen.) ....C 3
Cottian Alps (mts.) ....G 5
Creuse (river) ....D 4
Dordogne (river) ....D 5
Dore Alps (mts.) ....E 5
Doubs (river) ....G 4
Drôme (river) ....F 5
Dronne (river) ....D 5
Durance (river) ....F 6
Écrins, Les (mt.) ....G 5
English (channel) ....B 3
Eure (river) ....D 3
Faucilles (mts.) ....G 3
Forez (mts.) ....E 5
Fréjus (pass) ....G 5
Gard (river) ....F 5
Garonne (river) ....C 5
Gave-de-Pau (river) ....C 6
Geneva (lake) ....G 4
Gers (river) ....D 6
Gironde (river) ....C 5
Graian Alps (mts.) ....G 5
Grand-Lieu (lake) ....C 4
Gris-Nez (cape) ....D 2
Groix (isl.), 3,525 ....B 4
Hague (cape) ....C 3
Hérault (river) ....E 6
Hyères, d' (isls.) ....G 6
Incudine (mt.) ....B 7
Indre (river) ....D 4
Isère (river) ....
Isle (river) ....
Jura (mts.) ....
La Manche (English) (channel
Langres (plateau) ....
Limousin (mts.) ....
Lions (Lion) (gulf) ....
Little Saint Bernard (pass) ...
Loir (river) ....
Loire (river) ....
Lot (river) ....
Maritime Alps (mts.) ....
Marne (river) ....
Mayenne (river) ....
Mediterranean (sea) ....
Médoc (regn.) ....
Meuse (river) ....
Mont Cenis (tunnel) ....
Moselle (river) ....
Noirmoutier (isl.), 3,906............
North (sea) ....
Oise (river) ....
Oléron, d', 14,797 ....
Omaha (beach) ....
Orb (river) ....
Orne (river) ....
Ouessant (isl.), 1,938............
Penmarch (point) ....
Perche (regn.) ....
Plomb-du-Cantal (mt.) ....
Puy-de-Dôme (mt.) ....
Pyrenees (mts.) ....
Ré (isl.), 9,682 ....
Rhine (river) ....
Rhône (river) ....
Risle (river) ....
Saint-Florent (gulf) ....
Saint-Malo (gulf) ....
Saône (river) ....
Sarthe (river) ....
Sein (isl.), 1,094 ....
Seine (bay) ....
Seine (river) ....
Sologne (regn.) ....
Somme (river) ....
Tarn (river) ....
Tavignano (river) ....
Ushant (Ouessant)(isl.), 1,938....A
Utah (beach) C
Vaccarès (lake) ....F
Vienne (river) ....D
Vignemale (mt.) C
Vilaine (river) C
Vosges (mts.) ....G
Yeu, d' (isl.), 4,739 ....B
Yonne (river) ....E

MONACO

AREA 370 acres
POPULATION 22,297

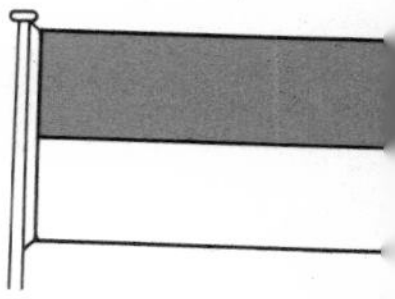

Monte Carlo, 9,516 ....G 6

AGRICULTURE, INDUSTRY and RESOURCES

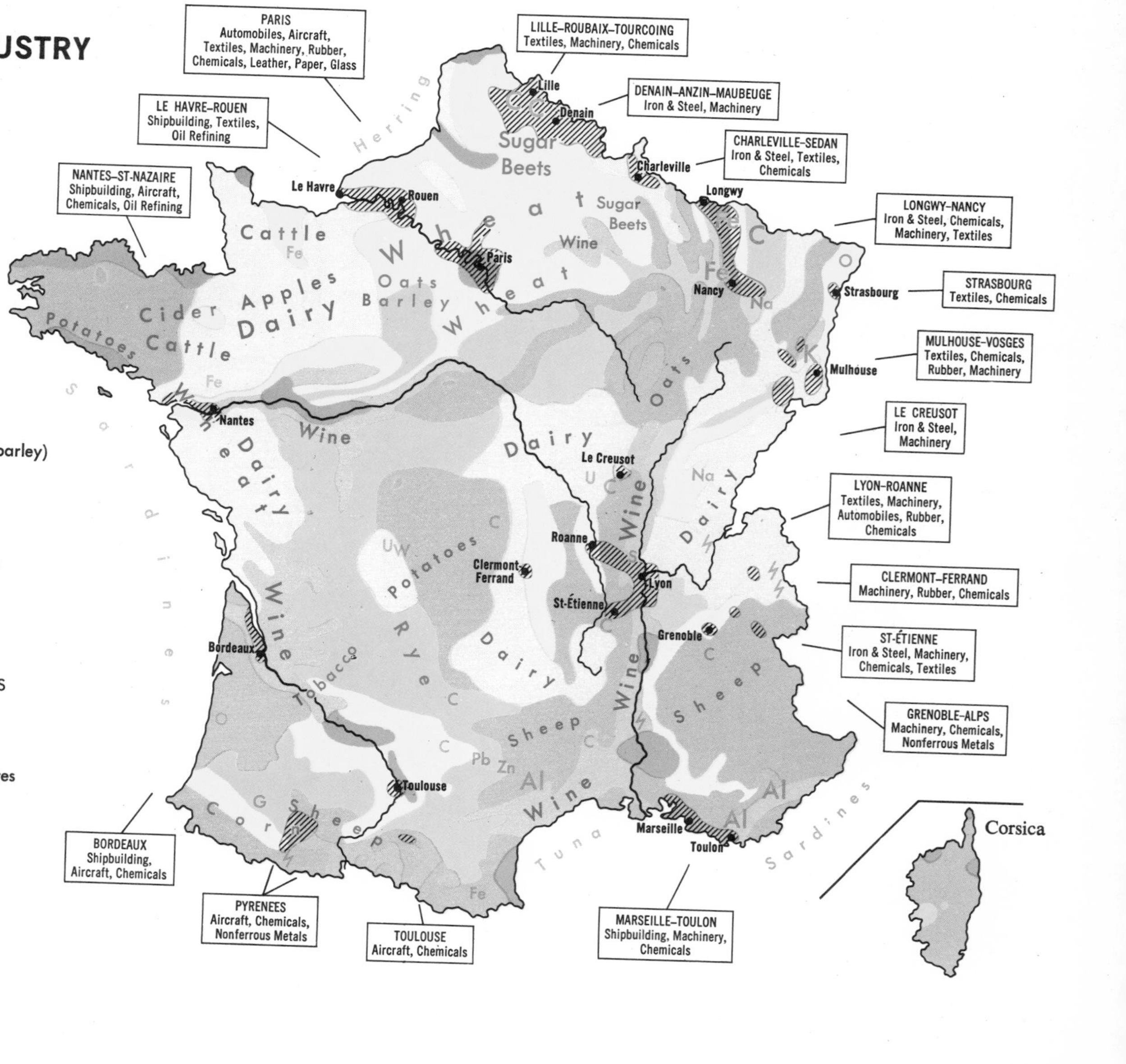

PARIS
Automobiles, Aircraft, Textiles, Machinery, Rubber, Chemicals, Leather, Paper, Glass
LILLE-ROUBAIX-TOURCOING
Textiles, Machinery, Chemicals
LE HAVRE-ROUEN
Shipbuilding, Textiles, Oil Refining
DENAIN-ANZIN-MAUBEUGE
Iron & Steel, Machinery
NANTES-ST-NAZAIRE
Shipbuilding, Aircraft, Chemicals, Oil Refining
CHARLEVILLE-SEDAN
Iron & Steel, Textiles, Chemicals
LONGWY-NANCY
Iron & Steel, Chemicals, Machinery, Textiles
STRASBOURG
Textiles, Chemicals
MULHOUSE-VOSGES
Textiles, Chemicals, Rubber, Machinery
LE CREUSOT
Iron & Steel, Machinery
LYON-ROANNE
Textiles, Machinery, Automobiles, Rubber, Chemicals
CLERMONT-FERRAND
Machinery, Rubber, Chemicals
ST-ÉTIENNE
Iron & Steel, Machinery, Chemicals, Textiles
GRENOBLE-ALPS
Machinery, Chemicals, Nonferrous Metals
BORDEAUX
Shipbuilding, Aircraft, Chemicals
PYRENEES
Aircraft, Chemicals, Nonferrous Metals
TOULOUSE
Aircraft, Chemicals
MARSEILLE-TOULON
Shipbuilding, Machinery, Chemicals
Lille
Denain
Le Havre
Rouen
Paris
Charleville
Longwy
Nancy
Strasbourg
Mulhouse
Nantes
Le Creusot
Roanne
Clermont-Ferrand
Lyon
St-Étienne
Grenoble
Bordeaux
Toulouse
Marseille
Toulon
Corsica
Herring
Sugar Beets
Wheat
Oats
Barley
Cattle
Cider Apples
Dairy
Potatoes
Wine
Tobacco
Rye
Sheep
Corn
Sardines
Tuna

DOMINANT LAND USE

- Cereals (chiefly wheat)
- Cereals (chiefly rye, oats, barley)
- Dairy
- Pasture Livestock
- Truck Farming, Horticulture
- Grapes, Wine
- Forests

MAJOR MINERAL OCCURRENCES

Al	Bauxite	O	Petroleum
C	Coal	Pb	Lead
Fe	Iron Ore	S	Sulfur, Pyrites
G	Natural Gas	U	Uranium
K	Potash	W	Tungsten
Na	Salt	Zn	Zinc

Water Power
Major Industrial Areas

SPAIN and PORTUGAL

ANDORRA

SPAIN

PORTUGAL

SPAIN
AREA 195,258 sq. mi.
POPULATION 31,339,000
CAPITAL Madrid
LARGEST CITY Madrid (greater) 2,443,152
HIGHEST POINT Pico de Teide 12,200 ft. (Canary Is.)
Mulhacén 11,417 ft. (mainland)
MONETARY UNIT peseta
MAJOR LANGUAGES Spanish, Catalan
MAJOR RELIGION Roman Catholic

ANDORRA
AREA 175 sq. mi.
POPULATION 11,000
CAPITAL Andorra la Vella
MONETARY UNIT French franc, Spanish peseta
MAJOR LANGUAGES Catalan
MAJOR RELIGION Roman Catholic

PORTUGAL
35,413 sq. mi.
9,123,000
Lisbon
Lisbon 802,230
Malhão da Estrêla 6,532 ft.
escudo
Portuguese
Roman Catholic

GIBRALTAR
2 sq. mi.
24,502
Gibraltar
pound sterling
English, Spanish
Roman Catholic

AGRICULTURE, INDUSTRY and RESOURCES

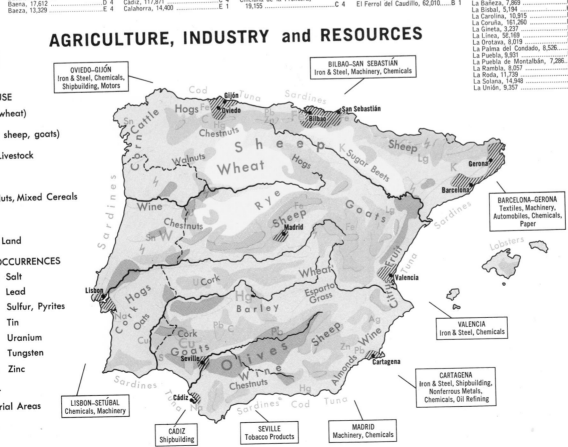

OVIEDO–GIJÓN
Iron & Steel, Chemicals, Shipbuilding, Motors

BILBAO–SAN SEBASTIÁN
Iron & Steel, Machinery, Chemicals

BARCELONA–GERONA
Textiles, Machinery, Automobiles, Chemicals, Paper

VALENCIA
Iron & Steel, Chemicals

CARTAGENA
Iron & Steel, Shipbuilding, Nonferrous Metals, Chemicals, Oil Refining

LISBON–SETÚBAL
Chemicals, Machinery

CÁDIZ
Shipbuilding

SEVILLE
Tobacco Products

MADRID
Machinery, Chemicals

DOMINANT LAND USE

Cereals (chiefly wheat)
Livestock (chiefly sheep, goats)
Mixed Cereals, Livestock
Olives, Fruit
Grapes, Fruit, Nuts, Mixed Cereals
Forests
Nonagricultural Land

MAJOR MINERAL OCCURRENCES

Ag Silver
C Coal
Cu Copper
Fe Iron
Hg Mercury
K Potash
Lg Lignite
Na Salt
Pb Lead
S Sulfur, Pyrites
Sn Tin
U Uranium
W Tungsten
Zn Zinc

⚡ Water Power
▨ Major Industrial Areas

Spain and Portugal
(continued)

TOPOGRAPHY

0 50 100
MILES

Below Sea Level | 100 m. 328 ft. | 200 m. 656 ft. | 500 m. 1,640 ft. | 1,000 m. 3,281 ft. | 2,000 m. 6,562 ft. | 5,000 m. 16,404 ft.

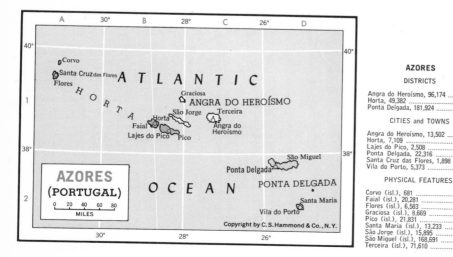

Spain and Portugal
(continued)

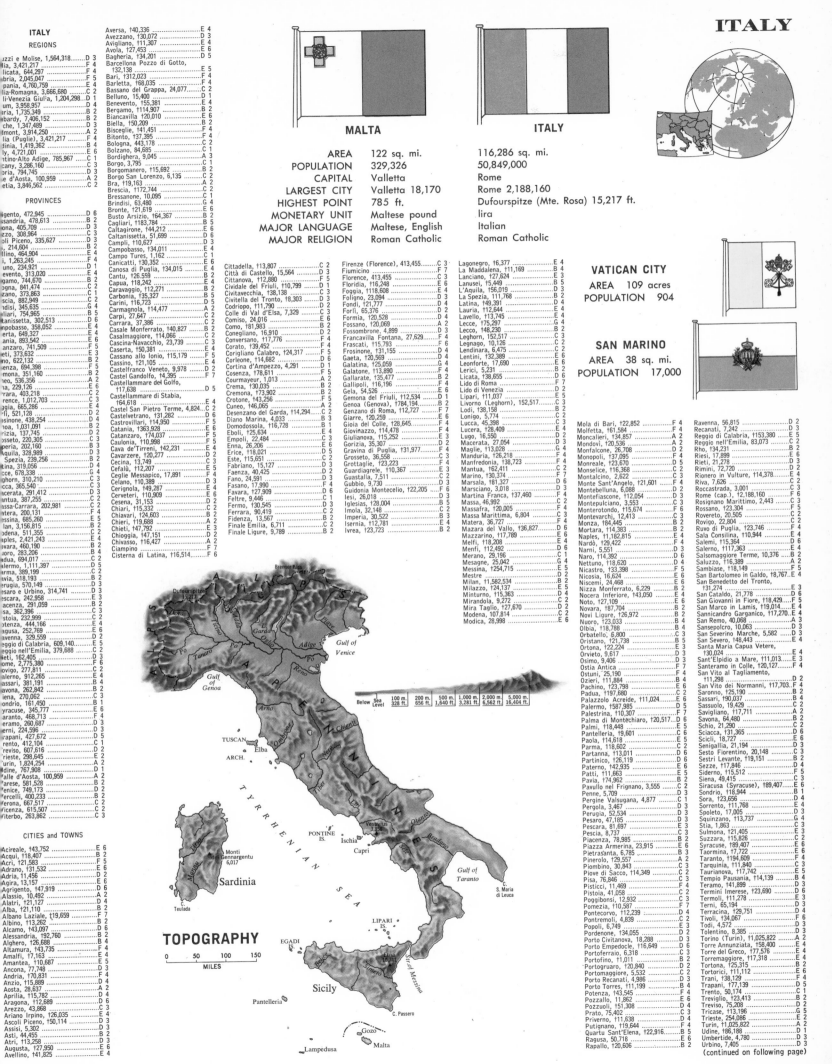

ITALY

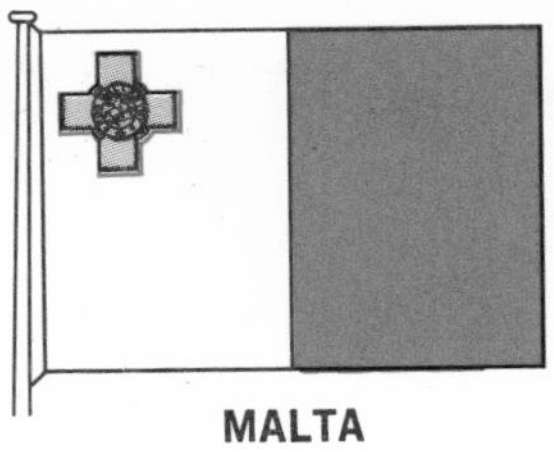

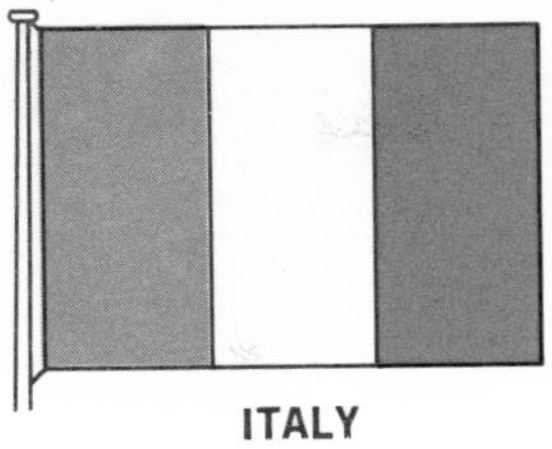

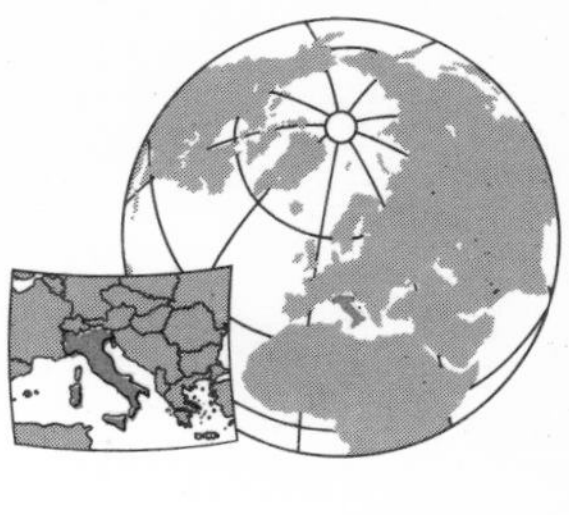

	MALTA	ITALY
AREA	122 sq. mi.	116,286 sq. mi.
POPULATION	329,326	50,849,000
CAPITAL	Valletta	Rome
LARGEST CITY	Valletta 18,170	Rome 2,188,160
HIGHEST POINT	785 ft.	Dufourspitze (Mte. Rosa) 15,217 ft.
MONETARY UNIT	Maltese pound	lira
MAJOR LANGUAGE	Maltese, English	Italian
MAJOR RELIGION	Roman Catholic	Roman Catholic

VATICAN CITY

AREA 109 acres
POPULATION 904

SAN MARINO

AREA 38 sq. mi.
POPULATION 17,000

ITALY

REGIONS

uzzi e Molise, 1,564,318 D 3
lia, 3,421,217 F 4
licata, 644,297 F 4
bria, 2,045,047 F 5
pania, 4,760,759 E 4
lia-Romagna, 3,666,680 C 2
li-Venezia Giulia, 1,204,298 D 1
um, 3,958,957 D 4
ria, 1,735,349 B 2
bardy, 7,406,152 B 2
che, 1,347,489 D 3
dmont, 3,914,250 A 2
lia (Puglie), 3,421,217 F 4
dinia, 1,419,362 B 4
ly, 4,721,001 E 6
ntino-Alto Adige, 785,967 C 1
cany, 3,286,160 C 3
oria, 794,745 D 3
e d'Aosta, 100,959 A 2
etia, 3,846,562 C 2

PROVINCES

igento, 472,945 D 6
ssandria, 478,613 B 2
ona, 405,709 D 3
zzo, 308,964 C 3
oli Piceno, 335,627 D 3
, 214,604 B 2
llino, 464,904 E 4
i, 1,263,245 F 4
uno, 234,921 D 1
evento, 313,020 E 4
gamo, 744,670 B 2
ogna, 841,474 C 2
zano, 373,863 C 1
scia, 882,949 C 2
ndisi, 345,635 G 4
liari, 754,965 B 5
tanissetta, 302,513 D 6
npobasso, 358,052 E 4
erta, 649,327 E 4
ania, 893,542 E 6
anzaro, 741,509 F 5
eti, 373,632 E 3
no, 622,132 B 2
enza, 694,398 F 5
mona, 351,160 B 2
neo, 536,356 A 2
na, 229,126 E 6
rrara, 403,218 C 2
rence, 1,012,703 C 3
ggia, 665,286 E 4
rlì, 521,128 D 2
osinone, 438,254 D 4
noa, 1,031,091 B 2
rizia, 137,745 D 2
osseto, 220,305 C 3
peria, 202,160 B 3
Aquila, 328,989 D 3
Spezia, 239,256 B 2
tina, 319,056 D 4
cce, 678,338 G 4
ghorn, 310,210 C 3
cca, 365,540 C 3
acerata, 291,412 D 3
antua, 387,255 C 2
assa-Carrara, 202,981 C 2
atera, 200,131 F 4
essina, 685,260 E 5
lan, 3,156,815 B 2
odena, 511,355 C 2
aples, 2,421,243 E 4
ovara, 460,190 B 2
uoro, 283,206 B 4
adua, 694,017 C 2
alermo, 1,111,397 D 5
arma, 389,199 C 2
avia, 518,193 B 2
erugia, 570,149 D 3
esaro e Urbino, 314,741 D 3
escara, 242,958 E 3
acenza, 291,059 B 2
sa, 362,396 C 3
stoia, 232,999 C 2
otenza, 444,166 E 4
agusa, 252,769 E 6
avenna, 329,559 D 2
eggio di Calabria, 609,140 E 5
eggio nell'Emilia, 379,688 C 2
ieti, 162,405 D 3
ome, 2,775,380 F 6
ovigo, 277,811 C 2
alerno, 912,265 E 4
assari, 381,191 B 4
avona, 262,842 B 2
iena, 270,062 C 3
ondrio, 161,450 B 1
yracuse, 345,777 E 6
aranto, 468,713 F 4
eramo, 260,687 D 3
erni, 224,596 D 3
rapani, 427,672 D 5
rento, 412,104 C 1
reviso, 607,616 D 2
rieste, 298,645 E 2
urin, 1,824,254 A 2
dine, 767,908 D 1
alle d'Aosta, 100,959 A 2
arese, 581,528 B 2
enice, 749,173 D 2
ercelli, 400,233 B 2
erona, 667,517 C 2
icenza, 615,507 C 2
iterbo, 263,862 C 3

CITIES and TOWNS

Acireale, †43,752 E 6
Acqui, †18,407 B 2
Acri, †21,583 F 5
Adrano, †31,532 E 6
Adria, 11,456 D 2
Agira, 13,157 E 6
Agrigento, †47,919 D 6
Alassio, 10,492 A 2
Alatri, †21,127 D 4
Alba, †21,110 B 2
Albano Laziale, †19,659 F 7
Albino, †13,262 B 2
Alcamo, †43,097 D 6
Alessandria, †92,760 B 2
Alghero, †26,688 B 4
Altamura, †43,735 F 4
Amalfi, †7,163 E 4
Amantea, †10,687 E 5
Ancona, 77,748 D 3
Andria, †70,831 F 4
Anzio, †15,889 D 4
Aosta, 28,637 A 2
Aprilia, †15,782 D 4
Aragona, †12,689 D 6
Arezzo, 43,868 C 3
Ariano Irpino, †26,035 E 4
Ascoli Piceno, †50,114 D 3
Assisi, 5,302 D 3
Asti, 44,455 B 2
Atri, †13,258 D 3
Augusta, †27,950 E 6
Avellino, †41,825 E 4
Aversa, †40,336 E 4
Avezzano, †30,072 D 3
Avigliano, †11,307 E 4
Avola, †27,453 E 6
Bagheria, †34,201 D 5
Barcellona Pozzo di Gotto, †32,138 E 5
Bari, †312,023 F 4
Barletta, †68,035 F 4
Bassano del Grappa, 24,077 C 2
Belluno, 15,400 D 1
Benevento, †55,381 E 4
Bergamo, †114,907 B 2
Biancavilla †20,010 E 6
Biella, †50,209 B 2
Bisceglie, †41,451 F 4
Bitonto, †37,395 F 4
Bologna, 443,178 C 2
Bolzano, 84,685 C 1
Bordighera, 9,045 A 3
Borgo, 3,795 C 1
Borgomanero, †15,692 B 2
Borgo San Lorenzo, 6,135 C 2
Bra, †19,163 A 2
Brescia, †172,744 C 2
Bressanone, 10,095 C 1
Brindisi, 63,480 G 4
Bronte, †21,619 E 6
Busto Arsizio, †64,367 B 2
Cagliari, †183,784 B 5
Caltagirone, †44,212 E 6
Caltanissetta, 51,699 D 6
Campli, †10,627 D 3
Campobasso, †34,011 E 4
Campo Tures, 1,162 C 1
Canicatti, †30,352 E 6
Canosa di Puglia, †34,015 E 4
Cantu, †26.559 B 2
Capua, †18,242 E 4
Caravaggio, †12,271 B 2
Carbonia, †35,327 B 5
Carini, †16,723 D 5
Carmagnola, †14,477 A 2
Carpi, 27,647 C 2
Carrara, 37,386 C 2
Casale Monferrato, †40,827 B 2
Casalmaggiore, †14,066 C 2
Cascina-Navacchio, 23,739 C 3
Caserta, †50,381 E 4
Cassano allo Ionio, †15,179 F 5
Cassino, †21,105 E 4
Castelfranco Veneto, 9,978 D 2
Castel Gandolfo, †4,395 F 7
Castellammare del Golfo, †17,638 D 5
Castellammare di Stabia, †64,618 E 4
Castel San Pietro Terme, 4,824 C 2
Castelvetrano, †31,282 D 6
Castrovillari, †14,950 F 5
Catania, †363,928 E 6
Catanzaro, †74,037 F 5
Caulonia, †10,998 F 5
Cava de'Tirreni, †42,231 E 4
Cavarzere, †20,277 D 2
Cecina, 13,749 C 3
Cefalù, †12,207 E 5
Ceglie Messapico, 17,891 F 4
Celano, †10,389 D 3
Cerignola, †49,287 E 4
Cerveteri, †10,909 E 6
Cesena, 31,153 D 2
Chiari, †15,332 C 2
Chiavari, †24,603 B 2
Chieri, †19,688 A 2
Chieti, †47,792 E 3
Chioggia, †47,151 D 2
Chivasso, †16,427 A 2
Ciampino F 7
Cisterna di Latina, †16,514 F 6
Cittadella, †13,807 C 2
Città di Castello, 15,564 D 3
Cittanova, †12,880 F 5
Cividale del Friuli, †10,799 D 1
Civitavecchia, †38,138 C 3
Civitella del Tronto, †8,303 D 3
Codriopo, †11,790 D 2
Colle di Val d'Elsa, 7,329 C 3
Comiso, 24,016 E 6
Como, †81,983 B 2
Conegliano, 16,910 D 2
Conversano, †17,776 F 4
Corato, †39,452 F 4
Corigliano Calabro, †24,317 F 5
Corleone, †14,682 D 6
Cortina d'Ampezzo, 4,291 D 1
Cosenza, †78,611 F 5
Courmayeur, 1,013 A 2
Crema, †30,035 B 2
Cremona, †73,902 B 2
Crotone, †43,256 F 5
Cuneo, †46,065 A 2
Desenzano del Garda, †14,294 C 2
Diano Marina, 4,033 B 3
Domodossola, †16,728 B 1
Eboli, †25,634 E 4
Empoli, 22,484 C 3
Enna, 26,206 E 6
Erice, †18,021 D 5
Este, †15,651 C 2
Fabriano, 15,127 D 3
Faenza, 40,425 D 2
Fano, 24,591 D 3
Fasano, 17,990 F 4
Favara, †27,909 D 6
Feltre, 9,446 C 1
Fermo, †30,545 D 3
Ferrara, 90,419 C 2
Fidenza, 13,567 B 2
Finale Emilia, 6,711 C 2
Finale Ligure, 9,789 B 2
Firenze (Florence), 413,455 C 3
Fiumicino F 7
Florence, 413,455 C 3
Floridia, †16,248 E 6
Foggia, †118,608 E 4
Foligno, 23,094 D 3
Fondi, †21,777 D 4
Forlì, 65,376 D 2
Formia, †20,528 D 4
Fossano, †20,069 A 2
Fossombrone, 4,899 D 3
Francavilla Fontana, 27,629 F 4
Frascati, †15,793 F 6
Frosinone, †31,155 D 4
Gaeta, †20,569 D 4
Galatina, †25,059 G 4
Galatone, †13,890 F 4
Gallarate, †35,477 B 2
Gallipoli, †16,196 F 4
Gela, 54,526 E 6
Gemona del Friuli, †12,534 D 1
Genoa (Genova), †784,194 B 2
Genzano di Roma, †12,727 F 7
Giarre, †20,259 E 6
Gioia del Colle, †28,645 F 4
Giovinazzo, †14,478 F 4
Giulianova, †15,252 E 3
Gorizia, 35,307 D 2
Gravina di Puglia, †31,977 F 4
Grosseto, 36,558 C 3
Grottaglie, †23,223 F 4
Guardiagrele, †10,367 E 3
Guastalla, 7,511 C 2
Gubbio, 9,730 D 3
Guidonia Montecelio, †22,205 F 6
Iesi, 26,018 D 3
Iglesias, †28,004 B 5
Imola, 32,148 C 2
Imperia, 30,522 B 3
Isernia, †12,781 E 4
Ivrea, †23,723 B 2
Lagonegro, †6,377 E 4
La Maddalena, †11,169 B 4
Lanciano, †27,624 E 3
Lanusei, †5,449 B 5
L'Aquila, †56,019 D 3
La Spezia, 111,768 B 2
Latina, †49,391 D 4
Lauria, †12,644 E 4
Lavello, †13,745 E 4
Lecce, †75,297 G 4
Lecco, †48,230 B 2
Leghorn, 152,517 C 3
Legnago, 10,126 C 2
Lendinara, 6,475 C 2
Lentini, †32,389 E 6
Leonforte, 17,690 E 6
Lerici, 5,231 B 2
Licata, †38,655 D 6
Lido di Roma F 7
Lido di Venezia D 2
Lipari, †11,037 E 5
Livorno (Leghorn), 152,517 C 3
Lodi, †38,158 B 2
Lonigo, 5,774 C 2
Lucca, 45,398 C 3
Lucera, †28,409 E 4
Lugo, 16,550 D 2
Macerata, 27,054 D 3
Maglie, †13,028 G 4
Manduria, †26,218 F 4
Manfredonia, †38,723 F 4
Mantua, †62,411 C 2
Marino, †30,374 F 7
Marsala, †81,327 D 6
Marsciano, 3,018 D 3
Martina Franca, †37,460 F 4
Massa, 46,992 C 2
Massafra, †20,005 F 4
Massa Marittima, 6,804 C 3
Matera, 36,727 F 4
Mazara del Vallo, †36,827 D 6
Mazzarino, †17,789 E 6
Melfi, †18,208 E 4
Menfi, †12,492 D 6
Merano, 29,196 C 1
Mesagne, 25,042 G 4
Messina, †254,715 E 5
Mestre D 2
Milan, †1,582,534 B 2
Milazzo, †24,137 E 5
Minturno, †15,363 D 4
Mirandola, 9,272 C 2
Mira Taglio, †27,670 D 2
Modena, 107,814 C 2
Modica, 28,998 E 6
Mola di Bari, †22,852 F 4
Molfetta, †61,584 F 4
Moncalieri, †34,857 A 2
Mondovì, †20,536 A 2
Monfalcone, 26,708 D 2
Monopoli, †37,095 F 4
Monreale, †23,670 D 5
Monselice, †16,368 C 2
Montalcino, 2,622 C 3
Monte Sant'Angelo, †21,601 F 4
Montebelluna, 6,088 D 2
Montefiascone, †12,054 D 3
Montepulciano, 3,553 C 3
Monterotondo, †15,674 F 6
Montevarchi, 12,413 C 3
Monza, †84,445 B 2
Mortara, †14,383 B 2
Naples, †1,182,815 E 4
Nardò, †29,422 F 4
Narni, 5,551 D 3
Naro, †14,392 D 6
Nettuno, †18,620 D 4
Nicastro, †33,398 F 5
Nicosia, 16,624 E 6
Niscemi, 24,468 E 6
Nizza Monferrato, 6,229 B 2
Nocera Inferiore, †43,050 E 4
Noto, †27,109 E 6
Novara, †87,704 B 2
Novi Ligure, †26,972 B 2
Nuoro, †23,033 B 4
Olbia, †18,788 B 4
Orbatello, 6,800 C 3
Oristano, †21,738 B 5
Ortona, †22,224 E 3
Orvieto, 9,617 D 3
Osimo, 9,406 D 3
Ostia Antica F 7
Ostuni, 25,190 F 4
Ozieri, †11,884 B 4
Pachino, †23,798 E 6
Padua, †197,680 C 2
Palazzolo Acreide, †11,024 E 6
Palermo, †587,985 D 5
Palestrina, †10,307 F 7
Palma di Montechiaro, †20,517 D 6
Palmi, †18,448 E 5
Pantelleria, †9,601 C 6
Paola, †14,618 E 5
Parma, 118,602 C 2
Partanna, †13,011 D 6
Partinico, †26,119 D 6
Paterno, †42,935 E 6
Patti, †11,663 E 5
Pavia, †74,962 B 2
Pavullo nel Frignano, 3,555 C 2
Penne, 5,709 D 3
Pergine Valsugana, 4,877 C 1
Pergola, 3,467 D 3
Perugia, 52,534 D 3
Pesaro, 47,185 D 3
Pescara, 81,697 E 3
Pescia, 8,737 C 3
Piacenza, 78,985 B 2
Piazza Armerina, 23,915 E 6
Pietrasanta, 6,785 B 3
Pinerolo, †29,557 A 2
Piombino, 30,843 C 3
Piove di Sacco, †14,349 C 2
Pisa, 76,846 C 3
Pisticci, 11,469 F 4
Pistoia, 41,058 C 2
Poggibonsi, 12,932 C 3
Pomezia, †10,587 F 7
Pontecorvo, †12,239 D 4
Pontremoli, 4,839 C 2
Popoli, 6,749 E 3
Pordenone, †34,055 D 2
Porto Civitanova, 18,288 D 3
Porto Empedocle, †16,649 D 6
Portoferraio, 6,318 C 3
Portofino, †1,011 B 2
Portogruaro, †20,840 D 2
Portomaggiore, 5,532 C 2
Porto Recanati, 4,986 D 3
Porto Torres, †11,199 B 4
Potenza, †43,545 F 4
Pozzallo, 11,862 E 6
Pozzuoli, †51,308 D 4
Prato, 75,402 C 3
Priverno, †11,638 D 4
Putignano, †19,644 F 4
Quartu Sant'Elena, †22,916 B 5
Ragusa, 50,718 E 6
Rapallo, †20,606 B 2
Ravenna, 56,815 D 2
Recanati, 7,242 D 3
Reggio di Calabria, †153,380 E 5
Reggio nell'Emilia, 83,073 C 2
Rho, †34,231 B 2
Riesi, 17,899 E 6
Rieti, 21,278 D 3
Rimini, 72,720 D 2
Rionero in Vulture, †14,378 E 4
Riva, 7,626 C 2
Roccastrada, 3,001 C 3
Rome (cap.), †2,188,160 F 6
Rosignano Marittimo, 2,443 C 3
Rossano, †23,304 F 5
Rovereto, 20,505 C 2
Rovigo, 22,804 C 2
Ruvo di Puglia, †23,746 F 4
Sala Consilina, †10,944 E 4
Salemi, †15,364 D 6
Salerno, †117,363 E 4
Salsomaggiore Terme, 10,376 B 2
Saluzzo, †16,389 A 2
Sambiase, †18,149 F 5
San Bartolomeo in Galdo, †8,767 E 4
San Benedetto del Tronto, †31,274 E 3
San Cataldo, 21,778 D 6
San Giovanni in Fiore, †18,429 F 5
San Marco in Lamis, †19,014 E 4
Sannicandro Garganico, †17,270 E 4
San Remo, 40,068 A 3
Sansepolcro, 10,063 D 3
San Severino Marche, 5,582 D 3
San Severo, †48,443 E 4
Santa Maria Capua Vetere, †30,024 E 4
Sant'Elpidio a Mare, †11,013 E 3
Santeramo in Colle, †20,127 F 4
San Vito al Tagliamento, †11,298 D 2
San Vito dei Normanni, †17,703 F 4
Saronno, †25,190 B 2
Sassari, †90,037 B 4
Sassuolo, 19,429 C 2
Savigliano, †17,711 A 2
Savona, 64,480 B 2
Schio, 21,290 C 2
Sciacca, †31,365 D 6
Scicli, 18,727 E 6
Senigallia, 21,194 D 3
Sesto Fiorentino, 20,148 C 3
Sestri Levante, †19,151 B 2
Sezze, †17,846 D 4
Siderno, †15,512 F 5
Siena, 49,415 C 3
Siracusa (Syracuse), †89,407 E 6
Sondrio, †18,944 B 1
Sora, †23,656 D 4
Sorrento, †11,768 E 4
Spoleto, 17,005 D 3
Squinzano, †13,737 G 4
Stia, 1,863 C 3
Sulmona, †21,405 E 3
Suzzara, †15,826 C 2
Syracuse, †89,407 E 6
Taormina, †7,722 E 6
Taranto, †194,609 F 4
Tarquinia, †11,840 C 3
Taurianova, †17,742 E 5
Tempio Pausania, †14,139 B 4
Teramo, †41,899 D 3
Termini Imerese, †23,690 D 6
Termoli, †11,278 E 3
Terni, 65,194 D 3
Terracina, †29,751 D 4
Tivoli, †34,067 F 6
Todi, 4,572 D 3
Tolentino, 8,385 D 3
Torino (Turin), †1,025,822 A 2
Torre Annunziata, †58,400 E 4
Torre del Greco, †77,576 E 4
Torremaggiore, †17,318 E 4
Tortona, †25,315 B 2
Tortorici, †11,112 E 6
Trani, †38,129 F 4
Trapani, †77,139 D 5
Trento, 50,174 C 1
Treviglio, †23,413 B 2
Treviso, 75,208 D 2
Tricase, †13,196 G 5
Trieste, 254,086 E 2
Turin, †1,025,822 A 2
Udine, †86,188 D 1
Umbertide, 4,780 D 3
Urbino, 7,405 D 3

(continued on following page)

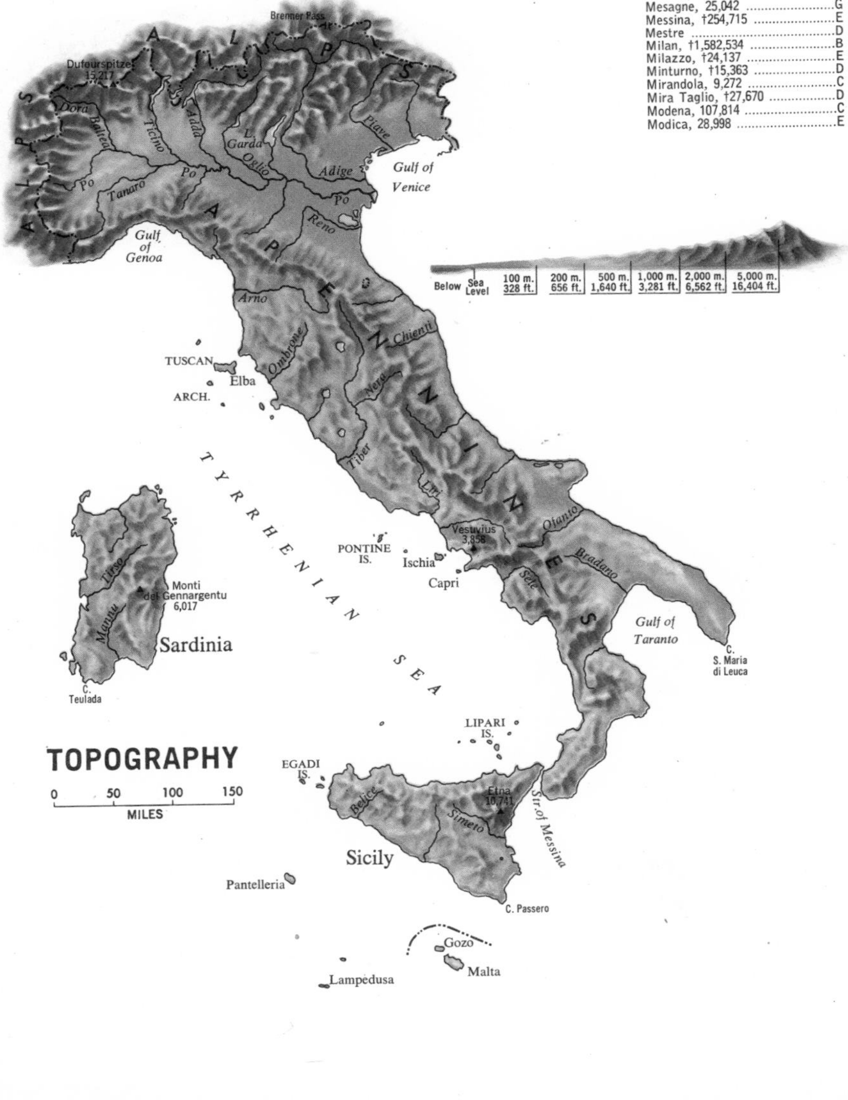

Italy
(continued)

DOMINANT LAND USE

- Wheat, Rice, Dairy
- Pasture Livestock
- Cereals, Livestock
- Fruit, Truck and Mixed Farming
- Grapes, Wine
- Forests
- Nonagricultural Land

MAJOR MINERAL OCCURRENCES

Al	Bauxite	Hg	Mercury	O	Petroleum
C	Coal	Lg	Lignite	Pb	Lead
Fe	Iron	Mr	Marble	S	Sulfur, Pyrites
G	Natural Gas	Na	Salt	Zn	Zinc

Water Power

Major Industrial Areas

AGRICULTURE, INDUSTRY and RESOURCES

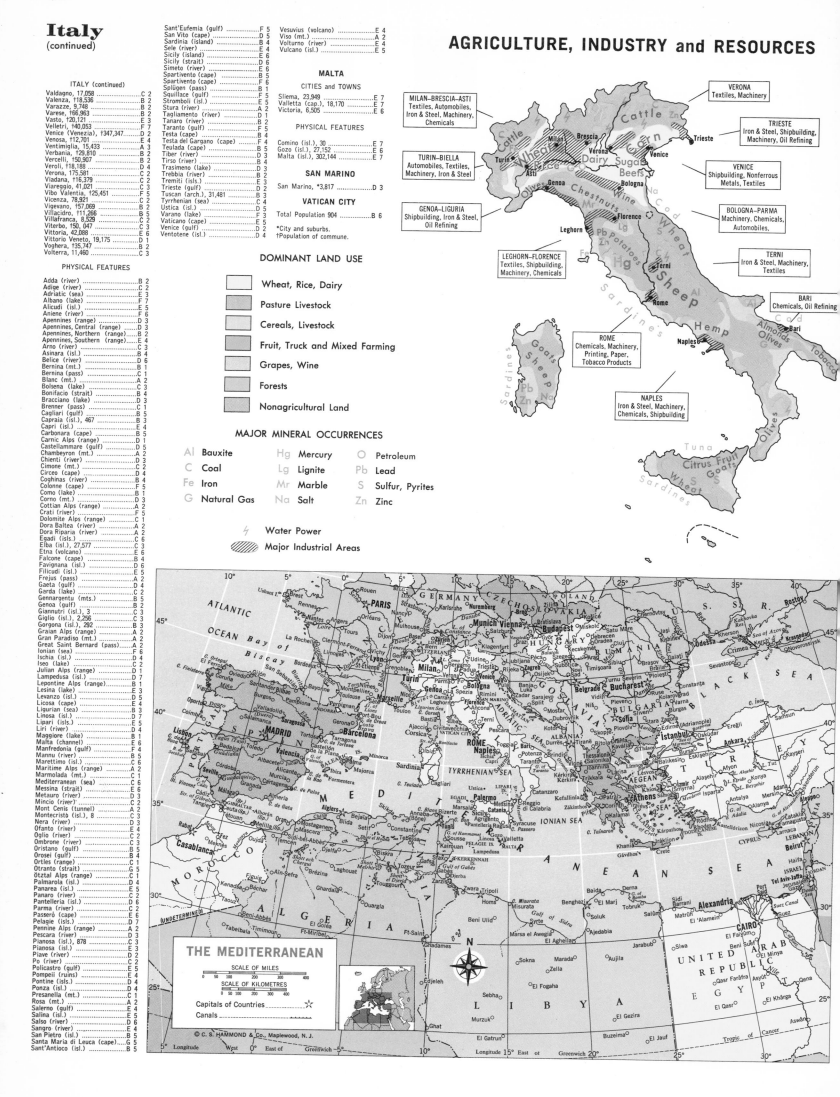

VERONA
Textiles, Machinery

TRIESTE
Iron & Steel, Shipbuilding, Machinery, Oil Refining

VENICE
Shipbuilding, Nonferrous Metals, Textiles

BOLOGNA–PARMA
Machinery, Chemicals, Automobiles.

TERNI
Iron & Steel, Machinery, Textiles

BARI
Chemicals, Oil Refining

MILAN–BRESCIA–ASTI
Textiles, Automobiles, Iron & Steel, Machinery, Chemicals

TURIN–BIELLA
Automobiles, Textiles, Machinery, Iron & Steel

GENOA–LIGURIA
Shipbuilding, Iron & Steel, Oil Refining

LEGHORN–FLORENCE
Textiles, Shipbuilding, Machinery, Chemicals

ROME
Chemicals, Machinery, Printing, Paper, Tobacco Products

NAPLES
Iron & Steel, Machinery, Chemicals, Shipbuilding

THE MEDITERRANEAN

SCALE OF MILES
0 50 100   200   300   400

SCALE OF KILOMETRES
0 50 100   200   300   400

Capitals of Countries ....☆
Canals ....

© C. S. HAMMOND & Co., Maplewood, N.J.

SWITZERLAND and LIECHTENSTEIN

SWITZERLAND

AREA	15,944 sq. mi.
POPULATION	6,030,000
CAPITAL	Bern
LARGEST CITY	Zürich 444,000
HIGHEST POINT	Dufourspitze (Mte. Rosa) 15,217 ft.
MONETARY UNIT	Swiss franc
MAJOR LANGUAGES	German, French, Italian, Romansch
MAJOR RELIGIONS	Protestant, Roman Catholic

LIECHTENSTEIN

65 sq. mi.
18,000
Vaduz
Vaduz 3,398
Naafkopf 8,445 ft.
Swiss franc
German
Roman Catholic

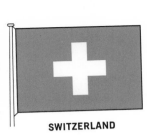

SWITZERLAND

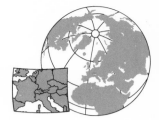

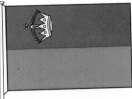

LIECHTENSTEIN

LANGUAGES

- German
- French
- Italian
- Romansch

Switzerland is a multilingual nation with four official languages. 70% of the people speak German, 19% French, 10% Italian and 1% Romansch.

SWITZERLAND

CANTONS

Aargau, 374,700	F 2
Appenzell, Ausser Rhoden, 49,800	H 2
Appenzell, Inner Rhoden, 13,300	H 2
Baselland, 160,800	E 1
Baselstadt, 230,800	D 2
Bern, 912,100	D 3
Fribourg, 161,000	C 3
Geneva (Genève), 275,900	B 4
Glarus, 41,400	H 3
Graubünden (Grisons), 155,100	J 3
Luzern (Lucerne), 260,500	F 2
Neuchâtel, 154,500	C 3
Nidwalden, 23,000	F 3
Obwalden, 23,600	F 3
Sankt Gallen, 348,100	H 2
Schaffhausen, 69,700	G 1
Schwyz, 80,600	G 2
Solothurn (Soleure), 209,200	E 2
Thurgau, 171,800	H 1
Ticino, 203,700	G 4
Unterwalden, 46,600	F 3
Uri, 32,400	G 3
Valais, 187,000	E 4
Vaud, 464,700	C 3
Zug, 55,300	G 2
Zürich, 1,001,000	G 2

CITIES and TOWNS

Aadorf, 2,258	G 2
Aarau, 17,300	F 2
Aarberg, 2,355	D 2
Aarburg, 5,302	E 2
Adelboden, 2,881	E 3
Aeschi bei Spiez, 1,319	E 3
Affoltern am Albis, 4,904	F 2
Affoltern im Emmental, 1,206	E 2
Aigle, 4,381	C 4
Airolo, 2,023	G 3
Alle, 1,471	D 2
Allschwil, 14,000	D 1
Alpnach, 3,211	F 3
Altdorf, 7,477	G 3
Altstätten, 8,751	H 1
Amriswil, 6,752	H 1
Andermatt, 1,523	G 3
Appenzell, 5,082	H 2
Arbedo-Castione, 1,467	G 4
Arbon, 12,500	H 1
Ardon, 1,432	D 4
Arlesheim, 5,219	E 2
Arosa, 2,600	J 3
Arth, 6,321	F 2
Ascona, 3,053	G 4
Attalens, 1,023	C 3
Aubonne, 1,766	B 3
Avenches, 1,776	C 3
Baar, 9,114	F 2
Bad Ragaz, 2,699	H 2
Baden, 14,900	F 2
Balerna, 3,040	G 5
Balsthal, 5,735	E 2
Bäretswil, 2,577	G 2
Basel (Bâle), 210,800	E 1
Bassecourt, 2,284	D 2
Bätterkinden, 1,916	E 2
Bauma, 3,214	G 2
Beatenberg, 1,303	E 3
Beckenried, 2,042	G 3
Beinwil am See, 2,346	F 2

Bellinzona, 13,400	H 4
Belp, 4,922	D 3
Bergün-Bravuogn, 551	J 3
Bern (Berne) (cap.), 168,900	D 3
Beromünster, 1,443	F 2
Bex, 4,667	D 4
Biasca, 3,349	G 3
Biberist, 7,188	D 2
Biel (Bienne), 64,000	D 2
Bière, 1,166	B 3
Binningen, 13,000	D 1
Bischofszell, 3,811	H 1
Blumenstein, 1,121	E 3
Bodio, 1,276	G 4
Bolligen, 17,900	E 3
Boltigen, 1,691	D 3
Boncourt, 1,493	C 2
Bönigen, 1,883	E 3
Boswil, 1,663	F 2
Boudry, 3,086	C 3
Bourg-Saint-Pierre, 524	D 5
Breil-Brigels, 1,272	H 3
Breitenbach, 1,851	E 2
Bremgarten, 4,555	F 2
Brienz, 2,864	E 3
Brig, 4,647	E 4
Brissago, 1,845	G 4
Brittnau, 3,070	E 2
Brugg, 6,683	F 2
Brusio, 1,445	K 4
Bubendorf, 1,690	E 2
Bubikon, 2,612	G 2
Buchs, 6,345	H 2
Bülach, 8,188	G 1
Bulle, 5,983	D 3
Buochs, 2,733	F 3
Büren an der Aare, 2,432	D 2
Burgdorf, 14,400	E 2
Bürglen, 3,175	G 3
Bürglen, 1,899	H 1
Bussigny-près-Lausanne, 2,381	B 3
Bütschwil, 3,414	H 2
Carouge, 14,600	B 4
Castagnola, 3,775	G 4
Cazis, 1,553	H 3
Cernier, 1,545	C 2
Chalais, 1,597	E 4
Cham, 6,483	F 2
Charmoson, 2,088	D 4
Charmey, 1,144	D 3
Châteaux-d'Oex, 3,378	D 4
Châtel-Saint-Denis, 2,666	C 3
Chavornay, 1,414	C 3
Chexbres, 1,449	C 3
Chiasso, 7,377	G 5
Chur (Coire), 26,700	J 3
Churwalden, 877	J 3
Coire (Chur), 26,700	J 3
Conthey, 3,563	D 4
Coppet, 774	B 4
Corcelles-près-Payerne, 1,253	C 3
Corgémont, 1,414	D 2
Cossonay, 1,284	B 3
Courgenay, 1,666	D 2
Courroux, 1,667	D 2
Court, 1,493	D 2
Courtelary, 1,330	C 2
Courtételle, 1,618	D 2
Couvet, 3,450	C 3
Cully, 1,375	C 3
Därstetten, 900	D 3
Davos (Dorf and Platz), 9,588	J 3
Degersheim, 3,221	H 2
Delémont, 9,542	D 2
Derendingen, 4,463	E 2
Diemtigen, 1,934	D 3
Diessenhofen, 2,222	G 1
Dietikon, 17,300	F 2
Disentis-Mustèr, 2,376	G 3
Dombresson, 1,040	C 2
Dornach, 4,260	E 2
Dübendorf, 15,200	G 2
Düdingen, 4,248	D 3
Dürnten, 4,271	G 2
Dürrenroth, 1,221	E 2
Ebnat-Kappel, 4,979	H 2
Echallens, 1,428	C 3
Egg, 3,018	G 2
Eggiwil, 2,591	E 3
Eglisau, 1,911	G 1
Egnach, 3,483	H 1
Einsiedeln, 8,792	G 2
Elgg, 2,643	G 2
Emmen, 18,200	F 2
Engelberg, 2,646	F 3
Engi, 1,064	H 2
Ennenda, 3,076	H 2
Entlebuch, 3,318	F 3
Erlenbach im Simmental, 1,471	E 3
Ermatingen, 1,857	H 1
Erstfeld, 4,126	G 3
Eschenbach, 2,866	G 2

(continued on following page)

AGRICULTURE, INDUSTRY and RESOURCES

DOMINANT LAND USE

- Cereals, Dairy
- Pasture Livestock
- General Farming, Livestock
- Fruit, Truck, Mixed Farming
- Forests
- Nonagricultural Land

⚡ Water Power
▨ Major Industrial Areas

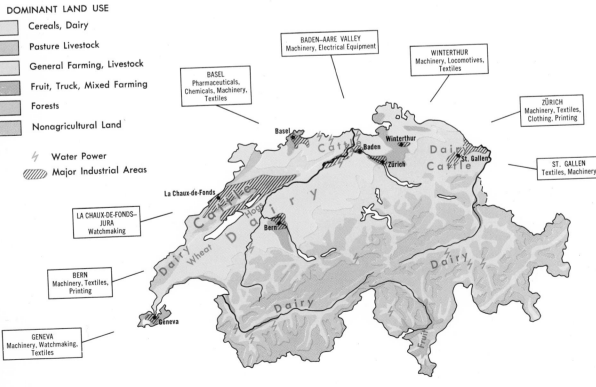

BADEN–AARE VALLEY
Machinery, Electrical Equipment

WINTERTHUR
Machinery, Locomotives, Textiles

BASEL
Pharmaceuticals, Chemicals, Machinery, Textiles

ZÜRICH
Machinery, Textiles, Clothing, Printing

ST. GALLEN
Textiles, Machinery

LA CHAUX-DE-FONDS–JURA
Watchmaking

BERN
Machinery, Textiles, Printing

GENEVA
Machinery, Watchmaking, Textiles

Switzerland and Liechtenstein
(continued)

TOPOGRAPHY

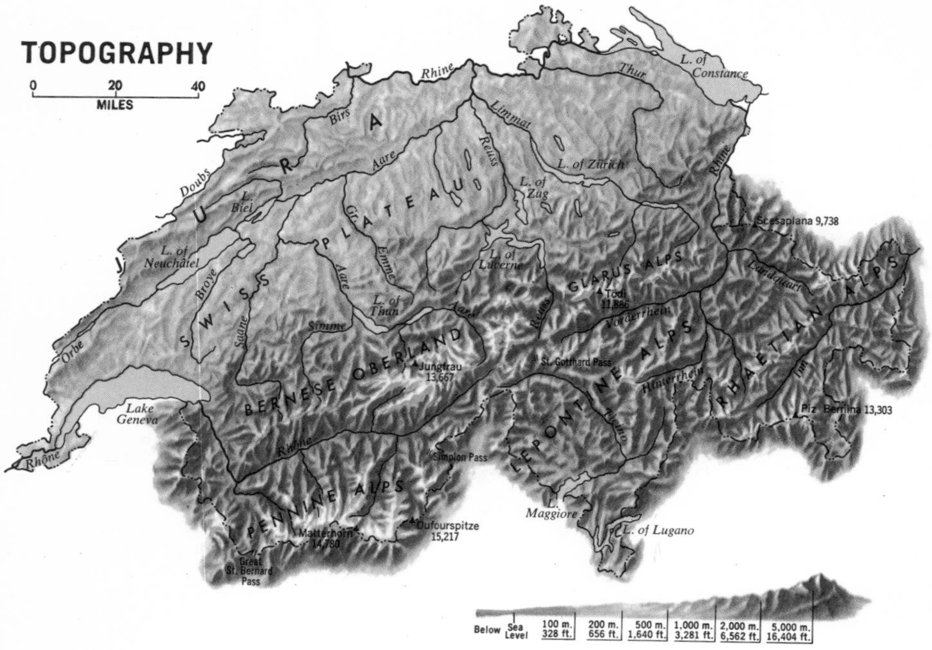

SWITZERLAND (continued)

Escholzmatt, 3,257 ....E 3
Estavayer-le-Lac, 2,583 ....C 3
Evolène, 1,786 ....D 4
Faido, 1,441 ....G 4
Flawil, 7,256 ....H 2
Fleurier, 3,814 ....C 3
Flims, 1,444 ....H 3
Flüelen, 1,717 ....G 3
Flums, 4,462 ....H 2
Frauenfeld, 15,900 ....G 1
Fribourg, 34,000 ....D 3
Frick, 2,123 ....E 1
Frutigen, 5,565 ....E 3
Fully, 3,419 ....D 4
Gais, 2,488 ....H 2
Gelterkinden, 3,870 ....E 2
Geneva (Genève), 181,400 ....B 4
Gersau, 1,754 ....G 2
Gimel, 1,091 ....B 3
Giornico, 1,063 ....G 4
Giswil, 2,656 ....F 3
Giubiasco, 4,281 ....H 4
Gland, 1,545 ....B 4
Glarus, 5,852 ....H 2
Glattfelden, 2,426 ....F 1
Gordola, 1,794 ....G 4
Göschenen, 1,284 ....G 3
Gossau, 9,731 ....H 2
Grabs, 4,218 ....H 2
Grandson, 2,091 ....C 3
Gränichen, 4,411 ....F 2
Grenchen, 18,800 ....D 2
Grindelwald, 3,244 ....E 3
Grossandelfingen, 1,102 ....G 1
Grosswangen, 2,373 ....F 2
Gruyères, 1,349 ....D 3
Gsteig, 937 ....D 4
Guggisberg, 2,021 ....D 3
Gurtnellen, 1,048 ....G 3
Hallau, 1,966 ....F 1
Heiden, 3,158 ....H 2
Heimberg, 2,125 ....E 3
Hemberg, 1,011 ....H 2
Henau, 7,828 ....H 2
Hérémence, 1,868 ....D 4
Herisau, 15,200 ....H 2
Hermance, 512 ....B 4
Herzogenbuchsee, 4,641 ....E 2
Hinwil, 4,811 ....G 2
Hochdorf, 4,452 ....F 2
Horgen, 14,500 ....G 2
Hospental, 289 ....F 3
Huttwil, 4,664 ....E 2
Igis, 3,902 ....J 3
Ilanz, 1,843 ....H 3
Illnau, 6,160 ....G 2
Ingenbohl, 5,046 ....G 2
Innertkirchen, 1,230 ....F 3
Ins, 2,486 ....D 2
Interlaken, 4,738 ....E 3
Jegenstorf, 1,397 ....D 2
Jenaz, 1,143 ....J 3
Jona, 5,686 ....G 2
Jungfraujoch ....E 3
Kaltbrunn, 2,527 ....H 2
Kandersteg, 937 ....E 4
Kerns, 3,553 ....F 3
Kerzers, 2,228 ....D 3
Kilchberg, 6,784 ....F 2
Kirchberg, 3,304 ....E 2
Kirchberg, 5,554 ....G 2
Kleinlützel, 1,269 ....D 2
Klingnau, 2,192 ....F 1
Klosters, 3,181 ....J 3
Kloten, 8,446 ....G 2
Koblenz, 1,114 ....F 1
Kölliken, 3,007 ....F 2
Köniz, 29,700 ....D 3
Kreuzlingen, 13,800 ....H 1
Kriens, 15,500 ....F 2
Küsnacht, 11,984 ....G 2
Küssnacht, 12,400 ....F 2
Küttigen, 3,457 ....F 2
La Chaux-de-Fonds, 41,200 ....C 2
La Neuveville, 3,216 ....D 2
La Roche, 1,043 ....D 3
La Sarraz, 1,026 ....C 3
La Tour-de-Peilz, 6,820 ....C 4
L'Abbaye, 1,124 ....B 3
Lachen, 3,913 ....G 2
Langenthal, 11,600 ....E 2
Langnau, 9,201 ....E 3
Langnau am Albis, 2,850 ....G 2
Läufelfingen, 1,176 ....E 2
Laufen, 3,955 ....D 2
Laufenburg, 1,850 ....F 1
Laupen, 1,607 ....D 3
Lauperswil, 2,652 ....E 3
Lausanne, 132,500 ....C 3
Lauterbrunnen, 3,216 ....E 3
Le Brassus (Le Chenit), 5,242 ....B 3
Le Châble, 4,237 ....D 4
Le Lieu, 970 ....B 3
Le Locle, 14,200 ....C 2
Le Mont, 1,719 ....C 3
Le Noirmont, 1,559 ....C 2
Lengnau, 3,524 ....D 2
Lenk, 1,900 ....D 4
Lens, 1,743 ....D 4
Lenzburg, 6,378 ....F 2
Les Bois, 1,098 ....C 2
Les Ponts-de-Martel, 1,429 ....C 2
Les Verrières, 1,084 ....B 3
Leuk, 2,546 ....E 4
Leukerbad, 619 ....E 4
Leysin, 2,241 ....C 4
Liestal, 11,000 ....E 2
Linthal, 2,645 ....H 3
Littau, 8,715 ....F 2
Locarno, 10,200 ....G 4
Lucens, 1,620 ....C 3
Lucerne (Luzern), 72,400 ....F 2
Lugano, 19,000 ....G 4
Lungern, 1,794 ....F 3
Luthern, 1,801 ....E 2
Lutry, 3,481 ....C 3
Lützelflüh, 3,960 ....E 3
Luzein, 1,013 ....J 3
Luzern (Lucerne), 72,400 ....F 2
Lyss, 5,616 ....D 2
Maienfeld, 1,488 ....J 2
Malans, 1,358 ....J 3
Malters, 4,579 ....F 2
Malvaglia, 1,120 ....H 4
Männedorf, 6,182 ....G 2
Marbach, 1,347 ....E 3
Martigny, 7,593 ....C 4
Meilen, 8,203 ....G 2
Meiringen, 3,749 ....F 3
Melchnau, 1,511 ....E 2
Melide, 1,046 ....G 5
Mellingen, 1,941 ....F 2
Mels, 5,254 ....H 2
Mendrisio, 5,100 ....G 5
Menzingen, 3,340 ....G 2
Menznau, 2,275 ....E 2
Mesocco, 1,324 ....H 4
Minusio, 3,663 ....G 4
Möhlin, 4,681 ....E 1
Mollis, 2,303 ....H 2
Montana-Vermala (Montana), 1,543 ....E 4
Monthey, 6,834 ....C 4
Montreux-Le Châtelard, 18,700 ....C 4
Morges, 8,420 ....B 3
Moudon, 2,806 ....C 3
Moutier, 7,472 ....D 2
Müllheim, 1,475 ....G 1
Mümliswil-Ramiswil, 2,714 ....E 2
Münchenbuchsee, 3,652 ....E 2
Münsingen, 6,051 ....E 3
Muotathal, 2,592 ....G 3
Muri, 3,957 ....F 2
Muri bei Bern, 7,855 ....E 3
Murten, 3,330 ....D 3
Müstair, 717 ....K 3
Muttenz, 12,600 ....E 1
Näfels, 3,617 ....H 2
Naters, 3,797 ....E 4
Nebikon, 1,206 ....F 2
Nesslau, 2,002 ....H 2
Netstal, 2,925 ....H 2
Neuchâtel, 34,800 ....C 3
Neuenegg, 2,921 ....D 3
Neuhausen am Rheinfall, 10,900 ....G 1
Neunkirch, 1,208 ....F 1
Niederbipp, 3,141 ....E 2
Niederurnen, 3,347 ....G 2
Niederweningen, 1,027 ....F 1
Nunningen, 1,372 ....E 2
Nyon, 7,643 ....B 4
Oberägeri, 2,656 ....G 2
Oberburg, 3,030 ....E 2
Oberdiessbach, 1,927 ....E 3
Oberdorf, 1,132 ....E 2
Oberriet, 5,498 ....J 2
Obersaxen, 710 ....H 3
Oberuzwil, 4,394 ....H 2
Oensingen, 2,907 ....E 2
Ollon, 4,126 ....D 4
Olten, 21,400 ....E 2
Orbe, 3,824 ....C 3
Ormont-Dessous, 996 ....D 4
Orsières, 2,281 ....D 4
Payerne, 6,024 ....C 3
Peseux, 4,933 ....C 3
Pfäffikon, 5,735 ....G 2
Pfaffnau, 2,575 ....E 2
Pieterlen, 2,978 ....D 2
Pontresina, 1,067 ....J 3
Porrentruy, 7,095 ....C 2
Poschiavo, 3,743 ....J 4
Pratteln, 9,492 ....E 1
Pully, 14,200 ....C 4
Quinto, 1,365 ....G 3
Rafz, 1,925 ....G 1
Ramsen, 1,181 ....G 1
Rapperswil, 7,585 ....G 2
Raron, 1,077 ....E 4
Rechthalten, 1,015 ....D 3
Regensdorf, 4,997 ....F 2
Reichenbach, 2,829 ....E 3
Reiden, 2,795 ....F 2
Reigoldswil, 1,192 ....E 2
Reinach, 5,174 ....F 2
Renens, 12,600 ....C 3
Rheinau, 2,363 ....G 1
Rheineck, 3,047 ....J 2
Rheinfelden, 5,197 ....E 1
Richterswil, 5,842 ....G 2
Riehen, 19,100 ....E 1
Riggisberg, 1,949 ....E 3
Riva San Vitale, 1,358 ....G 5
Rivera, 950 ....G 4
Roggwil, 3,420 ....E 2
Rohrbach, 1,534 ....E 2
Rolle, 2,942 ....B 4
Romanshorn, 7,755 ....H 1
Romont, 2,982 ....C 3
Rorschach, 13,000 ....H 2
Rosenlaui ....F 3
Rothrist, 5,048 ....E 2
Rougemont, 860 ....D 4
Roveredo, 1,878 ....H 4
Rüeggisberg, 2,035 ....E 3
Rüschegg, 1,628 ....D 3
Ruswil, 4,657 ....F 2
Rüthi, 1,521 ....J 2
Rüti, 8,282 ....G 2
Rüti, 738 ....H 3
Saanen, 5,649 ....D 4
Saas-Fee, 739 ....E 4
Sachseln, 2,721 ....F 3
Saignelégier, 1,636 ....D 2
Saint-Blaise, 2,412 ....D 2
Saint-Imier, 6,704 ....D 2
Saint-Martin, 1,155 ....E 4
Saint-Maurice, 3,196 ....C 4
Saint Moritz, 3,751 ....J 3
Saint Niklaus, 2,071 ....E 4
Saint-Prex, 1,897 ....B 4
Saint-Stephan, 1,227 ....D 3
Saint-Ursanne, 1,304 ....D 2
Sainte-Croix, 6,925 ....B 3
Samedan, 2,106 ....J 3
Sankt Gallen, 78,300 ....H 2
Sargans, 2,571 ....H 2
Sarnen, 6,554 ....F 3
Satigny, 1,594 ....A 4
Savièse, 3,203 ....D 4
Savognin, 632 ....J 3
Saxon, 2,305 ....D 4
Schaffhausen, 32,900 ....G 1
Schangnau, 1,031 ....E 3
Schänis, 2,328 ....H 2
Schiers, 2,363 ....J 3
Schinznach-Dorf, 1,081 ....F 2
Schlarigna-Celerina, 868 ....J 3
Schleitheim, 1,494 ....G 1
Schlieren, 10,700 ....F 2
Schönenwerd, 4,561 ....E 2
Schüpfheim, 3,771 ....F 3
Schwanden, 3,020 ....H 2
Schwyz, 11,400 ....G 2
Scuol-Schuls, 1,429 ....K 3
Sedrun, 1,855 ....G 3
Seewis, 969 ....J 3
Sembrancher, 710 ....D 4
Sempach, 1,345 ....F 2
Semsales, 762 ....C 3
Seon, 3,006 ....F 2
Sevelen, 2,370 ....H 2
Sierre, 8,690 ....D 4
Siggenthal, 7,376 ....F 1
Signau, 2,555 ....E 3
Sigriswil, 3,739 ....E 3
Silenen, 2,261 ....G 3
Sils im Domleschg, 737 ....H 3
Silvaplana, 346 ....J 4
Sins, 2,195 ....F 2
Sion, 17,100 ....D 4
Sirnach, 3,075 ....G 2
Sissach, 4,574 ....E 2
Solothurn (Soleure), 19,100 ....E 2
Somvix, 2,004 ....G 3
Sonvico, 1,005 ....G 4
Spiez, 8,168 ....E 3
Stäfa, 6,947 ....G 2
Stalden, 1,007 ....E 4
Stammheim, 1,460 ....G 1
Stans, 4,337 ....F 3
Steckborn, 3,514 ....G 1
Steffisburg, 11,000 ....E 3
Stein, 1,060 ....E 1
Stein am Rhein, 2,588 ....G 1
Sulgen, 1,252 ....H 1
Sulz, 1,022 ....F 1
Sumiswald, 5,525 ....E 2
Sursee, 5,324 ....F 2
Tafers, 1,621 ....D 3
Täuffelen, 1,500 ....D 2
Tavannes, 3,939 ....D 2
Thalwil, 12,500 ....G 2
Thayngen, 3,013 ....G 1
Therwil, 1,946 ....E 1
Thun, 31,300 ....E 3
Thusis, 1,998 ....H 3
Trachselwald, 1,269 ....E 2
Tramelan, 5,567 ....D 2
Trogen, 2,101 ....H 2
Trub, 1,981 ....E 3
Trun, 1,583 ....G 3
Turbenthal, 2,685 ....G 2
Turgi, 1,860 ....F 1
Ueberstorf, 1,536 ....D 3
Uetendorf, 2,810 ....E 3
Unterägeri, 3,832 ....G 2
Unterkulm, 2,149 ....F 2
Unterseen, 3,783 ....E 3
Untervaz, 1,142 ....H 3
Urnäsch, 2,330 ....H 2
Uster, 18,700 ....G 2
Utzenstorf, 2,821 ....E 2
Uznach, 3,173 ....H 2
Vallorbe, 3,990 ....B 3
Vals, 968 ....H 3
Vaz-Obervaz, 1,568 ....J 3
Vechigen, 3,153 ....E 3
Vernayaz, 1,188 ....D 4
Versoix, 3,426 ....B 4
Vevey, 17,900 ....C 4
Veyrier, 2,705 ....B 4
Villeneuve, 2,366 ....C 4
Visp, 3,658 ....E 4
Vouvry, 1,368 ....C 4
Wädenswil, 12,900 ....G 2
Wahlern, 4,723 ....D 3
Wald, 7,778 ....G 2
Waldenburg, 1,284 ....E 2
Waldkirch, 2,487 ....H 2
Wallenstadt, 3,296 ....H 2
Walzenhausen, 2,345 ....J 2
Wangen an der Aare, 1,936 ....E 2
Wängi, 1,681 ....H 1
Wartau, 3,284 ....H 2
Wattwil, 7,480 ....H 2
Weesen, 1,280 ....H 2
Weggis, 2,243 ....F 2
Weinfelden, 6,954 ....H 1
Wettingen, 18,600 ....F 2
Wetzikon, 11,500 ....G 2
Wil, 11,800 ....H 2
Wilchingen, 1,061 ....F 1
Wilderswil, 1,701 ....E 3
Wildhaus, 1,179 ....H 2
Willisau, 2,508 ....F 2
Wimmis, 1,756 ....E 3
Windisch, 5,377 ....F 1
Winterthur, 86,300 ....G 1
Wohlen, 8,636 ....F 2
Wohlen bei Bern, 2,985 ....D 3
Wolfenschiessen, 1,647 ....F 3
Wolhusen, 3,446 ....F 2
Wollerau, 2,415 ....G 2
Worb, 5,885 ....E 3
Wynigen, 2,221 ....E 2
Yverdon, 17,500 ....C 3
Yvonand, 1,290 ....C 3
Zäziwil, 1,265 ....E 3
Zell, 1,582 ....E 2
Zell, 3,347 ....G 2
Zermatt, 2,731 ....E 4
Zizers, 1,290 ....J 3
Zofingen, 1,290 ....F 2
Zollikofen, 6,237 ....E 3
Zollikon, 11,200 ....G 2
Zug, 21,100 ....G 2
Zuoz, 1,001 ....J 3
Zürich, 444,000 ....F 2
Zurzach, 2,694 ....F 1
Zweisimmen, 2,676 ....D 3

PHYSICAL FEATURES

Aa (river) ....F 3
Aare (river) ....E 3
Ägerisee (lake) ....G 2
Albristhorn (mt.) ....D 4
Aletschhorn (mt.) ....F 4
Allaine (river) ....D 2
Areuse (river) ....C 3
Aubert (mt.) ....C 3
Aul (mt.) ....H 3
Baldeggersee (lake) ....F 2
Balmhorn (mt.) ....E 4
Bärenhorn (mt.) ....H 3
Basodino (mt.) ....G 4
Bernese Oberland (region) ....E 3
Bernina (mts.) ....J 4
Bernina (pass) ....K 4
Bernina (river) ....J 4
Beverin (mt.) ....H 3
Biel (lake) ....D 2
Bietschhorn (mt.) ....E 4
Birs (river) ....D 2
Blas (mt.) ....G 3
Blindenhorn (mt.) ....F 4
Blümlisalp (mt.) ....E 3
Bodensee (Constance) (lake) ....H 1
Borgne (river) ....D 4
Breithorn (mt.) ....E 5
Breithorn (mt.) ....E 4
Brienz (lake) ....F 3
Brienzer Rothorn (mt.) ....F 3
Broye (river) ....C 3
Brulé (mt.) ....D 4
Buchegg (mts.) ....D 2
Bürkelkopf (mt.) ....K 3
Bütschelegg (mt.) ....D 3
Calancasca (river) ....H 4
Campo (mt.) ....K 4
Campo Tencia (mt.) ....G 4
Ceneri (mt.) ....G 4
Cheville (pass) ....D 4
Churfirsten (mt.) ....H 2
Claridenstock (mt.) ....G 3
Collon (mt.) ....D 5
Constance (Bodensee) (lake) ....H 1
Dammastock (mt.) ....F 3
Davos (valley) ....J 3
Dent Blanche (mt.) ....E 4
Dent d'Herens (mt.) ....E 5
Dent de Lys (mt.) ....D 4
Dent de Ruth (mt.) ....D 3
Dent du Midi (mt.) ....C 4
Diablerets (mt.) ....D 4
Doldenhorn (mt.) ....E 4
Dolent (mt.) ....C 5
Dom (mt.) ....E
Doubs (river) C
Drance (river) ....D
Dufourspitze (mt.) ....E
Emmental (valley) ....E
Err (mt.) ....J
Faulen (mt.) ....G
Finsteraarhorn (mt.) ....F
Finstermünz (pass) ....K
Fletschhorn (mt.) ....F
Flüela (pass) ....J
Fluhberg (mt.) ....G
Fort (mt.) ....D
Frienis (mt.) ....D
Furka (pass) ....F
Generoso (mt.) ....H
Geneva (Léman) (lake) C
Gestler (mt.) ....D
Giacomo (pass) ....G
Gibloux (mt.) ....D
Glâne (river) C
Glärnisch (mt.) ....H
Glarus Alps (mts.) ....H
Glatt (river) ....G
Goms (valley) ....F
Grand Combin (mt.) ....D
Grande Dixence (dam) ....D
Grauehörner (mts.) ....H

SWITZERLAND and LIECHTENSTEIN

CONIC PROJECTION

SCALE OF MILES

0 5 10 20 30

SCALE OF KILOMETRES

0 5 10 20 30 40 50

Capitals of Countries .... ☆
Capitals of Cantons .... ◉
International Boundaries .... — — —
Canals ....

Copyright by C.S. HAMMOND & Co., N.Y.

Austria, Czechoslovakia and Hungary

AUSTRIA

PROVINCES

Burgenland, 271,001 ....D 3
Carinthia, 495,226 ....B 3
Lower Austria, 1,374,012 ....C 2
Salzburg, 347,292 ....B 3
Styria, 1,137,865 ....C 3
Tirol, 462,899 ....A 3
Upper Austria, 1,131,623 ....B 2
Vienna (city), 1,631,423 ....D 2
Vorarlberg, 226,323 ....A 3

CITIES and TOWNS

Admont, 3,057 ....C 3
Aigen, 1,941 ....B 2
Alt Aussee, 2,026 ....B 3
Altheim, 4,271 ....B 2
Althofen, 3,221 ....C 3
Amstetten, 12,086 ....C 2
Andau, 3,011 ....D 3
Arnoldstein, 6,229 ....B 3
Aspang, 2,359 ....D 3
Attnang-Puchheim, 7,525 ....B 2
Bad Aussee, 5,144 ....B 3
Bad Hofgastein, 4,700 ....B 3
Bad Ischl, 12,703 ....B 3
Bad Sankt Leonhard, 1,939 ....C 3
Baden, 22,484 ....D 2
Badgastein, 5,742 ....B 3
Berndorf, 8,992 ....C 3
Bischofshofen, 8,287 ....B 3
Bludenz, 11,127 ....A 3
Bramberg, 2,620 ....B 3
Braunau, 14,449 ....B 2
Bregenz, 21,428 ....A 3
Bruck an der Leitha, 6,791 ....D 2
Bruck an der Mur, 16,087 ....C 3
Deutsch Feistritz, 3,427 ....C 3
Deutsch Landsberg, 5,227 ....C 3
Deutsch Wagram, 4,207 ....D 2
Deutschkreutz, 3,901 ....D 3
Dornbirn, 28,075 ....A 3
Ebenfurth, 2,342 ....D 3
Ebensee, 9,602 ....B 3
Eferding, 3,151 ....B 2
Eggenburg, 3,338 ....C 2
Eisenerz, 12,435 ....C 3
Eisenstadt, 7,167 ....D 3
Enns, 8,919 ....C 2
Feldbach, 3,687 ....C 3
Feldkirch, 17,343 ....A 3
Feldkirchen in Karnten, 3,181 ....B 3
Ferlach, 5,672 ....C 3
Fieberbrunn, 3,010 ....B 3
Fohnsdorf, 11,571 ....C 3
Frankenmarkt, 2,565 ....B 3
Frauenkirchen, 2,812 ....D 3
Friesach, 3,388 ....C 3
Freistadt, 5,375 ....C 2
Frohnleiten, 4,969 ....C 3
Fulpmes, 2,282 ....A 3
Fürstenfeld, 6,415 ....C 3
Gaming, 4,218 ....C 3
Gänserndorf, 3,378 ....D 2
Gleisdorf, 4,385 ....C 3
Gloggnitz, 7,228 ....D 3
Gmünd, Carinthia, 2,195 ....B 3
Gmünd, Lower Austria, 6,552 ....C 2
Gmunden, 12,518 ....B 3
Goisern, 6,028 ....B 3
Golling an der Salzach, 2,845 ....B 3
Götzis, 7,034 ....A 3
Gratwein, 2,515 ....C 3
Graz, 237,080 ....C 3
Grein, 2,518 ....C 2
Grieskirchen, 4,137 ....B 2
Gross Siegharts, 2,599 ....C 2
Grünburg, 3,609 ....C 3
Güssing, 2,715 ....D 3
Haag, 4,671 ....C 2
Hainburg, 6,437 ....D 2
Hainfeld, 3,883 ....C 2
Hallein, 13,329 ....B 3
Hallstatt, 1,373 ....B 3
Hartberg, 3,629 ....C 3
Haslach an der Muhl, 2,565 ....C 2
Heidenreichstein, 3,653 ....C 2
Heiligenblut, 1,195 ....B 3
Hermagor, 2,778 ....B 3
Herzogenburg, 5,166 ....C 2
Hieflau, 2,003 ....C 3
Hohenau an der March, 3,907 ....D 2
Hohenberg, 2,093 ....C 3
Hohenems, 9,188 ....A 3
Hollabrunn, 5,832 ....D 2
Hopfgarten in Nordtirol, 4,163 ....B 3
Horn, 4,705 ....C 2
Hüttenberg, 2,257 ....C 3
Imst, 5,057 ....A 3
Innsbruck, 100,695 ....A 3
Jenbach, 5,479 ....A 3
Judenburg, 9,869 ....C 3
Kapfenberg, 23,859 ....C 3
Kappl, 1,970 ....A 3
Kaprun, 2,164 ....B 3
Kindberg, 5,766 ....C 3
Kirchdorf an der Krems, 2,964 ....C 3
Kitzbühel, 7,744 ....B 3
Klagenfurt, 69,218 ....C 3
Klosterneuburg, 22,787 ....D 2
Knittelfeld, 14,259 ....C 3
Köflach, 12,367 ....C 3
Königswiesen, 2,707 ....C 2
Korneuburg, 8,276 ....D 2
Kössen, 2,361 ....B 3
Kotschach-Mauthen, 2,763 ....B 3
Krems, 21,046 ....C 2
Kufstein, 11,215 ....B 3
Kundl, 2,508 ....A 3
Laa an der Thaya, 4,925 ....D 2
Laakirchen, 6,722 ....B 3
Lambach, 3,019 ....C 2
Landeck, 6,514 ....A 3
Landskron, 9,058 ....B 3
Längenfeld, 2,314 ....A 3
Langenlois, 4,655 ....C 2
Langenwang, 3,734 ....C 3
Lavamünd, 2,506 ....C 3
Leibnitz, 6,356 ....C 3
Lenzing, 5,372 ....B 3
Leoben, 36,257 ....C 3
Leonfelden, 2,546 ....C 2
Lienz, 11,132 ....B 3
Liezen, 5,444 ....C 3
Lilienfeld, 3,307 ....C 3
Linz, 195,978 ....C 2
Lustenau, 12,582 ....A 3
Mannersdorf, 3,909 ....D 3
Marchegg, 2,159 ....D 2
Mariazell, 2,191 ....C 3
Matrei, 3,430 ....B 3
Mattersburg, 4,270 ....D 3
Mattighofen, 3,919 ....B 2
Mauerkirchen, 2,175 ....B 2
Mautern, 2,365 ....C 3
Mauthausen, 3,836 ....C 2
Mauthen-Kotschach, 2,763 ....B 3
Mayrhofen, 2,523 ....A 3
Melk, 3,534 ....C 2
Mistelbach an der Zaya, 5,434 ....D 2
Mittersill, 3,502 ....B 3
Mödling, 17,274 ....D 2
Mondsee, 2,050 ....B 3
Murau, 2,755 ....C 3
Mürzzuschlag, 11,586 ....C 3
Nassereith, 1,744 ....A 3
Neuberg an der Mürz, 2,411 ....C 3
Neumarkt, Styria, 1,880 ....C 3
Neumarkt am Wallersee, 2,877 ....B 3
Neunkirchen, 10,027 ....C 3
Neusiedl am See, 3,826 ....D 3
Neustift im Stubaital, 2,195 ....A 3
Ober Grafendorf, 3,825 ....C 2
Oberndorf bei Salzburg, 3,084 ....B 3
Obervellach, 2,371 ....B 3
Oberwart, 4,740 ....D 3
Paternion, 5,581 ....B 3
Perg, 4,106 ....C 2
Peuerbach, 2,105 ....B 2
Pinkafeld, 3,826 ....C 3
Pöchlarn, 2,921 ....C 2
Pörtschach, 2,449 ....C 3
Poysdorf, 2,738 ....D 2
Pregarten, 2,818 ....C 2
Radenthein, 5,651 ....B 3
Radstadt, 3,311 ....B 3
Rankweil, 6,451 ....A 3
Rechnitz, 3,374 ....D 3
Reichenau an der Rax, 4,441 ....C 3
Retz, 2,941 ....D 2
Reutte, 4,285 ....A 3
Ried im Innkreis, 9,471 ....B 2
Rottenmann, 4,139 ....C 3
Saalfelden, 8,901 ....B 3
Salzburg, 108,114 ....B 3
Sankt Aegyd am Neuwalde, 3,206 ....C 3
Sankt Anton am Arlberg, 1,741 ....A 3
Sankt Johann, 4,713 ....B 3
Sankt Michael, Styria, 3,433 ....C 3
Sankt Michael im Lungau, 2,422 ....B 3
Sankt Paul, 1,808 ....C 3
Sankt Pölten, 40,112 ....C 2
Sankt Valentin, 7,750 ....C 2
Sankt Veit an der Glan, 10,950 ....C 3
Sankt Wolfgang, 2,234 ....B 3
Schärding, 5,710 ....B 2
Scheibbs, 3,231 ....C 2
Schladming, 3,249 ....B 3
Schrems, 3,080 ....C 2
Schruns, 3,304 ....A 3
Schwarzach, 3,186 ....B 3
Schwaz, 9,455 ....A 3
Schwertberg, 3,369 ....C 2
Sierning, 7,527 ....C 2
Sillian, 1,948 ....B 3
Solbad Hall, 10,750 ....A 3
Spital, 2,421 ....C 3
Spittal, 10,045 ....B 3
Steinach, 2,155 ....A 3
Steyr, 38,306 ....C 2
Stockerau, 11,853 ....D 2
Strassburg, 2,972 ....C 3
Tamsweg, 4,431 ....B 3
Telfs, 5,438 ....A 3
Ternitz, 9,032 ....D 3
Traiskirchen, 7,026 ....D 2
Traun, 16,026 ....C 2
Trieben, 4,023 ....C 3
Trofaiach, 6,909 ....C 3
Tulln, 6,306 ....D 2
Velden, 2,039 ....C 3
Vienna (cap.), 1,631,423 ....D 2
Villach, 32,971 ....B 3
Vöcklabruck, 9,353 ....B 2
Voitsberg, 6,353 ....C 3
Völkermarkt, 3,678 ....C 3
Vordernberg, 2,896 ....C 3
Waidhofen an der Thaya, 3,748
Waidhofen an der Ybbs, 5,586.
Weitensfeld, 2,998 ....
Weiz, 8,146 ....
Wels, 41,060 ....
Weyer, 2,367 ....
Wiener-Neustadt, 33,845 ....
Wildon, 2,020 ....
Wilhelmsburg, 6,196 ....
Wolfsberg, 9,470 ....
Wörgl, 6,828 ....
Ybbs, 5,324 ....
Zams, 2,782 ....
Zell am See, 6,455 ....
Zeltweg, 7,340 ....
Zirl, 3,165 ....
Zistersdorf, 3,011 ....
Zwettl, 3,836 ....

PHYSICAL FEATURES

Allgäu Alps (mts.) ....
Atter (lake) ....
Brenner (pass) ....
Carnic Alps (mts.) ....
Constance (lake) ....
Danube (river) ....
Donau (Danube) (river) ....
Drau (river) ....
Enns (river) ....

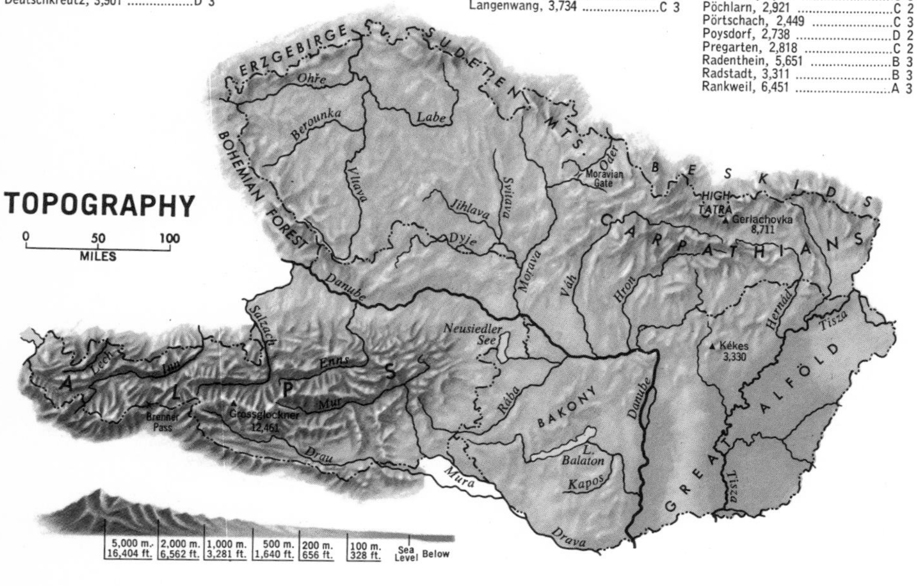

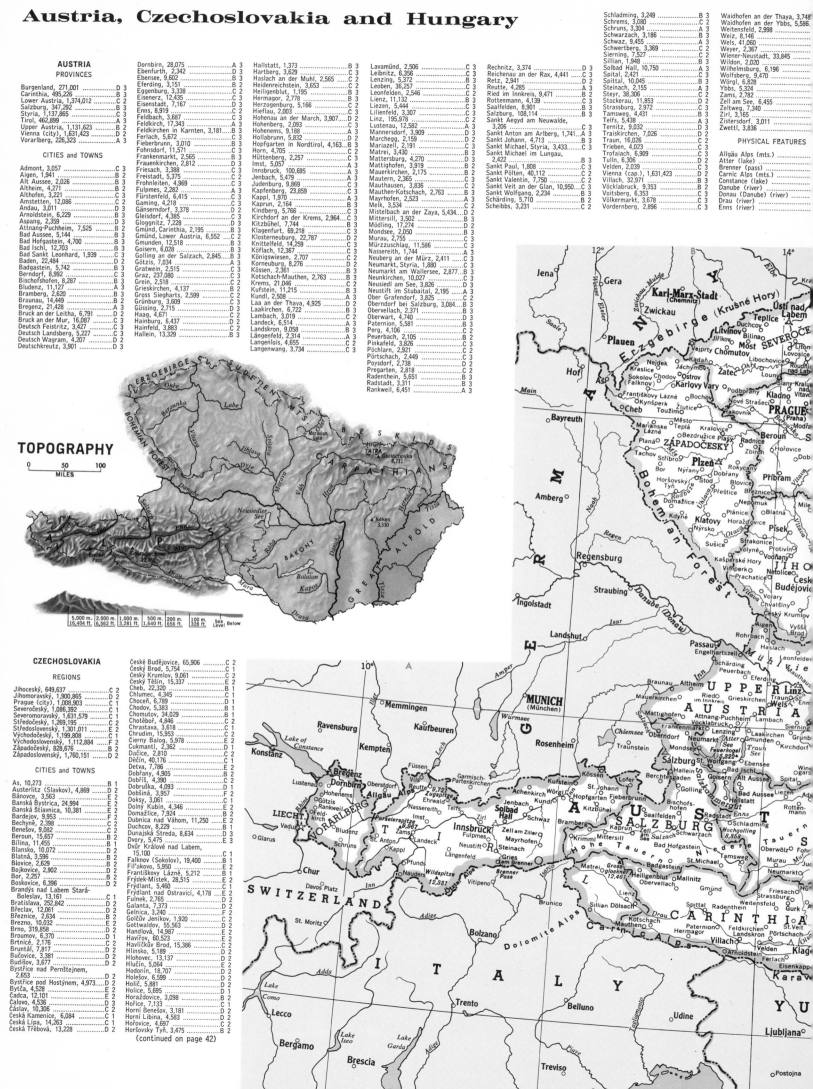

TOPOGRAPHY

0 50 100 MILES

CZECHOSLOVAKIA

REGIONS

Jihoceský, 649,637 ....C 2
Jihomoravský, 1,900,865 ....D 2
Prague (city), 1,008,903 ....C 1
Severočeský, 1,086,392 ....C 1
Severomoravský, 1,631,579 ....C 1
Středočeský, 1,269,195 ....C 2
Středoslovenský, 1,301,011 ....E 2
Východočeský, 1,199,808 ....C 1
Východoslovenský, 1,112,884 ....F 2
Západočeský, 828,676 ....B 2
Západoslovenský, 1,760,151 ....D 2

CITIES and TOWNS

As, 10,273 ....B 1
Austerlitz (Slavkov), 4,869 ....D 2
Bánovce, 3,563 ....E 2
Banská Bystrica, 24,994 ....E 2
Banská Štiavnica, 10,381 ....E 2
Bardejov, 9,953 ....F 2
Bechyně, 2,398 ....C 2
Benešov, 9,082 ....C 2
Beroun, 15,657 ....B 2
Bílina, 11,455 ....B 1
Blansko, 10,072 ....D 2
Blatná, 3,596 ....B 2
Blovice, 2,629 ....B 2
Bojkovice, 2,902 ....D 2
Bor, 2,257 ....B 2
Boskovice, 6,396 ....D 2
Brandýs nad Labem Stará-Boleslav, 13,161 ....C 1
Bratislava, 252,842 ....D 2
Břeclav, 12,061 ....D 2
Březnice, 2,634 ....B 2
Brezno, 10,032 ....E 2
Brno, 319,858 ....D 2
Broumov, 6,370 ....D 1
Brtnicé, 2,176 ....C 2
Bruntál, 7,817 ....D 2
Bučovice, 3,381 ....D 2
Budišov, 3,677 ....D 2
Bystřice nad Pernštejnem, 2,653 ....D 2
Bystřice pod Hostýnem, 4,973 ....D 2
Bytča, 4,528 ....E 2
Čadca, 12,101 ....E 2
Čalovo, 4,536 ....D 3
Čáslav, 10,306 ....C 2
Česká Kamenice, 6,084 ....C 1
Česká Lípa, 14,263 ....C 1
Česká Třěbová, 13,228 ....D 2
České Budějovice, 65,906 ....C 2
Český Brod, 5,754 ....C 1
Český Krumlov, 9,061 ....C 2
Český Těšín, 15,337 ....E 2
Cheb, 22,320 ....B 1
Chlumec, 4,345 ....C 1
Choceň, 6,789 ....D 1
Chodov, 5,383 ....B 1
Chomutov, 34,029 ....B 1
Chotěboř, 4,846 ....C 2
Chrastava, 3,618 ....C 1
Chrudim, 15,953 ....C 2
Čierny Balog, 5,978 ....E 2
Cukmantl, 2,362 ....D 1
Dačice, 2,810 ....C 2
Děčín, 40,176 ....C 1
Detva, 7,786 ....E 2
Dobřany, 4,905 ....B 2
Dobříš, 4,390 ....C 2
Dobruška, 4,093 ....D 1
Dobšiná, 3,957 ....F 2
Doksy, 3,061 ....C 1
Dolný Kubín, 4,346 ....E 2
Domažlice, 7,924 ....B 2
Dubnica nad Váhom, 11,250 ....E 2
Duchcov, 8,229 ....B 1
Dunajská Streda, 8,634 ....D 3
Dvory, 5,475 ....E 3
Dvůr Králové nad Labem, 15,100 ....C 1
Falknov (Sokolov), 19,400 ....B 1
Fiľakovo, 5,950 ....E 2
Františkovy Lázně, 5,212 ....B 1
Frýdek-Místek, 28,515 ....E 2
Frýdlant, 5,460 ....C 1
Frýdlant nad Ostravicí, 4,178 ....E 2
Fulnek, 2,765 ....D 2
Galanta, 7,373 ....D 2
Gelnica, 3,240 ....F 2
Golčův Jeníkov, 1,920 ....C 2
Gottwaldov, 55,563 ....D 2
Handlová, 14,987 ....E 2
Havířov, 60,523 ....E 2
Havlíčkův Brod, 15,386 ....C 2
Hlinsko, 5,189 ....D 2
Hlohovec, 13,137 ....D 2
Hlučín, 5,064 ....E 2
Hodonín, 18,707 ....D 2
Holešov, 6,599 ....D 2
Holič, 5,881 ....D 2
Holice, 5,695 ....D 1
Horaždovice, 3,098 ....B 2
Hořice, 7,133 ....C 1
Horní Benešov, 3,181 ....D 2
Horní Libina, 4,583 ....D 2
Hořovice, 4,697 ....C 2
Horšovsky Tyň, 3,475 ....B 2

(continued on page 42)

AUSTRIA, CZECHOSLOVAKIA and HUNGARY

	AUSTRIA	CZECHOSLOVAKIA	HUNGARY
AREA	32,369 sq. mi.	49,356 sq. mi.	35,875 sq. mi.
POPULATION	7,193,000	14,058,000	10,123,000
CAPITAL	Vienna	Prague	Budapest
LARGEST CITY	Vienna 1,631,423	Prague 1,008,903	Budapest 1,874,947
HIGHEST POINT	Grossglockner 12,461 ft.	Gerlachovka 8,711 ft.	Kékes 3,330 ft.
MONETARY UNIT	schilling	koruna (crown)	forint
MAJOR LANGUAGE	German	Czech, Slovak	Hungarian
MAJOR RELIGION	Roman Catholic	Roman Catholic	Roman Catholic, Protestant

AUSTRIA   CZECHOSLOVAKIA   HUNGARY

AUSTRIA, CZECHOSLOVAKIA and HUNGARY
CONIC PROJECTION

SCALE OF MILES
0 10 20 40 60 80

SCALE OF KILOMETRES
0 10 20 40 60 80

Capitals of Countries .... ☆
Administrative Centers .... ○
Canals
International Boundaries _____
Internal Boundaries _____

© C. S. HAMMOND & Co., N.Y.

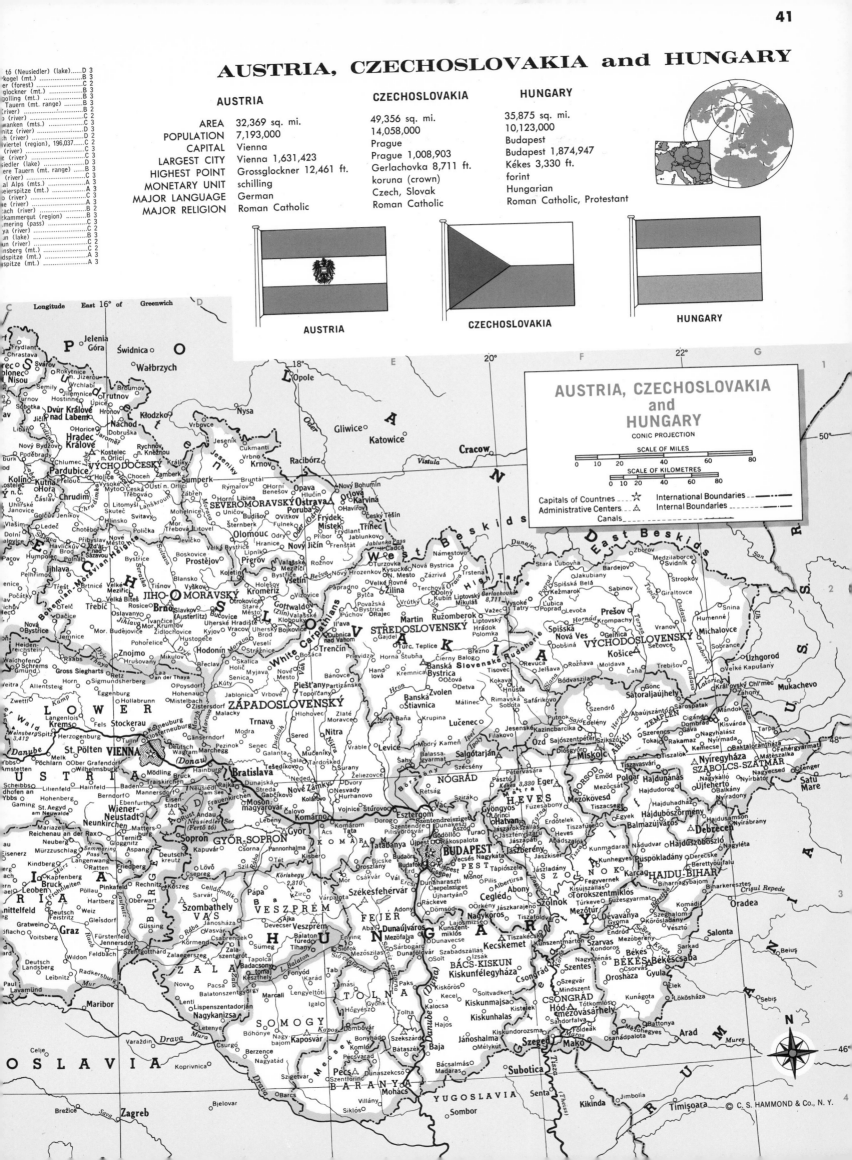

Austria, Czechoslovakia and Hungary
(continued)

CZECHOSLOVAKIA (continued)

Hostinné, 4,412 ....C 1
Hradec Králové, 57,074 ....C 1
Hranice, 11,071 ....D 2
Hronov, 10,500 ....D 1
Hrušovany, 3,128 ....D 2
Humenné, 12,031 ....G 2
Humpolec, 5,083 ....C 2
Hurbanovo, 3,578 ....E 3
Hustopeče, 2,698 ....D 2
Il'ava, 2,043 ....E 2
Ivančice, 4,742 ....D 2
Jablonec nad Nisou, 27,806 ....C 1
Jablunkov, 4,467 ....E 2
Jáchymov, 6,806 ....B 1
Jaroměř, 11,922 ....C 1
Jelšava, 2,456 ....F 2
Jemnice, 3,383 ....C 2
Jeseník, 5,873 ....D 1
Jesenské, 1,567 ....F 2
Jevíčko, 2,881 ....D 2
Jičín, 12,345 ....C 1
Jihlava, 35,566 ....C 2
Jilemnice, 3,362 ....C 1
Jindřichův Hradec, 10,585 ....C 2
Jiříkov, 11,741 ....B 1
Kadaň, 5,062 ....B 1
Kamenice, 2,692 ....C 2
Kaplice, 1,931 ....C 2
Karlovy Vary, 43,091 ....B 1
Karviná, 54,625 ....E 2
Kašperské Hory, 2,814 ....B 2
Kdyně, 2,609 ....B 2
Kežmarok, 7,372 ....F 2
Kladno, 50,796 ....B 1
Klatovy, 14,268 ....B 2
Kojetín, 5,292 ....D 2
Kokava, 5,398 ....E 2
Kolárovo, 10,895 ....D 3
Kolín, 23,530 ....C 1
Komárno, 24,854 ....D 3
Košice, 88,310 ....F 2
Kostelec nad Černými Lesy, 3,616 ....C 2
Kostelec nad Orlicí, 5,539 ....D 1
Králíky, 3,895 ....D 1
Kralovice, 2,268 ....B 2
Kráľovský Chlmec, 3,410 ....G 2
Kralupy nad Vltavou, 11,870 ....C 1
Kraslice, 6,294 ....B 1
Krásna Lípa, 5,041 ....C 1
Kremnica, 4,979 ....E 2
Krnov, 21,772 ....D 1
Kroměříž, 20,923 ....D 2
Krompachy, 3,340 ....F 2
Krupina, 5,418 ....E 2
Kutná Hora, 16,820 ....C 2
Kúty, 3,348 ....D 2
Kyjov, 5,620 ....D 2
Kynšperk, 5,398 ....B 1
Kysucké Nové Mesto, 2,318 ....E 2
Lanškroun, 6,558 ....D 2
Ledeč, 2,625 ....C 2
Levice, 14,190 ....E 2
Levoča, 7,584 ....F 2
Libáň, 2,261 ....C 1
Liberec, 66,365 ....C 1
Libochovice, 2,879 ....B 1
Lidice ....C 1
Lipník, 6,887 ....D 2
Liptovský Mikuláš, 12,455 ....E 2
Lišov, 2,691 ....C 2
Litoměřice, 17,234 ....C 1
Litomyšl, 6,384 ....D 2
Litovel, 4,496 ....D 2
Litvínov, 20,744 ....B 1
Lomnice, 2,228 ....C 2
Louny, 12,540 ....B 1
Lovosice, 4,962 ....C 1
L'ubica, 3,335 ....F 2
Lučenec, 16,349 ....E 2
Lysá, 6,500 ....C 1
Malacky, 10,067 ....D 2
Mariánské Lázně, 12,847 ....B 2
Martin, 25,201 ....E 2
Mělník, 13,775 ....C 1
Město Teplá, 2,500 ....B 2
Michalovce, 17,006 ....G 2
Mikulov, 5,220 ....D 2
Milevsko, 3,754 ....C 2
Mimoň, 5,349 ....C 1
Místek-Frýdek, 28,515 ....E 2
Mladá Boleslav, 26,171 ....C 1
Mladá Vožice, 1,732 ....C 2
Mnichovo Hradiště, 4,647 ....C 1
Modra, 6,239 ....D 2
Modřany, 10,229 ....C 1
Modrý Kameň, 1,836 ....E 2
Mohelnice, 4,949 ....D 2
Moldava, 2,241 ....F 2
Moravská Třebová, 5,844 ....D 2
Moravské Budějovice, 4,348 ....D 2
Moravský Krumlov, 2,897 ....D 2
Most, 51,374 ....B 1
Mučeníky, 5,207 ....D 2
Myjava, 9,935 ....D 2
Náchod, 17,996 ....D 1
Neded, 4,553 ....D 2
Nejdek, 5,748 ....B 1
Nepomuk, 1,860 ....B 2
Nesvady, 5,070 ....E 3
Netolice, 2,503 ....C 2
Nitra, 35,792 ....E 2
Nová Baňa, 5,113 ....E 2
Nová Bystřice, 2,418 ....C 2
Nové Město na Moravě, 3,250 ....D 2
Nové Město nad Váhom, 12,881 ....D 2
Nové Strašecí, 3,288 ....B 1
Nové Zamky, 22,642 ....D 3
Nový Bohumín, 11,600 ....E 2
Nový Bor, 5,994 ....C 1
Nový Bydžov, 6,120 ....C 1
Nový Hrozenkov, 5,302 ....E 2
Nový Jičín, 16,801 ....E 2
Nymburk, 12,580 ....C 1
Nýřany, 4,420 ....B 2
Nýrsko, 4,124 ....B 2
Odry, 5,340 ....D 2
Olomouc, 72,221 ....D 2
Opava, 43,622 ....E 2
Orlova, 21,255 ....E 2
Oslavany, 3,606 ....D 2
Ostrava, 244,899 ....E 2
Ostrov, 18,443 ....B 1
Otrokovice-Kvítkovice, 10,744 ....D 2
Pacov, 2,775 ....C 2
Pardubice, 55,331 ....C 1
Partizánske, 3,171 ....E 2
Pelhřimov, 7,548 ....C 2
Pezinok, 11,025 ....D 2
Piešťany, 19,489 ....D 2
Písek, 20,430 ....C 2
Planá, 5,216 ....B 2
Plánice, 1,718 ....B 2
Plasy, 1,472 ....B 2
Plzeň, 139,643 ....B 2
Počatky, 2,141 ....C 2
Podbořany, 3,893 ....B 1
Poděbrady, 12,062 ....C 1
Pohořelice, 3,068 ....D 2
Polička, 5,600 ....D 2
Polná, 4,005 ....C 2
Poprad, 15,069 ....F 2
Poruba, 21,179 ....D 2
Považská Bystrica, 12,106 ....E 2
Prachatice, 5,196 ....B 2
Prague (Praha) (cap.), 1,008,903 ....C 1
Přelouč, 4,228 ....C 1
Přerov, 31,431 ....D 2
Prešov, 36,306 ....F 2
Přeštice, 4,616 ....B 2
Příbor, 5,491 ....E 2
Příbram, 27,112 ....B 2
Přibyslav, 2,556 ....C 2
Prievidza, 19,778 ....E 2
Prostějov, 33,588 ....D 2
Protivín, 3,217 ....C 2
Púchov, 4,316 ....E 2
Radnice, 2,342 ....B 2
Rajec, 2,753 ....E 2
Rakovník, 12,106 ....B 1
Říčany, 6,376 ....C 2
Rimavská Sobota, 11,036 ....E 2
Rokycany, 12,184 ....B 2
Rokytnice nad Jizerou, 3,893 ....C 1
Rosice, 4,900 ....D 2
Roudnice nad Labem, 9,964 ....C 1
Rožňava, 10,578 ....F 2
Rožnov, 3,989 ....E 2
Rumburk, 6,759 ....C 1
Ružomberok, 19,063 ....E 2
Rychnov nad Kněžnou, 6,296 ....D 1
Rýmařov, 4,328 ....D 2
Sabinov, 3,909 ....F 2
Šafaríkovo, 3,180 ....F 2
Šahy, 4,019 ....E 2
Sal'a, 4,397 ....D 2
Sečovce, 3,354 ....F 2
Sedlčany, 2,083 ....C 2
Semily, 6,549 ....C 1
Senec, 6,184 ....D 2
Senica, 7,032 ....D 2
Sered, 6,208 ....D 2
Skalica, 5,440 ....D 2
Skuteč, 3,348 ....D 2
Slaný, 12,176 ....C 1
Slavkov, 4,869 ....D 2
Snina, 5,002 ....G 2
Sobešlav, 4,643 ....C 2
Sobotka, 2,147 ....C 1
Sokolov, 19,400 ....B 1
Spišská Belá, 3,072 ....F 2
Spišská Nová Ves, 18,324 ....F 2
Stará L'ubovňa, 1,989 ....F 2
Staré Město, 6,350 ....D 2
Šternberk, 11,338 ....D 2
Stod, 2,502 ....B 2
Strakonice, 14,953 ....B 2
Strážnice, 5,147 ....D 2
Stříbro, 4,659 ....B 2
Stropkov, 2,506 ....F 2
Šturovo, 4,082 ....E 3
Šumperk, 19,964 ....D 1
Šurany, 5,381 ....E 2
Sušice, 6,793 ....B 2
Svárov, 3,381 ....C 1
Svitavy, 13,743 ....D 2
Tábor, 19,885 ....C 2
Tachov, 5,935 ....B 2
Tardošked, 6,689 ....E 2
Telč, 4,381 ....C 2
Teplice, 43,997 ....B 1
Terchová, 4,400 ....E 2
Tišnov, 4,885 ....D 2
Tisovec, 3,988 ....E 2
Topol'čany, 11,107 ....E 2
Třebíč, 19,589 ....C 2
Trebišov, 9,627 ....F 2
Třeboň, 4,663 ....C 2
Trenčín, 23,119 ....E 2
Třešť, 4,900 ....C 2
Trhové Sviny, 2,953 ....C 2
Třinec, 23,516 ....E 2
Trnava, 33,011 ....D 2
Trstená, 2,468 ....E 2
Trutnov, 23,437 ....D 1
Turnov, 11,563 ....C 1
Turzovka, 9,823 ....E 2
Tyn, 4,135 ....C 2
Uherské Hradiště, 13,260 ....D 2
Uherský Brod, 6,457 ....D 2
Uhlířské Janovice, 1,979 ....C 2
Uničov, 3,325 ....D 2
Úpice, 5,498 ....C 1
Ústí nad Labem, 66,674 ....C 1
Ústí nad Orlicí, 10,978 ....D 2
Valašské Klobouky, 2,525 ....D 2
Valašské Meziříčí, 12,816 ....D 2
Varnsdorf, 13,607 ....C 1
Važec, 2,747 ....E 2
Vejprty, 5,476 ....B 1
Velká Bíteš, 1,714 ....D 2
Velká Bystřice, 4,459 ....D 2
Veľ'ké Kapušany, 2,371 ....G 2
Velké Meziříčí, 6,217 ....D 2
Veselí nad Lužnicí, 4,382 ....C 2
Veselí nad Moravou, 4,636 ....D 2
Vítkov, 2,685 ....D 2
Vizovice, 3,583 ....D 2
Vlašim, 5,066 ....C 2
Vodňany, 5,374 ....C 2
Volary, 5,034 ....B 2
Volyně, 3,019 ....B 2
Votice, 2,191 ....C 2
Vráble, 3,148 ....E 2
Vracov, 4,171 ....D 2
Vranov, 3,964 ....F 2
Vrchlabí, 10,177 ....C 1
Vrútky, 5,927 ....E 2
Vsetín, 18,999 ....D 2
Vyškov, 12,840 ....D 2
Vysoké Mýto, 7,983 ....D 2
Vysoké Tatry, 14,445 ....F 2
Vyšší Brod, 1,905 ....C 2
Zábřeh, 5,847 ....D 2
Žamberk, 4,278 ....D 1
Žatec, 15,301 ....B 1
Zbiroh, 1,718 ....B 2
Zborov, 1,551 ....F 2
Žd'ár nad Sázavou, 10,663 ....
Želiezovce, 3,748 ....
Židlochovice, 2,696 ....
Žilina, 34,269 ....
Zlaté Moravce, 4,003 ....
Zlín (Gottwaldov), 55,563 ....
Žlutice, 2,114 ....
Znojmo, 24,512 ....
Zvolen, 20,903 ....

PHYSICAL FEATURES

Berounka (river) ....
Beskids, East (mts.) ....
Beskids, West (mts.) ....
Bohemia (region), 6,039,087 ....
Bohemian (forest) ....
Bohemian-Moravian Heights ....
Dudváh (river) ....
Dunajec (river) ....
Dyje (river) ....
Erzgebirge (mts.) ....
Gerlachovka (mt.) ....
Hornád (river) ....
Hron (river) ....
Ipel' (river) ....
Jablunka (pass) ....
Jeseniky (mts.) ....
Jihlava (river) ....
Krušné Hory (Erzgebirge) (mts.) ....
Labe (river) ....
Laborec (river) ....
Lužnice (river) ....
Moldau (Vltava) (river) ....
Morava (river) ....
Moravia (region), 3,532,444 ....
Nitra (river) ....
Oder (Odra) (river) ....
Ohře (river) ....
Orava (river) ....
Orlice (river) ....
Otava (river) ....
Poprad (river) ....
Slana (river) ....
Slovakia (region), 4,239,588 ....
Slovenske Rudohorie (mts.) ....
Sudeten (mts.) ....
Tatra, High (mts.) ....
Uh (river) ....
Váh (river) ....
Vltava (river) ....
White Carpathians (mts.) ....

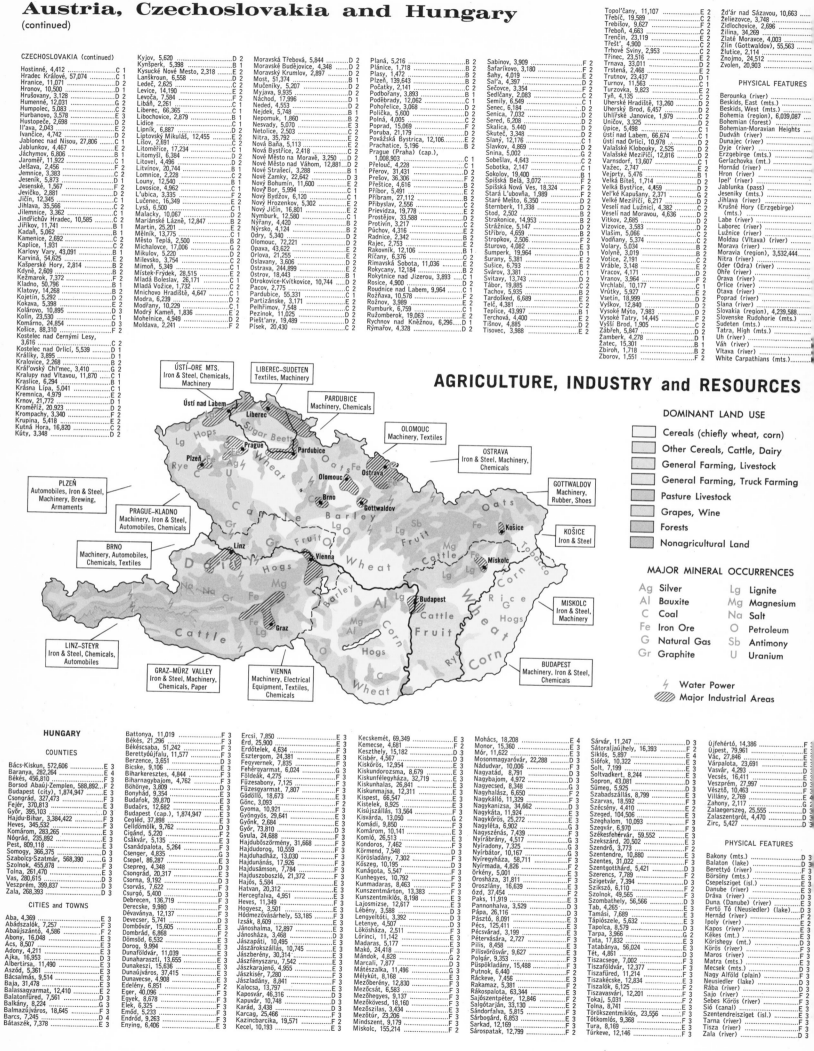

AGRICULTURE, INDUSTRY and RESOURCES

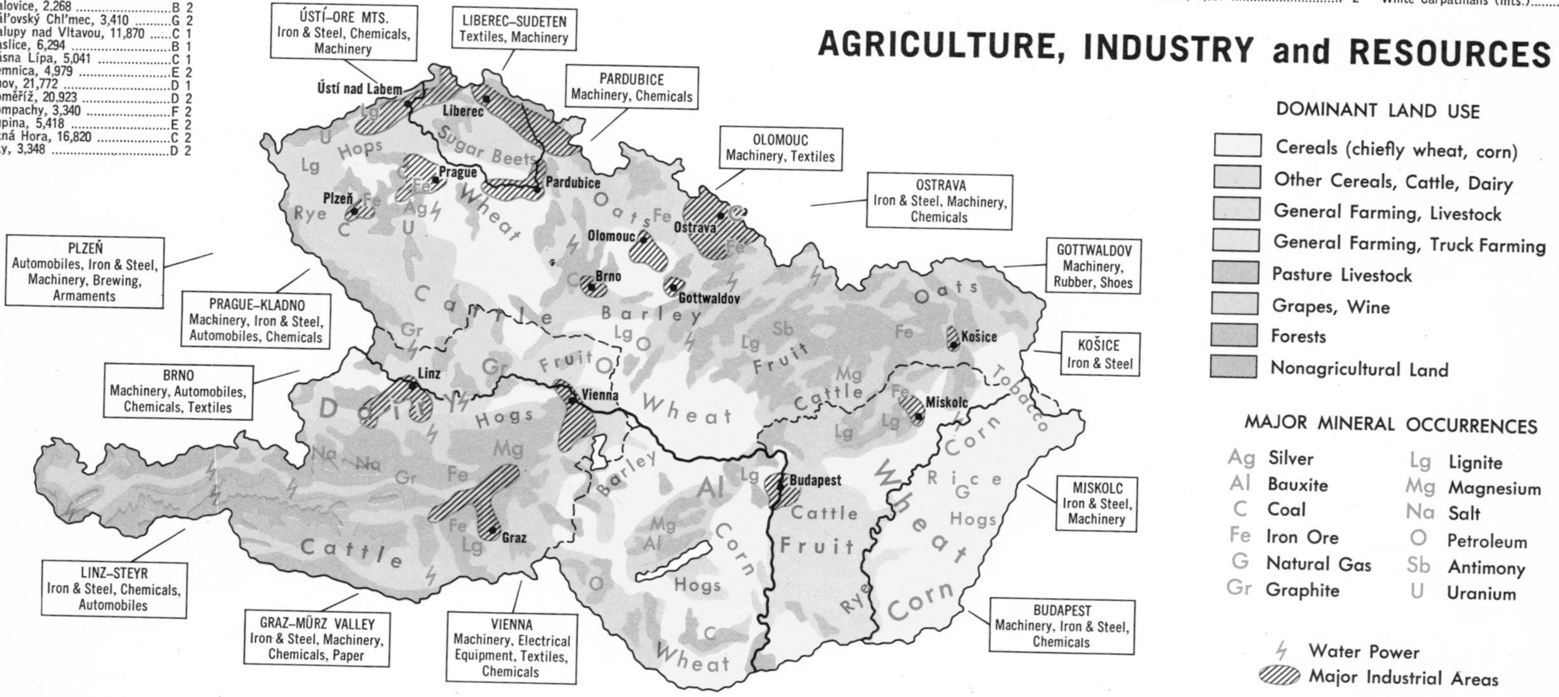

ÚSTÍ–ORE MTS. Iron & Steel, Chemicals, Machinery
LIBEREC–SUDETEN Textiles, Machinery
PARDUBICE Machinery, Chemicals
OLOMOUC Machinery, Textiles
OSTRAVA Iron & Steel, Machinery, Chemicals
PLZEŇ Automobiles, Iron & Steel, Machinery, Brewing, Armaments
PRAGUE–KLADNO Machinery, Iron & Steel, Automobiles, Chemicals
GOTTWALDOV Machinery, Rubber, Shoes
BRNO Machinery, Automobiles, Chemicals, Textiles
KOŠICE Iron & Steel
MISKOLC Iron & Steel, Machinery
LINZ–STEYR Iron & Steel, Chemicals, Automobiles
GRAZ–MÜRZ VALLEY Iron & Steel, Machinery, Chemicals, Paper
VIENNA Machinery, Electrical Equipment, Textiles, Chemicals
BUDAPEST Machinery, Iron & Steel, Chemicals
Ústí nad Labem
Liberec
Prague
Pardubice
Plzeň
Olomouc
Ostrava
Brno
Gottwaldov
Košice
Linz
Vienna
Miskolc
Budapest
Graz
Hops
Sugar Beets
Oats
Wheat
Rye
Cattle
Barley
Fruit
Dairy
Hogs
Tobacco
Corn
Rice
DOMINANT LAND USE
Cereals (chiefly wheat, corn)
Other Cereals, Cattle, Dairy
General Farming, Livestock
General Farming, Truck Farming
Pasture Livestock
Grapes, Wine
Forests
Nonagricultural Land
MAJOR MINERAL OCCURRENCES
Ag Silver
Al Bauxite
C Coal
Fe Iron Ore
G Natural Gas
Gr Graphite
Lg Lignite
Mg Magnesium
Na Salt
O Petroleum
Sb Antimony
U Uranium
Water Power
Major Industrial Areas

HUNGARY

COUNTIES

Bács-Kiskun, 572,606 ....E 3
Baranya, 282,264 ....E 4
Békés, 456,810 ....F 3
Borsod Abaúj-Zemplén, 588,892 ....F 2
Budapest (city), 1,874,947 ....E 3
Csongrád, 327,473 ....F 3
Fejér, 370,813 ....E 3
Győr, 395,103 ....D 3
Hajdu-Bihar, 3,384,422 ....F 3
Heves, 345,532 ....F 3
Komárom, 283,265 ....E 3
Nógrád, 235,892 ....E 3
Pest, 809,118 ....E 3
Somogy, 366,375 ....D 3
Szabolcs-Szatmár, 568,390 ....G 3
Szolnok, 455,878 ....F 3
Tolna, 261,470 ....E 3
Vas, 280,615 ....D 3
Veszprém, 399,837 ....D 3
Zala, 268,393 ....D 3

CITIES and TOWNS

Aba, 4,369 ....E 3
Abádszalók, 7,257 ....F 3
Abaújszántó, 4,586 ....F 2
Abony, 16,048 ....E 3
Ács, 8,507 ....E 3
Adony, 4,211 ....E 3
Ajka, 16,953 ....D 3
Albertirsa, 11,490 ....E 3
Aszód, 5,361 ....E 3
Bácsalmás, 9,514 ....E 3
Baja, 31,478 ....E 3
Balassagyarmat, 12,410 ....E 2
Balatonfüred, 7,561 ....D 3
Balkány, 8,224 ....G 3
Balmazújváros, 18,645 ....F 3
Barcs, 7,245 ....D 4
Bátaszék, 7,378 ....E 3
Battonya, 11,019 ....F 3
Békés, 21,296 ....F 3
Békéscsaba, 51,242 ....F 3
Berettyóújfalu, 11,577 ....F 3
Berzence, 3,651 ....D 3
Bicske, 9,106 ....E 3
Biharkeresztes, 4,844 ....F 3
Biharnagybajom, 4,762 ....F 3
Böhönye, 3,809 ....D 3
Bonyhád, 9,354 ....E 3
Budafok, 39,870 ....E 3
Budaörs, 12,682 ....E 3
Budapest (cap.), 1,874,947 ....E 3
Cegléd, 37,898 ....E 3
Celldömölk, 9,762 ....D 3
Cigánd, 5,220 ....F 2
Csákvár, 5,135 ....E 3
Csanádpalota, 5,264 ....F 3
Csenger, 4,835 ....G 3
Csepel, 86,287 ....E 3
Csepreg, 4,348 ....D 3
Csongrád, 20,317 ....F 3
Csorna, 9,192 ....D 3
Csorvás, 7,622 ....F 3
Csurgó, 5,400 ....D 3
Debrecen, 136,719 ....F 3
Derecske, 9,980 ....F 3
Dévaványa, 12,137 ....F 3
Devecser, 5,741 ....D 3
Dombóvár, 15,605 ....E 3
Dombrád, 6,868 ....F 2
Dömsöd, 6,532 ....E 3
Dorog, 9,994 ....E 3
Dunaföldvár, 11,039 ....E 3
Dunaharaszti, 13,655 ....E 3
Dunakeszi, 15,636 ....E 3
Dunaújváros, 37,415 ....E 3
Dunavecse, 4,908 ....E 3
Edelény, 6,851 ....F 2
Eger, 40,096 ....F 3
Egyek, 8,678 ....F 3
Elek, 6,325 ....F 3
Emőd, 5,233 ....F 3
Endrőd, 9,263 ....F 3
Enying, 6,406 ....E 3
Ercsi, 7,850 ....E 3
Érd, 25,900 ....E 3
Erdőtelek, 4,634 ....F 3
Esztergom, 24,381 ....E 3
Fegyvernek, 7,835 ....F 3
Fehérgyarmat, 6,024 ....G 3
Földeák, 4,275 ....F 3
Füzesabony, 7,125 ....F 3
Füzesgyarmat, 7,807 ....F 3
Gödöllő, 18,673 ....E 3
Gönc, 3,093 ....F 2
Gyoma, 10,921 ....F 3
Gyöngyös, 29,641 ....E 3
Gyönk, 2,684 ....E 3
Győr, 73,810 ....D 3
Gyula, 24,688 ....F 3
Hajdúböszörmény, 31,668 ....F 3
Hajdudorog, 10,559 ....F 3
Hajduhadház, 13,030 ....F 3
Hajdunánás, 17,926 ....F 3
Hajdusámson, 7,784 ....F 3
Hajduszoboszló, 21,372 ....F 3
Hajós, 5,584 ....E 3
Hatvan, 20,312 ....E 3
Hercegfalva, 4,951 ....E 3
Heves, 11,349 ....F 3
Hogyesz, 3,501 ....E 3
Hódmezővásárhely, 53,185 ....F 3
Izsák, 8,609 ....E 3
Jánoshalma, 12,897 ....E 3
Jánosháza, 3,468 ....D 3
Jászapáti, 10,495 ....F 3
Jászárokszállás, 10,745 ....E 3
Jászberény, 30,314 ....E 3
Jászfényszaru, 7,542 ....E 3
Jászkarajenő, 4,955 ....E 3
Jászkisér, 7,280 ....F 3
Jászladány, 8,841 ....F 3
Kalocsa, 13,797 ....E 3
Kaposvár, 46,316 ....D 3
Kapuvár, 10,748 ....D 3
Karád, 3,438 ....D 3
Karcag, 25,466 ....F 3
Kazincbarcika, 19,571 ....F 2
Kecel, 10,193 ....E 3
Kecskemét, 69,349 ....E 3
Kemecse, 4,681 ....F 2
Keszthely, 15,182 ....D 3
Kisbér, 4,567 ....D 3
Kiskőrös, 12,954 ....E 3
Kiskundorozsma, 8,679 ....E 3
Kiskunfélegyháza, 32,719 ....E 3
Kiskunhalas, 26,841 ....E 3
Kiskunmajsa, 12,311 ....E 3
Kispest, 66,547 ....E 3
Kistelek, 8,925 ....E 3
Kisújszállás, 13,564 ....F 3
Kisvárda, 13,050 ....G 2
Komádi, 9,850 ....F 3
Komárom, 10,141 ....E 3
Komló, 26,513 ....E 3
Kondoros, 7,462 ....F 3
Körmend, 7,548 ....D 3
Köröslađány, 7,302 ....F 3
Kőszeg, 10,195 ....D 3
Kunágota, 5,547 ....F 3
Kunhegyes, 10,792 ....F 3
Kunmadaras, 8,463 ....F 3
Kunszentmárton, 13,383 ....F 3
Kunszentmiklós, 8,198 ....E 3
Lajosmizse, 12,617 ....E 3
Lébény, 3,588 ....D 3
Lengyeltóti, 3,392 ....D 3
Letenye, 4,507 ....D 3
Lőkösháza, 2,511 ....F 3
Lőrinci, 11,142 ....E 3
Madaras, 5,177 ....E 3
Makó, 24,418 ....F 3
Mándok, 4,828 ....G 2
Marcali, 7,877 ....D 3
Mátészalka, 11,496 ....G 3
Mélykút, 8,168 ....E 3
Mezőberény, 12,830 ....F 3
Mezőcsát, 6,583 ....F 3
Mezőhegyes, 9,137 ....F 3
Mezőkövesd, 18,160 ....F 3
Mezőtúr, 23,206 ....F 3
Mindszent, 9,179 ....F 3
Miskolc, 155,214 ....F 2
Mohács, 18,208 ....E 4
Monor, 15,360 ....E 3
Mór, 11,622 ....E 3
Mosonmagyaróvár, 22,288 ....D 3
Nádudvar, 10,006 ....F 3
Nagyatád, 8,791 ....D 3
Nagybajom, 4,972 ....D 3
Nagyecsed, 8,348 ....G 3
Nagyhalász, 6,650 ....F 2
Nagykálló, 11,329 ....F 3
Nagykanizsa, 34,662 ....D 3
Nagykáta, 11,924 ....E 3
Nagykőrös, 25,272 ....E 3
Nagyléta, 6,902 ....F 3
Nagyszénás, 7,439 ....F 3
Nyírábrány, 4,517 ....G 3
Nyíradony, 7,325 ....G 3
Nyírbátor, 10,167 ....G 3
Nyíregyháza, 58,711 ....F 3
Nyírmada, 4,826 ....F 2
Örkény, 5,001 ....E 3
Orosháza, 31,811 ....F 3
Oroszlány, 16,639 ....E 3
Ózd, 37,454 ....F 2
Paks, 11,919 ....E 3
Pannonhalva, 3,529 ....D 3
Pápa, 26,116 ....D 3
Pásztó, 8,091 ....E 3
Pécs, 125,411 ....E 3
Pécsvárad, 3,199 ....E 3
Pétervására, 2,727 ....F 3
Pilis, 8,458 ....E 3
Pilisvörösvár, 9,627 ....E 3
Polgár, 9,353 ....F 3
Püspökladány, 15,488 ....F 3
Putnok, 6,440 ....F 2
Ráckeve, 7,456 ....E 3
Rakamaz, 5,381 ....F 2
Rákospalota, 63,344 ....E 3
Sajószentpéter, 12,846 ....F 2
Salgótarján, 33,130 ....E 2
Sándorfalva, 5,815 ....F 3
Sárbogárd, 6,853 ....E 3
Sarkad, 12,169 ....F 3
Sárospatak, 12,799 ....F 2
Sárvár, 11,247 ....D 3
Sátoraljaújhely, 16,393 ....F 2
Siklós, 5,897 ....E 4
Siófok, 10,322 ....E 3
Solt, 7,199 ....E 3
Soltvadkert, 8,244 ....E 3
Sopron, 43,081 ....D 3
Sümeg, 5,925 ....D 3
Szabadszállás, 8,799 ....E 3
Szarvas, 18,592 ....F 3
Szécsény, 4,410 ....E 2
Szeged, 104,506 ....F 3
Szeghalom, 10,093 ....F 3
Szegvár, 6,970 ....F 3
Székesfehérvár, 59,552 ....E 3
Szekszárd, 20,502 ....E 3
Szendrő, 3,773 ....F 2
Szentendre, 10,880 ....E 3
Szentes, 31,022 ....F 3
Szentgotthárd, 5,421 ....D 3
Szerencs, 7,789 ....F 2
Szigetvár, 7,394 ....D 3
Szikszó, 6,110 ....F 2
Szolnok, 49,565 ....F 3
Szombathely, 56,566 ....D 3
Tab, 4,265 ....D 3
Tamási, 7,689 ....E 3
Tápiószele, 5,632 ....E 3
Tapolca, 8,579 ....D 3
Tarpa, 3,966 ....G 2
Tata, 17,832 ....E 3
Tatabánya, 56,024 ....E 3
Tét, 4,861 ....D 3
Tiszacsege, 7,002 ....F 3
Tiszaföldvár, 12,377 ....F 3
Tiszafüred, 11,214 ....F 3
Tiszakécske, 12,834 ....F 3
Tiszalök, 6,125 ....F 2
Tiszavasvári, 12,201 ....F 3
Tokaj, 5,031 ....F 2
Tolna, 8,741 ....E 3
Törökszentmiklós, 23,556 ....F 3
Tótkomlós, 9,368 ....F 3
Tura, 8,169 ....E 3
Túrkeve, 12,146 ....F 3
Újfehértó, 14,386 ....F
Újpest, 79,961 ....E
Vác, 27,846 ....E
Várpalota, 23,691 ....E
Vásvár, 4,293 ....D
Vecsés, 16,411 ....E
Veszprém, 27,997 ....D
Vésztő, 10,463 ....F
Villány, 2,769 ....E
Zahony, 2,117 ....G
Zalaegerszeg, 25,555 ....D
Zalaszentgrót, 4,470 ....D
Zirc, 5,427 ....D

PHYSICAL FEATURES

Bakony (mts.) ....D 3
Balaton (lake) ....D 3
Berettyó (river) ....F 3
Börsöny (mts.) ....E 3
Csepelsziget (isl.) ....E 3
Danube (river) ....E 3
Dráva (river) ....D 3
Duna (Danube) (river) ....E 3
Fertő Tó (Neusiedler) (lake) ....D 3
Hernád (river) ....F 2
Ipoly (river) ....E 2
Kapos (river) ....E 3
Kékes (mt.) ....E 3
Kőrishegy (mt.) ....D 3
Körös (river) ....F 3
Maros (river) ....F 3
Matra (mts.) ....E 3
Mecsek (mts.) ....D 3
Nagy Alföld (plain) ....E 3
Neusiedler (lake) ....D 3
Rába (river) ....D 3
Sajo (river) ....F 2
Sebes Körös (river) ....F 3
Sió (canal) ....E 3
Szentendreisziget (isl.) ....E 3
Tarna (river) ....F 3
Tisza (river) ....F 3
Zala (river) ....D 3

BALKAN STATES

YUGOSLAVIA

AREA	99,079 sq. mi.
POPULATION	19,503,000
CAPITAL	Belgrade
LARGEST CITY	Belgrade 653,000
HIGHEST POINT	Triglav 9,393 ft.
MONETARY UNIT	Yugoslav dinar
MAJOR LANGUAGES	Serbian-Croatian, Slovenian, Macedonian
MAJOR RELIGIONS	Eastern Orthodox, Roman Catholic

BULGARIA

AREA	42,796 sq. mi.
POPULATION	8,211,000
CAPITAL	Sofia
LARGEST CITY	Sofia (greater) 724,600
HIGHEST POINT	Musala 9,596 ft.
MONETARY UNIT	lev
MAJOR LANGUAGE	Bulgarian
MAJOR RELIGION	Eastern Orthodox

ALBANIA

11,096 sq. mi.
1,867,000
Tiranë
Tiranë 152,500
Korab 9,068 ft.
lek
Albanian

Mohammedan, Eastern Orthodox, Roman Catholic

GREECE

51,182 sq. mi.
8,550,000
Athens
Athens (greater) 1,852,709
Olympus 9,550 ft.
drachma
Greek
Greek Orthodox

RUMANIA

91,671 sq. mi.
19,092,000
Bucharest
Bucharest (greater) 1,366,794
Moldoveanul 8,343 ft.
leu
Rumanian

Rumanian Orthodox

ALBANIA

RUMANIA

YUGOSLAVIA

BULGARIA

GREECE

DOMINANT LAND USE

- Cereals (chiefly wheat, corn)
- Mixed Farming, Horticulture
- Pasture Livestock
- Tobacco, Cotton
- Grapes, Wine
- Forests
- Nonagricultural Land

AGRICULTURE, INDUSTRY and RESOURCES

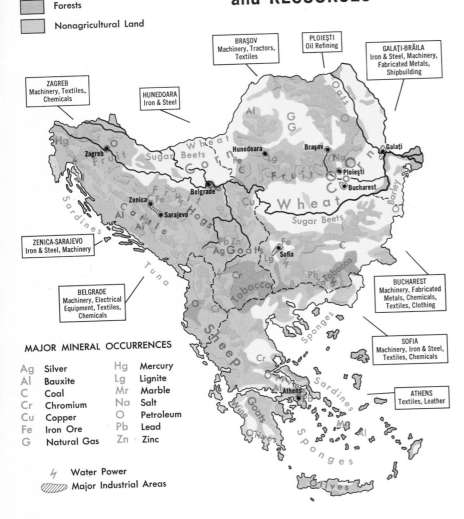

ZAGREB Machinery, Textiles, Chemicals

HUNEDOARA Iron & Steel

BRAŞOV Machinery, Tractors, Textiles

PLOIEŞTI Oil Refining

GALAŢI-BRĂILA Iron & Steel, Machinery, Fabricated Metals, Shipbuilding

ZENICA-SARAJEVO Iron & Steel, Machinery

BELGRADE Machinery, Electrical Equipment, Textiles, Chemicals

BUCHAREST Machinery, Fabricated Metals, Chemicals, Textiles, Clothing

SOFIA Machinery, Iron & Steel, Textiles, Chemicals

ATHENS Textiles, Leather

MAJOR MINERAL OCCURRENCES

Ag	Silver	Hg	Mercury
Al	Bauxite	Lg	Lignite
C	Coal	Mr	Marble
Cr	Chromium	Na	Salt
Cu	Copper	O	Petroleum
Fe	Iron Ore	Pb	Lead
G	Natural Gas	Zn	Zinc

Water Power
Major Industrial Areas

ALBANIA

CITIES and TOWNS

Berat, 21,000	D 5
Bicaj	D 6
Delvinë, 5,525	D 6
Durrës, 45,935	D 5
Elbasan, 34,100	E 5
Fier, 17,050	D 5
Frashër	E 5
Gjinokastër, 14,400	D 5
Himarë	D 5
Kavajë, 17,225	D 5
Klos	E 5
Konispol	E 6
Korçë, 42,550	E 5
Kruë, 6,575	D 5
Kucovë (Stalin), 11,700	D 5
Kukës, 3,425	E 4
Leskovik, 1,625	E 5
Lezh, 2,800	D 5
Lushnje, 15,050	D 5
Peqin, 3,700	D 5
Përmet, 3,900	E 5
Peshkopi, 4,975	E 5
Pogradec, 8,585	E 4
Pukë, 1,535	E 6
Sarandë, 7,375	D 5
Shëngjin, 900	D 5
Shijak, 4,850	D 5
Shkodër, 45,925	D 5
Stalin, 11,700	D 5
Tepelenë, 2,340	D 5
Tiranë (Tirana) (cap.), 152,500	E 5
Tropojë	D 4
Vlonë, 45,350	D 5

PHYSICAL FEATURES

Drin (riv.)	E 4
Korab (mt.)	E 5
Ohrid (lake)	E 5
Otranto (str.)	D 5
Prespa (lake)	E 5
Saseno (isl.)	D 5
Scutari (lake)	D 4
Tomor (mt.)	E 5
Vijosë (riv.)	D 5

BULGARIA

CITIES and TOWNS

Akhtopol, 1,049	H 4
Alfatar, 4,049	H 4
Ardino, 2,556	G 5
Asenovgrad, 25,319	H 4
Aytos, 14,003	H 4
Balchik, 7,990	J 4
Bansko, 6,842	F 5
Belogradchik, 3,452	F 4
Berkovitsa, 9,059	F 4
Blagoyevgrad, 21,936	F 5
Botevgrad, 8,683	F 4
Bregovo, 4,992	F 3
Breznik, 3,486	F 4
Burgas, 72,795	H 4
Byala, 7,884	G 4
Byala Slatina, 13,502	F 4
Chirpan, 15,501	G 4
Devin, 3,602	G 5
Dimitrovgrad, 34,389	G 4
Dobrich (Tolbukhin), 42,815	H 4
Dryanovo, 5,400	G 4
Elena, 4,092	G 4
Elkhovo, 10,339	H 4
Gabrovo, 38,032	G 4
General Toshevo, 5,982	H 4
Godech, 2,933	F 4
Gorna Dzhumaya (Blagoyevgrad), 21,936	F 5
Gorna Oryakhovitsa, 18,907	G 4
Gotse Delchev, 12,526	F 5
Grudevo, 7,733	G 4
Ikhtiman, 9,123	F 4
Isperikh, 6,788	H 4
Ivaylovgrad, 2,918	H 5
Kara-pelit, 2,033	H 4
Kavarna, 7,112	J 4
Kazanlŭk, 31,133	G 4
Kharmanlii, 12,577	H 5
Khaskovo, 39,006	G 5
Kolarovgrad, 41,670	H 4
Kotel, 5,881	H 4
Krumovgrad, 2,232	G 5
Kubrat, 6,559	H 4
Kula, 6,467	F 4
Kŭrdzhali, 21,018	G 5
Kyustendil, 24,876	F 4
Levskigrad, 12,679	G 4
Lom, 23,015	F 4
Lovech, 17,963	G 4
Lukovit, 8,812	G 4
Malko Tŭrnovo, 3,746	H 4
Maritsa, 7,167	H 4
Michurin, 2,794	H 4
Mikhaylovgrad, 13,434	F 4
Momchilgrad, 4,307	G 5
Nesebŭr, 2,340	H 4
Nikopol, 5,788	G 4
Nova Zagora, 14,913	G 4
Novi Pazar, 9,149	H 4
Novoseltsi, 4,060	H 4
Omortag, 6,145	H 4
Oryakhovo, 8,136	F 4
Panagyurishte, 14,038	F 4
Pazardzhik, 39,520	F 4
Pernik, 59,721	F 4
Peshtera, 13,921	G 4
Petrich, 16,462	F 5
Pirdop, 5,570	G 4
Pleven, 57,758	G 4
Plovdiv, 198,200	G 4
Polyanovgrad, 14,551	H 4
Pomorie, 6,020	H 4
Popina, 2,713	H 3
Popovo, 10,650	H 4
Provadiya, 12,426	H 4
Radomir, 6,709	F 4
Razgrad, 18,416	H 4
Razlog, 8,652	F 5
Rositsa, 1,514	H 4
Ruse, 117,500	H 4
Samokov, 16,919	F 4
Sandanski, 10,554	F 5
Sevlievo, 14,420	G 4
Shabla, 3,739	J 4
Shumen (Kolarovgrad), 41,670	H 4
Silistra, 20,491	H 3
Simeonovgrad (Maritsa), 7,167	H 4
Sliven, 46,383	H 4
Smedovo, 5,941	H 4
Smolyan, 5,095	G 5
Sofia (cap.), 591,685	F 4
Sofia, *724,600	F 4
Sozopol, 3,265	H 4
Stanke Dimitrov, 25,137	F 4
Stara Zagora, 55,322	G 4
Sveti Vrach (Sandanski), 10,554	F 5
Svilengrad, 11,001	G 5
Svishtov, 18,537	G 4
Teteven, 7,799	G 4
Tolbukhin, 42,815	H 4
Topolovgrad, 6,970	H 4
Troyan, 9,973	G 4
Trŭn, 2,923	F 4
Tŭrgovishte, 14,241	H 4
Tŭrnovo, 24,751	G 4
Tutrakan, 9,577	H 3
Vidin, 23,984	F 4
Vratsa, 26,592	F 4
Yambol, 42,038	H 4
Zimnitsa, 2,315	H 4
Zlatograd, 4,522	G 5

PHYSICAL FEATURES

Balkan (mts.)	G 4
Black (sea)	J 4
Bogdan (mt.)	G 4
Danube (Dunav) (riv.)	H 4
Emine (cape)	J 4
Iskŭr (riv.)	G 4
Kaliakra (cape)	J 4
Lom (riv.)	F 4
Maritsa (riv.)	H 5
Mesta (riv.)	F 5
Midzhur (mt.)	F 4
Murgash (mt.)	F 4
Musala (mt.)	F 4
Osŭm (riv.)	G 4
Perelik (mt.)	G 5
Rhodope (mts.)	F 4
Ruyen (mt.)	F 4
Struma (riv.)	F 5
Timok (riv.)	F 3
Tundzha (riv.)	G 4
Vit (riv.)	G 4

GREECE

REGIONS

Aegean Islands, 477,476	G 6
Áyion Óros, 2,687	G 5
Central Greece and Euboea, 2,823,658	F 6
Crete, 483,258	G 8
Epirus, 352,604	D 6
Ionian Islands, 212,573	D 6
Macedonia, 1,890,654	F 5
Pelopónnisos, 1,096,390	F 7
Thessalía, 695,385	F 6
Thrace, 356,555	G 5

CITIES and TOWNS

Agrínion, 24,763	E 6
Aíyina, 4,989	F 7
Áyion Óros, 17,762	F 6
Alexandroúpolis, 18,712	H 5
Alivérion, 3,523	G 6
Almirós, 6,010	F 6
Amaliás, 15,468	E 7
Amfilokhía, 5,408	E 6
Ámfissa, 6,076	F 6
Ándissa, 2,530	G 6
Andravídha, 3,155	E 6
Ándros, 2,032	G 7
Áno Viánnos, 1,820	G 8
Anóyia, 2,461	F 5
Ardhéa, 3,222	F 5
Areópolis, 834	F 7
Argalastí, 1,864	F 6
Argos, 16,712	F 7
Argostólion, 7,322	J 2
Arkhángelos, 2,918	J 2
Arnaía, 2,612	F 5
Árta, 16,899	E 7
Astipálaia, 1,205	H 7
Atalándi, 4,552	F 6
Athens, *627,564	F 7
Athens, *1,852,709	F 7
Ayiá, 3,067	F 6
Áyios Kírikos, 998	H 7
Áyios Matthaíos, 1,892	D 6
Áyios Nikólaos, 3,709	G 8
Candia (Iráklion), 63,458	G 8
Canea (Khaniá), 38,467	F 8
Chalcis (Khalkís), 24,745	F 6
Corinth, 15,892	F 7
Delvinákion, 1,076	E 6
Dhidhimótikhon, 7,287	H 5
Dhíkaia, 1,181	H 4
Dhimitsána, 1,300	F 7
Dhomokós, 2,017	F 6
Dráma, 32,195	G 5
Édhessa, 15,534	F 5
Elassón, 6,501	F 6
Eleftheroúpolis, 5,448	G 5
Ermoúpolis, 14,402	G 7
Fársala, 6,356	F 6
Filiátes, 3,065	E 6
Filiatrá, 6,753	E 7
Flórina, 11,933	E 5
Gargaliánoi, 6,637	E 7
Grevená, 6,892	E 6
Idhra, 2,546	F 7
Ierápetra, 6,488	G 8
Igoumenítsa, 3,235	E 6
Ioánnina, 34,997	E 6
Iráklion, 63,458	G 8
Istiaía, 3,882	F 6
Itháki, 2,632	E 6
Kalámai, 38,211	F 7
Kalampáka, 4,640	E 6
Kalávrita, 2,039	F 7
Kálimnos, 10,211	H 7
Kándanos, 337	F 8
Kardhítsa, 23,708	F 6
Kariá, 1,739	E 6
Karíai, 429	G 5
Káristos, 3,335	G 7
Karpeníson, 3,523	E 6
Kastéllion, 1,351	F 8
Kastéllion, 2,071	G 8
Kastoría, 10,162	E 5
Katákolon, 873	E 7
Katerini, 28,046	F 5

(continued on following page)

Balkan States

(continued)

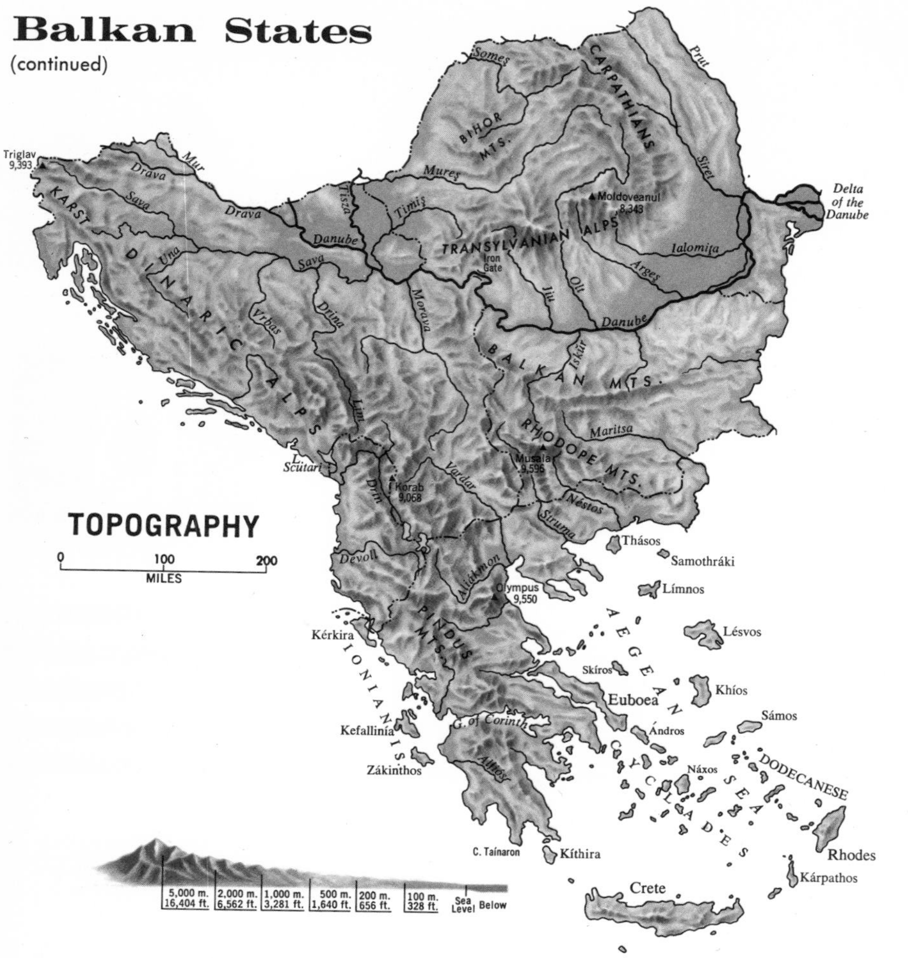

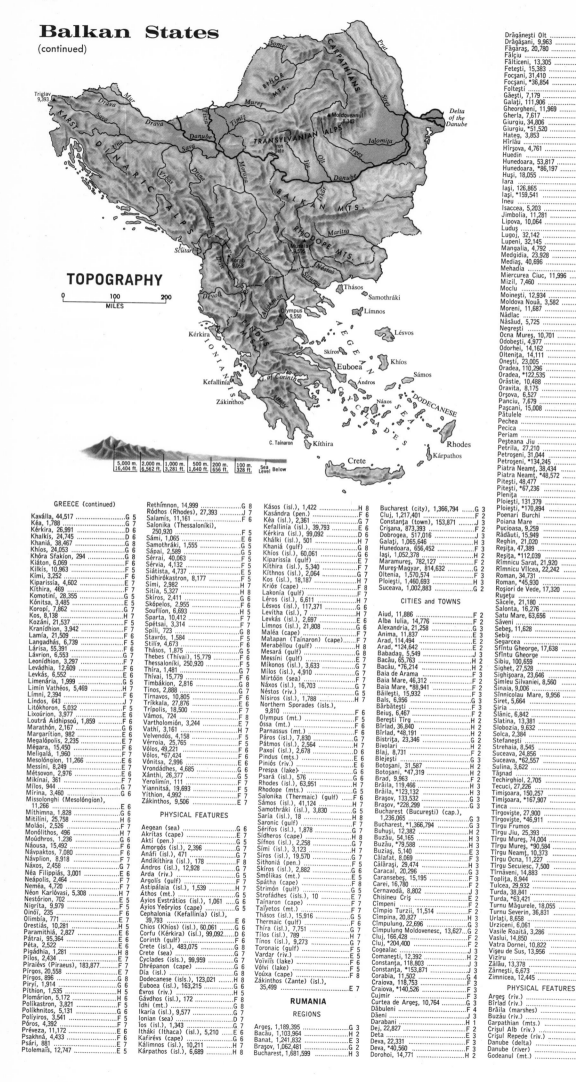

Triglav 9,393
Mur
Drava
Sava
KARST
DINARIC ALPS
Una
Vrbas
Drina
Danube
Tisza
Timiş
Mureş
Someş
BIHOR MTS.
CARPATHIANS
Prut
Siret
Moldoveanul 8,343
TRANSYLVANIAN ALPS
Ialomiţa
Argeş
Olt
Jiu
Iron Gate
Morava
Iskŭr
BALKAN MTS.
Maritsa
RHODOPE MTS.
Musala 9,596
Vardar
Lim
Scutari
Korab 9,068
Drin
Devoll
Nestos
Struma
Thásos
Samothráki
Límnos
Olympus 9,550
Aliákmon
PINDUS MTS.
Kérkira
IONIAN SEA
AEGEAN SEA
Lésvos
Skíros
Euboea
Khíos
Sámos
Kefallinía
Zákinthos
G. of Corinth
Ándros
Náxos
CYCLADES
DODECANESE
C. Taínaron
Kíthira
Rhodes
Kárpathos
Crete
Delta of the Danube
TOPOGRAPHY
0 100 200
MILES
5,000 m. 16,404 ft.
2,000 m. 6,562 ft.
1,000 m. 3,281 ft.
500 m. 1,640 ft.
200 m. 656 ft.
100 m. 328 ft.
Sea Level
Below

GREECE (continued)

Kaválla, 44,517 ....G 5
Kéa, 1,788 ....G 7
Kérkira, 26,991 ....D 6
Khalkís, 24,745 ....D 6
Khaniá, 38,467 ....G 8
Khíos, 24,053 ....G 6
Khóra Sfakíon, 294 ....G 8
Kiáton, 6,069 ....F 6
Kilkís, 10,963 ....F 5
Kími, 3,252 ....F 6
Kiparissía, 4,602 ....E 7
Kíthira, 469 ....F 7
Komotiní, 28,355 ....G 5
Kónitsa, 3,485 ....E 5
Koropí, 7,862 ....G 7
Kos, 8,138 ....H 7
Kozáni, 21,537 ....F 5
Kranídhion, 3,942 ....F 7
Lamía, 21,509 ....F 6
Langadhás, 6,739 ....F 5
Lárisa, 55,391 ....F 6
Lávrion, 6,553 ....G 7
Leonídhion, 3,297 ....F 7
Levádhia, 12,609 ....F 6
Levkás, 6,552 ....E 6
Limenária, 1,999 ....G 5
Limín Vathéos, 5,469 ....H 7
Límni, 2,394 ....F 6
Líndos, 643 ....J 7
Litókhoron, 5,032 ....F 5
Lixoúrion, 3,977 ....E 6
Loutrá Aidhipsoú, 1,859 ....F 6
Marathón, 2,167 ....G 6
Margarítion, 982 ....E 6
Megalópolis, 2,235 ....E 7
Mégara, 15,450 ....F 6
Meligalá, 1,960 ....F 7
Mesolóngion, 11,266 ....E 6
Messíni, 8,249 ....E 7
Métsovon, 2,976 ....E 6
Mikínai, 361 ....F 7
Mílos, 944 ....G 7
Mírina, 3,460 ....G 6
Missolonghi (Mesolóngion), 11,266 ....E 6
Míthimna, 1,828 ....G 6
Mitilíni, 25,758 ....H 6
Moláoi, 2,526 ....F 7
Monólithos, 496 ....H 7
Moúdhros, 1,236 ....G 6
Náousa, 15,492 ....F 6
Návpaktos, 7,080 ....F 6
Návplion, 8,918 ....F 7
Náxos, 2,458 ....G 7
Néa Filippiás, 3,001 ....E 6
Neápolis, 2,464 ....F 7
Neméa, 4,720 ....F 7
Néon Karlóvasi, 5,308 ....H 7
Nestórion, 702 ....E 5
Nigríta, 9,979 ....F 5
Oinóï, 235 ....F 6
Olimbía, 771 ....E 7
Orestiás, 10,281 ....H 5
Paramithiá, 2,827 ....E 6
Pátrai, 95,364 ....E 6
Péta, 2,522 ....E 6
Pigádhia, 1,281 ....H 8
Pílos, 2,434 ....E 7
Piraiévs (Piraeus), 183,877....F 7
Pírgos, 20,558 ....E 7
Pírgos, 896 ....G 8
Piryí, 1,914 ....G 6
Píthion, 1,535 ....H 5
Plomárion, 5,172 ....H 6
Políkastron, 3,821 ....F 5
Políkhnitos, 5,131 ....G 6
Políyiros, 3,541 ....F 5
Póros, 4,392 ....F 7
Préveza, 11,172 ....E 6
Psakhná, 4,433 ....F 6
Psári, 881 ....E 7
Ptolemaïs, 12,747 ....E 5
Rethímnon, 14,999 ....G 8
Ródhos (Rhodes), 27,393 ....J 7
Salamís, 11,161 ....F 6
Salonika (Thessaloníki), 250,920 ....F 5
Sámi, 1,065 ....E 6
Samothráki, 1,555 ....G 5
Sápai, 2,589 ....G 5
Sérrai, 40,063 ....F 5
Sérvia, 4,132 ....F 5
Siátista, 4,737 ....E 5
Sidhirókastron, 8,177 ....F 5
Sími, 2,982 ....H 7
Sitía, 5,327 ....H 8
Skíros, 2,411 ....G 6
Skópelos, 2,955 ....F 6
Souflíon, 6,693 ....H 5
Sparta, 10,412 ....F 7
Spétsai, 3,314 ....F 7
Spíli, 723 ....G 8
Stavrós, 1,584 ....F 5
Stilís, 4,673 ....F 6
Thásos, 1,875 ....G 5
Thebes (Thívai), 15,779 ....F 6
Thessaloníki, 250,920 ....F 5
Thíra, 1,481 ....G 7
Thívai, 15,779 ....F 6
Timbákion, 2,816 ....G 8
Tínos, 2,888 ....G 7
Tírnavos, 10,805 ....F 6
Tríkkala, 27,876 ....E 6
Trípolis, 18,500 ....F 7
Vámos, 724 ....F 8
Vartholomión, 3,244 ....E 7
Vathí, 3,161 ....H 7
Velvendós, 4,158 ....F 5
Vérroia, 25,765 ....F 5
Vólos, 49,221 ....F 6
Vólos, *67,424 ....F 6
Vónitsa, 2,996 ....E 6
Vrondádhes, 4,685 ....G 6
Xánthi, 26,377 ....G 5
Yerolimín, 111 ....F 7
Yiannitsá, 19,693 ....F 5
Yíthion, 4,992 ....F 7
Zákinthos, 9,506 ....E 7

PHYSICAL FEATURES

Aegean (sea) ....G 6
Akrítas (cape) ....E 7
Aktí (pen.) ....G 5
Amorgós (isl.), 2,396 ....G 7
Anáfi (isl.), 471 ....G 7
Andikíthira (isl.), 178 ....F 8
Ándros (isl.), 12,928 ....G 7
Arda (riv.) ....G 5
Argolís (gulf) ....F 7
Astipálaia (isl.), 1,539 ....H 7
Áthos (mt.) ....G 5
Áyios Evstrátios (isl.), 1,061 ....G 6
Áyios Yeóryios (cape) ....G 5
Cephalonia (Kefallinía) (isl.), 39,793 ....E 6
Chios (Khíos) (isl.), 60,061 ....G 6
Corfu (Kérkira) (isl.), 99,092....D 6
Corinth (gulf) ....F 6
Crete (isl.), 483,075 ....G 8
Crete (sea) ....G 7
Cyclades (isls.), 99,959 ....G 7
Dhrépanon (cape) ....G 6
Día (isl.) ....G 8
Dodecanese (isls.), 123,021 ....H 8
Euboea (isl.), 163,215 ....G 6
Évros (riv.) ....H 5
Gávdhos (isl.), 172 ....F 8
Ídhi (mt.) ....G 8
Ikaría (isl.), 9,577 ....G 7
Ionian (sea) ....D 7
Íos (isl.), 1,343 ....G 7
Itháki (Ithaca) (isl.), 5,210 ....E 6
Kafirévs (cape) ....G 6
Kálimnos (isl.), 10,211 ....H 7
Kárpathos (isl.), 6,689 ....H 8
Kásos (isl.), 1,422 ....H 8
Kasándra (pen.) ....F 6
Kéa (isl.), 2,361 ....G 7
Kefallinía (isl.), 39,793 ....E 6
Kérkira (isl.), 99,092 ....D 6
Khálki (isl.), 501 ....H 7
Khaniá (gulf) ....G 8
Khíos (isl.), 60,061 ....G 6
Kiparissía (gulf) ....E 7
Kíthira (isl.), 5,340 ....F 7
Kíthnos (isl.), 2,064 ....G 7
Kos (isl.), 18,187 ....H 7
Kriós (cape) ....F 8
Lakonía (gulf) ....F 7
Léros (isl.), 6,611 ....H 7
Lésvos (isl.), 117,371 ....G 6
Levítha (isl.), 7 ....H 7
Levkás (isl.), 2,697 ....E 6
Límnos (isl.), 21,808 ....G 6
Maléa (cape) ....F 7
Matapan (Taínaron) (cape)....F 7
Merabéllou (gulf) ....H 8
Mesará (gulf) ....G 8
Messíni (gulf) ....E 7
Míkonos (isl.), 3,633 ....G 7
Mílos (isl.), 4,910 ....G 7
Mirtóön (sea) ....F 7
Náxos (isl.), 16,703 ....G 7
Néstos (riv.) ....G 5
Nísiros (isl.), 1,788 ....H 7
Northern Sporades (isls.), 9,810 ....F 6
Olympus (mt.) ....F 5
Óssa (mt.) ....F 6
Parnassus (mt.) ....F 6
Páros (isl.), 7,830 ....G 7
Pátmos (isl.), 2,564 ....H 7
Paxoí (isl.), 2,678 ....D 6
Pindus (mts.) ....E 6
Piniós (riv.) ....E 6
Prespa (lake) ....G 6
Psará (isl.), 576 ....G 6
Rhodes (isl.), 63,951 ....H 7
Rhodope (mts.) ....G 5
Salonika (Thermaic) (gulf) ....F 6
Sámos (isl.), 41,124 ....H 7
Samothráki (isl.), 3,830 ....G 5
Saría (isl.), 18 ....H 8
Saronic (gulf) ....F 7
Sérifos (isl.), 1,878 ....G 7
Sídheros (cape) ....H 8
Sífnos (isl.), 2,258 ....G 7
Sími (isl.), 3,123 ....H 7
Síros (isl.), 19,570 ....G 7
Sithoniá (pen.) ....F 5
Skíros (isl.), 2,882 ....G 6
Smólikas (mt.) ....E 5
Spátha (cape) ....F 8
Strimón (gulf) ....G 5
Strofádhes (isls.), 10 ....E 7
Taínaron (cape) ....F 7
Taïyetos (mt.) ....F 7
Thásos (isl.), 15,916 ....G 5
Thermaic (gulf) ....F 6
Thíra (isl.), 7,751 ....G 7
Tílos (isl.), 789 ....H 7
Tínos (isl.), 9,273 ....G 7
Toronaic (gulf) ....F 5
Vardar (riv.) ....E 5
Voïviïs (lake) ....F 6
Vólvi (lake) ....F 5
Voúxa (cape) ....F 8
Zákinthos (Zante) (isl.), 35,499 ....E 7

RUMANIA

REGIONS

Argeş, 1,189,395 ....G 3
Bacău, 1,103,964 ....H 2
Banat, 1,241,832 ....E 3
Braşov, 1,062,481 ....G 2
Bucharest, 1,681,599 ....H 3
Bucharest (city), 1,366,794 ....G 3
Cluj, 1,217,401 ....F 2
Constanţa (town), 153,871 ....J 3
Crişana, 873,393 ....F 2
Dobrogea, 517,016 ....J 3
Galaţi, 1,065,646 ....H 3
Hunedoara, 656,452 ....F 3
Iaşi, 1,052,378 ....H 2
Maramureş, 782,127 ....F 2
Mureş-Magyar, 814,632 ....G 2
Oltenia, 1,570,574 ....F 3
Ploieşti, 1,460,693 ....H 3
Suceava, 1,002,883 ....G 2

CITIES and TOWNS

Aiud, 11,886 ....F 2
Alba Iulia, 14,776 ....F 2
Alexandria, 21,258 ....G 3
Anima, 11,837 ....E 3
Arad, 114,494 ....E 2
Arad, *124,642 ....E 2
Babadag, 5,549 ....J 3
Bacău, 65,763 ....H 2
Bacău, *76,214 ....H 2
Baia de Arama ....F 3
Baia Mare, 46,312 ....F 2
Baia Mare, *88,941 ....F 2
Băileşti, 15,932 ....F 3
Bals, 6,956 ....G 3
Bărbăteşti ....F 3
Beiuş, 6,467 ....F 2
Bereşti Tîrg ....H 2
Bîrlad, 36,840 ....H 2
Bîrlad, *48,191 ....H 2
Bistriţa, 23,346 ....G 2
Bivolari ....H 2
Blaj, 8,731 ....F 2
Blejeşti ....G 3
Botoşani, 31,587 ....H 2
Botoşani, *47,319 ....H 2
Brad, 9,963 ....F 2
Brăila, 119,466 ....H 3
Brăila, *123,132 ....H 3
Braşov, 133,532 ....G 3
Braşov, *228,299 ....G 3
Bucharest (Bucureşti) (cap.), 1,236,065 ....G 3
Bucharest, *1,366,794 ....G 3
Buhuşi, 12,382 ....H 2
Buzău, 54,165 ....H 3
Buzău, *79,588 ....H 3
Buziaş, 5,140 ....E 3
Călafat, 8,069 ....F 3
Călăraşi, 29,474 ....H 3
Caracal, 20,296 ....G 3
Caransebeş, 15,195 ....F 3
Carei, 16,780 ....F 2
Cernavodă, 8,802 ....J 3
Chisineu Criş ....E 2
Cîmpeni ....F 2
Cîmpio Turzii, 11,514 ....F 2
Cîmpina, 20,827 ....H 3
Cîmpulung, 22,696 ....G 3
Cîmpulung Moldovenesc, 13,627...G 2
Cluj, 166,428 ....F 2
Cluj, *204,400 ....F 2
Cogealac ....J 3
Comaneşti, 12,392 ....H 2
Constanţa, 118,803 ....J 3
Constanţa, *153,871 ....J 3
Corabia, 11,502 ....G 4
Craiova, 118,753 ....F 3
Craiova, *140,526 ....F 3
Cujmir ....F 3
Curtea de Argeş, 10,764 ....G 3
Dăbuleni ....F 4
Dăeni ....J 3
Darabani ....H 1
Dej, 22,827 ....F 2
Deta ....E 3
Deva, 22,331 ....F 3
Deva, *40,560 ....F 3
Dorohoi, 14,771 ....H 2
Drăgăneşti Olt ....G 3
Drăgăşani, 9,963 ....F 3
Făgăraş, 20,780 ....G 3
Fălçiu ....J 2
Fălticeni, 13,305 ....H 2
Feteşti, 15,383 ....H 3
Focşani, 31,410 ....H 3
Focşani, *36,854 ....H 3
Folteşti ....H 3
Găeşti, 7,179 ....G 3
Galaţi, 111,906 ....H 3
Gheorgheni, 11,969 ....G 2
Gherla, 7,617 ....G 2
Giurgiu, 34,806 ....G 3
Giurgiu, *51,520 ....G 3
Hateg, 3,853 ....F 3
Hîrlău ....H 2
Hîrşova, 4,761 ....J 3
Huedin ....F 2
Hunedoara, 53,817 ....F 3
Hunedoara, *86,197 ....F 3
Huşi, 18,055 ....J 2
Iara ....F 2
Iaşi, 126,865 ....H 2
Iaşi, *159,541 ....H 2
Ineu ....E 2
Isaccea, 5,203 ....J 3
Jimbolia, 11,281 ....E 3
Lipova, 10,064 ....E 2
Luduş ....G 2
Lugoj, 32,142 ....F 3
Lupeni, 32,145 ....F 3
Mangalia, 4,792 ....J 4
Medgidia, 23,928 ....J 3
Mediaş, 40,696 ....G 2
Mehadia ....F 3
Miercurea Ciuc, 11,996 ....G 2
Mizil, 7,460 ....H 3
Moclu ....G 2
Moineşti, 12,934 ....H 2
Moldova Nouă, 3,582 ....E 3
Moreni, 11,687 ....G 3
Nădlac ....F 2
Năsăud, 5,725 ....G 2
Negreşti ....H 2
Ocna Mureş, 10,701 ....G 2
Odobeşti, 4,977 ....H 3
Odorhei, 14,162 ....G 2
Olteniţa, 14,111 ....H 3
Oneşti, 23,005 ....H 2
Oradea, 110,296 ....E 2
Oradea, *122,535 ....E 2
Orăstie, 10,488 ....F 3
Oravita, 8,175 ....E 3
Orşova, 6,527 ....F 3
Panciu, 7,679 ....H 3
Paşcani, 15,008 ....H 2
Pătulele ....F 3
Pechea ....H 3
Pecica ....E 2
Periam ....E 2
Peşteana Jiu ....F 3
Petrila, 27,210 ....F 3
Petroşeni, 31,044 ....F 3
Petroşeni, *134,245 ....F 3
Piatra Neamţ, 38,434 ....G 2
Piatra Neamţ, *48,572 ....G 2
Piteşti, 48,477 ....G 3
Piteşti, *67,236 ....G 3
Pleniţa ....F 3
Ploieşti, 131,379 ....H 3
Ploieşti, *170,894 ....H 3
Poenari Burchi ....G 3
Poiana Mare ....F 4
Pucioasa, 9,259 ....G 3
Rădăuti, 15,949 ....G 2
Reghin, 21,020 ....G 2
Reşiţa, 47,389 ....E 3
Reşiţa, *112,039 ....E 3
Rîmnicu Sarat, 21,920 ....H 3
Rîmnicu Vîlcea, 22,242 ....F 3
Roman, 34,731 ....H 2
Roman, *45,930 ....H 2
Roşiori de Vede, 17,320 ....G 3
Ruşeţu ....H 3
Săcele, 21,180 ....G 3
Salonta, 16,276 ....E 3
Satu Mare, 63,656 ....F 2
Săveni ....H 1
Sebeş, 11,628 ....F 3
Sebiş ....F 2
Segarcea ....F 3
Sfîntu Gheorge, 17,638 ....G 3
Sfîntu Gheorge ....J 3
Sibiu, 100,659 ....G 3
Sighet, 27,528 ....F 2
Sighişoara, 23,646 ....G 2
Şimleu Silvaniei, 8,560 ....F 2
Sinaia, 9,006 ....G 3
Sînnicolau Mare, 9,956 ....E 2
Siret, 5,664 ....G 1
Şiria ....E 2
Slănic, 6,842 ....G 3
Slatina, 13,381 ....G 3
Slobozia, 9,632 ....H 3
Solca, 2,384 ....G 2
Stefaneşti ....H 2
Strehaia, 8,545 ....F 3
Suceava, 24,856 ....G 2
Suceava, *62,557 ....G 2
Sulina, 3,622 ....J 3
Tăşnad ....F 2
Techirghiol, 2,705 ....J 3
Tecuci, 27,226 ....H 3
Timişoara, 150,257 ....E 3
Timişoara, *167,907 ....E 3
Tinca ....F 2
Tîrgovişte, 27,900 ....G 3
Tîrgovişte, *46,911 ....G 3
Tîrgu Frumos ....H 2
Tîrgu Jiu, 25,393 ....F 3
Tîrgu Mureş, 74,004 ....G 2
Tîrgu Mureş, *90,584 ....G 2
Tîrgu Neamţ, 10,373 ....G 2
Tîrgu Ocna, 11,227 ....H 2
Tîrgu Secuiesc, 7,500 ....H 2
Tîrnăveni, 14,883 ....F 2
Topliţa, 8,944 ....G 2
Tulcea, 29,932 ....J 3
Turda, 38,841 ....G 2
Turda, *63,421 ....G 2
Turnu Măgurele, 18,055 ....G 4
Turnu Severin, 36,831 ....F 3
Urlaţi, 8,658 ....H 3
Urziceni, 6,061 ....H 3
Vasile Roaită, 3,286 ....J 3
Vaslui, 14,850 ....H 2
Vatra Dornei, 10,822 ....G 2
Vişeu de Sus, 13,956 ....F 2
Viziru ....H 3
Zălău, 13,378 ....F 2
Zărneşti, 6,673 ....G 3
Zimnicea, 12,445 ....G 4

PHYSICAL FEATURES

Argeş (riv.) ....G 3
Bîrlad (riv.) ....H 2
Brăila (marshes) ....H 3
Buzău (riv.) ....H 3
Carpathian (mts.) ....G 2
Crişul Alb (riv.) ....F 2
Crişul Repede (riv.) ....F 2
Danube (delta) ....J 3
Danube (river) ....H 4
Godeanul (mt.) ....F 3
Ialomiţa (marshes) ....J 3
Ialomiţa (riv.) ....H 3
Jijia (riv.) ....H 2
Jiu (riv.) ....F 3
La Omu (mt.) ....G 3
Moldoveanul (mt.) ....G 3
Mureş (riv.) ....E 2
Negoiul (mt.) ....G 3
Olt (riv.) ....G 3
Pietrosul (mt.) ....G 2
Prut (riv.) ....J 2
Retezat (mt.) ....F 3
Siret (riv.) ....H 2
Someş (riv.) ....F 2
Timiş (riv.) ....E 3
Tîrnava Mare (riv.) ....G 2
Transylvanian Alps (mts.) ....G 3

YUGOSLAVIA

INTERNAL DIVISIONS

Bosnia and Hercegovina (rep.), 3,277,948 ....C 3
Croatia (rep.), 4,159,696 ....C 3
Kosovo-Mitohiyan (aut. prov.), 963,988 ....E 4
Macedonia (rep.), 1,406,003 ....E 5
Montenegro (rep.), 471,894....D 4
Serbia (rep.), 7,642,227 ....E 3
Slovenia (rep.), 1,591,523 ....B 2
Voyvodina (aut. prov.), 1,854,965 ....D 3

CITIES and TOWNS

Aleksinac, 8,828 ....E 4
Apatin, 17,000 ....D 3
Bačka Topola, 14,000 ....D 3
Banja Luka, 55,000 ....C 3
Bar, 2,184 ....D 4
Bečej, 22,000 ....E 3
Bela Crkva, 11,000 ....E 3
Belgrade (Beograd) (cap.), 653,000 ....E 3
Bihać, 17,000 ....B 3
Bijeljina, 19,000 ....D 3
Bijelo Polje, 5,856 ....D 4
Bileća, 2,491 ....D 4
Biograd, 2,418 ....B 4
Bitola (Bitolj), 52,000 ....E 5
Bjelovar, 16,000 ....C 3
Bled, 4,156 ....A 2
Bor, 19,000 ....E 3
Bosanska Dubica, 6,259 ....C 3
Bosanska Gradiška, 6,363 ....C 3
Bosanska Kostajnica, 2,034 ....B 3
Bosanska Krupa, 6,191 ....C 3
Bosanski Brod, 7,350 ....D 3
Bosanski Novi, 7,023 ....C 3
Bosanski Petrovac, 3,473 ....C 3
Bosanski Šamac, 3,654 ....D 3
Brčko, 20,000 ....D 3
Brežice, 2,641 ....B 3
Brod, 30,000 ....D 3
Bugojno, 5,453 ....C 3
Buje, 1,955 ....A 3
Čačak, 30,000 ....F 4
Čapljina, 3,275 ....C 4
Caribrod (Dimitrovgrad), 3,665...F 4
Cazin, 795 ....B 3
Celje, 28,000 ....B 2
Cetinje, 9,359 ....D 4
Ćuprija, 12,000 ....E 4
Debar, 6,323 ....E 5
Derventa, 9,843 ....C 3
Dimitrovgrad, 3,665 ....F 4
Djakovica, 22,000 ....E 4
Djakovo, 13,000 ....D 3
Donji Vakuf, 3,764 ....C 3
Drvar, 3,646 ....C 3
Dubrovnik, 24,000 ....C 4
Fiume (Rijeka), 108,000 ....B 3
Foča, 6,763 ....D 4
Fojnica, 1,549 ....C 4
Gacko, 1,368 ....D 4
Gevgelija, 7,332 ....F 5
Glamoč, 1,626 ....C 3
Gnjilane, 14,000 ....E 4
Gornji Vakuf, 1,860 ....C 4
Gospić, 6,767 ....B 3
Gostivar, 14,000 ....E 5
Gračac, 2,183 ....B 3
Gračanica, 7,656 ....D 3
Gradačac, 5,878 ....D 3
Grubišno Polje, 2,655 ....C 3
Gusinje, 2,756 ....D 4
Hercegnovi, 3,797 ....D 4
Ivangrad, 6,969 ....E 4
Jajce, 6,853 ....C 3
Jesenice, 16,000 ....A 2
Kamnik, 5,062 ....B 2
Kanjiža, 10,000 ....D 2
Kardeljevo, 3,267 ....C 4
Karlovac, 35,000 ....B 3
Kastav, 776 ....B 3
Kavadarci, 13,000 ....E 5
Kičevo, 11,000 ....E 5
Kikinda, 32,000 ....E 3
Kladanj, 2,825 ....D 3
Ključ, 2,320 ....C 3
Knin, 5,116 ....C 3
Knjaževac, 7,448 ....F 4
Kočevje, 5,819 ....B 3
Konjic, 5,927 ....D 4
Koper, 12,000 ....A 3
Koprivnica, 12,000 ....C 2
Korčula, 2,458 ....C 4
Kosovska Mitrovica, 29,000....E 4
Kostajnica, 2,080 ....C 3
Kostanjevica, 548 ....B 3
Kotor, 4,764 ....D 4
Kragujevac, 56,000 ....E 3
Kraljevo (Rankovićevo), 26,000....E 4
Kranj, 23,000 ....B 2
Križevci, 6,642 ....C 2
Krk, 1,280 ....B 3
Krško, 3,518 ....B 3
Kruševac, 31,000 ....E 4
Kulen Vakuf, 923 ....B 3
Kumanovo, 33,000 ....E 4
Leskovac, 37,000 ....E 4
Livno, 5,181 ....C 4
Ljubinje, 621 ....D 4
Ljubljana, 153,000 ....B 3
Ljubuški, 2,168 ....C 4
Loznica, 12,000 ....D 3
Maglaj, 4,556 ....D 3
Makarska, 3,634 ....C 4
Maribor, 89,000 ....B 2
Mladenovac, 12,000 ....E 4
Modriča, 5,053 ....D 3
Mostar, 53,000 ....D 4
Našice, 4,187 ....C 3
Negotin, 8,635 ....F 3
Nevesinje, 2,349 ....D 4
Nikšić, 25,000 ....D 4
Nin, 1,823 ....B 3
Niš, 92,000 ....F 4
Nova Gradiška, 9,229 ....C 3
Novi, 2,075 ....B 3
Novi Pazar, 23,000 ....E 4
Novi Sad, 119,000 ....D 3
Novo Mesto, 6,885 ....B 3
Novska, 3,844 ....C 3
Ogulin, 3,522 ....B 3
Ohrid, 18,000 ....
Omiš, 2,171 ....
Opatija, 7,974 ....
Osijek, 78,000 ....
Pag, 2,431 ....
Pančevo, 49,000 ....
Paraćin, 17,000 ....
Peć, 30,000 ....
Petrinja, 7,366 ....
Piran, 5,474 ....
Pirot, 20,000 ....
Plav, 2,535 ....
Pljevlja, 12,000 ....
Podgorica (Titograd), 37,000 ....
Pola (Pula), 40,000 ....
Poreč, 3,006 ....
Postojna, 4,857 ....
Požarevac, 23,000 ....
Požega, 14,000 ....
Preševo, 5,680 ....
Priboj, 5,490 ....
Prijedor, 13,000 ....
Prijepolje, 4,566 ....
Prilep, 40,000 ....
Priština, 43,000 ....
Prizren, 29,000 ....
Prokuplje, 15,000 ....
Prozor, 1,052 ....
Ptuj, 7,392 ....
Pula, 40,000 ....
Rab, 1,548 ....
Rača, 1,351 ....
Radeče, 1,500 ....
Radoviš, 6,246 ....
Ragusa (Dubrovnik), 24,000 ....
Rankovićevo, 26,000 ....
Raška, 2,278 ....
Rijeka, 108,000 ....
Rogatica, 3,040 ....
Rovinj, 7,155 ....
Ruma, 21,000 ....
Šabac, 30,000 ....
Sanski Most, 5,096 ....
Sarajevo, 213,000 ....
Šavnik, 487 ....
Senj, 3,903 ....
Senta, 22,000 ....
Šibenik, 27,000 ....
Sinj, 4,134 ....
Sisak, 29,000 ....
Škofja Loka, 3,429 ....
Skopje, 206,000 ....
Skradin, 1,118 ....
Smederevo, 29,000 ....
Sombor, 31,000 ....
Split, 106,000 ....
Srebrenica, 1,859 ....
Sremska Mitrovica, 22,000 ....
Sremski Karlovci, 6,390 ....
Stari Majdan, 1,445 ....
Štip, 22,000 ....
Stolac, 2,970 ....
Ston, 562 ....
Struga, 6,857 ....
Strumica, 17,000 ....
Subotica, 76,000 ....
Surdulica, 5,007 ....
Svetozarevo, 22,000 ....
Svilajnac, 5,895 ....
Tešanj, 3,148 ....
Tetovo, 27,000 ....
Titograd, 37,000 ....
Titovo Užice, 26,000 ....
Titov Veles, 29,000 ....
Travnik, 12,000 ....
Trbovlje, 16,000 ....
Trebinje, 4,073 ....
Trogir, 5,003 ....
Tržič, 4,881 ....
Tuzla, 55,000 ....
Ulcinj, 5,705 ....
Valjevo, 27,000 ....
Varaždin, 28,000 ....
Vareš, 7,647 ....
Veliki Bečkerek (Zrenjanin), 56,000 ....E
Vinkovci, 24,000 ....D
Virovitica, 10,000 C
Višegrad, 3,309 ....D
Vranje, 18,000 ....F
Vrbas, 19,000 ....D
Vršac, 32,000 ....E
Vukovar, 25,000 ....D
Žabari, 1,984 ....E
Zadar, 28,000 ....B
Zagreb, 481,000 C
Zaječar, 18,000 ....E
Zara (Zadar), 28,000 ....B
Zenica, 50,000 C
Žepče, 2,709 ....D
Zrenjanin, 56,000 ....E
Zvornik, 5,444 ....D

PHYSICAL FEATURES

Adriatic (sea) ....B
Bosna (riv.) ....D
Brač (isl.), 14,227 C
Cazma (riv.) C
Cres (isl.), 4,949 ....B
Čursnica (mt.) C
Danube (riv.) ....E
Dinaric Alps (mts.) ....B
Drava (riv.) C
Drina (riv.) ....D
Dugi Otok (isl.), 4,873 ....B
Durmitor (mt.) ....D
Hvar (isl.), 12,147 C
Ibar (riv.) ....E
Ivancica (mt.) C
Kamenjak (cape) ....A
Komovi (mt.) ....D
Korab (mt.) ....E
Korčula (isl.), 10,245 C
Kornat (isl.), 6 ....B
Krk (isl.), 14,548 ....B
Kvarner (gulf) ....B
Lastovo (Lagosta) (isl.), 1,449....C
Lim (riv.) ....D
Lošinj (isl.), 5,068 ....B
Midzhur (mt.) ....F
Mljet (isl.), 1,963 C
Mokra Gora (mt.) ....E
Morava (riv.) ....E
Mur (riv.) ....B
Neretva (riv.) ....D
Ohrid (lake) ....E
Pag (isl.), 8,017 ....B
Pelagruž (Pelagosa) (isl.)....C
Prespa (lake) ....E
Rab (isl.), 8,400 ....B
Rajinac (mt.) ....B
Ruyen (mt.) ....F
Sava (riv.) ....D
Scutari (lake) ....D
Solta (isl.), 2,735 C
Solunska (mt.) ....E
Tara (riv.) ....D
Timok (riv.) ....F
Tisza (riv.) ....E
Triglav (mt.) ....A
Una (riv.) C
Vardar (riv.) ....E
Vis (isl.), 7,004 ....C 4
Vrbas (riv.) ....C 3
Žirje (isl.), 506 ....B 4

*City and suburbs.

THE BALKAN STATES

CONIC PROJECTION

SCALE OF MILES

0 25 50 75 100 125 150 175

SCALE OF KILOMETRES

0 25 50 75 100 125 150 175

Capitals of Countries ————— ☆
Administrative Centers ————— △
International Boundaries ——·—·—
Major Internal Boundaries ——— ——
Minor Internal Boundaries ————————
Canals ——————————

BULGARIA and GREECE are divided into counties and departments, respectively. Because of the scale no attempt has been made to delimit and name these subdivisions; their administrative centers have, however, been designated.

The larger divisions named in Greece are well-known geographical regions, without administrative function.

RUMANIA consists of sixteen regions and two independent administrative units, Bucharest City and Constanta Town.

ALBANIA is divided into prefectures, bearing the same names as their administrative centers.

YUGOSLAVIA is a federation of six republics. The Serbian republic includes an autonomous province (Voyvodina), and an autonomous region (Kosovo-Mitohiyan).

© C. S. HAMMOND & Co., N.Y.

Poland

TOPOGRAPHY

0 50 100
MILES

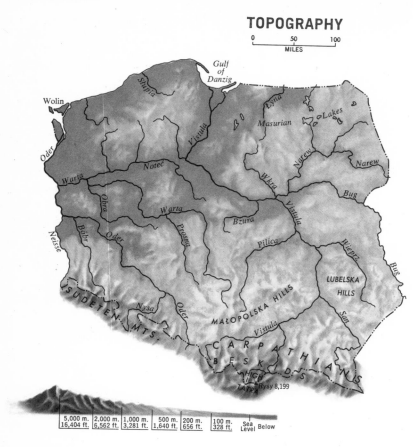

5,000 m. | 2,000 m. | 1,000 m. | 500 m. | 200 m. | 100 m. | Sea
16,404 ft. | 6,562 ft. | 3,281 ft. | 1,640 ft. | 656 ft. | 328 ft. | Level | Below

PROVINCES

Białystok, 1,139,300 ....F 2
Bydgoszcz, 1,803,500 ....D 2
Cracow, 2,088,400 ....D 4
Cracow (City), 505,400 ....E 3
Gdańsk, 1,312,300 ....C 1
Katowice, 3,458,600 ....D 3
Kielce, 1,882,600 ....E 3
Koszalin, 730,200 ....C 2
Łódź, 1,651,300 ....D 3
Łódź (City), 734,300 ....D 3
Lublin, 1,876,100 ....F 3
Olsztyn, 929,000 ....E 2
Opole, 987,700 ....C 3
Poznań, 2,090,200 ....C 2
Poznań (City), 429,300 ....C 2
Rzeszów, 1,664,600 ....E 4
Szczecin, 817,800 ....B 2
Warsaw, 2,415,900 ....E 2
Warsaw (City), 1,221,900 ....E 2
Wrocław, 1,914,700 ....C 3
Wrocław (City), 461,900 ....C 3
Zielona Góra, 824,700 ....B 2

CITIES and TOWNS

Aleksandrów Kujawski, 8,800 .....D 2
Aleksandrów Łódzki, 12,800 ....D 3
Allenstein (Olsztyn), 72,300 ....E 2
Augustów, 16,100 ....F 2
Auschwitz (Oświęcim), 34,100....D 3
Bartoszyce, 12,800 ....E 1
Będzin, 41,200 ....C 4
Belgard (Białogard), 19,000 ....B 2
Beuthen (Bytom), 191,400 ....B 4
Biała Podlaska, 22,200 ....F 2
Białogard (Belgard), 19,000.......B 2
Białystok, 132,100 ....F 2
Bielawa, 30,000 ....C 3
Bielsk Podlaski, 11,800 ....F 2
Bielsko-Biała, 80,500 ....D 4
Biłgoraj, 8,600 ....F 3
Bochnia, 13,000 ....E 4
Bogatynia, 12,300 ....B 3
Bolesławiec, 25,600 ....B 3
Braniewo, 10,600 ....E 1
Breslau (Wrocław), 461,900 ....C 3
Brieg (Brzeg), 26,900 ....C 3
Brodnica, 15,500 ....D 2
Bromberg (Bydgoszcz), 248,300..D 2
Brzeg (Brieg), 26,900 ....C 3
Brzeziny Śląskie, 8,400 ....B 4

Busko Zdrój, 9,100 ....E
Bydgoszcz (Bromberg), 248,300...
Bystrzyca Kłodzka, 8,600 ....
Bytom, 191,400 ....
Bytów, 9,500 ....
Chełm, 33,500 ....
Chełmno, 17,100 ....
Chełmża, 14,400 ....
Chodzież, 12,200 ....
Chojnice, 21,700 ....
Chojnów, 10,300 ....
Chorzów (Königshütte), 153,300..
Choszczno, 8,200 ....
Chrzanów, 22,500 ....
Ciechanów, 20,900 ....
Cieplice Śląskie-Zdrój, 15,100.....
Cieszyn (Teschen), 23,800 ....
Cracow, 505,400 ....
Czechowice-Dziedzice, 23,700....
Czeladź, 31,200 ....
Częstochowa, 171,800 ....
Dąbrowa Górnicza, 59,500 ....
Danzig (Gdańsk), 309,700 ....
Darłowo, 9,900 ....
Dębica, 18,300 ....
Dęblin, 11,300 ....
Dębno, 9,500 ....
Działdowo, 8,300 ....E

POLAND 1938

0 50 100
MILES

POLAND 1945

0 50 100
MILES

AGRICULTURE, INDUSTRY and RESOURCES

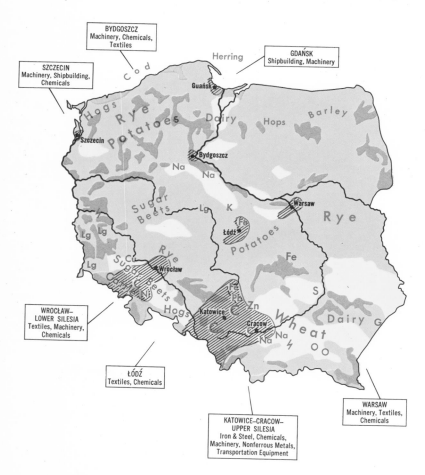

BYDGOSZCZ
Machinery, Chemicals, Textiles

SZCZECIN
Machinery, Shipbuilding, Chemicals

GDAŃSK
Shipbuilding, Machinery

WROCŁAW–LOWER SILESIA
Textiles, Machinery, Chemicals

ŁÓDŹ
Textiles, Chemicals

KATOWICE–CRACOW–UPPER SILESIA
Iron & Steel, Chemicals, Machinery, Nonferrous Metals, Transportation Equipment

WARSAW
Machinery, Textiles, Chemicals

DOMINANT LAND USE

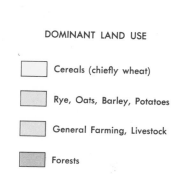

Cereals (chiefly wheat)

Rye, Oats, Barley, Potatoes

General Farming, Livestock

Forests

MAJOR MINERAL OCCURRENCES

C Coal
Cu Copper
Fe Iron
G Natural Gas
K Potash
Lg Lignite

Na Salt
Ni Nickel
O Petroleum
Pb Lead
S Sulfur
Zn Zinc

⚡ Water Power
▨ Major Industrial Areas

POLAND

AREA	119,734 sq. mi.
POPULATION	31,161,000
CAPITAL	Warsaw
LARGEST CITY	Warsaw 1,221,900
HIGHEST POINT	Rysy 8,199 ft.
MONETARY UNIT	zloty
MAJOR LANGUAGE	Polish
MAJOR RELIGION	Roman Catholic

erżoniów, 29,300 ... C 3
ąg (Elbing), 83,200 ... D 1
23,500 ... D 1
ńsk, 309,700 ... D 1
nia, 159,300 ... E 1
ycko, 15,800 ... E 2
z (Kłodzko), 24,800 ... C 3
wice (Gleiwitz), 145,900 ... B 3
gów, 10,400 ... B 3
wno, 12,100 ... D 2
bczyce, 9,700 ... D 3
chołazy, 12,500 ... C 3
ezno (Gnesen), 46,400 ... C 2
eniów, 11,900 ... E 4
lice, 12,800 ... B 2
rzów Wielkopolski, 64,500 ... B 2
stynin, 11,100 ... D 2
styń, 10,300 ... D 2
ajewo, 9,400 ... E 2
audenz (Grudziądz), 69,500 ... D 2
odziec, 10,900 ... B 3
odzisk Mazowiecki, 19,500 ... C 2
odzisk Wielkopolski, 8,300 ... C 2
ójec, 9,000 ... D 2
udziądz (Graudenz), 69,500 ... D 2
yfice, 12,100 ... B 3
jin, 13,400 ... F 2
aynów (Chojnów), 10,300 ... A 4
ndenburg (Zabrze), 199,400 ... A 4
rschberg (Jelenia Góra), 53,000 ... B 3
ohensalza (Inowrocław), 53,000 ... C 2
rubieszów, 13,100 ... F 3
awa, 13,800 ... C 3
nowrocław, 49,900 ... C 3
arocin, 17,100 ... C 3
asło, 12,800 ... E 4
awor (Jauer), 14,500 ... D 3
edrzejów, 13,400 ... D 3
elenia Góra, 53,000 ... B 3
Kalisz, 74,600 ... C 3
Kamienna Góra, 19,600 ... B 4
Katowice, 282,500 ... D 3
Kędzierzyn, 24,000 ... C 3
Kępno, 9,500 ... E 1
Kętrzyn, 17,000 ... E 1
Kielce, 97,900 ... D 3
Kłobuck, 10,100 ... D 3
Kłodzko (Glatz), 24,800 ... C 3
Kluczbork, 14,800 ... D 3
Knurów, 15,700 ... A 4
Koło, 11,600 ... D 2
Kołobrzeg, 20,400 ... B 1
Königshütte (Chorzów), 153,200 ... B 4
Konin, 20,800 ... C 2
Końskie, 10,500 ... D 3
Konstantynów, 11,800 ... D 3
Kościan, 16,600 ... C 2
Kościerzyna, 12,200 ... C 1
Kostrzyn, 8,200 ... B 2

Koszalin, 50,000 ... C 1
Kraków (Cracow), 505,400 ... E 3
Kraśnik, 13,300 ... F 3
Krasnystaw, 11,500 ... F 3
Krosno, 23,400 ... E 4
Krotoszyn, 19,800 ... C 2
Krynica, 9,300 ... E 4
Kutno, 26,900 ... D 2
Kwidzyn (Marienwerder), 21,700 ... D 2
Łabędy, 16,300 ... A 4
Łańcut, 10,900 ... E 4
Landeshut (Kamienna Góra), 19,600 ... C 3
Landsberg (Gorzów Wielkopolski), 64,500 ...
Langenbielau (Bielawa), 30,000 ... C 3
Lębork (Lauenburg), 22,700 ... D 1
Łęczyca, 12,600 ... D 2
Legionowo, 20,400 ... E 2
Legnica (Liegnitz), 69,800 ... C 3
Leszno, 30,900 ... C 2
Lidzbark Warmiński, 11,900 ... E 1
Lipno, 10,800 ... D 2
Łódź, 734,300 ... D 3
Łomża, 21,700 ... F 2
Łowicz, 18,300 ... E 2
Lubań, 16,200 ... B 3
Lubin, 8,200 ... F 3
Lublin, 197,100 ... F 3
Lubliniec, 17,000 ... D 3
Luboń, 15,100 ... C 2
Lubsko, 11,600 ... B 3
Łuków, 12,100 ... E 2
Lyck (Ełk), 23,500 ... F 2
Malbork (Marienburg), 27,200 ... D 2
Marienwerder (Kwidzyn), 21,700 ...
Międzyrzec Podlaski, 11,900 ... F 3
Międzyrzecz, 11,400 ... B 2
Mielec, 24,100 ... B 4
Mikołów, 19,500 ... D 3
Mińsk Mazowiecki, 21,000 ... E 2
Mława, 16,900 ... D 2
Morąg, 8,900 ...
Mrągowo, 11,600 ... E 1
Myślenice, 9,600 ... E 4
Myślibórz, 8,000 ... B 2
Mysłowice (Myslowitz), 42,700 ... B 4
Myszków, 15,500 ... D 3
Nakło nad Notecią, 15,000 ... C 2
Namysłów, 8,900 ... C 3
Neisse (Nysa), 26,400 ... C 3
Neustadt (Prudnik), 18,400 ... C 3
Neustettin (Szczecinek), 25,100 ... C 2
Nisko, 8,800 ...
Nowa Ruda, 18,100 ... B 3
Nowa Sól, 28,500 ... B 3
Nowy Dwór Mazowiecki, 14,100 ... E 3
Nowy Sącz, 36,400 ... E 4
Nowy Targ, 18,200 ... E 4
Nysa (Neisse), 26,400 ...

Oborniki, 8,800 ... C 2
Oels (Oleśnica), 22,300 ... C 3
Oława (Ohlau), 12,800 ... F 2
Olecko, 8,100 ...
Oleśnica, 22,300 ... D 3
Olkusz, 15,300 ... E 2
Olsztyn, 72,300 ... E 1
Opoczno, 10,700 ...
Opole (Oppeln), 68,800 ... E 1
Orneta, 8,000 ...
Ostróda (Osterode), 19,000 ... D 2
Ostrołęka, 17,100 ...
Ostrów Mazowiecka, 13,400 ... C 2
Ostrów Wielkopolski, 44,800 ... C 3
Ostrowiec Świętokrzyski, 41,700 ... E 3
Oświęcim (Auschwitz), 34,100 ... C 3
Otwock, 24,800 ...
Ozorków, 16,800 ...
Pabianice, 58,200 ... B 4
Piekary Śląskie, 34,700 ... B 4
Piła (Schneidemühl), 36,600 ... C 2
Pionki, 14,200 ...
Piotrków Trybunalski, 55,400 ... D 3
Pleszew, 11,700 ... C 2
Pisz, 8,000 ...
Płock, 50,000 ... D 2
Płońsk, 10,600 ... B 2
Police, 10,900 ...
Poznań (Posen), 429,300 ... C 2
Prudnik, 18,400 ...
Pruszków, 37,700 ... E 2
Przasnysz, 8,900 ...
Przemyśl, 49,300 ... F 4
Przeworsk, 8,100 ...
Puławy, 15,800 ...
Pułtusk, 11,400 ...
Pyskowice, 22,900 ... A 4
Racibórz (Ratibor), 35,500 ... C 3
Radom, 139,700 ...
Radomsko, 28,300 ... D 3
Ratibor (Racibórz), 35,500 ...
Rawa Mazowiecka, 9,200 ... E 3
Rawicz, 13,300 ...

Ruda Śląska, 138,700 ... B 4
Rumia, 18,000 ... D 1
Rybnik, 36,800 ... D 3
Rypin, 9,300 ...
Rzeszów, 67,200 ... E 4
Sandomierz, 14,200 ... E 3
Sanok, 18,300 ... F 4
Schneidemühl (Piła), 36,600 ...
Schweidnitz (Świdnica), 43,100 ... C 3
Siedlce, 34,900 ...
Siemianowice Śląskie, 65,200 ... B 3
Sieradz, 14,400 ... D 3
Sierpc, 11,700 ...
Skarżysko-Kamienna, 36,100 ... E 3
Skierniewice, 23,400 ... D 2
Sławno, 9,400 ... C 1
Słubice, 10,200 ...
Słupsk (Stolp), 57,400 ... C 1
Sochaczew, 17,300 ...
Sokółka, 8,000 ...
Sokołów Podlaski, 8,700 ... D 1
Sopot (Zoppot), 45,100 ... B 3
Sorau (Żary), 27,100 ...
Sosnowiec, 137,300 ... C 2
Śrem, 11,200 ...
Środa, 13,600 ... C 2
Stalowa Wola, 24,600 ... E 3
Starachowice, 38,100 ...
Stargard Szczeciński, 36,800 ... B 2
Starogard Gdański, 28,600 ... D 2
Stettin (Szczecin), 299,200 ... B 2
Stolp (Słupsk), 57,400 ...
Strzegom, 13,100 ...
Strzelce Opolskie, 13,000 ... C 3
Strzelin, 9,100 ...
Suchedniów, 8,400 ...
Sulechów, 9,200 ... B 2
Suwałki, 21,300 ... F 1
Świdnica (Schweidnitz), 43,100 ... C 3
Świdnik, 14,800 ... F 3
Świdwin, 10,900 ... B 2
Świebodzin, 13,000 ... B 2
Świecie, 14,500 ... D 2
Świętochłowice, 58,200 ... B 4

Świnoujście (Swinemünde), 20,100 ... B 2
Szamotuły, 12,200 ... C 2
Szczecin, 299,200 ... B 2
Szczecinek, 25,100 ... C 2
Szczytno, 13,900 ... E 2
Szprotawa, 10,200 ... B 3
Tarnobrzeg, 9,300 ... E 3
Tarnów, 75,100 ... E 3
Tarnowskie Góry, 30,500 ... B 3
Tczew (Dirschau), 36,000 ... D 1
Teschen (Cieszyn), 23,800 ... D 4
Thorn (Toruń), 111,300 ... D 2
Tomaszów Lubelski, 10,200 ... F 3
Tomaszów Mazowiecki, 51,200 ... E 3
Toruń (Thorn), 111,300 ... D 2
Trzcianka, 10,200 ... B 1
Trzebiatów (Treptow), 8,000 ... B 1
Tuchola, 8,300 ... D 2
Turek, 13,500 ... D 2
Tychy, 59,500 ... B 4
Wąbrzeźno, 11,700 ... D 2
Wadowice, 30,300 ... D 4
Wągrowiec, 13,400 ... C 2
Wałbrzych, 122,700 ... C 3
Wałcz, 16,600 ... C 2
Waldenburg (Wałbrzych), 122,700 ... C 3
Warsaw (Warszawa) (cap.), 1,221,900 ... E 2
Wejherowo, 27,400 ... D 1
Wieliczka, 12,300 ... E 3
Wieluń, 12,400 ... D 3
Włocławek, 66,900 ... D 2
Wołomin, 22,600 ... E 2
Wołów, 8,300 ... C 3
Wrocław, 461,900 ... C 3
Września, 14,800 ... C 2
Wschowa, 9,000 ... B 2
Ząbkowice Śląskie, 12,600 ... C 3
Zabrze (Hindenburg), 199,400 ... A 4

Żagań, 20,100 ... B 3
Zakopane, 25,800 ... D 4
Zambrów, 11,000 ... F 2
Zamość, 29,600 ... F 3
Żary, 27,100 ... B 3
Zawiercie, 34,700 ... D 3
Zduńska Wola, 26,900 ... D 3
Zgierz, 38,700 ... D 3
Zgorzelec, 20,300 ... B 3
Ziębice, 10,300 ... C 3
Zielona Góra, 59,700 ... B 3
Złocieniec, 9,300 ... C 3
Złotów, 9,700 ... C 2
Żnin, 8,800 ... C 2
Zoppot (Sopot), 45,100 ... D 1
Żyrardów, 30,900 ... D 2
Żywiec, 20,100 ... D 4

PHYSICAL FEATURES

Alle (Łyna) (river) ... E 1
Baltic (sea) ... B 1
Beskids (mts.) ... E 4
Brda (river) ... F 2
Bug (river) ... F 2
Bzura (river) ... D 2
Danzig (gulf) ... D 1
Drawa (river) ... B 2
Drwęca (river) ... E 4
Dukla (pass) ... E 4
Dunajec (river) ... D 4
Gwda (river) ... B 1

Hel (pen.) ... D 1
High Tatra (mts.) ... D 4
Kłodnica (river) ... B 4
Łyna (river) ... E 1
Mamry (Mauer) (lake) ... E 2
Narew (river) ... E 2
Neisse (Nysa Łużycka) (riv.) ... B 3
Noteć (Netze) (river) ... C 2
Nysa (river) ... C 3
Nysa Łużycka (Neisse) (riv.) ... B 3
Oder (Odra) (river) ... B 2
Odra (Oder) (river) ... B 2
Pilica (river) ... D 3
Pomerania (gulf) ... B 1

Prosna (river) ... C 2
Rysy (mt.) ... E 4
San (river) ... E 4
Śniardwy (Spirding) (lake) ... E 2
Sołokija (river) ... E 3
Sudeten (mt. range) ... C 3
Usnam (Usedom) (isl.), 20,100 ... B 1
Vistula (Wisła) (river) ... C 2
Warta (Warthe) (river) ... C 2
Wieprz (river) ... F 3
Wisła (Vistula) (river) ... D 2
Wkra (river) ... E 2
Wolin (Wollin) (isl.) ... B 2

POLAND
CONIC PROJECTION
SCALE OF MILES
SCALE OF KILOMETRES
International Boundaries ___ ___ ___
Internal Boundaries _____
Capitals of Countries ⭑
Administrative Centers ◉
Canals
© C. S. HAMMOND & Co., N.Y.

GLOSSARY

PRESENT POLISH	FORMER GERMAN	KEY
Brzeg	Brieg	C-3
Bytom	Beuthen	B-4
Elbląg	Elbing	D-1
Gdańsk	Danzig	D-1
Gliwice	Gleiwitz	A-4
Głogów	Glogau	C-3
Gorzów W.	Landsberg	B-2
Gubin	Guben	B-2
Jelenia Góra	Hirschberg	B-3
Kołobrzeg	Kolberg	B-1
Kostrzyn	Küstrin	B-2
Koszalin	Köslin	C-1
Legnica	Liegnitz	C-3
Malbork	Marienburg	D-2
Nysa	Neisse	C-3
Olsztyn	Allenstein	E-2
Opole	Oppeln	C-2
Piła	Schneidemühl	C-2
Racibórz	Ratibor	C-3
Słupsk	Stolp	C-1
Świdnica	Schweidnitz	C-3
Świnoujście	Swinemünde	B-2
Szczecin	Stettin	B-2
Wałbrzych	Waldenburg	C-3
Wrocław	Breslau	C-3
Zabrze	Hindenburg	D-3
Zielona Góra	Grünberg	B-3

Post-war territorial changes shown on this map do not necessarily represent the final status of such boundaries. Only after the signing of the Peace Treaties can changes be considered official and definite.

Union of Soviet Socialist Republics

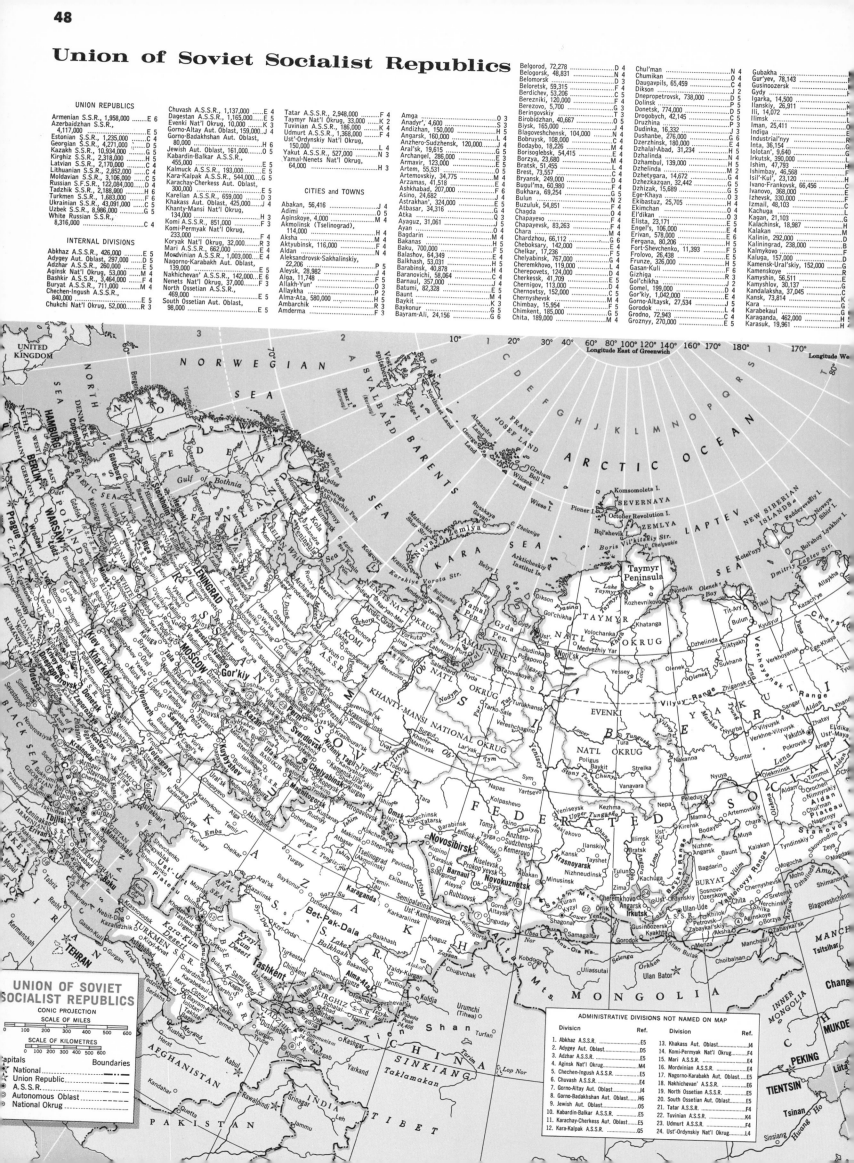

UNION OF SOVIET SOCIALIST REPUBLICS
CONIC PROJECTION
SCALE OF MILES
0 100 200 300 400 500 600
SCALE OF KILOMETRES
0 100 200 300 400 500 600

Capitals — Boundaries
National
Union Republic
A.S.S.R.
Autonomous Oblast
National Okrug

ADMINISTRATIVE DIVISIONS NOT NAMED ON MAP

Division	Ref.
1. Abkhaz A.S.S.R.	E5
2. Adygey Aut. Oblast	D5
3. Adzhar A.S.S.R.	E5
4. Aginsk Nat'l Okrug	M4
5. Chechen-Ingush A.S.S.R.	E5
6. Chuvash A.S.S.R.	E4
7. Gorno-Altay Aut. Oblast	J4
8. Gorno-Badakhshan Aut. Oblast	H6
9. Kabardin-Balkar A.S.S.R.	E5
10. Kara-Kalpak A.S.S.R.	G5
11. Karachay-Cherkess Aut. Oblast	E5
12. Kara-Kalpak A.S.S.R.	G5
13. Khakass Aut. Oblast	J4
14. Komi-Permyak Nat'l Okrug	F4
15. Mari A.S.S.R.	E4
16. Mordvinian A.S.S.R.	E4
17. Nagorno-Karabakh Aut. Oblast	E5
18. Nakhichevan' A.S.S.R.	E5
19. North Ossetian A.S.S.R.	E5
20. South Ossetian Aut. Oblast	E5
21. Tatar A.S.S.R.	F4
22. Tuvinian A.S.S.R.	K4
23. Udmurt A.S.S.R.	F4
24. Ust'-Ordynskiy Nat'l Okrug	L4

UNION OF SOVIET SOCIALIST REPUBLICS

AREA	8,570,600 sq. mi.
POPULATION	226,253,000
CAPITAL	Moscow
LARGEST CITY	Moscow (greater) 6,354,000
HIGHEST POINT	Mt. Communism 24,590 ft.
MONETARY UNIT	ruble
MAJOR LANGUAGES	Russian, Ukrainian, White Russian, Uzbek, Azerbaidzhani, Tatar, Georgian, Lithuanian, Armenian, Yiddish, Latvian, Mordvinian, Kirghiz, Tadzhik, Estonian, Kazakh, etc.
MAJOR RELIGIONS	Russian Orthodox, Moslem, Tribal Religions

UNION REPUBLICS

	AREA (sq. mi.)	POPULATION	CAPITAL and LARGEST CITY
RUSSIAN S.F.S.R.	6,501,500	122,084,000	Moscow (greater) 6,354,000
KAZAKH S.S.R.	1,061,600	10,934,000	Alma-Ata 580,000
UKRAINIAN S.S.R.	220,600	43,091,000	Kiev 1,248,000
TURKMEN S.S.R.	187,200	1,683,000	Ashkhabad 207,000
UZBEK S.S.R.	157,400	8,986,000	Tashkent 1,029,000
WHITE RUSSIAN S.S.R.	80,100	8,316,000	Minsk 644,000
KIRGHIZ S.S.R.	76,100	2,318,000	Frunze 326,000
TADZHIK S.S.R.	54,900	2,188,000	Dushanbe 276,000
AZERBAIDZHAN S.S.R.	33,100	4,117,000	Baku 700,000
GEORGIAN S.S.R.	29,400	4,271,000	Tbilisi 768,000
LITHUANIAN S.S.R.	25,200	2,852,000	Vilna 271,000
LATVIAN S.S.R.	24,600	2,170,000	Riga 632,000
ESTONIAN S.S.R.	17,400	1,235,000	Tallinn 311,000
MOLDAVIAN S.S.R.	13,100	3,106,000	Kishinev 254,000
ARMENIAN S.S.R.	11,500	1,958,000	Erivan 578,000

Columns of place-name index (left block):

rkaralinsk, 6,874	H 5
rshi, 19,709	G 6
unas, 247,000	C 4
azach'ye	O 2
zalinsk, 7,697	G 5
azan', 725,000	F 4
azandzhik, 7,807	F 6
em', 18,127	D 3
emerovo, 328,000	J 4
erki, 11,838	G 6
ezhma	K 4
nabarovsk, 349,000	O 5
nandyga	O 3
nanty-Mansiysk, 20,677	H 3
har'kov, 1,006,000	D 5
natanga	
nerson, 192,000	M 4
nilok, 15,855	
nodzheyli, 20,525	F 5

Kholmsk, 31,541	P 5
Khorog, 8,218	H 6
Kiev, 1,248,000	D 4
Kirensk	
Kirov, 284,000	F 4
Kirovabad, 126,000	E 5
Kirovograd, 142,000	D 5
Kiselevsk, 142,000	J 4
Kishinev, 254,000	C 4
Kizel, 60,687	F 4
Kizyl-Arvat, 16,199	F 6
Klaipéda, 105,000	B 4
Kokchetav, 39,694	H 4
Kolomna, 125,000	D 4
Kolpashevo, 22,595	J 4
Komsomol'sk, 192,000	O 4
Kondopoga, 16,060	D 3
Kopeysk, 168,000	G 4
Korf	R 3
Korkino, 84,962	G 4

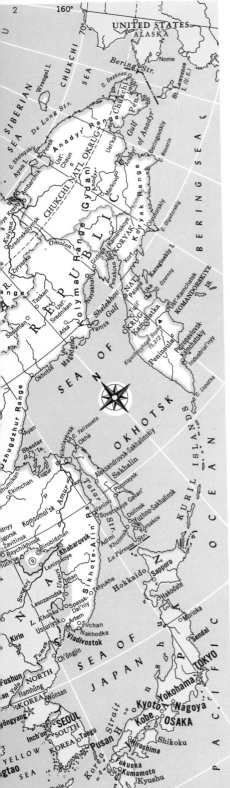

Second place-name index block:

Korsakov, 32,914	P 5
Koslan	E 3
Kostroma, 193,000	E 4
Kotlas, 39,162	E 3
Kovel', 24,666	C 4
Kovrov, 105,000	E 4
Kozhevnikovo	L 2
Krasino	
Krasnodar, 368,000	E 5
Krasnokamsk, 54,715	F 4
Krasnotur'insk, 61,990	G 3
Krasnoural'sk, 39,245	
Krasnovishersk, 15,207	F 3
Krasnovodsk, 39,272	F 5
Krasnoyarsk, 483,000	K 4
Kremenchug, 100,000	D 5
Krivoy Rog, 448,000	D 5
Kudymkar, 21,801	F 4
Kul'sary	F 5
Kungur, 64,796	F 4

Kupino, 23,185	H 4
Kurgan, 182,000	G 4
Kurgan-Tyube, 23,560	G 6
Kursk, 233,000	D 4
Kushka	G 6
Kustanay, 105,000	G 4
Kutaisi, 141,000	E 5
Kuybyshev, 901,000	F 4
Kyakhta, 10,000	L 4
Kyusyur	N 2
Kyzyl, 34,462	K 4
Kzyl-Orda, 65,902	G 5
Labytnangi	H 3
Lar'yak	J 3
Leninabad, 77,465	G 5
Leninakan, 117,000	E 5
Leningrad, 3,180,000	D 4
Leninogorsk, 66,812	J 5
Leninsk-Kuznetskiy, 140,000	J 4
Leninskoye	O 5

Lenkoran', 25,209	E 6
Lesozavodsk, 32,124	O 5
Liepāja, 71,464	B 4
Lipetsk, 205,000	E 4
Luga, 25,540	D 4
Lugansk, 314,000	E 5
Lutsk, 56,282	C 4
Luza	E 3
L'vov, 469,000	C 4
Lys'va, 72,989	F 4
Magadan, 62,225	N 4
Magdagachi	N 4
Magnitogorsk, 333,000	G 4
Makhachkala, 140,000	E 5
Makinsk	H 4
Maklakovo	K 4
Mama	M 4
Markovo	S 3
Mary, 48,125	G 6
Maykop, 82,135	D 5

Mednogorsk, 36,303	F 4
Medvezhiy Yar	K 2
Medvezh'yegorsk, 15,824	D 3
Melekess, 50,696	F 4
Menza	L 5
Mezen'	E 3
Michurinsk, 80,653	E 4
Millerovo, 30,005	E 5
Minsk, 644,000	C 4
Minusinsk, 38,318	K 4
Mogilev, 145,000	D 4
Mogocha	N 4
Molodechno, 26,275	C 4
Monchegorsk, 45,523	C 3
Moscow (cap.), 6,317,000	D 4
Moscow (greater), 6,354,000	D 4
Mozyr', 25,710	C 4
Murgab	H 6
Murmansk, 254,000	D 3
Muya	M 4

Muynak, 10,428	F 5
Nagornyy	N 4
Nakanna	L 3
Nakhichevan', 25,340	E 6
Nakhodka, 63,725	O 5
Nal'chik, 106,000	E 5
Namangan, 138,000	H 5
Napas	J 4
Nar'yan-Mar, 11,000	F 3
Naryn, 14,857	H 5
Nayakhan	Q 3
Nebit-Dag, 32,903	F 6
Nel'kan	O 4
Nepa	L 4
Nerchinsk, 11,600	M 4
Nikolayev, 263,000	D 5
Nikolayevsk, 30,923	P 4
Nimnyrskiy	N 4
Nizhne-Angarsk	M 4
Nizhneudinsk, 38,761	K 4

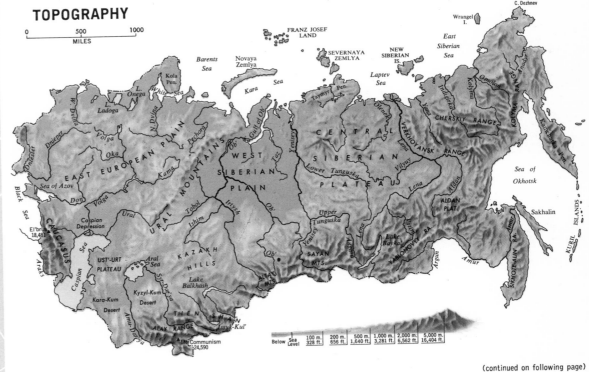

TOPOGRAPHY

0 — 500 — 1000 MILES

Below Sea Level | 100 m. 328 ft. | 200 m. 656 ft. | 500 m. 1,640 ft. | 1,000 m. 3,281 ft. | 2,000 m. 6,562 ft. | 5,000 m. 16,404 ft.

(continued on following page)

Union of Soviet Socialist Republics
(continued)

AGRICULTURE, INDUSTRY and RESOURCES

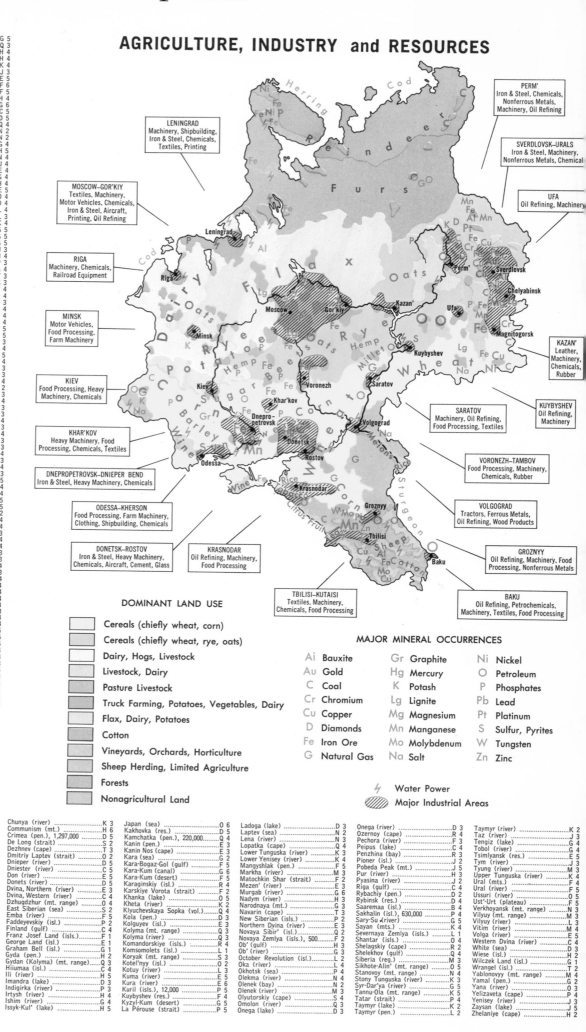

PERM'
Iron & Steel, Chemicals, Nonferrous Metals, Oil Refining

SVERDLOVSK–URALS
Iron & Steel, Machinery, Nonferrous Metals, Chemical

UFA
Oil Refining, Machinery

LENINGRAD
Machinery, Shipbuilding, Iron & Steel, Chemicals, Textiles, Printing

MOSCOW–GOR'KIY
Textiles, Machinery, Motor Vehicles, Chemicals, Iron & Steel, Aircraft, Printing, Oil Refining

RIGA
Machinery, Chemicals, Railroad Equipment

MINSK
Motor Vehicles, Food Processing, Farm Machinery

KIEV
Food Processing, Heavy Machinery, Chemicals

KHAR'KOV
Heavy Machinery, Food Processing, Chemicals, Textiles

DNEPROPETROVSK–DNIEPER BEND
Iron & Steel, Heavy Machinery, Chemicals

ODESSA–KHERSON
Food Processing, Farm Machinery, Clothing, Shipbuilding, Chemicals

DONETSK–ROSTOV
Iron & Steel, Heavy Machinery, Chemicals, Aircraft, Cement, Glass

KRASNODAR
Oil Refining, Machinery, Food Processing

TBILISI–KUTAISI
Textiles, Machinery, Chemicals, Food Processing

KAZAN'
Leather, Machinery, Chemicals, Rubber

SARATOV
Machinery, Oil Refining, Food Processing, Textiles

KUYBYSHEV
Oil Refining, Machinery

VORONEZH–TAMBOV
Food Processing, Machinery, Chemicals, Rubber

VOLGOGRAD
Tractors, Ferrous Metals, Oil Refining, Wood Products

GROZNYY
Oil Refining, Machinery, Food Processing, Nonferrous Metals

BAKU
Oil Refining, Petrochemicals, Machinery, Textiles, Food Processing

DOMINANT LAND USE

- Cereals (chiefly wheat, corn)
- Cereals (chiefly wheat, rye, oats)
- Dairy, Hogs, Livestock
- Livestock, Dairy
- Pasture Livestock
- Truck Farming, Potatoes, Vegetables, Dairy
- Flax, Dairy, Potatoes
- Cotton
- Vineyards, Orchards, Horticulture
- Sheep Herding, Limited Agriculture
- Forests
- Nonagricultural Land

MAJOR MINERAL OCCURRENCES

Ai	Bauxite	Gr	Graphite	Ni	Nickel
Au	Gold	Hg	Mercury	O	Petroleum
C	Coal	K	Potash	P	Phosphates
Cr	Chromium	Lg	Lignite	Pb	Lead
Cu	Copper	Mg	Magnesium	Pt	Platinum
D	Diamonds	Mn	Manganese	S	Sulfur, Pyrites
Fe	Iron Ore	Mo	Molybdenum	W	Tungsten
G	Natural Gas	Na	Salt	Zn	Zinc

⚡ Water Power

▨ Major Industrial Areas

Union of Soviet Socialist Republics
(continued)

AGRICULTURE, INDUSTRY and RESOURCES

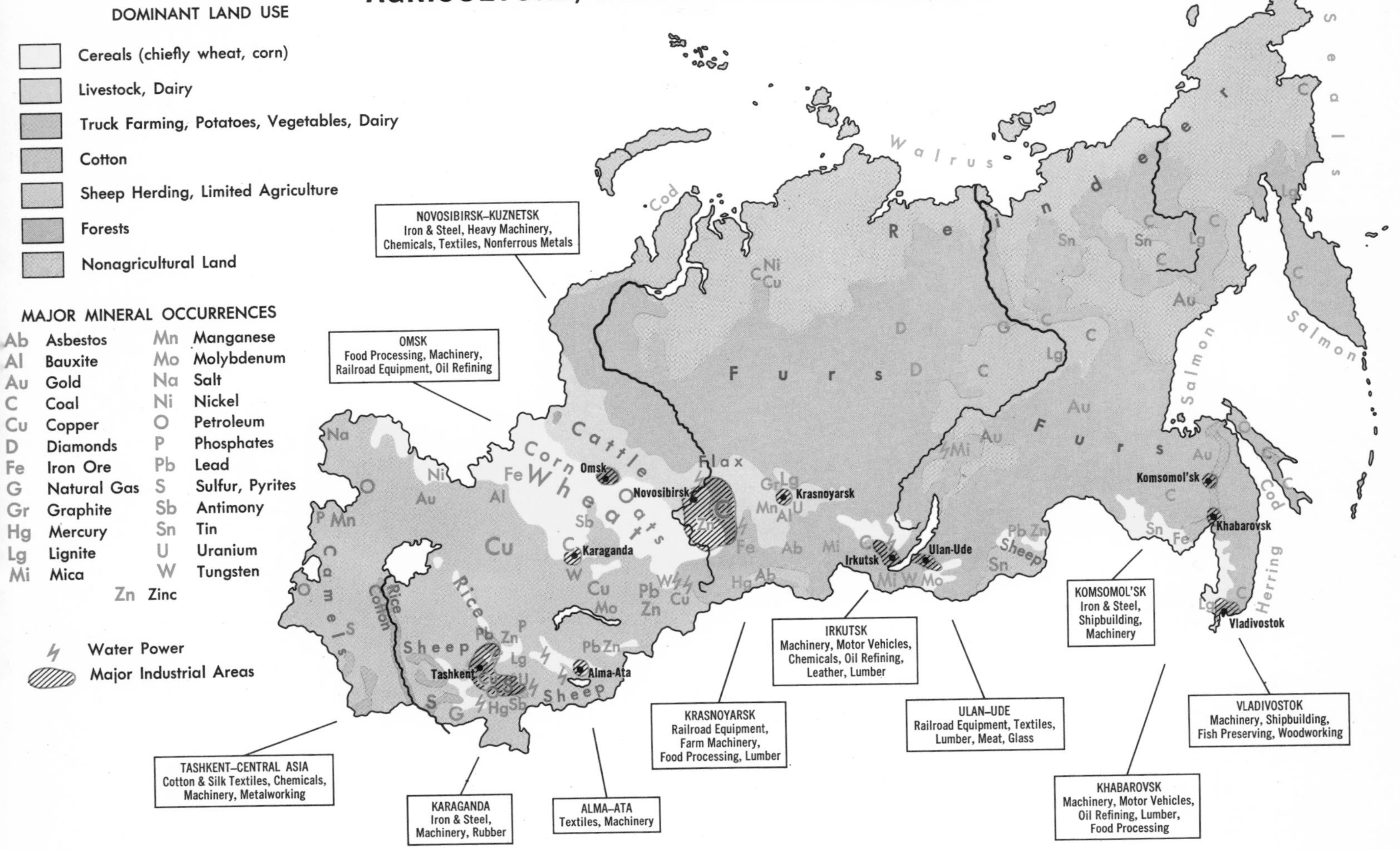

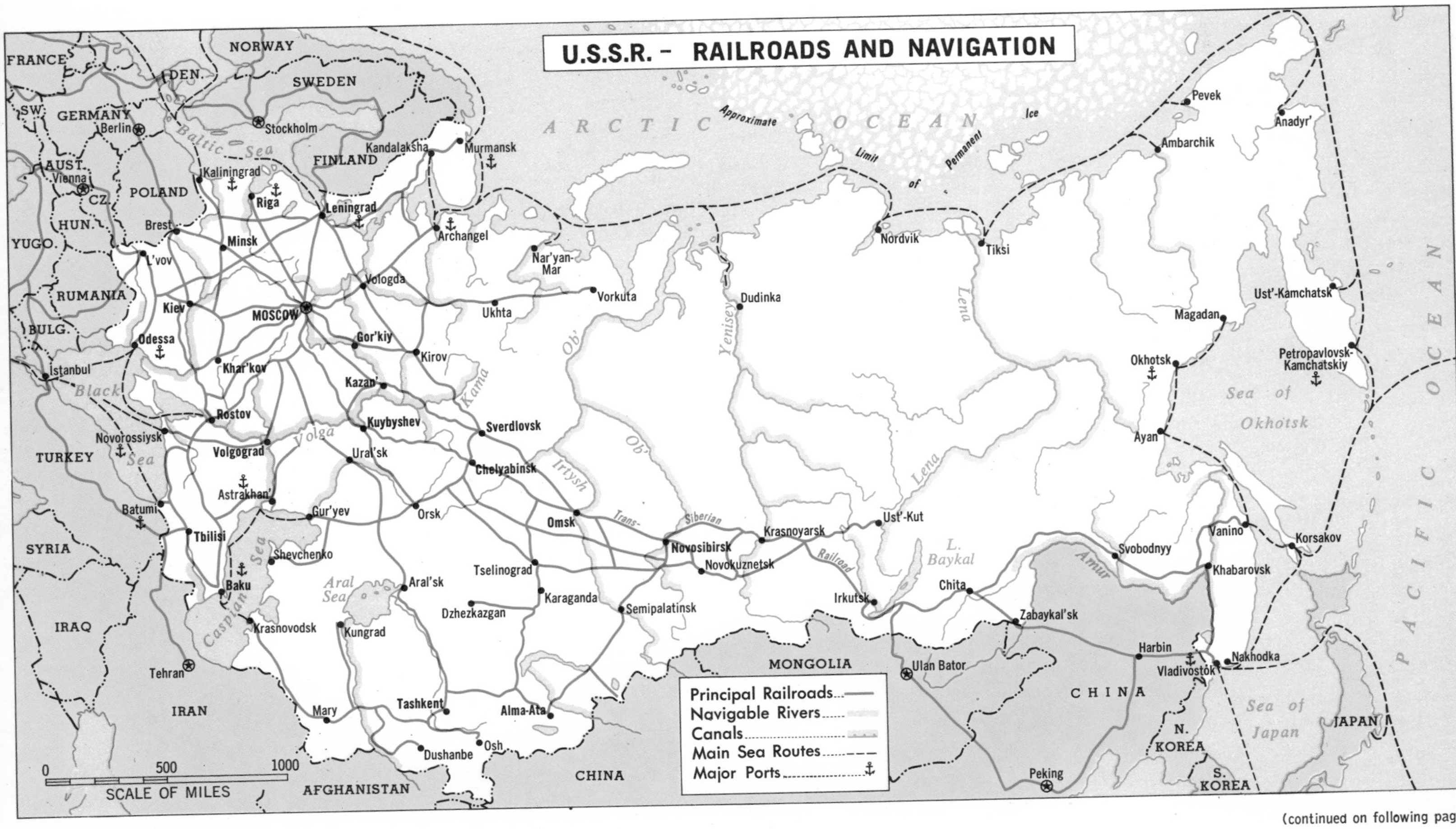

DOMINANT LAND USE
Cereals (chiefly wheat, corn)
Livestock, Dairy
Truck Farming, Potatoes, Vegetables, Dairy
Cotton
Sheep Herding, Limited Agriculture
Forests
Nonagricultural Land
MAJOR MINERAL OCCURRENCES
Ab Asbestos
Al Bauxite
Au Gold
C Coal
Cu Copper
D Diamonds
Fe Iron Ore
G Natural Gas
Gr Graphite
Hg Mercury
Lg Lignite
Mi Mica
Mn Manganese
Mo Molybdenum
Na Salt
Ni Nickel
O Petroleum
P Phosphates
Pb Lead
S Sulfur, Pyrites
Sb Antimony
Sn Tin
U Uranium
W Tungsten
Zn Zinc
Water Power
Major Industrial Areas
NOVOSIBIRSK–KUZNETSK
Iron & Steel, Heavy Machinery, Chemicals, Textiles, Nonferrous Metals
OMSK
Food Processing, Machinery, Railroad Equipment, Oil Refining
TASHKENT–CENTRAL ASIA
Cotton & Silk Textiles, Chemicals, Machinery, Metalworking
KARAGANDA
Iron & Steel, Machinery, Rubber
ALMA–ATA
Textiles, Machinery
KRASNOYARSK
Railroad Equipment, Farm Machinery, Food Processing, Lumber
IRKUTSK
Machinery, Motor Vehicles, Chemicals, Oil Refining, Leather, Lumber
ULAN–UDE
Railroad Equipment, Textiles, Lumber, Meat, Glass
KOMSOMOL'SK
Iron & Steel, Shipbuilding, Machinery
KHABAROVSK
Machinery, Motor Vehicles, Oil Refining, Lumber, Food Processing
VLADIVOSTOK
Machinery, Shipbuilding, Fish Preserving, Woodworking
Walrus
Reindeer
Seals
Cod
Furs
Salmon
Cattle
Corn
Wheat
Oats
Flax
Rice
Cotton
Camels
Sheep
Herring
Omsk
Novosibirsk
Karaganda
Krasnoyarsk
Irkutsk
Ulan-Ude
Komsomol'sk
Khabarovsk
Vladivostok
Tashkent
Alma-Ata

U.S.S.R. - RAILROADS AND NAVIGATION
ARCTIC OCEAN
Approximate Limit of Permanent Ice
PACIFIC OCEAN
Sea of Okhotsk
Sea of Japan
Black Sea
Baltic Sea
Caspian Sea
Aral Sea
L. Baykal
FRANCE
NORWAY
SWEDEN
FINLAND
DEN.
SW.
GERMANY
AUST.
CZ.
POLAND
HUN.
YUGO.
RUMANIA
BULG.
TURKEY
SYRIA
IRAQ
IRAN
AFGHANISTAN
CHINA
MONGOLIA
N. KOREA
S. KOREA
JAPAN
Berlin
Stockholm
Vienna
Kaliningrad
Riga
Leningrad
Kandalaksha
Murmansk
Archangel
Brest
Minsk
L'vov
Kiev
Odessa
Istanbul
Khar'kov
MOSCOW
Vologda
Gor'kiy
Kirov
Kazan'
Rostov
Novorossiysk
Volgograd
Kuybyshev
Ural'sk
Sverdlovsk
Chelyabinsk
Astrakhan'
Batumi
Tbilisi
Baku
Shevchenko
Gur'yev
Orsk
Krasnovodsk
Kungrad
Aral'sk
Tehran
Mary
Tashkent
Dushanbe
Osh
Alma-Ata
Dzhezkazgan
Tselinograd
Karaganda
Semipalatinsk
Omsk
Novosibirsk
Novokuznetsk
Krasnoyarsk
Ust'-Kut
Irkutsk
Ulan Bator
Chita
Zabaykal'sk
Harbin
Peking
Vladivostok
Nakhodka
Khabarovsk
Svobodnyy
Vanino
Korsakov
Ayan
Okhotsk
Magadan
Ust'-Kamchatsk
Petropavlovsk-Kamchatskiy
Anadyr'
Pevek
Ambarchik
Tiksi
Nordvik
Dudinka
Vorkuta
Ukhta
Nar'yan-Mar
Volga
Kama
Ob'
Irtysh
Yenisey
Lena
Amur
Trans-Siberian Railroad
Principal Railroads
Navigable Rivers
Canals
Main Sea Routes
Major Ports
0 500 1000
SCALE OF MILES

(continued on following page)

UNION OF SOVIET SOCIALIST REPUBLICS
European Part

CONIC PROJECTION

SCALE OF MILES

0   50   100   200   300

SCALE OF KILOMETRES

0   50 100   200   300

National Capitals .... ★
Capitals of Union Republics .... ⬡
Administrative Centers .... △
International boundaries ....
Union Republic boundaries ....
A.S.S.R., Oblast, Kray boundaries ....
Autonomous Oblast boundaries ....
National Okrug boundaries ....
Canals ....

The government of the United States has not recognized the
incorporation of Estonia, Latvia and Lithuania into the Soviet
Union, nor does it recognize as final the de facto western limit
of Polish administration in Germany (the Oder-Neisse line).

Copyright by C.S. Hammond & Co., N.Y.

Administrative Divisions bear same
names as their respective Capitals
or Centers, except:

Abkhaz A.S.S.R.	Sukhumi	F6
Adygey Aut. Oblast	Maykop	F6
Adzhar A.S.S.R.	Batumi	F6
Bashkir A.S.S.R.	Ufa	J4
Chechen-Ingush A.S.S.R.	Groznyy	G6
Chuvash A.S.S.R.	Cheboksary	G3
Crimean Oblast	Simferopol'	D6
Dagestan A.S.S.R.	Makhachkala	G6
Kabardin-Balkar A.S.S.R.	Nal'chik	F6
Kalmuck A.S.S.R.	Elista	F5
Karachay-Cherkess Aut. Obl.	Cherkessk	F6
Karelian A.S.S.R.	Petrozavodsk	D2
Komi A.S.S.R.	Syktyvkar	H2
Komi-Permyak Nat'l Okrug	Kudymkar	H3
Mari A.S.S.R.	Yoshkar-Ola	G3
Mordvinian A.S.S.R.	Saransk	G4
Nagorno-Karabakh Aut. Obl.	Stepanakert	G7
Nenets Nat'l Okrug	Nar'yan-Mar	H1
North Ossetian A.S.S.R.	Ordzhonikidze	F6
South Ossetian Aut. Obl.	Tskhinvali	F6
Tatar A.S.S.R.	Kazan'	G3
Trans-Carpathian Oblast	Uzhgorod	B5
Udmurt A.S.S.R.	Izhevsk	H3
Volyn Oblast	Lutsk	C4

Union of Soviet Socialist Republics
(continued)

U.S.S.R.-EUROPEAN

UNION REPUBLICS

rmenian S.S.R., 1,958,000 ....F 6
zerbaidzhan S.S.R., 4,117,000...G 6
stonian S.S.R., 1,235,000 ....C 3
eorgian S.S.R., 4,271,000 ....F 6
atvian S.S.R., 2,170,000 ....B 3
thuanian S.S.R., 2,852,000 ......B 3
oldavian S.S.R., 3,106,000 ....C 5
ussian S.F.S.R., 122,084,000 ....F 3
krainian S.S.R., 43,091,000 ......D 5
hite Russian S.S.R., 8,316,000..C 4

INTERNAL DIVISIONS

bkhaz A.S.S.R., 426,000 ....F 6
dygey Aut. Oblast, 297,000 ......F 6
dzhar A.S.S.R., 260,000 ....F 6
ashkir A.S.S.R., 3,464,000 ....J 4
hechen-Ingush A.S.S.R., 840,000 ....G 6
huvash A.S.S.R., 1,137,000 ....G 3
rimean Oblast, 1,297,000 ....D 6
agestan A.S.S.R., 1,165,000 ......G 6
Kabardin-Balkar A.S.S.R., 455,000 ....F 6
Kalmuck A.S.S.R., 193,000 ....F 5
Karachay-Cherkess Aut. Oblast, 300,000 ....F 6
Karelian A.S.S.R., 659,000 ....D 2
Komi A.S.S.R., 851,000 ....H 2
Komi-Permyak Nat'l Okrug, 233,000 ....H 3
Mari A.S.S.R., 662,000 ....G 3
Mordvinian A.S.S.R., 1,003,000...G 4
Nagorno-Karabakh Aut. Oblast, 139,000 ....G 7
Nakhichevan' A.S.S.R., 142,000...F 7
Nenets Nat'l Okrug, 37,000 ....H 1
North Ossetian A.S.S.R., 469,000 ....F 6
South Ossetian Aut. Oblast, 98,000 ....F 6
Tatar A.S.S.R., 2,948,000 ....G 3
Trans-Carpathian Oblast, 966,000 ....B 5
Udmurt A.S.S.R., 1,368,000.........H 3
Volyn Oblast, 925,000 ....C 4

CITIES and TOWNS

Abdulino, 29,976 ....H 4
Agdam, 16,061 ....G 6
Agryz, 20,270 ....H 3
Akhaltsikhe, 16,868 ....F 6
Akhtubinsk, 15,221 ....G 5
Akhtyrka, 31,563 ....E 4
Akkerman (Belgorod-Dnestrovskiy), 21,832 ....D 5
Alagir, 15,163 ....F 6
Alatyr', 36,933 ....G 4
Aleksandriya, 35,190 ....D 5
Aleksandrov, 36,738 ....E 3
Alekseyevka, 20,148 ....E 4
Aleksin, 46,313 ....E 4
Ali-Bayramly, 13,427 ....G 7
Al'met'yevsk, 48,611 ....H 3
Alushta, 12,337 ....D 6
Anapa, 18,512 ....E 6
Apatity, 19,938 ....D 1
Apsheronsk, 29,837 ....F 6
Archangel (Arkhangel'sk), 286,000 ....F 2
Armavir, 123,000 ....F 5
Artemovsk, 60,626 ....E 5
Arzamas, 41,518 ....F 3
Astara, 5,381 ....G 7
Astrakhan', 324,000 ....G 5
Atkarsk, 27,771 ....G 4
Azov, 39,931 ....E 5
Bakhchisaray, 10,852 ....D 6
Bakhmach, 13,066 ....D 4
Baku, 700,000 ....H 6
Baku, *1,086,000 ....H 6
Balakhna, 29,846 ....F 3
Balaklava ....D 6
Balakovo, 36,428 ....G 4
Balashov, 64,349 ....F 4
Baltiysk, 17,378 ....A 4
Baranovichi, 58,064 ....C 4
Barysh, 17,909 ....G 4
Bataysk, 52,242 ....E 5
Batumi, 82,328 ....F 6
Belaya Tserkov', 70,633 ....C 5
Belebey, 26,172 ....H 4
Belev, 17,153 ....E 4
Belgorod, 72,278 ....E 4
Belgorod-Dnestrovskiy, 21,832....D 5
Beloretsk, 59,315 ....J 4
Bel'tsy, 67,114 ....C 5
Bendery, 43,109 ....C 5
Berdichev, 53,206 ....C 5
Berdyansk, 65,249 ....E 5
Beregovo, 25,730 ....B 5
Berezniki, 120,000 ....J 3
Berislav, 10,507 ....D 5
Beslan, 19,385 ....F 6
Bezhetsk, 26,921 ....E 3
Birsk, 24,837 ....J 3
Bobrinets, 11,453 ....D 5
Bobruysk, 108,000 ....C 4
Bologoye, 30,301 ....D 3
Bol'shoy Tokmak, 28,575 ....D 5
Borisoglebsk, 54,415 ....F 4
Borislav, 28,603 ....B 5
Borisov, 59,280 ....C 4
Borovichi, 44,123 ....D 3
Borzhomi, 15,332 ....F 6
Brest, 73,557 ....B 4
Bryansk, 249,000 ....D 4
Bugul'ma, 60,980 ....H 4
Buguruslan, 42,476 ....H 4
Buy, 27,221 ....F 3
Buynaksk, 32,956 ....G 6
Buzuluk, 54,851 ....H 4
Bykhov, 13,227 ....C 4
Cēsis, 13,800 ....C 3
Chadyr-Lunga, 13,193 ....B 5
Chapayevsk, 83,263 ....G 4
Cheboksary, 142,000 ....G 3
Cherepovets, 124,000 ....E 3
Cherkassy, 103,000 ....D 5
Cherkessk, 41,709 ....F 6
Chernigov, 113,000 ....D 4
Chernovtsy, 152,000 ....C 5
Chervonograd, 12,241 ....B 4
Chiatura, 21,521 ....F 6
Chistopol', 51,864 ....H 3
Chkalov (Orenburg), 293,000 ....J 4
Chortkov, 15,294 ....B 5
Chusovoy, 60,658 ....J 3
Danilov, 16,902 ....E 3
Daugavpils, 65,459 ....C 3
Davlekanovo, 17,072 ....H 4
Derbent, 47,318 ....G 6
Dmitrov, 34,415 ....E 3
Dneprodzerzhinsk, 207,000 ....D 5
Dnepropetrovsk, 738,000 ....D 5
Dobrush, 14,270 ....D 4
Donetsk, 774,000 ....E 5
Drogobych, 42,145 ....B 5
Dubna, 32,626 ....E 3
Dubna ....E 4
Dvinsk (Daugavpils), 65,459 ....C 3
Dzerzhinsk, 180,000 ....F 3
Dzhankoy, 28,457 ....D 5
Dzhul'fa, 4,017 ....G 7
Elista, 23,171 ....F 5
Engel's, 106,000 ....G 4
Erivan, 578,000 ....F 6
Fastov, 30,240 ....C 4
Feodosiya, 46,327 ....D 5
Frolovo, 26,438 ....F 5
Furmanov, 38,225 ....F 3
Gadyach, 11,725 ....D 4
Gagra, 14,023 ....E 6
Galich, 16,119 ....F 3
Gandzha (Kirovabad), 126,000....G 6
Gaysin, 17,680 ....C 5
Genichesk, 14,420 ....E 5
Glazov, 59,012 ....H 3
Glukhov, 22,962 ....D 4
Gomel', 199,000 ....D 4
Gori, 35,061 ....F 6
Gorki, 15,099 ....D 4
Gor'kiy, 1,042,000 ....F 3
Gorlovka, 309,000 ....E 5
Gornyatskiy, 28,457 ....K 1
Gorodets, 27,019 ....F 3
Gremyachinsk, 38,014 ....J 3
Grodno, 72,943 ....B 4
Groznyy, 300,000 ....G 6
Gryazi, 34,425 ....F 4
Gubakha, 47,094 ....J 3
Gubkin, 21,333 ....E 4
Gudauta, 13,019 ....F 6
Gukovo, 52,969 ....F 5
Gus-Khrustal'nyy, 54,158 ....F 3
Ichnya, 13,131 ....D 4
Inta, 36,154 ....K 1
Inza, 18,612 ....G 4
Ishimbay, 46,568 ....J 4
Ivano-Frankovsk, 66,456 ....B 5
Ivanovo, 368,000 ....E 3
Izhevsk, 330,000 ....H 3
Izmail, 48,103 ....C 5
Izyaslav, 11,587 ....C 4
Izyum, 37,595 ....E 5
Jelgava, 36,300 ....B 3
Kadiyevka, 192,000 ....E 5
Kagul, 16,223 ....C 5
Kakhovka, 19,107 ....D 5
Kalach, 16,906 ....F 5
Kalinin, 292,000 ....E 3
Kaliningrad, 238,000 ....B 4
Kalinkovichi, 14,942 ....F 4
Kaluga, 157,000 ....E 4
Kamenets-Podold'skiy, 40,299 ....C 5
Kamenka, 27,634 ....F 4
Kamensk-Shakhtinskiy, 57,525 ....E 5
Kamyshin, 56,511 ....F 4
Kanash, 32,897 ....G 3
Kandalaksha, 37,045 ....D 1
Kapsukas, 19,600 ....B 4
Kashin, 16,162 ....E 3
Kasimov, 27,855 ....F 4
Kaspiysk, 25,178 ....G 6
Kaunas, 247,000 ....B 4
Kazan', 725,000 ....G 3
Kazatin, 22,784 ....C 5
Kem', 18,127 ....D 2
Kerch', 107,000 ....E 5
Khachmas, 17,123 ....G 6
Khar'kov, 1,006,000 ....E 5
Khasavyurt, 34,194 ....G 6
Kherson, 192,000 ....D 5
Khmel'nitskiy, 62,473 ....C 5
Khorol, 12,357 ....D 5
Khotin, 10,319 ....C 5
Khvalynsk, 17,036 ....G 4
Kiev, 1,248.000 ....D 4
Kiliya, 20,304 ....C 5
Kimovsk, 39,490 ....E 4
Kimry, 41,243 ....E 3
Kinel', 32,447 ....H 4
Kineshma, 85,418 ....F 3
Kirov, 16,647 ....D 4
Kirov, 284,000 ....G 3
Kirovabad, 126,000 ....G 6
Kirovakan, 49,423 ....G 6
Kirovo-Chepetsk, 28,726 ....H 3
Kirovograd, 142,000 ....D 5
Kirovsk, 39,047 ....D 1
Kirsanov, 15,654 ....F 4
Kishinev, 254,000 ....C 5
Kislovodsk, 79,097 ....F 6
Kizel, 60,687 ....J 3
Kizlyar, 25,573 ....G 6
Klaipėda, 105,000 ....B 3
Klimovichi, 11,586 ....D 4
Klintsy, 42,033 ....D 4
Kobrin, 13,686 ....B 4
Kobuleti, 12,598 ....F 6
Kohtla-Järve, 29,200 ....C 3
Kolomna, 125,000 ....E 4
Kommunarsk, 110,000 ....E 5
Komrat, 14,361 ....C 5
Kondopoga, 16,060 ....D 2
Königsberg (Kaliningrad), 238,000 ....B 4
Konotop, 54,097 ....D 4
Korosten', 38,041 ....C 4
Kostroma, 193,000 ....F 3
Kotel'nich, 27,640 ....G 3
Kotel'nikovo, 17,605 ....F 5
Kotlas, 39,162 ....G 2
Kotovsk, 25,511 ....F 4
Kotovsk, 27,383 ....C 5
Kovel', 24,666 ....C 4
Kovrov, 105,000 ....F 3
Kramatorsk, 126,000 ....E 5
Krasnodar, 368,000 ....E 6
Krasnograd, 14,941 ....E 5
Krasnokamsk, 54,715 ....H 3
Krasnoslobodsk, 18,993 ....F 4
Krasnovishersk, 15,207 ....J 2
Krasnyy Liman, 28,911 ....E 5
Kremenchug, 100,000 ....D 5
Krichev, 19,028 ....D 4
Krivoy Rog, 448,000 ....D 5
Krolevets, 13,996 ....D 4
Kronshtadt ....C 3
Kropotkin, 53,997 ....F 5
Krymsk, 32,803 ....E 6
Kuba, 15,947 ....G 6
Kudymkar, 21,801 ....H 3
Kulebaki, 44,720 ....F 3
Kumertau, 30.937 ....J 4
Kungur, 64,796 ....J 3
Kupyansk, 25,644 ....E 5
Kursk, 233,000 ....E 4
Kutaisi, 141,000 ....F 6
Kuvandyk, 21,383 ....J 4
Kuybyshev, 901,000 ....H 4
Kuznetsk, 56,880 ....G 4
Labinsk, 41,944 ....F 6
Lebedin, 24,741 ....D 4
Leninakan, 117,000 ....F 6
Leningrad, 3,180,000 ....C 3
Leningrad, *3,552,000 ....C 3
Leninogorsk, 38,565 ....H 4
Lenkoran', 25,209 ....G 7
L'gov, 21,328 ....E 4
Lida, 28,541 ....C 4
Liepāja, 71,464 ....B 3
Lipetsk, 205,000 ....E 4
Lisichansk, 37,878 ....E 5
Liski, 37,638 ....E 4

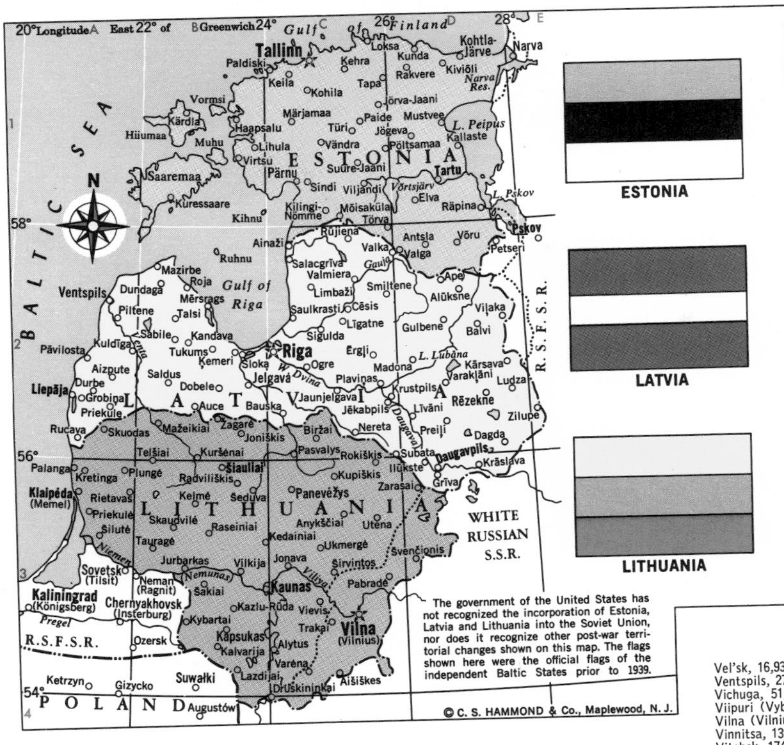

The government of the United States has not recognized the incorporation of Estonia, Latvia and Lithuania into the Soviet Union, nor does it recognize other post-war territorial changes shown on this map. The flags shown here were the official flags of the independent Baltic States prior to 1939.

© C. S. HAMMOND & Co., Maplewood, N. J.

THE BALTIC STATES

SCALE OF MILES: 0 25 50 75 100
SCALE OF KILOMETRES: 0 30 60 90 120 150 180

Capitals ....☆
International Boundaries ....
Union Republic Boundaries ....
Prewar boundaries of the Baltic States where divergent from present boundaries ....

Alytus, 12,300 ....C 3
Cēsis, 13,800 ....C 2
Daugavpils, 65,459 ....D 3
Dvina, Western (riv.)....C 2
Finland (gulf) ....D 1
Haapsalu ....B 1
Hiiumaa (isl.) ....B 1
Jaunjelgava ....C 2
Jēkabpils ....C 2
Jelgava, 36,300 ....B 2
Kapsukas, 19,600 ....B 3
Kaunas, 247,000 ....C 3
Kedainiai, 10,600 ....C 3
Klaipėda, 105,000 ....A 3
Kohtla-Järve, 29,200 ....D 1
Krustpils ....D 2
Kuldīga, 10,500 ....A 2
Kunda ....D 1
Kuressaare ....B 1
Liepāja, 71,464 ....A 2
Memel (Klaipėda), 105,000 ....A 3
Narva, 27,600 ....E 1
Niemen (Nemunas)(riv.) A 3
Panevėžys, 41,100 ....C 3
Pärnu, 36,100 ....C 1
Pāvilosta ....A 2
Peipus (lake) ....D 1
Pskov (lake) ....D 1
Radviliškis, 12,600 ....B 3
Rakvere, 14,300 ....D 1
Rēzekne, 21,400 ....D 2
Riga, 632,000 ....C 2
Riga (gulf) ....B 2
Saaremaa (isl.) ....B 1
Šiauliai, 59,722 ....B 3
Tallinn, 311,000 ....C 1
Tartu, 74,263 ....D 1
Tauragė, 12,000 ....B 3
Telšiai, 13,500 ....B 2
Tukums, 10,800 ....B 2
Ukmergė, 14,900 ....C 3
Utena ....C 3
Valga, 13,400 ....D 2
Valmiera, 11,600 ....C 2
Ventspils, 27,400 ....A 2
Viliya (riv.) ....C 3
Viljandi, 17,900 ....C 1
Vilna (Vilnius), 271,000...C 3
Virtsu ....B 1
Võru, 10,700 ....D 2
Western Dvina (riv.)....C 2

Livny, 23,900 ....E 4
Lodeynoye Pole, 17,485 ....D 2
Lozovaya, 27,144 ....E 5
Lubny, 29,442 ....D 4
Luga, 25,540 ....C 3
Lugansk, 314,000 ....E 5
Luninets, 10,328 ....C 4
Lutsk, 56,282 ....B 4
L'vov (Lwów), 469,000 ....B 5
Lyubotin, 31,540 ....E 4
Lyskovo, 16,167 ....F 3
Lys'va, 72,989 ....J 3
Lyudinovo, 26,433 ....D 4
Makeyevka, 381,000 ....E 5
Makhachkala, 140,000 ....G 6
Makharadze, 19,131 ....F 6
Malaya Vishera, 16,109 ....D 3
Manturovo, 16,345 ....F 3
Marganets, 34,422 ....E 5
Mariupol' (Zhdanov), 320,000....E 5
Maykop, 82,135 ....F 6
Mednogorsk, 36,303 ....J 4
Medvezh'yegorsk, 15,824 ....D 2
Melekess, 50,696 ....G 4
Melenki, 17,462 ....F 3
Meleuz, 17,772 ....J 4
Melitopol', 104,000 ....D 5
Memel (Klaipėda), 105,000....B 3
Merefa, 26,307 ....E 5
Michurinsk, 80,653 ....F 4
Mikhaylovka, 34,645 ....F 4
Millerovo, 30,005 ....F 5
Mineralnye Vody, 40,131 ....F 6
Mingechaur, 19,904 ....G 6
Minsk, 644,000 ....C 4
Mirgorod, 25,069 ....D 5
Mogilev, 145,000 ....C 4
Mogilev-Podol'skiy, 21,208 ....C 5
Molodechno, 26,275 ....C 4
Molotov (Perm'), 722,000 ....J 3
Molotovsk (Severodvinsk), 78,657 ....E 2
Monchegorsk, 45,523 ....D 1
Morozovsk, 26,952 ....F 5
Morshansk, 40,924 ....F 4
Moscow (Moskva) (cap.), 6,317,000 ....E 3
Moscow, *6,354,000 ....E 3
Mozhaysk, 15,697 ....E 3
Mozhga, 29,987 ....H 3
Mozyr', 25,710 ....C 4
Mukachevo, 46,423 ....B 5
Murmansk, 254,000 ....D 1
Murom, 71,567 ....F 3
Naberezhnye Chelny, 16,214 ....H 3
Nakhichevan', 25,340 ....F 7
Nal'chik, 106,000 ....F 6
Naro-Fominsk, 35,419 ....E 3
Narva, 27,600 ....C 3
Nar'yan-Mar, 11,000 ....H 1
Nelidovo, 26,465 ....D 3
Nerekhta, 22,310 ....F 3
Nevinnomyssk, 39,806 ....F 6
Nezhin, 46,211 ....D 4
Nikel', 16,305 ....C 1
Nikolayev, 263,000 ....D 5
Nikol'sk, 16,818 ....G 3
Nikopol', 82,992 ....D 5
Noginsk, 92,760 ....E 3
Novaya Kakhovka, 19,885 ....D 5
Novgorod, 60,669 ....D 3
Novgorod-Severskiy, 11,249 ....D 4
Novoanninskiy, 18,664 ....F 4
Novocherkassk, 104,000 ....F 5
Novograd-Volynskiy, 27,580 ....C 4
Novokuybyshevsk, 62,755 ....G 4
Novomoskovsk, 114,000 ....E 4
Novorossiysk, 104,000 ....E 6
Novoshakhtinsk, 108,000 ....E 5
Novotroitsk, 54,484 ....J 4
Novoukrainka, 16,098 ....D 5
Novovolynsk, 23,895 ....B 4
Novyy Bug, 15,354 ....D 5
Nukha, 34,348 ....G 6
Nyandoma, 21,668 ....F 2
Obruch, 11,536 ....C 4
Ochamchire, 16,500 ....F 6
Odessa, 709,000 ....D 5
Oktyabr'sk, 33,771 ....G 4
Oktyabr'skiy, 64,717 ....H 4
Omutninsk, 24,789 ....H 3
Onega, 21,306 ....E 2
Oni, 4,385 ....F 6
Ordzhonikidze, 194,000 ....F 6
Orekhovo-Zuyevo, 113,000 ....E 3
Orel, 183,000 ....E 4
Orenburg, 293,000 ....J 4
Orgeyev, 14,391 ....C 5
Orsha, 64,432 ....C 4
Orsk, 199,000 ....J 4
Osipenko (Berdyansk), 65,249....E 5
Osipovichi, 15,777 ....C 4
Ostashkov, 19,542 ....D 3
Ostrogozhsk, 28,403 ....E 4
Ostrov, 17,646 ....C 3
Otradnyy, 27,889 ....H 4
Panevėžys, 41,100 ....B 3
Pärnu, 36,100 ....C 3
Pavlovo, 47,890 ....F 3
Pechora, 30,586 ....J 1
Penza, 296,000 ....F 4
Perm', 722,000 ....J 3
Pervomaysk, 44,330 ....D 5
Pervomayskiy, 16,341 ....F 2
Petrovsk, 24,987 ....G 4
Petrozavodsk, 145,000 ....D 2
Pinsk, 41,548 ....C 4
Piryatin, 15,203 ....D 4
Pochep, 15,700 ....D 4
Podol'sk, 144,000 ....E 3
Polonnoye, 19,775 ....C 4
Polotsk, 41,308 ....C 3
Poltava, 158,000 ....D 5
Polyarnyy ....D 1
Postavy, 10,566 ....C 3
Poti, 42,068 ....F 6
Povorino, 19,274 ....F 4
Prikumsk, 27,895 ....F 6
Priluki, 43,719 ....D 4
Primorsko-Akhtarsk, 22,006 ....E 5
Privolzhskiy, 15,168 ....G 5
Priyutovo, 18,941 ....H 4
Promyshlennyy, 20,405 ....K 1
Pskov, 101,000 ....C 3
Pugachev, 32,725 ....G 4
Pushkin, 30,035 ....D 3
Pyatigorsk, 69,617 ....F 6
Pyatikhatki, 21,359 ....D 5
Radomyshl', 11,427 ....C 4
Rakhov, 10,849 ....B 5
Rakvere, 14,300 ....C 3
Rasskazovo, 33,785 ....F 4
Rechitsa, 30,602 ....C 4
Revel (Tallinn), 311,000 ....B 3
Rēzekne, 21,400 ....C 3
Riga, 632,000 ....B 3
Rogachev, 10,156 ....D 4
Romny, 35,792 ....D 4
Roslavl', 37,433 ....D 4
Rossosh', 30,184 ....E 4
Rostov, 29,230 ....E 3
Rostov, 689,000 ....F 5
Rovno, 56,163 ....C 4
Rtishchevo, 32,739 ....F 4
Rubezhnoye, 35,122 ....E 5
Rustavi, 62,395 ....G 6
Ruzayevka, 24,909 ....F 4
Ryazan', 262,000 ....E 4
Rybinsk, 195,000 ....E 3
Rybnitsa, 18,649 ....C 5
Rzhev, 48,971 ....D 3
Sabirabad, 8,872 ....G 6
Safonovo, 31,709 ....D 3
Saki, 18,122 ....D 5
Salavat, 60,667 ....H 4
Sal'sk, 36,983 ....F 5
Sal'yany, 17,197 ....G 7
Samara (Kuybyshev), 901,000....H 4
Saransk, 124,000 ....G 4
Sarapul, 68,741 ....H 3
Saratov, 644,000 ....G 4
Sarny, 10,174 ....C 4
Sasovo, 20,735 ....F 4
Segezha, 19,708 ....D 2
Semenov, 19,837 ....F 3
Serdobol (Sortavala), 17,611....D 2
Serdobsk, 26,119 ....F 4
Serpukhov, 113,000 ....E 4
Sevastopol', 169,000 ....D 6
Severodvinsk, 78,657 ....E 2
Severomorsk, 32,234 ....D 1
Shakhty, 201,000 ....F 5
Shakhun'ya, 21,305 ....G 3
Shar'ya, 22,268 ....G 3
Shatura, 19,629 ....E 3
Shcherbakov (Rybinsk), 195,000..E 3
Shemakha, 13,066 ....G 6
Shepetovka, 31,898 ....C 4
Shostka, 38,884 ....D 4
Shumerlya, 30,213 ....G 3
Shuya, 64,562 ....F 3
Šiauliai, 59,722 ....B 3
Sibay, 28,822 ....J 4
Simferopol', 203,000 ....D 6
Skopin, 17,957 ....F 4
Slantsy, 35,303 ....C 3
Slavgorod, 38,413 ....D 4
Slavuta, 20,216 ....C 4
Slavyansk, 82,784 ....E 5
Slavyansk-na-Kubani, 38,954 ....E 5
Slobodskoy, 30,836 ....H 3
Slutsk, 22,740 ....C 4
Smela, 44,534 ....D 5
Smolensk, 170,000 ....D 4
Sochi, 174,000 ....E 6
Sokol, 41,709 ....F 3
Sol'-Iletsk, 21,614 ....J 4
Solikamsk, 82,874 ....J 3
Sorochinsk, 19,359 ....H 4
Soroki, 15,195 ....C 5
Sortavala, 17,611 ....D 2
Sosnogorsk, 15,799 ....H 2
Sovetsk, 31,941 ....B 4
Stalingrad (Volgograd), 663,000..F 5
Stalino (Donetsk), 774,000 ....E 5
Staraya Russa, 25,409 ....D 3
Starobel'sk, 19,519 ....E 5
Staryy Oskol, 27,474 ....E 4
Stavropol', 158,000 ....F 5
Stepanakert, 19,703 ....G 7
Stepnoy (Elista), 23,171 ....G 5
Sterlitamak, 131,000 ....J 4
Stupino, 40,343 ....E 4
Sukhumi, 64,730 ....F 6
Sumgait, 52,186 ....G 6
Sumy, 117,000 ....E 4
Syktyvkar, 64,461 ....H 2
Syzran', 159,000 ....G 4
Taganrog, 220,000 ....E 5
Tallinn, 311,000 ....B 3
Tambov, 194,000 ....F 4
Tartu, 74,263 ....C 3
Tauragė, 12,000 ....B 3
Tbilisi, 768,000 ....F 6
Telavi, 15,328 ....G 6
Telšiai, 13,500 ....B 3
Temryuk, 22,182 ....E 5
Ternopol', 52,245 ....C 5
Teykovo, 28,298 ....E 3
Tiflis (Tbilisi), 768,000 ....F 6
Tighina (Bendery), 43,109....C 5
Tikhoretsk, 49,658 ....F 5
Tikhvin, 18,412 ....D 3
Tiraspol', 62,676 ....D 5
Togliatti, 61,281 ....G 4
Toropets, 15,154 ....D 3
Torzhok, 34,921 ....D 3
Tskhinvali, 21,641 ....F 6
Tuapse, 36,650 ....E 6
Tukums, 10,800 ....B 3
Tula, 351,000 ....E 4
Tul'chin, 12,492 ....C 5
Tutayev, 17,210 ....E 3
Tuymazy, 23,408 ....H 4
Ufa, 630,000 ....J 4
Ugleural'skiy, 31,369 ....J 3
Uglich, 28,890 ....E 3
Ukhta, 36,154 ....H 2
Ukmerge, 14,900 ....C 3
Ul'yanovsk, 247,000 ....G 4
Uman', 44,546 ....D 5
Uryupinsk, 31,546 ....F 4
Uzhgorod, 47,396 ....B 5
Uzlovaya, 53,912 ....E 4
Valga, 13,400 ....C 3
Valmiera, 11,600 ....C 3
Valuyki, 18,068 ....E 4
Vasil'kov, 20,450 ....D 4
Velikiy Ustyug, 37,026 ....F 2
Velikiye Luki, 58,939 ....D 3
Vel'sk, 16,938 ....F 2
Ventspils, 27,400 ....B 3
Vichuga, 51,676 ....F 3
Viipuri (Vyborg), 51,088 ....C 2
Vilna (Vilnius), 271,000 ....C 4
Vinnitsa, 139,000 ....C 5
Vitebsk, 174,300 ....C 3
Vladimir, 181,000 ....F 3
Volgodonsk, 15,710 ....F 5
Volgograd, 663,000 ....F 5
Volkhov, 36,630 ....D 3
Volkovysk, 18,283 ....B 4
Vologda, 152,000 ....F 3
Vol'sk, 61,792 ....G 4
Volzhsk, 33,412 ....G 3
Volzhskiy, 66,965 ....G 5
Vorkuta, 55,668 ....K 1
Voronezh, 535,000 ....E 4
Voroshilovgrad (Lugansk), 314,000 ....F 5
Votkinsk, 59,666 ....H 3
Voznesensk, 31,043 ....D 5
Vyatskiye Polyany, 25,717 ....H 3
Vyaz'ma, 31,883 ....D 3
Vyborg, 51,088 ....C 2
Vyksa, 40,275 ....F 3
Vyshniy Volochek, 66,360 ....D 3
Yalta, 43,994 ....D 6
Yanaul, 15,843 ....J 3
Yaroslavl', 454,000 ....E 3
Yartsevo, 25,558 ....D 3
Yefremov, 28,672 ....E 4
Yegor'yevsk, 59,341 ....E 3
Yelabuga, 21,992 ....H 3
Yelets, 77,900 ....E 4
Yenakiyevo, 92,306 ....E 5
Yershov, 19,977 ....G 4
Yessentuki, 48,101 ....F 6
Yevpatoria, 56,992 ....D 5
Yeysk, 55,324 ....E 5
Yoshkar-Ola, 116,000 ....G 3
Yur'yevets, 19,746 ....F 3
Zagorsk, 73,578 ....E 3
Zaporozh'ye, 507,000 ....E 5
Zelenodol'sk, 60,472 ....G 3
Zhdanov, 320,000 ....E 5
Zherdevka, 15,267 ....K 4
Zhigulevsk, 46,117 ....G 4
Zhitomir, 120,000 ....C 4
Zhlobin, 19,216 ....D 4
Zhmerinka, 29,368 ....C 5
Znamenka, 22,297 ....D 5
Zolotonosha, 24,603 ....D 5
Zugdidi, 31,081 ....F 6
Zvenigorodka, 17,154 ....D 5

PHYSICAL FEATURES

Apsheron (pen.) ....H 6
Araks (river) ....G 7
Azov (sea) ....E 5
Baltic (sea) ....B 3
Belaya (river) ....H 3
Beloye (lake) ....E 2
Berezina (river) ....C 4
Black (sea) ....D 6
Bolvanskiy Nos (cape) ....K 1
Bug (river) ....B 4
Bug (river) ....D 5
Caspian (sea) ....G 6
Caucasus (mts.) ....F 6
Central Ural (mts.) ....J 2
Cheshskaya (bay) ....G 1
Chir (river) ....F 5
Crimea (pen.), 1,297,000 ....D 5
Dagö (Hiiumaa) (isl.) ....B 3
Denezhkin Kamen' (mt.) ....J 2
Desna (river) ....D 4
Dnieper (river) ....D 5
Dniester (river) ....C 5
Dolgiy (isl.) ....J 1
Don (river) ....F 5
Donets (river) ....E 5
Dvina (bay) ....E 2
Dvina, Northern (river) ....F 2
Dvina, Western (river) ....C 3
Dykh-Tau (mt.) ....F 6
El'brus (mt.) ....F 6
Finland (gulf) ....C 3
Goryn' (river) ....C 4
Hiiumaa (isl.) ....B 3
Ilek (river) ....J 4
Il'men (lake) ....D 3
Imandra (lake) ....D 1
Izhma (river) ....H 2
Kakhovka (res.) ....D 5
Kama (river) ....H 2
Kandalaksha (gulf) ....D 1
Kanin (pen.) ....G 1
Kanin Nos (cape) ....F 1
Kapydzhik (mt.) ....G 7
Kara (sea) ....K 1
Karskiye Vorota (strait) ....J 1
Kazbek (mt.) ....F 6
Khoper (river) ....F 4
Kil'din (isl.) ....D 1
Kinel' (river) ....H 4
Kola (pen.) ....E 1
Kolguyev (isl.) ....G 1
Kolva (river) ....J 1
Kuban' (river) ....E 5
Kubeno (lake) ....E 3
Kuma (river) ....G 5
Kura (river) ....G 6
Kuybyshev (res.) ....G 4
Kuyto (lake) ....D 2
Lacha (lake) ....E 2
Ladoga (lake) ....D 2
Lovat' (river) ....D 3
Mansel'ka (mts.) ....C 1
Manych-Gudilo (lake) ....F 5
Matveyev (isl.) ....J 1
Medveditsa (river) ....F 4
Mezen' (bay) ....F 1
Mezen' ((river) ....G 1
Mezhdusharskiy (isl.) ....G 1
Moksha (river) ....F 4
Moskva (river) ....E 3
Msta (river)....D 3
Narodnaya (mt.) ....K 1
Niemen (river) ....B 4
North Ural (mts.) ....K 1
Northern Dvina (river) ....F 2
Novaya Zemlya (isls.), 500 ....H 1
Oka (river) ....F 4
Onega (bay) ....E 2
Onega (lake) ....E 2
Onega (river) ....E 2
ösel (Saaremaa) (isl.) ....B 3
Pay-Yer (mt.) ....K 1
Pechora (river) ....H 1
Peipus (lake) ....C 3
Pinega (river) ....G 2
Ponoy (river) ....E 1
Pripet (marsh) ....C 4
Pripyat' (river) ....C 4
Prut (river) ....C 5
Psel (river) ....D 4
Riga (gulf) ....B 3
Russkiy Zavorot (cape) ....H 1
Rybachiy (pen.) ....D 1
Rybinsk (res.) ....E 3
Saaremaa (isl.) ....B 3
Samara (river) ....H 4
Seg (lake) ....D 2
Sevan (lake) ....G 6
Seym (river) ....D 4
Solovetskiye (isls.) ....E 1
South Ural (mts.) ....J 4
Suda (river) ....E 3
Sukhona (river) ....F 2
Sura (river) ....G 4
Svir' (river) ....D 2
Sysola (river) ....H 2
Tel'pos-Iz (mt.) ....K 2
Timan Ridge (mts.) ....H 1
Top (lake) ....D 1
Tsimlyansk (res.) ....F 5
Tuloma (river) ....D 1
Ufa (river) ....J 3
Undzha (river) ....F 3
Ural (mts.) ....J 2
Ural (river) ....J 4
Usa (river) ....K 1
Vaga (river) ....F 2
Valday (hills) ....D 3
Vaygach (isl.) ....K 1
Velikaya (river) ....C 3
Vetluga (river) ....G 3
Vodl (lake) ....E 2
Volga (river) ....G 5
Volga-Don (canal) ....F 5
Volkhov (river) ....D 3
Vorona (river) ....F 4
Vorskla (river) ....E 4
Vozhe (lake) ....F 2
Vyatka (river) ....H 3
Vychegda (river) ....G 2
Vyg (lake) ....E 2
Vym' (river) ....H 2
Western Dvina (river) ....C 3
White (sea) ....E 1
Yamantau (mt.) ....J 4
Yug (river) ....G 2
Yugorskiy (pen.) ....K 1

*City and suburbs.

ASIA

LAMBERT AZIMUTHAL EQUAL-AREA PROJECTION

SCALE OF MILES

0   150   300   600   900   1200

SCALE OF KILOMETRES

0   300   600   900   1200

Capitals of Countries .... ☆   Canals ___

International Boundaries ___

Copyright by C. S. Hammond & Co., N.Y.

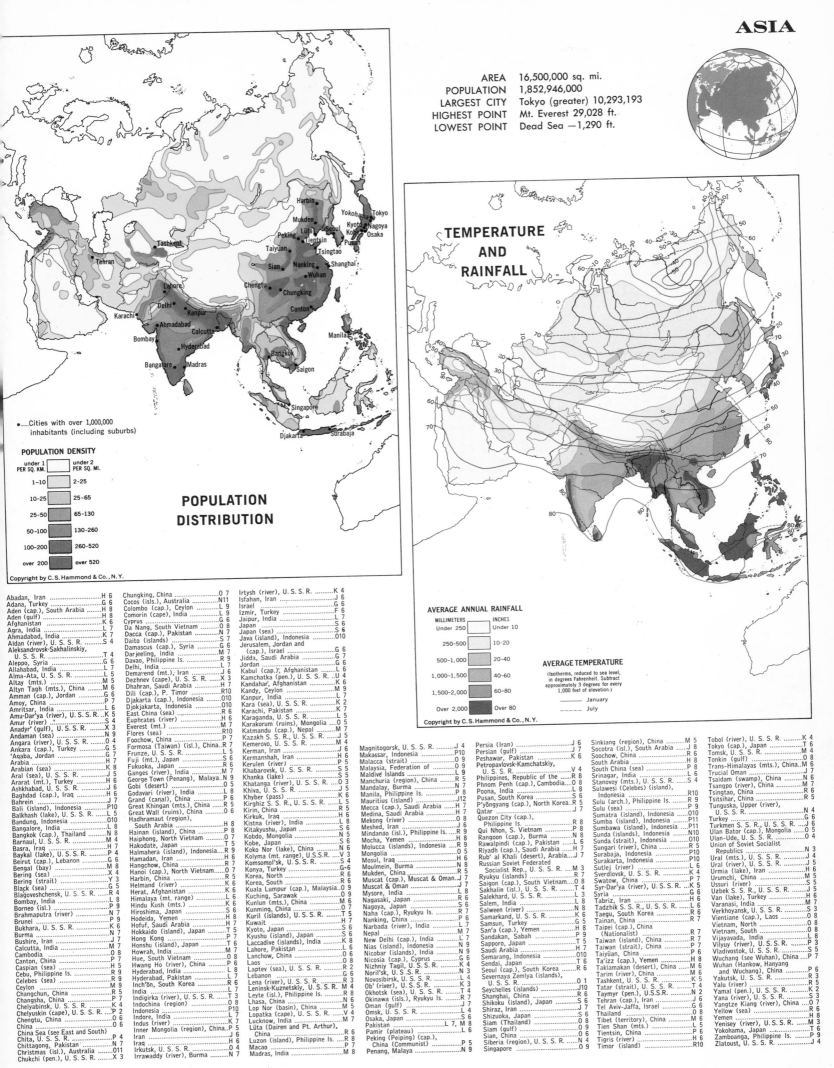

AREA 16,500,000 sq. mi.
POPULATION 1,852,946,000
LARGEST CITY Tokyo (greater) 10,293,193
HIGHEST POINT Mt. Everest 29,028 ft.
LOWEST POINT Dead Sea −1,290 ft.

POPULATION DISTRIBUTION

• Cities with over 1,000,000 inhabitants (including suburbs)

POPULATION DENSITY

PER SQ. KM.	PER SQ. MI.
under 1	under 2
1–10	2–25
10–25	25–65
25–50	65–130
50–100	130–260
100–200	260–520
over 200	over 520

Copyright by C. S. Hammond & Co., N.Y.

TEMPERATURE AND RAINFALL

AVERAGE ANNUAL RAINFALL

MILLIMETERS	INCHES
Under 250	Under 10
250–500	10–20
500–1,000	20–40
1,000–1,500	40–60
1,500–2,000	60–80
Over 2,000	Over 80

AVERAGE TEMPERATURE

(Isotherms, reduced to sea level, in degrees Fahrenheit. Subtract approximately 3 degrees for every 1,000 feet of elevation.)

—— January
----- July

Copyright by C. S. Hammond & Co., N.Y.

SOUTHERN ASIA
TRANSPORTATION

Principal Railroads.....................
　　Under Construction.....................
Connecting Roads.....................
　　Under Construction.....................
Desert Tracks, Caravan Routes.....................
Major Seaports.....................

SCALE OF MILES

0　100　200　　400　　600

SCALE OF KILOMETRES

0　100　200　400　　600

© C. S. HAMMOND & Co., Maplewood, N.J.

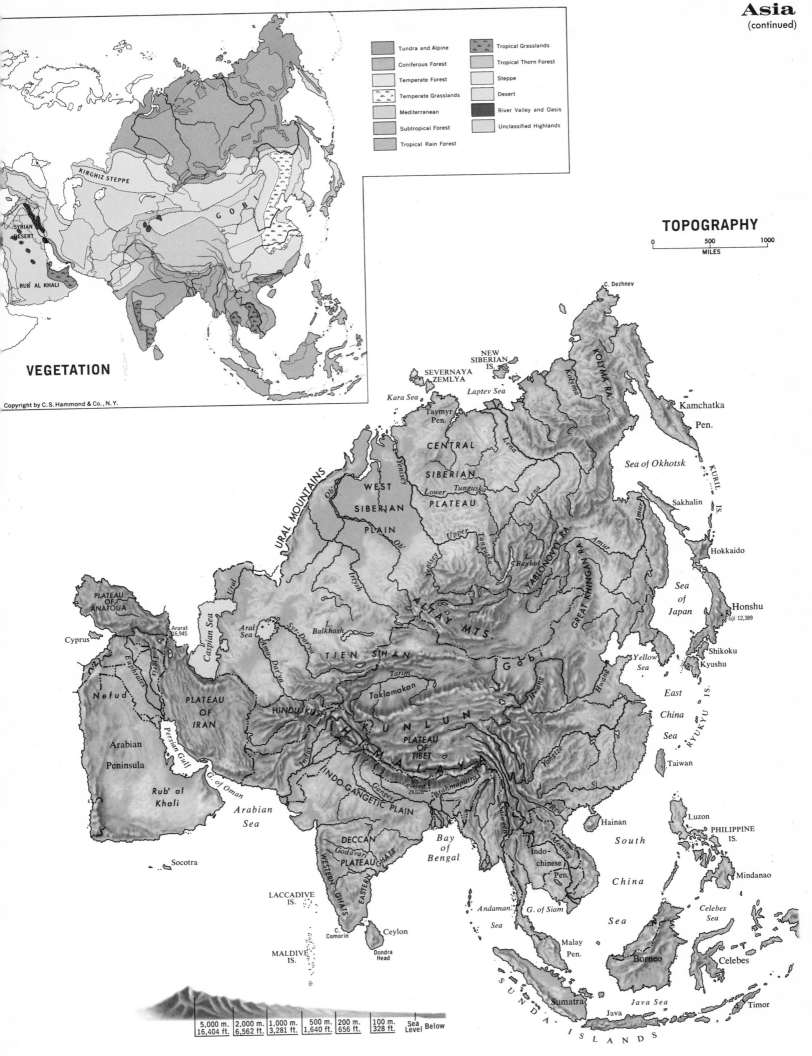

VEGETATION

Copyright by C.S. Hammond & Co., N.Y.

	Tundra and Alpine		Tropical Grasslands
	Coniferous Forest		Tropical Thorn Forest
	Temperate Forest		Steppe
	Temperate Grasslands		Desert
	Mediterranean		River Valley and Oasis
	Subtropical Forest		Unclassified Highlands
	Tropical Rain Forest		

TOPOGRAPHY

0   500   1000
MILES

5,000 m. | 2,000 m. | 1,000 m. | 500 m. | 200 m. | 100 m. | Sea | Below
16,404 ft. | 6,562 ft. | 3,281 ft. | 1,640 ft. | 656 ft. | 328 ft. | Level |

KIRGHIZ STEPPE

SYRIAN DESERT

RUB' AL KHALI

GOBI

C. Dezhnev

NEW SIBERIAN IS.

SEVERNAYA ZEMLYA

Kara Sea

Laptev Sea

Taymyr Pen.

CENTRAL SIBERIAN PLATEAU

Lena

Kolyma

KOLYMA RA.

Kamchatka Pen.

Sea of Okhotsk

WEST SIBERIAN PLAIN

Yenisey

Ob

Lower Tunguska

Upper Tunguska

Lena

Amur

KURIL IS.

Sakhalin

URAL MOUNTAINS

Ob

Irtysh

Yenisey

L. Baykal

YABLONOVYY RA.

GREAT KHINGAN RA.

Amur

Hokkaido

PLATEAU OF ANATOLIA

Ararat 16,945

Ural

Aral Sea

Syr Darya

L. Balkhash

ALTAY MTS.

Sea of Japan

Honshu

Fuji 12,389

Cyprus

Euphrates

Tigris

Caspian Sea

Amu Darya

TIEN SHAN

Tarim

Taklamakan

Gobi

Hwang

Yellow Sea

Shikoku

Kyushu

Nefud

PLATEAU OF IRAN

HINDU KUSH

KUNLUN

PLATEAU OF TIBET

Hwang

East China Sea

RYUKYU IS.

Persian Gulf

HIMALAYA

Indus

Mt. Everest 29,028

Brahmaputra

Yangtze

Taiwan

Arabian Peninsula

G. of Oman

INDO-GANGETIC PLAIN

Ganges

Si

Red

Rub' al Khali

Arabian Sea

Salween

Hainan

South

Luzon

PHILIPPINE IS.

Socotra

DECCAN PLATEAU

Godavari

WESTERN GHATS

EASTERN GHATS

Bay of Bengal

Indo-chinese Pen.

Mekong

China

Mindanao

LACCADIVE IS.

C. Comorin

Ceylon

Dondra Head

Andaman Sea

G. of Siam

Sea

Malay Pen.

Borneo

Celebes Sea

Celebes

MALDIVE IS.

SUNDA ISLANDS

Sumatra

Java

Java Sea

Timor

Near and Middle East

SAUDI ARABIA **KUWAIT** **YEMEN** **BAHREIN**

AFGHANISTAN
CITIES and TOWNS

Adin Khel	J 3
Anardarra	H 3
Andkhui, 30,000	J 2
Baghlan, 20,000	J 2
Bala Murghab, 10,000	H 2
Balkh, 15,000	J 2
Bamian, 10,000	J 3
Bara Khel	J 3
Belchiragh	J 2
Chahar Burjak, 500	H 3
Chahardeh	J 3
Charikar, 15,000	J 2
Daulat Yar, 2,000	J 3

Daulatabad, 15,000	H 3
Dilaram	H 3
Doshi, 5,000	J 2
Faizabad, 25,000	K 2
Farah, 10,000	H 3
Farsi	H 3
Gardez, 20,000	J 3
Ghazni, 25,000	J 3
Ghizao	J 3
Ghurian, 10,000	H 3
Girishk, 10,000	H 3
Haibak, 10,000	J 2
Herat, 61,760	H 3
Isfi Maidan	J 3
Ishkashim	K 2
Jalalabad, 44,290	K 3
Jurm, 10,000	K 2

Juwain, 2,000	H 3
Kabul (cap.), 400,000	J 3
Kabul, *480,000	J 3
Kala Bist, 500	H 3
Kala Kin	H 3
Kalat-i-Ghilzai, 10,000	J 3
Kandahar, 119,000	J 3
Khanabad, 30,000	J 2
Khash	J 3
Khugiani	J 3
Kuhsan	H 3
Kushk, 10,000	H 3
Landi Muhammad Amin Khan, 1,000	K 3
Maimana, 30,000	H 2
Maruf	J 3
Matun, 15,000	J 3

Mazar-i-Sharif, 39,695	J 2
Mirabad	H 3
Mukur, 10,000	J 3
Nauzad	H 3
Obeh, 5,000	H 3
Panjao, 3,000	J 3
Qala Panja, 1,000	K 2
Qaleh-i-Kang, 1,000	H 3
Rudbar, 1,000	H 3
Rustak, 10,000	J 2

Sabzawar, 5,000	H 3
Safar	H 3
Sangar	J 3
Sar-i-Pul, 5,000	J 2
Shahjui, 5,000	J 3
Shamalan	J 3
Shibarghan, 20,000	J 2
Shindand (Sabzawar), 5,000	H 3
Taiwara, 5,000	H 3
Tashkurghan	J 2

Tulak	H 3
Zebak, 3,000	K 2

PHYSICAL FEATURES

Farah Rud (river)	H 3
Gaud-i-Zirreh (marsh)	H 3
Hari Rud (river)	H 3
Helmand (river)	J 3

Hindu Kush (mts.)	J 2
Kabul (river)	K 3
Kunar (river)	K 2
Kunduz (river)	J 2
Lora (river)	J 3
Margo, Dasht-i- (desert)	H 3
Murghab (river)	H 2
Namaksar (salt lake)	H 3
Paropamisus (mts.)	H 2
Pyandzh (river)	J 2

NEAR and MIDDLE EAST

For facts and flags of nations other than Arabian states, see pages 61 to 69.

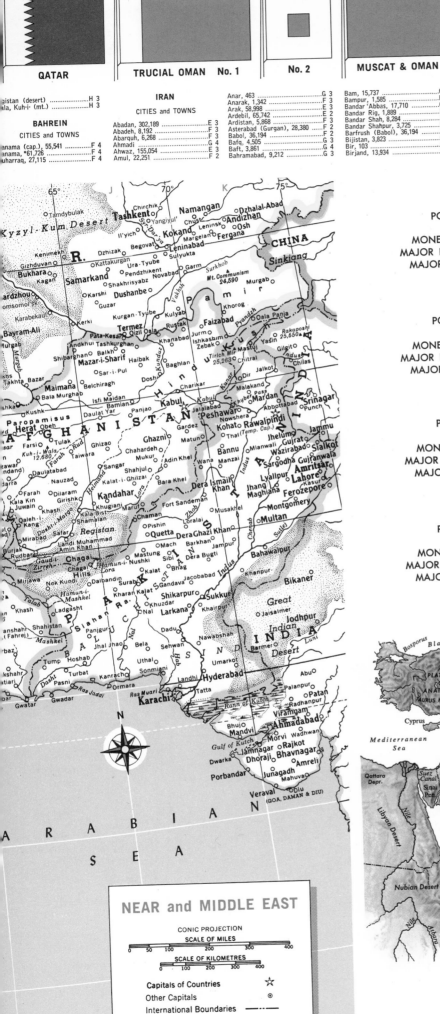

QATAR

TRUCIAL OMAN   No. 1

No. 2

MUSCAT & OMAN

gistan (desert) ....H 3
ala, Kuh-i- (mt.) ....H 3

BAHREIN
CITIES and TOWNS
anama (cap.), 55,541 ....F 4
anama, *61,726 ....F 4
uharraq, 27,115 ....F 4

IRAN
CITIES and TOWNS
Abadan, 302,189 ....E 3
Abadeh, 8,192 ....F 3
Abarquh, 6,268 ....F 3
Ahmadi ....E 3
Ahwaz, 155,054 ....E 3
Amul, 22,251 ....F 2

Anar, 463 ....G 3
Anarak, 1,342 ....F 3
Arak, 58,998 ....E 3
Ardebil, 65,742 ....E 2
Ardistan, 5,868 ....F 3
Asterabad (Gurgan), 28,380 ...F 2
Babol, 36,194 ....F 2
Bafq, 4,505 ....G 3
Baft, 3,861 ....G 4
Bahramabad, 9,212 ....G 3

Bam, 15,737 ....G 4
Bampur, 1,585 ....H 4
Bandar 'Abbas, 17,710 ....G 4
Bandar Rig, 1,889 ....F 4
Bandar Shah, 8,284 ....F 2
Bandar Shahpur, 3,725 ....E 3
Barfrush (Babol), 36,194 ....F 2
Bijistan, 3,823 ....G 3
Bir, 103 ....G 4
Birjand, 13,934 ....G 3

Borazjun, 10,233 ....F 4
Bujnurd, 19,253 ....G 2
Burujird, 49,186 ....E 3
Bushire, 18,412 ....F 4
Chahbar, 1,800 ....H 4
Chalus, 9,758 ....F 2
Damghan, 8,909 ....F 2
Darab, 9,106 ....F 4
Dashtiari ....H 4
Dezh-i-Shahpur, 1,384 ....E 2

	SAUDI ARABIA	KUWAIT
AREA	350,000 sq. mi.	8,000 sq. mi.
POPULATION	7,000,000	468,042
CAPITAL	Riyadh, Mecca	Al Kuwait
MONETARY UNIT	riyal	Kuwaiti dinar
MAJOR LANGUAGE	Arabic	Arabic
MAJOR RELIGION	Mohammedan	Mohammedan

	YEMEN	SOUTH ARABIA
AREA	75,000 sq. mi.	110,000 sq. mi.
POPULATION	5,000,000	1,613,000
CAPITAL	San'a, Ta'izz	Aden
MONETARY UNIT	bakcha	East African shilling
MAJOR LANGUAGE	Arabic	Arabic
MAJOR RELIGION	Mohammedan	Mohammedan

	BAHREIN	QATAR
AREA	231 sq. mi.	5,000 sq. mi.
POPULATION	182,203	60,000
CAPITAL	Manama	Doha
MONETARY UNIT	Indian rupee	Indian rupee
MAJOR LANGUAGE	Arabic	Arabic
MAJOR RELIGION	Mohammedan	Mohammedan

	TRUCIAL OMAN	MUSCAT & OMAN
AREA	12,000 sq. mi.	82,000 sq. mi.
POPULATION	111,000	565,000
CAPITAL	Dubai	Muscat
MONETARY UNIT	Indian rupee	rupee, Maria Theresa dollar
MAJOR LANGUAGE	Arabic	Arabic
MAJOR RELIGION	Mohammedan	Mohammedan

TOPOGRAPHY

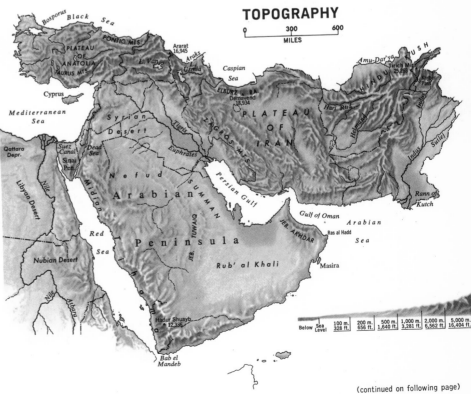

NEAR and MIDDLE EAST

CONIC PROJECTION
SCALE OF MILES
50 100   200   300   400
SCALE OF KILOMETRES
100   200   300   400

Capitals of Countries ....☆
Other Capitals ....◉
International Boundaries ....————

Copyright by C. S. Hammond & Co., N.Y.

(continued on following page)

Near and Middle East
(continued)

IRAN (continued)

Dizful, 52,121 E 3
Duruh H 3
Duzdab (Zahidan), 17,495 H 4
Enzeli (Pahlevi), 31,349 E 2
Estahbanat, 16,308 F 4
Fahrej (Iranshahr), 3,618 H 4
Fasa, 11,711 F 4
Firdaus, 6,834 G 3
Gach Saran F 3
Garmsar, 3,520 F 2
Geh H 4
Gulpaigan, 12,400 F 3
Gunabad, 7,555 G 3
Gurgan, 28,380 F 2
Gwatar H 4
Hamadan, 114,610 E 3
Iranshahr, 3,618 H 4
Isfahan, 339,909 F 3
Jahrum, 29,169 F 4
Jask, 1,078 G 4
Juimand (Gunabad), 7,555 G 3
Kangan, 2,682 F 4
Kangavar, 6,251 E 3
Kashan, 45,955 F 3
Kashmar, 13,299 G 2
Kazerun, 30,641 F 4
Kazvin, 66,420 E 2
Kerman, 62,157 G 3
Kermanshah, 166,720 E 3
Khaf, 4,144 H 3
Khash, 7,439 H 4
Khoi, 34,491 E 2
Khorramshahr, 43,850 E 3
Khur, 2,307 G 3
Khurramabad, 38,676 E 3
Lar, 14,188 F 4
Lingeh, 4,920 F 4
Mahabad, 20,332 E 2
Maragheh, 36,551 E 2
Marand, 13,822 E 2
Mehrabad, 1,695 F 2
Meshed, 312,186 H 2
Mianeh, 21,100 E 2
Minab, 4,228 G 4
Mirjawa, 883 H 4
Naband, 97 F 4
Naibandan G 3
Na'in, 4,681 F 3
Naishapur (Nishapur), 25,820 G 2
Nasratabad (Zabul), 12,221 H 3
Natanz, 2,090 F 3
Neh, 2,130 G 3
Nehavend, 20,972 E 3
Nejafabad, 30,422 F 3
Nikshahr, 1,879 H 4
Nishapur, 25,820 G 2
Pahlevi, 31,349 E 2
Qain, 4,414 G 3
Quchan, 21,250 G 2
Qum, 105,272 F 3
Ramishk G 4
Ravar, 5,074 G 3
Resht, 118,634 E 2
Reza'iyeh, 67,605 D 2
Sabzawar, 30,545 G 2
Sabzawaran, 2,480 G 4
Saidabad, 12,160 G 4
Samnan, 29,036 F 2
Sanandaj, 40,651 E 2
Saqqiz, 12,729 E 2
Sarbaz H 4
Sari, 26,278 F 2
Saveh, 14,537 F 2
Shahdad, 2,777 G 3
Shahistan, 4,012 H 4
Shahr-i-Tajan (Sari), 26,278 F 2
Shahriza, 29,311 F 3
Shahrud, 17,058 G 2
Shahsawar, 7,626 F 2
Shiraz, 229,761 F 4
Shirvan, 6,906 G 2
Shushtar, 18,527 E 3
Sultanabad (Arak), 58,998 E 3
Sultanabad (Kashmar), 13,299 G 2
Susangird, 6,025 E 3
Tabas, 466 G 3
Tabas, 7,413 H 3
Tabriz, 387,803 E 2
Tarum, 394 G 4
Tehran (Teheran) (cap.), 2,317,116 F 2
Tun (Firdaus), 6,834 G 3
Turbat-i-Haidari, 19,830 G 2
Turbat-i-Shaikh Jam, 6,756 H 2
Turshiz (Kashmar), 13,299 G 2
Turun G 2
Turut, 721 F 2
Urmia (Reza'iyeh), 67,605 D 2
Yazdan H 3
Yezd, 63,502 F 3
Zabul, 12,221 H 3
Zahidan, 17,495 H 4
Zarand, 4,099 G 3
Zenjan, 47,159 E 2

PHYSICAL FEATURES

Aj-i-Bala (mt.) F 3
'Aliabad (mt.) F 3
'Alijug (mt.) F 3
Araks (river) E 2
Atrek (river) G 2
Bazman (mt.) H 4
Demavend (mt.) F 2
Diz, Ab-i- (river) E 3
Elburz (mts.) F 2
Galvkhaneh (lake) F 3
Gurgan (river) F 2
Haliri (river) G 4
Jaz Murian, Hamun-i- (marsh) G 4
Karun (river) E 3
Kavir, Dasht-i- (salt desert) G 3
Kavir-i-Namak (salt desert) G 3
Lalehzar (mt.) G 4
Lut, Dasht-i- (desert) G 3
Maidani, Ras (cape) G 4
Mand Rud (river) F 4
Manisht (mt.) E 3
Mashkel (river) H 4
Mehran (river) F 4
Mihrabi (mt.) G 2
Namak, Darya-i- (salt lake) F 3
Namaksar (salt lake) H 3
Namakzar (marsh) G 3
Nezwar (mt.) F 2
Qais (isl.) F 4
Qishm (isl.) G 4
Qizil Uzun (river) E 2
Safidar (mt.) F 4
Savalan (mt.) E 2
Shaikh Shu'aib (isl.) F 4
Shir (mt.) F 3
Taftan (mt.) H 4
Talab (river) H 4
Tashk (lake) F 4
Urmia (lake) E 2
Zagros (mt. range) E 3

IRAQ

CITIES and TOWNS

Al 'Aziziya, 27,288 E 3
Al Falluja, 50,499 D 3
Al Fatha D 2
Al Musaiyib, 12,219 D 3
Al Qurna, 4,124 E 3
'Amadiya, 9,099 D 2
'Amara, 62,552 E 3
An Najaf, 125,424 D 3
An Nasiriya, 39,239 E 3
'Ana, 15,729 D 3
Ar Rahhaliya, 1,579 D 3
Arbela (Erbil), 39,913 D 2
As Salman, 3,584 E 3
Baghdad (cap.), 410,877 E 3
Baghdad, *784,763 E 3
Ba'quba, 56,616 D 3
Basra, 175,678 E 3
Erbil, 39,913 D 2
Habbaniya, 35,113 D 3
Haditha, 17,589 D 3
Hai, 45,205 E 3
Hilla, 72,943 D 3
Hit, 23,297 D 3
Karbala, 60,294 D 3
Khanaqin, 19,797 D 3
Kirkuk, *176,794 D 2
Kut, 71,360 E 3
Maidan, 7,939 E 3
Mosul, *215,882 D 2
Qal'a Sharqat, 35,367 D 2
Ramadi, 55,971 D 3
Rutba, 11,025 D 3
Samarra, 48,940 D 3
Samawa, 27,010 D 3
Shithatha, 2,083 D 3
Sulaimaniya, 48,812 E 2
Tikrit, 21,702 D 3

PHYSICAL FEATURES

Al Batin, Wadi (river) E 4
'Aneiza, Jebel (mt.) C 3
'Ar'ar, Wadi (dry river) D 3
El Hamad (desert) D 3
Hauran, Wadi (dry river) D 3
Mesopotamia (reg.) D 3

KUWAIT

CITIES and TOWNS

Al Kuwait (cap.), 99,633 E 4
Al Kuwait, *152,218 E 4
Mina al-Ahmadi E 4

PHYSICAL FEATURES

Bubiyan (isl.) E 4

MUSCAT AND OMAN

CITIES and TOWNS

Adam G 5
Dhank G 5
Ibra G 5
'Ibri G 5
Juwara G 6
Kamil G 5
Khaluf G 5
Khasab G 4
Manah G 5
Matrah, 11,100 G 5
Murbat G 6
Muscat (cap.), 5,080 G 5
Muscat, *6,208 G 5
Nizwa G 5
Quryat G 5
Risut F 6
Salala F 6
Sarur G 5
Shinas G 5
Sohar G 5
Sur G 5
Suwaiq G 5

PHYSICAL FEATURES

Akhdar, Jebel (mt. range) G 5
Batina (reg.) G 5
Dhofar (reg.) F 6
Hadd, Ras al (cape) G 5
Jibsh, Ras (cape) G 5
Madraka, Ras (cape) G 6
Masira (gulf) G 6
Masira (isl.) G 5
Musandam, Ras (cape) G 4
Nus, Ras (cape) G 6
Oman (reg.) G 5
Ruus al Jibal (dist.) G 4
Sauqira (bay) G 6
Sauqira, Ras (cape) G 6
Sham, Jebel (mt.) G 5
Sharbatat, Ras (cape) G 6

QATAR

CITIES and TOWNS

Doha (cap.), 45,000 F 4
Dukhan, 2,500 F 4
Umm Sa'id, 3,500 F 5

PHYSICAL FEATURES

Rakan, Ras (cape) F 4

SAUDI ARABIA

PROVINCES

'Asir, 900,000 D 6
Hasa, 2,250,000 E 4
Hejaz, 1,250,000 C 4
Nejd, 1,500,000 D 4

CITIES and TOWNS

'Abaila F 5
Abha D 6
Abqaiq E 4
Abu 'Arish D 6
Abu Hadriya E 4
'Ain al Mubarrak C 5
Akhdar C 4
Al 'Ain C 4
Al 'Ala C 4
Al 'Auda E 4
Al Lith C 5
Al Muadhdham C 4
Al Qahm D 6
Anaiza D 4
Artawiya E 4
Ashaira D 5
Ayun D 4
Badr C 5
Bisha D 5
Buraida D 4
Dam D 5
Dammam, 3,000 F 4
Dar al Hamra C 4
Debaba D 6
Dhaba C 4
Dhahran, 12,500 E 4
Dharma E 5
Dilam E 5
Doqa D 6
Duwadami D 5
Er Ras D 4
Faid D 4
Gail E 5
Haddar E 5
Hadiya C 4
Hafar al Batin E 4
Hail, 20,000 D 4
Halli D 6
Hamar E 5
Hanakiya D 5
Haql C 4
Haradh E 5
Haraja D 6
Hariq E 5
Hauta E 5
Hofuf, 83,000 E 4
Jabrin E 5
Jauf, 5,000 C 4
Jidda, 147,859 C 5
Jubail F 4
Jubba D 4
Junaina D 5
Kaf C 3
Khaibar D 6
Khamis Mushait D 6
Khurma D 5
Khurs D 5
Laila E 5
Majma'a D 4
Maqna C 4
Mastaba C 5
Mastura C 5
Mecca (cap.), 158,908 C 5
Medain Salih C 4
Medina, 72,000 D 5
Mendak D 5
Mina Sa'ud E 4
Mubarraz E 4
Mudhnib D 4
Muwaila C 4
Najran D 6
Nisab D 4
Oqair E 4
Qadhima C 5
Qafar D 4
Qasr al Haiyanya D 4
Qatif E 4
Qizan D 6
Qunfidha D 6
Qusaiba D 4
Rabigh C 5
Ras Tanura F 4
Riyadh (cap.), 169,185 E 5
Rumaihiya E 4
Sabya D 6
Sakaka D 4
Salwa F 5
Shaqra D 4
Shuqaiq D 6
Sufeina D 5
Sulaiyil E 5
Taif, 54,000 D 5
Taima C 4
Tamra D 5
Tebuk C 4
Truba D 4
Turaba D 5
Umm Lajj C 4
Wejh C 4
Yamama E 5
Yenbo C 5
Zilfi E 4

PHYSICAL FEATURES

Abu-mad (cape) C 5
Al Ahqaf (Bahr es Safi) (desert) E 6
'Aneiza, Jebel (mt.) C 3
'Aqaba (gulf) C 4
'Ar'ar, Wadi (dry river) D 3
Arafat, Jebel (mt.) D 5
Arma (plateau) E 4
Aswad, Ras al (cape) C 5
Bahr es Safi (desert) E 6
Barida, Ras (cape) C 5
Bisha, Wadi (dry river) D 5
Dahana (desert) E 4
Dawasir, Wadi (dry river) E 5
Dawasir, Hadb (mt. range) D 5
Farasan (isls.) D 6
Hatiba, Ras (cape) C 5
Jafura (desert) F 5
Mashabi (isl.) C 4
Midian (district) C 4
Misha'ab, Ras (cape) E 4
Nefud (desert) D 4
Nefud Dahi (desert) D 5
Ranya, Wadi (dry river) D 5
Red (Nefud) (desert) D 4
Rima, Wadi (river) D 4
Rimal, Ar (desert) F 5
Rub' al Khali (desert) F 5
Safaniya, Ras (cape) E 4
Salma, Jebel (mts.) D 4
Shaibara (isl.) C 4
Shammar, Jebel (plateau) D 4
Sirhan, Wadi (dry river) C 3
Subh, Jebel (mt.) C 5
Summan (plateau) E 4
Tiran (isl.) C 4
Tuwaiq, Jebel (mt. range) E 5

SOUTH ARABIA

CITIES and TOWNS

Aden (cap.), 99,285 E 7
Ahwar E 7
Al Ittihad, 29,897 E 7
Al Qatn E 6
Balhaf E 7
Bir 'Ali E 7
Damqut F 6
'Einat E 6
Ghaida F 6
Habban E 7
Hajarain E 6
Haura E 7
Hureidha E 6
'Irqa E 7
Lahej E 7
Leijun E 6
Lodar E 7
Maqatin E 7
Mukalla, 20,000 E 7
Nisab E 7
Nuqub E 6
Qishn F 6
Riyan E 7
Saihut F 6
Seiyun E 6
Shabwa E 6
Shibam E 6
Shihr E 7
Shuqra E 7
Taburkum E 6
Tarim
Yeshbum

PHYSICAL FEATURES

Asida, Ras (cape)
Fartak, Ras (cape)
Hadhramaut (dist.), 350,000
Hadhramaut, Wadi (dry river)
Hallaniya (isl.), 70
Kamaran (isl.), 2,200
Kuria Muria (isls.), 70
Perim (isl.), 381
Qamr (bay)

TRUCIAL OMAN

CITIES and TOWNS

Abu Dhabi, 4,000
'Ajman, 2,000
'Arada
Dubai, (cap.), 40,000
Dubai, *55,000
Fujaira, 2,000
Sharja, 9,000

PHYSICAL FEATURES

Das (isl.)
Yas (isl.)
Zirko (isl.)

YEMEN

CITIES and TOWNS

'Amram
Bait al Faqih
Dhamar
Harib
Hodeida, 40,000
Huth
Ibb
Luhaiya (Loheia)
Maida, 2,500
Manakha
Marib
Mocha
Sa'ada
Safir
San'a (cap.), 75,000
Sheikh Sa'id
Ta'izz (cap.), 25,000
Yarim, 5,000
Zabid, 8,000

PHYSICAL FEATURES

Hanish (isls.)
Manar, Jebel (mt.)
Sabir, Jebel (mt.)
Zuqar (isl.)

NEAR EAST

Arabian (sea) H
Buraimi G
Euphrates (river) E
Kurdistan (reg.) D
Mandeb, Bab el (strait) D
Oman (gulf) G
Persian (gulf) F
Red (sea) C
Tigris (river) E
Tihama (reg.) C

*City and suburbs.

AGRICULTURE, INDUSTRY and RESOURCES

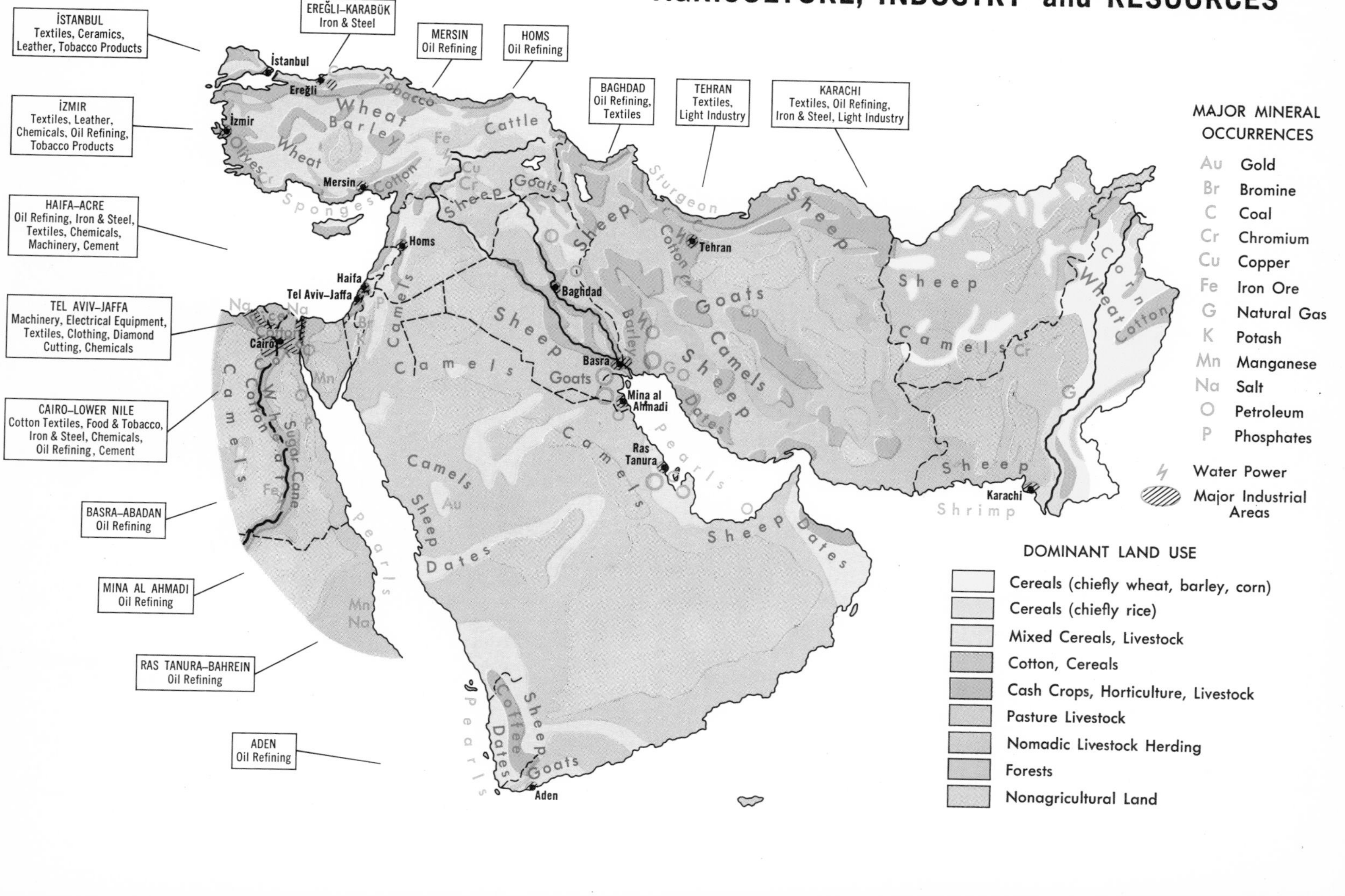

İSTANBUL Textiles, Ceramics, Leather, Tobacco Products
İZMIR Textiles, Leather, Chemicals, Oil Refining, Tobacco Products
HAIFA–ACRE Oil Refining, Iron & Steel, Textiles, Chemicals, Machinery, Cement
TEL AVIV–JAFFA Machinery, Electrical Equipment, Textiles, Clothing, Diamond Cutting, Chemicals
CAIRO–LOWER NILE Cotton Textiles, Food & Tobacco, Iron & Steel, Chemicals, Oil Refining, Cement
BASRA–ABADAN Oil Refining
MINA AL AHMADI Oil Refining
RAS TANURA–BAHREIN Oil Refining
ADEN Oil Refining
EREĞLI–KARABÜK Iron & Steel
MERSIN Oil Refining
HOMS Oil Refining
BAGHDAD Oil Refining, Textiles
TEHRAN Textiles, Light Industry
KARACHI Textiles, Oil Refining, Iron & Steel, Light Industry
İstanbul
Ereğli
İzmir
Mersin
Homs
Haifa
Tel Aviv–Jaffa
Cairo
Baghdad
Tehran
Basra
Mina al Ahmadi
Ras Tanura
Karachi
Aden
Wheat
Barley
Tobacco
Cattle
Olives
Cotton
Sponges
Sheep
Goats
Camels
Sturgeon
Dates
Pearls
Sugar Cane
Coffee
Corn
Shrimp
MAJOR MINERAL OCCURRENCES
Au Gold
Br Bromine
C Coal
Cr Chromium
Cu Copper
Fe Iron Ore
G Natural Gas
K Potash
Mn Manganese
Na Salt
O Petroleum
P Phosphates
Water Power
Major Industrial Areas
DOMINANT LAND USE
Cereals (chiefly wheat, barley, corn)
Cereals (chiefly rice)
Mixed Cereals, Livestock
Cotton, Cereals
Cash Crops, Horticulture, Livestock
Pasture Livestock
Nomadic Livestock Herding
Forests
Nonagricultural Land

TURKEY, SYRIA, LEBANON and CYPRUS

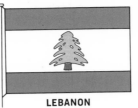
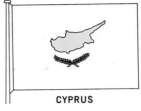

TURKEY **SYRIA** **LEBANON** **CYPRUS**

	TURKEY	SYRIA	LEBANON	CYPRUS
AREA	296,185 sq. mi.	72,587 sq. mi.	3,475 sq. mi.	3,572 sq. mi.
POPULATION	31,118,000	5,399,000	2,500,000	591,000
CAPITAL	Ankara	Damascus	Beirut	Nicosia
LARGEST CITY	İstanbul (greater) 1,466,525	Damascus (greater) 630,063	Beirut (greater) 500,000	Nicosia (greater) 100,000
HIGHEST POINT	Ararat 16,945 ft.	Hermon 9,232 ft.	Qurnet es Sauda 10,131 ft.	Troodos 6,406 ft.
MONETARY UNIT	Turkish pound (lira)	Syrian pound	Lebanese pound	Cypriot pound
MAJOR LANGUAGES	Turkish	Arabic, Turkish, Kurdish	Arabic, French	Greek, Turkish
MAJOR RELIGIONS	Mohammedan	Mohammedan, Christian	Christian, Mohammedan	Greek Orthodox, Mohammedan

AGRICULTURE, INDUSTRY and RESOURCES

DOMINANT LAND USE

- Cereals (chiefly wheat, barley), Livestock
- Cash Crops, Horticulture, Livestock
- Pasture Livestock
- Nomadic Livestock Herding
- Forests
- Nonagricultural Land

MAJOR MINERAL OCCURRENCES

Ab	Asbestos
C	Coal
Cr	Chromium
Cu	Copper
Fe	Iron Ore
Na	Salt
O	Petroleum
Pb	Lead
Zn	Zinc

⚡ Water Power
▨ Major Industrial Areas

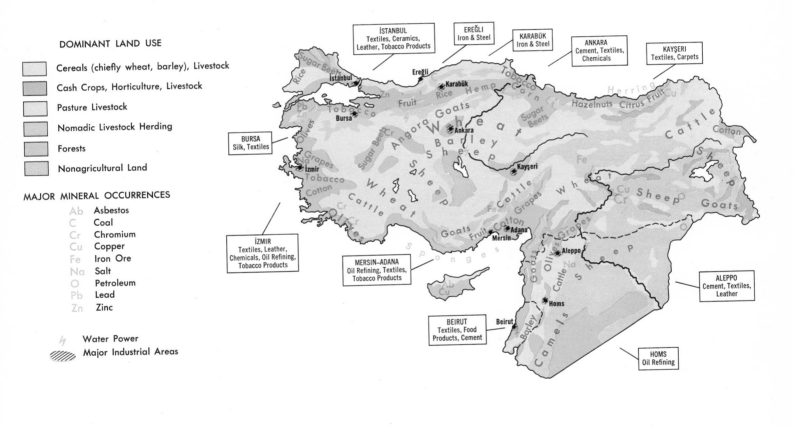

İSTANBUL
Textiles, Ceramics, Leather, Tobacco Products

EREĞLI
Iron & Steel

KARABÜK
Iron & Steel

ANKARA
Cement, Textiles, Chemicals

KAYŞERI
Textiles, Carpets

BURSA
Silk, Textiles

İZMIR
Textiles, Leather, Chemicals, Oil Refining, Tobacco Products

MERSIN–ADANA
Oil Refining, Textiles, Tobacco Products

ALEPPO
Cement, Textiles, Leather

BEIRUT
Textiles, Food Products, Cement

HOMS
Oil Refining

Turkey, Syria, Lebanon and Cyprus
(continued)

TURKEY (continued)

Ilgaz, 2,216	....	E 2
Ilgın, 8,116	....	D 3
Ilíc, 922	....	H 3
Incesu, 5,824	....	F 3
Inebolu, 5,873	....	D 1
Inegöl, 25,297	....	C 2
Inönü, 4,699	....	C 3
Intepe, 25,717	....	B 6
Ipsile, 1,787	....	G 2
Iskenderun, 62,061	....	G 4
Iskilip, 12,210	....	F 2
Islahiye, 11,560	....	G 4
Isparta, 35,981	....	D 4
Ispir, 2,025	....	J 2
İstanbul, 1,466,525	....	D 6
İzmir (Smyrna), 296,635	....	B 3
İzmir, *360,829	....	B 3

İzmit, 73,488	....	C 2
İznik, 6,290	....	C 2
Kadıköy, 129,918	....	D 6
Kadınhanı, 6,848	....	E 3
Kadirli, 10,964	....	F 4
Kağızman, 7,176	....	K 2
Kâhta, 3,866	....	H 4
Kalan, 3,818	....	H 3
Kale, 3,101	....	C 4
Kalecik, 4,112	....	E 2
Kaman, 8,871	....	E 3
Kandıra, 4,876	....	D 2
Karabük, 31,440	....	D 2
Karacabey, 15,969	....	C 2
Karahallı, 4,771	....	C 3
Karaköse, 19,776	....	K 3
Karaman, 21,668	....	E 4
Karapınar, 10,767	....	E 4
Karataş, 3,313	....	F 4

Karayazı, 950	....	J 3
Kars, 32,141	....	K 2
Karşıyaka, 64,194	....	K 2
Kartal, 14,815	....	D 6
Kas, 1,479	....	C 5
Kastamonu, 20,307	....	E 1
Kavak, 1,959	....	C 5
Kaymaz, 2,056	....	D 3
Kayseri, 102,596	....	F 3
Kelkit, 3,806	....	H 2
Kemah, 2,408	....	H 3
Kemaliye, 2,652	....	H 3
Kemalpaşa, 657	....	J 2
Kemer, 1,712	....	D 4
Kemerburgaz, 3,059	....	D 5
Kepsut, 3,980	....	C 3
Keşan, 15,061	....	B 2
Keskin, 6,438	....	E 3
Kığı, 1,430	....	J 3

Kilimli, 20,294	....	G 4
Kilis, 33,005	....	G 4
Kilitbahir, 865	....	B 6
Kilyos, 442	....	D 5
Kirikhan, 15,219	....	G 4
Kırıkkale, 42,904	....	E 3
Kırıkkağ, 11,345	....	E 2
Kırşehir, 20,196	....	E 3
Kırşehir, 20,248	....	F 3
Kızılcahamam, 4,124	....	D 2
Kızıltepe, 6,379	....	J 4
Kocaeli (İzmit), 73,488	....	C 2
Kömürcüpınar	....	C 5
Konya, 119,861	....	E 3
Korkuteli, 5,033	....	D 4
Kozan, 15,159	....	F 4
Kozlu, 17,533	....	D 2
Kozluk, 2,748	....	J 4
Kula, 8,532	....	C 3

Kulu, 7,198	....	E 3
Kumkale, 1,237	....	B 6
Küre, 1,765	....	E 2
Kuşadası, 7,008	....	B 4
Kütahya, 39,663	....	C 3
Ládik, 5,520	....	F 2
Lâpseki, 3,129	....	J 6
Lice, 6,725	....	J 3
Lüleburgaz, 22,362	....	H 3
Maden, 7,956	....	H 3
Mağara, 6,040	....	F 4
Malatya, 83,692	....	H 3
Malazgirt, 5,060	....	K 3
Malkara, 9,364	....	B 2
Manavgat, 3,218	....	D 4
Manisa, 59,675	....	B 3
Maraş, 54,447	....	G 4
Mardin, 28,382	....	J 4
Marmaris, 3,411	....	C 4
Mazgirt, 1,543	....	H 3
Mazıdağı, 1,999	....	J 4
Mecidiye, 1,134	....	B 5
Mecitözü, 5,217	....	F 2
Menemen, 15,155	....	B 3
Mersin, 68,485	....	F 4
Merzifon, 22,096	....	F 2
Midyat, 9,621	....	J 4

Mihalıçcık, 3,289	....	D 3
Milâs, 11,710	....	B 4
Misis, 999	....	F 4
Mucur, 5,289	....	E 3
Mudanya, 6,026	....	C 2
Mudurnu, 3,462	....	D 2
Muğla, 14,053	....	C 4
Müküs, 1,231	....	K 3
Muradiye, 1,864	....	K 3
Muş, 11,995	....	J 3
Mustafa Kemalpaşa, 20,886	....	C 2
Mut, 4,590	....	E 4
Nazilli, 36,660	....	C 3
Nevşehir, 18,662	....	F 3
Niğde, 18,042	....	F 4
Niksar, 10,534	....	G 2
Nizip, 19,336	....	G 4
Nusaybin, 5,011	....	J 4
Obruk, 737	....	E 3
Ödemiş, 28,482	....	B 3
Oltu, 4,306	....	J 2
Ordu, 20,029	....	G 2
Ortaköy, 2,025	....	F 3
Osmancık, 6,748	....	F 2
Osmaniye, 27,451	....	G 4
Ovacık, 904	....	E 4
Özalp, 1,930	....	K 3

Palu, 3,995	....	H 3
Pasinler, 7,926	....	J 2
Patnos, 3,478	....	K 3
Pazar, 4,846	....	H 2
Pazarcık, 5,812	....	G 4
Pera (Beyoğlu), 216,425	....	D 6
Pertek, 3,069	....	H 3
Pınarbaşı, 5,631	....	G 3
Polatlı, 20,169	....	E 3
Posof, 1,469	....	J 2
Pozantı, 2,470	....	F 4
Pülümür, 2,277	....	H 3
Pütürge, 2,532	....	H 3
Refahiye, 1,677	....	H 3
Reşadiye, 2,372	....	G 2
Reyhanlı, 12,371	....	G 4
Rize, 22,181	....	J 2
Rumelifeneri, 2,225	....	D 5
Safranbolu, 7,383	....	E 2
Saimbeyli, 2,188	....	F 4
Sakarya (Adapazarı), 79,420	....	D 2
Salihli, 24,109	....	C 3
Samandağı, 13,912	....	G 4
Samsat, 991	....	H 4
Samsun, 87,688	....	F 2
Sandıklı, 9,357	....	D 3
Sapanca, 5,788	....	D 2

Turkey is divided into provinces bearing the same names as their capital towns, except:

Province	Capital	
AFYON-KARAHISAR	Afyon	D 3
AĞRI	Karaköse	K 3
BİNGÖL	Çapakçur	J 3
HAKKÂRİ	Çölemerik	K 4
HATAY	Antákya	G 4
İÇEL	Mersin	F 4
KOCAELİ	İzmit	C 2
SAKARYA	Adapazarı	D 2
TUNCELİ	Kalan	H 3

Turkey, Syria, Lebanon and Cyprus
(continued)

ane, 3,245 ....C 3
ıköy, 6,984 ....C 4
ıönü, 5,783 ....E 3
amiş, 17,529 ....K 2
er, 43,991 ....D 5
ikaraağaç, 3,737 ....D 3
ısla, 6,647 ....G 3
at, 1,748 ....K 2
r, 3,379 ....J 4
ıkarahisar, 8,747 ....H 2
ülbahir, 466 ....B 6
rihisar, 4,416 ....B 3
ıdi, 2,135 ....C 3
niye, 1,944 ....B 4
dinli, 840 ....L 4
flikoçhisar, 8,656 ....E 3
k, 4,775 ....D 4
dişehir, 6,303 ....D 4
ıan (Adana), 231,548....................F 4
tgazi, 2,577 ....D 3
, 22,944 ....J 4
, 2,749 ....C 2
ke, 9,843 ....E 4
ri, 4,949 ....C 2
an, 6,492 ....J 3
av, 6,528 ....C 3
dirgi, 5,065 ....C 3
Sinop, 10,214 ....F 2
Şiran, 1,665 ....H 2
Şirnak, 4,058 ....K 4
Sivas, 93,368 ....G 3
Siverek, 26,134 ....H 4
Sivrihisar, 7,186 ....D 3
Smyrna (İzmir), 296,635 ....B 3
Söke, 23,593 ....B 4
Soma, 13,200 ....B 3
Şuhut, 5,922 ....D 3
Sungurlu, 10,619 ....F 2
Sürmene, 3,517 ....H 2
Sürüç, 6,800 ....H 4
Suşehri, 6,426 ....H 2
Susurluk, 11,450 ....C 3
Tarsus, 51,184 ....F 4
Taşkent, 4.998 ....E 4
Taşköprü, 5,715 ....F 4
Tatvan, 6,533 ....K 3
Tavas, 8,042 ....C 4
Tavşanlı, 11,622 ....C 3
Tefenni, 2,918 ....C 4
Tekirdağ, 23,987 ....B 2
Tercan, 2,234 ....J 3
Terme, 7,090 ....G 2
Tire, 26,643 ....B 3
Tirebolu, 4,705 ....H 2

TURKEY, SYRIA, LEBANON and CYPRUS
SCALE OF MILES
0 25 50 75 100 125 150
SCALE OF KILOMETRES
0 25 50 75 100 125 150
Capitals of Countries
Capitals of Provinces
Provincial Boundaries
Copyright by C. S. Hammond & Co., N. Y.
Kutaisi
Tbilisi
Batumi
Leninakan
Erivan
Kars
Erzurum
Mardin
Mosul
Kirkuk
Lake Van
Deir ez Zor
Euphrates
I R A Q

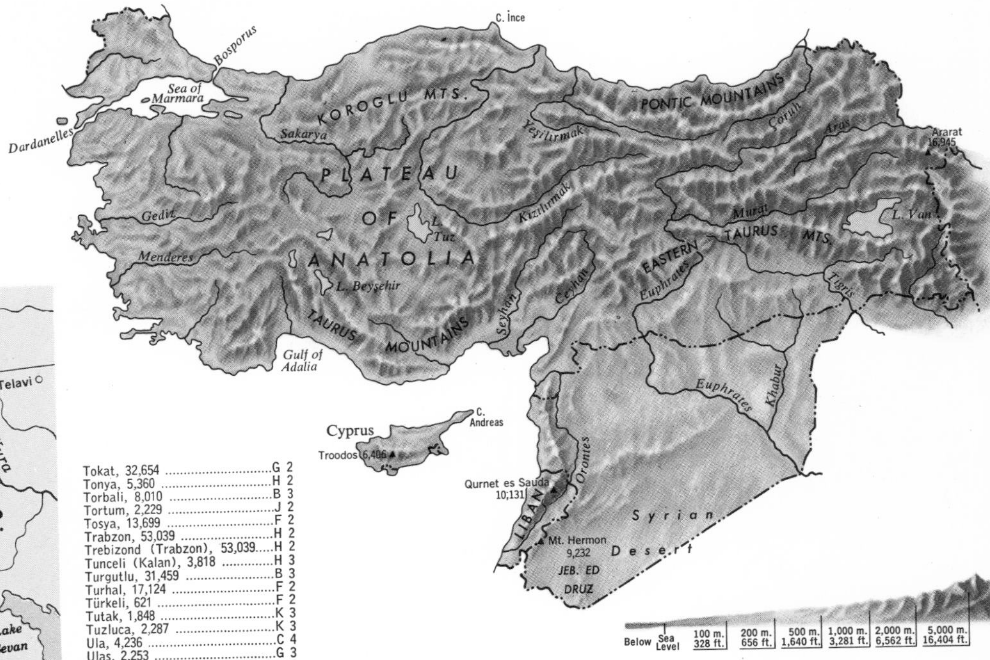

C. İnce
Bosporus
Sea of Marmara
Dardanelles
KOROGLU MTS.
PONTIC MOUNTAINS
Sakarya
Yeşilırmak
PLATEAU OF ANATOLIA
L. Tuz
Kızılırmak
Ararat 16,945
L. Van
Murat
EASTERN TAURUS MTS.
Gediz
Menderes
L. Beyşehir
TAURUS MOUNTAINS
Gulf of Adalia
Seyhan
Ceyhan
Euphrates
Tigris
Khabur
Cyprus
C. Andreas
Troodos 6,406
Qurnet es Sauda 10,131
Orontes
LIBAN
Mt. Hermon 9,232
JEB. ED DRUZ
Syrian Desert
Below Sea Level
100 m. 328 ft.
200 m. 656 ft.
500 m. 1,640 ft.
1,000 m. 3,281 ft.
2,000 m. 6,562 ft.
5,000 m. 16,404 ft.

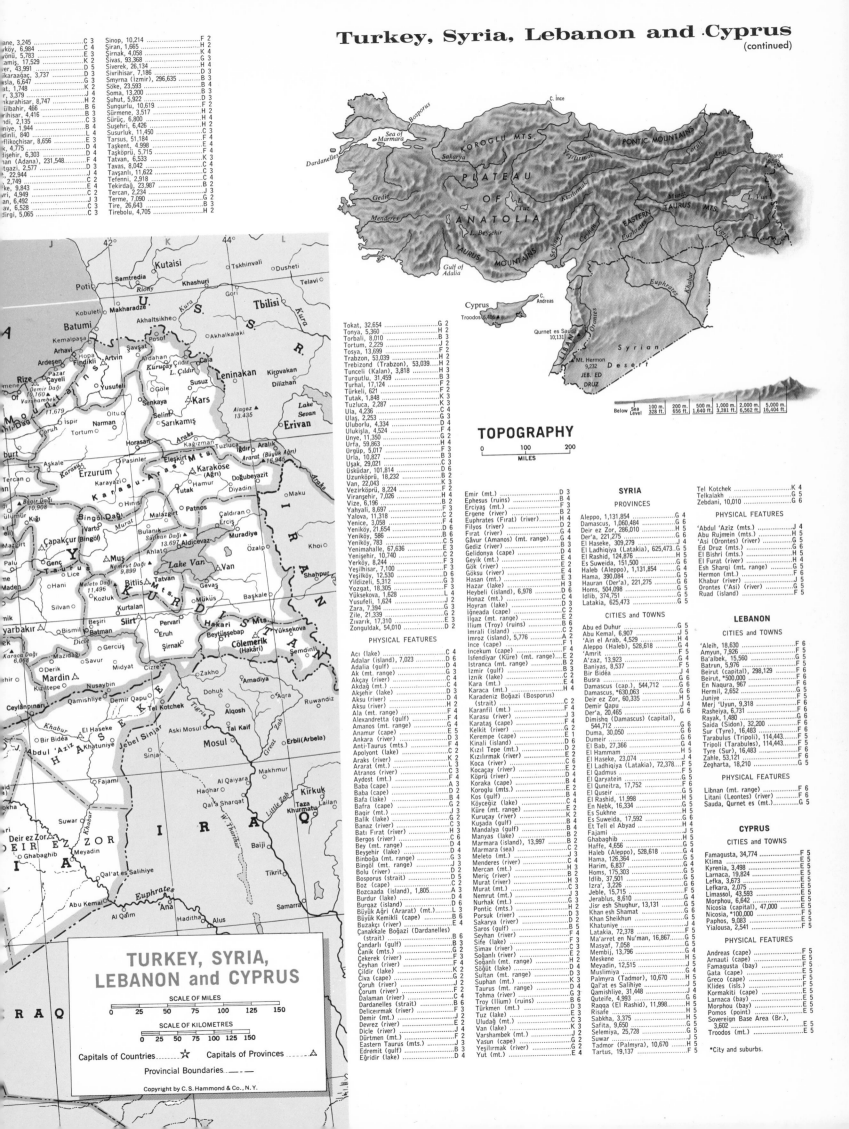

TOPOGRAPHY

0 100 200
MILES

Tokat, 32,654 ....G 2
Tonya, 5,360 ....H 2
Torbali, 8,010 ....B 3
Tortum, 2,229 ....J 2
Tosya, 13,699 ....F 2
Trabzon, 53,039 ....H 2
Trebizond (Trabzon), 53,039....................H 2
Tunceli (Kalan), 3,818 ....H 3
Turgutlu, 31,459 ....B 3
Turhal, 17,124 ....F 2
Türkeli, 621 ....F 2
Tutak, 1,848 ....K 3
Tuzluca, 2,287 ....K 3
Ula, 4,236 ....C 4
Ulaş, 2,253 ....G 3
Uluborlu, 4,334 ....D 4
Ulukişla, 4,524 ....F 4
Ünye, 11,350 ....G 2
Urfa, 59,863 ....H 4
Ürgüp, 5,017 ....F 3
Urla, 10,827 ....B 3
Uşak, 29,021 ....C 3
Üsküdar, 101,814 ....D 6
Uzunköprü, 18,232 ....B 2
Van, 22,043 ....K 3
Vezirköprü, 8,224 ....F 2
Viranşehir, 7,026 ....H 4
Vize, 6,196 ....B 2
Yahyali, 8,697 ....F 3
Yalova, 11,318 ....C 2
Yenice, 3,058 ....F 4
Yeniköy, 21,654 ....D 6
Yeniköy, 586 ....B 6
Yeniköy, 783 ....C 5
Yenimahalle, 67,636 ....E 3
Yenişehir, 10,740 ....C 2
Yerköy, 8,244 ....F 3
Yeşilhisar, 7,100 ....F 3
Yeşilköy, 12,530 ....D 6
Yildizeli, 5,312 ....G 3
Yozgat, 18,305 ....F 3
Yüksekova, 1,628 ....L 4
Yusufeli, 1,624 ....J 2
Zara, 7,394 ....G 3
Zile, 21,339 ....G 2
Zıvarık, 17,310 ....E 3
Zonguldak, 54,010 ....D 2

PHYSICAL FEATURES

Acı (lake) ....C 4
Adalar (island), 7,023 ....D 6
Adalia (gulf) ....D 4
Ak (mt. range) ....G 3
Akçay (river) ....C 4
Akdağ (mt.) ....C 4
Akşehir (lake) ....D 3
Aksu (river) ....D 4
Aksu (river) ....H 2
Ala (mt. range) ....F 4
Alexandretta (gulf) ....F 4
Amanos (mt. range) ....G 4
Anamur (cape) ....E 5
Ankara (river) ....D 3
Anti-Taurus (mts.) ....F 4
Apolyont (lake) ....C 2
Araks (river) ....K 2
Ararat (mt.) ....L 3
Atranos (river) ....C 3
Aydost (mt.) ....F 4
Baba (cape) ....A 3
Baba (cape) ....D 2
Bafa (lake) ....B 4
Bafra (cape) ....G 2
Bagir (mt.) ....J 3
Balik (lake) ....G 2
Banaz (river) ....C 3
Batı Fırat (river) ....H 3
Bergos (river) ....C 6
Bey (mt. range) ....D 4
Beyşehir (lake) ....D 4
Binboğa (mt. range) ....G 3
Bingöl (mt. range) ....J 3
Bolu (river) ....D 2
Bosporus (strait) ....D 5
Boz (cape) ....C 2
Bozcaada (island), 1,805....................A 3
Burdur (lake) ....D 4
Burgaz (island) ....D 6
Büyük Ağri (Ararat) (mt.)....................L 3
Büyük Kemikli (cape) ....B 6
Buzakçı (river) ....E 4
Çanakkale Boğazi (Dardanelles) (strait) ....B 6
Çandarlı (gulf) ....B 3
Čanik (mts.) ....G 2
Çekerek (river) ....F 3
Čeyhan (river) ....F 4
Çildir (lake) ....K 2
Čiva (cape) ....G 2
Çoruh (river) ....J 2
Çorum (river) ....F 2
Dalaman (river) ....C 4
Dardanelles (strait) ....B 6
Deliceırmak (river) ....F 3
Demir (mt.) ....J 2
Devrez (river) ....E 2
Dicle (river) ....J 4
Dürtmen (mt.) ....F 2
Eastern Taurus (mts.) ....J 3
Edremit (gulf) ....B 3
Eğridir (lake) ....D 4
Emir (mt.) ....D 3
Ephesus (ruins) ....B 4
Erciyaş (mt.) ....F 3
Ergene (river) ....B 2
Euphrates (Fırat) (river)....................H 4
Filyos (river) ....D 2
Fırat (river) ....G 4
Gâvur (Amanos) (mt. range)....................G 4
Gediz (river) ....B 3
Gelidonya (cape) ....D 4
Geyik (mt.) ....E 4
Gök (river) ....E 2
Göksu (river) ....E 4
Hasan (mt.) ....E 3
Hazar (lake) ....H 3
Heybeli (island), 6,978 ....D 6
Honaz (mt.) ....C 4
Hoyran (lake) ....D 3
İğneada (cape) ....C 2
İlgaz (mt. range) ....E 2
Ilium (Troy) (ruins) ....B 6
İmrali (island) ....C 2
İmroz (island), 5,776 ....A 2
İnce (cape) ....F 1
İncekum (cape) ....F 4
Isfendiyar (Küre) (mt. range)....................E 2
Istranca (mt. range) ....B 2
İzmir (gulf) ....B 3
İznik (lake) ....C 2
Kara (mt.) ....E 4
Karaca (mt.) ....H 4
Karadeniz Boğazi (Bosporus) (strait) ....C 2
Karanfil (mt.) ....F 4
Karasu (river) ....J 3
Karataş (cape) ....F 4
Kelkit (river) ....G 2
Kerempe (cape) ....E 1
Kinali (island) ....D 6
Kızıl Tepe (mt.) ....D 2
Kızılırmak (river) ....E 2
Koca (river) ....C 6
Kocaçay (river) ....E 2
Köprü (river) ....D 4
Koraka (cape) ....B 4
Koroglu (mts.) ....E 2
Kos (gulf) ....B 4
Köyceğiz (lake) ....C 4
Küre (mt. range) ....E 2
Kuruçay (river) ....K 2
Kuşada (gulf) ....B 4
Mandalya (gulf) ....B 4
Manyas (lake) ....B 2
Marmara (island), 13,997 ....B 2
Marmara (sea) ....C 2
Meleto (mt.) ....J 3
Menderes (river) ....C 4
Mercan (mt.) ....H 3
Meriç (river) ....B 2
Murat (river) ....H 3
Murat (mt.) ....C 3
Nemrut (mt.) ....J 3
Nurhak (mt.) ....G 3
Pontic (mts.) ....H 2
Porsuk (river) ....D 3
Sakarya (river) ....D 2
Saros (gulf) ....B 5
Seyhan (river) ....F 4
Sife (lake) ....F 3
Simav (river) ....C 3
Soğanlı (river) ....E 2
Soğanlı (mt. range) ....H 2
Söğüt (lake) ....D 4
Sultan (mt. range) ....D 3
Suphan (mt.) ....K 3
Taurus (mt. range) ....D 4
Tohma (river) ....G 3
Troy (Ilium) (ruins) ....B 6
Türkmen (mt.) ....D 3
Tuz (lake) ....E 3
Uludağ (mt.) ....C 3
Van (lake) ....K 3
Varshambek (mt.) ....J 2
Yasun (cape) ....G 2
Yeşilırmak (river) ....G 2
Yut (mt.) ....E 4

SYRIA

PROVINCES

Aleppo, 1,131,854 ....G 4
Damascus, 1,060,484 ....G 6
Deir ez Zor, 286,010 ....H 5
Der'a, 221,275 ....G 6
El Haseke, 309,279 ....J 4
El Ladhiqiya (Latakia), 625,473..G 5
El Rashid, 124,876 ....H 5
Es Suweida, 151,500 ....G 6
Haleb (Aleppo), 1,131,854 ....G 4
Hama, 390,084 ....G 5
Hauran (Der'a), 221,275 ....G 6
Homs, 504,098 ....G 5
Idlib, 374,751 ....G 5
Latakia, 625,473 ....G 5

CITIES and TOWNS

Abu ed Duhur ....G 5
Abu Kemal, 6,907 ....J 5
'Ain el Arab, 4,529 ....H 4
Aleppo (Haleb), 528,618 ....G 4
'Amrit ....F 5
A'zaz, 13,923 ....G 4
Baniyas, 8,537 ....F 5
Bir Bidéa ....J 4
Busra ....G 6
Damascus (cap.), 544,712 ....G 6
Damascus, *630,063 ....G 6
Deir ez Zor, 60,335 ....H 5
Demir Qapu ....J 4
Der'a, 20,465 ....G 6
Dimishq (Damascus) (capital), 544,712 ....G 6
Duma, 30,050 ....G 6
Dumeir ....G 6
El Bab, 27,366 ....G 4
El Hammam ....H 5
El Haseke, 23,074 ....J 4
El Ladhiqiya (Latakia), 72,378....F 5
El Qadmus ....F 5
El Qaryatein ....G 5
El Quneitra, 17,752 ....F 6
El Quseir ....G 5
El Rashid, 11,998 ....H 5
En Nebk, 16,334 ....G 5
Es Sukhne ....H 5
Es Suweida, 17,592 ....G 6
Et Tell el Abyad ....H 4
Fajami ....J 5
Ghabaghib ....H 5
Haffe, 4,656 ....G 5
Haleb (Aleppo), 528,618 ....G 4
Hama, 126,364 ....G 5
Harim, 6,837 ....G 4
Homs, 175,303 ....G 5
Idlib, 37,501 ....G 5
Izra', 3,226 ....G 6
Jeble, 15,715 ....F 5
Jerablus, 8,610 ....G 4
Jisr esh Shughur, 13,131 ....G 5
Khan esh Shamat ....G 6
Khan Sheikhun ....G 5
Khatuniye ....J 4
Latakia, 72,378 ....F 5
Ma'arret en Nu'man, 16,867....................G 5
Masyaf, 7,058 ....G 5
Membij, 13,796 ....G 4
Meskene ....H 5
Meyadin, 12,515 ....J 5
Muslimiya ....G 4
Palmyra (Tadmor), 10,670 ....H 5
Qal'at es Salihiye ....J 5
Qamishliye, 31,448 ....J 4
Quteife, 4,993 ....G 6
Raqqa (El Rashid), 11,998....................H 5
Risafe ....H 5
Sabkha, 3,375 ....H 5
Safita, 9,650 ....G 5
Selemiya, 25,728 ....G 5
Suwar ....J 5
Tadmor (Palmyra), 10,670 ....H 5
Tartus, 19,137 ....F 5
Tel Kotchek ....K 4
Telkalakh ....G 5
Zebdani, 10,010 ....G 6

PHYSICAL FEATURES

'Abdul 'Aziz (mts.) ....J 4
Abu Rujmein (mts.) ....H 5
'Asi (Orontes) (river) ....G 5
Ed Druz (mts.) ....G 6
El Bishri (mts.) ....H 5
El Furat (river) ....H 4
Esh Sharqi (mt. range) ....G 5
Hermon (mt.) ....F 6
Khabur (river) ....J 5
Orontes ('Asi) (river) ....G 5
Ruad (island) ....F 5

LEBANON

CITIES and TOWNS

'Aleih, 18,630 ....F 6
Amyun, 7,926 ....F 5
Ba'albek, 15,560 ....G 5
Batrun, 5,976 ....F 5
Beirut (capital), 298,129 ....F 6
Beirut, *500,000 ....F 6
En Naqura, 967 ....F 6
Hermil, 2,652 ....G 5
Juniye ....F 5
Merj 'Uyun, 9,318 ....F 6
Rasheiya, 6,731 ....F 6
Rayak, 1,480 ....G 6
Saida (Sidon), 32,200 ....F 6
Sur (Tyre), 16,483 ....F 6
Tarabulus (Tripoli), 114,443....................F 5
Tripoli (Tarabulus), 114,443....................F 5
Tyre (Sur), 16,483 ....F 6
Zahle, 53,121 ....F 6
Zegharta, 18,210 ....G 5

PHYSICAL FEATURES

Libnan (mt. range) ....F 6
Litani (Leontes) (river) ....F 6
Sauda, Qurnet es (mt.)....................G 5

CYPRUS

CITIES and TOWNS

Famagusta, 34,774 ....F 5
Ktima ....E 5
Kyrenia, 3,498 ....E 5
Larnaca, 19,824 ....E 5
Lefka, 3,673 ....E 5
Lefkara, 2,075 ....E 5
Limassol, 43,593 ....E 5
Morphou, 6,642 ....E 5
Nicosia (capital), 47,000 ....E 5
Nicosia, *100,000 ....F 5
Paphos, 9,083 ....E 5
Yialousa, 2,541 ....F 5

PHYSICAL FEATURES

Andreas (cape) ....F 5
Arnauti (cape) ....E 5
Famagusta (bay) ....F 5
Gata (cape) ....E 5
Greco (cape) ....F 5
Klides (isls.) ....F 5
Kormakiti (cape) ....E 5
Larnaca (bay) ....E 5
Morphou (bay) ....E 5
Pomos (point) ....E 5
Sovereign Base Area (Br.), 3,602 ....E 5
Troodos (mt.) ....E 5

*City and suburbs.

Israel and Jordan

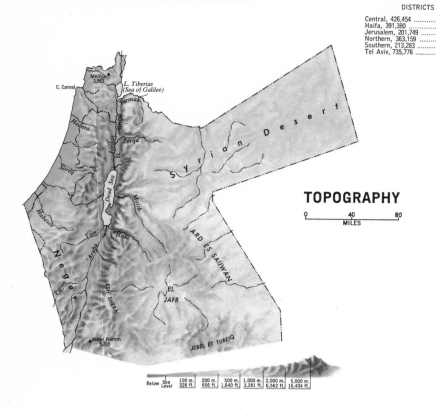

TOPOGRAPHY

0   40   80
MILES

Below Sea Level | 100 m. 328 ft. | 200 m. 656 ft. | 500 m. 1,640 ft. | 1,000 m. 3,281 ft. | 2,000 m. 6,562 ft. | 5,000 m. 16,404 ft.

ISRAEL

DISTRICTS

Central, 426,454 ....B 3
Haifa, 391,380 ....C 2
Jerusalem, 201,749 ....B 4
Northern, 363,159 ....C 2
Southern, 213,283 ......B, D 5
Tel Aviv, 735,776 ....B 3

CITIES and TOWNS

Acre, 28,100 ....C 2
Afiqim, 1,243 ....D 2
'Afula, 15,000 ....C 2
Ahuzzam, 407 ....B 4
Akko (Acre), 28,100 ....C 2
'Arrabe, 3,636 ....C 2
Ashdod, 11,700 ....B 4
Ashdot Ya'aqov, 1,197 ......D 2
Ashqelon, 28,400 ....A 4
Atlit, 1,516 ....B 2
Avihayil, 579 ....B 3
Bat Shelomo, 218 ....B 2
Bat Yam, 39,100 ....B 3
Beer Ora ....D 5
Be'er Tuveya, 602 ....B 4
Be'eri, 390 ....B 4
Beersheba, 51,600 ....D 4
Beit Guvrin ....B 4
Bene Beraq, 51,700 ....B 3
Bet Dagon, 2,932 ....B 4
Bet Hagaddi, 566 ....B 5
Bet Qama, 228 ....B 5
Bet She'an, 10,900 ....D 3
Binyamina, 2,950 ....B 2
Carmel ....C 2
Dafna, 577 ....D 1
Dalyat al-Karmel, 4,124 ....B 2
Dan, 498 ....D 1
Dimona, 12,100 ....D 4
Dor, 195 ....B 2
'Ein Harod, 1,372 ....C 2
El 'Auja ....D 5
Elath (Elat), 7,000 ....D 5
Elyakim, 568 ....C 2
Elyashiv, 435 ....B 3
Even Yehuda, 3,464 ....B 3
Gal'on, 356 ....B 4
Gan Yavne, 2,668 ....B 4
Gat, 430 ....B 4
Gedera, 4,561 ....B 4
Gesher, 360 ....D 2
Gesher Haziv, 238 ....C 1
Gevar'am, 283 ....B 4
Gilat, 561 ....B 5
Ginnosar, 473 ....D 2
Giv'at Brenner, 1,505 ......B 4
Giv'at Hayyim, 1,360 ....B 3
Giv'atayim, 30,932 ....B 3
Gosh Halav (Jish), 1,498 ...C 1
Habonim, 189 ....B 2
Hadar Ramatayim, 6,438 ...B 3
Hadera, 27,200 ....B 3
Haifa, 195,400 ....B 2
Hartuv, 8,200 ....B 4
Hazerim, 127 ....B 5
Helez, 466 ....B 4
Herzeliyya, 30,000 ....B 3
Hodiyya, 400 ....B 4
Holon, 55,200 ....B 3
Iksal, 2,156 ....C 2
Jerusalem (cap.), 181,100 ...C 4
Jish, 1,498 ....C 1
Kafar Kanna, 3,549 ....C 2
Kafar Yasif, 2,975 ....C 2
Karkur, 2,856 ....C 3
Kefar Atta, 16,300 ....C 2
Kefar Blum, 565 ....D 1
Kefar Gil'adi, 701 ....D 1
Kefar Ruppin, 306 ....D 3
Kefar Sava, 19,000 ....B 3
Kefar Vitkin, 808 ....B 3
Kefar Yona, 2,372 ....B 3
Kefar Zekhariya, 420 ....B 4
Kinneret, 909 ....D 2
Kurnub ....D 5
Lod (Lydda), 21,000 ....B 4
Lydda, 21,000 ....B 4
Magdi'el, 4,815 ....B 3
Magen, 149 ....A 5
Mash' Abbe Sade, 238 .....B 6
Mavqi'im, 177 ....B 4
Megiddo ....C 2
Me'ona, 317 ....C 1
Metula, 261 ....D 1
Migdal, 688 ....C 2
Mikhmoret, 608 ....B 3
Mishmar Hanegev, 336 .....B 5
Mivtahim, 398 ....A 5
Mizpe Ramon, 331 ....D 5
Moza Illit, 219 ....C 4
Mughar, 4,010 ....B 4
Muqeible, 459 ....C 2
Nahariyya, 15,900 ....C 1
Nazareth, 26,400 ....C 2
Negba, 435 ....B 4
Nes Ziyyona, 11,200 ....B 4
Nesher, 8,450 ....B 2
Netanya, 46,200 ....B 3
Nevatim, 436 ....B 5
Newe Yam, 211 ....B 2
Nir Am, 331 ....B 4
Nir Yitzhaq, 209 ....A 5
Nizzanim, 479 ....B 4
Oron ....C 6
Pardes Hanna, 8,200 ....B 2
Peduyim, 361 ....B 5
Petah Tiqwa, 58,700 ....B 3
Qadima, 2,937 ....B 3
Qedma, 157 ....B 4
Qiryat Bialik, 10,400 ....C 2
Qiryat Gat, 10,111 ....B 4
Qiryat Haayin, 9,256 ....B 2
Qiryat Motzkin, 10,300 .....C 2
Qiryat Shemona, 13,900 ...C 1
Qiryat Tiv'on, 9,518 ....C 2
Qiryat Yam, 11,600 ....C 2
Ra'anana, 10,000 ....B 3
Ramat Gan, 95,800 ....B 3
Ramat Hasharon, 11,100 ...B 3
Rame, 2,986 ....C 2
Ramla, 23,900 ....B 4
Rehovot, 30,400 ....A 4
Re'im, 155 ....A 5
Revadim, 175 ....B 4
Revivim, 258 ....D 5
Rishon Le Ziyyon, 30,000 ...B 4
Rosh Pinna, 700 ....D 2
Ruhama, 497 ....B 4
Sa'ad, 418 ....B 5
Safad (Zefat), 11,500 ....C 2
Sakhnin, 5,500 ....C 2
Sedom ....D 5
Sedot Yam, 511 ....B 3
Shave Ziyyon, 269 ....B 1
Shefar'am, 7,650 ....C 2
Shefayim, 614 ....B 3
Shoval, 393 ....B 4
Tayibe, 8,100 ....C 3
Tel Aviv-Jaffa, 394,400 .....B 3
Tiberias, 22,300 ....C 2
Tirat Hakarmel, 11,300 .....B 2
Tirat Zevi, 353 ....D 3
Tiv'on, 9,650 ....C 2
Tur'an, 2,304 ....C 2
Umm el Fahm, 8,100 ....C 3
Urim, 203 ....A 5
Uzza, 487 ....B 4
Yad Mordekhai, 416 ....A 4
Yagur, 1,266 ....C 2
Yavne, 6,200 ....B 4
Yavne'el, 1,580 ....C 2
Yehud, 7,000 ....B 3
Yeroham, 1,574 ....D 5
Yesodot, 293 ....B 4
Yesud Hama'ala, 428 ....D 2
Yirka, 2,715 ....C 2
Yoqne'am, 2,884 ....C 2
Zavdi'el, 396 ....B 4
Ze'elim, 148 ....B 5
Zefat, 11,500 ....C 2
Zikhron Ya'aqov, 4,393 ....B 2
Zippori, 241 ....C 2

PHYSICAL FEATURES

Acre (bay) ....
'Araba, Wadi (dry river) .....
Beer Ef'e (well) ....
Beer Sheva', Wadi (dry river) ...
Borot Kidod (well) ....
Carmel (cape) ....
Carmel (mt.) ....
Dead (sea) ....
'Ein Gedi (well) ....
'Ein Netafim (well) ....
Galilee (region) ....
Galilee, Sea of (sea) ....
Gerar, Wadi (dry river) ......
Habesor, Wadi (dry river) ...
Hadera (river) ....
Hatira (mt.) ....
Hayarqon, Wadi (dry river) ...
Hemar, Wadi (dry river) .....
Judaea (region) ....
Kishon, Wadi (dry river) ....
Lakhish, Wadi (dry river) ...
Meiron (mt.) ....
Negev (region) ....
Paran, Wadi (dry river) ......
Qarn (mt.) ....
Ramon (mt.) ....
Rubin, Wadi (dry river) ......
Shigma (river) ....
Tabor (mt.) ....
Tiberias (Galilee) (sea) .....
Tseelim, Wadi (dry river) ...
Tsin, Wadi (dry river) ....
Yarmuk (river) ....

ARCHAEOLOGICAL SITES IN PALESTINE

■ Major Excavations

0   10   20   30
Miles

LEBANON

SYRIA

Sur
Tyre

Meirun
Merom

Acre ○

Tell el-Qedah
Hazor

Tell Hum
Capernaum

Haifa ○ Tell Abu Hawam

Sheikh Sa'd
Karnaim

Sea of Galilee

Khirbet Kerak

'Athlit   Sheikh Abreiq

Nazareth

Wadi el-Murgharah

el-Hammeh

el-Burj

Tell el-Mutesellim
Megiddo

Caesarea

Mediterranean Sea

Tell Ta'annek
Taanach

Tell el-Husn
Beth-shan

Tell el-Qasileh

Tell el-Far'ah
Tirzah

Jarash
Gerasa

Sabastiya
Samaria

Balatah
Shechem

Tell Deir 'allah
Succoth

Tel Aviv-Jaffa ○

Ras el-'Ain
Aphek

JORDAN

Seilun
Shiloh

Jordan

Beitin
Bethel

Amman
Philadelphia

Tell Jezer
Gezer

Tell en-Nasbeh
Mizpah

et-Tell
Ai

Tell es-Sultan
Jericho

Jerusalem

Tell el-Ful
Gibeah

Tell er-Rumeileh
Beth-shemesh

Bethlehem

Khirbet Qumran

Ma'daba

Ascalon

Tell Sandahannah
Tell el-Hesi
Eglon

Kh. et-Tubeiqah
Beth-zur

Tell ed-Duweir
Lachish

Dhiban
Dibon

Gaza

Tell el-'Ajjul

Tell Beit Mirsim
Debir

Dead Sea

Tell Jemmeh

Tell el-Far'ah
Sharuhen

Tell Abu Matar

Masada

Bab edh Dra'

Ader

U.A.R. (EGYPT)

Kurnub

Khirbet et-Tannur

Isbeita
Subaita

© C.S. Hammond & Co.

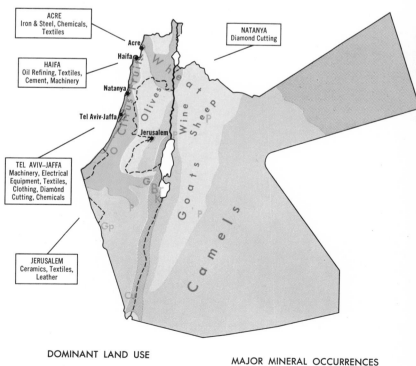

AGRICULTURE, INDUSTRY and RESOURCES

ACRE
Iron & Steel, Chemicals, Textiles

NATANYA
Diamond Cutting

HAIFA
Oil Refining, Textiles, Cement, Machinery

Acre
Haifa
Natanya

Tel Aviv-Jaffa

Jerusalem

TEL AVIV-JAFFA
Machinery, Electrical Equipment, Textiles, Clothing, Diamond Cutting, Chemicals

JERUSALEM
Ceramics, Textiles, Leather

Wheat
Citrus Fruit
Olives
Wheat
Wine
Sheep
Goats
Camels

DOMINANT LAND USE

Cereals, Livestock
Cash Crops, Horticulture
Nomadic Livestock Herding
Nonagricultural Land

MAJOR MINERAL OCCURRENCES

Br — Bromine
Cu — Copper
G — Natural Gas
Gp — Gypsum

K — Potash
O — Petroleum
P — Phosphates

▨ Major Industrial Areas

ISREAL and JORDAN

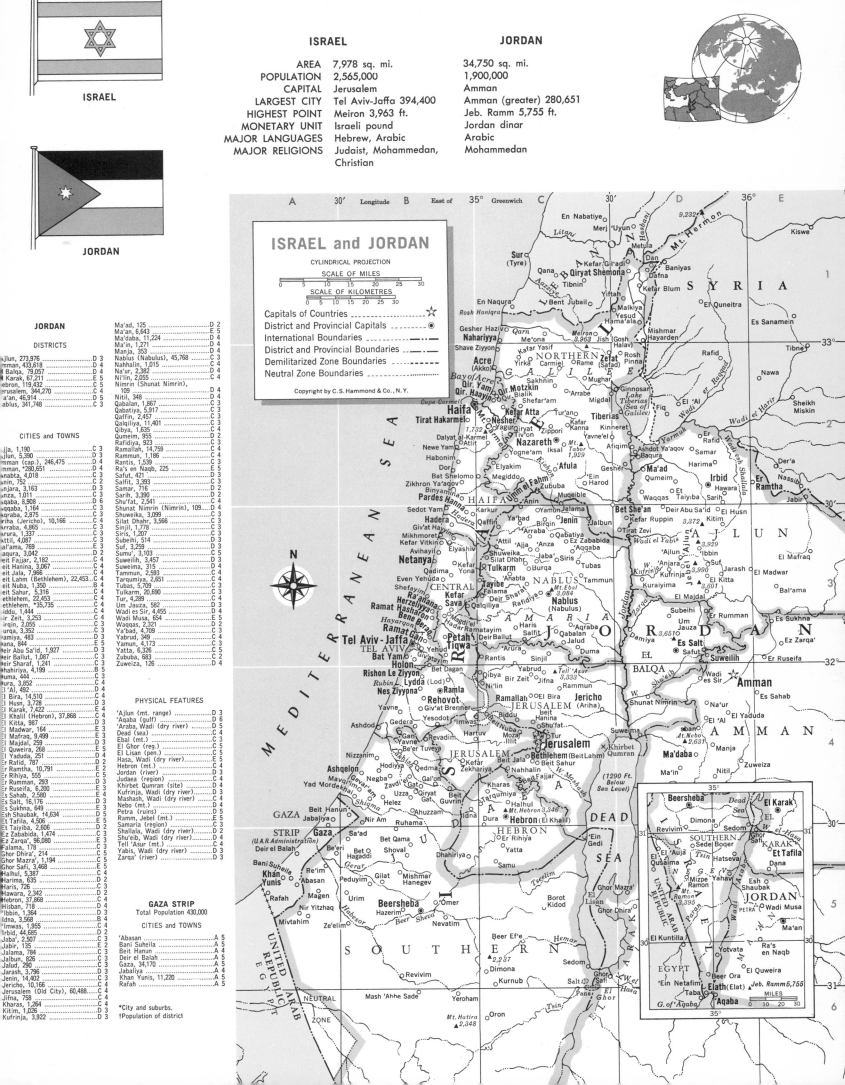

ISRAEL

JORDAN

	ISRAEL	JORDAN
AREA	7,978 sq. mi.	34,750 sq. mi.
POPULATION	2,565,000	1,900,000
CAPITAL	Jerusalem	Amman
LARGEST CITY	Tel Aviv-Jaffa 394,400	Amman (greater) 280,651
HIGHEST POINT	Meiron 3,963 ft.	Jeb. Ramm 5,755 ft.
MONETARY UNIT	Israeli pound	Jordan dinar
MAJOR LANGUAGES	Hebrew, Arabic	Arabic
MAJOR RELIGIONS	Judaist, Mohammedan, Christian	Mohammedan

ISRAEL and JORDAN

CYLINDRICAL PROJECTION

SCALE OF MILES

SCALE OF KILOMETRES

Capitals of Countries	☆
District and Provincial Capitals	◉
International Boundaries	
District and Provincial Boundaries	
Demilitarized Zone Boundaries	
Neutral Zone Boundaries	

Copyright by C.S. Hammond & Co., N.Y.

JORDAN

DISTRICTS

'Ajlun, 273,976 .... D 3
'Amman, 433,618 .... D 4
El Karak, 79,057 .... D 4
Hebron, 119,432 .... C 5
Jerusalem, 344,270 ...... C 4
Ma'an, 46,914 .... D 5
Nablus, 341,748 .... C 3

CITIES and TOWNS

'Ajja, 1,190 .... C 3
'Ajlun, 5,390 .... C 3
'Amman (cap.), 246,475 .. D 4
'Anabta, 4,018 .... C 2
'Anjara, 3,163 .... D 2
'Anza, 1,011 .... C 3
'Aqaba, 8,908 .... D 6
'Aqraba, 1,164 .... C 3
'Araba, 2,875 .... C 4
'Ariha (Jericho), 10,166 . C 4
'Arraba, 4,865 .... C 3
'Arura, 1,337 .... C 4
'Attil, 4,087 .... C 3
'Awarta, 769 .... E 3
Ba'qura, 3,042 .... D 2
Beit Fajjar, 2,182 .... C 4
Beit Hanina, 3,067 .... C 4
Beit Lahm (Bethlehem), 22,453 . C 4
Beit Nuba, 1,350 ...... B 4
Beit Sahur, 5,316 ..... C 4
Bethlehem, 22,453 ..... C 4
Bethlehem, *35,735 .... C 4
Biddu, 1,444 .... C 4
Bir Zeit, 3,253 .... C 4
Birqin, 2,055 .... C 3
Damiya, 3,352 .... D 3
Damiya, 483 .... D 3
Deir 'Alla, 844 .... E 5
Deir Abu Sa'id, 1,927 . D 3
Deir Ballut, 1,087 .... C 3
Deir Sharaf, 1,241 .... C 4
Dhahiriya, 4,199 ...... B 5
Duma, 444 .... C 4
Dura, 3,852 .... C 4
El Bira, 14,510 .... C 4
El Husn, 3,728 .... D 3
El Karak, 7,422 .... D 5
El Khalil (Hebron), 37,868 . C 4
El Kitta, 987 .... D 3
El Madwar, 164 .... E 3
El Majdal, 259 .... D 4
El Quweira, 268 .... D 5
El Yaduda, 251 .... D 4
Er Rafid, 787 .... E 2
Er Ramtha, 10,791 ..... E 2
Er Rihiya, 555 .... C 4
Er Rumman, 283 .... E 3
Er Ruseifa, 6,200 ..... D 4
Es Sabab, 2,580 .... E 4
Es Salt, 16,176 .... D 3
Es Sukhna, 649 .... E 4
Esh Shaubak, 14,634 ... D 5
Et Tafila, 4,506 ...... E 5
Et Taiyiba, 2,606 ..... C 4
Ez Zababida, 1,474 .... C 3
Ez Zarqa, 96,080 ...... D 4
Ghor Dhira', 214 ...... C 5
Ghor Mazra', 1,194 .... C 5
Ghor Safi, 3,468 ...... E 5
Halhul, 5,387 .... C 4
Harima, 625 .... C 3
Haris, 726 .... C 3
Hawara, 2,342 .... C 4
Hebron, 37,868 .... C 4
Hisban, 718 .... D 4
'Ibbin, 1,364 .... D 3
Idna, 3,568 .... B 4
'Imwas, 1,955 .... C 4
Irbid, 44,685 .... D 2
Jaba', 2,507 .... C 3
Jabir, 135 .... E 2
Jalama, 290 .... C 3
Jalbun, 826 .... D 3
Jarash, 3,796 .... D 3
Jenin, 14,402 .... C 3
Jericho, 10,166 .... C 4
Jerusalem (Old City), 60,488 . C 4
Jifna, 758 .... C 4
Kharas, 1,264 .... C 4
Kitim, 1,026 .... D 3
Kufrinja, 3,922 .... D 3

Ma'ad, 125 .... D 2
Ma'an, 6,643 .... D 5
Ma'daba, 11,224 ...... D 4
Ma'in, 1,271 .... D 4
Manja, 353 .... D 4
Nablus (Nabulus), 45,768 . C 3
Nahhalin, 1,015 ...... C 4
Na'ur, 2,382 .... D 4
Ni'lin, 2,055 .... C 4
Nimrin (Shunat Nimrin), 109 . D 4
Nitil, 348 .... D 4
Qabalan, 1,867 .... C 3
Qabatiya, 5,917 ...... C 3
Qaffin, 2,457 .... C 3
Qalqiliya, 11,401 .... C 4
Qibya, 1,635 .... C 4
Qumeim, 955 .... D 2
Rafidiya, 923 .... C 3
Ramallah, 14,759 ..... C 4
Rammun, 1,186 .... C 4
Rantis, 1,539 .... C 4
Ra's en Naqb, 225 .... E 5
Safut, 421 .... D 3
Salfit, 3,393 .... C 3
Samar, 716 .... D 2
Sarih, 3,390 .... D 2
Shu'fat, 2,541 .... C 4
Shunat Nimrin (Nimrin), 109 . D 4
Shuweika, 3,099 ...... C 3
Silat Dhahr, 3,566 ... C 3
Sinjil, 1,778 .... C 3
Siris, 1,207 .... C 3
Subeihi, 514 .... D 3
Suf, 3,259 .... D 3
Sumu', 3,103 .... C 5
Suweilih, 3,457 ...... D 3
Suweima, 315 .... D 4
Tammun, 2,593 .... C 4
Tarqumiya, 2,651 ..... C 4
Tubas, 5,709 .... C 3
Tulkarm, 20,690 ...... C 3
Tur, 4,289 .... C 4
Um Jauza, 582 .... D 3
Wadi es Sir, 4,455 ... D 4
Wadi Musa, 654 .... E 5
Waqqas, 2,321 .... D 2
Ya'bad, 4,709 .... C 3
Yabrud, 349 .... C 4
Yamun, 4,173 .... C 3
Yatta, 6,326 .... C 5
Zububa, 683 .... C 2
Zuweiza, 126 .... D 4

PHYSICAL FEATURES

'Ajlun (mt. range) ..... D 3
'Aqaba (gulf) .... D 6
'Araba, Wadi (dry river) . D 5
Dead (sea) .... C 4
Ebal (mt.) .... C 3
El Ghor (reg.) .... C 4
El Lisan (pen.) .... C 5
Hasa, Wadi (dry river) . E 5
Hebron (mt.) .... C 4
Jordan (river) .... D 4
Judaea (region) .... C 4
Khirbet Qumran (site) . D 4
Kufrinja, Wadi (dry river) . D 3
Mashash, Wadi (dry river) . C 4
Nebo (mt.) .... D 4
Petra (ruins) .... D 5
Ramm, Jebel (mt.) ..... E 5
Samaria (region) ...... C 3
Shallala, Wadi (dry river) . D 2
Shu'eib, Wadi (dry river) . D 4
Tell 'Asur (mt.) ...... C 4
Yabis, Wadi (dry river) . D 3
Zarqa' (river) .... D 3

GAZA STRIP

Total Population 430,000

CITIES and TOWNS

'Abasan .... A 5
Bani Suheila .... A 5
Beit Hanun .... A 4
Deir el Balah .... A 5
Gaza, 34,170 .... A 5
Jabaliya .... A 5
Khan Yunis, 11,220 .... A 5
Rafah .... A 5

*City and suburbs.
†Population of district

Iran and Iraq

IRAN
INTERNAL DIVISIONS

Bakhtiari (governorate),
 340,612 ....F 4
East Azerbaijan (prov.),
 2,012,134 ....E 1
Fars (prov.), 1,295,682 ......H 6
Gilan (prov.), 1,422,407 .....F 2
Hamadan (governorate),
 730,365 ....F 3
Isfahan (prov.), 1,682,781 ..H 4
Islands and Ports of the Sea of
 Oman (governorate),
 240,289 ....H 7
Kerman (prov.), 616,705 ....K 6
Kermanshah (prov.), 1,438,607 ..E 3
Khurasan (prov.), 2,023,612 ..K 3
Khuzistan (prov.), 1,855,162 ..F 5
Kurdistan (prov.), 490,244 ...E 3
Luristan (governorate),
 564,987 ....F 4
Mazanderan (prov.), 1,365,555 ..H 2
Persian Gulf (governorate),
 188,063 ....G 6
Samnan (governorate), 177,239 ..J 3
Seistan and Baluchistan (prov.),
 428,363 ....M 6
Tehran (prov.), 3,264,140 ....G 3
West Azerbaijan (prov.),
 719,023 ....D 1

CITIES and TOWNS

Abadan, 302,189 ....F 5
Abadeh, 8,192 ....H 5
Abarquh, 6,268 ....H 5
Abhar, 9,634 ....F 2
Agha Jari, 24,195 ....F 5
Ahar, 19,816 ....E 1
Ahwaz, 155,054 ....F 5
Alishtar, 294 ....E 4
Amar, 463 ....H 2
Anar, 463 ....J 5
Anarak, 1,342 ....H 4
Andimeshk, 7,324 ....F 4
Aq Darband, 104 ....M 2
Aradan, 2,401 ....H 3
Arak, 58,998 ....F 3
Ardal, 159 ....G 4
Ardebil, 65,742 ....F 1
Ardistan, 5,868 ....H 4
Arfa' Deh, 201 ....H 3
Asadabad (Gurgan), 28,380 ..J 2
Aveh, 200 ....F 3
Avroman, 1,024 ....E 3
Azarshahr, 12,687 ....D 2
Azna, 1,577 ....F 3
Babol, 36,194 ....H 2
Babulsar, 7,237 ....H 2
Bafq, 4,505 ....J 5
Baft, 3,861 ....K 6
Bagh Baqu, 254 ....M 3

Baghu, 80 ....K 7
Bahramabad, 9,212 ....K 5
Bajgiran, 1,151 ....L 2
Bam, 15,737 ....L 6
Bampur, 1,585 ....M 7
Bandar Abbas, 17,710 .....H 7
Bandar Dilam, 3,691 ......G 5
Bandar Ma'shur, 15,694 ..F 5
Bandar Rig, 1,889 ....G 6
Bandar Shah, 8,284 ....H 2
Bandar Shahpur, 3,725 ....F 5
Basht, 535 ....G 5
Bastak, 2,473 ....J 7
Behbehan, 29,886 ....G 5
Behshahr, 16,172 ....H 2
Bidukht, 226 ....L 3
Bijar, 9,090 ....F 3
Bijistan, 3,823 ....K 3
Bir, 103 ....M 3
Birjand, 13,934 ....L 4
Bostan, 4,619 ....F 5
Borazjun, 10,233 ....G 6
Bostan, 4,619 ....F 5
Bujnurd, 19,253 ....K 2
Bukan, 5,307 ....D 2
Buq, 68 ....M 6
Burujird, 49,186 ....F 4
Bushire, 18,412 ....G 6
Bustam, 329 ....J 2
Bustanabad, 1,297 ....E 2
Chahbar, 1,800 ....M 8
Chalus, 9,758 ....G 2
Charak, 453 ....J 7
Chehar Deh ....K 4
Dalijan, 4,887 ....G 4
Damghan, 8,909 ....J 2
Darab, 9,106 ....J 6
Daran, 3,331 ....G 4
Darreh Gaz, 8,541 ....L 2
Dashtab ....K 6
Dashtiari ....M 8

Daulatabad (Malayer), 21,105 ..F 3
Daulatabad, 1,129 ....F 3
Daulatabad, 1,235 ....M 2
Deh Bid, 556 ....H 5
Deh Diz, 268 ....F 4
Deh Haqq, 6,075 ....G 4
Demavend, 4,523 ....H 3
Dezh-i-Shahpur, 1,384 ...E 3
Dizful, 52,121 ....F 4
Duruh ....L 4
Duzdab (Zahidan), 17,495 ..M 6
Estahabad, 16,308 ....H 7
Evaz, 6,064 ....H 7
Fahrej (Iranshahr), 3,618 ..M 7
Fariman, 4,802 ....L 3
Farrashband, 3,342 ....G 6
Fasa, 11,711 ....H 6
Firdaus, 6,834 ....L 3
Firuzabad, 5,747 ....H 6
Firuzkuh, 3,487 ....H 3
Fumen, 6,692 ....F 2
Galand, 169 ....J 2
Ganaveh, 2,695 ....G 6
Garmsar, 3,520 ....H 3
Gazik, 51 ....M 4
Gifan, 896 ....M 2
Golshan (Tabas), 7,413 ...K 4
Gulpaigan, 12,400 ....G 4
Gumishan, 5,168 ....J 2
Gunabad, 7,555 ....L 3
Gunbad-i-Qabus ....K 3
Gunbadli, 531 ....M 2
Gurgan, 28,380 ....J 2
Gushi, 1,177 ....G 4
Gwatar ....M 8
Haft Kel, 7,693 ....F 5
Hamadan, 114,610 ....F 3
Hashtpar, 3,354 ....F 2

Havizeh, 4,722 ....F 5
Herauabad, 5,422 ....F 2
Hormuz ....J 7
Ilam, 8,346 ....E 4
Iranshahr, 3,618 ....M 7
Isfahan, 339,909 ....G 4
Isfandak, 265 ....N 7
Izeh, 1,983 ....F 5
Jahrum, 29,169 ....H 6
Jajarm, 3,641 ....K 2
Jalq ....N 7
Jamm ....H 6
Jandag, 1,361 ....J 3
Jask, 1,078 ....L 8
Jauri ....M 6
Kakhk ....L 3
Kalat, 1,114 ....L 2
Kangan, 2,682 ....G 7
Kangavar, 6,251 ....F 3
Karaj, 14,526 ....G 3
Kariz, 1,125 ....L 3
Kart, 320 ....M 3
Kashan, 45,955 ....G 3
Kashmar, 13,299 ....L 3
Kazerun, 30,641 ....G 6
Kazvin, 66,420 ....F 2
Kerman, 62,157 ....K 5
Kermanshah, 166,720 ....E 3
Khaf, 4,144 ....M 3
Khash, 7,439 ....M 7
Khorramshahr, 43,850 ...F 5
Khunsar, 10,669 ....G 4
Khur, 2,307 ....J 3
Khurramabad, 38,676 ....F 4
Kuhpayeh, 1,906 ....H 4
Kurd Kui, 9,855 ....J 2
Ladis ....M 6
Lahijan, 19,877 ....E 2
Lar, 14,188 ....J 7
Lingeh, 4,920 ....J 7
Mahabad, 20,332 ....D 2
Mahallat, 10,575 ....G 4
Mahan, 6,239 ....K 5
Maibud, 3,296 ....J 4
Maku, 5,306 ....D 1
Malamir (Izeh), 1,983 ....F 5
Malayer, 21,105 ....F 3
Maragheh, 36,551 ....E 2
Marand, 13,822 ....D 1
Marivan (Dezh-i-Shahpur),
 1,384 ....E 3

Masjid-i-Sulaiman, 44,651 ..F 5
Mehrabad, 1,695 ....G 3
Mehran, 664 ....E 4
Meshed, 312,186 ....L 2
Meshed-i-Sar (Babulsar), 7,237 ..H 2
Meshkinshahr, 7,221 ......F 1
Mianeh, 21,100 ....F 1
Minab, 4,228 ....K 7
Mirjawa, 883 ....M 6
Miyanduab, 14,796 ....E 2
Naband, 97 ....H 7
Naft-i-Shah, 2,825 ....D 4
Na'in, 4,681 ....H 4
Naraq, 2,725 ....G 4
Nasratabad (Zabul), 12,221 ..M 5
Nasratabad Sipi, 1,488 ...L 6
Natanz, 2,090 ....H 4
Nau Gumbaz ....H 6
Naushahr, 2,717 ....G 2
Neh, 2,130 ....M 5
Nehavend, 30,422 ....F 3
Nejafabad, 30,422 ....G 4
Nikshahr, 1,879 ....M 7
Niriz, 12,401 ....J 6
Nishapur, 25,820 ....L 2
Pahlevi (Enzeli), 31,349 ..F 2
Pazanun, 81 ....F 5
Pik, 802 ....G 3
Pishin, 1,660 ....M 7
Qain, 4,414 ....L 4
Qasr-i-Shirin, 23,901 .....D 3
Qasrqand (Nikshahr), 1,879 ..M 7
Qazian, 3,054 ....F 2
Quchan, 21,250 ....L 2
Qum, 105,272 ....G 3
Qurveh, 2,929 ....E 3
Qutur, 655 ....D 1
Rafsenjan (Bahramabad),
 9,212 ....K 5
Rai, 22,327 ....G 3
Ram Hormuz, 7,258 ......F 5
Ramsar, 1,105 ....G 2
Rask ....M 7
Ravar, 5,074 ....K 5
Resht, 118,634 ....F 2
Reza'iyeh, 67,605 ....D 1
Rigan, 8,255 ....L 6
Robat-i-Karim, 2,328 .....G 3
Rud-i-Sar, 4,222 ....G 2
Sabzawar, 30,545 ....K 2
Sabzawaran, 2,480 ....K 6
Samnan, 29,036 ....H 3

Sanandaj, 40,641 ....E 3
Sang-i-Sar, 9,109 ....H 3
Saqqiz, 12,729 ....E 2
Sarab, 13,086 ....F 1
Sarakhs, 3,461 ....M 2
Saraskand, 3,153 ....F 1
Saravan (Shahista), 4,012 ..N 7
Sarbaz ....N 7
Sardasht, 2,645 ....E 2
Savanat (Estahabad), 16,308 ..H 7
Sari, 26,278 ....H 2
Saveh, 14,537 ....G 3
Sehkuheh ....M 5
Shahabad, 4,346 ....E 3
Shahdad, 2,777 ....L 5
Shahdegan, 4,321 ....F 5
Shahi, 23,055 ....H 2
Shahin Dezh, 4,195 ....D 2
Shahistan, 4,012 ....N 7
Shahr-i-Kurd, 15,476 .....G 4
Shahrud, 17,058 ....J 2
Shahsawar, 7,626 ....G 2
Shamil, 666 ....K 7
Sharifabad, 760 ....H 3
Sharifkhaneh, 1,260 ......D 1
Shiraz, 229,761 ....H 6
Shirvan, 6,906 ....L 2
Shush, 1,433 ....F 4
Shushtar, 18,527 ....F 5
Sib, 1,249 ....N 7
Sinneh (Sanandaj), 40,641 ..E 3
Sirik, 1,365 ....L 7
Sirjan, 12,160 ....K 6
Sivand, 1,811 ....H 5
Soh, 1,012 ....H 4
Sufian, 2,914 ....D 1
Sultanabad (Kashmar), 13,299 ..L 3
Sunqur, 12,126 ....F 3
Susangird, 6,025 ....F 5
Tabas (Tabas-Masina), 466 ..L 3
Tabas (Golshan), 7,413 ...K 4
Tabriz, 387,803 ....E 1
Taft, 6,451 ....J 5
Tajabad, 269 ....H 3
Takistan, 10,534 ....F 3
Tarum, 394 ....J 7
Tehran (cap.), 2,317,116 ..G 3
Tuiserkan, 11,323 ....F 3

50°Longitude G East of 52°Greenwich H

IRAN and IRAQ
CONIC PROJECTION

SCALE OF MILES
0   25   50   100   150   200

SCALE OF KILOMETRES
0 25 50   100   150   200

Capitals of Countries ....☆
Capitals of Provinces ....△
Capitals of Governorates ......◉
International Boundaries ....___
Provincial Boundaries ....___
Governorate Boundaries ....___

Copyright by C.S. Hammond & Co., N.Y.

Iran consists of thirteen provinces
called ostans. Attached to six of these
provinces are six governates.

IRAN and IRAQ

IRAN

AREA	628,000 sq. mi.
POPULATION	22,860,000
CAPITAL	Tehran
LARGEST CITY	Tehran 2,317,116
HIGHEST POINT	Demavend 18,934 ft.
MONETARY UNIT	rial
MAJOR LANGUAGES	Persian, Arabic, Kurdish
MAJOR RELIGIONS	Mohammedan, Parsi

IRAQ

	116,000 sq. mi.
	7,004,000
	Baghdad
	Baghdad (greater) 784,763
	Haji Ibrahim 12,000 ft.
	Iraqi dinar
	Arabic, Turkish, Kurdish
	Mohammedan

TOPOGRAPHY

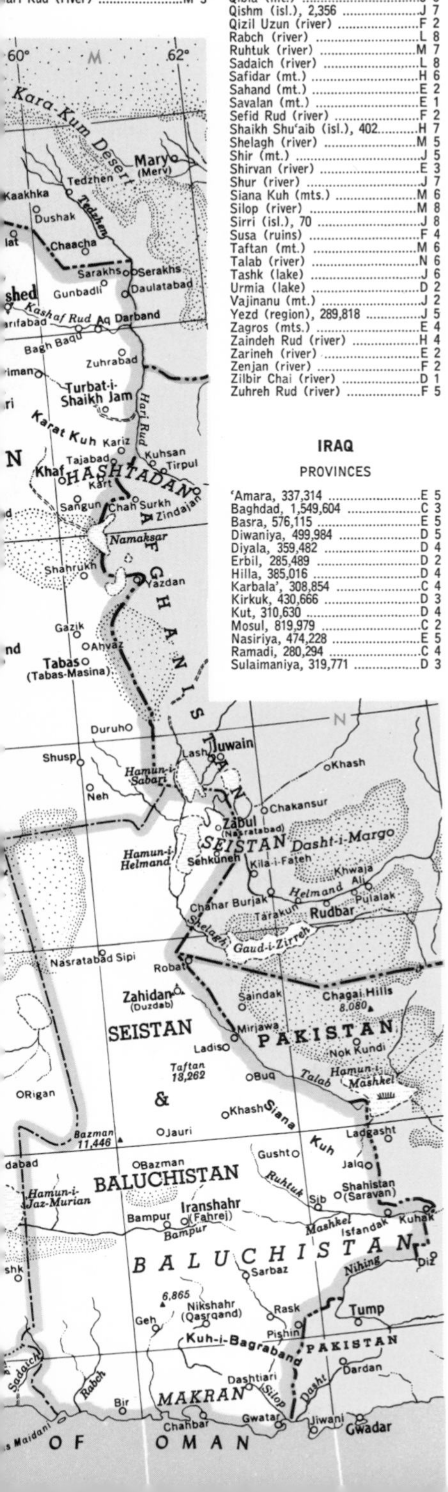

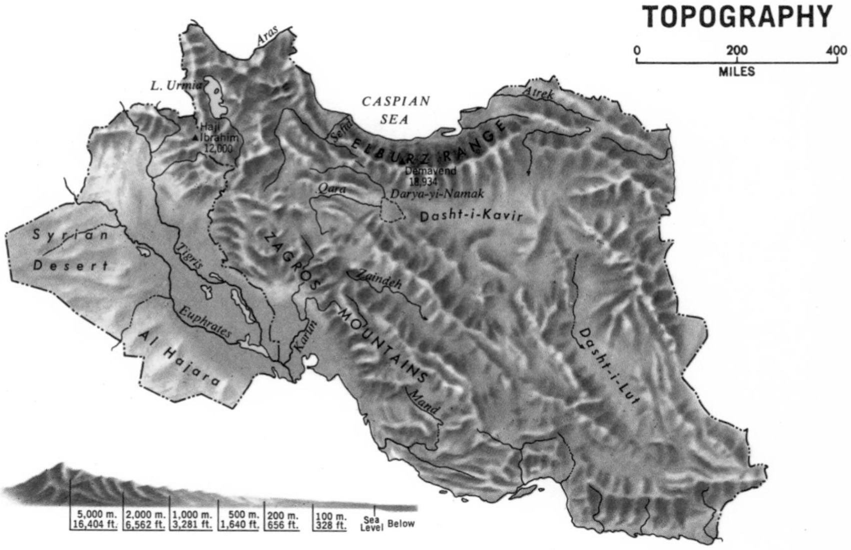

0 200 400
MILES

AGRICULTURE, INDUSTRY and RESOURCES

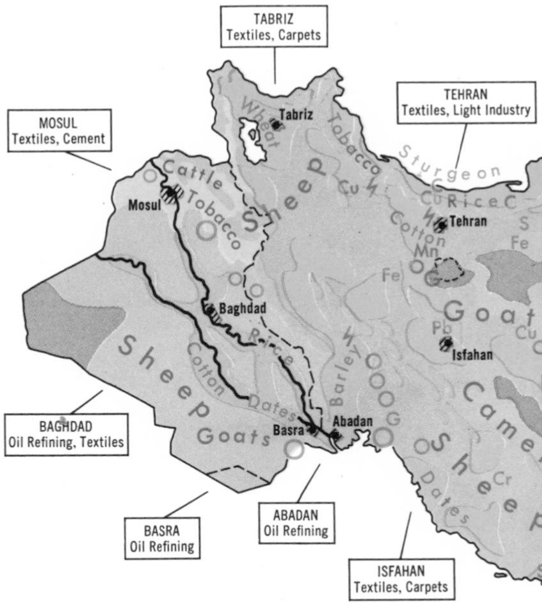

DOMINANT LAND USE

Cereals, Livestock
Cash Crops, Horticulture, Livestock
Pasture Livestock
Nomadic Livestock Herding
Forests
Nonagricultural Land

MAJOR MINERAL OCCURRENCES

C	Coal
Cr	Chromium
Cu	Copper
Fe	Iron
G	Natural Gas
Mn	Manganese
Na	Salt
O	Petroleum
Pb	Lead
S	Sulfur, Pyrites

Water Power
Major Industrial Areas

MOSUL
Textiles, Cement

TABRIZ
Textiles, Carpets

TEHRAN
Textiles, Light Industry

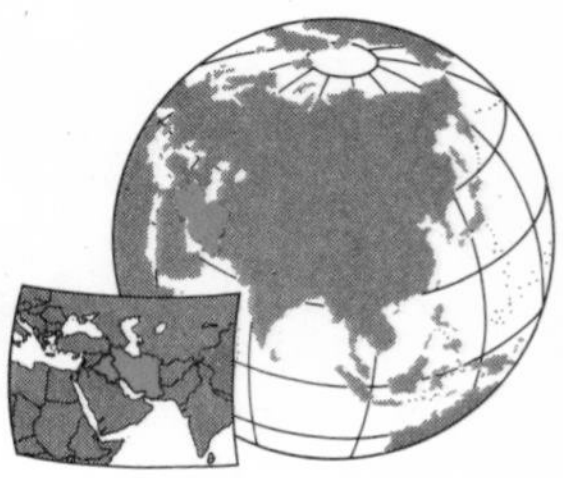

BAGHDAD
Oil Refining, Textiles

BASRA
Oil Refining

ABADAN
Oil Refining

ISFAHAN
Textiles, Carpets

INDIAN SUBCONTINENT and AFGHANISTAN

CONIC PROJECTION

SCALE OF MILES

0   50   100   200   300

SCALE OF KILOMETRES

0   50 100   200   300

Capitals of Countries .... ☆
Provincial and State Capitals .... ◉
International Boundaries .... — · — · —
Provincial and State Boundaries ... — — —
Canals ....

Copyright by C. S. HAMMOND & CO., N.Y.

INDIAN SUBCONTINENT and AFGHANISTAN

	INDIA	**PAKISTAN**	**CEYLON**
AREA	1,196,995 sq. mi.	364,218 sq. mi.	25,332 sq. mi.
POPULATION	476,278,000	100,762,000	10,965,000
CAPITAL	New Delhi	Rawalpindi	Colombo
LARGEST CITY	Calcutta (greater) 6,117,171	Karachi (greater) 3,360,017	Colombo 510,947
HIGHEST POINT	K2 (Godwin Austen) 28,250 ft.	Tirich Mir 25,263 ft.	Pidurutalagala 8,291 ft.
MONETARY UNIT	Indian rupee	Pakistani rupee	Celanese rupee
MAJOR LANGUAGES	Indo-Aryan (Hindi, Bengali, Urdu, Gujarati, Punjabi, etc.), Dravidian (Tamil, Kanarese, Telugan), English	Indo-Aryan (Urdu, Bengali, Punjabi, etc.)	Singhalese, Tamil
MAJOR RELIGIONS	Hindu, Buddhist, Mohammedan, Animist, Sikh, Jain, Parsi, Christian	Mohammedan, Hindu, Sikh, Christian	Buddhist, Hindu

	AFGHANISTAN	**NEPAL**	**MALDIVE ISLANDS**
AREA	250,000 sq. mi.	54,000 sq. mi.	115 sq. mi.
POPULATION	15,227,000	9,900,000	94,527
CAPITAL	Kabul	Katmandu	Malé
LARGEST CITY	Kabul (greater) 480,000	Katmandu 122,507	Malé (greater) 8,515
HIGHEST POINT	Hindu Kush 24,556 ft.	Mt. Everest 29,028 ft.	20 ft.
MONETARY UNIT	afghani	Nepalese rupee	Indian & Celanese rupees
MAJOR LANGUAGES	Afghan (Pushtu), Persian	Indo-Aryan languages, Tibetan	Maldivian, English
MAJOR RELIGIONS	Mohammedan	Hindu, Buddhist, Lamaist	Mohammedan

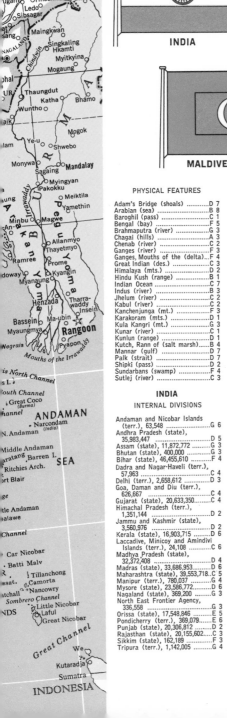

INDIA PAKISTAN CEYLON AFGHANISTAN NEPAL

MALDIVE ISLANDS

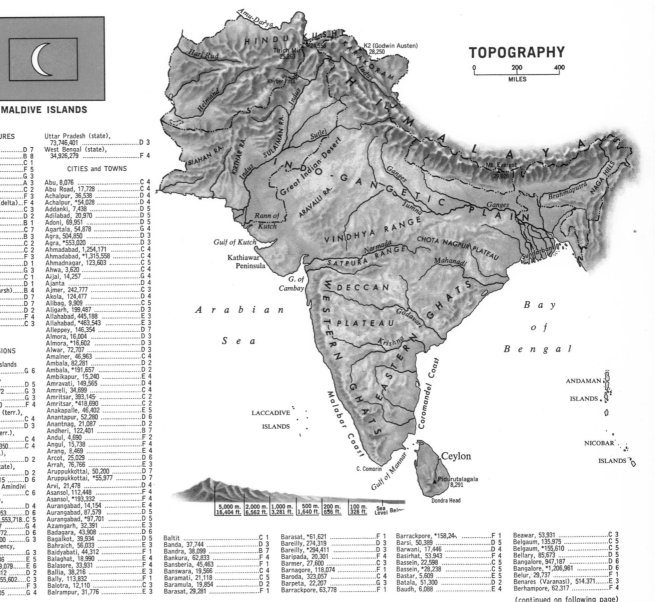

TOPOGRAPHY

0   200   400

MILES

5,000 m. | 2,000 m. | 1,000 m. | 500 m. | 200 m. | 100 m. | Sea
16,404 ft. | 6,562 ft. | 3,281 ft. | 1,640 ft. | 656 ft. | 328 ft. | Level Below

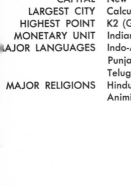

PHYSICAL FEATURES

Adam's Bridge (shoals)	D 7
Arabian (sea)	B 8
Baroghil (pass)	C 1
Bengal (bay)	F 5
Brahmaputra (river)	G 3
Chagai (hills)	A 3
Chenab (river)	C 2
Ganges (river)	F 3
Ganges, Mouths of the (delta)	F 4
Great Indian (des.)	C 3
Himalaya (mts.)	D 2
Hindu Kush (range)	B 1
Indian Ocean	C 7
Indus (river)	B 3
Jhelum (river)	C 2
Kabul (river)	C 2
Kanchenjunga (mt.)	F 3
Karakoram (mts.)	D 1
Kula Kangri (mt.)	F 3
Kunar (river)	C 1
Kunlun (range)	D 1
Kutch, Rann of (salt marsh)	B 4
Mannar (gulf)	D 7
Palk (strait)	D 7
Shipki (pass)	D 2
Sundarbans (swamp)	F 4
Sutlej (river)	C 3

INDIA
INTERNAL DIVISIONS

Andaman and Nicobar Islands (terr.), 63,548	G 6
Andhra Pradesh (state), 35,983,447	D 5
Assam (state), 11,872,772	G 3
Bhutan (state), 400,000	G 3
Bihar (state), 46,455,610	F 4
Dadra and Nagar-Haveli (terr.), 57,963	
Delhi (terr.), 2,658,612	D 3
Goa, Daman and Diu (terr.), 626,667	C 4
Gujarat (state), 20,633,350	C 4
Himachal Pradesh (terr.), 1,351,144	D 2
Jammu and Kashmir (state), 3,560,976	D 2
Kerala (state), 16,903,715	D 6
Laccadive, Minicoy and Amindivi Islands (terr.), 24,108	C 6
Madhya Pradesh (state), 32,372,408	D 4
Madras (state), 33,686,953	D 6
Maharashtra (state), 39,553,718	C 5
Manipur (terr.), 780,037	H 4
Mysore (state), 23,586,772	D 6
Nagaland (state), 369,200	G 3
North East Frontier Agency, 336,558	G 3
Orissa (state), 17,548,846	E 5
Pondicherry (terr.), 369,079	E 6
Punjab (state), 20,306,812	D 2
Rajasthan (state), 20,155,602	C 3
Sikkim (state), 162,189	F 3
Tripura (terr.), 1,142,005	G 4

Uttar Pradesh (state), 73,746,401	D 3
West Bengal (state), 34,926,279	F 4

CITIES and TOWNS

Abu, 8,076	C 4
Abu Road, 17,728	C 4
Achalpur, 36,538	D 4
Achalpur, *54,028	D 4
Addanki, 7,438	D 5
Adilabad, 20,970	D 5
Adoni, 69,951	D 5
Agartala, 54,878	G 4
Agra, 504,850	D 3
Agra, *553,020	D 3
Ahmadabad, 1,254,171	C 4
Ahmadabad, *1,315,558	C 4
Ahmadnagar, 123,603	C 5
Ahwa, 3,620	C 4
Aijal, 14,257	G 4
Ajanta	D 4
Ajmer, 242,777	C 3
Ajmer, 124,477	D 4
Alibag, 9,905	C 5
Aligarh, 199,487	D 3
Allahabad, 445,188	E 3
Allahabad, *463,543	E 3
Alleppey, 146,354	D 7
Almora, 16,004	D 3
Almora, *16,602	D 3
Alwar, 72,707	D 3
Amalner, 46,963	C 4
Ambala, 82,281	D 2
Ambala, *191,657	D 2
Ambikapur, 15,240	E 4
Amravati, 149,565	D 4
Amreli, 34,699	C 4
Amritsar, 393,145	C 2
Amritsar, *418,690	C 2
Anakapalle, 46,402	E 5
Anantapur, 52,280	D 6
Anantnag, 21,087	D 2
Andheri, 122,401	B 7
Andul, 4,690	F 2
Angul, 15,738	F 4
Arang, 8,469	E 4
Arcot, 25,029	D 6
Arrah, 76,766	E 3
Aruppukkottai, 50,200	D 7
Aruppukkottai, *55,977	D 7
Arvi, 21,478	D 4
Asansol, 112,448	F 4
Asansol, *193,332	F 4
Aurangabad, 14,154	E 4
Aurangabad, 87,579	D 5
Aurangabad, *97,701	D 5
Azamgarh, 32,391	E 3
Badagara, 43,908	D 6

Baltit	C 1	Barasat, *61,621	F 1	Barrackpore, *158,24...	F 1	Beawar, 53,931	C 3
Banda, 37,744	D 3	Banda, 37,744	D 3	Barsi, 50,389	D 5	Belgaum, 135,975	C 5
Bandra, 38,099	B 7	Bareilly, 274,319	D 3	Barwani, 17,446	D 4	Belgaum, *155,610	C 5
Bankura, 62,833	F 4	Bareilly, *294,411	D 3	Basirhat, 53,943	F 4	Bellary, 85,673	D 5
Bansberia, 45,463	F 1	Baripada, 20,301	F 4	Bassein, 22,598	C 5	Bangalore, 947,187	D 6
Banswara, 19,566	C 4	Barnagore, 118,074	F 1	Bassein, *28,238	C 5	Bangalore, *1,206,961	D 6
Baramati, 21,118	C 5	Baroda, 323,057	C 4	Bastar, 5,609	D 5	Belur, 29,737	F 1
Baramulla, 19,854	D 2	Barpeta, 22,207	G 3	Batala, 51,300	D 2	Benares (Varanasi), 514,371	E 3
Balrampur, 31,776	E 3	Barpeta, 63,778	F 1	Baudh, 6,088	E 4	Berhampore, 62,317	F 4
Balaghat, 18,990	D 4						
Balasore, 33,931	F 4						
Balotra, 12,110	C 3						
Bally, 113,832	F 1						
Balaghat, 18,990	D 4						
Baidyabati, 44,312	F 1						
Bahraich, 56,033	E 3						
Bagalkot, 39,934	D 5						
Badagara, 43,908	D 6						

(continued on following page)

Indian Subcontinent and Afghanistan
(continued)

BRITISH INDIA

British India. The provinces of British India were directly administered by Britain. A few areas were leased from the Indian princes.

Indian States. The Indian States, sometimes referred to as the "Native" or "Princely States," were under the nominal control of maharajas or other hereditary princes.

Possessions of Other Countries in India

State or Provincial Boundaries

Other Internal Boundaries

U.S.S.R.
AFGHANISTAN
IRAN
GILGIT AGENCY
KASHMIR & JAMMU
N.W. FRONTIER PROV.
PUNJAB
BALUCHISTAN
Gwadar (Oman)
SIND
PUNJAB STATES
PUNJ. ST.
BAHAWALPUR (PUNJ. ST.)
RAJPUTANA
AJMER-MERWARA
DELHI
RAMPUR
UNITED PROVINCES
TIBET
NEPAL
CHINA
SIKKIM
BHUTAN
Brahmaputra
ASSAM
KHASI HILLS
E. ST.
MANIPUR
TRIPURA (E. ST.)
BENGAL
BIHAR
BENARES
CENTRAL INDIA
GWALIOR
WESTERN INDIA
GUJARAT ST.
Diu (Port.)
Damão (Port.)
Arabian Sea
CENTRAL PROVINCES
BERAR
EASTERN STATES
ORISSA
Chandernagore (Fr.)
BURMA
HYDERABAD
DECCAN STATES
Gôa (Port.)
Yanaon (Fr.)
Bay of Bengal
MYSORE
Bangalore (Br.)
COORG
Mahé (Fr.)
Pondichéry (Fr.)
Karikal (Fr.)
M. ST.
MADRAS
MADRAS STATES
Cochin (Br.)
Laccadive Islands (Madras)
Andaman Islands (Br.)
Nicobar Islands (Br.)
CEYLON
Ganges
Indus

Indian Subcontinent and Afghanistan

(continued)

lore, 116,315 ....D 6
lore, *128,341 ....D 6
ıgurla, 12,061 ....C 5
ıkatagiri, 17,114 ....D 6
ʻaval, 46,637 ....C 4
ʻaval, *60,857 ....C 4
ıava, 14,580 ....B 7
lisha, 27,718 ....D 4
ayavada, 253,464 ....D 5
lupuram, 43,496 ....D 6
ıukonda, 11,374 ....D 5
ajpet, 8,138 ....D 6
amgam, 38,955 ....C 4
ıakhapatnam, 206,657 ....E 5
ınagar, 25,982 ....C 4
ıagapatam (Visakhapatnam), 206,657 ....E 5
ıianagaram, 76,808 ....E 5
ıltair ....E 5
ırangal, 163,766 ....D 5
ırdha, 49,113 ....D 4
ın, 18,176 ....D 5
ınam, 7,032 ....E 5
llamanchili, 13,556 ....E 5
llandlapad ....E 5
ola, 21,039 ....C 4
otmal, 45,587 ....D 4

PHYSICAL FEATURES

or (hills) ....G 3
ıatti (isl.), 2,411 ....C 6
nindivi (isls.), 7,854 ....C 6
nini (isl.), 3,530 ....C 6
ıai Mudi (mt.) ....D 6
daman (isls.) ....G 6
daman (sea) ....G 6
ıdroth (isl.), 4,183 ....C 6
ıck (bay) ....B 7
ıltistan (region) ....D 1
ınas (river) ....D 3
ırar (region), 4,580,302 ....D 4
ıtwa (river) ....D 4
ıima (river) ....D 5
dyadhari (river) ....F 2
ombay (harb.) ....B 7
ımbay (gulf) ....C 4
ımorta (isl.) ....G 7
ır Nicobar (isl.) ....G 7
ıambal (river) ....D 3
ıerial (river) ....F 2
ıetlat (isl.), 953 ....C 6
ıilka (lake) ....F 5
ıomo Lhari (mt.) ....F 3
ıco (channel) ....G 6
ılaba (pt.) ....B 7
ılair (lake) ....E 5
ımorin (cape) ....D 7
ıromandel Coast (reg.) ....E 6
ıman (dist.), 22,390 ....C 4
ımodar (river) ....F 4
ıccan (plateau) ....D 6
u (dist.), 14,280 ....C 4
ıncan (passage) ....G 6
ıstern Ghats (mts.) ....D 6
ephanta (isl.) ....B 7
ılse (pt.) ....F 4
ılse Divi (pt.) ....E 5
ıaghra (river) ....E 3
ıea (river) ....F 1
ıa (dist.), 589,997 ....C 5
ıdavari (river) ....D 5
ıdwin Austen (K2) (mt.) ....D 1
ılconda (ruins) ....D 5
ʻeat (channel) ....G 7
ʻeat Nicobar (isl.) ....G 7
ıgari (river) ....D 6
ıoghly (river) ....F 2
dravati (river) ....E 5
terview (isl.) ....G 6
ımna (river) ....E 3
2 (mt.) ....D 1
admat (isl.), 1,851 ....C 6
alpeni (isl.), 2,613 ....C 7

Kamet (mt.) ....D 2
Kaveri (riv.) ....D 6
Khasi (hills) ....G 3
Kiltan (isl.), 1,520 ....C 6
Krishna (river) ....D 5
Kutch (gulf) ....B 4
Laccadive (isls.), 12,115 ....C 6
Ladakh (region), 88,651 ....D 2
Landfall (isl.) ....G 6
Little Andaman (isl.) ....G 6
Little Nicobar (isl.) ....G 7
Luni (river) ....C 3
Lushai (hills) ....G 4
Mahanadi (river) ....E 4
Mahim (bay) ....B 7
Malabar Coast (reg.) ....C 6
Malabar (hill) ....B 7
Malabar (pt.) ....B 7
Malad (creek) ....B 7
Manori (creek) ....B 7
Middle Andaman (isl.) ....G 6
Minicoy (isl.), 4,139 ....C 7
Miri (hills) ....G 3
Mishmi (hills) ....H 3
Nancowry (isl.) ....G 7
Nanda Devi (mt.) ....D 2
Nanga Parbat (mt.) ....D 1
Narcondam (isl.) ....G 6
Narmada (river) ....D 4
Nicobar (isls.) ....G 7
Nine Degree (chan.) ....C 7
North Andaman (isl.) ....G 6
North Sentinel (isl.) ....G 6
Palmyras (pt.) ....F 4
Pangong Tso (lake) ....D 2
Penganga (river) ....D 5
Penner (river) ....D 6
Periyar (lake) ....D 7
Pitti (isl.), 80 ....C 6
Pulicat (lake) ....E 6
Rakaposhi (mt.) ....C 1
Ritchies (arch.) ....G 6
Rutland (isl.) ....G 6
Salsette (isl.), 1,566,572 ....B 7
Sambhar (lake) ....C 3
Saraswati (river) ....F 1
Sarsati (river) ....F 1
Satpura (range) ....D 4
Soda (plains) ....D 1
Sombrero (channel) ....G 7
Son (river) ....E 3
South Andaman (isl.) ....G 6
Suheli Par (isl.) ....C 6
Tapti (river) ....D 4
Tel (river) ....E 4
Ten Degree (chan.) ....G 7
Thana (creek) ....B 7
Tillanchong (isl.) ....G 7
Tolly's Nullah (river) ....F 2
Towers of Silence ....B 7
Tranvancore (region) ....D 7
Tulsi (lake) ....B 6
Tungabhadra (river) ....D 5
Vehar (lake) ....B 7
Vindhya (range) ....D 4
Wardha (river) ....D 4
Western Ghats (mts.) ....C 5
Zaskar (mts.) ....D 2

PAKISTAN

PROVINCES

East Pakistan, 50,840,235 ....G 4
West Pakistan, 42,880,378 ....B 2

CITIES and TOWNS

Abbottabad, 31,036 ....C 2
Ahmadpur East, 20,423 ....C 3
Attock ....C 2
Campbellpore, 19,041 ....C 2
Bahawalnagar, 36,290 ....C 2
Bahawalpur, 84,377 ....C 3
Bannu, 31,623 ....C 2
Barisal, 69,936 ....G 4
Barkhan ....B 3
Bela, 3,139 ....B 3
Bhag ....B 3
Bogra, 33,784 ....F 4
Bostan ....B 2
Campbellpore, 19,041 ....C 2
Chachro ....C 3
Chagai, ‡41,263 ....A 3
Chaman ....B 2
Chiniot ....C 2
Chitral ....C 1
Chittagong, 364,205 ....G 4
Comilla, 54,504 ....G 4
Cox's Bazar (Maheshkhali) ....G 4
Dacca (cap.), 556,712 ....G 4
Dacca, *918,718 ....G 4
Dadu, 19,142 ....B 3
Dalbandin ....A 3
Dera Bugti ....B 3
Dera Ghazi Khan, 47,105 ....C 3
Dera Ismail Khan, 46,140 ....C 2
Dinajpur, 37,711 ....F 3
Dir ....C 1
Duki ....B 2
English Bazar ....F 3
Faridpur, 28,333 ....F 4
Fort Sandeman, 8,058 ....B 2
Gandava ....B 3
Gujranwala, 196,154 ....C 2
Gujrat, 59,608 ....C 2
Gwadar ....A 4
Habiganj ....G 4
Hindubagh ....B 2
Hyderabad, 434,537 ....B 3
Hyderabad, *850,978 ....B 3
Islamabad (future cap.) ....C 2
Jacobabad, 35,278 ....B 3
Jamalpur ....F 4
Jessore, 46,366 ....F 4
Jhal Jhao ....B 3
Jhang-Maghiana, 94,971 ....C 2
Jhelum, 52,585 ....C 2
Jhudo ....B 3
Kalam ....C 1
Kalat, 5,321 ....B 3
Kanrach ....A 3
Karachi, 1,912,598 ....B 4
Karachi, *3,360,017 ....B 4
Kashmor ....C 3
Kasur ....C 2
Khairpur, 34,144 ....B 3
Khanewal ....C 2
Khanpur ....C 3
Kharan Kalat, 2,692 ....A 3
Khulna, 127,970 ....F 4
Khulna, *208,887 ....F 4
Khushab ....C 2
Khuzdar ....B 3
Kishorganj ....G 4
Kohat, 49,854 ....C 2
Ladgasht ....A 3
Lahore, 1,296,477 ....C 2
Lahore, *2,524,473 ....C 2
Lahri ....B 3
Landhi ....B 4
Larkana, 48,008 ....B 3
Leiah ....C 2
Loralai, 5,519 ....B 2
Lyallpur, 425,248 ....C 2
Mach ....B 3
Madaripur ....G 4
Maheshkhali ....G 4
Malakand ....C 2
Mardan, 77,932 ....C 2
Mastung ....B 3
Mianwali, 31,398 ....C 2
Miram Shah ....C 2
Mirpur Khas, 60,861 ....B 3
Montgomery, 15,180 ....C 2
Multan, 358,201 ....C 2
Multan, *698,600 ....C 2
Mungla Anchorage ....G 4
Murree ....C 2
Musa Khel Bazar ....B 2
Mymensingh, 53,256 ....G 4
Nagar Parkar ....C 4
Narayanganj, 162,054 ....G 4
Narayanganj, *287,846 ....G 4
Nawabganj ....F 4
Nawabshah, 45,651 ....B 3
Nazimabad ....B 3
Noakhali, 19,874 ....G 4
Nok Kundi ....A 3
Nowshera ....C 2
Nushki, 3,153 ....B 3
Ormara ....A 3
Pabna, 40,792 ....F 4
Parachinar, 22,953 ....B 2
Peshawar, 218,691 ....C 2
Peshawar, *384,964 ....C 2
Pindi Gheb ....C 2
Pishin ....B 2
Quetta, 106,633 ....B 2
Quetta, *186,126 ....B 2
Rahimyar Khan, 43,548 ....C 3
Rajshahi, 56,885 ....F 4
Rangamati, 6,416 ....G 4
Rangpur, 40,634 ....F 3
Rawalpindi (cap.), 340,175 ....C 2
Rawalpindi, *537,545 ....C 2
Risalpur ....C 2
Rohri ....B 3
Saidu, 15,920 ....C 2
Sargodha, 129,291 ....C 2
Sehwan ....B 3
Shahbandar ....B 4
Shikarpur ....B 3
Sialkot, 164,346 ....C 2
Sialkot, *308,235 ....C 2
Sibi, 13,327 ....B 3
Sirajganj ....F 4
Sonmiani ....B 3
Sui ....B 3
Sukkur, 103,216 ....B 3
Surab ....B 3
Sylhet, 37,740 ....G 4
Tando Adam ....B 3
Tatta, 12,786 ....B 4
Teknaf ....G 4
Tump ....A 3
Turbat, 4,578 ....A 3
Uch ....B 3
Umarkot ....B 3
Uthal ....B 3
Wana ....C 2

PHYSICAL FEATURES

Baluchistan (reg.), 1,251,837 ....B 3
Beji (river) ....B 3
Bolan (pass) ....B 3
Dasht (river) ....A 3
Hab (river) ....B 3
Indus, Mouths of the (delta) ....B 4
Jaddi, Ras (cape) ....A 4
Khyber (pass) ....B 1
Lora, Hamun-i- (swamp) ....B 3
Mashkel (river) ....A 3
Mashkel, Hamun-i- (swamp) ....A 3
Mohenjo Daro (ruins) ....B 3
Muari, Ras (cape) ....B 4
Nal (river) ....B 3
Punjab (reg.), 18,251,818 ....C 2
Ravi (river) ....C 2
Siahan (range) ....A 3
Sind (reg.), 5,952,531 ....B 3
Sulaiman (range) ....C 3
Talab (river) ....A 3
Taxila (ruins) ....C 2
Tirich Mir (mt.) ....C 1
Zhob (river) ....B 2

NEPAL

CITIES and TOWNS

Baitadi ....E 3
Bhaktapur, 37,075 ....F 3
Bhojpur ....F 3
Biratnagar, 33,293 ....F 3
Birganj, 10,759 ....F 3
Dailekh ....E 3
Dhangarhi ....E 3
Dhankuta ....F 3
Doti ....E 3
Ilam ....F 3
Jaleswar ....F 3
Janakpur, 7,037 ....F 3
Jumla ....E 3
Katmandu (cap.), 122,507 ....E 3
Laga ....E 3
Lalitpur, 48,577 ....E 3
Mukhtinath ....E 3
Mustang ....E 3
Nepalganj, 15,817 ....E 3
Palpa ....E 3
Pokhara ....E 3
Pyuthan ....E 3
Ramechhap ....F 3
Ridi ....E 3
Sallyana ....E 3

PHYSICAL FEATURES

Annapurna (mt.) ....E 3
Bheri (river) ....E 3
Dhaulagiri (mt.) ....E 3
Everest (mt.) ....F 3

AFGHANISTAN

CITIES and TOWNS

Anardarra ....A 2
Andkhui, 30,000 ....B 1
Baghlan, 20,000 ....B 1
Bala Murghab, 10,000 ....A 1
Balkh, 15,000 ....B 1
Bamian, 10,000 ....B 2
Belchiragh ....B 1
Chahar Burjak, 500 ....A 2
Chahardeh ....B 2
Charikar, 15,000 ....B 1
Daulatabad, 15,000 ....A 2
Daulat Yar, 2,000 ....B 2
Dilaram ....A 2
Faizabad, 25,000 ....C 1
Farah, 10,000 ....A 2
Farsi ....A 2
Gardez, 20,000 ....B 2
Ghazni, 25,000 ....B 2
Ghizao ....B 2
Ghurian, 10,000 ....A 2
Girishk, 10,000 ....A 2
Haibak, 10,000 ....B 1
Herat, 61,760 ....A 2
Jalalabad, 44,290 ....B 2
Jurm, 10,000 ....C 1
Juwain, 2,000 ....A 2
Kabul (cap.), 400,000 ....B 2
Kabul, *480,000 ....B 2
Kala Bist, 500 ....A 2
Kalat-i-Ghilzai, 10,000 ....B 2
Kandahar, 119,000 ....B 2
Kandahar, *142,000 ....B 2
Khanabad, 30,000 ....B 1
Khash ....A 2
Kuhsan ....A 2
Kushk, 10,000 ....A 1
Landi Muhammad Amin Khan, 1,000 ....A 2
Maimana, 30,000 ....A 1
Matun, 15,000 ....B 2
Mazar-i-Sharif, 39,695 ....B 1
Mukur, 10,000 ....B 2
Obeh, 5,000 ....A 2
Panjao, 3,000 ....B 2
Qala Panja, 1,000 ....C 1
Qaleh-i-Kang, 1,000 ....A 2
Rudbar, 1,000 ....A 2
Rustak, 10,000 ....B 1
Sabzawar, 5,000 ....A 2
Sar-i-Pul, 5,000 ....B 1
Shahjui, 5,000 ....B 2
Shibarghan, 20,000 ....B 1
Shindand (Sabzawar), 5,000 ....A 2
Taiwara, 5,000 ....A 2
Tashkurghan, 30,000 ....B 1
Zebak, 3,000 ....C 1

PHYSICAL FEATURES

Farah Rud (river) ....A 2
Hari Rud (river) ....A 1
Helmand (river) ....B 2
Kunduz (river) ....B 1
Lora (river) ....B 2
Margo, Dasht-i- (des.) ....A 2
Namaksar (salt lake) ....A 2
Paropamisus (range) ....A 2
Registan (desert) ....B 2
Tarnak (river) ....B 2
Wala, Kuh-i- (mt.) ....A 2
Zirreh, Gaud-i- (marsh) ....A 3

CEYLON

CITIES and TOWNS

Anuradhapura, 29,397 ....E 7
Badulla, 27,088 ....E 7
Batticaloa, 22,957 ....E 7
Colombo (cap.), 510,947 ....D 7
Galle, 64,942 ....D 7
Hambantota, 5,387 ....E 7
Jaffna, 94,248 ....E 7
Kalmunai, 16,488 ....E 7
Kalutara, 25,286 ....D 7
Kandy, 67,768 ....E 7
Kurunegala, 21,293 ....E 7
Mannar, 8,988 ....E 7
Matara, 32,284 ....E 7
Moratuwa, 77,632 ....D 7
Mullaittivu, 4,025 ....E 7
Negombo, 47,026 ....D 7
Nuwara Eliya, 19,988 ....E 7
Polgahawela, 5,293 ....D 7
Polonnaruwa, 5,921 ....E 7
Puttalam, 13,250 ....E 7
Ratnapura, 21,582 ....D 7
Tangalla, 7,920 ....E 7
Trincomalee, 34,872 ....E 7
Vavuniya, 7,176 ....E 7

PHYSICAL FEATURES

Adams (peak) ....E 7
Dondra (head) ....E 7
Kirigalpota (mt.) ....E 7
Pedro (pt.) ....E 6
Pidurutalagala (mt.) ....E 7

*City and suburbs.
†Population of sub-division.
‡Population of district.

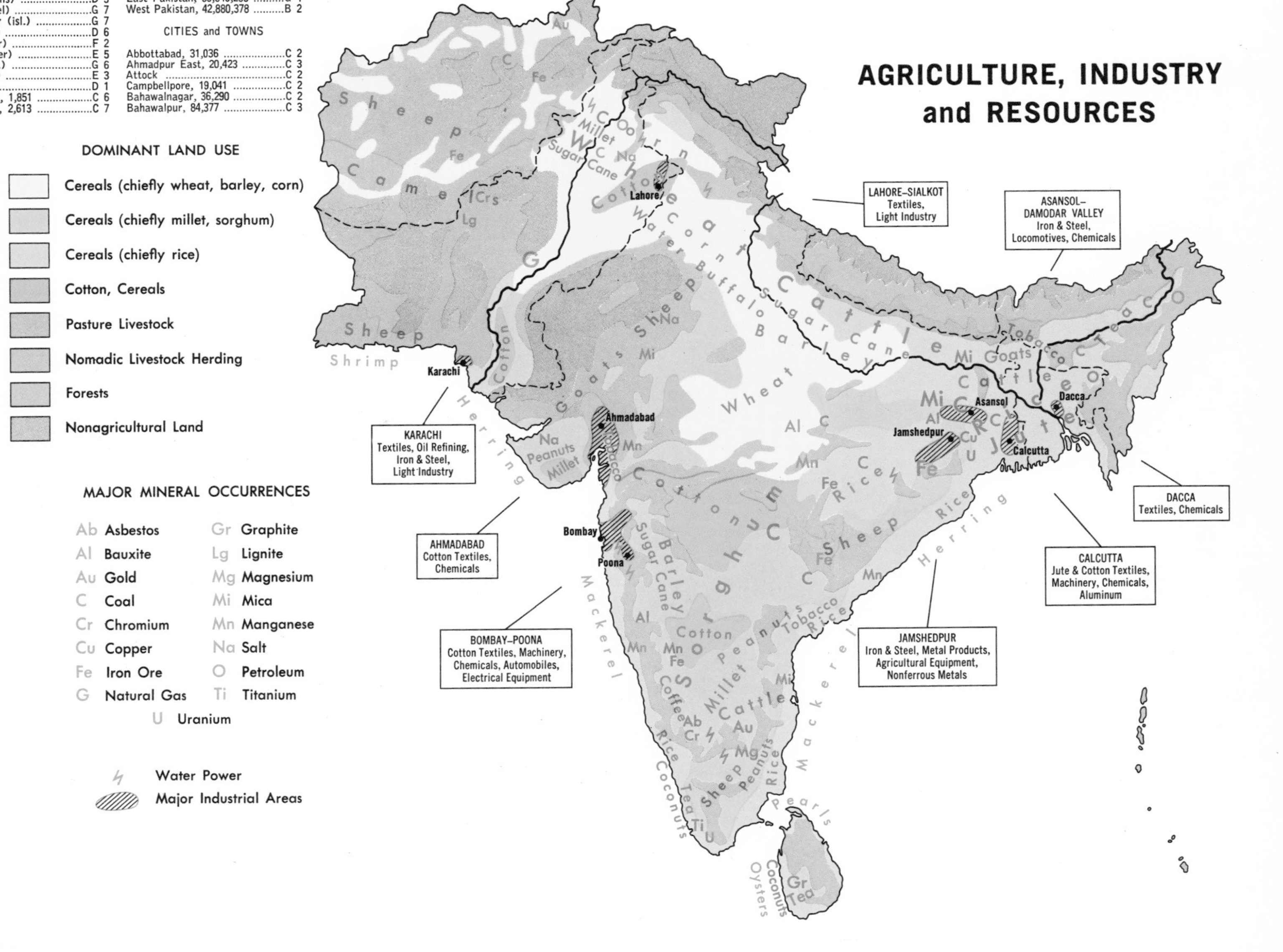
AGRICULTURE, INDUSTRY and RESOURCES
DOMINANT LAND USE
Cereals (chiefly wheat, barley, corn)
Cereals (chiefly millet, sorghum)
Cereals (chiefly rice)
Cotton, Cereals
Pasture Livestock
Nomadic Livestock Herding
Forests
Nonagricultural Land
MAJOR MINERAL OCCURRENCES
Ab Asbestos
Al Bauxite
Au Gold
C Coal
Cr Chromium
Cu Copper
Fe Iron Ore
G Natural Gas
Gr Graphite
Lg Lignite
Mg Magnesium
Mi Mica
Mn Manganese
Na Salt
O Petroleum
Ti Titanium
U Uranium
Water Power
Major Industrial Areas
LAHORE–SIALKOT Textiles, Light Industry
ASANSOL–DAMODAR VALLEY Iron & Steel, Locomotives, Chemicals
KARACHI Textiles, Oil Refining, Iron & Steel, Light Industry
AHMADABAD Cotton Textiles, Chemicals
BOMBAY–POONA Cotton Textiles, Machinery, Chemicals, Automobiles, Electrical Equipment
DACCA Textiles, Chemicals
CALCUTTA Jute & Cotton Textiles, Machinery, Chemicals, Aluminum
JAMSHEDPUR Iron & Steel, Metal Products, Agricultural Equipment, Nonferrous Metals
Lahore
Karachi
Ahmadabad
Bombay
Poona
Asansol
Jamshedpur
Calcutta
Dacca

BURMA, THAILAND, INDOCHINA and MALAYA

CONIC PROJECTION

SCALE OF MILES

SCALE OF KILOMETRES

International Boundaries
Provincial and State Boundaries
Capitals of Countries
Provincial and State Capitals

Copyright by C.S. HAMMOND & Co., N.Y.

BURMA, THAILAND, INDOCHINA and MALAYA

BURMA

AREA	261,610 sq. mi.
POPULATION	24,229,000
CAPITAL	Rangoon
LARGEST CITY	Rangoon 821,800
HIGHEST POINT	Hkakabo Razi 19,296 ft.
MONETARY UNIT	kyat
MAJOR LANGUAGES	Burmese, Karen, Shan
MAJOR RELIGIONS	Buddhist, Tribal religions

CAMBODIA

AREA	69,884 sq. mi.
POPULATION	6,200,000
CAPITAL	Phnom Penh
LARGEST CITY	Phnom Penh (greater) 403,500
HIGHEST POINT	5,948 ft.
MONETARY UNIT	riel
MAJOR LANGUAGES	Khmer (Cambodian), Lao
MAJOR RELIGIONS	Buddhist

MALAYSIA

AREA	129,374
POPULATION	9,148,000
CAPITAL	Kuala Lumpur
LARGEST CITY	Kuala Lumpur 316,230
HIGHEST POINT	Mt. Kinabalu 13,455 ft.
MONETARY UNIT	Malayan dollar
MAJOR LANGUAGES	Malay, Chinese, English, Indonesian, Hindi
MAJOR RELIGIONS	Mohammedan, Confucianist, Buddhist, Tribal religions, Hindu, Taoist

THAILAND

200,148 sq. mi.
30,591,000
Bangkok
Bangkok (greater) 1,608,305
Doi Inthanon 8,452 ft.
baht
Thai, Khmer
Buddhist, Tribal religions

NORTH VIETNAM

63,370 sq. mi.
17,900,000
Hanoi
Hanoi (greater) 643,576
Fan Si Pan 10.308 ft.
dong
Vietnamese, Lao
Buddhist, Taoist, Confucianist

SINGAPORE

220 sq. mi.
1,844,000
Singapore
Singapore (greater) 1,820,000
Bukit Timah 581 ft.
Malayan dollar
Malay, Chinese, Tamil, English

Confucianist, Buddhist, Taoist, Hindu, Mohammedan, Christian

LAOS

89,343 sq. mi.
1,960,000
Vientiane
Vientiane (greater) 162,297
Phu Bia 9,252 ft.
kip
Lao, Khmer (Annamese), French
Buddhist

SOUTH VIETNAM

65,726 sq. mi.
15,715,000
Saigon
Saigon 1,431,000
Ngoc Linh 8,524 ft.
piaster
Vietnamese, Lao
Buddhist, Taoist, Roman Catholic

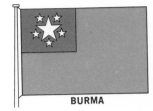
BURMA

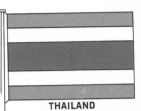
THAILAND

LAOS

CAMBODIA

NORTH VIETNAM

SOUTH VIETNAM

MALAYSIA

SINGAPORE

TOPOGRAPHY

0   200   400
MILES

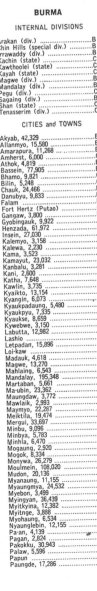

5,000 m. | 2,000 m. | 1,000 m. | 500 m. | 200 m. | 100 m. | Sea Level Below
16,404 ft. | 6,562 ft. | 3,281 ft. | 1,640 ft. | 656 ft. | 328 ft. |

Pegu, 47,378	C 3
Prome, 36,997	B 3
Putao	C 1
Pyapon, 19,174	C 3
Pyinmana, 22,025	C 3
Pyu, 10,443	C 3
Rangoon (cap.), 821,800	B 2
Rathedaung, 2,969	B 2
Sagaing, 15,382	B 2
Sandoway, 5,172	B 3
Shwebo, 17,827	B 2
Shwegyin, 5,439	C 3
Shwenyaung	C 2
Singkaling Hkamti	B 1
Singu, 4,027	B 2
Syriam, 15,296	C 3
Taungdwingyi, 16,233	B 2
Taunggyi	C 2
Taungup, 4,065	B 3
Tavoy, 40,312	C 5
Tenasserim, 1,086	C 5
Tharrawaddy, 8,977	C 3
Thaton, 38,047	C 3
Thayetmyo, 11,649	B 3
Thazi, 7,531	C 2
Thongwa, 10,829	C 3
Thonze, 14,443	C 3
Toungoo, 31,589	C 3
Victoria Point, 1,520	C 5
Wakema, 20,716	B 3
Yamethin, 11,167	C 2
Yandoon, 15,245	C 3
Ye, 12,852	C 4
Yenangyaung, 24,416	B 2
Yesagyo, 7,880	B 2
Ye-u, 5,307	B 2

BURMA

INTERNAL DIVISIONS

Arakan (div.)	B 3
Chin Hills (special div.)	B 2
Irrawaddy (div.)	B 3
Kachin (state)	C 1
Kawthoolei (state)	C 3
Kayah (state)	B 2
Magwe (div.)	B 2
Mandalay (div.)	C 3
Pegu (div.)	C 3
Sagaing (div.)	B 1
Shan (state)	C 2
Tenasserim (div.)	C 4

CITIES and TOWNS

Akyab, 42,329	B 2
Allanmyo, 15,580	B 3
Amarapura, 11,268	B 2
Amherst, 6,000	C 3
Athok, 4,819	B 3
Bassein, 77,905	B 3
Bhamo, 9,821	C 1
Bilin, 5,248	C 3
Chauk, 24,466	B 2
Danubyu, 9,833	B 3
Falam	B 2
Fort Hertz (Putao)	C 1
Gangaw, 3,800	B 2
Gyobingauk, 9,922	C 3
Henzada, 61,972	B 3
Insein, 27,030	C 3
Kalemyo, 3,158	B 2
Kalewa, 2,230	B 2
Kama, 3,523	C 3
Kamayut, 23,032	B 2
Kanbalu, 3,281	C 2
Kani, 2,600	B 2
Katha, 7,648	C 1
Kawlin, 3,735	B 2
Kyaikto, 13,154	C 3
Kyangin, 6,073	B 3
Kyaukpadaung, 5,480	B 2
Kyaukpyu, 7,335	B 3
Kyaukse, 8,659	C 2
Kywebwe, 3,150	C 3
Labutta, 12,982	B 3
Lashio	C 2
Letpadan, 15,896	C 3
Loi-kaw	C 3
Madauk, 4,618	C 3
Magwe, 13,270	B 2
Mahlaing, 6,543	C 2
Mandalay, 195,348	C 2
Martaban, 5,661	C 3
Ma-ubin, 23,362	B 3
Maungdaw, 3,772	B 2
Mawlaik, 2,993	B 2
Maymyo, 22,287	C 2
Meiktila, 19,474	C 2
Mergui, 33,697	C 4
Minbu, 9,096	B 2
Minbya, 5,783	B 3
Minhla, 6,470	C 2
Mogaung, 2,920	C 1
Mogok, 8,334	C 2
Monywa, 26,279	B 2
Moulmein, 108,020	C 3
Mudon, 20,136	C 3
Myanaung, 11,155	B 3
Myaungmya, 24,532	B 3
Myebon, 3,499	B 2
Myingyan, 36,439	C 2
Myitkyina, 12,382	C 1
Myitnge, 3,888	C 2
Myohaung, 6,534	B 2
Nyaunglebin, 12,155	C 3
Pa-an, 4,139	C 3
Pagan, 2,824	B 2
Pakokku, 30,943	B 2
Palaw, 5,596	C 4
Papun	B 3
Paungde, 17,286	B 3

PHYSICAL FEATURES

Amya (pass)	C 4
Andaman (sea)	B 4
Arakan Yoma (mts.)	B 3
Bengal (bay)	B 3
Bilauktaung (range)	C 4
Chauken (pass)	C 1
Cheduba (isl.), 2,621	B 3
Chin (hills)	B 2
Chindwin (river)	B 2
Coco (chan.)	A 4
Combermere (bay)	B 3
Dawna (range)	C 3
Great Coco (isl.)	A 4
Great Tenasserim (river)	C 4
Hkakabo Razi (mt.)	C 1
Indawgyi (lake)	C 1
Inle (lake)	C 2
Irrawaddy (river)	B 3
Irrawaddy, Mouths of the (delta)	B 4
Kaladan (river)	B 2
Khao Luang (mt.)	C 5
Loi Leng (mt.)	C 2
Manipur (river)	B 2
Martaban (gulf)	C 4
Mekong (river)	D 2
Mergui (arch.)	C 5
Mon (river)	B 2
Mu (river)	C 2
Nam Hka (river)	C 2
Nam Pawn (river)	C 2
Nam Teng (river)	C 2
Negrais (cape)	B 3
Pakchan (river)	C 5
Pangsau (pass)	B 1
Pegu Yoma (mts.)	B 3
Preparis (isl.)	B 4
Ramree (isl.), 11,133	B 3
Salween (river)	C 3
Shan (plateau)	C 2
Sittang (river)	C 3
Taungthonton (mt.)	C 4
Tavoy (point)	C 4
Tenasserim (isl.)	C 4
Three Pagodas (pass)	C 4
Victoria (mt.)	B 2

CAMBODIA

CITIES and TOWNS

Banam, †87,048	E 5
Battambang, 38,846	D 4
Cheom Ksan	D 4
Chhlong, †46,108	D 4
Chong Kal, †16,918	D 4
Kampot, 12,558	E 5

(continued on following page)

Burma, Thailand, Indochina and Malaya
(continued)

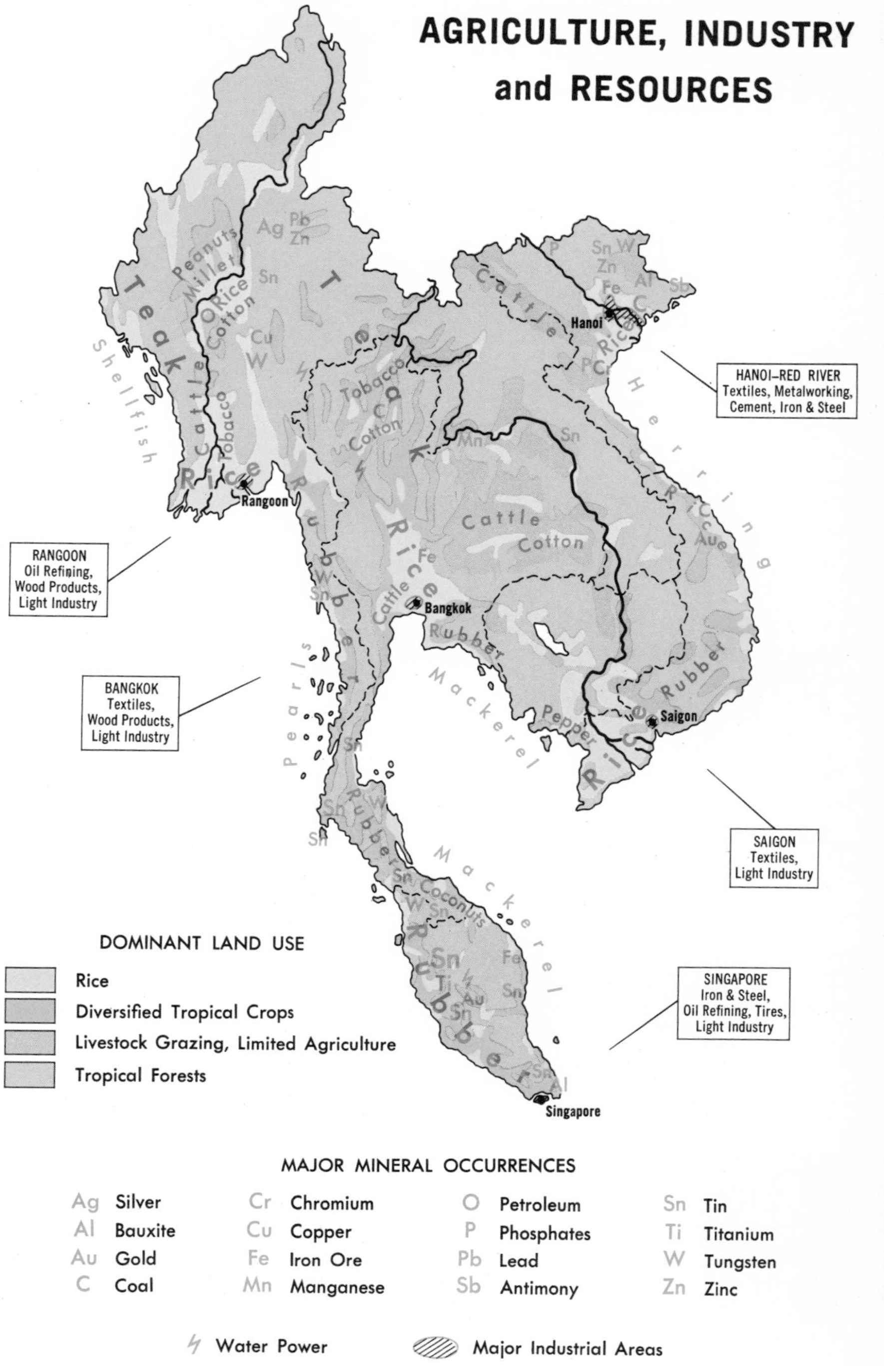
AGRICULTURE, INDUSTRY
and RESOURCES
Hanoi
HANOI–RED RIVER
Textiles, Metalworking,
Cement, Iron & Steel
Rangoon
RANGOON
Oil Refining,
Wood Products,
Light Industry
Bangkok
BANGKOK
Textiles,
Wood Products,
Light Industry
Saigon
SAIGON
Textiles,
Light Industry
Singapore
SINGAPORE
Iron & Steel,
Oil Refining, Tires,
Light Industry
Teak
Rice
Cattle
Cotton
Rubber
Tobacco
Shellfish
Herring
Mackerel
Pearls
Coconuts
Pepper
DOMINANT LAND USE
Rice
Diversified Tropical Crops
Livestock Grazing, Limited Agriculture
Tropical Forests
MAJOR MINERAL OCCURRENCES
Ag Silver
Al Bauxite
Au Gold
C Coal
Cr Chromium
Cu Copper
Fe Iron Ore
Mn Manganese
O Petroleum
P Phosphates
Pb Lead
Sb Antimony
Sn Tin
Ti Titanium
W Tungsten
Zn Zinc
Water Power
Major Industrial Areas

CAMBODIA (continued)

Kep, 7,565 ... E 5
Khemarak Phouinville ... D 5
Kohnieh ... E 4
Kompong Cham, 28,534 ... E 4
Kompong Chhnang, 12,847 ... D 4
Kompong Kleang ... E 4
Kompong Speu, 7,453 ... E 5
Kompong Thom, 9,682 ... E 4
Kompong Trabek, †108,227 ... E 5
Koulen ... E 4
Kratie, 11,908 ... E 4
Krauchmar, †63,262 ... E 4
Melouprey ... E 4
Moung, †88,321 ... D 4
Pailin, †15,536 ... D 4
Phnom Penh (cap.), *403,500 ... E 5
Phsar Babau ... D 4
Phsar Oudong, †50,456 ... E 5
Phum Rovieng, †21,151 ... E 4
Poipet ... D 4
Prek Po ... E 5
Prey Veng, 8,792 ... E 5
Pursat, 14,329 ... D 4
Ream ... D 5
Sambor, †11,213 ... E 4
Siem Pang, †8,959 ... E 4
Siem Reap, 10,230 ... D 4
Sihanoukville, 6,578 ... D 5
Sisophon, †29,581 ... D 4
Sre Khtum ... E 4
Stung Treng, 3,369 ... E 4
Suong ... E 5
Svay Rieng, 11,184 ... E 5
Takeo, 11,312 ... E 5
Voeune Sai, †16,912 ... E 4

PHYSICAL FEATURES

Angkor Wat (ruins) ... E 4
Dang Raek, Phanom (mts.) ... D 4
Joncs (plain) ... E 5
Kas Kong (isl.) ... D 5
Kas Rong (isl.) ... D 5
Kas Tang (isl.) ... D 5
Kong, Kas (isl.) ... D 5
Mekong (river) ... E 4
Phanom Dang Raek (mts.) ... D 4
Preapatang (rapids) ... E 4
Rong, Kas (isl.) ... D 5
Samit (point) ... D 5
Se Khong (river) ... E 4
Se San (river) ... E 4
Siam (gulf) ... D 5
Srepok (river) ... E 4
Stung Sen (river) ... E 4
Tang, Kas (isl.) ... D 5
Tonle Sap (lake) ... D 4

LAOS

CITIES and TOWNS

Attopeu, 2,750 ... E 4
Ban Bung Sai ... E 4
Borikhane ... D 3
Botene ... D 3
Boun Neua, 2,500 ... D 2
Boun Tai, †1,681 ... D 2
Champassak, 3,500 ... E 4
Houei Sai, 1,500 ... D 2
Hua Muong ... D 2
Keng Kok, 2,000 ... E 3
Kham Keut, †31,206 ... E 3
Khone ... E 4
Khong, 1,750 ... E 4
Khong Sédone, 2,000 ... E 4
Luang Prabang, 7,596 ... D 3
Mahaxay, 2,000 ... E 3
Muong Beng, †2,305 ... D 2
Muong Bo ... D 3
Muong Hai, †476 ... D 2
Muong Hôm ... D 3
Muong Lan, †836 ... D 3
Muong May ... E 4
Muong Phalane ... E 3
Muong Phine ... E 3
Muong Phong ... D 3
Muong Sai, 2,000 ... D 2
Muong Sing, 1,091 ... D 2
Muong Son ... D 2
Muong Song Khone, 2,000 ... E 3
Muong Wapi ... E 4
Muong Yo ... D 2
Nam Tha, 1,459 ... D 2
Napé ... E 3
Nong Het ... D 3
Ou Neua, †4,300 ... D 2
Pak Beng, †2,964 ... D 3
Pak Hin Boun, 1,750 ... E 3
Pak Sane, 2,500 ... D 3
Paklay, 2,000 ... D 3
Pakse, 8,000 ... E 4
Phiafay, †17,216 ... E 4
Phon Tiou ... E 3
Phong Saly, 2,500 ... D 2
Sam Neua, 3,000 ... E 2
Saravane, 2,350 ... E 4
Savannakhet, 8,500 ... E 3
Sayaboury, 2,500 ... D 3
Tchepone, 1,250 ... E 3
Tha-deua ... D 3
Thakhek, 5,500 ... E 3
Tourakom ... D 3
Vang Vieng, 1,250 ... D 3
Vien Phou Kha ... D 2
Vientiane (cap.), 68,206 ... D 3
Vientiane, *162,297 ... D 3
Xieng Khouang, 3,500 ... D 3

PHYSICAL FEATURES

Bolovens (plateau) ... E 4
Hou, Nam (river) ... D 2
Jars (plain) ... D 3
Mekong (river) ... D 3
Nam Hou (river) ... D 2
Nam Tha (river) ... D 2
Phu Bia (mt.) ... D 3
Phu Co Pi (mt.) ... E 3
Phu Loi (mt.) ... D 2
Rao Co (mt.) ... E 3
Se Khong (river) ... E 4
Tha, Nam (river) ... D 2
Tran Ninh (plateau) ... D 3

MALAYSIA, FEDERATION OF

STATES

Johore, 926,850 ... D 7
Kedah, 701,964 ... D 6
Kelantan, 505,522 ... D 6
Malacca, 291,211 ... D 7
Negri Sembilan, 364,524 ... D 7
Pahang, 313,058 ... D 7
Penang, 572,100 ... D 6
Perak, 1,221,446 ... D 6
Perlis, 90,885 ... D 6
Selangor, 1,012,929 ... D 7
Trengganu, 278,269 ... D 6

CITIES and TOWNS

Alor Gajah, 2,135* ... D 7
Alor Star, 52,915 ... D 6
Baling, 4,121 ... D 6
Bandar Maharani, 39,046 ... D 7
Bandar Penggaram, 39,294 ... D 7
Batu Gajah, 10,143 ... D 6
Bentong, 18,845 ... D 7
Butterworth, 42,504 ... D 6
Chukai, 10,803 ... D 6
Gemas, 4,873 ... D 7
George Town (Penang), 234,903 ... C 6
Ipoh, 125,770 ... D 6
Johore Bahru, 74,909 ... F 5
Kajang, 9,630 ... D 7
Kampar, 24,602 ... D 6
Kangar, 6,064 ... D 6
Klang, 75,649 ... D 7
Kluang, 31,181 ... D 7
Kota Bharu, 38,103 ... D 6
Kota Tinggi, 7,475 ... F 5
Kuala Dungun, 12,515 ... D 6
Kuala Lipis, 8,753 ... D 6
Kuala Lumpur (cap.), 316,230 ... D 7
Kuala Pilah, 12,024 ... D 7
Kuala Selangor, 2,285 ... D 7
Kuala Trengganu, 29,446 ... D 6
Kuantan, 23,034 ... D 7
Kulai, 7,759 ... F 5
Lumut, 2,947 ... D 6
Malacca, 69,848 ... D 7
Mentakab, 12,296 ... D 7
Mersing, 7,228 ... E 7
Pekan, 2,070 ... D 7
Pekan Nenas, 7,129 ... E 5
Penang, 234,903 ... C 6
Pontian Kechil, 8,459 ... E 5
Port Dickson, 4,416 ... D 7
Port Swettenham, 16,925 ... D 7
Port Weld, 2,260 ... D 6
Raub, 15,363 ... D 7
Segamat, 18,445 ... D 7
Seremban, 52,091 ... D 7
Sungei Patani, 22,916 ... C 6
Taiping, 48,206 ... D 6
Tanah Merah, 775 ... D 6
Teluk Anson, 37,042 ... D 6
Tumpat, 8,946 ... D 6

PHYSICAL FEATURES

Aur, Pulau (isl.), 415 ... E 7
Blumut, Gunong (mt.) ... D 7
Gelang, Tanjong (point) ... D 6
Johore (river) ... F 5
Johore (str.) ... E 6
Kelantan (river) ... D 6
Langkawi, Pulau (isl.), 16,535 ... C 6
Lima, Pulau (isl.) ... F 6
Malacca (str.) ... D 7
Malaya (reg.), 7,810,000 ... E 6
Ophir (mt.) ... D 7
Pahang (river) ... D 7
Pangkor, Pulau (isl.), 2,580 ... D 6
Penang (isl.), 338,898 ... C 6
Perak, Gunong (mt.) ... D 6
Perhentian (isls.), 447 ... D 6
Pulai (river) ... E 5
Ramunia, Tanjong (point) ... F 6
Redang, Pulau (isl.), 470 ... D 6
Sedili Kechil, Tanjong (point) ... F 5
Tahan, Gunong (mt.) ... D 6
Temiang, Bukit (mt.) ... D 6
Tenggol, Pulau (isl.), 2,386 ... D 6
Tinggi, Pulau (isl.), 440 ... E 7

SINGAPORE

CITIES and TOWNS

Nee Soon, 6,043 ... F 6
Paya Lebar, 45,440 ... F 6
Serangoon, 3,798 ... F 6
Singapore (cap.), 1,775,200 ... F 6
Singapore, *1,820,000 ... F 6
Woodlands, 737 ... F 6

PHYSICAL FEATURES

Keppel (harb.) ... F 6
Main (str.) ... F 6
Singapore (str.) ... F 6
Tekong Besar, Pulau (isl.), 4,074 ... F 6

THAILAND (SIAM)

CITIES and TOWNS

Amnat, 11,335 ... E 4
Ang Thong, 6,458 ... C 4
Ayutthaya, 24,597 ... D 4
Ban Aranyaprathet, 11,112 ... D 4
Ban Hat Yai, 35,504 ... C 6
Ban Kantang, 5,076 ... C 6
Ban Khlong Yai, 3,815 ... D 5
Ban Pak Phanang, 11,963 ... D 5
Ban Pua, 12,317 ... D 3
Ban Sattahip, 22,942 ... D 4
Ban Tha Uthen, 7,297 ... D 3
Bang Lamung, 9,087 ... D 4
Bang Saphan, 6,959 ... C 5
Bangkok (cap.), 1,299,528 ... D 4
Bangkok, *1,608,305 ... D 4
Banphot Phisai, 6,036 ... C 3
Buriram, 12,579 ... D 4
Chachoengsao, 19,809 ... G 4
Chai Badan, 6,158 ... D 4
Chai Buri, †31,135 ... D 3
Chainat, 4,652 ... D 4
Chaiya, 3,607 ... C 5
Chaiyaphum, 9,633 ... D 4
Chang Khoeng, 6,037 ... C 3
Chanthaburi, 10,780 ... D 4
Chiang Dao, 8,017 ... C 3
Chiang Khan, 5,810 ... D 3
Chiang Rai, 11,663 ... C 3
Chiang Saen, 5,443 ... C 2
Chiengmai, 65,600 ... C 3
Chon Buri, 32,496 ... D 4
Chumphon, 9,342 ... C 5
Dan Sai, 6,710 ... D 3
Den Chai, 12,732 ... C 3
Hua Hin, 17,078 ... D 4
Kabin Buri, 3,703 ... D 4
Kalasin, 11,043 ... D 3
Kamphaeng Phet, 7,171 ... C 3
Kanchanaburi, 12,957 ... C 4
Khemmarat, 5,426 ... E 4
Khon Kaen, 19,591 ... D 3
Khorat (Nakhon Ratchasima), 41,037 ... D 4
Khu Khan, †122,206 ... E 4
Kra Buri, 3,717 ... C 5
Krung Thep (Bangkok) (cap.), 1,299,528 ... D 4
Kumphawapi, 20,759 ... D 3
Lae, 5,743 ... D 3
Lampang, 36,488 ... C 3
Lamphun, 10,602 ... C 3
Lang Suan, 4,108 ... C 5
Loei, 7,301 ... D 3
Lom Sak, 8,386 ... D 3
Lop Buri, 21,244 ... D 4
Maha Sarakham, 15,680 ... D 3
Mukdahan, 17,738 ... E 3
Nakhon Nayok, 8,048 ... D 4
Nakhon Pathom, 28,426 ... C 4
Nakhon Phanom, 14,799 ... D 3
Nakhon Ratchasima, 41,037 ... D 4
Nakhon Sawan, 34,947 ... D 4
Nakhon Si Thammarat, 25,919 ... D 5
Nan, 13,843 ... D 3
Nang Rong, 15,623 ... D 4
Narathiwat, 17,508 ... D 6
Ngao, †32,643 ... D 3
Nong Khai, 21,120 ... D 3
Pattani, 16,804 ... D 6
Phanat Nikhom, 9,307 ... D 4
Phangnga, 4,782 ... C 5
Phatthalung, 10,420 ... D 6
Phayao, 17,959 ... C 3
Phet Buri, 24,654 ... C 4
Phetchabun, 5,947 ... D 3
Phichai, 5,258 ... D 3
Phichit, 9,258 ... D 3
Phitsanulok, 30,364 ... D 3
Phon Phisai, 6,745 ... D 3
Phrae, 16,005 ... D 3
Phuket, 28,163 ... C 6
Phutthaisong, 9,315 ... D 4
Prachin Buri, 13,420 ... D 4
Prachuap Khiri Khan, 6,303 ... D 5
Pran Buri, 7,795 ... D 4
Rahaeng (Tak), 13,274 ... C 3
Ranong, 5,993 ... C 5
Rat Buri, 20,383 ... C 4
Rayong, 9,680 ... D 4
Roi Et, 12,930 ... D 4
Rong Kwang, †39,375 ... D 3
Sakon Nakhon, 16,457 ... E 3
Samut Prakan, 21,769 ... D 4
Samut Sakhon, 27,802 ... D 4
Samut Songkhram, 12,801 ... C 4
Sara Buri, 17,572 ... D 4
Satun, 4,369 ... C 6
Sawankhalok, 7,880 ... C 3
Selaphum, 10,395 ... E 3
Sing Buri, 8,384 ... D 4
Singora (Songkhla), 31,014 ... D 6
Sisaket, 9,519 ... E 4
Songkhla, 31,014 ... D 6
Sukhothai, 8,627 ... D 3
Suphan Buri, 13,859 ... C 4
Surat Thani, 19,738 ... C 5
Surin, 13,860 ... D 4
Suwannaphum, 15,731 ... D 4
Tak, 13,274 ... C 3
Takua Pa, 6,308 ... C 5
Thoen, 17,283 ... C 3
Thonburi, 402,818 ... D 4
Thonburi, *459,555 ... D 4
Trang, 17,158 ... C 6
Trat, 3,813 ... D 4
Ubon, 27,092 ... E 4
Udon Thani, 29,965 ... D 3
Uthai Thani, 10,729 ... C 4
Uttaradit, 9,120 ... D 3
Warin Chamrap, 7,067 ... E 4
Yala, 18,083 ... D 6
Yasothon, 9,717 ... D 4

PHYSICAL FEATURES

Amya (pass) ... C 4
Bilauktaung (range) ... C 4
Chao Phraya, Mae Nam (river) ... D 4
Chi, Mae Nam (river) ... D 3
Chong Pak Phra (cape) ... C 5
Dang Raek, Phanom (mts.) ... D 4
Doi Inthanon (mt.) ... C 3
Doi Pha Hom Pok (mt.) ... C 2
Doi Pia Fai (mt.) ... D 4
Kao Prawa (mt.) ... C 3
Khao Luang (mt.) ... C 5
Khwae Noi, Mae Nam (river) ... C 4
Ko Chang (isl.) ... D 4
Ko Kut (isl.) ... D 5
Ko Lanta (isl.), 9,486 ... C 6
Ko Phangan (isl.) ... D 5
Ko Phuket (isl.), 75,652 ... C 5
Ko Samui (isl.), 30,818 ... D 5
Ko Tao (isl.) ... C 5
Ko Terutao (isl.) ... C 6
Ko Thalu (isls.) ... C 5
Kra (isthmus) ... C 5
Laem Pho (cape) ... D 6
Laem Talumphuk (cape) ... D 5
Luang (mt.) ... C 5
Mae Klong, Mae Nam (river) ... C 4
Mekong (river) ... E 3
Mulayit Taung (mt.) ... C 3
Mun, Mae Nam (river) ... D 4
Nan, Mae Nam (river) ... D 3
Nong Lahan (lake) ... D 3
Pa Sak, Mae Nam (river) ... D 4
Pakchan (river) ... C 5
Phanom Dang Raek (mts.) ... D 4
Ping, Mae Nam (river) ... C 3
Samui (str.) ... D 5
Siam (gulf) ... D 5
Tapi, Mae Nam (river) ... C 5
Tha Chin, Mae Nam (river) ... C 4
Thale Luang (lagoon) ... D 6
Three Pagodas (pass) ... C 4
Wang, Mae Nam (river) ... C 3

VIETNAM (NORTH)

CITIES and TOWNS

Ba Don ... E 3
Bac Can ... E 2
Bac Ninh, 22,560 ... E 2
Bai Thuong ... E 3
Bao Ha ... D 2
Bao Lac ... E 2
Ben Thuy ... E 3
Cao Bang ... E 2
Co Lieu ... E 3
Con Cuong ... E 3
Cua Rao ... E 3
Dien Bien Phu ... D 2
Dong Hoi ... E 3
Ha Giang ... E 2
Ha Tinh ... E 3
Haiphong, 182,496 ... E 2
Haiphong, *369,248 ... E 2
Hanoi (cap.), 414,620 ... E 2
Hanoi, *643,576 ... E 2
Hoa Binh ... E 2
Hoi Xuan ... E 2
Hon Gay, 35,412 ... E 2
Huong Khe ... E 3
Ke Bao ... E 2
Lai Chau ... D 2
Lang Mo ... E 3
Lang Son, 15,071 ... E 2
Lao Cai ... E 2
Luc An Chau ... E 2
Mon Cay ... E 2
Muong Khuong ... E 2
Nam Dinh, 86,132 ... E 2
Nghia Lo ... D 2
Ninh Binh ... E 2
Phu Dien ... E 3
Phu Lang Thuong ... E 2
Phuly ... E 2
Phu Qui ... E 3
Phu Tho, 10,888 ... E 2
Phu Tinh Gia ... E 3
Quang Khe ... E 3
Quang Yen ... E 2
Ron ... E 3
Son La ... D 2
Son Tay, 19,213 ... E 2
Thai Binh, 14,739 ... E 2
Thai Nguyen, 21,846 ... E 2
Thanh Hoa, 31,211 ... E 3
That Khe ... E 2
Tien Yen ... E 2
Trung Khanh Phu ... E 2
Tuyen Quang ... E 2
Van Hoa ... E 2
Van Yen ... E 2
Vinh, 43,954 ... E 3
Vinh Yen ... E 2
Vu Liet ... E 3
Yen Bai ... E 2
Yen Minh ... E 2

PHYSICAL FEATURES

Bach Long Vi, Dao (isl.) ... F 2
Black (river) ... D 2
Cat Ba, Dao (isl.) ... E 2
Dao Bach Long Vi (isl.) ... F 2
Fan Si Pan (mt.) ... D 2
Lay (cape) ... E 3
Mui Duong (cape) ... E 3
Nightingale (Bach Long Vi) (isl.) ... F 2
Rao Co (mt.) ... E 3
Red (river) ... E 2
Sip Song Chau Thai (mts.) ... D 2
Song Bo (Black) (river) ... D 2
Song Ca (river) ... E 3
Song Coi (Red) (river) ... E 2
Tigre (isl.) ... E 3
Tonkin (gulf) ... E 3

VIETNAM (SOUTH)

CITIES and TOWNS

An Khe ... F 4
An Loc, 5,600 ... E 5
Ba Ngoi ... F 5
Bac Lieu (Vinh Loi), 29,520 ... E 5
Ban Me Thuot, 29,610 ... F 4
Baria (Phuo Cle), 4,770 ... E 5
Bien Hoa, 37,810 ... E 5
Binh Dinh, 18,350 ... F 4
Binh Son ... F 4
Bong Son ... F 4
Bu Dop ... E 4
Can Tho, 49,310 ... E 5
Cao Lanh, 2,560 ... E 5
Cap Saint-Jacques (Vung Tau), 5,800 ... E 5
Chaudoc, 51,600 ... E 5
Cheo Reo ... E 4
Chu Lai ... F 4
Da Lat, 48,840 ... F 5
Da Nang, 110,784 ... E 3
Dak Bla ... E 4
Dam Doi ... E 5
Di Linh, 4,500 ... F 5
Duong Dong ... D 5
Go Cong, 7,570 ... E 5
Go Quao ... E 5
Ha Tien, 5,200 ... E 5
Ham Tan, 9,810 ... E 5
Hoa Da ... F 5
Hoi An, 16,590 ... F 4
Hon Chong ... E 5
Hue, 105,784 ... E 3
Khanh Hoa ... F 4
Khanh Hung, 39,690 ... E 5
Kontum, 8,760 ... E 4
Loc Ninh ... E 5
Long Xuyen, 23,300 ... E 5
Mo Duc ... F 4
Moc Hoa, 5,000 ... E 5
My Tho, 40,070 ... E 5
Nha Trang, 49,150 ... F 4
Phan Rang, 21,940 ... F 5
Phan Ri ... F 5
Phan Thiet, 55,180 ... F 5
Phu Cuong, 22,840 ... E 5
Phu Loc ... E 5
Phu My ... F 4
Phu Rieng ... E 5
Phu Vinh (Tra Vinh), 12,520 ... E 5
Phuoc Le, 4,770 ... E 5
Pleiku, 53,390 ... E 4
Pleime ... E 4
Quan Long, 17,980 ... E 5
Quang Nam ... E 4
Quang Ngai, 8,640 ... F 4
Quang Tri, 10,740 ... E 3
Qui Nhon, 30,900 ... F 4
Rach Gia, 36,960 ... E 5
Sa Dec, 35,410 ... E 5
Saigon (cap.), 1,431,000 ... E 5
Son Ha ... F 4
Song Cau ... F 4
Tam Ky ... F 4
Tam Quan, 3,820 ... F 4
Tan An, 12,840 ... E 5
Tay Ninh, 14,670 ... E 5
Tra Vinh, 12,520 ... E 5
Truc Giang, 15,610 ... E 5
Tuy Hoa, 17,210 ... F 4
Van Gia ... F 4
Vinh Loi, 29,520 ... E 5
Vinh Long, 26,920 ... E 5
Vo Dat ... E 5
Vung Tau, 5,800 ... E 5

PHYSICAL FEATURES

Batangan (cape) ... F 4
Bên Gôi (bay) ... F 4
Ca Mau (Mui Bai Bung) (pt.) ... E 5
Cam Ranh (bay) ... F 5
Chon May (bay) ... F 3
Chu Yang Sin (mt.) ... F 4
Con Son (isls.), 1,200 ... E 5
Cu Lao Hon (isls.), 7,070 ... F 5
Dama, Poulo (isls.) ... D 5
Dao Phu Quoc (isl.) ... D 5
Darlac (plateau) ... F 4
Dent du Tigre (mt.) ... E 3
Deux Frères, Les (isls.) ... E 5
Hon Khoai (isl.) ... E 5
Hon Panjang (isl.) ... D 5
Ia Drang (riv.) ... E 4
Joncs (plain) ... E 5
Ke Ga (point) ... F 5
Kontum (plateau) ... E 4
Lang Bian (mts.) ... E 4
Mekong, Mouths of the (delta) ... E 5
Mui Bai Bung (pt.) ... E 5
Mui Dinh (cape) ... F 5
Nam Tram (cape) ... F 4
Nui Ba Den (mt.) ... E 5
Phu Quoc, Dao (isl.) ... D 5
Poulo Dama (isls.) ... D 5
Poulo Way (isls.) ... D 5
Se San (river) ... E 4
Siam (gulf) ... D 5
Song Ba (river) ... F 4
Song Cai (river) ... E 4
South China (sea) ... F 4
Varella (cape) ... F 4
Way, Poulo (isls.) ... D 5

*City and suburbs.
†Population of district.

CHINA and MONGOLIA

CHINA (MAINLAND)
AREA	3,745,296 sq. mi.
POPULATION	700,000,000
CAPITAL	Peking
LARGEST CITY	Shanghai 6,977,000
HIGHEST POINT	Mt. Everest 29,028 ft.
MONETARY UNIT	yüan
MAJOR LANGUAGES	Chinese, Mongol, Turki
MAJOR RELIGIONS	Confucianist, Buddhist, Taoist, Mohammedan

CHINA (TAIWAN)
22,440 sq. mi.
12,429,000
Taipei
Taipei 1,027,648
Sinkao Shan 13,064 ft.
new Taiwan dollar
Chinese, Formosan
Confucianist, Buddhist, Taoist, Christian, Tribal religions

MONGOLIA
625,946 sq. mi.
1,044,000
Ulan Bator
Ulan Bator 203,000
Tabun Bogdo 15,266 ft.
tugrik
Mongolian, Russian
Lamaist, Tribal religions

HONG KONG
AREA	391 sq. mi.
POPULATION	3,982,100
CAPITAL	Victoria
MONETARY UNIT	Hong Kong dollar
MAJOR LANGUAGES	Chinese, English
MAJOR RELIGIONS	Confucianist, Buddhist, Christian

MACAO
6 sq. mi.
174,000
Macao
pataca
Chinese, Portuguese
Confucianist, Buddhist, Taoist, Christian

CHINA (MAINLAND)

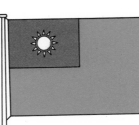

CHINA (TAIWAN)

MONGOLIA

CHINA
PROVINCES
Anhwei, 33,560,000 ....J 5
Chekiang, 25,280,000 ....J 6
Fukien, 14,650,000 ....J 6
Heilungkiang, 14,860,000 ......L 2
Honan, 48,670,000 ....H 5
Hopei, 44,720,000 ....J 4
Hunan, 36,220,000 ....H 6
Hupei, 30,790,000 ....H 5
Inner Mongolian Autonomous
  Region, 9,200,000 ....G 3
Kansu, 12,800,000 ....F 4
Kiangsi, 18,610,000 ....J 6
Kiangsu, 45,230,000 ....K 5
Kirin, 12,550,000 ....K 3
Kwangsi Chuang Autonomous
  Region, 19,390,000 ....G 7
Kwangtung, 37,960,000 ....H 7
Kweichow, 16,890,000 ....G 6
Liaoning, 24,090,000 ....K 3
Ningsia Hui Autonomous Region,
  1,810,000 ....G 4
Shansi, 15,960,000 ....H 4
Shantung, 54,030,000 ....J 4
Shensi, 18,130,000 ....G 5
Sinkiang-Uigur Autonomous
  Region, 5,640,000 ....B 3
Szechwan, 72,160,000 ....F 5
Taiwan, 12,429,000 ....K 7
Tibet, 1,270,000 ....C 5
Tsinghai, 2,050,000 ....E 4
Yünnan, 19,100,000 ....F 7

CITIES and TOWNS
Ahpa ....F 5
Aigun ....L 1
Aihsien ....G 8
Altai ....C 2
Amoy, 308,000 ....J 7
Anganchi ....K 2
Ankang ....G 5
Anking, 129,000 ....J 5
Anshan, 833,000 ....K 3
Anshun, 40,000 ....G 6
Ansi ....E 3
Anta ....K 2
Antung, 370,000 ....K 3
Anyang, 153,000 ....H 4
Aqsu ....B 3
Arshan ....J 2
Awati ....B 3
Baba Hatim ....B 4
Bai ....B 5
Barkha ....B 5
Barkhatu ....B 4
Barkol ....E 2
Batang ....E 6
Bayinhot ....F 4
Bulak ....B 2
Burchun ....C 2
Canton, 1,867,000 ....H 7
Chalainor ....J 2
Chamdo ....E 5
Changchih, 180,000 ....H 4
Changchow, 300,000 ....J 5
Changchow, 81,200 ....J 7
Changchun, 988,000 ....K 3
Changpeh ....H 3
Changsha, 709,000 ....H 6
Changteh, 94,800 ....H 6
Changting ....J 6
Changyeh, 45,000 ....F 4
Chanyi ....G 6
Chaochow, 101,000 ....J 7
Chaotung, 50,000 ....F 6
Chaoyang, 30,000 ....J 3
Charkhliq ....C 4
Chefoo, 140,000 ....K 4
Chendo ....E 5
Chengan ....G 6
Chengchow, 785,000 ....H 5
Chengkiang ....F 7
Chengteh, 120,000 ....J 3
Chengtu, 1,135,000 ....F 6
Chenhsien ....H 6
Chenpa ....G 5
Chenyüan ....G 6
Chenyieh ....F 7
Cherchen ....C 4
Chiai, 191,074 ....K 7
Chiehmo (Cherchen) ....C 4
Chihfeng, 49,000 ....J 3
Chihshui ....G 6
Chihtan ....G 5
Chikien ....K 5
Chimai ....E 5
Chimunai ....C 1
Chinchow, 400,000 ....J 3
Chinkiang, 190,000 ....K 5
Chinsi, 45,000 ....K 3
Chinwangtao, 210,000 ....K 4
Chira ....B 4
Chomo Dzong ....D 6
Chowkow, 85,500 ....J 5
Chüanchow, 110,000 ....J 7
Chüanhsien ....H 6
Chucheng ....J 4
Chuchow, 190,000 ....H 6
Chuguchak ....B 2
Chühsien ....J 6
Chumatien, 45,000 ....H 5
Chunghsin ....K 2
Chungking, 2,165,000 ....G 6
Chungning ....G 4
Chungtien ....F 6
Chushul ....D 6
Dairen, 766,400 ....K 4
Denchin ....E 5
Draya ....D 6
Drepung ....D 5
Durbuljin ....B 2
Ed Dzong ....C 6
Erhchiang (Charkhliq) ....C 4
Erhlien ....H 3
Fatshan, 120,000 ....H 7
Fengfeng, 45,000 ....H 4
Fenghsien ....G 5
Fengkieh ....G 5
Fengning ....J 3
Fenyang, 25,000 ....H 4
Foochow, 623,000 ....J 6
Fowyang, 75,000 ....J 5
Fuchin ....M 2
Fuchow, 45,000 ....J 5
Fuhai ....C 2
Fukang ....C 2
Fularki ....K 2
Fushun, 1,019,000 ....K 3
Fusin, 290,000 ....J 3
Fuyü, 62,969 ....L 2
Fuyüan ....M 2
Gartok ....B 5
Giamda Dzong (Taichao) ....D 5
Golmo ....D 4
Gulo Gomba ....B 5
Guma ....A 4
Gyangtse ....D 6
Gyatsa Dzong ....D 6
Hailar, 60,000 ....J 2
Hailun ....L 2
Hailung, 20,000 ....L 3
Hami, 20,000 ....D 3
Hanchung, 70,000 ....G 5
Hangchow, 794,000 ....J 6
Hankow, 749,952 ....H 5
Hanku, 75,000 ....J 4
Hantan, 380,000 ....H 4

(continued on following page)

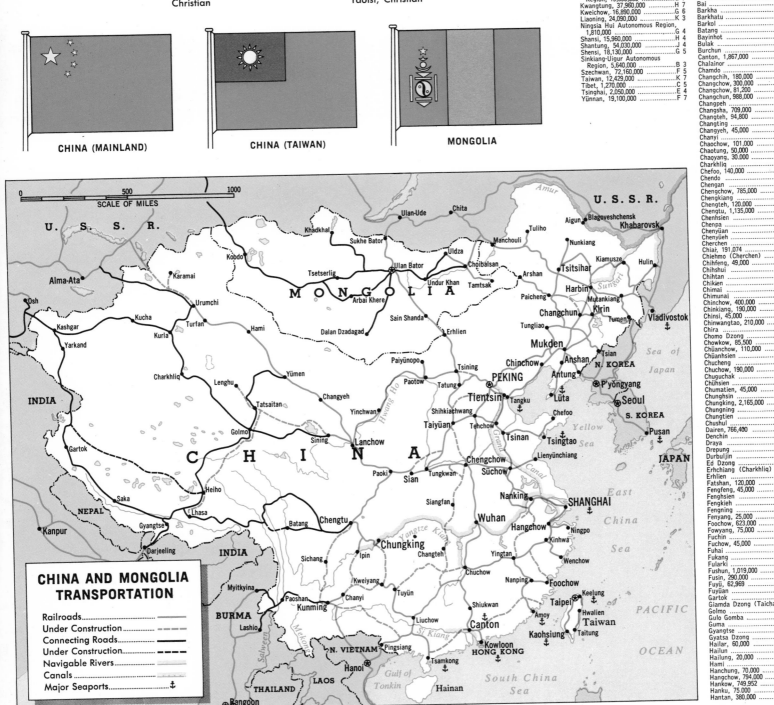

CHINA AND MONGOLIA TRANSPORTATION

Railroads	
Under Construction	
Connecting Roads	
Under Construction	
Navigable Rivers	
Canals	
Major Seaports	‡

China and Mongolia
(continued)

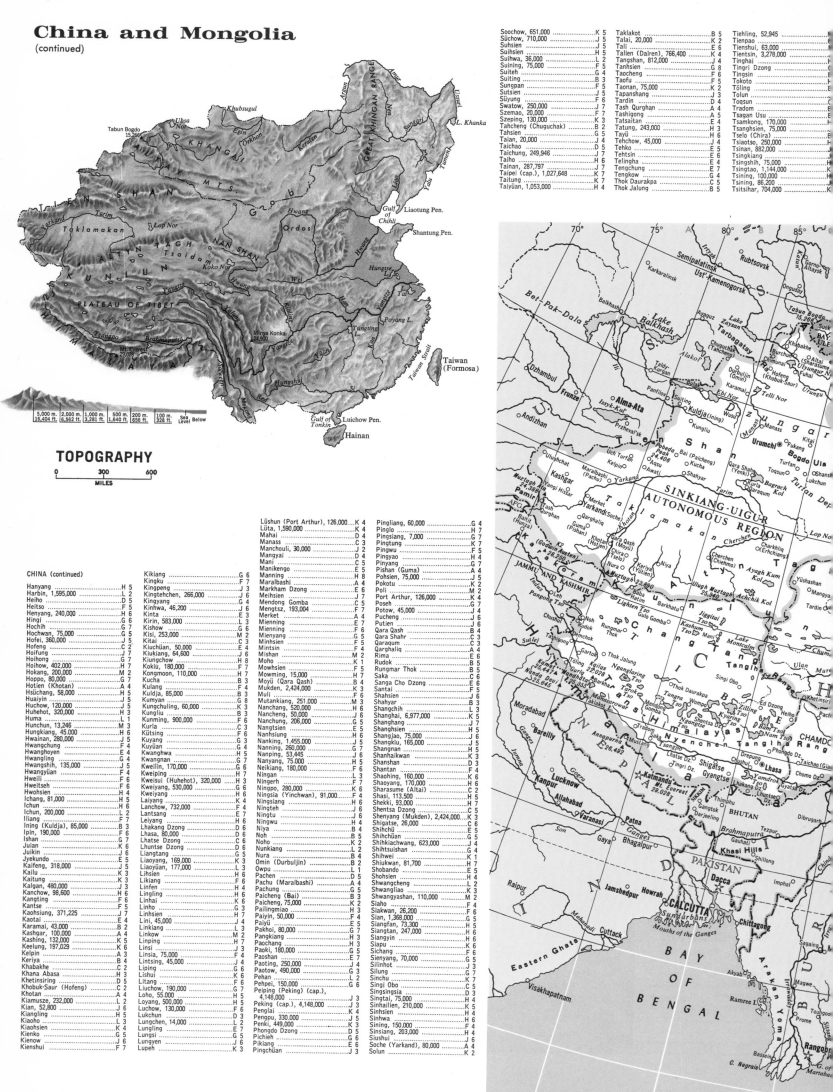

TOPOGRAPHY

0   300   600
MILES

5,000 m. | 2,000 m. | 1,000 m. | 500 m. | 200 m. | 100 m. | Sea Level | Below
16,404 ft. | 6,562 ft. | 3,281 ft. | 1,640 ft. | 656 ft. | 328 ft.

(continued on following page)

CHINA and MONGOLIA
CONIC PROJECTION
SCALE OF MILES
0 100 200 300 400 500
SCALE OF KILOMETRES
0 100 200 300 400 500

Capitals of Countries.... ☆ International Boundaries
Provincial Capitals........ ◉ Provincial Boundaries
Canals   Walls

Copyright by C. S. Hammond & Co., N.Y.

*Wuhan municipality consists of Hankow, Hanyang and Wuchang
†Lüta municipality includes Port Arthur and Dairen

China and Mongolia

(continued)

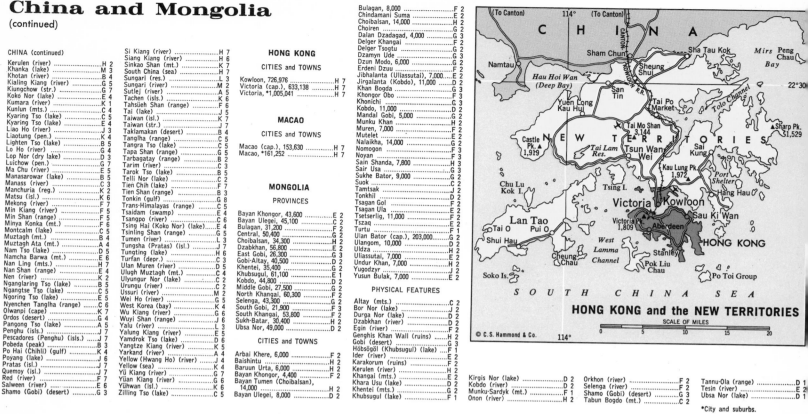

HONG KONG and the NEW TERRITORIES

© C.S. Hammond & Co.

SCALE OF MILES

AGRICULTURE, INDUSTRY and RESOURCES

DOMINANT LAND USE

- Cereals (chiefly wheat, millet)
- Cereals (chiefly wheat, rice, barley)
- Cereals (chiefly rice, barley)
- Livestock Herding, Limited Agriculture
- Forests
- Nonagricultural Land

MAJOR MINERAL OCCURRENCES

Ab Asbestos
Ag Silver
Al Bauxite
Au Gold
C Coal
Cu Copper
Fe Iron Ore
G Natural Gas
Gp Gypsum
Hg Mercury
J Jade
Mg Magnesium
Mn Manganese
Mo Molybdenum
Na Salt
O Petroleum
Pb Lead
Sb Antimony
Sn Tin
U Uranium
W Tungsten
Zn Zinc

⚡ Water Power
◩ Major Industrial Areas

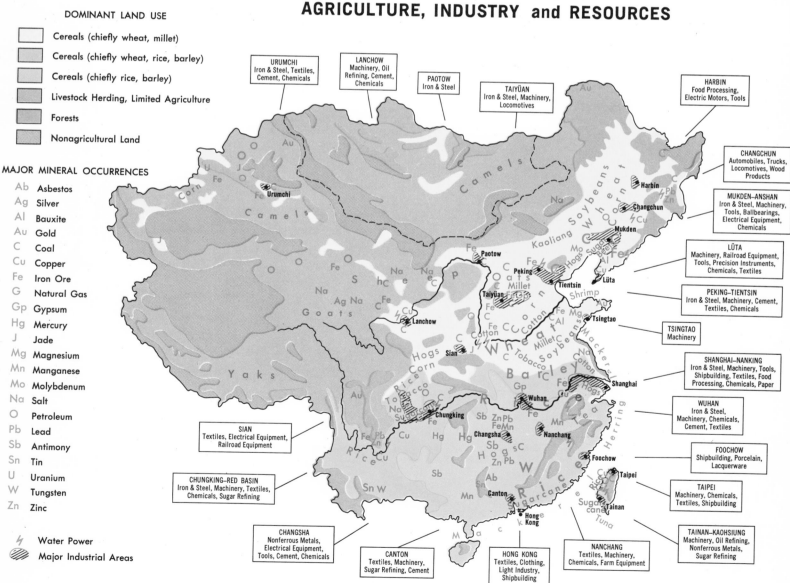

URUMCHI — Iron & Steel, Textiles, Cement, Chemicals

LANCHOW — Machinery, Oil Refining, Cement, Chemicals

PAOTOW — Iron & Steel

TAIYÜAN — Iron & Steel, Machinery, Locomotives

HARBIN — Food Processing, Electric Motors, Tools

CHANGCHUN — Automobiles, Trucks, Locomotives, Wood Products

MUKDEN–ANSHAN — Iron & Steel, Machinery, Tools, Ballbearings, Electrical Equipment, Chemicals

LÜTA — Machinery, Railroad Equipment, Tools, Precision Instruments, Chemicals, Textiles

PEKING–TIENTSIN — Iron & Steel, Machinery, Cement, Textiles, Chemicals

TSINGTAO — Machinery

SHANGHAI–NANKING — Iron & Steel, Machinery, Tools, Shipbuilding, Textiles, Food Processing, Chemicals, Paper

WUHAN — Iron & Steel, Machinery, Chemicals, Cement, Textiles

FOOCHOW — Shipbuilding, Porcelain, Lacquerware

TAIPEI — Machinery, Chemicals, Textiles, Shipbuilding

TAINAN–KAOHSIUNG — Machinery, Oil Refining, Nonferrous Metals, Sugar Refining

NANCHANG — Textiles, Machinery, Chemicals, Farm Equipment

HONG KONG — Textiles, Clothing, Light Industry, Shipbuilding

CANTON — Textiles, Machinery, Sugar Refining, Cement

CHANGSHA — Nonferrous Metals, Electrical Equipment, Tools, Cement, Chemicals

CHUNGKING–RED BASIN — Iron & Steel, Machinery, Textiles, Chemicals, Sugar Refining

SIAN — Textiles, Electrical Equipment, Railroad Equipment

JAPAN and KOREA

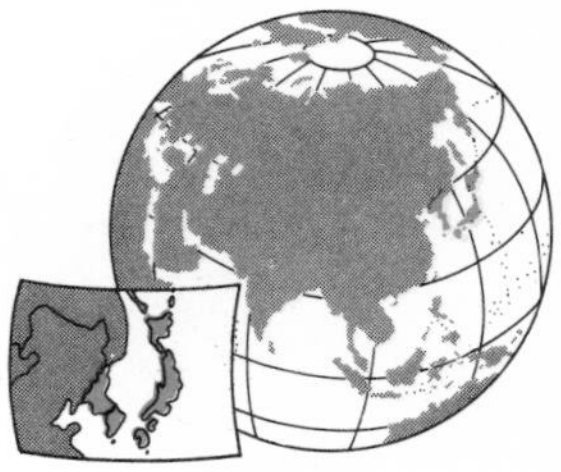

	JAPAN	NORTH KOREA	SOUTH KOREA
AREA	142,743 sq. mi.	49,096 sq. mi.	36,152 sq. mi.
POPULATION	98,399,074	10,930,000	28,155,000
CAPITAL	Tokyo	P'yŏngyang	Seoul
LARGEST CITY	Tokyo (greater) 10,428,000	P'yŏngyang 653,100	Seoul 3,108,894
HIGHEST POINT	Fuji 12,389 ft.	Paektu 9,003 ft.	Halla 6,398 ft.
MONETARY UNIT	yen	won	hwan
MAJOR LANGUAGE	Japanese	Korean	Korean
MAJOR RELIGIONS	Buddhist, Shinto	Confucianist, Buddhist, Christian	Confucianist, Buddhist, Christian

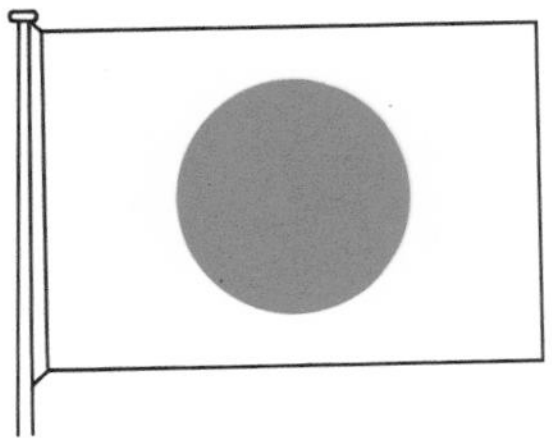

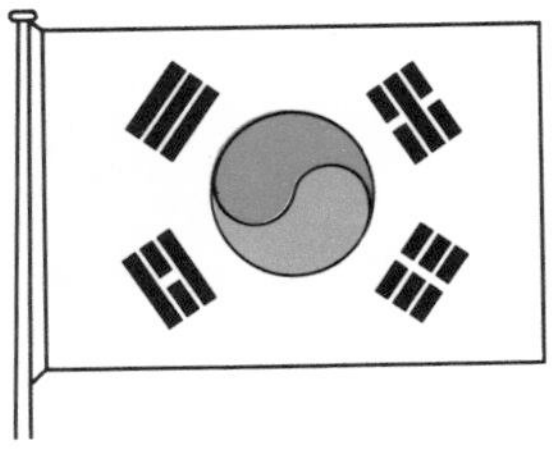

JAPAN

PREFECTURES

Aichi, 4,649,054 ....H 6
Akita, 1,356,288 ....J 4
Aomori, 1,507,020 ....K 3
Chiba, 2,591,600 ....P 2
Ehime, 1,516,210 ....F 7
Fukui, 760,179 ....G 5
Fukuoka, 4,119,350 ....D 7
Fukushima, 2,049,212 ....K 5
Gifu, 1,724,558 ....H 6
Gumma, 1,613,078 ....J 5
Hiroshima, 2,322,288 ....E 6
Hokkaido, 5,316,586 ....K 2
Hyogo, 4,251,560 ....H 7
Ibaraki, 2,110,911 ....K 5
Ishikawa, 990,832 ....H 5
Iwate, 1,488,136 ....K 4
Kagawa, 939,255 ....G 6
Kagoshima, 1,958,346 ....E 8
Kanagawa, 4,028,999 ....O 2
Kochi, 878,360 ....F 7
Kumamoto, 1,850,012 ....E 7
Kyoto, 2,104,097 ....J 7
Mie, 1,561,395 ....H 6
Miyagi, 1,814,749 ....F 4
Miyazaki, 1,151,293 ....E 8
Nagano, 2,000,616 ....J 5
Nagasaki, 1,768,818 ....D 7
Nara, 817,531 ....J 8
Niigata, 2,456,551 ....J 5
Oita, 1,290,711 ....E 7
Okayama, 1,720,380 ....F 6
Osaka, 6,258,251 ....J 8
Saga, 921,832 ....E 7
Saitama, 2,788,670 ....O 2
Shiga, 861,500 ....J 7
Shimane, 874,098 ....F 6
Shizuoka, 2,890,094 ....H 6
Tochigi, 1,540,440 ....K 5
Tokushima, 857,822 ....G 7
Tokyo, 10,293,193 ....O 2
Tottori, 604,669 ....G 6
Toyama, 1,040,430 ....H 5
Wakayama, 1,059,214 ....G 6
Yamagata, 1,301,464 ....K 4
Yamaguchi, 1,609,488 ....E 6
Yamanashi, 789,954 ....J 6

CITIES and TOWNS

Abashiri, 44,052 ....M 1
Ageo, 38,889 ....O 2
Aikawa, 19,057 ....H 4
Aizuwakamatsu, 102,000 ....J 5
Ajigasawa, 22,123 ....J 3
Akabiri, 54,635 ....K 2
Akashi, 149,000 ....H 8
Aki, 30,370 ....F 7
Akita, 217,000 ....J 4
Akkeshi, 20,185 ....M 2
Akune, 38,908 ....E 7
Amagasaki, 484,000 ....H 8
Amaha, 13,593 ....O 3
Anamizu, 18,179 ....H 5
Anan, 60,110 ....G 7
Anegasaki, 11,307 ....P 3
Anjo, 56,787 ....H 6
Aomori, 232,000 ....K 3
Asahi, 31,493 ....K 6
Asahikawa, 243,000 ....L 2
Ashibetsu, 67,137 ....L 2
Ashikaga, 150,000 ....J 5
Ashiya, 57,050 ....H 8
Atami, 52,163 ....J 6
Atsugi, 46,239 ....O 2
Awaji, 20.327 ....H 8
Ayabe, 51,258 ....G 6
Bekkai ....M 2
Beppu, 129,000 ....E 7
Bibai, 87,345 ....L 2
Biratori, 13,387 ....L 2
Chiba, 291,000 ....P 2
Chichibu, 59,796 ....J 6
Chigasaki, 68,054 ....O 3
Chitose, 44,522 ....K 2
Chofu, 68,621 ....O 2
Choshi, 91,470 ....K 6
Daito, 20,513 ....J 8
Ebetsu, 37,396 ....K 2
Esashi, Hokkaido, 15,366 ....J 3
Esashi, Hokkaido, 11,913 ....L 1
Esashi, Iwate, 47,363 ....K 4
Fuchu, Hiroshima, 40,691 ....F 6
Fuchu, Tokyo, 104,000 ....O 2
Fujisawa, 146,000 ....O 3
Fukuchiyama, 61,490 ....G 6
Fukue, 38,860 ....D 7
Fukui, 160,000 ....G 5
Fukuoka, 717,000 ....D 7
Fukushima, Fukushima, 149,000...K 5
Fukushima, Nagano, 9,217 ....H 6
Fukuyama, 161,000 ....F 6
Funabashi, 186,000 ....P 2
Furukawa, 53,953 ....K 4
Fuse, 230,000 ....J 8
Futtsu, 16,567 ....O 3
Gifu, 353,000 ....H 6
Gobo, 30,700 ....G 7
Goi, 21,560 ....P 2
Gose, 35,549 ....J 8
Gosen, 36,941 ....J 5
Goshogawara, 48,033 ....K 3
Gotsu, 33,485 ....F 6
Habikino, 36,982 ....J 8
Haboro, 28,168 ....K 1
Hachinohe, 188,000 ....K 3
Hachioji, 178,000 ....O 2
Hagi, 56,831 ....E 6
Hakodate, 251,000 ....K 3
Hakui, 29,556 ....H 5
Hamada, 46,626 ....E 6
Hamamatsu, 368,000 ....H 6
Hamasaka, 15,643 ....G 6
Hanamaki, 62,385 ....K 4
Hanno, 44,153 ....O 2
Haramachi, 41,006 ....K 5
Hayama, 15,762 ....O 3
Hikone, 60,864 ....H 6
Himeji, 360,000 ....G 6
Himi, 65,962 ....H 5
Hirakata, 107,000 ....J 7
Hiraoka, 50,115 ....J 8
Hirata, 34,799 ....F 6
Hiratsuka, 121,000 ....O 3
Hiroo, 12,592 ....L 2
Hirosaki, 157,000 ....K 3
Hiroshima, 485,000 ....E 6
Hitachi, 180,000 ....K 5
Hitachiota, 38,541 ....K 5
Hitoyoshi, 47,259 ....E 7
Hofu, 94,513 ....E 6
Hokota, 28,657 ....K 5
Hondo, 41,893 ....E 7
Honjo, 38,738 ....J 4
Hyuga, 40,685 ....E 7
Ibaraki, 71,859 ....J 7
Ibusuki, 33,623 ....E 8
Ichikawa, 181,000 ....P 2
Ichinohe, 26,228 ....K 3
Ichinomiya, 192,000 ....H 6
Ichinoseki, 57,585 ....K 4
Iida, 67,555 ....H 6
Iizuta, 60,431 ....E 7
Ikeda, Hokkaido, 16,731 ....L 2
Ikeda, Osaka, 59,688 ....H 7
Ikuno, 10,564 ....G 6
Imabari, 104,000 ....F 6
Imari, 78,397 ....D 7
Imazu, 11,347 ....G 6
Ina, 46,179 ....H 6
Isahaya, 64,506 ....D 7
Ise, 104,000 ....H 6
Ishige, 19,304 ....P 2
Ishinomaki, 83,947 ....K 4
Itami, 117,000 ....H 7
Ito, 54,564 ....J 6
Itoigawa, 41,910 ....H 5
Iwaki, 58,080 ....K 5
Iwakuni, 103,000 ....E 6
Iwamisawa, 60,650 ....L 2
Iwanai, 25,093 ....K 2
Iwasaki, 5,329 ....J 3
Iwatsuki, 35,169 ....O 2
Iyo, 30,047 ....F 7
Izuhara, 23,472 ....D 6
Izumi, 70,701 ....J 8
Izumiotsu, 42,304 ....J 8
Izumisano, 56,827 ....G 6
Izumo, 69,219 ....F 6
Kaga, 54,548 ....H 5
Kagoshima, 322,000 ....E 8
Kaizuka, 61,067 ....H 8
Kakogawa, 89,539 ....G 6
Kamaishi, 87,511 ....L 4
Kamakura, 110,000 ....O 3
Kameoka, 42,355 ....J 7
Kaminoyama, 40,383 ....J 4
Kamiyaku, 13,369 ....E 8
Kamo, 39,292 ....J 5
Kanazawa, 322,000 ....H 5
Kanonji, 46,731 ....F 6
Kanoya, 72,498 ....E 8
Kanuma, 77,927 ....J 5
Karatsu, 77,825 ....D 7
Kashihara, 35,645 ....J 8
Kashiwa, 63,745 ....P 2
Kashiwazaki, 74,139 ....J 5
Kasukabe, 34,280 ....O 2
Katsuura, 31,141 ....K 6
Kawachi, 55,132 ....J 8
Kawachinagano, 34,399 ....J 8
Kawagoe, 116,000 ....O 2
Kawaguchi, 213,000 ....O 2
Kawanishi, 41,916 ....H 7
Kawasaki, 764,000 ....O 2
Kazusa, 14,215 ....P 3
Kembuchi, 9,047 ....L 1
Kesennuma, 57,016 ....K 4
Kikonai, 11,914 ....K 3
Kiryu, 127,000 ....J 5
Kisarazu, 52,689 ....P 3
Kishiwada, 134,000 ....J 8
Kitaibaraki, 60,567 ....K 5
Kitakata, 42,338 ....J 5
Kitakyushu, 1,052,000 ....E 6
Kitami, 66,922 ....L 2
Kizu, 10,628 ....J 7
Kobayashi, 43,894 ....E 8
Kobe, 1,181,000 ....H 7
Kochi, 217,000 ....F 7
Kofu, 172,000 ....J 6
Kojima, 75,256 ....F 6
Kokubu, 34,256 ....E 8
Komatsu, 89,085 ....H 5
Komoro, 39,283 ....J 5
Koriyama, 112,000 ....K 5
Kosaka, 15,676 ....K 3
Kuji, 37,714 ....K 3
Kuki, 23,114 ....O 2
Kumagaya, 105,000 ....J 5
Kumamoto, 397,000 ....E 7
Kurashiki, 144,000 ....F 6
Kurayoshi, 51,528 ....F 6
Kure, 224,000 ....F 6
Kuroiso, 30,413 ....K 5
Kurume, 158,000 ....E 7
Kusatsu, 7,933 ....J 5
Kushikino, 33,104 ....E 8
Kushima, 41,143 ....E 8
Kushimoto, 22,000 ....G 7
Kushira, 17,495 ....E 8
Kushiro, 166,000 ....M 2
Kutchan, 18,195 ....K 2
Kyoto, 1,324,000 ....J 7
Machida, 71,269 ....O 2
Maebashi, 190,000 ....J 5
Maibara, 13,936 ....G 6
Maizuru, 104,000 ....G 6
Makurazaki, 33,511 ....D 8
Marugame, 61,403 ....G 6
Mashike, 14,657 ....K 2
Masuda, 56,053 ....E 6
Matsubara, 47,037 ....H 8
Matsudo, 131,000 ....P 2
Matsue, 108,000 ....F 6
Matsumae, 19,534 ....J 3
Matsumoto, 150,000 ....H 5
Matsusaka, 104,000 ....H 6
Matsuyama, 276,000 ....F 7
Mihara, 80,395 ....F 6
Miki, 38,264 ....H 7
Mikuni, 22,530 ....G 5
Minamata, 48,342 ....E 7
Minobu, 13,805 ....J 6
Minoo, 34,249 ....J 7
Misawa, 36,570 ....K 3
Mishima, 62,966 ....J 6
Mitaka, 119,000 ....O 2
Mito, 158,000 ....K 5
Mitsukaido, 37,577 ....P 2
Miura, 39,811 ....O 3
Miwa, 6,941 ....H 7
Miyako, 55,385 ....L 4
Miyakonojo, 92,230 ....E 8
Miyazaki, 185,000 ....E 8
Miyazu, 34,799 ....G 6
Miyoshi, 42,163 ....F 6
Mizusawa, 44,187 ....K 4
Mobara, 39,378 ....K 6
Mombetsu, 40,281 ....L 1
Mori, 20,010 ....K 2
Moriguchi, 121,000 ....J 7
Morioka, 171,000 ....K 4
Motegi, 26,786 ....K 5
Murakami, 32,878 ....J 4
Murayama, 39,057 ....J 4
Muroran, 170,000 ....K 2
Muroto, 30,498 ....G 7
Musashino, 129,000 ....O 2
Mutsu, 38,312 ....K 3
Nachikatsuura, 25,775 ....H 7
Nagahama, Ehime, 18,246 ....F 7
Nagahama, Shiga, 47,700 ....H 6
Nagano, 167,000 ....J 5
Nagaoka, 151,000 ....J 5
Nagareyama, 25,672 ....P 2
Nagasaki, 404,000 ....D 7
Nagato, 30,903 ....E 6
Nagoya, 1,859,000 ....H 6
Nakamura, 38,951 ....F 7
Nakasato, 16,842 ....K 3
Nakatsu, 61,667 ....E 7
Nakoso, 48,117 ....K 5
Nanao, 50,121 ....H 5
Nangoku, 41,798 ....F 7
Naoetsu, 43,304 ....H 5
Nara, 150,000 ....J 8
Nayoro, 35,859 ....L 1
Naze, 42,539 ....O 5
Nemuro, 42,740 ....M 2
Neyagawa, 45,633 ....J 7
Nichinan, 61,974 ....E 8
Niigata, 341,000 ....J 5
Niihama, 136,000 ....F 6
Niimi, 37,437 ....F 6
Niitsu, 56,110 ....J 5
Nikko, 33,348 ....J 5
Nishinomiya, 314,000 ....H 8
Nishinoomote, 32,645 ....E 8
Nobeoka, 130,000 ....E 7
Noda, 54,150 ....P 2
Noshiro, 63,002 ....J 3
Numata, 42,919 ....J 5
Numazu, 155,000 ....J 6
Obama, 36,236 ....G 6

(continued on following page)

AGRICULTURE, INDUSTRY and RESOURCES

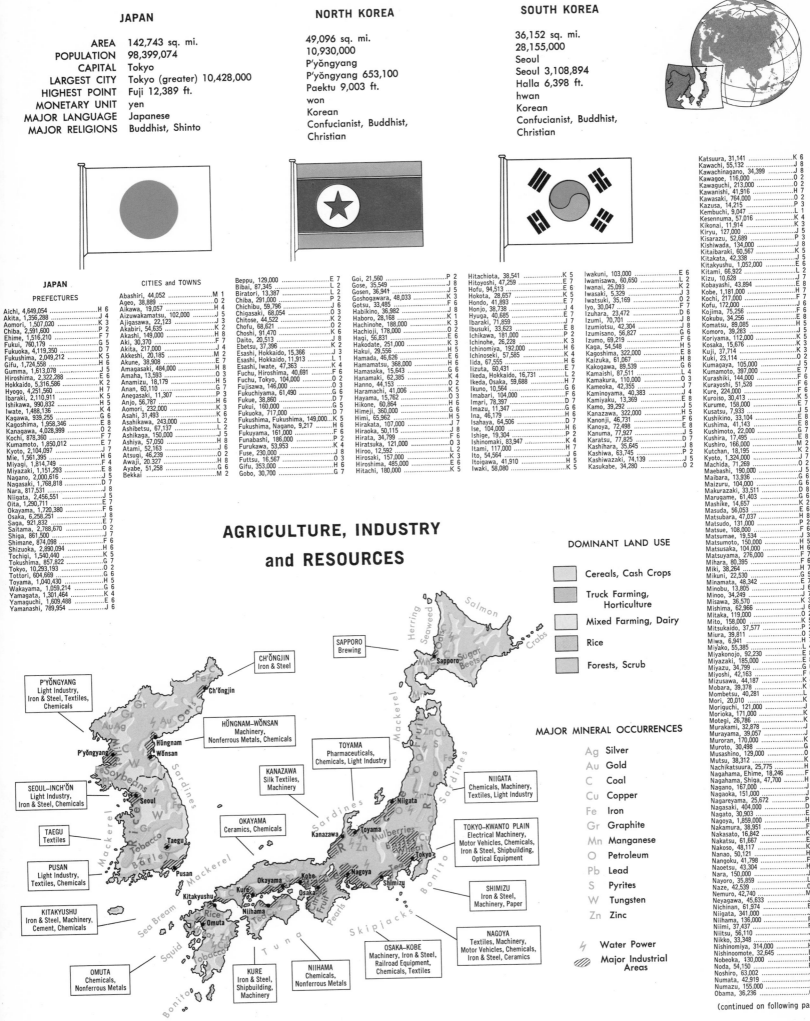

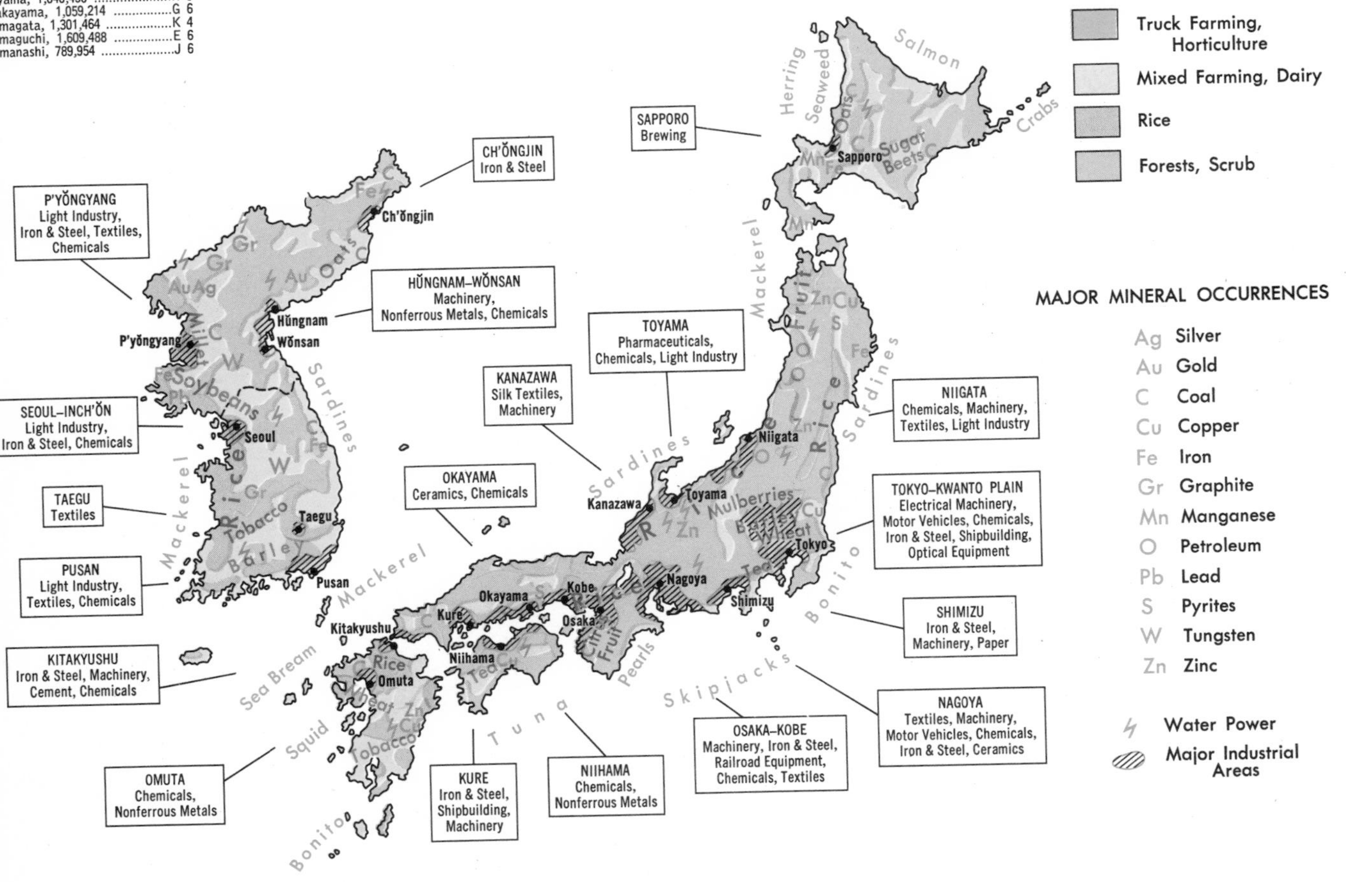
DOMINANT LAND USE
Cereals, Cash Crops
Truck Farming, Horticulture
Mixed Farming, Dairy
Rice
Forests, Scrub
MAJOR MINERAL OCCURRENCES
Ag Silver
Au Gold
C Coal
Cu Copper
Fe Iron
Gr Graphite
Mn Manganese
O Petroleum
Pb Lead
S Pyrites
W Tungsten
Zn Zinc
Water Power
Major Industrial Areas
SAPPORO Brewing
CH'ŎNGJIN Iron & Steel
P'YŎNGYANG Light Industry, Iron & Steel, Textiles, Chemicals
HŬNGNAM–WŎNSAN Machinery, Nonferrous Metals, Chemicals
TOYAMA Pharmaceuticals, Chemicals, Light Industry
KANAZAWA Silk Textiles, Machinery
SEOUL–INCH'ŎN Light Industry, Iron & Steel, Chemicals
NIIGATA Chemicals, Machinery, Textiles, Light Industry
OKAYAMA Ceramics, Chemicals
TAEGU Textiles
TOKYO–KWANTO PLAIN Electrical Machinery, Motor Vehicles, Chemicals, Iron & Steel, Shipbuilding, Optical Equipment
PUSAN Light Industry, Textiles, Chemicals
SHIMIZU Iron & Steel, Machinery, Paper
KITAKYUSHU Iron & Steel, Machinery, Cement, Chemicals
NAGOYA Textiles, Machinery, Motor Vehicles, Chemicals, Iron & Steel, Ceramics
OSAKA–KOBE Machinery, Iron & Steel, Railroad Equipment, Chemicals, Textiles
OMUTA Chemicals, Nonferrous Metals
KURE Iron & Steel, Shipbuilding, Machinery
NIIHAMA Chemicals, Nonferrous Metals
Salmon
Herring
Seaweed
Crabs
Sugar Beets
Sapporo
Ch'ŏngjin
Hŭngnam
Wŏnsan
P'yŏngyang
Seoul
Taegu
Pusan
Niigata
Kanazawa
Toyama
Tokyo
Nagoya
Shimizu
Kobe
Osaka
Okayama
Kure
Niihama
Kitakyushu
Omuta
Mackerel
Sardines
Soybeans
Millet
Rice
Tobacco
Barley
Fruit
Mulberries
Wheat
Tea
Citrus Fruit
Pearls
Skipjacks
Bonito
Tuna
Squid
Sea Bream

Japan and Korea
(continued)

TOPOGRAPHY

Unzen (mt.) ...... D 7
Unzen-Amakusa Nat'l Park ...... D 7
Wakasa (bay) ...... H 6
Yadaijin (mt.) ...... K 5
Yaku (isls.), 24,010 ...... E 8
Yariga (mt.) ...... H 5
Yodo (river) ...... J 7
Yoron (isl.), 7,792 ...... N 6
Yoshino (river) ...... G 6
Yoshino-Kumano Nat'l Park ...... H 7
Zao (mt.) ...... K 5

KOREA

CITIES and TOWNS

P'anmunjŏm ...... C 5

PHYSICAL FEATURES

Kanghwa (bay) ...... B 5
Yellow (sea) ...... B 6

NORTH KOREA

CITIES and TOWNS

Anak ...... B 4
Anju ...... B 4
Aoji-dong ...... D 4
Changjon ...... D 4
Ch'angsŏng ...... B 3
Changyŏn ...... B 4
Chasŏng ...... C 3
Chinnamp'o ...... B 4
Ch'ŏngjin ...... E 3
Chŏngju ...... B 4
Cho'san ...... B 3
Chuūronjang ...... E 2
Haeju ...... B 4
Hamhŭng ...... C 4
Hapsu ...... C 3
Hoeryŏng ...... D 2
Hongwŏn ...... C 4
Hu'chang ...... C 3
Hŭich'ŏn ...... C 3
Hŭngnam ...... C 4

Hwangju C
Hyesanjin C
Iwŏn C
Kaesŏng, 139,900 C
Kanggye C
Kapsan C
Kilchu C
Koksan C
Kosŏng C
Kunu-ri C
Kusŏng C
Kuŭp-tong C
Kyŏmip'o C
Manp'ojin C
Musan C
Myŏngch'ŏn C
Najin C
Namch'ŏnjom C
Nanam C
Ongjin C
Onsong C
Pak'chŏn C
Pukch'ong ...... D
P'ungsan ...... D

JAPAN (continued)
Obihiro, 111,000 ...... L 2
Oda, 47,211 ...... F 6
Odate, 57,775 ...... K 3
Odawara, 134,000 ...... J 6
Ofunato, 35,946 ...... L 4
Oga, 46,099 ...... J 4
Ogaki, 115,000 ...... H 6
Ogi, 5,948 ...... J 5
Oita, 228,000 ...... E 7
Ojiya, 49,445 ...... J 5
Okaya, 52,256 ...... H 5
Okayama, 300,000 ...... F C
Okazaki, 185,000 ...... H 6
Omagari, 41,090 ...... K 4
Ominato ...... K 3
Omiya, 198,000 ...... O 2
Omu, 10,518 ...... L 1
Omura, 59,498 ...... D 7
Omuta, 221,000 ...... E 7
Onagawa, 18,002 ...... M 4
Ono, 44,466 ...... H 6
Onoda, 55,192 ...... E 6
Onomichi, 91,003 ...... F 6
Osaka, 3,197,000 ...... J 8
Otaru, 207,000 ...... K 2
Otsu, 116,000 ...... J 7
Owase, 34,534 ...... H 7
Ozu, 43,583 ...... F 7
Rausu, 7,558 ...... M 1
Rikuzentakata, 31,839 ...... K 4
Rumoi, 35,818 ...... K 2
Ryotsu, 28,892 ...... J 4
Sabae, 49,045 ...... H 6
Saga, 140,000 ...... E 7
Sagamihara, 131,000 ...... O 2
Saigo, 15,865 ...... F 5
Saiki, 51,369 ...... E 7
Saito, 37,661 ...... E 7
Sakado, 23,569 ...... O 2
Sakai, Ibaraki, 22,587 ...... P 1
Sakai, Osaka, 426,000 ...... J 8
Sakaiminato, 32,714 ...... F 6
Sakata, 97,671 ...... J 4
Sakurai, 35,424 ...... J 7
Sanda, 32,528 ...... H 7
Sanjo, 71,594 ...... J 5
Sapporo, 690,000 ...... K 2
Sarufutsu, 8,319 ...... L 1
Sasebo, 284,000 ...... D 7
Satte, 23,378 ...... O 2
Sawara, 49,564 ...... K 6
Sayama, 32,785 ...... O 2
Sendai, Kagoshima, 61,322 ...... E 8
Sendai, Miyagi, 464,000 ...... K 4
Seto, 82,101 ...... H 6
Shari, 18,371 ...... M 2
Shibata, 73,886 ...... J 5
Shibetsu, 38,951 ...... M 2
Shimabara, 45,205 ...... E 7
Shimada, 53,900 ...... J 6
Shimizu, 208,000 ...... J 6
Shimoda, 27,387 ...... J 6
Shimonoseki, 255,000 ...... E 6
Shingu, 39,114 ...... H 7
Shinjo, 43,550 ...... K 4
Shiogama, 55,325 ...... K 4
Shirakawa, 41,196 ...... K 5
Shiroishi, 43,911 ...... K 4
Shizuoka, 355,000 ...... H 6
Shobara, 30,663 ...... F 6
Soka, 48,533 ...... O 2
Soma, 41,352 ...... K 5
Suita, 154,000 ...... J 7
Sukumo, 30,016 ...... F 7
Sumoto, 48,497 ...... G 6
Sunagawa, 31,750 ...... K 2
Susaki, 32,976 ...... F 7
Suttsu, 9,121 ...... J 2
Suwa, 44,035 ...... H 6
Suzu, 35,827 ...... H 5
Tachikawa, 67,949 ...... O 2
Taira, 71,115 ...... K 5
Takada, 73,238 ...... J 5

Takaishi, 34,104 ...... H 7
Takamatsu, 242,000 ...... G 6
Takaoka, 139,000 ...... H 5
Takarazuka, 66,491 ...... H 7
Takasaki, 157,000 ...... J 5
Takatsuki, 108,000 ...... J 7
Takawa, 101,000 ...... E 7
Takayama, 50,588 ...... H 5
Takefu, 62,610 ...... G 6
Tanabe, Kyoto, 15,793 ...... J 7
Tanabe, Wakayama, 48,673 ...... G 7
Tateyama, 57,643 ...... K 6
Tawaramoto, 19,769 ...... J 8
Tenri, 50,438 ...... J 8
Teradomari, 16,291 ...... J 5
Teshio, 9,365 ...... K 1
Toba, 30,521 ...... H 7
Tobetsu, 19,391 ...... K 2
Tochigi, 73,436 ...... J 5
Toi, 9,180 ...... F 6
Tojo, 20,017 ...... F 6
Toki, 55,198 ...... H 6
Tokiwa, 3,886 ...... L 1
Tokorosawa, 65,903 ...... O 2
Tokushima, 190,000 ...... G 7
Tokuyama, 77,246 ...... E 6
Tokyo (cap.), 8,733,000 ...... O 2
Tokyo, *10,428,000 ...... O 2
Tomakomai, 62,384 ...... K 2
Tomiyama, 8,463 ...... O 3
Tomo ...... F 6
Toride, 22,582 ...... P 2
Tosashimizu, 29,944 ...... F 7
Tosu, 41,870 ...... E 7
Towada, 45,362 ...... K 3
Toyama, 217,000 ...... H 5
Toyohashi, 233,000 ...... H 6
Toyonaka, 245,000 ...... J 7
Toyooka, 42,569 ...... G 6
Tsu, 118,000 ...... H 6
Tsubata, 21,836 ...... H 5
Tsuchiura, 71,474 ...... K 5
Tsuruga, 53,493 ...... G 6
Tsurugi ...... H 5
Tsuruoka, 83,149 ...... J 4
Tsuyama, 78,549 ...... F 6
Ube, 168,000 ...... E 6
Ueda, 70,186 ...... J 5
Ueno, 17,226 ...... H 6
Uji, 47,336 ...... J 7
Umi, 20,374 ...... E 7
Uozu, 47,309 ...... H 5
Uraga ...... O 3
Urakawa, 21,915 ...... L 2
Urawa, 198,000 ...... O 2
Urayasu ...... P 2
Ushibuka, 34,700 ...... D 7
Usuki, 45,421 ...... E 7
Utsunomiya, 254,000 ...... J 5
Uwajima, 68,106 ...... F 7
Wajima, 38,754 ...... H 5
Wakasa, 9,616 ...... G 6
Wakayama, 312,000 ...... J 8
Wakkanai, 55,113 ...... K 1
Warabi, 50,952 ...... O 2
Yagi, 11,042 ...... J 8
Yaizu, 72,118 ...... J 6
Yakumo, 25,111 ...... J 2
Yamagata, 188,000 ...... K 4
Yamaguchi, 104,000 ...... E 6
Yamamoto, 40,975 ...... J 8
Yamatokoriyama, 43,093 ...... J 8
Yamatotakada, 41,705 ...... J 8
Yanagawa, 48,691 ...... E 7
Yao, 142,000 ...... J 8
Yatabe, 20,570 ...... E 7
Yatsushiro, 107,000 ...... E 7
Yawata, 36,322 ...... J 7
Yawatahama, 52,527 ...... F 7
Yoichi, 28,659 ...... K 2
Yokkaichi, 218,000 ...... H 6
Yokohama, 1,590,000 ...... O 3
Yokosuka, 297,000 ...... O 3
Yokote, 46,950 ...... K 4

Yonago, 94,808 ...... F 6
Yonezawa, 96,991 ...... K 5
Yono, 40,840 ...... O 2
Yubari, 102,000 ...... K 2
Yubetsu, 12,192 ...... L 1
Yukuhashi, 47,188 ...... E 7
Yuzawa, 41,228 ...... K 4
Zushi, 39,571 ...... O 3

*City and suburbs.

PHYSICAL FEATURES

Abashiri (river) ...... M 1
Abukuma (river) ...... K 4
Agano (river) ...... J 5
Akan Nat'l Park ...... M 2
Amakusa (isls.), 248,103 ...... D 7
Amami (isls.), 157,909 ...... N 5
Amami-O-Shima (isl.), 61,673 ...... N 5
Ara (river) ...... O 2
Asahi (mt.) ...... J 4
Asama (mt.) ...... J 5
Ashizuri (point) ...... F 7
Aso (mt.) ...... E 7
Aso Nat'l Park ...... E 7
Atsumi (bay) ...... H 6
Awa (isl.), 825 ...... J 4
Awaji (isl.), 198,808 ...... H 7
Bandai (mt.) ...... K 5
Bandai-Asahi Nat'l Park ...... J 5
Biwa (lake) ...... H 6
Bungo (strait) ...... F 7
Chichibu-Tama Nat'l Park ...... J 6
Chokai (mt.) ...... J 4
Chubu Sangaku Nat'l Park ...... H 5
Daio (cape) ...... H 6
Daisen (mt.) ...... F 6
Daisen-Oki National Park ...... F 6
Daisetsu (mt.) ...... L 2
Daisetsu-Zan Nat'l Park ...... L 2
Dogo (isl.), 26,846 ...... F 5
Dozen (isl.), 14,793 ...... F 5
East China (sea) ...... D 7
Edo (river) ...... P 2
Erabu (isl.), 25,062 ...... N 5
Erimo (cape) ...... L 2
Esan (point) ...... K 3
Fuji (mt.) ...... J 6
Fuji (river) ...... J 6
Fuji-Hakone-Izu Nat'l Park ...... H 6
Gas (mt.) ...... J 4
Goto (isls.), 302,244 ...... D 7
Habomai (isls.) ...... N 2
Hachiro-Gata (lake) ...... J 3
Hakken (mt.) ...... J 7
Haku (mt.) ...... H 5
Hakusan Nat'l Park ...... H 5
Harima (sea) ...... G 6
Hida (river) ...... H 6
Hokkaido (isl.), 5,316,586 ...... L 2
Honshu (isl.), 75,830,479 ...... J 5
Iki (isl.), 50,497 ...... D 7
Inawashiro (lake) ...... K 5
Inubo (cape) ...... K 6
Iro (point) ...... J 6
Ise (bay) ...... H 6
Ise-Shima Nat'l Park ...... H 7
Ishikari (bay) ...... K 2
Ishikari (river) ...... K 2
Ishizuchi (mt.) ...... F 7
Iwaki (mt.) ...... K 3
Iwate (mt.) ...... K 4
Iyo (sea) ...... F 7
Izu (isls.), 38,681 ...... J 6
Japan (sea) ...... E 4
Joshinetsu-Kogen Nat'l Park ...... J 5
Kagoshima (bay) ...... E 8
Kamui (mt.) ...... K 2
Kariba (mt.) ...... J 2
Kasumiga-Ura (inlet) ...... P 2
Kii (channel) ...... G 7
Kikai (isl.), 14,738 ...... N 5
Kino (river) ...... J 7
Kirishima Nat'l Park ...... E 8

Kitakami (river) ...... K 4
Kita-Ura (lake) ...... L 5
Komaga (mt.) ...... K 2
Koshiki (isls.), 20,496 ...... D 8
Kuchino (isl.) ...... E 7
Kuju (mt.) ...... E 7
Kutcharo (lake) ...... M 2
Kyushu (isl.), 13,060,362 ...... E 7
Meakan (mt.) ...... L 2
Mikuni (mt.) ...... F 6
Mogami (river) ...... J 4
Motsutano (cape) ...... J 2
Muroto (point) ...... G 7
Mutsu (bay) ...... K 3
Naka (river) ...... K 5
Nantai (mt.) ...... J 5
Nasu (mt.) ...... J 5
Nemuto (mt.) ...... M 1
Nii (isl.), 4,438 ...... J 6
Nikko Nat'l Park ...... J 5
Nojima (cape) ...... K 6
Noshappu (point) ...... N 2
Noto (cape) ...... H 5
Nyudo (cape) ...... J 4
Oani (river) ...... K 3
Obitsu (river) ...... P 3
Oki (isls.), 41,639 ...... F 5
Okushiri (isl.), 7,908 ...... J 2
Oma (cape) ...... K 3
Omine (mt.) ...... J 7
Omono (river) ...... J 4
Ono (river) ...... E 7
Ontake (mt.) ...... H 6
Osaka (bay) ...... H 7
O-Shima (isl.), 12,090 ...... J 6
Osumi (isls.), 88,542 ...... E 8
Osumi (strait) ...... E 8
Rebun (isl.), 8,795 ...... K 1
Rikuchu-Kaigan Nat'l Park ...... L 4
Rishiri (isl.), 19,093 ...... K 1
Sado (isl.), 113,296 ...... J 4
Sagami (bay) ...... O 3
Sagami (river) ...... O 2
San'in Kaigan Nat'l Park ...... G 6
Sata (cape) ...... E 8
Shikoku (isl.), 4,191,647 ...... F 7
Shikotan (isl.) ...... N 2
Shikotsu (lake) ...... K 2
Shikotsu-Toya Nat'l Park ...... K 2
Shinano (river) ...... J 5
Shiono (cape) ...... H 7
Shirakami (cape) ...... J 4
Shirane (mt.) ...... J 6
Shirane (mt.) ...... H 6
Shiretoko (cape) ...... M 1
Shiriya (cape) ...... K 3
Soya (cape) ...... K 1
Suo (sea) ...... E 6
Suruga (bay) ...... J 6
Suwanose (isl.) ...... O 4
Suzu (isl.) ......
Takeshima (isls.) ...... F 5
Tama (river) ...... O 2
Tanega (isl.), 64,532 ...... E 8
Tappi (point) ...... K 3
Tazawa (lake) ...... K 4
Tenryu (river) ...... J 6
Teshio (river) ...... L 1
Tobi (isl.) ...... J 4
Tokachi (mt.) ...... L 2
Tokachi (river) ...... L 2
Tokara (arch.) ...... O 4
Tokuno (isl.), 19,804 ...... O 5
Tokyo (bay) ...... J 6
Tone (river) ...... J 5
Tosa (bay) ...... F 7
Towada (lake) ...... K 3
Towada-Hachimantai Nat'l Park ...... K 3
Toya (lake) ...... J 2
Toyama (bay) ...... H 5
Tsu (isl.), 69,556 ...... D 7
Tsugaru (strait) ...... K 3
Tsugaru (strait) ...... J 4
Tsushima (strait) ...... D 7
Uchiura (bay) ...... K 2

JAPAN is divided into prefectures bearing the same names as their capitals except:

Prefecture	Capital	Ref.
AICHI	NAGOYA	H 6
EHIME	MATSUYAMA	F 6
GUMMA	MAEBASHI	J 5
HOKKAIDO	SAPPORO	K 2
HYOGO	KOBE	H 7
IBARAKI	MITO	K 5
ISHIKAWA	KANAZAWA	H 5
IWATE	MORIOKA	K 4
KAGAWA	TAKAMATSU	G 6
KANAGAWA	YOKOHAMA	O 3
MIE	TSU	H 6
MIYAGI	SENDAI	K 4
SAITAMA	URAWA	O 2
SHIGA	OTSU	J 7
SHIMANE	MATSUE	F 6
TOCHIGI	UTSUNOMIYA	K 5
YAMANASHI	KOFU	J 6

Japan and Korea
(continued)

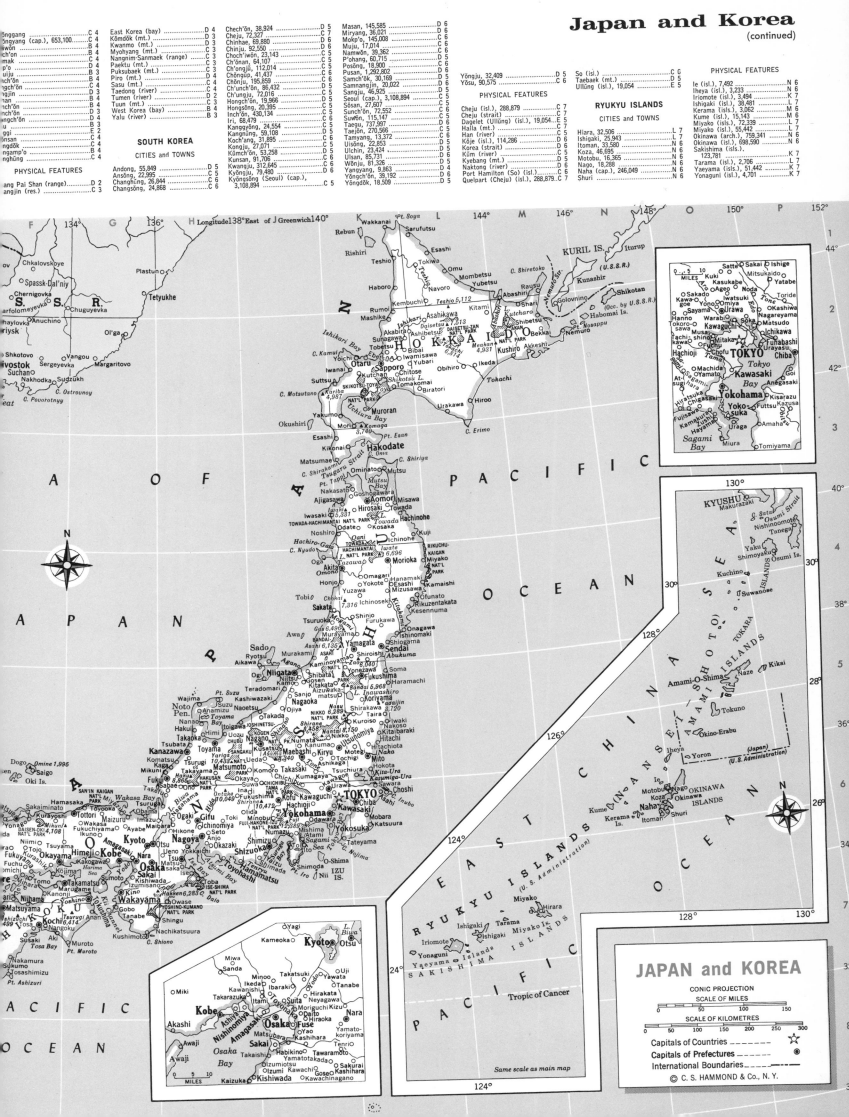

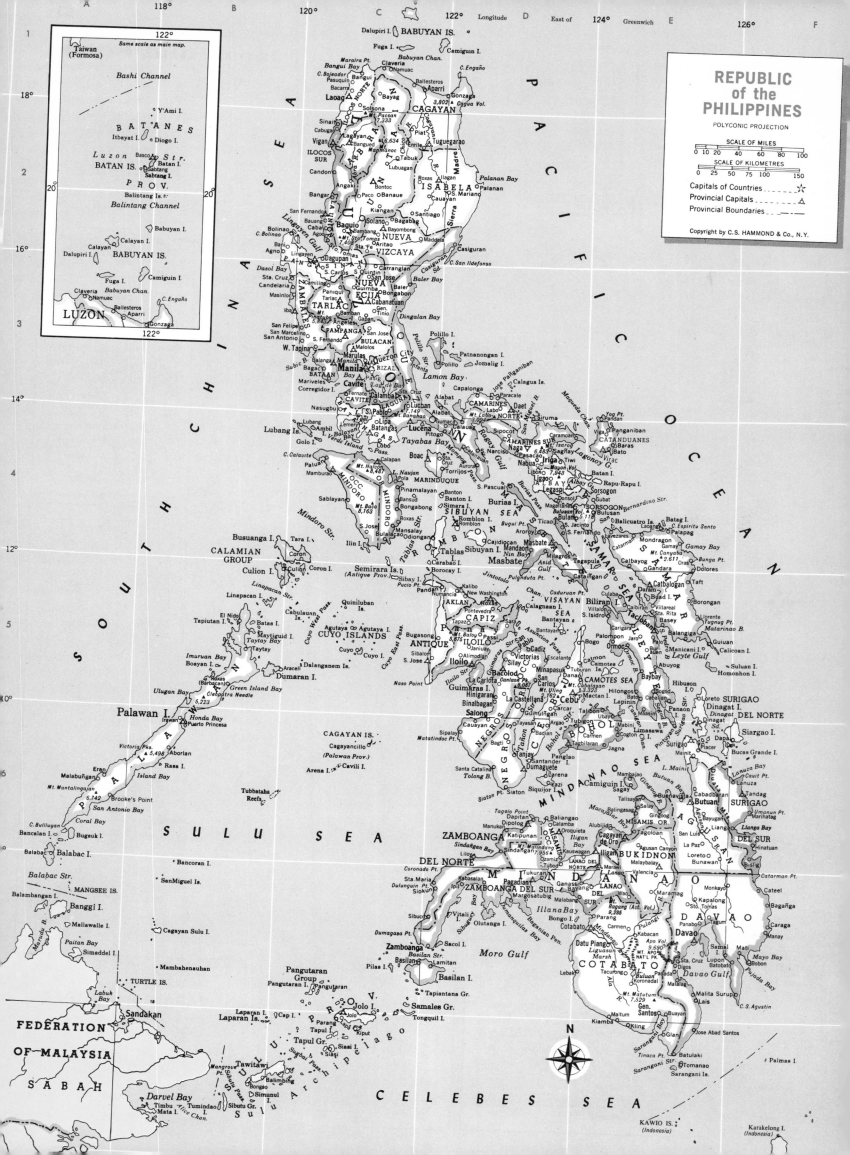

PHILIPPINES

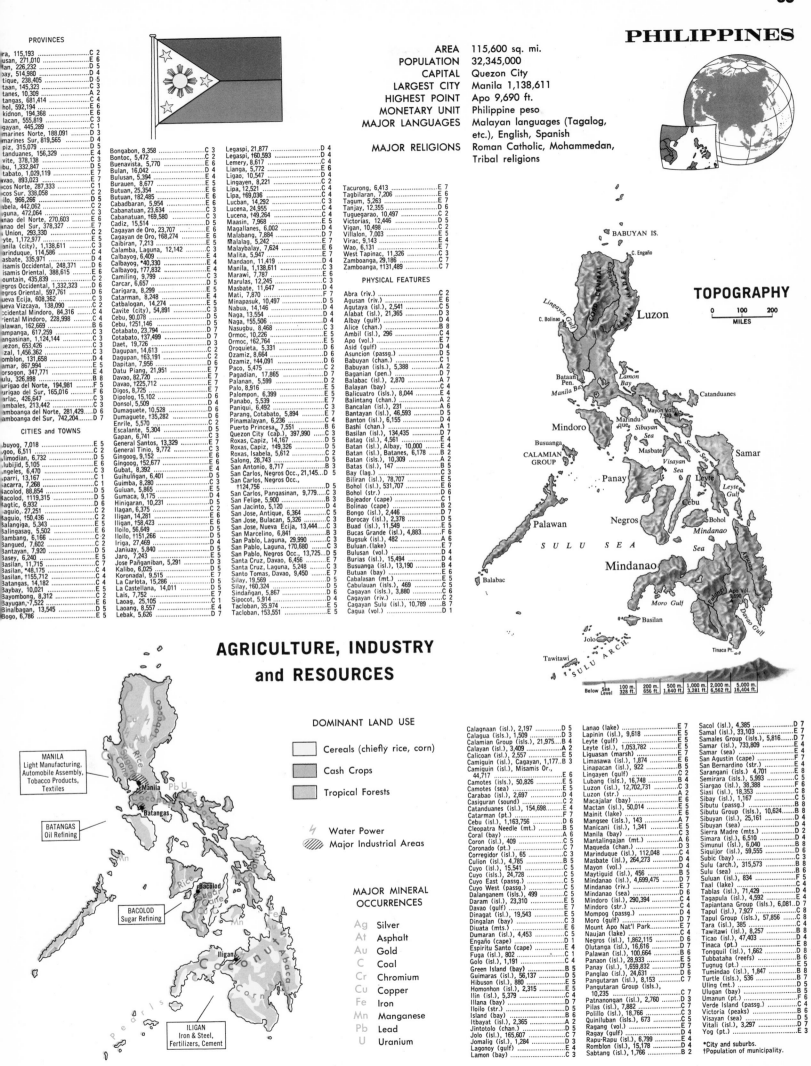

AREA	115,600 sq. mi.
POPULATION	32,345,000
CAPITAL	Quezon City
LARGEST CITY	Manila 1,138,611
HIGHEST POINT	Apo 9,690 ft.
MONETARY UNIT	Philippine peso
MAJOR LANGUAGES	Malayan languages (Tagalog, etc.), English, Spanish
MAJOR RELIGIONS	Roman Catholic, Mohammedan, Tribal religions

TOPOGRAPHY

AGRICULTURE, INDUSTRY and RESOURCES

DOMINANT LAND USE

- Cereals (chiefly rice, corn)
- Cash Crops
- Tropical Forests

Water Power
Major Industrial Areas

MANILA Light Manufacturing, Automobile Assembly, Tobacco Products, Textiles

BATANGAS Oil Refining

BACOLOD Sugar Refining

ILIGAN Iron & Steel, Fertilizers, Cement

MAJOR MINERAL OCCURRENCES

Ag Silver
At Asphalt
Au Gold
C Coal
Cr Chromium
Cu Copper
Fe Iron
Mn Manganese
Pb Lead
U Uranium

Southeast Asia

TOPOGRAPHY

0　300　600
MILES

| Below Sea Level | 100 m. 328 ft. | 200 m. 656 ft. | 500 m. 1,640 ft. | 1,000 m. 3,281 ft. | 2,000 m. 6,562 ft. | 5,000 m. 16,404 ft. |

Tanimbar (isls.), 41,233	J 7
Tidore (isl.), 24,064	H 5
Timor (sea)	H 7
Timor, Indonesian (reg.), 702,638	H 7
Toba (lake)	B 5
Tolo (gulf)	G 6
Tomini (gulf)	G 6
Tukangbesi (isls.), 59,775	G 7
Wangiwangi (isl.), 19,719	G 7
We (isl.)	B 4
Wetar (isl.), 11,383	H 7

Sibu, 29,630	E 5
Simanggang, 5,648	E 5
Tawau, 10,276	F 4
Victoria, 3,213	E 5

PHYSICAL FEATURES
Balambangan (isl.)	F 4
Banggi (isl.)	F 4
Iran (mts.)	E 5
Kinabalu (mt.)	F 4
Labuan (isl.), 1,490	E 4
Labuk (bay)	F 4
Rajang (river)	E 5
Sirik (cape)	E 5

FEDERATION OF MALAYSIA
STATES
North Borneo (Sabah), 518,000.	F 5
Sabah, 518,000	F 4
Sarawak, 820,000	E 5

CITIES and TOWNS
Beaufort, †25,408	F 4
Bintulu, 5,307	E 5
Jesselton, 21,719	F 4
Keningau, †14,645	F 4
Kuching, 50,579	E 5
Kudat, 3,660	F 4
Lahad Datu, †19,534	F 5
Marudi, 2,663	E 5
Miri, 13,350	E 5
Papar, †28,210	F 4
Ranau, †17,033	F 4
Sandakan, 28,806	F 4
Semporna, †16,895	F 5

TERRITORY OF NEW GUINEA
Total Population 1,575,966

CITIES and TOWNS
Aitape, ‡3,147	
Ambunti, ‡864	
Angoram, ‡836	
Bogia, ‡1,428	
Bulolo, ‡540	
Finschhafen, ‡3,052	
Goroka, ‡14,920	
Lae, ‡8,168	
Madang, ‡12,688	
Morobe, ‡2,912	
Saidor, ‡6,102	
Telefomin, ‡1,111	
Vanimo, ‡1,402	
Wau, ‡3,938	
Wewak, 1,819	

BRUNEI
CITIES and TOWNS
Brunei (cap.), 9,702 ....E 4

INDONESIA
CITIES and TOWNS
Amahai, †8,017	H 6
Ambarawa, †48,768	J 2
Amboina, 56,037	H 6
Ambon (Amboina), 56,037	H 6
Balikpapan, 91,706	F 6
Bandanaira, 13,686	H 6
Bandjarmasin, 214,096	F 6
Bandung, 972,566	H 2
Banggai, 144,747	G 6
Bangil, 34,112	K 2
Bangkahulu, 25,330	C 6
Bangkalan, †29,536	K 2
Banjuwangi, 53,576	L 2
Barus, †35,716	B 5
Batang, 67,561	J 2
Batavia (Djakarta), *2,973,052	H 1
Baturadja, 126,706	C 6
Bengkajang, †17,029	E 5
Bengkalis, †36,433	C 5
Bindjai, 45,235	B 5
Blitar, 62,972	K 2
Blora, 49,296	K 2
Bodjonegoro, †61,749	J 2
Bogor, 154,092	H 2
Bondowoso, †44,215	L 2
Bonthain, †40,289	F 7
Brebes, †72,971	H 2
Bukittinggi, 51,456	B 6
Bula, 3,116	J 6
Bumiaju, 152,790	H 2
Demak, †42,915	J 2
Denpasar, 152,000	E 7
Djailolo, 110,170	H 5
Djakarta (cap.), 2,906,533	H 1
Djakarta, *2,973,052	H 1
Djambi, 113,080	C 6
Djapara, 154,025	J 2
Djatinegara	
Djokjakarta, 312,698	J 2
Djombang, †57,370	K 2
Dumai, †13,770	C 5
Fort de Kock (Bukittinggi), 51,456	B 6
Galela, †7,384	H 5
Garut, †67,542	H 2
Gorontalo, 71,378	G 5
Gresik, 36,790	K 2
Gunungsitoli, †44,712	B 5
Indramaju, †56,117	H 2
Kädjang, †30,304	G 7
Kalianda, 131,073	D 7
Kampung Baru (Tolitoli), 8,333	
Kau, †7,497	H 5
Kebumen, †64,874	J 2
Kediri, 158,918	K 2
Kendal, 23,129	J 2
Kendari, †91,065	G 6

Kendawangan, 6,845	D 6
Ketapang, Madura, 146,245	K 2
Kolaka, †18,671	G 6
Kotaagung, †25,314	C 7
Kragan, 23,786	K 2
Kraksaan, †29,466	L 2
Kualakurun, 11,489	E 6
Kuandang, †15,379	G 5
Kudus, 62,130	J 2
Kumai, 8,835	E 6
Kuningan, †77,181	H 2
Kupang, 47,171	G 8
Kutaradja, 40,067	A 4
Kutoardjo, 44,962	J 2
Labuhan, 122,259	G 2
Lahat, †25,781	C 6
Langsa, †47,044	B 5
Lawang, †40,239	K 2
Longiram, 7,776	E 6
Longnawan, †16,234	F 5
Lumadjang, 55,700	L 2
Madiun, 122,373	K 2
Madjalengka, †47,055	H 2
Madjene, †37,727	F 6
Magelang, 96,454	J 2
Magetan, 154,159	K 2
Malang, 341,452	K 2
Malili, 5,735	G 6
Malinau, 9,677	F 5
Malingping, 141,284	G 2
Mamudju, †47,309	F 6
Manado, 129,912	G 5
Martapura, †53,216	F 6
Masamba, †15,152	G 6
Medan, 479,098	B 5
Menggala, 20,343	D 6
Meulaboh, 6,544	B 5
Merak, 136,293	G 1
Modjokerto, 51,732	K 2
Muaratewe, 6,135	F 6
Muntok, †25,883	D 6
Namlea, 16,018	H 6
Nangapinoh, †24,836	E 6
Nangatajap, 18,285	E 6
Natal, †16,478	B 5
Ngabang, 124,516	D 5
Padang, 143,699	B 6
Padangsidempuan, 171,704	B 5
Pajakumbuh, †74,393	C 6
Pakanbaru, 70,821	C 5
Palelah, 5,466	G 5
Palembang, 474,971	D 6
Pamangkat, †51,871	D 5
Pamekasan, 142,650	L 2
Pamenungpeuk, †24,662	H 2
Pandeglang, †24,823	G 1
Pangkalanbrandan, †23,806	B 5
Pangkalpinang, 60,283	D 6
Pare, †85,528	K 2
Parepare, 67,992	F 6
Pariaman, †45,812	B 6
Pasuruan, 63,408	K 2
Pati, 156,749	J 2
Patjitan, 44,383	J 2
Pekalongan, 102,380	J 2
Pemalang, †93,608	J 2

Pematangsiantar, 114,870	B 5
Piru, †23,633	H 6
Ponorogo, 49,993	J 2
Pontianak, 150,220	D 6
Poso, 141,292	G 6
Prapat, 5,552	B 5
Probolinggo, 68,828	K 2
Purbolinggo, 31,719	J 2
Purwakarta, †88,680	H 2
Purwodadi, 154,648	J 2
Purwokerto, 22,623	H 2
Purworedjo, 23,209	J 2
Putussibau, 18,357	E 5
Rambipudji, 145,521	K 2
Rangkasbitung, †51,176	G 2
Rapang, 54,996	F 6
Rembang, 39,939	K 2
Rengat, †22,982	C 6
Sabang, We, 6,747	B 4
Salatiga, 58,135	J 2
Samarinda, 69,715	F 6
Sambas, 153,290	D 5
Sampang, 47,596	L 2
Sanana, 23,388	H 6
Sanggau, †28,039	E 5
Sangkulirang, 6,108	F 5
Saparua, 53,390	H 6
Saumlaki, 122,732	J 7
Sawahlunto, 12,276	C 6
Semarang, 503,153	J 2
Semitau, 19,255	E 5
Serang, †43,661	G 1
Sibolga, 38,655	B 5
Siborongborong, 130,143	B 5
Sidoardjo, †40,591	K 2
Sigli, †4,050	B 4
Sindangbarang, 41,223	H 2
Singaradja	
Singkang, †17,948	F 6
Singkawang, †61,107	D 5
Sintang, 125,067	E 5
Situbondo, 30,000	L 2
Sragen, 32,310	J 2
Subang, †22,825	H 2
Sukabumi, 80,438	H 2
Sukadana, 6,899	E 6
Sumbawa, †22,308	F 7
Sumedang, †74,062	H 2
Sumenep, 33,628	L 2
Surabaja, 1,007,945	K 2
Surakarta, 367,626	J 2
Tandjungbalai, 29,152	C 5
Tandjungkarang, 133,901	C 7
Tandjungpandan, †39,253	D 6
Tandjungpriok, †140,573	H 1
Tandjungpura, †20,726	B 5
Tangerang, †81,042	G 1
Tarakan, 24,807	F 5
Tarutung, †41,041	B 5
Tasikmalaja, †101,466	H 2
Tegal, 89,016	J 2
Telukbetung, 101,801	D 7
Tenggarong, †15,516	F 6
Ternate, 23,500	H 5
Tjepu, 41,748	J 2
Tjiamis, †80,018	H 2
Tjiandjur, †77,927	H 2
Tjidulang, †32,475	H 2
Tjilatjap, 78,619	H 2

Tjimahi, †90,718	H 2
Tjirebon, 158,299	H 2
Tobelo, †14,430	H 5
Tolitoli, 8,333	G 5
Tondano, †29,584	H 5
Trenggalek, †37,762	K 2
Tuban, 48,123	K 2
Tulungagung, 43,115	K 2
Turen, 157,711	K 2
Wahai, 38,781	H 6
Wates, †33,514	J 2
Wonogiri, 145,704	J 2
Wonosobo, 33,917	J 2

PHYSICAL FEATURES
Alas (str.)	F 7
Anambas (isls.), 15,700	D 5
Arafura (sea)	J 7
Aru (isls.), 27,006	J 7
Asahan (river)	B 5
Babar (isls.), 14,133	H 7
Bali (isl.), 1,782,529	F 7
Bali (sea)	F 7
Banda (sea)	H 7
Bangka (isl.), 311,922	D 6
Banjak (isls.), 1,696	B 5
Barisan (mts.)	C 6
Barito (river)	E 6
Batjan (isl.), 21,861	H 6
Batu (isls.), 60,806	B 6
Bawean (isl.), 47,589	K 1
Belitung (Billiton) (isl.), 102,375	D 6
Bengalen (passage)	A 4
Billiton (isl.), 102,375	D 6
Bintan (isl.), 10,580	C 5
Bintan (isl.), 65,301	C 5
Blackwood (Ngundju) (cape)	G 7
Bone (gulf)	G 6
Borneo (isl.)	E 5
Borneo (Kalimantan) (reg.), 4,101,475	E 5
Bunguran (Natuna) (isls.), 15,261	D 5
Buru (isl.), 16,018	H 6
Butung (isl.), 253,262	G 6
Celebes (isl.), 6,288,043	G 6
Celebes (sea)	G 5
Ceram (isl.), 73,453	H 6
Damar (isls.)	H 7
Diamond (point)	B 4
Djemadja (isl.), 3,874	D 5
Enggano (isl.), 686	C 7
Ewab (isls.), 76,606	J 7
Flores (isl.), 901,772	G 7
Flores (sea)	F 7
Gebe (isl.), 5,410	H 6
Gorong (isls.), 33,241	J 6
Halmahera (isl.), 97,133	H 5
Indramaju (point)	H 1
Java (head)	C 7
Java (isl.), 60,909,381	J 2
Java (sea)	J 2
Kabaena (isl.), 14,380	G 7
Kai (Ewab) (isls.), 76,606	J 7
Kalao (isl.), 670	G 7
Kalaotoa (isl.), 2,031	G 7
Kalimantan (reg.), 4,101,475	E 5

Kangean (isls.), 52,893	F 7
Kapuas (river)	D 6
Karakelong (isl.), 15,276	H 5
Karimata (arch.), 1,623	D 6
Karimundjawa (isls.), 1,611	J 1
Kerintji (mt.)	C 6
Kisar (isl.), 16,569	H 7
Komodo (isl.)	F 7
Krakatau (isl.)	C 7
Laut (isl.), 42,099	F 6
Leuser (mt.)	B 5
Lingga (arch.), 39,307	D 5
Lingga (isl.), 14,309	D 5
Lombok (isl.), 1,300,234	F 7
Madura (isl.), 2,150,194	K 2
Mahakam (river)	F 6
Makassar (str.)	F 6
Malacca (str.)	C 5
Mentawai (isls.), 23,649	B 6
Molucca (sea)	H 6
Moluccas (isls.), 847,930	H 6
Morotai (isl.), 19,523	H 5
Müller (mts.)	E 5
Muna (isl.), 111,766	G 6
Musi (river)	C 6
Natuna (isls.), 15,261	D 5
Ngundju (cape)	G 7
Nias (isl.), 314,829	B 5
Obi (isls.), 6,358	H 6
Ombai (str.)	H 7
Puting (cape), Borneo	E 6
Puting (cape), Sumatra	C 7
Raja (mt.)	C 6
Rantekombola (mt.)	F 6
Riau (arch.), 278,966	C 5
Rokan (river)	C 5
Roti (isl.), 68,330	G 8
Salajar (isl.), 87,278	G 7
Sandalwood (Sumba) (isl.), 251,126	F 7
Sangihe (isl.), 83,585	H 5
Sangihe (isls.), 126,931	G 5
Sawu (isls.), 78,785	G 8
Sawu (sea)	G 7
Schwaner (mts.)	E 6
Seaflower (channel)	B 6
Sebuko (bay)	F 5
Selatan (cape)	E 6
Semeru (mt.)	K 2
Siau (isl.), 29,762	H 5
Siberut (str.)	B 6
Simeulue (isl.), 25,951	A 5
Singkep (isl.), 17,712	D 6
Sipora (isl.), 5,671	B 6
Slamet (mt.)	H 2
Sorik Merapi (mt.)	B 5
South Natuna (isls.), 3,318	D 5
Sula (isls.), 30,779	H 6
Sulawesi (Celebes) (isl.), 6,288,043	G 6
Sumatra (isl.), 14,982,910	B 5
Sumba (isl.), 251,126	F 7
Sumba (str.)	F 7
Sumbawa (isl.), 507,596	F 7
Sunda (str.)	C 7
Tahulandang (isl.), 13,584	H 5
Talaud (isls.), 28,738	H 5
Taliabu (isl.), 7,391	G 6
Tambelan (isls.), 3,551	D 5

AGRICULTURE, INDUSTRY and RESOURCES

SINGAPORE
Iron & Steel, Oil Refining, Tires, Light Industry

DJAKARTA
Textiles, Light Industry

DOMINANT LAND USE
Cereals (chiefly rice, corn)
Diversified Tropical Crops
Forests

MAJOR MINERAL OCCURRENCES
Al Bauxite　　C Coal　　Mn Manganese　　○ Petroleum
Au Gold　　Fe Iron Ore　　Ni Nickel　　Sn Tin
Major Industrial Areas

EASTERN NEW GUINEA
MILES
0　50　100　200

SOUTHEAST ASIA

INDONESIA

AREA	735,268 sq. mi.
POPULATION	102,200,000
CAPITAL	Djakarta
LARGEST CITY	Djakarta (greater) 2,973,052
HIGHEST POINT	Mt. Kerintji 12,484 ft.
MONETARY UNIT	rupiah
MAJOR LANGUAGES	Indonesian (Malay, Javanese, etc.)
MAJOR RELIGIONS	Mohammedan, Tribal religions, Christian, Hindu

PORTUGUESE TIMOR		BRUNEI
AREA	7,332 sq. mi.	2,226 sq. mi.
POPULATION	543,000	97,000
CAPITAL	Dili	Brunei

INDONESIA

SOUTHEAST ASIA

LAMBERT AZIMUTHAL EQUAL-AREA PROJECTION

SCALE OF MILES

SCALE OF KILOMETRES

Capitals of Countries
Administrative Center
International Boundaries
Other Boundaries

Copyright by C.S. HAMMOND & CO., N.Y.

JAVA
MILES

Pacific Ocean

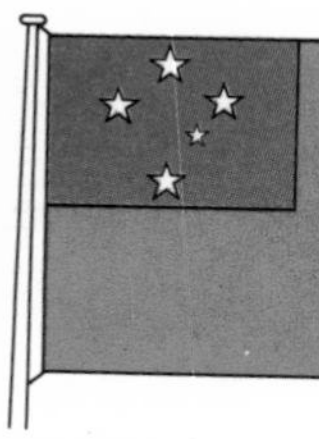

WESTERN SAMOA

AREA	1,133 sq. mi.
POPULATION	122,000
CAPITAL	Apia
LARGEST CITY	Apia 21,699
HIGHEST POINT	Mt. Silisili 6,094 ft.
MONETARY UNIT	West Samoan pound
MAJOR LANGUAGES	Samoan, English
MAJOR RELIGIONS	Protestant, Catholic

Abaiang (atoll), 3,370 ....H 5
Abemama (atoll), 2,060 ....H 5
Adamstown, 91 ....N 8
Adelaide, †600,200 ....D 9
Admiralty (isls.), 19,017 ....E 6
Agaña, 1,642 ....E 4
Agrihan (isl.), 127 ....E 4
Ahau, 436 ....H 7
Ahurei ....M 8
Ailinglapalap (atoll), 1,183 ....G 5
Ailuk (atoll), 410 ....H 4
Aitape, ‡3,147 ....E 6
Aitutaki (atoll), 2,726 ....K 7
Alamagan (isl.), 41 ....E 4
Albany, 10,526 ....B 9
Albury, 22,983 ....E 9
Alice Springs, 4,648 ....D 8
Alofi, 1,026 ....K 7
Amadeus (lake) ....D 8
Amanu (atoll), 146 ....N 7
Ambrym (isl.), 3,670 ....G 7
American Samoa, 26,000 ....J 7
Anaa (atoll), 420 ....M 7
Anatahan (isl.), 46 ....E 4
Aneityum (isl.), 246 ....H 9
Angaur (isl.), 459 ....D 5
Apataki (atoll), 137 ....M 7
Apia, 21,699 ....J 7
Arafura (sea) ....D 6
Armidale, 12,875 ....F 9
Arnhem (cape) ....D 7
Arnhem Land (reg.) ....D 7
Arno (atoll), 1,408 ....H 5
Arorae (atoll), 1,760 ....H 6
Asuncion (isl.) ....E 4
Ashburton (riv.) ....B 8
Atafu (atoll), 539 ....J 6
Atiu (isl.), 1,212 ....L 8
Atuona, 672 ....M 7
Auckland, 149,400 ....H 9
Auki ....G 6
Austral (isls.), 4,371 ....L 8
Australia, 11,359,510 ....C 8
Australian Capital Terr., 85,676 ....F 9
Avarua, 321 ....L 8
Babelthuap (isl.), 4,404 ....D 5
Bairiki, 979 ....H 6
Baker (isl.) ....J 5
Ballarat, 41,037 ....E 9
Banks (isls.), 3,059 ....G 7
Barkly Tableland (plat.) ....D 7
Barlee (lake) ....B 8
Barrow (isl.) ....B 8
Bass (isls.) ....M 8
Bass (strait) ....E 9
Bathurst (isl.) ....C 7
Belep (isls.), 573 ....G 7
Bellona (reefs) ....G 8
Bendigo, 30,195 ....E 9
Beru (atoll), 2,337 ....H 6
Bikar (atoll) ....H 4
Bikini (atoll) ....G 4
Bismarck (arch.), 163,634 ....E 6
Blackall, 2,217 ....E 8
Blue Mountains, 28,119 ....E 9
Bonin and Volcano (isls.), 205 ....E 3
Borabora (isl.), 1,723 ....L 7
Bougainville (isl.), 49,559 ....F 6
Boulder, 5,773 ....C 9
Bounty (isls.) H10
Bourail, 1,504 ....G 8
Bowen, 5,160 ....E 7
Brisbane, †649,500 ....F 8
Broken Hill, 31,267 ....E 9
Broome, 1,222 ....C 7
Bruce (mt.) ....C 8
Bunbury, 13,186 ....B 9
Bundaberg, 22,799 ....E 8
Butaritari (atoll), 2,611 ....H 5
Cairns, 25,204 ....E 7
Canberra, 85,676 ....F 9
Canton (isl.), 525 ....J 6
Cape York (pen.) ....E 7
Carnarvon, 1,809 ....B 8
Caroline (isl.) ....M 7
Caroline (isls.), 49,107 ....E 5
Carpentaria (gulf) ....D 7
Cato (isls.) ....F 8
Charleville, 5,154 ....E 8
Charters Towers, 7,633 ....E 7
Chatham (isls.), 510 ....F 7
Chesterfield (isls.) ....F 7
Chichi (isl.), 205 ....E 3
Choiseul (isl.), 6,600 ....F 6
Christchurch, 158,800 ....H10
Christmas (isl.), 477 ....L 5
Cloncurry, 2,438 ....E 8
Collie, 7,547 ....B 9
Cook (isls.), 20,000 ....K 7
Cook (mt.) H10
Cook (strait) H10
Cooktown, 429 ....E 7
Cooper (creek) ....D 8
Coral (sea) ....F 7
Coringa (isls.) ....F 7
Cunnamulla, 2,234 ....E 8
Daly Waters ....D 7
Danger (Pukapuka) (atoll), 746 ....K 7
Darling (riv.) ....E 9
Daru, ‡8,283 ....E 6
Darwin, 12,708 ....D 7
D'Entrecasteaux (isls.), 31,298 ....F 6
Derby, 994 ....C 7
Devonport, 13,068 ....E10
Dirk Hartogs (isl.) ....B 8
Disappointment (isls.) ....N 7
Disappointment (lake) ....C 8
Ducie (isl.) ....O 8
Duke of Gloucester (isls.) ....M 8
Dunedin, 77,500 ....H10
East (cape) ....H 9
Easter (isl.), 1,135 ....Q 8
Eauripik (atoll), 101 ....E 5
Ebon (atoll), 953 ....G 5
Efate (isl.), 5,000 ....G 7
Eiao (isl.) ....M 6
Elato (atoll), 36 ....E 5
Ellice (isls.), 5,444 ....H 6
Enderbury (isl.) ....J 6
Eniwetok (atoll) ....G 4
Erromanga (isl.), 975 ....H 7
Esperance, 1,111 ....C 9
Espiritu Santo (isl.), 5,124 ....G 7
Eyre (lake) ....D 8
Fais (isl.), 216 ....E 5
Fakaofo (isl.), 807 ....J 6
Fakarava (atoll), 286 ....M 7
Fanning (isl.), 521 ....L 5
Farallon de Pajaros (isl.) ....E 3
Faraulep (atoll), 158 ....E 5
Fatuhiva (isl.), 348 ....N 7
Fiji (isls.), 464,000 ....H 8
Fitzroy (riv.) ....C 7
Flinders (riv.) ....E 7
Flint (isl.) ....L 7
Fly (riv.) ....E 6
Fongafale, 669 ....H 6
Foveaux (strait) H10
Fraser (isl.) ....F 8
Fremantle, 24,343 ....B 9
French Frigate (shoal) ....K 3
French Polynesia, 86,000 ....L 8
Frome (lake) ....E 9
Funafuti (atoll), 687 ....H 6
Furneaux (isls.), 1,407 ....E 3
Gaferut (isl.) ....E 5
Gairdner (lake) ....D 9
Gambier (isls.), 563 ....N 8
Garapan ....E 4
Gardner (isl.), 230 ....J 6
Gardner Pinnacles (isl.) ....K 3
Gascoyne (riv.) ....B 8
Geelong, 18,019 ....E 9
Geraldton, 10,894 ....B 8
Gibson (desert) ....C 8
Gilbert (isls.), 37,973 ....H 6
Gilbert & Ellice Islands, 49,879 ....J 6
Gisborne, 24,100 ....H 9
Grafton, 15,526 ....F 8
Great Australian (bight) ....C 9
Great Barrier (reef) ....E 7
Great Sandy (desert) ....C 8
Great Victoria (desert) ....C 8
Greenwich (Kapingamarangi) (atoll), 491 ....F 5
Greymouth, 8,920 ....H10
Groote Eylandt (isl.) ....D 7
Guadalcanal (isl.), 20,000 ....F 7
Guam (isl.), 72,000 ....E 4
Gympie, 11,094 ....F 8
Ha'apai Group (isls.), 9,918 ....J 8
Haha (isl.) ....E 3
Hall (isls.), 491 ....F 5
Halls Creek, 161 ....C 7
Hamilton, 59,500 ....H 9
Hao (atoll), 194 ....N 7
Hastings, 26,900 ....H 9
Hawaii (state), 711,000 ....K 4
Hawaii (isl.), 61,332 ....L 3
Hawaiian (isls.), 713,355 ....J 3
Henderson (isl.) ....O 8
Hikueru (atoll), 187 ....M 7
Hilo, 25,966 ....L 4
Hivaoa (isl.), 1,004 ....N 6
Hobart, †121,275 ....E10
Honiara, 6,431 ....F 6
Honolulu, 294,194 ....L 3
Honolulu, *351,336 ....L 3
Hoorn (isls.), 2,900 ....J 7
Howe (cape) ....F 9
Howland (isl.) ....J 5
Huahine (isl.), 3,214 ....L 7
Hughenden, 2,329 ....E 8
Hull (isl.), 583 ....J 6
Huon (gulf) ....E 6
Huon (isls.) ....G 7
Ifalik (atoll), 323 ....E 5
Invercargill, 43,800 ....H10
Ipswich, 48,679 ....F 8
Iwo (isl.) ....E 3
Jaluit (atoll), 1,124 ....G 5
Jarvis (isl.) ....K 6
Johnston (atoll), 156 ....L 4
Joseph Bonaparte (gulf) ....C 7
Kahoolawe (isl.) ....L 4
Kalgoorlie, 9,696 ....B 9
Kandavu (isl.), 6,846 ....H 7
Kangaroo (isl.), 3,285 ....D 9
Kapingamarangi (atoll), 491 ....F 5
Katherine, 606 ....D 7
Kauai (isl.), 27,922 ....L 3
Kavieng, ‡2,464 ....E 6
Kermadec (isls.) ....J 9
Kieta, ‡1,528 ....F 6
Kili (atoll), 289 ....G 5
King (isl.), 2,784 ....E10
Kingman Reef (isl.) ....K 5
Kingston ....G 8
Kita Iwo (isl.) ....D 3
Koror, 4,296 ....D 5
Kosciusko (mt.) ....F 9
Kure (atoll) ....J 3
Kusaie (isl.), 3,060 ....G 5
Kwajalein (atoll), 2,388 ....G 5
La Grange ....C 7
Lae, ‡8,163 ....E 6
Lamotrek (atoll), 194 ....E 5
Lanai (isl.), 2,115 ....L 3
Lau Group (isls.), 12,954 ....J 7
Launceston, 38,118 ....E10
Laverton, 57 ....C 8
Laysan (isl.) ....J 3
Leeuwin (cape) ....B 9
Leveque (cape) ....C 7
Levuka, 1,535 ....H 7
Lifu (isl.), 6,082 ....G 8
Line (isls.), 1,691 ....K 5
Lisianski (isl.) ....J 3
Lismore, 18,935 ....F 8
Lithgow, 14,229 ....F 9
Little Makin (isl.), 1,292 ....H 5
Longreach, 3,806 ....E 8
Lord Howe (isl.), 249 ....G 9
Lord Howe (Ontong Java) (isl.), 900 ....G 6
Louisiade (archipelago), 8,398 ....F 7
Loyalty (isls.), 11,409 ....G 8
Luganville, 3,500 ....G 7
Macdonnell (ranges) ....D 8
Mackay, 16,809 ....F 8
Mackay (lake) ....D 8
Madang, ‡12,688 ....E 6
Maitland, 27,353 ....F 9
Majuro (atoll), 3,940 ....H 5
Makatea (isl.), 2,273 ....L 7
Makin (Butaritari) (atoll), 2,611 ....H 5
Malaita (isl.), 54,000 ....G 6
Malden (isl.) ....L 6
Malekula (isl.), 9,207 ....G 7
Maloelap (atoll), 509 ....H 5
Mangaia (isl.), 1,817 ....L 8
Mangareva (isl.), 563 ....N 8
Manihiki (atoll), 756 ....K 7
Manra (Sydney) (isl.) ....J 6
Manua (isls.), 2,695 ....K 7
Manuae (atoll), 18 ....K 7
Manus (isl.), 11,088 ....E 6
Marble Bar, 201 ....C 8
Marcus (isl.) ....F 3
Maré (isl.), 3,240 ....G 8
Maria (isl.) ....L 8
Mariana (isls.), 10,275 ....E 4
Mariana Trench ....E 4
Marquesas (isls.), 4,837 ....N 6
Marshall (isls.), 18,205 ....G 4
Marutea (atoll) ....N 8
Maryborough, 19,126 ....F 8
Matautu ....J 7
Maui (isl.), 35,717 ....L 3
Mauke (isl.), 722 ....L 8
Mauna Kea (volcano) ....L 4
Meekatharra, 640 ....B 8
Mehetia (isl.) ....M 7
Melanesia (reg.) ....E 5
Melbourne, †2,003,100 ....E 9
Melville (isl.) ....D 7
Merir (isl.) ....D 5
Micronesia (reg.) ....
Midway (isls.), 2,355 ....
Mili (atoll), 612 ....
Minami Iwo (isl.) ....
Mitiaro (isl.), 267 ....
Moen (isl.), 3,829 ....
Moerai, 811 ....
Mokil (atoll), 608 ....
Molokai (isl.), 5,023 ....
Monte Bello (isls.) ....
Moorea (isl.), 4,147 ....
Morane (isl.) ....
Morobe, ‡2,912 ....
Mount Gambier, 15,388 ....
Murray (riv.) ....
Mururoa (isl.) ....
Musgrave (ranges) ....
Nabari, 209 ....
Namatanai, ‡3,053 ....
Namonuito (atoll) ....
Namorik (atoll), 490 ....
Nandi, 1,653 ....
Nanumea (atoll), 1,051 ....
Napier, 28,000 ....
Nassau (isl.), 113 ....
Nauru (isl.), 5,000 ....
Ndeni (isl.) ....
Necker (isl.) ....
Neiafu, 2,873 ....
Nelson, 26,800 ....
New Britain (isl.), 116,588 ....
New Caledonia (isl.), 73,886 ....
New Georgia (isl.) ....
New Guinea (isl.) ....
New Guinea, Terr. of, 1,539,849 ....
New Hanover (isl.), 7,201 ....
New Hebrides (isls.), 66,000 ....G

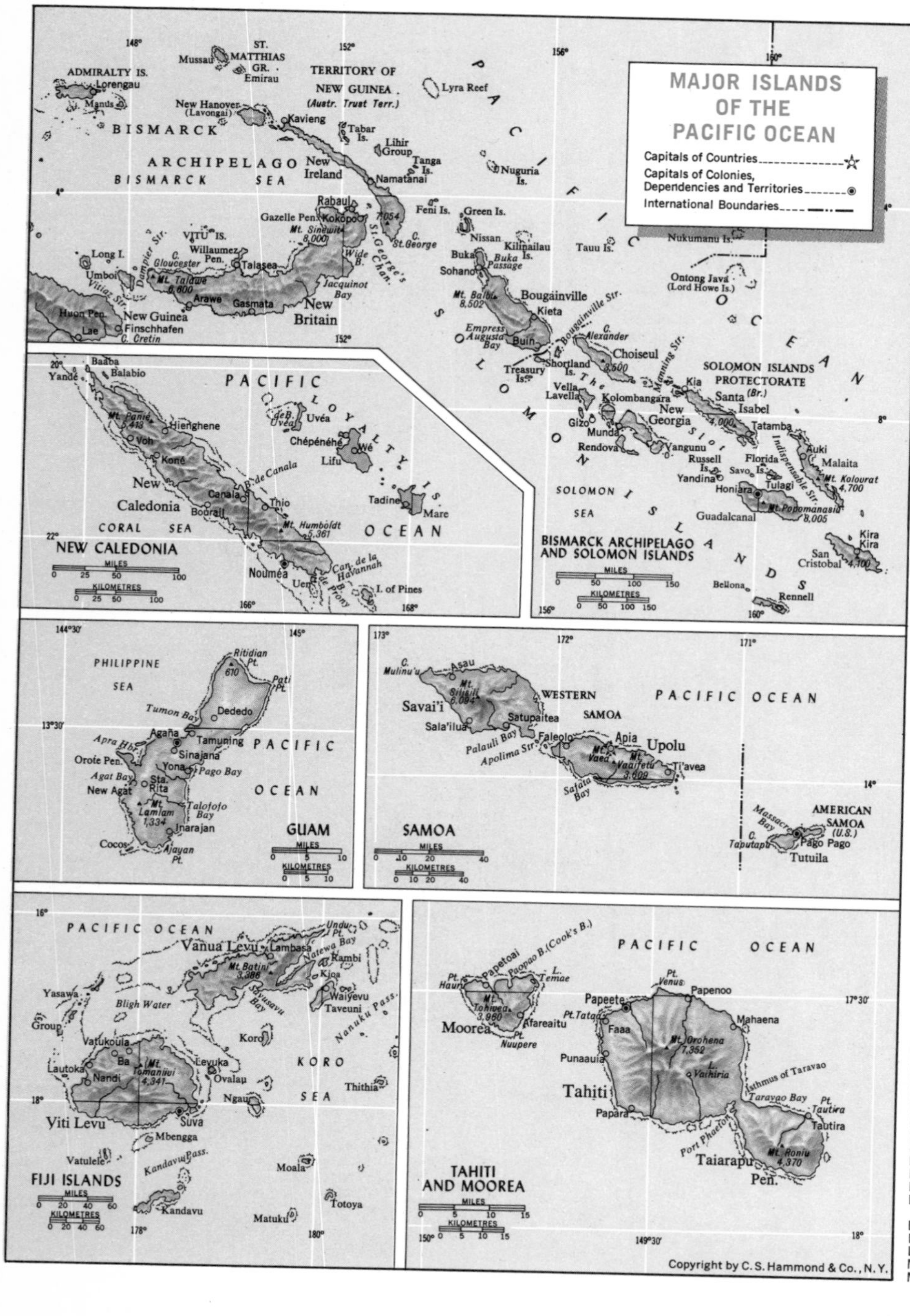
MAJOR ISLANDS OF THE PACIFIC OCEAN
Capitals of Countries
Capitals of Colonies, Dependencies and Territories
International Boundaries
BISMARCK ARCHIPELAGO AND SOLOMON ISLANDS
NEW CALEDONIA
GUAM
SAMOA
FIJI ISLANDS
TAHITI AND MOOREA

Copyright by C. S. Hammond & Co., N.Y.

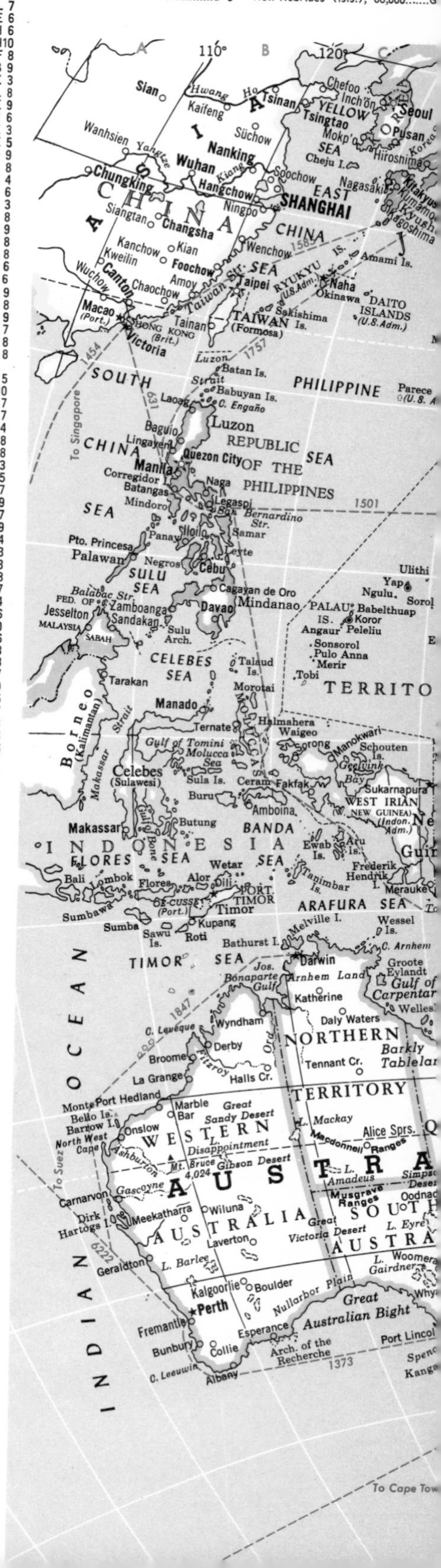

PACIFIC OCEAN

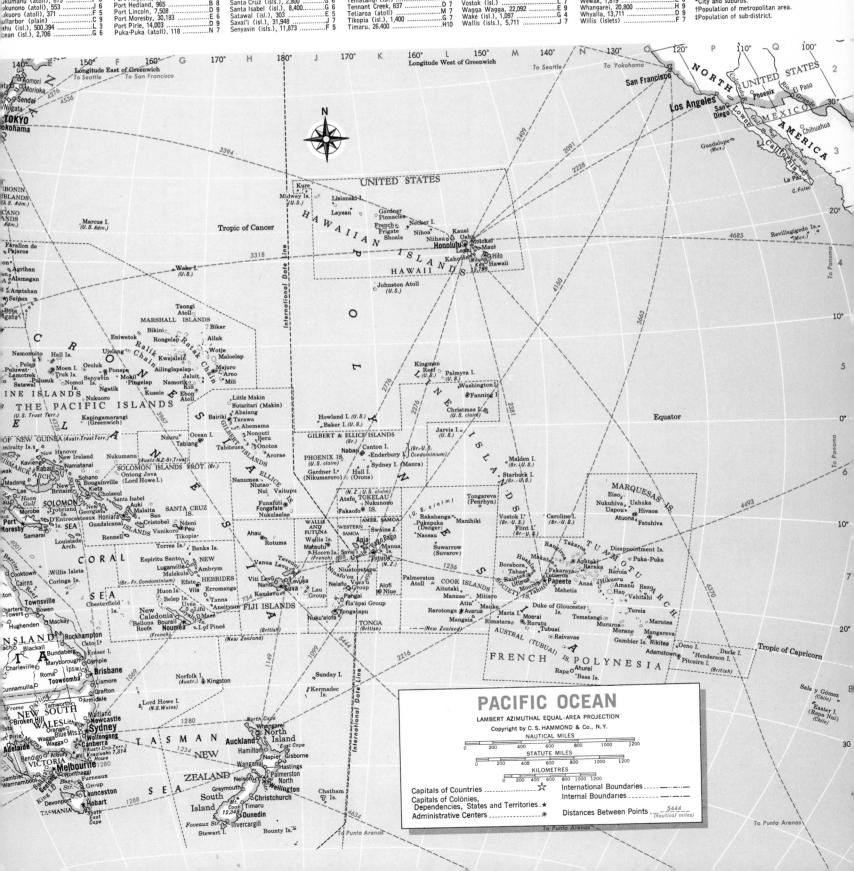

PACIFIC OCEAN
LAMBERT AZIMUTHAL EQUAL-AREA PROJECTION
Copyright by C. S. Hammond & Co., N.Y.
NAUTICAL MILES
STATUTE MILES
KILOMETRES

Capitals of Countries .... ☆
Capitals of Colònies,
Dependencies, States and Territories .. ★
Administrative Centers ....
International Boundaries ----------
Internal Boundaries ----------
Distances Between Points — 5444 (nautical miles)

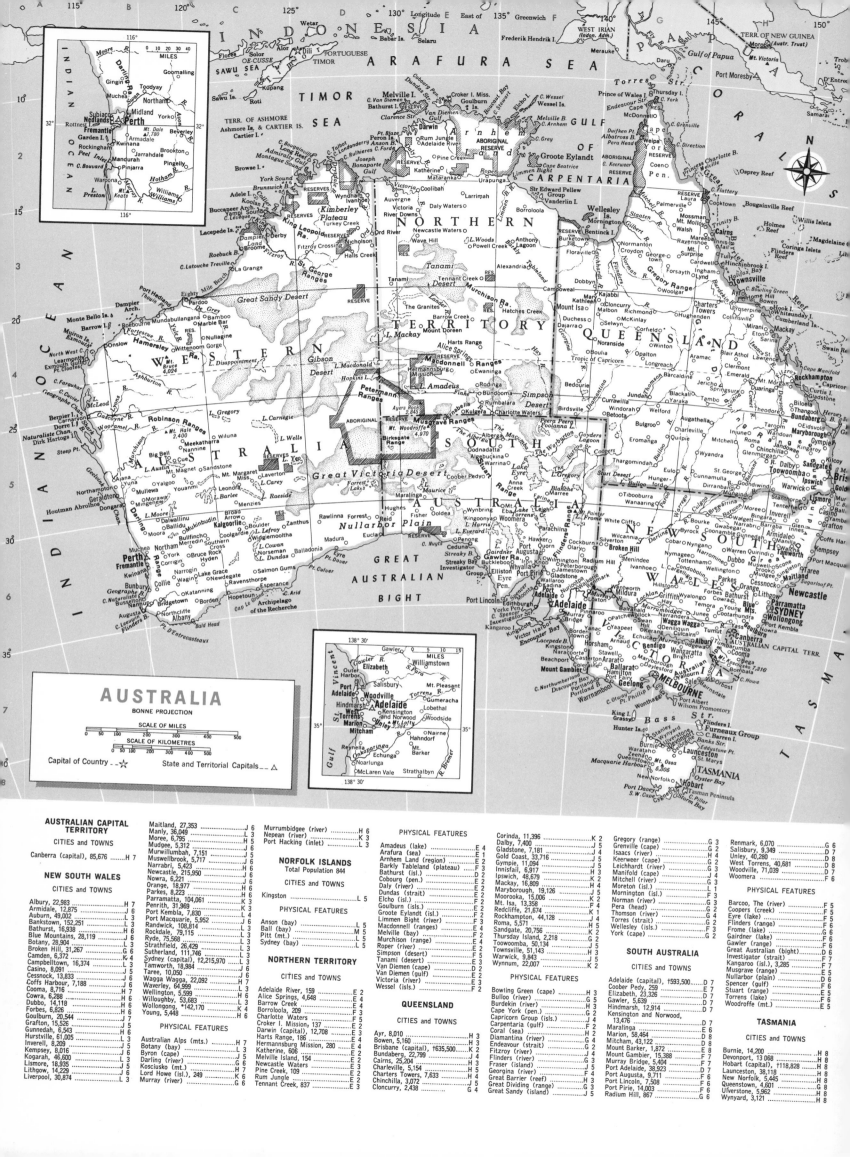

AUSTRALIA
BONNE PROJECTION

SCALE OF MILES

SCALE OF KILOMETRES

Capital of Country .... ☆   State and Territorial Capitals __ ▲

AUSTRALIA

AREA	2,974,581 sq. mi
POPULATION	11,002,811
CAPITAL	Canberra
LARGEST CITY	Sydney (greater) 2,215,970
HIGHEST POINT	Mt. Kosciusko 7,316 ft.
LOWEST POINT	Lake Eyre —39 ft.
MONETARY UNIT	Australian dollar
MAJOR LANGUAGE	English
MAJOR RELIGIONS	Protestant, Roman Catholic

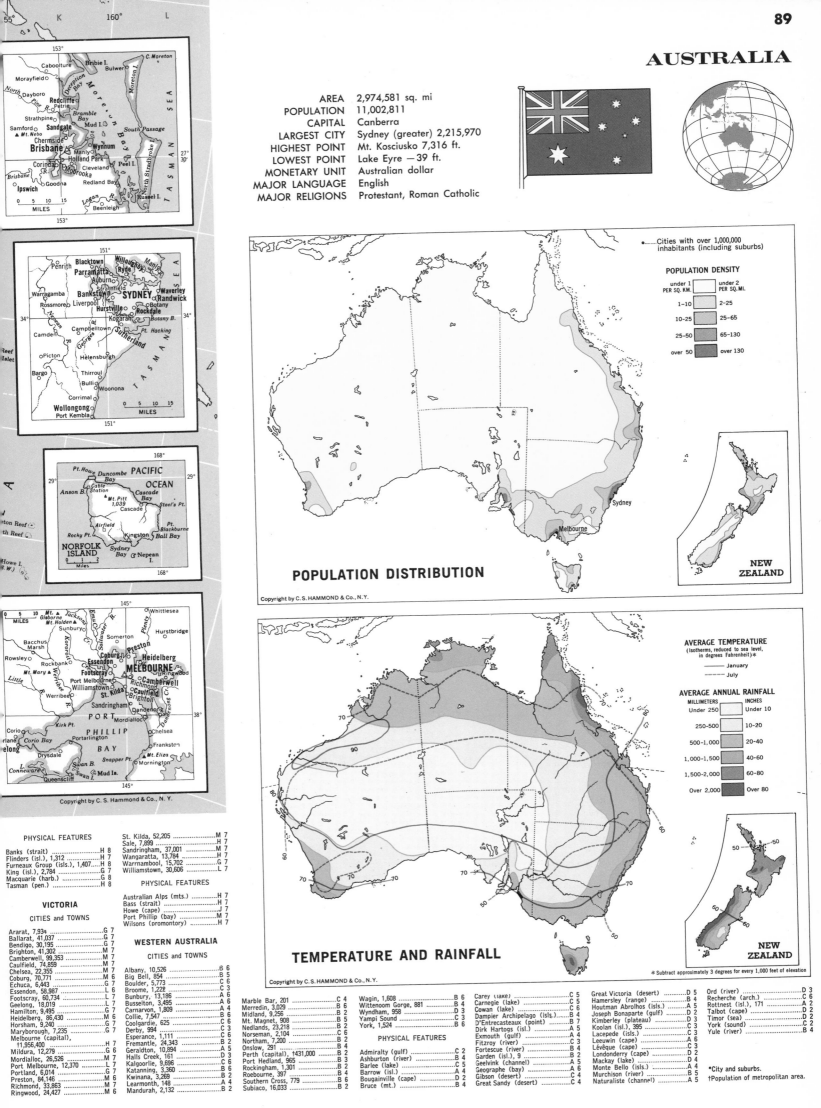

POPULATION DISTRIBUTION

Cities with over 1,000,000 inhabitants (including suburbs)

POPULATION DENSITY

under 1 PER SQ. KM.	under 2 PER SQ. MI.
1–10	2–25
10–25	25–65
25–50	65–130
over 50	over 130

NEW ZEALAND

Copyright by C. S. HAMMOND & Co., N.Y.

TEMPERATURE AND RAINFALL

AVERAGE TEMPERATURE
(Isotherms, reduced to sea level, in degrees Fahrenheit)*

— January
— July

AVERAGE ANNUAL RAINFALL

MILLIMETERS	INCHES
Under 250	Under 10
250–500	10–20
500–1,000	20–40
1,000–1,500	40–60
1,500–2,000	60–80
Over 2,000	Over 80

NEW ZEALAND

Copyright by C. S. HAMMOND & Co., N.Y.

* Subtract approximately 3 degrees for every 1,000 feet of elevation.

PHYSICAL FEATURES

Banks (strait) ....H 8
Flinders (isl.), 1,312 ....H 7
Furneaux Group (isls.), 1,407...H 8
King (isl.), 2,784 ....G 7
Macquarie (harb.) ....G 8
Tasman (pen.) ....H 8

VICTORIA

CITIES and TOWNS

Ararat, 7,934 ....G 7
Ballarat, 41,037 ....G 7
Bendigo, 30,195 ....G 7
Brighton, 41,302 ....M 7
Camberwell, 99,353 ....M 7
Caulfield, 74,859 ....M 7
Chelsea, 22,355 ....M 7
Coburg, 70,771 ....M 6
Echuca, 6,443 ....G 6
Essendon, 58,987 ....L 6
Footscray, 60,734 ....L 7
Geelong, 18,019 ....G 7
Hamilton, 9,495 ....G 7
Heidelberg, 86,430 ....M 6
Horsham, 9,240 ....G 7
Maryborough, 7,235 ....G 7
Melbourne (capital),
    11,956,400 ....H 7
Mildura, 12,279 ....G 6
Mordialloc, 26,526 ....M 7
Port Melbourne, 12,370 ....L 7
Portland, 6,014 ....G 7
Preston, 84,146 ....M 6
Richmond, 33,863 ....M 7
Ringwood, 24,427 ....M 6

St. Kilda, 52,205 ....M 7
Sale, 7,899 ....H 7
Sandringham, 37,001 ....M 7
Wangaratta, 13,784 ....H 7
Warrnambool, 15,702 ....G 7
Williamstown, 30,606 ....L 7

PHYSICAL FEATURES

Australian Alps (mts.) ....H 7
Bass (strait) ....H 7
Howe (cape) ....J 7
Port Phillip (bay) ....M 7
Wilsons (promontory) ....H 7

WESTERN AUSTRALIA

CITIES and TOWNS

Albany, 10,526 ....B 6
Big Bell, 854 ....B 2
Boulder, 5,773 ....C 5
Broome, 1,222 ....C 3
Bunbury, 13,186 ....A 6
Busselton, 3,495 ....A 6
Carnarvon, 1,809 ....A 4
Collie, 7,547 ....A 6
Coolgardie, 625 ....C 5
Derby, 994 ....C 3
Esperance, 1,111 ....C 6
Fremantle, 24,343 ....A 5
Geraldton, 10,894 ....A 5
Halls Creek, 161 ....D 3
Kalgoorlie, 9,696 ....C 5
Katanning, 3,360 ....B 6
Kwinana, 3,269 ....B 2
Learmonth, 148 ....A 4
Mandurah, 2,132 ....B 2

Marble Bar, 201 ....C 4
Merredin, 3,029 ....B 6
Midland, 9,256 ....B 2
Mt. Magnet, 908 ....B 5
Nedlands, 23,218 ....B 2
Northam, 7,200 ....B 5
Onslow, 291 ....B 4
Perth (capital, †431,000 ....B 2
Port Hedland, 965 ....B 3
Rockingham, 1,301 ....A 6
Roebourne, 397 ....B 4
Southern Cross, 779 ....B 6
Subiaco, 16,033 ....B 2

Wagin, 1,608 ....B 6
Wittenoom Gorge, 881 ....B 4
Wyndham, 958 ....D 3
Yampi Sound ....C 3
York, 1,524 ....B 6

PHYSICAL FEATURES

Admiralty (gulf) ....C 2
Ashburton (river) ....B 4
Barlee (lake) ....B 5
Barrow (isl.) ....A 4
Bougainville (cape) ....B 2
Bruce (mt.) ....B 4

Carey (lake) ....C 5
Carnegie (lake) ....C 5
Cowan (lake) ....C 6
Dampier Archipelago (isls.)....B 4
D'Entrecasteaux (point) ....B 7
Dirk Hartogs (isl.) ....A 5
Exmouth (gulf) ....A 4
Fitzroy (river) ....C 3
Fortescue (river) ....B 4
Garden (isl.), 9 ....B 2
Geelvink (channel) ....A 5
Geographe (bay) ....A 6
Gibson (desert) ....C 4
Great Sandy (desert) ....C 4

Great Victoria (desert) ....D 5
Hamersley (range) ....B 4
Houtman Abrolhos (isls.) ....A 5
Joseph Bonaparte (gulf) ....D 2
Kimberley (plateau) ....C 3
Koolan (isl.), 395 ....C 3
Lacepede (isls.) ....C 3
Leeuwin (cape) ....A 6
Lévêque (cape) ....C 3
Londonderry (cape) ....C 2
Mackay (lake) ....D 4
Monte Bello (isls.) ....A 4
Murchison (river) ....B 5
Naturaliste (channel) ....A 5

Ord (river) ....D 3
Recherche (arch.) ....C 6
Rottnest (isl.), 171 ....A 2
Talbot (cape) ....D 2
Timor (sea) ....C 2
York (sound) ....C 2
Yule (river) ....B 4

*City and suburbs.
†Population of metropolitan area.

Copyright by C. S. Hammond & Co., N. Y.

Australia
(continued)

DOMINANT LAND USE

- Cereals (chiefly wheat), Livestock
- Dairy, Truck Farming
- Cash Crops, Horticulture, Fruit
- Pasture Livestock
- Range Livestock
- Forests
- Nonagricultural Land

MAJOR MINERAL OCCURRENCES

Ab	Asbestos	Na	Salt
Ag	Silver	O	Petroleum
Al	Bauxite	Op	Opals
Au	Gold	Pb	Lead
C	Coal	S	Sulfur, Pyrites
Cu	Copper	Sb	Antimony
Fe	Iron Ore	Sn	Tin
Gp	Gypsum	Ti	Titanium
Lg	Lignite	U	Uranium
Mi	Mica	W	Tungsten
Mn	Manganese	Zn	Zinc

Water Power
Major Industrial Areas

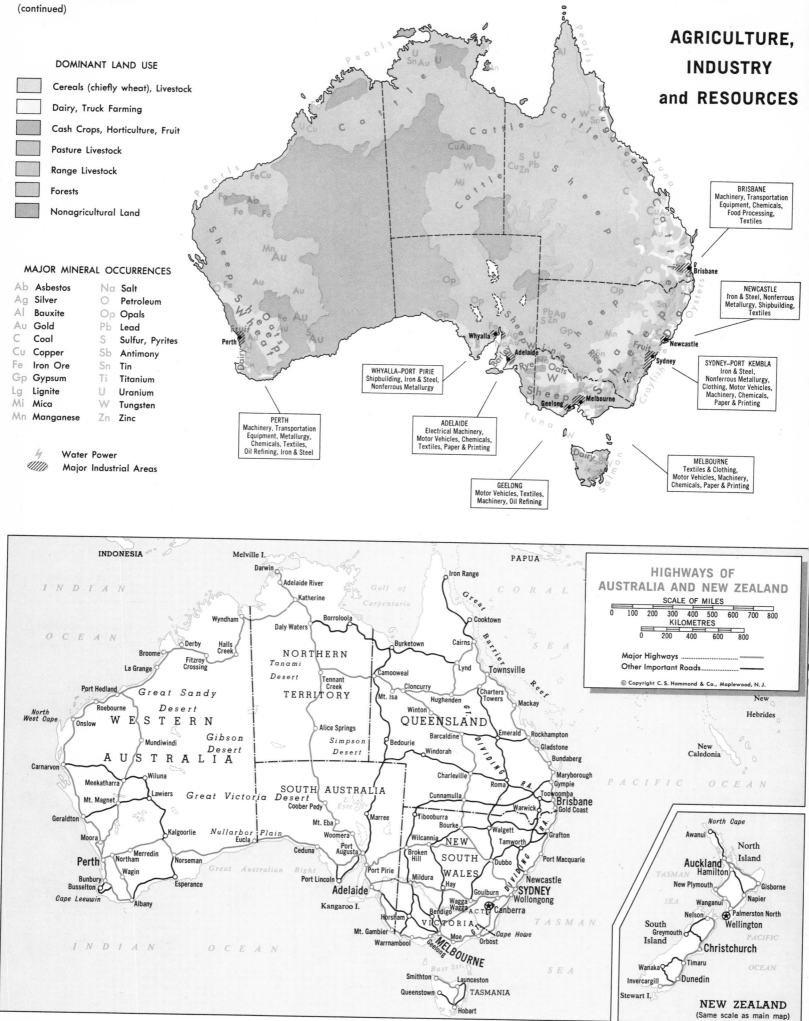

BRISBANE
Machinery, Transportation
Equipment, Chemicals,
Food Processing,
Textiles

NEWCASTLE
Iron & Steel, Nonferrous
Metallurgy, Shipbuilding,
Textiles

SYDNEY–PORT KEMBLA
Iron & Steel,
Nonferrous Metallurgy,
Clothing, Motor Vehicles,
Machinery, Chemicals,
Paper & Printing

WHYALLA–PORT PIRIE
Shipbuilding, Iron & Steel,
Nonferrous Metallurgy

PERTH
Machinery, Transportation
Equipment, Metallurgy,
Chemicals, Textiles,
Oil Refining, Iron & Steel

ADELAIDE
Electrical Machinery,
Motor Vehicles, Chemicals,
Textiles, Paper & Printing

MELBOURNE
Textiles & Clothing,
Motor Vehicles, Machinery,
Chemicals, Paper & Printing

GEELONG
Motor Vehicles, Textiles,
Machinery, Oil Refining

HIGHWAYS OF
AUSTRALIA AND NEW ZEALAND
SCALE OF MILES
0 100 200 300 400 500 600 700 800
KILOMETRES
0 200 400 600 800

Major Highways
Other Important Roads

© Copyright C. S. Hammond & Co., Maplewood, N.J.

NEW ZEALAND
(Same scale as main map)

Australia
(continued)

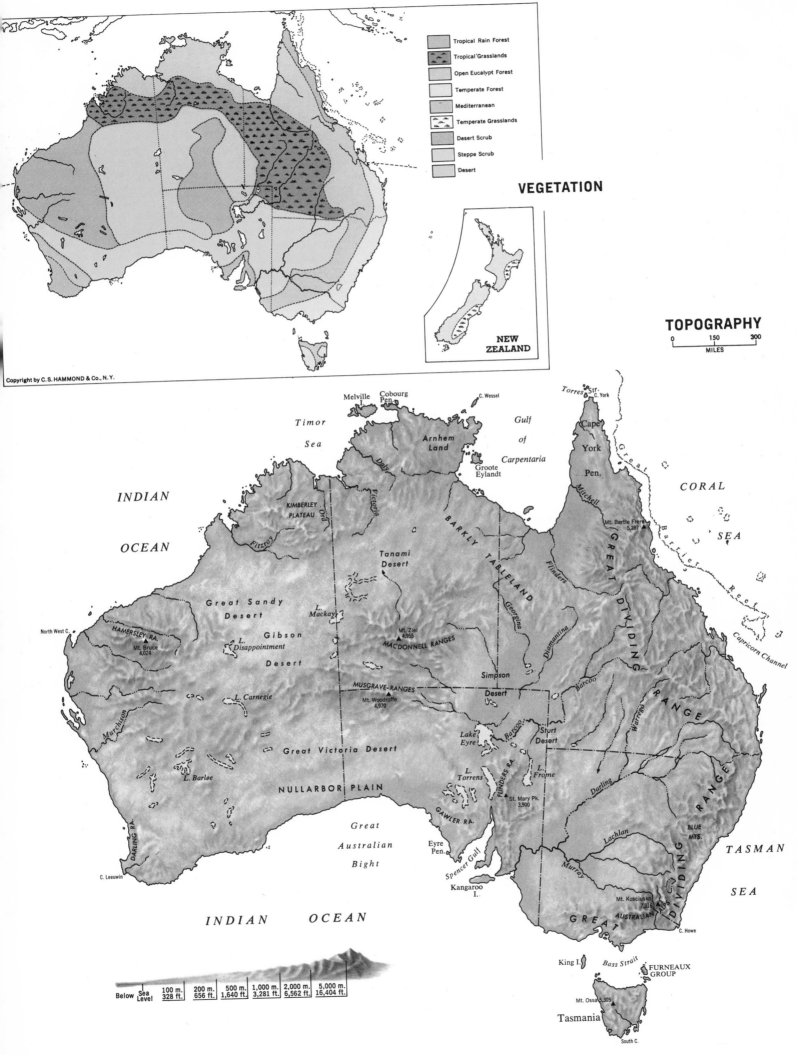

VEGETATION

Tropical Rain Forest
Tropical Grasslands
Open Eucalypt Forest
Temperate Forest
Mediterranean
Temperate Grasslands
Desert Scrub
Steppe Scrub
Desert

NEW ZEALAND

Copyright by C.S. HAMMOND & Co., N.Y.

TOPOGRAPHY

0   150   300
MILES

Timor Sea
Melville
Cobourg Pen.
C. Wessel
Torres Str.
C. York

Gulf of Carpentaria

Cape York Pen.

INDIAN OCEAN

Arnhem Land
Groote Eylandt

CORAL SEA

Daly
Victoria
KIMBERLEY PLATEAU
Fitzroy
Ord
Mt. Bartle Frere 5,287

Great Barrier Reef

North West C.

Great Sandy Desert
HAMERSLEY RA.
Mt. Bruce 4,024

L. Mackay
Tanami Desert

BARKLY TABLELAND

Mitchell
Flinders
Georgina

GREAT DIVIDING RANGE

L. Gibson Disappointment Desert

Mt. Ziel 4,955
MACDONNELL RANGES

L. Carnegie

MUSGRAVE RANGES
Mt. Woodroffe 4,970

Simpson Desert

Diamantina

Capricorn Channel

Murchison

Great Victoria Desert

Lake Eyre
Barcoo

Barcoo
Sturt Desert

L. Barlee

NULLARBOR PLAIN

L. Torrens

FLINDERS RA.
St. Mary Pk. 3,900

Darling

DARLING RA.

GAWLER RA.

Warrego

Lachlan

BLUE MTS.

C. Leeuwin

Great Australian Bight

Eyre Pen.

L. Frome

TASMAN SEA

INDIAN OCEAN

Spencer Gulf
Kangaroo I.

Murray

Mt. Kosciusko 7,316
AUSTRALIAN ALPS

GREAT DIVIDING RANGE

C. Howe

Below Sea Level   100 m. 328 ft.   200 m. 656 ft.   500 m. 1,640 ft.   1,000 m. 3,281 ft.   2,000 m. 6,562 ft.   5,000 m. 16,404 ft.

King I.
Bass Strait
FURNEAUX GROUP

Mt. Ossa 5,305

Tasmania

South C.

WESTERN AUSTRALIA

AREA	975,920 sq. mi.
POPULATION	784,107
CAPITAL	Perth
LARGEST CITY	Perth (greater) 431,000
HIGHEST POINT	Mt. Bruce 4,024 ft.

TOPOGRAPHY

CITIES and TOWNS

Ajana (A5)	126	Boulder (C5)	5,773	Cuballing (B2)	325
Albany (B6)	10,526	Boyanup (A2)	631	Cue (B4)	299
Anna Plains (C2)		Braeside (C3)		Cunderdin (B2)	738
Argyle Downs (E2)		Bridgetown (B6)	1,877	Dale West (B2)	511
Armadale (A1)	1,970	Broad Arrow (C5)	82	Dalwallinu (B5)	442
Ashburton Downs (B3)		Brookton (B2)	557	Dalyup (C6)	113
Augusta (A6)	280	Broome (C2)	1,222	Dampier Downs (C2)	
Balladonia (D6)		Bruce Rock (B5)	794	Dandaragan (A5)	324
Ballidu (B5)	482	Brunswick Jct. (A2)	870	Darkan (B2)	525
Balmoral (B3)		Bullfinch (B5)	727	De Grey (B3)	58
Bamboo (C3)		Bunbury (A2)	13,186	Denham (A4)	274
Bandya (C4)		Busselton (A6)	3,495	Denmark (B6)	845
Beagle Bay Mission (C2)	72	Capel (A2)	522	Derby (C2)	994
Bencubbin (B5)	414	Carnamah (A5)	743	Dongara (A5)	368
Beverley (B1)	851	Carnarvon (A4)	1,809	Donnybrook (A2)	1,011
Big Bell (B4)	854	Christmas Creek (D2)		Duranillin (B2)	199
Bindoon (B1)	352	Collie (B2)	7,547	Dwellingup (B2)	489
Boddington (B2)	497	Coolgardie (C5)	625	Ellendale (D2)	
Boolaloo (B3)		Coorow (B5)	308	Esperance (C6)	1,111
Borden (B6)	518	Copperfield (B5)	132	Ethel Creek (C3)	
		Corrigin (B6)	681	Eucla (E5)	
		Cowaramup (A6)	580	Exmouth Gulf (A3)	
		Cranbrook (B6)	697	Eyre (D6)	

Fitzroy Crossing (D2)	54	Ivanhoe (E1)	
Forrest (D5)	50	Jarrahdale (A1)	559
Forrest River Mission (D1)		Kalamunda-Gooseberry Hill (B1)	2,488
Fremantlet (A1)	24,343	Kalbarri (A4)	75
Gascoyne Junction (A4)		Kalgoorlie (C5)	9,696
Geraldton (A5)	10,894	Kalgoorlie (C5)	21,773
Gibb River (D2)		Kalumburu Mission (D1)	
Gibson (C6)	156	Karunjie (D2)	
Gingin (A1)	465	Katanning (B6)	3,360
Gnowangerup (B6)	740	Kellerberrin (B5)	1,191
Goomalling (B1)	619	Kimberley Research Station (E1)	52
Gordon Downs (E2)		Kojonup (B6)	863
Gosnells (A1)	1,987	Kwinana (A1)	3,269
Grass Patch (C6)	88	La Grange (C2)	
Gwalia and Leonora (C5)		Lake Grace (B6)	462
Halls Creek (D2)	970	Lake Way (C4)	153
Hamelin Pool (A4)	161	Laverton (C5)	57
Harvey (A2)	51	Lawlers (C5)	
Highbury (B2)	1,898	Learmonth (A3)	148
Hopetoun (C6)	211	Leonora and Gwalia (C5)	970
Hyden (B6)	65		
	302		

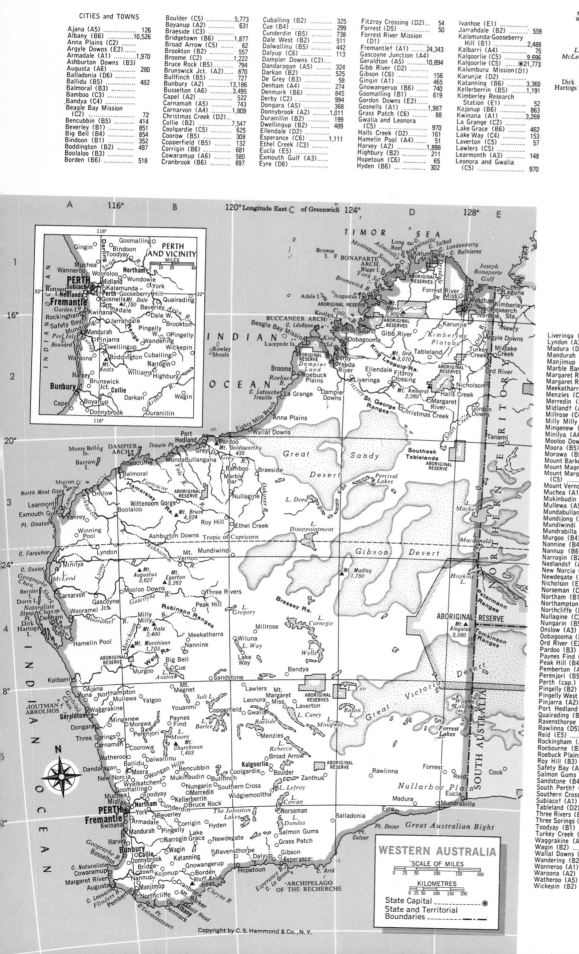

PHYSICAL FEATURES (map index)

Liveringa (D2)	114	Adele (isl.)	C 1
Lyndon (A3)		Admiralty (gulf)	D 1
Madura (D5)		Aloysius (mt.)	E 4
Mandurah (A2)	2,132	Amherst (mt.)	D 2
Manjimup (B6)	2,978	Arid (cape)	C 6
Marble Bar (C3)	201	Arthur (river)	A 1
Margaret River (D2)		Ashburton (river)	A 3
Margaret River (A6)	657	Augustus (isl.)	D 1
Meekatharra (B4)	640	Augustus (mt.)	A 4
Menzies (C5)	137	Austin (lake)	B 4
Merredin (B5)	3,029	Avon (river)	B 1
Midlandt (A1)	9,256	Bald (head)	B 6
Millrose (C4)		Barlee (lake)	B 5
Milly Milly (B4)		Barrow (isl.)	A 3
Mingenew (A5)	668	Bernier (isl.)	A 4
Minilya (A4)		Bigge (isl.)	D 1
Mooloo Downs (B4)		Bluff Knoll (mt.)	B 6
Moora (B5)	1,145	Bonaparte (arch.)	D 1
Morawa (B5)	469	Bougainville (cape)	D 1
Mount Barker (B6)		Bouvard (cape)	A 2
Mount Magnet (B5)	1,632	Brassey (range)	C 3
Mount Margaret Mission (C5)	908	Browse (isl.)	C 1
Mount Vernon (B3)	34	Bruce (mt.)	B 3
Muchea (A1)	210	Brunswick (bay)	C 1
Mukinbudin (B5)	594	Buccaneer (arch.)	C 2
Mullewa (A5)	799	Carey (lake)	C 5
Mundabullangana (B3)		Carnegie (lake)	C 4
Mundijong (A2)	540	Cheyne (bay)	B 6
Mundiwindi (B3)		Churchman (mt.)	B 5
Mundrabilla (E5)		Cloates (point)	A 3
Murgoo (B4)		Collier (bay)	C 1
Nannine (B4)		Cowan (lake)	C 5
Nannup (B2)	909	Culver (point)	D 6
Narrogin (B2)	4,620	Dale (mt.)	B 1
Nedlandst (A1)	23,218	Dampier (arch.)	A 3
New Norcia (B1)	731	Dampier Land (reg.)	C 2
Newdegate (B6)	316	Darling (range)	A 1
Nicholson (E2)		De Grey (river)	B 3
Norseman (C6)	2,104	D'Entrecasteaux (point)	B 6
Northam (B1)	7,200	Dirk Hartogs (isl.)	A 4
Northampton (A5)	714	Disappointment (lake)	C 3
Northcliffe (B6)	578	Dora (lake)	C 3
Nullagine (C3)	104	Dorre (isl.)	A 4
Nungarin (B5)	538	Dover (point)	D 6
Oobagooma (D2)	291	Drysdale (river)	D 1
Ord River (E2)		Dundas (lake)	C 6
Pardoo (B3)		Egerton (mt.)	B 4
Paynes Find (B5)		Eighty Mile (beach)	C 2
Peak Hill (B4)		Esperance (bay)	C 6
Pemberton (A6)	1,201	Exmouth (gulf)	A 3
Perénjori (B5)	577	Farquhar (cape)	A 3
Perth (cap.) (A1)	*431,000	Fitzroy (river)	D 2
Pingelly (B2)	939	Flinders (bay)	A 6
Pingelly West (B2)	387	Fortescue (river)	B 3
Pinjarra (A2)	956	Garden (isl.)	A 1
Port Hedland (B3)	965	Gascoyne (river)	B 4
Quairading (B1)	642	Geelvink (bay)	A 5
Ravensthorpe (B6)	509	Geographe (bay)	A 6
Rawlinna (D5)	142	Geographe (chan.)	A 4
Reid (E5)		Gibson (desert)	D 3
Rockingham (A2)	1,301	Goldsworthy (mt.)	C 3
Roebourne (B3)	397	Great Australian (bight)	E 6
Roebuck Plains (C2)		Great Sandy (desert)	C 3
Roy Hill (B3)		Great Victoria (desert)	D 5
Safety Bay (A2)	807	Gregory (lake)	C 4
Salmon Gums (C6)	188	Hale (mt.)	B 4
Sandstone (B4)	72	Hamersley (range)	B 3
South Perth† (A1)	29,941	Hann (mt.)	D 1
Southern Cross (B5)	779	Hopkins (lake)	E 4
Subiaco† (A1)	16,033	Houtman Abrolhos (isls.)	A 5
Tableland (D2)		Indian Ocean	A 5
Three Rivers (B4)		Johnston, The (lake)	C 6
Three Springs (A5)	701	Joseph Bonaparte (gulf)	E 1
Toodyay (B1)	663	Keats (mt.)	A 2
Turkey Creek (E2)		Kimberley (plateau)	D 1
Waggrakine (A5)	342	King (sound)	C 2
Wagin (B2)	1,608	King Leopold (range)	D 2
Wallal Downs (C2)		Koolan (isl.), 261	C 1
Wandering (B2)	283	Lacepede (isls.)	C 2
Wanneroo (A1)	1,265	Latouche Treville (cape)	C 2
Waroona (A2)	980	Le Grand (cape)	C 6
Watheroo (A5)	345	Leeuwin (cape)	A 6
Wickepin (B2)	577	Lefroy (lake)	C 5
		Lévêque (cape)	C 2
Widgiemooltha (C5)	117	Londonderry (cape)	D 1
Williams (B2)	490	Long (reef)	C 1
Wiluna (C4)	153	Lyons (river)	A 4
Winning Pool (A3)		Macdonald (lake)	E 3
Wittenoom Gorge (B3)	881	Mackay (lake)	E 3
Wongan Hills (B5)	601	Madley (mt.)	D 4
Wooramel (A4)		McLeod (lake)	A 4
Wooroloo (A1)	705	Minigwal (lake)	D 4
Wundowie (B1)	1,102	Montague (sound)	D 1
Wyalkatchem (B5)	760	Monte Bello (isls.)	A 3
Wyndham (E1)	958	Moore (lake)	B 5
Yalgoo (B5)	162	Muiron (isls.)	A 3
Yampi Sound (C2)		Murchison (mt.)	B 4
Yanrey (A3)		Murchison (river)	A 4
Yeeda River (C2)		Murray (river)	A 2
York (B1)	1,524	Naturaliste (cape)	A 6
Youanmi (B5)		Naturaliste (chan.)	A 4
Yuna (A5)	140	North West (cape)	A 3
Zanthus (C5)		Nullarbor (plain)	D 5
		Oakover (river)	C 3
		Ord (mt.)	C 2
		Ord (river)	E 2
		Peel (inlet)	A 2
		Percival (lakes)	D 3
		Peron (pen.)	A 4
		Petermann (ranges)	E 4
		Raeside (lake)	C 5
		Rason (lake)	D 5
		Rebecca (lake)	C 5
		Recherche (arch.)	C 6
		Robinson (ranges)	B 4
		Roebuck (bay)	C 2
		Rottnest (isl.), 171	A 1
		Rowley (shoals)	B 2
		Rulhieres (cape)	D 1
		Saint George (ranges)	D 2
		Salt (lake)	B 5
		Shark (bay)	A 4
		Southesk Tablelands	D 3
		Steep (point)	A 4
		Sturt (creek)	D 2
		Swan (river)	A 1
		Talbot (cape)	D 1
		The Johnston (lake)	C 6
		Thouin (point)	D 1
		Timor (sea)	C 1
		Tomkinson (ranges)	E 4
		Wanna (lakes)	D 5
		Way (lake)	C 4
		Weld (range)	B 4
		Wells (lake)	C 4
		Wooramel (river)	A 4
		Yeo (lake)	D 4
		York (sound)	D 1
		Yule (river)	B 3

*Population of metropolitan area.
⊙ Population of urban area.
†In Perth metropolitan area.

WESTERN AUSTRALIA

SCALE OF MILES

KILOMETRES

State Capital	⊙
State and Territorial Boundaries	

AREA 523,620 sq. mi.
POPULATION 28,822
CAPITAL Darwin
LARGEST CITY Darwin 12,708
HIGHEST POINT Mt. Ziel 4,955 ft.

CITIES and TOWNS

Adelaide River (B2).... 159
Aileron (C7)
Alexandria (E5)
Alice Springs (D7)....4,648
Alroy Downs (E5)
Andado (D8)
Angas Downs (C8)
Anthony Lagoon (D4)..
Areyonga (C8) 273
Argadargada (E6)
Arltunga (D7)
Auvergne (B3)
Avon Downs (E5)
Banka Banka (D5)
Barrow Creek (D6)
Batchelor (B2) 800
Bathurst Island Mission
(B1) 869
Birdum (C3)
Birrimbah (C3)
Birrindudu (A5)
Borroloola (E4) 209
Bundooma (D8)
Burramurra (E6)
Calvert Hills (E4)
Charlotte Waters (D8)..
Claravale (B3)
Coniston (C7)
Coolibah (B3)
Creswell Downs (E4)
Croker Island Mission
(C1) 137
Daly River (B2) 140

Daly Waters (C4)
Darwin (cap.) (B2)..12,708
Douglas (B2)
Elcho Island Mission
(D1) 579
Elliott (C4)
Epenarra (D6)
Erldunda (C8)
Eva Downs (D5)
Ewaninga (D8)
Fitzroy (B4)
Frewena (D5)
Gribbles Settlement
(B1) 239
Haasts Bluff (B7) 617
Harts Range (D7) 186
Hatches Creek (D6)... 7
Helen Springs (C5)
Henbury (C8)
Hermannsburg Mission
(C7) 280
Hooker Creek (B5) 277
Humpty Doo (B2)
Inverway (A4)
Katherine (B3) 606
Kildurk (A4)
Killarney (B4)
Koolpinyah (B2)
Kulgera (C8)
Kurundi (D6)
Lake Nash (E6)
Legune (A3)
Limbunya (B4)
Litchfield (B2)
Lucy Creek (E7)

Mainoru (C3)
Mataranka (C3)........... 70
Milingimbi Mission (D2) 481
Mistake Creek (A4)
Montejinni (C4)
Mount Cavanagh (C8)...
Mount Doreen (B7)....
Murray Downs (D6)
Napperby (C7)
Newcastle Waters (C4)
Newry (A3)
Numbulwar (D3) 223
Numbulwar (D3)
Nutwood Downs (D3)..
Oenpelli Mission (C2)... 299
O. T. Downs (D4)
Pine Creek (C2) 109
Plenty River Mine (D7)
Port Keats Mission (A3) 452
Powell Creek (C5)
Rankine Store (E5)
Ringwood (D7)
Robinson River (E4)
Rockhampton Downs
(D5)
Rodinga (D8)
Roper River Mission
(D3) 228
Roper Valley (D3)
Rosewood (A4)
Rum Jungle (B2)
Rumbalara (D8)
Soudan (E6)
Stirling (C6)
Tanami (A5)
Tarlton Downs (E7)

Tea Tree Well Store
(C7)
Tempe Downs (C8)....
Tennant Creek (C5)... 837
The Granites (B6)
Top Springs (C4)
Ucharonidge (D4)
Umbeara (C8)
Urapunga (D3)
Utopia (D7)
Victoria River Downs
(B4)
Waterloo (A4)
Wave Hill (B4)
White Quartz Hill (D7)
Willeroo (B3)
Willowra (C6)
Wollogorang (F4)
Yambah (C7)
Yirrakala Mission (E2) 501
Yuendumu (B7) 649

PHYSICAL FEATURES

Amadeus (lake)..........B 8
Arafura (sea)..............D 1
Arnhem (cape)............E 2
Arnhem Land (reg.),
3,231 ....D 2
Arnold (river)............D 3
Barkly Tableland........D 4
Bathurst (isl.), 869.....A 1
Beagle (gulf).............A 2
Beatrice (cape)..........E 3
Bennett (lake)...........B 7
Bickerton (isl.)..........E 2
Blaze (point).............A 2
Boucaut (bay)...........D 1
Carpentaria (gulf).......E 3
Central Wedge (mt.)....C 7
Clarence (str.)...........B 2
Cobourg (pen.)..........C 1
Conner (mt.).............B 8

Corker (cape)............C 1
Daly (river)..............B 2
Davenport (mt.)........E 7
Dobbie (mt.).............E 7
Drummond (mt.)........E 5
Dry (river)...............C 3
Dundas (str.)............B 1
East Alligator (river)...C 2
Ehrenberg (range).....B 7
Elcho (isl.), 579.........D 1
Ewing (mt.)..............E 7
Finke (river).............C 8
Fitzmaurice (river).....B 3
Flora (river).............B 3
Ford (cape)..............A 2
Georgina (river)........E 6
Goulburn (isls.), 212...C 1
Goyder (river)...........D 2
Grey (cape)..............E 2
Groote Eylandt (isl.),
637 ....E 2
Hale (river)..............D 8
Hanson (river)..........C 6
Hay (cape)...............A 3
Hay (dry river).........E 5
Hogarth (mt.)...........E 6
Hopkins (lake)..........A 8

Joseph Bonaparte (gulf)A 3
Katherine (river)........C 3
Lander (river)...........C 6
Leisler (mt.).............A 7
Limmen (bight)..........E 3
Limmen Bight (river)...D 4
Macdonald (lake)........A 8
Macdonnell (ranges)....C 7
Mackay (lake)...........B 7
Mann (river).............D 2
Marshall (river).........D 7
Melville (bay)............E 2
Melville (isl.), 343.......B 1
Murchison (range)......D 4
Napier (mt.).............A 4
Neale (lake)..............A 8
Newcastle (creek)......E 5
Nicholson (river)........E 5
Old Marsh Bed..........B 6
Olga (mt.)................B 8
Peron (isls.).............A 2
Petermann (ranges)....A 8
Port Darwin (inlet).....E 6
Ranken (river)...........E 6
Robinson (river)........C 3
Roper (river)............C 3
Rose (river).............D 2

Sandover (river)........D 6
Simpson (desert).......E 8
Singleton (mt.).........B 6
Sir Edward Pellew Group
(isls.).................E 3
South Alligator (river)..C 2
Stanley (mt.)............B 7
Stewart (cape)..........D 1
Stirling (creek).........A 4
Sturt (plain).............C 4
Sylvester (lake)........D 5
Tanami (desert)........C 5
Timor (sea)..............A 2
Todd (river).............D 8
Van Diemen (cape).....B 1
Van Diemen (gulf)......B 1
Vanderlin (isl.).........E 4
Victoria (river).........B 3
Warwick (chan.)........B 3
Wessel (cape)..........E 2
Wessel (isls.)...........E 1
West Baines (river)....A 4
White (lake)............A 6
Winnecke (creek)......B 5
Woods (lake)...........C 5
Young (mt.)............D 3
Ziel (mt.)...............C 7

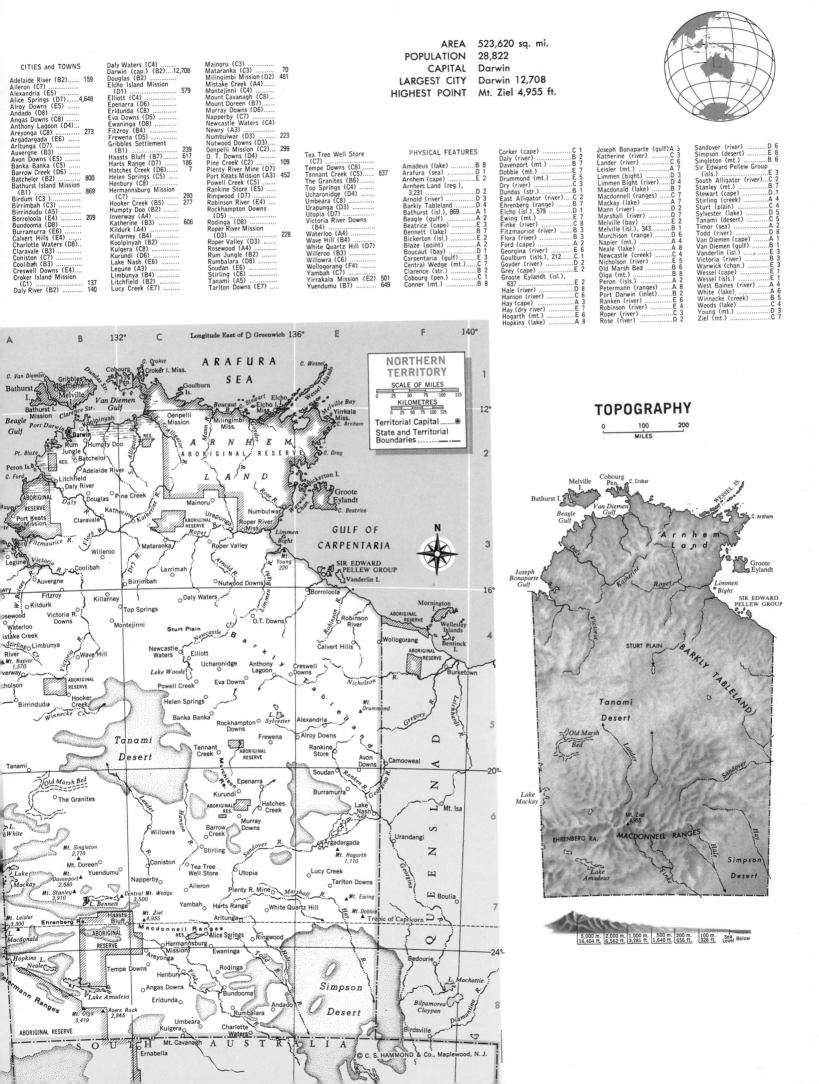

© C. S. HAMMOND & Co., Maplewood, N.J.

SOUTH AUSTRALIA

AREA	380,070 sq. mi.
POPULATION	1,020,174
CAPITAL	Adelaide
LARGEST CITY	Adelaide (greater) 593,500
HIGHEST POINT	Mt. Woodroffe 4,970 ft.

CITIES and TOWNS

Abminga (D2)
Adelaide (cap.) (B6) †593,500
Alberga (D2)
Alton Downs (F2)
Andamooka (E4) 380
Angaston (F6) 1,913
Anna Creek (D3)
Balaklava (F6) 1,301
Barmera (G6) 1,179
Beachport (F7) 495
Berri (G6) 1,680
Birdwood (C7) 394
Blinman (F4) 66
Bordertown (G7) 1,546

Brighton* (A8) 20,337
Burnside* (B8) 36,266
Burra (F5) 1,382
Campbelltown* (B7) 20,945
Ceduna (D5) 1,292
Clare (F5) 1,622
Cleve (E5) 674
Clifton Hills (F2)
Cockburn (G5) 131
Colonel Light Gardens* (A8) 3,671
Coober Pedy (D3) 259
Cook (B4) 128
Coorabie (B4) 76
Copley (F4) 95
Cordillo Downs (G2)
Coward Springs (E3)

Cowarie (F2)
Cowell (E5) 682
Crystal Brook (E5) 1,144
Cummins (D6) 768
Curnamona (F4)
Edithburgh (E6) 510
Elizabeth (B7) 23,326
Elliston (D5) 121
Enfield* (B7) 72,427
Ernabella (C2)
Etadunna (F3)
Fisher (B4)
Gawler (B6) 5,639
Gladstone (F5) 1,063
Glenelg* (A8) 14,492
Gumeracha (C7) 467
Hahndorf (C8) 705

Hawker (F4) 538
Hindmarsh* (A7) 12,914
Hope Valley-Teatree Gully (B7) 4,755
Hughes (A4)
Innamincka (G2)
Iron Knob (E5) 650
Jamestown (F5) 1,304
Kadina (F5) 1,866
Kangarilla (B8) 495
Kapunda (F6) 1,164
Keith (G7) 951
Kensington and Norwood* (B8) 13,476
Kimba (E5) 648
Kingoonya (D4) 112
Kingscote (E6) 949

Kingston (G7) 963
Koonibba (C4) 178
Kyancutta (D5) 159
Lameroo (G6) 568
Laura (F5) 598
Leigh Creek (F4) 1,020
Lenswood (C8) 495
Lobethal (C7) 1,085
Lock (D5) 186
Loxton (G6) 2,057
Loxton North (G6) 1,189
Lyndoch (C6) 562
Lyndhurst (E4) 57
Maitland (E6) 989
Mannahill (F5) 112
Mannum (F6) 1,841
Maralinga (and Woomera) (B3) 4,808
Marion* (A8) 58,464
Marree (E3) 278
Meadows (C8) 487
Meningie (F6) 569
Millicent (F7) 3,401
Minlaton (E6) 860
Minnipa (D5) 261
Mitcham* (B8) 43,122
Moonta (E5) 1,151
Morphett Vale (A8) 615
Mount Barker (C8) 1,872
Mount Eba (D4)
Mount Gambier (G7) 15,388
Murnpeowie (F3)
Murray Bridge (F6) 5,404
Nairne (C8) 553
Nangwarry (G7) 1,156
Naracoorte (G7) 4,410
Noarlunga (A8) 323
Nullarbor (B4)
Nuriootpa (F6) 1,761
Olary (G5) 107
Oodnadatta (D2) 137
Ooldea (D2) 137
Orroroo (F5) 687
Outer Harbor (A7)
Pandie Pandie (F2)
Parachilna (F4) 51
Parndana (E6) 824
Payneham* (B7) 14,930
Pedrika (D2)
Penola (G7) 1,355
Penong (C4) 212
Peterborough (F5) 3,430
Pinnaroo (G6) 904
Port Adelaide* (A7) 38,923
Port Augusta (E5) 9,711
Port Broughton (F5) 465
Port Kenny (D5) 170
Port Lincoln (E6) 7,508
Port Noarlunga-Christies Beach (A8) 2,509
Port Pirie (E5) 14,003
Prospect* (B7) 22,184
Quorn (F5) 566
Radium Hill (G5) 867
Renmark (G6) 6,070
Reynella (A8) 680
Robe (F7) 424
Roseworthy (B6) 174
Salisbury (B7) 9,349
Smoky Bay (D5) 146
Snowtown (E5) 642
Stirling-Bridgewater (B8) 4,084
Stirling North (E5) 685
Strathalbyn (F6) 1,465

Streaky Bay (D5) 766
Tailem Bend (F6) 2,049
Tanunda (C6) 1,863
Tarcoola (D4) 129
Terowie (F5) 616
Thebarton* (A7) 12,884
Tieyon (C2)
Tilcha (G3)
Tumby Bay (E6) 834
Unley* (B8) 40,280
Uraidla (B8) 587
Victor Harbor (B7) 2,036
Virginia (B7) 803
Waikerie (E5) 916
Wallaroo (E5) 2,237
Wanilla (D6) 176
Warrina (D3)
West Torrens* (A8) 40,681
Whyalla (E5) 13,711
William Creek (E3)
Williamstown (C7) 647
Willunga (F6) 569
Wilmington (F5) 365
Wirrulla (D5) 183
Woodside (C8) 569
Woodville* (A7) 71,039
Wooltana (F4) 58
Woomera (and Maralinga) (E4) 4,808
Wudinna (D5) 343
Wynbring (C4)
Yorketown (E6) 769
Yunta (F5) 179

PHYSICAL FEATURES

Acraman (lake) D5
Alberga, The (river) D2
Alexandrina (lake) F6
Anxious (bay) D5
Arckaringa (creek) D2
Barcoo (creek) F3
Barossa (res.) C6
Birksgate (range) A2
Blanche (lake) F3
Brady (mt.) D3
Cadibarrawirracanna (lake) D3
Callabonna (lake) D3
Catastrophe (cape) D6
Coffin (bay) D6
Coffin Bay (pen.) D6
Coopers (Barcoo) (creek) F3
Coorong, The (lag.) F6
Dey Dey (lake) B3
Encounter (bay) C7
Everard (lake) D4
Everard (ranges) C2
Eyre (pen.) D5
Eyre North (lake) E3
Eyre South (lake) E3
Finke (river) C1
Flinders (range) F4
Frome (lake) G4
Gairdner (lake) D4
Gawler (ranges) E5
Gawler (river) E5
Gilles (lake) E5
Goyders (lagoon) F3
Great Australian (bight) A5
Great Victoria (des.) B3
Gregory (lake) F3

Hack (mt.) F4
Hamilton, The (river) D2
Harris (lake) D4
Head of Bight (bay) B4
Indian Ocean E7
Investigator (str.) E6
Investigator Group (isls.) D5
Island (lagoon) E4
Jaffa (cape) F7
Kangaroo (isl.), 3,285 E7
Lacepede (bay) F7
Little Para (river) B7
Lofty (mt.) B8
Macfarlane (lake) E5
Macumba, The (river) E2
Maurice (lake) B3
Meramangye (lake) C3
Morris (mt.) B2
Mount Bold (res.) B8
Murray (river) F6
Musgrave (ranges) B2
Neales, The (river) E2
Neptune (isls.) D6
Northumberland (cape) F7
Nukey Bluff (mt.) D5
Nullarbor (plain) A4
Nurrari (lakes) B3
Nuyts (arch.) C5
Nuyts (cape) C5
Onkaparinga (river) B8
Peera Peera Poolanna (lake) F2
Saint Mary (peak) F4
Saint Vincent (gulf) F6
Serpentine (lakes) A3
Simpson (desert) E1
Sir Joseph Banks Group (isls.) E6
South Para (river) C7
Spencer (cape) E6
Spencer (gulf) E5
Stevenson, The (river) D2
Streaky (bay) D5
Strzelecki (creek) G3
Stuart (range) D3
Sturt (desert) G3
Sturt (river) G3
The Alberga (river) D2
The Coorong (lag.) F6
The Hamilton (river) D2
The Macumba (river) E2
The Neales (river) E2
The Stevenson (river) D2
The Warburton (river) F2
Thistle (isl.) E6
Torrens (lake) E4
Torrens (river) E4
Warburton, The (river) F2
Warren (res.) C7
Whidbey (isls.) D6
Wilkinson (lakes) B3
Wilson Bluff (prom.) A4
Woodroffe (mt.) A2
Wright (lake) A2
Yarle (lakes) B2
Yorke (pen.) E6

†Population of metropolitan area.

*In Adelaide metropolitan area.

TOPOGRAPHY

0 100 200 MILES

Below Sea Level | 100 m. 328 ft. | 200 m. 656 ft. | 500 m. 1,640 ft. | 1,000 m. 3,281 ft. | 2,000 m. 6,562 ft. | 5,000 m. 16,404 ft.

ADELAIDE AND VICINITY

SOUTH AUSTRALIA
SCALE OF MILES
KILOMETRES
State Capital ⊙
State and Territorial Boundaries

QUEENSLAND

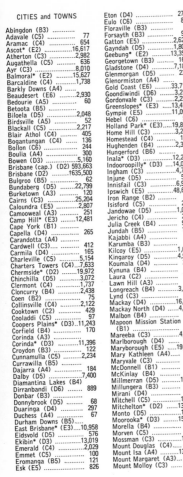

AREA	667,000 sq. mi.
POPULATION	1,571,982
CAPITAL	Brisbane
LARGEST CITY	Brisbane (greater) 635,500
HIGHEST POINT	Mt. Bartle Frere 5,287 ft.

CITIES and TOWNS

Abingdon (B3) ....
Adavale (C5) 77
Aramac (C4) 654
Ascot* (E2) 16,617
Atherton (C3) 2,982
Augathella (C5) 636
Ayr (C3) 8,010
Balmoral* (E2) 15,627
Barcaldine (C4) 1,738
Barkly Downs (A4)
Beaudesert (E6) 2,930
Bedourie (A5) 60
Betoota (B5)
Biloela (D5) 2,048
Birdsville (A5) 52
Blackall (C5) 2,217
Blair Athol (C4) 405
Bogantungan (C4) 136
Bollon (C6) 244
Boulia (A4) 300
Bowen (D3) 5,160
Brisbane (cap.) (D2) 593,663
Brisbane (D2) 1635,500
Bulgroo (B5)
Bundaberg (D5) 22,799
Burketown (A3) 120
Cairns (C3) 25,204
Caloundra (E5) 2,807
Camooweal (A3) 251
Camp Hill* (E3) 12,481
Cape York (B1)
Capella (D4) 265
Carandotti (A4)
Cardwell (C3) 412
Carmila (D4) 165
Charleville (C5) 5,154
Charters Towers (C4) ..7,633
Chermside* (D2) 19,972
Chinchilla (D5) 3,072
Clermont (C4) 1,737
Cloncurry (B4) 2,438
Coen (B2) 75
Collinsville (C3) 2,122
Cooktown (C2) 429
Cooladdi (C5) 97
Coopers Plains* (D3) ..11,243
Corfield (B4) 170
Corinda (E3) 11,396
Corinda* (D3)
Croydon (B3) 122
Cunnamulla (C5) 2,234
Currawilla (B5)
Dajarra (A4) 184
Dalby (D5) 7,400
Diamantina Lakes (B4)
Dirranbandi (D6) 889
Donbar (B3)
Donnybrook (D5) 68
Duaringa (D5) 297
Duchess (A4) 67
Durham Downs (B5)
East Brisbane* (E3) ..10,958
Eidsvold (D5) 576
Ekibin* (D3) 13,019
Emerald (C4) 2,029
Emmet (C5) 100
Eromanga (B5) 121
Esk (E5) 826

Eton (D4) 270
Eulo (C6) 83
Floraville (B3)
Forsayth (B3) 95
Gatton (E5) 2,623
Gayndah (D5) 1,805
Geebung* (E2) 13,358
Georgetown (B3) 167
Gladstone (D4) 7,181
Glenmorgan (D5) 234
Glenmorriston (A4)
Gold Coast (E6) 33,716
Goondiwindi (D6) 3,274
Gordonvale (C3) 2,234
Greenslopes* (E3) 13,411
Gympie (E5) 11,094
Hebel (C6) 94
Holland Park* (E3) ..19,852
Home Hill (C3) 3,217
Homestead (C4) 123
Hughenden (B4) 2,329
Hungerford (B6) 20
Inala* (D3) 12,278
Indooroopilly* (D3) ..14,032
Ingham (C3) 4,790
Injune (D5) 504
Innisfail (C3) 6,917
Iron Range (B2)
Ipswich (E3) 48,679
Isisford (C4) 293
Jandowae (D5) 1,020
Jericho (C4) 291
Julia Creek (B4) 905
Jundah (C4) 137
Kajabbi (A4) 70
Karumba (B3) 50
Kilcoy (E5) 1,033
Kingaroy (D5) 4,914
Koumala (D4) 228
Kynuna (B4) 51
Laura (C2)
Lawn Hill (A3) 116
Longreach (B4) 3,806
Lynd (C3)
Mackay (D4) 16,809
Mackay North (D4) ..4,602
Malbon (B4) 56
Mapoon Mission Station
(B1) 103
Mareeba (C3) 4,585
Marlborough (D4) 142
Maryborough (E5) 19,126
Mary Kathleen (A4) 982
Maryvale (C4) 171
McDonnell (B1)
McKinlay (B4) 71
Millmerran (D5) 1,060
Millungera (B3)
Mirani (D4) 413
Mitchell (D5) 1,822
Mitchelton* (D2) 13,183
Monto (D5) 1,795
Moorooka* (D3) 15,006
Morella (B4) 329
Morven (C5) 382
Mossman (C3) 1,491
Mount Douglas (C4)
Mount Isa (A4) 13,358
Mount Margaret (A3)
Mount Molloy (C3) 252

Mount Morgan (D4) ..4,000
Mount Surprise (C3) 68
Munbura (C2) 93
Mungindi (D6) 88
Murgon (D5) 2,099
Murra Murra (C6) 51
Musgrave (B2)
Muttaburra (C4) 304
Nambour (D5) 5,336
Nappamerry (B5)
Newmarket* (D2) ..12,464
Noccundra (B5)
Noranside (A4)
Normanton (B3) 334
Nundah* (E2) 15,615
Opalton (B4)
Palmerville (B3)
Pelham (B3)
Pialba (E5) 4,191
Prairie (C4) 120
Proserpine (D4) 2,523
Quilpie (C5) 859
Ravenshoe (C3) 1,086
Redcliffe* (E5) 21,674
Richmond (B4) 1,065
Rockhampton (D4) ..44,128
Roma (D5) 5,571
Rutland Plains (B2)
Saint George (D5) ..2,209
Saint Lawrence (D4) 232
Sandgate* (D2) 20,756
Sarina (D4) 2,119
Scottsville (C4) 2,122
Selwyn (B4)
Springfield (D5) 92
Springsure (D5) 814
Stafford* (D2) 12,467
Stanthorpe (D6) 3,234
Stonehenge (B5) 53
Tambo (D5) 586
Tara (D5) 990
Taroom (D5) 628
Tewantin (E5) 2,015
Thangool (D5) 198
Thargomindah (C5) 163
Theodore (D5) 714
Thursday Island (B1)..2,218
Toowoomba (D5) ..50,134
Townsville (C3) 51,143
Tully (C3) 2,678
Uanda (C4)
Vanrook (B3)
Vena Park (B3)
Walsh (B3)
Wandoan (D5) 500
Warenda (B4)
Warwick (D6) 9,843
Weipa (B2) 110
Welford (C5)
Westmoreland (A3)
Windorah (B5) 99
Windsor* (D2) 14,017
Winton (B4) 1,784
Woolgar (B3)
Wurong (B3)
Wyandra (C5) 160
Wynnum* (E5) 22,007
Yaraka (C4) 87
Yeppoon (D4) 2,869
Yeronga* (D3) 11,113

†Population of metropolitan area.

*In Brisbane area.

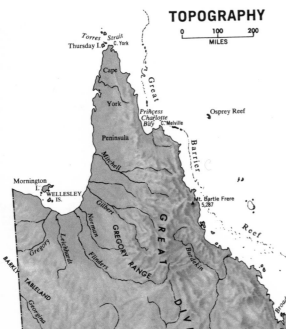

TOPOGRAPHY

0   100   200
MILES

5,000 m. | 2,000 m. | 1,000 m. | 500 m. | 200 m. | 100 m. | Sea Level | Below
16,404 ft. | 6,562 ft. | 3,281 ft. | 1,640 ft. | 656 ft. | 328 ft. |

Copyright by C.S. Hammond & Co., N.Y.

PHYSICAL FEATURES

Albatross (bay) ....B 2
Alice (river) ....C 4
Archer (river) ....B 2
Balonne (river) ....D 6
Banks (isl.), 299 ....B 1
Barcoo (river) ....B 5
Barkly Tableland ....A 4
Bartle Frere (mt.) ....C 3
Beal (range) ....B 5
Belyando (river) ....C 4
Bentinck (isl.) ....A 3
Bigge (range) ....D 5
Bougainville (reef) ....C 2
Bowling Green (cape)..C 3
Bramble (bay) ....E 2
Brisbane (river) ....D 5
Brisbane Airport ....E 2
Broad (sound) ....D 4
Bulimba (creek) ....E 3
Bulloo (lake) ....B 6
Bulloo (river) ....B 6
Bunker Group (isls.)..............D 5
Burdekin (river) ....C 3
Cabbage Tree (cr.) ....E 2
Cape York (pen.) ....B 1
Capricorn (chan.) ....D 4
Capricorn Group (isls.)..E 4
Carnarvon (range) ....D 5
Carpentaria (gulf) ....A 2

Caryapundy (swamp)....B 6
Clarke (range) ....C 4
Cloncurry (river) ....B 4
Coleman (river) ....B 2
Comet (river) ....D 5
Condamine (river) ....D 5
Coral (sea) ....C 1
Cumberland (isls.) ....D 4
Curtis (isl.) ....D 4
Darling Downs ....D 5
Dawson (river) ....D 5
Diamantina (river) ....B 4
Direction (cape) ....B 2
Downfall (creek) ....D 2
Drummond (range) ....C 5
Duifken (point) ....B 1
Endeavour (str.) ....B 1
Enoggera (creek) ....D 2
Fitzroy (river) ....D 4
Flattery (cape) ....C 2
Flinders (reefs) ....D 3
Flinders (river) ....B 3
Fraser (isl.) ....E 5
Galilee (lake) ....C 4
Georgina (river) ....A 4
Gilbert (river) ....B 3
Great Barrier (reef) ....C 2
Great Dividing (range)..C 4
Great Sandy (Fraser)
  (isl.) ....E 5
Gregory (range) ....B 3

Gregory (river) ....A 3
Grenville (cape) ....B 1
Grey (range) ....B 5
Halifax (bay) ....C 3
Hamilton (river) ....A 4
Herveys (cays) ....D 2
Hervey (bay) ....E 5
Hinchinbrook (isl.) ....C 3
Holmes (reef) ....D 3
Holroyd (river) ....B 2
Hook (isl.) ....D 3
Isaacs (river) ....D 4
Kedron (brook) ....D 2
Keerweer (cape) ....B 2
Leichhardt (range) ....C 4
Leichhardt (river) ....A 3
Machattie (lake) ....A 4
Macintyre (river) ....D 6
Manifold (cape) ....D 4
Maranoa (river) ....C 5
Marion (cape) ....D 4
Mary (river) ....E 5
McIlwraith (range) ....C 2
Melville (cape) ....C 2
Mitchell (river) ....B 3
Moreton (bay) ....E 5
Moreton (isl.) ....E 5
Mornington (isl.), 53..A 3
Nicholson (river) ....A 3
Nogoa (river) ....C 5
Norman (creek) ....D 3

Norman (river) ....B 3
Normandy (river) ....C 2
Northumberland (isls.)..D 4
Osprey (reef) ....D 1
Oxley (creek) ....D 3
Peak (range) ....C 4
Pera (head) ....B 2
Prince of Wales (isl.)..B 1
Princess Charlotte (bay).C 2
Sandy (cape) ....E 5
Saumarez (reef) ....E 4
Selwyn (range) ....B 4
Sidmouth (cape) ....C 2
Simpson (desert) ....A 5
Staaten (river) ....B 3
Sturt (desert) ....B 6
Suttor (river) ....C 4
Swain (reefs) ....E 4
Thompson (river) ....B 4
Torres (str.) ....B 1
Trinity (bay) ....C 3
Tully (falls) ....C 3
Warrego (range) ....C 5
Warrego (river) ....C 5
Wellesley (isls.) ....A 3
Whitsunday (isl.) ....D 4
Wide (bay) ....E 5
Willies (range) ....C 6
Wilson (river) ....C 5
Yamma Yamma (lake)..B 5
York (cape) ....B 1

New South Wales and Victoria

NEW SOUTH WALES and VICTORIA

	NEW SOUTH WALES	VICTORIA
AREA	309,433 sq. mi.	87,884 sq. mi.
POPULATION	4,086,293	3,080,215
CAPITAL	Sydney	Melbourne
LARGEST CITY	Sydney (greater)	Melbourne (greater)
	2,215,970	1,956,400
HIGHEST POINT	Mt. Kosciusko 7,316 ft.	Mt. Bogong 6,508 ft.

Coffs Harbour (G2) 7,188
Collarenebri (E1) 599
Collie (E2) 76
Comboyne (G2) 321
Come-by-Chance (E2) 128
Conargo (C4) 235
Concord■ (J3) 27,428
Condobolin (D3) 3,150
Conoble (C3) 50
Coogee (K3) .....
Coolabah (D2) 111
Coolah (E2) 911
Coolamon (D4) 988
Coolatai (F1) 82
Cooma (E5) 8,716
Coonabarabran (E2) 2,547
Coonamble (E2) 3,235
Cootamundra (D4) 5,939
Copmanhurst (G1) 150
Coraki (G1) 905

Coree South (C4) 68
Corowa (D4) 2,593
Cowra (E3) 6,288
Cronulla (J4) .....
Crookwell (E4) 2,340
Culcairn (D4) 932
Cumnock (E3) 355
Curlewis (F2) 438
Darlington Point (C4) 622
Darnick (B3) 165
Deepwater (F1) 334
Deewhy (K3) .....
Delegate (E5) 477
Delungra (F1) 508
Deniliquin (C4) 5,575
Denman (F3) 743
Dorrigo (G2) 1,027
Drummoyne■ (J3) 30,197
Dubbo (E3) 14,118
Dunedoo (E3) 766

Dungalear Station (D1) .....
Dungog (F3) 2,211
Dungowan (F2) 357
Duri (F2) 405
Eden (E5) 1,245
Emmaville (F1) 604
Enngonia (C1) 90
Ermeran Station (D3).....
Euabalong (D3) 196
Eugowra (E3) 669
Eumungerie (E2) 367
Euston (B4) 323
Evans Head (G1) 969
Fairfield■ (H3) 80,707
Fifield (C3) 122
Finley (C4) 1,505
Forbes (E3) 6,826
Fords Bridge (C1) 139
Forster (G2) 1,466
Frederickton (G2) 616

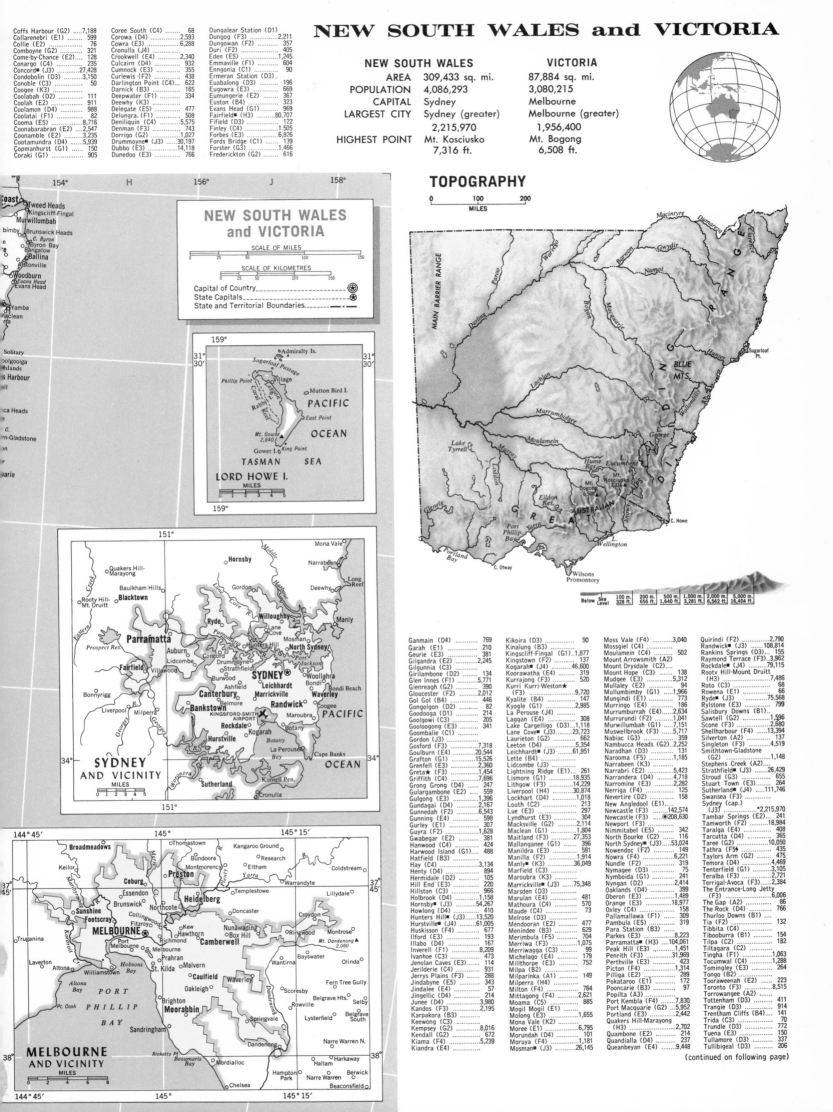

Ganmain (D4) 769
Garah (E1) 210
Geurie (E3) 381
Gilgandra (E2) 2,245
Gilgunnia (C3) .....
Girilambone (D2) 134
Glen Innes (F1) 5,771
Glenreagh (G2) 390
Gloucester (F2) 2,012
Gol Gol (B4) 446
Gongolgon (D2) 82
Goodooga (D1) 214
Goolgowi (C3) 205
Gooloogong (E3) 341
Goombalie (C1) .....
Gordon (J3) .....
Gosford (F3) 7,318
Goulburn (E4) 20,544
Grafton (G1) 15,526
Grenfell (E3) 2,360
Greta★ (F3) 1,454
Griffith (C4) 7,696
Grong Grong (D4) 247
Gulargambone (E2) 559
Gulgong (E3) 1,396
Gundagai (D4) 2,167
Gunnedah (F2) 6,543
Gunning (E4) 598
Gurley (E1) 307
Guyra (F2) 1,628
Gwabegar (E2) 381
Hanwood (C4) 424
Harwood Island (G1) 488
Hatfield (B3) .....
Hay (C4) 3,134
Henty (D4) 894
Hermidale (D2) 105
Hill End (E3) 220
Hillston (C3) 966
Holbrook (D4) 1,158
Hornsby■ (J3) 54,267
Howlong (D4) 410
Hunters Hill■ 13,520
Hurstville■ (J4) 61,005
Huskisson (F4) 677
Ilford (E3) 193
Illabo (D4) 167
Inverell (F1) 8,209
Ivanhoe (C3) 473
Jenolan Caves (E3) 114
Jerilderie (C4) 931
Jerrys Plains (F3) 288
Jindabyne (E5) 343
Jindalee (E4) 57
Jingellic (D4) 214
Junee (D4) 3,980
Kandos (F3) 2,195
Karpakora (B3) .....
Keewong (C3) .....
Kempsey (G2) 8,016
Kendall (G2) 672
Kiama (F4) 5,239
Kiandra (E4) .....

Kikoira (D3) 90
Kinalung (B3) .....
Kingscliff-Fingal (G1) 1,877
Kingstown (F2) 137
Kogarah■ (J4) 46,600
Koorawatha (E4) 319
Kurrajong (F3) 520
Kurri Kurri-Weston★ (F3) 9,720
Kyalite (B4) 147
Kyogle (G1) 2,985
La Perouse (J4) .....
Laggan (E4) 308
Lake Cargelligo (D3)...1,118
Lane Cove■ (J3) 23,723
Laurieton (G2) 662
Leeton (D4) 5,354
Leichhardt■ (J3) 61,951
Lette (B4) .....
Lidcombe (J3) .....
Lightning Ridge (E1) 261
Lismore (G1) 18,935
Lithgow (F3) 14,229
Liverpool (H4) 30,874
Lockhart (D4) 1,018
Louth (C2) 213
Lue (E3) 297
Lyndhurst (E3) 304
Macksville (G2) 2,114
Maclean (G1) 1,804
Maitland (F3) 27,353
Mallanganee (G1) 396
Manildra (E3) 591
Manilla (F2) 1,914
Manly■ (K3) 36,049
Marfield (C3) .....
Maroubra (K3) .....
Marrickville■ (J3) 75,348
Marsden (D3) .....
Marulan (E4) 481
Mathoura (C4) 570
Maude (C4) 73
Melrose (D3) .....
Mendooran (E2) 477
Menindee (B3) 629
Merimbula (F5) 704
Merriwa (F3) 1,075
Merriwagga (C3) 99
Michelago (E5) 179
Millthorpe (E3) 752
Milparinka (A1) 149
Milperra (H4) .....
Milton (F4) 764
Mittagong (F4) 2,621
Moama (C5) 885
Mogil Mogil (E1) .....
Molong (E3) 1,655
Mona Vale (K2) .....
Moree (E1) 6,795
Morundah (D4) 101
Moruya (F4) 1,181
Mosman■ (J3) 26,145

Moss Vale (F4) 3,040
Mossgiel (C4) .....
Moulamein (C4) 502
Mount Arrowsmith (A2) .....
Mount Drysdale (C2)...
Mount Hope (C3) 138
Mudgee (E3) 5,312
Mullaley (E2) 94
Mullumbimby (G1) 1,966
Mungindi (E1) 773
Murringo (E4) 186
Murrumburrah (E4)....2,634
Murrurundi (F2) 1,041
Murwillumbah (G1) 7,151
Muswellbrook (F3) 5,717
Nabiac (G3) 359
Nambucca Heads (G2)..2,252
Naradhan (D3) 131
Narooma (F5) 1,185
Narrabeen (K3) .....
Narrabri (E2) 5,423
Narrandera (D4) 4,718
Narromine (E3) 2,282
Nerriga (F4) 125
Nevertire (D2) 158
New Angledool (E1).....
Newcastle (F3) 142,574
Newcastle (F3) .....◎208,630
Newport (F3) .....
Nimmitabel (E5) 342
North Bourke (D1) 116
North Sydney■ (J3) 53,024
Nowendoc (F2) 149
Nowra (F4) 6,221
Nundle (F2) 319
Nymagee (D3) 75
Nymboida (G1) 241
Nyngan (D2) 2,414
Oaklands (D4) 399
Oberon (E3) 1,489
Orange (E3) 18,977
Oxley (C4) 158
Pallamallawa (F1) 309
Pambula (E5) 319
Para Station (B3) .....
Parkes (E3) 8,223
Parramatta■ (H3) 104,061
Peak Hill (E3) 1,451
Penrith (E3) 31,969
Perthville (E3) 423
Picton (F4) 2,384
Pilliga (E2) 289
Pokataroo (E1) 172
Pooncarie (B3) 97
Popilta (A3) .....
Port Kembla (F4) 7,830
Port Macquarie (G2) 5,952
Portland (F3) 2,442
Quakers Hill-Marayong (F3) .....
Quambone (E2) 214
Quandialla (D4) 237
Queanbeyan (E4) 9,448

Quirindi (F2) 2,790
Randwick■ (J3) 108,814
Rankins Springs (D3)...155
Raymond Terrace (F3)..3,962
Rockdale■ (J4) 79,115
Rooty Hill-Mount Druitt (H3) 7,486
Roto (C3) 68
Rowena (E1) 66
Ryde■ (J3) 75,568
Rylstone (E3) 799
Salisbury Downs (B1)...
Sawtell (G2) 1,596
Scone (F3) 2,680
Shellharbour (F4) 13,394
Silverton (A2) 137
Singleton (F3) 4,519
Smithtown-Gladstone (G2) 1,148
Stephens Creek (A2).....
Strathfield■ (J3) 26,429
Stroud (G3) 655
Stuart Town (E3) 264
Sutherland■ (J4) 111,746
Swansea (F3) .....
Sydney (cap.) (J3) *2,215,970
Tambar Springs (E2) 241
Tamworth (F2) 18,984
Taralga (E4) 408
Tarcutta (D4) 365
Taree (G2) 10,050
Tathra (F5) 435
Taylors Arm (G2) 475
Temora (D4) 4,469
Tenterfield (G1) 3,105
Teralba (F3) 2,721
Terrigal-Avoca (F3)....2,384
The Entrance-Long Jetty (F3) 6,006
The Gap (A2) 86
The Rock (D4) 766
Thurloo Downs (B1) .....
Tia (F2) 132
Tibbita (C4) .....
Tibooburra (B1) 154
Tilpa (C2) 182
Tiltagara (C2) .....
Tingha (F1) 1,063
Tocumwal (C4) 1,288
Tomingley (E3) 264
Tongo (B2) .....
Tooraweenah (E2) 223
Toronto (F3) 8,515
Torrowangee (A2) .....
Tottenham (D3) 411
Trangie (D3) 914
Trenthan Cliffs (B4)....141
Trida (C3) 70
Trundle (D3) 772
Tuena (E3) 150
Tullamore (E3) 337
Tullibigeal (D3) 206

(continued on following page)

New South Wales and Victoria
(continued)

NEW SOUTH WALES
(continued)

Tumbarumba (D4) 1,511
Tumblong (E4) 257
Tumut (E4) 3,489
Tuncurry (G3) 936
Tweed Heads (G1)........3,291
Ulladulla (F4) 1,458
Ulmarra (G1) 532
Ungarie (D3) 497
Upper Horton (F2) 139
Uralla (F2) 1,658
Urana (D4) 544
Urbenville (G1) 420
Urunga (G2) 787
Village (J2) ....
Villawood (H3) ....
Wagga Wagga (D4)....22,092
Wakool (C4) 258
Walbundrie (D4) 224
Walcha (F2) 1,585
Walgett (E2) 1,726
Walla Walla (D4) 547
Wallendbeen (E4)......... 284
Wallerawang (F3) 1,930
Wanaaring (B1) 81
Wanganella (C4) 172
Warialda (F1) 1,294
Warragamba (F3) 1,777
Warren (D2) 1,505
Wauchope (G2) 3,038
Waverley■ (K3) 64,999
Waverley Downs (B1)..
Wee Waa (E2) 1,099
Wellington (E3) 5,599
Wentworth (B4) 1,154
Werris Creek (F2).........2,299
West Wyalong (D3)......2,399
Wetuppa (B4) ....
White Cliffs (B2) 248
Whitton (D4) 306
Whyjonta (B1) ....
Wilcannia (B2) 839
Willoughby■ (J3) 53,683
Willow Tree (F2) 352
Windsor (F3) 12,047
Wingham (G2) 2.887
Wollomombi (G2) 299
Wollongong (F4)....◉131,754
Womboota (C4) 135
Woodburn (G1) 510
Woodenbong (G1) 469
Woodstock (E3) 381
Woolbrook (F2) 298
Woolgoolga (G2) 1,109
Wooli (G1) 160
Woollahra■ (K3) 47,977
Woy Woy-Ettalong
(F3) 12,206
Wyalong (D3) 578
Wyong (F3) 1,907
Yallock (C3) ....
Yalpunga (A1) ....
Yamba (G1) 853
Yancannia (B2) ....
Yanco (D4) 738
Yantabulla (C1) 69
Yantara (B1) ....
Yarrowyck (F2) 160
Yass (E4) 3,909
Yenda (D4) 666
Yeoval (E3) 574
Yetman (F1) 218
Yoogali (D4) 523
Young (E4) 5,448

PHYSICAL FEATURES

Admiralty (isls.) ....J 1
Ana Branch, Darling
(river) ....A 3
Australian Alps (mts.)...D 5
Bancannia (lake) ....A 2
Banks (cape) ....K 4
Baradine (creek) ....E 2
Barrington Tops (mt.)....F 2
Barwon (river) ....D 2
Birrie (river) ....D 1
Blue (mts.) ....F 3
Bogan (river) ....D 2
Bokhara (river) ....D 1
Bondi (beach) ....K 3
Botany (bay) ....J 4
Brewster (lake) ....D 3
Broken (bay) ....F 3
Burrinjuck (res.) ....E 4
Byron (cape) ....G 1
Capertee (river) ....F 3
Caryapundi (swamp) .....B 1
Castlereagh (river) ....E 2
Cawndilla (lake) ....A 3
Clarence (river) ....G 1
Colo (river) ....F 3
Cowal (lake) ....D 3
Crowdy (head) ....G 2
Crowl (creek) ....C 2
Culgoa (river) ....D 1
Cuttaburra (creek) ....C 1
Darling (river) ....B 3
Dumaresq (river) ....F 1
East (point) ....J 2
Eastern (creek) ....H 3
Eucumbene (lake) ....E 5
Evans (head) ....G 1
George (lake) ....E 4
Georges (river) ....H 4
Gower (isl.) ....J 2
Gower (mt.) ....J 2
Great Dividing (range)...E 3
Green (cape) ....F 5
Gunderbooka (ranges)....C 2
Gwydir (river) ....E 1
Horton (river) ....F 2
Howe (cape) ....F 5
Hume (res.) ....D 4
Hunter (river) ....F 3
Innes (lake) ....G 2
Irrara (creek) ....C 1
Jindabyne (res.) ....E 5
King (point) ....J 2
Kingsford-Smith Airport..J 4
Kosciusko (mt.) ....E 5
Kulkyne (creek) ....C 1
Kurnell (pen.) ....J 4
Lachlan (range) ....C 3
Lachlan (river) ....C 3
Lane Cove (river) ....J 3
Liverpool (range) ....F 2
Long Reef (point) ....K 3
Lord Howe (isl.), 249......J 2
Macintrye (river) ....E 1
Macquarie (lake) ....F 3
Macquarie (river) ....D 2
Main Barrier (range) ....A 2
Manning (river) ....F 2
Marra (creek) ....D 2
Marrowie (creek) ....C 3
Marthaguy (creek) ....D 2
McPherson (range) ....G 1
Medgun (creek) ....E 1
Menindee (lake) ....B 3
Middle Harbour (creek)..J 3
Monaro (range) ....E 5
Moomin (creek) ....E 1
Moonie (river) ....E 1
Moulamein (creek) ....C 4
Mount Royal (range) ....F 2
Murray (river) ....A 4
Murrumbidgee (river) ....C 4
Mutton Bird (isl.) ....J 2
Myall (lake) ....G 3
Namoi (river) ....E 2
Narran (lake) ....D 1
Narran (river) ....D 1
Nedgera (creek) ....E 2
New England (range).....F 1
Nymboida (river) ....G 1
Ottleys (creek) ....F 1
Paroo (chan.) ....B 2
Paroo (river) ....C 1
Parramatta (river) ....J 3
Peery (lake) ....B 2
Phillip (point) ....J 2
Pian (creek) ....E 1
Pitarpunga (lake) ....B 4
Plomer (point) ....G 2
Poopeloe (lake) ....C 2
Popilta (lake) ....A 3
Port Jackson (inlet) ......J 3
Port Stephens (inlet)......G 3
Prospect (res.) ....H 3
Rabbit (isl.) ....J 2
Richmond (range) ....G 1
Richmond (river) ....G 1
Riverina (reg.) ....C 4
Robe (mt.) ....A 2
Round, The (mt.) ....G 2
Salt, The (lake) ....B 2
Severn (river) ....F 1
Shoalhaven (river) ....E 4
Smoky (cape) ....G 2
Snowy (mts.) ....E 5
Snowy (river) ....E 5
Solitary (isls.) ....G 1
Stony (ranges) ....B 2
Sturt (mt.) ....A 1
Sugarloaf (passage) ....J 1
Sugarloaf (point) ....G 3
Talyawalka (creek) ....B 2
Talyawalka Ana Branch,
Darling (river) ....B 3
Tandou (lake) ....A 3
Tasman (sea) ....F 5
The Round (mt.) ....G 2
The Salt (lake) ....B 2
Timbarra (river) ....G 1
Tongo (lake) ....B 2
Travellers (lake) ....B 3
Tuggerah (lake) ....F 3
Tumut (res.) ....E 4
Twofold (bay) ....F 5
Urana (lake) ....D 4
Victoria (lake) ....A 3
Wallis (lake) ....G 3
Warrego (river) ....C 1
Whalan (creek) ....E 1
Willandra Billabong
(creek) ....C 3
Wollondilly (river) ....F 4
Wongallarra (lake) ....C 2
Woronora (river) ....J 4
Wyangala (res.) ....E 3
Yanko (creek) ....C 4
Yantara (lake) ....B 1

VICTORIA

CITIES and TOWNS

Alexandra (C5) 1,945
Altona‡ (H5) 16,167
Apollo Bay (B6) 982
Apsley (A5) 337
Ararat (B5) 7,934
Avoca (B5) 971
Bacchus Marsh (C5).....3.288
Bairnsdale (D5) 7,427
Ballarat☆ (C5) 41,037
Ballarat (C5) ....†54,880
Balmoral (A5) 304
Bayswater (K5) ....
Beaconsfield (K6) 592
Beaufort (B5) 1,240
Beechworth (D5) 3,508
Belgrave Heights (J5)...
Belgrave South (K5).....
Benalla (D5) 8,260
Bendigo• (C5) 30,195
Bendigo (C5) ....†40,327
Bendoc (E5) 111
Berwick‡ (K6) 10,884
Beulah (B4) 401
Birchip (B4) 1,058
Birregurra (B6) 489
Boort (B6) 836
Boundary Bend (B4)..... 170
Box Hill‡ (J5) 50,420
Branxholme (A5) 270
Bright (D5) 845
Brighton‡ (J5) 41,302
Broadford (C5) 1,678
Broadmeadows‡ (H4)..66,306
Brunswick‡ (H5) 53,093
Bruthen (D5) 767
Bundoora (J4) ....
Camberwell‡ (J5) 99,353
Camperdown (C6) 3,446
Cann River (E5) 315
Casterton (A5) 2,442
Castlemaine (C5) 7,216
Caulfield‡ (J5) 74,859
Charlton (B5) 1,527
Chelsea‡ (J6) 22,355
Clunes (B5) 836
Cobden (B6) 929
Cobram (C4) 2,538
Coburg‡ (H5) 70,771
Cohuna (C4) 1,815
Colac (B6) 9,252
Coldstream (K4) ....
Coleraine (A5) 1,503
Colignan (B4) 222
Collingwood‡ (J5) 25,413
Cororooke (B6) 517
Corryong (D5) 1,129
Cowangie (A4) 194
Creswick (B5) 1,730
Croydon‡ (K5) 15,694
Cudgewa (D5) 380
Dandenong‡ (K5) 24,909
Darby (D6) ....
Dartmoor (A5) 447
Daylesford (C5) 2,776
Derrinallum (B5) 662
Dimboola (B5) 1,923
Donald (B5) 1,517
Doncaster and Temple-
stowe‡ (J5) 19,061
Drouin (C6) 2,511
Dunkeld (B5) 442
Dunolly (B5) 753
Eaglehawk• (C5) 4,926
Echuca (C5) 6,443
Edenhope (A5) 863
Eildon (C5) 965
Eltham‡ (J4) 12,745
Erica (D5) 298
Essendon‡ (H5) 58,987
Euroa (C5) 3,040
Fern Tree Gully‡
(K5) 35,927
Fitzroy‡ (H5) 29,399
Footscray‡ (H5) 60,734
Geelong△ (C6) 18,019
Geelong (C6) ....†91,777
Geelong West△ (C6)....17,681
Goroke (A5) 522
Gunbower (C4) 902
Hallam (K5) ....
Hamilton (B5) 9,495
Hampton Park (K6)..... 380
Harkaway (K5) ....
Harrow (A5) 225
Hawthorn‡ (J5) 36,707
Healesville (C5) 2,687
Heathcote (C5) 1,287
Heidelberg‡ (J5) 86,430
Heyfield (D6) 1,917
Heywood (A6) 865
Hopetoun (B4) 973
Horsham (B5) 9,240
Inglewood (B5) 860
Kangaroo Ground (J4) 307
Kaniva (A5) 993
Keilor‡ (H5) 29,519
Kerang (B4) 3,727
Kew‡ (J5) 33,341
Kilmore (C5) 1,363
Koondrook (B4) 889
Koroit (B6) 1,466
Korumburra (D6) 3,237
Kyabram (C5) 3,936
Kyneton (C5) 3,366
Lake Boga (B4) 535
Lake Bolac (B5) 647
Lakes Entrance (E5)....1,602
Laverton (H5) 4,152
Leongatha (C6) 2,755
Lillydale‡ (J4) 12,894
Lysterfield (K5) ....
Macarthur (A6) 560
Maffra (D5) 3,404
Maldon (C5) 1,071
Mallacoota (E5) 215
Malvern‡ (J5) 47,870
Mansfield (D5) 1,944
Maryborough (B5) 7,235
Melbourne (cap.),
(H5) *1,956,400
Merbein (A4) 1,737
Merino (A5) 476
Mildura (A4) 12,279
Minyip (B5) 710
Moe□ (D6) 15,463
Mnotmorency (J4) ......
Montrose (K5) ....
Moorabbin‡ (J5) 95,669
Mooroopna (C5) 2,505
Mordialloc‡ (J6) 26,526
Morea (A5) ....
Mornington (C6) 4,886
Mortlake (B6) 1,297
Morwell□ (D5) 14,833
Mount Beauty (D5)......1,509
Murrayville (A4) 367
Murtoa (B5) 1,135
Myrtleford (D5) 2,123
Narre Warren (K6) ......
Narre Warren North
(K5) ....
Nathalia (C5) 1,276
Natimuk (A5) 490
Newmerella (E5) 283
Newton and Chilwell△
(C6) 11,783
Nhill (A5) 2,233
Northcote‡ (J5) 44,746
Nowa Nowa (E5) 365
Numurkah (C5) 2,687
Nunawading‡ (J5) 53,246
Nyah (B4) 459
Nyah West (B4) 755
Oakleigh‡ (J5) 48,017
Olinda (K5) ....
Omeo (D5) 417
Orbost (E5) 2,613
Ouyen (B4) 1,695
Patchewollock (A4) 174
Penshurst (B5) 657
Port Albert (D6) 283
Port Fairy (B6) 2,426
Port Melbourne‡
(H5) 12,370
Portland (A6) 6,014
Prahran‡ (J5) 52,554
Preston‡ (J4) 84,146
Quambatook (B4) 457
Rainbow (A4) 896
Red Cliffs (B4) 2,440
Research (J4) 732
Richmond‡ (J5) 33,863
Ringwood‡ (K5) 24,427
Robinvale (B4) 1,700
Rochester (C5) 1,965
Rosebud (C6) 3,726
Rowville (K5) ....
Rushworth (C5) 1,077
Rutherglen (D5) 1,292
Saint Arnaud (B5) 3,150
Saint Kilda‡ (J5)........52,205
Sale (D6) 7,899
Sandringham‡ (J5) 37,001
Scoresby (K5) ....
Sea Lake (B4) 948
Sebastopol☆ (B5) 4,663
Selby (K5) ....
Serviceton (A5) 355
Seymour (C5) 5,104
Shepparton (C5) 13,580
South Melbourne‡
(J5) 32,528
Springvale‡ (J5) 28,526
Stawell (B5) 5,506
Sunbury (C5) 3,131
Sunshine‡ (H5) 62,321
Swan Hill (B4) 6,186
Swifts Creek (D5) 356
Tallangatta (D5) 1,025
Tatura (C5) 2,166
Templestowe and Don-
caster‡ (J5) 19,061
Terang (B6) 2,380
Thomastown (J4) ....
Tongala (C5) 866
Traralgon□ (D6) 12,300
Truganina (H5) 69
Tyntynder Central (B4) 268
Underbool (A4) 340
Wangaratta (D5) 13,784
Wantirna (K5) ....
Warburton (C5) 1,630
Warracknabeal (B5) 3,061
Warragul (D6) 6,405
Warrandyte (J4) ....
Warrnambool (B6) 15,702
Waverley‡ (J5) 44,987
Wedderburn (B5) 958
Werribee (C5) 5,398
Werribee South (C5).....2,158
Werrimull (A4) 110
Whittlesea (C5) 535
Willaura (B5) 525
Williamstown‡ (H5)....30,606
Winchelsea (B6) 1,057
Wodonga (D5) 7,498
Wonthaggi (C6) 4,190
Woodend (C5) 1,224
Woods Point (D5) 229
Wycheproof (B5) 995
Yaapeet (B4) 168
Yallourn□ (D6) 5,010
Yanac (A5) 235
Yarram (D6) 2,053
Yarrawonga (C5) 3,022
Yea (C5) 1,113

PHYSICAL FEATURES

Altona (bay) ....H 5
Australian Alps (mts.)....D 5
Avoca (river) ....B 5
Barry (mts.) ....D 5
Beaumaris (bay) ....J 6
Bogong (mt.) ....D 5
Bridgewater (cape) ......A 6
Buller (mt.) ....D 5
Campaspe (river) ....C 5
Cook (point) ....H 5
Corangamite (lake) ....B 6
Corner (inlet) ....D 6
Dandenong (creek) ....K 5
Dandenong (mt.) . ...K 5
Difficult (mt.) ....B 5
Discovery (bay) ....A 6
Eildon (res.) ....C 5
French (isl.), 228 ....C 6
Gippsland (reg.) ....D 6
Glenelg (river) ....A 5
Goulburn (river) ....C 5
Hindmarsh (lake) ....A 5
Hobsons (bay) ....H 5
Hopkins (river) ....B 5
Hume (res.) ....D 4
Indian Ocean ....B 6
Kororoit (creek) ....H 5
Loddon (river) ....B 5
Maribyrnong (river) ......H 5
Mitchell (river) ....D 5
Mitta Mitta (river) ....D 5
Mornington (pen.) ....C 6
Mount Emu (creek) ....B 5
Murray (river) ....A 4
Nelson (cape) ....A 6
Ninety Mile (beach) ......D 6
Otway (cape) ....B 6
Ovens (river) ....D 5
Phillip (isl.) ....C 6
Plenty (riyer) ....J 4
Port Phillip (bay) ....C 6
Portland (bay) ....A 6
Ricketts (point) ....J 6
Rocklands (res.) ....B 5
Snake (isl.) ....D 6
South East (point) ......D 6
Tamboritha (mt.) ....D 5
Tasman (sea) ....F 5
Tyrrell (lake) ....B 4
Venus (bay) ....C 6
Waranga (res). ....C 5
Waratah (bay) ....C 6
Wellington (lake) ....D 6
Western Port (inlet)......C 6
Wilsons (prom.) ....D 6
Wimmera (river) ....A 5
Yarra (river) ....C 5

AUSTRALIAN CAPITAL TERRITORY
Total Population 77,578

CITIES and TOWNS

Canberra (cap.), Australia
(E4) *56,449
Jervis Bay (F4) 527

PHYSICAL FEATURES

Saint George (head)(F4)

*Population of metropolitan area. †Population of urban area. ◉City and suburbs. ■In Sydney metropolitan area. ★In Greater Cessnock municipality.
‡In Melbourne metropolitan area, ☆In Ballarat urban area. •In Bendigo urban area. △In Geelong urban area. □In Latrobe Valley urban area.

IRRIGATION AREAS AND ARTESIAN BASINS IN AUSTRALIA

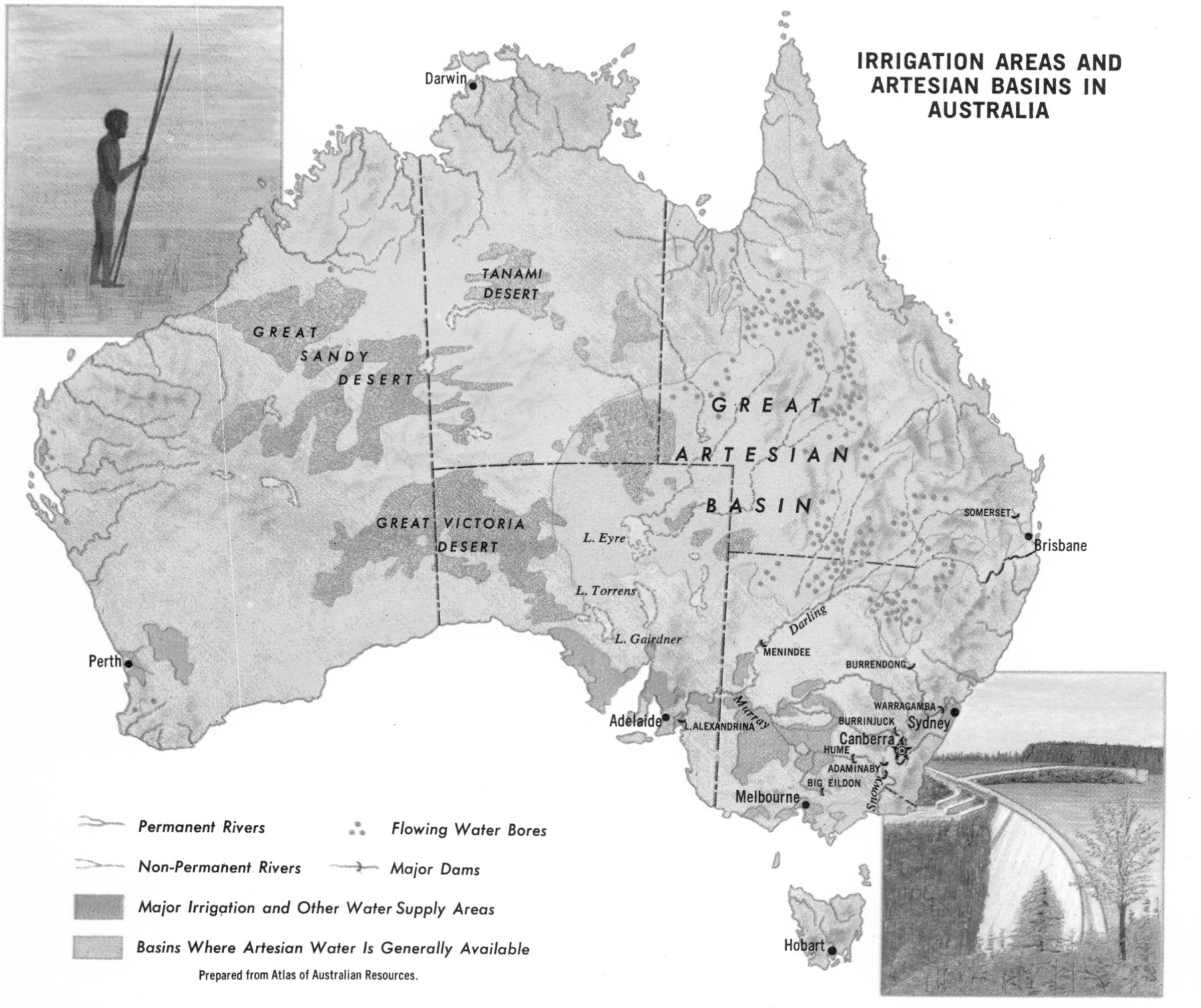

Darwin
TANAMI DESERT
GREAT SANDY DESERT
GREAT VICTORIA DESERT
GREAT ARTESIAN BASIN
L. Eyre
L. Torrens
L. Gairdner
Darling
Murray
Snowy
SOMERSET
Brisbane
MENINDEE
BURRENDONG
WARRAGAMBA
BURRINJUCK
Sydney
Canberra
HUME
ADAMINABY
BIG EILDON
Melbourne
Adelaide
L. ALEXANDRINA
Perth
Hobart

Permanent Rivers
Non-Permanent Rivers
Flowing Water Bores
Major Dams
Major Irrigation and Other Water Supply Areas
Basins Where Artesian Water Is Generally Available

Prepared from Atlas of Australian Resources.

TASMANIA

AREA 26,215 sq. mi.
POPULATION 373,640
CAPITAL Hobart
LARGEST CITY Hobart (greater) 118,828
HIGHEST POINT Mt. Ossa 5,305 ft.

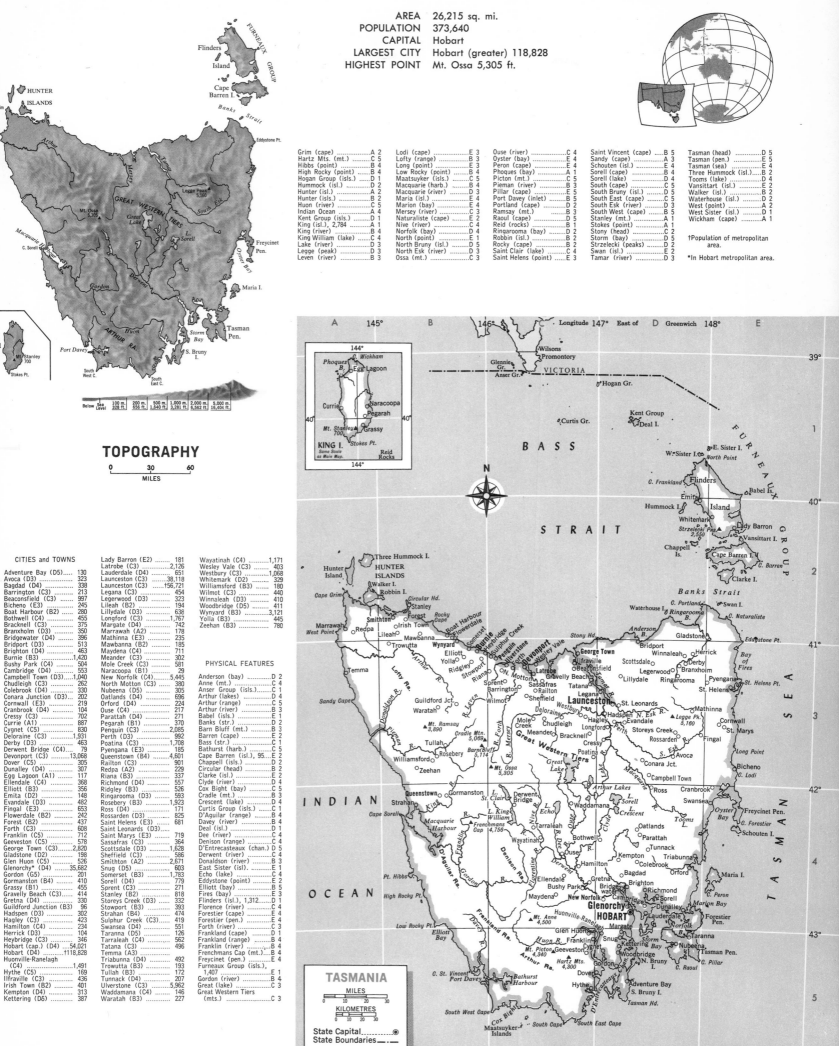

Grim (cape) ....A 2
Hartz Mts. (mt.) ......C 5
Hibbs (point) ....B 4
High Rocky (point) ...B 4
Hogan Group (isls.) ..D 1
Hummock (isl.) ....D 2
Hunter (isl.) ....A 2
Hunter (isls.) ....B 2
Huon (river) ....C 5
Indian Ocean ....A 4
Kent Group (isls.) .....D 1
King (isl.), 2,784 ....A 1
King (river) ....B 4
King William (lake) ...C 4
Lake (river) ....D 3
Legge (peak) ....D 3
Leven (river) ....B 3

Lodi (cape) ....E 3
Lofty (range) ....B 3
Long (point) ....E 3
Low Rocky (point) ....B 4
Maatsuyker (isls.) .....C 5
Macquarie (harb.) .....B 4
Macquarie (river) .....D 3
Maria (isl.) ....E 4
Marion (bay) ....E 4
Mersey (river) ....C 3
Naturaliste (cape) ....E 2
Nive (river) ....C 4
Norfolk (bay) ....D 4
North (point) ....E 1
North Bruny (isl.) .....D 5
North Esk (river) ......D 3
Ossa (mt.) ....C 3

Ouse (river) ....C 4
Oyster (bay) ....E 4
Peron (cape) ....E 4
Phoques (bay) ....C 1
Picton (mt.) ....C 5
Pieman (river) ....B 3
Pillar (cape) ....E 5
Port Davey (inlet) .....B 5
Portland (cape) ....D 2
Ramsay (mt.) ....B 3
Raoul (cape) ....D 5
Reid (rocks) ....B 1
Ringarooma (bay) ....D 2
Robbin (isl.) ....B 2
Rocky (cape) ....B 2
Saint Clair (lake) ......C 4
Saint Helens (point) ..E 3

Saint Vincent (cape) ..B 5
Sandy (cape) ....A 3
Schouten (isl.) ....E 4
Sorell (cape) ....B 4
Sorell (lake) ....D 4
South (cape) ....C 5
South Bruny (isl.) .....C 5
South East (cape) .....C 5
South Esk (river) ......D 3
South West (cape) ....B 5
Stanley (mt.) ....A 1
Stokes (point) ....A 1
Stony (head) ....C 2
Storm (bay) ....D 5
Strzelecki (peaks) ....D 2
Swan (isl.) ....E 2
Tamar (river) ....D 3

Tasman (head) ....D 5
Tasman (pen.) ....E 4
Tasman (sea) ....E 4
Three Hummock (isl.)..B 2
Tooms (lake) ....D 4
Vansittart (isl.) ....E 2
Walker (isl.) ....B 2
Waterhouse (isl.) .....D 2
West (point) ....A 2
West Sister (isl.) ......D 1
Wickham (cape) ......A 1

†Population of metropolitan
  area.

*In Hobart metropolitan area.

TOPOGRAPHY

0   30   60
MILES

CITIES and TOWNS

Adventure Bay (D5)	130
Avoca (D3)	323
Bagdad (D4)	338
Barrington (C3)	213
Beaconsfield (C3)	997
Bicheno (E3)	245
Boat Harbour (B2)	280
Bothwell (C4)	455
Bracknell (C3)	375
Branxholm (C3)	350
Bridgewater (D4)	396
Bridport (D3)	513
Brighton (D4)	463
Burnie (B3)	1,420
Bushy Park (C4)	504
Cambridge (D4)	553
Campbell Town (D3)	1,040
Chudleigh (C3)	262
Colebrook (D4)	330
Conara Junction (D3)	202
Cornwall (E3)	219
Cranbrook (D4)	104
Cressy (C3)	702
Currie (A1)	887
Cygnet (C5)	830
Deloraine (C3)	1,931
Derby (D3)	463
Derwent Bridge (C4)	79
Devonport (C3)	13,068
Dover (C5)	305
Dunalley (D4)	307
Egg Lagoon (A1)	117
Ellendale (C4)	368
Elliott (B3)	356
Emita (D2)	148
Evandale (D3)	482
Fingal (E3)	653
Flowerdale (B2)	242
Forest (B2)	437
Forth (C3)	608
Franklin (C5)	712
Geeveston (C5)	578
George Town (C3)	2,820
Gladstone (D2)	198
Glen Huon (C5)	526
Glenorchy* (D4)	35,682
Gordon (G5)	201
Gormanston (B4)	410
Grassy (B1)	455
Gravelly Beach (C3)	414
Gretna (C4)	330
Guildford Junction (B3)	96
Hadspen (C3)	302
Hagley (C3)	423
Hamilton (C4)	234
Herrick (D3)	104
Heybridge (C3)	346
Hobart (cap.) (D4)	54,021
Hobart (D4)	†118,828
Huonville-Ranelagh (C4)	1,491
Hythe (C5)	169
Ilfraville (C3)	436
Irish Town (B2)	401
Kempton (D4)	313
Kettering (D5)	387

Lady Barron (E2)	181
Latrobe (C3)	2,126
Lauderdale (D4)	651
Launceston (C3)	38,118
Launceston (C3)	†56,721
Legana (C3)	454
Legerwood (D3)	323
Lileah (B2)	194
Lillydale (D3)	638
Longford (D3)	1,767
Margate (D4)	742
Marrawah (A2)	178
Mathinna (E3)	235
Mawbanna (B2)	185
Maydena (C4)	711
Meander (C3)	302
Mole Creek (C3)	581
Naracoopa (B1)	29
New Norfolk (C4)	5,445
North Motton (C3)	380
Nubeena (D5)	305
Oatlands (D4)	696
Orford (D4)	224
Ouse (C4)	217
Parattah (D4)	271
Pegarah (B1)	370
Penguin (C3)	2,085
Perth (D3)	982
Poatina (C3)	1,708
Pyengana (E3)	185
Queenstown (B4)	4,601
Railton (C3)	901
Redpa (A2)	229
Riana (B3)	337
Richmond (D4)	557
Ridgley (B3)	526
Ringarooma (D3)	593
Rosebery (B3)	1,923
Ross (D4)	171
Rossarden (D3)	825
Saint Helens (E3)	681
Saint Leonards (D3)	
Saint Marys (E3)	719
Sassafras (C3)	364
Scottsdale (D3)	1,628
Sheffield (C3)	586
Smithton (A2)	2,671
Snug (D5)	603
Somerset (B3)	1,783
Sorell (D4)	779
Sprent (C3)	271
Stanley (B2)	818
Storeys Creek (D3)	332
Stowport (B3)	393
Strahan (B4)	474
Sulphur Creek (C3)	419
Swansea (D4)	551
Taranna (D5)	126
Tarraleah (C4)	562
Tatana (C3)	
Temma (A3)	
Triabunna (D4)	492
Trowutta (B3)	193
Tullah (B3)	172
Tunnack (D4)	207
Ulverstone (C3)	5,962
Waddamana (C4)	146
Waratah (B3)	227

Wayatinah (C4)	1,171
Wesley Vale (C3)	403
Westbury (C3)	1,068
Whitemark (D2)	329
Williamsford (B3)	180
Wilmot (B3)	440
Winnaleah (D3)	410
Woodbridge (D5)	411
Wynyard (B3)	3,121
Yolla (B3)	445
Zeehan (B3)	780

PHYSICAL FEATURES

Anderson (bay)	D 2
Anne (mt.)	C 4
Anser Group (isls.)	C 1
Arthur (lakes)	D 4
Arthur (range)	C 5
Arthur (river)	B 3
Babel (isls.)	E 1
Banks (str.)	D 2
Barn Bluff (mt.)	B 3
Barren (cape)	E 2
Bass (str.)	C 1
Bathurst (harb.)	B 4
Cape Barren (isl.), 95	E 2
Chappell (isls.)	D 2
Circular (head)	B 2
Clarke (isl.)	E 2
Clyde (river)	C 4
Cox Bight (bay)	C 5
Cradle (mt.)	B 3
Crescent (lake)	C 4
Curtis Group (isls.)	C 1
D'Aguilar (range)	B 4
Davey (river)	B 4
Deal (isl.)	D 1
Dee (river)	C 4
Denison (range)	C 4
D'Entrecasteaux (chan.)	D 5
Derwent (river)	C 4
Donaldson (river)	B 3
East Sister (isl.)	E 1
Echo (lake)	C 4
Eddystone (point)	E 2
Elliott (bay)	B 5
Fires (bay)	E 3
Flinders (isl.), 1,312	E 1
Florence (river)	C 4
Forestier (cape)	E 4
Forestier (pen.)	E 4
Forth (river)	C 3
Frankland (cape)	D 1
Frankland (range)	B 4
Franklin (river)	B 4
Frenchmans Cap (mt.)	B 4
Freycinet (pen.)	E 4
Furneaux Group (isls.)	E 1
	1,407	E 1
Gordon (lake)	B 4
Gordon (river)	B 4
Great (lake)	C 4
Great Western Tiers (mts.)	C 3

NEW ZEALAND

CONIC PROJECTION

SCALE OF MILES

SCALE OF KILOMETRES

Dominion Capital .... ☆
Provincial Capitals .... △
Provincial Boundaries .... _ _ _ _

Copyright by C. S. HAMMOND & CO., N.Y.

NEW ZEALAND

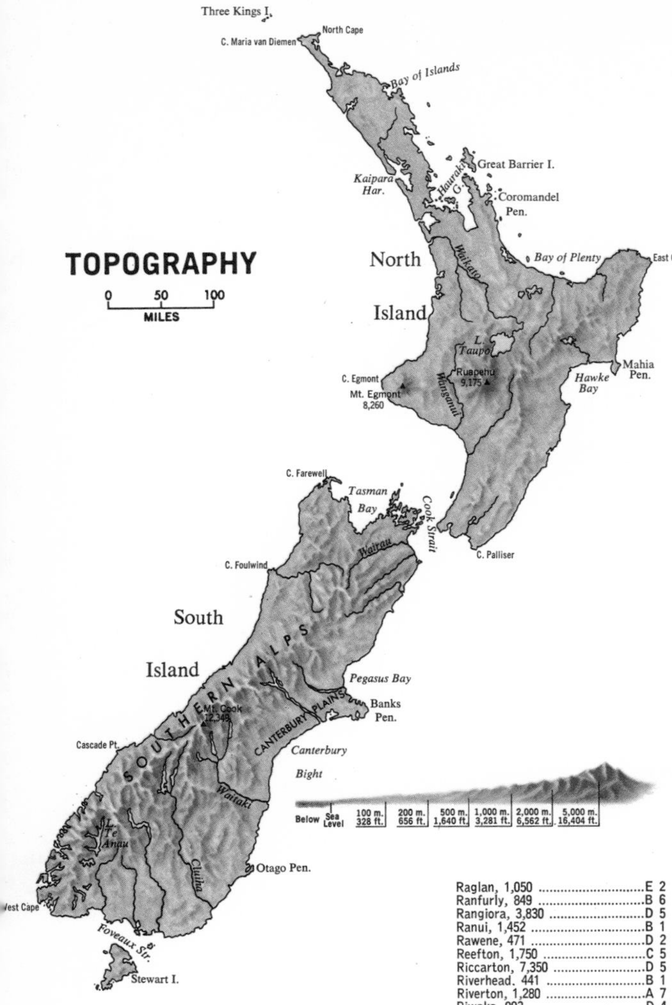

Three Kings I.
C. Maria van Diemen
North Cape
Bay of Islands
Great Barrier I.
Kaipara Har.
Hauraki G.
Coromandel Pen.
North
Island
Bay of Plenty
East Cape
Waikato
L. Taupo
Ruapehu 9,175
C. Egmont
Mt. Egmont 8,260
Wanganui
Mahia Pen.
Hawke Bay
C. Farewell
Tasman Bay
Cook Strait
Wairau
C. Palliser
C. Foulwind
South
Island
SOUTHERN ALPS
Pegasus Bay
Banks Pen.
Mt. Cook 12,349
CANTERBURY PLAINS
Canterbury Bight
Cascade Pt.
Waitaki
Anau
Clutha
Otago Pen.
West Cape
Foveaux Str.
Stewart I.
Below Sea Level
100 m. 328 ft.
200 m. 656 ft.
500 m. 1,640 ft.
1,000 m. 3,281 ft.
2,000 m. 6,562 ft.
5,000 m. 16,404 ft.

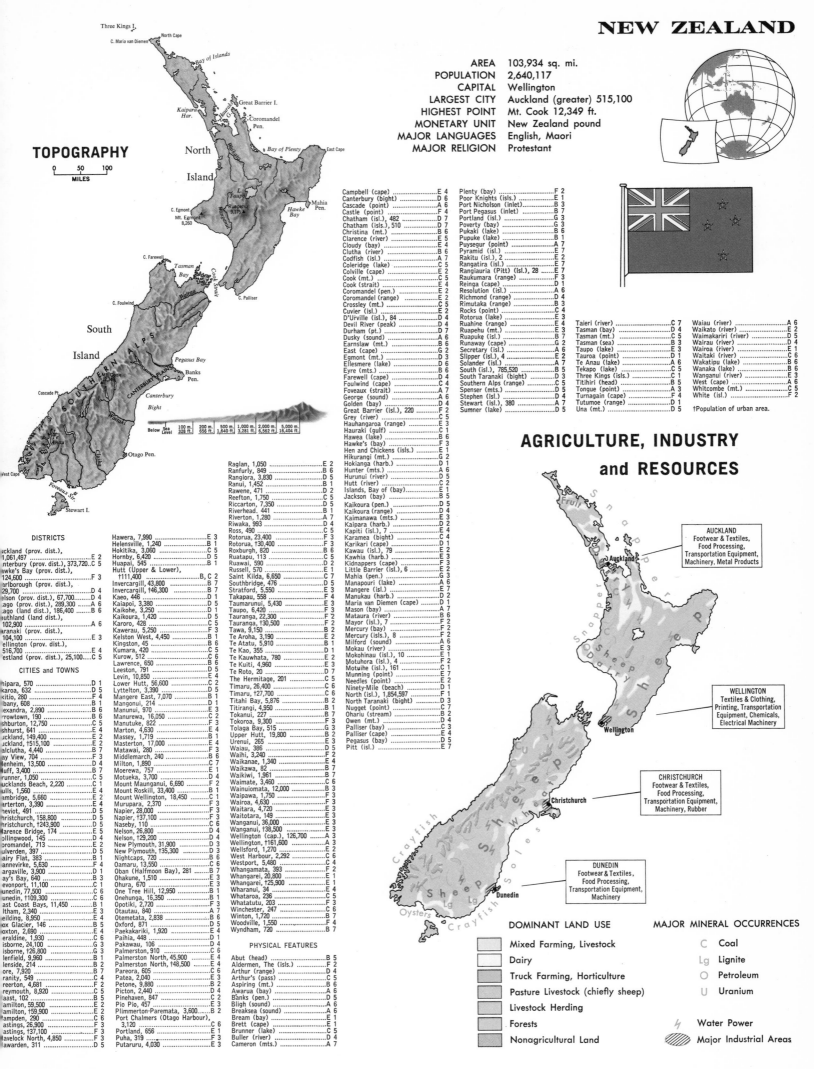

TOPOGRAPHY

0 50 100
MILES

AREA	103,934 sq. mi.
POPULATION	2,640,117
CAPITAL	Wellington
LARGEST CITY	Auckland (greater) 515,100
HIGHEST POINT	Mt. Cook 12,349 ft.
MONETARY UNIT	New Zealand pound
MAJOR LANGUAGES	English, Maori
MAJOR RELIGION	Protestant

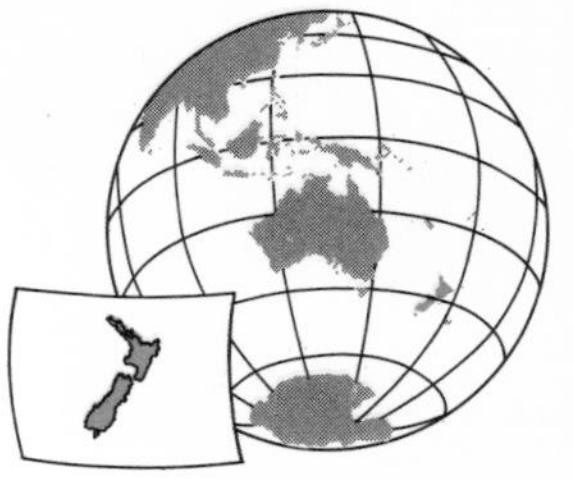

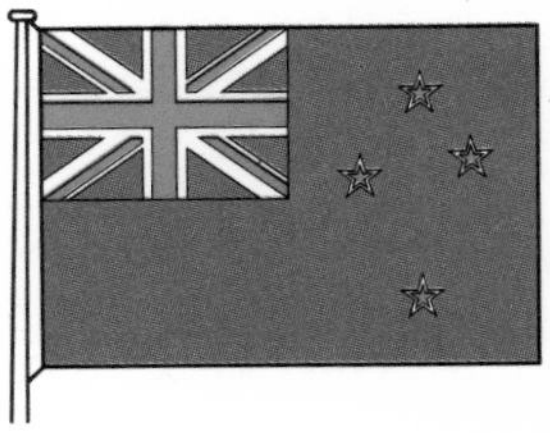

DISTRICTS

uckland (prov. dist.), 1,061,497 ... E 2
nterbury (prov. dist.), 373,720 .. C 5
awke's Bay (prov. dist.), 124,600 ... F 3
arlborough (prov. dist.), 29,700 ... D 4
elson (prov. dist.), 67,700 ... D 4
ago (prov. dist.), 289,300 ... A 6
ago (land dist.), 186,400 ... B 6
outhland (land dist.), 102,900 ... A 6
aranaki (prov. dist.), 104,100 ... E 3
ellington (prov. dist.), 516,700 ... E 4
estland (prov. dist.), 25,100 ... C 5

CITIES and TOWNS

hipara, 570 ... D 1
karoa, 632 ... D 5
kitio, 280 ... F 4
bany, 608 ... B 1
exandra, 2,890 ... B 6
rowtown, 190 ... B 6
shburton, 12,750 ... C 5
shhurst, 641 ... E 4
uckland, 149,400 ... E 2
uckland, †515,100 ... E 2
alclutha, 4,440 ... B 7
ay View, 704 ... F 3
enheim, 13,500 ... D 4
luff, 3,400 ... B 7
runner, 1,050 ... C 5
ucklands Beach, 2,220 ... C 1
ulls, 1,560 ... E 4
ambridge, 5,660 ... E 2
arterton, 3,390 ... E 4
heviot, 491 ... D 5
hristchurch, 158,800 ... D 5
hristchurch, †243,900 ... D 5
larence Bridge, 174 ... E 5
ollingwood, 145 ... D 4
oromandel, 713 ... E 2
ulverden, 397 ... D 5
airy Flat, 383 ... B 1
annevirke, 5,630 ... F 4
argaville, 3,900 ... D 1
ay's Bay, 640 ... B 3
evonport, 11,100 ... C 1
unedin, 77,500 ... C 6
unedin, †109,300 ... C 6
ast Coast Bays, 11,450 ... B 1
ltham, 2,340 ... E 3
eilding, 8,950 ... E 4
ox Glacier, 146 ... B 5
oxton, 2,690 ... E 4
eraldine, 1,930 ... C 6
isborne, 24,100 ... G 3
isborne, †26,800 ... G 3
lenfield, 9,960 ... B 1
lenside, 214 ... B 2
ore, 7,920 ... B 7
ranity, 549 ... C 4
reerton, 4,681 ... F 2
reymouth, 8,920 ... C 5
aast, 102 ... B 5
amilton, 59,500 ... E 2
amilton, †59,900 ... E 2
ampden, 290 ... C 6
astings, 26,900 ... F 3
astings, †37,100 ... F 3
avelock North, 4,850 ... F 3
awarden, 311 ... D 5
Hawera, 7,990 ... E 3
Helensville, 1,240 ... B 1
Hokitika, 3,060 ... C 5
Hornby, 6,420 ... D 5
Huapai, 545 ... B 1
Hutt (Upper & Lower), †111,400 ... B, C 2
Invercargill, 43,800 ... B 7
Invercargill, †46,300 ... B 7
Kaeo, 446 ... D 1
Kaiapoi, 3,380 ... D 5
Kaikohe, 3,250 ... D 1
Kaikoura, 1,420 ... D 5
Karoro, 428 ... C 5
Kawerau, 5,250 ... F 3
Kelston West, 4,450 ... B 1
Kingston, 45 ... B 6
Kumara, 420 ... C 5
Kurow, 512 ... C 6
Lawrence, 650 ... B 6
Leeston, 791 ... D 5
Levin, 10,850 ... E 4
Lower Hutt, 56,600 ... C 2
Lyttelton, 3,390 ... D 5
Mangere East, 7,070 ... B 1
Mangonui, 214 ... D 1
Manunui, 970 ... E 3
Manurewa, 16,050 ... C 2
Manutuke, 822 ... F 3
Marton, 4,630 ... E 4
Massey, 1,719 ... B 1
Masterton, 17,000 ... E 4
Matawai, 280 ... F 3
Middlemarch, 240 ... B 6
Milton, 1,890 ... C 7
Moerewa, 757 ... E 1
Motueka, 3,700 ... D 4
Mount Maunganui, 6,690 ... F 2
Mount Roskill, 33,400 ... B 1
Mount Wellington, 18,450 ... C 1
Murupara, 2,370 ... F 3
Napier, 28,000 ... F 3
Napier, †37,100 ... F 3
Naseby, 110 ... C 6
Nelson, 26,800 ... D 4
Nelson, †29,200 ... D 4
New Plymouth, 31,900 ... D 3
New Plymouth, †35,300 ... D 3
Nightcaps, 720 ... B 6
Oamaru, 13,550 ... C 6
Oban (Halfmoon Bay), 281 ... B 7
Ohakune, 1,510 ... E 3
Ohura, 670 ... E 3
One Tree Hill, 12,950 ... B 1
Onehunga, 16,350 ... B 1
Opotiki, 2,720 ... F 3
Otautau, 840 ... A 7
Otemetata, 2,838 ... B 6
Oxford, 871 ... D 5
Paekakariki, 1,920 ... E 4
Paihia, 448 ... D 1
Pakawau, 106 ... D 4
Palmerston, 910 ... C 6
Palmerston North, 45,900 ... E 4
Palmerston North, †48,500 ... E 4
Pareora, 605 ... C 6
Patea, 2,040 ... E 3
Petone, 9,880 ... B 2
Picton, 2,440 ... D 4
Pinehaven, 847 ... C 2
Pio Pio, 457 ... E 3
Plimmerton-Paremata, 3,600 ... B 2
Port Chalmers (Otago Harbour), 3,120 ... C 6
Portland, 656 ... E 1
Puha, 319 ... F 3
Putaruru, 4,030 ... E 3
Raglan, 1,050 ... E 2
Ranfurly, 849 ... B 6
Rangiora, 3,830 ... D 5
Ranui, 1,452 ... B 1
Rawene, 471 ... D 2
Reefton, 1,750 ... C 5
Riccarton, 7,350 ... D 5
Riverhead. 441 ... B 1
Riverton, 1,280 ... A 7
Riwaka, 993 ... D 4
Ross, 490 ... C 5
Rotorua, 23,400 ... F 3
Rotorua, †30,400 ... F 3
Roxburgh, 820 ... B 6
Ruatapu, 113 ... C 5
Ruawai, 590 ... D 2
Russell, 570 ... E 1
Saint Kilda, 6,650 ... C 7
Southbridge, 476 ... D 5
Stratford, 5,550 ... E 3
Takapau, 558 ... F 4
Taumarunui, 5,430 ... E 3
Taupo, 6,420 ... F 3
Tauranga, 22,300 ... F 2
Tauranga, †30,500 ... F 2
Tawa, 9,150 ... B 2
Te Aroha, 3,190 ... E 2
Te Atatu, 5,910 ... B 1
Te Kao, 355 ... D 1
Te Kauwhata, 780 ... E 2
Te Kuiti, 4,960 ... E 3
Te Roto, 20 ... D 7
The Hermitage, 201 ... C 5
Timaru, 26,400 ... C 6
Timaru, †27,700 ... C 6
Titahi Bay, 5,876 ... B 2
Titirangi, 4,950 ... B 1
Tokanui, 227 ... B 7
Tokoroa, 9,300 ... F 3
Tolaga Bay, 515 ... G 3
Upper Hutt, 19,800 ... B 2
Urenui, 265 ... E 3
Waiau, 386 ... D 5
Waihi, 3,240 ... F 2
Waikanae, 1,340 ... E 4
Waikawa, 82 ... B 7
Waikiwi, 1,961 ... B 7
Waimate, 3,460 ... C 6
Wainuiomata, 12,000 ... B 3
Waipawa, 1,750 ... F 3
Wairoa, 4,630 ... F 3
Waitara, 4,720 ... E 3
Waitotara, 149 ... E 3
Wanganui, 36,000 ... E 3
Wanganui, †38,500 ... E 3
Wellington (cap.), 126,700 ... A 3
Wellington, †161,600 ... A 3
Wellsford, 1,270 ... E 2
West Harbour, 2,292 ... C 6
Westport, 5,480 ... C 4
Whangamata, 393 ... F 2
Whangarei, 20,800 ... E 1
Whangarei, †25,900 ... E 1
Wharanui, 34 ... E 4
Whataroa, 236 ... C 5
Whatatutu, 203 ... F 3
Winchester, 247 ... C 6
Winton, 1,720 ... B 7
Woodville, 1,550 ... F 4
Wyndham, 720 ... B 7

PHYSICAL FEATURES

Abut (head) ... B 5
Aldermen, The (isls.) ... F 2
Arthur (range) ... D 4
Arthur's (pass) ... C 5
Aspiring (mt.) ... B 6
Awarua (bay) ... A 6
Banks (pen.) ... D 5
Bligh (sound) ... A 6
Breaksea (sound) ... A 6
Bream (bay) ... E 1
Brett (cape) ... E 1
Brunner (lake) ... C 5
Buller (river) ... D 4
Cameron (mts.) ... A 7
Campbell (cape) ... E 4
Canterbury (bight) ... D 6
Cascade (point) ... A 6
Castle (point) ... F 4
Chatham (isl.), 482 ... D 7
Chatham (isls.), 510 ... D 7
Christina (mt.) ... B 6
Clarence (river) ... E 5
Cloudy (bay) ... E 4
Clutha (river) ... B 6
Codfish (isl.) ... A 7
Coleridge (lake) ... C 5
Colville (cape) ... E 2
Cook (mt.) ... C 5
Cook (strait) ... E 4
Coromandel (pen.) ... E 2
Coromandel (range) ... E 2
Crossley (mt.) ... C 5
Cuvier (isl.) ... E 2
D'Urville (isl.), 84 ... D 4
Devil River (peak) ... D 4
Durham (pt.) ... D 7
Dusky (sound) ... A 6
Earnslaw (mt.) ... B 6
East (cape) ... G 2
Egmont (mt.) ... D 3
Ellesmere (lake) ... D 6
Eyre (mts.) ... B 6
Farewell (cape) ... D 4
Foulwind (cape) ... C 4
Foveaux (strait) ... A 7
George (sound) ... A 6
Golden (bay) ... D 4
Great Barrier (isl.), 220 ... F 2
Grey (river) ... C 5
Hauhangaroa (range) ... E 3
Hauraki (gulf) ... C 1
Hawea (lake) ... B 6
Hawke's (bay) ... F 3
Hen and Chickens (isls.) ... E 1
Hikurangi (mt.) ... G 2
Hokianga (harb.) ... D 1
Hunter (mts.) ... A 6
Hurunui (river) ... D 5
Hutt (river) ... C 2
Islands, Bay of (bay) ... E 1
Jackson (bay) ... B 5
Kaikoura (pen.) ... D 5
Kaikoura (range) ... D 4
Kaimanawa (mts.) ... E 3
Kaipara (harb.) ... D 2
Kapiti (isl.), 7 ... E 4
Karamea (bight) ... C 4
Karikari (cape) ... D 1
Kawau (isl.), 79 ... E 2
Kawhia (harb.) ... E 3
Kidnappers (cape) ... F 3
Little Barrier (isl.), 6 ... E 2
Mahia (pen.) ... G 3
Manapouri (lake) ... A 6
Mangere (isl.) ... E 7
Manukau (harb.) ... D 2
Maria van Diemen (cape) ... D 1
Mason (bay) ... A 7
Mataura (river) ... B 6
Mayor (isl.), 7 ... F 2
Mercury (bay) ... F 2
Mercury (isls.), 8 ... F 2
Milford (sound) ... A 6
Mokau (river) ... E 3
Mokohinau (isl.), 10 ... E 1
Motuhora (isl.), 4 ... F 2
Motuihe (isl.), 161 ... C 1
Munning (point) ... E 7
Needles (point) ... E 2
Ninety-Mile (beach) ... D 1
North (isl.), 1,854,597 ... F 1
North Taranaki (bight) ... D 3
Nugget (point) ... C 7
Ohariu (stream) ... B 2
Owen (mt.) ... D 4
Palliser (bay) ... C 3
Palliser (cape) ... E 4
Pegasus (bay) ... D 5
Pitt (isl.) ... E 7
Plenty (bay) ... F 2
Poor Knights (isls.) ... E 1
Port Nicholson (inlet) ... B 3
Port Pegasus (inlet) ... B 7
Portland (isl.) ... G 3
Poverty (bay) ... G 3
Pukaki (lake) ... B 6
Pupuke (lake) ... B 1
Puysegur (point) ... A 7
Pyramid (isl.) ... E 7
Rakitu (isl.), 2 ... E 2
Rangatira (isl.) ... E 7
Rangiauria (Pitt) (isl.), 28 ... E 7
Raukumara (range) ... F 3
Reinga (cape) ... D 1
Resolution (isl.) ... A 6
Richmond (range) ... D 4
Rimutaka (range) ... B 3
Rocks (point) ... C 4
Rotorua (lake) ... E 3
Ruahine (range) ... E 4
Ruapehu (mt.) ... E 3
Ruapuke (isl.) ... B 7
Runaway (cape) ... G 2
Secretary (isl.) ... A 6
Slipper (isl.), 4 ... E 2
Solander (isl.) ... A 7
South (isl.), 785,520 ... B 5
South Taranaki (bight) ... D 3
Southern Alps (range) ... C 5
Spenser (mts.) ... D 5
Stephen (isl.) ... D 4
Stewart (isl.), 380 ... A 7
Sumner (lake) ... D 5
Taieri (river) ... C 7
Tasman (bay) ... D 4
Tasman (mt.) ... C 5
Tasman (sea) ... B 3
Taupo (lake) ... E 3
Tauroa (point) ... D 1
Te Anau (lake) ... A 6
Tekapo (lake) ... C 5
Three Kings (isls.) ... C 1
Titihiri (head) ... B 5
Tongue (point) ... A 3
Turnagain (cape) ... F 4
Tutumoe (range) ... D 1
Una (mt.) ... D 5
Waiau (river) ... A 6
Waikato (river) ... E 2
Waimakariri (river) ... D 5
Wairau (river) ... D 4
Wairoa (river) ... E 1
Waitaki (river) ... C 6
Wakatipu (lake) ... B 6
Wanaka (lake) ... B 6
Wanganui (river) ... E 3
West (cape) ... A 6
Whitcombe (mt.) ... C 5
White (isl.) ... F 2

†Population of urban area.

AGRICULTURE, INDUSTRY and RESOURCES

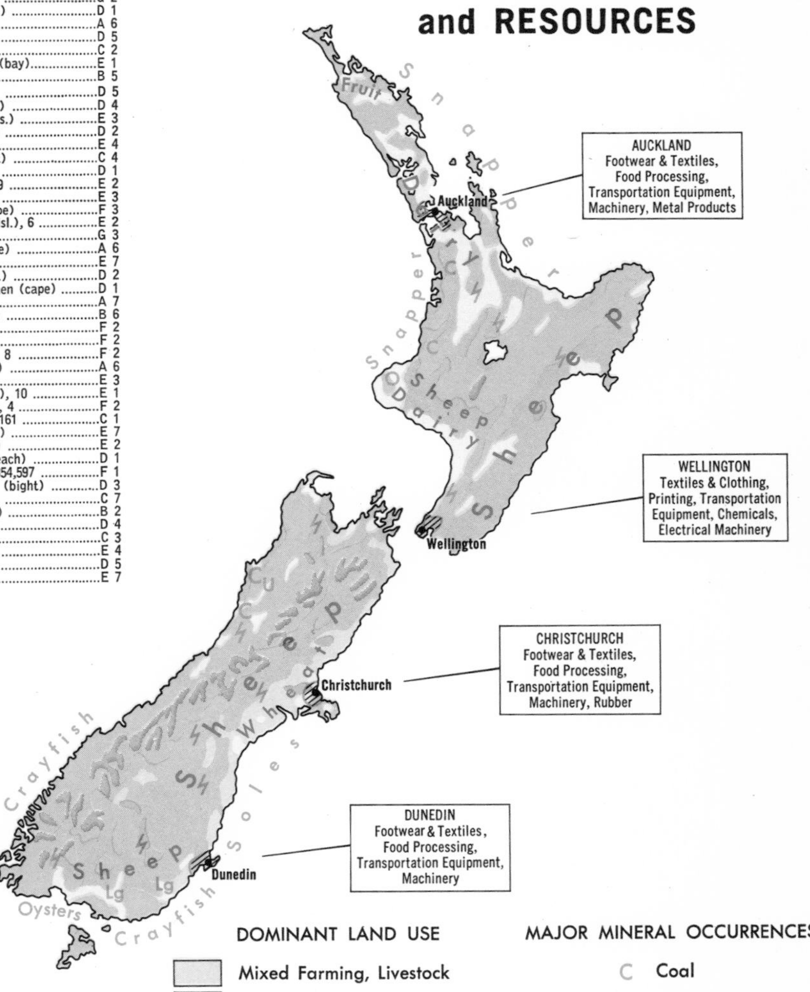

AUCKLAND
Footwear & Textiles, Food Processing, Transportation Equipment, Machinery, Metal Products
Auckland
WELLINGTON
Textiles & Clothing, Printing, Transportation Equipment, Chemicals, Electrical Machinery
Wellington
CHRISTCHURCH
Footwear & Textiles, Food Processing, Transportation Equipment, Machinery, Rubber
Christchurch
DUNEDIN
Footwear & Textiles, Food Processing, Transportation Equipment, Machinery
Dunedin
Fruit
Snapper
Sheep
Dairy
Wheat
Crayfish
Soles
Oysters

DOMINANT LAND USE

- Mixed Farming, Livestock
- Dairy
- Truck Farming, Horticulture
- Pasture Livestock (chiefly sheep)
- Livestock Herding
- Forests
- Nonagricultural Land

MAJOR MINERAL OCCURRENCES

- C Coal
- Lg Lignite
- O Petroleum
- U Uranium
- Water Power
- Major Industrial Areas

AFRICA

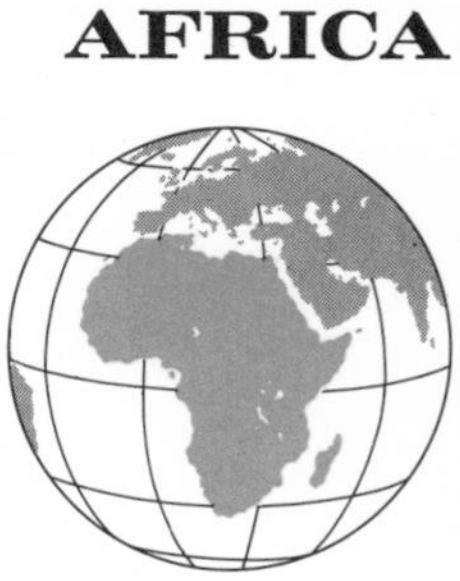

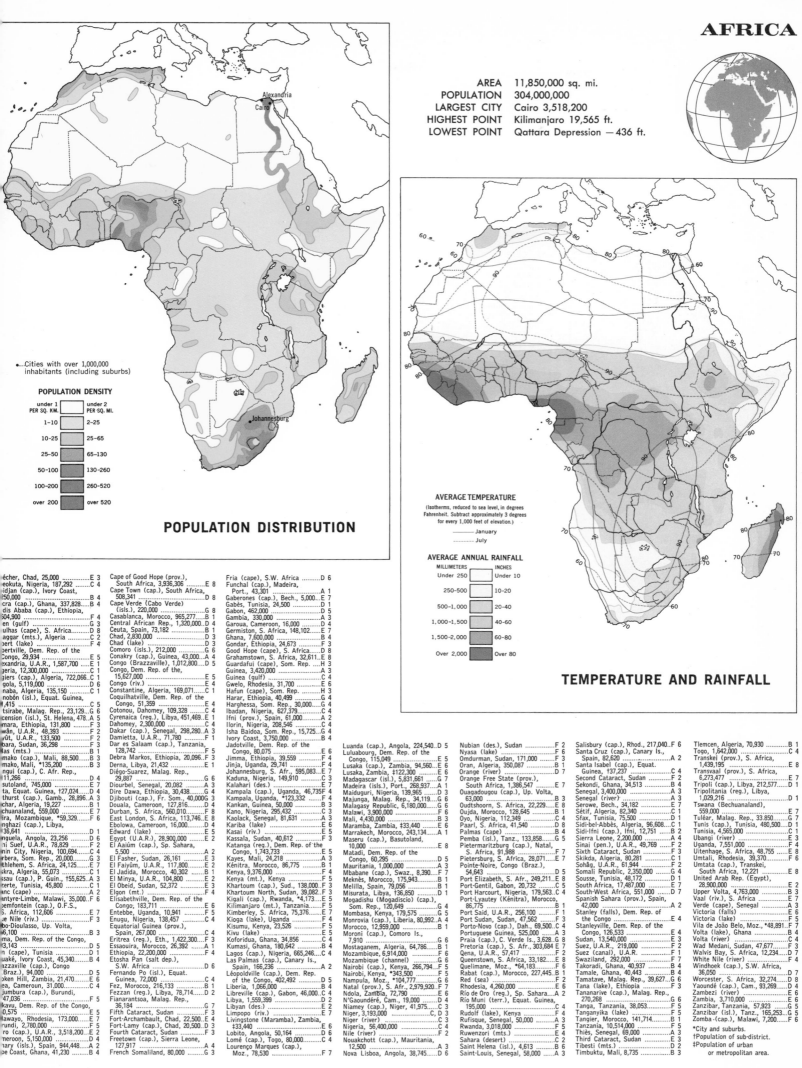

AREA	11,850,000 sq. mi.
POPULATION	304,000,000
LARGEST CITY	Cairo 3,518,200
HIGHEST POINT	Kilimanjaro 19,565 ft.
LOWEST POINT	Qattara Depression —436 ft.

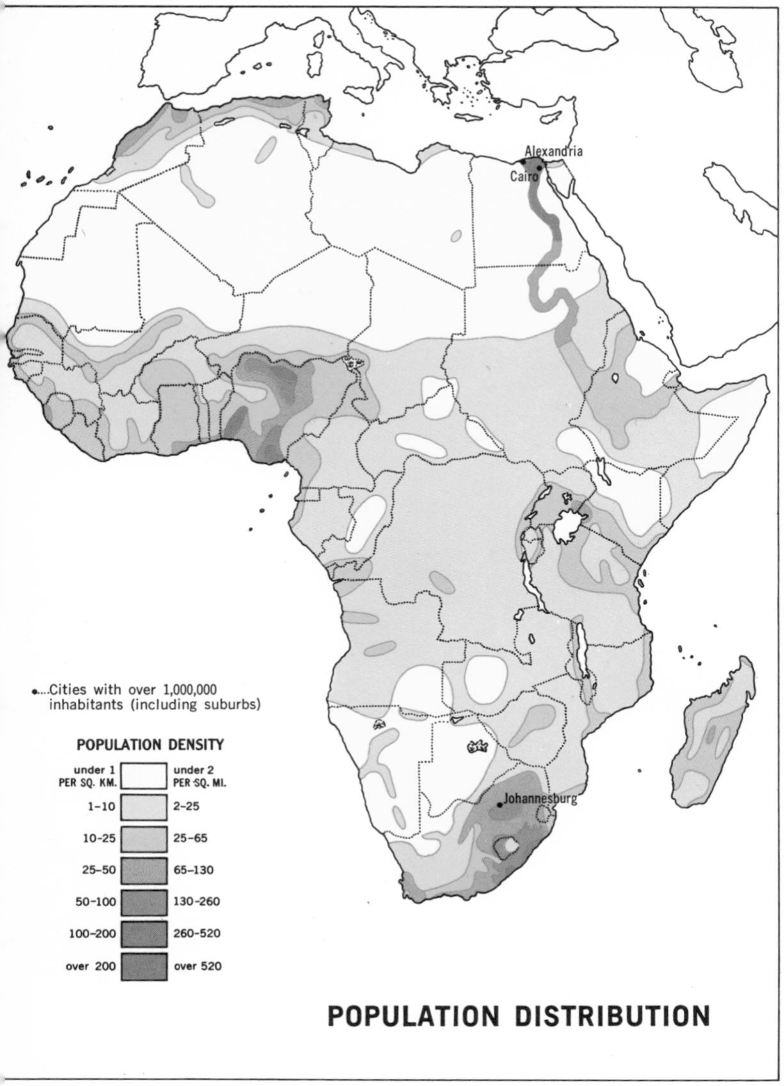
Alexandria
Cairo
Johannesburg
•...Cities with over 1,000,000 inhabitants (including suburbs)
POPULATION DENSITY
under 1 PER SQ. KM. — under 2 PER SQ. MI.
1-10 — 2-25
10-25 — 25-65
25-50 — 65-130
50-100 — 130-260
100-200 — 260-520
over 200 — over 520

POPULATION DISTRIBUTION

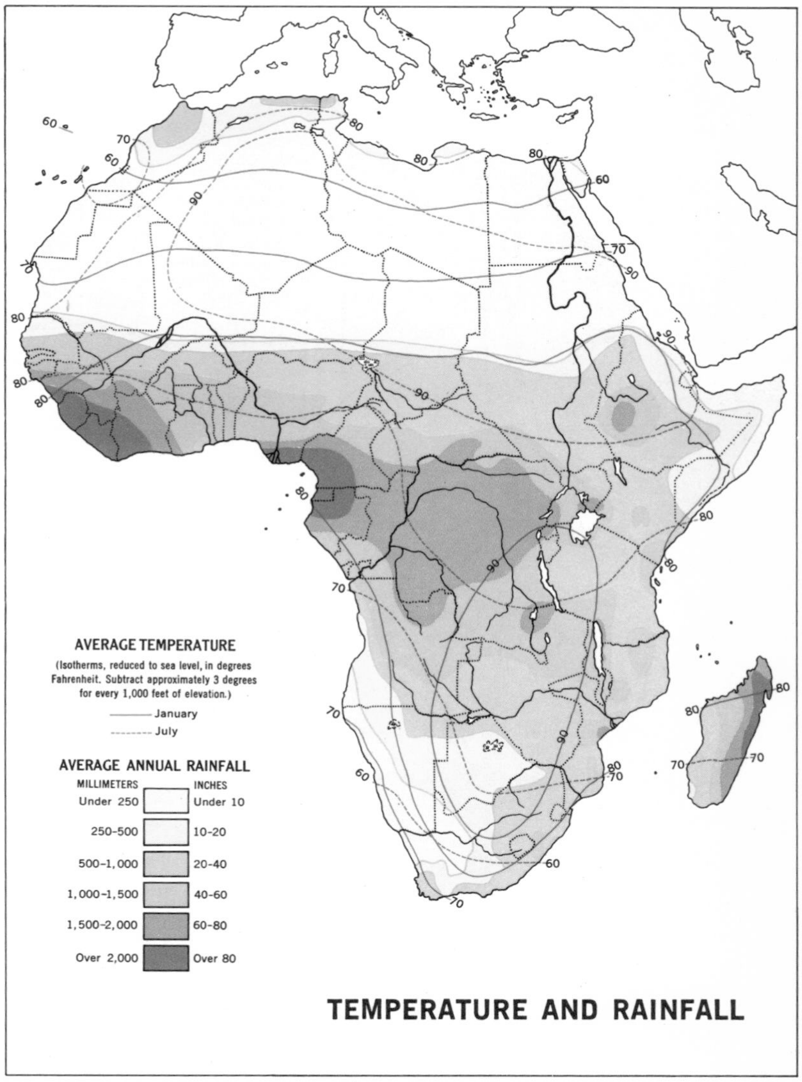
AVERAGE TEMPERATURE
(Isotherms, reduced to sea level, in degrees Fahrenheit. Subtract approximately 3 degrees for every 1,000 feet of elevation.)
January
July
AVERAGE ANNUAL RAINFALL
MILLIMETERS — INCHES
Under 250 — Under 10
250-500 — 10-20
500-1,000 — 20-40
1,000-1,500 — 40-60
1,500-2,000 — 60-80
Over 2,000 — Over 80

TEMPERATURE AND RAINFALL

échen, Chad, 25,000 ....E 3
eokuta, Nigeria, 187,292 ....C 4
idjan (cap.), Ivory Coast,
250,000 ....B 4
cra (cap.), Ghana, 337,828.....B 4
dis Ababa (cap.), Ethiopia,
504,900 ....F 4
en (gulf) ....G 3
ulhas (cape), S. Africa..........D 8
aggar (mts.), Algeria ....C 2
bert (lake) ....F 4
bertville, Dem. Rep. of the
Congo, 29,934 ....E 5
exandria, U.A.R., 1,587,700 .....E 1
geria, 12,300,000 ....C 1
giers (cap.), Algeria, 722,066..C 1
gola, 5,119,000 ....D 6
naba, Algeria, 135,150 ....C 1
nobón (isl.), Equat. Guinea,
,415 ....C 5
tsirabe, Malag. Rep., 23,129...G 6
cension (isl.), St. Helena, 478..A 5
mara, Ethiopia, 131,800 ....F 3
wân, U.A.R., 48,393 ....F 2
yût, U.A.R., 133,500 ....F 2
bara, Sudan, 36,298 ....F 3
las (mts.) ....B 1
mako (cap.), Mali, 88,500......B 3
mako, Mali, *135,200 ....B 3
ngui (cap.), C. Afr. Rep.,
111,266 ....D 4
sutoland, 745,000 ....E 7
ta, Equat. Guinea, †27,024......D 4
thurst (cap.), Gamb., 28,896..A 3
char, Algeria, 19,227 ....B 1
chuanaland, 559,000 ....E 7
ira, Mozambique, *59,329.......F 6
nghazi (cap.), Libya,
136,641 ....D 1
nguela, Angola, 23,256 ....D 6
ni Suef, U.A.R., 78,829 ....F 2
nin City, Nigeria, 100,694.......C 4
rbera, Som. Rep., 20,000.........G 3
thlehem, S. Africa, 24,125.......E 7
skra, Algeria, 55,073 ....C 1
ssau (cap.), P. Guin., †55,625..A 3
zerte, Tunisia, 45,800 ....C 1
anc (cape) ....A 2
antyre-Limbe, Malawi, 35,000..F 6
oemfontein (cap.), O.F.S.,
S. Africa, 112,606 ....E 7
ue Nile (riv.) ....F 3
bo-Dioulasso, Up. Volta,
6,100 ....B 3
ma, Dem. Rep. of the Congo,
3,143 ....D 5
n (cape), Tunisia ....D 1
uaké, Ivory Coast, 45,340........B 4
azzaville (cap.), Congo
(Braz.), 94,000 ....D 5
oken Hill, Zambia, 21,470........E 6
ea, Cameroun, 31,000..............C 4
jumbura (cap.), Burundi,
47,036 ....F 5
kavu, Dem. Rep. of the Congo,
0,575 ....E 5
lawayo, Rhodesia, 173,000......E 7
rundi, 2,780,000 ....F 5
ro (cap.), U.A.R., 3,518,200...E 2
meroon, 5,150,000 ....D 4
nary (isls.), Spain, 944,448.....A 2
pe Coast, Ghana, 41,230 ....B 4
Cape of Good Hope (prov.),
South Africa, 3,936,306 ....E 8
Cape Town (cap.), South Africa,
508,341 ....D 8
Cape Verde (Cabo Verde)
(isls.), 220,000 ....G 8
Casablanca, Morocco, 965,277.....B 1
Central African Rep., 1,320,000..D 4
Ceuta, Spain, 73,182 ....B 1
Chad, 2,830,000 ....D 3
Chad (lake) ....D 3
Comoro (isls.), 212,000 ....G 6
Conakry (cap.), Guinea, 43,000...A 4
Congo (Brazzaville), 1,012,800....D 5
Congo, Dem. Rep. of the,
15,627,000 ....E 5
Congo (riv.) ....E 4
Constantine, Algeria, 169,071......C 1
Coquilhatville, Dem. Rep. of the
Congo, 51,359 ....E 4
Cotonou, Dahomey, 109,328 ....C 4
Cyrenaica (reg.), Libya, 451,469..E 1
Dahomey, 2,300,000 ....C 4
Dakar (cap.), Senegal, 298,280..A 3
Damietta, U.A.R., 71,780 ....F 1
Dar es Salaam (cap.), Tanzania,
128,742 ....F 5
Debra Markos, Ethiopia, 20,096..F 3
Derna, Libya, 21,432 ....E 1
Diégo-Suarez, Malag. Rep.,
29,887 ....G 6
Diourbel, Senegal, 20,082 ....A 3
Dire Dawa, Ethiopia, 30,438........G 4
Djibouti (cap.), Fr. Som., 40,000G 3
Douala, Cameroon, 127,816.........D 4
Durban, S. Africa, 560,010..........F 8
East London, S. Africa, 113,746..E 8
Ebolowa, Cameroon, 16,000.........D 4
Edward (lake) ....E 5
Egypt (U.A.R.), 28,900,000 ....E 2
El Aaiúm (cap.), Sp. Sahara,
5,500 ....A 2
El Fasher, Sudan, 26,161 ....E 3
El Faiyûm, U.A.R., 117,800.........E 2
El Jadida, Morocco, 40,302 ....B 1
El Minya, U.A.R., 104,800 ....E 2
El Obeid, Sudan, 52,372 ....E 3
Elgon (mt.) ....F 4
Elisabethville, Dem. Rep. of the
Congo, 183,711 ....E 6
Entebbe, Uganda, 10,941 ....F 5
Enugu, Nigeria, 138,457 ....C 4
Equatorial Guinea (prov.),
Spain, 267,000 ....C 4
Eritrea (reg.), Eth., 1,422,300....F 3
Essaouira, Morocco, 26,392 ....A 1
Ethiopia, 22,200,000 ....F 4
Etosha Pan (salt dep.),
S.W. Africa ....D 6
Fernando Po (isl.), Equat.
Guinea, 72,000 ....C 4
Fez, Morocco, 216,133 ....B 1
Fezzan (reg.), Libya, 78,714......D 2
Fianarantsoa, Malag. Rep.,
36,184 ....G 7
Fifth Cataract, Sudan ....F 3
Fort-Archambault, Chad, 22,500..E 4
Fort-Lamy (cap.), Chad, 20,500..D 3
Fourth Cataract, Sudan ....F 3
Freetown (cap.), Sierra Leone,
127,917 ....A 4
French Somaliland, 80,000 ....G 3
Fria (cape), S.W. Africa ....D 6
Funchal (cap.), Madeira,
Port., 43,301 ....A 1
Gaberones (cap.), Bech., 5,000...E 7
Gabès, Tunisia, 24,500 ....D 1
Gabon, 462,000 ....D 5
Gambia, 330,000 ....A 3
Garoua, Cameroon, 16,000 ....D 4
Germiston, S. Africa, 148,102......E 7
Ghana, 7,600,000 ....B 4
Gondar, Ethiopia, 24,673 ....F 3
Good Hope (cape), S. Africa......D 8
Grahamstown, S. Africa, 32,611..E 8
Guardafui (cape), Som. Rep. ....H 3
Guinea, 3,420,000 ....A 3
Guinea (gulf) ....C 4
Gwelo, Rhodesia, 31,700 ....E 6
Hafun (cape), Som. Rep. ....H 3
Harar, Ethiopia, 40,499 ....G 4
Harghessa, Som. Rep., 30,000.....G 4
Ibadan, Nigeria, 627,379............C 4
Ifni (prov.), Spain, 61,000..........A 2
Ilorin, Nigeria, 208,546 ....C 4
Isha Baidoa, Som. Rep., 15,725...G 4
Ivory Coast, 3,750,000 ....B 4
Jadotville, Dem. Rep. of the
Congo, 80,075 ....E 6
Jimma, Ethiopia, 39,559 ....F 4
Jinja, Uganda, 29,741 ....F 4
Johannesburg, S. Afr., 595,083...E 7
Kaduna, Nigeria, 149,910 ....C 3
Kalahari (des.) ....E 7
Kampala (cap.), Uganda, 46,735F 4
Kampala, Uganda, *123,332 ....F 4
Kankan, Guinea, 50,000 ....B 3
Kano, Nigeria, 295,432 ....C 3
Kaolack, Senegal, 81,631 ....A 3
Kariba (lake) ....E 6
Kasai (riv.) ....E 5
Kassala, Sudan, 40,612 ....F 3
Katanga (reg.), Dem. Rep. of the
Congo, 1,743,733 ....E 5
Kayes, Mali, 24,218 ....A 3
Kénitra, Morocco, 86,775 ....B 1
Kenya, 9,376,000 ....F 4
Kenya (mt.), Kenya ....F 5
Khartoum (cap.), Sud., 138,000..F 3
Khartoum North, Sudan, 39,082..F 3
Kigali (cap.), Rwanda, *4,173....E 5
Kilimanjaro (mt.), Tanzania.......F 5
Kimberley, S. Africa, 75,376.......E 7
Kioga (lake), Uganda ....F 4
Kisumu, Kenya, 23,526 ....F 5
Kivu (lake) ....E 5
Koforidua, Ghana, 34,856 ....C 4
Kumasi, Ghana, 180,642 ....B 4
Lagos (cap.), Nigeria, 665,246....C 4
Las Palmas (cap.), Canary Is.,
Spain, 166,236 ....A 2
Léopoldville (cap.), Dem. Rep.
of the Congo, 402,492 ....D 5
Liberia, 1,066,000 ....B 4
Libreville (cap.), Gabon, 46,000..C 4
Libya, 1,559,399 ....D 2
Libyan (des.) ....E 2
Limpopo (riv.) ....E 7
Livingstone (Maramba), Zambia,
‡33,440 ....E 6
Lobito, Angola, 50,164 ....D 6
Lomé (cap.), Togo, 80,000..........C 4
Lourenço Marques (cap.),
Moz., 78,530 ....F 7
Luanda (cap.), Angola, 224,540..D 5
Luluabourg, Dem. Rep. of the
Congo, 115,049 ....E 5
Lusaka (cap.), Zambia, 94,560...E 6
Lusaka, Zambia, ‡122,300 ....E 6
Madagascar (isl.), 5,831,661 ......G 7
Madeira (isls.), Port., 268,937....A 1
Maiduguri, Nigeria, 139,965 ....D 3
Majunga, Malag. Rep., 34,119....G 6
Malagasy Republic, 6,180,000......G 6
Malawi, 3,900,000 ....F 6
Mali, 4,430,000 ....B 3
Maramba, Zambia, ‡33,440 ....E 6
Marrakech, Morocco, 243,134......A 1
Maseru (cap.), Basutoland,
10,000 ....E 8
Matadi, Dem. Rep. of the
Congo, 60,295 ....D 5
Mauritania, 1,000,000 ....A 3
Mbabane (cap.), Swaz., 8,390....F 7
Meknès, Morocco, 175,943...........B 1
Melilla, Spain, 79,056 ....B 1
Misurata, Libya, †36,850 ....D 1
Mogadishu (Mogadiscio) (cap.),
Som. Rep., 120,649 ....G 4
Mombasa, Kenya, 179,575 ....G 5
Monrovia (cap.), Liberia, 80,992..A 4
Morocco, 12,959,000 ....B 1
Moroni (cap.), Comoro Is.,
7,910 ....G 6
Mostaganem, Algeria, 64,786......B 1
Mozambique, 6,914,000 ....F 6
Mozambique (channel) ....G 6
Nairobi (cap.), Kenya, 266,794...F 5
Nairobi, Kenya, *343,500 ....F 5
Nampula, Moz., *104,777............G 6
Natal (prov.), S. Afr., 2,979,920..F 7
Ndola, Zambia, 72,790 ....E 6
N'Gaoundéré, Cam., 19,000 ....D 4
Niamey (cap.), Niger, 41,975......C 3
Niger, 3,193,000 ....C, D 3
Niger (river) ....C 3
Nigeria, 56,400,000 ....C 4
Nile (river) ....F 2
Nouakchott (cap.), Mauritania,
12,500 ....A 3
Nova Lisboa, Angola, 38,745......D 6
Nubian (des.), Sudan ....F 2
Nyasa (lake) ....F 6
Omdurman, Sudan, 171,000 ....F 3
Oran, Algeria, 350,087 ....B 1
Orange (river) ....D 7
Orange Free State (prov.),
South Africa, 1,386,547 ....E 7
Ouagadougou (cap.), Up. Volta,
63,000 ....B 3
Oudtshoorn, S. Africa, 22,229.....E 8
Oujda, Morocco, 128,645 ....B 1
Oyo, Nigeria, 112,349 ....C 4
Paarl, S. Africa, 41,540 ....D 8
Palmas (cape) ....B 4
Pemba (isl.), Tanz., 133,858.......G 5
Pietermaritzburg (cap.), Natal,
S. Africa, 91,988 ....F 7
Pietersburg, S. Africa, 28,071.....E 7
Pointe-Noire, Congo (Braz.),
54,643 ....D 5
Port Elizabeth, S. Afr., 249,211..E 8
Port-Gentil, Gabon, 20,732 ....C 5
Port Harcourt, Nigeria, 179,563..C 4
Port-Lyautey (Kénitra), Morocco,
86,775 ....B 1
Port Said, U.A.R., 256,100 ....F 1
Port Sudan, Sudan, 47,562 ....F 3
Porto-Novo (cap.), Dah., 69,500..C 4
Portuguese Guinea, 525,000 ....A 3
Praia (cap.), C. Verde Is., 3,628..G 8
Pretoria (cap.), S. Afr., 303,684 E 7
Qena, U.A.R., 57,417 ....F 2
Queenstown, S. Africa, 33,182.....E 8
Quelimane, Moz., *64,183...........F 6
Rabat (cap.), Morocco, 227,445..B 1
Red (sea) ....F 2
Rhodesia, 4,260,000 ....E 6
Río de Oro (reg.), Sp. Sahara....A 2
Río Muni (terr.), Equat. Guinea,
195,000 ....C 4
Rudolf (lake), Kenya ....F 4
Rufisque, Senegal, 50,000 ....A 3
Rwanda, 3,018,000 ....F 5
Ruwenzori (mts.) ....E 4
Sahara (desert) ....C 2
Saint Helena (isl.), 4,613 ....B 6
Saint-Louis, Senegal, 58,000 ......A 3
Salisbury (cap.), Rhod., 217,040..F 6
Santa Cruz (cap.), Canary Is.,
Spain, 82,620 ....A 2
Santa Isabel (cap.), Equat.
Guinea, †37,237 ....C 4
Second Cataract, Sudan ....F 2
Sekondi, Ghana, 34,513 ....B 4
Senegal, 3,400,000 ....A 3
Senegal (river) ....A 3
Serowe, Bech., 34,182 ....E 7
Sétif, Algeria, 82,340 ....C 1
Sfax, Tunisia, 75,500 ....D 1
Sidi-bel-Abbès, Algeria, 96,608....C 1
Sidi-Ifni (cap.), Ifni, 12,751 ......B 2
Sierra Leone, 2,200,000 ....A 4
Sinai (pen.), U.A.R., 49,769 ......F 2
Sixth Cataract, Sudan ....F 3
Skikda, Algeria, 80,281 ....C 1
Sohâg, U.A.R., 61,944 ....F 2
Somali Republic, 2,350,000 ....G 4
Sousse, Tunisia, 48,172 ....D 1
South Africa, 17,487,000 ....E 7
South-West Africa, 551,000 ....D 7
Spanish Sahara (prov.), Spain,
42,000 ....A 2
Stanley (falls), Dem. Rep. of
the Congo ....E 4
Stanleyville, Dem. Rep. of the
Congo, 126,533 ....E 4
Sudan, 13,540,000 ....E 3
Suez, U.A.R., 219,000 ....F 2
Suez (canal), U.A.R. ....F 1
Swaziland, 292,000 ....F 7
Takoradi, Ghana, 40,937 ....B 4
Tamale, Ghana, 40,443 ....B 4
Tamatave, Malag. Rep., 39,627...G 6
Tana (lake), Ethiopia ....F 3
Tananarive (cap.), Malag. Rep.,
270,268 ....G 6
Tanga, Tanzania, 38,053.............F 5
Tanganyika (lake) ....F 5
Tangier, Morocco, 141,714..........B 1
Tanzania, 10,514,000 ....F 5
Thiès, Senegal, 69,000 ....A 3
Third Cataract, Sudan ....E 3
Tibesti (mts.) ....D 2
Timbuktu, Mali, 8,735 ....B 3
Tlemcen, Algeria, 70,930 ....B 1
Togo, 1,642,000 ....C 4
Transkei (prov.), S. Africa,
1,439,195 ....E 8
Transvaal (prov.), S. Africa,
6,273,477 ....E 7
Tripoli (cap.), Libya, 212,577......D 1
Tripolitania (reg.), Libya,
1,029,216 ....D 1
Tswana (Bechuanaland),
559,000 ....E 7
Tuléar, Malag. Rep., 33.850........G 7
Tunis (cap.), Tunisia, 480,500....D 1
Tunisia, 4,565,000 ....C 1
Ubangi (river) ....E 3
Uganda, 7,551,000 ....F 4
Uitenhage, S. Africa, 48,755 ......E 8
Umtali, Rhodesia, 39,370............F 6
Umtata (cap.), Transkei,
South Africa, 12,221 ....E 8
United Arab Rep. (Egypt),
28,900,000 ....E 2
Upper Volta, 4,763,000 ....B 3
Vaal (riv.), S. Africa ....E 7
Verde (cape), Senegal ....A 3
Victoria (falls) ....E 6
Victoria (lake) ....F 5
Vila de João Belo, Moz., *48,891..F 7
Volta (lake), Ghana ....B 4
Volta (river) ....C 4
Wad Medani, Sudan, 47,677........F 3
Walvis Bay, S. Africa, 12,234.....D 7
White Nile (river) ....F 4
Windhoek (cap.), S.W. Africa,
36,050 ....D 7
Worcester, S. Africa, 32,274......D 8
Yaoundé (cap.), Cam., 93,269......D 4
Zambezi (river) ....E 6
Zambia, 3,710,000 ....E 6
Zanzibar, Tanzania, 57,923 ....G 5
Zanzibar (isl.), Tanz., 165,253...G 5
Zomba (cap.), Malawi, 7,200......F 6

*City and suburbs.
†Population of sub-district.
‡Population of urban or metropolitan area.

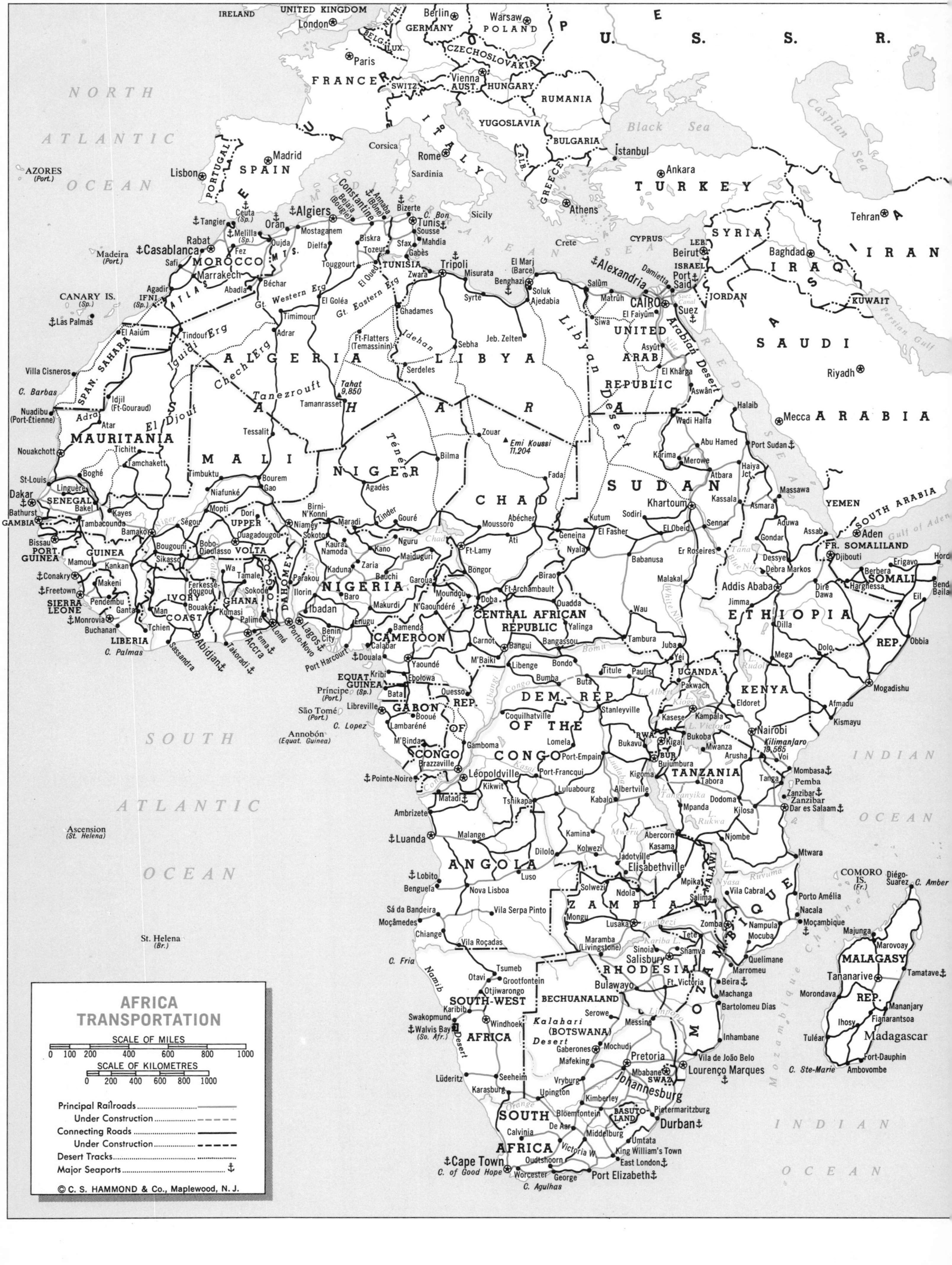

AFRICA TRANSPORTATION

SCALE OF MILES

0 100 200 400 600 800 1000

SCALE OF KILOMETRES

0 200 400 600 800 1000

Principal Railroads ....
Under Construction ....
Connecting Roads ....
Under Construction ....
Desert Tracks ....
Major Seaports .... ‡

© C. S. HAMMOND & Co., Maplewood, N. J.

Oceans and Seas: NORTH ATLANTIC OCEAN, SOUTH ATLANTIC OCEAN, INDIAN OCEAN, Mediterranean Sea, Black Sea, Caspian Sea, Red Sea, Gulf of Aden, Persian Gulf, Mozambique Channel

Countries: IRELAND, UNITED KINGDOM, FRANCE, SPAIN, PORTUGAL, GERMANY, POLAND, U.S.S.R., CZECHOSLOVAKIA, AUST., HUNGARY, RUMANIA, YUGOSLAVIA, BULGARIA, ITALY, GREECE, TURKEY, SYRIA, IRAQ, IRAN, ISRAEL, JORDAN, KUWAIT, SAUDI ARABIA, YEMEN, SOUTH ARABIA, MOROCCO, ALGERIA, TUNISIA, LIBYA, UNITED ARAB REPUBLIC, SPAN. SAHARA, MAURITANIA, MALI, NIGER, CHAD, SUDAN, SENEGAL, GAMBIA, PORT. GUINEA, GUINEA, SIERRA LEONE, LIBERIA, IVORY COAST, UPPER VOLTA, GHANA, DAHOMEY, NIGERIA, CAMEROON, CENTRAL AFRICAN REPUBLIC, ETHIOPIA, FR. SOMALILAND, SOMALI REP., EQUAT. GUINEA, GABON, REP. OF CONGO, DEM. REP. OF THE CONGO, UGANDA, KENYA, TANZANIA, RWANDA, BURUNDI, ANGOLA, ZAMBIA, MALAWI, MOZAMBIQUE, RHODESIA, SOUTH-WEST AFRICA, BECHUANALAND (BOTSWANA), SOUTH AFRICA, SWAZILAND, BASUTOLAND, MALAGASY REP.

Islands: AZORES (Port.), Madeira (Port.), CANARY IS. (Sp.), Corsica, Sardinia, Sicily, Crete, Cyprus, Ascension (St. Helena), St. Helena (Br.), Príncipe (Port.), São Tomé (Port.), Annobón (Equat. Guinea), COMORO IS. (Fr.), Madagascar

Selected cities: London, Paris, Madrid, Lisbon, Berlin, Warsaw, Vienna, Rome, Athens, Istanbul, Ankara, Tehran, Baghdad, Beirut, Riyadh, Mecca, Aden, Casablanca, Rabat, Tangier, Algiers, Oran, Tunis, Tripoli, Benghazi, Alexandria, Cairo, Suez, Port Said, Khartoum, Addis Ababa, Djibouti, Dakar, Bathurst, Bissau, Conakry, Freetown, Monrovia, Abidjan, Accra, Lagos, Ibadan, Yaoundé, Libreville, Léopoldville, Brazzaville, Luanda, Lobito, Nairobi, Mombasa, Dar es Salaam, Zanzibar, Lusaka, Salisbury, Bulawayo, Beira, Lourenço Marques, Johannesburg, Pretoria, Durban, Cape Town, Port Elizabeth, East London, Windhoek, Walvis Bay, Tananarive

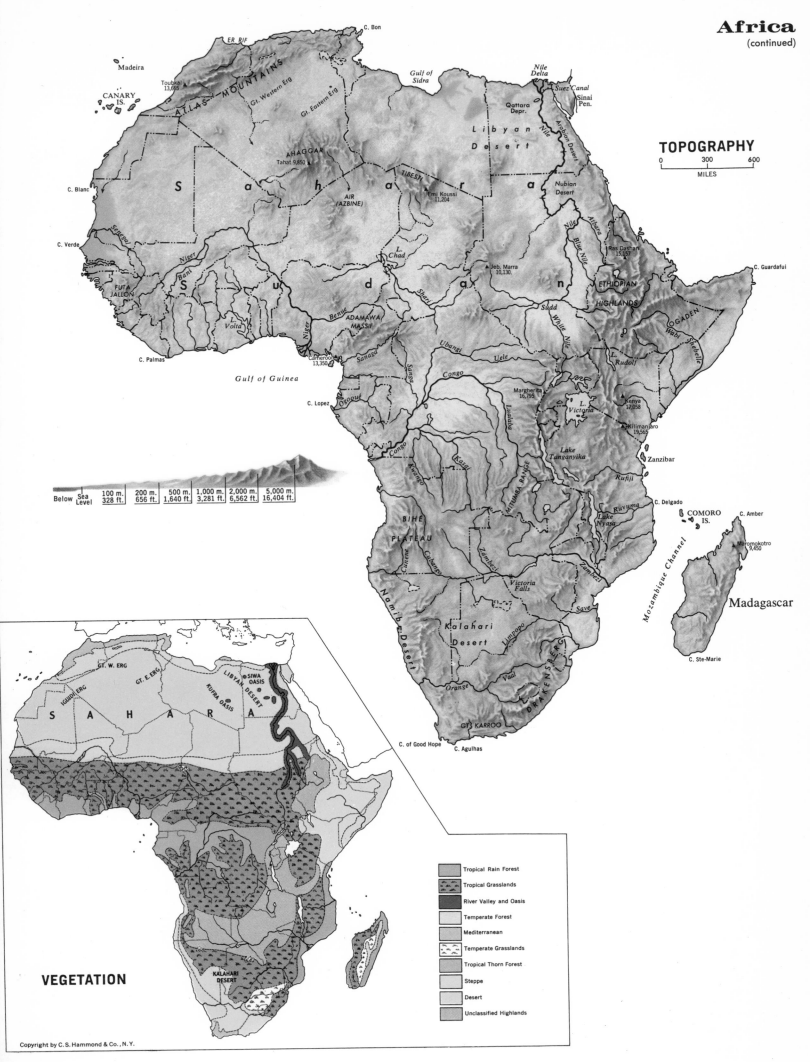

TOPOGRAPHY

0   300   600
MILES

Below Sea Level | 100 m. 328 ft. | 200 m. 656 ft. | 500 m. 1,640 ft. | 1,000 m. 3,281 ft. | 2,000 m. 6,562 ft. | 5,000 m. 16,404 ft.

Gulf of Guinea

Madagascar

Mozambique Channel

VEGETATION

	Tropical Rain Forest
	Tropical Grasslands
	River Valley and Oasis
	Temperate Forest
	Mediterranean
	Temperate Grasslands
	Tropical Thorn Forest
	Steppe
	Desert
	Unclassified Highlands

MOROCCO

AREA	171,583 sq. mi.
POPULATION	12,959,000
CAPITAL	Rabat
LARGEST CITY	Casablanca 965,277
HIGHEST POINT	Jeb. Toubkal 13,665 ft.
MONETARY UNIT	dirham
MAJOR LANGUAGES	Arabic, Berber, French
MAJOR RELIGIONS	Mohammedan, Christian, Jewish

ALGERIA

919,353 sq. mi.
12,300,000
Algiers
Algiers (greater) 883,879
Tahat 9,850 ft.
Algerian franc
Arabic, French, Berber
Mohammedan, Roman Catholic

TUNISIA

48,300 sq. mi.
4,565,000
Tunis
Tunis (greater) 632,100
Jeb. Chambi 5,066 ft.
Tunisian dinar
Arabic, French
Mohammedan, Roman Catholic

SPANISH SAHARA

AREA	103,243 sq. mi.
POPULATION	42,000
CAPITAL	El Aaiún
LARGEST CITY	El Aaiún 5,500
HIGHEST POINT	2,700 ft.
MONETARY UNIT	Spanish peseta
MAJOR LANGUAGES	Arabic, Spanish
MAJOR RELIGIONS	Mohammedan

MAURITANIA

328,185 sq. mi.
1,000,000
Nouakchott
Nouakchott 12,500
2,972 ft.
CFA franc
Arabic, French

Mohammedan

MALI

584,942 sq. mi.
4,430,000
Bamako
Bamako (greater) 135,200
Hombori Mts. 3,789 ft.
Malian franc
Sudanese, Hamitic, Arabic, French
Mohammedan, Tribal religions

NIGER

501,930 sq. mi.
3,193,000
Niamey
Niamey 41,975
Banguezane 6,234 ft.
CFA franc
Sudanese, Hamitic, Arabic, French
Mohammedan, Tribal religions

SENEGAL

AREA	77,401 sq. mi.
POPULATION	3,400,000
CAPITAL	Dakar
LARGEST CITY	Dakar (greater) 382,980
HIGHEST POINT	Futa Jallon, 1,640 ft.
MONETARY UNIT	CFA franc
MAJOR LANGUAGES	Sudanese, Arabic, French
MAJOR RELIGIONS	Mohammedan, Tribal religions, Roman Catholic

GAMBIA

4,033 sq. mi.
330,000
Bathurst
Bathurst 28,896
100 ft.
West African pound
Sudanese, English
Mohammedan, Tribal religions, Christian

PORTUGUESE GUINEA

13,948 sq. mi.
525,000
Bissau
Bissau
689 ft.
Portuguese escudo
Sudanese, Portuguese
Mohammedan, Tribal religions, Roman Catholic

GUINEA

96,525 sq. mi.
3,420,000
Conakry
Conakry (greater) 150,000
Nimba Mts. 6,070 ft.
Guinean franc
Sudanese, French, English
Mohammedan, Tribal religions

SIERRA LEONE

AREA	27,925 sq. mi.
POPULATION	2,200,000
CAPITAL	Freetown
LARGEST CITY	Freetown 127,917
HIGHEST POINT	Loma Mts. 6,390 ft.
MONETARY UNIT	leone
MAJOR LANGUAGES	Sudanese, English
MAJOR RELIGIONS	Tribal religions, Mohammedan, Christian

LIBERIA

43,000 sq. mi.
1,066,000
Monrovia
Monrovia 80,992
Wutivi 5,584 ft.
Liberian dollar
Sudanese, English
Christian, Tribal religions

IVORY COAST

183,397 sq. mi.
3,750,000
Abidjan
Abidjan (greater) 250,000
Nimba Mts. 5,745 ft.
CFA franc
Sudanese, French
Tribal religions, Mohammedan

UPPER VOLTA

105,841 sq. mi.
4,763,000
Ouagadougou
Ouagadougou (greater) 100,000
2,352 ft.
CFA franc
Sudanese, French
Mohammedan, Tribal religions, Roman Catholic

GHANA

AREA	91,844 sq. mi.
POPULATION	7,600,000
CAPITAL	Accra
LARGEST CITY	Accra (greater) 388,396
HIGHEST POINT	Togo Hills 2,900 ft.
MONETARY UNIT	cedi
MAJOR LANGUAGES	Sudanese, English
MAJOR RELIGIONS	Tribal religions, Christian

TOGO

AREA	20,733 sq. mi.
POPULATION	1,642,000
CAPITAL	Lomé
LARGEST CITY	Lomé (greater) 90,000
HIGHEST POINT	Agou 3,445 ft.
MONETARY UNIT	CFA franc
MAJOR LANGUAGES	Sudanese, French
MAJOR RELIGIONS	Tribal religions, Roman Catholic, Mohammedan

DAHOMEY

AREA	42,471 sq. mi.
POPULATION	2,300,000
CAPITAL	Porto-Novo
LARGEST CITY	Cotonou 109,328
HIGHEST POINT	Atakora Mts. 2,083 ft.
MONETARY UNIT	CFA franc
MAJOR LANGUAGES	French, Sudanese
	Tribal religions,
MAJOR RELIGIONS	Mohammedan, Roman Catholic

NIGERIA

356,093 sq. mi.
56,400,000
Lagos
Lagos 665,246
Vogel 6,700 ft.
Nigerian pound
Sudanese, Arabic, English
Mohammedan, Christian

TOPOGRAPHY

0 200 400 600
MILES

(continued on following page)

Western Africa
(continued)

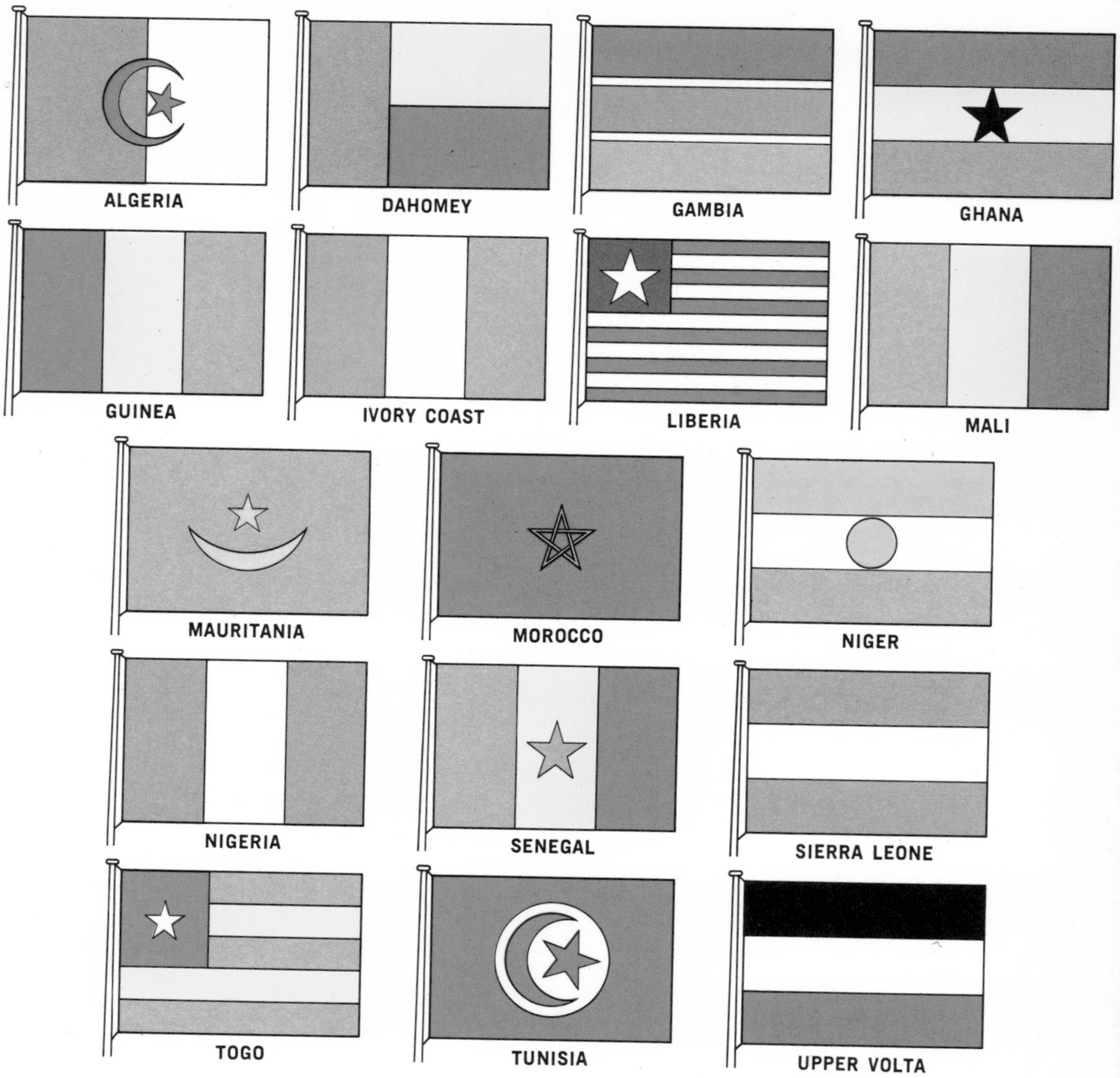

ALGERIA

CITIES and TOWNS

Abadla, 2,567 ... D 2
Adrar, 2,107 ... D 3
Aïn-Béïda, 26,976 ... F 1
Aïn-Salah, 5,374 ... E 3
Aïn-Sefra, 7,068 ... D 2
Aïn-Témouchent, 23,252 ... D 1
Algiers (cap.), 722,066 ... E 1
Algiers, *883,879 ... E 1
Amguid ... F 3
Annaba, 135,150 ... F 1
Annaba, *164,844 ... F 1
Aoulef, 3,406 ... E 3
Arak ... E 3
Batna, 18,114 ... F 1
Béchar, 19,227 ... D 2
Bejaïa, 57,572 ... F 1
Beni-Abbès, 1,900 ... D 2
Beni-Ounif, 3,336 ... D 2
Beni-Saf, 17,521 ... D 1
Berga ... E 3
Bidon 5 (Poste Maurice Cordier) ... E 4
Biskra, 55,073 ... F 2
Blida, 73,618 ... E 1
Boghari, 14,294 ... E 1
Bône (Annaba), 135,150 ... F 1
Bordj-Bou-Arréridj, 35,238 ... E 1
Bordj Fly Sainte-Marie ... D 3
Boufarik, 21,901 ... E 1
Bougie (Bejaïa), 57,572 ... F 1
Bou-Saâda, 21,059 ... E 1
Brézina, 896 ... E 2
Charouïn, 746 ... D 3
Cherchell, 10,943 ... E 1
Constantine, 169,071 ... F 1
Constantine, *223,259 ... F 1
Deldoul, 758 ... F 3
Dellys, 7,506 ... E 1
Djamaâ, 4,191 ... F 2
Djanet, 509 ... F 4
Djelfa, 27,067 ... E 2
Djidjelli, 26,570 ... F 1
Edjeleh ... F 3
El Abiod-Sidi-Cheikh, 2,292 ... E 2
El Asnam, 38,607 ... E 1
El Bayadh, 15,932 ... E 2
El Djezair (Algiers) (cap.), 722,066 ... E 1
El Goléa, 11,527 ... E 2
El Oued, 36,494 ... F 2
Fort-Flatters, 362 ... F 3
Fort-Lallemand ... F 2
Fort-Mac-Mahon ... E 3
Fort-Miribel ... E 3
Fort-Polignac, 645 ... F 3
Ghardaïa, 15,076 ... E 2
Ghazaouet, 12,625 ... D 2
Guelma, 33,312 ... F 1
Guémar, 4,170 ... F 2
Guerrara, 11,849 ... E 2
Guerzim, 936 ... D 3
Hassi-Messaoud ... F 2
Hassi-R'Mel ... E 2
Idelès ... F 4
Ighil Izane, 32,889 ... E 1
Igli, 1,497 ... D 2
In-Amenas, 34 ... F 3
In-Amguel ... E 4
In-Eker ... F 4
In-Rhar, 1,598 ... E 3
Kenadsa, 9,631 ... D 2
Kerzaz, 1,494 ... D 3
Khemis Miliana, 21,319 ... E 1
Laghouat, 20,594 ... E 2
Mascara, 44,839 ... D 1
Méchéria, 10,460 ... D 2
Médéa, 13,348 ... E 1
Metlili, 1,702 ... E 2
Miliana, 7,425 ... E 1
Mohammadia, 11,817 ... D 1
Mostaganem, 64,786 ... D 1
M'Sila, 17,521 ... E 1
Oran, 350,087 ... D 1
Oran, *392,637 ... D 1
Orléansville (El Asnam), 38,607 ... E 1
Ouallene ... E 4
Ouargla, 7,931 ... F 2
Ouled-Djellal, 11,971 ... F 2
Philippeville (Skikda), 80,281 ... F 1
Poste Maurice Cordier ... E 4
Poste Weygand ... D 4
Reggan, 508 ... D 3
Saïda, 21,396 ... E 2
Sba, 627 ... D 3
Sétif, 82,340 ... F 1
Sidi-bel-Abbès, 96,608 ... D 1
Sidi-bel-Abbès, *105,357 ... D 1
Silet ... E 4
Skikda, 80,281 ... F 1
Souk-Ahras, 23,210 ... F 1
Tabelbala, 447 ... D 3
Tamanrasset, 2,760 ... F 4
Tamentit, 931 ... D 3
Taourirt ... E 3
Tarat ... F 3
Tarhit, 555 ... D 2
Tébessa, 26,622 ... F 1
Temacine, 2,999 ... F 2
Temassinin (Fort-Flatters), 362 ... F 3
Ténès, 8,386 ... E 1
Tiaret, 36,322 ... E 1
Tiguentourine ... F 3
Timimoun, 4,345 ... E 3
Tindouf, 1,872 ... C 3
Tizi-Ouzou, 25,367 ... E 1
Tlemcen, 70,930 ... D 2
Touggourt, 18,353 ... F 2
Zaouïet-Kounta, 854 ... D 3

PHYSICAL FEATURES

Ahaggar (range) ... F 4
Aouïnet Legraa (well) ... C 3
Atlas (mts.) ... E 2
Aurés (mts.) ... F 1
Azzel Mati, Sebkra (lake) ... E 3
Bougaroun (cape) ... F 1
Chélia (mt.) ... F 1
Chéliff (riv.) ... E 1
Chenachane (well) ... D 3
Chergui, Shott Ech (salt lake) ... E 2
Gourara (oasis), 28,893 ... E 3
Great Western Erg (des.) ... E 2
In-Ezzane (well) ... G 4
In-Guezzam (well) ... F 5
Irharhar, Wadi (dry riv.) ... F 3
Issaouane Erg (des.) ... F 3
Kabylia (reg.) ... E 1
Mekerhane, Sebkra (salt lake) ... E 3
Melrhir, Shott (salt lake) ... F 2
Mouydir (mts.) ... E 3
Mya, Wadi (dry riv.) ... E 2
Mzab (oasis), 52,500 ... E 2
Raoui Erg (des.) ... D 3
Rhir, Wadi (dry riv.) ... F 2
Saoura, Wadi (dry riv.) ... D 3
Souf (oasis), 92,014 ... F 2
Tademait (plat.) ... E 3
Tahat (mt.) ... F 4
Tamanrasset, Wadi (dry riv.) ... E 4
Tassili n'Ahaggar (plat.) ... E 4
Tassili n'Ajjer (plat.) ... F 3
Tidikelt (oasis), 17,280 ... E 3
Timgad (ruins) ... F 1
Timmissao (well) ... E 4
Tindouf, Sebkra de (salt lake) ... C 3
Tinrhert Hamada (des.) ... F 3
Tni Haïa (well) ... D 4
Touat (oasis), 35,537 ... E 3

CAPE VERDE ISLANDS
Total Population 220,000

CITIES and TOWNS

Mindelo, 7,312 ... A 7
Praia (cap.), 3,628 ... B 8
Ribeira Grande, †17,573 ... B 7
Sal Rei, †3,309 ... B 8
Santa Maria, †2,626 ... B 8

PHYSICAL FEATURES

Boa Vista (isl.), 3,309 ... B 8
Brava (isl.), 8,646 ... B 8
Fogo (isl.), 25,457 ... B 8
Maio (isl.), 2,718 ... B 8
Sal (isl.), 2,626 ... B 7
Santa Luzia (isl.) ... B 8
Santo Antão (isl.), 36,703 ... A 7
São Nicolau (isl.), 13,894 ... B 8
São Tiago (isl.), 86,835 ... B 8
São Vicente (isl.), 21,361 ... B 7

DAHOMEY

CITIES and TOWNS

Abomey, 19,000 ... E 7
Athiémé, 1,782 ... E 7
Cotonou, 109,328 ... E 7
Djougou, 7,000 ... E 7
Grand-Popo, 2,545 ... E 7
Kandi, 5,100 ... E 6
Malanville, 1,900 ... E 6
Natitingou, 2,260 ... E 6
Nikki ... E 7
Ouidah, 18,915 ... E 7
Parakou, 10,600 ... E 7
Porto-Novo (cap.), 69,500 ... E 7
Savalou, 5,000 ... E 7
Savé, 6,262 ... E 7

PHYSICAL FEATURES

Atakora (mts.) ... E 6
Ouémé (riv.) ... E 7

GAMBIA

CITIES and TOWNS

Basse, 1,639 ... B 6
Bathurst (cap.), 28,896 ... A 6
Brikama, 4,195 ... A 6
Georgetown, 1,592 ... A 6

GHANA

CITIES and TOWNS

Accra (cap.), 337,828 ... D 7
Accra, *388,396 ... D 7
Ada Foah, 3,332 ... E 7
Akim Oda, 19,666 ... D 7
Amedika Akuse, 3,638 ... E 7
Attebubu, 4,216 ... D 7
Axim, 5,619 ... D 8
Bawku, 12,719 ... D 6
Bekwai, 9,093 ... D 7
Berekum, 11,148 ... D 7
Bole, 3,118 ... D 7
Bolgatanga, 5,515 ... D 6
Cape Coast, 41,230 ... D 7
Daboya, 1,579 ... D 7
Damongo, 6,575 ... D 7
Dunkwa, 12,689 ... D 7
Elmina, 8,534 ... D 8
Enkyi, 4,007 ... D 7
Gambaga, 2,936 ... D 6
Gyasikan, 4,989 ... D 7
Half Assini, 4,575 ... D 8
Ho, 14,519 ... E 7
Keta, 16,719 ... E 7
Kete Krakye, 3,928 ... E 7
Kintampo, 4,678 ... D 7
Koforidua, 34,856 ... D 7
Kpandu, 8,070 ... D 7
Kumasi, 180,642 ... D 7
Kumasi, *218,172 ... D 7
Lawra, 3,237 ... D 6
Mampong, 7,943 ... D 7
Mpraeso, 5,193 ... D 7
Navrongo, 5,274 ... D 6
Obuasi, 22,818 ... D 7
Prestea, 13,246 ... D 7
Salaga, 4,199 ... D 7
Sehwi Wiawso, 4,430 ... D 7
Sekondi, 34,513 ... D 8
Sekondi-Takoradi, *123,313 ... D 8
Sunyani, 12,160 ... D 7
Takoradi, 40,937 ... D 8
Tamale, 40,443 ... D 7
Tarkwa, 13,545 ... D 7
Tema, 14,937 ... E 7
Tumu, 2,773 ... D 6
Wa, 14,342 ... D 6
Wenchi, 10,672 ... D 7
Winneba, 25,376 ... D 7
Yapei, 515 ... D 7
Yendi, 16,096 ... D 7
Zuarungu, 1,278 ... D 6

PHYSICAL FEATURES

Ashanti (reg.), 1,109,133 ... D 7
Gold Coast (reg.) ... D 8
Saint Paul (cape) ... E 7
Three Points (cape) ... D 8
Volta (lake) ... D 7
Volta (riv.) ... E 7

GUINEA

CITIES and TOWNS

Beyla, 6,035 ... C 7
Boffa, 1,014 ... B 6
Boké, 6,000 ... B 6
Conakry (cap.), 43,000 ... B 7
Conakry, *150,000 ... B 7
Dabola, 5,600 ... B 6
Dalaba, 5,450 ... B 6
Dinguiraye, 2,600 ... B 6
Dubréka, 740 ... B 7
Faranah, 4,000 ... B 6
Forécariah, 5,250 ... B 7
Gaoual, 3,208 ... B 6
Guéckédou, 1,421 ... B 7
Kankan, 50,000 ... C 6
Kérouané ... C 7
Kindia, 25,000 ... B 6
Kissidougou, 12,000 ... B 7
Kouroussa, 6,100 ... C 6
Labé, 11,609 ... B 6
Macenta, 22,500 ... C 7
Mamou, 9,000 ... B 6
N'Zérékoré, 11,000 ... C 7
Siguiri, 12,000 ... C 6
Tougué, 9,810 ... B 6
Victoria, 1,913 ... B 6

PHYSICAL FEATURES

Los (isls.) ... B 7
Milo (riv.) ... C 7
Verga (cape) ... B 6

IFNI
Total Population 61,000

CITIES and TOWNS

Sidi Ifni (cap.), 12,751 ... B 3

IVORY COAST

CITIES and TOWNS

Abengourou, 18,000 ... D 7
Abidjan (cap.), 250,000 ... D 7
Aboisso, 3,310 ... D 7
Agboville, 15,475 ... D 7
Bingerville, 2,500 ... D 7
Bondoukou, 5,216 ... D 7
Bouaflé, 5,000 ... C 7
Bouaké, 45,340 ... D 7
Bouna, 3,410 ... D 7
Boundiali, 3,608 ... C 7
Dabakala, 1,500 ... D 7
Dabou, 4,500 ... D 7
Daloa, 20,000 ... C 7
Danané, 5,200 ... C 7
Dimbokro, 10,260 ... D 7
Ferkessédougou, 9,110 ... D 7
Fresco, 719 ... C 7
Gagnoa, 18,000 ... C 7
Grand-Bassam, 12,330 ... D 7
Grand-Lahou, 4,040 ... C 8
Guiglo, 3,867 ... C 7
Katiola, 7,778 ... C 7
Kong, 4,073 ... D 7
Korhogo, 10,139 ... C 7
Man, 24,000 ... C 7
Odienné, 6,000 ... C 7
Port-Bouet ... D 7
Sassandra, 5,300 ... D 7
Séguéla, 7,598 ... C 7
Sinfra, 5,965 ... C 7
Tabou, 3,030 ... C 8
Touba, 1,217 ... C 7
Toumodi, 3,000 ... D 7

PHYSICAL FEATURES

Aby (lag.) ... D 8
Bandama (riv.) ... C 7
Ebrié (lag.) ... D 8
Ivory Coast (reg.) ... C 8
Sassandra (riv.) ... C 7

LIBERIA

CITIES and TOWNS

Bomi Hills ... B 7
Buchanan ... B 7
Gbarnga ... C 7
Grand Bassa (Buchanan) ... B 7
Grand Cess ... C 8
Greenville, 3,628 ... C 8
Harper ... C 8
Kolahun ... C 7
Marshall ... B 7
Monrovia (cap.), 80,992 ... B 7
River Cess ... C 7
Roberts Field ... B 7
Robertsport ... B 7
Salala ... B 7
Sàss Town ... C 8
Sinoe (Greenville), 3,628 ... C 8
Tappita ... C 7
Tchien ... C 7
Zwedru (Tchien) ... C 7

PHYSICAL FEATURES

Bong (mts.) ... B 7
Grain Coast (reg.) ... B 8
Kru Coast (reg.) ... C 8
Mount (cape) ... B 7
Palmas (cape) ... C 8

MALI

CITIES and TOWNS

Anéfis ... E 5
Ansongo ... E 5
Araouane ... D 5
Badougou ... C 6
Bafoulabé, 800 ... B 6
Bamako (cap.), 88,500 ... C 6
Bamako, *135,200 ... C 6
Bamba ... D 5
Bandiagara, 4,500 ... D 6
Bou Djebeha ... D 5
Bougouni, 5,000 ... C 6
Bourem ... E 5
Dioila, 2,000 ... C 6
Dire, 4,000 ... D 5
Djenné, 8,042 ... D 6
Douentza, 5,570 ... D 6
Gao, 12,839 ... E 5
Goumbou, 5,000 ... C 6
Goundam, 6,842 ... D 5
Gourma-Rharous, 1,800 ... D 5
Hombori, 3,600 ... D 5
Kangaba, 4,909 ... C 6
Kati, 5,900 ... C 6
Kayes, 24,218 ... B 6
Ké-Macina, 2,102 ... C 6
Kéniéba, 1,690 ... B 6
Kerchoual ... E 5
Kidal ... E 5
Kita, 5,230 ... C 6
Kolokani, 4,248 ... C 6
Koulikoro, 6,144 ... C 6
Kourouba, 807 ... B 6
Koutiala, 8,047 ... C 6
Mabrouk ... D 5
Ménaka, 1,300 ... E 5
Mopti, 12,740 ... D 6
Nampala ... C 5
Nara, 4,000 ... C 5
Niafunké, 4,500 ... D 5
Niono, 4,000 ... C 6
Nioro, 10,000 ... C 5
San, 11,463 ... D 6
Satadougou, 180 ... B 6
Ségou, 20,200 ... C 6
Sikasso, 13,085 ... C 6
Sokolo, 3,457 ... C 6
Taoudenni ... D 4
Tessalit ... E 4
Timbuktu, 8,735 ... D 5
Tin-Zaouatene ... E 5
Yelimané, 1,150 ... B 5

PHYSICAL FEATURES

Achourat (well) ... D 4
Asselar (well) ... D 5
Azaouad (reg.) ... D 5
Azaouak (dry riv.) ... E 5
Bani (riv.) ... C 6
Baoulé (dry riv.) ... C 6
Bir Ounane (well) ... D 4
Debo (lake) ... D 5
El-Mraiti (well) ... D 5
Faguibine (lake) ... D 5
Haricha Hamada (des.) ... D 4
Hombori (mts.) ... D 5
In Dagouber (well) ... D 4
Macina (depr.) ... D 6
Mina (mt.) ... C 6
Oum el Asel (well) ... D 4
Sekkane (des.) ... D 4
Tadjnout Hagguerete (well) ... D 4
Terhazza (ruins) ... C 4
Tilemsi (valley) ... E 5
Toufourine (well) ... C 4

MAURITANIA

CITIES and TOWNS

Aïoun el Atrous, 3,054 ... C 5
Akjoujt, 2,360 ... B 5
Akreïjit ... C 5
Aleg, 1,000 ... B 5
Atar, 7,120 ... B 4
Bassikounou ... C 5
Boutilimit, 3,000 ... B 5
Boghé, 2,316 ... B 5
Chinguetti, 600 ... B 4
Fort-Gouraud (Idjil), †900 ... B 4
Idjil, †900 ... B 4
Kaédi, 8,037 ... B 5
Kankossa, †13,000 ... B 5
Kiffa, 2,600 ... B 5
Maghama, 3,157 ... B 5
Mal ... B 5
M'Bout, 1,400 ... B 5
Méderdra, 1,473 ... A 5
Moudjéria, 753 ... B 5
Néma, 2,946 ... C 5
Nouakchott (cap.), 12,500 ... A 5
Nuadibu, 7,680 ... A 4
Ouadane ... B 4
Oualata, 1,285 ... C 5
Oujaf ... C 5
Oujeft ... B 4
Port-Étienne (Nuadibu), 7,680 ... A 4
Rosso, 3,923 ... A 5
Sélibaby, 1,206 ... B 5
Tamchakett, 641 ... B 5
Tamsagout ... C 4
Tichitt, 1,000 ... C 5
Tidjikja, 5,900 ... B 5
Timbédra, 1,200 ... C 5

PHYSICAL FEATURES

Adafer (reg.) ... B 5
Adrar (reg.), 50,920 ... B 4
Affolé (reg.) ... B 5
Agmar (well) ... B 3
Aïn ben Tili (well) ... C 3
Arguin (bay) ... A 4
Assaba (reg.), 100,000 ... B 5
Ben Guerdane (well) ... B 3
Bir el Khzaim (well) ... C 4
Bir Moghrein (oasis), 1,052 ... B 4
Brakna (reg.), 82,020 ... B 5
Chegga (well) ... C 3
Djouf, El (des.) ... C 4
El Mrayer (well) ... C 4
El Mreïti (well) ... C 4
Fort-Trinquet (Bir Moghrein) (oasis), 1,052 ... B 4
Gorgol (reg.), 54,037 ... B 5
Hodh (reg.), 183,945 ... C 5
Inchiri (reg.), 15,443 ... A 5
Kumbi Saleh (ruins) ... C 5
Lévrier (bay) ... A 4
Makteïr (des.) ... B 4
Meraia (reg.) ... C 5
Mirik (Timiris) (cape) ... A 5
Ouarane (reg.) ... B 4
Tagant (reg.), 52,703 ... B 5
Tidra (isl.) ... A 5
Timiris (cape) ... A 5
Trarza (reg.), 105,737 ... A 5

MOROCCO

CITIES and TOWNS

Agadir, 16,695 ... C 2
Al Hoceima, 11,262 ... D 1
Asilah, 10,839 ... C 1
Azemmour, 12,449 ... C 2
Azrou, 14,143 ... C 2
Beni-Mellal, 28,933 ... C 2
Berguent, 2,607 ... D 2
Bouârfa, 8,775 ... D 2
Bou-Izakarn, 661 ... C 3
Boujad, 14,728 ... C 2
Casablanca, 965,277 ... C 2
Chechaouen, 13,712 ... D 1
Dar-el-Beida (Casablanca), 965,277 ... C 2
El Jadida, 40,302 ... C 2
El Kelâa des Srarhna, 10,187 ... C 2
Erfoud, 4,491 ... D 2
Essaouira, 26,392 ... B 2
Fédala (Mohammedia), 35,010 ... C 2
Fez, 216,133 ... D 2
Figuig, 12,108 ... D 2
Goulmima, 1,804 ... C 2
Inezgane, 6,917 ... C 2
Jerada, 18,872 ... D 2
Kénitra, 86,775 ... C 2
Khenifra, 18,503 ... C 2
Khouribga, 40,838 ... C 2
Ksar-el-Kebir, 34,035 ... C 2
Ksar-es-Souk, 6,554 ... D 2
Larache, 30,763 ... C 1
Marrakech, 243,134 ... C 2
Mazagan (El Jadida), 40,302 ... C 2
Meknès, 175,943 ... C 2
Mogador (Essaouira), 26,392 ... B 2
Mohammedia, 35,010 ... C 2
Nador, 17,583 ... D 1
Ouarzazate, 4,200 ... C 2
Oued-Zem, 18,640 ... C 2
Ouezzane, 26,203 ... C 2
Oujda, 128,645 ... D 2
Petitjean (Sidi-Kacem), 19,478 ... C 2
Port-Lyautey (Kénitra), 86,775 ... C 2
Rabat (cap.), 227,445 ... C 2
Safi, 81,072 ... C 2
Saïdia, 1,102 ... D 2
Salé, 75,799 ... C 2
Sefrou, 21,478 ... D 2
Settat, 29,617 ... C 2
Sidi-Kacem, 19,478 ... C 2
Tagounite, 354 ... C 3
Tangier (Tanger), 141,714 ... C 1
Tantan, 2,153 ... B 3
Taourirt, 7,343 ... D 2
Taouz, 641 ... D 2
Tarfaya, 1,521 ... B 3
Taroudant, 17,141 ... C 2
Taza, 31,667 ... D 2
Tendrara, 1,563 ... D 2
Tétouan (Tetuán), 101,352 ... C 1
Tinjoub ... C 3
Tiznit, 7,694 ... B 3
Youssoufia, 8,302 ... C 2
Zagora, 2,200 ... C 2

Western Africa
(continued)

PHYSICAL FEATURES

:i-Atlas (ranges) ..... C 3
as (mts.) ..... C 2
ni, Jebel (mts.) ..... C 3
ntin (cape) ..... C 2
a Hamada (des.) ..... C 3
a, Wadi (dry riv.) ..... C 3
Rif (range) ..... D 2
raltar (str.) ..... C 1
gh Atlas (ranges) ..... C 2
by (cape) ..... B 3
ddle Atlas (ranges) ..... C 2
ulouya (riv.) ..... D 2
éris, Wadi (dry riv.) ..... D 2
r (cape) ..... B 2
Er (range) ..... D 2
ro, Jebel (mts.) ..... C 2
bou (riv.) ..... C 2
n (cape) ..... B 2
ubkal, Jebel (mt.) ..... C 2
, Wadi (dry riv.) ..... D 2

NIGER

CITIES and TOWNS

adès, 6,600 ..... F 5
ma, 1,300 ..... G 5
ni-N'Konni, 7,930 ..... E 6
sso, 509 ..... G 6
rfa ..... G 4
koro, 2,380 ..... F 6
ssa ..... E 6
ado ..... G 4
gondoutchi, 7,456 ..... E 6
sso, 3,530 ..... E 6
chi, 1,060 ..... G 5
ingué, 5,215 ..... E 6
ngara ..... F 6
ya, 3,500 ..... E 6
uré, 1,500 ..... G 6
rouane, 2,000 ..... F 5
Gall, 1,555 ..... F 5
bi ..... G 6
adama ..... G 4
adaoua ..... F 6
agaria, 2,949 ..... F 6
ainé-Soroa, 1,490 ..... G 6
aradi, 11,653 ..... F 6
Guigmi, 3,300 ..... G 6
amey (cap.), 41,975 ..... E 6
y, 2,665 ..... E 6
houa, 13,000 ..... F 6
nout, 1,587 ..... F 6
ra, 5,827 ..... E 6
ssaoua, 5,860 ..... F 6
labéry, 1,632 ..... E 6
nder, 16,271 ..... F 6

PHYSICAL FEATURES

hégour (well) ..... G 5
adem (well) ..... G 5
r (mts.) ..... F 5
aye (well) ..... G 5
sakarai (dry riv.) ..... F 5
zaoua (reg.) ..... E 5
zbine (Air) (mts.) ..... F 5
agam (well) ..... F 5
nguezane (mt.) ..... F 5
douaram (well) ..... G 5
allol Bosso (dry riv.) ..... E 6
llia (dry riv.) ..... G 5
ado (plat.) ..... G 4
Azaoua (well) ..... F 4
antas (well) ..... E 5
lak (reg.) ..... E 5
néré (des.) ..... G 5
mboulaga (well) ..... F 5
o Baba (well) ..... G 5

NIGERIA

REGIONS

astern, 12,394,462 ..... F 7
agos (fed. cap.), 665,246 ..... E 7
id-West, 2,535,839 ..... F 7
orthern, 29,739,764 ..... F 6
estern, 10,265,992 ..... E 7

CITIES and TOWNS

ba, 131,003 ..... F 7
beokuta, 187,292 ..... E 7
buja ..... F 7
do, 157,519 ..... E 7
fikpo ..... F 7
ku, 20,809 ..... F 7
kure, 38,853 ..... F 7
rgungu ..... E 6
saba, 17,387 ..... F 7
zare ..... G 6
aga ..... G 6
ama ..... G 6
aro ..... F 7
auchi ..... F 6
enin City, 100,694 ..... F 7
ida ..... F 7
irnin Kebbi ..... E 6
iu ..... G 6
onny ..... F 8
rass ..... F 8
urutu, 6,784 ..... F 7
ussa ..... E 6
alabar, 46,705 ..... F 7
eba Habe ..... G 6
egema ..... F 8
ikwa ..... G 6
onga ..... G 7
de, 134,550 ..... E 7
ha Amufu, 29,434 ..... F 7
nugu, 138,457 ..... F 7
orcados ..... E 7
untua ..... F 6
ashaka ..... G 7
bogo ..... F 7
eidam ..... G 6
ombe ..... G 6
umel ..... F 6
ummi ..... F 6
usau, 40,202 ..... F 6
wadabawa ..... F 6
adejia ..... G 6
badan, 627,379 ..... E 7
bi ..... F 7
fe, 130,050 ..... E 7
jebu-Ode, 27,558 ..... E 7
kom ..... F 7
lesha, 165,822 ..... F 7
lorin, 208,546 ..... E 7
sa ..... F 6
seyin, 49,680 ..... E 7
wo, 158,583 ..... E 7
alingo ..... G 7
ebba ..... E 7
ega ..... E 6
os, 38,527 ..... F 7
Kabba, 7,305 ..... F 7
Kaduna, 149,910 ..... F 6
Kaiama ..... E 7
Kalmalo ..... F 6
Kano, 295,432 ..... F 6
Katsina, 52,672 ..... F 6
Katsina Ala ..... F 7
Kaura Namoda ..... F 6
Keffi ..... F 7
Kontagora ..... F 6
Kukawa ..... G 6
Kumo ..... G 7
Kuta ..... F 7
Lafia ..... F 7
Lafiagi ..... F 7
Lagos (cap.), 665,246 ..... E 7
Lere ..... F 7
Lokoja, 13,103 ..... F 7
Maiduguri, 139,965 ..... G 6
Maigatari ..... F 6
Makurdi ..... F 7
Minna ..... F 7
Mubi ..... G 6
Mushin, 189,755 ..... E 7
Nasarawa ..... F 7
Nguru, 23,084 ..... G 6
Nnewi, 28,777 ..... F 7
Nsukka ..... F 7
Numan ..... G 7
Offa, 20,668 ..... E 7
Ogbomosho, 319,881 ..... E 7
Ogoja ..... F 7
Okene, 32,602 ..... F 7
Ondo, 36,233 ..... F 7
Onitsha, 163,032 ..... F 7
Oron ..... F 8
Oshogbo, 210,384 ..... F 7
Owo, 30,662 ..... F 7
Oyo, 112,349 ..... E 7
Pankshin ..... F 7
Panyam ..... F 7
Port Harcourt, 179,563 ..... F 8
Ringim ..... F 6
Sapele, 33,638 ..... F 7
Shaki, 22,983 ..... E 7
Shendàm ..... F 7
Sokoto, 47,643 ..... F 6
Toungo ..... G 7
Uromi, 22,339 ..... F 7
Vom ..... F 7
Wamba ..... F 7
Warri, 19,526 ..... F 7
Wukari ..... F 7
Yan ..... G 7
Yelwa ..... F 6
Yola ..... G 7
Zaria, 166,170 ..... F 6
Zungeru ..... F 7

PHYSICAL FEATURES

Adamawa (reg.) ..... G 7
Benue (riv.) ..... F 7
Biafra (bight) ..... F 8
Bornu (reg.) ..... G 6
Cross (riv.) ..... F 7
Donga (riv.) ..... G 7
Foge (isl.) ..... E 6
Gongola (riv.) ..... G 6
Hadejia (riv.) ..... F 6
Kaduna (riv.) ..... F 7
Kebbi (riv.) ..... E 6
Niger (delta) ..... F 8
Osse (riv.) ..... F 7
Sokoto (riv.) ..... F 6
Vogel (peak) ..... G 7

PORTUGAL—Madeira

CITIES and TOWNS

Funchal, 43,301 ..... A 2

PHYSICAL FEATURES

Desertas (isls.) ..... A 2
Madeira (isls.), 268,937 ..... A 2
Madeira (isl.), 265,432 ..... A 2
Pôrto Santo (isl.), 3,505 ..... A 2
Salvage (isls.) ..... A 2

PORTUGUESE GUINEA

CITIES and TOWNS

Bissau (cap.), †55,625 ..... A 6
Bolama, †4,642 ..... A 6
Buba ..... B 6
Bubaque ..... A 6
Cacheu, †70,233 ..... A 6

PHYSICAL FEATURES

Bissagos (isls.), 9,332 ..... A 6

SÃO TOMÉ E PRÍNCIPE

Total Population 64,406

CITIES and TOWNS

Santo António, 882 ..... F 8
São Tomé (cap.), 5,714 ..... F 8

PHYSICAL FEATURES

Príncipe (isl.), 4,605 ..... F 8
São Tomé (isl.), 58,880 ..... F 8

SENEGAL

CITIES and TOWNS

Bakel, 2,400 ..... B 6
Bignona, 5,432 ..... A 6
Dagana, 4,156 ..... A 5
Dakar (cap.), 298,280 ..... A 6
Dakar, *382,980 ..... A 6
Diourbel, 20,082 ..... A 6
Kaolack, 81,631 ..... A 6
Kédougou, 1,938 ..... B 6
Louga, 15,000 ..... A 5
Matam, 6,000 ..... B 5
M'Bour, 15,000 ..... A 6
Nioro-du-Rip, 2,788 ..... A 6
Podor, 4,521 ..... B 5
Richard Toll, 894 ..... A 5
Rufisque, 50,000 ..... A 6
Saint-Louis, 58,000 ..... A 5
Sedhiou, 2,419 ..... A 6
Tambacounda, 10,027 ..... B 6
Thiès, 69,000 ..... A 5
Tivaouane, 8,000 ..... A 5
Touba, 2,575 ..... A 6
Yarboutenda ..... B 6
Ziguinchor, 23,495 ..... A 6

PHYSICAL FEATURES

Ferlo (reg.) ..... B 6
Verde (cape) ..... A 6

SIERRA LEONE

CITIES and TOWNS

Bo, 26,613 ..... B 7
Bonthe, 6,230 ..... B 7
Freetown (cap.), 127,917 ..... B 7
Kabala, 4,610 ..... B 7
Kambia, 3,700 ..... B 7
Kenema, 13,246 ..... B 7
Lungi, 2,170 ..... B 7
Makeni, 12,304 ..... B 7
Moyamba, 4,564 ..... B 7
Pendembu, 2,696 ..... B 7
Port Loko, 5,809 ..... B 7
Pujehun, 2,034 ..... B 7

PHYSICAL FEATURES

Sherbro (isl.), 6,894 ..... B 7
Yawri (bay) ..... B 7

SPAIN—Canary Islands, Ceuta and Melilla

CITIES and TOWNS

Arrecife, 12,748 ..... B 3
Ceuta, 73,182 ..... C 1
La Laguna, 15,899 ..... A 3
Las Palmas de Gran Canaria, 166,236 ..... B 3
Melilla, 79,056 ..... D 1
Santa Cruz de la Palma, 9,928 ..... A 3
Santa Cruz de Tenerife, 82,620 ..... A 3

PHYSICAL FEATURES

Canary (isls.), 944,448 ..... A 3
Fuerteventura (isl.), 18,138 ..... B 3
Gomera (isl.), 27,790 ..... A 3
Grand Canary (isl.), 400,837 ..... A 3
Hierro (isl.), 7,957 ..... A 3
Lanzarote (isl.), 34,805 ..... B 3
La Palma (isl.), 67,141 ..... A 3
Tenerife (isl.), 387,767 ..... A 3

SPANISH SAHARA

CITIES and TOWNS

El Aaiúm (cap.), 5,500 ..... B 3
Güera ..... A 4
Semara ..... B 3
Villa Cisneros, †1,961 ..... A 4

PHYSICAL FEATURES

Ausert (well) ..... B 4
Barbas (cape) ..... A 4
Bir Ganduz (well) ..... A 4
Bir Nzaran (well) ..... B 4
Bojador (cape) ..... B 3
Durnford (pt.) ..... A 4
Guelta de Zemmur (well) ..... B 3
Río de Oro (reg.) ..... B 4
Saguia el Hamra (dry riv.) ..... B 3
Saguia el Hamra (reg.) ..... B 3
Tichlá (well) ..... B 4

TOGO

CITIES and TOWNS

Anécho, 10,487 ..... E 7
Atakpamé, 9,672 ..... E 7
Lama-Kara, †13,017 ..... E 7
Lomé (cap.), 80,000 ..... E 7
Lomé, *90,000 ..... E 7
Palimé, 11,925 ..... E 7
Sansanné-Mango, 6,000 ..... E 6
Sokodé, 14,756 ..... E 7

TUNISIA

CITIES and TOWNS

Beja, 22,700 ..... F 1
Ben Gardane, 2,138 ..... G 2
Bizerte, 45,800 ..... F 1
El Djem, 6,800 ..... G 1
Fort-Saint ..... F 2
Gabès, 24,500 ..... F 2
Gafsa, 24,345 ..... F 2
Kairouan, 35,000 ..... F 1
Kalaa-Kebira, 16,800 ..... F 1
Kasserine, 2,800 ..... F 1
La Goulette, 27,500 ..... G 1
La Skhirra, 1,500 ..... G 2
Le Kef, 17,000 ..... F 1
Mahdia, 10,900 ..... G 1
Mareth, 153 ..... F 2
Mateur, 15,600 ..... F 1
Médenine, 5,500 ..... F 2
Menzel Bourguiba, 36,700 ..... F 1
Menzel-Temime, 12,500 ..... G 1
Moknine, 18,500 ..... G 1
Monastir, 16,500 ..... G 1
Msaken, 27,500 ..... G 1
Nabeul, 15,500 ..... G 1
Nefta, 15,000 ..... F 2
Remada, 1,866 ..... F 2
Sbeitla, 4,000 ..... F 1
Sfax, 75,500 ..... G 2
Souk-el-Arba, 13,000 ..... F 1
Sousse, 4,817 ..... G 1
Tabarka, 356 ..... F 1
Tatahouine, 3,100 ..... G 2
Tozeur, 11,820 ..... F 2
Tunis (cap.), 480,500 ..... G 1
Tunis, *632,100 ..... G 1
Zarzis, 30,080 ..... G 2

PHYSICAL FEATURES

Blanc (cape) ..... G 1
Bon (cape) ..... G 1
Chambi, Jebel (mt.) ..... F 2
Djerba (isl.), 62,445 ..... G 2
Djerid, Shott el (salt lake) ..... F 2
Gabès (gulf) ..... G 2
Hammamet (gulf) ..... G 1
Jefara (reg.) ..... G 2
Kerkennah (isls.), 13,074 ..... G 2
Tunis (gulf) ..... G 1

UPPER VOLTA

CITIES and TOWNS

Aribinda, 3,150 ..... D 6
Banfora, 4,511 ..... D 6
Batié, 1,335 ..... D 6
Bobo-Dioulasso, 56,100 ..... D 6
Bogandé, 3,125 ..... E 6
Dédougou, 3,680 ..... D 6
Diapaga, 3,050 ..... E 6
Djibo ..... D 6
Dori, 3,500 ..... D 6
Fada-N'Gourma, 4,867 ..... E 6
Gaoua, 5,907 ..... D 6
Houndé, 1,153 ..... D 6
Kaya, 10,304 ..... D 6
Koudougou, 7,940 ..... D 6
Koupela, 3,800 ..... D 6
Léo, 2,139 ..... D 6
Ouagadougou (cap.), 63,000 ..... D 6
Ouagadougou, *100,000 ..... D 6
Ouahigouya, 12,960 ..... D 6
Pama, 1,411 ..... E 6
Po, 4,000 ..... D 6
Tenkodogo, 6,561 ..... E 6
Tougan, 5,000 ..... D 6
Yako, 5,110 ..... D 6

WESTERN AFRICA

PHYSICAL FEATURES

Adrar des Iforas (plat.) ..... E 5
Agueraktem (well) ..... C 4
Atoui, Wadi (dry riv.) ..... B 4
Bafing (riv.) ..... B 6
Bagoé (riv.) ..... C 6
Bakoy (riv.) ..... B 6
Baoulé (riv.) ..... C 6
Benin (bight) ..... E 8
Bir Ksaib Ounane (well) ..... C 4
Black Volta (riv.) ..... D 6
Blanc (cape) ..... A 4
Chad (lake) ..... G 6
Cavally (riv.) ..... C 7
Chech Erg (des.) ..... D 3
Comoé (riv.) ..... D 7
El War (well) ..... G 4
Falémé (riv.) ..... B 6
Futa Jallon (mts.) ..... B 6
Gambia (riv.) ..... B 6
Great Eastern Erg (des.) ..... F 2
Guinea (gulf) ..... E 8
Guir Hamada (des.) ..... D 2
High Plateaus (ranges) ..... D 2
Iguidi Erg (des.) ..... C 3
Komadugu Yobe (riv.) ..... G 6
Loma (mts.) ..... B 7
Mediterranean (sea) ..... E 1
Medjerda (riv.) ..... F 1
Moa (riv.) ..... B 7
Mono (riv.) ..... B 7
Mono (riv.) ..... E 7
Niger (riv.) ..... F 7
Nimba (mts.) ..... C 7
North Atlantic Ocean ..... A 2
Oti (riv.) ..... E 7
Red Volta (riv.) ..... D 6
Rima (riv.) ..... F 6
Sahara (des.) ..... C 4
Saharan Atlas (ranges) ..... E 2
Senegal (riv.) ..... B 5
Slave Coast (reg.) ..... E 7
Sudan (reg.) ..... E 6
Tafassasset, Wadi (dry riv.) ..... F 4
Tanezrouft (des.) ..... E 4
Touila (well) ..... C 3
Tummo (El War) (well) ..... G 3
White Volta (riv.) ..... D 6

*City and suburbs.
†Population of subdistrict or division.

AGRICULTURE, INDUSTRY and RESOURCES

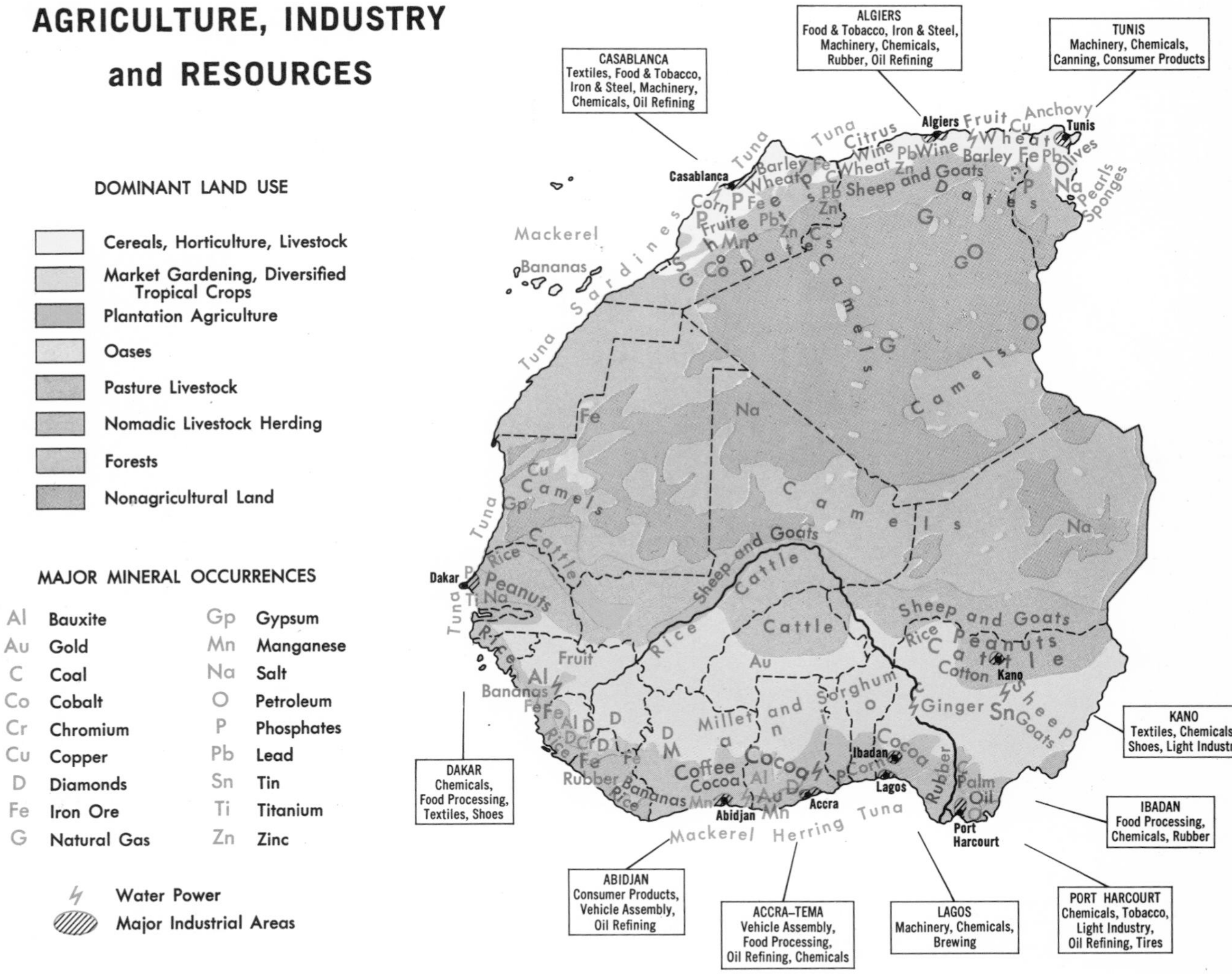
DOMINANT LAND USE
Cereals, Horticulture, Livestock
Market Gardening, Diversified Tropical Crops
Plantation Agriculture
Oases
Pasture Livestock
Nomadic Livestock Herding
Forests
Nonagricultural Land
MAJOR MINERAL OCCURRENCES
Al Bauxite
Au Gold
C Coal
Co Cobalt
Cr Chromium
Cu Copper
D Diamonds
Fe Iron Ore
G Natural Gas
Gp Gypsum
Mn Manganese
Na Salt
O Petroleum
P Phosphates
Pb Lead
Sn Tin
Ti Titanium
Zn Zinc
Water Power
Major Industrial Areas
ALGIERS
Food & Tobacco, Iron & Steel, Machinery, Chemicals, Rubber, Oil Refining
TUNIS
Machinery, Chemicals, Canning, Consumer Products
CASABLANCA
Textiles, Food & Tobacco, Iron & Steel, Machinery, Chemicals, Oil Refining
KANO
Textiles, Chemicals, Shoes, Light Industry
DAKAR
Chemicals, Food Processing, Textiles, Shoes
IBADAN
Food Processing, Chemicals, Rubber
ABIDJAN
Consumer Products, Vehicle Assembly, Oil Refining
ACCRA–TEMA
Vehicle Assembly, Food Processing, Oil Refining, Chemicals
LAGOS
Machinery, Chemicals, Brewing
PORT HARCOURT
Chemicals, Tobacco, Light Industry, Oil Refining, Tires
Algiers
Tunis
Casablanca
Dakar
Kano
Ibadan
Lagos
Accra
Abidjan
Port Harcourt
Mackerel
Bananas
Sardines
Tuna
Citrus
Wine
Wheat
Barley
Fruit
Anchovy
Olives
Pearls
Sponges
Sheep and Goats
Dates
Camels
Cattle
Rice
Peanuts
Millet and Sorghum
Cocoa
Coffee
Ginger
Cotton
Rubber
Palm Oil
Herring

Northeastern Africa

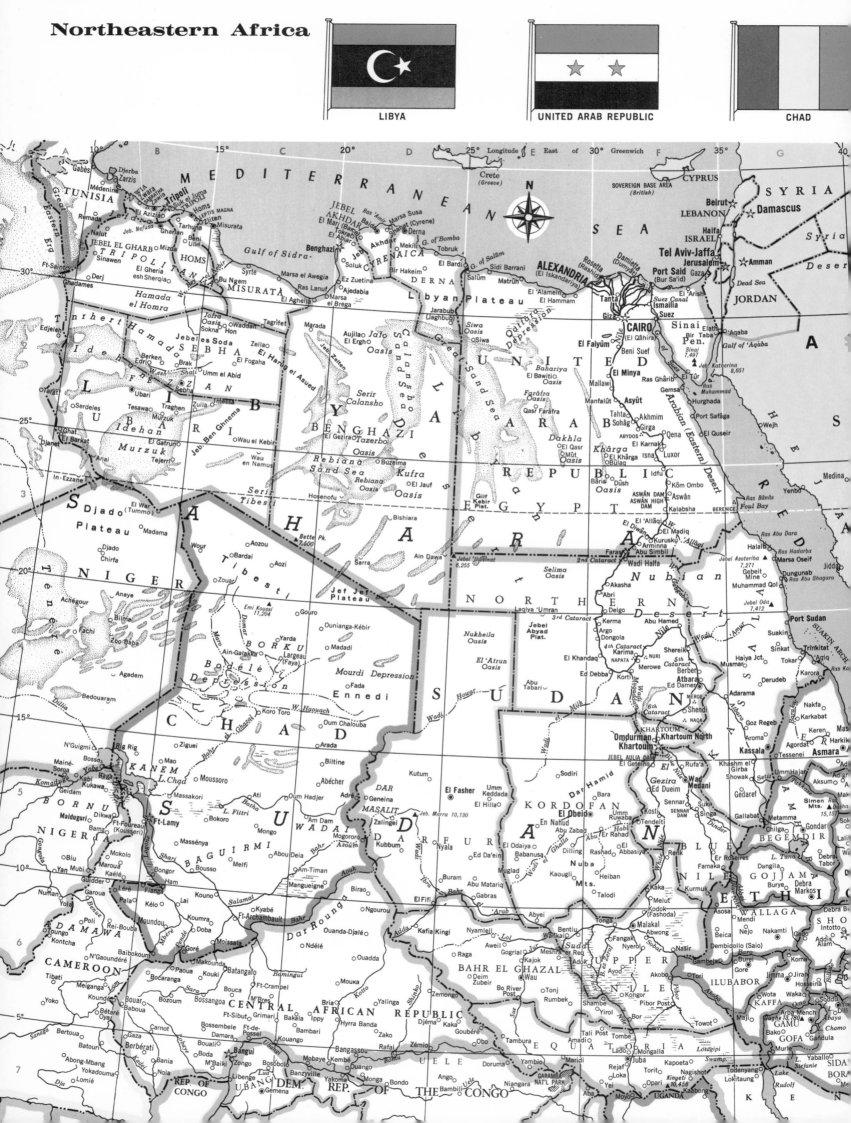

LIBYA

UNITED ARAB REPUBLIC

CHAD

SUDAN

ETHIOPIA

NORTHEASTERN AFRICA

LIBYA

AREA	679,358 sq. mi.
POPULATION	1,559,399
CAPITAL	Tripoli, Benghazi
LARGEST CITY	Tripoli 212,577
HIGHEST POINT	Bette Pk. 7,500 ft.
MONETARY UNIT	Libyan pound
MAJOR LANGUAGES	Arabic
MAJOR RELIGIONS	Mohammedan

UNITED ARAB REPUBLIC

AREA	386,000 sq. mi.
POPULATION	28,900,000
CAPITAL	Cairo
LARGEST CITY	Cairo 3,518,200
HIGHEST POINT	Jeb. Katherina 8,651 ft.
MONETARY UNIT	Egyptian pound
MAJOR LANGUAGES	Arabic
MAJOR RELIGIONS	Mohammedan, Christian

SUDAN

AREA	967,500 sq. mi.
POPULATION	13,540,000
CAPITAL	Khartoum
LARGEST CITY	Omdurman 171,000
HIGHEST POINT	Jeb. Marra 10,130 ft.
MONETARY UNIT	Sudanese pound
MAJOR LANGUAGES	Arabic, Sudanese
MAJOR RELIGIONS	Mohammedan, Tribal religions

CHAD

	455,598 sq. mi.
	2,830,000
	Fort-Lamy
	Fort-Lamy (greater) 91,688
	Emi Koussi 11,204 ft.
	CFA franc
	Bantu, Sudanese, Arabic, French
	Mohammedan, Tribal religions

ETHIOPIA

	457,148 sq. mi.
	22,200,000
	Addis Ababa
	Addis Ababa 504,900
	Ras Dashan 15,157 ft.
	Ethiopian dollar
	Amharic, Hamitic, Arabic
	Coptic Christian, Mohammedan

FRENCH SOMALILAND

AREA	8,492 sq. mi.
POPULATION	80,000
CAPITAL	Djibouti

CHAD

CITIES and TOWNS

Abécher, 25,000		D 5
Abou Deia, 1,100		C 5
Adré		D 5
Ain-Galakka		C 4
Am-Dam, 1,002		D 5
Am-Timan, 1,314		C 5
Aozi		C 3
Aozou		C 3
Arada		D 4
Ati, 4,000		C 5
Baibokoum, 3,138		C 6
Bardai		C 3
Biltine, 4,000		D 5
Bokoro, 4,700		C 5
Bongor, 4,397		C 5
Bousso, 1,800		C 5
Doba, 7,375		C 6
Fada, 206		D 4
Faya (Largeau), 5,385		C 4
Fianga, 923		C 6
Fort-Archambault, 22,500		C 6
Fort-Lamy (cap.), 20,500		C 5
Fort-Lamy, *91,688		C 5
Goré		C 6
Gouro		C 4
Ham		C 6
Kélo, 6,067		C 6
Koro Toro		C 4

Koumra, 6,351		C 6
Kouno		C 6
Kyabé, 3,000		C 6
Lai, 5,021		C 6
Largeau, 5,385		C 4
Léré, 3,332		B 6
Madadi		D 4
Mangueigne		D 5
Mao, 4,015		C 5
Massakori, 1,590		C 5
Massénya, 1,700		C 5
Melfi, 2,008		C 5
Mogororo		D 5
Moissala, 3,000		C 6
Mongo, 2,038		C 5
Moundou, 25,000		C 6
Moussoro, 5,000		C 5
Oum Chalouba		D 4
Oum Hadjer, 1,209		D 5
Ounianga-Kébir		D 4
Pala, 4,351		B 6
Rig Rig, 286		B 5
Wour		C 3
Yarda		C 4
Ziguei		C 5
Zouar		C 3

PHYSICAL FEATURES

Baguirmi (reg.), 81,666		C 5
Bahr el Ghazal (dry riv.)		C 5
Batha (riv.)		C 4
Bodélé (depr.)		C 4
Borku (reg.), 21,962		C 4
Chad (lake)		C 5
Domar (dry riv.)		C 4
Emi Koussi (mt.)		C 4
Ennedi (plat.)		D 4
Fittri (lake)		C 5
Haouach, Wadi		
(dry riv.)		D 4
Jef Jef (plat.)		D 3
Kanem (reg.), 261,108		C 5
Logone (riv.)		C 6
Maro (dry riv.)		C 4
Mbéré (riv.)		B 6
Mourdi (depr.)		D 4
Pendé (riv.)		C 6
Salamat (riv.)		C 6
Sara (riv.)		C 6
Shari (riv.)		C 5
Tibesti (mts.)		C 3
Wadai (reg.), 314,775		D 5

ETHIOPIA

PROVINCES

Arusi, 1,013,100		G 6
Begemdir, 1,229,900		G 5
Eritrea, 1,422,300		G 4
Gamu-Gofa, 766,700		G 6
Gojjam, 1,437,400		G 5
Harar, 3,198,600		H 6
Ilubabor, 598,400		F 6
Kaffa, 623,000		G 6
Shoa, 3,486,400		G 6
Sidamo-Borana, 1,438,400		G 7
Tigre, 2,104,100		H 5
Wallaga, 1,298,300		G 6
Wallo, 2,845,100		H 5

CITIES and TOWNS

Addis Ababa (cap.), 504,900		G 6
Addis Alam, 7,789		G 6
Adigrat		G 5
Adi Ugri		G 4
Adola		G 6
Adwa		G 5

TOPOGRAPHY

0 200 400 600
MILES

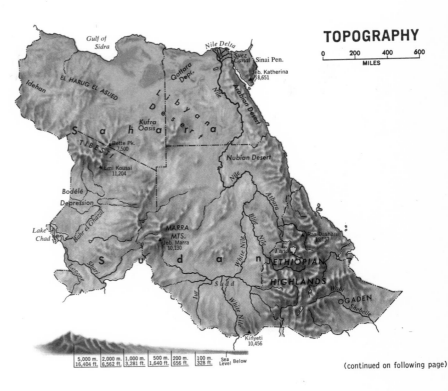

5,000 m. 16,404 ft.	2,000 m. 6,562 ft.	1,000 m. 3,281 ft.	500 m. 1,640 ft.	200 m. 656 ft.	100 m. 328 ft.	Sea Level Below

(continued on following page)

Northeastern Africa
(continued)

ETHIOPIA (continued)

Agordat G 4
Aksum, 11,596 G 5
Ankober, 12,871 H 6
Arba Mench G 6
Asmara, 131,800 G 4
Asosa F 5
Assab H 5
Asselle, 9,523 G 6
Awareh H 6
Awash H 6
Bako G 6
Bedessa H 6
Beica F 6
Burei G 6
Burye, 18,139 G 5
Callafo H 6
Chilga G 5
Dagabur H 6
Dallol G 5
Dangila, 2,351 G 5
Debra Birhan G 6
Debra Markos, 20,096 G 5
Debra Tabor G 5
Dembidollo F 6
Dessye, 43,145 G 5
Dilla G 6
Dire Dawa, 30,438 H 6
Dolo H 7
Domo J 6
Edd H 5
El Carre H 6
El Der H 6
Filtu H 6
Gabredarre H 6
Galadi J 6
Gambela, 9,955 F 6
Gardula G 6
Gedo G 6
Gerlogubi H 6
Ginir H 6
Goba, 6,389 H 6
Gondar, 24,673 G 5
Gore G 6
Gorrahei H 6
Hadama, 7,293 G 6
Harar, 40,499 H 6
Harkiko G 4
Hosseina, 5,803 G 6
Imi H 6
Jijiga H 6
Jimma, 39,559 G 6
Jiran G 6
Karkabat G 4
Keren G 4
Koma G 6
Lalibela G 5
Magdala G 5
Maji G 6
Makale, 16,873 G 5
Massawa G 4
Masslo G 6
Mega G 7
Mendi G 6
Mersa Fatma H 5
Metamma G 5
Miesso, 32,960 H 6
Murle G 6
Mustahil H 6
Nakamti, 5,889 G 6
Nakfa G 4
Negelli G 6
Nejo G 6
Saio (Dembidollo) F 6
Soddu, 5,595 G 6
Sokota G 5
Tessenei G 4
Thio H 5
Tori F 6
Umm Hajar G 5
Waka G 6
Waldia G 5
Wardere J 6
Wota G 6
Yaballo G 6
Yirga Alam G 6
Zula G 4

PHYSICAL FEATURES

Abaya (lake) G 6
Abbai (riv.) G 5
Amhara (reg.) G 5
Assale (lake) H 5
Awash (riv.) H 5
Bale (mt.) G 6
Billate (riv.) G 6
Buri (pen.) H 4
Chamo (lake) G 6
Dahlak (arch.) H 4
Dahlak (isl.) H 4
Danakil (reg.) H 5
Dawa (riv.) H 7
Fafan (riv.) H 6
Ganale Dorya (riv.) H 6
Gughe (mt.) G 6
Haud (reg.) J 6
Ogaden (reg.) H 6
Omo (riv.) G 6
Ras Dashan (mt.) G 5
Simen (mts.) G 5
Stefanie (lake) G 7
Takkaze (riv.) G 5
Tana (lake) G 5
Wabi (riv.) H 6
Wabi Shebelle (riv.) H 6
Zwai G 6

FRENCH SOMALILAND

CITIES and TOWNS

Ali Sabieh, 2,000 H 5
Dikhil, 1,000 H 5
Djibouti (cap.), 40,000 H 5
Obock, 582 H 5
Tadjoura, 2,000 H 5

LIBYA

PROVINCES

Benghazi, 279,665 D 2
Derna, 84,001 D 1
Homs, 137,205 B 1
Jebel el Akhdar, 87,803 D 1
Jebel el Gharb, 181,334 B 1
Misurata, 145,468 C 1
Sebha, 46,700 B 2
Tripoli, 376,177 B 1
Ubari, 32,014 B 2
Zawia, 189,032 B 1

CITIES and TOWNS

Ajedabia, 15,430 D 1
Aujila, †2,993 D 2
Baida, 12,799 D 1
Barce (El Marj), 10,645 D 1
Benghazi (cap.), 136,641 C 1
Beni Ulid, †4,293 B 1
Berken, †3,114 B 2
Bir Hakeim D 1
Brak, †7,042 B 2
Bu Ngem C 1
Buzeima D 3
Cyrene (Shahat), †6,266 D 1
Derj, †2,272 B 1
Derna, 21,432 D 1
El Abiar, †14,260 D 1
Edri, †4,271 B 2
El Agheila, †852 C 1
El Azizia B 1
El Bardi, †3,755 D 1
El Barkat, †1,476 B 3
El Ergh D 2
El Fogaha, †607 C 2
El Gatrun, †1,660 B 3
El Gezira D 2
El Gheria esh Shergia B 1
El Jauf, †4,330 D 3
El Marj, 10,645 D 1
Ez Zuetina, †2,430 D 1
Ghadames, †2,636 A 2
Gharian, †10,807 B 1
Ghat, †1,639 B 3
Homs, †13,864 B 1
Hon, †3,435 C 2
Jaghbub (Jarabub), †1,101 D 2
Jarabub, †1,101 D 2
Marada, †1,858 C 2
Marsa el Awegia C 1
Marsa el Brega, †2,797 D 1
Marsa Susa, †2,062 D 1
Mekili D 1
Misurata, †36,850 C 1
Mizda, †2,508 B 1
Murzuk, †3,863 B 2
Nalut, †9,010 B 1
Ras Lanuf C 1
Sebha, †9,804 B 2
Serdeles B 2
Shahat, †6,266 D 1
Sinawen, †715 B 1
Sokna, †1,873 C 2
Soluk, †12,395 D 1
Suk el Juma, †81,123 B 1
Syrte, †7,093 C 1
Tagrifet C 2
Tarhuna, †25,502 B 1
Tejerri B 3
Tesawa B 2
Tmessa C 2
Tobruk, 15,867 D 1
Tokra, †5,900 D 1
Traghen, †2,952 B 2
Tripoli (cap.), 212,577 B 1
Ubari, †1,711 B 2
Umm el Abid C 2
Waddan, †3,519 C 2
Wau el Kebir C 2
Zawia, †28,349 B 1
Zella, †2,560 C 2
Zliten, †17,950 C 1
Zuila, †1,839 C 2
Zwara, †14,578 B 1

PHYSICAL FEATURES

Ain Dawa (well) D 3
Akhdar, Jebel (mts.) D 1
'Amir, Ras (cape) D 1
Anai (well) B 3
Ben Ghnema, Jebel (mts.) C 2
Bette (peak) C 3
Bey el Kebir, Wadi (dry riv.) B 1
Bishiara (well) D 3
Bomba (gulf) D 1
Calansho Sand Sea (des.) D 2
Calansho, Serir (des.) D 2
Cyrenaica (reg.), 451,469 D 1
Fezzan (reg.), 78,714 B 2
Harug el Asued, El (mts.) C 2
Homra, Hamada el (des.) B 2
Hosenofu (well) D 3
Idehan (des.) B 2
Idehan Murzuk (des.) B 2
Jalo (oasis), 3,910 D 2
Jefara (reg.) B 1
Jofra (oasis), 8,827 C 2
Kufra (oasis), 5,509 D 3
Leptis Magna (ruins) B 1
Nefusa, Jebel (mts.) B 1
Rebiana (oasis), †666 D 3
Rebiana Sand Sea (des.) D 3
Sabratha (ruins) B 1
Sarra (well) D 3
Shati, Wadi esh (dry riv.) B 2
Sidra (gulf) C 1
Soda, Jebel es (mts.) C 2
Tazerbo (oasis), †1,307 D 2
Tinrhert Hamada (des.) B 2
Tripolitania (reg.), 1,029,216 B 1
Wau en Namus (well) C 3
Zelten, Jebel (mts.) D 2

SUDAN

PROVINCES

Bahr el Ghazal, 991,022 E 6
Blue Nile, 2,069,646 F 5
Darfur, 1,328,765 D 5
Equatoria, 903,503 E 6
Kassala, 941,039 G 4
Khartoum, 504,923 F 4
Kordofan, 1,761,968 E 5
Northern, 873,059 E 3
Upper Nile, 888,611 F 6

CITIES and TOWNS

'Abri F 3
Abu Hamed F 4
Abu Matariq E 5
Abu Zabad E 5
Abwong F 6
Abyei E 6
Adarama G 4
Adok F 6
Akasha F 3
Akobo F 6
Amadi F 6
'Aqiq G 4
Argo, 2,329 F 4
Aroma, 3,451 G 4
Atbara, 36,298 F 4
Aweil, 2,438 E 6
Ayod F 6
Babanusa E 5
Bara, 4,885 F 5
Bentiu E 6
Berber, 10,977 F 4
Bor F 6
Bo River Post E 6
Buram E 5
Deim Zubeir E 6
Delgo F 3
Derudeb G 4
Dilling, 5,596 E 5
Dongola, 3,350 F 4
Dungunab G 3
Ed Da'ein E 5
Ed Damer, 5,458 F 4
Ed Debba F 4
Ed Dueim, 12,319 F 5
El Abbasiya, 2,846 F 5
El Fasher, 26,161 E 5
El Fifi D 5
El Geteina F 5
El Hilla E 5
El Khandaq E 4
El Obeid, 52,372 E 5
El Odaiya E 5
En Nahud, 16,499 E 5
Er Rahad, 6,706 F 5
Er Roseires, 3,927 F 5
Famaka F 5
Fangak F 6
Faras F 3
Fashoda (Kodok), 9,100 F 6
Gabras E 5
Gallabat G 5
Gebeit Mine G 3
Gedaref, 17,537 G 5
Geneina, 11,817 D 5
Gogrial E 6
Goz Regeb G 4
Haiya Junction G 4
Halaib G 3
Heiban F 5
Juba, 10,660 F 7
Kadugli, 4,716 E 5
Kafia Kingi D 6
Kajok E 6
Kaka F 5
Kapoeta F 7
Karima, 5,989 F 4
Karora G 4
Kassala, 40,612 G 4
Kerma F 4
Khartoum (cap.), 138,000 F 4
Khartoum North, 39,082 F 4
Khashm el Girba G 5
Kodok, 9,100 F 6
Kongor F 6
Korti F 4
Kosti, 22,688 F 5
Kubbum D 5
Kurmuk, 1,647 F 5
Kutum D 5
Lado F 6
Loka F 7
Malakal, 9,680 F 6
Maridi, 839 E 7
Marsa Oseif G 3
Melut, 334 F 5
Merowe, 1,620 F 4
Meshra' er Req E 6
Mongalla F 6
Muglad, 3,735 E 5
Muhammad Qol G 3
Musmar G 4
Nagishot F 7
Nasir F 6
Nimule F 7
Nyala, 12,278 E 5
Nyamlell E 6
Nyerol F 6
Omdurman, 171,000 F 4
Opari F 7
Pibor Post F 6
Port Sudan, 47,562 G 4
Raga E 6
Rashad, 1,683 F 5
Rejaf F 7
Renk F 5
Rufa'a, 9,137 F 5
Rumbek, 2,944 E 6
Sennar, 8,093 F 5
Shambe F 6
Shendi, 11,031 F 4
Shereik F 4
Showak, 2,171 G 5
Singa, 9,436 F 5
Sinkat, 5,175 G 4
Sodiri, 1,804 E 5
Suakin, 4,228 G 4
Suki, 7,388 F 5
Tali Post F 6
Talodi, 2,736 F 5
Tambura E 6
Tendelti, 7,555 F 5
Tokar, 16,802 G 4
Tombe F 6
Tonga F 6
Tonj, 2,071 E 6
Torit, 2,353 F 7
Towot F 6
Trinkitat G 4
Umm Keddada E 5
Umm Ruwaba, 7,805 F 5
Wadi Halfa, 11,006 F 3
Wad Medani, 47,677 F 5
Wankai E 6
Wau, 8,009 E 6
Yambio, 3,890 E 7
Yei, 739 F 7
Yirol, 1,895 F 6
Zalingei, 3,314 D 5

PHYSICAL FEATURES

Abu Dara, Ras (cape) G 3
Abu Habl, Wadi (dry riv.) F 5
Abu Shagara, Ras (cape) G 3
Abu Tabari (well) E 4
Adda (riv.) D 6
'Amur, Wadi (dry riv.) G 4
Asoteriba, Jebel (mt.) G 3
Bahr Azoum (riv.) D 5
Bahr el 'Arab (riv.) E 6
Bahr ez Zeraf (riv.) F 6
Dar Hamid (reg.) F 5
Dar Masalit (reg.), 323,616 D 5
El 'Atrun (oasis) E 4
Fifth Cataract (rapids) F 4
Fourth Cataract (rapids) F 4
Gezira, El (reg.) F 5
Ghalla, Wadi el (dry riv.) E 5
Hadarba, Ras (cape) G 3
Howar, Wadi (dry riv.) E 4
Ibra, Wadi (dry riv.) D 5
Jebel Abyad (plat.) E 4
Jebel Aulia (dam) F 4
Jur (riv.) E 6
Kinyeti (mt.) F 7
Laqiya 'Umran (well) E 3
Lol (dry riv.) E 6
Lotagipi (swamp) F 6
Marra, Jebel (mt.) D 5
Meroe (ruins) F 4
Milk, Wadi el (dry riv.) E 4
Muqaddam, Wadi (dry riv.) F 4
Napata (ruins) F 4
Naqa (ruins) F 4
Nuba (mts.) F 5
Nubian (des.) F 3
Nukheila (oasis) E 4
Nuri (ruins) F 4
Oda, Jebel (mt.) G 3
Pibor (riv.) F 6
Second Cataract (rapids) F 3
Selima (oasis) E 3
Sennar (dam) F 5
Setit (riv.) G 5
Sixth Cataract (rapids) F 4
Sobat (riv.) F 6
Suakin (arch.) G 4
Sudd (swamp) E 6
Sue (riv.) E 6
Third Cataract (rapids) E 4
White Nile (riv.) F 5

UNITED ARAB REPUBLIC (Egypt)

CITIES and TOWNS

Abnûb, 27,751 J 4
Abu Qurqâs, 19,318 J 4
Abu Simbil, 2,630
Akhmin, 41,580
Alexandria, 1,587,700
Arminna, 1,321
Aswân, 43,393
Asyût, 133,500
Bâris, 1,347
Benha, 52,686
Beni Mazar, 30,583
Beni Suef, 78,829
Biba, 20,773
Bûlaq, 928
Bur Sa'id (Port Said), 256,100
Cairo (cap.), 3,518,200
Dairût, 24,364
Damanhur, 133,200
Damietta, 71,780
Disûq, 39,473
Dumyât (Damietta), 71,780
Dûsh, 794
El 'Alamein, 593
El 'Allâqi
El 'Arish, 26,669
El Bawiti, 2,478
El Diwân, 966
El Fashn, 25,961
El Faiyûm, 117,800
El Hammam, 3,664
El Iskandariya (Alexandria), 1,587,700
El Karnak, 14,121
El Khârga, 9,277
El Madiq
El Mahalla el Kubra, 198,900
El Mansûra, 172,600
El Minya, 104,800
El Qâhira (Cairo) (cap.), 3,518,200
El Qantara, 11,201
El Qasr, 1,789
El Quseir, 4,336
El Tûr, 418
El Wasta, 11,283
Gaza
Gemsa, 225
Girga, 42,017
Giza, 276,200
Heliopolis, 124,774
Helwân, 943,385
Hurghada, 2,012
Idfu, 25,105
Ismailia, 156,300
Isna, 25,342
Kalabsha, 707
Kôm Ombo, 21,783
Kurusku, 599
Luxor, 35,074
Maghâgha, 28,650
Mallawi, 52,614
Manfalût, 28,540
Matrûh, 9,254
Minûf, 41,914
Mût, 3,496
Port Fuad, 12,881
Port Safâga, 1,448
Port Sa'id, 256,100
Port Taufiq, 26,075
Qalyub, 43,202
Qasr Farâfra, 747
Qena, 57,417
Ras Ghârib, 5,857
Rashid (Rosetta), 32,368
Rosetta, 32,368
Salûm, 1,348
Samalût, 17,368
Shibin el Kom, 54,910
Sidi Barrani, 1,583
Sinnûris, 31,831
Siwa, 3,839
Sohâg, 61,944
Suez, 219,000
Tahta, 36,165
Tanta, 209,500
Zagazig, 131,200
Zifta, 31,421

PHYSICAL FEATURES

Abu Qir (bay) F
Abydos (ruins) F
'Aqaba (gulf) G
Arabian (des.) F
Aswân (dam) F
Aswân High (dam) F
Bahariya (oasis), 6,779 E
Bahr Yusef (stream)
Bânâs, Ras (cape) F
Berenice (ruins) F
Birket Qârûn (lake) E
Bir Taba (well) F
Bitter (lakes) K
Dakhla (oasis), 21,586 E
Eastern (Arabian) (des.) F
Farâfra (oasis), 747 E
Foul (bay) G
Ghard Abu Muharik (des.) E
Gilf Kebir (plat.) E
Katherina, Jebel (mt.) F
Khârga (oasis), 12,346 F
Memphis (ruins) J
Muhammad, Ras (cape) F
Pyramids (ruins) J
Qattâra (depr.) E
Salûm (gulf) E
Sinai (mt.) F
Sinai (pen.), 49,769 F
Siwa (oasis), 3,839 E
Suez (canal) K
Suez (gulf) F

NORTHEASTERN AFRICA

PHYSICAL FEATURES

Abbe (lake) H
Aden (gulf) K
Akobo (riv.) F
'Allaqi, Wadi (dry riv.) F
Atbara (riv.) G
Bab el Mandeb (str.) H
Baraka (dry riv.) G
Baro (riv.) G
Blue Nile (riv.) G
Dinder (riv.) G
Gabgaba, Wadi (dry riv.) F
Great Sand Sea (des.) D
Kasar, Ras (cape) G
Libyan (des.) D
Libyan (plat.) D
Mediterranean (sea) C
Nile (riv.) F
Red (sea) G
Sahara (des.) C
Sudan (reg.) C
Tibesti, Serir (des.) C
'Uweinat, Jebel (mt.) E

*City and suburbs.
†Population of sub-district or division.

AGRICULTURE, INDUSTRY and RESOURCES

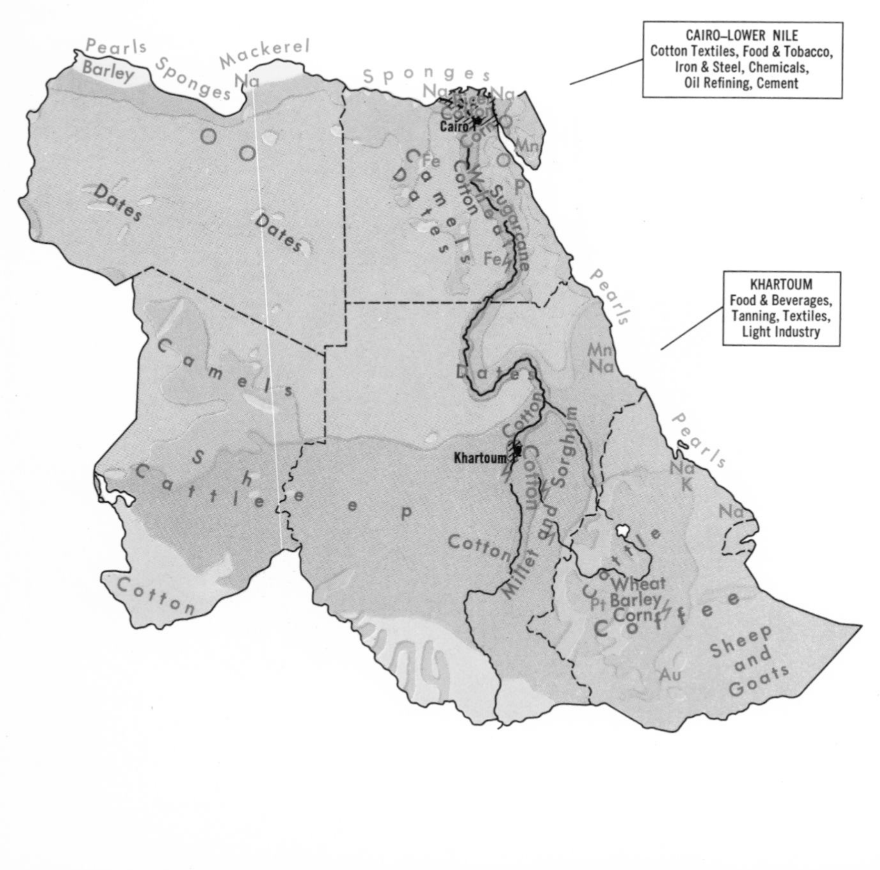

CAIRO–LOWER NILE
Cotton Textiles, Food & Tobacco, Iron & Steel, Chemicals, Oil Refining, Cement
KHARTOUM
Food & Beverages, Tanning, Textiles, Light Industry
Pearls
Mackerel
Barley
Sponges
Na
Cairo
Camels
Cotton
Dates
Sugarcane
Fe
Mn
Khartoum
Sorghum
Millet and Sorghum
Cattle
Sheep
Wheat
Barley
Corn
Coffee
Sheep and Goats
Pt
Au
K

DOMINANT LAND USE

- Cereals, Horticulture, Livestock
- Cash Crops, Mixed Cereals
- Cotton, Cereals
- Market Gardening, Diversified Tropical Crops
- Plantation Agriculture
- Oases
- Pasture Livestock
- Nomadic Livestock Herding
- Forests
- Nonagricultural Land

MAJOR MINERAL OCCURRENCES

- Au Gold
- Fe Iron Ore
- K Potash
- Mn Manganese
- Na Salt
- O Petroleum
- P Phosphates
- Pt Platinum

- Water Power
- Major Industrial Areas

CAMEROON

AREA	178,368 sq. mi.
POPULATION	5,150,000
CAPITAL	Yaoundé
LARGEST CITY	Douala (greater) 187,000
HIGHEST POINT	Cameroon 13,350 ft.
MONETARY UNIT	CFA franc
MAJOR LANGUAGES	Sudanese, Bantu, Arabic, French
MAJOR RELIGIONS	Tribal religions, Christian, Mohammedan

CENTRAL AFRICAN REP.

239,382 sq. mi.
1,320,000
Bangui
Bangui 111,266
Gao 4,659 ft.
CFA franc
Bantu, Sudanese, Arabic, French
Tribal religions, Christian, Mohammedan

SOMALI REP.

262,000 sq. mi.
2,350,000
Mogadishu
Mogadishu 120,649
Surud Ad 7,900 ft.
somalo
Somali, Arabic, Italian, English
Mohammedan, Roman Catholic

GABON

90,733 sq. mi.
462,000
Libreville
Libreville 46,000
Ibounzi 5,165 ft.
CFA franc
Bantu, Sudanese, Arabic, French
Tribal religions, Christian

REPUBLIC OF CONGO

AREA	902,274 sq. mi.
POPULATION	1,012,800
CAPITAL	Brazzaville
LARGEST CITY	Brazzaville (greater) 139,734
HIGHEST POINT	Leketi Mts. 3,412 ft.
MONETARY UNIT	CFA franc
MAJOR LANGUAGES	Bantu, Sudanese, Arabic, French
MAJOR RELIGIONS	Christian, Tribal religions

DEM. REP. OF THE CONGO

175,676 sq. mi.
15,627,000
Léopoldville
Léopoldville 402,492
Margherita 16,795 ft.
Congo franc
Bantu, French, Flemish
Tribal religions, Christian

UGANDA

80,301 sq. mi.
7,551,000
Kampala
Kampala (greater) 123,332
Margherita 16,795 ft.
East African shilling
Bantu, Sudanese, English
Tribal religions, Christian

KENYA

219,730 sq. mi.
9,376,000
Nairobi
Nairobi (greater) 343,500
Kenya 17,058 ft.
East African shilling
Swahili, English
Tribal religions, Christian

TANZANIA

343,726 sq. mi.
10,514,000
Dar es Salaam
Dar es Salaam 128,742
Kilimanjaro 19,565 ft.
East African shilling
Bantu, Swahili, English
Tribal religions, Christian, Mohammedan

RWANDA

AREA	10,169 sq. mi.
POPULATION	3,018,000
CAPITAL	Kigali
LARGEST CITY	Kigali (greater) 4,173
HIGHEST POINT	Karisimbi 14,780 ft.
MONETARY UNIT	Rwanda-Burundi franc
MAJOR LANGUAGES	Kinyarwanda, French
MAJOR RELIGIONS	Tribal religions, Roman Catholic

BURUNDI

10,747 sq. mi.
2,780,000
Bujumbura
Bujumbura (greater) 47,036
8,858 ft.
Rwanda-Burundi franc
Kirundi, French
Tribal religions, Roman Catholic

ANGOLA

481,351 sq. mi.
5,119,000
Luanda
Luanda 224,540
8,597 ft.
Portuguese escudo
Bantu, Portuguese
Tribal religions

MALAWI

36,829 sq. mi.
3,900,000
Zomba
Blantyre-Limbe (greater) 40,498
Mlanje 9,843 ft.
Malawi pound
Bantu, English
Tribal religions, Mohammedan

ZAMBIA

290,320 sq. mi.
3,710,000
Lusaka
Lusaka (greater) 122,300
Sunzu 6,782 ft.
Zambian pound
Bantu, English
Tribal religions

EQUATORIAL GUINEA

AREA	10,836 sq. mi.
POPULATION	267,000
CAPITAL	Santa Isabel

BURUNDI

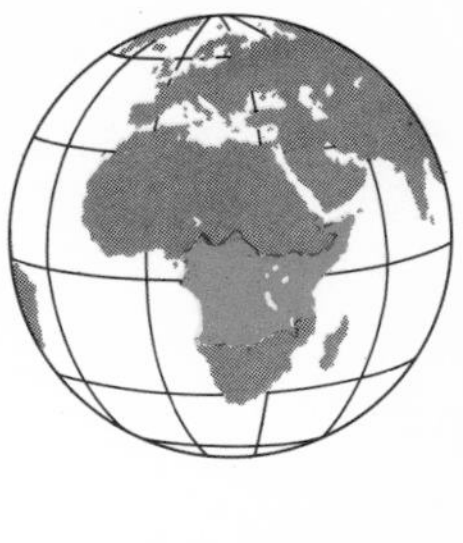

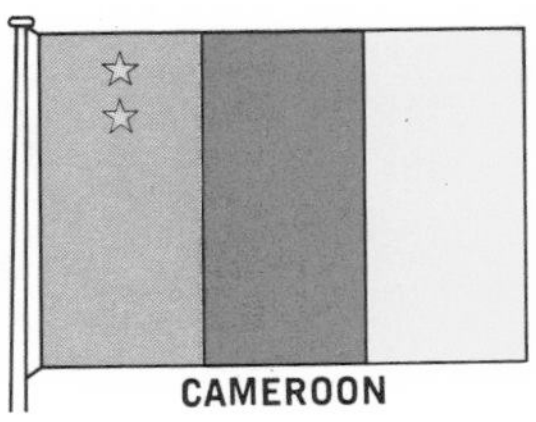

CAMEROON

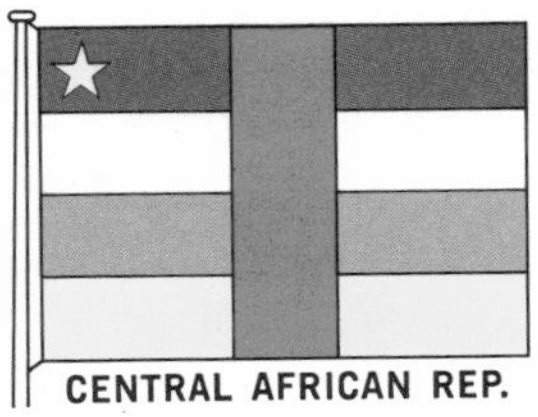

CENTRAL AFRICAN REP.

REPUBLIC OF CONGO

DEM. REP. OF THE CONGO

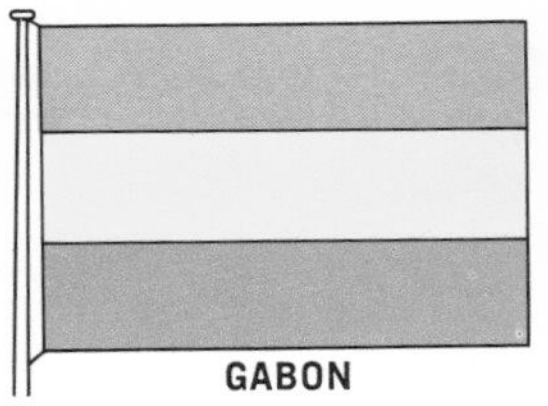

GABON

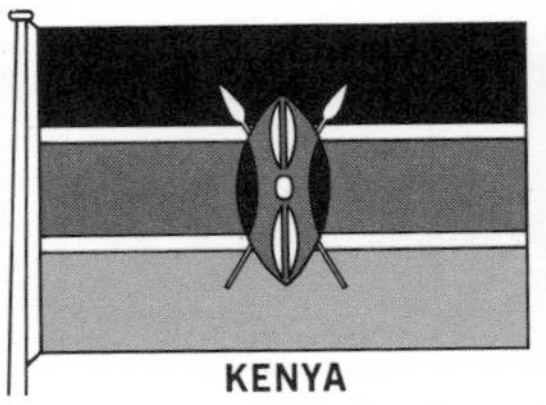

KENYA

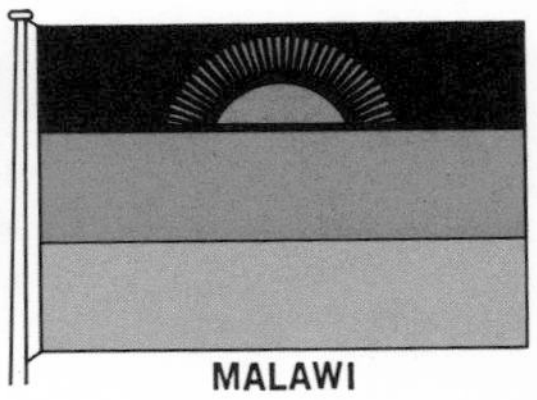

MALAWI

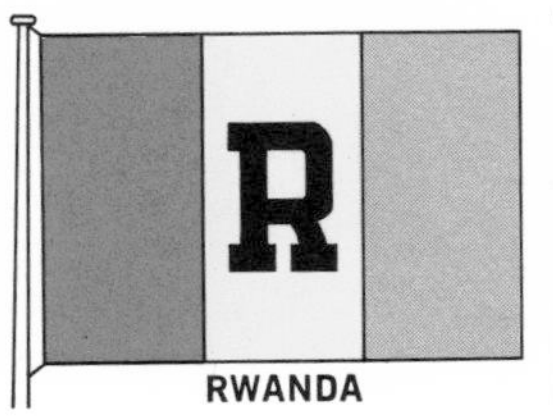

RWANDA

SOMALI REPUBLIC

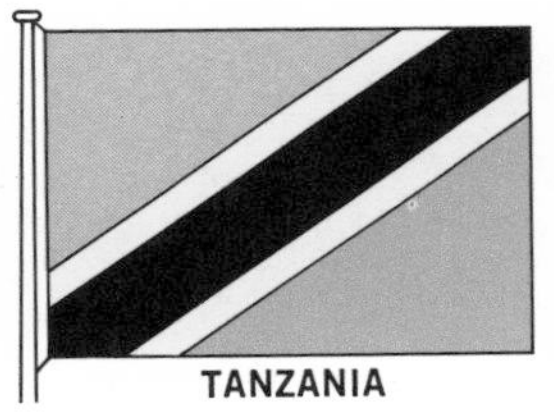

TANZANIA

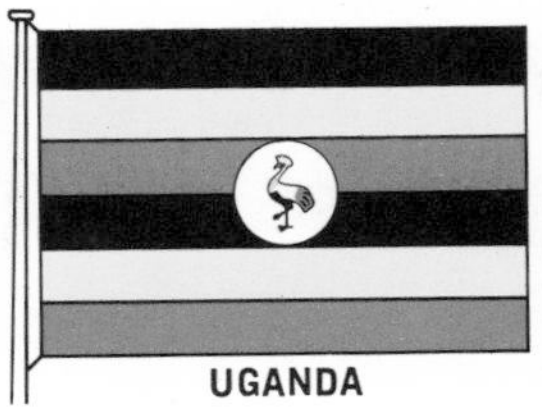

UGANDA

ZAMBIA

ANGOLA

DISTRICTS

Benguela, 487,873 ....B 6
Bié-Cuando Cubango, 565,731 ...C 6
Cabinda, 58,547 ....B 5
Cuanza-Norte, 263,051 ....B 5
Cuanza-Sul, 401,650 ....C 6
Huambo, 597,332 ....C 6
Huíla, 594,609 ....B 7
Luanda, 346,763 ....B 5
Lunda, 247,273 ....C 5
Malange, 451,849 ....C 6
Moçâmedes, 43,004 ....B 7
Moxico, 266,449 ....D 6
Uíge, 399,412 ....C 5
Zaire, 103,906 ....B 5

CITIES and TOWNS

Alto Chicapa ....C 6
Ambriz ....B 5
Ambrizete ....B 5
Andulo (Vila Macedo de
  Cavaleiros), 14,492 ....C 6
Baía dos Tigres ....B 7
Balombo (Vila Norton de
  Matos) ....B 6
Bela Vista ....B 6
Bembe ....B 5
Benguela, 23,256 ....B 6
Cabinda, 4,635 ....C 5
Cacolo ....C 5
Caconda, 5,331 ....B 6
Cacuso ....C 6
Calulo ....C 6
Camabatela, 4,516 ....C 5
Camacupa (Vila General
  Machado), 4,241 ....C 6
Cameia ....C 6
Cangamba (Vila de Aljustrel) ...C 6
Carmona, 6,251 ....C 5
Cassai ....C 6
Cassamba ....C 7
Cassinga ....B 5
Catete ....B 5
Catumbela, 11,149 ....B 6
Caúngula ....C 5
Cavungo (Nana Candundo) .....C 6
Caxito (Vila Oledo) ....B 5
Cazombo ....D 6
Cela ....C 6
Chiange (Vila de Almoster) ....B 7
Chinguar, 4,009 ....B 6
Chitado ....B 7
Chitato (Portugália) ....D 5
Chitembo ....C 6
Cuangar ....C 7
Cuango ....C 5
Cuilo ....C 5
Cuio ....C 6
Cuito Cuanavale ....C 7
Cuma ....B 6
Dala ....D 6
Damba ....B 5
Dirico ....D 7
Dombe Grande ....B 6
Dondo, 6,234 ....B 5
Duque de Bragança ....C 5
Folgares, 4,133 ....B 7
Foz do Cunene ....B 7
Gabela, 4,846 ....B 6
Golungo Alto, 2,250 ....B 5
Henrique de Carvalho, 3,092 ..D 5
Humbe ....B 7
Iona ....B 7
Lândana ....B 5
Léua ....D 6
Lobito, 50,164 ....D 5
Lóvua ....D 5
Luanda (cap.), 224,540 ....B 5
Lucira ....B 6
Lumege (Cameia) ....D 6
Luso, 3,777 ....C 6
Macondo ....D 6
Malange, 19,271 ....C 5
Maquela do Zombo ....C 5
Mavinga ....D 7
Moçâmedes, 7,963 ....B 7
Monteverde ....C 5
Mossâmedes (Moçâmedes),
  7,963 ....B 7
Mucusso ....D 7
Munhango ....C 6
Mupa ....C 7
Muxima ....B 5
Nana Candundo ....D 6
Nóqui ....B 5
Nova Chaves ....C 5
Nova Gaia ....C 6
Nova Lisboa, 38,745 ....B 6
Novo Redondo, 12,324 ....B 6
N'riquinha ....D 7
Porto Alexandre, 5,943 ....B 7
Porto Amboim, 10,711 ....B 6
Portugália ....D 5
Quela ....C 5
Quibaxe ....C 6
Quibaxe ....B 5
Quilengues ....B 6
Quimbele ....B 5
Quinzau ....B 5
Sá da Bandeira, 15,086 ......B 5
Salazar, 5,571 ....B 5
Santo António do Zaire ....B 5
Sanza Pombo ....C 5
São Salvador do Congo, 3,525 ..B 5
São Nicolau ....B 6
Saurimo (Henrique de Carvalho),
  3,092 ....D 5
Silva Porto, 5,606 ....C 6
Uíge (Carmona), 6,251 ....C 5
Vila Arriaga ....B 6
Vila Artur de Paiva, 2,861 ....C 6
Vila de Aljustrel ....C 6
Vila de Almoster ....B 7
Vila de Aviz ....B 7
Vila Gago Coutinho ....D 6
Vila General Machado, 4,241 ..C 6
Vila João de Almeida ....B 7
Vila Macedo de Cavaleiros,
  14,492 ....C 6
Vila Mariano Machado, 8,021 ..B 6
Vila Norton de Matos ....B 6
Vila Nova do Seles ....B 6
Vila Oledo ....B 5
Vila Paiva Couceiro ....B 6
Vila Pereira d'Eca ....C 7
Vila Robert Williams ....B 6
Vila Roçadas ....B 7
Vila Serpa Pinto ....C 6
Vila Teixeira da Silva ....B 6
Vila Teixeira de Sousa ....D 6
Vila Veríssimo Sarmento ....D 5

PHYSICAL FEATURES

Bero (riv.) ....B 7
Cambo (riv.) ....C 5
Coporolo (riv.) ....B 6
Cuango (riv.) ....C 5
Cuanza (riv.) ....B 6
Cubango (riv.) ....C 7
Cuito (riv.) ....C 7
Cunene (riv.) ....B 7
Cuvo (riv.) ....B 6
Loge (riv.) ....B 5
M'Bridge (riv.) ....B 5
Negro (cape) ....B 7
Palmeirinhas (pt.) ....B 5
Santa Maria (cape) ....B 6

BURUNDI

CITIES and TOWNS

Bujumbura (cap.), *47,036 ....E 4
Gitega, 3,579 ....F 4
Rutana ....F 4

CAMEROON

CITIES and TOWNS

Abong-Mbang, 2,037 ....B 3
Bafia ....A 2
Bali ....A 3
Bamenda, 1,455 ....A 2
Banyo, 3,000 ....B 2
Batouri, 5,120 ....B 3
Bertoua, 2,500 ....B 3
Bétaré-Oya, 1,400 ....B 2
Bonabéri ....A 3
Buea, 31,000 ....A 3
Campo, 2,159 ....A 3
Djoum ....B 3
Douala, 127,816 ....B 3
Douala, *187,000 ....B 3
Dschang, 6,000 ....A 3
Ebolowa, 16,000 ....B 3
Edéa, 12,000 ....B 3
Eséka ....B 3
Fort-Foureau, 2,000 ....B 1
Foumban, 20,000 ....B 2
Garoua, 16,000 ....B 2
Guidder, 4,500 ....B 2
Kaélé ....B 2
Kontcha ....B 2
Kousseri, 2,000 ....B 1
Kribi, 7,000 ....A 3
Kumba, 10,000 ....A 3
Kumbo ....B 2
Lomié, 10,127 ....B 3
Mamfé, 10,000 ....A 2
Maroua, 24,979 ....B 1
M'Balmayo, 5,500 ....B 3
Meiganga, 2,000 ....B 2
Mokolo, 3,000 ....B 1
Moloundou, 8,575 ....C 3
N'Gaoundéré, 19,000 ....B 2
N'Kambe, 2,145 ....B 2
N'Kongsamba, 31,991 ....B 3
Poli, 700 ....B 2
Rei-Bouba ....B 2
Sangmélima, 5,700 ....B 3
Tibati, 3,000 ....B 2
Tiko, 15,000 ....A 3
Victoria, 15,000 ....A 3
Wum, 9,710 ....A 2
Yabassi ....A 3
Yaoundé (cap.), 93,269 ......B 3
Yokadouma ....B 3
Yoko ....B 2

PHYSICAL FEATURES

Adamawa (reg.) ....B 2
Benue (riv.) ....A 2
Cameroon (mt.) ....A 3
Cross (riv.) ....A 2
Donga (riv.) ....B 2
Logone (riv.) ....C 2
Lom (riv.) ....B 2
Sanaga (riv.) ....B 3

CENTRAL AFRICAN REPUBLIC

CITIES and TOWNS

Baboua, 2,000 ....C 2
Bakala, 1,000 ....C 2
Bambari, 19,700 ....D 2
Bangassou, 7,300 ....D 3
Bangui (cap.), 111,266 ....C 3
Bania ....C 3
Batangafo, 7,500 ....C 2
Berbérati, 13,100 ....C 3
Birao ....D 2
Bocaranga, 4,000 ....C 2
Boda ....C 3
Bossangoa, 19,000 ....C 2
Bossembele, 1,700 ....C 2
Bouali ....C 3
Bouar, 20,700 ....C 2
Bouca, 3,000 ....C 2
Bozoum, 4,700 ....C 2
Bria, 2,596 ....D 2
Carnot, 4,000 ....C 2
Damara, 800 ....C 2
Djéma ....E 2
Fort-Crampel, 5,000 ....C 2
Fort-de-Possel, 500 ....C 2
Fort-Sibut, 526 ....C 2
Gaza ....E 2
Goubéré ....E 2
Grimari, 1,400 ....C 2
Hyrra Banda ....D 2
Ippy, 6,000 ....D 2
Kaka ....E 2
Kembé ....D 3
Kouango ....C 2
Kouki ....C 2
Koundé ....C 2
Makounda ....C 2
M'Baiki, 3,000 ....C 3
M'Bres, 7,000 ....C 2
Mobaye ....D 3
Mouka ....D 2
Ndélé, 2,500 ....D 2
Ngouro ....D 2
Nola, 700 ....C 3
Obo, 3,000 ....E 2
Ouanda-Djalé ....D 2
Ouango, 2,190 ....D 2
Paoua, 3,500 ....C 2
Rafaï, 8,891 ....D 2
Yalinga, 1,500 ....D 2
Zako ....D 2
Zémio, 1,500 ....E 2
Zemongo ....E 2

PHYSICAL FEATURES

Bamingui (riv.) ....C 2
Dar Rounga (reg.), 25,000 ...D 2
Gao (mt.) ....D 2
Kotto (riv.) ....C 2
Lobaye (riv.) ....C 2
Pendé (riv.) ....C 2
Sara (riv.) ....C 2
Shari (riv.) ....C 2
Shinko (riv.) ....D 2

CONGO, REP. OF (Brazzaville)

CITIES and TOWNS

Boko, 800 ....B 4
Brazzaville, 94,000 ....C 4
Brazzaville, *139,734 ....C 4
Djambala, 1,433 ....B 4
Dolisie, 12,487 ....B 4
Dongou, 2,190 ....C 3
Epéna, 8,446 ....C 3
Etoumbi ....B 3
Ewo, 700 ....B 4
Fort-Rousset, 5,082 ....C 4
Gamboma, 1,700 ....C 4
Ikelemba, 400 ....C 3
Impfondo, 2,000 ....C 3
Kayes, 1,500 ....B 4
Kellé, 1,282 ....B 4
Kibangou, 1,000 ....B 4

(continued on following page)

Central Africa
(continued)

ale, 142,228 .... D 3
a-abibele .... D 4
ni, †188,793 .... E 3
oro, 170,425 .... D 4
ote, 391 .... D 4
ungu, 181,747 .... C 4
ish, 155,806 .... C 3
oma, 33,143 .... B 5
nongo, †26,393 .... D 3
gandanga, 169,490 .... D 3

Bosobolo, 169,450 .... D 3
Budjala, †108,216 .... D 3
Bukama, 169,974 .... E 5
Bukavu, 60,575 .... E 4
Bumba, 10,838 .... D 3
Bunia, 12,410 .... E 3
Bunkeya .... D 6
Busanga .... D 6
Busanga, 197,508 .... D 3
Busu-Djanoa .... D 3
Buta, 10,845 .... D 3
Butembo, 9,980 .... E 3
Charlesville .... D 5
Coquilhatville, 51,359 .... D 4

Dekese, †32,416 .... D 4
Demba, 195,516 .... D 5
Dibaya, †157,404 .... D 4
Dibaya-Lubue .... D 4
Dilolo, †101,718 .... D 6
Dimbelenge, †82,196 .... D 5
Djolu, †62,468 .... D 3
Djugu, †229,631 .... F 3
Djuma .... C 4
Dongo .... D 3
Doruma .... E 3
Dungu, †121,548 .... E 3
Elila .... E 4
Elisabethville, 183,711 .... E 6

Equateur .... C 3
Etoile .... E 6
Faradje, 188,238 .... E 3
Feshi, †76,791 .... C 5
Fizi, †81,856 .... E 4
Gandajika, 188,170 .... D 5
Gemena, 11,551 .... C 3
Goma, 14,115 .... E 4
Gombari .... E 3
Gumba-Mobeka .... C 3
Gungu, †232,236 .... C 5
Idiofa, †287,841 .... C 4
Ikela, 195,810 .... D 4
Imese .... C 3

Ingende, †58,101 .... C 4
Inongo, †50,897 .... C 4
Irumu .... E 3
Isangi †143,721 .... D 3
Isangila .... B 5
Jadotville, 80,075 .... E 6
Kabalo, †43,704 .... E 4
Kabambare, †70,704 .... E 4
Kabare, †336,995 .... E 4
Kabinda, †91,482 .... D 5
Kabongo, 189,217 .... E 5
Kabunda, †47,680 .... E 6
Kahemba, †55,873 .... C 5
Kalehe, †116,877 .... E 4
Kalima .... E 4
Kaloko .... E 5
Kama .... E 4
Kambove (with Shinkolobwe),
  14,517 .... E 6
Kamina, 20,915 .... D 5
Kampene .... E 4
Kanda Kanda .... D 5
Kaniama, †30,421 .... D 5
Kapanga, 147,767 .... D 5
Kasaji .... D 6
Kasangulu, 141,176 .... C 4
Kasenga, †47,320 .... E 6
Kasenyi .... E 3
Kasese .... E 4
Kasongo, †119,708 .... E 4
Kasongo-Lunda, †124,105 .... C 5
Katako-Kombe, 183,068 .... D 4
Katana .... E 4
Katenga .... E 5
Kazumba, †170,714 .... D 5
Kenge, †133,567 .... C 4
Kiambi .... E 5
Kibombo, †39,248 .... E 4
Kikwit, 16,101 .... C 5
Kilwa .... E 5
Kilo .... E 3
Kindu-Port Empain, 19,385 .... E 4
Kiniama .... E 6
Kipushi, 22,602 .... E 6
Kiri, 150,239 .... C 4
Kirundu .... E 4
Kole, Haut-Congo .... D 4
Kole, Sankuru, 149,407 .... D 4
Kolwezi, 45,192 .... D 6
Komba .... D 3
Kongolo, 10,434 .... E 5
Kutu, †73,782 .... C 4
Kwamouth .... C 4
Léopoldville (cap.), 402,492 .... C 4
Libenge, †86,072 .... C 3
Lienartville .... E 3
Likati .... D 3
Lisala, †91,581 .... D 3
Lodja, 7,227 .... D 4
Lokolama .... C 4
Lolo .... D 4
Lomela, †45,874 .... D 4
Loto .... D 4
Lotumbe .... C 4
Luashi .... D 6
Lubefu, 147,363 .... D 4
Lubudi, 5,915 .... E 5
Lubutu, †28,214 .... E 4
Luebo, †65,638 .... D 5
Luisa, †136,181 .... D 5
Luishia .... E 6
Lukolela, Cuvette-Centrale .... C 4
Lukolela, Lomami .... D 5
Luluabourg, 115,049 .... D 5
Lufama .... E 4
Luofu .... E 4
Luozi, 193,123 .... B 5
Lusambo, 9,395 .... D 5
Lusangi .... E 4
Madimba, †139,517 .... C 5
Mahagi, †166,280 .... F 3
Malonga .... D 6
Mambasa, †54,432 .... E 4
Manono, 12,234 .... E 5
Masi-Manimba, †239,870 .... C 4
Masisi, †219,314 .... E 4
Matadi, 60,295 .... B 5
Mitwaba, †37,414 .... E 5
Moanda .... B 5
Moba .... E 5
Mogalo .... C 3
Moliro .... E 5

Monga .... D 3
Monkoto, †31,485 .... D 4
Monveda .... D 3
Moto .... E 3
Mulongo .... E 5
Mungbere .... E 3
Mushie, 12,118 .... C 4
Mutshatsha .... D 6
Muyumba .... E 5
Mwadingusha .... E 6
Mwanza .... E 5
Mweka, †134,011 .... D 4
Mwene Ditu, †103,423 .... D 5
Mwenga, 108,800 .... E 4
Niangara, 167,964 .... E 3
Niemba .... E 5
Nouvelle-Anvers .... C 3
Nyunzu, †36,228 .... E 4
Opala, 193,553 .... D 3
Oshwe, †46,689 .... C 4
Panda .... E 6
Pangi, 199,225 .... E 4
Paulis, 17,430 .... E 3
Penge .... E 4
Piana-Mwanga .... E 5
Poie .... D 4
Poko, †109,032 .... E 3
Ponthierville, 188,623 .... E 4
Popokabaka, †83,485 .... C 5
Port-Francqui, †72,387 .... D 5
Punia, †41,078 .... E 4
Pweto, 154,419 .... E 5
Rutshuru, †151,381 .... E 4
Sakania, †35,333 .... E 6
Samba .... E 4
Sampwe .... E 5
Sandoa, 172,010 .... D 5
Sentery, 180,037 .... E 4
Shabunda, †68,963 .... E 4
Shinkolobwe (with Kambove),
  14,517 .... E 6
Stanleyville, 126,533 .... E 3
Tenke .... E 6
Thysville, 1,601 .... C 5
Titule .... E 3
Tolo .... C 4
Tondo .... C 3
Tora .... E 3
Tshela, †147,288 .... B 4
Tshikapa, †192,646 .... D 5
Tshofa .... D 5
Uvira, †127,295 .... E 4
Vanga .... C 4
Wafania .... D 4
Waka .... D 3
Walikale, †56,345 .... E 4
Wamba, †137,455 .... E 3
Watsa, 6,077 .... E 3
Yahuma, †35,771 .... D 3
Yakoma .... D 3
Yangambi, 18,849 .... D 3
Zongo .... C 3

PHYSICAL FEATURES

Albert Nat'l Park .... E 4
Aruwimi (riv.) .... D 3
Elila (riv.) .... E 4
Fimi (riv.) .... C 4
Garamba Nat'l Park .... E 3
Giri (riv.) .... C 3
Itimbiri (riv.) .... D 3
Ituri (for.) .... E 3
Kwa (riv.) .... C 4
Kwango (riv.) .... C 5
Léopold II (lake) .... C 4
Lindi (riv.) .... E 3
Livingstone (falls) .... B 5
Lokoro (riv.) .... C 4
Lomami (riv.) .... D 4
Lomela (riv.) .... D 4
Lowa (riv.) .... E 4
Lua (riv.) .... C 3
Lualaba (riv.) .... E 4
Lubilash (riv.) .... D 5
Lufira (riv.) .... E 5
Luilaka (riv.) .... D 4

Lukenie (riv.) .... D 4
Lukuga (riv.) .... E 5
Lulua (riv.) .... D 5
Luvua (riv.) .... E 5
Marungu (mts.) .... E 5
Mitumba (range) .... E 5
Sankuru (riv.) .... D 4
Stanley (falls) .... E 3
Stanley Pool (lake) .... C 4
Tshuapa (riv.) .... D 4
Tumba (lake) .... C 4
Uele (riv.) .... D 3
Ulindi (riv.) .... E 4
Upemba (lake) .... E 5
Upemba Nat'l Park .... E 5

EQUATORIAL GUINEA

TERRITORIES

Fernando Po, 72,000 .... A 3
Río Muni, 195,000 .... B 3

CITIES and TOWNS

Bata, †27,024 .... B 3
Kogo .... A 3
Río Benito, †14,503 .... A 3
San Carlos, †19,933 .... A 3
Santa Isabel (cap.), †37,237 .... A 3

PHYSICAL FEATURES

Corisco (isl.) .... A 3
Elobey (isls.) .... A 3
Fernando Po (isl.), 72,000 .... A 3

GABON

CITIES and TOWNS

Banda .... B 4
Bitam, 2,080 .... B 3
Booué, 114 .... B 3
Chinchoua .... A 4
Cocobeach, 100 .... A 3
Franceville, 2,790 .... B 4
Iguéla .... A 4
Kango, 300 .... B 3
Kémboma .... B 4
Koula-Moutou, 3,170 .... B 4
Lalara, 1,333 .... B 3
Lambaréné, 3,750 .... B 4
Lastoursville, 2,000 .... B 4
Lekoni, 3,020 .... B 4
Libreville (cap.), 46,000 .... A 3
Makokou, 1,150 .... B 3
Mayumba, 1,000 .... A 4
M'Bigou, 1,500 .... B 4
Mekambo, 800 .... B 3
Mimongo, 350 .... B 4
Mimvoul, 200 .... B 3
Mitzic, 1,180 .... B 3
Moanda, 2,700 .... B 4
Mouila, 4,240 .... B 4
Myadhi .... B 3
N'Dendé, 1,560 .... B 4
N'Djolé, 500 .... B 4
Nyanga .... A 4
Okondja, 2,470 .... B 4
Omboué .... A 4
Owendo .... A 3
Oyem, 3,050 .... B 3
Port-Gentil, 20,732 .... A 4
Setté-Cama, 1,609 .... A 4
Tchibanga, 2,080 .... B 4

PHYSICAL FEATURES

Ibounzi (mt.) .... B 4
Lopez (cape) .... A 4
N'Dogo (lag.) .... A 4
N'Komi (lag.) .... A 4
Onangué (lake) .... A 4
Pongara (pt.) .... A 3

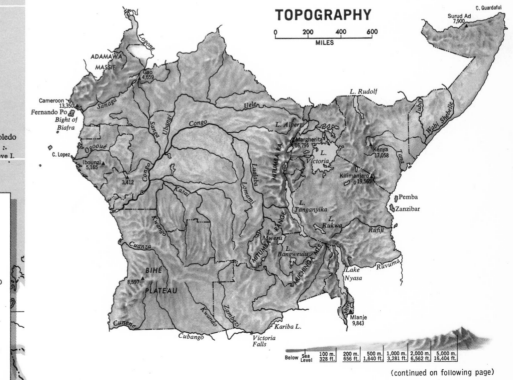

TOPOGRAPHY

0 200 400 600
MILES

Below Sea Level | 100 m. 328 ft. | 200 m. 656 ft. | 500 m. 1,640 ft. | 1,000 m. 3,281 ft. | 2,000 m. 6,562 ft. | 5,000 m. 16,404 ft.

(continued on following page)

CENTRAL AFRICA

CYLINDRICAL EQUAL-AREA PROJECTION

SCALE OF MILES
0 50 100 200 300

SCALE OF KILOMETERS
0 50 100 200 300

Capitals of Countries .... ☆
Other Capitals .... ⊙
International Boundaries _____
Internal Boundaries _____

© C. S. HAMMOND & Co., Maplewood, N.J.

Central Africa
(continued)

KENYA

PROVINCES

Central, 1,323,600 G 4
Coast, 741,100 G 4
Eastern, 1,557,500 G 4
Nairobi (dist.), 343,500 G 4
North Eastern, 268,900 G 3
Nyanza, 1,634,100 F 4
Rift Valley, 1,750,500 G 3
Western, 1,014,500 G 3

CITIES and TOWNS

Baragoi G 3
Buna G 3
Bura H 4
Eldoret, 19,605 G 3
El Wak H 3
Embu, 5,213 G 4
Fort Hall, 5,389 G 4
Garba Tula G 3
Garissa G 4
Garsen G 4
Gazi, 6,452 G 4
Gilgil G 4
Hadu G 4
Isiolo, 5,445 G 3
Kajiado G 4
Kakamega F 3
Kaningo G 4
Karungu F 4
Kericho, 7,692 F 4
Kiambu G 4
Kibwezi G 4
Kilifi G 4
Kipini H 4
Kisii F 4
Kisumu, 23,526 F 4
Kitale, 9,342 G 3
Kitui G 4
Kolbio H 4
Konza G 4
Kwale G 4
Laisamis G 3
Lamu, 5,828 H 4
Lodwar G 3
Lokitaung G 3
Lolgorien G 4
Machakos G 4
Magadi G 4
Malindi, 5,818 H 4
Mambrui H 4
Mandera H 3
Mararal G 3
Marsabit G 3
Meru G 3
Mombasa, 179,575 G 4
Moyale G 3
Muddo Gashi G 3
Nairobi (cap.), 266,794 G 4
Nairobi, *343,500 G 4
Naivasha G 4
Nakuru, 38,181 G 4
Namanga G 4
Nanyuki, 10,448 G 3
Narok G 4
Ngong G 4
North Horr G 3
Nyeri, 7,857 G 4
Port Victoria F 3
Rumuruti G 3
South Horr G 3
Toveta G 4
Thika, 13,952 G 4
Thomson's Falls, 5,316 G 3
Todenyang G 3
Tsavo G 4
Vanga G 4
Voi G 4
Wajir H 3
Witu H 4

PHYSICAL FEATURES

Dawa (riv.) H 3
Formosa (bay) H 4
Galana (riv.) G 4
Gedi (ruins) G 4
Kavirondo (gulf) F 4
Kenya (mt.) G 4
Lorian (swamp) G 3
Lotagipi (swamp) F 2
Nyira (mt.) G 3
Patta (isl.) H 4
Royal Tsavo Nat'l Park G 4
Rudolf (lake) G 3
Tana (riv.) G 4

MALAWI

CITIES and TOWNS

Bandawe F 6
Blantyre-Limbe, 35,000 F 7
Blantyre-Limbe, *40,498 F 7
Chilumbe F 6
Chinteche F 6
Chipoka F 6
Chiromo F 7
Chitipa F 5
Cholo F 7
Dedza, 1,630 F 6
Dowa, 750 F 6
Fort Johnston, 680 G 6
Karonga, 2,310 F 5
Kasungu F 6
Lilongwe, 8,100 F 6
Livingstonia F 6
Mchinji F 6
Mzimba, 940 F 6
Ncheu F 6
Nkhata Bay F 6
Nkhota Kota, 2,240 F 6
Nsanje, 3,790 G 7
Salima, 1,030 F 6
Zomba (cap.), 7,200 G 7
Zomba, *22,000 G 7

PHYSICAL FEATURES

Chilwa (lake) G 7
Mlanje (mt.) G 7
Shire (riv.) G 7

RWANDA

CITIES and TOWNS

Astrida, 3,714 E 4
Kigali (cap.), *4,173 F 4
Kisenyi, 3,956 E 4
Nyanza, 1,010 F 4
Shangugu, 284 E 4

PHYSICAL FEATURES

Kagera Nat'l Park F 4

SOMALI REPUBLIC

PROVINCES

Benadir, 392,109 H 3
Eastern J 2
Hiran, 176,603 J 3
Lower Juba, 113,774 H 3
Mijirtein, 82,710 J 2
Mudugh, 141,197 J 2
Upper Juba, 362,397 H 3
Western H 2

CITIES and TOWNS

Adadle H 2
Afgoi, ◉14,798 J 3
Afmadu, ◉2,051 H 3
Ainabo J 2
Alula, ◉2,175 K 1
Ankhor J 1
Audegle, ◉7,881 J 3
Baduen J 2
Balad, ◉1,198 J 3
Barawa (Brava), ◉7,160 H 3
Bardera, ◉7,134 H 3
Bargal, ◉2,148 K 1
Beira J 2
Belet Uen, 8,515 J 3
Bender Beila, ◉1,975 K 2
Bender Kassim (Bosaso), 6,359 J 1
Berbera, 20,000 J 2
Bereda, ◉2,011 K 1
Birikao (Bur Gavo) H 4
Bohotleh J 2
Borama, 4,000 H 2
Bosaso, 6,359 J 1
Brava, ◉7,160 H 3
Bulhar H 2
Bulo Burti, ◉3,852 J 3
Bur Acaba, ◉10,657 H 3
Burao, 12,000 J 2
Bur Gavo H 4
Callis J 2
Candala, ◉2,771 J 1
Dante (Hafun) K 1
Dif H 3
Dinsor, ◉3,589 H 3
Dusa Mareb, ◉2,337 J 2
Eil, ◉2,067 J 2
El Athale (Itala), ◉844 J 3
El Bur, ◉2,371 J 3
El Dere, ◉565 J 3
El Hamurre J 2
Erigavo, 2,500 J 1
Ferfer J 2
Galkayu, 8,550 J 2
Garad J 2
Gardo, ◉4,076 J 2
Garoe, ◉3,462 J 2
Gobwen H 4
Hafun K 1
Halin J 2
Harardera, ◉508 J 3
Harghessa, 30,000 H 2
Hodur, ◉2,820 H 3
Hordio K 1
Iddan J 2
Iet H 3
Isha Baidoa, 15,725 H 3
Itala, ◉844 J 3
Jelib, ◉10,200 H 3
Karin J 1
Kismayu, 10,386 H 4
Las Anod, 3,000 J 2
Las Dureh J 1
Lugh, ◉2,810 H 3
Marek J 3
Margherita, ◉19,209 H 3
Merka, ◉60,371 H 3
Mogadishu (cap.), 120,649 J 3
Obbia, ◉1,989 J 2
Odweina J 2
Skushuban, ◉1,184 J 1
Taleh J 2
Tijeglo, ◉1,204 H 3
Uanle Uen, ◉6,098 H 3
Upper Sheikh J 2
Villabruzzi, ◉16,014 J 3
Vittorio d'Africa H 3
Zeila H 1

PHYSICAL FEATURES

Aden (gulf) J 1
Guardafui (cape) K 1
Guban (reg.) H 1
Hafun, Ras (cape) K 1
Haud (plat.) J 2
Juba (riv.) H 3
Negro (bay) J 2
Nogal (reg.) J 2
Surud Ad (mt.) J 1
Wabi Shebelle (riv.) H 3

TANZANIA

PROVINCES

Central, 886,962 G 5
Dar es Salaam (city), 128,742 G 5
Eastern, 955,828 G 5
Lake, 1,731,794 F 4
Northern, 772,434 G 4
Southern, 1,014,265 G 6
Southern Highlands, 1,030,269 F 5
Tanga, 688,290 G 4
Western ,1,062,598 F 5
West Lake, 514,431 F 4
Zanzibar, 299,111 H 5

CITIES and TOWNS

Arusha, 10,038 G 4
Bahati G 4
Bagamoyo, 3,445 G 5
Biharamulo F 4
Bukene F 4
Bukoba, 3,760 F 4
Chake Chake, 7,167 G 5
Chunya, †2,663 F 5
Dar es Salaam (cap.), 128,742 G 5
Dodoma, 13,435 G 5
Geita, 1,663 F 4
Handeni G 5
Ifakara G 5
Iringa, 9,587 G 5
Itigi, †7,513 F 5
Kahama, 1,478 F 4
Kaliua, †7,657 F 5
Kanga G 5
Karema, †4,210 F 5
Kasanga, †19,451 F 5
Kasulu F 4
Kibara F 4
Kibaya, †15,662 G 5
Kibondo F 4
Kigoma, 3,466 E 4
Kilosa, 3,209 G 5
Kilwa Kisiwani G 5
Kilwa Kivinje, 2,790 G 5
Kinyangiri, †8,724 G 4
Kipili, †2,964 F 5
Kisiju, †17,710 G 5
Kitunda F 5
Kizimkazi, 992 G 5
Kondoa, 2,816 G 4
Kongwa, 1,364 G 5
Korogwe, 3,536 G 5
Lindi, 10,315 G 5
Liuli F 6
Liwale, †23,192 G 5
Longido, †11,486 G 4
Lushoto, 995 G 4
Mahenge, †5,884 G 5
Makumbako G 5
Manda F 6
Manyoni, 1,388 G 5
Masasi G 6
Mbamba Bay G 6
Mbeya, 6,932 F 5
Mbulu G 4
Mchinga, †16,169 H 5
Mikindani, 4,807 G 6
Mkokotoni, 1,735 G 5
Mohoro, †9,325 G 5
Mombo, †27,767 G 4
Morogoro, 14,507 G 5
Moshi, 13,726 G 4
Mpanda, †21,248 F 5
Mpwapwa, 1,612 G 5
Mtakuja F 5
Mtwara, 10,459 H 6
Murongo, †4,624 F 4
Musoma, 6,057 F 4
Muwale F 5
Mwadui, †11,636 F 4
Mwanza, 19,877 F 4
Mwaya, †15,940 F 5
Nachingwea, 3,792 G 6
Newala, †36,622 G 6
Ngara F 4
Njombe F 5
Nzega F 4
Pangani, 2,052 G 5
Rungwa, †2,812 F 5
Sadani G 5
Same, †4,428 G 4
Sekenke F 4
Shinyanga, 2,113 F 4
Singida, 2,943 F 4
Songea, 1,033 G 6
Sumbawanga, †32,146 F 5
Tabora, 15,361 F 5
Tanga, 38,053 G 4
Tukuyu F 5
Tunduru G 6
Ujiji, 11,739 E 5
Urambo, †4,133 F 4
Utete, 1,622 G 5
Uvinza, †3,792 F 5
Wete, 7,507 G 4
Zanzibar, 57,923 G 5
Zanzibar, *62,636 G 5

PHYSICAL FEATURES

Eyasi (lake) F 4
Gombe (riv.) F 4
Great Ruaha (riv.) G 5
Juani (isl.) G 5
Kanzi (cape) G 5
Kilimanjaro (mt.) G 4
Kilombero (riv.) G 5
Kungwe (mt.) F 5
Mafia (isl.), 12,199 H 5
Manyara (lake) G 4
Masai (steppe) G 4
Mbarangandu (riv.) G 5
Mbemkuru (riv.) G 5
Meru (mt.) G 4
Ngorongoro (crater) F 4
Njombe (riv.) F 5
Olduvai Gorge (canyon) G 4
Pangani (riv.) G 4
Pemba (isl.), 133,858 H 5
Rufiji (riv.) G 5
Rukwa (lake) F 5
Rungwa (riv.) F 5
Rungwe (mt.) F 5
Ruvuma (riv.) G 4
Serengeti Nat'l Park F 4
Wami (riv.) G 5
Wembere (riv.) F 4
Zanzibar (isl.), 165,253 G 5

UGANDA

PROVINCES

Buganda, 1,881,149 F 3
Eastern, 1,902,697 F 3
Northern, 1,249,310 F 3
Western, 1,503,375 F 3

CITIES and TOWNS

Arua, 4,645 F 3
Atura, 119 F 3
Butiaba, 1,216 F 3
Entebbe, 10,941 F 4
Fort Portal, 8,317 F 3
Gulu, 4,770 F 3
Hoima, 1,056 F 3
Jinja, 29,741 F 3
Kaabong F 3
Kabale, 10,919 E 4
Kampala (cap.), 44,735 F 3
Kampala, *123,332 F 3
Kasese, 1,564 F 3
Katwe, 2,057 F 4
Kilembe F 3
Kitgum, 3,454 F 3
Lira, 2,929 F 3
Masaka, 4,785 F 4
Masindi, 1,571 F 3
Mbale, 13,569 F 3
Mbarara, 3,844 F 4
Moroto, 2,082 F 3
Moyo, 2,009 F 3
Mubende, 1,878 F
Namasagali F
Pakwach, 1,467 F
Rhino Camp, 3,478 F
Soroti, 6,645 F
Tororo, 6,365 F
Yumbe, 949 F

PHYSICAL FEATURES

George (lake) F
Kioga (lake) F
Murchison (falls) F
Owen Falls (dam) F
Queen Elizabeth Nat'l Park F
Sese (isls.) F

ZAMBIA

CITIES and TOWNS

Abercorn, 3,660 F
Balovale, 2,260 D
Bancroft, ‡28,170 E
Broken Hill, 21,470 E
Broken Hill, ‡44,730 E
Chibwe E
Chilanga, 2,510 E
Chingola, 16,890 E
Chingola, ‡52,350 E
Chinsali, 1,110 F
Chisamba, 790 E
Choma, 6,940 E
Feira, 310 E
Fort Jameson, 8,520 F
Fort Rosebery, 5,180 F
Isoka, 1,370 F
Kabompo, 990 D
Kafue, 2,490 E
Kalabo, 2,420 D
Kalomo, 2,560 E
Kapiri Mposhi, 440 E
Kasama, 6,720 F
Kasempa, 670 E
Katanino E
Kawambwa, 1,430 E
Kitwe, 54,590 E
Lealui D
Livingstone (Maramba), ‡33,440 E
Luanshya, 19,950 E
Luanshya, ‡72,070 E
Lukulu D
Lundazi, 1,750 F
Lusaka (cap.), 94,560 E
Lusaka, ‡122,300 E
Luwingu, 850 E
Mankoya, 1,600 D
Maramba, ‡33,440 E
Mazabuka, 5,510 E
Mongu, 4,950 D
Monze, 3,230 E
Mpika, 660 F
Mporokoso, 790 F
Mpulungu, 1,830 F
Mufulira, 20,740 E
Mufulira, ‡76,150 E
Mulobezi E
Mumbwa, 1,400 E
Mwinilunga, 700 D
Namwala, 880 E
Nchanga, 35,030 E
Ndola, 72,790 E
Ndola, ‡88,370 E
Nkana, 54,500 E
Nkana-Kitwe, ‡111,450 E
Petauke, 1,640 F
Roan Antelope, 36,300 E
Senanga, 1,500 D
Serenje, 1,650 F
Sesheke, 910 D
Solwezi, 1,930 E
Tunduma F

PHYSICAL FEATURES

Bangweulu (lake) F
Barotseland (reg.), 364,060 D
Chambeshi (riv.) F
Dongwe (riv.) D
Kabompa (riv.) D
Kafue (riv.) E
Kariba (dam) E
Kariba (lake) E
Luangwa (riv.) F
Mosi-Ao-Tunya (Victoria) (falls) E
Muchinga (mts.) F
Mulungushi (dam) E
Sunzu (mt.) F
Victoria (falls) E

CENTRAL AFRICA

PHYSICAL FEATURES

Albert (lake) F
Biafra (bight) A
Bomu (riv.) D
Chiamboni, Ras (cape) H
Chicapa (riv.) D
Congo (riv.) C
Dick's Head (Chiamboni) (cape) H
Dja (riv.) B
Edward (lake) E
Elgon (mt.) F
Indian Ocean H
Ivinda (riv.) B
Kadei (riv.) C
Kalambo (falls) F
Karisimbi (mt.) E
Kasai (riv.) C
Kivu (lake) E
Kwando (riv.) D
Kwilu (riv.) C
Lak Dera (dry riv.) H
Loange (riv.) C
Luapula (riv.) E
Lungwebungu (riv.) D
Margherita (mt.) E
Mbéré (riv.) B
Mweru (lake) E
Natron (lake) G 4
N'Gounié (riv.) B 4
Nyasa (lake) F
Ogooué (riv.) A 4
Ruwenzori (range) E
Ruzizi (riv.) E 4
Sanga (riv.) C
South Atlantic Ocean B
Tanganyika (lake) E
Ubangi (riv.) C
Victoria (lake) F 4
Virunga (range) E
Zambezi (riv.) F 7

*City and suburbs.
†Population of sub-district or division
‡Population of urban area.
◉Population of municipality.

AGRICULTURE, INDUSTRY and RESOURCES

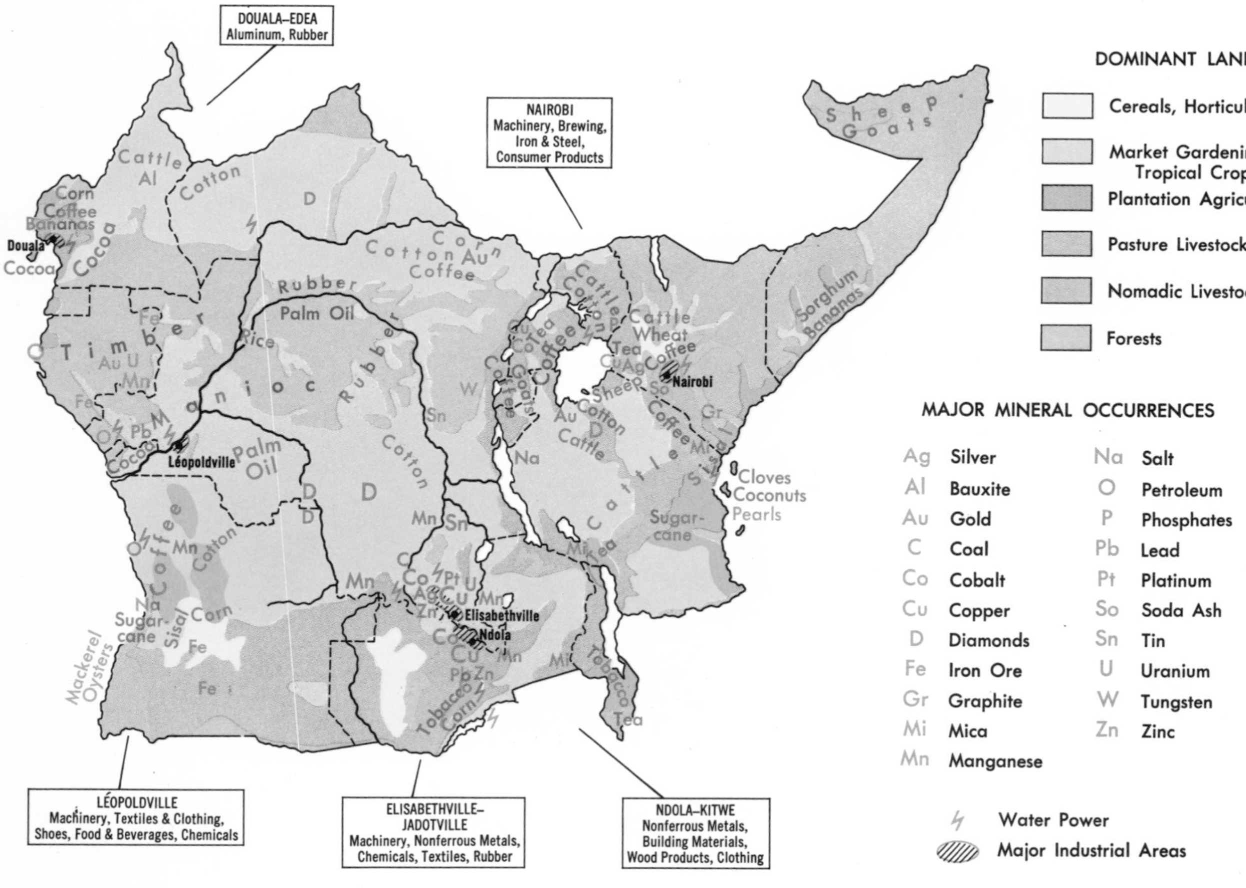
DOUALA–EDEA
Aluminum, Rubber
NAIROBI
Machinery, Brewing, Iron & Steel, Consumer Products
LÉOPOLDVILLE
Machinery, Textiles & Clothing, Shoes, Food & Beverages, Chemicals
ELISABETHVILLE–JADOTVILLE
Machinery, Nonferrous Metals, Chemicals, Textiles, Rubber
NDOLA–KITWE
Nonferrous Metals, Building Materials, Wood Products, Clothing
Douala
Léopoldville
Elisabethville
Ndola
Nairobi
Cloves
Coconuts
Pearls
Mackerel
Oysters
DOMINANT LAND USE
Cereals, Horticulture, Livestock
Market Gardening, Diversified Tropical Crops
Plantation Agriculture
Pasture Livestock
Nomadic Livestock Herding
Forests
MAJOR MINERAL OCCURRENCES
Ag Silver
Al Bauxite
Au Gold
C Coal
Co Cobalt
Cu Copper
D Diamonds
Fe Iron Ore
Gr Graphite
Mi Mica
Mn Manganese
Na Salt
O Petroleum
P Phosphates
Pb Lead
Pt Platinum
So Soda Ash
Sn Tin
U Uranium
W Tungsten
Zn Zinc
Water Power
Major Industrial Areas

SOUTH-WEST AFRICA
AREA	317,725 sq. mi.
POPULATION	551,000
CAPITAL	Windhoek
LARGEST CITY	Windhoek 36,050
HIGHEST POINT	Brandberg 8,550 ft.
MONETARY UNIT	rand
MAJOR LANGUAGES	Bantu, Afrikaans
MAJOR RELIGIONS	Tribal religions, Protestant

MOZAMBIQUE
AREA	297,731 sq. mi.
POPULATION	6,914,000
CAPITAL	Lourenço Marques
LARGEST CITY	Lourenço Marques (greater) 183,798
HIGHEST POINT	Mt. Binga 7,992 ft.
MONETARY UNIT	Portuguese escudo
MAJOR LANGUAGES	Bantu, Portuguese
MAJOR RELIGIONS	Tribal religions, Roman Catholic

BECHUANALAND
	222,000 sq. mi.
	559,000
	Gaberones
	Serowe 34,182
	Tsodilo Hill 5,922 ft.
	pound sterling
	Bantu, Bushman, English
	Tribal religions, Protestant

SOUTH AFRICA
	472,733 sq. mi.
	17,487,000
	Cape Town, Pretoria
	Johannesburg (greater) 1,152,525
	Mont-aux-Sources 10,822 ft.
	rand
	Afrikaans, English, Bantu
	Protestant, Roman Catholic, Mohammedan, Hindu, Buddhist

RHODESIA
	150,333 sq. mi.
	4,260,000
	Salisbury
	Salisbury (greater) 314,800
	Mt. Inyangani 8,517 ft.
	Rhodesian pound
	Bantu, English
	Tribal religions, Protestant

MALAGASY REPUBLIC
	241,094 sq. mi.
	6,180,000
	Tananarive
	Tananarive (greater) 392,153
	Maromokotro 9,450 ft.
	CFA franc
	French, Malagasy
	Tribal religions, Roman Catholic, Protestant

	BASUTOLAND	COMORO ISLANDS	MAURITIUS	RÉUNION	SEYCHELLES	SWAZILAND
AREA	11,716 sq. mi.	849 sq. mi.	720 sq. mi.	970 sq. mi.	157 sq. mi.	6,704 sq. mi.
POPULATION	745,000	212,000	734,000	387,000	46,000	292,000
CAPITAL	Maseru	Moroni	Port Louis	St-Denis	Victoria	Mbabane

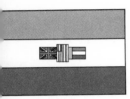

SOUTH AFRICA   RHODESIA   MALAGASY REPUBLIC

AGRICULTURE, INDUSTRY and RESOURCES

DOMINANT LAND USE

- Cereals, Horticulture, Livestock
- Market Gardening, Diversified Tropical Crops
- Plantation Agriculture
- Pasture Livestock
- Nomadic Livestock Herding
- Forests
- Nonagricultural Land

MAJOR MINERAL OCCURRENCES

Ab	Asbestos		Na	Salt
Ag	Silver		Ni	Nickel
Au	Gold		P	Phosphates
Be	Beryl		Pb	Lead
C	Coal		Pt	Platinum
Cr	Chromium		Sb	Antimony
Cu	Copper		Sn	Tin
D	Diamonds		U	Uranium
Fe	Iron Ore		V	Vanadium
Gr	Graphite		W	Tungsten
Mi	Mica		Zn	Zinc
Mn	Manganese			

⚡ Water Power
▨ Major Industrial Areas

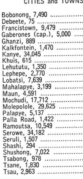

SALISBURY–GWELO Metal Products, Machinery, Transportation Equipment, Building Materials, Wood Products, Chemicals, Clothing, Iron & Steel

BULAWAYO Metal Products, Machinery, Clothing, Wood Products, Chemicals, Building Materials

CAPE TOWN Food & Tobacco, Textiles, Clothing, Machinery, Chemicals, Leather

JOHANNESBURG–WITWATERSRAND Iron & Steel, Machinery, Electrical Goods, Chemicals, Building Materials, Textiles, Food Processing, Printing

DURBAN–PIETERMARITZBURG Oil Refining, Machinery, Sugar Refining, Rubber, Chemicals

PORT ELIZABETH Automobile Assembly, Textiles, Rubber, Leather

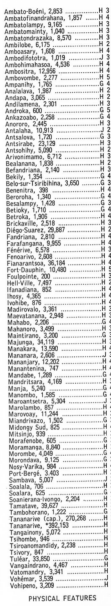

(continued on following page)

Southern Africa
(continued)

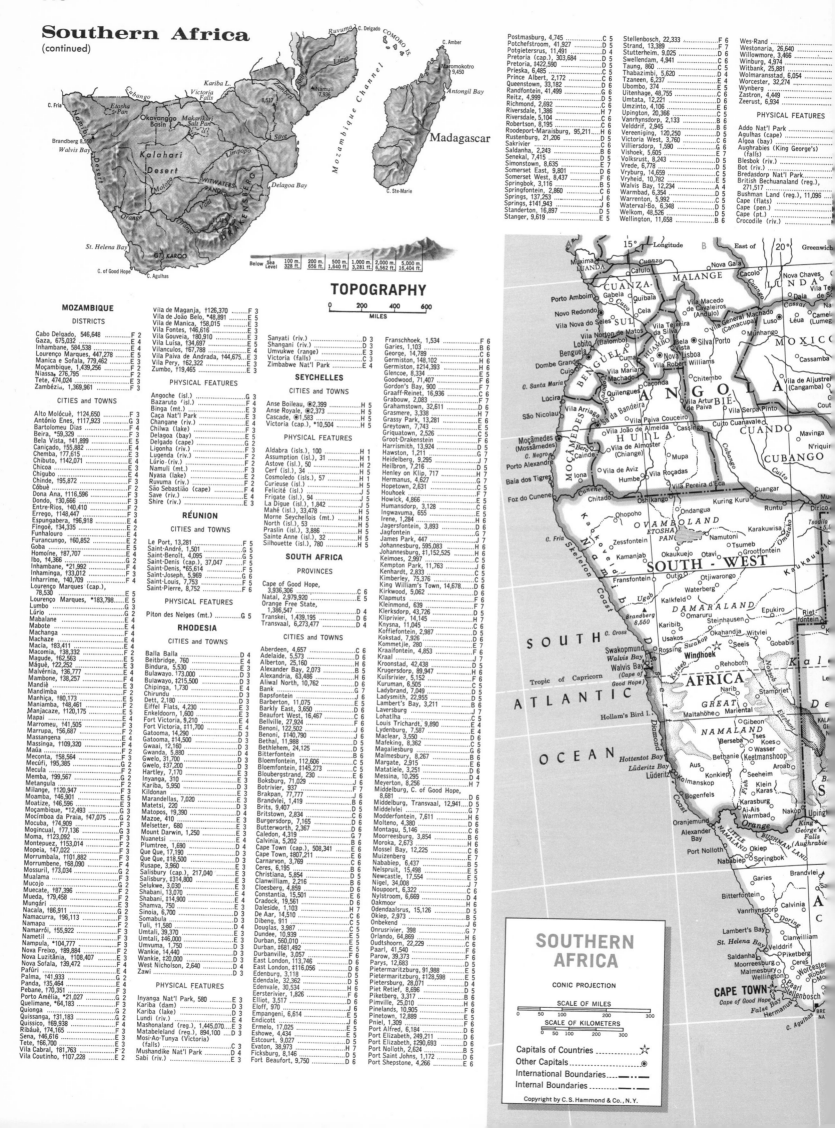

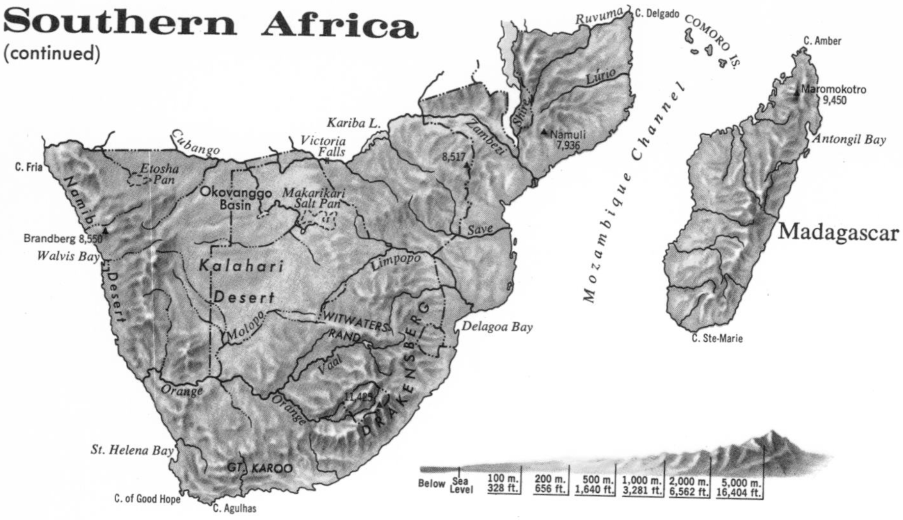
Ruvuma
C. Delgado
COMORO IS.
C. Amber
Maromokotro 9,450
Antongil Bay
Madagascar
C. Ste-Marie
Mozambique Channel
Lúrio
Namuli 7,936
Shire
Zambezi
Kariba L.
Victoria Falls
Cubango
C. Fria
Etosha Pan
Okovanggo Basin
Makarikari Salt Pan
Brandberg 8,550
Walvis Bay
Namib Desert
Kalahari Desert
Limpopo
Save
Molopo
WITWATERSRAND
Delagoa Bay
Vaal
Orange
DRAKENSBERG
St. Helena Bay
GT. KAROO
C. of Good Hope
C. Agulhas
Below Sea Level
100 m. 328 ft.
200 m. 656 ft.
500 m. 1,640 ft.
1,000 m. 3,281 ft.
2,000 m. 6,562 ft.
5,000 m. 16,404 ft.

TOPOGRAPHY

0 200 400 600
MILES

MOZAMBIQUE

DISTRICTS

Cabo Delgado, 546,648 ....F 2
Gaza, 675,032 ....E 4
Inhambane, 584,538 ....E 4
Lourenço Marques, 447,278 ....E 5
Manica e Sofala, 779,462 ....E 3
Moçambique, 1,439,256 ....F 2
Niassa, 276,795 ....F 2
Tete, 474,024 ....E 3
Zambézia, 1,369,961 ....F 3

CITIES and TOWNS

Alto Molócuè, †124,650 ....F 3
António Enes, †117,923 ....G 3
Bartolomeu Dias ....F 4
Beira, *59,329 ....F 3
Bela Vista, †41,899 ....E 5
Caniçado, †55,882 ....E 4
Chemba, †77,615 ....E 3
Chibuto, †142,071 ....E 4
Chicoa ....E 3
Chigubo ....E 4
Chinde, †95,872 ....F 3
Cóbuè ....F 2
Dona Ana, †116,596 ....F 3
Dondo, †30,666 ....F 3
Entre-Rios, †40,410 ....F 2
Errego, †148,447 ....F 3
Espungabera, †96,918 ....E 4
Fíngoè, †34,335 ....E 2
Funhalouro ....E 4
Furancungo, †60,852 ....E 2
Goba ....E 5
Homoíne, †87,707 ....E 4
Ibo, †4,366 ....G 2
Inhambane, *21,992 ....F 4
Inhaminga, †33,012 ....F 3
Inharrime, †40,709 ....F 4
Lourenço Marques (cap.), 78,530 ....E 5
Lourenço Marques, *183,798............E 5
Lumbo ....G 3
Lúrio ....G 2
Mabalane ....E 4
Mabote ....E 4
Machanga ....F 4
Machaze ....E 4
Macia, †83,411 ....E 4
Macomia, †38,332 ....F 2
Magude, †62,563 ....E 5
Máguè, †22,252 ....E 3
Malvérnia, †36,777 ....E 4
Mambone, †38,257 ....F 4
Mandiè ....E 3
Mandimba ....F 2
Manhiça, †80,173 ....E 5
Maniamba, †48,461 ....F 2
Manjacaze, †120,175 ....E 5
Mapai ....E 4
Marromeu, †41,505 ....F 3
Marrupa, †56,687 ....F 2
Massangena ....E 4
Massinga, †109,320 ....F 4
Maúa ....F 2
Meconta, †58,564 ....F 3
Mecúfi, †95,385 ....G 2
Mecula ....F 2
Memba, †99,567 ....G 2
Metangula ....F 2
Milange, †120,947 ....F 3
Moamba, †46,901 ....E 5
Moatize, †46,596 ....E 3
Moçambique, *12,493 ....G 3
Mocímboa da Praia, †47,075 ....G 2
Mocuba, †74,909 ....F 3
Mogincual, †77,136 ....G 3
Moma, †123,092 ....F 3
Montepuez, †153,014 ....F 2
Mopeia, †47,022 ....F 3
Morrumbala, †101,882 ....F 3
Morrumbene, †68,090 ....F 4
Mossuril, †73,034 ....G 2
Mualama ....F 3
Mucojo ....G 2
Muecate, †87,396 ....F 2
Mueda, †79,458 ....F 2
Mungári ....E 3
Nacala, †86,911 ....G 2
Namacurra, †96,113 ....F 3
Namapa ....F 2
Namarrói, †55,922 ....F 3
Nametil ....F 3
Nampula, *104,777 ....F 3
Nova Freixo, †89,884 ....F 2
Nova Luzitânia, †108,407 ....E 3
Nova Sofala, †39,472 ....F 4
Pafúri ....E 4
Palma, †41,933 ....G 2
Panda, †35,464 ....E 4
Pebane, †70,351 ....F 3
Porto Amélia, *21,027 ....G 2
Quelimane, *64,183 ....F 3
Quionga ....G 2
Quissanga, †31,183 ....G 2
Quissico, †69,938 ....F 4
Ribáuè, †74,165 ....F 3
Sena, †46,616 ....E 3
Tete, †66,700 ....E 3
Vila Cabral, †81,763 ....F 2
Vila Coutinho, †107,228 ....E 2
Vila de Maganja, †126,370 ....F 3
Vila de João Belo, *48,891 ....E 5
Vila de Manica, †58,015 ....E 3
Vila Fontes, †46,616 ....E 3
Vila Gouveia, †80,910 ....E 3
Vila Luísa, †34,697 ....E 5
Vilanculos, †67,788 ....E 4
Vila Paiva de Andrada, †44,675...E 3
Vila Pery, †62,322 ....E 3
Zumbo, †19,465 ....E 3

PHYSICAL FEATURES

Angoche (isl.) ....G 3
Bazaruto (isl.) ....F 4
Binga (mt.) ....E 3
Caça Nat'l Park ....E 3
Changane (riv.) ....E 4
Chilwa (lake) ....F 3
Delagoa (bay) ....E 5
Delgado (cape) ....G 2
Ligonha (riv.) ....F 3
Lugenda (riv.) ....F 2
Lúrio (riv.) ....F 2
Namuli (mt.) ....F 3
Nyasa (lake) ....E 2
Ruvuma (riv.) ....F 2
São Sebastião (cape) ....F 4
Save (riv.) ....E 4
Shire (riv.) ....E 3

RÉUNION

CITIES and TOWNS

Le Port, 13,281 ....F 5
Saint-André, 1,501 ....G 5
Saint-Benoît, 4,095 ....G 5
Saint-Denis (cap.), 37,047 ....F 5
Saint-Denis, *65,614 ....F 5
Saint-Joseph, 5,969 ....G 6
Saint-Louis, 7,753 ....F 5
Saint-Pierre, 8,752 ....F 6

PHYSICAL FEATURES

Piton des Neiges (mt.) ....G 5

RHODESIA

CITIES and TOWNS

Balla Balla ....D 4
Beitbridge, 760 ....E 4
Bindura, 5,530 ....E 3
Bulawayo. 173,000 ....D 3
Bulawayo, ‡215,500 ....D 3
Chipinga, 1,730 ....E 4
Chirundu ....D 3
Dett, 2,180 ....D 3
Eiffel Flats, 4,230 ....E 3
Enkeldoorn, 1,600 ....E 3
Fort Victoria, 9,210 ....E 4
Fort Victoria, ‡11,700 ....E 4
Gatooma, 14,290 ....D 3
Gatooma, ‡14,500 ....D 3
Gwaai, †2,160 ....D 3
Gwanda, 5,880 ....D 4
Gwelo, 31,700 ....D 3
Gwelo, ‡37,200 ....D 3
Hartley, 7,170 ....E 3
Inyanga, 310 ....E 3
Kariba, 5,950 ....D 3
Kildonan ....E 3
Marandellas, 7,020 ....E 3
Matetsi, 220 ....D 3
Matopos, †9,390 ....D 4
Mazoe, 410 ....E 3
Melsetter, 680 ....E 3
Mount Darwin, 1,250 ....E 3
Nuanetsi ....E 4
Plumtree, 1,690 ....D 4
Que Que, 17,190 ....D 3
Que Que, ‡18,500 ....D 3
Rusape, 3,960 ....E 3
Salisbury (cap.), 217,040 ....E 3
Salisbury, ‡314,800 ....E 3
Selukwe, 3,030 ....E 3
Shabani, 13,070 ....E 4
Shabani, ‡14,900 ....E 4
Shamva, 750 ....E 3
Sinoia, 6,700 ....D 3
Somabula ....D 3
Tuli, †1,580 ....D 4
Umtali, 39,370 ....E 3
Umtali, ‡46,000 ....E 3
Umvuma, 1,750 ....D 3
Wankie, 14,440 ....D 3
Wankie, ‡20,000 ....D 3
West Nicholson, 2,640 ....D 4
Zawi ....D 3

PHYSICAL FEATURES

Inyanga Nat'l Park, 580 ....E 3
Kariba (dam) ....D 3
Kariba (lake) ....D 3
Lundi (riv.) ....E 4
Mashonaland (reg.), 1,445,070....E 3
Matabeleland (reg.), 894,100 ....D 3
Mosi-Ao-Tunya (Victoria) (falls) ....C 3
Mushandike Nat'l Park ....D 4
Sabi (riv.) ....E 3
Sanyati (riv.) ....D 3
Shangani (riv.) ....D 3
Umvukwe (range) ....E 3
Victoria (falls) ....C 3
Zimbabwe Nat'l Park ....E 4

SEYCHELLES

CITIES and TOWNS

Anse Boileau, ◉2,399 ....H 5
Anse Royale, ◉2,373 ....H 5
Cascade, ◉1,583 ....H 5
Victoria (cap.), *10,504 ....H 5

PHYSICAL FEATURES

Aldabra (isls.), 100 ....H 1
Assumption (isl.), 31 ....H 1
Astove (isl.), 50 ....H 2
Cerf (isl.), 34 ....H 5
Cosmoledo (isls.), 57 ....H 1
Curieuse (isl.) ....H 5
Felicité (isl.) ....J 5
Frigate (isl.), 94 ....J 5
La Digue (isl.), 1,842 ....J 5
Mahé (isl.), 33,478 ....H 5
Morne Seychellois (mt.) ....H 5
North (isl.), 53 ....H 5
Praslin (isl.), 3,886 ....H 5
Sainte Anne (isl.), 32 ....H 5
Silhouette (isl.), 780 ....H 5

SOUTH AFRICA

PROVINCES

Cape of Good Hope, 3,936,306 ....C 6
Natal, 2,979,920 ....E 5
Orange Free State, 1,386,547 ....D 4
Transkei, 1,439,195 ....D 6
Transvaal, 6,273,477 ....D 4

CITIES and TOWNS

Aberdeen, 4,657 ....C 6
Adelaide, 5,573 ....D 6
Alberton, 25,160 ....H 6
Alexander Bay, 2,073 ....B 5
Alexandria, 63,486 ....H 6
Aliwal North, 10,762 ....D 6
Bank ....G 7
Bapsfontein ....J 6
Barberton, 11,075 ....E 5
Barkly East, 3,650 ....D 6
Beaufort West, 16,467 ....C 6
Bellville, 27,924 ....F 6
Benoni, 122,502 ....J 6
Benoni, ‡140,790 ....J 6
Bethal, 11,988 ....D 5
Bethlehem, 24,125 ....D 5
Bitterfontein ....B 6
Bloemfontein, 112,606 ....C 5
Bloemfontein, ‡145,273 ....C 5
Bloubergstrand, 230 ....E 6
Boksburg, 71,029 ....J 6
Botrivier, 937 ....F 7
Brakpan, 77,777 ....J 6
Brandvlei, 1,419 ....B 6
Brits, 9,407 ....D 5
Britstown, 2,834 ....C 6
Burgersdorp, 7,165 ....D 6
Butterworth, 2,367 ....D 6
Caledon, 4,319 ....G 7
Calvinia, 5,202 ....B 6
Cape Town (cap.), 508,341 ....E 6
Cape Town, ‡807,211 ....E 6
Carnarvon, 3,769 ....C 6
Ceres, 6,195 ....B 6
Christiana, 5,854 ....D 5
Clanwilliam, 2,216 ....B 6
Cloesberg, 4,859 ....D 6
Constantia, 15,501 ....E 6
Cradock, 19,561 ....D 6
Daleside, 1,103 ....H 7
De Aar, 14,510 ....C 6
Dibeng, 911 ....C 5
Douglas, 3,987 ....C 5
Dundee, 10,939 ....E 5
Durban, 560,010 ....E 5
Durban, ‡681,492 ....E 5
Durbanville, 3,057 ....F 6
East London, 113,746 ....D 6
East London, ‡116,056 ....D 6
Edenburg, 3,118 ....D 5
Edendale, 32,362 ....D 5
Edenvale, 30,534 ....H 6
Eersterivier, 1,826 ....F 6
Elliot, 3,517 ....D 6
Eloff, 970 ....J 6
Empangeni, 6,614 ....E 5
Endicott ....J 6
Ermelo, 17,025 ....E 5
Eshowe, 4,434 ....E 5
Estcourt, 9,027 ....D 5
Evaton, 38,973 ....H 7
Ficksburg, 8,146 ....D 5
Fort Beaufort, 9,750 ....D 6
Franschhoek, 1,534 ....F 6
Garies, 1,103 ....B 6
George, 14,789 ....C 6
Germiston, 148,102 ....H 6
Germiston, ‡214,393 ....H 6
Glencoe, 8,334 ....E 5
Goodwood, 71,407 ....F 6
Gordon's Bay, 900 ....F 7
Graaff-Reinet, 16,936 ....C 6
Grabouw, 2,083 ....F 7
Grahamstown, 32,611 ....D 6
Grasmere, 3,338 ....H 7
Grassy Park, 13,281 ....E 6
Greytown, 7,743 ....E 5
Griquatown, 2,526 ....C 5
Groot-Drakenstein ....F 6
Harrismith, 13,924 ....D 5
Hawston, 1,211 ....G 7
Heidelberg, 9,295 ....J 7
Heilbron, 7,216 ....D 5
Henley on Klip, 717 ....H 7
Hermanus, 4,627 ....G 7
Hopetown, 2,631 ....C 5
Houhoek ....F 7
Howick, 4,866 ....E 5
Humansdorp, 3,128 ....C 6
Ingwavuma, 655 ....E 5
Irene, 1,284 ....H 6
Jagersfontein, 3,893 ....D 6
Jagfontein ....G 7
James Park, 447 ....J 7
Johannesburg, 595,083 ....H 6
Johannesburg, ‡1,152,525 ....H 6
Keimoes, 2,997 ....C 5
Kempton Park, 11,763 ....J 6
Kenhardt, 2,833 ....C 5
Kimberley, 75,376 ....C 5
King William's Town, 14,678............D 6
Kirkwood, 5,062 ....D 6
Klapmuts ....F 6
Kleinmond, 639 ....F 7
Klerksdorp, 43,726 ....D 5
Kliprivier, 14,145 ....H 7
Knysna, 11,045 ....C 6
Koffiefontein, 2,987 ....D 5
Kokstad, 7,926 ....D 6
Kommetjie, 280 ....E 7
Kraaifontein, 4,853 ....F 6
Kraal ....J 7
Kroonstad, 42,438 ....D 5
Krugersdorp, 89,947 ....H 6
Kuilsrivier, 5,152 ....F 6
Kuruman, 6,505 ....C 5
Ladybrand, 7,049 ....D 5
Ladysmith, 22,955 ....D 5
Lambert's Bay, 3,211 ....B 6
Laversburg ....J 7
Lohatlha ....C 5
Louis Trichardt, 9,890 ....E 4
Lydenburg, 7,587 ....E 4
Maclear, 3,550 ....D 6
Mafeking, 8,362 ....C 5
Magaliesburg ....G 6
Malmesbury, 8,267 ....B 6
Margate, 2,915 ....E 6
Matatiele, 3,251 ....D 6
Messina, 10,295 ....D 4
Meyerton, 8,256 ....H 7
Middelburg, C. of Good Hope, 8,681 ....D 6
Middelburg, Transvaal, 12,941....D 5
Middelvlei ....G 7
Modderfontein, 7,611 ....H 6
Molteno, 4,380 ....D 6
Montagu, 5,146 ....C 6
Moorreesburg, 3,854 ....B 6
Moroka, 2,673 ....H 6
Mossel Bay, 12,225 ....C 6
Muizenberg ....E 7
Nababiep, 6,437 ....B 5
Nelspruit, 15,498 ....E 5
Newcastle, 17,554 ....E 5
Nigel, 34,008 ....J 7
Noupoort, 6,322 ....C 6
Nylstroom, 6,669 ....D 4
Oakmoor ....H 6
Odendaalsrus, 15,126 ....D 5
Okiep, 2,973 ....B 5
Onbekend ....J 6
Onrusrivier, 398 ....G 7
Orlando, 64,869 ....H 6
Oudtshoorn, 22,229 ....C 6
Paarl, 41,540 ....F 6
Parow, 39,373 ....F 6
Parys, 12,683 ....D 5
Pietermaritzburg, 91,988 ....E 5
Pietermaritzburg, ‡128,598 ....E 5
Pietersburg, 28,071 ....D 4
Piet Retief, 8,696 ....D 5
Piketberg, 3,317 ....B 6
Pimville, 25,010 ....H 6
Pinelands, 10,905 ....F 6
Pinetown, 12,889 ....E 5
Pniel, 1,309 ....F 6
Port Alfred, 6,184 ....D 6
Port Elizabeth, 249,211 ....D 6
Port Elizabeth, ‡290,693 ....D 6
Port Nolloth, 2,624 ....B 5
Port Saint Johns, 1,172 ....D 6
Port Shepstone, 4,266 ....E 6
Postmasburg, 4,745 ....C 5
Potchefstroom, 41,927 ....D 5
Potgietersrus, 11,491 ....D 4
Pretoria (cap.), 303,684 ....D 5
Pretoria, ‡422,590 ....D 5
Prieska, 6,485 ....C 5
Prince Albert, 2,172 ....C 6
Queenstown, 33,182 ....D 6
Randfontein, 41,499 ....G 6
Reitz, 4,999 ....D 5
Richmond, 2,692 ....C 6
Riversdale, 1,386 ....H 7
Riversdale, 5,104 ....C 6
Robertson, 8,195 ....C 6
Roodeport-Maraisburg, 95,211.....H 6
Rustenburg, 21,206 ....D 5
Sakrivier ....C 6
Saldanha, 2,243 ....B 6
Senekal, 7,415 ....D 5
Simonstown, 8,635 ....E 7
Somerset East, 9,801 ....D 6
Somerset West, 8,437 ....F 6
Springbok, 3,116 ....B 5
Springfontein, 2,860 ....C 6
Springs, 137,253 ....J 6
Springs, ‡141,943 ....J 6
Standerton, 16,897 ....D 5
Stanger, 9,619 ....E 5
Stellenbosch, 22,333 ....F 6
Strand, 13,389 ....F 7
Stutterheim. 9,025 ....D 6
Swellendam, 4,941 ....C 6
Taung, 860 ....C 5
Thabazimbi, 5,620 ....D 4
Tzaneen, 6,237 ....E 4
Ubombo, 374 ....E 5
Uitenhage, 48,755 ....C 6
Umtata, 12,221 ....D 6
Umzinto, 4,106 ....E 6
Upington, 20,366 ....C 5
Vanrhynsdorp, 2,133 ....B 6
Velddrif, 2,945 ....B 6
Vereeniging, 120,250 ....D 5
Victoria West, 3,760 ....C 6
Villiersdorp, 1,590 ....G 6
Vishoek, 5,605 ....E 7
Volksrust, 8,243 ....D 5
Vrede, 6,778 ....D 5
Vryburg, 14,659 ....C 5
Vryheid, 10,782 ....E 5
Walvis Bay, 12,234 ....A 4
Warmbad, 6,354 ....D 5
Warrenton, 5,992 ....C 5
Waterval-Bo, 6,348 ....D 5
Welkom, 48,526 ....D 5
Wellington, 11,658 ....B 6
Wes-Rand ....
Westonaria, 26,640 ....
Willowmore, 3,466 ....
Winburg, 4,974 ....
Witbank, 25,881 ....
Wolmaransstad, 6,054 ....
Worcester, 32,274 ....
Wynberg ....
Zastron, 4,449 ....
Zeerust, 6,934 ....

PHYSICAL FEATURES

Addo Nat'l Park ....
Agulhas (cape) ....
Algoa (bay) ....
Aughrabies (King George's) (falls) ....
Blesbok (riv.) ....
Bot (riv.) ....
Bredasdorp Nat'l Park............
British Bechuanaland (reg.), 271,517 ....
Bushman Land (reg.), 11,096 ....
Cape (flats) ....
Cape (pen.) ....
Cape (pt.) ....
Crocodile (riv.) ....

15° Longitude
B
East of
20°
Greenwich
LUANDA
MALANGE
CUANZA-SUL
LUNDA
MOXICO
BENGUELA
HUAMBO
BIÉ
ANGOLA
HUILA
MOÇÂMEDES
CUANDO CUBANGO
OVAMBOLAND
ETOSHA PAN
SOUTH-WEST AFRICA
DAMARALAND
Windhoek
NAMALAND
GREAT
Swakopmund
Walvis Bay
Lüderitz
Keetmanshoop
SOUTH ATLANTIC OCEAN
Tropic of Capricorn
Skeleton Coast
Namib Desert
Diamond Coast
Orange
LITTLE NAMALAND
BUSHMAN LAND
Port Nolloth
Springbok
St. Helena Bay
CAPE TOWN
Cape of Good Hope
False Bay
Stellenbosch
C. Agulhas
SOUTHERN AFRICA
CONIC PROJECTION
SCALE OF MILES
0 50 100 200 300
SCALE OF KILOMETERS
0 50 100 200 300
Capitals of Countries
Other Capitals
International Boundaries
Internal Boundaries
Copyright by C. S. Hammond & Co., N.Y.

SOUTH AMERICA

POPULATION DISTRIBUTION

AREA	6,894,000 sq. mi.
POPULATION	162,000,000
LARGEST CITY	Buenos Aires (greater) 6,762,629
HIGHEST POINT	Cerro Aconcagua 22,834 ft.
LOWEST POINT	Salina Grande —131 ft.

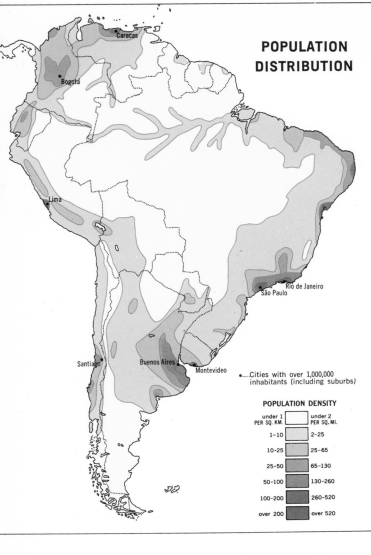

•..Cities with over 1,000,000
inhabitants (including suburbs)

POPULATION DENSITY

under 1 PER SQ. KM.	under 2 PER SQ. MI.
1–10	2–25
10–25	25–65
25–50	65–130
50–100	130–260
100–200	260–520
over 200	over 520

TEMPERATURE AND RAINFALL

AVERAGE TEMPERATURE
(Isotherms, reduced to sea level, in degrees Fahrenheit. Subtract approximately 3 degrees for every 1,000 feet of elevation.)

—————— January
- - - - - - July

AVERAGE ANNUAL RAINFALL

MILLIMETERS	INCHES
Under 250	Under 10
250–500	10–20
500–1,000	20–40
1,000–1,500	40–60
1,500–2,000	60–80
Over 2,000	Over 80

Copyright by C.S. HAMMOND & Co., N.Y.

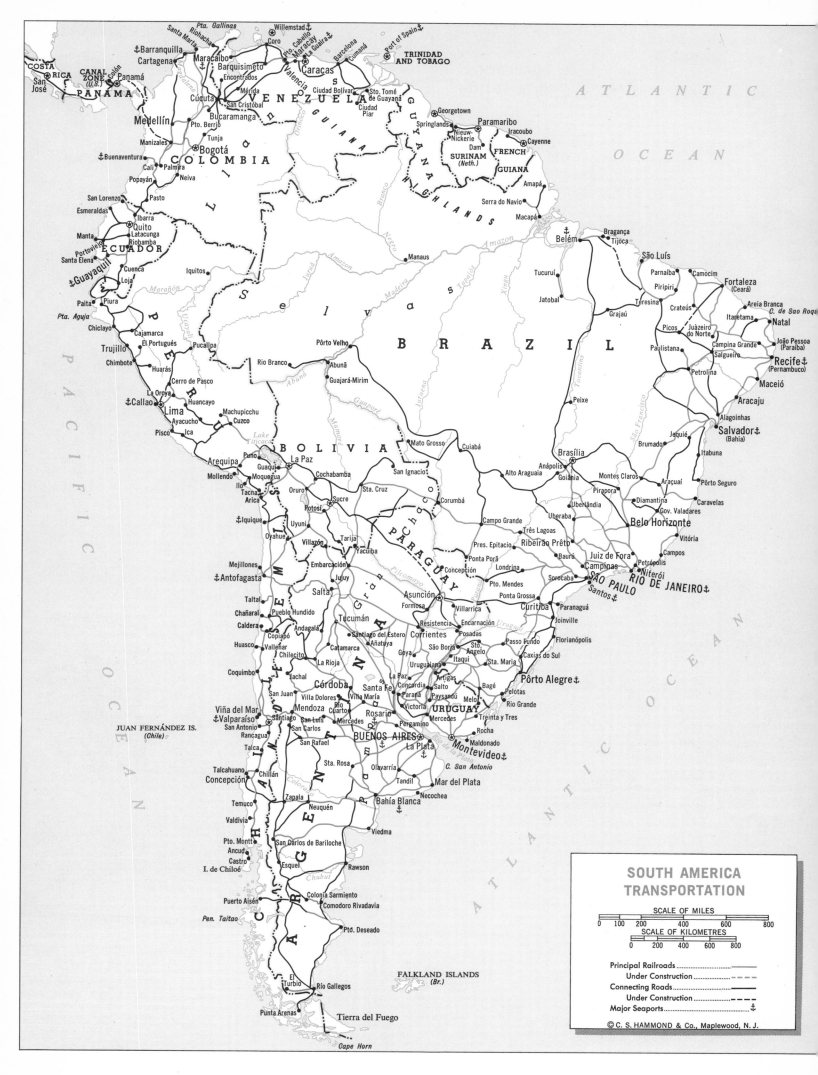

SOUTH AMERICA
TRANSPORTATION

SCALE OF MILES

0 100 200   400   600   800

SCALE OF KILOMETRES

0   200   400   600   800

Principal Railroads ....
Under Construction ....
Connecting Roads ....
Under Construction ....
Major Seaports ....⚓

© C. S. HAMMOND & Co., Maplewood, N. J.

5,000 m. | 2,000 m. | 1,000 m. | 500 m. | 200 m. | 100 m. | Sea
16,404 ft. | 6,562 ft. | 3,281 ft. | 1,640 ft. | 656 ft. | 328 ft. | Level | Below

Pta. Gallinas

Pico Cristóbal Colón 19,029

Lake Maracaibo

Delta del Orinoco

Orinoco

Meta

Cauca

Magdalena

L L A N O S

Guaviare

Orinoco

Negro

G U I A N A

Angel Fall

H I G H L A N D S

Essequibo

I. de Marajó

Putumayo

Japurá

Amazon

Amazon

Xingu

Tocantins

Tapajós

C. de São Roque

Gulf of Guayaquil

Marañón

S e l v a s

Parnaíba

Pta. Aguja

Juruá

Purus

Madeira

Araguaia

Tocantins

São Francisco

C a a t i n g a s

Huascarán 22,205

Ucayali

Beni

Guaporé

Mamoré

PLANALTO DE MATO GROSSO

B R A Z I L I A N

L A   M O N T A Ñ A

L. Titicaca

A N D E S

L. Poopó

Pilcomayo

Rio Grande

H I G H L A N D S

C a m p o s

Vol. Llullaillaco 22,057

Bermejo

G R A N   C H A C O

Paraná

Paraguay

Iguassú Falls

TOPOGRAPHY

Ojos del Salado 22,539

Salado

Paraná

Uruguay

L. dos Patos

M O U N T A I N S

Aconcagua 22,834

P A M P A S

Salado

Rio de la Plata

C. San Antonio

JUAN FERNÁNDEZ IS.

Colorado

Colorado

Negro

I. de Chiloé

P A T A G O N I A

Chubut

G. San Matías

Pen. Valdés

G. San Jorge

Pen. Taitao

ARCH. REINA ADELAIDA

Str. of Magellan

Tierra del Fuego

FALKLAND ISLANDS

Cape Horn

0 | 300 | 600
MILES

L L A N O S

S E L V A S

C A A T I N G A S

ATACAMA DESERT

C A M P O S

C H A C O

P A M P A S

Tropical Rain Forest

Tropical Grasslands

Subtropical Forest

Temperate Forest

Mediterranean

Temperate Grasslands

Tropical Thorn Forest

Temperate Steppe

Desert

Unclassified Highlands

VEGETATION

Venezuela

INTERNAL DIVISIONS		CITIES and TOWNS	

INTERNAL DIVISIONS

Amazonas (terr.), 31,757 ....E 5
Anzoátegui (state), 382,002 ....F 3
Apure (state), 121,077 ....D 4
Aragua (state), 313,274 ....E 3
Barinas (state), 139,271 ....D 3
Bolívar (state), 213,543 ....F 4
Carabobo (state), 381,636 ....D 2
Cojedes (state), 72,652 ....D 3
Delta Amacuro (terr.), 33,979 ......H 3
Dependencias Federales (terr.),
  861 ....E 2
Distrito Federal, 1,257,515 ....E 2
Falcón (state), 340,450 ....D 2
Guárico (state), 244,966 ....E 3
Lara (state), 489,140 ....C 2
Mérida (state), 270,668 ....C 3
Miranda (state), 492,349 ....E 2
Monagas (state), 246,217 ....G 3
Nueva Esparta (state),
  89,492 ....G 2
Portuguesa (state), 203,707 ....D 3
Sucre (state), 401,992 ....G 2
Táchira (state), 399,163 ....B 3
Trujillo (state), 326,634 ....C 3
Yaracuy (state), 175,291 ....D 2
Zulia (state), 919,863 ....B 2

CITIES and TOWNS

Acarigua, 30,635 ....D 3
Achaguas, 1,928 ....D 4
Adícora, 563 ....D 2
Agua Fría ....D 2
Agua Linda ....E 5
Aguada Grande, 1,601 ....G 3
Aguasay, 1,451 ....G 3
Altagracia, 7,362 ....C 2
Altagracia de Orituco, 13,141 ....E 3
Amuay ....C 2
Anaco, 22,733 ....F 3
Apurito, 739 ....D 4
Araborpo ....G 5
Aragua de Barcelona, 8,255 ......F 3
Aragua de Maturín, 2,632 ....G 3
Araquita ....E 4
Araure, 12,299 ....D 3
Aricagua, 237 ....C 3
Arichuna, 983 ....E 4
Aripao, 400 ....F 4
Arismendi, 1,248 ....D 4
Aroa, 6,356 ....D 2
Atapirire, 202 ....F 3
Bachaquero ....C 2
Baragua, 831 ....D 2

Barbacoas, 1,582 ....E 3
Barcelona, 42,267 ....F 2
Barinas, 25,895 ....C 3
Barinitas, 5,897 ....C 3
Barquisimeto, 227,357 ....D 2
Barrancas, Barinas, 3,169 ....C 3
Barrancas, Monagas, 4,210 ....G 3
Betijoque, 3,912 ....C 3
Biruaca, 631 ....E 4
Biscucuy, 3,906 ....D 3
Bobare, 970 ....D 2
Bobures, 2,159 ....C 3
Boca de Aroa, 1,273 ....D 2
Boca de Mangle ....D 2
Boca del Pao, 282 ....F 3
Bocoñó, 10,434 ....C 3
Borbón ....F 4
Borojó, 367 ....C 2
Bruno ....E 7
Bruzual, 556 ....D 4
Buena Vista, Anzoátegui ....F 3
Buena Vista, Falcón, 786 ....D 2
Cabimas, 111,382 ....C 2
Cabruta, 826 ....E 4
Cabudare, 4,480 ....D 3
Cabure, 1,443 ....D 2
Cagua, 16,230 ....E 3
Caicara, Bolívar, 3,281 ....E 4
Caicara, Monagas, 4,759 ....G 3
Calabozo, 15,738 ....E 3
Calderas, 883 ....C 3
Camaguán, 1,934 ....E 3

Camatagua, 1,419 ....E 3
Campo Claro, 1,620 ....G 2
Cantaura, 14,794 ....F 3
Capatárida, 1,281 ....C 2
Capibara ....E 6
Capure ....H 2
Carabobo, Bolívar ....H 4
Carabobo, Carabobo ....D 2
Caracas (cap.), 786,863 ....E 2
Caracas, *1,589,411 ....E 2
Carache, 2,623 ....C 3
Carapa, 108 ....G 3
Cariaco, 4,281 ....G 2
Cariben ....E 4
Caripe, 3,748 ....G 2
Caripito, 21,106 ....G 2
Carirubana, 1,030 ....C 2
Carmelo, 1,944 ....D 2
Carora, 23,227 ....C 2
Carrasquero, 1,353 ....B 2
Carúpano, 38,197 ....G 2
Casanay, 3,561 ....G 2
Casigua, Falcón, 406 ....C 2
Casigua, Zulia ....B 3
Castaña ....F 5
Castillos ....H 2
Caucagua, 4,705 ....E 2
Cazorla, 523 ....E 3
Chaguaramas, 1,363 ....E 3
Chichiriviche, 2,578 ....D 2
Chivacoa, 12,871 ....D 2
Choroní, 353 ....E 2
Churuguara, 4,498 ....D 2
Ciudad Bolívar, 63,266 ....G 4

Ciudad Bolivia, 2,106 ....C 3
Ciudad de Nutrias, 529 ....D 3
Ciudad Ojeda, 53,745 ....C 2
Ciudad Piar ....G 4
Clarines, 2,018 ....F 3
Clavial ....C 2
Cojoro ....C 2
Colón ....E 6
Coloradito ....B 3
Comunidad ....E 6
Coporito ....H 3
Coro, 45,368 ....D 2
Corozo Pando ....E 3
Cúa, 5,567 ....E 2
Cubiro, 1,742 ....D 3
Cuchivero ....F 4
Cucurital ....G 4
Cumaná, 69,937 ....F 2
Cumanacoa, 7,354 ....G 2
Cunaviche, 596 ....E 4
Curiapo, 375 ....H 3
Dabajuro, 3,902 ....C 2
Dolores, 1,130 ....E 4
Duaca, 5,771 ....D 2
Ejido, 5,360 ....C 3
El Almacén ....C 4
El Amparo, 1,090 ....C 4
El Baúl, 1,550 ....D 3
El Callao, 5,039 ....G 4
El Calvario, 577 ....E 3
El Carmen ....E 7
El Chaparro, 1,709 ....F 3
El Cristo ....G 4
El Dorado, 2,094 ....H 4

El Empedrado, 1,739 ....C 3
El Guapo, 842 ....E 2
El Manteco, 999 ....G 4
El Miamo, 269 ....H 4
El Murciélago ....E 7
El Negro ....G 4
El Oso, Amazonas ....F 5
El Oso, Bolívar ....H 5
El Palmar, 1,986 ....G 4
El Pao, Anzoátegui, 686 ....F 3
El Pao, Bolívar ....G 4
El Pao, Cojedes, 1,081 ....D 3
El Peru ....H 4
El Pilar, 3,326 ....G 2
El Rastro, 746 ....E 3
El Roque ....D 3
El Samán de Apure, 1,109 ....D 4
El Socorro, 3,167 ....E 3
El Sombrero, 5,748 ....E 3
El Terror ....H 3
El Tigre, 42,028 ....F 3
El Tigrito, 20,753 ....F 3
El Tocuyo, 14,560 ....D 2
El Toro ....H 3
El Vigía, 8,938 ....C 3
El Vinculo ....D 1
El Yagual, 435 ....D 4
Elorza, 2,112 ....D 4
Encontrados, 2,991 ....B 3
Espino, 441 ....F 3
Evegüí ....G 5
Garcitas, 1,224 ....D 4
Guacara, 11,343 ....D 2
Guachara, 462 ....D 4

Guadarrama, 461 ....E 3
Guaina ....
Guanajuña ....
Guanare, 18,476 ....D 3
Guanarito, 1,047 ....D 3
Guanoco ....
Guanta, 7,825 ....F 2
Guaraguao ....
Guardatinajas, 706 ....E 3
Guarero ....
Guarico, 3,653 ....D 2
Guariquén, 633 ....
Guasdualito, 4,580 ....C 4
Guasimal, 303 ....
Guasipati, 3,446 ....H 4
Guatisimina ....
Guayabal ....
Guayabal, 844 ....E 3
Güiria, 11,061 ....H 2
Guri ....
Gusmán Blanco ....
Higuerote, 3,852 ....E 2
Iasauutedi ....
Icabarú ....
Independencia, 3,658 ....D 1
Irapa, 4,532 ....
Juangriego, 4,483 ....
Judibana ....
Jusepin ....
Kavanayen ....
La Asunción, 5,517 ....G 2
La Campanita ....
La Canoa, 256 ....
La Ceiba, Apure ....

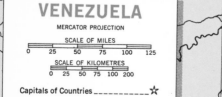

VENEZUELA

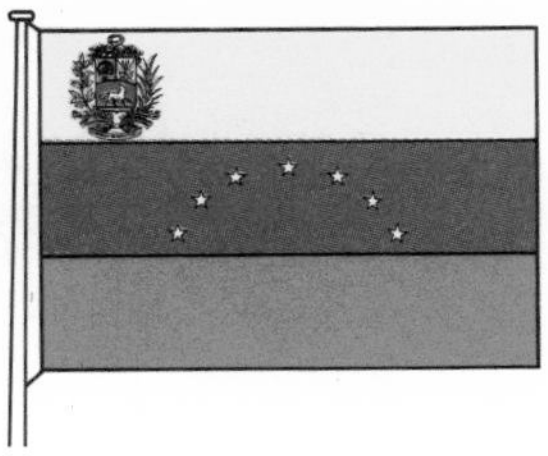

AREA	352,143 sq. mi.
POPULATION	8,722,000
CAPITAL	Caracas
LARGEST CITY	Caracas (greater) 1,589,411
HIGHEST POINT	Pico Bolívar 16,427 ft.
MONETARY UNIT	bolívar
MAJOR LANGUAGE	Spanish
MAJOR RELIGION	Roman Catholic

Ceiba, Trujillo, 199 ....C 3
Concepción ....B 2
Concepción, 9,488 ....B 2
Cruz de Taratara, 1,339 ....D 2
Democracia ....E 6
Esmeralda ....F 6
Esperanza, Amazonas ....E 6
Esperanza, Delta Amacuro ....H 3
Fría, 4,771 ....B 3
Grita, 7,866 ....C 3
Guaira, 20,497 ....E 2
Horqueta ....G 3
Inglesa ....G 3
Leona ....G 3
Lucha ....E 3
Luz, 414 ....D 3
Margarita ....H 3
Paragua, 833 ....G 4
Tigra ....H 4
Trinidad, Apure ....D 4
Trinidad, Portuguesa, 145 ....D 3
Trinidad de Orichuna, 820 ....D 4
Unión, 1,077 ....E 3
Urbana, 444 ....E 4
Vela, 4,971 ....D 2
Victoria, Apure, 303 ....D 4
Victoria, Aragua, 22,291 ....E 2
guna Sucia ....F 4
gunetas ....C 3
s Bonitas, 306 ....F 4
s Cruces ....B 3
s Lajitas ....F 4
s Loras ....B 3
s Mercedes, 5,422 ....E 3

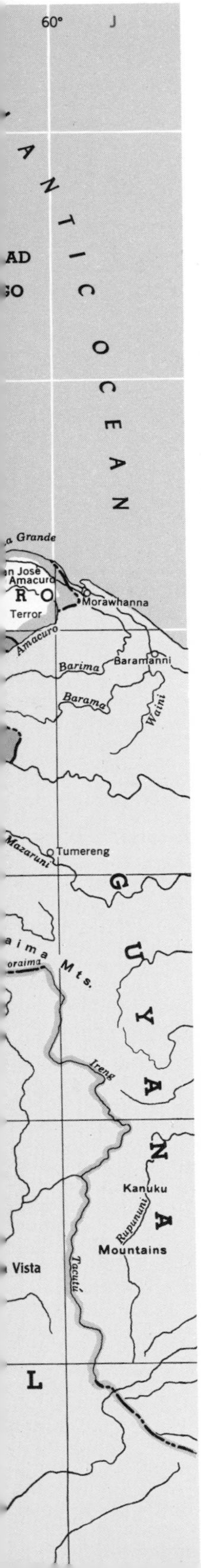

60°
J
AD
O
A
N
T
I
C
O
C
E
A
N
a Grande
an José
Amacuro
R O
Morawhanna
Terror
Amacuro
Barima
Baramanni
Barama
Waini
Mazaruni
Tumereng
G
aima
oraima
Mts.
U
Y
Ireng
A
N
Kanuku
Rupununi
A
Mountains
Vista
Tacutu
L

Las Piedras, Falcón, 1,834 ....C 2
Las Piedras, Zulia ....B 2
Las Trincheras ....F 4
Las Vegas, 1,190 ....D 3
Libertad, Barinas, 1,238 ....D 3
Libertad, Cojedes, 1,000 ....D 3
Los Taques, 3,095 ....C 2
Los Teques, 36,073 ....E 2
Luepa ....H 5
Macareo Santo Niño ....H 3
Machiques, 11,115 ....B 3
Macuro, 899 ....H 2
Macuto, 7,041 ....E 2
Maiquetía, 75,687 ....E 2
Manoa ....H 3
Mantecal, Apure, 987 ....D 4
Mantecal, Bolívar ....F 4
Maparari, 1,339 ....D 2
Mapire, 658 ....F 4
Maporal, 224 ....C 4
Maracaibo, 502,693 ....C 2
Maracay, 153,724 ....E 2
Marigüitar, 3,075 ....G 2
Maripa, 802 ....F 4
Maroa, 417 ....E 6
Matú ....F 4
Maturín, 54,250 ....G 3
Mauacunya ....F 5
Mene de Mauroa, 3,606 ....C 2
Mene Grande, 11,673 ....C 3
Mérida, 46,409 ....C 3
Mesa Bolívar, 1,237 ....C 3
Mirimire, 1,473 ....D 2
Moitaco, 364 ....F 4
Morganito ....E 5
Morón, 7,126 ....D 2
Mucuchachí, 396 ....C 3
Mucuchíes, 1,036 ....C 3
Naricual, 595 ....F 2
Nirgua, 7,371 ....D 2
Nuevo Mamo ....G 3
Obispos, 652 ....D 3
Ocumare de la Costa, 1,343 ....E 2
Ocumare del Tuy, 15,006 ....E 2
Onoto, 1,091 ....F 3
Ortiz, 1,317 ....E 3
Ospino, 1,624 ....D 3
Palmarejo ....C 2
Palmarito, Apure, 1,176 ....D 4
Palmarito, Mérida, 903 ....C 3
Papelón, 411 ....D 3
Paraguaipoa, 1,443 ....C 2
Paraíso de Chabasquén, 2,321 ....D 3
Pariaguán, 6,241 ....F 3
Parmana ....F 4
Pedernales, 788 ....G 3
Pedregal, 1,474 ....C 2
Peraitepuí ....H 5
Piacoa ....H 3
Piedra Mapaya ....F 6
Pimichin ....E 6
Píritu, Anzoátegui, 1,445 ....F 2
Píritu, Falcón, 1,868 ....D 2
Píritu, Portuguesa, 4,882 ....D 3
Porlamar, 21,754 ....G 2
Pregonero, 2,894 ....C 3
Pueblo Nuevo, 2,867 ....D 1
Puedpa ....G 4
Puerto Ayacucho, 5,462 ....E 5
Puerto Cabello, 52,222 ....E 2
Puerto Cumarebo, 8,033 ....D 2
Puerto Hierro ....H 2
Puerto La Cruz, 59,099 ....F 2
Puerto Miranda ....E 4
Puerto Nutrias, 565 ....D 3
Puerto Páez, 767 ....E 4
Puerto Píritu, 2,404 ....F 2
Punta Cardón, 11,246 ....C 2
Punta de Mata ....G 3
Punta de Piedras, 2,250 ....F 2
Punto Fijo ....D 2
Puruey, 343 ....F 4
Puruname ....E 6
Quibor, 7,046 ....D 3
Quiriquire, 7,405 ....G 3
Quisiro, 816 ....C 2
Rajunya ....F 5
Rincón Hondo ....D 4
Río Caribe, 7,774 ....G 2
Río Chico, 2,612 ....F 2

Río Claro, 1,374 ....D 3
Río Tocuyo, 1,650 ....C 2
Rosario, 10,442 ....B 2
Rubio, 11,774 ....B 4
Sabaneta, 2,009 ....D 3
Sabaneta, 414 ....D 2
San Antonio, Amazonas ....E 6
San Antonio, Monagas, 3,355 ....G 2
San Antonio, Táchira, 14,247 ....B 4
San Antonio, Zulia, 510 ....C 3
San Antonio de Caparo, 1,412 ....C 4
San Antonio de Tabasca, 435 ....G 3
San Carlos, Cojedes, 11,934 ....D 3
San Carlos, Zulia, 686 ....C 2
San Carlos de Río Negro, 474 ....E 7
San Carlos del Zulia, 14,480 ....C 3
San Casimiro, 3,469 ....E 3
San Cristóbal, 116,176 ....B 4
San Diego de Cabrutica, 459 ....F 3
San Felipe, Yaracuy, 28,744 ....D 2
San Felipe, Zulia ....B 3
San Félix, 424 ....C 2
San Fernando de Apure, 24,443 ....E 4
San Fernando de Atabapo, 898 ....E 5
San Francisco, Lara, 967 ....C 2
San Francisco, Zulia, 33,152 ....C 2
San Ignacio ....B 2
San José, Amazonas ....E 5
San José, Zulia, 2,991 ....B 3
San José de Amacuro ....H 3
San José de Areocuar, 1,000 ....G 2
San José de la Costa ....D 2
San José de Río Chico, 3,368 ....F 2
San José de Tiznados, 504 ....E 3
San Juan de Colón, 8,944 ....B 3
San Juan de Las Galdonas, 1,104 G 2
San Juan de los Cayos, 1,191 ....D 2
San Juan de los Morros, 27,062 ....E 3
San Juan de Payara, 945 ....E 4
San Lorenzo, Falcón, 527 ....D 2
San Lorenzo, Zulia ....C 3
San Mateo, 1,850 ....F 3
San Mauricio ....E 3
San Pedro de las Bocas ....G 4
San Rafael, 6,390 ....C 2
San Rafael de Atamaica, 597 ....E 4
San Rafael de Orituco, 991 ....E 3
San Sebastián, 4,104 ....E 2
San Timoteo, 2,823 ....C 3
San Tomé ....F 3
San Vicente, Amazonas ....E 5
San Vicente, Apure, 252 ....D 4
Sanare, 3,599 ....D 3
Sanariapo ....E 5
Santa Ana, Anzoátegui, 3,613 ....F 3
Santa Ana, Táchira, 3,677 ....B 4
Santa Bárbara, Amazonas ....E 6
Santa Bárbara, Barinas, 2,079 ....C 4
Santa Bárbara, Bolívar ....H 4
Santa Bárbara, Monagas, 1,725 ..G 3
Santa Bárbara, Zulia ....C 3
Santa Catalina, Barinas, 420 ....D 4
Santa Calatina, Delta Amacuro ..H 3
Santa Clara ....G 4
Santa Cruz, Anzoátegui, 420 ....F 3
Santa Cruz, Mérida, 3,125 ....C 3
Santa Cruz de Bucaral, 1,871 ....D 2
Santa Cruz de Mara, 1,919 ....C 2
Santa Cruz del Zulia, 2,041 ....B 3
Santa Elena de Uairén, 752 ....H 5
Santa Inés, Anzoátegui, 920 ....F 3
Santa Inés, Barinas, 257 ....C 3

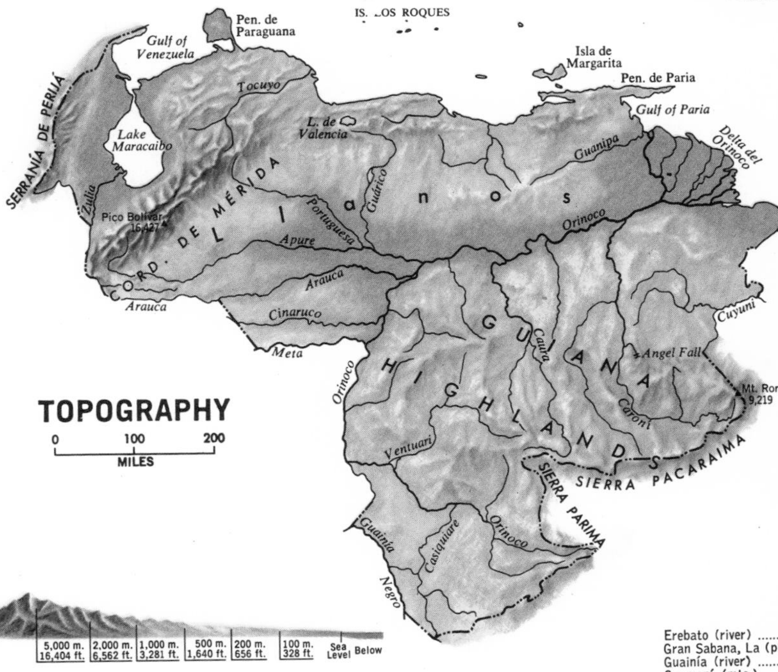

Pen. de Paraguana
IS. LOS ROQUES
Gulf of Venezuela
Isla de Margarita
Pen. de Paria
Gulf of Paria
Delta del Orinoco
SERRANIA DE PERIJA
Tocuyo
L. de Valencia
Lake Maracaibo
Guanipa
Zulia
Pico Bolívar 16,427
CORD. DE MERIDA
Portuguesa
Guárico
L l a n o s
Orinoco
Apure
Arauca
Arauca
Cinaruco
Cuyuni
Meta
Orinoco
Caura
G U I A N A
H I G H L A N D S
Angel Fall
Caroni
Mt. Roraima 9,219
Ventuari
SIERRA PACARAIMA
SIERRA PARIMA
Orinoco
Casiquiare
Guainia
Negro
5,000 m. 16,404 ft.
2,000 m. 6,562 ft.
1,000 m. 3,281 ft.
500 m. 1,640 ft.
200 m. 656 ft.
100 m. 328 ft.
Sea Level
Below

TOPOGRAPHY

0 100 200
MILES

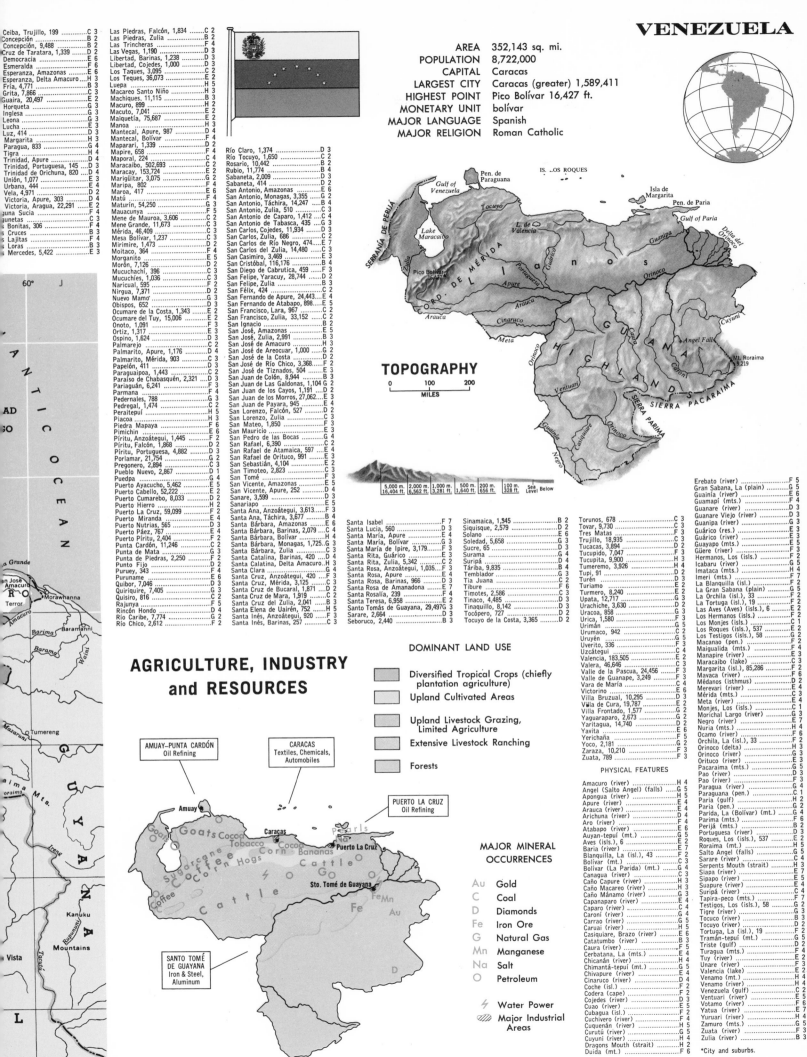

Santa Isabel ....F 7
Santa Lucia, 560 ....D 3
Santa María, Apure ....E 4
Santa María, Bolívar ....G 3
Santa María de Ipire, 3,179 ....F 3
Santa Rita, Guárico ....E 3
Santa Rita, Zulia, 5,342 ....C 2
Santa Rosa, Anzoátegui, 1,035 ....F 3
Santa Rosa, Apure ....E 4
Santa Rosa, Barinas, 966 ....D 3
Santa Rosa de Amanadona ....E 7
Santa Rosalía, 239 ....F 4
Santa Teresa, 6,958 ....E 2
Santo Tomás de Guayana, 29,497 G 3
Sarare, 2,664 ....D 3
Seboruco, 2,440 ....B 3

Sinamaica, 1,345 ....B 2
Siquisque, 2,579 ....D 2
Solano ....E 6
Soledad, 5,658 ....G 3
Sucre, 65 ....D 3
Surama ....G 4
Suripá ....D 4
Táriba, 9,835 ....B 4
Temblador ....G 3
Tia Juana ....C 2
Tibure ....F 6
Timotes, 2,586 ....C 3
Tinaco, 4,485 ....D 3
Tinaquillo, 8,142 ....D 3
Tocópero, 727 ....D 2
Tocuyo de la Costa, 3,365 ....D 2

Torunos, 678 ....C 3
Tovar, 9,730 ....C 3
Tres Matas ....F 3
Trujillo, 18,935 ....C 3
Tucacas, 3,894 ....D 2
Tucupido, 7,047 ....F 3
Tucupita, 9,900 ....H 3
Tumeremo, 3,926 ....H 4
Tupi, 91 ....D 2
Turén ....D 3
Turiamo ....E 2
Turmero, 8,240 ....E 2
Upata, 12,717 ....G 3
Urachiche, 3,630 ....D 2
Uracoa, 858 ....G 3
Urica, 1,580 ....F 3
Urimán ....G 5
Urumaco, 942 ....C 2
Uruyén ....G 5
Uverito, 336 ....F 3
Uzcátegui ....C 4
Valencia, 183,505 ....E 2
Valera, 46,646 ....C 3
Valle de la Pascua, 24,456 ....F 3
Valle de Guanape, 3,249 ....F 3
Vara de María ....C 4
Victorino ....E 6
Villa Bruzual, 10,295 ....D 3
Villa de Cura, 19,787 ....E 2
Villa Frontado, 1,577 ....G 2
Yaguaraparo, 2,673 ....G 2
Yaritagua, 14,740 ....D 2
Yavita ....E 6
Yerichaña ....F 5
Yoco, 2,181 ....G 2
Zaraza, 10,210 ....F 3
Zuata, 789 ....F 3

PHYSICAL FEATURES

Amacuro (river) ....H 4
Angel (Salto Angel) (falls) ....G 5
Apongua (river) ....H 5
Apure (river) ....E 4
Arauca (river) ....E 4
Arichuna (river) ....D 4
Aro (river) ....F 4
Atabapo (river) ....E 6
Auyan-tepuí (mt.) ....G 5
Aves (isls.), 6 ....E 2
Baria (river) ....E 7
Blanquilla, La (isl.), 43 ....F 2
Bolívar (mt.) ....C 3
Bolívar (La Parida) (mt.) ....G 4
Canagua (river) ....C 3
Caño Capure (river) ....H 3
Caño Macareo (river) ....H 3
Caño Mánamo (river) ....G 3
Capanaparo (river) ....E 4
Caparo (river) ....C 4
Caroní (river) ....G 4
Carrao (river) ....G 5
Caruai (river) ....H 5
Casiquiare, Brazo (river) ....E 6
Catatumbo (river) ....B 3
Caura (river) ....F 5
Cerbatana, La (mts.) ....E 4
Chicanán (river) ....H 4
Chimantá-tepuí (mt.) ....G 5
Chivapure (river) ....E 4
Cinaruco (river) ....D 4
Coche (isl.) ....F 2
Codera (cape) ....F 2
Cojedes (river) ....D 3
Cuao (river) ....E 5
Cubagua (isl.) ....F 2
Cuchivero (river) ....F 4
Cuquenán (river) ....H 5
Curutú (river) ....G 5
Cuyuni (river) ....H 4
Dragons Mouth (strait) ....H 2
Duida (mt.) ....F 6

Erebato (river) ....F 5
Gran Sabana, La (plain) ....G 5
Guainía (river) ....E 6
Guamapí (mts.) ....F 4
Guanare (river) ....D 3
Guanare Viejo (river) ....D 3
Guanipa (river) ....G 3
Guárico (res.) ....E 3
Guárico (river) ....E 3
Guayapo (mts.) ....E 5
Güere (river) ....F 3
Hermanos, Los (isls.) ....F 2
Icabaru (river) ....G 5
Imataca (mts.) ....H 4
Imeri (mts.) ....F 7
La Blanquilla (isl.) ....F 2
La Gran Sabana (plain) ....G 5
La Orchila (isl.), 33 ....F 2
La Tortuga (isl.), 19 ....F 2
Las Aves (Aves) (isls.), 6 ....E 2
Los Hermanos (isls.) ....F 2
Los Monjes (isls.) ....C 1
Los Roques (isls.), 537 ....E 2
Los Testigos (isls.), 58 ....G 2
Macanao (pen.) ....F 2
Maigualida (mts.) ....F 4
Manapire (river) ....E 3
Maracaibo (lake) ....C 3
Margarita (isl.), 85,286 ....F 2
Mavaca (river) ....F 6
Médanos (isthmus) ....D 2
Merevari (river) ....E 4
Mérida (mts.) ....C 3
Meta (river) ....E 4
Monjes, Los (isls.) ....C 1
Morichal Largo (river) ....G 3
Negro (river) ....E 7
Nuria (mts.) ....H 4
Ocamo (river) ....F 6
Orchila, La (isl.), 33 ....F 2
Orinoco (delta) ....H 3
Orinoco (river) ....G 3
Orituco (river) ....E 3
Pacaraima (mts.) ....G 5
Pao (river) ....D 3
Pao (river) ....F 3
Paragua (river) ....G 4
Paraguana (pen.) ....C 1
Paria (gulf) ....H 2
Paria (pen.) ....G 2
Parida, La (Bolívar) (mt.) ....G 4
Parima (mts.) ....F 6
Perijá (mts.) ....B 2
Portuguesa (river) ....D 3
Roques, Los (isls.), 537 ....E 2
Roraima (mt.) ....H 5
Salto Angel (falls) ....G 5
Sarare (river) ....C 4
Serpents Mouth (strait) ....H 3
Siapa (river) ....E 7
Sipapo (river) ....E 5
Suapure (river) ....E 4
Suripá (river) ....C 4
Tapira-peco (mts.) ....F 7
Testigos, Los (isls.), 58 ....G 2
Tigre (river) ....G 3
Tocuco (river) ....B 3
Tocuyo (river) ....D 2
Tortuga, La (isl.), 19 ....F 2
Tramán-tepuí (mt.) ....G 5
Triste (gulf) ....D 2
Turagua (mts.) ....F 4
Tuy (river) ....E 2
Unare (river) ....F 3
Valencia (lake) ....E 2
Venamo (mt.) ....H 4
Venamo (river) ....H 4
Venezuela (gulf) ....C 2
Ventuari (river) ....E 5
Votamo (river) ....F 6
Yatua (river) ....E 7
Yuruari (river) ....H 4
Zamuro (mts.) ....G 5
Zuata (river) ....F 3
Zulia (river) ....B 3

*City and suburbs.

AGRICULTURE, INDUSTRY and RESOURCES

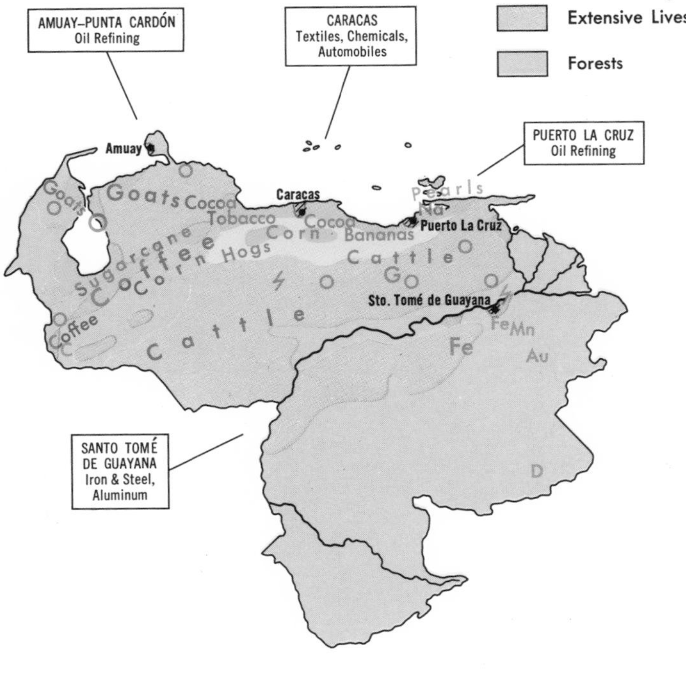

AMUAY–PUNTA CARDÓN
Oil Refining
CARACAS
Textiles, Chemicals, Automobiles
PUERTO LA CRUZ
Oil Refining
SANTO TOMÉ DE GUAYANA
Iron & Steel, Aluminum
Amuay
Caracas
Puerto La Cruz
Sto. Tomé de Guayana
Goats
Goats
Cocoa
Tobacco
Cocoa
Pearls
Na
Sugarcane
Coffee
Corn
Bananas
Corn
Hogs
Cattle
Coffee
Cattle
Fe
Mn
Fe
Au
D

DOMINANT LAND USE

- Diversified Tropical Crops (chiefly plantation agriculture)
- Upland Cultivated Areas
- Upland Livestock Grazing, Limited Agriculture
- Extensive Livestock Ranching
- Forests

MAJOR MINERAL OCCURRENCES

- Au Gold
- C Coal
- D Diamonds
- Fe Iron Ore
- G Natural Gas
- Mn Manganese
- Na Salt
- O Petroleum
- Water Power
- Major Industrial Areas

COLOMBIA

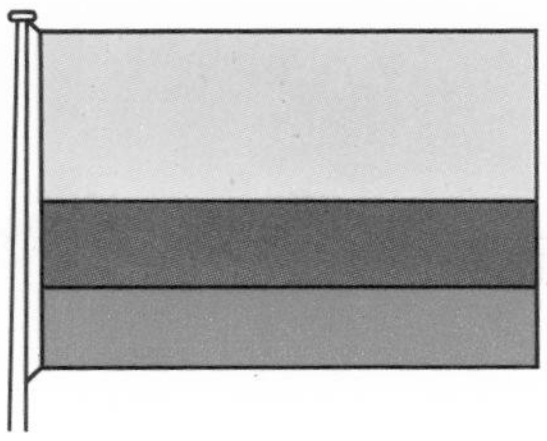

AREA	439,828 sq. mi.
POPULATION	17,787,000
CAPITAL	Bogotá
LARGEST CITY	Bogotá (greater) 1,654,876
HIGHEST POINT	Pico Cristóbal Colón 19,029 ft.
MONETARY UNIT	Colombian peso
MAJOR LANGUAGE	Spanish
MAJOR RELIGION	Roman Catholic

INTERNAL DIVISIONS

onas (commissary), 8,920...D 8
quia (dept.), 2,049,800 ......C 4
a (intendency), 15,440.......E 4
tico (dept.), 678,960 ....C 2
ar (dept.), 826,850 ....C 3
á (dept.), 856,600 ....D 5
s (dept.), 1,466,160 ....C 5
ta (intendency), 91,320.....C 7
(dept.), 544,960 ....B 6
(dept.), 152,280 ....B 4
ba (dept.), 441,980 ....C 3
namarca (dept.),
21,420 ....C 5
to Especial, 1,680,758.........C 5
ía (intendency)◉ ....F 6
ra, La (intendency),
,810 ....D 2
(dept.), 393,630 ....C 6
ajira (intendency),
,810 ....D 2
alena (dept.), 532,650 ....D 3
(dept.), 87,080 ....D 6
o (dept.), 633,570 ....B 7
de Santander (dept.),
,750 ....D 4
mayo (commissary),
440 ....C 7
Andrés y Providencia
tendency), 11,620 ....B10
ander (dept.), 895,380 ....D 4
a (dept.), 915,390 ....C 5
del Cauca (dept.),
39,880 ....B 6
és (commissary), 10,670......E 7
da (commissary), 16,530.....F 5

CITIES and TOWNS

ías, 2,712 ....D 6
dí, 1,201 ....B 3
do, 2,546 ....C 6
de Dios, 5,627 ....C 5
das, 8,064 ....C 5
2,221 ....C 6
ciras, 2.559 ....C 6
guer, 921 ....B 7
fi, 2,592 ....C 4
s, 6,905 ....C 5
rma, 7,767 ....B 5
oquia, 3,998 ....B 4
, 610 ....C 4
ataca, 4,336 ....D 2
ca, 4,300 ....E 4
quita, 269 ....E 4
a, 12,361 ....C 2
enia, 57,098 ....B 5
ero, 10,258 ....C 5
el, 2,426 ....C 3
do, 683 ....B 5
noa, 8,143 ....C 2
ya, 1,736 ....C 6
acoas, 3,349 ....A 7
osa, 2,448 ....D 5
chara, 2,513 ....D 4
ancabermeja, 25,046 ....C 4
ancas, 1,438 ....D 2
anco de Loba, 1,561 ....C 3
anquilla, 521,070 ....C 2
ló, 205 ....B 5
n, 641 ....C 7
, 28,398 ....C 4
otá (cap.), 1,325,080 ....D 5
otá, *1,654,876 ....D 5
var, Antioquia, 6,121 ....C 5
var, Cauca, 2,310 ....B 7
aramanga, 250,550 ....D 4
aventura, 35,087 ....B 6
saco, 1,928 ....B 7
a, 32,016 ....B 6
eres, 305 ....C 4
edonia, 10,681 ....C 5
mar, 5,393 ....C 2

Calarcá, 15,707 ....C 5
Cali, 813,240 ....B 6
Campo de la Cruz, 4,912...............C 2
Campoalegre, 5,997 ....C 6
Cañasgordas, 3,137 ....B 4
Carmen, 9,647 ....C 3
Cartagena, 197,590 ....C 2
Cartago, 31,051 ....B 5
Caucasia, 897 ....C 4
Cereté, 6,161 ....C 3
Cerrito, 4,786 ....B 6
Cerro San Antonio, 2,265 ....C 2
Chaparral, 11,705 ....C 6
Chimichagua, 3,322 ....D 3
Chinácota, 2,596 ....D 4
Chinchiná, 7,577 ....C 5
Chinú, 4,987 ....C 3
Chiquinquirá, 10,143 ....C 5
Chiriguaná, 3,302 ....D 3
Ciénaga, 24,358 ....C 2
Ciénaga de Oro, 6,108 ....C 3
Cisneros, 5,489 ....C 4
Colombia, 1,217 ....C 6
Colón, 480 ....B 7
Condoto, 1,710 ....B 5
Contratación, 3,303 ....D 4
Convención, 4,526 ....D 3
Corinto, 3,344 ....B 6
Corozal, 7,240 ....C 3
Cúcuta, 147,250 ....D 4
Cumbal, 1,963 ....B 7
Dabeiba, 2,832 ....B 4
Dagua, 3,114 ....B 6
Duitama, 7,723 ....D 5
El Banco, 9,636 ....D 3
El Carmen, Chocó, 1,161 ....B 5
El Carmen, Nariño ....A 6
El Carmen, Norte de Santander,
2,587 ....D 3
El Cocuy 2,973 ....D 4
El Tambo, 1,914 ....B 6
Envigado, 13,392 ....C 4
Espinal, 9,389 ....C 5
Facatativa, 13,479 ....C 5
Florencia, 21,770 ....C 7
Fonseca, 2,987 ....D 2
Fontibón, 13,871 ....C 5
Fresno, 5,019 ....C 5
Fundación, 6,620 ....D 2
Fusagasugá, 8,345 ....C 5
Gachalá, 856 ....D 5
Gamarra, 2,576 ....D 3
Garzón, 5,750 ....C 6
Gigante, 2,607 ....C 6
Girardot, 35,665 ....C 5
Gramalote, 2,776 ....D 4
Guacamaya ....C 6
Guamal, 2,458 ....C 3
Guapi, 1,882 ....B 6
Guateque, 2,408 ....D 5
Honda, 16,051 ....C 5
Ibagué, 160,400 ....C 5
Ipiales, 11,569 ....B 7
Iscuandé, 887 ....A 6
Itaguí, 11,027 ....C 4
Itsmina, 2,755 ....B 5
Ituango, 2,673 ....C 4
La Cruz, 2,745 ....B 7
La Dorada, 14,577 ....C 5
La Gloria, 1,277 ....D 3
La Palma, 3,843 ....C 5
La Plata, 2,416 ....C 6
La Unión, 2,796 ....B 7
Leticia, 2,200 ....F10
Líbano, 12,090 ....C 5
Lorica, 8,420 ....C 3
Los Andes, 1,075 ....B 7
Magangué, 17,114 ....C 3
Majagual, 1,516 ....C 3
Málaga, 6,022 ....D 4
Manare, 39 ....E 4
Maní, 150 ....D 5
Manizales, 186,910 ....C 5
Matanza, 735 ....D 4

Medellín, 776,970 ....C 4
Medina, 639 ....D 5
Mercaderes, 824 ....B 7
Miraflores, Boyacá, 2,456 ....D 5
Miraflores, Vaupés ....E 7
Miranda, 4,082 ....B 6
Mitú, 250 ....E 7
Mocoa, 4,950 ....B 7
Mompós, 9,192 ....C 3
Moniquirá, 3,230 ....D 5
Montería, 108,800 ....B 3
Murindó, 280 ....B 4
Muzo, 337 ....D 5
Natagaima, 4,107 ....C 6
Neiva, 87,820 ....C 6
Nóvita, 680 ....B 5
Nueva Antioquia ....F 5
Nunchía, 579 ....D 5
Nuquí, 576 ....B 5
Ocaña, 15,214 ....D 3
Orocué, 645 ....E 5
Ortega, 2,874 ....C 6
Pacho, 4,118 ....C 5
Páez, 514 ....C 6
Paipa, 1,293 ....D 5
Palmira, 54,293 ....B 6
Pamplona, 16,396 ....D 4
Pasto, 134,130 ....B 7
Patía, 1,475 ....B 6
Paz de Aripara, 222 ....E 5
Paz del Río, 650 ....D 4
Pedraza, 4,073 ....C 2
Pereira, 76,262 ....C 5
Piedecuesta, 7,720 ....D 4
Piendamó, 1,615 ....B 6
Pitalito, 3,616 ....B 7
Pivijay, 4,789 ....C 2
Planeta Rica ....C 3
Plato, 8,039 ....C 3
Popayán, 67,510 ....B 6
Potosí ....C 7
Pradera, 6,092 ....B 6
Puente Nacional, 1,808 ....D 5
Puerto Berrío, 8,947 ....C 4
Puerto Carranza ....F 9
Puerto Carreño, 720 ....G 4
Puerto Colombia, 5,689 ....C 2
Puerto Escondido ....B 3
Puerto Leguízamo, 1,433 ....C 8
Puerto López, La Guajira ....E 2
Puerto López, Meta ....D 5
Puerto Mercedes ....D 7
Puerto Mutis ....B 4
Puerto Nariño ....F 5
Puerto Niño ....C 5
Puerto Nuevo ....F 5
Puerto Ospina ....C 7
Puerto Paulina ....D 7
Puerto Pizarro, Caquetá ....D 8
Puerto Pizarro, Chocó ....B 5
Puerto Reyes ....B 5
Puerto Rico, Caquetá ....C 7
Puerto Rico, Meta ....C 6
Puerto Salgar, 3,621 ....C 5
Puerto Tejada, 8,535 ....B 6
Puerto Toledo ....C 8

AGRICULTURE, INDUSTRY and RESOURCES

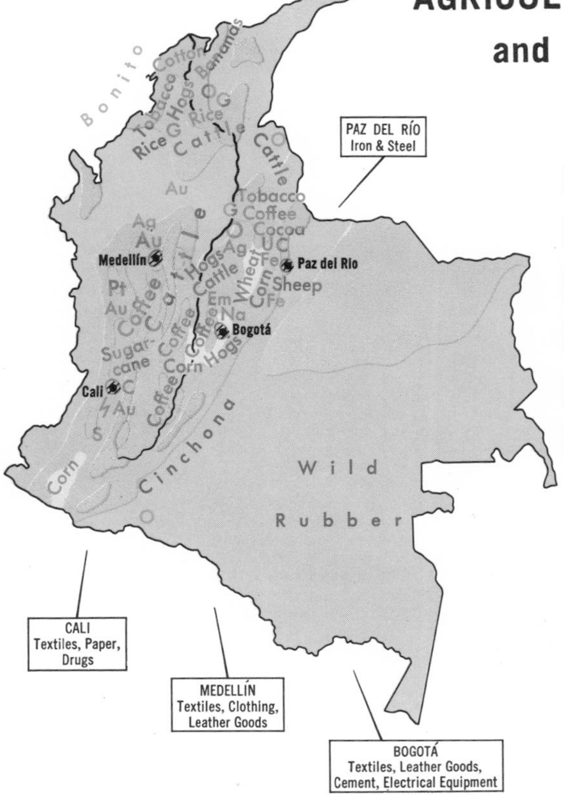
Bonito
Cotton
Tobacco
Rice
Hogs
Bananas
Cattle
Au
Ag
Coffee
Cocoa
Wheat
Sheep
Corn
Sugar cane
Cinchona
Wild Rubber
Medellín
Paz del Río
Bogotá
Cali
PAZ DEL RÍO
Iron & Steel
CALI
Textiles, Paper, Drugs
MEDELLÍN
Textiles, Clothing, Leather Goods
BOGOTÁ
Textiles, Leather Goods, Cement, Electrical Equipment

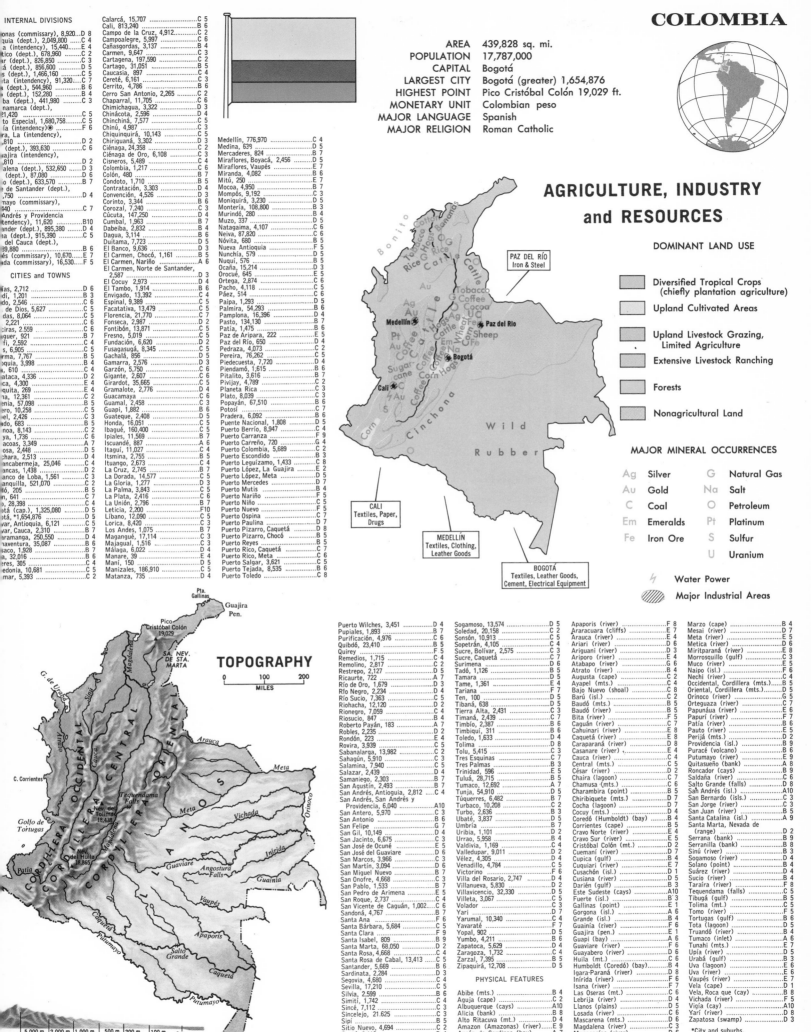

DOMINANT LAND USE

- Diversified Tropical Crops (chiefly plantation agriculture)
- Upland Cultivated Areas
- Upland Livestock Grazing, Limited Agriculture
- Extensive Livestock Ranching
- Forests
- Nonagricultural Land

MAJOR MINERAL OCCURRENCES

Ag	Silver	G	Natural Gas
Au	Gold	Na	Salt
C	Coal	O	Petroleum
Em	Emeralds	Pt	Platinum
Fe	Iron Ore	S	Sulfur
		U	Uranium

Water Power

Major Industrial Areas

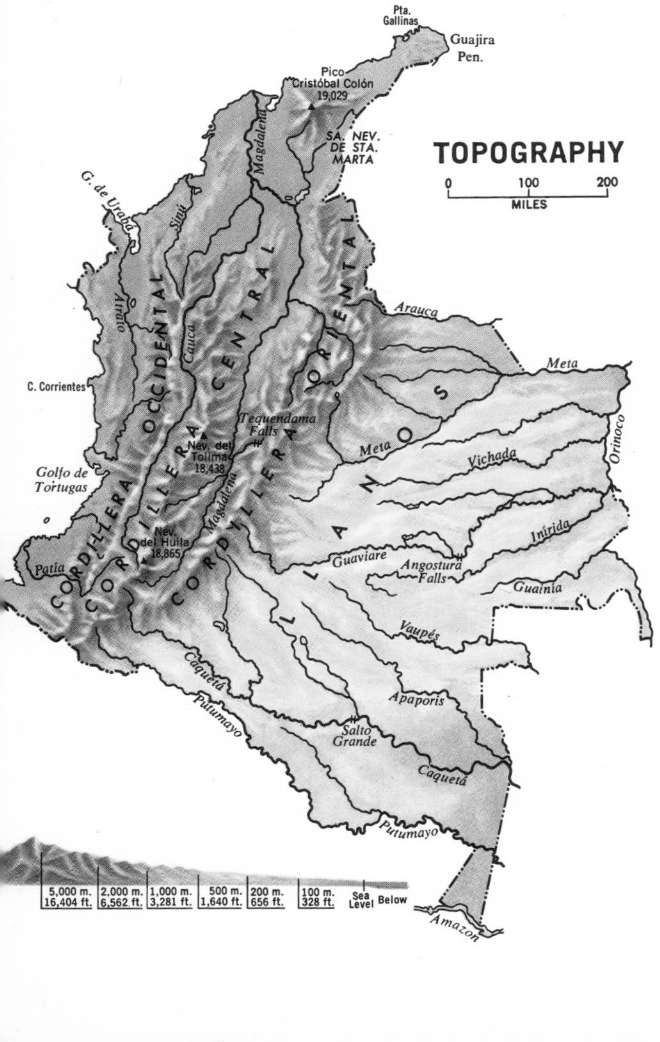
TOPOGRAPHY
0 100 200
MILES
Pta. Gallinas
Guajira Pen.
Pico Cristóbal Colón 19,029
SA. NEV. DE STA. MARTA
Magdalena
G. de Urabá
Sinú
C. Corrientes
Atrato
Cauca
Arauca
Meta
CORDILLERA OCCIDENTAL
CORDILLERA CENTRAL
CORDILLERA ORIENTAL
Tequendama Falls
Nev. del Tolima 18,438
Nev. del Huila 18,865
Golfo de Tortugas
Patía
LLANOS
Vichada
Orinoco
Guaviare
Angostura Falls
Inírida
Guainía
Vaupés
Caquetá
Apaporis
Putumayo
Salto Grande
Amazon
5,000 m. 16,404 ft.
2,000 m. 6,562 ft.
1,000 m. 3,281 ft.
500 m. 1,640 ft.
200 m. 656 ft.
100 m. 328 ft.
Sea Level
Below

Puerto Wilches, 3,451 ....D 4
Pupiales, 1,893 ....B 7
Purificación, 4,976 ....C 6
Quibdó, 23,410 ....B 5
Quirey ....F 5
Remedios, 1,715 ....C 4
Remolino, 2,817 ....C 2
Restrepo, 2,127 ....D 5
Ricaurte, 722 ....A 7
Río de Oro, 1,679 ....D 3
Río Negro, 2,234 ....D 4
Río Sucio, 7,363 ....C 5
Riohacha, 12,120 ....D 2
Rionegro, 7,059 ....C 4
Riosucio, 847 ....B 4
Roberto Payán, 183 ....A 7
Robles, 2,235 ....D 2
Rondón, 223 ....E 4
Rovira, 3,939 ....C 5
Sabanalarga, 13,982 ....C 2
Sahagún, 5,910 ....C 3
Salamina, 7,940 ....C 5
Salazar, 2,439 ....D 4
Samaniego, 2,303 ....B 7
San Agustín, 2,493 ....B 7
San Andrés, Antioguia, 2,812 ....C 4
San Andrés, San Andrés y
Providencia, 6,040 ....A10
San Antero, 5,970 ....C 3
San Antonio ....B 6
San Felipe ....G 7
San Gil, 10,149 ....D 4
San Jacinto, 6,675 ....C 3
San José de Ocuné ....E 5
San José del Guaviare ....D 6
San Marcos, 3,966 ....C 3
San Martín, 3,094 ....D 6
San Miguel Nuevo ....B 7
San Onofre, 4,668 ....C 3
San Pablo, 1,533 ....B 7
San Pedro de Arimena ....E 5
San Roque, 2,737 ....C 4
San Vicente de Caguán, 1,002...................C 6
Sandoná, 4,767 ....B 7
Santa Ana ....F 6
Santa Bárbara, 5,684 ....C 5
Santa Clara ....F 9
Santa Isabel, 809 ....B 9
Santa Marta, 68,050 ....D 2
Santa Rosa, 4,668 ....C 4
Santa Rosa de Cabal, 13,413 ....C 5
Santander, 5,669 ....B 6
Sardinata, 2,284 ....D 3
Segovia, 4,680 ....C 4
Sevilla, 17,210 ....C 5
Silvia, 2,599 ....B 6
Simití, 1,742 ....C 4
Sincé, 7,112 ....C 3
Sincelejo, 21.625 ....C 3
Sipí ....B 5
Sitio Nuevo, 4,694 ....C 2
Soatá, 3,116 ....D 4
Socorro, 11,842 ....D 4

Sogamoso, 13,574 ....D 5
Soledad, 20,158 ....C 2
Sonsón, 10,913 ....C 5
Sopetrán, 4,105 ....C 4
Sucre, Bolívar, 2,575 ....C 3
Sucre, Caquetá ....C 7
Surimena ....D 6
Tadó, 1,126 ....B 5
Tamara ....D 5
Tame, 1,361 ....E 4
Tariana ....F 7
Ten, 100 ....D 5
Tibaná, 638 ....D 5
Tierra Alta, 2,431 ....C 3
Timaná, 2,439 ....C 7
Timbío, 2,387 ....B 6
Timbiquí, 311 ....B 6
Toledo, 1,633 ....D 4
Tolima ....D 8
Tolu, 5,415 ....C 3
Tres Esquinas ....C 7
Tres Palmas ....B 3
Trinidad, 596 ....E 5
Tuluá, 28,715 ....B 5
Tumaco, 12,692 ....A 7
Tunja, 54,910 ....D 5
Túquerres, 6,482 ....B 7
Turbaco, 10,208 ....C 2
Turbo, 2,636 ....B 3
Ubaté, 3,837 ....D 5
Umbría ....B 7
Uribia, 1,101 ....D 2
Urrao, 5,958 ....B 4
Valdivia, 1,169 ....C 4
Valledupar, 9,011 ....D 2
Vélez, 4,305 ....D 4
Venadillo, 4,784 ....C 5
Victorino ....F 6
Villa del Rosario, 2,747 ....D 4
Villanueva, 5,830 ....D 2
Villavicencio, 32,330 ....D 5
Villeta, 3,067 ....C 5
Volador ....C 3
Yari ....D 7
Yarumal, 10,340 ....C 4
Yavaraté ....F 7
Yopal, 902 ....D 5
Yumbo, 4,211 ....B 6
Zapatoca, 5,629 ....D 4
Zaragoza, 1,732 ....C 4
Zarzal, 7,395 ....B 5
Zipaquirá, 12,708 ....D 5

PHYSICAL FEATURES

Abibe (mts.) ....B 4
Aguja (cape) ....C 2
Albuquerque (cays) A10
Alicia (bank) ....B 8
Alto Ritacuva (mt.) ....D 4
Amazon (Amazonas) (river)...............................E 9
Ancón de Sardinas (bay)....................................A 7
Angostura (falls) ....E 6
Apaporis (river) ....F 8
Araracuara (cliffs) ....E 7
Arauca (river) ....E 4
Ariari (river) ....D 6
Ariguani (river) ....D 3
Ariporo (river) ....E 4
Atabapo (river) ....G 6
Atrato (river) ....B 4
Augusta (cape) ....C 2
Ayapel (mts.) ....C 4
Bajo Nuevo (shoal) ....C 8
Barú (isl.) ....C 2
Baudó (mts.) ....B 5
Baudó (river) ....B 5
Bita (river) ....F 5
Caguán (river) ....C 7
Cahuinari (river) ....E 8
Caquetá (river) ....E 8
Caraparaná (river) ....D 8
Casanare (river) ....E 4
Cauca (river) ....C 4
Central (mts.) ....C 5
César (river) ....D 2
Chaira (lagoon) ....C 7
Chamusa (mts.) ....C 6
Charambira (point) ....B 5
Chiribiquete (mts.) ....D 7
Cocha (lagoon) ....D 7
Cocuy (mts.) ....D 4
Coredó (Humboldt) (bay) ....B 4
Corrientes (cape) ....B 5
Cravo Norte (river) ....E 4
Cravo Sur (river) ....E 5
Cristóbal Colón (mt.) ....D 2
Cuemaní (river) ....D 7
Cupica (gulf) ....B 4
Cuquiari (river) ....E 7
Cusachón (isl.) ....D 1
Cusiana (river) ....D 5
Darién (gulf) ....B 3
Este Sudeste (cays) A10
Fuerte (isl.) ....B 3
Gallinas (point) ....E 1
Gorgona (isl.) ....A 6
Grande (isl.) ....B 4
Guainía (river) ....F 6
Guajira (pen.) ....E 1
Guapi (bay) ....A 6
Guaviare (river) ....F 6
Guayabero (river) ....D 6
Huila (mt.) ....C 6
Humboldt (Coredó) (bay).....................................B 4
Igara-Paraná (river) ....D 8
Inírida (river) ....F 6
Isana (river) ....F 7
Las Oseras (mt.) ....C 6
Lebrija (river) ....D 4
Llanos (plains) ....D 5
Losada (river) ....C 6
Mascarena (mts.) ....D 6
Magdalena (river) ....C 3
Manacacías (river) ....D 6
Mapiripán (lagoon) ....E 6
Marzo (cape) ....B 4
Mesai (river) ....D 7
Meta (river) ....E 5
Metica (river) ....D 6
Miritparaná (river) ....E 8
Morrosquillo (gulf) ....C 3
Muco (river) ....E 5
Naipo (isl.) ....F 6
Nechi (river) ....C 4
Occidental, Cordillera (mts.).................................B 5
Oriental, Cordillera (mts.).....................................D 5
Orinoco (river) ....G 5
Orteguaza (river) ....C 7
Papunáua (river) ....E 6
Papurí (river) ....F 7
Patía (river) ....B 6
Pauto (river) ....E 5
Perijá (mts.) ....D 2
Providencia (isl.) ....B 9
Puracé (volcano) ....B 6
Putumayo (river) ....E 9
Quitasueño (bank) ....A 8
Roncador (cays) ....B 9
Saldaña (river) ....C 6
Salto Grande (falls) ....D 8
San Andrés (isl.) A10
San Bernardo (isls.) ....C 3
San Jorge (river) ....C 3
San Juan (river) ....B 5
Santa Catalina (isl.) ....A 9
Santa Marta, Nevada de
(range) ....D 2
Serrana (bank) ....B 9
Serranilla (bank) ....B 8
Sinú (river) ....B 3
Sogamoso (river) ....D 4
Solano (point) ....B 4
Suárez (river) ....D 4
Sucio (river) ....B 4
Taraíra (river) ....F 8
Tequendama (falls) ....C 5
Tibugá (gulf) ....B 5
Tolima (mt.) ....C 5
Tomo (river) ....F 5
Tortugas (gulf) ....B 6
Tota (lagoon) ....D 5
Truandó (river) ....B 4
Tumaco (inlet) ....A 6
Tunahi (mts.) ....E 7
Upía (river) ....D 5
Urabá (gulf) ....B 3
Uva (lagoon) ....E 6
Uva (river) ....E 6
Vaupés (river) ....E 7
Vela (cape) ....D 1
Vela, Roca que (cay) ....B 8
Vichada (river) ....F 5
Vigía (cay) A10
Yarí (river) ....D 8
Zapatosa (swamp) ....D 3

*City and suburbs.
◉Population included in Vaupés.

PERU and ECUADOR

PERU

	PERU	**ECUADOR**
AREA	513,000 sq. mi.	115,000 sq. mi.
POPULATION	11,649,600	5,084,000
CAPITAL	Lima	Quito
LARGEST CITY	Lima (greater) 1,436,231	Guayaquil 506,037
HIGHEST POINT	Huascarán 22,205 ft.	Chimborazo 20,561 ft.
MONETARY UNIT	sol	sucre
MAJOR LANGUAGES	Spanish, Indian	Spanish, Indian
MAJOR RELIGION	Roman Catholic	Roman Catholic

ECUADOR

TOPOGRAPHY

0 100 200
MILES

5,000 m. 2,000 m. 1,000 m. 500 m. 200 m. 100 m. Sea Below
16,404 ft. 6,562 ft. 3,281 ft. 1,640 ft. 656 ft. 328 ft. Level

(continued on following page)

Peru and Ecuador

(continued)

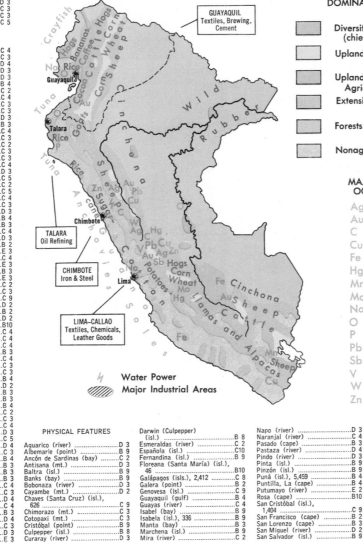

ECUADOR (continued)

Napo, 24,253 ....D 3
Pastaza, 13,693 ....D 3
Pichincha, 587,835 ....C 3
Tungurahua, 178,709 ....C 3
Zamora-Chinchipe, 11,464 ....C 5

CITIES and TOWNS

Alausí, 6,676 ....C 4
Ambato, 53,372 ....C 3
Andoas Nuevo ....D 4
Arapicos ....D 3
Archidona ....D 3
Arenillas, 3,925 ....B 4
Atuntaqui, 8,759 ....C 2
Azogues, 8,075 ....C 4
Baba, 693 ....C 3
Babahoyo, 16,444 ....C 3
Baeza, 213 ....D 3
Bahía de Caráquez, 8,845 ....B 3
Balao, 1,415 ....C 4
Balzar, 6,588 ....C 3
Bolívar, 410 ....C 2
Cajabamba, 2,094 ....C 3
Calceta, 4,946 ....C 3
Cañar, 4,935 ....C 4
Canelos ....D 3
Cariamanga, 5,381 ....C 5
Carondelet, 318 ....C 2
Catacocha, 3,796 ....C 5
Catamayo, 4,097 ....C 4
Catarama, 2,424 ....C 3
Cayambe, 8,101 ....D 3
Celica, 3,467 ....B 4
Chone, 12,832 ....B 3
Chunchi, 2,388 ....C 4
Coca ....D 3
Cojimíes, 1,538 ....B 2
Cononaco ....E 3
Cuenca, 60,402 ....C 4
Cuyabeno ....E 3
Daule, 7,428 ....B 3
Edén ....E 3
El Ángel, 4,009 ....C 2
El Corazón, 1,118 ....C 3
El Progreso ....C 9
El Pun, 612 ....D 2
Esmeraldas, 33,403 ....B 2
Farfán ....D 2
Floreana B10
Girón, 1,914 ....C 4
Gualaceo, 3,065 ....C 4
Gualaquiza, 635 ....C 4
Guale ....B 3
Guamote, 2,640 ....C 4
Guano, 4,455 ....C 3
Guaranda, 9,900 ....C 3
Guayaquil, 506,037 ....B 4
Ibarra, 25,835 ....D 2
Jama, 1,743 ....B 3
Jipijapa, 13,367 ....B 3
La Libertad, 13,565 ....B 4
La Tola, 650 ....C 2
Latacunga, 14,856 ....C 3
Loja, 26,785 ....C 4
Loreto ....D 3
Macará, 5,027 ....C 5
Macas, 1,355 ....D 4
Machachi, 3,951 ....C 3
Machala, 29,036 ....B 4
Machalilla, 615 ....B 3
Manglaralto, 799 ....B 3
Manta, 33,622 ....B 3
Méndez, 527 ....C 4
Mera ....C 3
Miazal ....D 4
Milagro, 28,148 ....C 4
Montecristi, 4,540 ....B 3
Morona ....D 4
Mulaló, 427 ....C 3
Napo ....D 3
Nuevo Rocafuerte, 435 ....E 3
Otavalo, 8,630 ....C 2
Paján, 1,818 ....B 3
Palanda ....C 5
Papallacta ....D 3
Pasaje, 13,215 ....C 4
Paute, 1,511 ....C 4
Pedernales, 610 ....B 2
Pelileo, 2,545 ....C 3
Píllaro, 2,714 ....C 3
Piñas, 3,344 ....C 4
Playas, 5,067 ....B 4
Portoviejo, 32,228 ....B 3
Posorja, 2,086 ....B 4
Puerto Baquerizo Moreno ....C 9
Puerto Bolívar ....B 4
Puerto de Cayo, 713 ....B 3
Pujilí, 2,534 ....C 3
Putumayo ....E 3
Puyo, 2,290 ....D 3
Quevedo, 20,602 ....C 3
Quito (cap.), 368,217 ....C 3
Río Tigre ....D 4
Riobamba, 41,625 ....C 3
Rocafuerte, 4,349 ....B 3
Rosa Zárate, 1,662 ....C 2
Salinas, 5,460 ....B 4
San Gabriel, 6,803 ....D 2
San Lorenzo, 575 ....C 2
San Miguel, 2,410 ....C 3
San Miguel de Salcedo, 3,442 ....C 3
Sangolquí, 5,501 ....C 3
Santa Ana, 3,940 ....B 3
Santa Cruz ....B 9
Santa Elena, 4,241 ....B 4
Santa Isabel, 1,602 ....C 4
Santa Rosa, 8,935 ....C 4
Santa Rosa de Sucumbíos, 132....D 2
Santo Domingo de los Colorados, 6,951 ....C 3
Saraguro, 1,562 ....C 4
Sarayacu ....D 3
Sigsig, 1,228 ....C 4
Sigüe ....D 2
Sucre, 2,578 ....B 3
Sucúa, 1,153 ....C 4
Tabacundo, 2,009 ....C 2
Tachina ....C 2
Tena, 1,029 ....D 3
Tulcán, 16,448 ....D 2
Valdez, 3,358 ....C 2
Viche, 230 ....C 2
Villamil ....B 9
Vinces, 5,901 ....C 3
Yacuambí, 405 ....C 4
Yaguachi, 2,996 ....C 4
Yaupi ....D 4
Zamora, 1,030 ....C 5
Zapotillo, 460 ....B 5
Zaruma, 9.000 ....C 4
Zumba, 450 ....C 5

AGRICULTURE, INDUSTRY and RESOURCES

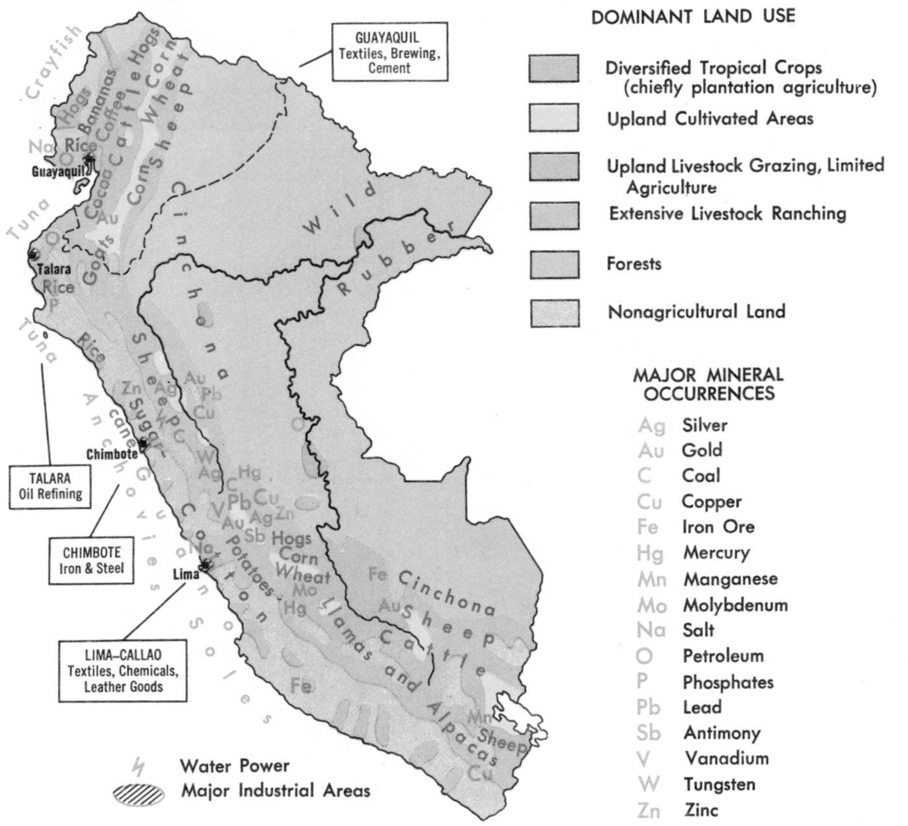
GUAYAQUIL
Textiles, Brewing, Cement
TALARA
Oil Refining
CHIMBOTE
Iron & Steel
LIMA-CALLAO
Textiles, Chemicals, Leather Goods
Guayaquil
Talara
Chimbote
Lima
DOMINANT LAND USE
Diversified Tropical Crops (chiefly plantation agriculture)
Upland Cultivated Areas
Upland Livestock Grazing, Limited Agriculture
Extensive Livestock Ranching
Forests
Nonagricultural Land
MAJOR MINERAL OCCURRENCES
Ag Silver
Au Gold
C Coal
Cu Copper
Fe Iron Ore
Hg Mercury
Mn Manganese
Mo Molybdenum
Na Salt
O Petroleum
P Phosphates
Pb Lead
Sb Antimony
V Vanadium
W Tungsten
Zn Zinc
Water Power
Major Industrial Areas

PHYSICAL FEATURES

Aguarico (river) ....D 3
Albemarle (point) ....B 9
Ancón de Sardinas (bay) ....C 2
Antisana (mt.) ....D 3
Baltra (isl.) ....B 9
Banks (bay) ....B 9
Bobonaza (river) ....D 3
Cayambe (mt.) ....D 2
Chaves (Santa Cruz) (isl.), 626 ....C 9
Chimorazo (mt.) ....C 3
Cotopaxi (mt.) ....C 3
Cristóbal (point) ....B 9
Culpepper (isl.) ....B 8
Curaray (river) ....D 3
Darwin (Culpepper) (isl.) ....B 8
Esmeraldas (river) ....C 2
Española (isl.) C10
Fernandina (isl.) ....B 9
Floreana (Santa María) (isl.), 46 ....B10
Galápagos (isls.), 2,412 ....C 8
Galera (point) ....B 2
Genovesa (isl.) ....C 9
Guayaquil (gulf) ....B 4
Guayas (river) ....C 4
Isabel (bay) ....B 9
Isabela (isl.), 336 ....B 9
Manta (bay) ....B 3
Marchena (isl.) ....B 9
Mira (river) ....C 2
Napo (river) ....D 3
Naranjal (river) ....C 4
Pasado (cape) ....B 3
Pastaza (river) ....D 4
Pindo (river) ....D 3
Pinta (isl.) ....B 9
Pinzón (isl.) ....B 9
Puná (isl.), 5,459 ....B 4
Puntilla, La (cape) ....B 4
Putumayo (river) ....E 2
Rosa (cape) B10
San Cristóbal (isl.), 1,404 ....C 9
San Francisco (cape) ....B 2
San Lorenzo (cape) ....B 3
San Miguel (river) ....D 2
San Salvador (isl.) ....B 9
Sangay (mt.) ....C 4
Santa Cruz (isl.), 626 ....C 9
Santa Elena (bay) ....B 3
Santa Fé (isl.) ....C 9
Santa María (isl.), 46 ....B10
Santiago (San Salvador) (isl.) ....C 9
Tumbes (river) ....B 4
Wenman (isl.) ....B 8
Wolf (Wenman) (isl.) ....B 8
Zamora (river) ....B 4

*City and suburbs.

†Population of district.

AGRICULTURE, INDUSTRY and RESOURCES

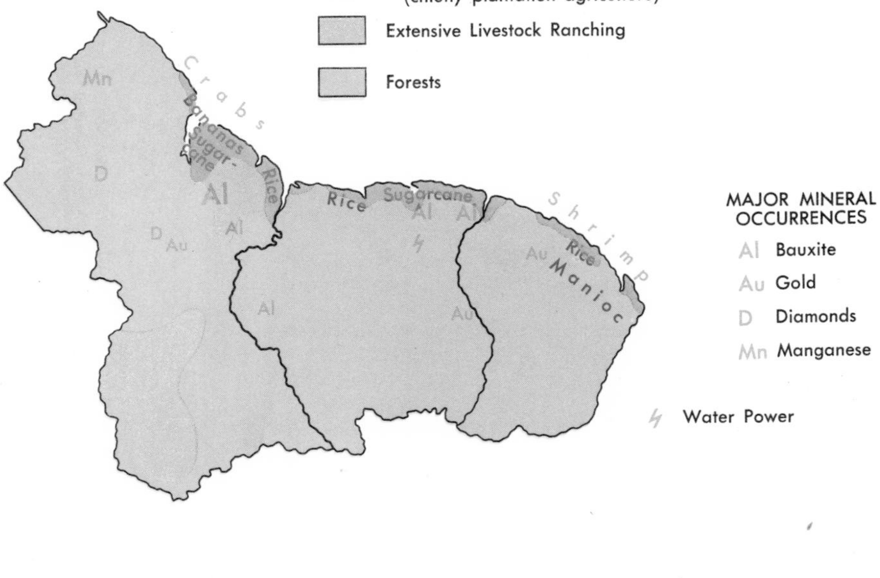
DOMINANT LAND USE
Diversified Tropical Crops (chiefly plantation agriculture)
Extensive Livestock Ranching
Forests
MAJOR MINERAL OCCURRENCES
Al Bauxite
Au Gold
D Diamonds
Mn Manganese
Water Power
Rice
Sugarcane
Shrimp
Manioc

GUYANA

COUNTIES

Berbice, 96,623 ....
Demerara, 220,639 ....
Essequibo, 58,439 ....

CITIES and TOWNS

Adventure, 507 ....
Anna Regina, 848 ....
Annai ....
Apoteri ....
Arakaka ....
Atkinson Field ....
Aurora ....
Baramanni ....
Baramita ....
Bartica, 2,352 ....
Biloku ....
Charity, 838 ....
Dadanawa ....
Danielstown, 478 ....
Epira ....
Five Stars ....
Georgetown (cap.), 78,000 ....
Georgetown, *162,000 ....
Imbaimadai ....
Issano ....
Issineru ....
Ituni ....
Kamakusa ....
Kamarang, 510 ....
Karasabai ....
Kumaka ....
Kurupukari ....
Kwakwani ....
Lethem ....
Lumid Pau ....
Mabaruma, 343 ....
Mackenzie ....
Mahaica, 8,646 ....
Mahaicony, 8,272 ....
Mahdia ....
Mara ....
Morawhanna, 305 ....
Mount Everard ....
New Amsterdam, 14,300 ....
Orealla ....
Paradise ....
Parika, 577 ....
Pickersgill, 334 ....
Queenstown, 1,067 ....
Rockstone ....
Rosignol, 1,204 ....
Skeldon, 4,367 ....
Springlands, 181 ....
Suddie, 512 ....
Takama ....
Towakaima ....
Tumatumari ....
Tumereng ....
Vreed-en-Hoop, 3,156 ....
Wichabai ....
Wismar ....
Yupukari ....

PHYSICAL FEATURES

Akarai (mts.) ....
Amakara (river) ....
Amuku (mts.) ....
Ariwa (mt.) ....
Barama (river) ....
Barima (river) ....
Berbice (river) ....
Burro-Burro (river) ....
Caburai (mt.) ....
Canje (river) ....
Courantyne (river) ....
Cuyuni (river) ....
Demerara (river) ....
Essequibo (river) ....
Great (falls) ....
Ireng (river) ....
Kaieteur (falls) ....
Kamaria (falls) ....
Kamoa (river) ....
Kanuku (mts.) ....
Kukui (river) ....
Kurungiku (mts.) ....
Kuyuwini (river) ....
Kwitaro (river) ....
Leguan (isl.), 6,567 ....
Marudi (mts.) ....
Mazaruni (river) ....
Moruka (river) ....
New (river) ....
Pakaraima (mts.) ....
Playa (point) ....
Pomeroon (river) ....
Potaro (river) ....
Puruni (river) ....
Roraima (mt.) ....
Rupununi (river) ....
Serikoeng (falls) ....
Sororieng (mt.) ....
Takutu (river) ....
Venamo (mt.) ....
Waini (river) ....
Wakenaam (isl.), 6,718 ....
Wenamu (river) ....

SURINAM

DISTRICTS

Brokopondo, 1,376 ....
Commewijne, 18,796 ....
Coronie, 4,069 ....
Marowijne, 10,074 ....
Nickerie, 24,730 ....
Paramaribo, 122,634 ....
Saramacca, 10,979 ....
Suriname, 80,870 ....

CITIES and TOWNS

Ajoewa ....
Albina, 482 ....
Asidonhoppi ....
Batavia ....
Berg-en-Dal, 191 ....
Brokopondo ....
Burnside, 313 ....
Cottica, 8 ....
Dam ....
Domburg, 2,852 ....
Groningen, 256 ....
Intelewa ....
Jamaiké ....
Kwakoegron, 55 ....
Kwatta, 6,378 ....
Lelydorp, 5,948 ....
Majoli ....
Marienburg, 2,524 ....
Moengo ....
Nassau ....
Nieuw-Amsterdam, 1,078 ....

GUIANAS

	GUYANA	SURINAM	FRENCH GUIANA
AREA	89,480 sq. mi.	54,300 sq. mi.	35,135 sq. mi.
POPULATION	628,000	362,000	36,000
CAPITAL	Georgetown	Paramaribo	Cayenne
LARGEST CITY	Georgetown (greater) 162,000	Paramaribo 122,634	Cayenne 18,010
HIGHEST POINT	Mt. Roraima 9,219 ft.	Wilhelmina Mts. 4,200 ft.	2,723 ft.
MONETARY UNIT	British West Indian dollar	Surinam guilder	French franc
MAJOR LANGUAGES	English, East Indian	Dutch	French
MAJOR RELIGIONS	Christian, Hindu, Mohammedan	Christian, Mohammedan, Hindu	Roman Catholic, Protestant

TOPOGRAPHY

0 50 100
MILES

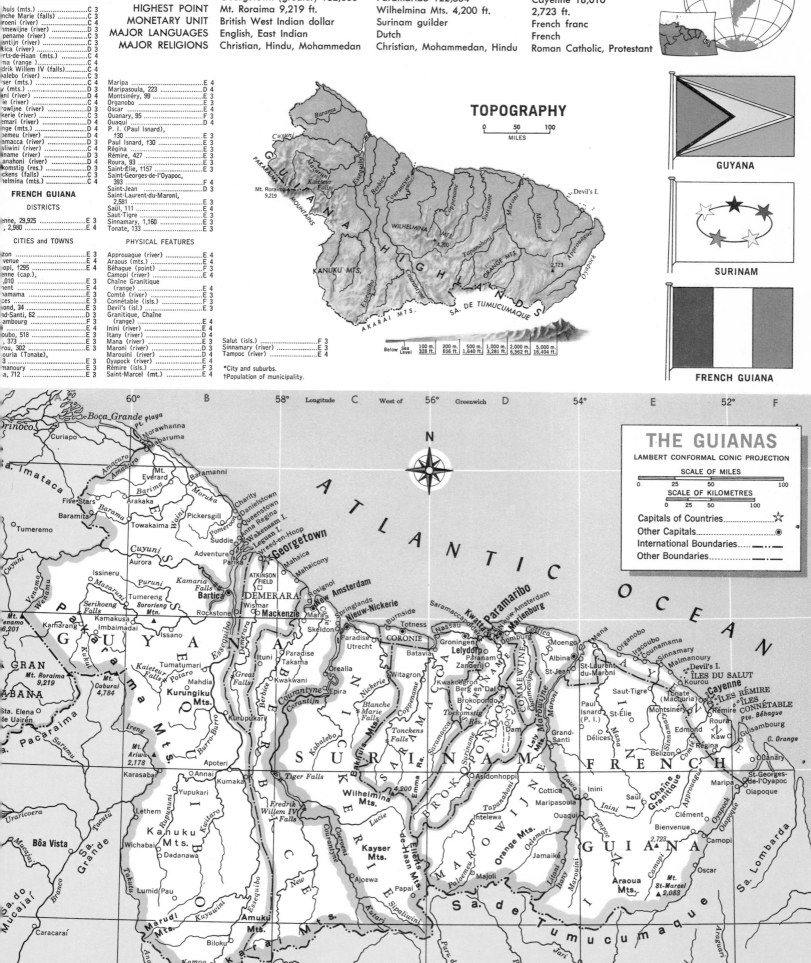

*City and suburbs.
†Population of municipality.

Below Sea Level	100 m. 328 ft.	200 m. 656 ft.	500 m. 1,640 ft.	1,000 m. 3,281 ft.	2,000 m. 6,562 ft.	5,000 m. 16,404 ft.

GUYANA

SURINAM

FRENCH GUIANA

THE GUIANAS
LAMBERT CONFORMAL CONIC PROJECTION

SCALE OF MILES
0 25 50 100

SCALE OF KILOMETRES
0 25 50 100

Capitals of Countries .... ☆
Other Capitals .... ◉
International Boundaries ____ ._ _
Other Boundaries .... _ _ _

BRAZIL

BIPOLAR OBLIQUE CONIC CONFORMAL PROJECTION

SCALE OF MILES

SCALE OF KILOMETRES

Capitals of Countries .... ⊛
State Capitals .... ◉
International Boundaries .... —·—·—
State Boundaries .... —··—··—

Copyright by C.S. HAMMOND & CO., N.Y.

BRAZIL
WESTERN PART

BRAZIL

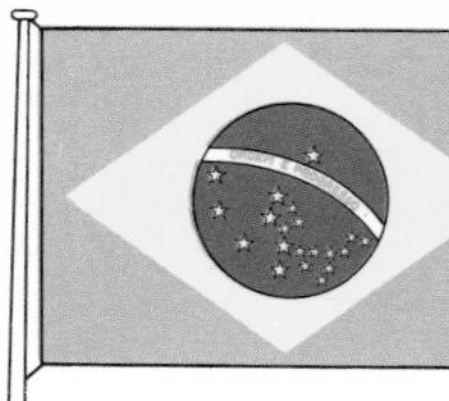

AREA 3,286,170 sq. mi.
POPULATION 82,222,000
CAPITAL Brasília
LARGEST CITY Rio de Janeiro 3,223,408
HIGHEST POINT Pico da Bandeira 9,462 ft.
MONETARY UNIT cruzeiro
MAJOR LANGUAGE Portuguese
MAJOR RELIGION Roman Catholic

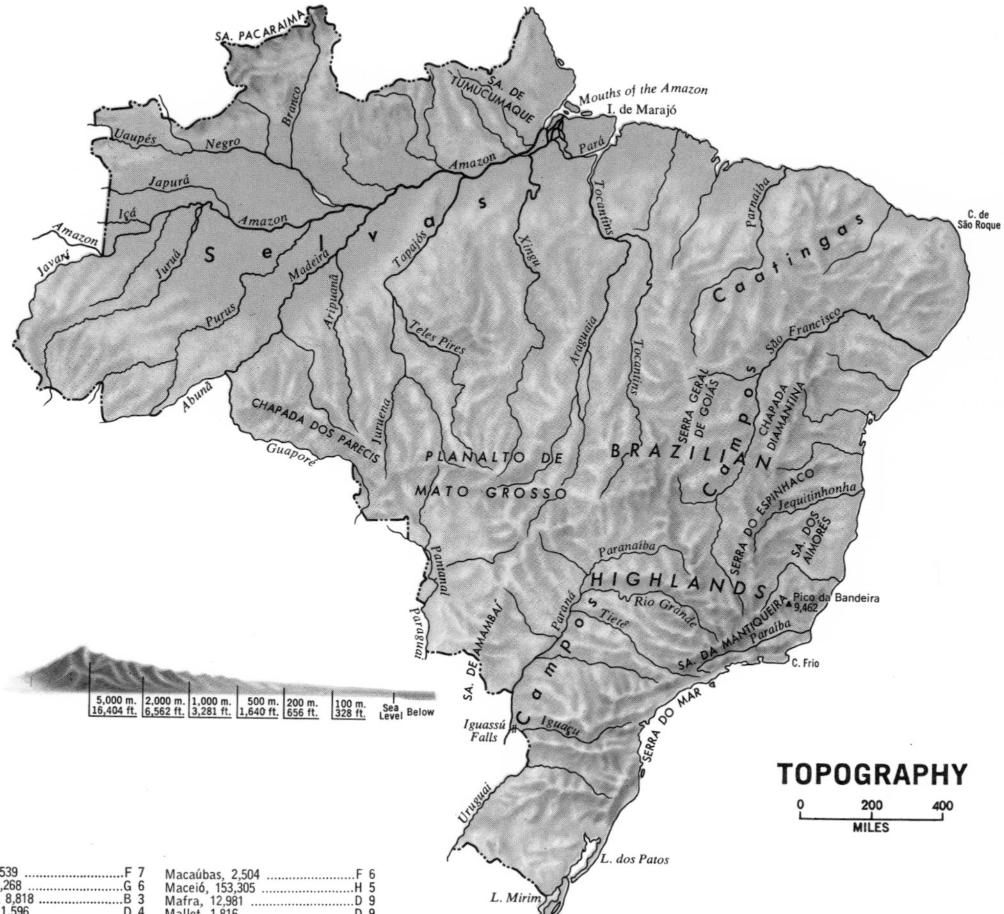
SA. PACARAIMA
SA. DE TUMUCUMAQUE
Mouths of the Amazon
I. de Marajó
Branco
Uaupés
Negro
Amazon
Pará
Japurá
Içá
Amazon
Javari
Juruá
Purus
Madeira
Aripuanã
Tapajós
Xingu
Tocantins
Parnaíba
C. de São Roque
S e l v a s
C a a t i n g a s
Teles Pires
Araguaia
Tocantins
São Francisco
Abunã
CHAPADA DOS PARECIS
Guaporé
Juruena
SERRA GERAL DE GOIÁS
CHAPADA DIAMANTINA
P L A N A L T O D E
M A T O G R O S S O
B R A Z I L I A N
Campos
SERRA DO ESPINHAÇO
Jequitinhonha
SA. DOS AIMORES
Paranaíba
H I G H L A N D S
Pico da Bandeira 9,462
Rio Grande
Paraíba
Tietê
Paraná
Pantanal
Paraguai
SA. DE AMAMBAÍ
SA. DA MANTIQUEIRA
C. Frio
SERRA DO MAR
Campos
Iguassú Falls
Iguaçu
Uruguai
L. dos Patos
L. Mirim
5,000 m. 16,404 ft.
2,000 m. 6,562 ft.
1,000 m. 3,281 ft.
500 m. 1,640 ft.
200 m. 656 ft.
100 m. 328 ft.
Sea Level
Below

TOPOGRAPHY

0 200 400 MILES

STATES and TERRITORIES

cre, 187,000 G10
lagoas, 1,362,000 G 5
napá (terr.), 92,000 D 2
mazonas, 843,000 G 9
ahia, 6,617,000 F 6
eará, 3,682,000 G 4
spírito Santo, 1,384,000 F 7
ederal District, 141,742 E 6
oiás, 2,452,000 D 6
uanabara, 3,857,000 F 8
uaporé (Rondônia) (terr.), 97,000 H10
aranhão, 3,097,000 E 4
ato Grosso, 1,189,000 B 6
inas Gerais, 10,945,000 E 7
ará, 1,802,000 C 4
araíba, 2,177,000 G 4
araná, 6,024,000 D 9
ernambuco, 4,536,000 G 5
auí, 1,374,000 F 4
o de Janeiro, 4,103,000 F 8
o Grande do Norte, 1,254,000 G 4
o Grande do Sul, 6,182,000 C10
ondônia (terr.), 97,000 H10
oraima (terr.), 37,000 H 8
nta Catarina, 2,502,000 D 9
o Paulo, 15,326,000 D 8
rgipe, 821,000 G 5

CITIES and TOWNS

aeté, 7,988 E 7
aetetuba, 11,196 D 3
araú, 3,042 F 3
opiara, 3,953 G 4
orizal, 892 C 6
u, 8,158 G 4
agoa Grande, 12,115 H 4
agoinhas, 38,246 G 6
cobaça, 1,812 G 7
egre, 7,487 F 8
egrete, 33,735 B10
enquer, 7,027 C 3
enas, 16,051 E 8
fredo Chaves, 1,209 F 8
tamira, 2,939 C 3
to Araguaia, 2,077 C 7
to Parnaíba, 1,300 E 5
os, 5,056 F 4
nambaí, 2,601 C 8
napá, 1,591 D 2
narante, 3,199 F 4
nargosa, 6,059 F 6
ápolis, 48,847 D 7
chieta, 1,535 F 8
darai, 2,510 F 6
gicos, 1,551 G 4
icuns, 3,642 D 7
tenor Navarro, 2,705 G 4
uidauana, 11,997 C 8
acaju, 112,516 G 5
acati, 11,016 G 4
açatuba, 53,563 D 8
açuaí, 6,763 F 7
aguacema, 1,745 D 5
aguari, 35,520 D 7
aioses, 1,487 F 3
aranguá, 7,775 D10
araquara, 58,076 E 8
ari, 4,004 E 3
axá, 24,041 E 7
coverde, 18,008 G 5
eia Branca, 8,904 G 4
aias, 1,446 E 6
sis, 30,207 D 8
aré, 20,334 D 8
cabal, 15,531 E 4
gé, 47,930 C10
hia (Salvador), 630,878 G 6
ão, 2,265 D 3
xo Guandu, 6,975 F 7
sas, 1,946 E 4
nbuí, 8,148 E 8
bacena, 41,931 F 8
rcelos, 1,904 H 9
ra, 7,237 F 5
ra-do-Corda, 3,723 E 4
ra-do-Piraí, 29,398 E 8
ras, 3,388 F 4
reiras, 7,175 E 6
reirinhas, 2,184 F 3
reiros, 10,402 H 5
retos, 39,950 D 8
alha, 15,559 F 3
urité, 7,198 G 4
uru, 85,237 D 8
edouro, 18,249 D 8
a Vista, 8,878 C 8
a Vista de Goiás, 2,687 D 7
ém, 359,988 D 3
monte, 7,897 G 6
o Horizonte, 642,912 F 7
njamin Constant, 3,224 G 9
nto Gonçalves, 13,662 C10
menau, 46,591 D 9
a Vista, 10,180 H 8
ca do Acre, 2,994 G10
caiúva, 5,952 E 7
m Conselho, 6,840 G 5
m Despacho, 13,568 E 7
m Jesus, 1,431 E 5
m Jesus da Lapa, 6,107 F 6
m Retiro, 1,601 D10
ba, 1,304 H 9
ucatu, 33,878 D 8
gança, 12,848 E 3
gança Paulista, 27,328 E 8
siléia, 1,902 G10
sília, 3,182 F 7
sília (cap.), 130,968 E 6
jo, 3,084 F 3
ves, 2,051 D 3
mado, 7,054 F 6
sque, 16,127 D 9
iti, 1,951 F 3
iti Alegre, 5,042 D 7
iti dos Lopes, 1,812 F 3
edelo, 10,738 H 4
o Frio, 13,117 F 8
ador, 10,480 D 9
apava do Sul, 6,712 C10
eres, 8,246 B 7
hoeira, 11,415 G 6
hoeira de Itapemirim, 8,470 G 8
hoeira do Arari, 2,532 D 3
hoeira do Sul, 38,661 C10
tité, 4,823 F 6
apônia, 2,476 C 7
ó, 15,826 G 4
azeiras, 15,884 G 4
das Novas, 1,377 D 7
naquã, 9,732 C10
nbará, 6,028 D 8
netá, 5,695 D 3
nocim, 10,788 F 3
npina Grande, 116,226 G 4
npina Verde, 4,464 D 7
npinas, 179,797 E 8
npo Belo, 15,742 E 8
npo Formoso, 3,925 F 5
npo Grande, 64,477 C 8
npo Maior, 13,939 F 4

Campos, 90,601 F 8
Cananéia, 1,948 E 9
Canavieiras, 10,264 G 6
Canguaretama, 4,261 H 4
Canindé, 5,854 G 4
Canoinhas, 9,252 D 9
Canto do Buriti, 1,636 F 5
Capanema, 9,678 E 3
Capão Bonito, 6,829 D 9
Capela, 5,172 G 5
Carangola, 11,896 F 8
Caratinga, 22,275 F 7
Carauari, 1,345 G 9
Caraúbas, 3,066 G 4
Caravelas, 3,096 G 7
Carinhanha, 2,163 E 6
Carolina, 8,137 E 4
Caruaru, 64,471 G 5
Carutapera, 2,477 E 3
Casa Nova, 1,525 F 5
Cascavel, 3,336 G 4
Castanhal, 9,528 E 3
Castelo, 5,729 F 8
Castelo do Piauí, 1,185 F 4
Castro, 9,249 D 9
Castro Alves, 7,388 G 6
Catalão, 11,471 D 7
Catanduva, 37,307 D 8
Catolé do Rocha, 5,217 G 4
Caxambu, 10,491 E 8
Caxias, 19,092 F 4
Caxias do Sul, 60,607 D10
Ceará (Fortaleza), 354,942 G 3
Ceará-Mirim, 8,290 H 4
Cícero Dantas, 2,972 G 5
Clevelândia do Norte, 1,010 D 2
Coari, 5,908 H 9
Codajás, 1,505 H 9
Codó, 11,089 E 4
Colatina, 26,757 F 7
Colinas, 2,972 F 4
Conceição da Barra, 2,229 G 7
Conceição do Araguaia, 2,332 D 5
Concórdia, 5,864 D 9
Conde, 4,190 G 5
Conselheiro Lafaiete, 29,208 E 8
Corinto, 12,247 E 7
Cornélio Procópio, 17,524 D 8
Coroatá, 7,720 F 3
Coromandel, 5,148 E 7
Corrente, 2,214 E 5
Correntina, 2,636 E 6
Corumbá, 36,744 B 7
Corumbá de Goiás, 1,704 D 7
Coxim, 1,371 C 7
Crateús, 14,572 F 4
Crato, 27,649 G 4
Criciúma, 25,331 D10
Cristalina, 3,810 E 7
Cruz Alta, 33,190 C10
Cruzeiro do Sul, 2,826 G10
Cuiabá, 43,112 C 6
Curaça, 1,264 G 5
Curitiba, 344,560 D 9
Currais Novos, 7,782 G 4
Curuçá, 3,871 E 3
Cururupu, 4,822 E 3
Curvelo, 21,772 E 7
Diamantina, 14,252 F 7
Dianópolis, 2,145 E 5
Divinópolis, 41,544 E 8
Dom Pedrito, 15,429 C10
Dores do Indaiá, 10,354 E 7
Dourados, 10,757 C 8
Eirunepé, 3,023 G10
Erechim, 24,941 C 9
Erval, 1,404 C11
Escada, 13,761 H 5
Esperança, 9,105 G 4
Esplanada, 3,792 G 5
Estância, 16,106 G 5
Exu, 2,549 G 4
Faro, 1,434 B 3
Feira de Santana, 61,612 G 5
Ferros, 2,456 F 7
Flores, 2,102 G 4
Floriano, 16,063 F 4
Florianópolis, 74,323 E 9
Fonte Boa, 1,154 G 9
Formiga, 18,763 E 8
Formosa, 9,449 E 6
Fortaleza, 354,942 G 3
Foz do Iguaçu, 7,407 C 9
França, 47,244 E 8
Fronteiras, 1,320 F 4
Frutal, 8,252 D 7
Garanhuns, 34,050 G 5
Glória, 1,062 G 5
Goiana, 19,026 H 4
Goiandira, 3,169 E 7
Goiânia, 132,577 D 7
Goiás, 7,121 D 6
Governador Valadares, 70,494 F 7
Grajaú, 2,539 E 4
Granja, 5,074 F 3
Guajará-Mirim, 7,115 H10
Guamá, 2,470 E 3
Guarabira, 15,848 H 4
Guarapuava, 13,546 C 9
Guaratinguetá, 38,293 E 8
Guaxupé, 14,168 E 8
Guimarães, 1,512 E 3
Guiratinga, 4,203 C 7
Humaitá, 1,192 H10
Ibiá, 6,999 E 7
Ibipetuba, 2,288 F 5
Icó, 5,586 G 4
Icoraci, 11,512 D 3
Igarapé-Miri, 2,591 D 3
Iguatu, 16,540 G 4
Ijuí, 19,671 C10
Ilhéus, 45,712 G 6
Imbituba, 6,638 D10
Imperatriz, 9,004 E 4
Inhumas, 8,298 D 7
Ipameri, 8,987 E 7
Ipiaú, 13,164 G 6
Ipu, 7,724 F 4
Irati, 12,764 D 9
Itabaiana, Paraíba, 11,847 H 4
Itabaiana, Sergipe, 11,050 G 5
Itaberaba, 8,555 F 6

Itabira, 15,539 F 7
Itabuna, 54,268 G 6
Itacoatiara, 8,818 B 3
Itaguatins, 1,596 D 4
Itaituba, 1,187 C 4
Itajaí, 38,889 D 9
Itajubá, 31,262 E 8
Itamarandiba, 2,404 F 7
Itapecuru-Mirim, 3,385 F 3
Itapemirim, 4,095 F 8
Itapetininga, 29,468 D 8
Itapeva, 13,510 D 8
Itapipoca, 7,186 G 3
Itápolis, 7,430 D 8
Itaporanga, 5,328 G 4
Itaqui, 13,223 B10
Itararé, 12,812 D 9
Itauçu, 1,431 F 6
Ituberá, 4,097 G 6
Ituiutaba, 29,724 D 7
Itumbiara, 12,575 D 7
Jaboticabal, 20,231 D 8
Jacareí, 28,131 E 8
Jacarèzinho, 14,813 D 8
Jacobina, 12,373 F 5
Jaguaquara, 5,363 F 6
Jaguarão, 12,336 C11
Jaguariaíva, 6,465 D 9
Jaicós, 1,308 F 4
Januária, 9,741 E 6
Jardim, 3,104 G 4
Jataí, 14,022 D 7
Jaú, 31,229 D 8
Jequié, 40,158 F 6
Jequitinhonha, 5,410 F 7
Jeremoabo, 3,177 G 5
Jerumenha, 1,473 F 4
Joaçaba, 7,921 D 9
João Pessoa, 135,820 H 4
João Pinheiro, 3,433 E 7
Joinville, 44,255 D 9
Juàzeiro, 21,196 G 5
Juàzeiro do Norte, 53,421 F 4
Juiz de Fora, 124,979 F 8
Jundiaí, 79,536 E 8
Lábrea, 2,080 G10
Laguna, 17,451 D10
Lajes, 35,112 D 9
Lapa, 7,167 D 9
Laranjeiras, 4,296 G 5
Laranjeiras do Sul, 3,802 C 9
Lavras, 23,793 E 8
Lençóis, 2,483 F 6
Limeira, 45,256 E 8
Limoeiro, 21,252 H 4
Limoeiro do Norte, 5,705 G 4
Linhares, 5,751 F 7
Lins, 32,204 D 8
Londrina, 74,110 D 8
Luís Correia, 1,523 F 3
Luziânia, 4,849 E 7
Luzilândia, 3,434 F 3
Macaé, 19,830 F 8
Macapá, 27,585 D 2
Macau, 11,876 G 4

Macaúbas, 2,504 F 6
Maceió, 153,305 H 5
Mafra, 12,981 D 9
Mallet, 1,816 D 9
Manacapuru, 2,584 H 9
Manaus, 154,040 H 9
Manga, 2,000 E 6
Manhuaçu, 10,546 F 8
Manicoré, 2,268 H 9
Marabá, 8,533 D 4
Maracaju, 1,848 C 8
Maragogipe, 12,575 G 6
Maranguape, 8,715 G 3
Marapanim, 3,542 E 3
Marechal-Deodoro, 5,269 H 5
Marília, 51,789 D 8
Massapê, 4,760 G 3
Mata de São João, 8,117 G 6
Maués, 4,161 B 3
Miguel Alves, 4,537 F 4
Minas Novas, 1,708 F 7
Mineiros, 5,105 C 7
Miracema, 9,810 F 8
Miranda, 2,075 C 8
Mocajuba, 1,352 D 3
Mogi das Cruzes, 63,748 E 8
Monte-Alegre, 3,911 C 3
Monte Alegre de Minas, 4,464 D 7
Monte Azul, 4,860 F 6
Monte Santo, 1,607 G 5
Monteiro, 6,028 G 4
Montenegro, 14,491 D10
Montes Claros, 40,545 E 7
Morrinhos, 9,879 D 7
Morro do Chapéu, 2,039 F 5
Morros, 1,887 F 3
Mossoró, 38,833 G 4
Mundo Novo, 3,237 F 5
Muqui, 4,262 F 8
Muriaé, 22,571 F 8
Natal, 154,276 H 4
Natividade, 1,243 E 5
Nazaré, 14,644 G 6
Neópolis, 7,356 G 5
Neves, 85,741 F 8
Nioaque, 2,578 C 8
Niquelândia, 1,262 D 6
Niterói, 288,826 F 8
Nova Cruz, 6,780 H 4
Nova Friburgo, 49,901 F 8
Nova Iguaçu, 134,708 F 8
Nova Russas, 4,666 F 4
Óbidos, 5,901 C 3
Oeiras, 6,098 F 4
Olinda, 100,545 H 4
Oliveira, 12,919 E 8
Oriximiná, 3,974 C 3
Orleães, 3,070 D10
Ourinhos, 25,717 D 8
Ouro Fino, 9,610 E 8
Ouro Prêto, 14,722 E 8
Palmares, 17,327 H 5
Palmas, 5,540 C 9
Palmeira, 5,916 D 9
Palmeira das Missões, 8,017 C 9

Palmeiras, 2,040 F 6
Palmeiras de Goiás, 2,378 D 7
Pará (Belém), 359,988 E 3
Pará de Minas, 15,858 E 7
Paracatu, 10,677 E 7
Paraguaçu Paulista, 11,391 D 8
Paranaguá, 27,728 E 9
Paranaíba, 3,853 D 7
Paratinga, 2,403 F 6
Parintins, 9,068 B 3
Parnaíba, 39,951 F 3
Parnamirim, 1,589 F 4
Passagem Franca, 1,703 E 4
Passo Fundo, 47,299 D10
Passos, 28,555 E 8
Pastos Bons, 1,258 E 4
Patos, 27,275 G 4
Patos de Minas, 31,471 E 7
Pau dos Ferros, 4,298 G 4
Patrocínio, 13,933 E 7
Paulistana, 1,105 F 4
Peçanha, 3,602 F 7
Pedra Azul, 8,238 F 6
Pedreiras, 10,189 E 4
Pedro Afonso, 3,175 E 5
Pedro Segundo, 3,160 F 4
Pelotas, 121,280 C10
Penalva, 5,339 E 3
Penedo, 17,084 G 5
Pernambuco (Recife), 788,569 H 5
Petrolina, 14,652 G 5
Petrópolis, 93,849 F 8
Piaçabuçu, 4,864 H 5
Picos, 8,176 F 4
Pilão Arcado, 1,457 F 5
Pilar, 7,201 H 5
Pinheiro, 6,537 E 3
Piracanjuba, 3,869 D 7
Piracicaba, 80,670 E 8
Piracuruca, 4,320 F 3
Piraí do Sul, 4,842 D 9
Pirapora, 13,772 E 7
Pirenópolis, 3,088 D 6
Pires do Rio, 8,390 E 7
Piripiri, 9,635 F 4
Piuí, 9,164 E 8
Poções, 6,115 F 6
Poconé, 4,702 B 7
Poços de Caldas, 32,291 E 8
Ponta de Pedras, 1,907 D 3
Ponta Grossa, 77,803 D 9
Ponta Porã, 9,610 C 8
Ponte Nova, 22,536 F 8
Portel, 1,821 D 3
Pôrto, 1,234 F 3
Pôrto Alegre, 617,629 D10
Pôrto Franco, 1,750 E 4

Pôrto Murtinho, 4,476 B 8
Pôrto Nacional, 4,926 E 5
Pôrto Seguro, 2,697 G 7
Pôrto União, 9,954 D 9
Pôrto Velho, 19,387 H10
Posse, 1,953 E 6
Pouso Alegre, 18,852 E 8
Poxoréu, 3,315 C 6
Prata, 4,725 D 7
Presidente Dutra, 3,349 E 4
Presidente Prudente, 54,055 D 8
Presidente Venceslau, 13,140 D 8
Propriá, 15,947 G 5
Prudentópolis, 4,524 D 9
Quaraí, 10,575 C10
Queimadas, 3,553 F 5
Quipapá, 3,421 G 5
Quixadá, 8,747 G 4
Quixeramobim, 6,384 F 4
Recife, 788,569 H 5
Regeneração, 1,672 F 4
Remanso, 5,125 F 5
Riachão, 1,907 E 4
Ribas do Rio Pardo, 1,175 C 8
Ribeirão Prêto, 116,153 E 8
Rio Branco, 17,245 G10
Rio Brilhante, 876 C 8
Rio Claro, 48,548 E 8
Rio de Janeiro, 3,223,408 F 8
Rio do Sul, 13,433 D 9
Rio Grande, 83,189 D11
Rio Negro, 10,225 D 9
Rio Pardo, 14,412 C10
Rio Pardo de Minas, 1,169 F 6
Rio Real, 3,171 G 5
Rio Tinto, 16,811 H 4
Rio Verde, 11,268 D 7
Rolândia, 10,023 D 8
Rosário, 6,999 F 3
Rosário-do-Sul, 15,786 C10
Rosário-Oeste, 2,607 C 6
Russas, 7,102 G 4
Sabinópolis, 4,101 F 7
Sacramento, 5,872 D 7
Salgueiro, 8,936 G 5
Salinas, 5,186 F 7
Salinópolis, 4,101 E 3
Salvador, 630,878 G 6
Santa Cruz, 5,286 G 4
Santa Cruz do Sul, 18,898 C10
Santa Leopoldina, 1,174 G 7
Santa Maria, 78,682 C10
Santa Maria da Vitória, 3,208 F 6
Santa Vitória do Palmar, 8,224 C11
Santana, 4,357 E 6
Santana do Ipanema, 8,139 G 5
Santana do Livramento, 37,666 C10

Santarém, 24,924 C 3
Santiago, 15,140 C10
Santo Amaro, 17,226 G 6
Santo Ângelo, 25,415 C10
Santo Antônio da Platina, 9,378 D 8
Santo Antônio do Leverger, 2,028 C 6
Santos, 262,048 E 9
Santos Dumont, 20,414 F 8
São Bento, 7,094 E 3
São Borja, 20,339 C10
São Cristóvão, 7,624 G 5
São Félix, 5,993 G 6
São Fidélis, 6,145 F 8
São Francisco, 4,074 E 6
São Francisco do Sul, 11,593 E 9
São Gabriel, 22,967 C10
São João da Boa Vista, 25,226 E 8
São João del Rei, 34,654 E 8
São João do Piauí, 2,688 F 5
São João dos Patos, 2,590 F 4
São José, 3,295 D 9
São José da Laje, 5,822 H 5
São José de Mipibu, 5,179 H 4
São José do Rio Prêto, 66,476 D 8
São José dos Pinhais, 7,574 D 9
São Leopoldo, 41,023 D10
São Lourenço do Sul, 6,877 C10
São Luís (Maranhão), 124,606 F 3
São Luís Gonzaga, 12,926 C10
São Mateus, 6,075 G 7
São Miguel dos Campos, 6,511 G 5
São Paulo, 3,164,804 E 8
São Paulo de Olivença, 1,157 G 9
São Pedro do Piauí, 2,139 F 4
São Raimundo das Mangabeiras, 1,736 E 4
São Raimundo Nonato, 3,751 F 5
São Romão, 1,438 E 7
São Sebastião do Paraíso, 14,451 E 8
São Vicente Ferrer, 1,095 E 3
Sena Madureira, 1,962 G10
Senador Pompeu, 8,210 G 4
Senhor do Bonfim, 13,958 F 5
Serra Talhada, 12,164 G 4
Serrinha, 10,284 G 5
Sertânia, 7,556 G 5
Sertanópolis, 6,469 D 8
Sete Lagoas, 36,302 E 7
Silvânia, 2,920 D 7
Simplício Mendes, 1,682 F 4
Sobral, 32,281 G 3
Sorocaba, 109,258 D 8
Soure, 6,666 D 3
Taguatinga, 1,496 E 6
Taquara, 11,282 D10

(continued on following page)

Brazil
(continued)

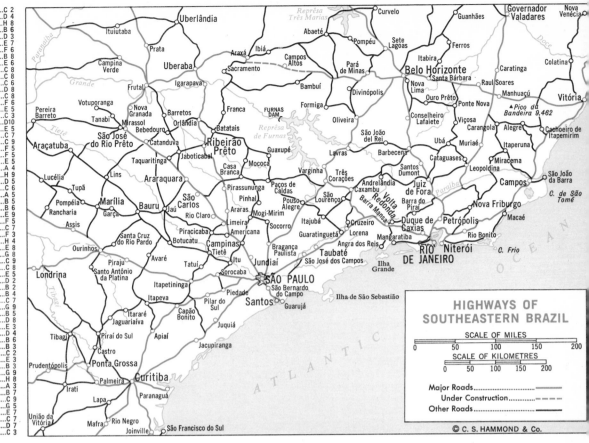

HIGHWAYS OF SOUTHEASTERN BRAZIL

SCALE OF MILES
0 50 100 150 200

SCALE OF KILOMETRES
0 50 100 150 200

Major Roads _____
Under Construction ___ ___ ___
Other Roads _____

© C. S. HAMMOND & Co.

AGRICULTURE, INDUSTRY and RESOURCES

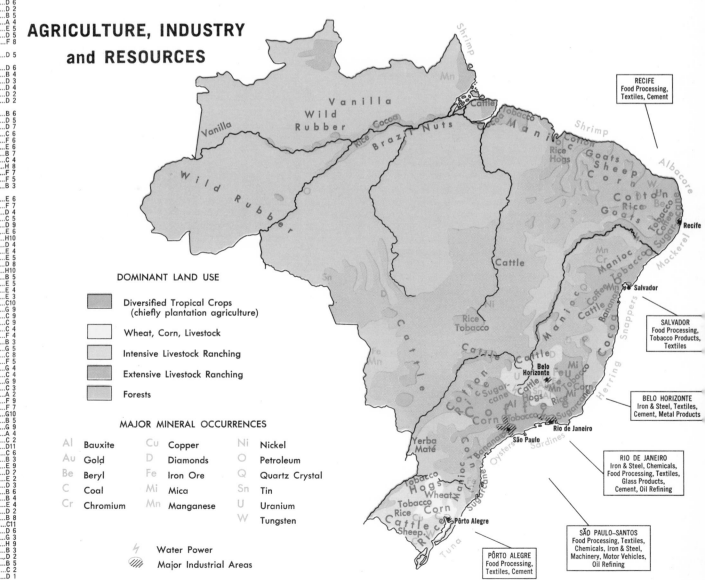

DOMINANT LAND USE

- Diversified Tropical Crops (chiefly plantation agriculture)
- Wheat, Corn, Livestock
- Intensive Livestock Ranching
- Extensive Livestock Ranching
- Forests

MAJOR MINERAL OCCURRENCES

Al	Bauxite	Cu	Copper	Ni	Nickel
Au	Gold	D	Diamonds	O	Petroleum
Be	Beryl	Fe	Iron Ore	Q	Quartz Crystal
C	Coal	Mi	Mica	Sn	Tin
Cr	Chromium	Mn	Manganese	U	Uranium
				W	Tungsten

Water Power

Major Industrial Areas

RECIFE
Food Processing, Textiles, Cement

SALVADOR
Food Processing, Tobacco Products, Textiles

BELO HORIZONTE
Iron & Steel, Textiles, Cement, Metal Products

RIO DE JANEIRO
Iron & Steel, Chemicals, Food Processing, Textiles, Glass Products, Cement, Oil Refining

SÃO PAULO–SANTOS
Food Processing, Textiles, Chemicals, Iron & Steel, Machinery, Motor Vehicles, Oil Refining

PÔRTO ALEGRE
Food Processing, Textiles, Cement

SOUTHEASTERN BRAZIL

STATES

...pírito Santo, 1,384,000	F 2
...anabara, 3,857,000	E 3
...nas Gerais, 10,945,000	D 2
...raná, 6,024,000	D 2
...o de Janeiro, 4,103,000	E 3
...o Paulo, 15,326,000	B 3

CITIES and TOWNS

...udos, 6,564	B 3
... 7,487	E 2
...m Paraíba, 18,399	E 2
...enas, 16,051	C 2
...ericana, 32,000	C 3
...amparo, 14,348	C 3
...drelândia, 4,617	D 2
...ntonina, 8,520	B 4
...arecida, 15,290	D 3
...iaí, 2,728	B 4
... 53,563	A 2
...araquara, 58,076	B 2
...aras, 23,898	C 3
...is, 30,207	A 3
...mbuí, 8,148	C 2
...rão de Cocais, 7,223	E 1
...bacena, 41,931	E 2
...riri, 8,403	B 3
...rra do Piraí, 29,398	D 3
...rra Mansa, 47,398	D 3
...rretos, 38,950	B 2
...tatais, 15,266	C 2
...uru, 85,237	B 3
...bedouro, 18,249	B 2
...lo Horizonte, 642,912	D 1
...tim, 18,963	D 2
...cas, 7,463	A 2
...gui, 18,721	A 2
...a Esperança, 9,263	D 2
...m Despacho, 13,568	D 1
...m Sucesso, 6,173	C 4
...tucatu, 33,878	A 2
...agança Paulista, 27,328	C 3
...rí, 2,666	B 3
...bo Frio, 13,117	F 3
...raguatatuba, 7,987	D 3
...eté, 10,840	E 1
...felândia, 6,573	C 2
...juru, 4,971	C 2
...ampo, 6,028	A 3
...mpanha, 6,178	D 2
...mpinas, 179,797	C 3
...mpo Belo, 15,742	C 2
...mpo Florido, 1,307	B 1
...mpo Largo, 7,915	B 4
...mpos, 90,601	F 2
...mpos Altos, 5,243	C 1
...ananéia, 1,948	C 4
...pao Bonito, 3,479	E 3
...raguatatuba, 6,829	D 3
...randaí, 4,655	D 3
... 2,792	D 2
...rangola, 11,896	E 2

Caratinga, 22,275	E 2
Casa Branca, 8,980	C 2
Cascatinha, 19,497	E 3
Cássia, 7,034	C 2
Castro, 9,242	B 4
Cataguases, 21,476	E 2
Catanduva, 37,307	B 2
Caxambu, 10,491	D 2
Cêrro Azul, 1,460	B 4
Conselheiro Lafaiete, 29,208	E 2
Cruzeiro, 27,005	D 3
Cubatão, 18,885	C 3
Curitiba, 344,560	B 4
Divinópolis, 41,544	D 2
Dois Córregos, 7,272	B 3
Duque de Caxias, 173,077	E 3
Eldorado, 1,524	B 4
Fernandópolis, 14,375	A 2
Formiga, 18,736	C 2
Franca, 47,244	C 2
Frutal, 8,252	B 1
Garça, 18,155	B 3
Guacuí, 7,724	F 2
Guaratinguetá, 38,293	D 3
Guarujá, 6,506	C 4
Guarulhos, 77,980	C 3
Guaxupé, 14,168	C 2
Ibaiti, 3,828	A 4
Ibitinga, 8,881	B 2
Igarapava, 9,083	C 2
Iguape, 5,465	C 4
Imbituva, 3,290	A 4
Irati, 12,764	A 4
Itabirito, 10,511	E 2
Itaí, 1,601	B 3
Itajubá, 31,262	D 2
Itanhaém, 5,376	C 4
Itapecerica, 7,696	D 2
Itaperuna, 18,095	F 2
Itapetininga, 29,468	B 3
Itapeva, 13,510	B 3
Itapira, 16,859	C 3
Itápolis, 7,430	B 2
Itararé, 12,812	B 4
Itariri, 1,318	C 4
Itatiba, 12,336	D 2
Itaúna, 22,319	D 2
Itu, 23,435	C 3
Iturama, 1,518	A 1
Ituverava, 11,890	C 2
Jaboticabal, 20,231	B 2
Jacareí, 28,131	D 3
Jacarèzinho, 14,813	A 3
Jacupiranga, 2,144	B 4
Jaguariaíva, 6,465	A 4
Jaú, 31,229	B 3
Joaquim Távora, 3,574	A 3
Juiz de Fora, 124,979	E 2
Jundiaí, 79,536	C 3
Juquiá, 2,573	C 4
Lambari, 6,825	D 2
Lavras, 23,793	D 2
Leme, 11,785	C 3
Leopoldina, 17,726	E 2
Lima Duarte, 3,554	E 2
Limeira, 45,256	C 3
Lins, 32,204	B 2

Lorena, 26,068	D 3
Luz, 5,633	D 1
Macaé, 19,830	F 3
Machado, 8,373	C 2
Magé, 10,712	E 3
Manhuaçu, 10,546	E 2
Manhumirim, 9,477	E 2
Mariana, 6,378	E 2
Marília, 51,789	A 3
Marquês de Valença, 18,935	E 2
Mimoso do Sul, 5,278	F 2
Miracema, 13,674	E 2
Mirassol, 13,674	B 2
Mococa, 14,306	C 2
Mogi das Cruzes, 63,748	C 3
Mogi Mirim, 18,345	C 3
Monte Aprazível, 7,235	B 2
Muriaé, 22,571	E 2
Muzambinho, 18,073	C 2
Neves, 85,741	E 1
Niterói, 288,826	E 3
Nova Era, 7,326	E 1
Nova Friburgo, 49,901	E 3
Nova Granada, 5,134	B 2
Nova Iguaçu, 134,708	E 3
Nova Lima, 21,135	E 2
Novo Horizonte, 8,581	B 2
Olímpia, 14,629	B 2
Oliveira, 12,919	D 2
Orlândia, 6,898	C 2
Ourinhos, 25,717	B 3
Ouro Fino, 8,044	C 3
Ouro Prêto, 14,722	E 2
Palmeira, 5,916	B 4
Pará de Minas, 15,858	D 1
Paraíba do Sul, 7,675	E 2
Paranaguá, 27,728	B 4
Parati, 3,046	D 3
Passos, 28,555	C 2
Paulo de Faria, 2,722	B 2
Pederneiras, 8,053	B 3
Penápolis, 14,400	A 2
Petrópolis, 93,849	E 3
Piedade, 4,812	C 3
Pindamonhangaba, 19,144	D 3
Pinhal, 14,260	C 3
Piquete, 9,810	D 3
Piracicaba, 80,670	C 3
Piraí do Sul, 4,842	B 4
Piraju, 10,658	B 3
Pirajuí, 6,465	B 3
Pirassununga, 16,784	C 3
Pitangui, 7,421	D 1
Piuí, 9,164	C 2
Poços de Caldas, 32,291	C 2
Pompéia, 7,462	A 3
Ponta Grossa, 77,803	A 4
Ponte Nova, 22,536	E 2
Porciúncula, 4,868	F 2
Pôrto Féliz, 11,786	C 3
Pouso Alegre, 18,852	D 3
Promissão, 9,683	B 2
Raposos, 7,631	E 2
Raul Soares, 6,194	E 2
Registro, 4,913	C 4
Resende, 13,544	D 3
Ribeira, 603	B 4
Ribeirão Prêto, 116,153	C 2

Rio Bonito, 11,916	E 3
Rio Claro, 48,548	C 3
Rio de Janeiro, 3,223,408	E 3
Rio Pomba, 6,083	E 2
Sabará, 10,004	E 1
Sacramento, 5,872	C 2
Salto, 12,643	C 3
Santa Cruz do Rio Pardo, 13,889	B 3
Santa Rita do Sapucaí 8,464	D 2
Santo André, 230,196	C 3
Santo Antônio da Platina, 9,378	A 3
Santos, 262,048	C 3
Santos Dumont, 20,414	E 2
São Bernardo do Campo, 61,645	C 3
São Caetano do Sul, 114,039	C 3
São Carlos, 50,010	C 3
São Fidélis, 6,145	F 2
São João da Boa Vista, 25,226	C 2
São João del Rei, 34,654	D 2
São João Nepomuceno, 9,436	E 2
São Joaquim da Barra, 13,853	C 2
São José do Rio Pardo, 14,186	C 2
São José do Rio Prêto, 66,476	B 2
São José dos Campos, 55,349	D 3
São Lourenço, 14,680	D 2
São Manuel, 10,009	B 3
São Miguel Arcanjo, 3,633	C 3
São Miguel Paulista, 39,644	C 3
São Paulo, 3,164,804	C 3
São Pedro, 4,474	C 3
São Roque, 12,409	C 3
São Sebastião, 3,490	D 3
São Sebastião do Paraíso, 14,451	C 2
São Simão, 5,742	C 2
São Vicente, 73,578	C 3
Socorro, 6,402	C 3
Sorocaba, 109,258	C 3
Taquaritinga, 11,624	B 2
Tatuí, 22,550	C 3
Taubaté, 64,863	D 3
Teresópolis, 29,540	E 3
Tibagi, 1,746	A 4
Tietê, 8,729	C 3
Três Corações, 17,498	D 2
Três Pontas, 11,534	D 2
Três Rios, 22,246	E 2
Tupã, 28,723	A 2
Ubá, 21,767	E 2
Ubatuba, 3,748	D 3
Uberaba, 72,053	C 1
Varginha, 24,944	D 2
Vera Cruz, 5,535	B 2
Viçosa, 9,342	E 2
Visconde do Rio Branco, 12,363	E 2
Volta Redonda, 83,973	D 3
Votuporanga, 18,722	B 2

PHYSICAL FEATURES

Araruama (lagoon)	E 3
Bandeira (mt.)	F 2
Buzios (cape)	F 3
Cardoso (isl.)	C 4
Comprida (isl.)	C 4
Doce (river)	E 2
Feia (lake)	F 3
Feio (river)	B 2
Frio (cape)	F 3
Furnas (dam)	C 2
Furnas (res.)	C 2
Grande (river)	D 3
Grande (river)	B 1

Guanabara (bay)	E 3
Ilha Grande (bay)	D 3
Itararé (river)	B 3
Mantiqueira (range)	D 2
Mar (range)	C 4
Moji Guaçu (river)	C 2
Orgãos (range)	E 2
Paraíba (river)	E 2
Paranapanema (river)	B 3
Paranapiacaba (range)	B 4

Pardo (river)	B 2
Peixoto (dam)	C 2
Ribeira (river)	B 4
São Francisco (river)	D 2
São Sebastião (isl.)	D 3
Sapucaí (river)	D 2
Sepetiba (bay)	D 3
Tibagi (river)	A 4
Tietê (river)	B 2
Turvo (river)	B 2

BRASÍLIA — MILES

© C. S. Hammond & Co., Maplewood, N. J.

SOUTHEASTERN BRAZIL
POLYCONIC PROJECTION
SCALE OF MILES
SCALE OF KILOMETRES
State Capitals ... ◉
State Boundaries ... —·—·—
© Copyright by C. S. HAMMOND & CO., Maplewood, N. J.

Bolivia

La Paz, 1,157,400	A 4	Alcalá	C 6	Arcopongo	B 5
Oruro, 265,400	A 6	Alto Seco	D 6	Aroma	B 6
Pando, 24,400	B 2	Amarete	A 4	Arque, 1,254	B 5
Potosí, 619,600	B 7	Ananea, 302	A 4	Arroyo Grande	A 2
Santa Cruz, 326,900	E 5	Ancoraimes, 769	A 5	Ascensión	D 4
Tarija, 142,600	D 7	Andamarca	B 6	Ascensión	B 5
		Anzaldo	B 5	Asunción	B 2
DEPARTMENTS		Apolo, 1,043	A 4	Atén, 199	A 4
		Aquío	D 6	Atocha	C 7
Beni, 161,800	C 3	Araca	B 5	Ayacucho, 729	D 5
Chuquisaca, 307,600	C 6	Arampampa	B 5	Ayata	A 4
Cochabamba, 550,300	C 5	Arani, 2,200	C 5	Azurduy, 1,234	C 6
				Barrera	B 3
CITIES and TOWNS				Baures, 592	B 3
Abapó, 466	D 6				
Acchilla, 208	C 7				
Achacachi, 3,621	A 5				
Aiquile, 3,465	C 6				

Bella Vista	E 3	Calamarca, 802	A 5	Carandaití, 1,403	D
Berenguela	A 5	Calcha	B 7	Carangas	
Betanzos, 1,097	B 7	Calcha	C 7	Caraparí, 351	D 7
Bolívar	B 3	Callapa, 636	A 5	Carmen	
Boyuibe, 537	D 7	Calacoto	A 5	Carrizal	
Buena Hora	E 4	Camargo, 1,609	C 7	Cavari, 249	
Buena Vista	B 2	Camatindi	D 7	Cavinas	
Buena Vista, 435	D 5	Camiri, 4,969	D 7	Chaguaya	
Cabezas, 2,980	C 7	Cañas	C 8	Chachacomani, 159	
Cachuela Esperanza, 1,073	C 2	Cañas	A 7	Chaguaya	
Caiza, 838	C 7	Canquella	B 7	Challacollo, 284	C 7
Cajuata, 447	B 5	Capinota, 1,734	B 5	Challacota	
Calacoto, 415	A 5	Capirenda	D 7	Challana	
		Caracollo, 909	B 5	Challapata, 2,529	C 6

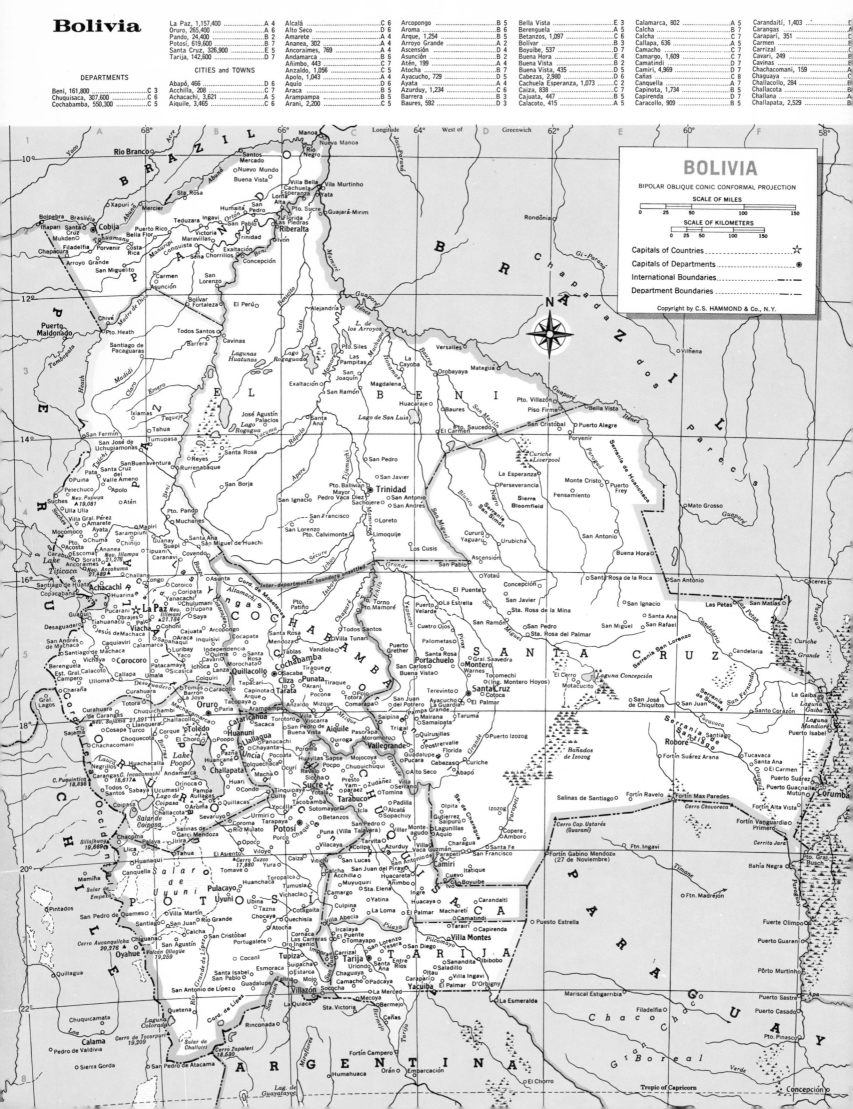

BOLIVIA

AREA	412,777 sq. mi.
POPULATION	3,702,000
CAPITAL	La Paz, Sucre
LARGEST CITY	La Paz 352,912
HIGHEST POINT	Nevada Ancohuma 21,489 ft.
MONETARY UNIT	Bolivian peso
AJOR LANGUAGES	Spanish, Indian
MAJOR RELIGION	Roman Catholic

TOPOGRAPHY

0   100   200
MILES

Below Sea Level	100 m. 328 ft.	200 m. 656 ft.	500 m. 1,640 ft.	1,000 m. 3,281 ft.	2,000 m. 6,562 ft.	5,000 m. 16,404 ft.

AGRICULTURE, INDUSTRY and RESOURCES

DOMINANT LAND USE

- Diversified Tropical Crops (chiefly plantation agriculture)
- Upland Cultivated Areas
- Upland Livestock Grazing, Limited Agriculture
- Extensive Livestock Ranching
- Forests
- Nonagricultural Land

MAJOR MINERAL OCCURRENCES

Ag	Silver	O	Petroleum
Au	Gold	Pb	Lead
Cu	Copper	S	Sulfur
		Sb	Antimony
Sn	Tin		
W	Tungsten		
Zn	Zinc		

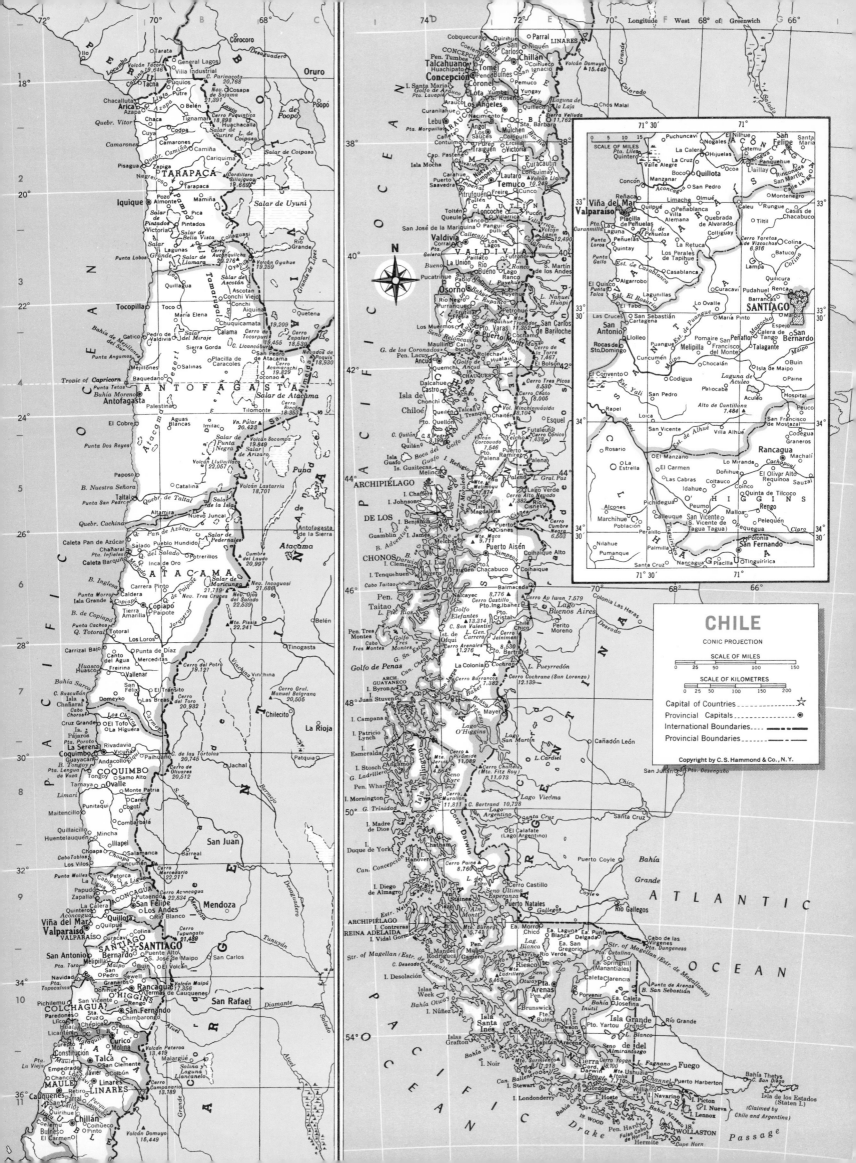

CHILE

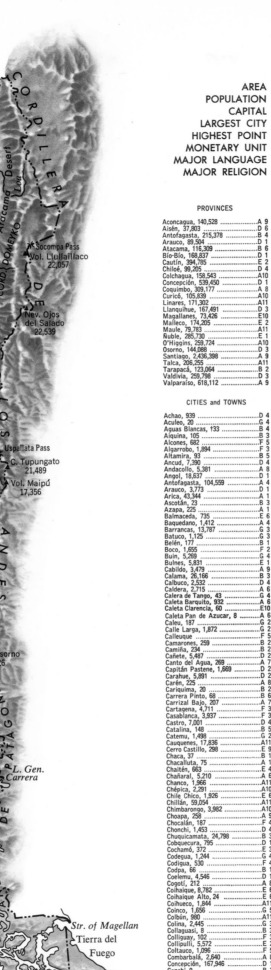

TOPOGRAPHY

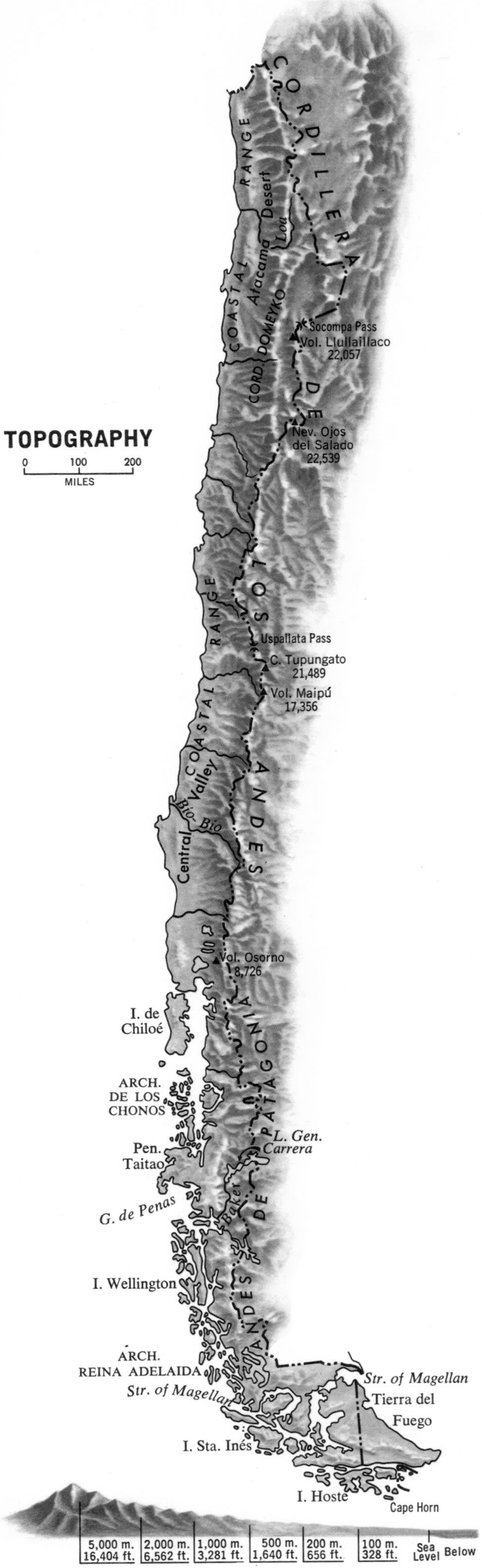
0 100 200
MILES
CORDILLERA DE LOS ANDES
COASTAL RANGE
Atacama Desert
Loa
CORD. DOMEYKO
Socompa Pass
Vol. Llullaillaco 22,057
Nev. Ojos del Salado 22,539
Uspallata Pass
C. Tupungato 21,489
Vol. Maipú 17,356
COASTAL RANGE
Central Valley
Bío Bío
Vol. Osorno 8,726
I. de Chiloé
ARCH. DE LOS CHONOS
Pen. Taitao
L. Gen. Carrera
G. de Penas
Baker
ANDES DE PATAGONIA
I. Wellington
ARCH. REINA ADELAIDA
Str. of Magellan
Str. of Magellan
Tierra del Fuego
I. Sta. Inés
I. Hoste
Cape Horn
5,000 m. 16,404 ft.
2,000 m. 6,562 ft.
1,000 m. 3,281 ft.
500 m. 1,640 ft.
200 m. 656 ft.
100 m. 328 ft.
Sea Level
Below

AREA	286,396 sq. mi.
POPULATION	8,567,000
CAPITAL	Santiago
LARGEST CITY	Santiago (greater) 2,270,738
HIGHEST POINT	Ojos del Salado 22,539 ft.
MONETARY UNIT	Chilean escudo
MAJOR LANGUAGE	Spanish
MAJOR RELIGION	Roman Catholic

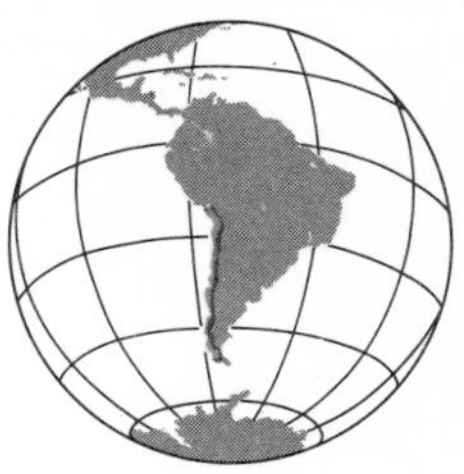

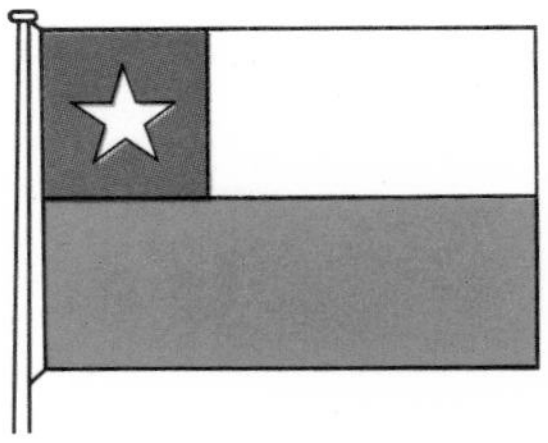

PROVINCES

Aconcagua, 140,528	A 9
Aisén, 37,803	D 6
Antofagasta, 215,378	B 4
Arauco, 89,504	D 1
Atacama, 116,309	B 6
Bío-Bío, 168,837	D 1
Cautín, 394,785	E 2
Chiloé, 99,205	D 4
Colchagua, 158,543	A10
Concepción, 539,450	D 1
Coquimbo, 309,177	A 8
Curicó, 105,839	A10
Linares, 171,302	A11
Llanquihue, 167,491	D 3
Magallanes, 73,426	E10
Malleco, 174,205	E 2
Maule, 79,783	A11
Ñuble, 285,730	E 1
O'Higgins, 259,724	A10
Osorno, 144,088	D 3
Santiago, 2,436,398	A 9
Talca, 206,255	A11
Tarapacá, 123,064	B 2
Valdivia, 259,798	D 3
Valparaíso, 618,112	A 9

CITIES and TOWNS

Achao, 939	D 4
Aculeo, 20	G 4
Aguas Blancas, †33	B 4
Aiquina, 105	B 3
Alcones, 682	F 5
Algarrobo, 1,894	F 3
Altamira, 93	B 5
Ancud, 7,390	D 4
Andacollo, 5,381	A 8
Angol, 18,637	D 1
Antofagasta, 104,559	A 4
Arauco, 3,773	D 1
Arica, 43,344	A 1
Ascotán, 23	B 3
Azapa, 225	A 1
Balmaceda, 735	E 6
Baquedano, 1,412	A 4
Barrancas, 13,787	G 3
Batuco, 1,125	G 3
Belén, 177	B 1
Boco, 1,655	F 2
Buin, 5,269	G 4
Bulnes, 5,831	E 1
Cabildo, 3,479	A 9
Calama, 26,166	B 3
Calbuco, 2,532	D 4
Caldera, 2,715	A 6
Calera de Tango, 43	G 4
Caleta Barquito, 932	A 6
Caleta Clarencia, 60	E10
Caleta Pan de Azucar, 8	A 6
Caleu, 187	G 2
Calle Larga, 1,872	G 2
Calleuque	F 5
Camarones, 259	B 2
Camiña, 234	B 2
Cañete, 5,487	D 2
Canto del Agua, 269	A 7
Capitán Pastene, 1,669	D 2
Carahue, 5,891	D 2
Carén, 225	A 8
Cariquima, 20	B 2
Carrera Pinto, 68	B 6
Carrizal Bajo, 207	A 7
Cartagena, 4,711	F 3
Casablanca, 3,937	F 3
Castro, 7,001	D 4
Catalina, 148	B 5
Catemu, 1,498	G 2
Cauquenes, 17,836	A11
Cerro Castillo, 298	E 9
Chaca, 37	B 1
Chacalluta, 75	A 1
Chaitén, 663	E 4
Chañaral, 5,210	A 6
Chanco, 1,966	A11
Chépica, 2,291	A10
Chile Chico, 1,926	E 6
Chillán, 59,054	A11
Chimbarongo, 3,982	A10
Choapa, 258	A 9
Chocalán, 187	F 4
Chonchi, 1,453	D 4
Chuquicamata, 24,798	B 3
Cobquecura, 795	D 1
Cochamó, 372	E 3
Codegua, 1,244	G 4
Codigua, 530	F 4
Codpa, 66	B 1
Coelemu, 4,546	D 1
Cogotí, 212	A 8
Coihaique, 8,782	E 6
Coihaique Alto, 24	E 6
Coihueco, 1,844	A11
Coinco, 1,656	G 5
Colbún, 980	A11
Colina, 2,445	G 3
Collaguasi, 8	B 3
Colliguay, 102	F 3
Collipulli, 5,572	E 2
Coltauco, 1,096	F 5
Combarbalá, 2,640	A 8
Concepción, 167,946	D 1
Conchi, 9	B 3
Conchi Viejo, 17	B 3
Concón, 5,381	F 2
Constitución, 9,536	A11
Contulmo, 978	D 2
Copiapó, 30,123	B 6
Coquimbo, 33,749	A 8
Coronel, 33,870	D 1
Corral, 3,740	D 3
Cruz Grande, 478	A 7
Cunco, 3,342	E 2
Cuncumén, Coquimbo, 1,052	A 9
Cuncumén, Santiago	F 4
Curacautin, 9,601	E 2
Curacaví, 4,116	G 3
Curanilahue, 12,117	D 1
Curepto, 1,699	A10
Curicó, 32,562	A10
Cuya, 86	B 2
Dalcahue, 451	D 4
Domeyko, 1,814	A 7
Doñihue, 1,622	G 5
El Carmen, Ñuble, 2,263	A11
El Carmen, O'Higgins, 625	F 5
El Cobre, 7	A 4
El Convento, 733	F 4
El Manzano, 1,073	F 5
El Ñilhue, 341	G 1
El Olivar Alto, 1,084	G 5
El Quisco, 1,019	E 3
El Tabo, 714	F 3
El Tofo, 1,175	A 7
El Tránsito, 235	B 7
El Volcán, 250	B10
Empedrado, 574	A11
Ercilla, 1,311	E 2
Espejo, 3,481	G 3
Estancia Caleta Josefina, 166	F10
Estancia Laguna Blanca, 119	E 9
Estancia Morro Chico, 32	E 9
Estancia Punta Delgada, 233	E 9
Estancia San Gregorio, 59	E 9
Estancia Springhill (Manantiales), 291	F10
Freire, 2,006	E 2
Freirina, 1,831	A 7
Fresia, 3,571	D 3
Frutillar, 686	D 3
Fuerte Bulnes, 18	E10
Futaleufú, 616	E 4
Futrono, 981	E 3
Galvarino, 1,735	D 2
Gatico, 16	A 4
General Lagos, 6	B 1
Graneros, 5,644	G 5
Guayacán, 1,514	A 8
Hijuelas, 897	F 2
Hospital, 460	G 4
Huachipato, †16,336	D 1
Hualaihué, 391	E 4
Hualañé, 1,712	A10
Huara, 885	B 2
Huasco, 1,902	A 7
Huentelauquén, 355	A 8
Idahue, 1,832	F 5
Illapel, 10,395	A 8
Imilac, 27	B 4
Inca de Oro, 1,406	B 6
Iquique, 50,655	A 2
Isla de Maipo, 3,580	G 4
La Calera, 18,134	F 2
La Colonia, 41	D 7
La Cruz, 3,000	F 2
La Estrella, 319	F 5
La Higuera, 889	A 7
La Laguna, 316	F 2
La Ligua, 5,095	A 9
La Retuca, 173	F 3
La Serena, 40,854	A 8
La Unión, 11,558	D 3
Lago Ranco, 1,541	D 3
Lago Verde, 193	E 5
Lagunas, 30	B 3
Lagunillas, 468	F 3
Lampa, 1,698	G 3
Lanco, 4,948	D 2
Las Breas, 14	B 7
Las Cabras, 1,668	F 5
Las Cruces, 612	F 3
Lautaro, 10,448	E 2
Lebu, 6,248	D 1
Licantén, 1,368	A10
Limache, 14,488	F 2
Linares, 27,568	A11
Llaillay, 7,049	G 2
Llico, 330	A10
Llolleo, 9,846	F 4
Lo Miranda, 2,270	G 5
Lo Ovalle, 129	F 3
Loica, 446	F 4
Loncoche, 6,619	D 2
Longaví 2,625	A11
Lonquimay, 1,320	E 2
Los Andes, 20,448	B 9
Los Ángeles, 35,511	D 1
Los Lagos, 3,897	D 3
Los Loros, 269	A 6
Los Muermos, 1,616	D 3
Los Perales de Tapihue, 176	F 3
Los Sauces, 2,717	D 2
Los Vilos, 3,027	A 9
Lota, 27,739	D 1
Machalí, 3,008	G 5
Maipú, 16,740	G 3
Maitencillo, 31	A 8
Malloa, 926	G 5
Mamiña, 341	B 2
Manantiales, 291	F10
Manzanar, 248	F 2
Marchihue, 924	F 5
María Elena, 9,572	B 3
María Pinto, 416	G 3
Maullín, 1,789	D 4
Mayer, 29	E 7
Mejillones, 3,363	A 4
Melinca, 166	D 5
Melipilla, 15,593	F 4
Merceditas, 33	B 7
Mincha, 301	A 8
Molina, 7,621	A10
Monte Patria, 798	A 8
Montenegro, 327	G 2
Mulchén, 10,729	E 1
Nacimiento, 3,823	D 1
Nancagua, 1,961	F 6
Navidad, 629	A10
Negreiros, 2	B 2
Nilahue, 428	E 6
Ñiquén, 296	E 1
Nogales, 2,797	F 2
Nueva Imperial, 6,442	D 2
Nuevo Juncal, 2	B 5
Ocoa, 871	G 2
Olmué, 1,905	F 2
Osorno, 55,091	D 3
Ovalle, 25,282	A 8
Oyahue, 333	B 3
Paihuano, 639	B 8
Paillaco, 3,539	D 3
Paine, 2,720	G 4
Paipote, 2,278	B 6
Palena, 462	E 5
Palestina, 7	B 4
Paliocabe, 77	F 4
Palmilla, 1,136	F 6
Panguipulli, 4,708	E 2
Panquehue, 235	G 2
Paposo, 87	A 5
Papudo, 1,292	A 9
Paredones, 462	A10
Parral, 14,610	A11
Pedro de Valdivia, 11,028	B 4
Pelequen, 1,068	G 5
Pemuco, 1,667	E 1
Peñablanca, 5,586	F 2
Peñaflor, 10.699	G 4
Penco, 15,483	D 1
Peñuelas, 359	F 3
Petorca, 1,395	A 9
Petrohué, 40	E 3
Peuco, 211	G 4
Peumo, 2,574	F 5
Pica, 1,646	B 2
Pichidegua, 841	F 5
Pichilemu, 2,227	A10
Pintados, 144	B 2
Pinto, 958	A11
Pisagua, 118	A 2
Pitrufquén, 6,472	D 2
Placilla, 1,047	F 6
Placilla de Caracoles, 2	B 4
Placilla de Peñuelas, 1,495	F 2
Población, 1,026	F 5
Polonia	G 6
Pomaire, 1,366	F 4
Porvenir, 1,956	E10
Potrerillos, 6,168	B 6
Pozo Almonte, 1,174	B 2
Puangue	F 4
Pucatrihue, 60	D 3
Puchuncaví, 588	F 2
Pucón, 2,508	E 2
Pudahuel, 172	G 3
Pueblo Hundido, 2,123	B 6
Puente Alto, 43,557	B10
Puerto Aisén, 5,488	E 6
Puerto Bertrand, 52	E 7
Puerto Chacabuco, 130	D 6
Puerto Cisnes, 369	E 5
Puerto Cristal, 698	E 6
Puerto Ingeniero Ibáñez, 750	E 6
Puerto Montt, 41,681	E 4
Puerto Natales, 9,399	E 9
Puerto Palena, 105	D 5
Puerto Quellón, 795	D 4
Puerto Ramírez, 82	E 5
Puerto Saavedra, 805	D 2
Puerto Varas, 10,305	E 3
Puerto Williams, 302	F11
Puerto Yartou, 14	E10
Pumanque, 346	F 6
Punitaqui, 1,716	A 8
Punta Arenas, 49,504	E10
Punta de Díaz, 11	B 7
Puquios, 105	B 1
Purén, 3,525	D 2
Purranque, 4,706	D 3
Putaendo, 3,997	A 9
Putre, 459	B 1
Puyehue, 39	E 3
Quebrada de Alvarado, 429	F 2
Queilén, 438	D 4
Quemchi, 696	D 4
Queule, 235	D 2
Quilicura, 2,739	G 3
Quillagua, 288	B 3
Quillaicillo, 195	A 8
Quilleco, 1,005	E 1
Quillota, 29,447	F 2
Quilpué, 26,588	F 2
Quinta de Tilcoco, 410	G 5
Quintay, 166	F 3
Quintero, 6,486	F 2
Quirihue, 3,462	E 1
Rancagua, 53,318	G 5
Rapel, 699	F 4
Reñaca, 1,267	F 2
Renca, 376	G 3
Rengo, 10,989	G 5
Requegua, 1,699	G 5
Requíhoa, 1,646	G 5
Retiro, 601	A11
Rinconada San Martín, 1,466	G 2
Río Blanco, 456	B 9
Río Bueno, 7,544	D 3
Río Cisnes, 244	E 5
Río Negro, 3,661	D 3
Río Verde, 68	E10
Rivadavia, 443	A 7
Rocas de Santo Domingo, 809	F 3
Rolecha, 573	D 4
Rosario, 423	F 5
Rungue, 312	G 2
Salado, 1,375	A 6
Salamanca, 3,197	A 9
Salinas, 7	B 4
Samo Alto, 244	A 8
San Antonio, 26,917	F 3
San Bernardo, 45,207	G 4
San Carlos, 13,598	E 1
San Clemente, 2,507	A11
San Felipe, 19,048	G 2
San Félix, 495	A 7
San Fernando, 21,774	G 6
San Francisco de Mostazal, 3,257	G 4
San Francisco del Monte, 5,079	G 4
San Ignacio, 1,489	E 1
San Javier, 8,541	A11
San José de la Mariquina, 2,878	D 2
San José de Maipo, 2,854	B10
San Pablo, 1,112	D 3
San Pedro, Santiago, 572	F 4
San Pedro, Valparaíso, 1,420	F 2
San Pedro de Atacama, 515	C 4
San Rosendo, 3,744	E 1
San Sebastián, 494	F 3
San Vicente, 230	F 4
San Vicente (San Vicente de Tagua Tagua), 4,447	F 5
Santa Bárbara, 2,920	E 1
Santa Cruz, 5,905	F 6
Santa María, 1,580	G 2
Santiago (cap.), 1,907,378	G 3
Santiago, *2,270,738	G 3
Sewell, 10,866	A10
Sierra Gorda, 126	B 4
Talagante, 11,560	G 4
Talca, 68,148	A11
Talcahuano, 102,323	D 1
Taltal, 5,291	A 5
Tamaya, 248	A 8
Tarapacá, 130	B 2
Temuco, 72,132	E 2
Teno, 2,501	A10
Termas de Cauquenes, 210	B10
Tierra Amarilla, 1,830	A 6
Tignamar, 226	B 1
Tilomonte, 3	B 4
Tiltil, 1,825	G 2
Tinguiririca, 1,012	G 6
Toco, 24	B 3
Toconao, 452	C 4
Tocopilla, 21,580	A 3
Toltén, 299	D 2
Tomé, 26.942	D 1
Tongoy, 935	A 8
Totoral, 109	A 6
Traiguén, 9,990	D 2
Valdivia, 61,334	D 3
Valle Alegre, 241	F 2
Vallenar, 15,693	A 7
Valparaíso, 280, 236	E 2
Victoria, 4,943	B 3
Victoria, 14,215	E 2
Vicuña, 4,144	A 8
Villa Alemana, 15,659	F 2
Villa Alhué, 882	G 4
Villa Industrial, 28	B 1
Villarrica, 9,122	E 2
Viña del Mar, 135,782	F 2
Yumbel, 3,495	E 1
Yungay, 3,301	E 1
Zapallar, 717	A 9

PHYSICAL FEATURES

Acamarachi (mt.)	C 4
Aconcagua (river)	F 2
Aculeo (lagoon)	G 4
Adventure (bay)	D 5
Alhué (river)	F 4
Almirantazgo (bay)	F11
Almeida (mts.)	C 4
Almirante Montt (gulf)	D 9
Alto Nevado (mt.)	E 5
Ancho (channel)	D 8
Ancud (gulf)	D 4
Angamos (isl.)	D 8
Angamos (point)	A 4
Ap Iwan (mt.)	E 6
Arauco (gulf)	D 1
Arenales (mt.)	D 7
Ascotán (salt deposit)	B 3
Atacama (desert)	B 4
Atacama (salt deposit)	C 4
Aucanquilcha (mt.)	B 3
Azapa (river)	B 1
Baker (river)	D 7
Ballenero (channel)	E11
Barrancos (mt.)	D 7
Bascuñán (cape)	A 7
Beagle (channel)	E11
Bella Vista (salt deposit)	B 3
Benjamín (isl.), 16	D 5
Bertrand (mt.)	D 8
Bío-Bío (river)	E 2
Blanca (lagoon)	E10
Blanco (lake)	F10
Bravo (river)	D 7
Brunswick (pen.)	E10
Bueno (river)	D 3
Buenos Aires (lake)	E 6
Burney (mt.)	D 9
Byron (isl.)	D 7
Cachapoal (river)	G 5
Cachina (river)	A 5

(continued on following page)

Chile
(continued)

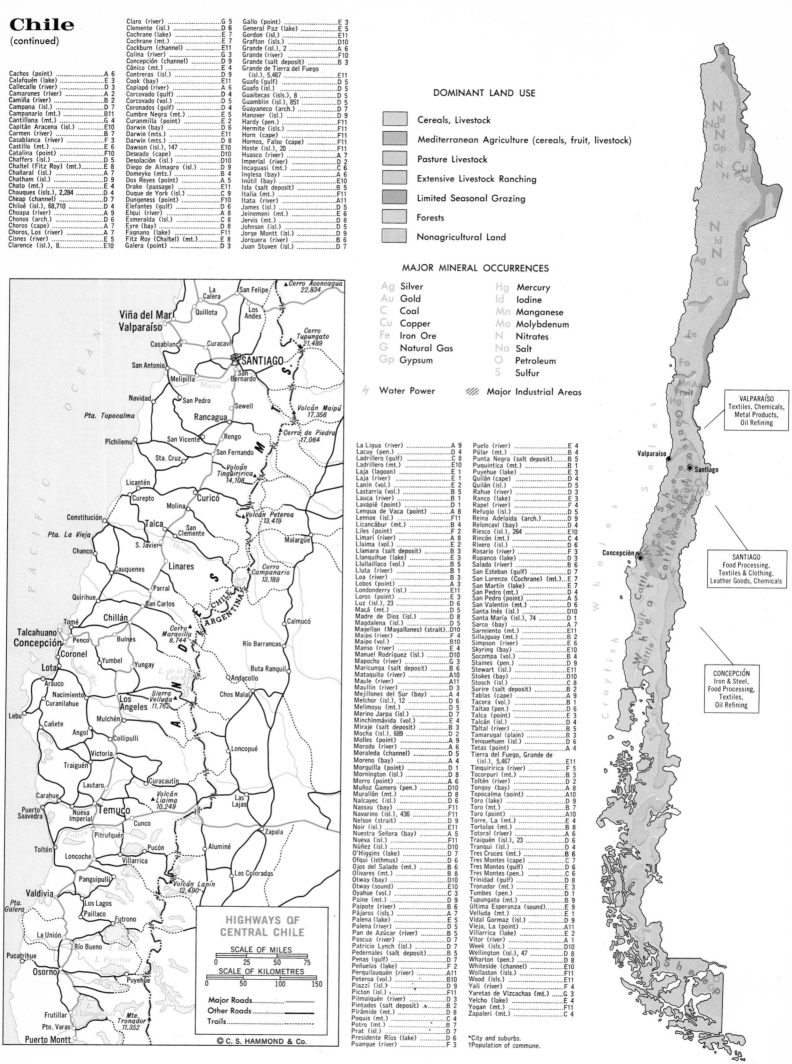

DOMINANT LAND USE

- Cereals, Livestock
- Mediterranean Agriculture (cereals, fruit, livestock)
- Pasture Livestock
- Extensive Livestock Ranching
- Limited Seasonal Grazing
- Forests
- Nonagricultural Land

MAJOR MINERAL OCCURRENCES

Ag	Silver	Hg	Mercury
Au	Gold	Id	Iodine
C	Coal	Mn	Manganese
Cu	Copper	Mo	Molybdenum
Fe	Iron Ore	N	Nitrates
G	Natural Gas	Na	Salt
Gp	Gypsum	O	Petroleum
		S	Sulfur

⚡ Water Power   ▨ Major Industrial Areas

*City and suburbs.
†Population of commune.

HIGHWAYS OF CENTRAL CHILE

SCALE OF MILES
0   25   50   75

SCALE OF KILOMETRES
0   50   100   150

Major Roads ————
Other Roads ————
Trails ·············

© C. S. HAMMOND & Co.

Map labels (Highways of Central Chile): Cerro Aconcagua 22,834, La Calera, San Felipe, Viña del Mar, Valparaíso, Quillota, Los Andes, Casablanca, Curacaví, Cerro Tupungato 21,489, San Antonio, SANTIAGO, San Bernardo, Melipilla, Maipo, Navidad, San Pedro, Sewell, Volcán Maipú 17,356, Pta. Topocalma, Rancagua, Pichilemu, San Vicente, Rengo, Cerro de Piedra 17,064, Sta. Cruz, San Fernando, Licantén, Volcán Tinguiririca 14,108, Curepto, Curicó, Molina, Constitución, Talca, Volcán Peteroa 13,419, Pta. La Vieja, San Clemente, S. Javier, Chanco, Maule, Malargüe, Cauquenes, Linares, Volcán Lastarria, Parral, Quirihue, San Carlos, Cerro Campanario 13,189, Tomé, Chillán, Cerro Maravilla 8,744, Talcahuano, Concepción, Penco, Bulnes, Río Barrancas, Coronel, Yumbel, Yungay, Buta Ranquil, Lota, Andacollo, Arauco, Bío Bío, Nacimiento, L. de la Laja, Chos Malal, Curanilahue, Los Angeles, Sierra Velluda 11,762, Lebu, Cañete, Mulchén, Angol, Collipulli, Loncopué, Victoria, Traiguén, Curacautín, Lautaro, Carahue, Volcán Llaima 10,249, Las Lajas, Puerto Saavedra, Nueva Imperial, Temuco, Cunco, Pitrufquén, Pucón, Zapala, Pta. Galera, Toltén, Loncoche, Villarrica, Aluminé, Panguipulli, Las Coloradas, Valdivia, Volcán Lanín 12,490, Los Lagos, Paillaco, Futrono, La Unión, Río Bueno, L. Ranco, Pucatrihue, Osorno, L. Puyehue, Puyehue, Frutillar, Llanquihue, Mte. Tronador 11,352, Pto. Varas, Puerto Montt

Side profile map labels: N, Id, Na, Gp, Cu, Ag, Fe, Mn, Hg, Au, Coal, Rice, Wine, Fruit, Corn, Wheat, Cattle, Sheep, Whales, Soles, Crayfish

VALPARAÍSO — Textiles, Chemicals, Metal Products, Oil Refining

SANTIAGO — Food Processing, Textiles & Clothing, Leather Goods, Chemicals

CONCEPCIÓN — Iron & Steel, Food Processing, Textiles, Oil Refining

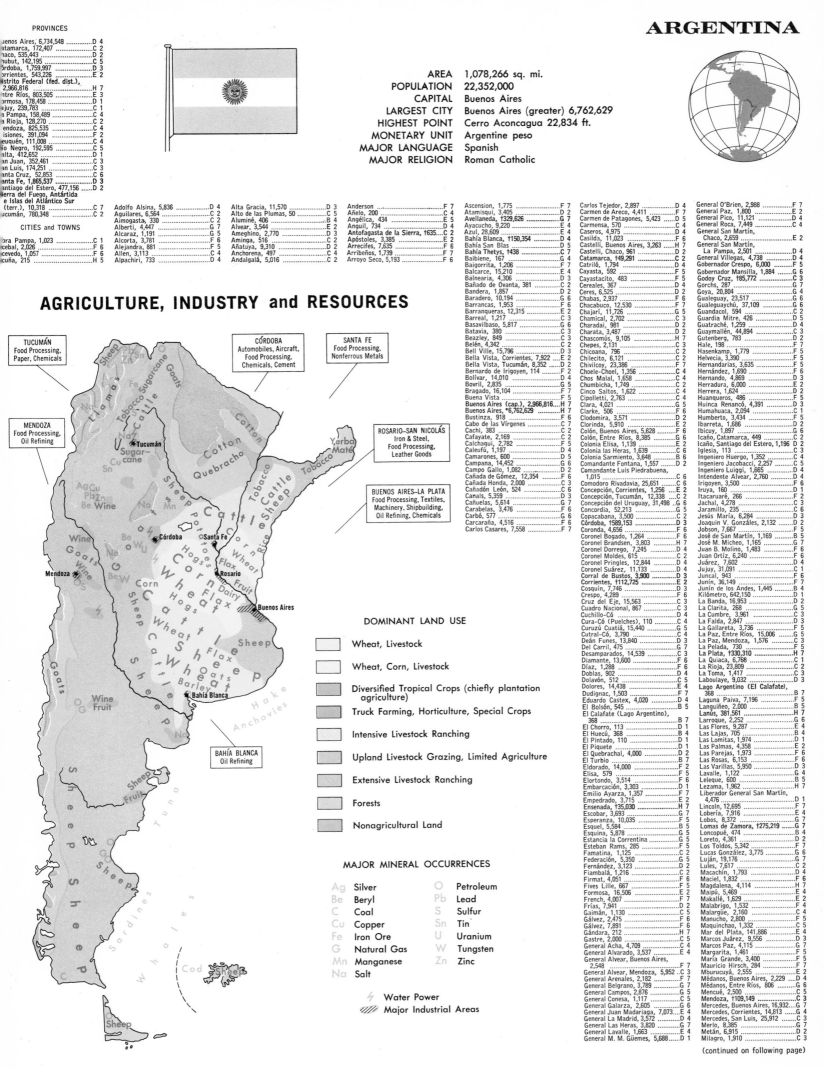

ARGENTINA

AREA 1,078,266 sq. mi.
POPULATION 22,352,000
CAPITAL Buenos Aires
LARGEST CITY Buenos Aires (greater) 6,762,629
HIGHEST POINT Cerro Aconcagua 22,834 ft.
MONETARY UNIT Argentine peso
MAJOR LANGUAGE Spanish
MAJOR RELIGION Roman Catholic

AGRICULTURE, INDUSTRY and RESOURCES

TUCUMÁN Food Processing, Paper, Chemicals

CÓRDOBA Automobiles, Aircraft, Food Processing, Chemicals, Cement

SANTA FE Food Processing, Nonferrous Metals

MENDOZA Food Processing, Oil Refining

ROSARIO–SAN NICOLÁS Iron & Steel, Food Processing, Leather Goods

BUENOS AIRES–LA PLATA Food Processing, Textiles, Machinery, Shipbuilding, Oil Refining, Chemicals

BAHÍA BLANCA Oil Refining

DOMINANT LAND USE

Wheat, Livestock

Wheat, Corn, Livestock

Diversified Tropical Crops (chiefly plantation agriculture)

Truck Farming, Horticulture, Special Crops

Intensive Livestock Ranching

Upland Livestock Grazing, Limited Agriculture

Extensive Livestock Ranching

Forests

Nonagricultural Land

MAJOR MINERAL OCCURRENCES

Ag	Silver	O	Petroleum
Be	Beryl	Pb	Lead
C	Coal	S	Sulfur
Cu	Copper	Sn	Tin
Fe	Iron Ore	U	Uranium
G	Natural Gas	W	Tungsten
Mn	Manganese	Zn	Zinc
Na	Salt		

⚡ Water Power

▨ Major Industrial Areas

(continued on following page)

Argentina

(continued)

Miñones, 800 ....G 5
Miramar (General Alvarado), 3,537 ....E 4
Moisés Ville, 3,166 ....E 5
Molinos, 151 ....C 2
Monte, 2,491 ....G 7
Monte Caseros, 11,409 ....G 5
Monte Comán, 2,112 ....C 3
Monte Quemado, 2,512 ....D 2
Monteros, 7,745 ....C 2
Morteros, 5,993 ....D 3
Mosconi, 333 ....F 7
Naré, 346 ....F 5
Navarro, 2,547 ....G 7
Necochea, 17,808 ....E 4
Nelson, 866 ....F 5
Neuquén, 7,498 ....C 4
Niquivil, 154 ....C 3
Nogoyá, 12,051 ....F 6
Norberto de la Riestra, 2,809 ....G 7
Ñorquincó ....B 5
Norumbega, 114 ....F 7
Nueva Pompeya, 2,500 ....D 2
Nueve de Julio, 13,678 ....F 7
Oberá, 4,823 ....F 2
Ojo de Agua, 1,201 ....D 2
Olavarría, 24,204 ....D 4
Oliva, 8,701 ....D 3
Olta, 656 ....C 3
Orán, 6,706 ....D 1
Ordoqui, 402 ....F 7
Palo Santo, 1,868 ....E 2
Pampa del Chañar, 325 ....C 2
Pampa del Infierno, 604 ....D 2
Parada Labougle ....G 5
Paraná, †174,272 ....F 5
Paso de Indios, 200 ....C 5
Paso de los Libres, 11,665 ....E 2
Paso Flores, 1,000 ....C 5
Patquia, 620 ....C 3
Paz, 2,495 ....F 6
Pedernal, 282 ....G 5
Pedro Diáz Colodrero, 2,000 ......G 5
Pehuajó, 13,537 ....D 4
Pellegrini, 2,310 ....D 4
Pérez, 3,433 ....F 6
Pergamino, 32,382 ....F 6
Perito Moreno ....B 6
Perugorria, 1,053 ....G 4
Pico Truncado, 326 ....C 6
Pigüé, 5,869 ....D 4
Pila, 1,009 ....H 7
Pilar, 2,508 ....F 5
Pipinas, 658 ....H 7
Pirané, 3,561 ....E 2
Plaza Huincul, 2,662 ....B 4
Pomán, 1,098 ....C 2
Posadas, 37,588 ....E 2
Pozo Hondo, 100 ....D 2
Presidencia de la Plaza, 4,305 ....D 2
Presidencia Roque (Sáenz Peña), 23,100 ....D 2
Puán, 3,191 ....D 4
Pueblo Domínguez, 1,465 ....G 6
Puelches (Cura-Có), 110 ....C 4
Puelén, 168 ....C 4
Puerto Algarrobo, 800 ....G 5
Puerto Deseado, 3,392 ....D 6
Puerto Harberton ....C 7
Puerto Irigoyen, 900 ....D 1
Puerto Madryn, 3,441 ....C 5
Puerto Pirámides, 200 ....D 5
Puerto Ruiz, 464 ....G 6
Punta Alta, 19,852 ....D 4
Quemú-Quemú, 2,735 ....D 4
Quequén, 4,760 ....E 4
Quimilí, 3,686 ....D 2
Quines, 3,038 ....C 3
Quiroga, 1,827 ....F 7
Quitilipí, 3,298 ....D 2
Rafaela, 23,665 ....F 5
Ramallo, 4,824 ....F 6
Ramírez, 2,971 ....F 6
Ranchos, 2,475 ....H 7
Rauch, 5,274 ....E 4
Rawson, Buenos Aires, 2,425 ......F 7
Rawson, Chubut, 1,890 ....D 5
Rawson, S. Juan, 10,492 ....C 3
Reconquista, 12,729 ....D 2
Recreo, 2,656 ....C 2
Resistencia, 52,385 ....E 2
Rigby, 737 ....F 6
Rinconada, 157 ....C 1
Río Colorado, La Pampa ....D 4
Río Colorado, Río Negro, 3,304 ....D 4
Río Cuarto, 48,706 ....D 3
Río Gallegos, 5,880 ....C 7
Río Grande, 1,401 ....C 7
Río Segundo, 5,873 ....D 3
Río Tercero, 10,683 ....D 3
Rivadavia, Mendoza, 5,643 ....C 3
Rivadavia, Salta ....D 1
Rivas, 429 ....G 7
Rojas, 6,608 ....F 7
Roldán, 3,402 ....F 6
Romang, 1,906 ....F 4
Roque Pérez, 2,841 ....G 7
Rosario, †671,852 ....F 6
Rosario de la Frontera, 4,927 ......D 2
Rosario de Lerma, 2,594 ....C 1
Rosario del Tala, 10,584 ....G 6
Rufino, 10,987 ....D 3
Saforcada, 146 ....F 7
Saladas, 3,900 ....E 2
Saladillo, 7,586 ....G 7
Salta, †121,491 ....C 1
Salto, 7,771 ....F 7
San Andrés de Giles, 5,392 ....G 7
San Antonio de Areco, 7,436 ......G 7
San Antonio de los Cobres, 794....C 1
San Antonio Oeste, 3,847 ....C 5
San Carlos, Corrientes, 852 ....E 2
San Carlos, Mendoza, 440 ....C 3
San Carlos, Santa Fé, 3,126 ....F 5
San Carlos de Bariloche, 6,562 ....B 5
San Cristóbal, 9,071 ....F 5
San Fernando, †91,644 ....G 7
San Francisco, Córdoba, 24,354....D 3
San Francisco, San Luis, 2,345 ....C 3
San Francisco del Chañar, 817 ....C 2
San Genaro, 1,522 ....F 6
San Ignacio, 1,727 ....E 2
San Isidro, 521 ....C 2
San Jaime, 1,662 ....G 5
San Javier, Río Negro, 1,500 ......D 5
San Javier, Santa Fé, 2,961 ....F 5
San José de Feliciano, 7,643 ......G 5
San Juan, †106,746 ....C 3
San Julián, 3,050 ....C 6
San Justo, 6,571 ....F 5
San Lorenzo, 11,109 ....F 6
San Luis, 25,147 ....C 3
San Martín, 8,747 ....C 3
San Martín de los Andes, 2,366....C 5
San Martín Norte, 485 ....F 5
San Miguel, 1,138 ....E 2
San Nicolás, 25,029 ....G 6
San Pedro, Buenos Aires, 12,778..F 6
San Pedro, Jujuy, 6,105 ....D 1
San Rafael, 28,847 ....C 3
San Salvador, 3,532 ....G 5
San Sebastián, †3,154 ....C 7
San Urbano, 1,721 ....F 6
Santa Catalina, 149 ....C 1
Santa Clara, 3,700 ....F 6
Santa Cruz, 1,153 ....C 7
Santa Elena, 7,757 ....F 5
Santa Fe, †259,560 ....F 5
Santa Lucia, Buenos Aires, 1,831..F 6
Santa Lucia, Corrientes, 3,163 ....E 2
Santa Mariá, 2,052 ....C 2
Santa Rosa, Córdoba, 2,999 ....D 3
Santa Rosa, La Pampa, 14,623 ....C 4
Santa Rosa, San Luis, 3,564 ....C 3
Santa Victoria, 250 ....D 1
Santiago del Estero, †103,115.....D 2
Santo Tomé, Corrientes, 8,348 ....E 2
Santo Tomé, Santa Fé, 4,446 ......F 5
Sauce, 3,017 ....G 5
Sauce Luna, 922 ....G 5
Seguí, 1,604 ....G 6
Selva, 911 ....D 2
Sierra Colorada, 450 ....C 5
Solari, 1,377 ....G 4
Soledad, 794 ....F 5
Suipacha, 3,006 ....G 7
Sunchales, 5,048 ....F 5
Suncho Corral, 3,020 ....D 2
Susana, 484 ....F 5
Tafí Viejo, 15,374 ....C 2
Tamberías, 182 ....C 3
Tandil, 32,309 ....E 4
Tapalquén, 3,018 ....E 4
Tartagal, 8,539 ....D 1
Telsen, 165 ....C 5
Tigre, †91,824 ....G 7
Tilcara, 1,380 ....C 1
Tinogasta, 2,169 ....C 2
Tintina, 2,219 ....D 2
Toay, 2,457 ....D 4
Toba, 174 ....F 4
Tornquist, 2,782 ....D 4
Tostado, 5,234 ....D 2
Trelew, 5,880 ....C 5
Trenel, 1,206 ....D 4
Trenque Lauquen, 10,887 ....D 4
Tres Arroyos, 29,996 ....D 4
Tres Lomas, 3,425 ....D 4
Tricao Malal, 2,500 ....C 4
Tucumán, †287,004 ....D 2
Tunuyán, 2,437 ....C 3
Ulapes, 285 ....C 3
Unión, 365 ....C 3
Urdinarrain, 4,832 ....G 6
Ushuaia, †3,472 ....C 7
Valcheta, 841 ....C 5
Valle Fértil, 745 ....C 3
Vedia, 3,676 ....F 7
Veinticinco de Mayo, 9,063 ....F 7
Venado Tuerto, 15,947 ....D 3
Vergara, 1,077 ....H 7
Verónica, 2,405 ....H 7
Victoria, 17,711 ....F 6
Victorica, 2,475 ....C 4
Vicuña Mackenna, 3,032 ....D 3
Viedma, 4,683 ....D 5
Vieytes, 180 ....H 7
Villa Ana, 5,413 ....E 2
Villa Ángela, 7,375 ....D 2
Villa Atuel, 2,536 ....C 3
Villa Bustos, 1,302 ....C 2
Villa Cañas, 7,099 ....F 6
Villa Constitución, 9,183 ....F 6
Villa del Rosario, 4,461 ....D 3
Villa Dolores, 13,835 ....C 2
Villa Elisa, 3,969 ....G 6
Villa Federal, 9,158 ....G 5
Villa General Roca, 258 ....C 3
Villa Guillermina, 7,471 ....D 2
Villa Mantero, 1,605 ....G 6
Villa María, 30,362 ....D 3
Villa Ocampo, 4,897 ....D 2
Villa Regina, 2,154 ....C 4
Villa San José, 6,176 ....G 6
Villa Unión, 713 ....C 2
Villaguay, 17,607 ....G 5
Villalonga, 392 ....D 5
Vinchina, 138 ....C 2
Winifreda, 1,063 ....D 4
Yofré, 800 ....G 4
Zapala, 3,387 ....B 4
Zárate, 35,197 ....G 6
Zavalla, 1,799 ....F 6

PHYSICAL FEATURES

Aconcagua (mt.) ....C 3
Alerces, Los (park) ....C 5
Andes (mts.) ....C 2
Arenas (point) ....C 7
Argentino (lake) ....B 7
Arizaro (s. dep.) ....C 2
Arrecifes (river) ....G 6
Atacama, Puna de (reg.) ....C 2
Atuel (river) ....C 4
Barrancas (river) ....G 5
Bermeja (point) ....D 5
Bermejo (river) ....E 2
Blanca (bay) ....D 4
Blanco (river) ....C 2
Brazo Sur (river) ....E 1
Buenos Aires (lake) ....B 6
Campanario (mt.) ....C 4
Carcaraña (river) ....D 3
Cardiel (lake) ....B 6
Chaco Austral (reg.) ....D 2
Chaco Central (reg.) ....D 1
Chato (mt.) ....B 5
Chico (river) ....C 5
Chico (river) ....C 6
Chubut (river) ....C 5
Colhué Huapí (lake) ....C 6
Colorado (river) ....D 4
Cónico (mt.) ....B 5
Corrientes (river) ....E 2
Coyle (river) ....B 7

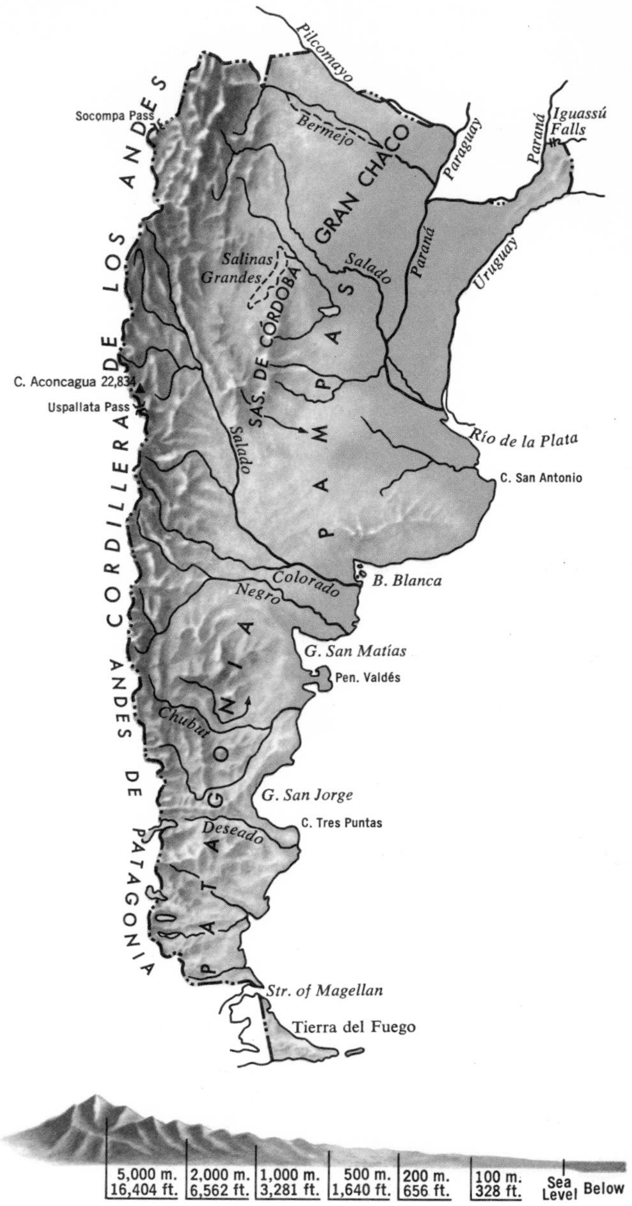

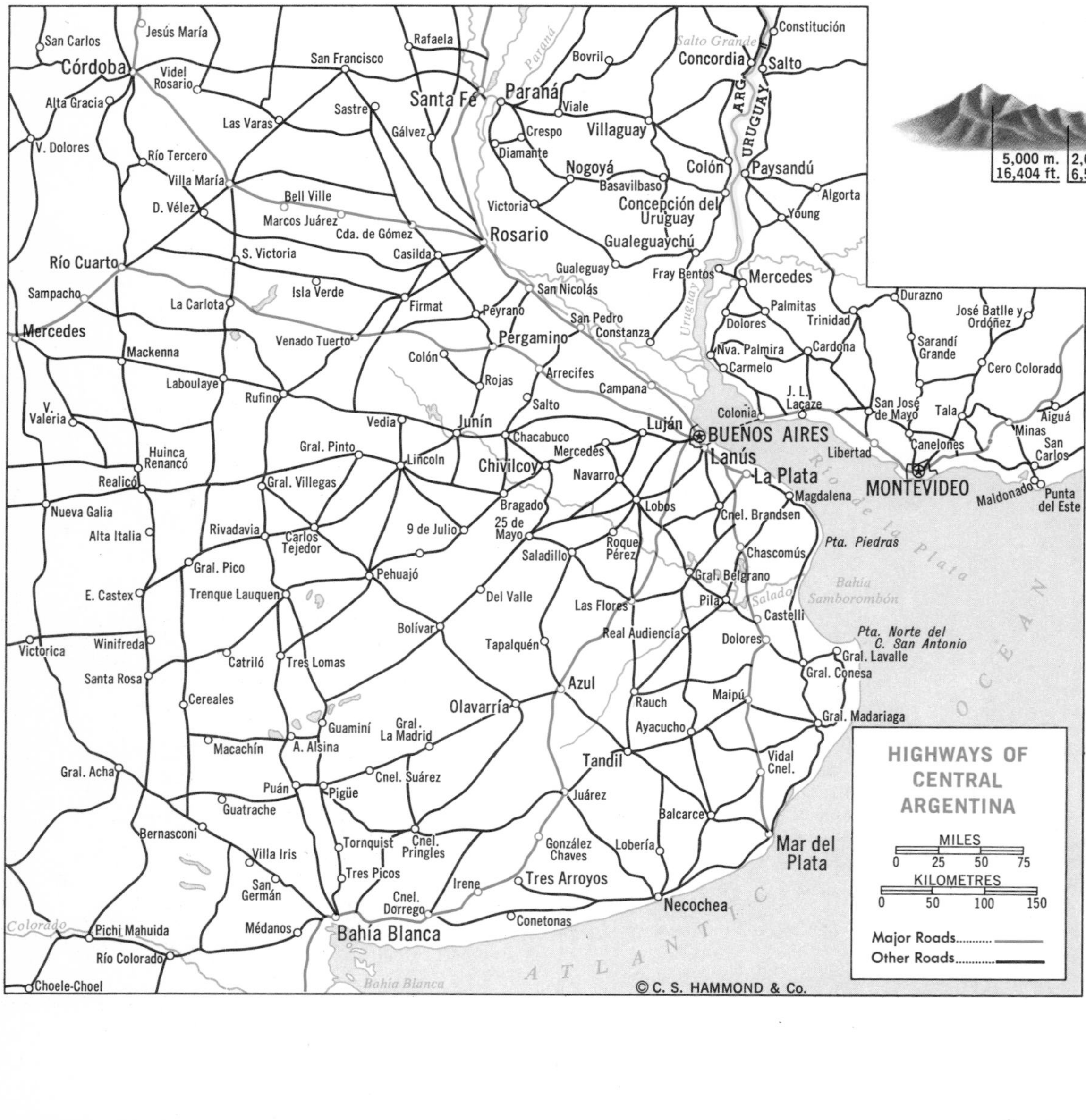

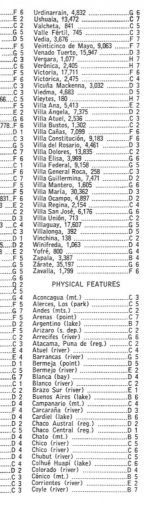

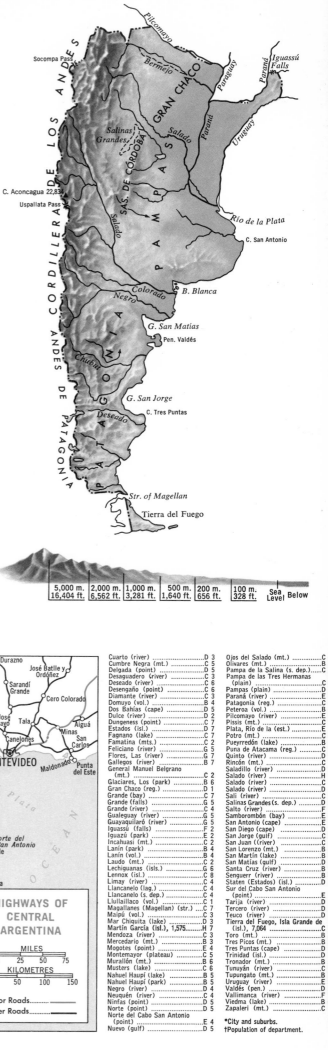

Cuarto (river) ....D 3
Cumbre Negra (mt.) ....C 5
Delgada (point) ....D 5
Desaguadero (river) ....C 3
Deseado (river) ....C 6
Desengaño (point) ....C 6
Diamante (river) ....C 3
Domuyo (vol.) ....B 4
Dos Bahías (cape) ....D 5
Dulce (river) ....D 2
Dungeness (point) ....C 7
Estados (isl.) ....D 7
Fagnano (lake) ....C 7
Famatina (mts.) ....C 2
Feliciano (river) ....G 5
Flores, Las (river) ....G 7
Gallegos (river) ....B 7
General Manuel Belgrano (mt.) ....C 2
Glaciares, Los (park) ....B 6
Gran Chaco (reg.) ....D 1
Grande (bay) ....C 7
Grande (falls) ....G 5
Grande (river) ....C 4
Gualeguay (river) ....G 5
Guayaquilaró (river) ....G 5
Iguassú (falls) ....F 2
Iguazú (park) ....E 2
Incahuasi (mt.) ....C 2
Lanín (park) ....B 4
Lanín (vol.) ....B 4
Laudo (mt.) ....C 2
Lechiguanas (isls.) ....G 6
Lennox (isl.) ....C 8
Limay (river) ....C 4
Llancanelo (lag.) ....C 4
Llancanelo (s. dep.) ....C 4
Llullaillaco (vol.) ....C 1
Magallanes (Magellan) (str.) ....C 7
Maipú (vol.) ....C 3
Mar Chiquita (lake) ....D 3
Martín García (isl.), 1,575.........H 7
Mendoza (river) ....C 3
Mercedario (mt.) ....B 3
Mogotes (point) ....E 4
Montemayor (plateau) ....C 5
Murallón (mt.) ....B 6
Musters (lake) ....C 6
Nahuel Haupí (lake) ....B 5
Nahuel Haupí (park) ....B 5
Negro (river) ....D 4
Neuquén (river) ....C 4
Ninfas (point) ....D 5
Norte (point) ....D 5
Norte del Cabo San Antonio (point) ....E 4
Nuevo (gulf) ....D 5
Ojos del Salado (mt.) C
Olivares (mt.) ....B
Pampa de la Salina (s. dep.)......C
Pampa de las Tres Hermanas (plain) C
Pampas (plain) ....D
Paraná (river) ....E
Patagonia (reg.) C
Peteroa (vol.) ....B
Pilcomayo (river) ....E
Pissis (mt.) C
Plata, Río de la (est.) ....E
Potro (mt.) C
Pueyrredón (lake) ....B
Puna de Atacama (reg.) C
Quinto (river) ....D
Rincón (mt.) C
Saladillo (river) ....D
Salado (river) ....H
Salado (river) C
Salado (river) ....D
Sali (river) C
Salinas Grandes (s. dep.) ....D
Salto (river) ....F
Samborombón (bay) ....E
San Antonio (cape) ....E
San Diego (cape) ....D
San Jorge (gulf) C
San Juan ((river) C
San Lorenzo (mt.) ....B
San Martín (lake) ....B
San Matías (gulf) ....D
Santa Cruz (river) ....B
Senguerr (river) ....B
Staten (Estados) (isl.) ....D
Sur del Cabo San Antonio (point) ....E
Tarija (river) ....D
Tercero (river) ....D
Teuco (river) ....D
Tierra del Fuego, Isla Grande de (isl.), 7,064 C
Toro (mt.) ....B
Tres Picos (mt.) ....B
Tres Puntas (cape) ....D
Trinidad (isl.) ....D
Tronador (mt.) ....B
Tunuyán (river) C
Tupungato (mt.) ....B
Uruguay (river) ....E
Valdés (pen.) ....D
Vallimanca (river) ....F
Viedma (lake) ....B
Zapaleri (mt.) C

*City and suburbs.
†Population of department.

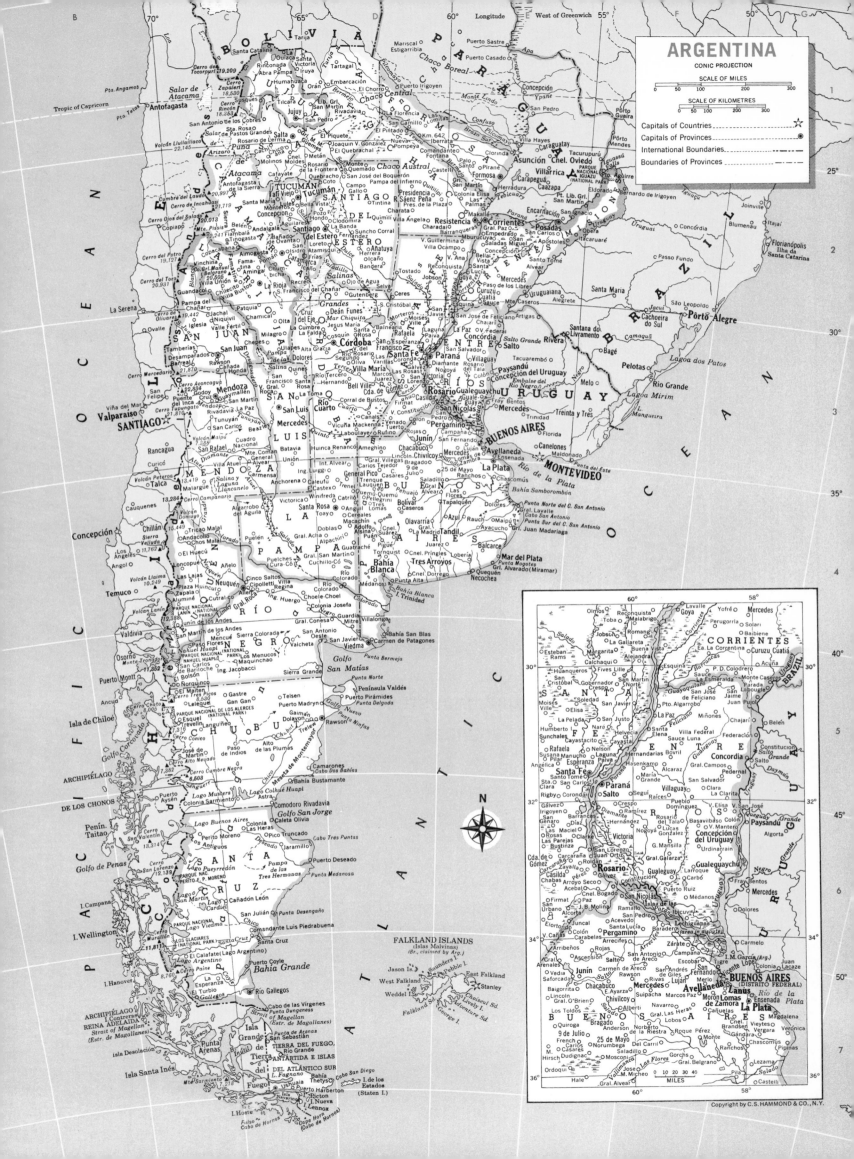

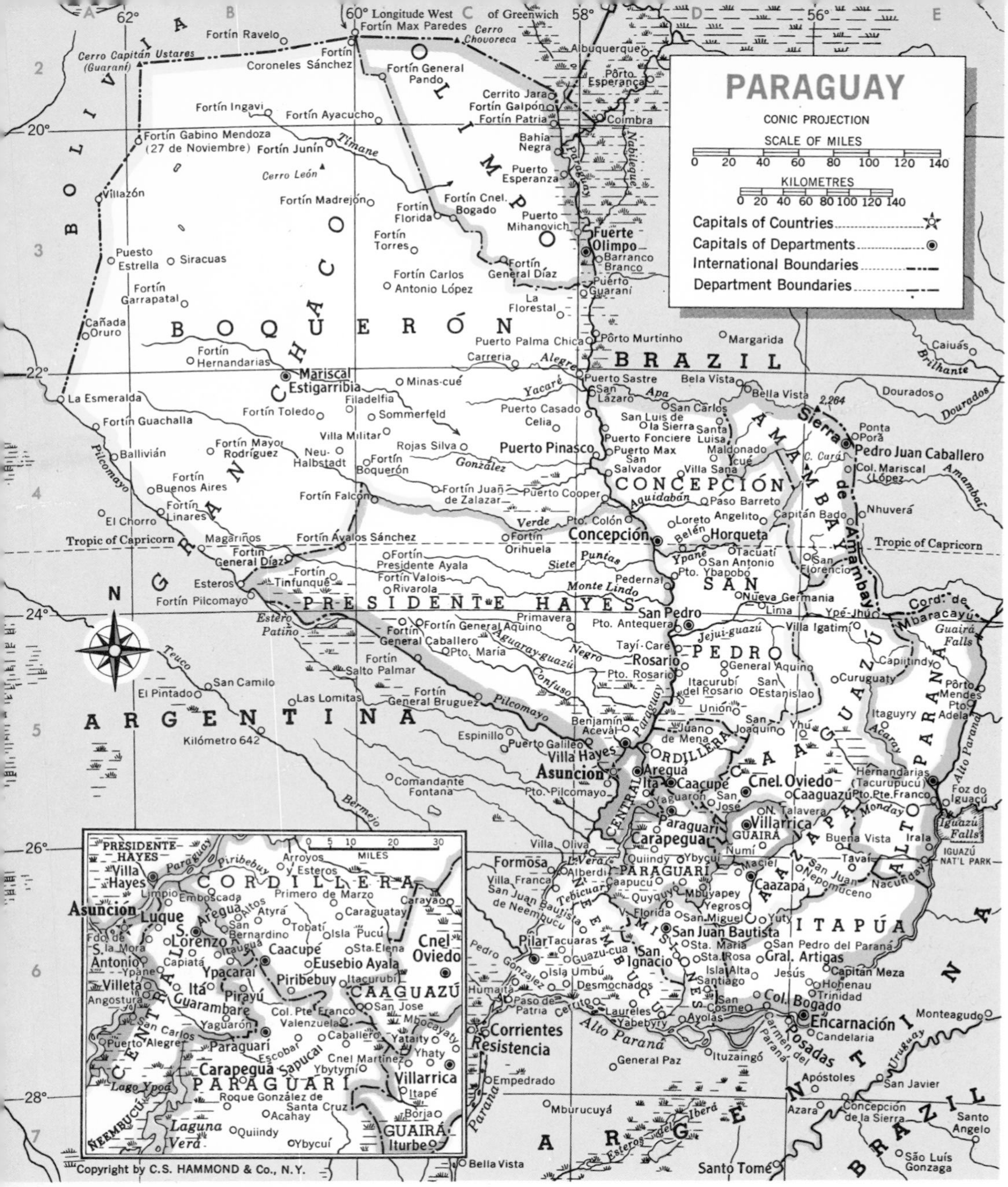
PARAGUAY
CONIC PROJECTION
SCALE OF MILES
0 20 40 60 80 100 120 140
KILOMETRES
0 20 40 60 80 100 120 140
Capitals of Countries
Capitals of Departments
International Boundaries
Department Boundaries
BOLIVIA
BRAZIL
ARGENTINA
Tropic of Capricorn
60° Longitude West of Greenwich
Asunción
Concepción
Villarrica
Encarnación
Copyright by C.S. HAMMOND & Co., N.Y.

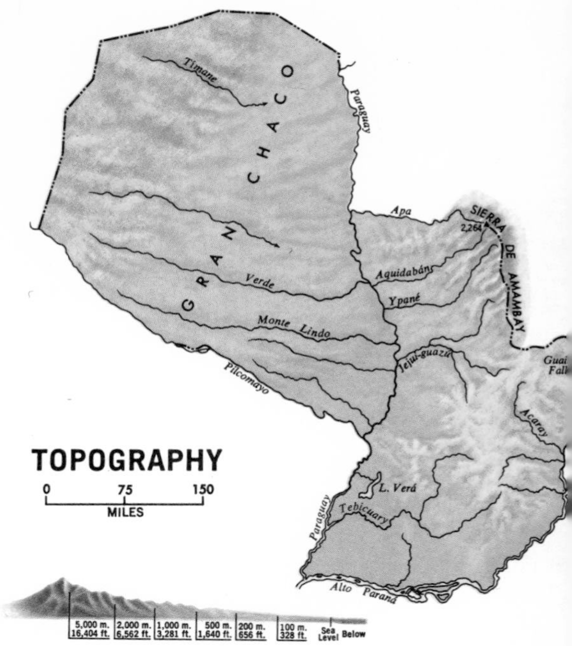
GRAN CHACO
TOPOGRAPHY
0 75 150
MILES
5,000 m. 16,404 ft.
2,000 m. 6,562 ft.
1,000 m. 3,281 ft.
500 m. 1,640 ft.
200 m. 656 ft.
100 m. 328 ft.
Sea Level
Below

AGRICULTURE, INDUSTRY and RESOURCES

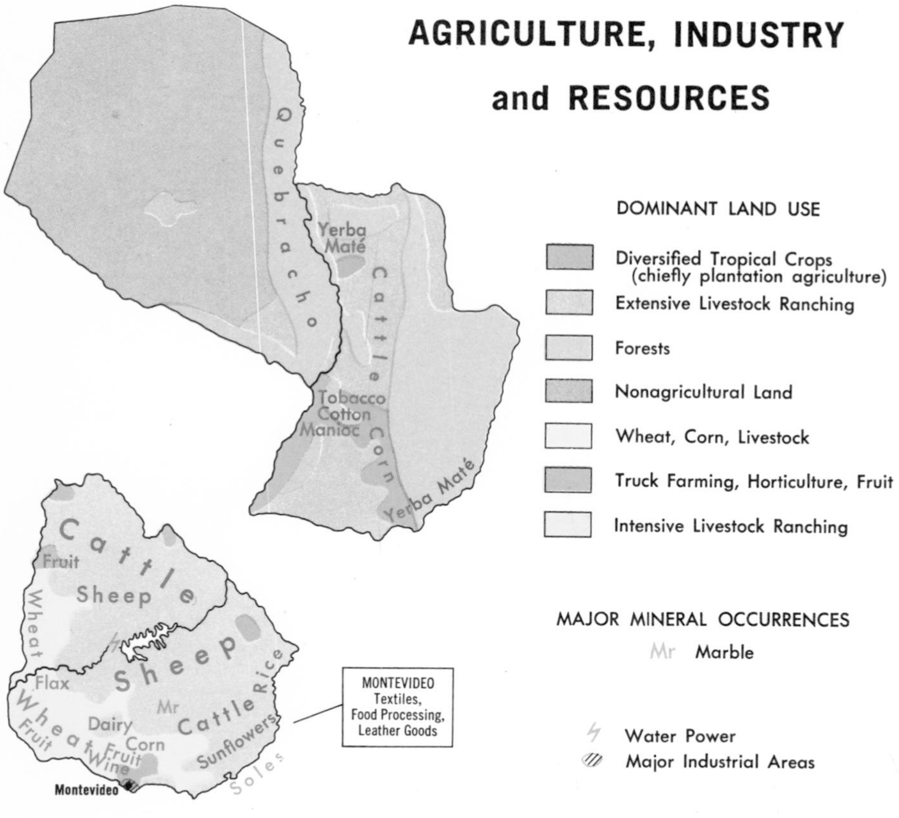
DOMINANT LAND USE
Diversified Tropical Crops (chiefly plantation agriculture)
Extensive Livestock Ranching
Forests
Nonagricultural Land
Wheat, Corn, Livestock
Truck Farming, Horticulture, Fruit
Intensive Livestock Ranching
MAJOR MINERAL OCCURRENCES
Mr Marble
Water Power
Major Industrial Areas
MONTEVIDEO
Textiles,
Food Processing,
Leather Goods
Montevideo

PARAGUAY

DEPARTMENTS

Alto Paraná, 26,680 ....E 5
Amambay, 33,782 ....E 4
Boquerón, 42,223 ....B 3
Caaguazú, 123,590 ....E 5
Caazapá, 91,807 ....D 6
Capital (dist.), 311,301 ....A 6
Central, 204,719 ....D 5
Concepción, 86,336 ....D 4
Cordillera, 189,041 ....D 5
Guairá, 114,297 ....D 5
Itapúa, 151,035 ....E 6
Misiones, 59,454 ....D 6
Ñeembucú, 58,621 ....D 6
Olimpo, 3,362 ....C 3
Paraguarí, 204,220 ....D 6
Presidente Hayes, 31,572 ....C 4
San Pedro, 90,991 ....D 5

CITIES and TOWNS

Acahay, 2,502 ....B 7
Alberdi, 1,542 ....D 6
Altos, 1,445 ....B 6
Angelito ....D 4
Angostura ....A 6
Aregúa, 3,734 ....B 6
Arroyos y Esteros, 1,149 ....B 6
Asunción (cap.), 350,000 ....A 6
Atyrá, 1,245 ....B 6
Ayolas, 297 ....D 6
Bahía Negra ....C 3
Ballivián ....B 4
Belén, 1,414 ....D 4
Bella Vista, 2,292 ....D 4
Benjamín Aceval, 3,115 ....D 5
Borja, 1,114 ....C 7
Buena Vista, 1,924 ....E 5
Caacupé, 4,329 ....B 6
Caaguazú, 2,154 ....E 5
Caapucu, 1,468 ....D 6
Caazapá, 3,588 ....D 6
Caballero, 1,552 ....B 6
Cañada Oruro ....A 3
Capiatá, 1,929 ....B 6
Capiitindy ....E 5
Capitán Bado, 257 ....E 4
Capitán Meza, 1,337 ....E 6
Caraguatay, 1,872 ....C 6
Carapegúa, 2,645 ....B 6
Carayaó, 1,184 ....C 6
Carmen del Paraná, 1,881 ....D 6
Carreria ....C 3
Celia ....C 4
Cerrito, 771 ....D 6
Cerrito Jara ....C 2
Colonia Mariscal López ....E 4
Colonia Presidente Franco ....B 6
Concepción, 33,500 ....D 4
Coronel Bogado, 3,839 ....E 6
Coronel Martínez, 1,255 ....C 6
Coronel Oviedo, 9,503 ....C 6
Curuguaty, 511 ....E 5
Desmochados, 209 ....D 6
Emboscada, 954 ....B 6
Encarnación, 35,000 ....E 6
Escobar, 558 ....B 6
Esteros, ...B 4
Eusebio Ayala, 2,268 ....B 6
Fernando de la Mora, 8,638....A 6
Filadelfia ....C 4
Fortín 27 de Noviembre ....B 3
Fortín Ávalos Sánchez ....B 4
Fortín Ayacucho ....B 2
Fortín Boquerón ....C 4
Fortín Buenos Aires ....B 4
Fortín Carlos Antonio López ....C 3
Fortín Coronel Bogado ....C 3
Fortín Coroneles Sánchez ....B 2
Fortín Falcón ....B 4
Fortín Florida ....C 3
Fortín Gabino Mendoza ....B 3
Fortín Galpón ....C 2
Fortín Garrapatal ....B 3
Fortín General Aquino ....C 5
Fortín General Bruguez ....C 5
Fortín General Caballero ....C 5
Fortín General Díaz (Boquerón) ..B 4
Fortín General Díaz (Olimpo) ....C 3
Fortín General Pando ....C 2
Fortín Guachalla ....A 4
Fortín Hernandarias ....B 3
Fortín Ingavi ....B 2
Fortín Juan de Zalazar ....C 4
Fortín Junín ....B 3
Fortín Linares ....B 4
Fortín Madrejón ....B 3
Fortín Mayor Rodríguez ....B 4
Fortín Orihuela ....C 4
Fortín Patria ....C 2
Fortín Presidente Ayala ....C 4
Fortín Salto Palmar ....C 5
Fortín Tinfunqué ....B 4
Fortín Toledo ....B 4
Fortín Torres ....C 3
Fortín Valois Rivarola ....C 4
Fuerte Olimpo, 1,666 ....D 3
General Artigas, 3,106 ....E 6
General Aquino, 1,130 ....D 5
Guarambaré, 3,779 ....B 6
Guazú-cuá, 153 ....D 6
Hernandarias, 2,311 ....E 5
Hohenau, 697 ....E 6
Horqueta, 4,785 ....D 4
Humaitá, 714 ....C 6
Irala, 295 ....E 5
Isla Alta ....D 6
Isla Pucú, 1,680 ....B 6
Isla Umbú, 200 ....C 6
Itá, 6,223 ....B 6
Itacurubí de la Cordillera, 2,154 ....C 6
Itacurubí del Rosario, 1,700....D 5
Itaguyry ....E 5
Itapé, 1,178 ....C 6
Itauguá, 3,053 ....B 6
Iturbe, 3,239 ....C 7
Jesús, 1,759 ....E 6
Juan de Mena, 1,037 ....D 6
La Esmeralda ....A 4
La Florestal ....C 3
Laureles, 362 ....D 6
Lima, 609 ....D 4
Limpio, 1,778 ....B 6
Loreto, 792 ....D 4
Luque, 10,834 ....B 6
Maciel, 396 ....D 6
Magariños ....B 4
Maldonado-cué ....D 4
Mariscal Estigarribia, 1,508....B 4
Mbocayaty, 677 ....C 6
Mbuyapey, 1,290 ....D 6
Minas-cué ....C 4
Ñacunday, 166 ....E 6
Natalicio Talavera, 911 ....D 5
Neu Halbstadt ....B 4
Nueva Germania, 509 ....D 4
Ñumí, 1,053 ....D 5
Paraguarí, 4,968 ....B 6
Paso Barreto ....D 4
Paso de Patria, 613 ....C 6
Pedernal ....D 4
Pedro González, 449 ....C 6
Pedro Juan Caballero, 10,187....E 4
Pilar, 10,500 ....C 6
Pirayú, 2,733 ....B 6
Piribebuy, 3,769 ....B 6
Primavera ....C 5
Primero de Marzo, 635 ....B 6
Puerto Adela ....E 5
Puerto Alegre ....A 6
Puerto Antequera, 1,064 ....D 5
Puerto Casado ....C 4
Puerto Colón ....D 4
Puerto Cooper ....C 4
Puerto Esperanza ....C 3
Puerto Fonciere ....D 4
Puerto Galileo ....C 5
Puerto Guaraní ....D 3
Puerto María ....C 5
Puerto Max ....D 4
Puerto Mihanovich C
Puerto Palma Chica C
Puerto Pinasco, 4,495 C
Puerto Presidente Franco ....E
Puerto Rosario ....D
Puerto Sastre ....D
Puerto Ybapobó ....D
Puesto Estrella ....B
Quiindy, 2,732 ....B
Quyquyó, 1,172 ....D
Rojas Silva C
Roque González de Santa Cruz, 1,401 ....B
Rosario, 4,580 ....D
San Antonio, Central, 2,889....A
San Antonio, San Pedro ....D
San Bernardino, 569 ....B
San Carlos, Central ....B
San Carlos, Concepción, 360 ....D
San Cosme, 553 ....D
San Estanislao, 2,894 ....D
San Florencio ....E
San Ignacio, 5,344 ....D
San Joaquín, 415 ....D
San José, 2,418 C
San Juan Bautista, 5,351 ....D
San Juan Bautista de Ñeembucú, 440 C
San Juan Nepomuceno, 1,772 ....E
San Lázaro, 276 ....D
San Lorenzo, 7,620 ....B
San Luis de la Sierra ....D
San Miguel, 1,045 ....D 6
San Pedro, 3,317 ....D 5
San Pedro del Paraná, 1,961 ....E 6
San Salvador, 1,536 ....D 4
Santa Elena, 1,373 ....C 6
Santa Luisa ....D 4
Santa María, 747 ....D 6
Santa Rosa, 2,630 ....D 6
Santiago, 1,557 ....D 6
Sapucaí, 2,298 ....B 6
Siracuas ....B 3
Sommerfeld ....C 4
Tacuaras, 80 ....C 6
Tacuatí, 449 ....D 4
Tacurupucú (Hernandarias), 2,311 ....E 5
Tavaí, 266 ....E 6
Tayí-Caré ....D 5
Tobatí, 2,397 ....B 6
Trinidad, 597 ....E 6
Unión, 779 ....D 5
Valenzuela, 977 ....B 6
Villa Florida, 1,026 ....D 6
Villa Franca, 374 ....C 6
Villa Hayes, 4,330 ....A 6
Villa Igatimí ....E 5
Villa Militar ....C 4
Villa Oliva, 950 ....C 5
Villa Sana ....D 4
Villarrica, 30,500 ....C 6
Villazón ....A 3
Villeta, 2,904 ....A 6
Yabebyry, 495 ....D 6
Yaguarón, 1,290 ....B 6
Yataity, 1,042 ....C 6
Ybycuí, 3,072 ....B 7
Ybytimí, 1,240 ....B 6
Yegros, 1,423 ....D 6
Yhaty ....C 6
Yhú, 1,136 ....E 5
Ypacaraí, 5,330 ....B 6
Ypané, 1,413 ....A 6
Ypé-Jhú, 275 ....E 4
Yuty (Yyty), 2,403 ....D 6

PHYSICAL FEATURES

Acaray (river) ....E 5
Aguaray-guazú (river) ....C 5
Alegre (river) ....C 3
Alto Paraná (river) ....D 6
Amambay (mts.) ....E 4
Apa (river) ....D 4
Aquidabán, (river) ....D 4
Capitán Ustarés (hill) ....B 2
Cará (mt.) ....E 4
Chovoreca (hill) ....C 2
Confuso (river) ....C 5
González (river) ....C 4
Gran Chaco (reg.) ....B 4
Guairá (falls) ....E 5
Guaraní (Capitán Ustarés) (hill) ....B 2
León (mt.) ....B 3
Mbaracayú (mts.) ....E 4
Monday (river) ....E 5
Monte Lindo (river) ....D 4
Negro (river) ....D 5
Paraguay (river) ....D 5
Pilcomayo (river) ....C 5
Siete Puntas (river) ....D 4
Tebicuary (river) ....D 6
Tímane (river) ....C 3
Verá (lagoon) ....B 7
Verde (river) ....C 4
Yacaré (river) ....C 4
Ypané (river) ....D 4
Ypoá (lake) ....B 6

PARAGUAY and URUGUAY

	PARAGUAY	URUGUAY
AREA	150,518 sq. mi.	72,172 sq. mi.
POPULATION	1,996,000	2,682,000
CAPITAL	Asunción	Montevideo
LARGEST CITY	Asunción 350,000	Montevideo (greater) 1,202,890
HIGHEST POINT	Amambay Range 2,264 ft.	Mira Nacional 1,644 ft.
MONETARY UNIT	guaraní	Uruguayan peso
MAJOR LANGUAGES	Spanish, Indian	Spanish
MAJOR RELIGION	Roman Catholic	Roman Catholic

URUGUAY

DEPARTMENTS

Artigas, 52,261 ..... B 1
Canelones, 211,644 ..... D 5
Cerro Largo, 118,880 ..... E 3
Colonia, 135,185 ..... B 5
Durazno, 113,797 ..... C 4
Flores, 35,457 ..... C 4
Florida, 104,739 ..... D 4
Montevideo (cap.), 777,885 ..... B 7
Montevideo,* 1,202,890 ..... B 7
Lavalleja, 114,090 ..... D 5
Maldonado, 62,344 ..... E 5
Montevideo, 1,173,114 ..... B 7
Paysandú, 89,908 ..... B 3
Río Negro, 49,258 ..... B 3
Rivera, 86,430 ..... D 2
Rocha, 84,210 ..... E 4
Salto, 105,698 ..... B 2
San José, 94,541 ..... C 5
Soriano, 78,234 ..... B 4
Tacuarembó, 119,690 ..... D 2
Treinta y Tres, 81,887 ..... E 4

CITIES and TOWNS

Aceguá ..... E 2
Achar ..... C 3
Aguas Corrientes ..... C 4
Aiguá, 2,715 ..... E 5
Algorta ..... B 3
Arapey ..... B 2
Artigas, 23,429 ..... C 1
Atlántida ..... D 5
Balneario Solís, 225 ..... D 5
Baltasar Brum, 1,764 ..... B 2
Bañado de Medina ..... E 3
Bañado de Rocha ..... E 4
Belén, 2,933 ..... B 2
Bella Unión, 4,955 ..... B 1
Bizcocho, 117 ..... B 4
Cañada Nieto, 407 ..... B 4
Canelones, 8,041 ..... D 5
Cardona, 4,110 ..... C 4
Carlos Reyles ..... C 3
Carmelo, 11,923 ..... A 4
Carmen, 1,687 ..... D 4
Castillos, 5,345 ..... F 5
Casupá, 1,652 ..... D 4
Cerro Chato, 2,045 ..... D 4
Chamberlain ..... C 3
Colonia, 9,825 ..... B 5
Colonia Arrué ..... B 5
Colonia Lavalleja ..... C 2
Colonia Rossel y Rius ..... D 4
Colonia Valdense, 1,126 ..... D 5
Conchillas ..... B 5
Constancia ..... A 2
Costa Azul ..... E 5
Cuaró ..... C 2
Cuaymán ..... B 3
Diez y Nueve de Abril ..... E 5
Diez y Ocho de Julio ..... F 5
Dolores, 12,480 ..... A 4
Durazno, 19,486 ..... C 3
Estación Atlántida, 1,007 ..... B 6
Estación Paso Ignacio, 131 ..... C 4
Estación Rincón ..... F 3
Estación Villasboas ..... C 3
Estanzuela ..... B 5
Florida, 17,243 ..... D 4
Fortaleza de Santa Teresa ..... F 5
Fraile Muerto, 1,876 ..... E 3
Francia ..... C 3
Fray Marcos ..... D 4
Fray Bentos, 14,625 ..... A 4
General Enrique Martínez ..... F 4
Getulio Vargas ..... E 3
Grecco ..... B 3
Guichón, 4,625 ..... B 3
Ituzaingó ..... A 6
Javier de Viana, 317 ..... C 1
Joaquín Suárez, Canelones, 1,752 ..... B 6
Joaquín Suárez, Colonia ..... B 5
José Batlle y Ordóñez ..... D 4
José Enrique Rodó, 1,319 ..... B 4
José Pedro Varela, 2,955 ..... E 4
Juan D. Jackson, 163 ..... C 4
Juan L. Lacaze, 9,916 ..... B 5
Julio María Sanz ..... F 4
La Coronilla ..... F 5
La Cruz ..... D 4
La Floresta ..... D 5
La Paloma ..... F 5
La Paz, Canelones ..... B 6
La Paz, Colonia ..... B 5
La Pedrera ..... F 5
La Sierra, 241 ..... D 5
Las Flores, 404 ..... D 5
Las Piedras, 15,724 ..... B 6
Lascano, 4,204 ..... E 4
Libertad, 4,622 ..... C 5
Lorenzo Geyres ..... B 3
Los Novillos ..... B 2
Mal Abrigo ..... C 5
Maldonado, 15,005 ..... D 6
Manga ..... B 7
Manguera Azul ..... D 5
María Albina ..... E 4
Mariscala, 1,305 ..... E 4
Martín Chico ..... A 5
Masoller ..... C 2
Mazangano ..... E 3
Melo, 28,673 ..... E 3
Mendoza ..... C 5
Mercedes, 31,325 ..... B 4
Merinos ..... C 3
Miguelete ..... B 5
Migues ..... C 6
Minas, 21,133 ..... D 5
Minas de Corrales ..... D 2
Montes ..... D 5
Nando ..... F 3
Nico Pérez ..... D 4
Nueva Helvecia ..... B 5
Nueva Palmira, 4,611 ..... A 4
Nuevo Berlín, 1,531 ..... B 3
Olimar ..... E 3
Ombúes de Lavalle ..... C 4
Ombúes de Oribe ..... C 4
Palermo ..... C 5
Palmitas, 1,288 ..... B 4
Palomas ..... B 2
Pan de Azúcar, 4,190 ..... D 5
Pando, 11,623 ..... B 6
Parada Esperanza ..... B 3
Parada Liebigs ..... B 4
Parada Rivas ..... B 6
Parish ..... C 3
Paso Ataques ..... D 1
Paso de Andrés Pérez ..... B 3
Paso de la Laguna, Salto ..... B 2
Paso de la Laguna, Tacuarembó ..... D 3
Paso de las Piedras ..... D 3
Paso de León, 184 ..... B 1
Paso de los Toros, 10,524 ..... C 3
Paso de Ramos, 23 ..... C 1
Paso de Ulestes ..... B 3
Paso del Borracho ..... D 2
Paso del Horno ..... C 2
Paso del Parque ..... B 2
Paso Hondo ..... B 4
Paso Potrero ..... C 2
Paysandú, 47,875 ..... A 3
Pedrera ..... C 6
Peralta ..... C 3
Piedra Sola ..... C 3
Piedras Coloradas ..... B 3
Piñera ..... C 3
Pintado, Artigas ..... C 1
Pintado, Florida ..... D 4
Pirarajá, 160 ..... E 4
Piriápolis, 4,546 ..... D 5
Polanco del Yí ..... D 4
Polonio ..... F 5
Porvenir ..... B 3
Progreso ..... B 6
Pueblo del Sauce ..... B 6
Puerto Amaro ..... F 3
Puerto Arazatí ..... C 5
Punta del Este, 5,272 ..... E 6
Puntas de Maciel ..... C 4
Quebracho, 1,002 ..... B 2
Ramón Trigo ..... E 3
Real de San Carlos ..... A 5
Retamosa ..... E 4
Río Branco, 3,345 ..... F 3
Rivera, 42,623 ..... D 1
Rocha, 19,895 ..... E 5
Rodríguez, 1,097 ..... C 5
Rosario, 6,398 ..... B 5
Salto, 55,425 ..... B 2
San Bautista ..... D 5
San Carlos, 13,695 ..... E 5
San Gregorio, San José ..... C 4
San Gregorio, Tacuarembó, 1,606 ..... D 3
San Jacinto ..... D 5
San Javier ..... A 3
San José de Mayo, 21,048 ..... C 5
San Ramón, 3,983 ..... D 5
San Servando ..... F 3
Santa Ana ..... C 1
Santa Catalina, 824 ..... B 4
Santa Clara de Olimar ..... D 3
Santa Lucía, 9,126 ..... B 6
Santa Rosa ..... B 6
Santiago Vázquez ..... A 7
Sarandí de Navarro ..... B 3
Sarandí del Yí, 5,900 ..... D 4
Sarandí Grande, 5,620 ..... C 4
Sauce, Canelones ..... B 6
Sauce, Rocha ..... E 5
Sauce del Yí ..... D 4
Saucedo ..... C 2
Sequeira, 880 ..... C 1
Siete Cerros ..... C 6
Soca ..... C 6
Solís, 1,531 ..... D 5
Solís de Matajo ..... D 5
Soriano, 1,036 ..... B 4
Tala, 3,340 ..... D 5
Talita ..... D 4
Tambores, 1,273 ..... C 2
Tiatucurá ..... C 3
Timote ..... C 3
Toledo ..... B 6
Tomás Gomensoro, 2,144 ..... B 1
Totoral ..... C 3
Tranqueras, 3,340 ..... D 2
Treinta y Tres, 18,856 ..... E 4
Tres Árboles ..... C 3
Tres Bocas ..... C 2
Tres Islas ..... E 3
Trinidad, 17,233 ..... C 4
Tupambaé, 1,359 ..... E 3
Unión ..... B 7
Valentines ..... E 4

PARAGUAY

CITIES and TOWNS

Veinticinco de Agosto, 1,139 ..... A 6
Veinticinco de Mayo ..... C 5
Velázquez, 1,199 ..... D 5
Veras ..... C 2
Verdún ..... D 5
Vergara, 2,480 ..... E 3
Vichadero ..... D 2
Villa del Cerro ..... A 7
Young, 6,485 ..... B 3
Zapicán ..... E 4
Zapucay ..... D 2

PHYSICAL FEATURES

Aiguá (river) ..... E 4
Alférez (river) ..... E 5
Arapey Chico (river) ..... B 1
Arapey Grande (river) ..... B 2
Belén (river) ..... B 2
Bonete (dam) ..... D 3
Brava (river) ..... B 7
Cañas (range) ..... C 2
Caraguatá (river) ..... C 2
Castillos (lagoon) ..... F 5
Cebollatí (river) ..... F 4
Cordobés (river) ..... D 3
Cuareim (river) ..... B 1
Cuñapirú (river) ..... D 2
Daymán (range) ..... B 2
Daymán (river) ..... B 2
Durazno (range) ..... D 3
Espinillo (point) ..... A 7
Este (point) ..... D 6
Flores (isl.) ..... D 5
Garzón (lagoon) ..... E 5
Grande (range) ..... D 4
Grande (river) ..... D 4
Grande Inferior (range) ..... C 4
Haedo (range) ..... C 2
India Muerta (river) ..... E 4
José Ignacio (lagoon) ..... E 5
La Plata (river) ..... B 5
Lobos (isl.), 11 ..... E 6
Maciel (river) ..... C 4
Mira Nacional (mt.) ..... D 5
Mirim (lagoon) ..... F 4
Negra (lagoon) ..... F 5
Negra (range) ..... C 3
Negro (river) ..... B 4
Negro (river) ..... B 3
Olimar Grande (river) ..... E 4
Pando (river) ..... B 6
Parao (river) ..... E 3
Plata, La (river) ..... B 5
Polonio (cape) ..... F 5
Queguay Chico (river) ..... B 3
Queguay Grande (river) ..... B 3
Río Negro (res.) ..... C 3
Rocha (lagoon) ..... E 5
Salto Grande (falls) ..... A 2
San José (river) ..... C 5
San Miguel (swamp) ..... F 4
San Salvador (river) ..... B 4
Santa Ana (range) ..... D 2
Santa Lucía (river) ..... C 5
Santa Lucía Chico (river) ..... D 4
Santa María (cape) ..... F 5
Sauce (lagoon) ..... D 5
Sopas (river) ..... C 2
Tacuarembó (river) ..... D 2
Tacuarí (river) ..... F 3
Tigre (isl.) ..... A 7
Uruguay (river) ..... A 3
Yaguarón (river) ..... F 3
Yí (river) ..... B 4

*City and suburbs.

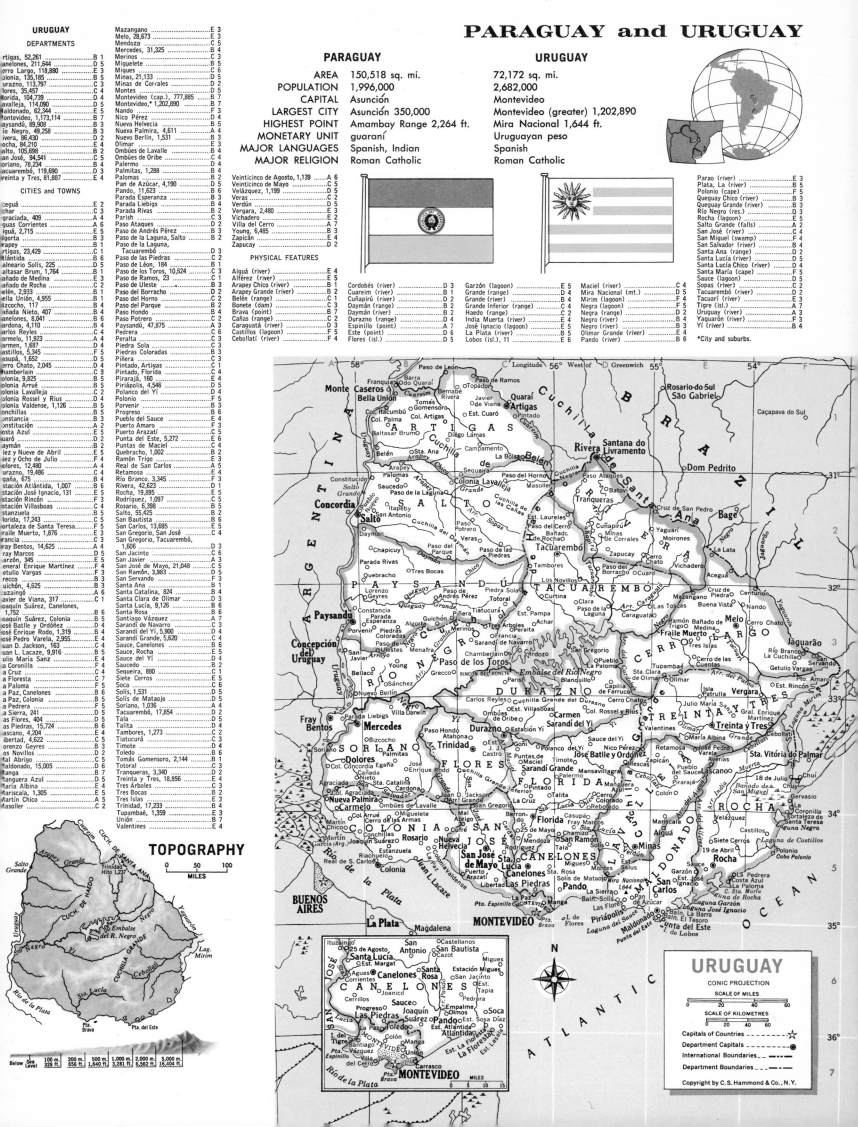

TOPOGRAPHY
0   50   100
MILES

URUGUAY
CONIC PROJECTION
SCALE OF MILES
0   20   40   60
SCALE OF KILOMETRES
0   20   40   60
Capitals of Countries .... ★
Department Capitals .... ◉
International Boundaries .... ____
Department Boundaries .... ____

Copyright by C. S. Hammond & Co., N.Y.

NORTH AMERICA

LAMBERT AZIMUTHAL EQUAL-AREA PROJECTION

SCALE OF MILES
0   100   200   400   600   800

SCALE OF KILOMETRES
0   200   400   600   800

Capitals of Countries _____ ☆
International Boundaries ___ __ ___ __
Other Boundaries _____ __ __ __
Canals _____ _ _ _ _

© C.S. HAMMOND & Co., N.Y.

POPULATION DISTRIBUTION

Montréal
Toronto
Buffalo
Boston
Minneapolis
Milwaukee
Detroit Cleveland
New York
Chicago
Pittsburgh
Philadelphia
Washington
Baltimore
St. Louis
San Francisco
Los Angeles
Houston
Havana
Mexico City

• ......Cities with over 1,000,000 inhabitants (including suburbs)

POPULATION DENSITY

under 1 PER SQ. KM.	under 2 PER SQ. MI.	50-100	130-260
1-10	2-25	100-200	260-520
10-25	25-65	over 200	over 520
25-50	65-130		

Copyright by C.S. HAMMOND & Co., N.Y.

NORTH AMERICA

AREA	9,124,000 sq. mi.
POPULATION	286,000,000
LARGEST CITY	New York (greater) 14,114,927
HIGHEST POINT	Mt. McKinley 20,320 ft.
LOWEST POINT	Death Valley −282 ft.

TEMPERATURE AND RAINFALL

AVERAGE ANNUAL RAINFALL

MILLIMETERS	INCHES
Under 250	Under 10
250-500	10-20
500-1,000	20-40
1,000-1,500	40-60
1,500-2,000	60-80
Over 2,000	Over 80

AVERAGE TEMPERATURE

(Isotherms, reduced to sea level, in degrees Fahrenheit. Subtract approximately 3 degrees for every 1,000 feet of elevation.)

—— January
----- July

Copyright by C.S. HAMMOND & Co., N.Y.

North America
(continued)

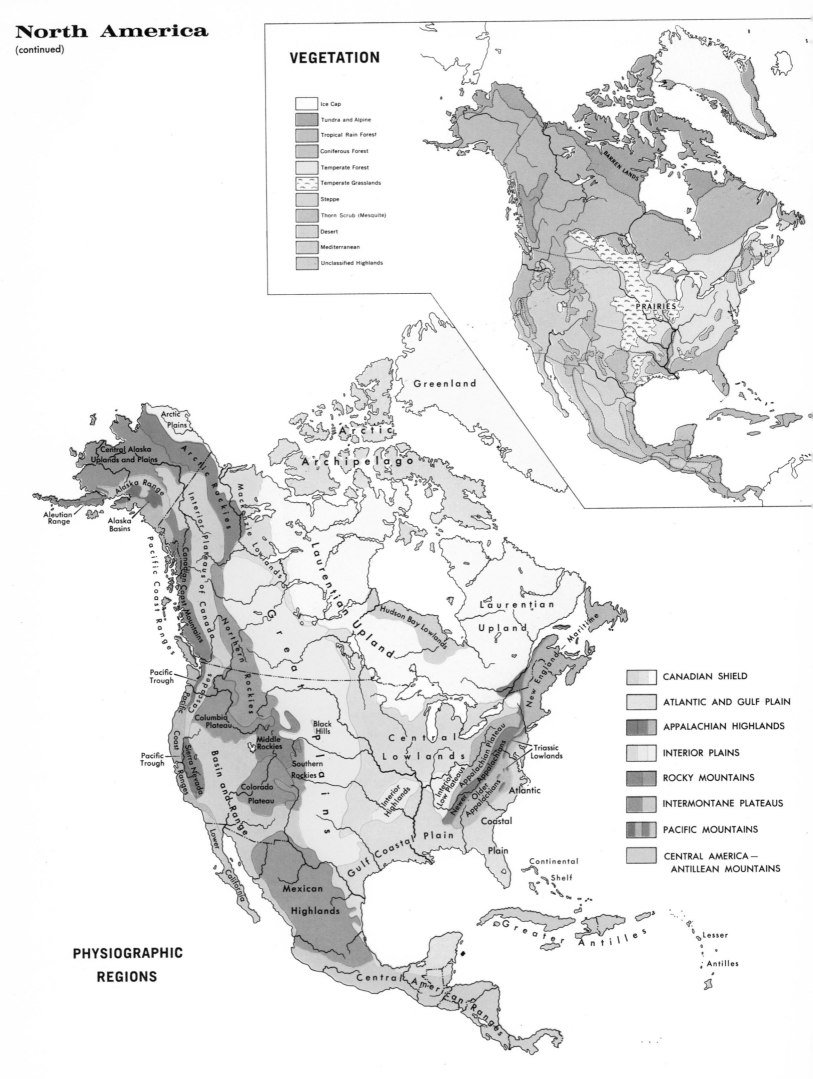

VEGETATION

- Ice Cap
- Tundra and Alpine
- Tropical Rain Forest
- Coniferous Forest
- Temperate Forest
- Temperate Grasslands
- Steppe
- Thorn Scrub (Mesquite)
- Desert
- Mediterranean
- Unclassified Highlands

BARREN LANDS

PRAIRIES

Greenland

Arctic

Archipelago

Arctic Plains

Central Alaska Uplands and Plains

Aleutian Range

Alaska Basins

Alaska Range

Arctic Rockies

Mackenzie Lowlands

Laurentian Upland

Pacific Coast Ranges

Interior Plateaus of Canada

Canadian Coast Mountains

Northern Rockies

Pacific Trough

Columbia Plateau

Middle Rockies

Pacific Trough

Sierra Nevada

Coast Ranges

Basin and Range

Colorado Plateau

Lower California

Black Hills

Southern Rockies

Great Plains

Hudson Bay Lowlands

Laurentian Upland

New England — Maritime

Central Lowlands

Interior Highlands

Interior Low Plateaus

Appalachian Plateau

Newer Appalachians

Older Appalachians

Triassic Lowlands

Atlantic

Coastal Plain

Gulf Coastal Plain

Continental Shelf

Mexican Highlands

Greater Antilles

Lesser Antilles

Central American Ranges

- CANADIAN SHIELD
- ATLANTIC AND GULF PLAIN
- APPALACHIAN HIGHLANDS
- INTERIOR PLAINS
- ROCKY MOUNTAINS
- INTERMONTANE PLATEAUS
- PACIFIC MOUNTAINS
- CENTRAL AMERICA — ANTILLEAN MOUNTAINS

PHYSIOGRAPHIC REGIONS

TOPOGRAPHY

```
0        400       800
         MILES
```

ARCTIC OCEAN

QUEEN
ELIZABETH
SVERDRUP
ISLANDS IS.

Greenland

C. Morris Jesup

Beaufort
Sea

Pt. Barrow

Banks
I.

Parry

Victoria
I.

Baffin
Bay

Disko I.

Baffin
Island

Davis Strait

C. Farewell

ALEUTIAN
ISLANDS

Bering
Sea

St. Lawrence
I.

Bering Strait

Seward
Pen.

Yukon

BROOKS RANGE

Mt. McKinley
20,320

Alaska
Pen.

Kenai
Pen.

Kodiak
I.

Gulf
of
Alaska

Mt.
Logan
19,850

ALEXANDER
ARCH.

QUEEN
CHARLOTTE
IS.

Great Bear
L.

Mackenzie

Great
Slave L.

Athabasca

Peace

Athabasca

Foxe
Basin

Southampton
I.

Hudson Str.

Hudson
Bay

Ungava
Peninsula

Labrador
Sea

C. Chidley

Churchill

Newfoundland

C. Race

PACIFIC

Vancouver
I.

Mt.
Rainier
14,410

C. Mendocino

COAST RANGES

COAST MOUNTAINS

ROCKY

Fraser

Columbia

COLUMBIA
PLATEAU

Great
Basin

Mt. Whitney
14,495

Snake

Columbia

MOUNTAINS

Nelson

Saskatchewan

Missouri

Red

L.
Winnipeg

Albany

L.
Superior

LAURENTIAN

Eastmain

PLATEAU

Cape Breton
I.

Nova
Scotia

OCEAN

Cod C.

Colorado

COLORADO
PLATEAU

Missouri

Platte

GREAT

Arkansas

OZARK
PLATEAU

Mississippi

L.
Michigan

L.
Huron

L.
Erie

Ontario

St. Lawrence

APPALACHIAN MTS.

Long I.

C. Hatteras

ATLANTIC

Bermuda

C. Falso

Lower California

Gulf of California

SIERRA MADRE OCCIDENTAL

MEXICAN PLATEAU

SIERRA MADRE ORIENTAL

Rio Grande

Grande

PLAINS

Red

Ohio

Tennessee

Mississippi

PLAIN

GULF

COASTAL

ATLANTIC COASTAL PLAIN

Florida
Pen.

C. Kennedy

BAHAMA IS.

Puerto
Rico

OCEAN

Citlaltépetl
18,700

Gulf of
Campeche

Yucatán
Pen.

Gulf of Mexico

Cuba

GREATER

Jamaica

Hispaniola

ANTILLES

LESSER ANTILLES

Trinidad

Isthmus
of
Tehuantepec

L.
Nicaragua

Isthmus of
Panama

Caribbean   Sea

Chirripó Grande
12,467

5,000 m.	2,000 m.	1,000 m.	500 m.	200 m.	100 m.	Sea	
16,404 ft.	6,562 ft.	3,281 ft.	1,640 ft.	656 ft.	328 ft.	Level	Below

Mexico

STATES and TERRITORIES

Aguascalientes, 243,363 ....H 6
Baja California, 520,165 ....B 1
Baja California Sur (terr.), 81,594 ....C 3
Campeche, 168,219 ....O 7
Chiapas, 1,210,870 ....N 8
Chihuahua, 1,226,793 ....F 2
Coahuila, 907,734 ....H 3
Colima, 164,450 ....G 7
Distrito Federal, 4,870,876 ....L 1
Durango, 760,836 ....G 4
Guanajuato, 1,735,490 ....J 6
Guerrero, 1,186,716 ....J 8
Hidalgo, 994,598 ....K 6
Jalisco, 2,443,261 ....H 6
México, 1,897,851 ....K 7
Michoacán, 1,851,876 ....H 7
Morelos, 387,264 ....K 7
Nayarit, 389,929 ....G 6
Nuevo León, 1,078,848 ....K 4
Oaxaca, 1,727,266 ....L 8
Puebla, 1,973,837 ....L 7
Querétaro, 355,045 ....J 6
Quintana Roo (terr.), 50,169............P 7
San Luis Potosí, 1,048,297 ....J 5
Sinaloa, 838,404 ....F 4
Sonora, 783,378 ....D 2
Tabasco, 496,340 ....N 7
Tamaulipas, 1,024,182 ....K 4
Tlaxcala, 346,699 ....N 1
Veracruz, 2,727,899 ....L 7
Yucatán, 614,049 ....P 6
Zacatecas, 817,831 ....H 5

CITIES and TOWNS

Acámbaro, 26,187 ....J 7
Acaponeta, 8,462 ....G 5
Acapulco de Juárez, 49,149............J 8
Acatlán, 7,268 ....K 7
Acatzingo, 6,672 ....N 2
Acayucan, 12,831 ....M 8
Aconchi, 1,384 ....D 2
Actopan, 1,242 ....Q 1
Agua Dulce, 9,295 ....M 7
Agua Prieta, 15,339 ....E 1
Agualeguas, 2,426 ....J 3
Aguascalientes, 143,293 ....H 6
Aguililla, 4,036 ....H 7
Ahuacatlán, 4,982 ....G 6
Ajalpan, 6,492 ....L 7
Alamo, 6,438 ....L 6
Alamos, 3,602 ....E 3
Aldama, Chihuahua, 5,294 ....G 2
Aldama, Tamaulipas, 2,067 ....L 5
Aljojuca, 2,642 ....O 1
Allende, Chihuahua, 3,104 ....G 3
Allende, Coahuila, 9,418 ....J 2
Allende, Nuevo León, 6,497............J 4
Almoloya del Río, 3,387 ....K 1
Altamira, 2,620 ....K 5
Altar, 1,116 ....D 1
Altotonga, 5,584 ....P 1
Alvarado, 12,548 ....M 7
Amatlán de los Reyes, 3,041............P 2
Amealco, 2,201 ....K 6
Ameca, 17,588 ....H 6
Amecameca de Juárez, 12,291............L 1
Amozoc de Mota, 7,019 ....N 2
Angostura, 1,372 ....E 4
Apan, 8,640 ....M 1
Apatzingán de la Constitución, 19,568 ....J 7
Apizaco, 15,705 ....N 1
Aquiles Serdán, 4,357 ....G 2
Aramberri, 1,311 ....J 5
Arandas, 17,071 ....H 6
Arcelia, 6,292 ....J 7
Arizpe, 1,410 ....D 1
Armería, 4,852 ....G 7
Arteaga, 2,960 ....H 7
Ascensión, 2,807 ....E 1
Asunción Nochixtlan, 3,172 ....L 8
Atlixco, 30,650 ....M 2
Atotonilco, 14,430 ....H 6
Autlan de Navarro, 17,017 ....G 7
Ayutla de los Libres, 2,658............K 8
Azcapotzalco, 63,857 ....L 1
Azoyú, 2,545 ....K 8
Bacadéhuachi, 1,406 ....E 2
Bacerac, 1,016 ....E 1
Bácum, 1,508 ....D 3
Balancán, 2,554 ....O 8
Bamoa, 1,934 ....E 4
Batuc, 1,267 ....E 2
Baviácora, 1,317 ....E 2
Benjamín Hill, 4,392 ....D 1
Boca del Río, 2,660 ....Q 1
Bolonchen de Rejón, 1,540 ....P 7
Buenaventura, 2,780 ....F 2
Cadereyta, 1,635 ....K 6
Cadereyta Jiménez, 8,042 ....K 4
Calera, 5,504 ....H 5
Calkiní, 5,611 ....O 6
Calpulalpam, 6,551 ....M 1
Calvillo, 5,735 ....H 6
Campeche, 43,874 ....O 7
Cananea, 19,683 ....D 1
Canatlán, 5,077 ....G 4
Candela, 2,240 ....J 3
Carbo, 2,428 ....D 2
Cárdenas, S. Luis Potosí, 12,461 ....K 6
Cárdenas, Tabasco, 4,583 ....N 8
Caritas de Felipe Pescador, 5,107 ....H 5
Carmen, 21,164 ....N 7
Catemaco, 8,702 ....M 7
Ceballos, 2,508 ....G 3
Cedral, 4,221 ....J 5
Celaya, 58,851 ....J 6
Celestún, 840 ....O 6
Cerralvo, 4,057 ....J 3
Cerritos, 9,989 ....K 5
Chalchihuites, 3,951 ....G 5
Chalco, 7,595 ....M 1
Champotón, 4,694 ....O 7
Chapulco, 1,520 ....O 2
Charcas, 9,105 ....J 5
Chetumal, 12,855 ....Q 7
Chiapa, 6,960 ....N 8
Chiautempan, 11,296 ....N 1
Chicoloapan de Juárez, 3,672............M 1
Chietla, 4,651 ....M 2
Chignahuapan, 3,081 ....N 1
Chignautla, 1,937 ....N 1
Chihuahua, 187,886 ....G 2
Chilapa, 7,368 ....K 8
Chilpancingo, 18,022 ....K 8
China, 2,494 ....K 4
Chocamán, 4,512 ....P 2
Choix, 1,923 ....E 3
Cholula, 12,833 ....M 1
Cihuatlán, 4,125 ....G 7
Cintalapa, 8,150 ....M 8
Ciudad Acuña, 20,048 ....J 2
Ciudad Altamirano, 6,014 ....J 7
Ciudad Camargo, 18,951 ....G 3
Ciudad Camargo, 7,902 ....K 3
Ciudad del Maíz, 4,767 ....K 5
Ciudad de Valles, 23,823 ....K 5
Ciudad Guerrero, 2,719 ....F 2
Ciudad Guzmán, 30,941 ....H 7
Ciudad Juárez, 356,895 ....F 1
Ciudad Lerdo, 17,682 ....H 4
Ciudad Madero, 53,628 ....L 5
Ciudad Mante, 22,919 ....K 5
Ciudad Mendoza, 16,051 ....O 2
Ciudad Miguel Alemán, 6,535............K 3
Ciudad Obregón, 67,956 ....E 3
Ciudad Serdán, 9,942 ....O 2
Ciudad Victoria, 50,797 ....K 5
Coalcomán de Matamoros, 7,695 H 7
Coatepec, 18,022 ....P 1
Coatetelco, 4,614 ....L 2
Coatzacoalcos (Puerto México), 37,300 ....M 7
Cocorit, 3,819 ....E 3
Cocula, 10,119 ....G 6
Colima, 43,518 ....H 7
Colón, 2,716 ....K 6
Colotlán, 6,337 ....H 5
Comala, 4,943 ....G 7
Comalcalco, 7,745 ....N 7
Comitán, 15,409 ....O 8
Comondú, 540 ....D 3
Compostela, 7,658 ....G 6
Concepción del Oro, 8,452 ....J 4
Concordia, 4,099 ....G 5
Córdoba, 47,448 ....P 2
Cosalá, 1,692 ....F 4
Cosamaloapan de Carpio, 16,944 ....M 7
Cosautlán de Carvajal, 1,659 ....P 1
Coscomatepec de Bravo, 5,187............P 2
Cosío, 1,350 ....H 5
Cosoleacaque, 5,665 ....M 7
Costa Rica, 6,649 ....F 4
Cotija, 8,059 ....H 7
Coyame, 791 ....G 2
Coyoacán, 54,866 ....L 1
Coyotepec, 5,967 ....L 1
Coyuca, 3,124 ....J 7
Coyuca de Benítez, 4,486 ....J 8
Coyutla, 3,880 ....L 6
Cozumel, 2,085 ....Q 6
Cristóbal de las Casas, 23,343............O 8
Cruillas, 415 ....K 4
Cuatrociénegas de Carranza, 3,931 ....H 3
Cuauhtémoc, 14,686 ....F 2
Cuautitlán, 8,378 ....L 1
Cuautla Morelos, 12,427 ....L 2
Cuencamé, 2,982 ....H 4
Cuernavaca, 37,144 ....L 2
Cuicatlán, 1,978 ....L 8
Cuitlahuac, 3,634 ....P 2
Culiacán, 85,024 ....F 4
Cumpas, 2,314 ....E 1
Cunduacán, 1,792 ....N 7
Delicias, 39,919 ....G 2
Distrito Federal, 4,870,876 ....L 1
Doctor Arroyo, 3,085 ....K 5
Dolores Hidalgo, 12,311 ....J 6
Durango, 118,506 ....G 4
Dzitbalché, 3,666 ....P 6
Ejutla de Crespo, 5,194 ....L 8
El Carmen, 4,857 ....N 1
El Dorado, 6,423 ....F 4
El Ebano, 5,564 ....K 5
El Fuerte, 5,331 ....E 3
El Oro, Durango, 4,224 ....G 4
El Oro, México, 3,507 ....K 7
El Salto, 6,947 ....G 5
Empalme, 18,964 ....D 2
Encarnación de Díaz, 8,710 ....H 6
Ensenada, 42,561 ....A 1
Escuinapa de Hidalgo, 9,920............G 5
Escuintla, 3,468 ....N 9
Esperanza, 3,550 ....O 2
Espita, 5,161 ....Q 6
Etchojoa, 4,075 ....E 3
Fortín de las Flores, 6,328............P 2
Fresnillo, 35,582 ....H 5
Frontera, 8,375 ....N 7
Fronteras, 548 ....E 1
Galeana, Chihuahua, 744 ....F 1
Galeana, Nuevo León, 3,127............J 4
García de la Cadena, 1,754............H 6
General Bravo, 1,718 ....K 4
General Cepeda, 3,832 ....J 4
Gómez Palacio, 61,174 ....G 4
González, 3,270 ....K 5
Granados, 1,124 ....E 2
Guadalajara, 977,779 ....H 6
Guadalupe, Nvo. León, 27,020............J 4
Guadalupe, Zacatecas, 7,888 ....H 5
Guadalupe-Bravos, 2,392 ....F 1
Guadalupe Victoria, 6,520 ....G 4
Guadalupe y Calvo, 1,864 ....F 2
Guamúchil, 7,878 ....E 4
Guanacevi, 1,148 ....G 4
Guanajuato, 28,212 ....J 6
Guasave, 17,510 ....E 4
Guaymas, 34,865 ....D 3
Guazapares, 430 ....E 3
Guitérrez Zamora, 6,518 ....L 6
Halachó, 4,543 ....O 6
Hecelchakán, 3,879 ....O 6
Hermosillo, 132,324 ....D 2
Heroica Caborca, 9,338 ....C 1
Heroica Huamantla, 10,154 ....N 1
Hidalgo, 3,394 ....K 4
Hopelchén, 3,006 ....P 7
Huajuapan de León, 8,531 ....L 8
Huaquechula, 1,929 ....M 2
Huatabampo, 10,228 ....D 3
Huatusco de Chicuellar, 8,680............P 2
Huauchinango, 12,317 ....L 6
Huautla, 6,862 ....L 7
Huehuetlán, 2,924 ....M 2
Huejotzingo, 7,390 ....M 1
Huejutla de Reyes, 3,849............K 6
Huetamo de Núñez, 6,191 ....J 7
Hueyotlipan, 1,520 ....M 1
Huimanguillo, 4,537 ....N 8
Huitzuco, 6,354 ....K 7
Huixtla, 12,327 ....N 9
Hunucmá, 6,616 ....O 6
Ignacio de la Llave, 2,629 ....Q 2
Iguala, 26,845 ....K 7
Imuris, 1,003 ....D 1
Indé, 1,278 ....G 4
Irapuato, 83,768 ....J 6
Isla Mujeres, 557 ....Q 6
Iturbide, 752 ....P 7
Ixmiquilpan, 1,752 ....K 6
Ixtacalco, 25,546 ....L 1
Ixtapalapa, 25,517 ....L 1
Ixtepec, 12,087 ....M 8
Ixtlán del Río, 8,330 ....G 6
Izamal, 8,633 ....P 6
Izúcar de Matamoros, 16,556 ...M 2
Jala, 3,803 ....G 6
Jalacingo, 2,831 ....P 1
Jalapa Enríquez, 66,269 ....P 1
Jalpa, Tabasco, 5,133 ....N 7
Jalpa, Zacatecas, 6,213 ....H 6
Jalpan, 1,008 ....K 6
Jáltipan, 8,588 ....M 8
Jantetelco, 1,351 ....L 2
Jaumave, 1,884 ....K 5
Jerez de García Salinas, 15,016..H 5
Jico, 6,965 ....P 1
Jiquilpan, 2,689 ....K 7
Jiménez, Chihuahua, 14,904 ....G 3
Jiménez, Coahuila, 1,003 ....J 2
Jojutla de Juárez, 11,555 ....L 2
Jonacatepec, 3,250 ....M 2
Jonuta, 1,482 ....N 7
Juan Aldama, 7,742 ....H 4
Juárez, 1,152 ....J 3
Juchipila, 3,459 ....H 6
Juchique de Ferrer, 983............Q 1
Juchitán de Zaragoza, 19,797....M 8
La Babia, 28 ....H 2
La Barca, 16,273 ....H 6
La Concordia, 1,879 ....N 9
La Cruz, Chihuahua, 1,049 ....G 3
La Cruz, Sinaloa, 2,740 ....F 5
La Junta, 3,234 ....F 2
La Paz, 24,253 ....D 5
La Piedad, 24,337 ....H 6
La Potosí, 1,755 ....J 4
La Purísima, 598 ....D 3
La Trinitaria, 2,370 ....N 9
La Yesca, 508 ....G 6
Lagos, 23,636 ....J 6
Las Nieves, 1,455 ....G 3
Las Vigas, 4,762 ....P 1
León, 260,952 ....J 6
Libres, 2,443 ....O 1
Linares, 13,592 ....K 4
Llera de Canales, 1,653 ....K 5
Loma Bonita, 9,789 ....M 7
Loreto, 4,969 ....J 5
Los Algodones, 5,542 ....B 1
Los Mochis, 38,307 ....E 4
Los Reyes, 9,796 ....H 7
Macuspana, 6,597 ....N 8
Madera, 7,314 ....F 2
Magdalena, 9,445 ....D 1
Mamantel, 89 ....O 7
Manuel Benavides, 801 ....H 2
Manzanillo, 19,950 ....G 7
Mapastepec, 4,664 ....N 9
Mapimí, 2,998 ....G 4
Martínez de la Torre, 14,615 ....L 6
Mascota, 5,267 ....G 6
Matamoros, Coahuila, 13,770........H 4
Matamoros, Tamaulipas, 122,680 ....L 4
Matehuala, 19,927 ....J 5
Matías Romero, 10,187 ....M 8
Maxcanú, 5,139 ....O 6
Mazapil, 1,777 ....J 4
Mazatán, 644 ....E 2
Mazatlán, 75,751 ....F 5
Melchor Múzquiz, 12,971 ....J 3
Melchor Ocampo, 647 ....H 4
Melchor Ocampo del Balsas, 1,906 ....H 8
Meoqui, 10,287 ....G 2
Mérida, 183,701 ....P 6
Metepec, 6,839 ....M 2
Mexicali, 261,299 ....B 1
Mexico City (México) (capital), 3,118,059 ....L 1
Mezquital, 837 ....G 5
Miacatlán, 4,149 ....L 2
Miahuatlán de Porfirio Díaz, 7,518 ....L 8
Mier, 4,120 ....K 3
Miguel Azua, 7,173 ....H 4
Minatitlán, 35,350 ....M 8
Mineral del Monte, 10,061 ....K 6
Miquihuana, 1,777 ....K 5
Misantla, 9,201 ....P 1
Mocorito, 4,223 ....F 4
Moctezuma, S. L. Potosí, 1,333 ....J 5
Moctezuma, Sonora, 2,148 ....E 2
Monclova, 43,077 ....J 3
Montemorelos, 11,641 ....K 4
Monterrey, 774,059 ....J 4
Morelia, 121,964 ....J 7
Morelos, 3,096 ....J 2
Morelos Cañada, 2,709 ....O 2
Moroleón, 17,954 ....J 6
Motozintla de Mendoza, 4,084....N 9
Motul, 10,351 ....P 6
Mulegé, 846 ....C 3
Muna, 4,443 ....P 6
Naco, 2,864 ....D 1
Nacozari de García, 2,745............E 1
Nadadores, 1,890 ....J 3
Nanacamilpa, 5,427 ....M 1
Naolinco de Victoria, 3,658 ....P 1
Naranjos, 8,354 ....L 6
Naucalpan, 10,365 ....L 1
Nautla, 1,432 ....L 6
Nava, 3,118 ....J 2
Navojoa, 30,560 ....E 3
Navolato, 9,188 ....E 4
Nazas, 2,738 ....G 4
Nieves, 3,147 ....H 5
Nochistlán, 7,293 ....H 6
Nogales, Sonora, 37,657 ....D 1
Nogales, Veracruz, 11,219 ....P 2
Nombre de Dios, 3,159 ....G 5
Nonoava, 1,582 ....F 3
Nopalucan, 2,783 ....O 1
Nueva Casas Grandes, 11,687............F 1
Nueva Ciudad Guerrero, 3,409............K 3
Nueva Rosita, 34,302 ....J 2
Nuevo Laredo, 112,280 ....J 3
Nuevo Morelos, 580 ....K 5
Nuri, 808 ....E 3
Oaxaca, 72,370 ....L 8
Ocampo, Chihuahua, 375 ....E 2
Ocampo, Coahuila, 1,298 ....H 3
Ocampo, Tamaulipas, 3,348 ....K 5
Ocotlán, 25,416 ....H 6
Ocotlán de Morelos, 5,298 ....L 8
Ojinaga, 8,252 ....G 2
Ojocaliente, 6,779 ....H 5
Ometepec, 4,990 ....K 8
Opodepe, 1,050............
Oputo, 1,962 ....
Oriental, 5,097 ....
Orizaba, 69,706 ....
Otuma de Gómez Farías, 1,701 ....
Oxkutzcab, 6,252 ....
Ozuluama, 1,833 ....
Ozumba, 5,305 ....
Pachuca, 64,571 ....
Padilla, 2,898 ....
Palenque, 942 ....
Palizada, 2,333 ....
Palmar de Bravo, 1,584 ....
Palmillas, 1,165 ....
Pánuco, 8,818 ....
Papantla de Olarte, 18,865 ....
Paraíso, 4,094 ....
Parral, 41,474 ....
Parras, 19,768 ....
Pátzcuaro, 14,324 ....
Pedro Antonio Santos, 76 ....
Pedro Montoya, 4,844 ....
Pénjamo, 11,429 ....
Peñón Blanco, 3,277 ....

MEXICO

AREA 760,373 sq. mi.
POPULATION 40,913,000
CAPITAL Mexico City
LARGEST CITY Mexico City 3,118,059
HIGHEST POINT Citlaltépetl 18,700 ft.
MONETARY UNIT Mexican peso
MAJOR LANGUAGE Spanish
MAJOR RELIGION Roman Catholic

States Indicated by Numbers

1	Tlaxcala	6 Querétaro
2	Morelos	7 Guanajuato
3	Distrito Federal	8 Aguascalientes
4	México	9 Nayarit
5	Hidalgo	10 Colima

Mexico

(continued)

AGRICULTURE, INDUSTRY and RESOURCES

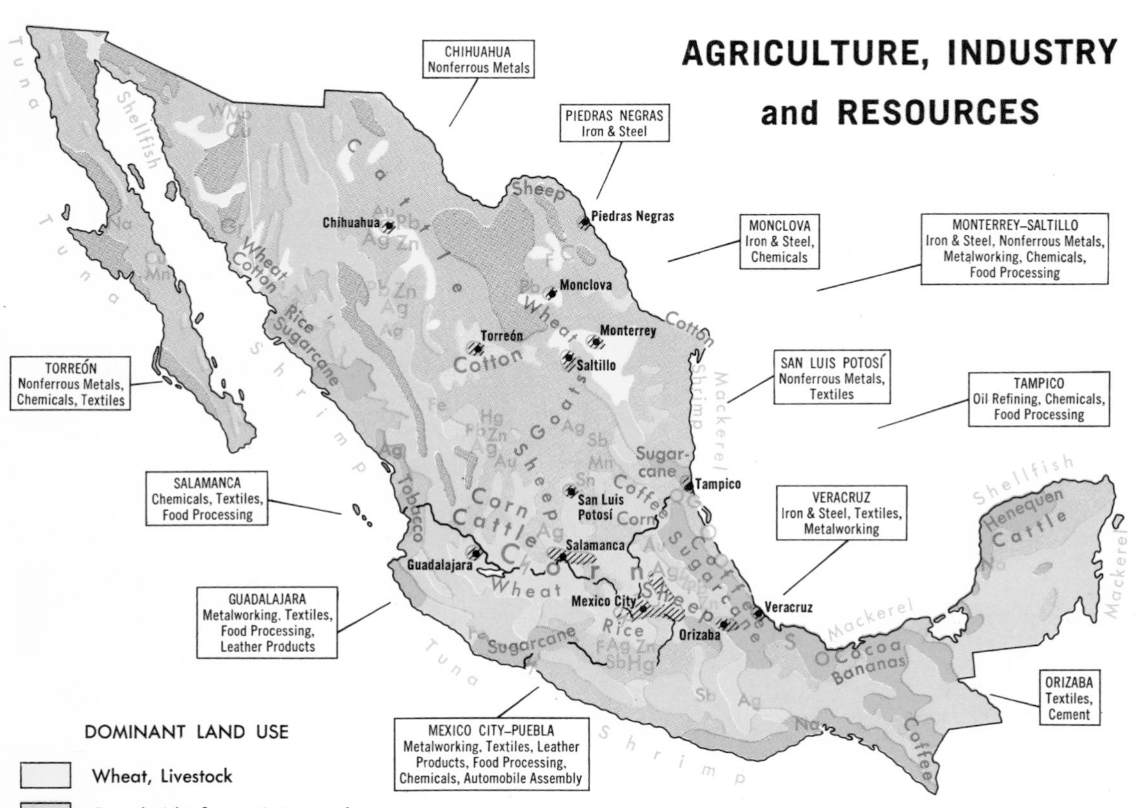

CHIHUAHUA
Nonferrous Metals

PIEDRAS NEGRAS
Iron & Steel

MONCLOVA
Iron & Steel,
Chemicals

MONTERREY-SALTILLO
Iron & Steel, Nonferrous Metals,
Metalworking, Chemicals,
Food Processing

TORREÓN
Nonferrous Metals,
Chemicals, Textiles

SAN LUIS POTOSÍ
Nonferrous Metals,
Textiles

TAMPICO
Oil Refining, Chemicals,
Food Processing

SALAMANCA
Chemicals, Textiles,
Food Processing

VERACRUZ
Iron & Steel, Textiles,
Metalworking

GUADALAJARA
Metalworking, Textiles,
Food Processing,
Leather Products

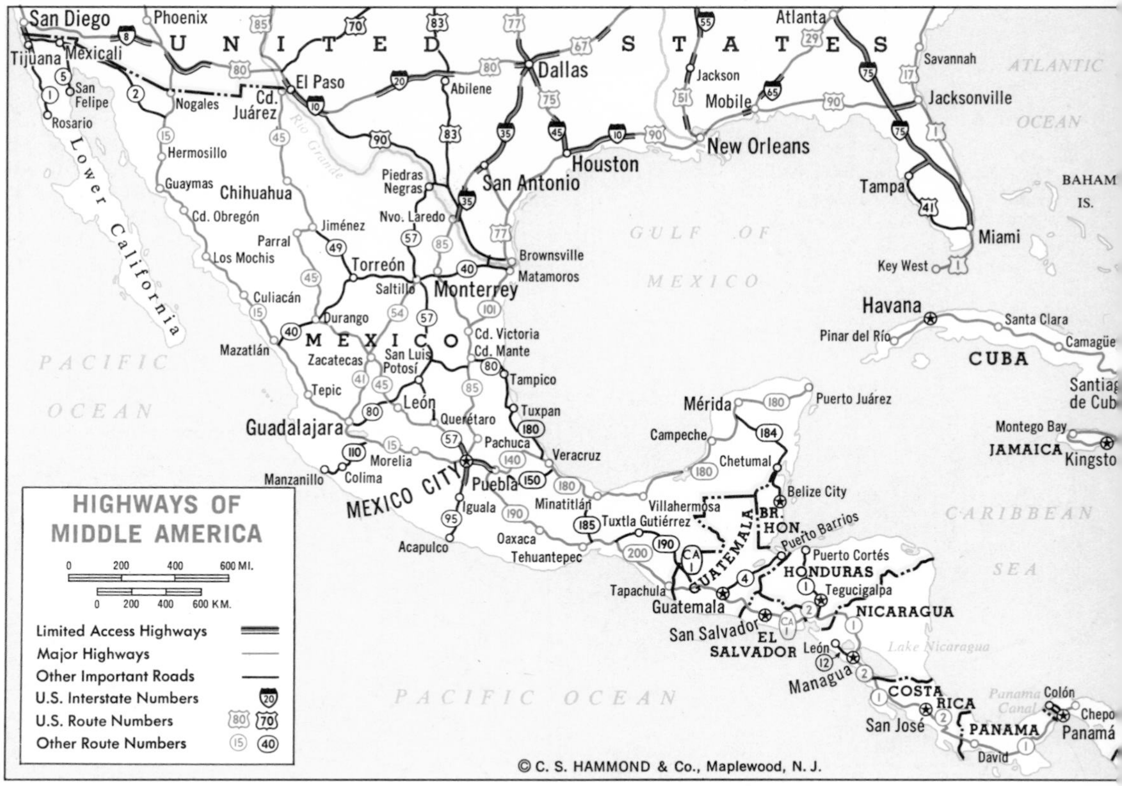

MEXICO CITY–PUEBLA
Metalworking, Textiles, Leather
Products, Food Processing,
Chemicals, Automobile Assembly

ORIZABA
Textiles, Cement

DOMINANT LAND USE

- Wheat, Livestock
- Cereals (chiefly corn), Livestock
- Diversified Tropical Cash Crops
- Cotton, Mixed Cereals
- Livestock, Limited Agriculture
- Range Livestock
- Forests
- Nonagricultural Land

⚡ Water Power
▨ Major Industrial Areas

MAJOR MINERAL OCCURRENCES

Ag	Silver	G	Natural Gas	O	Petroleum
Au	Gold	Gr	Graphite	Pb	Lead
C	Coal	Hg	Mercury	S	Sulfur
Cu	Copper	Mn	Manganese	Sb	Antimony
F	Fluorspar	Mo	Molybdenum	Sn	Tin
Fe	Iron Ore	Na	Salt	W	Tungsten
				Zn	Zinc

HIGHWAYS OF MIDDLE AMERICA

0   200   400   600 MI.

0   200   400   600 KM.

Limited Access Highways
Major Highways
Other Important Roads
U.S. Interstate Numbers
U.S. Route Numbers
Other Route Numbers

© C. S. HAMMOND & Co., Maplewood, N.J.

GUATEMALA

AREA	45,452 sq. mi.
POPULATION	4,343,000
CAPITAL	Guatemala
LARGEST CITY	Guatemala 572,937
HIGHEST POINT	Tajumulco 13,814 ft.
MONETARY UNIT	quetzal
MAJOR LANGUAGES	Spanish
MAJOR RELIGIONS	Roman Catholic

BRITISH HONDURAS

	8,867 sq. mi.
	106,000
	Belize City
	Belize City (greater) 41,444
	Victoria Peak 3,681 ft.
	British Honduras dollar
	English, Spanish
	Protestant, Roman Catholic

EL SALVADOR

	8,060 sq. mi.
	2,859,000
	San Salvador
	San Salvador 281,122
	Santa Ana 7,825 ft.
	colón
	Spanish
	Roman Catholic

HONDURAS

AREA	45,000 sq. mi.
POPULATION	2,315,000
CAPITAL	Tegucigalpa
LARGEST CITY	Tegucigalpa (greater) 134,075
HIGHEST POINT	Las Minas 9,403 ft.
MONETARY UNIT	lempira
MAJOR LANGUAGES	Spanish
MAJOR RELIGIONS	Roman Catholic

NICARAGUA

	57,143 sq. mi.
	1,754,000
	Managua
	Managua (greater) 274,278
	Saslaya 5,413 ft.
	córdoba
	Spanish
	Roman Catholic

COSTA RICA

	19,238 sq. mi.
	1,467,000
	San José
	San José (greater) 322,208
	Chirripó Grande 12,467 ft.
	colón
	Spanish
	Roman Catholic

PANAMA

	28,575 sq. mi.
	1,244,000
	Panamá
	Panamá 318,536
	Vol. Chiriquí 11,410
	balboa
	Spanish
	Roman Catholic

CANAL ZONE

AREA	362 sq. mi.
POPULATION	53,900
CAPITAL	Balboa Heights

AGRICULTURE, INDUSTRY and RESOURCES

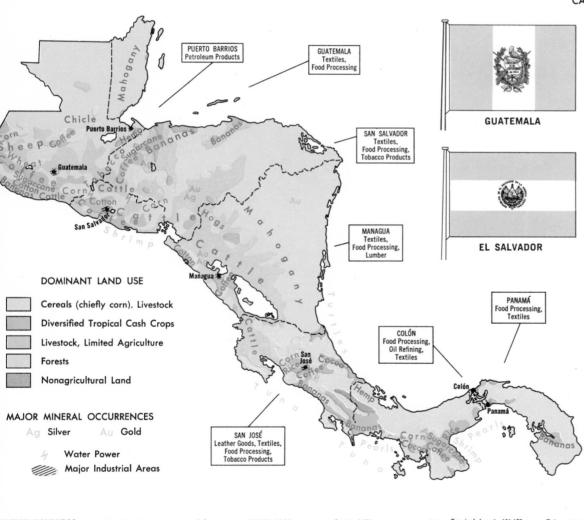

PUERTO BARRIOS
Petroleum Products

GUATEMALA
Textiles,
Food Processing

SAN SALVADOR
Textiles,
Food Processing,
Tobacco Products

MANAGUA
Textiles,
Food Processing,
Lumber

PANAMÁ
Food Processing,
Textiles

COLÓN
Food Processing,
Oil Refining,
Textiles

SAN JOSÉ
Leather Goods, Textiles,
Food Processing,
Tobacco Products

DOMINANT LAND USE

- Cereals (chiefly corn), Livestock
- Diversified Tropical Cash Crops
- Livestock, Limited Agriculture
- Forests
- Nonagricultural Land

MAJOR MINERAL OCCURRENCES

Ag Silver   Au Gold

⚡ Water Power

▨ Major Industrial Areas

GUATEMALA

EL SALVADOR

HONDURAS

NICARAGUA

COSTA RICA

PANAMA

BRITISH HONDURAS

CITIES and TOWNS

Belize City (cap.), 32,867		C 2
Belize City *41,444		C 2
Benque Viejo, 1,607		C 2
Bullyo, 1,890		C 2
Corozal, 3,171		C 1
Hill Bank, 78		C 2
Monkey River, 417		C 2
Orange Walk, 2,157		C 1
Punta Gorda, 1,789		C 3
San José, 365		C 2
San Pedro, 170		D 2
Stann Creek, 5,287		C 2

PHYSICAL FEATURES

Ambergris (cay), †572		D 1

Belize (river)		C 2
Bokel (cay)		D 2
Cockscomb (mts.)		C 2
Corker (cay), †360		D 2
Glovers (reef)		D 2
Half Moon (cay)		D 2
Hondo (river)		C 1
Honduras (gulf)		D 2
Mauger (cay)		D 2
New (river)		C 1
Saint Georges (cay), 134		D 2
Sarstún (river)		C 3
Turneffe (isl.), 99		D 2

CANAL ZONE

CITIES and TOWNS

Balboa, 3,139		H 6
Cristóbal, 817		G 6

COSTA RICA

CITIES and TOWNS

Alajuela, 19,620		E 6
Atenas, 963		E 6
Atlanta		E 5
Bagaces, 1,175		E 5
Beverly		F 6
Boruca, ‡1,049		F 6
Buenos Aires, ‡4,624		F 6
Cañas, 2,991		E 5
Carmen		F 5
Cartago, 18,084		F 6
Chomes, ‡1,991		E 5
Ciudad Quesada, 3,696		E 5
El Salvador		E 5
Esparta, 2,860		E 5
Filadelfia, 1,574		E 5
Golfito, 6,859		F 6

Grecia, 4,862		E 5
Guácimo, 5,731		F 5
Guápiles, 983		E 6
Heredia, 19,249		E 5
Las Juntas, 827		E 5
Liberia, 6,087		E 5
Limón, 19,432		F 5
Miramar, 1,122		E 5
Nicoya, 3,196		E 5
Orotina, 1,749		E 6
Palmares, 1,529		F 6
Paquera		F 6
Paraíso, 4,427		F 6
Pejivalle		F 6
Platanilla		F 6
Playa Bonita		F 5
Puerto Cortés, 1,757		F 6
Puntarenas, 19,582		E 6
Quepos, 1,858		E 6
San Ignacio, 315		E 6

San José (cap.), 101,162		F 5
San José, *322,208		F 5
San Marcos, 411		E 6
San Ramón, 6,444		E 5
Santa Cruz, 3,849		E 5
Santa Rosa, ‡1,750		E 5
Santo Domingo, 3,333		F 5
Sibube		F 6
Siquirres, 2,157		F 5
Turrialba, 8,629		F 6
Vesta		F 6

PHYSICAL FEATURES

Blanca (point)		F 5
Blanco (cape)		E 6
Blanco (mt.)		F 6
Burica (point)		F 6
Cahuita (point)		F 6
Caño (isl.)		F 6

Carreta (point)		F 6
Chirripó Grande (mt.)		F 6
Coronada (bay)		F 6
Cuilapa Miravalles (volcano)		E 5
Dulce (gulf)		F 6
Góngora (mt.)		E 6
Guionos (point)		E 6
Irazú (mt.)		F 6
Judas (point)		E 5
Llerena (point)		F 6
Matapalo (cape)		E 6
Nicoya (gulf)		E 6
Nicoya (pen.)		E 6
Papagayo (gulf)		E 5
Salinas (bay)		D 5
San Juan (river)		E, F 5
Santa Elena (cape)		D 5
Talamanca (mt. range)		F 6
Velas (cape)		D 5

EL SALVADOR

CITIES and TOWNS

Acajutla, 3,662		B 4
Ahuachapán, 13,261		B 4
Atiquizaya, 6,346		C 3
Chalatenango, 5,332		C 3
Chinameca, 5,778		C 4
Cojutepeque, 11,415		C 4
Estanzuelas, 2,083		C 4
Ilobasco, 4,716		C 4
Intipucá, 2,401		D 4
Jucuarán, 1,103		C 4
La Libertad, 4,943		C 4
La Palma, 1,464		C 3
La Unión, 11,432		D 4
Metapán, 3,435		C 3
Nueva San Salvador (Santa Tecla), 27,039		C 4

(continued on following page)

Central America

(continued)

EL SALVADOR (continued)

Puerto de la Concordia..............C 4
San Francisco Gotera,
3,668...C 4
San Miguel, 40,432.....................D 4
San Salvador (cap.),
281,122......................................C 4
San Vicente, 15,433...................C 4
Santa Ana, 72,839......................C 4
Santa Rosa de Lima,
4,618...D 4
Santa Tecla (Nueva San
Salvador), 27,039....................C 4
Sensuntepeque, 5,063................C 4
Sonsonate, 23,666......................C 4
Suchitoto, 4,447..........................C 4
Texistepeque, 1,339...................C 3

Usulután, 12,467.........................C 4
Zacatecoluca, 12,232................C 4

PHYSICAL FEATURES

Fonseca (gulf)...............................D 4
Güija (lake)...................................C 3
Lempa (river)................................C 4
Remedios (point).........................B 4
Santa Ana (mt.)...........................C 4

GUATEMALA

CITIES and TOWNS

Amatitlán, 12,225........................B 3
Antigua, 13,576...........................B 3

Asunción Mita, 6,341.................C 3
Cahabón, 939...............................C 3
Chahal, 323...................................C 3
Chajul, 4,187.................................B 3
Champerico, 3,823.......................A 3
Chichicastenango, 2,099...........B 3
Chimaltenango, 9,077.................B 3
Chinaja...B 2
Chiquimula, 14,760.....................C 3
Chisec, 812....................................B 3
Coatepeque, 13,657....................A 3
Cobán, 9,073.................................B 3
Comalapa, 9,202..........................B 3
Cuilapa, 3,657...............................B 3
Cuilco, 728.....................................B 3
Dolores, 630..................................C 2
El Cambio.......................................C 2
El Porvenir.....................................B 2
El Progreso, 3,458.......................B 3
Escuintla, 24,832.........................B 3
Flores, 1,503.................................C 2
Guatemala (cap.), 572,937.......B 3
Huehuetenango, 10,185.............B 3
Ipala, 3,190...................................C 3

Izabal...C 3
Iztapa, 751....................................B 4
Jacaltenango, 3,873...................B 3
Jalapa, 10,035.............................B 3
Jutiapa, 7,747..............................B 3
La Gomera, 1,397........................B 3
La Libertad, 770...........................B 2
Livingston, 3,026.........................B 3
Los Amates, 1,131......................C 3
Masagua, 1,100...........................B 3
Matías de Gálvez.........................C 3
Mazatenango, 19,506.................B 3
Momostenango, 3,148................B 3
Morales, 1,710.............................C 3
Nejapa..B 3
Ocós, 576......................................A 3
Panzós, 1,803...............................C 3
Puerto Barrios, 22,242...............C 3
Quezaltenango, 45,195..............B 3
Quezaltepeque, 2,578................C 3
Rabinal, 4,155..............................B 3
Retalhuleu, 14,366.....................B 3
Río Hondo, 1,300........................C 3
Sacapulas, 1,407.........................B 3
Salamá, 4,442..............................B 3
San Andrés, 939..........................B 2

San Felipe, 2,916........................B 3
San José, 5,771............................B 4
San Juan de Dios.........................B 4
San Luis, 763................................C 2
San Luis Jilotepeque, 5,795......C 3
San Marcos, 5,569......................B 3
San Martín Jilotepeque,
2,806...B 3
San Mateo Ixtatán, 2,892..........B 2
San Miguel.....................................C 2
San Pedro Carchá, 3,966...........C 3
Santa Ana, 239.............................C 2
Santa Ana Mixtán........................B 4
Santa Cruz del Quiché, 6,472....B 3
Santa Rosa de Lima, 734...........B 3
Sipacate...B 4
Sololá, 3,957.................................B 3
Tacaná, 900..................................A 3
Tejutla, 973...................................B 3
Totonicapán, 7,292.....................B 3
Yaloch...C 2
Zacapa, 11,173............................C 3

PHYSICAL FEATURES

Atitlán (lake).................................B 3

Atitlán (volcano)..........................B 3
Azul (river)....................................C 2
Chixoy (river)...............................B 3
Dulce (Izabal) (lake)..................C 3
Güija (lake)...................................C 3
Honduras (gulf)............................C 3
Izabal (lake).................................C 3
Minas (mts.).................................C 3
Motagua (river)...........................B 3
Pasión (river)...............................B 2
Petén-Itzá (lake)..........................B 2
San Pedro (river).........................B 2
Sarstún (river)..............................C 3
Tacaná (volcano).........................A 3
Tres Puntas (cape)......................C 3
Usumacinta (river)......................B 2

HONDURAS

CITIES and TOWNS

Ahuás..E 3
Amapala, 2,940............................D 4
Balana...E 3

Balfate, 451...................................D 3
Belén, 191......................................C 2
Brus Laguna, 928.........................E 3
Caratasca.......................................E 3
Catacamas, 3,873........................D 3
Cedros, 895....................................D 3
Chichicaste.....................................D 3
Choloma, 4,600............................C 3
Choluteca, 11,483.......................D 4
Colorado, 1,538............................C 3
Comayagua, 8,473.......................D 3
Comayagüela, 65,352.................D 3
Concepción de María, 481.........D 4
Concordia, 525..............................D 3
Copán, 1,837..................................C 3
Corquín, 2,458...............................C 3
Cruta..E 3
Cedros, 6,325................................
Donei..
El Dulce Nombre, 118.................
El Paraíso, Copán, 1,150............
El Paraíso, El Paraíso,
4,159...
El Porvenir, 461............................
El Progreso, 13,797.....................
El Triunfo, 1,499...........................

Central America
(continued)

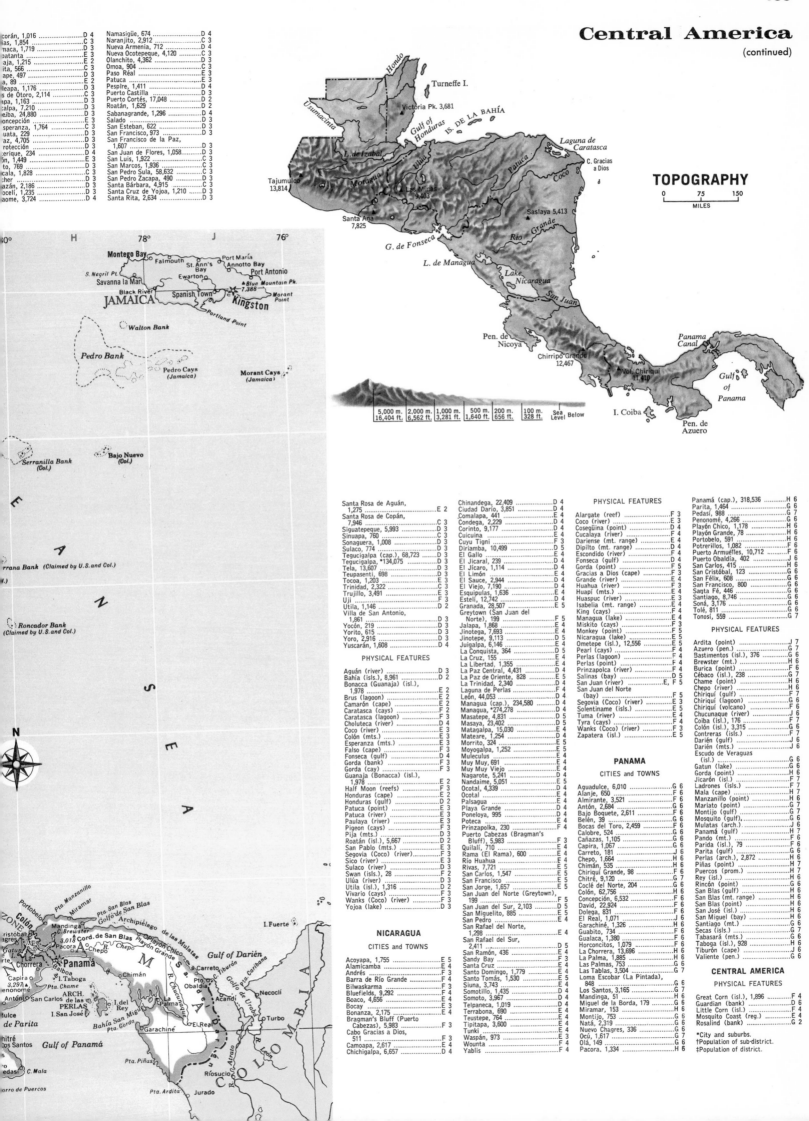

TOPOGRAPHY

0	75	150

MILES

| 5,000 m. 16,404 ft. | 2,000 m. 6,562 ft. | 1,000 m. 3,281 ft. | 500 m. 1,640 ft. | 200 m. 656 ft. | 100 m. 328 ft. | Sea Level | Below |

...corán, 1,016 .... D 4
...as, 1,854 .... C 3
...maca, 1,719 .... E 3
...patata ....
...aja, 1,215 .... D 3
...ta, 566 .... D 3
...ape, 497 .... D 3
...a, 89 .... E 2
...eapa, 1,176 .... C 3
...s de Otoro, 2,114 .... C 3
...apa, 1,163 .... D 3
...alpa, 7,210 .... D 3
...eiba, 24,880 .... D 3
...oncepción ....
...speranza, 1,764 .... C 3
...uata, 229 .... D 3
...z, 4,705 .... D 3
...rotección, 234 .... D 4
...n, 1,449 .... E 3
...to, 769 .... D 3
...cala, 1,828 .... D 3
...cher .... D 3
...azán, 2,186 .... D 3
...oceli, 1,235 .... D 3
...aome, 3,724 .... D 4

Namasigüe, 674 .... D 4
Naranjito, 2,912 .... C 3
Nueva Armenia, 712 .... D 4
Nueva Ocotepeque, 4,120 .... C 3
Olanchito, 4,362 .... D 3
Omoa, 904 .... C 2
Paso Real .... E 3
Patuca .... E 3
Pespire, 1,411 .... D 4
Puerto Castilla .... D 3
Puerto Cortés, 17,048 .... D 2
Roatán, 1,629 .... D 2
Sabanagrande, 1,296 .... D 4
Salado .... D 3
San Esteban, 622 .... D 3
San Francisco, 973 .... D 3
San Francisco de la Paz, 1,607 .... D 3
San Juan de Flores, 1,058 .... D 3
San Luis, 1,922 .... C 3
San Marcos, 1,936 .... C 3
San Pedro Sula, 58,632 .... C 3
San Pedro Zacapa, 490 .... D 3
Santa Bárbara, 4,915 .... C 3
Santa Cruz de Yojoa, 1,210 .... D 3
Santa Rita, 2,634 .... D 3

Santa Rosa de Aguán, 1,275 .... E 2
Santa Rosa de Copán, 7,946 .... C 3
Siguatepeque, 5,993 .... D 3
Sinuapa, 760 .... C 3
Sonaguera, 1,008 .... D 3
Tegucigalpa (cap.), 68,723 .... D 3
Tegucigalpa, *134,075 .... D 3
Tela, 13,607 .... D 3
Teupasenti, 698 .... D 3
Tocoa, 1,203 .... E 3
Trinidad, 2,322 .... C 3
Trujillo, 3,491 .... E 3
Uji .... F 3
Villa de San Antonio, 1,861 .... D 3
Yocón, 219 .... D 3
Yorito, 615 .... D 3
Yoro, 2,916 .... D 3
Yuscarán, 1,608 .... D 4

PHYSICAL FEATURES

Aguán (river) .... D 3
Bahía (isls.), 8,961 .... D 2
Bonacca (Guanaja) (isl.), 1,978 .... E 2
Brus (lagoon) .... E 2
Camarón (cape) .... E 2
Caratasca (cays) .... F 2
Caratasca (lagoon) .... F 2
Choluteca (river) .... D 4
Coco (river) .... E 3
Colón (mts.) .... E 3
Esperanza (mts.) .... E 3
Falso (cape) .... F 3
Fonseca (gulf) .... D 4
Gorda (bank) .... F 3
Gorda (cay) .... F 3
Guanaja (Bonacca) (isl.), 1,978 .... E 2
Half Moon (reefs) .... F 3
Honduras (cape) .... E 3
Honduras (gulf) .... D 2
Patuca (point) .... E 3
Patuca (river) .... E 3
Paulaya (river) .... E 3
Pigeon (cays) .... F 3
Pija (mts.) .... D 3
Roatán (isl.), 5,667 .... D 2
San Pablo (mts.) .... D 3
Segovia (Coco) (river) .... F 3
Sico (river) .... E 3
Sulaco (river) .... D 3
Swan (isls.), 28 .... D 2
Ulúa (river) .... D 3
Utila (isl.), 1,316 .... D 2
Vivario (cays) .... F 3
Wanks (Coco) (river) .... F 3
Yojoa (lake) .... D 3

NICARAGUA
CITIES and TOWNS

Acoyapa, 1,755 .... E 5
Alamicamba .... F 3
Andrés .... F 3
Barra de Río Grande .... F 4
Bilwaskarma .... F 3
Bluefields, 9,292 .... F 4
Boaco, 4,656 .... E 4
Bocay .... E 4
Bonanza, 2,175 .... E 4
Bragman's Bluff (Puerto Cabezas), 5,983 .... F 3
Cabo Gracias a Dios, 511 .... F 3
Camoapa, 2,617 .... E 4
Chichigalpa, 6,657 .... D 4

Chinandega, 22,409 .... D 4
Ciudad Darío, 3,851 .... D 4
Comalapa, 441 .... E 4
Condega, 2,229 .... D 4
Corinto, 9,177 .... D 4
Cuicuina .... F 3
Cuyu Tigni .... F 3
Diriamba, 10,499 .... D 5
El Gallo .... E 4
El Jicaral, 239 .... D 4
El Jícaro, 1,114 .... E 4
El Limón .... E 4
El Sauce, 2,944 .... D 4
El Viejo, 7,190 .... D 4
Esquipulas, 1,636 .... E 4
Estelí, 12,742 .... D 4
Granada, 28,507 .... E 5
Greytown (San Juan del Norte), 199 .... F 5
Jalapa, 1,868 .... E 4
Jinotega, 7,693 .... E 4
Jinotepe, 9,113 .... D 5
Juigalpa, 6,146 .... E 4
La Conquista, 364 .... D 5
La Cruz, 155 .... E 4
La Libertad, 1,355 .... E 4
La Paz Central, 4,431 .... D 4
La Paz de Oriente, 828 .... E 5
La Trinidad, 2,340 .... D 4
Laguna de Perlas .... F 4
León, 44,053 .... D 4
Managua (cap.), 234,580 .... D 4
Managua, *274,278 .... D 4
Masatepe, 4,831 .... D 5
Masaya, 23,402 .... D 5
Matagalpa, 15,030 .... E 4
Mateare, 1,254 .... D 4
Morrito, 324 .... E 5
Moyogalpa, 1,252 .... E 5
Muleculus .... E 4
Muy Muy, 691 .... E 4
Muy Muy Viejo .... E 4
Nagarote, 5,241 .... D 4
Nandaime, 5,051 .... E 5
Ocotal, 4,339 .... E 4
Ocotal .... E 4
Palsagua .... E 4
Playa Grande .... D 4
Poneloya, 995 .... D 4
Poteca .... E 4
Prinzapolka, 230 .... F 4
Puerto Cabezas (Bragman's Bluff), 5,983 .... F 3
Quilalí, 710 .... E 4
Rama (El Rama), 600 .... E 4
Río Huahua .... F 3
Rivas, 7,721 .... D 5
San Carlos, 1,547 .... E 5
San Francisco .... E 5
San Jorge, 1,657 .... E 5
San Juan del Norte (Greytown), 199 .... F 5
San Juan del Sur, 2,103 .... D 5
San Miguelito, 885 .... E 5
San Pedro .... E 4
San Rafael del Norte, 1,298 .... E 4
San Rafael del Sur, 2,411 .... D 5
San Ramón, 436 .... E 4
Sandy Bay .... F 3
Santa Cruz .... E 4
Santo Domingo, 1,779 .... E 4
Santo Tomás, 1,530 .... E 4
Siuna, 3,743 .... E 4
Somotillo, 1,435 .... D 4
Somoto, 3,967 .... D 4
Telpaneca, 1,019 .... D 4
Terrabona, 690 .... E 4
Teustepe, 764 .... E 4
Tipitapa, 3,600 .... D 4
Tunki .... E 4
Waspán, 973 .... F 3
Wounta .... F 4
Yablis .... F 4

PHYSICAL FEATURES

Alargate (reef) .... F 3
Coco (river) .... E 3
Coseguina (point) .... D 4
Cucalaya (river) .... F 4
Dariense (mt. range) .... E 4
Dipilto (mt. range) .... D 4
Escondido (river) .... F 4
Fonseca (gulf) .... D 4
Gorda (point) .... F 5
Gracias a Dios (cape) .... F 3
Grande (river) .... E 4
Huahua (river) .... F 3
Huapí (mts.) .... E 5
Huaspuc (river) .... E 3
Isabelia (mt. range) .... E 4
King (cays) .... F 4
Managua (lake) .... D 4
Miskito (cays) .... F 3
Monkey (point) .... F 5
Nicaragua (lake) .... E 5
Ometepe (isl.), 12,556 .... E 5
Pearl (cays) .... F 4
Perlas (lagoon) .... F 4
Perlas (point) .... F 4
Prinzapolca (river) .... F 4
Salinas (bay) .... D 5
San Juan (river) .... E, F 5
San Juan del Norte (bay) .... F 5
Segovia (Coco) (river) .... E 3
Solentiname (isls.) .... E 5
Tuma (river) .... E 4
Tyra (cays) .... F 4
Wanks (Coco) (river) .... F 3
Zapatera (isl.) .... E 5

PANAMA
CITIES and TOWNS

Aguadulce, 6,010 .... G 6
Alanje, 650 .... F 6
Almirante, 3,521 .... F 6
Antón, 2,684 .... G 6
Bajo Boquete, 2,611 .... F 6
Belén, 39 .... F 6
Bocas del Toro, 2,459 .... F 6
Calobre, 524 .... G 6
Cañazas, 1,105 .... G 6
Capira, 1,067 .... G 6
Carreto, 181 .... J 6
Chepo, 1,664 .... H 6
Chimán, 535 .... H 6
Chiriquí Grande, 98 .... F 6
Chitré, 9,120 .... G 6
Coclé del Norte, 204 .... G 6
Colón, 62,756 .... H 6
Concepción, 6,532 .... F 6
David, 22,924 .... F 6
Dolega, 831 .... F 6
El Real, 1,071 .... J 6
Garachiné, 1,326 .... H 6
Guabito, 734 .... F 6
Gualaca, 1,380 .... F 6
Horconcitos, 1,079 .... F 6
La Chorrera, 13,696 .... H 6
La Palma, 1,885 .... H 6
Las Tablas, 3,504 .... G 7
Loma Escobar (La Pintada), 848 .... G 6
Los Santos, 3,165 .... G 7
Mandinga, 51 .... H 6
Miguel de la Borda, 179 .... G 6
Miramar, 153 .... G 6
Montijo, 753 .... G 6
Natá, 2,319 .... G 6
Nuevo Chagres, 336 .... G 6
Ocú, 1,617 .... G 7
Olá, 149 .... G 6
Pacora, 1,334 .... H 6

Panamá (cap.), 318,536 .... H 6
Parita, 1,464 .... G 6
Pedasí, 988 .... G 7
Penonomé, 4,266 .... G 6
Playón Chico, 1,178 .... H 6
Playón Grande, 78 .... H 6
Portobelo, 591 .... H 6
Potrerillos, 1,082 .... F 6
Puerto Armuelles, 10,712 .... F 6
Puerto Obaldía, 402 .... J 6
San Carlos, 415 .... H 6
San Cristóbal, 123 .... G 6
San Félix, 608 .... G 6
San Francisco, 800 .... G 6
Santa Fé, 446 .... G 6
Santiago, 8,746 .... G 6
Soná, 3,176 .... G 6
Tolé, 811 .... G 6
Tonosí, 559 .... G 7

PHYSICAL FEATURES

Ardita (point) .... J 7
Azuero (pen.) .... G 7
Bastimentos (isl.), 376 .... F 6
Brewster (mt.) .... H 6
Burica (point) .... F 6
Cébaco (isl.), 238 .... G 7
Chame (point) .... H 6
Chepo (river) .... H 6
Chiriquí (gulf) .... F 7
Chiriquí (lagoon) .... G 6
Chiriquí (volcano) .... F 6
Chucunaque (river) .... J 6
Coiba (isl.), 176 .... F 7
Colón (isl.), 3,315 .... F 6
Contreras (isls.) .... F 7
Darién (gulf) .... J 6
Darién (mts.) .... J 6
Escudo de Veraguas (isl.) .... G 6
Gatún (lake) .... H 6
Gorda (point) .... H 6
Jicarón (isl.) .... F 7
Ladrones (isls.) .... F 7
Mala (cape) .... G 7
Manzanillo (point) .... H 6
Mariato (point) .... G 7
Montijo (gulf) .... G 7
Mosquito (gulf) .... G 6
Mulatas (arch.) .... H 6
Panamá (gulf) .... H 7
Pando (mt.) .... F 6
Parida (isl.), 79 .... F 6
Parita (gulf) .... G 6
Perlas (arch.), 2,872 .... H 6
Piñas (point) .... H 7
Puercos (prom.) .... G 7
Rey (isl.) .... H 6
Rincón (point) .... G 6
San Blas (isl.) .... H 6
San Blas (mt. range) .... H 6
San José (isl.) .... H 6
San Miguel (bay) .... H 6
Santiago (mt.) .... G 7
Secas (isls.) .... G 7
Tabasará (mts.) .... G 6
Taboga (isl.), 928 .... H 6
Tiburón (cape) .... J 6
Valiente (pen.) .... G 6

CENTRAL AMERICA
PHYSICAL FEATURES

Great Corn (isl.), 1,896 .... F 4
Guardian (isl.) .... F 4
Little Corn (isl.) .... F 4
Mosquito Coast (reg.) .... E 4
Rosalind (bank) .... G 2

*City and suburbs.
†Population of sub-district.
‡Population of district.

West Indies

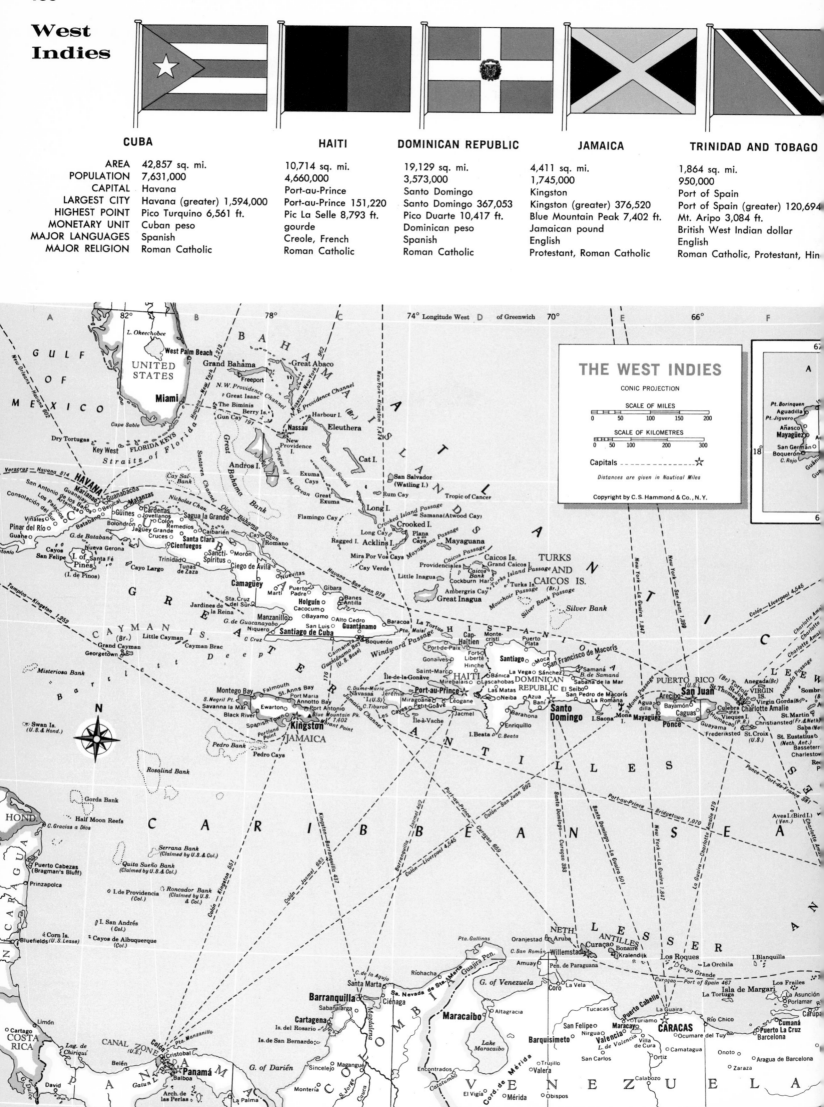

	CUBA	HAITI	DOMINICAN REPUBLIC	JAMAICA	TRINIDAD AND TOBAGO
AREA	42,857 sq. mi.	10,714 sq. mi.	19,129 sq. mi.	4,411 sq. mi.	1,864 sq. mi.
POPULATION	7,631,000	4,660,000	3,573,000	1,745,000	950,000
CAPITAL	Havana	Port-au-Prince	Santo Domingo	Kingston	Port of Spain
LARGEST CITY	Havana (greater) 1,594,000	Port-au-Prince 151,220	Santo Domingo 367,053	Kingston (greater) 376,520	Port of Spain (greater) 120,694
HIGHEST POINT	Pico Turquino 6,561 ft.	Pic La Selle 8,793 ft.	Pico Duarte 10,417 ft.	Blue Mountain Peak 7,402 ft.	Mt. Aripo 3,084 ft.
MONETARY UNIT	Cuban peso	gourde	Dominican peso	Jamaican pound	British West Indian dollar
MAJOR LANGUAGES	Spanish	Creole, French	Spanish	English	English
MAJOR RELIGION	Roman Catholic	Roman Catholic	Roman Catholic	Protestant, Roman Catholic	Roman Catholic, Protestant, Hin

WEST INDIES

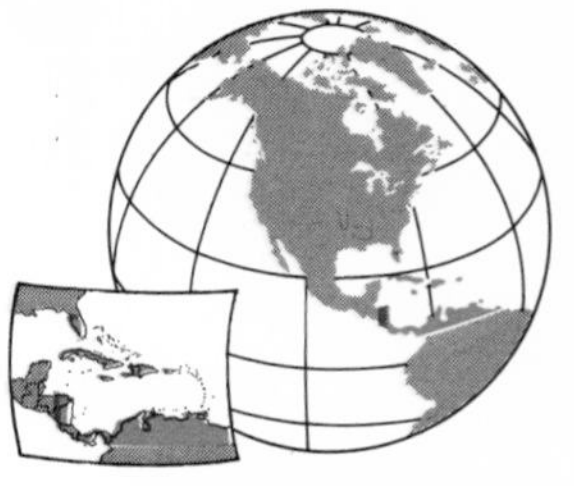

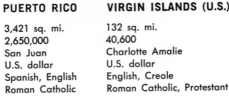

	BERMUDA	BAHAMA ISLANDS	PUERTO RICO	VIRGIN ISLANDS (U.S.)
AREA	21 sq. mi.	4,404 sq. mi.	3,421 sq. mi.	132 sq. mi.
POPULATION	49,000	133,000	2,650,000	40,600
CAPITAL	Hamilton	Nassau	San Juan	Charlotte Amalie
MONETARY UNIT	Bermuda pound	Bahaman dollar	U.S. dollar	U.S. dollar
MAJOR LANGUAGES	English	English	Spanish, English	English, Creole
MAJOR RELIGIONS	Protestant	Roman Catholic, Protestant	Roman Catholic	Roman Catholic, Protestant

	VIRGIN ISLANDS (BRITISH)	NETHERLANDS ANTILLES
AREA	58 sq. mi.	383 sq. mi.
POPULATION	8,000	207,000
CAPITAL	Road Town	Willemstad
MONETARY UNIT	British West Indian dollar	Antilles guilder
MAJOR LANGUAGES	English, Creole	Dutch, Spanish, English
MAJOR RELIGIONS	Protestant	Roman Catholic, Protestant

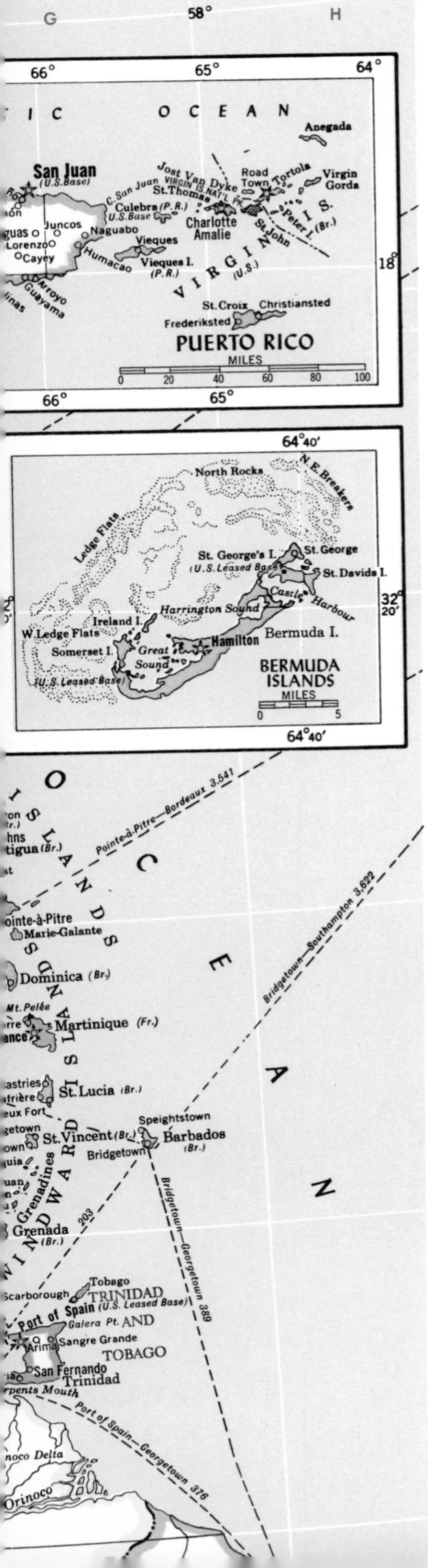

OCEAN
Anegada
San Juan (U.S. Base)
Jost Van Dyke
Road Town
Tortola
Virgin Gorda
St. Thomas
Culebra (P.R.)
Charlotte Amalie
St. John
Juncos
Naguabo
Vieques
Humacao
Vieques I. (P.R.)
VIRGIN IS. (U.S.)
St. Croix
Christiansted
Frederiksted
PUERTO RICO
MILES
North Rocks
N.E. Breakers
Ledge Flats
St. George's I. (U.S. Leased Base)
St. George
St. Davids I.
Castle Harbour
Harrington Sound
Ireland I.
W. Ledge Flats
Great Sound
Hamilton
Bermuda I.
Somerset I.
(U.S. Leased Base)
BERMUDA ISLANDS
MILES
Pointe-à-Pitre—Bordeaux 3,541
Bridgetown—Southampton 3,622
Bridgetown—Georgetown 389
Port of Spain—Georgetown 376
Pointe-à-Pitre
Marie-Galante
Dominica (Br.)
Mt. Pelée
Martinique (Fr.)
St. Lucia (Br.)
Speightstown
St. Vincent (Br.)
Barbados (Br.)
Bridgetown
Grenada (Br.)
Tobago
Scarborough
TRINIDAD (U.S. Leased Base)
Port of Spain
Galera Pt.
AND TOBAGO
Arima
Sangre Grande
San Fernando
Trinidad
Orinoco Delta
Orinoco

ANTIGUA

Antigua (isl.), 54,304 ....G 3
Barbuda (isl.), 1,145 ....G 3
Codrington, 1,145 ....G 3
Falmouth, 239 ....F 3
Redonda (isl.) ....F 3
Saint Johns (cap.), 21,396.........G 3

BAHAMA ISLANDS

Acklins (isl.), 1,235 ....C 2
Andros (isl.), 7,560 ....B 1
Atwood (Samana) (cay) ....D 2
Berry (isls.), 266 ....B 1
Biminis, The (isls.), 1,699..........B 1
Cat (isl.), 3,146 ....C 1
Cay Sal (bank) ....B 2
Crooked (isl.), 794 ....D 2
Crooked Island (passage) ....C 2
Eleuthera (isl.), 7,283 ....C 1
Exuma (cays) ....C 1
Exuma (Great Exuma) (isl.), 3,441 ....C 2
Exuma (sound) ....C 1
Flamingo (cay) ....C 2
Grand Bahama (isl.), 8,454.........B 1
Great Abaco (isl.), 6,514 ....C 1
Great Bahama (bank) ....B 1
Great Exuma (isl.), 3,441 ....C 2
Great Inagua (isl.), 1,275 ....D 2
Great Isaac (isl.) ....B 1
Gun (cay) ....B 1
Harbour (isl.), 1,005 ....C 1
Little Inagua (isl.) ....D 2
Long (cay), 34 ....C 2
Long (isl.), 4,177 ....C 2
Mayaguana (isl.), 708 ....D 2
Mayaguana (pasage) ....D 2
Mira Por Vos (cays) ....C 2
Nassau (cap.), 81,591 ....C 1
New Providence (isl.), 81,591......C 1
North East Providence (chan.)...C 1
North West Providence (chan.)...B 1
Plana (cays) ....D 2
Ragged (isl.), 389 ....C 2
Rum (cay), 81 ....C 2
Samana (cay) ....D 2
San Salvador (isl.), 971 ....C 1
Santaren (chan.) ....B 1
Tongue of the Ocean (chan.)......C 1
Verde (cay) ....C 2
Watling (San Salvador) (isl.), 971 ....C 1

BARBADOS

Bridgetown (cap.), 11,452 ....G 4
Speightstown, 2,415 ....G 4

BERMUDA

CITIES and TOWNS

Hamilton (cap.), 2,800 ....H 3
Hamilton, *14,156 ....H 3
Saint George, 1,335 ....H 2

PHYSICAL FEATURES

Bermuda (isl.) ....H 3
Castle (harb.) ....H 2
Great (sound) ....G 3
Harrington (sound) ....G 3
Ireland (isl.) ....G 3
Ledge Flats ....G 2
North East Breakers ....H 2
North Rocks ....H 2
Saint Davids (isl.) ....H 2
Saint George's (isl.) ....H 2
Somerset (isl.) ....G 3
West Ledge Flats ....G 3

CAYMAN ISLANDS

Total Population 9,000

Cayman Brac (isl.), 1,240 ....B 3
Georgetown (cap.), 2,573 ....B 3
Grand Cayman (isl.), 6,359 ....B 3
Little Cayman (isl.), 23 ....B 3

CUBA

CITIES and TOWNS

Alto Cedro, 679 ....C 2
Antilla, 6,481 ....C 2
Artemisa, 23,200 ....A 2
Banes, 28,200 ....C 2
Baracoa, 11,459 ....C 2
Batabanó, 5,075 ....A 2
Bayamo, 37,200 ....C 2
Bejucal, 9,582 ....A 2
Bolondrón, 3,444 ....B 2
Boquerón ....C 3
Cacocum, 2,724 ....C 2
Caibarién, 22,900 ....B 2
Caimanera, 5,647 ....C 3
Camagüey, 157,700 ....B 2
Cárdenas, 44,000 ....B 2
Ciego de Ávila, 47,500 ....B 2
Cienfuegos, 72,200 ....B 2
Colón, 15,755 ....B 2
Consolación del Sur, 6,146 ....A 2
Cruces, 10,704 ....B 2
Gibara, 8,144 ....C 2
Guanabacoa, 32,490 ....B 2
Guanajay, 12,908 ....A 2
Guane, 4,070 ....A 2
Guantánamo, 87,200 ....C 2
Güines, 35,300 ....B 2
Havana (cap.), 940,100 ....A 2
Havana, *1,594,000 ....A 2
Holguín, 82,200 ....C 2
Jagüey Grande, 5,244 ....B 2
Jovellanos, 10,444 ....B 2
Los Palacios, 5,210 ....A 2
Manzanillo, 50,900 ....C 2
Marianao, †315,600 ....A 2
Martí, 2,605 ....C 2
Matanzas, 79,900 ....B 2
Morón, 18,629 ....B 2
Niquero, 7,204 ....C 2
Nueva Gerona, 3,203 ....A 2
Nuevitas 12,300 ....C 2
Pinar del Río, 50,600 ....A 2
Puerto Padre, 9,705 ....C 2
Remedios, 10,602 ....B 2
Sagua la Grande, 30,400 ....B 2
San Antonio de los Baños, 22,200 ....A 2
San Luis, 11,110 ....C 2
Sancti-Spíritus, 55,000 ....B 2
Santa Clara, 101,900 ....B 2
Santa Cruz del Sur, 2,781 ....B 2
Santa Fé, 5,370 ....A 2
Santiago de Cuba, 213,400 ....B 2
Trinidad, 22,600 ....B 2
Tunas de Zaza, 1,380 ....B 2
Viñales, 1,602 ....A 2

PHYSICAL FEATURES

Batabanó (gulf) ....A 2
Cruz (cape) ....C 3
Florida (straits) ....B 1
Guacanayabo (gulf) ....C 2
Jardines de la Reina (isls.)........B 2
Largo (cay) ....B 2
Maisí (point) ....D 2
Nicolas (chan.) ....B 2
Pines (Pinos) (isl.), 11,000........A 2
Romano (cay) ....C 2
San Antonio (cape) ....A 2
San Felipe (cay), 391 ....A 2

DOMINICA

Portsmouth, 2,238 ....G 4
Roseau (cap.), 10,417 ....G 4
Roseau, *13,883 ....G 4

DOMINICAN REPUBLIC

CITIES and TOWNS

Azua, 12,350 ....D 3
Baní, 14,472 ....D 3
Bánica, 633 ....D 3
Barahona, 20,398 ....D 3
Ciudad Trujillo (Santo Domingo) (cap.), 367,053 ....E 3
Enriquillo, 3,485 ....D 3
La Romana, 24,058 ....E 3
La Vega, 19,884 ....D 3
Las Matas de Farfán, 3,585 ....D 3
Moca, 13,829 ....D 3
Monte Cristi, 5,912 ....D 2
Neiba, 7,322 ....D 3
Puerto Plata, 19,073 ....D 3
Sabana de la Mar, 4,032..............E 3
Samaná, 3,309 ....E 3
San Francisco de Macorís, 26,000 ....E 3
San Pedro de Macorís, 22,935.....E 3
Sánchez, 4,587 ....E 3
Santiago de los Caballeros, 83,523 ....D 3
Santo Domingo (cap.), 367,053...E 3
Seibo, 4,621 ....E 3

PHYSICAL FEATURES

Beata (cape) ....D 3
Beata (isl.) ....D 3
Samaná (bay) ....E 3
Saona (isl.), 409 ....E 3

GRENADA

Carriacou (isl.), 6,958 ....G 4
Gouyave, 2,356 ....F 4
Saint George's (cap.), 7,303 ......F 5
Saint George's, *26,843 ....F 5

GUADELOUPE

Basse-Terre (cap.), 12,317 ....F 4
Marie-Galante (isl.), 16,341 ......G 4
Pointe-à-Pitre, 27,737 ....G 3
Port-Louis, 4,057 ....G 3
Saint-Barthélémy (isl.), 2,176.....F 3
Saint-Martin (isl.), 4,502 ....F 3

HAITI

CITIES and TOWNS

Cap-Haïtien, 27,538 ....D 3
Fort-Liberté, 1,637 ....D 3
Gonaïves, 15,373 ....D 3
Hinche, 5,847 ....D 3
Jacmel, 9,397 ....D 3
Jérémie, 12,456 ....C 3
Lascahobas, 2,356 ....D 3
Léogane, 3,922 ....D 3
Les Cayes, 13,088 ....C 3
Miragoâne, 2,711 ....D 3
Mirebalais, 1,995 ....D 3
Petit-Goâve, 5,847 ....D 3
Port-au-Prince (cap.), 151,220....D 3
Port-de-Paix, 6,964 ....D 3
Saint-Marc, 10,222 ....D 3

PHYSICAL FEATURES

Dame-Marie (cape) ....C 3
Gonâve (isl.), 26,860 ....D 3
Tiburon (cape) ....C 3
Tortue, La (Tortuga) (isl.), 12,501 ....D 2
Vache (isl.), 3,463 ....D 3

JAMAICA

CITIES and TOWNS

Annotto Bay, 3,559 ....C 3
Black River, 3,077 ....B 3
Falmouth, 3,727 ....C 3
Ewarton ....C 3
Kingston (cap.), 123,403 ....C 3
Kingston, *376,520 ....C 3
Montego Bay, 23,610 ....B 3
Port Antonio, 7,830 ....C 3
Port Maria, 3,998 ....C 3
Saint Anns Bay, 5,087 ....C 3
Savanna la Mar, 9,789 ....B 3
Spanish Town, 14,706 ....C 3

PHYSICAL FEATURES

Blue Mountain (peak)...................C 3
Morant (point) ....C 3
Pedro (bank) ....B 3
Pedro (cays) ....C 3
Portland (point) ....C 3
South Negril (point) ....B 3

MARTINIQUE

Fort-de-France (cap.), 74,673 ....G 4
Pelée (vol.) ....G 4
Saint-Pierre, 5,434 ....G 4

MONTSERRAT

Total Population 13,000

Plymouth (cap.), 1,911 ....F 3

NETHERLANDS ANTILLES

Aruba (isl.), 58,506 ....E 4
Bonaire (isl.), 6,086 ....E 4
Curaçao (isl.), 129,676 ....E 4
Kralendijk, 839 ....E 4
Oranjestad, 15,398 ....D 4
Saba (isl.), 1,020 ....F 3
Saint Eustatius (isl.), 1,069 ....F 3
Saint Maarten (Saint Martin) (isl.). 3,250 ....F 3
Willemstad (cap.), 43,547 ....E 4
Willemstad, *94,133 ....E 4

PUERTO RICO

CITIES and TOWNS

Adjuntas, 5,318 ....F 1
Aguadilla, 15,943 ....F 1
Añasco, 2,068 ....F 1
Arecibo, 28,828 ....G 1
Arroyo, 3,741 ....G 1
Bayamón, 15,109 ....G 1
Boquerón, †2,580 ....F 1
Caguas, 32,015 ....G 1
Camuy, 2,341 ....F 1
Cataño, 8,276 ....G 1
Cayey, 19,738 ....G 1
Coamo, 12,146 ....G 1
Guanica, 4,100 ....F 1
Guayama, 19,183 ....G 1
Guayanilla, 3,067 ....F 5
Humacao, 8,005 ....G 1
Isabela, 7,302 ....F 1
Jayuya, 2,344 ....G 1
Juncos, 6,247 ....G 1
Lares, 4,216 ....F 1
Manatí, 9,682 ....G 1
Mayagüez, 50,147 ....F 1
Naguabo, 3,396 ....G 1
Ponce, 114,286 ....F 1
Salinas, 3,666 ....G 1
San Germán, 7,790 ....F 1
San Juan (cap.), 432,377 ....G 1
San Juan, *542,156 ....G 1
San Lorenzo, 5,551 ....G 1
Utuado, 9,870 ....F 1
Vieques, 2,487 ....G 1
Yauco, 8,996 ....F 1

PHYSICAL FEATURES

Borinquen (point) ....F 1
Culebra (isl.), 573 ....G 1
Jiguero (point) ....F 1
Mona (isl.) ....E 3
Rojo (cape) ....F 1
San Juan (cape) ....G 1
Vieques (isl.), 7,210 ....G 1

SAINT CHRISTOPHER, NEVIS AND ANGUILLA

Anguilla (isl.), 5,605 ....F 3
Basseterre (cap.), 15,726 ....F 3
Charlestown, 2,852 ....F 3
Nevis (isl.), 12,762 ....F 3
Saint Christopher (Saint Kitts) (isl.), 38,291 ....F 3
Sombrero (isl.), 5 ....F 3

SAINT LUCIA

Castries (cap.), 4,353 ....G 4
Castries, *15,291 ....G 4
Soufrière, 2,692 ....G 4
Vieux Fort, 3,228 ....G 4

SAINT VINCENT

Bequia (isl.), 3,148 ....G 4
Canouan (isl.), 542 ....G 4
Georgetown, 1,213 ....G 4
Kingstown (cap.), 4,308 ....G 4
Kingstown, *20,688 ....G 4
Union (isl.), 1,274 ....G 4

TRINIDAD AND TOBAGO

CITIES and TOWNS

Arima, 10,982 ....G 5
Port of Spain (cap.), 93,954 ....G 5
Port of Spain, *120,694 ....G 5

(continued on following page)

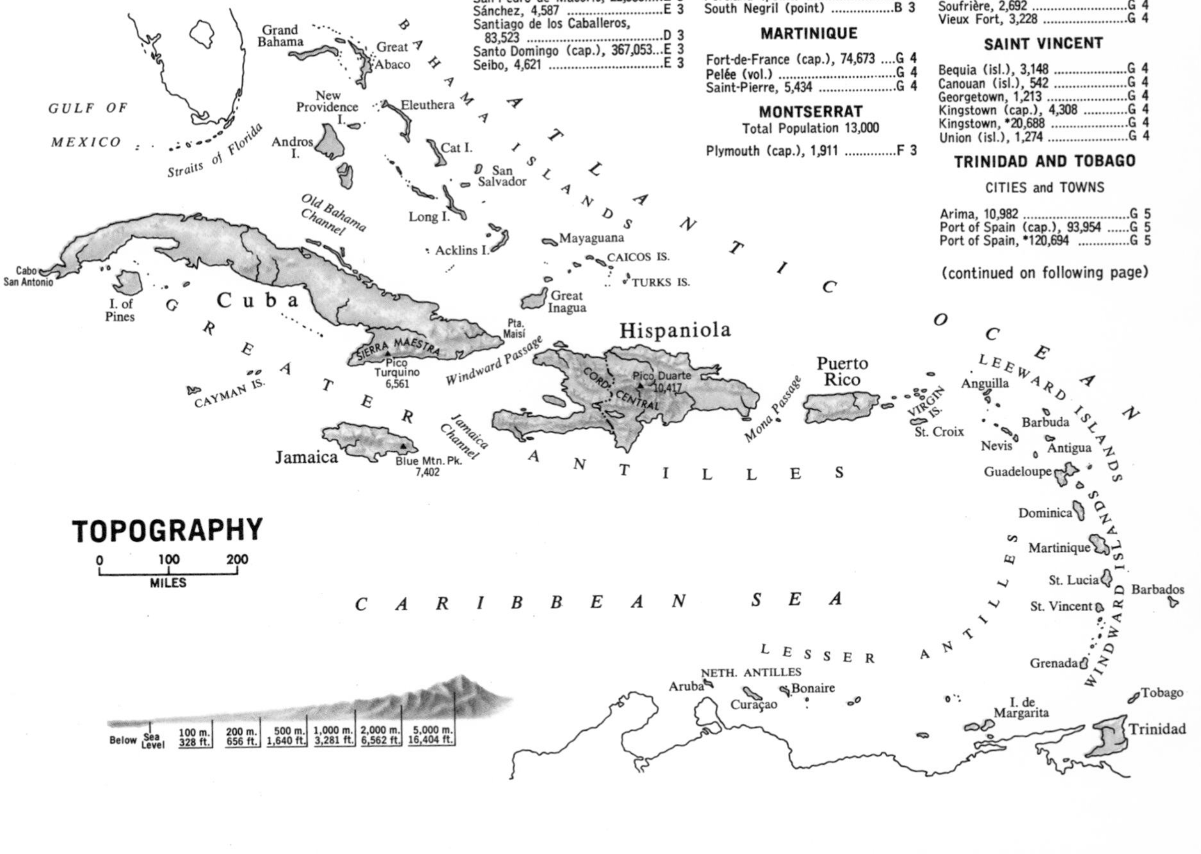

Grand Bahama
Great Abaco
BAHAMA ISLANDS
GULF OF MEXICO
Straits of Florida
New Providence I.
Eleuthera
Andros I.
Cat I.
San Salvador
Old Bahama Channel
Long I.
Acklins I.
Mayaguana
CAICOS IS.
TURKS IS.
Cabo San Antonio
I. of Pines
Cuba
Great Inagua
Pta. Maisí
SIERRA MAESTRA
Pico Turquino 6,561
Windward Passage
Hispaniola
CORD. CENTRAL
Pico Duarte 10,417
Puerto Rico
Mona Passage
VIRGIN IS.
St. Croix
CAYMAN IS.
Jamaica Channel
Jamaica
Blue Mtn. Pk. 7,402
GREATER ANTILLES
ATLANTIC OCEAN
LEEWARD ISLANDS
Anguilla
Barbuda
Nevis
Antigua
Guadeloupe
Dominica
Martinique
St. Lucia
Barbados
St. Vincent
WINDWARD ISLANDS
Grenada
CARIBBEAN SEA
LESSER ANTILLES
NETH. ANTILLES
Aruba
Curaçao
Bonaire
I. de Margarita
Tobago
Trinidad
0 100 200 MILES
Below Sea Level
100 m. 328 ft.
200 m. 656 ft.
500 m. 1,640 ft.
1,000 m. 3,281 ft.
2,000 m. 6,562 ft.
5,000 m. 16,404 ft.

TOPOGRAPHY

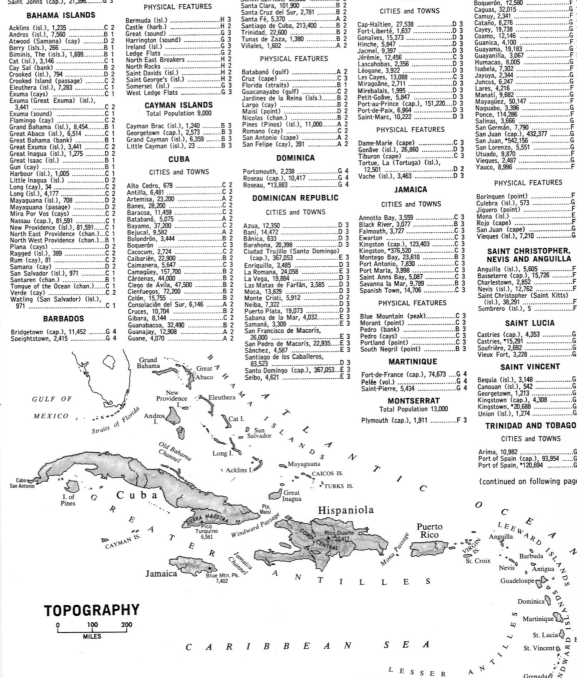

West Indies
(continued)

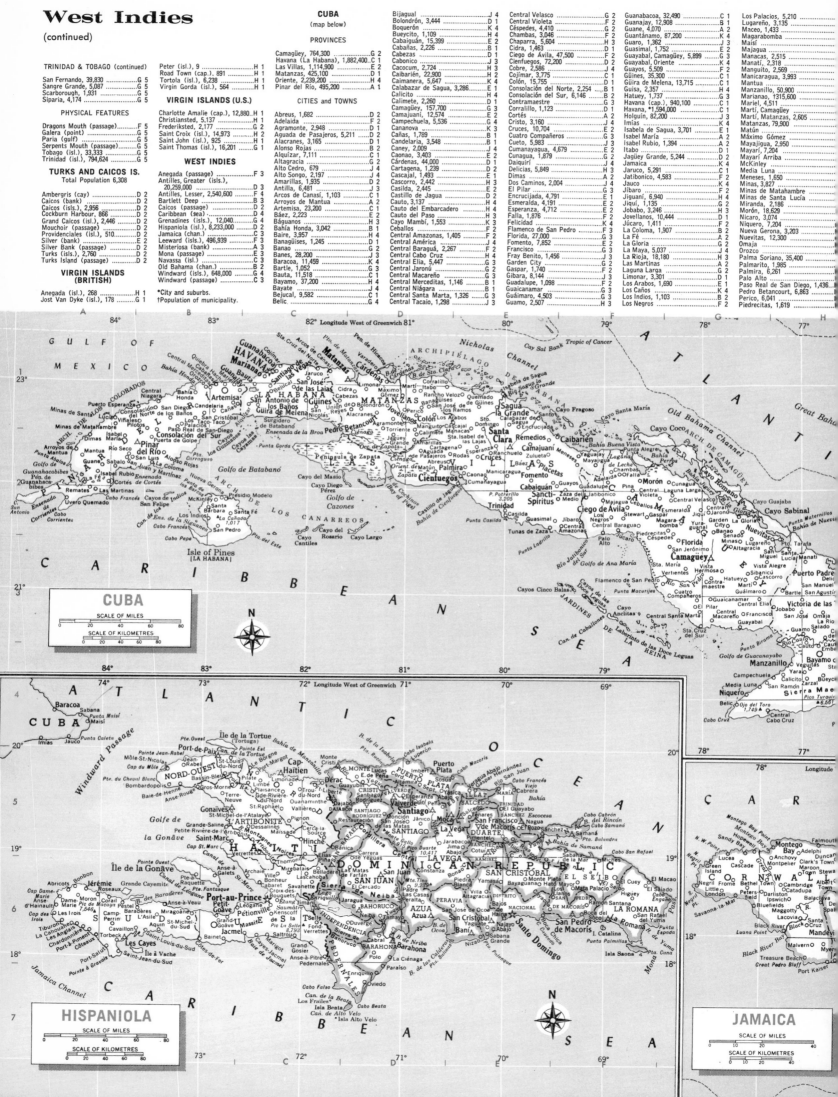

CUBA
SCALE OF MILES
0 20 40 60 80
SCALE OF KILOMETRES
0 20 40 60 80

HISPANIOLA
SCALE OF MILES
0 20 40 60 80
SCALE OF KILOMETRES
0 20 40 60 80

JAMAICA
SCALE OF MILES
0 10 20 30 40
SCALE OF KILOMETRES
0 10 20 30 40

West Indies
(continued)

…os .... B 1
… 3,667 .... F 2
… del Río, 50,600 .... B 2
…tas, 29,900 .... E 2
…dio Modelo .... C 2
…on, 3,827 .... J 3
…a de Golpe, 1,512 .... B 2
…o Esperanza, 1,867 .... A 1
…o Padre, 9,705 .... H 3
…o Samá .... J 3
…o Tarafa .... H 3
…o Vita .... J 4
…a Alegre, 4,068 .... F 2
…ado de Güines, 4,840 .... E 1
…ra Hacha, 1,584 .... B 1
…ón de las Yaguas .... J 4
…ho Veloz, 2,789 .... D 1
…huelo, 4,288 .... E 2
…tes .... A 2
…dios, 10,602 .... E 2
…Seco, 1,615 .... A 2
…s, 4,569 .... E 2
…lo .... A 2
…na .... K 4
…a de Tánamo, 7,604 .... K 3
…a la Grande, 30,400 .... E 1
…lo .... H 3
…Agustín .... H 3
…Andrés, 1,655 .... H 3
…Antonio, 1,300 .... K 4
…Antonio de los Baños, …200 .... C 1
…Cristóbal, 4,638 .... B 1
…Germán, 5,802 .... J 3
…Jerónimo .... G 3
…José de la Plata .... H 3
…José de las Lajas, 13,011 .... C 1
…José de los Ramos, 1,269 .... D 1
…Juan y Martínez, 4,865 .... B 2
…Luis, Oriente, 11,110 .... J 4
…Luis, Pinar del Río, 2,735 .... B 2
…Manuel, 2,105 .... H 3
…Miguel .... H 3
…Nicolás, 5,734 .... C 1

San Pedro .... B 2
San Ramón, 1,037 .... H 4
Sancti-Spíritus, 55,000 .... E 2
Santa Bárbara .... B 2
Santa Clara, 101,900 .... E 2
Santa Cruz del Norte, 3,537 .... C 1
Santa Cruz del Sur, 2,781 .... G 3
Santa Fé, 5,372 .... C 2
Santa Isabel de las Lajas .... E 2
Santa Lucía, Camagüey .... H 2
Santa Lucía, Oriente .... J 3
Santa María .... G 3
Santa Rita, 1,655 .... H 4
Santiago de Cuba, 213,400 .... J 4
Santiago de las Vegas, 10,974 .... C 1
Santo, 2,210 .... E 1
Santo Domingo .... E 1
Senado, 1,314 .... G 2
Sibanicú, 3,378 .... G 3
Siboney .... J 4
Stewart, 1,943 .... F 2
Surgidero de Batabanó, 5,075 .... C 1
Taco-Taco .... B 1
Tánamo, 2,032 .... J 3
Tiguabos, 1,286 .... J 4
Torriente .... D 1
Trinidad, 22,600 .... E 2
Tunas de Zaza, 1,380 .... E 2
Unión de Reyes, 5,351 .... C 1
Uvero Quemado .... A 2
Varadero, 2,640 .... D 1
Veguitas, 2,014 .... H 4
Velasco, 1,444 .... H 3
Vertientes .... G 3
Victoria de las Tunas, 28,400 .... H 3
Viñales, 1,602 .... A 1
Vista Alegre .... H 3
Vista Hermosa .... G 3
Yaguajay, 5,191 .... F 2
Yara, 3,246 .... H 4
Yuraguanal .... G 2
Zarzal, 1,421 .... H 4
Zaza del Medio, 4,252 .... F 2
Zulueta, 4,254 .... E 2

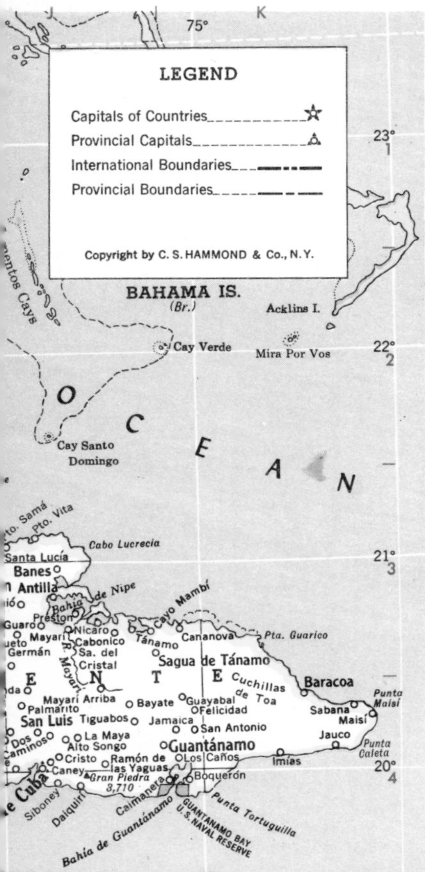

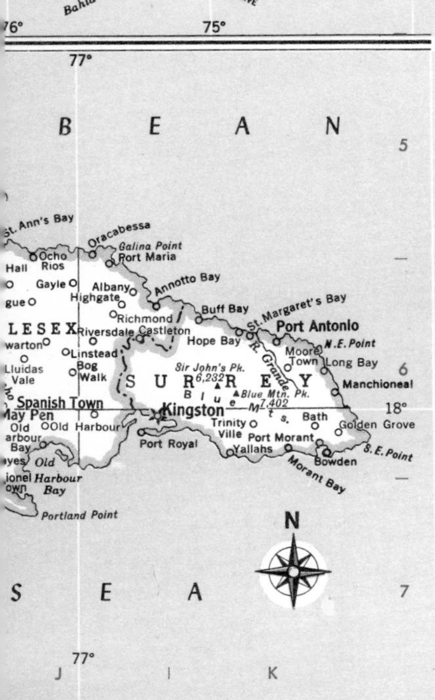

PHYSICAL FEATURES

Abalos (point) .... A 2
Ana María (gulf) .... F 3
Anclitas (cay) .... F 3
Batabanó (gulf) .... C 2
Birama (point) .... G 3
Broa (inlet) .... C 1
Buena Vista (bay) .... F 2
Caballones (chan.) .... F 3
Caleta (point) .... K 4
Camagüey (arch.) .... G 2
Cantiles (cay) .... C 3
Cárdenas (bay) .... D 1
Carraguao (point) .... B 2
Casilda (point) .... E 2
Cauto (river) .... H 3
Cayamas (cays) .... C 2
Cazones (gulf) .... C 2
Cienfuegos (bay) .... D 2
Cinco Balas (cays) .... E 3
Cochinos (bay) .... D 2
Coco (cay) .... G 1
Corrientes (cape) .... A 2
Corrientes (inlet) .... A 2
Cortés (inlet) .... B 2
Cristal, Sierra del (mts.) .... J 4
Cruz (cape) .... G 4
Diego Pérez (cay) .... C 2
Doce Leguas (cays) .... F 3
Este (point) .... C 3
Fragoso (cay) .... F 1
Francés (cape) .... A 2
Gorda (point) .... C 2
Gran Piedra (mt.) .... J 4
Guacanayabo (gulf) .... G 4
Guajaba (cay) .... H 2
Guanahacabibes (gulf) .... A 2
Guanahacabibes (pen.) .... A 2
Guantánamo (bay) .... J 4
Guantánamo Bay U.S. Naval Reserve .... J 4
Guarico (point) .... K 3
Guzmanes (cays) .... B 2
Hicacos (pen.) .... D 1
Honda (bay) .... B 1
Indios (chan.) .... B 2
Jardines de la Reina (arch.) .... F 3
Jatibonico del Sur (river) .... F 3
Jigüey (bay) .... G 2
Laberinto de las Doce Leguas (cays) .... F 3
La Cañada (mt.) .... B 2
La Gloria (bay) .... G 2
Ladrillo (point) .... E 2
Largo (cay) .... D 2
Leche (lagoon) .... F 2
Los Barcos (point) .... B 2
Los Canarreos (arch.) .... C 2
Los Colorados (arch.) .... A 1
Lucrecia (cape) .... J 3
Macurijes (point) .... F 3
Maestra, Sierra (mts.) .... H 4
Maisí (point) .... K 4
Mangle (point) .... J 3
Masio (cay) .... C 2
Matanzas (bay) .... D 1
Matanzas (point) .... H 2
Mayarí (river) .... J 4
Nicholas (chan.) .... E 1
Nipe (bay) .... J 3
Nuevitas (bay) .... H 2
Ojo del Toro (mt.) .... G 4
Old Bahama (chan.) .... G 1
Pepe (cape) .... B 1
Perros (bay) .... G 2
Pigs (Cochinos) (bay) .... D 2
Pines (isl.), 11,000 .... G 3
Potrerillo (peak) .... E 2
Romano (cay) .... G 2
Rosario (cay) .... C 2
Sabana (arch.) .... E 1
Sabinal (cay) .... H 2
Sagua la Grande (river) .... E 1
San Antonio (cape) .... A 2
San Felipe (cays) .... B 2
San Pedro (river) .... G 3
Santa Clara (bay) .... D 1
Santa María (cay) .... F 1
Siguanea (bay) .... B 2
Tabacal (point) .... H 4
Toa, Cuchillas de (mts.) .... K 4
Tortuguilla (point) .... K 4
Turquino (peak) .... H 4
Zapata (pen.) .... C 2
Zapata Occidental (swamp) .... D 2
Zapata Oriental (swamp) .... D 2

DOMINICAN REPUBLIC

PROVINCES

Azua, 75,147 .... D 6
Baoruco, 52,343 .... D 6
Barahona, 79,880 .... D 6
Dajabón, 40,822 .... D 5
Distrito Nacional, 462,192 .... E 6
Duarte, 161,326 .... E 5
Elías Piña, 43,266 .... D 5
El Seibo, 115,604 .... F 6
Espaillat, 117,126 .... E 5
Independencia, 27,475 .... D 6
La Romana, 104,987 .... F 6
La Vega, 248,069 .... D 6
María Trinidad Sánchez, 85,185 .... E 5
Monte Cristi, 59,240 .... D 5
Pedernales, 8,652 .... D 7
Peravia, 106,736 .... E 6
Puerto Plata, 163,896 .... D 5
Salcedo, 68,656 .... E 5
Samaná, 44,592 .... E 5
San Cristóbal, 249,776 .... E 6
San Juan, 148,206 .... D 6
San Pedro de Macorís, 68,953 .... F 6
Sánchez Ramírez, 93,498 .... E 5
Santiago, 287,941 .... D 5
Santiago Rodríguez, 40,399 .... D 5
Valverde, 59,558 .... D 5

CITIES and TOWNS

Altamira, 1,336 .... D 5
Azua, 12,350 .... D 6
Bajos de Haina, 4,614 .... E 6
Baní, 14,472 .... E 6
Bánica, 633 .... D 5
Barahona, 20,398 .... D 6
Bayaguana, 1,848 .... E 6
Boca Chica, 7,692 .... E 6
Boca del Soco, 7,647 .... F 6
Bonao, 12,951 .... E 6
Cabral, 4,149 .... D 6
Cabrera, 1,072 .... E 5
Carrera de Yeguas, 6,393 .... D 6
Castillo, 2,021 .... E 5
Cayacoa, 3,478 .... E 6
Ciudad Trujillo (Santo Domingo) (cap.), 367,053 .... E 6
Constanza, 3,162 .... D 6
Cotuí, 4,706 .... E 5
Dajabón, 3,230 .... D 5
Duverge, 6,701 .... D 6
El Cercado, 2,302 .... D 6
El Cuey, 6,310 .... F 6
El Guayabo, 8,684 .... E 5
El Macao .... F 6
El Pozo, 8,887 .... E 5
El Salado, 5,170 .... F 6
El Seibo, 4,621 .... F 6
Elías Piña, 2,890 .... C 6
Enriquillo, 3,485 .... D 7
Esperanza, 3,899 .... D 5
Gaspar Hernández, 1,327 .... E 5
Guayubín, 1,291 .... D 5
Hato Mayor, 5,775 .... F 6
Higüey, 10,084 .... F 6
Imbert, 2,325 .... D 5
Jánico, 986 .... D 5
Jarabacoa, 3,710 .... E 5
Jaragua, 3,828 .... D 6
Jima Abajo, 8,573 .... E 5
Jimaní, 1,503 .... C 6
La Ciénaga, 4,424 .... D 6
La Romana, 24,058 .... F 6
La Vega, 19,884 .... D 5
Las Matas de Farfán, 3,585 .... D 6
Los Llanos, 1,009 .... F 6
Lucas E. de Peña, 5,638 .... D 5
Luperón, 1,548 .... D 5
Mata Palacio, 7,148 .... F 6
Miches, 3,110 .... F 6
Moca, 13,829 .... D 5
Monción, 1,137 .... D 5
Monte Cristi, 5,912 .... C 5
Monte Plata, 2,202 .... E 6
Nagua, 9,337 .... E 5
Najayo Abajo, 3,183 .... E 6
Neiba, 7,322 .... D 6
Nizao, 2,574 .... E 6
Oviedo, 1,493 .... D 7
Padre Las Casas, 3,026 .... D 6
Paraíso, 1,665 .... D 7
Pedernales, 2,466 .... C 7
Peña, 2,286 .... D 5
Peralta, 5,521 .... D 6
Piedra Blanca, 7,984 .... E 6
Pimentel, 5,258 .... E 5
Polo, 3,470 .... D 6
Puerto Plata, 19,073 .... D 5
Ramón Santana, 936 .... F 6
Restauración, 1,369 .... D 5
Río San Juan, 1,912 .... E 5
Sabana de la Mar, 4,032 .... F 5
Sabana Grande, 2,857 .... E 6
Salcedo, 6,175 .... E 5
Samaná, 3,309 .... F 5
San Cristóbal, 15,525 .... E 6
San Francisco de Macorís, 26,000 .... E 5
San José de las Matas, 2,305 .... D 5
San José de Ocoa, 5,591 .... E 6
San Juan, 20,449 .... D 6
San Pedro de Macorís, 22,935 .... E 6
San Rafael del Yuma, 948 .... F 6
Sánchez, 4,587 .... E 5
Santiago, 83,523 .... D 5
Santo Domingo (cap.), 367,053 .... E 6
Sosua, 1,808 .... E 5
Tamao, 3,613 .... D 6
Tenares, 1,980 .... E 5
Valverde, 17,885 .... D 5
Veragua Abajo, 3,765 .... E 5
Villa Altagracia, 4,344 .... E 6
Villa Riva, 1,215 .... E 5
Yaguate, 1,440 .... E 6
Yamasá, 1,511 .... E 6
Yásica Abajo, 13,080 .... E 5

PHYSICAL FEATURES

Alto Velo (chan.) .... C 7
Alto Velo (isl.) .... D 7
Bahoruco, Sierra de (mts.) .... D 6
Balandra (point) .... F 5
Beata (cape) .... D 7
Beata (chan.) .... C 7
Beata (isl.) .... C 7
Cabrón (cape) .... F 5
Calderas (bay) .... D 6
Cana (point) .... F 6
Catalina (isl.) .... F 6
Caucedo (cape) .... E 6
Central, Cordillera (range) .... D 5
Duarte (peak) .... D 5
Engaño (cape) .... F 5
Enriquillo (lake) .... C 6
Escocesa (bay) .... E 5
Espada (point) .... F 6
Falso (cape) .... C 7
Francés Viejo (cape) .... E 5
Gallo (mt.) .... D 5
Isabela (bay) .... D 5
Isabela (cape) .... D 5
Los Frailes (isl.) .... C 7
Macorís (cape) .... E 5
Manzanillo (bay) .... C 5
Mona (passage) .... F 6
Neiba (bay) .... D 6
Neiba (mt.) .... D 6
Ocoa (bay) .... D 6
Oriental, Cordillera (range) .... F 6
Palenque (point) .... E 6
Palmillas (point) .... F 6
Rincón (bay) .... F 5
Rucia (point) .... D 5
Salinas (point) .... E 6
Samaná (bay) .... F 5
Samaná (cape) .... F 5
San Rafael (cape) .... F 5
Saona (isl.), 409 .... F 6
Septentrional, Cordillera (range) .... D 5
Tina (mt.) .... D 6
Yaque del Norte (river) .... D 5
Yaque del Sur (river) .... D 6
Yuma (bay) .... F 6
Yuma (river) .... E 5

HAITI

DEPARTMENTS

Artibonite, 567,221 .... C 5
Nord, 539,049 .... C 5
Nord-Ouest, 168,279 .... B 5
Ouest, 1,083,069 .... C 6
Sud, 739,602 .... A 6

CITIES and TOWNS

Abricots, 618 .... B 6
Anse-à-Galets, 484 .... B 6
Anse-à-Pitre, 549 .... C 6
Anse-à-Veau, 893 .... B 6
Anse-d'Hainault, 2,468 .... A 6
Anse-Rouge, 665 .... B 5
Aquin, 2,880 .... B 6
Archaie, 1,962 .... C 6
Baie-de-Henne, 430 .... B 5
Bainet, 1,039 .... B 6
Baradères, 902 .... B 6
Bassin-Bleu, 404 .... B 5
Belladère, 1,342 .... C 6
Bombardopolis, 602 .... B 5
Bonbon, 545 .... A 6
Cabaret, 522 .... C 6
Camp-Perrin, 1,561 .... A 6
Cap-Haïtien, 27,538 .... C 5
Cavaillon, 828 .... A 6
Cayes-Jacmel, 1,043 .... C 6
Cerca-la-Source, 818 .... C 5
Chardonnière, 1,431 .... A 6
Corail, 1,313 .... A 6
Côteaux, 3,146 .... A 6
Côtes-de-Fer, 736 .... B 6
Croix-des-Bouquets, 1,581 .... C 6
Dame-Marie, 2,085 .... A 2
Dérac, 4,767 .... C 5
Dessalines, 4,073 .... C 5
Fond-Verrettes, 480 .... C 6
Fort-Liberté, 1,637 .... C 5
Gonaïves, 15,373 .... B 5
Grand-Goâve, 2,022 .... B 6
Grand-Gosier, 532 .... C 6
Grande-Rivière-du-Nord, 2,931 .... C 5
Grande-Saline, 807 .... B 5
Gros-Morne, 2,451 .... B 4
Hinche, 5,847 .... C 5
Jacmel, 9,397 .... C 6
Jean-Rabel, 1,181 .... B 5
Jérémie, 12,456 .... A 6
Kenscoff, 1,071 .... C 6
La Cahouane .... A 6
Lascahobas, 2,356 .... C 6
L'Asile, 299 .... B 6
Le Borgne, 1,325 .... C 5
Léogane, 3,922 .... C 6
Les Anglais, 1,048 .... A 6
Les Cayes, 13,088 .... B 6
Les Irois, 500 .... A 6
Limbé, 3,488 .... C 5
Limonade, 1,313 .... C 5
Maissade, 1,318 .... C 5
Marigot, 1,191 .... C 6
Miragoâne, 2,711 .... B 6
Mirebalais, 1,995 .... C 6
Môle-Saint-Nicolas, 471 .... B 5
Moron, 1,138 .... A 6
Ouanaminthe, 2,586 .... C 5
Pestel, 721 .... A 6
Pétionville, 10,239 .... C 6
Petit-Goâve, 5,847 .... B 6
Petite-Rivière-de-l'Artibonite, 4,766 .... B 5
Pignon, 1,681 .... C 5
Pilate, 1,392 .... C 5
Plaisance, 1,840 .... C 5
Pointe-à-Raquette .... B 6
Port-à-Piment, 2,525 .... A 6
Port-au-Prince (cap.), 151,220 .... C 6
Port-de-Paix, 6,964 .... B 5
Port-Margot, 1,697 .... C 5
Port-Salut, 899 .... A 6
Roseaux, 442 .... A 6
Saint-Jean-du-Sud, 272 .... B 6
Saint-Louis-du-Nord, 3,130 .... B 5
Saint-Louis-du-Sud, 1,400 .... B 6
Saint-Marc, 10,222 .... B 5
Saint-Michel-de-l'Atalaye, 2,431 .... C 5
Saint-Michel-du-Sud .... B 6
Saint-Raphaël, 1,586 .... C 5
Saltrou, 1,203 .... C 6
Savanette, 627 .... C 6
Terre-Neuve .... B 5
Thomonde, 1,175 .... C 6
Tiburon, 1,468 .... A 6
Torbeck .... A 6
Trou-du-Nord, 2,879 .... C 5
Vallière, 364 .... C 5
Verrettes, 1,503 .... C 5
Ville-Bonheur .... C 6

PHYSICAL FEATURES

Artibonite (river) .... C 5
Baradères (bay) .... B 6
Cheval Blanc (point) .... B 5
Dame-Marie (cape) .... A 6
Est (point) .... C 4
Fantasque (point) .... B 6
Gonâve (gulf) .... B 5
Gonâve (isl.), 26,860 .... B 6
Grande Cayemite (isl.), 1,951 .... B 6
Gravois (point) .... A 6
Irois (cape) .... A 6
Jean-Rabel (point) .... B 5
La Selle (mts.) .... C 6
La Selle (peak) .... C 6
Macaya (peak) .... A 6
Manzanillo (bay) .... C 5
Môle (cape) .... B 5
Noires (mts.) .... C 5
Ouest (point) .... B 4
Ouest (point) .... B 6
Saint-Marc (cape) .... B 5
Saint-Marc (chan.) .... B 6
Saumâtre (lake) .... C 6
Tortue (chan.) .... C 5
Tortue, La (isl.), 12,501 .... C 4
Tortuga (Tortue) (isl.), 12,501 .... C 4
Trois-Rivières (river) .... B 5
Vache (isl.), 3,463 .... B 6
Windward (passage) .... A 5

JAMAICA

COUNTIES

Cornwall, 419,297 .... H 6
Middlesex, 637,866 .... J 6
Surrey, 552,651 .... K 6

(continued on following page)

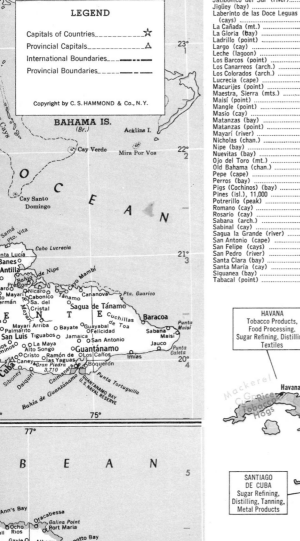

AGRICULTURE, INDUSTRY and RESOURCES

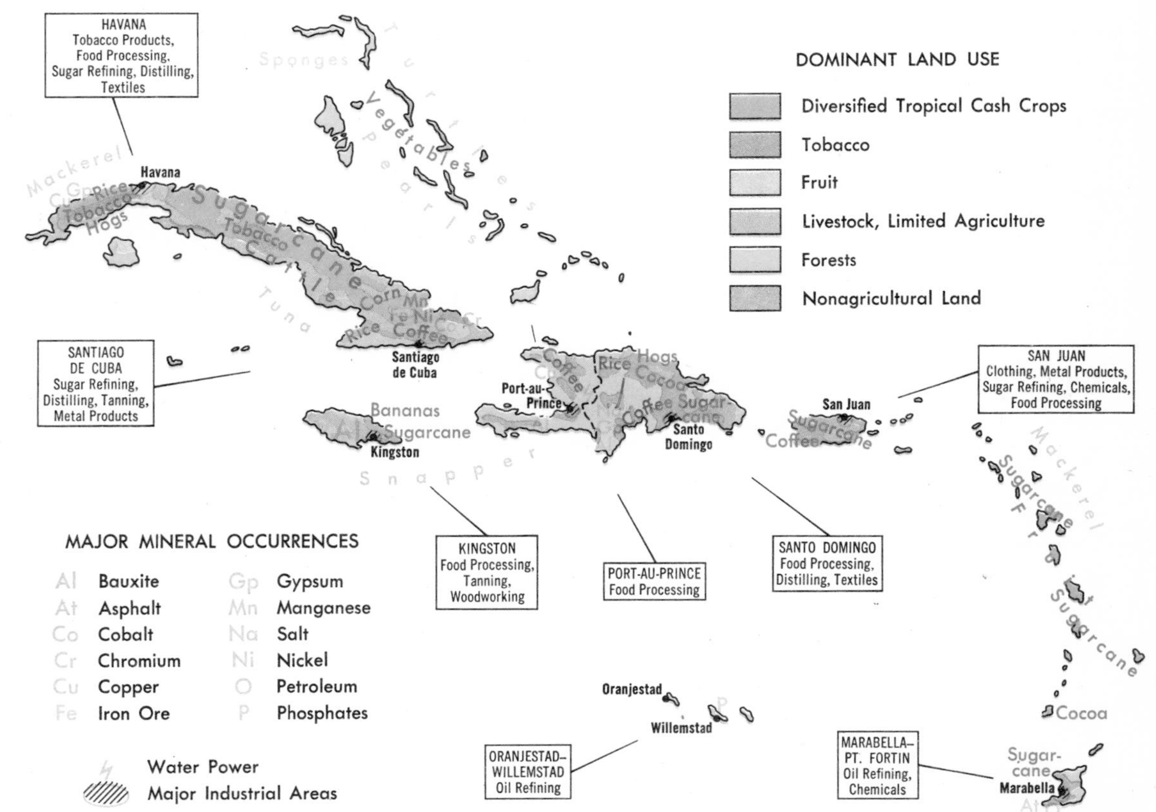

West Indies
(continued)

JAMAICA (continued)

CITIES and TOWNS

Adelphi ... H 5
Albany, 1,590 ... J 6
Albert Town, 1,650 ... H 6
Alley ... J 7
Alligator Pond ... H 6
Anchovy ... H 5
Annotto Bay, 3,559 ... K 6
Balaclava, 1,153 ... H 6
Bath, 1,979 ... K 6
Bethel Town ... G 6
Black River, 3,077 ... H 6
Bluefields ... H 6
Bog Walk, 2,808 ... J 6
Bowden ... K 6
Brown's Town, 3,899 ... H 6
Buff Bay, 2,821 ... K 6
Cambridge ... H 6
Cascade ... G 6
Castleton ... J 6
Catadupa ... H 6
Chapelton, 4,417 ... J 6
Christiana, 4,404 ... H 6
Claremont, 1,417 ... J 6
Clark's Town, 1,543 ... H 6
Darliston ... H 6
Devon ... H 6
Discovery Bay ... J 5
Dry Harbour (Discovery Bay) ... J 5
Duncans ... H 5
Ewarton ... J 6
Falmouth, 3,727 ... H 5
Four Paths ... J 6
Frankfield, 2,123 ... H 6
Frome ... G 6
Gayle ... J 6
Golden Grove ... K 6
Green Island ... G 6
Hayes ... J 6
Highgate, 3,313 ... J 6
Hope Bay ... K 6
Hopewell ... G 5
Ipswich ... H 6
Kingston (cap.), 123,403 ... K 6
Kingston, *376,520 ... K 6
Lacovia ... H 6
Lime Hall ... J 6
Linstead, 3,781 ... J 6
Lionel Town, 2,664 ... J 7
Little London ... G 6
Lluidas Vale ... J 6
Lucea, 2,803 ... G 5
Maggotty ... H 6
Malvern ... H 6
Manchioneal ... K 6
Mandeville, 8,416 ... H 6
Maroon Town ... H 6
May Pen, 14,085 ... J 6
Moneague ... J 6
Montego Bay, 23,610 ... H 5
Montpelier ... H 6
Moore Town ... K 6
Morant Bay, 5,054 ... K 7
Myersville ... H 6
Negril ... G 6
Ocho Rios, 4,570 ... J 6
Old England ... H 6
Old Harbour, 4,192 ... J 6
Oracabessa, 1,313 ... J 5
Petersfield ... G 6
Port Antonio, 7,830 ... K 6
Port Kaiser ... H 7
Port Maria, 3,998 ... J 6
Port Morant, 2,284 ... K 6
Port Royal, 37,673 ... J 6
Porus, 2,723 ... H 6
Richmond ... J 6
Rio Bueno ... H 5
Riversdale ... J 6
Runaway Bay ... J 5
Saint Anns Bay, 5,087 ... J 5
Saint Margaret's Bay ... K 6
Sandy Bay ... G 5
Santa Cruz, 1,426 ... H 6
Savanna-la-Mar, 9,789 ... G 6
Spaldings, 2,003 ... H 6
Spanish Town, 14,706 ... J 6
Spur Tree ... H 6
Stewart Town ... H 6
Treasure Beach ... H 6
Trinityville ... K 6
Trout Hall ... J 6
Ulster Spring ... H 6
Williamsfield ... H 6
Yallahs ... K 6

PHYSICAL FEATURES

Black (river) ... H 6
Black River (bay) ... G 6
Blue (mts.) ... K 6
Blue Mountain (peak) ... K 6
Galina (point) ... J 6
Grande (river) ... K 6
Great (river) ... H 6
Great Pedro Bluff (prom.) ... H 6
Long (bay) ... H 7
Luana (point) ... G 6
Minho (river) ... J 6
Montego (bay) ... G 5
Montego Bay (point) ... G 5
North East (point) ... K 6
North Negril (point) ... G 6
North West (point) ... G 5
Old Harbour (bay) ... J 6
Portland (point) ... J 7
Sir John's (peak) ... K 6
South East (point) ... K 6
South Negril (point) ... G 6

*City and suburbs.
†Population of municipality.

PUERTO RICO

DISTRICTS

Aguadilla, 277,400 ... A 1
Arecibo, 256,468 ... C 1
Bayamón, 364,414 ... D 1
Guayama, 296,022 ... D 2
Humacao, 252,579 ... F 2
Mayagüez, 255,653 ... B 2
Ponce, 287,145 ... C 2
San Juan, 359,863 ... E 1

CITIES and TOWNS

Adjuntas, 5,318 ... B 2
Aguada, 3,759 ... A 1
Aguadilla, 15,943 ... A 1
Aguas Buenas, 2,470 ... E 2
Aibonito, 5,477 ... D 2
Añasco, 2,068 ... A 1
Ángeles, †3,520 ... B 2
Arecibo, 28,828 ... B 1
Arroyo, 3,741 ... E 3
Arus ... C 3
Bahomamey ... A 1
Bajadero ... C 1
Barceloneta, 762 ... C 1
Barranquitas, 4,684 ... D 2
Bayamón, 15,109 ... D 1
Boquerón, †2,580 ... A 3
Cabo Rojo, 3,086 ... A 2
Caguas, 32,015 ... E 2
Camuy, 2,341 ... B 1
Carolina, 3,075 ... E 1
Cataño, 8,276 ... D 1
Cayey, 19,738 ... D 2
Ceiba, 1,644 ... F 2
Central Aguirre, 1,689 ... D 3
Ciales, 3,275 ... C 1
Cidra, 3,191 ... D 2
Coamo, 12,146 ... D 2
Comerío, 5,232 ... D 2
Coquí ... D 3
Corozal, 3,166 ... D 1
Corral Viejo ... C 2
Coto Laurel, †3,907 ... C 2
Culebra, 498 ... G 1
Dewey (Culebra), 498 ... G 1
Dorado, 2,120 ... D 1
Ensenada, 3,229 ... B 3
Esperanza ... G 2
Fajardo, 12,409 ... F 1
Florida, 2,955 ... C 1
Guánica, 4,100 ... B 3
Guayama, 19,183 ... E 3
Guayanilla, 3,067 ... B 3
Guaynabo, 3,343 ... D 1
Gurabo, 3,957 ... E 2
Hatillo, 2,582 ... B 1
Hato Rey, 98,630 ... E 1
Hormigüeros, 1,647 ... A 2
Humacao, 8,005 ... E 2
Isabel Segunda, 2,487 ... G 2
Isabela, 7,302 ... A 1
Jayuya, 2,344 ... C 2
Jobos, 815 ... D 3
Juana Díaz, 4,618 ... C 2
Juncos, 6,247 ... E 2
Lajas, 914 ... A 3
Lares, 4,216 ... B 2
Las Marias, 511 ... B 2
Las Piedras, 3,147 ... E 2
Loíza, 3,097 ... E 1
Loíza Aldea, 2,330 ... E 1
Luquillo, 2,107 ... F 1
Manatí, 9,682 ... C 1
Maricao, 1,475 ... B 2
Maunabo, 1,027 ... E 3
Mayagüez, 50,147 ... A 2
Moca, 1,938 ... A 1
Morovis, 2,428 ... D 1
Naguabo, 3,396 ... F 2
Naranjito, 2,719 ... D 1
Orocovis, 3,005 ... C 2
Palmer, †1,435 ... F 1
Palo Seco, †709 ... D 1
Parguera, †1,030 ... A 3
Patillas, 1,888 ... E 3
Peñuelas, 2,261 ... B 2
Playa de Fajardo, 2,143 ... F 1
Playa de Humacao, †2,433 ... F 2
Playa de Ponce ... C 3
Ponce, 114,286 ... C 3
Puerto Nuevo ... D 1
Puerto Real, †3,766 ... A 2
Puerto Real (Playa de Fajardo), 2,143 ... F 1
Punta Santiago (Playa de Humacao), †2,433 ... F 2
Quebradillas, 2,131 ... B 1
Rincón, 1,094 ... A 1
Río Blanco, †2,665 ... F 2
Río Grande, 2,763 ... E 1
Río Piedras ... E 1
Rosario, †715 ... A 2
Sabana Grande, 3,318 ... B 2
Sabana Seca, †7,755 ... D 1
Salinas, 3,666 ... D 3
San Antonio ... A 1
San Germán, 7,790 ... A 2
San Juan (cap.), 432,377 ... E 1
San Juan, *542,156 ... E 1
San Lorenzo, 5,551 ... E 2
San Sebastián, 4,019 ... B 1
Santa Isabel, 4,712 ... C 3
Santurce, 178,179 ... E 1
Tallaboa, †773 ... B 3
Toa Alta, 1,284 ... D 1
Toa Baja, 1,084 ... D 1
Trujillo Alto, 1,297 ... E 1
Utuado, 9,870 ... B 2
Vega Alta, 3,182 ... D 1
Vega Baja, 3,718 ... C 1
Vieques (Isabel Segunda), 2,487 ... G 2
Villalba, 1,892 ... C 2
Yabucoa, 3,734 ... E 2
Yauco, 8,996 ... B 2

PHYSICAL FEATURES

Aguadillo (bay) ... A 1
Algarrobo (pt.) ... A 2
Añasco (bay) ... A 1
Arenas (pt.) ... F 2
Bauta (river) ... C 2
Bayamón (river) ... D 1
Boquerón (bay) ... A 3
Borinquen (pt.) ... A 1
Cabullón (pt.) ... C 3
Caja de Muertos (isl.) ... C 3
Camuy (river) ... B 1
Candelero (pt.) ... F 2
Canovanas (river) ... E 1
Caonillas (lake) ... C 2
Carite (lake) ... E 2
Carraízo (lake) ... E 1
Cayey, Sierra de (mts.) ... D 2
Central, Cordillera (range) ... C 2
Cerro Gordo (pt.) ... D 1
Coamo (res.) ... D 3
Coamo (river) ... D 3
Culebra (isl.), 573 ... G 1
Culebrinas (river) ... A 1
Culebrita (isl.) ... G 2
El Toro (mt.) ... F 2
El Yunque (mt.) ... F 1
Este (pt.) ... G 2
Fajardo (river) ... F 1
Figuras (pt.) ... E 3
Fosforescente (bay) ... A 3
Grande de Añasco (river) ... B 2
Grande de Arecibo (river) ... C 1
Grande de Loíza (river) ... E 1
Grande de Manatí (river) ... C 1
Guajataca (lake) ... B 1
Guanajibo (pt.) ... A 2
Guanajibo (river) ... A 2
Guánica (lake) ... B 3
Guaniquilla (pt.) ... A 2
Guayabal (lake) ... C 2
Guayanés (pt.) ... F 2
Guayanés (river) ... E 2
Guayanilla (bay) ... B 3
Guayo (lake) ... B 2
Guilarte (mt.) ... B 2
Honda (bay) ... F 2
Humacao (river) ... E 2
Jacaguas (river) ... C 2
Jaicoa (mts.) ... B 1
Jiguero (pt.) ... A 1
Jobos (bay) ... D 3
La Bandera (pt.) ... F 1
Lima (pt.) ... F 2
Lobo (cay) ... G 1
Luquillo, Sierra de (mts.) ... E 2
Majada (river) ... D 2
Manglillo (pt.) ... B 3
Mayagüez (bay) ... A 2
Miquillo (pt.) ... F 1
Molinos (pt.) ... G 1
Mona (passage) ... A 2
Negra (pt.) ... G 2
Ola Grande (pt.) ... D 3
Palmas Altas (pt.) ... C 1
Patillas (lake) ... E 2
Peñón (pt.) ... B 1
Petrona (pt.) ... D 3
Pirata (mt.) ... F 2
Plata (river) ... D 2
Puerca (pt.) ... F 2
Puerto Medio Mundo (bay) ... F 2
Puerto Nuevo (pt.) ... C 1
Puntas, Cerro de (mt.) ... C 2
Ramey A.F.B. ... A 1
Rincón (bay) ... D 3
Rojo (cape) ... A 3
Salinas (pt.) ... D 1
San José (lake) ... E 1
San Juan, Cabezas de (prom.) ... F 1
San Juan Nat'l Hist. Site ... D 1
Sardina (pt.) ... A 1
Soldado (pt.) ... G 2
Sucia (bay) ... A 3
Tanamá (river) ... B 1
Torrecilla (lagoon) ... E 1
Tortuguero (lake) ... D 1
Tuna (pt.) ... E 3
Vacía Talega (pt.) ... E 1
Viento (pt.) ... E 3
Vieques (isl.), 7,210 ... G 2
Vieques (passage) ... F 2
Vieques (sound) ... G 2
Yagüez (river) ... A 2
Yauco (lake) ... B 2
Yeguas (pt.) ... F 3

ANTIGUA
Total Population 62,000

CITIES and TOWNS

All Saints, 2,077 ... D11
Cedar Grove, 899 ... E11
Falmouth, 239 ... E11
Freetown, 1,026 ... E11
Jennings, 850 ... D11
Johnsons Point, 339 ... D11
Liberta, 1,988 ... E11
Old Road, 1,178 ... D11
Parham, 1,123 ... E11
Saint Johns (cap.), 21,396 ... E11
Willkies Village, 1,330 ... E11

PHYSICAL FEATURES

Antigua (isl.), 54,060 ... E11
Boggy (peak) ... D11
Boon (pt.) ... E11
Green (isl.) ... E11
Guana (isl.) ... E11
Long (isl.) ... E11
Saint Johns (harb.) ... D11
Standfast (pt.) ... E11
Willoughby (bay) ... E11

BARBADOS
Total Population 244,000

CITIES and TOWNS

Bathsheba ... B 8
Belleplaine ... B 8
Bridgetown (cap.), 11,452 ... B 9
Carlton ... B 8
Cave Hill ... B 9
Checker Hall ... B 8
Codrington ... B 8
Crab Hill ... B 8
Crane ... C 9
Drax Hall ... B 8
Ellerton ... B 9
Greenland ... B 8
Hastings ... B 9
Holetown ... B 8
Kendal ... B 8
Lodge Hill ... B 8
Marchfield ... B 9
Maxwell ... B 9
Maxwell Hill ... B 9
Mount Standfast ... B 8
Oistins ... B 9
Portland ... B 8
Rose Hill ... B 8
Rouen ... B 9
Saint Lawrence ... B 9
Saint Martins ... B 9
Seawell ... B 9
Six Mens ... B 8
Speightstown, 2,415 ... B 8
Spring Hall ... B 8
Welchman Hall ... B 8
Worthing ... B 9

PHYSICAL FEATURES

Carlisle (bay) ... B 9
Hillaby (mt.) ... B 8
Long (bay) ... B 9
North (pt.) ... B 8
Oistins (bay) ... B 9
Pelican (isl.) ... B 9
Ragged (pt.) ... C 8
Sam Lord's Castle ... C 9
South (pt.) ... B 9

DOMINICA
Total Population 65,000

CITIES and TOWNS

Barroui ... E 6
Castle Bruce, 1,340 ... F 6
Coulihaut, 978 ... E 6
Delice, 1,211 ... F 7
Grand Bay, 3,467 ... F 7
Hampstead ... E 5
La Plaine, 1,201 ... F 6
Laudat, 308 ... E 6
Mahaut, 1,583 ... E 6
Marigot, 2,797 ... E 6
Petit Soufrière ... F 6
Portsmouth, 2,238 ... E 5
Rosalie ... F 6
Roseau (cap.), 10,417 ... E 7
Roseau, *13,883 ... E 7
Saint Joseph, 2,045 ... E 6
Salybia ... F 6
Soufrière, 667 ... E 7
Vieille Case, 1,146 ... E 5
Wesley, 1,444 ... F 5

PHYSICAL FEATURES

Capuchin (cape) ... E 5
Carib Reserve, 1,415 ... F 6
Clyde (river) ... F 6
Crampton (pt.) ... F 5
Diablotin, Morne (mt.) ... E 6
Dominica (passage) ... E 5
Douglas (bay) ... E 5
Grand (bay) ... F 7
Jaquet (pt.) ... E 5
Layou (river) ... E 6
Martinique (passage) ... E 7
Micotrin (mt.) ... F 6
Pagoua (bay) ... F 6
Prince Rupert (bay) ... E 5
Roseau (river) ... E 7
Scotts (head) ... E 7
Soufrière (bay) ... E 7
Trois Pitons, Morne (mt.) ... E 6

GRENADA
Total Population 93,000

CITIES and TOWNS

Crochu ... D 8
Gouyave, 2,356 ... C 8
Grand Anse ... C 9
Grand Roy ... C 8
Grenville, 1,747 ... D 8
Hermitage ... D 8
La Taste ... D 8
Marquis ... D 8
Mount Tivoli ... D 8
Providence ... D 9
Saint George's (cap.), 7,303 ... C 9
Saint George's, *26,843 ... C 9
Sauteurs, 925 ... D 8
Union ... D 8
Victoria, 1,692 ... D 8
Woburn ... C 9
Woodford ... C 8

PHYSICAL FEATURES

Bedford (pt.) ... D 8
David (pt.) ... D 8
Great Bacolet (pt.) ... D 8
Green (isl.) ... D 8
Grenville (bay) ... D 8
Gros (pt.) ... C 8
Halifax (harb.) ... C 8
Irvins (bay) ... D 8
Les Tantes (isls.) ... D 7
Molinière (pt.) ... C 8
Prickly (pt.) ... C 9
Ronde (isl.) ... D 7
Saint Catherine (mt.) ... D 8
Saline (pt.) ... C 9
Sinai (mt.) ... D 8
Telescope (pt.) ... D 8

GUADELOUPE
Total Population 306,000

CITIES and TOWNS

Anse-Bertrand, 1,500 ... B 5
Baie-Mahault, 2,304 ... A 6
Bailiff, 1,902 ... A 7
Baninier ... A 7
Basse-Terre (cap.), 12,317 ... A 7
Bouillante, 553 ... A 6
Bourg-des-Saintes, 1,208 ... A 7
Capesterre, 6,255 ... A 7
Capesterre, 1,117 ... B 7
Deshaies, 866 ... A 6
Ferry ... A 6
Gosier, 2,560 ... B 6
Gourbeyre, 1,449 ... A 7
Goyave, 703 ... A 6
Grand-Bourg, 2,489 ... B 7
Grippon ... B 6
Lamentin, 1,292 ... A 6
Le Moule, 8,189 ... B 6
Les Abymes, 2,292 ... B 6
Morne-à-l'Eau, 5,749 ... A 6
Petit-Bourg, 3,191 ... A 6
Petit-Cânal, 1,148 ... A 6
Pigeon ... A 6
Pointe-à-Pitre, 27,737 ... B 6
Pointe-Noire, 2,364 ... A 6
Port-Louis, 4,057 ... B 5
Saint-Claude, 2,407 ... A 7
Saint-François, 3,374 ... B 6
Saint-Louis, 1,391 ... B 7
Sainte-Anne, 3,190 ... B 6
Sainte-Marguerite ... B 6
Sainte-Marie ... A 6
Sainte-Rose, 2,237 ... A 6
Trois-Rivières, 1,007 ... A 7
Vieux-Fort, 214 ... B 7
Vieux-Habitants, 921 ... A 7

PHYSICAL FEATURES

Allègre (pt.) ... A 6
Antigues (pt.) ... A 5
Basse-Terre (isl.), 133,332 ... A 6
Châteaux (pt.) ... B 6
Constant, Morne (hill) ... B 7
Désirade (isl.), 1,592 ... B 6
Fajou (isl.) ... A 6
Grand Cul-de-Sac Marin (bay) ... A 6
Grand Îlet (isl.) ... A 7
Grand-Terre (isl.), 122,508 ... B 5
Grande Vigie (pt.) ... B 5
Guadeloupe (isl.), 255,840 ... B 6
Guadeloupe (passage) ... A 5
Kahouanne (isl.) ... A 6
Marie-Galante (isl.), 16,341 ... B 7
Nord (pt.) ... B 7
Nord-Est (bay) ... B 6
Petit Cul-de-Sac Marin (bay) ... A 6
Petite-Terre (isls.) ... B 6
Saintes (isls.), 2,772 ... A 7
Saintes, Canal des (chan.) ... A 7
Salée (river) ... A 6
Sans Toucher (mt.) ... A 6
Soufrière (mt.) ... A 7
Terre-de-Bas (isl.), 1,508 ... A 7
Terre-de-Haut (isl.), 1,264 ... A 7
Vieux-Fort (pt.) ... A 7

MARTINIQUE
Total Population 310,000

CITIES and TOWNS

Ajoupa-Bouillon, 771 ... C 5
Anses-d'Arlet, 1,172 ... C 7
Basse-Pointe, 2,022 ... C 5
Belle-Fontaine, 1,047 ... C 6
Carbet, 2,447 ... C 6
Case-Pilote, 1,432 ... C 6
Diamant, 760 ... D 7
Ducos, 874 ... D 6
Fond-Lahaye ... C 6
Fonds-Saint-Denis, 579 ... C 6
Fort-de-France (cap.), 74,673 ... C 6
Fort-Desaix ... D 6
François, 2,849 ... D 6
Grande-Rivière, 1,386 ... C 5
Gros-Morne, 904 ... D 6
Lemantin, 4,625 ... D 6
Lorrain, 1,994 ... D 5
Macouba, 324 ... C 5
Marigot, 608 ... D 5
Marin, 2,004 ... D 7
Morne-Rouge, 1,629 ... C 5
Morne-Vert, 353 ... C 6
Prêcheur, 1,495 ... C 5
Rivière-Pilote, 1,691 ... D 7
Rivière-Salée, 1,535 ... D 7
Robert, 2,131 ... D 6
Saint-Esprit, 2,603 ... D 6
Saint-Joseph, 1,720 ... C 6
Saint-Pierre, 5,434 ... C 6
Sainte-Anne, 964 ... D 7
Sainte-Luce, 907 ... D 7
Sainte-Marie, 2,436 ... D 5
Schoelcher, 3,879 ... C 6
Trinité, 3,571 ... D 6
Trois-Îlets, 1,132 ... D 6
Vauclin, 2,657 ... D 6
Vert-Pré ... D 6

PHYSICAL FEATURES

Cabet, Pitons du (mt.) ... C 6
Cabri (isl.) ... D 7
Caravelle (pen.) ... D 6
Cul-de-Sac du Marin (bay) ... D 7
Diable (pt.) ... D 5
Ferré (cape) ... E 7
Fort-de-France (bay) ... C 6
Galion (bay) ... D 6
Lézarde (river) ... D 6
Long, Îlet (isl.) ... D 6
Lorrain (river) ... D 5
Martinique (passage) ... C 5
Pelée (vol.) ... C 5
Pilote (river) ... D 7
Ramièrs, Îlet-à- (isl.) ... C 6
Ramville, Îlet (isl.) ... D 6
Robert (harb.) ... D 6
Rocher du Diamant (isl.) ... C 7
Rose (pt.) ... D 6
Saint-Martin (cape) ... C 5
Saint-Pierre (bay) ... C 6
Salines (pt.) ... D 7
Salomon (pt.) ... C 7
Vauclin (mt.) ... D 6

NETHERLANDS ANTILLES

CITIES and TOWNS

Aresji ... D 9
Ascension ... F 8
Bacuna ... E 8
Balashi ... E10
Boven Bolivia ... E 8
Bubali ... D10
Bushiribana ... E10
Dokterstuin ... D 8
Druif ... D10
Emmastad ... G 9
Entrejo ... E 8
Fontein ... E 8
Fuik ... G 9
Groot Sint Joris ... G 9
Hato ... G 8
Kralendijk (cap.), Bonaire, 839 ... E 8
Lago ... E10
Lagoen ... F 8
Montanja di Reij ... G 9
New Port ... G 9
Noord di Salinja ... E 8
Onima ... E 8
Oranjestad (cap.), Aruba, 15,398 ... D10
Otrabanda ... F 9
Patrick ... F 8
Rincon ... E 8
Rooi ... E 8
Sabana Westpunt ... F 8
Santa Barbara ... G 9
Santa Catharina ... G 9
Savaneta ... E10
Savonet ... F 8
Sint Anna ... D10
Sint Jan ... D 8
Sint Kruis ... F 8
Sint Martha ... F 8
Sint Michiel ... F 9
Sint Nicolaas ... E10
Sint Willebrordus ... F 8
Terra Corra ... E 8
Westpunt ... D10
Willemstad (cap.), 43,547 ... F 9
Willemstad, *94,133 ... F 9

PHYSICAL FEATURES

Aruba (isl.), 58,506 ... E 9
Basora (pt.) ... E10
Bonaire (isl.), 6,086 ... E 9
Bullen (bay) ... F 8
Caracas (bay) ... G 9
Curaçao (isl.), 129,676 ... G 7
Goto (lake) ... D 8
Jamanota (mt.) ... E10
Kanon (pt.) ... G 9
Klein (isl.) ... E 8
Kudarebe (pt.) ... D 9
Lac (bay) ... D 9
Lacre (pt.) ... E 9
Malmok (mt.) ... E 8
Noord (pt.) ... D 8
Noord (pt.) ... F 8
Paarden (bay) ... D10
Palm (beach) ... D10
Pekelmeer (lake) ... E 9
Piscadera (bay) ... F 9
Schottegat (bay) ... G 9
Sint Anna (bay) ... F 9
Sint Christoffel Berg (mt.) ... F 8
Sint Joris (bay) ... G 9
Slag (bay) ... D 8
Vierkant (pt.) ... E 8

SAINT CHRISTOPHER, NEVIS and ANGUILLA
Total Population 62,000

CITIES and TOWNS

Basseterre (cap.), 15,726 ... C10
Cayon, 1,524 ... C10
Charlestown, 2,852 ... C11
Cotton Ground, 747 ... C11
Dieppe Bay, 949 ... C10
Gingerland ... D11
Golden Rock ... C10
Newcastle, 361 ... D11
Old Road, 1,206 ... C10
Sadlers Village, 1,091 ... C10
Sandy Point, 3,608 ... C10
Tabernacle, 1,250 ... C10
Zion Hill ... D11

PHYSICAL FEATURES

Brimstone (hill) ... C10
Dogwood (pt.) ... D11
Fort (pt.) ... C11
Great Salt (pond) ... D10
Heldens (pt.) ... C10
Horse Shoe (pt.) ... C11
Misery (mt.) ... C10
Monkey (hill) ... C10
Muddy (pt.) ... C10
Narrows, The (str.) ... D11
Nevis (isl.), 12,762 ... D11
Nevis (peak) ... D11
North Friars (bay) ... D10
Palmetto (pt.) ... C10
Saint Christopher (isl.), 38,291 ... D10
Saint Kitts (Saint Christopher) (isl.), 38,291 ... D10
South Friars (bay) ... C10

SAINT LUCIA
Total Population 94,000

CITIES and TOWNS

Anse la Raye, 2,053 ... F 6
Canaries, 1,676 ... G 6
Castries (cap.), 4,353 ... G 6
Castries, *15,291 ... G 6
Choc ... G 5
Choiseul, 513 ... F 7
Dauphin ... G 5
Dennery, 2,252 ... G 6
Gros Islet, 1,016 ... G 5
Laborie, 1,591 ... G 7
Marigot ... G 6
Marquis ... G 6
Micoud, 2,040 ... G 6
Praslin ... G 6
Soufrière, 2,692 ... F 6
Vieux Fort, 3,228 ... G 7

PHYSICAL FEATURES

Beaumont (pt.) ... F 6
Canaries, Piton (mt.) ... G 6
Cannelles (pt.) ... G 7
Cannelles (river) ... G 6
Cap (pt.) ... G 5
Choc (bay) ... G 5
Fond d'Or (bay) ... G 6
Gimie (mt.) ... G 6
Grand Caille (pt.) ... F 6
Grand Cul de Sac (river) ... G 6
Gros Islet (bay) ... G 5
Gros Piton (mt.) ... G 6
Maria (isl.) ... G 7
Ministre (pt.) ... G 7
Moule à Chique (cape) ... G 7
Petit Piton (mt.) ... G 6
Pigeon (isl.) ... G 5
Port Castries (harb.) ... G 6
Port Praslin (bay) ... G 6
Roseau (river) ... G 6
Saint Lucia (chan.) ... G 5
Saint Vincent (passage) ... G 7
Savannes (bay) ... G 7
Sorcière, La (mt.) ... G 6
Soufrière (bay) ... F 6
Vierge (pt.) ... G 6
Vieux Fort (river) ... G 6

SAINT VINCENT
Total Population 86,000

CITIES and TOWNS

Barrouallie, 1,119 ... A 9
Calliaqua, 636 ... A 9
Camden Park ... A 9
Chateaubelair, 463 ... A 8
Colonarie ... A 9
Georgetown, 1,213 ... A 8
Kingstown (cap.), 4,308 ... A 9
Kingstown, *20,688 ... A 9
Layou, 1,149 ... A 9
Turema ... A 8
Wallibu ... A 8

PHYSICAL FEATURES

Colonarie (pt.) ... A 9
Cumberland (bay) ... A 8
Dark (head) ... A 8
De Volet (pt.) ... A 8
Espagnol (pt.) ... A 8
Greathead (bay) ... A 9
Kingstown (bay) ... A 9
Owia (bay) ... A 8
Porter (pt.) ... A 8
Richmond (peak) ... A 8
Saint Andrew (mt.) ... A 9
Saint Vincent (passage) ... A 8
Soufrière (mt.) ... A 8
Yambu (head) ... A 9

TRINIDAD and TOBAGO

CITIES and TOWNS

Arima, 10,982 ... B10
Arouca, 4,781 ... B10
Basse Terre ... B11
Biche, 1,986 ... B10
Blanchisseuse, 205 ... B10
California ... A11
Carapichaima ... B10
Caroni, 678 ... B10
Cedros, 1,388 ... A11
Chaguanas, 3,509 ... A10
Chaguaramas ... A10
Couva, 3,567 ... B10
Cunapo ... B10
Débé, 2,189 ... B11
Ecclesville ... B11
Flanagin Town ... B10
Fullarton ... A11
Fyzabad, 1,869 ... A11
Gran Couva ... B11
Grande Rivière, 301 ... B10
Guaico ... B10
Guayaguayare, 287 ... B11
La Brea, 4,828 ... A11
La Lune, 252 ... B11
Marabella, 8,937 ... A11
Matelot, 289 ... B10
Matura ... B10
Mayaro, 1,828 ... B11
Moruga, 656 ... B11
Mucurapo, 2,851 ... A10
Nestor ... B10
Palo Seco ... A11
Peñal, 3,594 ... B11
Piarco ... B10
Point Fortin, 8,753 ... A11
Port-of-Spain (cap.), 93,954 ... A10
Port-of-Spain, *120,694 ... A10
Princes Town, 6,681 ... B11
Redhead, 302 ... B10
Rio Claro, 2,174 ... B11
Sadhoowa ... B11
Saint Joseph, 4,079 ... B10
Saint Joseph ... B11
San Fernando, 39,830 ... A11
San Francique ...
San Juan, 19,064 ...
Sangre Grande, 5,087 ...
Sans Souci, 295 ...
Siparia, 4,174 ...
Tabaquite ...
Tableland ...
Tacarigua, 6,704 ...
Talparo ...
Toco, 979 ...
Tunapuna, 11,287 ...
Upper Manzanilla ...
Valencia, 370 ...
Waterloo ...

PHYSICAL FEATURES

Aripo, El Cerro del (mt.) ...
Boca Grande (passage) ...
Casa Cruz (cape) ...
Chacachacare (isl.) ...
Chupara (pt.) ...
Cocos (bay) ...
Dragons Mouth (passage) ...
Erin (bay) ...
Erin (pt.) ...
Galeota (pt.) ...
Galera (pt.) ...
Guapo (bay) ...
Guatuaro (pt.) ...
Icacos (pt.) ...
Matura (bay) ...
Mayaro (bay) ...
Monos (isl.) ...
Nariva (swamp) ...
Oropuche (river) ...
Ortoire (river) ...
Paria (gulf) ...
Pitch (lake) ...
Serpents Mouth (passage) ...
Tamana (mt.) ...
Trinidad (isl.), 794,624 ...
Tucuche, El (mt.) ...
U.S. Naval Base ...

VIRGIN ISLANDS (BRITISH)

CITIES and TOWNS

Road Town (cap.), 891 ...
West End, 105 ...

PHYSICAL FEATURES

Flanagan (passage) ...
Frenchman (cay), 56 ...
Great Thatch (isl.) ...
Great Tobago (isl.) ...
Jost Van Dyke (isl.), 178 ...
Little Tobago (isl.) ...
Narrow, The (str.) ...
Norman (isl.) ...
Peter (isl.), 9 ...
Road (bay) ...
Sage (mt.) ...
Sir Francis Drake (chan.) ...
Tortola (isl.), 6,238 ...

VIRGIN ISLANDS (U. S.)

CITIES and TOWNS

Bethlehem ...
Canebay ...
Charlotte Amalie (cap.), 12,880 ...
Christiansted, 5,137 ...
Cruz Bay, 599 ...
Diamond ...
East End, 32 ...
Emmaus ...
Fredensdal ...
Frederiksted, 2,177 ...
Grove Place ...
Kingshill ...
Longford ...
Negro Bay ...

PHYSICAL FEATURES

Altona (lagoon) ...
Annaly (bay) ...
Baron Bluff (prom.) ...
Bordeaux (mt.) ...
Brass (isls.) ... A
Buck (isl.) ...
Buck Island (chan.) ...
Buck Island Reef Nat'l Mon. ...
Butler (bay) ...
Caneel (bay) ... B
Capella (isls.) ... B
Coral (bay) ... C
Crown (mt.) ... A
Dutchcap (cay) ... A
Eagle (mt.) ... B
East (pt.) ...
Flanagan (passage) ... D
Flat (cays) ... A
Grass (pt.) ... C
Great (pond) ... F
Great Pond (bay) ... F
Green (cay) ... F
Hams Bluff (prom.) ... E
Hans Lollik (isls.) ... B
Hassel (isl.) ... B
Jersey (bay) ... B
Krause (lagoon) ... F
Leeward (passage) ... B
Long (pt.) ... B
Long (pt.) ... E
Lovango (cay) ... C
Magens (bay) ... B
Maho (bay) ... C
Narrows, The (str.) ... C
Nulliberg (mt.) ... B
Perseverance (bay) ... A
Picara (pt.) ... B
Pillsbury (sound) ... B
Privateer (pt.) ... D
Pull (pt.) ... F
Ram (head) ... C
Red (pt.) ... D
Reef (bay) ... C
Saba (isl.) ... A
Saint Croix (isl.), 14,973 ... G
Saint James (isls.) ... B
Saint John (isl.), 925 ... C
Saint Thomas (harb.) ... B
Saint Thomas (isl.), 16,201 ... A
Salt (cay) ... A
Salt (river) ... F
Salt River (bay) ... F
Sandy (pt.) ... D
Savana (isl.) ... A
Southwest (cape) ... E
Tague (bay) ... G
Thatch (cay) ... B
Turner Hole (bay) ... G
U.S. Naval Air Sta. ... A
Vagthus (pt.) ... F
Virgin (passage) ... A
Virgin Islands Nat'l Hist. Site ... F
Virgin Islands Nat'l Park ... C
Water (isl.) ... A
Westend Saltpond (lagoon) ... E

*City and suburbs.
†Population of municipality.

PUERTO RICO AND THE LESSER ANTILLES

Copyright by C.S. HAMMOND & CO., N.Y.

National, Territorial and Colonial Capitals ⋯ ⭐   International Boundaries ⋯⋯⋯

Lesser Administrative Centers ⋯⋯⋯ ◉   Senatorial District Boundaries ⋯⋯⋯

ISLANDS	POLITICAL UNITS
Puerto Rico	Commonwealth of the United States
St. Thomas & St. John } St. Croix	Virgin Islands – U. S. Territory
Curaçao, Aruba } Bonaire	Neth. Antilles-Integral Part of Neth. Realm
Guadeloupe	French Overseas Department
Martinique	French Overseas Department
Dominica, St. Lucia, St. Vincent, Barbados, Grenada, St. Christopher & Nevis, Antigua	British Colonies
Trinidad	Trinidad and Tobago — Independent Member of the British Commonwealth

CANADA

CONIC PROJECTION

SCALE OF MILES

50   100   200   300

SCALE OF KILOMETRES

50 100 200   300   400   500

Capitals of Countries .... ☆
Provincial Capitals .... △
International Boundaries .... —·—·—
Provincial Boundaries .... —·—·—
Canals .... ═══

Copyright by C.S. HAMMOND & Co., N.Y.

CANADA

AREA	3,851,809 sq. mi.
POPULATION	19,785,000
CAPITAL	Ottawa
LARGEST CITY	Montréal (greater) 2,321,000
HIGHEST POINT	Mt. Logan 19,850 ft.
MONETARY UNIT	Canadian dollar
MAJOR LANGUAGES	English, French
MAJOR RELIGIONS	Protestant, Roman Catholic

VEGETATION

BARREN LANDS

PRAIRIES

Tundra and Alpine

Coniferous Forest

Temperate Forest

Temperate Grasslands

Steppe

Copyright by C. S. HAMMOND & Co., N. Y.

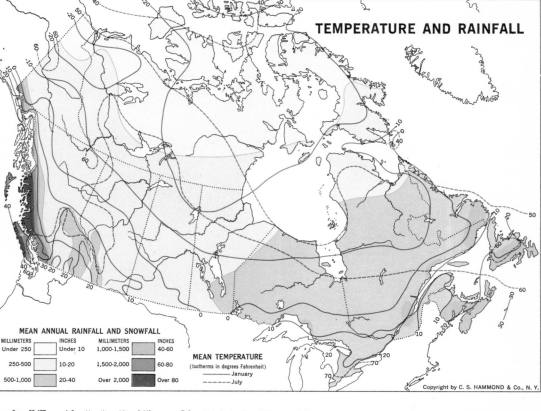

TEMPERATURE AND RAINFALL

MEAN ANNUAL RAINFALL AND SNOWFALL

MILLIMETERS	INCHES	MILLIMETERS	INCHES
Under 250	Under 10	1,000-1,500	40-60
250-500	10-20	1,500-2,000	60-80
500-1,000	20-40	Over 2,000	Over 80

MEAN TEMPERATURE
(Isotherms in degrees Fahrenheit)
—— January
--- July

Copyright by C. S. HAMMOND & Co., N. Y.

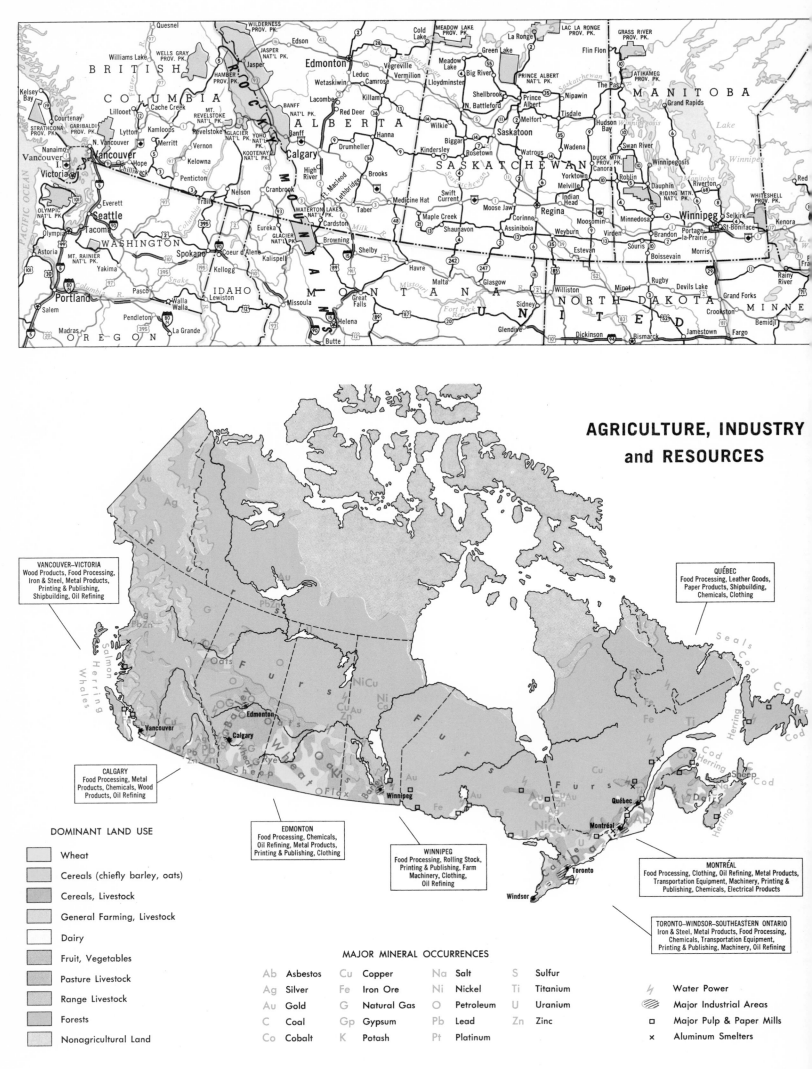

AGRICULTURE, INDUSTRY and RESOURCES

VANCOUVER–VICTORIA
Wood Products, Food Processing,
Iron & Steel, Metal Products,
Printing & Publishing,
Shipbuilding, Oil Refining

QUÉBEC
Food Processing, Leather Goods,
Paper Products, Shipbuilding,
Chemicals, Clothing

CALGARY
Food Processing, Metal
Products, Chemicals, Wood
Products, Oil Refining

EDMONTON
Food Processing, Chemicals,
Oil Refining, Metal Products,
Printing & Publishing, Clothing

WINNIPEG
Food Processing, Rolling Stock,
Printing & Publishing, Farm
Machinery, Clothing,
Oil Refining

MONTRÉAL
Food Processing, Clothing, Oil Refining, Metal Products,
Transportation Equipment, Machinery, Printing &
Publishing, Chemicals, Electrical Products

TORONTO–WINDSOR–SOUTHEASTERN ONTARIO
Iron & Steel, Metal Products, Food Processing,
Chemicals, Transportation Equipment,
Printing & Publishing, Machinery, Oil Refining

DOMINANT LAND USE

- Wheat
- Cereals (chiefly barley, oats)
- Cereals, Livestock
- General Farming, Livestock
- Dairy
- Fruit, Vegetables
- Pasture Livestock
- Range Livestock
- Forests
- Nonagricultural Land

MAJOR MINERAL OCCURRENCES

Ab	Asbestos	Cu	Copper	Na	Salt	S	Sulfur
Ag	Silver	Fe	Iron Ore	Ni	Nickel	Ti	Titanium
Au	Gold	G	Natural Gas	O	Petroleum	U	Uranium
C	Coal	Gp	Gypsum	Pb	Lead	Zn	Zinc
Co	Cobalt	K	Potash	Pt	Platinum		

- Water Power
- Major Industrial Areas
- Major Pulp & Paper Mills
- Aluminum Smelters

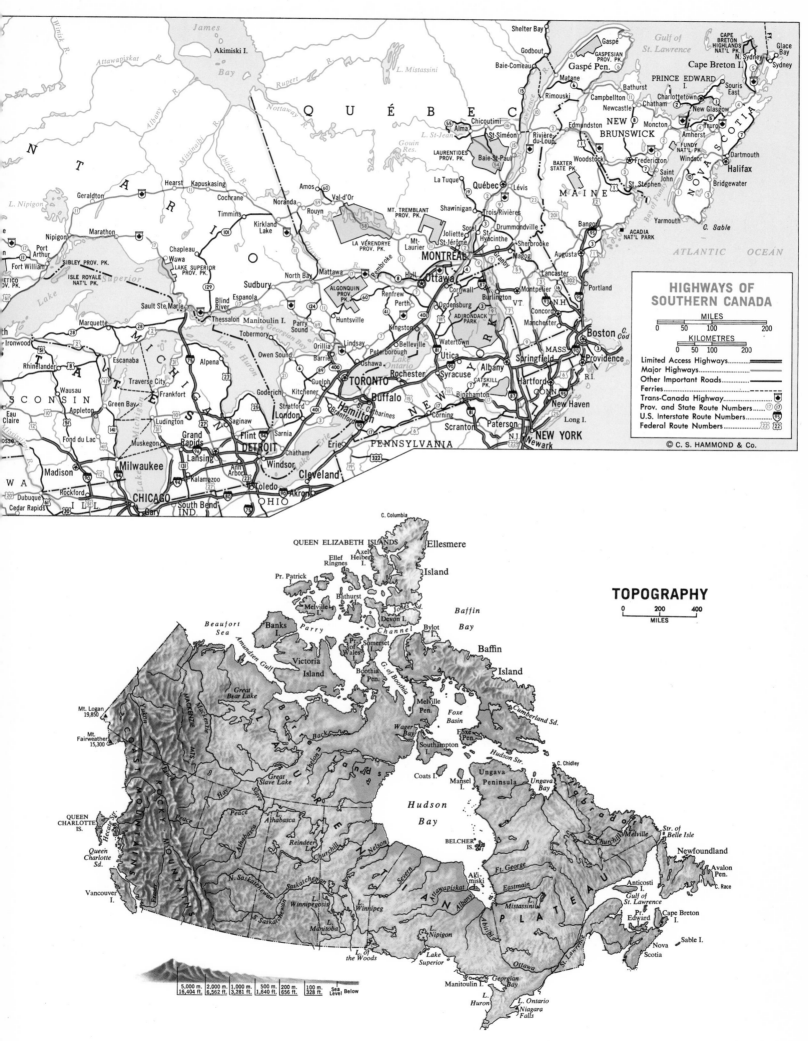

HIGHWAYS OF SOUTHERN CANADA

MILES
0   50   100   200

KILOMETRES
0   50   100   200

Limited Access Highways............
Major Highways............
Other Important Roads............
Ferries............
Trans-Canada Highway............
Prov. and State Route Numbers............ 17 17
U.S. Interstate Route Numbers............ 95 95
Federal Route Numbers............ 22 22

© C. S. HAMMOND & Co.

TOPOGRAPHY

0   200   400
MILES

5,000 m. 2,000 m. 1,000 m. 500 m. 200 m. 100 m. Sea Below
16,404 ft. 6,562 ft. 3,281 ft. 1,640 ft. 656 ft. 328 ft. Level

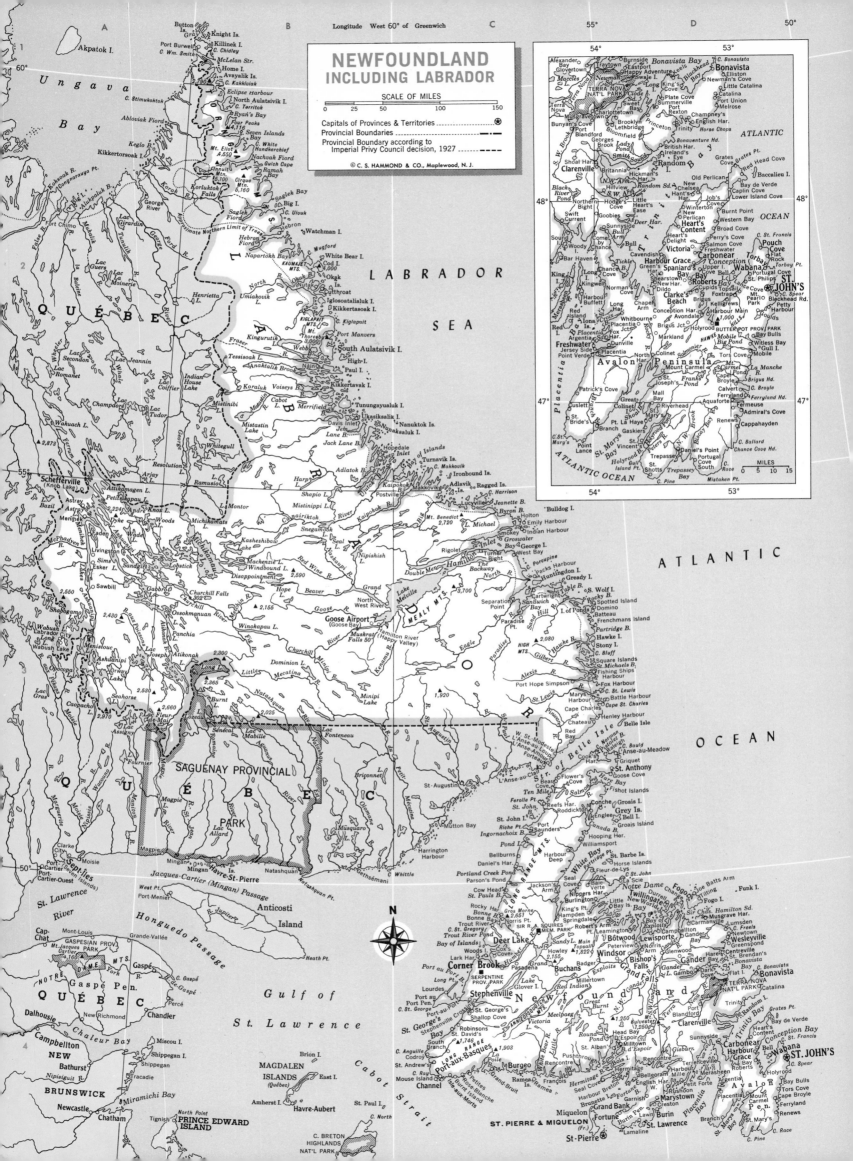

NEWFOUNDLAND INCLUDING LABRADOR

SCALE OF MILES

0   25   50   100   150

Capitals of Provinces & Territories ················ ⊛
Provincial Boundaries ·····························
Provincial Boundary according to
Imperial Privy Council decision, 1927 ·····

© C. S. HAMMOND & CO., Maplewood, N. J.

NEWFOUNDLAND

AREA 156,185 sq. mi.
POPULATION 501,000
CAPITAL St. John's
LARGEST CITY St. John's (greater) 90,838
HIGHEST POINT Cirque Mtn. 5,160 ft.
SETTLED IN 1610
ADMITTED TO CONFEDERATION 1949
PROVINCIAL FLOWER Pitcher Plant

CITIES and TOWNS

Admiral's Cove (D2)..... 177
Alexander Bay (C1) 25
Aquaforte (D2) 208
Argentia (C2) 493
Astray (A3) ....
Avondale (D2) 511
Badger (C4) 1,036
Baie-Verte (C4) 958
Bar Haven (C2) 197
Batteau (C3) 63
Battle Harbour (C3)..... 87
Bay Bulls (D2) 697
Bay de Verde (D2) 884
Bay Roberts (D2) 1,328
Bear Cove (C3) 169
Bellburns (C3) 172
Belleoram (C4) 577
Bell Island (D2) 8,026
Bishop's Falls (C4).......4,099
Blackhead Road (D2)...1,200
Bloomfield (D2) 537
Bonavista (D2) 4,186
Bonne Bay (C4) 509
Botwood (C4) 3,680
Branch (D2) 556
Brigus (D2) 704
Brigus Junction (D2).... 110
Britannia (D2) 89
British Harbour (D2).... 90
Broad Cove (D2) 257
Brooklyn (D2) 192
Buchans (C4) 2,463
Bunyan's Cove (C2) 405
Burgeo (C4) 1,454
Burin (C4) 1,144
Burnside (D1) 213
Burnt Island (C4) 678
Burnt Point (D2) 258
Calvert (D2) 468
Campbellton (D4) 636
Cape Broyle (D2) 630
Cape Charles (C3) ....
Caplin Cove (D2) 193
Cappahayden (D2) 82
Carbonear (D2) 4,234
Carmanville (D4) 855
Cartwright (C3) 493
Catalina (D2) 1,110
Cavendish (D2) 306
Centreville (Fair Island) (D4) 186
Champney's (D2) 136
Chance Cove (D2) 478
Change Islands (D4).... 50
Channel—Port-aux-Basques (C4) 4,141
Chapel Arm (D2) 561
Charlottetown (D2) 302
Chateau (C3) ....
Clarenville (C2) 1,541
Clarke's Beach (D2)..... 669
Codroy (C4) 258
Colinet (D2) 261
Come by Chance (C2)... 197
Conception Harbour (D2) 585
Cook's Harbour (C3)..... 342
Corner Brook (C4)......25,185
Cow Head (C4) 544
Cox's Cove (C4) 630
Creston (C4) 837
Cupids (D2) 485
Cuslett (C2) 127
Cut Throat Harbor (B2)
Daniel's Harbour (C3).. 403
Dark Cove (D4) 955
Davis Inlet (B2) 98
Deer Lake (C4) 3,998
Dildo (D2) 687
Domino Harbour (C3)...
Dunville (D2) 1,121
Durrell (D4) 273
Eastport (D1) 438
Elliston (D2) 678
Emily Harbour (C3)......
Englee (C3) 802
English Harbour (D2) .. 155
English Harbour West (C4) 371
Esker (A3) ....
Faden (A3) ....
Fair Island (D4).......... 186
Fermeuse (D2) 311
Ferryland (D2) 713
Fishing Ships Harbour (C3) ....
Fishot Islands (C3)...... 173
Flat Island (D4) 78
Flat Rock (D2) 632
Fleur-de-Lys (C3) 457
Flowers Cove (C3)........ 312
Fogo (D4) 1,152
Forteau (C3) 232
Fortune (C4) 1,360
Fox Harbour (C3) 232
Fox Harbour (D2) 746
François (C4) 341
Frenchmans Island (C3)
Freshwater (C2) 1,396
Freshwater (D2) 365
Gambo (D4) 480
Gander (D4) 5,725
Gander Bay (D4) 500
Garnish (C4) 500
Gaskiers (D2) 328
Georges Brook (D2) 252
Glenwood (D4) 1,130
Glovertown (C1) 1,197
Goobies (D2) 120
Goose Airport (Goose Bay) (B3) 3,040
Goose Cove (C3) 260
Goulds (D2) ....
Grand Bank (C4) 2,703
Grand-Bruit (C4) 132
Grand Falls (C4) 6,606
Grates Cove (D2) 382
Green's Harbour (D2).. 713
Greenspond (D4) 728
Griquet (C3) 423
Groais Island (C3)........ 86
Hamilton River (B3) 2,861
Hampden (C4) 682
Hant's Harbour (D2).... 487
Happy Valley (Hamilton River) (B3) 2,861
Harbour Breton (C4).....1,076
Harbour Buffett (C2).... 285
Harbour Deep (C3) 304
Harbour Grace (D2)......2,650
Harbour Main (D2) 469
Harbour Mille (D4) 345
Hare Bay (D4) 1,467
Head Bay D'Espoir (C4) 413
Heart's Content (D2).... 607
Heart's Delight (D2)..... 631
Hebron (B2) 189
Henley Harbour (C3).... 80
Hermitage (C4) 417
Hickman's Harbour (D2) 419
Hillview (D2) 246
Hodge's Cove (D2) 375
Holton (C3) ....
Holyrood (D2) 350
Hooping Harbour (C3).. 166
Hopedale (B2) 218
Horse Islands (C3) 156
Howley (C4) 452
Indian Harbour (C3)..... 21
Ireland's Eye (D2) 64
Îsle-aux-Morts (C4) 884
Jackson's Arm (C4) 422
Jersey Side (C2) 923
Job's Cove (D2) 226
Joe Batt's Arm (D4)....1,058
Keels (D1) 185
Kelligrews (D2) 444
King's Cove (D1) 201
King's Point (C4) 546
Kingwell (C2) 159
La Scie (C4) 939
Lamaline (C4) 500
Lance Cove (D2) 654
Lanse-Amour (C3) ....
L'Anse-au-Clair (C3) 202
L'Anse-au-Loup (C3) 343
L'Anse-au-Meadow (C3) 60
Lark Harbour (C4) 335
Lawn (C4) 716
Lethbridge (D2) 532
Lewisporte (C4) 2,702
Little Bay Islands (C4) 426
Little Catalina (D2) 752
Little Heart's Ease (D2) 427
Livingston (A3) ....
Long Harbour (D2) 356
Lourdes (C4) 975
Lower Island Cove (D2) 494
Lucyville (C3) ....
Lumsden (D4) 269
Makkovik (C2) 168
Mall Bay (D2) 120
Markland (D2) 322
Mary's Harbour (C3).... 264
Marystown (D4) 1,691
Melrose (D2) 346
Menihek (A3) ....
Merasheen (D4) 291
Millertown (C4) 365
Mobile (D2) 80
Mount Carmel (D2) 673
Mount Pearl Park (D2) 2,785
Mouse Island (C4) 507
Mud Lake (B3) 117
Musgravetown (C2) 597
Nain (B2) 465
New Chelsea (D2) 283
New Harbour (D2) 756
New Perlican (D2) 427
Newman's Cove (D2).... 329
Newtown (D4) 585
Nippers Harbour (C4)... 236
Norman's Cove (D2) 571
Norris Arm (C4) 1,226
Norris Point (C4) 711
North Harbour (D2) 141
North West River (B3) 753
Northern Bight (C2) 50
Nutak (B2) 66
Old Perlican (D2) 599
Orway (A3) ....
Packs Harbour (C3) .....
Paradise Point (C3) .....
Parson's Pond (C3) 337
Patrick's Cove (C2)...... 135
Perry's Cove (D2) 271
Peterview (C4) 726
Petit Forte (D4) 176
Petites (C4) 118
Petty Harbour (D2) 908
Placentia (C2) 1,610
Placentia Junction (D2)
Plate Cove (Plate Cove East) (D2) 214
Point La Haye (D2) 178
Point Lance (C2) 154
Point Leamington (C4).. 901
Point Verde (C2) 323
Port-au-Port (C4) 482
Port-aux-Basques—Channel (C4) 4,141
Port Blandford (C2)..... 716
Port Hope Simpson (C3) 402
Port Rexton (D2) 438
Port Saunders (C3) 504
Port Union (D2) 645
Portugal Cove (D2) 1,141
Portugal Cove South (D2) 304
Postville (B3) 84
Pouch Cove (D2) 1,324
Princeton (D2) 174
Pushthrough (C4) 247
Raleigh (C3) 307
Ramea (C4) 970
Red Bay (C3) 261
Red Head Cove (D2) 194
Red Island (C2) 243
Reefs Harbour (C3) 163
Rencontre East (C4) 293
Rencontre West (C4).... 161
Renews (D2) 567
Rigolet (C3) 108
Riverhead (D2) 292
Robinsons (C4) 322
Rocky Harbour (C4) 620
Roddickton (C3) 1,185
Rose-Blanche (C4) 626
Rushoon (D4) 336
Saint Alban's (C4) 1,547
Saint Andrew's (C4) 294
Saint Anthony (C3) 1,820
Saint Brendan's (D4).... 387
Saint Bride's (C2) 397
Saint David's (C4) 317
Saint George's (C4) 1,181
SAINT JOHN'S (D2)..63,633
Saint John's (D2)......†90,838
Saint Joseph's (D2) 301
Saint Lawrence (C4).....2,095
Saint Mary's (D2) 434
Saint Phillips (D2) 792
Saint Shotts (D2) 189
Saint Vincent's (D2)..... 599
Salmon Cove (D2)......... 655
Sawbill (A3) ....
Seal Cove (C3) 462
Seal Cove (C4) 436
Separation Point (C3).. 51
Shallop Cove (C4) 406
Shearstown (D2) 680
Shoal Harbour (C2) 544
Smokey (C3) ....
Sound Island (C2) ....
South Branch (C4) 311
Spaniard's Bay (D2).....1,289
Spotted Island (C3) 64
Springdale (C4) 1,638
Square Islands (C3)......
Stephenville (C4) 6,043
Stephenville Crossing (C4) 2,209
Summerville (D2) 393
Sunnyside (D2) 533
Sweet Bay (D2) 193
Swift Current (C2) 402
Terra Nova (C2) 194
Terrenceville (D4) 616
Tilting (D4) 432
Topsail (D2) 1,066
Torbay (D2) 1,445
Tors Cove (D2) 303
Traytown (D1) 355
Trepassey (D2) 495
Trinity (D2) 692
Trout River (C4) 696
Turner's Bight (C3) .....
Twillingate (C4) 947
Upper Island Cove (D2)1,668
Victoria (D2) 1,506
Wabana (Bell Island) (D2) 8,026
Wabush Lake (A3) 151
Wesleyville (D4) 1,285
West Bay (C3) ....
West Saint-Modeste (C3) 141
Western Bay (D2) 484
Whitbourne (D2) 1,085
Williamsport (C3) 151
Windsor (C4) 5,505
Winterton (D2) 808
Witless Bay (D2) 498
Woody Island (C2) ......

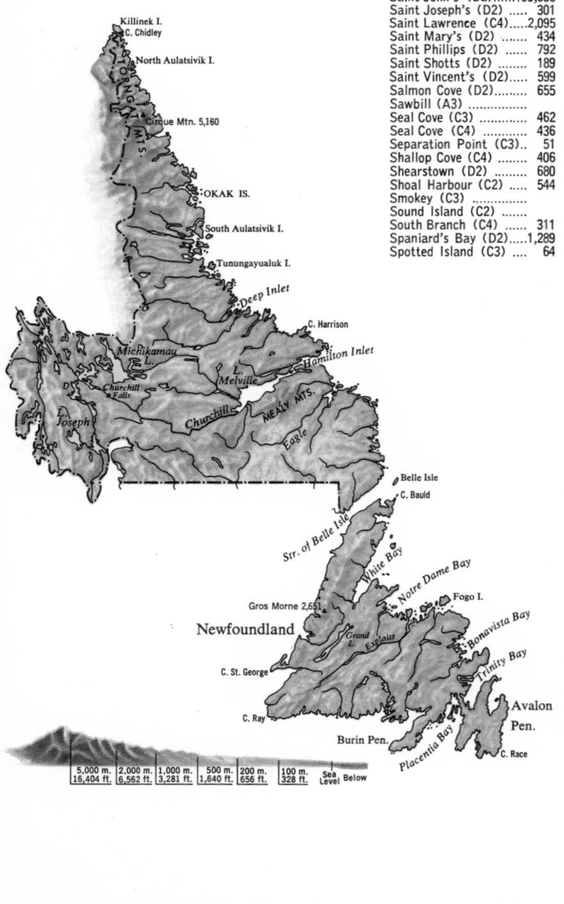

Killinek I.
C. Chidley
North Aulatsivik I.
Cirque Mtn. 5,160
OKAK IS.
South Aulatsivik I.
Tunungayualuk I.
Deep Inlet
C. Harrison
Michikamau
Hamilton Inlet
L. Melville
Churchill Falls
MEALY MTS.
Joseph
Churchill
Eagle
Belle Isle
C. Bauld
Str. of Belle Isle
White Bay
Notre Dame Bay
Fogo I.
Gros Morne 2,651
Newfoundland
Bonavista Bay
Trinity Bay
C. St. George
Avalon Pen.
C. Ray
Burin Pen.
Placentia Bay
C. Race
5,000 m. 16,404 ft.
2,000 m. 6,562 ft.
1,000 m. 3,281 ft.
500 m. 1,640 ft.
200 m. 656 ft.
100 m. 328 ft.
Sea Level
Below

OTHER FEATURES

Adlatok (bay) ....B 2
Adlavik (isls.) ....C 2
Aguanus (river) ....B 3
Alexis (river) ....C 3
Anaktalik Brook (river)..B 2
Andre (lake) ....A 3
Anguille (cape) ....C 4
Annieopsquotch (mts.)....C 4
Ashuanipi (lake) ....A 3
Ashuanipi (river) ....A 3
Astray (lake) ....A 3
Atikonak (lake) ....B 3
Atikonak (river) ....B 3
Attikamagen (lake) ....A 3
Avalon (peninsula) ....D 2
Avayalik (isls.) ....B 1
Baccalieu (isl.) ....D 2
Backway, The (inlet)......C 3
Ballard (cape) ....D 2
Bauld (cape) ....C 3
Beaver (river) ....B 3
Bell (isl.) ....C 3
Bell (isl.), 12,281 ....D 2
Belle Isle (isl.) ....C 3
Belle Isle (strait) ....C 3
Benedict (mt.) ....C 3
Big (isl.) ....B 2
Big (river) ....C 3
Biscay Bay (river) ....D 2
Black River (pond) ....C 2
Blackhead (bay) ....D 2
Bluff (cape) ....C 3
Bois (isl.) ....C 4
Bonaventure (cape) ......D 2
Bonavista (bay) ....D 1
Bonavista (cape) ....D 1
Bonne (bay) ....C 4
Branch (river) ....C 2
Brigus (cape) ....D 2
Broyle (cape) ....D 2
Brunette (isl.) ....C 4
Bull (isl.) ....D 2
Bull Arm (inlet) ....D 2
Bulldog (isl.) ....C 3
Burin (peninsula) ....C 4
Burnt (lake) ....B 3
Byron (bay) ....C 3
Cabot (lake) ....B 2
Cabot (strait) ....B 4
Canada (bay) ....C 3
Canairiktok (river)..........B 3
Chance Cove (cape) ....D 2
Chidley (cape) ....B 1
Churchill (falls) ....B 3
Churchill (riv.) ....B 3
Cirque (mt.) ....B 2
Clode (sound) ....D 2
Cod (isl.) ....B 2
Conception (bay) ....D 2
Deep (inlet) ....B 2
Deer (harbor) ....D 2
Disappointment (lake)....B 3
Dominion (lake) ....B 3
Double Mer (lake) ....C 3
Dyke (lake) ....A 3
Eagle (river) ....C 3
Eclipse (harbor) ....B 2
Eliot (mt.) ....B 2
Espoir (bay) ....C 4
Exploits (bay) ....C 4
Exploits (river) ....C 4
Ferolle (point) ....C 3
Ferryland (cape) ....D 2
Fig (river) ....B 3
Fogo (isl.), 4,546 ....D 4
Fonteneau (lake) ....B 3
Fortune (bay) ....C 4
Four (peaks) ....B 2
Franks (pond) ....D 2
Fraser (river) ....B 2
Freels (cape) ....D 4
Funk (isl.) ....D 4
Gabbro (lake) ....A 3
Gander (lake) ....D 4
Gander (river) ....D 4
George (isl.) ....C 3
Gilbert (river) ....C 3
Gisburn (lake) ....D 4
Glover (isl.) ....C 4
Goose (river) ....B 3
Grand (lake) ....B 3
Grand (lake) ....C 4
Grates (point) ....D 2
Gready (isl.) ....C 3
Great Burnt (lake) ....C 4
Great Colinet (isl.) ....D 2
Grey (isls.) ....C 3
Groais (isl.) ....C 3
Gros Morne (mt.) ....C 4
Groswater (bay) ....C 3
Gulch (cape) ....B 2
Gull (isl.) ....D 2
Gull Island (point) ....D 2
Hamilton (inlet) ....C 3
Hare (bay) ....C 3
Harp (lake) ....B 2
Harrison (cape) ....C 3
Hawke (hills) ....D 2
Hawke (isl.) ....C 3
Hawke (river) ....C 3
Hebron (fjord) ....B 2
Hermitage (bay) ....C 4
High (isl.) ....B 2
High (mts.) ....C 3
Holyrood (bay) ....D 2
Holyrood (pond) ....D 2
Home (isl.) ....B 1
Hope (lake) ....B 3
Horse Chops (channel)....D 2
Humber (river) ....C 4
Huntingdon (isl.) ....C 3
Iglosoatalialuk (isl.) ......B 2
Ingornachoix (bay) ....C 3
Innuit (mt.) ....B 2
Iona (isls.) ....C 2
Ironbound (isls.) ....C 2
Islands (bay) ....C 2
Islands (bay) ....C 4
Jack Lane (bay) ....B 2
Jeanette (bay) ....C 3
Jem Lane (bay) ....B 2
Joseph (lake) ....B 3
Kaipokok (bay) ....B 2
Kaipokok (river) ....B 3
Kakkiviak (cape) ....B 1
Kasheshibaw (lake) ....B 3
Kaumajet (mts.) ....B 2
Kenamu (river) ....B 3
Kiglapait (cape) ....B 2
Kiglapait (mts.) ....B 2
Kikkertasoak (isl.) ....B 2
Kikkertavak (isl.) ....B 2
Killinek (isl.) ....B 1
King (isl.) ....C 2
Kingurutik (lake) ....B 2
Knox (lake) ....A 3
Koraluk (river) ....B 2
Labrador (district), 13,534 ....B 2
Labrador (sea) ....C 2
Lady (pond) ....D 2
La Poile (bay) ....C 4
Little (river) ....C 4
Little Mecatina (river)...B 3
Lobstick (lake) ....B 3
Long (isl.) ....C 2
Long (isl.) ....D 2
Long (lake) ....B 3
Long (point) ....C 4
Long (range) ....C 4
Lozeau (lake) ....B 3
Mabille (lake) ....B 3
Maccles (lake) ....C 1
Mackenzie (lake) ....B 3
Main Topsail (mt.) ....C 4
Makkovik (cape) ....C 2
Manche, La (river) ....D 2
McLelan (strait) ....B 1
McPhadyen (river) ....A 3
Mealy (mts.) ....C 3
Meelpaeg (lake) ....C 4
Melville (lake) ....C 3
Menihek (lakes) ....A 3
Menistouc (lake) ....A 3
Merasheen (isl.) ....C 2
Merrifield (bay) ....B 2
Metchin (river) ....B 3
Michael (lake) ....C 3
Michikamats (lake) ....B 3
Michikamau (lake) ....B 3
Minipi (lake) ....B 3
Minipi (river) ....B 3
Mistaken (point) ....D 2
Mistastin (lake) ....B 2
Mistastin (river) ....B 2
Mistinippi (lake) ....B 3
Mobile Big (pond) ....D 2
Mount Carmel (pond) ....D 2
Mugford (cape) ....B 2
Muskrat (falls) ....B 3
Nachvak (fjord) ....B 2
Nanuktok (isls.) ....C 2
Napartokh (bay) ....B 2
Naskaupi (river) ....B 3
Natashquan (river) ....B 3
Natashquan-Est (riv.) ....B 3
New World (isl.), 4,443...C 4
Newman (sound) ....D 2
Nipishish (lake) ....B 3
Norman (cape) ....C 3
North (river) ....B 2
North (river) ....C 3
North Aulatsivik (isl.).....B 2
North West Arm (inlet)..D 2
North West Brook (river) D 2
North West Gander (river) ....C 4
Notre Dame (bay) ....C 4
Nunaksaluk (isl.) ....B 2
Okak (bay) ....B 2
Okak (isls.) ....B 2
Ossokmanuan (lake) ......B 3
Panchia (lake) ....B 3
Paradise (river) ....C 3
Partridge (bay) ....C 3
Paul (isl.) ....B 2
Peters (river) ....D 2
Petitsikapau (lake) ....A 3
Pine (cape) ....D 2
Pinware (river) ....C 3
Pistolet (bay) ....C 3
Placentia (bay) ....C 2
Placentia (sound) ....C 2
Poissons (river) ....A 3
Pond (lake) ....C 3
Ponds (isl.) ....C 3
Porcupine (cape) ....C 3
Port au Port (bay) ....C 4
Port au Port (peninsula)..C 4
Port Manvers (harbor)....B 2
Portland Creek (pond) ...C 3
Race (cape) ....D 2
Ragged (isls.) ....C 2
Ramah (bay) ....B 2
Ramea (isls.) ....C 4
Random (isl.), 1,644 ......D 2
Random (sound) ....D 2
Ray (cape) ....C 4
Red (isl.) ....C 2
Red Indian (lake) ....C 4
Red Wine (river) ....B 3
Riche (point) ....C 3
Rocky (bay) ....C 3
Rocky (river) ....D 2
Romaine (river) ....B 3
Round (pond) ....C 4
Ryan's (bay) ....B 2
Saglek (fjord) ....B 2
Saglek (bay) ....B 2
Saint-Augustin (river) ....C 3
Saint Barbe (isls.) ....C 3
Saint Charles (cape) ......C 3
Saint Croix (bay) ....D 2
Saint Francis (cape) .....D 2
Saint George (cape) ....C 4
Saint Georges (bay) ....C 4
Saint John (bay) ....C 3
Saint John (cape) ....C 3
Saint John (isl.) ....C 3
Saint Lewis (cape) ....C 3
Saint Lewis (river) ....C 3
Saint Marys (bay) ....C 2
Saint Mary's (cape) ....C 2
Saint Michaels (bay) .....C 3
Saint Paul (river) ....C 3
Saint Pauls (bay) ....C 4
Salmon (river) ....C 3
Salmonier (river) ....D 2
Sand Hill (river) ....C 3
Sandgirt (lake) ....A 3
Sandwich (bay) ....C 3
Sandy (lake) ....C 4
Seahorse (lake) ....A 3
Seal (lake) ....B 3
Sénécal (lake) ....B 3
Seven Islands (bay) ....B 2
Shabogamo (lake) ....A 3
Shapio (lake) ....B 3
Shoal (bay) ....D 2
Sims (lake) ....A 3
Sir Charles Hamilton (sound) ....D 4
Smith (sound) ....D 2
Snegamook (lake) ....B 3
South Aulatsivik (isl.) ...B 2
South West Arm (inlet)..D 2
South West Brook (river)C 2
South West Gander (river) ....C 4
South Wolf (isl.) ....C 3
Spear (cape) ....D 2
Stony (isl.) ....C 3
Swale (isl.) ....D 1
Sylvester (mt.) ....C 4
Table (bay) ....C 3
Ten Mile (lake) ....C 3
Terra Nova (river) ....C 2
Terra Nova Nat'l Park ...D 2
Territok (cape) ....B 2
Tessisoak (lake) ....B 2
Thoresby (mt.) ....B 2
Tickle (bay) ....D 2
Torbay (point) ....D 2
Torngat (mts.) ....B 2
Trepassey (bay) ....D 2
Trinity (bay) ....D 2
Trout River (pond) ....C 4
Tunungayualuk (isl.) ....B 2
Turnavik (isls.) ....C 2
Uivuk (cape) ....B 2
Ujutok (bay) ....B 2
Ukasiksalik (isl.) ....B 2
Umiakovik (lake) ....B 2
Victoria (lake) ....C 4
Voiseys (bay) ....B 2
Wabush (lake) ....A 3
Wade (lake) ....A 3
Watchman (isl.) ....B 2
Webb (bay) ....B 2
White (bay) ....C 3
White Bear (isl.) ....B 2
White Bear (river) ....C 4
White Handkerchief (cape) ....B 2
Windbound (lake) ....B 3
Winokapau (lake) ....B 3
Woods (lake) ....B 3

†Population of metropolitan area.

AGRICULTURE, INDUSTRY and RESOURCES

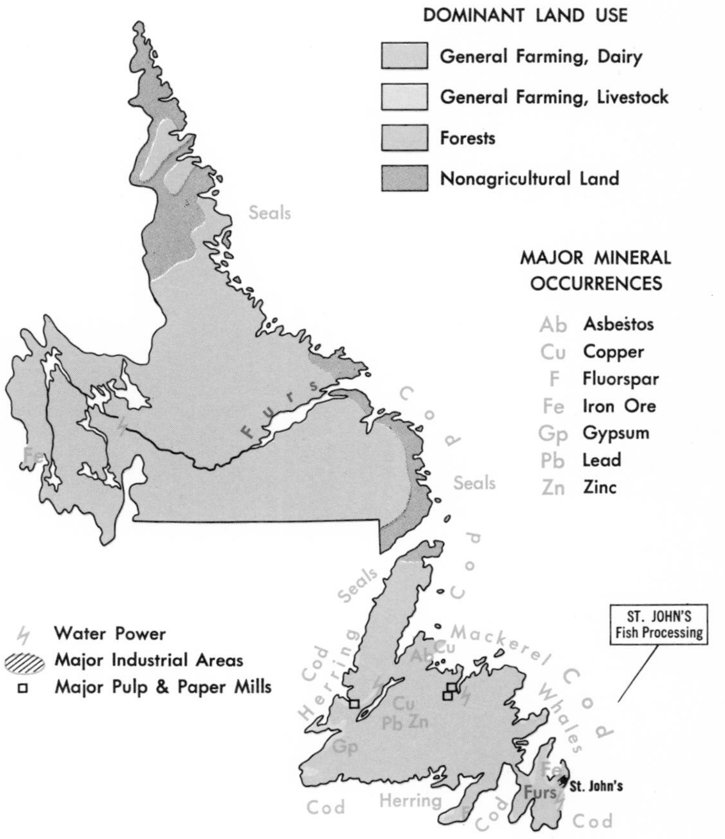

DOMINANT LAND USE
General Farming, Dairy
General Farming, Livestock
Forests
Nonagricultural Land
MAJOR MINERAL OCCURRENCES
Ab Asbestos
Cu Copper
F Fluorspar
Fe Iron Ore
Gp Gypsum
Pb Lead
Zn Zinc
Water Power
Major Industrial Areas
Major Pulp & Paper Mills
ST. JOHN'S Fish Processing
Seals
Furs
Cod
Mackerel
Herring
Whales
Fe
Ab
Cu
Pb Zn
Gp
St. John's

Nova Scotia and Prince Edward Island

NOVA SCOTIA and PRINCE EDWARD ISLAND

NOVA SCOTIA

AREA	21,425 sq. mi.
POPULATION	759,000
CAPITAL	Halifax
LARGEST CITY	Halifax (greater) 183,946
HIGHEST POINT	Cape Breton Highlands 1,747 ft.
SETTLED IN	1605
ADMITTED TO CONFEDERATION	1867
PROVINCIAL FLOWER	Trailing Arbutus or Mayflower

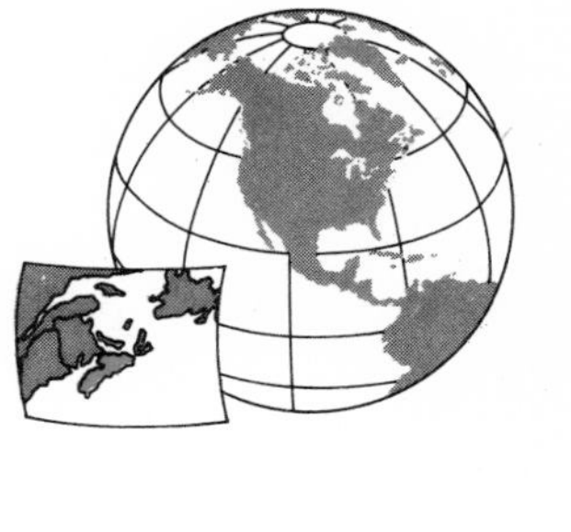

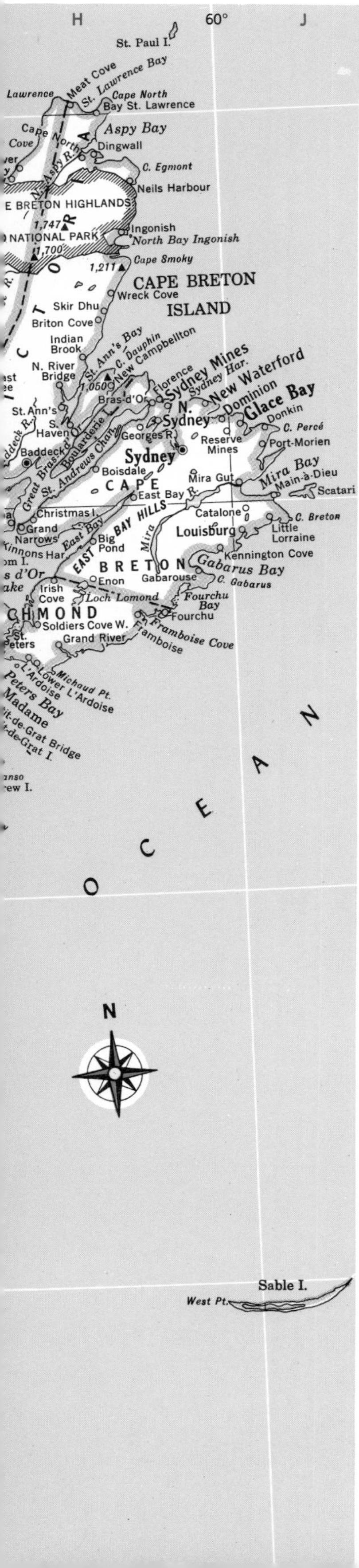

PRINCE EDWARD ISLAND

	2,184 sq. mi.
	108,000
	Charlottetown
	Charlottetown 18,318
	465 ft.
	1720
	1873
	Lady's Slipper

TOPOGRAPHY

0 30 60
MILES

AGRICULTURE, INDUSTRY and RESOURCES

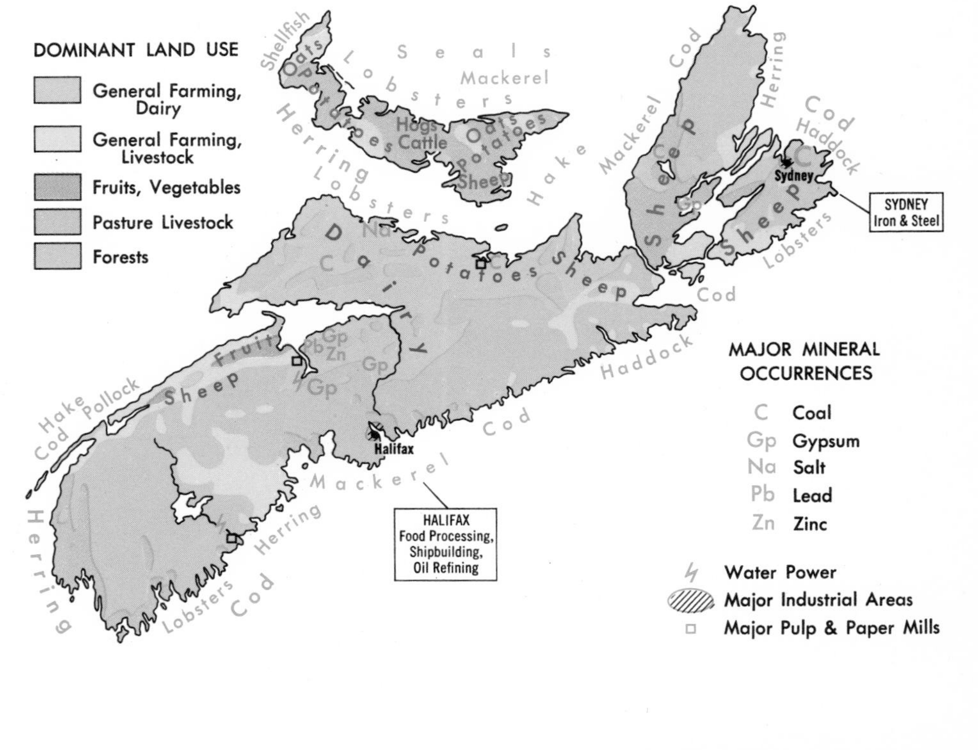

DOMINANT LAND USE

- General Farming, Dairy
- General Farming, Livestock
- Fruits, Vegetables
- Pasture Livestock
- Forests

SYDNEY
Iron & Steel

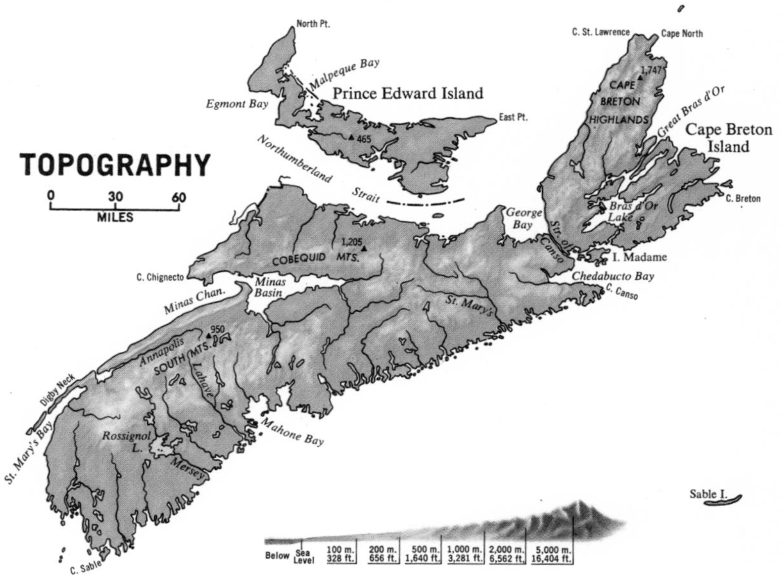

HALIFAX
Food Processing, Shipbuilding, Oil Refining

MAJOR MINERAL OCCURRENCES

C	Coal
Gp	Gypsum
Na	Salt
Pb	Lead
Zn	Zinc

⚡ Water Power
/// Major Industrial Areas
□ Major Pulp & Paper Mills

New Brunswick

COUNTIES

Albert (F3)	12,485
Carleton (C2)	23,507
Charlotte (C3)	23,285
Gloucester (E1)	66,343
Kent (E2)	26,667
Kings (E3)	25,908
Madawaska (B1)	38,983
Northumberland (D2)	50,035
Queens (D3)	11,640
Restigouche (C1)	40,973
Saint John (E3)	89,251
Sunbury (D3)	22,796
Victoria (C2)	19,712
Westmorland (F2)	93,679
York (C3)	52,672

CITIES and TOWNS

Acadie Siding (E2)	177
Adamsville (E2)	133
Albert (F3)	250
Albert Mines (F3)	154
Albertine (B1)	133

Aldouane (E2)	111
Allainville (E1)	80
Allandale (C3)	
Allardville (E1)	280
Alma (F3)	474
Alward (F3)	
Anagance (E3)	129
Andover⊛ (C2)	848
Annidale (E3)	
Anse-Bleue (E1)	516
Apohaqui (E3)	343
Aroostook Junction (E1)	
Argyle (C2)	64
Arthurette (C2)	303
Astle (D2)	252
Atholville (D1)	2,145
Aulac (F2)	194
Back Bay (D3)	725
Baie-Sainte-Anne (F1)	246
Baie-Verte (E1)	133
Baker Brook (B1)	371
Balmoral (D1)	898
Bantalor (D3)	
Barber Dam (C3)	
Barker (C3)	
Barnaby River (E2)	204

Barnesville (E3)	210
Bartibog Bridge (E1)	214
Barton (C3)	
Bas-Caraquet (F1)	786
Bass River (E2)	172
Bath (C2)	767
Bathurst⊛ (E1)	5,494
Bathurst Mines (E1)	64
Bayfield (F3)	188
Bayside (C3)	78
Beaubois (E2)	172
Beaver Brook Station (E1)	264
Beaver Harbour (D3)	387
Beersville (E2)	123
Belledune (E1)	252
Belledune River (E1)	117
Bellefleur (C1)	142
Belleisle Creek (E3)	75
Belleville (C2)	50
Ben Lomond (E3)	418
Benton (C3)	183
Beresford (E1)	699
Berry Mills (E2)	318
Bertrand (E1)	468
Black Point (D1)	133
Black River (E3)	50

Black River Bridge (E2)	
Blacks Harbour (D3)	1,297
Blackville (E2)	484
Bloomfield Station (E3)	68
Blue Bell (C2)	170
Bocabec (C3)	181
Boiestown (D2)	343
Bonny River (D3)	107
Bossé (B1)	306
Bourgoin (B1)	61
Brantville (E1)	800
Brest (E2)	
Bristol (C2)	643
Brockway (C3)	87
Brookville (E3)	193
Browns Flat (D3)	284
Bruce (E1)	
Buctouche (F2)	1,537
Burnsville (E1)	209
Burnt Church (E1)	99
Burton⊛ (D3)	433
Burtts Corner (D2)	389
Butte-d'Or (E1)	140
Calhoun (F2)	70
Cambridge (E3)	122
Campbellton (D1)	9,873
Canaan Station (E3)	88
Canterbury Station (C3)	595
Cap-Pelé (F2)	859
Cape Station (F3)	56
Cape Tormentine (G2)	345
Caraquet (E1)	1,214
Caron Brook (B1)	149
Carr (C2)	

Carrolls Crossing (D2)	194
Castalia (D4)	241
Central Blissville (D3)	45
Centre-Acadie (E2)	103
Centre-Saint-Simon (E1)	550
Centreville (C2)	352
Chamcook (C3)	327
Chance Harbour (D3)	183
Charlo Station (D1)	409
Chatham⊛ (E1)	7,109
Chatham Head (E1)	1,610
Chipman (E2)	1,490
Clair (B1)	770
Clarendon (D3)	424
Cliffordvale (C2)	139
Clifton (E1)	192
Clifton Royal (D3)	122
Cloverdale (C2)	104
Coal Branch Station (E2)	569
Coal Creek (E2)	113
Cocagne (E3)	113
Codys (E3)	55
Coldbrook (E3)	507
Coldstream (C2)	187
Coles Island (E3)	
College Bridge (F3)	621
Collette (E2)	333
Connors (B1)	244
Cork Station (D3)	105
Corn-Village (E3)	84
Corn Hill (E3)	93
Cross Creek (D2)	252
Cross Creek Station (D2)	50

Cumberland Bay (E2)	320
Dalhousie⊛ (D1)	5,856
Dalhousie Junction (D1)	172
Daulnay (E1)	550
Dauversière (E1)	164
Dawsonville (C1)	228
Debec (C2)	263
Deer Lake (C3)	
Derby (E2)	75
Derby Junction (E2)	116
Devereaux (E1)	108
Dieppe (F2)	4,032
Dipper Harbour (D3)	150
Doaktown (D2)	595
Dorchester⊛ (F3)	1,779
Dorchester Crossing (F2)	569
Douglas Harbour (D3)	86
Douglastown (E1)	615
Duguayville (E1)	273
Dumbarton Station (D3)	51
Dumfries (C3)	83
Durham Bridge (D3)	193
Durham Centre (D1)	348
East Bathurst (E1)	1,876
East Brighton (C2)	76
East Galloway (E2)	64
Edmundston⊛ (B1)	12,791
Eel River Bridge (F1)	518
Eel River Crossing (D1)	636
Elgin (E3)	315

Enniskillen Station (D3)	47
Escuminac (F1)	317
Evandale (D3)	80
Evangeline (E1)	124
Fairhaven (C4)	174
Fairvale Station (E3)	759
Ferry Road (E1)	438
Fielding (C2)	
Flatlands (D1)	282
Flemington (C2)	
Florenceville (C2)	229
Fontaine (F2)	273
Forest City (E1)	51
Fort Beauséjour (F3)	
Fosterville (C3)	103
Fox Creek (F2)	305
Francoeur (B1)	
FREDERICTON⊛ (D3)	19,683
Fredericton Junction (D3)	641
Gagetown⊛ (D3)	572
Gardners Creek (E3)	71
Gaspereau Forks (E2)	
Geary (D3)	938
Germantown (F3)	75
Gilks (F2)	404
Glassville (C2)	128
Glencoe (D1)	192
Glenlivet (D1)	309
Gloucester Junction (E1)	
Goshen (E3)	
Grand Bay (E3)	725
Grand Falls (C1)	3,983
Grand Harbour (D4)	439
Grand River (C1)	

Grande-Anse (E1)	522
Grande-Digue (F2)	183
Grandmaison (B1)	54
Gray Rapids (E2)	191
Green Road (C2)	
Greenwich Hill (D3)	73
Gunningsville (F2)	1,254
Hampstead (D3)	116
Hampton⊛ (E3)	571
Hampton Station (E3)	593
Hanford Brook (E3)	
Harcourt (E2)	231
Hardwicke (E1)	125
Hardwood Ridge (D2)	237
Hartland (C2)	1,025
Harvey (F3)	231
Harvey Station (C3)	323
Hatfield Point (E3)	
Havelock (E3)	190
Hawkshaw (C3)	
Hayesville (D2)	131
Head of Millstream (E3)	92
Heath Steele (D1)	
Hillsborough (F3)	679
Hillsdale (E3)	110
Holmesville (C2)	
Honeydale (C3)	68
Hopewell Cape⊛ (F3)	141
Hopewell Hill (F3)	217
Howard (F2)	176
Hoyt (D3)	327
Inkerman (F1)	468
Irishtown (F2)	
Jacksonville (C2)	360

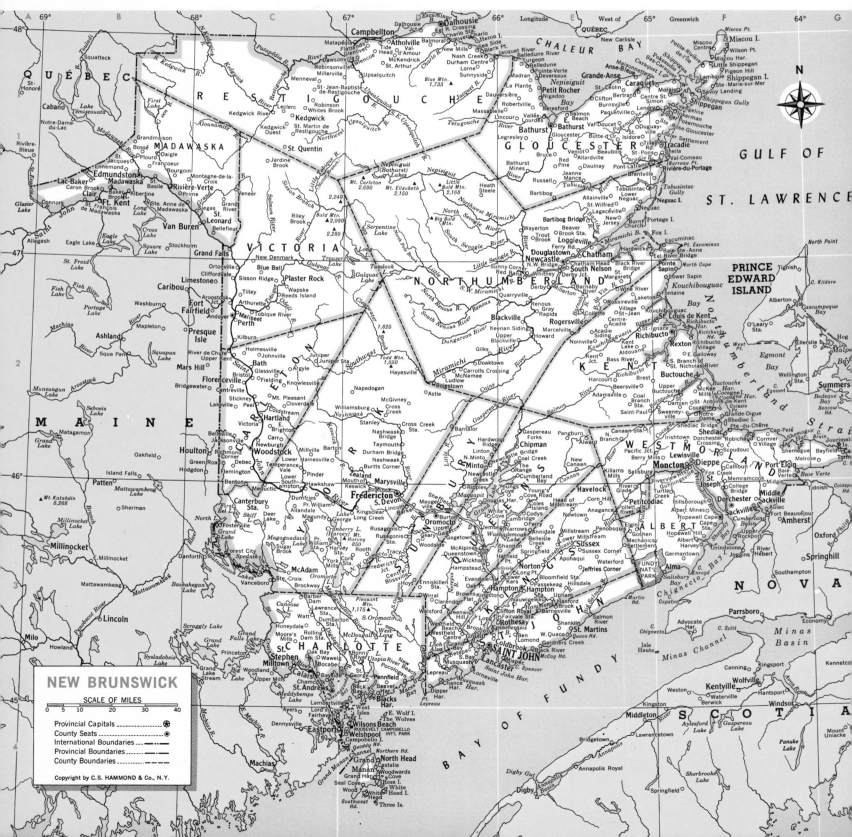

NEW BRUNSWICK

AREA	28,354 sq. mi.
POPULATION	626,000
CAPITAL	Fredericton
LARGEST CITY	Saint John (greater) 95,563
HIGHEST POINT	Mt. Carleton 2,690 ft.
SETTLED IN	1611
ADMITTED TO CONFEDERATION	1867
PROVINCIAL FLOWER	Purple Violet

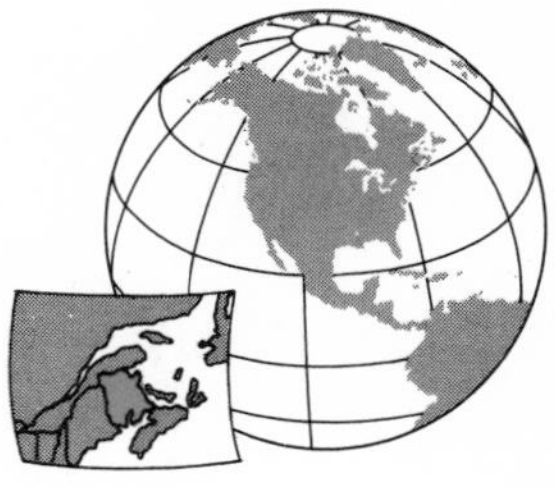

Jacquet River (E1)....... 500
Jardine Brook (C1).......
Jeanne-Mance (E1) .....
Jeffries Corner (E3)..... 106
Jemseg (D3) 172
Johnville (C2) 120
Juniper (C2) 691
Juniper Station (C2) 77
Kedgwick (C1) 1,095
Kedgwick-Ouest (C1).... 173
Kedgwick River (C1)..... 66
Keenan Siding (E2) 122
Kent Junction (E2) 182
Kent Lake (E2) 52
Ketepec (D3) 310
Kilburn (C2) 137
Killams Mills (E2) 55
Kingsclear (D3) 200
Kingston (D3) 74
Knowlesville (C2) 180
Kouchibouguac (F2) 57
Lac-Baker (B1) 338
Lagacéville (E1) 263
Laketon (E2) 89
Lakeville (C2) 148
Lambertville (C3) 350
Lamèque (F1) 1,082
Lancaster (D3) 13,848
Landry (E1) 399
La Plante (E1) ....
Lawrence Station (C3).. 210
Leclerc (C1) ....
Legresley (E1) ....
Lepreau (D3) 94
Lewisville (F2) 3,094
Lincoln (D3) 809
Lincour (E1) 144
Linton (D2) 77
Little Shippegan (F1).. 30
Loggieville (E1) 691
Long Creek (D3) ....
Long Point (E3) 61
Lord's Cove (C4) 250
Lorne (D1) 890
Lorneville (D3) 666
Lower Mainesville (C2).. 183
Lower Kars (E3) ....
Lower Millstream (E3).. 80
Lower Neguac (E1) 324
Lower Sapin (F2) 310
Lower Southampton (C3) 130
Lozier Settlement (F1) 236
Ludlow (D2) 240
Madran (E1) 223
Magundy (C3) 62
Maisonette (E1) 627
Maliseet (C2) ....
Marcelville (E2) 96
Marysville (D2) 3,233
Massabielle (D1) ....
Maugerville (D3) 631
McAdam (C3) 2,472
McAlpines (D3) ....
McGivney (D2) 235
McKee Mills (F2) 152
McKendrick (D1) 523
McNamee (D2) 257
Mechanics Settlement (E3) ....
Meductic (C3) 232
Melrose (F2) 178
Memramcook (F2) 402
Menneval (C1) 178
Middle Sackville (F3)... 442
Midgic (F3) 272
Millerton (E2) 232
Millerville (C1) ....
Millstrèam (E3) 181
Milltown (C3) 1,892
Millville (C2) 390
Minto (D2) 1,319
Miscou Centre (F1) 513
Miscou Harbour (F1).... 106
Mispec (E3) 183
Moncton (F2) 43,840
Montagne-de-la-Croix (C1) ....
Moore's Mills (C3) 116
Morais (F1) 258
Mount Pleasant (C2).....
Mouth of Keswick (D2) 210
Musquash (D3) 88
Napadogan (D2) 167
Narrows (E3) 97
Nash Creek (D1) 250
Nashwaak (D2) 127
Nashwaak Bridge (D2).. 195
Nawigewauk (E3) 83
Neguac (E1) 559
New Canaan (E2) 58
New Denmark (C1)....... 90
New Jersey (E1) 128
New Mills (D1) 230
New River (D3) ....
Newburg (C2) 137
Newcastle ◉(E1) 5,236
Newcastle Bridge (E2).. 483
Newcastle Creek (D2)... 347
Newtown (E3) ....
Nigadoo (E1) 361
Noinville (E2) 109
North Branch (E2) ......
North Head (D4) 609
North Minto (D2) 422
Northern Head (D4) ....
Northwest Bridge (E2)
Norton (E3) 846
Notre-Dame (F2) 317
Oak Bay (C3) 287
Oak Point (D3) 118
Oromocto (D3) 12,170
Ortonville (C2) 72
Pacific Junction (E2)..
Pangburn (E2) ....
Paquetville (E1) 380
Passekeag (E3) 180
Peel (C2) 139
Pelletier Mills (B1)...... 156
Pennfield (D3) 160
Penobsquis (E3) 259
Perry (E3) ....
Perth (C2) 909
Petit-Rocher (E1) 500
Petitcodiac (E3) 902
Petite-Rivière-de-l'Île (F1) 607
Pigeon Hill (F1) 431
Pinder (C2) 53
Plaster Rock (C2) 1,267
Plourd (B1) 482
Pocologan (D3) 127
Pointe-du-Chêne (F2).... 534
Pointe Sapin (F2) 638
Pointe-Verte (E1) 350
Pollett River (E3) 71
Pont-Lafrance (E1)...... 469
Port Elgin (F2) 661
Prime (B1) 265
Prince William (C3) 80
Prince William Station (C3) ....
Quarryville (E2) 256
Queenstown (D3) 138
Red Bank (E2) 331
Red Pine (E1) ....
Reeds Island (C2) ....
Renous (E2) 350
Rexton (F2) 668
Richibucto◉ (E2) 1,375
Richibucto Village (F2) 345
Richmond Corner (C2)..
Riley Brook (C1).......... 178
Ripples (D3) 233
River Charlo (D1) 164
River de Chute (C2) 84
River Glade (E3) 289
Riverview Heights (F2)..2,666
Rivière-du-Portage (F1) 586
Rivière-Verte (B1) 918
Robertville (E1) 680
Robichaud (F2) 371
Robinson (C1) ....
Robinsonville (C1) 233
Rogersville (E2) 1,040
Rolling Dam Station (C3) 132
Rooth (D3) 55
Rosaireville (E2) 123
Rothesay (E3) 782
Rusagonis (D3) 262
Rusagonis Station (D3) 84
Russell (E1) ....
Sackville (F3) 3,038
Saint Andrews◉ (C3)...1,531
Saint-Arthur (D1) 605
Saint-Antoine-de-Kent (F2) 300
Saint-Basile (B1) 1,733
Saint-Damien (F2) 162
Saint-François-de-Madawaska (B1) 561
Saint George (D3) 1,133
Saint-Ignace (F2) 515
Saint-Isidore (E1) 614
Saint-Jacques (B1) 892
Saint-Jean-Baptiste-de-Restigouche (C1) 346
Saint John◉ (E3) 55,153
Saint John (E3) ......†95,563
Saint Joseph (F3) 748
Saint-Léolin (E1) 607
Saint-Léonard (C1) 1,666
Saint-Louis-de-Kent (F2) 861
Saint Margarets (E2)...
Saint-Martin-de-Restigouche (C1) 239
Saint Martins (E3) 509
Saint-Paul (E2) 446
Saint-Pons (E1) 433
Saint-Quentin (C1)........2,089
Saint Stephen (C3) 3,380
Saint Wilfred (E1) 299
Sainte-Anne-de-Madawaska (B1) 1,122
Sainte-Croix (C3) 173
Sainte-Marie-sur-Mer (F1) 435
Sainte-Rose-Gloucester (F1) 404
Salisbury (E2) 589
Salmon Beach (E1) 295
Salmon River (E3) ......
Savoy Landing (F1) 100
Scoudouc (F2) 175
Sea Side (D1) 78
Seal Cove (D4) 549
Shanklin (E3) ....
Shannon (E3) 142
Shediac (F2) 2,159
Shediac Bridge (F2) 382
Sheffield (D3) 169
Sheila (F1) 553
Shemogue (F2) 93
Shippegan (F1) 1,631
Siegas (C1) 255
Sisson Ridge (C2) 149
South Bay (D3) 166
South Branch of Saint Nicholas River (F2)..
South Devon (D3) 1,070
South Nelson (E2) 792
Springfield (E3) 109
Stanley (D2) 301
Stickney (C2) 313
Sugar Broook (C3) ......
Sunny Corner (E2) 468
Sunnyside (D1) 99
Sussex (E3) 3,457
Sussex Corner (E3) 359
Sweeneyville (F2) 78
Tabusintac (E1) 263
Taymouth (D2) 299
Temperance Valε (C2).. 264
The Range (E2) 100
Tide Head (D1) 702
Tilley (C2) 218
Tilley Road (E1) 360
Tobique River (C2).......
Tracadie (F1) 1,651
Tracy (D3) 655
Trout Brook (E1) 185
Turgeon (E1) 237
Turtle Creek (F3) 101
Upham (E3) 166
Upper Blackville (E2)... 438
Upper Buctouche (F2)... 184
Upper Gagetown (D3)... 244
Upper Kent (C2) 174
Upper Mills (C3) 153
Upper Pokemouche (F1) 191
Upper Rockport (F3).... 50
Upsalquitch (D1) 165
Val-Comeau (F1) 444
Val-d'Amour (D1) 474
Val-Doucet (E1) 457
Vallée-Lourdes (E1) 331
Veneer (C1) ....
Veniot (E1) ....
Victoria (C2) 182
Village-Saint-Jean (E2)..
Wapske (C2) 182
Waterford (E3) 116
Watt (C3) 40
Waweig (C3) 179
Wayerton (E1) 129
Welsford (D3) 424
Welshpool (D4) 199
West Quaco (E3) 108
Westfield Beach (D3)... 80
Westfield Centre (D3) .. 114
White Head (D4) 272
Whites Brook (C1) ......
White's Cove (D3) 268
Whitney (E2) 336
Wickham (D3) 121
Williamsburg (D2) 369
Wilson Point (F1)........ 88
Wilsons Beach (D4) 768
Wine River (E2) ....
Wirral (D3) 123
Wood Island (D4) ....
Woodside (D3) 98
Woodstock◉ (C2) 4,305
Woodwards Cove (D4).. 188
York Mills (C3) 94
Youngs Cove (E3) 134
Youngs Cove Road (E3) 67
Zealand (D2) 442

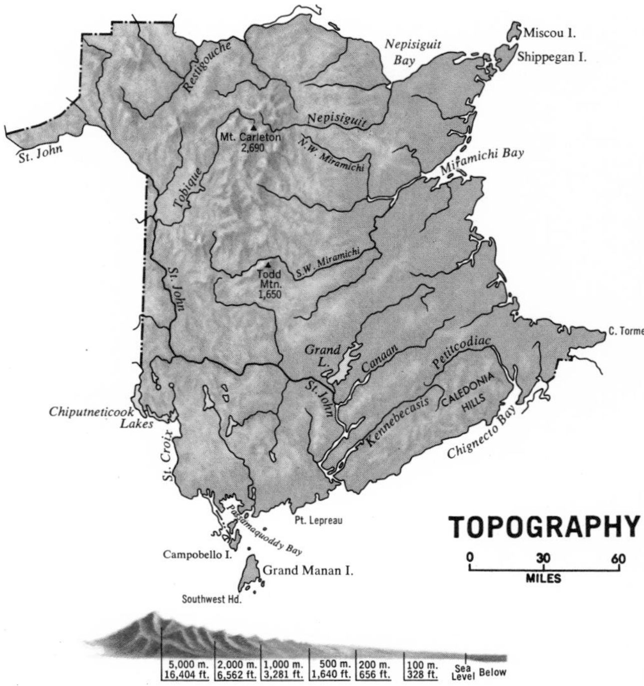

Miscou I.
Shippegan I.
Nepisiguit Bay
Restigouche
Nepisiguit
Mt. Carleton 2,690
N.W. Miramichi
Miramichi Bay
St. John
Tobique
St. John
Todd Mtn. 1,650
S.W. Miramichi
C. Tormentine
Grand L.
Canaan
Petitcodiac
Chiputneticook Lakes
St. Croix
St. John
Kennebecasis
CALEDONIA HILLS
Chignecto Bay
Passamaquoddy Bay
Pt. Lepreau
Campobello I.
Grand Manan I.
Southwest Hd.
0 30 60
MILES
5,000 m. 16,404 ft.
2,000 m. 6,562 ft.
1,000 m. 3,281 ft.
500 m. 1,640 ft.
200 m. 656 ft.
100 m. 328 ft.
Sea Level
Below

TOPOGRAPHY

AGRICULTURE, INDUSTRY and RESOURCES

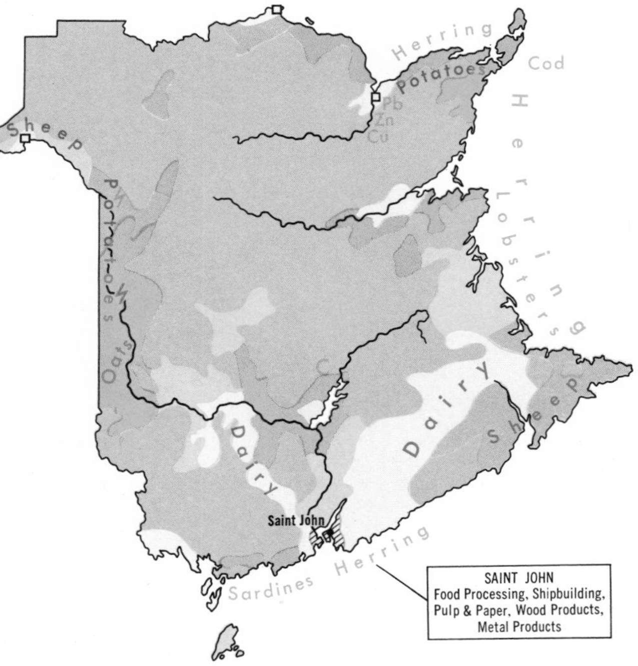

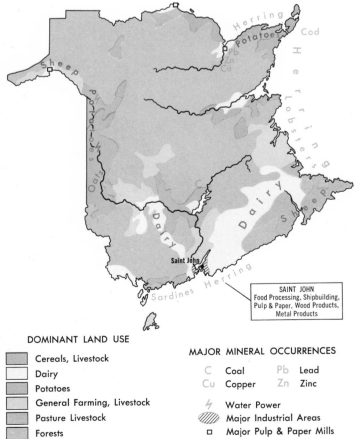

Herring
Cod
Potatoes
Pb
Zn
Cu
Sheep
Herring
Lobsters
Potatoes
Oats
Dairy
Dairy
Sheep
Dairy
Saint John
Herring
Sardines
SAINT JOHN
Food Processing, Shipbuilding, Pulp & Paper, Wood Products, Metal Products

DOMINANT LAND USE

- Cereals, Livestock
- Dairy
- Potatoes
- General Farming, Livestock
- Pasture Livestock
- Forests

MAJOR MINERAL OCCURRENCES

- C Coal
- Pb Lead
- Cu Copper
- Zn Zinc
- Water Power
- Major Industrial Areas
- □ Major Pulp & Paper Mills

OTHER FEATURES

Alva (lake) ....D 3
Bald (mt.) ....C 1
Barnaby (river) ....E 2
Barreau (point) ....F 1
Bartibog (river) ....E 1
Bathurst (Nepisiguit) (lakes) ....D 1
Bay du Vin (river) ....E 2
Belleisle (bay) ....E 3
Big Bald (mt.) ....D 1
Big Salmon (river) ....E 3
Blue (mt.) ....D 1
Bruin (cape) ....G 2
Buctouche (harbor) ....F 2
Buctouche (river) ....F 2
Cains (river) ....D 2
Caissie (point) ....F 2
Campobello (isl.), 1,137..D 4
Canaan (river) ....E 2
Canoose (lake) ....C 3
Caraquet (isl.) ....F 1
Carleton (mt.) ....D 1
Chaleur (bay) ....E 1
Charlo (river) ....D 1
Chignecto (bay) ....F 3
Chiputneticook (lakes) ...C 3
Clearwater Brook (river)D 2
Cocagne (harbor) ....F 2
Cocagne (isl.) ....F 2
Cocagne (river) ....F 2
Cranberry (lake) ....D 3
Cumberland (basin) ....F 3
Deer (isl.) ....D 4
Digdeguash (river) ....C 3
Dungarvon (river) ....D 2
East Wolf (isl.) ....D 4
Elizabeth (mt.) ....D 1
Enragé (cape) ....F 3
Escuminac (bay) ....D 1
Escuminac (point) ....F 1
First (lake) ....B 1
First Eel (lake) ....C 3
Fox (isl.) ....F 1
Fundy (bay) ....E 3
Fundy Nat'l Park ....E 3
Gaspereau (river) ....D 2
George (lake) ....C 3
Gounamitz (river) ....C 1
Grand (bay) ....D 3
Grand (lake) ....C 3
Grand (lake) ....D 3
Grand (river) ....C 1
Grand Manan (channel) C 4
Grand Manan (isl.), 2,564 ....D 4
Green (river) ....B 1
Grindstone (isl.) ....F 3
Gulquac (lake) ....D 2
Gulquac (river) ....C 2
Hammond (river) ....E 3
Harvey (mt.) ....D 3
Harvey (Cranberry) (lake) ....D 3
Heron (isl.) ....D 1
Jacquet (river) ....D 1
Jourimain (isls.) ....G 2
Kedgwick (river) ....C 1
Kennebecasis (bay) ....E 3
Kennebecasis (river) .....E 3
Keswick (river) ....C 2
Kouchibouguac (bay) .....F 2
Kouchibouguacis (river)..E 2
Lepreau (point) ....D 3
Lepreau (river) ....D 3
Little (river) ....D 2
Little Bald (mt.) ....D 1
Little Sevogle (river) ....D 1
Little Southwest Miramichi (river) ....D 2
Little Tobique (river) ....C 1
Long (isl.) ....D 3
Long (lake) ....D 1
Long Reach (inlet) ....D 3
Maces (bay) ....D 3
Madawaska (river) ....B 1
Magaguadavic (lake) .....C 3
Magaguadavic (river) ....C 3
Maquapit (lake) ....D 3
Martin (head) ....E 3
McCoy (head) ....E 3
McDougall (lake) ....D 3
Miramichi (bay) ....E 1
Miscou (isl.) ....F 1
Miscou (point) ....F 1
Musquash (harbor) ....D 3
Nashwaak (river) ....D 2
Neguac (isl.) ....F 1
Nepisiguit (bay) ....E 1
Nepisiguit (lakes) ....D 1
Nepisiguit (river) ....D 1
Nerepis (river) ....D 3
Nictor Branch, Tobique (river) ....C 1
North (cape) ....F 2
North (lake) ....C 3
North Kedgwick (river)..C 1
North Pole Brook (river)D 1
North Renous (river) ....D 2
North Sevogle (river) ....D 1
Northern (head) ....D 4
Northumberland (strait) F 2
Northwest Miramichi (river).........................D 1
Northwest Oromocto (river) ....D 3
Northwest Upsalquitch (river) ....D 1
Odell (river) ....C 2
Oromocto (lake) ....C 3
Oromocto (river) ....D 3
Passamaquoddy (bay) ....C 3
Patapédia (river) ....C 1
Petitcodiac (river) ....F 3
Pleasant (mt.) ....D 3
Pokemouche (river) ......E 1
Pokesudie (isl.) ....F 1
Pollett (river) ....E 3
Portage (isl.) ....F 1
Quaco (head) ....E 3
Renous (river) ....D 2
Restigouche (river) ....C 1
Richibucto (harbor) ......F 2
Richibucto (head) ....F 2
Richibucto (river) ....E 2
Ross (isl.) ....D 4
Saint Croix (river) ....C 3
Saint John (harbor) ......E 3
Saint John (river) ....C 2
Saint Lawrence (gulf) ...F 1
Salisbury (bay) ....F 3
Salmon (river) ....C 1
Salmon (river) ....E 2
Serpentine (lake) ....D 1
Shediac (isl.) ....F 2
Shemogue (harbor) ....F 2
Shepody (bay) ....F 3
Shippegan (gully) ....F 1
Shippegan (isl.) ....F 1
Shippegan (sound) ....F 1
Sisson Branch, Tobique (river) ....C 1
Skiff (lake) ....C 3
South Kedgwick (river)..B 1
South Oromocto (lake)...D 3
South Oromocto (river)..D 3
South Renous (river) .....D 2
South Sevogle (river) ....D 1
Southeast Upsalquitch (river) ....D 1
Southwest (head) ....D 4
Southwest Miramichi (river) ....D 2
Spear (cape) ....G 2
Spednik (lake) ....C 3
Spencer (cape) ....E 3
Tabusintac (gully) ....F 1
Tabusintac (river) ....E 1
Tetagouche (river) ....D 1
Three (isls.) ....D 4
Tobique (river) ....C 2
Todd (mt.) ....D 2
Tracadie (river) ....E 1
Trousers (lake) ....C 1
Tuadook (lake) ....D 2
Upsalquitch (river) ....D 1
Utopia (lake) ....D 3
Verte (bay) ....G 2
Washademoak (lake) .....E 3
West (isls.), 976 ....D 4
West Long (lake) ....D 3
White Head (isl.) ....D 4
Wolves, The (isls.).........D 4

◉County Seat.
†Population of metropolitan area.

Quebec

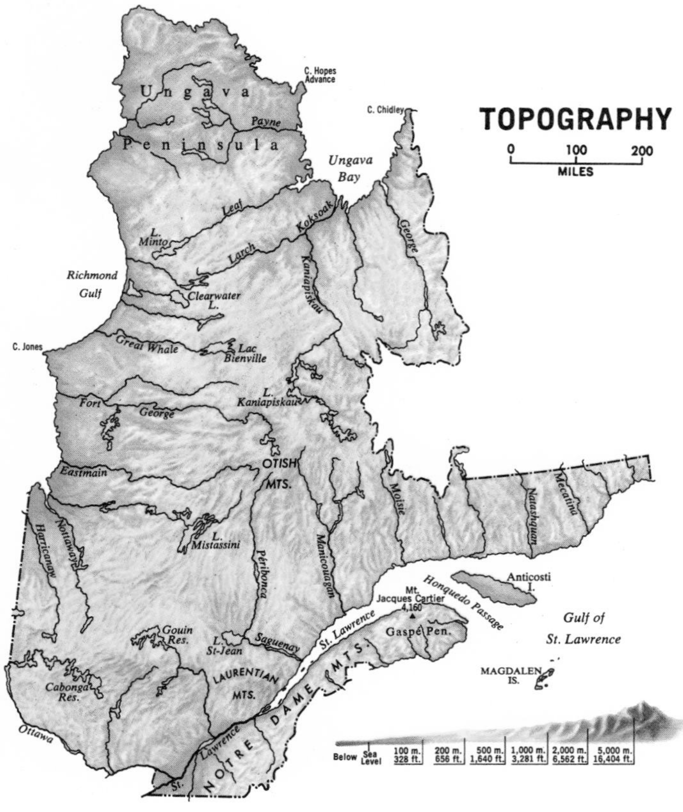
TOPOGRAPHY
0 100 200
MILES
Ungava
Peninsula
C. Hopes Advance
C. Chidley
Payne
Ungava Bay
Leaf
Koksoak
George
L. Minto
Larch
Kaniapiskau
Richmond Gulf
Clearwater L.
C. Jones
Great Whale
Lac Bienville
L. Kaniapiskau
Fort George
Eastmain
OTISH MTS.
Moisie
Natashquan
Mecatina
Nottaway
Harricana
L. Mistassini
Péribonca
Manicouagan
Mt. Jacques Cartier 4,160
Honguedo Passage
Anticosti I.
Gulf of St. Lawrence
Gaspé Pen.
Gouin Res.
L. St-Jean
Saguenay
LAURENTIAN MTS.
St. Lawrence
NOTRE DAME MTS.
MAGDALEN IS.
Cabonga Res.
Ottawa
Below Sea Level
100 m. 328 ft.
200 m. 656 ft.
500 m. 1,640 ft.
1,000 m. 3,281 ft.
2,000 m. 6,562 ft.
5,000 m. 16,404 ft.

SOUTHERN QUEBEC

COUNTIES

Argenteuil (C4) 31,830
Arthabaska (E4) 45,301
Bagot (E4) 21,390
Beauce (G3) 62,264
Beauharnois (C4) 49,667
Bellechasse (G3) 26,054
Berthier (C3) 27,325
Bonaventure (C2) 42,962
Brome (E4) 13,691
Chambly (J4) 146,745
Champlain (E2) 111,953
Charlevoix-Est (G2).....16,450
Charlevoix-Ouest (G2)..14,562
Châteauguay (D4) 34,042
Chicoutimi (G1) 157,196
Compton (F4) 24,410
Deux-Montagnes (C4) 32,837
Dorchester (G3) 34,711
Drummond (E4) 58,220
Frontenac (G4) 30,600
Gaspé-Est (D1) 41,333
Gaspé-Ouest (C1) 20,529
Gatineau (B3) 44,308
Hochelaga (H4) 1,179,205
Hull (B4) 84,803
Huntingdon (C4) 14,752
Iberville (D4) 18,080
Jacques-Cartier (H4) 568,491
Joliette (C3) 44,969
Kamouraska (H2) 27,138
L'Assomption (D4) 39,440
L'Islet (G2) 24,798
Labelle (B3) 29,084
Lac-Saint-Jean-Est (F1) 43,920
Lac-Saint-Jean-Ouest (E1) 61,310
Laprairie (H4) 31,157
Laval (H4) 21,4741
Lévis (J3) 51,842
Lotbinière (F3) 30,234
Maskinongé (D3) 21,274
Matane (B1) 35,078
Matapédia (B2) 35,586
Mégantic (F3) 57,400
Missisquoi (E4) 29,526
Montcalm (C3) 18,766
Montmagny (G3) 26,450
Montmorency No. 1 (F2) 20,734
Montmorency No. 2 (G3) 4,974
Napierville (D4) 11,216
Nicolet (E3) 30,8227
Papineau (B4) 32,697
Portneuf (E3) 50,711
Québec (F3) 331,307
Richelieu (D4) 38,565
Richmond (F4) 42,232
Rimouski (J1) 65,295
Rivière-du-Loup (H2)...40,239
Rouville (D4) 25,979
Saguenay (H1) 81,900
Saint-Hyacinthe (D4) 44,993
Saint-Jean (D4) 38,470
Saint-Maurice (D3) ..109,873
Shefford (E4) 54,963
Sherbrooke (E4) 80,490
Soulanges (C4) 10,075
Stanstead (F4) 36,095
Témiscouata (J2) 29,079
Terrebonne (H4) 102,275
Vaudreuil (C4) 28,681
Verchères (J4) 25,697
Wolfe (F4) 18,335
Yamaska (E3) 16,058

CITIES and TOWNS

Abbotsford (E4) 619
Acton Vale (E4)...........3,957
Alma (F1) 13,309
Amqui◉ (B2) 3,659
Ancienne-Lorette (H3)..3,958
Ange-Gardien-de-Rouville (E4) 474
Anjou (H4) 9,511
Anse-au-Griffon (D1)..... 204
Armagh (G3) 914
Arthabaska◉ (F3) 2,977
Arundel (C4) 409
Arvida (F1) 14,460
Asbestos (F4) 11,083
Aston Junction (E3)..... 396
Athelstan (C4) 167
Ayers Cliff◉ (E4) 747
Aylmer East (B4).........6,286
Bagotville (G1) 5,629
Baie-Comeau (A1) 7,956
Baie-des-Sables (B1).... 927
Baie-d'Urfé (G4) 3,549
Baie-Saint-Paul◉ (G2)..4,674
Baie-Trinité (B1) 968
Baieville (E3) 558
Barachois-de-Malbaie (D1) 495
Barré (G3) 353
Batiscan (E3) 231
Beaconsfield (H4) 10,064
Beauceville-Est◉ (G3)..1,920
Beauceville-Ouest (G3)..1,645
Beauharnois◉ (D4) 8,704
Beauport (J3) 9,192
Beaupré (G2) 2,587
Beaurivage (F3) 518
Bécancour◉ (E3) 320
Bedford (E4) 2,855
Beebe (E4) 1,363
Beloeil (D4) 6,283
Berthierville◉ (D3) 3,708
Bic (J1) 1,177
Black Lake (F3) 4,180
Boischatel (J3) 1,579
Bolduc (G4) 1,176
Bonaventure (C2) 804
Boucherville (J4) 7,403
Bouchette (A3) 464
Breakeyville (J3) 500
Brébeuf (C3) 194
Bromptonville (F4) 2,726
Brownsburg (C4) 3,617
Buckingham (B4) 7,421
Buckland (G3) 314
Bury (F4) 440
Cabano (J2) 2,695
Cacouna (H2) 834
Calumet (C4) 889
Candiac (H4) 1,050
Canton-Bégin (F1) 1,000
Cap-à-l'Aigle (G2) 659
Cap-Chat (B1) 2,035
Cap-de-la-Madeleine (E3) 26,925
Cap-Rouge (H3) 350
Cap-Saint-Ignace (G2)..1,247
Cap-Santé◉ (F3) 546
Caughnawaga (H4) 2,240
Causapscal (B2) 3,463
Chambly (J4) 3,737
Chambord (E1) 1,188
Champlain (E3) 750
Chandler (D2) 3,406
Charette (D3) 583
Charlemagne (H4) 3,068
Charlesbourg (J3) 14,308
Charny (J3) 4,189
Château-Richer◉ (F3)..1,837
Châteauguay Basin (H4)7,591
Chénéville (B4) 746
Chicoutimi◉ (G1) 31,657
Chomedey (H4) 30,445
Clermont (G2) 3,114
Cloridorme (D1) 350
Coaticook (F4) 6,906
Coaticook-Nord (F4) 500
Compton (F4) 543
Contrecoeur (D4) 2,007
Cookshire◉ (F4) 1,412
Corner of the Beach (D1) 300
Côte-St-Michel (H4)....55,978
Coteau-Landing◉ (C4).. 544
Courcelles (G4) 773
Cowansville (E4) 7,050
Crabtree Mills (D4)......1,313
Danville (E4) 2,562
Daveluyville (E3) 733
Delisle (F1) 1,302
Delson Village (H4)......2,075
Desbiens (F1) 1,970
Deschaillons (E3) 415
Deschambault (E3) 1,056
Deux-Rivières (St-Stanislas-de-Champlain) (E3) 590
Disraeli (F4) 3,079
Dixville (F4) 521
Donnacona (F3) 4,812
Dorion-Vaudreuil (D4)..4,996
Dosquet (F3) 394
Douglastown (D1) 416
Drummondville◉ (E4) 27,909
Dunham (E4) 434
Duvernay (H4) 10,939
East Angus (F4) 5,756
East Broughton (F3).....1,099
East Broughton Sta. (F3) 1,136
Eastman (E4) 637
Farnham (E4) 6,354
Fassett (C4) 434
Ferme-Neuve (B3) 1,971
Fontenelle (D1) 358
Forestville (H1) 1,529
Fort-Chambly (J4) 1,987
Fortierville (F3) 558
Foster (E4) 453
Frampton (G3) 526
Garthby Sta. (F4) 507
Gaspé (D1) 2,603
Gatineau (B4) 13,022
Gentilly (E3) 677
Giffard (J3) 10,129
Godbout (B1) 824
Gracefield (A3) 670
Granby (E4) 31,463
Grand'Mère (E3) 15,806
Grande-Rivière (D2) 1,176
Grande-Vallée (D1) 824
Grandes-Bergeronnes (H1) 779
Grandes-Piles (E3)........ 580
Grenville (C4) 1,330
Grosses-Roches (B1) 501
Ham-Nord (F4) 573
Ham-Sud◉ (F4) 59
Hébertville (F1) 1,604
Hébertville-Sta. (F1)....1,257
Hemmingford (D4) 778
Henryville (D4) 711
Hérouxville (E3) 591
Howick (D4) 647
Huberdeau (C4) 605
Hudson (C4) 1,671
Hull◉ (B4) 56,929
Huntingdon◉ (C4) 3,134
Iberville ◉(D4) 7,588
Île-Bizard (H4) 1,350
Île-Perrot-Nord (G4) 450
Île-Perrot-Sud (H4) 3,106
Inverness◉ (F3) 296
Isle-aux-Grues (H1) 280
Isle-Maligne (F1) 2,070
Isle-Verte (H1) 1,517
Jacques-Cartier (J4)...40,807
Joliette◉ (D3) 18,088
Jonquière (F1) 28,588
Kamouraska (H2) 518
Kenogami (F1) 11,816
Kiamika (B3) 168
Kildare (D3) 450
Kingsey Falls (E4) 531
Knowlton◉ (E4) 1,396
La Durantaye (G3) 412
La Guadeloupe (F4) 1,728
La Malbaie◉ (G2) 2,580
La Minerve (C3) 344
La Patrie (F4) 519
La Pocatière (H2) 3,086
La Salle (H4) 30,904
La Tuque (E2) 13,023
Labelle (C3) 1,224
Lac-au-Saumon (B2) 1,548
Lac-aux-Sables (E3) 857
Lac-Bouchette (E1) 911
Lac-Carré (C3) 687
Lac-Édouard (E2) 250
Lac-Etchemin (G3) 2,297
Lac-Frontière (H3) 264
Lac-Humqui (B2) 338
Lac-Masson (D3) 650
Lac-Mégantic◉ (G4)....7,015
Lac-Saguay (B3) 187
Lac-Sainte-Marie (B4).. 450
L'Acadie (J4) 327
Lachine (H4) 38,630
Lachute◉ (C4) 7,560
Lacolle (D4) 1,187
Laflèche (J4) 10,984
Lamartine (G2) 1,000
Lambton (F4) 699
L'Ange-Gardien (F3).... 333
Langevin (G3) 552
L'Annonciation (C3) 1,042
Lanoraie (D4) 1,060
L'Anse-Saint-Jean (G1) 250
Laprairie◉ (J4) 7,328
Larouche (F1) 518
L'Assomption◉ (D4).....4,448
Laterrière (F1) 651
Laurierville (F3) 872
Lauzon (F3) 11,533
Laval-des-Rapides (H4)19,227
Lavatrie (D4) 1,034
L'Avenir (E4) 350
Leeds Village (F3) 434
Lennoxville (F4) 3,699
L'Épiphanie (D4) 2,663
Les-Éboulements (G2)... 619
Les Escoumins (H1) 993
Les Étroits (J2) 291
Les Hauteurs-de-Rimouski (J1) 281
Les Méchins (B1) 1,455
Lévis (J3) 15,112
Linière (G3) 1,269
L'Islet (G2) 816
Longueuil◉ (J4) 24,131
Loretteville◉ (H3 6,522
Lotbinière (F6) 561
Louiseville◉ (E3) 4,138
Low (B4) 422
Luceville (J1) 1,419
Lyster Station (F3)..... 912
Magog (E4) 13,139
Maniwaki◉ (B3)...........6,349
Manseau (E3) 837
Mansonville (E4) 481
Marbleton (F4) 661
Maria (C2) 500
Marieville◉ (D4) 3,809
Mascouche (H4) 1,152
Maskinongé (E3) 893
Masson (B4) 1,933
Massueville (St-Aimé) (E4) 574
Matane◉ (B1) 9,190
Matapédia (B2) 596
Mégantic (Lac-Mégantic)◉ (G4)......7,015
Melocheville (C4) 1,666
Mont-Joli (J1) 6,178
Mont-Laurier◉ (B3) 5,859
Mont-Louis (C1) 585
Mont-Rolland (C4) 1,457
Mont-Saint-Grégoire (D4) 667
Montauban (E3) 620
Montebello (B4) 1,486
Montmagny◉ (G3) 6,850
Montmorency (J3) 5,985
Montréal◉ (H4) 1,191,062
Montréal (H4) .....†2,321,000
Mount Royal (H4) 21,182
Namur (C4) 224
Napierville◉ (D4) 1,812
Neuville (F3) 802
New Carlisle◉ (D2) 1,333
New Richmond (C2) 411
Newport (D2) 510
Nicolet (E3) 4,441
Nominingue (B3) 744
Normandin (E1) 1,838
North Hatley (E4) 719
Notre-Dame-de-Ham (F4) 170
Notre-Dame-des-Bois (G4) 243
Notre-Dame-du-Lac◉ (J2) 1,695
Notre-Dame-du-Laus (B3) 565
Notre-Dame-du-Rosaire (G3) 800
Oka (C4) 1,243
Omerville (E4) 1,094
Ormstown (D4) 1,527
Outremont (H4) 30,753
Panet (G3) 571
Papineauville◉ (C4).....1,300
Parisville (F3) 500
Paspébiac (D2) 800
Percé◉ (D1) 594
Péribonca (E1) 496
Petit-Saguenay (G1).....1,068
Pierrefonds (H4) 12,171
Pierreville (E3) 1,559
Plaisance (B4) 451
Plessisville (F3) 6,570
Pointe-au-Pic (G2)........1,333
Pointe-aux-Trembles (J4) 21,926
Pointe-Claire◉ (H4)...22,709
Pointe-Gatineau (B4)....8,854
Poltimore (B4) 156
Pont-Rouge (F3) 2,988
Pont-Viau (H4) 16,077
Pontbriand (F3) 349
Port-Alfred (G1) 9,066
Port-Daniel (D2) 218
Portneuf (F3) 1,372
Price (A1) 3,094
Princeville (F3) 3,174
QUÉBEC◉ (H3) 171,979
Québec (H3) ....†357,568
Ravignan (G3) 807
Rawdon (D3) 2,388
Repentigny (J4) 9,139
Restigouche (C2) 165
Richelieu (Village-Richelieu) (D4) 1,612
Richmond◉ (E4) 4,072
Rigaud (C4) 1,990
Rimouski◉ (J1) 17,739
Rimouski-Est (J1) 1,581

AGRICULTURE, INDUSTRY and RESOURCES

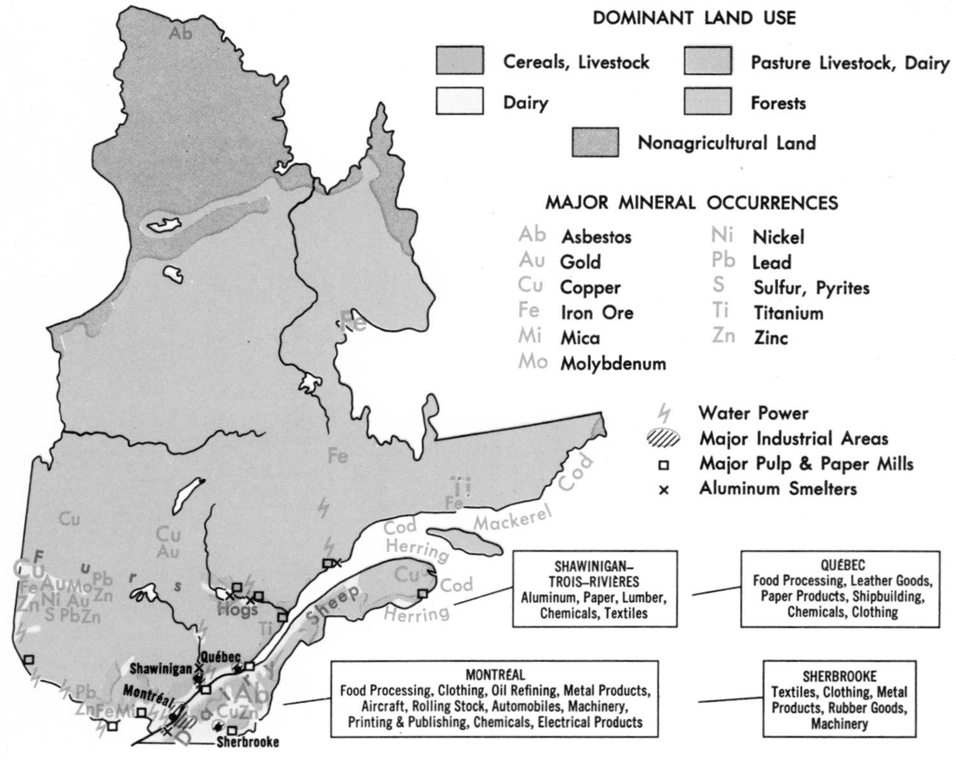
DOMINANT LAND USE
Cereals, Livestock
Pasture Livestock, Dairy
Dairy
Forests
Nonagricultural Land
MAJOR MINERAL OCCURRENCES
Ab Asbestos
Au Gold
Cu Copper
Fe Iron Ore
Mi Mica
Mo Molybdenum
Ni Nickel
Pb Lead
S Sulfur, Pyrites
Ti Titanium
Zn Zinc
Water Power
Major Industrial Areas
Major Pulp & Paper Mills
Aluminum Smelters
Cod
Mackerel
Herring
Sheep
Hogs
Shawinigan
Québec
Montréal
Sherbrooke
SHAWINIGAN–TROIS-RIVIÈRES
Aluminum, Paper, Lumber, Chemicals, Textiles
QUÉBEC
Food Processing, Leather Goods, Paper Products, Shipbuilding, Chemicals, Clothing
MONTRÉAL
Food Processing, Clothing, Oil Refining, Metal Products, Aircraft, Rolling Stock, Automobiles, Machinery, Printing & Publishing, Chemicals, Electrical Products
SHERBROOKE
Textiles, Clothing, Metal Products, Rubber Goods, Machinery

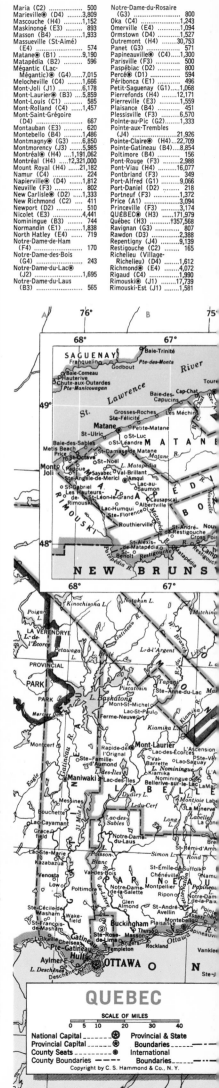

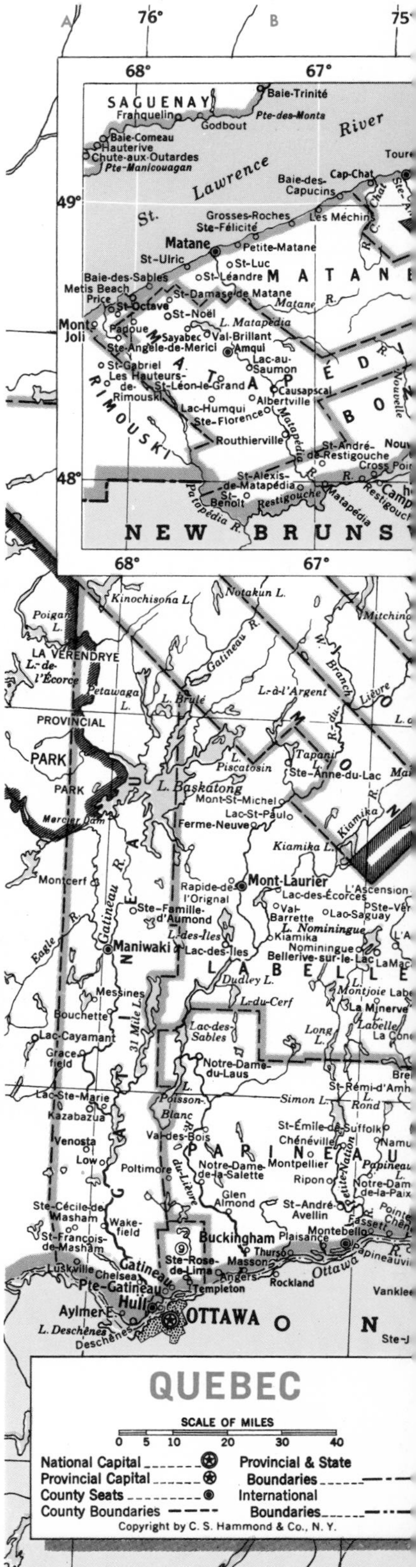
SAGUENAY
Baie-Trinité
Godbout
Pte-des-Monts
St. Lawrence River
Matane
MATANE
Rimouski
RIMOUSKI
NEW BRUNSWICK
Mont-Laurier
Maniwaki
LABELLE
Buckingham
Hull
OTTAWA
QUEBEC
SCALE OF MILES
0 5 10 20 30 40
National Capital
Provincial Capital
County Seats
County Boundaries
Provincial & State Boundaries
International Boundaries
Copyright by C. S. Hammond & Co., N. Y.

QUEBEC

AREA	594,860 sq. mi.
POPULATION	5,712,000
CAPITAL	Québec
LARGEST CITY	Montréal (greater) 2,321,000
HIGHEST POINT	Mt. Jacques Cartier 4,160 ft.
SETTLED IN	1608
ADMITTED TO CONFEDERATION	1867
PROVINCIAL FLOWER	White Garden Lily

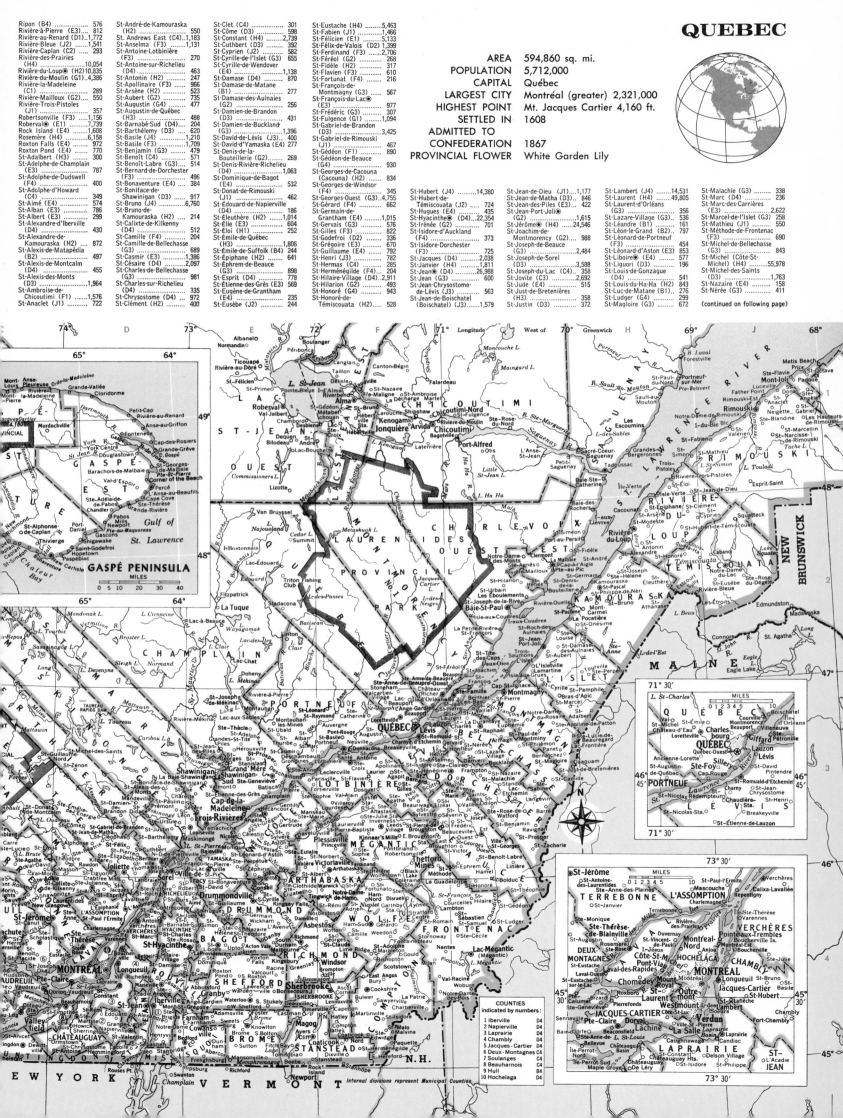

COUNTIES
indicated by numbers:

1 Iberville	D4
2 Napierville	D4
3 Laprairie	D4
4 Chambly	D4
5 Jacques-Cartier	D4
6 Deux-Montagnes	C4
7 Soulanges	C4
8 Beauharnois	C4
9 Hull	D4
10 Hochelaga	D4

Internal divisions represent Municipal Counties

Quebec
(continued)

St-Nicolas (H3) 424
St-Noël (B1) 1,124
St-Norbert-d'Arthabaska (F3) 292
St-Octave (B1) 211
St-Odilon (G3) 686
St-Omer (C3) 470
St-Ours (D4) 711
St-Pacôme (G2) 1,242
St-Pamphile (H3) 1,839
St-Pascal◉ (H2) 2,144
St-Paul-de-Chester (F4) 318
St-Paul-de-Montminy (G3) 850
St-Paul-du-Nord (H1) 337
St-Paul-l'Ermite (J4) 2,935
St-Paulin (D3) 920
St-Philémon (G3) 539
St-Philippe-de-Laprairie (J4) 424
St-Philippe-de-Néri (H2) 746
St-Pie (E4) 1,434
St-Pierre-Baptiste (F3) 100
St-Pierre-de-Broughton (F3) 389
St-Pierre-les-Becquets (E3) 451
St-Pierre-Montmagny (G3) 281
St-Placide (C4) 336
St-Polycarpe (C4) 560
St-Prime (E1) 659
St-Prosper (E3) 158
St-Prosper-de-Dorchester (G3) 1,357
St-Raphaël-Bellechasse◉ (G3) 1,134
St-Raymond (F3) 3,931
St-Rémi (D4) 2,276
St-Rémi-d'Amherst (C3) 396
St-Robert (E4) 301
St-Roch-de-l'Achigan (D4) 614
St-Roch-de-Richelieu (D4) 614
St-Roch-des-Aulnaies (G2) 350
St-Romain (F4) 465
St-Romauld-d'Etchemin (J4) 5,183
St-Samuel-de-Gayhurst (G4) 511
St-Sauveur-des-Monts (C4) 1,702
St-Sébastian-de-Frontenac (G4) 516
St-Siméon (G2) 1,197
St-Simon (E4) 215
St-Simon (H1) 528
St-Stanislas-de-Champlain (E3) 590
St-Sylvestre (F3) 652
St-Télesphore (C4) 275
St-Théophile (G4) 510
St-Thuribe (E3) 208
St-Timothée (D4) 1,003
St-Tite (E3) 3,250
St-Tite-des-Caps (G2) 1,227
St-Ubald (E3) 764
St-Ulric (B1) 1,021
St-Urbain-de-Charlevoix (G2) 878
St-Valère-de-Bulstrode (E3) 197
St-Valérien (E4) 226
St-Valérien-de-Rimouski (J1) 310
St-Vallier (G3) 540
St-Victor-de-Beauce (G3) 931
St-Vincent-de-Paul (H4) 11,214
St-Wenceslas (E3) 358
St-Zacharie (G3) 1,361
St-Zénon (D3) 598
St-Zéphirin (E3) 247
Ste-Adélaïde-de-Pabos (D2) 726
Ste-Adèle (C4) 1,331
Ste-Agathe-de-Lotbinière (F3) 600
Ste-Agathe-des-Monts (C3) 5,725
Ste-Angèle-de-Laval (E3) 484
Ste-Angèle-de-Merici (J1) 666
Ste-Angèle-de-Monnoir (D4) 314
Ste-Anne-de-Beaupré (F2) 1,878
Ste-Anne-de-Bellevue (H4) 4,044
Ste-Anne-de-la-Pérade (E3) 1,184
Ste-Anne-des-Monts (C1) 1,906
Ste-Anne-des-Plaines (H4) 1,256
Ste-Anne-du-Lac (B3) 423
Ste-Apolline-de-Patton (H3) 353
Ste-Béatrix (D3) 375
Ste-Blandine (J1) 508
Ste-Catherine (F3) 893
Ste-Cécile-de-Frontenac (G4) 141
Ste-Cécile-de-Masham (B4) 399
Ste-Claire (G3) 1,338
Ste-Clothilde (E4) 256
Ste-Croix◉ (F3) 1,363
Ste-Edwidge (F4) 205
Ste-Élizabeth (D3) 557
Ste-Émélie-de-l'Énergie (D3) 721
Ste-Eulalie (E3) 193
Ste-Euphémie (G3) 158
Ste-Famille (G3) 300
Ste-Félicité (B1) 1,057
Ste-Flore (E3) 622
Ste-Florence (B2) 450
Ste-Foy (H3) 29,716
Ste-Geneviève-de-Batiscan◉ (E3) 532
Ste-Geneviève-de-Pierrefonds (H4) 2,397
Ste-Gertrude (E3) 362
Ste-Hélène-de-Bagot (E4) 342
Ste-Hélène-de-Kamouraska (H2) 529
Ste-Hénédine◉ (F3) 518
Ste-Julie-de-Verchères (J4) 434
Ste-Julienne◉ (D4) 753
Ste-Justine-de-Newton (C4) 513
Ste-Louise (G2) 493
Ste-Lucie-de-Beauregard (H3) 297
Ste-Lucie-de-Doncaster (C3) 178
Ste-Marguerite-de-Dorchester (G3) 324
Ste-Marie-Beauce (G3) 3,662
Ste-Marthe (C4) 261
Ste-Martine (D4) 1,695
Ste-Perpétue (E3) 203
Ste-Perpétue-de-l'Islet (H2) 674
Ste-Pudentienne (Roxton Pond) (E4) 770
Ste-Rosalie (D4) 1,255
Ste-Rose◉ (H4) 7,571
Ste-Rose-de-Lima (B4) 2,961
Ste-Rose-de-Watford (G3) 258
Ste-Rose-du-Dégelé (J2) 1,943
Ste-Sabine (G3) 444
Ste-Scholastique◉ (C4) 838
Ste-Sophie-de-Lévrard (E3) 398
Ste-Sophie-de-Mégantic (F3) 267
Ste-Thérèse-de-Blainville (H4) 11,771
Ste-Ursule (D3) 422
Ste-Véronique (C3) 250
Ste-Victoire (D4) 163
Sault-au-Mouton (H1) 876
Sawyerville (F4) 789
Sayabec (B2) 2,314
Scotstown (F4) 1,038
Scott-Jonction (F3) 665
Senneville (G4) 1,262
Shawbridge (C4) 1,034
Shawinigan (D3) 32,169
Sherbrooke◉ (E4) 66,554
Sillery (J3) 14,109
Sorel◉ (D4) 17,147
South Durham (E4) 438
Squatteck (J2) 1,088
Stanstead (Stanstead Plain) (F4) 1,116
Stoneham (F2) 472
Stratford Centre (F4) 461
Sully (H2) 8 33
Sutton (E4) 1,755
Sweetsburg (E4) 958
Tadoussac◉ (H1) 1,083
Templeton (B4) 2,965
Terrebonne (H4) 6,207
Thetford Mines (F3) 21,618
Thurso (B4) 3,310
Ticouapé (E1) 600
Tingwick (F4) 581
Tourelle (C1) 700
Tourville (H2) 645
Tring-Jonction (F3) 1,214
Trois-Pistoles (H1) 4,349
Trois-Rivières (E3) 53,477
Upton (E4) 830
Val-Alain (F3) 301
Val-Barrette (B3) 557
Val-Brillant (B1) 879
Val-David (C3) 1,118
Valcartier-Village (F3) 163
Valcourt (E4) 843
Vallée-Jonction (G3) 1,405
Valleyfield (C4) 27,297
Valmont (E3) 520
Varennes (J4) 2,240
Vaudreuil◉ (C4) 897
Verchères◉ (J4) 1,768
Verdun (H4) 78,317
Victoriaville (E3) 18,720
Village-Richelieu (D4) 1,612
Ville-St-Georges (G3) 4,082
Villeneuve (J3) 1,934
Villers (Ste-Gertrude) (E3) 362
Wakefield (B4) 381
Warwick (F4) 2,487
Waterloo◉ (E4) 4,543
Waterville (F4) 1,330
Weedon (F4) 1,426
West Shefford (E4) 406
Westmount (H4) 25,012
Wickham-Ouest (E4) 378
Windsor (F4) 6,589
Wotton (F4) 726
Yamachiche◉ (E3) 1,186

OTHER FEATURES

Aylmer (lake) F 4
Baskatong (lake) B 3
Batiscan (riv.) E 2
Boisvert (point) J 1
Brome (lake) E 4
Brompton (lake) E 4
Cascapédia (riv.) C 1
Chaleur (bay) C 2
Champlain (lake) D 4
Chaudière (riv.) G 4
Chicoutimi (riv.) F 2
Commissioners (lake) E 1
Coudres (isl.), 1,391 G 2
Dartmouth (riv.) D 1
Deschênes (lake) A 4
Édouard (lake) E 2
Gaspé (bay) D 1
Gaspé (cape) D 1
Gaspé (pen.) D 2
Gaspesian Prov. Park C 1
Gatineau (riv.) B 3
Ha Ha (riv.) G 1
Îles (lake) B 3
Jacques-Cartier (mt.) C 1
Jacques-Cartier (riv.) F 2
Jésus (isl.), 124,741 H 4
Kenogami (lake) F 1
Kiamika (lake) B 3
L'Assomption (riv.) D 3
Laurentides Prov. Park F 2
Lièvre (riv.) B 4
Loup (riv.) H 2
Madeleine (cape) D 1
Malbaie (riv.) G 2
Manicouagan (point) B 1
Maskinongé (riv.) D 3
Matapédia (lake) B 1
Mattawin (riv.) D 3
Mégantic (lake) G 4
Mékinac (lake) E 2
Memphremagog (lake) E 4
Métabetchouan (riv.) F 1
Mille-Îles (riv.) H 4
Mistassini (riv.) E 1
Mont-Tremblant Prov. Park C 3
Montmorency (riv.) F 2
Nicolet (riv.) E 3
North (riv.) C 4
Oies (isl.), 364 G 2
Orléans (isl.), 4,974 F 3
Ouareau (riv.) D 3
Papineau (lake) C 4
Patapédia (riv.) B 2
Petite-Nation (riv.) B 4
Prairies (riv.) H 4
Restigouche (riv.) B 2
Rimouski (riv.) J 1
Rouge (riv.) C 3
Saguenay (riv.) G 1
St. Francis (lake) C 4
St-Francis (riv.) E 4
St-François (lake) F 4
St-Jean (lake) E 1
St-Joseph (lake) F 3
St. Lawrence (riv.) H 1
St-Louis (lake) H 4
St-Maurice (riv.) E 2
St-Pierre (lake) E 3
St-Pierre (point) D 1
Ste-Anne (riv.) G 2
Ste-Anne (riv.) F 3
Ste-Thérèse (isl.) J 4
Salmon (riv.) F 4
Shawinigan (riv.) E 3
Taureau (res.) D 3
Témiscouata (lake) H 2
Thirty One Mile (lake) B 3
Two Mountains (lake) C 4
Yamaska (riv.) E 4

NORTHERN QUEBEC

INTERNAL DIVISIONS

Abitibi (county) (B3) 108,313
Abitibi (district) (B2) 11,321
Île-Anticosti (county) (E3) 532
Mistassini (dist.) (B2) 1,796
Nouveau Québec (Ungava) (dist.) (E1) 8,121
Témiscamingue (county) (B3) 60,288

CITIES and TOWNS

Aguanish (E2) 560
Amos◉ (B3) 6,080
Angliers (B3) 488
Baie-Johan-Beetz (E2) 237
Barraute (B3) 1,199
Barville (B3) 304
Belleterre (B3) 638
Betsiamites (D3) 400
Blanc-Sablon (F2) 252
Bourlamaque (B3) 3,344
Cadillac (B3) 1,077
Cann (C3) 250
Casey (C3)
Chapais (B3) 2,363
Chibougamau (C3) 4,765
Clarke City (D2) 816
Clova (B3) 240
Dolbeau (C3) 6,052
Duparquet (B3) 978
Dupuy (B3) 466
Eastmain (B2) 212
Factory River (B2) 378
Fort Chimo (F2) 480
Fort George (B2) 1,074
Gagnon (D2) 1,900
Great Whale River (B1) 718
Harrington Harbour (F2) 457
Hauterive (D3) 5,980
Havre-St-Pierre (E2) 2,407
Kipawa (B3) 272
Knob Lake (Schefferville) (D2) 3,178
La Sarre (B3) 3,944
La Tabatière (F2) 326
Labrieville (C3) 519
Macamic (B3) 1,614
Magpie (E2) 359
Malartic (B3) 6,998
Mistassini (C3) 3,461
Moisie (D2) 511
Mutton Bay (F2) 235
Natashquan (E3) 300
Noranda (B3) 11,477
Normetal (B3) 2,284
Parent (C3) 1,298
Perron (B3) 206
Port-Cartier (D2) 3,458
Port-Menier◉ (E3) 475
Povungnituk (E1) 434
Ragueneau (D3) 300
Rapide-Blanc (C3) 319
Rivière-au-Tonnerre (D2) 716
Rivière-Pentecôte (D3) 776
Rouyn (B3) 18,716
Rupert House (B2) 528
Saint-Augustin (F2) 444
Schefferville (D2) 3,178
Senneterre (B3) 3,246
Sept-Îles (Seven Islands) (D2) 14,196
Shelter Bay (D3) 1,171
Sugluk (E1) 255
Taschereau (B3) 1,000
Témiscaming (B3) 2,517
Tête-à-la-Baleine (E2) 311
Val-d'Or (B3) 10,983
Ville-Marie◉ (B3) 1,710

OTHER FEATURES

Aguanus (river) E 2
Albanel (lake) C 2
Allard (lake) E 2
Anticosti (isl.), 532 E 3
Assinica (lake) C 2
Baleine (river) D 1
Bell (river) B 3
Bermen (lake) D 2
Betsiamites (river) C 2
Bienville (lake) C 2
Broadback (river) B 2
Burnt (lake) E 2
Cabonga (res.) B 3
Clearwater (lake) C 1
Delorme (lake) C 2
Dozois (res.) B 3
Duncan (lake) B 2
Eastmain (river) B 2
Erlandson (lake) D 1
Evans (lake) B 2
Fort George (river) B 2
George (river) F 2
Goéland (lake) B 3
Gouin (res.) C 3
Great Whale (river) B 1
Gué (river) C 1
Harricanaw (river) B 2
Heath (point) E 3
Honguedo (passage) E 3
Hopes Advance (cape) F 1
Iberville (lake) C 1
Indian House (lake) E 1
Jacques Cartier (pass.) E 3
James (bay) A 2
Jones (cape) B 2
Kanaaupscow (river) B 2
Kaniapiskau (lake) D 2
Kaniapiskau (river) D 1
Kogaluk (river) E 1
Koksoak (river) D 1
La Vérendrye Prov. Park B 3
Larch (river) F 2
Leaf (river) F 2
Little Mecatina (isl.) F 2
Little Whale (river) B 1
Magpie (lake) E 2
Manicouagan (lake) D 2
Manicouagan (river) D 2
Manouane (lake) C 2
Marguerite (river) D 2
Marie Victorin (mts.) C 2
Mattagami (lake) B 3
Mecatina (river) E 2
Mingan (Jacques Cartier) (passage) E 3
Minto (lake) E 2
Mistassibi (river) C 2
Mistassini (lake) C 2
Moisie (river) D 2
Naococane (lake) C 2
Natashquan (river) E 2
New Quebec (crater) F 1
Nottaway (river) B 2
Opinaca (river) B 2
Opiscoteo (lake) D 2
Ottawa (river) B 3
Outardes (river) D 2
Pas (river) D 1
Payne (lake) E 1
Payne (river) F 1
Péribonca (river) C 3
Petit-Mécatina (river) E 2
Pipmuacan (lake) D 3
Pletipi (lake) C 2
Reed (mt.) D 2
Richmond (gulf) B 1
Romaine (river) E 2
Rupert (river) B 2
Saguenay Prov. Park E 2
Saint-Augustin (river) F 2
Saint Lawrence (gulf) E 3
Saint-Paul (river) F 2
Sakami (lake) B 2
Sakami (river) B 2
Sandy (river) D 1
Sérigny (river) D 1
Toulnustouc (river) D 2
Tudor (lake) D 1
Ungava (bay) F 1
Ungava (peninsula) E 1
Vérendrye Prov. Park B 3
Weggs (cape) F 1
West (point) E 3
Wheeler (river) D 1
Whitegull (lake) E 1
Whittle (cape) F 2
Wolstenholme (cape) E 1
Wright (mt.) D 2

◉County Seat.
†Population of metropolitan area.

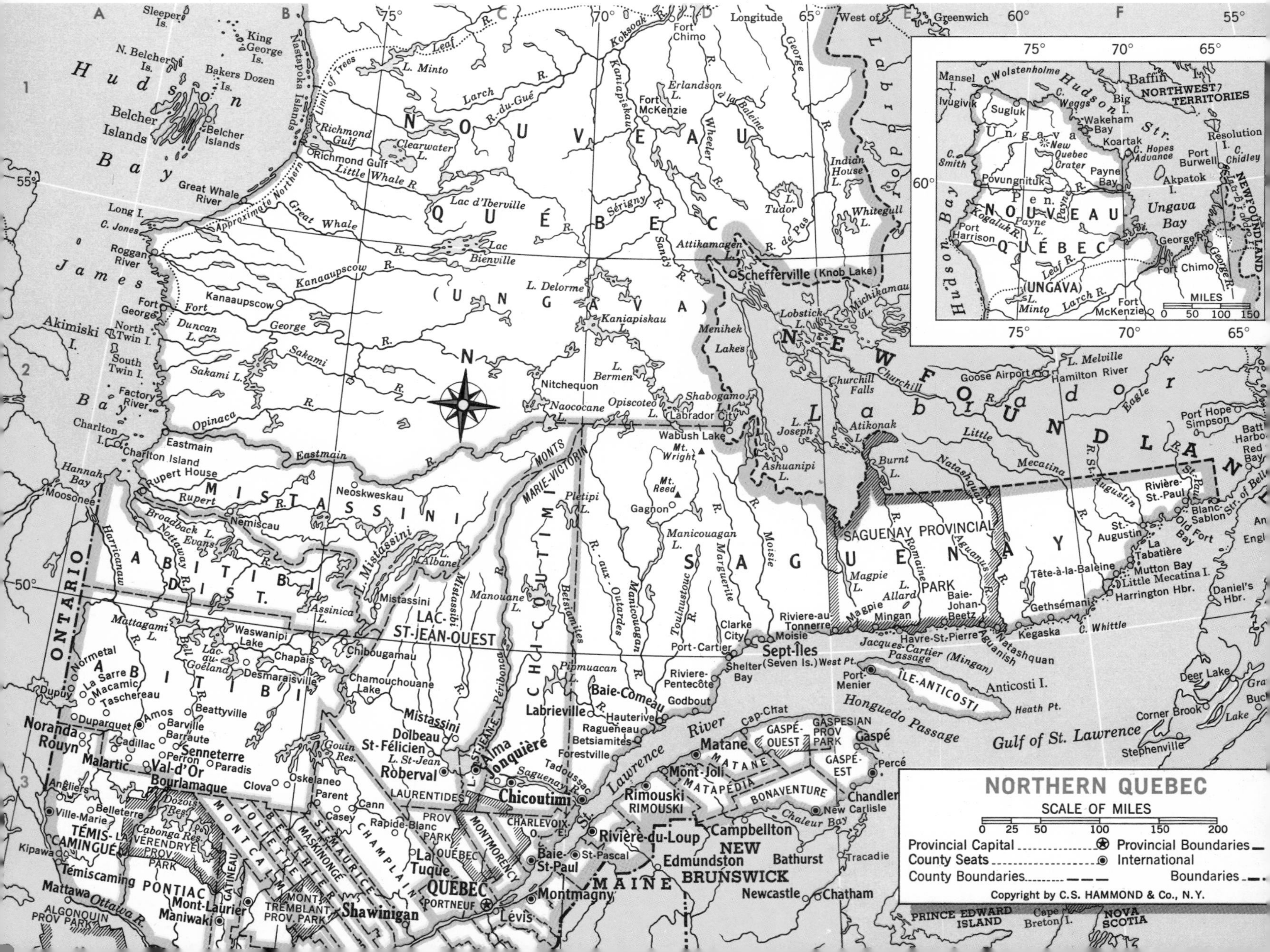
NORTHERN QUEBEC
SCALE OF MILES
0 25 50 100 150 200
Provincial Capital
County Seats
County Boundaries
Provincial Boundaries
International Boundaries
Copyright by C.S. HAMMOND & Co., N.Y.
Hudson Bay
James Bay
NOUVEAU QUÉBEC
(UNGAVA)
MISTASSINI
SAGUENAY
ABITIBI
NEWFOUNDLAND
Labrador
Gulf of St. Lawrence
ÎLE-ANTICOSTI
Honguedo Passage
Jacques-Cartier (Mingan) Passage
SAGUENAY PROVINCIAL PARK
LAC-ST-JEAN-OUEST
CHICOUTIMI
NEW BRUNSWICK
MAINE
ONTARIO
NORTHWEST TERRITORIES
Ungava Bay
Hudson Str.
Schefferville (Knob Lake)
Fort Chimo
Sept-Îles
Noranda
Rouyn
Val-d'Or
Chicoutimi
Jonquière
Québec
Rimouski

NORTHERN ONTARIO

DISTRICT

Kenora (Patricia Portion), (C2) ...12,341

CITIES and TOWNS

Allan Water (C2)
Ansonville (D3) ...3,080
Armstrong Station ...375
Atikokan (B3) ...6,674
Attawapiskat (D2)
Auden (C2) ...188
Balmertown (B2) ...1,421
Barwick (B3) ...154
Beardmore (C3) ...1,043
Bearskin Lake (B2)
Big Beaver House (B2)
Biscotasing (D3) ...147
Blind River (D3) ...4,093
Bruce Mines (D3) ...484
Byng Inlet (D3) ...217
Capreol (D3) ...3,003
Caramat (C3) ...368
Cat Lake (B2)
Central Patricia (C2) ...51
Chalk River (E3) ...1,135
Chapleau (D3) ...3,350
Cobalt (D3) ...2,209
Cochrane (D3) ...4,521
Coniston (D3) ...2,692
Coppell (D3) ...221
Copper Cliff (D3) ...3,600
Coral (D2) ...51
Deep River (E3) ...5,377
Deer Lake (B2) ...67
Dinorwic (B3) ...98
Dryden (B3) ...5,728
Dyment (B3) ...158
Ebamet Lake (Fort Hope) (C2)
Echo Bay (D3) ...577
Elk Lake (D3) ...701
Elliot Lake (D3) ...9,950
Emo (B3) ...630
Englehart (E3) ...1,786
English River (B3)
Espanola (D3) ...5,353
Fauquier (D3) ...490
Favourable Lake (B2)
Flanders (B3) ...57
Foleyet (D3) ...504
Fort Albany (D2)
Fort Frances (B3) ...9,481
Fort Hope (Ebamet Lake) (C2)
Fort Severn (C1)
Fort William (B3) ...45,214
Franz (D3) ...70
Fraserdale (D3) ...215

Frater (D3)
Geraldton (C3) ...3,375
Ghost River (D2)
Gogama (D3) ...653
Goldpines (B2) ...53
Goudreau (C3) ...60
Graham (B3) ...52
Haileybury (D3) ...2,638
Hawk Junction (D3) ...378
Hearst (D3) ...2,373
Heron Bay (C3) ...167
Hornepayne (C3) ...1,692
Hudson (B2) ...65
Huntsville (E3) ...3,189
Ignace (B3) ...517
Iroquois Falls (D3) ...1,681
Island Falls (D3) ...111
Jackfish (C3) ...77
Kakabeka Falls (B3) ...296
Kapuskasing (D3) ...6,870
Keewatin (A3) ...2,197
Kenora (B3) ...10,904
Kirkland Lake (D3) ...15,366
Lac Seul (B2) ...65
Lake River (D2)
Lansdowne House (C2)
Larder Lake (E3) ...2,030
Levack (D3) ...3,178
Lingman Lake (B2)
Longlac (C3) ...1,125
Low Bush River (E3) ...52
Manitouwadge (C3) ...2,006
Marathon (C3) ...2,568
Matachewan (D3) ...923
Matawa (E3) ...3,314
Mattice (B3) ...711
Michipicoten Harbour (C3) ...159
Minaki (B3) ...207
Mine Center (B3) ...88
Missanabie (D3) ...98
Moose Factory (D2) ...689
Moosonee (D2) ...975
Nakina (C2) ...747
New Liskeard (E3) ...4,896
Nicholson (D3) ...66
Nipigon (C3) ...2,105
North Bay (E3) ...23,781
Oba (C3) ...129
Opasatika (D3) ...520
Osnaburgh House (C2)
Otter Rapids (D2) ...528
Pagwa River (D3) ...111
Palmquist (D3) ...100
Parry Sound (D3) ...6,004
Pembroke (E3) ...16,791
Peterbell (D3) ...104
Pikangikum (B2)

Pickle Crow (C2) ...281
Port Arthur (B3) ...45,276
Quetico (B3)
Quibell (B3) ...170
Rainy River (A3) ...1,168
Raith (C3) ...128
Rat Rapids (C2)
Red Lake (B2) ...2,051
Red Rock (B3) ...1,316
Redditt (B2) ...300
Renfrew (E3) ...8,935
Root Portage (B2)
Sault Sainte Marie (D3) ...43,088
Savanne (B3)
Savant Lake (B2) ...115
Schreiber (C3) ...2,230
Schumacher (D3) ...3,017
Sioux Lookout (B2) ...2,453
Smoky Falls (D3) ...83
Smooth Rock Falls (D3) ...1,131
South Porcupine (D3) ...5,144
Steep Rock Lake (B3) ...80
Stratton (B3) ...112
Sturgeon Falls (E3) ...6,288
Sudbury (D3) ...80,120
Sultan (D3) ...511
Terrace Bay (C3) ...1,901
Thessalon (D3) ...1,725
Timmins (D3) ...29,270
Trout Lake (C2)
Upsala (B3) ...190
Vermilion Bay (B3) ...503
Wawa (D3) ...2,749
White River (C3) ...836
Windigo Lake (B2)
Winisk (C1)

OTHER FEATURES

Abitibi (lake) ...E3
Abitibi (river) ...D2
Albany (river) ...C2
Algonquin Provincial Park ...E3
Asheweig (river) ...C2
Attawapiskat (lake) ...C2
Attawapiskat (river) ...C2
Basswood (lake) ...B3
Berens (river) ...A2
Big Trout (lake) ...B2
Black Duck (river) ...C1
Bloodvein (river) ...A2
Caribou (isl.) ...C3
Cobham (river) ...A2
Ekwan (river) ...C2
English (river) ...B2
Fawn (river) ...C2
Finger (lake) ...B2

Georgian (bay) ...D3
Groundhog (river) ...D2
Hannah (bay) ...D2
Henrietta Maria (cape) ...D1
Hudson (bay) ...D1
Huron (lake) ...D3
James (bay) ...D2
Kapiskau (river) ...C2
Kapuskasing (river) ...D2
Kenogami (river) ...C2
Kesagami (lake) ...D2
Lake of the Woods ...B3
Lake Superior Prov. Park (D3) ...43,088
Little Current (river) ...C2
Manitoulin (isl.) ...D3
Mattagami (river) ...D2
Michipicoten (isl.) ...C3
Mille Lacs (lake) ...B3
Missinaibi (lake) ...D2
Missinaibi (river) ...D2
Missisa (lake) ...D2
Nipigon (lake) ...C3
Nipissing (lake) ...E3
North (channel) ...D3
North Caribou (lake) ...C2
Nungesser (lake) ...B2
Ogoki (river) ...C2
Opazatika (river) ...D3
Opinnagau (river) ...D2
Otoskwin (river) ...C2
Otter (head) ...C3
Partridge (isl.) ...C1
Pipestone (river) ...B2
Quetico Prov. Park ...B3
Rainy (lake) ...B3
Red (lake) ...B2
Sachigo (river) ...B2
Saganaga (lake) ...B3
Saint Ignace (isl.) ...C3
Saint Joseph (lake) ...B2
Sandy (lake) ...B2
Savant (lake) ...B2
Seine (river) ...B3
Seul (lake) ...B2
Severn (lake) ...B2
Severn (river) ...B2
Shamattawa (river) ...C2
Shibogama (lake) ...C2
Sibley Provincial Park ...C3
Slate (isls.) ...C3
Sutton (lake) ...D2
Superior (lake) ...D2
Sutton (river) ...D2
Thunder (bay) ...C3
Timagami (lake) ...D3
Timiskaming (lake) ...E3
Tip Top Hill (mt.) ...C3
Trout (lake) ...C3
Wabuk (point) ...D1
Winisk (lake) ...C2
Winisk (river) ...C2
Wunnummin (lake) ...C2

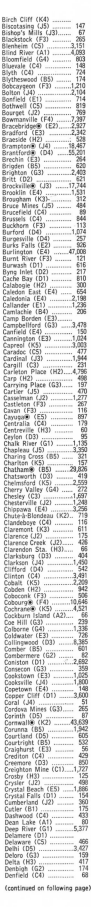

AREA	412,582 sq. mi.
POPULATION	6,832,000
CAPITAL	Toronto
LARGEST CITY	Toronto (greater) 2,066,000
HIGHEST POINT	Tip Top Hill 2,120 ft.
SETTLED IN	1749
ADMITTED TO CONFEDERATION	1867
PROVINCIAL FLOWER	White Trillium

SOUTHERN ONTARIO

COUNTIES and DISTRICTS

Algoma (J5) ...111,408
Brant (D4) ...83,839
Bruce (C4) ...43,036
Carleton (J2) ...352,932
Cochrane (J4) ...95,666
Dufferin (D3) ...16,095
Dundas (J2) ...17,162
Durham (D4) ...39,916
Elgin (C5) ...62,682
Essex (B5) ...258,218
Frontenac (H3) ...87,534
Glengarry (K2) ...19,217
Grenville (J3) ...22,864
Grey (D3) ...62,005
Haldimand (E5) ...28,197
Haliburton (F3) ...6,928
Halton (E4) ...106,967
Hastings (G3) ...93,377
Huron (C4) ...53,805
Kenora (G5) ...51,474
Kent (B5) ...102,131
Lambton (B5) ...109,011
Lanark (H3) ...40,313
Leeds (H3) ...46,889
Lennox and Addington (G3) ...23,717
Lincoln (E4) ...126,674
Manitoulin (B3) ...11,176
Middlesex (C4) ...221,422
Muskoka (E3) ...26,705
Nipissing (F2) ...70,568
Norfolk (D5) ...50,475
Northumberland (F3) ...41,892
Ontario (D3) ...135,895
Oxford (D4) ...70,499
Parry Sound (E3) ...29,632
Peel (D4) ...111,575
Perth (C4) ...57,452

Peterborough (F3) ...76,375
Prescott (K2) ...27,226
Prince Edward (G3) ...21,108
Rainy River (G5) ...26,531
Renfrew (G2) ...89,635
Russell (J2) ...20,892
Simcoe (E3) ...141,271
Stormont (K2) ...57,867
Sudbury (J5) ...165,862
Thunder Bay (H5) ...138,518
Timiskaming (K5) ...50,971
Victoria (F3) ...29,750
Waterloo (D4) ...176,754
Welland (E4) ...164,741
Wellington (D4) ...84,702
Wentworth (D4) ...358,837
York (E4) ...1,733,108

CITIES and TOWNS

Actinolite (G3) ...104
Acton (D4) ...4,144
Agincourt (J4) ...1,738
Ailsa Craig (C4) ...544
Ajax (F4) ...7,755
Alexandria (K2) ...2,597
Alfred (K2) ...1,195
Algoma Mills (B1) ...373
Algonquin Park (F2) ...100
Allenford (C3) ...209
Alliston (E3) ...2,884
Alma (D4) ...167
Almonte (H2) ...3,267
Alton (E4) ...438
Alvinston (B5) ...660
Amherstburg (A5) ...4,452
Angus (E3) ...1,180
Ansonville (K5) ...3,080
Appin (C5) ...169
Apple Hill (K2) ...384
Apsley (G3) ...295
Arden (G3) ...227

Arkona (C4) ...504
Armstrong Station (H4) ...375
Arnprior (H2) ...5,474
Arthur (D4) ...1,200
Athens (J3) ...1,015
Atherley (E3) ...348
Atikokan (G5) ...6,674
Atwood (D4) ...418
Auburn (C4) ...216
Auden (H4) ...188
Aurora (J3) ...8,791
Avening (D3) ...51
Avonmore (K2) ...308
Aylmer West (C5) ...4,705
Ayr (D4) ...1,016
Ayton (D3) ...375
Baden (D4) ...977
Bala (E3) ...495
Baltimore (F3) ...220
Bancroft (G2) ...2,615
Bannockburn (G3) ...186
Barrie (E3) ...21,169
Barrys Bay (G2) ...1,439
Bath (H3) ...692
Bayfield (C4) ...395
Baysville (E2) ...199
Beachburg (H2) ...542
Beachville (D4) ...849
Beamsville (E4) ...2,537
Beardmore (H5) ...1,043
Beaverton (E3) ...1,217
Beeton (E3) ...810
Belgrave (C4) ...143
Bellamys (J3) ...96
Belle River (B5) ...1,854
Belleville (G3) ...30,655
Belmont (C5) ...649
Belwood (D4) ...117
Berkeley (D3) ...116
Bervie (C4) ...82
Bethany (F3) ...279

Birch Cliff (K4)
Biscotasing (J5) ...147
Bishop's Mills (J3) ...67
Blackstock (F3) ...265
Blenheim (C5) ...3,151
Blind River (A1) ...4,093
Bloomfield (G3) ...803
Bluevale (C4) ...148
Blyth (C4) ...724
Blytheswood (B5) ...174
Bobcaygeon (F3) ...1,210
Bolton (D4) ...2,104
Bonfield (E1) ...714
Bothwell (C5) ...819
Bourget (J2) ...769
Bowmanville (F4) ...7,397
Bracebridge (E2) ...2,927
Bradford (E3) ...2,342
Braeside (H2) ...528
Brampton (J4) ...18,467
Brantford (D4) ...55,201
Brechin (E3) ...264
Brigden (B5) ...620
Brighton (G3) ...2,403
Britt (E2) ...621
Brockville (J3) ...17,744
Brooklin (E4) ...1,531
Brougham (K3) ...312
Bruce Mines (J5) ...484
Brucefield (C4) ...89
Brussels (C4) ...844
Buckhorn (F3) ...113
Burford (D4) ...1,074
Burgessville (D4) ...257
Burks Falls (E2) ...926
Burlington (E4) ...47,008
Burnt River (F3) ...121
Burwash (D1) ...616
Byng Inlet (D2) ...217
Cache Bay (D1) ...810
Calabogie (H2) ...300
Caledon East (E4) ...654
Caledonia (E4) ...2,198
Callander (E1) ...1,236
Camlachie (B4) ...206
Camp Borden (E3)
Campbellford (G3) ...3,478
Canfield (E4) ...150
Cannington (E3) ...1,024
Capreol (K5) ...3,003
Caradoc (C5) ...477
Cardinal (J3) ...1,944
Cargill (C3) ...231
Carleton Place (H2) ...4,796
Carp (H2) ...498
Carrying Place (G3) ...197
Cartier (J5) ...470
Casselman (J2) ...1,277
Castleton (F3) ...267
Cavan (F3) ...116
Cayuga (E5) ...897
Centralia (C4) ...179
Centreville (H3) ...60
Ceylon (D3) ...95
Chalk River (G1) ...1,135
Chapleau (J5) ...3,350
Charing Cross (B5) ...321
Charlton (K5) ...157
Chatham (C5) ...29,826
Chatsworth (D3) ...419
Chelmsford (K5) ...2,559
Cherry Valley (G4) ...272
Chesley (C3) ...1,697
Chesterville (J2) ...1,248
Chippawa (E4) ...3,256
Chute-à-Blondeau (K2) ...719
Clandeboye (C4) ...116
Claremont (K3) ...611
Clarence (J2) ...175
Clarence Creek (J2) ...426
Clarendon Sta. (H3) ...66
Clarksburg (D3) ...404
Clarkson (J4) ...1,450
Clifford (D4) ...542
Clinton (C4) ...3,491
Cobalt (K5) ...2,209
Cobden (H2) ...942
Coboconk (F3) ...506
Cobourg (F4) ...10,646
Cochrane (K5) ...4,521
Coe Hill (G2) ...239
Colborne (G4) ...1,336
Coldwater (E3) ...726
Collingwood (D3) ...8,385
Comber (B5) ...601
Combermere (G2) ...82
Coniston (D1) ...2,692
Consecon (G3) ...359
Cookstown (E3) ...1,025
Cooksville (J4) ...1,800
Copetown (E4) ...148
Copper Cliff (D1) ...3,600
Coral (J4) ...51
Cordova Mines (G3) ...265
Corinth (D5) ...87
Cornwall (K2) ...43,639
Corunna (B5) ...1,942
Courtland (D5) ...605
Courtright (B5) ...532
Craighurst (E3) ...429
Creemore (D3) ...850
Creighton Mine (C1) ...1,727
Crosby (H3) ...125
Crysler (J2) ...498
Crystal Beach (E5) ...1,886
Crystal Falls (D1) ...154
Cumberland (J2) ...360
Cutler (B1) ...175
Dashwood (C4) ...433
Dean Lake (A1) ...80
Deep River (G1) ...5,377
Delamere (D1)
Delaware (C5) ...466
Delhi (D5) ...3,427
Deloro (H3) ...159
Delta (H3) ...417
Denbigh (G2) ...174
Denfield (C4) ...68

(continued on following page)

NORTHERN ONTARIO

SCALE OF MILES

0 25 50 100 150 200

Provincial Capital ....
County Seats .... Provincial and State Boundaries
International Boundaries .... County Boundaries

Copyright by C.S. HAMMOND & Co., N.Y.

Ontario
(continued)

Place (grid)	Pop.
Depot Harbour (D2)..	457
Desbarats (J5)	154
Desboro (C3)	160
Deseronto (G3)	1,797
Detlor (G2)	65
Deux-Rivières (F1)	163
Devlin (J5)	262
Dixie (J4)	551
Dorchester (C5)	1,183
Dorion (F5)	200
Dorset (F2)	220
Douglas (H2)	365
Drayton (D4)	646
Dresden (B5)	2,346
Drumbo (D4)	416
Dryden (G4)	5,728
Dublin (C4)	301
Dunchurch (H2)	91
Dundalk (D3)	852
Dundas (E4)	12,912
Dungannon (C4)	166
Dunnville (E5)	5,181
Duntroon (D3)	67
Durham (D3)	2,180
Dutton (C5)	815
Dyment (G5)	158
Eastview (J2)	24,555
Eastwood (D4)	135
Eau Claire (F1)	83
Echo Bay (J5)	577
Edy's Mills (B5)	75
Eganville (G2)	1,549
Elgin (H3)	279
Elk Lake (K5)	701
Elliot Lake (B1)	9,950
Elmira (D4)	3,337
Elmvale (E3)	957
Elmwood (C3)	357
Elora (D4)	1,486
Elsas (J5)	150
Embro (D4)	552
Embrun (J2)	1,112
Emo (F5)	630
Emsdale (E2)	149
Englehart (K5)	1,786
English River (G5)	60
Enterprise (H3)	222
Erieau (C5)	497
Erin (D4)	1,005
Espanola (C1)	5,353
Essex (B5)	3,428
Ethel (C4)	134
Everett (E3)	426
Exeter (C4)	3,047
Falkenburg Station (E2)	60
Fallbrook (H3)	250
Fauquier (J5)	490
Fenelon Falls (F3)	1,359
Fergus (D4)	3,831
Fesserton (E3)	189
Feversham (E3)	151
Field (E1)	647
Fingal (C5)	346
Finch (J2)	386
Fisherville (E5)	234
Fitzroy Harbour (H2)..	253
Flanders (G5)	57
Flesherton (D3)	515
Florence (B5)	202
Foleyet (J5)	504
Fonthill (E4)	2,324
Fordwich (C4)	267
Forest (C4)	2,188
Foresters Falls (H2)	159
Formosa (C3)	370
Fort Erie (E5)	9,027
Fort Frances (F5)	9,481
Fort Hill (J4)	20,849
Fort William (G5)	45,214
Fournier (K2)	227
Foxboro (G3)	494
Frankford (G3)	1,642
Frankton (J2)	109
Fraserdale (J5)	215
Galetta (H2)	142
Galt (D4)	27,830
Gananoque (H3)	5,096
Gelert (F3)	200
Georgetown (E4)	10,298
Geraldton (H5)	3,375
Glammis (C3)	64
Glen Huron (D3)	101
Glen Robertson (K2)	409
Glen Williams (D4)	874
Glencoe (C5)	1,156
Goderich (C4)	6,411
Gogama (J5)	653
Golden Lake (G2)	254
Gooderham (F2)	275
Goodwood (E3)	304
Gore Bay (B2)	716
Gormley (J3)	108
Gorrie (C4)	319
Goudreau (J5)	60
Grafton (G4)	348
Grand Bend (C4)	928
Grand Valley (D4)	634
Granton (C4)	303
Gravenhurst (E4)	3,007
Grimsby (D4)	5,148
Guelph (D4)	39,838
Hagersville (D5)	2,075
Haileybury (K5)	2,638
Haley Sta. (H2)	186
Haliburton (F2)	853
Hamilton (E4)	273,991
Hamilton (E4)	1431,000
Hammond (J2)	84
Hanover (C3)	4,401
Harriston (C4)	1,631
Harrow (B5)	1,787
Harrowsmith (H3)	469
Harty (J5)	110
Harwood (F3)	185
Hastings (G3)	897
Hatchley (D4)	62
Havelock (G3)	1,260
Hawk Jct. (J5)	378
Hawkesbury (K2)	8,661
Hawkestone (E3)	202
Hearst (J5)	2,373
Heathcote (D3)	101
Hensall (C4)	926
Hepworth (C3)	258
Heron Bay (H5)	167
Hespeler (D4)	4,519
Hickson (D4)	151
Highgate (C5)	374
Highland Creek (K4)	2,400
Hillsburgh (D4)	440
Hillsdale (E3)	255
Holland Centre (D3)	72
Holland Landing (E3)	508
Holstein (D3)	185
Hornepayne (J4)	1,692
Hornings' Mills (D3)	211
Hudson (G4)	65
Huntsville (E2)	3,189
Hyde Park (C4)	250
Ignace (G5)	517
Idington (C4)	289
Ingersoll (C4)	6,874
Inglewood (F4)	419
Inkerman (J2)	68
Innerkip (D4)	371
Inwood (C5)	201
Iona (C5)	104
Iron Bridge (A1)	867
Iroquois (J3)	1,136
Iroquois Falls (K5)	1,681
Islington (J4)	
Ivanhoe (G3)	130
Jarvis (D5)	783
Jasper (H3)	221
Jeannettes Creek (B5)	196
Jellicoe (H5)	203
Kagawong (B2)	58
Kakabeka Falls (G5)	296
Kaladar (H3)	251
Kaministikwia (G5)	81
Kapuskasing (J5)	6,870
Kearney (F3)	365
Keene (F3)	324
Keewatin (G5)	2,197
Kemptville (J2)	1,959
Kenilworth (C4)	200
Kenmore (J2)	128
Kenora (F4)	10,904
Kent Bridge (B5)	118
Kerwood (C5)	113
Keswick (E3)	699
Killaloe Sta. (G2)	932
Kimberley (D3)	71
Kinburn (H2)	172
Kincardine (C3)	2,841
King City (J3)	1,864
Kingston (H3)	53,526
Kingsville (D5)	3,041
Kinmount (F3)	256
Kippen (C4)	112
Kirkfield (E3)	211
Kirkland Lake	15,366
Kitchener (D4)	74,485
Kitchener (D4)	154,864
Kleinburg (J4)	275
Komoka (C5)	465
La Passe (H2)	105
Lakefield (F3)	2,167
Lakeport (G4)	173
Lakeview (J4)	15,201
L'Amable (G3)	88
Lanark (H2)	918
Lancaster (K2)	584
Lansdowne (H3)	522
Lansing (J4)	
Latchford (K5)	479
Laurel (D4)	74
Leamington (B5)	9,030
Leaside (J4)	18,579
Lefaivre (K2)	194
Levack (J5)	3,178
Limoges (J2)	396
Lindsay (F3)	11,399
Linwood (D4)	374
Lion's Head (C2)	416
Listowel (D4)	4,022
Little Britain (F3)	290
Little Current (B2)	1,527
Lloydtown (J3)	140
Lochalsh (J5)	53
Lombardy (H3)	82
London (C5)	169,569
London (C5)	196,000
Long Branch (J4)	11,039
Longford Mills (E3)	360
Longlac (H5)	1,125
L'Orignal (K2)	1,189
Loring (D2)	200
Lorne Park (J4)	540
Low Bush River (K5)	67
Lucan (C4)	986
Lucknow (C3)	1,031
Lyn (J3)	554
Lynden (D4)	532
Lyndhurst (H3)	192
MacTier (F2)	851
Madawaska (F2)	429
Madoc (G3)	1,347
Magnetawan (E2)	205
Maidstone (B5)	153
Mallorytown (J3)	335
Malton (J4)	2,148
Malvern (K4)	658
Manitouwadge (H5)	2,006
Manitowaning (C2)	400
Manotick (J2)	434
Maple (J3)	1,552
Marathon (H5)	2,568
Markdale (D3)	1,090
Markham (K4)	4,294
Markstay (D1)	326
Marlbank (D3)	237
Marmora (G3)	1,381
Martintown (K2)	409
Massey (C1)	1,324
Matachewan (J5)	923
Matheson (K5)	853
Mattawa (F1)	3,314
Mattice (J5)	711
Maxville (K2)	804
Maynooth (G2)	290
McGregor (B5)	397
McKellar (F2)	163
McKerrow (C1)	221
Meadowvale (J4)	333
Meaford (D3)	3,834
Melbourne (C5)	333
Merlin (B5)	595
Merricgville (J3)	947
Metcalfe (J3)	385
Michipicoten Harbour (H5)	159
Middleville (H2)	84
Midhurst (E3)	340
Midland (E3)	8,656
Mildmay (C3)	847
Mill Bridge (G3)	51
Millbank (D4)	235
Millbrook (F3)	891
Milton (E4)	5,629
Milverton (C4)	1,111
Mimico (J4)	18,212
Minaki (F4)	207
Minden (F2)	658
Mississippi Station (H3)	88
Mitchell (C4)	2,247
Monkton (C4)	422
Moonbeam (J5)	253
Moorefield (D4)	253
Moose Creek (K2)	429
Morewood (J2)	189
Morpeth (C5)	211
Morrisburg (J3)	1,820
Morton (H3)	94
Mount Albert (E3)	561
Mount Brydges (C5)	1,016
Mount Dennis (J4)	
Mount Forest (D4)	2,623
Mount Pleasant (D4)	809
Mountain Grove (H3)	135
Muncey (C5)	83
Myrtle (H4)	130
Nakina (H4)	747
Nanticoke (E5)	121
Napanee (G3)	4,550

Copyright by C. S. HAMMOND & CO., N.Y.

ONTARIO
CENTRAL PART
SCALE OF MILES

Ontario
(continued)

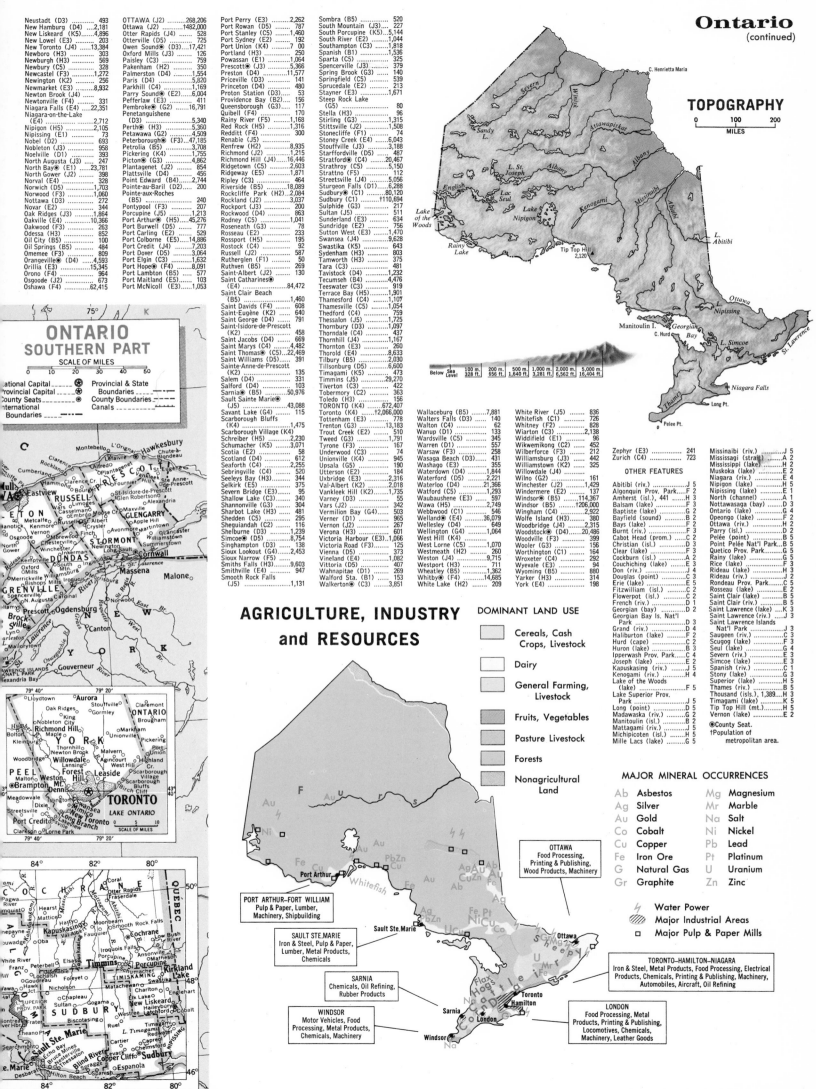

TOPOGRAPHY

0   100   200
MILES

Below Sea Level | 100 m. 328 ft. | 200 m. 656 ft. | 500 m. 1,640 ft. | 1,000 m. 3,281 ft. | 2,000 m. 6,562 ft. | 5,000 m. 16,404 ft.

ONTARIO SOUTHERN PART

SCALE OF MILES
0   10   20   30   40   50

National Capital ⊛
Provincial Capital ⊛
County Seats ⊙
International Boundaries
Provincial & State Boundaries
County Boundaries
Canals

TORONTO
LAKE ONTARIO
SCALE OF MILES
0   5   10

AGRICULTURE, INDUSTRY and RESOURCES

DOMINANT LAND USE

Cereals, Cash Crops, Livestock
Dairy
General Farming, Livestock
Fruits, Vegetables
Pasture Livestock
Forests
Nonagricultural Land

MAJOR MINERAL OCCURRENCES

Ab	Asbestos	Mg	Magnesium
Ag	Silver	Mr	Marble
Au	Gold	Na	Salt
Co	Cobalt	Ni	Nickel
Cu	Copper	Pb	Lead
Fe	Iron Ore	Pt	Platinum
G	Natural Gas	U	Uranium
Gr	Graphite	Zn	Zinc

⚡ Water Power
▨ Major Industrial Areas
□ Major Pulp & Paper Mills

OTTAWA
Food Processing, Printing & Publishing, Wood Products, Machinery

PORT ARTHUR–FORT WILLIAM
Pulp & Paper, Lumber, Machinery, Shipbuilding

SAULT STE. MARIE
Iron & Steel, Pulp & Paper, Lumber, Metal Products, Chemicals

SARNIA
Chemicals, Oil Refining, Rubber Products

WINDSOR
Motor Vehicles, Food Processing, Metal Products, Chemicals, Machinery

TORONTO–HAMILTON–NIAGARA
Iron & Steel, Metal Products, Food Processing, Electrical Products, Chemicals, Printing & Publishing, Machinery, Automobiles, Aircraft, Oil Refining

LONDON
Food Processing, Metal Products, Printing & Publishing, Locomotives, Chemicals, Machinery, Leather Goods

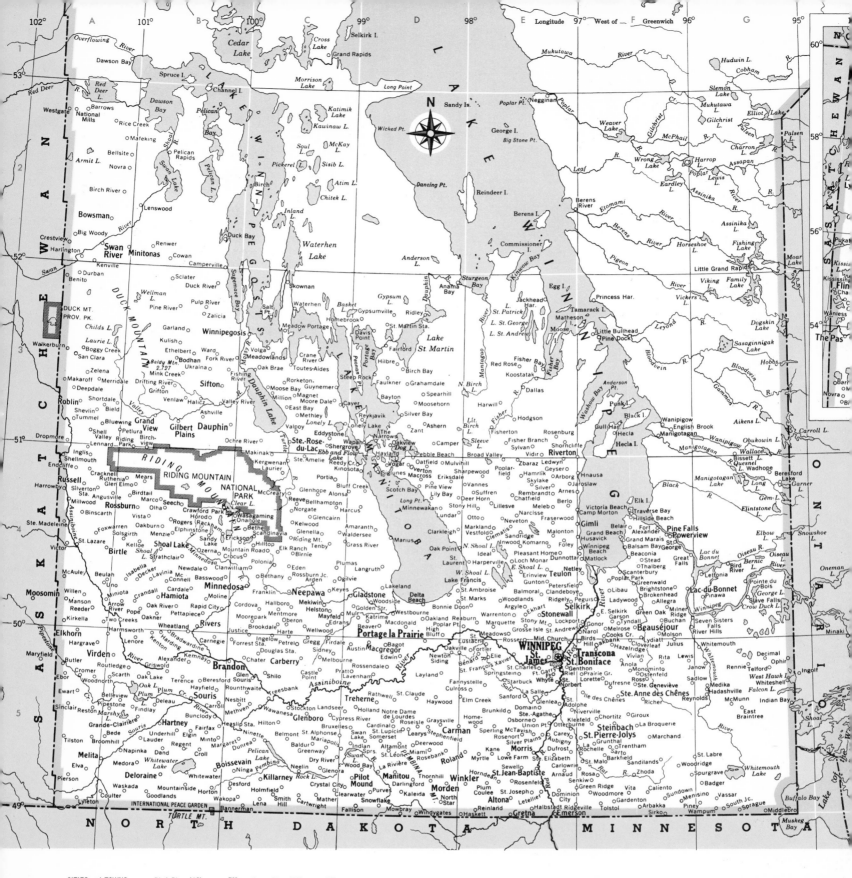

CITIES and TOWNS

Alexander (B5) 269
Alonsa (C4) 133
Altamont (D5) 123
Altona (E5) 2,026
Amaranth (D4) 294
Angusville (A4) 208
Anola (F5) 100
Arborg (E4) 811
Arden (C4) 188
Arnaud (E5) 88
Arrow River (B4) 150
Ashern (D3) 374
Aubigny (E5) 117
Austin (D5) 384
Baden (A2) 89
Badger (G5) 110
Baulur (C5) 370
Balmoral (E4) 103
Balsam Bay (F4) 100
Bannerman (C5) 118
Barrows (A2) 123
Basswood (B4) 121
Beauséjour (F4) 1,177
Bellsite (A2) 85
Belmont (C5) 378
Benito (A3) 427
Berens River (F2) 169
Bethany (A3) 80
Beulah (A4) 74
Binscarth (A4) 456

Birch River (A2) 799
Birnie (C4) 88
Birtle (B4) 857
Bissett (G4) 770
Boggy Creek (A3) 350
Boissevain (C5) 1,303
Bowsman (A2) 504
Bradwardine (B5) 75
Brandon (C5) 28,166
Brochet (H2) 158
Brookdale (C4) 108
Brooklands (E5) 4,369
Brunkild (E5) 120
Camp Morton (F4) 350
Camperville (B2) 627
Carberry (C5) 1,113
Cardale (B4) 91
Carman (D5) 1,930
Carroll (C5) 88
Cartwright (C5) 482
Channing (H3) 509
Chatfield (E4) 158
Chortitz (E5) 77
Churchill (K2) 1,878
Clandeboye (E5) 119
Clanwilliam (C4) 182
Clearwater (D5) 121
Cormorant (H3) 272
Cowan (B2) 124
Cranberry Portage (H3) 838
Crandall (B4) 105

Crane River (C3) 147
Cromer (A5) 71
Crystal City (C5) 541
Cypress River (D5) 288
Dallas (E3) 480
Darlingford (D5) 189
Dauphin (B3) 7,374
Deepdale (A3) 77
Deleau (B5) 188
Deloraine (B5) 916
Delta Beach (D4) 74
Dominion City (E5) 534
Douglas Sta. (C5) 289
Dufrost (E5) 96
Dunnottar (E4) 232
Dunrea (C5) 196
Durban (A3) 118
East Kildonan (E5) 27,305
East Selkirk (F4) 401
Eden (C4) 146
Elgin (C5) 259
Elie (E5) 370
Elkhorn (A5) 666
Elm Creek (E5) 337
Elphinstone (B4) 386
Emerson (E5) 932
Erickson (C4) 531
Eriksdale (D3) 242
Ethelbert (B3) 556
Fannystelle (E5) 153
Fisher Branch (E3) 369
Flin Flon (H3) 11,104

Fork River (B3) 174
Fort Garry (E5) 1,485
Fort Whyte (E5) 800
Foxwarren (A4) 272
Franklin (C4) 73
Fraserwood (E4) 78
Gardenton (F5) 104
Garland (B3) 128
Garson (F4) 330
Gilbert Plains (B3) 849
Gillam (K2) 332
Gimli (E4) 1,841
Gladstone (D4) 944
Glenboro (C5) 797
Glenella (C4) 219
Gods Lake (J3) 80
Gonor (F4) 323
Goodlands (B5) 138
Grand Beach (F4) 259
Grand Marais (F4) 280
Grand Rapids (C1) 986
Grand View (C4) 1,057
Graysville (D5) 115
Great Falls (F4) 164
Greenway (C5) 133
Gretna (E5) 575
Griswold (B5) 137
Grunthal (E5) 287
Gunton (E4) 88
Gypsumville (D3) 235
Halbstadt (E5) 83

Hallboro (C4) 86
Hamiota (B4) 779
Hargrave (A5) 75
Harrowby (A4) 70
Hartney (B5) 592
Haskett (E5) 71
Hayfield (B5) 87
Haywood (D5) 146
Hazelridge (F5) 70
High Bluff (D4) 77
Hnausa (F4) 102
Hodgson (E3) 222
Holland (D5) 433
Holmfield (C5) 122
Horndean (E5) 161
Ile-des-Chênes (F5) 211
Ilford (J2) 165
Inglis (A4) 295
Inwood (E4) 183
Janow (G5) 172
Kelloe (B4) 86
Kelwood (C4) 323
Kemnay (C5) 81
Kenton (B5) 222
Kenville (A3) 144
Killarney (C5) 1,729
Kississing (H3) 183
Klefeld (F5) 102
Komarno (E4) 101
La Broquerie (F5) 386
La Rivière (D5) 232
La Rochelle (F5) 120

La Salle (E5) 128
Lac-du-Bonnet (G4) 569
Langruth (D4) 249
Lauder (B5) 72
Laurier (C4) 262
Lavenham (D5) 71
Lenore (B5) 98
Lenswood (B2) 300
Letellier (E5) 266
Libau (F4) 84
Lockport (E4) 405
Lorette (F5) 700
Lowe Farm (E5) 310
Lundar (D4) 713
Lyleton (C5) 123
Macdonald (D4) 118
MacGregor (D5) 642
Mafeking (B2) 385
Manigotagan (F3) 213
Manitou (D5) 863
Marchand (F5) 99
Margaret (C5) 78
Mariapolis (C5) 258
Marius (D4) 800
Marquette (E4) 87
Mather (C5) 125
Matheson Island (E3) 176
Matlock (F4) 500
McAuley (A4) 199
McConnell (B4) 65
McCreary (C4) 579

McTavish (E5) 139
Meadow Portage (C3) 61
Meadows (C4) 65
Medika (G5) 450
Medora (B5) 90
Melbourne (C5) 78
Meleb (E4) 97
Melita (A5) 1,038
Melrose (E5) 300
Miami (D5) 349
Middlebro (G5) 147
Milner Ridge (F4) 63
Miniota (B4) 248
Minitonas (B2) 606
Minnedosa (B4) 2,211
Minto (B5) 171
Moorepark (C4) 166
Moose Lake (H3) 283
Moosehorn (D3) 108
Morden (D5) 2,793
Morris (D5) 1,370
Mowbray (D5) 75
Mulvihill (D4) 169
Myrtle (D5) 110
Napinka (B5) 178
Narol (F4) 592
Neelin (C5) 86
Neepawa (C4) 3,197
Nesbitt (C5) 86
Newdale (B4) 350
Ninette (C5) 673
Ninga (C5) 129

Niverville (F5) 474
Norway House (J3) 543
Notre-Dame-de-Lourdes (D5) 511
Oak Lake (B5) 430
Oak Point (D4) 238
Oak River (B4) 357
Oakburn (B4) ....
Oakner (B4) 120
Oakview (D3) ....
Oakville (D5) 377
Ochre River (C3) 321
Onanole (C4) 348
Otterburne (F5) 258
Pelican Rapids (B2) 213
Petersfield (F4) 157
Pierson (A5) 229
Pikwitonei (J3) 175
Pilot Mound (D5) 802
Pinawa (F4) 75
Pine Falls (F4) 1,244
Pine River (B3) 351
Piney (F5) 197
Pipestone (B5) 226
Plum Coulee (E5) 510
Plumas (C4) 344
Pointe-du-Bois (G4) 284
Poplar Park (F4) 300
Poplar Point (D4) 257
Poplarfield (E3) 142
Portage-la-Prairie (D4) 12,388

MANITOBA
Northern Part
SCALE OF MILES
0 40 80 120

MANITOBA
SOUTHERN PART
SCALE OF MILES
0 5 10 20 40 60

Provincial Capital .... ⊛
International Boundaries ___.___.
Provincial Boundaries ___ ___

Copyright by C.S. HAMMOND & Co., N.Y.

MANITOBA

AREA	251,000 sq. mi.
POPULATION	959,000
CAPITAL	Winnipeg
LARGEST CITY	Winnipeg (greater) 490,000
HIGHEST POINT	Duck Mtn. 2,727 ft.
SETTLED IN	1812
ADMITTED TO CONFEDERATION	1870
PROVINCIAL FLOWER	Prairie Crocus

Saint James (E5) 33,977
Saint-Jean-Baptiste (E5) 521
Saint-Joseph (E5) 109
Saint-Laurent (D4) 869
Saint-Lazare (D4) 869
Saint-Lupicin (D5) 268
Saint-Malo (F5) 574
Saint Marks (F4) 80
Saint-Norbert (E5) 695
Saint-Pierre-Jolys (F5).. 856
Sainte-Agathe (E5) 298
Sainte-Amélie (C4) 66
Sainte-Anne-des-Chênes (F5) 653
Sainte-Elisabeth (E5)... 300
Sainte-Rose-du-Lac (C3) 790
San Clara (A3) 94
Sandilands (F5) 133
Sandy Lake (B4) 383
Sanford (E5) 103
Scanterbury (F4) 97
Scarth (B5) 94
Selkirk (F4) 8,576
Senkiw (F5) 150
Seven Sisters Falls (G4) 131
Shellmouth (A4) 98
Shergrove (C3) 150
Sherridon (H3) 1,500
Shoal Lake (B4) 774
Shorncliffe (E3) 173
Sidney (C5) 154
Sifton (B3) 245
Sinclair (A5) 85
Skownan (C3) 61
Skylake (E4) 140
Snowflake (D5) 73
Solsgirth (B4) 78
Somerset (D5) 587
Souris (B5) 1,841
South Junction (G5).... 233
Spearhill (D3) 75
Sperling (E5) 172
Split Lake (J2) 500
Sprague (G5) 364
Springstein (E5) 84
Spurgrave (G5) 140
Starbuck (E5) 240
Steep Rock (D3) 168
Steinbach (F5) 3,739
Stockton (C5) 61
Stonewall (E4) 1,420
Stony Mountain (E4)..1,130
Strathclair (B4) 465
Sundown (F5) 196
Swan Lake (D5) 307
Swan River (A2) 3,163
Sylvan (E3) 250
Teulon (E4) 749
Thalberg (F4) 288

The Narrows (D3) ....
The Pas (H3) 4,671
Thicket Portage (J3).... 275
Thornhill (D5) 105
Tilston (A5) 101
Tolstoi (F5) 99
Transcona (F5) 14,248
Traverse Bay (F4) 120
Treherne (D5) 569
Trentham (F5) 500
Tuxedo (E5) 1,627
Two Creeks (B4) 86
Tyndall (F4) 241
Union Point (E5) 78
Vassar (G5) 243
Victoria Beach (F4).... 74
Virden (A5) 2,708
Vista (B4) 79
Vita (F5) 316
Wabowden (J3) 327
Wakopa (C5) 62
Wanless (H3) 156
Warrenton (E4) 122
Wasagaming (C4) 146
Waskada (B5) 297
Wawanesa (C5) 456
Wekusko (H3) 81
Wellwood (C4) 73
West Kildonan (E5) ...20,077
Westbourne (D4) 123
Westgate (A2) 69
Wheatland (D4) 195
Whitemouth (G5) 385
Whitewater (B5) 93
Winkler (E5) 2,529
WINNIPEG (E5)......265,429
Winnipeg (E5) 1490,000
Winnipeg Beach (F4)... 807
Winnipegosis (B3) 980
Woodlands (E4) 124
Woodridge (E5) 289
York Factory (K2) 76

OTHER FEATURES

Aikens (lake) ....G 3
Alexander Slough (marsh) ....B 5
Anderson (lake) ....D 2
Armit (lake) ....A 2
Assapan (riv.) ....G 2
Assiniboine (riv.) ....C 5
Assinika (riv.) ....G 2
Baralzon (lake) ....J 1
Basket (lake) ....C 3
Beaverhill (lake) ....J 3
Berens (isl.) ....E 2
Berens (riv.) ....F 2

TOPOGRAPHY
0 75 150
MILES

Below Sea Level | 100 m. 328 ft. | 200 m. 656 ft. | 500 m. 1,640 ft. | 1,000 m. 3,281 ft. | 2,000 m. 6,562 ft. | 5,000 m. 16,404 ft.

Powerview (F4) 902
Prairie Grove (F5)....... 300
Purves (D5) 66
Rackham (B4) 56
Rapid City (B4) 467
Rathwell (D5) 197
Reinland (E5) 231
Rennie (G5) 135
Reston (A5) 529
Richer (F5) 339
Ridgeville (E5) 86
Riding Mountain (C4).. 212

Rita (F5) 102
Rivers (B4) 1,574
Riverton (E3) 808
Roblin (A3) 1,368
Roland (D5) 374
Rorketon (C3) 273
Roseisle (D5) 66
Rosenfeld (E5) 316
Rosenort (E5) 110
Ross (F5) 77
Rossburn (B4) 591
Rossendale (D5) 137

Rosser (E5) 67
Russell (A4) 1,263
Saint-Adolphe (E5) 217
Saint-Amboise (E4) 359
Saint Andrews (E4)..... 850
Saint-Boniface (F5)..37,600
Saint-Charles (E5) 500
Saint-Claude (D5) 609
Saint-Eustache (E5) ... 332
Saint-François-Xavier (E5) 450
Saint George (F4) 288

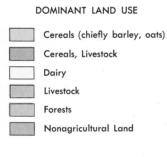

AGRICULTURE, INDUSTRY
and RESOURCES

DOMINANT LAND USE

Cereals (chiefly barley, oats)
Cereals, Livestock
Dairy
Livestock
Forests
Nonagricultural Land

MAJOR MINERAL OCCURRENCES

Au	Gold	Ni	Nickel
Co	Cobalt	O	Petroleum
Cu	Copper	Pt	Platinum
Na	Salt	Zn	Zinc

⚡ Water Power
Major Industrial Areas
□ Major Pulp & Paper Mills

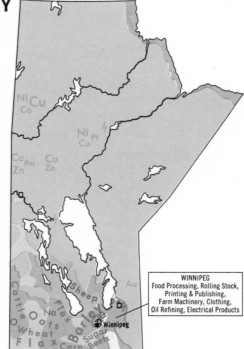

WINNIPEG
Food Processing, Rolling Stock,
Printing & Publishing,
Farm Machinery, Clothing,
Oil Refining, Electrical Products

Big Stone (point) ....E 2
Bigstone (riv.) ....J 3
Birch (isl.) ....C 2
Black (isl.) ....F 3
Bloodvein (riv.) ....F 3
Bonnet (lake) ....G 4
Buffalo (bay) ....G 5
Burntwood (riv.) ......J 2
Carroll (lake) ....G 3
Cedar (lake) ....B 1
Channel (isl.) ....B 2
Charron (lake) ....G 2
Childs (lake) ....A 3
Chitek (lake) ....C 2
Churchill (riv.) ....J 2
Clear (lake) ....C 4
Cochrane (riv.) ....H 2
Commissioner (isl.) ...E 3
Cormorant (lake) .....H 3
Cross (lake) ....C 1
Cross (lake) ....J 3
Crow Duck (lake) .....G 4
Dauphin (lake) ....C 3
Dawson (bay) ....B 2
Dennis (lake) ....D 3
Dog (lake) ....D 3
Dogskin (lake) ....G 3
Eardley (lake) ....F 2
East Shoal (lake) ......E 4
Ebb and Flow (lake)...C 3
Egg (isl.) ....E 3
Elbow (lake) ....G 2
Elk (isl.) ....F 4
Elliot (lake) ....G 2
Etawney (lake) ....J 2
Falcon (lake) ....G 5
Family (lake) ....G 2
Fisher (bay) ....E 3
Fishing (lake) ....G 2
Flintstone (lake) ......G 2
Fox (riv.) ....J 2
Gammon (riv.) ....G 3
Garner (lake) ....G 4
Gem (lake) ....G 2
George (isl.) ....E 2
George (lake) ....G 4
Gilchrist (lake) ....G 4
Gods (riv.) ....K 2
Granville (lake) ....H 2
Grass (riv.) ....J 3
Gypsum (lake) ....D 3
Harrop (lake) ....F 2
Hayes (riv.) ....K 3
Hecla (isl.) ....E 3
Horseshoe (lake) ......F 2
Hubbart (point) ....K 2
Hudson (bay) ....K 2

Hudwin (lake) ....G 1
Inland (lake) ....C 2
International Peace Garden ....B 5
Island (lake) ....K 3
Katimik (lake) ....C 2
Kawinaw (lake) ......C 2
Kazanjerri (lake) .....H 2
Kinwow (bay) ....E 2
Kississing (lake) .....H 2
Knee (lake) ....J 3
Laurie (lake) ....A 3
Lewis (lake) ....G 2
Lonely (lake) ....C 3
Long (lake) ....G 4
Long (lake) ....D 1
Long (point) ....D 4
Manigotagan (lake) ..G 4
Manitoba (lake) ....D 4
Mantagao (riv.) ....E 3
Marshy (lake) ....B 5
McKay (lake) ....C 2
McPhail (riv.) ....F 2
Minnedosa (riv.) ......B 4
Moar (lake) ....G 2
Molson (lake) ....J 3
Moose (isl.) ....E 3
Moose (lake) ....H 3
Morrison (lake) ....C 1
Mossy (riv.) ....C 3
Mukutawa (riv.) ......E 1
Nejanilini (lake) ......J 2
Nelson (riv.) ....J 2
North Birch (lake) ....E 3
North Indian (lake) ...J 2
North Shoal (lake) ....E 4
Nueltin (lake) ....J 1
Oak (lake) ....B 5
Obukowin (lake) ......G 2
Oiseau (riv.) ....G 4
Overflowing (riv.) ....A 2
Owl (riv.) ....K 2
Oxford (lake) ....J 3
Paint (lake) ....J 2
Palsen (riv.) ....J 2
Pelican (lake) ....B 2
Pelican (lake) ....C 5
Pembina (mt.) ....D 5
Pembina (riv.) ....C 5
Peonan (point) ....D 3
Pickerel (lake) ....D 3
Pigeon (riv.) ....F 2
Pipestone (creek) .....A 5
Plum (lake) ....B 5
Poplar (point) ....D 4
Portage (bay) ....D 3
Punk (isl.) ....F 3

Quesnel (lake) ....G 4
Rat (riv.) ....F 5
Red (riv.) ....F 5
Red Deer (lake) ....A 2
Reindeer (isl.) ....E 2
Reindeer (lake) ....H 2
Riding Mountain Nat'l Park, 253 ....B 4
Rock (lake) ....C 5
Saint Andrew (lake) ..E 3
Saint George (lake) ...E 3
Saint Martin (lake) ...D 3
Sale (riv.) ....E 5
Sasaginnigak (lake) ..G 3
Seal (riv.) ....J 2
Setting (lake) ....H 3
Shoal (lake) ....G 4
Shoal (lake) ....G 5
Sipiwesk (lake) ....J 3
Sisib (lake) ....C 2
Sleeve (lake) ....E 3
Slemon (lake) ....G 1
Snowshoe (lake) ......G 4
Souris (riv.) ....B 5
Southern Indian (lake)..H 2
Split (lake) ....J 2
Spruce (isl.) ....B 1
Stevenson (lake) ......J 3
Sturgeon (bay) ....E 3
Swan (lake) ....B 2
Swan (lake) ....D 5
Tamarac (isl.) ....F 3
Tatnam (cape) ....K 2
Turtle (mt.) ....B 5
Turtle (riv.) ....C 3
Valley (riv.) ....B 3
Vickers (lake) ....F 3
Viking (lake) ....G 2
Wallace (lake) ....G 3
Wanipigow (riv.) .....G 3
Washow (bay) ....F 3
Waterhen (lake) ......C 2
Weaver (lake) ....B 3
Wellman (lake) ....B 3
West Hawk (lake) .....G 5
West Shoal (lake) .....E 4
Whitemouth (lake) ...G 5
Whitewater (lake) ....B 5
Wicked (point) ....D 2
Winnipeg (lake) ....E 2
Winnipeg (riv.) ....G 4
Winnipegosis (lake) ...C 2
Woods (lake) ....H 5
Wrong (lake) ....F 2

†Population of metropolitan area.

TOPOGRAPHY

0 60 120
MILES

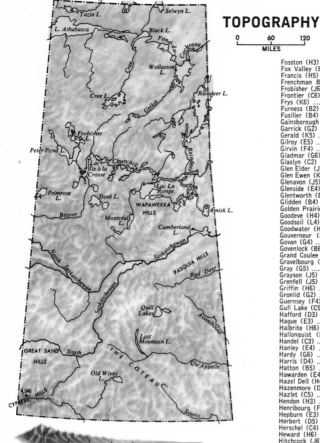

5,000 m. | 2,000 m. | 1,000 m. | 500 m. | 200 m. | 100 m. | Sea Level / Below
16,404 ft. | 6,562 ft. | 3,281 ft. | 1,640 ft. | 656 ft. | 328 ft.

CITIES and TOWNS

AGRICULTURE, INDUSTRY and RESOURCES

DOMINANT LAND USE

- Wheat
- Cereals (chiefly barley, oats)
- Cereals, Livestock
- Livestock
- Forests

MAJOR MINERAL OCCURRENCES

Au Gold
Cu Copper
G Natural Gas
K Potash
Lg Lignite
Na Salt
O Petroleum
S Sulfur
U Uranium
Zn Zinc

⚡ Water Power
▨ Major Industrial Areas

REGINA
Food Processing, Machinery, Oil Refining

SASKATCHEWAN

AREA	251,700 sq. mi.
POPULATION	953,000
CAPITAL	Regina
LARGEST CITY	Regina 126,000
HIGHEST POINT	Cypress Hills 4,546 ft.
SETTLED IN	1774
ADMITTED TO CONFEDERATION	1905
PROVINCIAL FLOWER	Prairie Lily

Tisdale (H3) 2,402
Togo (K4) 263
Tompkins (C5) 453
Torquay (H6) 462
Tramping Lake (B3) 288
Traynor (C3) 92
Tribune (H6) 153
Trossachs (G6) 89
Truax (G6) 76
Tuffnell (H4) 88
Tugaske (E5) 267
Turtleford (B2) 352
Tuxford (F5) 141
Tway (F3) 97
Tyvan (H5) 84
Unity (B3) 1,902
Uranium City (L2) 1,665
Val-Marie (D6) 443
Valley Centre (D4) 98
Valparaiso (G3) 71
Vanguard (D6) 433
Vanscoy (D4) 136
Vawn (C2) 102
Verigin (K4) 238
Verlo (C5) 134
Verwood (F6) 84
Vibank (H5) 308
Viceroy (F6) 225
Vidora (D6) 75
Viscount (F4) 303
Vonda (F3) 238
Wadena (H4) 1,311
Wakaw (F3) 974
Waldeck (D5) 237
Waldheim (E3) 515
Waldron (J5) 99
Walpole (K6) 70
Wapella (K5) 584
Warman (E3) 659
Wartime (C4) 96

Waseca (B2) 103
Waskesiu Lake (E2) 100
Watrous (F4) 1,461
Watson (G3) 910
Wauchope (K6) 83
Wawota (J6) 453
Webb (C5) 168
Weekes (J3) 294
Weirdale (F2) 98
Weldon (F2) 227
Welwyn (K5) 182
West Bend (H4) 91
Westerham (B5) 75
Weyburn (H6) 9,101
White Bear (C5) 139
White Fox (H2) 396
Whitewood (D3) 900
Whitkow (D3) 93
Wilcox (G5) 258
Wilkie (C3) 1,612
Willow Bunch (F6) 698
Willowbrook (J4) 86
Windthorst (J5) 202
Wiseton (D4) 246
Wishart (H4) 270
Wolseley (H5) 1,031
Wood Mountain Station (E6) 135
Woodrow (E6) 155
Wordsworth (J6) 72
Wroxton (K4) 127
Wymark (D5) 257
Wynyard (F4) 1,686
Yellow Creek (F3) 182
Yellow Grass (H6) 527
Yorkton (J4) 9,995
Young (F4) 341
Zealandia (D4) 192
Zelma (E4) 81
Zenon Park (H2) 384

OTHER FEATURES

Amisk (lake) ....M 4
Arm (riv.) ....F 5
Assiniboine (riv.) ....J 3
Athabasca (lake) ....L 1
Bad (lake) ....C 5
Basin (lake) ....F 3
Battle (creek) ....B 6
Battle (riv.) ....A 2
Bear (hills) ....B 3
Beaver (hills) ....H 4
Beaver (riv.) ....B 1
Beaver Lodge (lake) ....L 2
Big Muddy (lake) ....G 6
Bigstick (lake) ....B 5
Birch (lake) ....B 3
Bitter (lake) ....B 5
Black (lake) ....M 1
Brightsand (lake) ....B 2
Bronson (lake) ....B 1
Candle (lake) ....F 2
Canoe (lake) ....L 3
Carrot (riv.) ....J 2
Chipman (riv.) ....L 2
Chitek (lake) ....D 2
Churchill (riv.) ....M 3
Clearwater (riv.) ....L 3
Cochrane (riv.) ....N 2
Coteau, The (hills) ....D 5
Cowan (lake) ....B 2
Crane (lake) ....B 5
Crean (lake) ....E 1
Cree (lake) ....L 2
Cumberland (lake) ....J 1
Cypress Hills Prov.
  Park ....B 6
Delaronde (lake) ....E 1
Doré (lake) ....L 2

Duck Mountain Prov.
  Park ....K 4
Eagle (lake) ....C 3
Eaglehill (creek) ....D 3
Ear (lake) ....B 3
Etomami (riv.) ....J 3
Eyehill (creek) ....B 3
File (hills) ....H 5
Fir (riv.) ....J 3
Forrest (lake) ....L 3
Foster (lake) ....M 3
Frenchman (riv.) ....C 6
Frobisher (lake) ....L 1
Gap (lake) ....A 5
Geikie (riv.) ....M 3
Good Spirit Lake Prov.
  Park ....J 4
Great Sand (hills) ....B 5
Green (lake) ....D 1
Greenwater Lake Prov.
  Park ....H 3
Haultain (riv.) ....L 2
Ironspring (creek) ....G 3
Jackfish (lake) ....C 2
Kingsmere (lake) ....E 1
Kiyiu (lake) ....C 4
Last Mountain (lake) ....F 4
Leaf (lake) ....L 3
Leech (lake) ....J 3
Lenore (lake) ....G 3
Little Manitou (lake) ....F 4
Lodge (creek) ....B 5
Long (creek) ....H 6
Loon (creek) ....G 6
Makwa (lake) ....B 1
Manito (lake) ....B 3
McFarlane (riv.) ....L 2
Ministikwan (lake) ....B 1
Missouri Coteau
  (hills) ....F 6

Moose Mountain Prov.
  Park ....J 6
Mossy (riv.) ....H 1
Muddy (lake) ....B 3
Mudjatik (riv.) ....L 3
Nipawin Prov. Park ....G 1
North Saskatchewan
  (riv.) ....D 3
Notukeu (creek) ....D 6
Old Wives (lake) ....E 5
Oldman (riv.) ....F 2
Opuntia (lake) ....C 4
Overflowing (riv.) ....K 2
Pasquia (hills) ....J 3
Pelican (lake) ....E 5
Peter Pond (lake) ....L 3

Pheasant (hills) ....J 5
Pinto (creek) ....D 6
Pipestone (creek) ....K 6
Pipestone (riv.) ....L 2
Ponass (lake) ....H 3
Poplar (riv.) ....E 6
Porcupine (mt.) ....K 3
Primrose (lake) ....L 3
Prince Albert Nat'l
  Park, 109 ....E 1
Qu'Appelle (riv.) ....J 5
Red Deer (lake) ....A 5
Red Deer (riv.) ....J 3
Redberry (lake) ....D 3
Reflex (lake) ....A 1
Reindeer (lake) ....N 3

Reindeer (riv.) ....M 3
Riou (lake) ....M 2
Rivers (lake) ....F 6
Salt (lake) ....K 2
Saskatchewan (riv.) ....K 2
Saskeram (riv.) ....K 2
Scott (lake) ....M 2
Selwyn (lake) ....M 2
Souris (riv.) ....H 6
South Saskatchewan
  (riv.) ....C 5
Stripe (lake) ....C 4
Sturgeon (riv.) ....E 2
Swan (riv.) ....J 3
Tazin (riv.) ....L 1
Thickwood (hills) ....D 2

Torch (riv.) ....H 2
Touchwood (hills) ....G 4
Trout (riv.) ....C 2
Turtle (lake) ....C 2
Twelvemile (lake) ....E 6
Wapawekka (hills) ....M 4
Waskana (creek) ....G 5
Watham (riv.) ....M 3
Weed (lake) ....J 5
White Gull (creek) ....G 2
Westmore (lake) ....L 3
Whiteswan (lakes) ....F 1
William (riv.) ....L 2
Witchekan (lake) ....D 3
Wollaston (lake) ....N 2
Wood (riv.) ....E 6

SASKATCHEWAN Northern Part

SASKATCHEWAN SOUTHERN PART
SCALE OF MILES
0 5 10 20 40 60
Provincial Capital ⊛
International Boundaries
Provincial Boundaries

Copyright by C.S. HAMMOND & CO., N.Y.

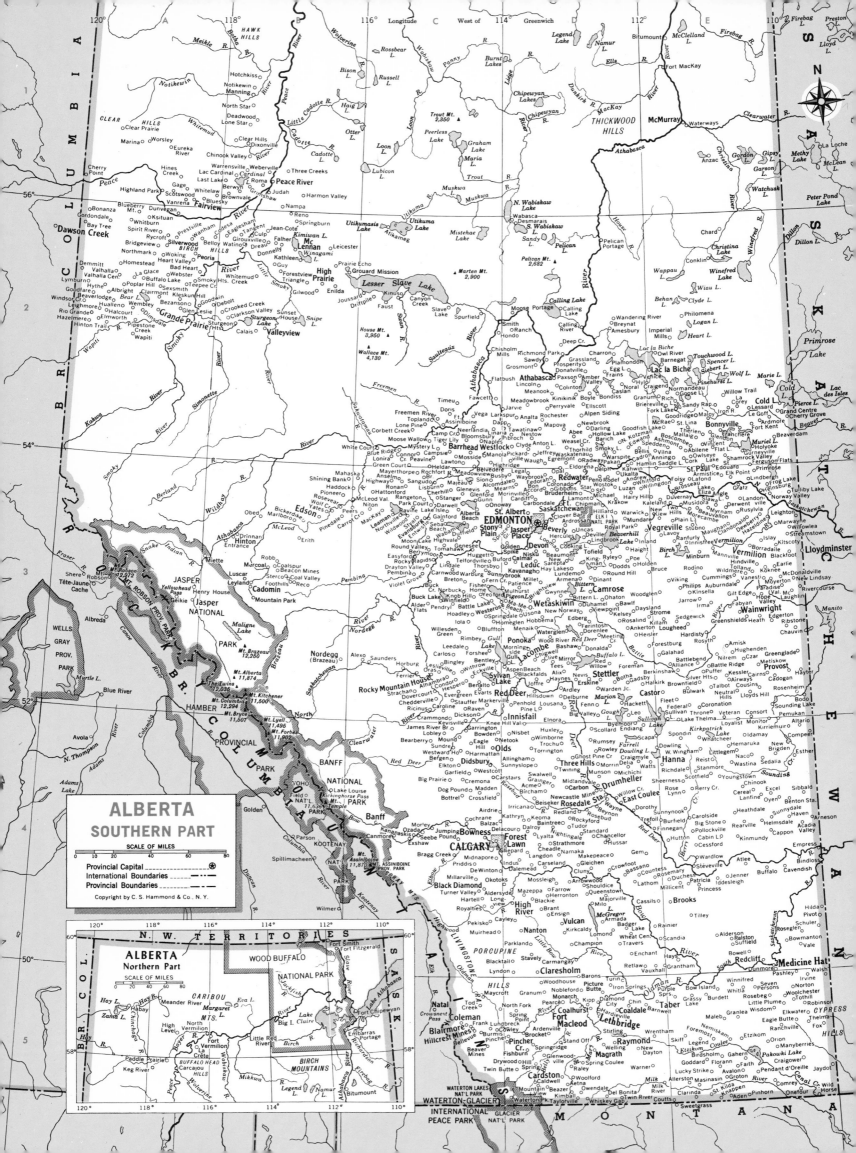

ALBERTA
SOUTHERN PART

SCALE OF MILES

Provincial Capital .... ⊗
International Boundaries ......
Provincial Boundaries ....

Copyright by C. S. Hammond & Co., N.Y.

ALBERTA
Northern Part
SCALE OF MILES

ALBERTA

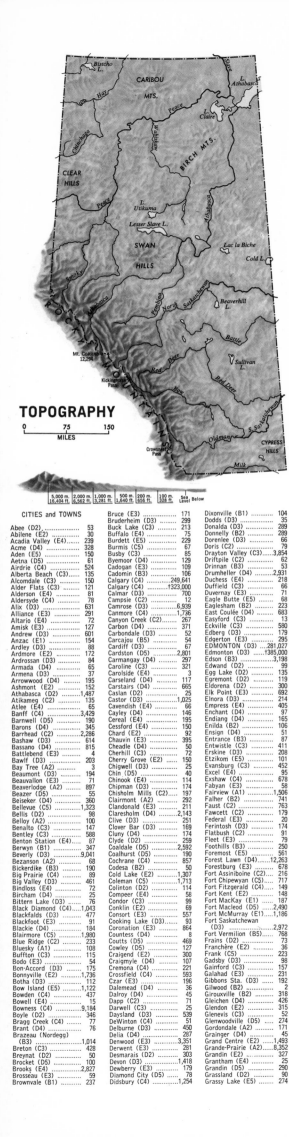

AREA	255,285 sq. mi.
POPULATION	1,456,000
CAPITAL	Edmonton
LARGEST CITY	Edmonton (greater) 385,000
HIGHEST POINT	Mt. Columbia 12,294 ft.
SETTLED IN	1861
ADMITTED TO CONFEDERATION	1905
PROVINCIAL FLOWER	Wild Rose

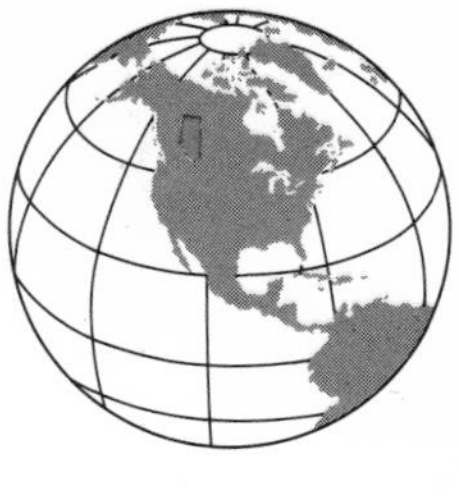

TOPOGRAPHY

0   75   150
MILES

5,000 m. 2,000 m. 1,000 m. 500 m. 200 m. 100 m. Sea Level
16,404 ft. 6,562 ft. 3,281 ft. 1,640 ft. 656 ft. 328 ft. Below

CITIES and TOWNS

Abee (D2) 53
Abilene (E2) 30
Acadia Valley (E4) 239
Acme (D4) 328
Aden (E5) 150
Aetna (D5) 61
Airdrie (C4) 524
Alberta Beach (C3) 135
Alcomdale (C3) 150
Alder Flats (C3) 121
Alderson (E4) 81
Aldersyde (C4) 78
Alix (D3) 631
Alliance (E3) 291
Altario (E4) 72
Amisk (E3) 127
Andrew (D3) 601
Anzac (E1) 154
Ardley (D3) 88
Ardmore (E2) 172
Ardrossan (D3) 84
Armada (D4) 65
Armena (D3) 37
Arrowwood (D4) 195
Ashmont (E2) 152
Athabasca (D2) 1,487
Atikameg (C2) 135
Atlee (E4) 81
Banff (C4) 3,429
Barnwell (D5) 190
Barons (D4) 345
Barrhead (C2) 2,286
Bashaw (D3) 614
Bassano (D4) 815
Battlebend (E3) 4
Bawlf (D3) 203
Bay Tree (A2) 3
Beaumont (D3) 194
Beauvallon (E3) 71
Beaverlodge (A2) 897
Beazer (D5) 55
Beiseker (D4) 360
Bellevue (C5) 1,323
Bellis (D2) 98
Belloy (C3) 100
Benalto (C3) 147
Bentley (C3) 588
Benton Station (E4) ... 8
Berwyn (B1) 347
Beverly (D3) 9,041
Bezanson (A2) 68
Bickerdike (B3) 190
Big Prairie (C4) 89
Big Valley (D3) 461
Bindloss (E4) 72
Bircham (D4) 25
Bittern Lake (D3) 76
Black Diamond (C4) .. 1,043
Blackfalds (D3) 477
Blackfoot (E3) 91
Blackie (D4) 184
Blairmore (C5) 1,900
Blue Ridge (C2) 233
Bluesky (A1) 108
Buffton (C5) 115
Bodo (E3) 54
Bon-Accord (D3) 175
Bonnyville (E2) 1,736
Botha (D3) 112
Bow Island (E5) 1,122
Bowden (C4) 437
Bowell (E4) 15
Bowness (C4) 9,184
Boyle (D2) 346
Bragg Creek (C4) 77
Brant (D4) 76
Brazeau (Nordegg) (B3) 1,014
Breton (C3) 428
Breynat (D2) 50
Brocket (D5) 100
Brooks (E4) 2,827
Brosseau (E3) 59
Brownvale (B1) 237

Bruce (E3) 171
Bruderheim (D3) 299
Buck Lake (C3) 213
Buffalo (E4) 75
Burdett (E5) 229
Burmis (C5) 67
Busby (C3) 85
Byemoor (D4) 129
Cadogan (E3) 109
Cadomin (B3) 106
Calgary (C4) 249,641
Calgary (C4) ... 1323,000
Calmar (D3) 700
Campsie (C2) 12
Camrose (D3) 6,939
Canmore (C4) 1,736
Canyon Creek (C2) .. 267
Carbon (D4) 371
Carbondale (C3) 52
Carcajou (B5) 54
Cardiff (D3) 67
Cardston (D5) 2,801
Carmangay (D4) 297
Caroline (C3) 321
Carolside (C4) 3
Carseland (D4) 117
Carstairs (D4) 665
Caslan (D2) 25
Castor (D3) 1,025
Cavendish (E4) 66
Cayley (D4) 146
Cereal (E4) 195
Cessford (E4) 150
Chard (D2) 92
Chauvin (E3) 395
Cheadle (D4) 50
Cherhill (C3) 72
Cherry Grove (E2) 150
Chigwell (D3) 25
Chin (D5) 40
Chinook (E4) 114
Chipman (D3) 174
Chisholm Mills (C2) .. 197
Clairmont (A2) 292
Clandonald (E3) 211
Claresholm (D4) 2,143
Clive (D3) 251
Clover Bar (D3) 169
Cluny (D4) 174
Clyde (D2) 259
Coaldale (D5) 2,592
Coalhurst (D5) 190
Cochrane (C4) 857
Codesa (B2) 50
Cold Lake (E2) 1,307
Coleman (C5) 1,713
Colinton (D2) 114
Compeer (E4) 58
Condor (C3) 99
Conklin (E2) 69
Consort (E3) 557
Cooking Lake (D3) ... 863
Coronation (E3) 864
Countess (D4) 8
Coutts (D5) 469
Cowley (D5) 127
Craigend (C2) 300
Craigmyle (D4) 107
Cremona (C4) 221
Crossfield (C4) 593
Czar (E3) 196
Dalemead (D4) 36
Dalroy (D4) 45
Dapp (C2) 71
Darwell (C3) 25
Daysland (D3) 539
DeWinton (C4) 51
Delburne (D3) 450
Delia (D4) 287
Denwood (E3) 3,351
Derwent (E3) 281
Desmarais (D2) 303
Devon (D3) 1,418
Dewberry (E3) 179
Diamond City (D5) ... 78
Didsbury (C4) 1,254

Dixonville (B1) 104
Dodds (D3) 35
Donalda (D3) 289
Donnelly (B2) 289
Dorenlee (D3) 66
Doris (C2) 79
Drayton Valley (C3) 3,854
Driftpile (C2) 62
Drinnan (B3) 53
Drumheller (D4) 2,931
Duchess (E4) 218
Duffield (C3) 66
Duvernay (E3) 71
Eagle Butte (E5) 68
Eaglesham (B2) 223
East Coulée (D4) 683
Easyford (C3) 13
Eckville (C3) 580
Edberg (D3) 179
Edgerton (E3) 67
Edmonton (D3) .. 281,027
Edmonton (D3) . 1385,000
Edson (B3) 3,198
Edward (D2) 99
Egg Lake (D2) 135
Egremont (D2) 119
Eldorena (D2) 29
Elk Point (E3) 692
Elnora (D3) 214
Empress (E4) 405
Enchant (D4) 97
Endiang (D4) 165
Enilda (B2) 106
Ensign (D4) 51
Entrance (B3) 87
Entwistle (C3) 411
Erskine (D3) 208
Etzikom (E5) 101
Evansburg (C3) 452
Excel (E4) 95
Exshaw (C4) 678
Fabyan (E3) 58
Fairview (A1) 1,506
Falher (B2) 741
Faust (B2) 763
Fawcett (C2) 179
Federal (E3) 20
Ferintosh (D3) 174
Flatbush (C2) 91
Fleet (E3) 79
Foothills (B3) 250
Foremost (E5) 561
Forest Lawn (D4) . 12,263
Forestburg (E3) 678
Fort Assiniboine (C2) . 216
Fort Chipewyan (C1) . 717
Fort Fitzgerald (C4) . 149
Fort Kent (E2) 148
Fort MacKay (E1) 187
Fort Macleod (D5) .. 2,490
Fort McMurray (E1) 1,186
Fort Saskatchewan
(D3) 2,972
Fort Vermilion (B5) .. 768
Frains (C2) 73
Franchère (E2) 36
Frank (C5) 223
Gadsby (D3) 98
Gainford (C3) 157
Galahad (E3) 231
Gibbons Sta. (D3) ... 192
Gilwood (B2) 2
Girouxville (B2) 318
Gleichen (D4) 426
Glendon (E2) 315
Glenevis (C3) 52
Glenwoodville (D5) .. 274
Gordondale (A2) 171
Grainger (D4) 45
Grand Centre (E2) . 1,493
Grande-Prairie (A2) 8,352
Grandin (C3) 221
Grandin (E4) 25
Grandin (D3) 290
Grassland (D2) 90
Grassy Lake (E5) 274

Green Court (C2) 59
Grimshaw (B1) 1,095
Grouard Mission (C2).. 328
Gwynne (D3) 109
Habay (A5) 450
Hairy Hill (H3) 173
Halkirk (D3) 172
Hanna (E4) 2,645
Hardieville (D5) 472
Hardisty (E3) 582
Harmattan (C4) 266
Hartell (C4) 500
Hay Lakes (D3) 233
Haynes (D3) 94
Hays (E4) 62
Hayter (E3) 50
Hazeldine (E3) 75
Heath (E3) 31
Heinsburg (E3) 135
Heisler (D3) 214
Heldar (C2) 100
Hemaruka (E4) 61
Hercules (D3) 18
High Level (A5) 90
High Prairie (B2) .. 1,756
High River (D4) 2,276
Highridge (D2) 50
Hilda (E4) 194
Hill Spring (D5) 243
Hillcrest Mines (C5) . 594
Hilliard (D3) 85
Hines Creek (A1) 398
Hinton (B3) 3,529
Hobbema (D3) 122
Holden (D3) 556
Hondo (D2) 102
Hughenden (E3) 294
Hussar (D4) 213
Huxley (D4) 102
Hythe (A2) 494
Iddesleigh (E4) 35
Imperial Mills (E2) .. 211
Indus (D4) 46
Innisfail (D3) 2,270
Innisfree (E3) 291
Irma (E3) 425
Iron Springs (D5) 64
Irricana (D4) 167
Irvine (E5) 240
Islay (E3) 107
James River Bridge (C4) 10
Jarrow (E3) 66
Jarvie (D2) 147
Jasper (B3) 2,360
Jasper Place (D3) .. 30,530
Jean-Côté (B2) 64
Jenner (E4) 24
Joffre (D3) 56
Kathleen (B2) 72
Kathryn (D4) 44
Keg River (A5) 279
Kelsey (D3) 55
Killam (D3) 552
Kingman (D3) 108
Kinsella (E3) 91
Kinuso (C2) 323
Kipp (D5) 88
Kirkcaldy (D4) 47
Kirriemuir (E4) 77
Kitscoty (E3) 326
La Crête (B5) 277
La Glace (A2) 95
Lac-la-Biche (E2) .. 1,314
Lacombe (D3) 3,029
Lafond (E3) 54
Lake Louise (C4) 178
Lamont (D3) 705
Lanfine (E4) 44
Langdon (D4) 98
Leduc (D3) 2,356
Leicester (B2) 68
Leslieville (C3) 178
Lethbridge (D5) .. 35,454
Leyland (B3) 53
Lindbergh (E3) 85
Lloydminster (E3) . 2,944
Lodgepole (C3) 508
Lomond (D4) 244
Longview (C4) 246
Lougheed (E3) 217
Lousana (D3) 74
Loyalist (E4) 69
Lundbreck (C5) 112
Luscar (B3) 301
Ma-Me-O Beach (D3) 142
MacKay (D3) 53
Magrath (D5) 1,338
Mallaig (E2) 205
Manning (B1) 896
Mannville (E3) 632
Manola (C2) 59
Manyberries (E5) 103
Marlboro (B3) 289
Marwayne (E3) 379
Mayerthorpe (C3) ... 663

Mazeppa (D4) 48
McLaughlin (E3) 52
McLennan (B2) 1,078
Meander River (A5) . 244
Medicine Hat (E4). 24,484
Meeting Creek (D3)... 71
Mercoal (B3) 972
Metiskow (E3) 99
Michichi (D4) 52
Midlandvale (D4) ... 449
Midnapore (C4) 399
Milk River (D5) 801
Millet (D3) 403
Millicent (E4) 77
Milo (D4) 167
Minburn (E3) 164
Mirror (D3) 577
Monarch (D5) 109
Monitor (E4) 86
Montgomery (C4) .. 5,077
Morecambe (E3) 53
Morinville (D3) 935
Morley (C4) 75
Morningside (D3) 72
Morrin (D4) 316
Mossleigh (D4) 50
Mountain Park (B3) . 400
Mountain View (D5) . 84
Mundare (D3) 603
Munson (D3) 82
Myrnam (E3) 441
Nampay (B1) 271
Nanton (D4) 1,054
Neerlandia (C2) 71
Nemiskam (E5) 54
Nevis (D3) 75
New Brigden (E4) ... 96
New Dayton (D5) .. 102
New Norway (D3) .. 263
New Sarepta (D3) .. 184
Newbrook (D2) 202
Newcastle Mine (D4). 949
Nisku (D3) 58
Nobleford (D5) 309
Noral (D2) 81
Nordegg (B3) 1,014
North Star (B1) 87
Obed (B3) 73
Ohaton (D3) 88
Okotoks (C4) 1,046
Olds (D4) 2,433
Onoway (C3) 302
Opal (D3) 128
Orion (E5) 51
Oyen (E4) 780
Ozada (C4) 250
Paradise Valley (E3). 182
Parkland (D4) 96
Patricia (E4) 130
Peace River (B1) .. 2,543
Pearce (D5) 60
Peers (B3) 128
Penhold (D3) 319
Philomena (E2) 58
Pibroach (D2) 118
Pickardville (D2) 140
Picture Butte (D5) .. 978
Pincher (C5) 80
Pincher Creek (D5) 2,961
Pine Lake (D3) 60
Plamondon (D2) 133
Pollockville (E4) 66
Ponoka (D3) 3,938
Provost (E3) 1,022
Purple Springs (E5).. 40
Queenstown (D4) 67
Radway (D2) 183
Rainier (E4) 51
Ranfurly (E3) 147
Raymond (D5) 2,362

Red Deer (D3) 19,612
Red Willow (D3) 95
Redcliffe (E4) 2,226
Redland (D3) 39
Redwater (D3) 1,135
Reno (B2) 52
Retlaw (D4) 99
Ribstone (E3) 68
Richdale (E4) 38
Rimbey (C3) 1,266
Rochester (D2) 83
Rochfort Bridge (C3). 85
Rocky Mountain House
(C3) 2,360
Rocky Rapids (C3) ... 50
Rockyford (D4) 282
Rosalind (D3) 197
Rosebud (D4) 99
Rosedale Sta. (D4) . 301
Rosemary (E4) 210
Round Hill (D3) 160
Rowley (D4) 65
Royalties (C4) 156
Rumsey (D3) 123
Rycroft (A2) 520
Ryley (D3) 469
Saint-Albert (D3) . 4,059
Saint Lina (E2) 80
Saint Michael (D3) . 129
Saint Paul (D3) ... 2,823
Sangudo (C3) 325
Saunders (C3) 159
Sawdy (D2) 130
Scandia (E4) 51
Schuler (E4) 156
Scollard (D4) 66
Seba Beach (C3) 113
Sedalia (E4) 66
Sedgewick (E3) 655
Seebe (C4) 137
Seven Persons (E5)... 97
Sexsmith (A2) 531
Sheerness (E4) 93
Shepard (D4) 66
Sibbald (E4) 75
Smith (D2) 86
Smoky Lake (J2) 626
Spedden (E2) 123
Spirit River (A2) 890
Spring Coulee (D5) .. 76
Spruce Grove (C3) . 465
Standard (D4) 266
Stanmore (E4) 45
Stavely (D4) 349
Stettler (D3) 3,638
Stirling (D5) 468
Stony Plain (C3) .. 1,311
Strathmore (D4) 924
Streamstown (E3) 55
Strome (D3) 311
Sturgeon Heights (B2) 73
Sundre (C4) 853
Sunnybrook (C3) 200
Sunnynook (E4) 76
Sunnyslope (C4) 61
Swalwell (D4) 85
Swan Hills (C2) 643
Sylvan Lake (D3) . 1,381

Taber (E3) 3,951
Talbot (E3) 50
Tawatinaw (D2) 125
Tees (D3) 63
Thérien (E2) 83
Thorhild (D2) 312
Thorsby (D3) 491
Three Hills (D4) .. 1,491
Tilley (E4) 257
Timeu (C2) 53
Tofield (D3) 905
Tomahawk (C3) 106
Torrington (D4) 149
Travers (D4) 50
Trochu (D4) 671
Turin (D5) 99
Turner Valley (C4).. 702
Vauxhall (D4) 942
Vègreville (E3) 2,908
Vermilion (E3) 2,449
Veteran (E3) 239
Viking (E3) 1,043
Vilna (E2) 400
Violet Grove (C3) .. 200
Vulcan (D4) 1,310
Wabamun (C3) 198
Wabasca (D2) 381
Walsh (E5) 67
Wanham (A2) 251
Warburg (C3) 285
Warden Jct. (D3) ... 106
Warner (D5) 472
Warspite (D2) 153
Waskatenau (D2) ... 300
Waterton Park (D5). 300
Waterways (E1) 400
Watina (B2) 93
Wayne (D4) 116
Weasel Creek (D2) .. 20
Welling (D5) 291
Wembley (A2) 303
Westcott (C4) 95
Westlock (C2) 1,838
Westward Ho (C4).. 51
Wetaskiwin (D3) . 5,300
Whiskey Gap (D5).. 100
Whitecourt (C2) .. 1,054
Whitelaw (A1) 264
Whitla (E5) 67
Wildwood (C3) 479
Willingdon (E3) 429
Wimborne (D4) 80
Winfield (C3) 238
Winnifred (E5) 96
Woking (A2) 157
Wolf Creek (B3) ... 103
Wostok (D3) 150
Wrentham (D5) 111
Youngstown (E4) .. 321

OTHER FEATURES

Alberta (mt.) .... D 3
Assiniboine (mt.) .... C 4
Athabasca (lake) .... C 5
Athabasca (riv.) .... D 1
Banff Nat'l Park,
4,101 .... B 4

Battle (riv.) .... D 3
Beaverhill (lake) .... D 3
Biche (lake) .... E 2
Birch (lake) .... E 3
Birch (mt.) .... B 5
Bittern (lake) .... D 3
Bow (riv.) .... D 4
Brazeau (riv.) .... D 3
Buffalo (lake) ...... D 3
Buffalo Head (hills) . B 5
Calling (lake) ...... D 2
Caribou (mts.) ..... B 5
Claire (lake) .... B 5
Cold (lake) .... E 2
Columbia (mt.) ..... B 3
Crowsnest (pass) ... C 5
Cypress Hills Prov.
Park .... E 5
Eisenhower (mt.) ... C 4
Elk Island Nat'l Park,
69 .... D 3
Etzikom Coulee (riv.) E 5
Forbes (mt.) .... B 4
Gordon (lake) ...... E 1
Graham (lake) ..... C 3
Gull (lake) .... C 3
Hay (lake) .... A 5
Hay (riv.) .... A 5
Jasper Nat'l Park,
2,902 .... A 3
Kickinghorse (pass) . B 4
Kitchener (mt.) .... B 3
Legend (lake) ..... D 1
Lesser Slave (lake) . C 2
Lyell (mt.) .... B 3
Mackenzie Highway . B 1
Maligne (lake) ..... B 3
Muriel (lake) ...... E 2
N. Saskatchewan (riv.) E 4
N. Wabiskaw (lake) . D 1
Oldman (riv.) ...... D 5
Peace (riv.) .... B 1
Peerless (lake) .... C 1
Pembina (riv.) ..... C 3
Pigeon (lake) ..... D 3
Porcupine (hills) ... C 4
Red Deer (riv.) .... D 3
Rocky (mts.) ...... A 3
Slave (riv.) .... C 5
Smoky (riv.) ...... A 2
S. Saskatchewan (riv.) E 4
S. Wabiskaw (lake) . D 2
Sullivan (lake) .... D 3
Temple (mt.) ...... B 4
The Twins (mt.) ... B 3
Thickwood (hills) .. D 1
Utikuma (lake) .... C 2
Wabiskaw (riv.) ... C 1
Wallace (mt.) ..... C 2
Waterton Lakes Nat'l
Park, 300 .... C 4
Winefred (lake) .... E 2
Wood Buffalo Nat'l Park,
86 .... B 5
Yellowhead (pass) .. A 3

†Population of
metropolitan area.

AGRICULTURE, INDUSTRY and RESOURCES

DOMINANT LAND USE

Wheat
Cereals (chiefly barley, oats)
Cereals, Livestock
Dairy
Pasture Livestock
Range Livestock
Forests
Nonagricultural Land

MAJOR MINERAL OCCURRENCES

C Coal
G Natural Gas
Na Salt

O Petroleum
S Sulfur

⚡ Water Power
░ Major Industrial Areas

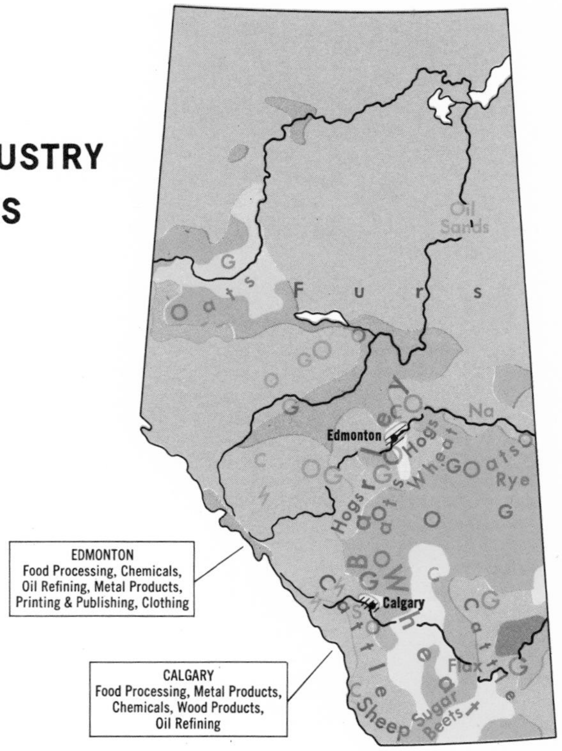

EDMONTON
Food Processing, Chemicals,
Oil Refining, Metal Products,
Printing & Publishing, Clothing

CALGARY
Food Processing, Metal Products,
Chemicals, Wood Products,
Oil Refining

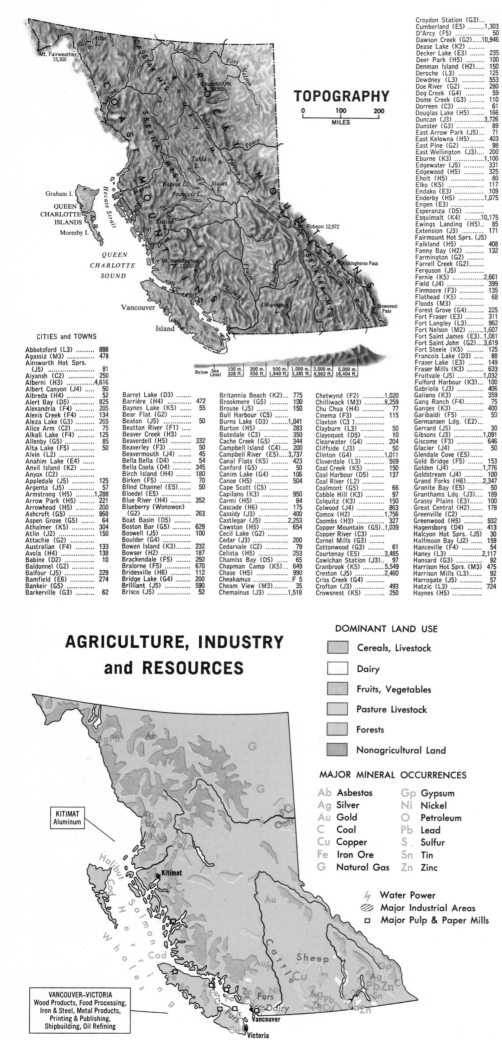

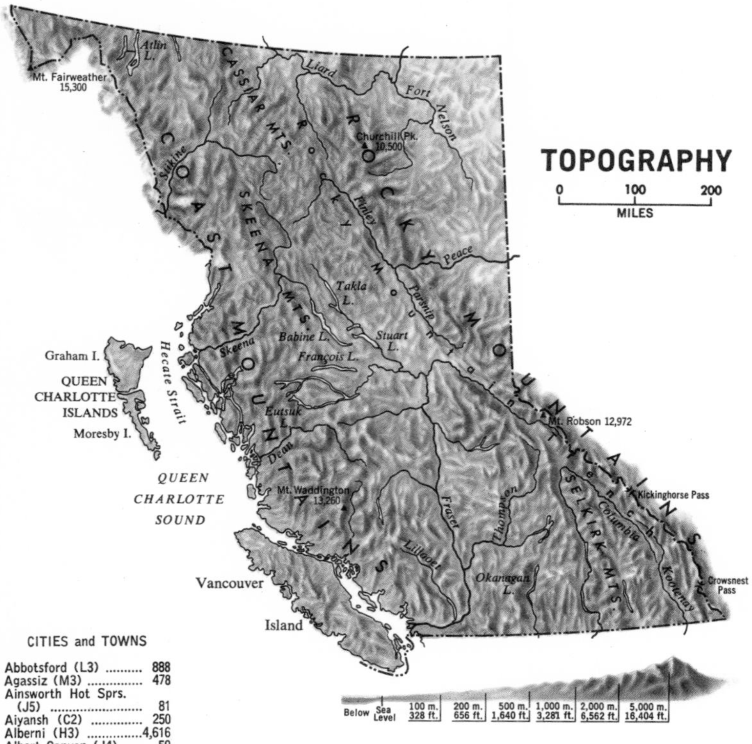
TOPOGRAPHY
0 100 200
MILES
Atlin L.
Mt. Fairweather 15,300
CASSIAR MTS.
Liard
Fort Nelson
Churchill Pk. 10,500
ROCKY MOUNTAINS
Stikine
COAST MOUNTAINS
SKEENA MTS.
Finlay
Peace
Takla L.
Parsnip
Babine L.
Stuart L.
Skeena
François L.
Graham I.
QUEEN CHARLOTTE ISLANDS
Moresby I.
Hecate Strait
Eutsuk
Mt. Robson 12,972
Dean
Fraser
Thompson
Columbia
SELKIRK MTS.
Kickinghorse Pass
Mt. Waddington 13,260
QUEEN CHARLOTTE SOUND
Lillooet
Okanagan L.
Kootenay
Crowsnest Pass
Vancouver
Island
Below
Sea Level
100 m. 328 ft.
200 m. 656 ft.
500 m. 1,640 ft.
1,000 m. 3,281 ft.
2,000 m. 6,562 ft.
5,000 m. 16,404 ft.

CITIES and TOWNS

Abbotsford (L3) 888
Agassiz (M3) 478
Ainsworth Hot Sprs. (J5) 81
Aiyansh (C2) 250
Alberni (H3) 4,616
Albert Canyon (J4) 50
Albreda (H4) 52
Alert Bay (D5) 825
Alexandria (F4) 205
Alexis Creek (F4) 134
Aleza Lake (G3) 265
Alice Arm (C2) 75
Alkali Lake (F4) 125
Allenby (G5) 85
Alta Lake (F5) 50
Alvin (L2) ....
Anahim Lake (E4) ......
Anvil Island (K2) ....
Anyox (C2) ....
Appledale (J5) 125
Argenta (J5) 57
Armstrong (H5) 1,288
Arrow Park (H5) 221
Arrowhead (H5) 200
Ashcroft (G5) 868
Aspen Grove (G5) 64
Athalmer (K5) 304
Atlin (J2) 150
Attachie (G2) ....
Australian (F4) 133
Avola (H4) 138
Babine (D2) 10
Baldonnel (G2) ....
Balfour (J5) 229
Bamfield (E6) 274
Bankeir (G5) ....
Barkerville (G3) 62
Barret Lake (D3) ....
Barrière (H4) 472
Baynes Lake (K5) 55
Bear Flat (G2) ....
Beaton (J5) 50
Beatton River (F1) .....
Beaver Creek (H3) ......
Beaverdell (H5) 332
Beaverley (F3) 50
Beavermouth (J4) 45
Bella Bella (D4) 54
Bella Coola (D4) 345
Birch Island (H4) 180
Birken (F5) 70
Blind Channel (E5)...... 50
Bloedel (E5) ....
Blue River (H4) 352
Blueberry (Wonowon) (G2) 263
Boat Basin (D5) ....
Boston Bar (G5) 629
Boswell (J5) 100
Boulder (G4) ....
Bowen Island (K3)........ 232
Bowser (H2) 187
Brackendale (F5) 292
Bralorne (F5) 670
Bridesville (H6) 112
Bridge Lake (G4) 200
Brilliant (J5) 590
Brisco (J5) 52
Britannia Beach (K2)... 775
Brookmere (G5) 100
Brouse (J5) 150
Bull Harbour (C5) ....
Burns Lake (D3) 1,041
Burton (H5) 283
Butedale (C3) 350
Cache Creek (G5) 344
Campbell Island (C4).... 200
Campbell River (E5).....3,737
Canal Flats (K5) 423
Canford (G5) 50
Canim Lake (G4) 106
Canoe (H5) 504
Cape Scott (C5) ....
Capilano (K3) 950
Carmi (H5) 84
Cascade (H6) 175
Cassidy (J3) 400
Castlegar (J5) 2,253
Cawston (H5) 654
Cecil Lake (G2) ....
Cedar (J3) 200
Cedarvale (C2) 79
Celista (H5) 253
Chamiss Bay (D5) 65
Chapman Camp (K5)... 649
Chase (H5) 990
Cheakamus ....F 5
Cheam View (M3)........ 35
Chemainus (J3) 1,518
Chetwynd (F2) 1,020
Chilliwack (M3) 8,259
Chu Chua (H4) 77
Cinema (F3) 115
Claxton (C3)...............
Clayburn (L3) 50
Clayoquot (D5) 10
Clearwater (G4) 204
Cliffside (J3) 50
Clinton (G4) 1,011
Cloverdale (L3) 569
Coal Creek (K5) 150
Coal Harbour (D5) 137
Coal River (L2) ....
Coalmont (G5) 66
Cobble Hill (K3) 97
Colquitz (K3) 150
Colwood (J4) 863
Comox (H2) 1,756
Coombs (H3) 327
Copper Mountain (G5)..1,039
Copper River (C3) ....
Cornel Mills (G3) ....
Cottonwood (G3) 61
Courtenay (E5) 3,485
Cowichan Station (J3).. 97
Cranbrook (K5) 5,549
Creston (J5) 2,460
Criss Creek (G4) ....
Crofton (J3) 493
Crowsnest (K5) 250
Croydon Station (G3)...
Cumberland (E5) 1,303
D'Arcy (F5) 50
Dawson Creek (G2).....10,946
Dease Lake (K2) ....
Decker Lake (E3) 235
Deer Park (H5) 100
Denman Island (H2)..... 150
Deroche (L3) 125
Dewdney (L3) 553
Doe River (G2) 280
Dog Creek (G4) 59
Dome Creek (G3) 110
Dorreen (C3) 61
Douglas Lake (H5)........ 166
Duncan (J3) 3,726
Dunster (G3) 89
East Arrow Park (J5)... 71
East Kelowna (H5)........ 403
East Pine (G2) 98
East Wellington (J3).... 200
Eburne (K3) 1,100
Edgewater (J5) 331
Edgewood (H5) 325
Eholt (H5) 80
Elko (K5) 117
Endako (E3) 109
Enderby (H5) 1,075
Engen (E3) ....
Esperanza (D5) ....
Esquimalt (K4) 10,175
Ewings Landing (H5).. 85
Extension (J3) 171
Fairmount Hot Sprs. (J5)
Falkland (H5) 408
Fanny Bay (H2) 132
Farmington (G2) ....
Farrell Creek (G2)........
Ferguson (J5) ....
Fernie (K5) 2,661
Field (J4) 399
Finmoore (F3) 135
Flathead (K5) 68
Floods (M3) ....
Forest Grove (G4)......... 225
Fort Fraser (E3) 311
Fort Langley (L3)......... 962
Fort Nelson (M2) 1,607
Fort Saint James (E3)..1,081
Fort Saint John (G2)....3,619
Fort Steele (K5) 125
Francois Lake (D3) 88
Fraser Lake (E3) 149
Fraser Mills (K3) 633
Fruitvale (J5) 1,032
Fulford Harbour (K3)... 100
Gabriola (J3) 406
Galiano (K3) 359
Gang Ranch (F4).......... 75
Ganges (K3) 400
Garibaldi (F5) 50
Germansen Ldg. (E2)...
Gerrard (J5) 30
Gibsons (J3) 1,091
Giscome (F3) 646
Glacier (J4) 50
Glendale Cove (E5).......
Gold Bridge (F5) 153
Golden (J4) 1,776
Goldstream (J4) 100
Grand Forks (H6).........2,347
Granite Bay (E5) 50
Granthams Ldg. (J3).... 189
Grassy Plains (E3)....... 100
Great Central (H2)....... 178
Greenville (C2) ....
Greenwood (H5) 932
Hagensborg (D4) 413
Halcyon Hot Sprs. (J5) 30
Halfmoon Bay (J2) 159
Hanceville (F4) 54
Haney (L3) 2,117
Hansard (G3) 92
Harrison Hot Sprs. (M3) 475
Harrison Mills (L3)....... 92
Harrogate (J5) 57
Hatzic (L3) 724
Haynes (H5) ....
Haysport (C3) 50
Hazelton (D2) 410
Headquarters (E5) 182
Hedley (G5) 425
Heffley Creek (G5) 143
Holberg (C5) 177
Honeymoon Bay (J3).... 518
Hope (M3) 2,751
Hopkins Landing (K2).. 135
Hornby Island (H2)...... 119
Horsefly (G4) 54
Horseshoe Bay (K3) 150
Hosmer (K5) 104
Hot Springs Cove (D5) 66
Houston (D3) 699
Howser (J5) 36
Hudson Hope (F2)........ 66
Hulatt (F3) 50
Huntingdon (L3) 122
Hutton (G3) 75
Hydraulic (F4) 50
Invermere (J5) 744
Ioco (K3) 294
Irvine's Landing (J2).... 83
Isle-Pierre (F3) 63
Jaffray (K5) 282
James Island (K3) 163
Johnson's Landing (J5) 35
Kaleden (H5) 350
Kamloops (G5) 10,076
Kaslo (J5) 646
Keefer's (G5) 50
Keithley Creek (G4)...... 75
Kelowna (H5) 13,188
Kemano (D3) 255
Keremeos (G5) 563
Kettle Valley (H5) 128
Kimberley (K5) 6,013
Kincolith (B2) 125
Kingsgate (K5) 71
Kinnaird (J5) 2,123
Kisgegas (D2) ....
Kitchener (J5) 75
Kitimat (C3) 8,000
Kitwanga (D2) 167
Klemtu (C4) 150
Koksilah (J3) 382
Kyuquot (D5) 184
Lac-la-Hache (G4) 775
Ladner (K3) 2,000
Ladysmith (J3) 2,173
Laidlaw (M3) 78
Lake Cowichan (J3)......2,149
Lake Hill (K3) ....
Langford (J3) 1,024
Langley (L3) 2,365
Lantzville (J3) 135
Lardeau (J5) 175
Lavington (H5) 131
Lempriere (H4) ....
Liard River (L2) ....
Lillooet (G5) 1,304
Lister (J5) 163
Little Fort (G4) 186
Lone Butte (G4) 163
Longworth (G3) 175
Loos (G3) 50
Louis Creek (H4) 274
Lower Post (K1) 160
Lumby (H5) 842
Lund (E5) 198
Lynn Creek (K3) 1,000
Lytton (G5) 442
Mabel Lake (H5) 123
Macalister (F4) 175
Magna Bay (H4) 92
Malakwa (H5) 336
Manson Creek (E2)....... 285
Mapes (E3) ....
Mara (H5) 232
Margaret Bay (D4)...... 50
Marguerite (F4) 83
Marysville (K5) 1,057
Masset (B3) 547
Matsqui (L3) 275
Mayne (K3) 139
McBride (G3) 590
McDame (K2) ....
McGuire (F5) ....
McLeod Lake (F2) 123
McLure (H4) 69
McMurdo (J4) 114
McMurphy (H4) ....
Merritt (G5) 3,039
Merville (E5) 326
Metchosin (K4) 370
Metlakatla (B3) 30
Michel (K5) 417
Midway (H5) 391
Milner (L3) 324
Milne's Landing (J4).... 50
Minstrel Island (D5)..... 50
Minto Mine (F5) 50
Miocene (G4) 99
Miocene (G4) 99
Mission City (L3)..........3,251
Monte Creek (G5) 53
Monte Creek (G5) 278
Montney (G2) ....
Moose Heights (F3)...... 164
Mount Cartier (J5)....... 95
Mount Currie (F5) 105
Mount Lehman (L3)...... 150
Mount Robson (H3) .....
Moyie (K5) 137
Mud River (F3) 129
Murrayville (L3) 431
Nadina River (D3)........ 100
Nakusp (J5) 992
Namu (D4) 159
Nanaimo (J3) 14,135
Nanoose Bay (J3) 56
Naramata (H5) 346
Nass Harbour (C3) ......
Natal (K5) 829
Nazko (F3) 61
Needles (H5) 130
Nelson (J5) 7,074
Nelson Forks (M2)........
New Brighton (K2)......
New Denver (J5) 564
New Hazelton (D2) 200
New Westminster (K3) 33,654
Newgate (K5) 60
Newlands (F3) 51
Newton (K3) 178
Nicola (G5) 159
Nithi River (E3)...........
North Bend (G5).......... 340
North Galiano (K3) 50
North Kamloops (G5)....6,456
North Pine (G2) ....
North Vancouver (K3) 23,656
Northfield (J3) 610
Notch Hill (H5) 104
Ocean Falls (D4)..........3,056
Okanagan Centre (H5).. 265
Okanagan Falls (H5)..... 353
Okanagan Ldg. (H5)..... 535
Okanagan Mission (H5) 103
Oliver (H5) 1,774
150 Mile House (G4)..... 124
Oona River (C3) ....
Oosta Lake (E3) 50
Osoyoos (H6) 1,022
Oyama (H5) 197
Pacific (C3) 74
Parksville (J3) 1,183
Parson (J4) 252
Pavilion (G5) 93
Peachland (G5) 500
Pemberton (F5) 181
Pemberton Meadows (F5) 265
Pender Island (K3)....... 300
Penny (G3) 151
Penticton (H5) 13,859
Perow (D3) 50
Pink Mountain (F1) ....
Pioneer Mine (F5) 226
Poplar Creek (J5) 33
Port Alberni (H3) 11,560
Port Albion (E6) 65
Port Alice (D5) 1,065
Port Clements (B3) 250
Port Coquitlam (L3).....8,111
Port Edward (B3) 887
Port Essington (C3)...... 225
Port Hammond (L3).....1,267
Port Hardy (D5) 606
Port Mann (L3) 500
Port Moody (L3) 4,789
Port Renfrew (J3)........ 279
Port Simpson (B3) 750
Pouce-Coupé (G2) 669
Powell River (E5) 9,700
Premier (C2) 400
Prince George (F3).....13,877
Prince Rupert (B3).....11,987
Princeton (G5) 2,163
Procter (J5) 213
Provincial Cannery (C4)
Punchaw (F3) ....
Quathiaski Cove (E5).... 76
Quatsina (D5) 87
Queen Charlotte (A3)... 283
Quesnel (F4) 4,673
Quick (D3) 200
Quilchena (G5) 101
Radium Hot Sprs. (J5)
Red Pass (J5) 70
Redstoe (F4) 10
Refuge Cove (E5)......... 300
Reid Lake (F3) 100
Remo (C3) 55
Renata (H5) 131
Revelstoke (J5) 3,624
Riske Creek (F4) 201
Rivers Inlet (D4) 250
Roberts Creek (J3)...... 353
Robson (J5) 909
Rock Bay (E5) 100
Rock Creek (H6) 222
Rolla (G2) 69
Rose Lake (E3) 50
Rosebery (J5) 52
Rosedale (M3) 654
Rossland (H6) 4,354
Royal Oak (K3) 100
Royston (H2) 700
Ruby Creek (M3) 73
Ruskin (L3) 447
Rutland (H5) 1,495
Ryder Lake (M3) 282
Saanichton (K3) 500
Salmo (J5) 889
Salmon Arm (H5) 1,506
Salmon Valley (F3) 309
Saltair (J3) 338
San Josef Bay (C5)......
Sandon (J5) 200
Sandspit (B3) 466
Sardis (M3) 898
Saturna (K3) 135
Savona (G5) 532
Sayward (D5) 299
Sechelt (J2) 488
Seton Portage (F5)...... 107
Seventy Mile House (G4) 512

AGRICULTURE, INDUSTRY and RESOURCES

DOMINANT LAND USE

- Cereals, Livestock
- Dairy
- Fruits, Vegetables
- Pasture Livestock
- Forests
- Nonagricultural Land

MAJOR MINERAL OCCURRENCES

Ab	Asbestos	Gp	Gypsum
Ag	Silver	Ni	Nickel
Au	Gold	O	Petroleum
C	Coal	Pb	Lead
Cu	Copper	S	Sulfur
Fe	Iron Ore	Sn	Tin
G	Natural Gas	Zn	Zinc

- Water Power
- Major Industrial Areas
- Major Pulp & Paper Mills

KITIMAT
Aluminum
Kitimat
Halibut
Cod
Herring
Salmon
Whales
Cattle
Sheep
Furs
Dairy
Vancouver
Victoria
VANCOUVER–VICTORIA
Wood Products, Food Processing, Iron & Steel, Metal Products, Printing & Publishing, Shipbuilding, Oil Refining

134°
132°
Frederick Sd.
Kake
Kupreanof
Petersburg
Devils Thumb
Kates Needle
Stikine R.
Iskut
Wrangell
Etolin I.
Prince of Wales Island
Craig
Ketchikan
Revillagigedo Island
Hydaburg
Dall Island
Annette I.
Duke I.
Dixon Entrance
Langara I.
Masset
Graham Island
Port Clements
Tlell
Prince Rupert
Port Edward
Port Simpson
Stephens I.
Porcher I.
Oona River
QUEEN CHARLOTTE
Skidegate
Queen Charlotte
Sandspit
Louise I.
Lyell I.
ISLANDS
Burnaby I.
Kunghit I.
Rose Harbour
C. St. James
HECATE STRAIT
PACIFIC
QUEEN CHARLOTTE SOUND
Aristazabal Island
Caamaño Sd.
Banks Island
Pitt Island

BRITISH COLUMBIA

SCALE OF MILES

0 15 30 60 90 120

Provincial Capital
State Capital
International Boundaries
Provincial Boundaries

Copyright by C. S. Hammond & Co., N. Y.

BRITISH COLUMBIA

AREA	366,255 sq. mi.
POPULATION	1,838,000
CAPITAL	Victoria
LARGEST CITY	Vancouver (greater) 850,000
HIGHEST POINT	Mt. Fairweather 15,300 ft.
SETTLED IN	1806
ADMITTED TO CONFEDERATION	1871
PROVINCIAL FLOWER	Dogwood

Seymour Arm (H4) ......
Shalalth (F5) 182
Shawnigan Lake (J3) .. 438
Shelley (F3) 148
Shere (H4) ....
Shoreacres (J5) 80
Shushartie Bay (C5) ... 25
Shuswap (H5) 90
Sicamous (J5) 588
Sidmouth (J5) 106
Sidney (J5) 1,558
Sikanni River (F1) ....
Silverdale (L3) 280
Silverton (J5) 285
Similkameen (J5) .....
Simoon Sound (D5) 244
Sinclair Mills (G3) ... 200
Sirdar (J5) 76
Skeena Crossing (D2) .. 15
Skidgate (B3) 400
Slocan (J5) 293
Slocan Park (J5) 278
Smith River (L1) .....
Smithers (D3) 2,487
Snowshoe (G3) ....
Soda Creek (G4) 113
Sointula (D5) 682
Solsqua (H5) 148
Somenos (J3) 207
Sooke (J4) 1,121
South Fort George (F3) 1,964
South Hazelton (D2) .. 150
South Pender (K3) 25
South Slocan (J5) 168
South Wellington (J3) . 409
Southbank (E3) 149
Spences Bridge (G5) .. 239
Spuzzum (H5) 74
Squamish (F5) 1,557
Squilax (H5) 200
Steveston (K3) 2,207
Stewart (C2) 327

Stillwater (E5) 165
Stoner (F3) 163
Strathnaver (F3) 191
Sullivan Bay (D5) 150
Summerland (G5) 3,893
Summit Lake (F3) 117
Taft (H4) 40
Tahsis (D5) 686
Takla Landing (E2) ...
Tatla Lake (E4) ......
Taylor (F2) 438
Telegraph Creek (K2).. 132
Telkwa (D3) 576
Terrace (C3) 4,682
Tête-Jaune-Cache (H4) 75
Thetis Island (J3) ... 114
Thurlow (E5) 75
Tintagel (E3) 83
Tlell (B3) ....
Tofina (E5) 440
Topley (D3) 75
Trail (J6) 11,580
Trout Lake (J5) 100
Tsawwassen (K3) ......
Tulameen (G5) 100
Tupper (D3) 67
Two Rivers (G2) ......
Ucluelet (E6) 782
Union Bay (H2) 600
Usk (C3) 73
Valemount (H4) 631
Vallican (J5) 106
Vananda (E5) 511
Vancouver (K3) 384,522
Vancouver (K3) .. 1850,000
VICTORIA (K4) 54,941
Victoria (K4) 1154,152
Wadhams (D4) ....
Waldo (K5) 117

Walhachin (G5) 65
Waneta (J5) 75
Wardner (K5) 171
Ware (E1) 75
Warfield (J5) 2,212
Wellington (J3) 599
Wells (J5) 740
West Vancouver (K3)...
Westbank (H5) 284
Westbridge (H5) 285
Westholme (J3) 74
Westwold (G5) 327
Whaletown (E5) 72
White Rock (K3) 6,453
Whonock (L3) 1,062
Williams Lake (F4).. 2,120
Willow River (F3) 331
Wilmer (J5) 244
Wilson Creek (J2) 333
Windermere (K5) 391
Winlaw (J5) 392
Wonowon (Blueberry) (G2) 263
Woodfibre (K2) 524
Woodpecker (F3) 75
Wynndel (J5) 631
Yahk (M2) 297
Yale (H5) 72
Ymir (J5) 323
Youbou (J3) 1,513
Zeballos (D5) 235

Beatton (riv.) ....G 1
Bella Coola (river.) ...D 4
Brooks (pen.) ....D 5
Bryce (mt.) ....D 3
Bulkley (riv.) ....D 2
Bute (inlet) ....D 3
Caamaño (sound) ......C 4
Calvert (isl.) ....C 4
Cariboo (mts.) ....G 2
Cassiar (mts.) ....K 2
Chatham (sound) ......B 3
Chilkat (mt.) ....H 1
Chilko (lake) ....F 4
Chilkoot (pass) ....J 1
Coast (mts.) ....J 4
Columbia (mt.) ....J 4
Columbia (riv.) ....H 4
Crowsnest (pass) .....K 5
Dean (chan.) ....D 4
Dean (riv.) ....D 4
Dease (lake) ....K 2
Devil's Thumb (mt.) ..A 1
Dixon Entrance (str.)..A 4
Eutsuk (lake) ....D 3
Fairweather (mt.) ....H 1
Finlay (riv.) ....E 1
François (lake) ....D 3
Fraser (riv.) ....F 4
Gardner (canal) ......C 3
Garibaldi Prov. Pk. ...L 2
Georgia (strait) ......J 3
Glacier Nat'l Pk. .....J 4
Graham (isl.) ....A 3
Hamber Prov. Pk. .....J 4
Harrison (lake) ......M 2
Hecate (strait) ....B 3
Iskut (riv.) ....B 2
Juan de Fuca (strait) .J 4
Kates Needle (mt.)....A 1
Kickinghorse (pass) ..J 4
King (isl.) ....D 4
Klinaklini (riv.) ......E 4

Knight (inlet) ....E 5
Kokanee Glacier Prov.
  Pk. ....J 5
Kootenay (lake) ......J 5
Kootenay Nat'l Pk. ...J 4
Kootenay (riv.) ....K 5
Liard (riv.) ....H 2
Lower Arrow (lake)...J 4
Manning, E. C. Prov.
  Park ....G 5
Monashee (mts.) .....H 4
Moresby (isl.), 139.....A 4
Mount Assiniboine Prov.
  Park ....K 5
Mt. Revelstoke Nat'l
  Park ....H 4

Mount Robson Prov. Park H 4
Nanika (dam) ....H 3
Nass (riv.) ....C 2
Observatory (inlet) ..C 2
Okanagan (lake) .....H 5
Parsnip (riv.) ....F 2
Peace (riv.) ....G 3
Pitt (isl.) ....C 3
Pitt (lake) ....L 3
Porcher (isl.) ....B 3
Portland (canal) .....B 2
Price (isl.) ....C 3
Princess Royal (isl.)..C 3
Purcell (mts.) ....J 5
Quatsino (sound) ....C 5
Queen Charlotte (isls.)..B 3

Queen Charlotte (sound) ....C 4
Queen Charlotte (strait) ....D 5
Quesnel Lake ....G 4
Robson (mt.) ....H 3
Rocky (mts.) ....G 3
Seechelt (pen.) ......J 2
Selkirk (mts.) ....J 4
Seymour (inlet) ......D 5
Shuswap (lake) ......H 4
Sir Sandford (mt.)....H 4
Skeena (riv.) ....C 3
Smith (sound) ....C 4
Stave (lake) ....L 3
Stikine (mts.) ....K 2
Stikine (riv.) ....B 1

Strathcona Prov. Pk. ...E 5
Stuart (lake) ....E 3
Tagish (lake) ....J 1
Takla (lake) ....D 2
Taku (riv.) ....J 2
Teidemann (peak) ....E 4
Texada (isl.) ....J 3
Thompson (riv.) .....G 4
Tweedsmuir Prov. Pk. .D 3
Upper Arrow (lake)...H 5
Vancouver (isl.) .....J 3
Waddington (mt.) ....E 4
Yellowhead (pass) ...H 4
Yoho Nat'l Park .....J 4

†Population of metropolitan area.

OTHER FEATURES

Alberni (inlet) ....H 3
Aristazabal (isl.) ....C 4
Assiniboine (mt.) ....K 5
Atlin (lake) ....J 1
Babine (lake) ....D 2
Babine (riv.) ....D 2
Banks (isl.) ....B 3
Barkley (sound) ......E 6

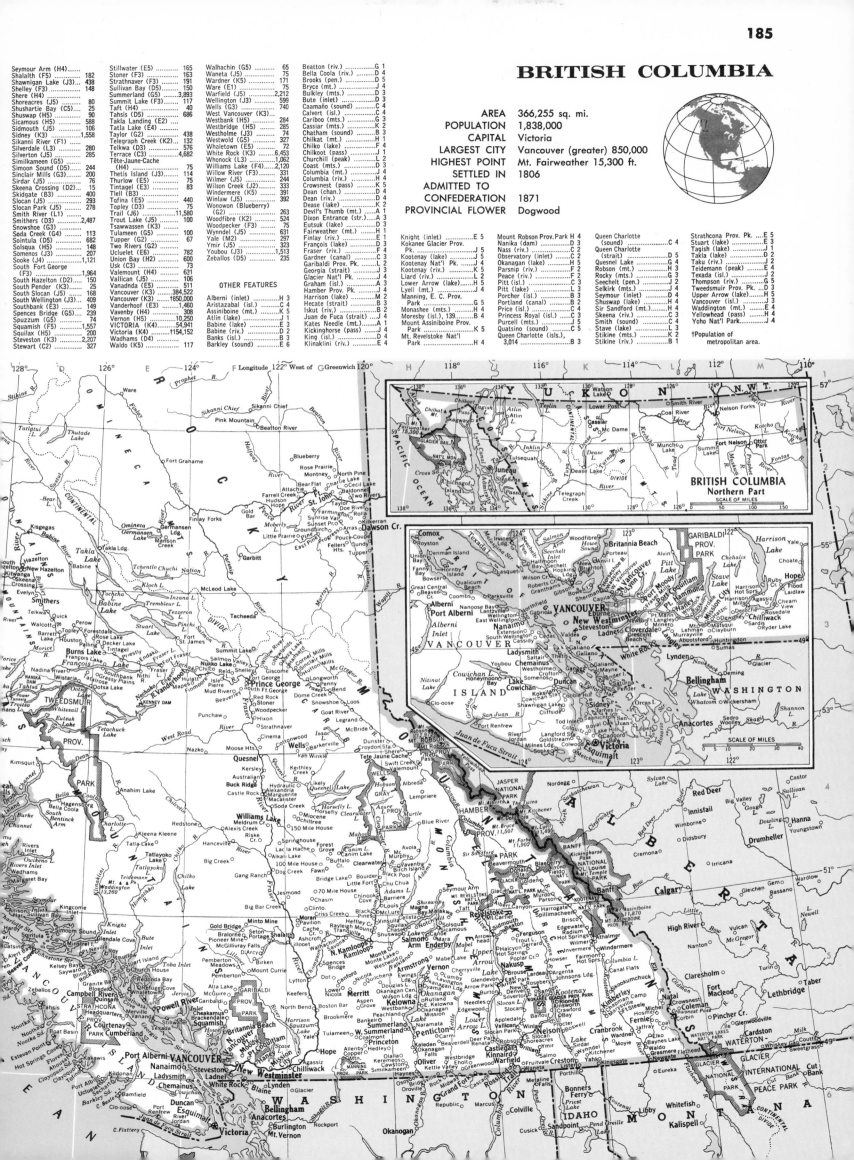

Yukon and Northwest Territories

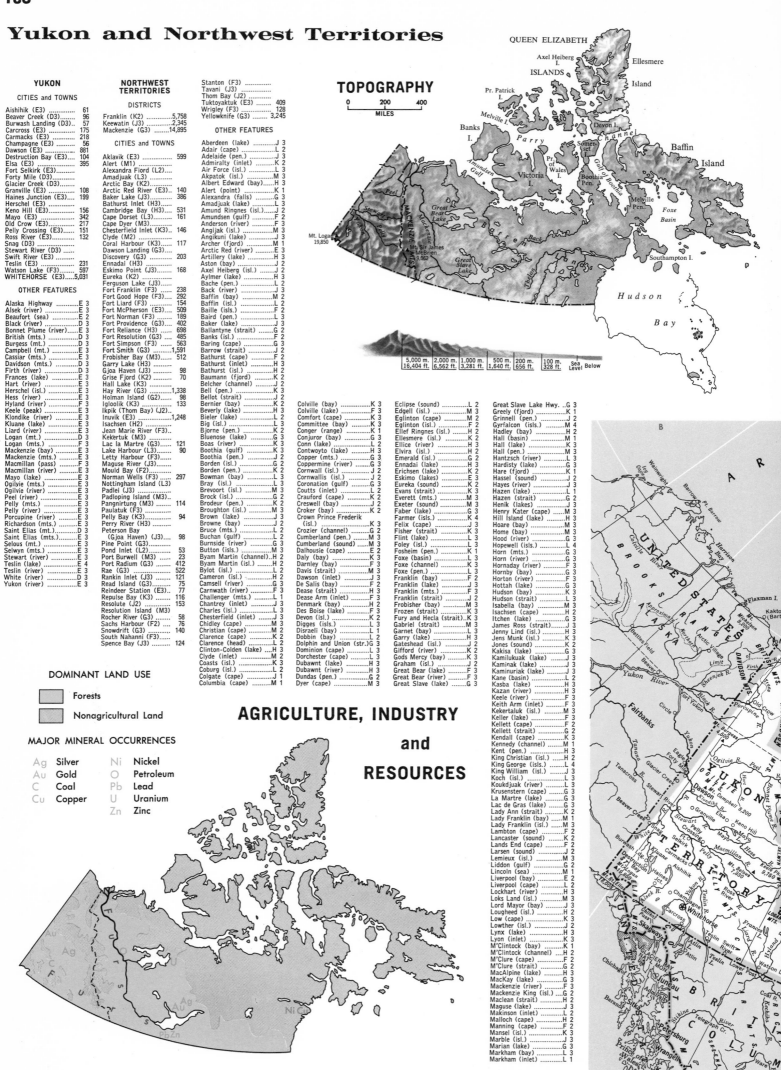

YUKON

CITIES and TOWNS

Aishihik (E3) 61
Beaver Creek (D3)........ 96
Burwash Landing (D3).. 57
Carcross (E3) 175
Carmacks (E3) 218
Champagne (E3) 56
Dawson (E3) 881
Destruction Bay (E3).... 104
Elsa (E3) 395
Fort Selkirk (E3)..........
Forty Mile (D3)............
Glacier Creek (D3)........
Granville (E3) 108
Haines Junction (E3).... 199
Herschel (E3) ....
Keno Hill (E3).............. 156
Mayo (E3) 342
Old Crow (E3).............. 217
Pelly Crossing (E3)...... 151
Ross River (E3)............ 132
Snag (D3) ....
Stewart River (D3) ......
Swift River (E3) ....
Teslin (E3) 231
Watson Lake (F3)........ 597
WHITEHORSE (E3).....5,031

OTHER FEATURES

Alaska Highway ....E 3
Alsek (river) ....E 3
Beaufort (sea) ....E 2
Black (river) ....D 3
Bonnet Plume (river)......E 3
British (mts.) ....D 3
Burgess (mt.) ....D 3
Campbell (mt.) ....E 3
Cassiar (mts.) ....E 3
Davidson (mts.) ....D 3
Firth (river) ....D 3
Frances (lake) ....E 3
Hart (river) ....E 3
Herschel (isl.) ....E 3
Hess (river) ....E 3
Hyland (river) ....F 3
Keele (peak) ....E 3
Klondike (river) ....E 3
Kluane (lake) ....E 3
Liard (river) ....E 3
Logan (mt.) ....D 3
Logan (mts.) ....F 3
Mackenzie (bay) ....E 3
Mackenzie (mts.) ....E 3
Macmillan (pass) ....F 3
Macmillan (river) ....E 3
Mayo (lake) ....E 3
Ogilvie (mts.) ....E 3
Ogilvie (river) ....E 3
Peel (river) ....E 3
Pelly (mts.) ....E 3
Pelly (river) ....E 3
Porcupine (river) ....E 3
Richardson (mts.) ....E 3
Saint Elias (mt.)............D 3
Saint Elias (mts.)..........E 3
Selous (mt.) ....E 3
Selwyn (mts.) ....E 3
Stewart (river) ....E 3
Teslin (lake) ....E 4
Teslin (river) ....E 3
White (river) ....D 3
Yukon (river) ....E 3

NORTHWEST TERRITORIES

DISTRICTS

Franklin (K2) 5,758
Keewatin (J3) 2,345
Mackenzie (G3) 14,895

CITIES and TOWNS

Aklavik (E3) 599
Alert (M1) ....
Alexandra Fiord (L2)....
Amadjuak (L3) ....
Arctic Bay (K2)............
Arctic Red River (E3).. 140
Baker Lake (J3)............ 386
Bathurst Inlet (H3)......
Cambridge Bay (H3).... 531
Cape Dorset (L3).......... 161
Cape Dyer (M3)............
Chesterfield Inlet (K3).. 146
Clyde (M2) ....
Coral Harbour (K3)...... 117
Dawson Landing (G3)....
Discovery (G3) 203
Ennadai (H3) ....
Eskimo Point (J3)........ 168
Eureka (K2) ....
Ferguson Lake (J3)......
Fort Franklin (F3) 238
Fort Good Hope (F3).... 292
Fort Liard (F3) 154
Fort McPherson (E3).... 509
Fort Norman (F3) 189
Fort Providence (G3).... 402
Fort Reliance (H3) 698
Fort Resolution (G3) 485
Fort Simpson (F3) 563
Fort Smith (G3) 1,591
Frobisher Bay (M3)...... 512
Garry Lake (H3) ....
Gjoa Haven (J3) 98
Grise Fjord (K2) 70
Hall Lake (K3) ....
Hay River (G3) 1,338
Holman Island (G2)...... 98
Igloolik (K3) 133
Ikpik (Thom Bay) (J2)..
Inuvik (E3) 1,248
Isachsen (H2) ....
Jean Marie River (F3)..
Kekertuk (M3) ....
Lac la Martre (G3)...... 121
Lake Harbour (L3)........ 90
Letty Harbour (F3)......
Maguse River (J3)........
Mould Bay (F2)............
Norman Wells (F3) 297
Nottingham Island (L3)
Padlei (J3) ....
Padloping Island (M3)..
Pangnirtung (M3) 114
Paulatuk (F3) ....
Pelly Bay (K3).............. 94
Perry River (H3) ....
Peterson Bay
(Gjoa Haven) (J3).... 98
Pine Point (G3)............
Pond Inlet (L2)............ 53
Port Burwell (M3) 23
Port Radium (G3) 412
Rae (G3) 522
Rankin Inlet (J3) 121
Read Island (G3).......... 75
Reindeer Station (E3).. 77
Repulse Bay (K3) 116
Resolute (J2) 153
Resolution Island (M3)
Rocher River (G3) 58
Sachs Harbour (F2) 76
Snowdrift (G3) 140
South Nahanni (F3)......
Spence Bay (J3) 124
Stanton (F3) ....
Tavani (J3) ....
Thom Bay (J2) ....
Tuktoyaktuk (E3) 409
Wrigley (F3) 128
Yellowknife (G3) 3,245

OTHER FEATURES

Aberdeen (lake) ....J 3
Adair (cape) ....L 2
Adelaide (pen.) ....J 3
Admiralty (inlet) ....K 2
Air Force (isl.) ....L 3
Akpatok (isl.) ....M 3
Albert Edward (bay)......H 3
Alert (point) ....K 1
Alexandra (falls) ....G 3
Amadjuak (lake) ....L 3
Amund Ringnes (isl.)......J 2
Amundsen (gulf) ....F 2
Anderson (river) ....F 3
Angijak (isl.) ....M 3
Angikuni (lake) ....J 3
Archer (fjord) ....M 1
Arctic Red (river) ....E 3
Artillery (lake) ....H 3
Aston (bay) ....J 2
Axel Heiberg (isl.) ....J 2
Aylmer (lake) ....H 3
Bache (pen.) ....L 2
Back (river) ....J 3
Baffin (bay) ....M 2
Baffin (isl.) ....L 2
Baille (isls.) ....F 2
Baird (pen.) ....L 3
Baker (lake) ....J 3
Ballantyne (strait) ....G 2
Banks (isl.) ....F 2
Baring (cape) ....G 3
Barrow (strait) ....J 2
Bathurst (cape) ....F 2
Bathurst (inlet) ....H 3
Bathurst (isl.) ....H 2
Baumann (fjord) ....K 2
Belcher (channel) ....J 2
Bell (pen.) ....K 3
Bellot (strait) ....J 2
Bernier (bay) ....K 2
Beverly (lake) ....H 3
Bieler (lake) ....L 2
Big (isl.) ....L 3
Bjorne (pen.) ....K 2
Bluenose (lake) ....G 3
Boas (river) ....K 3
Boothia (gulf) ....K 3
Boothia (pen.) ....J 2
Borden (isl.) ....G 2
Borden (pen.) ....K 2
Bowman (bay) ....L 3
Bray (isl.) ....L 3
Brevoort (isl.) ....M 3
Brock (isl.) ....G 2
Brodeur (pen.) ....K 2
Broughton (isl.) ....M 3
Brown (lake) ....J 3
Browne (bay) ....J 2
Bruce (mts.) ....L 2
Buchan (gulf) ....L 2
Burnside (river) ....G 3
Button (isls.) ....M 3
Byam Martin (channel)..H 2
Byam Martin (isl.) ....H 2
Bylot (isl.) ....L 2
Cameron (isl.) ....H 2
Camsell (river) ....G 3
Carnwath (river) ....F 3
Challenger (mts.) ....L 1
Chantrey (inlet) ....J 3
Charles (isl.) ....L 3
Chesterfield (inlet) ....J 3
Chidley (cape) ....M 3
Christian (cape) ....M 2
Clarence (cape) ....K 2
Clarence (head) ....L 2
Clinton-Colden (lake) ....H 3
Clyde (inlet) ....M 2
Coasts (isl.) ....K 3
Coburg (isl.) ....L 2
Colgate (cape) ....J 1
Columbia (cape) ....M 1
Colville (bay) ....K 3
Colville (lake) ....F 3
Comfort (cape) ....K 3
Committee (bay) ....K 3
Conger (range) ....K 1
Conjuror (bay) ....G 3
Conn (lake) ....L 2
Contwoyto (lake) ....H 3
Copper (mts.) ....G 3
Coppermine (river) ....G 3
Cornwall (isl.) .... J 2
Cornwallis (isl.) .... J 2
Coronation (gulf) ....G 3
Coutts (inlet) ....L 2
Crauford (cape) ....K 2
Creswell (bay) ....J 2
Croker (bay) ....K 2
Crown Prince Frederik
(isl.) ....K 3
Crozier (channel) ....G 2
Cumberland (pen.) ....M 3
Cumberland (sound) ......M 3
Dalhousie (cape) ....E 2
Daly (bay) ....K 3
Darnley (bay) ....F 3
Davis (strait) ....M 3
Dawson (inlet) ....J 3
De Salis (bay) ....F 2
Dease (strait) ....H 3
Dease Arm (inlet) ....F 3
Denmark (bay) ....H 2
Des Boise (lake) ....F 3
Devon (isl.) ....K 2
Digges (isls.) ....L 3
Disraeli (bay) ....L 1
Dobbin (bay) ....L 2
Dolphin and Union (str.)G 3
Dominion (cape) ....L 3
Dorchester (cape) ....L 3
Dubawnt (lake) ....H 3
Dubawnt (river) ....H 3
Dundas (pen.) ....G 2
Dyer (cape) ....M 3
Eclipse (sound) ....L 2
Edgell (isl.) ....M 3
Eglinton (cape) ....M 2
Eglinton (isl.) ....F 2
Ellef Ringnes (isl.) ....H 2
Ellesmere (isl.) ....K 2
Ellice (river) ....H 3
Elvira (isl.) ....H 2
Emerald (isl.) ....G 2
Ennadai (lake) ....H 3
Erichsen (lake) ....K 2
Eskimo (lakes) ....E 3
Eureka (sound) ....K 2
Evans (strait) ....K 3
Everett (mts.) ....M 3
Exeter (sound) ....M 3
Faber (lake) ....G 3
Farmer (isls.) ....K 4
Felix (cape) ....J 3
Fisher (strait) ....K 3
Flint (lake) ....L 3
Foley (isl.) ....L 3
Fosheim (pen.) ....K 1
Foxe (basin) ....L 3
Foxe (channel) ....K 3
Foxe (pen.) ....L 3
Franklin (bay) ....F 2
Franklin (lake) ....J 3
Franklin (mts.) ....F 3
Franklin (strait) ....J 2
Frobisher (bay) ....M 3
Frozen (strait) ....K 3
Fury and Hecla (strait)..K 3
Gabriel (strait) ....M 3
Garnet (bay) ....L 3
Garry (lake) ....H 3
Gateshead (isl.) ....J 2
Gifford (river) ....K 2
Gods Mercy (bay) ....K 3
Graham (isl.) ....J 2
Great Bear (lake) ....F 3
Great Bear (river) ....F 3
Great Slave (lake) ....G 3
Great Slave Lake Hwy. ..G 3
Greely (fjord) ....K 1
Grinnell (pen.) ....J 2
Gyrfalcon (isls.) ....M 4
Hadley (bay) ....H 2
Hall (basin) ....M 1
Hall (lake) ....K 3
Hall (pen.) ....M 3
Hantzsch (river) ....L 3
Hardisty (lake) ....G 3
Hare (fjord) ....K 1
Hassel (sound) ....J 2
Hayes (river) ....J 3
Hazen (lake) ....L 1
Hazen (strait) ....G 2
Henik (lakes) ....J 3
Henry Kater (cape) ......M 3
Hill Island (lake) ....H 3
Hoare (bay) ....M 3
Home (bay) ....M 3
Hood (river) ....G 3
Hopewell (isls.) ....L 4
Horn (mts.) ....G 3
Horn (river) ....G 3
Hornaday (river) ....F 3
Hornby (bay) ....G 3
Horton (river) ....F 3
Hottah (lake) ....G 3
Hudson (bay) ....K 3
Hudson (strait) ....L 3
Isabella (bay) ....M 3
Isachsen (cape) ....H 2
Itchen (lake) ....G 3
James Ross (strait)........J 3
Jenny Lind (isl.) ....H 3
Jens Munk (isl.) ....K 3
Jones (sound) ....K 2
Kakisa (lake) ....G 3
Kamilukuak (lake) ....J 3
Kaminak (lake) ....J 3
Kaminuriak (lake) ....J 3
Kane (basin) ....L 2
Kasba (lake) ....H 3
Kazan (river) ....H 3
Keele (river) ....F 3
Keith Arm (inlet) ....F 3
Kekertaluk (isl.) ....M 3
Keller (lake) ....F 3
Kellett (cape) ....F 2
Kellett (strait) ....G 2
Kendall (cape) ....K 3
Kennedy (channel) ....M 1
Kent (pen.) ....H 3
King Christian (isl.) ......H 2
King George (isls.) ....L 4
King William (isl.) ....J 3
Koch (isl.) ....L 3
Koukdjuak (river) ....L 3
Krusenstern (cape) ....G 3
La Martre (lake) ....G 3
Lac de Gras (lake) ....G 3
Lady Ann (strait) ....K 2
Lady Franklin (bay) ......M 1
Lady Franklin (isl.) ......M 3
Lambton (cape) ....F 2
Lancaster (sound) ....K 2
Lands End (cape) ....F 2
Larsen (sound) ....J 2
Lemieux (isl.) ....M 3
Liddon (gulf) ....G 2
Lincoln (sea) ....M 1
Liverpool (bay) ....E 2
Liverpool (cape) ....L 2
Lockhart (river) ....H 3
Loks Land (isl.) ....M 3
Lord Mayor (bay) ....J 3
Lougheed (isl.) ....H 2
Low (cape) ....K 3
Lowther (isl.) ....J 2
Lynx (lake) ....H 3
Lyon (inlet) ....K 3
M'Clintock (bay) ....K 1
M'Clintock (channel) ....H 2
M'Clure (cape) ....F 2
M'Clure (strait) ....G 2
MacAlpine (lake) ....H 3
MacKay (lake) ....G 3
Mackenzie (river) ....F 3
Mackenzie King (isl.) ....G 2
Maclean (strait) ....H 2
Maguse (lake) ....J 3
Makinson (inlet) ....L 2
Malloch (cape) ....H 2
Manning (cape) ....F 2
Mansel (isl.) ....K 3
Marble (isl.) ....J 3
Marian (lake) ....G 3
Markham (bay) ....L 3
Markham (inlet) ....L 1

TOPOGRAPHY

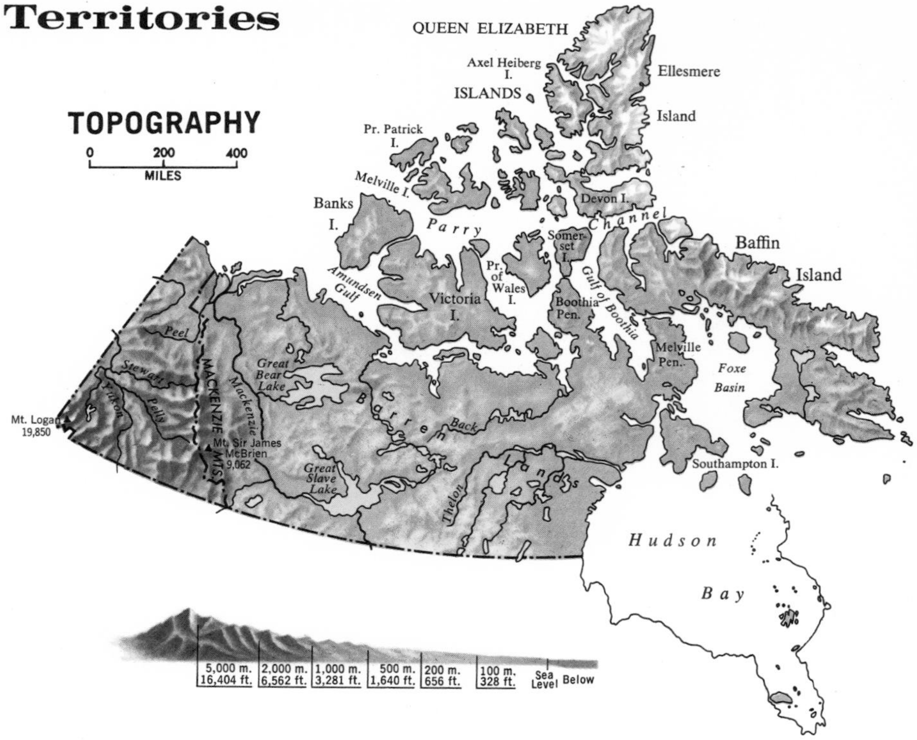

0 200 400
MILES
QUEEN ELIZABETH
ISLANDS
Axel Heiberg I.
Ellesmere Island
Pr. Patrick I.
Melville I.
Banks I.
Parry
Channel
Devon I.
Somerset I.
Baffin Island
Amundsen Gulf
Victoria I.
Pr. of Wales I.
Gulf of Boothia
Boothia Pen.
Melville Pen.
Foxe Basin
Peel
MACKENZIE MTS.
Mackenzie
Great Bear Lake
Back
Mt. Logan 19,850
Mt. Sir James McBrien 9,062
Great Slave Lake
Thelon
Southampton I.
Hudson
Bay
5,000 m. 16,404 ft.
2,000 m. 6,562 ft.
1,000 m. 3,281 ft.
500 m. 1,640 ft.
200 m. 656 ft.
100 m. 328 ft.
Sea Level
Below

DOMINANT LAND USE

Forests

Nonagricultural Land

MAJOR MINERAL OCCURRENCES

Ag Silver
Au Gold
C Coal
Cu Copper
Ni Nickel
O Petroleum
Pb Lead
U Uranium
Zn Zinc

AGRICULTURE, INDUSTRY and RESOURCES

Ag
Au
C
F
U
Ni Cu
Pb Zn

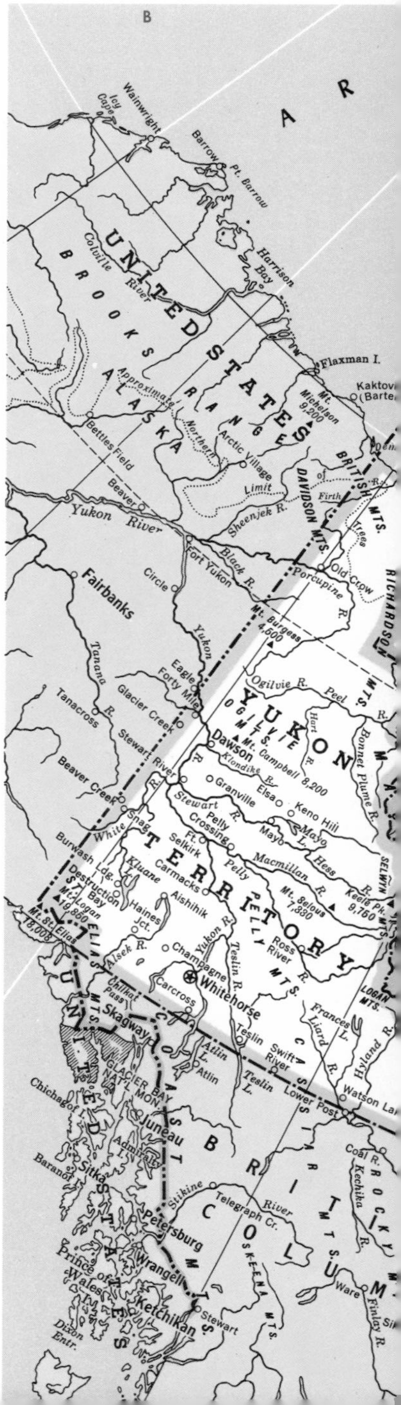

UNITED STATES
BROOKS RANGE
ALASKA
Barrow
Pt. Barrow
Wainwright
Harrison Bay
Flaxman I.
Colville River
Bettles Field
Arctic Village
Fairbanks
Yukon River
Fort Yukon
Circle
Eagle
Forty Mile
Dawson
Klondike
YUKON
TERRITORY
Granville
Elsa
Keno Hill
Mayo
Pelly Crossing
Ft. Selkirk
Carmacks
Aishihik
Haines Jct.
Destruction Bay
Burwash Lde.
Champagne
Whitehorse
Carcross
Skagway
Atlin
Juneau
Sitka
Petersburg
Wrangell
Ketchikan
Teslin
Watson Lake
BRITISH COLUMBIA

YUKON and NORTHWEST TERRITORIES

	NORTHWEST TERRITORIES	YUKON
AREA	1,304,903	207,076 sq. mi.
POPULATION	26,000	15,000
CAPITAL	Fort Smith (Admin. Center)	Whitehorse
LARGEST CITY	Yellowknife 3,245	Whitehorse 5,031
HIGHEST POINT	United States Range 9,600 ft.	Mt. Logan 19,850 ft.
SETTLED IN	1800	1897
ADMITTED TO CONFEDERATION	1870	1898
PROVINCIAL FLOWER	Mountain Avens	Fireweed

Maxwell (bay) ....K 2
McKeand (river) ....M 3
McLeod (bay) ....G 3
McTavish Arm (inlet) ....G 3
McVicar Arm (inlet) .....F 3
Meighen (isl.) ....H 2
Melbourne (isl.) ....H 3
Melville (isl.) ....G 2
Melville (pen.) ....K 3
Mercy (bay) ....G 2
Mercy (cape) ....M 3
Mill (isl.) ....L 3
Mills (lake) ....G 3
Milne (inlet) ....K 2
Mingo (lake) ....L 3
Minto (inlet) ....G 2
Mistake (bay) ....M 3
Moodie (isl.) ....M 3
Mountain (river) ....F 3
Nansen (sound) ....J 1
Nares (strait) ....L 2
Navy Board (inlet) ......K 2
Nelson (head) ....F 2
Nettilling (fjord) ....L 3
Nettilling (lake) ....L 3
Nonacho (lake) ....H 3
North Arm (inlet) ....G 3
North Kent (isl.) ....J 2
North Magnetic Pole ....H 2
Norway (bay) ....H 2
Norwegian (bay) ....J 2
Nueltin (lake) ....H 3
Ogden (bay) ....H 3
Ommanney (bay) ....H 2
Ottawa (isls.) ....K 4
Otto (fjord) ....K 1
Parry (bay) ....F 2
Parry (cape) ....F 2
Parry (channel) ....G 2
Parry (isls.) ....G 2
Parry (pen.) ....F 2

Pasley (bay) ....J 2
Peary (channel) ....H 2
Peel (sound) ....J 2
Pelly (bay) ....J 3
Pelly (lake) ....H 3
Penny (strait) ....J 2
Petitot (river) ....F 4
Phillips (isl.) ....J 1
Philpots (isl.) ....K 3
Pinger (point) ....K 3
Point (lake) ....G 3
Pond (inlet) ....K 2
Prince Albert (pen.) ...G 2
Prince Albert (sound) ..G 2
Prince Alfred (cape) ...F 2
Prince Charles (isl.) ..L 3
Prince Gustav Adolf (sea) ...H 2
Prince of Wales (strait) ...J 3
Prince of Wales (strait) ...G 2
Prince Patrick (isl.) ...F 2
Prince Regent (inlet) ..J 2
Queen (cape) ....L 3
Queen Elizabeth (isls.) ...H 1
Queen Maud (gulf) .....H 3
Queens (channel) ......J 2
Quoich (river) ....J 3
Raanes (pen.) ....L 2
Rae (isthmus) ....K 3
Rae (river) ....G 3
Rae (strait) ....J 3
Ramparts (river) ......E 3
Raper (cape) ....M 3
Redstone (river) ......F 3
Rennie (river) ....J 3
Resolution (isl.) ......M 3
Richard Collinson (inlet) Q...G 2
Richards (isl.) ....E 3
Richardson (isl.) .....J 3
Robeson (channel) ....M 1
Roes Welcome (sound) ...K 3

Rowley (isl.) ....K 3
Royal Geographical Society (isls.) ...J 3
Russell (cape) ....G 2
Russell (point) ....G 2
Sabine (pen.) ....G 2
Salisbury (isl.) ....L 3
Schultz (lake) ....J 3
Seahorse (point) .....L 3
Selwyn (lake) ....H 4
Shaler (mts.) ....G 2
Shepherd (bay) ....J 3

Sherard (cape) ....L 2
Sherman (inlet) ......J 3
Simpson (pen.) ....K 3
Sir James McBrien (mt.) F 3
Slave (river) ....F 3
Smith (bay) ....L 3
Smith (cape) ....L 3
Smith (sound) ....L 2
Smith Arm (inlet) .....F 3
Snare (river) ....G 3
Snowbird (lake) ......H 3
Somerset (isl.) ....J 2
South (bay) ....K 3

South Nahanni (river) ...F 3
Southampton (cape) ...K 3
Southampton (isl.) ....K 3
Spicer (isls.) ....L 3
Stallworthy (cape) ....L 1
Stapylton (bay) ....G 3
Steensby (inlet) ......L 2
Stefansson (isl.) .....H 2
Storkerson (bay) ......H 2
Sverdrup (channel) ...J 1
Sverdrup (isls.) ......J 2
Swinburne (cape) .....J 2
Tahiryuak (lake) ......G 2

Talbot (inlet) ....L 2
Taltson (river) ....G 3
Tathlina (lake) ....G 3
Tehek (lake) ....J 3
Tha-Anne (river) .....J 3
Thelon (river) ....H 3
Thesiger (bay) ....F 2
Thlewiaza (river) .....J 3
Thoa (river) ....H 3
Thomsen (river) ......G 2
Trout (lake) ....F 3
Truter (mts.) ....K 2
Ungava (bay) ....M 4

United States (range) ...L 1
Vansittart (isl.) ......K 3
Victoria (isl.) ....G 2
Victoria (strait) ......J 3
Virginia (falls) ....F 3
Viscount Melville (sound) ...G 2
Wager (bay) ....J 3
Wales (isl.) ....J 3
Walker (bay) ....G 2
Walsingham (cape) ...M 3
Wellington (bay) ......G 2
Wellington (channel) ...J 2

Wharton (lake) ....H 3
White (isl.) ....K 3
Wholdaia (lake) ......H 3
Willowlake (river) ....F 3
Wilson (bay) ....H 2
Winter (harbor) ......H 2
Winter (isl.) ....K 3
Wollaston (pen.) .....G 3
Wood Buffalo Nat'l Park G 3
Wynniatt (bay) ....G 2
Yathkyed (lake) ......J 3
Yellowknife (river) ...G 3
Yelverton (bay) ......K 1

YUKON AND NORTHWEST TERRITORIES

SCALE OF MILES

0 50 100 200 300 400

Territorial Capitals ....⊛
Administrative Center (N. W. Terr.) ....⊙
International Boundaries
Provincial & Territorial Boundaries
District Boundaries

All islands in Hudson and James Bays lie within the District of Keewatin.

© Copyright by C. S. HAMMOND & Co.

UNITED STATES

AREA	3,615,211 sq. mi.
POPULATION	196,164,000
CAPITAL	Washington
LARGEST CITY	New York (greater) 14,114,927
HIGHEST POINT	Mt. McKinley 20,320 ft.
MONETARY UNIT	dollar
MAJOR LANGUAGE	English
MAJOR RELIGIONS	Protestant, Roman Catholic

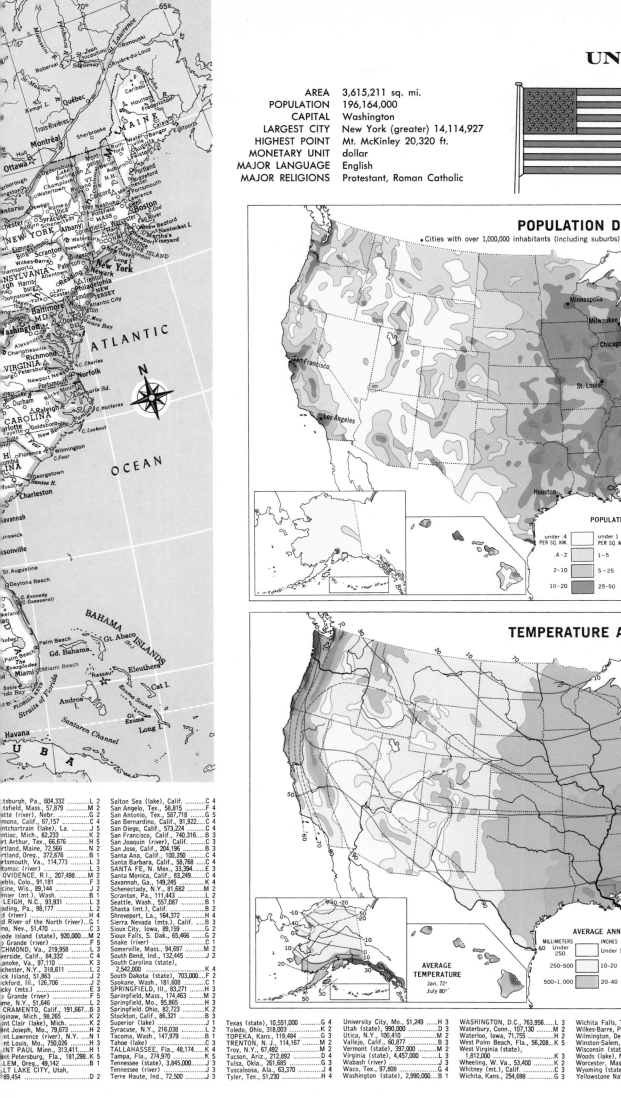

POPULATION DISTRIBUTION

• Cities with over 1,000,000 inhabitants (including suburbs)

POPULATION DENSITY

under .4 PER SQ. KM.	under 1 PER SQ. MI.	20-58	50-150
.4 - 2	1-5	58-386	150-1,000
2-10	5-25	over 386	over 1,000
10-20	25-50		

Copyright by C.S. HAMMOND & Co., N.Y.

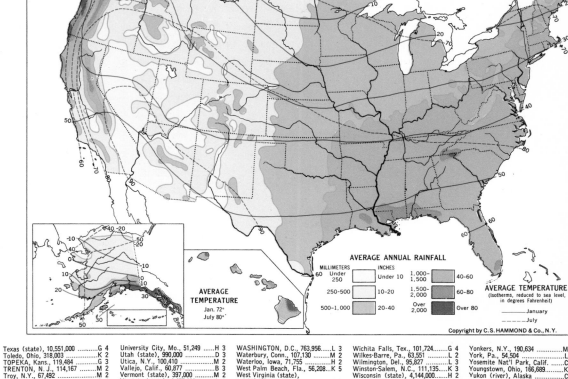

TEMPERATURE AND RAINFALL

AVERAGE TEMPERATURE
Jan. 72°
July 80°

AVERAGE ANNUAL RAINFALL

MILLIMETERS	INCHES		
Under 250	Under 10	1,000-1,500	40-60
250-500	10-20	1,500-2,000	60-80
500-1,000	20-40	Over 2,000	Over 80

AVERAGE TEMPERATURE
(Isotherms, reduced to sea level, in degrees Fahrenheit)
——— January
- - - - July

Copyright by C.S. HAMMOND & Co., N.Y.

United States
(continued)

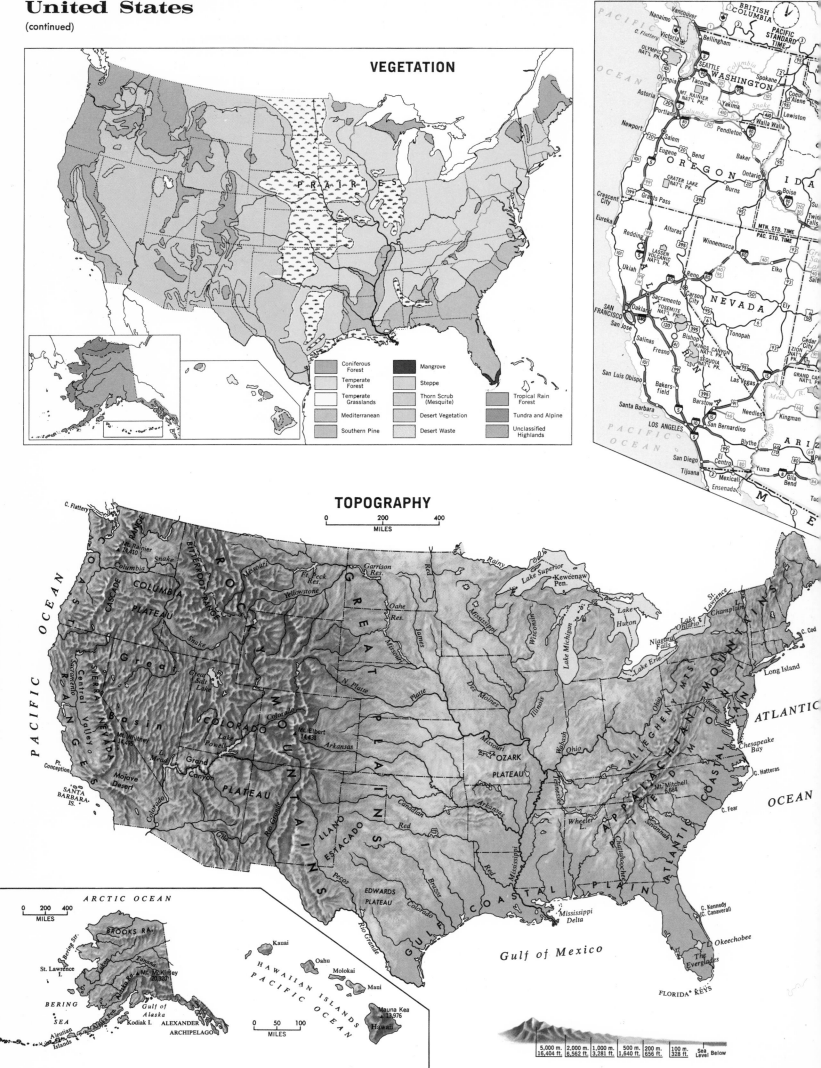

VEGETATION

Coniferous Forest
Temperate Forest
Temperate Grasslands
Mediterranean
Southern Pine
Mangrove
Steppe
Thorn Scrub (Mesquite)
Desert Vegetation
Desert Waste
Tropical Rain Forest
Tundra and Alpine
Unclassified Highlands

TOPOGRAPHY

0   200   400
MILES

5,000 m.   2,000 m.   1,000 m.   500 m.   200 m.   100 m.   Sea
16,404 ft.   6,562 ft.   3,281 ft.   1,640 ft.   656 ft.   328 ft.   Level   Below

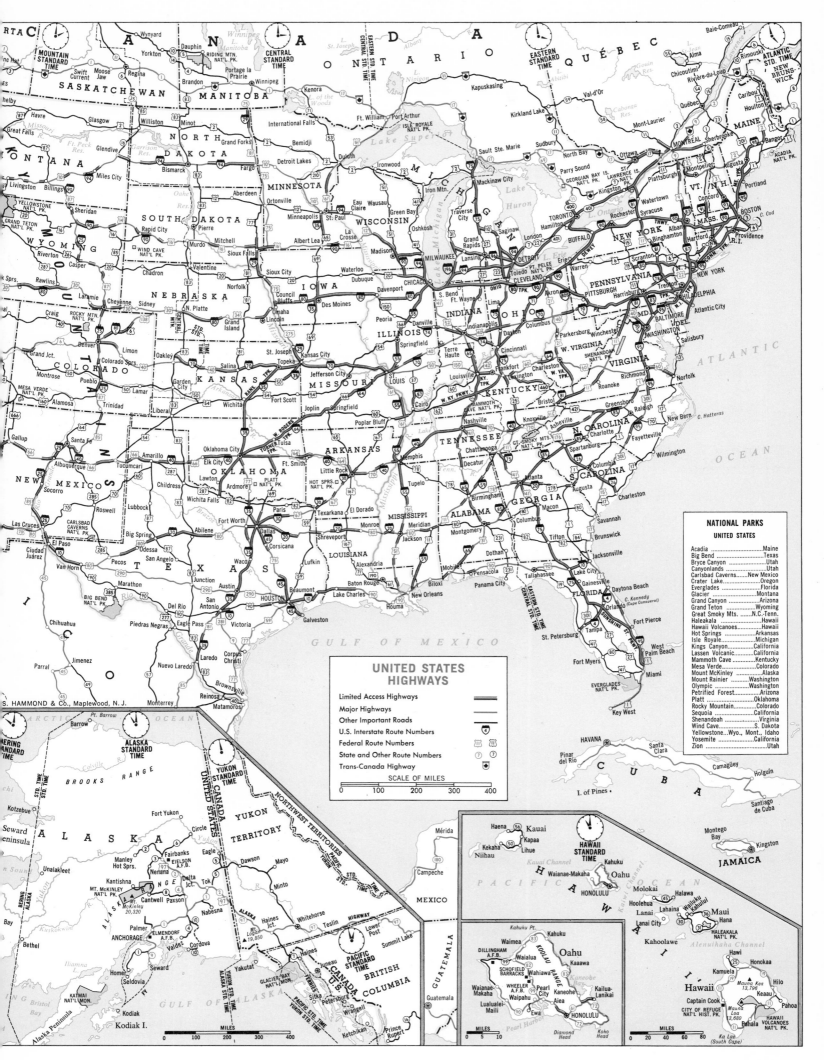

UNITED STATES
HIGHWAYS

Limited Access Highways
Major Highways
Other Important Roads
U.S. Interstate Route Numbers
Federal Route Numbers
State and Other Route Numbers
Trans-Canada Highway

SCALE OF MILES
0   100   200   300   400

NATIONAL PARKS
UNITED STATES

Acadia .... Maine
Big Bend .... Texas
Bryce Canyon .... Utah
Canyonlands .... Utah
Carlsbad Caverns .... New Mexico
Crater Lake .... Oregon
Everglades .... Florida
Glacier .... Montana
Grand Canyon .... Arizona
Grand Teton .... Wyoming
Great Smoky Mts. ...... N.C.-Tenn.
Haleakala .... Hawaii
Hawaii Volcanoes .... Hawaii
Hot Springs .... Arkansas
Isle Royale .... Michigan
Kings Canyon .... California
Lassen Volcanic .... California
Mammoth Cave .... Kentucky
Mesa Verde .... Colorado
Mount McKinley .... Alaska
Mount Rainier .... Washington
Olympic .... Washington
Petrified Forest .... Arizona
Platt .... Oklahoma
Rocky Mountain .... Colorado
Sequoia .... California
Shenandoah .... Virginia
Wind Cave .... S. Dakota
Yellowstone ...Wyo., Mont., Idaho
Yosemite .... California
Zion .... Utah

S. HAMMOND & Co., Maplewood, N.J.

United States
(continued)

LAND USE

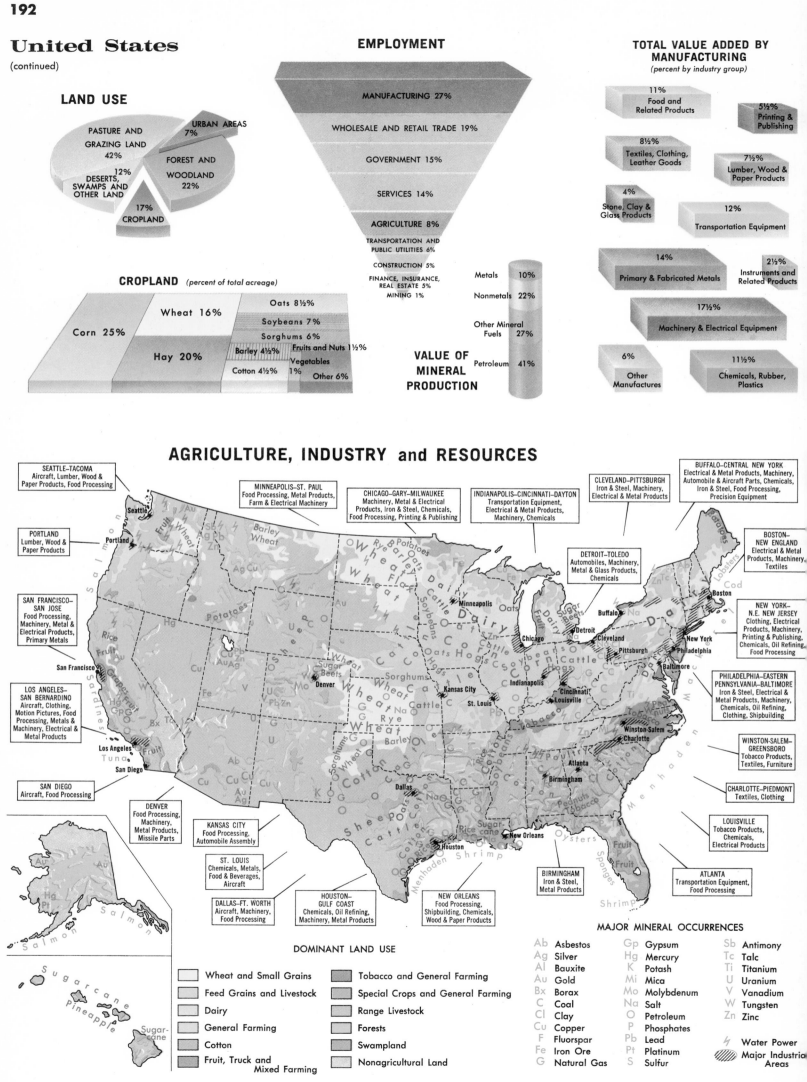

PASTURE AND GRAZING LAND 42%

URBAN AREAS 7%

FOREST AND WOODLAND 22%

DESERTS, SWAMPS AND OTHER LAND 12%

CROPLAND 17%

CROPLAND (percent of total acreage)

Corn 25%

Wheat 16%

Hay 20%

Oats 8½%

Soybeans 7%

Sorghums 6%

Barley 4½%

Cotton 4½%

Fruits and Nuts 1½%

Vegetables 1%

Other 6%

EMPLOYMENT

MANUFACTURING 27%

WHOLESALE AND RETAIL TRADE 19%

GOVERNMENT 15%

SERVICES 14%

AGRICULTURE 8%

TRANSPORTATION AND PUBLIC UTILITIES 6%

CONSTRUCTION 5%

FINANCE, INSURANCE, REAL ESTATE 5%

MINING 1%

VALUE OF MINERAL PRODUCTION

Metals 10%

Nonmetals 22%

Other Mineral Fuels 27%

Petroleum 41%

TOTAL VALUE ADDED BY MANUFACTURING
(percent by industry group)

11% Food and Related Products

5½% Printing & Publishing

8½% Textiles, Clothing, Leather Goods

7½% Lumber, Wood & Paper Products

4% Stone, Clay & Glass Products

12% Transportation Equipment

14% Primary & Fabricated Metals

2½% Instruments and Related Products

17½% Machinery & Electrical Equipment

6% Other Manufactures

11½% Chemicals, Rubber, Plastics

AGRICULTURE, INDUSTRY and RESOURCES

SEATTLE–TACOMA
Aircraft, Lumber, Wood & Paper Products, Food Processing

MINNEAPOLIS–ST. PAUL
Food Processing, Metal Products, Farm & Electrical Machinery

CHICAGO–GARY–MILWAUKEE
Machinery, Metal & Electrical Products, Iron & Steel, Chemicals, Food Processing, Printing & Publishing

INDIANAPOLIS–CINCINNATI–DAYTON
Transportation Equipment, Electrical & Metal Products, Machinery, Chemicals

CLEVELAND–PITTSBURGH
Iron & Steel, Machinery, Electrical & Metal Products

BUFFALO–CENTRAL NEW YORK
Electrical & Metal Products, Machinery, Automobile & Aircraft Parts, Chemicals, Iron & Steel, Food Processing, Precision Equipment

PORTLAND
Lumber, Wood & Paper Products

DETROIT–TOLEDO
Automobiles, Machinery, Metal & Glass Products, Chemicals

BOSTON–NEW ENGLAND
Electrical & Metal Products, Machinery, Textiles

SAN FRANCISCO–SAN JOSE
Food Processing, Machinery, Metal & Electrical Products, Primary Metals

NEW YORK–N.E. NEW JERSEY
Clothing, Electrical Products, Machinery, Printing & Publishing, Chemicals, Oil Refining, Food Processing

LOS ANGELES–SAN BERNARDINO
Aircraft, Clothing, Motion Pictures, Food Processing, Metals & Machinery, Electrical & Metal Products

PHILADELPHIA–EASTERN PENNSYLVANIA–BALTIMORE
Iron & Steel, Electrical & Metal Products, Machinery, Chemicals, Oil Refining, Clothing, Shipbuilding

WINSTON-SALEM–GREENSBORO
Tobacco Products, Textiles, Furniture

SAN DIEGO
Aircraft, Food Processing

CHARLOTTE–PIEDMONT
Textiles, Clothing

DENVER
Food Processing, Machinery, Metal Products, Missile Parts

LOUISVILLE
Tobacco Products, Chemicals, Electrical Products

KANSAS CITY
Food Processing, Automobile Assembly

ST. LOUIS
Chemicals, Metals, Food & Beverages, Aircraft

DALLAS–FT. WORTH
Aircraft, Machinery, Food Processing

HOUSTON–GULF COAST
Chemicals, Oil Refining, Machinery, Metal Products

NEW ORLEANS
Food Processing, Shipbuilding, Chemicals, Wood & Paper Products

BIRMINGHAM
Iron & Steel, Metal Products

ATLANTA
Transportation Equipment, Food Processing

DOMINANT LAND USE

- Wheat and Small Grains
- Feed Grains and Livestock
- Dairy
- General Farming
- Cotton
- Fruit, Truck and Mixed Farming
- Tobacco and General Farming
- Special Crops and General Farming
- Range Livestock
- Forests
- Swampland
- Nonagricultural Land

MAJOR MINERAL OCCURRENCES

Ab	Asbestos	Gp	Gypsum	Sb	Antimony
Ag	Silver	Hg	Mercury	Tc	Talc
Al	Bauxite	K	Potash	Ti	Titanium
Au	Gold	Mi	Mica	U	Uranium
Bx	Borax	Mo	Molybdenum	V	Vanadium
C	Coal	Na	Salt	W	Tungsten
Cl	Clay	O	Petroleum	Zn	Zinc
Cu	Copper	P	Phosphates		
F	Fluorspar	Pb	Lead	⚡	Water Power
Fe	Iron Ore	Pt	Platinum	▨	Major Industrial Areas
G	Natural Gas	S	Sulfur		

ALABAMA

AREA 51,609 sq. mi.
POPULATION 3,462,000
CAPITAL Montgomery
LARGEST CITY Birmingham 340,887
HIGHEST POINT Cheaha Mtn. 2,407 ft.
SETTLED IN 1702
ADMITTED TO UNION December 14, 1819
POPULAR NAMES Heart of Dixie; Cotton State
STATE FLOWER Camellia
STATE BIRD Yellowhammer

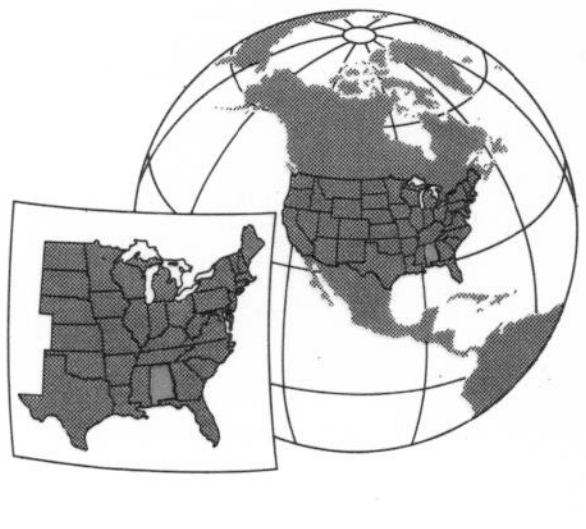

COUNTIES

Autauga (E5) 18,739
Baldwin (C9) 49,088
Barbour (H7) 24,700
Bibb (D5) 14,357
Blount (E2) 25,449
Bullock (G6) 13,462
Butler (E7) 24,560
Calhoun (G3) 95,878
Chambers (H5) 37,828
Cherokee (G2) 16,303
Chilton (E5) 25,693
Choctaw (B6) 17,870
Clarke (C7) 25,738
Clay (G4) 12,400
Cleburne (G3) 10,911
Coffee (G8) 30,583
Colbert (C1) 46,506
Conecuh (E8) 17,762
Coosa (F5) 10,726
Covington (F8) 35,631
Crenshaw (F7) 14,909
Cullman (E2) 45,572
Dale (G8) 31,066
Dallas (D6) 56,667
De Kalb (G2) 41,417
Elmore (F5) 30,524
Escambia (D8) 33,511
Etowah (F2) 96,980
Fayette (C3) 16,148
Franklin (C2) 21,988
Geneva (G8) 22,310
Greene (C5) 13,600
Hale (C5) 19,537
Henry (H8) 15,286
Houston (H8) 50,718
Jackson (F1) 36,681
Jefferson (E3) 634,864
Lamar (B3) 14,271
Lauderdale (C1) 61,622
Lawrence (D1) 24,501
Lee (H5) 49,754
Limestone (E1) 36,513
Lowndes (E6) 15,417
Macon (G6) 26,717
Madison (E1) 117,348
Marengo (C6) 27,098
Marion (C2) 21,837
Marshall (F2) 48,018
Mobile (B9) 314,301
Monroe (D7) 22,372
Montgomery (F6) 169,210
Morgan (E2) 60,454
Perry (D5) 17,358
Pickens (B4) 21,882
Pike (G7) 25,987
Randolph (H4) 19,477
Russell (H6) 46,351
Saint Clair (F3) 25,388
Shelby (E4) 32,132
Sumter (B5) 20,041
Talladega (F4) 65,495
Tallapoosa (G5) 35,007
Tuscaloosa (C4) 109,047
Walker (D3) 54,211
Washington (B8) 15,372
Wilcox (D7) 18,739
Winston (D2) 14,858

CITIES and TOWNS

Abanda (H4) 130
Abbeville◉ (H7) 2,524
Abernant (D4) 200
Acmar (E3) 900
Adamsville (D3) 2,095
Addison (D2) 343
Adger (D4) 600
Akron (C5) 604
Alabaster (E4) 1,623
Alberta (D6) 600
Albertville (F2) 8,250
Aldrich (E4) 950
Alexander City (G5) 13,140
Alexandria (G3) 500
Aliceville (B4) 3,194
Allen· (C7) 145
Allgood (F3) 147
Allsboro (B1) 150
Alma (C8) 600
Alpine (F4) 156
Alton (E3) 500
Altoona (F2) 744
Andalusia◉ (E8) 10,263
Anderson (D1) 350
Annemanie (D6) 100
Anniston◉ (G3) 33,657
Ansley (F7) 125
Arab (E2) 2,989
Ardmore (E1) 439
Argo (E3) 197
Ariton (G7) 687
Arkadelphia (E3) 350
Arley (D2) 400
Arlington (C6) 200
Ashby (E4) 98
Ashford (H8) 1,511
Ashland◉ (G4) 1,610
Ashville (F3) 973
Athens◉ (E1) 9,330
Atmore (C8) 8,173
Attalla (F2) 8,257
Auburn (H5) 16,261
Autaugaville (E6) 440
Avon (H8) 132
Axis (B9) 350
Babbie (F8) 60
Baileyton (E2) 300
Bakerhill (H7) 265
Banks (G7) 201
Barlow Bend (C8) 150
Barton (C1) 250
Bashi (C7) 150
Battles Wharf (C10) 500
Bay Minette◉ (C9) 5,197
Bayou La Batre (B10) 2,572
Bear Creek (C2) 243
Beatrice (D7) 506
Beaverton (B3) 162
Belgreen (C2) 500
Belk (C3) 150
Bellamy (B6) 750
Belle Mina (E1) 300
Bellwood (G8) 273
Belmont (C5) 153
Beloit (D6) 125
Benton (E6) 150
Bermuda (D8) 500
Berry (C3) 645
Bessemer (D4) 33,054
Beulah (H5) 350
Billingsley (E5) 179
Birmingham◉ (D3) 340,887
Birmingham (urban area) 521,330
Black (G8) 133
Blacksher (C8) 100
Bladon Springs (B7) 300
Blanton (H5) 100
Bleecker (H5) 250
Blount Springs (E3) 100
Blountsville (E2) 672
Blue Mountain (G3) 446
Blue Springs (G7) 94
Boaz (F2) 4,654
Boligee (C5) 134
Bolinger (B7) 200
Bolling (E7) 250
Bon Air (F4) 297
Bon Secour (C10) 500
Booth (E6) 250
Borden Springs (H3) 100
Boyd (B5) 250
Boylston (F6) 1,200
Braggs (E6) 300
Branchville (F3) 150
Brantley (F7) 1,014
Bremen (E3) 250
Brent (D5) 1,879
Brewton◉ (D8) 6,309
Brickyard (H6) 150
Bridgeport (G1) 2,906
Brierfield (E4) 146
Brighton (D4) 2,884
Brilliant (C2) 749
Bromley (C9) 585
Brompton (F3) 115
Brooklyn (E8) 100
Brookside (E3) 999
Brooksville (F2) 175
Brookwood (D4) 650
Browns (D6) 700
Brownsboro (F1) 100
Brownville (C4) 250
Brownville ‡(E4) 534
Brundidge (G7) 2,523
Buena Vista (D7) 200
Buhl (C4) 500
Burkville (E6) 200
Burnsville (E6) 300
Burnt Corn (D7) 250
Butler◉ (B6) 1,765
Butler Springs (E7) 200
Calcis (E4) 200
Caledonia (D7) 150
Calera (E4) 1,928
Calhoun (F6) 500
Calvert (B8) 500
Camden◉ (D7) 1,121
Camp Hill (G5) 1,270
Campbell (C7) 100
Canoe (D8) 500
Capps (H8) 100
Capshaw (E1) 650
Carbon Hill (D3) 1,944
Cardiff (E3) 202
Carlowville (D6) 100
Carlton (C8) 200
Carrollton◉ (B4) 894
Carrville (G5) 1,081
Carson (C8) 200
Castleberry (D8) 669
Catherine (D6) 350
Cecil (F6) 250
Cedar Bluff (G2) 687
Cedar Cove (D4) 100
Central (F5) 175
Centre◉ (G2) 2,392
Centreville◉ (D5) 1,981
Chancellor (G8) 200
Chandler Springs (F4) 200
Chapman (E7) 617
Chase (E1) 275
Chastang (B8) 200
Chatom◉ (B8) 993
Chelsea (E4) 300
Cherokee (C1) 1,349
Chestnut (D7) 200
Chickasaw (B9) 10,002
Childersburg (F4) 4,884
China Grove (G7) 200
Choccolocco (G3) 300
Choctaw (B6) 600
Choctaw Bluff (C8) 500
Chunchula (B9) 500
Citronelle (B8) 1,918
Claiborne (D7) 150
Clanton◉ (E5) 5,683
Claud (F5) 500
Clayton◉ (G7) 1,313
Cleveland (E3) 300
Clinton (C5) 200
Clio (G7) 929
Clopton (G7) 140
Cloverdale (C1) 600
Coaling (D4) 150
Coatopa (B6) 100
Coden (B10) 500
Coffee Springs (G8) 205
Coffeeville (B7) 250
Coker (C4) 500
Collinsville (G2) 1,199
Collirene (E6) 100
Columbia (H8) 783
Columbiana◉ (E4) 2,264
Comer (H6) 100
Cooks Springs (F3) 200
Cooper (E5) 400
Coosada (F5) 250
Copeland (B7) 160
Cordova (D3) 3,184
Corona (C3) 207
Cottage Grove (F5) 200
Cottondale (D4) 500
Cottonton (H6) 100
Cottonwood (H8) 953
County Line (E3) 278
Courtland (D1) 495
Covin (C3) 100
Cowarts (H8) 200
Coy (D7) 950
Cragford (G4) 160
Creola (B9) 500
Crews (B3) 150
Cromwell (B6) 500
Cropwell (F3) 200
Crossville (G2) 579
Cuba (B6) 390
Cullman◉ (E2) 10,883
Cullomburg (B7) 300
Cusseta (H5) 250
Cypress (C5) 150
Dadeville◉ (G5) 2,940
Daleville (G8) 693
Dancy (B4) 200
Danville (D2) 100
Daphne (C9) 1,527
Darlington (D7) 150
Dauphin Island (B10) 600
Daviston (G4) 129
Dayton (C6) 99
De Armanville (G3) 375
Deatsville (F5) 275
Decatur◉ (D1) 29,217
Deer Park (B8) 250

AGRICULTURE, INDUSTRY and RESOURCES

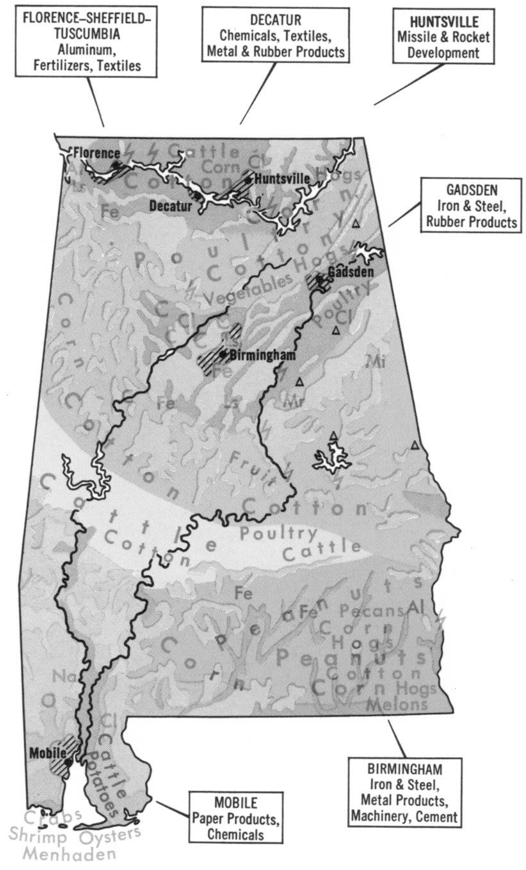

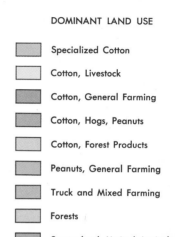

FLORENCE–SHEFFIELD–TUSCUMBIA Aluminum, Fertilizers, Textiles
DECATUR Chemicals, Textiles, Metal & Rubber Products
HUNTSVILLE Missile & Rocket Development
GADSDEN Iron & Steel, Rubber Products
BIRMINGHAM Iron & Steel, Metal Products, Machinery, Cement
MOBILE Paper Products, Chemicals
Florence
Huntsville
Decatur
Gadsden
Birmingham
Mobile
Cattle
Corn
Hogs
Poultry
Cotton
Vegetables
Fruit
Peanuts
Pecans
Melons
Potatoes
Crabs
Shrimp
Oysters
Menhaden

DOMINANT LAND USE

- Specialized Cotton
- Cotton, Livestock
- Cotton, General Farming
- Cotton, Hogs, Peanuts
- Cotton, Forest Products
- Peanuts, General Farming
- Truck and Mixed Farming
- Forests
- Swampland, Limited Agriculture

MAJOR MINERAL OCCURRENCES

Al	Bauxite	Ls	Limestone
At	Asphalt	Mi	Mica
C	Coal	Mr	Marble
Cl	Clay	Na	Salt
Fe	Iron Ore	O	Petroleum

Water Power
Major Industrial Areas
Major Textile Manufacturing Centers

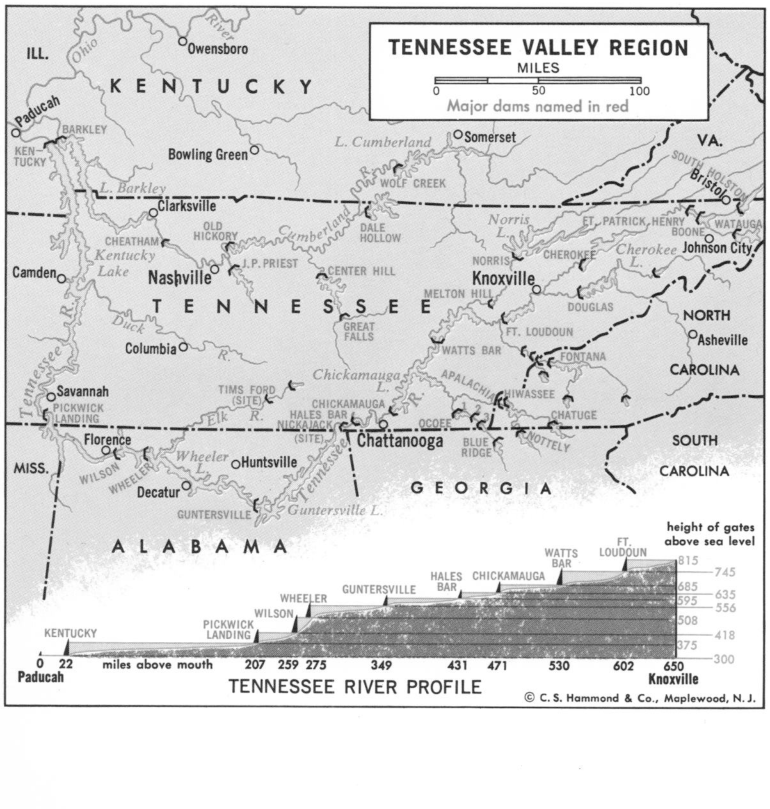

TENNESSEE VALLEY REGION
MILES
0 50 100
Major dams named in red
ILL.
KENTUCKY
Owensboro
Paducah
Bowling Green
Somerset
VA.
Clarksville
Nashville
Knoxville
Johnson City
Bristol
Camden
Columbia
Asheville
Savannah
Chattanooga
Florence
Huntsville
Decatur
TENNESSEE
NORTH CAROLINA
SOUTH CAROLINA
GEORGIA
ALABAMA
MISS.
KENTUCKY
BARKLEY
CHEATHAM
OLD HICKORY
J.P. PRIEST
CENTER HILL
DALE HOLLOW
WOLF CREEK
NORRIS
CHEROKEE
DOUGLAS
FT. PATRICK HENRY
BOONE
WATAUGA
SOUTH HOLSTON
MELTON HILL
FT. LOUDOUN
FONTANA
WATTS BAR
GREAT FALLS
TIMS FORD (SITE)
PICKWICK LANDING
WILSON
WHEELER
GUNTERSVILLE
NICKAJACK (SITE)
HALES BAR
CHICKAMAUGA
OCOEE
HIWASSEE
CHATUGE
BLUE RIDGE
NOTTELY
APALACHIA
L. Cumberland
L. Barkley
Kentucky Lake
Cherokee L.
Norris L.
Chickamauga L.
Wheeler L.
Guntersville L.
Tennessee R.
Cumberland R.
Duck R.
Elk R.
Ohio River
TENNESSEE RIVER PROFILE
height of gates above sea level
815 745 685 635 595 556 508 418 300
miles above mouth
0 22 207 259 275 349 431 471 530 602 650
Paducah
Knoxville

Delta (G4) 150
Demopolis (C6) 7,377
Detroit (B2) 113
Devenport (F6) 125
Dickinson (C7) 300
Dixons Mills (C6) 350
Dixonville (E8) 300
Dolomite (D4) 4,500
Dora (D3) 1,776
Dothan◉ (H8) 31,440
Double Springs◉ (D2) 811
Douglas (F2) 200
Dozier (F7) 335
Drewry (D8) 200
Duke (G3) 200
Dunavant (F4) 100
Duncanville (D4) 300
Dutton (G1) 350
Easonville (F3) 200
East Brewton (E8) 2,511
Eastaboga (F3) 600
Echo (G8) 150
Echola (C4) 250
Eclectic (F5) 926
Edna (B6) 500
Edwardsville (H3) 168
Edwin (H7) 150
Elamville (G7) 150
Elba◉ (F8) 4,321
Elberta (C10) 384
Eldridge (C3) 350
Elkmont (E1) 169
Elmore (F5) 350
Elon (F1) 300
Elrod (C4) 500
Emelle (B5) 300
Enterprise (G8) 11,410
Eoline (D4) 100
Epes (B5) 337
Equality (F5) 100
Estillfork (F1) 196
Ethelsville (B4) 62
Eufaula (H7) 8,357
Eunola (G8) 124
Eutaw◉ (C5) 2,784
Eva (E2) 180
Evergreen◉ (E8) 3,703
Excel (D8) 313
Fabius (G1) 100
Fackler (G1) 300
Fairfax (H5) 3,107
Fairfield (E3) 15,816
Fairford (B8) 400
Fairhope (C10) 4,858
Falkville (E2) 682
Farmersville (E6) 100
Faunsdale (C6) 124
Fayette◉ (C3) 4,227
Fayetteville (F4) 300
Finchburg (D7) 500
Five Points (H4) 285
Flat Creek (D3) 570
Flat Rock (G1) 500
Flatwood (C6) 250
Fleta (F6) 350
Flint City (D1) 432
Flomaton (D8) 1,454
Florala (F8) 3,011
Florence◉ (C1) 31,649
Foley (C10) 2,889
Forest Home (E7) 500
Forkland (C5) 250
Forney (H2) 100
Fort Davis (G6) 300
Fort Deposit (E7) 1,466
Fort Mitchell (H6) 950
Fort Payne◉ (G2) 7,029
Fostoria (E6) 150
Fountain (D7) 150
Francisco (F1) 150
Frankfort (C1) 130
Franklin (D7) 350
Frankville (B7) 500
Freemanville (D8) 100
Frisco City (D8) 1,177
Fruitdale (B8) 800
Fruithurst (G3) 255
Fulton (C7) 688
Fultondale (E3) 2,001
Furman (E6) 300
Fyffe (G2) 230
Gadsden◉ (G2) 58,088
Gadsden (urb. area) 68,944
Gainestown (C8) 160
Gainesville (B5) 214
Gallant (F2) 855
Gallion (C6) 300
Gantt (E8) 500
Gantts Quarry (F4) 238
Garden City (E2) 536
Gardendale (E3) 4,712
Garland (E7) 225
Gastonburg (C6) 175
Gaylesville (G2) 144
Geiger (B5) 104
Geneva◉ (G8) 3,840
Georgiana (E7) 2,093
Geraldine (G2) 340
Gilbertown (B7) 270
Glen Allen (C3) 131
Glencoe (G3) 2,592
Glenwood (F7) 416
Gold Hill (G5) 160
Goodsprings (D3) 300
Goodwater (F4) 2,023
Gordo (C4) 1,714
Gordon (H8) 222
Gordonsville (E6) 100
Gorgas (D3) 300
Goshen (F7) 260
Gosport (C7) 300
Grady (F7) 150
Graham (H4) 214
Grand Bay (B10) 500
Grant (F1) 274
Graysville (D3) 2,870
Green Pond (D4) 1,750
Greenbrier (E1) 200
Greensboro◉ (C5) 3,081
Greenville◉ (E7) 6,894
Greenwood (G6) 3,561
Grimes (H8) 175
Grove Hill◉ (C7) 1,834
Groveoak (F2) 250
Gu-win (C3) 80
Guin (C3) 1,462
Gulf Shores (C10) 356
Gulfcrest (B8) 100
Guntersville◉ (F2) 6,592
Gurley (F1) 750
Hackleburg (C2) 527
Haleburg (H8) 250
Haleyville (C2) 3,740
Halsell (B6) 500
Hamilton◉ (C2) 1,934
Hammondville (G1) 134
Hamner (B5) 100
Hanceville (E2) 1,174
Hardaway (G6) 300
Harpersville (F4) 667
Hartford (G8) 1,956
Hartselle (E2) 5,000
Harvest (E1) 250
Hatchechubbee (H6) 250
Hatton (D1) 550
Havana (C5) 180
Hayden (E3) 187
Hayneville◉ (E6) 950
Hazel Green (E1) 200
Headland (H8) 2,650
Healing Springs (B7) 150
Heath (F8) 125
Heflin◉ (G3) 2,400
Heiberger (D5) 100
Helena (E4) 523
Henagar (G1) 500
Higdon (G1) 350
Hightower (H3) 200
Hillsboro (D1) 218
Hissop (F5) 200
Hobbs Island (F1) 200
Hobson City (G3) 770
Hodges (C2) 194
Hodgesville (H8) 100
Hokes Bluff (G3) 1,619
Hollins (F4) 200
Holly Pond (E2) 193
Hollytree (F1) 239
Hollywood (G1) 246
Holt (D4) 2,400
Holy Trinity (H6) 350
Homewood (E4) 20,289
Honoraville (F7) 200
Hopewell (H3) 150
Horton (F2) 300
Houston (D2) 220
Hueytown (D4) 5,997
Hulaco (E2) 160
Hull (C4) 125
Huntsville◉ (E1) 72,365
Huntsville (urb. area) 74,970
Hurtsboro (H6) 1,056
Huxford (D8) 350
Hybart (D7) 200
Hytop (F1) 145
Ider (G1) 300
Inverness (G6) 140
Irondale (E3) 3,501
Irvington (B9) 200
Isbell (C2) 225
Isney (B7) 102
Jachin (B6) 250
Jack (F7) 100
Jackson (C8) 4,959
Jacksons Gap (G5) 600
Jacksonville (G3) 5,678
Jasper◉ (D3) 10,799
Jeff (E1) 100
Jefferson (C6) 600
Jemison (E5) 977
Johns (D4) 338
Jones (E5) 150

(continued on following page)

ALABAMA

SCALE OF MILES

0 5 10 20 30 40

⊛ State Capitals
○ County Seats

© C. S. HAMMOND & Co., N. Y.

Alabama
(continued)

Joppa (E2) 178
Kansas (C3) 211
Keener (G2) 150
Kellerman (D4) 214
Kellyton (F5) 475
Kennedy (B3) 379
Kent (G5) 500
Key (G2) 175
Killen (D1) 620
Kimberly (E3) 763
Kimbrough (C6) 158
Kings Landing (D6) 200
Kinsey (H8) 283
Kinston (F8) 470
Knoxville (C4) 300
Laceys Spring (E1) 350
Lafayette◉ (H5) 2,605
Lamison (C6) 350
Land (B6) 200
Landersville (D2) 150
Lanett (H5) 7,674
Langdale (H5) 2,528
Langston (G1) 250
Lapine (F7) 400
Larkinsville (F1) 300
Latham (B6) 200
Laurendine (B9) 300
Lavaca (B6) 350
Leeds (E3) 6,162
Leesburg (G2) 350
Leighton (D1) 1,158
Lenox (D8) 100
Leroy (B8) 300
Letohatchee (E6) 325
Lexington (D1) 315
Lillian (D10) 650
Lim Rock (F1) 200
Lincoln (F3) 629
Linden◉ (C6) 2,516
Lineville (G4) 1,612
Linwood (G5) 150
Lipscomb (E4) 2,811
Lisman (B5) 909
Little River (C8) 100
Littleville (C1) 460
Livingston◉ (B5) 1,544
Loachapoka (G5) 500
Lockhart (F8) 799
Logan (E2) 100
Lomax (E5) 100
Long Island (G1) 250
Longview (E4) 150
Lottie (C8) 150
Louisville (G7) 890
Lower Peach Tree (C7) 725
Lowndesboro (E6) 375
Loxley (C9) 831
Luverne◉ (F7) 2,238
Lynn (C2) 531
Macedonia (E6) 150
Madison (E1) 1,435
Madrid (H8) 245

Magnolia (C6) 150
Magnolia Springs (C10) 250
Malvern (G8) 213
Manchester (D3) 200
Manila (C7) 150
Mantua (C4) 150
Maplesville (E5) 679
Marbury (E5) 300
Margaret (F3) 715
Margerum (B1) 150
Marion◉ (D5) 3,807
Marion Junction (D6) 400
Marlow (C10) 100
Marvyn (H6) 200
Maud (B1) 100
Maylene (E4) 200
Maytown ‡(D3) 297
McCullough (D8) 600
McDowell (C5) 275
McIntosh (B9) 500
McKenzie (E7) 558
McShan (B4) 200
McWilliams (D7) 250
Megargel (D8) 410
Mehama (D1) 120
Melvin (B7) 300
Mentone (G1) 250
Meridianville (F1) 500
Mexia (D8) 150
Midfield (E4) 3,556
Midland City (H8) 854
Midway (H6) 594
Miflin (C10) 135
Mignon (F4) 2,271
Millbrook (F6) 700
Millers Ferry (D6) 425
Millerville (G4) 150
Millport (B3) 943
Milly (B7) 645
Milltown (H4) 125
Milstead (G6) 200
Minter (D6) 450
Mobile◉ (B9) 202,779
Mobile (urb. area) 268,139
Monroeville◉ (D7) 3,632
Monrovia (E1) 500
Monterey (E7) 150
Montevallo (E4) 2,755
MONTGOMERY◉ (F6) 134,393
Montgomery (urban area) 142,893
Montrose (C9) 750
Moores Bridge (C4) 300
Mooresville (E1) 93
Morganville (F6) 300
Morris (E3) 638
Morvin (C7) 100
Moulton◉ (D2) 1,716
Moundville (C5) 922
Mount Carmel (F6) 350

Mount Hope (D2) 600
Mount Meigs (F6) 200
Mount Sterling (B6) 350
Mount Vernon (B8) 553
Mount Willing (E6) 172
Mountain Brook (E4) 12,680
Mountain Creek (E5) 100
Mulga ‡(E3) 482
Munford (F3) 750
Murrycross (G2) 300
Muscadine (H3) 150
Muscle Shoals (C1) 4,084
Myrtlewood (C6) 403
Nanafalia (B6) 400
Natchez (D7) 203
Natural Bridge (C2) 100
Nauvoo (D3) 318
Needham (B7) 108
New Brockton (G8) 1,093
New Hope (F1) 953
New Market (F1) 500
New Site (G4) 500
Newbern (C5) 316
Newell (H4) 150
Newton (G8) 958
Newville (H8) 546
Nicholsville (C6) 225
Nixburg (F5) 200
Normal (E1) 1,400
North Johns (Johns) (D4) 338
Northport (C4) 5,245
Notasulga (G5) 884
Nottingham (F4) 100
Oakhill (D7) 116
Oakman (D3) 849
Odenville (F3) 300
Ohatchee (G3) 437
Old Spring Hill (C6) 100
Omega (F7) 400
Oneonta◉ (E3) 4,136
Opelika◉ (H5) 15,678
Opp (F8) 5,535
Orange Beach (C10) 500
Orrville (D6) 422
Owens Cross Rds. (E1) 800
Oxford (G3) 3,603
Ozark◉ (G8) 9,534
Paint Rock (F1) 264
Painter (E7) 250
Palestine (H3) 100
Panola (B5) 400
Pansey (H8) 200
Parrish (D3) 1,608
Paul (E8) 200
Peachburg (G6) 150
Pelham (E4) 400
Pennington (B6) 300
Perdido (B8) 300
Perdido Beach (C10) 128
Perdue Hill (C8) 275

Peterman (D7) 600
Peterson (D4) 900
Petrey (F7) 165
Phenix City◉ (H6) 27,630
Phil Campbell (C2) 898
Pickensville (B4) 175
Piedmont (G3) 4,794
Pigeon Creek (E7) 110
Pike Road (F6) 150
Pinckard (G8) 578
Pine Apple (E7) 355
Pine Hill (C7) 367
Pine Level (F6) 250
Pinson (E3) 950
Pisgah (G1) 214
Pittsview (H6) 300
Plantersville (E5) 650
Pleasant Grove ‡(E4) 3,097
Pleasant Hill (E6) 100
Plevna (F1) 100
Point Clear (C10) 750
Pollard (D8) 210
Prairie (D6) 150
Prattmont ‡(E6) 350
Prattville◉ (E6) 6,616
Prichard (B9) 47,371
Princeton (F1) 233
Prospect (D6) 80
Pushmataha (B6) 400
Putnam (B6) 289
Pyriton (G4) 100
Ragland (F3) 1,166
Rainbow City (F3) 1,625
Rainsville (G2) 398
Ralph (C4) 300
Ramer (F6) 500
Ranburne (H3) 317
Randolph (H5) 200
Range (D7) 140
Reads Mill (G3) 100
Red Bay (B2) 1,954
Red Level (E8) 327
Reece City (F2) 470
Reform (C4) 1,241
Rehoboth (D6) 175
Rembert (C6) 200
Remlap (E3) 102
Renfroe (F4) 400
Repton (D8) 314
Republic (E3) 500
Richmond (D6) 100
Riderwood (B6) 250
River Falls (E8) 401
River View (H5) 1,171
Riverside (F3) 159
Roanoke (H4) 5,288
Robertsdale (C9) 1,474
Rock Mills (H4) 500
Rock Run (G3) 120
Rock Spring (G3) 350
Rockford◉ (F5) 328
Rockwood (C2) 145

TOPOGRAPHY

0 30 60
MILES

Below Sea Level	100 m. 328 ft.	200 m. 656 ft.	500 m. 1,640 ft.	1,000 m. 3,281 ft.	2,000 m. 6,562 ft.	5,000 m. 16,404 ft.

HIGHWAYS

MILES
0 40 80

Limited Access Highways
Major Highways
Other Important Roads
Interstate Route Numbers 95
Federal Route Numbers 9
State and Other Route Numbers 4

Rogersville (D1) 766
Rosser (B6) 200
Russell (B8) 300
Russellville◉ (C2) 6,628
Rutherford (H6) 200
Ruthven (E7) 100
Rutledge (F7) 276
Safford (D6) 125
Saginaw (E4) 225
Saint Bernard (E2) 180
Saint Clair (E6) 125
Saint Clair Spgs. (F3) 125
Saint Elmo (B10) 500
Saint Florian (C1) 150
Saint Stephens (B7) 125
Salem (H5) 350
Salitpa (C7) 150
Samantha (C4) 163
Samson (F8) 1,932
Sandy Ridge (E6) 325
Sanford (F8) 247
Saragossa (D3) 300
Saraland (B9) 4,595
Sardis (E6) 750
Satsuma (B9) 1,491
Sawyerville (C5) 125
Sayre (E3) 500
Sayreton (E3) 950
Scottsboro◉ (F1) 6,449
Scranage (C8) 100
Scyrene (C7) 100
Seale (H6) 343
Searight (F8) 64
Section (G1) 595
Sellers (F6) 400
Selma◉ (E6) 28,385
Seman (F6) 152
Seminole (D10) 250
Semmes (B9) 660
Shady Grove (F7) 125
Shannon (E4) 592
Shawmut (H5) 1,898
Sheffield (C1) 13,491
Shelby (E4) 650
Shorter (G6) 600
Shorterville (H7) 400
Shortleaf (C6) 125
Silas (B7) 353
Siluria (E4) 736
Silver Run (G3) 125
Silverhill (C9) 417
Simmsville (E4) 500
Sims Chapel (B8) 200
Sipsey (B3) 320
Skipperville (G7) 100
Slapout (F5) 100
Slocomb (G8) 1,368
Smiths (H5) 950
Snead (F2) 150
Snowdoun (F6) 375
Society Hill (G6) 200
Somerville (E2) 166
Southside (E3) 150
Speigner (F5) 160
Sprague (F6) 150
Spring Garden (G3) 85
Spring Valley (C1) 300
Springville (E3) 822
Sprott (D5) 100
Spruce Pine (C2) 495
Standing Rock (H4) 425
Stanton (E5) 270

Stapleton (C9) 865
Steele (F3) 625
Sterrett (E4) 375
Stevenson (G1) 1,456
Stewart (C5) 200
Stewartsville (F4) 350
Stockton (C9) 950
Stroud (H4) 79
Suggsville (C7) 100
Sulligent (B3) 1,346
Sumiton (D3) 1,287
Summerdale (C10) 533
Summerfield (E5) 300
Sumter (D4) 300
Sumterville (B5) 100
Sunflower (B8) 100
Sunny South (C7) 200
Suttle (D5) 256
Swaim (F1) 136
Sweet Water (C6) 400
Sycamore (F4) 750
Sylacauga (F4) 12,857
Sylvan Springs ‡(D3) 245
Sylvania (G1) 500
Taits Gap (F3) 300
Talladega◉ (F4) 17,742
Talladega Spgs. (F4) 177
Tallahatta Spgs. (C7) 50
Tallassee (G5) 4,934
Tallaweka ‡(F5) 609
Tanner (E1) 600
Tarrant (E3) 7,810
Taylor (H8) 150
Tennille (G7) 100
Theodore (B9) 950
Thomaston (D6) 857
Thomasville (C7) 3,182
Thompson (G6) 150
Thorsby (E5) 968
Three Notch (G6) 125
Tibbie (B8) 200
Titus (F5) 100
Toney (E1) 300
Town Creek (D1) 810
Townley (D3) 660
Toxey (B7) 157
Trafford (E3) 529
Trenton (F1) 200
Triana (E1) 454
Trinity (D1) 454
Troy◉ (F7) 10,234
Trussville (E3) 2,510
Tunnel Springs (D7) 150
Tuscaloosa◉ (C4) 63,370
Tuscaloosa (urb. area) 76,815
Tuscumbia◉ (C1) 8,994
Tuskegee◉ (G6) 1,750
Tuskegee Ins'tute (G6) 5,000
Tyler (E6) 250
Uniform (B8) 100
Union (C5) 120
Union Grove (E2) 225
Union Springs◉ (G6) 3,704
Uniontown (D6) 1,993
Uriah (B8) 711
Valhermoso Spgs. (E2) 200
Valley Head (G1) 424
Vance (D4) 125
Vandiver (F3) 500
Verbena (E5) 500
Vernon◉ (B3) 1,492
Vestavia Hills (E4) 4,029

Vina (B2) 184
Vincent (F3) 1,402
Vinegar Bend (B8) 75
Vinemont (E2) 600
Vredenburgh (D7) 632
Wadley (G4) 605
Wadsworth (E5) 80
Walker Springs (C7) 200
Wallace (D8) 155
Walnut Grove (F2) 237
Ward (B6) 150
Warrior (E3) 2,448
Waterloo (B1) 215
Wattsville (F3) 500
Waugh (F6) 135
Waverly (G5) 250
Wayne (C6) 200
Weaver (G3) 1,401
Webb (H8) 331
Wedgeworth (C5) 300
Wedowee◉ (H4) 917
Wegra (D3) 570
Wellington (F4) 175
Weogufka (F4) 257
West Blocton (D4) 1,156
West Greene (B5) 300
Westover (E4) 600
Wetumpka◉ (F5) 3,672
Whatley (C7) 500
Wheeler (D1) 300
White Hall (E6) 100
White Plains (G3) 350
Whitfield (B6) 500
Whitney (F3) 400
Wicksburg (G8) 400
Wilmer (D9) 300
Wilsonville (E4) 683
Wilton (E4) 428
Winfield (C3) 2,907
Wing (E8) 135
Winn (C7) 110
Womack Hill (B7) 306
Woodland (H4) 250
Woodstock (D4) 300
Woodville (F1) 196
Wren (D2) 100
Wright (C1) 125
Yantley (B6) 250
Yellow Pine (B8) 215
York (B6) 2,932
Youngblood (G7) 150

OTHER FEATURES

Alabama (river) D 6
Anniston Army Depot. F 3
Bankhead (lake) D 4
Bartletts Ferry (dam) F 3
Big Canoe (creek) F 3
Black Warrior (river) E 3
Bon Secour (bay) C10
Brookley A.F.B. B 9
Cahaba (river) D 5
Cedar (point) B10
Chattahoochee (river) H 8
Chattooga (river) H 2
Cheaha (mt.) G 4
Choctawhatchee (river) H 8
Conecuh (river) D 8
Coosa (river) F 4

Cowikee, N. Fork (creek) H 6
Craig A.F.B. D 6
Cumberland (plateau) F 1
Demopolis (dam) C 5
Elk (river) D 1
Escambia (river) D 8
Fort Gaines B10
Fort McClellan Mil. Res. G 3
Fort Morgan C10
Fort Rucker G 8
Gaines, Fort B10
Goat Rock (dam) H 5
Grants Pass (channel) B10
Gunter A.F.B. F 6
Guntersville (dam) F 2
Harding (lake) H 5
Herbes (isl.) B 9
Horseshoe Nat'l Mil. Pk. G 5
Inland (lake) E 3
Jordan (dam) F 5
Lay (dam) E 5
Lewis Smith (lake) D 2
Little (river) G 2
Locust Fork (river) E 3
Logan Martin (res.) F 4
Lookout (mt.) G 1
Martin (lake) G 5
Maxwell A.F.B. F 6
Mississippi (sound) B10
Mitchell (dam) E 5
Mobile (bay) C10
Morgan, Fort C10
Mulberry (creek) E 5
Oakmulgee (creek) D 5
Oliver (dam) J 5
Paint Rock (river) F 1
Patsaliga (creek) F 7
Pea (river) G 7
Perdido (bay) D10
Perdido (river) C 9
Pickwick (lake) B 1
Pigeon (creek) E 7
Pleasure (isl.) C 9
Redstone Arsenal E 1
Rucker, Fort G 8
Russell Cave Nat'l Mon. G 1
Sand (mt.) G 1
Sandy (creek) H 7
Sepulga (river) D 8
Sipsey (river) B 4
Sipsey (river) G 2
Tallapoosa (river) G 4
Tallassee (creek) G 5
Tennessee (river) C 1
Tensaw (river) C 9
Thurlow (dam) G 6
Tombigbee (river) C 7
Town (creek) B 1
Walter F. George (dam) H 7
Walter F. George (lake) H 7
Warrior (dam) C 5
Weiss (res.) G 2
Wheeler (dam) D 3
Wilburn (dam) D 3
Wilson (dam) C 1

◉ County Seat.
‡ Name not on map.

AGRICULTURE, INDUSTRY and RESOURCES

DOMINANT LAND USE

- General Farming, Dairy, Vegetables
- General Farming, Livestock, Dairy
- Forests
- Nonagricultural Land

□ Pulp Mills
⚡ Water Power

MAJOR MINERAL OCCURRENCES

Au	Gold	G	Natural Gas
Be	Beryl	Hg	Mercury
C	Coal	O	Petroleum
Fe	Iron Ore	Pt	Platinum
U	Uranium		

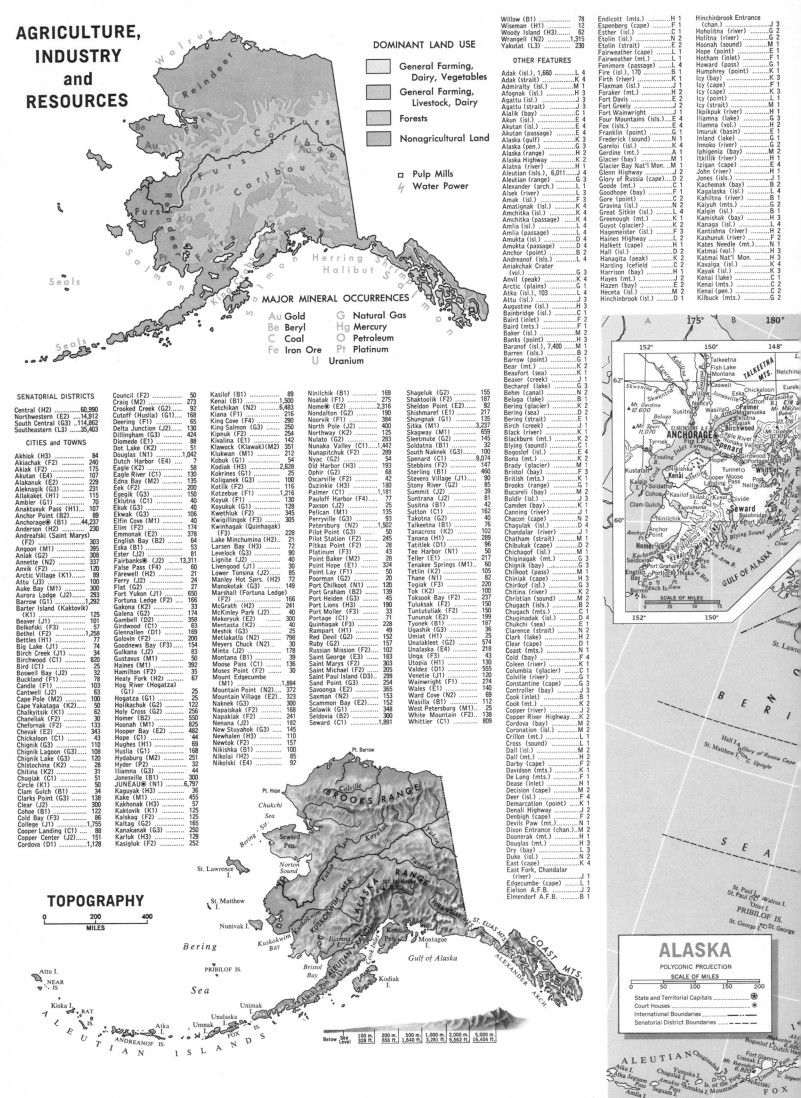

TOPOGRAPHY

0	200	400

MILES

Below Sea Level / 100 m. 328 ft. / 200 m. 656 ft. / 500 m. 1,640 ft. / 1,000 m. 3,281 ft. / 2,000 m. 6,562 ft. / 5,000 m. 16,404 ft.

ALASKA

POLYCONIC PROJECTION

SCALE OF MILES
0 50 100 150 200

- ⊛ State and Territorial Capitals
- ⊙ Court Houses
- International Boundaries
- Senatorial District Boundaries

ALASKA

AREA	586,400 sq. mi.
POPULATION	253,000
CAPITAL	Juneau
LARGEST CITY	Anchorage 44,237
HIGHEST POINT	Mt. McKinley 20,320 ft.
SETTLED IN	1801
ADMITTED TO UNION	January 3, 1959
POPULAR NAME	Great Land
STATE FLOWER	Forget-me-not
STATE BIRD	Willow Ptarmigan

See page 191 for highway map of Alaska

C. S. Hammond & Co., Maplewood, N.J.

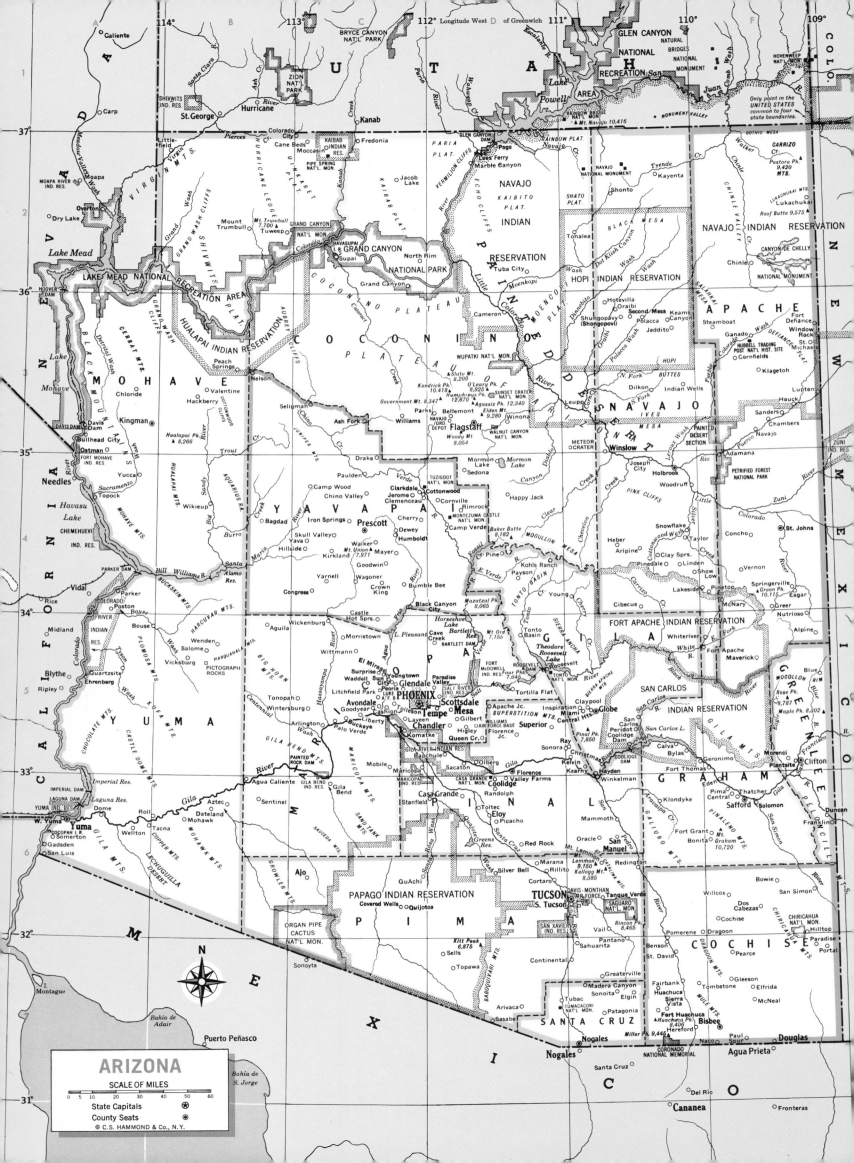

ARIZONA

(continued on following page)

COUNTIES

Apache (F3)	30,438
Cochise (F7)	55,039
Coconino (C3)	41,857
Gila (E5)	25,745
Graham (E6)	14,045
Greenlee (F5)	11,509
Maricopa (C5)	663,510
Mohave (A3)	7,736
Navajo (E3)	37,994
Pima (D6)	265,660
Pinal (D5)	62,673
Santa Cruz (E7)	10,808
Yavapai (C4)	28,912
Yuma (A5)	46,235

CITIES and TOWNS

Adamana (F4)	25
Agua Caliente (B6)	75
Aguila (B5)	450
Ajo (C6)	7,049
Alpine (F5)	500
Apache Junction (D5)	2,500
Aripine (E4)	25
Arivaca (D7)	52
Arlington (C5)	400
Ash Fork (C3)	800
Avondale (C5)	6,151
Aztec (B6)	49
Bagdad (B4)	1,462
Bapchule (D5)	800
Bellemont (D3)	150
Benson (E7)	2,494
Bisbee⊙ (F7)	9,914
Black Canyon City (C4)	250
Blue (F5)	55
Bonita (E6)	100
Bouse (A5)	150
Bowie (F6)	600
Buckeye (C5)	2,286
Bullhead City (A3)	750
Bumble Bee (C4)	21
Bylas (E5)	1,015
Calva (E5)	30
Cameron (D3)	100
Camp Verde (D4)	1,200
Camp Wood (C4)	50
Cane Beds (B2)	17
Casa Grande (D6)	8,311
Cashion (C5)	500
Castle Hot Sprs. (C5)	30
Cave Creek (D5)	500
Central (F6)	240
Central Heights (E5)	2,486
Chambers (F3)	500
Chandler (D5)	9,531
Cherry (C4)	45
Chinle (F2)	400
Chino Valley (C4)	600
Chloride (A3)	150
Christmas (E5)	250
Cibecue (E4)	35
Clarkdale (C4)	1,095
Clay Springs (E4)	199
Claypool (E5)	2,505
Clemenceau (C4)	300
Clifton⊙ (F5)	4,191
Cochise (F6)	240
Colorado City (B2)	350
Concho (F4)	175
Congress (C4)	300
Continental (D7)	12
Coolidge (D6)	4,990
Coolidge Dam (E5)	35
Cornfields (F3)	204
Cornville (D4)	422
Cortaro (D6)	75
Cottonwood (C4)	2,120
Covered Wells (C6)	100
Crown King (C4)	100
Dateland (B6)	40
Davis Dam (A3)	100
Dewey (C4)	95
Dilkon (E3)	63
Dome (A6)	100
Dos Cabezas (F6)	51
Douglas (F7)	11,925
Dragoon (F6)	250
Drake (C4)	25
Duncan (F6)	862
Eagar (F4)	873
Eden (F6)	80
Ehrenberg (A5)	75
El Mirage ‡(C5)	1,723
Elfrida (F7)	250
Elgin (E7)	51
Eloy (D6)	4,899
Fairbank (E7)	75
Flagstaff⊙ (D3)	18,214
Florence⊙ (E5)	2,143
Florence Junction (D5)	48
Fort Apache (F5)	500
Fort Defiance (F3)	800
Fort Grant (E6)	250
Fort Huachuca (E7)	100
Fort Thomas (E5)	475
Franklin (F6)	200
Fredonia (C2)	643
Gadsden (A6)	250
Ganado (F3)	500
Geronimo (F5)	23
Gila Bend (C6)	1,813
Gilbert (D5)	1,833
Gleeson (F7)	27
Glendale (C5)	15,696
Globe⊙ (E5)	6,217
Goodwin (C4)	20
Goodyear (C5)	1,654
Grand Canyon (C2)	1,300
Greaterville (E7)	30
Greer (F4)	50
Hackberry (B3)	92
Happy Jack (D4)	350
Hayden (E5)	1,760
Heber (E4)	500
Hereford (E7)	37
Higley (D5)	496
Hillside (B4)	100
Hilltop (F6)	23
Holbrook⊙ (E4)	3,438
Hotevilla (E3)	577
Houck (F3)	680
Huachuca (E7)	1,330
Humboldt (C4)	400
Indian Wells (E3)	11
Inspiration (D5)	300
Iron Springs (C4)	200
Jacob Lake (C2)	9
Jeddito (E3)	130
Jerome (C4)	243
Joseph City (E4)	500
Kayenta (E2)	500
Keams Canyon (E3)	600
Kearny (E5)	902
Kelvin (E5)	35
Kingman⊙ (A3)	4,525
Kirkland (C4)	150
Klagetoh (F3)	200

Klondyke (E6)	220
Kohls Ranch (D4)	100
Komatke (C5)	200
Lakeside (E4)	750
Laveen (C5)	500
Lees Ferry (D2)	13
Leupp (E3)	150
Liberty (C5)	150
Linden (E4)	98
Litchfield Pk.)C5)	3,500
Littlefield (B2)	100
Lukachukai (F2)	500
Lukeville (C7)	27
Lupton (F3)	125
Madera Canyon (E7)	60
Mammoth (E6)	1,913
Marana (D6)	950
Marble Canyon (D2)	5
Maricopa (C5)	150
Maverick (F5)	500
Mayer (C4)	700
McNary (F4)	1,608
McNeal (F7)	50
Mesa (D5)	33,772
Miami (E5)	3,350
Mobile (C5)	74
Moccasin (C2)	65
Mohawk (B6)	18
Morenci (F5)	2,431
Mormon Lake (D4)	26
Morristown (C5)	100
Mount Lemmon (E6)	50
Mount Trumbull (B2)	36
Naco (E7)	750
Navajo (F3)	100
Nelson (B3)	121
Nogales⊙ (E7)	7,286
Nutrioso (F5)	100
Oatman (A3)	74
Olberg (D5)	300
Oracle (E6)	950
Oraibi (E3)	300
Page (D2)	2,960
Palo Verde (C5)	500
Pantano (E7)	40
Paradise (F7)	9
Paradise Valley (D5)	2,368
Parker (A4)	1,642
Parks (C3)	50
Patagonia (E7)	540
Paul Spur (F7)	300
Paulden (C4)	12
Payson (D4)	1,200
Peach Springs (B3)	500
Pearce (F7)	25
Peoria (C5)	2,593
Peridot (E5)	800
Phoenix⊙ (C5)	439,170
Phoenix (urb. area)	552,043
Picacho (D6)	800
Pima (F6)	806
Pine (D4)	175
Pinedale (E4)	74
Pinetop (F4)	300
Plantsite (F5)	1,552
Polacca (E3)	500
Pomerene (E6)	300
Portal (F7)	50
Poston (A4)	320
Prescott⊙ (C4)	12,861
Quartzsite (A5)	266
Queen Creek (D5)	700
Randolph (D6)	290
Ray (E5)	1,468
Red Rock (D6)	80

Redington (E6)	35
Rillito (D6)	200
Roll (A6)	350
Roosevelt (D5)	100
Sacaton (D5)	750
Safford⊙ (F6)	4,648
Sahuarita (E7)	600
Saint David (E7)	850
Saint Johns⊙ (F4)	1,310
Saint Michaels (F3)	215
Salome (B5)	200
San Carlos (E5)	950
San Luis (A6)	30
San Manuel (E6)	4,524
San Simon (F6)	175
Sanders (F3)	325
Sasabe (D7)	47
Scottsdale (D5)	10,026
Second Mesa (E3)	30
Sedona (D4)	350
Seligman (B3)	850
Sells (D7)	850
Sentinel (B6)	35
Shonto (E2)	20
Show Low (F4)	1,625
Shungopavi (Shungopovi) (E3)	802
Sierra Vista (E7)	3,121
Silver Bell (D6)	350
Skull Valley (C4)	250
Snowflake (E4)	982
Solomon (F6)	600
Sombrero Butte (E6)	1
Somerton (A6)	1,613
Sonoita (E7)	100
Sonora (D5)	1,244
South Tucson (D6)	7,004
Springerville (F4)	719
Stanfield (C6)	150
Steamboat (F3)	100
Sun City (C5)	8,000
Supai (C2)	200
Superior (D5)	4,875
Surprise (C5)	1,574
Tacna (B6)	595
Tanque Verde (E6)	1,053
Taylor (E4)	500

ARIZONA FACTS

AREA	113,909 sq. mi.
POPULATION	1,608,000
CAPITAL	Phoenix
LARGEST CITY	Phoenix 439,170
HIGHEST POINT	Humphreys Pk. 12,670 ft.
SETTLED IN	1580
ADMITTED TO UNION	February 14, 1912
POPULAR NAME	Grand Canyon State
STATE FLOWER	Saguaro Cactus Blossom
STATE BIRD	Cactus Wren

TOPOGRAPHY

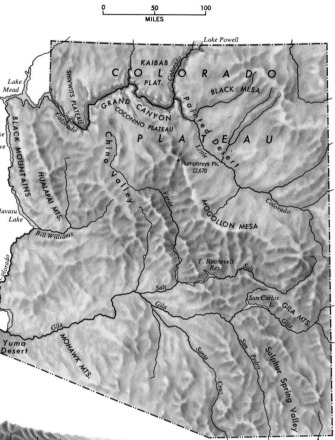

0   50   100
MILES

5,000 m. 16,404 ft. | 2,000 m. 6,562 ft. | 1,000 m. 3,281 ft. | 500 m. 1,640 ft. | 200 m. 656 ft. | 100 m. 328 ft. | Sea Level | Below

AGRICULTURE, INDUSTRY and RESOURCES

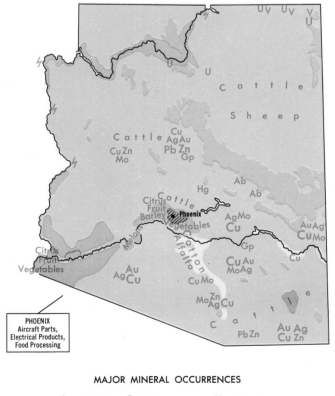

PHOENIX
Aircraft Parts,
Electrical Products,
Food Processing

MAJOR MINERAL OCCURRENCES

Ab	Asbestos	Gp	Gypsum	U	Uranium
Ag	Silver	Hg	Mercury	V	Vanadium
Au	Gold	Mo	Molybdenum	Zn	Zinc
Cu	Copper	Pb	Lead		

Tempe (D5)	24,897
Thatcher (F6)	1,581
Tolleson (C5)	3,886
Toltec (D6)	50
Tombstone (F7)	1,283
Tonalea (E2)	50
Tonopah (B5)	56
Tonto Basin (D5)	91
Topawa (D7)	342
Topock (A4)	125
Tortilla Flat (D5)	65
Tuba City (D2)	600
Tubac (E7)	125
Tucson⊙ (D6)	212,892
Tucson (urban area)	227,433
Tuweep (B2)	9

Vail (E6)	150
Valentine (B3)	127
Valley Farms (D6)	220
Vernon (F4)	150
Waddell (C5)	30
Wagoner (C4)	25
Walker (C4)	12
Wellton (A6)	800
Wenden (B5)	245
Whiteriver (E5)	950
Wickenburg (C5)	2,445
Wikieup (B4)	6
Willcox (F6)	2,441
Williams (C3)	3,559
Window Rock (F3)	1,800
Winkelman (E6)	1,123

Winona (D3)	100
Winslow (E3)	8,862
Wintersburg (B5)	50
Wittmann (C5)	300
Woodruff (E4)	116
Yarnell (C4)	500
Yava (C4)	20
Young (D4)	250
Youngtown (C5)	1,599
Yucca (C4)	40
Yuma⊙ (A6)	23,974

OTHER FEATURES

Chocolate (mts.)		A 5
Clear (creek)		D 4
Coconino (plateau)		C 3
Cocopah Indian Res.		A 6
Colorado (river)		A 6
Colorado River Ind. Res.		A 5
Coolidge (dam)		E 5
Copper (mts.)		B 6
Corn (creek)		E 3
Coronado Nat'l Mem.		E 7
Cottonwood (cliffs)		B 3
Cottonwood Wash (dry river)		E 4
Davis (dam)		A 3
Davis-Monthan A.F.B.		E 6
Defiance (plateau)		F 3
Detrital Wash (dry river)		A 3
Diablo (canyon)		D 4
Dinnebito Wash (dry river)		E 2
Dot Klish (canyon)		E 2
Dragoon (mts.)		F 7
Eagle (creek)		F 5
East Verde (river)		D 4
Echo (cliffs)		D 2
Elden (mts.)		D 3
Fort Apache Ind. Res.		E 5
Fort McDowell Ind. Res.		D 5
Fort Mohave Ind. Res.		A 4
Fossil (creek)		D 4
Four (peaks)		D 5
Galiuro (mts.)		E 6
Gila (mts.)		A 6
Gila (mts.)		F 5
Gila (river)		B 6
Gila Bend (mts.)		B 5
Gila Bend Ind. Res.		C 6
Gila River Ind. Res.		C 5
Glen Canyon (dam)		D 2
Gothic (mesa)		F 2
Government (mt.)		C 3
Graham (mt.)		F 6
Grand Canyon Nat'l Mon.		C 2
Grand Canyon Nat'l Park		C 2
Grand Wash (cliffs)		B 3
Grand Wash (dry river)		B 2
Green (peak)		F 4
Greens (res.)		D 6

Agassiz (peak)		D 3
Agua Fria (river)		C 5
Alamo (creek)		B 4
Aquarius (range)		B 4
Aravaipa (creek)		E 6
Aubrey (cliffs)		B 3
Baboquivari (mts.)		D 7
Baker (butte)		D 4
Bartlett (dam)		D 5
Bartlett (res.)		D 5
Big Horn (mts.)		B 5
Big Sandy (river)		B 4
Bill Williams (river)		B 4
Black (mts.)		A 3
Black (river)		E 5
Black (mesa)		E 2
Blue (river)		F 5
Bouse Wash (dry river)		A 4
Buckskin (mts.)		A 4
Burro (creek)		B 4
Canyon de Chelly Nat'l Mon.		F 2
Carrizo (creek)		E 4
Carrizo (mts.)		F 2
Casa Grande Nat'l Mon.		D 6
Castle Dome (mts.)		A 5
Cataract (creek)		C 3
Centennial Wash (dry river)		B 5
Cerbat (mts.)		A 3
Cherry (creek)		E 4
Chevelon (creek)		E 4
Chinle (creek)		F 2
Chinle (valley)		F 2
Chino (valley)		C 3
Chiricahua (mts.)		F 6
Chiricahua Nat'l Mon.		F 6

DOMINANT LAND USE

- Fruit, Truck and Mixed Farming
- Cotton and Alfalfa
- General Farming, Livestock, Special Crops
- Range Livestock
- Forests
- Nonagricultural Land

⚡ Water Power

▨ Major Industrial Areas

Arizona
(continued)

HIGHWAYS

Scale: 0 — 40 — 80 MILES

◉ County Seat.
‡ Name not on map.

Limited Access Highways ....
Major Highways ....
Other Important Roads ....
Interstate Route Numbers 95
Federal Route Numbers 9
State and Other Route Numbers ... 4

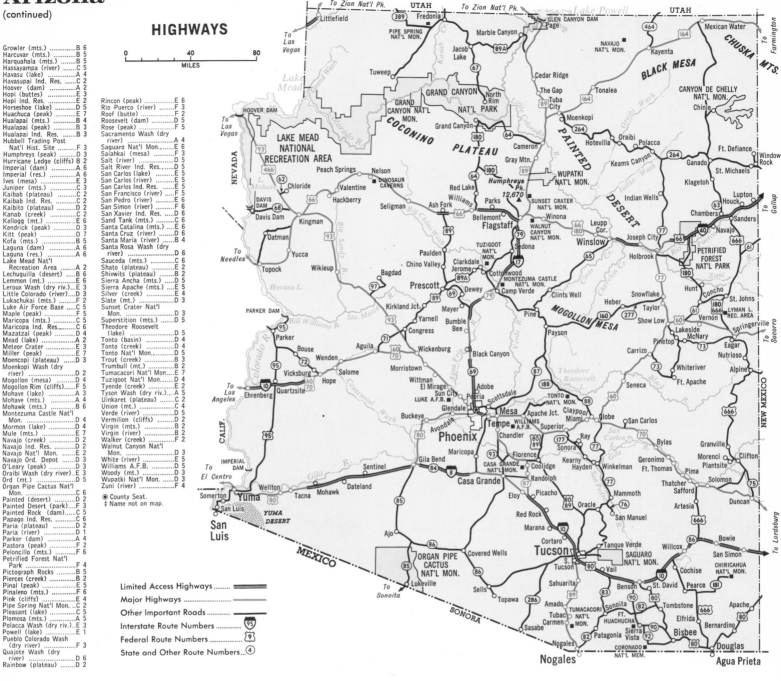

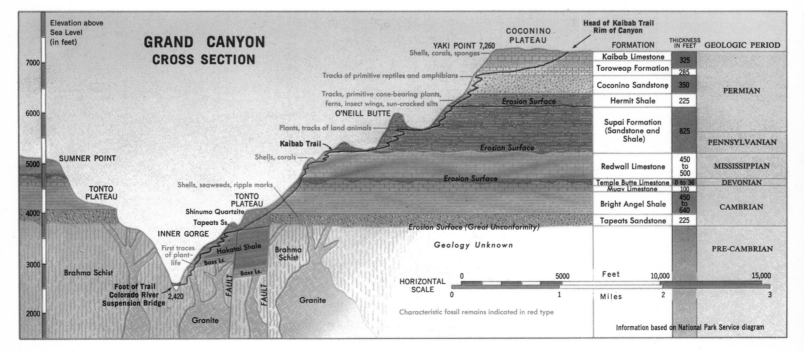

GRAND CANYON CROSS SECTION

FORMATION	THICKNESS IN FEET	GEOLOGIC PERIOD
Kaibab Limestone	325	
Toroweap Formation	285	PERMIAN
Coconino Sandstone	350	
Hermit Shale	225	
Supai Formation (Sandstone and Shale)	825	PENNSYLVANIAN
Redwall Limestone	450 to 500	MISSISSIPPIAN
Temple Butte Limestone	0 to 36	DEVONIAN
Muav Limestone	100	
Bright Angel Shale	450 to 640	CAMBRIAN
Tapeats Sandstone	225	
Geology Unknown		PRE-CAMBRIAN

Elevation above Sea Level (in feet)

YAKI POINT 7,260 — Shells, corals, sponges
Head of Kaibab Trail — Rim of Canyon
COCONINO PLATEAU

Tracks of primitive reptiles and amphibians
Tracks, primitive cone-bearing plants, ferns, insect wings, sun-cracked silts
O'NEILL BUTTE — Plants, tracks of land animals
Kaibab Trail
Shells, corals
SUMNER POINT
TONTO PLATEAU
Shells, seaweeds, ripple marks
Shinumo Quartzite
Tapeats Ss.
INNER GORGE
First traces of plant-life
Brahma Schist
Bass Ls.
Hakatai Shale
Brahma Schist
Foot of Trail — Colorado River Suspension Bridge — 2,420
FAULT
FAULT
Granite
Granite

Erosion Surface
Erosion Surface
Erosion Surface
Erosion Surface
Erosion Surface (Great Unconformity)

HORIZONTAL SCALE
0 — 5000 — Feet — 10,000 — 15,000
0 — 1 — Miles — 2 — 3

Characteristic fossil remains indicated in red type

Information based on National Park Service diagram

ARKANSAS

AREA	53,104 sq. mi.
POPULATION	1,960,000
CAPITAL	Little Rock
LARGEST CITY	Little Rock 107,813
HIGHEST POINT	Magazine Mtn. 2,823 ft.
SETTLED IN	1685
ADMITTED TO UNION	June 15, 1836
POPULAR NAMES	Land of Opportunity; Wonder State
STATE FLOWER	Apple Blossom
STATE BIRD	Mockingbird

COUNTIES

Arkansas (H5) 23,355
Ashley (G7) 24,220
Baxter (F1) 9,943
Benton (B1) 36,272
Boone (D1) 16,116
Bradley (F7) 14,029
Calhoun (E6) 5,991
Carroll (C1) 11,284
Chicot (H7) 18,990
Clark (D5) 20,950
Clay (K1) 21,258
Cleburne (F2) 9,059
Cleveland (F6) 6,944
Columbia (D7) 26,400
Conway (E3) 15,430
Craighead (J2) 47,303
Crawford (B2) 21,318
Crittenden (K3) 47,564
Cross (J3) 19,551
Dallas (E6) 10,522
Desha (H6) 20,770
Drew (G6) 15,213
Faulkner (E4) 24,303
Franklin (C2) 10,213
Fulton (G1) 6,657
Garland (D4) 46,697
Grant (F5) 8,294
Greene (J1) 25,198
Hempstead (C6) 19,661
Hot Spring (E5) 21,893
Howard (C5) 10,878
Independence (G2) 20,048
Izard (G1) 6,766
Jackson (H2) 22,843
Jefferson (G5) 81,373
Johnson (C2) 12,421
Lafayette (C7) 11,030
Lawrence (H1) 17,267
Lee (J4) 21,001
Lincoln (G6) 14,447
Little River (B6) 9,211
Logan (C3) 15,957
Lonoke (G4) 24,551
Madison (C1) 9,068
Marion (E1) 6,041
Miller (C7) 31,686
Mississippi (K2) 70,174
Monroe (H4) 17,327
Montgomery (C4) 5,370
Nevada (D6) 10,700
Newton (D2) 5,963
Ouachita (E6) 31,641
Perry (E4) 4,927
Phillips (J5) 43,997
Pike (C5) 7,864
Poinsett (J2) 30,834
Polk (B5) 11,981
Pope (D3) 21,177
Prairie (G4) 10,515
Pulaski (F4) 242,980
Randolph (H1) 12,520
Saint Francis (J3) 33,303
Saline (E4) 28,956
Scott (B4) 7,297
Searcy (E2) 8,124
Sebastian (B3) 66,685
Sevier (B6) 10,156
Sharp (G1) 6,319
Stone (F2) 6,294
Union (E7) 49,518
Van Buren (E2) 7,228
Washington (B2) 55,797
White (G3) 32,745
Woodruff (H3) 13,954
Yell (D3) 11,940

CITIES and TOWNS

Abbott (B3) 180
Adona (E3) 154
Agnos (G1) 140
Alabam (C1) 15
Alco (F2) 55
Alexander (F4) 177
Algoa (H2) 57
Alicia (H2) 236
Alix (C3) 200
Alleene (B6) 150
Alma (B3) 1,370
Almond (G2) 150
Almyra (H5) 240
Alpena (D1) 283
Alpine (D5) 85
Altheimer (G5) 979
Altus (C3) 392
Aly (D4) 105
Amagon (H2) 234
Amity (D5) 543
Antoine (D5) 163
Aplin (E4) 50
Appleton (E3) 200
Arden (B6) 100
Arkadelphia⦿ (D5) ... 8,069
Arkansas City⦿ (H6) ... 783
Arkansas Post (H5) 30
Arkinda (B6) 150
Armorel (L2) 500
Ash Flat (G1) 192
Ashdown⦿ (B6) 2,725
Athens (C5) 67
Atkins (E3) 1,391
Atlanta (D7) 40
Aubrey (J4) 560
Augusta⦿ (H3) 2,272
Aurora (C2) 100
Austin (G4) 210
Auvergne (H2) 116
Avoca (B1) 110
Bald Knob (G3) 1,705
Banks (F6) 233
Barber (B3) 36
Barfield (L2) 50
Barling (B3) 770
Barton (J4) 100
Bates (B4) 106
Batesville⦿ (G2) 6,207
Bauxite (F4) 800
Bay (J2) 627
Bayou Meto (H5) 300
Bearden (E6) 1,268
Beaver (C1) 24
Bee Branch (F3) 63
Beebe (G3) 1,697
Beirne (D6) 1,300
Bella Vista (B1) 50
Bellefonte (D1) 250
Belleville (D3) 273
Belton (C6) 100
Ben Lomond (B6) 157
Benton⦿ (E4) 10,399
Bentonville⦿ (B1) ... 3,649
Bergman (E1) 133
Berryville⦿ (C1) 1,999
Bestwater (B2) 180
Bethesda (G2) 432
Big Fork (B5) 50
Bigelow (E3) 231
Bigflat (F1) 217
Biggers (J1) 274
Bingen (C6) 175
Birdsong (K3) 100

AGRICULTURE, INDUSTRY and RESOURCES

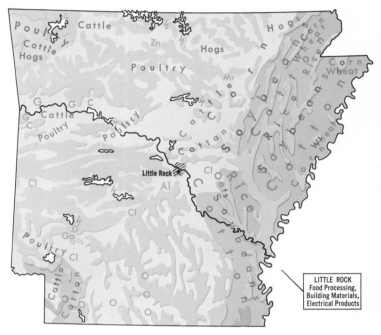

DOMINANT LAND USE

- Fruit and Mixed Farming
- Specialized Cotton
- Cotton, General Farming
- Rice, General Farming
- General Farming, Livestock, Truck Farming, Cotton
- Forests
- Swampland, Limited Agriculture

MAJOR MINERAL OCCURRENCES

Al	Bauxite	G	Natural Gas
C	Coal	Gp	Gypsum
Cl	Clay	Mr	Marble
D	Diamonds	O	Petroleum
		Zn	Zinc

⚡ Water Power   ▨ Major Industrial Areas

LITTLE ROCK
Food Processing,
Building Materials,
Electrical Products

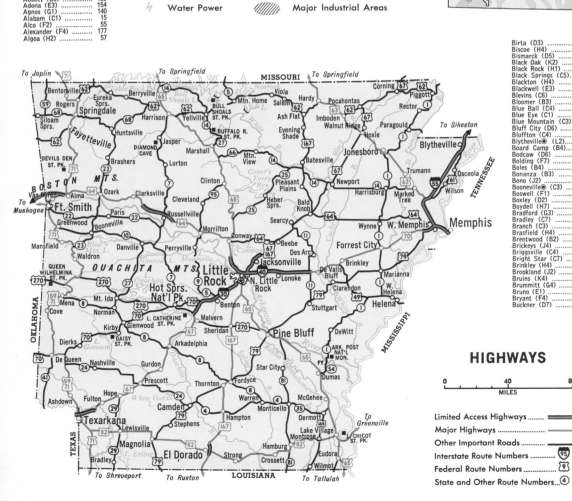

HIGHWAYS

0 ——— 40 ——— 80
MILES

Limited Access Highways	▬▬
Major Highways	▭▭
Other Important Roads	▬
Interstate Route Numbers	95
Federal Route Numbers	9
State and Other Route Numbers	4

Birta (D3) 52
Biscoe (H4) 350
Bismarck (D5) 118
Black Oak (K2) 220
Black Rock (H1) 554
Black Springs (C5) 90
Blackton (H4) 300
Blackwell (E3) 75
Blevins (C6) 198
Bloomer (B3) 100
Blue Ball (C4) 94
Blue Eye (C1) 69
Blue Mountain (C3) 94
Bluff City (D6) 300
Bluffton (C4) 280
Blytheville⦿ (L2) ... 20,797
Board Camp (B4) 75
Bodcaw (D6) 200
Boding (F7) 75
Boles (B4) 178
Bonanza (B3) 247
Bono (J2) 339
Booneville⦿ (C3) ... 2,690
Boswell (F1) 66
Boxley (D2) 44
Boydell (H7) 114
Bradford (G3) 779
Bradley (C7) 712
Branch (C3) 258
Brasfield (H4) 100
Brentwood (B2) 75
Brickeys (J4) 62
Briggsville (C4) 250
Bright Star (C7) 42
Brinkley (H4) 4,636
Brookland (J2) 301
Bruins (K4) 300
Brummitt (G4) 50
Bruno (E1) 50
Bryant (F4) 737
Buckner (D7) 289
Buckville (D4) 225
Buena Vista (D7) 280
Buffalo (E1) 30
Bull Shoals (E1) 268
Burdette (L2) 115
Butlerville (G4) 50
Butterfield (E5) 160
Cabot (F4) 1,321
Caddo Gap (C5) 230
Calamine (H1) 18
Cale (C6) 125
Caldwell (J3) 256
Calico Rock (F1) 773
Calion (E7) 544
Calmer (F6) 50
Camden⦿ (E6) 15,823
Cammack Village (E4) . 1,355
Canehill (B2) 50
Canfield (C7) 400
Caraway (K2) 821
Carlisle (G4) 1,514
Carryville (K1) 85
Carson (K2) 150
Carthage (E5) 528
Casa (D3) 184
Cash (J2) 141
Cass (C2) 75
Casscoe (H4) 175
Cato (F4) 100
Cauthron (B4) 50
Cave City (G2) 540
Cave Springs (B1) 281
Cedar Creek (C4) 75
Cedarville (B2) 52
Center Hill (J1) 306
Center Hill (G3) 150
Center Point (C5) 50
Center Ridge (E3) 170
Centerton (B1) 177
Centerville (D3) 185
Central City (B3) 125
Cerrogordo (B6) 50
Chapel Hill (B5) 75
Charleston⦿ (B3) ... 1,036
Chatfield (K3) 275
Cherokee City (A1) 30
Cherry Hill (B4) 200
Cherry Valley (J3) 455
Chester (B2) 99
Chickalah (D3) 60
Chicot (H7) 100
Chidester (D6) 348
Chismville (C3) 50
Choctaw (F2) 150
Chula (C4) 28
Cincinnati (B1) 50
Clarendon⦿ (H4) ... 2,293
Clarkedale (K3) 250
Clarksville⦿ (D3) ... 3,919
Cleveland (E3) 50
Clifty (C1) 50
Clinton⦿ (F2) 744
Clover Bend (H2) 100
Coal Hill (C3) 704
College City (J1) 358
College Heights (G6) .. 950
Collins (G6) 107
Colt (J3) 394
Columbus (C6) 300
Combs (C2) 200
Conway⦿ (F3) 9,791
Cord (H2) 75
Cornerstone (G5) 130
Cornerville (G6) 100
Corning⦿ (J1) 2,192
Cotter (E1) 683
Cotton Plant (H3) ... 1,704
Cove (B5) 320
Coy (G4) 206
Crawfordsville (K3) ... 744
Crocketts Bluff (H5) ... 95
Crossett (F7) 5,370
Crumrod (H5) 350
Crystal Springs (D5) ... 68
Curtis (D6) 600
Cushman (G2) 241
Cypert (J5) 55
Daisy (C5) 86
Dalark (E5) 123
Dalton (H1) 50
Damascus (F3) 500
Danville⦿ (D3) 955
Dardanelle⦿ (D3) .. 2,098
Datto (J1) 167
De Queen⦿ (B5) ... 2,859
De Valls Bluff⦿ (H4) .. 654
De Witt⦿ (H5) 3,019
Decatur (A1) 415
Deckerville (K3) 27
Deer (D2) 150
Delaney (C2) 200
Delaplaine (J1) 186
Delaware (D3) 450
Delight (C5) 446
Dell (K2) 383
Denning (C3) 227
Denton (D1) 40
Dermott (H7) 3,665
Des Arc⦿ (G4) 1,482
Diaz (H2) 348
Dierks (B5) 1,276
Dillen (D2) 21
Doddridge (C7) 700
Donaldson (E5) 400
Dover (D3) 525
Drasco (G2) 110
Driggs (C3) 115
Dryden (C2) 18
Dublin (D3) 50
Dumas (G6) 3,540
Durham (C2) 76
Dutch Mills (B2) 150
Dutton (C2) 35
Dyer (B3) 450
Dyess (K2) 409
Eagle Mills (E6) 245
Earle (K3) 2,391
Edgemont (F2) 75
Edmondson (K3) 288
El Dorado⦿ (E7) ... 25,292
El Paso (F3) 200
Elaine (J5) 898
Elba (E2) 52
Elizabeth (F1) 75
Elkins (C1) 332

(continued on following page)

Arkansas
(continued)

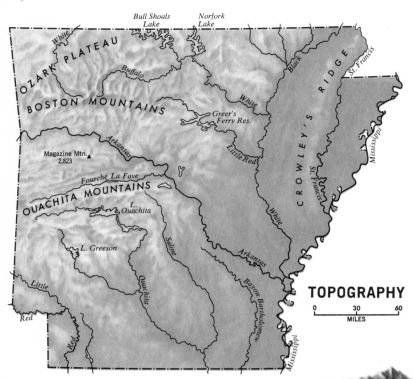

TOPOGRAPHY

0   30   60 MILES

Below Sea Level | 100 m. 328 ft. | 200 m. 656 ft. | 500 m. 1,640 ft. | 1,000 m. 3,281 ft. | 2,000 m. 6,562 ft. | 5,000 m. 16,404 ft.

Roland (E4) 525	Schaal (C6) 150	Strickler (B2) 50
Rolla (E5) 55	Scotland (E2) 140	Strong (F7) 741
Romance (F3) 50	Scott (F4) 240	Stuttgart● (H4) 9,661
Rondo (J4) 219	Scottsville (D3) 150	Subiaco (C3) 290
Rosboro (C5) 50	Scranton (C3) 229	Success (J1) 50
Rose Bud (F3) 150	Searcy● (G3) 7,272	Sugar Grove (C3) 225
Roseland (K2) 68	Sedgwick (J2) 206	Sugar Loaf (E1) 49
Rosie (G2) 300	Selma (G6) 350	Sulphur City (B2) 35
Rosston (D6) 250	Seyppel (K4) 100	Sulphur Rock (H2) 225
Round Pond (J3) 200	Sheridan● (F5) 1,938	Sulphur Springs (B1) 460
Rover (D4) 180	Sherrill (G5) 241	Snyder (E7) 30
Rowell (F6) 50	Sherwood (F4) 1,222	Solgohachia (E3) 135
Rudy (B2) 113	Shiloh (E7) 6	Soudan (J4) 25
Russell (G3) 203	Shirley (F2) 197	Sparkman (E6) 787
Russellville● (D3) 8,921	Shoffner (H2)	Spotville (D7) 62
Rye (F6) 220	Sidney (G1) 97	Spring Hill (C6) 150
Saddle (G1) 47	Sidon (G3) 70	Springdale (B1) 10,076
Sage (G1) 105	Siloam Springs (B1) 3,953	Springfield (E3) 160
Saint Charles (H5) 255	Sims (C4) 90	Springtown (B1) 92
Saint Francis (K1) 224	Simsboro (K3) 175	Stamps (D7) 2,591
Saint James (F2) 66	Sitka (H1) 27	Star City● (G6) 2,511
Saint Joe (E1)	Smackover (E7) 2,434	State Sanatorium (C3) 1,700
Saint Paul (C2) 118	Smale (H4) 26	Stephens (E7) 1,275
Salado (G1) 450	Smithville (H1) 75	Steprock (G3) 124
Salem● (G1) 713	Snow Hill (E7) 100	Steve (D4) 30
Salus (D2) 75	Snow Lake (H5) 119	Stonewall (J1) 164
Saratoga (C6) 62	Snowball (E2) 108	Strawberry (H2) 200

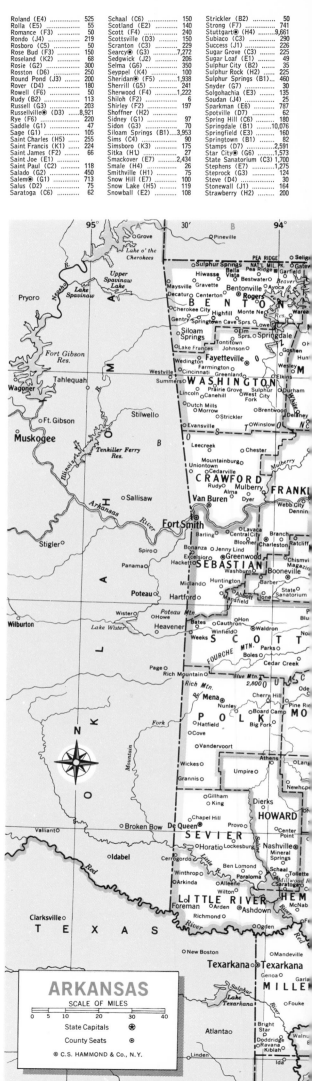

ARKANSAS

SCALE OF MILES

0   5   10   20   30   40

State Capitals ⊛
County Seats ●

© C.S. HAMMOND & Co., N.Y.

Elliott (E7) 100	Hampton● (F6) 1,011	Kingsland (F6) 249	McRae (G3) 428	Oxford (G1) 191
Elm Springs (B1) 238	Hardy● (H1) 555	Kingston (C1) 210	Melbourne● (G1) 571	Ozan (C6) 95
Emerson (D7) 350	Harmony (D2) 31	Kirby (C5) 300	Mellwood (H5) 400	Ozark● (C3) 1,965
Emmet (D6) 474	Harrell (F7) 267	Knobel (J1) 339	Mena● (B4) 4,388	Ozone (D2) 100
England (G4) 2,861	Harrisburg● (J2) 1,481	Knoxville (D3) 186	Menifee (E3) 300	Palarm (F4) 25
Enola (F3) 250	Harrison● (D1) 6,580	La Grange (J4) 500	Midland (B3) 261	Palatka (J1) 40
Ethel (H5) 500	Hartford (B3) 531	Lacey (G7) 225	Mineral Springs (C6) 616	Palestine (H4) 532
Etowah (K2) 200	Hartman (C3) 299	Ladelle (G7) 23	Minturn (H2) 61	Pangburn (G3) 489
Euclid Heights (D4) 2,030	Haskell (E4) 215	Lafe (J1) 258	Mist (G7) 40	Paragould● (J2) 9,947
Eudora (H7) 3,598	Hasty (D1) 25	Lake City● (K2) 850	Mitchell (G7) 44	Paraloma (B6) 94
Eureka Springs● (C1) 1,437	Hatfield (B5) 337	Lake Frances (B1) 22	Mitchellville (H6) 527	Paris● (C3) 3,007
Evansville (B2) 150	Hattieville (E3) 110	Lake Village (H7) 2,998	Moark (J1) 200	Parkdale (G7) 448
Evening Shade● (G1) 232	Havana (D3) 277	Lakeview (E1) 103	Monette (K2) 981	Parkin (J3) 1,489
Everton (E1) 118	Haynes (J4) 514	Lamar (D3) 514	Monroe (H4) 265	Parks (B4) 144
Excelsior (B3) 50	Hazen (G4) 1,456	Lambert (D5) 250	Monte Ne (B1) 175	Paron (E4) 100
Fair Oaks (J3) 250	Heber Springs● (G2) 2,265	Laneburg (D6) 500	Monticello● (G6) 4,412	Patmos (C7) 73
Fallsville (D2) 25	Hector (E3) 250	Langley (C5) 56	Montrose (H7) 399	Patterson (H3) 324
Fargo (H4) 269	Helena● (J4) 11,500	Lavaca (B3) 392	Moorefield (H2) 185	Pea Ridge (B1) 380
Farmington (B1) 216	Hensley (F4) 500	Lawson (F7) 300	Moreland (E3) 73	Peach Orchard (J1) 348
Fayetteville● (B1) 20,274	Hermitage (F7) 379	Leachville (K2) 1,507	Moro (H4) 182	Pearcy (D4) 100
Felsenthal (F7) 221	Heth (K3) 56	Lead Hill (E1) 102	Morobay (F7) 77	Pearson (F3) 80
Felton (J4) 75	Hickman (L2) 100	Leecreek (B2) 41	Morganton (F3) 100	Pecan Point (L3) 280
Fisher (J2) 303	Hickory Plains (G3) 225	Leola (E5) 321	Morrilton● (E3) 5,997	Penrose (H3) 35
Flippin (E1) 433	Hickory Ridge (J3) 364	Lepanto (K2) 1,585	Morriston (G1) 81	Perla (E5) 279
Floral (G3) 150	Higden (F2) 40	Leslie (E2) 506	Morrow (B2) 200	Perry (B3) 224
Florence (G6) 200	Higginson (G3) 183	Letona (G3) 141	Moscow (G5) 375	Perryton (C6) 71
Fordyce● (F6) 3,890	Highfill (B1) 92	Lewisville● (C7) 1,373	Mount Holly (E7) 300	Perryville● (E3) 719
Foreman (B6) 1,001	Highland (C5) 50	Lexa (J4) 500	Mount Ida● (C4) 564	Pettigrew (C2) 121
Formosa (E3) 150	Hillemann (H3) 40	Lexington (F2) 100	Mount Judea (D2) 250	Pfeiffer (G2) 76
Forrest City● (J3) 10,544	Hindsville (C1) 63	Limestone (D2) 20	Mount Pleasant (G2) 175	Pickens (H6) 191
Fort Smith (B3) 52,991	Hiwasse (B1) 175	Lincoln (B2) 820	Mount Sherman (D1) 130	Piggott● (K1) 2,776
Fort Smith (urban area) 61,640	Hollis (D4) 263	Lisbon (E7) 30	Mount Vernon (F3) 200	Pike (C5) 70
Forum (C7) 65	Holly Grove (H4) 672	LITTLE ROCK● (F4) 107,813	Mountain Home● (F1) 2,105	Pindall (E1) 150
Fouke (C7) 394	Holly Springs (E6) 77	Little Rock-North	Mountain Pine (D4) 1,279	Pine Bluff● (F5) 44,037
Fountain Hill (G7) 230	Hollywood (D5) 100	Little Rock (urban area) 185,017	Mountain Valley (D4) 160	Pine City (H4) 75
Fourche (E4) 48	Hon (B4) 200	Lockesburg (B6) 511	Mountain View● (F2) 983	Pine Grove (E6) 50
Fox (F2) 200	Hope● (C6) 8,399	Locust Bayou (E6) 150	Mountainburg (B2) 402	Pine Ridge (C4) 60
Franklin (G1) 75	Hopper (C5) 200	London (D3) 282	Mulberry (B2) 934	Piney (D3) 85
Fredonia (Biscoe) (H4) 350	Hopper (H4) 70	Lonoke● (G4) 2,359	Murfreesboro● (C5) 1,096	Pitts (J2) 77
Friendship (E5) 162	Horatio (B6) 722	Lonsdale (E4) 95	Nashville● (C6) 3,579	Plainfield (D7) 100
Fulton (C6) 309	Hot Springs National Park● (D4) 28,337	Louann (E7) 261	Nathan (C5) 150	Plainview (D4) 548
Galloway (F4) 350	Houston (E3) 206	Lowell (B1) 277	Natural Steps (E4) 100	Pleasant Plains (G2) 112
Garfield (C1) 48	Howell (H3) 98	Luna (H7) 20	Nelsonville (H1) 37	Plumerville (E3) 586
Garland (C7) 377	Hoxie (H1) 1,886	Lundell (H5) 175	New Blaine (D3) 100	Pocahontas● (H1) 3,665
Garner (G3) 150	Huffman (L2) 100	Lunsford (K2) 50	New Edinburg (F6) 300	Point Cedar (D5) 63
Gasville (F1) 233	Hulbert (K3) 500	Lurton (D2) 176	New London (F7) 50	Pollard (K1) 170
Gateway (B1) 63	Humnoke (G4) 319	Luxora (K2) 1,236	New Rocky Comfort	Ponca (D1) 62
Genoa (C7) 100	Humphrey (G5) 649	Lynn (H2) 263	(Foreman) (B6) 1,001	Poplar Grove (J4) 169
Gentry (A1) 686	Hunter (H3) 202	Mabelvale (F4) 350	New Spadra (C2) 101	Portia (H1) 333
Georgetown (G2) 250	Huntington (B3) 560	Macedonia (D7) 100	Newark (H2) 728	Portland (G7) 566
Gilbert (E2) 52	Huntsville● (C1) 1,050	Macks (H2) 96	Newburg (G1) 41	Postelle (J4) 42
Gillett (H5) 674	Huttig (F7) 936	Madison (J4) 750	Newhope (C5) 126	Pottsville (D3) 250
Gillham (B5) 177	Imboden (H1) 400	Magazine (D3) 463	Newport● (H2) 7,007	Poughkeepsie (H1) 190
Gilmore (K3) 438	Ingalls (F7) 110	Magness (H2) 140	Nimmons (K1) 154	Powhatan (H1) 136
Glenwood (C5) 840	Ione (B3) 78	Magnet (E5) 220	Nimrod (D4) 100	Poyen (E5) 312
Goldman (G5) 30	Ivan (F6) 100	Magnolia● (D7) 10,651	Noble Lake (G5) 100	Prague (E5) 220
Goodwin (J4) 50	Ivy (E5) 150	Malvern● (E5) 9,566	Nola (C4) 130	Prairie Grove (B2) 1,056
Goshen (C1) 75	Jacksonport (H2) 271	Mammoth Spring (G1) 825	Norfork (F1) 283	Prairie View (C3) 165
Gould (G6) 1,210	Jacksonville (F4) 14,488	Mandalay (K2) 200	Norman (C5) 482	Prattsville (F5) 336
Grady (G5) 622	Jamestown (G2) 61	Mandeville (C7) 500	Norphlet (E7) 459	Prescott● (D6) 3,533
Grand Glaise (G2) 200	Jasper● (D1) 273	Manila (K2) 1,753	North Little Rk. (F4) 58,032	Princeton (E6) 57
Grand Lake (H7)	Jefferson (F5) 100	Manning (E5) 225	North Little Rock-	Proctor (K3) 500
Grandview (C1) 40	Jennie (H7) 273	Mansfield (B3) 881	Little Rock	Provo (B5) 61
Grannis (B5) 185	Jenny Lind (B3) 513	Marble (C1) 100	(urban area) 185,017	Pyatt (E1) 144
Grapevine (F5) 309	Jericho (K3) 150	Marcella (G2) 152	Norvell (K3) 362	Quitman (F3) 305
Gravelly (C4) 150	Jerome (G7) 76	Marche (F4) 881	Nunley (B4) 50	Ratcliff (C3) 147
Gravette (B1) 855	Jersey (F7) 115	Marianna● (J4) 5,134	Oakgrove (C1) 151	Ratio (J5) 150
Grays (H3) 25	Jerusalem (E3) 200	Marion● (K3) 881	Oakhaven (C6) 87	Ravana (C7) 50
Graysonia (D5)	Jessieville (D4) 75	Marked Tree (K2) 3,216	Oden (C4) 90	Ravenden (H1) 231
Green Forest (D1) 1,038	Johnson (B1) 221	Marmaduke (K1) 657	Ogden (B6) 282	Ravenden Springs (H1) 126
Greenbrier (F3) 401	Johnsville (F7) 35	Marshall● (E2) 1,095	Ogemaw (E7) 200	Reader (D6) 229
Greenland (B1) 127	Joiner (K2) 748	Martinville (F3) 137	Oil Trough (G2) 237	Readland (H7) 75
Greenway (K1) 179	Jones Mills (E5) 600	Marvell (J4) 1,690	O'Kean (J1) 137	Rector (K1) 1,757
Greenwood● (B3) 1,558	Jonesboro● (J2) 21,418	Maumee (E1)	Okolona (D5) 344	Redfield (F5) 242
Gregory (H3) 515	Judsonia (G3) 977	Mayflower (F4) 355	Ola (D3) 805	Redstar (C2) 50
Griffithville (G3) 172	Junction City (E7) 749	Maynard (J1) 201	Olvey (E1) 100	Reed (H6) 357
Grubbs (H2) 360		Maysville (A1) 100	Olyphant (H2) 75	Reydell (G5) 70
Guion (G2) 222		McCaskill (C6) 62	Omaha (D1) 195	Reyno (J1) 195
Gum Springs (D5) 350		McClelland (H3) 80	Oneida (J5) 250	Rich Mountain (B4) 57
Gurdon (D6) 2,166		McCrory (H3) 1,053	Onyx (D4) 60	Richmond (B6) 100
Guy (F3) 66		McDougal (K1) 200	Optimus (F1) 49	Rison● (F6) 889
Hackett (B3) 328		McGehee (H6) 4,448	Osage (D1) 30	Rivervale (K2) 215
Hagarville (D2) 195		McKamie (C7) 45	Osceola● (K2) 6,189	Rockport (E5) 162
Halley (H6) 213		McNab (C6) 142	Otwell (J2) 100	Roe (H4) 300
Hamburg● (G7) 2,904		McNeil (D7) 746	Ouachita (E6) 40	Rogers (B1) 5,700
			Owensville (E4) 100	Rohwer (H6) 86

Summers (A2)	110	Tulip (E5)	105	Wabash (J5)	250	Wesson (E7)	260	Winthrop (B6)	225	Blue Mountain (lake)	C 3
Summit (E1)	239	Tulot (K2)	350	Wabbaseka (G5)	432	West Crossett (F7)	255	Wirth (H1)	35	Blytheville A.F.B.	L 2
Sumpter (F7)	40	Tupelo (H3)	201	Walcott (J1)	80	West End (F5)	2,208	Wiseman (G1)	275	Boston (mts.)	E 2
Sutton (D6)	80	Turner (H5)	200	Waldenburg (J2)	113	West Fork (B2)	350	Witter (C2)	50	Buffalo (river)	E 2
Swan Lake (G5)	100	Turrell (K3)	794	Waldo (D7)	1,722	West Helena (J4)	8,385	Witts Springs (E2)	34	Bull Shoals (lake)	E 1
Sweet Home (F4)	300	Tyro (G6)	15	Waldron® (B4)	1,619	West Memphis (K3)	19,374	Wiville (H3)	50	Cache (river)	H 3
Swifton (H2)	601	Tyronza (K3)	601	Walnut Hill (D7)	75	West Point (G3)	97	Wolf Bayou (G2)	146	Caddo (river)	D 5
Tamo (G5)	150	Ulm (H4)	140	Walnut Ridge® (J1)	3,547	West Ridge (K2)	178	Woodberry (E6)	44	Cadron (creek)	F 3
Taylor (D7)	734	Umpire (C4)	41	Waltreak (C4)	41	Western Grove (D1)	148	Woodson (F4)	500	Catherine (lake)	C 5
Texarkana® (C7)	19,788	Union (G1)	50	Ward (F3)	470	Wheatley (H4)	443	Wooster (F3)	161	Chinkapin Knob (mt.)	E 2
Thornton (F6)	658	Unionhill (H2)	32	Warm Springs (H1)	80	White (G7)	88	Worden (H3)	60	Conway (lake)	F 3
Three Creeks (E7)	100	Uniontown (B2)	200	Warren® (F6)	6,752	White Hall (F5)	1,257	Wrightsville (F4)	400	Crowleys Ridge (mt.)	J 2
Tichnor (H5)	65	Urbana (E7)	600	Washburn (B3)	175	Whitehall (J3)	200	Wynne® (J3)	4,922	Current (river)	H 1
Tillar® (H6)	232	Urbanette (D1)	50	Washington (C6)	321	Wideman (G1)	65	Yellville® (E1)	636	Dardanelle (res.)	D 3
Tilton (J3)	25	Vaden (E6)		Washita (D4)	90	Wickes (B5)	368	Yorktown (G5)	100	De View (river)	H 3
Timbo (F2)	130	Valley Springs (D1)	234	Ward (F3)	470	Widener (J3)	203	Zent (H4)	30	Des Arc (bayou)	G 3
Tinsman (F6)	110	Van Buren® (B3)	6,787	Washington (C6)		Wild Cherry (F1)	70	Zinc (E1)	68	Dutch (creek)	C 4
Tipperary (J1)	50	Vandervoort (B5)	144	Waterloo (D6)	200	Williford (H1)	195	Zion (G1)	125	Erling (lake)	C 7
Tokio (C5)	50	Vanndale (J3)	50	Watson (H6)	312	Willow (E5)	150			Fourche (river)	C 4
Tollville (G4)	65	Vick (F7)	35	Wattensaw (G4)	150	Wilmar (G6)	718	**OTHER FEATURES**		Fourche la Fave (river)	D 4
Toltec (F4)	120	Victoria (K2)	205	Waveland (C3)	110	Wilmot (G7)	732			Greer's Ferry (res.)	F 2
Tomtitown (A2)	209	Village (D7)	150	Webb City (C3)	100	Wilson (K2)	1,191	Arkansas (river)	G 5	Greeson (lake)	C 5
Traskwood (E5)	205	Vilonia (F3)	234	Wedington (B1)	303	Wilton (B6)	329	Bartholomew (bayou)	G 7	Hamilton (lake)	D 5
Trumann (J2)	4,511	Vimy Ridge (F4)	400	Weiner (J2)	669	Winchester (G6)	185	Bayou Bodcau (res.)	C 7	Illinois (bayou)	D 3
Tucker (G5)	350	Vincent (K3)	511	Weldon (H3)	150	Winfield (B4)	150	Beaver (res.)	C 1	L'Anguille (river)	J 3
Tuckerman (H2)	1,539	Viola (G1)	196	Weona (J2)	500	Winslow (B2)	183	Big Maumelle (lake)	E 4	Lagrue (bayou)	H 5
		Violet Hill (G1)	75	Wesley (C1)	100			Black (river)	H 2		

Little (river)	B 6	Peckerwood (lake)	H 4
Little Missouri (river)	D 6	Petit Jean (mt.)	C 3
Little Red (river)	G 3	Poteau (mt.)	B 4
Little Rock A.F.B.	F 4	Red (river)	C 6
Magazine (mt.)	C 3	Reeves Knob (mt.)	E 2
Meto (bayou)	H 5	Rich (mt.)	B 4
Millwood (res.)	C 6	Saint Francis (river)	J 4
Mississippi (river)	L 2	Saline (river)	B 6
Moro (creek)	F 7	Saline (river)	F 5
Mulberry (river)	C 3	Spring (river)	H 1
Nebo (mt.)	D 3	Sulphur (river)	B 7
Nimrod (lake)	D 4	Table Rock (lake)	D 1
Norfork (lake)	F 1	Tyronza (river)	K 2
Ouachita (mts.)	C 4	Walker (mt.)	E 2
Ouachita (mts.)	C 4	Wattensaw (bayou)	G 4
Ouachita (river)	E 7	White (river)	F 1
Ozark (plateau)	C 1	Winona (lake)	E 4
Pea Ridge Nat'l Mil.			
Park	B 1	® County Seat.	

CALIFORNIA

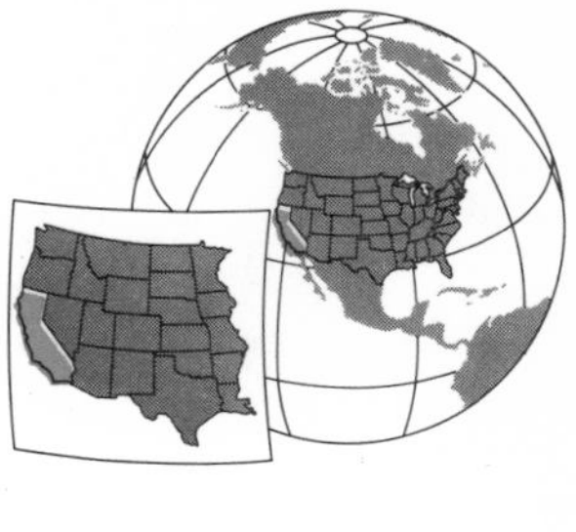

AREA	158,693 sq. mi.
POPULATION	18,602,000
CAPITAL	Sacramento
LARGEST CITY	Los Angeles 2,479,015
HIGHEST POINT	Mt. Whitney 14,495 ft.
SETTLED IN	1769
ADMITTED TO UNION	September 9, 1850
POPULAR NAME	Golden State
STATE FLOWER	Golden Poppy
STATE BIRD	California Valley Quail

COUNTIES

Alameda (D6) 908,209
Alpine (F5) 397
Amador (E5) 9,990
Butte (D4) 82,030
Calaveras (E5) 10,289
Colusa (C4) 12,075
Contra Costa (D6) 409,030
Del Norte (B2) 17,771
El Dorado (E5) 29,390
Fresno (F6) 365,945
Glenn (C4) 17,245
Humboldt (B3) 104,892
Imperial (K10) 72,105
Inyo (H7) 11,684
Kern (G8) 291,984
Kings (F8) 49,954
Lake (C4) 13,786
Lassen (E3) 13,597
Los Angeles (F9) 6,038,771
Madera (F6) 40,468
Marin (C5) 146,820
Mariposa (F6) 5,064
Mendocino (B4) 51,059
Merced (E6) 90,446
Modoc (E2) 8,308
Mono (F6) 2,213
Monterey (D7) 198,351
Napa (C5) 65,890
Nevada (E4) 20,911
Orange (F9) 703,925
Placer (E4) 56,998
Plumas (E4) 11,620
Riverside (J10) 306,191
Sacramento (D5) 502,778
San Benito (D7) 15,396
San Bernardino (J9) 503,591
San Diego (J11) 1,033,011
San Francisco (J2) 740,316
San Joaquin (E6) 249,989
San Luis Obispo (E8) 81,044
San Mateo (C6) 444,387
Santa Barbara (E9) 168,962
Santa Clara (D6) 642,315
Santa Cruz (C6) 84,219
Shasta (C3) 59,468
Sierra (E4) 2,247
Siskiyou (C2) 32,885
Solano (D5) 134,597
Sonoma (C5) 147,375
Stanislaus (D6) 157,294
Sutter (D4) 33,380
Tehama (C3) 25,305
Trinity (B3) 9,706
Tulare (G7) 168,403
Tuolumne (E5) 14,404
Ventura (F9) 199,138
Yolo (D5) 65,727
Yuba (D4) 33,859

CITIES and TOWNS

Adelanto (H9) 6,257
Alameda (J2) 63,855
Alamo (K2) 1,791
Albany (J2) 14,804
Alhambra (C10) 54,807
Alisal (D7) 16,473
Alpine (J11) 1,044
Alta Loma (E10) 1,821
Altadena (C10) 40,568
Alturas◉ (E2) 2,819
Alum Rock (L3) 18,942
Alviso (K3) 1,174
Anaheim (D10) 104,184
Anderson (C3) 4,492
Angels Camp (E5) 1,121
Angwin (C5) 995
Antioch (L1) 17,305
Apple Valley (H9) 5,836
Aptos (K4) 2,000
Arcadia (D10) 41,005
Arcata (A3) 5,235
Arlington (E11) 7,000
Armona (F7) 1,302
Arroyo Grande (E8) 3,291
Artesia (C11) 9,993
Arvin (G8) 5,310
Atascadero (E8) 5,983
Atherton (K3) 7,717
Atwater (E6) 7,318
Auburn◉ (C8) 5,586
Avalon (G10) 1,536
Avenal (E8) 3,147
Azusa (D10) 20,497
Bakersfield◉ (G8) 56,848
Bakersfield (urban area) 141,763
Baldwin Park (D10) 33,951
Banning (J10) 10,250
Barstow (H9) 11,644
Bayshore (J2) 900
Bayside (B3) 900
Beaumont (J10) 4,288
Bell (C11) 19,450
Bellflower (C11) 45,909
Belmont (J3) 15,996
Belvedere (H2) 2,148
Ben Lomond (K4) 1,814
Benicia (K1) 6,070
Berkeley (J2) 111,268
Beverly Hills (C10) 30,817
Big Bear City (J9) 588
Big Bear Lake (J9) 1,562
Big Pine (G6) 800
Biggs (D4) 831
Biola (E7) 651
Bishop (G6) 2,875
Black Point (J1) 644
Bloomington (E10) 9,995
Blue Lake (A3) 1,234
Bly (E10) 1,554
Blythe (L10) 6,023
Boonville (B5) 1,113
Boron (H8) 800
Boulder Creek (J4) 1,306
Bradbury (D10) 618
Brawley (K11) 12,703
Brea (D11) 8,487
Brentwood (L2) 2,186
Bridgeport◉ (F5) 250
Brisbane (J2) 4,500
Broderick (B8) 1,721
Bryte (B8) 3,000
Buena Park (D11) 46,401
Burbank (C10) 90,155
Burlingame (J3) 24,036
Burney (D3) 1,294
Buttonwillow (F8) 985
Byron (L2) 850
Calexico (K11) 7,992
California City (H8) 850
Calipatria (K10) 2,548
Calistoga (C5) 1,514
Camarillo (F9) 13,500
Cambria (D8) 1,600
Camino (E5) 950
Campbell (K3) 11,863
Campo (J11) 800
Canoga Park (B10) 64,200
Capistrano Beach (H10) 2,026

Capitola (K4) 2,021
Cardiff-by-the-Sea (H10) 3,149
Carlsbad (H10) 9,253
Carmel (C7) 4,580
Carmel Valley (D7) 1,143
Carmichael (C8) 20,455
Carpinteria (F9) 4,998
Caruthers (E7) 1,260
Castaic (G9) 750
Castro Valley (K2) 37,120
Castroville (C7) 2,838
Cathedral City (J10) 1,855
Cayucos (E7) 2,000
Cedarville (E2) 850
Central Valley (C3) 2,854
Ceres (D6) 4,406
Chatsworth (B10) 13,250
Chester (D3) 1,553
Chico (D4) 14,757
Chico Vecino (D4) 11,400
China Lake (H8) 11,400
Chino (D10) 10,305
Chowchilla (E6) 4,525
Chrisman (F9) 3,923
Chualar (D7) 800
Chula Vista (J11) 42,034
Claremont (D10) 12,633
Clearlake Highlands (C5) 850
Clearlake Oaks (C4) 850
Cloverdale (B5) 2,848
Clovis (F7) 5,546
Coachella (J10) 4,854
Coalinga (E7) 5,965
Colfax (E4) 915
Colma (J2) 500
Colton (E10) 18,666
Colusa◉ (C4) 3,518
Commerce ‡(C11) 9,555
Compton (C11) 71,812
Concord (K1) 36,208
Corcoran (F7) 4,976
Corning (C4) 3,006
Corona (E11) 13,336
Corona del Mar (G10) 4,500
Coronado (H11) 18,039
Corte Madera (J2) 5,962
Costa Mesa (D11) 37,550
Cotati (K5) 1,434
Cottonwood (C3) 950
Covina (D10) 20,124
Crescent City◉ (A2) 2,958
Crestline (H9) 1,290
Cucamonga (E10) 7,528
Culver City (B10) 32,163
Cupertino (K3) 3,664
Cutler (F7) 2,191
Cutten (A3) 1,572
Cypress (D11) 1,753
Daggett (H9) 1,780
Dairy Valley (C11) 3,508
Daly City (H2) 44,791
Dana Point (H10) 1,186
Danville (K2) 3,585
Davis (D8) 8,910
Del Mar (H11) 3,124
Del Rey (F7) 937
Del Rey Oaks (D7) 1,831
Delano (F8) 11,913
Delhi (E6) 1,175
Denair (E6) 860
Descanso (J11) 800
Desert Hot Springs (J9) 2,979
Diablo (K2) 2,096
Diamond Springs (D8) 895
Dixon (B5) 2,970
Dorris (D2) 973
Dos Palos (E6) 2,028
Dover Shores (D11) 500
Downey (C10) 82,505
Downieville◉ (E4) 350
Duarte (D10) 13,962
Dunsmuir (C2) 2,873
Durham (D4) 950
Eagle Mountain (K10) 650
Earlimart (F8) 2,897
East Bakersfield (G8) 11,995
East Irvine (D11) 316
East Los Angeles (C10) 104,270
Eastbluff (D11) 2,500
Edgemont (E11) 1,628
Edwards (G9) 1,000
El Cajon (J11) 37,618
El Centro◉ (K11) 16,811
El Cerrito (J2) 25,437
El Dorado (C8) 525
El Dorado Hills (C8) 2,000
El Granada (H3) 850
El Modeno (D11) 1,434
El Monte (D10) 13,163
El Nido (E6) 825
El Rio (F9) 6,966
El Segundo (B11) 14,219
Elk Grove (B9) 2,205
Elsinore (F11) 2,432
Emeryville (J2) 2,686
Empire (D6) 1,635
Encinitas (H10) 2,786
Encino (B10) 29,500
Escalon (E6) 1,763
Escondido (H10) 16,377
Etiwanda (E10) 787
Etna (C2) 596
Eureka◉ (A3) 28,137
Evergreen (L3) 950
Exeter (F7) 4,264
Fair Oaks (C8) 1,622
Fairfax (H1) 5,813
Fairfield◉ (K1) 14,968
Fallbrook (H10) 4,814
Farmersville (F7) 3,101
Fawnskin (J9) 640
Feather Falls (D4) 900
Fellows (F8) 900
Felton (K4) 1,380
Ferndale (A3) 1,371
Fillmore (F9) 4,808
Firebaugh (E7) 2,070
Folsom (C8) 3,925
Fontana (E10) 14,659
Ford City (F8) 3,926
Forest Knolls (H1) 1,500
Fort Bragg (B4) 4,433
Fort Dick (A2) 750
Fortuna (A3) 3,523
Fountain Valley (D11) 2,068
Fowler (F7) 1,892
Freedom (L4) 4,206
Fremont (K3) 43,790
Fresno◉ (E7) 133,929
Fresno (urb. area) 213,444
Fullerton (D11) 56,180
Galt (C9) 1,868
Garberville (B3) 1,350
Garden Grove (D11) 84,238
Gardena (C11) 35,943
Georgetown (E5) 900
Gerber (C3) 850
Geyserville (B5) 813
Gilroy (D6) 7,348
Glen Avon Hts. (E10) 3,416
Glendale (C10) 119,442

Glendora (D10) 20,752
Goleta (F9) 6,857
Gonzales (D7) 2,138
Goshen (F7) 1,061
Granada Hills (B10) 31,162
Grass Valley (D4) 4,876
Graton (C5) 1,055
Greenfield (D7) 1,680
Greenville (E3) 1,140
Gridley (D4) 3,343
Grover City (E8) 5,210
Guadalupe (E9) 2,614
Guerneville (B5) 1,400
Gustine (D6) 2,300
Half Moon Bay (H3) 1,957
Hamilton City (C4) 800
Happy Camp (B2) 800
Hanford◉ (F7) 10,133
Harbor City (B11) 10,000
Hawthorne (B11) 33,035
Hayfork (B3) 800
Hayward (J2) 72,700
Healdsburg (B5) 4,816
Hemet (J10) 5,416
Herlong (E3) 2,377
Hermosa Beach (B11) 16,115
Hesperia (H9) 3,226
Highgrove (E10) 1,900
Highland (H9) 7,772
Hillsborough (J2) 7,554
Hinkley (H9) 1,327
Hollister◉ (D7) 6,071
Hollywood (C10) 100,000
Holtville (K11) 3,080
Home Gardens (E11) 1,541
Hoopa (B2) 850
Hopland (B5) 1,250
Hughson (E6) 1,898
Huntington Beach (D11) 11,492
Huntington Pk. (C10) 29,920
Huron (F7) 1,269
Idyllwild (J10) 850
Imperial (K11) 2,658
Imperial Beach (H11) 17,773
Independence◉ (H7) 350
Indio (J10) 9,745
Industry‡ (D10) 778
Inglewood (B11) 63,390
Inyokern (H8) 660
Ione (C9) 1,118
Irwindale‡ (D10) 1,518
Isleton (L1) 1,039
Ivanhoe (F7) 1,616
Jackson◉ (C9) 1,852
Jacumba (J11) 700
Jamestown (E5) 875
Johannesburg (H8) 300
Kelseyville (C5) 800
Kerman (E7) 1,970
Kettleman City (E7) 500
King City (D7) 2,937
Kingsburg (F7) 3,093
Kings Beach (F4) 629
Klamath (B3) 725
Knights Landing (B8) 725
La Canada (C10) 18,338
La Crescenta (C10) 16,000
La Habra (D11) 25,136
La Jolla (H11) 28,000
La Mesa (H11) 30,441
La Mirada (C11) 22,444
La Puente (D10) 24,723
La Sierra (E11) 19,239
La Verne (D10) 6,516
Lafayette (K2) 7,114
Laguna Beach (G10) 9,288
Lagunitas (H1) 750
Lake Arrowhead (H9) 2,008
Lake Isabella (G8) 850
Lakeland Village (E11) 3,539
Lakeport◉ (C4) 2,303
Lakeside (J11) 4,400
Lakewood (C11) 67,126
Lamont (G8) 6,177
Lancaster (G9) 26,012
Larkspur (H1) 5,710
Lathrop (D6) 1,123
Laton (F7) 1,052
Lawndale (B11) 21,740
Lemon Grove (J11) 19,348
Lemoncove (G7) 700
Lemoore (F7) 2,561
Lennox (C11) 31,224
Lenwood (H9) 2,407
Leucadia (H10) 5,665
Lincoln (B8) 3,197
Linda (D4) 6,129
Linden (D5) 875
Lindsay (G7) 5,397
Live Oak (D4) 2,276
Livermore (L2) 16,058
Livingston (E6) 2,188
Lodi (C9) 22,229
Loleta (A3) 900
Loma Linda (E10) 5,000
Lomita (C11) 18,000
Lompoc (F9) 14,415
Lone Pine (H7) 1,310
Long Beach (C11) 344,168
Long Beach-Los Angeles (urban area) 6,488,791
Los Alamitos (D11) 4,312
Los Alamos (E9) 630
Los Altos (K3) 19,696
Los Altos Hills (J3) 3,412
Los Angeles◉ (C10) 2,479,015
Los Angeles-Long Beach (urban area) 6,488,791
Los Banos (E7) 5,272
Los Gatos (K4) 9,036
Los Molinos (D3) 1,060
Loyalton (E4) 936
Lucerne (C4) 850
Lucerne Valley (J9) 1,402
Lynwood (C11) 31,614
Madera◉ (E7) 14,430
Malibu (B10) 10,000
Manhattan Beach (B11) 33,934
Manteca (D6) 8,242
Maricopa (F6) 648
Mariposa◉ (F6) 700
Markleeville◉ (F5) 128
Martinez◉ (K1) 9,604
Marysville◉ (D4) 9,553
Maxwell (C4) 400
Maywood (C10) 14,588
McCloud (C2) 2,140
McFarland (F8) 3,686
Meiners Oaks (F9) 3,513
Mendocino (B4) 930
Mendota (E7) 2,099
Menlo Park (J3) 26,957
Mentone (H9) 3,218
Merced◉ (E6) 20,068
Midway City (D11) 5,000
Mill Valley (H2) 10,411
Millbrae (J2) 15,873

Milpitas (L3) 6,572
Mira Loma (E10) 3,982
Modesto◉ (D6) 36,585
Mojave (G8) 1,845
Mokelumne Hill (E5) 700
Monrovia (D10) 27,079
Montague (C2) 782
Montalvo (F9) 2,028
Montclair (D10) 13,546
Monte Sereno (K4) 1,506
Montebello (C10) 32,097
Montecito (F9) 9,000
Monterey (D7) 22,618
Monterey Park (C10) 37,821
Montrose (C10) 8,500
Moorpark (G9) 2,902
Morgan Hill (K4) 3,151
Morro Bay (D8) 7,700
Mount Aukum (E5) 50
Mount Shasta (C2) 1,936
Mountain View (K3) 30,889
Murphys (E5) 775
Napa◉ (C5) 22,170
National City (J11) 32,771
Needles (M9) 4,590
Nevada City◉ (D4) 2,353
Newark (K3) 9,884
Newhall (G9) 4,705
Newman (D6) 2,148
Newport Beach (D11) 26,564
Nipomo (E8) 950
Norco (E11) 10,000
North Highlands (B8) 21,271
North Hollywood (B10) 173,341
Norwalk (C11) 88,739
Novato (H1) 17,881
Oak View (F9) 2,448
Oakdale (E6) 4,980
Oakhurst (F6) 850
Oakland◉ (J2) 367,548
Oakland-San Francisco (urban area) 2,430,663
Oakley (L1) 2,000
Oceano (E8) 1,317
Oceanside (H10) 24,971
Oildale (G8) 6,382
Ojai (F9) 4,495
Olive (D11) 789

Olympic Valley (E4) 250
Ontario (D10) 46,617
Ontario-Pomona (urban area) 186,547
Opal Cliffs (K4) 3,825
Orange (D11) 26,444
Orange Cove (F7) 2,885
Orcutt (E9) 1,414
Orick (A2) 900
Orinda (J2) 4,712
Orland (C4) 2,534
Oro Grande (H9) 1,859
Orosi (F7) 1,048
Oroville◉ (D4) 6,115
Oxnard (F9) 40,265
Pacheco (K1) 1,518
Pacific Beach (H11) 43,000
Pacific Grove (C7) 12,121
Pacifica (H2) 20,995
Pajaro (D7) 1,273
Palermo (D4) 1,762
Palm Desert (J10) 1,295
Palm Springs (J10) 13,468
Palmdale (G9) 11,522
Palo Alto (K3) 52,287
Palos Verdes Peninsula (B11) 9,564
Paradise (D4) 8,268
Paramount (C11) 27,249
Parker Dam (L9) 500
Parlier (F7) 1,366
Pasadena (C10) 116,407
Paso Robles (E8) 6,677
Patterson (D6) 2,246
Pebble Beach (C7) 250
Perris (F11) 2,950
Pescadero (J4) 500
Petaluma (H1) 14,035
Philo (B4) 850
Pico Rivera (C10) 49,150
Piedmont (J2) 11,117
Pinedale (F7) 2,220
Pinole (J1) 6,064
Piru (G9) 1,500
Pismo Beach (E8) 1,762
Pittsburg (L1) 19,062
Pixley (F8) 1,327
Placentia (D11) 5,861
Placerville◉ (C8) 4,439
Planada (E6) 1,704
Pleasant Hill (K2) 26,001
Pleasanton (L2) 4,203
Plymouth (C8) 489
Point Arena (B5) 596
Pollock Pines (E5) 850
Pomona (C10) 67,157
Pomona-Ontario (urban area) 186,547
Poplar (F7) 1,478
Port Chicago (K1) 1,746
Port Hueneme (F9) 11,067
Porterville (F7) 7,991
Portola (E4) 1,874
Portola Valley (J3) 3,500
Potter Valley (B4) 995
Poway (J11) 1,921
Project City (C3) 1,200
Quartz Hill (G9) 3,325
Quincy◉ (E4) 2,723
Ramona (J10) 2,449
Rancho Cordova (C8) 7,429
Rancho Santa Fe (H10) 950
Red Bluff◉ (C3) 7,202
Redcrest (A3) 500
Redding◉ (C3) 12,773
Redlands (H9) 26,829
Redondo Beach (B11) 46,986
Redwood City◉ (J3) 46,290
Redwood Estates (K4) 1,284
Reedley (F7) 5,850
Reseda (B10) 52,000
Rialto (E10) 18,567

Richmond (J1) 71,854
Ridgecrest (H8) 6,400
Rio Dell (A3) 3,222
Rio Linda (B8) 2,189
Rio Vista (L1) 2,616
Ripon (D6) 1,852
Riverbank (E6) 2,786
Riverdale (F7) 1,012
Riverside◉ (E10) 84,332
Riverside-San Bernardino (urban area) 377,531
Rocklin (B8) 1,495
Rodeo (J1) 6,350
Rohnerville (B3) 2,268
Rolling Hills (B11) 1,664
Rolling Hills Estates (B11) 3,941
Rosamond (G9) 950
Rosemead (D10) 15,476
Roseville (B8) 13,421
Ross (H1) 2,551
SACRAMENTO◉ (B8) 191,667
Sacramento (urban area) 451,920
Saint Helena (C5) 2,832
Salinas◉ (D7) 28,957
Salyer (B3) 850
Samoa (A3) 600
San Andreas◉ (E5) 1,416
San Anselmo (H1) 11,584
San Ardo (E7) 800
San Bernardino◉ (E10) 91,922
San Bernardino-Riverside (urban area) 377,531
San Bruno (J2) 29,063
San Carlos (J3) 21,370
San Clemente (H10) 8,527
San Diego◉ (J11) 573,224
San Diego (urb. area) 836,175
San Dimas (D10) 11,520
San Fernando (C10) 16,093
San Francisco◉ (H2) 740,316
San Francisco-Oakland (urban area) 2,430,663
San Gabriel (C10) 22,561
San Jacinto (F11) 4,385
San Joaquin (E7) 879
San Jose◉ (L3) 204,196
San Jose (urb. area) 602,805
San Juan Bautista (D7) 1,046
San Juan Capistrano (H10) 1,848
San Leandro (J2) 65,962
San Lorenzo (K2) 23,773
San Luis Obispo◉ (E8) 20,437
San Marino (C10) 13,658
San Martin (L4) 1,162
San Mateo◉ (J3) 69,870
San Pablo (J1) 19,687
San Pedro (C11) 60,000
San Quentin (H1) 215
San Rafael◉ (H1) 20,460
San Ramon (J2) 862
Sanger (F7) 8,072
Sanitarium (C5) 862
Santa Ana◉ (D11) 100,350
Santa Barbara◉ (F9) 58,768
Santa Barbara (urban area) 72,740
Santa Clara (K3) 58,880
Santa Cruz◉ (K4) 25,596
Santa Fe Sprs. (C11) 16,342
Santa Margarita (E8) 975
Santa Maria (B10) 20,027
Santa Monica (B10) 83,249
Santa Paula (F9) 13,279
Santa Rosa◉ (C5) 31,027
Santa Susana (B10) 2,310
Saranap (K4) 6,450
Saratoga (K4) 14,861
Saticoy (F9) 2,283
Sausalito (H2) 5,331
Scotia (A3) 1,122
Seal Beach (C11) 6,994
Searles (H8) 2,450
Seaside (D7) 19,353
Sebastopol (C5) 2,694
Seeley (K11) 700
Selma (F7) 6,934
Sepulveda (B10) 28,339
Shafter (F8) 4,576
Shasta (C3) 800
Shell Beach (E8) 1,820
Shingle Springs (C8) 750

Shore Acres (K1) 3,093
Sierra Madre (C10) 9,732
Signal Hill (C11) 4,627
Simi (G9) 2,107
Smith River (A2) 800
Solana Beach (H11) 4,489
Soledad (D7) 2,837
Solvang (E9) 1,325
Sonoma (C5) 3,023
Sonora◉ (E5) 2,725
Soquel (K4) 950
South Bakersfield (G8) 5,384
South Dos Palos (E7) 750
South El Monte‡ (D10) 4,850
South Gate (C11) 53,831
South Oroville (D4) 3,704
South Pasadena (C10) 19,706
South Sacramento (B8) 16,443
South San Francisco (J2) 39,418
South San Gabriel (C10) 26,213
South Taft (F8) 1,910
Springville (G7) 683
Stanford (J3) 12,309
Stanton (D11) 11,163
Stockton◉ (D6) 86,321
Stockton (urb. area) 141,604
Stratford (F7) 800
Strathmore (F7) 1,095
Suisun City (K1) 2,470
Summit City (C3) 725
Sunland (C10) 17,614
Sunnymead (F11) 3,404
Sunnyvale (K3) 52,898
Sunol (L3) 650
Sunset Beach (C11) 2,000
Susanville◉ (E3) 5,598
Sutter (D4) 1,219
Sutter Creek (C9) 1,161
Taft (F8) 3,822
Tahoe City (E4) 791
Tahoe Valley (E5) 950
Tarzana (B10) 15,000
Tehachapi (G8) 3,161
Temple City (C10) 31,838
Templeton (E8) 750
Thermal (J10) 975
Thornton (B9) 850
Thousand Oaks (G9) 22,000
Tiburon (J2) 4,704
Tipton (F7) 950
Topanga (B10) 4,000
Torrance (C11) 100,991
Tracy (D6) 11,289
Trona (H8) 1,138
Truckee (E4) 1,800
Tujunga (C10) 21,000
Tulare (F7) 13,824
Tulelake (D2) 950
Tuolumne (E6) 1,403
Turlock (D6) 9,116
Tustin (D11) 2,006
Twentynine Palms (K9) 5,584
Ukiah◉ (B4) 9,900
Union City (J2) 6,618
University Park (D11) 950
Upland (E10) 15,918
Upper Lake (C4) 900
Vacaville (D5) 10,898
Vallejo (J1) 60,877
Valley Center (J10) 750
Van Nuys (B10) 168,475
Venice (B11) 40,000
Ventura◉ (F9) 29,114
Victorville (H9) 8,931
Visalia◉ (F7) 15,791
Vista (H10) 19,625
Walnut‡ (D10) 934
Walnut Creek (K2) 9,903
Walnut Grove (B9) 1,250
Wasco (F8) 6,841
Waterford (E6) 1,780
Watsonville (C5) 13,293
Weaverville◉ (B3) 1,736
Weed (C2) 3,223
West Covina (D10) 50,645
West Hollywood (B10) 28,870
West Los Angeles (B10) 43,167
West Pittsburg (K1) 5,188
West Point (E5) 750
West Sacramento (B8) 18,000
Westminster (D11) 25,750
Westmorland (K10) 1,404
Westwood (D3) 1,209
Westwood (B10) 45,670
Wheatland (D4) 813
Whittier (D11) 33,663
Williams (C4) 1,370
Willits (B4) 3,410
Willows◉ (C4) 4,139
Wilmington (C11) 45,000
Winterhaven (L11) 290
Winters (D5) 1,700
Woodbridge (B9) 800
Woodlake (G7) 2,623
Woodland◉ (B8) 13,524
Woodland Hills (B10) 36,038
Woodside (J3) 3,592
Yermo (J9) 1,139
Yolo (B8) 800
Yorba Linda (D11) 1,198
Yosemite Nat'l Pk. (F6) 950
Yountville (C5) 800
Yreka◉ (C2) 4,759
Yuba City◉ (D4) 11,507
Yucaipa (J9) 12,420

OTHER FEATURES

Agua Caliente Ind. Res., 78 .... J10
Alamo (river) K10
Alcatraz (isl.) .... J 2

(continued on following page)

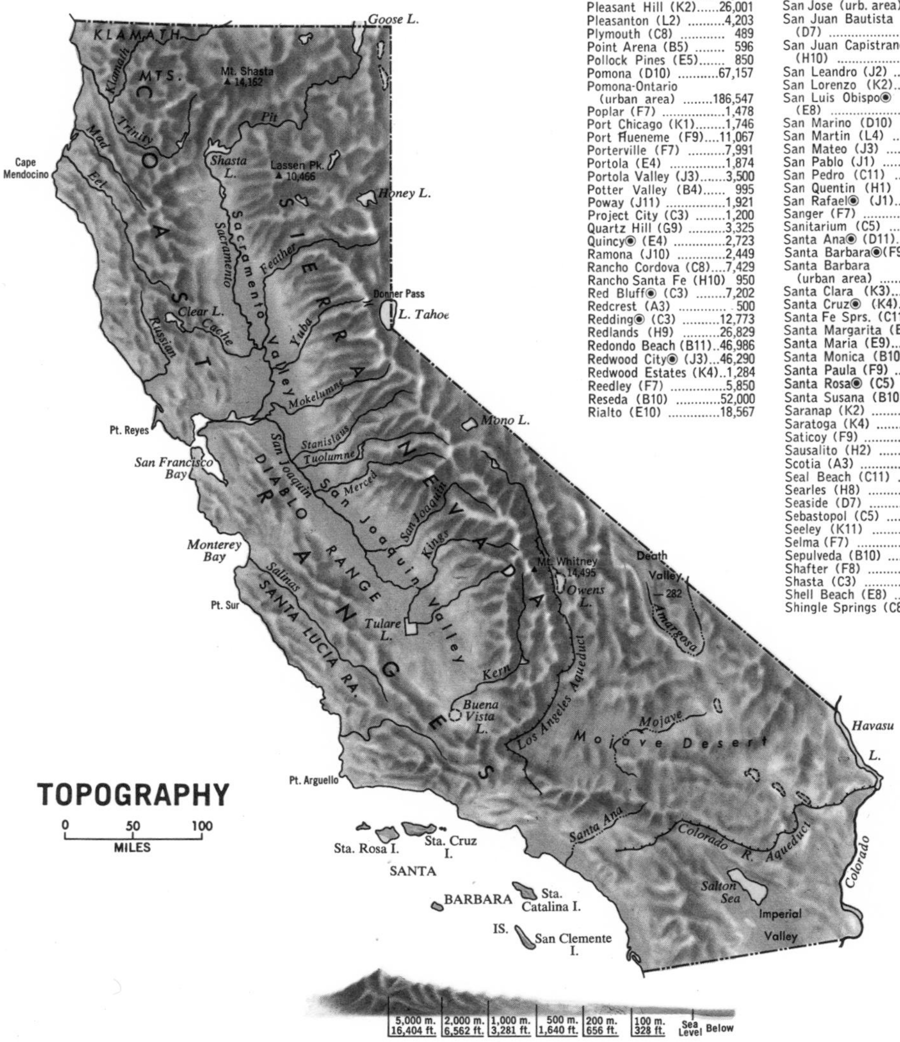

TOPOGRAPHY

MILES 0 50 100

| 5,000 m. | 2,000 m. | 1,000 m. | 500 m. | 200 m. | 100 m. | Sea Level |
| 16,404 ft. | 6,562 ft. | 3,281 ft. | 1,640 ft. | 656 ft. | 328 ft. | Level Below |

Map labels: Goose L.; KLAMATH MTS.; Mt. Shasta ▲14,162; Lassen Pk. ▲10,466; Honey L.; Cape Mendocino; Shasta; Trinity; COAST RANGE; Donner Pass; Clear L.; L. Tahoe; Pt. Reyes; San Francisco Bay; Monterey Bay; Pt. Sur; SANTA LUCIA RA.; Pt. Arguello; SIERRA NEVADA; Mono L.; DIABLO RANGE; Mt. Whitney ▲14,495; Owens; Death Valley −282; Mojave Desert; Buena Vista; Tulare L.; Salton Sea; Imperial Valley; Colorado R.; Havasu L.; Sta. Rosa I.; Sta. Cruz I.; SANTA BARBARA IS.; San Catalina I.; San Clemente I.; Los Angeles Aqueduct; Colorado R. Aqueduct

California
(continued)

All American (canal).....K11
Almanor (lake).....D 3
Amargosa (river).....J 7
American (river).....C 8
Anacapa (isl.).....F10
Angel (isl.).....J 2
Ano Nuevo (point).....J 3
Arena (point).....B 5
Arguello (point).....E 9
Argus (range).....H 7
Beale A.F.B......D 4
Berryessa (lake).....D 5
Big Sage (res.).....E 2
Black Butte (res.).....C 4
Bodega (bay).....B 5
Bonita (point).....H 2
Bristol (lake).....K 9
Buena Vista (lake).....F 8
Cabrillo Nat'l Mon......H11
Cadiz (lake).....K 9
Cahuilla Ind. Res......J10
Calaveras (res.).....L 3
Campo Ind. Res......J11
Capitan Grande Ind. Res. J11
Carnadero (creek).....L 4
Cascade (range).....D 1
Castle A.F.B......E 6
Channel Is. Nat'l Mon...F10
Chemehuevi Valley I. R. L 9
Chocolate (mts.).....K10
Clair Engle (lake).....C 3
Clear (lake).....A 2
Clear Lake (res.).....D 2
Coachella (canal).....K10
Coast (range).....L 8
Colorado (river).....L 8
Colorado River Aqueduct K10
Colorado River Ind. Res. L10
Conception (point).....E 9
Cooper (point).....D 7
Copco (lake).....C 3
Cosumnes (river).....C 3
Cottonwood (creek).....C 3
Coyote (res.).....L 4
Crowley (lake).....G 6
Crystal Springs (res.)...J 3
Cuddeback (lake).....H 8
Cuyama (river).....E 8

Cuyapaipe Ind. Res......J11
Danby (lake).....K 9
Death Valley Nat'l Mon. H 7
Delgada (point).....A 3
Devil's Postpile N. Mon. F 6
Dume (point).....G10
Duxbury (point).....H 2
Eagle (lake).....E 2
Eagle Crags (mt.).....J 8
Earl (lake).....A 2
East Park (res.).....C 4
Edison (lake).....F 6
Edwards A.F.B......H 9
Eel (river).....B 4
El Toro Marine Air Sta. D11
Elsinore (lake).....E11
Estero (bay).....D 7
Estrella (river).....E 8
Farallon (isls.).....B 6
Farallons (gulf).....H 2
Feather (river).....D 4
Florence (lake).....G 6
Folsom (res.).....C 3
Fort Baker.....J 2
Fort Bidwell I.R., 104...E 2
Fort Independence I. R. G 7
Fort Irwin.....J 8
Fort MacArthur.....C11
Fort Mohave Ind. Res.,
  277.....L 9
Fort Ord.....D 7
Fort Winfield Scott.....J 2
Forts Barry & Cronkhite..H 2
Freel (peak).....F 5
Fremont (peak).....H 8
Fresno (river).....E 7
General Grant Grove
  Park.....G 7
George A.F.B......H 9
Golden Gate (channel)...H 2
Goose (lake).....E 1
Grapevine (mts.).....H 7
Grizzly (bay).....K 1
Guadalupe (river).....K 3
Haiwee (res.).....H 7
Hamilton (mt.).....L 3
Hamilton A.F.B......J 1
Hat (peak).....E 2

Havasu (lake).....L 9
Hetch Hetchy (res.).....F 6
Hoffmann (mt.).....D 2
Honey (lake).....E 3
Hoopa Valley Ind. Res.,
  992.....A 2
Horse (lake).....E 3
Humboldt (bay).....A 3
Hunter Liggett Mil. Res. D 8
Imperial (res.).....L10
Imperial (valley).....K10
Ingalls (mt.).....E 3
Inyo (mts.).....G 6
Inyokern Nav. Test Sta. H 8
Isabella (res.).....G 8
Joshua Tree Nat'l Mon. J10
Kern (river).....G 8
Kings (river).....G 7
Kings Canyon Nat'l Park G 7
Klamath (river).....B 2
La Jolla Ind. Res......J10
Laguna (lake).....L11
Lassen (peak).....D 3
Lassen Vol. Nat'l Pk. ...D 3
Lava Beds Nat'l Mon...D 2
Leroy Anderson (res.)...L 4
Lopez (point).....D 7
Los Angeles Aqueduct...G 8
Los Coyotes Ind. Res. ...J10
Lost (river).....D 1
Mad (river).....B 3
Manzanita Ind. Res......J11
March A.F.B......E11
Mare Island Navy Yard...J 1
Mathews (lake).....E11
McClellan A.F.B......B 8
Mendocino (cape).....A 3
Merced (river).....E 6
Millerton (lake).....F 6
Moffett Naval Air Sta. K 3
Mojave (desert).....H 9
Mojave (river).....J 9
Mokelumne (river) ....C 3
Mono (lake).....G 5
Monterey (bay).....K 4
Morongo Ind. Res., 257...J10
Morris (res.).....D10
Mountain Meadows
  (res.).....E 3
Muir Woods Nat'l Mon. H 2
Nacimiento (river).....D 8
Navarro (river).....B 4
New (river).....K11
Norton A.F.B......F10
Noyo (river).....B 4

AGRICULTURE, INDUSTRY and RESOURCES

DOMINANT LAND USE

Wheat, Small Grains
Specialized Dairy
Fruit and Mixed Farming
Fruit, Truck and Mixed Farming
General Farming, Livestock, Special Crops
Cotton, Alfalfa
Potatoes, General Farming
Range Livestock
Forests
Urban Areas
Nonagricultural Land

SACRAMENTO
Food Processing,
Missile Parts

STOCKTON
Food Processing

SAN FRANCISCO–OAKLAND
Food Processing, Machinery,
Metal Products, Primary
Metals, Chemicals, Shipbuilding,
Printing & Publishing

SAN JOSE
Food Processing, Electrical
Products, Agricultural Equipment

FRESNO
Food Processing

LOS ANGELES
Aircraft, Clothing, Motion Pictures,
Food Processing, Electrical & Metal
Products, Machinery, Chemicals,
Printing & Publishing, Oil Refining,
Primary Metals, Spacecraft,
Electronic Equipment

SAN BERNARDINO–RIVERSIDE
Food Processing,
Iron & Steel

SAN DIEGO
Aircraft,
Food Processing

MAJOR MINERAL OCCURRENCES

Ab Asbestos
Ag Silver
Au Gold
Bx Borax
Cl Clay
Cu Copper
Fe Iron Ore
G   Natural Gas
Gp Gypsum
Hg Mercury
K   Potash
Mg Magnesium
Mo Molybdenum
Mr Marble
Na Salt
O   Petroleum
Pb Lead
Pt Platinum
Tc Talc
W   Tungsten
Zn Zinc

Water Power
Major Industrial Areas

HIGHWAYS

| 0   60   120 |
| MILES |

Limited Access Highways.........
Major Highways ....
Other Important Roads ....
Interstate Route Numbers ....
Federal Route Numbers ....
State and Other Route Numbers...

Old (river) ....L 1
Owens (lake) ....H 7
Owens (river) ....G 6
Paiute Ind. Res............G 6
Pala Ind. Res., 215....H10
Palomar (mt.)...........J10
Panamint (range) ...H 7
Pardee (res.)...........C 9
Pendleton, Camp...H10
Pescadero (point)....J 3
Picacho (mt.)...........L11
Piedras Blancas (pt.)..D 8
Pillar (point)..........H 3
Pillsbury (lake)........C 4
Pine (creek)............D 3
Pine Flat (res.)........F 7
Pinnacles Nat'l Mon. ...D 7
Pit (river)...............D 2
Point Mugu Naval Missile
  Center................F 9
Point Reyes Nat'l
  Seashore.............H 1
Presidio................J 2
Providence (mts.)....K 8
Punta Gorda (point)....A 3
Railroad Canyon (res.)..E11
Reyes (point)..........B 6
Rogers (lake)..........H 9
Rosamond (lake)....G 9
Round Valley I.R., 360...B 4
Russian (river)........B 4
Sacramento (river)....D 5
Saint George (point)....A 2
Salinas (river)........D 7
Salmon (river)........B 2
Salton Sea (lake)....K10
San Andreas (lake)....H 2
San Benito (river)....D 7
San Bernardino (mts.)..J10
San Clemente (isl.)....G11
San Diego (bay)....H11
San Francisco (bay)....J2
San Gabriel (res.)....D10
San Joaquin (river)....E 6
San Juan (creek)....E 8
San Lorenzo (river)....K 4
San Martin (cape)....D 8
San Miguel (cape)....E 9
San Nicolas (isl.)....F10
San Pablo (bay)....J 2
San Pedro (bay)....C11
Santa Ana (river)....E11

Santa Barbara (isl.)....G10
Santa Barbara (isls.)....F10
Santa Cruz (isl.)....F10
Santa Maria (river)....E10
Santa Rosa (isl.)....E10
Santa Rosa Ind. Res. ...J10
Santa Ynez (river)....E 9
Santa Ysabel Ind. Res.,
  136.................J10
Scott (river)..........B 2
Searles (lake)........H 8
Sequoia National Park...G 7
Shasta (lake)........C 3
Shasta (mt.).........C 2
Shasta (river).......C 2
Sierra Nevada (mts.)....E 4
Sierra Ordnance Depot...E 3
Siskiyou (mts.).....A 2
Smith River I.R., 102....A 2
Stony Gorge (res.)....C 4
Suisun (bay)........K 1
Sur (point)..........D 7
Susan (river)........D 3
Tahoe (lake)........F 4
Tamalpais (mt.)....H 1
Tehachapi (mts.)....G 8
Telescope (peak)....H 7
Tomales (point)....B 5
Torres Martinez I.R. ...J10
Travis A.F.B......E 9
Trinidad (head)....A 2
Trinity (river)......B 3
Truckee (river)....D 3
Tulare (lake)........F 7
Tule Lake (res.)....D 1
Tule River I.R., 325....G 7
Twitchell (res.)....E 8
Vandenberg A.F.B......E 9
Vizcaino (cape)....A 3
Walnut (creek)....K 1
Wheeler (peak)....F 5
Whipple (mts.)....L 9
Whitney (mt.)....G 7
Willow (creek)....E 3
Wilson (mt.)....D10
Yosemite Nat'l Park....F 6
Yuba (river)....D 4
Yuma Ind. Res., 965....L11

⊙ County Seat.
‡ Name not on map.

COLORADO

AREA	104,247 sq. mi.
POPULATION	1,969,000
CAPITAL	Denver
LARGEST CITY	Denver 493,887
HIGHEST POINT	Mt. Elbert 14,431 ft.
SETTLED IN	1858
ADMITTED TO UNION	August 1, 1876
POPULAR NAME	Centennial State
STATE FLOWER	Mountain Columbine
STATE BIRD	Lark Bunting

COUNTIES

County		Population
Adams (L3)		120,296
Alamosa (H7)		10,000
Arapahoe (L3)		113,426
Archuleta (E8)		2,629
Baca (O8)		6,310
Bent (N7)		7,419
Boulder (J2)		74,254
Chaffee (G5)		8,298
Cheyenne (O5)		2,789
Clear Creek (H3)		2,793
Conejos (G8)		8,428
Costilla (J8)		4,219
Crowley (M6)		3,978
Custer (J6)		1,305
Delta (D5)		15,602
Denver (K3)		493,887
Dolores (C7)		2,196
Douglas (K4)		4,816
Eagle (F3)		4,677
El Paso (K5)		143,742
Elbert (L4)		3,708
Fremont (J5)		20,196
Garfield (C3)		12,017
Gilpin (H3)		685
Grand (G2)		3,557
Gunnison (E5)		5,477
Hinsdale (E7)		208
Huerfano (K7)		7,867
Jackson (G1)		1,758
Jefferson (J3)		127,520
Kiowa (O6)		2,425
Kit Carson (O4)		6,957
La Plata (D8)		19,225
Lake (G4)		7,101
Larimer (H1)		53,343
Las Animas (L8)		19,983
Lincoln (M5)		5,310
Logan (N1)		20,302
Mesa (B5)		50,715
Mineral (F7)		424
Moffat (C1)		7,061
Montezuma (B8)		14,024
Montrose (C6)		18,286
Morgan (M2)		21,192
Otero (M7)		24,128
Ouray (D6)		1,601
Park (H4)		1,822
Phillips (P1)		4,440
Pitkin (F4)		2,381
Prowers (P7)		13,296
Pueblo (K6)		118,707
Rio Blanco (C3)		5,150
Rio Grande (G7)		11,160
Routt (E1)		5,900
Saguache (G6)		4,473
San Juan (D7)		849
San Miguel (C6)		2,944
Sedgwick (P1)		4,242
Summit (J3)		2,073
Teller (J5)		2,495
Washington (N3)		6,625
Weld (L1)		72,344
Yuma (P2)		8,912

CITIES and TOWNS

Agate (M4)	120
Aguilar (K8)	777
Akron◉ (N2)	1,890
Alamosa◉ (H8)	6,205
Allenspark (J2)	40
Alma (G4)	107
Almont (F5)	12
Amherst (P1)	95
Andrix (N8)	10
Anton (N3)	48
Antonito (H8)	1,045
Arapahoe (P5)	100
Arickaree (N3)	3
Arlington (N6)	25
Aroya (N5)	
Arriba (N4)	296
Arriola (B8)	142
Arvada (J3)	19,242
Aspen◉ (F4)	1,101
Atwood (N1)	250
Ault (K1)	799
Aurora (K3)	48,548
Austin (D5)	200
Avon (F3)	50
Avondale (L6)	500
Axial (D2)	75
Bailey (H4)	200
Barnesville (L2)	35
Basalt (E4)	213
Bayfield (D8)	322
Bedrock (B6)	60
Beecher Island (P3)	9
Bellvue (H1)	250
Bennett (L3)	287
Berthoud (J2)	1,014
Berthoud Pass (H3)	
Bethune (P4)	70
Beulah (K6)	950
Big Bend (O4)	75
Black Forest (K4)	3,000
Black Hawk (J3)	171
Blanca (H8)	233
Blende (K6)	300
Bonanza (E5)	19
Boncarbo (K8)	41
Bond (F3)	82
Boone (L6)	548
Boulder◉ (J2)	37,718
Bow Mar ‡(J3)	748
Bowie (D5)	250
Boyero (N5)	36
Brandon (P6)	50
Branson (M8)	124
Breckenridge◉ (G4)	393
Briggsdale (L1)	75
Brighton◉ (K3)	7,055
Bristol (P6)	400
Brookside (J6)	163
Brookvale (H3)	35
Broomfield (J3)	4,924
Brush (M2)	3,621
Buckingham (L1)	36
Buena Vista (G5)	1,806
Buffalo Creek (J4)	75
Buford (D2)	57
Burlington◉ (P4)	2,090
Burns (F3)	150
Byers (L3)	500
Cahone (B7)	72
Calhan (L4)	347
Campo (O8)	235
Canon City◉ (J6)	8,973
Capulin (G8)	500
Carbondale (E4)	612
Carlton (P6)	55
Carr (K1)	68
Cascade (K5)	300
Castle Rock◉ (K4)	1,152
Cedaredge (D5)	549
Center (G7)	1,600
Central City◉ (J3)	250
Chama (J8)	760
Cheraw (N6)	173
Cherry Hills Village ‡(K3)	1,931
Cheyenne Wells◉ (P5)	1,020
Chimney Rock (E8)	100
Chivington (O6)	20
Chromo (F8)	160
Cimmaron (D6)	75
Clark (F1)	64
Clarkville (P2)	10
Clifton (C4)	764
Climax (G4)	1,609
Coal Creek (J6)	206
Coaldale (H6)	103
Coalmont (F1)	26
Cokedale (K8)	219
Collbran (C4)	310
Colona (D6)	125
Colorado City (K7)	100
Colorado Springs◉ (K5)	70,194
Colorado Springs (urban area)	100,220
Columbine (E1)	12
Columbine Valley ‡(J3)	385
Commerce City (K3)	10,124
Commerce Town (K3)	8,970
Como (H4)	39
Conejos (G8)	105
Cope (O3)	125
Cornish (L2)	11
Cortez◉ (B8)	6,764
Cotopaxi (H6)	100
Cowdrey (G1)	60
Crawford (D5)	147
Craig◉ (D2)	3,984
Creede◉ (E7)	350
Crested Butte (E5)	289
Crestone (H7)	51
Cripple Creek◉ (J5)	614
Crook (O1)	209
Crowley (M6)	265
Cuchara (J8)	258
Dacona (K2)	302
Dailey (O1)	50
De Beque (C4)	172
Deckers (J4)	5
Deer Trail (M3)	764
Del Norte◉ (G7)	1,856
Delagua (K8)	239
Delcarbon (K7)	200
Delhi (M7)	20
Delta◉ (D5)	3,832
DENVER◉ (K3)	493,887
Denver (urb. area)	803,624
Dillon (H3)	814
Dinosaur (B2)	318
Divide (J5)	150
Dolores (C8)	805
Dove Creek◉ (A7)	986
Doyleville (F6)	100
Drake (J2)	70
Durango◉ (D8)	10,530
Eads◉ (N6)	929
Eagle◉ (F3)	546
East Canon (J6)	1,101
Eaton (K1)	1,267
Eckley (P2)	207
Edgewater (J3)	4,314
Edwards (F3)	100
Egnar (B7)	50
Elbert (L4)	176
Eldora (H3)	27
Elizabeth (K4)	326
Elk Springs (C2)	33
Empire (H3)	110
Englewood (K3)	33,398
Erie (K2)	875
Estes Park (J2)	1,175
Eureka (D7)	13
Evans (K2)	1,453
Evergreen (J3)	2,500
Fairplay◉ (H4)	404
Farisita (J7)	125
Federal Heights ‡(J3)	391
Firestone (K2)	276
Firstview (O5)	2
Flagler (N4)	693
Fleming (O1)	384
Florence (J6)	2,821
Florissant (J5)	53
Fort Collins◉ (J1)	25,027
Fort Garland (J8)	
Fort Lupton (K2)	2,194
Fort Lyon (N6)	900
Fort Morgan◉ (M2)	7,379
Fountain (K5)	1,602
Fowler (L6)	1,240
Foxton (J4)	35
Franktown (K4)	50
Fraser (H3)	253
Frederick (K2)	595
Freeman (G7)	65
Freshwater (Guffey) (H5)	15
Frisco (J3)	316
Fruita (B4)	1,830
Fruitvale (B4)	3,302
Galeton (K1)	300
Garcia (J8)	250
Garden City ‡(K2)	129
Gardner (J7)	175
Garfield (J5)	17
Gateway (B5)	300
Genoa (N4)	185
Georgetown◉ (H3)	307
Gilcrest (K2)	357
Gill (L2)	250
Gilman (G3)	375
Glade Park (B5)	281
Glen Haven (H2)	54
Glendale ‡(K3)	468
Glendevey (H1)	5
Glenwood Springs◉ (E4)	3,637
Golden◉ (J3)	7,118
Goodrich (M2)	15
Gould (G2)	105
Granada (P6)	593
Granby (H2)	503
Grand Junction◉ (C4)	18,694
Grand Lake (H2)	170
Grand Valley (D4)	245
Granite (G4)	55
Grant (H4)	300
Greeley◉ (K2)	26,314
Green Mountain Falls (K5)	179
Greenland (K4)	53
Greenwood Village ‡(K3)	572
Greystone (B1)	2
Grover (L1)	133
Guffey (H5)	15
Guinare (K8)	200
Gunnison◉ (E5)	3,477
Gypsum (F3)	358
Hale (P3)	6
Hamilton (D2)	50
Hartman (P6)	164
Hartsel (H4)	50
Hasty (O6)	200
Haswell (N6)	169
Haxtun (O1)	990
Hayden (E2)	764
Henderson (K3)	200
Hereford (L1)	75
Hesperus (C8)	100
Hillrose (N2)	157
Hillside (H6)	17
Hoehne (K8)	500
Holly (P6)	1,108
Holyoke◉ (P1)	1,555
Hooper (H7)	58
Hot Sulphur Springs◉ (H2)	237
Hotchkiss (D5)	626
Howard (H6)	25
Howardsville (E7)	20
Hoyt (L2)	37
Hudson (K2)	430
Hugo◉ (N4)	811
Hygiene (J2)	200
Idaho Springs (H3)	1,480
Idalia (P3)	87
Ignacio (D8)	609
Iliff (N1)	204
Ironton (D7)	1
Ivywild (K5)	11,065
Jamestown (J2)	107
Jansen (K8)	230
Jaroso (H8)	125
Jefferson (H4)	75
Joes (O3)	125
Johnstown (K2)	976
Julesburg◉ (P1)	1,840
Karval (N5)	90
Keenesburg (L2)	409
Keota (L1)	13
Kersey (K2)	378
Kim (N8)	275
Kiowa◉ (L4)	195
Kirk (P3)	113
Kit Carson (O5)	356
Kokomo (G4)	74
Kremmling (G2)	576
Kutch (M5)	2
La Garita (G7)	
La Jara (H8)	724
La Junta◉ (M7)	8,026
La Salle (K2)	1,070
La Sauces (H8)	257
La Veta (J8)	632
Lafayette (K3)	2,612
Laird (P2)	245
Lake City◉ (E6)	106
Lake George (J5)	39
Lakeside ‡(J3)	28
Lakewood (J3)	19,338
Lamar◉ (O6)	7,369
Laporte (J1)	700
Larkspur (K4)	200
Las Animas◉ (N6)	3,402
Lavalley (J8)	
Lawson (H3)	125
Lay (D2)	21
Lazear (D5)	69
Leadville◉ (G4)	4,008
Lebanon (B8)	137
Lewis (B8)	236
Limon (M4)	1,811
Lincoln Park (J6)	2,085
Lindon (N3)	33
Littleton◉ (K3)	13,670
Livermore (J1)	35
Log Lane Village (M2)	310
Loma (B4)	535
Longmont (J2)	11,489
Longview (J4)	21
Louisville (J3)	2,073
Louviers (K3)	305
Loveland (J2)	9,734
Lucerne (K2)	100
Lycan (P7)	4
Lyons (J2)	706
Mack (B4)	200
Maher (D5)	100
Malta (G4)	45
Manassa (H8)	831
Mancos (C8)	832
Manitou Springs (J5)	3,626
Manzanola (M6)	562
Marble (E4)	100
Marvel (C8)	100
Masonville (J2)	90
Massadona (B2)	3
Masters (L2)	6
Matheson (M4)	100
Maybell (C2)	137
McClave (M6)	175
McCoy (F3)	10
Mead (D2)	192
Meeker◉ (D2)	1,655
Meredith (F4)	30
Merino (N2)	268
Mesa (C4)	317
Mesa Verde National Park (C8)	86
Mesita (H8)	30
Messex (N2)	78
Milliken (K2)	630
Milner (F2)	112
Minturn (G3)	662
Model (L8)	30
Moffat (H6)	104
Molina (D4)	14
Monte Vista (G7)	3,385
Montezuma (J3)	17
Montrose◉ (D6)	5,044
Monument (K4)	204
Morrison (J3)	426
Mosca (H7)	130
Mountain View ‡(J3)	826
Nathrop (H5)	45

(continued on following page)

HIGHWAYS

Limited Access Highways	═══
Major Highways	━━━
Other Important Roads	━━━

Interstate Route Numbers	🛡95
Federal Route Numbers	9
State and Other Route Numbers	4

0　40　80
MILES

Colorado
(continued)

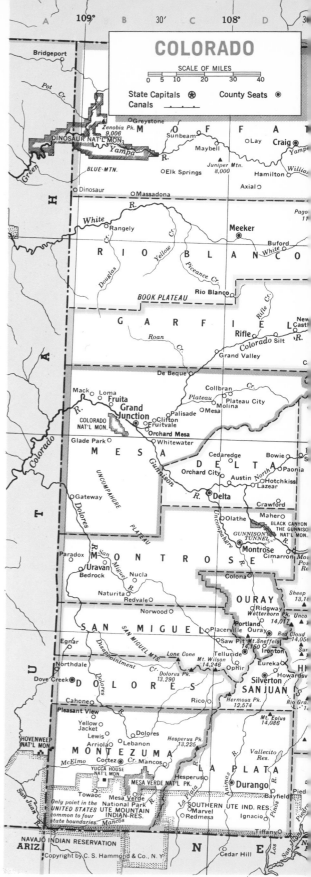

TOPOGRAPHY

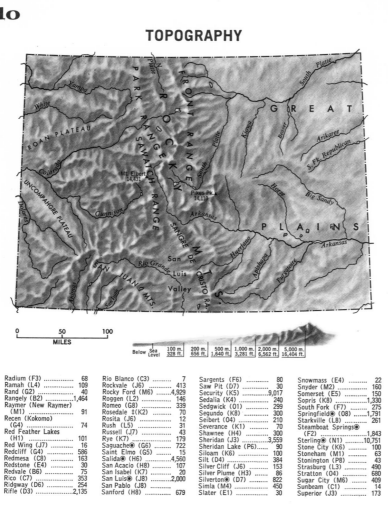

MILES
0   50   100

Below Sea Level | 100 m. 328 ft. | 200 m. 656 ft. | 500 m. 1,640 ft. | 1,000 m. 3,281 ft. | 2,000 m. 6,562 ft. | 5,000 m. 16,404 ft.

AGRICULTURE, INDUSTRY and RESOURCES

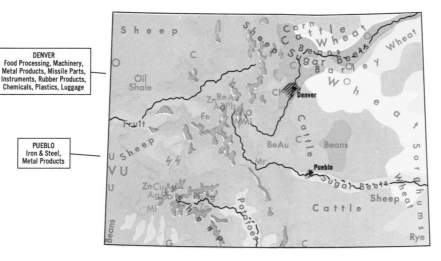

DENVER
Food Processing, Machinery, Metal Products, Missile Parts, Instruments, Rubber Products, Chemicals, Plastics, Luggage

PUEBLO
Iron & Steel, Metal Products

DOMINANT LAND USE

- Specialized Wheat
- Wheat, Range Livestock
- Wheat, Grain Sorghums, Range Livestock
- Dry Beans, General Farming
- Sugar Beets, Dry Beans, Livestock, General Farming
- Fruit, Mixed Farming
- General Farming, Livestock, Special Crops
- Range Livestock
- Forests
- Urban Areas
- Nonagricultural Land

MAJOR MINERAL OCCURRENCES

Ag	Silver	Mi	Mica
Au	Gold	Mo	Molybdenum
Be	Beryl	Mr	Marble
C	Coal	O	Petroleum
Cl	Clay	Pb	Lead
Cu	Copper	U	Uranium
F	Fluorspar	V	Vanadium
Fe	Iron Ore	W	Tungsten
G	Natural Gas	Zn	Zinc

Water Power
Major Industrial Areas

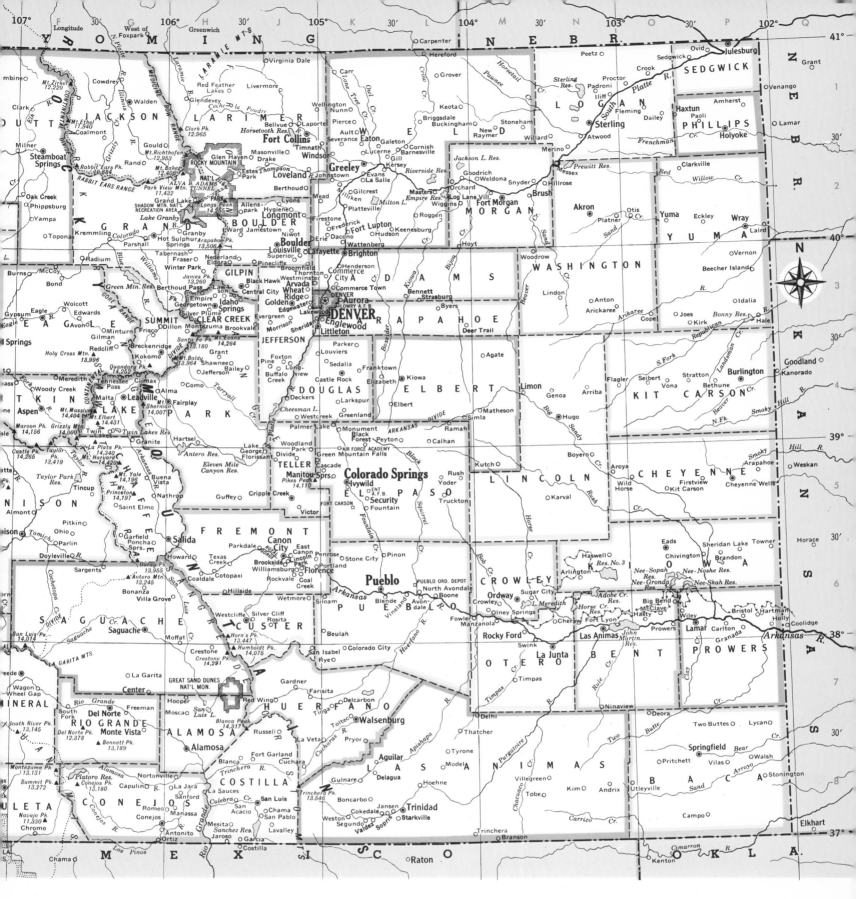

Map of Colorado

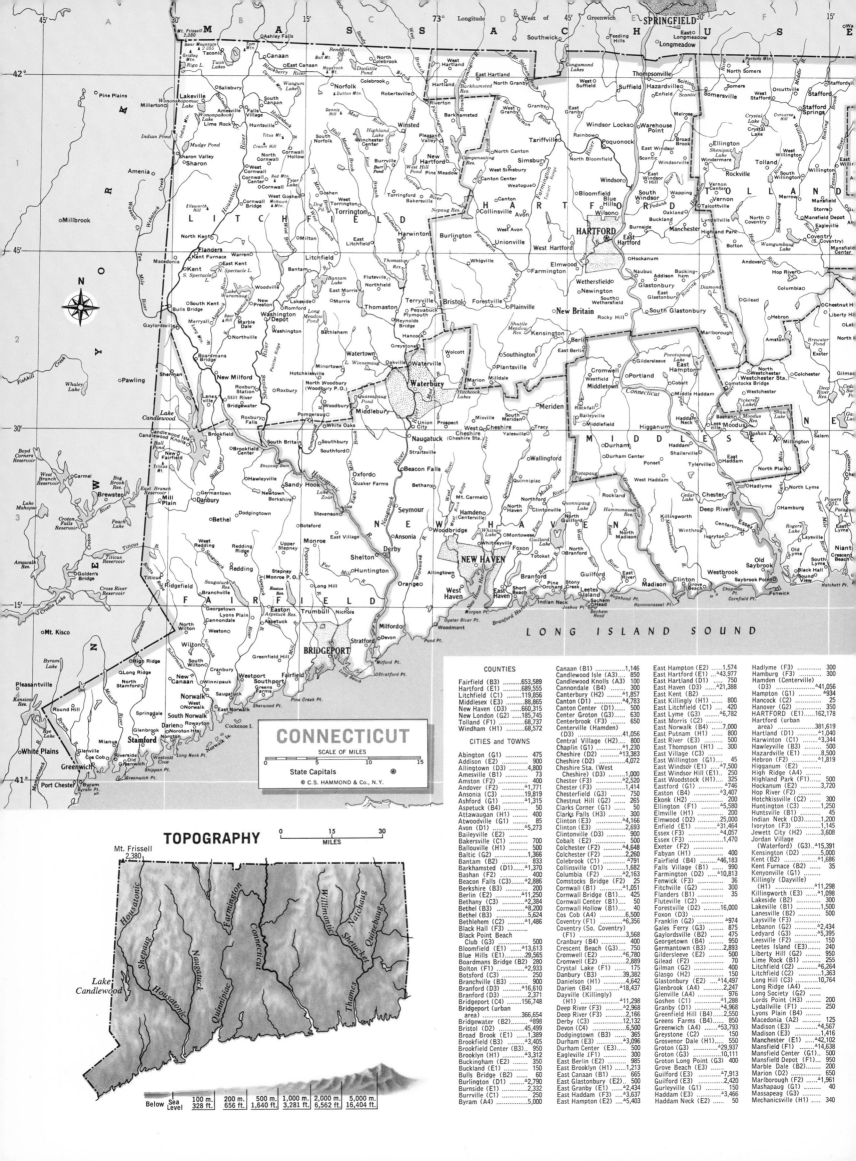

CONNECTICUT
SCALE OF MILES
0 5 10 15
● State Capitals
© C.S. HAMMOND & Co., N.Y.

TOPOGRAPHY
0 15 30 MILES
Mt. Frissell 2,380
Lake Candlewood

Below Sea Level	100 m. 328 ft.	200 m. 656 ft.	500 m. 1,640 ft.	1,000 m. 3,281 ft.	2,000 m. 6,562 ft.	5,000 m. 16,404 ft.

COUNTIES

County	Pop.
Fairfield (B3)	653,589
Hartford (E1)	689,555
Litchfield (C1)	119,856
Middlesex (E3)	88,865
New Haven (D3)	660,315
New London (G2)	185,745
Tolland (F1)	68,737
Windham (H1)	68,572

CITIES and TOWNS

Place	Pop.
Abington (G1)	475
Addison (E2)	900
Allingtown (D3)	4,800
Amesville (B1)	73
Amston (F2)	400
Andover (F2)	△1,771
Ansonia (C3)	19,819
Ashford (G1)	△1,315
Aspetuck (B4)	50
Attawaugan (H1)	400
Atwoodville (G1)	85
Avon (D1)	△5,273
Bakersville (C1)	700
Balouville (H1)	500
Baltic (G2)	1,366
Bantam (B2)	833
Barkhamsted (D1)	△1,370
Bashan (F2)	400
Beacon Falls (C3)	△2,886
Berkshire (B3)	200
Berlin (E2)	△11,250
Bethany (C3)	△2,384
Bethel (B3)	△8,200
Bethel (B3)	5,624
Bethlehem (H1)	△1,486
Black Hall (F3)	
Black Point Beach Club (G3)	500
Bloomfield (E1)	△13,613
Blue Hills (E1)	29,565
Boardmans Bridge (B2)	280
Bolton (F1)	△2,933
Botsford (B3)	250
Branchville (B3)	900
Branford (D3)	△16,610
Branford (D3)	2,371
Bridgeport (C4)	156,748
Bridgeport (urban area)	366,654
Bridgewater (B2)	△800
Bristol (D2)	45,499
Broad Brook (E1)	1,389
Brookfield (B3)	△3,405
Brookfield Center (B3)	950
Brooklyn (H1)	△3,312
Buckingham (E2)	350
Buckland (E1)	150
Bulls Bridge (B2)	60
Burlington (D1)	△2,790
Burnside (E1)	△2,332
Burrville (C1)	250
Byram (A4)	5,000
Canaan (B1)	1,146
Candlewood Isle (A3)	850
Candlewood Knolls (A3)	100
Cannondale (B4)	300
Canterbury (H2)	△1,857
Canton (D1)	△4,783
Canton Center (D1)	500
Center Groton (G3)	630
Centerbrook (F3)	650
Centerville (Hamden) (D3)	41,056
Central Village (H2)	800
Chaplin (G1)	△1,230
Cheshire (D2)	△13,383
Cheshire (D2)	4,072
Cheshire Sta. (West Cheshire) (D3)	1,000
Chester (F3)	△2,520
Chester (F3)	1,414
Chesterfield (G3)	750
Chestnut Hill (G2)	265
Clarks Corner (G1)	300
Clarks Falls (H3)	300
Clinton (E3)	△4,166
Clinton (E3)	2,693
Clintonville (D3)	900
Cobalt (E2)	500
Colchester (F2)	△4,648
Colchester (F2)	2,260
Colebrook (C1)	△791
Collinsville (D1)	1,682
Columbia (F2)	△2,163
Comstocks Bridge (F2)	25
Cornwall (B1)	△1,051
Cornwall Bridge (B1)	425
Cornwall Center (B1)	500
Cornwall Hollow (B1)	40
Cos Cob (A4)	6,500
Coventry (F1)	△6,356
Coventry (So. Coventry) (F1)	3,568
Cranbury (B4)	400
Crescent Beach (G3)	750
Cromwell (E2)	△6,780
Cromwell (E2)	2,889
Crystal Lake (F1)	175
Danbury (B3)	39,382
Danielson (H1)	4,642
Dayville (Killingly) (H1)	△11,298
Deep River (F3)	△2,968
Deep River (F3)	2,166
Derby (C3)	12,132
Devon (C4)	6,500
Dodgingtown (B3)	300
Durham (E3)	△3,096
Durham Center (E3)	500
Eagleville (F1)	300
East Berlin (E2)	985
East Brooklyn (H1)	1,213
East Canaan (B1)	500
East Glastonbury (E2)	500
East Granby (E1)	△2,434
East Haddam (F3)	△3,637
East Hampton (E2)	△5,403
East Hampton (E2)	1,574
East Hartford (E1)	△43,977
East Hartland (D1)	750
East Haven (D3)	△21,388
East Kent (B2)	
East Killingly (H1)	800
East Litchfield (C1)	420
East Lyme (G3)	△6,782
East Morris (C2)	
East Norwalk (B4)	7,000
East Putnam (H1)	800
East River (E3)	500
East Thompson (H1)	300
East Village (C3)	
East Wallingford (D3)	45
East Willington (F1)	250
East Windsor (E1)	△7,500
East Windsor Hill (E1)	250
East Woodstock (H1)	325
Eastford (G1)	△746
Easton (B4)	△3,407
Ekonk (H2)	200
Ellington (F1)	△5,580
Elmville (H1)	200
Elmwood (E1)	25,000
Enfield (E1)	△31,464
Essex (F3)	△4,057
Essex (F3)	1,470
Exeter (F2)	400
Fabyan (H1)	400
Fairfield (B4)	△46,183
Falls Village (B1)	990
Farmington (D2)	△10,813
Fenwick (F3)	36
Fitchville (G2)	300
Flanders (B1)	35
Fluteville (C2)	
Forestville (D2)	16,000
Foxon (D3)	
Franklin (G2)	△974
Gales Ferry (G3)	875
Gaylordsville (B2)	475
Georgetown (B4)	950
Germantown (B3)	2,893
Gildersleeve (E2)	500
Gilman (F2)	70
Gilman (G2)	400
Glasgo (H2)	150
Glastonbury (E2)	△14,497
Glenbrook (A4)	
Glenville (A4)	976
Goshen (C1)	△1,288
Granby (D1)	△4,968
Greenfield Hill (B4)	2,550
Greens Farms (B4)	850
Greenwich (A4)	△53,793
Greystone (C2)	150
Grosvenor Dale (H1)	550
Groton (G3)	29,937
Groton (G3)	10,111
Groton Long Point (G3)	400
Hadlyme (F3)	300
Hamburg (F3)	300
Hamden (Centerville) (D3)	△41,056
Hampton (G1)	△934
Hancock (C3)	25
Hanover (G2)	350
HARTFORD (E1)	162,178
Hartford (urban area)	381,619
Hartland (D1)	△1,040
Harwinton (C1)	△3,344
Hawleyville (B3)	500
Hazardville (E1)	8,500
Hebron (F2)	△1,819
Higganum (E2)	
High Ridge (F1)	
Highland Park (E1)	
Hockanum (E2)	3,720
Hop River (F2)	
Hotchkissville (C2)	300
Huntington (C3)	△1,250
Huntsville (B1)	45
Indian Neck (D3)	1,200
Ivoryton (F3)	1,145
Jewett City (H2)	3,608
Jordan Village (Waterford) (G3)	△15,391
Kensington (D2)	5,000
Kent (B2)	△1,686
Kent Furnace (B2)	35
Kenyonville (G1)	
Killingly (Dayville) (H1)	△11,298
Killingworth (E3)	△1,098
Lakeside (B2)	300
Lakeville (B1)	1,500
Lanesville (B2)	500
Laysville (F3)	
Lebanon (G2)	△2,434
Ledyard (G3)	△5,395
Leesville (F2)	150
Leetes Island (E3)	240
Liberty Hill (G2)	950
Lime Rock (B1)	250
Litchfield (C2)	△6,264
Litchfield (C2)	1,363
Long Hill (C3)	10,764
Long Ridge (A4)	
Long Society (G2)	
Lords Point (H3)	200
Lydallville (F1)	300
Lyons Plain (B4)	
Macedonia (A2)	125
Madison (E3)	△4,567
Madison (E3)	1,416
Manchester (E1)	△42,102
Mansfield (F1)	△14,638
Mansfield Center (G1)	500
Mansfield Depot (F1)	950
Marble Dale (B2)	200
Marion (D2)	650
Marlborough (F2)	△1,961
Mashapaug (G1)	40
Massapeag (G3)	
Mechanicsville (H1)	340

CONNECTICUT

AREA	5,009 sq. mi.
POPULATION	2,832,000
CAPITAL	Hartford
LARGEST CITY	Hartford 162,178
HIGHEST POINT	Mt. Frissell (S. Slope) 2,380 ft.
SETTLED IN	1635
ADMITTED TO UNION	January 9, 1788
POPULAR NAMES	Constitution State; Nutmeg State
STATE FLOWER	Mountain Laurel
STATE BIRD	Robin

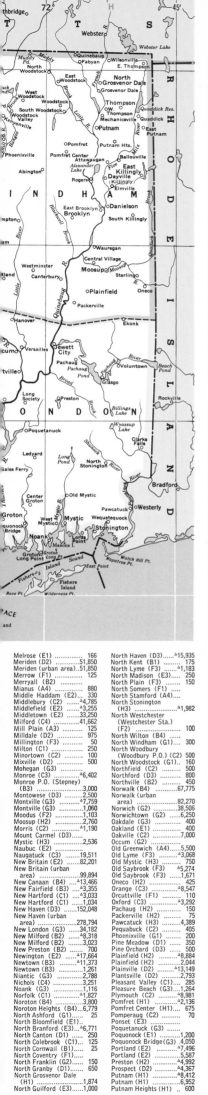

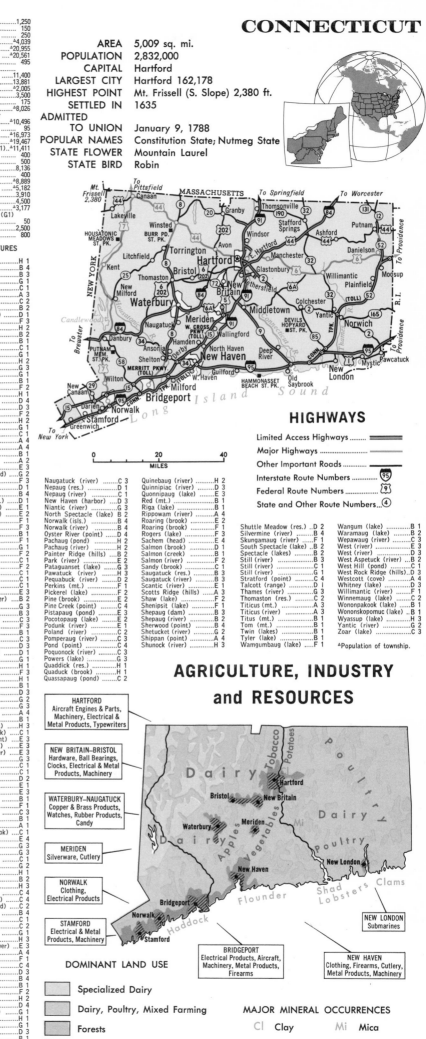

Quaddick (H1)	75	Westfield (E2)	1,250
Quaker Farms (C3)	187	Westford (G1)	150
Quaker Hill (G3)	1,671	Westminster (G2)	250
Quinebaug (H1)	625	Weston (B4)	▲4,039
Quinnipiac (D3)		Westport (B4)	▲20,955
Rainbow (E1)	200	Wethersfield (E2)	▲20,561
Redding (B3)	▲3,359	Whigville (D2)	495
Redding Ridge (B3)	500	White Oaks (C2)	
Reynolds Bridge (C2)	600	Whitneyville (D3)	▲11,400
Ridgefield (B3)	▲8,165	Willimantic (C2)	▲13,881
Ridgefield (B3)	2,954	Willington (F1)	▲2,005
Riverside (A4)	▲9,845	Wilson (E1)	3,500
Riverton (D1)	250	Wilsonville (H1)	175
Robertsville (C1)	150	Wilton (B4)	▲8,026
Rockfall (E2)	975	Winchester Center	
Rockland (E3)	400	(C1)	▲10,496
Rockville (F1)	9,478	Windermere (F1)	95
Rocky Hill (E2)	▲7,404	Windham (G2)	▲16,973
Rogers (H1)	700	Windsor (E1)	▲19,467
Romford (B2)	30	Windsor Locks (E1)	▲11,411
Round Hill (A4)	600	Windsorville (E1)	400
Rowayton (B4)	3,200	Winnipauk (B4)	500
Roxbury (B2)	▲912	Winsted (C1)	8,136
Roxbury Falls (B2)		Winthrop (E3)	400
Roxbury Station (B2)		Wolcott (H1)	▲8,889
Sachem Head (E3)		Woodbridge (D3)	▲5,182
Salem (F3)	▲925	Woodbury (C2)	3,910
Salisbury (B1)	▲3,309	Woodmont (D4)	4,500
Sandy Hook (B3)	1,600	Woodstock (H1)	▲3,177
Saugatuck (B4)	1,500	Woodstock Valley (G1)	
Saybrook Point (F3)	250	Woodville (B2)	50
Scantic (E1)	200	Yalesville (D3)	2,500
Scitico (E1)	125	Yantic (G2)	800
Scotland (G2)	▲684	
Seymour (C3)	▲10,100	**OTHER FEATURES**
Shailerville (E3)		
Sharon (B1)	▲2,141	Alexander (lake)	H 1
Sharon Valley (B1)	174	Aspetuck (res.)	B 4
Shelton (C3)	18,190	Aspetuck (river)	B 3
Sherman (B2)	▲825	Bald (hill)	C 1
Short Beach (D3)	1,200	Ball (mt.)	C 1
Simsbury (D1)	▲10,138	Ball (pond)	A 3
Simsbury (D1)	2,745	Bantam (lake)	C 2
Somers (F1)	▲3,702	Bantam (river)	B 2
Somersville (F1)	750	Barkhamsted (res.)	D 1
Sound View (E3)		Bashan (lake)	F 3
South Britain (B3)	420	Beach (pond)	H 2
South Canaan (B1)	65	Bear (hill)	B 2
South Coventry		Bear (mt.)	B 1
(Coventry) (F1)	3,568	Benedict (pond)	C 1
South Glastonbury		Bigelow (brook)	G 1
(E2)	2,500	Billings (lake)	H 2
South Kent (B2)	328	Black (pond)	G 3
South Killingly (H1)	350	Black (pond)	E 1
South Lyme (F3)	300	Blackberry (river)	B 1
South Meriden (D2)	1,600	Blackledge (river)	F 2
South Norfolk (C1)	350	Blackwell (brook)	H 1
South Norwalk (B4)	18,000	Branford (harbor)	D 4
South Wethersfield (E2)	200	Branford (river)	D 3
South Willington (F1)		Brewster (pond)	F 2
South Wilton (B4)		Broad (brook)	H 2
South Windham (G2)	450	Bungee (brook)	G 1
South Windsor (E1)	▲9,460	Burr (pond)	C 1
South Woodstock (G1)	500	Byram (point)	A 4
Southbury (C3)	▲5,186	Byram (river)	A 4
Southford (C3)		Canaan (mt.)	B 1
Southington (D2)	▲22,797	Candlewood (lake)	A 2
Southington (D2)	9,952	Cedar (lake)	E 3
Southport (B4)	3,500	Cedar Swamp (pond)	G 2
Springdale (A4)	5,280	Chapman (point)	F 3
Stafford (F1)	▲7,476	Cherry (brook)	D 1
Stafford Springs (F1)	3,322	Cockenoe (isl.)	B 4
Staffordville (G1)	980	Compensating (res.)	D 1
Stamford (A4)	92,713	Congamond (lakes)	E 1
Stepney (B3)	3,000	Connecticut (river)	E 2
Sterling (H2)	▲1,397	Converse (hill)	C 1
Stevenson (C3)	460	Cornfield (point)	E 3
Still River (B2)	100	Cream (hill)	B 1
Stonington (H3)	▲13,969	Crystal (lake)	F 1
Stonington (H3)	1,622	Crystal (pond)	G 1
Stony Creek (E3)	1,200	Deep River (res.)	F 2
Storrs (F1)	6,054	Dennis (hill)	C 1
Straitsville (D3)	242	Diamond (lake)	F 2
Stratford (C4)	▲45,012	Dog (pond)	C 1
Suffield (E1)	▲6,779	Doolittle (pond)	C 1
Suffield (E1)	1,069	Dutton (mt.)	C 1
Taconic (B1)	150	East (river)	E 3
Taftville (G2)	5,000	East Aspetuck (river)	B 2
Talcottville (F1)	950	Eastern (point)	G 3
Tariffville (D1)	800	Easton (res.)	B 3
Terryville (C2)	5,231	Eight Mile (brook)	C 3
Thamesville (G3)		Eight Mile (river)	F 2
Thomaston (C2)	▲5,850	Ellsworth (hill)	B 1
Thomaston (C2)	3,579	Far Mill (river)	C 3
Thompson (H1)	▲6,217	Farm (river)	D 3
Thompsonville (E1)	18,000	Farmington (river)	G 1
Titicus (A3)	275	Fenton (river)	F 1
Tolland (F1)	▲2,950	Five Mile (river)	H 1
Torrington (C1)		Four Mile (river)	F 3
Torrington (C1)	30,045	French (river)	H 1
Totoket (D3)	21,000	Frisbie (lake)	D 1
Tracy (D2)	200	Gaillard (lake)	D 3
Trumbull (C4)	▲20,379	Gardner (lake)	G 3
Tylerville (E3)		Goshen (point)	G 3
Uncasville (G3)	1,381	Greenwich (point)	A 4
Union (G1)	▲383	Gridley (mt.)	B 1
Union City (C3)	5,000	Groton Long (point)	H 3
Unionville (D1)	2,246	Hall Meadow (brook)	C 1
Upper Stepney (B3)		Hammonasset (point)	E 3
Vernon (F1)	▲16,961	Hammonasset (river)	E 3
Vernon Center (F1)	500	Hammonasset (river)	E 3
Versailles (G2)	600	Hatchett (point)	E 3
Voluntown (H2)	▲1,028	Haystack (mt.)	C 1
Wallingford (D3)	▲29,920	Highland (lake)	C 1
Wapping (E1)	900	Hitchcock (lakes)	D 2
Warehouse Point (E1)	1,936	Hockanum (river)	E 1
Warren (B2)	▲600	Hogshead (point)	E 3
Warrenville (G1)	110	Hollenbeck (river)	B 1
Washington (B2)	▲2,603	Hop (river)	F 1
Washington Depot (B2)	489	Housatonic (river)	B 1
Waterbury (C2)	107,130	Indian (mt.)	B 1
Waterbury (urban		Indian (river)	D 3
area)	141,626	Ivy Mountain (brook)	C 1
Waterford (Jordan		Joshua (pt.)	E 4
Village) (G3)	▲15,391	Konomoc (lake)	G 3
Watertown (C2)	▲14,837	Latimers (brook)	G 3
Waterville (C2)	5,088	Leadmine (brook)	C 1
Wauregan (H2)	900	Little (river)	G 1
Weatogue (D1)	750	Little (river)	G 2
Wequetequock (H3)	540	Long (mt.)	B 2
West Avon (D1)		Long (pond)	H 2
West Cheshire (Cheshire		Long Beach (pen.)	C 4
Sta.) (D3)	1,000	Long Island (sound)	C 4
West Cornwall (B1)	160	Long Meadow (pond)	C 2
West Goshen (B1)	600	Long Neck (point)	B 4
West Granby (D1)	600	Mad (river)	C 1
West Haddam (E3)		Mad (river)	C 2
West Hartford (D1)	▲62,382	Mashapaug (lake)	G 1
West Hartland (D1)		Masons (isl.)	H 3
West Haven (D3)	▲43,002	Menunketesuck (river)	E 3
West Mystic (H3)	3,268	Mianus (river)	A 4
West Norwalk (B4)	724	Middle (river)	C 4
West Redding (B3)	1,000	Milford (point)	C 4
West Simsbury (D1)	300	Mill (river)	D 3
West Stafford (F1)	480	Mill (river)	B 4
West Suffield (E1)	700	Mohawk (mt.)	B 1
West Thompson (H1)	100	Moodus (res.)	F 2
West Torrington (C1)	240	Morgan (point)	D 2
West Willington (F1)	350	Mount Hope (river)	G 1
West Woodstock (G1)	100	Muddy (brook)	H 1
Westbrook (F3)	▲2,399	Muddy (pond)	G 1
Westchester (F2)	100	Mudge (pond)	B 1
Westchester Sta.		Mystic (river)	H 3
(North Westchester)		Natchaug (river)	G 1
(F2)	100	

Naugatuck (river)	C 3	Quinebaug (river)	H 2
Nepaug (res.)	D 1	Quinnipiac (river)	D 3
Nepaug (river)	C 1	Quonnipaug (lake)	E 3
New Haven (harbor)	D 3	Red (mt.)	B 1
Niantic (river)	G 3	Riga (lake)	B 1
North Spectacle (lake)	B 2	Rippowam (river)	A 4
Norwalk (islands)	B 4	Roaring (brook)	C 2
Norwalk (river)	B 4	Roaring (brook)	F 1
Oyster River (point)	D 4	Rogers (lake)	F 3
Pachaug (pond)	H 2	Sachem (head)	E 4
Pachaug (river)	H 2	Salmon (brook)	D 1
Painter Ridge (hills)	B 2	Salmon (creek)	B 1
Park (river)	E 2	Salmon (river)	F 2
Pataguanset (lake)	G 3	Sandy (brook)	C 1
Pawcatuck (river)	H 3	Saugatuck (res.)	B 3
Pequabuck (river)	D 2	Saugatuck (river)	B 3
Perkins (mt.)	C 1	Scantic (river)	E 1
Pickerel (lake)	F 2	Scotts Ridge (hills)	A 3
Pine (brook)	C 1	Shaw (river)	F 2
Pine Creek (point)	C 4	Shenipsit (lake)	F 1
Pistapaug (lake)	E 3	Shepaug (dam)	B 3
Pocotopaug (lake)	E 2	Shepaug (river)	B 2
Podunk (river)	C 2	Sherwood (point)	B 4
Poland (river)	C 2	Shetucket (river)	G 2
Pomperaug (river)	C 3	Shippan (point)	A 4
Pond (point)	C 4	Shunock (river)	H 3
Poquonock (river)	G 3	
Powers (lake)	F 3	
Quaddick (res.)	H 1	
Quaduck (brook)	H 1	
Quassapaug (pond)	C 2	

Shuttle Meadow (res.)	D 2	Wangum (lake)	B 1
Silvermine (river)	B 4	Waramaug (lake)	B 2
Skungamaug (river)	F 1	Wepawaug (river)	C 3
South Spectacle (lake)	B 2	West (river)	E 3
Spectacle (lakes)	B 2	West (river)	D 3
Still (river)	C 1	West Aspetuck (river)	B 2
Still (river)	B 2	West Hill (pond)	C 1
Still (river)	C 1	West Rock Ridge (hills)	D 3
Still (river)	G 1	Westcott (cove)	A 4
Stratford (point)	C 4	Whitney (lake)	D 3
Talcott (range)	D 1	Willimantic (river)	F 1
Thames (river)	G 3	Winnemaug (lake)	C 2
Thomaston (res.)	C 2	Wononpakook (lake)	B 1
Titicus (mt.)	B 1	Wononskopomuc (lake)	B 1
Titicus (river)	A 3	Wyassup (lake)	H 3
Titus (mt.)	B 1	Yantic (river)	G 2
Tom (mt.)	B 1	Zoar (lake)	C 3
Twin (lakes)	B 1	
Tyler (lake)	C 1	
Wamgumbaug (lake)	F 1	

▲Population of township.

HIGHWAYS

Limited Access Highways	
Major Highways	
Other Important Roads	
Interstate Route Numbers	95
Federal Route Numbers	9
State and Other Route Numbers	4

0 20 40
MILES

Melrose (E1)	166	North Haven (D3)	▲15,935
Meriden (D2)	51,850	North Kent (B1)	175
Meriden (urban area)	51,850	North Lyme (F3)	▲1,183
Merrow (F1)	125	North Madison (E3)	250
Merryall (B2)		North Plain (F3)	150
Mianus (A4)	880	North Somers (F1)	
Middle Haddam (E2)	330	North Stamford (A4)	
Middlebury (C2)	▲4,785	North Stonington	
Middlefield (E2)	▲3,255	(H3)	▲1,982
Middletown (E2)	33,250	North Westchester	
Milford (C4)	41,662	(Westchester Sta.)	
Mill Plain (A3)	125	(F2)	100
Milldale (D2)	975	North Wilton (B4)	
Millington (F3)	50	North Windham (G1)	300
Milton (C1)	250	North Woodbury	
Minortown (C2)	100	(Woodbury P.O.) (C2)	500
Mixville (D2)	500	North Woodstock (G1)	160
Mohegan (G3)		Northfield (C2)	500
Monroe (C3)	▲6,402	Northford (D3)	800
Monroe P.O. (Stepney)		Northville (B2)	450
(B3)	3,000	Norwalk (B4)	67,775
Montowese (D3)	2,500	Norwalk (urban	
Montville (G3)	▲7,759	area)	82,070
Montville (G3)	1,060	Norwich (G2)	38,506
Moodus (F2)	1,103	Norwichtown (G2)	6,250
Moosup (H2)	2,760	Oakdale (G3)	400
Morris (C2)	▲1,190	Oakland (E1)	400
Mount Carmel (D3)		Oakville (C2)	7,000
Mystic (H3)	2,536	Occum (G2)	
Naubuc (E2)		Old Greenwich (A4)	5,500
Naugatuck (C3)	19,511	Old Lyme (F3)	▲3,068
New Britain (D2)	82,201	Old Mystic (H3)	750
New Britain (urban		Old Saybrook (F3)	▲5,274
area)	99,894	Old Saybrook (F3)	1,671
New Canaan (B4)	▲13,466	Oneco (H2)	425
New Fairfield (B3)	▲3,355	Orange (C3)	▲8,547
New Hartford (C1)	▲3,033	Orcuttville (F1)	110
New Hartford (C1)	1,034	Oxford (C3)	▲3,292
New Haven (D3)	152,048	Pachaug (H2)	150
New Haven (urban		Packerville (H2)	75
area)	278,794	Pawcatuck (H3)	4,389
New London (G3)	34,182	Pequabuck (C2)	405
New Milford (B2)	▲8,318	Phoenixville (G1)	200
New Milford (B2)	3,023	Pine Meadow (D1)	350
New Preston (B2)	700	Pine Orchard (D3)	500
Newington (E2)	▲17,664	Plainfield (H2)	▲8,884
Newtown (B3)	▲11,373	Plainfield (H2)	2,044
Newtown (B3)	1,261	Plainville (D2)	▲13,149
Niantic (G3)	2,788	Plantsville (D2)	2,793
Nichols (C4)	3,251	Pleasant Valley (C1)	285
Noank (G3)	1,116	Pleasure Beach (G3)	1,264
Norfolk (C1)	▲1,827	Plymouth (C2)	▲8,981
Noroton (B4)	3,800	Pomfret (H1)	▲2,136
Noroton Heights (B4)	6,779	Pomfret Center (H1)	675
North Ashford (G1)	25	Pomperaug (C3)	70
North Bloomfield (E1)		Ponset (E3)	
North Branford (E3)	▲6,771	Poquetanuck (G3)	
North Canton (D1)	250	Poquonock (E1)	1,200
North Colebrook (C1)	125	Poquonock Bridge (G3)	4,050
North Cornwall (B1)	25	Portland (E2)	▲7,496
North Coventry (F1)		Portland (E2)	5,587
North Franklin (G2)	150	Preston (H2)	▲4,992
North Granby (D1)	650	Prospect (D2)	▲4,367
North Grosvenor Dale		Putnam (H1)	▲8,412
(H1)	1,874	Putnam (H1)	6,952
North Guilford (E3)	1,000	Putnam Heights (H1)	600

AGRICULTURE, INDUSTRY and RESOURCES

HARTFORD
Aircraft Engines & Parts, Machinery, Electrical & Metal Products, Typewriters

NEW BRITAIN–BRISTOL
Hardware, Ball Bearings, Clocks, Electrical & Metal Products, Machinery

WATERBURY–NAUGATUCK
Copper & Brass Products, Watches, Rubber Products, Candy

MERIDEN
Silverware, Cutlery

NORWALK
Clothing, Electrical Products

STAMFORD
Electrical & Metal Products, Machinery

NEW LONDON
Submarines

BRIDGEPORT
Electrical Products, Aircraft, Machinery, Metal Products, Firearms

NEW HAVEN
Clothing, Firearms, Cutlery, Metal Products, Machinery

DOMINANT LAND USE

- Specialized Dairy
- Dairy, Poultry, Mixed Farming
- Forests
- Urban Areas

MAJOR MINERAL OCCURRENCES

Cl Clay   Mi Mica

Major Industrial Areas

FLORIDA

AREA	58,560 sq. mi.
POPULATION	5,805,000
CAPITAL	Tallahassee
LARGEST CITY	Miami 291,688
HIGHEST POINT	345 ft. (Walton County)
SETTLED IN	1565
ADMITTED TO UNION	March 3, 1845
POPULAR NAMES	Sunshine State; Peninsula State
STATE FLOWER	Orange Blossom
STATE BIRD	Mockingbird

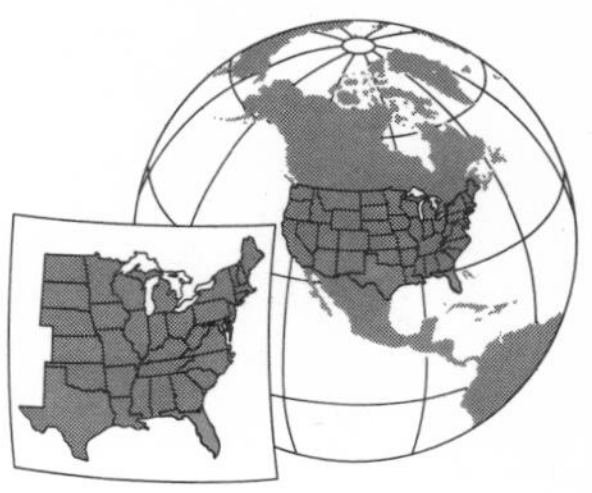

TOPOGRAPHY

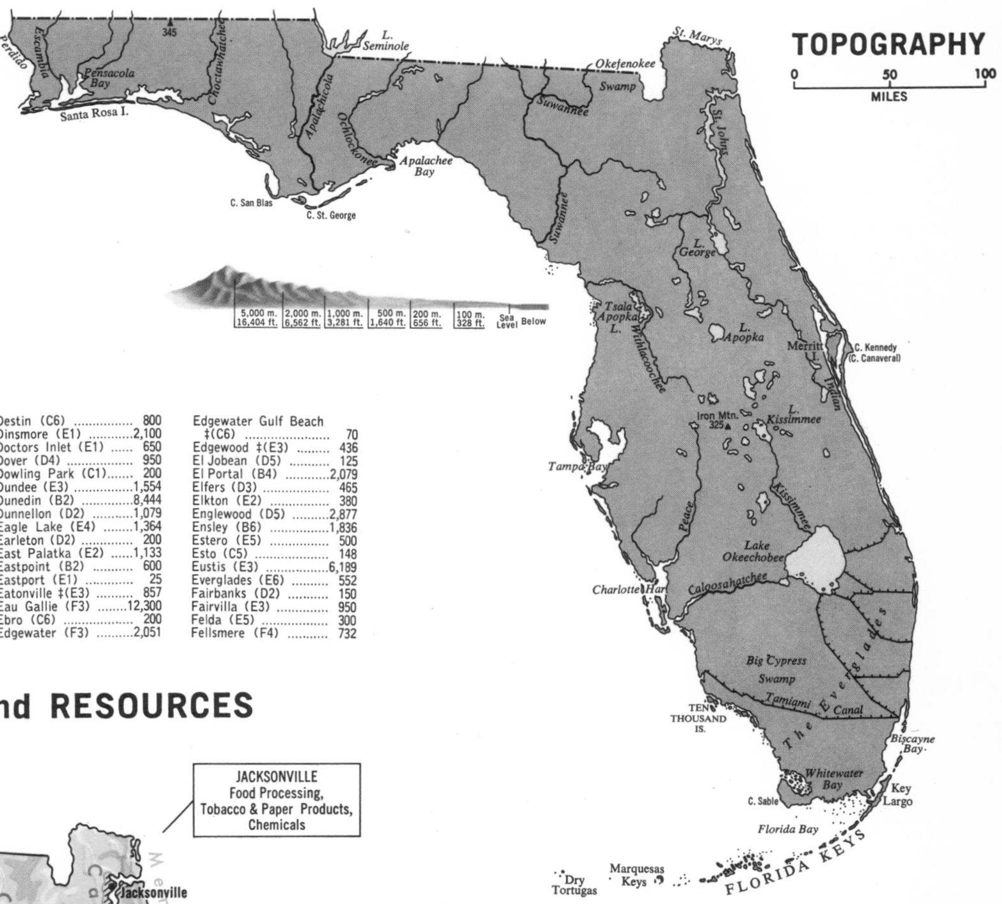

0 50 100
MILES
Perdido
Escambia
Pensacola Bay
Santa Rosa I.
345
Choctawhatchee
Apalachicola
Ochlockonee
L. Seminole
Apalachee Bay
C. San Blas
C. St. George
Okefenokee Swamp
St. Marys
Suwannee
St. Johns
L. George
Tsala Apopka L.
Withlacoochee
L. Apopka
Merritt I.
C. Kennedy (C. Canaveral)
Indian
Iron Mtn. 325
L. Kissimmee
Kissimmee
Tampa Bay
Peace
Lake Okeechobee
Charlotte Har.
Caloosahatchee
Big Cypress Swamp
Tamiami Canal
The Everglades
TEN THOUSAND IS.
Biscayne Bay
Whitewater Bay
C. Sable
Key Largo
Florida Bay
Marquesas Keys
Dry Tortugas
FLORIDA KEYS
5,000 m. 16,404 ft.
2,000 m. 6,562 ft.
1,000 m. 3,281 ft.
500 m. 1,640 ft.
200 m. 656 ft.
100 m. 328 ft.
Sea Level
Below

COUNTIES

Alachua (D2) 74,074
Baker (D1) 7,363
Bay (C6) 67,131
Bradford (D2) 12,446
Brevard (F3) 111,435
Broward (F5) 333,946
Calhoun (D6) 7,422
Charlotte (E5) 12,594
Citrus (D3) 9,268
Clay (E2) 19,535
Collier (E5) 15,753
Columbia (D1) 20,077
Dade (F6) 935,047
De Soto (E4) 11,683
Dixie (C2) 4,479
Duval (E1) 455,411
Escambia (B6) 173,829
Flagler (E2) 4,566
Franklin (B2) 6,576
Gadsden (B1) 41,989
Gilchrist (D2) 2,868
Glades (E5) 2,950
Gulf (D7) 9,937
Hamilton (D1) 7,705
Hardee (E4) 12,370
Hendry (E5) 8,119
Hernando (D3) 11,205
Highlands (E4) 21,338
Hillsborough (D4) 397,788
Holmes (C5) 10,844
Indian River (F4) 25,309
Jackson (D5) 36,208
Jefferson (C1) 9,543
Lafayette (C2) 2,889
Lake (E3) 57,383
Lee (E5) 54,539
Leon (B1) 74,225
Levy (D2) 10,364
Liberty (B1) 3,138
Madison (C1) 14,154
Manatee (D4) 69,168
Marion (D2) 51,616
Martin (F4) 16,932
Monroe (E7) 47,921
Nassau (E1) 17,189
Okaloosa (C6) 61,175
Okeechobee (F4) 6,424
Orange (E3) 263,540
Osceola (E3) 19,029
Palm Beach (F5).......228,106
Pasco (D3) 36,785
Pinellas (D4) 374,665
Polk (E4) 195,139
Putnam (E2) 32,212
Saint Johns (E2) 30,034
Saint Lucie (F4) 39,294
Santa Rosa (B6) 29,547
Sarasota (D4) 76,895
Seminole (E3) 54,947
Sumter (D3) 11,869
Suwannee (C1) 14,961
Taylor (C1) 13,168
Union (D1) 6,043
Volusia (E2) 125,319
Wakulla (B1) 5,257
Walton (C6) 15,576
Washington (C6) 11,249

CITIES and TOWNS

Alachua (D2) 1,974
Alford (D6) 380
Allenhurst (F3) 100
Alliance (A1) 100
Altamonte Sprs. (E3)...1,212
Altha (A1) 413
Altoona (E3) 750
Alturas (E4) 600
Alva (E5) 500
Anna Maria (D4) 690
Anthony (D2) 400
Apalachicola◉ (A2) 3,099
Apollo Beach (C3) ....
Apopka (E3) 3,578
Arcadia◉ (E4) 5,889
Archer (D2) 707
Argyle (C6) 110
Aripeka (D3) 250
Arlington (E1) 7,000
Arran (B1) 150
Astatula (E3) 357
Astor (E2) 125
Atlantic Beach (E1)....3,125
Atlantis ‡(F5) 2
Auburndale (E3) 5,595
Aucilla (C1) 300
Avon Park (E4) 6,073
Babson Park (E4) 950
Bagdad (B6) 1,500
Baker (C5) 800
Bal Harbour (C4) 727
Baldwin (E1) 1,272
Barberville (E2) 300
Barrineau Park (B6).... 200
Barth (B6) 200
Bartow◉ (E4) 12,849
Bascom (A1) 175
Basinger (F4) 200
Bay Harbour Isls. (C4) 3,249
Bay Pines (B3) ....
Bay Sprs. (B6) 125
Bayard (E1) 300
Bayview ‡(C6) 422
Bean City (F5) 400
Bee Ridge (D4) 2,043
Bell (D2) 134
Belle Glade (F5) 11,273
Belle Isle (E3) 2,344
Belleair (B2) 2,456
Belleair Beach (B2)...... 563
Belleair Shores (B3)..... 61
Belleview (D2) 864
Belleville (C1) 100
Bennett (D6) 125
Beverly Beach (E2) 9
Biscayne Park (B4)......2,911
Bithlo (E3) 168
Blountstown◉ (A1) 2,375
Boca Grande (D5) 500
Boca Raton (F5) 6,961
Bokeelia (D5) 350
Bonifay◉ (C5) 2,222
Bonita Springs (E5) 900
Bostwick (E2) 476
Boulogne (E1) 46
Bowling Green (E4)......1,171
Boyd (C1) 102
Boynton Beach (F5)....10,467
Bradenton◉ (D4) 19,380
Bradenton Beach (D4)..1,124
Bradley (D4) 1,035
Brandon (D4) 1,665
Branford (D2) 663
Brewster (E4) 100
Briny Breezes ‡(F5).....
Bristol◉ (B1) 614
Bronson◉ (D2) 707
Brooker (D2) 292
Brooksville◉ (D3) 3,301
Brownsville (B6) 38,417
Brownville (E4) 206
Bruce (C6) 200
Bryant (F5) 1,215
Bryceville (D1) 150
Bunnell◉ (E2) 1,860
Bushnell◉ (D3) 644
Callahan (E1) 782
Campbellton (D5) 309
Campville (D2) 160
Canal Point (F5) 832
Candler (E2) 182
Cantonment (B6) 2,499
Cape Canaveral (F3).....4,000
Capitola (B1) 250
Captiva (D5) 101
Carol City (B4) 21,749
Carrabelle (B2) 1,146
Caryville (C6) 730
Cassadaga (E3) 300
Casselberry ‡(E3) 2,463
Cedar Grove (D6) 676
Cedar Key (C2) 668
Center Hill (D3) 529
Century (B5) 2,046
Chaires (B1) 200
Charlotte Harbor (E5)..1,200
Chattahoochee (B1)......9,699
Cherry L. Farms (C1)... 400
Chiefland (D2) 1,459
Chipley◉ (D6) 3,159
Chokoloskee (E6) 190
Chosen (F5) 1,858
Christmas (E3) 250
Cinco Bayou (B6) 643
Citra (D2) 500
City Point (F3) 400
Clarksville (D6) 250
Clearwater◉ (B2) 34,653
Clermont (E3) 3,313
Cleveland (E5) 200
Clewiston (E5) 3,114
Cloud Lake ‡(F5)......... 148
Cocoa (F3) 12,294
Cocoa Beach (F3) 3,475
Coleman (D3) 921
Compass Lake (D6) 200
Concord (B1) 400
Cooper City (F5) 550
Coral Gables (B5)......34,793
Coronado (F2) 3,500
Cortez (D4) 2,000
Cottagehill (B6) 500
Cottondale (D6) 849
Crawfordville◉ (B1)..... 650
Crescent City (E2) 1,629
Crestview◉ (C6) 7,467
Cross City◉ (C2) 1,857
Crystal Lake (D6) 250
Crystal River (D3) 1,423
Crystal Springs (D3).... 300
Cutler Ridge (F6) 7,005
Cypress (A1) 260
Dade City◉ (D3) 4,759
Dania (B4) 7,065
Davenport (E3) 1,209
Davie (B4) 950
Day (C1) 350
Daytona Beach (F2)....37,395
Daytona Beach Shores (F2) 3,741
De Bary (E3) 2,362
De Funiak Sprs.◉ (C6)5,282
De Land◉ (E2) 10,775
De Leon Springs (E2)... 900
De Soto City (E4) 245
Deer Park (F3) 200
Deerfield Beach (F5)....9,573
Delray Beach (F5)......12,230
Denaud (E5) 125
Destin (C6) 800
Dinsmore (E1) 2,100
Doctors Inlet (E1) 650
Dover (D4) 950
Dowling Park (C1)....... 200
Dundee (E3) 1,554
Dunedin (B2) 8,444
Dunnellon (D2) 1,079
Eagle Lake (E4) 1,364
Earleton (D2) 200
East Palatka (E2) 1,133
Eastpoint (B2) 600
Eastport (E1) 25
Eatonville ‡(E3) 857
Eau Gallie (F3) 12,300
Ebro (C6) 200
Edgewater (F3) 2,051
Edgewater Gulf Beach ‡(C6) 70
Edgewood ‡(E3) 436
El Jobean (D5) 125
El Portal (B4) 2,079
Elfers (D3) 465
Elkton (E2) 380
Englewood (D5) 2,877
Ensley (B6) 1,836
Estero (E5) 500
Esto (C5) 148
Eustis (E3) 6,189
Everglades (E6) 552
Fairbanks (D2) 150
Fairvilla (E3) 950
Felda (E5) 300
Fellsmere (F4) 732
Fern Crest Vill. (B4).... 93
Fernandina Beach◉(E1)7,276
Flagler Beach (E2)...... 970
Floral City (D3) 925
Florida City (F6) 4,114
Floridatown (B6) 200
Florosa (B6) 350
Foley (C1) 2,000
Fort Drum (F4) 70
Fort George Isl. (E1).... 150
Fort Green (E4) 375
Ft. Lauderdale◉ (C4) 83,648
Fort Lauderdale-Hollywood (urban area)..319,951
Fort McCoy (E2) 600
Fort Meade (E4) 4,014
Fort Myers◉ (E5) 22,523
Ft. Myers Beach (E5)..2,463
Fort Ogden (E4) 500
Fort Pierce◉ (F4) 25,256
Ft. Walton Beach (C6)12,147
Fort White (D2) 425
Fountain (D6) 110
Freeport (C6) 900
Frink (D6) 300
Frostproof (E4) 2,664
Fruitland Park (D3).... 774
Fruitville (D4) 2,131
Gainesville◉ (D2) 29,701
Garden City (E1) 500
Gardner (E4) 125
Geneva (E3) 600
Georgetown (E2) 575
Gibsonton (C3) 1,673
Gifford (F4) 3,509
Glen Ridge ‡(F5) 226
Glen Saint Mary (D1).. 329
Glenwood (E2) 200
Golden Beach (C4) 413
Golf (F5) 35
Golfview ‡(F5) 131
Gonzalez (B6) 700
Goodland (E6) 300
Gotha (E3) 600
Goulding (B6) 300
Goulds (F6) 5,121
Graceville (D5) 2,307
Graham (D2) 115
Grand Ridge (A1) 415
Grandin (E2) 200
Grant (F4) 500
Green Cove Sprs.◉(E2)4,233
Greenacres City (F5)....1,026
Greensboro (B1) 709
Greenville (C1) 1,318
Greenwood (A1) 500
Gretna (B1) 647
Groveland (E3) 1,747
Gulf Breeze (B6) 2,500
Gulf Hammock (D2) 360
Gulf Stream (F5) 176
Gulfport (B3) 9,730
Hacienda (B4) 125
Haines City (E3) 9,135
Hallandale (B4) 10,483
Hampton (D2) 340
Harbor Bluffs (B3) .....
Harlem (F5) 1,256
Harold (B6) 250
Hastings (E2) 617
Havana (B1) 2,090
Haverhill ‡(F5) 442
Hawthorne (D2) 1,167
Hernando (D3) 301
Hialeah (B4) 66,972
Hialeah Gardens (B4).... 172
High Point (B3) ....
High Springs (D2) 2,329
Highland Beach (F5).... 65
Highland City (E4) 1,020
Highland Park (E4) 94
Hillcrest Heights (E4).. 138
Hilliard (E1) 1,075
Hilliardville (B1) 150
Hillsboro Beach ‡(F5).. 437
Hines (C2) 450
Hinson (B1) 600
Hobe Sound (F4) 950
Holder (D3) 160
Holly Hill (E2) 4,182
Hollywood (B4) 35,237
Hollywood-Fort Lauderdale (urban area)..319,951
Hollywood Ridge Farms (B4) 108
Holmes Beach (D4) 1,143
Holt (C6) 800
Homestead (F6) 9,152
Homosassa (D3) 650
Homosassa Sprs. (D3)... 300
Horseshoe Beach (C2).. 300
Howey in the Hills (E3) 402
Hudson (D3) 250
Hull (E4) 100
Hypoluxo (F5) 114
Immokalee (E5) 3,224
Indialantic (F3) 1,653
Indian Creek (B4) 60
Indian Hbr. Bch. (F3)..
Indian River City (F3).. 980
Indian R. Shores (F4)... 19
Indian Rocks Bch. (B3)1,940
Indian Rocks Bch. So. Shr. (B3) 296
Indiantown (F4) 1,411
Inglis (D2) 250
Intercession City (E3).. 400
Interlachen (E2) 349
Inverness◉ (D3) 1,878
Islamorada (F7) 800
Island Grove (D2) 175
Islandia ‡(F6) ....
Jacksonville◉ (E1)...201,030
Jacksonville (urban area) 372,569
Jacksonville Bch. (E1)12,049
Jamieson (B1) 250
Jasper◉ (D1) 2,103
Jay (B5) 672
Jennings (C1) 516
Jensen Beach (F4) 1,800
Johnson (E2) 150
Juno Beach (F5) 249
Jupiter (F5) 1,058
Jupiter Inlet Col. ‡(F5) 242
Jupiter Island (F4) 114
Kathleen (D3) 900
Kenansville (F4) 200
Kendall (B5) 2,100
Kendrick (D2) 500
Kenneth City (B3)........2,114
Key Biscayne (B5)........
Key Colony Beach (F7).. 66
Key Largo (F6) 900
Key West◉ (E7) 33,956
Keystone Heights (E2).. 655
Kinard (D6) 400
Kissimmee◉ (E3) 6,845
Kynesville (D6) 200
La Belle◉ (E5) 1,262
La Crosse (D2) 165
Lacoochee (D3) 1,523
Lady Lake (E3) 335
Lake Alfred (E3) 2,191
Lake Butler◉ (D1) 1,311
Lake City◉ (D1) 9,465
Lake Clarke Shrs. ‡(F5)1,297
Lake Como (E2) 250
Lake Hamilton (E3)...... 930
Lake Harbor (F5) 800
Lake Helen (E3) 1,096
Lake Jem (E3) 300
Lake Mary (E3) 800
Lake Monroe (E3) 975
Lake Park (F5) 3,589
Lake Placid (E4) 1,007
Lake Wales (E4) 8,346
Lake Worth (G5) 20,758
Lakeland (D3) 41,350
Lakeport (E5) 200
Lakeview ‡(F5) 20

(continued on following page)

AGRICULTURE, INDUSTRY and RESOURCES

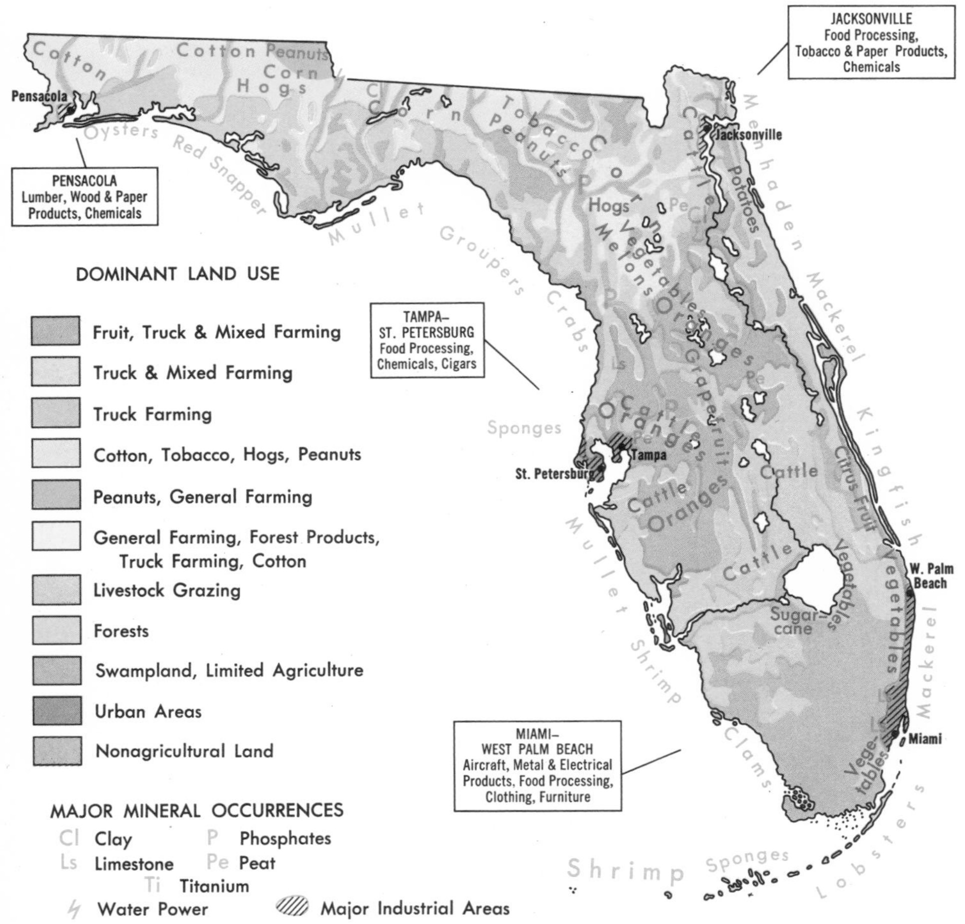

JACKSONVILLE
Food Processing, Tobacco & Paper Products, Chemicals
PENSACOLA
Lumber, Wood & Paper Products, Chemicals
TAMPA–ST. PETERSBURG
Food Processing, Chemicals, Cigars
MIAMI–WEST PALM BEACH
Aircraft, Metal & Electrical Products, Food Processing, Clothing, Furniture
Pensacola
Jacksonville
Tampa
St. Petersburg
W. Palm Beach
Miami
Cotton
Peanuts
Corn
Hogs
Tobacco
Cattle
Potatoes
Melons
Vegetables
Oranges
Grapefruit
Citrus Fruit
Sugar-cane
Oysters
Red Snapper
Mullet
Groupers
Crabs
Sponges
Shrimp
Clams
Lobsters
Menhaden
Mackerel
Kingfish
DOMINANT LAND USE
Fruit, Truck & Mixed Farming
Truck & Mixed Farming
Truck Farming
Cotton, Tobacco, Hogs, Peanuts
Peanuts, General Farming
General Farming, Forest Products, Truck Farming, Cotton
Livestock Grazing
Forests
Swampland, Limited Agriculture
Urban Areas
Nonagricultural Land
MAJOR MINERAL OCCURRENCES
Cl Clay
P Phosphates
Ls Limestone
Pe Peat
Ti Titanium
Water Power
Major Industrial Areas

Florida
(continued)

Lakewood (C5) 150
Lamont (C1) 500
Land O'Lakes (D3) 825
Lantana (F5) 5,021
Largo (B3) 5,302
Lauderdale-by-the-Sea (C3) 1,327
Lauderhill (B4) 132
Laurel (D4) 850
Laurel Hill (C5) 411
Lawtey (D1) 623
Lazy Lake (B3) 49
Lecanto (D3) 238
Lee (C1) 243
Leesburg (E3) 11,172
Leisure City (F6) 3,001
Lighthouse Point (F5)..2,453
Limestone (E4) 150
Live Oak◉ (D1) 6,544
Lloyd (C1) 300
Lochloosa (E2) 110
Long Bch. Resort ‡(C6) 66
Long Key (F7) 50
Longboat Key (D4).......1,000
Longwood (E3) 1,689
Lorida (E4) 302
Loughman (E3) 650
Lowell (D2) 150
Loxahatchee (F5) 500
Lulu (D1) 100
Lutz (D3) 1,800
Lynn Haven (C6) 3,078
Macclenny◉ (D1) 2,671
Madeira Beach (B3)....3,943
Madison◉ (C1) 3,239
Maitland (E3) 3,570
Malabar (F3) 650
Malone (A1) 661
Manalapan ‡(F5) 62
Mandarin (E1) 800
Mango (D4) 350
Mangonia Park ‡(F5)... 594
Mannville (E2) 100
Marathon (E7) 995
Marco (E6) 250
Margate ‡(F5) 2,646
Marianna◉ (A1) 7,152
Marineland (E2) 9
Martin (D2) 150
Mary Esther (B6) 780
Masaryktown (D3) 500
Mascotte (E3) 702
Maxville (E1) 800
Mayo◉ (C1) 687
Mayport (E1) 656
McAlpin (D1) 300
McDavid (B5) 700
McIntosh (D2) 258
McNeal (A1) 500
Medley (B4) 112
Melbourne (F3) 11,982
Melbourne Beach (F3)..1,004
Melbourne Vill. ‡(F3)... 458
Melrose (D2) 750
Memphis (D4) 2,647
Merritt Island (F3)......3,554
Miami◉ (B5) 291,688
Miami (urb. area) 852,705
Miami Beach (C5) 63,145
Miami Shores (B4) 8,865
Miami Springs (B5)....11,229
Micanopy (D2) 658
Micco (F4) 400
Miccosukee (B1) 225
Middleburg (E1) 900
Milligan (C6) 950
Milton◉ (B6) 4,108
Mims (F3) 1,307
Minneola (E3) 684
Miramar (B4) 5,485
Molino (B6) 750
Montbrook (D2) 200
Monticello ◉(C1) 2,490
Montverde (E3) 374
Moore Haven◉ (E5) 790
Morriston (D2) 100
Mossy Head (C6) 110
Mount Dora (E3) 3,756
Mount Pleasant (B1).... 102
Mulberry (E4) 2,922
Murdock (D4) 150
Myakka City (D4) 150
Myrtle Grove (B6) 950
Naples◉ (E5) 4,655
Naranja (F6) 2,509
Narcoossee (E3) 110
National Gardens (E2).. 100
Neptune Beach (E1).....2,868
New Port Richey (D3)..3,520
New Smyrna Bch. (F2)8,781
Newberry (D2) 1,105
Niceville (C6) 4,517
Nichols (E4) 350
Nocatee (E4) 1,200
Nokomis (D4) 1,400
Noma (C5) 200
North Bay Vill. ‡(F6)...2,006
North Miami (B4) 28,708
North Miami Beach (C4) 21,405
N. Orlando ‡(E3) 609
North Palm Bch. (F5)..2,684
N. Port Charlotte (D4) 178
N. Redington Beach(B3) 346
Oak Hill (F3) 758
Oakland (E3) 821

Oakland Park (B3) 5,331
O'Brien (D1) 200
Ocala◉ (D2) 13,598
Ocean Breeze Pk. ‡(F4)..
Ocean Ridge (F5) 209
Ochopee (E6) 150
Ocoee (E3) 2,628
Odessa (D3) 138
Ojus (B4) 3,791
Okahumpka (D3) 500
Okeechobee◉ (F4) 2,947
Oklawaha (E2) 500
Old Town (C2) 200
Oldsmar (B2) 878
Olustee (D1) 385
Ona (E4) 134
Oneco (D4) 1,530
Opa-locka (B4) 9,810
Orange City (E3) 1,598
Orange Lake (D2) 400
Orange Park (E1) 2,624
Orange Springs (E2)..... 500
Orlando◉ (E3) 88,135
Orlando (urb. area)...200,995
Ormond Beach (E2)......8,658
Orsino (F3) 244
Osprey (D4) 875
Osteen (E3) 600
Otter Creek (D2) 500
Overstreet (D6) 112
Oviedo (E3) 1,926
Oxford (D3) 287
Ozona (D3) 800
Pahokee (F5) 4,709
Palatka◉ (E2) 11,028
Palm Bay (F3) 2,808
Palm Beach (G5) 6,055
Palm Beach Gdns. ‡(F5) 1
Palm Beach Shrs. (G5).. 885
Palm City (F4) 750
Palm Harbor (D3) 1,600
Palm Shores ‡(F3).......
Palm Springs (F5) 2,503
Palmdale (E5) 82
Palmetto (D4) 5,556
Panacea (B1) 625
Panama City◉ (C6) ...33,275
Panama City Bch. ‡(C6) 36
Parker (D6) 2,669
Parrish (D4) 850
Paxton (C5) 215
Pembroke (B4) 569
Pembroke Pines (B4)....1,429
Penney Farms (E2) 545
Pennsuco (B4) 117
Pensacola◉ (B6) 56,752
Pensacola (urban area) 128,049
Perrine (F6) 6,424
Perry◉ (C1) 8,030
Pierce (E4) 550
Pierson (E2) 716
Pineland (D5) 250
Pinellas Park (B3)......10,848
Pinetta (C1) 210
Placida (D5) 150
Plant City (D3) 15,711
Plantation (B4) 4,772
Plymouth (E3) 750
Point Washington (C6).. 180
Polk City (E3) 203
Pomona Park (E2) 516
Pompano Beach (F5)..15,992
Ponce de Leon (C6)...... 500
Ponte Vedra Bch. (E1)1,000
Port Charlotte (D5) 3,197
Port Mayaca (F5) 112
Port Orange (F2) 1,801
Port Richey (D3) 1,931
Port Saint Joe (D6)......4,217
Port St. Lucie ‡(F4)....
Port Salerno (F4) 950
Portland (C6) 200
Princeton (F6) 1,719
Punta Gorda◉ (E5) 3,157
Quincy◉ (B1) 8,874
Raiford (D1) 500
Raleigh (D2) 200
Redbay (C6) 450
Reddick (D2) 594
Redington Beach (B3)..1,368
Redington Shores (B3).. 917
Richland (D3) 150
Richmond Hts. (F6).....4,311
Riverview (D4) 750
Riviera Beach (G5) 13,046
Rock Bluff (B1) 250
Rockledge (F3) 3,481
Roseland (F4) 400
Round Lake (D6) 400
Royal Palm Bch. ‡(F5) 11
Ruskin (C3) 1,894
Safety Harbor (B2)......1,787
St. Augustine◉ (E2)...14,734
St. Augustine Beach(E2) 396
Saint Catherine (D3).... 135
Saint Cloud (E3) 4,353
Saint James City (D5).. 300
Saint Leo (D3) 278
Saint Lucie (F4) 300
Saint Marks (B1) 484
St. Petersburg (B3)..181,298
St. Petersburg (urban area) 324,842
St. Petersburg Bch. (B3) 6,268

Salem (C2) 200
Samoset (D4) 4,824
Samsula (E2) 280
San Antonio (D3) 479
San Mateo (E2) 975
Sanderson (D1) 100
Sanford◉ (E3) 19,175
Sanibel (D5) 650
Santa Fe (D2) 300
Santa Rosa Beach (C6) 300
Santos (D2) 300
Sarasota◉ (D4) 34,083
Satellite Beach (F3).... 825
Satsuma (E2) 500
Scottsmoor (F3) 400
Sea Ranch Lakes (C3).. 170
Sebastian (F4) 698
Sebring◉ (E4) 6,939
Seffner (D4) 850
Seminole (B3) ....
Seville (E2) 623
Sewalls Point (F4) 151
Shalimar (C6) 754
Shamrock (C2) 450
Sharpes (F3) 700
Shiloh (F3) 150
Silver Springs (D2) 342
Sneads (B1) 1,399
Sopchoppy (B1) 450
Sorrento (E3) 500
South Bay (F5) 1,631
South Daytona (F2).....1,954
South Flomaton (B5).... 462
South Miami (B5) 9,846
South Palm Beach ‡(F5) 113
South Pasadena (B3)... 651
Southport (C6) 985
Sparr (D2) 500
Springfield (D6) 4,628
Starke◉ (D2) 4,806
Steinhatchee (C2) 600
Stuart◉ (F4) 4,791
Sumatra (B1) 125
Summerfield (D2) 350
Sun City (D4) 425
Sunland Gardens (F4)..1,417
Sunny Isles (C4)..........
Sunnyland (D4) 4,761
Sunnyside (C6) 250
Surfside (B4) 3,157
Suwannee (C2) 250
Sweetwater (B5) 645
Switzerland (E1) 500
Taft (E3) 1,214
TALLAHASSEE◉ (B1) 48,174
Tampa◉ (C2) 274,970
Tampa (urban area)..301,790
Tarpon Springs (D3)....6,768
Tavares◉ (E3) 2,724
Tavernier (F6) 600
Telogia (B1) 275
Temple Terrace (C2)....3,812
Tequesta (F5) 199
Terra Ceia (D4) 1,500
Thonotosassa (D3) 500
Tice (E5) 4,377
Titusville◉ (F3) 6,410
Treasure Island (B3)....3,506
Trenton◉ (D2) 941
Trilby (D3) 500
Umatilla (E3) 1,717
University Park ‡(F5).. 13
Valparaiso (C6) 5,975
Venice (D4) 3,444
Venus (E4) 225
Vernon (C6) 624
Vero Beach◉ (F4).......8,849
Virginia Gardens (B5)..2,159
Wabasso (F4) 850
Wacissa (B1) 450
Wakulla (B1) 350
Waldo (D2) 735
Walnut Hill (B5) 500
Ward Ridge (D6) 45
Warrington (B6) 16,752
Watertown (D1) 2,109
Wauchula◉ (E4) 3,411
Wausau (D6) 300
Waverly (E4) 1,160
Webster (D3) 366
Weirsdale (D3) 995
Welaka (E2) 526
Wellborn (D1) 350
West Hollywood (B4)....
West Melbourne (F3)....2,266
West Miami (B5) 5,296
W. Palm Beach◉ (F5)56,208
W. Palm Beach (urban area) 172,835
W. Panama Cy.Bch.(C6) 617
Westbay (C6) 400
Westville (C6) 425
Westwood Lakes (B5)22,517
Wewahitchka◉ (D6) 1,436
Whispering Hills ‡(F3) 834
White City (F4) 750
White Springs (D1) 633
Whitehouse (E1) 500
Wildwood (D3) 2,170
Williston (D2) 1,582
Wilton Manor (B3)......8,257
Wimauma (D4) 583
Windermere (E3) 576
Winter Beach (F4) 390
Winter Garden (E3)......5,513

Winter Haven (E3) 16,277
Winter Park (E3) 17,162
Woodville (B1) 700
Worthington (D2) 300
Yalaha (E3) 675
Yankeetown (D2) 425
Youngstown (D6) 350
Yukon (E1) 1,700
Yulee (E1) 750
Zellwood (E3) 1,750
Zephyrhills (D3) 2,887
Zolfo Springs (E4) 838

OTHER FEATURES

Alapaha (river) ....C 1
Alaqua (creek) ....C 6
Alligator (lake) ....E 3
Amelia (isl.) ....E 1
Anclote (keys) ....D 3
Apalachee (bay) ....B 2
Apalachicola (bay) ....B 2
Apalachicola (river) ......A 1
Apopka (lake) ....E 3
Arbuckle (lake) ....E 4
Aucilla (river) ....C 1
Banana (river) ....F 3
Barnes (sound) ....F 6
Big Cypress (swamp)......E 5
Big Pine (key) ....E 7
Biscayne (bay) ....F 6
Biscayne (key) ....B 5
Blackwater (river) ....B 6
Blue Cypress (lake) ......F 4
Boca Chica (key) ....E 7
Boca Ciega (bay) ....B 3
Boca Grande (key) ....D 7
Beresford (lake) ....E 3
Black (creek) ....E 1
Bryant (lake) ....E 2
Caladesi (isl.) ....B 2
Caloosahatchee (river) ..E 5
Canaveral (Kennedy) (cape) ....F 3
Captiva (isl.) ....D 5
Casey (key) ....D 4
Castillo de San Marcos Nat'l Mon. ....E 2
Charlotte (harbor) ....D 5
Chattahoochee (river).....B 1
Chipola (river) ....D 6
Choctawhatchee (bay) ...C 6
Choctawhatchee (river) ..C 6
Clearwater Beach (isl.)..B 2
Coldwater (creek) ....B 5
Crescent (lake) ....E 2
Crooked (lake) ....E 4
Crystal (bay) ....D 3
Cudjoe (key) ....E 7
Cypress (lake) ....E 3
Davis (isl.) ....C 3
DeSoto Nat'l Mem. ....D 4
Dead (lake) ....D 6
Dexter (lake) ....E 2
Disston (lake) ....E 2
Dog (isl.) ....B 2
Dorr (lake) ....E 2
Dry Tortugas (keys)......D 7
Dumfoundling (bay) ......C 4
East (cape) ....E 6
East Tohopekaliga (lake)E 3
Eglin A.F.B. ....C 6
Egmont (key) ....D 4
Elliott (key) ....F 6
Escambia (river) ....B 6
Estero (isl.) ....E 5
Eureka (res.) ....E 2
Everglades, The (swamp)F 6
Everglades Nat'l Park....F 6
Fenholloway (river) ....C 1
Fisher (isl.) ....B 5
Florida (bay) ....F 6
Florida (cape) ....F 6
Florida (keys) ....E 7
Florida (straits) ....F 7
Forbes (isl.) ....A 2
Ft. Caroline Nat'l Mem. E 1
Ft. Jefferson Nat'l Mon. C 7
Ft. Matanzas Nat'l Mon. ....E 2
Gadston (point) ....C 3
Gasparilla (isl.) ....D 5
George (lake) ....E 2
Grassy (key) ....F 7
Harney (lake) ....F 3
Hart (lake) ....E 3
Hatchineha (lake) ....E 3
Highland (point) ....E 6
Hillsborough (bay) ....C 3
Hillsborough (canal) .....F 5
Hillsborough (river) ......C 2
Holmes (creek) ....D 5
Homosassa (isls.) ....D 3
Homestead A.F.B. ....F 6
Horse (creek) ....E 4
Horseshoe (point) ....C 2
Iamonia (lake) ....B 1
Indian (river) ....F 3
Ingraham (lake) ....E 6
Iron (mt.) ....E 4
Istokpoga (lake) ....E 4
Jackson (lake) ....B 1
Jackson (lake) ....E 4
Jacksonville N.A.S. ....E 1
John F. Kennedy Space Center ....F 3

Johnston (key) ....E 7
June in Winter (lake).....E 4
Kennedy (Canaveral) (cape) ....F 3
Kerr (lake) ....E 2
Key Biscayne ....B 5
Key Largo ....F 6
Key Vaca ....E 7
Key West N.A.S. ....E 7
Kingsley (lake) ....E 2
Kissimmee (lake) ....E 4
Kissimmee (river) ....E 4
Lacosta (isl.) ....D 5
Largo (key) ....F 6
Levy (lake) ....D 2
Lewis (isl.) ....B 3
Lighthouse (point) ....B 2
Lochloosa (lake) ....D 2
Long (key) ....B 3
Long (key) ....F 7
Long (pond) ....D 2
Longboat (key) ....D 4
Lower Matecumbe (key)F 7
Lowery (lake) ....E 3
MacDill A.F.B. ....C 3
Maggiore (lake) ....B 3
Manatee (river) ....D 4
Marian (lake) ....E 4
Marquesas (keys) ....D 7
Matanzas (inlet) ....E 2
Merritt (isl.) ....F 3
Mexico (gulf) ....C 4
Miami (canal) ....F 5
Miami (river) ....B 5
Miccosukee (lake) ....B 1
Middle (cape) ....E 6
Monroe (lake) ....E 3

Mosquito (lagoon) ....F 3
Mullet (key) ....D 4
Myakka (river) ....D 4
Nassau (river) ....E 1
Nassau (sound) ....E 1
New (river) ....B 1
New (river) ....D 1
Newnans (lake) ....D 2
North Merritt (isl.) ......F 3
North New River (canal)F 5
Northwest (cape) ....E 6
Ocean (pond) ....D 1
Ochlockonee (river) ....B 1
Okaloacoochee Slough (swamp) ....E 5
Okeechobee (lake) ....F 5
Okefenokee (swamp) .....D 1
Oklawaha (river) ....E 2
Old Rhodes (key) ....F 6
Old Tampa (bay) ....B 3
Olustee (river) ....D 1
Orange (lake) ....D 2
Orlando A.F.B. ....E 3
Patrick A.F.B. ....F 3
Pavilion (key) ....E 6
Peace (river) ....E 4
Pensacola (bay) ....B 6
Pensacola N.A.S. ....B 6
Perdido (river) ....B 6
Pine (isl.) ....D 5
Pine (point) ....C 2
Pine Island (sound) ......D 5
Pine Log (creek) ....C 6
Pinellas (point) ....C 3
Piney (isl.) ....B 1
Piney (point) ....C 2
Placid (lake) ....E 4

Plantation (key) ....F 7
Poinsett (lake) ....F 3
Ponce de Leon (bay)......E 6
Port Everglades (harbor)C 4
Raccoon (point) ....D 3
Reedy (lake) ....E 4
Port Tampa (harbor) ....B 3
Rodman (res.) ....E 2
Romano (cape) ....E 6
Royal Glades (canal)......B 4
Sable (cape) ....E 6
Saint Andrew (point) ....D 6
Saint George (cape) ......A 2
Saint George (isl.) ....B 2
Saint George (sound) .....B 2
Saint Johns (river) ....E 2
Saint Joseph (bay) ....D 6
Saint Joseph (point) ......D 6
Saint Lucie (canal) ....F 4
Saint Lucie (inlet) ....F 4
Saint Marys (river) ....D 1
Saint Marys Entrance (inlet) ....E 1
Saint Vincent (isl.) ....D 7
San Blas (cape) ....D 7
Sand (key) ....B 3
Sands (key) ....F 6
Sanibel (isl.) ....D 5
Santa Fe (lake) ....D 2
Santa Fe (river) ....D 2
Santa Rosa (isl.) ....B 6
Santa Rosa (sound) ....B 6
Sarasota (point) ....D 4
Seminole (lake) ....B 1
Seminole Ind. Res. ...E 4,F 5
Shark (point) ....E 6
Shell (point) ....B 1

Shoal (river) ....C 6
Siesta (key) ....D 4
South New River (canal)F 5
Stafford (lake) ....D 2
Sugarloaf (key) ....E 7
Suwannee (river) ....C 2
Suwannee (sound) ....C 2
Talbot (isl.) ....E 1
Talquin (lake) ....B 1
Tamiami (canal) ....E 6
Tampa (bay) ....D 4
Ten Thousand (isls.) .....E 6
Tohopekaliga (lake) ......E 3
Torch (key) ....E 7
Treasure (isl.) ....B 3
Tsala Apopka (lake) .....D 3
Tyndall A.F.B. ....C 6
Upper Matecumbe (key) F 7
Vaca, Key ....E 7
Virginia (key) ....B 5
Waccasassa (bay) ....D 2
Waccasassa (river) ....D 2
Washington (lake) ....F 3
Weir (lake) ....E 2
Weohyakapka (lake) ......E 4
West Palm Bch. (canal)..F 5
Whitewater (bay) ....F 6
Wimico (lake) ....A 2
Winder (lake) ....F 3
Withlacoochee (river) ....C 1
Withlacoochee (river) ....D 2
Yale (lake) ....E 3
Yellow (river) ....B 6

◉ County Seat.
‡ Name not on map.

GEORGIA

AREA	58,876 sq. mi.
POPULATION	4,357,000
CAPITAL	Atlanta
LARGEST CITY	Atlanta 487,455
HIGHEST POINT	Brasstown Bald 4,784 ft.
SETTLED IN	1733
ADMITTED TO UNION	January 2, 1788
POPULAR NAMES	Empire State of the South; Peach State
STATE FLOWER	Cherokee Rose
STATE BIRD	Brown Thrasher

COUNTIES

Appling (H7) 13,246
Atkinson (G8) 6,188
Bacon (G7) 8,359
Baker (D8) 4,543
Baldwin (F4) 34,064
Banks (E2) 6,497
Barrow (E2) 14,485
Bartow (C2) 28,267
Ben Hill (F7) 13,633
Berrien (F8) 12,038
Bibb (E5) 141,249
Bleckley (F6) 9,642
Brantley (J8) 5,891
Brooks (E9) 15,292
Bryan (K6) 6,226
Bulloch (J6) 24,263
Burke (J4) 20,596
Butts (E4) 8,976
Calhoun (C7) 7,341
Camden (J9) 9,975
Candler (H6) 6,672
Carroll (B3) 36,451
Catoosa (B1) 21,101
Charlton (H9) 5,313
Chatham (K6) 188,299
Chattahoochee (C6)....13,011
Chattooga (B1) 19,954
Cherokee (D2) 23,001
Clarke (F3) 45,363
Clay (B7) 4,551
Clayton (D3) 46,365
Clinch (G9) 6,545
Cobb (C3) 114,174
Coffee (G8) 21,953
Colquitt (E8) 34,048
Columbia (H3) 13,423
Cook (F8) 11,822
Coweta (C4) 28,893
Crawford (E5) 5,816
Crisp (E7) 17,768
Dade (A1) 8,666
Dawson (D2) 3,590
De Kalb (D3) 256,782
Decatur (C9) 25,203
Dodge (F6) 16,483
Dooly (E6) 11,474
Dougherty (D7) 75,680
Douglas (C3) 16,741
Early (C8) 13,151
Echols (G9) 1,876
Effingham (K6) 10,144
Elbert (G2) 17,835
Emanuel (H5) 17,815
Evans (J6) 6,952
Fannin (D1) 13,620
Fayette (C4) 8,199
Floyd (B2) 69,130
Forsyth (D2) 12,170
Franklin (F2) 13,274
Fulton (D3) 556,326
Gilmer (D1) 8,922
Glascock (G4) 2,672
Glynn (J8) 41,954
Gordon (C2) 19,228
Grady (D9) 18,015
Greene (F3) 11,193
Gwinnett (D2) 43,541
Habersham (E1) 18,116
Hall (E2) 49,739
Hancock (G4) 9,979
Haralson (B3) 14,543
Harris (C5) 11,167
Hart (G2) 15,229
Heard (B4) 5,333
Henry (D4) 17,619
Houston (E6) 39,154
Irwin (F7) 9,211
Jackson (E2) 18,499
Jasper (E4) 6,135
Jeff Davis (G7) 8,914
Jefferson (H4) 17,468
Jenkins (J5) 9,148
Johnson (G5) 8,048
Jones (E5) 8,468
Lamar (D4) 10,240
Lanier (F8) 5,097
Laurens (G6) 32,313
Lee (D7) 6,204
Liberty (J7) 14,487
Lincoln (H3) 5,906
Long (J7) 3,874
Lowndes (F9) 49,270
Lumpkin (D1) 7,241
Macon (D6) 13,170
Madison (F2) 11,246
Marion (C6) 5,477
McDuffie (H4) 12,627
McIntosh (K7) 6,364
Meriwether (C4) 19,756
Miller (C8) 6,908
Mitchell (D8) 19,652
Monroe (E4) 10,495
Montgomery (G6) 6,284
Morgan (F3) 10,280
Murray (C1) 10,447
Muscogee (C6) 158,623
Newton (E3) 20,999
Oconee (F3) 6,304
Oglethorpe (F3) 7,926
Paulding (C3) 13,101
Peach (E5) 13,846
Pickens (D2) 8,903
Pierce (H8) 9,678
Pike (D4) 7,138
Polk (B3) 28,015
Pulaski (E6) 8,204
Putnam (F4) 7,798
Quitman (B7) 2,432
Rabun (F1) 7,456
Randolph (C7) 11,078
Richmond (H4) 135,601
Rockdale (D3) 10,572
Schley (D6) 3,256
Screven (J5) 14,919
Seminole (C9) 6,802
Spalding (D4) 35,404
Stephens (F1) 18,391
Stewart (C6) 7,371
Sumter (D6) 24,652
Talbot (C5) 7,127
Taliaferro (G3) 3,370
Tattnall (J6) 15,837
Taylor (D5) 8,311
Telfair (G7) 11,715
Terrell (D7) 12,742
Thomas (E9) 34,319
Tift (E8) 23,487
Toombs (H6) 16,837
Towns (E1) 4,538
Treutlen (G6) 5,874
Troup (B4) 47,189
Turner (E7) 8,439
Twiggs (F5) 7,935
Union (E1) 6,510
Upson (D5) 23,800
Walker (B1) 45,264
Walton (E3) 20,481
Ware (H8) 34,219
Warren (G4) 7,360
Washington (G4) 18,903
Wayne (J7) 17,921
Webster (C6) 3,247
Wheeler (G6) 5,342
White (E1) 6,935
Whitfield (B1) 42,109
Wilcox (F7) 7,905
Wilkes (G3) 10,961
Wilkinson (F5) 9,250
Worth (E8) 16,682

CITIES and TOWNS

Abbeville◉ (F7) 872
Acworth (C2) 2,359
Adairsville (C2) 1,026
Adel◉ (F8) 4,321
Adrian (G5) 568
Ailey (G6) 469
Alamo◉ (G6) 822
Alapaha (F8) 631
Albany◉ (D7) 55,890
Albany (urban area)...58,353
Aldora (D4) 535
Allentown (F5) 450
Alma◉ (G7) 3,515
Almon (E3) 300
Alpharetta (D2) 1,349
Alston (H6) 154
Alto (E2) 275
Alto Park (B2) 2,526
Alvaton (C4) 24
Ambrose (G7) 244
Americus◉ (D6) 13,472
Amsterdam (D9) 400
Andersonville (D6) 263
Apalachee (E3) 158
Appling◉ (H3) 200
Arabi (E7) 303
Aragon (B2) 1,023
Arcade (E2) 108
Argyle (G8) 225
Arlington (C8) 1,462
Armuchee (B2) 400
Ashburn◉ (E7) 3,291
Athens◉ (F3) 31,355
ATLANTA◉ (D3) 487,455
Atlanta (urban area)768,125
Attapulgus (D9) 567
Auburn (E2) 374
Augusta◉ (J4) 70,626
Augusta (urb. area)..123,698
Auraria (E1) 83
Austell (C3) 1,867
Avalon (F1) 194
Avans (A1) 500
Avera (H4) 197
Avondale Estates (D3)..1,646
Axson (G8) 350
Baconton (D8) 564
Bainbridge◉ (C9) 12,714
Baldwin (E2) 698
Ball Ground (D2) 707
Barnesville◉ (D4) 4,919
Barney (E8) 165
Barretts (F8) 300
Bartow (G5) 366
Barwick (E9) 400
Baxley◉ (H7) 4,268
Beach (G8) 53
Belleville (H6) 300
Benevolence (C7) 123
Berkeley Lake ‡(D3).... 94
Berlin (E8) 419
Berryton (B2) 600
Bethlehem (E3) 297
Bibb City (B5) 1,213
Bishop (F3) 214
Blackshear◉ (H8) 2,482
Blairsville◉ (E1) 437
Blakely◉ (C8) 3,580
Bloomingdale (K6) 350
Blue Ridge◉ (D1) 1,406
Bluffton (C7) 176
Blythe (H4) 172
Bogart (E3) 403
Boston (E9) 1,357
Bostwick (E3) 272
Bowdon (B3) 1,548
Bowersville (G2) 293
Bowman (G2) 654
Box Springs (C5) 570
Boykin (C8) 601
Bradley (E4) 400
Braselton (E2) 255
Bremen (B3) 3,132
Brinson (C9) 246
Bristol (H8) 162
Bronwood (D7) 400
Brookfield (F8) 500
Brooklet (J6) 557
Brooks (D4) 158
Broxton (G7) 907
Brunswick◉ (K8) 21,703
Buchanan◉ (B3) 753
Buckhead (F3) 169
Buena Vista◉ (C6) 1,574
Buford (D2) 4,168
Bullard (F5) 250
Butler◉ (D5) 1,346
Byromville (E6) 349
Byron (E5) 1,138
Cadwell (G6) 360
Cairo◉ (D9) 7,427
Calhoun◉ (B1) 3,587
Calvary (D9) 600
Camak (G4) 285
Camilla◉ (D8) 4,753
Campania (H4) 185
Campton (E3) 200
Canon (F2) 626
Canoochee (H5) 30
Canton◉ (C2) 2,411
Carl (E3) 204
Carlton (F2) 321
Carnegie (C7) 113
Carnesville◉ (F2) 481
Carrollton◉ (C3) 10,973
Carsonville◉ (D5) 52
Cartersville (C2) 8,668
Cassville (C2) 300
Cataula (C5) 250
Cave Spring (B2) 1,153
Cecil (F8) 279
Cedartown◉ (B2) 9,340
Celanese Village (B2)..1,500
Center (F2) 137
Centerville (E5) 290
Centralhatchee (B4) 174
Chalybeate Sprs. (C5).. 295
Chamblee (D3) 6,635
Charles (H6) 50
Chatsworth◉ (C1) 1,184
Chauncey (F6) 330
Cherrylog (D1) 318
Chester (F6) 377
Chickamauga (B1) 1,824
Choestoe (E1) 800
Chula (E7) 200
Cisco (C1) 300
Clarkesville◉ (F1) 1,352
Clarkston (D3) 1,524
Claxton◉ (J6) 2,672
Clayton◉ (F1) 1,507
Clem (B3) 400
Clermont (E2) 268
Cleveland◉ (E1) 657
Climax (D9) 329
Cloudland (A1) 300
Clyattville (F9) 340
Clyo (K6) 600
Cobb (E7) 90
Cobbtown (H6) 280
Cochran◉ (F6) 4,714
Cogdell (G8) 250
Cohutta (C1) 453
Colbert (F2) 425
Coleman (C7) 220
Colemans Lake ‡(H5)... 34
College Park (C3) 23,469
Collins (H6) 565
Colquitt◉ (C8) 1,556
Columbus◉ (C6) 116,779
Columbus (urban area) 158,382
Comer (F2) 882
Commerce (E2) 3,551
Concord (D4) 333
Conyers◉ (D3) 2,881
Coolidge (E8) 679
Coosa (B2) 200
Cordele◉ (E7) 10,609
Corinth (B4) 105
Cornelia (E1) 2,936
Cotton (D8) 108
Coverdale (E7) 162
Covington◉ (E3) 8,167
Covington Mills (E3).... 500
Crandall (C1) 208
Crawford (F3) 541
Crawfordville◉ (G3)..... 786
Crosland (E8) 95
Crystal Springs (B2).... 300
Culloden (D5) 260
Cumming◉ (D2) 1,561
Cusseta◉ (C6) 768
Cuthbert◉ (C7) 4,300
Dacula (E3) 440
Dahlonega◉ (D1) 2,604
Daisy (J6) 229
Dallas◉ (C3) 2,065
Dalton◉ (C1) 17,868
Damascus (C8) 297
Danburg (G3) 108
Danielsville◉ (F2) 362
Danville (F5) 264
Darien◉ (K8) 1,569
Dasher (F9) 300
Davisboro (G5) 417
Dawson◉ (D7) 5,062
Dawsonville◉ (D2) 307
De Soto (D7) 282
Dearing (H4) 403
Decatur◉ (D3) 22,026
Deepstep (G4) 139
Demorest (F1) 1,029
Denton (G7) 255
Devereux (F4) 500
Dewy Rose (G2) 200
Dexter (G6) 359
Dial (D1) 300
Dickey (C7) 76
Dillard (F1) 204
Dixie (E9) 220
Dock Jct. (J8) 5,417
Doctortown (J7) 350
Doerun (E8) 1,037
Donalsonville◉ (C8).....2,621
Dooling (E6) 300
Doraville (D3) 4,437
Double Branches (H3).. 300
Douglas◉ (G7) 8,736
Douglasville◉ (C3) 4,462
Dover (J5) 200
Doyle (D6) 10
Dry Branch (F5) 700
Du Pont (G9) 210
Dublin◉ (G5) 13,814
Ducktown (D2) 49
Dudley (F5) 360
Duluth (D2) 1,483
Durand (C5) 195
East Dublin (G5) 1,677
East Ellijay (C1) 501
East Juliette (E4) 201
East Point (C3) 35,633
East Thomaston (D5)....2,237
Eastanollee (F1) 300
Eastman◉ (F6) 5,118
Eastville (F3) 107
Eatonton◉ (F4) 3,612
Eden (K6) 200
Edge Hill (G4) 55
Edison (C7) 1,232
Edith (G9) 200
Elberta (E5) 644
Elberton◉ (G2) 7,107
Eldorendo (C8) 250
Elko (E6) 165
Ellabell (K6) 1,800
Ellaville◉ (D6) 905
Ellenton (E8) 385
Ellerslie (C5) 550
Ellijay◉ (C1) 1,320
Emerson (C2) 666
Enigma (F8) 525
Epworth (D1) 350
Esom Hill (B3) 200
Eton (C1) 275
Evans (H3) 900
Everett (J8) 350
Experiment (D4) 2,497
Faceville (C9) 700
Fair Oaks (D3) 7,969
Fairburn (C3) 2,470
Fairfax (G8) 200
Fairmount (C2) 619
Fargo (G9) 950
Farmington (F3) 151
Farrar (E4) 42
Fayetteville◉ (C4) 1,389
Felton (B3) 200
Finleyson (F6) 82
Fitzgerald◉ (F7) 8,781
Fleming (K7) 312
Flemington (J7) 149
Flintstone (B1) 275
Flippen (D3) 490
Flovilla (E4) 284
Flowery Branch (E2).... 741
Folkston◉ (H9) 1,810
Forest Park (D3) 14,201
Forsyth◉ (E4) 3,697
Fort Gaines◉ (C7)........1,320
Fort Oglethorpe (B1)....2,251

(continued on following page)

HIGHWAYS

0 30 60
MILES

Limited Access Highways
Major Highways
Other Important Roads
Interstate Route Numbers (95)
Federal Route Numbers (9)
State and Other Route Numbers (4)

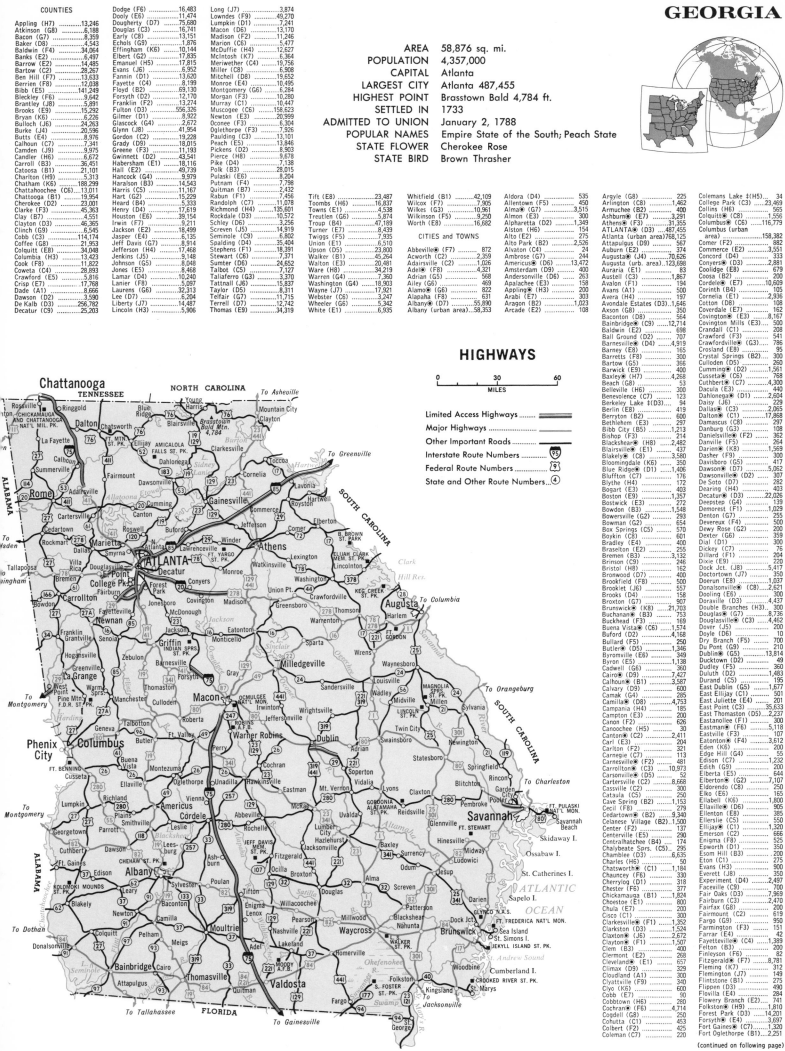

OTHER FEATURES

◉ County Seat
‡ Name not on map.

TOPOGRAPHY

0   40   80
MILES

AGRICULTURE, INDUSTRY and RESOURCES

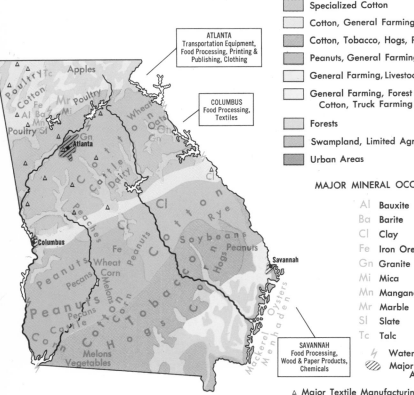

ATLANTA
Transportation Equipment,
Food Processing, Printing &
Publishing, Clothing

COLUMBUS
Food Processing,
Textiles

SAVANNAH
Food Processing,
Wood & Paper Products,
Chemicals

DOMINANT LAND USE

- Specialized Cotton
- Cotton, General Farming
- Cotton, Tobacco, Hogs, Peanuts
- Peanuts, General Farming
- General Farming, Livestock, Fruit, Tobacco
- General Farming, Forest Products, Cotton, Truck Farming
- Forests
- Swampland, Limited Agriculture
- Urban Areas

MAJOR MINERAL OCCURRENCES

- Al Bauxite
- Ba Barite
- Cl Clay
- Fe Iron Ore
- Gn Granite
- Mi Mica
- Mn Manganese
- Mr Marble
- Sl Slate
- Tc Talc
- ⚡ Water Power
- ▨ Major Industrial Areas
- △ Major Textile Manufacturing Centers

Hawaii

TOPOGRAPHY

0   40   80
MILES

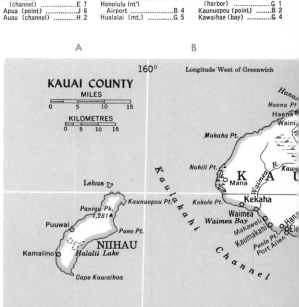

5,000 m. 16,404 ft.	2,000 m. 6,562 ft.	1,000 m. 3,281 ft.	500 m. 1,640 ft.	200 m. 656 ft.	100 m. 328 ft.	Sea Level	Below

AGRICULTURE, INDUSTRY and RESOURCES

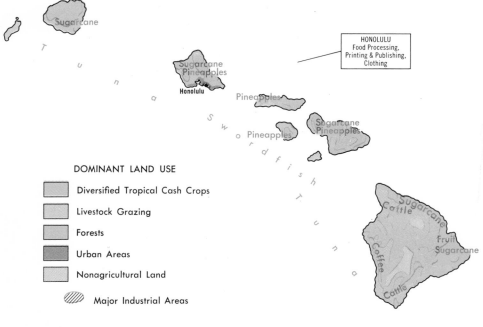

HONOLULU
Food Processing,
Printing & Publishing,
Clothing

DOMINANT LAND USE

Diversified Tropical Cash Crops

Livestock Grazing

Forests

Urban Areas

Nonagricultural Land

Major Industrial Areas

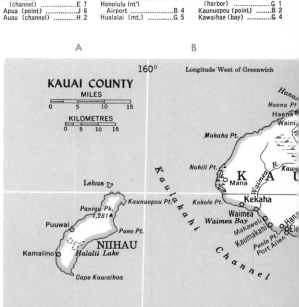

KAUAI COUNTY

MILES
0   5   10   15
KILOMETRES
0   5   10   15

160° Longitude West of Greenwich

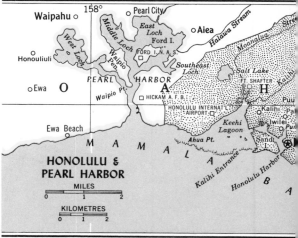

HONOLULU & PEARL HARBOR

158°

MILES
0   1   2
KILOMETRES
0   1   2

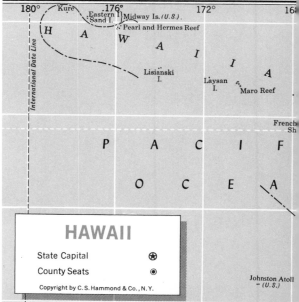

180°   176°   172°

HAWAII

State Capital ⊛

County Seats ◉

Copyright by C.S. Hammond & Co., N.Y.

HAWAII

AREA 6,424 sq. mi.
POPULATION 711,000
CAPITAL Honolulu
LARGEST CITY Honolulu 294,194
HIGHEST POINT Mauna Kea 13,796 ft.
SETTLED IN —
ADMITTED TO UNION August 21, 1959
POPULAR NAMES Aloha State; Paradise of the Pacific
STATE FLOWER Red Hibiscus
STATE BIRD Nene (Hawaiian Goose)

See page 191 for highway map of Hawaii

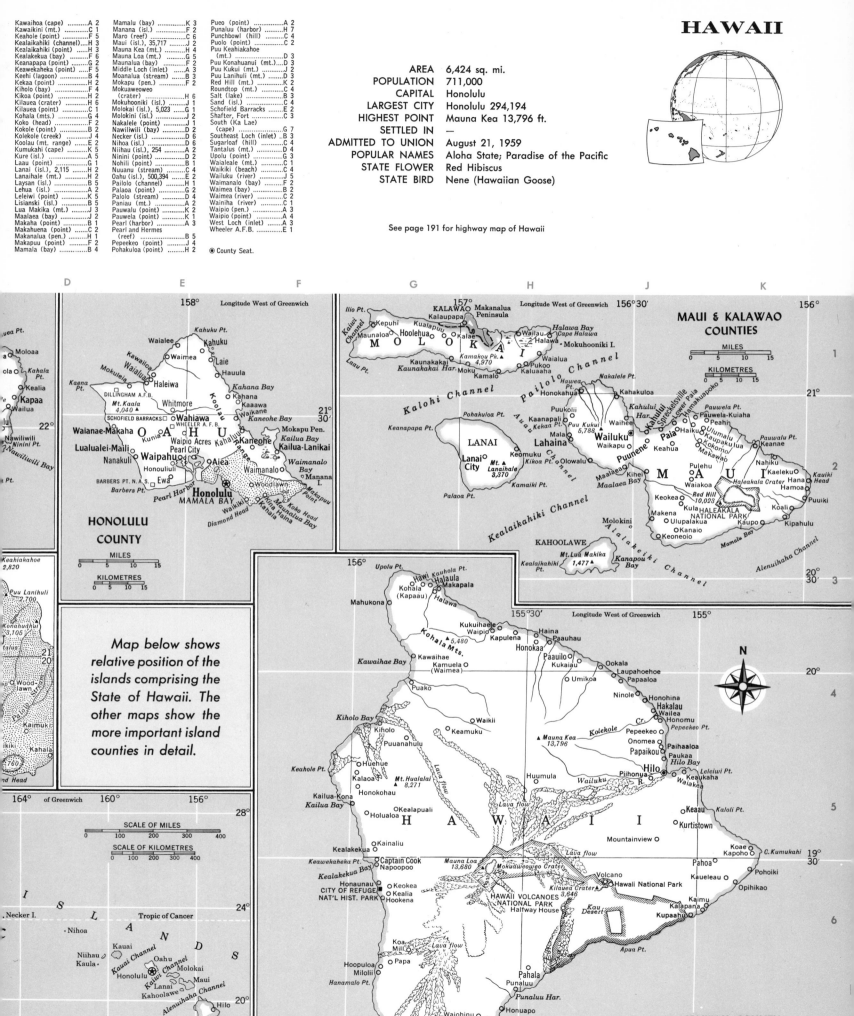

Map below shows relative position of the islands comprising the State of Hawaii. The other maps show the more important island counties in detail.

IDAHO

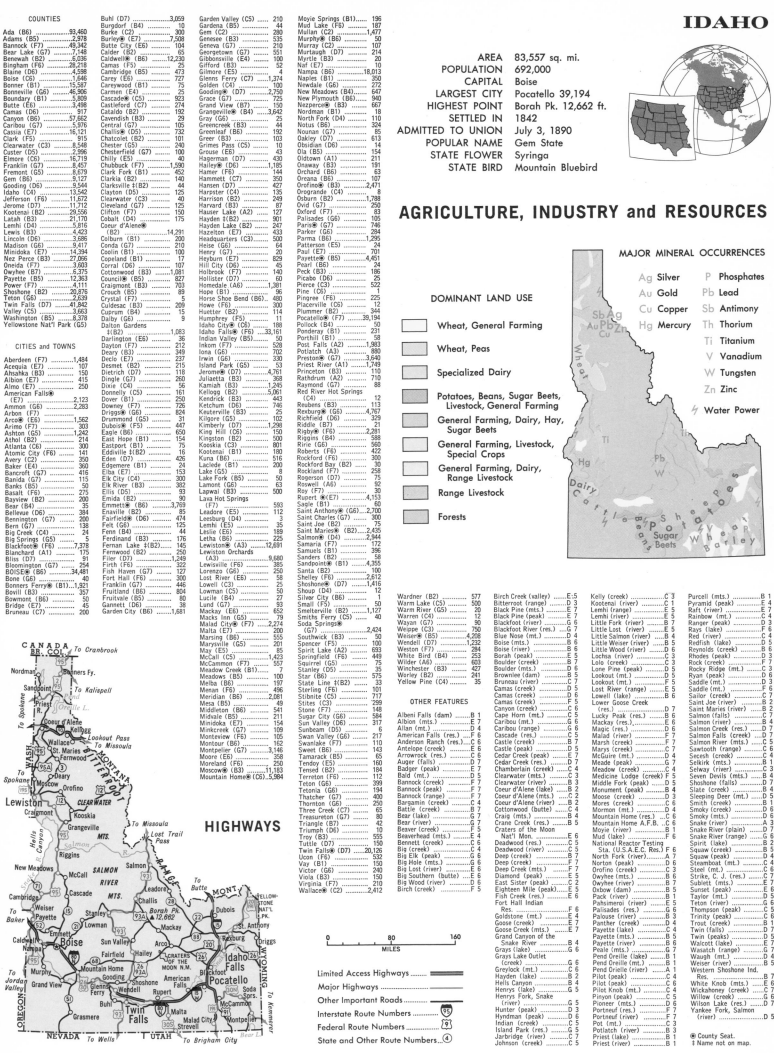

AREA 83,557 sq. mi.
POPULATION 692,000
CAPITAL Boise
LARGEST CITY Pocatello 39,194
HIGHEST POINT Borah Pk. 12,662 ft.
SETTLED IN 1842
ADMITTED TO UNION July 3, 1890
POPULAR NAME Gem State
STATE FLOWER Syringa
STATE BIRD Mountain Bluebird

AGRICULTURE, INDUSTRY and RESOURCES

DOMINANT LAND USE

Wheat, General Farming
Wheat, Peas
Specialized Dairy
Potatoes, Beans, Sugar Beets, Livestock, General Farming
General Farming, Dairy, Hay, Sugar Beets
General Farming, Livestock, Special Crops
General Farming, Dairy, Range Livestock
Range Livestock
Forests

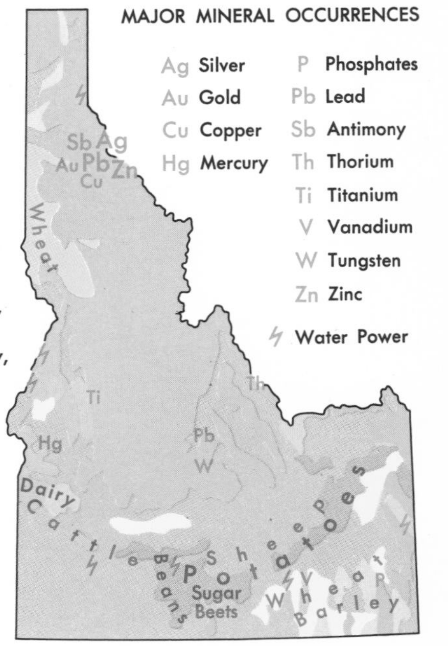
MAJOR MINERAL OCCURRENCES
Ag Silver
Au Gold
Cu Copper
Hg Mercury
P Phosphates
Pb Lead
Sb Antimony
Th Thorium
Ti Titanium
V Vanadium
W Tungsten
Zn Zinc
Water Power
Wheat
Dairy
Cattle
Sheep
Potatoes
Beans
Sugar Beets
Wheat
Barley

COUNTIES

Ada (B6) 93,460
Adams (B5) 2,978
Bannock (F7) 49,342
Bear Lake (G7) 7,148
Benewah (B2) 6,036
Bingham (F6) 28,218
Blaine (D6) 4,598
Boise (C6) 1,646
Bonner (B1) 15,587
Bonneville (G6) 46,906
Boundary (B1) 5,809
Butte (E6) 3,498
Camas (D6) 917
Canyon (B6) 57,662
Caribou (G7) 5,976
Cassia (E7) 16,121
Clark (F5) 915
Clearwater (C3) 8,548
Custer (D5) 2,996
Elmore (C6) 16,719
Franklin (G7) 8,457
Fremont (G5) 8,679
Gem (B6) 9,127
Gooding (D6) 9,544
Idaho (C4) 13,542
Jefferson (F6) 11,672
Jerome (D7) 11,712
Kootenai (B2) 29,556
Latah (B3) 21,170
Lemhi (D4) 5,816
Lewis (B3) 4,423
Lincoln (D6) 3,686
Madison (G6) 9,417
Minidoka (E7) 14,394
Nez Perce (B3) 27,066
Oneida (F7) 3,603
Owyhee (B7) 6,375
Payette (B5) 12,363
Power (F7) 4,111
Shoshone (B2) 20,876
Teton (G6) 2,639
Twin Falls (D7) 41,842
Valley (C5) 3,663
Washington (B5) 8,378
Yellowstone Nat'l Park (G5)

CITIES and TOWNS

Aberdeen (F7) 1,484
Acequia (E7) 107
Ahsahka (B3) 150
Albion (E7) 415
Almo (E7) 250
American Falls◉ (E7) 2,123
Ammon (G6) 2,283
Arbon (F7)
Arco◉ (E6) 1,562
Arimo (F7) 303
Ashton (G5) 1,242
Athol (B2) 214
Atlanta (C6) 300
Atomic City (F6) 141
Avery (C2) 350
Baker (E4) 360
Bancroft (G7) 416
Banida (G7) 115
Banks (B5) 50
Basalt (F6) 275
Bayview (B2) 200
Bear (B4) 35
Bellevue (D6) 384
Bennington (G7) 200
Bern (G7) 138
Big Creek (C4) 24
Big Springs (G5) 5
Blackfoot◉ (F6) 7,378
Blanchard (A1) 175
Bliss (D7) 91
Bloomington (G7) 254
BOISE◉ (B6) 34,481
Bone (G6) 40
Bonners Ferry◉ (B1) 1,921
Bovill (B3) 357
Bowmont (B6) 50
Bridge (E7) 45
Bruneau (C7) 200
Buhl (D7) 3,059
Burgdorf (B4) 10
Burke (C2) 300
Burley◉ (E7) 7,508
Butte City (E6) 104
Calder (B2) 65
Caldwell◉ (B6) 12,230
Camas (F5) 25
Cambridge (B5) 473
Carey (E6) 727
Careywood (B1) 75
Carmen (E4) 25
Cascade◉ (C5) 923
Castleford (C7) 274
Cataldo (B2) 192
Cavendish (B3) 29
Central (G7) 105
Challis◉ (D5) 732
Chatcolet (B2) 101
Chester (G5) 240
Chesterfield (G7) 100
Chilly (E5) 40
Chubbuck (F7) 1,590
Clark Fork (B1) 452
Clarkia (B2) 140
Clarksville ‡(B2) 44
Clayton (D5) 125
Clearwater (C3) 40
Cleveland (G7) 125
Clifton (F7) 150
Cobalt (D4) 175
Coeur d'Alene◉ (B2) 14,291
Colburn (B1) 200
Conda (G7) 210
Coolin (B1) 100
Copeland (B1) 17
Corral (D6) 107
Cottonwood (B3) 1,081
Council◉ (B5) 827
Craigmont (B3) 703
Crouch (B5) 89
Crystal (F7) 5
Culdesac (B3) 209
Cuprum (B4) 15
Dalby (G6) 9
Dalton Gardens ‡(B2) 1,083
Darlington (E6) 36
Dayton (F7) 212
Deary (B3) 349
Declo (E7) 237
Desmet (B2) 215
Dietrich (D7) 118
Dingle (G7) 260
Dixie (C4) 56
Donnelly (C5) 161
Dover (B1) 250
Downey (F7) 726
Driggs◉ (G6) 824
Drummond (G5) 31
Dubois◉ (F5) 447
Eagle (B6) 650
East Hope (B1) 154
Eastport (B1) 75
Eddiville ‡(B2) 16
Eden (D7) 426
Edgemere (B1) 24
Elba (E7) 153
Elk City (C4) 300
Elk River (B3) 382
Ellis (D5) 93
Emida (B2) 90
Emmett◉ (B6) 3,769
Enaville (B2) 85
Fairfield◉ (D6) 474
Felt (G6) 125
Fenn (B4) 44
Ferdinand (B3) 176
Fernan Lake ‡(B2) 145
Fernwood (B2) 250
Filer (D7) 1,249
Firth (F6) 322
Fish Haven (G7) 127
Fort Hall (F6) 300
Franklin (G7) 446
Fruitland (B6) 804
Fruitvale (B5) 80
Gannett (D6) 38
Garden City (B6) 1,681
Garden Valley (C5) 210
Gardena (B5) 44
Gem (C2) 280
Genesee (B3) 535
Geneva (G7) 210
Georgetown (G7) 551
Gibbonsville (E4) 100
Gifford (B3) 52
Gilmore (E5) 4
Glenns Ferry (C7) 1,374
Golden (C4) 100
Gooding◉ (D7) 2,750
Grace (G7) 725
Grand View (B7) 150
Grangeville◉ (B4) 3,642
Gray (G6) 25
Greencreek (B3) 44
Greenleaf (B6) 192
Greer (B3) 103
Grimes Pass (C5) 10
Grouse (E6) 43
Hagerman (D7) 430
Hailey◉ (D6) 1,185
Hamer (F6) 144
Hammett (C7) 350
Hansen (D7) 427
Harpster (C4) 135
Harrison (B2) 249
Harvard (B3) 87
Hauser Lake (A2) 127
Hayden ‡(B2) 901
Hayden Lake (B2) 247
Hazelton (E7) 433
Headquarters (C3) 500
Heise (G6) 64
Henry (G7) 20
Heyburn (E7) 829
Hill City (D6) 45
Holbrook (F7) 140
Hollister (D7) 60
Homedale (A6) 1,381
Hope (B1) 96
Horse Shoe Bend (B6) 480
Howe (F6) 300
Huetter (B2) 114
Humphrey (F5) 11
Idaho City◉ (C6) 188
Idaho Falls◉ (F6) 33,161
Indian Valley (B5) 50
Inkom (F7) 528
Iona (G6) 702
Irwin (G6) 330
Island Park (G5) 53
Jerome◉ (D7) 4,761
Juliaetta (B3) 368
Kamiah (B3) 1,245
Kellogg (B2) 5,061
Kendrick (B3) 443
Ketchum (D6) 746
Keuterville (B3) 25
Kilgore (G5) 102
Kimberly (D7) 1,298
King Hill (C6) 150
Kingston (B2) 500
Kooskia (C3) 801
Kootenai (B1) 180
Kuna (B6) 516
Laclede (B1) 200
Lake (G5) 8
Lake Fork (B5) 50
Lamont (G6) 63
Lapwai (B3) 500
Lava Hot Springs (F7) 593
Leadore (E5) 112
Leesburg (D4) 3
Lemhi (E5) 35
Leslie (E6) 189
Letha (B6) 225
Lewiston◉ (A3) 12,691
Lewiston Orchards (A3) 9,680
Lewisville (F6) 385
Lorenzo (G6) 250
Lost River (E6) 58
Lowell (C3) 25
Lowman (C5) 50
Lucile (B4) 27
Lund (G7) 93
Mackay (E6) 652
Macks Inn (G5) 79
Malad City◉ (F7) 2,274
Malta (E7) 200
Marsing (B6) 555
Marysville (G5) 201
May (E5) 85
McCall (C5) 1,423
McCammon (F7) 557
Meadow Creek (B1) 7
Meadows (B5) 100
Melba (B6) 197
Menan (F6) 496
Meridian (B6) 2,081
Mesa (B5) 49
Middleton (B6) 541
Midvale (B5) 211
Minidoka (E7) 154
Minkcreek (G7) 109
Monteview (F6) 105
Montour (B6) 162
Montpelier (G7) 3,146
Moore (E6) 358
Moreland (F6) 250
Moscow◉ (B3) 11,183
Mountain Home◉ (C6) 5,984
Moyie Springs (B1) 196
Mud Lake (F6) 187
Mullan (C2) 1,477
Murphy◉ (B6) 50
Murray (C2) 107
Murtaugh (D7) 214
Myrtle (B3) 20
Naf (E7) 10
Nampa (B6) 18,013
Naples (B1) 350
Newdale (G6) 272
New Meadows (B4) 647
New Plymouth (B6) 940
Nezperce◉ (B3) 667
Nordman (B1) 18
North Fork (D4) 110
Notus (B6) 324
Nounan (G7) 85
Oakley (D7) 613
Obsidian (D6) 14
Ola (B5) 154
Oldtown (A1) 211
Onaway (B3) 191
Orchard (B6) 63
Oreana (B6) 107
Orofino◉ (B3) 2,471
Orogrande (C4) 8
Osburn (B2) 1,788
Ovid (G7) 250
Oxford (F7) 83
Palisades (G6) 105
Paris◉ (G7) 746
Parker (G6) 284
Parma (B6) 1,295
Patterson (E5) 24
Paul (E7) 701
Payette◉ (B5) 4,451
Pearl (B6) 24
Peck (B3) 186
Picabo (D6) 25
Pierce (C3) 522
Pine (C6) 1
Pingree (F6) 225
Placerville (C6) 12
Plummer (B2) 344
Pocatello◉ (F7) 39,194
Pollock (B4) 50
Ponderay (B1) 231
Porthill (B1) 58
Post Falls (A2) 1,983
Potlatch (A3) 880
Preston◉ (G7) 3,640
Priest River (A1) 1,749
Princeton (B3) 110
Rathdrum (A2) 710
Raymond (G7) 88
Red River Hot Springs (C4) 12
Reubens (B3) 113
Rexburg◉ (G6) 4,767
Richfield (D6) 329
Riddle (B7) 21
Rigby◉ (F6) 2,281
Riggins (B4) 588
Ririe (G6) 560
Roberts (F6) 422
Rockford (F6) 300
Rockford Bay (B2) 30
Rockland (F7) 258
Rogerson (D7) 75
Roswell (A6) 92
Roy (F7) 30
Rupert ◉(E7) 4,153
Sagle (B1) 60
Saint Anthony◉ (G6) 2,700
Saint Charles (G7) 300
Saint Joe (B2) 75
Saint Maries◉ (B2) 2,435
Salmon◉ (D4) 2,944
Samaria (F7) 172
Samuels (B1) 396
Sanders (B2) 58
Sandpoint◉ (B1) 4,355
Santa (B2) 100
Shelley (F6) 2,612
Shoshone◉ (D7) 1,416
Shoup (D4) 12
Silver City (B6) 1
Small (F5) 50
Smelterville (B2) 1,127
Smiths Ferry (C5) 40
Soda Springs◉ (G7) 2,424
Southwick (B3) 50
Spencer (F5) 100
Spirit Lake (A2) 693
Springfield (F6) 449
Squirrel (G5) 75
Stanley (D5) 35
Star (B6) 575
State Line ‡(B2) 33
Sterling (F6) 101
Stibnite (C5) 717
Stites (C3) 299
Stone (F7) 148
Sugar City (G6) 584
Sun Valley (D6) 317
Sunbeam (D5) 6
Swan Valley (G6) 217
Swanlake (F7) 110
Sweet (B6) 143
Tamarack (B5) 65
Tendoy (E5) 160
Tensed (B2) 184
Terreton (F6) 112
Teton (G6) 399
Tetonia (G6) 194
Thatcher (G7) 400
Thornton (G6) 250
Three Creek (C7) 65
Treasureton (G7) 80
Triangle (B7) 42
Triumph (D6) 10
Troy (B3) 555
Tuttle (D7) 150
Twin Falls◉ (D7) 20,126
Ucon (F6) 532
Vay (B1) 150
Victor (G6) 240
Viola (B3) 150
Virginia (F7) 210
Wallace◉ (C2) 2,412
Wardner (B2) 577
Warm Lake (C5) 500
Warm River (G5) 20
Warren (C4) 12
Wayan (G7) 90
Weippe (C3) 750
Weiser◉ (B5) 4,208
Wendell (D7) 1,232
Weston (F7) 284
White Bird (B4) 253
Wilder (A6) 603
Winchester (B3) 427
Worley (B2) 241
Yellow Pine (C4) 35

OTHER FEATURES

Albeni Falls (dam) B 1
Albion (mts.) E 7
Allan (mt.) D 4
American Falls (res.) F 6
Anderson Ranch (res.) C 6
Antelope (creek) E 6
Arrowrock (res.) C 6
Auger (falls) D 7
Badger (peak) E 7
Bald (mt.) D 5
Bannock (creek) F 7
Bannock (peak) F 7
Bannock (range) F 7
Bargamin (creek) C 4
Battle (creek) B 7
Bear (lake) G 7
Bear (river) G 7
Beaver (creek) F 5
Beaverhead (mts.) E 4
Bennett (creek) C 6
Big (creek) C 4
Big Elk (peak) G 6
Big Hole (mts.) G 6
Big Lost (river) E 6
Big Southern (butte) E 6
Big Wood (river) D 6
Birch (creek) F 5
Birch Creek (valley) E 5
Bitterroot (range) D 3
Black Pine (mts.) E 7
Black Pine (peak) E 7
Blackfoot (river) G 6
Blackfoot River (res.) G 7
Blue Nose (mt.) D 4
Boise (mts.) B 6
Boise (river) B 6
Borah (peak) E 5
Boulder (creek) B 7
Boulder (mts.) D 6
Brownlee (dam) B 5
Bruneau (river) C 7
Camas (creek) D 5
Camas (creek) D 6
Camas (creek) F 5
Canyon (creek) C 6
Cape Horn (mt.) C 5
Caribou (mt.) G 6
Caribou (range) G 6
Cascade (res.) C 5
Castle (creek) B 7
Castle (peak) D 5
Cedar Creek (peak) E 7
Cedar Creek (res.) D 7
Chamberlain (creek) C 4
Clearwater (mts.) C 3
Clearwater (river) B 3
Coeur d'Alene (lake) B 2
Coeur d'Alene (mts.) C 2
Coeur d'Alene (river) B 2
Cottonwood (butte) C 4
Craig (mts.) B 4
Crane Creek (res.) B 5
Craters of the Moon Nat'l Mon. E 6
Deadwood (res.) C 5
Deadwood (river) C 5
Deep (creek) B 7
Deep (creek) F 7
Deep Creek (mts.) F 7
Diamond (peak) E 5
East Sister (peak) C 2
Eighteen Mile (peak) E 5
Fish Creek (res.) E 6
Fort Hall Indian Res. F 6
Goldstone (mt.) E 4
Goose (creek) E 7
Goose Creek (mts.) E 7
Grand Canyon of the Snake River B 4
Grays (lake) G 6
Grays Lake Outlet (creek) G 6
Greylock (mt.) C 6
Hayden (lake) B 2
Hells Canyon B 4
Henrys (lake) G 5
Henrys Fork, Snake (river) G 5
Hunter (peak) D 3
Hyndman (peak) D 6
Indian (creek) C 5
Island Park (res.) G 5
Jarbridge (river) C 7
Johnson (creek) C 5
Kelly (creek) C 3
Kootenai (river) C 1
Lemhi (range) E 5
Lemhi (river) E 5
Little Fork (river) B 7
Little Lost (river) E 5
Little Salmon (river) B 4
Little Weiser (river) B 5
Little Wood (river) D 6
Lochsa (river) C 3
Lolo (creek) C 3
Lone Pine (peak) D 5
Lookout (mt.) D 5
Lookout (mt.) F 5
Lost River (range) E 5
Lowell (lake) B 6
Lower Goose Creek (res.) D 7
Lucky Peak (res.) B 6
Mackay (res.) E 6
Magic (res.) D 6
Malad (river) F 7
Marsh (creek) F 7
Marys (creek) C 7
McGuire (mt.) D 4
Meade (peak) G 7
Meadow (creek) C 4
Medicine Lodge (creek) F 5
Middle Fork (peak) D 5
Monument (peak) B 4
Moose (creek) D 3
Mores (creek) C 6
Mormon (mt.) D 4
Mountain Home (res.) C 6
Mountain Home A.F.B. C 6
Moyie (river) B 1
Mud (lake) F 6
National Reactor Testing Sta. (U.S.A.E.C. Res.) F 6
North Fork (river) A 7
Norton (peak) D 6
Orofino (creek) C 3
Owyhee (mts.) B 6
Owyhee (river) B 7
Oxbow (dam) B 5
Pack (river) B 1
Pahsimeroi (river) E 5
Palisades (res.) G 6
Palouse (river) B 3
Panther (creek) D 4
Payette (lake) C 4
Payette (mts.) B 5
Payette (river) B 6
Peale (mts.) G 7
Pend Oreille (lake) B 1
Pend Oreille (mt.) B 1
Pend Orielle (river) A 1
Pilot (peak) C 4
Pilot (peak) C 6
Pilot Knob (mt.) C 4
Pinyon (peak) C 5
Pioneer (mts.) D 6
Portneuf (res.) F 7
Portneuf (river) F 7
Pot (mt.) C 3
Potlatch (river) B 3
Priest (lake) B 1
Priest (river) B 1
Purcell (mts.) B 1
Pyramid (peak) E 4
Raft (river) E 7
Rainbow (mt.) C 4
Ranger (peak) D 3
Rays (lake) F 6
Red (river) C 4
Redfish (lake) D 5
Reynolds (creek) B 6
Rhodes (peak) D 3
Rock (creek) F 7
Rocky Ridge (mt.) C 3
Ryan (peak) D 6
Saddle (mt.) D 3
Saddle (mt.) F 6
Sailor (creek) C 7
Saint Joe (river) B 2
Saint Maries (river) B 2
Salmon (falls) C 7
Salmon (river) B 4
Salmon Creek (res.) D 7
Salmon Falls (creek) D 7
Salmon River (mts.) C 5
Sawtooth (range) C 6
Secesh (creek) C 4
Selkirk (mts.) B 1
Selway (river) C 3
Seven Devils (mts.) B 4
Shoshone (falls) D 7
Slate (creek) B 4
Sleeping Deer (mt.) D 5
Smith (creek) B 1
Smoky (creek) D 6
Smoky (mts.) D 6
Snake (river) A 3
Snake River (plain) D 7
Snake River (range) G 6
Spirit (lake) B 2
Squaw (creek) B 5
Squaw (peak) D 4
Steamboat (mt.) C 4
Steel (mt.) C 6
Strike, C. J. (res.) C 7
Sublett (mts.) E 7
Sunset (peak) E 6
Taylor (mt.) D 5
Teton (river) G 6
Thompson (peak) C 5
Trinity (peak) C 6
Trout (creek) B 1
Twin (falls) D 7
Twin (peaks) D 5
Walcott (lake) E 7
Wasatch (range) G 7
Waugh (mt.) D 4
Weiser (river) B 5
Western Shoshone Ind. Res. B 7
White Knob (mts.) E 6
Wickahoney (creek) C 7
Willow (creek) G 6
Wilson Lake (res.) D 7
Yankee Fork, Salmon (river) D 5

◉ County Seat.
‡ Name not on map.

HIGHWAYS

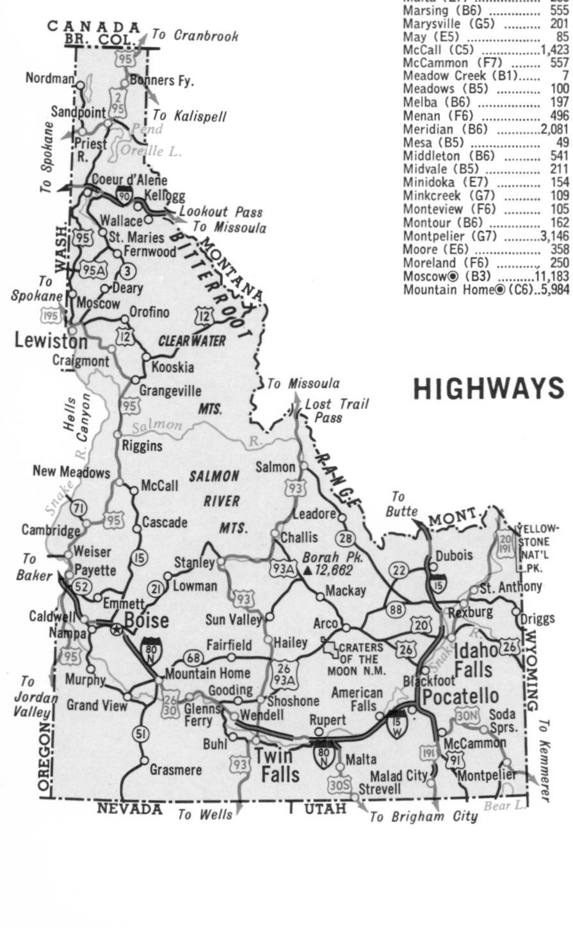
CANADA
BR. COL.
To Cranbrook
Nordman
Bonners Fy.
Sandpoint
To Kalispell
Priest R.
To Spokane
Coeur d'Alene
Kellogg
Lookout Pass
To Missoula
Wallace
St. Maries
Fernwood
MONTANA
BITTERROOT
WASH.
To Spokane
Deary
Moscow
Orofino
Lewiston
CLEARWATER
Craigmont
Kooskia
Grangeville
MTS.
To Missoula
Lost Trail Pass
Hells Canyon
Salmon
Riggins
New Meadows
McCall
SALMON RIVER MTS.
Salmon
RANGE
Cascade
Leadore
To Butte
MONT.
YELLOW-STONE NAT'L PK.
Cambridge
Challis
Weiser
Borah Pk. 12,662
Dubois
To Baker
Payette
Stanley
St. Anthony
Lowman
Mackay
Rexburg
Driggs
Emmett
Caldwell
Boise
Sun Valley
Arco
Nampa
Fairfield
Hailey
CRATERS OF THE MOON N.M.
Idaho Falls
To Jordan Valley
Murphy
Mountain Home
Blackfoot
WYOMING
Grand View
Gooding
Shoshone
American Falls
Pocatello
Soda Sprs.
To Kemmerer
Glenns Ferry
Wendell
Rupert
McCammon
OREGON
Buhl
Twin Falls
Malta
Montpelier
Grasmere
Malad City
Strevell
Bear L.
NEVADA
To Wells
UTAH
To Brigham City

0 80 160
MILES

Limited Access Highways
Major Highways
Other Important Roads
Interstate Route Numbers 95
Federal Route Numbers 9
State and Other Route Numbers 4

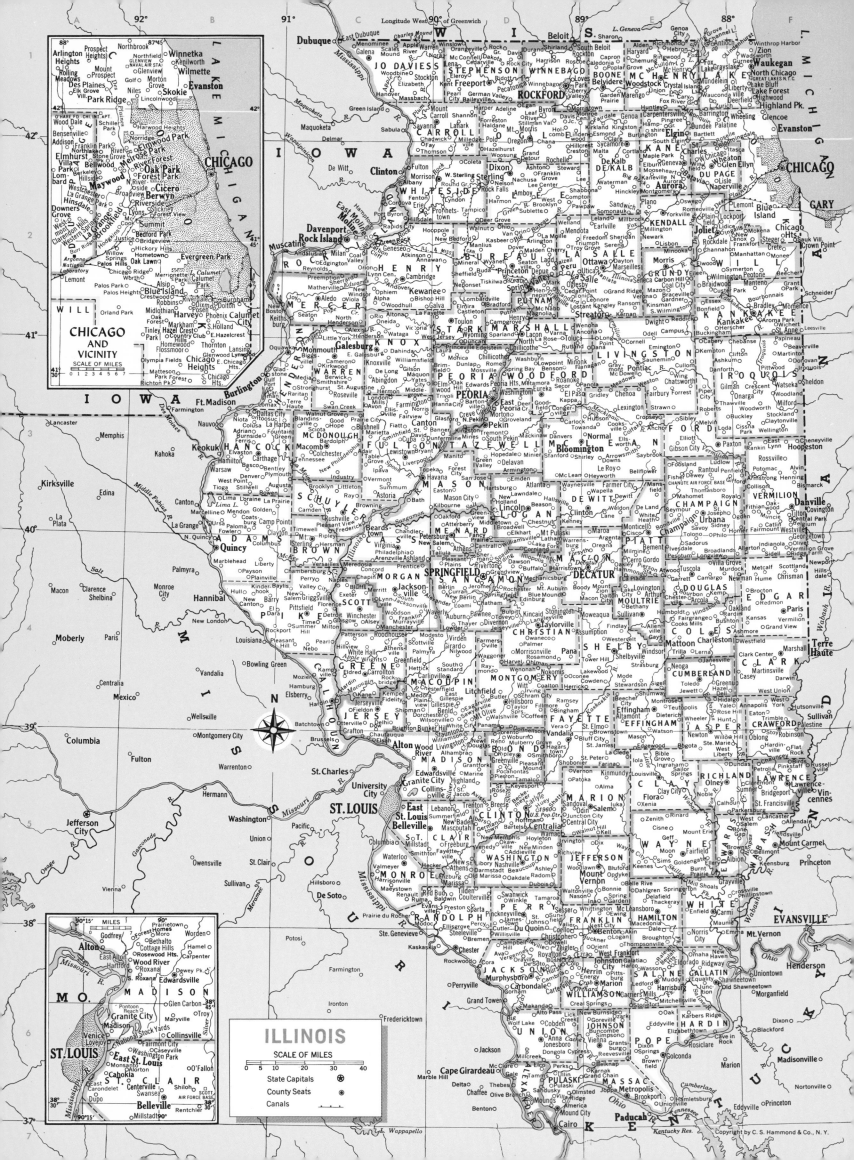

ILLINOIS

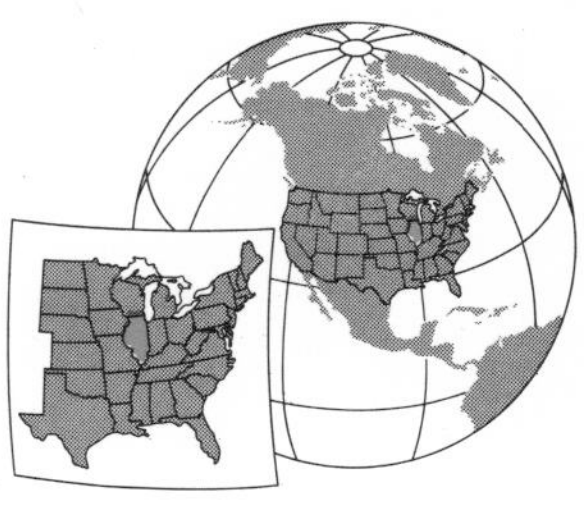

AREA 56,400 sq. mi.
POPULATION 10,644,000
CAPITAL Springfield
LARGEST CITY Chicago 3,550,404
HIGHEST POINT Charles Mound 1,241 ft.
SETTLED IN 1720
ADMITTED TO UNION December 3, 1818
POPULAR NAME Prairie State
STATE FLOWER Violet
STATE BIRD Cardinal

COUNTIES

Adams (B4) 68,467
Alexander (D6) 16,061
Bond (D5) 14,060
Boone (E1) 20,326
Brown (C4) 6,210
Bureau (D2) 37,594
Calhoun (C4) 5,933
Carroll (D1) 19,507
Cass (C4) 14,539
Champaign (E3) 132,436
Christian (D4) 37,207
Clark (F4) 16,546
Clay (E5) 15,815
Clinton (D5) 24,029
Coles (E4) 42,860
Cook (F2) 5,129,725
Crawford (F4) 20,751
Cumberland (E4) 9,936
De Kalb (E2) 51,714
De Witt (E3) 17,253
Douglas (E4) 19,243
Du Page (E2) 313,459
Edgar (F4) 22,550
Edwards (E5) 7,940
Effingham (E4) 23,107
Fayette (D4) 21,946
Ford (E3) 16,606
Franklin (E5) 39,281
Fulton (C3) 41,954
Gallatin (E6) 7,638
Greene (C4) 17,460
Grundy (E2) 22,350
Hamilton (E5) 10,010
Hancock (B3) 24,574
Hardin (E6) 5,879
Henderson (C3) 8,237
Henry (C2) 49,317
Iroquois (F3) 33,562
Jackson (D6) 42,151
Jasper (E4) 11,346
Jefferson (E5) 32,315
Jersey (C4) 17,023
Jo Daviess (C1) 21,821
Johnson (E6) 6,928
Kane (E2) 208,246
Kankakee (F2) 92,063
Kendall (E2) 17,540
Knox (C3) 61,280
La Salle (E2) 110,800
Lake (E1) 293,656
Lawrence (F5) 18,540
Lee (D2) 38,749
Livingston (E3) 40,341
Logan (D3) 33,656
Macon (E4) 118,257
Macoupin (D4) 43,524
Madison (D5) 224,689
Marion (E5) 39,349
Marshall (D2) 13,334
Mason (D3) 15,193
Massac (E6) 14,341
McDonough (C3) 28,928
McHenry (E1) 84,210
McLean (E3) 83,877
Menard (D3) 9,248
Mercer (C2) 17,149
Monroe (C5) 15,507
Montgomery (D4) 31,244
Morgan (C4) 36,571
Moultrie (E4) 13,635
Ogle (D1) 38,106
Peoria (D3) 189,044
Perry (D5) 19,184
Piatt (E4) 14,960
Pike (C4) 20,552
Pope (E6) 4,061
Pulaski (D6) 10,490
Putnam (D2) 4,570
Randolph (D5) 29,988
Richland (E5) 16,299
Rock Island (C2) 150,991
Saint Clair (D5) 262,509
Saline (E6) 26,227
Sangamon (D4) 146,539
Schuyler (C3) 8,746
Scott (C4) 6,377
Shelby (E4) 23,404
Stark (D2) 8,152
Stephenson (D1) 46,207
Tazewell (D3) 99,789
Union (D6) 17,645
Vermilion (F3) 96,176
Wabash (F5) 14,047
Warren (C3) 21,587
Washington (D5) 13,569
Wayne (E5) 19,008
White (E5) 19,373
Whiteside (D2) 59,887
Will (F2) 191,617
Williamson (E6) 46,117
Winnebago (D1) 209,765
Woodford (D3) 24,579

CITIES and TOWNS

Abingdon (C3) 3,469
Addison (A2) 6,741
Albany (C2) 637
Albers (D5) 566
Albion◉ (E5) 2,025
Aledo◉ (C2) 3,080
Alexis (C2) 878
Algonquin (E1) 2,014
Alhambra (D5) 537
Allendale (F5) 465
Alorton (B6) 3,282
Alpha (C2) 637
Alsip (B2) 3,770
Altamont (E4) 1,656
Alton (A6) 43,047
Altona (C2) 505
Amboy (D2) 2,067
Andalusia (C2) 560
Anna (D6) 4,280
Annawan (C2) 701
Antioch (E1) 2,268
Apple River (C1) 477
Arcola (E4) 2,273
Arenzville (C4) 417
Argenta (E4) 860
Arlington Hts. (A1)....27,878
Aroma Park (F2) 744
Arthur (E4) 2,120
Ashkum (E3) 601
Ashland (C4) 1,064
Ashley (D5) 662
Ashmore (F4) 447
Ashton (D2) 1,024
Assumption (E4) 1,439
Astoria (C3) 1,206
Athens (D4) 1,035
Atkinson (C2) 944
Atlanta (D3) 1,568
Atwood (E4) 1,258
Auburn (D4) 2,209
Augusta (C3) 915
Aurora (E2) 63,715
Aurora (urban area)..85,522
Ava (D6) 665
Aviston (D5) 717
Avon (C3) 996
Bannockburn ‡(F1) 466
Barrington (E1) 5,434
Barrington Hills ‡(E1)..1,726
Barry (B4) 1,422
Bartlett (E1) 1,540
Bartonville (D3) 7,253
Batavia (E2) 7,496
Beardstown (C3) 6,294
Beaverville (F3) 430
Beckemeyer (D5) 1,056
Bedford Park (B2) 737
Beecher (F2) 1,367
Beecher City (E4) 452
Belgium (F3) 494
Belleville◉ (B6) 37,264
Bellevue ‡(D3) 1,561
Bellwood (A2) 20,729
Belvidere◉ (E1) 11,223
Bement (E4) 1,558
Benld (D4) 1,848
Bensenville (A1) 9,141
Benson (D3) 427
Benton◉ (E6) 7,023
Berkeley (A2) 5,792
Berwyn (B2) 54,224
Bethalto (B6) 3,235
Bethany (E4) 1,118
Blandinsville (C3) 853
Bloomingdale (E2) 1,262
Bloomington◉ (D3)....36,271
Blue Island (B2) 19,618
Blue Mound (D4) 1,038
Bluffs (C4) 779
Bourbonnais (F2) 3,336
Bowen (B3) 559
Braceville (E2) 558
Bradford (D2) 857
Bradley (F2) 8,082
Braidwood (E2) 1,944
Breese (D5) 2,461
Bridgeport (F5) 2,260
Bridgeview (B2) 7,334
Brighton (C4) 1,248
Brimfield (D3) 656
Broadview (A2) 8,588
Brookfield (A2) 20,429
Brooklyn (Lovejoy) (A6) 1,922
Brookport (E6) 1,154
Brownstown (E5) 659
Buckley (F3) 690
Buckner (E6) 610
Buda (D2) 732
Buffalo Grove ‡(F1)....1,492
Bunker Hill (D4) 1,524
Burnham (B2) 2,478
Bush (D6) 459
Bushnell (C3) 3,710
Byron (D1) 1,578
Cahokia (B6) 15,829
Cairo◉ (D6) 9,348
Calumet City (B2) 25,000
Calumet Park (B2) 8,448
Cambria (D6) 568
Cambridge◉ (C2) 1,665
Camp Point (B3) 1,092
Canton (C3) 13,588
Capron (E1) 656
Carbon Cliff (C2) 1,268
Carbondale (D6) 14,670
Carlinville◉ (D4) 5,440
Carlyle◉ (D5) 2,903
Carmi◉ (E5) 6,152
Carol Stream ‡(E2) 836
Carpentersville (E1)....17,424
Carriers Mills (E6)....2,006
Carrollton◉ (C4) 2,558
Carterville (D6) 2,643
Carthage◉ (B3) 3,325
Cary (E1) 2,530
Casey (F4) 2,890
Caseyvile (B6) 2,455
Catlin (F3) 1,263
Cave in Rock (E6).... 495
Cedarville (D1) 570
Centerville (B6) 12,769
Central City (D5) 1,422
Central Park (F3) 2,676
Centralia (D5) 13,904
Cerro Gordo (E4) 1,067
Chadwick (D1) 602
Champaign (E3) 49,583
Champaign-Urbana (urban area) 78,014
Chandlerville (C3) 718
Channahon (E2) 1,122
Channel Lake (E1) 1,969
Chapin (C4) 477
Charleston◉ (E4) 10,505
Chatham (D4) 1,069
Chatsworth (E3) 1,330
Chebanse (F3) 995
Chenoa (E3) 1,523
Cherry (D2) 501
Cherry Valley (D1).... 875
Chester◉ (D6) 4,460
Chicago◉ (B2) 3,550,404
Chicago (urban area) 5,959,213
Chicago Heights (B3)..34,331
Chicago Ridge (A2) 5,748
Chillicothe (D3) 3,054
Chrisman (F4) 1,221
Christopher (D6) 2,854
Cicero (B2) 69,130
Cisne (E5) 615
Cissna Park (F3) 803
Clarendon Hills (A2)....5,885
Clay City (E5) 1,144
Clayton (B3) 774
Clifton (F3) 1,018
Clinton◉ (E3) 7,355
Coal City (E2) 2,852
Cobden (D6) 918
Coffeen (D4) 502
Colchester (C3) 1,495
Colfax (E3) 894
Collinsville (B6) 14,217
Colona ‡(C2) 491
Columbia (C5) 3,174
Cordova (C2) 502
Cornell (E3) 524
Cortland (E2) 461

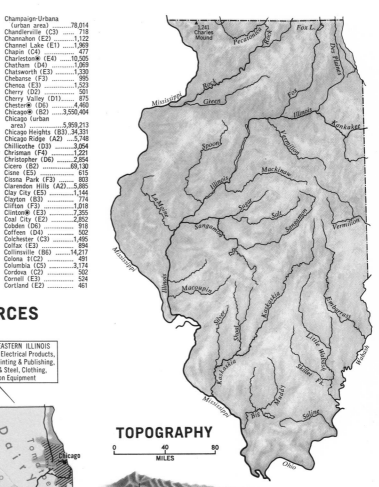

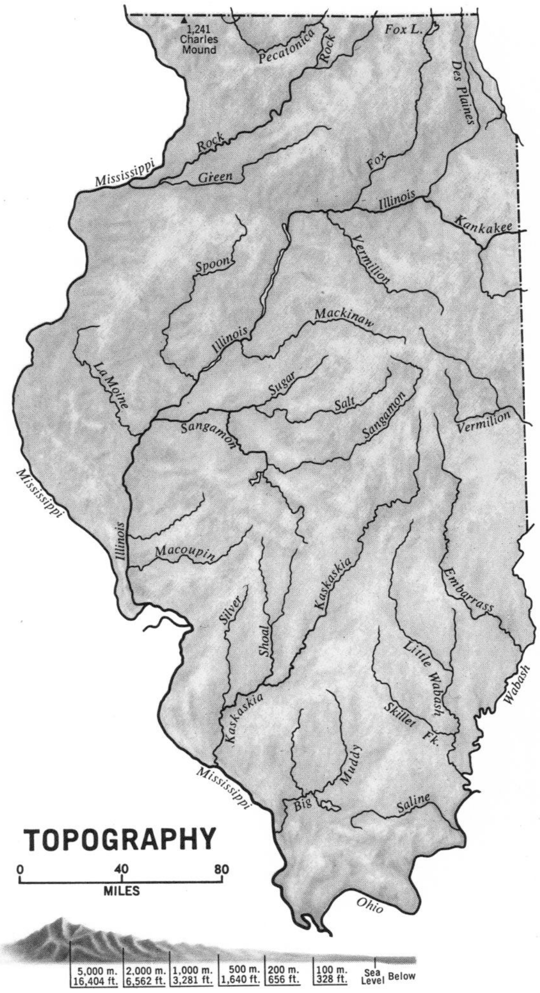
1,241
Charles Mound
Pecatonica
Rock
Fox L.
Des Plaines
Mississippi
Rock
Green
Fox
Illinois
Kankakee
Spoon
Vermilion
Mackinaw
La Moine
Illinois
Sugar
Salt
Sangamon
Sangamon
Vermilion
Mississippi
Illinois
Macoupin
Silver
Shoal
Kaskaskia
Embarrass
Little Wabash
Wabash
Kaskaskia
Skillet Fk.
Muddy
Mississippi
Big
Saline
Ohio
TOPOGRAPHY
0
40
80
MILES
5,000 m. 16,404 ft.
2,000 m. 6,562 ft.
1,000 m. 3,281 ft.
500 m. 1,640 ft.
200 m. 656 ft.
100 m. 328 ft.
Sea Level
Below

AGRICULTURE, INDUSTRY and RESOURCES

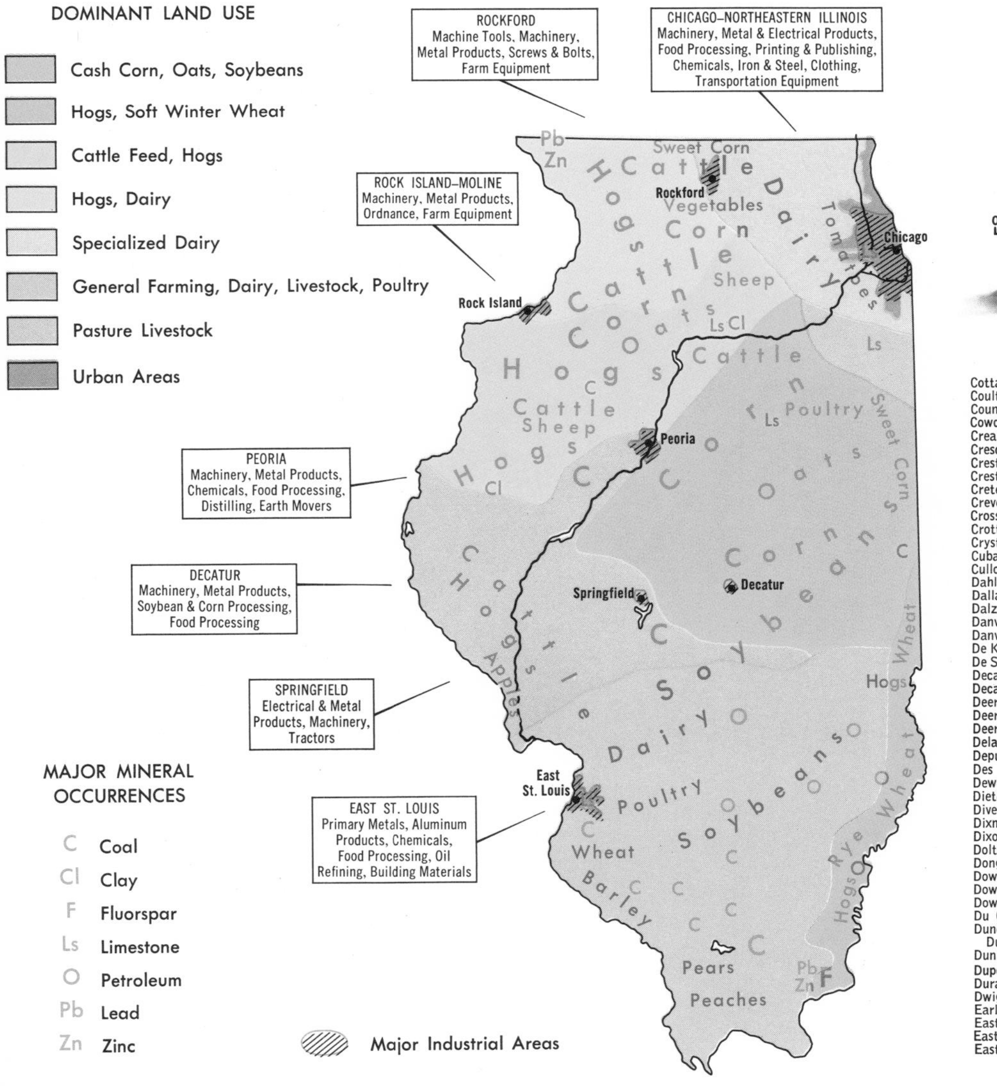
DOMINANT LAND USE
Cash Corn, Oats, Soybeans
Hogs, Soft Winter Wheat
Cattle Feed, Hogs
Hogs, Dairy
Specialized Dairy
General Farming, Dairy, Livestock, Poultry
Pasture Livestock
Urban Areas
ROCKFORD
Machine Tools, Machinery, Metal Products, Screws & Bolts, Farm Equipment
CHICAGO-NORTHEASTERN ILLINOIS
Machinery, Metal & Electrical Products, Food Processing, Printing & Publishing, Chemicals, Iron & Steel, Clothing, Transportation Equipment
ROCK ISLAND-MOLINE
Machinery, Metal Products, Ordnance, Farm Equipment
PEORIA
Machinery, Metal Products, Chemicals, Food Processing, Distilling, Earth Movers
DECATUR
Machinery, Metal Products, Soybean & Corn Processing, Food Processing
SPRINGFIELD
Electrical & Metal Products, Machinery, Tractors
EAST ST. LOUIS
Primary Metals, Aluminum Products, Chemicals, Food Processing, Oil Refining, Building Materials
Rockford
Chicago
Rock Island
Peoria
Springfield
Decatur
East St. Louis
Sweet Corn
Vegetables
Tomatoes
Sheep
Apples
Pears
Peaches
Barley
MAJOR MINERAL OCCURRENCES
C Coal
Cl Clay
F Fluorspar
Ls Limestone
O Petroleum
Pb Lead
Zn Zinc
Major Industrial Areas

Cottage Hills (B6) 3,976
Coulterville (D5) 1,022
Country Club Hills (B3)3,421
Cowden (E4) 575
Creal Springs (E6) 784
Crescent City (F3) 393
Crest Hill ‡(E2) 5,887
Crestwood (B2)....1,213
Crete (F2) 3,463
Creve Coeur (D3) 6,684
Crossville (F5) 874
Crotty (Seneca) (E2)...1,719
Crystal Lake (E1)....8,314
Cuba (C3) 1,380
Cullom (E3) 555
Dahlgren (E5) 480
Dallas City (B3) 1,276
Dalzell (D2) 496
Danvers (D3) 783
Danville◉ (F3) 41,856
De Kalb (E2) 18,486
De Soto (D6) 723
Decatur◉ (E4) 78,004
Decatur (urb. area)....89,516
Deer Creek (D3) 583
Deer Park ‡(E1) 476
Deerfield (F1) 11,786
Delavan (D3) 1,377
Depue (D2) 1,920
Des Plaines (A1) 34,886
Dewey Park (B6) 1,747
Dieterich (E4) 591
Divernon (D4) 997
Dixmoor (B2) 3,076
Dixon◉ (D2) 19,565
Dolton (B2) 18,746
Dongola (D6) 757
Dowell (D6) 453
Downers Grove (A2)...21,154
Downs (E3) 497
Du Quoin (D5) 6,558
Dundee (E. & W. Dundee) (E1) 4,751
Dunlap (D3) 564
Dupo (A6) 2,937
Durand (D1) 797
Dwight (E2) 3,086
Earlville (E2) 1,420
East Alton (B6) 7,630
East Carondelet (A6).... 463
East Chicago Hts. (B3) 3,270
East Dubuque (C1)....2,082
East Dundee (Dundee) (E1) 2,221
East Galesburg (C3).... 660
East Hazelcrest (B2)....1,457
East Moline (C2) 16,732
East Peoria (D3) 12,310
East Saint Louis (B6)..81,712
Edgewood (E5) 515
Edinburg (D4) 1,003
Edwardsville◉ (B6)....9,996
Effingham◉ (E4) 8,172
El Paso (D3) 1,964
Elburn (E2) 960
Eldorado (E6) 3,573
Elgin (E1) 49,447
Elizabeth (C1) 729
Elizabethtown◉ (E6)... 524
Elk Grove Village (A1)..6,608
Elkville (D6) 743
Elmhurst (A2) 36,991
Elmwood (D3) 1,882
Elmwood Park (B2)....23,866
Elwood (E2) 746
Emden (D3) 502
Energy (E6) 507
Enfield (E5) 791
Equality (E6) 665
Erie (C2) 1,215
Eureka◉ (D3) 2,538
Evanston (B1) 79,283
Evansville (D5) 829
Evergreen Park (B2)..24,178
Fairbury (E3) 2,937
Fairfield◉ (E5) 6,362
Fairmont City (B6) 2,688
Fairmount (F3) 725
Fairview (C3) 544
Farina (E5) 692
Farmer City (E3) 1,838
Farmersville (D4) 495
Farmington (C3) 2,831
Findlay (E4) 759
Fisher (E3) 1,155
Fithian (F3) 495
Flanagan (E3) 841
Flat Rock (F5) 497
Flora (E5) 5,331
Flossmoor (B3) 4,624
Forest Homes (B6) 2,025
Forest Park (B2) 14,452
Forest View (B2) 1,042
Forrest (E3) 1,220
Forreston (D1) 1,153
Fox Lake (E1) 3,700
Fox River Grove (E1)....1,866
Frankfort (F2) 1,135
Franklin (C4) 500
Franklin Grove (D2).... 773
Franklin Park (A2)....18,322
Freeburg (D5) 1,908
Freeport◉ (D1) 26,628
Fulton (C2) 3,387
Galatia (E6) 830
Galena◉ (C1) 4,410
Galesburg◉ (C3) 37,243
Galva (D2) 3,060
Gardner (E2) 1,041
Geneseo (C2) 5,169
Geneva◉ (E2) 7,646
Genoa (E1) 2,330
Georgetown (F4) 3,544
Germantown (D5) 983
Gibson City (E3) 3,453
Gifford (E3) 609
Gillespie (D4) 3,569
Gilman (E3) 1,704
Girard (D4) 1,734
Glasford (D3) 1,012
Glen Carbon (B6) 1,241
Glen Ellyn (F2) 15,972
Glencoe (F1) 10,472
Glendale Hts. ‡(E2)....5,244
Glenview (B1) 18,132
Glenwood (B3) 882
Godfrey (A6) 1,231
Golconda◉ (E6) 864
Golden (B3) 491
Goreville (E6) 625
Grafton (C5) 1,084
Grand Ridge (E2) 659
Grand Tower (D6) 847
Grandview (D4) 2,214
Granite City (B6) 40,073
Grant Park (F2) 757
Granville (D2) 1,048
Grayslake (E1) 3,762
Grayville (E5) 2,280
Green Rock (C2) 2,677
Green Valley (D3) 552
Greenfield (C4) 1,064
Greenup (E4) 1,477

(continued on following page)

Illinois
(continued)

Greenview (D3) 796
Greenville◉ (D5) 4,569
Gridley (E3) 889
Griggsville (C4) 1,240
Gurnee (F1) 1,831
Hamilton (B3) 2,228
Hammond (E4) 471
Hampshire (E1) 1,309
Hampton (C2) 742
Hanaford (Logan) (E5) 289
Hanna City (D3) 1,056
Hanover (C1) 1,396
Hardin◉ (C4) 356
Harrisburg◉ (E6) 9,171
Hartford (B6) 2,355
Harvard (E1) 4,248
Harvey (B2) 29,071
Harwood Heights (B1)..5,688
Havana◉ (D3) 4,363
Hazel Crest (B2) 6,205
Hebron (E1) 701
Hennepin◉ (D2) 391
Henry (D2) 2,278
Herrin (E6) 9,474
Herscher (E2) 658
Heyworth (E3) 1,196
Hickory Hills (B2)........2,707
Highland (D5) 4,943
Highland Park (F1)....25,532
Highwood (F1) 4,499
Hillsboro◉ (D4) 4,232
Hillsdale (C2) 490
Hillside (A2) 7,794
Hinckley (E2) 940
Hinsdale (A2) 12,859
Hodgkins (A2) 1,126
Homer (F3) 1,276
Hometown (B2) 7,479
Homewood (B3) 13,371
Hoopeston (F3) 6,606
Hopedale (D3) 737
Hoyleton (D5) 475
Hudson (E3) 493
Hull (B4) 535
Huntley (E1) 1,143
Hurst (D6) 863
Hutsonville (F4) 583
Illiopolis (D4) 995
Industry (C3) 514
Ingalls Park (F2) 4,035
Ipava (C3) 623
Irving (D4) 570
Island Lake (E1) 1,639
Itasca (F2) 3,564
Jacksonville◉ (C4) 21,690
Jerome (D4) 1,666
Jerseyville◉ (C4) 7,420
Johnston City (E6) 3,891
Joliet◉ (E2) 66,780
Joliet (urban area)...116,585
Jonesboro◉ (D6) 1,636
Joppa (E6) 578
Joy (C2) 503
Justice (A2) 2,803
Kampsville (C4) 453
Kane (C4) 469
Kankakee◉ (F2) 27,666
Kansas (F4) 815
Karnak (E6) 667
Keithsburg (B2) 963
Kenilworth (B1) 2,959
Kewanee (C2) 16,324
Kincaid (D4) 1,544
Kinmundy (E5) 813
Kirkland (E1) 928
Kirkwood (C3) 771
Knoxville (C3) 2,560
La Grange (A2) 15,285
La Grange Park (A2)..13,793
La Harpe (C3) 1,322
La Moille (D2) 655
La Salle (E2) 11,897
Lacon◉ (D2) 2,175
Ladd (D2) 1,255
Lake Bluff (F1) 3,494
Lake Forest (F1) 10,687
Lake in the Hills ‡(E1)..2,046
Lake Villa ‡(F1) 903
Lake Zurich (E1) 3,458
Lakemoor ‡(E1) 736
Lakewood ‡(E1) 635
Lanark (D1) 1,473
Lansing (B3) 18,098
Lawrenceville◉ (F5)....5,492
Le Roy (E3) 2,088
Leaf River (D1) 546
Lebanon (D5) 2,863
Leesville (F2) 492
Leland (E2) 642
Leland Grove ‡(D4) 1,731
Lemont (A2) 3,397
Lena (D1) 1,552
Lewistown◉ (C3) 2,603
Lexington (E3) 1,244
Libertyville (F1) 8,560
Lincoln◉ (D3) 16,890
Lincolnshire ‡(F1) 555
Lincolnwood (B1) 11,744
Lindenhurst (E1) 1,259
Lisle (E2) 4,219
Litchfield (D4) 7,330
Livingston (D5) 964
Loami (D4) 450
Lockport (F2) 7,560
Loda (E3) 585
Lomax (B3) 535
Lombard (A2) 22,561
London Mills (C3) 617
Long Grove ‡(E1) 640
Lostant (D2) 460
Louisville◉ (E5) 906
Lovejoy (A6) 1,922
Loves Park (E1) 9,086
Lovington (E4) 1,200
Ludlow (E3) 460
Lyndon (D2) 677
Lyons (B2) 9,936
Mackinaw (D3) 1,163
Macomb◉ (C3) 12,135
Macon (E4) 1,229
Madison (B6) 6,861
Mahomet (E3) 1,367
Malta (E2) 782
Manhattan (F2) 1,117
Manito (D3) 1,093
Mansfield (E3) 743
Manteno (F2) 2,225
Maple Park (E2) 592
Marengo (E1) 3,568
Marine (D5) 813
Marion◉ (E6) 11,274
Marissa (D5) 1,722
Mark (D2) 445
Markham (B2) 11,704
Maroa (E3) 1,235
Marquette Hts. ‡(D3)..2,517
Marseilles (E2) 4,347
Marshall◉ (F4) 3,270
Martinsville (F4) 1,351
Maryville (B6) 675
Mascoutah (D5) 3,625
Mason City (D3) 2,160
Matherville (C2) 612
Matteson (B3) 3,225
Mattoon (E4) 19,088
Maywood (A2) 27,330
Mazon (E2) 683
McCullom Lake (E1)..... 759
McHenry (E1) 3,336
McLean (D3) 758
McLeansboro◉ (E5)....2,951
Medora (C4) 447
Melrose Park (A2)........22,291
Melvin (E3) 559
Mendon (B3) 784
Mendota (D2) 6,154
Meredosia (C4) 1,034
Merrionette Park (B2)..2,354
Metamora (D3) 1,808
Metropolis◉ (E6) 7,339
Middletown (D3) 543
Midlothian (B2) 6,605
Milan (C2) 3,065
Milford (F3) 1,699
Milledgeville (D1) 1,208
Millstadt (B6) 1,830
Minier (D3) 847
Minonk (D3) 2,001
Minooka (E2) 539
Mokena (F2) 1,332
Moline (C2) 42,705
Moline-Davenport-Rock Island (urb. area)..227,176
Momence (F2) 2,949
Monee (F2) 646
Monmouth◉ (C3) 10,372
Montgomery (E2) 2,122
Monticello◉ (E3) 3,219
Morris◉ (E2) 7,935
Morrison◉ (C2) 4,159
Morrisonville (D4) 1,129
Morton (D3) 5,325
Morton Grove (B1)........20,533
Mound City◉ (D6)........1,669
Mounds (D6) 1,835
Mount Auburn (D4) 502
Mount Carmel◉ (F5)....8,594
Mount Carroll◉ (D1)....2,056
Mount Clare ‡(D4) 320
Mount Morris (D1) 3,075
Mount Olive (D4) 2,295
Mount Prospect (A1)..18,906
Mount Pulaski (D3)........1,689
Mount Sterling◉ (C4)..2,262
Mount Vernon◉ (E5)..15,566
Mount Zion (E4) 925
Moweaqua (E4) 1,614
Mulberry Grove (D5).... 745
Mundelein (E1) 10,526
Murphysboro◉ (D6) 8,673
Murrayville (C4) 442
Naperville (E2) 12,933
Naplate (E2) 738
Nashville◉ (D5) 2,606
Nauvoo (B3) 1,039
Nebo (C4) 441
Neoga (E4) 1,145
Neponset (D2) 495
New Athens (D5) 1,923
New Baden (D5) 1,464
New Berlin (D4) 627
New Boston (B2) 726
New Canton (B4) 449
New Haven (E6) 642
New Lenox (F2) 1,750
Newark (E2) 489
Newman (F4) 1,097
Newton◉ (E5) 2,901
Niantic (D4) 629
Niles (A1) 20,393
Noble (E5) 761
Nokomis (D4) 2,476
Normal (E3) 13,357
Norridge (B1) 14,087
Norris City (E6) 1,243
North Aurora (E2) 2,088
North Chicago (F1)....20,517
North Chillicothe (D3)..2,259
North Pekin (D3) 2,025
North Quincy (B4) 2,256
North Riverside (B2)....7,989
Northbrook (A1) 11,635
Northfield (B1) 4,005
Northlake (A2) 12,318
Norwood ‡(D3) 626
Oak Forest (B2) 3,724
Oak Lawn (B2) 27,471
Oak Park (B2) 61,093
Oakbrook Terr. ‡(A2)....1,121
Oakland (F4) 939
Oakwood (F3) 861
Oblong (F5) 1,817
Odell (E2) 936
Odin (D5) 1,242
O'Fallon (B6) 4,018
Ogden (F3) 515
Oglesby (D2) 4,215
Ohio (D2) 489
Okawville (D5) 931
Old Shawneetown (E6).. 433
Olmstead (D6) 475
Olney◉ (E5) 8,780
Olympia Fields (B3) 1,503
Onarga (F3) 1,397
Oneida (C2) 672
Oquawka◉ (C3) 1,090
Orangeville (D1) 491
Oreana (E4) 464
Oregon◉ (D1) 3,732
Orient (E6) 588
Orion (C2) 1,269
Orland Park (A2) 2,592
Oswego (E2) 1,510
Ottawa◉ (E2) 19,408
Palatine (E1) 11,504
Palestine (F4) 1,564
Palmyra (C4) 811
Palos Heights (A2) 3,775
Palos Hills (A2) 3,766
Palos Park (A2) 2,169
Pana (D4) 6,432
Panama (D4) 487
Paris◉ (F4) 9,823
Park City ‡(F1) 1,408
Park Forest (B3) 29,993
Park Ridge (A1) 32,659
Patoka (D5) 601
Pawnee (D4) 1,517
Pawpaw (E2) 725
Paxton◉ (E3) 4,370
Payson (B4) 502
Pearl City (D1) 488
Pecatonica (D1) 1,659
Pekin◉ (D3) 28,146
Peoria◉ (D3) 103,162
Peoria (urban area)..181,432
Peoria Heights (D3)....7,064
Peotone (F2) 1,788
Percy (D5) 810
Perry (C4) 442
Peru (D2) 10,460
Pesotum (E4) 468
Petersburg◉ (D4) 2,359
Philo (E3) 740
Phoenix (B2) 4,203
Pierron (D5) 451
Pinckneyville◉ (D5) 3,085
Piper City (E3) 807
Pittsburg (E6) 485
Pittsfield◉ (C4) 4,089
Plainfield (E2) 2,183
Plano (E2) 3,343
Pleasant Hills (C4) 950
Pleasant Plains (D4).... 518
Plymouth (C3) 781
Pocahontas (D5) 718
Polo (D1) 2,551
Pontiac◉ (E3) 8,435
Pontoon Beach (B6)..... 756
Poplar Grove (E1) 460
Port Byron (C2) 1,153
Posen (B2) 4,517
Potomac (F3) 661
Prairie City (C3) 613
Prairie du Rocher (C5).. 679
Princeton◉ (D2) 6,250
Princeville (D3) 1,281
Prophetstown (D2)........1,802
Quincy◉ (B4) 43,793
Ramsey (D4) 815
Rankin (F3) 761
Rantoul (E3) 22,116
Rapids City (C2) 675
Raymond (D4) 871
Red Bud (D5) 1,942
Reynolds (C2) 494
Richmond (E1) 855
Richton Park (B3) 933
Ridge Farm (F4) 894
Ridgway (E6) 1,055
River Forest (B2) 12,695
River Grove (A2) 8,464
Riverdale (B2) 12,008
Riverside (B2) 9,750
Riverton (D4) 1,536
Roanoke (D3) 1,821
Robbins (B2) 7,511
Roberts (E3) 504
Robinson◉ (F5) 7,226
Rochelle (D2) 7,008
Rochester (D4) 742
Rock Falls (D2) 10,261
Rock Island◉ (C2)......51,863
Rock Island-Davenport-Moline (urban area) 227,176
Rockdale (E2) 1,272
Rockford◉ (D1) 126,706
Rockford (urb. area)171,681
Rockton (E1) 1,833
Rolling Meadows (A1) 10,879
Rome (D3) 1,347
Romeoville (E2) 3,574
Roodhouse (C4) 2,352
Roselle (E1) 3,581
Rosemont ‡(A1) 978
Roseville (C3) 1,065
Rosewood Hts. (B6)......4,572
Rosiclare (E6) 1,700
Rossville (F3) 1,470
Round Lake ‡(E1) 997
Round Lake Bch. ‡(E1) 5,011
Round Lake Park ‡(E1) 2,565
Roxana (B6) 2,090
Royalton (D6) 1,225
Rushville◉ (C3) 2,819
Rutland (D3) 509
Saint Anne (F2) 1,378
Saint Charles (E2) 9,269
Saint David (C3) 862
Saint Elmo (E4) 1,503
Saint Francisville (F5)..1,040
Saint Jacob (D5) 529
Saint Joseph (E3) 1,210
Salem◉ (E5) 6,165
San Jose (D3) 1,093
Sandoval (D5) 1,356
Sandwich (E2) 3,842
Sauk Village (F2) 4,687
Savanna (C1) 4,950
Saybrook (E3) 859
Schaumburg ‡(E1) 986
Schiller Park (A1) 5,687
Schram City (D4) 698
Seneca (E2) 1,719
Sesser (D5) 1,764
Shabbona (E2) 690
Shannon (D1) 766
Shawneetown◉ (E6)....1,280
Sheffield (D2) 1,078
Shelbyville◉ (E4) 4,821
Sheldon (F3) 1,137
Sheridan (E2) 704
Sherrard (C2) 574
Shiloh (B6) 701
Sidell (F4) 614
Sidney (E3) 686
Silvis (C2) 3,973
Skokie (B1) 59,364
Smithton (C5) 629
Somonauk (E2) 899
Sorento (D5) 681
South Beloit (E1) 3,781
South Chicago Hts.(B3)4,043
South Elgin (E2) 2,624
South Holland (B2)....10,412
South Jacksonville (C4)2,340
South Pekin (D3) 1,007
South Roxana (B6) 2,010
South Wilmington (E2) 730
Southern View ‡(D4)....1,485
Sparland (D2) 534
Sparta (D5) 3,452
Spring Valley (D2) 5,371
SPRINGFIELD◉ (D4)83,271
Springfield (urban area) 111,403
Stanford (D3) 479
Staunton (D5) 4,228
Steeleville (D6) 1,569
Steger (F2) 6,432
Sterling (D2) 15,688
Stewardson (E4) 656
Stickney (B2) 6,239
Stillman Valley (D1).... 598
Stockton (C1) 1,800
Stone Park (A2) 3,038
Stonington (D4) 1,076
Strasburg (E4) 467
Streamwood ‡(E1) 4,821
Streator (E2) 16,868
Stronghurst (C3) 815
Sullivan◉ (E4) 3,946
Summit (B2) 10,374
Sumner (F5) 1,035
Swansea (B6) 3,018
Sycamore◉ (E2) 6,961
Table Grove (C3) 500
Tallula (D4) 547
Tamaroa (D5) 696
Tamms (D6) 548
Tampico (D2) 790
Taylor Springs (D4)..... 550
Taylorville◉ (D4) 8,801
Teutopolis (E4) 1,140
Thayer (D4) 649
Thebes (D6) 471
Thomasboro (E3) 458
Thomson (C2) 543
Thornton (B3) 2,895
Tilden (D5) 808
Tilton (F3) 2,598
Tinley Park (B2) 6,392
Tiskilwa (D2) 951
Toledo◉ (E4) 998
Tolono (E3) 1,539
Toluca (D2) 1,352
Tonica (E2) 750
Toulon◉ (D2) 1,213
Tovey (D4) 646
Towanda (E3) 586
Tower Hill (E4) 700
Tremont (D3) 1,558
Trenton (D5) 1,866
Troy (B6) 1,778
Tuscola◉ (E4) 3,875
Ullin (D6) 577
Union (E1) 480
Urbana◉ (E3) 27,294
Urbana-Champaign (urban area) 78,014
Valier (D5) 649
Valley View ‡(E2) 1,741
Valmeyer (C5) 709
Vandalia◉ (D5) 5,537
Venice (A6) 5,380
Vermont (C3) 903
Versailles (C4) 427
Victoria (C2) 453
Vienna◉ (E6) 1,094
Villa Grove (E4) 2,308
Villa Park (A2) 20,391
Viola (C2) 812
Virden (D4) 3,309
Virginia◉ (C4) 1,669
Wadsworth (F1) 558
Walnut (D2) 1,192
Wamac (D5) 1,394
Wapella (E3) 526
Warren (C1) 1,470
Warrensburg (D4) 681
Warrenville ‡(E2) 3,134
Warsaw (B3) 1,938
Washburn (D3) 1,064
Washington (D3) 5,919
Washington Park (B6)..6,601
Waterloo◉ (C5) 3,739
Waterman (E2) 916
Watseka◉ (F3) 5,219
Wauconda (E1) 3,227
Waukegan◉ (F1) 55,719
Waverly (D4) 1,375
Wayne City (E5) 903
Waynesville (D3) 510
Weldon (E3) 449
Wenona (E2) 1,005
West Chicago (E2) 6,854
West City (E5) 814
West Dundee (Dundee) (E1) 2,530
West Frankfort (E6)......9,027
West Salem (F5) 956
West Sterling (D2) 1,430
Westchester (A2) 18,092
Western Sprs. (A2)......10,838
Westfield (F4) 636
Westmont (A2) 5,997
Westville (F3) 3,497
Wheaton◉ (E2) 24,312
Wheeling (F1) 7,169
White Hall (C4) 3,012
Williamsfield (C3) 548
Williamsville (D4) 735
Willisville (D6) 532
Willow Springs (A2)......2,348
Wilmette (B1) 28,268
Wilmington (E2) 4,210
Wilsonville (D4) 688
Winchester◉ (C4) 1,657
Windsor (E4) 1,021
Winfield (E2) 1,575
Winnebago (D1) 1,059
Winnetka (B1) 13,368
Winthrop Harbor (F1)..3,848
Witt (D4) 1,101
Wood Dale (A1) 3,071
Wood River (B6) 11,694
Woodhull (C2) 779
Woodridge ‡(E2) 542
Woodstock◉ (E1) 8,897
Worden (B6) 1,060
Worth (A2) 8,196
Wyanet (D2) 938
Wyoming (D2) 1,559
Xenia (E5) 491
Yates City (C3) 802
Yorkville◉ (E2) 1,568
Zeigler (D6) 2,133
Zion (F1) 11,941

OTHER FEATURES

Apple (creek) ....C 4
Apple (river) ....C 1
Argonne Nat'l Lab. ....A 2
Big Bureau (river) ....D 2
Big Muddy (river) ....D 6
Bonpas (creek) ....F 5
Cache (river) ....D 6
Calumet (lake) ....B 2
Chanute A.F.B. ....E 3
Charles Mound (hill) ....C 1
Crab Orchard (lake) ....E 6
Decatur (lake) ....E 4
Des Plaines (river) ....F 2
Du Page (river) ....E 2
Edwards (river) ....C 2
Embarras (river) ....E 4
Fox (lake) ....E 1
Fox (river) ....E 2
Fox (river) ....E 5
Glenview N.A.S. ....A 1
Great Lakes Naval Training Center ....F 1
Green (river) ....D 2
Henderson (river) ....C 2
Illinois (river) ....C 4
Illinois-Mississippi (canal) ....C 2
Iroquois (river) ....F 3
Kankakee (river) ....E 2
Kaskaskia (river) ....E 4
La Moine (river) ....C 3
Lima (lake) ....B 3
Little Wabash (river)........E 5
Mackinaw (river) ....E 3
Macoupin (creek) ....C 4
McKee (creek) ....C 4
Michigan (lake) ....F 1
Mississippi (river) ....C 5
Ohio (river) ....E 6
Plum (river) ....C 1
Pope (creek) ....C 2
Rock (creek) ....D 2
Rock (river) ....C 2
Saline (river) ....E 6
Salt (creek) ....D 3
Sangamon (river) ....C 3
Scott A.F.B. ....B 6
Shoal (creek) ....D 5
Silver (creek) ....C 5
Skillet Fork (river) ....E 5
Spoon (river) ....C 3
Springfield (lake) ....D 4
Vermilion (river) ....E 2
Vermilion (river) ....E 3
Wabash (river) ....F 5

◉ County Seat.
‡ Name not on map.

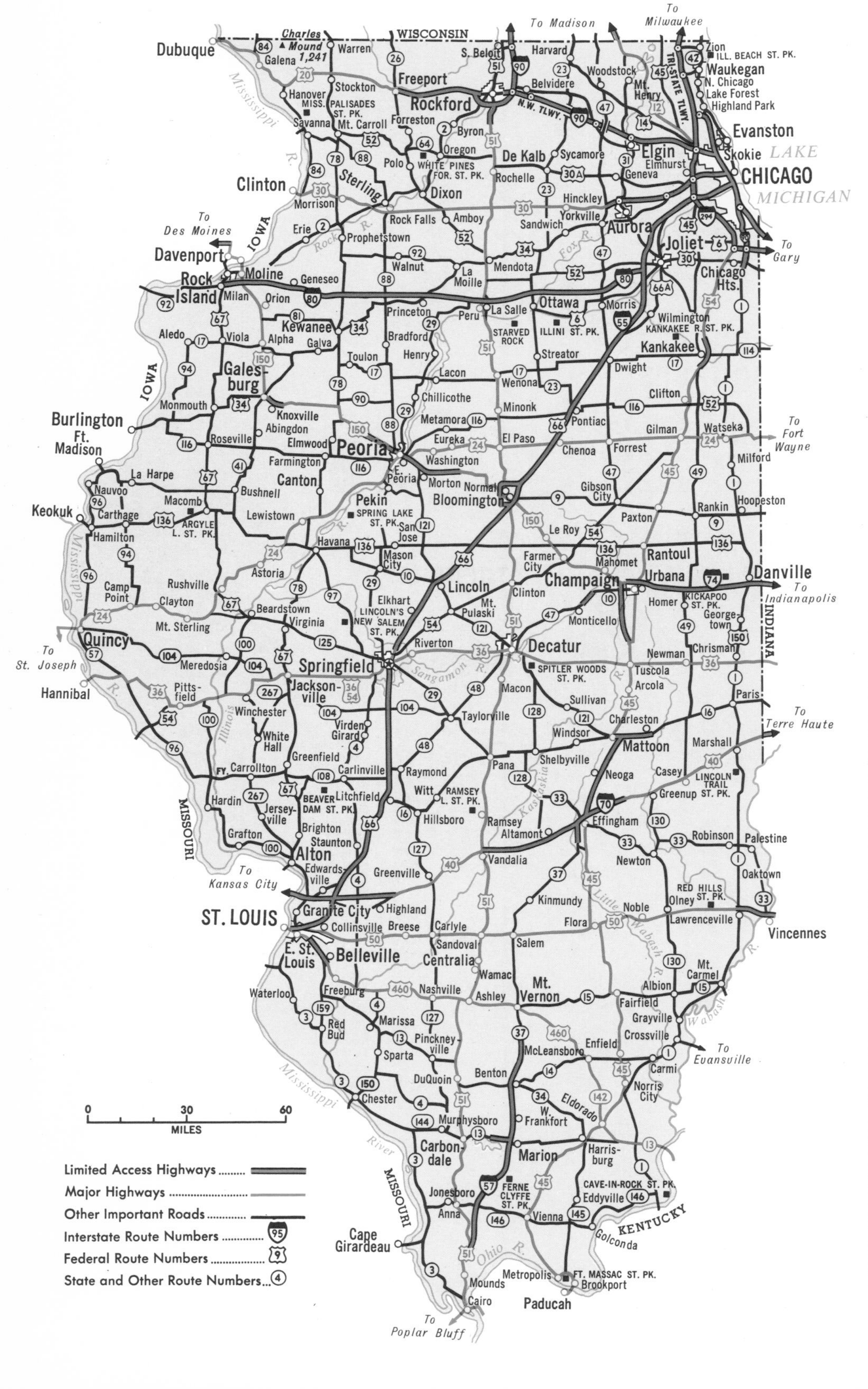

INDIANA

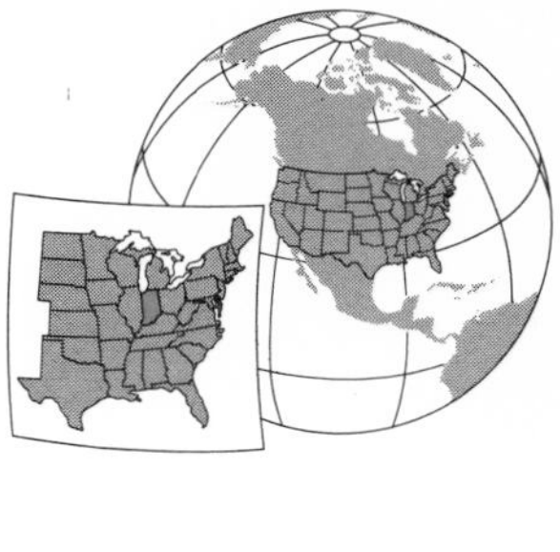

AREA	36,291 sq. mi.
POPULATION	4,885,000
CAPITAL	Indianapolis
LARGEST CITY	Indianapolis 476,258
HIGHEST POINT	1,257 ft. (Wayne County)
SETTLED IN	1730
ADMITTED TO UNION	December 11, 1816
POPULAR NAME	Hoosier State
STATE FLOWER	Peony
STATE BIRD	Cardinal

COUNTIES

Adams (H3) 24,643
Allen (G2) 232,196
Bartholomew (F6) 48,198
Benton (C3) 11,912
Blackford (G4) 14,792
Boone (E4) 27,543
Brown (E6) 7,024
Carroll (D3) 16,934
Cass (E3) 40,931
Clark (F8) 62,795
Clay (C6) 24,207
Clinton (E4) 30,765
Crawford (E8) 8,379
Daviess (C7) 26,636
De Kalb (H2) 28,271
Dearborn (H6) 28,674
Decatur (G6) 20,019
Delaware (G4) 110,938
Dubois (D8) 27,463
Elkhart (F1) 106,790
Fayette (G5) 24,454
Floyd (F8) 51,397
Fountain (C4) 18,706
Franklin (G6) 17,015
Fulton (E2) 16,957
Gibson (B8) 29,949
Grant (F3) 75,741
Greene (D6) 26,327
Hamilton (E4) 40,132
Hancock (F5) 26,665
Harrison (E8) 19,207
Hendricks (D5) 40,896
Henry (G5) 48,899
Howard (E4) 69,509
Huntington (G3) 33,814
Jackson (E7) 30,556
Jasper (C2) 18,842
Jay (G4) 22,572
Jefferson (G7) 24,061
Jennings (F7) 17,267
Johnson (E6) 43,704
Knox (C7) 41,561
Kosciusko (F2) 40,373
Lagrange (G1) 17,380
Lake (C2) 513,269
LaPorte (D1) 95,111
Lawrence (E7) 36,564
Madison (F4) 125,819
Marion (E5) 697,567
Marshall (E2) 32,443
Martin (D7) 10,608
Miami (E3) 38,000
Monroe (D6) 59,225
Montgomery (D4) 32,089
Morgan (E6) 33,875
Newton (C3) 11,502
Noble (G2) 28,162
Ohio (H7) 4,165
Orange (E7) 16,877
Owen (D6) 11,400
Parke (C5) 14,804
Perry (D8) 17,232
Pike (C8) 12,797
Porter (C2) 60,279
Posey (B8) 19,214
Pulaski (D2) 12,837
Putnam (D5) 24,927
Randolph (G4) 28,434
Ripley (G6) 20,641
Rush (G5) 20,393
Saint Joseph (E1) 238,614
Scott (F7) 14,643
Shelby (F5) 34,093
Spencer (C9) 16,074
Starke (D2) 17,911
Steuben (G1) 17,184
Sullivan (C6) 21,721
Switzerland (G7) 7,092
Tippecanoe (D4) 89,122
Tipton (E4) 15,856
Union (H5) 6,457
Vanderburgh (B8) 165,794
Vermillion (C5) 17,683
Vigo (C6) 108,458
Wabash (F3) 32,605
Warren (C4) 8,545
Warrick (C8) 23,577
Washington (E7) 17,819
Wayne (G5) 74,039
Wells (G3) 21,220
White (D3) 19,709
Whitley (F2) 20,954

CITIES and TOWNS

Abington (H5) 250
Acton (E5) 740
Adams (F6) 350
Advance (D5) 463
Akron (E2) 958
Alamo (C5) 144
Albany (G4) 2,132
Albion◉ (G2) 1,325
Alexandria (F4) 5,582
Alfordsville (C7) 121
Altona (G2) 313
Ambia (C4) 351
Amboy (F3) 446
Amo (D5) 437
Anderson◉ (F4) 49,061
Andrews (F3) 1,132
Angola◉ (G1) 4,746
Arcadia (E4) 1,271
Arcola (G2) 300
Ardmore (E1) 6,000
Argos (E2) 1,339
Arlington (F5) 380
Ashley (G1) 721
Atlanta (E4) 602
Attica (C4) 4,341
Atwood (F2) 253
Auburn◉ (G2) 6,350
Aurora (H6) 4,119
Austin (F7) 3,838
Avilla (G2) 919
Avoca (D7) 400
Bainbridge (D5) 603
Bargersville (E5) 586
Batesville (G6) 3,349
Battle Ground (D3) 804
Bedford◉ (E7) 13,024
Beech Grove (E5) 10,973
Benton (F2) 260
Berne (H3) 2,644
Bethany (E5) 119
Beverly Shores (C1) 773
Bicknell (C7) 3,878
Birdseye (D8) 366
Blackoak (C1) 3,000
Blanford (B5) 700
Blocher (F7) 275
Bloomfield◉ (D6) 2,224
Bloomingdale (C5) 455
Bloomington◉ (D6) 31,357
Blountsville (G4) 218
Blue Ridge (F5) 250
Bluffside (D1) 1,372
Bluffton◉ (G3) 6,238
Boonville◉ (C8) 4,801
Borden (F8) 327
Boston (H5) 240
Boswell (C3) 957
Bourbon (E2) 1,522
Bowling Green (D6) 229
Bradford (E8) 214
Brazil◉ (C5) 8,853
Bremen (E2) 3,052
Bridgeport (E5) 700
Bright (H6) 300
Brimfield (G2) 230
Bringhurst (E3) 250
Bristol (F1) 991
Bronson (Losantville) (G4) 868
Brook (C3) 845
Brooklyn (E5) 866
Brooksburg (G7) 129
Brookston (D3) 1,202
Brookville◉ (G6) 2,596
Brownsburg (E5) 4,478
Brownstown◉ (F7) 2,158
Brownsville (H5) 240
Bruce Lake (E2) 250
Bruceville (C7) 623
Bryant (G3) 316
Buck Creek (D4) 300
Buckskin (C8) 280
Bud (E6) 20
Buffalo (D3) 215
Bunker Hill (E3) 1,049
Burket (F2) 259
Burlington (E4) 800
Burnettsville (D3) 452
Burney (F6) 260
Burnsville (F6) 200
Burrows (E3) 350
Butler (H2) 2,176
Butlerville (F6) 250
Cadiz (G5) 198
Cambridge City (G5) 2,569
Camden (D3) 601
Campbellsburg (E7) 612
Cannelburg (C7) 124
Cannelton◉ (D9) 1,829
Cape Sandy (E8) 65
Carbon (C5) 409
Carlisle (C7) 755
Carmel (E5) 1,442
Cartersburg (E5) 260
Carthage (F5) 1,043
Cass (C6) 250
Castleton (E5) 267
Cato (C8) 383
Cayuga (C5) 904
Cedar Grove (H6) 232
Cedar Lake (C2) 5,766
Cedarville (G2) 250
Centenary (B5) 250
Center (E4) 289
Centerpoint (C6) 268
Centerton (E5) 500
Centerville (H5) 2,378
Chalmers (D3) 548
Chandler (C8) 1,784
Charlestown (F8) 5,726
Charlottesville (F5) 500
Chesterfield (F4) 2,588
Chesterton (D1) 4,335
Chrisney (C8) 380
Churubusco (G2) 1,284
Cicero (E4) 1,284
Clarks Hill (D4) 654
Clarksburg (G6) 300
Clarksville (F8) 8,088
Clay City (C6) 950
Claypool (F2) 452
Clayton (D5) 653
Clear Creek (E6) 300
Clear Lake (H1) 147
Clermont (E5) 1,058
Clifford (F6) 241
Clifty (F6) 1,167
Clinton (C5) 5,843
Cloverdale (D5) 741
Clymers (E3) 227
Coal City (D6) 250
Coalmont (C6) 400
Coatesville (D5) 497
Colburn (D3) 275
Colfax (D4) 725
Collegeville (C3) 600
Columbia City◉ (G2) 4,803
Columbus◉ (E6) 20,778
Connersville◉ (G5) 17,698
Converse (F3) 1,044
Cook (C2) 360
Correct (G7) 300
Corunna (G2) 361
Corydon◉ (E8) 2,701
Covington◉ (C4) 2,759
Cowan (G4) 250
Crandall (E8) 166
Crane (D7) 525
Crawfordsville◉ (D4) 14,231
Cromwell (F2) 451
Cross Plains (G7) 200
Crothersville (F7) 1,449
Crown Point◉ (C2) 8,443
Crows Nest ‡(E5) 122
Culver (E2) 1,558
Cumberland (E5) 872
Cynthiana (B8) 663
Dale (D8) 900
Daleville (F4) 1,548
Dana (C5) 811
Danville◉ (D5) 3,287
Darlington (D4) 668
Daylight (B8) 250
Dayton (D4) 650
Decatur◉ (H3) 8,327
Decker (B7) 317
Deer Creek (E3) 279
Delphi◉ (D3) 2,517
Demotte (C2) 900
Denver (E3) 565
Deputy (F7) 320
Desoto (G4) 250
Dillsboro (G6) 745
Dublin (G5) 1,021
Dubois (D8) 500
Dudleytown (F7) 250
Dugger (C6) 1,062
Dune Acres (C1) 238
Dunkirk (G4) 3,117
Dunlap (F1) 1,935
Dunreith (G5) 236
Dupont (G7) 325
Dyer (C1) 3,993
Earl Park (C3) 551
East Chicago (C1) 57,669
East Columbus (F6) 1,912
East Enterprise (H7) 250
East Gary (C1) 9,309
East Germantown (Pershing) (G5) 367
Eaton (G4) 1,529
Eckerty (D8) 225
Economy (G5) 280
Edgewood (F4) 2,119
Edinburg (E6) 3,664
Edwardsport (C7) 533
Edwardsville (F8) 300
Elberfeld (C8) 485
Elizabeth (F8) 214
Elizabethtown (F6) 417
Elkhart (F1) 40,274
Ellettsville (D6) 1,222
Elnora (C7) 824
Elwood (F4) 11,793
English◉ (E8) 698
Etna Green (E2) 483
Eugene (B5) 300
Evansville◉ (C9) 141,543
Evansville (urb. area) 143,660
Everton (G5) 180
Fairbanks (B6) 500
Fairland (F5) 790
Fairmount (F4) 3,080
Fairview Park (C5) 1,039
Farmersburg (C6) 1,027
Farmland (G4) 1,102
Ferdinand (D8) 1,427
Fillmore (D5) 550
Finly (F5) 325
Fishers (E5) 344
Flat Rock (F6) 276
Flora (E3) 1,742
Floyds Knobs (F8) 350
Fontanet (C5) 400
Forest (E4) 450
Fort Branch (B8) 1,983
Fort Wayne◉ (G2) 161,776
Fort Wayne (urban area) 179,571
Fortville (F5) 2,209
Fountain City (H5) 833
Fountaintown (F5) 400
Fowler◉ (C3) 2,491
Fowlerton (F4) 297
Francesville (D3) 1,002
Francisco (B8) 565
Frankfort◉ (E4) 15,302
Franklin◉ (E6) 9,453
Frankton (F4) 1,445
Fredericksburg (E8) 207
Freelandville (C7) 730
Freetown (E7) 350
Fremont (H1) 937
French Lick (D7) 1,954
Fulton (E3) 410
Galena (F8) 400
Galveston (E3) 1,111
Garrett (G2) 4,364
Gary (C1) 178,320
Gas City (F4) 4,469
Gaston (G4) 801
Gatchel (D8) 750
Geneva (H3) 1,053
Gentryville (C8) 297
Georgetown (F8) 643
Glenwood (G5) 382
Glezen (C8) 250
Goldsmith (E4) 225
Goodland (C3) 1,202
Goshen◉ (F1) 13,718
Gosport (D6) 646
Grabill (H2) 495
Grandview (C9) 599
Greencastle◉ (D5) 8,506
Greendale (H6) 2,861
Greenfield◉ (F5) 9,049
Greens Fork (H5) 474
Greensboro (G5) 232
Greensburg◉ (G6) 6,605
Greentown (E4) 1,266
Greenville (F8) 453
Greenwood (E5) 7,169
Griffin (B8) 212
Griffith (C1) 9,483
Grovertown (D2) 220
Guilford (H6) 200
Gwynneville (F5) 275
Hagerstown (G5) 1,730
Hamilton (H1) 380
Hamlet (D2) 688
Hammond (B1) 111,698
Hanna (D2) 450
Hanover (F7) 1,170
Hardinsburg (E8) 218
Harlan (H2) 550
Harmony (C5) 750
Harrodsburg (D6) 400
Hartford City◉ (G4) 8,053
Hartsville (F6) 399
Hatfield (C9) 610
Haubstadt (B8) 1,029
Hayden (F7) 300
Haysville (D8) 400
Hazleton (B8) 507
Hebron (C2) 1,401
Heltonville (E7) 500
Hemlock (F4) 205
Henryville (F7) 950
Highland (B1) 16,284
Hillisburg (E4) 225
Hillsboro (C4) 517
Hillsdale (C5) 500
Hoagland (H3) 600
Hobart (C1) 18,680
Holland (C8) 661
Holton (G6) 650
Home Corner (F3) 2,636
Homecroft (E5) 959
Homestead (H6) 465
Hope (F6) 1,489
Hortonville (E4) 250
Howe (G1) 520
Hudson (G1) 428
Huntertown (G2) 625
Huntingburg (D8) 4,146
Huntington◉ (G3) 16,185
Huntsville (F4) 228
Huron (D7) 414
Hymera (C6) 1,015
Idaville (D3) 608
Independence Hill (C2) 1,824
Indian Village (E1) 82
INDIANAPOLIS◉ (E5) 476,258
Indianapolis (urban area) 639,340
Ingalls (F5) 873
Inglefield (B8) 250
Inwood (E2) 265
Ireland (C8) 335
Jamestown (D5) 827
Jasonville (C6) 2,436
Jasper◉ (D8) 6,737
Jeffersonville◉ (F8) 19,522
Johnson (B8) 235
Jonesboro (F4) 2,260
Jonesville (F6) 196
Kempton (E4) 480
Kendallville (G2) 6,765
Kennard (G5) 466
Kent (F7) 200
Kentland◉ (C3) 1,783
Kewanna (E2) 683
Keystone (G3) 225
Kimmell (F2) 300
Kingman (C5) 461
Kingsbury (D1) 281
Kingsford Heights (D2) 1,276
Kirklin (E4) 767
Knightstown (F5) 2,496
Knightsville (C5) 722
Knox◉ (D2) 3,458
Kokomo◉ (E4) 47,197
Koontz Lake (D2) 729
Kouts (C2) 1,007
Kramer (C4) 225
Kurtz (E7) 225
La Crosse (D2) 632
La Fontaine (F3) 779
Ladoga (D5) 974
Lafayette◉ (D4) 42,330
Lagrange◉ (F1) 1,990
Lagro (F3) 763
Lake James (H1) 400
Lake Village (C2) 580
Laketon (F3) 650
Lakeville (E1) 757
Lanesville (E8) 346
Laotto (G2) 328
Lapaz (E2) 545
Lapel (F4) 1,772
LaPorte◉ (D1) 21,157
Larwill (F2) 994
Laurel (G6) 848
Lawrence (E5) 10,103
Lawrenceburg◉ (H6) 5,004
Leavenworth (E8) 387
Lebanon◉ (D4) 9,523
Leesburg (F2) 427
Leiters Ford (E2) 300
Leo (G2) 550
Leroy (C2) 350
Letts (F6) 200
Lewis (C6) 400
Lewisville (G5) 592
Lexington (F7) 350
Liberty◉ (H5) 1,745
Liberty Center (G3) 300
Liberty Mills (F2) 250
Ligonier (F2) 2,595
Linden (D4) 619
Linn Grove (H3) 250
Linton (C6) 5,736
Linwood (F4) 126
Little York (F7) 180
Livonia (E7) 150
Lizton (D5) 366
Logansport◉ (E3) 21,106
Long Beach (D1) 2,007
Loogootee (D7) 2,858
Losantville (G4) 868
Lowell (C2) 2,270
Lucerne (E3) 210
Lydick (E1) 1,217
Lyford (C5) 293
Lynhurst ‡(E5) 183
Lynn (H4) 1,260
Lynnville (C8) 409
Lyons (C7) 651
Macy (E3) 328
Madison◉ (G7) 10,488
Malden (C2) 190
Manilla (F5) 450
Marco (C7) 195
Marengo (E8) 803
Mariah Hill (D8) 257
Marietta (F6) 250
Marion◉ (F3) 37,854
Markland (G7) 200
Markle (G3) 789
Markleville (F5) 402
Marshall (C5) 360
Martinsville◉ (D6) 7,525
Matthews (F4) 627
Mauckport (E8) 107
Maxinkuckee (E2) 200
Maxwell (F5) 300
Mays (G5) 200

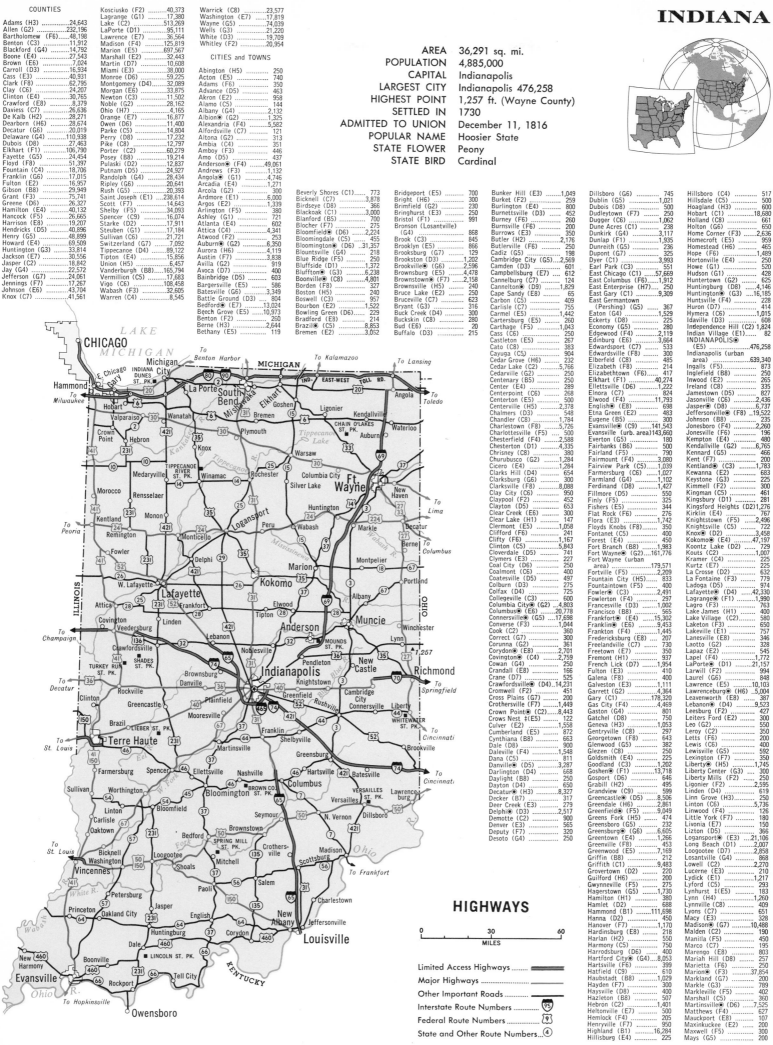

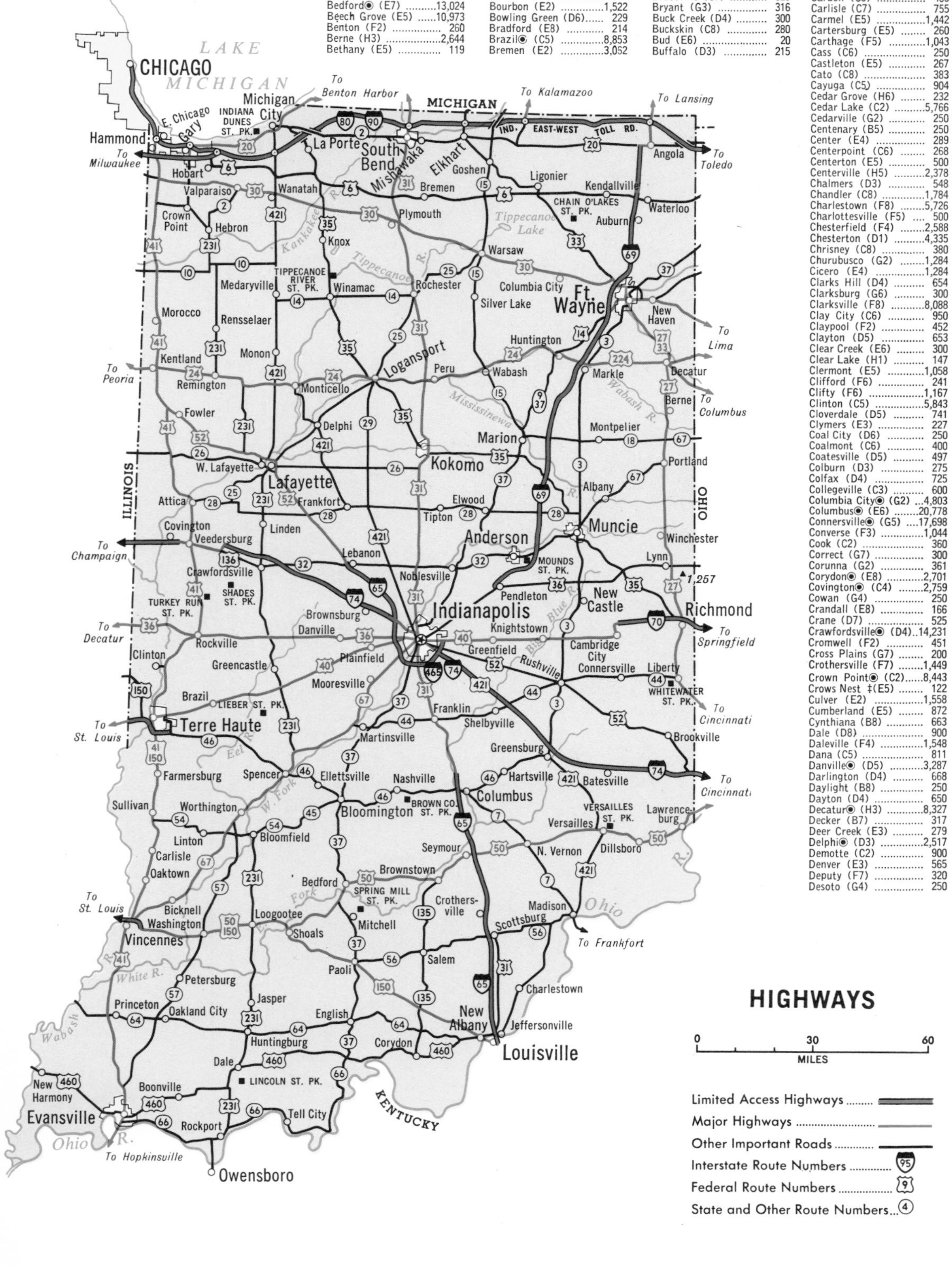
LAKE MICHIGAN
CHICAGO
Hammond
Gary
Michigan City
INDIANA DUNES ST. PK.
La Porte
South Bend
Mishawaka
Elkhart
Goshen
Angola
Kendallville
Auburn
Ft. Wayne
New Haven
Decatur
Berne
Portland
Winchester
Muncie
Anderson
Kokomo
Marion
Logansport
Peru
Wabash
Huntington
Lafayette
W. Lafayette
Frankfort
Lebanon
Noblesville
Indianapolis
Crawfordsville
Greencastle
Brazil
Terre Haute
Richmond
New Castle
Connersville
Shelbyville
Greensburg
Columbus
Franklin
Martinsville
Bloomington
Bedford
Seymour
Madison
Vincennes
Washington
Jasper
New Albany
Jeffersonville
Louisville
Evansville
Owensboro
Tell City
Rockport
Boonville
MICHIGAN
ILLINOIS
OHIO
KENTUCKY
Ohio R.
Wabash R.
To Milwaukee
To Benton Harbor
To Kalamazoo
To Lansing
To Toledo
To Lima
To Columbus
To Springfield
To Cincinnati
To Frankfort
To Hopkinsville
To St. Louis
To Decatur
To Champaign
To Peoria
1,257
HIGHWAYS
0 30 60
MILES
Limited Access Highways
Major Highways
Other Important Roads
Interstate Route Numbers
Federal Route Numbers
State and Other Route Numbers

(continued on following page)

Indiana
(continued)

Maywood (E5) 525
McCordsville (F5) 500
Mecca (C5) 800
Medaryville (D2) 758
Medora (E7) 716
Mellott (C4) 312
Memphis (F8) 300
Mentone (E2) 813
Meridian Hills (E5)......1,807
Merom (B6) 352
Metamora (G6) 450
Mexico (E3) 800
Miami (E3) 300
Michiana Shores ‡(D1).. 229
Michigan City (C1).....36,653
Michigantown (E4) 513
Middlebury (F1) 917
Middletown (F4) 2,033
Midland (C6) 200
Milan (G6) 1,174
Milford (F2) 197
Milford (Clifty) (F6)....1,167
Millersburg (F1) 489
Millhousen (G6) 212
Milltown (E8) 793
Milroy (G6) 800
Milton (G5) 700
Mishawaka (E1) 33,361
Mitchell (E7) 3,552
Modoc (G4) 238
Mongo (G1) 225
Monitor (D4) 300
Monon (D3) 1,417
Monroe (H3) 499
Monroe City (C7) 505
Monroeville (H3) 1,294
Monrovia (E5) 450
Monterey (D2) 278
Montezuma (C5) 1,231
Montgomery (C7) 446
Monticello◉ (D3).......4,035
Montmorenci (D4) 275
Montpelier (G3) 1,954
Mooreland (G5) 477
Moores Hill (G6) 476
Mooresville (E5) 3,856
Morgantown (E6) 971
Morocco (C3) 1,341
Morris (G6) 475
Morristown (F5) 704
Mount Auburn ‡(G5).... 144
Mount Ayr (C3) 186
Mount Carmel (H6)....... 142
Mount Etna (F3) 192
Mount Summit (G4) 424
Mount Vernon◉ (B9)...5,970
Mulberry (D4) 1,062
Muncie◉ (G4) 68,603

Muncie (urban area)..77,504
Munster (B1) 10,313
Napoleon (G6) 290
Nappanee (F2) 3,895
Nashville◉ (E6) 489
New Albany◉ (F8) 37,812
New Amsterdam (E8)... 43
New Augusta (E5) 300
New Carlisle (E1) 1,376
New Castle◉ (G5) 20,349
New Chicago (C1) 2,312
New Goshen (B5) 500
New Harmony (B8) 1,121
New Haven (H2) 3,396
New Lisbon (G5) 300
New London (E4) 200
New Marion (G6) 350
New Market (D5) 578
New Middletown (E8).. 132
New Palestine (F5) 725
New Paris (F2) 800
New Pekin (F7) 661
New Point (G6) 319
New Providence
(Borden) (F8) 327
New Richmond (D4) 394
New Ross (D5) 332
New Salisbury (E8) 190
New Trenton (H6) 218
New Washington (F7)... 750
New Waverly (E3) 200
New Whiteland (E5).....3,488
Newberry (C7) 256
Newburgh (C9) 1,450
Newport◉ (C5) 627
Newtown (C4) 321
Noblesville◉ (F4) 7,664
North Crows Nest ‡(E5) 60
North Grove (F3) 127
North Judson (D2) 1,942
North Liberty (E1)........1,241
North Manchester (F3) 4,377
North Salem (D5) 626
North Terre Haute (C5) 700
North Vernon (F6) 4,062
North Webster (F2) 494
Norway (D3) 200
Notre Dame (E1) 6,385
Oakford (E4) 250
Oakland City (C8) 3,016
Oaklandon (F5) 750
Oaktown (C7) 798
Oakville (G4) 235
Odon (C7) 1,192
Ogden Dunes (C1) 947
Oldenburg (G6) 694
Onward (E3) 153
Oolitic (E7) 1,140

Orestes (F4) 507
Orland (G1) 424
Orleans (D7) 1,659
Osceola (E1) 1,350
Osgood (G6) 1,434
Ossian (G3) 1,108
Otis (D1) 200
Otisco (F7) 450
Otterbein (C4) 788
Otwell (C8) 400
Owensburg (D7) 400
Owensville (B8) 1,121
Oxford (C3) 1,108
Palmyra (E8) 470
Paoli◉ (E7) 2,754
Paragon (D6) 560
Parker (G4) 1,181
Patoka (B8) 579
Patricksburg (D6) 258
Patriot (H7) 277
Paxton (C6) 250
Pekin (E7) 500
Pelzer (C8) 200
Pendleton (F5) 2,472
Pennville (G4) 730
Perkinsville (F4) 185
Perrysville (C4) 497
Pershing (G5) 367
Peru◉ (E3) 14,453
Petersburg◉ (C7) 2,939
Petroleum (G3) 250
Pierceton (F2) 1,186
Pilot Knob (E8) 200
Pimento (C6) 225
Pine Village (C4) 309
Pittsboro (D5) 826
Pittsburg (D3) 200
Plainfield (E5) 5,460
Plainville (C7) 545
Pleasant Lake (H1) 700
Plymouth◉ (E2) 7,558
Poland (C6) 300
Poneto (G3) 289
Portage (C1) 11,822
Porter (C1) 2,189
Portland◉ (H4) 6,999
Poseyville (B8) 997
Pottawatamie Park
(C1) 292
Powers (G4) 200
Prairie Creek (C6) 225
Prairieton (B6) 400
Preble (H3) 295
Princes Lakes (E6)...... 374
Princeton◉ (B8) 7,906
Putnamville (D5) 334
Quincy (D6) 300
Ragsdale (C7) 200
Ramsey (E8) 612
Ravenswood ‡(E5) 618
Ray (H1) 200
Reddington (F6) 285
Redkey (G4) 1,746
Reelsville (D5) 190
Remington (C3) 1,207
Rensselaer◉ (C3) 4,740

Reynolds (D3) 547
Richland (C9) 500
Richmond◉ (H5) 44,149
Ridgeville (G4) 950
Riley (C6) 248
Rising Sun◉ (H7) 2,230
River Forest (F4) 23
Roachdale (D5) 927
Roann (F3) 478
Roanoke (G3) 935
Rochester◉ (E2) 4,883
Rockfield (D3) 325
Rockport◉ (C9) 2,474
Rockville◉ (C5) 2,756
Rocky Ripple (E5)....... 967
Rolling Prairie (D1)..... 500
Rome City (G1) 995
Romney (D4) 400
Rosedale (C5) 726
Roseland (E1) 971
Roselawn (C2) 195
Rossville (D4) 831
Royal Center (E3) 966
Royerton (G4) 350
Rushville◉ (G5) 7,264
Russellville (D5) 372
Russiaville (E4) 1,064
Saint Anthony (D8)...... 725
Saint Bernice (C5) 950
Saint Joe (H2) 499
Saint John (C2) 1,128
Saint Leon (H6) 319
Saint Mary of the Woods
(B6) 600
Saint Marys (E1) 1,290
Saint Meinrad (D8) 710
Saint Paul (F6) 702
Saint Philip (B9) 275
Saint Wendel (B8)....... 150
Salamonia (H4) 142
Salem◉ (E7) 4,546
Saltillo (E7) 121
San Pierre (D2) 300
Sandborn (C7) 547
Sanders (E6) 185
Sandusky (G6) 200
Saratoga (H4) 363
Sardinia (F6) 212
Schererville (C2) 2,875
Schneider (C2) 405
Schnellville (D8) 300
Scipio (F6) 200
Scircleville (E4) 180
Scottsburg◉ (F7) 3,810
Seelyville (C6) 1,114
Sellersburg (F8) 2,679
Selma (G4) 562
Selvin (C8) 250
Servia (F3) 180
Seymour (F7) 11,629
Sharpsville (E4) 663
Shelburn (C6) 1,299
Shelby (C2) 500
Shelbyville◉ (F6) 14,317
Shepardsville (B5) 332
Sheridan (E4) 2,165
Shideler (G4) 210
Shipshewana (F1) 312
Shirley (F5) 1,038
Shirley City
(Woodburn) (H2) 585
Shoals◉ (D7) 1,022

Shooters Hill ‡(E5)...... 20
Shore Acres ‡(E5)...... 15
Sidney (F2) 208
Silver Lake (F2) 514
Sims (F3) 300
Smith Valley (E5) 425
Smithville (D6) 400
Somerset (F3) 265
Somerville (C8) 317
South Bend◉ (E1)....132,445
South Bend (urban
area) 218,933
South Milford (G1) 400
South Whitley (F2) 1,325
Southport (E5) 892
Speed (F8) 975
Speedway (E5) 9,624
Spelterville (C5) 450
Spencer◉ (D6) 2,557
Spencerville (G2) 400
Spiceland (F5) 863
Spring Grove (H5) 471
Spring Hills ‡(E5) 25
Spring Lake Park (F5).. 206
Springport (G4) 253
Spurgeon (C8) 269
Stanford (D6) 180
Star City (D3) 520
State Line (C4) 171
Staunton (C6) 490
Stendal (C8) 250
Stewartsville (B8) 300
Stilesville (D5) 361
Stillwell (D1) 275
Stinesville (D6) 288
Stockwell (D4) 632
Straughn (G5) 349
Stroh (G1) 800
Sullivan◉ (C6) 4,979
Sulphur Springs (G4).. 400
Summitville (F4) 1,048
Sunman (G6) 446
Swayzee (F4) 863
Sweetser (F3) 896
Switz City (C6) 339
Syracuse (F2) 1,595
Tangier (C5) 395
Taylorsville (F6) 565
Teegarden (E2) 192
Tell City (D9) 6,609
Tennyson (C8) 312
Terre Haute◉ (C6) 72,500
Terre Haute (urban
area) 81,415
Thayer (C2) 245
Thorntown (D4) 1,486
Tippecanoe (E2) 300
Tipton◉ (E4) 5,604
Topeka (F1) 600
Toto (D2) 200
Town of Pines ‡(D1).... 939
Trafalgar (E6) 459
Trail Creek (D1) 1,552
Trevlac (E6) 250
Tri Lakes (G2) 1,089
Troy (D9) 528
Tunnelton (E7) 180
Twelve Mile (E3) 250
Tyner (E2) 220
Ulen (E4) 130
Underwood (F7) 300
Union (C8) 210

Union City (H4) 4,047
Union Mills (D2) 370
Uniondale (G3) 311
Uniontown (D8) 187
Unionville (E6) 225

Universal (C5) 424
Upland (F4) 1,999
Urbana (F3) 400
Utica (F8) 600
Vallonia (E7) 800
Valparaiso◉ (C2) 15,227
Van Buren (F3) 929
Veedersburg (C4) 1,762
Velpen (C8) 197
Vera Cruz (G3) 176
Vernon◉ (F7) 461
Versailles◉ (G6) 1,158
Vevay◉ (G7) 1,503
Vicksburg (C6) 160
Vincennes◉ (C7) 18,046
Vistula (F1) 80
Wabash◉ (F3) 12,621
Wadesville (B8) 250
Wakarusa (F1) 1,145
Waldron (F6) 800
Walkerton (E2) 2,044
Wallace (C5) 122
Walton (E3) 1,079
Wanatah (D2) 689
Warren (G3) 1,241
Warren Park (F5) 852
Warsaw◉ (F2) 7,234
Washington◉ (C7) 10,846
Waterloo (G2) 1,432
Watson (F8) 300
Waveland (D5) 549
Wawaka (F2) 370
Wawasee (F2) 400
Waymansville (E6) 100
Waynetown (C4) 933
Webster (H5) 182
Wellsboro (D1) 134
West Baden Sprs.
(D7) 879
West College Corner
(H5) 613
West Harrison (H6)...... 341
West Lafayette (D4)...12,680
West Lebanon (C4)....... 720
West Middleton (E4).... 305
West Newton (E5)........ 500
West Terre Haute (B6)..3,006
Westfield (E4) 1,217
Westpoint (C4) 290
Westport (F6) 833
Westville (D1) 789
Wheatfield (C2) 679
Wheatland (C7) 614
Wheeler (C1) 425
Whiteland (E5) 1,368
Whitestown (E5) 613
Whitewater (H5) 102
Whiting (C1) 8,137
Wilkinson (F5) 388
Williams (D7) 400
Williams Creek (E5)..... 454
Williamsport◉ (C4)......1,353
Willow Branch (F5)...... 230
Winamac◉ (D2) 2,375
Winchester◉ (G4) 5,742
Windfall (F4) 1,135
Wingate (C4) 431
Winona Lake (F2) 1,928
Winslow (C8) 1,089
Wolcott (C3) 877
Wolcottville (G1) 720
Wolflake (F2) 300
Woodburn (H2) 585
Woodlawn Heights (F4) 29
Woodruff Place (E5)....1,501
Woodstock ‡(E5) 33
Worthington (C6) 1,635
Wyatt (E1) 275
Wynnedale ‡(E5) 174
Yankeetown (C9) 240
Yeoman (D3) 172
Yoder (G3) 211
Yorktown (G4) 1,137
Young America (E3).... 276
Youngstown (C6) 200
Zanesville (G3) 345
Zionsville (E5) 1,822

TOPOGRAPHY

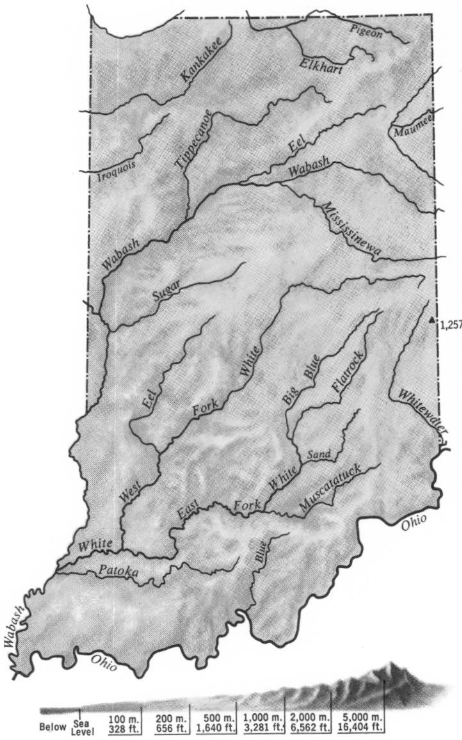

0 40 80
MILES
Kankakee
Pigeon
Elkhart
Maumee
Tippecanoe
Iroquois
Eel
Wabash
Mississinewa
Wabash
Sugar
1,257
White
Eel
Fork
Big Blue
Flatrock
Whitewater
Sand
White
Muscatatuck
West
East
Fork
Ohio
White
Patoka
Blue
Wabash
Ohio
Below Sea Level
100 m. 328 ft.
200 m. 656 ft.
500 m. 1,640 ft.
1,000 m. 3,281 ft.
2,000 m. 6,562 ft.
5,000 m. 16,404 ft.

OTHER FEATURES

Anderson (river) ....D 8
Bakalar A.F.B. ....E 6
Bass (lake) ....D 2
Bean Blossom (creek)....D 6
Benjamin Harrison,
Fort ....E 5
Big (creek) ....B 8
Big Blue (river) ....F 5
Big Pine (creek) ....C 3
Big Raccoon (creek).......C 5
Big Walnut (creek) ....D 5
Blue (river) ....E 8
Buck (creek) ....E 8
Bunker Hill A.F.B. ....E 3
Buseron (creek) ....C 7
Camp (creek) ....E 6
Cataract (lake) ....D 6
Cedar (creek) ....G 2
Clifty (creek) ....F 6
Coal (creek) ....C 4
Crane Nav. Amm. Depot D 7
Crooked (creek) ....D 2
Deer (creek) ....E 3
Deer (creek) ....D 5
Eagle (creek) ....E 4
Eel (river) ....C 6
Eel (river) ....F 3
Elkhart (river) ....F 1
Fawn (river) ....G 1
Fish (creek) ....H 2
Flatrock (creek) ....F 5
Fort Benjamin Harrison...E 5
Freeman (lake) ....D 3
Geist (res.) ....F 5
Graham (creek) ....F 7
Honey (creek) ....C 6
Hudson (lake) ....D 1
Indian (creek) ....E 8
Indian (creek) ....D 6
Iroquois (river) ....B 3
Kankakee (river) ....C 2
Laughery (creek) ....G 6
Little (river) ....G 3
Little Elkhart (river)......F 1
Little Pigeon (creek).......C 9
Little Vermilion (river)...B 5
Lost (river) ....D 7
Maria (creek) ....C 7
Maumee (river) ....H 2
Maxinkuckee (lake) ....E 2
Michigan (lake) ....C 1
Mill (creek) ....D 5
Mississinewa (river) ....F 3
Monroe (res.) ....E 6
Morse (res.) ....E 4
Muscatatuck (river)........E 7
Ohio (river) ....B 9
Patoka (river) ....C 8
Pigeon (creek) ....C 8
Pigeon (river) ....F 1
Pipe (creek) ....F 4
Prairie (creek) ....C 7
Richland (creek) ....D 6
Saint Joseph (river) ....E 1
Saint Joseph (river) ....H 2
Saint Marys (river) ....H 3
Salamonie (river) ....G 4
Salt (creek) ....E 6
Shafer (lake) ....D 3
Silver (creek) ....F 8
Sugar (creek) ....C 5
Sugar (creek) ....F 5
Sugar (creek) ....B 3
Tippecanoe (river) ....E 2
Vermilion (river) ....B 4
Vernon (creek) ....F 7
Wabash (river) ....B 7
Wawasee (lake) ....F 2
White (river) ....B 8
Whitewater (river) ....H 6
Wildcat (creek) ....E 4
Woods (lake) ....D 2
Yellow (river) ....D 2

◉ County Seat.
‡ Name not on map.

AGRICULTURE, INDUSTRY and RESOURCES

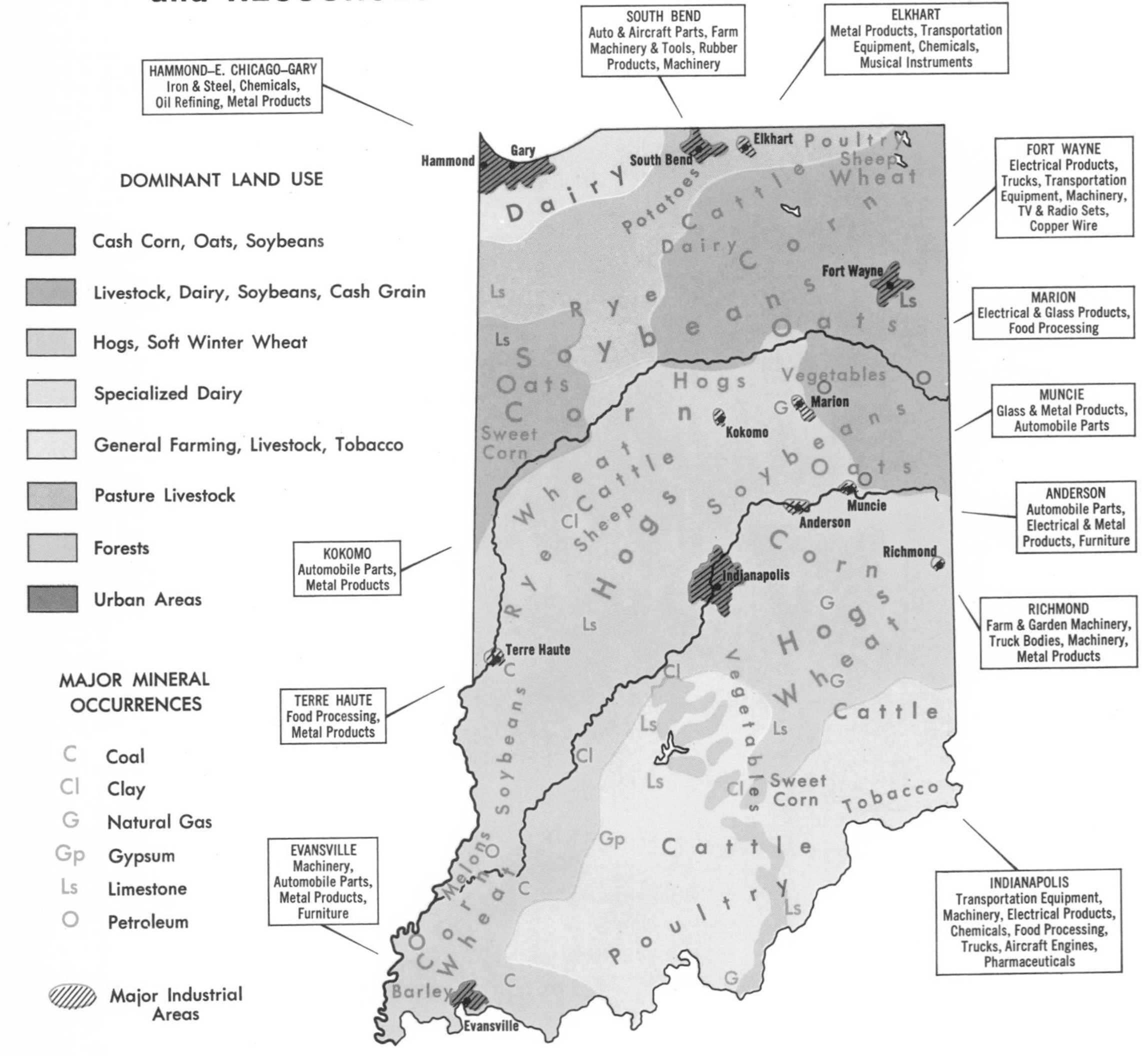

DOMINANT LAND USE
Cash Corn, Oats, Soybeans
Livestock, Dairy, Soybeans, Cash Grain
Hogs, Soft Winter Wheat
Specialized Dairy
General Farming, Livestock, Tobacco
Pasture Livestock
Forests
Urban Areas
MAJOR MINERAL OCCURRENCES
C Coal
Cl Clay
G Natural Gas
Gp Gypsum
Ls Limestone
O Petroleum
Major Industrial Areas
HAMMOND–E. CHICAGO–GARY
Iron & Steel, Chemicals, Oil Refining, Metal Products
SOUTH BEND
Auto & Aircraft Parts, Farm Machinery & Tools, Rubber Products, Machinery
ELKHART
Metal Products, Transportation Equipment, Chemicals, Musical Instruments
FORT WAYNE
Electrical Products, Trucks, Transportation Equipment, Machinery, TV & Radio Sets, Copper Wire
MARION
Electrical & Glass Products, Food Processing
MUNCIE
Glass & Metal Products, Automobile Parts
ANDERSON
Automobile Parts, Electrical & Metal Products, Furniture
RICHMOND
Farm & Garden Machinery, Truck Bodies, Machinery, Metal Products
KOKOMO
Automobile Parts, Metal Products
TERRE HAUTE
Food Processing, Metal Products
EVANSVILLE
Machinery, Automobile Parts, Metal Products, Furniture
INDIANAPOLIS
Transportation Equipment, Machinery, Electrical Products, Chemicals, Food Processing, Trucks, Aircraft Engines, Pharmaceuticals
Hammond
Gary
South Bend
Elkhart
Fort Wayne
Marion
Kokomo
Anderson
Muncie
Richmond
Indianapolis
Terre Haute
Evansville
Dairy
Potatoes
Cattle
Poultry
Sheep
Wheat
Dairy
Corn
Soybeans
Rye
Oats
Hogs
Vegetables
Corn
Sweet Corn
Wheat
Cattle
Sheep
Soybeans
Oats
Hogs
Corn
Rye
Soybeans
Hogs
Wheat
Cattle
Vegetables
Sweet Corn
Tobacco
Cattle
Melons
Corn
Wheat
Poultry
Barley

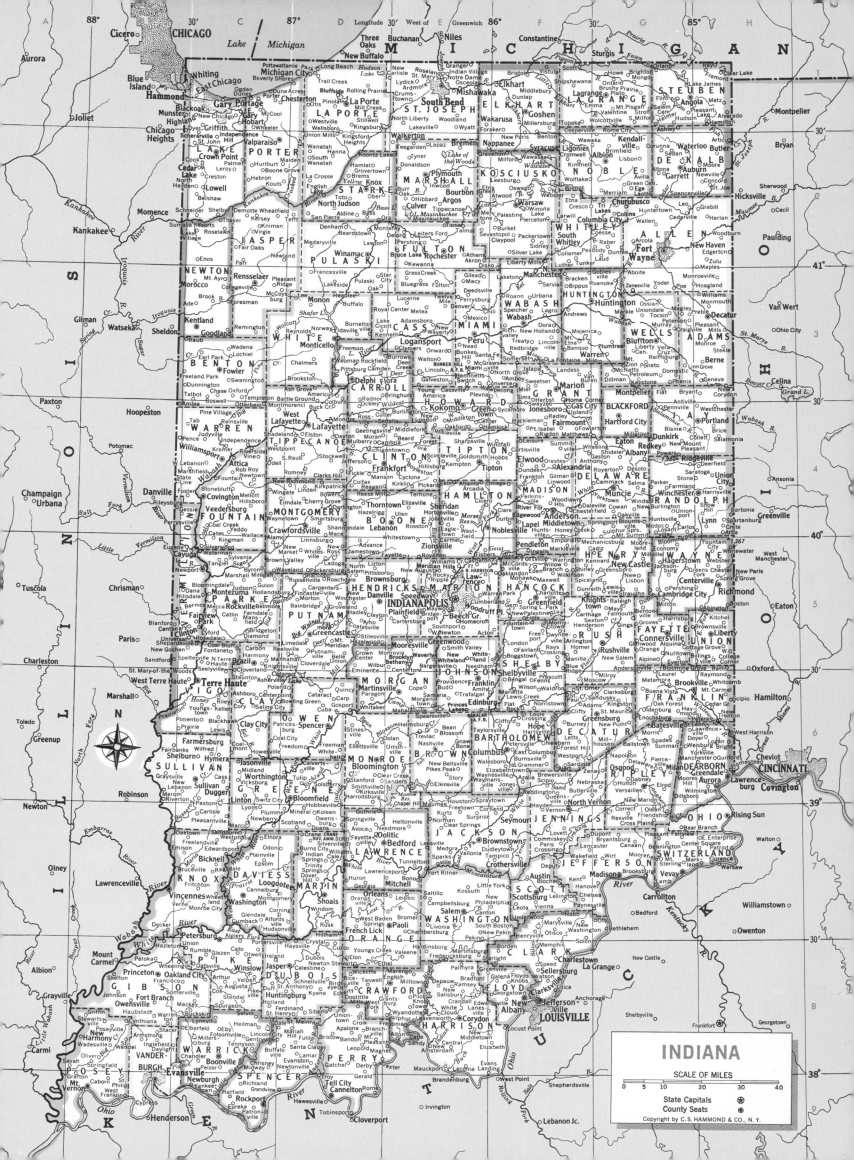

INDIANA

SCALE OF MILES

0 5 10 20 30 40

⊛ State Capitals
⊙ County Seats

Copyright by C.S. HAMMOND & CO., N.Y.

Iowa

COUNTIES

Adair (E6)	10,893
Adams (D6)	7,468
Allamakee (L2)	15,982
Appanoose (H7)	16,015
Audubon (D5)	10,919
Benton (J4)	23,422
Black Hawk (J4)	122,482
Boone (F5)	28,037
Bremer (J3)	21,108
Buchanan (K4)	22,293
Buena Vista (C3)	21,189
Butler (H3)	17,467
Calhoun (D4)	15,923
Carroll (D4)	23,431
Cass (D6)	17,919
Cedar (L5)	17,791
Cerro Gordo (G2)	49,894
Cherokee (B3)	18,598
Chickasaw (J2)	15,034
Clarke (F6)	8,222
Clay (C2)	18,504
Clayton (L3)	21,962
Clinton (M5)	55,060
Crawford (C4)	18,569
Dallas (E5)	24,123
Davis (J7)	9,199
Decatur (F7)	10,539
Delaware (L4)	18,483
Des Moines (L7)	44,605
Dickinson (C2)	12,574
Dubuque (M4)	80,048
Emmet (D2)	14,871
Fayette (K3)	28,581
Floyd (H2)	21,102
Franklin (G3)	15,472
Fremont (B7)	10,282
Greene (E5)	14,379
Grundy (H4)	14,132
Guthrie (D5)	13,607
Hamilton (F4)	20,032
Hancock (F2)	14,604
Hardin (G3)	22,533
Harrison (B5)	17,600
Henry (K6)	18,187
Howard (J2)	12,734
Humboldt (E3)	13,156
Ida (C4)	10,269
Iowa (J5)	16,396
Jackson (M4)	20,754
Jasper (G5)	35,282
Jefferson (K6)	15,818
Johnson (K5)	53,663
Jones (L4)	20,693
Keokuk (J6)	15,492
Kossuth (E2)	25,314
Lee (L7)	44,207
Linn (K4)	136,899
Louisa (L6)	10,290
Lucas (L6)	10,923
Lyon (A2)	14,468
Madison (E6)	12,295
Mahaska (H6)	23,602
Marion (G6)	25,886
Marshall (G4)	37,984
Mills (B6)	13,050
Mitchell (H2)	14,043
Monona (B4)	13,916
Monroe (H7)	10,463
Montgomery (C6)	14,467
Muscatine (L5)	33,840
O'Brien (B2)	18,840
Osceola (B2)	10,064
Page (C7)	21,023
Palo Alto (D2)	14,736
Plymouth (A3)	23,906
Pocahontas (D3)	14,234
Polk (F5)	266,315
Pottawattamie (B6)	83,102
Poweshiek (H5)	19,300
Ringgold (E7)	7,910
Sac (C4)	17,007
Scott (M5)	119,067
Shelby (C5)	15,825
Sioux (A2)	26,375
Story (G4)	49,327
Tama (H4)	21,413
Taylor (D7)	10,288
Union (E6)	13,712
Van Buren (K7)	9,778
Wapello (J6)	46,126
Warren (F6)	20,829
Washington (K6)	19,406
Wayne (G7)	9,800
Webster (E4)	47,810
Winnebago (F2)	13,099
Winneshiek (K2)	21,651
Woodbury (B4)	107,849
Worth (G2)	10,259
Wright (F3)	19,447

CITIES and TOWNS

Ackley (G3)	1,731
Ackworth (G6)	77
Adair (D6)	742
Adel (E5)	2,060
Afton (E6)	773
Agency (J7)	702
Ainsworth (K6)	371
Akron (A3)	1,351
Albert City (C3)	722
Albia (H6)	4,582
Albion (H4)	588
Alburnett (K4)	341
Alden (G3)	838
Alexander (G3)	294
Algona (E2)	5,702
Allerton (G7)	692
Allison (H3)	952
Alta (C3)	1,393
Alta Vista (J2)	276
Alton (A3)	1,048
Altoona (G5)	1,458
Alvord (A2)	238
Ames (F4)	27,003
Anamosa (L4)	4,616
Andover (N5)	91
Andrew (M4)	349
Anita (D6)	1,233
Ankeny (F5)	2,964
Anthon (B4)	681
Aplington (H3)	840
Arcadia (C4)	437
Archer (B2)	209
Aredale (H3)	153
Arion (B5)	201
Arispe (E7)	125
Arlington (K3)	614
Armstrong (D2)	958
Arnolds Park (C2)	953
Arthur (C4)	265
Asbury (M4)	71
Ashton (B2)	615
Aspinwall (C4)	95
Atalissa (L5)	212
Athelstan (D7)	75
Atkins (K4)	527
Atlantic (D6)	6,890
Auburn (D4)	367
Audubon (D5)	2,928
Aurelia (C3)	904
Aurora (K3)	223
Avoca (C6)	1,540
Ayrshire (D2)	298
Badger (E3)	340
Bagley (E5)	406
Baldwin (M4)	228
Bancroft (E2)	1,000
Bankston (L3)	36
Barnes City (H6)	273
Barnum (E3)	154
Bassett (J2)	130
Batavia (J7)	533
Baxter (G5)	681
Bayard (D5)	597
Beacon (H6)	718
Beaconsfield (E7)	71
Beaman (H4)	247
Beaver (E4)	115
Bedford (D7)	1,807
Belle Plaine (J4)	2,923
Bellevue (M4)	2,181
Belmond (F3)	2,506
Bennett (L5)	374
Benton (E7)	84
Berkley (E5)	58
Bernard (M4)	173
Bertram (K5)	170
Bettendorf (N5)	11,534
Bevington (F6)	55
Birmingham (K7)	441
Blairsburg (F4)	287
Blairstown (J5)	583
Blakesburg (H7)	401
Blanchard (C7)	174
Blencoe (A5)	286
Blockton (D7)	343
Bloomfield (J7)	2,771
Blue Grass (M5)	568
Bode (E3)	430
Bonaparte (K7)	574
Bondurant (G5)	395
Boone (F4)	12,468
Bouton (E5)	145
Boxholm (E4)	250
Boyden (B2)	562
Braddyville (D7)	176
Bradgate (E3)	166
Brandon (K4)	322
Brayton (D6)	225
Breda (C4)	535
Bridgewater (D6)	225
Brighton (K6)	724
Bristow (H3)	268
Britt (F2)	2,042
Brooklyn (J5)	1,415
Brunsville (A3)	128
Buckeye (G4)	190
Buffalo (M4)	1,088
Buffalo Center (F2)	1,140
Burlington (L7)	32,430
Burt (E2)	620
Bussey (H6)	557
Calamus (M5)	435
Callender (E4)	358
Calmar (K2)	1,061
Calumet (B3)	225
Camanche (N5)	2,225
Cambridge (G5)	587
Cantril (J7)	299
Carbon (D6)	162
Carlisle (G6)	1,317
Carpenter (H2)	177
Carroll (D4)	7,682
Carson (C6)	583
Carter Lake (B6)	2,287
Cascade (L4)	1,601
Casey (D5)	589
Castalia (K2)	216
Castana (B4)	230
Cedar Falls (H3)	21,195
Cedar Rapids (K5)	92,035
Cedar Rapids (urban area)	105,118
Center Junction (L4)	201
Center Point (K4)	1,236
Centerville (H7)	6,629
Central City (K4)	1,087
Centralia (M4)	85
Chariton (G6)	5,042
Charles City (H2)	9,964
Charlotte (M5)	417
Charter Oak (C4)	665
Chatsworth (A3)	84
Chelsea (J5)	453
Cherokee (B3)	7,724
Chester (J2)	211
Chillicothe (J6)	148
Churdan (D4)	586
Cincinnati (G7)	583
Clare (E3)	245
Clarence (M5)	859

IOWA

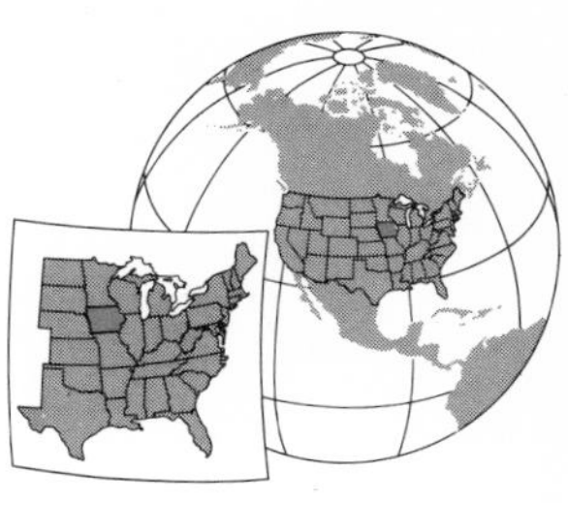

AREA	56,290 sq. mi.
POPULATION	2,760,000
CAPITAL	Des Moines
LARGEST CITY	Des Moines 208,982
HIGHEST POINT	Ocheyedan Mound 1,675 ft.
SETTLED IN	1788
ADMITTED TO UNION	December 28, 1846
POPULAR NAME	Hawkeye State
STATE FLOWER	Wild Rose
STATE BIRD	Eastern Goldfinch

Clarinda◉ (C7) 5,901
Clarion◉ (F3) 3,232
Clarksville (H3) 1,328
Clayton (L3) 130
Clear Lake (G2) 6,158
Clearfield (D7) 504
Cleghorn (B3) 228
Clemons (G4) 198
Clermont (K3) 570
Clinton◉ (N5) 33,589
Clio (G7) 120
Clive (F5) 752
Clutier (J4) 292
Coburg (C7) 54
Coggon (L4) 672
Coin (C7) 346
Colesburg (L3) 365
Colfax (G5) 2,331
College Springs (C7) 290
Collins (G5) 435
Colo (G4) 574
Columbus City (L6) 327
Columbus Jct. (L6) 1,016
Colwell (H2) 119
Conesville (L6) 248
Conrad (H4) 799
Conway (D7) 82
Coon Rapids (D5) 1,560
Coppock (K6) 61
Coralville (K5) 2,357
Corning◉ (D7) 2,041
Correctionville (B4) 912
Corwith (F3) 488
Corydon◉ (G7) 1,687
Cotter (L6) 52
Coulter (G3) 315
Council Bluffs◉ (B6) 55,641
Covington (K5) 80
Craig (A3) 117
Crawfordsville (K6) 317
Crescent (B6) 296
Cresco◉ (J2) 3,809
Creston◉ (E6) 7,667
Cromwell (E6) 138
Crystal Lake (F2) 267
Cumberland (D6) 425
Cumming (F6) 148
Curlew (D3) 134
Cushing (B4) 261
Cylinder (D2) 161
Dakota City◉ (E3) 706
Dallas (G6) 392
Dallas Center (E5) 1,083
Dana (E4) 123
Danbury (B4) 510
Danville (L7) 579
Davenport◉ (M5) 88,981
Davenport-Rock Island-Moline (urb. area) 227,176
Davis City (F7) 346
Dawson (E5) 257
Dayton (E4) 820
De Soto (E5) 273
De Witt (N5) 3,224
Decatur (F7) 203
Decorah◉ (K2) 6,435
Dedham (D5) 322
Deep River (J5) 329
Defiance (C5) 386
Delaware (L4) 167
Delhi (L4) 464
Delmar (M4) 556
Deloit (C4) 222
Delphos (E7) 48
Delta (J6) 514
Denison◉ (C4) 4,930
Denver (J3) 831
Derby (G7) 151
DES MOINES⊛ (G5) 208,982
Des Moines (urban area) 241,115
Dexter (E5) 670
Diagonal (E7) 443
Dickens (C2) 241
Dike (H4) 630
Dixon (M5) 280
Dolliver (D2) 122
Donahue (M5) 133
Donnellson (K7) 709
Doon (A2) 436
Douds (J7) 150
Dougherty (G3) 398
Dow City (B5) 531
Dows (F3) 882
Drakesville (J7) 197
Dubuque◉ (M3) 56,606
Dumont (H3) 719
Duncombe (E4) 355
Dundee (L3) 185

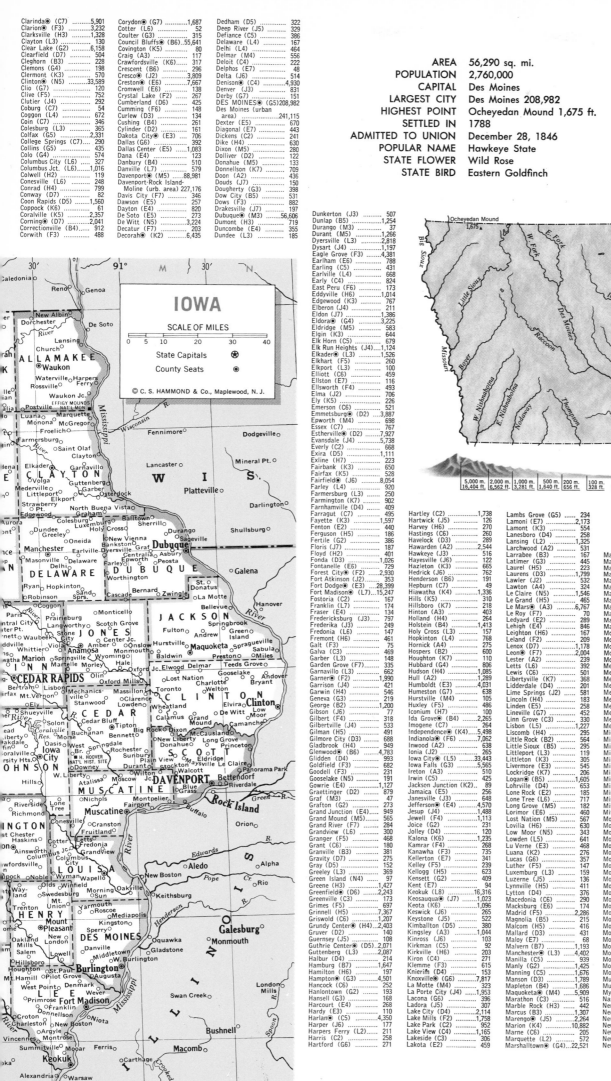

Dunkerton (J3) 507
Dunlap (B5) 1,254
Durango (M3) 37
Durant (M5) 1,266
Dyersville (L3) 2,818
Dysart (J4) 1,197
Eagle Grove (F3) 4,381
Earlham (E6) 788
Earling (C5) 431
Earlville (L4) 668
Early (C4) 824
East Peru (F6) 173
Eddyville (H6) 1,014
Edgewood (K3) 767
Elberon (J4) 211
Eldon (J7) 1,386
Eldora◉ (G4) 3,225
Eldridge (M5) 583
Elgin (K3) 644
Elk Horn (C5) 679
Elk Run Heights (J4) 1,124
Elkader◉ (L3) 1,526
Elkhart (F5) 260
Elkport (L3) 100
Elliott (C6) 459
Ellston (E7) 116
Ellsworth (F4) 493
Elma (J2) 706
Ely (K5) 226
Emerson (C6) 521
Emmetsburg◉ (D2) 3,887
Epworth (M4) 698
Essex (C7) 767
Estherville◉ (D2) 7,927
Evansdale (J4) 5,738
Everly (C2) 668
Exira (D5) 1,111
Exline (H7) 223
Fairbank (K3) 650
Fairfax (K5) 528
Fairfield◉ (J6) 8,054
Farley (L4) 920
Farmersburg (L3) 250
Farmington (K7) 902
Farnhamville (D4) 409
Farragut (C7) 495
Fayette (K3) 1,597
Fenton (E2) 440
Ferguson (H5) 186
Fertile (G2) 386
Floris (J7) 187
Floyd (H2) 401
Fonda (D3) 1,026
Fontanelle (E6) 729
Forest City◉ (F2) 2,930
Fort Atkinson (J2) 353
Fort Dodge◉ (E3) 28,399
Fort Madison◉ (L7) 15,247
Fostoria (C2) 167
Franklin (L7) 174
Fraser (E4) 134
Fredericksburg (J3) 797
Frederika (J3) 249
Fredonia (L6) 147
Fremont (H6) 461
Galt (F3) 75
Galva (C3) 469
Garber (L3) 148
Garden Grove (F7) 335
Garnavillo (L3) 662
Garner◉ (F2) 1,990
Garrison (J4) 421
Garwin (H4) 546
Geneva (G3) 219
George (B2) 1,200
Gibson (J6) 77
Gilbert (F4) 318
Gilbertville (J4) 533
Gilman (H5) 491
Gilmore City (D3) 688
Gladbrook (H4) 949
Glenwood◉ (B6) 4,783
Glidden (D4) 993
Goldfield (F3) 682
Goodell (F3) 231
Gooselake (N5) 191
Gowrie (E4) 1,127
Graettinger (D2) 879
Graf (M3) 47
Grafton (G2) 273
Grand Junction (E4) 949
Grand Mound (M5) 565
Grand River (F7) 284
Grandview (L6) 300
Granger (F5) 468
Grant (C6) 180
Granville (B3) 381
Gravity (D7) 275
Gray (D5) 152
Greeley (L3) 369
Green Island (N4) 97
Greene (H3) 1,427
Greenfield◉ (D6) 2,243
Greenville (C3) 173
Grimes (F5) 697
Grinnell (H5) 7,367
Griswold (C6) 1,207
Grundy Center◉ (H4) 2,403
Gruver (D2) 140
Guernsey (J5) 108
Guthrie Center◉ (D5) 2,071
Guttenberg (L3) 2,087
Halbur (D4) 214
Hamburg (B7) 1,647
Hamilton (H6) 197
Hampton◉ (G3) 4,501
Hancock (C6) 252
Hanlontown (G2) 193
Hansell (G3) 168
Harcourt (E4) 268
Hardy (E3) 110
Harlan◉ (C5) 4,350
Harper (J6) 177
Harpers Ferry (L2) 211
Harris (C2) 258
Hartford (G6) 271

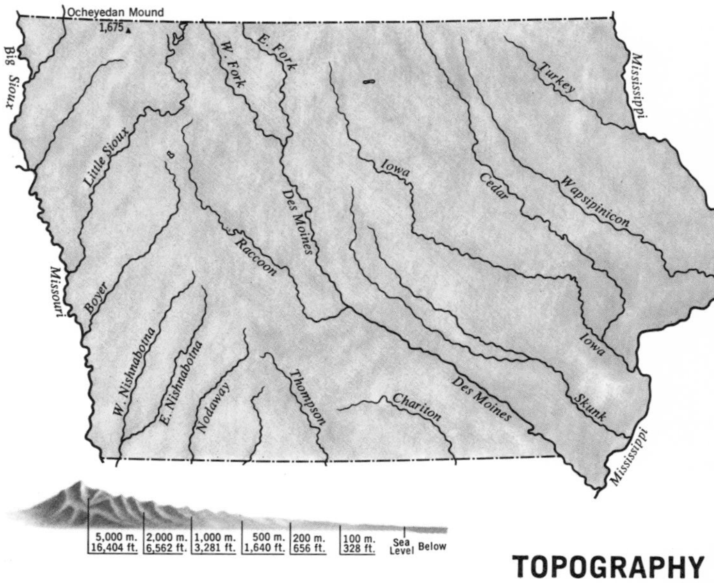

TOPOGRAPHY

0 40 80
MILES

Hartley (C2) 1,738
Hartwick (J5) 126
Harvey (H6) 270
Hastings (C6) 260
Havelock (D3) 289
Hawarden (A2) 2,544
Hawkeye (J3) 516
Hayesville (J6) 122
Hazleton (K3) 665
Hedrick (J6) 762
Henderson (B6) 191
Hepburn (C7) 49
Hiawatha (K4) 1,336
Hills (K5) 310
Hillsboro (K7) 218
Hinton (A3) 403
Holland (H4) 264
Holstein (B4) 1,413
Holy Cross (L3) 157
Hopkinton (L4) 768
Hornick (A4) 275
Hospers (B2) 600
Houghton (K7) 110
Hubbard (G4) 806
Hudson (H4) 1,085
Hull (A2) 1,289
Humboldt (E3) 4,031
Humeston (G7) 638
Hurstville (M4) 105
Huxley (F5) 486
Iconium (H7) 100
Ida Grove◉ (B4) 2,265
Imogene (C7) 264
Independence◉ (K4) 5,498
Indianola◉ (F6) 7,062
Inwood (A2) 638
Ionia (J2) 265
Iowa City◉ (L5) 33,443
Iowa Falls (G3) 5,565
Ireton (A3) 510
Irwin (C5) 425
Jackson Junction (K2) 89
Jamaica (E5) 256
Janesville (J3) 648
Jefferson◉ (E4) 4,570
Jesup (J4) 1,488
Jewell (F4) 1,113
Joice (G2) 231
Jolley (D4) 120
Kalona (K6) 1,235
Kamrar (F4) 268
Kanawha (F3) 735
Kellerton (E7) 341
Kelley (F5) 239
Kellogg (H5) 623
Kensett (G2) 409
Kent (E7) 94
Keokuk (L8) 16,316
Keosauqua◉ (J7) 1,023
Keota (K6) 1,096
Keswick (J6) 265
Keystone (J5) 522
Kimballton (D5) 380
Kingsley (A3) 1,044
Kinross (J6) 103
Kirkman (C5) 92
Kirkville (H6) 203
Kiron (C4) 271
Klemme (F3) 615
Knierim (D4) 153
Knoxville◉ (G6) 7,817
La Motte (M4) 323
La Porte City (J4) 1,953
Lacona (G6) 396
Ladora (J5) 307
Lake City (D4) 2,114
Lake Mills (F2) 1,758
Lake Park (C2) 952
Lake View (C4) 1,165
Lakeside (C3) 306
Lakota (E2) 459
Lambs Grove (G5) 234
Lamoni (E7) 2,173
Lamont (K3) 554
Lanesboro (D4) 258
Lansing (L2) 1,325
Larchwood (A2) 531
Larrabee (B3) 167
Latimer (G3) 445
Laurel (H5) 223
Laurens (D3) 1,799
Lawler (J2) 532
Lawton (A4) 324
Le Claire (N5) 1,546
Le Grand (H5) 465
Le Mars◉ (A3) 6,767
Le Roy (F7) 70
Ledyard (E2) 289
Lehigh (E4) 846
Leighton (H6) 167
Leland (F2) 209
Lenox (D7) 1,178
Leon◉ (F7) 2,004
Lester (A2) 239
Letts (L6) 392
Lewis (C6) 501
Libertyville (K7) 368
Lidderdale (D4) 201
Lime Springs (J2) 581
Lincoln (H4) 183
Linden (E5) 258
Lineville (G7) 452
Linn Grove (C3) 330
Lisbon (L5) 1,227
Liscomb (H4) 295
Little Rock (B2) 564
Little Sioux (B5) 295
Littleport (L3) 119
Littleton (K3) 305
Livermore (E3) 545
Lockridge (K7) 206
Logan◉ (B5) 1,605
Lohrville (D4) 653
Lone Rock (E2) 185
Lone Tree (L6) 717
Long Grove (M5) 182
Lorimor (E6) 460
Lost Nation (M5) 567
Lovilia (H6) 630
Low Moor (N5) 343
Lowden (L5) 641
Lu Verne (E3) 468
Luana (K2) 276
Lucas (G6) 357
Luther (F5) 147
Luxemburg (L3) 159
Luzerne (J5) 136
Lynnville (H5) 411
Lytton (D4) 376
Macedonia (C6) 290
Macksburg (E6) 174
Madrid (F5) 2,286
Magnolia (B5) 215
Malcom (H5) 416
Mallard (D3) 431
Maloy (E7) 68
Malvern (B7) 1,193
Manchester◉ (L3) 4,402
Manilla (C5) 939
Manly (G2) 1,425
Manning (C5) 1,676
Manson (D3) 1,789
Mapleton (B4) 1,686
Maquoketa◉ (M4) 5,909
Marathon (C3) 516
Marble Rock (H3) 442
Marcus (B3) 1,307
Marengo◉ (J5) 2,264
Marion (K4) 10,882
Marne (C6) 205
Marquette (L2) 572
Marshalltown◉ (G4) 22,521
Martelle (L4) 247
Martensdale (F6) 316
Martinsburg (J6) 172
Marysville (G6) 113
Mason City◉ (G2) 30,642
Masonville (K4) 168
Massena (D6) 456
Matlock (A2) 103
Maurice (A3) 237
Maxwell (G5) 773
Maynard (K3) 515
Maysville (M5) 126
McCallsburg (G4) 272
McCausland (M5) 173
McClelland (B6) 150
McGregor (L2) 1,040
McIntire (H2) 270
Mechanicsville (L5) 1,010
Mediapolis (L6) 1,040
Melbourne (G5) 517
Melcher (G6) 867
Melrose (G7) 214
Melvin (B2) 364
Menlo (E5) 421
Meriden (B3) 192
Merrill (A3) 645
Meservey (G3) 331
Middletown (L7) 245
Miles (N4) 376
Milford (C2) 1,476
Millersburg (J5) 186
Millerton (G7) 90
Milo (G6) 468
Milton (J7) 609
Minburn (E5) 357
Minden (C6) 355
Mingo (G5) 260
Missouri Valley (B5) 3,567
Mitchell (H2) 237
Mitchellville (G5) 957
Modale (B5) 276
Mondamin (B5) 436
Moneta (C2) 76
Monmouth (M4) 291
Monona (L2) 1,346
Monroe (G5) 1,366
Montezuma◉ (H5) 1,416
Monticello (L4) 3,190
Montour (H5) 452
Montrose (L7) 632
Moorhead (B5) 313
Moorland (E4) 281
Moravia (H7) 621
Morley (L4) 124
Morning Sun (L6) 875
Morrison (H4) 139
Moulton (H7) 773
Mount Auburn (J4) 186
Mount Ayr◉ (E7) 1,738
Mount Pleasant◉ (L7) 7,339
Mount Sterling (J7) 86
Mount Union (L6) 176
Mount Vernon (K5) 2,593
Moville (A4) 1,156
Murray (F6) 613
Muscatine◉ (L6) 20,997
Mystic (H7) 761
Nashua (J3) 1,737
Nemaha (C3) 151
Neola (B6) 870
Nevada◉ (G5) 4,227
New Albin (L2) 643
New Hampton◉ (J2) 3,456
New Hartford (H3) 649
New Liberty (M5) 145
New London (L7) 1,694
New Market (D7) 506
New Providence (G4) 206
New Sharon (H6) 1,063
New Vienna (L3) 265
New Virginia (F6) 381
Newell (D3) 893
Newhall (K5) 495
Newton◉ (H5) 15,381
Nichols (L6) 329
Nodaway (D7) 204
Nora Springs (H2) 1,275
North Buena Vista (L3) 150
North English (J5) 1,004
North Liberty (K5) 334
North Washington (J2) 156
Northboro (C7) 135
Northwood◉ (G2) 1,768
Norwalk (F6) 1,328
Norway (K5) 516
Numa (G7) 202
Oakland (C6) 1,340
Oakville (L6) 346
Ocheyedan (B2) 662
Odebolt (C4) 1,331
Oelwein (K3) 8,282
Ogden (E4) 1,525
Okoboji (C2) 330
Olds (K6) 189
Olin (L5) 703
Ollie (J6) 291
Onawa◉ (A4) 3,176
Oneida (L3) 76
Onslow (M4) 269
Orange City◉ (A2) 2,707
Orchard (H2) 116
Orient (E6) 341
Orleans (C2) 280
Osage◉ (H2) 3,753
Osceola◉ (F6) 3,350
Oskaloosa◉ (H6) 11,053
Ossian (K2) 827
Osterdock (L3) 45
Otho (E4) 593
Oto (B4) 221
Ottosen (E3) 92
Ottumwa◉ (J6) 33,871
Owasa (G4) 104
Oxford (K5) 633
Oxford Junction (M4) 725
Oyens (A3) 114
Pacific Junction (B6) 560
Packwood (J6) 215
Palmer (D3) 271
Palo (K4) 387
Panama (B5) 257
Panora (E5) 1,019
Panorama Park (N5) 140
Parkersburg (H3) 1,468
Parnell (J5) 200
Paton (E4) 370
Patterson (F6) 157
Paullina (B3) 1,329
Pella (H6) 5,198
Peosta (M4) 50
Perry (E5) 6,442
Persia (B5) 322
Peterson (C3) 565
Pierson (B3) 425
Pilot Mound (F4) 196
Pioneer (E3) 448
Pisgah (B5) 343
Plainfield (J3) 445
Plano (G7) 87
Pleasant Hill ‡(F5) 397

(continued on following page)

Iowa
(continued)

AGRICULTURE, INDUSTRY and RESOURCES

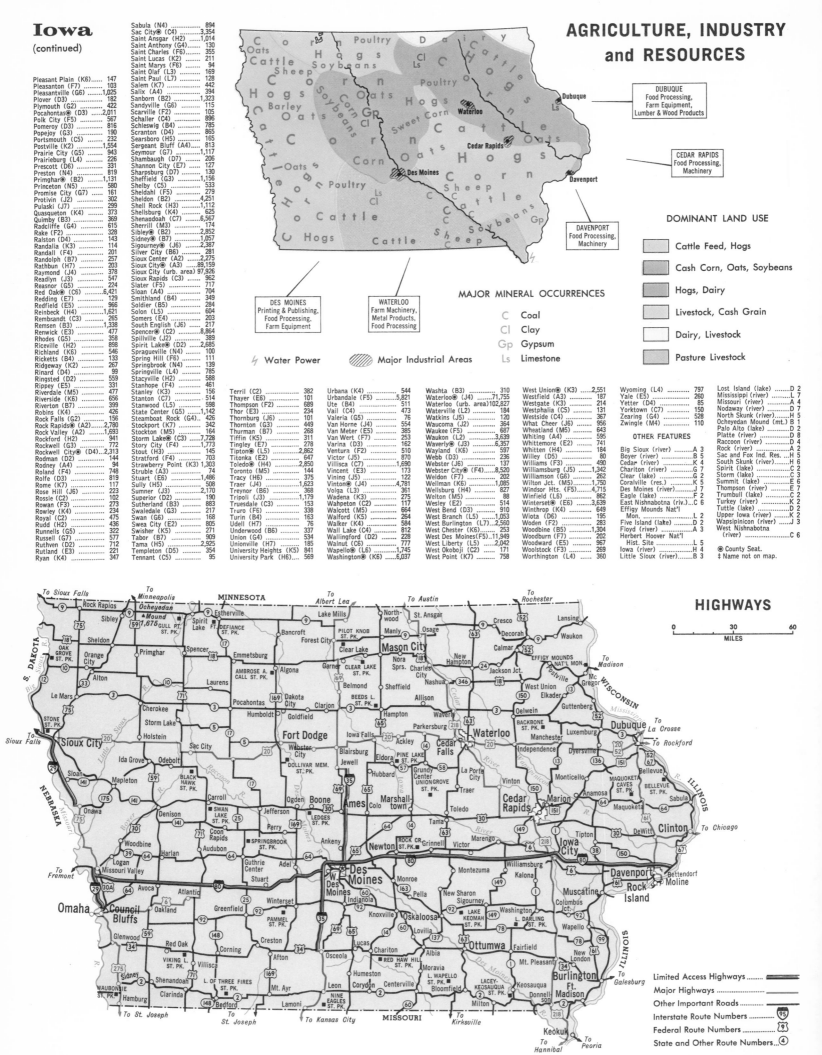

DOMINANT LAND USE

- Cattle Feed, Hogs
- Cash Corn, Oats, Soybeans
- Hogs, Dairy
- Livestock, Cash Grain
- Dairy, Livestock
- Pasture Livestock

DUBUQUE
Food Processing,
Farm Equipment,
Lumber & Wood Products

CEDAR RAPIDS
Food Processing,
Machinery

DAVENPORT
Food Processing,
Machinery

DES MOINES
Printing & Publishing,
Food Processing,
Farm Equipment

WATERLOO
Farm Machinery,
Metal Products,
Food Processing

MAJOR MINERAL OCCURRENCES

- C Coal
- Cl Clay
- Gp Gypsum
- Ls Limestone

⚡ Water Power   ▨ Major Industrial Areas

HIGHWAYS

0   30   60
MILES

- Limited Access Highways
- Major Highways
- Other Important Roads
- Interstate Route Numbers
- Federal Route Numbers
- State and Other Route Numbers

KANSAS

AGRICULTURE, INDUSTRY and RESOURCES

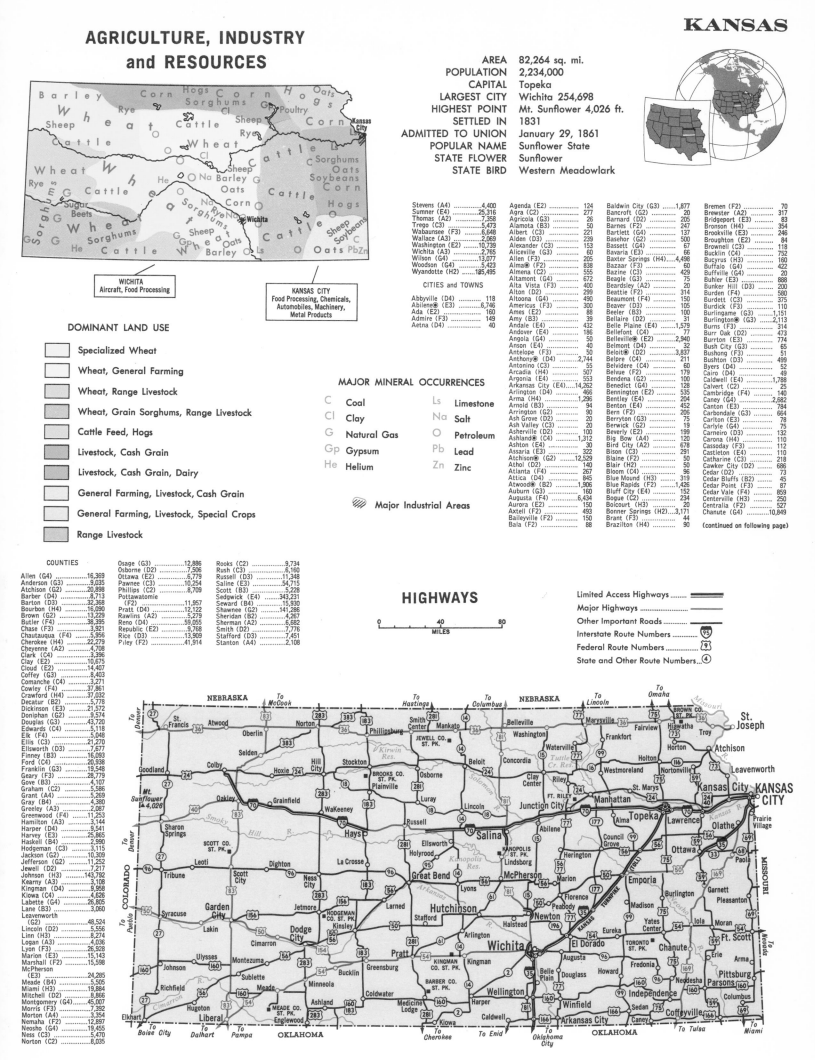

AREA	82,264 sq. mi.
POPULATION	2,234,000
CAPITAL	Topeka
LARGEST CITY	Wichita 254,698
HIGHEST POINT	Mt. Sunflower 4,026 ft.
SETTLED IN	1831
ADMITTED TO UNION	January 29, 1861
POPULAR NAME	Sunflower State
STATE FLOWER	Sunflower
STATE BIRD	Western Meadowlark

WICHITA
Aircraft, Food Processing

KANSAS CITY
Food Processing, Chemicals,
Automobiles, Machinery,
Metal Products

DOMINANT LAND USE

- Specialized Wheat
- Wheat, General Farming
- Wheat, Range Livestock
- Wheat, Grain Sorghums, Range Livestock
- Cattle Feed, Hogs
- Livestock, Cash Grain
- Livestock, Cash Grain, Dairy
- General Farming, Livestock, Cash Grain
- General Farming, Livestock, Special Crops
- Range Livestock

MAJOR MINERAL OCCURRENCES

C	Coal	Ls	Limestone
Cl	Clay	Na	Salt
G	Natural Gas	O	Petroleum
Gp	Gypsum	Pb	Lead
He	Helium	Zn	Zinc

▨ Major Industrial Areas

Stevens (A4)	4,400	Agenda (E2)	124	Baldwin City (G3)	1,877
Sumner (E4)	25,316	Agra (C2)	277	Bancroft (G2)	20
Thomas (A2)	7,358	Agricola (G3)	26	Barnard (D2)	205
Trego (C3)	5,473	Alamota (B3)	50	Barnes (F2)	247
Wabaunsee (F3)	6,648	Albert (C3)	221	Bartlett (G4)	137
Wallace (A3)	2,069	Alden (D3)	239	Basehor (G2)	500
Washington (E2)	10,739	Alexander (C3)	153	Bassett (G4)	67
Wichita (A3)	2,765	Aliceville (G3)	60	Bavaria (E3)	66
Wilson (G4)	13,077	Allen (F3)	205	Baxter Springs (H4)	4,498
Woodson (G4)	5,423	Alma⊙ (F2)	838	Bazaar (F3)	60
Wyandotte (H2)	185,495	Almena (C2)	555	Bazine (C3)	429
		Altamont (G4)	672	Beagle (G3)	75
CITIES and TOWNS		Alta Vista (F3)	400	Beardsley (A2)	30
		Alton (D2)	299	Beattie (F2)	314
Abbyville (D4)	118	Altoona (G4)	490	Beaumont (F4)	150
Abilene⊙ (E3)	6,746	Americus (F3)	300	Beaver (D3)	105
Ada (E2)	160	Ames (E2)	88	Beeler (B3)	100
Admire (F3)	149	Amy (B3)	39	Bellaire (D2)	31
Aetna (D4)	40	Andale (E4)	432	Belle Plaine (E4)	1,579
		Andover (E4)	186	Bellefont (C3)	77
		Angola (G4)	50	Belleville⊙ (E2)	2,940
		Anson (E4)	40	Belmont (D4)	32
		Antelope (F3)	50	Beloit⊙ (D2)	3,837
		Antonino (C3)	55	Belpre (C4)	211
		Anthony⊙ (D4)	2,744	Belvidere (C4)	60
		Arcadia (H4)	507	Belvue (F2)	179
		Argonia (E4)	553	Bendena (F2)	100
		Arkansas City (E4)	14,262	Benedict (G4)	128
		Arlington (D4)	466	Bennington (E2)	535
		Arma (H4)	1,296	Bentley (E4)	204
		Arnold (B3)	94	Benton (E4)	452
		Arrington (G2)	90	Bern (F2)	206
		Ash Grove (D2)	20	Berryton (G3)	75
		Ash Valley (C3)	20	Berwick (G2)	19
		Asherville (D2)	100	Beverly (E2)	199
		Ashland⊙ (C4)	1,312	Big Bow (A4)	120
		Ashton (E4)	30	Bird City (A2)	678
		Assaria (E3)	322	Bison (C3)	291
		Athol (D2)	140	Blaine (F2)	50
		Atlanta (F4)	267	Blair (H2)	50
		Attica (D4)	845	Bloom (C4)	96
		Atwood⊙ (B2)	1,906	Blue Mound (H3)	319
		Auburn (G3)	160	Blue Rapids (F2)	1,426
		Augusta (F4)	6,434	Bluff City (E4)	152
		Aurora (E2)	150	Bogue (C2)	234
		Axtell (F2)	493	Boicourt (H3)	20
		Baileyville (F2)	150	Bonner Springs (H2)	3,171
		Bala (F2)	88	Brant (F3)	44
				Brazilton (H4)	90

Bremen (F2)	70		
Brewster (A2)	317		
Bridgeport (E3)	83		
Bronson (H4)	354		
Brookville (E3)	246		
Broughton (E2)	84		
Brownell (C3)	118		
Bucklin (C4)	752		
Bucyrus (H3)	160		
Buffalo (G4)	422		
Buffville (G2)	20		
Buhler (E3)	888		
Bunker Hill (D3)	200		
Burden (F4)	580		
Burdett (C3)	375		
Burdick (F3)	110		
Burlingame (G3)	1,151		
Burlington⊙ (G3)	2,113		
Burns (E3)	314		
Burr Oak (D2)	473		
Burrton (E3)	774		
Bush City (G4)	65		
Bushong (F3)	51		
Bushton (D3)	499		
Byers (D4)	52		
Cairo (D4)	49		
Caldwell (E4)	1,788		
Calvert (C2)	25		
Cambridge (F4)	140		
Caney (G4)	2,682		
Canton (E3)	784		
Carbondale (G3)	664		
Carlton (E3)	78		
Carlyle (G4)	75		
Carneiro (D3)	132		
Carona (H4)	110		
Cassoday (F3)	112		
Castleton (E4)	110		
Catharine (C3)	218		
Cawker City (D2)	686		
Cedar (D2)	73		
Cedar Bluffs (B2)	45		
Cedar Point (F3)	87		
Cedar Vale (G4)	859		
Centerville (H3)	250		
Centralia (F2)	527		
Chanute (G4)	10,849		

(continued on following page)

COUNTIES

Allen (G4)	16,369	Osage (G3)	12,886	Rooks (C2)	9,734
Anderson (G3)	9,035	Osborne (D2)	7,506	Rush (C3)	6,160
Atchison (G2)	20,898	Ottawa (E2)	6,779	Russell (D3)	11,348
Barber (D4)	8,713	Pawnee (C3)	10,254	Saline (E3)	54,715
Barton (D3)	32,368	Phillips (D2)	8,709	Scott (B3)	5,228
Bourbon (H4)	16,090	Pottawatomie (F2)	11,957	Sedgwick (E4)	343,231
Brown (G2)	13,229	Pratt (D4)	12,122	Seward (B4)	15,930
Butler (F4)	38,395	Rawlins (A2)	5,279	Shawnee (G2)	141,286
Chase (F3)	3,921	Reno (D4)	59,055	Sheridan (B2)	4,267
Chautauqua (F4)	5,956	Republic (E2)	9,768	Sherman (A2)	6,682
Cherokee (H4)	22,279	Rice (D3)	13,909	Smith (D2)	7,776
Cheyenne (A2)	4,708	Riley (F2)	41,914	Stafford (D3)	7,451
Clark (C4)	3,396			Stanton (A4)	2,108
Clay (E2)	10,675				
Cloud (E2)	14,407				
Coffey (G3)	8,403				
Comanche (C4)	3,271				
Cowley (F4)	37,861				
Crawford (H4)	37,032				
Decatur (B2)	5,778				
Dickinson (E3)	21,572				
Doniphan (G2)	9,574				
Douglas (G3)	43,720				
Edwards (C4)	5,118				
Elk (F4)	5,048				
Ellis (C3)	21,270				
Ellsworth (D3)	7,677				
Finney (B3)	16,093				
Ford (C4)	20,938				
Franklin (G3)	19,548				
Geary (F3)	28,779				
Gove (B3)	4,107				
Graham (C2)	5,586				
Grant (A4)	5,269				
Gray (B4)	4,380				
Greeley (A3)	2,087				
Greenwood (F4)	11,253				
Hamilton (A3)	3,144				
Harper (D4)	9,541				
Harvey (E3)	25,865				
Haskell (B4)	2,990				
Hodgeman (C3)	3,115				
Jackson (G2)	10,309				
Jefferson (G2)	11,252				
Jewell (D2)	7,217				
Johnson (H3)	143,792				
Kearny (A3)	3,108				
Kingman (D4)	9,958				
Kiowa (C4)	4,626				
Labette (G4)	26,805				
Lane (B3)	3,060				
Leavenworth (G2)	48,524				
Lincoln (D2)	5,556				
Linn (H3)	8,274				
Logan (A3)	5,542				
Lyon (F3)	26,928				
Marion (E3)	15,143				
Marshall (F2)	15,598				
McPherson (E3)	24,285				
Meade (B4)	5,505				
Miami (H3)	19,884				
Mitchell (D2)	8,866				
Montgomery (G4)	45,007				
Morris (F3)	7,392				
Morton (A4)	3,354				
Nemaha (F2)	12,897				
Neosho (G4)	19,455				
Ness (C3)	5,470				
Norton (C2)	8,035				

HIGHWAYS

0	40	80
	MILES	

Limited Access Highways	═══
Major Highways	──
Other Important Roads	──
Interstate Route Numbers	95
Federal Route Numbers	9
State and Other Route Numbers	4

Kansas
(continued)

Chapman (E3)	1,095	Codell (C2)	125	Crawford (E3)	50	Dorrance (D3)	331	Elmont (G2)	100	Fort Scott⊙ (H4)	9,410	Glen Elder (D2)	444	Hammond (H4)	50

Chapman (E3) 1,095
Charleston (B4) 28
Chase (D3) 922
Chautauqua (F4) 205
Cheney (E4) 1,101
Cherokee (H4) 797
Cherryvale (G4) 2,783
Chetopa (G4) 1,538
Chicopee (H4) 125
Chiles (H3) 20
Cimarron⊙ (B4) 1,115
Circleville (G2) 151
Claflin (D3) 891
Claudell (C2) 20
Clay Center⊙ (E2) 4,613
Clayton (C3) 161
Clearwater (E4) 1,073
Cleburne (F2) 40
Clements (F3) 100
Clifton (E2) 746
Climax (F4) 81
Clyde (E2) 1,025
Coats (D4) 152

Codell (C2) 125
Coffeyville (G4) 17,382
Colby⊙ (A2) 4,210
Coldwater⊙ (C4) 1,164
Collyer (B2) 233
Colony (G3) 419
Columbus⊙ (H4) 3,395
Colwich (E4) 703
Concordia⊙ (E2) 7,022
Conway (E3) 78
Conway Springs (E4) 1,057
Coolidge (A3) 117
Copeland (B4) 247
Corbin (E4) 100
Corinth (D2) 29
Corning (F2) 240
Corwin (D4) 54
Cottonwood Falls⊙ (F3) 971
Council Grove⊙ (F3) 2,664
Countryside ‡(H2) 428
Courtland (E2) 384
Covert (D2) 75
Coville (G4) 133

Crawford (E3) 50
Crestline (H4) 125
Crystal Springs (D4) 59
Cuba (E2) 336
Cullison (D4) 128
Culver (E3) 200
Cummings (G2) 85
Cunningham (D4) 618
Damar (C2) 361
Danville (D4) 118
DeSoto (H3) 1,271
Dearing (G4) 249
Deerfield (A4) 442
Delavan (F3) 65
Delia (G2) 163
Dellvale (B2) 20
Delphos (E2) 619
Denison (F2) 184
Denmark (D2) 100
Dennis (G4) 200
Densmore (C2) 57
Denton (G2) 161
Detroit (E3) 85
Devon (H4) 100
Dexter (F4) 291
Dighton⊙ (B3) 1,526
Dillon (E3) 29
Dodge City⊙ (B4) 13,520
Doniphan (G2) 25

Dorrance (D3) 331
Douglass (F4) 1,058
Dover (G3) 136
Downs (D2) 1,206
Dresden (B2) 134
Dubuque (D3) 65
Duluth (F2) 64
Dunlap (F3) 134
Duquoin (D4) 20
Durham (D4) 183
Dwight (F3) 281
Earlton (G4) 104
Eastborough (E4) 1,001
Easton (G2) 320
Edgerton (H3) 414
Edmood (C2) 91
Edna (G4) 442
Edson (A2) 90
Edwardsville (H2) 513
Effingham (G2) 564
Elbing (E3) 105
El Dorado⊙ (F4) 12,523
Elgin (F4) 148
Elk City (G4) 498
Elk Falls (F4) 179
Elkhart⊙ (A4) 1,780
Ellinwood (D3) 2,729
Ellis (C3) 2,218
Ellsworth⊙ (D3) 2,361
Elmdale (F3) 114
Elmo (E3) 52

Elmont (G2) 100
Elsmore (G4) 128
Elwood (H2) 1,191
Elyria (E3) 40
Emmett (F2) 128
Emporia⊙ (F3) 18,190
Englevale (H4) 25
Englewood (C4) 243
Ensign (B4) 255
Enterprise (E3) 1,015
Erie⊙ (G4) 1,309
Esbon (D2) 237
Eskridge (F3) 519
Eudora (H3) 1,526
Eureka⊙ (F4) 4,055
Everest (G2) 348
Fairport (C2) 40
Fairview (F2) 272
Fairway ‡(H2) 5,398
Fall River (G4) 226
Falun (E3) 105
Farlington (H4) 100
Farlinville (H3) 100
Faulkner (H4) 65
Fellsburg (C4) 30
Florence (E3) 853
Flush (F2) 65
Fontana (H3) 138
Ford (C4) 252
Formoso (D2) 192
Fort Dodge (C4) 550

Fort Scott⊙ (H4) 9,410
Fostoria (F2) 100
Fowler (B4) 717
Frankfort (F2) 1,106
Franklin (H4) 600
Frederick (D3) 48
Fredonia⊙ (G4) 3,233
Freeport (E4) 31
Friend (B3) 51
Frontenac (H4) 1,713
Fulton (H4) 207
Galatia (D3) 73
Galena (H4) 3,827
Galesburg (G4) 128
Galva (F3) 442
Garden City⊙ (B4) 11,811
Garden Plain (E4) 560
Gardner (H3) 1,619
Garfield (C3) 278
Garfield Center (E2) 27
Garland (H4) 100
Garnett⊙ (G3) 3,034
Garrison (F2) 80
Gas (G4) 342
Gaylord (D2) 239
Gem (B2) 116
Geneseo (E3) 558
Geuda Springs (E4) 223
Girard⊙ (H4) 2,350
Glade (C2) 133
Glasco (E2) 812

Glen Elder (D2) 444
Glendale (E3) 17
Goddard (E4) 415
Goessel (E3) 327
Goff (G2) 259
Goodland⊙ (A2) 4,459
Goodrich (G3) 60
Gordon (F4) 50
Gorham (B3) 429
Gove⊙ (B3) 228
Grainfield (B2) 389
Grandview Plaza ‡(F2) 450
Grantville (G2) 168
Great Bend⊙ (D3) 16,670
Greeley (G3) 415
Green (E2) 190
Greenleaf (F2) 562
Greensburg⊙ (C4) 1,988
Grenola (F4) 349
Gridley (G3) 321
Grinnell (B2) 396
Gypsum (E3) 593
Haddam (E2) 311
Hale (F4) 20
Hallowell (H4) 174
Halls Summit (G3) 15
Halstead (E3) 1,598
Hamilton (F4) 400
Hamlin (G2) 99

Hammond (H4) 50
Hanover (F2) 773
Hanston (C3) 279
Hardtner (D4) 372
Harlan (D2) 91
Harper (D4) 1,899
Harris (G3) 36
Hartford (F3) 337
Harveyville (F3) 204
Havana (G4) 162
Haven (E4) 982
Havensville (F2) 166
Haviland (C4) 725
Hays⊙ (C3) 11,947
Haysville (E4) 5,836
Hazelton (D4) 246
Healy (B3) 251
Hedville (E3) 89
Heizer (D3) 178
Hepler (H4) 178
Herington (E3) 3,702
Herkimer (F2) 91
Herndon (B2) 339
Hesston (E3) 1,103
Hewins (F4) 75
Hiattville (H4) 150
Hiawatha⊙ (G2) 3,391
Hickok (A4) 45
Highland (H2) 755
Hill City⊙ (C2) 2,421
Hillsboro (E3) 2,441

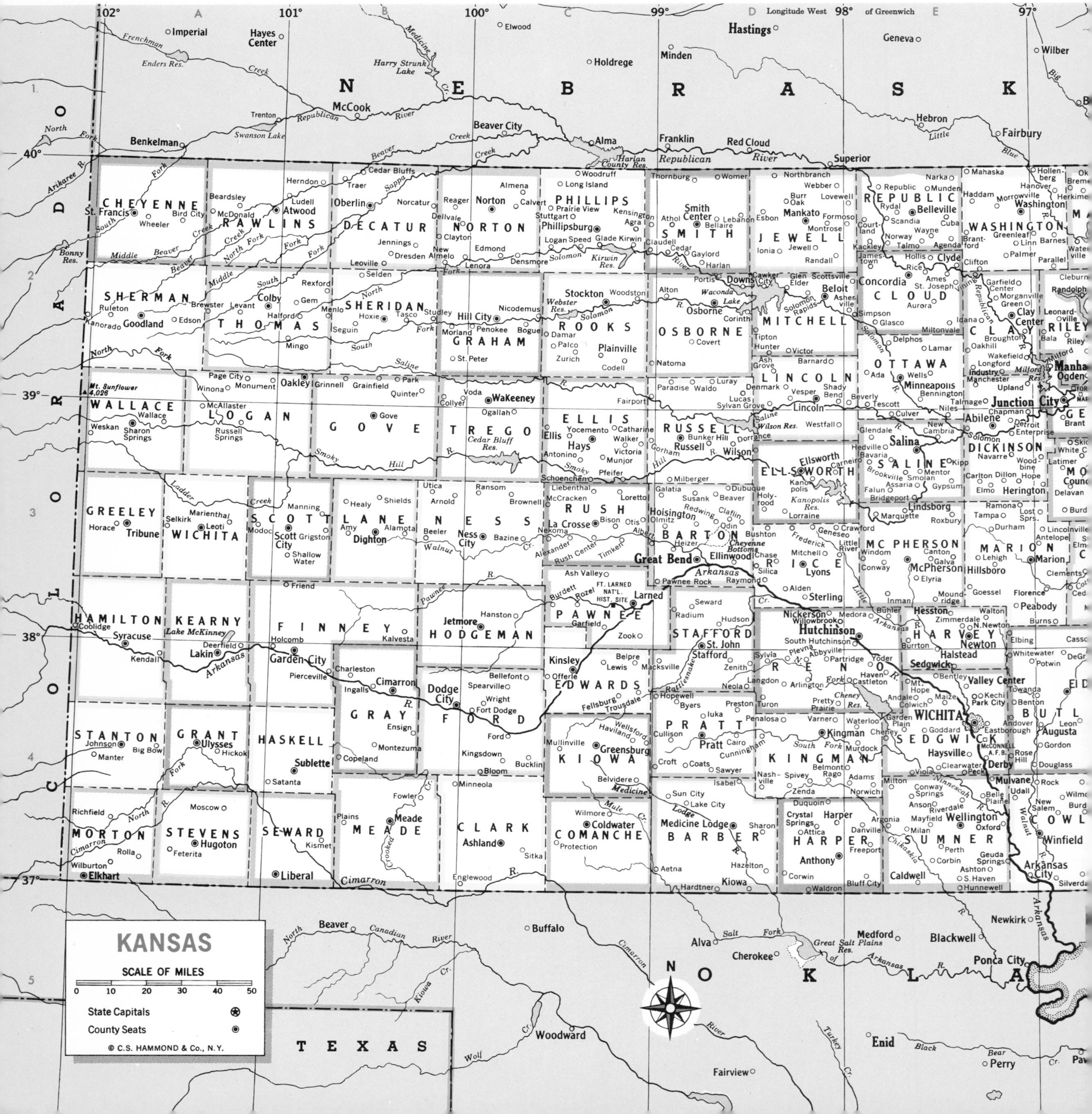

Kansas
(continued)

TOPOGRAPHY

0 50 100 MILES

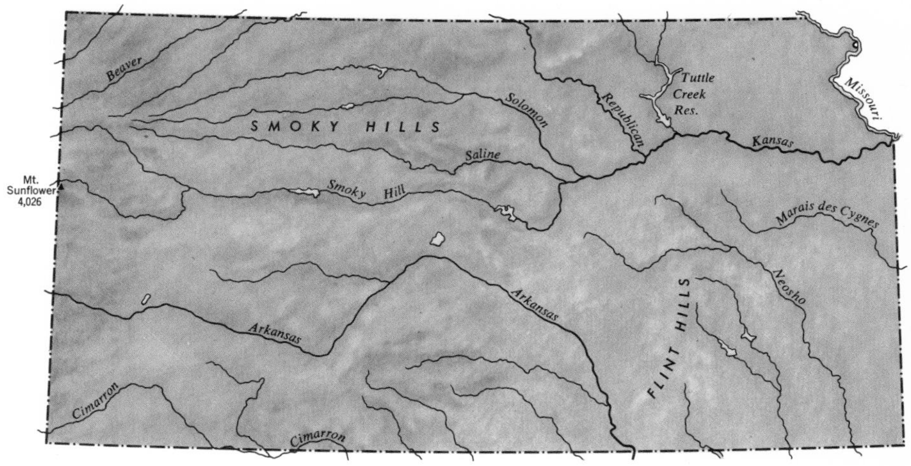

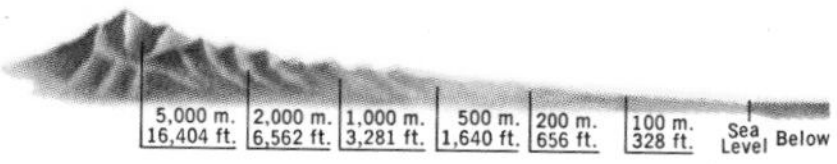

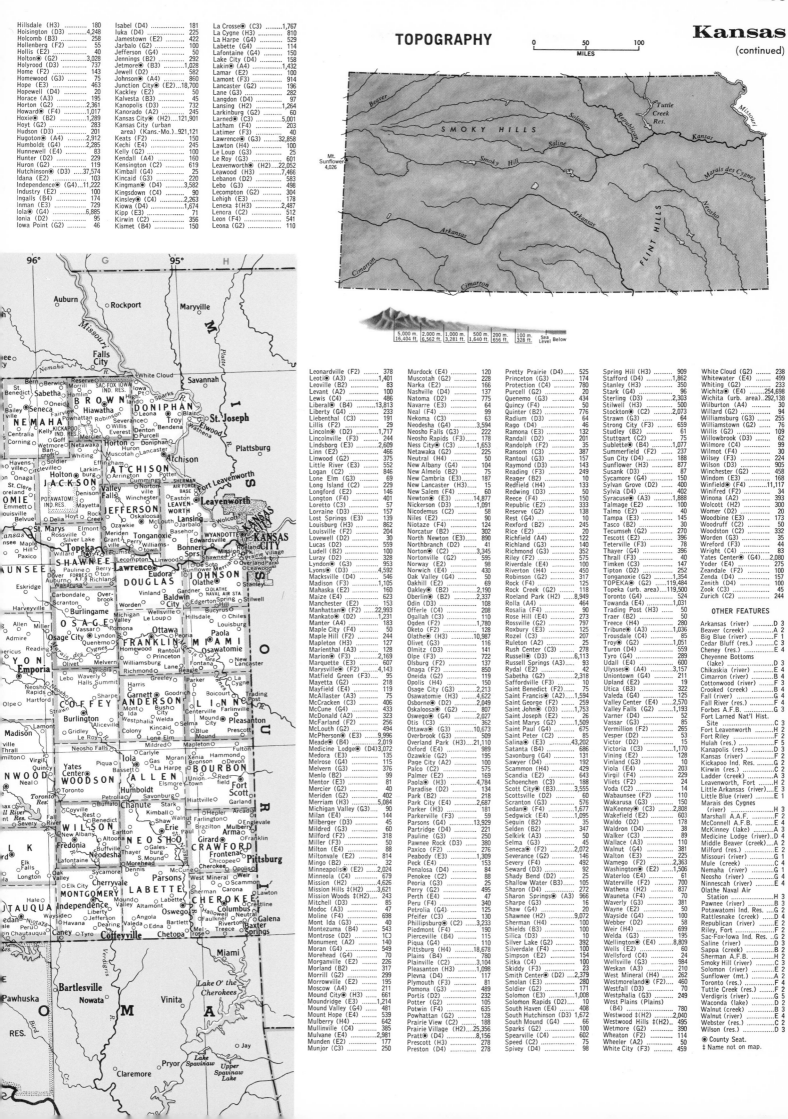

Hillsdale (H3) 180
Hoisington (D3) 4,248
Holcomb (B3) 258
Hollenberg (F2) 55
Hollis (E2) 40
Holton◉ (G2) 3,028
Holyrood (D3) 737
Home (F2) 143
Homewood (G3) 75
Hope (E3) 463
Hopewell (D4) 20
Horace (A3) 195
Horton (G2) 2,361
Howard◉ (F4) 1,017
Hoxie◉ (B2) 1,289
Hoyt (G2) 283
Hudson (D3) 201
Hugoton◉ (A4) 2,912
Humboldt (G4) 2,285
Hunnewell (E4) 83
Hunter (D2) 229
Huron (G2) 119
Hutchinson◉ (D3) 37,574
Idana (E2) 103
Independence◉ (G4)...11,222
Industry (E2) 100
Ingalls (B4) 174
Inman (E3) 729
Iola◉ (G4) 6,885
Ionia (D2) 95
Iowa Point (G2) 46
Isabel (D4) 181
Iuka (D4) 225
Jamestown (E2) 422
Jarbalo (G2) 100
Jefferson (G4) 50
Jennings (B2) 292
Jetmore◉ (B3) 1,028
Jewell (D2) 582
Johnson◉ (A4) 860
Junction City◉ (E2)...18,700
Kackley (E2) 50
Kalvesta (B3) 45
Kanopolis (D3) 732
Kanorado (A2) 245
Kansas City◉ (H2)....121,901
Kansas City (urban area) (Kans.-Mo.)..921,121
Keats (F2) 150
Kechi (E4) 245
Kelly (G2) 100
Kendall (A4) 160
Kensington (C2) 619
Kimball (G4) 25
Kincaid (G3) 220
Kingman◉ (D4) 3,582
Kingsdown (C4) 90
Kinsley◉ (C4) 2,263
Kiowa (D4) 1,674
Kipp (E3) 71
Kirwin (C2) 356
Kismet (B4) 150
La Crosse◉ (C3) 1,767
La Cygne (H3) 810
La Harpe (G4) 529
Labette (G4) 114
Lafontaine (G4) 150
Lake City (D4) 158
Lakin◉ (A4) 1,432
Lamar (E2) 100
Lamont (F3) 914
Lancaster (G2) 196
Lane (G3) 282
Langdon (D4) 97
Lansing (H2) 1,264
Larkinburg (G2) 60
Larned◉ (C3) 5,001
Latham (F4) 203
Latimer (F3) 40
Lawrence◉ (G3) 32,858
Lawton (H4) 100
Le Loup (G3) 25
Le Roy (G3) 601
Leavenworth◉ (H2)....22,052
Leawood (H3) 7,466
Lebanon (D2) 583
Lebo (G3) 498
Lecompton (G2) 304
Lehigh (E3) 178
Lenexa ‡(H3) 2,487
Lenora (C2) 512
Leon (F4) 541
Leona (G2) 110

Leonardville (F2) 378
Leoti◉ (A3) 1,401
Leoville (B2) 83
Levant (A2) 100
Lewis (C4) 486
Liberal◉ (B4) 13,813
Liberty (G4) 233
Liebenthal (C3) 191
Lillis (F2) 29
Lincoln◉ (D2) 1,717
Lincolnville (F3) 244
Lindsborg (E3) 2,609
Linn (E2) 466
Linwood (G2) 375
Little River (E3) 552
Logan (C2) 846
Lone Elm (G3) 69
Long Island (C2) 229
Longford (E2) 146
Longton (F4) 401
Loretto (C3) 57
Lorraine (D3) 157
Lost Springs (E3) 139
Louisburg (H3) 862
Louisville (F2) 204
Lovewell (D2) 30
Lucas (D2) 559
Ludell (B2) 100
Luray (D2) 328
Lyndon◉ (G3) 953
Lyons◉ (D3) 4,592
Macksville (D4) 546
Madison (F3) 1,105
Mahaska (E2) 160
Maize (E4) 623
Manchester (E2) 153
Manhattan◉ (F2) 22,993
Mankato◉ (D2) 1,231
Manter (A4) 183
Maple City (F4) 50
Maple Hill (F2) 244
Mapleton (H3) 127
Marienthal (A3) 128
Marion◉ (F3) 2,169
Marquette (E3) 607
Marysville◉ (F2) 4,143
Matfield Green (F3).... 95
Mayetta (G2) 218
Mayfield (E4) 119
McAllaster (A3) 75
McCracken (C3) 406
McCune (G4) 433
McDonald (A2) 323
McFarland (F2) 256
McLouth (G2) 494
McPherson◉ (E3) 9,996
Meade◉ (B4) 2,019
Medicine Lodge◉ (D4)3,072
Medora (E3) 135
Melrose (G4) 115
Melvern (G3) 376
Menlo (B2) 99
Mentor (E3) 81
Mercier (G2) 40
Meriden (G2) 402
Merriam (H3) 5,084
Michigan Valley (G3).... 90
Milan (E4) 144
Milberger (D3) 45
Mildred (G3) 60
Milford (F2) 318
Miller (F3) 50
Milton (E4) 88
Miltonvale (E2) 814
Mingo (B2) 32
Minneapolis◉ (E2) 2,024
Minneola (C4) 679
Mission (H2) 4,626
Mission Hills ‡(H2) 3,621
Mission Woods ‡(H2).... 243
Mitchell (D3) 85
Modoc (A3) 47
Moline (F4) 698
Mont Ida (G3) 40
Montezuma (B4) 543
Montrose (D2) .... 1C)
Monument (A2) 140
Moran (G4) 549
Morehead (G4) 70
Morganville (E2) 226
Morland (B2) 317
Morrill (G2) 299
Morrowville (E2) 195
Moscow (A4) 211
Mound City◉ (H3) 661
Moundridge (E3) 1,214
Mound Valley (G4) 481
Mount Hope (E4) 539
Mulberry (H4) 642
Mullinville (C4) 385
Mulvane (E4) 2,981
Munden (E2) 177
Munjor (C3) 250
Murdock (E4) 120
Muscotah (G2) 228
Narka (E2) 166
Nashville (D4) 137
Natoma (D2) 775
Navarre (E3) 64
Neal (F4) 99
Nekoma (C3) 63
Neodesha (G4) 3,594
Neosho Falls (G3) 222
Neosho Rapids (F3)...... 178
Ness City◉ (C3) 1,653
Netawaka (G2) 225
Neutral (H4) 50
New Albany (G4) 104
New Almelo (B2) 75
New Cambria (E3)........ 187
New Lancaster (H3)..... 15
New Salem (F4) 60
Newton◉ (E3) 14,877
Nickerson (D3) 1,091
Nicodemus (C2) 58
Niles (E2) 90
Niotaze (F4) 124
Norcatur (B2) 302
North Newton (E3)...... 890
Northbranch (D2) 41
Norton◉ (C2) 3,345
Nortonville (G2) 595
Norway (E2) 98
Norwich (E4) 430
Oak Valley (G4) 50
Oakhill (E2) 69
Oakley◉ (B2) 2,190
Oberlin◉ (B2) 2,337
Odin (D3) 108
Offerle (C4) 208
Ogallah (C3) 110
Ogden (F2) 1,780
Oketo (F2) 128
Olathe◉ (H3) 10,987
Olivet (G3) 116
Olmitz (D3) 141
Olpe (F3) 722
Olsburg (F2) 137
Onaga (F2) 850
Oneida (G2) 119
Opolis (H4) 150
Osage City (G3) 2,213
Osawatomie (H3) 4,622
Osborne◉ (D2) 2,049
Oskaloosa◉ (G2) 807
Oswego◉ (G4) 2,027
Otis (C3) 362
Ottawa◉ (G3) 10,673
Overbrook (G3) 509
Overland Park (H3)....21,110
Oxford (E4) 989
Ozawkie (G2) 195
Page City (A2) 100
Palco (C2) 575
Palmer (E2) 169
Paola◉ (H3) 4,784
Paradise (D2) 134
Park (B2) 218
Park City (E4) 2,687
Parker (H3) 181
Parkerville (F3) 59
Parsons (G4) 13,929
Partridge (D4) 221
Pauline (G3) 250
Pawnee Rock (D3) 380
Paxico (F2) 276
Peabody (E3) 1,309
Peck (E4) 153
Penalosa (D4) 84
Penokee (C2) 88
Peoria (G3) 25
Perry (G2) 495
Perth (E4) 47
Peru (F4) 340
Petrolia (G4) 125
Pfeifer (C3) 130
Phillipsburg◉ (C2) 3,233
Piedmont (F4) 190
Pierceville (B4) 115
Piqua (G4) 110
Pittsburg (H4) 18,678
Plains (B4) 780
Plainville (C2) 3,104
Pleasanton (H3) 1,098
Plevna (D4) 117
Plymouth (F3) 81
Pomona (G3) 489
Portis (D2) 232
Potter (G2) 105
Potwin (F4) 635
Powhattan (G2) 128
Prairie View (C2) 188
Prairie Village (H2)....25,356
Pratt◉ (D4) 8,156
Prescott (H3) 278
Preston (D4) 278
Pretty Prairie (D4)...... 525
Princeton (G3) 174
Protection (C4) 780
Purcell (G2) 20
Quenemo (G3) 434
Quincy (F4) 50
Quinter (B2) 776
Radium (D3) 64
Rago (D4) 46
Ramona (E3) 132
Randall (D2) 201
Randolph (F2) 35
Ransom (C3) 387
Rantoul (G3) 157
Raymond (D3) 143
Reading (F3) 249
Reager (B2) 10
Redfield (H4) 133
Redwing (D3) 50
Reece (F4) 150
Republic (E2) 333
Reserve (G2) 138
Rest (G4) 10
Rexford (B2) 245
Rice (E2) 20
Richfield (A4) 122
Richland (G3) 140
Richmond (G3) 352
Riley (F2) 575
Riverdale (E4) 100
Riverton (H4) 450
Robinson (G2) 317
Rock (F4) 125
Rock Creek (G2) 118
Roeland Park (H2) 8,949
Rolla (A4) 464
Rosalia (F4) 90
Rose Hill (E4) 273
Rossville (G2) 797
Roxbury (E3) 125
Rozel (C3) 207
Ruleton (A2) 25
Rush Center (C3) 278
Russell◉ (D3) 6,113
Russell Springs (A3)..... 93
Rydal (E2) 42
Sabetha (G2) 2,318
Saffordville (F3) 10
Saint Benedict (F2)...... 75
Saint Francis◉ (A2).....1,594
Saint George (F2) 259
Saint John◉ (D3) 1,753
Saint Joseph (E2) 26
Saint Marys (G2) 1,509
Saint Paul (G4) 675
Saint Peter (C2) 85
Salina◉ (E3) 43,202
Satanta (B4) 686
Savonburg (G4) 131
Sawyer (D4) 192
Scammon (H4) 429
Scandia (E2) 643
Schoenchen (C3) 188
Scott City◉ (B3)..........3,555
Scottsville (D2) 60
Scranton (G3) 576
Sedan◉ (F4) 1,677
Sedgwick (E4) 1,095
Seguin (B2) 35
Selden (B2) 347
Selkirk (A3) 50
Selma (G3) 45
Seneca◉ (F2) 2,072
Severance (G2) 146
Severy (F4) 492
Seward (D3) 92
Shady Bend (D2) 25
Shallow Water (B3)...... 105
Sharon (D4) 272
Sharon Springs◉ (A3) 966
Sharpe (G3) 16
Shaw (G4) 20
Shawnee (H2) 9,072
Sherman (H4) 100
Shields (B3) 100
Silica (D3) 10
Silver Lake (G2) 392
Silverdale (F4) 100
Simpson (E2) 154
Sitka (C4) 100
Skiddy (F3) 23
Smith Center◉ (D2) 2,379
Smolan (E3) 280
Soldier (G2) 171
Solomon (E3) 1,008
Solomon Rapids (D2).... 10
South Haven (E4) 408
South Hutchinson (D3) 1,672
South Mound (G4) 66
Sparks (G2) 100
Spearville (C4) 602
Speed (C2) 75
Spivey (D4) 98
Spring Hill (H3) 909
Stafford (D4) 1,862
Stanley (H3) 350
Stark (G4) 96
Sterling (D3) 2,303
Stilwell (H3) 500
Stockton◉ (C2) 2,073
Strawn (G3) 64
Strong City (F3) 659
Studley (B2) 61
Stuttgart (C2) 75
Sublette◉ (B4) 1,077
Summerfield (F2) 237
Sun City (D4) 188
Sunflower (H3) 877
Susank (D3) 87
Sycamore (G4) 150
Sylvan Grove (D2) 400
Sylvia (D4) 402
Syracuse◉ (A3) 1,888
Talmage (E2) 100
Talmo (E2) 40
Tampa (E3) 145
Tasco (B2) 30
Tecumseh (G2) 270
Tescott (E2) 396
Teterville (F3) 78
Thayer (G4) 396
Thrall (F3) 40
Timken (C3) 147
Tipton (D2) 252
Tonganoxie (G2) 1,354
TOPEKA◉ (G2) 119,484
Topeka (urb. area)....119,500
Toronto (G4) 524
Towanda (E4) 1,031
Trading Post (H3) 50
Traer (B2) 50
Treece (H4) 280
Tribune◉ (A3) 1,036
Trousdale (C4) 85
Troy◉ (G2) 1,051
Turon (D4) 559
Tyro (G4) 289
Udall (E4) 600
Ulysses◉ (A4) 3,157
Uniontown (G4) 211
Upland (E2) 19
Utica (B3) 322
Valeda (G4) 125
Valley Center (E4) 2,570
Valley Falls (G2) 1,193
Varner (D4) 52
Vassar (G3) 85
Vermillion (F2) 265
Vesper (D2) 53
Victor (D2) 15
Victoria (C3) 1,170
Vining (E2) 128
Vinland (G3) 10
Viola (E4) 203
Virgil (F4) 229
Vliets (F2) 24
Voda (C2) 14
Wabaunsee (F2) 110
Wakarusa (G3) 150
WaKeeney◉ (C3) 2,808
Wakefield (E2) 603
Waldo (D2) 178
Waldron (D4) 38
Walker (C3) 89
Wallace (A3) 110
Walnut (G4) 381
Walton (E3) 225
Wamego (F2) 2,363
Washington◉ (E2) 1,506
Waterloo (E4) 61
Waterville (F2) 700
Wathena (H2) 837
Wauneta (F4) 70
Waverly (G3) 381
Wayne (E2) 50
Wayside (G4) 100
Webber (D2) 58
Weir (H4) 699
Welda (G3) 195
Wellington◉ (E4) 8,809
Wells (E2) 60
Wellsford (C4) 24
Wellsville (G3) 984
Weskan (A3) 210
West Mineral (H4) 262
Westmoreland◉ (F2).... 460
Westfall (D3) 70
Westphalia (G3) 249
West Plains (Plains) (B4) 780
Westwood ‡(H2) 2,040
Westwood Hills ‡(H2).. 495
Wetmore (G2) 390
Wheaton (F2) 114
Wheeler (A2) 50
White City (F3) 459
White Cloud (G2) 238
Whitewater (E4) 499
Whiting (G2) 233
Wichita◉ (E4) 254,698
Wichita (urb. area)..292,138
Wilburton (A4) 30
Willard (G2) 94
Williamsburg (G3) 255
Williamstown (G2) 76
Willis (G2) 109
Willowbrook (D3) 62
Wilmore (C4) 99
Wilmot (F4) 30
Wilsey (F3) 224
Wilson (D3) 905
Winchester (G2) 458
Windom (E3) 168
Winfield◉ (F4) 11,117
Winifred (F2) 34
Winona (A2) 393
Wolcott (H2) 300
Womer (D2) 20
Woodbine (E3) 173
Woodruff (C2) 50
Woodston (C2) 332
Worden (G3) 35
Wreford (F3) 44
Wright (C4) 83
Yates Center◉ (G4).....2,080
Yoder (E4) 275
Zeandale (F2) 100
Zenda (D4) 157
Zenith (D4) 100
Zook (C3) 45
Zurich (C2) 244

OTHER FEATURES

Arkansas (river) ....D 3
Beaver (creek) ....A 2
Big Blue (river) ....F 1
Cedar Bluff (res.) ....C 3
Cheney (res.) ....E 4
Cheyenne Bottoms (lake) ....D 3
Chikaskia (river) ....E 4
Cimarron (river) ....B 4
Cottonwood (river) ....F 3
Crooked (creek) ....B 4
Fall (river) ....G 4
Fall River (res.) ....F 4
Forbes A.F.B. ....G 3
Fort Larned Nat'l Hist. Site ....C 3
Fort Leavenworth ....H 2
Fort Riley ....F 2
Hulah (res.) ....F 5
Kanapolis (res.) ....D 3
Kansas (river) ....F 2
Kickapoo Ind. Res. ....G 2
Kirwin (res.) ....C 2
Ladder (creek) ....A 3
Leavenworth, Fort ....H 2
Little Arkansas (river)....E 3
Little Blue (river) ....E 1
Marais des Cygnes (river) ....H 3
Marshall A.A.F. ....F 2
McConnell A.F.B. ....E 4
McKinney (lake) ....A 3
Medicine Lodge (river)..D 4
Middle Beaver (creek)....A 2
Milford (res.) ....E 2
Missouri (river) ....G 1
Mule (creek) ....C 4
Nemaha (river) ....G 1
Neosho (river) ....G 4
Ninnescah (river) ....E 4
Olathe Naval Air Station ....H 3
Pawnee (river) ....B 3
Potawatomi Ind. Res. ....G 2
Rattlesnake (creek) ......D 4
Republican (river) ....E 2
Riley, Fort ....F 2
Sac-Fox-Iowa Ind. Res. ..G 2
Saline (river) ....D 3
Sappa (creek) ....B 2
Sherman A.F.B. ....H 2
Smoky Hill (river) ....C 3
Solomon (river) ....E 2
Sunflower (mt.) ....A 2
Toronto (res.) ....F 4
Tuttle Creek (res.) ....F 2
Verdigris (river) ....G 5
Waconda (lake) ....D 2
Walnut (creek) ....B 3
Walnut (river) ....E 4
Webster (res.) ....C 2
Wilson (res.) ....D 3

◉ County Seat.
‡ Name not on map.

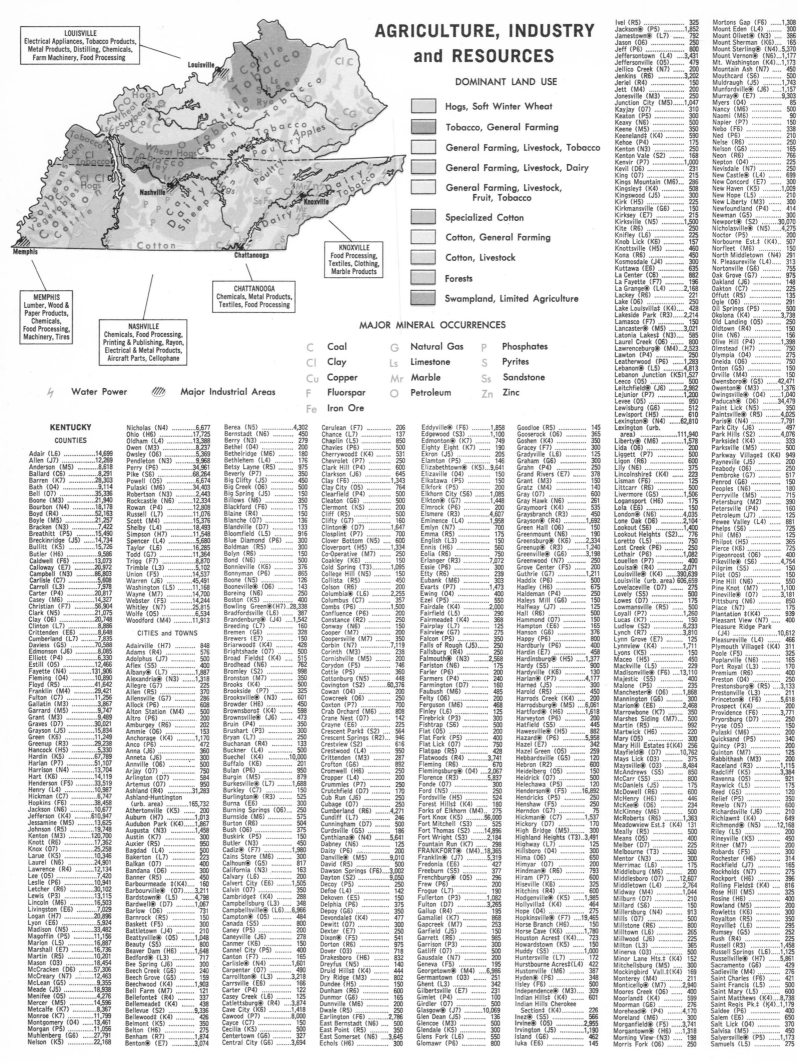

AGRICULTURE, INDUSTRY and RESOURCES

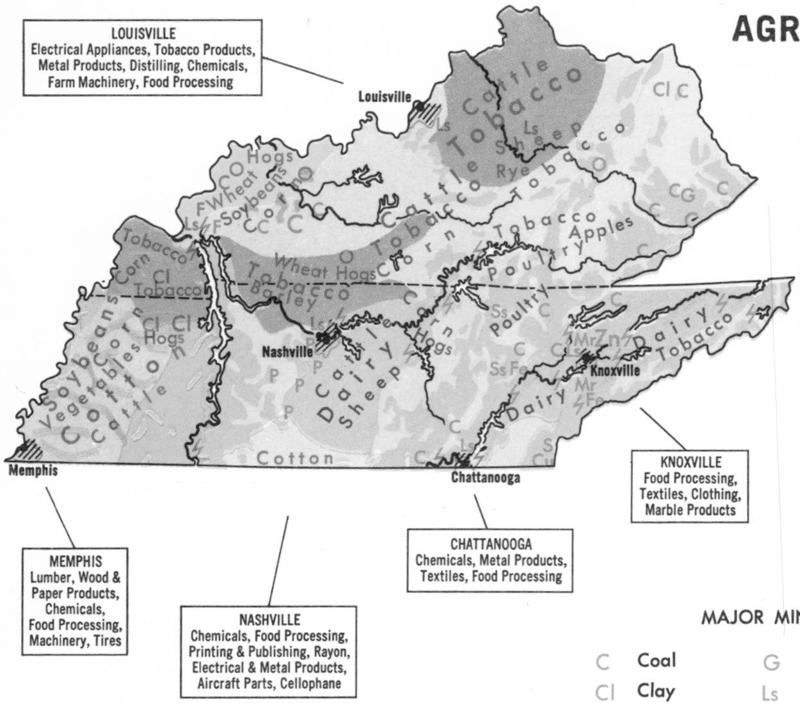
LOUISVILLE
Electrical Appliances, Tobacco Products, Metal Products, Distilling, Chemicals, Farm Machinery, Food Processing
Louisville
Nashville
Knoxville
Memphis
Chattanooga
KNOXVILLE
Food Processing, Textiles, Clothing, Marble Products
CHATTANOOGA
Chemicals, Metal Products, Textiles, Food Processing
MEMPHIS
Lumber, Wood & Paper Products, Chemicals, Food Processing, Machinery, Tires
NASHVILLE
Chemicals, Food Processing, Printing & Publishing, Rayon, Electrical & Metal Products, Aircraft Parts, Cellophane

DOMINANT LAND USE

- Hogs, Soft Winter Wheat
- Tobacco, General Farming
- General Farming, Livestock, Tobacco
- General Farming, Livestock, Dairy
- General Farming, Livestock, Fruit, Tobacco
- Specialized Cotton
- Cotton, General Farming
- Cotton, Livestock
- Forests
- Swampland, Limited Agriculture

MAJOR MINERAL OCCURRENCES

C Coal
Cl Clay
Cu Copper
F Fluorspar
Fe Iron Ore
G Natural Gas
Ls Limestone
Mr Marble
O Petroleum
P Phosphates
S Pyrites
Ss Sandstone
Zn Zinc

Water Power
Major Industrial Areas

KENTUCKY

COUNTIES

Adair (L6) 14,699
Allen (J7) 12,269
Anderson (M5) 8,618
Ballard (C6) 8,291
Barren (K7) 28,303
Bath (O4) 9,114
Bell (O7) 35,336
Boone (M3) 21,940
Bourbon (N4) 18,178
Boyd (R4) 52,163
Boyle (M5) 21,257
Bracken (N3) 7,422
Breathitt (P5) 15,490
Breckinridge (J5) 14,734
Bullitt (K5) 15,726
Butler (H6) 9,586
Caldwell (F6) 13,073
Calloway (E7) 20,972
Campbell (N3) 86,803
Carlisle (C7) 5,608
Carroll (L3) 7,978
Carter (P4) 20,817
Casey (M6) 14,327
Christian (F7) 56,904
Clark (N5) 21,075
Clay (O6) 20,748
Clinton (L7) 8,886
Crittenden (E6) 8,648
Cumberland (L7) 7,835
Daviess (G5) 70,588
Edmonson (J6) 8,085
Elliott (P4) 6,330
Estill (O5) 12,466
Fayette (N4) 131,906
Fleming (O4) 10,890
Floyd (R5) 41,642
Franklin (M4) 29,421
Fulton (C7) 11,256
Gallatin (M3) 3,867
Garrard (M5) 9,747
Grant (M3) 9,489
Graves (D7) 30,021
Grayson (J5) 15,834
Green (K6) 11,249
Greenup (R3) 29,238
Hancock (H5) 5,330
Hardin (K5) 67,789
Harlan (P7) 51,107
Harrison (N4) 13,704
Hart (K6) 14,119
Henderson (F5) 33,519
Henry (L4) 10,987
Hickman (C7) 6,747
Hopkins (F6) 38,458
Jackson (N6) 10,677
Jefferson (K4) 610,947
Jessamine (M5) 13,625
Johnson (R5) 19,748
Kenton (M3) 120,700
Knott (R6) 17,362
Knox (O7) 25,258
Larue (K5) 10,346
Laurel (N6) 24,901
Lawrence (R4) 12,134
Lee (O5) 7,420
Leslie (P6) 10,941
Letcher (R6) 30,102
Lewis (P3) 13,115
Lincoln (M6) 16,503
Livingston (E6) 7,029
Logan (H7) 20,896
Lyon (E6) 5,924
Madison (N5) 33,482
Magoffin (P5) 11,156
Marion (L5) 16,887
Marshall (E7) 16,736
Martin (R5) 10,201
Mason (O3) 18,454
McCracken (D6) 57,306
McCreary (N7) 12,463
McLean (G5) 9,355
Meade (J5) 18,938
Menifee (O5) 4,276
Mercer (M5) 14,596
Metcalfe (K7) 8,367
Monroe (K7) 11,799
Montgomery (O4) 13,461
Morgan (P5) 11,056
Muhlenberg (G6) 27,791
Nelson (K5) 22,168
Nicholas (N4) 6,677
Ohio (H6) 17,725
Oldham (L4) 13,388
Owen (M3) 8,237
Owsley (O6) 5,369
Pendleton (N3) 9,968
Perry (P6) 34,961
Pike (S6) 68,264
Powell (O5) 6,674
Pulaski (M6) 34,403
Robertson (N3) 2,443
Rockcastle (N6) 12,334
Rowan (P4) 12,808
Russell (L7) 11,076
Scott (M4) 15,376
Shelby (L4) 18,493
Simpson (H7) 11,548
Spencer (L4) 5,680
Taylor (L6) 16,285
Todd (G7) 11,364
Trigg (F7) 8,870
Trimble (L3) 5,102
Union (F5) 14,537
Warren (J6) 45,491
Washington (L5) 11,168
Wayne (M7) 14,700
Webster (F5) 14,244
Whitley (N7) 25,815
Wolfe (O5) 6,534
Woodford (M4) 11,913

CITIES and TOWNS

Adairville (H7) 848
Adams (R4) 576
Adolphus (J7) 500
Aflex (S5) 400
Albany◉ (L7) 1,887
Alexandria◉ (N3) 1,318
Allegre (G7) 225
Allen (R5) 370
Allensville (G7) 286
Allock (P6) 608
Alton Station (M4) 500
Altro (P6) 200
Amburgey (R6) 202
Ammie (O6) 153
Anchorage (K4) 1,170
Anco (P6) 472
Anna (J6) 360
Anneta (J6) 300
Annville (O6) 500
Arjay (O7) 750
Arlington (D7) 584
Artemus (O7) 950
Ashland (R4) 31,283
Ashland-Huntington (urb. area) 165,732
Athertonville (K5) 200
Auburn (H7) 1,013
Audubon Park (K4) 1,867
Augusta (N3) 1,458
Austin (K7) 300
Auxier (R5) 950
Bagdad (L4) 500
Bakerton (L7) 223
Balkan (O7) 400
Bandana (D6) 300
Banner (R5) 450
Barbourmeade ‡(K4) 160
Barbourville◉ (O7) 3,211
Bardstown◉ (L5) 4,798
Bardwell◉ (D7) 1,067
Barlow (D6) 731
Barnrock (R5) 150
Baskett (F5) 300
Battletown (J4) 210
Beattyville◉ (O5) 1,048
Beauty (S5) 800
Beaver Dam (H6) 1,648
Bedford◉ (L3) 717
Bee Spring (J6) 300
Beech Creek (G6) 240
Beech Grove (G5) 159
Beechwood (K4) 1,903
Bell Farm (M7) 121
Bellefonte‡ (R4) 337
Bellemeade‡ (K4) 438
Bellevue (S2) 9,336
Bellewood‡ (K4) 426
Belmont (K5) 350
Belton (H6) 275
Benham (R7) 1,874
Benton◉ (E7) 3,074
Berea (N5) 4,302
Bernstadt (N6) 450
Berry (N3) 279
Bethel (O4) 200
Bethelridge (M6) 180
Bethlehem (L4) 176
Betsy Layne (R5) 975
Beverly (P7) 350
Big Clifty (J5) 450
Big Creek (O6) 500
Big Spring (J5) 150
Billows (N6) 350
Blackford (F6) 175
Blaine (R4) 150
Blanche (O7) 136
Blandville (D7) 133
Bloomfield (L5) 916
Blue Diamond (P6) 300
Boldman (R5) 300
Bolyn (R6) 150
Bond (N6) 500
Bonnieville (K6) 376
Bonnyman (P6) 865
Boone (N5) 126
Booneville◉ (O6) 143
Boreing (N6) 250
Boston (K5) 400
Bowling Green◉(H7) 28,338
Bradfordsville (L6) 387
Brandenburg◉ (J4) 1,542
Breeding (L7) 160
Bremen (G6) 328
Brewers (E7) 150
Briarwood‡ (K4) 428
Brightshade (O7) 500
Broad Fields‡ (K4) 515
Brodhead (N6) 762
Bromley (S2) 998
Bronston (M7) 350
Brooks (K4) 500
Brookside (P7) 325
Brooksville◉ (N3) 601
Browder (H6) 450
Brownsboro‡ (K4) 598
Brownsville◉ (J6) 473
Bruin (P4) 350
Brushart (P3) 300
Bryan (L7) 250
Buchanan (R4) 133
Buckner (L4) 500
Buechel (K4) 10,000
Buffalo (K6) 201
Bulan (P6) 950
Burgin (M5) 879
Burkesville◉ (L7) 1,688
Burkley (C7) 150
Burlington◉ (R3) 525
Burna (E6) 300
Burning Springs (O6) 250
Burnside (M6) 575
Burton (R6) 504
Bush (O6) 375
Buskirk (P5) 150
Butler (N3) 450
Cadiz◉ (F7) 1,980
Cains Store (M6) 300
Calhoun◉ (G5) 817
California (N3) 163
Calvary (L6) 200
Calvert City (E6) 1,505
Calvin (O7) 350
Cambridge‡ (K4) 288
Campbellsburg (L3) 348
Campbellsville◉ (L6) 6,966
Campton◉ (O5) 484
Canada (S5) 800
Caney (P5) 200
Caneyville (J6) 278
Canmer (K6) 150
Cannel City (P5) 400
Canton (F7) 165
Carlisle◉ (N4) 1,601
Carpenter (O7) 490
Carrollton◉ (L3) 3,218
Carrsville (E6) 166
Carter (P4) 122
Casey Creek (L6) 125
Catlettsburg◉ (R4) 3,874
Cave City (K6) 1,418
Cawood (P7) 8,000
Cayce (C7) 150
Cecilia (K5) 500
Centertown (G6) 327
Central City (G6) 3,694
Cerulean (F7) 206
Chance (L7) 137
Chaplin (L5) 850
Chavies (P6) 500
Cherrywood‡ (K4) 531
Chevrolet (P7) 250
Clark Hill (P4) 600
Clarkson (J6) 645
Clay (F6) 1,343
Clay City (O5) 764
Clearfield (P4) 500
Cleaton (G6) 500
Clermont (K5) 200
Cliff (R5) 500
Clifty (G7) 160
Clinton◉ (D7) 1,647
Closplint (P7) 700
Clover Bottom (N5) 600
Cloverport (H5) 1,334
Co-Operative (M7) 250
Coakley (K6) 150
Cold Spring (T3) 1,095
College Hill (N5) 150
Collista (R5) 450
Colson (R6) 200
Columbia◉ (L6) 2,255
Columbus (C7) 357
Combs (P6) 1,500
Confluence (P6) 200
Constance (R2) 250
Conway (N6) 150
Cooper (M7) 200
Coopersville (M7) 350
Corbin (N7) 7,119
Corinth (M3) 238
Cornishville (M5) 200
Corydon (F5) 746
Cottle (P5) 360
Cottonburg (N5) 448
Covington (S2) 60,376
Cowan (O4) 200
Cowcreek (O6) 250
Coxton (P7) 700
Crab Orchard (M6) 808
Crane Nest (O7) 142
Crayne (E6) 225
Crescent Park‡ (S2) 564
Crescent Springs (R2) 946
Crestview (S2) 616
Crestwood (L4) 950
Crittenden (M3) 287
Crofton (G6) 892
Cromwell (H6) 250
Cropper (L4) 200
Crummies (P7) 250
Crutchfield (D7) 170
Cub Run (J6) 250
Cubage (O7) 250
Cumberland (R6) 4,271
Cundiff (L7) 246
Cunningham (D7) 500
Curdsville (G5) 186
Cynthiana◉ (N4) 5,641
Dabney (N6) 125
Daisy (P6) 200
Danville◉ (M5) 9,010
David (R5) 500
Dawson Springs (F6) 3,002
Dayton (S2) 9,050
Decoy (P5) 250
Defoe (L4) 142
Dekoven (E5) 150
Delphia (P6) 375
Depoy (G6) 350
Devondale‡ (K4) 477
Dewitt (O7) 300
Dexter (E7) 250
Dixon◉ (F5) 541
Dorton (R6) 975
Dover (O3) 718
Drakesboro (H6) 832
Dreyfus (N5) 140
Druid Hills‡ (K4) 444
Dry Ridge (M3) 802
Dundee (H5) 150
Dunham (R6) 600
Dunmor (G6) 165
Dunnville (M6) 200
Dwale (R5) 250
Earlington (F6) 2,786
East Bernstadt (N6) 500
East Point (R5) 350
East Somerset (N6) 3,645
Echols (H6) 300
Eddyville◉ (F6) 1,858
Edgewood (S3) 1,100
Edmonton◉ (K7) 749
Eighty Eight (K7) 190
Ekron (J5) 205
Elamton (P5) 146
Elizabethtown◉ (K5) 9,641
Elizaville (O4) 150
Elkatawa (P5) 150
Elkfork (P5) 200
Elkhorn City (S6) 1,085
Elkton◉ (G7) 1,448
Elmrock (P6) 200
Elsmere (R3) 4,607
Eminence (L4) 1,958
Emlyn (N7) 700
Emma (R5) 175
English (L3) 150
Ennis (H6) 560
Eolia (R6) 750
Erlanger (R3) 7,072
Essie (P6) 300
Etty (R6) 239
Eubank (M6) 303
Evarts (P7) 1,473
Ewing (O4) 400
Ezel (P5) 550
Fairdale (K4) 2,000
Fairfield (L5) 290
Fairmeade‡ (K4) 368
Fairplay (L7) 125
Fairview (G7) 275
Falcon (P5) 350
Falls of Rough (J5) 250
Fallsburg (R4) 250
Falmouth◉ (N3) 2,568
Fariston (N6) 175
Farler (P6) 200
Farmers (P4) 240
Farmington (D7) 160
Faubush (M6) 485
Felty (O6) 200
Ferguson (M6) 468
Finley (L6) 125
Firebrick (P3) 300
Fishtrap (S6) 500
Flat (O5) 200
Flat Fork (P5) 400
Flat Lick (O7) 750
Flatgap (R5) 428
Flatwoods (R4) 3,741
Fleming (R6) 670
Flemingsburg◉ (O4) 2,067
Florence (R3) 5,837
Fonde (O7) 300
Ford (N5) 250
Fordsville (H5) 524
Forest Hills‡ (K4) 180
Forks of Elkhorn (M4) 275
Fort Knox (K5) 56,000
Fort Mitchell (S3) 525
Fort Thomas (S2) 14,896
Fort Wright (S3) 2,184
Fountain Run (K7) 298
FRANKFORT◉ (M4) 18,365
Franklin◉ (J7) 5,319
Fredonia (E6) 427
Freeburn (S5) 377
Frenchburg◉ (O5) 296
Frew (P6) 200
Frogue (L7) 190
Fullerton (P3) 1,082
Fulton (D7) 3,265
Gallup (R4) 195
Gamaliel (K7) 868
Gapcreek (M7) 253
Garfield (J5) 150
Garrett (R6) 985
Garrison (P3) 300
Gatliff (O7) 500
Gausdale (N7) 200
Geneva (F5) 195
Georgetown◉ (M4) 6,986
Germantown (O3) 251
Ghent (L3) 342
Gilbertsville (E7) 231
Gimlet (P4) 100
Girdler (O7) 500
Glasgow◉ (J7) 10,069
Glen Dean (J5) 136
Glencoe (M3) 500
Glendale (K5) 300
Glens Fork (L6) 550
Glomawr (P6) 800
Goodloe (R5) 145
Gooserock (O6) 365
Goshen (K4) 350
Gracey (F7) 300
Gradyville (L6) 125
Graham (G6) 300
Grahn (P4) 250
Grand Rivers (E7) 378
Grant (M3) 150
Gratz (M4) 140
Gray (O7) 600
Gray Hawk (N6) 261
Graymoor‡ (K4) 535
Graysbranch (R3) 450
Grayson◉ (R4) 1,692
Green Hall (O6) 150
Greenmount (N6) 190
Greensburg◉ (K6) 2,334
Greenup◉ (R3) 1,240
Greenville◉ (G6) 3,198
Greenwood (N7) 250
Grove Center (F5) 200
Guthrie (G7) 1,211
Haddix (P6) 500
Hadley (H6) 675
Haldeman (P4) 250
Haleys Mill (G6) 150
Halfway (J7) 125
Hall (R6) 500
Hammond (O7) 150
Hampton (E6) 165
Hanson (G6) 376
Happy (P6) 800
Hardburly (P6) 400
Hardin (E7) 458
Hardinsburg◉ (H5) 1,377
Hardy (S5) 900
Hardyville (K6) 130
Harlan◉ (P7) 4,177
Harned (J5) 300
Harold (R5) 450
Harrods Creek (K4) 200
Harrodsburg◉ (M5) 6,061
Hartford◉ (H6) 1,618
Harveyton (P6) 200
Hatfield (S5) 445
Hawesville◉ (H5) 882
Hazard◉ (P6) 5,958
Hazel (E7) 342
Hazel Green (O5) 259
Hebbardsville (G5) 120
Hebron (R2) 600
Heidelberg (O5) 150
Heidrick (O7) 500
Helechawa (P5) 120
Henderson◉ (F5) 16,892
Hendricks (P5) 250
Henshaw (F5) 250
Herndon (G7) 75
Hickman◉ (C7) 1,537
Hickory (D7) 170
High Bridge (M5) 300
Highland Heights (T3) 3,491
Highway (L7) 125
Hillsboro (O4) 300
Hima (O6) 650
Himyar (O7) 200
Hindman◉ (R6) 793
Hiram (P7) 600
Hiseville (K6) 325
Hitchins (R4) 600
Hodgenville◉ (K5) 1,985
Hollyvilla‡ (K4) 464
Hope (O4) 275
Hopkinsville◉ (F7) 19,465
Horse Branch (H6) 150
Horse Cave (K6) 1,780
Houston Acres‡ (K4) 723
Howardstown (K5) 150
Huddy (S5) 1,000
Huntersville (L7) 172
Hurstbourne Acres‡(L4) 422
Hustonville (M6) 387
Hyden◉ (P6) 348
Ilsley (F6) 500
Independence◉ (M3) 309
Indian Hills‡ (K4) 601
Indian Hills Cherokee Section‡ (K4) 226
Inez◉ (S5) 566
Irvine◉ (O5) 2,955
Irvington (J5) 1,190
Island (G6) 462
Iuka (E6) 145
Ivel (R5) 325
Jackson◉ (P5) 1,852
Jamestown◉ (L7) 792
Jason (O6) 250
Jeff (P6) 800
Jeffersontown (L4) 3,431
Jeffersonville (O5) 479
Jellico Creek (N7) 200
Jenkins (R6) 3,202
Jeriel (R4) 150
Jett (M4) 200
Jonesville (M3) 250
Junction City (M5) 1,047
Kayjay (O7) 310
Keaton (P5) 300
Keavy (N6) 500
Keene (M5) 350
Keeneland‡ (K4) 590
Kehoe (P4) 175
Kenton (N3) 250
Kenton Vale (S2) 168
Kenvir (P7) 1,000
Kevil (D6) 231
King (O7) 215
Kings Mountain (M6) 286
Kingsley‡ (K4) 508
Kingswood (J5) 300
Kirk (H5) 225
Kirkmansville (G6) 150
Kirksey (E7) 215
Kirksville (N5) 1,500
Kite (R6) 250
Knifley (L6) 225
Knob Lick (K6) 157
Knottsville (H5) 460
Kona (R6) 450
Kosmosdale (J4) 300
Kuttawa (E6) 635
La Center (C6) 882
La Fayette (F7) 196
La Grange◉ (L4) 2,168
Lackey (R6) 221
Lake (O6) 250
Lake Louisvilla‡ (K4) 428
Lakeside Park (R3) 2,214
Lamasco (F7) 150
Lancaster◉ (M5) 3,021
Latonia Lakes‡ (N3) 585
Laurel Creek (O6) 800
Lawrenceburg◉ (M4) 2,523
Lawton (P4) 250
Leatherwood (P6) 1,283
Lebanon◉ (L5) 4,813
Lebanon Junction (K5) 1,527
Leeco (O5) 500
Leitchfield◉ (J6) 2,982
Lejunior (P7) 1,200
Levee (O5) 950
Lewisburg (G6) 512
Lewisport (H5) 610
Lexington◉ (N4) 62,810
Lexington (urb. area) 111,940
Liberty◉ (M6) 1,578
Lida (O6) 200
Liggett (P7) 500
Ligon (R6) 600
Lily (N6) 375
Lincolnshire‡ (K4) 223
Lisman (F6) 125
Littcarr (R6) 500
Livermore (G5) 1,506
Logansport (H6) 175
Lola (E6) 150
London◉ (N6) 4,035
Lone Oak (D6) 2,104
Lookout (S6) 1,400
Lookout Heights (S2) 776
Loretto (L5) 750
Lost Creek (P6) 250
Lothair (P6) 1,082
Louellen (P7) 400
Louisa◉ (R4) 2,071
Louisville◉ (K4) 390,639
Louisville (urb. area) 606,659
Lovelaceville (D7) 275
Lovely (S5) 500
Lowes (D7) 175
Lowmansville (R5) 500
Loyall (P7) 1,260
Lucas (K7) 150
Ludlow (S2) 6,233
Lynch (R7) 3,810
Lynn Grove (E7) 125
Lynnview (K4) 1,711
Lyons (K5) 150
Maceo (H5) 450
Mackville (L5) 229
Madisonville◉ (F6) 13,110
Majestic (S5) 400
Malone (P5) 235
Manchester◉ (O6) 1,868
Mannington (G6) 300
Marion◉ (E6) 2,468
Marrowbone (K7) 350
Marshes Siding (M7) 500
Martin (R5) 992
Martwick (H6) 220
Mary (O5) 300
Mary Hill Estates ‡(K4) 256
Mayfield◉ (D7) 10,762
Mays Lick (O3) 375
Maysville◉ (O3) 8,484
McAndrews (S5) 850
McCarr (S5) 800
McDaniels (J5) 175
McDowell (R6) 600
McHenry (H6) 446
McKee◉ (O6) 234
McKinney (M6) 500
McRoberts (R6) 1,363
Meadowview Est.‡ (K4) 131
Meally (R5) 500
Means (O5) 400
Melber (D7) 225
Melbourne (T3) 500
Mentor (N3) 300
Merrimac (L6) 175
Middleburg (M6) 200
Middlesboro (O7) 12,607
Middletown (L4) 2,764
Midway (M4) 1,044
Milburn (D7) 210
Millard (S6) 150
Millersburg (N4) 913
Mills (O7) 500
Millstone (R6) 800
Milltown (L6) 265
Millwood (J6) 225
Milton (L3) 365
Minerva (O3) 500
Minor Lane Hts.‡ (K4) 152
Mitchellsburg (M5) 300
Mockingbird Vall.‡(K4) 169
Monterey (M4) 211
Monticello◉ (M7) 2,940
Moores Creek (O6) 400
Moorland‡ (K4) 599
Moorman (G6) 276
Morehead◉ (P4) 4,170
Moreland (M6) 300
Morganfield◉ (F5) 3,741
Morgantown◉ (H6) 1,318
Morning View (N3) 198
Morris Fork (O6) 250
Mortons Gap (F6) 1,308
Mount Eden (L4) 300
Mount Olivet◉ (N3) 386
Mount Sherman (K6) 165
Mount Sterling◉ (N4) 5,370
Mount Vernon◉ (N6) 1,177
Mt. Washington (K4) 1,173
Mountain Ash (N7) 450
Mouthcard (S6) 500
Muldraugh (J5) 1,743
Munfordville◉ (J6) 1,157
Murray◉ (E7) 9,303
Myers (O4) 85
Nancy (M6) 500
Naomi (M6) 90
Napier (P7) 150
Nebo (F6) 338
Ned (P6) 210
Nelse (R6) 250
Nelson (G6) 165
Neon (R6) 766
Nepton (O4) 225
Nevisdale (N7) 250
New Castle◉ (L4) 699
New Concord (E7) 300
New Haven (K5) 1,009
New Hope (L5) 210
New Liberty (M3) 300
Newfoundland (P4) 414
Newman (G5) 300
Newport◉ (S2) 30,070
Nicholasville◉ (N5) 4,275
Noctor (P5) 200
Norbourne Est.‡ (K4) 507
Norfleet (M6) 150
North Middletown (N4) 291
N. Pleasureville (L4) 313
Nortonville (G6) 755
Oak Grove (G7) 975
Oakland (J6) 148
Oakton (C7) 225
Offutt (R5) 135
Ogle (O6) 291
Oil Springs (P5) 500
Okolona (K4) 3,738
Old Landing (O5) 250
Oldtown (R4) 150
Olin (N6) 156
Olive Hill (P4) 1,398
Olmstead (H7) 750
Olympia (O4) 275
Oneida (O6) 750
Onton (G5) 150
Orville (M4) 150
Owensboro◉ (G5) 42,471
Owenton◉ (M3) 1,376
Owingsville◉ (O4) 1,040
Paducah◉ (D6) 34,479
Paint Lick (N5) 350
Paintsville◉ (R5) 4,025
Paris◉ (N4) 7,791
Park City (J6) 497
Park Hills (S2) 4,076
Parkside‡ (K4) 333
Parksville (M5) 500
Parkway Village‡ (K4) 949
Payneville (J5) 200
Peabody (O6) 250
Pembroke (G7) 517
Penrod (G6) 150
Peoples (N6) 180
Perryville (M5) 715
Petersburg (M2) 390
Petersville (P4) 160
Petroleum (J7) 125
Pewee Valley (L4) 881
Phelps (S6) 725
Phil (M6) 125
Philpot (H5) 365
Pierce (K6) 725
Pigeonroost (O6) 400
Pikeville◉ (S6) 4,754
Pilgrim (S5) 150
Pilot (O5) 150
Pine Hill (N6) 550
Pine Knot (M7) 1,100
Pineville◉ (O7) 3,181
Pittsburg (N6) 850
Place (N7) 175
Plantation ‡(K4) 939
Pleasant View (N7) 400
Pleasure Ridge Park (J4) 10,612
Pleasureville (L4) 466
Plymouth Village‡ (K4) 311
Poole (F5) 325
Poplarville (N6) 165
Port Royal (L3) 170
Premium (R6) 400
Preston (O4) 250
Prestonsburg◉ (R5) 3,133
Prestonville (L3) 211
Princeton◉ (F6) 5,618
Prospect (K4) 200
Providence (F6) 3,771
Pryorsburg (D7) 250
Pryse (O5) 150
Pulaski (M6) 200
Quicksand (P5) 340
Quincy (P3) 200
Quinton (M7) 125
Rabbithash (M3) 200
Raceland (R3) 1,115
Radcliff (K5) 3,384
Ravenna (O5) 921
Raywick (L5) 175
Reed (G5) 120
Relief (P5) 350
Revelo (N7) 600
Richardsville (J6) 210
Richlawn‡ (K4) 649
Richmond◉ (N5) 12,168
Riley (L5) 200
Rineyville (K5) 450
Ritner (M7) 200
Robards (F5) 300
Rochester (H6) 314
Rockfield (J7) 165
Rockholds (N7) 275
Rockport (H6) 396
Rolling Fields‡ (K4) 816
Rose Hill (M5) 325
Rosine (H6) 400
Rowland (M5) 200
Rowletts (K6) 300
Royalton (R5) 350
Royville‡ (L6) 295
Rumsey (G5) 252
Rush (R4) 225
Russell (R3) 1,458
Russell Springs (L6) 1,125
Russellville◉ (H7) 5,861
Sacramento (G6) 429
Sadieville (M4) 276
Saint Charles (F6) 421
Saint Francis (L5) 500
Saint Mary (L5) 600
Saint Matthews (K4) 8,738
Saint Regis Pk.‡ (K4) 1,179
Saldee (P6) 400
Salem (E6) 650
Salt Lick (O4) 370
Salvisa (M5) 450
Salyersville◉ (P5) 1,173
Samuels (L5) 275

Sand Springs (N6) 200
Sanders (M3) 203
Sandgap (N6) 800
Sandy Hook◉ (P4) 195
Sardis (O3) 190
Savoy (N7) 600
Sawyer (N7) 400
Saxton (N7) 525
Scalf (O7) 200
Science Hill (M6) 463
Scottsville◉ (J7) 3,324
Scranton (O5) 250
Sebree (F5) 1,139
Seco (R6) 531
Sedalia (D7) 258
Seneca Gardens‡ (K4).. 928
Sewell (P5) 200
Sextons Creek (O6) 1,030
Sharon Grove (G7) 235
Sharpsburg (O4) 311
Shelbiana (R6) 500
Shelbyville◉ (L4) 4,525
Shepherdsville◉ (K4)...1,525
Sherman (M3) 150
Shively (K4) 15,155
Sibert (O6) 650
Siloam (R3) 500
Silver Grove (T3).........1,207
Silverhill (P5) 200
Simpson (P5) 150
Simpsonville (L4) 220
Sizerock (P6) 290
Skaggs (P4) 171
Slade (O5) 200
Slaughters (F6) 284
Slemp (P6) 750
Slickford (M7) 450
Sloans Valley (N7) 225
Smilax (P6) 630
Smith Mills (F5) 350
Smith Town (M7) 500
Smithfield (L4) 160
Smithland◉ (E6) 541
Smiths Grove (J6) 613
Soft Shell (P6) 252
Soldier (P4) 150
Somerset◉ (M6) 7,112
Sonora (K5) 268
South Carrollton (G6)... 234
South Ft. Mitchell (S3)4,086
South Irvine (N5) 300
South Park View (K4).. 317
South Pleasureville
(Pleasureville) (L4).. 466
South Portsmouth (P3) 950
South Shore (R3) 658
South Union (H7) 150
Southgate (S2) 2,070
Sparta (M3) 235
Spottsville (G5) 500
South Williamson (S5)..1,097
Spring Lick (H6) 150
Springfield◉ (L5) 2,382
Springlee‡ (K4) 987
Stab (N6) 300
Staffordsville (R5) 700
Stamping Ground (M4) 353
Stanford◉ (M5) 2,019
Stanley (G5) 431
Stanton◉ (O5) 753
State Line (C7) 200
Station Camp (N5) 150
Stearns (N7) 900
Stephensburg (J5) 203
Stephensport (H5) 150
Stillwater (O5) 800
Stone (S5) 750
Strathmoor Gdns.‡ (K4) 329
Strathmoor Man.‡ (K4) 434
Strathmoor Vill.‡ (K4) 498
Strunk (N7) 750
Sturgis (F5) 2,209
Sudith (O4) 250
Sullivan (E6) 260
Sulphur (L4) 350
Sulphur Well (K6) 350
Summer Shade (K7).... 350
Summersville (K6) 700
Sunny Acres (S3) 844
Susie (M7) 400
Switzer (M4) 150
Tateville (M7) 700
Taylor Mill‡ (M3) 710
Taylorsville◉ (L4) 937
Texas (L5) 135
Thealka (R5) 500
Tiline (E6) 200
Tinsley (O7) 500
Tiptop (P5) 200
Tollesboro (O3) 480
Tolu (E6) 200
Tompkinsville◉ (K7)....2,091
Tongs (R3) 200
Travellers Rest (O6) 268
Trenton (G7) 542

Trimble (M6) 150
Turkey (P6) 150
Turners Station (L3).. 125
Twila (P7) 550
Tyner (O6) 520
Tyrone (M4) 215
Ulysses (R5) 710
Union (M3) 340
Uniontown (F5) 1,255
Upper Tygart (P4) 150
Upton (K6) 547
Urban (O6) 125
Utica (G5) 300
Vada (O5) 300
Valley Station (K4).....10,553
Valley View (N5) 200
Van Lear (R5) 921
Vanceburg◉ (P3) 1,881
Verona (M3) 300
Versailles◉ (M4) 4,060
Vicco (P6) 995
Victory (N6) 160
Vine Grove (K5) 2,435
Virgie (R6) 1,500
Visalia (N3) 253
Waco (N5) 500
Waddy (L4) 300
Walker (O7) 400
Wallins Creek (O7) 468
Wallonia (F7) 150
Waltersville (N5) 250
Walton (M3) 1,530
Warfield (S5) 295
Warsaw◉ (M3) 981
Washington (O3) 500
Water Valley (D7) 267
Watergap (R5) 300
Waverly (F5) 331
Wayland (R6) 1,340
Waynesburg (M6)......... 500
Webbs Cross Rds. (L6) 750
Webbville (R4) 500
Webster (J5) 159
Wellington‡ (K4) 804
Wellington (O5) 300
West Buechel‡ (K4) 504
West Irvine (N5) 200
West Liberty◉ (P5) 1,165
West Louisville (G5) 250
West Paducah (D6) 135
West Point (J4) 1,957
West Somerset (M6).... 850
West Van Lear (R5) 750
Westbend (N5) 250
Westport (K4) 250
Westwood (R4) 7,500
Wheatcroft (F5) 317
Wheelwright (R6) 1,518
Whick (P6) 155
White Plains (G6) 359
Whitehouse (R5) 350
Whitesburg◉ (R6) 1,774
Whitesville (H5) 713
Whitley City◉ (N7) 1,034
Wickliffe◉ (C7) 917
Wild Cat (O6) 170
Wilders (S3) 239
Willard (R4) 164
Williamsburg◉ (N7) 3,478
Williamsport (R5) 300
Williamstown◉ (M3)....1,611
Willisburg (L5) 265
Wilmore (M5) 2,773
Winchester◉ (N4) 10,187
Windy Hills‡ (K4) 1,371
Wingo (D7) 340
Winston (N5) 191
Winston Park (S3) 744
Wolf Creek (J4) 200
Wolverine (P5) 156
Woodbine (N7) 500
Woodburn (J7) 291
Woodbury (H6) 122
Woodland Hills ‡(L4)... 769
Woodlawn (D6) 1,688
Woodlawn (S2) 387
Woodlawn Park‡ (K4)...1,137
Woodsbend (P5) 125
Woollum (O6) 200
Wooton (P6) 1,480
Worthington (R3) 1,000
Worthville (L3) 247
Wrigley (P4) 325
Wurtland (R3) 950
Yancey (P7) 550
Yeaddiss (P6) 300
Yosemite (M6) 250
Youngs Creek (N7) 150
Zebulon (R5) 350
Zula (M7) 1,383

OTHER FEATURES

Abraham Lincoln Nat'l
Hist. Park ....K 5
Barkley (lake) ....F 7
Barren (res.) ....J 7
Barren (river) ....H 6
Beech Fork (river).........L 5
Big Sandy (river) ....R 4
Black (mt.) ....R 7
Buckhorn (res.) ....O 6
Chaplin (river) ....L 5
Clarks, E. Fork (river)...E 7
Cumberland (lake) ....M 7
Cumberland (mt.) ....P 7
Cumberland (river) ....K 8
Cumberland Gap Nat'l
Hist. Park ....P 7
Dale Hollow (res.) ....L 7
Dewey (lake) ....R 5
Dix (river) ....M 5
Herrington (lake) ....M 5
Kentucky (lake) ....E 8
Kentucky (river) ....M 3
Licking (river) ....N 3
Little (river) ....F 7
Mammoth Cave Nat'l
Park ....J 6
Mud (river) ....H 7
Nolin (river) ....J 6
Ohio (river) ....F 5
Paint Lick (river) ....M 5
Pond (river) ....G 6
Red (river) ....O 5
Red (river) ....G 7
Rockcastle (river) ....N 6
Rolling Fork (river) ......L 5
Rough (river) ....H 5
Salt (river) ....K 5
Tennessee (river) ....D 6
Tradewater (river) ....F 6
Tug Fork (river) ....S 5

KENTUCKY and TENNESSEE

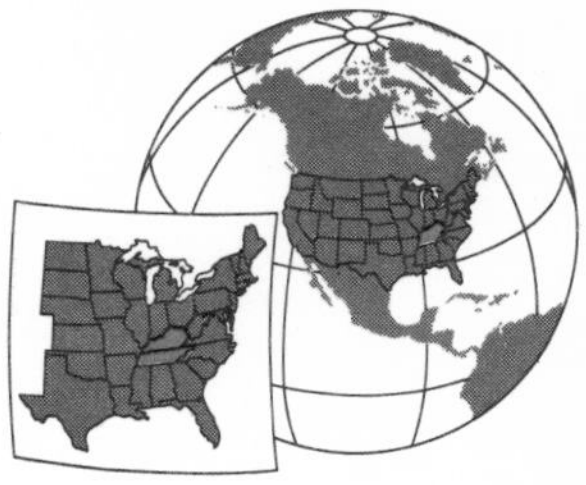

	KENTUCKY	TENNESSEE
AREA	40,395 sq. mi.	42,244 sq. mi.
POPULATION	3,179,000	3,845,000
CAPITAL	Frankfort	Nashville
LARGEST CITY	Louisville 390,639	Memphis 497,524
HIGHEST POINT	Black Mtn. 4,145 ft.	Clingmans Dome 6,642 ft.
SETTLED IN	1774	1757
ADMITTED TO UNION	June 1, 1792	June 1, 1796
POPULAR NAME	Blue Grass State	Volunteer State
STATE FLOWER	Goldenrod	Iris
STATE BIRD	Cardinal	Mockingbird

TENNESSEE

COUNTIES

Anderson (N8) 60,032
Bedford (J9) 23,150
Benton (E8) 10,662
Bledsoe (L9) 7,811
Blount (O9) 57,525
Bradley (M10) 38,324
Campbell (N8) 27,936
Cannon (J9) 8,537
Carroll (E9) 23,476
Carter (S8) 41,578
Cheatham (G8) 9,428
Chester (D10) 9,569
Claiborne (O8) 19,067
Clay (K7) 7,289
Cocke (P9) 23,390
Coffee (J9) 28,603
Crockett (C9) 14,594
Cumberland (L9) 19,135
Davidson (H8) 399,743
De Kalb (K9) 10,774
Decatur (E9) 8,324
Dickson (G8) 18,839
Dyer (C8) 29,537
Fayette (C10) 24,577
Fentress (M8) 13,288
Franklin (J10) 25,528
Gibson (D9) 44,699
Giles (G10) 22,410
Grainger (O8) 12,506
Greene (R8) 42,163
Grundy (K10) 11,512
Hamblen (P8) 33,092
Hamilton (L10) 237,905
Hancock (P7) 7,757
Hardeman (C10) 21,517
Hardin (E10) 17,397
Hawkins (P8) 30,468
Haywood (C9) 23,393
Henderson (E9) 16,115
Henry (E8) 22,275
Hickman (G9) 11,862
Houston (F8) 4,794
Humphreys (F8) 11,511
Jackson (K8) 9,233
Jefferson (P8) 21,493
Johnson (T7) 10,765
Knox (O9) 250,523
Lake (B8) 9,572
Lauderdale (B9) 21,844
Lawrence (G10) 28,049
Lewis (F9) 6,269
Lincoln (H10) 23,829
Loudon (N9) 23,757
Macon (J7) 12,197
Madison (D9) 60,655
Marion (K10) 21,036
Marshall (H10) 16,859
Maury (G9) 41,699
McMinn (M10) 33,662
McNairy (D10) 18,085
Meigs (M9) 5,160
Monroe (N10) 23,316
Montgomery (G8) 55,645
Moore (J10) 3,454
Morgan (M8) 14,304
Obion (C8) 26,957
Overton (L8) 14,661
Perry (F9) 5,273
Pickett (M7) 4,431
Polk (N10) 12,160
Putnam (K8) 29,236
Rhea (M9) 15,863
Roane (M9) 39,133
Robertson (H7) 27,335
Rutherford (J9) 52,368
Scott (M8) 15,413
Sequatchie (L10) 5,915
Sevier (O9) 24,251
Shelby (B10) 627,019
Smith (J8) 12,059
Stewart (F7) 7,851
Sullivan (S7) 114,139
Sumner (J8) 36,217
Tipton (B9) 28,564
Trousdale (J8) 4,914
Unicoi (S8) 15,082
Union (O8) 8,498
Van Buren (L9) 3,671
Warren (K9) 23,102
Washington (R8) 64,832
Wayne (F10) 11,908
Weakley (D8) 24,227
White (L9) 15,577
Williamson (H9) 25,267
Wilson (J8) 27,668

CITIES and TOWNS

Abiff (G9) 140
Adams (G7) 517
Adamsville (E10) 1,046
Afton (R8) 150
Alamo◉ (C9) 1,665
Alcoa (N9) 6,395
Alexandria (J8) 599
Algood (K8) 886
Allardt (M8) 800
Allons (L8) 200
Allred (L8) 472
Alpine (L8) 200
Altamont◉ (K10) 552
Anderson (K10) 160
Andersonville (O8) 420
Annadel (M8) 160
Ardmore (H10) 195
Arlington (B10) 620
Armathwaite (M8) 750
Arrington (H9) 500
Arthur (O7) 500
Ashland City◉ (G8) 1,400
Aspen Hill (G10) 225
Athens◉ (M10) 12,103
Atoka (B10) 357
Atwood (D9) 461
Auburntown (J9) 256
Bailey (B10) 207
Baileyton (R8) 206
Bakewell (L10) 300
Banner Hill (R8) 2,132
Banner Springs (M8).... 406
Bartlett (B10) 508
Bath Springs (E10) 725
Baxter (K8) 853
Beacon (E9) 300
Bean Station (P8) 300
Bearden (N9) 1,600
Beechgrove (J9) 200
Beersheba Sprs. (K10).. 577
Belfast (H10) 250
Bell Buckle (J9) 318
Belle Meade (H8) 3,082
Bells (C9) 1,232
Belvidere (J10) 200
Bemis (D9) 3,127
Benton◉ (M10) 638
Berry Hill (H8) 1,551
Bethel Springs (D10).... 533
Bethpage (J7) 315
Big Lick (L9) 363
Big Rock (F7) 275
Big Sandy (E8) 492
Big Spring (M10) 596
Birchwood (M10) 800
Blaine (O8) 900
Blanche (H10) 225
Bloomington Sprs. (K8) 300
Blountville◉ (S7) 975
Bluff City (S8) 948
Bogota (C8) 200
Bolivar◉ (C10) 3,338
Bon Air (L9) 300
Bon Aqua (G9) 800
Boothspoint (B8) 200
Braden (B10) 435
Bradford (D8) 763
Brazil (C9) 340
Briceville (N8) 1,217
Brighton (B10) 652
Bristol (S7) 17,582
Brotherton (L8) 600
Brownsville◉ (C9) 5,424
Bruceton (E8) 1,158
Brunswick (B10) 500
Brush Creek (J8) 450
Buena Vista (E9) 500
Buffalo Valley (K8) 150
Bullsgap (P8)............... 682
Bumpus Mills (F7) 200
Bunker Hill (H10) 150
Burlison (B9) 300
Burns (G8) 386
Burrville (M8) 180
Butler (T8) 450
Bybee (P8) 125
Byrdstown◉ (L7) 613
Cades (D9) 113
Cagle (L10) 400
Cainsville (J9) 150
Calderwood (N9) 245
Calhoun (M10) 706
Camden◉ (E8) 2,774
Campaign (K9) 500
Capleville (B10) 300
Carter (S8) 200
Carthage◉ (K8) 2,021
Caryville (N8) 500
Castalian Springs (J8).. 129
Cedar Hill (H7) 414
Celina◉ (K7) 1,228
Centertown (K9) 169
Centerville◉ (G9) 1,678
Chapel Hill (H9) 630
Chapmansboro (G8) 237
Charleston (M10) 764
Charlotte◉ (G8) 551
Chaska (N7) 150
Chattanooga◉ (K10) 130,009
Chattanooga (urb.
area) 205,143
Chesterfield (E9) 158
Chestnut Mound (K8)... 185
Christiana (J9) 300
Chuckey (R8) 300
Church Hill (R7) 769
Clairfield (O7) 950
Clarkrange (L8) 600
Clarksburg (E9) 300
Clarksville◉ (G7) 22,021
Cleveland◉ (M10) 16,196
Clifton (F10) 708
Clinton◉ (N8) 4,943
Coalmont (K10) 458
Cokercreek (N10) 366
Colesburg (G8) 220
College Grove (H9) 325
Collegedale (M10) 1,800
Collierville (B10) 2,020
Collinwood (F10) 596
Colonial Heights (R8)...2,312
Columbia◉ (G9) 17,624
Como (E8) 140
Conasauga (M10) 350
Concord (N9) 294
Cookeville◉ (L8) 7,805
Copperhill (N10) 631
Cordova (B10) 250
Cornersville (H10) 314
Corryton (O8) 400
Cosby (P9) 600
Cottagegrove (E8) 130
Cottontown (H8) 450
Counce (E10) 2,000
Covington◉ (B9) 5,298
Cowan (K10) 1,979
Crab Orchard (M9) 315
Crestview (G10) 250
Crockett Mills (C9)...... 125
Cross Plains (H7) 350
Crossville◉ (L9) 4,668
Crump (E10) 225
Culleoka (G10) 350
Cumberland City (F8)... 314
Cumberland Furn. (G8) 500
Cumberland Gap (O7)... 291
Cummingsville (L9) 150
Cunningham (G8) 250
Curve (B9) 160
Cypress Inn (F10) 1,000
Daisy (L10) 1,508
Dandridge◉ (O8) 829
Darden (E9) 200
Daus (L10) 300
Dayton◉ (L9) 3,500
De Rossett (L9) 250
Decatur◉ (M9) 681
Decaturville◉ (E9) 571
Decherd (J10) 1,704
Deer Lodge (M8) 300
Delano (M10) 325
Dellrose (H10) 175
Denver (F8) 120
Devonia (N8) 225
Dickson (G8) 5,028
Dixon Springs (J8) 200
Donelson (H8) 17,195
Dover◉ (F8) 736
Dowelltown (K8) 279
Doyle (K9) 484
Dresden◉ (D8) 1,510
Drummonds (A10) 215
Duck River (G9) 150
Ducktown (N10) 741
Duff (N8) 326
Dukedom (D8) 125
Dunlap◉ (L10) 1,026
Dyer (D8) 1,909
Dyersburg◉ (C8) 12,499
Eads (B10) 250
Eagan (O7) 550
Eagle Creek (E9) 100
Eagleville (H9) 363
East Ridge (L11) 19,570
Edenwold (H8) 1,091
Eidson (P7) 150
Elgin (M8) 550
Elizabethton◉ (S8)....10,896
Elk Valley (N7) 780
Elkton (H10) 199
Ellendale (B10) 700
Embreeville Jct. (R8)..1,204
Emory Gap (M9) 500
Englewood (M10) 1,574
Enville (E10) 250
Erin◉ (F8) 1,097
Erwin◉ (S8) 3,210
Estill Springs (J10) 734
Ethridge (G10) 550
Etowah (M10) 3,223
Eva (E8) 250
Evensville (M9) 250
Fairview (G9) 1,017
Fall Branch (R8) 850
Fall River (G10) 150
Farner (N10) 200
Fayetteville◉ (H10).....6,804
Finger (D10) 175
Finley (B8) 700
Five Points (G10) 200
Flag Pond (R8) 300
Flat Creek (H10) 300
Flat Woods (F10) 200
Flintville (J10) 500
Flynns Lick (K8) 300
Forbus (M7) 275
Fordtown (R8) 375
Forest Hill (B10) 574
Forest Hills (H8) 2,101
Fork Mountain (N8) 900
Fort Pillow (B9) 150
Fosterville (J9) 150
Fountain Head (J7) 252
Fowlkes (C9) 200
Franklin◉ (H9) 6,977
Friendship (C9) 399
Friendsville (N9) 606
Fruitland (D9) 150
Fruitvale (C9) 120
Gadsden (D9) 222
Gainesboro◉ (K8) 1,021
Gallatin◉ (H8) 7,901
Gardner (D8) 185
Garland (B9) 168
Gates (C9) 291
Gatlinburg (O9) 1,764
Germantown (B10) 1,104
Gibson (D9) 297
Gladeville (J8) 450
Gleason (D8) 900
Glen Alice (M9) 220
Glenmary (M8) 300
Goin (O8) 300
Goodlettsville (H8) 3,163
Gordonsville (K8) 249
Gorman (F8) 125
Grand Junction (C10) ... 446
Grandview (M9) 700
Granville (K8) 130
Graysville (L10) 838
Green Brier (H8) 1,238
Greenback (N9) 285
Greeneville◉ (R8) 11,759
Greenfield (D8) 1,779
Gruetli (K10) 600
Habersham (N8) 250
Halls (C9) 1,890
Hampshire (G9) 250
Hampton (S8) 1,048
Harriman (M9) 5,931
Harris (C8) 203
Harrison (L10) 300
Hartford (P9) 200
Hartsville◉ (J8) 1,712
Heiskell (O8) 130
Helenwood (M8) 500
Henderson◉ (D10) 2,691
Hendersonville (H8) 995
Henning (B9) 466
Henry (E8) 178
Henryville (G10) 265
Hermitage (H8) 240
Hermitage Springs (K7) 300
Hickman (K8) 213
Hickory Valley (C10)..... 179
Hilham (L8) 164
Hillsboro (K10) 200
Hillside (D8) 200
Hixson (L10) 2,100
Hohenwald◉ (F9) 2,194
Holladay (E9) 160
Hollow Rock (E8) 568
Holston Valley (S7) 450
Holtland (H9) 185
Hopson (S8) 225
Hornbeak (C8) 307
Hornsby (D10) 228
Humboldt (D9) 8,482
Huntingdon◉ (E8) 2,119
Huntland (J10) 500
Huntsville◉ (N8) 500
Hurricane Mills (F9).... 420
Idlewild (D8) 300
Indian Mound (F7) 300
Indian Springs (S7) 950
Inglewood (H8) 26,527
Iron City (F10) 511
Isabella (N10) 300
Isoline (L8) 275
Ivyton (L8) 210
Jacks Creek (D10) 200
Jacksboro◉ (N8) 1,125
Jackson◉ (D9) 34,376
Jamestown◉ (M8) 1,727
Jasper◉ (K10) 1,450
Jefferson City (P8) 4,550
Jellico (N7) 2,210
Joelton (H8) 350
Johnson City (S8) 31,187
Jonesboro◉ (R8) 1,148
Karns (N9) 350
Kenton (C8) 1,095
Kerrville (B10) 300
Kimball ‡(K4) 716
Kimberlin Heights (O9) 400
Kingsport (R7) 26,314
Kingston◉ (N9) 2,010
Kingston Springs (G8).. 380
Knoxville◉ (O9) 111,827
Knoxville (urb.
area) 172,734
Kodak (O9) 500
Kyles Ford (R7) 148
La Follette (N8) 6,204
La Grange (C10) 217
La Vergne (H9) 675
Laager (K10) 500
Lafayette◉ (J7) 1,590
Lake City (N8) 1,914

(continued on following page)

HIGHWAYS

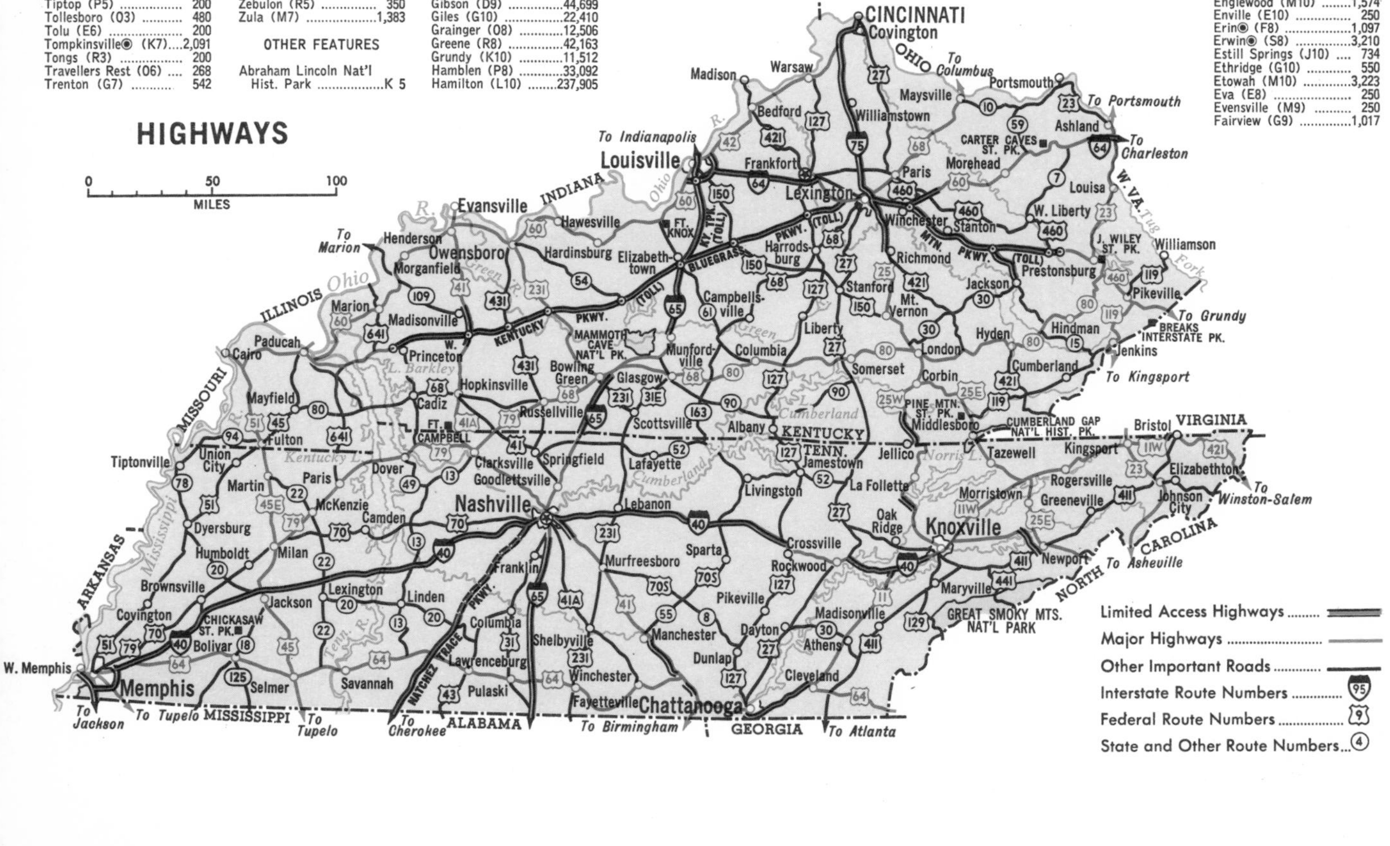
0 50 100
MILES
CINCINNATI
Covington
Louisville
Lexington
Frankfort
Evansville
Owensboro
Paducah
Nashville
Knoxville
Chattanooga
Memphis
W. Memphis
Bristol
Jackson
Limited Access Highways
Major Highways
Other Important Roads
Interstate Route Numbers
Federal Route Numbers
State and Other Route Numbers

TOPOGRAPHY

0   50   100
MILES

Below Sea 100 m. 200 m. 500 m. 1,000 m. 2,000 m. 5,000 m.
Level 328 ft. 656 ft. 1,640 ft. 3,281 ft. 6,562 ft. 16,404 ft.

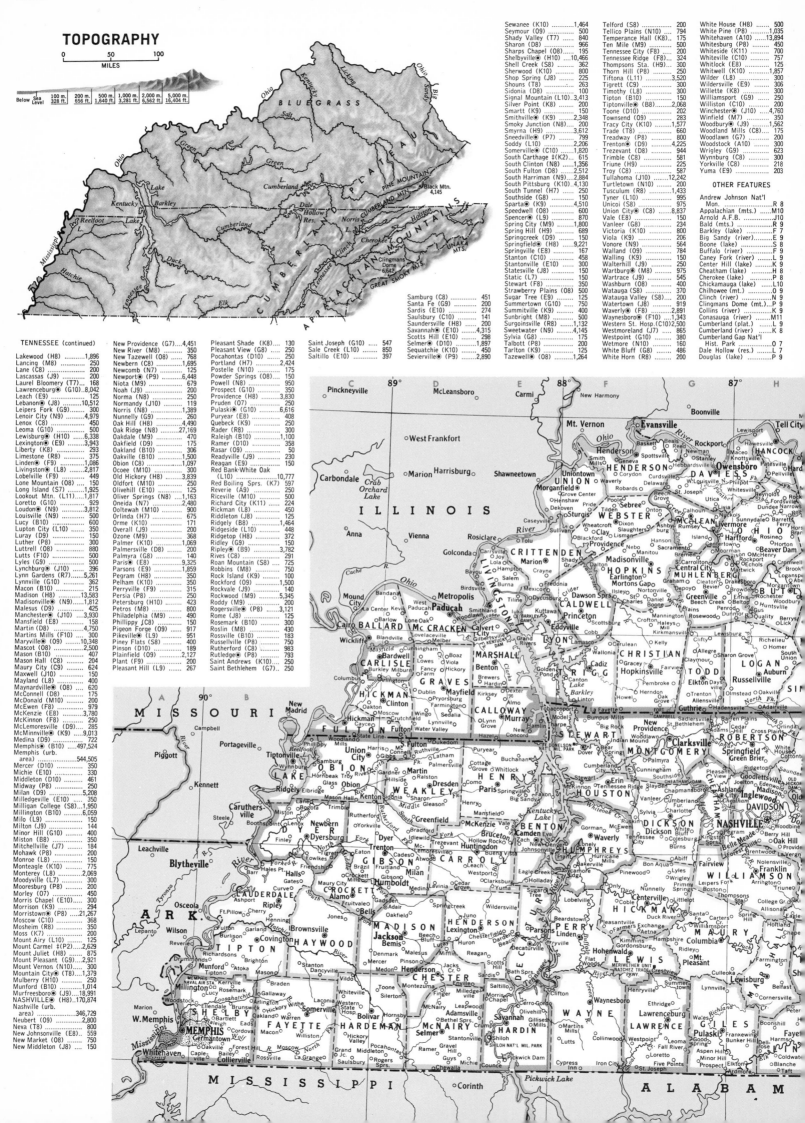

Sewanee (K10) ...1,464	Telford (S8) ...200	White House (H8) ...500
Seymour (09) ...500	Tellico Plains (N10) ...794	White Pine (P8) ...1,035
Shady Valley (T7) ...840	Temperance Hall (K8) ...175	Whitehaven (A10) ...13,894
Sharon (D8) ...966	Ten Mile (M9) ...500	Whitesburg (P8) ...450
Sharps Chapel (08) ...195	Tennessee City (H9) ...200	Whiteside (K11) ...700
Shelbyville (H10) ...10,466	Tennessee Ridge (F8) ...324	Whiteville (C10) ...757
Shell Creek (S8) ...362	Thompsons Sta. (H9) ...300	Whitlock (E8) ...125
Sherwood (K10) ...800	Thorn Hill (P8) ...250	Whitwell (K10) ...1,857
Shop Spring (J8) ...225	Tiftona (L11) ...3,520	Wilder (L8) ...300
Shouns (T8) ...263	Tigrett (D8) ...300	Wildersville (E9) ...300
Sidonia (D8) ...100	Timothy (L8) ...300	Willette (K8) ...300
Signal Mountain (L10).3,413	Tipton (B10) ...150	Williamsport (G9) ...250
Silver Point (K8) ...200	Tiptonville (B8) ...2,068	Williston (C10) ...200
Smartt (K9) ...150	Toone (C10) ...202	Winchester (J10) ...4,760
Smithville (K9) ...2,348	Townsend (09) ...283	Winfield (M7) ...350
Smoky Junction (N8)...200	Tracy City (K10) ...1,577	Woodbury (J9) ...1,562
Smyrna (H9) ...3,612	Trade (T8) ...660	Woodland Mills (C8)...175
Sneedville (P7) ...799	Treadway (P8) ...800	Woodlawn (G7) ...200
Soddy (L10) ...2,206	Trenton (D9) ...4,225	Woodstock (A10) ...300
Somerville (C10) ...1,820	Trezevant (D8) ...944	Wrigley (F9) ...623
South Carthage (K2)...615	Trimble (C8) ...500	Wynnburg (C8) ...300
South Clinton (N8) ...1,356	Triune (H9) ...225	Yorkville (D9) ...300
South Fulton (D8) ...2,512	Troy (C8) ...500	Yuma (E9) ...203
South Harriman (N9)...2,884	Tullahoma (J10) ...12,242	
South Pittsburg (K10).4,130	Turtletown (N10) ...200	**OTHER FEATURES**
South Tunnel (H7) ...250	Tusculum (R8) ...1,433	
Southside (G8) ...150	Tyner (L10) ...995	Andrew Johnson Nat'l Mon. ...R 8
Sparta (K9) ...4,510	Unicoi (S8) ...975	Appalachian (mts.) ...M10
Speedwell (08) ...600	Union City (C8) ...8,837	Arnold A.F.B. ...J10
Spencer (L9) ...870	Vale (G7) ...150	Bald (mts.) ...R 9
Spring City (M9) ...1,800	Vanleer (G8) ...234	Barkley (lake) ...F 7
Spring Hill (H9) ...689	Victoria (K10) ...800	Big Sandy (river) ...E 9
Springcreek (D9) ...150	Viola (K9) ...206	Boone (lake) ...S 8
Springfield (H8) ...9,221	Vonore (N9) ...564	Buffalo (river) ...F 9
Springville (E9) ...167	Walland (N9) ...784	Caney Fork (river) ...L 9
Stanton (C10) ...458	Walling (K9) ...150	Center Hill (lake) ...K 9
Stantonville (E10) ...300	Walterhill (J9) ...250	Cheatham (lake) ...H 8
Statesville (J8) ...150	Wartburg (M8) ...975	Cherokee (lake) ...P 8
Static (L7) ...150	Wartrace (J9) ...545	Chickamauga (lake) ...L10
Stewart (F8) ...350	Washburn (08) ...400	Chilhowee (mt.) ...0 9
Strawberry Plains (08) ...500	Watauga (S8) ...370	Clinch (river) ...N 9
Sugar Tree (E9) ...125	Watauga Valley (S8)...200	Clingmans Dome (mt.). P 9
Summertown (G10) ...750	Watertown (J8) ...919	Collins (river) ...K 9
Summitville (K9) ...400	Waverly (F9) ...2,891	Conasauga (river) ...M11
Sunbright (M8) ...500	Waynesboro (F10) ...1,343	Cumberland (plat.) ...L 9
Surgoinsville (P8) ...1,132	Western St. Hosp. (C10)2,500	Cumberland (river) ...K 8
Sweetwater (N9) ...4,145	Westmoreland (J7) ...865	Cumberland Gap Nat'l Hist. Park ...0 7
Sylvia (H8) ...175	Westport (G10) ...380	Dale Hollow (res.) ...L 7
Talbott (P8) ...300	Wetmore (N10) ...160	Douglas (lake) ...P 9
Tarlton (K9) ...125	White Bluff (G8) ...486	
	White Horn (R8) ...200	

	Samburg (C8) ...451		
	Santa Fe (G9) ...200		
	Sardis (E10) ...274		
	Saulsbury (C10) ...141		
	Saundersville (H8) ...200		
	Savannah (E10) ...4,315		
	Scotts Hill (E10) ...298		
	Selmer (E10) ...1,897		
	Sequatchie (K10) ...450		
	Sevierville (P9) ...2,890		

TENNESSEE (continued)			
Lakewood (H8) ...1,896	New Providence (G7) ...4,451	Pleasant Shade (K8) ...130	Saint Joseph (G10) ...547
Lancing (M8) ...250	New River (M8) ...350	Pleasant View (G8) ...250	Sale Creek (L10) ...850
Lane (C8) ...200	New Tazewell (08) ...768	Pocahontas (D10) ...250	Saltillo (E10) ...397
Lascassas (J9) ...200	Newbern (C8) ...1,695	Portland (H7) ...2,424	Saint Bethlehem (G7)...250
Laurel Bloomery (T7)...168	Newcomb (N7) ...125	Postelle (N10) ...175	
Lawrenceburg (G10)...8,042	Newport (P9) ...6,448	Powder Springs (08)...150	
Leach (E9) ...125	Noah (J9) ...200	Powell (N8) ...950	
Lebanon (J8) ...10,512	Norma (N8) ...250	Prospect (G10) ...350	
Leipers Fork (G9) ...300	Normandy (J10) ...119	Providence (H8) ...3,830	
Lenoir City (N9) ...4,979	Norris (N8) ...1,389	Pruden (07) ...250	
Lenox (C8) ...450	Nunnelly (G9) ...260	Pulaski (G10) ...6,616	
Leoma (G10) ...500	Oak Hill (H8) ...4,490	Puryear (E8) ...408	
Lewisburg (H10) ...6,338	Oak Ridge (N8) ...27,169	Quebeck (K9) ...250	
Lexington (E9) ...3,943	Oakdale (M9) ...470	Rader (R8) ...300	
Liberty (K8) ...293	Oakfield (D9) ...175	Raleigh (B10) ...1,100	
Limestone (R8) ...375	Oakland (B10) ...306	Ramer (D10) ...358	
Linden (F9) ...1,086	Oakville (B10) ...1,500	Rasar (09) ...50	
Livingston (L8) ...2,817	Obion (C8) ...1,097	Readyville (J9) ...230	
Lobelville (F9) ...449	Ocoee (M10) ...300	Reagan (E9) ...150	
Lone Mountain (08) ...150	Old Hickory (H8) ...3,839	Red Bank-White Oak (L10) ...10,777	
Long Island (S7) ...1,925	Oldfort (M10) ...250	Red Boiling Sprs. (K7) ...597	
Lookout Mtn. (L11)...1,817	Olivehill (E9) ...125	Reverie (A9) ...250	
Loretto (G10) ...929	Oliver Springs (N8)...1,163	Riceville (N10) ...500	
Loudon (N9) ...3,812	Oneida (N7) ...2,480	Richard City (K11) ...224	
Louisville (N9) ...500	Ooltewah (M10) ...900	Rickman (L8) ...450	
Lucy (B10) ...600	Orlinda (H7) ...675	Riddleton (J8) ...125	
Lupton City (L10) ...350	Orme (K10) ...171	Ridgely (B8) ...1,464	
Luray (D9) ...150	Overall (J9) ...200	Ridgeside (L10) ...448	
Luther (P8) ...300	Ozone (M9) ...368	Ridgetop (H8) ...372	
Luttrell (08) ...880	Palmer (K10) ...1,069	Ridley (G9) ...150	
Lutts (F10) ...500	Palmersville (D8) ...200	Ripley (B9) ...3,782	
Lyles (G9) ...500	Palmyra (G8) ...140	Rives (D8) ...291	
Lynchburg (J10) ...396	Paris (E8) ...9,325	Roan Mountain (S8) ...725	
Lynn Gardens (R7)...5,261	Parsons (E9) ...1,859	Robbins (M8) ...750	
Lynnville (G10) ...362	Pegram (H8) ...350	Rock Island (K9) ...100	
Macon (B10) ...215	Pelham (K10) ...350	Rockford (09) ...1,500	
Madison (H8) ...13,583	Perryville (F9) ...315	Rockvale (J9) ...140	
Madisonville (N9)...1,812	Persia (P8) ...250	Rockwood (M9) ...5,345	
Malesus (D9) ...425	Petersburg (H10) ...423	Roddy (M9) ...200	
Manchester (J10) ...3,930	Petros (M8) ...800	Rogersville (P8) ...3,121	
Mansfield (H8) ...158	Philadelphia (M9) ...490	Rome (J8) ...125	
Martin (D8) ...4,750	Phillippy (C8) ...150	Rosemark (B10) ...300	
Martins Mills (F10) ...300	Pigeon Forge (09) ...917	Rossin (N8) ...430	
Maryville (09) ...10,348	Pikeville (L9) ...951	Rossville (B10) ...183	
Mascot (08) ...2,500	Piney Flats (S8) ...400	Russellville (P8) ...750	
Mason (B10) ...407	Pinson (D10) ...189	Rutherford (C8) ...983	
Mason Hall (C8) ...204	Plainfield (09) ...2,127	Rutledge (P8) ...793	
Maury City (C9) ...624	Plant (F9) ...200	Saint Andrews (K10)...250	
Maxwell (J10) ...150	Pleasant Hill (L9) ...267		
Mayland (L8) ...400			
Maynardville (08) ...620			
McConnell (D8) ...175			
McDonald (M10) ...200			
McEwen (H8) ...879			
McKenzie (E8) ...3,780			
McKinnon (F8) ...250			
McLemoresville (D9)...285			
McMinnville (K9) ...9,013			
Medina (D9) ...722			
Memphis (B10) ...497,524			
Memphis (urb. area)...544,505			
Mercer (D10) ...350			
Michie (E10) ...330			
Middleton (D10) ...461			
Midway (P8) ...250			
Milan (D9) ...5,208			
Milledgeville (E10) ...350			
Milligan College (S8)...1,950			
Millington (B10) ...6,059			
Milo (D9) ...150			
Milton (J9) ...144			
Minor Hill (G10) ...400			
Miston (B8) ...350			
Mitchellville (J7) ...184			
Mohawk (P8) ...200			
Monroe (L8) ...150			
Monteagle (K10) ...775			
Monterey (L8) ...2,069			
Moodyville (L7) ...200			
Mooresburg (P8) ...200			
Morley (K9) ...200			
Morris Chapel (E10) ...300			
Morrison (K9) ...294			
Morristown (P8) ...21,267			
Moscow (C10) ...368			
Mosheim (R8) ...350			
Moss (K7) ...200			
Mount Airy (L10) ...125			
Mount Carmel ‡(P2)...2,629			
Mount Juliet (H8) ...875			
Mount Pleasant (G9)...2,921			
Mount Vernon (N10) ...300			
Mountain City (T8)...1,379			
Mulberry (H10) ...200			
Munford (B10) ...1,014			
Murfreesboro (J9)...18,991			
NASHVILLE (H8)...170,874			
Nashville (urb. area)...346,729			
Neubert (09) ...2,800			
Neva (T8) ...800			
New Johnsonville (E8)...559			
New Market (08) ...750			
New Middleton (J8) ...150			

Kentucky and Tennessee
(continued)

See page 193 for map of Tennessee Valley

Louisiana

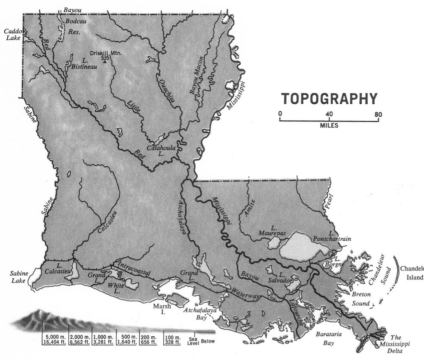

TOPOGRAPHY

0   40   80

MILES

5,000 m. 2,000 m. 1,000 m. 500 m. 200 m. 100 m. Sea
16,404 ft. 6,562 ft. 3,281 ft. 1,640 ft. 656 ft. 328 ft. Level Below

(continued on following page)

LOUISIANA

AREA	48,523
POPULATION	3,534,000
CAPITAL	Baton Rouge
LARGEST CITY	New Orleans 627,525
HIGHEST POINT	Driskill Mtn. 535 ft.
SETTLED IN	1699
ADMITTED TO UNION	April 30, 1812
POPULAR NAME	Pelican State
STATE FLOWER	Magnolia
STATE BIRD	Eastern Brown Pelican

Louisiana
(continued)

AGRICULTURE, INDUSTRY and RESOURCES

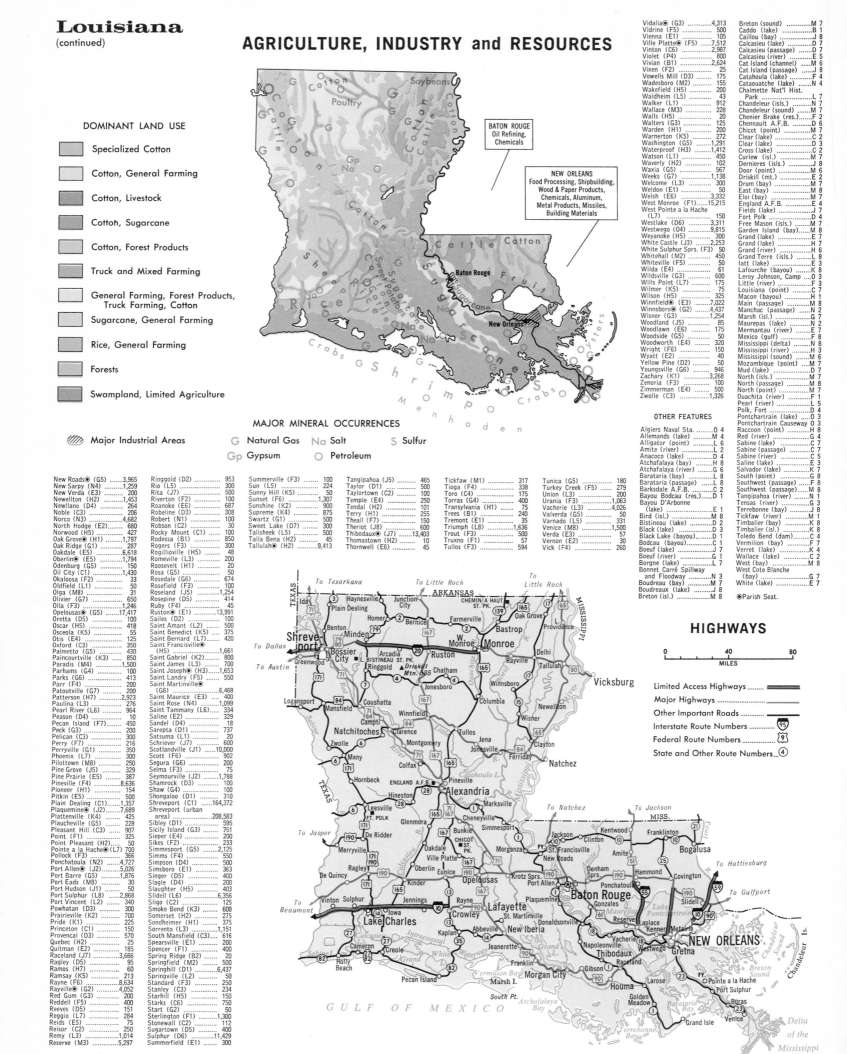

DOMINANT LAND USE

- Specialized Cotton
- Cotton, General Farming
- Cotton, Livestock
- Cotton, Sugarcane
- Cotton, Forest Products
- Truck and Mixed Farming
- General Farming, Forest Products, Truck Farming, Cotton
- Sugarcane, General Farming
- Rice, General Farming
- Forests
- Swampland, Limited Agriculture

Major Industrial Areas

BATON ROUGE
Oil Refining, Chemicals

NEW ORLEANS
Food Processing, Shipbuilding, Wood & Paper Products, Chemicals, Aluminum, Metal Products, Missiles, Building Materials

MAJOR MINERAL OCCURRENCES

- G Natural Gas
- Na Salt
- S Sulfur
- Gp Gypsum
- O Petroleum

HIGHWAYS

0 — 40 — 80
MILES

- Limited Access Highways
- Major Highways
- Other Important Roads
- Interstate Route Numbers
- Federal Route Numbers
- State and Other Route Numbers

Place	Pop.
New Roads◉ (G5)	3,965
New Sarpy (N4)	1,259
New Verda (E3)	200
Newellton (H2)	1,453
Newllano (D4)	264
Noble (C3)	206
Norco (N3)	4,682
North Hodge (E2)	680
Norwood (H5)	427
Oak Grove◉ (H1)	1,797
Oak Ridge (G1)	287
Oakdale (E5)	6,618
Oberlin◉ (E5)	1,794
Odenburg (G5)	150
Oil City (C1)	1,430
Okalosa (F2)	33
Oldfield (L1)	50
Olga (M8)	31
Olivier (G7)	650
Olla (F3)	1,246
Opelousas◉ (G5)	17,417
Oretta (D5)	100
Oscar (H5)	418
Osceola (K5)	55
Otis (E4)	125
Oxford (C3)	350
Palmetto (G5)	430
Paincourtville (K3)	850
Paradis (M4)	1,500
Parhams (G4)	100
Parks (G6)	413
Parr (F4)	200
Patoutville (G7)	200
Patterson (H7)	2,923
Paulina (L3)	276
Pearl River (L6)	964
Peason (D4)	10
Pecan Island (F7)	450
Peck (G3)	200
Pelican (C3)	300
Perry (F7)	216
Perryville (G1)	350
Phoenix (L7)	300
Pilottown (M8)	250
Pine Grove (J5)	329
Pine Prairie (F5)	387
Pineville (F4)	8,636
Pioneer (H1)	154
Pitkin (E5)	500
Plain Dealing (C1)	1,357
Plaquemine◉ (J2)	7,689
Plattenville (K4)	425
Plauchville (G5)	228
Pleasant Hill (C3)	907
Point (F1)	325
Point Pleasant (H2)	50
Pointe a la Hache◉ (L7)	700
Pollock (F3)	366
Ponchatoula (N2)	4,727
Port Allen◉ (J2)	5,026
Port Barre (G6)	1,876
Port Eads (M8)	30
Port Hudson (L1)	50
Port Sulphur (L8)	2,868
Port Vincent (L2)	340
Powhatan (D3)	300
Prairieville (K2)	700
Pride (K1)	225
Princeton (C1)	150
Provencal (D3)	570
Quebec (H2)	25
Quitman (F2)	185
Raceland (J7)	3,666
Ragley (D5)	95
Ramos (H7)	60
Ramsay (K5)	213
Rayne (F6)	8,634
Rayville◉ (G2)	4,052
Red Gum (G3)	200
Reddell (F5)	400
Reeves (D5)	151
Reggio (L7)	284
Reids (E5)	75
Reisor (C2)	250
Remy (L3)	1,014
Reserve (M3)	5,297

Place	Pop.
Ringgold (D2)	953
Rio (L5)	300
Rita (J7)	500
Riverton (F2)	100
Roanoke (E6)	687
Robeline (D3)	308
Robert (N1)	100
Robson (C3)	30
Rocky Mount (C1)	100
Rodessa (B1)	850
Rogers (F3)	300
Rogillioville (H5)	48
Romeville (L3)	200
Roosevelt (H1)	20
Rosa (L5)	50
Rosedale (G6)	674
Rosefield (F3)	100
Roseland (J5)	1,254
Rosepine (D5)	414
Ruby (F4)	45
Ruston◉ (E1)	13,991
Sailes (D2)	100
Saint Amant (L2)	500
Saint Benedict (K5)	375
Saint Bernard (L7)	420
Saint Francisville◉ (H5)	1,661
Saint Gabriel (K2)	800
Saint James (L3)	700
Saint Joseph◉ (H3)	1,653
Saint Landry (F5)	550
Saint Martinville◉ (G6)	6,468
Saint Maurice (E3)	400
Saint Rose (N4)	1,099
Saint Tammany (L6)	334
Saline (E2)	329
Sandel (D4)	18
Sarepta (D1)	737
Satsuma (L1)	20
Schriever (J7)	600
Scotlandville (J1)	10,000
Scott (F6)	902
Segura (G6)	200
Selma (F3)	75
Seymourville (J2)	1,788
Shamrock (D3)	100
Shaw (G4)	100
Shongaloo (D1)	310
Shreveport◉ (C1)	164,372
Shreveport (urban area)	208,583
Sibley (D1)	595
Sicily Island (G3)	761
Sieper (E4)	200
Sikes (F2)	233
Simmesport (G5)	2,125
Simms (F4)	550
Simpson (D4)	500
Simsboro (E1)	363
Singer (D5)	400
Slagle (D4)	200
Slaughter (H5)	403
Slidell (L6)	6,356
Sligo (C2)	125
Smoke Bend (K3)	600
Somerset (H2)	275
Sondheimer (H1)	375
Sorrento (L3)	1,151
South Mansfield (C3)	616
Spearsville (E1)	200
Spencer (F1)	400
Spring Ridge (B2)	20
Springfield (M2)	500
Springhill (D1)	6,437
Springville (L2)	50
Standard (F3)	250
Stanley (C3)	234
Starhill (H5)	150
Starks (C6)	750
Start (G2)	200
Sterlington (F1)	1,300
Stonewall (C2)	112
Sugartown (D5)	400
Sulphur (D6)	11,429
Summerfield (E1)	300

Place	Pop.
Summerville (F3)	100
Sun (L5)	224
Sunny Hill (K5)	50
Sunset (F6)	1,307
Sunshine (K2)	900
Supreme (K4)	875
Swartz (G1)	500
Sweet Lake (D7)	300
Talisheek (L5)	500
Tala Bena (H2)	45
Tallulah◉ (H2)	9,413

Place	Pop.
Tangipahoa (J5)	465
Taylor (D1)	100
Taylortown (C2)	100
Temple (E4)	250
Tendal (H2)	101
Terry (H1)	150
Theall (F7)	150
Theriot (J8)	600
Thibodaux◉ (J7)	13,403
Thomastown (H2)	10
Thornwell (E6)	45

Place	Pop.
Tickfaw (M1)	317
Tioga (F4)	338
Toro (C4)	175
Torras (G4)	450
Transylvania (H1)	75
Trees (B1)	240
Tremont (E2)	35
Triumph (L8)	1,636
Trout (F3)	500
Truxno (F1)	57
Tullos (F3)	594

Place	Pop.
Tunica (G5)	180
Turkey Creek (F5)	279
Union (D3)	200
Urania (F3)	1,063
Vacherie (L3)	4,026
Valverda (G5)	50
Varnado (L5)	331
Venice (M8)	1,500
Verda (E3)	57
Vernon (E2)	30
Vick (F4)	260

Place	Pop.
Vidalia◉ (G3)	4,313
Vidrine (F5)	500
Vienna (E1)	105
Ville Platte◉ (F5)	7,512
Vinton (C6)	2,987
Violet (P4)	800
Vivian (B1)	2,624
Vixen (F2)	25
Vowells Mill (D3)	175
Wadesboro (M2)	155
Wakefield (H5)	200
Waldheim (L5)	43
Walker (L1)	912
Wallace (M3)	228
Walls (H5)	20
Walters (G3)	125
Warden (H1)	200
Warnerton (K5)	272
Washington (G5)	1,291
Waterproof (H3)	1,412
Watson (L1)	450
Waverly (H2)	102
Waxia (G5)	567
Weeks (G7)	1,138
Welcome (L3)	300
Weldon (E1)	50
Welsh (E6)	3,332
West Monroe (F1)	15,215
West Pointe a la Hache (L7)	150
Westlake (D6)	3,311
Westwego (O4)	9,815
Weyanoke (H5)	300
White Castle (J3)	2,253
White Sulphur Sprs. (F3)	50
Whitehall (M2)	450
Whiteville (F5)	50
Wilda (G3)	61
Wildsville (G3)	600
Wills Point (L7)	175
Wilmer (K5)	75
Wilson (H5)	325
Winnfield◉ (E3)	7,022
Winnsboro◉ (G2)	4,437
Wisner (G3)	1,254
Woodland (J5)	85
Woodlawn (E6)	175
Woodside (G5)	50
Woodworth (E4)	320
Wright (F6)	150
Wyatt (E2)	40
Yellow Pine (D2)	50
Youngsville (G6)	946
Zachary (K1)	3,268
Zenoria (F3)	100
Zimmerman (E4)	500
Zwolle (C3)	1,326

OTHER FEATURES

Algiers Naval Sta.	O 4
Allemands (lake)	M 4
Alligator (point)	L 6
Amite (river)	L 2
Anacoco (lake)	D 4
Atchafalaya (bay)	H 8
Atchafalaya (river)	G 6
Barataria (bay)	L 8
Barataria (passage)	L 8
Barksdale A.F.B.	C 2
Bayou Bodcau (res.)	D 1
Bayou D'Arbonne (lake)	E 1
Bird (isl.)	M 8
Bistineau (lake)	D 1
Black (lake)	D 3
Black Lake (bayou)	D 1
Bodcau (bayou)	C 1
Boeuf (lake)	J 7
Boeuf (river)	G 2
Borgne (lake)	L 7
Bonnet Carré Spillway and Floodway	N 3
Boudreau (bay)	M 7
Boudreaux (lake)	J 8
Breton (isl.)	M 8

Breton (sound)	M 7
Caddo (lake)	B 1
Caillou (bay)	J 8
Calcasieu (lake)	D 7
Calcasieu (passage)	D 7
Calcasieu (river)	E 5
Cat Island (channel)	M 6
Cat Island (passage)	J 8
Catahoula (lake)	F 4
Cataouatche (lake)	N 4
Chalmette Nat'l Hist. Park	L 7
Chandeleur (isls.)	N 7
Chandeleur (sound)	M 7
Chenier Brake (res.)	F 2
Chennault A.F.B.	D 6
Chicot (point)	M 7
Clear (isl.)	C 2
Clear (lake)	C 3
Cross (lake)	C 1
Curlew (isl.)	M 7
Dernieres (isls.)	H 8
Door (point)	M 6
Driskill (mt.)	E 3
Drum (bay)	M 7
East (bay)	M 8
Eloi (bay)	M 7
England A.F.B.	E 4
Fields (lake)	J 7
Fort Polk	D 4
Free Mason (isls.)	N 7
Garden Island (bay)	M 8
Grand (isle)	L 8
Grand (lake)	H 7
Grand (river)	J 6
Grand Terre (isls.)	L 8
Iatt (lake)	E 3
Lafourche (bayou)	K 8
Leroy Johnson, Camp	K 3
Little (river)	F 3
Louisiana (point)	C 7
Macon (bayou)	H 1
Main (passage)	M 8
Manchac (passage)	M 7
Marsh (isl.)	G 7
Maurepas (lake)	M 2
Mermantau (river)	E 7
Mexico (gulf)	F 8
Mississippi (delta)	N 8
Mississippi (river)	H 3
Mississippi (sound)	M 7
Mozambique (point)	M 7
Mud (lake)	D 7
North (isls.)	N 7
North (passage)	M 8
North (point)	F 1
Ouachita (river)	G 2
Pearl (river)	L 5
Polk, Fort	D 4
Pontchartrain (lake)	O 3
Pontchartrain Causeway	O 3
Raccoon (point)	H 8
Red (river)	G 4
Sabine (lake)	C 7
Sabine (passage)	C 7
Sabine (river)	D 3
Saline (lake)	E 3
Salvador (lake)	M 4
South (point)	G 8
Southwest (passage)	F 8
Southwest (passage)	M 8
Tangipahoa (river)	N 1
Tensas (river)	G 3
Terrebonne (bay)	J 8
Tickfaw (river)	M 1
Timbalier (bay)	K 8
Timbalier (isl.)	J 8
Toledo Bend (dam)	C 4
Vermilion (bay)	F 7
Verret (lake)	J 7
Wallace (lake)	C 2
West (bay)	M 8
West Cote Blanche (bay)	G 7
White (lake)	E 7

◉Parish Seat.

MAINE

AREA	33,215 sq. mi.
POPULATION	993,000
CAPITAL	Augusta
LARGEST CITY	Portland 72,566
HIGHEST POINT	Mt. Katahdin 5,268 ft.
SETTLED IN	1624
ADMITTED TO UNION	March 15, 1820
POPULAR NAME	Pine Tree State
STATE FLOWER	Pine Cone & Tassel
STATE BIRD	Chickadee

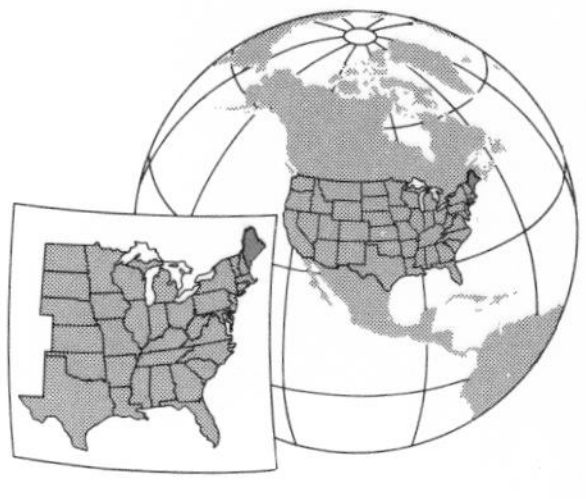

COUNTIES

- Androscoggin (C7) 86,312
- Aroostook (F2) 106,064
- Cumberland (C8) 182,751
- Franklin (B5) 20,069
- Hancock (G6) 32,293
- Kennebec (D7) 89,150
- Knox (E7) 28,575
- Lincoln (D7) 18,497
- Oxford (B7) 44,345
- Penobscot (F5) 126,346
- Piscataquis (E4) 17,379
- Sagadahoc (D7) 22,793
- Somerset (C4) 39,749
- Waldo (E6) 22,632
- Washington (H6) 32,908
- York (B9) 99,402

CITIES and TOWNS

- Abbot Village (D5) ...... △404
- Acton (B8) .... △501
- Addison (H6) .... △744
- Albion (E6) .... △974
- Alexander (H5) .... △220
- Alfred◉ (B9) .... △1,201
- Allagash (F1) .... △557
- Allens Mills (C6) 320
- Alna (D7) .... △347
- Alton (F5) .... △303
- Amherst (G6) .... △168
- Andover (B6) .... △762
- Anson (D6) .... △2,252
- Appleton (E7) .... △672
- Argyle (F5) 95
- Ashdale (D8) 60
- Ashland (G2) .... △1,980
- Ashville (G7) 100
- Athens (D6) .... △602
- Atkinson (E5) .... △280
- Atlantic (G7) 98
- Auburn◉ (C7) 24,449
- Auburn-Lewiston (urban area) 65,253
- AUGUSTA◉ (D7) 21,680
- Aurora (G6) .... △75
- Ayers (J6) 50
- Bailey Island (D8) 220
- Bancroft (H4) .... △94
- Bangor◉ (F6) 38,912
- Bar Harbor (G7) .... △3,807
- Bar Harbor (G7) 2,444
- Bar Mills (C8) 600
- Baring (J5) 175
- Bath◉ (D8) 10,717
- Bay Point (D8) 30
- Bayside (F7) 100
- Beals (H7) .... △640
- Beddington (H6) .... △14
- Belfast◉ (F7) 6,140
- Belgrade (D7) .... △1,102
- Belgrade Lakes (D6).... 600
- Belmont (E7) .... △295
- Benedicta (G4) .... △200
- Benton (D6) .... △1,521
- Berry Mills (C6) 150
- Berwick (B9) .... △2,738
- Berwick (B9) 1,557
- Bethel (B7) .... △2,408
- Bethel (B7) 1,117
- Biddeford (B9) 19,255
- Biddeford Pool (C9)..... 400
- Bingham (D5) .... △1,308
- Bingham (D5) 1,180
- Birch Harbor (H7) 170
- Blaine (H2) .... △945
- Blanchard (D5) .... △57
- Blue Hill (F7) .... △1,270
- Bolsters Mills (B7)...... 125
- Boothbay (D8) .... △1,617
- Boothbay Harbor (D8).. 2,252
- Bowdoinham (D7) .... △1,131
- Bowerbank (E5) .... △17
- Boyd Lake (F5) 50
- Bradford (F5) .... △690
- Bradford Center (F5)... 109
- Bradley (F6) .... △951
- Bremen ‡(E8) .... △438
- Brewer (F6) 9,009
- Bridgewater (H3) .... △999
- Bridgton (B7) .... △2,707
- Bridgton (B7) 1,715
- Brighton (D5) .... △62
- Bristol (D8) .... △1,441
- Brooklin (F7) .... △525
- Brooks (E6) .... △758
- Brooksville (F7) .... △603
- Brookton (H4) 225
- Brownfield (B8) .... △538
- Brownville (E5) .... △1,641
- Brownville Junction (E5) 850
- Brunswick (C8) .... △15,797
- Brunswick (C8) 9,444
- Bryant Pond (B7) 65
- Buckfield (C7) .... △982
- Bucks Harbor (J6) 169
- Bucksport (F6) .... △3,466
- Bucksport (F6) 2,327
- Burkettville (E7) 160
- Burlington (G5) .... △353
- Burnham (E6) .... △755
- Buxton ‡(C8) .... △2,339
- Buxton Center (B8)...... 93
- Byron (B6) .... △108
- Calais (J5) 4,223
- Cambridge (E5) .... △354
- Camden (F7) .... △3,988
- Camden (F7) 3,523
- Canaan (D6) .... △800
- Canton (C7) .... △728
- Cape Porpoise (C9)....... 450
- Caratunk (C5) .... △90
- Cardville (F5) 160
- Caribou (G2) .... △12,464
- Caribou (G2) 8,305
- Carmel (E6) .... △1,206
- Carrabassett (C5) 25
- Carroll (G5) .... △147
- Carthage (C6) .... △370
- Cary (H4) .... △208
- Casco (B7) .... △947
- Castine (F7) .... △824
- Center Lovell (B7)........ 250
- Center Montville (E7).. 40
- Centerville (H6) .... △47
- Chapman (G2) .... △376
- Charleston (F5) .... △750
- Charlotte (J5) .... △260
- Chebeague Island (C8).. 247
- Chelsea (D7) 1,893
- Cherryfield (H6) .... △780
- Chester (F5) .... △261
- Chesterville (C6) .... △505
- Chesuncook (D3) 20
- China (E7) .... △1,561
- Chisholm (C7) 1,193
- Citypoint (E7) 75
- Clark Island (E8) 100
- Clarks Mill (B8) 75
- Clayton Lake (E2) 39
- Cliff Island (C8) 100
- Clifton (G6) .... △227
- Clinton (D6) .... △1,729
- Columbia (H6) .... △219
- Columbia Falls (H6)..... △442
- Cooper (H6) .... △106
- Coopers Mills (E7) 150
- Corea (H7) 300
- Corinna (E6) .... △1,895
- Cornish (B8) .... △816
- Cornville (D6) .... △585
- Costigan (F5) 140
- Cranberry Isles (G7).... △181
- Crawford (H5) .... △83
- Crescent Lake (C7) 150
- Criehaven (F8) 25
- Crouseville (G2) 250
- Crystal (G4) .... △285
- Cumberland Ctr. (C8) △2,765
- Cundys Harbor (D8).... 80
- Cushing (E7) .... △479
- Cutler (J6) .... △654
- Damariscotta (E7) .... △1,093
- Danforth (H4) .... △821
- Danville (C7) 700
- Darkharbor (F7) 132
- Dayton ‡(B8) .... △451
- Deblois (H6) .... △26
- Dedham (F6) .... △438
- Deer Isle (F7) .... △1,129
- Denmark (B8) .... △376
- Dennysville (J6) .... △303
- Derby (E5) 500
- Detroit (E6) .... △564
- Dexter (E5) .... △3,951
- Dexter (E5) 2,720
- Dixfield (C6) .... △2,323
- Dixfield (C6) 1,334
- Dixmont (E6) .... △551
- Dover-Foxcroft (E5)... △4,173
- Dover-Foxcroft◉ (E5)... 2,481
- Dover South Mills (E5) 25
- Dresden (D7) .... △766
- Dry Mills (C8) 220
- Dryden (C6) 650
- Dyer Brook (G3) .... △180
- Eagle Lake (F1) .... △1,138
- East Andover (B6) 165
- East Baldwin (B8) 188
- East Blue Hill (G7) 200
- East Boothbay (D8) 510
- East Brownfield (B8)... 70
- East Corinth (F5) 200
- East Dixfield (C6) 225
- East Dixmont (E6) 100
- East Eddington (F6).... 200
- East Franklin (G6) 75
- East Hiram (B8) 400
- East Holden (F6) 350
- East Jackson (E6) 125
- East Knox (E7) 200
- East Lebanon (B9) 1,100
- East Limington (B8)..... 150
- East Livermore (C7)..... 350
- East Machias (J6) .... △1,198
- East Madison (D6) 300
- East Millinocket (F4).. △2,392
- East Millinocket (F4)... 2,295
- East New Portland(D6) 43
- East Orland (F6) 190
- East Otisfield (B7) 50
- East Parsonfield (B8).. 125
- East Peru (C7) 130
- East Poland (C7) 500
- East Stoneham (B7)..... 316
- East Sullivan (G6) 350
- East Sumner (C7) 114
- East Union (E7) 100
- East Vassalboro (D7)... 270
- East Waterboro (B8).... 179
- East Wilton (C6) 550
- East Winn (G5) 70
- Easton (H2) .... △1,389
- Eastport (K6) 2,537
- Eaton (H4) 85
- Eddington (F6) .... △958
- Edgecomb (D8) .... △453
- Edmunds (J6) 290
- Eliot (B9) .... △3,133
- Ellsworth◉ (F6) 4,444
- Ellsworth Falls (G6).... 550
- Emery Mills (B8) 95
- Enfield (F5) .... △1,098
- Etna (E6) .... △486
- Eustis (B5) .... △666
- Exeter (E6) .... △707
- Fairbanks (C6) 197
- Fairfield (D6) .... △5,829
- Fairfield (D6) 3,766
- Fairfield Center (D6).... 500
- Falmouth ‡(C8) .... △5,976
- Falmouth Foreside (C8) 1,062
- Farmington (C6) .... △5,001
- Farmington◉ (C6) 2,749
- Farmington Falls (C6).. 450
- Fayette (C7) .... △328
- Five Islands (D8) 154
- Forest City (H4) 24
- Forest Station (H4) 16
- Fort Fairfield (H2) .... △5,876
- Fort Fairfield (H2) 3,082
- Fort Kent (F1) .... △4,761
- Fort Kent (F1) 2,787
- Fort Kent Mills (F1)..... 422
- Frankfort (F6) .... △692
- Franklin (G6) .... △627
- Freedom (E7) .... △406
- Freeport (C8) .... △4,055
- Freeport (C8) 1,801
- Frenchboro (G7) 70
- Frenchville (G1) .... △1,421
- Friendship (E7) .... △806
- Frye (B6) 131
- Fryeburg (A7) .... △1,874
- Gardiner (D7) 6,897
- Garland (E5) .... △568
- Georgetown (D8) .... △790
- Gilead (B7) .... △136
- Glen Cove (E7) 285
- Glenburn (F6) .... △965
- Goodrich (H2) 400
- Goodwins Mills (B8)..... 125
- Goose Rocks Beach (C9) 275
- Gorham (C8) .... △5,767
- Gorham (C8) 2,322
- Gouldsboro (H7) .... △1,100
- Grand Isle (G1) .... △978
- Grand Lake Stream (H5) .... △219
- Gray (C8) .... △2,184
- Great Pond (G6) 50
- Great Works (F6) 450
- Green Lake (F6) 50
- Greene (C7) .... △1,226
- Greenville (D5) .... △2,025
- Greenville (D5) 1,893
- Greenville Jct. (D5) 400
- Grindstone (F4) 60
- Grove (J5) 125
- Guilford (E5) .... △1,880
- Guilford (E5) 1,372
- Haines Landing (B6).... 9
- Hallowell (D7) 3,169
- Hamlin (H1) .... △374
- Hampden (F6) .... △4,583
- Hampden Highlands (F6) 800
- Hancock (G6) .... △806
- Hanover (B7) .... △240
- Harmony (D6) .... △712
- Harpswell Center (D8).. 100
- Harrington (H6) .... △717
- Harrison (B7) .... △1,014
- Hartford (C7) .... △325
- Hartland (D6) .... △1,447
- Hartland (D6) 1,016
- Haynesville (G4) .... △187
- Hebron (C7) .... △465
- Hermon (F6) .... △2,087
- Highland Lake (C8)...... 600
- Highpine (B9) 125
- Hinckley (D6) 500
- Hiram (B8) .... △699
- Hodgdon (H3) .... △926
- Hollis Center (B8) .... △1,195
- Hope (E7) .... △525
- Houghton (B6) 15
- Houlton◉ (H3) .... △8,289
- Houlton (H3) 5,976
- Howland (F5) .... △1,362
- Howland (F5) 1,313
- Hudson (F5) .... △542
- Hulls Cove (G7) 250
- Indian River (H6) 74
- Intervale (C8) 45
- Island Falls (G3) ...... △1,018
- Isle au Haut (F7) .... △68
- Isleboro (F7) .... △444
- Islesford (G7) 95
- Jackman (C4) .... △984
- Jackman Station (C4).. 350
- Jacksonville (J6) 200
- Jay (C7) .... △3,247
- Jefferson (D7) .... △1,048
- Jemtland (G1) 30
- Jimpond (B5) 8
- Jonesboro (J6) .... △428
- Jonesport (H6) .... △1,563
- Jonesport (H6) 914
- Keegan (G1) 900
- Kenduskeag (E6) .... △584
- Kennebago Lake (B5).. 4
- Kennebunk (B9) .... △4,551
- Kennebunk (B9) 2,804
- Kennebunk Beach (C9).. 125
- Kennebunkport (C9)... △1,851
- Kents Hill (D7) 180
- Kezar Falls (B8) 850
- Kingfield (C6) .... △864
- Kingman (G4) 336
- Kingsbury (D5) .... △8
- Kittery (B9) .... △10,689
- Kittery (B9) 8,051
- Kittery Point (B9) 1,259
- Knox (E6) 439
- Kokadjo (E4) 25
- La Grange (F5) .... △424
- Lake Moxie (D5) 36
- Lake View (F5) .... △18
- Lambert Lake (H4)...... 178
- Lamoine (G7) .... △484
- Lebanon (B9) .... △1,534
- Lee (G5) .... △555
- Leeds (C7) .... △807
- Leeds Junction (C7) 81
- Levant (F6) .... △765
- Lewiston (C7) 40,804
- Lewiston-Auburn (urban area) 65,253
- Liberty (E7) .... △458
- Lille (G1) 200
- Limerick (B8) .... △907
- Limestone (H2) .... △13,102
- Limestone (H2) 1,772
- Limington (B8) .... △839
- Lincoln (G5) .... △4,541
- Lincoln (G5) 3,616
- Lincoln Center (G5)...... 300
- Lincolnville (E7) .... △867
- Lincolnville Center (E7) 300
- Linneus (H3) .... △607
- Lisbon (C7) .... △5,042
- Lisbon (C7) 1,542
- Lisbon Center (C7) 200
- Lisbon Falls (D7) 2,640
- Litchfield (D7) .... △1,011
- Little Deer Isle (F7).... 215
- Littleton (H3) .... △982
- Livermore (C7) .... △1,363
- Livermore Falls (C7)... △3,343
- Livermore Falls (C7)..... 2,882
- Locke Mills (B7) 380
- Long Cove (E8) 79
- Long Island (C8) .... △57
- Long Pond (C4) 30
- Lovell (B7) .... △588
- Lowell (F5) .... △132
- Lubec (K6) .... △2,684
- Lubec (K6) 1,289
- Ludlow (G3) .... △274
- Machias (J6) .... △2,614
- Machias◉ (J6) 1,523
- Machiasport (H6) .... △980
- Macwahoc (G4) .... △165
- Madawaska (G1) .... △5,507
- Madawaska (G1) 4,035
- Madison (D6) .... △3,935
- Madison (D6) 2,761
- Madrid (B6) .... △108
- Mainstream (D6) 200
- Manchester (D7) ...... △1,068
- Mapleton (G2) .... △1,514
- Mars Hill (H2) .... △2,062
- Mars Hill (H2) 1,458
- Masardis (G3) .... △408
- Matinicus (F8) .... △100
- Mattawamkeag (G5)..... △945
- McKinley (G7) 450
- Mechanic Falls (C7).... △2,195
- Mechanic Falls (C7)...... 1,992
- Meddybemps (J5) 86
- Medford (F5) 18
- Medford Center (F5).... 77
- Medway (G4) .... △1,266
- Mercer (D6) .... △272
- Mexico (B6) .... △5,043
- Mexico (B6) 3,951
- Milbridge (H6) .... △1,101
- Milford (F6) .... △1,572
- Millinocket (F4) .... △7,453
- Millinocket (F4) 7,318
- Milo (F5) .... △2,756
- Milo (F5) 1,802
- Minot (C7) .... △780
- Minturn (G7) 55
- Monarda (G4) 143
- Monhegan (E8) .... △65
- Monmouth (D7) .... △1,884
- Monroe (E6) .... △497
- Monson (E5) .... △852
- Monticello (H3) .... △1,109
- Montville (E7) .... △366
- Moody (B9) 100
- Moose River (C4) .... △205
- Moosehead (D4) 4
- Morrill (E7) .... △355
- Mount Desert (G7)...... △1,663
- Mount Vernon (D7) ..... △596
- Naples (B8) .... △735
- New Gloucester (C8)... △3,047

(continued on following page)

HIGHWAYS
CANADA
QUÉBEC
NEW BRUNSWICK
N.H.
To Edmundston
Edmundston
To Edmundston
To Campbellton
Ft. Kent
Van Buren
Long L.
Square L.
LORING A.F.B.
Caribou
Ft. Fairfield
Presque Isle
To Perth
AROOSTOOK ST. PK.
Mars Hill
Ashland
Round Mtn. 2,147
Peaked Mtn. 2,114
Eagle L.
Chamberlain L.
Grand L.
BAXTER STATE PARK
Mt. Katahdin 5,268
Houlton
To Woodstock
Patten
Island Falls
Seeboomook L.
To Québec
Chesuncook L.
Moosehead L.
Rockwood
LILY BAY ST. PK.
White Cap Mtn. 3,707
Millinocket
E. Millinocket
Danforth
Chiputneticook Lakes
Jackman Sta.
Coburn Mtn. 3,718
Greenville
Vanceboro
To Fredericton
To Thetford Mines
Snow Mtn. 3,948
Flagstaff L.
Bald Mtn. 2,630
Monson
Sebec L.
Lincoln
Topsfield
Guilford
Dover-Foxcroft
Milo
Howland
Lower Sysladobsis L.
Grand L.
To Saint John
Sugarloaf Mtn. 4,237
Rangeley
Bingham
Dexter
Corinna
Milford
Old Town
Woodland
Calais
Wesley
Perry
To Colebrook
Mooselookmeguntic L.
MT. BLUE ST. PK.
Madison
Skowhegan
Newport
Bangor
Aurora
Eastport
Campobello I.
ROOSEVELT CAMPOBELLO INTERNATIONAL PARK
Farmington
Pittsfield
Brewer
Machias
Mexico
Rumford
Livermore Falls
Fairfield
Waterville
Bucksport
Graham L.
Cherryfield
Jonesport
Milbridge
Ellsworth
To Gorham
Bethel
L. ST. GEORGE ST. PK.
Searsport
Bar Harbor
S. Paris
Winthrop
Augusta
Belfast
ACADIA NAT'L PARK
Norway
Southwest Har.
Long L.
CAMDEN HILLS ST. PK.
Camden
Lewiston
Auburn
Gardiner
To Littleton
Bridgton
ME. TPK.
Rockland
Isle au Haut
ACADIA NAT'L PARK
Fryeburg
SEBAGO L. ST. PK.
Sebago L.
Damariscotta
Brunswick
Cornish
Bath
Yarmouth
Boothbay Har.
REID ST. PK.
Westbrook
Portland
S. Portland
TWO LIGHTS ST. PK.
OCEAN
Sanford
TOLL
Saco
Biddeford
Rochester
Kennebunk
ATLANTIC
Ogunquit
Kittery
Portsmouth
0 30 60
MILES
Limited Access Highways
Major Highways
Other Important Roads
Interstate Route Numbers
Federal Route Numbers
State and Other Route Numbers

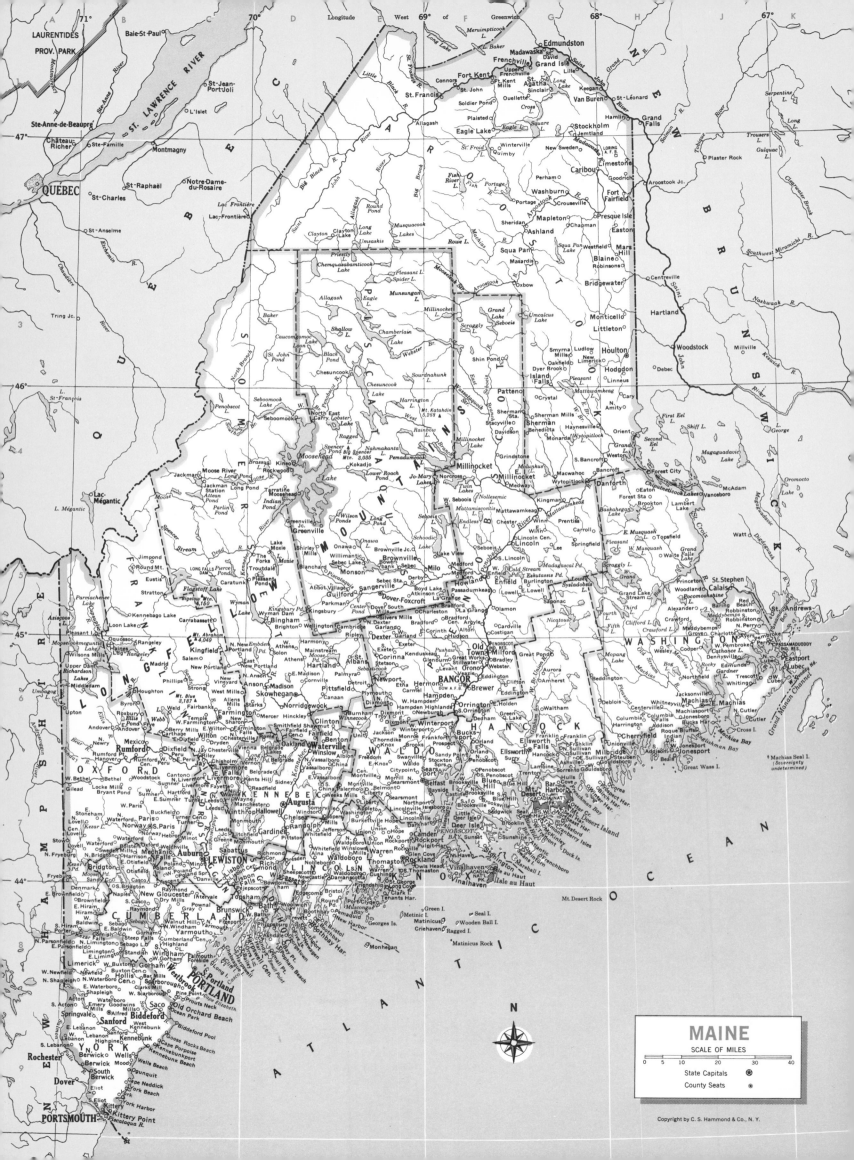

MAINE

SCALE OF MILES

0   5   10   20   30   40

State Capitals ⊛
County Seats ⊙

Maine
(continued)

New Harbor (E8) 525
New Limerick (G3) ...... ▲394
New Portland (C6) ...... ▲620
New Sharon (C6) .... ▲712
New Sweden (G2) ...... ▲713
New Vineyard (C6) ...... ▲357
Newagen (D8) 75
Newburgh (F6) .... ▲636
Newcastle (D7) ....▲1,101
Newfield (B8) .... ▲319
Newport (E6) ....▲2,322
Newport (E6) 1,589
Nobleboro (D7) .... ▲679
Norcross (F4) 60
Norridgewock (D6).....▲1,634
North Amity (H4) 325
North Anson (D6) 750
North Belgrade (D7).... 300
North Berwick (B9)....▲1,884
North Berwick (B9)......1,295
North Bradford (F5).... 70
North Bridgton (B7)..... 600
North Brooksville (F7).. 200
North Chesterville (C6) 150
North Cutler (J6) 100
North Dexter (E5) 100
North Dixmont (E6) 100
North East Carry (D4).. 5
North Fryeburg (B7).... 185
North Gorham (B8) 80
North Haven (F7) .... ▲384
North Jay (C6) 600
North Leeds (C7) 47
North Limington (B8).. 350
North Livermore (C7)... 165
North Lovell (B7) 72
North Lubec (J6) 380
North New Portland (C6) 250
North Newry (B6) 79
North Parsonfield (A8) 60
North Penobscot (F7)... 150
North Perry (J5) 100
North Raymond (C8).... 90
North Searsmont (E7).. 100
North Shapleigh (B8)... 90
North Sullivan (G6) 200
North Turner (C7) 350
North Vassalboro (D7).. 700
North Waldoboro (E7).. 160
North Waterboro (B8).. 150
North Waterford (B7).. 550
North Wayne (C7) 91
North Whitefield (D7).. 200
North Windham (C8).... 500
North Woodstock (B7).. 75
North Yarmouth (C8)..▲1,140
Northeast Hbr. (G7)..... 700
Northfield (H6) .... ▲79
Northport (E7) .... ▲648
Norway (B7) ....▲3,733
Norway (B7) 2,654
Norway Lake (B7) 350
Oakfield (G3) .... ▲848
Oakland (D6) ....▲3,075
Oakland (D6) 1,880
Ocean Park (C9) 165
Ogunquit (B9) 550
Olamon (F5) 600
Old Orchard Beach (C9) ....▲4,580
Old Orchard Beach (C9) 4,431
Old Town (F6) 8,626
Onawa (E5) 23
Oquossoc (B6) 150
Orient (H4) .... ▲124
Orland (F6) ....▲1,195
Orono (F6) ....▲8,341
Orono (F6) 3,234
Orrington (F6) ....▲2,539
Orrs Island (D8) 350
Otisfield (B7) .... ▲549
Otter Creek (G7) 250
Ouellette (G1) 100
Owls Head (F7) .... ▲994
Oxbow (G3) .... ▲137
Oxford (B7) ....▲1,658
Palermo (E7) .... ▲528
Palmyra (E6) ....▲1,009
Paris (B7) ....▲3,601
Parkman (D5) .... ▲530
Passadumkeag (F5)...... ▲355
Patten (F4) ....▲1,312
Patten (F4) 1,099
Pejepscot (D8) ....
Pemaquid (E8) 210
Pembroke (J6) .... ▲871
Penobscot (F7) .... ▲706
Perham (G2) .... ▲512
Perry (J6) .... ▲564
Peru (C6) ....▲1,229
Phillips (C6) ....▲1,021
Phippsburg (D8) ....▲1,121
Pine Point (C8) 650
Pittsfield (E6) ....▲4,010
Pittsfield (E6) 3,232
Pittston (D7) ....▲1,311
Plaisted (F1) 112
Pleasant Pond (D5) 11
Plymouth (E6) .... ▲494
Poland (C7) ....▲1,537
Poland Spring (C7) 500
Popham Beach (D8).... 100
Port Clyde (E8) 400
Portage (G2) .... ▲458
Porter (B8) .... ▲975
Portland◉ (C8) 72,566
Portland (urban area) 111,701
Pownal (C8) .... ▲778
Prentiss (G5) .... ▲227
Presque Isle (H2) 12,886
Princeton (H5) .... ▲829
Prospect (F6) .... ▲412
Prospect Harbor (H7)... 400
Prouts Neck (C8) 12
Pulpit Harbor (F7) 25
Quimby (F2) 357
Randolph (D7) ....▲1,724
Randolph (D7) 1,585
Rangeley (B6) ....▲1,087
Raymond (B8) .... ▲732
Readfield (D7) ....▲1,029
Red Beach (J5) 200
Richmond (D7) ....▲2,185
Richmond (D7) 1,412
Richmond Corner (D7).. 125
Riley (C6) 175
Ripley (E5) .... ▲317
Robbinston (J5) .... ▲476
Robinsons (H3) 543
Rockland◉ (E7) 8,769
Rockport (F7) ....▲1,893
Rockville (E7) 196
Rockwood (D4) 300
Rome (D6) .... ▲367
Roque Bluffs (H6) ...... ▲152
Round Mountain (B5)... 15
Round Pond (E8) 500
Roxbury (B6) .... ▲344
Rumford (B6) ....▲10,005
Rumford (B6) 7,233
Rumford Center (B7).... 325
Rumford Point (B6)..... 125
Sabattus (C7) 1,620
Saco (C8) 10,515
Saint Agatha (G1) ....▲1,137
Saint Albans (E6) ...... ▲927
Saint David (G1) 1,000
Saint Francis (E1) ....▲1,058
Saint George (E7) ......▲1,588
Saint John (F1) .... ▲407
Salem (C6) 75
Sandy Creek (B7) 150
Sandy Point (F7) 300
Sanford (B9) ....▲14,962
Sanford (B9) 10,936
Sangerville (E5) ....▲1,157
Scarborough (C8) ......▲6,418
Seal Cove (G7) 190
Seal Harbor (G7) 325
Searsmont (E7) .... ▲628
Searsport (F7) ....▲1,838
Sebago Lake (B8) 383
Sebec (E5) .... ▲384
Sebec Lake (E5) 108
Sebec Station (E5) ....
Seboeis (F5) .... ▲77
Seboomook (D4) 18
Sedgwick (F7) .... ▲574
Shapleigh (B8) .... ▲515
Shawmut (D6) 225
Sheepscott (D7) 100
Sheridan (F2) 385
Sherman (G4) ....▲1,034
Sherman Mills (G4) 600
Sherman Station (F4).. 250
Shin Pond (F3) 28
Shirley Mills (D5) ......
Sidney (D7) .... ▲988
Silvers Mills (E5) 52
Sinclair (G1) 320
Skowhegan (D6) ....▲7,661
Skowhegan◉ (D6) 6,667
Small Point (D8) 34
Smithfield (D6) .... ▲382
Smyrna Mills (G3) .... ▲331
Smyrna Mills (G3) 212
Soldier Pond (F1) 816
Solon (D6) .... ▲669
Somerville (D7) .... ▲254
Sorrento (G7) .... ▲196
South Acton (B8) 200
South Addison (H6) 170
South Bancroft (G4)..... 9
South Berwick (B9) ...▲3,112
South Berwick (B9) 1,773
South Blue Hill (F7).... 113
South Bridgton (B8).... 125
South Bristol (D8) ...... ▲610
South Brooksville (F7).. 99
South Casco (B8) 100
South China (D7) 205
South Eliot (B9) 1,730
South Exeter (E6) 40
South Harpswell (C8)... 300
South Hiram (B8) 150
South Hope (E7) 100
South La Grange (F5).. 71
South Lebanon (B9) 190
South Liberty (E7) 47
South Lincoln (F5) 141
South Orrington (F6).... 300
South Paris◉ (C7) 2,063
South Penobscot (F7)... 171
South Portland (C8) 22,788
South Robbinston (J5).. 150
South Sanford (B9)...... 600
South Thomaston (E7)..▲732
South Union (E7) 100
South Waldoboro (E7).. 400
South Warren (E7) 150
South Waterford (B7)... 110
South Windham (C8) ..1,142
Southport (D8) .... ▲416
Southwest Harbor (G7) ....▲1,480
Springfield (G5) .... ▲426
Springvale (B9) 2,379
Squa Pan (G2) 75
Stacyville (F4) .... ▲673
Standish (B8) ....▲2,095
Starks (D6) .... ▲306
Steep Falls (B8) 400
Stetson (E6) .... ▲420
Steuben (H6) .... ▲673
Stillwater (F6) 800
Stockholm (G1) .... ▲649
Stockton Springs (F7).. ▲980
Stonington (F7) ....▲1,408
Stow (A7) .... ▲108
Stratton (B5) 650
Strong (C6) .... ▲976
Sullivan (G6) .... ▲709
Sumner (C7) .... ▲481
Sunset (F7) 450
Sunshine (G7) 70
Surry (F7) .... ▲547
Swans Island (G7) ...... ▲402
Swanville (E6) .... ▲514
Sweden (B7) .... ▲119
Tarratine (D4) 2
Temple (C6) .... ▲314
Tenants Harbor (E8).... 800
The Forks (D5) .... ▲53
Thomaston (E7) ....▲2,780
Thomaston (E7) 2,342
Thorndike (E6) .... ▲457
Topsfield (H5) 210
Topsham (D8) ....▲3,818
Topsham (D8) 2,240
Tremont (G7) ....▲1,044
Trenton (G7) .... ▲375
Trescott (J6) 125
Trevett (D8) 245
Troutdale (D5) 19
Troy (E6) .... ▲469
Turner (C7) ....▲1,890
Turner Center (C7) 300
Union (E7) ....▲1,196
Unionville (H6) 78
Unity (E6) .... ▲983
Upper Dam (B6) 2
Upper Frenchville (G1).. 500
Upton (B6) .... ▲35
Van Buren (G1) ....▲4,679
Van Buren (G1) 3,589
Vanceboro (J4) .... ▲389
Vassalboro (D7) ....▲2,446
Veazie (F6) ....▲1,354
Vienna (D6) .... ▲160
Vinalhaven (F7) ....▲1,273
Waite (H5) .... ▲73
Waldo (E7) .... ▲395
Waldoboro (E7) ....▲2,882
Walnut Hill (C8) 350
Waltham (G6) .... ▲153
Warren (E7) ....▲1,678
Washburn (G2) ....▲2,083
Washburn (G2) 1,055
Washington (E7) .... ▲636
Waterboro (B8) ....▲1,059
Waterford (B7) .... ▲834
Waterville (D6) 18,695
Wayne (D7) .... ▲498
Webster (F6) 4,747
Weeks Mills (E7) 100
Welchville (C7) 400
Weld (C6) .... ▲348
Wellington (D5) .... ▲231
Wells (B9) ....▲3,528
Wells Beach (B9) 550
Wesley (H6) .... ▲145
West Athens (D6) 200
West Bath (D8) .... ▲766
West Bethel (B7) 300
West Brooksville (F7)... 145
West Buxton (B8) 254
West Enfield (F5) 546
West Farmington (C6).. 500
West Franklin (G6) 135
West Gardiner (D7) ....▲1,144
West Garland (E5) 50
West Gouldsboro (G7) 105
West Hampden (E6).....
West Jonesport (H6).... 425
West Kennebunk (B9)... 375
West Lebanon (B9) 150
West Lubec (J6) 320
West Mills (C6) 342
West Minot (C7) 300
West Newfield (B8) 175
West Paris (B7) ....▲1,050
West Pembroke (J6).... 485
West Peru (C7) 300
West Poland (C7) 275
West Rockport (E7) 300
West Scarborough (C8) 875
West Sumner (B7) 161
West Tremont (G7) 250
West Winterport (E6) 30
Westbrook (C8) 13,820
Westfield (G2) .... ▲569
Weston (H4) .... ▲202
Whitefield (D7) ....▲1,068
Whiting (J6) .... ▲339
Whitneyville (H6) .... ▲229
Willimantic (E5) .... ▲137
Wilsons Mills (B6) 95
Wilton (C6) ....▲3,274
Wilton (C6) 1,761
Windsor (D7) .... ▲878
Winn (G5) .... ▲526
Winslow (D6) ....▲5,891
Winslow (D6) 3,640
Winslows Mills (E7).... 200
Winter Harbor (G7)..... ▲756
Winterport (F6) ....▲2,088
Winterville (F2) .... ▲215
Winthrop (C7) ....▲3,537
Winthrop (C7) 2,260
Wiscasset◉ (D7) ......▲1,800
Woodland (H5) 1,393
Woolwich (D8) ....▲1,417
Wyman Dam (D5) 451
Wytopitlock (G4) 260
Yarmouth (C8) ....▲3,517
Yarmouth (C8) 2,913
York (B9) ....▲4,663
York Beach (B9) 500
York Harbor (B9) 950

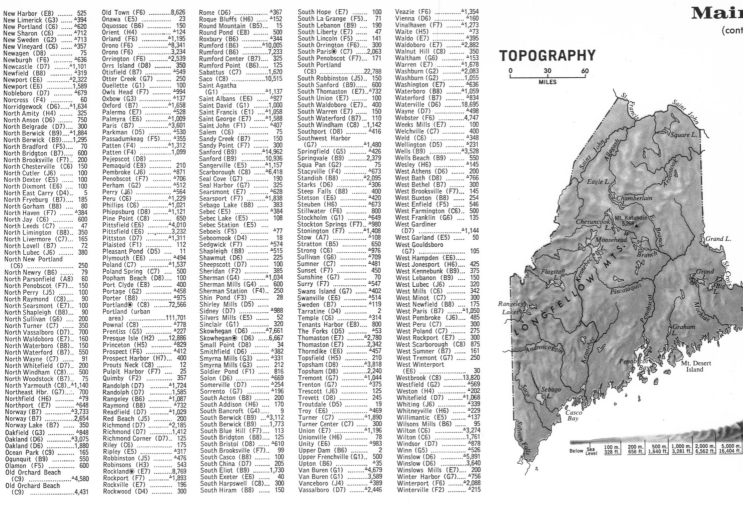

TOPOGRAPHY

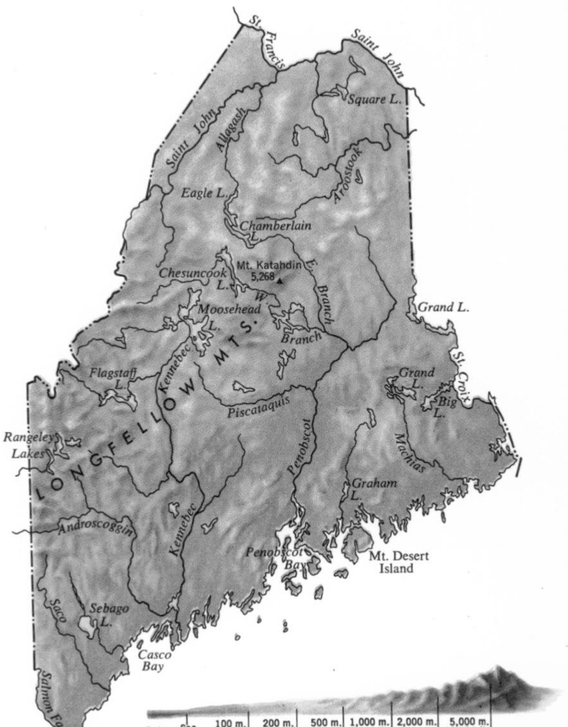

0
30
60
MILES
St. Francis
Saint John
Square L.
Saint John
Allagash
Aroostook
Eagle L.
Chamberlain
Mt. Katahdin 5,268
Chesuncook L.
E. Branch
Moosehead L.
W. Branch
Grand L.
LONGFELLOW MTS.
Flagstaff L.
Kennebec
St. Croix
Piscataquis
Grand L.
Big L.
Rangeley Lakes
Penobscot
Machias
Graham L.
Androscoggin
Kennebec
Penobscot Bay
Mt. Desert Island
Sebago L.
Saco
Casco Bay
Salmon Falls
Below Sea Level
100 m. 328 ft.
200 m. 656 ft.
500 m. 1,640 ft.
1,000 m. 3,281 ft.
2,000 m. 6,562 ft.
5,000 m. 16,404 ft.

AGRICULTURE, INDUSTRY and RESOURCES

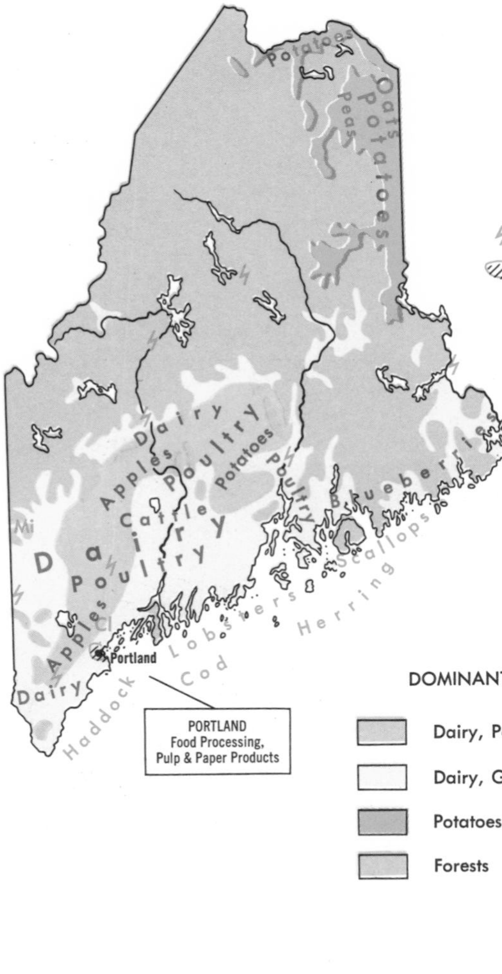

Potatoes
Oats
Potatoes
Peas
Dairy
Apples
Poultry
Potatoes
Poultry
Cattle
Blueberries
Dairy
Mi
Dairy
Poultry
Scallops
Lobsters
Herring
Apples
Portland
Dairy
Haddock
Cod
PORTLAND
Food Processing,
Pulp & Paper Products

MAJOR MINERAL OCCURRENCES

Cl Clay
Mi Mica

Water Power
Major Industrial Areas

DOMINANT LAND USE

Dairy, Poultry, Mixed Farming
Dairy, General Farming
Potatoes, General Farming
Forests

OTHER FEATURES

Abraham (mt.) ....C 5
Acadia National Park....G 7
Allagash (lake) ....D 3
Allagash (river) ....E 2
Androscoggin (river) .....C 7
Aroostook (river) ....G 2
Attean (pond) ....C 4
Aziscoos (lake) ....A 5
Baker (lake) ....D 3
Baskahegan (lake) ....H 4
Bear (river) ....B 6
Bigelow (mt.) ....C 5
Big (brook) ....E 2
Big (lake) ....H 5
Big Black (river) ....D 2
Big Spencer (mt.) ....D 4
Black (pond) ....D 3
Blue (mt.) ....C 6
Blue Hill (bay) ....G 7
Bog (lake) ....H 6
Brassua (lake) ....D 4
Casco (bay) ....C 8
Cathance (lake) ....J 6
Caucomgomoc (lake)......D 3
Center (pond) ....E 5
Chamberlain (lake) ....E 3
Chemquasabamticook (lake) ....D 3
Chesuncook (lake) ....E 3
Chiputneticook (lakes) ....H 4
Clayton (lake) ....D 2
Clifford (lake) ....H 5
Cold Stream (pond) ......G 5
Crawford (lake) ....H 5
Cross (isl.) ....J 6
Cross (lake) ....G 1
Cupsuptic (river) ....B 5
Dead (river) ....C 5
Deer (isl.) ....F 7
Dow A.F.B. ....F 6
Duck (isls.) ....G 7
Eagle (lake) ....E 3
Eagle (lake) ....F 1
East Machias (river) ....H 6
East Musquash (lake)....H 5
Elizabeth (cape) ....C 8
Ellis (pond) ....B 6
Ellis (river) ....B 6
Embden (pond) ....D 6
Endless (lake) ....F 5
Englishman (bay) ....J 6
Eskutassis (pond) ....G 5
Fifth (lake) ....H 5
Fish (river) ....F 2
Fish River (lake) ....F 2
Flagstaff (lake) ....C 5
Fourth (lake) ....H 5
Frenchman (bay) ....G 7
Gardner (lake) ....J 6
Georges (isls.) ....E 8
Graham (lake) ....G 6
Grand (lake) ....H 4
Grand Falls (lake) ....H 5
Grand Lake Seboeis (lake) ....F 3
Grand Manan (channel) ....K 6
Great Wass (isl.) ....J 7
Green (isl.) ....F 8
Harrington (lake) ....E 4
Haut (isl.) ....G 7
Indian Pond (lake) ....D 4
Islesboro (isl.) ....F 7
Jo Mary (lakes) ....E 4
Katahdin (mt.) ....F 4
Kennebec (river) ....D 7
Kezar (lake) ....B 7
Kezar (pond) ....B 7
Kingsbury (pond) ....D 5
Little Black (river).........E 1
Little Madawaska (river) ....G 2
Lobster (lake) ....D 4
Long (lake) ....B 7
Long (lake) ....E 2
Long (lake) ....G 1
Long (pond) ....C 4
Long (pond) ....D 6
Long (pond) ....E 5
Long Falls (dam) ....C 5
Longfellow (mts.) ....B 6
Loon (lake) ....D 3
Loring A.F.B. ....H 2
Lower Roach (pond) ......E 4
Lower Sysladobsis (lake) ....G 5
Machias (bay) ....J 6
Machias (river) ....F 2
Machias (river) ....H 6
Machias Seal (isl.)..........J 7
Madagascal (pond) ....G 5
Marshall (isl.) ....G 7
Matinicus Rock (isl.)......F 8
Mattamiscontis (lake)....F 4
Mattawamkeag (lake) ....G 4
Mattawamkeag (river) ....G 4
Meddybemps (lake) ....J 5
Metinic (isl.) ....E 8
Millinocket (lake) ....F 4
Millinocket (lake) ....F 3
Molunkus (lake) ....G 4
Monhegan (isl.) ....E 8
Moose (pond) ....B 7
Moose (pond) ....D 6
Moose (river) ....D 4
Moosehead (lake) ....D 4
Mooseleuk (stream) ......F 2
Mooselookmeguntic (lake) ....B 6
Mopang (lake) ....H 6
Mount Desert (isl.) ......G 7
Mount Desert Rock (isl.) ....G 8
Moxie (lake) ....D 5
Munsungan (lake) ....E 3
Muscongus (bay) ....E 8
Musquacook (lakes)........E 2
Nahmakanta (lake) ....E 4
Nicatous (lake) ....G 5
Nollesemic (lake) ....F 4
Old (stream) ....H 6
Onawa (lake) ....E 5
Parlin (pond) ....C 4
Parmachenee (lake)........B 5
Passamaquoddy (bay) ...J 5
Passamaquoddy Ind. Res. ....J 5
Pemadumcook (lake) ....E 4
Penobscot (bay) ....F 7
Penobscot (lake) ....C 4
Penobscot (river) ....F 5
Penobscot Ind. Res. ....F 6
Pierce (pond) ....C 5
Piscataqua (river) ....B 9
Piscataquis (river) ....E 5
Pleasant (lake) ....E 3
Pleasant (lake) ....G 3
Pleasant (lake) ....H 5
Pleasant (river) ....H 6
Pocomoonshine (lake) ...H 5
Portage (lake) ....F 2
Priestly (lake) ....E 2
Pushaw (lake) ....F 6
Ragged (isl.) ....F 8
Ragged (lake) ....E 4
Rainbow (lake) ....E 4
Rangeley (lake) ....B 6
Richardson (lakes) ....B 6
Rocky (lake) ....J 6
Round (pond) ....E 2
Rowe (lake) ....F 2
Saco (river) ....B 8
Saint Croix (river)..........J 5
Saint Francis (river) ....E 1
Saint Froid (lake) ....F 2
Saint John (pond) ....D 3
Saint John (river) ....G 1
Salmon Falls (river) ......B 9
Sandy (river) ....C 6
Schoodic (lake) ....F 5
Scraggly (lake) ....F 3
Scraggly (lake) ....H 5
Seal (isl.) ....F 8
Sebago (lake) ....B 8
Sebasticook (lake) ....E 6
Seboeis (lake) ....E 4
Seboeis (river) ....F 3
Seboomook (lake) ....D 4
Shallow (lake) ....E 3
Small (point) ....D 8
Sourdnahunk (lake) ......F 3
Spencer (pond) ....D 4
Spencer (stream) ....C 5
Spider (lake) ....E 3
Squa Pan (lake) ....G 2
Square (lake) ....G 1
Sunday (river) ....B 6
Swift (river) ....B 6
Third (lake) ....H 5
Twin (lakes) ....F 4
Umbagog (lake) ....A 6
Umcalcus (lake) ....G 3
Umsaskis (lake) ....E 2
Union, West Branch (river) ....G 6
Vinalhaven (isl.) ....F 7
Wassataquoik (stream)..F 4
Webb (lake) ....B 6
Webster (brook) ....E 3
West Grand (lake) ....H 5
West Musquash (lake)....H 5
West Quoddy (head) ......K 6
Wilson (ponds) ....E 5
Winnecook (lake) ....E 6
Wooden Ball (isl.) ....F 8
Wyman (lake) ....C 5
Wytopitlock (lake) ....G 4

◉County Seat.
▲Population of township.
‡Name not on map.

Maryland and Delaware

MARYLAND

COUNTIES

Allegany (C2) 84,169
Anne Arundel (M4) 206,634
Baltimore (M3) 492,428
Baltimore (city) (M3) 939,024
Calvert (M6) 15,826
Caroline (P5) 19,462
Carroll (K2) 52,785
Cecil (P2) 48,408
Charles (K6) 32,572
Dorchester (M7) 29,666
Frederick (J3) 71,930
Garrett (A2) 20,420
Harford (N2) 76,722
Howard (L4) 36,152
Kent (O3) 15,481
Montgomery (J4) 340,928
Prince Georges (L5) 357,395
Queen Annes (P4) 16,569
Saint Marys (M7) 38,915
Somerset (R8) 19,623
Talbot (O5) 21,578
Washington (G2) 91,219
Wicomico (R7) 49,050
Worcester (S8) 23,733

CITIES and TOWNS

Abell (M8) 400
Aberdeen (O2) 9,679
Abingdon (N3) 650
Accident (A2) 237
Accokeek (L6) 1,637
Adamstown (H3) 220
Aikin (O2) ....
Airey (O6) 110
Allen (R7) 250
American Corner (P5) 40
ANNAPOLIS◉ (M5) 23,385
Annapolis Jct. (M4) 750
Antietam (H3) 100
Aquasco (L6) 900
Arbutus-Halethorpe-Relay (M4) 22,402
Ardmore (G4) 1,330
Arlington (M3) 71,750
Baden (M6) 100
Baldwin (N3) 350
Baltimore (M3) 939,024
Barclay (P4) 142
Barnesville (J4) 145
Barstow (M6) 151
Barton (B2) 731
Bayview (P2) 150
Beaver Creek (H2) 50
Bel Air◉ (N2) 4,300
Bel Alton (L7) 700
Bellevue (O6) 289
Beltsville (G3) 4,589
Benedict (M6) 450
Bentley Spgs. (M2) 150
Berlin (T7) 2,046
Berwyn Hts. (G4) 2,376
Bethesda (E4) 56,527
Bethlehem (P6) ....
Betterton (O3) 328
Big Pool (G2) 950
Big Spring (G2) 125
Bishop (S7) 100
Bishops Head (O7) 300
Bishopville (T7) 300
Bivalve (P7) 290
Bladensburg (G4) 3,103
Bloomington (B3) 354
Blythedale (O2) 100
Boonsboro (H2) 1,211
Borden Shaft (B2) 200
Boring (L2) 197
Boulevard Hts. (F5) 500
Bowens (M6) 220
Bowie (L4) 1,072
Boyds (J4) 100
Bozman (N5) 450
Bradbury Park (G5) 200
Bradshaw (N3) 650
Brandywine (L6) 459
Brentwood (F4) 3,693
Bridgetown (P4) 39
Bristol (M5) 300
Brookeville (K4) 140
Brookview (P6) 83
Brownsville (H3) 205
Brunswick (H3) 3,555
Burkittsville (H3) 208
Burrsville (P5) 50
Bushwood (L7) 300
Butler (M2) 100
Cabin John (E4) 2,000
California (M7) 250
Calvert (O2) 125
Cambridge◉ (O6) 12,239
Camp Springs (F6) 900
Capitol Heights (G5) 3,138
Cardiff (N2) 325
Carney-Parkville (M3) 27,236
Carrollton (G4) 3,385
Carrollton (L2) 168
Castleton (N2) 343
Catoctin Furnace (J2) 233
Catonsville (M3) 37,372
Cavetown (H2) 325
Cecilton (P3) 596
Cedar Grove (K4) 350
Cedar Hts. (G5) 1,231
Cedartown (S8) 53
Cedarville (L6) 200
Centreville◉ (O4) 1,863
Chance (P8) 509
Chaptico (M7) 185
Charlestown (P2) 711
Charlotte Hall (M7) 200
Chase (N3) 900
Cheltenham (L6) 484
Cherry Hill (P2) 200
Chesapeake Beach (N6) 731
Chesapeake City (P2) 1,104
Chester (N5) 1,100
Chestertown◉ (O4) 3,602
Chesterville (P3) 60
Cheverly (G4) 5,223
Chevy Chase (E4) 2,405
Chewsville (H2) 350
Childs (P2) 275
Chillum (F4) 6,338
Church Creek (O6) 146
Church Hill (O4) 263
Churchton (N5) 1,000
Churchville (N2) 450
Claiborne (N5) 150
Clarksburg (J4) 448
Clarksville (L4) 200
Clear Spring (G2) 488
Clements (L7) 300
Clinton (G6) 1,578
Cockeysville (M3) 2,582
College Park (G4) 18,482
Colmar Manor (F4) 1,772
Colora (O2) 80
Compton (M7) 750
Conowingo (O2) 100
Cooksville (K3) 336
Cordova (O5) 300
Cornersville (O6) 200
Corriganville (C2) 1,200
Cottage City (F4) 1,099
Crapo (O7) 64
Creagerstown (J2) 325
Crellin (A3) 475
Cresaptown (C2) 1,680
Crisfield (P9) 3,540
Crocheron (O8) 165
Crownsville (M4) 80
Crumpton (P4) 281
Cumberland◉ (D2) 33,415
Damascus (K3) 1,120
Dameron (N8) 250
Dames Quarter (P8) 300
Daniels (L3) 460
Dargan (H3) 200
Darlington (N2) 500
Darnestown (J4) 300
Davidsonville (M5) 50
Deal Island (P8) 700
Deer Park (A3) 379
Delmar (R7) 1,291
Denton◉ (P5) 1,938
Derwood (K4) 200
Dickerson (J4) 350
District Hts. (G5) 7,524
Doncaster (K7) 75
Doubs (J3) 250
Downsville (G2) 250
Drayden (N8) 360
Dublin (N2) 300
Dundalk (N3) 82,428
Earleigh Hts. (M4) 850
Earleville (P3) 60
E. New Market (P6) 225
Easton◉ (O5) 6,337
Eckhart Mines (C2) 1,800
Eden (R7) 300
Edgemere-Fort Howard-Sparrows Pt. (N4) 11,775
Edgewood (N3) 1,670
Edmonston (G4) 1,197
Eldersburg (L3) 500
Eldorado (P6) 80
Elk Mills (P2) 500
Elk Neck (P2) 800
Elkridge (M4) 3,000
Elkton◉ (P2) 5,989
Ellerslie (C2) 850
Ellerton (H2) 54
Ellicott City◉ (L3) 1,500
Elliott (P7) 120
Emmitsburg (J2) 1,369
Essex (N3) 35,205
Ewell (O9) 360
Fair Hill (P2) 100
Fairbank (N6) 300
Fairlee (O4) 175
Fairmont Hts. (G5) 2,308
Fairmount (P8) 600
Fallston (N2) 600
Farmington (O2) 35
Fearer (A2) 150
Federalsburg (P6) 2,060
Ferndale (M4) 2,500
Finksburg (L3) 500
Fishing Creek (N7) 800
Flintstone (E2) 500
Forest Glen (F4) 1,500
Forest Hts. (F5) 3,524
Forest Hill (N2) 300
Forestville (G5) 5,144
Fort Foote (F6) 300
Fort Howard-Edgemere-Sparrows Pt. (N4) 11,775
Fort Washington (L6) 940
Foxville (J2) 450
Frederick◉ (J3) 21,744
Freeland (M2) 200
Friendship (M6) 275
Friendship Hts. (E4) 390
Friendsville (A2) 580
Frizzellburg (K2) 193
Frostburg (C2) 6,722
Fruitland (R7) 1,147
Funkstown (H2) 968
Gaithersburg (K4) 3,847
Galena (P3) 299
Galestown (P6) 151
Galesville (M5) 600
Gamber (L3) 300
Gambrills (M4) 500
Garrett Park (E3) 965
Garrison (L3) 800
Germantown (J4) 200
Girdletree (S8) 400
Glen Arm (N3) 350
Glen Burnie (M4) 3,900
Glen Echo (E4) 310
Glen Echo Hts. (E4) 900
Glenarden (G4) 1,336
Glenelg (L3) 40
Glenn Dale (G4) 2,094
Glyndon-Reisterstown (L3) 4,216
Golden Hill (O7) 98
Goldsboro (P4) 204
Golts (P3) 100
Graceham (J2) 202
Granite (L3) 600
Grantsville (B2) 446
Grasonville (O5) 1,200
Green Haven (M4) 1,302
Greenbelt (G4) 7,479
Greenmount (L2) 225
Greensboro (P5) 1,160
Hagerstown◉ (G2) 36,660
Halethorpe-Arbutus-Relay (M4) 22,402
Halfway (G2) 4,256
Hall (L5) 125
Hampstead (L2) 696
Hancock (F2) 2,004
Hanover (L4) 975
Harmans (M4) 750
Harney (K2) 450
Havre de Grace (O2) 8,510
Hebron (R7) 754
Helen (M7) 125
Henderson (P4) 129
Henryton (L3) 250
Hereford (M2) 400
Highfield (J2) 650
Hillcrest Hts. (F5) 15,295
Hillsboro (P5) 201
Hillside (G5) 5,528
Hobbs (P5) 95
Hollywood (M7) 3,841
Hood (F2) 53
Hoopersville (O7) 300
Hopewell (P8) 200
Hudson (N6) 125
Hughesville (L6) 1,550
Huntingtown (M6) 350
Hurlock (P6) 1,035
Hutton (A3) 300
Hyattstown (J3) 157
Hyattsville (F4) 15,168
Ijamsville (J3) 150
Ilchester (L4) 200
Indian Head (K6) 780
Ingleside (P4) 154
Ironshire (T7) 100
Island Creek (M7) 408
Issue (L7) 200
Jacksonville (M2) 150
Jarrettsville (M2) 400
Jefferson (H3) 267
Jennings (B2) 300
Jesterville (P7) 160
Johnsville (K2) 210
Keedysville (H3) 433
Kempton (A4) 12
Kemptown (J3) 225
Kennedyville (P3) 300
Kensington (E4) 2,175
Keymar (K2) 200
Kingston (R8) 75
Kingsville (N3) 3,230
Kitzmiller (B3) 535
Knoxville (H3) 500
La Plata◉ (L6) 1,214
LaVale-Narrows Park (C2) 4,031
Ladiesburg (J2) 71
Lakesville (O7) 37
Landover (G4) 800
Landover Hills (G4) 1,850
Langley Park (F4) 11,510
Lanham (G4) 2,621
Lansdowne-Baltimore Highlands (M3) 13,134
Lantz (J2) 75
Largo (G5) 25
Laurel (L4) 8,503
Laytonsville (K4) 196
Le Gore (J2) 500
Leeds (P2) 175
Leitersburg (H2) 500
Leonardtown◉ (M7) 1,281
Level (O2) 325
Lewistown (J2) 500
Lexington Park (M7) 7,039
Liberty Grove (O2) 125
Libertytown (J3) 500
Lime Kiln (J3) 176
Lineboro (L2) 250
Linkwood (P6) 176
Linthicum Hts. (M4) 1,400
Linwood (K2) 272
Lisbon (K3) 182
Little Orleans (E2) 132
Loch Lynn Hts. (A3) 476
Lonaconing (C2) 2,077
Long Green (M3) 500
Lothian (M5) 70
Love Point (N4) 120
Loveville (M7) 500
Lower Marlboro (M6) 156
Luke (B3) 587
Lusby (N7) 75
Lutherville-Timonium (M3) 12,265
Lynch (O3) 150
Mackall (M7) ....
Madison (O6) 400
Madonna (M2) 128
Magnolia (N3) 200
Manchester (L2) 1,108
Manokin (P8) 400
Mapleville (H2) 175
Marbury (K6) 750
Mardela Springs (P7) 380
Marion Station (R8) 270
Marshall Hall (K6) 365
Marydel (P4) 130
Maryland Line (M2) 175
Maryland Park (G5) 992
Mason Springs (K6) 50
Massey (P3) 210
Maugansville (H2) 950
Mayberry (K2) 108
Mayo (M5) 583
McDaniel (N5) 190
Meadows (G5) 150
Mechanicsville (M7) 500
Medford (K2) 25
Melitota (O4) 100
Melrose (L2) 58
Middle River (N3) 10,825
Middleburg (K2) 160
Middletown (J3) 1,036
Midland (C2) 737
Milestown (M7) 400
Milford (M3) ....
Millers (L2) 170
Millersville (M4) 750
Millington (P3) 408
Monie (P8) 250
Monkton (M2) 147
Monrovia (J3) 300
Morningside (G5) 1,708
Moscow Mills (B2) 350
Mt. Airy (K3) 1,352
Mt. Pleasant (J3) 260
Mt. Rainier (F4) 9,855
Mt. Savage (C2) 1,639
Mt. Vernon (P8) 400
Mountain Lake Park (A3) 975
Mountaindale (J2) 490
Muirkirk (L4) 500
Myersville (H3) 355
Nanjemoy (K7) 243
Nanticoke (P7) 500
Narrows Park-LaVale (C2) 4,031
Neavitt (N6) 250
New Glatz (F6) 50
New Market (J3) 358
New Windsor (K2) 738
Newark (S7) 265
Newburg (L7) ....
Newport (L7) 100
Nikep (C2) 210
Norrisville (N2) 206
N. Beach (M6) 606
N. Branch (D2) 70
N. Brentwood (F4) 864
N. East (O2) 1,628
Oakland◉ (A3) 1,977
Ocean City (T7) 983
Odenton (M4) 1,914
Oella (L3) 500
Oldtown (D2) 450
Oliver Beach-Twin Rivers Beach (N3) 1,426
Olivet (N7) 150
Olney (K4) 645
Orchard Beach (M4) 1,691
Oriole (P8) 268
Overlea (M3) 10,795
Owings (M6) 720
Owings Mills (L3) 3,810
Oxford (O6) 852
Oxon Hill (F6) 1,000
Park Hill (N8) 250
Parkton (M2) 500
Parkville-Carney (M3) 27,236
Parran (M6) ....
Parsonsburg (R7) 500
Pasadena (M4) 300
Patapsco (L2) 150

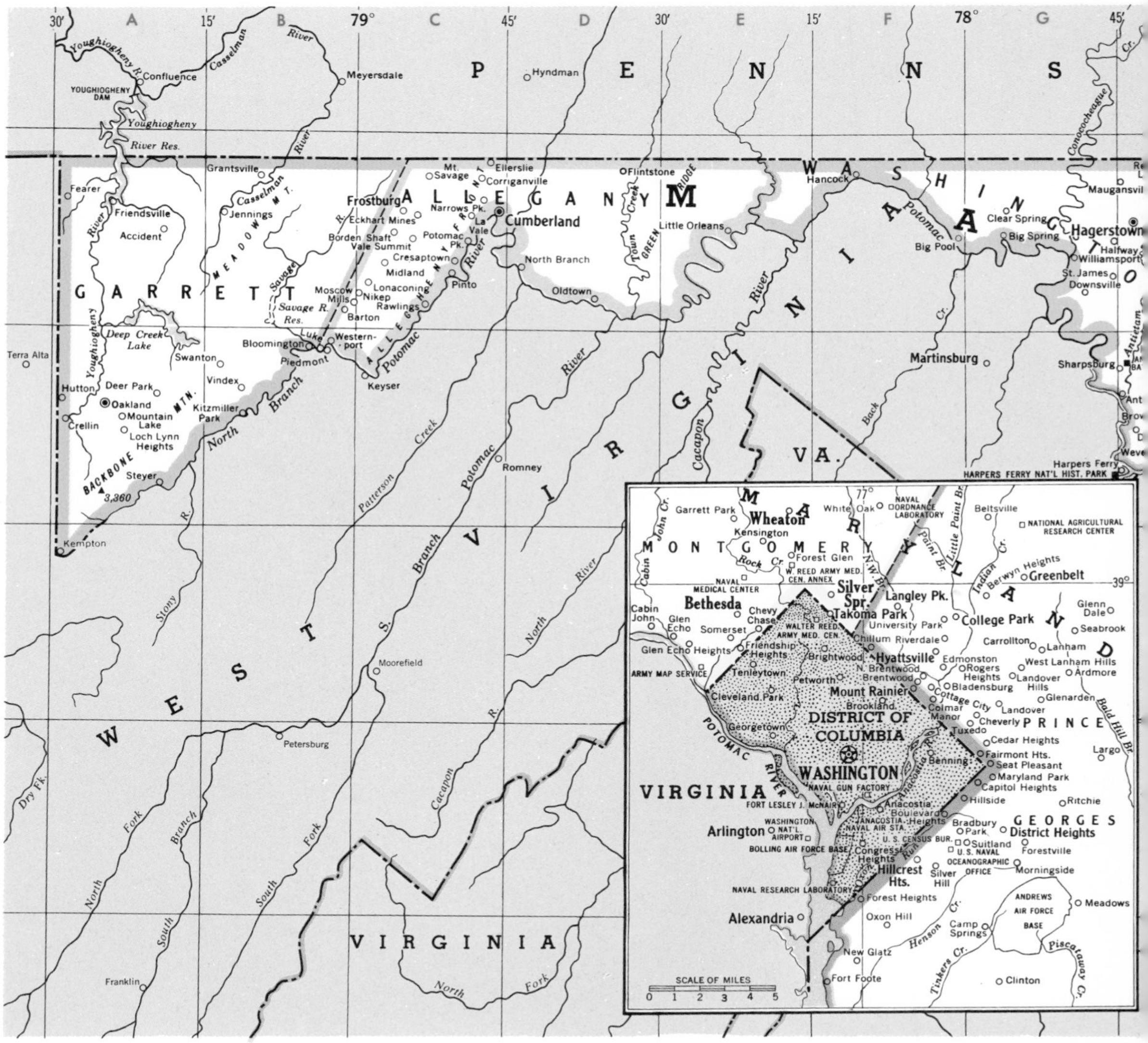

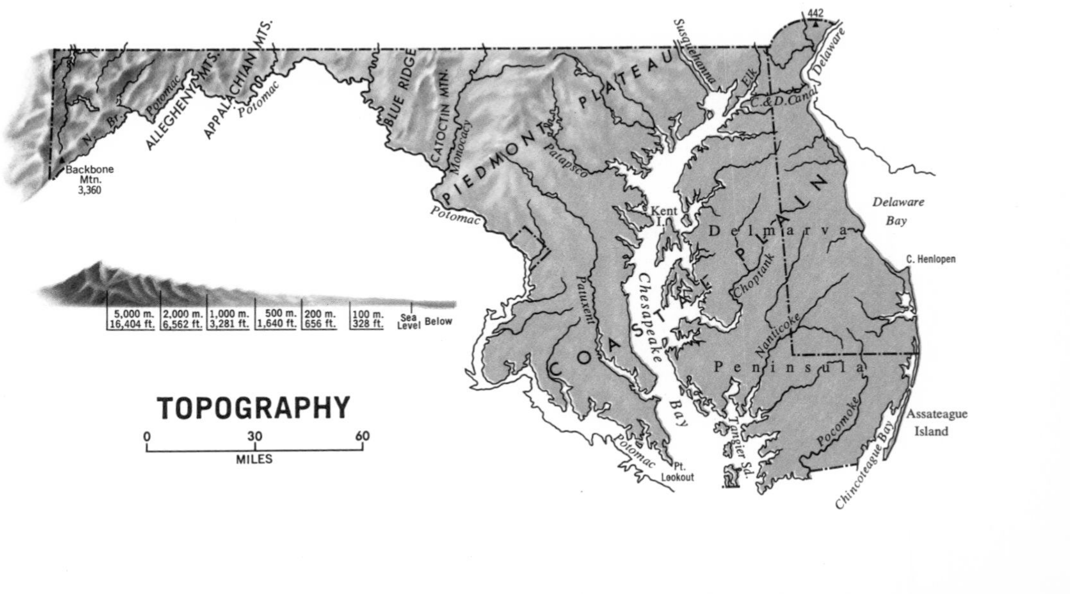

MARYLAND and DELAWARE

MARYLAND

AREA	10,577 sq. mi.
POPULATION	3,519,000
CAPITAL	Annapolis
LARGEST CITY	Baltimore 939,024
HIGHEST POINT	Backbone Mtn. 3,360 ft.
SETTLED IN	1634
ADMITTED TO UNION	April 28, 1788
POPULAR NAMES	Old Line State; Free State
STATE FLOWER	Black-eyed Susan
STATE BIRD	Baltimore Oriole

DELAWARE

AREA	2,057 sq. mi.
POPULATION	505,000
CAPITAL	Dover
LARGEST CITY	Wilmington 95,827
HIGHEST POINT	Ebright Road 442 ft.
SETTLED IN	1627
ADMITTED TO UNION	December 7, 1787
POPULAR NAMES	First State; Diamond State
STATE FLOWER	Peach Blossom
STATE BIRD	Blue Hen Chicken

MARYLAND and DELAWARE

SCALE OF MILES

0   10   20   30

National Capital ⊛   State Capital ⊛

County Seats ⊙   Canals

Copyright by C. S. Hammond & Co. Inc., N.Y.

Maryland and Delaware
(continued)

HIGHWAYS

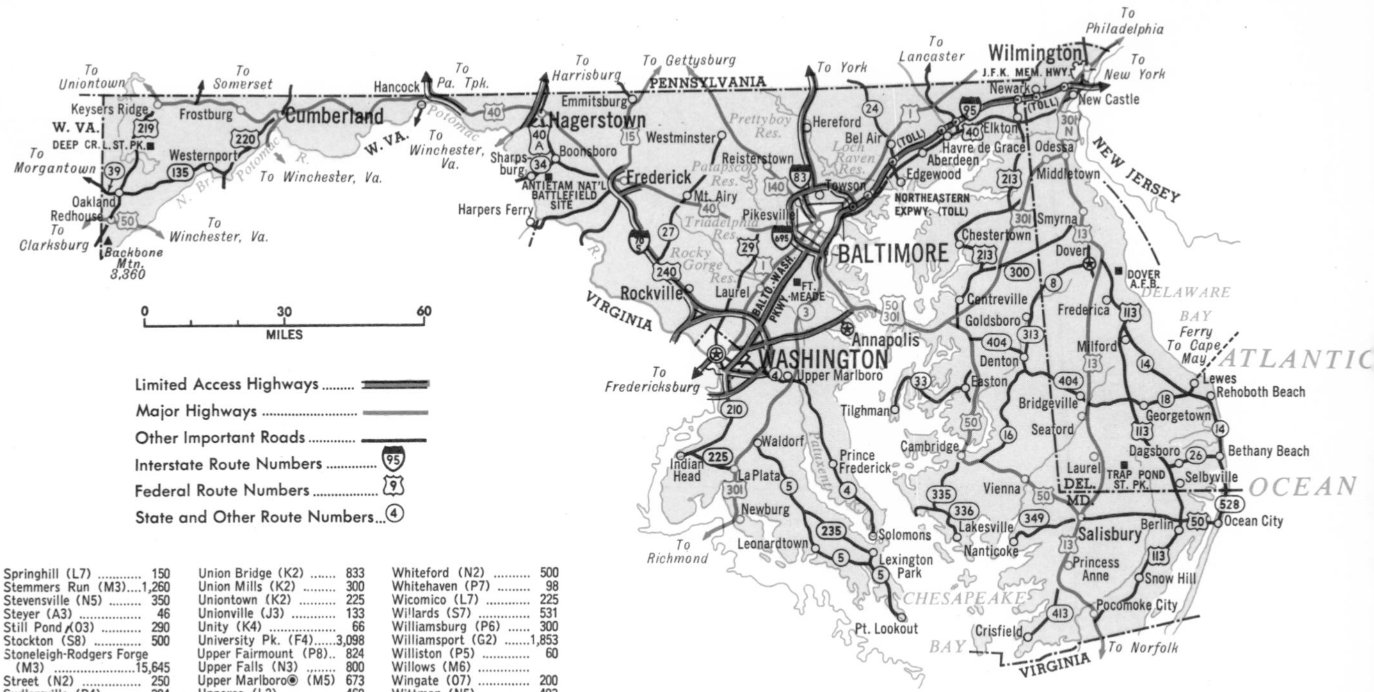

To Philadelphia
To Lancaster
Wilmington
To New York
To Harrisburg
To Gettysburg
To York
PENNSYLVANIA
To Uniontown
To Somerset
Hancock
To Pa. Tpk.
Newark
New Castle
Keysers Ridge
Frostburg
Cumberland
Emmitsburg
Hagerstown
Westminster
Hereford
Bel Air
Elkton
W. VA.
DEEP CR. L. ST. PK.
Westernport
W. VA.
To Winchester, Va.
Sharpsburg
Boonsboro
Reisterstown
Havre de Grace
Odessa
Aberdeen
Edgewood
Middletown
NEW JERSEY
To Morgantown
To Winchester, Va.
ANTIETAM NAT'L BATTLEFIELD SITE
Frederick
Mt. Airy
Towson
NORTHEASTERN EXPWY. (TOLL)
Smyrna
Oakland
Redhouse
To Clarksburg
Backbone Mtn. 3,360
To Winchester, Va.
Harpers Ferry
Pikesville
Chestertown
Dover
DOVER A.F.B.
BALTIMORE
DELAWARE BAY
VIRGINIA
Rockville
Laurel
FT. MEADE
Centreville
Goldsboro
Frederica
Ferry To Cape May
ATLANTIC
Annapolis
WASHINGTON
To Fredericksburg
Upper Marlboro
Denton
Milford
Easton
Lewes
Rehoboth Beach
Bridgeville
Georgetown
Tilghman
Seaford
Waldorf
Cambridge
Dagsboro
Bethany Beach
Indian Head
La Plata
Prince Frederick
Laurel
TRAP POND ST. PK.
Selbyville
DEL.
MD.
OCEAN
Newburg
Vienna
Berlin
Ocean City
Lakesville
Salisbury
To Richmond
Leonardtown
Solomons
Nanticoke
Lexington Park
Princess Anne
Snow Hill
CHESAPEAKE
Pocomoke City
Pt. Lookout
Crisfield
BAY
VIRGINIA
To Norfolk
0 30 60
MILES
Limited Access Highways
Major Highways
Other Important Roads
Interstate Route Numbers
Federal Route Numbers
State and Other Route Numbers

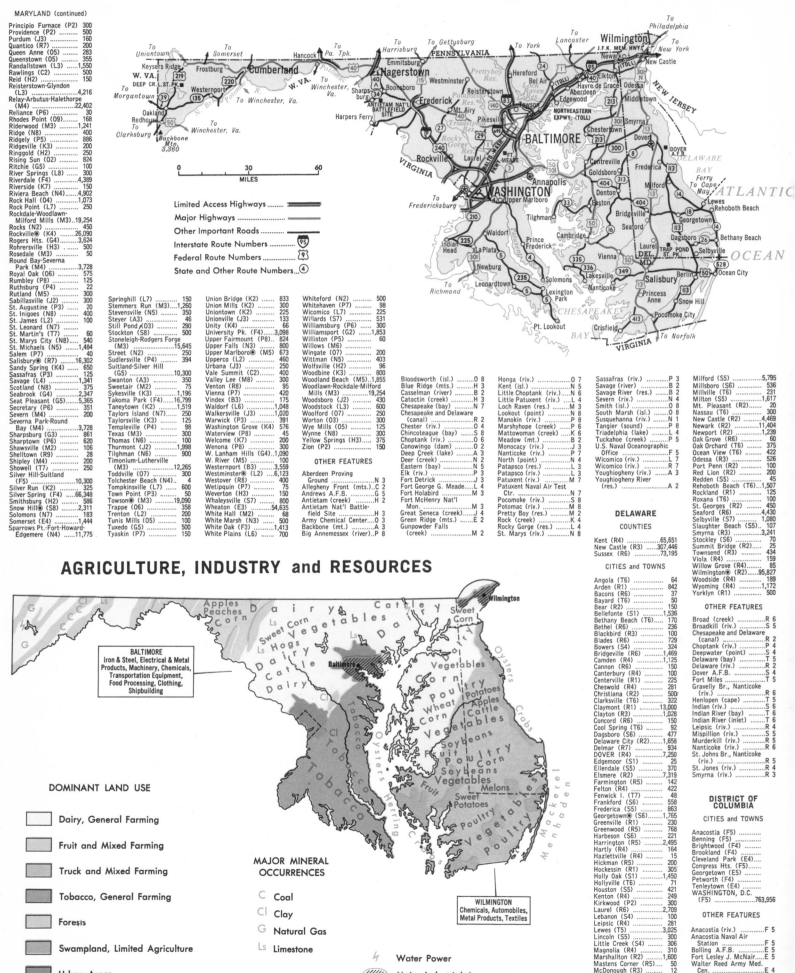

MARYLAND (continued)

Principio Furnace (P2) 300
Providence (P2) 500
Purdum (J3) 160
Quantico (R7) 200
Queen Anne (O5) 283
Queenstown (O5) 355
Randallstown (L3) 1,550
Rawlings (C2) 500
Reid (H2) 150
Reisterstown-Glyndon (L3) 4,216
Relay-Arbutus-Halethorpe (M4) 22,402
Reliance (P6) 30
Rhodes Point (O9)........ 168
Riderwood (M3) 1,241
Ridge (N8) 400
Ridgely (P5) 886
Ridgeville (K3) 200
Ringgold (H2) 250
Rising Sun (O2) 824
Ritchie (G5) 100
River Springs (L8) 300
Riverdale (F4) 4,389
Riverside (K7) 150
Riviera Beach (N4).......4,902
Rock Hall (O4) 1,073
Rock Point (L7) 250
Rockdale-Woodlawn-Milford Mills (M3)..19,254
Rocks (N2) 450
Rockville◉ (K4) 26,090
Rogers Hts. (G4)..........3,624
Rohrersville (H3) 500
Rosedale (M3) 50
Round Bay-Severna Park (M4) 3,728
Royal Oak (O6) 575
Rumbley (P8) 125
Ruthsburg (P4) 22
Rutland (M5) 300
Sabillasville (J2) 300
St. Augustine (P3) 20
St. Inigoes (N8) 400
St. James (L2) 100
St. Leonard (N7) ....
St. Martin's (T7) 60
St. Marys City (N8)..... 540
St. Michaels (N5) 1,484
Salem (P7) 40
Salisbury◉ (R7) 16,302
Sandy Spring (K4) 650
Sassafras (P3) 125
Savage (L4) 1,341
Scotland (N8) 375
Seabrook (G4) 2,347
Seat Pleasant (G5).......5,365
Secretary (P6) 351
Severn (M4) 200
Severna Park-Round Bay (M4) 3,728
Sharpsburg (G3) 861
Sharptown (P6) 620
Shawsville (M2) 106
Shelltown (R9) 28
Shipley (M4) 200
Showell (T7) 250
Silver Hill-Suitland (F5) 10,300
Silver Run (K2) 325
Silver Spring (F4) 66,348
Smithsburg (H2) 586
Snow Hill◉ (S8) 2,311
Solomons (N7) 183
Somerset (E4) 1,444
Sparrows Pt.-Fort-Howard-Edgemere (N4) 11,775
Springhill (L7) 150
Stemmers Run (M3)....1,260
Stevensville (N5) 350
Steyer (A3) 46
Still Pond (O3) 290
Stockton (S8) 500
Stoneleigh-Rodgers Forge (M3) 15,645
Street (N2) 250
Sudlersville (P4) 394
Suitland-Silver Hill (G5) 10,300
Swanton (A3) 350
Sweetair (M2) 75
Sykesville (K3) 1,196
Takoma Park (F4)......16,799
Taneytown (K2) 1,519
Taylors Island (N7)...... 250
Taylorsville (K3) 125
Templeville (P4) 98
Texas (M3) 300
Thomas (N6) 100
Thurmont (J2) 1,998
Tilghman (N6) 900
Timonium-Lutherville (M3) 12,265
Toddville (O7) 300
Tolchester Beach (N4).. 4
Tompkinsville (L7) 600
Town Point (P3) 50
Towson◉ (M3) 19,090
Trappe (O6) 358
Trenton (L2) 200
Tunis Mills (O5) 100
Tuxedo (G5) 500
Tyaskin (P7) 150
Union Bridge (K2) 833
Union Mills (K2) 300
Uniontown (K2) 225
Unionville (J3) 133
Unity (K4) 66
University Pk. (F4)......3,098
Upper Fairmount (P8).. 824
Upper Falls (N3) 800
Upper Marlboro◉ (M5) 673
Upperco (L2) 460
Urbana (J3) 250
Vale Summit (C2)........ 400
Valley Lee (M8) 300
Venton (R8) 95
Vienna (P7) 420
Vindex (B3) 175
Waldorf (L6) 1,048
Walkersville (J3) 1,020
Warwick (P3) 391
Washington Grove (K4) 576
Waterview (P8) 45
Welcome (K7) 200
Wenona (P8) 300
W. Lanham Hills (G4)..1,090
W. River (M5) 100
Westernport (B3) 3,559
Westminster◉ (L2) 6,123
Westover (R8) 400
Wetipquin (P7) 75
Weverton (H3) 150
Whaleysville (S7) 800
Wheaton (E3) 54,635
White Hall (M2) 68
White Marsh (N3) 500
White Oak (F3) 1,413
White Plains (L6) 700
Whiteford (N2) 500
Whitehaven (P7) 98
Wicomico (L7) 225
Willards (S7) 531
Williamsburg (P6) 300
Williamsport (G2) 1,853
Williston (P5) 60
Willows (M6) ....
Wingate (O7) 200
Wittman (N5) 403
Wolfsville (H2) 96
Woodbine (K3) 800
Woodland Beach (M5)..1,855
Woodlawn-Rockdale-Milford Mills (M3) 19,254
Woodsboro (J2) 430
Woodstock (L3) 600
Woolford (O7) 250
Worton (O3) 300
Wye Mills (O5) 125
Wynne (N8) 300
Yellow Springs (H3)..... 375
Zion (P2) 150

OTHER FEATURES

Aberdeen Proving Ground ....N 3
Allegheny Front (mts.)..C 2
Andrews A.F.B. ....G 5
Antietam (creek) ....H 2
Antietam Nat'l Battlefield Site ....H 3
Army Chemical Center....O 3
Backbone (mt.) ....A 3
Big Annemessex (river)..P 8
Bloodsworth (isl.) ....O 8
Blue Ridge (mts.) ....H 3
Casselman (river) ....B 2
Catoctin (creek) ....H 3
Chesapeake (bay) ....N 7
Chesapeake and Delaware (canal) ....R 2
Chester (riv.) ....O 4
Chincoteague (bay) ....S 8
Choptank (riv.) ....O 6
Conowingo (dam) ....O 2
Deep Creek (lake) ....A 3
Deer (creek) ....N 2
Eastern (bay) ....N 5
Elk (riv.) ....P 3
Fort Detrick ....J 3
Fort George G. Meade.....L 4
Fort Holabird ....M 3
Fort McHenry Nat'l Mon. ....M 3
Great Seneca (creek)......J 4
Green Ridge (mts.) ....E 2
Gunpowder Falls (creek) ....M 2
Honga (riv.) ....O 7
Kent (isl.) ....N 5
Little Choptank (riv.).....N 6
Little Patuxent (riv.) ....L 4
Loch Raven (res.) ....M 3
Lookout (point) ....N 8
Manokin (riv.) ....P 8
Marshyhope (creek) ......P 6
Mattowoman (creek) .....K 6
Meadow (mt.) ....B 2
Monocacy (riv.) ....J 3
Nanticoke (riv.) ....P 7
North (point) ....N 4
Patapsco (res.) ....L 3
Patapsco (riv.) ....L 3
Patuxent (riv.) ....M 7
Patuxent Naval Air Test Ctr. ....N 7
Pocomoke (riv.) ....S 8
Potomac (riv.) ....M 8
Pretty Boy (res.) ....M 2
Rock (creek) ....K 4
Rocky Gorge (res.) ....L 4
St. Marys (riv.) ....N 8
Sassafras (riv.) ....P 3
Savage (river) ....B 2
Savage River (res.) ....B 2
Severn (riv.) ....N 4
Smith (isl.) ....O 8
South Marsh (isl.) ....O 8
Susquehanna (riv.) ....N 1
Tangier (sound) ....P 8
Triadelphia (lake) ....L 4
Tuckahoe (creek) ....P 5
U.S. Naval Oceanographic Office ....F 5
Wicomico (riv.) ....L 7
Wicomico (riv.) ....R 7
Youghiogheny (riv.) ....A 3
Youghiogheny River (res.) ....A 2

DELAWARE

COUNTIES

Kent (R4) 65,651
New Castle (R3) 307,446
Sussex (R6) 73,195

CITIES and TOWNS

Angola (T6) 64
Arden (R1) 842
Bacons (R6) 37
Bayard (T6) 50
Bear (R2) 150
Bellefonte (S1) 1,536
Bethany Beach (T6)..... 170
Bethel (R6) 236
Blackbird (R3) 100
Blades (R6) 729
Bowers (S4) 324
Bridgeville (R6) 1,469
Camden (R4) 1,125
Cannon (R6) 150
Canterbury (R4) 100
Centerville (R1) 225
Cheswold (R4) 281
Christiana (R2) 500
Clarksville (T6) 322
Claymont (R1) 13,000
Clayton (R3) 1,028
Concord (R6) 150
Cool Spring (T6) 92
Dagsboro (S6) 477
Delaware City (R2).......1,658
Delmar (R7) 934
DOVER (R4) 7,250
Edgemoor (S1) 25
Ellendale (S5) 370
Elsmere (R2) 7,319
Farmington (R5) 142
Felton (R4) 422
Fenwick I. (T7) 48
Frankford (S6) 558
Frederica (S5) 863
Georgetown◉ (S6)........1,765
Greenville (R1) 230
Greenwood (R5) 768
Harbeson (S6) 221
Harrington (R5) 2,495
Hartly (R4) 164
Hazlettville (R4) 15
Hickman (R5) 200
Hockessin (R1) 305
Holly Oak (S1) 1,450
Hollyville (T6) 71
Houston (S5) 421
Kenton (R4) 249
Kirkwood (P2) 300
Laurel (R6) 2,709
Lebanon (S4) 100
Leipsic (R4) 281
Lewes (T5) 3,025
Lincoln (S5) 300
Little Creek (S4) 306
Magnolia (R4) 310
Marshallton (R2) 1,600
Mastens Corner (R5).... 50
McDonough (R3) 12
Middletown (R3) 2,191
Midway (T6) 50
Milford (S5) 5,795
Millsboro (S6) 536
Millville (T6) 231
Milton (S5) 1,617
Mt. Pleasant (R2)....... 20
Nassau (T6) 300
New Castle (R2) 4,469
Newark (R2) 11,404
Newport (R2) 1,239
Oak Grove (R6) 60
Oak Orchard (T6) 375
Ocean View (T6) 422
Odessa (R3) 526
Port Penn (R2) 100
Red Lion (R2) 200
Redden (S5) 45
Rehoboth Beach (T6)...1,507
Rockland (R1) 125
Roxana (T6) 100
St. Georges (R2) 450
Seaford (R6) 4,430
Selbyville (S7) 1,080
Slaughter Beach (S5).. 107
Smyrna (R3) 3,241
Stockley (S6) 70
Summit Bridge (R2)..... 25
Townsend (R3) 434
Viola (R4) 159
Willow Grove (R4)........ 85
Wilmington◉ (R2)......95,827
Woodside (R4) 189
Wyoming (R4) 1,172
Yorklyn (R1) 500

OTHER FEATURES

Broad (creek) ....R 6
Broadkill (riv.) ....S 5
Chesapeake and Delaware (canal) ....R 2
Choptank (riv.) ....P 4
Deepwater (point) ....S 4
Delaware (bay) ....T 5
Delaware (riv.) ....R 2
Dover A.F.B. ....S 4
Fort Miles ....T 5
Gravelly Br., Nanticoke (riv.) ....R 6
Henlopen (cape) ....T 5
Indian (riv.) ....S 6
Indian River (bay) ....T 6
Indian River (inlet) ....T 6
Leipsic (riv.) ....R 4
Mispillion (riv.) ....S 5
Murderkill (riv.) ....R 5
Nanticoke (riv.) ....R 6
St. Johns Br., Nanticoke (riv.) ....R 5
St. Jones (riv.) ....R 4
Smyrna (riv.) ....R 3

DISTRICT OF COLUMBIA

CITIES and TOWNS

Anacostia (F5) ....
Benning (F5) ....
Brightwood (F4) ....
Brookland (F4) ....
Cleveland Park (E4)....
Congress Hts. (F5).......
Georgetown (E5) ....
Petworth (F4) ....
Tenleytown (E4) ....
WASHINGTON, D.C. (F5) 763,956

OTHER FEATURES

Anacostia (riv.) ....F 5
Anacostia Naval Air Station ....F 5
Bolling A.F.B. ....E 5
Fort Lesley J. McNair.....E 5
Walter Reed Army Med. Cen. ....E 4

◉ County Seat.

AGRICULTURE, INDUSTRY and RESOURCES

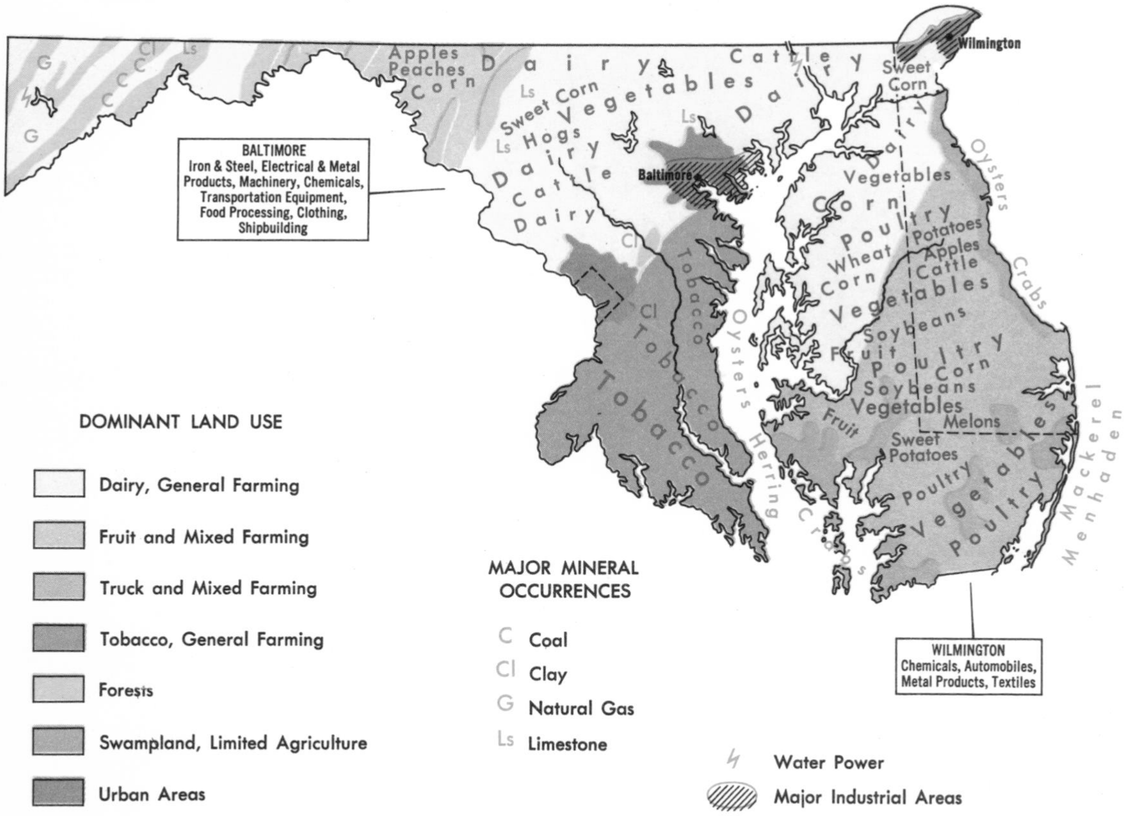

Apples
Peaches
Corn
Dairy
Cattle
Sweet Corn
Vegetables
Hogs
Wilmington
Baltimore
BALTIMORE
Iron & Steel, Electrical & Metal Products, Machinery, Chemicals, Transportation Equipment, Food Processing, Clothing, Shipbuilding
Oysters
Crabs
Poultry
Potatoes
Wheat
Soybeans
Fruit
Tobacco
Melons
Sweet Potatoes
Herring
Mackerel
Menhaden
WILMINGTON
Chemicals, Automobiles, Metal Products, Textiles
DOMINANT LAND USE
Dairy, General Farming
Fruit and Mixed Farming
Truck and Mixed Farming
Tobacco, General Farming
Forests
Swampland, Limited Agriculture
Urban Areas
MAJOR MINERAL OCCURRENCES
C Coal
Cl Clay
G Natural Gas
Ls Limestone
Water Power
Major Industrial Areas

MASSACHUSETTS and RHODE ISLAND

MASSACHUSETTS
COUNTIES

Barnstable (N6)	70,286
Berkshire (B3)	142,135
Bristol (K5)	398,488
Dukes (M7)	5,829
Essex (L2)	568,831
Franklin (D2)	54,864
Hampden (D4)	429,353
Middlesex (J3)	1,238,742
Nantucket (O7)	3,559
Norfolk (K4)	510,256
Plymouth (L5)	248,449
Suffolk (K3)	791,329
Worcester (G3)	583,228

CITIES and TOWNS

Abington (L4)	ᴬ10,607
Accord (E8)	256
Acton (J3)	ᴬ7,238
Acushnet (L6)	ᴬ5,755
Adams (B2)	11,949
Agawam (D4)	ᴬ15,718
Allerton (E7)	500
Amesbury (L1)	9,625
Amherst (E3)	10,306
Andover (K2)	ᴬ15,878
Arlington (C6)	49,953
Ashburnham (G2)	ᴬ2,758
Ashby (G2)	ᴬ1,883
Ashfield (C2)	ᴬ1,131
Ashland (J3)	ᴬ7,779
Ashley Falls (A4)	5,000
Assinippi (E8)	500
Assonet (K5)	1,075
Athol (F2)	10,161
Attleboro (J5)	27,118
Auburn (G4)	ᴬ14,047
Auburndale (B7)	8,000
Avon (K4)	ᴬ4,301
Ayer (H2)	3,323
Baldwinville (F2)	ᴬ1,631
Ballard Vale (K2)	1,100
Barnstable⊙ (N6)	ᴬ13,465
Barre (F3)	1,065
Barre Plains (F3)	532
Barrowsville (K5)	500
Becket (B3)	ᴬ770
Bedford (B6)	ᴬ10,969
Beechwood (F8)	200
Belchertown (E3)	ᴬ5,186
Bellingham (J4)	ᴬ6,774
Belmont (C6)	28,715
Berkley (K5)	ᴬ1,609
Berlin (H3)	ᴬ1,742
Bernardston (D2)	ᴬ1,370
Beverly (E5)	36,108
Beverly Farms (E5)	2,000
Billerica (J2)	ᴬ17,867
Blackinton (B2)	440
Blackstone (H4)	ᴬ5,130
Blandford (C4)	ᴬ636
Bolton (H3)	ᴬ1,264
Bondsville (E4)	1,200
BOSTON⊙ (D7)	697,197
Bourne (M6)	ᴬ14,011
Boxford (L2)	ᴬ2,010
Boylston (H3)	ᴬ2,367
Braintree (D8)	31,069
Brant Rock (M4)	500
Brewster (O5)	ᴬ1,236
Bridgewater (K5)	ᴬ4,296
Brimfield (F4)	ᴬ1,414
Brockton (K4)	72,813
Brookfield (F4)	ᴬ1,751
Brookline (C7)	54,044
Brookville (K4)	1,300
Buckland (C2)	ᴬ1,664
Burlington (C5)	ᴬ12,852
Buzzards Bay (M5)	2,170
Byfield (L1)	900

MASSACHUSETTS

AREA	8,257 sq. mi.
POPULATION	5,348,000
CAPITAL	Boston
LARGEST CITY	Boston 697,197
HIGHEST POINT	Mt. Greylock 3,491 ft.
SETTLED IN	1620
ADMITTED TO UNION	February 6, 1788
POPULAR NAMES	Bay State; Old Colony
STATE FLOWER	Mayflower
STATE BIRD	Chickadee

RHODE ISLAND

AREA	1,214 sq. mi.
POPULATION	920,000
CAPITAL	Providence
LARGEST CITY	Providence 207,498
HIGHEST POINT	Jerimoth Hill 812 ft.
SETTLED IN	1636
ADMITTED TO UNION	May 29, 1790
POPULAR NAME	Little Rhody
STATE FLOWER	Violet
STATE BIRD	Rhode Island Red

AGRICULTURE, INDUSTRY and RESOURCES

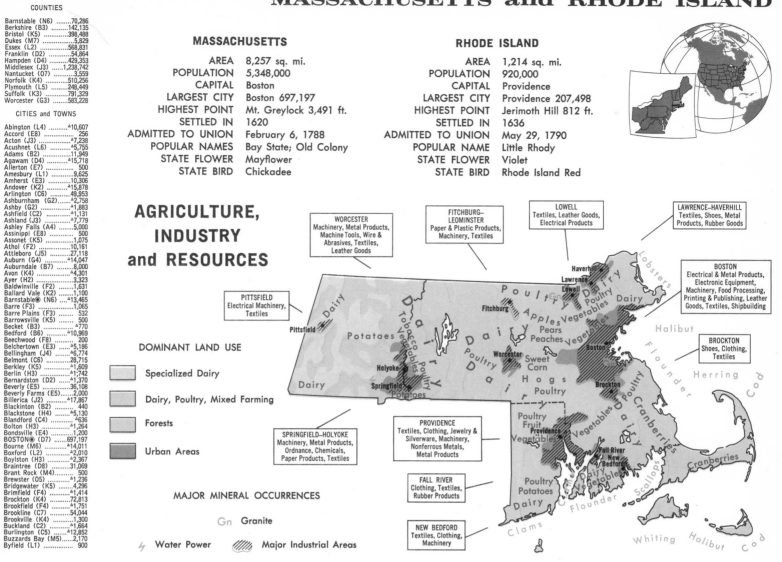

WORCESTER Machinery, Metal Products, Machine Tools, Wire & Abrasives, Textiles, Leather Goods

FITCHBURG–LEOMINSTER Paper & Plastic Products, Machinery, Textiles

LOWELL Textiles, Leather Goods, Electrical Products

LAWRENCE–HAVERHILL Textiles, Shoes, Metal Products, Rubber Goods

PITTSFIELD Electrical Machinery, Textiles

BOSTON Electrical & Metal Products, Electronic Equipment, Machinery, Food Processing, Printing & Publishing, Leather Goods, Textiles, Shipbuilding

BROCKTON Shoes, Clothing, Textiles

SPRINGFIELD–HOLYOKE Machinery, Metal Products, Ordnance, Chemicals, Paper Products, Textiles

PROVIDENCE Textiles, Clothing, Jewelry & Silverware, Machinery, Nonferrous Metals, Metal Products

FALL RIVER Clothing, Textiles, Rubber Products

NEW BEDFORD Textiles, Clothing, Machinery

DOMINANT LAND USE

- Specialized Dairy
- Dairy, Poultry, Mixed Farming
- Forests
- Urban Areas

MAJOR MINERAL OCCURRENCES

Gn Granite

⚡ Water Power   ⫽ Major Industrial Areas

HIGHWAYS

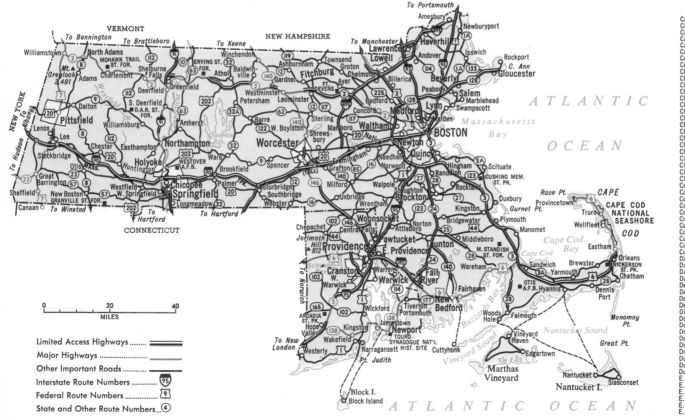

Limited Access Highways ═══
Major Highways ────
Other Important Roads
Interstate Route Numbers ⑨⑤
Federal Route Numbers ⑨
State and Other Route Numbers ④

0 20 40
MILES

Cambridge⊙ (C7)	107,716
Canton (C8)	ᴬ12,771
Carlisle (J2)	ᴬ1,488
Carver (M5)	ᴬ1,949
Caryville (J4)	150
Cataumet (M6)	500
Centerville (N6)	1,518
Central Village (K6)	800
Charlemont (C2)	ᴬ897
Charlton (F4)	ᴬ3,685
Charlton City (F4)	1,070
Chartley (K5)	800
Chatham (P6)	1,479
Chelmsford (J2)	ᴬ15,130
Chelsea (D6)	33,749
Cheshire (B2)	1,078
Chester (C3)	ᴬ1,155
Chesterfield (C3)	ᴬ556
Chicopee (D4)	61,553
Chicopee Falls (D4)	27,000
Chilmark (M7)	ᴬ238
City Mills (J4)	500
Clicquot-Millis (A8)	ᴬ2,588
Clifton (E6)	5,000
Clinton (H3)	12,848
Cochituate (A7)	4,500
Cohasset (F7)	2,748
Collinsville (J2)	2,500
Colrain (D2)	ᴬ1,426
Concord (B6)	3,188
Conway (D2)	ᴬ875
Cordaville (H3)	500
Cotuit (N6)	1,200
Cummaquid (N6)	300
Cummington (C3)	ᴬ550
Cushman (D3)	250
Dalton (B3)	ᴬ6,436
Danvers (D5)	21,926
Danversport (E5)	1,500
Dartmouth (K6)	ᴬ14,607
Dedham⊙ (C7)	23,869
Deerfield (D2)	ᴬ3,727
Dennis (O5)	ᴬ3,338
Dennis Port (O6)	ᴬ2,271
Dighton (K5)	ᴬ3,769
Dodge (G4)	1,083
Dodgeville (J5)	750
Dorchester (D7)	150,000
Douglas (H4)	ᴬ2,559
Dover (B7)	ᴬ2,846
Dracut (J2)	ᴬ13,674
Dudley (G4)	ᴬ6,510
Dunstable (J2)	ᴬ824
Duxbury (M4)	ᴬ1,069
E. Braintree (D8)	10,000
E. Brewster (O5)	500
E. Bridgewater (K4)	ᴬ6,139
E. Brookfield (L4)	ᴬ1,150
E. Dedham (C8)	1,500
E. Dennis (O5)	450

(continued on following page)

Massachusetts and Rhode Island

(continued)

MASSACHUSETTS (continued)

E. Douglas (G4)	1,695
E. Falmouth (M6)	1,655
E. Foxboro (K4)	600
E. Freetown (L5)	1,200
E. Harwich (O6)	650
E. Longmeadow (E4)	10,294
E. Milton (D7)	7,500
E. Northfield (E2)	1,500
E. Norton (K5)	800
E. Orleans (O6)	383
E. Pembroke (M4)	275
E. Pepperell (H2)	2,500
E. Sandwich (N6)	325
E. Saugus (D6)	4,000
E. Taunton (K5)	5,000
E. Templeton (G2)	1,200
E. Village (G4)	621
E. Walpole (C8)	2,000
E. Wareham (M5)	975
E. Weymouth (E8)	10,000
E. Whately (D3)	425
Eastham (O5)	^1,200
Easthampton (D3)	^12,326
Easton (K4)	^9,078
Edgartown (K4)	600
Edgartown (M7)	1,181
Egypt (F8)	600
Elmwood (L4)	350
Erving (E2)	^1,272
Essex (L2)	1,178
Fairhaven (L6)	^14,339
Fairview (D4)	2,108
Fall River⊙ (K6)	99,942
Falmouth (M6)	3,308
Farnams (B2)	144
Farnumsville (H4)	1,041
Fayville (H3)	975
Feeding Hills (D4)	4,000
Fiskdale (F4)	^1,200
Fitchburg⊙ (G2)	43,021
Florence (D3)	5,000
Florida (B2)	^569
Forge Village (H2)	1,191
Foxboro (J4)	3,169
Framingham (H3)	44,526
Framingham Ctr. (J3)	4,500
Franklin (J4)	6,391
Gardner (G2)	19,038
Gay Head (L7)	^103
Georgetown (L2)	2,005
Gilbertville (F3)	1,202
Gill (D2)	^1,203
Gleasondale (J3)	300
Glendale (A3)	300
Gloucester (M2)	25,789
Goshen (C3)	^385
Grafton (H4)	^10,627
Granby (E3)	^4,221
Graniteville (J2)	975
Granville (C4)	^874
Great Barrington (A4)	2,943
Green Harbor (M4)	650
Greenbush (F8)	650
Greenfield⊙ (D2)	14,389
Greenwood (D6)	5,000
Griswoldville (D2)	675
Groton (H2)	^1,178
Groveland (L1)	^3,297
Hadley (D3)	^3,099
Halifax (L5)	^1,599
Hamilton (L2)	^5,488
Hampden (E4)	^2,345
Hancock (A2)	^455
Hanover (L4)	^5,923
Hanson (L4)	^4,370
Hardwick (F3)	2,340
Harvard (H2)	^2,563
Harwich (O6)	3,747
Harwich Port (O6)	1,592
Hatfield (D3)	^1,330
Haverhill (K1)	46,346
Haydenville (C3)	950
Heath (C2)	^304
Hingham (E8)	^15,378
Hinsdale (B3)	^1,414
Holbrook (D8)	^10,104
Holden (G3)	1,704
Holland (F4)	^561
Holliston (A8)	2,447
Holyoke (D4)	52,689
Hoosac Tunnel (C2)	200
Hopedale (H4)	2,904
Hopkinton (H4)	2,754
Housatonic (A3)	1,370
Hubbardston (F3)	^1,217
Hudson (H3)	7,897
Hull (E7)	7,055
Humarock (M4)	200
Huntington (C4)	^1,392
Hyannis (N6)	5,139
Hyannis Port (N6)	300
Interlaken (A3)	350
Ipswich (L2)	4,617
Islington (C8)	2,300
Jamaica Plain (C7)	36,476
Kingston (M5)	1,301
Lakeville (L5)	^3,209
Lancaster (H3)	^3,958
Lanesboro (A2)	^2,933
Lanesville (M2)	1,046
Lawrence (K2)	70,933
Lee (B3)	^3,078
Leeds (B3)	1,200
Leicester (G4)	^1,750
Lenox (A3)	^1,713
Lenox Dale (B3)	500
Leominster (G2)	27,929
Leverett (E3)	^914
Lexington (B6)	27,691
Leyden (D2)	^343
Lincoln (B6)	^5,613
Lincoln Center (B6)	
Linwood (H4)	995
Littleton (H2)	^5,109
Littleton Common (J2)	2,277
Longmeadow (D4)	^10,565
Lowell (J2)	92,107
Ludlow (E4)	^13,805
Lunenburg (H2)	^6,334
Lynn (D6)	94,478
Lynnfield (D5)	^8,398
Lynnfield Center (C5)	^2,600
Malden (D6)	57,676
Manchaug (G4)	1,800
Manchester (F5)	^3,932
Manomet (M5)	1,800
Mansfield (J4)	^4,674
Marblehead (E5)	18,521
Marion (L6)	1,160
Marlborough (H3)	18,819
Marshfield (M4)	^6,748
Marshfield Hills (M4)	875
Marstons Mills (N6)	900
Mashpee (M6)	^867
Mattapan (C7)	19,086
Mattapoisett (L6)	1,640
Maynard (J3)	7,695
Medfield (B8)	2,424
Medford (C6)	64,971
Medway (J4)	1,602
Melrose (D6)	29,619
Mendon (H4)	^2,068
Merino Village (D4)	3,099
Merrimac (L1)	3,261
Merrimacport (L1)	300
Methuen (K2)	^28,114
Middleboro (L5)	^6,003
Middlefield (B3)	^315
Middleton (K2)	^3,718
Milford (H4)	^15,749
Mill River (A4)	350
Millbury (G4)	9,623
Millers Falls (E2)	1,199
Millis-Clicquot (A8)	^2,588
Millville (H4)	1,141
Milton (D7)	26,375
Minot (F8)	300
Monson (E4)	^2,413
Montague (E2)	^7,836
Montague City (D2)	609
Monterey (B4)	^480
Monument Beach (M6)	650

Massachusetts and Rhode Island
(continued)

Mount Hermon (D2)..... 760
Mt. Hope (C7) 5,000
Mt. Tom (D3) 210
Mt. Washington (A4)... △34
Myricks (K5) 500
Nabnasset (J2) 1,381
Nahant (E6) 3,960
Nantasket Beach (E7)..1,900
Nantucket◉ (O7).........2,804
Natick (A7) 28,831
Needham (B7) 25,793
Needham Hts. (B7) 8,000
Neponset (D7) 5,573
New Bedford◉ (K6)..102,477
New Braintree (F3)...... △509
New Marlboro (B4) ....△1,083
New Salem (E2)........... △397
Newbury (L1) ....△2,519
Newburyport◉ (L1)..△14,004
Newton (C7) 92,384
Newton Center (C7)....18,850
Newton Highlands (C7) 7,500
Newton Lower Falls (B7) 1,215
Newton Upper Falls (C7) 3,451
Newtonville (C7) 15,000
Noquochoke P.O. (Westport)(K6) .....△6,641
Norfolk (J4) ....△3,471
N. Abington (L4) 3,906
N. Acton (J2) 300
N. Adams (B2) 19,905
N. Amherst (E3) 1,009
N. Andover (K2)........△10,908
N. Attleboro◉ (J5)...△14,777
N. Bellingham (J4) 300
N. Billerica (J2) 4,500
N. Brookfield (F3) 2,615
N. Chelmsford (J2) 4,670
N. Dartmouth (K6).......6,500
N. Dighton (K5) 1,167
N. Eastham (O5) 600
N. Easton (K4) 3,800
N. Egremont (A4) 265
N. Falmouth (M6) 700
N. Grafton (H4) 2,800
N. Hadley (D3) 750
N. Hanover (L4) 800
N. Marshfield (M4)...... 500
N. Middleboro (L5) 500
N. Oxford (G4) 1,466
N. Pembroke (M4) 600
N. Plymouth (L5) 3,467
N. Reading (C5) ....△8,331
N. Scituate (F8) 3,421
N. Truro (O4) 500
N. Uxbridge (H4) 1,882
N. Westport (K6) 4,000
N. Weymouth (D8)....... 700
N. Wilbraham (E4) 3,000
Northampton◉ (D3)...30,058
Northboro (H3) 2,516
Northbridge (H4) 2,128
Northfield (E2) ....△1,179
Norton (K5) 1,501
Norwell (F8) ....△5,207
Norwood (B8) 24,898
Oak Bluffs (M7) 1,027
Oakham (F3) .... △524
Ocean Bluff (M4) 300
Ocean Grove (K6) 1,500
Old Sturbridge Vill.(F4)
Onset (M6) 1,714
Orange (E2) 3,689
Orleans (O5) ....△2,342
Osterville (N6) 1,094
Otis (B4) .... △473
Otter River (F2) 660
Oxford (G4) 6,985

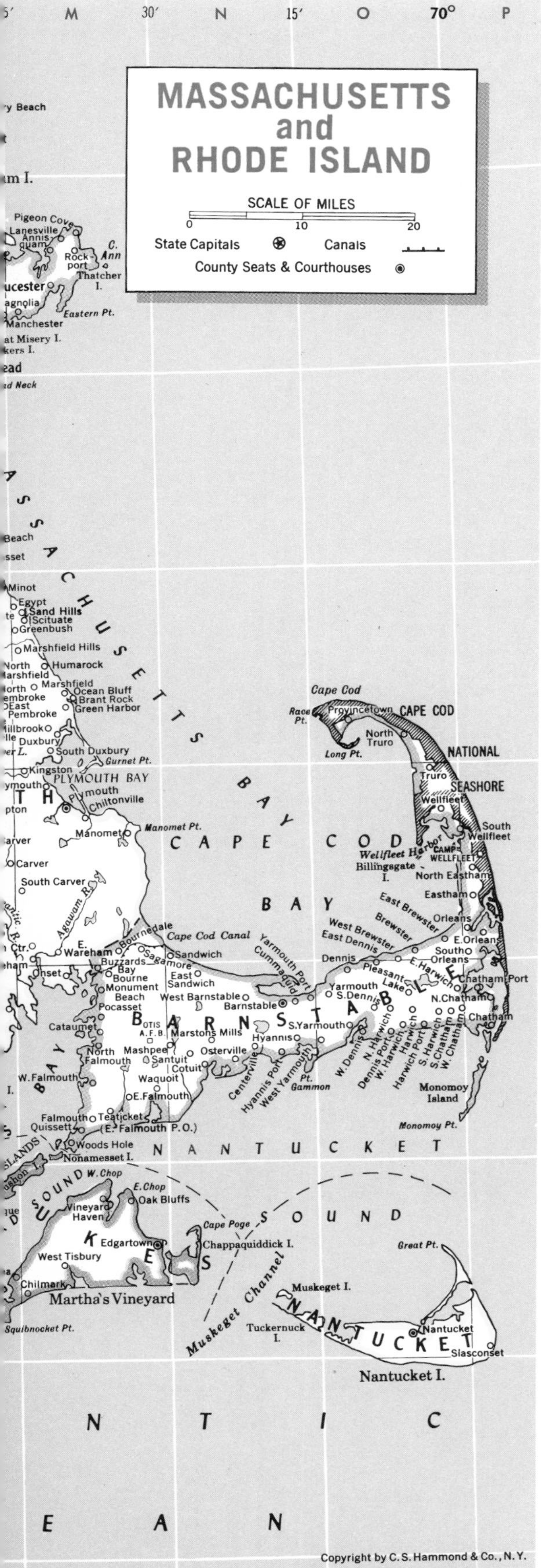
MASSACHUSETTS and RHODE ISLAND
SCALE OF MILES
0
10
20
State Capitals
Canals
County Seats & Courthouses
M
30′
N
15′
O
70°
P
Pigeon Cove
Lanesville
C. Ann
Rockport
Thatcher I.
Eastern Pt.
Manchester
Minot
Egypt
Sand Hills
Scituate
Greenbush
Marshfield Hills
Humarock
Marshfield
Ocean Bluff
Brant Rock
Green Harbor
Duxbury
South Duxbury
Gurnet Pt.
Kingston
PLYMOUTH BAY
Plymouth
Chiltonville
Manomet
Manomet Pt.
Carver
South Carver
Wareham
Buzzards Bay
Bourne
Monument Beach
Pocasset
Sagamore
Sandwich
Cape Cod Canal
East Sandwich
West Barnstable
Barnstable
Cataumet
North Falmouth
Mashpee
Santuit
Cotuit
Osterville
Waquoit
E. Falmouth
W. Falmouth
Falmouth
Teaticket
Quissett
(E. Falmouth P.O.)
Woods Hole
Nonamesset I.
W. Chop
E. Chop
Oak Bluffs
Vineyard Haven
Edgartown
West Tisbury
Chilmark
Martha's Vineyard
Squibnocket Pt.
Cape Poge
Chappaquiddick I.
Great Pt.
Muskeget I.
Muskeget Channel
Tuckernuck I.
Nantucket
Siasconset
Nantucket I.
Cape Cod
Race Pt.
Provincetown
CAPE COD
NATIONAL
SEASHORE
North Truro
Long Pt.
Truro
Wellfleet
South Wellfleet
Wellfleet Harbor
Billingsgate I.
North Eastham
Eastham
Orleans
E. Orleans
South Orleans
Chatham Port
N. Chatham
Chatham
Brewster
West Brewster
East Brewster
East Dennis
Dennis
Yarmouth Port
Yarmouth
S. Yarmouth
S. Dennis
Hyannis
Centerville
Hyannis Port
West Yarmouth
Pt. Gammon
W. Dennis
Dennis Port
Harwich Port
Harwich
S. Harwich
W. Harwich
W. Chatham
E. Harwich
Pleasant Lake
Monomoy Island
Monomoy Point
Marstons Mills
CAPE COD BAY
NANTUCKET SOUND
ATLANTIC OCEAN
BARNSTABLE

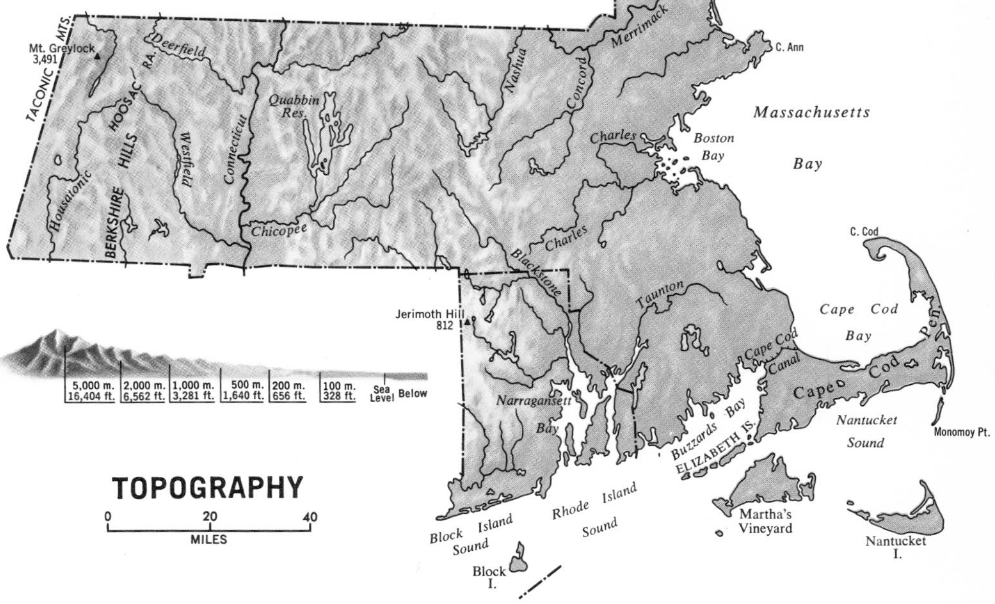
Mt. Greylock 3,491
TACONIC MTS.
Deerfield
HOOSAC RA.
Housatonic
BERKSHIRE HILLS
Westfield
Connecticut
Quabbin Res.
Chicopee
Nashua
Concord
Merrimack
C. Ann
Massachusetts Bay
Charles
Boston Bay
Blackstone
Taunton
Jerimoth Hill 812
C. Cod
Cape Cod Bay
Cape Cod Canal
Cape Cod Pen.
Narragansett Bay
Buzzards Bay
ELIZABETH IS.
Nantucket Sound
Monomoy Pt.
Martha's Vineyard
Nantucket I.
Rhode Island Sound
Block Island Sound
Block I.
5,000 m. 16,404 ft.
2,000 m. 6,562 ft.
1,000 m. 3,281 ft.
500 m. 1,640 ft.
200 m. 656 ft.
100 m. 328 ft.
Sea Level
Below
TOPOGRAPHY
0
20
40
MILES

Palmer (E4) 3,888
Paxton (G3) ....△2,399
Peabody (E5) 32,202
Pembroke (L4) ....△4,919
Pepperell (H2) ....△4,336
Petersham (F3) .... △890
Phillipston (F2) .... △695
Pigeon Cove (M2).........1,064
Pinehurst (B5) 1,991
Pittsfield◉ (A3) 57,879
Plainfield (C2) .... △237
Plainville (J4) ....△3,810
Pleasant Lake (O6)....... 200
Plymouth◉ (M5) 6,488
Plympton (L5) .... △821
Pocasset (M6) 1,035
Pottersville (K6) 2,700
Prides Crossing (E5)..... 450
Princeton (G3) ....△1,360
Provincetown (O4) 3,346
Quincy (D8) 87,409
Quisett (M6) 300
Randolph (D8) 18,900
Raynham (K5) ....△4,150
Raynham Center (K5)...2,500
Reading (C5) 19,259
Readville (C8) 33,123
Rehoboth (K5) ....△4,953
Revere (D6) 40,080
Richmond (A3) .... △890
Richmond Furnace (A3) 200
Rochdale (G4) 1,058
Rochester (L6) ....△1,559
Rock (L5) 487
Rockland (L4) ....△13,119
Rockport (M2) 3,511
Rockville (A8) 500
Rowe (C2) .... △231
Rowley (L2) 1,223
Royalston (F2) .... △800
Russell (C4) ....△1,366
Rutland (G3) 1,774
Sagamore (M5) 900
Salem◉ (E5) 39,211
Salisbury (L1) ....△3,154
Salisbury Beach (L1).... 550
Sand Hills-Shore Acres (M4) 1,778
Sandisfield (B4) .... △536
Sandwich (N5) ....△1,099
Santuit (N6) 320
Saugus (D6) 20,666
Saundersville (G4) 950
Savoy (B2) .... △277
Saxonville (A7) 3,200
Scituate (F8) 3,229
Seekonk (J5) ....△8,399
Sharon (K4) 5,888
Shawsheen Vill. (K2..)..2,100
Sheffield (A4) ....△2,138
Shelburne Falls (D2)....2,097
Sheldonville (J4) 300
Sherborn (A8) ....△1,806
Shirley (H2) 1,762
Shirley Center (H2)......2,000
Shore Acres-Sand Hills (M4) 1,778
Shrewsbury (H3) ......△16,622
Shutesbury (E3) .... △265
Siasconset (P7) 200
Silver Lake (L5) 4,654
Somerset (K5) 12,196
Somerville (C6) 94,697
S. Acton (J3) 1,114
S. Amherst (E3) 975
S. Ashburnham (G2)..... 975
S. Attleboro (J5) 6,000
S. Barre (F3) 1,800
S. Berlin (H3) 300
S. Braintree (D8) 5,600
S. Bridgewater (L5)......2,000
S. Carver (M5) 500
S. Chatham (O6) 500
S. Dartmouth (L6) 6,300
S. Deerfield (D3) 1,253
S. Dennis (O6) 500
S. Duxbury (M4) 950
S. Easton (K4) 3,500
S. Egremont (A4) 425
S. Grafton (H4) 1,663
S. Groveland (L2)......... 900
S. Hadley (D4) ....△14,956
S. Hadley Falls (D4).....5,000
S. Hanover (L4) 800
S. Harwich (O6) 400
S. Lancaster (H3) 1,891
S. Lee (A3) 375
S. Middleboro (L5) 486
S. Natick (A7) 1,500
S. Royalston (F2) 450
S. Sudbury (J3) 3,000
S. Walpole (K4) 1,450
S. Wellfleet (P5) 450
S. Weymouth (E8) 10,000
S. Yarmouth (O6).........2,029
Southampton (C4)......△2,192
Southboro (H3) 1,114
Southbridge (G4) 15,889
Southville (H3) 500
Southwick (C4) 1,242
Spencer (F3) 5,593
Springfield◉ (D4).....174,463
State Line (A3) 300
Sterling (G3) ....△3,193
Stockbridge (A3) ......△2,161
Stoneham (C6) 17,821
Stoughton (K4) ....△16,328
Stow (H3) ....△2,573
Straits Pond (F7) 250
Sturbridge (F4) ....△3,604
Sudbury (A6) ....△7,447
Sunderland (D3) ....△1,279
Sutton (G4) ....△3,638
Swampscott (E6) 13,294
Swansea (K5) ....△9,916
Taunton◉ (K5) 41,132
Teaticket (M6) 950
Templeton (F2) ....△5,371
Tewksbury (K2) 1,151
Thorndike (E4) 1,552
Three Rivers (E4) 3,082
Tolland (B4) .... △101
Topsfield (K2) ....△3,351
Townsend (H2) ....△3,650
Truro (O5) ....△1,002
Turners Falls (D2)........4,917
Twin Village (J5)......... 950
Tyngsboro (J2) ....△3,302
Tyringham (A4) .... △197
Upton (H4) ....△3,127
Upton-W. Upton (H4)..1,991
Uxbridge (H4) 3,377
Vineyard Haven (M7)...1,701
Waban (B7) 7,300
Wakefield (C5) 24,295
Wales (F4) .... △659
Walpole (B8) ....△14,068
Waltham (B6) 55,413
Waquoit (M6) 400
Ware (E3) 6,650
Wareham (L5) ....△9,461
Warren (F4) 1,616
Warwick (E2) 426
Washington (B3) .... △290
Watertown (C6) ....△39,092
Waterville (F2) 296
Waverley (B6) 10,000
Wayland (A7) ....△10,444
Webster (G4) 12,072
Wellesley (B7) 26,071
Wellesley Hills (B7)....15,600
Wellfleet (O5) ....△1,404
Wendell (E2) .... △292
Wenham (L2) ....△2,798
W. Barnstable (N6)...... 695
W. Berlin (H3) 300
W. Boxford (K2) 700
W. Boylston (G3)........△5,526
W. Bridgewater (K4)....5,061
W. Brookfield (F4).......1,250
W. Chatham (O6) 400
W. Chelmsford (J2) 300
W. Concord (A6) 1,556
W. Dennis (O6) 782
W. Falmouth (M6) 700
W. Groton (H2) 1,100
W. Hanover (L4) 1,200
W. Harwich (O6) 450
W. Mansfield (K5) 900
W. Medway (J4) 1,818
W. Millbury (G4) 450
W. Newbury (L1)........△1,844
W. Newton (B7) 15,000
W. Peabody (D5) 1,100
W. Springfield (D4)..△24,924
W. Stockbridge (A3)...△1,244
W. Tisbury (M7) .... △360
W. Townsend (H2) 1,300
W. Upton-Upton (H4)...1,991
W. Wareham (L5) 1,000
W. Warren (F4) 1,124
W. Yarmouth (N6) 1,365
Westboro (H3) 4,011
Westfield (D4) 26,302
Westford (J2) ....△6,261
Westhampton (C3) ...... △583
Westminster (G2) 1,047
Weston (B6) ....△8,261
Westport (K6) ....△6,641
Westport P.O. (North Westport) (K6) 4,000
Westwood (B8) ....△10,354
Weymouth (D8) 48,177
Whately (D3) ....△1,037
Wheelwright (F3) 350
Whitinsville (H4) 5,102
Whitman (L4) 10,485
Wilbraham (E4) ....△7,387
Williamsburg (C3) .....△2,186
Williamstown (B2) 5,428
Willimansett (D4) 10,181
Wilmington (C5) 2,250
Winchendon (F2) 3,839
Winchendon Sprs. (G2).. 333
Winchester (C6) 19,376
Windsor (B2) .... △384
Winthrop (D6) 20,303
Woburn (C6) 31,214
Woods Hole (M6) 975
Woodville (H4) 450
Worcester◉ (H3) 186,587
Woronoco (C4) 425
Worthington (C3) .... △597
Wrentham (J4) 1,790
Yarmouth (O6) ....△5,504
Yarmouth Port (N6)..... 450

OTHER FEATURES

Agawam (riv.) ....M 5
Ann (cape) ....M 2
Assabet (riv.) ....H 3
Assawompset (pond) .....L 5
Berkshire (hills) ....B 4
Birch Hill (res.) ....F 2
Blackstone (riv.) ....G 3
Blue (hills) ....C 8
Brewster (isls.) ....E 7
Buzzards (bay) ....L 7
Cape Cod (bay) ....N 5
Cape Cod (canal) ....N 5
Chappaquiddick (isl.) ....N 7
Charles (riv.) ....C 7
Cobble Mountain (res.)...C 4
Cod (cape) ....O 4
Concord (riv.) ....J 2
Congamond (lakes) ....D 4
Connecticut (riv.) ....D 2
Cuttyhunk (isl.) ....L 7
Elizabeth (isls.) ....L 7
Everett (mt.) ....A 4
Falls (riv.) ....D 2
Farmington (riv.) ....B 4
Great (point) ....O 7
Great Misery (isl.) ....F 5
Greylock (mt.) ....B 2
Hoosac (mt.) ....B 2
Hoosic (riv.) ....A 1
Housatonic (riv.) ....A 4
Manhan (riv.) ....D 4
Martha's Vineyard (isl.) ....M 7
Massachusetts (bay) ....M 4
Merrimack (riv.) ....K 1
Monomoy (isl.) ....O 6
Muskeget (channel) ......N 7
Mystic (riv.) ....C 6
Nantucket (isl.) ....O 8
Nantucket (sound) ....N 6
Nashua (riv.) ....H 3
Nomans Land (isl.) ....L 7
Otis A.F.B. ....M 6
Pontoosuc (lake) ....A 3
Quabbin (res.) ....E 3
Quaboag (riv.) ....F 4
Quinebaug (riv.) ....F 4
Race (point) ....N 4
Shawshine (riv.) ....K 2
Spy (pond) ....C 6
Squantum N.A.S. ....D 7
Stillwater (riv.) ....G 3
Swift (riv.) ....E 4
Taconic (mts.) ....A 2
Toby (mt.) ....E 3
Tom (mt.) ....D 4
Vineyard (sound) ....L 7
Wachusett (res.) ....G 3
Watuppa (pond) ....K 6
West (riv.) ....H 4
Westover A.F.B. ....D 4
Weweantic (riv.) ....L 5
Whitman (riv.) ....G 2
Winter Island C.G. Air Sta. ....E 5

RHODE ISLAND

COUNTIES

Bristol (J6) 37,146
Kent (H6) 112,619
Newport (J6) 81,891
Providence (H5) 568,778
Washington (H7).........59,054

CITIES and TOWNS

Adamsville (K6) ....
Albion (J5) 800
Allenton (H6) 975
Alton (H7) ....
Anthony (H6) 2,000
Apponaug (J6) 3,647
Arcadia (H6) 100
Arctic (H6) 5,000
Arnold Mills (J5) ....
Ashaway (G7) 1,298
Ashton (J5) 2,000
Barrington (J6) 13,826
Block Island (H8) 486
Bradford (H7) 900
Bristol◉ (J6) 14,570
Canonchet (H7) 120
Carolina (H7) 200
Centerdale (H5) ....
Central Falls (J5) 19,858
Charlestown (H7) ......△1,966
Chepachet (H5) 1,100
Clayville (H5) 550
Conimicut (J6) 3,198
Coventry (H6) ....△15,432
Coventry (Washington) (H6) 2,400
Coventry Ctr. (H6) ......
Cranston (J5) 66,766
Davisville (H6) 1,500
E. Greenwich◉ (J6)....△6,100
E. Providence (J5) 41,955
Esmond (H5) 2,535
Exeter (H6) ....△2,298
Fiskeville (H6) ....
Forestdale (H5) 715
Foster (H5) ....△2,097
Foster Center (Foster P.O.) (H5) 185
Georgiaville (H5) ....
Glendale (H5) 800
Greene (H6) 100
Greenville (H5) 3,500
Hamilton (J6) 900
Harmony (H5) 800
Harrisville (H5) 1,024
Hillsgrove (J6) 1,370
Hope (H6) 800
Hope Valley (H6) 1,250
Hopkinton (G7) ....△4,174
Howard (J5) 6,000
Island Park (J6) 1,147
Jamestown (J6) 1,843
Kenyon (H7) 400
Kingston (H7) 2,616
La Fayette (H6) 1,200
Little Compton (K6)..△1,702
Lonsdale (J5) ....
Manton (J5) ....
Manville (H5) 3,429
Mapleville (H5) ....
Middletown (J6).......△12,675
Narragansett (J7) 1,741
Nasonville (H5) 200
Natick (H6) 2,000
Newport◉ (J7) 47,049
North Kingstown (J6)△18,977
North Providence (J5) 18,220
North Scituate (H5)..... 800
North Tiverton (K6)......
Norwood (J6) 4,250
Oakland (H5) 900
Oakland Beach (J6) 3,559
Pascoag (H5) 2,983
Pawtucket (J5) 81,001
Peace Dale (J7) 2,000
Pontiac (J6) 861
Portsmouth (J6) ....△8,251
Potter Hill (G7) ....
PROVIDENCE◉ (H5) 207,498
Prudence Isl. (J6) 60
Riverside (J5) 14,000
Rockville (G6) 260
Rumford (J5) 6,500
Saunderstown (J6) 950
Saylesville (J5) 3,500
Shannock (H7) 400
Shawomet (J6) 793
Slatersville (H4) 1,780
Slocum (H6) 100
S. Foster (H5) 300
Summit (H6) 175
Thornton (H5) ....
Tiverton (K6) ....△9,461
Tiverton Four Cor's (K6)
Usquepaug (H6) 247
Valley Falls (J5) ....
Wakefield (H7) 4,000
Warren (J6) ....△8,750
Warwick (J6) 68,504
Washington (Coventry) (H6) 2,400
Watch Hill (G7) 200
Weekapaug (G7) 300
W. Barrington (J5) 3,484
W. Glocester (G5) 450
W. Kingston◉ (H7) 760
W. Warwick (H6)........21,414
Westerly◉ (G7) 9,698
Wood River Junction (H7) 98
Woonsocket◉ (J4)......47,080
Wyoming (H6) 500

OTHER FEATURES

Block (isl.) ....H 8
Block Island (sound) .....H 8
Brenton (point) ....J 7
Conanicut (isl.) ....J 6
Dickens (point) ....H 8
Durfee (hill) ....G 5
Grace (point) ....H 8
Jerimoth (hill) ....G 5
Judith (point) ....J 7
Mount Hope (bay) ....K 6
Narragansett (bay) ....J 7
Noyes (point) ....H 7
Pawcatuck (riv.) ....G 7
Quonset Point N.A.S. ....J 6
Rhode (isl.) ....J 6
Rhode Island (sound) ....J 7
Sakonnet (point) ....K 7
Sakonnet (riv.) ....K 7
Scituate (res.) ....H 5
Watch Hill (point) ....G 7

◉County Seat or Courthouse.
△Population of township.

MICHIGAN

AREA 58,216 sq. mi.
POPULATION 8,218,000
CAPITAL Lansing
LARGEST CITY Detroit 1,670,144
HIGHEST POINT Mt. Curwood 1,980 ft.
SETTLED IN 1650
ADMITTED TO UNION January 26, 1837
POPULAR NAME Wolverine State
STATE FLOWER Apple Blossom
STATE BIRD Robin

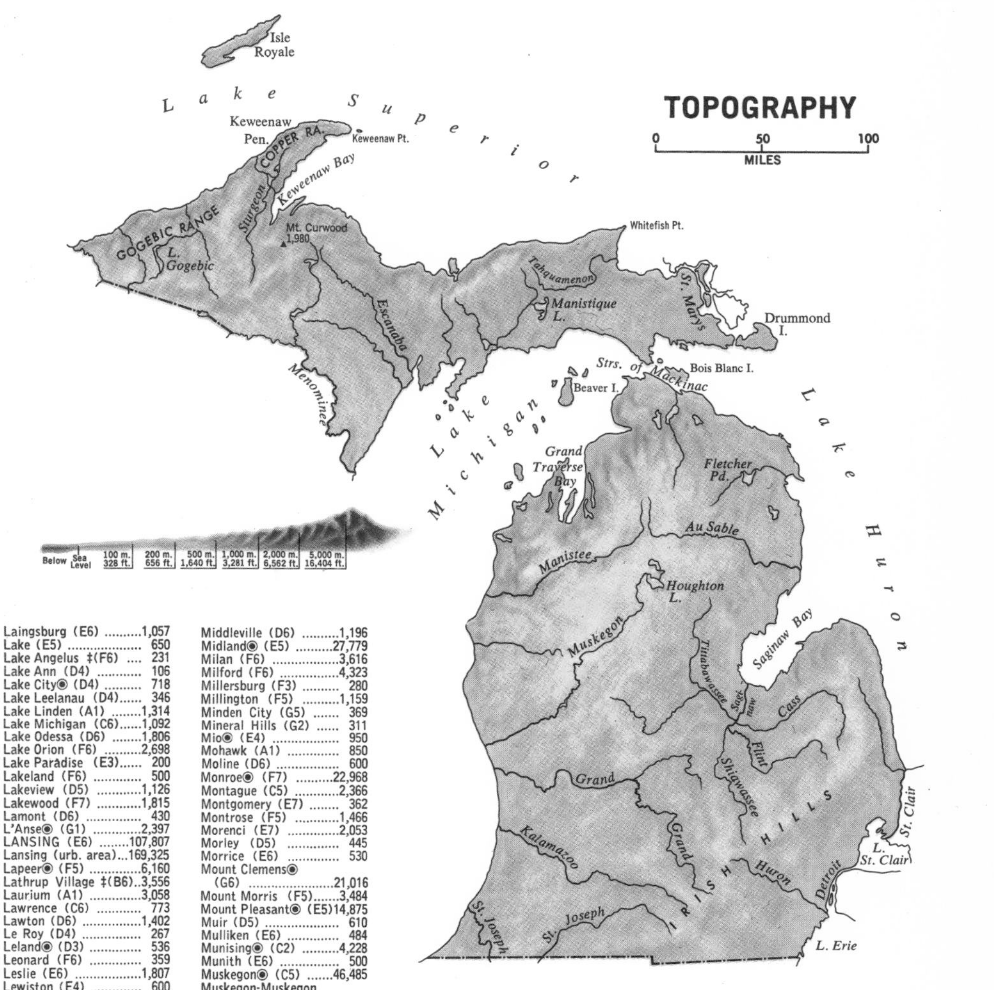
TOPOGRAPHY
0 50 100
MILES
Isle Royale
Lake Superior
Keweenaw Pen.
Keweenaw Pt.
COPPER RA.
Keweenaw Bay
GOGEBIC RANGE
L. Gogebic
Sturgeon
Mt. Curwood 1,980
Whitefish Pt.
Tahquamenon
Manistique L.
St. Marys
Drummond I.
Escanaba
Menominee
Strs. of Mackinac
Bois Blanc I.
Beaver I.
Lake Michigan
Lake Huron
Grand Traverse Bay
Fletcher Pd.
Au Sable
Manistee
Houghton L.
Muskegon
Tittabawassee
Saginaw Bay
Saginaw
Cass
Flint
Shiawassee
Grand
Kalamazoo
IRISH HILLS
Huron
Detroit
L. St. Clair
St. Clair
St. Joseph
L. Erie
Below Sea Level
100 m. 328 ft.
200 m. 656 ft.
500 m. 1,640 ft.
1,000 m. 3,281 ft.
2,000 m. 6,562 ft.
5,000 m. 16,404 ft.

COUNTIES

Alcona (F4) 6,352
Alger (C2) 9,250
Allegan (D6) 57,729
Alpena (F4) 28,556
Antrim (D3) 10,373
Arenac (F4) 9,860
Baraga (A2) 7,151
Barry (D6) 31,738
Bay (E5) 107,042
Benzie (C4) 7,834
Berrien (C7) 149,865
Branch (D7) 34,903
Calhoun (D6) 138,858
Cass (C7) 36,932
Charlevoix (D3) 13,421
Cheboygan (E3) 14,550
Chippewa (E2) 32,655
Clare (E5) 11,647
Clinton (E6) 37,969
Crawford (E4) 4,971
Delta (C2) 34,298
Dickinson (B2) 23,917
Eaton (E6) 49,684
Emmet (E3) 15,904
Genesee (F5) 374,313
Gladwin (E4) 10,769
Gogebic (F2) 24,370
Grand Traverse (D4)..33.490
Gratiot (E5) 37,012
Hillsdale (E7) 34,742
Houghton (G1) 35,654
Huron (F5) 34,006
Ingham (E6) 211,296
Ionia (D6) 43,132
Iosco (F4) 16,505
Iron (G2) 17,184
Isabella (E5) 35,348
Jackson (E6) 131,994
Kalamazoo (D6) 169,712
Kalkaska (D4) 4,382
Kent (D5) 363,187
Keweenaw (A1) 2,417
Lake (D5) 5,338
Lapeer (F5) 41,926
Leelanau (D4) 9,321
Lenawee (E7) 77,789
Livingston (F6) 38,233
Luce (D2) 7,827
Mackinac (D2) 10,853
Macomb (G6) 405,804
Manistee (C4) 19,042
Marquette (B2) 56,154
Mason (C4) 21,929
Mecosta (D5) 21,051
Menominee (B3) 24,685
Midland (E5) 51,450
Missaukee (D4) 6,784
Monroe (F7) 101,120
Montcalm (D5) 35,795
Montmorency (E3)....4,424
Muskegon (C5) 149,943
Newaygo (D5) 24,160
Oakland (F6) 690,259
Oceana (C5) 16,547
Ogemaw (E4) 9,680
Ontonagon (F1) 10,584
Osceola (D5) 13,595
Oscoda (E4) 3,447
Otsego (E3) 7,545
Ottawa (C6) 98,719
Presque Isle (F3)....13,117
Roscommon (E4) 7,200
Saginaw (E5) 190,752
Saint Clair (G6) 107,201
Saint Joseph (D7)....42,332
Sanilac (G5) 32,314
Schoolcraft (C2) 8,953
Shiawassee (E6) 53,446
Tuscola (F5) 43,305
Van Buren (C6) 48,395
Washtenaw (F6) 172,440
Wayne (F6) 2,666,297
Wexford (D4) 18,466

CITIES and TOWNS

Acme (D4) 450
Ada (D6) 400
Addison (E7) 575
Adrian◉ (F7) 20,347
Afton (E3) 450
Ahmeek (A1) 265
Akron (F5) 503
Alanson (E3) 290
Alba (E4) 400
Albion (E6) 12,749
Alden (D4) 350
Algonac (G6) 3,190
Allegan◉ (D6) 4,822
Allen (E7) 325
Allen Park (B7) 37,052
Alma (E5) 8,978
Almont (F6) 1,279
Alpena◉ (F3) 14,682
Alpha (A2) 317
Alston (G1) 475
Amasa (G2) 600
Anchorville (G6) 380
Ann Arbor◉ (F6) 67,340
Ann Arbor (urban area) 115,282
Applegate (G5) 252
Arcadia (C4) 462
Argyle (G5) 400
Armada (G6) 1,111
Ashley (E5) 448
Athens (D6) 966
Atlanta◉ (E3) 450
Atlantic Mine (G1).... 450
Au Gres (F4).. 584
Au Sable (F4) 300
Auburn (F5) 1,497
Auburn Heights (F6)....2,500
Augusta (D6) 972
Austin Lake (D6) 3,520
Bad Axe◉ (G5) 2,998
Bailey (D5) 275
Baldwin◉ (D5) 835
Baltic (G1) 400
Bancroft (E6) 636
Bangor (C6) 2,109
Bannister (E5) 350
Baraga (G1) 991
Bark River (B3) 450
Baroda (C7) 488
Barryton (D5) 418
Barton City (F4) 500
Batavia (D7) 33
Bath (E6) 575
Battle Creek (D6)....44,169
Bay City◉ (F5) 53,604
Bay City (urb. area)...72,763
Bay Port (F5) 550
Bear Lake (C4) 323
Beaverton (E5) 926
Bedford (D6) 750
Belding (D5) 4,887
Bellaire◉ (D4) 689
Belleville (F6) 1,921
Bellevue (E6) 1,277
Benton Harbor (C6)....19,136
Benton Heights (C6)....6,112
Benzonia (D4) 407
Bergland (F1) 650
Berkley (B6) 23,275
Berrien Springs (C7)....1,953
Bessemer◉ (F2) 3,304
Beulah◉ (C4) 436
Beverly Hills ‡(B6)....8,633
Big Bay (B2) 373
Big Rapids◉ (D5) 8,686
Bingham Farms ‡(F6).. 394
Birch Run (F5) 844
Birmingham (B6) 25,525
Bitely (D5) 202
Blissfield (F7) 2,653
Bloomfield Hills (B6)....2,378
Bloomingdale (C6).... 471
Boyne City (E3) 2,797
Boyne Falls (E3) 260
Brant (E5) 120
Breckenridge (E5) 1,131
Breedsville (C6) 245
Brethren (D4) 400
Bridgeport (F5) 1,326
Bridgman (C7) 1,454
Brighton (F6) 2,282
Brimley (E2) 400
Britton (F6) 622
Bronson (D7) 2,267
Brooklyn (E6) 986
Brown City (G5) 993
Buchanan (C7) 5,341
Buckley (D4) 247
Burlington (D6) 366
Burr Oak (D7) 867
Burt (F5) 350
Byron (E6) 542
Byron Center (D6) 712
Cadillac◉ (D4) 10,112
Caledonia (D6) 739
Calumet (A1) 1,139
Cambria (E7) 125
Camden (E7) 434
Capac (G5) 1,235
Carleton (F6) 1,379
Carney (B3) 400
Caro◉ (F5) 3,534
Carrollton (E5) 5,000
Carson City (E5) 1,201
Carsonville (G5) 502
Caseville (F5) 659
Casnovia (D5) 371
Caspian (G2) 1,493
Cass City (F5) 1,945
Cassopolis◉ (C7) 2,027
Cedar (D4) 300
Cedar Springs (D5)....1,768
Cedarville (E2) 700
Cement City (E6) 471
Center Line (B6) 10,164
Central Lake (D3) 692
Centreville◉ (D7) 971
Champion (B2) 512
Channing (B2) 600
Charlevoix◉ (D3) 2,751
Charlotte◉ (E6) 7,657
Chatham (B2) 275
Cheboygan◉ (E3) 5,859
Chelsea (E6) 3,355
Chesaning (E5) 2,770
Clair Haven (B6) 1,356
Clare (E5) 2,442
Clarklake (E6) 500
Clarkston (F6) 769
Clarksville (D6) 371
Clawson (B6) 14,795
Clayton (E7) 470
Clifford (F5) 389
Climax (D6) 587
Clinton (F6) 1,481
Clio (F5) 2,212
Coldwater◉ (D7) 8,880
Coleman (E5) 1,264
Coloma (C6) 1,473
Colon (D7) 1,055
Columbiaville (F5) 878
Comstock (D6) 3,000
Concord (E6) 990
Constantine (D7) 1,710
Coopersville (C5) 1,584
Copemish (D4) 232
Copper City (A1) 293
Cornell (B3) 538
Corunna◉ (E6) 2,764
Covert (C6) 700
Covington (G2) 500
Croswell (G5) 1,817
Crystal (E5) 350
Crystal Falls◉ (A2)....2,203
Curtis (D2) 750
Custer (C5) 365
Dafter (E2) 600
Daggett (B3) 296
Dalton (C5) 400
Dansville (E6) 453
Davison (F5) 3,761
De Tour Village (E3).... 669
De Witt (E6) 1,238
Dearborn (B7) 112,007
Dearborn Hts. ‡(B7)...71,551
Decatur (C6) 1,827
Deckerville (G5) 798
Deerfield (F7) 866
Delton (D6) 450
Detroit◉ (B7) 1,670,144
Detroit (urb. area) 3,537,709
Detroit Beach (F7)....1,571
Dexter (F6) 1,702
Dimondale (E6) 866
Dollar Bay (G1) 500
Dorr (D6) 400
Douglas (C6) 602
Dowagiac (D6) 7,208
Drayton Plains (F6)....13,500
Drummond Island (F3) 550
Dryden (F6) 531
Dundee (F7) 2,377
Durand (E6) 3,312
Eagle (E6) 141
Eagle River◉ (A1).... 62
East Detroit (B6)....45,756
East Grand Rapids (D6) 10,924
East Jordan (D3) 1,919
East Kingsford (A3)....1,063
East Lansing (E6) 30,198
East Tawas (F4) 2,462
Eastlake (C4) 436
Eaton Rapids (E6) 4,052
Eau Claire (C6) 562
Eben Junction (B2).... 460
Ecorse (B7) 17,328
Edenville (E5) 500
Edmore (E5) 1,234
Edwardsburg (C7) 902
Elba (F5) 400
Elberta (C4) 552
Elk Rapids (D4) 1,015
Elkton (F5) 1,014
Ellsworth (D3) 386
Eloise (F6) 900
Elsie (E5) 933
Emmett (G6) 283
Empire (C4) 448
Engadine (D2) 420
Ensign (C3) 551
Erie (F7) 998
Escanaba◉ (C3) 15,391
Essexville (F5) 4,590
Estral Beach (F7) 254
Evart (D5) 1,775
Ewen (F2) 822
Fair Haven (G6) 1,200
Fairgrove (F5) 609
Farmington (F6) 6,881
Farwell (E5) 737
Fennville (C6) 713
Fenton (F6) 8,067
Ferndale (B6) 31,347
Ferrysburg (C5) 1,550
Fife Lake (D4) 218
Filer City (C4) 375
Flat Rock (F6) 4,696
Flint◉ (F6) 196,940
Flint (urban area)....277,786
Flushing (F5) 3,761
Forestville (G5) 121
Fountain (C4) 194
Fowler (E5) 854
Fowlerville (F6) 1,674
Frankenmuth (F5) 1,728
Frankfort (C4) 1,690
Franklin (B6) 2,262
Fraser (B6) 7,027
Frederic (E4) 400
Free Soil (C4) 209
Freeland (E5) 987
Freeport (D6) 495
Fremont (D5) 3,384
Fruitport (C5) 1,037
Fulton (D6) 500
Gaastra (G2) 582
Gagetown (F5) 376
Gaines (F6) 387
Galesburg (D6) 1,410
Galien (C7) 750
Garden (C3) 380
Garden City (B7) 38,017
Gaylord◉ (E3) 2,568
Genesee (F5) 500
Germfask (C2) 500
Gibraltar (F6) 2,196
Gladstone (C3) 5,267
Gladwin◉ (E5) 2,226
Glen Arbor (C4) 800
Gobles (D6) 816
Goodrich (F6) 701
Gould City (D2) 400
Grand Beach (C7) 86
Grand Blanc (F6) 1,565
Grand Haven◉ (C5)....11,066
Grand Ledge (E6) 5,165
Grand Marais (D2) 600
Grand Rapids◉ (D5) 177,313
Grand Rapids (urban area) 294,230
Grandville (D6) 7,975
Grant (D5) 732
Grass Lake (E6) 1,037
Grayling◉ (E4) 2,015
Greenland (G1) 365
Greenville (D5) 7,440
Gregory (E6) 400
Grosse Ile (B7) 6,500
Grosse Pointe (B7)....6,631
Grosse Pointe Farms (B6) 12,172
Groose Pointe Pk. (B7)15,457
Grosse Pointe Shores (B6) 2,301
Grosse Pointe Woods (B6) 18,580
Gulliver (D2) 860
Gwinn (B2) 1,009
Hale (F4) 500
Hamilton (C6) 900
Hamtramck (B6) 34,137
Hancock (G1) 5,022
Hanover (E6) 449
Harbor Beach (G5)....2,282
Harbor Springs (D3)....1,433
Harper Woods (B6)....19,995
Harrietta (D4) 119
Harrison◉ (E4) 1,072
Harrisville◉ (F4) 487
Harsens Island (G6).... 500
Hart◉ (C5) 1,990
Hartford (C6) 2,305
Haslett (E6) 1,000
Hastings◉ (D6) 6,375
Hazel Park (B6) 25,631
Hemlock (E5) 794
Hermansville (B3) 350
Herron (F3) 800
Hersey (D5) 246
Hesperia (D5) 822
Hessel (E2) 480
Hickory Corners (D6)... 575
Highland Park (B6)....38,063
Hillman (F3) 445
Hillsdale◉ (E7) 7,629
Holland (C6) 24,777
Holly (F6) 3,269
Holt (E6) 4,818
Holton (C5) 350
Homer (E6) 1,629
Honor (D4) 278
Hope (E5) 760
Hopkins (D6) 556
Horton (E6) 390
Houghton◉ (G1) 3,393
Houghton Lake (E4).... 450
Houghton L. Hts. (E4) 1,195
Howard City (D5)....1,004
Howell◉ (E6) 4,861
Hubbardston (E5) 381
Hubbell (A1) 1,429
Hudson (E7) 2,546
Hudsonville (D6) 2,649
Hulbert (D2) 511
Huntington Woods ‡(F6) 8,746
Ida (F7) 975
Idlewild (D5) 486
Imlay City (F5) 1,968
Indian River (E3) 600
Inkster (B7) 36,149
Ionia◉ (D6) 6,754
Iron Mountain◉ (B3)....9,299
Iron River (G2) 3,754
Ironwood (F2) 10,265
Ishpeming (B2) 8,857
Ithaca◉ (E5) 2,920
Jackson◉ (E6) 50,720
Jackson (urban area)..71,412
Jamestown (D6) 500
Jasper (E7) 400
Jenison (D6) 4,000
Jonesville (E6) 1,896
Kalamazoo◉ (D6) 82,089
Kalamazoo (urban area) 115,659
Kaleva (C4) 348
Kalkaska◉ (D4) 1,321
Kawkawlin (F5) 650
Keego Harbor (F6) 2,761
Kent City (D5) 617
Kenton (G2) 350
Kinde (G5) 624
Kingsford (A3) 5,084
Kingsley (D4) 586
Kingston (F5) 456
Laingsburg (E6) 1,057
Lake (E5) 650
Lake Angelus ‡(F6) 231
Lake Ann (D4) 106
Lake City◉ (D4) 718
Lake Leelanau (D4).... 346
Lake Linden (A1) 1,314
Lake Michigan (C6)....1,092
Lake Odessa (D6) 1,806
Lake Orion (F6) 2,698
Lake Paradise (E3).... 200
Lakeland (F6) 500
Lakeview (D5) 1,126
Lakewood (F7) 1,815
Lamont (D6) 430
L'Anse◉ (G1) 2,397
LANSING (E6) 107,807
Lansing (urb. area)...169,325
Lapeer◉ (F5) 6,160
Lathrup Village ‡(B6)..3,556
Laurium (A1) 3,058
Lawrence (C6) 773
Lawton (D6) 1,402
Le Roy (D4) 267
Leland◉ (D3) 536
Leonard (F6) 359
Leslie (E6) 1,807
Lewiston (E4) 600
Lexington (G5) 722
Lincoln (F4) 441
Lincoln Park (B7)....53,933
Linden (F6) 1,146
Linwood (F5) 425
Litchfield (E6) 993
Little Lake (B2).... 800
Livonia (F6) 66,702
Lowell (D6) 2,545
Ludington◉ (C5) 9,421
Luna Pier ‡(F7) 1,344
Luther (D4) 325
Lyons (E6) 687
Mackinac Island (E3)... 942
Mackinaw City (E3).... 934
Madison Heights (F6) 33,343
Mancelona (E4) 1,141
Manchester (E6) 1,568
Manistee◉ (C4) 8,324
Manistique◉ (C3) 4,875
Manton (D4) 1,050
Maple Rapids (E5) 683
Marcellus (D6) 1,073
Marenisco (F2) 820
Marine City (G6)....4,404
Marion (D4) 898
Marlette (G5) 1,640
Marne (D5) 800
Marquette◉ (B2) 19,824
Marshall◉ (E6) 6,736
Martin (D6) 483
Marysville (G6) 4,065
Mason◉ (E6) 4,522
Mass (G1) 475
Mattawan ‡(D6) 769
Maybee (F6) 459
Mayville (F5) 896
McBain (D4) 551
McBrides (D5) 265
McMillan (D2) 800
Mecosta (D5) 303
Melvin (G5) 196
Melvindale (B7) 13,089
Memphis (G6) 996
Mendon (D7) 867
Menominee◉ (B3) 11,289
Merrill (E5) 963
Mesick (D4) 304
Metamora (F6) 452
Michiana (C7) 135
Michigamme (A2) 409
Michigan Center (E6)...4,611
Middleton (E5) 560
Middleville (D6) 1,196
Midland◉ (E5) 27,779
Milan (F6) 3,616
Milford (F6) 4,323
Millersburg (F3) 280
Millington (F5) 1,159
Minden City (G5) 369
Mineral Hills (G2) 311
Mio◉ (E4) 950
Mohawk (A1) 850
Moline (D6) 600
Monroe◉ (F7) 22,968
Montague (C5) 2,366
Montgomery (E7) 362
Montrose (F5) 1,466
Morenci (E7) 2,053
Morley (D5) 445
Morrice (E6) 530
Mount Clemens◉ (G6) 21,016
Mount Morris (F5)....3,484
Mount Pleasant◉ (E5)14,875
Muir (D5) 610
Mulliken (E6) 484
Munising◉ (C2) 4,228
Munith (E6) 500
Muskegon◉ (C5) 46,485
Muskegon-Muskegon Heights (urb. area)..95,350
Muskegon Hts. (C5)....19,552
Nahma (C3) 400
Napoleon (E6) 700
Nashville (D6) 1,525
National Mine (B2).... 950
Nazareth (D6) 850
Negaunee (B2) 6,126
New Baltimore (G6)....3,159
New Boston (F6) 900
New Buffalo (C7) 2,128
New Era (C5) 403
New Haven (G6) 1,198
New Lothrop (F5) 510
New Troy (C7) 385
Newaygo (D5) 1,447
Newberry (D2) 2,612
Niles (C7) 13,842
North Adams (E7) 494
North Bradley (E5).... 350
North Branch (F5) 901
North Muskegon (C5)...3,855
Northport (D3) 530
Northville (F6) 3,967
Norway (B3) 3,171
Novi (F6) 6,390
Oak Park (B6) 36,632
Oakley (E5) 417
Ocqueoc (F3) 475
Okemos (E6) 950
Olivet (E6) 1,185
Omer (F4) 322
Onaway (E3) 1,388
Onekama (C4) 469
Onondaga (E6) 505
Onsted (E6) 526
Ontonagon◉ (F1) 2,358
Orchard Lake (F6) 1,127
Ortonville (F6) 771
Oscoda (F4) 3,375
Oshtemo (D6) 500
Osseo (E7) 500
Ossineke (F4) 150
Otisville (F5) 701
Otsego (D6) 4,142
Otter Lake (F5) 562
Ovid (E5) 1,505
Owendale (F5) 298
Owosso (E5) 17,006
Oxford (F6) 2,357
Painesdale (G1) 743
Palmer (B2) 975
Palmyra (E7) 500
Parchment (D6) 1,565
Parma (E6) 770
Paw Paw◉ (D6) 2,970
Pearl Beach (G6) 1,224
Peck (G5) 548
Pellston (E3) 429
Pentwater (C5) 1,030
Perkins (B3) 380
Perrinton (E5) 424
Perry (E6) 1,370
Petersburg (F7) 1,018
Petoskey◉ (E3) 6,138
Pewamo (E5) 415
Pickford (E2) 875
Pierson (D5) 219
Pigeon (F5) 1,191
Pinckney (F6) 732
Pinconning (F5) 1,329
Pittsford (E7) 575
Plainwell (D6) 3 125
Pleasant Ridge (B6)....3,807
Plymouth (F6) 8,766
Pontiac◉ (F6) 82,233
Port Austin (F4) 706
Port Hope (G5) 349
Port Huron◉ (G6) 36,084
Port Sanilac (G5) 361
Portage (D6) 27,642
Portland (E6) 3,330
Posen (F3) 341
Potterville (E6) 1,028
Powers (B3) 415
Prescott (F4) 308
Prudenville (E4) 800
Quakertown ‡(F6) 482
Quincy (E7) 1,602
Quinnesec (A3) 500
Ramsay (F2) 1,158
Rapid River (C3) 650
Ravenna (D5) 801
Reading (E7) 1,128
Reed City◉ (D5) 2,184
Reese (F5) 711
Remus (D5) 600
Richland (D6) 511
Richmond (G6) 2,667
Richville (F5) 700
River Rouge (B7) 18,147
Riverdale (E5) 375
Riverside (C6) 650
Riverview (B7) 7,237
Rives Junction (E6).... 350
Rochester (F6) 5,431
Rockford (D5) 2 074
Rockland (G1) 550
Rockwood (F6) 2,026
Rogers City◉ (F3) 4,722
Romeo (F6) 3,327
Romulus (F6) 1,798
Roosevelt Park (C5)....2,578
Roscommon◉ (E4) 867
Rose City (E4) 435
Rosebush (E5) 400
Roseville (G6) 50,195
Royal Oak (B6)....80,612
Rudyard (E2) 925
Saginaw◉ (F5) 98,265
Saginaw (urb. area)..129,215
Sagola (B2) 350
Saint Charles (E5)....1,959
Saint Clair (G6) 4,538
Saint Clair Shores (G6) 76,657
Saint Helen (E4) 400
Saint Ignace◉ (E3) 3,334
Saint Johns◉ (E6) 5,629
Saint Joseph◉ (C6)....11,755
Saint Louis (E5) 3 808
Saline (F6) 2,334
Samaria (F7) 400
Sand Lake (D5) 394
Sandusky◉ (G5) 2,066
Sanford (E5) 666
Saranac (D6) 1,081
Saugatuck (C6) 927
Sault Sainte Marie◉ (E2) 18,722
Sawyer (C7) 558
Schoolcraft (D6) 1,205
Scottville (C5) 1,245
Sebewaing (F5) 2,026
Seney (C2) 275
Shelby (C5) 1,603
Shepherd (E5) 1,293
Sheridan (D5) 606
Sherwood (D6) 356
Shingleton (C2) 400
Shoreham (C6) 443
Silverwood (F5) 125
Sister Lakes (C6) 500
Six Lakes (D5) 300
Smiths Creek (G6) 400
Snover (G5) 350
Sodus (C6) 300
South Haven (C6) 6,149
South Lyon (F6) 1,753
South Range (G1).... 760
South Rockwood (F7)...1,337
Southfield (F6) 31,501
Southgate (F6) 29,404
Spalding (B3) 523
Sparlingville (G6) 1,877
Sparta (D5) 2 749
Spring Arbor (E6) 850
Spring Lake (C5) 2,063
Springfield (D6) 4,605
Springport (E6) 693
Stambaugh (G2) 1,876
Standish◉ (F5) 1,214
Stanton◉ (D5) 1,139
Stanwood (D5) 205
Stephenson (B3) 820
Sterling (E4) 470
Stevensville (C6) 697
Stockbridge (E6) 1,097
Stonington (C3) 408
Stronach (C4) 500
Sturgis (D7) 8,915
Sunfield (D6) 626
Suttons Bay (D3) 421
Swartz Creek (F6)....3,006
Sylvan Lake (F6) 2,004
Tawas City◉ (F4) 1,810
Taylor (B7) 55,000
Tecumseh (E7) 7,045
Tekonsha (E6) 744
Temperance (F7) 2,215
Thompsonville (C4) 243
Three Oaks (C7) 1,763
Three Rivers (D7)....7,092
Traverse City◉ (D4)...18 432
Trenary (C2) 350
Trenton (B7) 18,439
Trout Creek (G2) 818
Trout Lake (E2) 425
Troy (B6) 19,382
Trufant (D5) 900
Turner (F4) 206
Tustin (D4) 248
Twin Lake (C5) 350
Twining (F4) 199
Ubly (G5) 819
Union City (D6) 1,669
Union Pier (C7) 925
Unionville (F5) 629
Utica (F6) 1,454

(continued on following page)

Michigan

(continued)

HIGHWAYS

0   50   100
MILES

- Limited Access Highways ....
- Major Highways ....
- Other Important Roads ....
- Interstate Route Numbers 95
- Federal Route Numbers 9
- State and Other Route Numbers... 4

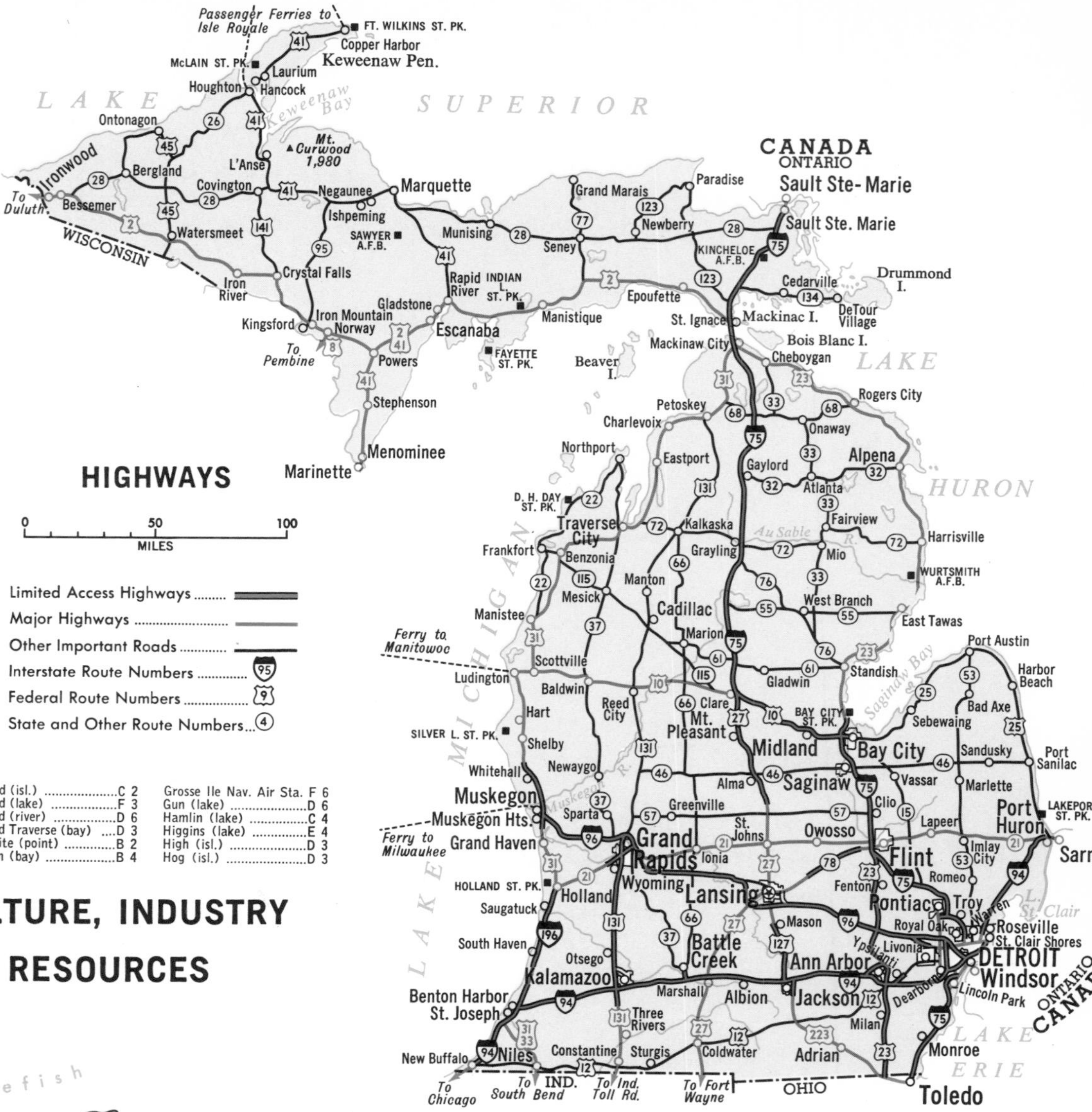

AGRICULTURE, INDUSTRY and RESOURCES

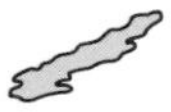

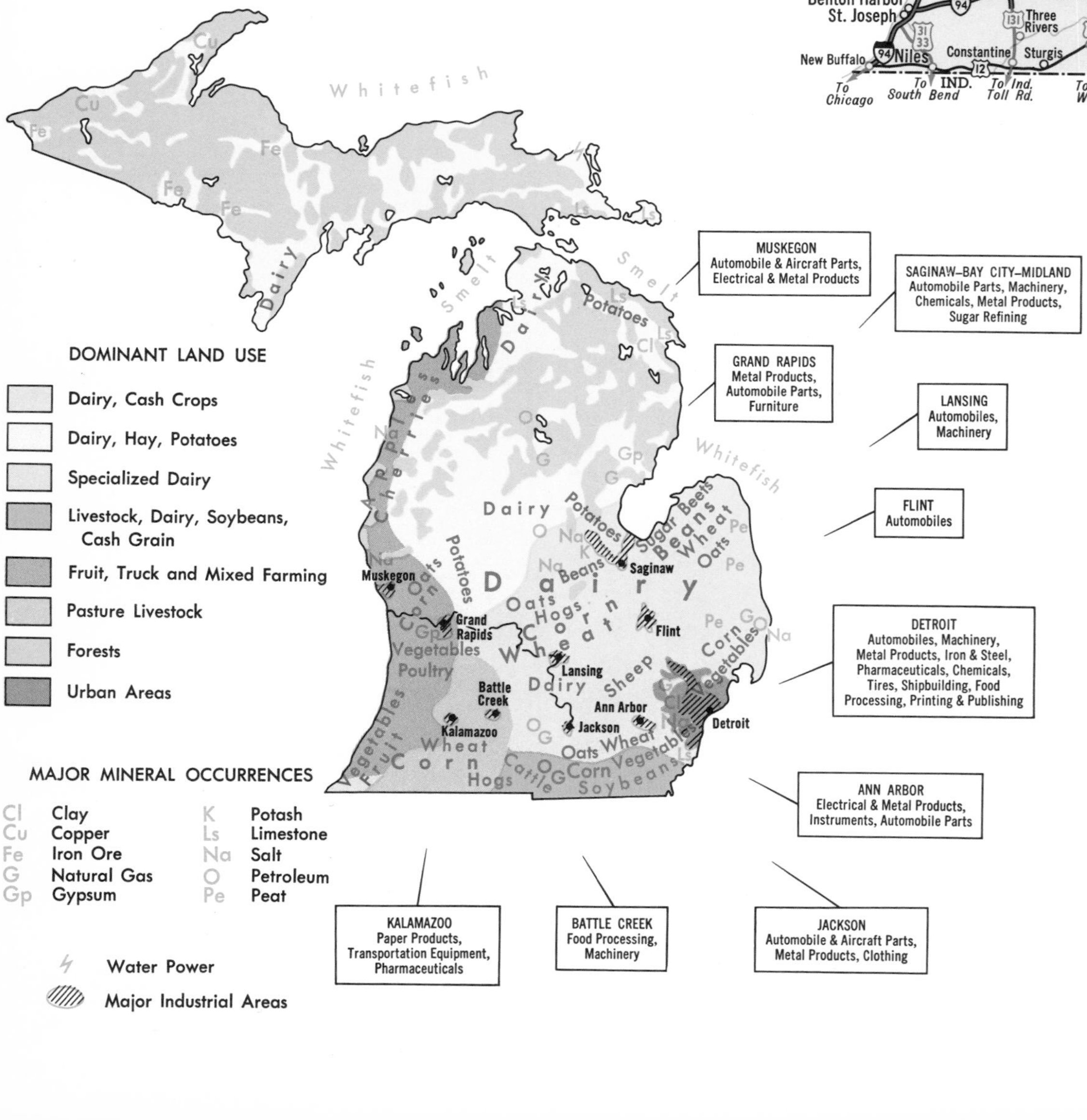

DOMINANT LAND USE

- Dairy, Cash Crops
- Dairy, Hay, Potatoes
- Specialized Dairy
- Livestock, Dairy, Soybeans, Cash Grain
- Fruit, Truck and Mixed Farming
- Pasture Livestock
- Forests
- Urban Areas

MAJOR MINERAL OCCURRENCES

Cl	Clay	K	Potash
Cu	Copper	Ls	Limestone
Fe	Iron Ore	Na	Salt
G	Natural Gas	O	Petroleum
Gp	Gypsum	Pe	Peat

⚡ Water Power

▨ Major Industrial Areas

MUSKEGON
Automobile & Aircraft Parts,
Electrical & Metal Products

SAGINAW–BAY CITY–MIDLAND
Automobile Parts, Machinery,
Chemicals, Metal Products,
Sugar Refining

GRAND RAPIDS
Metal Products,
Automobile Parts,
Furniture

LANSING
Automobiles,
Machinery

FLINT
Automobiles

DETROIT
Automobiles, Machinery,
Metal Products, Iron & Steel,
Pharmaceuticals, Chemicals,
Tires, Shipbuilding, Food
Processing, Printing & Publishing

ANN ARBOR
Electrical & Metal Products,
Instruments, Automobile Parts

KALAMAZOO
Paper Products,
Transportation Equipment,
Pharmaceuticals

BATTLE CREEK
Food Processing,
Machinery

JACKSON
Automobile & Aircraft Parts,
Metal Products, Clothing

MINNESOTA

AREA 84,068 sq. mi.
POPULATION 3,554,000
CAPITAL St. Paul
LARGEST CITY Minneapolis 482,872
HIGHEST POINT Eagle Mtn. 2,301 ft.
SETTLED IN 1805
ADMITTED TO UNION May 11, 1858
POPULAR NAMES North Star State; Gopher State
STATE FLOWER Lady-slipper
STATE BIRD Loon

COUNTIES

Aitkin (E4) 12,162
Anoka (E5) 85,916
Becker (C4) 23,959
Beltrami (C2) 23,425
Benton (D5) 17,287
Big Stone (B5) 8,954
Blue Earth (D6) 44,385
Brown (D6) 27,676
Carlton (F4) 27,932
Carver (E6) 21,358
Cass (D4) 16,720
Chippewa (C5) 16,320
Chisago (F5) 13,419
Clay (B4) 39,080
Clearwater (C3) 8,864
Cook (H3) 3,377
Cottonwood (C6) 16,166
Crow Wing (D4) 32,134
Dakota (E6) 78,303
Dodge (F7) 13,259
Douglas (C5) 21,313
Faribault (D7) 23,685
Fillmore (F7) 23,768
Freeborn (E7) 37,891
Goodhue (F6) 33,035
Grant (B5) 8,870
Hennepin (E5) 842,854
Houston (G7) 16,588
Hubbard (D3) 9,962
Isanti (E5) 13,530
Itasca (E3) 38,006
Jackson (C7) 15,501
Kanabec (E5) 9,007
Kandiyohi (C5) 29,987
Kittson (B2) 8,343
Koochiching (E2) 18,190
Lac qui Parle (B6) 13,330
Lake (G3) 13,702
Lake of the Woods (D2) 4,304
Le Sueur (E6) 19,906
Lincoln (B6) 9,651
Lyon (C6) 22,655
Mahnomen (C3) 6,341
Marshall (B2) 14,262
Martin (D7) 26,986
McLeod (D6) 24,401
Meeker (D5) 18,887
Mille Lacs (E5) 14,560
Morrison (D4) 26,641
Mower (F7) 48,498
Murray (C6) 14,743
Nicollet (D6) 23,196
Nobles (C7) 23,365
Norman (B3) 11,253
Olmsted (F7) 65,532
Otter Tail (C4) 48,960
Pennington (B2) 12,468
Pine (F4) 17,004
Pipestone (B6) 13,605
Polk (B3) 36,182
Pope (C5) 11,914
Ramsey (E5) 422,525
Red Lake (B3) 5,830
Redwood (C6) 21,718
Renville (C6) 23,249
Rice (E6) 38,988
Rock (B7) 11,864
Roseau (C2) 12,154
Saint Louis (F3) 231,588
Scott (E6) 21,909
Sherburne (E5) 12,861
Sibley (D6) 16,228
Stearns (D5) 80,345
Steele (E7) 25,029
Stevens (B5) 11,262
Swift (C5) 14,936
Todd (D4) 23,119
Traverse (B5) 7,503
Wabasha (F6) 17,007
Wadena (D4) 12,199
Waseca (E6) 16,041
Washington (F5) 52,432
Watonwan (D7) 14,460
Wilkin (B4) 10,650
Winona (G6) 40,937
Wright (D5) 29,935
Yellow Medicine (B6) 15,523

CITIES and TOWNS

Ada◉ (B3) 2,064
Adams (F7) 806
Adrian (C7) 1,215
Afton (F6) 158
Aitkin◉ (E4) 1,829
Akeley (D3) 434
Albany (D5) 1,375
Albert Lea◉ (E7) 17,108
Alberta (B5) 149
Albertville (E5) 279
Alden (E7) 694
Alexandria◉ (C5) 6,713
Alpha (D7) 207
Altura (G6) 320
Alvarado (B2) 282
Amboy (D7) 629
Annandale (D5) 984
Anoka◉ (E5) 10,562
Appleton (C5) 2,172
Arco (B6) 140
Arden Hills ‡(G5) 3,930
Argyle (B2) 789
Arlington (D6) 1,601
Ashby (C4) 426
Askov (F4) 331
Atwater (D5) 899
Audubon (C4) 245
Aurora (F3) 2,799
Austin◉ (E7) 27,908
Avoca (C7) 226
Avon (D5) 443
Babbitt (G3) 2,587
Backus (D4) 317
Badger (B2) 338
Bagley◉ (C3) 1,385
Balaton (C6) 723
Barnesville (B4) 1,632
Barnum (F4) 417
Barrett (B5) 345
Battle Lake (C4) 733
Baudette◉ (D2) 1,597
Baxter (D4) 1,037
Bayport (F5) 3,205
Beardsley (B5) 410
Beaver Bay (G3) 287
Beaver Creek (B7) 250
Becker (E5) 279
Bejou (B3) 164
Belgrade (C5) 666
Belle Plaine (E6) 1,931
Bellechester (F6) 184
Bellingham (B5) 327
Beltrami (B3) 186
Belview (C6) 400
Bemidji◉ (D3) 9,958
Bena (D3) 286
Benson◉ (C5) 3,678
Bertha (C4) 562
Bethel (E5) 302
Big Falls (E2) 526
Big Lake (E5) 610
Bigelow (C7) 256
Bigfork (E3) 464
Bingham Lake (C7) 254
Birchwood ‡(G5) 598
Bird Island (D6) 1,384
Biwabik (F3) 1,836
Blackduck (D3) 765
Blaine (G5) 7,570
Blomkest (D6) 171
Blooming Prairie (E7) 1,778
Bloomington (G6) 50,498
Blue Earth◉ (D7) 4,200
Bluffton (C4) 211
Borup (B3) 145
Bovey (E3) 1,086
Bowlus (D5) 263
Boyd (C6) 419
Braham (E5) 728
Brainerd◉ (D4) 12,898
Branch (F5) 583
Brandon (C5) 353
Breckenridge◉ (B4) 4,335
Brewster (C7) 500
Bricelyn (E7) 542
Brooklyn Center (G5) 24,356
Brooklyn Park (G5) 10,197
Brooks (B3) 148
Brookston (F4) 144
Brooten (C5) 661
Browerville (D4) 744
Browns Valley (B5) 1,033
Brownsdale (F7) 622
Brownsville (G7) 382
Brownton (D6) 698
Bruno (F4) 116
Buckman (D5) 166
Buffalo◉ (E5) 2,322
Buffalo Lake (D6) 707
Buhl (F3) 1,526
Burnsville ‡(E6) 3,908
Burtrum (D5) 160
Butterfield (D7) 601
Byron (F6) 660
Caledonia◉ (G7) 2,563
Callaway (C3) 235
Calumet (E3) 799
Cambridge◉ (E5) 2,728
Campbell (B4) 365
Canby (B6) 2,146
Cannon Falls (F6) 2,055
Canton (F7) 467
Carlos (C5) 262
Carlton◉ (F4) 862
Carver (E6) 467
Cass Lake (D3) 1,586
Center City◉ (F5) 293
Centerville (E5) 338
Ceylon (D7) 554
Champlin (E5) 1,271
Chandler (C7) 388
Chanhassen (F6) 244
Chaska◉ (E6) 2,501
Chatfield (F7) 1,841
Chisago City (E5) 772
Chisholm (E3) 7,144
Chokio (B5) 498
Circle Pines (G5) 2,789
Clara City (C6) 1,358
Claremont (E6) 466
Clarissa (C4) 569
Clarkfield (C6) 1,100
Clarks Grove (E7) 353
Clear Lake (E5) 316
Clearbrook (C3) 650
Clearwater (D5) 274
Clements (D6) 269
Cleveland (E6) 389
Climax (B3) 310
Clinton (B5) 565
Clitherall (C4) 138
Clontarf (C5) 139
Cloquet (F4) 9,013
Coates ‡(E6) 202
Cohassett (E3) 605
Cokato (D5) 1,356
Cold Spring (D5) 1,760
Coleraine (E3) 1,346
Cologne (E6) 454
Columbia Hgts. (G5) 17,533
Comfrey (D6) 616
Comstock (B4) 138
Conger (E7) 215
Cook (F3) 527
Coon Rapids (G5) 14,931
Corcoran (E5) 1,237
Cosmos (D6) 487
Cottonwood (C6) 717
Courtland (D6) 239
Cromwell (F4) 187
Crookston◉ (B3) 8,546
Crosby (D4) 2,629
Crosslake (E4) 165
Crystal (G5) 24,283
Currie (C6) 438
Cyrus (C5) 362
Dakota (G7) 339
Dalton (C4) 239
Danube (C6) 494
Danvers (C5) 132
Darfur (D6) 191
Darwin (D5) 273
Dassel (D5) 863
Dawson (B6) 1,766
Dayton (E5) 456
De Graff (C5) 196
Deephaven (G5) 3,286
Deer Creek (C4) 312
Deer River (E3) 992
Deerwood (E4) 527
Delano (E5) 1,612
Delavan (D7) 322
Dellwood (F5) 310
Dennison (E6) 179
Dent (C4) 176
Detroit Lakes◉ (C4) 5,633
Dexter (F7) 313
Dilworth (B4) 2,102
Dodge Center (F6) 1,441
Donnelly (B5) 358
Doran (B4) 136
Dover (F7) 312
Duluth◉ (F4) 106,884
Duluth-Superior (urban area) 144,763
Dumont (B5) 226
Dundas (E6) 488
Dundee (C7) 148
Dunnell (D7) 260
Eagle Bend (D4) 611
Eagle Lake (E6) 506
East Grand Forks (B3) 6,998
East Gull Lake (D4) 311
Easton (E7) 411
Echo (C6) 459
Eden Prairie (G6) 3,228
Eden Valley (D5) 793
Edgerton (B7) 1,019
Edina (E6) 28,501
Effie (E3) 195
Eitzen (G7) 181
Elba (F6) 152
Elbow Lake◉ (B4) 1,521
Elgin (F6) 521
Elizabeth (B4) 168
Elk River◉ (E5) 1,763
Elkton (F7) 147
Ellendale (E7) 501
Ellsworth (C7) 634
Elmore (D7) 1,078
Elrosa (C5) 205
Ely (G3) 5,438
Elysian (E6) 382
Emily (E4) 351
Emmons (E7) 408
Erhard (B4) 150
Erskine (B3) 614
Evan (D6) 153
Evansville (C4) 411
Eveleth (F3) 5,721
Excelsior (E6) 2,020
Eyota (F7) 558
Fairfax (D6) 1,489
Fairmont◉ (D7) 9,745
Falcon Heights (G5) 5,927
Faribault◉ (E6) 16,926
Farmington (E6) 2,300
Federal Dam (D3) 185
Felton (B3) 201
Fergus Falls◉ (B4) 13,733
Fertile (B3) 968
Fifty Lakes (D4) 143
Finlayson (F4) 213
Fisher (B3) 326
Flensburg (D5) 280
Floodwood (E4) 677
Foley◉ (D5) 1,112
Forest Lake (F5) 2,347
Foreston (E5) 266
Fosston (C3) 1,704
Fountain (F7) 297
Foxhome (B4) 181
Franklin (F3) 548
Frazee (C4) 1,083
Freeborn (E7) 314
Freeport (D5) 615
Fridley (G5) 15,173
Frost (D7) 381
Fulda (C7) 1,202
Garfield (C5) 240
Garvin (C6) 205
Gary (B3) 262
Gaylord◉ (D6) 1,631
Gem Lake ‡(G5) 305
Geneva (E7) 347
Georgetown (B3) 178
Ghent (C6) 326
Gibbon (D6) 896
Gilbert (F3) 2,591
Gilman (E5) 146
Glencoe◉ (D6) 3,216
Glenville (E7) 643
Glenwood◉ (C5) 2,631
Glyndon (B4) 489
Golden Valley (G5) 14,559
Gonvick (C3) 363
Good Thunder (D6) 468
Goodhue (F6) 566
Goodridge (C2) 134
Goodview (G6) 1,348
Graceville (B5) 823
Granada (D7) 418
Grand Marais◉ (G2) 1,301
Grand Meadow (F7) 837
Grand Rapids◉ (E3) 7,265
Granite Falls◉ (C6) 2,728
Grasston (E5) 146
Green Isle (E6) 331
Greenbush (B2) 706
Greenfield ‡(G6) 639
Greenwald (D5) 266
Greenwood ‡(F5) 520
Grey Eagle (D5) 372
Grove City (D5) 466
Grygla (C2) 192
Gully (C3) 168
Hackensack (D4) 204
Hadley (C7) 151
Hallock◉ (A2) 1,527
Halstad (B3) 639
Hamburg (D6) 288
Hamel (Medina) (F5) 1,472
Hammond (F6) 205
Hampton (E6) 305
Hancock (C5) 942
Hanley Falls (C6) 334
Hanover (E5) 263
Hanska (D6) 491
Hardwick (B7) 328
Harmony (F7) 1,214
Harris (F5) 552
Hartland (E7) 330
Hastings◉ (F6) 8,965
Hatfield (B7) 95
Hawley (B4) 1,270
Hayfield (F7) 889
Hayward (E7) 258
Hector (D6) 1,297
Henderson (E6) 728
Hendricks (B6) 797
Hendrum (B3) 305
Henning (C4) 980
Herman (B5) 764
Heron Lake (C7) 852
Hewitt (C4) 267
Hibbing (F3) 17,731
Hill City (E4) 429
Hills (B7) 516
Hilltop ‡(G5) 607
Hinckley (E4) 851
Hitterdal (B4) 235
Hoffman (C5) 605
Hokah (G7) 685
Holdingford (D5) 526
Holland (B6) 264
Hollandale (E7) 363

(continued on following page)

HIGHWAYS
0 40 80
MILES
Limited Access Highways
Major Highways
Other Important Roads
Interstate Route Numbers
Federal Route Numbers
State and Other Route Numbers
MANITOBA
ONTARIO
CANADA
NORTH DAKOTA
SOUTH DAKOTA
IOWA
WISCONSIN
Lake of the Woods
LAKE SUPERIOR
Eagle Mtn. 2,301
MESABI IRON RANGE
To Winnipeg
To Fort William
To Aberdeen
To Sioux Falls
To Sioux City
To Mason City
To Waterloo
To Dubuque
To Eau Claire
Fort Frances
International Falls
Fargo
Moorhead
Duluth
Superior
MINNEAPOLIS
St. Paul
Bloomington
St. Cloud
Rochester
Mankato
La Crosse
Brainerd
Bemidji
Hibbing
Virginia
Fergus Falls
Willmar
Austin
Albert Lea
Winona
Red Wing
Grand Marais
Ely
Crookston
Thief River Falls
Detroit Lakes
Alexandria
New Ulm
Owatonna
Faribault
Worthington

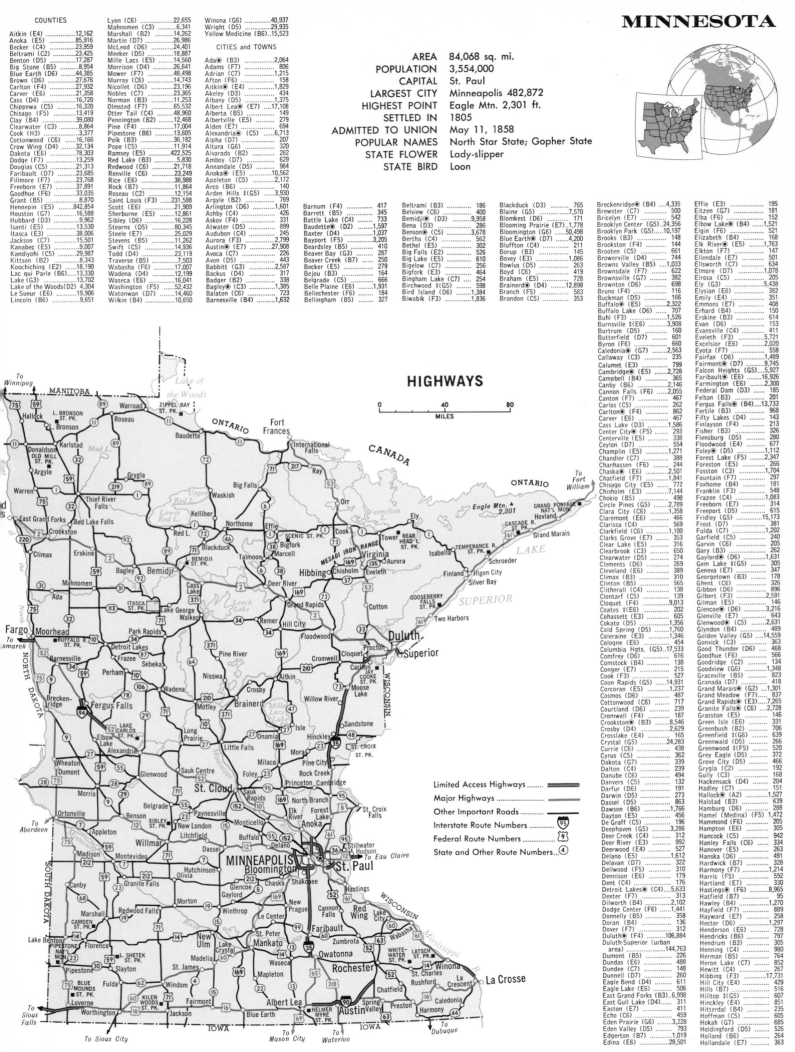

Minnesota
(continued)

TOPOGRAPHY

0   50   100
MILES

Below Sea Level / 100 m. 328 ft. / 200 m. 656 ft. / 500 m. 1,640 ft. / 1,000 m. 3,281 ft. / 2,000 m. 6,562 ft. / 5,000 m. 16,404 ft.

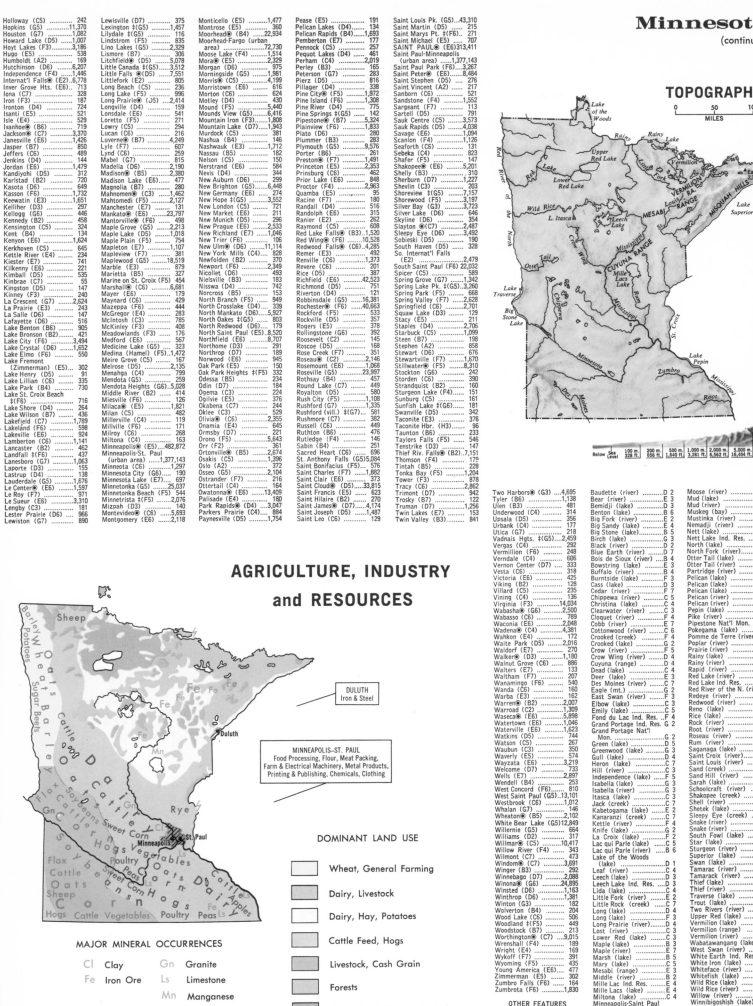

AGRICULTURE, INDUSTRY and RESOURCES

DULUTH
Iron & Steel

MINNEAPOLIS–ST. PAUL
Food Processing, Flour, Meat Packing,
Farm & Electrical Machinery, Metal Products,
Printing & Publishing, Chemicals, Clothing

DOMINANT LAND USE

- Wheat, General Farming
- Dairy, Livestock
- Dairy, Hay, Potatoes
- Cattle Feed, Hogs
- Livestock, Cash Grain
- Forests
- Swampland, Limited Agriculture
- Urban Areas

MAJOR MINERAL OCCURRENCES

Cl Clay   Gn Granite
Fe Iron Ore   Ls Limestone
  Mn Manganese
⚡ Water Power
▨ Major Industrial Areas

◉ County Seat.
‡ Name not on map.

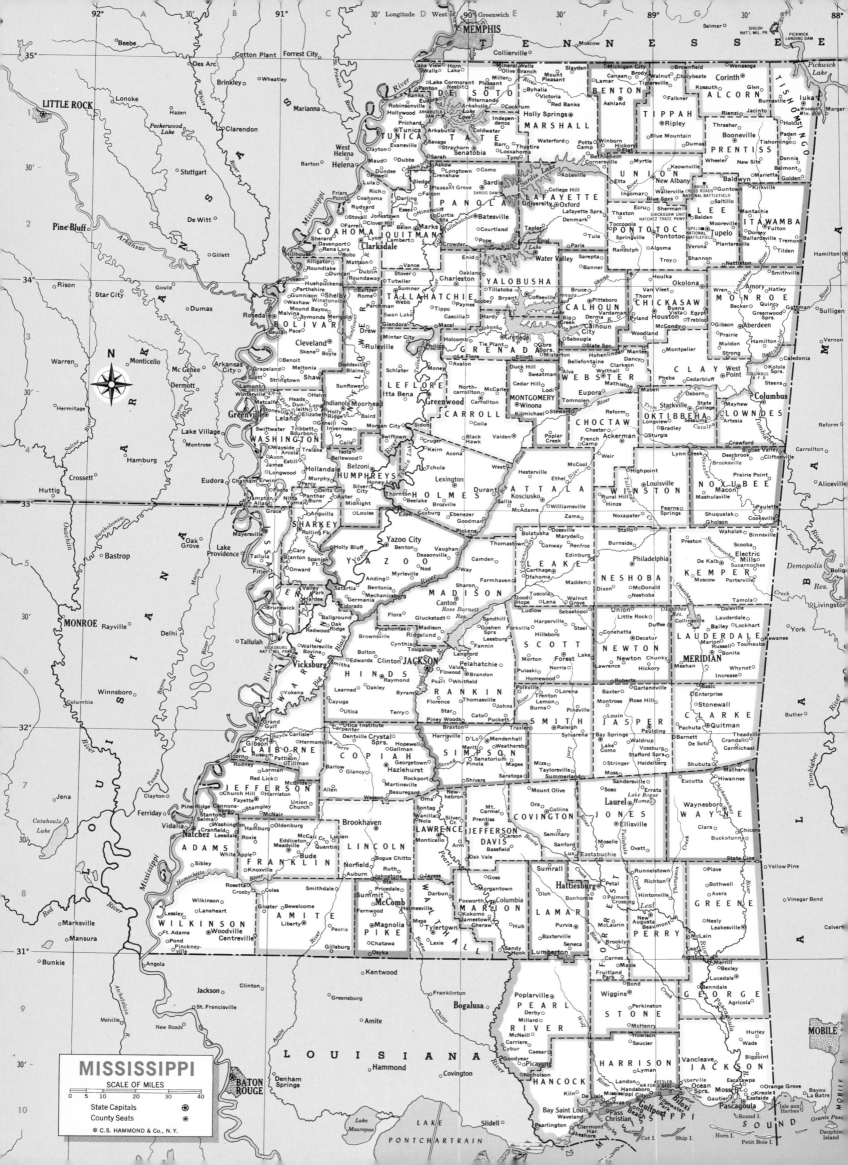

MISSISSIPPI

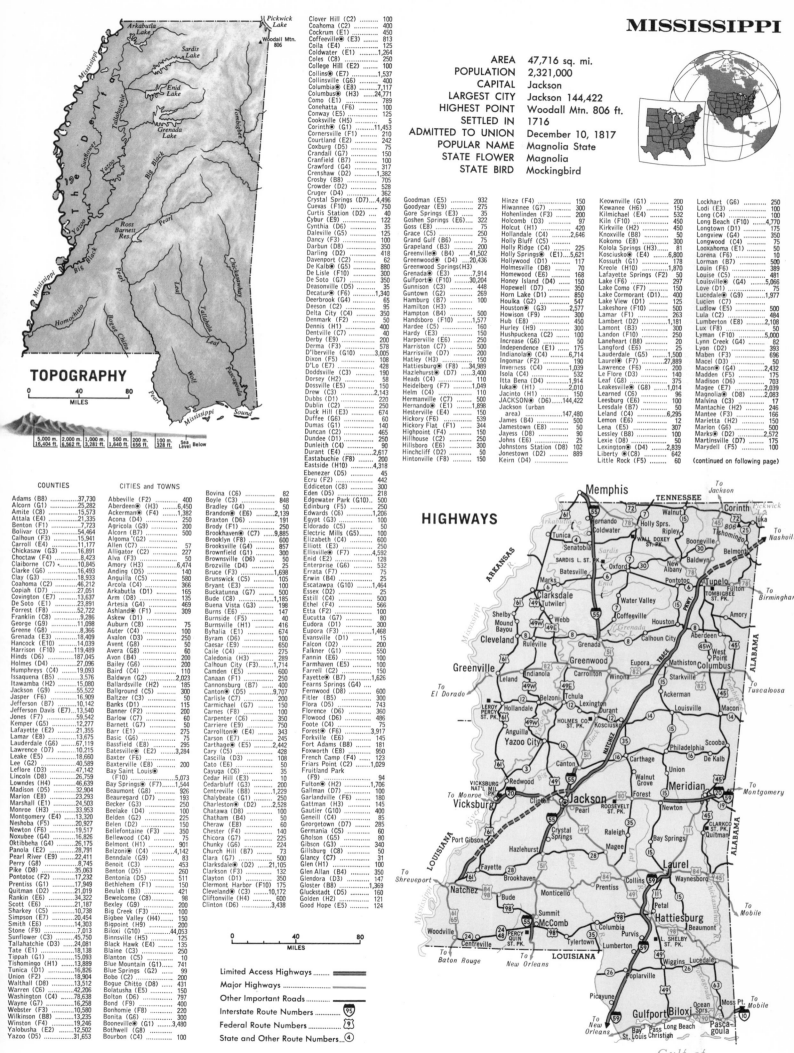

AREA	47,716 sq. mi.
POPULATION	2,321,000
CAPITAL	Jackson
LARGEST CITY	Jackson 144,422
HIGHEST POINT	Woodall Mtn. 806 ft.
SETTLED IN	1716
ADMITTED TO UNION	December 10, 1817
POPULAR NAME	Magnolia State
STATE FLOWER	Magnolia
STATE BIRD	Mockingbird

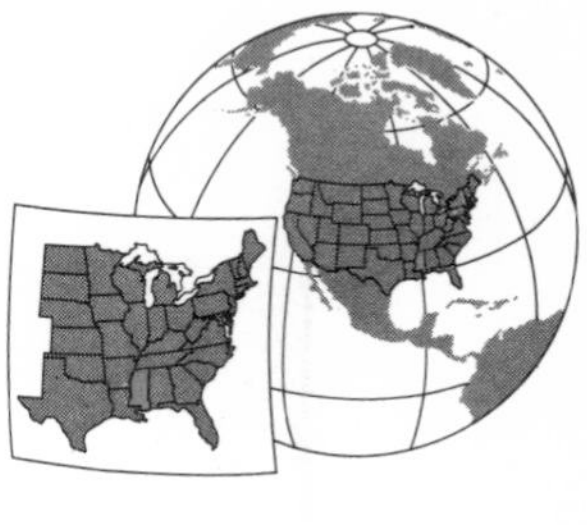

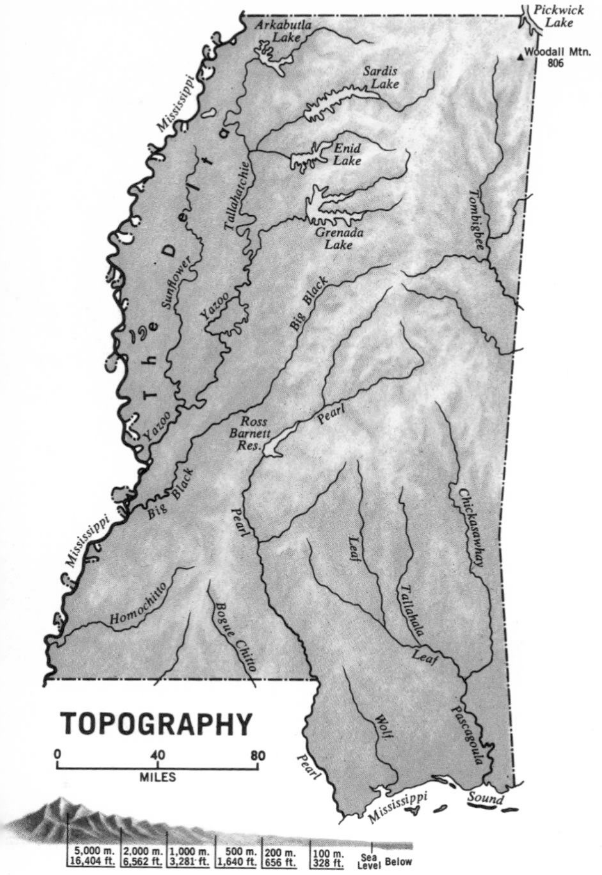
Pickwick Lake
Woodall Mtn. 806
Arkabutla Lake
Sardis Lake
Enid Lake
Grenada Lake
Mississippi
The Delta
Tallahatchie
Yazoo
Sunflower
Big Black
Tombigbee
Ross Barnett Res.
Pearl
Chickasawhay
Leaf
Tallahala
Homochitto
Bogue Chitto
Wolf
Pascagoula
Sound
TOPOGRAPHY
0 40 80
MILES
5,000 m. 16,404 ft.
2,000 m. 6,562 ft.
1,000 m. 3,281 ft.
500 m. 1,640 ft.
200 m. 656 ft.
100 m. 328 ft.
Sea Level
Below

COUNTIES

Adams (B8) 37,730
Alcorn (G1) 25,282
Amite (C8) 15,573
Attala (E4) 21,335
Benton (F1) 7,723
Bolivar (C3) 54,464
Calhoun (F3) 15,941
Carroll (E4) 11,177
Chickasaw (G3) 16,891
Choctaw (F4) 8,423
Claiborne (C7) 10,845
Clarke (G6) 16,493
Clay (G3) 18,933
Coahoma (C2) 46,212
Copiah (D7) 27,051
Covington (E7) 13,637
De Soto (E1) 23,891
Forrest (F8) 52,722
Franklin (C8) 9,286
George (G9) 11,098
Greene (G8) 8,366
Grenada (E3) 18,409
Hancock (E10) 14,039
Harrison (F10) 119,489
Hinds (D6) 187,045
Holmes (D4) 27,096
Humphreys (C4) 19,093
Issaquena (B5) 3,576
Itawamba (H2) 15,080
Jackson (G9) 55,522
Jasper (F6) 16,909
Jefferson (B7) 10,142
Jefferson Davis (E7)...13,540
Jones (F7) 59,542
Kemper (G5) 12,277
Lafayette (E2) 21,355
Lamar (E8) 13,675
Lauderdale (G6) 67,119
Lawrence (D7) 10,215
Leake (E5) 18,660
Lee (G2) 40,589
Leflore (D3) 47,142
Lincoln (D8) 26,759
Lowndes (H4) 46,639
Madison (D5) 32,904
Marion (E8) 23,293
Marshall (E1) 24,503
Monroe (H3) 33,953
Montgomery (E4) 13,320
Neshoba (F5) 20,927
Newton (F6) 19,517
Noxubee (G4) 16,826
Oktibbeha (G4) 26,175
Panola (E2) 28,791
Pearl River (E9) 22,411
Perry (G8) 8,745
Pike (D8) 35,063
Pontotoc (F2) 17,232
Prentiss (G1) 17,949
Quitman (D2) 21,019
Rankin (E6) 34,322
Scott (E6) 21,187
Sharkey (C5) 10,738
Simpson (E7) 20,454
Smith (E6) 14,303
Stone (F9) 7,013
Sunflower (C3) 45,750
Tallahatchie (D3) 24,081
Tate (E1) 18,138
Tippah (G1) 15,093
Tishomingo (H1) 13,889
Tunica (D1) 16,826
Union (F2) 18,904
Walthall (D8) 13,512
Warren (C6) 42,206
Washington (C4) 78,638
Wayne (G7) 16,258
Webster (F3) 10,580
Wilkinson (B8) 13,235
Winston (F4) 19,246
Yalobusha (E2) 12,502
Yazoo (D5) 31,653

CITIES and TOWNS

Abbeville (F2) 400
Aberdeen◉ (H3) 6,450
Ackerman◉ (F4) 1,382
Acona (D4) 250
Agricola (G9) 200
Alcorn (B7) 500
Algoma (G2) ....
Allen (C7) 57
Alligator (C2) 227
Alva (F3) 50
Amory (H3) 6,474
Anding (D5) 140
Anguilla (C5) 580
Arcola (C4) 366
Arkabutla (D1) 165
Arm (D8) 135
Artesia (G4) 469
Ashland◉ (F1) 309
Askew (D1) ....
Auburn (C8) 75
Auter (C4) 100
Avalon (D3) 250
Avent (G8) 50
Avera (G8) 60
Avon (B4) 200
Bailey (G6) 200
Baird (C4) 110
Baldwyn (G2) 2,023
Ballardsville (H2) 185
Ballground (C5) 300
Baltzer (C3) 50
Banks (D1) 115
Banner (F2) 200
Barlow (C7) 60
Barnett (G7) 50
Barr (E1) 275
Basic (G6) 75
Bassfield (E8) 295
Batesville◉ (E2) 3,284
Baxter (F6) ....
Baxterville (E8) 200
Bay Saint Louis◉ (F10) 5,073
Bay Springs◉ (F7) 1,544
Beaumont (G8) 926
Beauregard (D7) 193
Becker (G3) 250
Beelake (D4) 100
Belden (G2) 225
Belen (D2) 150
Bellefontaine (F3) 350
Bellewood (C4) 75
Belmont (H1) 901
Belzoni◉ (C4) 4,142
Benndale (G9) 83
Benoit (C3) 453
Benton (D5) 260
Bentonia (D5) 511
Bethlehem (F1) 150
Beulah (B3) 421
Bewelcome (C8) 98
Bexley (G9) 200
Big Creek (F3) 100
Bigbee Valley (H4) 150
Bigpoint (H9) 200
Biloxi (G10) 44,053
Binnsville (H5) 125
Black Hawk (E4) 135
Blaine (C3) 250
Blanton (C5) 10
Blue Mountain (G1) 741
Blue Springs (G2) 99
Bobo (C2) 200
Bogue Chitto (D8) 431
Bolatusha (E5) 150
Bolton (D6) 797
Bond (F9) 400
Bonhomie (F8) 220
Bonita (G6) 300
Booneville◉ (G1) 3,480
Bothwell (G8) ....
Bourbon (C4) 100
Bovina (C6) 82
Boyle (C3) 848
Bradley (G4) 50
Brandon◉ (E6) 2,139
Braxton (D6) 191
Brody (F1) 250
Brookhaven◉ (C7) 9,885
Brooklyn (F8) 600
Brooksville (G4) 857
Brownfield (G1) 300
Brownsville (D6) 50
Brozville (D4) 25
Bruce (F3) 1,698
Brunswick (C5) 105
Bryant (E3) 100
Buckatunna (G7) 500
Bude (C8) 1,185
Buena Vista (G3) 198
Burns (E6) 147
Burnside (F5) 40
Burnsville (H1) 416
Byhalia (E1) 674
Byram (D6) 100
Caesar (E9) 650
Caile (C4) 275
Caledonia (H3) 289
Calhoun City (F3) 1,714
Camden (E5) 600
Canaan (F1) 250
Cannonsburg (B7) 400
Canton◉ (D5) 9,707
Carlisle (C7) 200
Carmichael (G7) 150
Carnes (F8) 100
Carpenter (C6) 350
Carriere (E9) 750
Carrollton◉ (E4) 343
Carson (E7) 245
Carthage◉ (E5) 2,442
Cary (C5) 428
Cascilla (D3) 108
Cato (E6) 50
Cayuga (C6) 35
Cedar Hill (E3) 10
Cedarbluff (G3) 200
Centreville (B8) 1,229
Chalybeate (G1) 250
Charleston◉ (D2) 2,528
Chatawa (D8) 100
Chatham (B4) 50
Cheraw (E8) 60
Chester (F4) 140
Chicora (G7) 225
Chunky (G6) 224
Church Hill (B7) 73
Clara (G7) 500
Clarksdale◉ (D2) 21,105
Clarkson (F3) 132
Clayton (D1) 350
Clermont Harbor (F10) 175
Cleveland◉ (C3) 10,172
Cliftonville (H4) 600
Clinton (D6) 3,438
Clover Hill (C2) 100
Coahoma (C2) 400
Cockrum (E1) 450
Coffeeville◉ (E3) 813
Coila (E4) 125
Coldwater (E1) 1,264
Coles (C8) 250
College Hill (E2) 100
Collins◉ (E7) 1,537
Collinsville (G6) 400
Columbia◉ (E8) 7,117
Columbus◉ (H3) 24,771
Como (E1) 789
Conehatta (F6) 100
Conway (E5) 125
Cooksville (H5) 5
Corinth◉ (G1) 11,453
Cornersville (F1) 210
Courtland (E2) 242
Coxburg (D5) 75
Crandall (G7) 150
Cranfield (B7) 100
Crawford (G4) 317
Crenshaw (D2) 1,382
Crosby (B8) 705
Crowder (D2) 528
Cruger (D4) 362
Crystal Springs (D7)....4,496
Cuevas (F10) 750
Curtis Station (D2) 40
Cybur (E9) 122
Cynthia (D6) 35
Daleville (G5) 125
Dancy (F3) 100
Darbun (D8) 350
Darling (D2) 418
Davenport (C2) 62
De Kalb◉ (G5) 880
De Lisle (F10) 300
De Soto (G7) 350
Deasonville (D5) 35
Decatur◉ (F6) 1,340
Deerbrook (G4) 65
Deeson (C2) 95
Delta City (C4) 350
Denmark (F2) 50
Dennis (H1) 400
Dentville (C7) 40
Derby (E9) 200
Derma (F3) 578
D'Iberville (G10) 3,005
Dixon (F5) 108
D'Lo (E7) 428
Doddsville (C3) 190
Dorsey (H2) 58
Dossville (E5) 150
Drew (C3) 2,143
Dubbs (D1) 220
Dublin (C2) 250
Duck Hill (E3) 674
Duffee (G6) 60
Dumas (G1) 140
Duncan (C2) 465
Dundee (D1) 250
Dunleith (C4) 90
Durant (E4) 2,617
Eastabuchie (F8) 200
Eastside (H10) 4,318
Ebenezer (D5) 45
Ecru (F2) 442
Eddiceton (C8) 300
Eden (D5) 218
Edgewater Park (G10).. 500
Edinburg (F5) 250
Edwards (C6) 1,206
Egypt (G3) 100
Eldorado (C5) 50
Electric Mills (G5).... 100
Elizabeth (C4) 600
Elliott (E3) 250
Ellisville◉ (F7) 4,592
Enid (E2) 128
Enterprise (G6) 532
Errata (F7) 75
Erwin (B4) 25
Escatawpa (G10) 1,464
Essex (D2) 25
Estill (C4) 500
Ethel (F4) 566
Etta (F2) 100
Eucutta (G7) 80
Eudora (D1) 300
Eupora (F3) 1,468
Evansville (D1) 15
Falcon (D2) 200
Falkner (G1) 550
Fannin (E6) 100
Farmhaven (E5) 100
Farrell (C2) 150
Fayette◉ (B7) 1,626
Fearns Springs (G4) ....
Fernwood (D8) 600
Fitler (B5) 300
Flora (D5) 743
Florence (D6) 360
Flowood (D6) 486
Foote (C4) 75
Forest◉ (F6) 3,917
Forkville (E6) 145
Fort Adams (B8) 181
Foxworth (E8) 950
French Camp (F4) 123
Friars Point (C2) 1,029
Fruitland Park (F9) 94
Fulton◉ (H2) 1,706
Gallman (D7) 100
Garlandville (F6) 180
Gattman (H3) 145
Gautier (G10) 400
Geneill (C4) 85
Georgetown (D7) 285
Germania (C5) 60
Gholson (G5) 80
Gibson (G3) 340
Gillsburg (C8) 50
Glancy (C7) 31
Glen (H1) 100
Glen Allan (B4) 350
Glendora (D3) 147
Gloster (B8) 1,369
Gluckstadt (D5) 160
Golden (H2) 121
Good Hope (E5) 124
Goodman (E5) 932
Goodyear (E9) 275
Gore Springs (E3) 35
Goshen Springs (E6).... 322
Goss (E8) 75
Grace (C5) 250
Grand Gulf (B6) 75
Grapeland (B3) 200
Greenville◉ (B4) 41,502
Greenwood◉ (D4) 20,436
Greenwood Springs(H3)
Grenada◉ (E3) 7,914
Gulfport◉ (F10) 30,204
Gunnison (C3) 448
Guntown (G2) 269
Hamburg (B7) 100
Hamilton (H3) ....
Hampton (B4) 500
Handsboro (F10) 1,577
Hardee (C5) 160
Hardy (E3) 150
Harperville (E6) 250
Harriston (C7) 500
Harrisville (D7) 200
Hatley (H3) 150
Hattiesburg◉ (F8) 34,989
Hazlehurst◉ (D7) 3,400
Heads (C4) 110
Heidelberg (F7) 1,049
Helm (C4) 110
Hermanville (C7) 500
Hernando◉ (E1) 1,898
Hesterville (E4) 150
Hickory (F6) 539
Hickory Flat (F1) 344
Highpoint (F4) 150
Hillhouse (C2) 250
Hillsboro (E6) 300
Hinchcliff (D2) 50
Hintonville (F8) 150
Hinze (F4) 150
Hiwannee (G7) 300
Hohenlinden (F3) 200
Holcomb (D3) 97
Holcut (H1) 420
Hollandale (C4) 2,646
Holly Bluff (C5) ....
Holly Ridge (C4) 225
Holly Springs◉ (E1)....5,621
Hollywood (D1) 117
Holmesville (D8) 70
Homewood (E6) 168
Honey Island (D4) 150
Hopewell (D7) 350
Horn Lake (D1) 850
Houlka (G2) 547
Houston◉ (G3) 2,577
Howison (F9) 300
Hub (E8) 450
Hurley (H9) 300
Hushpuckena (C2) 100
Increase (G6) 50
Independence (E1) 175
Indianola◉ (C4) 6,714
Ingomar (F2) 190
Inverness (C4) 1,039
Isola (C4) 532
Itta Bena (D4) 1,914
Iuka◉ (H1) 2,010
Jacinto (H1) 150
JACKSON◉ (D6)....144,422
Jackson (urban area) 147,480
James (B4) 500
Jamestown (E8) 50
Jayess (D8) 90
Johns (E6) 25
Johnstons Station (D8) 102
Jonestown (D2) 889
Keirn (D4) ....
Keownville (G1) 200
Kewanee (H6) 150
Kilmichael (E4) 532
Kiln (F10) 450
Kirkville (H2) 450
Knoxville (B8) 50
Kokomo (E8) 300
Kolola Springs (H3).... 81
Kosciusko◉ (E4) 6,800
Kossuth (G1) 178
Kreole (H10) 1,870
Lafayette Springs (F2) 50
Lake (F6) 297
Lake Como (F7) 150
Lake Cormorant (D1).... 400
Lake View (D1) 125
Lakeshore (F10) 500
Lamar (F1) 263
Lambert (D2) 1,181
Lamont (B3) 300
Landon (F10) 250
Laneheart (B8) 20
Langford (E6) 25
Lauderdale (G5) 1,500
Laurel◉ (F7) 27,889
Lawrence (F6) 200
Le Flore (D3) 140
Leaf (G8) 375
Leakesville◉ (G8) 1,014
Learned (C6) 96
Leesburg (E6) 100
Leesdale (B7) 50
Leland (C4) 6,295
Lemon (E6) 12
Lena (E5) 307
Lessley (B8) 100
Lexie (D8) 50
Lexington◉ (D4) 2,839
Liberty ◉(C8) 642
Little Rock (F5) 60
Lockhart (G6) 250
Lodi (E3) 100
Long (C4) 100
Long Beach (F10) 4,770
Longtown (D1) 175
Longview (G4) 350
Longwood (C4) 75
Looxahoma (E1) 50
Lorena (F6) 10
Lorman (B7) 500
Louin (F6) 389
Louise (C5) 481
Louisville◉ (G4) 5,066
Love (D1) 75
Lucedale◉ (G9) 1,977
Lucien (C7) ....
Ludlow (E5) 500
Lula (C2) 484
Lumberton (E8) 2,108
Lux (F8) 50
Lyman (F10) 5,000
Lynn Creek (G4) 82
Lyon (D2) 393
Maben (F3) 696
Macel (D3) 50
Macon◉ (G4) 2,432
Madden (F5) 175
Madison (D6) 703
Magee (E7) 2,039
Magnolia◉ (D8) 2,083
Malvina (C3) 17
Mantachie (H2) 246
Mantee (F3) 166
Marietta (H2) 150
Marion (G6) 500
Marks◉ (D2) 2,572
Martinsville (D7) 175
Marydell (F5) 100

(continued on following page)

HIGHWAYS

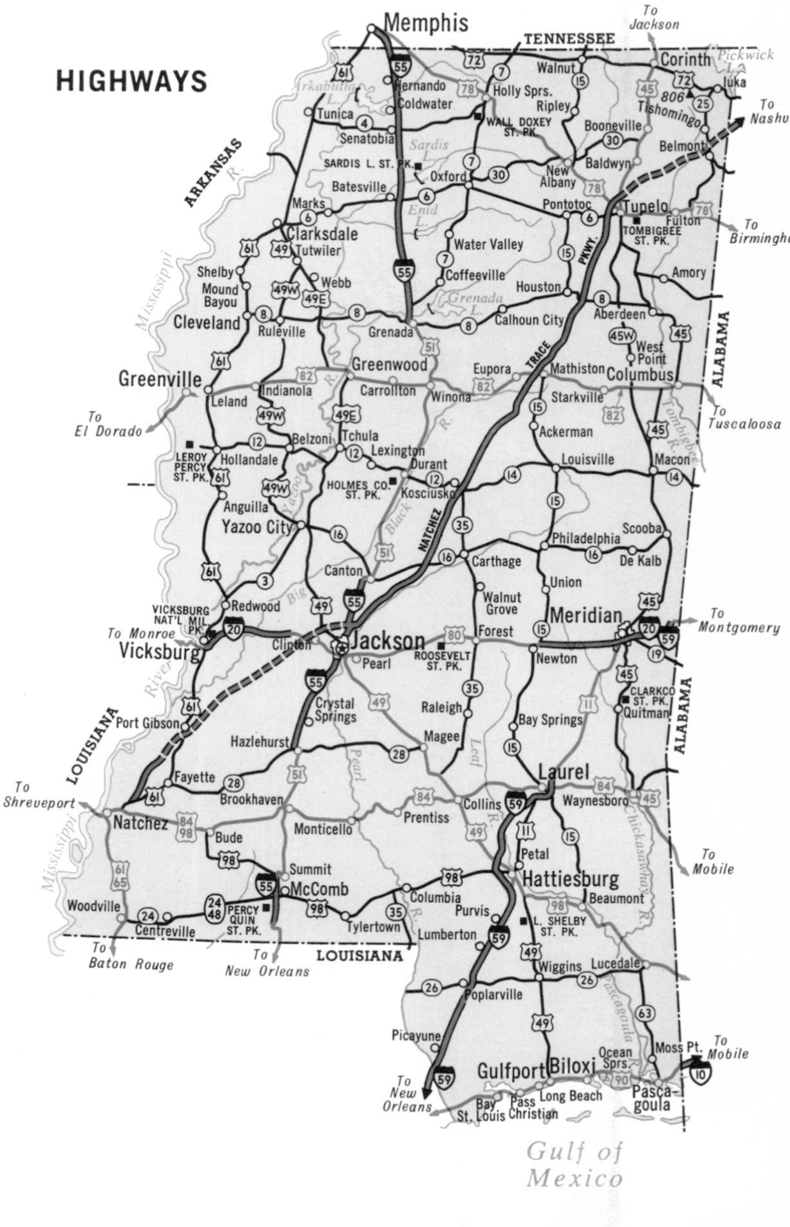
Memphis
TENNESSEE
To Jackson
Corinth
Pickwick L.
Iuka
To Nashville
Tunica
Hernando
Coldwater
Holly Sprs.
Ripley
Walnut
Booneville
Belmont
Senatobia
Sardis L.
Batesville
Oxford
New Albany
Baldwyn
Tupelo
Fulton
To Birmingham
ARKANSAS
Marks
Enid L.
Pontotoc
Clarksdale
Tutwiler
Water Valley
Coffeeville
Houston
Amory
Shelby
Mound Bayou
Cleveland
Webb
Grenada L.
Calhoun City
Aberdeen
West Point
Ruleville
Grenada
Greenwood
Eupora
Mathiston
Columbus
ALABAMA
Greenville
Leland
Indianola
Carrollton
Winona
Starkville
To Tuscaloosa
To El Dorado
Belzoni
Tchula
Ackerman
Hollandale
Lexington
Durant
Louisville
Macon
Anguilla
Kosciusko
Yazoo City
Philadelphia
Scooba
Carthage
De Kalb
Canton
Union
NATCHEZ TRACE PKWY.
Redwood
Meridian
To Monroe
Vicksburg
Clinton
Jackson
Pearl
Forest
To Montgomery
Newton
Crystal Springs
Raleigh
Port Gibson
Bay Springs
Quitman
LOUISIANA
Hazlehurst
Magee
Fayette
Brookhaven
Laurel
Prentiss
Collins
Waynesboro
To Shreveport
Natchez
Monticello
Bude
Petal
Hattiesburg
To Mobile
Summit
McComb
Columbia
Purvis
Beaumont
Woodville
Centreville
Tylertown
Lumberton
To Baton Rouge
To New Orleans
LOUISIANA
Wiggins
Lucedale
Poplarville
Picayune
Gulfport
Biloxi
Ocean Sprs.
Moss Pt.
To Mobile
To New Orleans
Bay St. Louis
Pass Christian
Long Beach
Pascagoula
Gulf of Mexico

0 40 80
MILES

Limited Access Highways ....
Major Highways ....
Other Important Roads ....
Interstate Route Numbers 95
Federal Route Numbers 9
State and Other Route Numbers... 4

Mississippi
(continued)

Name	Pop.
Mashulaville (G4)	50
Matherville (G7)	178
Mathiston (F3)	597
Mattson (C2)	240
Maud (D1)	102
Maxie (F9)	100
Mayersville● (B5)	250
Mayhew (G4)	200
McAdams (E4)	240
McBride (C7)	200
McCall Creek (C7)	149
McCarley (E3)	200
McComb (D8)	12,020
McCondy (G3)	135
McCool (F4)	211
McDonald (F5)	35
McHenry (F9)	525
McLain (G5)	635
McLaurin (F8)	200
McNair (E7)	100
McNeill (E9)	500
Meadville● (C8)	611
Mechanicsburg (D5)	15
Meehan (G6)	150
Meltonia (C3)	10
Mendenhall● (E7)	1,946
Meridian● (G6)	49,374
Merigold (C3)	602
Merit (E7)	10
Merrill (G9)	100
Mesa (D2)	35
Metcalfe (B4)	100
Michigan City (F1)	135
Midnight (C4)	500
Millard (E9)	3
Miller (E1)	200
Mineral Wells (E1)	275
Minter City (D3)	238
Mississippi City (F10)	4,169
Misterton (E3)	10
Mize (E7)	371
Money (D3)	200
Monticello● (D7)	1,432
Montpelier (G3)	250
Montrose (F6)	169
Mooreville (G2)	—
Moorhead (C4)	1,754
Morgan City (B4)	300
Morgantown (E8)	600
Morton (E6)	2,260
Moscow (G5)	32
Moselle (F8)	500
Moss (F7)	—
Moss Point (G10)	6,631
Mound Bayou (C3)	1,354
Mount Carmel (E7)	100
Mount Olive (E7)	841
Mount Pleasant (E1)	300
Muldon (D2)	60
Murphy (C4)	125
Myrleville (D5)	20
Myrtle (F1)	313
Natchez● (B7)	23,791
Neely (G8)	300
Nesbit (D1)	300
Neshoba (F5)	250
Nettleton (G2)	1,389
New Albany● (G2)	5,151
New Augusta● (F8)	275
New Site (H1)	80
Newhebron (D7)	271
Newton (F6)	3,178

Name	Pop.
Nicholson (E10)	400
Nitta Yuma (C4)	300
Nod (D5)	120
Nola (D7)	95
Norfield (C8)	75
Norris (F6)	12
Northcarrollton (E3)	521
Noxapater (F5)	549
Oak Ridge (C6)	475
Oak Vale (E8)	99
Oakland (E2)	488
Oakley (D6)	500
Ocean Springs (G10)	5,025
Ofahoma (E5)	900
Okolona● (G2)	2,622
Oldenburg (C7)	20
Olive Branch (E1)	642
Oloh (E8)	87
Oma (D7)	200
Onward (C5)	75
Ora (E7)	95
Orange Grove (H10)	300
Osborn (G3)	50
Osyka (D8)	712
Ovett (F8)	290
Oxford● (F2)	5,283
Pace (C3)	420
Pachuta (G6)	271
Paden (H1)	134
Palmers Crossing (F8)	440
Panther Burn (C4)	800
Parchman (D3)	250
Paris (F2)	200
Pascagoula● (G10)	17,155
Pass Christian (F10)	3,881
Pattison (C7)	400
Paulding● (F6)	250
Paulette (H4)	250
Paynes (D3)	200
Pearl (D6)	5,081
Pearlington (E10)	300
Pelahatchie (E6)	1,066
Penton (D1)	200
Peoria (C8)	160
Percy (C4)	75
Perkinston (F9)	900
Perthshire (C3)	600
Petal (F8)	4,007
Pheba (G3)	425
Philadelphia● (F5)	5,017
Philipp (D3)	700
Piave (G8)	—
Picayune (E9)	7,834
Pickens (E5)	727
Pinckneyville (B8)	100
Pine Ridge (B7)	200
Pineville (F9)	14
Piney Woods (D6)	500
Pinola (E7)	116
Pittsboro● (F3)	205
Plantersville (G2)	500
Pleasant Grove (D2)	50
Pleasant Hill (E1)	250
Pocahontas (D6)	300
Polkville (E6)	150
Pond (B8)	25
Pontotoc● (G2)	2,108
Pope (E2)	246
Poplar Creek (E4)	150
Poplarville● (E9)	2,136
Port Gibson● (B7)	2,861
Porterville (G5)	125

Name	Pop.
Potts Camp (F1)	429
Powell (D2)	80
Prairie (G3)	112
Prairie Point (H4)	50
Prentiss● (E7)	1,321
Preston (G5)	150
Pricedale (D8)	300
Prichard (D1)	70
Puckett (E6)	302
Pulaski (E6)	750
Purvis (F8)	1,614
Pyland (F3)	100
Quentin (C8)	300
Quincy (H3)	—
Quitman● (G7)	2,030
Raleigh● (F6)	614
Randolph (F2)	131
Raymond● (D6)	1,381
Red Banks (F1)	350
Red Lick (B7)	250
Redwood (C6)	50
Reform (F4)	350
Rena Lara (C2)	200
Renfroe (F5)	138
Rich (D2)	60
Richton (E8)	1,089
Ridgeland (D6)	875
Rienzi (G1)	375
Ripley● (G1)	2,668
Roberts (F6)	50
Robinsonville (D1)	300
Rockport (D7)	100
Rodney (B7)	200
Rolling Fork● (C5)	1,619
Rome (C3)	279
Rose Hill (F6)	300
Rosedale● (B3)	2,339
Rosetta (B8)	160
Roundaway (C4)	200
Roundlake (C2)	200
Roxie (B8)	585
Rudyard (C2)	110
Ruleville (D3)	1,902
Runnelstown (F8)	80
Rural Hill (F4)	125
Russell (G6)	500
Russum (B7)	350
Ruth (D8)	60
Sabougla (F3)	90
Sallis (E4)	223
Saltillo (G2)	536
Sanatorium (E7)	950
Sandersville (F7)	657
Sandhill (E5)	365
Sandy Hook (E8)	143
Sanford (F8)	250
Sarah (D1)	200
Saratoga (E7)	90
Sardis● (E2)	2,098
Sarepta (F3)	172
Satartia (C5)	126
Saucier (F9)	—
Savage (D1)	125
Schlater (D3)	400
Scobey (E3)	100
Scooba (G5)	513
Scott (B3)	1,050
Sebastopol (F5)	343
Selma (B7)	2
Seminary (E7)	288
Senatobia● (E1)	3,253
Seneca (F8)	136
Sessums (G4)	200
Shannon (G2)	554
Sharon (E5)	117
Shaw (C3)	2,062
Shelby (C3)	2,384
Sherard (C2)	100
Sherman (G2)	403
Shivers (E7)	100

Name	Pop.
Shubuta (G7)	718
Shuqualak (G5)	550
Sibley (B8)	400
Sidon (D4)	410
Silver City (C4)	431
Silver Creek (D7)	229
Skene (C3)	250
Slate Spring (F3)	123
Slayden (F1)	181
Sledge (D2)	440
Smithdale (C8)	—
Smiths (C6)	50
Smithville (H2)	489

Name	Pop.
Sontag (D7)	150
Soso (F7)	—
Spanish Fort (C5)	20
Springville (F2)	400
Stafford Springs (F7)	20
Stallo (F5)	500
Stampley (B7)	200
Stanton (B7)	260
Star (D6)	300
Starkville● (G4)	9,041
State College (G4)	7,500
State Line (G8)	653
Steel (F6)	125

Name	Pop.
Steens (H3)	148
Stewart (F4)	162
Stoneville (C4)	700
Stonewall (G6)	1,126
Stovall (C2)	125
Stover (D2)	75
Strayhorn (D1)	250
Stringer (F7)	150
Stringtown (C3)	450
Strong (G4)	300
Sturgis (G4)	358
Sucarnoochee (H5)	35
Summerland (F7)	112

Name	Pop.
Summit (D8)	1,663
Sumner● (D3)	551
Sumrall (E8)	797
Sunflower (C3)	662
Swan Lake (D3)	150
Sweatman (E4)	45
Swiftown (D4)	150
Swiftwater (B4)	64
Sylvarena (F6)	69
Symonds (C3)	10
Tallula (B5)	200
Tamola (G5)	150
Taylor (E2)	122
Taylorsville (F7)	1,132
Tchula (D4)	882
Terry (D6)	585
Thaxton (F2)	150
Theadville (G7)	75
Thomastown (E5)	300
Thomasville (E6)	15
Thorn (F3)	56
Thornton (D4)	300
Thrasher (G1)	200
Thyatira (E1)	—
Tie Plant (E3)	1,491
Tilden (H2)	250
Tillatoba (E3)	102
Tillman (C7)	150
Tiplersville (G1)	125
Tippo (D3)	55
Tishomingo (H1)	415
Toccopola (F2)	198
Tomnolen (F4)	200
Toomsuba (G6)	400
Tougaloo (D6)	1,800
Tralake (C4)	300
Traxler (E6)	70
Trebloc (G3)	500
Tremont (H2)	150
Trenton (E6)	50
Tribbett (C4)	100
Troy (G2)	—
Tula (F2)	150
Tunica● (D1)	1,445
Tupelo● (G2)	17,221
Tuscola (E5)	75
Tutwiler (D2)	912
Tylertown● (D8)	1,532
Tyro (E1)	—
Union (F5)	1,726
Union Church (C7)	194
University (E2)	3,597
Utica (C6)	764
Utica Institute (C6)	—
Valden● (E4)	475
Valley Park (C5)	495
Value (D6)	300
Van Vleet (G3)	275
Vance (D2)	500
Vancleave (G9)	700
Vardaman (F3)	637
Vaughan (D5)	150
Verona (G2)	824
Vicksburg● (C6)	29,143
Vossburg (F7)	700
Wade (G9)	300
Wahalak (G5)	75
Waldrup (F7)	125
Walkersville (G2)	100
Walls (D1)	250
Walnut (D1)	390
Walnut Grove (F5)	433
Waltersville (C6)	475
Walthall● (F3)	153
Wanilla (D7)	45
Washington (B7)	—
Water Valley● (E2)	3,206
Waterford (E1)	125
Waveland (F10)	1,106
Waxhaw (C3)	10
Way (E5)	50
Waynesboro● (G7)	3,892
Wayside (C4)	475
Weathersby (E7)	80
Webb (D3)	686
Weir (D4)	522
Wenasoga (G1)	100
Wesson (D7)	1,157

Name	Pop.
West (E4)	282
West Point● (G3)	8,550
Wheeler (G1)	500
White Apple (B8)	86
Whitfield (E6)	500
Whynot (G6)	25
Wiggins● (F9)	1,591
Wilkinson (B8)	300
Williamsville (F4)	500
Winborn (F1)	77
Winona● (E4)	4,282
Winstonville (C3)	327
Winterville (B4)	300
Woodland (F3)	135
Woodville● (B8)	1,856
Wren (G3)	90
Yazoo City● (D5)	11,236
Yokena (C6)	25
Zama (F5)	250

OTHER FEATURES

Amite (river)	C 8
Arkabutla (dam)	D 1
Arkabutla (lake)	E 1
Big Black (river)	F 8
Black (river)	E 7
Bogue Chitto (river)	D 8
Bogue Homo (lake)	F 7
Bowie (creek)	E 7
Brices Cross Roads Nat'l Battlefield Site	G 2
Buttahatchie (river)	H 3
Cat (isl.)	F10
Catalpa (creek)	G 4
Chickasaw Unit, Natchez Trace Parkway	G 2
Chickasawhay (river)	G 7
Coldwater (river)	D 1
Columbus A.F.B.	H 3
Deer (creek)	C 4
Enid (lake)	E 2
Greenville A.F.B.	B 3
Grenada (lake)	E 3
Homochitto (river)	B 8
Horn (isl.)	G10
Keesler A.F.B.	G10
Leaf (river)	F 8
Little Tallahatchie (riv.)	D 2
Mississippi (river)	A 8
Mississippi (sound)	F10
Noxubee (river)	G 4
Okatibbee (creek)	G 5
Okatibbee (res.)	G 6
Pascagoula (river)	G 9
Pearl (river)	D 8
Petit Bois (isl.)	H10
Pickwick (lake)	H 1
Pierre (bayou)	C 7
Ross Barnett (res.)	D 6
Round (isl.)	G10
Saint Louis (bay)	F10
Sardis (dam)	E 2
Sardis (lake)	E 2
Ship (isl.)	G10
Skuna (river)	E 3
Strong (river)	E 7
Sucarnoochee (creek)	G 5
Sunflower (river)	C 4
Tallahaga (creek)	F 6
Tallahala (creek)	F 7
Tallahatchie (river)	D 2
Tchula (lake)	D 4
Thompson (creek)	G 8
Tombigbee (river)	H 4
Trim Cane (creek)	G 4
Tupelo Nat'l Battlefield Site	G 2
Vicksburg Nat'l Mil. Park	C 6
Wolf (river)	F 9
Woodall (mt.)	H 1
Yalobusha (river)	E 3
Yazoo (river)	C 4
Yockanookany (river)	E 5

● County Seat.

AGRICULTURE, INDUSTRY and RESOURCES

DOMINANT LAND USE

- Specialized Cotton
- Cotton, Livestock
- Cotton, General Farming
- Cotton, Forest Products
- Truck and Mixed Farming
- Forests
- Swampland, Limited Agriculture

MAJOR MINERAL OCCURRENCES

- Cl Clay
- G Natural Gas
- O Petroleum

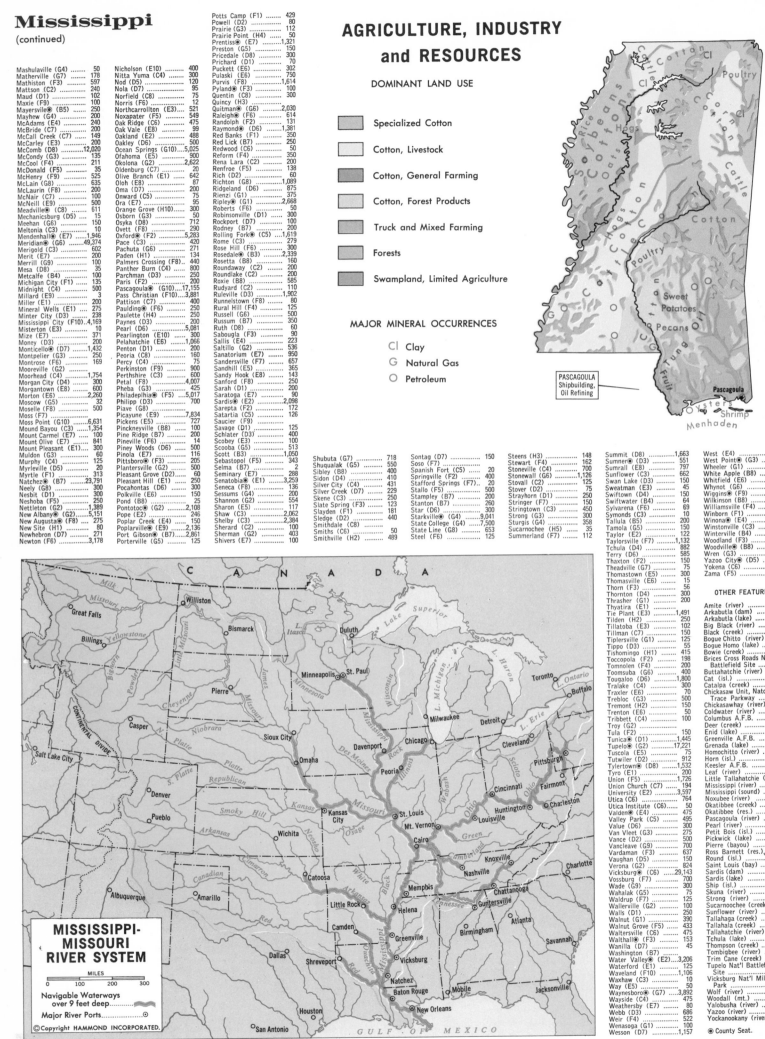

PASCAGOULA
Shipbuilding,
Oil Refining

MISSISSIPPI-MISSOURI RIVER SYSTEM

MILES
0   100   200   300

Navigable Waterways over 9 feet deep ....
Major River Ports .... ◉

MISSOURI

AREA 69,686 sq. mi.
POPULATION 4,497,000
CAPITAL Jefferson City
LARGEST CITY St. Louis 750,026
HIGHEST POINT Taum Sauk Mtn. 1,772 ft.
SETTLED IN 1764
ADMITTED TO UNION August 10, 1821
POPULAR NAME Show Me State
STATE FLOWER Hawthorn
STATE BIRD Bluebird

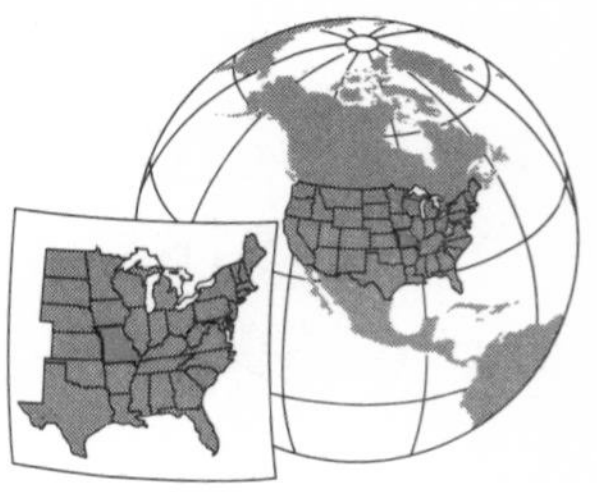

COUNTIES

Adair (G2) 20,105
Andrew (C3) 11,062
Atchison (B2) 9,213
Audrain (J4) 26,079
Barry (E9) 18,921
Barton (D7) 11,113
Bates (D6) 15,905
Benton (F6) 8,737
Bollinger (M8) 9,167
Boone (H4) 55,202
Buchanan (C3) 90,581
Butler (M9) 34,656
Caldwell (E3) 8,830
Callaway (J5) 23,858
Camden (G6) 9,116
Cape Girardeau (N8) 42,020
Carroll (F4) 13,847
Carter (L9) 3,973
Cass (D5) 29,702
Cedar (E7) 9,185
Chariton (G3) 12,720
Christian (F9) 12,359
Clark (J2) 8,725
Clay (D4) 87,474
Clinton (D3) 11,588
Cole (H6) 40,761
Cooper (G5) 15,448
Crawford (K7) 12,647
Dade (E8) 7,577
Dallas (F7) 9,314
Daviess (E3) 9,502
De Kalb (D3) 7,226
Dent (J7) 10,445
Douglas (G9) 9,653
Dunklin (M10) 39,139
Franklin (K6) 44,566
Gasconade (J6) 12,195
Gentry (D2) 8,793
Greene (F8) 126,276
Grundy (E2) 12,220
Harrison (E2) 11,603
Henry (E6) 19,226
Hickory (F7) 4,516
Holt (B2) 7,885
Howard (G4) 10,859
Howell (J9) 22,027
Iron (L7) 8,041
Jackson (D5) 622,732
Jasper (D8) 78,863
Jefferson (L6) 66,377
Johnson (E5) 28,981
Knox (H2) 6,558
Laclede (G7) 18,991
Lafayette (E4) 25,274
Lawrence (E8) 23,260
Lewis (J2) 10,984
Lincoln (L4) 14,783
Linn (F3) 16,815
Livingston (E3) 15,771
Macon (G3) 16,473
Madison (M8) 9,366
Maries (J6) 7,282
Marion (J3) 29,522
McDonald (D9) 11,798
Mercer (E2) 5,750
Miller (H6) 13,800
Mississippi (O9) 20,695
Moniteau (G5) 10,500
Monroe (H3) 10,688
Montgomery (K5) 11,097
Morgan (G6) 9,476
New Madrid (N9) 31,350
Newton (D9) 30,093
Nodaway (C2) 22,215
Oregon (K9) 9,845
Osage (J6) 10,867
Ozark (H9) 6,744
Pemiscot (N10) 38,095
Perry (N7) 14,642
Pettis (F5) 35,120
Phelps (J7) 25,396
Pike (K4) 16,706
Platte (C4) 23,350
Polk (F7) 13,753
Pulaski (H7) 46,567
Putnam (F2) 6,999
Ralls (J3) 8,078
Randolph (G3) 22,014
Ray (E4) 16,075
Reynolds (L8) 5,161
Ripley (L9) 9,096
Saint Charles (L5) 52,970
Saint Clair (E6) 8,421
Saint Francois (M7) 36,516
Saint Louis (M5) 703,532
Saint Louis (city) (M5) 750,026
Sainte Genevieve (M7) 12,116
Saline (F4) 25,148
Schuyler (G2) 5,052
Scotland (H2) 6,484
Scott (N8) 32,748
Shannon (K8) 7,087
Shelby (H3) 9,063
Stoddard (N9) 29,490
Stone (F9) 8,176
Sullivan (F2) 8,783
Taney (F9) 10,238
Texas (J8) 17,758
Vernon (D7) 20,540
Warren (K5) 8,750
Washington (L7) 14,346
Wayne (L8) 8,638
Webster (G8) 13,753
Worth (D2) 3,936
Wright (H8) 14,183

CITIES and TOWNS

Adrian (D6) 1,082
Advance (N8) 692
Agency (C3) 240
Airport Drive (C8) 292
Alba (D8) 336
Albany◉ (D2) 1,662
Aldrich (F7) 181
Alexandria (K2) 452
Allendale (D2) 136
Alma (E4) 390
Altamont (D3) 190
Altenburg (O7) 260
Alton◉ (K9) 677
Amazonia (C3) 326
Amity (D3) 111
Amoret (C6) 261
Amsterdam (C6) 118
Anderson (D9) 992
Annada (L4) 105
Annapolis (L8) 334
Anniston (O9) 307
Appleton (N7) 75
Appleton City (E6) 1,075
Arbela (H2) 70
Arbor Terrace ‡(P3) 1,225
Arbyrd (M10) 667
Arcadia (L7) 489
Archie (D5) 348
Argyle (J6) 99
Armstrong (G4) 387
Arrow Rock (F4) 245
Asbury (C8) 186
Ash Grove (E8) 886
Ashburn (K3) 124
Ashland (H5) 495
Atlanta (H3) 386
Augusta (M3) 206
Aullville (E4) 90
Aurora (E9) 4,683
Austin (D5) 80
Auxvasse (J4) 534
Ava◉ (G9) 1,581
Avilla (D8) 135
Avondale (P5) 663
Bagnell (G6) 62
Baker ‡(N9) 114
Ballwin (O3) 5,710
Baring (H2) 213
Barnard (C2) 237
Barnett (G6) 200
Bates City (E5) 110
Bel-Nor ‡(P3) 2,388
Bel-Ridge ‡(P3) 4,395
Belgique (N7) 61
Bell City (N8) 409
Bella Villa ‡(P3) 779
Belle (J6) 1,016
Bellefontaine Neighbors (R2) 13,650
Bellerive ‡(P3) 314
Bellflower (K4) 245
Belton (C5) 4,897
Benton◉ (O8) 554
Benton City (J4) 155
Berdell Hills ‡(P3) 533
Berger (K5) 187
Berkeley (P2) 18,676
Bernie (M9) 1,578
Bertrand (O9) 465
Bethany◉ (E2) 2,771
Bethel (J3) 152
Beverly Hills ‡(P3) 849
Bevier (G3) 781
Bigelow (B2) 100
Billings (F8) 602
Birch Tree (K9) 420
Birmingham (P5) 201
Bismarck (L7) 1,237
Blackburn (F4) 310
Blackwater (G5) 284
Blairstown (E5) 177
Bland (J6) 654
Blodgett (O8) 203
Bloomfield◉ (M9) 1,330
Blue Eye (F9) 74
Blue Lick (F4) 75
Blue Springs (R6) 2,555
Blythedale (E2) 179
Bogard (E4) 277
Bolckow (C2) 232
Bolivar◉ (F7) 3,512
Bonne Terre (L7) 3,219
Boonville◉ (G5) 7,090
Bosworth (F4) 465
Bourbon (K6) 779
Bowling Green◉ (K4) 2,650
Bradleyville (F9) 91
Bragg City (N10) 274
Brandsville (J9) 128
Branson (F9) 1,887
Brashear (H2) 309
Brasher (N10) 135
Braymer (E3) 874
Breckenridge (E3) 605
Breckenridge Hills (O2) 6,299
Brentwood (P3) 12,250
Bridgeton (O2) 7,820
Bridgeton Terr. ‡(P3) 625
Brimson (E2) 107
Bronaugh (C7) 173
Brookfield (F3) 5,694
Browning (F2) 412
Brownington (E6) 130
Brumley (H6) 74
Brunswick (F4) 1,493
Bucklin (G3) 639
Buckner (R5) 1,198
Buell (K4) 53
Buffalo◉ (F7) 1,477
Bunceton (G5) 468
Bunker (K8) 300
Burgess (C7) 86
Burlington Jct. (B2) 650
Butler◉ (D6) 3,791
Butterfield (E9) 125
Cabool (H8) 1,284
Cainsville (E2) 495
Cairo (H4) 210
Caledonia (L7) 119
Calhoun (E6) 374
California◉ (H5) 2,788
Callao (G3) 329
Calverton Park ‡(P2) 1,714
Camden (D4) 310
Camden Point (C4) 171
Camdenton◉ (G6) 1,405
Cameron (D3) 3,674
Campbell (M9) 1,964
Canalou (N9) 447
Canton (J2) 2,562
Cape Girardeau (O8) 24,947
Cardwell (M10) 815
Carl Junction (C8) 1,220
Carrollton◉ (E4) 4,554
Carterville (D8) 1,443
Carthage◉ (D8) 11,264
Caruthersville◉ (N10) 8,643
Cassville◉ (E9) 1,451
Catron (N9) 177
Center (J3) 484
Centertown (H5) 190
Centerview (E5) 208
Centerville◉ (L8) 163
Centralia (H4) 3,200
Chaffee (N8) 2,862
Chamois (J5) 658
Champ ‡(O2) 50
Charlack ‡(P3) 1,493
Charleston◉ (O9) 5,911
Chilhowee (E5) 339
Chillicothe◉ (E3) 9,236
Chula (F3) 285
Clarence (H3) 1,103
Clark (H4) 260
Clarksburg (G5) 357
Clarksdale (D3) 242
Clarkson Valley (N3) 137
Clarksville (K4) 638
Clarkton (M10) 1,049
Claycomo (P5) 1,423
Clayton◉ (P3) 15,245
Clearmont (C1) 292
Cleveland (C5) 216
Clever (F8) 283
Clifton Hill (G4) 207
Climax Springs (G6) 93
Clinton◉ (E6) 6,925
Clyde (G2) 90
Cobalt City ‡(M7) 434
Coffey (E2) 190
Cole Camp (F6) 853
Collins (E7) 177
Columbia◉ (H5) 36,650
Commerce (O8) 247
Conception Jct. (C2) 253
Concordia (E5) 1,471
Conway (G7) 500
Cool Valley ‡(P2) 1,492
Cooter (N10) 477
Corder (E4) 506
Corning (B2) 128
Cosby (C3) 119
Country Club Hills ‡(P3) 1,763
Country Club Vill. (C3) 395
Country Life Acres ‡(O3) 66
Cowgill (E3) 259
Craig (B2) 488
Crane (E9) 954
Creighton (D6) 228
Crestwood (O3) 11,106
Creve Coeur (O3) 5,122
Crocker (H7) 821
Cross Timbers (F6) 186
Crosstown (N7) 83
Crowder (N9) 115
Crystal City (M6) 3,678
Crystal Lake Park ‡(P3) 307
Cuba (K6) 1,672
Curryville (K4) 287
Dadeville (E8) 142
Dalton (F4) 197
Danville (J5) 69
Darlington (D2) 169
De Kalb (C3) 304
De Soto (M6) 5,804
De Witt (F4) 174
Dearborn (C3) 444
Deepwater (E6) 712
Deering (N10) 122
Dellwood ‡(P2) 4,720
Delta (N8) 416
Dennis Acres ‡(D8) 99
Denton (N10) 97
Denver (D2) 116
Des Arc (L8) 275
Des Peres (O3) 4,362
Desloge (M7) 2,308
Dexter (N9) 5,519
Diamond (D9) 453
Diehlstadt (N9) 141
Diggins (G8) 101
Dixon (H6) 1,473
Doniphan ◉(L9) 1,421
Doolittle (J7) 499
Dover (E4) 172
Downing (H2) 463
Drexel (C6) 651
Dudley (M9) 287
Duenweg (D8) 529
Dunlap (F2) 50
Duquesne (D8) 699
Eagleville (D2) 341
East Kansas City (P5) 219
East Lynne (D5) 243
East Prairie (O9) 3,449
Easton (C3) 198
Edgerton (C4) 449
Edina◉ (H2) 1,457
Edmundson ‡(P2) 1,428
El Dorado Sprs. (E7) 2,864
Eldon (G6) 3,158
Ellington (L8) 812
Ellisville (N3) 2,732
Ellsinore (L9) 311
Elmdale Village ‡(P2) 712
Elmer (G3) 266
Elmira (D3) 123
Elmo (B1) 213
Elsberry (L4) 1,491
Elvins (L7) 1,818
Eminence◉ (K8) 516
Emma (F5) 202
Essex (N9) 511
Esther (M7) 1,033
Ethel (G3) 149
Eugene (H6) 151
Eureka (N3) 1,134
Everton (E8) 261
Ewing (J2) 324
Excelsior Springs (R4) 6,473
Exeter (D9) 294
Fair Play (E7) 335
Fairfax (B2) 736
Fairview (D9) 249
Farber (J4) 451
Farley (O4) 120
Farmington◉ (M7) 5,618
Fayette◉ (G4) 3,294
Fenton (O3) 207
Ferguson (P2) 22,149
Ferrelview (O4) 158
Festus (M6) 7,021
Fillmore (C2) 254
Fisk (M9) 498
Flat River (M7) 4,515
Flemington (F7) 142
Flordell Hills ‡(P2) 1,119
Florissant (P2) 38,166
Foley (L4) 183
Ford City (C2) 63
Fordland (G8) 338
Forest City (B3) 435
Forsyth◉ (F9) 489
Fort Wyman Hts. ‡(J7) 193
Fortescue (B2) 78
Foster (D6) 153
Frankford (K4) 474
Franklin (G4) 355
Fredericktown◉ (M7) 3,484
Freeburg (J6) 399
Freeman (C5) 391
Freistatt (E8) 172
Fremont (K9) 131
Frohna (N7) 216
Frontenac (O3) 3,089
Fulton◉ (J5) 11,131
Gainesville◉ (G9) 266
Galena◉ (F9) 389
Gallatin◉ (E3) 1,658
Galt (F2) 373
Garden City (D5) 600
Gasconade (J5) 333
Gentry (D2) 98
Gerald (K6) 474
Gibbs (H2) 158
Gibson (M10) 100
Gideon (N10) 1,411
Gilliam (F4) 249
Gilman City (D2) 379
Gladstone (P5) 14,502
Glasgow (G4) 1,200
Glen Echo Park ‡(P3) 333
Glenaire (R5) 341
Glenallen (M8) 113
Glendale (P3) 7,048
Glenwood (G1) 242
Gobler (N10) 78
Golden City (D8) 714
Goodfellow Terr. ‡(P3) 824
Goodman (C9) 540
Gordonville (N8) 92
Gower (C3) 406
Graham (C2) 215
Grain Valley (S6) 552
Granby (D9) 1,808
Grandin (L9) 259
Grandview (P6) 6,027
Granger (H2) 146
Grant City◉ (D2) 1,061
Grantwood ‡(P3) 676
Green Acres ‡(E4) 154
Green Castle (G2) 250
Green City (F2) 628
Green Ridge (F5) 375
Greendale ‡(P3) 1,107
Greenfield◉ (E8) 1,172
Greentop (H2) 311
Greenville ◉(M8) 282
Greenwood (R6) 488
Grover (O3) 380
Grovespring (G8) 92
Guilford (C2) 125
Gunn City (D5) 63
Hale (F3) 504
Hallsville (H4) 363
Halltown (E8) 86
Hamilton (E3) 1,701
Hanley Hills ‡(P3) 3,308
Hannibal (K3) 20,028
Hardin (E4) 727
Harris (F2) 171
Harrisburg (H4) 124
Harrisonville◉ (D5) 3,510
Hartsburg (H5) 158
Hartville◉ (G8) 486
Harviell (M9) 177
Harwood (D7) 89
Hawk Point (K5) 270
Hayti (N10) 3,737
Hazelwood (P2) 6,045
Henley (H6) 73
Henrietta (E4) 497
Herculaneum (M6) 1,767
Hermann◉ (K5) 2,536
Hermitage◉ (F7) 328
Higbee (H4) 646
Higginsville (E4) 4,003
High Hill (K5) 173
High Ridge (O4) 2,642
Highlandville (F9) 84
Highley Heights ‡(L7) 132
Hillhouse Add. ‡(H7) 144
Hillsboro◉ (L6) 457
Hillsdale ‡(P3) 2,788
Hoberg (E8) 75
Holcomb (N10) 436
Holden (E5) 1,951
Holland (N10) 403
Holliday (H3) 181
Hollister (F9) 600
Hollywood (M10) 104
Holt (D4) 281
Hopkins (C1) 710
Hornersville (M10) 752
Houston◉ (J8) 1,660
Houston Lake ‡(O5) 289
Houstonia (F5) 261
Howardville ‡(N9) 190
Hughesville (F5) 134
Humansville (E7) 745
Hume (C6) 369
Humphreys (F2) 163
Hunnewell (J3) 284
Hunter (L9) 105
Huntleigh ‡(P3) 375
Huntsville◉ (H4) 1,526
Hurdland (H2) 205
Hurley (F9) 117
Hurricane Deck (G6) 117
Iberia (H6) 694
Illmo (O8) 1,174
Independence ◉(R5) 62,328
Ionia (F6) 114
Iron Gates ‡(D8) 312
Irondale (L7) 335
Ironton◉ (L7) 1,310
Jackson◉ (N8) 4,875
Jacksonville (G3) 153
Jameson (E2) 177
Jamesport (E3) 622
Jamestown (G5) 216
Jasper (D8) 746
JEFFERSON CITY◉ (H5) 28,228
Jennings (P2) 19,965
Jerico Springs (E7) 179
Jonesburg (K5) 415
Joplin (D8) 38,958
Junction City ‡(M7) 260
Kahoka◉ (J2) 2,160
Kansas City (P5) 475,539
Kansas City (urban area) (Mo.-Kans.) 921,121
Kearney (D4) 678
Kelso (O8) 258
Kennett◉ (M10) 9,098
Keytesville◉ (G4) 644
Kidder (D3) 224
Kimmswick (M6) 303
King City (D2) 1,009
Kingston◉ (E3) 311
Kingsville (D5) 225
Kinloch (P2) 6,501
Kirksville ◉(H2) 13,123
Kirkwood (O3) 29,421
Knob Noster (E5) 2,292
Knox City (H2) 330
Koshkonong (J9) 478
La Belle (J2) 866
La Due (E6) 175
La Grange (K2) 1,347
La Monte (F5) 801
La Plata (H2) 1,365
La Russell (D8) 129
Laclede (F3) 428
Laddonia (J4) 671
Ladue (P3) 9,466
Lake Lotawana (R6) 1,499
Lake Tapawingo (R8) 1,000
Lake Waukomis ‡(P5) 506
Lakeshire ‡(P3) 487
Lamar◉ (D8) 3,608
Lamar Heights ‡(D8) 113
Lanagan (C9) 357
Lancaster◉ (H1) 740
Laredo (E2) 370
Latham (G5) 131
Lathrop (D3) 1,006
Latour (D5) 68
Lawson (D4) 778
Leadington (M7) 365
Leadwood (L7) 1,343
Leasburg (K6) 176
Leawood ‡(D8) 152
Lebanon◉ (G7) 8,220
Lee's Summit (R6) 8,267
Leeton (E5) 371
Leonard (H3) 142
Leslie (K6) 104
Levasy (S5) 140
Lewistown (J2) 454
Lexington ◉(E4) 4,845
Liberal (D7) 612
Liberty◉ (R5) 8,909
Licking (J8) 954
Liege (K5) 78
Lilbourn (N9) 1,216
Lincoln (F6) 446
Linn◉ (J5) 1,050
Linn Creek (G6) 174
Linneus◉ (F3) 471
Lithium (N7) 54
Livonia (G1) 154
Lock Springs (E3) 117
Lockwood (E8) 835
Lohman (H5) 128
Lone Jack (S6) 272
Longtown (N7) 113
Louisburg (F7) 175
Louisiana (K4) 4,286
Lowry City (E6) 437
Lucerne (F2) 157
Ludlow (E3) 235
Lupus (H5) 75
Luray (J2) 154
Lutesville (M8) 658
Mackenzie ‡(P3) 283
Macks Creek (G7) 123
Macon◉ (H3) 4,547
Madison (H4) 528
Maitland (B2) 427
Malden (M9) 5,007
Malta Bend (F4) 338
Manchester ‡(O3) 2,021
Mansfield (G8) 949
Maplewood (P3) 12,552
Marble Hill◉ (N8) 497
Marceline (F3) 2,872
Margona Vill. ‡(P3) 320
Marionville (E8) 1,251
Marlborough ‡(P3) 650
Marquand (M8) 392
Marshall◉ (F4) 9,572
Marshfield◉ (G8) 2,221
Marston (N9) 631
Marthasville (L5) 339
Martinsburg (J4) 330
Martinsville (D2) 79
Marvin Terrace ‡(P2) 1,260
Mary Ridge ‡(P2) 631
Maryville◉ (C2) 7,807
Matthews (N9) 450
Maysville◉ (D3) 942
Mayview (E4) 270
McFall (D2) 206

(continued on following page)

HIGHWAYS

0 50 100
MILES

Limited Access Highways
Major Highways
Other Important Roads
Interstate Route Numbers 95
Federal Route Numbers 9
State and Other Route Numbers 4

Missouri
(continued)

AGRICULTURE, INDUSTRY and RESOURCES

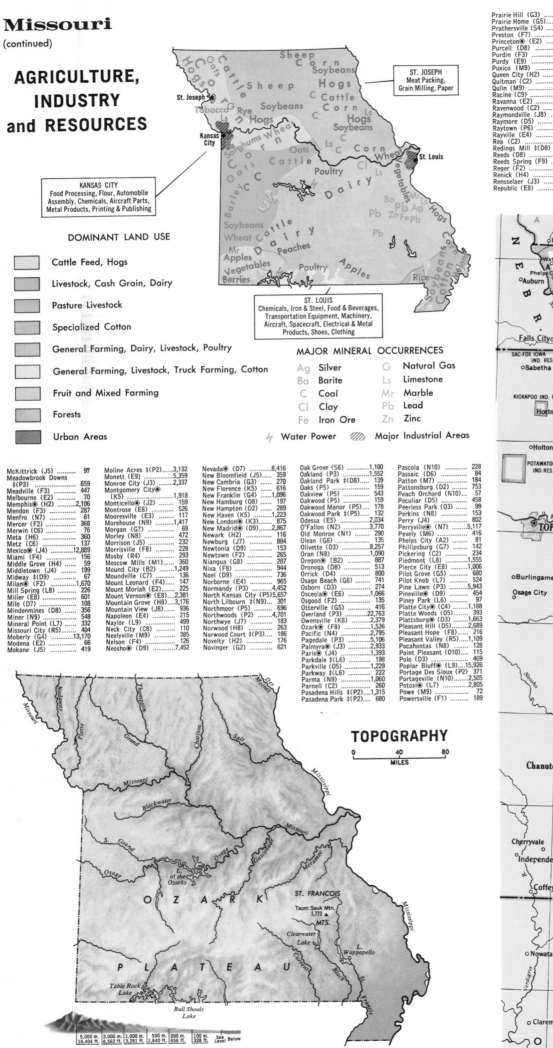

ST. JOSEPH — Meat Packing, Grain Milling, Paper

KANSAS CITY — Food Processing, Flour, Automobile Assembly, Chemicals, Aircraft Parts, Metal Products, Printing & Publishing

ST. LOUIS — Chemicals, Iron & Steel, Food & Beverages, Transportation Equipment, Machinery, Aircraft, Spacecraft, Electrical & Metal Products, Shoes, Clothing

DOMINANT LAND USE
- Cattle Feed, Hogs
- Livestock, Cash Grain, Dairy
- Pasture Livestock
- Specialized Cotton
- General Farming, Dairy, Livestock, Poultry
- General Farming, Livestock, Truck Farming, Cotton
- Fruit and Mixed Farming
- Forests
- Urban Areas

MAJOR MINERAL OCCURRENCES
Ag	Silver	G	Natural Gas
Ba	Barite	Ls	Limestone
C	Coal	Mr	Marble
Cl	Clay	Pb	Lead
Fe	Iron Ore	Zn	Zinc

⚡ Water Power   ▨ Major Industrial Areas

TOPOGRAPHY

MILES 0 — 40 — 80

5,000 m.	2,000 m.	1,000 m.	500 m.	200 m.	100 m.	Sea Level	Below
16,404 ft.	6,562 ft.	3,281 ft.	1,640 ft.	656 ft.	328 ft.		

Montana

COUNTIES

Beaverhead (C5) 7,194
Big Horn (J5) 10,007
Blaine (G2) 8,091
Broadwater (E4) 2,804
Carbon (G5) 8,317
Carter (M5) 2,493
Cascade (E3) 73,418
Chouteau (F3) 7,348
Custer (L4) 13,227
Daniels (L2) 3,755
Dawson (M3) 12,314
Deer Lodge (C5) 18,640
Fallon (M4) 3,997
Fergus (G3) 14,018
Flathead (B2) 32,965
Gallatin (E5) 26,045
Garfield (J3) 1,981
Glacier (C2) 11,565
Golden Valley (G4) 1,203
Granite (C4) 3,014
Hill (F2) 18,653
Jefferson (D4) 4,297
Judith Basin (F4) 3,085
Lake (B3) 13,104
Lewis and Clark (D3) 28,006
Liberty (E2) 2,624
Lincoln (A2) 12,537
Madison (D5) 5,211
McCone (L3) 3,321
Meagher (F4) 2,616
Mineral (B3) 3,037
Missoula (C3) 44,663
Musselshell (H4) 4,888
Park (F5) 13,168
Petroleum (H3) 894
Phillips (J2) 6,027
Pondera (D2) 2,653
Powder River (L5) 2,485
Powell (C4) 7,002
Prairie (L4) 2,318
Ravalli (B4) 12,341
Richland (M3) 10,504
Roosevelt (L2) 11,731
Rosebud (K4) 6,187
Sanders (A3) 6,880
Sheridan (L2) 6,458
Silver Bow (D5) 46,454
Stillwater (G4) 5,526
Sweet Grass (G5) 3,290
Teton (D3) 7,295
Toole (E2) 7,904
Treasure (J4) 1,345
Valley (K2) 17,080
Wheatland (G4) 3,026
Wibaux (M4) 1,698
Yellowstone (H4) 79,016
Yellowstone Nat'l Park (F6) 47

CITIES and TOWNS

Absarokee (G5) 667
Acton (H5) 10
Agawam (D2) 25
Alberton (B3) 356
Albion (M5) 6
Alder (D5) 100
Alhambra (E4) 55
Alzada (M5) 75
Amsterdam (E5) 75
Anaconda◉ (C4) 12,054
Anceney (E5) 9
Andes (M3) 18
Angela (K4) 5
Antelope (M2) 116
Apgar (B2) 76
Archer (M2) 5
Armington (F3) 120
Armstead (D6) 102
Arrow Creek (F3) 20
Ashland (K5) 150
Augusta (D3) 500
Austin (D4) 42
Avon (D4) 200
Babb (C2) 25
Bainville (M2) 285
Baker◉ (M4) 2,365
Ballantine (J5) 350
Bannack (D5) 23
Barber (G4) 60
Basin (D4) 280
Bearcreek (G5) 61
Bearmouth (C4) 10
Becket (K5) 16
Beehive (G5) 12
Belfry (H5) 250
Belgrade (E5) 1,057
Belknap (A3) 18
Belmont (G4) 18
Belt (E3) 757
Benchland (F3) 100
Biddle (L5) 5
Big Arm (B3) 100
Big Sandy (G2) 954
Big Timber◉ (G5) 1,660
Bigfork (C2) 400
Bighorn (J4) 20

Billings◉ (H5) 52,851
Billings (urban area) 60,712
Birney (K5) 31
Black Eagle (E3) 1,395
Blackfoot (D2) 200
Blackleaf (D2) 25
Bloomfield (M3) 38
Bonner (C4) 450
Boulder◉ (D4) 1,394
Box Elder (F2) 275
Boyd (G5) 30
Boyes (M5) 25
Bozeman◉ (F5) 13,361
Brady (E2) 235
Brandenberg (K5) 5
Bridger (H5) 824
Broadus◉ (L5) 628
Broadview (H4) 160
Brockton (M2) 367
Brockway (L3) 90
Brooks (G3) 10
Browning (C2) 2,011
Brusett (J3) 15
Buffalo (G4) 36
Busby (J5) 400
Butte◉ (D5) 27,877
Bynum (D3) 50

Camas (B3) 125
Camas Prairie (B3) 300
Cameron (E5) 10
Canyon Creek (D4) 130
Canyon Ferry (E4) 117
Capitol (M5) 4
Cardwell (E5) 297
Carlyle (M4) 41
Carter (F3) 100
Cartersville (K4) 35
Cascade (E3) 604
Cat Creek (H3) 74
Centerville (D4) 2,000
Chapman (J2) 35
Charlo (B3) 350
Chester◉ (E2) 1,158
Chico (F5) 20
Chinook◉ (G2) 2,326
Choteau◉ (D3) 1,966
Christina (G3) 15
Circle◉ (L3) 1,117
Clancy (E4) 300
Clarkston (E4) 20
Clasoil (E4) 8
Cleveland (G3) 25
Clinton (C4) 250
Clyde Park (F5) 253
Coalridge (M2) 36
Coalwood (L5) 5
Coffee Creek (F3) 100
Cohagen (K3) 36
Collins (E3) 29
Colstrip (K5) 150
Columbia Falls (B2) 2,132
Columbus◉ (G5) 1,281

Comanche (H4) 12
Comertown (M2) 50
Condon (C3) 30
Conner (B5) 150
Conrad◉ (D2) 2,665
Cooke City (G5) 25
Coram (B2) 440
Corvallis (B4) 950
Corwin Springs (F5) 16
Craig (D3) 100
Crane (M3) 75
Creston (C2) 25
Crow Agency (J5) 700
Crow Rock (L4) 5
Culbertson (M2) 919
Custer (J4) 236
Cut Bank◉ (D2) 4,539
Dagmar (M2) 62
Danvers (H3) 19
Darby (B4) 398
Dayton (B3) 60
De Borgia (A3) 150
Dean (G5) 92

Decker (K5) 14
Deer Lodge◉ (D4) 4,681
Dell (D6) 40
Delpine (H4) 35
Denton (G3) 410
Devon (E2) 58
Dillon◉ (D5) 3,690
Divide (D5) 100
Dixon (B3) 207
Dodson (H2) 313
Dooley (M2) 17
Drummond (D4) 577
Dunkirk (E2) 25
Dupuyer (D2) 125
Dutton (E3) 504
East Glacier Park (C2) 300
East Helena (E4) 1,490
Eddy (A3) 41
Eden (E3) 5
Edgar (H5) 200
Ekalaka◉ (M5) 738
Elk Park (D4) 75

Elliston (D4) 200
Elmo (B3) 150
Emigrant (F5) 25
Enid (M3) 8
Ennis (E5) 525
Epsie (L5) 53
Essex (B2) 75
Ethridge (D2) 50
Evaro (C3) 135
Eureka (A2) 1,229
Fairfield (D3) 752
Fairview (M3) 1,006
Fallon (L4) 251
Ferdig (E2) 14
Fergus (H3) 11
Finch (K4) 22
Findon (F4) 22
Fishtail (G5) 75
Flaxville (L2) 262
Florence (B4) 350
Flowerree (E3) 60
Forestgrove (H3) 24
Forsyth◉ (K4) 2,032
Fort Belknap (H2) 12
Fort Benton◉ (F3) 1,887
Fort Logan (E4) 8
Fort Peck (K2) 1,214
Fort Shaw (E3) 120

Fort Smith (J5) 2,100
Fort Union (M2) 6
Fortine (A2) 378
Four Buttes (L2) 40
Francis (F4) 16
Franklin (G4) 7
Frazer (K2) 450
Frenchtown (B3) 225
Fresno (G2) 10
Froid (M2) 418
Fromberg (H5) 367
Galata (E2) 64
Galen (D5) 677
Gallatin Gateway (E5) 200
Gardiner (F5) 800
Garland (L4) 3
Garneill (G4) 88
Garnet (C4) 20
Garrison (D4) 300
Garryowen (J5) 50
Geraldine (F3) 364
Geyser (F3) 105
Gildford (F2) 350
Giltedge (G3) 15
Glasgow◉ (K2) 6,398
Glen (D5) 75
Glendive◉ (M3) 7,058

Glengarry (G3) 10
Glentana (K2) 61
Gold Stone (F2) 8
Goldcreek (D4) 215
Grant (C5) 40
Grantsdale (B4) 50
Grassrange (H3) 222
Great Falls◉ (E3) 55,357
Great Falls (urban area) 57,629
Greenough (C4) 50
Gregson (D4) 50
Greycliff (G5) 88
Hall (C4) 320
Hamilton◉ (B4) 2,475
Hammond (M5) 10
Hanover (F3) 50
Hardin◉ (J5) 2,789
Harlem (H2) 1,417
Harlowton◉ (F4) 1,734
Harrison (E5) 46
Hathaway (K4) 25
Haugan (A3) 75
Havre◉ (G2) 10,740
Haxby (K3) 25
Hays (H2) 700
Heart Butte (C2) 150
Heath (G3) 10
Hedgesville (G4) 25
HELENA★ (E4) 20,227
Helmville (C4) 175
Heron (A2) 200
Highwood (F3) 200
Hilger (F3) 42
Hingham (F2) 254
Hinsdale (K2) 400
Hobson (G4) 207
Hodges (M4) 35
Hogeland (H2) 75
Homestead (M2) 150
Horton (L4) 10
Hot Springs (B3) 585
Hungry Horse (B2) 450
Huntley (H5) 400
Huson (B3) 75
Hysham◉ (J4) 494
Inga (F2) 100
Ingomar (J4) 50
Intake (M3) 30
Inverness (F2) 176
Ismay (M4) 59
Jackson (C5) 50
Jardine (F5) 110
Jeffers (F5) 65
Jefferson City (E4) 100
Jefferson Island (E5) 5
Jennings (A2) 4
Joliet (G5) 452
Joplin (F2) 368
Jordan◉ (J3) 557
Judith Gap (G4) 185
Kalispell◉ (B2) 10,151
Kenilworth (F2) 100
Kevin (D2) 375

TOPOGRAPHY

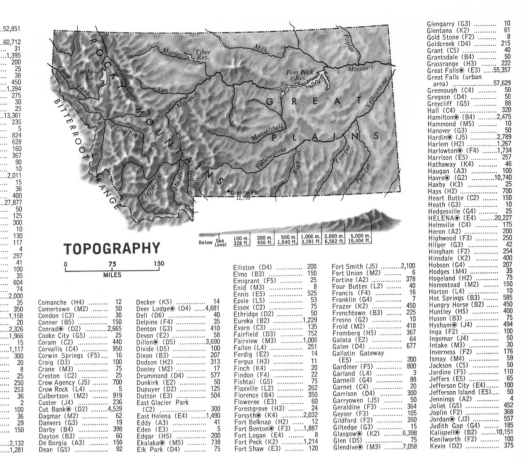

0 — 75 — 150
MILES

| Below Sea Level | 100 m. 328 ft. | 200 m. 656 ft. | 500 m. 1,640 ft. | 1,000 m. 3,281 ft. | 2,000 m. 6,562 ft. | 5,000 m. 16,404 ft. |

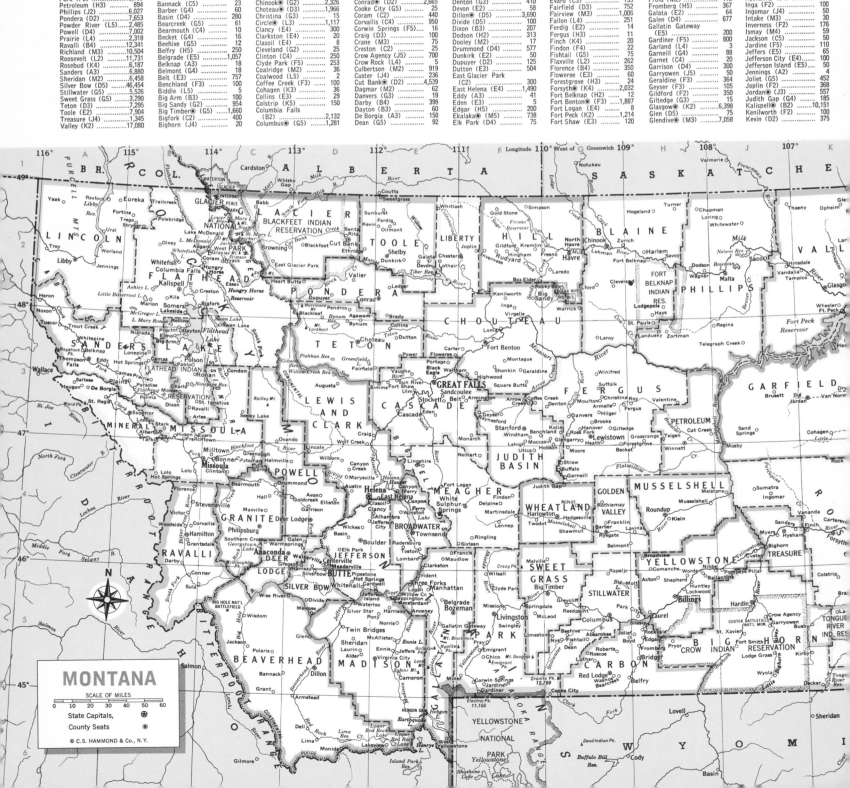

MONTANA

SCALE OF MILES
0 10 20 30 40 50 60

◉ State Capitals,
◉ County Seats

© C.S. HAMMOND & Co., N.Y.

MONTANA

AREA	147,138 sq. mi.
POPULATION	706,000
CAPITAL	Helena
LARGEST CITY	Great Falls 55,357
HIGHEST POINT	Granite Pk. 12,799 ft.
SETTLED IN	1809
ADMITTED TO UNION	November 8, 1889
POPULAR NAME	Treasure State
STATE FLOWER	Bitterroot
STATE BIRD	Western Meadowlark

Place Index

Kila (B2) 46
Kinsey (L4) 10
Kirby (J5) 5
Klein (H4) 60
Knobs (M5) 4
Knowlton (L4) 10
Kolin (G3) 9
Kremlin (F2) 125
Lake McDonald (B2) 2
Lakeside (B2) 500
Lakeview (E6) 18
Lambert (M3) 359
Lame Deer (K5) 400
Lanark (M2) 2
Landusky (H3) 165
Laredo (G2) 10
Larslan (K2) 100
Laurel (D5) 4,601
Laurin (D4) 48
Lavina (H4) 212
Ledger (E2) 19
Lee (K5) 13
Lehigh (F3) 6
Lennep (F4) 60
Leroy (G3) 55
Lewistown● (G3) 7,408
Libby● (A2) 2,828
Lima (D6) 397
Limestone (F5) 43
Lincoln (D4) 540
Lindsay (L3) 57
Lingshire (E4) 6
Livingston● (F5) 8,229
Lloyd (G2) 75
Locate (L4) 25
Lockwood (H5) 800
Lodge Grass (J5) 687
Lodgepole (H2) 5
Loesch (L5) 10
Logan (E5) 196
Lohman (G2) 20
Lolo (B4) 300
Lolo Hot Springs (B4) 20
Loma (F3) 175
Lombard (E4) 26
Lonepine (B3) 14
Loring (J2) 35
Lothair (E2) 83
Lozeau (B3) 43
Lustre (K2) 25
Luther (G5) 42
Madoc (L2) 22
Malta● (J2) 2,239
Manhattan (E5) 889
Marion (B2) 40
Marsh (M4) 25
Martinsdale (H4) 250
Marysville (D4) 60
Maudlow (E4) 35
Maxville (C4) 60
McAllister (E5) 70
McCabe (M2) 37

McLeod (G5) 7
Meaderville (D4) 600
Medicine Lake (M2) 452
Melrose (D5) 330
Melstone (H4) 266
Melville (F4) 425
Mildred (M4) 75
Miles City● (L4) 9,665
Mill Iron (M5) 2
Milltown (C4) 750
Miner (E5) 35
Mission (F5) 12
Missoula● (C4) 27,090
Mizpah (L4) 5
Moccasin (F3) 100
Molese (J4) 2
Molt (H5) 20
Monarch (F3) 33
Monida (D6) 18
Montague (F3) 4
Moon Creek (L4) 3
Moore (G4) 216
Moorhead (K5) 15
Mosby (J4) 3
Moulton (D3) 4
Musselshell (H4) 125
Myers (J4) 6
Nashua (K2) 796
Navajo (M2) 7
Neihart (F4) 150
Niarada (B3) 7
Nibbe (H4) 20
Nihill (G4) 2
Nohly (M3) 13
North Havre (G2) 1,168
Norris (E5) 75
Noxon (A3) 250
Nyack (C2) 15
Nye (G5) 500
Oilmont (D2) 250
Olive (L5) 7
Ollie (M4) 10
Olney (B2) 200
Opheim (K2) 457
Oswego (L2) 100
Otter (K5) 57
Outlook (M2) 226
Ovando (D3) 100
Pablo (B3) 300
Paradise (B3) 250
Park City (H5) 850
Peerless (L2) 179
Pendroy (D2) 50
Perma (B3) 30
Philipsburg● (C4) 1,107
Pipestone Hot Sprs. (D5) 8
Plains (B3) 769
Plentywood● (M2) 2,121
Plevna (M4) 263
Polaris (C5) 56
Polebridge (B2) 17
Polson● (B3) 2,314
Pompeys Pillar (J5) 102

Pony (E5) 150
Poplar (L2) 1,565
Portage (E3) 25
Potomac (C4) 72
Powderville (L5) 4
Power (E3) 160
Pray (F5) 50
Proctor (B3) 86
Pryor (H5) 100
Quietus (K5) 37
Radersburg (E4) 100
Ramsay (E5) 350
Rapelje (G5) 150
Ravalli (B3) 120
Raymond (M2) 40
Raynesford (F4) 40
Red Lodge● (G5) 2,278
Redstone (M2) 74
Reedpoint (G5) 150
Regina (J3) 29
Reserve (M2) 175
Rexford (A2) 365
Richey (L3) 480
Richland (K2) 55
Ridge (M5) 5
Ringling (F4) 65
Roberts (G5) 275
Rock Springs (K4) 15
Rockvale (H5) 15
Rocky Boy (G2) 60
Rollins (B3) 150
Ronan (C3) 1,334
Roscoe (G5) 42
Rosebud (K4) 144
Ross Fork (G3) 13
Rothiemay (G4) 55
Roundup● (H4) 2,842
Roy (H3) 175
Rudyard (F2) 628
Ryegate● (G4) 314
Saco (J2) 490
Saint Ignatius (C3) 940
Saint Pauls (H3) 50
Saint Phillips (M4) 6
Saint Regis (A3) 500
Saint Xavier (J5) 150
Saltese (A3) 100
Sand Coulee (E3) 500
Sand Springs (J3) 19
Sanders (J4) 50
Santa Rita (D2) 123
Sappington (E5) 15
Savage (M3) 350
Savoy (H2) 102
Scobey● (L2) 1,726
Seeley Lake (C3) 625
Shawmut (G4) 122
Sheffield (K4) 30
Shelby● (E2) 4,017
Shepherd (H5) 125
Sheridan (D5) 539
Shonkin (F3) 6
Sidney● (M3) 4,564
Silesia (H5) 150
Silver Star (D5) 130
Silverbow (D5) 41
Silverbok (D5) 41
Simms (E3) 295
Simpson (F2) 80
Sioux Pass (M3) 40
Sixteen (F4) 1
Snowden (M2) 16
Somers (B2) 831
Sonnette (K5) 5
Southern Cross (C4) 30
Springdale (F5) 24
Square Butte (F3) 85
Stacey (L5) 7
Stanford● (F3) 615
Stark (B3) 25
Stevensville (C4) 784
Stockett (E3) 249
Straw (G4) 30
Stryker (B2) 54
Suffolk (G3) 26
Sula (B5) 28
Sumatra (J4) 28
Sun River (E3) 165
Sunburst (E2) 882
Superior● (B3) 1,242
Swan Lake (C3) 200
Sweetgrass (E2) 200
Swingley (F5) 10
Tampico (K2) 75
Tarkio (B4) 75
Teigen (H3) 2
Telegraph Creek (J3) 3
Terry● (L4) 1,140
Thoeny (K2) 10
Thompson Falls● (A3) 1,274
Three Forks (E5) 1,161
Thurlow (K4) 12
Toston (E4) 75
Townsend● (E4) 1,528
Trailcreek (B2) 22
Trego (B2) 150
Trident (E5) 100
Trout Creek (A3) 118
Troy (A2) 855
Turner (H2) 175
Tuscor (A3) 4
Twin Bridges (D5) 509
Twodot (F4) 65
Ulm (E3) 250
Ural (A2) 50
Utica (F4) 65
Valentine (H3) 8
Valier (D2) 724
Van Norman (K3) 3
Vananda (K4) 50
Vandalia (J2) 25
Vaughn (E3) 205
Victor (B4) 795
Vida (L3) 95
Virgelle (E3) 36
Virginia City● (E5) 194
Volborg (L5) 50
Wagner (H2) 71
Walkerville (D4) 1,453
Waltham (E3) 4
Warland (A2) 90
Warmsprings (D4) 400
Warrick (G2) 3
Washoe (G5) 5
Waterloo (D5) 138
Watkins (K3) 2
Webster (M4) 1
Weldon (L3) 1
West Glacier (C2) 440
West Yellowstone (E6) 500
Westby (M2) 309
Wheeler (K2) 20
White Sulphur Springs● (E4) 1,519
Whitefish (B2) 2,965
Whitehall (D5) 898
Whitepine (A3) 52
Whitetail (J2) 206
Whitewater (J2) 85
Whitlash (E2) 20
Wibaux● (M3) 766
Wickes (D4) 44
Wilborn (D4) 14

Willard (M4) 4
Willow Creek (E5) 300
Wilsall (F5) 275
Windham (F3) 165
Winifred (G3) 220
Winnett● (H4) 360
Winston (E4) 53
Wisdom (C5) 175
Wise River (C5) 75
Wolf Creek (D3) 624
Wolf Point● (L2) 3,585
Woodside (B4) 60
Worden (H5) 310
Wyola (J5) 110
Yaak (B2) 25
Zortman (H3) 180
Zurich (G2) 85

OTHER FEATURES

Absaroka (range) F5
Allen (mt.) C2
Arrow (creek) F3
Ashley (lake) B2
Battle (creek) G1
Bearhat (mt.) C2
Beaver (creek) J4
Beaver (creek) L2
Beaverhead (river) D5
Big (lake) H5
Big Belt (mts.) E4
Big Dry (creek) K3
Big Hole (river) C5
Big Hole Nat'l Battlefield C5
Big Muddy (river) M2
Bighorn (river) J5
Birch (creek) D2
Bitterroot (range) B4
Bitterroot (river) B4
Blackfeet Ind. Res. D2
Blackfoot (river) C4
Blackmore (mt.) F5
Bowdoin (lake) J2
Boxelder (creek) M3
Boxelder (creek) H5
Bynum (creek) M5
Cabinet (mts.) A2
Canyon Ferry (lake) E4
Clark Fork (river) A3
Clark Fork, Yellowstone (river) G6
Cottonwood (creek) G2
Cow (creek) G2
Crazy (peak) F4
Crow Ind. Res. H5
Custer Battlefield Nat'l Mon. J5
Cut Bank (creek) D2
Douglas (creek) F5
Earthquake (lake) E6
Electric (peak) F6
Emigrant (peak) F5
Ennis (lake) E5
Flathead (lake) C3
Flathead (river) B2
Flathead (river) C3
Flathead Ind. Res. B3
Flatwillow (creek) H4
Fort Belknap Ind. Res. H2
Fort Peck (dam) K3
Fort Peck (res.) K3
Frenchman (river) J2
Fresno (res.) F2
Gallatin (peak) E5
Gallatin (river) E5
Georgetown (lake) C4
Gibson (res.) D3
Glacier National Park C2
Granite (peak) G5
Greenfield (lake) D3
Hauser (lake) E4
Haystack (peak) A3
Hebgen (dam) E6
Hebgen (lake) E6
Helena (lake) E4
Hungry Horse (res.) C2
Hurricane (mt.) D2
Hyalite (lake) E5
Jackson (mt.) C2
Jefferson (river) D5
Judith (river) G3
Kootenai (river) A2
Lewis (range) C2
Libby (res.) A2
Lima (res.) D6
Little Bighorn (river) J5
Little Bitterroot (lake) B2
Little Dry (creek) K3
Little Missouri (river) M5
Lockhart (mt.) C2
Lodge (creek) G2
Lone (mt.) E5

Lower Red Rock (lake) E6
Lower Saint Mary (lake) C2
Madison (river) E5
Marias (river) D2
Mary Ronan (lake) B3
McDonald (lake) B2
McGloughlin (peak) C4
McGregor (lake) B3
Medicine (lake) M2
Milk (river) G2
Mission (range) C3
Musselshell (river) J3
Nelson (res.) G2
Ninepipe (res.) C3

O'Fallon (creek) L4
Pishkun (res.) D3
Poplar (river) L2
Porcupine (creek) J4
Porcupine (creek) K4
Powder (river) L4
Purcell (mts.) A2
Railey (mt.) C3
Red Rock (creek) D6
Red Rock (lakes) E6
Redwater (creek) L3
Rock (creek) C4
Rocky (mts.) D4
Rocky Boy's Indian Res. G2
Rosebud (creek) K4

Sage (creek) F2
Saint Mary (river) C2
Saint Mary (river) C1
Sandy (creek) F2
Sheep (mt.) C2
Shields (river) F4
Siyeh (mt.) C2
Smith (river) E3
Sphinx (mt.) E5
Stillwater (river) G5
Stimson (mt.) C2
Swan (lake) C3
Swan (river) C3
Sun (river) D3
Teton (river) E2
Tiber (res.) E2

Tongue (river) K5
Tongue River (res.) K5
Tongue River Indian Res. K5
Upper Red Rock (lake) E6
Ward (peak) A3
Waterton-Glacier Int'l Peace Park C2
Whitefish (lake) B2
Willow (creek) E2
Willow Creek (res.) M3
Yellowstone (river) M3
Yellowstone National Park F6

● County Seat.

AGRICULTURE, INDUSTRY and RESOURCES

DOMINANT LAND USE

- Specialized Wheat
- Wheat, Range Livestock
- General Farming, Dairy, Range Livestock
- General Farming, Livestock, Special Crops
- Range Livestock
- Sugar Beets, Beans, Livestock, General Farming
- Forests

MAJOR MINERAL OCCURRENCES

Ag	Silver	O	Petroleum
Au	Gold	P	Phosphates
Cu	Copper	Pb	Lead
G	Natural Gas	Th	Thorium
Gp	Gypsum	Zn	Zinc

⚡ Water Power

HIGHWAYS

0 80 160
MILES

Limited Access Highways
Major Highways
Other Important Roads

Interstate Route Numbers
Federal Route Numbers
State and Other Route Numbers

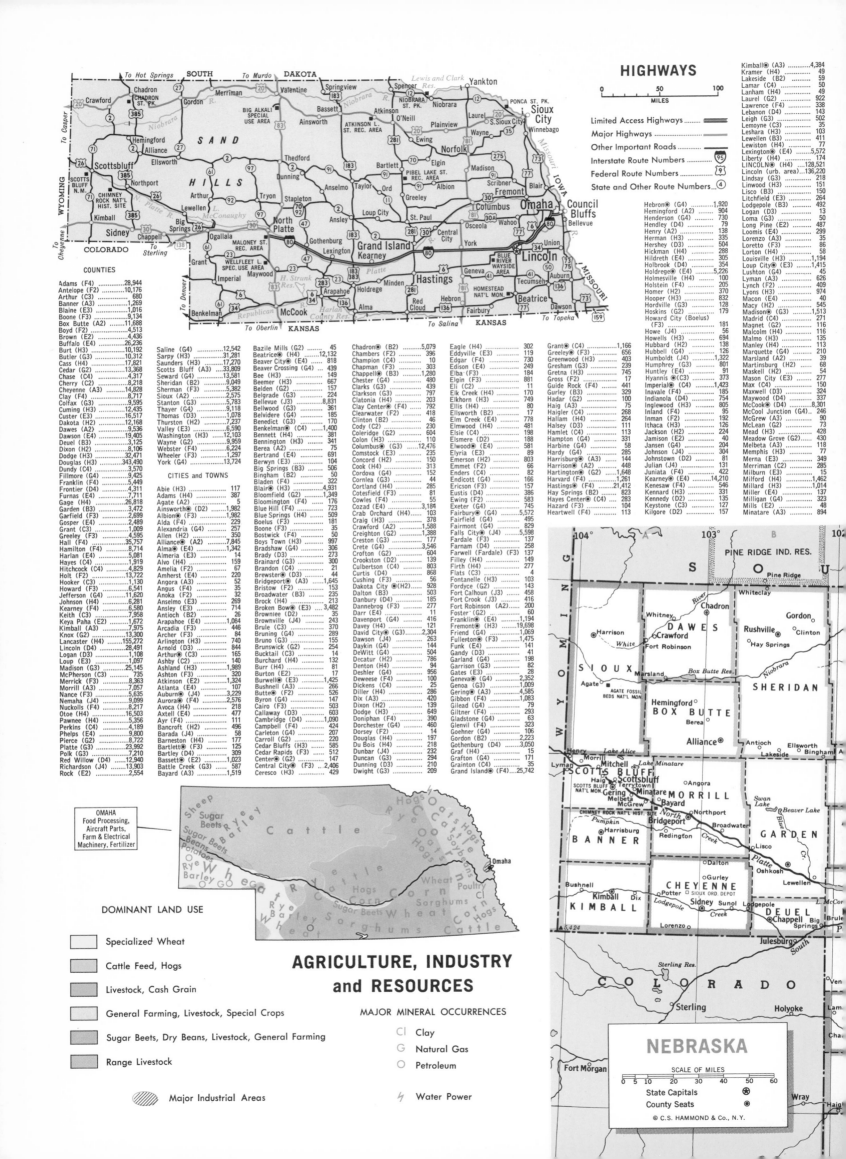

Minden⊙ (F4) 2,383	Pickrell (H4) 130	Silver Creek (G3) 431	Waco (G4) 166
Mitchell (A3) 1,920	Pierce⊙ (G2) 1,216	Smithfield (E4) 85	Wahoo⊙ (H3) 3,610
Monowi (F2) 40	Pilger (G2) 491	Snyder (H3) 325	Wakefield (H2) 1,068
Monroe (G3) 261	Plainview (G2) 1,467	South Bend (H4) 86	Wallace (C4) 293
Moorefield (D4) 55	Platte Center (G3) 402	South Sioux City (H2)..........7,200	Walthill (H2) 844
Morrill (A3) 684	Plattsmouth⊙ (J3)..........6,244	Spalding (F3) 683	Walton (H4) 100
Morse Bluff (H3) 119	Pleasant Dale (G4) 190	Sparks (D2) 5	Washington (H3) 44
Mullen⊙ (C2) 811	Pleasanton (E4) 199	Spencer (F2) 671	Waterbury (H2) 81
Murdock (H4) 247	Plymouth (G4) 372	Springfield (H3) 506	Waterloo ‡(H3) 516
Murray (J4) 279	Polk (G3) 433	Springview⊙ (E2) 281	Wauneta (C4) 794
Naper (E2) 198	Ponca⊙ (H2) 932	Stamford (E4) 220	Wausa (G2) 724
Naponee (E4) 206	Potter (A3) 554	Stanton⊙ (G3) 1,317	Waverly (H4) 511
Nebraska City⊙ (J4) 7,252	Powell (G4) 60	Staplehurst (G4) 240	Wayne⊙ (H2) 4,217
Nehawka (H4) 262	Prague (H3) 372	Stapleton⊙ (D3) 359	Weeping Water (J4)..........1,048
Neligh⊙ (G2) 1,776	Preston (J4) 66	Star (F2) 4	Weissert (F3) 61
Nelson⊙ (F4) 695	Primrose (F3) 117	Steele City (G4) 173	Wellfleet (D4) 67
Nemaha (J4) 232	Prosser (F4) 70	Steinauer (H4) 124	Wells (C2) 3
Nenzel (C2) 43	Purdum (D2) 90	Stella (J4) 262	West Lincoln (H4) 507
Newcastle (H2) 357	Raeville (F3) 100	Sterling (H4) 471	West Point⊙ (H3)..........2,921
Newman Grove (G3) 860	Ragan (G4) 131	Stockham (F4) 69	Western (G4) 351
Newport (E2) 162	Ralston (J3) 2,977	Stockville⊙ (D4) 91	Westerville (E3) 45
Nickerson (H3) 168	Randolph (G2) 1,063	Stratton (C4) 492	Weston (H3) 340
Niobrara (F2) 736	Ravenna (G4) 1,417	Stromsburg (G3) 1,244	Whiteclay (B2) 108
Nora (E4) 60	Raymond (H4) 223	Stuart (E2) 794	Whitman (C2) 98
Norden (D2) 20	Red Cloud⊙ (F4) 1,525	Sumner (E4) 254	Whitney (G2) 260
Norfolk⊙ (G2) 13,640	Redbird (F2) 121	Sunol (B3) 100	Wilcox (E4) 260
Norman (F4) 57	Reynolds (G4) 131	Superior (G4) 2,935	Willow Island (D4)..........70
North Bend (H3) 1,174	Republican City (E4)..........189	Surprise (G3) 79	Wilsonville (D4) 289
North Loup (F3) 453	Richland (G3) 139	Sutherland (C3) 867	Winnebago (H2) 682
North Platte⊙ (D3)..........17,184	Rising City (G3) 308	Sutton (G4) 1,252	Winnetoon (F2) 85
Northport (B3) 128	Riverdale (E4) 144	Swanton (H4) 190	Winside (G2) 416
Oak (G4) 125	Riverton (F4) 303	Swedeburg (H3) 75	Winslow (H3) 136
Oakdale (F2) 397	Roca (H4) 123	Sweetwater (E3) 20	Wisner (G2) 1,192
Oakland (H3) 1,429	Rockville (F3) 153	Syracuse (H4) 1,261	Wolbach (F3) 382
Obert (G2) 42	Rogers (H3) 162	Table Rock (H4) 422	Wood Lake (D2) 197
Oconto (E3) 219	Rosalie (H2) 182	Talmage (H4) 361	Wood River (F4) 828
Octavia (G3) 94	Roscoe (C3) 86	Tamora (G4) 88	Wymore (H4) 1,975
Odell (H4) 358	Rose (E2) 9	Tarnov (G3) 70	Wynot (G2) 209
Odessa (E4) 150	Roseland (F4) 163	Taylor⊙ (E3) 280	York⊙ (G4) 6,173
Ogallala⊙ (C3) 4,250	Royal (F2) 93	Tecumseh⊙ (H4) 1,887	Yutan (H3) 335
Ohiowa (F4) 195	Rulo (J4) 412	Tekamah⊙ (H3) 1,788	
Omaha⊙ (J3) 301,598	Rushville⊙ (B2) 1,228	Terrytown (A3) 164	**Other Features**
Omaha (urb. area)..........389,881	Ruskin (G4) 203	Thayer (G4) 78	
O'Neill⊙ (F2) 3,181	Saint Edward (G3) 777	Thedford⊙ (D3) 303	Agate Fossil Beds Nat'l Mon. ....A 2
Ong (G4) 128	Saint Helena (G2) 63	Thurston (H2) 140	Alice (lake) ....A 2
Orchard (F2) 421	Saint Libory (F3) 175	Tilden (G2) 917	Beaver (creek) ....B 5
Ord⊙ (F3) 2,413	Saint Mary (H4) 65	Tobias (G4) 202	Beaver (lake) ....B 3
Orleans (E4) 608	Saint Paul⊙ (F3) 1,714	Trenton⊙ (C4) 914	Big Blue (river) ....H 4
Osceola⊙ (G3) 1,013	Salem (J4) 261	Trumbull (F4) 173	Blue (creek) ....B 3
Oshkosh⊙ (B3) 1,025	Santee (G2) 150	Tryon⊙ (C3) 193	Box Butte (res.) ....A 2
Osmond (G2) 719	Sargent (E3) 876	Uehling (H3) 231	Cedar (river) ....F 3
Otoe (H4) 225	Saronville (G4) 71	Ulysses (G3) 357	Chimney Rock Nat'l Hist. Site ....A 3
Overton (E4) 523	Schuyler⊙ (G3) 3,096	Unadilla (H4) 254	Colamus (river) ....E 2
Oxford (E4) 1,090	Scotia (F3) 350	Union (J4) 303	Dismal (river) ....D 2
Page (F2) 230	Scottsbluff (A3) 13,377	Upland (F4) 237	Dods (lake) ....G 2
Palisade (C4) 544	Scribner (H3) 1,021	Utica (G4) 564	Elkhorn (river) ....G 3
Palmer (F3) 418	Seneca (D2) 160	Valentine⊙ (D2) 2,875	Enders (res.) ....C 4
Palmyra (H4) 377	Seward⊙ (G4) 4,208	Valley (H3) 1,452	Frenchman (creek) ....C 4
Panama (H4) 155	Shelby (G3) 613	Valparaiso (H3) 394	Gavins Point (dam) ....F 2
Papillion⊙ (J3) 2,235	Shelton (F4) 904	Venango (C4) 227	Harlan County (res.) ....E 4
Parks (C4) 65	Shickley (G4) 371	Venus (F2) 5	Harry Strunk (lake) ....D 4
Pauline (F4) 88	Sholes (H3) 26	Verdel (F2) 123	Homestead Nat'l Mon. ....H 4
Pawnee City⊙ (H4) 1,343	Shubert (J4) 231	Verdigre (F2) 584	Jeffrey (res.) ....D 4
Paxton (C3) 566	Sidney⊙ (B3) 8,004	Verdon (J4) 267	Johnson (res.) ....E 4
Pender⊙ (H2) 1,165		Vesta (H4) 75	Keya Paha (river) ....D 1
Peru (J4) 1,151		Virginia (H4) 88	
Petersburg (G3) 400			
Phillips (F4) 192			

Kingsley (dam) ....C 3	Medicine Creek (dam)....D 4	Omaha Ind. Res. ....H 2	South Loup (river) ....D 3
Lewis and Clark (lake)..F 2	Middle Loup (river) ....D 3	Pelican (lake) ....D 2	South Platte (river) ....C 3
Little Blue (river) ....H 5	Minatare (lake) ....A 3	Platte (river) ....E 4	Sutherland (res.) ....C 3
Lodgepole (creek) ....A 3	Missouri (river) ....H 3	Pumpkin (creek) ....A 3	Swan (lake) ....B 3
Logan (creek) ....H 2	Moon (lake) ....E 2	Republican (river) ....G 5	Swanson (lake) ....C 4
Loup (river) ....F 3	Niobrara (river) ....E 2	Scotts Bluff Nat'l Mon. ....A 3	White (river) ....A 2
Maloney (res.) ....D 3	North Loup (river) ....E 3	Sherman (res.) ....E 3	Winnebago Ind. Res. ...H 2
McConaughy (lake) ....C 3	North Platte (river) ....B 3	Sioux Ordnance Depot ...A 3	
Medicine (creek) ....D 4	Offutt A.F.B. ....J 3	Snake (river) ....C 2	

⊙ County Seat.

NEBRASKA

AREA	77,227 sq. mi.
POPULATION	1,477,000
CAPITAL	Lincoln
LARGEST CITY	Omaha 301,598
HIGHEST POINT	5,424 ft. (Kimball Co.)
SETTLED IN	1847
ADMITTED TO UNION	March 1, 1867
POPULAR NAME	Cornhusker State
STATE FLOWER	Goldenrod
STATE BIRD	Western Meadowlark

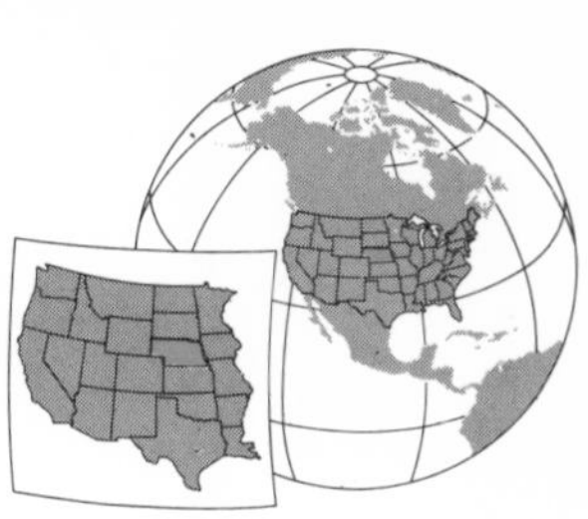

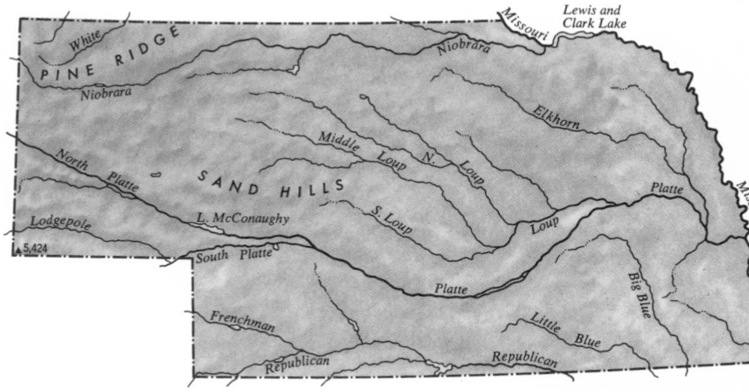

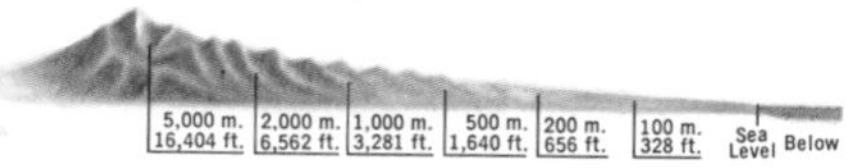

TOPOGRAPHY

5,000 m.	2,000 m.	1,000 m.	500 m.	200 m.	100 m.	Sea Level	Below
16,404 ft.	6,562 ft.	3,281 ft.	1,640 ft.	656 ft.	328 ft.		

0   50   100 MILES

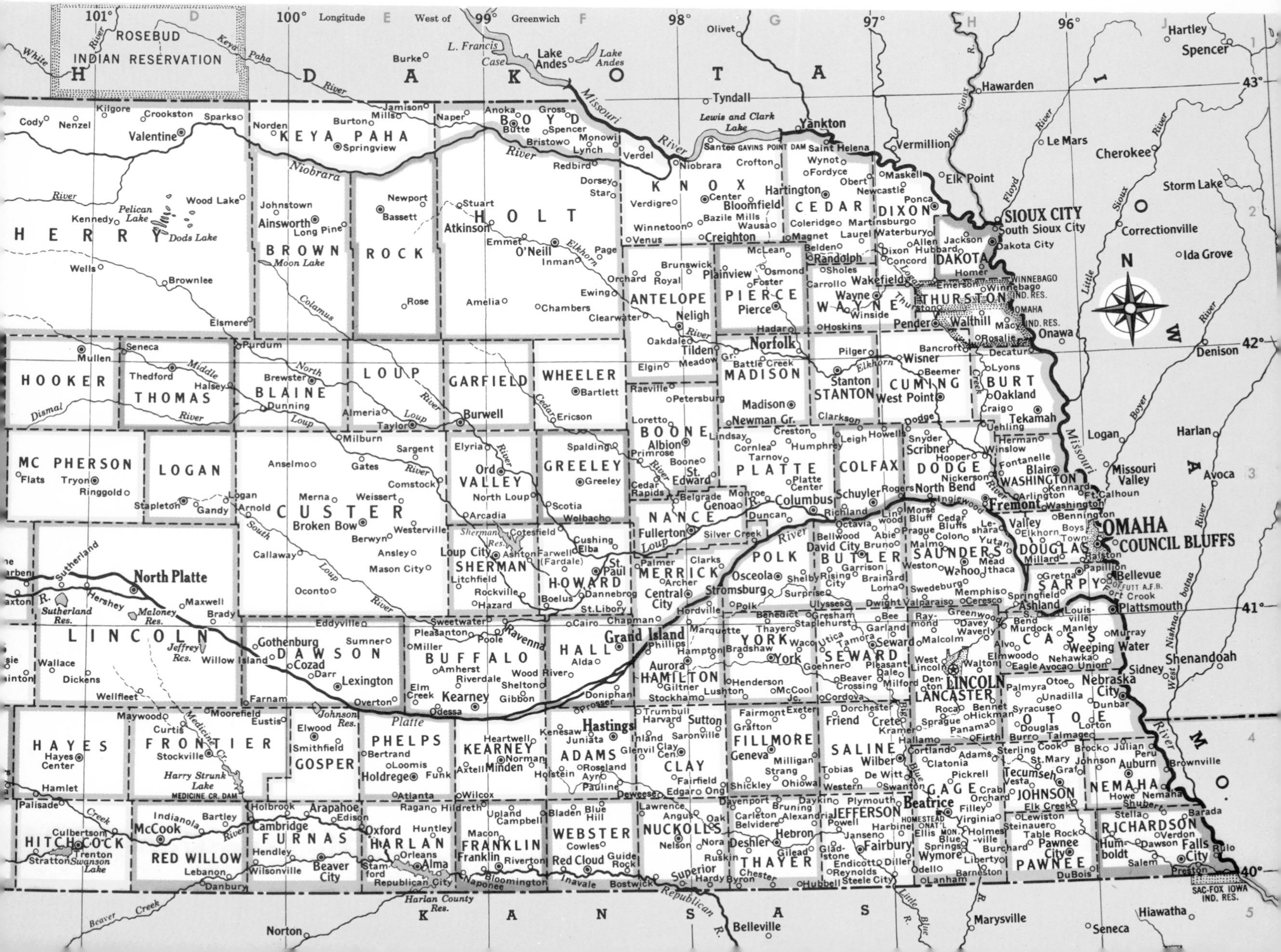

NEVADA

SCALE OF MILES

0 5 10 20 30 40 50 60

◉ State Capitals
◉ County Seats

GREAT SALT LAKE DESERT

Copyright by C. S. Hammond & Co., N.Y.

NEVADA

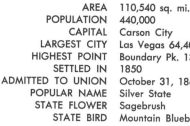

AREA	110,540 sq. mi.
POPULATION	440,000
CAPITAL	Carson City
LARGEST CITY	Las Vegas 64,405
HIGHEST POINT	Boundary Pk. 13,140 ft.
SETTLED IN	1850
ADMITTED TO UNION	October 31, 1864
POPULAR NAME	Silver State
STATE FLOWER	Sagebrush
STATE BIRD	Mountain Bluebird

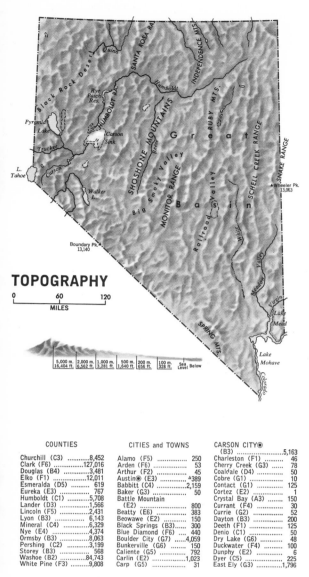

TOPOGRAPHY

0 — 60 — 120
MILES

5,000 m. / 2,000 m. / 1,000 m. / 500 m. / 200 m. / 100 m. / Sea Level
16,404 ft. / 6,562 ft. / 3,281 ft. / 1,640 ft. / 656 ft. / 328 ft. / Below

COUNTIES

Churchill (C3)	8,452
Clark (F6)	127,016
Douglas (B4)	3,481
Elko (F1)	12,011
Esmeralda (D5)	619
Eureka (E3)	767
Humboldt (C1)	5,708
Lander (D3)	1,566
Lincoln (F5)	2,431
Lyon (B3)	6,143
Mineral (C4)	6,923
Nye (E4)	4,374
Ormsby (B3)	8,063
Pershing (C2)	3,199
Storey (B3)	568
Washoe (B2)	84,743
White Pine (F3)	9,808

CITIES and TOWNS

Alamo (F5)	250
Arden (B3)	53
Arthur (F2)	45
Austin⊙ (E3)	^389
Babbitt (C4)	2,159
Baker (G3)	50
Battle Mountain (E2)	800
Beatty (E4)	383
Beowawe (E2)	150
Black Springs (B3)	300
Blue Diamond (F6)	440
Boulder City (F6)	4,059
Bunkerville (G6)	150
Caliente (G5)	792
Carlin (E2)	1,023
Carp (G5)	31

CARSON CITY⊙

(B3)	5,163
Charleston (F1)	46
Cherry Creek (G3)	78
Coaldale (D4)	50
Cobre (G1)	10
Contact (G1)	125
Cortez (E2)	1
Crystal Bay (A3)	150
Currant (F4)	30
Currie (G2)	52
Dayton (B3)	200
Deeth (F1)	125
Denio (C1)	50
Dry Lake (G6)	48
Duckwater (F4)	100
Dunphy (E2)	6
Dyer (C5)	225

East Las Vegas (F6)	200
Eastgate (D3)	12
Elgin (G5)	25
Elko⊙ (F2)	6,298
Ely⊙ (G3)	4,018
Eureka⊙ (E3)	^496
Fallon⊙ (C3)	2,734
Fernley (B3)	700
Flanigan (B2)	14
Gabbs (D4)	770
Gardnerville (B4)	900
Genoa (B4)	150
Gerlach (B2)	350
Glenbrook (B3)	95
Glendale (G6)	20
Golconda (D2)	350
Gold Hill (B3)	41
Gold Point (D5)	38
Goldfield⊙ (D5)	184
Goodsprings (F7)	90
Halleck (F2)	45
Hawthorne⊙ (C4)	2,838
Hazen (C3)	50
Henderson (G6)	12,525
Hiko (F5)	23
Hudson (B4)	2
Humboldt (C2)	3
Imlay (C2)	300
Indian Springs (F6)	450
Ione (D4)	50
Jarbidge (F1)	40
Jean (F7)	75
Jiggs (F2)	150
Jungo (C2)	30
Kimberly (F3)	300
Lamoille (F2)	65
Las Vegas⊙ (F6)	64,405
Las Vegas (urban area)	89,427
Lee (F2)	152
Logandale (G6)	350
Lovelock⊙ (C2)	1,948
Lund (F4)	365
Luning (C4)	55
Manhattan (E4)	25
Mason (B4)	89
McDermitt (D1)	215
McGill (G3)	2,195
Mercury (E6)	2,200
Mesquite (G6)	516
Metropolis (G1)	58
Midas (E1)	50
Mill City (D2)	20
Mina (C4)	350
Minden⊙ (B4)	250
Moapa (G6)	150
Montello (G1)	185
Mount Montgomery (C4)	13
Mountain City (F1)	130
Nelson (G7)	36
Nivloc (D5)	4
Nixon (B3)	250
North Las Vegas (F6)	18,422
Oasis (G1)	10
Oreana (C2)	24
Orovada (D1)	300
Overton (G6)	1,169
Owyhee (F1)	150
Pahrump (E6)	325
Palisade (E2)	15
Panaca (G5)	499
Paradise Valley (D1)	60
Pioche⊙ (G5)	^696
Pittman (F6)	150
Preston (G4)	45
Pyramid (B2)	27
Rawhide (C4)	20
Red House (D2)	10
Reno⊙ (B3)	51,470
Reno (urban area)	70,189
Rhyolite (E6)	5
Rio Tinto (E1)	6
Rochester (C2)	12
Round Mountain (E4)	180
Rowland (F1)	11
Rox (G6)	51
Ruby Valley (F2)	200
Ruth (F3)	800
San Jacinto (G1)	10
Schurz (C4)	300
Searchlight (F7)	217
Shafter (G2)	15
Shoshone (G4)	40
Silver City (B3)	125
Silverpeak (D5)	63
Sloan (F7)	27
Smith (B4)	200
Sparks (B3)	16,618
Steamboat (B3)	250
Stillwater (C3)	8
Sulphur (C2)	33
Tonopah⊙ (D4)	1,679
Tungsten (C2)	60
Tuscarora (E1)	40
Unionville (G5)	32
Ursine (G5)	60
Valmy (D2)	50
Verdi (B3)	50
Virginia City⊙ (B3)	^515
Vya (B1)	6
Wabuska (B3)	125
Wadsworth (B3)	250
Weed Heights (B4)	1,092
Weeks (B3)	6
Wellington (B4)	300
Wells (G1)	1,071
Wilkins (G1)	40
Winnemucca⊙ (D2)	3,453
Yerington⊙ (B4)	1,764
Zephyr Cove (A3)	50

OTHER FEATURES

Alkali (lake)	B 1
Antelope (range)	E 4
Arc Dome (mt.)	D 4
Arrow Canyon (range)	G 6
Beaver Creek Fork (river)	F 1
Belted (range)	E 5
Berlin (mt.)	D 4
Big Smoky (valley)	D 4
Bishops (creek)	F 1
Black Rock (desert)	B 2
Black Rock (range)	B 1
Boundary (peak)	C 5
Buffalo (creek)	E 1
Butte (mts.)	F 2
Cactus (range)	E 5
Carson (lake)	C 3
Carson (river)	B 3
Carson Sink (depression)	C 3
Cedar (mt.)	D 4
Charleston (peak)	F 6
Clan Alpine (mts.)	D 3
Columbus (salt marsh)	C 4
Cortez (mts.)	E 2
Crescent (valley)	E 2
Davis (dam)	G 7
Death Valley Nat'l Mon. (Devil's Hole)	E 6
Delamar (mts.)	G 5
Desatoya (mts.)	D 3
Desert (range)	F 6
Desert (valley)	C 1
Desert Rock, Camp	E 6
Division (peak)	B 1
Duck (creek)	G 3
East (range)	D 2
East Walker (river)	B 4
Egan (range)	G 3
Ely (range)	B 1
Emigrant (peak)	C 5
Excelsior (mts.)	C 4
Fallon Ind. Res.	C 3
Fort Mohave Indian Res.	G 7
Franklin (lake)	F 2
Frenchman Flat (basin)	F 6
Gillis (range)	C 4
Golden Gate (range)	F 5
Goshute (mts.)	G 2
Goshute Ind. Res.	G 2
Granite (peak)	B 2
Granite (range)	B 2
Grant (range)	F 4
Great Salt Lake (desert)	H 2
Hawthorne Nav. Amm. Depot	C 4
High Rock (creek)	B 1
Highland (peak)	G 5
Hoover (dam)	G 7
Hot Creek (range)	E 4
Hot Creek (valley)	E 4
Humboldt (range)	C 2
Humboldt (river)	E 2
Humboldt (salt marsh)	D 3
Humboldt Sink (depression)	C 3
Huntington (creek)	F 2
Independence (mts.)	E 1
Indian Springs A.F.B.	F 6
Jackson (mts.)	C 1
Job (peak)	C 3
Kawich (peak)	E 5
Kawich (range)	E 5
Kelley (creek)	D 1
Kings (river)	C 1
Lahontan (res.)	B 3
Lake Mead Nat'l Recreation Area	G 6
Las Vegas (range)	F 6
Las Vegas Bombing and Gunnery Range	E 5
Lehman Caves Nat'l Mon.	G 4
Little Humboldt (river)	D 1
Little Smoky (valley)	E 4
Lone (mt.)	D 4
Long (valley)	B 1
Marys (river)	F 1
Mason (mt.)	F 1
Massacre (lake)	B 1
Mead (lake)	G 6
Meadow Valley Wash (dry river)	G 5
Moapa River Indian Res.	G 6
Mohave (lake)	G 7
Monitor (range)	E 4
Monte Cristo (range)	D 4
Mormon (mts.)	G 6
Mount Airy (range)	D 3
Muddy (mts.)	G 6
Nellis A.F.B.	F 6
Nelson (creek)	G 2
New Pass (range)	D 3
Nightingale (mts.)	B 2
Owyhee (river)	E 1
Pah-rum (peak)	B 2
Pahranagat (range)	F 5
Pahrock (range)	F 5
Pahrump (valley)	F 6
Pahute (mesa)	E 5
Pahute (peak)	B 1
Pancake (range)	E 4
Pequop (mts.)	G 2
Pilot (peak)	C 4
Pine (creek)	E 2
Pine Forest (range)	C 1
Pintwater (range)	F 6
Piper (peak)	D 5
Potosi (mt.)	F 7
Pyramid (lake)	B 2
Pyramid Lake Indian Res.	B 2
Quinn (river)	C 1
Quinn Canyon (range)	F 4
Railroad (valley)	F 4
Reese (river)	D 3
Reveille (peak)	E 5
Reveille (range)	E 4
Rock (creek)	E 2
Ruby (lake)	F 2
Ruby (mts.)	F 2
Rye Patch (res.)	C 2
Sand Springs (salt depression)	C 3
Santa Rosa (range)	D 1
Schell Creek (range)	G 3
Sheep (range)	F 6
Shoshone (mts.)	D 3
Silver Peak (range)	D 5
Simpson Park (mts.)	E 3
Smith Creek (valley)	D 3
Smoke Creek (desert)	B 2
Snake (range)	G 3
Snow Water (lake)	G 2
Sonoma (range)	D 2
Specter (range)	E 6
Spotted (range)	F 6
Spring (creek)	D 2
Spring (mts.)	F 6
Spring (valley)	G 3
Stead A.F.B.	B 3
Stillwater (range)	C 3
Sulphur Spring (range)	E 3
Summit (lake)	C 1
Summit Lake Indian Res.	B 1
Table (mt.)	C 3
Tahoe (lake)	B 3
Thousand Spring (creek)	G 1
Timber (mts.)	E 5
Timber (mt.)	F 5
Timpahute (range)	F 5
Toana (range)	G 2
Toiyabe (range)	D 3
Topaz Lake (res.)	B 4
Toquima (range)	E 4
Trident (peak)	C 1
Trinity (range)	C 2
Truckee (river)	B 3
Tule (desert)	G 5
Tuscarora (mts.)	E 1
Virgin (mts.)	G 6
Virgin (peak)	G 6
Virgin (river)	G 6
Virginia (range)	B 3
Walker (lake)	C 4
Walker (river)	C 4
Walker River Indian Res.	C 3
Washoe (lake)	B 3
Wassuk (range)	C 4
West Fork, Bruneau (river)	F 1
Western Shoshone Ind. Res.	E 1
Wheeler (peak)	G 4
White Pine (mts.)	F 3
Wild Horse (res.)	E 1
Winnemucca (lake)	B 2
Winnemucca Ind. Res.	D 2
Yucca Flat (basin)	E 6

⊙County Seat.
^Population of township.

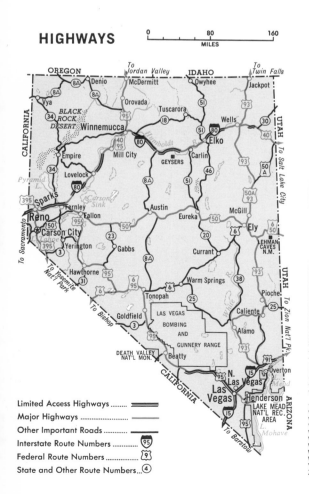

HIGHWAYS

0 — 80 — 160
MILES

Limited Access Highways	═══
Major Highways	───
Other Important Roads	───
Interstate Route Numbers	95
Federal Route Numbers	9
State and Other Route Numbers	4

AGRICULTURE, INDUSTRY and RESOURCES

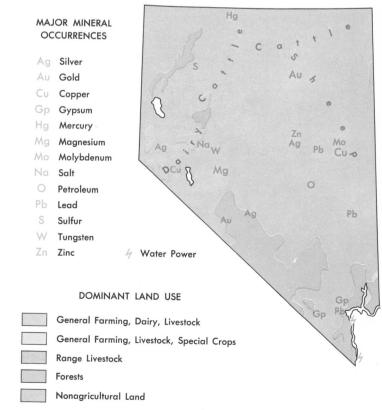

MAJOR MINERAL OCCURRENCES

Ag	Silver
Au	Gold
Cu	Copper
Gp	Gypsum
Hg	Mercury
Mg	Magnesium
Mo	Molybdenum
Na	Salt
O	Petroleum
Pb	Lead
S	Sulfur
W	Tungsten
Zn	Zinc
⚡	Water Power

DOMINANT LAND USE

- General Farming, Dairy, Livestock
- General Farming, Livestock, Special Crops
- Range Livestock
- Forests
- Nonagricultural Land

NEW HAMPSHIRE and VERMONT

AGRICULTURE, INDUSTRY and RESOURCES

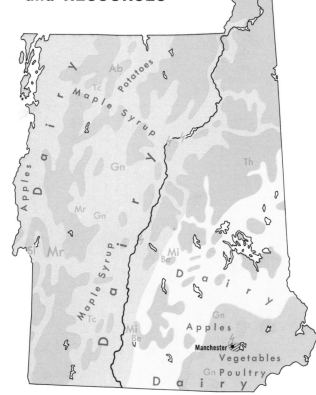

DOMINANT LAND USE

- ☐ Specialized Dairy
- ☐ Dairy, General Farming
- ☐ Dairy, Poultry, Mixed Farming
- ☐ Forests
- ⚡ Water Power
- ▨ Major Industrial Areas

MANCHESTER
Leather Goods, Textiles,
Electrical Products

MAJOR MINERAL OCCURRENCES

Ab	Asbestos		Mr	Marble
Be	Beryl		Sl	Slate
Gn	Granite		Tc	Talc
Mi	Mica		Th	Thorium

NEW HAMPSHIRE

AREA	9,304 sq. mi.
POPULATION	669,000
CAPITAL	Concord
LARGEST CITY	Manchester 88,282
HIGHEST POINT	Mt. Washington 6,288 ft.
SETTLED IN	1623
ADMITTED TO UNION	June 21, 1788
POPULAR NAME	Granite State
STATE FLOWER	Purple Lilac
STATE BIRD	Purple Finch

VERMONT

9,609 sq. mi.

397,000

Montpelier

Burlington 35,531

Mt. Mansfield 4,393 ft.

1764

March 4, 1791

Green Mountain State

Red Clover

Hermit Thrush

TOPOGRAPHY

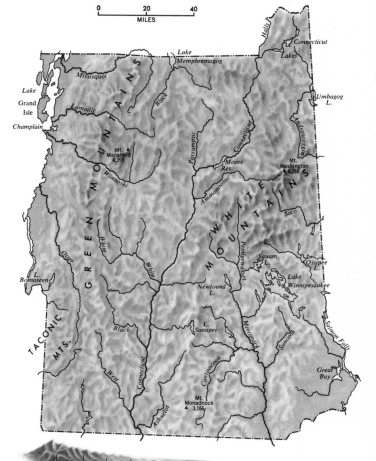

(continued on following page)

New Hampshire and Vermont
(continued)

NEW HAMPSHIRE
(continued)

Unity (C5) ... Δ708
Wakefield (E4) ... Δ1,223
Walpole (C5) ... Δ2,825
Warner (D5) ... Δ1,004
Warren (D4) ... Δ548
Washington (C5) ... Δ162
Weare (D5) ... Δ1,420
Webster (D5) ... Δ457
Weirs Beach (E4) ... 356
Wentworth (D4) ... Δ300
Wentworth Location (E2) Δ58
West Brentwood (E6) ... 150
West Campton (D4) ... 200
West Canaan (C4) ... 200
West Derry (E6) ... 4,468
West Epping (E5) ... 175
West Hampstead (E6) .. 153
West Henniker (D5) ... 300
West Lebanon (C4) ... 3,333
West Milan (E2) ... 300
West Nottingham (E5) .. 225
West Ossipee (E4) ... 200
West Peterborough (C6) 255
West Rindge (C6) ... 230
West Rumney (D4) ... 299
West Rye (F6) ... 300
West Stewartstown (E2) ... 890
West Swanzey (C6) ... 4,400
West Thornton (D4) ... 450
Westmoreland (C6) ... Δ921
Westport (C6) ... 417
Westville (E6) ... 450
Whitefield (D3) ... Δ1,581
Whitefield (D3) ... 1,244
Wilmot (D5) ... Δ391
Wilton (D6) ... Δ2,025
Wilton (D6) ... 1,425
Winchester (C6) ... Δ2,411
Windham (E6) ... Δ1,317
Winnisquam (E5) ... 400
Wolfeboro (E4) ... Δ2,689
Wolfeboro (E4) ... 1,557
Wolfeboro Falls (E4) ... 600
Woodstock (D4) ... Δ827
Woodsville◉ (C3) ... 1,596

OTHER FEATURES

Adams (mt.) ... E 3
Ammonoosuc (river) ... D 3
Androscoggin (riv.) ... E 2
Ashuelot (riv.) ... C 6
Back (lake) ... E 1
Baker (river) ... D 4
Bearcamp (river) ... E 4
Beaver (brook) ... E 6
Belknap (mt.) ... E 5
Blackwater (res.) ... D 5
Blue (mt.) ... E 2
Bond (mt.) ... E 3
Bow (lake) ... E 5
Cabot (mt.) ... E 2
Cardigan (mt.) ... D 4
Carrigain (mt.) ... E 3
Carter Dome (mt.) ... E 3
Cocheco (river) ... E 5
Cold (river) ... C 5
Connecticut (river) ... B 6
Crawford Notch (pass) ... E 3
Crystal (lake) ... E 5
Cube (mt.) ... C 4
Dixville (peak) ... E 2
Dixville Notch (pass) ... E 2
Ellis (river) ... E 3
Everett (dam) ... D 5
First Connecticut (lake) .. E 1
Francis (lake) ... E 1
Franconia Notch (pass) ... D 3
Gale (river) ... D 3
Great (bay) ... F 5
Grenier Air Force Base ... E 6
Halls (strm.) ... E 1
Hancock (mt.) ... D 3
Highland (lake) ... C 5
Hutchins (mt.) ... E 2
Indian (strm.) ... E 1
Jefferson (mt.) ... E 3
Kearsarge (mt.) ... D 5
Kingman Notch (pass) ... D 3
Lafayette (mt.) ... D 3
Lamprey (river) ... E 5
Liberty (mt.) ... D 3
Long (mt.) ... E 2
MacDowell, Edward (res.) ... D 6
Mad (river) ... D 4
Madison (mt.) ... E 3
Magalloway (mt.) ... E 1
Mascoma (lake) ... C 4
Massabesic (lake) ... E 6
Merrimack (river) ... D 5
Merrymeeting (lake) ... E 5
Mohawk (river) ... E 2
Monadnock (mt.) ... C 6
Monroe (mt.) ... E 3
Moosilauke (mt.) ... D 3
Newfound (lake) ... D 4
North Carter (mt.) ... E 3
North Twin (mt.) ... D 3
Nubanusit (lake) ... C 5
Osceola (mt.) ... E 3
Ossipee (lake) ... E 4
Ossipee (river) ... F 4
Passaconaway (mt.) ... E 4
Pawtuckaway (pond) ... E 5
Pemigewasset (river) ... D 4
Pine (river) ... E 4
Pinkham Notch (pass) ... E 3
Piscataqua (river) ... F 5
Piscataquag (river) ... D 5
Presidential (range) ... E 3
Rice (mt.) ... E 2
Saco (river) ... E 3
Salmon Falls (river) ... F 5
Sandwich (mt.) ... E 4
Sandwich (range) ... E 4
Second (lake) ... E 1
Shaw (mt.) ... E 4
Shoals (isls.) ... F 6
Smarts (mt.) ... C 4
Southegan (river) ... D 6
South Twin (mt.) ... D 3
Squam (lake) ... E 4
Starr King (mt.) ... E 3
Sugar (river) ... C 5
Sunapee (lake) ... C 5
Suncook (lakes) ... E 5
Surry Mountain (res.) ... C 5
Tarleton (lake) ... D 4
Tecumseh (mt.) ... D 4
Third (lake) ... E 1
Tom (mt.) ... E 3
Umbagog (lake) ... E 2
Upper Ammonoosuc (river) ... E 2
Warner (river) ... D 5
Washington (mt.) ... E 3
Waumbek (mt.) ... E 3
Wentworth (lake) ... E 4
White (mts.) ... E 3
Whiteface (mt.) ... E 4
Wild Ammonoosuc (river) ... D 3
Wilder (dam) ... C 4
Winnipesaukee (lake) ... E 4
Winnipesaukee (river) ... D 5
Winnisquam (lake) ... D 4

VERMONT

COUNTIES

Addison (A3) ... 20,076
Bennington (A6) ... 25,088
Caledonia (C2) ... 22,786
Chittenden (A3) ... 74,425
Essex (D2) ... 6,083
Franklin (B2) ... 29,474
Grand Isle (A2) ... 2,927
Lamoille (B2) ... 11,027
Orange (C3) ... 16,014
Orleans (C2) ... 20,143
Rutland (A4) ... 46,719
Washington (B3) ... 42,860
Windham (B5) ... 29,776
Windsor (B4) ... 42,483

CITIES and TOWNS

Addison (A3) ... Δ645
Albany (C2) ... Δ560
Albany (C2) ... 169
Alburg (A2) ... Δ1,123
Alburg (A2) ... 426
Andover (B5) ... Δ215
Arlington (A5) ... Δ1,605
Arlington (A5) ... 1,111
Ascutney (C5) ... 250
Averhill (D2) ... Δ16
Bakersfield (B2) ... Δ664
Barnard (B4) ... Δ435
Barnet (C3) ... Δ1,445
Barre (C3) ... 10,387
Barton (C2) ... Δ3,066
Barton (C2) ... 1,169
Beebe Plain (C2) ... 185
Beecher Falls (D2) ... 600
Bellows Falls (C5) ... 3,831
Belvidere Junction (B2) 7
Bennington (A6) ... Δ13,002
Bennington◉ (A6) ... 8,023
Benson (A4) ... 549
Berkshire (B2) ... Δ965
Bethel (B4) ... Δ1,356
Bolton (B3) ... Δ237
Bomoseen (A4) ... 500
Bondville (B5) ... 350
Bradford (C3) ... Δ1,619
Bradford (C3) ... 760
Braintree (B4) ... Δ536
Brandon (A4) ... Δ3,329
Brattleboro (B6) ... Δ11,734
Brattleboro (B6) ... 9,135
Bread Loaf (B4) ... 11
Bridgewater (B4) ... Δ776
Bridgewater Corners (B4) ... 175
Bridport (A4) ... Δ653
Bristol (A3) ... Δ2,159
Bristol (A3) ... 1,421
Brookfield (B3) ... Δ597
Brownington (C2) ... Δ599
Brownsville (C5) ... 209
Burke (D2) ... Δ9,922
Burlington (A3) ... 35,531
Cabot (C3) ... Δ763
Cabot (C3) ... 244
Calais (B3) ... Δ684
Cambridge (B2) ... Δ1,295
Cambridge (B2) ... 217
Canaan (D2) ... Δ1,094
Castleton (A4) ... Δ1,902
Cavendish (B5) ... 1,223
Center Rutland (A4) ... 438
Charlotte (A3) ... Δ1,271
Chelsea◉ (C4) ... Δ957
Chester (B5) ... Δ2,318
Chester (B5) ... 923
Chester Depot (B5) ... 500
Chittenden (B4) ... Δ460
Colchester (A2) ... Δ4,718
Concord (D3) ... Δ956
Concord (D3) ... 389
Corinth (C3) ... Δ775
Cornwall (A4) ... Δ756
Coventry (C2) ... Δ458
Craftsbury (C2) ... 150
Cuttingsville (B4) ... 177
Danby (B5) ... Δ891
Danville (C3) ... 1,368
Derby (Derby Center) (C2) ... 433
Derby Line (C2) ... 849
Dorset (A5) ... Δ1,150
Duxbury (B3) ... Δ546
East Arlington (A5) ... 500
East Barre (B3) ... 700
East Berkshire (B2) ... 300
East Brookfield (C3) ... 175
East Burke (D2) ... 250
East Calais (C3) ... 225
East Charleston (D2) ... 225
East Concord (D3) ... 225
East Dorset (A5) ... 270
East Dover (B6) ... 170
East Fairfield (B2) ... 500
East Hardwick (B2) ... 214
East Haven (D2) ... 159
East Middlebury (A4) ... 500
East Montpelier (B3) .. Δ1,200
East Poultney (A4) ... 275
East Richford (B2) ... 160
East Ryegate (C3) ... 225
East Thetford (C4) ... 275
East Wallingford (B5) .. 250
Eden (B2) ... Δ430
Eden Mills (B2) ... 225
Ely (C4) ... 56
Enosburg Falls (B2) ... 1,321
Essex (A2) ... Δ7,090
Essex Junction (A3) ... 5,340
Fair Haven (A4) ... 2,378
Fairfax (B2) ... Δ1,244
Fairfield (B2) ... Δ1,225
Fairlee (C4) ... Δ569
Ferrisburg (A3) ... Δ1,426
Florence (A4) ... 500
Forest Dale (A4) ... 400
Franklin (B2) ... Δ796
Gaysville (B4) ... 150
Georgia Center (A2) ... Δ1,079
Gilman (D3) ... 650
Glover (C2) ... Δ683
Glover (C2) ... 230
Grafton (B5) ... Δ426
Granby (D2) ... Δ56
Grand Isle (A2) ... Δ624
Graniteville (C3) ... 1,200
Granville (B4) ... Δ215
Greensboro (C2) ... Δ600
Groton (C3) ... Δ631
Groton (C3) ... 387
Guildhall◉ (D2) ... Δ248
Guilford (B6) ... Δ823
Halifax Center (B6) ... Δ268
Hancock (B4) ... Δ323
Hardwick (C2) ... Δ2,349
Hardwick (C2) ... 1,521
Hartford (C4) ... Δ6,355
Hartland (C4) ... Δ1,592
Heartwellville (A6) ... 75
Highgate Center (B2) ... 350
Highgate Falls (A2) ... 650
Highgate Springs (A2) .. 300
Hinesburg (A3) ... Δ1,180
Hubbardton (A4) ... 238
Huntington (B3) ... Δ518
Huntington Center (B3) 150
Hyde Park (B2) ... Δ1,219
Hyde Park◉ (B2) ... 474
Hydeville (A4) ... 500
Ira (A4) ... Δ220
Irasburg (C2) ... 711
Island Pond (D2) ... 1,319
Isle La Motte (A2) ... Δ238
Jacksonville (B6) ... 240
Jamaica (B5) ... Δ496
Jay (C2) ... Δ197
Jeffersonville (B2) ... 346
Jericho (A2) ... 500
Jericho Center (B3) ... 225
Johnson (B2) ... Δ1,478
Johnson (B2) ... 941
Killington (B4) ... 266
Lake Dunmore (A4) ... 25
Lake Elmore (B2) ... 250
Lincoln (B3) ... Δ481
Londonderry (B5) ... Δ898
Lowell (C2) ... Δ617
Ludlow (B5) ... Δ2,386
Ludlow (B5) ... 1,658
Lunenburg (D3) ... Δ1,237
Lyndon (C2) ... 350
Lyndon Center (C2) ... 274
Lyndonville (D2) ... 1,477
Maidstone (D2) ... Δ78
Manchester (A5) ... Δ2,470
Manchester◉ (A5) ... 403
Manchester Center (A5) 900
Manchester Depot (B5) ... 1,387
Marlboro (B6) ... Δ347
Marshfield (C3) ... Δ891
Marshfield (C3) ... 313
McIndoe Falls (C3) ... 300
Middlebury (A3) ... Δ5,305
Middlebury◉ (A3) ... 3,688
Middlesex (B3) ... Δ770
Middletown Springs (A5) ... Δ381
Milton (A2) ... Δ2,022
Milton (A2) ... 817
Monkton (A3) ... Δ551
Montgomery (B2) ... Δ876
MONTPELIER (B3) ... 8,782
Moretown (B3) ... Δ788
Morgan (D2) ... 261
Morgan Center (D2) ... 300
Morrisville (B2) ... 2,047
Moscow (B3) ... 240
Mount Holly (B5) ... Δ517
New Haven (A3) ... Δ922
Newbury (C3) ... 1,452
Newfane (B6) ... Δ714
Newfane◉ (B6) ... 146
Newport (C2) ... Δ1,010
Newport◉ (C2) ... 5,019
Newport Center (C2) ... 375
North Bennington (A6) ... 1,437
North Clarendon (B4) ... 600
North Danville (C3) ... 212
North Ferrisburg (A3) .. 230
North Hartland (C4) ... 400
North Hero◉ (A2) ... Δ328
North Hyde Park (B2) .. 300
North Montpelier (C3) .. 225
North Pomfret (B4) ... 200
North Pownal (A6) ... 775
North Springfield (B5) .. 600
North Thetford (C4) ... 110
North Troy (C2) ... 961
North Tunbridge (C4) ... 50
North Westminster (B5) ... 368
North Williston (A3) ... 120
Northfield (B3) ... Δ4,511
Northfield (B3) ... 2,159
Northfield Falls (B3) ... 500
Norton (D2) ... Δ241
Norwich (C4) ... Δ1,790
Old Bennington (A6) ... 205
Orange (C3) ... Δ430
Orleans (C2) ... 1,240
Orwell (A4) ... Δ826
Panton (A3) ... Δ352
Passumpsic (D3) ... 204
Pawlet (A5) ... Δ1,112
Peacham (C3) ... Δ433
Perkinsville (B5) ... 167
Peru (B5) ... Δ194
Pittsfield (B4) ... Δ254
Pittsford (A4) ... Δ2,225
Pittsford (A4) ... 671
Plainfield (C3) ... Δ966
Plainfield (C3) ... 507
Plymouth (B4) ... Δ308
Pomfret (B4) ... Δ600
Post Mills (C4) ... 272
Poultney (A4) ... Δ3,009
Poultney (A4) ... 1,810
Pownal (A6) ... Δ1,509
Pownal Center (A6) ... 300
Proctor (A4) ... Δ2,102
Proctor (A4) ... 1,978
Proctorsville (B5) ... 476
Putney (B6) ... Δ1,177
Quechee (C4) ... 500
Randolph (B4) ... Δ3,414
Randolph (B4) ... 2,122
Reading (B5) ... Δ472
Readsboro (B6) ... Δ783
Readsboro (B6) ... 577
Richford (B2) ... Δ2,316
Richford (B2) ... 1,663
Richmond (A3) ... Δ1,303
Richmond (A3) ... 765
Ripton (A4) ... Δ131
Rochester (B4) ... Δ879
Roxbury (B3) ... 364
Royalton (B4) ... 1,388
Rupert (A5) ... Δ603
Rutland◉ (B4) ... 18,325
Ryegate (C3) ... Δ894
Saint Albans◉ (A2) ... 8,806
Saint Albans Bay (A2) .. 335
Saint Johnsbury (D3) .. Δ8,869
Saint Johnsbury◉ (D3) ... 6,809
Saint Johnsbury Center (D3) ... 400
Salisbury (A4) ... Δ575
Sandgate (A5) ... Δ93
Saxtons River (B5) ... 725
Shaftsbury (A6) ... 480
Sharon (C4) ... Δ485
Sheffield (C2) ... Δ342
Shelburne (A3) ... Δ1,805
Sheldon (B2) ... Δ1,281
Sheldon Springs (A2) ... 650
Sherburne Center (B4) .. 266
Shoreham (A4) ... Δ786
South Barre (B3) ... 700
South Burlington (A3) ... Δ6,903
South Dorset (A5) ... 185
South Hero (A2) ... Δ614
South Londonderry (B5) ... 900
South Newbury (C3) ... 140
South Royalton (C4) ... 975
South Ryegate (C3) ... 360
South Shaftsbury (A6) ... 480
South Wallingford (B5) 150
Springfield (C5) ... Δ9,934
Springfield (C5) ... 6,600
Stamford (A6) ... Δ600
Starksboro (A3) ... Δ502
Stockbridge (B4) ... Δ392
Stowe (B3) ... Δ1,901
Stowe (B3) ... 534
Strafford (C4) ... Δ548
Sudbury (A4) ... Δ249
Sutton (C2) ... Δ476
Swanton (A2) ... 2,390
Taftsville (C4) ... 200
Thetford (C4) ... Δ1,049
Thetford Center (C4) ... 400
Tinmouth (A5) ... Δ228
Topsham (C3) ... Δ638
Townshend (B5) ... Δ643
Townshend (B5) ... 170
Troy (C2) ... Δ1,613
Tunbridge (C4) ... Δ743
Tyson (B5) ... 175
Underhill (B2) ... 695
Underhill Center (B2) ... Δ730
Vergennes (A3) ... 1,921
Vernon (B6) ... Δ865
Vershire (C4) ... Δ236
Waitsfield (B3) ... Δ658
Walden (C3) ... Δ427
Wallingford (B5) ... Δ1,439
Wardsboro (B5) ... Δ322
Warren (B3) ... Δ469
Washington (C3) ... Δ565
Waterbury (B3) ... 2,984
Waterbury Center (B3) 630
Waterville (B2) ... Δ332
Websterville (B3) ... 800
Wells (A5) ... Δ419
Wells River (C3) ... 472
West Brattleboro (B6) .. 1,500
West Burke (C2) ... 369
West Charleston (C2) ... 185
West Dummerston (B6) 200
West Fairlee (C4) ... Δ333
West Halifax (B6) ... 200
West Hartford (C4) ... 300
West Pawlet (A5) ... 500
West Rupert (A5) ... 300
West Rutland (A4) ... Δ2,302
West Rutland (A4) ... 1,991
West Salisbury (A4) ... 145
West Townshend (B5) .. 150
West Woodstock (B4) ... 165
Westfield (C2) ... Δ347
Westford (A2) ... Δ680
Westminster (C5) ... Δ1,602
Westminster (C5) ... 333
Westminster Station (C5) ... 150
Westmore (C2) ... Δ179
Weston (B5) ... Δ442
Weybridge (A3) ... 427
Wheelock (C2) ... 246
White River Junction (C4) ... 2,546
Whiting (A4) ... 290
Whitingham (B6) ... Δ838
Wilder (C4) ... 1,322
Williamstown (B3) ... Δ1,553
Williamsville (B6) ... 150
Williston (A3) ... Δ1,484
Wilmington (B6) ... Δ1,245
Wilmington (B6) ... 591
Windham (B5) ... Δ135
Windsor (C5) ... Δ4,468
Winooski (A3) ... 7,420
Wolcott (C2) ... Δ633
Woodbury (C3) ... Δ317
Woodford (A6) ... Δ207
Woodstock (B4) ... Δ2,786
Woodstock◉ (B4) ... 1,415
Worcester (B3) ... Δ417

OTHER FEATURES

Abraham (mt.) ... B 3
Ascutney (mt.) ... C 5
Bald (mt.) ... C 2
Batten Kill (creek) ... A 5
Belvidere (mt.) ... B 2
Black (river) ... B 5
Black (river) ... C 2
Bloodroot (mt.) ... B 4
Bomoseen (lake) ... A 4
Bread Loaf (mt.) ... A 3
Bromley (mt.) ... B 5
Camels Hump (mt.) ... B 3
Carmi (lake) ... B 2
Caspian (lake) ... C 2
Champlain (lake) ... A 2
Clyde (river) ... C 2
Comerford (dam) ... D 3
Connecticut (river) ... C 4
Crystal (lake) ... C 2
Deerfield (river) ... B 6
Dunmore (lake) ... A 4
Ellen (mt.) ... B 3
Equinox (mt.) ... A 5
Ethan Allen Air Force Base ... A 2
Glastenbury (mt.) ... A 6
Gore (mt.) ... D 2
Green (mts.) ... B 4
Haystack (mt.) ... B 6
Hoosic (river) ... A 6
Hortonia (lake) ... A 4
Hunger (mt.) ... B 3
Jay (peak) ... B 2
Killington (peak) ... B 4
Lamoille (river) ... A 2
Lewis (creek) ... A 3
Lincoln Gap (pass) ... B 3
Little (river) ... B 3
Mad (river) ... B 3
Mansfield (mt.) ... B 2
Mettawee (river) ... A 5
Middlebury Gap (pass) .. B 4
Mill (river) ... B 4
Missisquoi (river) ... B 2
Moore (dam) ... D 3
Moose (river) ... D 2
Norton (pond) ... D 2
Nulhegan (river) ... D 2
Okemo (mt.) ... B 5
Ottauquechee (river) ... B 4
Passumpsic (river) ... D 2
Pico (peak) ... B 4
Saint Catherine (lake) ... A 5
Salem Pond (lake) ... C 2
Seymour (lake) ... D 2
Smugglers Notch (pass) ... B 2
Somerset (res.) ... A 5
Spruce (mt.) ... C 3
Stratton (mt.) ... B 5
Tabor (mt.) ... B 5
Trout (river) ... B 2
Waits (river) ... C 3
Wells (river) ... C 3
West (river) ... B 5
White (river) ... C 4
Whiteface (mt.) ... B 2
Whitingham (lake) ... B 6
Wilder (dam) ... C 4
Willoughby (lake) ... D 2
Winooski (river) ... B 3

◉County Seat.
ΔPopulation of township.

HIGHWAYS

0 — 20 — 40 MILES

Limited Access Highways
Major Highways
Other Important Roads
Interstate Route Numbers (95)
Federal Route Numbers (9)
State and Other Route Numbers (4)

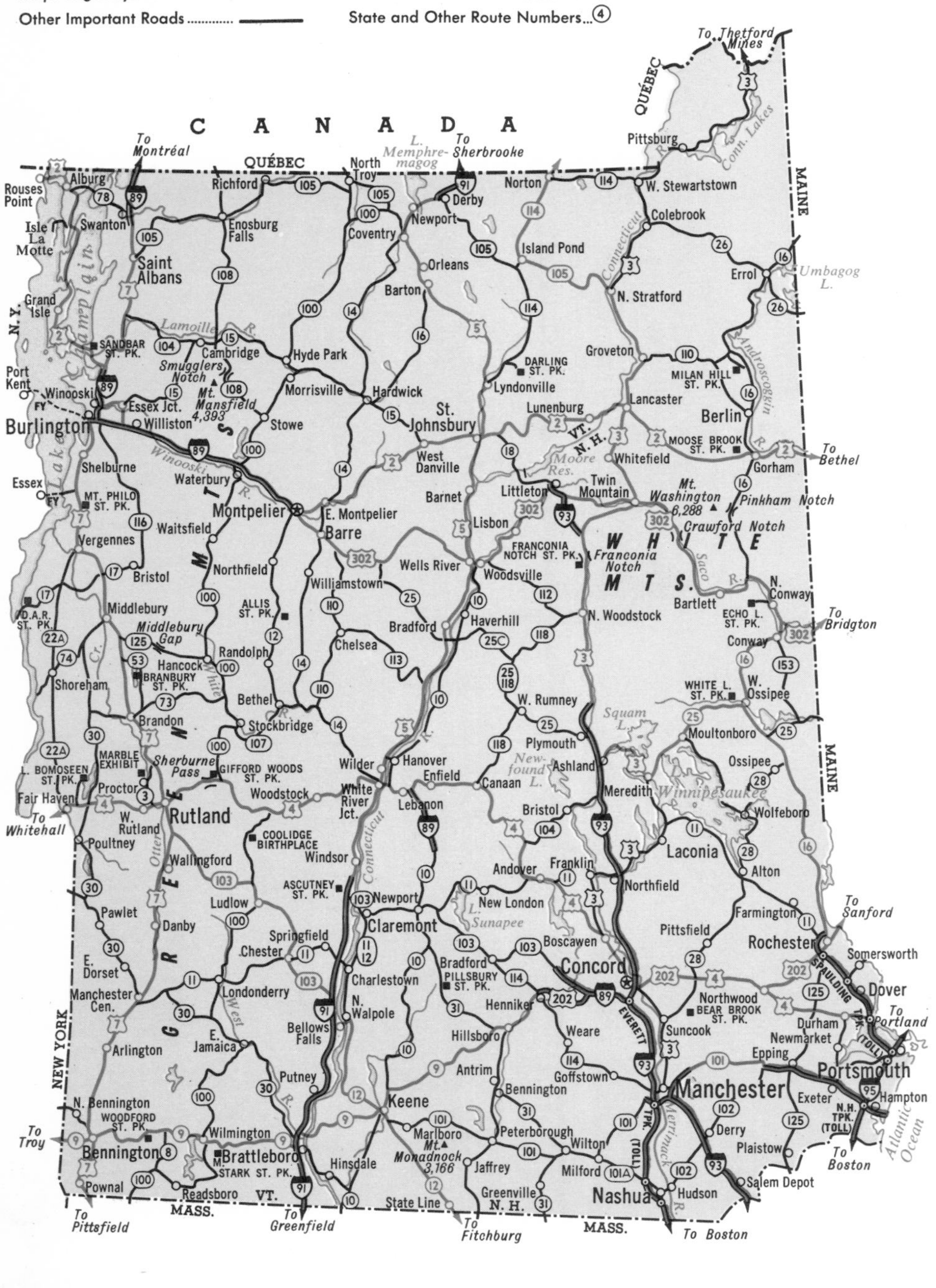

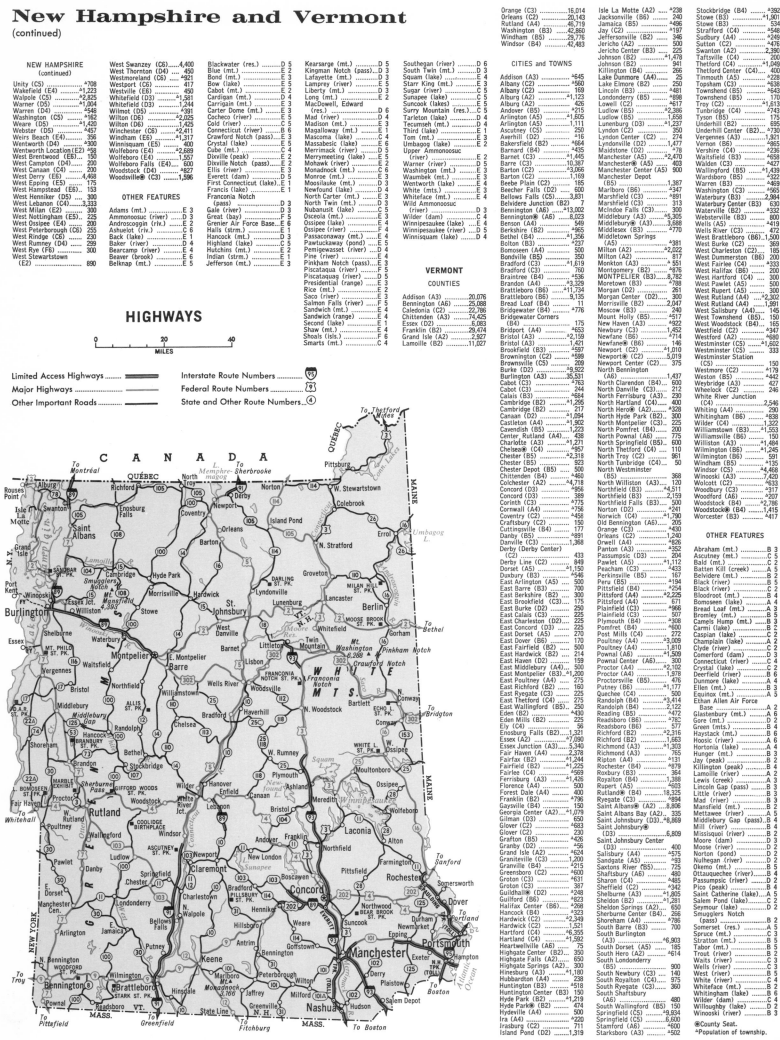

NEW JERSEY

AREA	7,836 sq. mi.
POPULATION	6,774,000
CAPITAL	Trenton
LARGEST CITY	Newark 405,220
HIGHEST POINT	High Point 1,803 ft.
SETTLED IN	1617
ADMITTED TO UNION	December 18, 1787
POPULAR NAME	Garden State
STATE FLOWER	Violet
STATE BIRD	Eastern Goldfinch

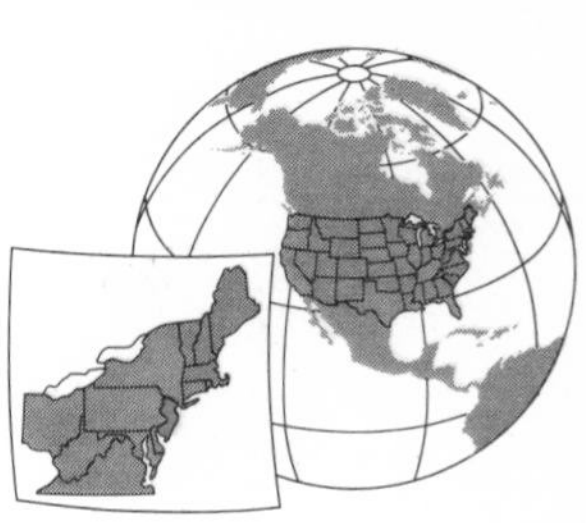

COUNTIES

Atlantic (D5) 160,880
Bergen (E2) 780,255
Burlington (D4) 24,499
Camden (D4) 392,035
Cape May (D5) 48,555
Cumberland (C5) 106,850
Essex (E2) 923,545
Gloucester (C4) 134,840
Hudson (E2) 610,734
Hunterdon (D2) 54,107
Mercer (D3) 266,392
Middlesex (E3) 433,856
Monmouth (E3) 334,401
Morris (D2) 261,620
Ocean (E4) 108,241
Passaic (E1) 406,618
Salem (C4) 58,711
Somerset (D2) 143,913
Sussex (D1) 49,255
Union (E2) 504,255
Warren (C2) 63,220

CITIES and TOWNS

Absecon (D5) 4,320
Adelphia (E3) 500
Allamuchy (D2) 247
Allendale (B1) 4,092
Allenhurst (F3) 795
Allentown (D3) 1,393
Allenwood (E3) 500
Alloway (C4) 950
Alpha (C2) 2,406
Alpine (C1) 921
Andover (D2) 734
Annandale (D2) 600
Arlington (B2) 16,000
Asbury (C2) 350
Asbury Park (F3) 17,366
Ashland (D4) 1,500
Atco (D4) 2,500
Atlantic City (E5) 59.544
Atlantic City (urban area) 124,902
Atlantic Hi'lands (F3)..4,119
Audubon (C4) 10,440
Audubon Park (B3)......1,713
Augusta (D1) 878
Aura (C4) 225
Avalon (D5) 695
Avenel (E2) 10,000
Avon by the Sea (F3)..1,707
Awosting (E1) 144
Baptistown (D2) 350
Barnegat (E4) 1,150
Barnegat Light (E4)..... 287
Barrington (B3) 7,943
Bartley (D2) 500
Basking Ridge (D2) 2,438
Bay Head (E3) 824
Bayonne (B2) 74,215
Bayville (E4) 2,000
Beach Haven (E4) 1,041
Beach Haven Crest (E4) 100
Beach Haven Terr. (E4) 400
Beachwood (E4) 2,765
Beaver Lake (D1) 175
Bedminster (D2) 650
Beesleys Point (D5).... 200
Belford (E3) 6,800
Belle Mead (D3) 650
Belleplain (D5) 450
Belleville (B2) 35,005
Bellmawr (B3) 11,853
Belmar (E3) 5,190
Belvidere◉ (C2) 2,636
Bergenfield (C1) 27,203
Berkeley Hts. (E2)........8,721
Berlin (D4) 3,578
Bernardsville (D2) 5,515
Bevans (D1) 100
Beverly (D3) 3,400
Birmingham (D4) 500
Bivalve (C5) 150
Blackwood (C4) 5,000
Blackwood Terr. (C4)....2,500
Blairstown (C2) 950
Blansingburg (E3) 1,702
Blawenburg (D3) 250
Bloomfield (B2) 51,867
Bloomingdale (E1) 5,293
Bloomsbury (C2) 838
Bogota (B2) 7,965
Boonton (E2) 7,981
Bordentown (D3) 4,974
Bound Brook (D2) 10,263
Bradley Beach (F3)......4,204
Brainards (C2) 350
Branchburg Park (D2)..1,468
Branchville (D1) 963
Brant Beach (E4) 200
Breton Woods (E3)......1,292
Brick Town (E3) 800
Bridgeboro (D3) 900
Bridgeport (C4) 800
Bridgeton◉ (C5) 20,966
Brielle (E3) 2,619
Brigantine (E5) 4,201
Broadway (C2) 300
Brooklawn (B3) 2,504
Brookside (D2) ....
Browns Mills (D4) 1,500
Budd Lake (D2) 1,520
Buena (D4) 3,243
Burlington (D3) 12,687
Butler (E2) 5,414
Buttzville (D2) 375
Caldwell (E2) 6,942
Califon (D2) 777
Camden◉ (C4) 117,159
Canton (C5) 75
Cape May (D6) 4,477
Cape May Court House◉ (D5) 1,749
Cape May Point (D6).... 263
Carlstadt (B2) 6,042
Carneys Point (C4)......1,850
Carpentersville (C2)...... 150
Carteret (E2) 20,502
Cedar Brook (D4) 600
Cedar Grove (B2) 14,603
Cedar Knolls (E2) 1,900
Cedar Run (E4) 260
Cedarville (C5) 1,095
Cedarwood Park (E3)..1,052
Centerton (C4) 150
Changewater (D2) 320
Chatham (E2) 9,517
Chatsworth (D4) 639
Cheesequake (E3) 1,800
Cherry Hill (B3) ......▲31,522
Chesilhurst (D4) 384
Chester (D2) 1,074
Chesterfield (D3) 500
Clark (A3) 12,195
Clarksboro (C4) 2,500
Clarksburg (E3) 800
Clayton (C4) 4,711
Clementon (D4) 3,766
Cliffside Park (F2,....17,642
Cliffwood (E3) 4,000
Clifton (E2) 82,084
Clinton (D2) 1,158
Closter (C1) 7,767
Cold Spring (C6) 100
Colesville (D1) 196
Collingswood (C4) 17,370
Cologne (D4) 600
Colonia (E2) 6,450
Colts Neck (E3) 500
Columbia (C2) 350
Columbus (D3) 650
Convent Station (E2)....1,450
Cookstown (D3) 200
Corbin City (D5) 271
Coytesville (C2) 3,600
Cranberry Lake (D2).... 200
Cranbury (E3) 1,038
Cranford (E2) 26,424
Creamridge (E3) 55
Cresskill (C1) 7,290
Crosswicks (D3) 475
Daretown (C4) 150
Dayton (D3) 750
Deal (F3) 1,889
Deans (D3) 480
Deepwater (C4) 800
Deerfield Street (C4).... 500
Delair (C4) 2,500
Delanco (D3) 4,011
Delaware (C2) 250
Delmont (C5) 390
Demarest (C1) 4,231
Dennisville (D5) 850
Denville (E2) 10,500
Deptford (B4) 3,000
Dias Creek (D5) 500
Dividing Creek (C5) 500
Dorchester (D5) 400
Dorothy (D5) 950
Dover (D2) 13,034
Dumont (F2) 18,882
Dunellen (D2) 6,840
Dutch Neck (D3) 200
East Keansburg (E3)....3,000
East Millstone (D3) 612
East Newark (B2) 1,872
East Orange (B2) 77,259
East Paterson (B2)....19,344
East Rutherford (B2) ..7,769
Eatontown (E3) 10,334
Echo Lake (E1) 300
Edgewater (C2) 4,113
Edgewater Park (D3).... 300
Edison (E2) 44,799
Egg Harbor City (D4)..4,416
Elberon (E3) 990
Eldora (D5) 230
Elizabeth◉ (E2) 107,698
Elmer (C4) 1,505
Elwood (D4) 600
Emerson (B1) 6,849
Englewood (C2) 26,057
Englewood Cliffs (C2). 2,913
English Creek (D5) 600
Englishtown (E3) 1,143
Erlton (B3) 4,800
Essex Fells (B2) 2,174
Estell Manor (D5) 496
Ewan (C4) 300
Fair Haven (E3) 5,678
Fair Lawn (B1) 36,421
Fairfield (A2) 3,310
Fairton (C5) 350
Fairview (C2) 9,399
Fanwood (E2) 7,963
Far Hills (D2) 702
Farmingdale (E3) 959
Fieldsboro (D3) 583
Finesville (C2) 274
Flagtown (D2) 400
Flanders (D2) 750
Flatbrookville (D1) 50
Flemington◉ (D2) 3,232
Florence (D3) 4,215
Florham Park (E2)......7,222
Folsom (D4) 482
Fords (E2) 16,500
Forked River (E4) 25
Fort Lee (C2) 21,815
Fortescue (C5) 300
Franklin (D1) 3,624
Franklin Lakes (B1) 3,316
Franklin Park (D3)....... 715
Franklinville (C4) 1,226
Freehold◉ (E3) 9,140
Frenchtown (C2) 1,340
Garfield (E2) 29,253
Garwood (E2) 5,426
Gibbsboro (D4) 2,141
Gibbstown (C4) 2,820
Gilford Park (E4) 1,560
Gillette (E2) 1,300
Gladstone-Peapack (D2) 1,804
Glassboro (C4) 10,253
Glasser (D2) 300
Glen Gardner (D2) 787
Glen Ridge (B2) 8,322
Glen Rock (B1) 12,896
Glendora (B4) 4,750

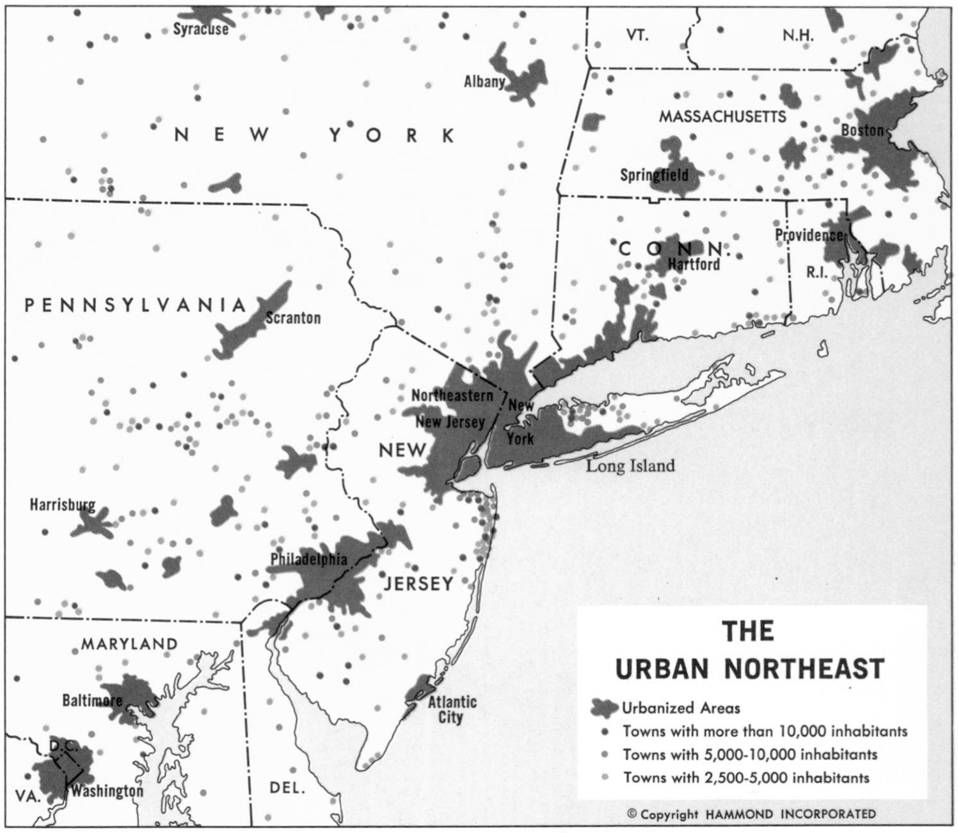
Syracuse
VT.
N.H.
Albany
NEW YORK
MASSACHUSETTS
Boston
Springfield
CONN.
Hartford
Providence
R.I.
PENNSYLVANIA
Scranton
Northeastern New Jersey
New York
Long Island
NEW JERSEY
Harrisburg
Philadelphia
MARYLAND
Baltimore
Atlantic City
D.C.
Washington
VA.
DEL.
THE URBAN NORTHEAST
Urbanized Areas
Towns with more than 10,000 inhabitants
Towns with 5,000-10,000 inhabitants
Towns with 2,500-5,000 inhabitants

AGRICULTURE, INDUSTRY and RESOURCES

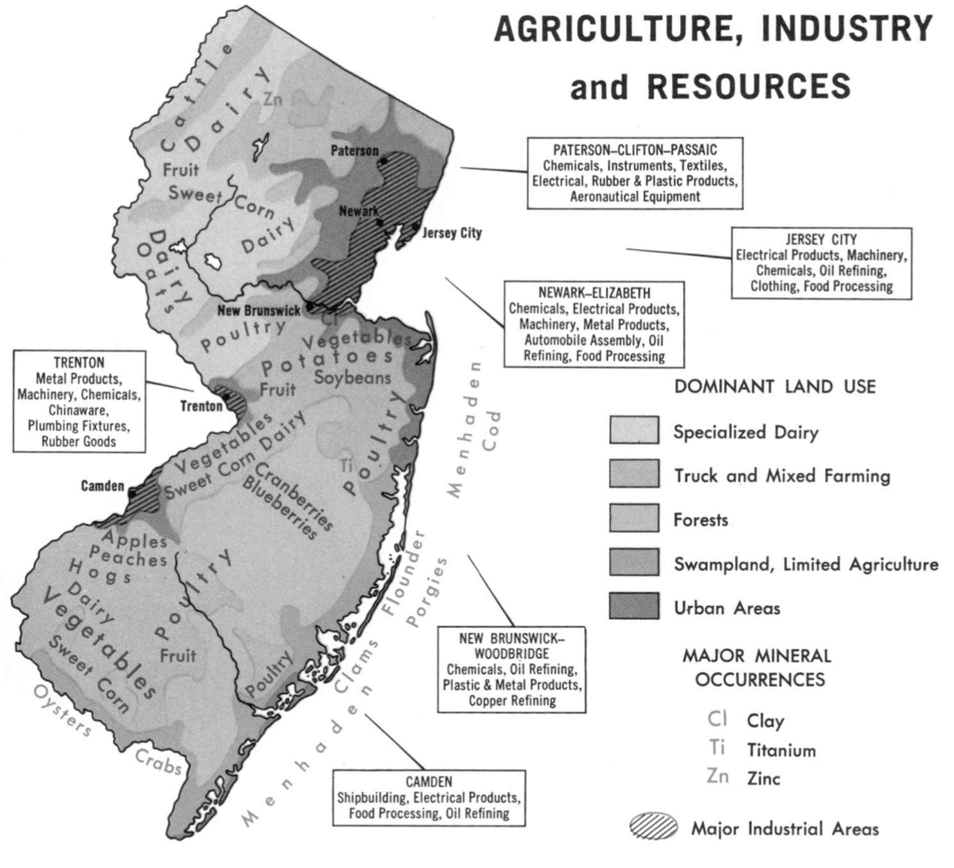
Cattle
Dairy
Zn
Fruit
Sweet Corn
Dairy
Dairy
Oats
Paterson
Newark
Jersey City
New Brunswick
Poultry
Vegetables
Potatoes
Soybeans
Fruit
Trenton
Vegetables
Sweet Corn
Dairy
Cranberries
Blueberries
Ti
Poultry
Camden
Apples
Peaches
Hogs
Dairy
Vegetables
Sweet Corn
Fruit
Poultry
Poultry
Oysters
Crabs
Clams
Menhaden
Flounder
Porgies
Menhaden
Cod
PATERSON-CLIFTON-PASSAIC
Chemicals, Instruments, Textiles, Electrical, Rubber & Plastic Products, Aeronautical Equipment
JERSEY CITY
Electrical Products, Machinery, Chemicals, Oil Refining, Clothing, Food Processing
NEWARK-ELIZABETH
Chemicals, Electrical Products, Machinery, Metal Products, Automobile Assembly, Oil Refining, Food Processing
TRENTON
Metal Products, Machinery, Chemicals, Chinaware, Plumbing Fixtures, Rubber Goods
NEW BRUNSWICK-WOODBRIDGE
Chemicals, Oil Refining, Plastic & Metal Products, Copper Refining
CAMDEN
Shipbuilding, Electrical Products, Food Processing, Oil Refining
DOMINANT LAND USE
Specialized Dairy
Truck and Mixed Farming
Forests
Swampland, Limited Agriculture
Urban Areas
MAJOR MINERAL OCCURRENCES
Cl Clay
Ti Titanium
Zn Zinc
Major Industrial Areas

Glenwood (D1) 450
Gloucester City (C4)..15,511
Goshen (D5) 350
Great Meadows (D2).... 825
Green Bank (D4) 200
Green Creek (D5) 950
Green Pond (E1) 250
Green Village (D2) 800
Greendell (D2) 75
Greenwich (C5) 950
Grenloch (C4) 850
Greystone Park (D2)....6,400
Groveville (D3) 700
Guttenberg (C2) 5,118
Hackensack◉ (F2) 30,521
Hackettstown (D2) 5,276
Haddon Heights (C4)....9,260
Haddonfield (D4) 13,201
Hainesburg (C2) 100
Hainesport (D4) 1,600
Hainesville (D1) 100
Haledon (B1) 6,161
Haleyville (C5) 120
Hamburg (D1) 1,532
Hamilton Square (D3)..3,500
Hammonton (D4) 9,854
Hampton (D2) 1,135
Hancocks Bridge (C4)... 500
Hanover (E2) 1,500
Harbourton (D3) 110
Hardingville (C4) 165
Harlingen (D3) 300
Harrington Park (C1)..3,581
Harrison (B2) 11,743
Harrisonville (C4) 190
Hartford (D4) 500
Harvey Cedars (E4) 134
Hasbrouck Hts. (B2)..13,046
Haskell (A1) 3,000
Haworth (C1) 3,215
Hawthorne (E2) 17,735
Hazlet (E3) 12,000
Heislerville (D5) 504
Helmetta (E3) 779
Hewitt (E1) 861
Hi-Nella (B4) 474
Hibernia (E2) 350
High Bridge (D2) 2,148
Highland Park (E2)....11,049
Highlands (F3) 3,536
Hightstown (D3) 4,317
Hillcrest (C2) 1,922
Hillsdale (E2) 8,734
Hillside (B2) 22,304
Hoboken (C2) 48,441
Ho-Ho-Kus (B1) 3,988
Holmdel (E3) 250
Holmeson (E3) 160
Hopatcong (D2) 3,391
Hope (D2) 750
Hopewell (D3) 1,928
Hornerstown (E3) 180
Huntington (C2) 1,879
Imlaystown (D3) 252
Interlaken (E3) 1,168
Iona (C4) 500
Ironia (D2) 900
Irvington (B2) 59,379
Iselin (E2) 11,000
Island Heights (E4)....1,150
Jackson (E3) ....▲5,939
Jacobstown (D3) 150
Jamesburg (E3) 2,853
Jersey City◉ (F2) 276,101
Jobstown (D3) 250
Johnsonburg (D2) 375
Juliustown (D3) 425
Jutland (D2) 150
Keansburg (E3) 6,854
Kearny (B2) 37,472
Keasbey (E2) 1,200
Kenilworth (E2) 8,379
Kenvil (D2) 2,200
Keswick Grove (E4) 150
Keyport (E3) 6,440
Kingston (D3) 900
Kinnelon (E2) 4,431
Kirkwood (B4) 900
Lafayette (D1) 950
Lake Hiawatha (E2)......5,000
Lake Hopatcong (D2)...3,000
Lake Mohawk (D1) 4,647
Lakehurst (E3) 2,780
Lakewood (E3) 13,004
Lambertville (D3) 4,269
Lamington (D2) 70
Landing (D2) 1,500
Landisville (D4) 1,500
Lanoka Harbor (E4).... 555
Laurel Springs (B4)....2,028
Laurence Harbor (E3)..3,000
Lavallette (E4) 832
Lawnside (B3) 2,155
Lawrenceville (D3) 1,950
Layton (D1) 250
Lebanon (D2) 880
Ledgewood (D2) 800
Leeds Point (E4) 200
Leesburg (D5) 600
Leonardo (E3) 3,200
Leonia (C2) 8,384
Liberty Corner (D2)....1,400
Lincoln Park (A1) 6,048
Lincroft (E3) 2,650
Linden (E2) 39,931
Lindenwold (B4) 7,335
Linwood (D5) 3,847
Little Falls (E2) 9,730
Little Ferry (B2) 6,175
Little Silver (F3) 5,202
Little York (C2) 125
Livingston (E2) 23,124
Loch Arbour ‡(F3)....... 297
Lodi (B2) 23,502
Long Branch (F3).......26,228
Long Valley (D2) 1,220
Longport (D5) 1,077
Lower Bank (E4) 537
Lumberton (D4) 900
Lyndhurst (B2) 21,867
Lyons (D2) 2,750
Madison (E2) 15,122
Magnolia (C4) 4,199
Mahwah (E1) 3,800
Malaga (C4) 650
Manahawkin (E4) 1,200
Manalapan (E3) ....▲3,990
Manasquan (E3) 4,022
Mantoloking (E3) 160
Mantua (C4) 1,800
Manville (D2) 10,995
Maple Shade (D4) 12,947
Maplewood (E2) 23,977
Marcella (E2) 500
Margate City (E5) 9,474
Marlboro (E3) 618
Marlton (D4) 950
Marmora (D5) 500
Martinsville (D2) 2,700
Masonville (D4) 850
Matawan (E3) 5,097
Mauricetown (D5) 362
Mayetta (E4) 150
Mays Landing◉ (D5)...1,404
Maywood (B2) 11,460
McAfee (D1) 800
McKee City (D5) 700
Medford (D4) 1,480
Medford Lakes (D4).....2,876
Mendham (D2) 2,371
Menlo Park (E2) 6,200
Mercerville (D3) 5,000
Merchantville (B3) 4,075
Metuchen (E2) 14,041
Mickleton (C4) 900
Middle Valley (D2) 225
Middlebush (D3) 882
Middlesex (E2) 10,520
Middletown (E3) 39,675
Middleville (D1) 85
Midland Park (B1)......7,543
Midvale (A1) 2,000
Milford (C2) 1,114
Millburn (E2) 18,799
Millington (D2) 1,182
Millstone (D2) 409
Milltown (E3) 5,435
Millville (C5) 19,096
Milmay (D5) 456
Milton (D1) 1,100

(continued on following page)

New Jersey
(continued)

Mine Hill (D2) 2,297
Minotola (D4) 950
Mizpah (D5) 875
Monmouth Beach (F3)..1,363
Monmouth Jct. (D3)....1,500
Monroe (D1) 225
Monroeville (C4) 170
Montague (D1) 650
Montclair (E2) 43,129
Montvale (E1) 3,699
Montville (E2) 2,000
Moonachie (B2) 3,052
Moorestown (D4) 9,175
Morganville (E3) 650
Morris Plains (D2) 4,703
Morristown◉ (D2) 17,712
Mount Arlington (D2)...1,246
Mount Ephraim (B3)....5,447
Mount Freedom (D2)....1,328
Mount Holly◉ (D4).....13,271
Mount Hope (D2) 1,500
Mount Royal (C4) 850
Mountain Lakes (E2)....4,037
Mountain View (B2).....5,000
Mountainside (E2)........6,325
Mullica Hill (C4) 900
Mystic Islands (E4)......2,500
National Park (B3)......3,380
Navesink (E3) 1,400
Neptune (E3) 21,487
Neptune City (E3)........4,013
Neshanic (D3) 500
Netcong (D2) 2,765
New Brunswick◉
(E3) 40,139
New Egypt (E3) 1,737
New Gretna (E4) 800
New Hampton (D2) 100
New Lisbon (D4) 400
New Milford (B1) 18,810
New Monmouth (E3).... 700
New Providence (E2)..10,243
New Sharon (D3) 50
New Shrewsbury (E3)...7,313
New Vernon (D2) 1,100
Newark◉ (E2) 405,220
Newfield (D4) 1,299
Newfoundland (D1) 1,130
Newport (C5) 650
Newton◉ (D1) 6,563
Newtonville (D4) 750
Nixon (E2) 6,000
Norma (C4) 800
Normandy Beach (E3).. 50
North Arlington (B2)..17,477
North Bergen (B2)......42,387
North Branch (D2) 600
North Caldwell (B2).....4,163
North Cape May (C6)...1,650
North Haledon (B1)......6,026
North Plainfield (E2)..16,993
North Wildwood (D6)...3,598
Northfield (D5) 5,849
Northvale (F1) 2,892
Norwood (C1) 2,852
Nutley (B2) 29,513
Oak Ridge (E1) 600
Oakhurst (E3) 4,374
Oakland (E1) 9,446
Oaklyn (B3) 4,778
Ocean City (D5) 7,618
Ocean Gate (E4) 706
Ocean Grove (F3) 5,000
Ocean View (D5) 350
Oceanport (E3) 4,937
Oceanville (D5) 950
Ogdensburg (D1) 1,212
Old Bridge (E3) 7,000
Old Tappan (C1) 2,330
Oldwick (D2) 600
Oradell (B1) 7,487
Orange (B2) 35,789
Osbornsville (E3) 1,500
Oxford (C2) ....^1,657
Packanack Lake (B1)..3,000
Palermo (D5) 375
Palisades Park (C2)....11,943
Palmyra (D4) 7,036
Paramus (B1) 23,238
Park Ridge (B1) 6,389
Parkertown (E4) 425
Parlin (E3) 8,000
Parsippany (E2) 25,557
Passaic (E2) 53,963
Paterson◉ (E2) 143,663
Pattenburg (C2) 462
Paulsboro (C4) 8,121
Peapack-Gladstone
(D2) 1,804
Pedricktown (C4) 700
Pemberton (D4) 1,250
Pennington (D3) 2,063
Penns Grove (C4) 6,176
Pennsauken (B3) 33,771
Pennsville (C4) 3,500
Pequannock (E2) 3,700
Perrineville (E3) 491
Perth Amboy (E2) 38,007
Petersburg (D5) 350
Phillipsburg (C2) 18,502
Pine Beach (E4) 985
Pine Brook (E2) 1,200
Pine Hill (D4) 3,939
Pine Valley (D4) 20
Piscataway (D2) 5,700
Pitman (C4) 8,644
Pittstown (C2) 200
Plainfield (E2) 45,330
Plainsboro (D3) 1,118
Pleasant Grove (D2).... 75
Pleasantville (D5) 15,172
Pluckemin (D2) 350
Point Pleasant (E3)....10,182
Point Pleasant Beach
‡(E3) 3,873
Pomona (D5) 900
Pompton Lakes (A1).....9,445
Pompton Plains (E2)....7,150
Port Elizabeth (D5)...... 974
Port Monmouth (E3)....3,500
Port Morris (D2) 600
Port Murray (D2) 750
Port Norris (C5) 1,789
Port Reading (E2) 4,200
Port Republic (D4) 561
Pottersville (D2) 350
Princeton (D3) 11,890
Princeton Jct. (D3)....... 950
Prospect Park (E2)......5,201
Quakertown (D2) 245
Quinton (C4) 700
Rahway (E2) 27,699
Ralston (D2) 500
Ramsey (E1) 9,527
Rancocas (D3) 500
Raritan (D2) 6,137
Readington (D2) 500
Reaville (D3) 206
Red Bank (E3) 12,482
Richland (D5) 800
Richwood (C4) 450
Ridgefield (B2) 10,788
Ridgefield Park (F2)...12,701
Ridgewood (E2) 25,391
Riegelsville (C2) 400
Ringoes (D3) 500
Ringwood (E1) 4,182
Rio Grande (D5) 900
River Edge (B1) 13,264
Riverdale (E2) 2,596
Riverside (D3) 8,474
Riverton (D3) 3,324
Roadstown (C5) 225
Robbinsville (D3) 2,038
Rochelle Park (B2)......6,119
Rockaway (D2) 5,413
Rockleigh (C1) 430
Rocky Hill (D3) 528
Roebling (D3) 3,272
Roosevelt (E3) 764
Roseland (A2) 2,804
Roselle (B2) 21,032
Roselle Park (A2) 12,546
Rosemont (D3) 149
Rosenhayn (C5) 450
Rumson (F3) 6,405
Runnemede (C4) 8,396
Rutherford (B2) 20,473
Saddle Brook (B1)......13,834
Saddle River (B1).........1,776
Salem◉ (C4) 8,941
Sand Brook (D3) 150
Sayreville (E3) 22,553
Schooleys Mountain
(D2) 525
Scotch Plains (E2)......18,491
Sea Bright (F3) 1,138
Sea Girt (E3) 1,798
Sea Isle City (D5) 1,393
Seabrook (C5) 1,798
Seaside Heights (E4).... 954
Seaside Park (E4) 1,054
Secaucus (B2) 12,154
Sergeantsville (D3) 230
Sewaren (E2) 2,000
Sewell (C4) 975
Sharptown (C4) 200
Shiloh (C5) 554
Ship Bottom (E4) 717
Short Hills (E2) 6,500
Shrewsbury (E3) 3,222
Sicklerville (D4) 950
Singac (B2) 1,200
Skillman (D3) 3,500
Smithburg (E3) 25
Smiths Mills (E1) 250
Smithville (D4) 300
Somerdale (D4) 4,839
Somers Point (D5) 4,504
Somerville◉ (D2) 12,458
South Amboy (E3) 8,422
South Belmar (E3) 1,537
South Bound Brook
(E2) 3,626
South Branch (D2) 600
South Dennis (D5) 300
South Orange (A2).....16,175
South Plainfield (E2)..17,879
South River (E3) 13,397
South Seaville (D5) 90
South Toms River (E4) 1,603
Southard (E3) 1,500
Sparta (D1) 3,300
Sperry Springs (D2) 800
Spotswood (E3) 5,788
Spring Lake (F3) 2,922
Spring Lake Heights
(E3) 3,309
Springfield (E2) 14,467
Squankum (E3) 300
Staffordville (E4) 250
Stanhope (D2) 1,814
Stanton (D2) 350
Steelmanville (D5) 500
Stephensburg (D2) 100
Stewartsville (C2) 950
Stillwater (D1) 375
Stirling (E2) 1,382
Stockholm (D1) 800
Stockton (D3) 520
Stone Harbor (D5) 834
Stratford (C4) 4,308
Strathmere (D5) 75
Succasunna (D2) 2,500
Summit (E2) 23,677
Surf City (E4) 419
Sussex (D1) 1,656
Swartswood (D1) 125
Swedesboro (C4) 2,449
Tabor (E2) 1,320
Tavistock (B3) 10
Teaneck (B2) 42,085
Tenafly (F2) 14,264
Tennent (E3) 200
Teterboro (B2) 22
Thorofare (B4) 1,850
Three Bridges (D2) 700
Titusville (D3) 2,500
Toms River◉ (E4) 6,062
Totowa (B1) 10,897
Towaco (E2) 1,500
Townsends Inlet (D5)... 250
Tranquility (D2) 150
TRENTON◉ (D3) 114,167
Trenton (urban
area) 242,401
Tuckahoe (D5) 800
Tuckerton (E4) 1,536
Union (E2) 51,499
Union Beach (E3) 5,862
Union City (C2) 52,180
Upper Macopin (E1)..... 300
Upper Saddle River
(B1) 3,570
Vail (C2) 50
Vail Homes (E3) 1,204
Van Hiseville (E3) 250
Vauxhall (A2) 9,000
Ventnor City (E5) 8,688
Vernon (E1) 400
Verona (E2) 13,782
Victory Gardens ‡(D2)..1,085
Vienna (D2) 275
Villas (D5) 2,085
Vincentown (D4) 700
Vineland (C5) 37,685
Waldwick (E1) 10,495
Wallington (B2) 9,261
Wallpack Center (D1)... 210
Wanamassa (E3) 3,928
Wanaque (B1) 7,126
Waretown (E4) 921
Washington (D2) 5,723
Watchung (E2) 3,312
Waterford Works (D4)..1,200
Wayne (A1) 29,353
Weehawken (C2) 13,504
Wenonah (C4) 2,100
West Belmar (E3) 2,511
West Berlin (D4) 3,500
West Caldwell (A2) 8,314
West Cape May (D6)....1,030
West Creek (E4) 753
West Englewood (C2)..16,000
West Long Branch
(F3) 5,337
West Milford (E1) 2,500
West New York (C2)...35,547
West Orange (A2).......39,895
West Paterson (B2) 7,602
West Portal (D2) 200
West Trenton (D3) 4,500
West Wildwood (D6).... 207
Westfield (E2) 31,447
Westville (C4) 4,951
Westwood (B1) 9,046
Wharton (D2) 5,006
Whippany (E2) 7,500
White House Sta. (D2) 750
Whitehouse (D2) 500
Whitesbog (E4) 200
Whitesboro (D5) 800
Whitesville (E3) 450
Whiting (E4) 450
Wickatunk (E3) 500
Wildwood (D6) 4,690
Wildwood Crest (D6)....3,011
Williamstown (D4) 2,722
Willingboro (D3) 11,861
Windsor (D3) 400
Winfield (B3) 2,459
Winslow (D4) 900
Wood-Lynne (B3) 3,128
Wood-Ridge (B2) 7,964
Woodbine (D5) 2,823
Woodbridge (E2) 78,846
Woodbury◉ (C4) 12,453
Woodbury Hgts. (B4)...1,723
Woodcliff Lake (B1)....2,742
Woodport (D2) 2,000
Woodstown (C4) 2,942
Wrightstown (D3) 4,846
Wyckoff (E2) 11,205
Yardville (D3) 1,600
Yorktown (C4) 100
Zarephath (D2) 200
Zion (D3) 75

OTHER FEATURES

Absecon (inlet) ....E 5
Alloways (creek) ....C 4
Arthur Kill (strait) ......B 3
Atlantic Highlands ....E 3
Barnegat (bay) ....E 4
Barnegat (inlet) ....E 4
Batsto (river) ....D 4
Bayonne Naval Base .....B 2
Beach Haven (inlet) ......E 4
Beaver (brook) ....C 2
Ben Davis (point) ....C 5
Big Flat (brook) ....D 1
Big Timber (creek) ....C 4
Boonton (res.) ....E 2
Brigantine (inlet) ....E 5
Budd (lake) ....D 2
Canistear (res.) ....E 1
Cape May Coast Guard
Center ....D 6
Cedar (creek) ....E 4
Clinton (res.) ....E 1
Cohansey (river) ....C 5
Cold Spring (inlet) ......D 6
Cooper (river) ....B 3
Corson (inlet) ....D 5
Crosswicks (creek) ....D 3
Culvers (lake) ....D 1
Delaware (bay) ....C 5
Delaware (river) ....D 3
Dix, Fort ....D 3
Earle Naval Amm. Dep. E 3
Echo (lake) ....E 1
Edison Lab. Nat'l Mon. A 2
Egg Island (point) ....C 5
Fort Dix ....D 3
Fort Hancock ....F 3
Fort Monmouth ....E 3
Great (bay) ....E 4
Great Egg Harbor (inlet) E 5
Great Egg Harbor (river) D 4
Greenwood (lake) ....E 1
Hackensack (river) ....F 1
Hancock, Fort ....F 3
Hereford (inlet) ....D 5
High Point (mt.) ....D 1
Hopatcong (lake) ....D 2
Hudson (river) ....C 1
Island (beach) ....E 4
Kill Van Kull (strait) ....B 2
Kittatinny (mts.) ....D 1
Lakehurst N.A.S. ....E 3
Lamington (river) ....D 2
Landing (creek) ....D 4
Little Egg (harbor) ....E 4
Little Egg (inlet) ....E 5
Lockatong (creek) ....C 3
Long (beach) ....E 4
Lower New York (bay)...E 2
Manasquan (river) ....E 3
Manumuskin (river) ......D 5
May (cape) ....C 6
Maurice (river) ....C 4
McGuire A.F.B. ....D 3
Metedeconk (river) ....E 3
Mill (creek) ....E 4
Millstone (river) ....D 3
Mohawk (lake) ....D 1
Monmouth, Fort ....E 3
Morristown Nat'l Park ..D 2
Mullica (river) ....D 4
Musconetcong (river) ....C 2
Narrows, The (strait) ....E 2
Navesink (river) ....E 3
Newark (bay) ....B 2
Newark Airport ....B 2
Oak Ridge (res.) ....D 1
Oldmans (creek) ....C 4
Oradell (res.) ....B 1
Oswego (river) ....E 4
Owassa (lake) ....D 1
Palisades ....C 1
Passaic (river) ....E 2
Paulins Kill (river) ......D 1
Pennsauken (creek) ......B 3
Pequest (river) ....D 2
Picatinny Arsenal ....D 2
Pines (lake) ....B 1
Pohatcong (creek) ....C 2
Pompton (lakes) ....B 1
Raccoon (creek) ....C 4
Ramapo (river) ....E 1
Rancocas (creek) ....D 3
Raritan (bay) ....E 3
Raritan (river) ....D 2
Raritan Arsenal ....E 3
Ridgeway Branch, Toms
(river) ....E 3
Saddle (river) ....B 1
Salem (river) ....C 4
Sandy Hook (spit) ....F 3
Shoal Branch, Wading
(river) ....D 4
Stony (brook) ....D 3
Stow (creek) ....C 5
Swartswood (lake) ....D 1
Tocks Island Nat'l
Recreation Area ....C 1
Toms (river) ....E 3
Townsend (inlet) ....D 5
Tuckahoe (river) ....D 5
Union (lake) ....C 5
Upper New York (bay)..E 2
Wading (river) ....D 4
Wallkill (river) ....D 1
Wanaque (res.) ....E 1
Wawayanda (lake) ....E 1
Yellow (brook) ....E 3

◉County Seat.
^Population of township.
‡Name not on map.

TOPOGRAPHY

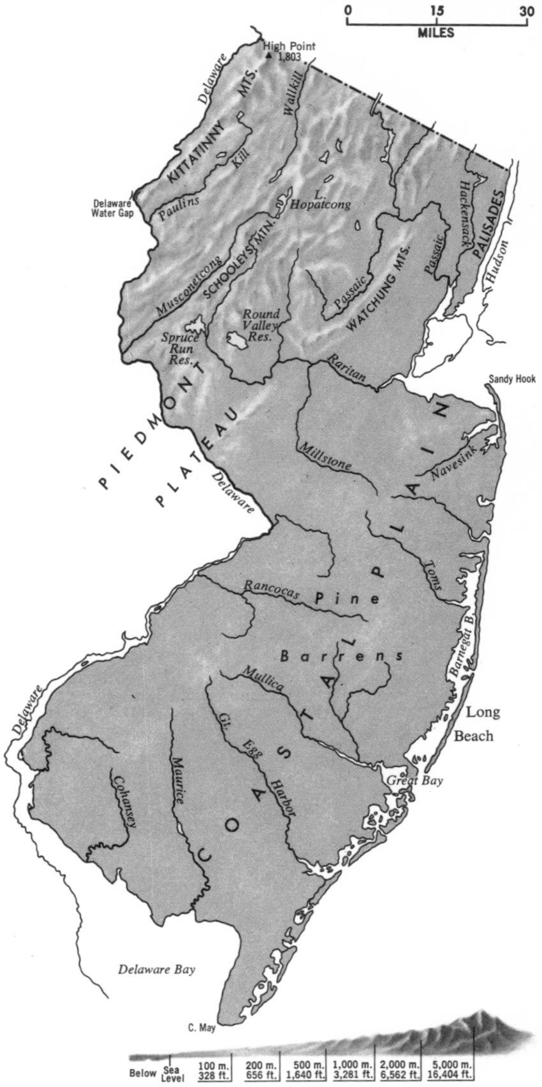

0 15 30
MILES
High Point 1,803
Delaware
KITTATINNY MTS.
Wallkill
Paulins Kill
Delaware Water Gap
L. Hopatcong
SCHOOLEYS MTN.
Musconetcong
Passaic
WATCHUNG MTS.
Hackensack
PALISADES
Hudson
Round Valley Res.
Spruce Run Res.
Raritan
Sandy Hook
PIEDMONT
PLATEAU
Millstone
Navesink
Delaware
COASTAL PLAIN
Rancocas
Pine
Barrens
Toms
Barnegat B.
Mullica
Long Beach
Gt. Egg Harbor
Great Bay
Maurice
Cohansey
Delaware Bay
C. May
Below Sea Level
100 m. 328 ft.
200 m. 656 ft.
500 m. 1,640 ft.
1,000 m. 3,281 ft.
2,000 m. 6,562 ft.
5,000 m. 16,404 ft.

HIGHWAYS

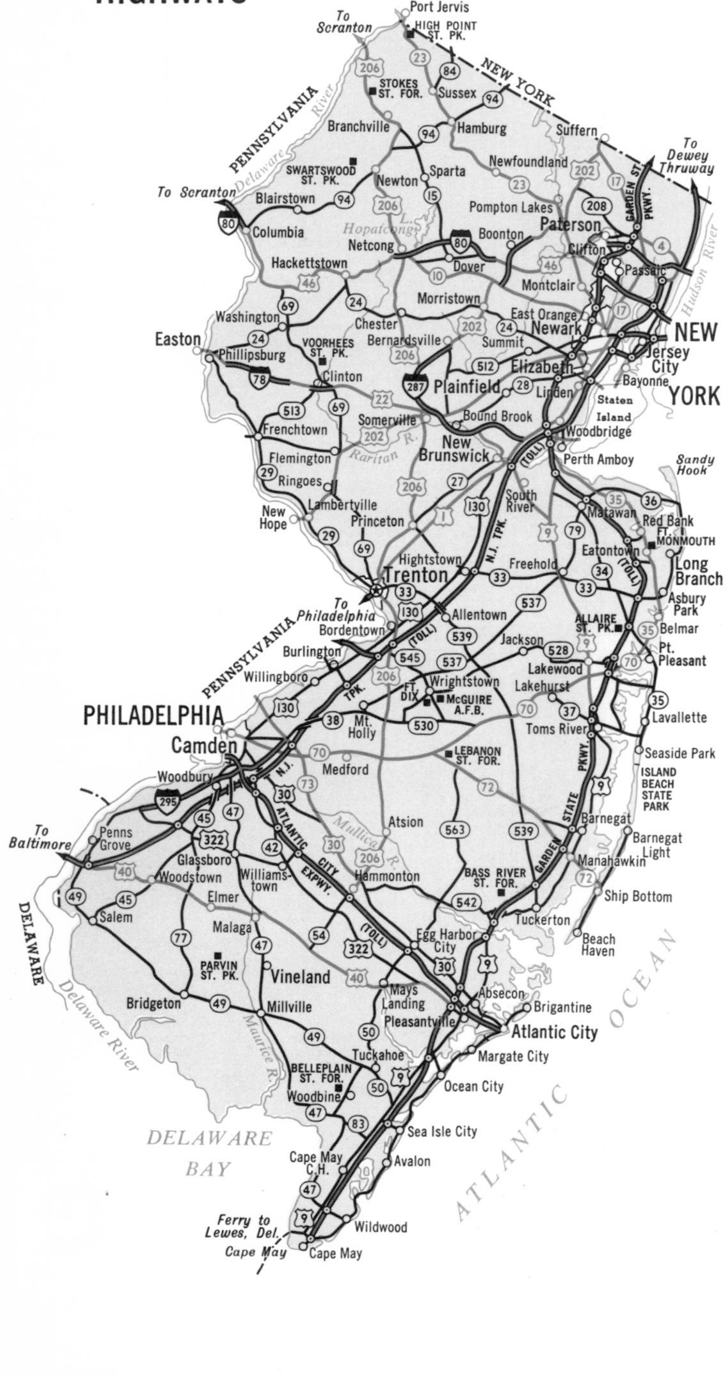

To Scranton
Port Jervis
HIGH POINT ST. PK.
STOKES ST. FOR.
NEW YORK
PENNSYLVANIA
Sussex
Branchville
Hamburg
Suffern
To Dewey Thruway
SWARTSWOOD ST. PK.
Newton
Sparta
Newfoundland
To Scranton
Blairstown
Pompton Lakes
Paterson
GARDEN ST. PKWY.
Columbia
Hopatcong
Netcong
Boonton
Clifton
Passaic
Hackettstown
Dover
Montclair
Hudson River
Morristown
East Orange
Newark
NEW
Washington
Chester
Bernardsville
Summit
Jersey City
Easton
Phillipsburg
VOORHEES ST. PK.
Elizabeth
Bayonne
Clinton
Plainfield
Linden
Staten Island
YORK
Somerville
Bound Brook
Frenchtown
Woodbridge
New Brunswick
Flemington
Perth Amboy
Sandy Hook
Ringoes
Raritan R.
South River
Matawan
New Hope
Lambertville
Red Bank
FT. MONMOUTH
Princeton
Eatontown
Long Branch
Hightstown
Freehold
Trenton
Asbury Park
To Philadelphia
Bordentown
Allentown
ALLAIRE ST. PK.
Belmar
Burlington
Jackson
Pt. Pleasant
Willingboro
Lakewood
Wrightstown
Lakehurst
PHILADELPHIA
FT. DIX
McGUIRE A.F.B.
Lavallette
Camden
Mt. Holly
Toms River
LEBANON ST. FOR.
Seaside Park
Medford
Woodbury
ISLAND BEACH STATE PARK
To Baltimore
Penns Grove
Glassboro
Barnegat
Woodstown
Williamstown
Atsion
Hammonton
Barnegat Light
Salem
Elmer
BASS RIVER ST. FOR.
Manahawkin
Ship Bottom
Malaga
PARVIN ST. PK.
Vineland
Egg Harbor City
Tuckerton
Beach Haven
DELAWARE
Bridgeton
Millville
Mays Landing
Absecon
Brigantine
Pleasantville
Atlantic City
Delaware River
Maurice R.
Tuckahoe
Margate City
BELLEPLAIN ST. FOR.
Ocean City
Woodbine
ATLANTIC OCEAN
DELAWARE BAY
Sea Isle City
Cape May C.H.
Avalon
Ferry to Lewes, Del.
Wildwood
Cape May

0 20 40
MILES

Limited Access Highways ....
Major Highways ....
Other Important Roads ....
Interstate Route Numbers .... (95)
Federal Route Numbers .... (9)
State and Other Route Numbers... (4)

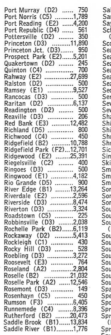

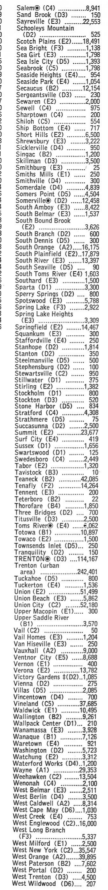

NEW JERSEY

SCALE OF MILES

State Capitals ⊛   Canals

County Seats ⊙

Copyright by C.S. HAMMOND & CO., N.Y.

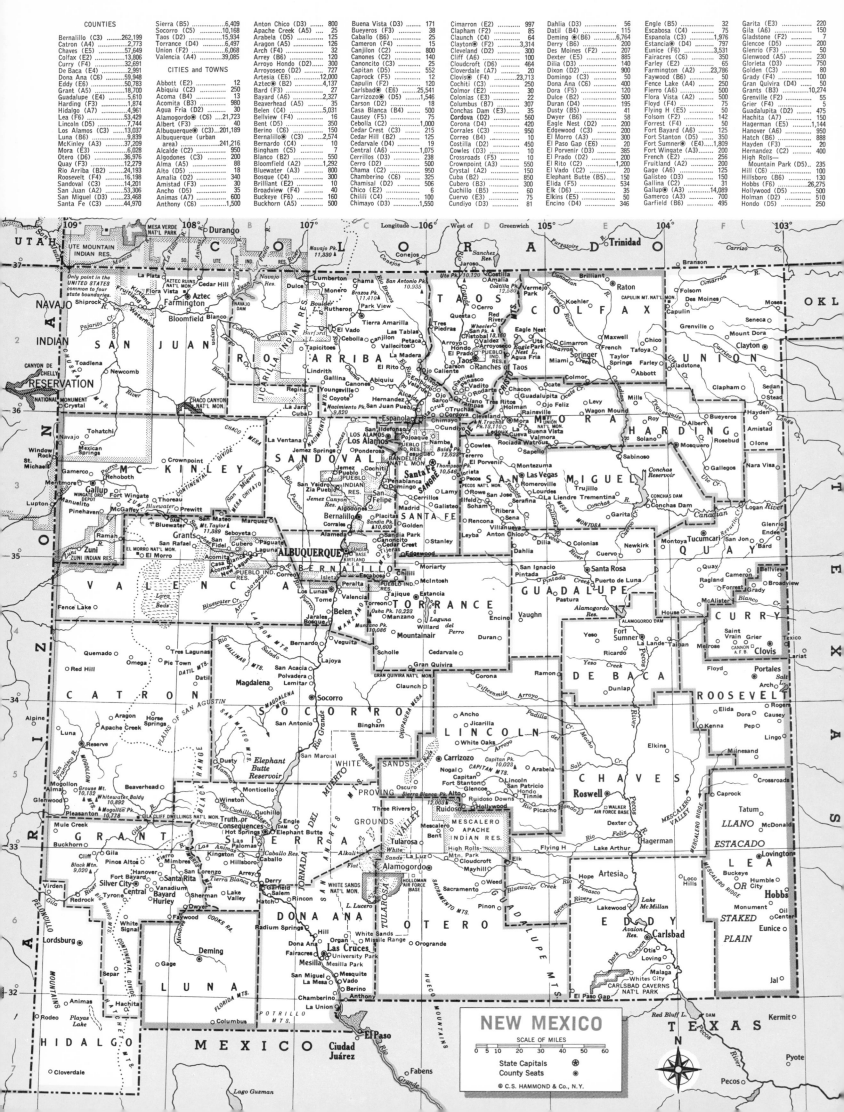

NEW MEXICO

SCALE OF MILES

0 5 10 20 30 40 50 60

⊛ State Capitals
⊙ County Seats

© C.S. Hammond & Co., N.Y.

NEW MEXICO

AREA	121,666 sq. mi.
POPULATION	1,029,000
CAPITAL	Santa Fe
LARGEST CITY	Albuquerque 201,189
HIGHEST POINT	Wheeler Pk. 13,160 ft.
SETTLED IN	1605
ADMITTED TO UNION	January 6, 1912
POPULAR NAME	Land of Enchantment
STATE FLOWER	Yucca
STATE BIRD	Road Runner

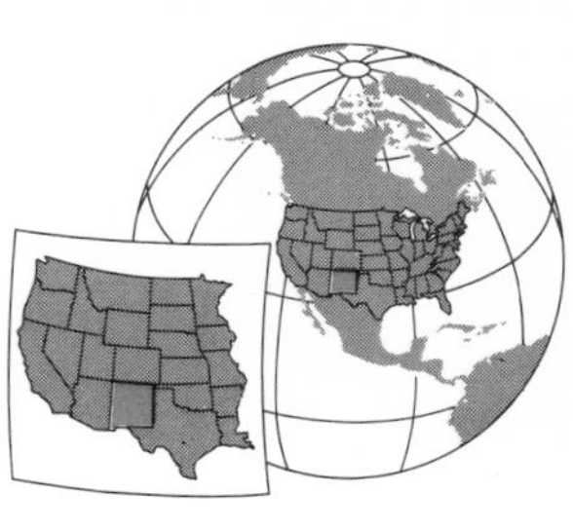

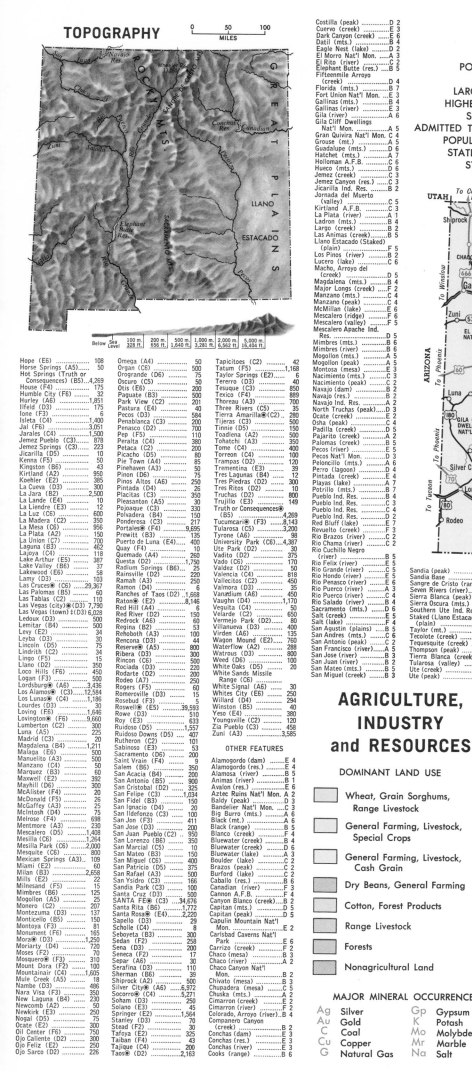

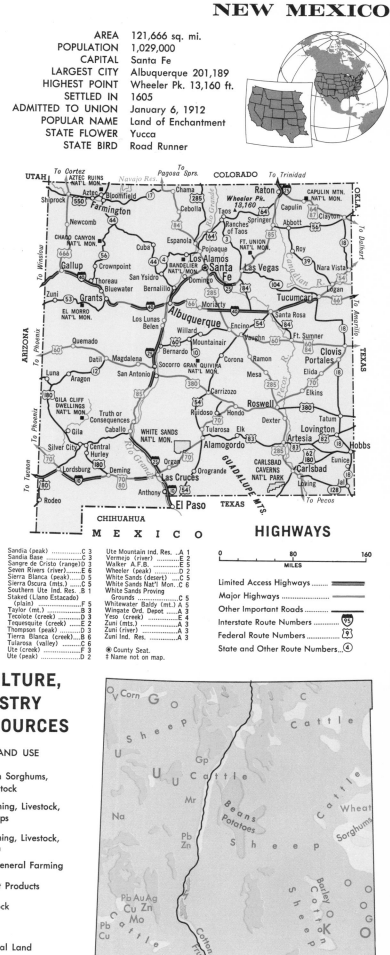

TOPOGRAPHY

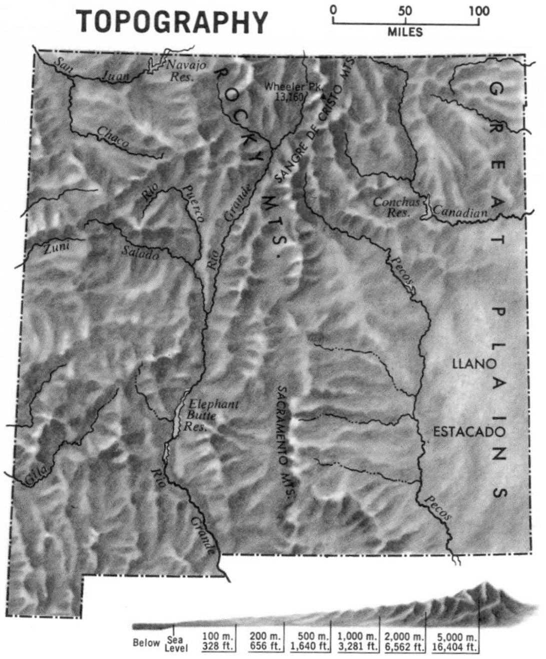

0 50 100
MILES
Navajo Res.
San Juan
Wheeler Pk. 13,160
ROCKY MTS.
SANGRE DE CRISTO MTS.
GREAT PLAINS
Chaco
Rio Puerco
Rio Grande
Conchas Res.
Canadian
Zuni
Salado
Pecos
LLANO
ESTACADO
Elephant Butte Res.
SACRAMENTO MTS.
Gila
Below Sea Level
100 m. 328 ft.
200 m. 656 ft.
500 m. 1,640 ft.
1,000 m. 3,281 ft.
2,000 m. 6,562 ft.
5,000 m. 16,404 ft.

Hope (E6) 108
Horse Springs (A5)...... 50
Hot Springs (Truth or Consequences) (B5)...4,269
House (F4) 175
Humble City (F6) 32
Hurley (A6) 1,851
Ilfeld (D3) 175
Ione (F3) 6
Isleta (C4) 1,400
Jal (F6) 3,051
Jarales (C4) 1,500
Jemez Pueblo (C3)....... 878
Jemez Springs (C3)...... 223
Jicarilla (D5) 10
Kenna (F5) 50
Kingston (B6) 43
Kirtland (A2) 950
Koehler (E2) 385
La Cueva (D3) 300
La Jara (B2) 2,500
La Lande (E4) 10
La Liendre (E3) 12
La Luz (C6) 600
La Madera (C2) 350
La Mesa (C6) 956
La Plata (A2) 150
La Union (C7) 700
Laguna (B3) 462
Lajoya (C4) 118
Lake Arthur (E5) 387
Lake Valley (B6) 37
Lakewood (E6) 58
Lamy (D3) 103
Las Cruces◉ (C6) 29,367
Las Palomas (B5) 60
Las Tablas (C2) 110
Las Vegas (city)◉(D3) 7,790
Las Vegas (town) ‡(D3) 6,028
Ledoux (D3) 500
Lemitar (B4) 500
Levy (E2) 34
Leyba (D3) 30
Lincoln (D5) 75
Lindrith (C2) 34
Lingo (F5) 15
Llano (D2) 350
Loco Hills (F6) 450
Logan (F3) 500
Lordsburg◉ (A6) 3,436
Los Alamos◉ (C3)......12,584
Los Lunas◉ (C4) 1,186
Lourdes (D3) 30
Loving (F6) 1,646
Lovington◉ (F6) 9,660
Lumberton (C2) 300
Luna (A5) 225
Madrid (C3) 20
Magdalena (B4) 1,211
Malaga (E6) 500
Manuelito (A3) 500
Manzano (C4) 50
Marquez (B3) 60
Maxwell (E2) 392
Mayhill (D6) 300
McAlister (F4) 20
McDonald (F5) 26
McGaffey (A3) 25
McIntosh (D4) 75
Melrose (F4) 698
Mentmore (A3) 230
Mescalero (D5) 1,408
Mesilla (C6) 1,264
Mesilla Park (C6) 2,000
Mesquite (C6) 800
Mexican Springs (A3).. 109
Miami (E2) 60
Milan (B3) 2,658
Mills (E2) 22
Milnesand (F5) 15
Mimbres (B6) 125
Mogollon (A5) 25
Monero (C2) 207
Montezuma (D3) 137
Monticello (B5) 150
Montoya (F3) 81
Monument (F6) 165
Mora◉ (D3) 1,250
Moriarty (D4) 720
Moses (F2) 70
Mosquero◉ (F3) 310
Mount Dora (F2) 100
Mountainair (C4) 1,605
Mule Creek (A5) 18
Nambe (D3) 486
Nara Visa (F3) 350
New Laguna (B4) 230
Newcomb (A2) 50
Newkirk (E3) 250
Nogal (D5) 75
Ocate (E2) 300
Oil Center (F6) 750
Ojo Caliente (D2) 300
Ojo Feliz (E2) 250
Ojo Sarco (D2) 226
Omega (A4) 50
Organ (C6) 500
Orogrande (D6) 75
Oscuro (C5) 50
Otis (E6) 200
Paguate (B3) 500
Park View (C2) 201
Pastura (E4) 40
Pecos (D3) 584
Penablanca (C3) 200
Penasco (D2) 700
Pep (F5) 110
Peralta (C4) 380
Petaca (C2) 200
Picacho (D5) 80
Pie Town (A4) 85
Pinehaven (A3) 50
Pinon (D6) 75
Pinos Altos (A6) 250
Pintada (D4) 26
Placitas (C3) 350
Pleasanton (A5) 30
Pojoaque (C3) 330
Polvadera (B4) 150
Ponderosa (C3) 217
Portales◉ (F4) 9,695
Prewitt (B3) 135
Puerto de Luna (E4)..... 400
Quay (F4) 10
Quemado (A4) 260
Questa (D2) 1,750
Radium Springs (B6)... 25
Rainsville (D2) 220
Ramah (A3) 250
Ramon (D4) 6
Ranches of Taos (D2) ..1,668
Raton◉ (E2) 8,146
Red Hill (A4) 6
Red River (D2) 150
Redrock (A6) 60
Regina (B2) 53
Rehoboth (A3) 100
Rencona (D3) 44
Reserve◉ (A5) 800
Ribera (D3) 300
Rincon (C6) 500
Rociada (D3) 220
Rodarte (D2) 200
Rodeo (A7) 250
Rogers (F5) 60
Romeroville (D3) 15
Rosebud (F3) 5
Roswell◉ (E5) 39,593
Rowe (D3) 510
Roy (E3) 633
Ruidoso (D5) 1,557
Ruidoso Downs (D5) 407
Rutheron (C2) 101
Sabinoso (E3) 53
Sacramento (D6) 200
Saint Vrain (F4) 9
Salem (B6) 350
San Acacia (B4) 200
San Antonio (B5) 900
San Cristobal (D2) 325
San Felipe (C3) 1,034
San Fidel (B3) 150
San Ignacio (D4) 20
San Ildefonzo (C3) 100
San Jon (F3) 411
San Jose (D3) 200
San Juan Pueblo (C2) .. 950
San Lorenzo (B6) 350
San Marcial (C5) 10
San Mateo (B3) 150
San Miguel (C6) 400
San Patricio (D5) 375
San Rafael (A3) 500
San Ysidro (C3) 166
Sandia Park (C3) 100
Santa Cruz (D3) 500
SANTA FE◉ (C3) 34,676
Santa Rita (B6) 1,772
Santa Rosa◉ (E4)........2,220
Sapello (D3) 29
Scholle (C4) 8
Seboyeta (B3) 300
Sedan (F2) 258
Sena (D3) 200
Seneca (F2) 17
Separ (A6) 30
Serafina (D3) 110
Sherman (B6) 39
Shiprock (A2) 500
Silver City◉ (A6) 6,972
Socorro◉ (C4) 5,271
Soham (D3) 250
Solano (E3) 45
Springer (E2) 1,564
Stanley (D3) 70
Stead (F2) 30
Tafoya (E2) 325
Taiban (F4) 43
Tajique (C4) 200
Taos◉ (D2) 2,163
Tapicitoes (C2) 42
Tatum (F5) 1,168
Taylor Springs (E2)...... 6
Tererro (D3) 40
Tesuque (C3) 850
Texico (F4) 889
Thoreau (A3) 700
Three Rivers (C5) 35
Tierra Amarilla◉(C2).. 280
Tijeras (C3) 500
Tinnie (D5) 150
Toadlena (A2) 500
Tohatchi (A3) 350
Tome (C4) 400
Torreon (C4) 100
Trampas (D2) 120
Trementina (E3) 39
Tres Lagunas (B4) 12
Tres Piedras (D2) 300
Tres Ritos (D2) 10
Truchas (D2) 800
Trujillo (E3) 149
Truth or Consequences◉ (B5) 4,269
Tucumcari◉ (F3) 8,143
Tularosa (C5) 3,200
Tyrone (A6) 98
University Park (C6)....4,387
Ute Park (D2) 30
Vadito (D2) 375
Vado (C6) 170
Valdez (D2) 50
Valencia (C4) 818
Vallecitos (C2) 450
Valmora (D3) 35
Vanadium (A6) 450
Vaughn (D4) 1,170
Veguita (C4) 50
Velarde (C2) 650
Vermejo Park (D2)...... 80
Villanueva (D3) 400
Virden (A6) 135
Wagon Mound (E2)..... 760
Waterflow (A2) 288
Watrous (D3) 800
Weed (D6) 100
White Oaks (D5) 20
White Sands Missile Range (C6) ....
White Signal (A6) 30
Whites City (E6) 250
Willard (D4) 294
Winston (B5) 40
Yeso (E4) 380
Youngsville (C2) 120
Zia Pueblo (C3) 458
Zuni (A3) 3,585

OTHER FEATURES

Alamogordo (dam) ....E 4
Alamogordo (res.) ....E 4
Alamosa (river) ....B 5
Animas (river) ....B 1
Avalon (res.) ....E 6
Aztec Ruins Nat'l Mon. A 2
Baldy (peak) ....D 3
Bandelier Nat'l Mon. ....C 3
Big Burro (mts.) ....A 6
Black (mt.) ....A 6
Black (range) ....B 5
Blanco (creek) ....F 4
Bluewater (creek) ....B 4
Bluewater (creek) ....D 6
Bluewater (lake) ....A 3
Boulder (lake) ....C 2
Brazos (peak) ....C 2
Burford (lake) ....C 2
Caballo (res.) ....B 6
Canadian (river) ....F 3
Cannon A.F.B. ....F 4
Canyon Blanco (creek)....B 2
Capitan (mts.) ....D 5
Capitan (peak) ....D 5
Capulin Mountain Nat'l Mon. ....E 2
Carlsbad Caverns Nat'l Park ....E 6
Carrizo (creek) ....F 2
Chaco (mesa) ....B 3
Chaco (river) ....A 2
Chaco Canyon Nat'l Mon. ....B 2
Chivato (mesa) ....B 3
Chupadera (mesa) ....C 5
Chuska (mts.) ....A 2
Cimarron (creek) ....E 2
Cimarron (river) ....F 2
Colorado, Arroyo (river)..B 4
Companero Canyon (creek) ....B 2
Conchas (dam) ....E 3
Conchas (res.) ....E 3
Conchas (river) ....E 3
Cooks (range) ....B 6
Costilla (peak) ....D 2
Cuervo (creek) ....E 3
Dark Canyon (creek) ......E 6
Datil (mts.) ....B 4
Eagle Nest (lake) ....D 2
El Morro Nat'l Mon. .....A 3
El Rito (river) ....C 2
Elephant Butte (res.) ....B 5
Fifteenmile Arroyo (creek) ....D 4
Florida (mts.) ....B 7
Fort Union Nat'l Mon. ...E 3
Gallinas (mts.) ....B 4
Gallinas (river) ....E 3
Gila (river) ....A 6
Gila Cliff Dwellings Nat'l Mon. ....A 5
Gran Quivira Nat'l Mon. C 4
Grouse (mt.) ....A 5
Guadalupe (mts.) ....D 6
Hatchet (mts.) ....A 7
Holloman A.F.B. ....C 6
Hueco (mts.) ....D 6
Jemez (creek) ....C 3
Jemez Canyon (res.) ......C 3
Jicarilla Ind. Res. ....B 2
Jornada del Muerto (valley) ....C 5
Kirtland A.F.B. ....C 3
La Plata (river) ....A 1
Ladron (mts.) ....B 4
Largo (creek) ....B 2
Las Animas (creek).........B 5
Llano Estacado (Staked) (plain) ....F 5
Los Pinos (river) ....B 2
Lucero (lake) ....C 6
Macho, Arroyo del (creek) ....D 5
Magdalena (mts.) ....B 4
Major Longs (creek) .....F 2
Manzano (mts.) ....C 4
Manzano (peak) ....C 4
McMillan (lake) ....E 6
Mescalero (ridge) ....F 6
Mescalero (valley) ....F 5
Mescalero Apache Ind. Res. ....D 5
Mimbres (mts.) ....B 6
Mimbres (river) ....B 6
Mogollon (mts.) ....A 5
Mogollon (peak) ....A 5
Montosa (mesa) ....E 3
Nacimiento (mts.) ....C 3
Nacimiento (peak) ....C 2
Navajo (dam) ....B 2
Navajo (res.) ....B 2
Navajo Ind. Res. ....A 2
North Truchas (peak).....D 3
Ocate (creek) ....E 2
Osha (peak) ....C 4
Padilla (creek) ....D 5
Pajarito (creek) ....A 2
Palomas (creek) ....B 5
Pecos (river) ....E 5
Pecos Nat'l Mon. ....D 3
Peloncillo (mts.) ....A 6
Perro (lagoon) ....D 4
Pintada (creek) ....E 4
Playas (lake) ....A 7
Potrillo (mts.) ....B 7
Pueblo Ind. Res. ....B 4
Pueblo Ind. Res. ....C 3
Pueblo Ind. Res. ....C 4
Pueblo Ind. Res. ....D 2
Red Bluff (lake) ....E 7
Revuelto (creek) ....F 3
Rio Brazos (river) ....C 2
Rio Chama (river) ....C 2
Rio Cuchillo Negro (river) ....B 5
Rio Felix (river) ....E 5
Rio Grande (river) ....C 5
Rio Hondo (river) ....E 5
Rio Penasco (river) ....E 6
Rio Puerco (river) ....A 3
Rio Puerco (river) ....C 4
Rio Salado (river) ....B 4
Sacramento (mts.) ....D 6
Salt (creek) ....E 5
Salt (lake) ....F 4
San Agustin (plains) .....B 5
San Andres (mts.) ....C 6
San Antonio (peak) ....C 2
San Francisco (river)......A 5
San Jose (river) ....B 3
San Juan (river) ....B 2
San Mateo (mts.) ....B 5
San Miguel (creek) ....B 3
Sandia (peak) ....C 3
Sandia Base ....C 3
Sangre de Cristo (range)D 3
Seven Rivers (river)........E 6
Sierra Blanca (peak)......D 5
Sierra Oscura (mts.) ......C 5
Southern Ute Ind. Res. .B 1
Staked (Llano Estacado) (plain) ....F 5
Taylor (mt.) ....B 3
Tecolote (creek) ....D 3
Tequesquite (creek) ......E 2
Thompson (peak) ....D 3
Tierra Blanca (creek)....B 6
Tularosa (valley) ....C 6
Ute (creek) ....F 3
Ute (peak) ....D 2
Ute Mountain Ind. Res. ..A 1
Vermejo (river) ....E 2
Walker A.F.B. ....E 5
Wheeler (peak) ....D 2
White Sands (desert) ....C 5
White Sands Nat'l Mon. .C 6
White Sands Proving Grounds ....C 5
Whitewater Baldy (mt.) A 5
Wingate Ord. Depot ......A 3
Yeso (creek) ....E 4
Zuni (mts.) ....A 3
Zuni (river) ....A 3
Zuni Ind. Res. ....A 3

◉ County Seat.
‡ Name not on map.

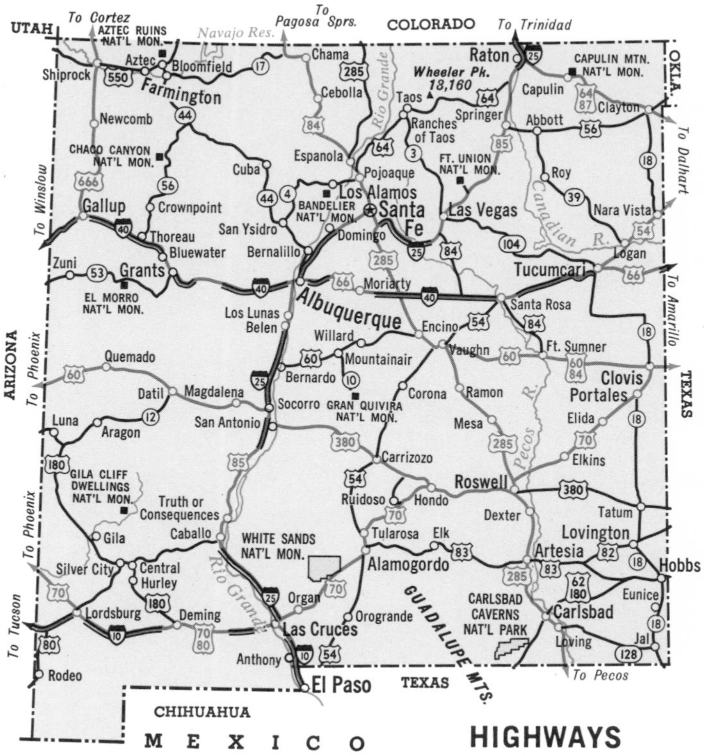

UTAH
COLORADO
OKLA.
TEXAS
ARIZONA
CHIHUAHUA
MEXICO
To Cortez
To Pagosa Sprs.
To Trinidad
To Dalhart
To Amarillo
To Winslow
To Phoenix
To Tucson
To Pecos
Navajo Res.
AZTEC RUINS NAT'L MON.
Aztec
Bloomfield
Shiprock
Farmington
Chama
Cebolla
Raton
Wheeler Pk. 13,160
Taos
CAPULIN MTN. NAT'L MON.
Capulin
Clayton
Springer
Abbott
Ranches of Taos
Newcomb
CHACO CANYON NAT'L MON.
Espanola
FT. UNION NAT'L MON.
Roy
Cuba
Pojoaque
Los Alamos
BANDELIER NAT'L MON.
Santa Fe
Las Vegas
Nara Visa
Gallup
Crownpoint
San Ysidro
Domingo
Thoreau
Bluewater
Bernalillo
Tucumcari
Logan
Zuni
Grants
EL MORRO NAT'L MON.
Moriarty
Albuquerque
Santa Rosa
Los Lunas
Belen
Willard
Encino
Quemado
Mountainair
Vaughn
Ft. Sumner
Bernardo
Clovis
Datil
Magdalena
Socorro
GRAN QUIVIRA NAT'L MON.
Corona
Ramon
Portales
Luna
San Antonio
Mesa
Elida
Aragon
Carrizozo
Elkins
GILA CLIFF DWELLINGS NAT'L MON.
Truth or Consequences
Roswell
Ruidoso
Hondo
Dexter
Tatum
Gila
Caballo
WHITE SANDS NAT'L MON.
Tularosa
Elk
Lovington
Silver City
Central
Hurley
Alamogordo
Artesia
Hobbs
Eunice
Lordsburg
Deming
Organ
Orogrande
CARLSBAD CAVERNS NAT'L PARK
Carlsbad
Las Cruces
GUADALUPE MTS.
Jal
Loving
Rodeo
Anthony
El Paso
TEXAS
Rio Grande
Pecos R.
Canadian R.

HIGHWAYS

0 80 160
MILES

Limited Access Highways
Major Highways
Other Important Roads
Interstate Route Numbers
Federal Route Numbers
State and Other Route Numbers

AGRICULTURE, INDUSTRY and RESOURCES

DOMINANT LAND USE

- Wheat, Grain Sorghums, Range Livestock
- General Farming, Livestock, Special Crops
- General Farming, Livestock, Cash Grain
- Dry Beans, General Farming
- Cotton, Forest Products
- Range Livestock
- Forests
- Nonagricultural Land

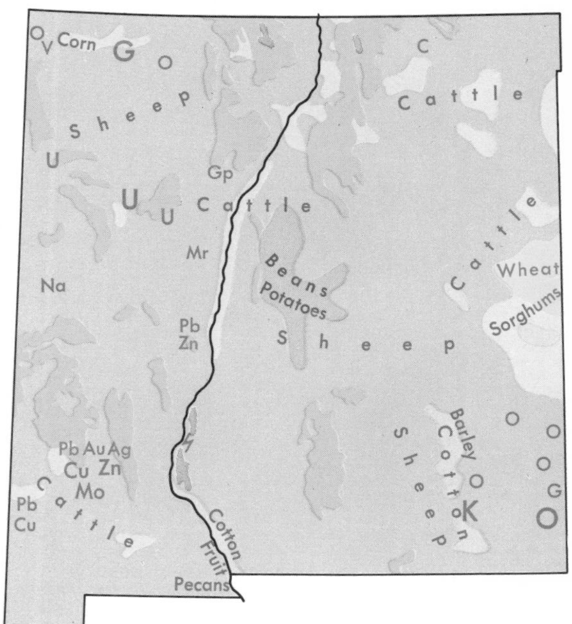

Corn
Sheep
Cattle
Wheat
Sorghums
Beans
Potatoes
Barley
Cotton
Fruit
Pecans

MAJOR MINERAL OCCURRENCES

Ag	Silver	Gp	Gypsum			U	Uranium		
Au	Gold	K	Potash						
C	Coal	Mo	Molybdenum						
Cu	Copper	Mr	Marble	O	Petroleum	V	Vanadium	ϟ	Water Power
G	Natural Gas	Na	Salt	Pb	Lead	Zn	Zinc		

NEW YORK

AREA	49,576 sq. mi.
POPULATION	18,073,000
CAPITAL	Albany
LARGEST CITY	New York (greater) 14,114,927
HIGHEST POINT	Mt. Marcy 5,344 ft.
SETTLED IN	1614
ADMITTED TO UNION	July 26, 1788
POPULAR NAME	Empire State
STATE FLOWER	Rose
STATE BIRD	Bluebird

TOPOGRAPHY

0   50   100
MILES

5,000 m. 2,000 m. 1,000 m. 500 m. 200 m. 100 m. Sea
16,404 ft. 6,562 ft. 3,281 ft. 1,640 ft. 656 ft. 328 ft. Level Below

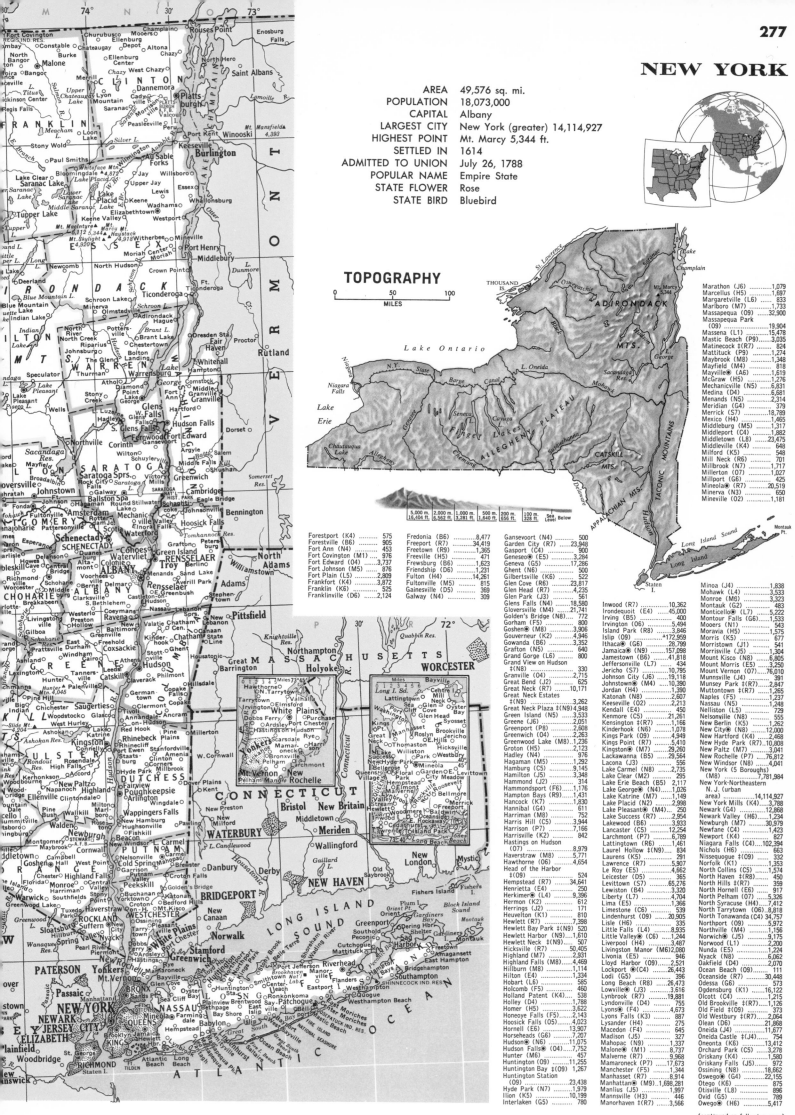

Forestport (K4)	575	Fredonia (B6)	8,477
Forestville (B6)	905	Freeport (R7)	34,419
Fort Ann (N4)	453	Freetown (R9)	1,365
Fort Covington (M1)	976	Freeville (H5)	471
Fort Edward (O4)	3,737	Frewsburg (B6)	1,623
Fort Johnson (M5)	876	Friendship (D6)	1,231
Fort Plain (L5)	2,809	Fulton (H4)	14,261
Frankfort (K4)	3,872	Fultonville (M5)	815
Franklin (K6)	525	Gainesville (D5)	369
Franklinville (D6)	2,124	Galway (N4)	309

Gansevoort (N4)	500
Garden City (R7)	23,948
Gasport (C4)	900
Geneseo◉ (E5)	3,284
Geneva (G5)	17,286
Ghent (N6)	500
Gilbertsville (K6)	522
Glen Cove (R6)	23,817
Glen Head (R7)	4,235
Glen Park (J3)	561
Glens Falls (N4)	18,580
Gloversville (M4)	21,741
Golden's Bridge (N8)	772
Gorham (F5)	800
Gouverneur (K2)	4,946
Gowanda (B6)	3,352
Grafton (N6)	640
Grand Gorge (L6)	800
Grand View on Hudson ‡(N8)	330
Granville (O4)	2,715
Great Bend (J2)	625
Great Neck (R7)	10,171
Great Neck Estates ‡(N9)	3,262
Great Neck Plaza ‡(N9)	4,948
Green Island (N5)	3,533
Greene (J6)	2,051
Greenport (P8)	2,608
Greenwich (O4)	2,263
Greenwood Lake (M8)	1,236
Groton (H5)	2,123
Hadley (N4)	976
Hagaman (M5)	1,292
Hamburg (C5)	9,145
Hamilton (J5)	3,348
Hammond (J2)	314
Hammondsport (F6)	1,176
Hampton Bays (R9)	1,431
Hancock (K7)	1,830
Hannibal (G4)	611
Harriman (M8)	752
Harris Hill (C5)	3,944
Harrison (O7)	7,166
Harrisville (K2)	842
Hastings on Hudson (O7)	8,979
Haverstraw (M8)	5,771
Hawthorne (O6)	4,654
Head of the Harbor ‡(O9)	524
Hempstead (R7)	34,641
Henrietta (E4)	250
Herkimer◉ (L4)	9,396
Hermon (K2)	612
Herrings (J2)	171
Heuvelton (K1)	810
Hewlett (R7)	7,398
Hewlett Bay Park ‡(N9)	520
Hewlett Harbor (N9)	1,610
Hewlett Neck ‡(N9)	507
Hicksville (R7)	50,405
Highland (N7)	2,931
Highland Falls (M8)	4,469
Hillburn (M8)	1,114
Hilton (E4)	1,334
Hobart (L6)	585
Holcomb (F5)	460
Holland Patent (K4)	538
Holley (D4)	1,788
Homer (H5)	3,622
Honeoye Falls (F5)	2,143
Hoosick Falls (O5)	4,023
Hornell (E6)	13,907
Horseheads (G6)	7,207
Hudson◉ (N6)	11,075
Hudson Falls◉ (O4)	7,752
Hunter (M6)	457
Huntington (O9)	11,255
Huntington Bay ‡(O9)	1,267
Huntington Station (O9)	23,438
Hyde Park (N7)	1,979
Ilion (K5)	10,199
Interlaken (G5)	780

Inwood (R7)	10,362
Irondequoit (E4)	45,000
Irving (B5)	400
Irvington (O6)	5,494
Island Park (R8)	3,846
Islip (O9)	*172,959
Ithaca◉ (G6)	28,799
Jamaica (O9)	157,088
Jamestown (B6)	41,818
Jeffersonville (J7)	434
Jericho (S7)	10,795
Johnson City (J6)	19,118
Johnstown◉ (M4)	10,390
Jordan (H4)	1,390
Katonah (N8)	2,607
Keeseville (O2)	2,213
Kendall (E4)	450
Kenmore (C5)	21,261
Kensington ‡(R7)	1,166
Kinderhook (N6)	1,078
Kings Park (O9)	4,949
Kings Point (R7)	5,410
Kingston◉ (M7)	29,260
Lackawanna (B5)	29,564
Lacona (J3)	556
Lake Carmel (N8)	2,735
Lake Clear (M2)	295
Lake Erie Beach (B5)	2,117
Lake George◉ (N4)	1,026
Lake Katrine (M7)	1,149
Lake Placid (N2)	2,998
Lake Pleasant◉ (M4)	250
Lake Success (R7)	2,954
Lakewood (B6)	3,933
Lancaster (C5)	12,254
Larchmont (P7)	6,789
Lattingtown (R6)	1,461
Laurel Hollow ‡(N9)	834
Laurens (K5)	291
Lawrence (R7)	5,907
Le Roy (D5)	4,662
Leicester (D5)	365
Levittown (S7)	65,276
Lewiston (B4)	3,320
Liberty (L7)	4,704
Lima (E5)	1,366
Limestone (C6)	460
Lindenhurst (O9)	20,905
Lisle (H6)	335
Little Falls (L4)	8,935
Little Valley◉ (C6)	1,244
Liverpool (H4)	3,487
Livingston Manor (M6)	2,080
Livonia (E5)	946
Lloyd Harbor (O9)	2,521
Lockport◉ (C4)	26,443
Lodi (G5)	396
Long Beach (R8)	26,473
Lowville◉ (J3)	3,616
Lynbrook (R7)	19,881
Lyndonville (D4)	755
Lyons◉ (F4)	4,673
Lyons Falls (K3)	887
Lysander (H4)	275
Macedon (F4)	645
Madison (J5)	327
Mahopac (N8)	1,337
Malone◉ (M1)	8,737
Malverne (R7)	9,968
Mamaroneck (P7)	17,673
Manchester (F5)	1,348
Manhasset (R7)	8,914
Manhattan◉ (M9)	1,698,281
Manlius (J5)	1,997
Mannsville (H3)	446
Manorhaven (R7)	3,566

Marathon (J6)	1,079
Marcellus (H5)	1,697
Margaretville (L6)	833
Marlboro (M7)	1,733
Massapequa (O9)	32,900
Massapequa Park (O9)	19,904
Massena (L1)	15,478
Mastic Beach (P9)	3,035
Matinecock ‡(R7)	824
Mattituck (P9)	1,274
Maybrook (M8)	1,348
Mayfield (M4)	818
Mayville◉ (A6)	1,619
McGraw (H5)	1,276
Mechanicville (N5)	6,831
Medina (D4)	6,681
Menands (N5)	2,314
Meridian (G2)	379
Merrick (S7)	18,789
Mexico (H4)	1,465
Middleburg (M4)	1,317
Middleport (C4)	1,882
Middletown (L8)	23,475
Middleville (K4)	648
Milford (K5)	548
Mill Neck (R6)	701
Millbrook (N7)	1,717
Millerton (O7)	1,027
Millport (G6)	425
Mineola◉ (R7)	20,519
Minerva (N3)	650
Mineville (O2)	1,181

Minoa (J4)	1,838
Mohawk (L4)	3,533
Monroe (M8)	3,323
Montauk (G2)	483
Monticello◉ (L7)	5,222
Montour Falls (G6)	1,533
Mooers (N1)	543
Moravia (H5)	1,575
Morris (H5)	677
Morristown (J1)	541
Morrisville (J5)	1,304
Mount Kisco (N8)	6,805
Mount Morris (E5)	3,250
Mount Vernon (O7)	76,010
Munnsville (J4)	391
Munsey Park ‡(R7)	2,847
Muttontown ‡(R7)	1,265
Naples (F5)	1,237
Nassau (N5)	1,248
Nelliston (J5)	729
Nelsonville (N8)	555
New Berlin (K5)	1,262
New City◉ (N8)	12,000
New Hartford (K4)	2,468
New Hyde Park (R7)	10,808
New Paltz (M7)	3,041
New Rochelle (P7)	76,812
New Windsor (M8)	4,041
New York (5 Boroughs) (M8)	7,781,984
New York-Northeastern N. J. (urban area)	14,114,927
New York Mills (K4)	3,788
Newark (G4)	12,868
Newark Valley (H6)	1,234
Newburgh (M8)	30,979
Newfane (C4)	1,423
Newport (K4)	827
Niagara Falls (A4)	102,394
Nichols (H6)	663
Nissequogue ‡(O9)	332
Norfolk (K1)	1,353
North Collins (B5)	1,574
North Haven ‡(R8)	450
North Hills ‡(R7)	359
North Hornell (E6)	917
North Pelham (O7)	5,326
North Syracuse (H4)	7,412
North Tarrytown (O6)	8,818
North Tonawanda (A4)	34,757
Northport (O9)	5,972
Northville (M4)	1,156
Norwich◉ (J5)	9,175
Norwood (L1)	2,200
Nunda (E5)	1,224
Nyack (N8)	6,062
Oakfield (D4)	2,070
Ocean Beach (O9)	111
Oceanside (R7)	30,448
Odessa (G6)	573
Ogdensburg (K1)	16,122
Olcott (C4)	1,215
Old Brookville ‡(R7)	1,126
Old Westbury ‡(R7)	2,064
Olean (D6)	21,868
Oneida (J4)	11,677
Oneida Castle ‡(J4)	754
Oneonta (K6)	13,412
Orchard Park (C5)	3,278
Oriskany (K4)	1,580
Oriskany Falls (J5)	972
Ossining (N8)	18,662
Oswego◉ (G4)	22,155
Otego (K6)	875
Otisville (L8)	896
Ovid (G5)	789
Owego◉ (H6)	5,417

(continued on following page)

New York
(continued)

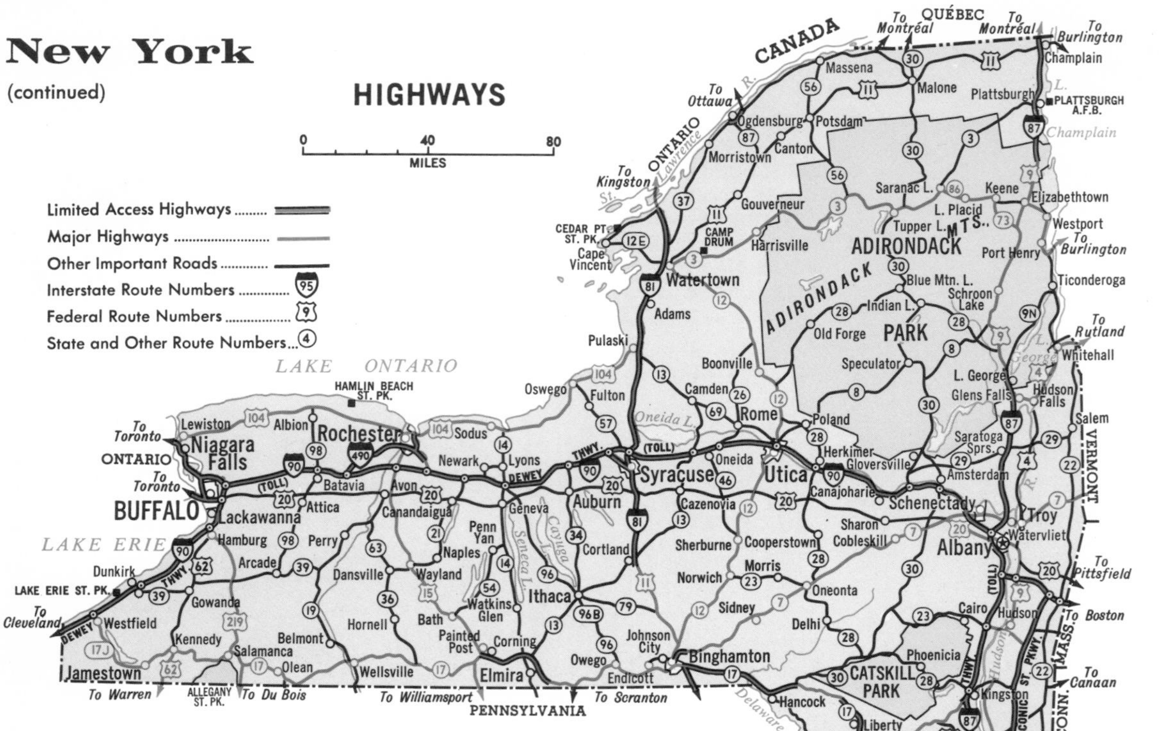
HIGHWAYS
0 40 80
MILES
Limited Access Highways
Major Highways
Other Important Roads
Interstate Route Numbers 95
Federal Route Numbers 9
State and Other Route Numbers 4
CANADA
To Montréal
QUÉBEC
To Montréal
To Burlington
Champlain
Massena
Malone
Plattsburgh
PLATTSBURGH A.F.B.
To Ottawa
Ogdensburg
Potsdam
Canton
Morristown
To Kingston
ONTARIO
Gouverneur
CEDAR PT. ST. PK.
Cape Vincent
CAMP DRUM
Harrisville
Watertown
Adams
Saranac L.
L. Placid
Keene
Elizabethtown
Tupper L.
ADIRONDACK
MTS.
Westport
To Burlington
Port Henry
Ticonderoga
Blue Mtn. L.
Schroon Lake
Indian L.
Old Forge
PARK
To Rutland
Whitehall
Pulaski
LAKE ONTARIO
HAMLIN BEACH ST. PK.
Oswego
Fulton
Boonville
Speculator
L. George
Glens Falls
Hudson Falls
Camden
Rome
Oneida L.
Poland
Salem
To Toronto
Lewiston
Albion
Rochester
Sodus
Niagara Falls
ONTARIO
To Toronto
Batavia
Newark
Lyons
Syracuse
Oneida
Utica
Herkimer
Gloversville
Saratoga Sprs.
Amsterdam
VERMONT
BUFFALO
Lackawanna
Attica
Avon
Canandaigua
Geneva
Auburn
Cazenovia
Canajoharie
Schenectady
Troy
Watervliet
LAKE ERIE
Hamburg
Perry
Penn Yan
Naples
Cortland
Sherburne
Cooperstown
Sharon
Cobleskill
Albany
Dunkirk
Arcade
Dansville
Wayland
Norwich
Morris
Oneonta
To Pittsfield
LAKE ERIE ST. PK.
Gowanda
Watkins Glen
Ithaca
Sidney
Delhi
Cairo
Hudson
To Boston
To Cleveland
Westfield
Belmont
Hornell
Bath
Painted Post
Corning
Owego
Johnson City
Binghamton
Phoenicia
Kennedy
Salamanca
Olean
Wellsville
Elmira
Endicott
CATSKILL PARK
Kingston
Jamestown
To Warren
ALLEGANY ST. PK.
To Du Bois
To Williamsport
PENNSYLVANIA
To Scranton
Hancock
Liberty
MASS.
CONN.
To Canaan
Monticello
Poughkeepsie
Middletown
Newburgh
Beacon
Brewster
To Danbury
Port Jervis
To Stroudsburg
N.J.
Peekskill
Suffern
To New Haven
Long Island Sound
Greenport
Southampton
To Newark
Eastport
To Newark
Babylon
Long Island
Freeport
NEW YORK
ATLANTIC OCEAN

Oxford (J6) 1,871
Oyster Bay (S6) 6,066
Oyster Bay Cove ‡(N9).. 988
Painted Post (F6)........2,570
Palatine Bridge ‡(L5).. 578
Palmyra (F4) 3,476
Panama (A6) 450
Parish (H4) 567
Patchogue (P9) 8,838
Patterson (N8) 2,250
Pawling (N7) 1,734
Pearl River (M8)........12,500
Peekskill (N8) 18,737
Pelham (O7) 1,964
Pelham Manor (R6) 6,114
Penn Yan◉ (F5) 5,770
Perry (D5) 4,629
Perrysburg (B6) 434
Phelps (F5) 1,887
Philadelphia (J2) 868
Philmont (N6) 1,750
Phoenix (H4) 2,408
Piermont (M8) 1,906
Pike (D5) 345
Pine Bush (M7) 1,016
Pine Hill (M6) 180
Pine Island (L8) 800
Pittsford (E4) 1,749
Plainview (O9) 27,710
Plandome ‡(R7) 1,379
Plandome Heights
‡(R7) 1,025
Plandome Manor ‡(R7) 705
Plattsburgh◉ (O1).....20,172
Pleasantville (N8) 5,877
Poland (L4) 564
Poquott ‡(O9) 295
Port Byron (G4) 1,201
Port Chester (P7).........24,960
Port Dickinson (J6) 2,295
Port Ewen (N7) 2,622
Port Henry (O2) 1,767
Port Jefferson (P9) 2,336
Port Jervis (L8) 9,268
Port Leyden (K3) 898
Port Washington (R6)15,657
Port Washington North
‡(R7) 722
Portville (D6) 1,336
Potsdam (K1) 7,765
Poughkeepsie◉ (N7)...38,330
Prattsburg (F5) 690
Preble (H5) 800
Preston Hollow (M6)... 525
Prospect (K4) 348
Pulaski (H3) 2,256
Purchase (P7) 2,160
Putnam Valley (N8)...△3,070
Queens Village (R7)...70,000
Quogue (P9) 692
Randolph (C6) 1,414
Ravena (N6) 2,410
Red Creek (G4) 689
Red Hook (N7) 1,719
Remsen (K4) 567
Rensselaer (N5) 10,506
Rensselaer Falls (K1).... 375
Rhinebeck (N7) 2,093
Richburg (D6) 493
Richfield Springs (K5) 1,630
Richmondville (M5) 743
Ripley (A6) 1,247
Riverhead◉ (P9) 5,830
Riverside (F6) 1,030
Rochester◉ (E4) 318,611
Rochester (urban
area) 493,402
Rock City Falls (M4).... 350
Rockville Centre (R7)..26,355
Rome (J4) 51,646
Rome-Utica (urban
area) 187,779
Ronkonkoma (O9) 4,220
Roosevelt (R7) 12,883
Rosendale (M7) 1,033
Roseton (M7) 300
Roslyn (R7) 2,681
Roslyn Estates ‡(R7)....1,289
Roslyn Harbor ‡(R7)..... 925
Rotterdam Junction
(N5) 950
Rouses Point (O1) 2,160
Rushville (F5) 465
Russell Gardens ‡(R7)..1,156
Rye (P7) 14,225
Sackets Harbor (H3)....1,279
Saddle Rock ‡(N9) 1,109
Sag Harbor (R8) 2,346
Saint George◉ (M9).....9,000
Saint Johnsville (L5)....2,196
Salamanca (C6) 8,480
Salem (O4) 1,076
Sands Point (N9) 2,161
Sandy Creek (H3) 697

Saranac Lake (M2)......6,421
Saratoga Springs (N4) 16,630
Saugerties (M6) 4,286
Sauquoit (K5) 1,715
Savannah (G4) 602
Savona (F6) 904
Sayville (O9) 6,485
Scarsdale (P7) 17,968
Schaghticoke (N5) 720
Schenectady◉ (M5)....81,682
Schenectady-Albany-
Troy (urban area)..455,447
Schenevus (L5) 493
Schoharie◉ (M5) 1,168
Schuylerville (N4) 1,361
Scotia (N5) 7,625
Scottsville (E4) 1,863
Scranton (C5) 1,078
Sea Cliff (R6) 5,669
Seneca Falls (G5).........7,439
Sharon Springs (L5).... 351
Sherburne (K5) 1,647
Sherman (A6) 873
Sherrill (J4) 2,922
Shortsville (F5) 1,382
Sidney (K6) 5,157
Silver Creek (B5) 3,310
Silver Springs (E5) 726
Sinclairville (B6) 726
Skaneateles (H5) 2,921
Sloan (C5) 5,803
Sloatsburg (M8) 2,565
Smithtown (O9) 7,094
Smyrna (J5) 286
Sodus (G4) 1,645
Sodus Point (G4) 868
Solvay (H4) 8,732
South Corning (F6).......1,448
South Dayton (C6) 696
South Fallsburg (L7)....1,290
South Floral Park
‡(N9) 1,090
South Glens Falls (N4) 4,129
South Nyack ‡(N8) 3,113
Southampton (R9) 4,582
Southold (P8) 982
Speculator (M3) 372
Spencer (H6) 767
Spencerport (E4) 2,461
Spring Valley (M8)......6,538
Springville (C5) 3,852
Stamford (L6) 1,166
Stewart Manor ‡(R7)...2,422
Stillwater (N5) 1,398
Stony Brook (O9) 3,548
Stony Point (M8) 3,330
Stottville (N6) 1,040
Suffern (M8) 5,094
Syosset (S7) 8,560
Syracuse◉ (H4) 216,038
Syracuse (urban
area) 333,286
Tannersville (M6) 580
Tarrytown (O6) 11,109
Theresa (J2) 956
Thomaston (R7) 2,767
Ticonderoga (N3) 3,568
Tivoli (N6) 732
Tonawanda (B4) 21,561
Trenton (Barneveld)
(K4) 363
Troy◉ (N5) 67,492
Troy-Albany-Schenectady
(urban area) 455,447
Trumansburg (G5) 1,768
Tuckahoe (O7) 6,423
Tully (H5) 803
Tupper Lake (M2) 5,200
Turin (K3) 323
Tuxedo Park (M8) 723
Unadilla (K6) 1,586
Union Springs (G5)......1,066
Unionville (L8) 511
Upper Brookville ‡(R7) 1,045
Upper Nyack ‡(N9) 1,833
Utica◉ (K4) 100,410
Utica-Rome (urban
area) 187,779
Valatie (N6) 1,237
Valhalla (P6) 3,829
Valley Falls (N5) 589
Valley Stream (N9).....38,629
Van Etten (G6) 507
Vernon ‡(J4) 913
Victor (F5) 1,180
Victory Mills (Victory)
(N4) 497
Village of the Branch
‡(O9) 886
Voorheesville (M5) 1,228
Waddington (K1) 921
Walden (M7) 4,851
Wallkill (M7) 1,215
Walton (K6) 3,855

Wampsville◉ (J4) 564
Wantagh (N9) 34,172
Wappingers Falls (N7)4,447
Warrensburg (N3) 2,240
Warsaw◉ (D5) 3,653
Warwick (M8) 3,218
Washingtonville ‡(M8) 1,178
Waterford (N5) 2,915
Waterloo◉ (G5) 5,098
Watertown◉ (J3) 33,306
Waterville (K5) 1,901
Watervliet (N5) 13,917
Watkins Glen◉ (G6)....2,813
Waverly (G7) 5,950
Wayland (E5) 2,003
Webster (F4) 3,060
Weedsport (G4) 1,731
Wellsburg (G6) 643
Wellsville (E6) 5,967
West Carthage (J3) 2,167
West Elmira (G6) 5,763
West Glens Falls (N4) 2,725
West Haverstraw ‡(M8) 5,020
West Point (M8) 5,700
West Seneca (C5) 23,138
West Winfield (K5) 960
Westbury (R7) 14,757
Westfield (A6) 3,878
Westhampton (P9) 773
Westhampton Beach
(P9) 1,460
Westport (N2) 723
White Plains◉ (P6)....50,485
Whitehall (O3) 4,016
Whitesboro (K4) 4,784
Whitney Point (J6) 1,049
Williamson (F4) 1,690
Williamsville (C5) 6,316
Williston Park (R7)......8,255
Wilson (C4) 1,320

Windsor (J6) 1,026
Wolcott (G4) 1,641
Woodhull (F6) 321
Woodmere (R7) 14,011
Woodridge (L7) 1,034
Woodsburgh ‡(R7) 907
Wurtsboro (L7) 655
Wyoming (D5) 526
Yonkers (O7) 190,634
Yorktown (N8) 3,576
Yorkville (K4) 3,749
Youngstown (C4) 1,848

OTHER FEATURES

Adirondack (mts.) ....M 3
Allegheny (res.) ....C 7
Allegheny (river) ....C 6
Allegany Indian Res.,
1,059 ....C 6
Ashokan (res.) ....M 7
Ausable (river) ....N 2
Batten Kill (river) ....O 4
Beaver (river) ....K 3
Beaver River Flow
(lake) ....K 3
Big Moose (lake) ....L 3
Black (lake) ....J 1
Black (river) ....K 3
Block Island (sound) .....S 8
Blue Mountain (lake)....M 3
Bonaparte (lake) ....K 2
Brandreth (lake) ....L 3
Brant (lake) ....N 3
Brookhaven Nat'l Lab. ...P 9
Butterfield (lake) ....J 2
Canadice (lake) ....F 5
Canandaigua (lake) ....F 5
Canisteo (river) ....F 6
Cannonsville (res.) ....K 6

Catskill (mts.) ....L 6
Cattaraugus (creek) ......C 6
Cattaraugus Indian Res.,
1,688 ....C 5
Cayuga (lake) ....G 5
Cayuta (creek) ....G 6
Champlain (lake) ....O 1
Chautauqua (lake) ....A 6
Chazy (lake) ....N 1
Chenango (river) ....J 6
Cohocton (river) ....F 6
Conesus (lake) ....E 5
Conewango (creek) ....B 6
Cranberry (lake) ....L 2

Deer (river) ....J 3
Deer (river) ....L 1
Delaware (river) ....K 7
East (river) ....N 9
Erie (lake) ....A 4
Fire Island National
Seashore ....P 9
Fishers (isl.) ....S 8
Forked (lake) ....L 3
Fort Niagara ....C 4
Fort Tilden ....N 9
Fort Totten ....N 9
Fulton Chain (lakes)......K 3
Galloo (isl.) ....H 2
Gardiners (bay) ....R 8
Gardiners (isl.) ....R 8
Genesee (river) ....E 5
George (lake) ....N 4
Grand (isl.) ....C 5
Grass (river) ....K 1
Great South (bay) ....O 9
Great South (beach) ......O 9
Greenwood (lake) ....M 8
Grenadier (isl.) ....H 2
Griffiss A.F.B. ....K 4
Haystack (mt.) ....N 2
Hemlock (lake) ....F 5
Hinckley (res.) ....K 4
Honeoye (lake) ....F 5
Honnedaga (lake) ....L 3
Hudson (river) ....N 7
Hunter (mt.) ....M 6
Indian (lake) ....M 3
Jones (beach) ....S 8
Keuka (lake) ....F 5
Lila (lake) ....L 2
Little Tupper (lake) .....L 2
Long (isl.) ....O 9
Long (lake) ....M 2
Long Island (sound) ......P 8
Lower Saranac (lake)...M 2
MacIntyre (mt.) ....M 2
Manhattan (isl.),
1,698,281 ....M 9
Marcy (mt.) ....N 2
Meacham (lake) ....M 1
Middle Saranac (lake)...M 2
Mohawk (river) ....L 5
Montauk (pt.) ....S 8
Moose (river) ....K 3
Neversink (res.) ....L 7
New York State Barge
(canal) ....C 4
Niagara (river) ....B 4
Oil Spring Indian Res. ..D 6
Oneida (lake) ....J 4
Onondaga Ind. Res., 941 H 5
Ontario (lake) ....F 3
Orient (pt.) ....R 8

Oswegatchie (river) ......K 2
Oswego (river) ....H 4
Otisco (lake) ....H 5
Otsego (lake) ....L 5
Otselic (river) ....J 5
Owasco (lake) ....G 5
Peconic (bay) ....R 9
Peninsula (point) ....H 3
Pepacton (res.) ....L 6
Piseco (lake) ....M 4
Placid (lake) ....N 2
Plattsburgh A.F.B. ....N 1
Pleasant (lake) ....M 4
Plum (isl.) ....R 8
Poosepatuck Indian Res. F 2
Raquette (lake) ....L 3
Raquette (river) ....L 1
Rondout (res.) ....M 7
Round (lake) ....L 2
Sacandaga (lake) ....L 3
Sacandaga (res.) ....M 4
Sackets (harbor) ....H 3
Saint Lawrence (lake) ...K 1
Saint Lawrence (river) ...J 2
Saint Regis (river) ....L 1
Saint Regis Indian Res.,
1,774 ....M 1
Salmon (res.) ....J 3
Salmon (river) ....H 3
Salmon (river) ....M 1
Saranac (lakes) ....M 2
Saranac (river) ....N 1
Saratoga (lake) ....N 4
Saratoga Nat'l Historic
Park ....N 4
Schoharie (creek) ....M 6
Schoharie (res.) ....M 6
Schroon (lake) ....N 3
Schroon (river) ....N 3
Seneca (lake) ....G 5
Seneca (river) ....G 5
Seneca Ordnance Depot...F 5
Shelter (isl.) ....R 8
Shinnecock Indian Res.,
234 ....R 9
Silver (lake) ....N 1
Skaneateles (lake) ....H 5
Skylight (mt.) ....M 2
Slide (mt.) ....L 6
Staten (isl.), 221,991.....M 9
Stewart A.F.B. ....M 7
Stony (isl.) ....H 3
Stony (point) ....H 3
Susquehanna (river) .....H 6
Thousand (isls.) ....H 2
Tioughnioga (river) ......H 6
Titus (lake) ....M 1
Tomhannock (res.) ....O 5
Tonawanda Ind. Res., 30 D 4
Toronto (res.) ....L 7
Tupper (lake) ....M 2
Tuscarora Indian Res.,
1,934 ....B 4
Unadilla (river) ....K 5
Upper Chateaugay
(lake) ....M 1
Upper Saranac (lake).....M 2
Valcour (isl.) ....N 1
Walkill (river) ....M 7
Whiteface (mt.) ....N 2
Whitney Point (res.)......J 6
Woodhull (lake) ....L 3

◉ County Seat.
‡ Name not on map.

AGRICULTURE, INDUSTRY and RESOURCES

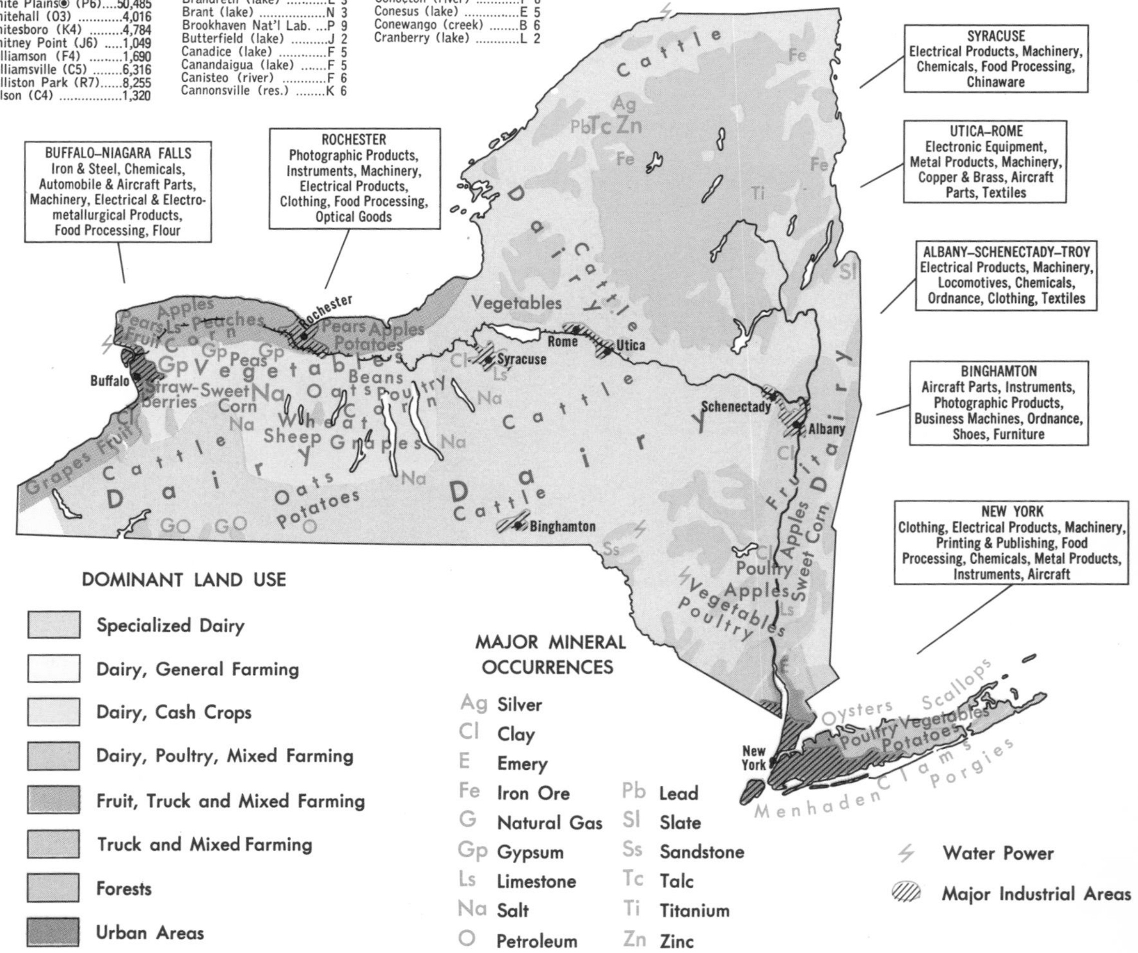
BUFFALO–NIAGARA FALLS
Iron & Steel, Chemicals, Automobile & Aircraft Parts, Machinery, Electrical & Electro-metallurgical Products, Food Processing, Flour
ROCHESTER
Photographic Products, Instruments, Machinery, Electrical Products, Clothing, Food Processing, Optical Goods
SYRACUSE
Electrical Products, Machinery, Chemicals, Food Processing, Chinaware
UTICA–ROME
Electronic Equipment, Metal Products, Machinery, Copper & Brass, Aircraft Parts, Textiles
ALBANY–SCHENECTADY–TROY
Electrical Products, Machinery, Locomotives, Chemicals, Ordnance, Clothing, Textiles
BINGHAMTON
Aircraft Parts, Instruments, Photographic Products, Business Machines, Ordnance, Shoes, Furniture
NEW YORK
Clothing, Electrical Products, Machinery, Printing & Publishing, Food Processing, Chemicals, Metal Products, Instruments, Aircraft
Cattle
Dairy
Vegetables
Rochester
Rome
Utica
Syracuse
Buffalo
Schenectady
Albany
Binghamton
Grapes
Fruit
Corn
Straw-berries
Sheep
Wheat
Oats
Potatoes
Beans
Poultry
Apples
Pears
Peaches
Sweet Corn
Oysters
Scallops
Clams
Porgies
Menhaden
New York
DOMINANT LAND USE
Specialized Dairy
Dairy, General Farming
Dairy, Cash Crops
Dairy, Poultry, Mixed Farming
Fruit, Truck and Mixed Farming
Truck and Mixed Farming
Forests
Urban Areas
MAJOR MINERAL OCCURRENCES
Ag Silver
Cl Clay
E Emery
Fe Iron Ore
G Natural Gas
Gp Gypsum
Ls Limestone
Na Salt
O Petroleum
Pb Lead
Sl Slate
Ss Sandstone
Tc Talc
Ti Titanium
Zn Zinc
Water Power
Major Industrial Areas

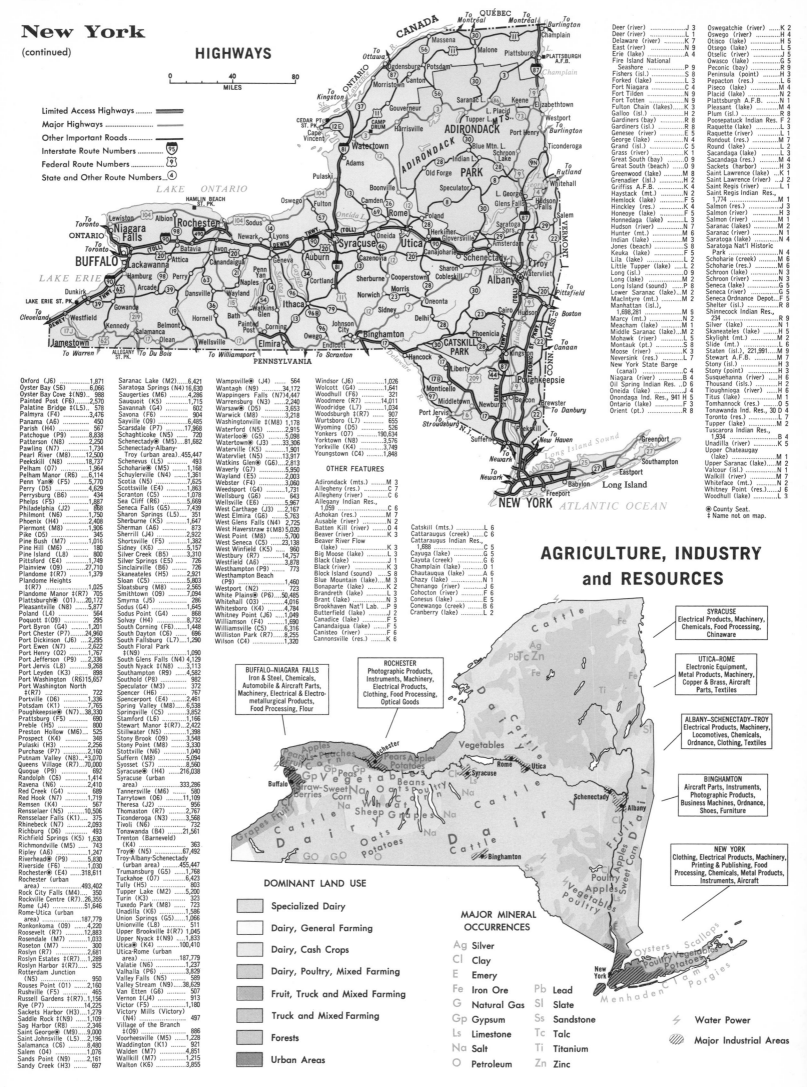

NORTH CAROLINA

AREA 52,712 sq. mi.
POPULATION 4,914,000
CAPITAL Raleigh
LARGEST CITY Charlotte 201,564
HIGHEST POINT Mt. Mitchell 6,684 ft.
SETTLED IN 1650
ADMITTED TO UNION November 21, 1789
POPULAR NAME Tarheel State
STATE FLOWER Flowering Dogwood
STATE BIRD Cardinal

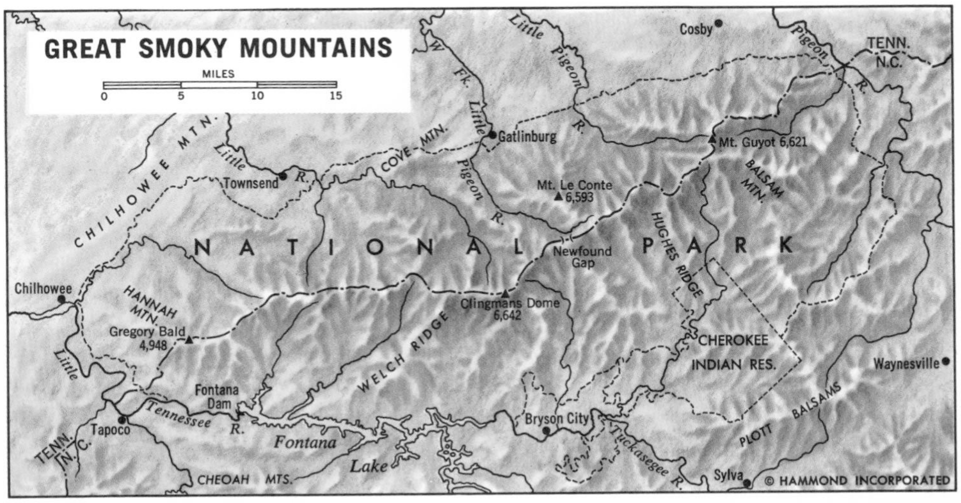
GREAT SMOKY MOUNTAINS
MILES
0 5 10 15
NATIONAL PARK
Cosby
TENN.
N.C.
Little Pigeon R.
W. Fk. Little Pigeon R.
Pigeon R.
Gatlinburg
Mt. Guyot 6,621
BALSAM MTN.
CHILHOWEE MTN.
COVE MTN.
Little R.
Townsend
Mt. Le Conte 6,593
Newfound Gap
HUGHES RIDGE
Chilhowee
HANNAH MTN.
Gregory Bald 4,948
Clingmans Dome 6,642
WELCH RIDGE
CHEROKEE INDIAN RES.
Waynesville
Little
Fontana Dam
Tapoco
TENN. N.C.
Tennessee R.
Fontana Lake
Bryson City
PLOTT BALSAMS
Tuckasegee R.
CHEOAH MTS.
Sylva
© HAMMOND INCORPORATED

COUNTIES

Alamance (L3) 85,674
Alexander (G3) 15,625
Alleghany (G1) 7,734
Anson (J4) 24,962
Ashe (F2) 19,768
Avery (F2) 12,009
Beaufort (R4) 36,014
Bertie (P2) 24,350
Bladen (M5) 28,881
Brunswick (N6) 20,278
Buncombe (D3) 130,074
Burke (F3) 52,701
Cabarrus (H4) 68,137
Caldwell (F3) 49,552
Camden (S2) 5,598
Carteret (R5) 30,940
Caswell (L2) 19,912
Catawba (G3) 73,191
Chatham (L3) 26,785
Cherokee (A4) 16,335
Chowan (R2) 11,729
Clay (B4) 5,526
Cleveland (F4) 66,048
Columbus (M6) 48,973
Craven (P4) 58,773
Cumberland (M4) 148,418
Currituck (S2) 6,601
Dare (T3) 5,935
Davidson (J3) 79,493
Davie (H3) 16,728
Duplin (O5) 40,270
Durham (M3) 111,995
Edgecombe (O3) 54,226
Forsyth (J2) 189,428
Franklin (N2) 28,755
Gaston (G4) 127,074
Gates (R2) 9,254
Graham (B4) 6,432
Granville (M2) 33,110
Greene (O3) 16,741
Guilford (K3) 246,520
Halifax (O2) 58,956
Harnett (M4) 48,236
Haywood (C3) 39,711
Henderson (D4) 36,163
Hertford (P2) 22,718
Hoke (L4) 16,356
Hyde (S3) 5,765
Iredell (H3) 62,526
Jackson (C4) 17,780
Johnston (N4) 62,936
Jones (P4) 11,005
Lee (L4) 26,561
Lenoir (O4) 55,276
Lincoln (G3) 28,814
Macon (B4) 14,935
Madison (D3) 17,217
Martin (P3) 27,139
McDowell (E3) 26,742
Mecklenburg (H4) 272,111
Mitchell (E2) 13,906
Montgomery (K4) 18,408
Moore (L4) 36,733
Nash (O2) 61,002
New Hanover (O6) 71,742
Northampton (P2) 26,811
Onslow (P5) 82,706
Orange (L2) 42,970
Pamlico (R4) 9,850
Pasquotank (S2) 25,630
Pender (O5) 18,508
Perquimans (S2) 9,178
Person (M2) 26,394
Pitt (P3) 69,942
Polk (E4) 11,395
Randolph (K3) 61,497
Richmond (K4) 39,202
Robeson (L5) 89,102
Rockingham (K2) 69,629
Rowan (H3) 82,817
Rutherford (E4) 45,091
Sampson (N4) 48,013
Scotland (L5) 25,183
Stanly (J4) 40,873
Stokes (J2) 22,314
Surry (H2) 48,205
Swain (B3) 8,387
Transylvania (D4) 16,372
Tyrrell (R3) 4,520
Union (H4) 44,670
Vance (N2) 32,002
Wake (M3) 169,082
Warren (N2) 19,652
Washington (R3) 13,488
Watauga (F2) 17,529
Wayne (N4) 82,059
Wilkes (G2) 45,269
Wilson (O3) 57,716
Yadkin (H2) 22,804
Yancey (E3) 14,008

CITIES and TOWNS

Abbottsburg (M5) 450
Aberdeen (L4) 1,531
Addor (L4) 118
Advance (J3) 197
Ahoskie (P2) 4,583
Alamance (K2) 500
Alarka (C4) 560
Albemarle◉ (J4) 12,261
Alert (N2) 250
Alexander (D3) 150
Alliance (R4) 650
Alma (L5) 250
Almond (B4) 250
Altamahaw (L2) 800
Andrews (B4) 1,404
Angier (M4) 1,249
Ansonville (J4) 558
Apex (M3) 1,368
Arapahoe (R4) 274
Archdale (K3) 1,520
Arden (D4) 600
Arlington (H2) 590
Asheboro◉ (K3) 9,449
Asheville◉ (D3) 60,192
Asheville (urban area) 68,592
Ashford (F3) 18
Askewville (R2) 195
Atkinson (N5) 302
Atlantic (S5) 800
Atlantic Beach (R5) 76
Aulander (P2) 1,083
Aurora (R4) 449
Autryville (M4) 192
Avon (U4) 300
Avondale (F4) 700
Ayden (P4) 3,108
Aydlett (T2) 250
Bachelor (R5) 200
Badin (J4) 1,905
Bahama (M2) 250
Bailey (J3) 795
Bakersville◉ (E2) 393
Balfour (E4) 1,106
Balfours (K3) 3,805
Balsam (C4) 400
Bannertown (H1) 1,096
Barco (T2) 300
Barker Heights (D4) 2,184
Barnard (D3) 200
Barnardsville (E3) 199
Bat Cave (E4) 300
Bath (R4) 346
Battleboro (O2) 364
Bayboro◉ (R4) 545
Bear Creek (L3) 250
Beargrass (P3) 103
Beaufort◉ (R5) 2,922
Bee Log (E3) 200
Belcross (S2) 200
Belhaven (R3) 2,386
Bellarthur (O3) 204
Belmont (H4) 5,007
Belvidere (S2) 280
Belwood (F4) 300
Benham (G2) 200
Bennett (K3) 222
Benson (N4) 2,355
Bessemer City (G4) 4,017
Beta (C4) 675
Bethel (P3) 1,578
Beulaville (O5) 1,062
Big Pine (D3) 150
Biltmore Forest (E3) 1,004
Biscoe (K4) 1,053
Black Creek (E3) 310
Black Mountain (K8) 1,313
Bladenboro (M5) 774
Blounts Creek (P4) 300
Blowing Rock (F2) 711
Bluff (D3) 100
Boardman (M6) 200
Boger City (G4) 1,728
Bogue (R5) 600
Boiling Springs (F4) 1,311
Bolivia (N6) 201
Bolton (N6) 617
Bonlee (L3) 275
Bonnie Doon (L4) 4,481
Boone◉ (F2) 3,686
Boonville (H2) 539
Bowdens (N4) 300
Brevard◉ (D4) 4,857
Bricks (O2) 250
Bridgeton (R4) 638
Broadway (L4) 466
Brookford (G3) 596
Browns Summit (K2) 500
Brunswick (M6) 169
Bryson City◉ (C4) 1,084
Buckner (D3) 50
Buies (L5) 300
Buies Creek (M4) 800
Bullock (M2) 600
Bunn (N3) 332
Bunnlevel (M4) 187
Burgaw◉ (N5) 1,750
Burlington (K2) 33,199
Burnsville◉ (E3) 1,388
Busick (E3) 150
Butters (M5) 250
Buxton (U4) 700
Bynum (L3) 450
Calypso (N4) 633
Camden◉ (S2) 200
Cameron (L4) 298
Candler (D3) 300
Candor (K4) 593
Canton (D3) 5,068
Cape Carteret ‡(P5) 52
Caroleen (F4) 1,168
Carolina Beach (O6) 1,192
Carrboro (L3) 1,997
Carthage◉ (K4) 1,190
Cary (M3) 3,356
Casar (F3) 350
Cashiers (C4) 342
Castalia (O2) 267
Castle Hayne (O6) 600
Catawba (G3) 504
Catharine Lake (O5) 200
Cedar Falls (K3) 600
Cedar Island (S5) 245
Cedar Mountain (D4) 250
Cerro Gordo (M6) 306
Chadbourn (M6) 2,323
Chadwick Acres ‡(R3) 5
Chalybeate Spgs. (M3) 200
Chapel Hill (M3) 12,573
Charlotte◉ (H4) 201,564
Charlotte (urban area) 209,551
Cherokee (C4) 600
Cherry (R3) 61
Cherryville (G4) 3,607
China Grove (H3) 1,500
Chinquapin (O5) 800
Chocowinity (P4) 580
Claremont (G3) 728
Clarendon (M6) 250
Clark (P4) 175
Clarkton (M6) 662
Clayton (N3) 3,302
Clemmons (J2) 2,152
Cleveland (H3) 594
Cliffside (F4) 1,275
Climax (K3) 225
Clinton◉ (N5) 7,461
Clyde (D3) 680
Coats (M4) 1,049
Cofield (R2) 500
Coinjock (S2) 300
Colerain (R2) 340
Coleridge (K3) 500
Colington (T3) 200
Collettsville (F3) 275
Columbia◉ (S3) 1,099
Columbus◉ (E4) 725
Comfort (O5) 300
Como (P1) 250
Concord◉ (H4) 17,799
Conetoe (O3) 147
Connellys Springs (F3) 500
Conover (G3) 2,281
Conway (P2) 662
Cooleemee (H3) 1,609
Cornelius (H4) 1,444
Council (M6) 56
Cove City (P4) 551
Cove Creek (D3) 50
Cramerton (G4) 3,123
Creedmoor (M2) 862
Creswell (S3) 402
Crisp (O3) 300
Crouse (G4) 901
Cruso (D4) 200
Culberson (A4) 106
Cullasaja (C4) 200
Cullowhee (C4) 300
Cumberland (M5) 700
Cumnock (L3) 250
Currie (N6) 200
Currituck◉ (S2) 300
Cycle (H2) 300
Dallas (G4) 3,270
Danbury◉ (J2) 175
Davidson (H4) 2,573
Davis (R5) 600
Day Book (E3) 150
Deep Gap (F2) 125
Deep Run (O4) 183
Delco (N6) 466
Dellview ‡(G4) 4
Dellwood (C3) 75
Denton (J3) 852
Denver (G3) 113
Dillsboro (C4) 140
Dobson◉ (H2) 684
Dockery (G2) 600
Dover (P4) 651
Draper (K1) 3,382
Drexel (F3) 1,146
Dublin (M5) 366
Dudley (N4) 158
Dundarrach (L5) 109
Dunn (M4) 7.566
Durham◉ (M2) 78,302
Durham (urban area) 84,642
Dysartsville (F3) 159
Eagle Springs (K4) 650
Earl (F4) 300
East Bend (H2) 446
East Flat Rock (E4) 2,100
East Laport (C4) 240
East Laurinburg (L5) 695
East Lumberton (M5) 1,200
East Spencer (J3) 2,171
East Wilmington (N6) 5,520
Edenton◉ (R2) 4,458
Edneyville (K8) 650
Edward (R4) 112
Efland (L2) 800
Eldorado (K4) 200
Elizabeth City◉ (S2) 14,062
Elizabethtown◉ (M5) 1,625
Elk Park (F2) 460
Elkin (H2) 2,868
Ellenboro (F4) 492
Ellerbe (K4) 843
Elm City (O3) 729
Elon College (L2) 1,284
Emerald Isle (P5) 14
Enfield (O2) 2,978
Englehard (T3) 600
Enka (D3) 1,500
Ernul (P4) 311
Erwin (M4) 3,183
Etowah (D4) 400
Eure (R2) 200
Eureka (O3) 246
Everetts (P3) 225
Evergreen (M6) 300
Fair Bluff (M6) 1,030
Fairfield (S3) 250
Fairmont (L6) 2,286
Fairview (D3) 300
Faison (N4) 666
Faith (J3) 494
Falcon (M4) 235
Falkland (O3) 140
Fallston (F4) 600
Farmville (O3) 3,997
Fayetteville◉ (M4) 47,106
Flat Rock (E4) 1,808
Flats (B4) 150
Fletcher (E4) 700
Forest City (E4) 6,556
Fountain (O3) 496
Four Oaks (M4) 1,010
Francisco (J2) 500
Franklin◉ (C4) 2,173
Franklinton (N2) 1,513
Franklinville (K3) 686
Freeland (N6) 320
Fremont (N3) 1,609
Fuquay-Varina (M3) 3,389
Garland (N5) 642
Garner (M3) 3,451
Garysburg (O2) 181
Gaston (O1) 1,214
Gastonia◉ (G4) 37,276
Gates (R2) 300
Gatesville◉ (R2) 460
Germanton (J2) 162
Gibson (K5) 501
Gibsonville (K2) 1,784
Glade Valley (G2) 200
Glen Alpine (F3) 734
Glen Raven (L2) 2,418
Glendon (L4) 200
Glenville (C4) 750
Glenwood (E3) 500
Godwin (M4) 149
Gold Hill (J3) 300
Gold Point (P3) 98
Goldsboro◉ (O4) 28,873
Goldston (L3) 374
Graham◉ (L2) 7,723
Graingers (O4) 188
Grandy (T2) 396
Granite Falls (G3) 2,644
Granite Quarry (H3) 1,059
Grantsboro (R4) 750
Greenmountain (E3) 600
Greensboro◉ (K2) 119,574
Greensboro (urban area) 123,334
Greenville◉ (P3) 22,860
Grifton (P4) 1,816
Grimesland (P3) 362
Grover (G4) 538
Guilford College (K2) 3,500
Gulf (L3) 300
Halifax◉ (O2) 370
Hallsboro (M6) 500
Hamilton (P3) 565
Hamlet (K5) 4,460
Hampstead (O6) 400
Hamptonville (H2) 170
Harbinger (T2) 500
Harkers Island (R5) 1,362
Harmony (H3) 322
Harrells (N5) 259
Harrellsville (R2) 171
Harrisburg (H4) 200
Hassell (P3) 147
Hatteras (T4) 750
Havelock (P5) 2,433
Haw River (L2) 1,410
Hayesville◉ (B4) 428
Hayne (M5) 250
Hays (G2) 750
Haywood (L3) 713
Hazelwood (C4) 1,925
Helton (G1) 50
Henderson◉ (N2) 12,740
Hendersonville◉ (E4) 5,911
Henrietta (F4) 950
Hertford◉ (S2) 2,068
Hickory (G3) 19,328
Hiddenite (G3) 600
High Point (J3) 62,063
High Point (urban area) 66,543
Highfalls (K4) 300
Highlands (C4) 597
Highshoals (G4) 750
Hildebran (F3) 518
Hillsborough◉ (L2) 1,349
Hobgood (P2) 630
Hobucken (S4) 500
Hoffman (K4) 344
Hollister (O2) 500
Holly Ridge (P6) 731
Holly Springs (M3) 558
Hookerton (O4) 358
Hope Mills (M5) 1,109
Hot Springs (D3) 723
Hudson (G3) 1,536
Huntersville (H4) 1,004
Hurdle Mills (L2) 250
Husk (F1) 202
Icard (G3) 1,400
Indian Trail (H4) 364
Ingold (N5) 250
Iron Station (G4) 279
Ivanhoe (N5) 350
Jackson◉ (P2) 765
Jackson Springs (K4) 244
Jacksonville◉ (O5) 13,491
James City (R4) 1,474
Jamestown (K3) 1,247
Jamesville (R3) 538
Jefferson◉ (G2) 814
Johns (K5) 300
Jonesville (H2) 1,895
Julian (K3) 250
Jupiter (D3) 174
Kannapolis (H4) 34,647
Kelford (P2) 362
Kelly (N6) 700
Kenansville◉ (O5) 724
Kenly (N3) 1,147
Kernersville (J2) 2,942
Kerr (N5) 150
Kill Devil Hills (T3) 268
King (J2) 950
Kings Creek (G3) 150
Kings Mountain (G4) 8,008
Kinston◉ (O4) 24,819
Kipling (M4) 185
Kittrell (M2) 121
Kitty Hawk (T2) 350
Knightdale (N3) 622
Knotts Island (S2) 420
Kure Beach (O7) 293
La Grange (O4) 2,133
Lake Landing (T4) 350
Lake Toxaway (D4) 1,200
Lake Waccamaw (N6) 780
Lakeview (L4) 450
Landis (H3) 1,763
Lansing (F1) 278
Lasker (P2) 119
Lattimore (F4) 257
Laurel Hill (K5) 750
Laurel Park (D4) 421
Laurinburg◉ (K5) 8,242
Lawndale (F4) 723
Lawsonville (J2) 200
Leaksville (K2) 6,427
Leasburg (L2) 400
Leggett (O3) 300
Leicester (D3) 225
Leland (N6) 150
Lemon Springs (L4) 300

(continued on following page)

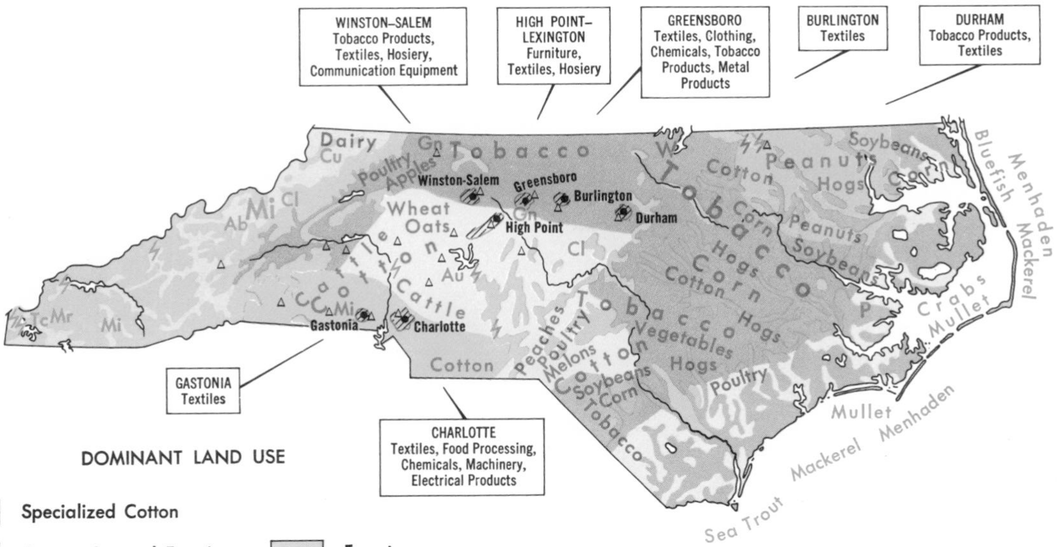
WINSTON-SALEM
Tobacco Products, Textiles, Hosiery, Communication Equipment
HIGH POINT–LEXINGTON
Furniture, Textiles, Hosiery
GREENSBORO
Textiles, Clothing, Chemicals, Tobacco Products, Metal Products
BURLINGTON
Textiles
DURHAM
Tobacco Products, Textiles
GASTONIA
Textiles
CHARLOTTE
Textiles, Food Processing, Chemicals, Machinery, Electrical Products
Dairy
Tobacco
Poultry
Apples
Winston-Salem
Greensboro
Burlington
Durham
High Point
Wheat
Oats
Cattle
Cotton
Corn
Peanuts
Hogs
Soybeans
Bluefish
Menhaden
Mackerel
Crabs
Mullet
Gastonia
Charlotte
Peaches
Melons
Vegetables
Sea Trout

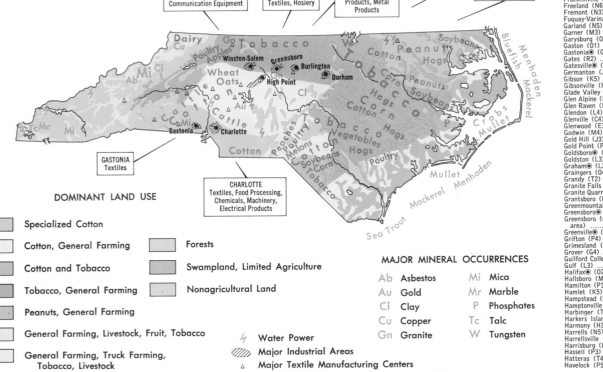

DOMINANT LAND USE

Specialized Cotton
Cotton, General Farming
Cotton and Tobacco
Tobacco, General Farming
Peanuts, General Farming
General Farming, Livestock, Fruit, Tobacco
General Farming, Truck Farming, Tobacco, Livestock
Forests
Swampland, Limited Agriculture
Nonagricultural Land

Water Power
Major Industrial Areas
Major Textile Manufacturing Centers

MAJOR MINERAL OCCURRENCES

Ab Asbestos
Au Gold
Cl Clay
Cu Copper
Gn Granite
Mi Mica
Mr Marble
P Phosphates
Tc Talc
W Tungsten

North Carolina
(continued)

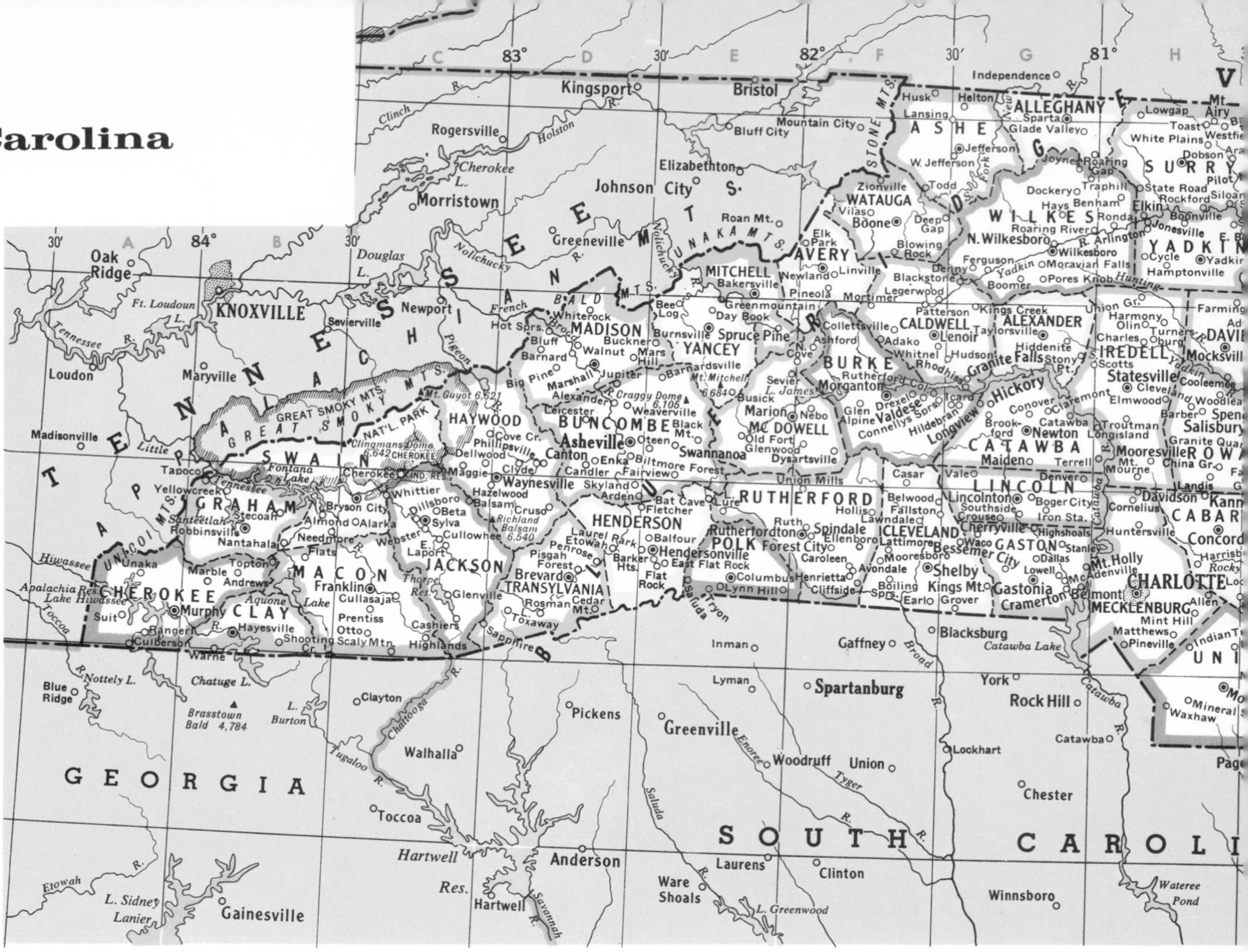

Lenoir● (G3) 10,257
Lewarae (K5) 425
Lewiston (P2) 360
Lexington● (J3) 16,093
Liberty (K3) 1,438
Lilesville (K5) 635
Lillington● (M4) 1,242
Lincolnton● (G4) 5,699
Linden (M4) 157
Linville (F2) 500
Linwood (J3) 200
Littleton (O2) 1,024
Locust (J4) 211
Long Beach (N7) 102
Longhurst (L2) 1,546
Longisland (H3) 350
Longview (F3) 2,997
Longwood (N6) 600
Longwood Park (K5)...1,144
Louisburg● (N2) 2,862
Love Valley ‡(H3)........78
Lowell (G4) 2,784
Lowgap (H1) 700
Lowland (S4) 547
Lucama (N3) 498
Lumber Bridge (L5)....100
Lumberton● (L5) ...15,305
Lynn (E4) 500
Macclesfield (O3) 473
Mackeys (R3) 250
Macon (N2) 187
Madison (K2) 1,912
Maggie (C3) 400
Magnolia (O5) 629
Maiden (G3) 2,039
Mamers (L4) 425
Manly (M4) 239
Manns Harbor (T3).....300
Manson (N2) 210
Manteo● (T3) 587
Maple Hill (O5) 250
Marble (B4) 625
Margarettsville (P1)....106
Marietta (L6) 239
Marion● (E3) 3,345
Marshall● (D3) 926
Marshallberg (S5) 800
Marshville (J4) 1,360
Marston (K5) 159
Matthews (H4) 609
Maury (O4) 285
Maxton (L5) 1,755
Mayodan (K2) 2,366
Maysville (P5) 892
McAdenville (H4) 748
McCain (L4) 700
McDonalds (L5) 79
McFarlan (J5) 161
Mebane (L2) 2,364
Merrimon (R5) 150
Merry Hill (R2) 150
Merry Oaks (L3) 77
Method (M3) 350

Micro (N3) 350
Middleburg (N2) 170
Middlesex (N3) 588
Middletown (T4) 250
Midland (J4) 250
Midstate Mill (L1) 78
Midway Park (O5)....4,164
Milton (L1) 235
Milwaukee (P2) 311
Mineral Springs (H5)...111
Mint Hill (H4) 1,500
Misenheimer (J4) 160
Mocksville● (H3) 2,379
Momeyer (N3) 150
Moncure (L3) 500
Monroe● (J5) 10,882
Mooresboro (F4) 400
Mooresville● (H3) ...6,918
Moravian Falls (G2)....375
Morehead City (R5)...5,583
Morganton● (F3) 9,186
Morrisville (M3) 222
Mortimer (F2) 3
Morven (J5) 518
Mount Airy (H1) 7,055
Mount Gilead (K4) ...1,229
Mount Holly (H4) 4,037
Mount Mourne (H3)...210
Mount Olive (O4) 4,673
Mount Pleasant (J4)..1,041
Mount Vernon Springs
  (L3) 140
Moyock (S1) 300
Murfreesboro (R2) ...2,643
Murphy● (B4) 2,235
Nags Head (T3) 728
Nakina (M6) 100
Nantahala (B4) 100
Nashville● (O3) 1,423
Nebo (F3) 710
Needmore (B4) 200
Neuse (M3) 500

New Bern● (P4) 15,717
New Hill (M3) 125
New Holland (S4) 500
New London (J4) 223
Newland● (F2) 564
Newport (R5) 861
Newton● (G3) 6,658
Newton Grove (N4)....477
Norlina (N2) 927
Norman (K4) 220
North Cove (F3) 500
North Harlowe (R5)....500
North Wilkesboro (G2).4,197
Northside (M2) 300
Norwood (J4) 1,844
Oak City (P3) 574
Oak Ridge (K2) 650
Oakboro (J4) 581
Oakley (P3) 17
Ocean Isle Beach (N7)...5
Ocracoke (T4) 700
Old Fort (E3) 787
Old Trap (T2) 475
Olivia (L4) 450
Oriental (R4) 522
Orrum (L6) 139
Oteen (E3) 1,500
Otto (C4) 200
Owens (M4) 5,207
Oxford● (M2) 6,978
Pactolus (P3) 211
Palmyra (P2) 50
Pantego (R3) 262
Parkersburg (N5) 65
Parkton (M5) 906
Parmele (P3) 323
Patterson (F3) 265
Peachland (J5) 563
Pelham (L1) 800
Pembroke (L5) 1,372
Penrose (D4) 900
Phillipsville (D3) 311
Pike Road (R3) 125
Pikeville (N4) 525
Pilot Mountain (H2)..1,310
Pine Hall (K2) 400

Pine Level (N4) 833
Pinebluff (K4) 509
Pinehurst (K4) 1,124
Pineola (F2) 375
Pinetops (O3) 1,372
Pinetown (R3) 215
Pineview (L4) 175
Pineville (H4) 1,514
Pink Hill (O4) 457
Pinnacle (J2) 700
Pisgah Forest (D4)...1,200
Pittsboro● (L3) 1,215
Pleasant Hill (O1) 210
Plymouth● (R3) 4,666
Point Harbor (T2) 225
Polkton (J4) 530
Pollocksville (P5) 416
Ponzer (S3) 200
Poplar Branch (T2) 287
Powells Point (T2) 210
Powellsville (R2) 259
Prentiss (C4) 225
Princeton (N4) 948
Princeville (P3) 797
Proctorville (M6) 188
Quitsna (P3) 210
Raeford● (L5) 3,058
RALEIGH● (M3)...93,931
Ramseur (K3) 1,258
Randleman (K3) 2,232
Ranger (L4) 40
Ranlo ‡(G4) 2,067
Red Oak (N2) 334
Red Springs (L5) 2,767
Reidsville (L2) 14,267
Rex (M5) 1,515
Rhodhiss (F3) 937
Rich Square (P2) 1,134
Richfield (J4) 293
Richlands (O5) 1,079
Ridgeway (N2) 500
Riegelwood (N6) 159
Roanoke Rapids (O2).13,320

Roaring Gap (H2) 600
Roaring River (G2) 185
Robbins (K4) 1,294
Robbinsville● (B4) 587
Roberdell (K5) 379
Robersonville (P3) ...1,684
Rockfish (L5) 150
Rockingham● (K5) ..5,512
Rockwell (J3) 948
Rocky Mount (O3) ..32,147
Rocky Point (O6) 850
Rolesville (N3) 358
Ronda (H2) 510
Roper (R3) 771
Rose Hill (O5) 1,727
Roseboro (N5) 1,354
Rosman (D4) 419
Rougemont (L2) 500
Rowland (L5) 1,408
Roxboro● (M2) 5,147
Roxobel (P2) 452
Royal (R4) 135
Royal Cotton Mills
  (M2) 500
Ruffin (K2) 500
Rural Hall (J2) 1,503
Ruth (E4) 529
Rutherford College (F3)800
Rutherfordton● (E4)..3,392
Saint Pauls (M5) 2,249
Salemburg (N4) 569
Salisbury● (H3) 21,297
Salter Path (R5) 500
Saluda (E4) 570
Sandy Ridge (J1) 200
Sanford● (L4) 12,253
Sapphire (D4) 200
Saratoga (O3) 409
Saxapahaw (L3) 750
Scaly Mtn. (C4) 225
Scotland Neck (P2)..2,974
Scotts Hill (O6) 150
Scranton (S4) 975
Seaboard (O1) 624

Seagrove (K3) 323
Sealevel (S5) 350
Selma (N3) 3,102
Semora (L2) 250
Seven Springs (O4)....207
Severn (P2) 310
Sevier (E3) 100
Shallotte (N7) 480
Shannon (L5) 350
Sharpsburg (O3) 490
Shawboro (S2) 500
Shelby● (G4) 17,698
Shelmerdine (P4) 29
Shooting Creek (B4)...200
Siler City (L3) 4,455
Silverdale (P5) 500
Simpson (Chicod) (P3).302
Sims (N3) 205
Skyland (D4) 1,100
Smithfield● (N3) 6,117
Smithtown (J2) 199
Smyrna (R5) 500
Sneads Ferry (P5).......500
Snow Camp (L3) 134
Snow Hill● (O4) 1,043
Sophia (K3) 550
South Creek (R4) 82
South Mills (S2) 700
South Wadesboro (J5)..189
Southern Pines (L4)..5,198
Southmont (J3) 800
Southport● (N7) 2,034
Southside (G4) 500
Sparta● (G1) 1,047
Speed (P3) 142
Spencer (H3) 2,904
Spencer Mtn. ‡(G4)....100
Spindale (F4) 4,082
Spring Hope (O3) 1,336
Spring Lake (M4) 4,110
Spruce Pine (E3) 2,504
Stacy (S5) 425
Staley (K3) 260

Stanfield (J4) 471
Stanley (G4) 1,980
Stanleyville (J2) 1,138
Stantonsburg (O3) 897
Star (K4) 745
State Road (H2) 775
Statesville● (H3) ..19,844
Stecoah (B4) 88
Stedman (M4) 458
Steeds (K4) 100
Stella (P5) 500
Stem (N2) 221
Stokes (P3) 195
Stokesdale (K2) 900
Stoneville (K2) 951
Stonewall (R4) 214
Stony Point (G3) 1,015
Stovall (M2) 570
Straits (R5) 150
Stumpy Point (T3) 170
Suit (A4) 75
Summerfield (K2) 923
Sunbury (R2) 500
Sunset Beach ‡(N7)....39
Supply (N6) 136
Swan Station (L4) 190
Swannanoa (E3) 2,189
Swanquarter● (S4) ...300
Swansboro (P5) 1,104
Sylva● (C4) 1,564
Tabor City (M6) 2,338
Tapoco (A4) 100
Tarboro● (O3) 8,411
Tarheel (M5) 77
Taylorsville● (G3) ..1,470
Teachey (N5) 187
Terrell (G3) 192
Thomasville (J3) ...15,190
Tillery (O2) 200
Timberlake (M2) 200
Toast (H2) 2,023
Todd (F2) 52
Topsail Beach ‡(O6)...972
Topton (B4) 125

Townsville (N1) 195
Traphill (H2) 175
Trent Woods (P4) 517
Trenton● (P4) 404
Trinity (K3) 881
Troutman (H3) 648
Troy● (K4) 2,346
Tryon (E4) 2,223
Tunis (P2) 250
Turkey (N4) 199
Tyner (R2) 450
Ulah (K3) 400
Unaka (A4) 50
Union Grove (H2) 493
Union Mills (F3) 350
University (L2) 119
Valdese (F3) 2,941
Vale (G3) 200
Vanceboro (P4) 806
Vandemere (R4) 452
Vass (L4) 767
Vaughan (N2) 122
Verona (O5) 500
Vilas (F2) 100
Waco (G4) 529
Wade (M4) 750
Wadesboro● (J5) ...3,744
Wadeville (L4) 300
Wagram (L5) 562
Wake Forest (M3) ...2,664
Walkertown (J2) 1,240
Wallace (N5) 2,285
Wallburg (J3) 205
Walnut (D3) 400
Walnut Cove (J2) 1,288
Walstonburg (O3) 191
Wanchese (T3) 975
Warne (B5) 250
Warren Plains (N2) 205
Warrensville (G6) 116
Warrenton● (N2) 1,124
Warsaw (N4) 2,221
Washington● (R3) ..9,939

Washington Park (R3)..574
Watha (O5) 174
Waxhaw (H5) 729
Waynesville● (D4) ...6,159
Weaverville (D3) 1,041
Webster (C4) 166
Weeksville (S2) 350
Welcome (J3) 600
Weldon (O2) 2,165
Wendell (N3) 1,620
Wentworth● (K2) 140
West Jefferson (F2)..1,000
Westfield (H2) 500
Whitakers (O2) 1,004
White Lake (M5) 130
White Oak (M5) 250
White Plains (H2) 500
Whitehall (Seven Spgs.)
  (O4) 207
Whiterock (D3) 150
Whiteville● (M6) 4,683
Whitnel (F3) 1,232
Whittier (C4) 400
Wilkesboro● (G2) ...1,568
Willard (O5) 600
Williamston● (R3) ...6,924
Wilmington● (N6)..44,013
Wilson● (O3) 28,753
Wilson Mills (M3).......280
Windsor● (R2) 1,813
Winfall (S2) 269
Wingate (J5) 1,304
Winnabow (N6) 650
Winston-Salem●
  (J2) 111,135
Winston-Salem (urban
  area) 128,762
Winterville (P3) 1,418
Winton● (P2) 835
Wise (N2) 500
Wood (N2) 94
Woodland (P2) 651
Woodleaf (H3) 750
Woodville (P2) 344
Worthville (K3) 600
Wrightsville Beach (O6).723
Yadkin College (J3).....75
Yadkinville● (H2) 1,644
Yanceyville● (L2) 1,113
Yaupon Beach (N7).....89
Yellowcreek (A4) 300
Youngsville (N2) 596
Zebulon (N3) 1,534
Zionville (F2) 565

OTHER FEATURES

Albemarle (sound) ....S 2
Alligator (lake) ....S 3
Alligator (river) ....S 3
Angola (swamp) ....O 5
Apalachia (res.) ....A 4
Appalachian (mts.) ......D 2
Aquone (lake) ....B 4
Ashe (isl.) ....P 6
Bald (mts.) ....D 3
Black (river) ....N 5
Blue Ridge (mts.) ....D 2
Bogue (inlet) ....P 5
Bogue (sound) ....P 5
Bragg, Fort ....M 4
Broad (river) ....E 4
Buggs Island (lake) .....M 1
Cape Fear (river) ....M 5
Cape Hatteras Nat'l
  Seashore ....T 4
Catawba (lake) ....G 4
Catawba (river) ....H 4
Catfish (lake) ....P 5
Chatuge (lake) ....B 5
Cherokee Indian Res. ..C 3
Cherry Point Marine
  Corps Air Station........R 5

TOPOGRAPHY

0   40   80
MILES

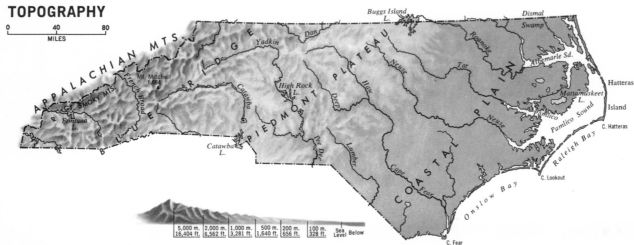

5,000 m. | 2,000 m. | 1,000 m. | 500 m. | 200 m. | 100 m. | Sea Level | Below
16,404 ft. | 6,562 ft. | 3,281 ft. | 1,640 ft. | 656 ft. | 328 ft.

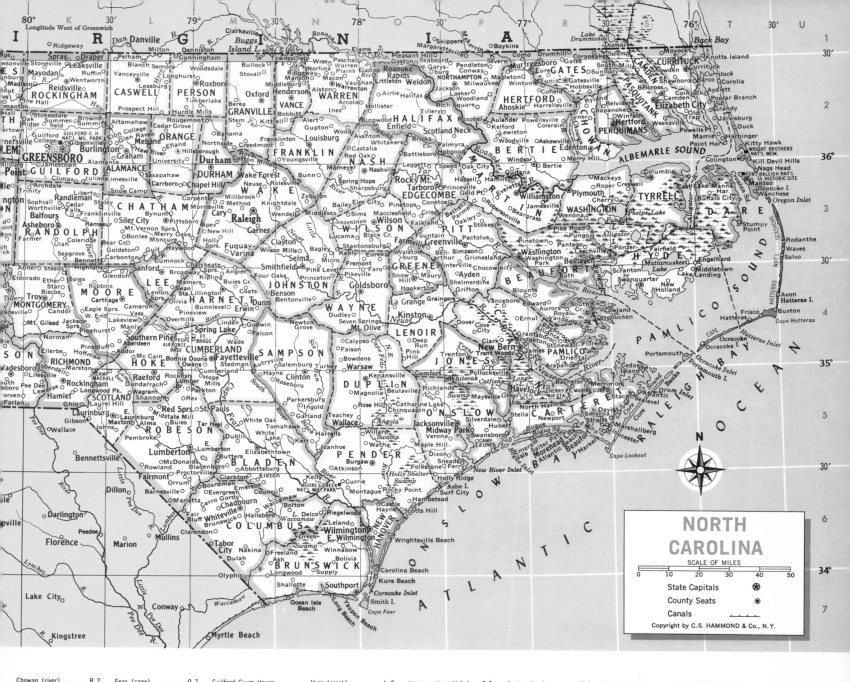

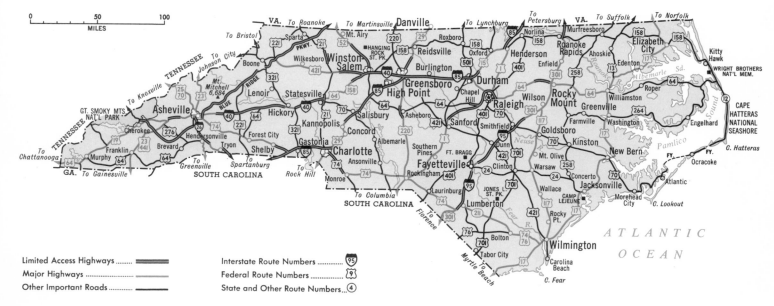

Chowan (river)	R 2	
Clingmans Dome (mt.)	C 3	
Contentnea (creek)	N 3	
Core (banks)	S 5	
Core (sound)	S 5	
Corncake (inlet)	O 7	
Craggy Dome (mt.)	D 3	
Croatan (sound)	T 3	
Currituck (sound)	T 2	
Dan (river)	L 1	
Deep (river)	K 3	
Dismal (swamp)	S 1	
Drum (inlet)	S 5	

Fear (cape)	O 7
Fishing (creek)	O 2
Fontana (lake)	B 4
Fort Bragg	M 4
Fort Raleigh Nat'l Hist. Site	T 3
French Broad (river)	D 3
Gaston (res.)	M 1
Great (lake)	R 4
Great Smoky (mts.)	B 3
Hiwassee (lake)	A 4
Hiwassee (river)	A 4
Holly Shelter (swamp)	O 6
Hunting (river)	H 2

Guilford Court House Nat'l Mil. Park	K 2
Guyot (mt.)	C 3
Hatteras (cape)	U 4
Hatteras (inlet)	T 4
Hatteras (isl.)	U 4
Haw (river)	K 2
High Rock (lake)	J 3
Hyco (creek)	L 2
James (lake)	E 3
Lanes (creek)	J 5
Lejeune, Camp	P 5
Little (river)	N 3
Little (river)	L 4
Little Pee Dee (river)	L 6

Hyco (creek)	L 2
James (lake)	E 3
Lanes (creek)	J 5
Lejeune, Camp	P 5
Little (river)	N 3
Little (river)	L 4
Little Pee Dee (river)	L 6
Little Tennessee (river)	B 4
Long (lake)	P 5
Lookout (cape)	S 5
Lumber (river)	L 6
Mackall, Camp	K 5

Mattamuskeet (lake)	S 3
Meherrin (river)	P 1
Mitchell (mt.)	D 3
Moores Creek Nat'l Mil. Park	N 6
Neuse (river)	R 5
New (river)	O 5
New River (inlet)	P 6
Nolichucky (river)	E 2
North East Cape Fear (river)	O 4
Ocracoke (inlet)	T 5
Ocracoke (isl.)	T 4

Onslow (bay)	P 6
Oregon (inlet)	U 3
Pamlico (river)	R 4
Pamlico (sound)	S 4
Pee Dee (river)	K 5
Phelps (lake)	S 3
Pigeon (river)	C 3
Pope A.F.B.	L 4
Portsmouth (isl.)	T 5
Pungo (lake)	S 3
Pungo (river)	R 4
Raleigh (bay)	S 5
Richland Balsam (mt.)	D 4

Roanoke (isl.)	T 3
Roanoke (river)	P 2
Rocky (river)	H 4
Santeetlah (lake)	B 4
Six Run (creek)	N 4
Smith (isl.)	O 7
South (river)	M 4
South Fork, New (riv.)	G 2
South Yadkin (river)	H 3
Stone (mt.)	F 2
Tar (river)	O 3
Thorpe (res.)	C 4
Tillery (lake)	J 4

Trent (river)	P 4
Unaka (mts.)	E 2
Unicoi (mts.)	A 4
Waccamaw (lake)	N 6
Waccamaw (river)	L 7
Watauga (river)	F 6
Whiteoak (swamp)	P 5
Wright Brothers Nat'l Mem.	U 2
Yadkin (river)	J 3

⊙ County Seat.
‡ Name not on map.

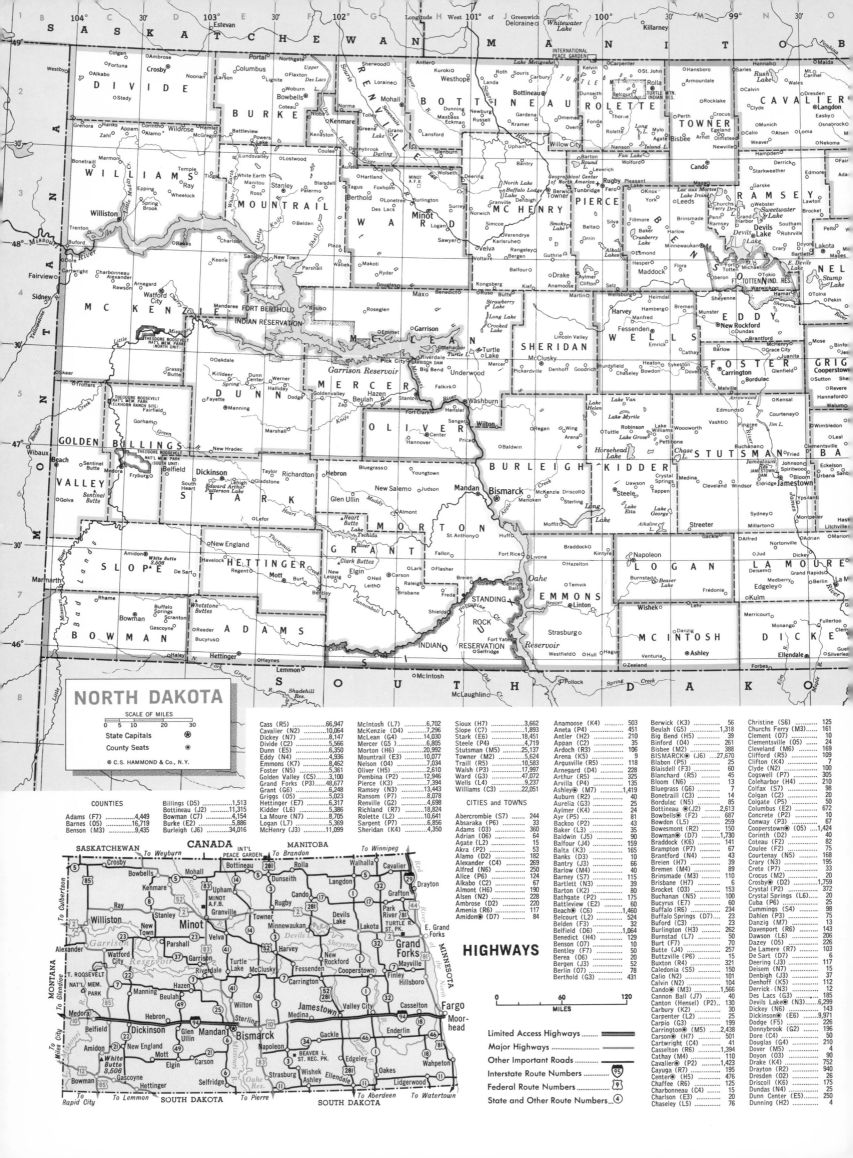

NORTH DAKOTA

SCALE OF MILES 0 5 10 20 30

⊛ State Capitals
◉ County Seats

COUNTIES

County		Population
Adams	(F7)	4,449
Barnes	(O5)	16,719
Benson	(M3)	9,435
Billings	(D5)	1,513
Bottineau	(J2)	11,315
Bowman	(C7)	4,154
Burke	(E2)	5,886
Burleigh	(J6)	34,016
Cass	(R5)	66,947
Cavalier	(N2)	10,064
Dickey	(N7)	8,147
Divide	(C2)	5,566
Dunn	(E5)	6,350
Eddy	(N4)	4,936
Emmons	(K7)	8,462
Foster	(N5)	5,361
Golden Valley	(C5)	3,100
Grand Forks	(P3)	48,677
Grant	(G6)	6,248
Griggs	(O5)	5,023
Hettinger	(E7)	6,317
Kidder	(L6)	5,386
La Moure	(N7)	7,296
Logan	(L7)	5,369
McHenry	(J3)	11,099
McIntosh	(L7)	6,702
McKenzie	(D4)	7,296
McLean	(G4)	14,030
Mercer	(G5)	6,805
Morton	(H6)	20,992
Mountrail	(E3)	10,077
Nelson	(O4)	7,034
Oliver	(H5)	2,610
Pembina	(P2)	12,946
Pierce	(K3)	7,394
Ramsey	(N3)	13,443
Ransom	(P7)	8,078
Renville	(G2)	4,698
Richland	(R7)	18,824
Rolette	(L2)	10,641
Sargent	(P7)	6,856
Sheridan	(K4)	4,350
Sioux	(H7)	3,662
Slope	(C7)	1,893
Stark	(E6)	18,451
Steele	(P4)	
Stutsman	(M5)	25,137
Towner	(M2)	5,624
Traill	(R5)	10,583
Walsh	(P3)	17,997
Ward	(G3)	47,072
Wells	(L4)	9,237
Williams	(C3)	22,051

CITIES and TOWNS

Place		Pop.
Abercrombie	(S7)	244
Absaraka	(P6)	33
Adams	(O3)	360
Adrian	(O6)	64
Agate	(L2)	15
Akra	(P2)	53
Alamo	(D2)	182
Alexander	(C4)	269
Alfred	(N6)	250
Alice	(P6)	124
Alkabo	(C2)	67
Almont	(H6)	190
Alsen	(N2)	228
Ambrose	(D2)	220
Amenia	(R6)	117
Amidon◉	(D7)	84
Anamoose	(K4)	503
Aneta	(P4)	451
Antler	(H2)	210
Appan	(C2)	35
Ardoch	(R3)	106
Argusville	(R5)	118
Arnegard	(D4)	228
Arthur	(R5)	325
Arvilla	(P4)	135
Ashley◉	(M7)	1,419
Auburn	(R2)	40
Aurelia	(G3)	25
Aylmer	(P4)	24
Ayr	(P5)	81
Backoo	(P2)	43
Baker	(K3)	35
Baldwin	(J5)	90
Balfour	(J4)	159
Balta	(K3)	165
Banks	(D3)	9
Bantry	(J3)	66
Barlow	(N5)	39
Barney	(S7)	115
Bartlett	(N3)	39
Barton	(K2)	80
Bathgate	(P2)	175
Battleview	(E2)	40
Beach◉	(C6)	1,460
Belcourt	(L2)	524
Belden	(F3)	32
Belfield	(D6)	1,064
Benedict	(H4)	129
Benson	(O7)	10
Bentley	(F7)	10
Berea	(O6)	10
Bergen	(J3)	52
Berlin	(O7)	78
Berthold	(G3)	431
Berwick	(K3)	56
Beulah	(G5)	1,318
Big Bend	(H5)	39
Binford	(O4)	261
Bisbee	(M2)	388
Blabon	(P5)	25
Blaisdell	(F3)	60
Blanchard	(R5)	45
Bloom	(N6)	13
Bluegrass	(G6)	7
Bonetrail	(C3)	14
Bordulac	(M5)	85
Bottineau◉	(J2)	2,613
Bowbells◉	(F2)	687
Bowdon	(L5)	259
Bowesmont	(R2)	150
Bowman◉	(C7)	1,730
Braddock	(K6)	141
Brampton	(P7)	67
Brantford	(N4)	43
Breien	(H7)	39
Bremen	(M4)	89
Brinsmade	(M3)	110
Brisbane	(H7)	6
Brocket	(O3)	687
Buchanan	(N5)	100
Bucyrus	(F7)	60
Buffalo	(R6)	234
Buffalo Springs	(D7)	23
Buford	(D4)	23
Burlington	(H3)	262
Burnstad	(L7)	50
Burt	(F7)	70
Butte	(J4)	257
Buttzville	(P6)	15
Buxton	(R4)	321
Christine	(S6)	125
Churchs Ferry	(M3)	161
Clement	(O7)	10
Clementsville	(O5)	24
Cleveland	(M6)	169
Clifford	(R5)	109
Clifton	(K4)	7
Clyde	(N2)	100
Cogswell	(P7)	98
Coleharbor	(H4)	210
Colfax	(S7)	98
Colgan	(C2)	20
Colgate	(P5)	50
Columbus	(E2)	672
Concrete	(P2)	10
Conway	(P3)	67
Cooperstown◉	(O5)	1,424
Corinth	(D2)	40
Coteau	(F2)	82
Coulee	(F2)	75
Courtenay	(N5)	168
Crary	(N3)	195
Crete	(P7)	33
Crocus	(M2)	20
Crosby◉	(D2)	1,759
Crystal	(P2)	372
Crystal Springs	(L6)	25
Cuba	(P6)	25
Cummings	(S4)	98
Dahlen	(P3)	75
Danzig	(M7)	20
Davenport	(R6)	143
Dawson	(L6)	206
Dazey	(O5)	226
De Lamere	(R7)	103
De Sart	(C7)	6
Deering	(J3)	117
Deisem	(N3)	15
Denbigh	(J3)	37
Denhoff	(K5)	112
Derrick	(K3)	12
Des Lacs	(G3)	185
Devils Lake◉	(N3)	6,299
Dickey	(N6)	143
Dickinson◉	(E6)	9,971
Dodge	(F5)	226
Donnybrook	(G2)	196
Dore	(C4)	50
Douglas	(G4)	210
Dover	(M5)	30
Doyon	(N3)	90
Drake	(K4)	752
Drayton	(R2)	940
Dresden	(O2)	26
Driscoll	(K6)	175
Dundas	(N4)	25
Dunn Center	(E5)	250
Dunning	(H2)	4

HIGHWAYS

0 60 120 MILES

Limited Access Highways	═══
Major Highways	───
Other Important Roads	───
Interstate Route Numbers	(95)
Federal Route Numbers	(81)
State and Other Route Numbers	(4)

Dunseith (K2) 1,017
Durbin (R6) 35
Dwight (S7) 101
Easby (O2) 15
Eckelson (O6) 100
Eckman (H2) 5
Edgeley (N7) 992
Edinburg (P3) 330
Edmore (O3) 405
Edmunds (M5) 34
Egeland (M2) 190
Eldridge (N6) 63
Elgin (G7) 944
Ellendale◉ (N7) 1,800
Elliott (P7) 62
Embden (R6) 126
Emerado (R4) 328
Emmet (G4) 100
Emrick (L4) 22
Enderlin (P6) 1,596
Englevale (P7) 70
Epping (D3) 151
Erie (R5) 150
Esmond (L3) 420
Everest (R6) 10
Fairdale (O3) 126
Fairfield (D5) 10
Fairmount (S7) 503
Falkirk (H5) 30
Fallon (H6) 3
Fargo◉ (S6) 46,662
Fargo-Moorhead (urban area) 72,730
Fayette (E5) 15
Fero (L3) 4
Fessenden◉ (L4) 920
Fillmore (L3) 74
Fingal (P6) 190
Finley◉ (P4) 808
Flasher (H7) 515
Flaxton (F2) 375
Flora (M4) 40
Fonda (K2) 20
Forbes (N8) 138
Fordville (P3) 367
Forest River (P3) 191
Forman◉ (P7) 530
Fort Clark (H5) 13
Fort Ransom (P6) 100
Fort Rice (J6) 25
Fort Totten (M4) 215
Fort Yates◉ (J7) 484
Fortuna (C2) 185
Foxholm (G3) 150
Freda (H7) 5
Fredonia (M7) 141
Fried (N5) 16
Fryburg (D6) 35
Fullerton (O7) 181
Gackle (M6) 523
Galchutt (S7) 100
Galesburg (R5) 166
Gardar (P2) 75
Gardena (J2) 113
Gardner (R5) 107
Garrison (H4) 1,794
Garske (N3) 50
Gascoyne (D7) 50
Geneseo (R7) 12
Gilby (R3) 281
Gladstone (F6) 185
Glasston (R2) 375
Glen Ullin (G6) 1,210
Glenburn (H2) 363
Glenfield (N5) 129
Glover (O7) 50
Goldenvalley (F5) 286
Golva (C6) 162
Goodrich (K5) 392
Gorham (D5) 15
Grace City (N4) 104
Grafton◉ (R3) 5,885
Grand Forks◉ (R4) 34,451
Grand Harbor (N3) 38
Grand Rapids (N7) 50
Grandin (R5) 147
Grano (G2) 14
Granville (J3) 400
Grassy Butte (D5) 75
Great Bend (S7) 164
Greene (G2) 16
Grenora (C2) 448
Guelph (O7) 59
Guthrie (K3) 24
Gwinner (P7) 242
Hague (L7) 197
Haley (D8) 14
Halliday (F5) 509
Hallson (P2) 3
Hamar (N4) 81
Hamberg (L4) 64
Hamilton (R2) 217
Hamlet (E2) 25
Hampden (N2) 71
Hankinson (S7) 1,285
Hanks (C2) 78
Hannaford (O5) 277
Hannah (N2) 253
Hannover (H5) 28
Hansboro (M2) 143
Harlow (M3) 95
Hartland (G3) 40
Harvey (L4) 2,365
Harwood (S6) 150
Hastings (O6) 102
Hatton (R4) 856
Havana (P8) 206
Havelock (E7) 15
Haynes (F8) 111
Hazelton (K7) 451
Hazen (G5) 1,222
Heaton (L5) 62
Hebron (G6) 1,340
Heil (G7) 50
Heimdal (L4) 148
Hensel (P2) 130
Hensler (H5) 65
Hesper (L4) 15
Hettinger◉ (E8) 1,769
Hickson (S6) 49
Hillsboro◉ (S5) 1,278
Holmes (R4) 11
Honeyford (R3) 30
Hoople (P2) 334
Hope (P5) 390
Horace (S6) 178
Hoving (P7) 2
Huff (J6) 150
Hull (K7) 50
Hunter (R5) 446
Hurdsfield (L5) 183
Inkster (P3) 282
Jamestown◉ (N6) 15,163
Jessie (O4) 81
Johnson (N6) 15
Johnstown (R3) 50
Joliette (R2) 36
Juanita (N4) 40
Jud (N6) 156
Judson (H6) 75
Karlsruhe (J3) 221
Karnak (O5) 9
Kathryn (P6) 142
Keene (E4) 250
Kellys (R4) 11
Kelso (R5) 51
Kelvin (K2) 10
Kempton (P4) 50
Kenaston (F2) 50
Kenmare (G2) 1,696
Kensal (N5) 334
Kief (J4) 97
Killdeer (E5) 765
Kindred (R6) 580
Kintyre (L6) 78
Kloten (O4) 110
Knox (L3) 122
Kongsberg (J4) 20
Kramer (J2) 175
Kulm (N7) 664
Kuroki (H2) 10
La Moure◉ (O7) 1,068
Lake Williams (L5) 6
Lakota◉ (O3) 1,066
Landa (J2) 110
Langdon◉ (O2) 2,151
Lankin (P3) 303
Lansford (H2) 382
Larimore (P4) 1,714
Lark (H7) 11
Larson (E2) 62
Lawton (O3) 159
Leal (O5) 70
Leeds (N3) 797
Lefor (F6) 112
Lehigh (E6) 55
Lehr (M7) 381
Leith (G7) 100
Leonard (R6) 232
Leroy (P2) 70
Leverich (L3) 5
Lidgerwood (R7) 1,081
Lignite (F2) 355
Lincoln Valley (K4) 79
Linton◉ (K7) 1,826
Lisbon◉ (P7) 2,093
Litchville (O6) 345
Livona (K6) 150
Logan (H3) 560
Loma (O2) 20
Lonetree (G3) 37
Loraine (G2) 54
Lostwood (F3) 39
Lucca (P6) 50
Ludden (O7) 59
Lundsvalley (E3) 11
Luverne (P5) 109
Lynchburg (R6) 30
Maddock (L4) 740
Maida (O2) 19
Makoti (G4) 214
Mandan◉ (J6) 10,525
Mandaree (E4) 115
Manfred (L4) 70
Manitou (E3) 35
Manning◉ (E5) 85
Mantador (R7) 98
Manvel (R3) 313
Mapes (O3) 55
Mapleton (S6) 180
Marion (O6) 309
Marmarth (B7) 319
Marmon (C3) 30
Marshall (F5) 17
Martin (K4) 146
Max (H4) 410
Maxbass (H2) 218
Mayville (R4) 2,168
Maza (M3) 31
McCanna (P3) 40
McClusky◉ (K4) 751
McGregor (D2) 150
McHenry (N4) 155
McKenzie (K6) 81
McLeod (R7) 87
McVille (O4) 551
Medberry (N7) 5
Medina (M6) 545
Medora◉ (C6) 133
Mekinock (R4) 115
Melville (M5) 38
Menoken (J6) 60
Mercer (J5) 154
Merricourt (N7) 66
Merrifield (R4) 20
Michigan (O3) 451
Millarton (N6) 28
Milnor (R7) 658
Milton (O2) 264
Minnewaukan◉ (M3) 420
Minot◉ (H3) 30,604
Minto (R3) 642
Moffit (K6) 126
Mohall◉ (G2) 956
Monango (N7) 133
Montpelier (O6) 97
Mooreton (S7) 164
Mott◉ (F7) 1,463
Mount Carmel (O2) 42
Mountain (P2) 218
Munich (N2) 213
Munster (M4) 25
Murray (R5) 5
Mylo (L2) 103
Nanson (L2) 12
Napoleon◉ (L6) 1,078
Nash (P3) 45
Neche (P2) 545
Nekoma (O2) 143
New England (E6) 1,095
New Hradec (E5) 62
New Leipzig (G7) 390
New Rockford◉ (N4) 2,177
New Salem (G6) 986
New Town (F4) 1,586
Newburg (J2) 158
Newville (M2) 10
Niagara (P4) 157
Niobe (F2) 50
Nolan (P5) 8
Nome (P6) 145
Noonan (D2) 625
Norma (G2) 100
Northgate (F2) 65
Northwood (R4) 1,195
Norton (O3) 200
Nortonville (N6) 110
Norwich (J3) 75
Oakdale (E5) 6
Oakes (O7) 1,650
Oakwood (R3) 63
Oberon (M4) 248
Olga (O2) 50
Olmstead (M2) 9
Omemee (K2) 11
Oriska (P6) 148
Orr (P3) 58
Orrin (K3) 125
Osgood (S6) 2
Osnabrock (O2) 289
Overly (K2) 65
Page (P5) 432
Palermo (F3) 188
Park River (P3) 1,813
Parshall (F4) 1,216
Pekin (O4) 180
Pelto (O3) 211
Pembina (R2) 625
Penn (M3) 72
Perth (M2) 73
Petersburg (P3) 272
Pettibone (L5) 205
Pick City (G5) 101
Pickardville (J5) 20
Pickert (P5) 25
Pillsbury (P5) 76
Pingree (N5) 151
Pisek (P3) 176
Plaza (G3) 385
Pleasant Lake (L3) 12
Portal (E2) 351
Portland (R5) 606
Portland Junction (R4) 15
Powers Lake (E2) 633
Prosper (R6) 28
Raleigh (H7) 100
Ramsey (M3) 12
Rangeley (J3) 9
Raub (F4) 25
Rawson (C4) 28
Ray (D3) 1,049
Reeder (E7) 321
Regan (K5) 104
Regent (E7) 388
Revere (O5) 22
Reynolds (R4) 269
Rhame (C7) 254
Richardton (F6) 792
Riverdale (H4) 1,055
Robinson (L5) 155
Rocklake (M2) 350
Rogers (O5) 119
Rohrville (N3) 18
Rolette (L2) 524
Rolla◉ (L2) 1,398
Roseglen (G4) 30
Ross (E3) 167
Roth (J2) 28
Rugby◉ (L3) 2,972
Ruso (J4) 31
Russell (J2) 25
Rutland (P7) 308
Ryder (G4) 264
Saint Anthony (H6) 90
Saint John (L2) 420
Saint Michael (N4) 50
Saint Thomas (R2) 660
Sanborn (O6) 263
Sanger (H5) 13
Sanish (E4) 63
Sarles (N2) 225
Saunders (S6)
Sawyer (H3) 390
Scranton (D7) 358
Selfridge (J7) 371
Selz (L4) 175
Sentinel Butte (C6) 160
Sharon (P4) 251
Sheldon (P6) 221
Shepard (O5) 4
Sherwood (G2) 360
Sheyenne (M4) 423
Shields (H7) 73
Sibley (P5) 22
Silva (L3) 50
Silverleaf (O7) 6
Simcoe (J3) 24
Skaar (C5) 2
Solen (J7) 300
Souris (J2) 213
South Heart (D6) 105
South West Fargo (S6) 3,328
Southam (N3) 75
Spiritwood (N6) 100
Spring Brook (D3) 35
Stady (C2) 25
Stanley◉ (F3) 1,795
Stanton◉ (H5) 409
Starkweather (N3) 223
Steele◉ (L6) 847
Sterling (K6) 59
Stirum (P7) 75
Strasburg (K7) 612
Straubville (O7) 12
Streeter (M6) 491
Surrey (H3) 309
Sutton (O5) 110
Sydney (N6) 10
Sykeston (M5) 236
Taft (R5) 8
Tagus (G3) 72
Tappen (L6) 326
Taylor (F6) 215
Temple (D3) 23
Temvik (K7) 50
Thompson (R4) 211
Thorne (L2) 37
Tioga (E3) 2,087
Tokio (N4) 125
Tolley (G2) 189
Tolna (O4) 291
Tower City (P6) 300
Towner◉ (K3) 948
Trenton (C3) 169
Turtle Lake (J4) 792
Tuttle (L5) 255
Tyler (S7) 25
Underwood (H5) 819
Union (O2) 22
Upham (J2) 333
Urbana (O6) 25
Valley City◉ (P6) 7,809
Vashti (M5) 10
Velva (J3) 1,330
Venturia (L7) 148
Verendrye (J3) 19
Verona (O7) 162
Veseleyville (R3) 74
Voltaire (J3) 70
Voss (R3) 45
Wabek (G4) 14
Wahpeton◉ (S7) 5,876
Walcott (R6) 250
Walden (P5) 5
Wales (N2) 151
Walhalla (P2) 1,432
Walum (O5) 38
Warren (S6) 150
Warsaw (R3) 96
Warwick (N4) 204
Washburn◉ (J5) 993
Watford City◉ (D4) 1,865
Weaver (N2) 12
Webster (N3) 70
Wellsburg (L4) 17
Werner (F5) 59
West Fargo (S6) 93
Westfield (K7) 40
Westhope (H2) 824
Wheatland (R6) 119
Wheelock (D3) 82
White Earth (E3) 208
Whitman (O3) 80
Wild Rice (S6) 26
Wildrose (D2) 361
Williston◉ (C3) 11,866
Willow City (K2) 494
Wilton (J5) 739
Wimbledon (O5) 402
Windsor (N6) 47
Wing (K5) 303
Wishek (L7) 1,290
Woburn (F2) 10
Wolford (L3) 136
Wolseth (H3) 20
Woods (R6) 3
Woodworth (M5) 221
Wyndmere (R7) 644
York (L3) 148
Youngtown (H6) 8
Ypsilanti (O6) 550
Zahl (C2) 70
Zap (G5) 339
Zeeland (L8) 427

OTHER FEATURES

Alkali (lakes) L 3
Alkaline (lake) L 6
Apple (creek) J 6
Arrowwood (lake) N 5
Arthur (lake) L 6
Ashtabula (lake) P 5
Bad Lands (region) C 7
Baldhill (Ashtabula) (res.) P 5
Bear (creek) O 7
Beaver (creek) B 5
Beaver (creek) K 7
Beaver (creek) L 7
Buffalo Lodge (lake) J 3
Cannonball (river) G 7
Cedar (creek) G 7
Chase (lake) M 5
Cherry (creek) D 4
Clark (butte) G 7
Coteau du Missouri (plain) G 3
Cranberry (lake) L 3
Crooked (lake) J 4
Darling (lake) G 2
Deep (river) H 2
Des Lacs (river) G 3
Devils (lake) N 3
Dry (lake) M 3
East Devils (lake) N 4
Edward A. Patterson (lake) E 6
Egg (creek) H 3
Elm (river) N 8
Elm (river) R 5
Etta (lake) L 6
Fan (lake) L 2
Forest (river) P 3
Fort Berthold Ind. Res. E 4
Fort Totten Ind. Res. N 4
Garrison (dam) H 5
Garrison (res.) G 5
George (lake) L 6
Goose (river) P 4
Grand Forks A.F.B. R 4
Green (river) D 5
Grove (lake) L 5
Heart (river) F 6
Heart (butte) G 6
Helen (lake) K 5
Horsehead (lake) L 5
International Peace Garden K 1
Irvine (lake) M 3
Island (lake) L 2
James (river) N 6
Jamestown (dam) N 5
Jamestown (res.) N 6
Jim (lake) N 5
Knife (river) G 5
Little Knife (river) F 3
Little Missouri (river) D 4
Little Muddy (creek) C 3
Long (lake) J 4, K 6, L 2
Maple (river) O 8, R 6
Metigoshe (lake) K 2
Minot A.F.B. H 3
Missouri (river) H 5
Mortes (lake) M 3
Muddy (creek) G 6
Myrtle (lake) L 5
North (lake) J 3
North Fork, Grand (riv.) E 8
Oahe (res.) J 7
Oak (creek) J 8
Park (river) R 3
Pembina (river) O 1
Pipestem (river) M 5
Porcupine (creek) J 7
Red River of the North (river) S 4
Round (lake) K 3
Rush (lake) N 2
Rush (river) R 5
Sentinel (butte) C 6
Sevenmile (creek) G 2
Shell (creek) F 3
Sheyenne (river) O 6
Smoky (lake) K 3
Souris (river) J 2
Spring (creek) E 5
Standing Rock Ind. Res. J 7
Strawberry (lake) J 4
Stump (lake) O 4
Sweetwater (lake) N 3
Theodore Roosevelt Mem. Park C 5, D 4, D 6
Thirtymile (creek) F 6
Tongue (river) P 2
Tschida (lake) G 6
Turtle (lake) H 4
Turtle (mts.) K 2
Turtle Mt. Ind. Res. L 2
Upper Des Lacs (lake) F 2
Van (lake) L 5
Whetstone (buttes) E 7
White (butte) D 7
White Earth (river) E 3
Wild Rice (river) R 7
Yellowstone (river) B 4

◉ County Seat.

NORTH DAKOTA

AREA 70,665 sq. mi.
POPULATION 652,000
CAPITAL Bismarck
LARGEST CITY Fargo 46,662
HIGHEST POINT White Butte 3,506 ft.
SETTLED IN 1780
ADMITTED TO UNION November 2, 1889
POPULAR NAMES Flickertail State; Sioux State
STATE FLOWER Prairie Rose
STATE BIRD Meadowlark

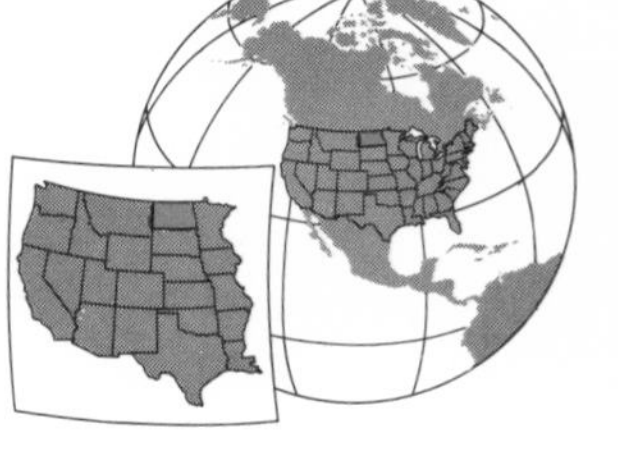

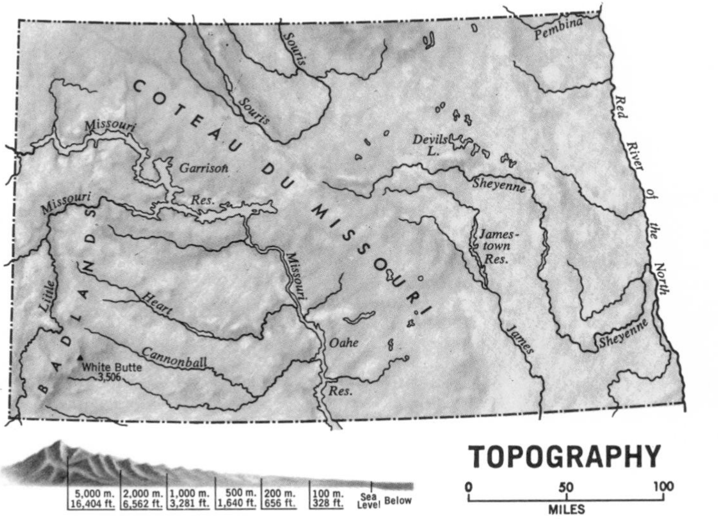

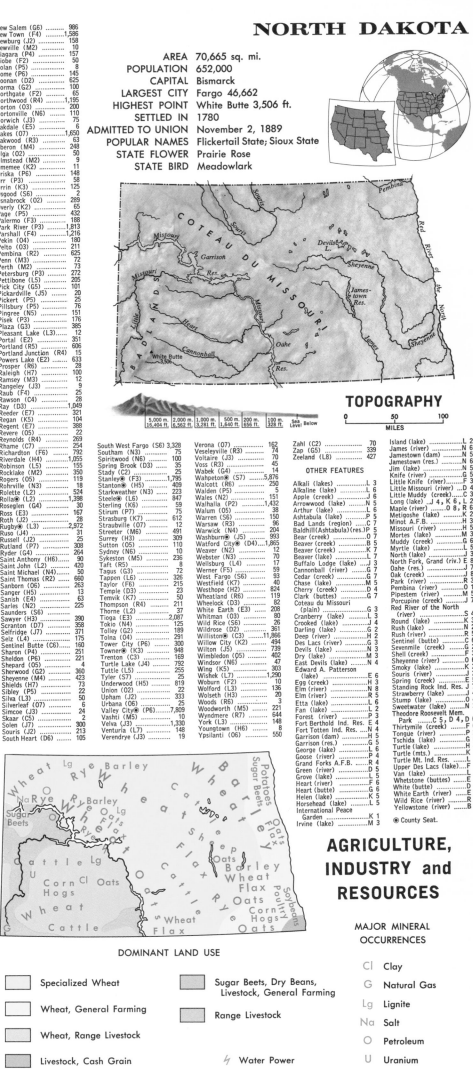

TOPOGRAPHY

DOMINANT LAND USE

- Specialized Wheat
- Wheat, General Farming
- Wheat, Range Livestock
- Livestock, Cash Grain
- Sugar Beets, Dry Beans, Livestock, General Farming
- Range Livestock
- ϟ Water Power

AGRICULTURE, INDUSTRY and RESOURCES

MAJOR MINERAL OCCURRENCES

- Cl Clay
- G Natural Gas
- Lg Lignite
- Na Salt
- O Petroleum
- U Uranium

OHIO

SCALE OF MILES

0 5 10   20   30   40

⊛ State Capitals
◉ County Seats

OHIO

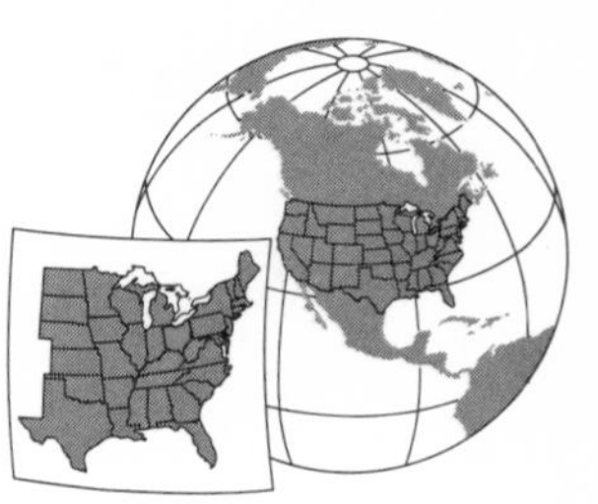

AREA	41,222 sq. mi.
POPULATION	10,245,000
CAPITAL	Columbus
LARGEST CITY	Cleveland 876,050
HIGHEST POINT	Campbell Hill 1,550 ft.
SETTLED IN	1788
ADMITTED TO UNION	March 1, 1803
POPULAR NAME	Buckeye State
STATE FLOWER	Scarlet Carnation
STATE BIRD	Cardinal

COUNTIES

Adams (D8) 19,982
Allen (B4) 103,691
Ashland (F4) 38,771
Ashtabula (J2) 93,067
Athens (F7) 46,998
Auglaize (B4) 36,147
Belmont (J5) 83,864
Brown (C8) 25,178
Butler (A7) 199,076
Carroll (H4) 20,857
Champaign (C5) 29,714
Clark (C6) 131,440
Clermont (B7) 80,530
Clinton (C7) 30,004
Columbiana (J4) 107,004
Coshocton (G5) 32,224
Crawford (E4) 46,775
Cuyahoga (G3) 1,647,895
Darke (A5) 45,612
Defiance (A3) 31,508
Delaware (D5) 36,107
Erie (E3) 68,000
Fairfield (E6) 63,912
Fayette (D6) 24,775
Franklin (E5) 682,962
Fulton (B2) 29,301
Gallia (F8) 26,120
Geauga (H3) 47,573
Greene (C6) 94,642
Guernsey (H5) 38,579
Hamilton (A7) 864,121
Hancock (C3) 53,686
Hardin (C4) 29,633
Harrison (H5) 17,995
Henry (B3) 25,392
Highland (C7) 29,716
Hocking (F6) 20,168
Holmes (G4) 21,591
Huron (E3) 47,326
Jackson (E7) 29,372
Jefferson (J5) 99,201
Knox (F5) 38,808
Lake (H2) 148,700
Lawrence (E8) 55,438
Licking (F5) 90,242
Logan (C5) 34,803
Lorain (F3) 217,500
Lucas (C2) 456,931
Madison (D6) 26,454
Mahoning (J4) 300,480
Marion (D4) 60,221
Medina (G3) 65,315
Meigs (F7) 22,159
Mercer (A4) 32,559
Miami (B5) 72,901
Monroe (H6) 15,268
Montgomery (B6) 527,080
Morgan (G6) 12,747
Morrow (E4) 19,405
Muskingum (G5) 75,159
Noble (G6) 10,982
Ottawa (D2) 35,323
Paulding (A3) 16,792
Perry (F6) 27,864
Pickaway (D6) 35,855
Pike (D7) 19,380
Portage (H3) 91,798
Preble (A6) 32,498
Putnam (B3) 28,331
Richland (E4) 117,761
Ross (D7) 61,215
Sandusky (D3) 56,486
Scioto (D8) 84,216
Seneca (D3) 59,326
Shelby (B5) 33,586
Stark (H4) 340,345
Summit (G3) 513,569
Trumbull (J3) 208,526
Tuscarawas (H5) 76,789
Union (D5) 22,853
Van Wert (A4) 28,840
Vinton (E7) 10,274
Warren (B7) 65,711
Washington (H7) 51,689
Wayne (G4) 75,497
Williams (A2) 29,968
Wood (C3) 72,596
Wyandot (D4) 21,648

CITIES and TOWNS

Aberdeen (C8) 774
Ada (C4) 3,918
Addyston (B9) 1,376
Adelphi (E7) 441
Adena (J5) 1,317
Akron◉ (G3) 290,351
Akron (urban area)...458,253
Albany (F7) 629
Alexandria (E5) 452
Alger (C4) 1,068
Alliance (H4) 28,362
Alvordton (A2) 388
Amanda (E6) 732
Amberley (C9) 2,951
Amelia (D10) 913
Amherst (F3) 6,750
Amsterdam (J5) 931
Andover (J2) 1,116
Anna (B5) 701
Ansonia (A5) 1,002
Antwerp (A3) 1,465
Apple Creek (G4) 722
Aquilla (H2) 459
Arcadia (D3) 610
Arcanum (A6) 1,678
Archbold (B2) 2,348
Arlington (C4) 955
Arlington Heights (C9) 1,355
Ashland◉ (F4) 17,419
Ashley (E5) 907
Ashtabula (J2) 24,559
Ashville (E6) 1,639
Athalia (F8) 341
Athens◉ (F7) 16,470
Attica (E3) 965
Aurora (H3) 4,049
Avon (F3) 6,002
Avon Lake (F2) 9,403
Bailey Lakes ‡(F4)....... 445
Bainbridge (D7) 1,001
Ballville (D3) 1,424
Baltic (G5) 537
Baltimore (E6) 2,116
Barberton (G4) 33,805
Barnesville (H6) 4,425
Batavia◉ (B7) 1,729
Bay View (E3) 802
Bay Village (G9) 14,489
Beach City (G4) 1,151
Beachwood (J9) 6,089
Beallsville (J6) 441
Beaver (E7) 341
Beaverdam (C4) 514
Bedford (H9) 15,223
Bedford Heights (J9)...5,275
Bellaire (J5) 11,502
Bellbrook (C6) 941
Belle Center (C4) 949
Belle Valley (G6) 438
Bellefontaine◉ (C5)....11,424
Bellevue (E3) 8,286
Bellville (E4) 1,621
Belmont (J5) 563
Beloit (J4) 877
Belpre (G7) 5,418
Berea (G10) 16,592
Bergholz (J4) 955
Berlin (G4) 475
Berlin Heights (F3)...... 721
Bethel (B8) 2,019
Bethesda (H5) 1,178
Bettsville (D3) 776
Beverly (G6) 1,194
Bexley (E6) 14,319
Blanchester (B7) 2,944
Bloomdale (D3) 669
Bloomingburg (D6) 719
Bloomville (D3) 836
Blue Ash (C9) 8,341
Bluffton (C4) 2,591
Bolivar (G4) 932
Boston Heights (H3).... 831
Botkins (B5) 854
Bowerston (H5) 463
Bowersville (C6) 327
Bowling Green◉ (C3)..13,574
Bradford (B5) 2,148
Bradner (C3) 994
Brady Lake (H3) 544
Bratenahl (H9) 1,332
Brecksville (H10) 5,435
Bremen (F6) 1,417
Brewster (G4) 2,025
Briarwood Beach (G3).. 359
Bridgeport (J5) 3,824
Brilliant (J5) 2,174
Broadview Hgts. (H10) 6,209
Brook Park (G9) 12,856
Brooklyn (H9) 10,733
Brooklyn Heights (H9)..1,449
Brookside (J5) 831
Brookville (B6) 3,184
Brunswick (G3) 11,725
Bryan◉ (A3) 7,361
Buchtel (F7) 499
Buckeye Lake (F6) 2,129
Bucyrus◉ (E4) 12,276
Burton (H3) 1,085
Butler (F4) 976
Byesville (G6) 2,447
Cadiz◉ (J5) 3,259
Cairo (B4) 566
Calcutta (J4) 2,221
Caldwell◉ (G6) 1,999
Caledonia (D4) 673
Cambridge◉ (G5) 14,562
Camden (A6) 1,308
Camp Dennison (D9).... 600
Campbell (J3) 13,406
Canal Fulton (H4) 1,555
Canal Winchester (E6)..1,976
Canfield (J3) 3,252
Canton◉ (H4) 113,631
Canton (urb. area)....213,574
Cardington (E5) 1,613
Carey (D4) 3,722
Carlisle (B6) 671
Carroll (E6) 444
Carrollton◉ (J4) 2,786
Casstown (B5) 366
Castalia (E3) 954
Catawba (C6) 355
Cecil (A3) 288
Cedarville (C6) 1,702
Celina◉ (A4) 7,659
Centerburg (E5) 963
Centerville (B6) 3,490
Chagrin Falls (J9) 3,458
Chardon◉ (H2) 3,154
Chatfield (E4) 263
Chauncey (F7) 996
Chesapeake (E9) 1,396
Cheshire (F8) 369
Chesterhill (G6) 376
Cheviot (B9) 10,701
Chillicothe◉ (E7).......24,957
Christiansburg (C5) 788
Cincinnati◉ (B9) 502,550
Cincinnati (urban
area) 993,568
Circleville◉ (D6) 11,059
Clarington (J6) 394
Clarksburg (D7) 438
Clarksville (C7) 583
Clay Center (D2) 446
Clayton (B6) 550
Cleveland◉ (H9) 876,050
Cleveland (urban
area) 1,784,991
Cleveland Hgts. (H9)..61,813
Cleves (B9) 2,076
Clinton (G4) 924
Clyde (E3) 4,826
Coal Grove (E9) 2,961
Coalton (E7) 648
Coldwater (A5) 2,766
College Corner (A6) 439
Columbiana (J4) 4,164
COLUMBUS◉ (E6)...471,316
Columbus (urban
area) 616,743
Columbus Grove (B4)....2,104
Conesville (G5) 451
Conneaut (J2) 10,557
Continental (B3) 1,147
Convoy (A4) 976
Coolville (G7) 443
Corning (F6) 1,065
Cortland (J3) 1,957
Corwin (B6) 447
Coshocton◉ (G5) 13,106
Covington (B5) 2,473
Craig Beach (H3 1,139
Crestline (E4) 5,521
Creston (G3) 1,522
Cridersville (B4) 1,053
Crooksville (F6) 2,958
Croton (E5) 397
Cumberland (G6) 493
Cuyahoga Falls (G3)....47,922
Cuyahoga Heights (H9) 796
Cygnet (C3) 593
Dalton (G4) 1,067
Danville (F5) 926
Darbydale (D6) 740
Dayton◉ (B6) 262,332
Dayton (urb. area)....501,664
Deer Park (C9) 8,423
Defiance◉ (B3) 14,553
Degraff (C5) 996
Delaware◉ (E5) 13,282
Dellroy (H4) 391
Delphos (B4) 6,961
Delta (B2) 2,376
Dennison (H5) 4,158
Deshler (C3) 1,824
Dillonvale (J5) 1,232
Dover (G4) 11,300
Doylestown (G4) 1,873
Dresden (G5) 1,338
Dublin (D5) 552
Dunkirk (C4) 1,006
East Ashtabula (J2).....4,179
East Canton (H4) 1,521
East Cleveland (J9).....37,991
East Liverpool (J4).....22,306
East Palestine (J4) 5,232
East Sparta (H4) 961
Eastlake (J8) 12,467
Eaton◉ (A6) 5,034
Eaton Estates (F3)......1,733
Edgerton (A3) 1,566
Edison (E4) 559
Edon (A2) 757
Eldorado (A6) 449
Elida (B4) 1,215
Elmore (D3) 1,302
Elmwood Place (B9)....3,813
Elyria◉ (F3) 43,782
Elyria-Lorain (urban
area) 142,860
Empire (J5) 551
Englewood (B6) 1,515
Enon (C6) 1,227
Etna (E6) 382
Euclid (J9) 62,998
Evendale (C9) 773
Fairborn (B6) 19,453
Fairfax (C9) 2,430
Fairport Harbor (H2)...4,267
Fairview Park (G9)....14,624
Farmersville (A6) 797
Fayette (B2) 1,090
Fayetteville (C7) 389
Felicity (B8) 678
Findlay◉ (C3) 30,344
Fletcher (B5) 569
Flushing (J5) 1,189
Forest (C4) 1,314
Forest Park (B9)..........5,350
Fort Jennings (B4) 436
Fort Loramie (B5) 687
Fort Recovery (A5) 1,336
Fostoria (D3) 15,732
Frankfort (D7) 871
Franklin (B6) 7,917
Frazeysburg (F5) 842
Fredericksburg (G4) 565
Fredericktown (F5) 1,531
Freeport (H5) 503
Fremont◉ (D3) 17,573
Fulton (E5) 292
Fultonham (Uniontown)
(F6) 213
Gahanna (E5) 2,717
Galena (E5) 411
Galion (E4) 12,650
Gallipolis◉ (F8) 8,775
Gambier (F5) 1,148
Garfield Heights (J9)..38,455
Garrettsville (H3) 1,662
Gates Mills (J9) 1,588
Geneva (J2) 5,677
Geneva-on-the-Lake
(H2) 631
Genoa (D2) 1,957
Georgetown◉ (C8) 2,674
Germantown (B6) 3,399
Gettysburg (A5) 443
Gibsonburg (D3) 2,540
Gilboa (C3) 207
Girard (J3) 12,997
Glandorf (B3) 747
Glencoe (J6) 720
Glendale (C9) 2,823
Glenwillow (J10) 359
Glouster (F6) 2,255
Gnadenhutten (G5) 1,257
Golf Manor (C9) 4,648
Grafton (F3) 1,683
Grand Rapids (C3) 670
Grand River (H2) 477

(continued on following page)

TOPOGRAPHY

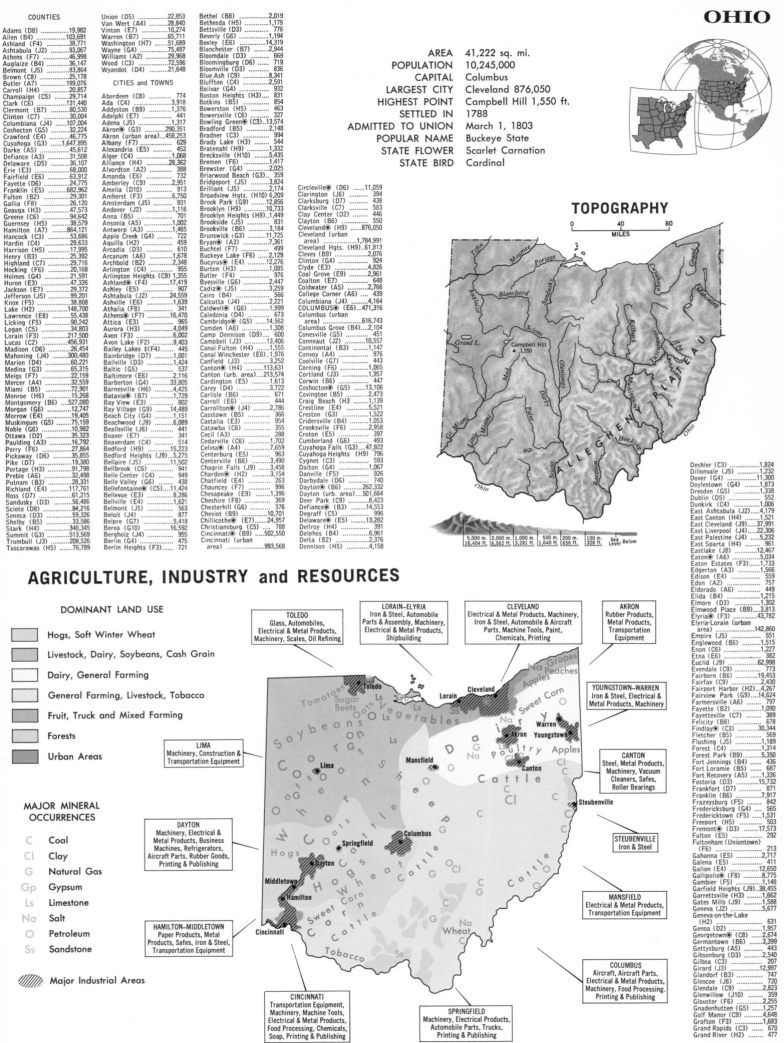

0 40 80
MILES
Tiffin
Maumee
Portage
Auglaize
Blanchard
Sandusky
Cuyahoga
Grand
Mahoning
Killbuck
Scioto
Tuscarawas
Grand L.
Campbell Hill
1,550
Mad
Olentangy
Muskingum
ALLEGHENY PLATEAU
Darby
Paint
Gt. Miami
Little Miami
Hocking
Raccoon
Ohio
5,000 m. 16,404 ft.
2,000 m. 6,562 ft.
1,000 m. 3,281 ft.
500 m. 1,640 ft.
200 m. 656 ft.
100 m. 328 ft.
Sea Level
Below

AGRICULTURE, INDUSTRY and RESOURCES

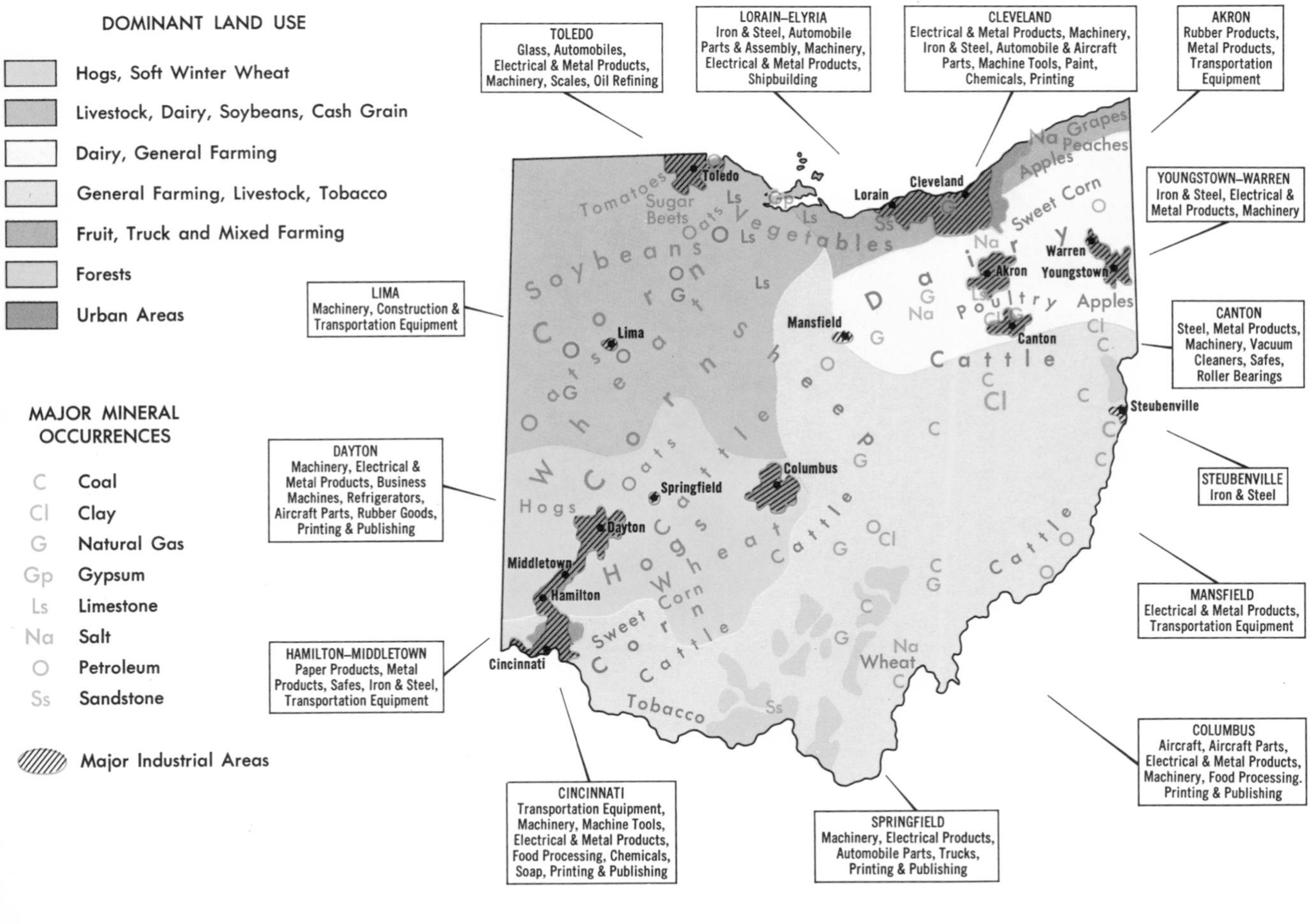
DOMINANT LAND USE
Hogs, Soft Winter Wheat
Livestock, Dairy, Soybeans, Cash Grain
Dairy, General Farming
General Farming, Livestock, Tobacco
Fruit, Truck and Mixed Farming
Forests
Urban Areas
MAJOR MINERAL OCCURRENCES
C Coal
Cl Clay
G Natural Gas
Gp Gypsum
Ls Limestone
Na Salt
O Petroleum
Ss Sandstone
Major Industrial Areas
TOLEDO
Glass, Automobiles, Electrical & Metal Products, Machinery, Scales, Oil Refining
LORAIN–ELYRIA
Iron & Steel, Automobile Parts & Assembly, Machinery, Electrical & Metal Products, Shipbuilding
CLEVELAND
Electrical & Metal Products, Machinery, Iron & Steel, Automobile & Aircraft Parts, Machine Tools, Paint, Chemicals, Printing
AKRON
Rubber Products, Metal Products, Transportation Equipment
YOUNGSTOWN–WARREN
Iron & Steel, Electrical & Metal Products, Machinery
LIMA
Machinery, Construction & Transportation Equipment
CANTON
Steel, Metal Products, Machinery, Vacuum Cleaners, Safes, Roller Bearings
DAYTON
Machinery, Electrical & Metal Products, Business Machines, Refrigerators, Aircraft Parts, Rubber Goods, Printing & Publishing
STEUBENVILLE
Iron & Steel
MANSFIELD
Electrical & Metal Products, Transportation Equipment
HAMILTON–MIDDLETOWN
Paper Products, Metal Products, Safes, Iron & Steel, Transportation Equipment
COLUMBUS
Aircraft, Aircraft Parts, Electrical & Metal Products, Machinery, Food Processing, Printing & Publishing
CINCINNATI
Transportation Equipment, Machinery, Machine Tools, Electrical & Metal Products, Food Processing, Chemicals, Soap, Printing & Publishing
SPRINGFIELD
Machinery, Electrical Products, Automobile Parts, Trucks, Printing & Publishing
Toledo
Lorain
Cleveland
Warren
Youngstown
Akron
Canton
Lima
Mansfield
Steubenville
Columbus
Springfield
Dayton
Middletown
Hamilton
Cincinnati
Tomatoes
Sugar Beets
Vegetables
Oats
Soybeans
Corn
Hogs
Sheep
Cattle
Dairy
Poultry
Apples
Grapes
Peaches
Sweet Corn
Wheat
Tobacco

Ohio

(continued)

Grandview Hgts. (D6)...8,270
Granville (E5) 2,868
Gratis (A6) 586
Green Camp (D4) 492
Green Springs (E3) 1,262
Greenfield (D7) 5,422
Greenhills (B9) 5,407
Greenville◉ (A5) 10,585
Greenwich (E3) 1,371
Groesbeck (B9) 2,200
Grove City (D6) 8,107
Groveport (E6) 2,043
Grover Hill (B3) 547
Hamden (F7) 1,035
Hamersville (C8) 524
Hamilton◉ (A7) 72,354
Hamilton (urban area) 89,778
Hamler (B3) 588
Hanging Rock (E8)...... 352
Hanoverton (J4) 442
Harrisburg (D6) 359
Harrison (A9) 3,878
Harrisville (J5) 343
Harrod (C4) 563
Hartford (Croton) (E5) 397
Hartville (H4) 1,353
Harveysburg (C7) 514
Haskins (C3) 521
Hayesville (F4) 435
Heath (F5) 2,426
Hebron (E6) 1,260
Hicksville (A3) 3,116
Higginsport (C8) 412
Highland (C7) 265
Highland Hgts. (J9).....2,929
Hilliards (D5) 5,633
Hills and Dales ‡(H4)... 320
Hillsboro◉ (C7) 5,474
Hiram (H3) 1,011
Holgate (B3) 1,374
Holland (C2) 924
Holloway (H5) 541
Holmesville (G4) 422
Hopedale (J5) 932
Hoytville (C3) 334
Hubbard (J3) 7,137
Hudson (H3) 2,438
Hunting Valley (J9) 629
Huntsville (C5) 511
Huron (E3) 5,197
Independence (H9) 6,868
Indian Hill (C9) 4,526
Irondale (J4) 705
Ironton◉ (E8) 15,745
Jackson◉ (E7) 6,980
Jackson Center (B5)..... 980
Jacksonville (F7) 580
Jamestown (C6) 1,730
Jefferson ‡(F4) 2,774
Jefferson◉ (J2) 2,116
Jeffersonville (C6) 897
Jeromesville (F4) 540
Jerry City (C3) 386
Jewett (H5) 925
Johnstown (E5) 2,881
Junction City (F6) 763
Kalida (B4) 705
Kent (H3) 17,836
Kenton◉ (C4) 8,747
Kettering (B6) 54,462
Killbuck (G5) 865
Kingston (E7) 1,066
Kipton (F3) 353
Kirkersville (E6) 417
La Fayette (C4) 476
La Rue (D4) 842
Lagrange (F3) 1,007
Lakemore (H3) 2,765
Lakeview (C4) 1,008
Lakeville (F4) 4,181
Lakewood (G9) 66,154
Lancaster◉ (E6) 29,916
Laura (B6) 526
Laurelville (E7) 539
Lebanon ◉(B7) 5,993
Leesburg (D7) 932
Leesville (H5) 287
Leetonia (J4) 2,543
Leipsic (C3) 1,802
Leroy (G3) 504
Lewis Center (D5) 400
Lewisburg (A6) 1,415
Lexington (E4) 1,311
Liberty Center (B3) 867
Lima◉ (B4) 51,037
Lima (urban area).......62,963
Lincoln Heights (C9).....7,798
Lincoln Heights (F4)....8,004
Lindenwald (A7) 9,734
Lindsey (D3) 581
Linndale (G9) 381
Lisbon◉ (J4) 3,579
Lithopolis (E6) 411
Lockbourne (E6) 460
Lockland (C9) 5,292
Lodi (F3) 2,213
Logan◉ (F6) 6,417
London◉ (C6) 6,379
Lorain (F3) 68,932
Lorain-Elyria (urban area) 142,860
Lore City (H6) 458
Loudonville (F4) 2,611
Louisville (H4) 5,116
Loveland (D9) 5,008
Lowell (H6) 783
Lowellville (J3) 2,055
Lucas (F4) 719
Lucasville (E8) 1,277
Luckey (D3) 946
Lynchburg (C7) 1,022
Lyndhurst (J9) 16,805
Lyons (B2) 590
Macedonia (J10) 5,391
Madeira (C9) 6,744
Madison (H2) 1,347
Madisonburg (G4) 850
Magnetic Springs (D5) 344
Magnolia (H4) 1,596
Maineville (C9) 343
Malinta (B3) 339
Malta (G6) 983
Malvern (H4) 1,320
Manchester (C8) 2,172
Mansfield◉ (F4) 47,325
Mantua (H3) 1,194
Maple Heights (H9)...31,667
Marble Cliff ‡(D6) 622
Marblehead (E2) 858
Mariemont (C9) 4,120
Marietta◉ (G7) 16,847
Marion◉ (D4) 37,079
Marshallville (G4) 611
Martins Ferry (J5) 11,919
Martinsville (C7) 488
Marysville◉ (D5) 4,952

Mason (B7) 4,727
Massillon (H4) 31,236
Masury (J3) 2,512
Maumee (C2) 12,063
Mayfield (J9) 1,977
Mayfield Heights (J9) 13,478
McArthur◉ (F7) 1,529
McClure (C3) 651
McComb (C3) 1,176
McConnelsville◉ (G6)...2,257
McDonald (J3) 2,727
McGuffey (C4) 647
Mechanicsburg (C5)......1,810
Medina◉ (G3) 8,235
Mendon (A4) 663
Mentor (H2) 27,441
Mentor-on-the-Lake (G2) 3,290
Metamora (C2) 598
Miamisburg (B6) 9,893
Middleburg Hts. (G10) 7,282
Middlefield (H3) 1,467
Middleport (F7) 3,373
Middletown (A6) 42,115
Midland (C7) 367
Midvale (H5) 683
Midway (Sedalia) (D6) 341
Milan (E3) 1,309
Milford (D9) 4,131
Milford Center (D5).... 794
Millbury (D2) 730
Milledgeville (C6) 222
Millersburg◉ (F4) 3,101
Millersport (E6) 752
Millville (A7) 676
Mineral City (H4) 917
Minerva (H4) 3,833
Minerva Park (E5).......1,169
Mingo Junction (J5).....4,987
Minster (B5) 2,193
Mogadore (H3) 3,851
Monroe (B7) 1,475
Monroeville (E3) 1,371
Montgomery (C9) 3,075
Montpelier (A2) 4,131
Moraine (B6) 2,262
Moreland Hills (J9).....2,188
Morral (D4) 493
Morristown (H5) 396
Morrow (B7) 1,477
Moscow (B8) 438
Mount Blanchard (D4).. 432
Mount Gilead◉ (E4).....2,788
Mount Healthy (B9).....6,553
Mount Orab (C7) 1,058
Mount Pleasant (J5).... 656
Mount Sterling (D6).....1,338
Mount Vernon◉ (E5)..13,284
Mount Victory (D4) 598
Mowrystown (C7) 416
Munroe Falls (H3) 1,828
Murray City (F6) 717
Napoleon◉ (B3) 6,739
Navarre (H4) 1,698
Nelsonville (F7) 4,834
Nevada (D4) 919
New Alexandria (J5)..... 396
New Athens (H5) 472
New Bloomington (D4).. 368
New Boston (E8) 3,984
New Bremen (B5) 1,972
New Carlisle (C6) 4,107
New Concord (G6) 2,127
New Holland (D6) 798
New Knoxville (B5) 792
New Lebanon (B6) 1,459
New Lexington◉ (F6)..4,514
New London (F3) 2,392
New Madison (A6) 910
New Matamoras (J6).... 925
New Miami (A7) 2,360
New Middletown (J4)... 500
New Paris (A6) 1,679
New Philadelphia◉ (G5) 14,241
New Richmond (B8).....2,834
New Riegel (D3) 349
New Straitsville (F6)....1,019
New Vienna (C7) 858
New Washington (E4)...1,162
New Waterford (J4)..... 711
Newark◉ (F5) 41,790
Newburgh Hgts. (H9)...3,512
Newcomerstown (G5)....4,273
Newport (H7) 700
Newton Falls (J3) 5,038
Newtonsville (B7) 339
Newtown (C10) 1,750
Ney (B3) 338
Niles (J3) 19,545
North Baltimore (C3)....3,011
North Bend (B9) 622
North Canton (H4) 7,727
North College Hill (B9)12,035
North Fairfield (E3)..... 547
North Hampton (C5)..... 495
North Kingsville (J2)....1,854
North Lewisburg (C5)... 879
North Olmsted (G9)....16,290
North Perry (H2) 658
North Randall (H9) 688
North Ridgeville (F3)....8,057
North Royalton (H10)...9,290
Northfield (J10) 1,055
Northwood (D2) 3,768
Norwalk◉ (E3) 12,900
Norwood (C9) 34,580
Oak Harbor (D2)..........2,903
Oak Hill (E8) 1,748
Oakwood (B6) 10,493
Oakwood (H9) 3,283
Oakwood (B3) 686
Oberlin (F3) 8,198
Obetz (E6) 1,984
Ohio City (A4) 851
Old Washington (H5).... 369
Olmsted Falls (G9).......2,144
Ontario (E4) 3,049
Orange (J9) 2,006
Orangeville (J3) 397
Oregon (D2) 13,319
Orrville (G4) 6,511
Orwell (J2) 819
Ostrander (D5) 438
Ottawa◉ (B3) 3,245
Ottawa Hills (C2) 3,870
Ottoville (B4) 793
Owensville (B7) 609
Oxford (A6) 7,828
Painesville◉ (H2) 16,116
Pandora (C4) 782
Parkview (G9) 2,018
Parma (H9) 82,845
Parma Heights (G9)...18,100
Pataskala (E5) 1,046
Paulding◉ (A3) 2,936
Payne (A3) 1,287
Peebles (D8) 1,601
Pemberville (C3) 1,237
Peninsula (G3) 644
Pepper Pike (J9) 3,217
Perry (H2) 885
Perrysburg (C2) 5,519
Perrysville (F4) 769
Phillipsburg (B6) 715

HIGHWAYS

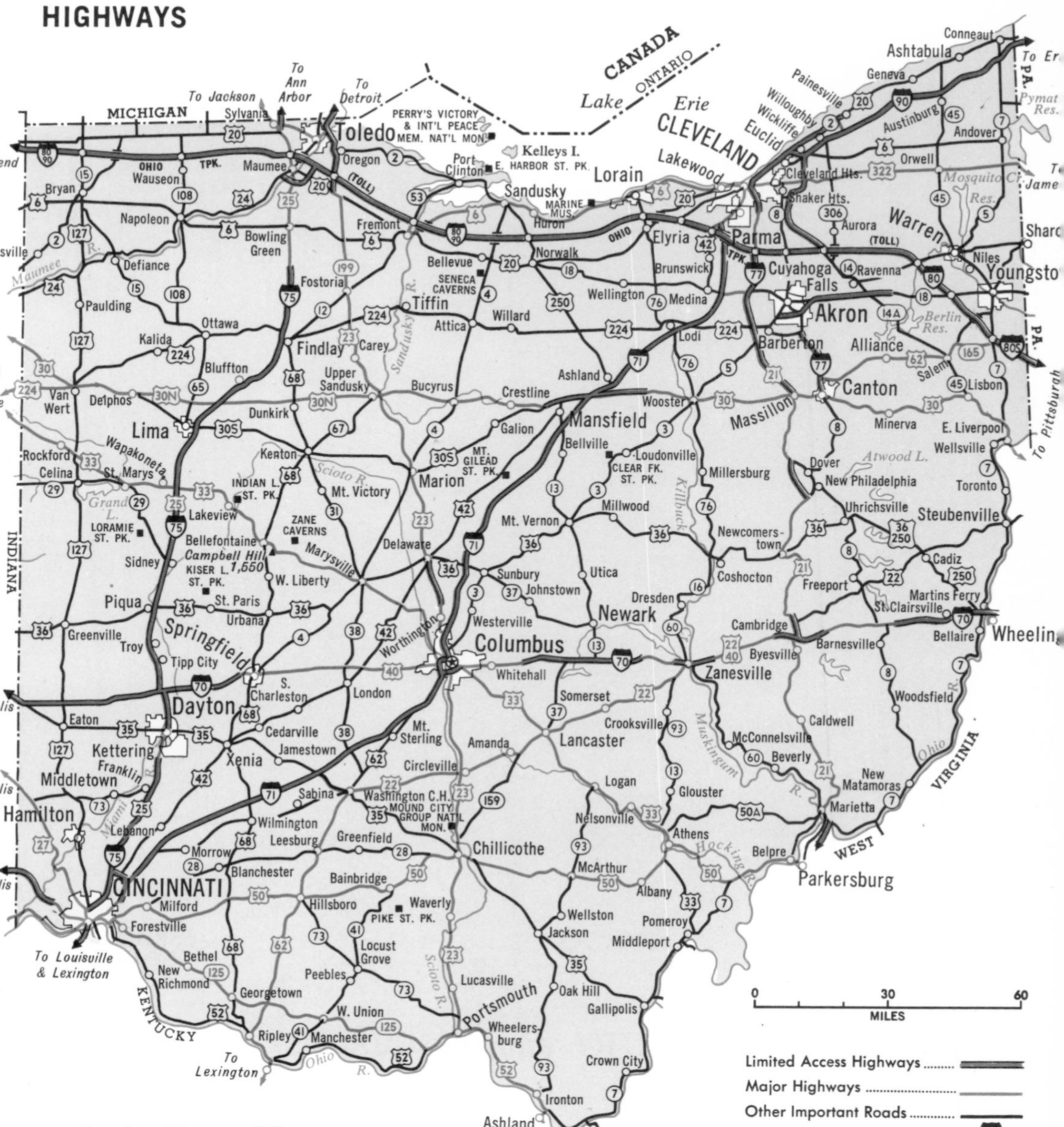

0 30 60
MILES

Limited Access Highways ....
Major Highways ....
Other Important Roads ....
Interstate Route Numbers 95
Federal Route Numbers 9
State and Other Route Numbers... 4

Philo (G6) 913
Pickerington (E6) 634
Piketon (E7) 1,244
Pioneer (A2) 855
Piqua (B5) 19,219
Pitsburg (A6) 394
Plain City (D5) 2,146
Pleasant City (G6) 491
Pleasant Hill (B5) 1,060
Pleasantville (F6) 741
Plymouth (E4) 1,822
Poland (J3) 2,766
Pomeroy◉ (G7) 3,345
Port Clinton◉ (E2) 6,870
Port Jefferson (C5) 438
Port Washington (G5).. 526
Port William (C6) 360
Portage (C3) 420
Portsmouth◉ (D8) 33,637
Powell (D5) 390
Powhatan Point (J6)....2,147
Proctorville (F9) 831
Prospect (D5) 1,067
Put-in-Bay (E2) 357
Quaker City (H6) 583
Quincy (C5) 668
Racine (G8) 499
Ravenna◉ (H3) 10,918
Rawson (C4) 407
Rayland (J5) 694
Reading (C9) 12,832
Republic (D3) 729
Reynoldsburg (E6) 7,793
Richmond (J5) 728
Richmond (Grand River) (H2) 477
Richmond Hgts. (H9)...5,068
Richwood (D5) 2,137
Ridgeway (C4) 448
Ripley (C8) 2,174
Risingsun (C3) 815
Rittman (G4) 5,410
Riverlea (D5) 625
Rock Creek (J2) 673
Rockford (A4) 1,155
Rocky River (G9) 18,097
Rockyridge (D2) 441
Rosedale (E4) 8,204
Roseville (F6) 1,749
Ross (B9) 800
Rossford (C2) 4,406
Roswell (H5) 379
Rushsylvania (C5) 601
Russells Point (C5) 1,111
Russellville (C8) 412
Rutland (F7) 687
Sabina (C7) 2,313
Saint Bernard (B9) 6,778
Saint Clairsville◉ (J5)..3,865
Saint Henry (A5) 978
Saint Louisville (F5).... 349
Saint Marys (B4) 7,737
Saint Paris (C5) 1,460

Salem (J4) 13,854
Salineville (J4) 1,898
Sandusky◉ (E3) 31,989
Sardinia (C7) 799
Savannah (F4) 409
Scio (H5) 1,135
Sciotodale (E8) 1,113
Scott (A4) 365
Seaman (C8) 714
Sebring (H4) 4,439
Sedalia (Midway)(D6).. 341
Senecaville (H6) 575
Seven Hills (G3) 5,708
Seven Mile (A7) 690
Seville (G3) 1,190
Shadyside (J6) 5,028
Shaker Heights (H9)..36,460
Shanesville (G4) 510
Sharonville (C9) 7,629
Shawnee (F6) 1,000
Shawnee Hills (D5) 394
Sheffield (F3) 1,664
Sheffield Lake (F3).....6,884
Shelby (E4) 9,106
Sherrodsville (H4) 480
Sherwood (A3) 578
Shiloh (E4) 724
Shreve (F4) 1,617
Sidney◉ (B5) 14,663
Silver Lake (G3) 2,655
Silverton (C9) 6,682
Smithfield (J5) 1,312
Smithville (G4) 1,024
Solon (J9) 6,333
Somerset (F6) 1,361
Somerville (A6) 478
South Amherst (F3) 1,657
South Bloomfield (D6).. 424
South Charleston (C6)..1,505
South Euclid (H9) 27,569
South Lebanon (B7).....2,720
South Point (E9) 1,663
South Russell (H3) 1,276
South Solon (C6) 414
South Vienna (C6) 440
South Webster (E8) 803
South Zanesville (F6)...1,557
Spencer (F3) 742
Spencerville (B4) 2,061
Spring Valley (C6) 678
Springboro (B6) 917
Springdale (B9) 3,556
Springfield◉ (C6) 82,723
Springfield (urban area) 90,157
Steubenville◉ (J5) 32,495
Steubenville-Weirton (urban area) 81,613
Stockport (G6) 458
Stow (H3) 12,194
Strasburg (G4) 1,687
Strongsville (G10) 8,504
Struthers (J3) 15,631

Stryker (B3) 1,205
Sugar Bush Knolls ‡(H3) 68
Sugar Grove (E6) 479
Sugarcreek (G5) 982
Summerfield (H6) 352
Sunbury (E5) 1,360
Swanton (C2) 2,306
Sycamore (D4) 998
Sylvania (C2) 5,187
Syracuse (G7) 731
Tallmadge (H3) 10,246
Tarlton (E6) 377
Taylorsville (Philo)(G6) 913
Terrace Park (D9) 2,023
The Plains (F7) 1,148
Thornville (F6) 521
Thurston (E6) 429
Tiffin◉ (D3) 21,478
Tiltonsville (J5) 2,454
Timberlake (J8) 670
Tipp City (B6) 4,267
Toledo◉ (D2) 318,003
Toledo (urban area)..438,283
Tontogany (C3) 380
Toronto (J5) 7,780
Tremont City (C5) 414
Trenton (B7) 3,064
Trimble (F7) 481
Trotwood (B6) 4,992
Troy◉ (B5) 13,685
Tuscarawas (H5) 817
Twinsburg (J10) 4,098
Uhrichsville (H5) 6,201
Union (B6) 1,072
Union City (A5) 1,657
Uniontown (H4) 1,668
Uniontown (Fultonham) (F6) 213
University Hgts. (H9)..16,641
Upper Arlington (D6)..28,486
Upper Sandusky◉ (D4) 4,941
Urbana◉ (C5) 10,461
Urbancrest (D6) 1,029
Utica (F5) 1,854
Valley View (H10) 1,221
Valley View (D6) 790
Van Wert◉ (A4) 11,323
Vanburen (C3) 374
Vandalia (B6) 6,342
Vanlue (C4) 386
Vermilion (F3) 7,612
Vermilion-on-the-Lake (F3) 1,273
Verona (A6) 527
Versailles (A5) 2,159
Vienna (J3) 950
Vinton (F8) 374
Wadsworth (G3) 10,635

Wakeman (F3) 728
Walbridge (C2) 2,142
Waldo (D5) 374
Walton Hills (H10)......1,776
Wapakoneta◉ (B4) 6,756
Warren◉ (J3) 59,648
Warren-Youngstown (urban area) 372,748
Warrensville Hts. (H9)10,609
Warsaw (G5) 594
Washington (Old Washington) (H5) 369
Washington Court House◉ (D6) 12,388
Washingtonville (J4)..... 810
Waterville (C3) 1,856
Wauseon◉ (B2) 4,311
Waverly◉ (D7) 3,830
Wayne (C3) 949
Waynesburg (H4) 1,442
Waynesfield (C4) 765
Waynesville (B6) 1,298
Wellington (F3) 3,599
Wellston (F7) 5,728
Wellsville (J4) 7,117
West Alexandria (A6)...1,524
West Carrollton (B6)....4,749
West Elkton (A6) 345
West Farmington (J3).. 614
West Jefferson (D6) 2,774
West Lafayette (G5).....1,476
West Liberty (C5) 1,522
West Manchester (A6).. 460
West Mansfield (C5)..... 791
West Milton (B6) 2,972
West Portsmouth (D8)..3,100
West Salem (F4) 1,017
West Union◉ (C8) 1,762
West Unity (B2) 1,192
Westerville (D5) 7,011
Westlake (G9) 12,906
Weston (C3) 1,075
Westview (G10) 1,303
Wharton (D4) 463
Wheelersburg (E8) 2,682
Whitehall (E6) 20,818
Whitehouse (C2) 1,135
Wickliffe (J9) 15,760
Willard (E3) 5,457
Williamsburg (B7) 1,956
Williamsport (D6) 840
Willoughby (J8) 15,058
Willoughby Hills (J9)...4,241
Willowick (J8) 18,749
Willshire (A4) 601
Wilmington◉ (C7) 8,915
Wilmot (G4) 402
Winchester (C8) 788
Windham (H3) 3,777

Wintersville (J5) 3,597
Withamsville (D10) 2,811
Woodlawn (C9) 3,007
Woodmere (J9) 398
Woodsfield◉ (H6) 2,956
Woodville (D3) 1,700
Wooster◉ (G4) 17,046
Worthington (E5) 9,239
Wyoming (C9) 7,736
Xenia◉ (C6) 20,445
Yellow Springs (C6)......4,167
Yorkville (J5) 1,801
Youngstown◉ (J3)....166,689
Youngstown-Warren (urban area) 372,748
Zanesville◉ (G6) 39,077

OTHER FEATURES

Atwood (res.) ....H 4
Auglaize (river) ....B 4
Berlin (res.) ....H 4
Big Walnut (creek) ....E 5
Black (river) ....F 3
Black Fork, Mohican (river) ....F 4
Blanchard (river) ....C 4
Blennerhassett (isl.) ....G 7
Buckeye (lake) ....F 6
Campbell (hill) ....C 5
Captina (creek) ....J 6
Cedar (point) ....D 2
Chagrin (river) ....J 8
Clear Fork, Mohican (river) ....F 4
Clearfork (res.) ....E 4
Clendening (res.) ....H 5
Cleveland Hopkins Municipal Airport........G 9
Cuyahoga (river) H10
Darby (creek) ....D 5
Deer (creek) ....D 6
Delaware (res.) ....E 5
Dillon (res.) ....F 5
Dover (res.) ....H 4
Duck (creek) ....H 6
Erie (lake) ....H 1
Grand (river) ....H 2
Grand (lake) ....A 4
Great Miami (river).......A 7
Hocking (river) ....F 7
Hoover (res.) ....E 5
Huron (river) ....E 3
Indian (lake) ....C 5
International Peace Memorial Nat'l Mon. ..E 2

Kelleys (isl.) ....E 2
Killbuck (creek) ....G 4
Kokosing (river) ....E 5
Leesville (res.) ....H 5
Little Beaver (creek).......J 4
Little Miami (river).........C 9
Little Muskingum (riv.)..H 6
Loramie (lake) ....B 5
Mad (river) ....C 6
Maumee (bay) ....D 2
Maumee (river) ....A 3
Middle Bass (isl.) ....E 2
Mohican (river) ....F 4
Mosquito Creek (res.) ....J 3
Mound City Group Nat'l Mon. ....E 7
Muskingum (river) ....G 6
North Bass (isl.) ....E 2
Ohio (river) ....B 8
Ohio Brush (creek) ....D 8
Olentangy (river) ....D 4
Paint (creek) ....D 7
Perrys Victory Nat'l Mon. ....E 2
Piedmont (res.) ....H 5
Portage (river) ....D 3
Pymatuning (res.) ....J 2
Raccoon (creek) ....F 8
Rattlesnake (creek) ......C 7
Rocky (river) ....G 9
Rocky Fork (lake) ....D 7
Saint Joseph (river) ......A 3
Saint Marys (river) ....A 4
Salt (creek) ....E 7
Salt Fork (creek) ....H 5
Sandusky (bay) ....E 3
Sandusky (river) ....D 3
Scioto (river) ....D 8
Senecaville (res.) ....H 6
Sevenmile (creek) ....A 6
South Bass (isl.) ....E 2
Stillwater (river) ....B 5
Symmes (creek) ....F 8
Tappan (res.) ....H 5
Tiffin (river) ....B 3
Tuscarawas (river) ....H 5
Vermilion (river) ....F 3
Wabash (river) ....A 5
West Sister (isl.) ....D 2
Whiteoak (creek) ....C 7
Wills (creek) ....G 5
Wills Creek (res.) ....G 5
Yellow (creek) ....J 4

◉ County Seat.
‡ Name not on map.

OKLAHOMA

AREA	69,919 sq. mi.
POPULATION	2,482,000
CAPITAL	Oklahoma City
LARGEST CITY	Oklahoma City 324,253
HIGHEST POINT	Black Mesa 4,978 ft.
SETTLED IN	1889
ADMITTED TO UNION	November 16, 1907
POPULAR NAME	Sooner State
STATE FLOWER	Mistletoe
STATE BIRD	Scissor-tailed Flycatcher

COUNTIES

Adair (S3) 13,112
Alfalfa (K1) 8,445
Atoka (O6) 10,352
Beaver (E1) 6,965
Beckham (G4) 17,782
Blaine (K3) 12,077
Bryan (O7) 24,252
Caddo (K4) 28,621
Canadian (K3) 24,727
Carter (M6) 39,044
Cherokee (R3) 17,762
Choctaw (P6) 15,637
Cimarron (A1) 4,496
Cleveland (M4) 47,600
Coal (O5) 5,546
Comanche (K5) 90,803
Cotton (K6) 8,031
Craig (R1) 16,303
Creek (O3) 40,495
Custer (H3) 21,040
Delaware (S2) 13,198
Dewey (H2) 6,051
Ellis (G2) 5,457
Garfield (L2) 52,975
Garvin (M5) 28,290
Grady (L5) 29,590
Grant (L1) 8,140
Greer (G5) 8,877
Harmon (G5) 5,852
Harper (G1) 5,956
Haskell (R4) 9,121
Hughes (O4) 15,144
Jackson (H5) 29,736
Jefferson (L6) 8,192
Johnston (N6) 8,517
Kay (M1) 51,042
Kingfisher (L3) 10,635
Kiowa (J5) 14,825
Latimer (R5) 7,738
Le Flore (S5) 29,106
Lincoln (N3) 18,783
Logan (M3) 18,662
Love (M7) 5,862
Major (K2) 7,808
Marshall (N6) 7,263
Mayes (R2) 20,073
McClain (M5) 12,740
McCurtain (S6) 25,851
McIntosh (P4) 12,371
Murray (M6) 10,622
Muskogee (R3) 61,866
Noble (M2) 10,376
Nowata (P1) 10,848
Okfuskee (O3) 11,706
Oklahoma (M3) 439,506
Okmulgee (P3) 36,945
Osage (O1) 32,441
Ottawa (S1) 28,301
Pawnee (N2) 10,884
Payne (N3) 44,231
Pittsburg (P5) 34,360
Pontotoc (N5) 28,089
Pottawatomie (N4) ..41,486
Pushmataha (R6) 9,088
Roger Mills (G3) 5,090
Rogers (P2) 20,614
Seminole (N4) 28,066
Sequoyah (S3) 18,001
Stephens (L6) 37,990
Texas (C1) 14,162
Tillman (J6) 14,654
Tulsa (P2) 346,038
Wagoner (P3) 15,673
Washington (P1) 42,347
Washita (J4) 18,121
Woods (J1) 11,932
Woodward (H2) 13,902

CITIES and TOWNS

Achille (O7) 294
Ada◉ (N5) 14,347
Adair (R2) 434
Adams (D1) 180
Adamson (P5) 200
Addington (L6) 144
Adel (P5) 10
Afton (S1) 1,111
Agra (N3) 265
Akins (S3) 100
Albany (O7) 250
Albert (K4) 121
Albion (R5) 161
Alderson (P5) 207
Alex (L5) 545
Alfalfa (J4) 110
Aline (K1) 314
Allen (O5) 1,005
Alluwe (R1) 500

Alma (L6) 175
Altus◉ (H5) 21,225
Alva◉ (J1) 6,258
Amber (L4) 250
America (S7) 10
Ames (K2) 211
Amorita (K1) 74
Anadarko◉ (K4) 6,299
Antlers◉ (P6) 2,085
Apache (K5) 1,455
Apperson (N1) 40
Arapaho◉ (H3) 351
Arcadia (M3) 410
Ardmore◉ (M6) 20,184
Arkoma (T4) 1,862
Arnett◉ (G2) 547
Asher (N5) 343
Ashland (O5) 87
Atoka◉ (O6) 2,877
Atwood (O5) 200
Avant (O2) 381
Avard (J1) 56
Avery (N3) 20
Bache (P5) 100
Bacone (R3) 250
Baker (D1) 78
Balko (E1) 60
Barnsdall (O1) 1,663
Baron (S3) 150
Bartlesville◉ (O1)....27,893
Battiest (S6) 150
Bearden (O4) 250
Beaver◉ (F1) 2,087
Bebee (N5) 98
Beggs (P3) 1,114
Belzoni (R6) 25
Bengal (R5) 62
Bennington (P7) 226
Bentley (O6) 128
Berlin (G4) 48
Bernice (S1) 100
Bessie (H4) 226
Bethany (L3) 12,342
Bethel (S6) 225
Big Cabin (R1) 228
Big Canyon (N6) 105
Billings (M1) 510
Binger (K4) 603
Bison (L2) 90
Bixby (P3) 1,711
Blackburn (N2) 129
Blackgum (S3) 125
Blackwell (M1) 9,588
Blair (H5) 893
Blanchard (L4) 1,377
Blanco (P5) 200
Blocker (P4) 84
Blue (P4) 155
Bluejacket (R1) 245
Boatman (R2) 115
Boggy Depot (O6) 130
Boise City◉ (B1) 1,978
Bokchito (O6) 620
Bokhoma (S7) 200
Bokoshe (S4) 431
Boley (O4) 573
Boswell (P6) 753
Bowden (O2) 175
Bowlegs (N4) 300
Bowring (O1) 85
Boyd (E1) 10
Boynton (P3) 604
Braden (S4) 25
Bradley (L5) 294
Braggs (R3) 279
Braman (M1) 336
Bray (L5) 110
Breckinridge (L2) 42
Briartown (R4) 182
Bridgeport (K3) 139
Brinkman (G4) 14
Bristow (O3) 4,795
Broken Arrow (P2) 5,928
Broken Bow (S7) 2,087
Bromide (N6) 264
Brooksville (M4) 175
Bryant (P4) 72
Buffalo◉ (G1) 1,618
Bunch (S3) 60
Burbank (N1) 238
Burlington (K1) 174
Burneyville (M7) 55
Burns Flat (H4) 2,280
Bushyhead (P2) 42
Butler (H3) 351
Byars (N5) 256
Byng (N5) 250
Byron (K1) 82
Cache (J5) 1,003
Caddo (O6) 814
Cairo (O5) 23

Calera (O7) 692
Calumet (K3) 354
Calvin (O5) 331
Camargo (H2) 254
Cameron (T4) 211
Canadian (P4) 255
Caney (O6) 128
Canton (J2) 887
Canute (H4) 370
Capron (J1) 102
Cardin (S1) 850
Carlton (K2) 16
Carmen (J1) 533
Carnegie (J4) 1,500
Carney (N3) 227
Carrier (K2) 80
Carter (H4) 364
Carter Nine (N1) 87
Cartersville (S4) 75
Cashion (L3) 221
Castle (O4) 149
Catesby (G2) 3
Catoosa (P2) 638
Cement (K5) 959
Center (N5) 200
Centrahoma (O5) 148
Centralia (R1) 80
Cestos (H2) 16
Chandler◉ (N3) 2,524
Chattanooga (J6) 356
Checotah (R4) 2,614
Chelsea (P1) 1,541
Cherokee◉ (K1) 2,410
Chester (J2) 98
Cheyenne◉ (G3) 930
Chickasha◉ (L4) 14,866
Chilocco (M1) 775
Choctaw (M4) 623
Chouteau (R2) 958
Christie (S3) 50
Claremore◉ (R2) 6,639
Clarita (O6) 114
Clarksville (P3) 150
Clayton (R5) 615
Clearview (O4) 500
Clemscot (L6) 200
Cleo Springs (K2) 236
Cleora (S1) 60
Cleveland (O2) 2,519
Clinton (H3) 9,617
Cloud Chief (J4) 60
Cloudy (R6) 150
Coalgate◉ (O5) 1,689
Cogar (K4) 67
Colbert (O7) 671
Colcord (S2) 173
Cold Springs
    (J5) 30
Cole (L4) 100
Coleman (N6) 200
Collinsville (P2) 2,526
Colony (L4) 200
Comanche (L6) 2,082
Commerce (R1) 2,378
Concho (L3) 150
Connerville (N6) 250
Cooperton (J5) 106
Copan (P1) 617
Cordell◉ (J4) 3,589
Corinne (R6) 65
Corn (J4) 317
Cornish (L6) 127
Council Hill (P3) 130
Countyline (M6) 575
Courtney (L7) 50
Covington (L2) 687
Coweta (P3) 1,858
Cowlington (S4) 74
Cox City (L5) 200
Coyle (M3) 292
Crawford (G3) 75
Crescent (L3) 1,264
Cromwell (N4) 269
Crowder (P4) 254
Cumberland (N6) 200
Curtis (H2) 125
Cushing (N3) 8,619
Custer (J3) 448
Cyril (K5) 1,284
Dacoma (J1) 219
Daisy (P5) 100
Dale (M4) 300
Darwin (P6) 50
Davenport (N3) 813
Davidson (J6) 429
Davis (M5) 2,203
Deer Creek (L1) 215
Del City (L4) 12,934
Dela (P6) 20
Dow (P5) 315
Doxey (G4) 75

Driftwood (K1) 32
Drummond (L2) 281
Drumright (O3) 4,190
Duke (G5) 400
Dunbar (P6) 85
Duncan◉ (L5) 20,009
Durant◉ (O6) 10,467
Durham (G3) 36

Dustin (O4) 457
Eagle City (J3) 76
Eagletown (S6) 505
Eakly (J4) 217
Earlsboro (N4) 257
East Duke (H5) 333
Echota (S3) 14
Edmond (M3) 8,577

Edna (O3) 20
El Reno◉ (K3) 11,015
Eldorado (G6) 708
Elgin (K5) 540
Elk City (G4) 8,196
Elmer (H6) 120
Elmore City (M5) 982
Elmwood (F1) 19

Enid◉ (L2) 38,859
Enterprise (R4) 75
Erick (G4) 1,342
Estella (R1) 10
Eucha (S2) 140
Eufaula◉ (P4) 2,382
Eva (C1) 24
Fairfax (N1) 2,076

Fairland (S1) 646
Fairmont (L2) 115
Fairview◉ (J2) 2,213
Follis (K4) 42
Fanshawe (S5) 150
Fargo (G2) 291

(continued on following page)

AGRICULTURE, INDUSTRY and RESOURCES

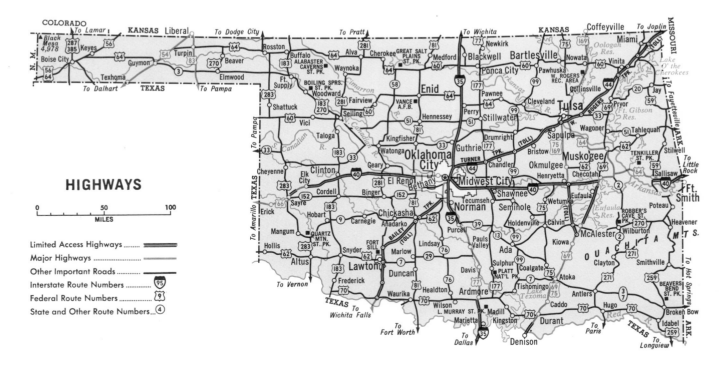

OKLAHOMA CITY
Food Processing, Meat Packing, Electrical & Metal Products, Machinery, Transportation Equipment, Oil Refining

TULSA
Oil Refining, Aircraft, Electrical & Metal Products, Chemicals, Machinery

DOMINANT LAND USE

- Wheat, General Farming
- Wheat, Grain Sorghums, Range Livestock
- Wheat, Range Livestock
- General Farming, Livestock, Cash Grain
- General Farming, Livestock, Truck Farming, Cotton
- Cotton, General Farming
- Cotton, Wheat
- Fruit and Mixed Farming
- Range Livestock
- Forests

MAJOR MINERAL OCCURRENCES

C	Coal	Ls	Limestone
G	Natural Gas	O	Petroleum
Gp	Gypsum	Pb	Lead
He	Helium	Zn	Zinc

⚡ Water Power   ▨ Major Industrial Areas

HIGHWAYS

0 ——— 50 ——— 100
MILES

Limited Access Highways ....
Major Highways ....
Other Important Roads ....
Interstate Route Numbers 95
Federal Route Numbers 9
State and Other Route Numbers 4

Oklahoma
(continued)

Farris (P6) 100
Faxon (J6) 137
Fay (J3) 107
Featherston (P4) 50
Felt (A1) 57
Fillmore (N6) 200
Finley (R6) 220
Fittstown (N5) 450
Fitzhugh (N5) 122
Fleetwood (L7) 55
Fletcher (K5) 884
Flint (S2) 100
Foraker (O1) 74
Forest Park (M3) 766
Forgan (E1) 532
Fort Cobb (K4) 687
Fort Gibson (R3) 1,407
Fort Sill (K5) 22,500
Fort Supply (G1) 394
Fort Towson (R7) 474
Foss (H4) 289
Foster (M5) 65
Fox (N6) 300
Foyil (R2) 127
Francis (N5) 286
Frederick⊙ (H6) 5,879
Freedom (H1) 268
Gage (G2) 482
Gans (S4) 234
Garber (M2) 905
Garvin (S7) 109
Gate (F1) 130
Geary (K3) 1,416
Gene Autry (N6) 110
Geronimo (K6) 199
Gerty (O5) 135
Gideon (R2) 100
Glencoe (M2) 264
Glenpool (P3) 353
Glover (S6) 100
Golden (S6) 150
Goltry (K1) 313
Goodland (P7) 73
Goodwater (S7) 25
Goodwell (C1) 771
Gore (R3) 334
Gotebo (J4) 538
Gould (G5) 241
Gowen (R5) 525
Gracemont (K4) 306
Grady (L6) 98
Graham (M6) 250
Grainola (N1) 67
Grand Lake Towne (R1) 16
Grandfield (J6) 1,606
Granite (H5) 952
Grant (R7) 286
Gray (E1) 9
Gray Horse (N1) 225
Greenfield (K3) 128
Griggs (B1) 16
Grimes (G4) 25
Grove (S1) 975
Guthrie⊙ (M3) 9,502
Guymon⊙ (D1) 5,768
Gypsy (N3) 53
Haileyville (P5) 922
Hallett (O2) 132
Hammon (H3) 656
Hanna (P4) 233
Hanson (S4) 100
Harden City (N5) 300
Hardesty (D1) 187
Hardy (N1) 6
Harjo (N4) 112
Harmon (G2) 15
Harrah (M4) 934
Harris (S7) 210
Hartshorne (R5) 1,903
Haskell (P3) 1,887
Hastings (K6) 200
Haworth (S7) 351
Hayward (L2) 42
Haywood (P5) 100
Headrick (H5) 152
Healdton (M6) 2,898
Heavener (S5) 1,891
Helena (K1) 580
Hendrix (Kemp City) (O7) 142
Hennepin (M5) 256
Hennessey (L2) 1,228
Henryetta (O4) 6,551
Herd (O1) 19
Hess (H6) 50
Hester (H5) 22
Hickory (N5) 112
Highland Beach ‡(L3) 35
Hillsdale (K1) 60
Hinton (K4) 907

Hitchcock (K3) 134
Hitchita (P3) 120
Hobart⊙ (J5) 5,132
Hochatown (S6) 175
Hockerville (S1) 250
Hodgen (S5) 100
Hoffman (P4) 248
Holdenville⊙ (O4) 5,712
Hollis⊙ (G5) 3,006
Hollister (J6) 166
Homestead (K2) 60
Hominy (O2) 2,866
Honobia (R5) 285
Hooker (D1) 1,684
Hopeton (J1) 65
Howe (S5) 390
Hoyt (R4) 165
Hugo⊙ (R6) 6,287
Hulbert (R3) 500
Humphreys (H5) 97
Hunter (L1) 203
Hydro (K3) 697
Idabel⊙ (S7) 4,967
Indiahoma (J5) 378
Indianola (P4) 234
Ingersoll (K1) 30
Inola (P2) 584
Isabella (K2) 100
Jay⊙ (S2) 1,120
Jefferson (L1) 119
Jenks (P2) 1,734
Jennings (N2) 306
Jet (K1) 339

Jones (M3) 794
Jumbo (P6) 50
Kansas (S2) 400
Karen Park ‡(M3) 6
Kaw (N1) 457
Keefeton (R3) 150
Kellyville (O3) 501
Kemp (O7) 153
Kemp City (Hendrix) (O7) 142
Kendrick (N3) 155
Kenefic (O6) 125
Kenton (A1) 35
Kenwood (S2) 115
Keota (S4) 579
Ketchum (R1) 255
Keyes (B1) 627
Keystone (O2) 151
Kiamichi (R5) 114
Kildare (M1) 124
Kingfisher⊙ (L3) 3,249
Kingston (N7) 639
Kinta (R4) 233
Kiowa (P5) 607
Knowles (F1) 62
Konawa (N5) 1,555
Kosoma (P6) 50
Krebs (P5) 1,342
Kremlin (L1) 128
Lahoma (K2) 160
Lake Aluma ‡(M3) 82
Lamar (O4) 150
Lambert (J1) 21
Lamont (L1) 543
Lane (O6) 100
Langley (N2) 205
Langston (M3) 136
Laverne (G1) 1,137
Lawton⊙ (K5) 61,697
Lawton (urban area) 61,941

Leach (S2) 53
Lebanon (N7) 150
Leedey (H3) 451
Leflore (H3) 350
Lehigh (O6) 296
Lela (N2) ....
Lenapah (P1) 322
Leon (M7) 109
Leonard (P3) 130
Lequire (R4) 100
Lexington (M4) 1,216
Lindsay (L5) 4,258
Little Chief (N1) 400
Little City (N6) 102
Loco (L6) 268
Lodi (R4) 83
Locust Grove (R2) 828
Logan (F1) 21
Lone Grove (M6) 285
Lone Wolf (H5) 617
Longdale (K2) 218
Lookeba (K4) 158
Lookout (H1) 5
Loveland (L6) 90
Lovell (L2) 27
Loyal (K3) 87
Lucien (M2) 200
Lugert (H5) 25
Lula (O5) 80
Luther (M3) 517
Lutie (R5) 250
Macomb (M4) 76
Madill⊙ (N6) 3,084
Manchester (L1) 162
Mangum⊙ (G5) 3,950
Manitou (J5) 269
Mannford (O2) 358
Mannsville (N6) 297
Maramec (N2) 169
Marble City (S3) 271
Marietta⊙ (M7) 1,933
Marland (M1) 191

Marlow (K5) 4,027
Marshall (L2) 363
Martha (H5) 243
Mason (O3) 100
Maud (N4) 1,137
May (G1) 114
Mayfield (G4) 21
Maysville (M5) 1,530
Mazie (R2) 100
McAlester⊙ (P5) 17,419
McBride ‡(N6) 14
McCurtain (R4) 528
McLemore (L4) 528
McLoud (M4) 837
McMan (G5) 125
McMillan (M6) 53
McQueen (G5) 18
Mead (O7) 200
Medford⊙ (L1) 1,223
Medicine Park (J5) 825
Meeker (N4) 664
Meers (J5) 84
Mehan (M2) 44
Meno (K2) 118
Meridian (M3) 160
Miami⊙ (S1) 12,869
Micawber (N3) 90
Midway (M4) 2,292
Midwest City (M4) 36,058
Milburn (O6) 228
Milfay (N3) 150
Mill Creek (N6) 287
Millerton (S7) 200
Milo (M6) 109
Milton (S4) 100
Minco (L4) 1,021
Mocane (F1) 10
Moffett (S4) 357
Monroe (S4) 150
Moodys (S2) 260
Moon (S7) 150
Moore (M4) 1,783

Mooreland (H2) 871
Moorewood (H3) 7
Morris (P3) 982
Morrison (M2) 256
Mountain Park (J5) 403
Mountain View (J4) 864
Moyers (P6) 100
Muldrow (S4) 1,137
Mulhall (M2) 253
Murphy (R2) 66
Muse (S5) 100
Muskogee⊙ (R3) 38,059
Mustang (L4) 198
Mutual (H2) 84
Narcissa (S1) 45
Nardin (M1) 142
Nash (K1) 230
Nashoba (R6) 125
Navina (L3) 11
Nelagoney (O1) 100
Nelson (P6) 45
New Cordell (Cordell) (J4) 3,589
New Lima (O4) 125
New Marshall (Marshall) (L2) 363
New Woodville (Woodville) (N7) 98
Newalla (M4) 150
Newcastle (L4) 175
Newkirk⊙ (N1) 2,092
Newport (M6) 27
Nichols Hills (L3) 4,897
Nicoma Park (M4) 1,263
Ninnekah (L5) 250
Noble (M4) 995
North Enid (L2) 286
North Miami (R1) 472
Nowata⊙ (P1) 4,163
Oakhurst (P2) 400

Oakland (N6) 288
Oaks (S2) 199
Oakwood (J3) 122
Oberlin (P7) 125
Ochelata (P1) 312
Octavia (S5) 55
Oilton (N2) 1,100
Okarche (L3) 584
Okay (R3) 419
Okeene (K2) 1,164
Okemah⊙ (O4) 2,836
Okesa (O1) 25
OKLAHOMA CITY (L4) 324,253
Oklahoma City (urban area) 429,188
Okmulgee⊙ (O3) 15,951
Oktaha (R3) 199
Oleta (R6) 50
Olive (O3) 83
Olney (O6) 75
Olustee (H5) 463
Omega (K3) 40
Oologah (P2) 299
Optima (D1) 64
Orienta (J2) 10
Orlando (M2) 194
Orr (M6) 70
Osage (O2) 220
Oscar (L7) 20
Overbrook (M6) 60
Owasso (P2) 2,032
Paden (N3) 417
Page (S5) 20
Panama (S4) 937
Panola (R5) 120
Paoli (M5) 358
Park Hill (R3) 150
Parkland (S3) 50
Pauls Valley⊙ (M5) 6,856
Pawhuska⊙ (O1) 5,414

Pawnee⊙ (N2) 2,303
Pearson (N4) 140
Peckham (M1) 55
Peggs (R2) 28
Pensacola (R2) 55
Peoria (S1) 156
Perkins (M3) 769
Pernell (M5) 250
Perry⊙ (M2) 5,210
Pershing (O1) ....
Pharoah (O4) 100
Phillips (O6) 91
Picher (S1) 2,553
Pickens (S6) 300
Piedmont (L3) 146
Pierce (P4) 16
Pittsburg (P5) 195
Platter (O7) 300
Pleasant Valley (M3) 16
Plunkettville (S6) 100
Pocasset (L4) 215
Ponca City (M1) 24,411
Pondcreek (L1) 935
Pontotoc (N6) 40
Pooleville (M6) 100
Porter (R4) 492
Porum (R4) 551
Poteau⊙ (S4) 4,428
Prague (N4) 1,545
Preston (P3) 250
Proctor (S3) 175
Prue (O2) 300
Pryor⊙ (R2) 6,476
Purcell⊙ (M5) 3,729
Putnam (J3) 83
Quapaw (S1) 850
Quay (N2) 51
Quinlan (J2) 75
Quinton (R4) 898
Ralston (N2) 411
Ramona (P2) 546
Randlett (K6) 356

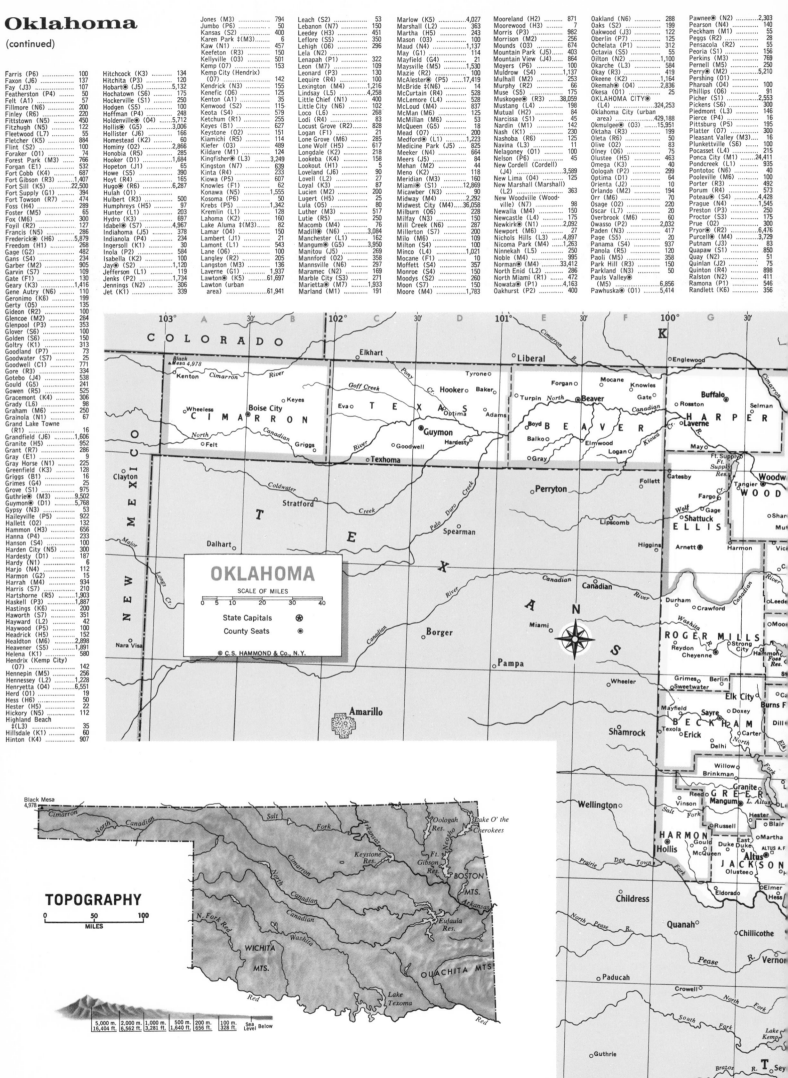

OKLAHOMA
SCALE OF MILES
0 5 10 20 40

State Capitals ⊛
County Seats ⊙

© C. S. HAMMOND & Co., N.Y.

TOPOGRAPHY

0   50   100
MILES

5,000 m. | 2,000 m. | 1,000 m. | 500 m. | 200 m. | 100 m. | Sea | Below
16,404 ft. | 6,562 ft. | 3,281 ft. | 1,640 ft. | 656 ft. | 328 ft. | Level

Place	Ref	Pop.	Place	Ref	Pop.
Rattan	(R6)	300	Sawyer	(R7)	220
Ravia	(N6)	307	Sayre ⦿	(G4)	2,913
Reagan	(N6)	100	Schulter	(P3)	500
Red Oak	(R5)	453	Scipio	(P4)	250
Redbird	(P3)	310	Scraper	(S2)	110
Redden	(P5)	112	Scullin	(N5)	27
Redrock	(M2)	262	Seiling	(J2)	910
Reed	(G5)	70	Selman	(H1)	64
Renfrow	(L1)	38	Seminole	(N4)	11,464
Rentiesville	(R4)	122	Sentinel	(H4)	1,154
Reydon	(G3)	183	Seward	(M3)	49
Ringling	(L6)	1,170	Shadypoint	(S4)	350
Ringold	(R6)	95	Shamrock	(O3)	211
Ringwood	(K2)	232	Sharon	(H2)	97
Ripley	(N2)	263	Shattuck	(G2)	1,625
Roberta	(O7)	40	Shawnee ⦿	(N4)	24,326
Rock Island	(T4)	120	Sherwood	(S6)	50
Rocky	(J4)	343	Shidler	(N1)	870
Roff	(N5)	638	Short	(S3)	
Roland	(S4)	100	Skedee	(N2)	128
Roosevelt	(J5)	495	Skiatook	(O2)	2,503
Rose	(R2)	350	Slick	(O3)	151
Rosedale	(M5)	88	Smith ‡	(M4)	93
Rosston	(G1)	58	Smithville	(R6)	110
Rubottom	(M7)	100	Snow	(R6)	200
Rufe	(R6)	75	Snyder	(J5)	1,663
Rush Springs	(L5)	1,303	Soper	(R5)	309
Russell	(G5)	63	South Coffeyville	(P1)	622
Ryan	(L6)	978	Southard	(K2)	246
Saddle Mountain	(J5)	10	Sparks	(N3)	186
Sageeyah	(P2)	50	Spaulding	(O4)	75
Saint Louis	(N4)	76	Spavinaw	(R2)	319
Salina	(R2)	972	Spencer	(M3)	1,189
Sallisaw ⦿	(S4)	3,351	Spencerville	(R6)	256
Salt Fork	(L1)	27	Sperry	(P2)	883
Sand Creek	(K1)	15	Spiro	(S4)	1,450
Sand Springs	(O2)	7,754	Springer	(M6)	212
Sapulpa ⦿	(O3)	14,282	Springlake Park ‡	(M4)	11
Sardis	(R5)	107	Stafford	(H3)	150
Sasakwa	(N5)	253	Stanley	(R5)	50
Savanna	(P5)	620	Stapp	(S5)	25

Place	Ref	Pop.	Place	Ref	Pop.
Stecker	(K5)	60	Tipton	(H6)	1,117
Sterling	(K5)	562	Tishomingo ⦿	(N6)	2,381
Stidham	(P4)	200	Tom	(S7)	500
Stigler ⦿	(R4)	1,923	Tonkawa	(M1)	3,415
Stillwater ⦿	(N2)	23,965	Tribbey	(M4)	100
Stilwell ⦿	(S3)	1,916	Trousdale	(M4)	50
Stonebluff	(P3)	300	Troy	(N6)	150
Stonewall	(O5)	584	Tryon	(N3)	254
Strang	(R2)	176	Tullahassee	(P3)	199
Stratford	(M5)	1,058	Tulsa ⦿	(O2)	261,685
Stringtown	(P6)	414	Tulsa (urban area)		298,922
Stroud	(N3)	2,456	Tupelo	(O5)	261
Stuart	(O5)	271	Turley	(P2)	1,200
Sugden	(L6)	68	Turpin	(E1)	195
Sulphur ⦿	(N5)	4,737	Tushka	(O6)	248
Summerfield	(S5)	300	Tuskahoma	(R5)	300
Sumner	(M2)	27	Tussy	(L6)	165
Sweetwater	(G4)	44	Tuttle	(L4)	855
Swink	(R6)	86	Tyrone	(D1)	456
Tabler	(L4)	25	Uncas	(M1)	90
Taft	(R4)	386	Union	(L4)	329
Tahlequah ⦿	(R3)	5,840	Utica	(O7)	100
Talala	(P1)	258	Valley Brook	(M4)	1,378
Talihina	(S5)	1,048	Valliant	(R6)	477
Taloga ⦿	(J2)	322	Vamoosa	(N5)	111
Tamaha	(S4)	80	Velma	(L6)	775
Tangier	(G2)	25	Vera	(P2)	125
Tatums	(M6)	319	Verden	(K4)	405
Tecumseh ⦿	(N4)	2,630	Verdigris	(P2)	120
Tegarden	(J1)	14	Vernon	(P4)	158
Temple	(K6)	1,282	Vian	(S4)	930
Terlton	(O2)	90	Vici	(H2)	601
Terral	(L7)	585	Vinco	(M3)	50
Texhoma	(C1)	911	Vinita ⦿	(R1)	6,027
Thackerville	(M7)	185	Vinson	(G5)	137
The Village	(L3)	12,118	Virgil	(R6)	115
Thomas	(J3)	1,211	Vivian	(P4)	50
Three Sands	(M2)	25	Wade	(O7)	65
Tiawah	(P2)		Wagoner ⦿	(R3)	4,469
			Wainwright	(R3)	114
			Wakita	(L1)	452

Place	Ref	Pop.	Place	Ref	Pop.
Walters ⦿	(K6)	2,825	Wirt	(L6)	400
Wanette	(M5)	381	Wister	(S5)	592
Wann	(P1)	157	Wolco	(O1)	30
Wapanucka	(N6)	459	Woodford	(M6)	44
Wardville	(P6)	150	Woodlawn Park ‡	(M4)	129
Warner	(R4)	881	Woodville	(N7)	98
Warr Acres	(L3)	7,135	Woodward ⦿	(H2)	7,747
Warwick	(M3)	95	Wright City	(R6)	1,161
Washington	(M4)	278	Wyandotte	(S1)	226
Washunga	(N1)	60	Wynnewood	(M5)	2,509
Watonga ⦿	(K3)	3,252	Wynona	(O1)	652
Watova	(P1)	250	Yahola	(P3)	12
Watson	(S6)	60	Yale	(N2)	1,369
Watts	(R2)	268	Yanush	(R5)	150
Waukomis	(K2)	516	Yeager	(O4)	129
Waurika ⦿	(L6)	1,933	Yonkers	(P2)	20
Wayne	(M5)	517	Yuba	(O7)	92
Waynoka	(J1)	1,794	Yukon	(L3)	3,076
Weatherford	(J4)	4,499	Zafra	(S5)	
Weathers	(P5)	125	Zena	(S2)	25
Webb City	(N1)	233	Zincville	(S1)	40
Webbers Falls	(R4)	441	Zoe	(S5)	80
Welch	(R1)	557			
Weleetka	(O4)	1,231			
Welling	(S3)	75			
Wellston	(M3)	630			
Welty	(O3)	63			
Westville	(S3)	727			
Wetumka	(O4)	1,756			
Wewoka ⦿	(O4)	5,954			
Wheeless	(A1)	50			
Whitefield	(R4)	300			
Whiteoak	(R1)	50			
Whitesboro	(S5)	750			
Wilburton ⦿	(R5)	1,772			
Wildcat	(P3)	142			
Williams	(T4)	200			
Willis	(N7)	100			
Willow	(G4)	187			
Wilson	(M6)	1,647			

OTHER FEATURES

Altus (lake)	H 5
Altus A.F.B.	H 5
Arkansas (river)	S 4
Atoka (res.)	P 5
Beaver (creek)	K 6
Bird (creek)	O 1
Black Bear (creek)	M 2
Black Mesa (mt.)	A 1
Blue (river)	O 6
Boston (mts.)	S 3
Broken Bow (res.)	S 6
Cache (creek)	K 6
Canadian (river)	L 4
Caney (river)	O 1
Canton (res.)	J 2
Carl Blackwell (lake)	M 2

Feature	Ref	Feature	Ref
Cherokees, Lake O' the (lake)	S 1	Neosho (river)	R 1
Cimarron (river)	N 2	North Canadian (river)	K 3
Clear Boggy (creek)	O 6	Oologah (res.)	P 1
Clinton Sherman A.F.B.	J 3	Osage Indian Res.	O 1
Deep Fork, North Canadian (river)	N 3	Ouachita (mts.)	R 5
Denison (dam)	O 7	Platt National Park	N 6
Elk (creek)	H 4	Pony (creek)	C 1
Eufaula (res.)	P 4	Poteau (river)	S 4
Fort Cobb (res.)	J 4	Prairie Dog Town Fork, Red (river)	F 5
Fort Gibson (res.)	R 2	Red (river)	R 7
Fort Sill Mil. Res.	K 5	Salt Fork, Arkansas (river)	J 1
Fort Supply (res.)	G 1	Salt Fork, Red (river)	J 5
Foss (res.)	H 3	Sanbois (mts.)	R 4
Goff (creek)	C 1	Scott (mt.)	K 5
Great Salt Plains (res.)	K 1	Short Mountain (res.)	R 4
Heyburn (res.)	N 3	Spavinaw (lake)	S 2
Hulah (res.)	O 1	Tenkiller Ferry (res.)	S 3
Illinois (river)	S 3	Texoma (lake)	N 7
Jackfork (mts.)	P 5	Tinker A.F.B.	M 4
Keystone (res.)	N 2	Turkey (creek)	L 2
Kiamichi (mts.)	R 5	Upper Spavinaw (lake)	L 2
Kiamichi (river)	R 6	Vance A.F.B.	K 2
Kiowa (creek)	J 1	Verdigris (river)	P 2
Lawtonka (lake)	K 5	Washita (river)	M 5
Little (river)	R 6	Webbers Falls (res.)	M 5
Markham Ferry (res.)	R 2	Wichita (mts.)	J 5
McAlester (lake)	P 4	Wildhorse (creek)	L 5
Mountain Fork (river)	L 6	Wister (lake)	S 5
Mud (creek)	L 6	Wolf (creek)	G 2
Muddy Boggy (creek)	O 5		
Murray (lake)	M 6		

⦿ County Seat.
‡ Name not on map.

Oregon

COUNTIES

Baker (K3)	17,295
Benton (D3)	39,165
Clackamas (E2)	113,038
Clatsop (D1)	27,380
Columbia (D2)	22,379
Coos (C4)	54,955
Crook (G3)	9,430
Curry (C5)	13,983
Deschutes (F4)	23,100
Douglas (E4)	68,458
Gilliam (G2)	3,069
Grant (J3)	7,726
Harney (H4)	6,744
Hood River (F2)	13,395
Jackson (E5)	73,962
Jefferson (F3)	7,130
Josephine (D5)	29,917
Klamath (F5)	47,475
Lake (G5)	7,158
Lane (E4)	162,890
Lincoln (D3)	24,635
Linn (E3)	58,867
Malheur (K4)	22,764
Marion (E3)	120,888
Morrow (H2)	4,871
Multnomah (E2)	522,813
Polk (D3)	26,523
Sherman (G2)	2,446
Tillamook (D2)	18,955
Umatilla (J2)	44,352
Union (J2)	18,180
Wallowa (K2)	7,102
Wasco (F2)	20,205
Washington (D2)	92,237
Wheeler (G3)	2,722
Yamhill (D2)	32,478

CITIES and TOWNS

Adams (J2)	192
Adel (H5)	40
Adrian (K4)	300
Agate Beach (C3)	606
Agness (D5)	100
Airlie (D3)	81
Albany (D3)	12,926
Algoma (F5)	50
Alicel (J2)	35
Allegany (D4)	450
Aloha (D2)	675
Alpine (D3)	130
Alsea (D3)	200
Altamont (F5)	10,811
Alvadore (D3)	230
Amity (D2)	620
Andrews (J5)	100
Anlauf (J4)	100
Antelope (E2)	46
Antone (H3)	18
Arago (C4)	190
Arlington (G2)	643
Arock (K5)	43
Ash (J4)	99
Ashland (E5)	9,119
Ashwood (G3)	13
Astoria (D1)	11,239
Athena (J2)	950
Aumsville (E3)	300
Aurora (A2)	274
Austin (J3)	200
Azalea (D5)	25
Baker (K3)	9,986
Ballston (D2)	150
Bancroft (D5)	90
Bandon (C4)	1,653
Banks (A1)	347
Bar View (C3)	75
Barlow (B2)	85
Barnes (D4)	5,076
Barton (B2)	268
Bates (J3)	500
Bay City (D2)	996
Beatty (F5)	50
Beaver (D3)	567
Beavercreek (B2)	60
Beaverton (A2)	5,937
Belknap Springs (F3)	6
Bellfountain (D3)	36
Bend (F3)	11,936
Beulah (J4)	6
Biggs (G2)	50
Birkenfeld (D1)	50
Blachly (J4)	131
Blackbutte (E4)	8
Blaine (D2)	210
Blodgett (D3)	400
Blue River (E3)	500
Bly (J4)	300
Boardman (H2)	153
Bonanza (F5)	297
Bonneville (F2)	550
Boring (E2)	800
Boyd (F2)	64
Breitenbush (F3)	50
Bridal Veil (E2)	150
Bridge (D4)	200
Bridgeport (K3)	75
Brighton (C2)	50
Brightwood (E2)	200
Broadacres (A3)	60
Broadbent (C4)	425
Brogan (K3)	75
Brookings (C5)	2,637
Brooks (A3)	400
Brothers (G4)	25
Brownlee (L3)	200
Brownsboro (E5)	40
Brownsville (E3)	875
Buena Vista (D3)	128
Bunker Hill (C4)	1,655
Burlington (A1)	200
Burns (H4)	3,523
Butte Falls (E5)	384
Butteville (A2)	70
Buxton (D2)	140
Camas Valley (D4)	550
Camp Sherman (F3)	200
Canary (E3)	50
Canby (B2)	2,168
Cannon Beach (D2)	495
Canyon City (J3)	654
Canyonville (D5)	1,089
Carlton (D2)	959
Carpenterville (C5)	25
Carson (K3)	14
Carver (B2)	215
Cascade Locks (E2)	660
Cascade Summit (F4)	15
Cascadia (E3)	200
Cayuse (J2)	80
Cecil (H2)	88
Cedar Hills (A2)	1,200
Cedar Mill (A2)	215
Celilo (E2)	35
Central Point (D5)	2,289
Charleston (C4)	700
Chemawa (A3)	825
Chemult (F4)	310
Cherry Grove (D2)	300
Cherryville (E2)	220
Cheshire (D3)	85
Chiloquin (F5)	945
Clackamas (B2)	3,141
Clarno (G3)	11
Clatskanie (D1)	797
Cloverdale (D2)	183
Coburg (D3)	754
Cochran (D2)	5
Colestin (E5)	10
Colton (B3)	300
Columbia City (B2)	423
Condon (G2)	1,149
Coos Bay (C4)	7,084
Coquille (C4)	4,730
Cornelius (A2)	1,146
Cornucopia (K3)	2
Corvallis (D3)	20,669
Cottage Grove (D4)	3,895
Cove (K2)	311
Cove Junction (D5)	248
Cove Orchard (D2)	60
Crabtree (E3)	550
Crane (J4)	21
Crater Lake (E5)	80
Crawfordsville (E3)	300
Crescent (F4)	400
Crescent Lake (F4)	50
Creston (K4)	10
Creswell (D3)	760
Crow (D4)	150
Culver (F3)	301
Curtin (D4)	150
Cushman (D4)	214
Dairy (F5)	70
Dale (J3)	35
Danner (K5)	20
Days Creek (D5)	200
Dayton (A3)	673
Dayville (H3)	234
Denmark (C5)	400
Depoe Bay (C3)	750
Detroit (E3)	206
Dexter (E3)	300
Diamond (J4)	8
Diamond Lake (E4)	77
Dillard (A2)	500
Dilley (A2)	280
Disston (E4)	232
Donald (A3)	201
Dora (D4)	125
Dorena (E4)	375
Drain (D4)	1,052
Drew (E5)	7
Drewsey (J4)	39
Dryden (D5)	2
Dufur (F2)	488
Dundee (A2)	318
Dunes City (Westlake) (C4)	629
Durham (A3)	500
Durkee (K3)	250
Eagle Creek (E2)	75
Eagle Point (E5)	752
Eastside (C4)	1,380
Echo (H2)	456
Eddyville (D3)	30
Elgarose (D4)	210

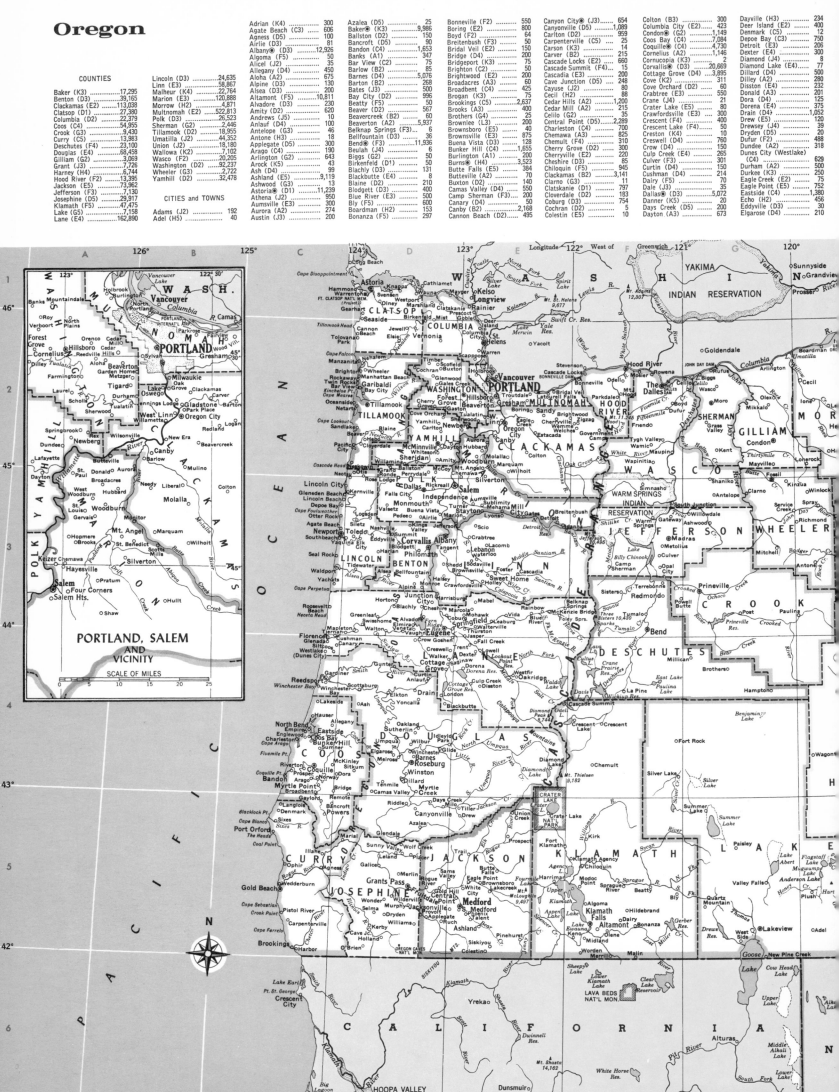

PORTLAND, SALEM AND VICINITY

SCALE OF MILES
0 5 10 15 20 25

OREGON

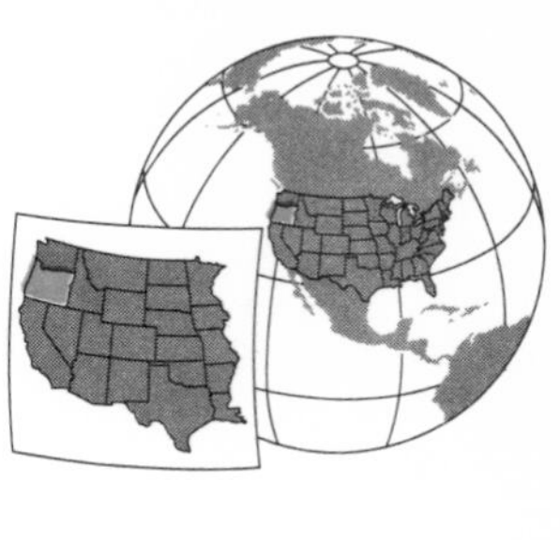

AREA 96,981 sq. mi.
POPULATION 1,899,000
CAPITAL Salem
LARGEST CITY Portland 372,676
HIGHEST POINT Mt. Hood 11,245 ft.
SETTLED IN 1810
ADMITTED TO UNION February 14, 1859
POPULAR NAME Beaver State
STATE FLOWER Oregon Grape
STATE BIRD Western Meadowlark

Elgin (K2) 1,315
Elk City (D3) 50
Elkton (D4) 146
Elmira (D3) 2,000
Elsie (D2) 50
Empire (C4) 3,781
Englewood (C4) 1,382
Enterprise◉ (K2) 1,932
Estacada (E2) 957
Eugene◉ (D3) 50,977
Eugene (urban area) 95,686
Fairview (B2) 578
Fall Creek (E4) 200
Falls City (D3) 653
Farmington (A2) 15
Fields (J5) 7
Flora (K2) 45
Florence (C4) 1,642
Foley Springs (E3)...... 180
Forest Grove (A2) 5,628
Fort Klamath (E5) 450
Fort Rock (G4) 17
Fossil◉ (G2) 672
Foster (E3) 350
Four Corners (A3) 4,743
Fox (H3) 65
Frenchglen (H5) 46
Friend (F2) 15
Fruitdale (D5) 2,158
Gales Creek (D2) 200
Galice (D5) 18
Garden Home (A2) 2,200
Gardiner (C4) 350
Garibaldi (D2) 1,163
Gaston (D2) 320
Gates (E3) 189
Gateway (F3) 25
Gaylord (C5) 75
Gearhart (C1) 725
Gervais (A3) 438
Gibbon (J2) 60
Gladstone (B2) 3,854
Glenada (C4) 110
Glendale (D5) 748
Gleneden Beach (C3).... 185
Glenwood (D2) 750
Glide (D4) 200
Goble (E1) 70
Gold Beach◉ (C5) 1,765
Gold Hill (D5) 608
Goshen (D4) 300
Government Camp (F2) 88
Grand Ronde (D2) 150
Granite (J3) 3
Grants Pass◉ (D5)....10,118
Grass Valley (G2) 234
Greenleaf (D3) 41
Gresham (B2) 3,944
Gunter (D4) 10
Haines (J3) 331
Halfway (K3) 505
Halsey (D3) 404
Hamilton (H3) 58
Hammond (C1) 480
Hampton (G4) 10
Harbor (C5) 600
Hardman (H2) 30
Harlan (D3) 160
Harney (J4) 3
Harper (K4) 140
Harriman (E5) 250
Harrisburg (D3) 939
Hauser (C4) 233
Hayesville (A3) 4,568
Hebo (D2) 350
Helix (J2) 148
Heppner◉ (H2) 1,661
Hereford (K3) 65
Hermiston (H2) 4,402
Hildebrand (F5) 100
Hillsboro◉ (A2) 8,232
Hines (H4) 1,207
Holbrook (A1) 100
Holdman (J2) 25
Holland (D5) 100
Holley (E3) 85
Hood River◉ (F2) 3,657
Hopmere (A3) 50
Horton (D3) 235
Hot Lake (K2) 75
Hubbard (A3) 526
Hullt (B3) ....
Huntington (K3) 689
Idanha (E3) 295
Idleyld Park (D4)........ 100
Illahe (C5) 25
Imbler (J2) 137
Imnaha (L2) 35
Independence (D3) 1,930
Ione (H2) 350
Ironside (K3) 40
Irrigon (H2) 232
Island City (K2) 158
Jacksonville (D5) 1,172
Jamieson (K3) 145
Jasper (E3) 300
Jefferson (D3) 716
Jennings Lodge (B2)....2,867
Jewell (D2) 150
John Day (J3) 1,520
Jordan Valley (K5)...... 204
Joseph (K2) 788
Junction City (D3) 1,614
Juntura (K4) 98
Kamela (J2) 25
Keating (K3) 11
Keizer (A3) 5,288
Keno (F5) 350
Kent (G2) 60
Kerby (D5) 800
Kernville (D3) 73
Kimberly (H3) 11
Kings Valley (D3) 150
Kinzua (H3) 900
Kirk (F5) 25
Klamath Agency (F5)... 250
Klamath Falls◉ (F5)..16,949
Knappa (D1) 200
La Grande◉ (J2) 9,014
La Pine (F4) 750
Lacomb (E3) 800
Lafayette (A2) 553
Lake Oswego (B2)........8,906
Lakecreek (E5) 224
Lakeside (C4) 950
Lakeview◉ (G5) 3,260
Langlois (C5) 150
Latourell Falls (E2)..... 60
Laurel (A2) 12
Lawen (J4) 15
Leaburg (E3) 106
Lebanon (E3) 5,858
Leland (D5) 152
Lexington (H2) 240
Liberal (B3) 40
Lime (K3) 100
Lincoln Beach (C3) 100
Lincoln City (C3) 3,400
Logan (B2) 50
Logsden (D3) ....
London (D4) 45
Lonerock (H2) 31
Long Creek (H3) 295
Lostine (K2) 240
Lowell (E4) 503
Lyons (E3) 463
Mabel (E3) 85
Madras◉ (F3) 1,515
Malin (F5) 568
Manhattan Beach (D2) 100
Manzanita (C2) 363
Mapleton (C3) 600
Marcola (E3) 360
Marial (D5) 9
Marion (D3) 250
Marquam (B3) 75
Marshland (D1) 150
Maupin (F2) 381
May Park (J2) 1,071
Mayger (D1) 100
Mayville (G2) 30
McCoy (D2) 75
McKenzie Bridge (E3).. 225
McKinley (D4) 50
McMinnville◉ (D2) 7,656
McNary (H2) 412
Meacham (J2) 55
Medford◉ (E5) 24,425
Medical Springs (K2)... 25
Mehama (E3) 300
Melrose (D4) 80
Merlin (D5) 255
Merrill (F5) 804
Metolius (F3) 270
Metzger (A2) 1,450
Midland (F5) 100
Mikkalo (G2) 80
Mill City (E3) 1,289
Millican (F4) 8
Milo (E5) 500
Milton-Freewater (J2)..4,110
Milwaukie (B2) 9,099
Minam (K2) 75
Mist (D1) 130
Mitchell (G3) 236
Modoc Point (F5) 100
Mohawk (E3) 60
Molalla (B3) 1,501
Monitor (B3) 100
Monmouth (D3) 2,229
Monroe (D3) 374
Monument (H3) 214
Moro◉ (G2) 327
Mosier (F2) 252
Mount Angel (B3) 1,428
Mount Hood (F2) 225
Mount Vernon (H3)....... 502
Mountaindale (A1) 95
Mulino (B2) 323
Murphy (D5) 50
Myrtle Creek (D4) 2,231
Myrtle Point (C4) 2,886
Narrows (H4) 7
Nashville (D3) 38
Needy (B3) 115
Nehalem (D2) 233
Neotsu (C2) 160
Neskowin (D2) 150
Netarts (C2) 850
New Bridge (K3) 96
New Era (B2) 50
New Pine Creek (G5).... 275
Newberg (A2) 4,204
Newport◉ (C3) 5,344
North Bend (C4) 7,512
North Plains (A2) 580
North Portland (B1)..... 126
North Powder (K2) 399
Norway (C4) 250
Nyssa (K4) 2,611
Oak Grove (B2) 3,404
Oakland (D4) 856
Oakridge (E4) 1,973
O'Brien (D5) 235
Oceanside (C2) 225
Odell (F2) 450
Olene (F5) 130
Olex (G2) 33
Olney (D1) 100
Ontario (K3) 5,101
Opal City (F3) 50
Ophir (C5) 100
Oregon City◉ (B2) 7,996
Orenco (A2) 400
Otis (D2) 200
Otter Rock (C3) 138
Owyhee Corner (K4).... 60
Oxbow (K2) 50
Pacific City (C2) 200
Paisley (G5) 219
Paradise (K2) 5
Park Place (B2) 950
Parkdale (F2) 275
Parkrose (B2) 9,900
Paulina (G3) 300
Pedee (D3) 123
Pendleton◉ (J2) 14,434
Perry (J2) 100
Perrydale (D2) 100
Philomath (D3) 1,359
Phoenix (E5) 769
Pilot Rock (J2) 1,695
Pine (K3) 73
Pinehurst (E5) 6
Pistol River (C5) 160
Placer (D5) 192
Pleasant Valley (K3).... 25
Plush (H5) 110
Port Orford (C5) 1,171
Portland◉ (B2) 372,676
Portland (urban area) 651,685
Post (G3) 1
Powell Butte (G3) 580
Powers (D5) 1,366
Prairie City (J3) 801
Pratum (A3) 107
Prescott (D1) 129
Princeton (J4) 6
Prineville◉ (G3) 3,263
Promise (K2) 7
Prospect (E5) 500
Prosper (C4) 55
Provolt (D5) 50
Quartz Mountain (G5) 12
Rainbow (E3) 150
Rainier (E1) 1,152
Redland (B2) 100
Redmond (F3) 3,340
Reedsport (C4) 2,998
Reedville (A2) 168
Remote (D5) 40
Rex (A2) 5
Richland (K3) 228
Richmond (H3) 8
Rickreall (D3) 120
Riddle (D5) 992
Rieth (J2) 325
Riley (H4) 6
Ritter (H3) 2
Riverside (J4) 10
Riverton (C4) 125
Rockaway (C2) 771
Rogue River (D5) 520
Rome (K5) 42
Roosevelt Beach (C3)... 6
Rose Lodge (D3) 150
Roseburg◉ (D4) 11,467
Rowena (F2) 100
Roy (A2) 78
Ruch (E5) 50
Rufus (G2) 30
Rye Valley (K3) 12
Saginaw (E4) 60
Saint Benedict (B3)..... 102
Saint Helens◉ (E2)......5,022
Saint Louis (A3) 135
Saint Paul (A3) 254
SALEM◉ (A3) 49,142
Salem Heights (A3)....10,770
Sams Valley (E5) 800
Sandlake (C2) 278
Sandy (E2) 1,147
Scappoose (E2) 923
Scholls (A2) 50
Scio (E3) 441
Scofield (D2) 101
Scotts Mills (B3) 155
Scottsburg (D4) 250
Seal Rock (C3) 500
Seaside (D2) 3,877
Selma (D5) 125
Seneca (J3) 450
Service Creek (G3) 6
Shaniko (G3) 39
Shaw (A3) 35
Sheaville (K4) 6
Shedd (D3) 152
Sheridan (D2) 1,763
Sherwood (A2) 680
Siletz (D3) 583
Siltcoos (C4) 28
Silver Lake (F4) 150
Silverton (B3) 3,081
Silvies (H3) 9
Simnasho (F3) 90
Siskiyou (E5) 15
Sisters (F3) 602
Sitkum (D4) 50
Sixes (C5) 250
Sodaville (E3) 145
South Junction (G3)..... 30
South Medford (E5).....2,306
Southbeach (C3) 250
Sparta (K3) 10
Sprague River (F5)...... 208
Spray (H3) 194
Springbrook (A2) 75
Springfield (E3) 19,616
Stanfield (H2) 745
Starkey (J2) 25
Stayton (E3) 2,108
Sublimity (E3) 490
Summer Lake (G5) 34
Summerville (K2) 76
Summit (D3) 115
Sumner (C4) 40
Sumpter (J3) 96
Sunny Valley (D5) 350
Sutherlin (D4) 2,452
Svensen (D1) 500
Sweet Home (E3) 3,353
Swisshome (D3) 500
Sylvan (B2) 1,200
Talent (E5) 868
Tangent (D3) 220
Telocaset (K2) 49
Tenmile (D4) 150
Terrebonne (F3) 378
The Dalles◉ (F2) 10,493
Thurston (E3) 600
Tidewater (D3) 175
Tiernan (C3) 200
Tigard (A2) 1,980
Tillamook◉ (D2) 4,244
Tiller (E5) 350
Timber (D2) 216
Toledo (D3) 3,053
Tolovana Park (C2)...... 195
Trail (E5) 88
Trent (E4) 400
Troutdale (E2) 522
Troy (K2) 12
Tualatin (A2) 359
Tumalo (F3) 125
Turner (E3) 770
Twin Rocks (C2) 200
Tygh Valley (F2) 410
Ukiah (J2) 200
Umapine (J2) 100
Umatilla (H2) 617
Umpqua (D4) 59
Union (K2) 1,490
Union Creek (E5) 100
Unity (J3) 288
Vale◉ (K4) 1,491
Valley Falls (G5) 14
Valsetz (D3) 675
Van (J4) 5
Vaughn (D3) 300
Veneta (D3) 1,150
Verboort (A2) 400
Vernonia (D2) 1,089
Vida (E3) 250
Wagontire (H4) 5
Waldport (C3) 667
Walker (D4) 100
Wallowa (K2) 989
Walterville (E3) 98
Walton (D3) 200
Wamic (F2) 213
Wapinitia (F2) 15
Warm Springs (F3)...... 450
Warren (E2) 500
Warrenton (C1) 1,717
Wasco (G2) 348
Waterloo (E3) 151
Wauna (D1) 125
Wedderburn (C5) 350
Welches (E2) 150
Wemme (E2) 109
West Linn (B2) 3,933
West Side (G5) 16
West Woodburn (A3) 250
Westfall (K3) 8
Westfir (E4) 492
Westlake (C4) 629
Weston (J2) 783
Westport (D1) 200
Wheeler (D2) 237
White City (E5) 200
Whiteson (D2) 80
Wilbur (D4) 150
Wilderville (D5) 150
Wilhoit (B3) 22
Willamina (D2) 960
Williams (D5) 500
Willowcreek (K3) 35
Willowdale (G3) 35
Wilsonville (A2) 229
Winchester (D4) 631
Winchester Bay (C4) 450
Winlock (H3) 10
Winston (D4) 2,395
Wolf Creek (D5) 500
Wonder (D5) 55
Wood Village (B2) 822
Woodburn (A3) 3,120
Worden (F5) 100
Yachats (C3) 500
Yamhill (D2) 407
Yaquina (C3) 76
Yoncalla (D4) 698
Zigzag (F2) 150
Zumwalt (L2) 2

OTHER FEATURES

Abert (lake) ....G 5
Abiqua (creek) ....B 3
Agency (lake) ....E 5
Agency Valley (res.) ......J 4
Alsea (river) ....D 3
Alvord (lake) ....J 5
Anderson (lake) ....H 5
Antelope (creek) ....K 5
Antelope (res.) ....K 5
Arago (cape) ....C 4
Aspen (lake) ....E 5
Badger (creek) ....H 3
Battle (creek) ....K 5
Bear (creek) ....E 5
Bear (creek) ....K 2
Bear (creek) ....G 4
Benjamin (lake) ....G 4
Billy Chinook (lake) ....F 3
Birch (creek) ....J 2
Blacklock (point) ....C 5
Blanco (cape) ....C 5
Blue (mts.) ....J 3
Bonneville (dam) ....E 2

(continued on following page)

TOPOGRAPHY

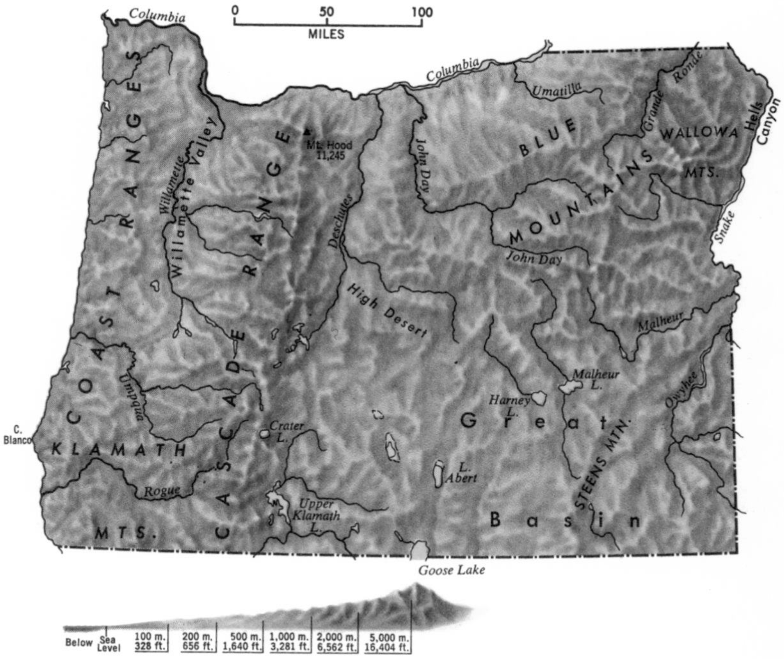
0 50 100
MILES
Columbia
COAST RANGES
CASCADE RANGE
BLUE MOUNTAINS
WALLOWA MTS.
KLAMATH MTS.
Mt. Hood 11,245
Willamette Valley
High Desert
Great Basin
STEENS MTN.
Malheur L.
Harney L.
Crater L.
Upper Klamath L.
L. Abert
Goose Lake
C. Blanco
Below Sea Level
100 m. 328 ft.
200 m. 656 ft.
500 m. 1,640 ft.
1,000 m. 3,281 ft.
2,000 m. 6,562 ft.
5,000 m. 16,404 ft.

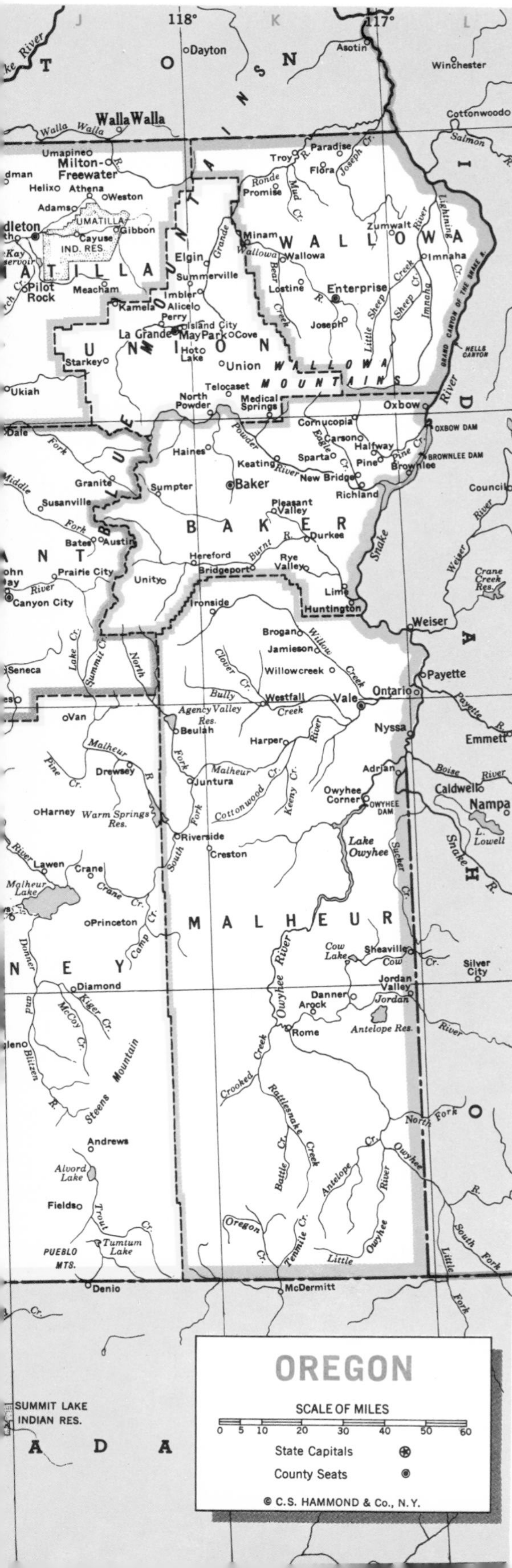
OREGON
SCALE OF MILES
0 5 10 20 30 40 50 60
State Capitals
County Seats
© C.S. HAMMOND & Co., N.Y.

Oregon
(continued)

AGRICULTURE, INDUSTRY and RESOURCES

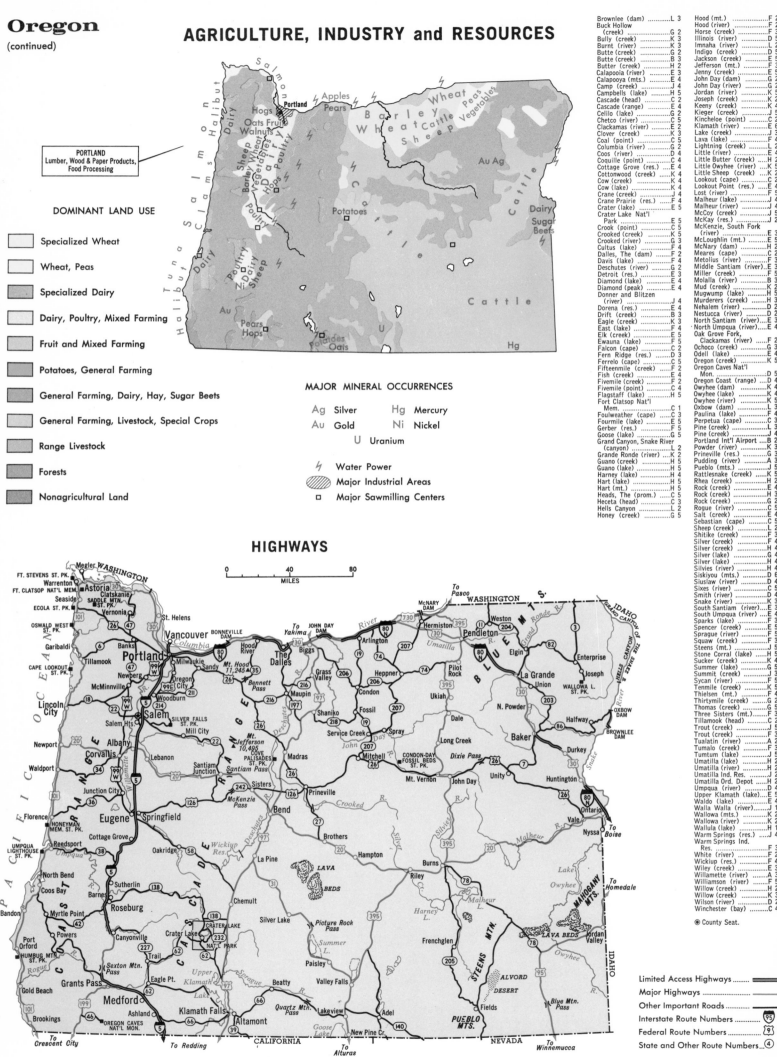

PORTLAND
Lumber, Wood & Paper Products,
Food Processing

DOMINANT LAND USE

- Specialized Wheat
- Wheat, Peas
- Specialized Dairy
- Dairy, Poultry, Mixed Farming
- Fruit and Mixed Farming
- Potatoes, General Farming
- General Farming, Dairy, Hay, Sugar Beets
- General Farming, Livestock, Special Crops
- Range Livestock
- Forests
- Nonagricultural Land

MAJOR MINERAL OCCURRENCES

Ag Silver   Hg Mercury
Au Gold   Ni Nickel
         U Uranium

⚡ Water Power
▨ Major Industrial Areas
☐ Major Sawmilling Centers

HIGHWAYS

Limited Access Highways
Major Highways
Other Important Roads
Interstate Route Numbers
Federal Route Numbers
State and Other Route Numbers

PENNSYLVANIA

AGRICULTURE, INDUSTRY and RESOURCES

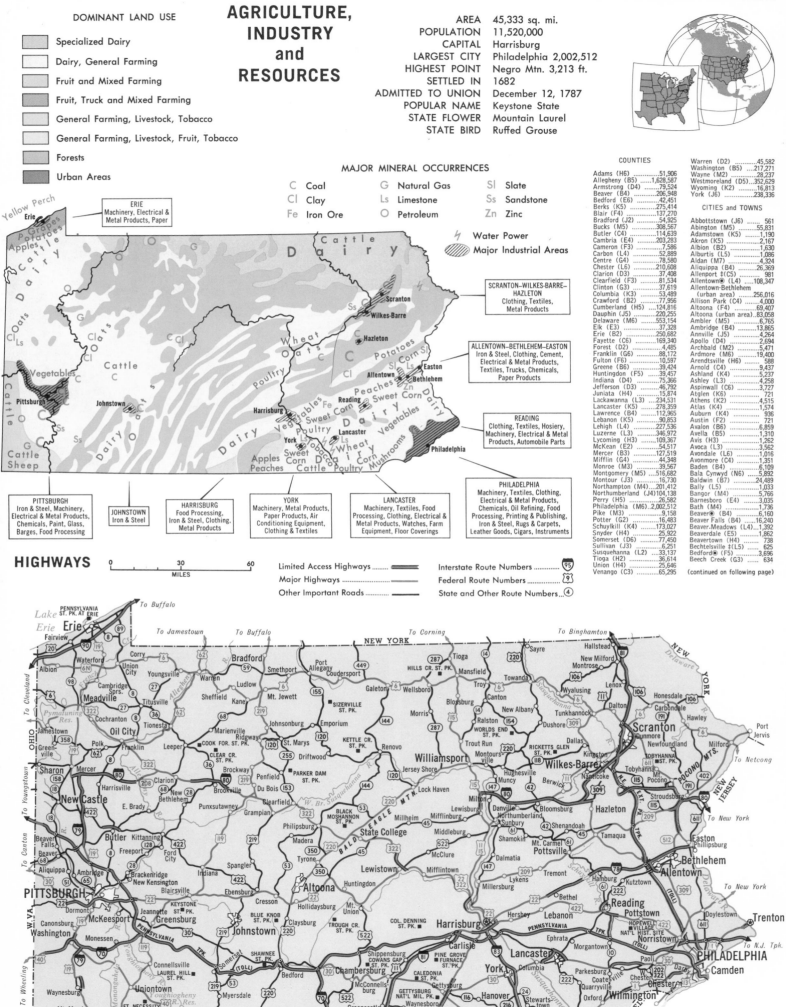

DOMINANT LAND USE

- Specialized Dairy
- Dairy, General Farming
- Fruit and Mixed Farming
- Fruit, Truck and Mixed Farming
- General Farming, Livestock, Tobacco
- General Farming, Livestock, Fruit, Tobacco
- Forests
- Urban Areas

AREA	45,333 sq. mi.
POPULATION	11,520,000
CAPITAL	Harrisburg
LARGEST CITY	Philadelphia 2,002,512
HIGHEST POINT	Negro Mtn. 3,213 ft.
SETTLED IN	1682
ADMITTED TO UNION	December 12, 1787
POPULAR NAME	Keystone State
STATE FLOWER	Mountain Laurel
STATE BIRD	Ruffed Grouse

MAJOR MINERAL OCCURRENCES

- C Coal
- Cl Clay
- Fe Iron Ore
- G Natural Gas
- Ls Limestone
- O Petroleum
- Sl Slate
- Ss Sandstone
- Zn Zinc
- Water Power
- Major Industrial Areas

ERIE
Machinery, Electrical & Metal Products, Paper

SCRANTON–WILKES-BARRE–HAZLETON
Clothing, Textiles, Metal Products

ALLENTOWN–BETHLEHEM–EASTON
Iron & Steel, Clothing, Cement, Electrical & Metal Products, Textiles, Trucks, Chemicals, Paper Products

READING
Clothing, Textiles, Hosiery, Machinery, Electrical & Metal Products, Automobile Parts

PITTSBURGH
Iron & Steel, Machinery, Electrical & Metal Products, Chemicals, Paint, Glass, Barges, Food Processing

JOHNSTOWN
Iron & Steel

HARRISBURG
Food Processing, Iron & Steel, Clothing, Metal Products

YORK
Machinery, Metal Products, Paper Products, Air Conditioning Equipment, Clothing & Textiles

LANCASTER
Machinery, Textiles, Food Processing, Clothing, Electrical & Metal Products, Watches, Farm Equipment, Floor Coverings

PHILADELPHIA
Machinery, Textiles, Clothing, Electrical & Metal Products, Chemicals, Oil Refining, Food Processing, Printing & Publishing, Iron & Steel, Rugs & Carpets, Leather Goods, Cigars, Instruments

COUNTIES

County	Population
Adams (H6)	51,906
Allegheny (B5)	1,628,587
Armstrong (D4)	79,524
Beaver (B4)	206,948
Bedford (E6)	42,451
Berks (K5)	275,414
Blair (F4)	137,270
Bradford (J2)	54,925
Bucks (M5)	308,567
Butler (C4)	114,639
Cambria (E4)	203,283
Cameron (F3)	7,586
Carbon (L4)	52,889
Centre (G4)	78,580
Chester (L6)	210,608
Clarion (D3)	37,408
Clearfield (F3)	81,534
Clinton (G3)	37,619
Columbia (K3)	53,489
Crawford (B2)	77,956
Cumberland (H5)	124,816
Dauphin (J5)	220,255
Delaware (M6)	553,154
Elk (E3)	37,328
Erie (B2)	250,682
Fayette (C6)	169,340
Forest (D2)	4,485
Franklin (G6)	88,172
Fulton (F6)	10,597
Greene (B6)	39,424
Huntingdon (F5)	39,457
Indiana (D4)	75,366
Jefferson (D3)	46,792
Juniata (H4)	15,874
Lackawanna (L3)	234,531
Lancaster (K5)	278,359
Lawrence (B4)	112,965
Lebanon (K5)	90,853
Lehigh (L4)	227,536
Luzerne (L3)	346,972
Lycoming (H3)	109,367
McKean (E2)	54,517
Mercer (B3)	127,519
Mifflin (G4)	44,348
Monroe (M3)	39,567
Montgomery (M5)	516,682
Montour (J3)	16,730
Northampton (M4)	201,412
Northumberland (J4)	104,138
Perry (H5)	26,582
Philadelphia (M6)	2,002,512
Pike (M3)	9,158
Potter (G2)	16,483
Schuylkill (K4)	173,027
Snyder (H4)	25,922
Somerset (D6)	77,450
Sullivan (J3)	6,251
Susquehanna (L2)	33,137
Tioga (H2)	36,614
Union (H4)	25,646
Venango (C3)	65,295
Warren (D2)	45,582
Washington (B5)	217,271
Wayne (M2)	28,237
Westmoreland (D5)	352,629
Wyoming (K2)	16,813
York (J6)	238,336

CITIES and TOWNS

City/Town	Population
Abbottstown (J6)	561
Abington (M5)	55,831
Adamstown (K5)	1,190
Akron (K5)	2,167
Albion (B2)	1,630
Alburtis (L5)	1,086
Aldan (M7)	4,324
Aliquippa (B4)	26,369
Allenport ‡(C5)	981
Allentown⊙ (L4)	108,347
Allentown-Bethlehem (urban area)	256,016
Alison Park (C4)	4,000
Altoona (F4)	69,407
Altoona (urban area)	83,058
Ambler (M5)	6,765
Ambridge (B4)	13,865
Annville (J5)	4,264
Apollo (D4)	2,694
Archbald (M2)	5,471
Ardmore (M6)	19,400
Arendtsville (H6)	588
Arnold (C4)	9,437
Ashland (K4)	5,237
Ashley (L3)	4,258
Aspinwall (C4)	3,727
Atglen (K6)	721
Athens (K2)	4,515
Atlas (K4)	1,574
Auburn (K4)	936
Austin (F2)	721
Avalon (B6)	6,859
Avella (B5)	1,310
Avis (H3)	1,262
Avoca (L3)	3,562
Avondale (L6)	1,016
Avonmore (C4)	1,351
Baden (B4)	6,109
Bala Cynwyd (N6)	5,892
Baldwin (B7)	24,489
Bally (L5)	1,033
Bangor (M4)	5,766
Barnesboro (E4)	3,035
Bath (M4)	1,736
Beaver⊙ (B4)	6,160
Beaver Falls (B4)	16,240
Beaver-Meadows (L4)	1,392
Beaverdale (E5)	1,862
Beavertown (H4)	738
Bechtelsville ‡(L5)	625
Bedford⊙ (F5)	3,696
Beech Creek (G3)	634

(continued on following page)

HIGHWAYS

MILES: 0 — 30 — 60

- Limited Access Highways
- Major Highways
- Other Important Roads
- Interstate Route Numbers — 95
- Federal Route Numbers — 9
- State and Other Route Numbers — 4

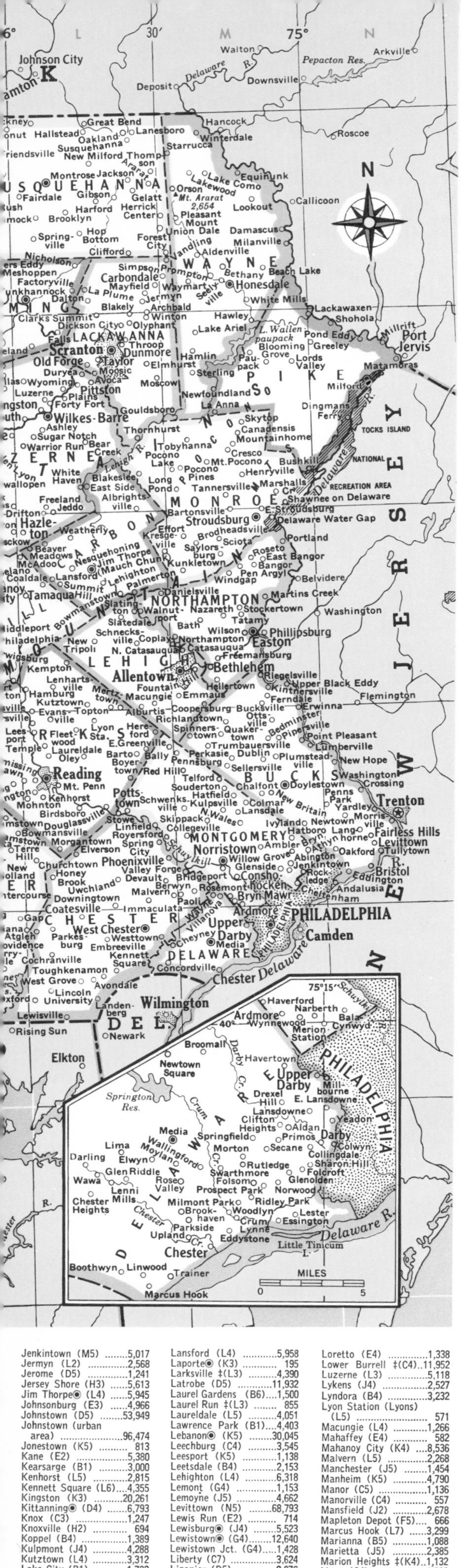
Johnson City
Deposit
Walton
Pepacton Res.
Arkville
Downsville
Delaware R.
Great Bend
Hallstead
Lanesboro
Hancock
Winterdale
Roscoe
Oakland
Susquehanna
Starrucca
New Milford
Thompson
Montrose
Jackson
Equinunk
Lake Como
SUSQUEHANNA
Orson
Mt. Ararat 2,654
Callicoon
Fairdale
Gibson
Gelatt
Herrick Center
Lakewood
Lookout
Brooklyn
Harford
Pleasant Mount
Damascus
Milanville
Hop Bottom
Forest City
Union Dale
Clifford
Aldenville
WAYNE
Nicholson
Carbondale
Prompton
Bethany
Beach Lake
Honesdale
Factoryville
Mayfield
Waymart
Seelyville
White Mills
Dalton
La Plume
Jermyn
Blakely
Archbald
Lackawaxen
Shohola
Clarks Summit
Dickson City
Olyphant
Winton
Hawley
Lake Ariel
L. Wallenpaupack
Pond Eddy
Port Jervis
Millrift
LACKAWANNA
Scranton
Dunmore
Throop
Hamlin
Blooming Grove
Greeley
Lords Valley
Old Forge
Taylor
Moosic
Avoca
Elmhurst
Duryea
Wyoming
Pittston
Moscow
Sterling
PIKE
Matamoras
Milford
Luzerne
Plains
Newfoundland
La Anna
Dingmans Ferry
Wilkes-Barre
Gouldsboro
Forty Fort
Skytop
Canadensis
Mountainhome
Sugar Notch
Ashley
Thornhurst
Tobyhanna
Warrior Run
Bear Creek
Pocono Lake
Cresco
Mt. Pocono
Bushkill
TOCKS ISLAND
NATIONAL RECREATION AREA
White Haven
Blakeslee
Pocono Pines
Henryville
East Side
Long Pond
Tannersville
Marshalls Creek
Freeland
Jeddo
Albrightsville
MONROE
E. Stroudsburg
Shawnee on Delaware
Hazleton
Bartonsville
Stroudsburg
Delaware Water Gap
Weatherly
Effort
Kresgeville
Brodheadsville
Portland
Beaver Meadows
McAdoo
Nesquehoning
Jim Thorpe (Mauch Chunk)
Saylorsburg
Sciota
Kunkletown
Roseto
Bangor
East Bangor
Pen Argyl
Wind Gap
Belvidere
Coaldale
Lansford
Summit Hill
Lehighton
Palmerton
Tamaqua
Danielsville
Martins Creek
NORTHAMPTON
Stockertown
Slatington
Walnut-port
Nazareth
Tatamy
Washington
Slatedale
Bath
Wilson
Phillipsburg
Easton
Schnecksville
Coplay
Northampton
Catasauqua
N. Catasauqua
Freemansburg
Philadelphia
New Tripoli
LEHIGH
Bethlehem
Kempton
Allentown
Hellertown
Riegelsville
Upper Black Eddy
Lenharts
Fountain Hill
Kintnersville
Ferndale
Hamburg
Kutztown
Macungie
Emmaus
Erwinna
Flemington
Topton
Alburtis
Coopersburg
Bucksville
Ottsville
Richlandtown
Lyon Sta.
Fleetwood
Spinnerstown
Quakertown
Pipersville
Point Pleasant
Bedminster
Hereford
Trumbauersville
Lumberville
Laureldale
Oley
Bally
Perkasie
Dublin
Plumsteadville
Boyertown
Red Hill
Pennsburg
Sellersville
Reading
Mt. Penn
Telford
Souderton
Chalfont
Doylestown
Washington Crossing
New Hope
BUCKS
Penns Park
Yardley
Trenton
Kenhorst
Mohnton
Birdsboro
Pottstown
Schwenksville
Hatfield
Kulpsville
N. Wales
Lansdale
Colmar
New Britain
Morrisville
Levittown
Fairless Hills
Douglassville
Stowe
Linfield
Royersford
Skippack
Collegeville
Ivyland
Newtown
Hatboro
Langhorne
Bowmansville
Morgantown
Spring City
MONTGOMERY
Norristown
Bryn Athyn
Oakford
Tullytown
Bristol
Terre Hill
Churchtown
Elverson
Phoenixville
Willow Grove
Abington
Glenside
Jenkintown
Eddington
Andalusia
Honey Brook
Uwchland
Valley Forge
Devault
Rosemont
Conshohocken
Bryn Mawr
Cheltenham
Downingtown
Coatesville
Malvern
Paoli
Ardmore
Berwyn
Immaculata
PHILADELPHIA
CHESTER
West Chester
Westtown
Upper Darby
Media
Camden
Gap
Atglen
Parkesburg
Embreeville
Kennett Square
DELAWARE
Concordville
Cochranville
Toughkenamon
Avondale
Chester
West Grove
Lincoln University
Landenberg
Wilmington
Oxford
Lewisville
Rising Sun
Newark
DEL.
Elkton
75°15'
Schuylkill
Haverford
Narberth
Ardmore
Wynnewood
Bala Cynwyd
Broomall
Merion Station
Newtown Square
Havertown
Springton Res.
Crum
Upper Darby
Drexel Hill
Millbourne
E. Lansdowne
Lansdowne
Clifton Heights
Aldan
Yeadon
Darby
Colwyn
Primos
Secane
Springfield
Morton
Rutledge
Collingdale
Sharon Hill
Folcroft
Glenolden
Swarthmore
Lima
Moylan
Wallingford
Darling
Elwyn
Glen Riddle
Rose Valley
Prospect Park
Norwood
Wawa
Lenni
Chester Heights
Milmont Park
Ridley Park
Brookhaven
Woodlyn
Crum Lynne
Lester
Essington
Parkside
Upland
Eddystone
Chester
Little Tinicum I.
Delaware R.
Boothwyn
Linwood
Trainer
Marcus Hook
MILES
0
5

McEwensville ‡(J3)...... 795
McKees Rocks (B7)....13,185
McKeesport (C7) 45,489
McSherrystown (H6)....2,839
Meadow Lands (B5) 1,967
Meadville◉ (B2) 16,671
Mechanicsburg (H5)......8,123
Mechanicsville ‡(K4).... 588
Media◉ (L7) 5,803
Mercer◉ (B3) 2,800
Mercersburg (G6) 1,759
Merion Station (M6)....7,300
Meyersdale (E6) 2,901
Middleburg◉ (H4) 1,366
Middleport (L4) 775
Middletown (J5) 11,182
Midland (A4) 5,425
Midway (B5) 1,012
Mifflin (H4) 745
Mifflinburg (H4) 2,476
Mifflintown◉ (H4)........ 887
Milesburg (G4) 729
Milford◉ (N3) 1,198
Mill Hall (G3) 1,891
Millbourne (M6) 793
Millersburg (J4) 2,984
Millerstown (H4) 675
Millersville (K6) 3,883
Millheim (G4) 780
Millsboro (B6) 1,179
Millvale (B7) 6,624
Millville (J3) 952
Milmont Park (M7)....2,208
Milroy (G4) 1,666
Milton (J3) 7,972
Minersville (K4) 6,606
Mocanaqua (K3) 1,104
Modena ‡(L6) 859
Mohnton (L5) 2,223
Monaca (B4) 8,394
Monessen (C5) 18,424
Monongahela (B5) 8,388
Monroeville (C7) 22,446
Mont Alto (G6) 1,039
Montgomery (H3) 2,150
Montoursville (J3) 5,211
Montrose◉ (L2) 2,363
Moosic (L3) 4,243
Morrisville (N5) 7,790
Morton (M7) 2,207
Moscow (L3) 1,212
Mount Carmel (K4) 10,760
Mount Holly Sprs. (H5)1,840
Mount Jewett (E2) 1,226
Mount Joy (K5) 3,292
Mount Lebanon (B7)..35,361
Mount Oliver (B7) 5,980
Mount Penn (L5) 3,574
Mount Pleasant (D5)....6,107
Mount Pocono (M3)....... 935
Mount Union (G5) 4,091
Mount Wolf (J5) 1,514
Mountville (K5) 1,411
Muncy (J3) 2,830
Munhall (C7) 17,312
Murrysville (C5) 2,500
Myerstown (K5) 3,268
Nanticoke (K3) 15,601
Nanty Glo (E5) 4,608
Narberth (M6) 5,109
Natrona (C4) 5,000
Nazareth (M4) 6,209
Nemacolin (B6) 1,404
Nescopeck (K3) 1,934
Nesquehoning (L4) 3,511
New Alexandria (C5).... 685
New Beaver ‡(B4) 1,338
New Berlin (J4) 654
New Bethlehem (D3)....1,599
New Bloomfield◉ (H5) 987
New Brighton (B4) 8,397
New Britain (M5) 1,109
New Castle◉ (B3) 44,790
New Cumberland (J5)..9,257
New Eagle (B5) 2,670
New Florence (D5) 958
New Freedom (J6) 1,395
New Galilee (A4) 593
New Holland (K5) 3,425
New Hope (N5) 958
New Kensington (C4)..23,485
New Milford (L2) 1,129
New Oxford (H6) 1,407
New Philadelphia (K4) 1,702
New Salem (C6) 1,834
New Salem (Delmont)
(D5) 1,313
New Wilmington (B3)..2,203
Newell ‡(C5) 746
Newport (H5) 1,861
Newtown (N5) 2,323
Newtown Square (L6) 11,600
Newville (H5) 1,656
Nicholson (L2) 942
Norristown◉ (M5) 38,925
North Apollo (D4) 1,741
North Belle Vernon
‡(C5) 3,148

North Braddock (C7)..13,204
North Catasauqua (L4) 2,805
North Charleroi ‡(C5)..2,259
North East (C1) 4,217
North Irwin ‡(C5) 1,143
North Wales (M5) 3,673
North Warren (D2) 1,458
North York ‡(J5) 2,290
Northampton (M4) 8,866
Northumberland (J4)....4,156
Norvelt (C5) 1,211
Norwood (M7) 6,729
Oakdale (B5) 1,695
Oakford (N5) 2,300
Oakland (L2) 889
Oakmont (C6) 7,504
Ohioville ‡(B4) 3,050
Oil City (C3) 17,692
Oklahoma ‡(C4) 983
Old Forge (L3) 8,928
Oliver (C6) 3,015
Olyphant (L3) 5,864
Orbisonia (G5) 643
Orwigsburg (K4) 2,131
Osborne (B4) 609
Osceola Mills (Osceola)
‡(F4) 1,777
Oxford (K6) 3,376
Paint (E5) 1,275
Palmerton (L4) 5,942
Palmyra (J5) 6,999
Palo Alto ‡(K4) 1,445
Paoli (M5) 11,500
Parker (C3) 945
Parkesburg (L6) 2,759
Parkside (M7) 2,426
Parkville (J6) 4,516
Parryville ‡(L4) 580
Patterson Heights‡(B4) 816
Patton (E4) 2,880
Paxtang (J5) 1,916
Pen Argyl (M4) 3,693
Penbrook (J5) 3,671
Penn (C5) 858
Penndel ‡(N5) 2,158
Pennsburg (M5) 1,698
Perkasie (M5) 4,650
Perryopolis (C5) 1,799
Petersburg (G4) 552
Philadelphia◉ (N6)2,002,512
Philadelphia (urban
area) 3,635,228
Philipsburg (F4) 3,872
Phoenixville (L5) 13,797
Picture Rocks (J3) 594
Pine Grove (K4) 2,267
Pitcairn (C5) 5,383
Pittsburgh◉ (B7) 604,332
Pittsburgh (urban
area) 1,804,400
Pittston (L3) 12,407
Plains (L3) 6,325
Pleasant Gap (G4) 1,389
Pleasant Hills (B7) 8,573
Pleasantville (C2) 940
Plum (C5) 10,241
Plymouth (K3) 10,401
Point Marion (C6) 1,853
Polk (C3) 3,574
Port Allegany (F2) 2,742
Port Carbon (K4) 2,775
Port Clinton (K4) 739
Port Matilda (F4) 697
Port Royal (H4) 805
Port Vue (C7) 6,635
Portage (E5) 3,933
Portland (M4) 589
Pottstown (L5) 26,144
Pottsville◉ (K4) 21,659
Pringle ‡(L3) 1,418
Prospect (B4) 903
Prospect Park (M7) 6,596
Punxsutawney (E4) 8,805
Quakertown (M5) 6,305
Quarryville (K6) 1,427
Ramey (F4) 558
Rankin (C7) 5,164
Reading◉ (L5) 98,177
Reading (urb. area)..160,297
Red Hill (L5) 1,086
Red Lion (J6) 5,594
Renovo (G3) 3,316
Reynoldsville (D3) 3,158
Rices Landing (C6) 693
Richland (K5) 1,276
Richlandtown (M5) 741
Ridgway◉ (E3) 6,387
Ridley Park (M7) 7,387
Riegelsville (M4) 953
Rimersburg (D3) 1,323
Ringtown (K4) 849
Riverside (J4) 1,580
Roaring Spring (F5) ...2,937
Robesonia (K5) 1,579
Rochester (B4) 5,952
Rockhill ‡(G5) 566
Rockledge (M5) 2,587
Rockwood (D6) 1,101

Roscoe (C5) 1,315
Rose Valley (L7) 626
Rosemont (M5) 2,000
Roseto (M4) 1,630
Rosslyn Farms (B7)...... 555
Rouseville (C3) 923
Royalton (J5) 1,128
Royersford (L5) 3,969
Rural Valley (D4) 860
Russellton (C4) 1,613
Rutledge (M7) 947
Saegertown (B2) 1,131
Saint Clair (K4) 5,159
Saint Lawrence ‡(E4).. 929
Saint Marys (E3) 8,065
Salisbury (D6) 862
Saltsburg (D4) 1,054
Sandy (E3) 2,070
Sandy Lake (B3) 838
Sankertown ‡(E5) 828
Saxonburg (C4) 876
Sayre (K2) 7,917
Scalp Level (E5) 1,445
Schnecksville (L4) 800
Schuylkill Haven (K4)..6,470
Schwenksville (L5) 620
Scottdale (C5) 6,244
Scranton◉ (L3) 111,443
Scranton (urban
area) 210,676
Secane (M7) 2,000
Selinsgrove (J4) 3,948
Sellersville (M5) 2,497
Seven Springs (D5)....... 30
Seward (E5) 754
Sewickley (B4) 6,157
Sewickley Heights ‡(B4) 931
Shamokin (J4) 13,674
Shamokin Dam (J4) 1,093
Sharon (B3) 25,267
Sharon Hill (N7) 7,123
Sharpsburg (B6) 6,096
Sharpsville (A3) 6,061
Sheffield (D2) 1,971
Shenandoah (K4) 11,073
Shickshinny (K3) 1,843
Shillington (K5) 5,639
Shinglehouse (F2) 1,298
Shippensburg (H5) 6,138
Shippenville (D3) 599
Shiremanstown ‡(J5) ..1,212
Shoemakersville (K4)....1,464
Shrewsbury (J6) 943
Simpson (L2) 2,700
Sinking Spring (K5).......2,244
Slatington (L4) 4,316
Sligo (C3) 814
Slippery Rock (B3) 2,563
Smethport◉ (F2) 1,725
Smithfield (C6) 939
Smithton (C5) 649
Snow Shoe (G3) 714
Somerset◉ (D6) 6,347
Souderton (M5) 5,381
South Bethlehem (D4).. 510
South Coatesville ‡(L6) 2,032
South Connellsville (C6)2,434
South Fork (E5) 2,053
South Greensburg ‡(C5)3,058
South Heights (B4) 740
South Mountain (H6)....2,000
South New Castle ‡(B4) 955
South Renovo (G3) 777
South Waverly (J2)......1,382
South Williamsport
(J3) 6,972
Southmont ‡(E5) 2,857
Southwest Greensburg
‡(C5) 3,264
Spangler (E4) 2,658
Speers ‡(C5) 1,479
Spring City (L5) 3,162
Spring Grove (J6) 1,675
Springboro (B2) 583
Springdale (C4) 5,602
Springfield (M7) 26,733
State College (G4) 22,409
Steelton (J5) 11,266
Stewartstown (K6) 1,164
Stockdale ‡(C5) 815
Stockertown (M4) 777
Stoneboro (B3) 1,267
Stowe (L5) 2,765
Strasburg (K6) 1,416
Stroudsburg◉ (M4)........6,070
Sugar Notch (L3) 1,524
Sugargrove (D1) 636
Summerhill (E5) 870
Summerville (D3) 895
Summit Hill (L4) 4,386
Sunbury◉ (J4) 13,687
Susquehanna (L2) 2,591
Sutersville ‡(C5) 964
Swarthmore (M7) 5,753
Swissvale (C7) 15,089
Swoyersville ‡(L3) 6,751
Sykesville (E3) 1,479
Tamaqua (L4) 10,173

Pennsylvania
(continued)

Tarentum (C4) 8,232
Tatamy (M4) 762
Taylor (L3) 6,148
Telford (M5) 2,763
Temple (L5) 1,633
Terre Hill (L5) 1,129
Thompsontown (H4)...... 713
Throop (L3) 4,732
Tidioute (D2) 860
Tioga (H2) 597
Tionesta◉ (C2) 778
Titusville (C2) 8,356
Topton (L5) 1,684
Towanda◉ (J2) 4,293
Tower City (J4) 1,968
Trafford (C5) 4,330
Trainer (L7) 2,358
Trappe ‡(M5) 1,264
Tremont (K4) 1,893
Tresckow (K4) 1,145
Trevorton (J4) 2,597
Troy (J2) 1,478
Trumbauersville (M5)... 785
Tullytown (N5) 2,452
Tunkhannock◉ (L2) 2,297
Turbotville (J3) 612
Turtle Creek (C7) 10,607
Tyrone (F4) 7,792
Union City (C2) 3,819
Uniontown◉ (C6) 17,942
United (D5) 2,044
Universal (C7) 3,200
Upland (L7) 4,343
Upper Darby (M6).....93,158
Valley View (J4) 1,540
Vanderbilt (C5) 826
Vandergrift (D4) 8,742
Vandling (M2) 578
Vanport (B4) 2,500
Verona (C6) 4,032
Versailles (C7) 2,297
Villanova (M6) 4,250
Vintondale (E5) 938
Wall (C5) 1,493
Wallingford (L7) 2,500
Walnutport (L4) 1,609
Wampum (B4) 1,085
Warren◉ (D2) 14,505
Warren Center (K2) 800
Warrior Run (L3) 833
Washington◉ (B5) 23,545
Waterford (B2) 1,390
Watsontown (J3) 2,431
Waymart (M2) 1,106
Wayne (M6) 8,000
Waynesboro (G6) 10,427
Waynesburg◉ (B6) 5,188
Weatherly (L4) 2,591
Weissport ‡(L4) 625
Wellsboro◉ (H2) 4,369
Wernersville (K5) 1,462
Wesleyville (C1) 3,534
West Brownsville (C5)..1,907
West Chester◉ (L6)....15,705
West Conshohocken
‡(M5) 2,254
West Easton ‡(M4) 1,228
West Elizabeth (C5)...... 921
West Fairview ‡(J5).....1,718
West Grove (L6) 1,607
West Hazleton (K4).....6,278
West Homestead
‡(B7) 4,155
West Kittanning (C4)...1,101
West Lawn (K5) 2,059
West Leechburg
(C4) 1,323
West Mayfield ‡(B4)....2,201
West Middlesex (B3)....1,301
West Mifflin (C7).......27,289
West Newton (C5) 3,982
West Pittston ‡(L3)......6,998
West Reading ‡(L5) 4,938
West View (B6) 8,079
West Wyoming
‡(L3) 3,166
West York (J6) 5,526
Westfield (H2) 1,333
Westmont (E5) 6,573
Westtown (L6) 1,500
Wheatland (B3) 1,813
Whitaker (C7) 2,130
White Haven (L3) 1,778
White Oak (C7) 9,047
Whitehall (B7) 16,075
Wiconisco (J4) 1,402
Wilkes-Barre◉ (L3)....63,551
Wilkes-Barre (urban
area) 233,932
Wilkinsburg (C7) 30,066

Williamsburg (F5) 1,792
Williamsport ◉(H3)....41,967
Williamstown (J4) 2,097
Willow Grove (M5) ...12,000
Wilmerding (C7) 4,349
Wilson (M4) 8,465
Windber (E5) 6,994
Windgap (M4) 1,930
Windsor (J6) 1,029
Winton (M3) 5,456
Womelsdorf (K5) 1,471
Woodlyn (M7) 6,000
Woodville (B7) 3,745
Wormleysburg ‡(J5) ...1,794
Worthington (C4) 772
Wrightsville (J5) 2,345
Wyalusing (K2) 685
Wynnewood (M6) 8,500
Wyoming (L3) 4,127
Wyomissing (K5) 5,044
Wyomissing Hills ‡(L5) 1,644
Yardley (N5) 2,271
Yeadon (N7) 11,610
Yeagertown (G4) 1,349
Yoe ‡(J6) 731
York◉ (J6) 54,504
York (urban area)....100,872
York Haven (J5) 736
Youngstown ‡(D5) 590
Youngsville (D2) 2,211
Youngwood (D5) 2,813
Yukon (C5) 1,062
Zelienople (B4) 3,284

OTHER FEATURES

Allegheny (res.) ....E 2
Allegheny (river) ....D 2
Allegheny Front (mts.)...E 5
Appalachian (mts.) ....H 4
Ararat (mt.) ....M 2
Beaver (river) ....B 4
Blue (mt.) ....G 5
Blue Knob (mt.) ....E 5
Casselman (river) ....D 6
Chester (creek) ....L 7
Clarion (river) ....D 3
Conemaugh (river) ....D 5
Conewango (creek) ....D 1
Cornplanter Ind. Res. ....E 2
Crum (creek) ....M 7
Darby (creek) ....M 6
Delaware (river) ....N 3
Erie (lake) ....B 1
Fort Necessity National
Battlefield ....C 6
French (creek) ....C 2
George B. Stevenson
(dam) ....G 3
Gettysburg National
Military Park ....H 6
Juniata (river) ....G 5
Laurel Hill (mt.) ....D 5
Lehigh (river) ....L 3
Letterkenny Ord. Depot..G 6
Licking (creek) ....F 6
Little Tinicum (isl.) ....M 7
Lycoming (creek) ....H 3
Monongahela (river) ....C 6
Negro (Davis) (mt.)........D 6
North (mt.) ....K 3
Ohio (river) ....A 4
Oil (creek) ....C 2
Pine (creek) ....H 2
Pine Grove (res.) ....K 6
Pocono (mts.) ....M 3
Pymatuning (res.) ....A 2
Raystown Branch,
Juniata (river) ....F 5
Redbank (creek) ....E 3
Schuylkill (river) ....M 5
Shenango River (res.)....B 3
Sinnemahoning (creek) ..F 3
South (mt.) ....H 6
South Park Mil. Res. ......B 7
Springton (res.) ....L 6
Sugar (creek) ....J 2
Susquehanna (river) ....K 6
Tioga (river) ....H 1
Tocks Island Nat'l Rec.
Area ....N 3
Towanda (creek) ....J 2
Tuscarora (mt.) ....G 5
Wallenpaupack (lake).....M 3
Youghiogheny (dam) .....D 6
Youghiogheny River
(res.) ....D 6

◉ County Seat.
‡ Name not on map.

Jenkintown (M5) 5,017
Jermyn (L2) 2,568
Jerome (D5) 1,241
Jersey Shore (H3) 5,613
Jim Thorpe◉ (L4) 5,945
Johnsonburg (E3) 4,966
Johnstown (D5) 53,949
Johnstown (urban
area) 96,474
Jonestown (K5) 813
Kane (E2) 5,380
Kearsarge (B1) 3,000
Kenhorst (L5) 2,815
Kennett Square (L6)....4,355
Kingston (K3) 20,261
Kittanning◉ (D4) 6,793
Knox (C3) 1,247
Knoxville (H2) 694
Koppel (B4) 1,389
Kulpmont (J4) 4,288
Kutztown (L4) 3,312
Lake City (B1) 1,722
Lakemont (F5) 1,300
Lancaster◉ (K5) 61,055
Lancaster (urban
area) 93,855
Landisville (K5) 1,690
Langeloth (A5) 1,112
Langhorne (N5) 1,461
Langhorne Manor
‡(N5) 1,506
Lansdale (M5) 12,612
Lansdowne (M7) 12,601

Lansford (L4) 5,958
Laporte◉ (K3) 195
Larksville ‡(L3) 4,390
Latrobe (D5) 11,932
Laurel Gardens (B6)...1,500
Laurel Run ‡(L3) 855
Laureldale (L5) 4,051
Lawrence Park (B1)....4,403
Lebanon◉ (K5) 30,045
Leechburg (C4) 3,545
Leesport (K5) 1,138
Leetsdale (B4) 2,153
Lehighton (L4) 6,318
Lemont ‡(G4) 1,153
Lemoyne (J5) 4,662
Levittown (N5) 68,793
Lewis Run (E2) 714
Lewisburg◉ (J4) 5,523
Lewistown◉ (G4) 12,640
Lewistown Jct. (G4).....1,428
Liberty (C7) 3,624
Ligonier (D5) 2,276
Lilly (E5) 1,642
Lincoln (C7) 1,686
Linesville (A2) 1,255
Linntown (J4) 1,628
Linwood (L7) 4,500
Lititz (K5) 5,987
Littlestown (H6) 2,756
Liverpool (H4) 894
Lock Haven◉ (H3) 11,748
Loganville (J6) 742
Lorain ‡(E5) 1,324

Loretto (E4) 1,338
Lower Burrell ‡(C4)..11,952
Luzerne (L3) 5,118
Lykens (J4) 2,527
Lyndora (B4) 3,232
Lyon Station (Lyons)
(L5) 571
Macungie (L4) 1,266
Mahaffey (E4) 582
Mahanoy City (K4) 8,536
Malvern (L5) 2,268
Manchester (J5) 1,454
Manheim (K5) 4,790
Manor (C5) 1,136
Manorville (C4) 557
Mansfield (J2) 2,678
Mapleton Depot (F5)...... 666
Marcus Hook (L7) 3,299
Marianna (B5) 1,088
Marietta (J5) 2,385
Marion Heights ‡(K4)..1,132
Mars (C4) 1,522
Martinsburg (F5) 1,772
Marysville (H5) 2,580
Masontown (C6) 4,730
Matamoras (N3) 2,087
Mauch Chunk (Jim
Thorpe) (L4) 5,945
Mayfield (L2) 1,996
McAdoo (L4) 3,560
McClure (H4) 1,001
McConnellsburg◉ (F6) 1,245
McDonald (B5) 3,141

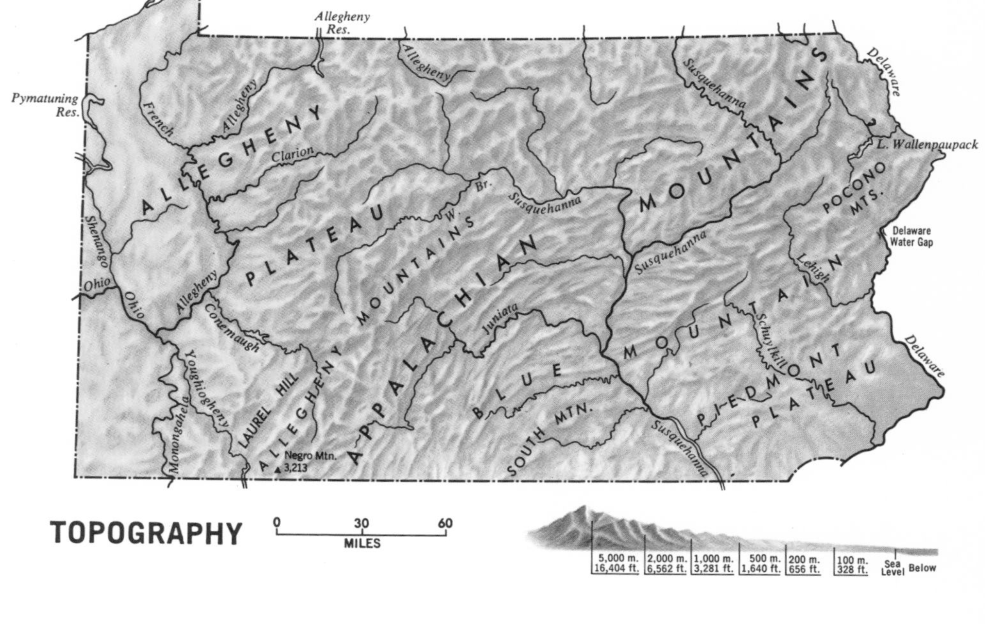
Allegheny Res.
Allegheny
Pymatuning Res.
French
Allegheny
ALLEGHENY
Clarion
PLATEAU
Shenango
Ohio
Allegheny
Conemaugh
Youghiogheny
Monongahela
LAUREL HILL
ALLEGHENY
Negro Mtn. 3,213
W. Br.
Susquehanna
MOUNTAINS
APPALACHIAN
Juniata
BLUE
SOUTH MTN.
MOUNTAIN
Susquehanna
Schuylkill
PIEDMONT
PLATEAU
Lehigh
Delaware
Delaware Water Gap
POCONO MTS.
L. Wallenpaupack
0
30
60
MILES
5,000 m. 16,404 ft.
2,000 m. 6,562 ft.
1,000 m. 3,281 ft.
500 m. 1,640 ft.
200 m. 656 ft.
100 m. 328 ft.
Sea Level
Below

TOPOGRAPHY

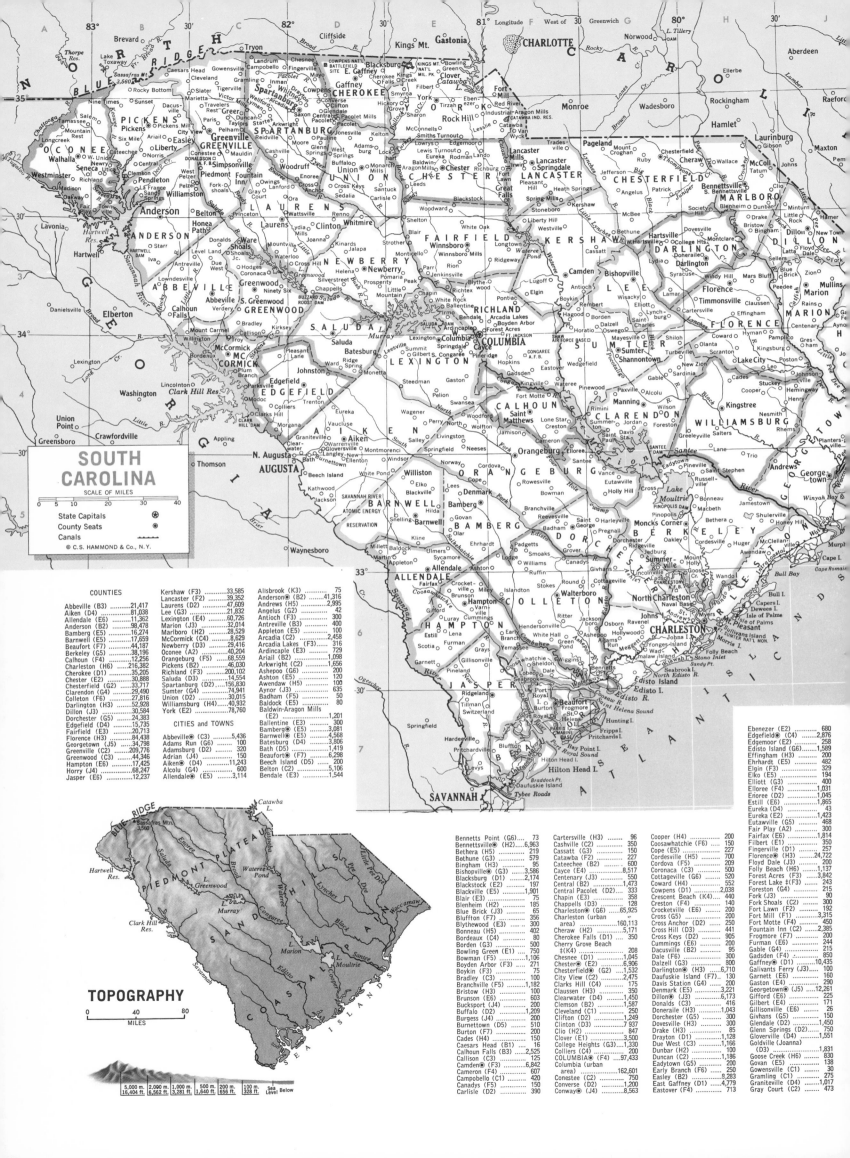

30'
K
L
teville
South
R.
Fear
Elizabethtown
R.
White
hiteville
L. Waccamaw
Marsh
Longs
Little River
Little R. Inlet
Cherry Grove Beach
Ocean Drive Beach
Crescent Beach
Windy Hill Beach
Waterway
ampee
yrtle Beach
N

SOUTH CAROLINA

AREA	31,055 sq. mi.
POPULATION	2,542,000
CAPITAL	Columbia
LARGEST CITY	Columbia 97,433
HIGHEST POINT	Sassafras Mtn. 3,560 ft.
SETTLED IN	1670
ADMITTED TO UNION	May 23, 1788
POPULAR NAME	Palmetto State
STATE FLOWER	Yellow Jessamine
STATE BIRD	Carolina Wren

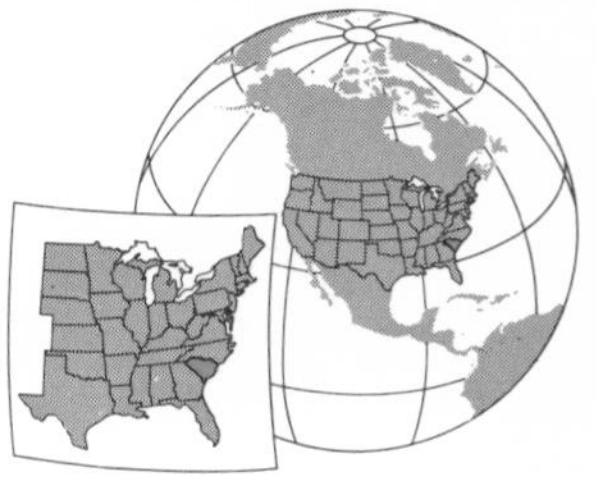

Grays (E6) 100
Great Falls (F2) 3,030
Greeleyville (H4) 504
Green Pond (F6)
Green Sea (J3) 500
Greenville◉ (C2) 66,188
Greenville (urban area) 126,887
Greenwood◉ (C3) 16,644
Greer (C2) 8,967
Gresham (J4) 100
Grover (F5) 500
Gurley (J3) 300
Hagood (F3) 9
Hamer (J3) 325
Hampton◉ (E6) 2,486
Hardeeville (E7) 700
Harleyville (G5) 561
Hartsville (G3) 6,392
Heath Springs (F2) 832
Helena (D3) 300
Hemingway (J4) 951
Hendersonville (F6) 100
Henry (J4) 100
Hickory Grove (E2) 287
Hilda (E5) 259
Hilton Head Island (F7) 1,600
Hodges (C3) 209
Holly Hill (G5) 1,235
Hollywood (G6) 334
Honea Path (C3) 3,453
Honey Hill (H5) 75
Hopkins (F4) 300
Horatio (G3) 600
Huger (H5) 225
Hyman (H4) 150
Inman (C1) 1,714
Irmo (E3) 359
Irwin (F2) 1,113
Islandton (F6) 30
Isle of Palms (H6) 1,186
Iva (B3) 1,357
Jackson (D5) 1,746
Jacksonboro (G6) 600
Jalapa (D3) 50
Jamestown (H5) 184
Jamison (F4) 220
Jedburg (G5) 500
Jefferson (G2) 493
Jenkinsville (E3) 500
Joanna (D3) 1,831
Johns Island (G6) 3,500
Johnsonville (J4) 882
Johnston (D4) 2,119
Jonesville (D2) 1,439
Jordan (G4) 15
Jordanville (J4) 100
Kathwood (D5) 500
Kelton (D2) 100
Kershaw (G2) 1,567
Kinards (D3) 300
Kings Creek (E1) 150
Kingsburg (H4) 50
Kingstree◉ (H4) 3,847
Kingville (F4) 500
Kirksey (C3) 125
Kline (E5) 213
La France (B2) 800
Ladson (G6) 500
Lake City (H4) 6,059
Lake View (J3) 865
Lamar (G3) 1,121
Lancaster◉ (F2) 7,999
Lancaster Mills (F2) 3,274
Lando (E2) 800
Landrum (C1) 1,930
Lane (H5) 497
Lanford (C2) 200
Langley (D4) 1,216
Latta (J3) 1,901
Laurens◉ (C3) 9,598
Leeds (E2) 150
Lees (E5) 100
Leesville (E4) 1,619
Lena (E6) 150
Leo (H4) 350
Lesslie (E2) 250
Level Land (C3) 230
Levys (E7) 150
Lewis Turnout (E2) 150
Lexington◉ (E4) 1,127
Liberty (B2) 2,657
Liberty Hill (F3) 250
Lincolnville (G6) 420
Little Mountain (E3) 238
Little River (K4) 350
Little Rock (J3) 150
Livingston (E4) 208
Lobeco (F6) 137
Lockhart (D2) 128
Lodge (F5) 181
Lone Star (F4) 50
Longcreek (A2) 200
Longs (K4) 85
Longtown (F3) 75
Loris (K3) 1,702
Lowndesville (B3) 274
Lowrys (E2) 298
Lugoff (F3)
Luray (E6) 102
Lydia (G3) 300
Lydia Mills (D3) 1,177
Lyman (C2) 1,261
Lynchburg (G3) 544
Macbeth (H5) 150
Madison (A2) 1,904
Manning◉ (G4) 3,917
Marietta (C1) 1,600
Marion◉ (J3) 7,174
Mars Bluff (H3) 350
Martin (D5) 100
Mauldin (C2) 1,462
Mayesville (G4) 750
Mayo (D1) 500
McBee (G3) 512
McClellanville (H5) 354
McColl (H2) 2,479
McConnells (E2) 266
McCormick◉ (C4) 1,998
Meggett (G6) 188
Miley (E6) 500
Millett (D5) 150
Minturn (J2) 47
Modoc (C4) 150
Monarch Mills (D2) 1,990
Moncks Corner◉ (G5) 2,030
Monetta (D4) 750
Montclare (H3) 150
Monticello (E3) 106
Montmorenci (D4) 700
Moore (D2) 200
Morgana (D4) 50
Mount Carmel (C3) 109
Mount Croghan (G2) 145
Mount Holly (H5) 175
Mount Pleasant (H6) 5,116
Mountain Rest (A2) 200
Mountville (C3) 260
Mullins (J3) 6,229
Murrells Inlet (K4) 950
Myers (H6) 2,785
Myrtle Beach (K4) 7,834
Naval Base (G6) 1,686
Neeses (E4) 347
Nesmith (H4) 232
New Ellenton (D5) 2,309
New Town (J3) 650
New Zion (H4) 250
Newberry◉ (D3) 8,208
Newry (B2) 400
Nichols (J3) 617
Nine Times (B2) 20
Ninety Six (D3) 1,435
Nixonville (K4) 150
Norris (B2) 594
North (E4) 1,047
North Augusta (C5) 10,348
North Charleston (G6) 25,000
Norway (E5) 525
Oakley (G5) 150
Oakway (A2) 500
Ocean Drive Beach (K4) 313
Olanta (H4) 568
Olar (E5) 467
Ora (D2) 185
Orangeburg◉ (F4) 13,852
Osborn (G6) 100
Oswego (G3) 300
Owings (C2) 250
Pacolet (D2) 1,252
Pacolet Mills (D2) 1,476
Pacolet Park ‡(D2) 117
Padgetts (F5) 75
Pageland (G2) 2,020
Pamplico (H4) 988
Paris (C2) 750
Parksville (C4) 164
Parr (E3) 20
Patrick (G2) 393
Pauline (D2) 500
Pawleys Island (J5) 2,000
Paxville (G4) 216
Peak (E3) 86
Peedee (H3) 400
Pelham (C2) 500
Pelion (E4) 233
Pelzer (B2) 106
Pendleton (B2) 2,358
Perry (E4) 196
Pickens◉ (B2) 2,198
Pickens Mill (B2) 675
Piedmont (C2) 2,108
Pineland (E6) 100
Pineridge (E4) 329
Pineville (H5) 250
Pinewood (G4) 570
Pinopolis (G5) 300
Plantersville (J4) 800
Pleasant Hill (F2) 250
Pleasant Lane (D4) 50
Plum Branch (C4) 139
Pomaria (E3) 230
Pontiac (F3) 75
Port Royal (F7) 686
Poston (J4) 300
Pregnall (G5) 100
Princeton (C2) 250
Pritchardville (E7) 200
Prosperity (D3) 757
Rains (J3) 600
Ravenel (G6) 527
Red River (F2) 255
Reevesville (F5) 268
Reidville (C2) 242
Rembert (G3) 300
Renno (D2) 65
Rhems (H4) 25
Richburg (E2) 235
Richland (A2) 75
Richtex (E3) 120
Ridge Spring (D4) 649
Ridgeland◉ (E7) 1,192
Ridgeville (G5) 611
Ridgeway (F3) 417
Rimini (G4) 450
Rion (E3) 500
Ritter (F6) 200
Rock Hill (E2) 29,404
Rocky Bottom (B1) 150
Rodman (E2) 750
Round O (F6) 75
Rowesville (F5) 398
Ruby (G2) 284
Ruffin (F6) 500
Russellville (H5) 300
Saint Andrews (G6) 20,000
Saint Charles (G3) 300
Saint George◉ (F5) 1,833
Saint Matthews◉ (F4) 2,433
Saint Paul (G4) 50
Saint Stephen (H5) 1,462
Salem (A2) 206
Salley (E4) 403
Salters (H4) 100
Saluda◉ (D4) 2,089
Sandy Springs (B2) 174
Santee (F5) 105
Santuck (D2) 300
Sardinia (G4) 150
Saxon (D2) 3,917
Scotia (E6) 102
Scranton (H4) 613
Seabrook (F6) 500
Sedalia (D2) 300
Sellers (H3) 431
Seneca (A2) 5,227
Shannontown (G4) 7,064
Sharon (E2) 280
Sheldon (F6) 300
Shelton (E3) 50
Shiloh (G4) 100
Shoals Junction (C3) 80
Shulerville (H5) 75
Silverstreet (D3) 181
Simpsonville (C2) 2,282
Six Mile (B2) 218
Slater (C1) 950
Smiths Turnout (E2) 110
Smoaks (F5) 145
Smyrna (E1) 52
Snelling (E5) 100
Society Hill (H2) 677
South Bennettsville (H2) 1,025
South Congaree (E4) 650
South Greenwood (C3) 2,520
Spartanburg◉ (C1) 44,352
Spring Mills (F2) 1,069
Springdale (E4) 1,002
Springdale (F2) 2,981
Springfield (E4) 787
Starr (B3) 243
Startex (C2) 1,800
Steedman (E4) 100
Stokes (F6) 80
Stoneboro (F2) 100
Strother (E3) 25
Stuckey (H4) 199
Sullivans Island (H6) 1,358
Summerton (G4) 1,504
Summerville (G5) 3,633
Summit (E4) 108
Sumter◉ (G4) 23,062
Sunset (B2) 200
Surfside Beach (K4) 933
Swansea (E4) 776
Switzerland (E7) 235
Sycamore (E5) 401
Syracuse (G3) 25
Tamassee (A2) 300
Tatum (H2) 132
Taylors (C2) 1,071
Tigerville (C1) 950
Tillman (E7) 350
Timmonsville (H3) 2,178
Tirzah (E2) 100
Toddville (J4) 200
Townville (B2) 250
Tradesville (F2) 150
Travelers Rest (C2) 1,973
Trenton (D4) 314
Trio (H5) 125
Troy (C4) 260
Turbeville (G4) 355
Ulmers (E5) 168
Union◉ (D2) 10,191
Utica (B2) 1,294
Van Wyck (F2) 485
Vance (G5) 85
Varnville (E6) 1,461
Vaucluse (D4) 750
Verdery (C3) 119
Victor Mills (C2) 2,018
Wadmalaw Island (G6) 2,500
Wagener (E4) 614
Walhalla◉ (A2) 3,431
Wallace (H2) 200
Walterboro◉ (F6) 5,417
Wampee (K4) 162
Wando (H6) 500
Ward (D4) 162
Ware Shoals (C3) 2,671
Warrenville (D4) 1,128
Wateree (F4) 117
Waterloo (C3) 148
Wattsville (D3) 1,438
Wedgefield (F4) 500
Wellford (C2) 1,040
West Columbia (E4) 6,410
West Hartsville (G3) 2,427
West Pelzer (B2) 687
West Springs (D2) 300
West Union (B2) 443
Westminster (A2) 2,413
Westville (F3) 175
White Hall (F6) 50
White Oak (E3) 200
White Pond (D5) 275
White Rock (E3) 200
Whitmire (D3) 2,663
Whitney (D1) 2,502
Wiggins (F6) 50
Williams (F5) 194
Williamston (B2) 3,721
Willington (C4) 75
Williston (E5) 2,722
Wilson (G4) 300
Windsor (E5) 250
Windy Hill (H3) 2,201
Windy Hill Beach (K4) 273
Winnsboro ◉(E3) 3,479
Winnsboro Mills (E3) 2,411
Wisacky (G3) 151
Wolfton (E4) 150
Woodford (E4) 172
Woodruff (D2) 3,679
Woodward (E2) 150
Yemassee (F6) 473
Yonges Island (G6) 300
York◉ (E1) 4,758
Zion (J3) 100

OTHER FEATURES

Ashepoo (river) F 6
Ashley (river) G 6
Bay Point (isl.) F 7
Big Black (creek) G 2
Black (river) H 4
Blue Ridge (mts.) B 1
Braddock (point) F 7
Broad (river) E 2
Broad (river) F 7
Buck (creek) J 3
Bull (bay) H 6
Bull (isl.) H 6
Bullock (creek) E 2
Bush (river) D 3
Buzzard Roost (dam) D 3
Cape (isl.) J 5
Capers (isl.) H 6
Catawba (lake) E 1
Catawba (river) F 2
Catawba Ind. Res. F 2
Catfish (creek) J 3
Charleston A.F.B. G 6
Chattooga (river) A 2
Clark Hill (dam) C 4
Clark Hill (res.) C 4
Combahee (river) F 6
Congaree (river) F 4
Congaree A.F.B. F 4
Cooper (river) H 6
Coosaw (river) G 7
Coosawhatchie (river) E 6
Cowpens Nat'l Battlefield Site D 1
Crooked (creek) H 2
Deep (creek) B 2
Dewees (isl.) H 6
Edisto (isl.) G 7
Edisto (river) G 6
Enoree (river) C 2
Fort Jackson F 4
Fort Sumter Nat'l Mon. H 6
Four Hole Swamp (creek) F 5
Fripps (isl.) G 7
Greenwood (lake) D 3
Hartwell (dam) B 3
Hartwell (res.) A 3
Hilton Head (isl.) F 7
Hunting (isl.) G 7
Intracoastal Waterway (canal) H 5
Jackson, Fort F 4
James (isl.) H 6
Johns (isl.) G 6
Juniper (creek) H 2
Keowee (river) B 2
Kiawah (isl.) G 6
Kings Mountain Nat'l Mil. Park E 1
Little (river) C 3
Little (river) D 3
Little Lynches (river) G 3
Little Pee Dee (river) J 4
Little River (inlet) L 4
Lumber (river) J 3
Lynches (river) H 3
Marion (lake) G 5
Morris (isl.) H 6
Moultrie (lake) G 5
Murphy (isl.) J 5
Murray (lake) D 4
Myrtle Beach A.F.B. K 4
New (river) E 6
North (inlet) J 5
North (isl.) J 5
North Edisto (river) G 6
Pacolet (river) D 1
Palms, Isle of (isl.) H 6
Parris Island Marine Base F 7
Pee Dee (river) J 4
Pinopolis (dam) G 5
Pocotaligo (river) G 4
Port Royal (isl.) F 7
Port Royal (sound) F 7
Pritchards (isl.) G 7
Reedy (river) C 2
Rocky (river) B 3
Romain (cape) J 6
Saint Helena (isl.) F 7
Saint Helena (sound) G 7
Salkehatchie (river) E 5
Saluda (dam) E 3
Saluda (river) D 3
Sandy (point) H 6
Sandy (river) E 2
Santee (dam) G 4
Santee (river) H 5
Sassafras (mt.) B 1
Savannah (river) E 6
Savannah River Atomic Energy Res. D 5
Sea (isls.) G 7
Seabrook (isl.) G 6
Seneca (river) B 2
Shaw A.F.B. F 4
South (isl.) J 5
Stevens (creek) C 4
Stono (inlet) H 6
Thompsons (creek) G 2
Tugaloo (river) A 2
Turkey (creek) E 2
Tybee Roads (channel) F 7
Tyger (river) D 2
Waccamaw (river) J 5
Wando (river) H 6
Wateree (pond) F 3
Wateree (river) F 3
Winyah (bay) J 5

◉ County Seat.
‡ Name not on map.

AGRICULTURE, INDUSTRY and RESOURCES

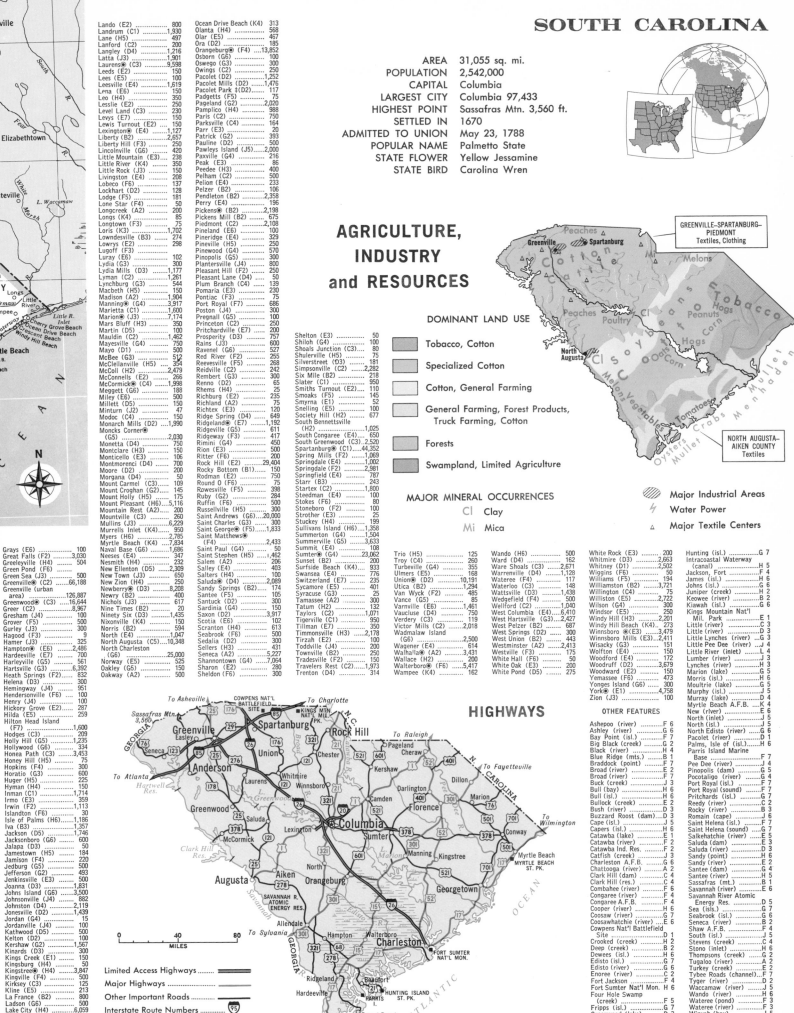

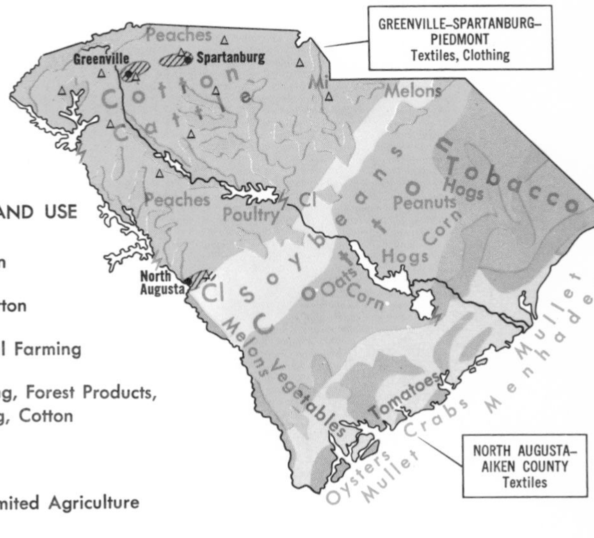
GREENVILLE–SPARTANBURG–PIEDMONT
Textiles, Clothing
Greenville
Spartanburg
Peaches
Cotton
Cattle
Melons
Tobacco
Hogs
Peanuts
Corn
Soybeans
Peaches
Poultry
Cl
Mi
North Augusta
Oats
Corn
Hogs
Melons
Vegetables
Tomatoes
Crabs
Menhaden
Mullet
Oysters
Mullet
NORTH AUGUSTA–AIKEN COUNTY
Textiles

DOMINANT LAND USE

- Tobacco, Cotton
- Specialized Cotton
- Cotton, General Farming
- General Farming, Forest Products, Truck Farming, Cotton
- Forests
- Swampland, Limited Agriculture

MAJOR MINERAL OCCURRENCES

Cl Clay
Mi Mica

Major Industrial Areas
Water Power
Major Textile Centers

HIGHWAYS

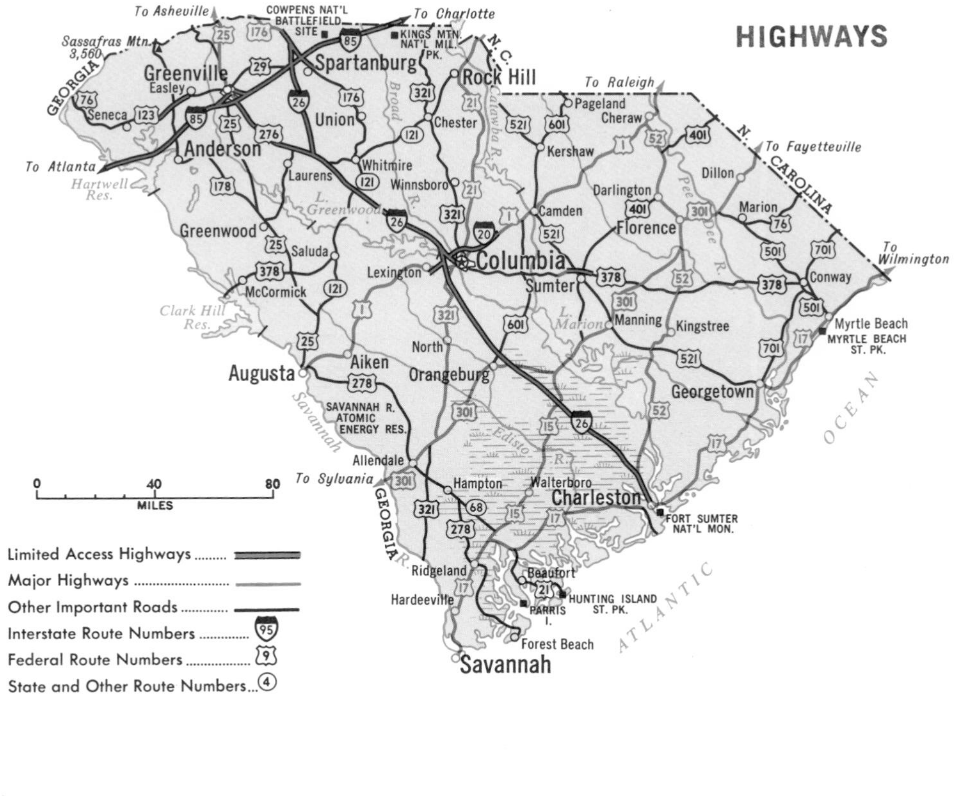
To Asheville
COWPENS NAT'L BATTLEFIELD SITE
To Charlotte
KINGS MTN. NAT'L MIL. PK.
Sassafras Mtn. 3,560
Greenville
Easley
Spartanburg
Rock Hill
N.C.
To Raleigh
GEORGIA
Seneca
Anderson
Union
Chester
Pageland
Cheraw
Kershaw
To Fayetteville
N. CAROLINA
To Atlanta
Hartwell Res.
Laurens
Whitmire
Winnsboro
Darlington
Dillon
Marion
Greenwood
L. Greenwood
Camden
Florence
Saluda
Columbia
Lexington
Sumter
Conway
To Wilmington
Clark Hill Res.
McCormick
L. Marion
Manning
Kingstree
Myrtle Beach
MYRTLE BEACH ST. PK.
Augusta
Aiken
North
Orangeburg
Georgetown
OCEAN
Savannah
SAVANNAH R. ATOMIC ENERGY RES.
Allendale
Edisto
To Sylvania
Hampton
Walterboro
Charleston
FORT SUMTER NAT'L MON.
GEORGIA
Ridgeland
Beaufort
HUNTING ISLAND ST. PK.
Hardeeville
PARRIS I.
Forest Beach
ATLANTIC
Savannah
0 40 80
MILES
Limited Access Highways
Major Highways
Other Important Roads
Interstate Route Numbers
Federal Route Numbers
State and Other Route Numbers

South Dakota

COUNTIES

Aurora (M6) 4,749
Beadle (N5) 21,682
Bennett (F7) 3 053
Bon Homme (O7) 9,229
Brookings (R5) 20,046
Brown (N2) 34,106
Brule (L6) 6,319
Buffalo (L5) 1,547
Butte (B4) 8,592
Campbell (J2) 3,531
Charles Mix (M7) 11,785
Clark (O4) 7,134
Clay (P8) 10,810
Codington (P4) 20,220
Corson (G2) 5,798
Custer (B6) 4,906
Davison (N6) 16,681
Day (O3) 10,516
Deuel (R4) 6 782
Dewey (G3) 5,257
Douglas (N7) 5,113
Edmunds (L3) 6,079
Fall River (B7) 10,688
Faulk (L3) 4,397
Grant (R3) 9,913
Gregory (L7) 7,399
Haakon (F5) 3,303
Hamlin (P4) 6,303
Hand (L4) 6,712
Hanson (N6) 4,584
Harding (B2) 2,371
Hughes (J5) 12,725
Hutchinson (O7) 11,085
Hyde (K4) 2,602
Jackson (F6) 1,985
Jerauld (M5) 4,048
Jones (H6) 2,066
Kingsbury (O5) 9,227
Lake (P5) 11,764
Lawrence (B5) 17,075
Lincoln (R7) 12,371
Lyman (J6) 4,428
Marshall (O2) 6,663
McCook (P6) 8,268

McPherson (L2) 5,821
Meade (D5) 12,044
Mellette (H6) 2,664
Miner (O5) 5,398
Minnehaha (R6) 86,575
Moody (R5) 8,810
Pennington (C6) 58,195
Perkins (D3) 5,977
Potter (J3) 4,926
Roberts (P2) 13,190
Sanborn (N5) 4,641
Shannon (D7) 6,000
Spink (N4) 11,706
Stanley (H5) 4,085
Sully (J4) 2,607
Todd (H7) 4,661
Tripp (K7) 8,761
Turner (P7) 11,159
Union (R8) 10,197
Walworth (J3) 8,097
Washabaugh (F6) 1,042
Yankton (P7) 17,551
Ziebach (F4) 2,495

CITIES and TOWNS

Aberdeen (M3) 23,073
Academy (M7) 25
Agar (J4) 139
Ahnberg (P5) 2
Akaska (J3) 90

Albee (S3) 42
Alcester (R7) 479
Alexandria (O6) 614
Allen (F7) 100
Alpena (N5) 407
Alsen (R8) 25
Altamont (R4) 77
Amherst (O2) 71
Andover (O3) 224
Appleby (R4) 8
Ardmore (B7) 73
Argonne (O5) 8
Arlington (P5) 996
Armour (N7) 875
Arpan (B4) 50
Artas (K2) 87
Artesian (N3) 330
Ashton (N3) 182
Astoria (S4) 176
Athboy (F2) 4
Athol (M3) 120
Aurora (R5) 232
Avon (N8) 637
Badger (P5) 117
Baltic (R6) 278
Bancroft (O4) 86
Barnard (N2) 65
Batesland (E7) 100
Bath (N3) 90
Bear Butte (C5) 50
Beebe (L3) 4

Belle Fourche (B4) 4,087
Belvidere (G6) 232
Bemis (R4) 50
Benclare (S6) 15
Beresford (R7) 1,794
Betts (N6) 5
Big Springs (S8) 21
Big Stone City (S3) 718
Bijou Hills (L6) 10
Bison (E2) 457
Black Hawk (C5) 375
Blue Bell (C6) 4
Blunt (H5) 532
Bonesteel (M7) 452
Bonilla (N4) 60
Bovee (M7) 5
Bowdle (K3) 673
Box Elder (D5) 550
Bradley (O3) 188
Brandon (R6) 720
Brandt (R4) 148
Brentford (N3) 96
Bridgewater (P6) 694
Bristol (O3) 562
Britton (O2) 1,442
Broadland (N4) 33
Brookings (R5) 10,558
Bruce (R5) 272
Bryant (P4) 522
Buffalo (B2) 652
Buffalo Gap (C6) 194

Bullhead (G2) 400
Burbank (R8) 125
Burdette (M4) 6
Burdock (B7) 4
Burke (L7) 811
Burkmere (L3) 2
Bushnell (R5) 92
Butler (O3) 62
Camp Crook (B2) 90
Canistota (N6) 627
Canning (K5) 49
Canova (O6) 247
Canton (R7) 2,511
Capa (H5) 11
Caputa (D5) 45
Carlock (L7) 2
Carpenter (O4) 50
Carter (J7) 18
Carthage (O5) 368
Castle Rock (B4) 12
Castlewood (R4) 500
Cavour (N5) 140
Cedarbutte (H6) 3
Center (P6) 8
Center Point (P7) 25
Centerville (R7) 887
Central City (B5) 784
Chamberlain (L6) 2,598
Chance (E3) 16
Chancellor (R7) 214
Chelsea (M3) 53

Cherry Creek (F4) 290
Chester (R6) 223
Claire City (P2) 86
Claremont (N2) 247
Clark (O4) 1,484
Clayton (O7) 22
Clear Lake (R4) 1,137
Clearfield (K7) 24
Colman (R6) 505
Colome (K7) 398
Colton (P6) 593
Columbia (N2) 272
Conata (E6) 50
Conde (N3) 388
Corona (R3) 150
Corsica (N7) 479
Cottonwood (F6) 38
Crandall (O3) 16
Crandon (N4) 4
Creighton (E5) 4
Cresbard (M3) 229
Crocker (O3) 65
Crooks (R6) 200
Crow Lake (M6) 11
Custer (B6) 2,105
Cuthbert (N6) 28
Dalesburg (P8) 35
Dallas (K7) 212
Dante (N7) 102

Davis (P7) 124
De Grey (K5) 6
De Smet (O5) 1,324
Deadwood (B5) 3,045
Deerfield (B5) 38
Dell Rapids (R6) 1,863
Delmont (N7) 363
Dempster (R4) 150
Denby (E7) 13
Denver (R4) 25
Dimock (O7) 198
Dixon (L7) 17
Doland (N4) 481
Dolton (P7) 71
Draper (J6) 215
Dupree (F3) 548
Eagle Butte (G3) 495
East Mobridge (J2) .....
Eden (P2) 136
Edgemont (B7) 1,772
Egan (R6) 310
Elk Point (R8) 1,378
Elkton (S5) 621
Elm Springs (D5) 3
Emery (O6) 502
Epiphany (O6) 40
Erwin (P5) 157
Esmond (O5) 19
Estelline (R4) 722

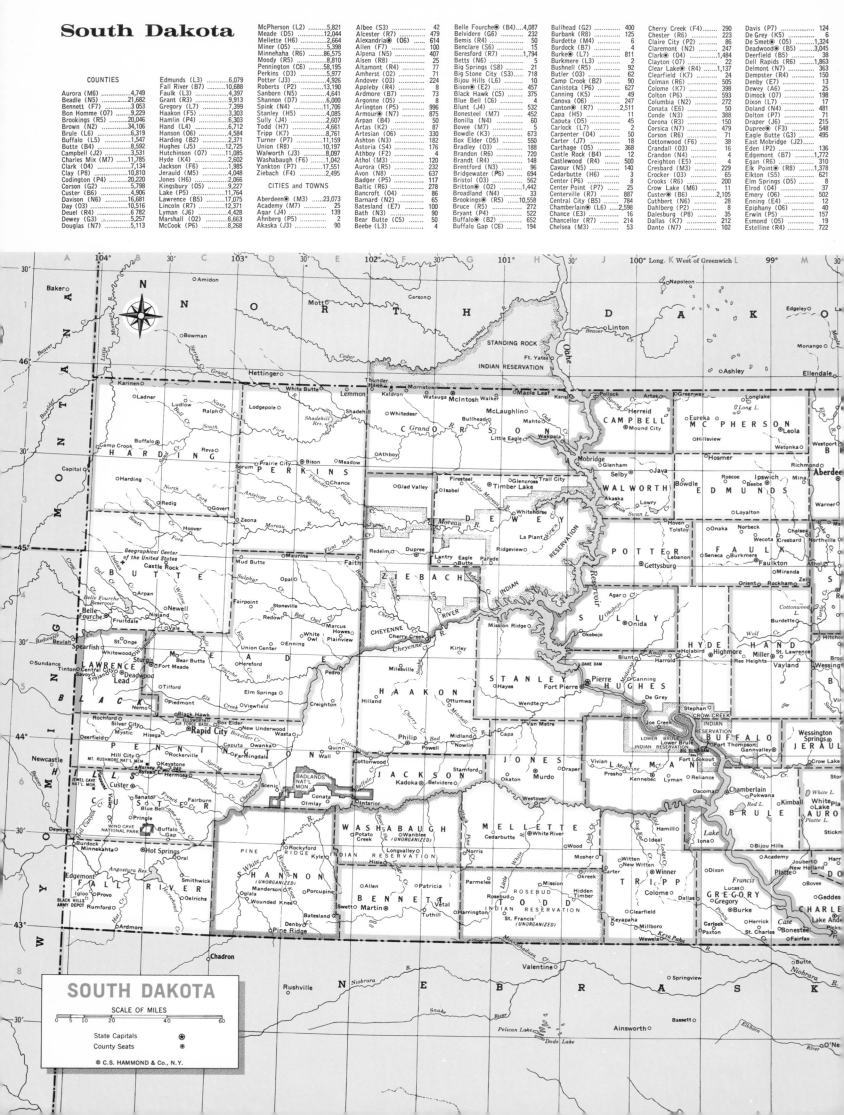

SOUTH DAKOTA
SCALE OF MILES
0 5 10 20   40   60

State Capitals ....⊛
County Seats ....◉

© C.S. HAMMOND & Co., N.Y.

SOUTH DAKOTA

AREA	77,047 sq. mi.
POPULATION	703,000
CAPITAL	Pierre
LARGEST CITY	Sioux Falls 65,466
HIGHEST POINT	Harney Pk. 7,242 ft.
SETTLED IN	1856
ADMITTED TO UNION	November 2, 1889
POPULAR NAMES	Coyote State; Sunshine State
STATE FLOWER	Pasqueflower
STATE BIRD	Ring-necked Pheasant

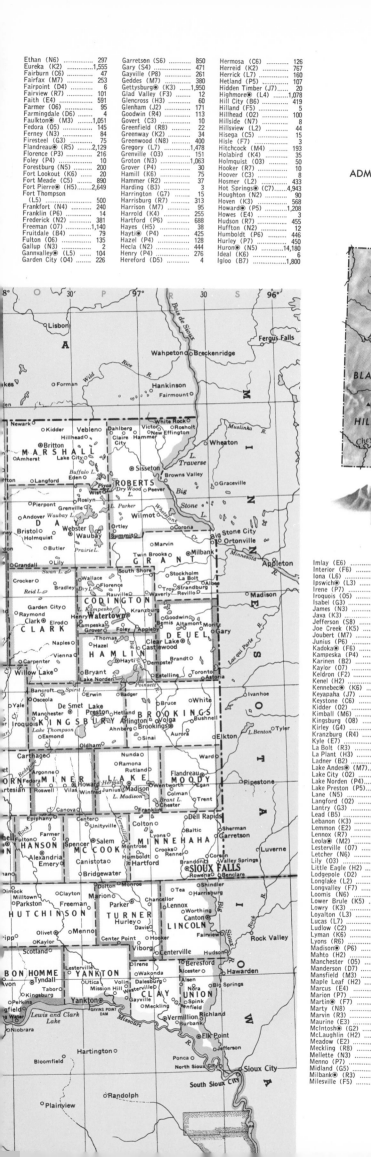

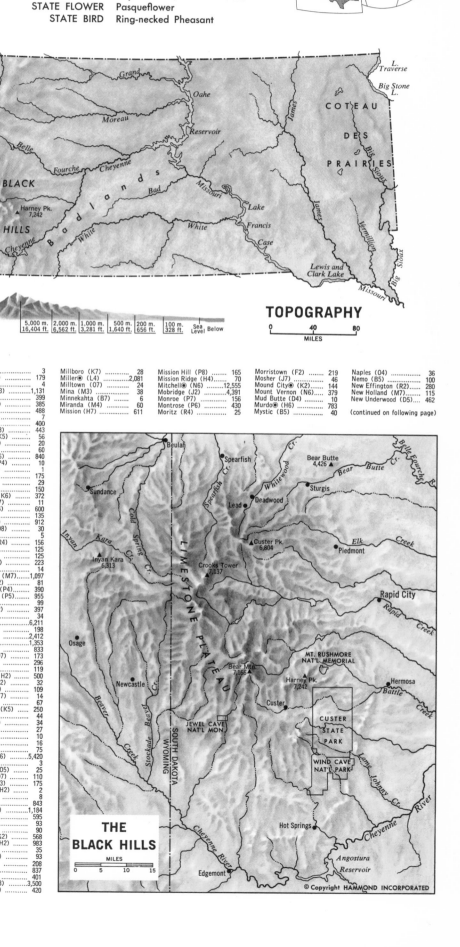

TOPOGRAPHY

5,000 m. 16,404 ft. | 2,000 m. 6,562 ft. | 1,000 m. 3,281 ft. | 500 m. 1,640 ft. | 200 m. 656 ft. | 100 m. 328 ft. | Sea Level | Below

0 — 40 — 80 MILES

(continued on following page)

THE BLACK HILLS

MILES
0 — 5 — 10 — 15

South Dakota
(continued)

New Witten (K7)	146	Ree Heights (L4)	188
Newark (O2)	39	Reliance (K6)	201
Newell (C4)	797	Renner (R6)	180
Nisland (C4)	211	Reva (C2)	6
Nora (R8)	35	Revillo (R3)	202
Norbeck (L3)	15	Richland (R8)	30
Norris (G7)	52	Richmond (M2)	7
North Shore ‡(P4)	171	Ridgeview (H3)	60
North Sioux City (R8)	736	Rochford (B5)	102
Northville (M3)	153	Rockerville (C6)	30
Nowlin (G5)	25	Rockham (M4)	197
Nunda (P5)	106	Rockyford (E7)	11
Oacoma (L6)	312	Roscoe (L3)	532
Oelrichs (C7)	132	Rosebud (H7)	537
Oglala (D7)	300	Rosholt (R2)	423
Okaton (H6)	65	Roslyn (P2)	256
Okobojo (J4)	2	Roswell (O6)	39
Okreek (J7)	250	Rowena (R6)	68
Oldham (P5)	291	Rumford (B7)	8
Olivet⊙ (O7)	135	Running Water (N8)	12
Onaka (L3)	85	Rutland (P5)	100
Onida⊙ (K4)	843	Saint Charles (L7)	50
Opal (D4)	50	Saint Francis (H7)	421
Oral (C7)	65	Saint Lawrence (M4)	290
Ordway (N2)	8	Saint Onge (B4)	108
Orient (L4)	133	Salem⊙ (P6)	1,188
Ortley (P3)	127	Sanator (B6)	130
Osceola (O5)	22	Savoy (B5)	10
Ottumwa (G5)	8	Scenic (D6)	125
Owanka (D5)	30	Scotland (O7)	1,077
Parade (G3)	7	Selby⊙ (J3)	979
Parker⊙ (P7)	1,142	Seneca (L3)	161
Parkston (O7)	1,514	Shadehill (E2)	19
Parmelee (G7)	302	Sherman (S6)	116
Patricia (G7)	10	Shindler (R7)	61
Paxton (L7)	4	Silver City (B5)	50
Pedro (E5)	19	Sinai (P5)	166
Peever (R2)	208	Sioux Falls⊙ (R6)	65,466
Perkins (O8)	9	Sioux Falls (urban	
Philip⊙ (F5)	1,114	area)	66,582
Pickstown (M7)	500	Sisseton⊙ (R2)	3,218
Piedmont (C5)	200	Smithwick (C7)	45
Pierpont (O3)	258	Sorum (D3)	3
PIERRE⊙ (J5)	10,088	South Shore (P3)	259
Pine Ridge (E7)	1,256	Spearfish (B5)	3,682
Plainview (E4)	17	Spencer (O6)	460
Plankinton⊙ (N6)	644	Spink (R8)	41
Platte (M7)	1,167	Springfield (N8)	1,194
Pollock (J2)	417	Stamford (G6)	2
Porcupine (E7)	25	Stephan (K5)	40
Potato Creek (F6)	50	Stickney (M6)	456
Powell (G5)	15	Stockholm (R3)	155
Prairie City (D2)	69	Stoneville (D4)	6
Presho (J6)	881	Storla (M6)	101
Pringle (B6)	145	Strandburg (R3)	105
Provo (B7)	250	Stratford (N3)	109
Pukwana (L6)	247	Sturgis⊙ (B5)	4,539
Putney (N2)	16	Summit (P3)	283
Quinn (F5)	162	Swett (E7)	20
Ralph (F3)	4	Sylvan Lake (B6)	5
Ramona (P5)	247	Tabor (O8)	378
Randolph (N3)	3	Tacoma Park (N2)	19
Rapid City⊙ (C5)	42,399	Tea (R7)	188
Rauville (P3)	8	Thomas (R4)	2
Ravinia (N7)	164	Thunder Hawk (F2)	65
Raymond (O4)	168	Tilford (C5)	85
Redelm (F3)	7	Timber Lake⊙ (H3)	624
Redfield⊙ (N4)	2,952	Tinton (C5)	10
Redig (C3)	23	Tolstoy (K3)	142
Redowl (D4)	9	Toronto (R4)	268

Trail City (H3)	150	Virgil (N5)	81
Trent (R6)	232	Vivian (J6)	250
Tripp (N7)	837	Volga (R5)	780
Trojan (B5)	15	Volin (P8)	171
Troy (R3)	44	Wagner (N7)	1,586
Tulare (N4)	225	Wakonda (P7)	382
Turton (N3)	140	Wakpala (P3)	424
Tuthill (G7)	75	Walker (G2)	27
Twin Brooks (R3)	86	Wall (L6)	629
Tyndall⊙ (O8)	1,262	Wallace (P3)	132
Union Center (D4)	29	Wanblee (F6)	300
Unityville (P6)	48	Ward (R5)	74
Utica (P8)	70	Warner (M3)	150
Vale (C4)	140	Wasta (L6)	196
Valley Springs		Watauga (F2)	144
(S6)	472	Watertown⊙ (P4)	14,077
Van Metre (H5)	10	Waubay (P3)	851
Vayland (M5)	75	Waverly (R3)	40
Veblen (P2)	437	Webster⊙ (P3)	2,409
Verdon (N3)	28	Wecota (L3)	55
Vermillion⊙ (R8)	6,102	Wendte (H5)	56
Vetal (G7)	16	Wentworth (R6)	211
Viborg (P7)	699	Wessington (M5)	378
Victor (R2)	17	Wessington Springs⊙	
Vienna (O4)	191	(M5)	1,488
Viewfield (D5)	1	Westerville (P8)	45
Vilas (O6)	49	Westover (H6)	5

Westport (M2)	150		
Wetonka (M2)	46		
Wewela (K7)	23		
White (R5)	417		
White Butte (E2)	154		
White Lake (M6)	397		
White Owl (E4)	8		
White River⊙ (H6)	583		
White Rock (R2)	76		
Whitewater (F2)	6		
Whitehorse (H3)	100		
Whitewood (B5)	470		
Willow Lake (O4)	467		
Wilmot (R3)	545		
Winfred (P6)	137		
Winner⊙ (K7)	3,705		
Wist (P2)	5		
Witten (J7)	150		
Wolsey (N5)	354		
Wood (J6)	267		
Woonsocket⊙ (N5)	1,035		
Worthing (R7)	304		
Wounded Knee (D7)	500		
Yale (O5)	171		
Yankton⊙ (P8)	9,279		
Ze\l (M4)	100		
Zeona (D3)	5		

AGRICULTURE, INDUSTRY and RESOURCES

DOMINANT LAND USE

Specialized Wheat

Wheat, General Farming

Wheat, Range Livestock

Cattle Feed, Hogs

Livestock, Cash Grain

General Farming, Livestock, Special Crops

Range Livestock

Forests

Water Power

MAJOR MINERAL OCCURRENCES

Ag	Silver	Mi	Mica
Au	Gold	O	Petroleum
Be	Beryl	U	Uranium
Gn	Granite	V	Vanadium

OTHER FEATURES

Aeber (creek)	G 4
Andes (lake)	N 7
Angostura (res.)	B 7
Antelope (creek)	D 3
Bad (river)	G 5
Badlands Nat'l Mon.	E 6
Battle (creek)	C 6
Bear in the Lodge	
(creek)	F 6
Beaver (creek)	A 6
Beaver (creek)	E 4
Belle Fourche (res.)	B 4
Belle Fourche (river)	C 4
Big Bend (dam)	L 5
Big Sioux (river)	S 7
Big Stone (lake)	R 3
Black Hills (mts.)	B 5
Black Hills Army Depot	B 7
Black Pine (creek)	B 6
Bois de Sioux (river)	R 1
Boxelder (creek)	D 5
Brant (lake)	R 6
Buffalo (creek)	F 6
Buffalo (lake)	P 2
Bull (creek)	C 2
Bull (creek)	K 6
Byron (lake)	N 4
Cain (creek)	N 5
Cherry (creek)	F 4
Cherry (creek)	F 5
Cheyenne (river)	F 4
Cheyenne River Indian	
Res.	F 4
Choteau (creek)	N 7
Cottonwood (creek)	E 5
Cottonwood (lake)	M 4
Crow (creek)	A 4
Crow Creek Ind. Res.	L 5
Dog Ear (creek)	K 6
Dry (creek)	G 4
Dry (lake)	P 3
Dry Wood (lake)	G 3
Elk (creek)	C 5
Ellsworth A.F.B.	C 5
Elm (creek)	D 4
Elm (creek)	M 2
Firesteel (creek)	N 6
Flint Rock (creek)	E 3
Fort Randall (dam)	N 7
Fort Randall (res.)	L 7
Foster (creek)	N 4
French (creek)	C 6
Gavins Point (dam)	P 8
Grand (river)	F 2
Harney (peak)	B 6
Hat (creek)	B 7
Hell Canyon (creek)	B 6
Herman (lake)	P 5
Horsehead (creek)	C 7
Indian (creek)	B 4
James (river)	N 5
Jewel Cave National	
Monument	B 6
Kampeska (lake)	P 4
Keyapaha (river)	K 7
Lame Johnny (creek)	C 6
Lewis and Clark (lake)	O 8
Little Missouri (river)	A 2
Little Moreau (river)	G 3
Little White (river)	H 7
Long (lake)	L 2
Lower Brule Indian	
Res.	K 5
Madison (lake)	P 6
Maple (lake)	M 1
Medicine (creek)	J 6
Medicine Knoll (creek)	J 5
Minnechaduza (creek)	H 7
Minnesota (river)	S 3
Missouri (river)	J 3
Mitchell (creek)	N 5
Moreau (river)	G 3
Mount Rushmore Nat'l	
Mem.	B 6
Mud (creek)	N 3
Nasty (creek)	C 2
Oahe (dam)	J 5
Oahe (res.)	H 2
Oak (creek)	G 2
Oak (creek)	H 2
Okobojo (creek)	J 4
Old Lodge (creek)	K 6
Owl (creek)	B 4
Parker (lake)	P 3
Pearl (creek)	N 5
Pine Ridge Ind. Res.	D 7
Piyas (lake)	P 2
Platte (lake)	M 6
Pleasant Valley (creek)	B 6
Poinsett (lake)	P 4
Ponca (creek)	L 7
Prairie (lake)	E 3
Rabbit (creek)	D 3
Red (lake)	O 3
Red Owl (creek)	E 4
Redstone (creek)	A 3
Redwater (creek)	A 4
Reid (lake)	O 3
Rock (creek)	O 7
Rosebud Ind. Res.	H 7
Sand (creek)	N 3
Sand (creek)	M 3
Sand (creek)	M 5
Sand (creek)	M 4
Shadehill (res.)	E 2
Shue (creek)	N 5
Smith (creek)	L 6
Snake (creek)	F 5
Snake (creek)	M 3
Snake (creek)	M 3
Spirit (lake)	O 3
Spring (creek)	C 6
Spring (creek)	G 3
Sulphur (creek)	D 4
Swan (lake)	O 3
Swan (lake)	K 3
Thompson (lake)	O 5
Thunder (lake)	N 3
Thunder Butte (creek)	E 3
Traverse (lake)	R 2
Turtle (creek)	M 4
Vermillion (river)	P 6
Virgin (creek)	H 3
Waubay (lake)	P 3
Whetstone (creek)	R 3
White (lake)	M 6
White (river)	D 7
Whitewood (creek)	B 4
Willow (creek)	C 4
Wind Cave National	
Park	B 6
Wolf (creek)	L 4
Wounded Knee (creek)	E 7

HIGHWAYS

0 — 40 — 80
MILES

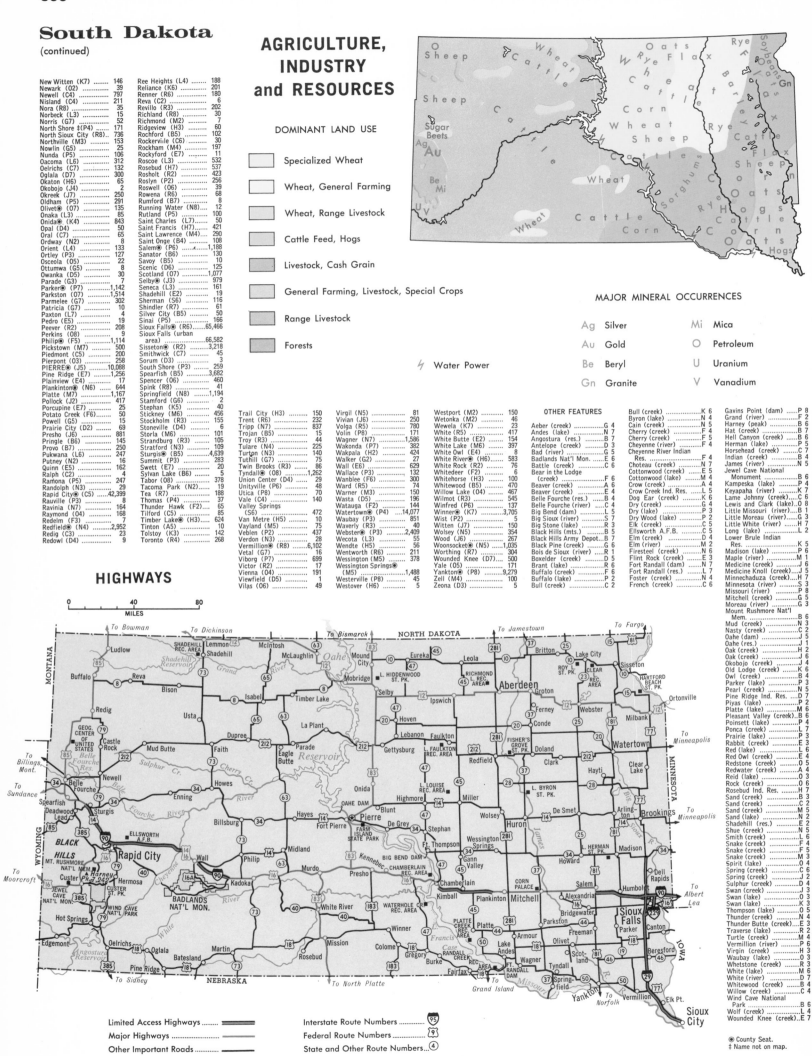

Limited Access Highways ....

Major Highways ....

Other Important Roads ....

Interstate Route Numbers

Federal Route Numbers

State and Other Route Numbers

⊙ County Seat.
‡ Name not on map.

TEXAS

AREA	267,339 sq. mi.
POPULATION	10,551,000
CAPITAL	Austin
LARGEST CITY	Houston 938,219
HIGHEST POINT	Guadalupe Pk. 8,751 ft.
SETTLED IN	1686
ADMITTED TO UNION	December 29, 1845
POPULAR NAME	Lone Star State
STATE FLOWER	Bluebonnet
STATE BIRD	Mockingbird

COUNTIES

Anderson (J6)	28,162
Andrews (B5)	13,450
Angelina (K6)	39,814
Aransas (H10)	7,006
Archer (F4)	6,110
Armstrong (C3)	1,966
Atascosa (F9)	18,828
Austin (H8)	13,777
Bailey (B3)	9,090
Bandera (E8)	3,892
Bastrop (G7)	16,925
Baylor (E4)	5,893
Bee (G9)	23,755
Bell (G6)	94,097
Bexar (F8)	687,151
Blanco (F7)	3,657
Borden (C5)	1,076
Bosque (G6)	10,809
Bowie (K4)	59,971
Brazoria (J3)	76,204
Brazos (H7)	44,895
Brewster (A8)	6,434
Briscoe (C3)	3,577
Brooks (F11)	8,609
Brown (F6)	24,728
Burleson (H7)	11,177
Burnet (F7)	9,265
Caldwell (G8)	17,222
Calhoun (H9)	16,592
Callahan (E5)	7,929
Cameron (G11)	151,098
Camp (K5)	7,849
Carson (C2)	7,781
Cass (K4)	23,496
Castro (B3)	8,923
Chambers (L1)	10,379
Cherokee (J6)	33,120
Childress (D3)	8,421
Clay (F4)	8,351
Cochran (B4)	6,417
Coke (D6)	3,589
Coleman (E6)	12,458
Collin (H4)	41,247
Collingsworth (D3)	6,276
Colorado (H8)	18,463
Comal (F8)	19,844
Comanche (F5)	11,865
Concho (E6)	3,672
Cooke (G4)	22,560
Coryell (G6)	23,961
Cottle (D3)	4,207
Crane (B6)	4,699
Crockett (C7)	4,209
Crosby (C4)	10,347
Culberson (C11)	2,794
Dallam (B1)	6,302
Dallas (G2)	951,527
Dawson (C5)	19,185
De Witt (G9)	20,683
Deaf Smith (B3)	13,187
Delta (J4)	5,860
Denton (G4)	47,432
Dickens (D4)	4,963
Dimmit (E9)	10,095
Donley (D2)	4,449
Duval (F10)	13,398
Eastland (F5)	19,526
Ector (B6)	90,995
Edwards (D7)	2,317
El Paso (A10)	314,070
Ellis (H5)	43,395
Erath (F5)	16,236
Falls (H6)	21,263
Fannin (H4)	23,880
Fayette (H8)	20,384
Fisher (D5)	7,865
Floyd (C3)	12,369
Foard (E3)	3,125
Fort Bend (J2)	40,527
Franklin (J4)	5,101
Freestone (H6)	12,525
Frio (E9)	10,112
Gaines (B5)	12,267
Galveston (K3)	140,364
Garza (C4)	6,611
Gillespie (F7)	10,048
Glasscock (C6)	1,118
Goliad (G9)	5,429
Gonzales (G8)	17,845
Gray (D2)	31,535
Grayson (H4)	73,043
Gregg (K5)	69,436
Grimes (J7)	12,709
Guadalupe (G8)	29,017
Hale (C3)	36,798
Hall (D3)	7,322
Hamilton (F6)	8,488
Hansford (C1)	6,208
Hardeman (E3)	8,275
Hardin (K7)	24,629
Harris (J1)	1,243,158
Harrison (K5)	45,594
Hartley (B2)	2,171
Haskell (E4)	11,174
Hays (F7)	19,934
Hemphill (D2)	3,185
Henderson (J5)	21,786
Hidalgo (F11)	180,904
Hill (G5)	23,650
Hockley (B4)	22,340
Hood (G5)	5,443
Hopkins (J4)	18,594
Houston (J6)	19,376
Howard (C5)	40,139
Hudspeth (B10)	3,343
Hunt (H4)	39,399
Hutchinson (C2)	34,419
Irion (C6)	1,183
Jack (F4)	7,418
Jackson (H9)	14,040
Jasper (K7)	22,100
Jeff Davis (C11)	1,582
Jefferson (K8)	245,659
Jim Hogg (F11)	5,022
Jim Wells (F10)	34,548
Johnson (G5)	34,720
Jones (E5)	19,299
Karnes (G9)	14,995
Kaufman (H5)	29,931
Kendall (F8)	5,889
Kenedy (G11)	884
Kent (D4)	1,727
Kerr (E7)	16,800
Kimble (E7)	3,943
King (D4)	640
Kinney (D8)	2,452
Kleberg (G10)	30,052
Knox (E4)	7,857
La Salle (E9)	5,972
Lamar (J4)	34,234
Lamb (B3)	21,896
Lampasas (F6)	9,418
Lavaca (H8)	20,174
Lee (H7)	8,949
Leon (J6)	9,951
Liberty (K7)	31,595
Limestone (H6)	20,413
Lipscomb (D1)	3,406
Live Oak (F9)	7,846
Llano◉ (F7)	5,240
Loving (D10)	226
Lubbock (C4)	156,271
Lynn (C4)	10,914
Madison (J6)	6,749
Marion (K5)	8,049
Martin (C5)	5,068
Mason (E7)	3,780
Matagorda (H9)	25,744
Maverick (D9)	14,508
McCulloch (E6)	8,815
McLennan (G6)	150,091
McMullen (F9)	1,116
Medina (E8)	18,904
Menard (E7)	2,964
Midland (B6).	67,717
Milam (H7)	22,263
Mills (F6)	4,467
Mitchell (D5)	11,255
Montague (G4)	14,893
Montgomery (J7)	26,839
Moore (C2)	14,773
Morris (K4)	12,576
Motley (D3)	2,870
Nacogdoches (K6)	28,046
Navarro (H5)	34,423
Newton (L7)	10,372
Nolan (D5)	18,963
Nueces (G10)	221,573
Ochiltree (D1)	9,380
Oldham (B2)	1,928
Orange (L7)	60,357
Palo Pinto (F5)	20,516
Panola (K5)	16,870
Parker (G5)	22,880
Parmer (B3)	9,583
Pecos (B7)	11,957
Polk (K7)	13,861
Potter (C2)	115,580
Presidio (C12)	5,460
Rains (J5)	2,993
Randall (C2)	33,913
Reagan (C6)	3,782
Real (E8)	2,079
Red River (J4)	15,682
Reeves (D11)	17,644
Refugio (G9)	10,975
Roberts (D2)	1,075
Robertson (H6)	16,157
Rockwall (H5)	5,878
Runnels (E6)	15,016
Rusk (K5)	36,421
Sabine (L6)	7,302
San Augustine (K6)	7,722
San Jacinto (J7)	6,153
San Patricio (G10)	45,021
San Saba (F6)	6,381
Schleicher (D7)	2,791
Scurry (D5)	20,369
Shackelford (E5)	3,990
Shelby (K6)	20,479
Sherman (C1)	2,605
Smith (J5)	86,350
Somervell (G5)	2,577
Starr (F11)	17,137
Stephens (F5)	8,885
Sterling (C6)	1,177
Stonewall (D4)	3,017
Sutton (D7)	3,738
Swisher (C3)	10,607
Tarrant (F2)	538,495
Taylor (E5)	101,078
Terrell (B7)	2,600
Terry (B4)	16,286
Throckmorton (E4)	2,767
Titus (K4)	16,785
Tom Green (D6)	64,630
Travis (G7)	212,136
Trinity (J6)	7,539
Tyler (K7)	10,666
Upshur (K5)	19,793
Upton (B6)	6,239
Uvalde (E8)	16,814
Val Verde (C8)	24,461
Van Zandt (J5)	19,091
Victoria (H9)	46,475
Walker (J7)	21,475
Waller (J8)	12,071
Ward (A6)	14,917
Washington (H7)	19,145
Webb (E10)	64,791
Wharton (H8)	38,152
Wheeler (D2)	7,947
Wichita (F3)	123,528
Wilbarger (E3)	17,748
Willacy (G11)	20,084
Williamson (G7)	35,044
Wilson (F8)	13,267
Winkler (A6)	13,652
Wise (G4)	17,012
Wood (J5)	17,653
Yoakum (B4)	8,032
Young (F4)	17,254
Zapata (E11)	4,393
Zavala (E9)	12,696

CITIES and TOWNS

Abernathy (B4)	2,491
Abilene◉ (E5)	90,368
Abilene (urban area)	91,566
Alamo (F11)	4,121
Alamo Heights (F8)	7,552
Albany◉ (E5)	2,174
Alice◉ (F10)	20,861
Alpine◉ (D11)	4,740
Alvarado (G5)	1,907
Alvin (J3)	5,643
Amarillo◉ (C2)	137,969
Amarillo (urban area)	137,969
Anahuac◉ (K8)	1,985
Anderson◉ (J7)	500
Andrews◉ (B5)	11,135
Angleton◉ (J8)	7,312
Anson (E5)	2,890
Aransas Pass (G10)	6,956
Arcadia (K3)	1,500
Archer City◉ (F4)	1,974
Arlington (F2)	44,775
Asherton (E9)	1,890
Aspermont◉ (D4)	1,286
Athens◉ (J5)	7,086
Atlanta (K4)	4,076
AUSTIN◉ (G7)	186,545
Austin (urban area)	187,157
Azle (E1)	2,969
Bacliff (K2)	1,707
Baird◉ (E5)	1,633
Balch Springs (H2)	6,821
Ballinger◉ (E6)	5,043
Bandera◉ (F8)	1,185
Barrett (K1)	2,364
Bartlett (G7)	1,540
Bastrop◉ (G7)	3,001
Bay City◉ (H9)	11,656
Baytown (L2)	28,159
Beaumont◉ (K7)	119,175
Beaumont (urban area)	119,178
Bedford (F2)	2,706
Beeville◉ (G9)	13,811
Bellaire (J2)	19,872
Bellmead (H6)	5,127
Bellville◉ (H8)	2,218
Belton◉ (G7)	8,163
Benavides (F10)	2,459
Benbrook (E2)	3,254
Benjamin◉ (E4)	338
Beverly Hills ‡(G6)	1,728
Big Lake◉ (C6)	2,668
Big Spring◉ (C5)	31,230
Bishop (G10)	3,722
Bloomington (H9)	1,756
Blue Mound (E1)	1,253
Boerne◉ (F8)	2,169
Boling (H8)	1,412
Bonham◉ (H4)	7,357
Borger (C2)	20,911
Boston◉ (K4)	100
Bowie (G4)	4,566
Brackettville◉ (D8)	1,662
Brady◉ (E6)	5,338
Brazoria (J9)	1,291
Breckenridge◉ (F5)	6,273
Brenham◉ (H7)	7,740
Bridgeport (G4)	3,218
Bronte (D6)	999
Brookshire (J8)	1,339
Brownfield◉ (B4)	10,286
Brownsville◉ (G12)	48,040
Brownwood◉ (F6)	16,974
Bryan◉ (H7)	27,542
Bunker Hill (J1)	2,216
Burkburnett (F3)	7,621
Burleson (F2)	2,345
Burnet◉ (F7)	2,214
Caldwell◉ (H7)	2,204
Call (L7)	1,500
Calvert (H7)	2,073
Cameron◉ (H7)	5,640
Canadian◉ (D2)	2,239
Canton◉ (J5)	1,114
Canutillo (A10)	1,377
Canyon◉ (C3)	5,864
Carrizo Springs◉ (E9)	5,699
Carrollton (G1)	4,242
Carthage◉ (K5)	5,262
Castle Hills ‡(F8)	2,622
Castroville (E8)	1,508
Cedar Hill (G2)	1,848
Celina (H4)	1,204
Center◉ (K6)	4,510
Centerville◉ (H6)	836
Channelview (K1)	10,000
Channing◉ (B2)	351
Charlotte (F9)	1,465
Childress◉ (D3)	6,399
Cisco (E5)	4,499
Clarendon◉ (C3)	2,172
Clarksville◉ (K4)	3,851
Claude◉ (C2)	895
Clear Lake Shores (K2)	600
Cleburne◉ (G5)	15,381
Cleveland (K7)	5,838
Clifton (G6)	2,335
Clute (J8)	4,501
Coahoma (C5)	1,239
Cockrell Hill (G2)	3,104
Coldspring◉ (J7)	400
Coleman◉ (E6)	6,371
College Station (H7)	11,396
Colleyville (F1)	1,491
Colorado City◉ (C5)	6,457
Columbus◉ (H8)	3,656
Comanche◉ (F6)	3,415
Commerce (J4)	5,789
Conroe◉ (J7)	9,192
Cooper◉ (J4)	2,213
Copperas Cove (G6)	4,567
Corpus Christi◉ (G10)	167,690
Corpus Christi (urban area)	177,380
Corsicana◉ (H5)	20,344
Cotulla◉ (E9)	3,960
Crane◉ (B6)	3,796
Crockett◉ (J6)	5,356
Crosbyton◉ (C4)	2,088
Crowell◉ (E4)	1,703
Crystal City◉ (E9)	9,101
Cuero◉ (G8)	7,338
Daingerfield◉ (K4)	3,133
Daisetta (K7)	1,500
Dalhart◉ (B1)	5,160
Dallas◉ (H2)	679,684
Dallas (urban area)	932,349
Dayton (J7)	3,367
De Kalb (K4)	2,042
De Leon (F5)	2,022
De Soto (G2)	1,969
Decatur◉ (G4)	3,563
Deer Park (K2)	4,865
Del Rio◉ (D8)	18,612
Denison (H4)	22,748
Denton◉ (G4)	26,844
Denver City (B4)	4,302
Devine (E8)	2,522
Diboll (K6)	2,506
Dickens◉ (D4)	302
Dickinson (K3)	4,715
Dilley (E9)	2,118
Dimmitt◉ (B3)	2,935
Donna (F11)	7,522
Dublin (F5)	2,443
Dumas◉ (C2)	8,477
Duncanville (G2)	3,774
Eagle Lake (H8)	3,565
Eagle Pass◉ (D9)	12,094
East Bernard (H8)	1,276
Eastland (F5)	3,292
Edcouch ‡(G11)	2,814
Eden (E6)	1,486
Edinburg◉ (F11)	18,706
Edna◉ (H9)	5,038
El Campo (H8)	7,700
El Paso◉ (A10)	276,687
El Paso (urban area)	277,128
Eldorado◉ (D7)	1,815
Electra (F4)	4,759
Elgin (G7)	3,511
Elsa (G11)	3,847
Emory◉ (J5)	559
Ennis (H5)	9,347
Euless (F2)	2,062
Fabens (B10)	3,134
Fairfield◉ (H6)	1,781
Falfurrias◉ (F10)	6,515
Farmers Branch (G1)	13,441
Farmersville (H4)	2,021
Farwell◉ (A3)	1,009
Ferris (H3)	1,807
Floresville◉ (F8)	2,126
Floydada◉ (C3)	3,769
Forest Hill (F2)	3,221
Forney (H5)	1,544
Fort Davis◉ (D11)	750
Fort Stockton◉ (A7)	6,373
Fort Worth◉ (E2)	356,268
Fort Worth (urban area)	502,682
Franklin◉ (H7)	1,065
Frankston (J5)	953
Fredericksburg◉ (E7)	4,629
Freeport (J9)	11,619
Freer (F10)	2,724
Friona (B3)	2,048
Fritch (C2)	1,846
Fruitdale (G2)	1,418
Gail◉ (C5)	130
Gainesville◉ (G4)	13,083
Galena Park (J2)	10,852
Galveston◉ (L3)	67,175
Galveston-Texas City (urban area)	118,482
Ganado (H8)	1,626
Garden City◉ (C6)	300
Garland (H1)	38,501
Gatesville◉ (G6)	4,626
George West◉ (F9)	1,878
Georgetown◉ (G7)	5,218
Giddings◉ (H7)	2,821
Gilmer◉ (J5)	4,312
Gladewater (K5)	5,742
Glen Rose◉ (G5)	1,422
Goldthwaite◉ (F6)	1,383
Goliad◉ (G9)	1,782
Gonzales◉ (G8)	5,829
Graham◉ (F4)	8,505
Granbury◉ (G5)	2,227
Grand Prairie (G2)	30,386
Grand Saline (J5)	2,006
Granger (G7)	1,339
Grapevine (F1)	2,821
Greenville◉ (H4)	19,087
Gregory ‡(G10)	1,970
Griffing Park ‡(L8)	2,267
Groesbeck◉ (H6)	2,498
Groves (L8)	17,304
Groveton◉ (J7)	1,148
Grulla (F11)	1,436
Guthrie◉ (D4)	200
Hale Center (C3)	2,196
Hallettsville◉ (G8)	2,808
Haltom City (F2)	23,133
Hamilton◉ (G6)	3,106
Hamlin (E5)	3,791
Harlingen (G11)	41,207
Harlingen-San Benito (urban area)	61,658
Haskell◉ (E4)	4,016
Hearne (H7)	5,072
Hebbronville◉ (F10)	3,987
Hemphill◉ (L6)	913
Hempstead◉ (J7)	1,505
Henderson◉ (K5)	9,666
Henrietta◉ (F4)	3,062
Hereford◉ (B3)	7,652
Highland Park (G2)	10,411
Highlands (K1)	4,336
Hillsboro◉ (G5)	7,402
Hitchcock (K3)	5,216
Hondo◉ (E8)	4,992
Honey Grove (J4)	2,071
Honey Island (K7)	1,250
Hooks (K4)	2,048
Houston◉ (J2)	938,219
Houston (urban area)	1,139,678
Hubbard (H6)	1,628
Hughes Springs (K5)	1,813
Humble (J7)	1,711
Hunters Creek Village (J1)	2,478
Huntsville◉ (J7)	11,999
Hurst ‡(F2)	10,165
Idalou (C4)	1,274
Ingleside ‡(G10)	3,022
Iowa Park (F4)	3,295
Iraan (B7)	1,255
Irving (G2)	45,985
Itasca (G5)	1,383
Jacinto City ‡(J1)	9,547
Jacksboro◉ (F4)	3,816
Jacksonville (J5)	9,590
Jasper◉ (L7)	4,889
Jayton◉ (D4)	649
Jefferson◉ (K5)	3,082
Johnson City◉ (F7)	611
Jourdanton◉ (F9)	1,504
Junction◉ (E7)	2,441
Karnes City◉ (G9)	2,693
Katy (J8)	1,569
Kaufman◉ (H5)	3,087
Keene (G5)	1,532
Kenedy (G9)	4,301
Kennedale (F2)	1,521
Kermit◉ (B6)	10,465
Kerrville◉ (E7)	8,901
Kilgore (K5)	10,092
Killeen (G6)	23,377
Kingsville◉ (G10)	25,297
Kirbyville (K7)	1,660
Kleberg (H2)	3,572
Knox City (E4)	1,805
Kountze◉ (K7)	1,768
La Feria (G11)	3,047
La Grange◉ (G8)	3,623
La Marque (K3)	13,969
La Porte (K2)	4,512
La Villa ‡(G11)	1,261
Lacy-Lakeview ‡(G6)	2,272
Lake Jackson (J9)	9,651
Lake Worth (E2)	3,833
Lakeview ‡(L8)	3,849
Lakewood (K1)	1,882
Lamesa◉ (C5)	12,438
Lampasas◉ (F6)	5,061
Lancaster (G2)	7,501
Laredo◉ (E10)	60,678
Laredo (urban area)	60,678
League City (K2)	2,622
Leakey◉ (E8)	587
Legion (F7)	1,691
Levelland◉ (B4)	10,153
Lewisville (G5)	3,956
Liberty◉ (K7)	6,127
Lindale (J5)	1,285
Linden◉ (K4)	1,832
Lipscomb◉ (D1)	90
Littlefield◉ (B4)	7,236
Livingston◉ (K7)	3,398
Llano◉ (F7)	2,656

(continued on following page)

AGRICULTURE, INDUSTRY and RESOURCES

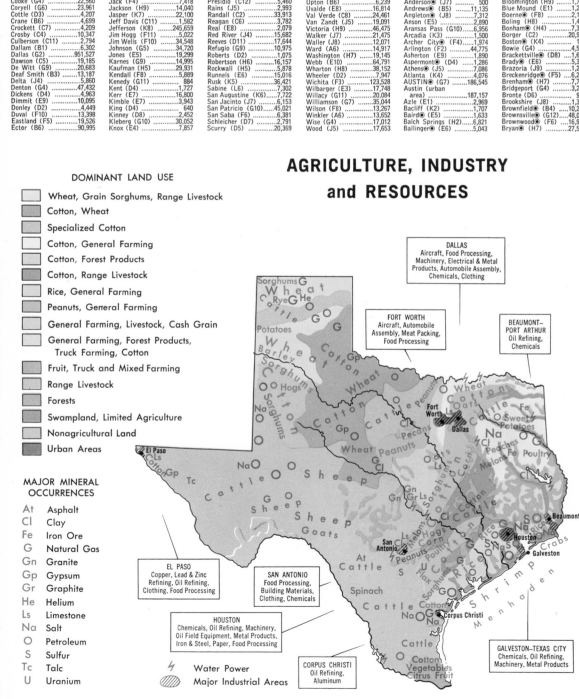

DOMINANT LAND USE

- Wheat, Grain Sorghums, Range Livestock
- Cotton, Wheat
- Specialized Cotton
- Cotton, General Farming
- Cotton, Forest Products
- Cotton, Range Livestock
- Rice, General Farming
- Peanuts, General Farming
- General Farming, Livestock, Cash Grain
- General Farming, Forest Products, Truck Farming, Cotton
- Fruit, Truck and Mixed Farming
- Range Livestock
- Forests
- Swampland, Limited Agriculture
- Nonagricultural Land
- Urban Areas

MAJOR MINERAL OCCURRENCES

- At Asphalt
- Cl Clay
- Fe Iron Ore
- G Natural Gas
- Gn Granite
- Gp Gypsum
- Gr Graphite
- He Helium
- Ls Limestone
- Na Salt
- O Petroleum
- S Sulfur
- Tc Talc
- U Uranium

- Water Power
- Major Industrial Areas

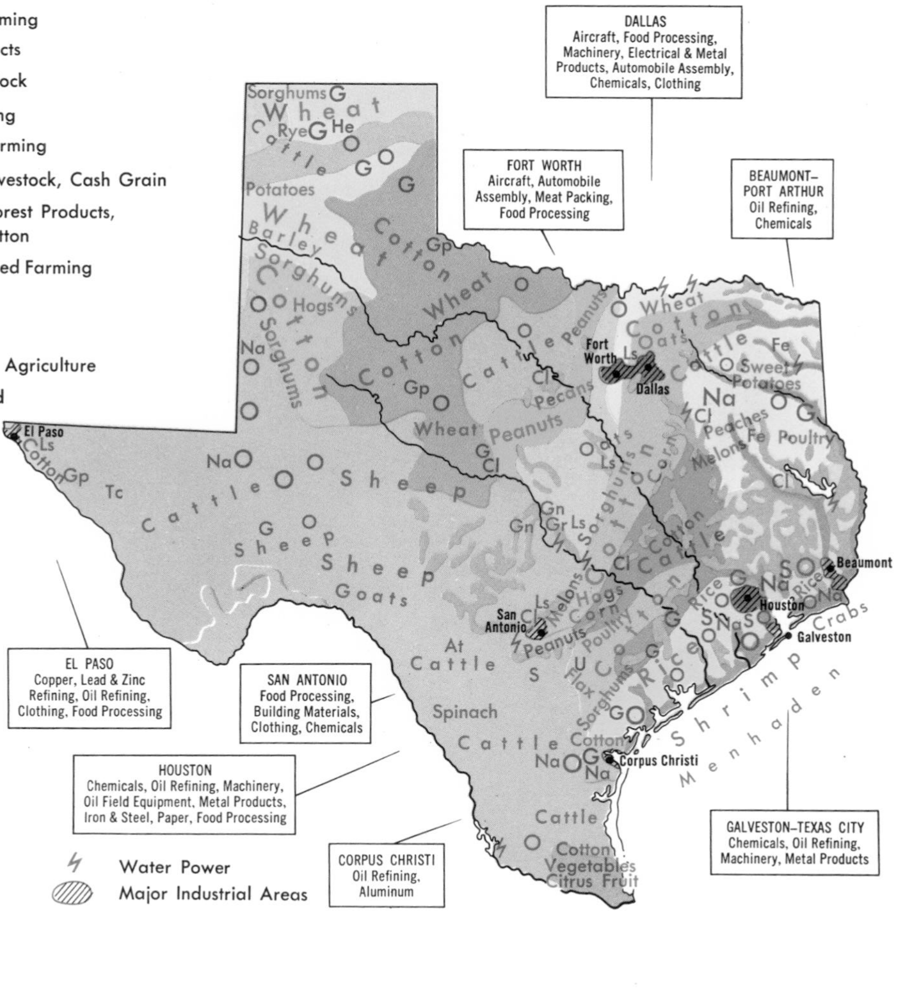
DALLAS
Aircraft, Food Processing, Machinery, Electrical & Metal Products, Automobile Assembly, Chemicals, Clothing
FORT WORTH
Aircraft, Automobile Assembly, Meat Packing, Food Processing
BEAUMONT–PORT ARTHUR
Oil Refining, Chemicals
EL PASO
Copper, Lead & Zinc Refining, Oil Refining, Clothing, Food Processing
SAN ANTONIO
Food Processing, Building Materials, Clothing, Chemicals
HOUSTON
Chemicals, Oil Refining, Machinery, Oil Field Equipment, Metal Products, Iron & Steel, Paper, Food Processing
CORPUS CHRISTI
Oil Refining, Aluminum
GALVESTON–TEXAS CITY
Chemicals, Oil Refining, Machinery, Metal Products
Fort Worth
Dallas
El Paso
San Antonio
Houston
Beaumont
Galveston
Corpus Christi
Sorghums
Wheat
Rye
Cattle
Potatoes
Barley
Cotton
Hogs
Sheep
Goats
Peanuts
Pecans
Oats
Sweet Potatoes
Peaches
Melons
Poultry
Corn
Rice
Flax
Spinach
Shrimp
Crabs
Menhaden
Vegetables
Citrus Fruit

Lockhart◉ (G8) 6,084
Lockney (C3) 2,141
Lone Star ‡(K5) 1,513
Longview◉ (K5) 40,050
Los Fresnos (G11) 1,289
Lubbock◉ (C4) 128,691
Lubbock (urban area) 129,289
Lufkin◉ (K6) 17,641
Luling (G8) 4,412
Lyford (G11) 1,554
Mabank (H5) 944
Madisonville◉ (J7) 2,324
Malakoff (H5) 1,657
Mansfield (F2) 1,375
Marble Falls (F7) 2,161
Marfa◉ (C12) 2,799
Marlin◉ (H6) 6,918
Marshall◉ (K5) 23,846
Mart (H6) 2,197
Mason◉ (E7) 1,910
Matador◉ (D3) 1,217
Mathis (G9) 6,075
McAllen (F11) 32,728
McCamey (B6) 3,375
McGregor (G6) 4,642
McKinney◉ (H4) 13,763
McLean (D2) 1,330
McNair (K1) 1,880
Memphis◉ (D3) 3,332
Menard◉ (E7) 1,914
Mentone◉ (D10) 226
Mercedes (F12) 10,943
Meridian◉ (G6) 993
Merkel (E5) 2,312
Mertzon◉ (C6) 584
Mesquite (H2) 27,526
Mexia (H6) 6,121
Miami◉ (D2) 656
Midland◉ (C6) 62,625
Midland (urban area) 63,274
Midlothian (G5) 1,521
Mineola (J5) 3,810
Mineral Wells (F5)..11,053
Mission (F11) 14,081
Monahans◉ (B6) 8,567
Mont Belvieu (L1) 1,230
Montague◉ (G4) 420
Morton◉ (B4) 2,731
Mount Pleasant◉ (K4) 8,027
Mount Vernon◉ (J4)..1,338
Muleshoe◉ (B3) 3,871
Munday (E4) 1,978
Nacogdoches◉ (J6)..12,674
Naples (K4) 1,692
Navasota (J7) 4,937
Nederland (K8) 12,036
New Boston (K4) 2,773
New Braunfels◉ (F8)..15,631
Newgulf (J8) 1,419
Newton◉ (L7) 1,233
Nixon (G8) 1,751
Nocona (G4) 3,127
North Richland Hills (F2) 8,662
Odem ‡(G10) 2,088
Odessa◉ (B6) 80,338
Odessa (urban area)..84,265
O'Donnell (C5) 1,356
Olmos Park ‡(F8) 2,457
Olney (F4) 3,872
Olton (B3) 1,917
Orange◉ (L7) 25,605
Overton (K5) 1,950
Ozona◉ (C7) 3,361
Paducah◉ (D4) 2,392
Paint Rock◉ (E6) 500
Palacios (H9) 3,676
Palestine◉ (J6) 13,974
Palo Pinto◉ (F5) 500
Pampa◉ (D2) 24,664
Panhandle◉ (C2) 1,958
Paris◉ (J4) 20,977
Pasadena (J2) 58,737
Pear Ridge ‡(L8) 3,470
Pearland (J2) 1,497
Pearsall◉ (E9) 4,957
Pecos◉ (D10) 12,728
Perryton◉ (D1) 7,903
Petersburg (C4) 1,400
Pharr (F11) 14,106
Phillips (C2) 3,605
Pilot Point (H4) 1,254
Pinehurst ‡(J7) 1,703
Pineland (L6) 1,236
Piney Point (J11) 1,790
Pittsburg◉ (J4) 3,796
Plains◉ (B4) 1,195

Plainview◉ (C3) 18,735
Plano (H4) 3,695
Pleasanton (F9) 3,467
Point Comfort (F9) 1,453
Port Arthur◉ (K8)..66,676
Port Arthur (urban area) 116,365
Port Isabel (G11) 3,575
Port Lavaca◉ (H9) 8,864
Port Neches (K7) 8,696
Portland (G10) 2,538
Post◉ (C4) 4,663
Poteet (F8) 2,811
Prairie View (J7) 2,326
Premont (F10) 3,049
Quanah◉ (E3) 4,564
Quitaque (C3) 586
Quitman (J5) 1,237
Ralls (C4) 2,229
Ranger (F5) 3,313
Rankin◉ (B6) 1,214
Raymondville◉ (G11)..9,385
Reese Village (B4) 1,433
Refugio◉ (G9) 4,944
Richardson (H1) 16,810
Richland Hills (F2)..7,804
Richmond◉ (J8) 4,686
Rio Grande City◉ (F11) 5,835
Rio Hondo (G11) 1,344
River Oaks (E2) 8,444
Robert Lee◉ (D5) 990
Robinson ‡(G6) 2,211
Robstown (G10) 10,266
Roby (D5) 913
Rockdale (G7) 4,481
Rockport◉ (H9) 2,989
Rocksprings◉ (D8) 1,182
Rockwall◉ (H5) 2,166
Roma-Los Saenz (E11) 1,496
Roscoe (D5) 1,490
Rosebud (G7) 1,644
Rosenberg (J8) 9,698
Rotan (D5) 2,788
Round Rock (G7) 1,878
Royse City (H4) 1,274
Rule (E4) 1,347
Rusk◉ (J6) 4,900
Sabinal (E8) 1,747
San Angelo◉ (D6)..58,815
San Angelo (urban area) 58,815
San Antonio◉ (F8)..587,718
San Antonio (urban area) 641,965
San Augustine◉ (K6)..2,584
San Benito (G12) 16,422
San Benito-Harlingen (urban area) 61,658
San Diego◉ (F10)..4,351
San Juan (F11) 4,371
San Marcos◉ (F8)..12,713
San Saba◉ (F6) 2,728
Sanderson◉ (B7) 2,189
Sansom Park Village (E2) 4,175
Santa Anna (E6) 1,320
Santa Rosa ‡(G11)..1,572
Sarita◉ (G10) 250
Schulenburg (H8) 2,207
Seabrook (K2) 2,600
Seagoville (H2) 3,745
Seagraves (B5) 2,307
Sealy (H8) 2,328
Seguin◉ (G8) 14,299
Seminole◉ (B5) 5,737
Seth Ward (C3) 1,328
Seymour◉ (E4) 3,789
Shamrock (D2) 3,113

Sherman◉ (H4) 24,988
Shiner (G8) 1,945
Sierra Blanca (B11)..786
Silsbee (K7) 6,277
Silverton◉ (C3) 1,098
Sinton◉ (G9) 6,008
Slaton (C4) 6,568
Smithville (G7) 2,933
Snyder◉ (D5) 13,850
Sonora◉ (D7) 2,619
Sourlake (K7) 1,602
South Houston (J2)..7,523
Southside Place (J2)..1,282
Spearman◉ (C1) 3,555
Spring Valley (J1) 3,004
Spur (D4) 2,170
Stafford (J2) 1,485
Stamford (E5) 5,259
Stanton◉ (C5) 2,228
Stephenville◉ (F5)..7,359
Sterling City◉ (D6)..854
Stinnett◉ (C2) 2,695
Stratford◉ (C1) 1,380
Sudan (B3) 1,235
Sugar Land (J8) 2,802
Sulphur Sprs.◉ (J4)..9,160
Sunray (C1) 1,967
Sweeny (J8) 3,087
Sweetwater◉ (D5)..13,914
Taft (G9) 3,463
Tahoka◉ (C4) 3,012
Taylor (G7) 9,434
Teague (H6) 2,728
Temple (G6) 30,419
Terrell (H5) 13,803
Terrell Hills (F8) 5,572
Texarkana◉ (L4) 30,218
Texarkana (urban area) 53,420
Texas City (K3) 32,065
Texas City-Galveston (urban area) 118,482
Three Rivers (F9) 1,932
Throckmorton◉ (F4)..1,299
Tilden◉ (F9) 325
Tomball (J7) 1,713
Trinity (J7) 1,787
Troup (J5) 1,667
Tulia◉ (C3) 4,410
Tyler◉ (J5) 51,230
Tyler (urban area) 51,739
Universal City ‡(F8)..3,377
University Park (H2)..23,202
Uvalde◉ (E8) 10,293
Van Alstyne (H4) 1,608
Van Horn◉ (C11) 1,953
Vega◉ (B2) 658
Vernon◉ (E3) 12,141
Victoria◉ (H9) 33,047
Vidor (K7) 4,938
Waco◉ (H6) 97,808
Waco (urban area)..116,163
Waelder (G8) 1,270
Waskom (L5) 1,336
Waxahachie◉ (H5)..12,749
Weatherford◉ (G5)..9,759
Weimar (H8) 2,006
Wellington◉ (D3) 3,137

Whitewright (H4) 1,315
Wichita Falls◉ (F4)..101,724
Wichita Falls (urban area) 102,104
Wills Point (J5) 2,281
Wilmer (H2) 1,785
Wink (A6) 1,863
Winnsboro (J5) 2,675
Winters (E6) 3,266
Wolfe City (J4) 1,317
Woodsboro◉ (G9) 2,081
Woodville◉ (K7) 1,920

Woodway ‡(G6) 1,244
Wooster (K2) 2,500
Wylie (H5) 1,804
Yoakum (G8) 5,761
Yorktown (G9) 2,527
Zapata◉ (E11) 2,031

OTHER FEATURES

Amarillo A.F.B. ....C 2
Alabama Coushatta Ind. Res. ....K 7

Amistad (dam) ....C 8
Angelina (river) ....K 6
Apache (mts.) C11
Aransas (passage) H10
Arlington (lake) ....F 2
Baffin (bay) G10
Balcones Escarpment (plateau) ....E 8
Beals (creek) ....C 5
Benbrook (res.) ....E 2
Bergstrom A.F.B. ....G 7
Big Bend Nat'l Park ....A 8

Biggs A.F.B. A10
Bolivar (peninsula) ....K 8
Brazos (river) ....H 7
Brownwood (lake) ....E 6
Buchanan (lake) ....F 7
Buck (creek) ....D 3
Cactus Ord. Works ....B 2
Caddo (lake) ....L 5
Canadian (river) ....B 2
Carrizo (creek) ....A 1
Carswell A.F.B. ....E 2
Cathedral (mt.) D12
Cavallo (passage) ....H 9
Cedar (lake) ....B 5
Cerro Alto (mt.) B10
Chinati (mts.) C12
Chinati (peak) C12
Chisos (mts.) ....A 8
Cibolo (creek) C12
Clear Fork (river) ....E 2
Clear Fk., Brazos (riv.)..D 5
Coldwater (creek) ....B 1
Colorado (river) ....F 7
Copano (bay) ....G 9
Corpus Christi (lake) ....F 9
Corpus Christi (passage)..G10
Corpus Christi N.A.S. G10
Cottonwood Draw (creek) C10
Davis (mts.) C11
Deep (creek) ....C 5
Delaware (creek) C10
Delaware (mts.) C10
Denison (dam) ....H 4
Devils (lake) ....D 8
Devils (river) ....C 7
Double Mountain Fork, Brazos (river) ....C 4
Eagle (peak) C11
Eagle Mountain (lake)..E 1
Edwards (plateau) D12
Elephant (mt.) D12
Ellington A.F.B. ....K 2
Elm Fork (river) ....H 4
Emory (peak) ....A 8
Falcon (dam) E11
Falcon (res.) E11
Finlay (mts.) B10
Fort Bliss A10
Fort Davis Nat'l Hist. Site D11
Fort Hood ....G 6
Frio (river) ....E 8
Galveston (bay) ....L 2
Galveston (isl.) ....K 8
Glass (mts.) ....A 7
Goodfellow A.F.B. ....D 6
Grapevine (res.) ....F 1
Guadalupe (mts.) C10
Guadalupe (peak) C10
Guadalupe (river) ....G 8
Houston (lake) ....J 8
Houston Ship (canal) ....K 2
Howard (creek) ....C 7
Hubbard Creek (res.)..E 5
Hueco (mts.) B10
Intracoastal Waterway..J 9
Johnson (creek) ....C 7
Kemp (lake) ....E 4
Kingsville N.A.S. G10
Kiowa (creek) ....D 1
Lampasas (river) ....G 6
Laredo A.F.B. E10
Lavaca (bay) ....H 9
Leon (river) ....F 6
Livermore (mt.) C11
Livingston (dam) ....K 7
Llano (river) ....D 7
Llano Estacado (Staked (plain) ....B 3
Locke (mt.) D11
Los Olmos (creek) F10
Los Olmos (creek) F11
Madre (lagoon) G11
Maravillas (creek) ....A 7
Matagorda (bay) ....H 9

Matagorda (peninsula)...J 9
Matagorda Isl. Bombing & Gunnery Range..H 9
Medina (lake) ....E 8
Medina (river) ....F 8
Middle Concho (river)..C 6
Mountain Creek (lake)..G 2
Mustang (creek) ....A 1
Mustang Draw (creek)..B 5
Navasota (river) ....H 7
N.A.S.A. Space Center..K 2
Navidad (river) ....H 8
Neches (river) ....K 6
North Bosque (river) ....G 6
North Concho (river) ....C 6
North Pease (river) ....D 3
Nueces (river) ....F 9
Padre (isl.) G10
Padre Is. Nat'l Seashore G11
Palo Duro (creek) ....D 5
Palo Duro (creek) ....C 1
Pease (river) ....D 3
Pecos (river) ....C 7
Pedernales (river) ....F 7
Possum Kingdom (res.)..F 5
Prairie Dog Town Fork (river) ....C 3
Pyote A.F.B. ....B 6
Quitman (mts.) B11
Red (river) ....F 3
Red Bluff (lake) D10
Rio Grande (river) ....D 9
Rita Blanca (river) ....C 1
Sabine (lake) ....L 8
Sabine (pass) ....L 7
Sabine (river) ....L 7
Saint Joseph (isl.) H10
Salt Fork, Red (river)..D 3
Sam Rayburn (res.) ....K 6
San Antonio (bay) ....H 9
San Antonio (mt.) B10
San Francisco (creek)..B 8
San Luis (passage) ....K 8
San Martine Draw (creek) C11
San Saba (river) ....D 7
Santa Isabel (creek)..E10
Santiago (mts.) ....A 8
Santiago (peak) D12
Shafter (lake) ....B 5
Sheppard A.F.B. ....F 3
Sierra Diablo (mts.)..C10
Sierra Vieja (mts.) C11
Spring (creek) ....D 6
Staked (Llano Estacado) (plain) ....B 3
Stockton (plateau) ....B 7
Sulphur (river) ....J 4
Sulphur Draw (creek)..B 4
Sulphur Springs (creek)..B 4
Tenmile (creek) ....G 2
Terlingua (creek) D12
Texarkana (res.) ....J 4
Texoma (lake) ....H 3
Tierra Blanca (creek)..B 3
Toledo Bend (dam) ....L 6
Toyah (creek) D11
Toyah (lake) ....A 6
Travis (lake) ....G 7
Trinity (bay) ....L 2
Trinity (river) ....H 5
Trujillo (creek) ....C 3
Walk (lake) ....C 8
Walnut (creek) ....F 2
Washita (river) ....D 2
Webb A.F.B. ....C 5
West (bay) ....K 8
White (lake) ....C 3
White Rock (creek) ....G 1
Wichita (river) ....F 4
Wolf (creek) ....D 1
Worth (lake) ....E 2

◉ County Seat.
‡ Name not on map.

TOPOGRAPHY

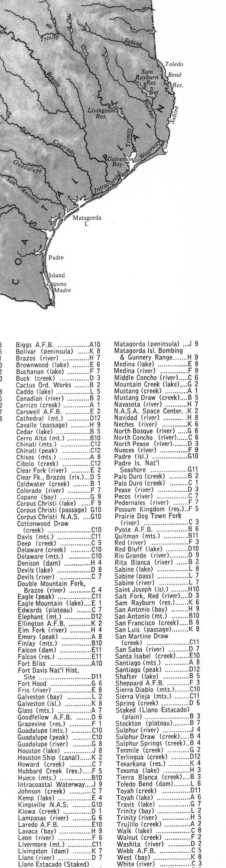

0   90   180
MILES

5,000 m. / 16,404 ft. — 2,000 m. / 6,562 ft. — 1,000 m. / 3,281 ft. — 500 m. / 1,640 ft. — 200 m. / 656 ft. — 100 m. / 328 ft. — Sea Level — Below

HIGHWAYS

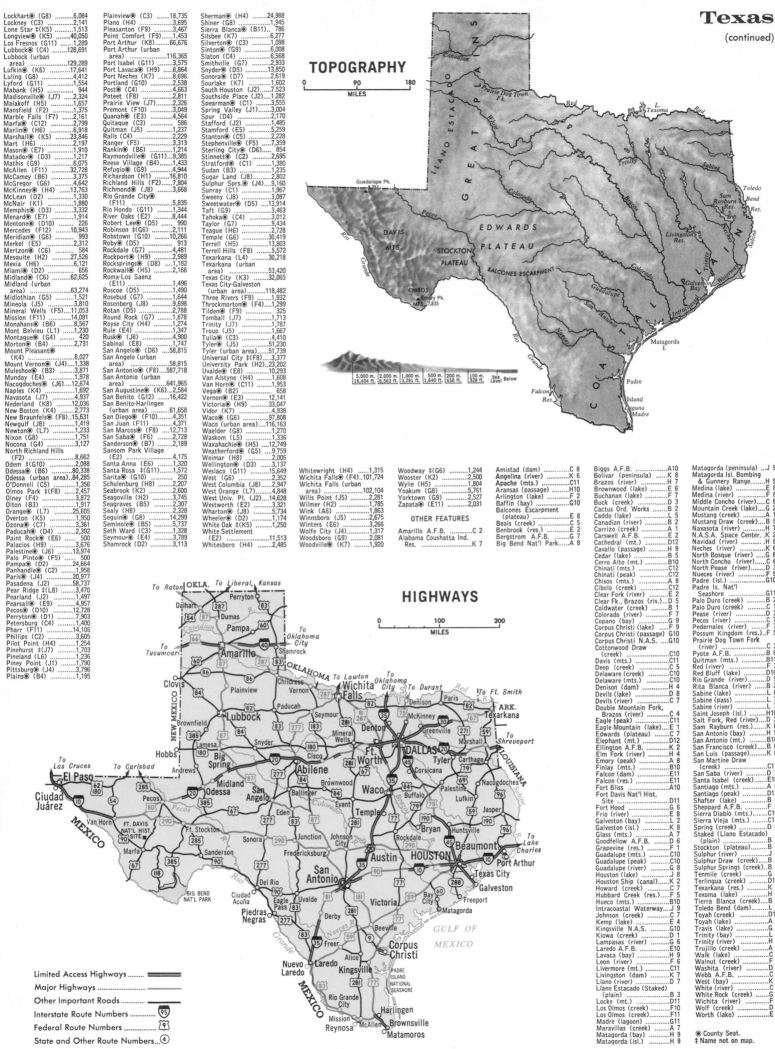

0   100   200
MILES

Limited Access Highways
Major Highways
Other Important Roads
Interstate Route Numbers ....[95]
Federal Route Numbers ....[9]
State and Other Route Numbers ....(4)

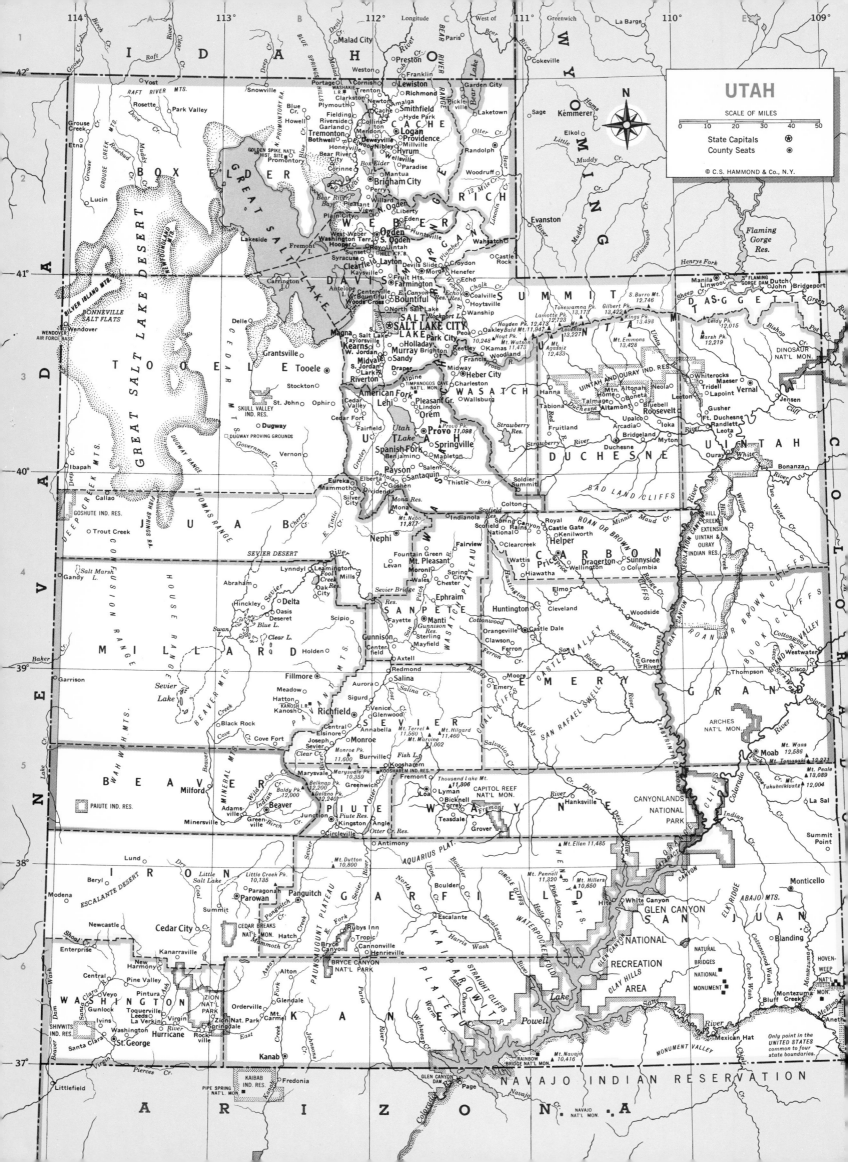

UTAH

SCALE OF MILES

0 10 20 30 40 50

⊛ State Capitals
⊙ County Seats

© C.S. Hammond & Co., N.Y.

UTAH

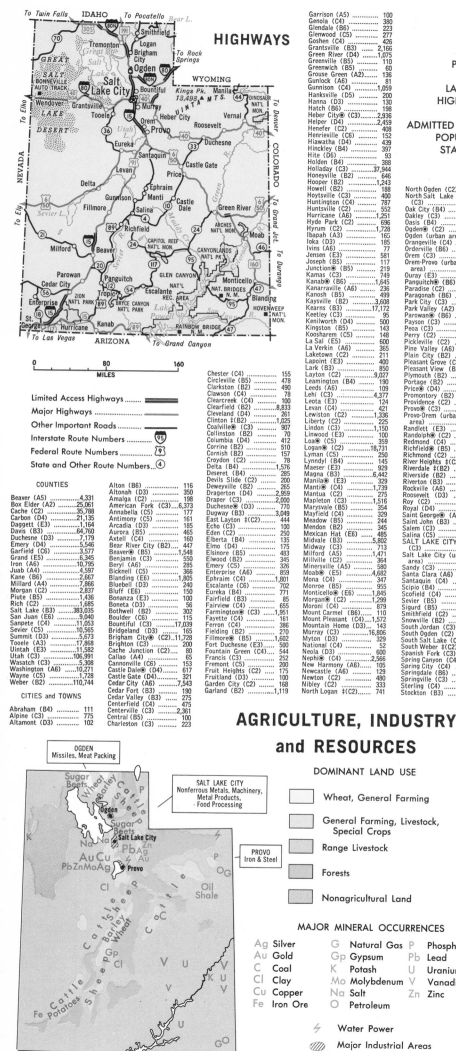

AREA	84,916 sq. mi.
POPULATION	990,000
CAPITAL	Salt Lake City
LARGEST CITY	Salt Lake City 189,454
HIGHEST POINT	Kings Pk. 13,498 ft.
SETTLED IN	1847
ADMITTED TO UNION	January 4, 1896
POPULAR NAME	Beehive State
STATE FLOWER	Sego Lily
STATE BIRD	Sea Gull

HIGHWAYS

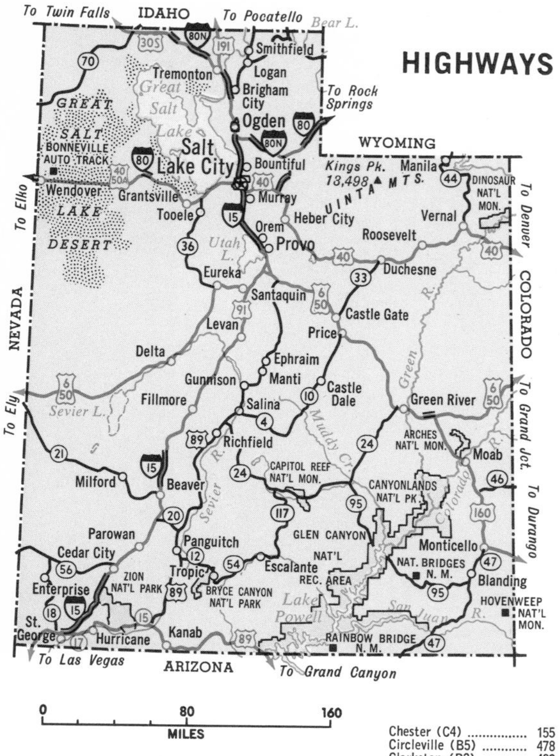
To Twin Falls
IDAHO
To Pocatello
Bear L.
Smithfield
Tremonton
Logan
Brigham City
To Rock Springs
Ogden
GREAT SALT LAKE DESERT
BONNEVILLE AUTO TRACK
Salt Lake City
Bountiful
WYOMING
Kings Pk. 13,498
Manila
DINOSAUR NAT'L MON.
Wendover
Grantsville
Murray
UINTA MTS.
To Elko
Tooele
Heber City
Vernal
Orem
Provo
Roosevelt
To Denver
Utah L.
Eureka
Duchesne
Santaquin
Castle Gate
NEVADA
Levan
Price
COLORADO
Delta
Ephraim
Gunnison
Manti
Castle Dale
Fillmore
Salina
Green River
Sevier L.
To Ely
Richfield
ARCHES NAT'L MON.
To Grand Jct.
CAPITOL REEF NAT'L MON.
Moab
Milford
Beaver
CANYONLANDS NAT'L PK.
To Durango
GLEN CANYON NAT'L REC. AREA
Parowan
Panguitch
Monticello
Cedar City
NAT. BRIDGES N.M.
Tropic
Escalante
Blanding
ZION NAT'L PARK
BRYCE CANYON NAT'L PARK
Enterprise
HOVENWEEP NAT'L MON.
St. George
Hurricane
Kanab
RAINBOW BRIDGE N.M.
To Las Vegas
ARIZONA
To Grand Canyon
0 80 160
MILES

Limited Access Highways	
Major Highways	
Other Important Roads	
Interstate Route Numbers	95
Federal Route Numbers	9
State and Other Route Numbers	4

COUNTIES

Beaver (A5)	4,331
Box Elder (A2)	25,061
Cache (C2)	35,788
Carbon (D4)	21,135
Daggett (E3)	1,164
Davis (B3)	64,760
Duchesne (D3)	7,179
Emery (D4)	5,546
Garfield (C6)	3,577
Grand (E5)	6,345
Iron (A6)	10,795
Juab (A4)	4,597
Kane (B6)	2,667
Millard (A4)	7,866
Morgan (C2)	2,837
Piute (B5)	1,436
Rich (C2)	1,685
Salt Lake (B3)	383,035
San Juan (E6)	9,040
Sanpete (C4)	11,053
Sevier (C5)	10,565
Summit (D3)	5,673
Tooele (A3)	17,868
Uintah (E3)	11,582
Utah (C3)	106,991
Wasatch (C3)	5,308
Washington (A6)	10,271
Wayne (C5)	1,728
Weber (B2)	110,744

CITIES and TOWNS

Abraham (B4)	111
Alpine (C3)	775
Altamont (D3)	102
Alton (B6)	116
Altonah (D3)	350
Amalga (C2)	198
American Fork (C3)	6,373
Annabella (C5)	177
Antimony (C5)	161
Arcadia (D3)	185
Aurora (B5)	465
Axtell (C4)	160
Bear River City (B2)	447
Beaver◉ (B5)	1,548
Benjamin (C3)	550
Beryl (A6)	285
Bicknell (C5)	366
Blanding (E6)	1,805
Bluebell (D3)	240
Bluff (E6)	150
Bonanza (E3)	100
Boneta (D3)	56
Bothwell (B2)	302
Boulder (C6)	115
Bountiful (C3)	17,039
Bridgeland (D3)	165
Brigham City◉ (C2)	11,728
Brighton (C3)	200
Cache Junction (C2)	80
Callao (A4)	65
Cannonville (C6)	153
Castle Dale◉ (D4)	617
Castle Gate (D4)	321
Cedar City (A6)	7,543
Cedar Fort (B3)	190
Cedar Valley (B3)	275
Centerfield (C4)	475
Centerville (C3)	2,361
Central (B5)	100
Charleston (C3)	223
Chester (C4)	155
Circleville (B5)	478
Clarkston (B2)	490
Clawson (C4)	78
Clearcreek (C4)	100
Clearfield (B2)	8,833
Cleveland (D4)	261
Clinton ‡(B2)	1,025
Coalville◉ (C3)	907
Collinston (B2)	70
Columbia (D4)	412
Corrine (B2)	510
Cornish (B2)	157
Croydon (C2)	78
Delta (B4)	1,576
Deseret (B4)	285
Devils Slide (C2)	200
Deweyville (B2)	265
Dragerton (D4)	2,959
Draper (C3)	2,000
Duchesne◉ (D3)	770
Dugway (B3)	3,049
East Layton ‡(C2)	444
Echo (C3)	100
Eden (C2)	250
Elberta (B4)	135
Elmo (D4)	175
Elsinore (B5)	483
Elwood (B2)	345
Emery (C5)	326
Enterprise (A6)	859
Ephraim (C4)	1,801
Escalante (C6)	702
Eureka (B4)	771
Fairfield (B3)	85
Fairview (C4)	655
Farmington◉ (C3)	1,951
Fayette (C4)	161
Ferron (C4)	386
Fielding (B2)	270
Fillmore◉ (B5)	1,602
Fort Duchesne (E3)	500
Fountain Green (C4)	544
Francis (C3)	252
Fremont (C5)	200
Fruit Heights (C2)	175
Fruitland (D3)	100
Garden City (C2)	168
Garland (B2)	1,119
Garrison (A5)	100
Genola (C4)	380
Glendale (B6)	223
Glenwood (C5)	277
Goshen (C4)	426
Grantsville (B3)	2,166
Green River (D4)	1,075
Greenville (B5)	110
Greenwich (B5)	60
Grouse Green (A2)	136
Gunlock (A6)	81
Gunnison (C4)	1,059
Hanksville (D5)	200
Hanna (D3)	130
Hatch (B6)	198
Heber City◉ (C3)	2,936
Helper (D4)	2,459
Henefer (C2)	408
Henrieville (C6)	152
Hiawatha (D4)	439
Hinckley (B4)	397
Hite (D6)	93
Holden (B4)	388
Holladay (C3)	37,944
Honeyville (B2)	646
Hooper (B2)	1,243
Howell (B2)	188
Hoytsville (C3)	400
Huntington (C4)	787
Huntsville (C2)	552
Hurricane (A6)	1,251
Hyde Park (C2)	696
Hyrum (C2)	1,728
Ibapah (A3)	165
Ioka (D3)	185
Ivins (A6)	77
Jensen (E3)	581
Joseph (B5)	117
Junction◉ (B5)	219
Kamas (C3)	749
Kanab◉ (B6)	1,645
Kanarraville (A6)	236
Kanosh (B5)	499
Kaysville (B2)	3,608
Kearns (B3)	17,172
Keetley (C3)	95
Kenilworth (D4)	500
Kingston (B5)	143
Koosharem (C5)	148
La Sal (E5)	600
La Verkin (A6)	365
Laketown (C2)	211
Lapoint (E3)	400
Lark (B3)	850
Layton (C2)	9,027
Leamington (B4)	190
Leeds (A6)	109
Lehi (C3)	4,377
Leota (E3)	124
Levan (C4)	421
Lewiston (C2)	1,336
Liberty (C2)	225
Lindon (C3)	1,150
Linwood (E3)	100
Loa◉ (C5)	359
Logan◉ (C2)	18,731
Lyman (C5)	250
Lynndyl (B4)	145
Maeser (E3)	929
Magna (B3)	6,442
Manila◉ (E3)	329
Manti◉ (C4)	1,739
Mantua (C2)	275
Mapleton (C3)	1,516
Marysvale (B5)	354
Mayfield (C4)	329
Meadow (B5)	244
Mendon (B2)	345
Mexican Hat (E6)	485
Midvale (B3)	5,802
Midway (C3)	713
Milford (A5)	1,471
Millville (C2)	364
Minersville (A5)	580
Moab◉ (E5)	4,682
Mona (C4)	347
Monroe (B5)	955
Monticello◉ (E6)	1,845
Morgan◉ (C2)	1,299
Moroni (C4)	879
Mount Carmel (B6)	110
Mount Pleasant (C4)	1,572
Mountain Home (D3)	143
Murray (C3)	16,806
Myton (D3)	329
National (C4)	52
Neola (D3)	600
Nephi◉ (C4)	2,566
New Harmony (A6)	105
Newcastle (A6)	129
Newton (C2)	480
Nibley (C2)	333
North Logan ‡(C2)	741
North Ogden (C2)	2,621
North Salt Lake (C3)	1,655
Oak City (B4)	312
Oakley (C3)	247
Oasis (B4)	190
Ogden◉ (C2)	70,197
Ogden (urban area)	121,927
Orangeville (C4)	571
Orderville (B6)	398
Orem (C3)	18,394
Orem-Provo (urban area)	60,795
Ouray (E3)	130
Panguitch◉ (B6)	1,435
Paradise (C2)	368
Paragonah (B6)	300
Park City (C3)	1,366
Park Valley (A2)	100
Parowan◉ (B6)	1,486
Payson (C3)	4,237
Peoa (C3)	200
Perry (C2)	587
Pickleville (C2)	94
Pine Valley (A6)	54
Plain City (B2)	1,152
Pleasant Grove (C3)	4,772
Pleasant View (B2)	927
Plymouth (B2)	231
Portage (B2)	189
Price◉ (D4)	6,802
Promontory (B2)	70
Providence (C2)	1,189
Provo◉ (C3)	36,047
Provo-Orem (urban area)	60,795
Randlett (E3)	400
Randolph◉ (C2)	537
Redmond (C4)	413
Richfield◉ (B5)	4,412
Richmond (C2)	977
River Heights ‡(C2)	880
Riverdale ‡(B2)	1,848
Riverside (B2)	295
Riverton (B3)	1,993
Rockville (A6)	138
Roosevelt (D3)	1,812
Roy (C2)	9,239
Royal (D4)	195
Saint George◉ (A6)	5,130
Saint John (B3)	168
Salem (C3)	920
Salina (C5)	1,618
SALT LAKE CITY◉ (C3)	189,454
Salt Lake City (urban area)	348,661
Sandy (C3)	3,322
Santa Clara (A6)	291
Santaquin (C4)	1,183
Scipio (B4)	328
Scofield (C4)	158
Sevier (B5)	65
Sigurd (B5)	339
Smithfield (C2)	2,512
Snowville (B2)	159
South Jordan (C3)	1,354
South Ogden (C2)	7,405
South Salt Lake (C3)	9,520
South Weber ‡(C2)	382
Spanish Fork (C3)	6,472
Spring Canyon (C4)	458
Spring City (C4)	463
Springdale (B6)	248
Springville (C3)	7,913
Sterling (C4)	137
Stockton (B3)	362
Summit (B6)	158
Sunnyside (D4)	1,740
Sunset (B2)	4,235
Syracuse (B2)	1,061
Tabiona (D3)	167
Talmage (D3)	175
Taylorsville (B3)	3,340
Teasdale (C5)	196
Thistle (C4)	86
Thompson (E5)	110
Tooele◉ (B3)	9,133
Toquerville (A6)	197
Torrey (C5)	128
Tremonton (B2)	2,115
Trenton (B2)	448
Tridell (E3)	250
Tropic (B6)	382
Uintah (C2)	344
Upalco (D3)	110
Venice (C5)	220
Vernal◉ (E3)	3,655
Vernon (B3)	160
Veyo (A6)	125
Virgin (A6)	124
Wales (C4)	130
Wallsburg (C3)	180
Wanship (C3)	150
Washington (A6)	445
Washington Terr. (B2)	6,441
Wattis (C4)	63
Wellington (D4)	1,066
Wellsville (C2)	1,106
Wendover (A3)	609
West Bountiful (B3)	945
West Jordan (B3)	3,009
West Point ‡(B2)	599
West Weber (B2)	500
Whiterocks (E3)	395
Willard (C2)	814
Woodland (C3)	200
Woodruff (C2)	169
Woods Cross (B3)	1,098
Yost (A2)	87
Zion Nat'l Park (B6)	63

OTHER FEATURES

Abajo (mts.)	E 6
Agassiz (mt.)	D 3
Antelope (isl.)	B 3
Aquarius (plateau)	C 5
Arches Nat'l Mon.	E 5
Bad Land (cliffs)	D 4
Bald (mt.)	C 3
Baldy (peak)	B 5
Bear (lake)	C 2
Bear (river)	B 2
Bear River (bay)	B 2
Bear River (range)	C 1
Beaver (mts.)	A 5
Belknap (peak)	B 5
Blue (lake)	B 4
Blue Springs (hills)	B 1
Bonneville Flats (salt deposit)	A 3
Book (cliffs)	E 4
Box Elder (lake)	B 2
Brown (Roan) (cliffs)	E 4
Bryce Canyon Nat'l Park	B 6
Canyonlands Nat'l Park	D 5
Capitol Reef Nat'l Mon.	C 5
Carrington (isl.)	B 3
Castle (valley)	D 4
Cataract (canyon)	D 5
Cedar (mts.)	B 3
Cedar Breaks Nat'l Mon.	B 6
Circle (cliffs)	C 6
Clay (hills)	D 6
Clear (lake)	B 4
Coal (cliffs)	C 5
Colorado (river)	C 7
Confusion (range)	A 4
Deep Creek (mts.)	A 4
Delano (peak)	B 5
Desolation (canyon)	E 4
Dinosaur Nat'l Mon.	E 3
Dirty Devil (river)	D 5
Dolores (river)	E 5
Duchesne (river)	D 3
Dugway (range)	A 3
Dugway Proving Grounds	B 3
Dutton (mt.)	B 5
East Canyon (res.)	C 3
Echo (res.)	C 3
Elk (ridge)	E 6
Ellen (mt.)	D 5
Escalante (desert)	A 6
Escalante (river)	C 6
Fish (lake)	C 5
Fish Springs (range)	A 4
Flaming Gorge (res.)	E 3
Fool Creek (res.)	B 4
Fremont (river)	C 5
Glen (canyon)	D 6
Glen Canyon Nat'l Rec. Area	D 6
Golden Spike Nat'l Hist. Site	B 2
Goshute Ind. Res.	A 4
Grand River (valley)	E 4
Gray (canyon)	D 4
Great Salt (lake)	B 2
Great Salt Lake (desert)	A 3
Green (river)	D 4
Grouse Creek (mts.)	A 2
Gunnison (res.)	C 4
Hayden (peak)	C 3
Henry (mts.)	D 6
Henrys Fork, Green (river)	E 2
Hilgard (mt.)	C 5
Hill A.F.B.	C 2
Hill Creek Ext., Uintah & Ouray Ind. Res.	E 4
Hillers (mt.)	D 6
House (range)	A 4
Hovenweep Nat'l Mon.	E 6
Hoyt (peak)	C 3
Indian (creek)	E 5
Indian (creek)	B 5
Jordan (river)	C 3
Kaiparowits (plateau)	C 6
Kanab (creek)	B 7
Kanosh Ind. Res.	B 5
Kings (peak)	D 3
Koosharem Ind. Res.	C 5
Labyrinth (canyon)	D 5
Lamotte (peak)	D 3
Leidy (peak)	E 3
Little Salt (lake)	A 6
Lovenia (mt.)	D 3
Malad (river)	B 1
Marsh (peak)	E 3
Marvine (mt.)	C 5
Marysvale (peak)	B 5
Mineral (mts.)	B 5
Minnie Maud (creek)	D 4
Mona (res.)	C 4
Monroe (peak)	B 5
Montezuma (creek)	E 6
Monument (valley)	D 6
Natural Bridges Nat'l Mon.	D 6
Navajo (mt.)	D 6
Navajo Ind. Res.	D 7
Nebo (mt.)	C 4
Newfoundland (mts.)	A 2
North Promontory (range)	B 2
Orange (cliffs)	D 5
Otter Creek (res.)	C 5
Paiute Ind. Res.	A 5
Panguitch (creek)	B 6
Paria (river)	B 6
Paunsaugunt (plateau)	B 6
Pavant (mts.)	B 5
Peale (mt.)	E 5
Pennell (mt.)	D 6
Pine (creek)	C 6
Pine Alcove (creek)	D 6
Piute (res.)	B 5
Powell (lake)	D 6
Price (river)	D 4
Provo (peak)	C 3
Provo (river)	C 3
Raft (river)	A 1
Raft River (mts.)	A 2
Rainbow Bridge Nat'l Mon.	C 6
Red (river)	D 3
Roan (Brown) (cliffs)	E 4
Rockport (lake)	C 3
Salaratus Wash (creek)	D 4
Salt Marsh (lake)	A 4
San Juan (river)	D 6
San Pitch (river)	C 4
San Rafael (river)	D 4
San Rafael Swell (cliffs)	D 5
Santa Clara (river)	A 6
Scofield (res.)	C 4
Sevier (desert)	B 4
Sevier (lake)	A 5
Sevier (river)	B 4
Sevier, East Fork (river)	B 6
Sevier Bridge (res.)	C 4
Shivwits Ind. Res.	A 6
Silver Island (mts.)	A 3
Skull Valley Ind. Res.	B 3
Spanish Fork (river)	C 3
Strait (cliffs)	C 6
Strawberry (river)	D 3
Swan (lake)	B 4
Thomas (range)	A 4
Thousand Lake (mt.)	C 5
Timpanogos Cave Nat'l Mon.	C 3
Tomasaki (mt.)	E 5
Tukuhnikivatz (mt.)	E 5
Uinta (mts.)	D 3
Uinta (river)	D 3
Uintah and Ouray Ind. Res.	D 3
Utah (lake)	C 3
Virgin (river)	A 6
Virgin, East Fork (river)	B 6
Wah Wah (mts.)	A 5
Wahweap (creek)	C 6
Wasatch (plateau)	C 4
Wasatch (range)	C 3
Washakie Ind. Res.	B 2
Waterpocket Fold (cliffs)	D 6
Weber (river)	C 3
Wendover A.F.B.	A 3
White (river)	E 3
Wild Cat (creek)	B 5
Zion Nat'l Park	A 6

◉ County Seat.
‡ Name not on map.

TOPOGRAPHY

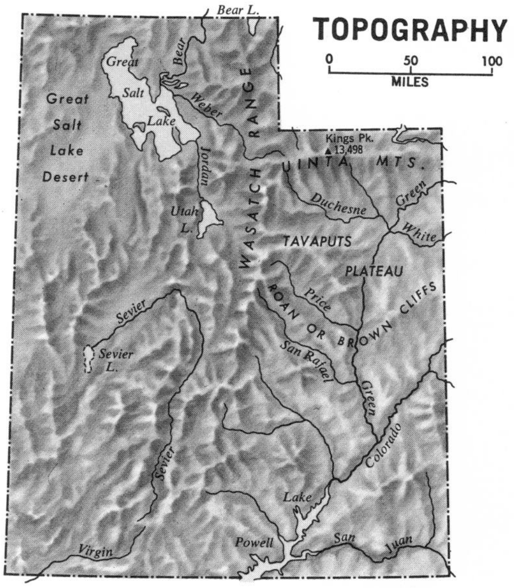
0 50 100
MILES
Bear L.
Great Salt Lake
Great Salt Lake Desert
Weber
Bear
Jordan
WASATCH RANGE
Kings Pk. 13,498
UINTA MTS.
Duchesne
Green
White
Utah L.
TAVAPUTS PLATEAU
Price
ROAN OR BROWN CLIFFS
San Rafael
Sevier
Sevier L.
Green
Colorado
Lake
Powell
San Juan
Virgin

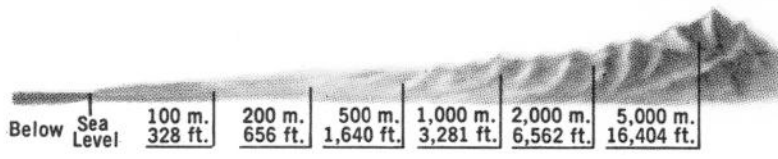
Below
Sea Level
100 m. 328 ft.
200 m. 656 ft.
500 m. 1,640 ft.
1,000 m. 3,281 ft.
2,000 m. 6,562 ft.
5,000 m. 16,404 ft.

AGRICULTURE, INDUSTRY and RESOURCES

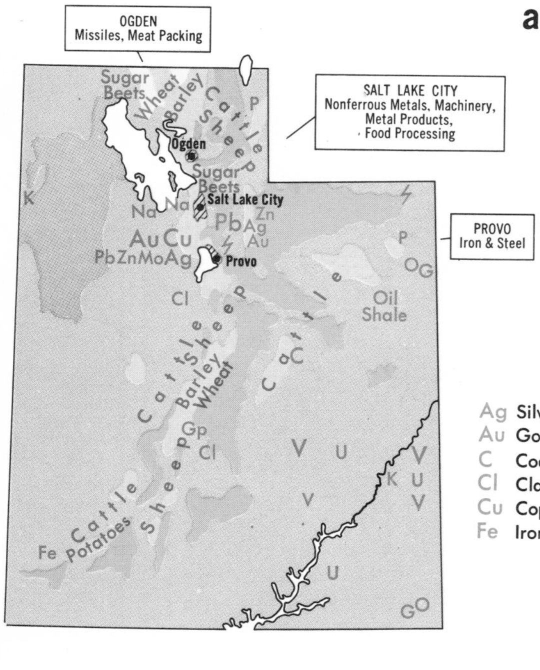
OGDEN
Missiles, Meat Packing
SALT LAKE CITY
Nonferrous Metals, Machinery, Metal Products, Food Processing
PROVO
Iron & Steel
Sugar Beets
Wheat
Barley
Cattle
Sheep
Ogden
Salt Lake City
Provo
Au Cu
Pb Ag
PbZnMoAg
Oil Shale
Cattle
Sheep
Wheat
Barley
Potatoes
Gp
Cl
V
U
K
O G
GO

DOMINANT LAND USE

- Wheat, General Farming
- General Farming, Livestock, Special Crops
- Range Livestock
- Forests
- Nonagricultural Land

MAJOR MINERAL OCCURRENCES

Ag	Silver	G	Natural Gas	P	Phosphates
Au	Gold	Gp	Gypsum	Pb	Lead
C	Coal	K	Potash	U	Uranium
Cl	Clay	Mo	Molybdenum	V	Vanadium
Cu	Copper	Na	Salt	Zn	Zinc
Fe	Iron Ore	O	Petroleum		

Water Power

Major Industrial Areas

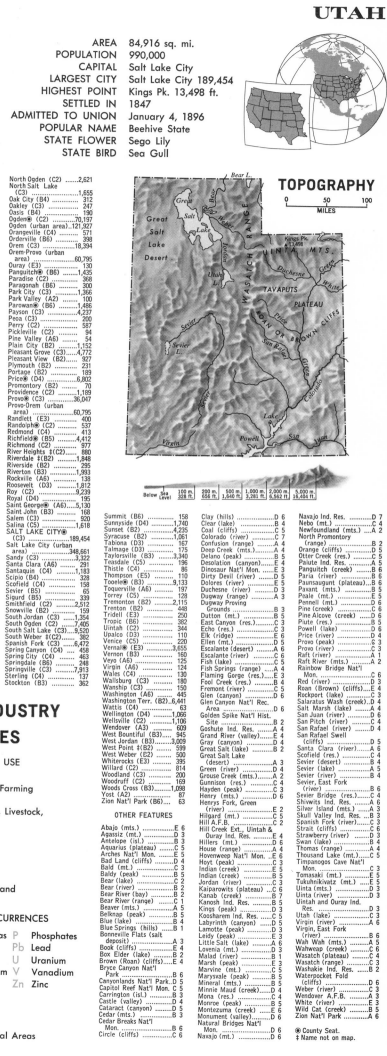

Virginia

TOPOGRAPHY

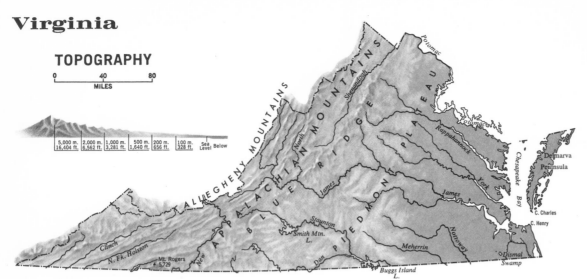

0　40　80
MILES

5,000 m.	2,000 m.	1,000 m.	500 m.	200 m.	100 m.	Sea Level
16,404 ft.	6,562 ft.	3,281 ft.	1,640 ft.	656 ft.	328 ft.	Below

COUNTIES

Accomack (S5) 30,635
Albemarle (L5) 30,969
Alleghany (H5) 12,128
Amelia (M6) 7,815
Amherst (K5) 22,953
Appomattox (L6) 9,148
Arlington (O3) 163,401
Augusta (K4) 37,363
Bath (J4) 5,335
Bedford (J6) 31,028
Bland (F6) 5,982
Botetourt (J5) 16,715
Brunswick (N7) 17,779
Buchanan (D6) 36,724
Buckingham (L5) 10,877
Campbell (K6) 32,958
Caroline (O4) 12,725
Carroll (G7) 23,178
Charles City (O6) 5,492
Charlotte (L7) 13,368
Chesterfield (N6) ...71,197
Clarke (M2) 7,942
Craig (H6) 3,356
Culpeper (M3) 15,088
Cumberland (M6) 6,360
Dickenson (D6) 20,211
Dinwiddie (N6) 22,183
Essex (P5) 6,690
Fairfax (O3) 275,002
Fauquier (N3) 24,066
Floyd (H7) 10,462
Fluvanna (M5) 7,227
Franklin (H7) 25,925
Frederick (M2) 21,941
Giles (G6) 17,219
Gloucester (P6) 11,919
Goochland (N5) 9,206
Grayson (F7) 17,390
Greene (M4) 4,715
Greensville (N7) 16,155
Halifax (L7) 33,637
Hanover (N5) 27,550
Henrico (O6) 117,339
Henry (J7) 40,335
Highland (J4) 3,221
Isle of Wight (O7) ..17,164
James City (P6) 11,539
King and Queen (P5)...5,889
King George (O4) 7,243
King William (O5) 7,563
Lancaster (R5) 9,174
Lee (B7) 25,824
Loudoun (N2) 24,549
Louisa (N5) 12,959
Lunenburg (M7) 12,523
Madison (M4) 8,187
Mathews (R6) 7,121
Mecklenburg (M7) 31,428
Middlesex (R5) 6,319
Montgomery (H6) 32,923
Nansemond (P7) 31,366
Nelson (L5) 12,752
New Kent (P5) 4,504
Northampton (S6) 16,966
Northumberland (R5)..10,185
Nottoway (M6) 15,141
Orange (M4) 12,900
Page (M3) 15,572
Patrick (H7) 15,282
Pittsylvania (K7) ...58,296
Powhatan (N5) 6,747
Prince Edward (M6)...14,121
Prince George (O6)...20,270
Prince William (O3)..50,164
Pulaski (G6) 27,258
Rappahannock (M3)....5,368
Richmond (P5) 6,375
Roanoke (H6) 61,693
Rockbridge (K5) 24,039
Rockingham (L4) 40,485
Russell (D7) 26,290
Scott (C7) 25,813
Shenandoah (L3) 21,825
Smyth (E7) 31,066
Southampton (O7) 27,195
Spotsylvania (N4) ...13,819
Stafford (N4) 16,876
Surry (P6) 6,220
Sussex (O7) 12,411
Tazewell (E6) 44,791
Warren (M3) 14,655
Washington (D7) 38,076
Westmoreland (P4)....11,042
Wise (C6) 43,579
Wythe (F7) 21,975
York (P6) 21,583

CITIES and TOWNS

Abingdon◉ (D7) 4,758
Accomac◉ (S5) 414
Acorn (P4) 71
Adner (P5) 71
Advance Mills (L4) 100
Afton (M4) 200
Agricola (K5) 125
Alberene (L5) 300
Alberta (N7) 430

Alexandria* (P3) ...91,023
Alleghany (H5) 165
Allisonia (G7) 329
Altavista (K6) 3,299
Alton (K7) 53
Alvarado (E7) 50
Amelia C.H.◉ (N6)......775
Amherst◉ (K5) 1,200
Amissville (M3) 100
Ammon (N6) 65
Amonate (E6) 250
Andersonville (L6) 80
Andover (C7) 400
Appalachia (C7) 2,456
Appomattox◉ (L6) ...1,184
Ararat (G7) 500
Arcadia (J5) 100
Arrington (L5) 325
Artrip (D7) 200
Arvonia (M5) 400
Ashburn (O2) 231
Ashland (N5) 2,773
Atkins (F7) 500
Atlee (O5) 140
Augusta Springs (K4)...400
Austinville (F7) 900
Axton (J7) 175
Aylett (O5) 496
Ballsville (M6) 250
Banco (M4) 120
Banner (D7) 450
Barboursville (M4) 250
Barren Springs (G7) ...125
Baskerville (M7) 715
Bassett (J7) 3,148
Bastian (F6) 800
Batesville (L5) 400
Baywood (G7) 125
Bealeton (N3) 500
Beaverdam (N5) 500
Beaverlett (R6) 188
Bedford◉ (J6) 5,921
Belle Haven (S5) 371
Belspring (G6) 354
Ben Hur (B7) 500
Benhams (D7) 250
Benns Church (P7) 100
Bent Creek (L5) 80
Bent Mountain (H6) 88
Bentonville (M3) 700
Berea (N4) 350
Bergton (L3) 105
Berryville◉ (M2) ...1,645
Big Island (K5) 500
Big Rock (D6) 100
Big Stone Gap (C7)...4,688
Birchleaf (D6) 650

Birdsnest (S6) 375
Blacksburg (H6) 7,070
Blackstone (N6) 3,659
Blackwater (B7) 500
Blairs (K7) 186
Bland◉ (F6) 500
Bloxom (S5) 349
Blue Grass (J3) 105
Blue Ridge (J6) 400
Bluefield (F6) 4,235
Bluemont (N2) 250
Bluff City (R6) 350
Bohannon (R6) 150
Boissevain (E6) 400
Bon Air (N5) 700
Bonny Blue (B7) 285
Boones Mill (J6) 371
Boonesville (M4) 125
Boulevard (P6) 100
Bowling Green◉ (O4)....528
Boxwood (J7) 55
Boyce (M2) 384
Boydton◉ (M7) 449
Boykins (O7) 710
Branchville (O7) 158
Brandon (O6) 100
Brandy Station (N4)....275
Breaks (D6) 312
Bremo Bluff (M5) 850
Bridgewater (K4) 1,815
Brightwood (M4) 650
Bristol* (D7) 17,144
Bristow (N3) 75
Broadford (E7) 900
Broadway (L3) 646
Brodnax (N7) 561
Brokenburg (N4) 200
Brooke (O4) 300
Brookland (N5) 38,845
Brookneal (L6) 1,070
Brownsburg (K5) 200
Browntown (M3) 300
Brucetown (M2) 200
Buchanan (J5) 1,349
Buckhorn (P7) 100
Buckingham◉ (L5) 218
Buena Vista* (K5) ...6,300
Buffalo Junction (L7)..80
Bumpass (N5) 110
Burgess (R5) 613
Burges Garden (F6)....380
Burkeville (M6) 705
Caledonia (M5) 100
Callands (J7) 118
Callao (P5) 450
Callaville (N7) 45
Callaway (H7) 275
Calverton (N3) 250

Cambria (H6) 722
Camp (F7) 200
Cana (G7) 150
Cape Charles (R6)....2,041
Capeville (R6) 350
Capron (O7) 327
Cardwell (N5) 150
Carloover (J5) 75
Carrie (D6) 500
Carrsville (P7) 100
Carson (O6) 100
Cartersville (M5) 103
Carysbrook (M5) 62
Casanova (N3) 350
Cascade (J7) 200
Castlewood (D7) 250
Catawba (H6) 150
Catlett (N3) 420
Cedar Bluff (E6) 995
Cedar Springs (F7) 150
Cedarville (M3) 150
Cedon (O4) 75
Center Cross (P5) 100
Champlain (O4) 400
Chancellor (N4) 263
Charles City◉ (O6) 30
Charlotte C.H.◉ (L6)...555
Charlottesville◉ (M4)29,427
Chase City (M7) 3,207
Chatham◉ (K7) 1,822
Check (H6) 125
Cheriton (R6) 761
Cherry Hill (O3) 500
Chesapeake* (R7)....73,647
Chester (O6) 1,290
Chesterfield◉ (N6) 174
Chilhowie (E7) 1,169
Chincoteague (T5)....2,131
Christiansburg◉ (H6)..3,653
Chuckatuck (P7) 500
Chula (N6) 111
Church Road (N6) 120
Church View (P5) 150
Churchville (K4) 300
Cismont (M4) 400
Claremont (P6) 377
Clarksville (M7) 1,530
Claudville (H7) 156
Clay Bank (P6) 120
Clayville (N6) 150
Cleveland (E6) 415
Clifford (K5) 125
Clifton (O3) 230
Clifton Forge* (J5)..5,268
Clinchburg (E7) 425
Clinchco (D6) 1,390
Clinchport (C7) 302

Clintwood◉ (D6) 1,400
Clover (L7) 261
Cloverdale (J6) 750
Cluster Springs (L7)...200
Cobbs Creek (R6) 350
Cobham (M4) 350
Coburn (D7) 2,471
Cohasset (M5) 100
Collierstown (J5) 150
Collinsville (J7) ...3,586
Colonial Beach (P4)..1,769
Colonial Heights* (O6).9,587
Colony (N5) 100
Columbia (M5) 200
Columbia Furnace (L3)..100
Comers Rock (F7) 250
Comorn (O4) 88
Concord (K6) 700
Coniceville (L3) 59
Cootes Store (L3) 225
Copper Valley (G7)....450
Courtland◉ (O7) 855
Covesville (L5) 400
Covington◉* (H5) ...11,062
Craigsville (J4) 978
Crandon (G6) 135
Crewe (M6) 2,012
Criglersville (M4) 65
Crimora (L4) 500
Cripple Creek (F7) 200
Critz (H7) 199
Crockett (F7) 125
Cross Junction (M2)....100
Crozet (L4) 1,500
Crozier (N5) 200
Crystal Hill (L7) 325
Cullen (L6) 167
Culpeper◉ (M4) 2,412
Cumberland◉ (M6) 400
Dahlgren (O4) 300
Daleville (J6) 200
Damascus (E7) 1,485
Dante (D7) 1,436
Darwin (C6) 200
Davenport (D6) 484
Dayton (L4) 930
De Jarnette (O5) 75
Delaplane (N3) 188
Deltaville (R5) 800
Dendron (P6) 403
Denniston (L7) 100
Deskins (D6) 375
DeWitt (N6) 452
Dillwyn (M5) 515
Dinwiddie◉ (N6) 350
Disputanta (O6) 400
Dorchester (C7) 90

Doswell (N5) 200
Downings (P5) 110
Drakes Branch (L7)....759
Draper (G7) 233
Drewrys Bluff (N6) 210
Drewryville (O7) 195
Drill (E6) 275
Dry Fork (K7) 250
Dryden (B7) 425
Dublin (G6) 1,427
Duffield (C7) 97
Dumfries (O3) 1,368
Dunbar (C6) 200
Dunbrooke (P5) 150
Dundas (M7) 250
Dungannon (D7) 444
Dunnsville (P5) 250
Eagle Rock (J5) 500
Earls (N6) 100
Earlysville (M4) 450
East Lexington (K5)....245
East Stone Gap (C7)....500
Eastville◉ (R6) 261
Eclipse (R7) 350
Edgehill (O4) 200
Edgerton (N7) 165
Edinburg (M3) 517
Edom (L3) 185
Eggleston (G6) 400
Elk Creek (F7) 150
Elk Garden (E7) 125
Elkton (L4) 1,506
Elliston (H6) 700
Emmerton (P5) 165
Emory (E7) 300
Emporia◉ (N7) 5,535
Esmont (L5) 750
Esserville (G2) 1,000
Etlan (M3) 300
Ettrick (N6) 2,998
Evergreen (L6) 256
Evington (K6) 100
Ewing (B7) 600
Exmore (S6) 1,566
Faber (L5) 100
Fair Port (R6) 100
Fairfax◉* (O3) 13,585
Fairfield (K5) 265
Fairlawn (G6) 1,325
Fairview (C7) 125
Falls Church* (O3)..10,192
Falls Mills (F6) 100
Falmouth (O4) 1,478
Farmville◉ (M6) 4,293
Farnham (P5) 200
Ferrum (H7) 600
Fieldale (H7) 1,499
Fincastle◉ (J6) 403

Fishersville (K4) 475
Flint Hill (M3) 250
Floyd◉ (H7) 487
Ford (N6) 350
Fordwick (K4) 600
Forest (K6) 350
Fork Union (M5) 250
Forks of Buffalo (K5)..110
Fort Blackmore (C7)....250
Fort Defiance (L4) 100
Fort Mitchell (M7) 64
Fosters Falls (G7) 152
Fox (F7) 5
Franklin* (P7) 7,264
Franktown (S6) 100
Fredericks Hall (N4)...125
Fredericksburg* (N4).13,639
Free Union (M4) 65
Fremont (D6) 65
Fries (F7) 1,039
Front Royal◉ (M3) ...7,949
Gainesboro (M2) 110
Gainesville (N3) 200
Galax* (G7) 5,254
Gasburg (N7) 300
Gate City◉ (C7) 2,142
Georges Fork (C6) 500
Gibson Station (A7)....500
Glade Spring (E7) ...1,407
Gladehill (J7) 200
Gladys (K6) 175
Glamorgan (C6) 100
Glasgow (K5) 1,091
Glen Allen (N5) 728
Glen Lyn (G6) 222
Glen Wilton (J5) 350
Glenwood (K7) 1,857
Gloucester◉ (P6) 600
Gloucester Point (R6)..800
Goldbond (G6) 343
Goochland◉ (N5) 125
Goode (K6) 350
Gordonsville (M4) ...1,109
Gore (M2) 500
Goshen (K5) 99
Grafton (P6) 500
Green Bay (M6) 500
Greenbackville (T5)....100
Greenbush (S5) 125
Greenfield (L5) 100
Greenville (K5) 450
Greenwood (L4) 650
Gretna (K7) 900
Grimstead (R5) 250
Grottoes (L4) 969
Grundy◉ (D6) 2,287
Guinea (O4) 325
Gum Spring (N5) 120
Hacksneck (S5) 185
Hague (P5) 75
Halifax◉ (L7) 792
Hallsboro (N6) 100
Hallwood (S5) 269
Hamilton (N2) 403
Hampden-Sydney (L6)....650
Hampton* (P7) 89,258
Hampton-Newport News
  (urban area) 208,874
Handsom (O7) 100
Hanover◉ (O5) 500
Hansonville (D7) 100
Harborton (S5) 350
Harman-Maxie (D6) 100
Harrisonburg◉ (K4)..11,916
Harriston (L4) 98
Haymarket (N3) 257
Haysi (D6) 485
Healing Springs (J5)...250
Healys (R5) 75
Heathsville◉ (P5) 300
Henry (J7) 250
Herndon (O3) 1,960
Hewlett (O5) 200
Highland Springs (O5).5,497
Hillsboro (N2) 124
Hillsville◉ (G7) 905
Hiltons (D7) 300
Hiwassee (G6) 500
Hoadly (O3) 350
Hobson (P7) 500
Holland (P7) 338
Hollins (J6) 800
Holston (D7) 89
Honaker (D6) 851
Hopeton (S5) 316
Hopewell* (O6) 17,895
Hopkins (S5) 80
Horntown (T5) 400
Hot Springs (J4) 800
Huddleston (J6) 75
Hume (N3) 275
Huntly (M3) 100

Hurley (D6) 900
Hurt (K6) 800
Hylas (N5) 64
Independence◉ (F7)....679
Indian Neck (O5) 203
Indian Valley (G7) 112
Iron Gate (J5) 716
Irvington (R5) 570
Irwin (N5) 50
Isle of Wight◉ (P7)...150
Ivanhoe (G7) 900
Ivor (P7) 398
Jamestown (P6) 5
Jarratt (O7) 608
Java (K7) 150
Jeffersonton (N3) 400
Jeffress (L7) 69
Jennings Ordinary (M6).125
Jericho (P7) 2,300
Jerome (L3) 250
Jetersville (M6) 150
Jewell Ridge (E6) 250
Jonesville◉ (B7) 710
Joyner (O7) 75
Keeling (K7) 250
Keezletown (L4) 275
Keller (S5) 263
Kenbridge (M7) 1,188
Keokee (C7) 410
Keswick (M4) 500
Keysville (M6) 733
Kilmarnock (R5) 927
King George◉ (O4) 350
King William◉ (O5)....200
Kinsale (P4) 250
Konnarock (E7) 125
La Crosse (M7) 726
Lacey Spring (L3) 100
Ladysmith (N4) 350
Lafayette (H6) 250
Lahore (M4) 12
Lambsburg (G7) 300
Lancaster◉ (R5) 150
Lanesville (P5) 57
Laurel Fork (G7) 938
Lawrenceville◉ (N7)..1,941
Lebanon◉ (D7) 2,085
Lebanon Church (L2)....50
Leesburg◉ (N2) 2,869
Leesville (K6) 75
Lexington◉ (J5) 7,537
Lightfoot (P6) 950
Lilian (R5) 200
Limeton (M3) 400
Linden (M3) 700
Little Plymouth (P5)...210
Littleton (D7) 123
Lively (P5) 275
Locustville (S5) 175
Long Island (K6) 90
Longshoal (G7) 100
Lorton (O3) 500
Lottsburg (P5) 650
Louisa◉ (N5) 576
Lovettsville (N2) 217
Lowesville (K5) 100
Lowmoor (J5) 900

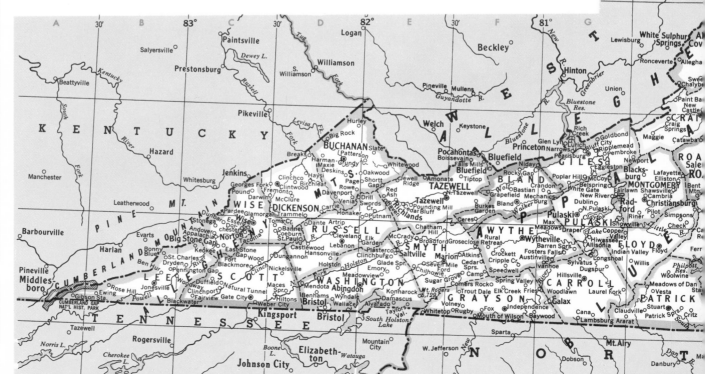

A　30′　83°　B　30′　C　82°　D　30′　E　81°　F　G

VIRGINIA

AREA	40,815 sq. mi.
POPULATION	4,457,000
CAPITAL	Richmond
LARGEST CITY	Norfolk 304,869
HIGHEST POINT	Mt. Rogers 5,729 ft.
SETTLED IN	1607
ADMITTED TO UNION	June 26, 1788
POPULAR NAME	Old Dominion
STATE FLOWER	Dogwood
STATE BIRD	Cardinal

(continued on following page)

Virginia
(continued)

AGRICULTURE, INDUSTRY and RESOURCES

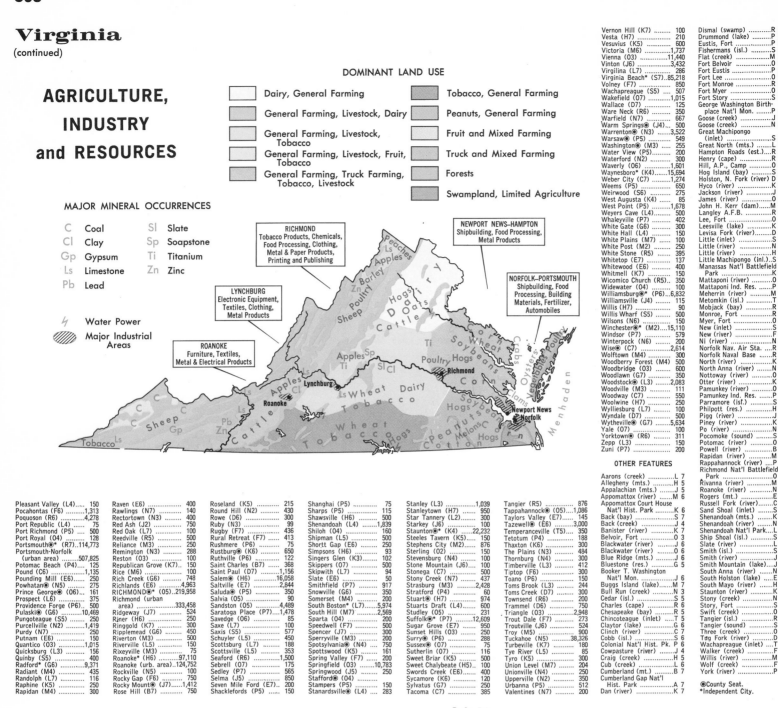

DOMINANT LAND USE

- Dairy, General Farming
- General Farming, Livestock, Dairy
- General Farming, Livestock, Tobacco
- General Farming, Livestock, Fruit, Tobacco
- General Farming, Truck Farming, Tobacco, Livestock
- Tobacco, General Farming
- Peanuts, General Farming
- Fruit and Mixed Farming
- Truck and Mixed Farming
- Forests
- Swampland, Limited Agriculture

MAJOR MINERAL OCCURRENCES

C	Coal	Sl	Slate
Cl	Clay	Sp	Soapstone
Gp	Gypsum	Ti	Titanium
Ls	Limestone	Zn	Zinc
Pb	Lead		

Water Power
Major Industrial Areas

RICHMOND Tobacco Products, Chemicals, Food Processing, Clothing, Metal & Paper Products, Printing and Publishing

NEWPORT NEWS–HAMPTON Shipbuilding, Food Processing, Metal Products

LYNCHBURG Electronic Equipment, Textiles, Clothing, Metal Products

NORFOLK–PORTSMOUTH Shipbuilding, Food Processing, Building Materials, Fertilizer, Automobiles

ROANOKE Furniture, Textiles, Metal & Electrical Products

Index (upper right)

Vernon Hill (K7) 100
Vesta (H7) 210
Vesuvius (K5) 600
Victoria (M6) 1,737
Vienna (O3) 11,440
Vinton (J6) 3,432
Virgilina (L7) 286
Virginia Beach* (S7) 85,218
Volney (F7) 850
Wachapreague (S5) 507
Wakefield (O7) 1,015
Wallace (E6) 275
Ware Neck (R6) 350
Warfield (N7) 667
Warm Springs⊙ (J4)
Warrenton⊙ (N3) 3,522
Warsaw⊙ (P5) 549
Washington⊙ (M3) 255
Water View (P5) 200
Waterford (N2) 300
Waverly (O6) 1,601
Waynesboro* (K4) 15,694
Weber City (C7) 1,274
Weems (P5) 650
Weirwood (S6) 275
West Augusta (K4) 85
West Point (P5) 1,678
Weyers Cave (L4) 500
Whaleyville (P7) 402
White Gate (G6) 300
White Hall (L4) 150
White Plains (M7) 100
White Post (M2) 250
White Stone (R5) 395
Whitetop (E7) 137
Whitewood (E6) 400
Whitmell (K7) 150
Wicomico Church (R5) 350
Widewater (O4) 100
Williamsburg⊙* (P6) 6,832
Williamsville (J4) 115
Willis (H7) 90
Willis Wharf (S5) 500
Wilsons (N6) 150
Winchester⊙* (M2) 15,110
Windsor (P7) 579
Winterpock (N6) 200
Wise⊙ (C7) 2,614
Wolftown (M4) 300
Woodberry Forest (M4) 500
Woodbridge (O3) 600
Woodlawn (G7) 350
Woodstock⊙ (L3) 2,083
Woodville (M3) 111
Woodway (G7) 550
Woolwine (H7) 250
Wylliesburg (L7) 100
Wyndale (D7) 500
Wytheville⊙ (G7) 5,634
Yale (O7) 150
Yorktown⊙ (R6) 311
Zepp (L3) 150
Zuni (P7) 200

OTHER FEATURES

Aarons (creek) L7
Alleghany (mts.) H5
Appalachian (mts.) J5
Appomattox (river) M6
Appomattox Court House Nat'l Hist. Park J6
Back (bay) S7
Back (creek) J4
Banister (river) K7
Belvoir, Fort O3
Blackwater (river) J6
Blackwater (river) O6
Blue Ridge (mts.) J4
Bluestone (res.) G5
Booker T. Washington Nat'l Mon. J6
Buggs Island (lake) M7
Bull Run (creek) N3
Cedar (isl.) S5
Charles (cape) R6
Chesapeake (bay) R5
Chincoteague (inlet) T5
Claytor (lake) G6
Clinch (river) C7
Cobb (isl.) S6
Colonial Nat'l Hist. Pk. R6
Cowpasture (river) J4
Craig (creek) H5
Cub (creek) L6
Cumberland (mt.) B7
Cumberland Gap Nat'l Hist. Park A7
Dan (river) K7
Dismal (swamp) R8
Drummond (lake) P7
Eustis, Fort P6
Fishermans (isl.) S6
Flat (creek) M6
Fort Belvoir O3
Fort Eustis P6
Fort Lee O6
Fort Monroe O3
Fort Myer O3
Fort Story S7
George Washington Birthplace Nat'l Mon. P4
Goose (creek) J6
Goose (creek) N3
Great Machipongo (inlet) S6
Great North (mts.) L3
Hampton Roads (est.) R7
Henry (cape) O4
Hill, A.P., Camp O4
Hog Island (bay) S6
Holston, N. Fork (river) D7
Hyco (river) K8
Jackson (river) J4
James (river) M7
John H. Kerr (dam) M7
Langley A.F.B. R6
Lee, Fort O6
Leesville (lake) K6
Levisa Fork (river) B6
Little (inlet) S6
Little (river) G6
Little (river) N5
Little (river) J7
Little Machipongo (inl.) S6
Manassas Nat'l Battlefield Park K3
Mattaponi (river) O5
Mattaponi Ind. Res. O5
Meherrin (river) M7
Metomkin (isl.) T5
Mobjack (bay) R6
Monroe, Fort O3
Myer, Fort O3
New (inlet) S6
New (river) F6
Ni (river) N4
Norfolk Nav. Air Sta. R7
Norfolk Naval Base R7
North (river) K4
North Anna (river) N4
Nottoway (river) O4
Otter (river) K6
Pamunkey (river) O5
Pamunkey Ind. Res. P5
Parramore (isl.) S6
Philpott (res.) H7
Pigg (river) J7
Piney (river) K5
Po (river) N4
Pocomoke (sound) S5
Potomac (river) O3
Powell (river) B7
Rapidan (river) M4
Rappahannock (river) P4
Richmond Nat'l Battlefield Park O6
Rivanna (river) M5
Roanoke (river) N8
Rogers (mt.) F7
Russell Fork (river) C5
Sand Shoal (inlet) S6
Shenandoah (mts.) N2
Shenandoah (river) M3
Shenandoah Nat'l Park L3
Ship Shoal (isl.) S6
Slate (river) L5
Smith (isl.) S6
Smith (river) J7
Smith Mountain (lake) J6
South Anna (river) N5
South Holston (lake) E7
Staunton (river) K6
Stony (creek) N6
Story, Fort S7
Swift (creek) N6
Tangier (isl.) R5
Tangier (sound) S5
Three (creek) O7
Ttg Fork (river) D7
Wachapreague (inlet) T6
Walker (river) J7
Willis (river) K5
Wolf (creek) F6
York (river) P6

⊙County Seat.
*Independent City.

Lower index (alphabetical, multi-column)

Pleasant Valley (L4) 150
Pocahontas (F6) 1,313
Poquoson (R6) 4,278
Port Republic (L4) 75
Port Richmond (P5) 500
Port Royal (L4) 128
Portsmouth⊙* (R7) 114,773
Portsmouth-Norfolk (urban area) 507,825
Potomac Beach (P4) 125
Pound (C6) 1,135
Pounding Mill (E6) 250
Powhatan⊙ (N5) 275
Prince George⊙ (O6) 161
Prospect (L6) 375
Providence Forge (P6) 500
Pulaski⊙ (G6) 10,469
Pungoteague (S5) 250
Purcellville (N2) 1,419
Purdy (N7) 250
Putnam (E6) 150
Quantico (O3) 1,015
Quicksburg (L3) 156
Quinby (S5) 400
Radford* (G6) 9,371
Radiant (M4) 435
Randolph (L7) 116
Raphine (K5) 250
Rapidan (M4) 300

Raven (E6) 400
Rawlings (N7) 140
Rectortown (N3) 400
Red Ash (J2) 750
Red Oak (L7) 100
Reedville (R5) 500
Reliance (M3) 250
Remington (N3) 288
Reston (O3) 100
Republican Grove (K7) 150
Rice (O3) 100
Rich Creek (G6) 748
Richlands (E6) 4,963
RICHMOND⊙* (O5) 219,958
Richmond (urban area) 333,458
Ridgeway (J7) 524
Riner (H6) 250
Ringgold (K7) 300
Ripplemead (G6) 450
Riverton (M3) 500
Riverville (L5) 150
Rixeyville (M3) 75
Roanoke* (H6) 97,110
Roanoke (urb. area) 124,752
Rockville (N5) 100
Rocky Gap (F6) 750
Rocky Mount⊙ (J7) 1,412
Rose Hill (B7) 750

Roseland (K5) 215
Round Hill (N2) 430
Rowe (D6) 300
Ruby (N3) 99
Rugby (F7) 436
Rural Retreat (F7) 413
Rushmere (P6) 75
Rustburg⊙ (K6) 650
Ruthville (P6) 122
Saint Charles (B7) 368
Saint Paul (D7) 1,156
Salem⊙* (H6) 16,058
Saltville (E7) 2,844
Saluda⊙ (P5) 350
Salvia (O5) 90
Sandston (O5) 4,489
Saratoga Place (P7) 1,478
Savedge (O6) 85
Saxe (L7) 100
Saxis (S5) 577
Schuyler (L5) 450
Scottsburg (L7) 188
Scottsville (L5) 353
Seaford (R6) 1,500
Sebrell (O7) 175
Sedley (P7) 565
Selma (J5) 850
Seven Mile Ford (E7) 200
Shacklefords (P5) 150

Shanghai (P5) 75
Sharps (P5) 115
Shawsville (H6) 250
Shenandoah (L4) 1,839
Shiloh (O4) 160
Shipman (L5) 500
Shortt Gap (E6) 250
Simpsons (H6) 93
Singers Glen (K3) 102
Skippers (O7) 500
Skipwith (L7) 94
Slate (E6) 50
Smithfield (P7) 917
Snowville (G6) 300
Somerset (M4) 200
South Boston* (L7) 5,974
South Hill (M7) 2,565
Sparta (O4) 200
Speedwell (F7) 500
Spencer (J7) 300
Sperryville (M3) 200
Spotsylvania⊙ (N4) 750
Spottswood (K5) 161
Spring Valley (F7) 200
Springfield (O3) 10,783
Springwood (J5) 250
Stafford⊙ (O4)
Stampers (P5) 150
Stanardsville⊙ (L4) 283

Stanley (L3) 1,039
Stanleytown (H7) 950
Star Tannery (L2) 300
Starkey (J6) 100
Staunton⊙* (K4) 22,232
Steeles Tavern (K5) 150
Stephens City (M2) 876
Sterling (O2) 150
Stevensburg (N4) 100
Stone Mountain (J6) 100
Stonega (C7) 500
Stony Creek (N7) 437
Strasburg (M3) 2,428
Stratford (P4) 60
Stuart⊙ (H7) 974
Stuarts Draft (L4) 600
Studley (O5) 231
Suffolk⊙* (P7) 12,609
Sugar Grove (E7) 950
Sunset Hills (O3) 250
Surry⊙ (P6) 288
Sussex⊙ (O7) 75
Sutherlin (O7) 116
Sweet Briar (K5) 500
Sweet Chalybeate (H5)
Swords Creek (E6) 400
Sycamore (K6) 120
Sylvatus (G7) 250
Tacoma (O7) 385

Tangier (R5) 876
Tappahannock⊙ (O5) 1,086
Taylors Valley (E7) 145
Tazewell⊙ (E6) 3,000
Temperanceville (T5) 350
Tetotum (P4) 188
Thaxton (K6) 300
The Plains (N3) 484
Thornburg (N4) 300
Timberville (L3) 412
Tiptop (F6) 300
Toano (P6) 150
Toms Brook (L3) 244
Toms Creek (D7) 300
Townsend (R6) 200
Trammel (D6) 750
Triangle (O3) 2,948
Trout Dale (F7) 273
Troutville (J6) 524
Troy (M5) 900
Tuckahoe (N5) 38,326
Turbeville (K7) 180
Tye River (L5) 85
Tyro (K5) 300
Union Level (M7) 204
Unionville (N4) 250
Upperville (N2) 350
Urbanna (P5) 512
Valentines (N7) 200

HIGHWAYS

Scale:
0 — 40 — 80 MILES

- Limited Access Highways
- Major Highways
- Other Important Roads
- Interstate Route Numbers ⑨⑤
- Federal Route Numbers ⑨
- State and Other Route Numbers ④

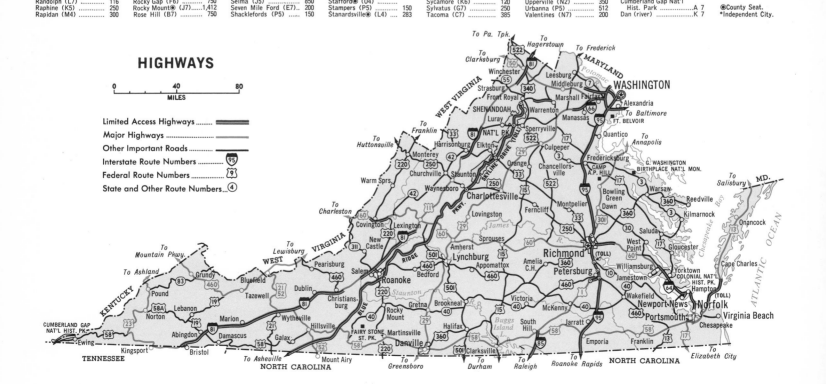

AGRICULTURE, INDUSTRY and RESOURCES

WASHINGTON

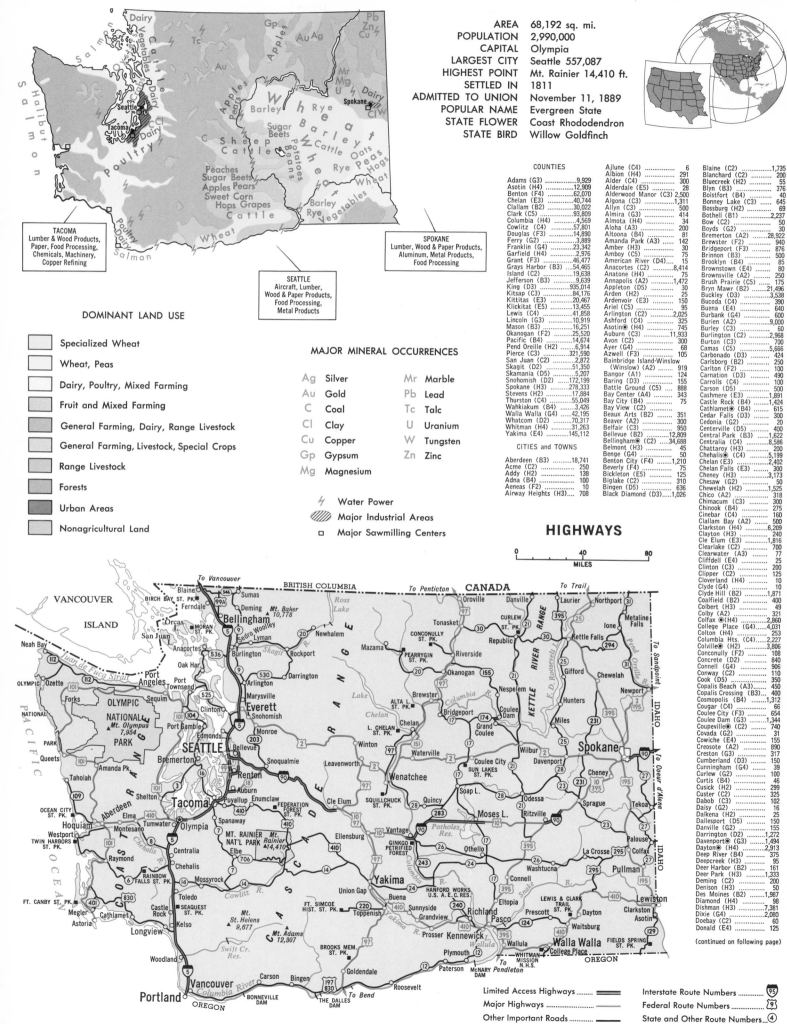

AREA	68,192 sq. mi.
POPULATION	2,990,000
CAPITAL	Olympia
LARGEST CITY	Seattle 557,087
HIGHEST POINT	Mt. Rainier 14,410 ft.
SETTLED IN	1811
ADMITTED TO UNION	November 11, 1889
POPULAR NAME	Evergreen State
STATE FLOWER	Coast Rhododendron
STATE BIRD	Willow Goldfinch

TACOMA
Lumber & Wood Products, Paper, Food Processing, Chemicals, Machinery, Copper Refining

SEATTLE
Aircraft, Lumber, Wood & Paper Products, Food Processing, Metal Products

SPOKANE
Lumber, Wood & Paper Products, Aluminum, Metal Products, Food Processing

DOMINANT LAND USE

- Specialized Wheat
- Wheat, Peas
- Dairy, Poultry, Mixed Farming
- Fruit and Mixed Farming
- General Farming, Dairy, Range Livestock
- General Farming, Livestock, Special Crops
- Range Livestock
- Forests
- Urban Areas
- Nonagricultural Land

MAJOR MINERAL OCCURRENCES

Ag	Silver		Mr	Marble
Au	Gold		Pb	Lead
C	Coal		Tc	Talc
Cl	Clay		U	Uranium
Cu	Copper		W	Tungsten
Gp	Gypsum		Zn	Zinc
Mg	Magnesium			

- ⚡ Water Power
- ▨ Major Industrial Areas
- ▫ Major Sawmilling Centers

COUNTIES

Adams (G3)	9,929
Asotin (H4)	12,909
Benton (F4)	62,070
Chelan (E3)	40,744
Clallam (B2)	30,022
Clark (C5)	93,809
Columbia (H4)	4,569
Cowlitz (C4)	57,801
Douglas (F3)	14,890
Ferry (G2)	3,889
Franklin (G4)	23,342
Garfield (H4)	2,976
Grant (F3)	46,477
Grays Harbor (B3)	54,465
Island (C2)	19,638
Jefferson (B3)	9,639
King (D3)	935,014
Kitsap (C3)	84,176
Kittitas (E3)	20,467
Klickitat (E5)	13,455
Lewis (C4)	41,858
Lincoln (G3)	10,919
Mason (B3)	16,251
Okanogan (F2)	25,520
Pacific (B4)	14,674
Pend Oreille (H2)	6,914
Pierce (C3)	321,590
San Juan (C2)	2,872
Skagit (D2)	51,350
Skamania (D5)	5,207
Snohomish (D2)	172,199
Spokane (H3)	278,333
Stevens (H2)	17,884
Thurston (C4)	55,049
Wahkiakum (B4)	3,426
Walla Walla (G4)	42,195
Whatcom (D2)	70,317
Whitman (H4)	31,263
Yakima (E4)	145,112

CITIES and TOWNS

Aberdeen (B3)	18,741
Acme (C2)	250
Addy (H2)	138
Adna (B4)	100
Aeneas (F2)	10
Airway Heights (H3)	708

Ajlune (C4)	6
Albion (H4)	291
Alder (C4)	300
Alderdale (E5)	28
Alderwood Manor (C3)	2,500
Algona (C3)	1,311
Allyn (C3)	500
Almira (G3)	414
Almota (H4)	34
Aloha (A3)	200
Altoona (B4)	81
Amanda Park (A3)	142
Amber (H3)	30
Amboy (C5)	75
American River (D4)	15
Anacortes (C2)	8,414
Anatone (H4)	75
Annapolis (A2)	1,472
Appleton (D5)	30
Arden (H2)	25
Ardenvoir (E3)	150
Ariel (C5)	95
Arlington (C2)	2,025
Ashford (C4)	325
Asotin⊙ (H4)	745
Auburn (C3)	11,933
Avon (C2)	300
Ayer (G4)	68
Azwell (F3)	105
Bainbridge Island-Winslow (Winslow) (A2)	919
Bangor (A1)	124
Baring (D3)	155
Battle Ground (C5)	888
Bay Center (A4)	343
Bay City (B4)	75
Bay View (C2)	50
Beaux Arts (B2)	351
Beaver (A2)	300
Belfair (C3)	950
Bellevue (B2)	12,809
Bellingham⊙ (C2)	34,688
Belmont (H3)	45
Benge (G4)	50
Benton City (F4)	1,210
Beverly (F4)	75
Bickleton (E5)	125
Biglake (D3)	310
Bingen (D5)	636
Black Diamond (D3)	1,026

Blaine (C2)	1,735
Blanchard (C2)	200
Bluecreek (H2)	55
Blyn (B3)	376
Boistfort (B4)	40
Bonney Lake (C3)	645
Bossburg (H2)	69
Bothell (B1)	2,237
Bow (C2)	50
Boyds (G2)	30
Bremerton (A2)	28,922
Brewster (F2)	940
Bridgeport (F3)	876
Brinnon (B3)	500
Brooklyn (B4)	85
Brownstown (E4)	80
Brownsville (A2)	250
Brush Prairie (C5)	175
Bryn Mawr (B2)	21,496
Buckley (D3)	3,538
Bucoda (C4)	390
Buena (E4)	640
Burbank (G4)	600
Burien (A2)	9,000
Burley (C3)	60
Burlington (C2)	2,968
Burton (C3)	700
Camas (C5)	5,666
Carbonado (D3)	424
Carlsborg (C2)	250
Carlton (F2)	100
Carnation (D3)	490
Carrolls (C4)	100
Cashmere (E3)	1,891
Castle Rock (B4)	1,424
Cathlamet⊙ (B4)	615
Cedar Falls (D3)	300
Cedonia (G2)	20
Centerville (D5)	400
Central Park (B3)	1,622
Centralia (C4)	8,586
Chattaroy (H3)	200
Chehalis⊙ (C4)	5,199
Chelan (E3)	2,402
Chelan Falls (E3)	300
Cheney (H3)	3,173
Chesaw (G2)	50
Chewelah (H2)	1,525
Chico (A2)	318
Chimacum (C3)	300
Chinook (B4)	275
Cinebar (C4)	160
Clallam Bay (A2)	500
Clarkston (H4)	6,209
Clayton (H3)	240
Cle Elum (E3)	1,816
Clearlake (C2)	700
Clearwater (A3)	77
Cliffdell (E4)	25
Clinton (C3)	200
Clipper (C2)	125
Cloverland (H4)	10
Clyde (G4)	10
Clyde Hill (B2)	1,871
Coalfield (B2)	400
Colbert (H3)	49
Colby (A2)	321
Colfax⊙ (H4)	2,860
College Place (G4)	4,031
Colton (H4)	253
Columbia Hts. (C4)	2,227
Colville⊙ (H2)	3,806
Conconully (F2)	108
Concrete (D2)	840
Connell (G4)	906
Conway (C2)	110
Cook (D5)	350
Copalis Beach (A3)	450
Copalis Crossing (B3)	400
Cosmopolis (B4)	1,312
Cougar (C4)	66
Coulee City (F3)	654
Coulee Dam (G2)	1,344
Coupeville⊙ (C2)	740
Covada (G2)	31
Cowiche (E4)	155
Creosote (A2)	890
Creston (H3)	317
Cumberland (D3)	150
Cunningham (G4)	39
Curlew (G2)	100
Curtis (B4)	46
Cusick (H2)	299
Custer (C2)	325
Dabob (C3)	102
Daisy (H2)	16
Dalkena (H2)	25
Dallesport (D5)	150
Danville (G2)	75
Darrington (D2)	1,272
Davenport⊙ (G3)	1,494
Dayton⊙ (H4)	2,913
Deep River (B4)	375
Deepcreek (H3)	95
Deer Harbor (B2)	161
Deer Park (H3)	1,333
Deming (H3)	200
Denison (H3)	50
Des Moines (B2)	1,987
Diamond (H4)	98
Dishman (H3)	7,381
Dixie (G4)	2,080
Doebay (C2)	60
Donald (E4)	125

(continued on following page)

HIGHWAYS

0   40   80
MILES

Limited Access Highways ═══
Major Highways ────
Other Important Roads ━━━

Interstate Route Numbers 〔95〕
Federal Route Numbers 〔9〕
State and Other Route Numbers ④

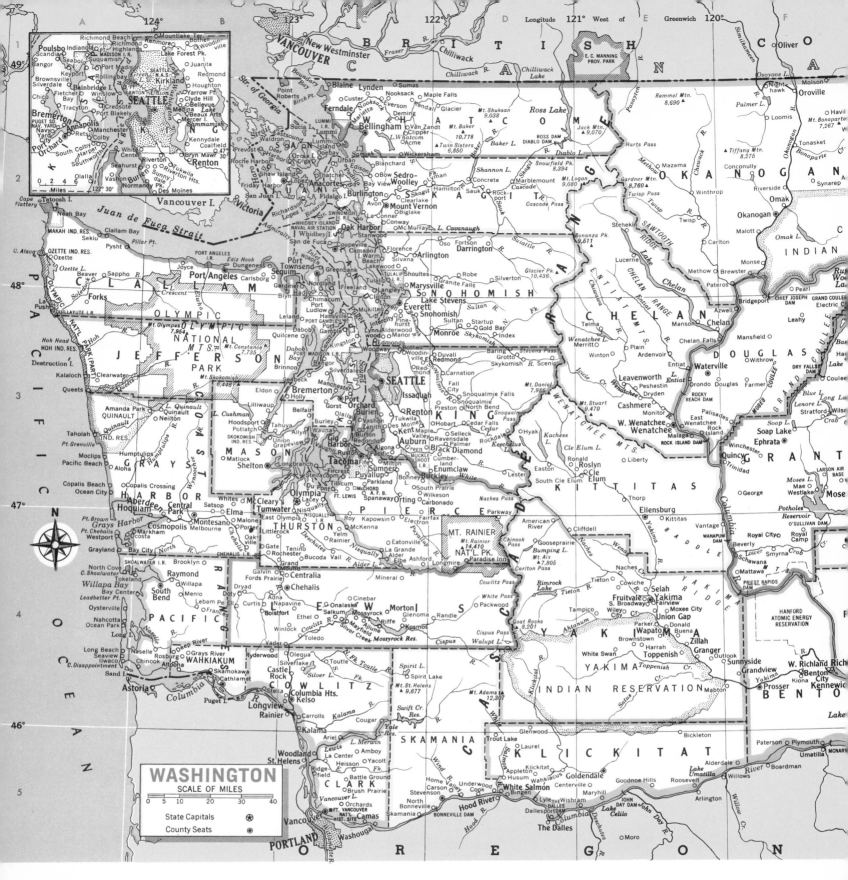

WASHINGTON
SCALE OF MILES
0 5 10 20 30 40
⊛ State Capitals
◉ County Seats

Washington
(continued)

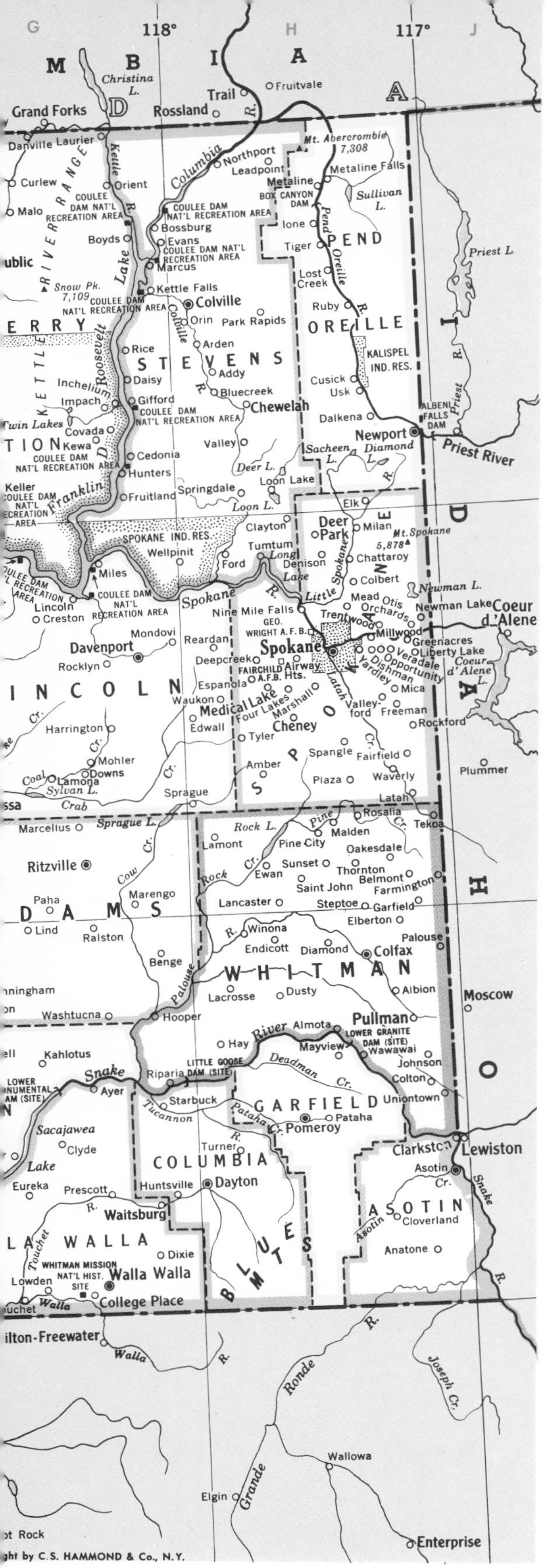

118°
117°
G H J
M B I A
C O L U M B I A
Christina L.
Fruitvale
Trail
Grand Forks
Rossland
Danville
Laurier
Curlew
Orient
Malo
Northport
Leadpoint
Mt. Abercrombie 7,308
Metaline
Metaline Falls
BOX CANYON DAM
Sullivan L.
Ione
COULEE DAM NAT'L RECREATION AREA
Bossburg
Boyds
Evans
Tiger
P E N D
O R E I L L E
KALISPEL IND. RES.
Marcus
Kettle Falls
Colville
Snow Pk. 7,109
Lost Creek
Ruby
F E R R Y
Orin
Park Rapids
Rice
Arden
S T E V E N S
Daisy
Addy
Inchelium
Bluecreek
Cusick
Usk
Impach
Gifford
Chewelah
Dalkena
Twin Lakes
Covada
Kewa
Valley
Newport
Priest River
ALBENI FALLS DAM
Cedonia
Hunters
Deer L.
Sacheen L.
Diamond L.
Loon Lake
Keller
Fruitland
Springdale
Loon L.
Elk
SPOKANE IND. RES.
Clayton
Deer Park
Milan
Mt. Spokane 5,878
Wellpinit
Tumtum
Ford
Denison
Chattaroy
Miles
Colbert
Newman L.
Newman Lake
Lincoln
Creston
Mead
Otis Orchards
Coeur d'Alene
Nine Mile Falls
GEO. WRIGHT A.F.B.
Trentwood
Millwood
Greenacres
Liberty Lake
Davenport
Mondovi
Reardan
Spokane
Veradale
Dishman
Opportunity
Rocklyn
Deepcreek
FAIRCHILD A.F.B.
Airway Hts.
Espanola
Yardley
Mica
L I N C O L N
Waukon
Medical Lake
Four Lakes
Marshall
Valleyford
Freeman
Edwall
Rockford
Harrington
Cheney
Tyler
S P O K A N E
Mohler
Amber
Spangle
Fairfield
Downs
Lamona
Sylvan L.
Plaza
Waverly
Plummer
Sprague
Latah
Marcellus
Sprague L.
Rock L.
Rosalia
Tekoa
Malden
Lamont
Pine City
Oakesdale
Ritzville
Sunset
Thornton
Ewan
Belmont
Saint John
Farmington
Paha
Marengo
A D A M S
Lancaster
Steptoe
Garfield
Lind
Ralston
Elberton
Winona
Palouse
Endicott
Diamond
Colfax
Benge
W H I T M A N
Cunningham
Lacrosse
Dusty
Albion
Moscow
Washtucna
Hooper
Almota
Pullman
Hay
Mayview
LOWER GRANITE DAM (SITE)
Wawawai
Kahlotus
Johnson
LITTLE GOOSE DAM (SITE)
Riparia
LOWER MONUMENTAL DAM (SITE)
Ayer
Colton
Uniontown
Starbuck
G A R F I E L D
Pataha
Pomeroy
Sacajawea
Clyde
Clarkston
Lewiston
Turner
C O L U M B I A
Asotin
Eureka
Prescott
Huntsville
Dayton
A S O T I N
Cloverland
Waitsburg
W A L L A   W A L L A
Dixie
Anatone
B L U E   M T S.
WHITMAN MISSION NAT'L HIST. SITE
Lowden
Walla Walla
Touchet
College Place
Milton-Freewater
Wallowa
Elgin
Enterprise
Pilot Rock
Copyright by C.S. HAMMOND & Co., N.Y.

TOPOGRAPHY

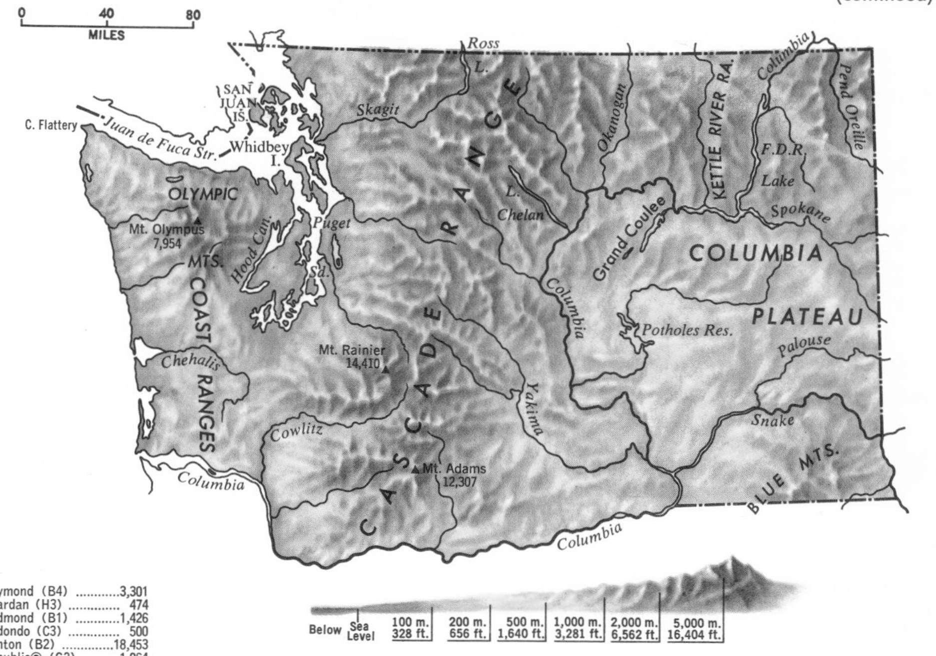

0 40 80
MILES
C. Flattery
Juan de Fuca Str.
SAN JUAN IS.
Whidbey I.
Ross L.
Skagit
Okanogan
KETTLE RIVER RA.
Columbia
Pend Oreille
F.D.R. Lake
OLYMPIC MTS.
Mt. Olympus 7,954
Hood Can.
Puget Sd.
C A S C A D E   R A N G E
L. Chelan
Grand Coulee
Spokane
COLUMBIA PLATEAU
COAST RANGES
Chehalis
Mt. Rainier 14,410
Potholes Res.
Palouse
Yakima
Snake
Cowlitz
Mt. Adams 12,307
BLUE MTS.
Columbia
Below Sea Level
100 m. 328 ft.
200 m. 656 ft.
500 m. 1,640 ft.
1,000 m. 3,281 ft.
2,000 m. 6,562 ft.
5,000 m. 16,404 ft.

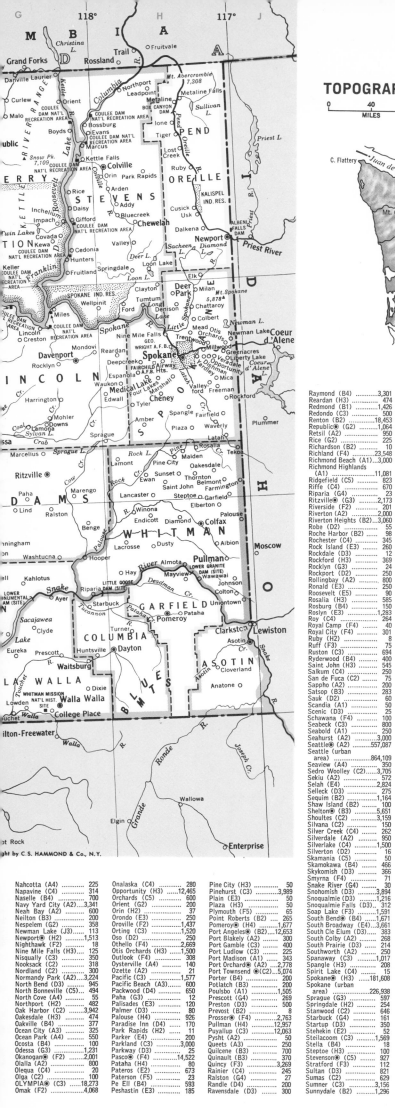

Nahcotta (A4) 225
Napavine (C4) 314
Naselle (B4) 700
Navy Yard City (A2)....3,341
Neah Bay (A2) 600
Neilton (B3) 200
Nespelem (G2) 358
Newman Lake (J3)...... 113
Newport◉ (H2) 1,513
Nighthawk (F2) 18
Nine Mile Falls (H3).... 125
Nisqually (C3) 350
Nooksack (C2) 318
Nordland (C2) 300
Normandy Park (A2)....3,224
North Bend (D3) 945
North Bonneville (C5)... 494
North Cove (A4) 55
Northport (H2) 482
Oak Harbor (C2) 3,942
Oakesdale (H3) 474
Oakville (B4) 377
Ocean City (A3) 325
Ocean Park (A4) 550
Ocosta (B4) 100
Odessa (G3) 1,231
Okanogan◉ (F2) 2,001
Olalla (A2) 800
Olequa (C4) 20
Olga (C2) 100
OLYMPIA◉ (C3) 18,273
Omak (F2) 4,068
Onalaska (C4) 280
Opportunity (H3) 12,465
Orchards (C5) 600
Orient (G2) 200
Orin (H2) 37
Orondo (E3) 250
Oroville (F2) 1,437
Orting (C3) 1,520
Oso (D2) 250
Othello (F4) 2,669
Otis Orchards (H3) 1,500
Outlook (F4) 308
Oysterville (A4) 140
Ozette (A2) 21
Pacific (C3) 1,577
Pacific Beach (A3)....... 600
Packwood (D4) 650
Paha (G3) 12
Palisades (E3) 120
Palmer (D3) 80
Palouse (H4) 926
Paradise Inn (D4) 170
Park Rapids (H2) 11
Parker (E4) 200
Parkland (C3) 3,000
Parkway (D3) 25
Pasco◉ (F4) 14,522
Pataha (H4) 80
Pateros (E2) 673
Paterson (F5) 23
Pe Ell (B4) 593
Peshastin (E3) 185
Pine City (H3) 50
Pinehurst (C3) 3,989
Plain (E3) 50
Plaza (H3) 50
Plymouth (F5) 65
Point Roberts (B2) 265
Pomeroy◉ (H4) 1,677
Port Angeles◉ (B2)....12,653
Port Blakely (A2) 300
Port Gamble (C3) 400
Port Ludlow (C3) 225
Port Madison (A1) 343
Port Orchard◉ (A2) 2,778
Port Townsend ◉(C2)...5,074
Porter (B4) 200
Potlatch (B3) 200
Poulsbo (A1) 1,505
Prescott (G4) 269
Preston (D3) 500
Prevost (B2) 8
Prosser◉ (F4) 2,763
Pullman (H4) 12,957
Puyallup (C3) 12,063
Pysht (A2) 50
Queets (A3) 250
Quilcene (B3) 700
Quinault (B3) 370
Quincy (F3) 3,269
Rainier (C4) 245
Ralston (G4) 27
Randle (D4) 200
Ravensdale (D3) 300
Raymond (B4) 3,301
Reardan (H3) 474
Redmond (B1) 1,426
Redondo (C3) 500
Renton (B2) 18,453
Republic◉ (G2) 1,064
Retsil (A2) 950
Rice (G2) 225
Richardson (B2) 10
Richland (F4) 23,548
Richmond Beach (A1)...3,000
Richmond Highlands (A1) 11,081
Ridgefield (C5) 823
Riffe (C4) 670
Riparia (G4) 23
Ritzville◉ (G3) 2,173
Riverside (F2) 201
Riverton (A2) 2,000
Riverton Heights (B2)...3,060
Robe (D2) 55
Roche Harbor (B2) 98
Rochester (C4) 345
Rock Island (E3) 260
Rockdale (D3) 12
Rockford (H3) 369
Rocklyn (G3) 24
Rockport (D2) 250
Rollingbay (A2) 800
Ronald (E3) 250
Roosevelt (E5) 90
Rosalia (H3) 585
Rosburg (B4) 150
Roslyn (E3) 1,283
Roy (C4) 264
Royal Camp (F4) 40
Royal City (F4) 301
Ruby (H2) 8
Ruff (F3) 75
Ruston (C3) 694
Ryderwood (B4) 400
Saint John (H3) 545
Salkum (C4) 250
San de Fuca (C2) 75
Sappho (A2) 200
Satsop (B3) 283
Sauk (D2) 60
Scandia (A1) 50
Scenic (D3) 25
Schawana (F4) 100
Seabeck (C3) 800
Seabold (A1) 250
Seahurst (A2) 3,000
Seattle◉ (A2) 557,087
Seattle (urban area) 864,109
Seaview (A4) 350
Sedro Woolley (C2)......3,705
Sekiu (A2) 572
Selah (E4) 2,824
Selleck (D3) 275
Sequim (B2) 1,164
Shaw Island (B2) 100
Shelton◉ (B3) 5,651
Shoultes (C2) 3,159
Silvana (C2) 150
Silver Creek (C4) 262
Silverdale (A2) 950
Silverlake (C4) 1,500
Silverton (D2) 16
Skamania (C5) 50
Skamokawa (B4) 466
Skykomish (D3) 366
Smyrna (F4) 71
Snake River (G4) 30
Snohomish (D3) 3,894
Snoqualmie (D3) 1,216
Snoqualmie Falls (D3).. 312
Soap Lake (F3) 1,591
South Bend◉ (B4) 1,671
South Broadway (E4)...3,661
South Cle Elum (D3)..... 383
South Colby (A2) 268
South Prairie (D3) 214
Southworth (A2) 250
Spanaway (C3) 1,017
Spangle (H3) 208
Spirit Lake (C4) 15
Spokane◉ (H3) 181,608
Spokane (urban area) 226,938
Sprague (G3) 597
Springdale (H2) 254
Stanwood (C2) 646
Starbuck (G4) 161
Startup (D3) 350
Stehekin (E2) 52
Steilacoom (C3) 1,569
Stella (B4) 18
Steptoe (H3) 100
Stevenson◉ (C5) 927
Stratford (F3) 112
Sultan (D3) 821
Sumas (C2) 629
Sumner (C3) 3,156
Sunnydale (B2) 1,296
Sunnyside (F4) 6,208
Sunset (H3) 65
Suquamish (A1) 900
Synarep (F2) 8
Tacoma◉ (C3) 147,979
Tacoma (urb. area)...214,930
Taholah (A3) 350
Tahuya (B3) 150
Tampico (E4) 50
Tekoa (H3) 911
Telma (E3) 100
Tenino (C4) 836
Thatcher (C2) 4
Thornton (H3) 225
Thorp (E3) 300
Tieton (E4) 479
Tiger (H2) 60
Tillicum (C3) 1,500
Tokeland (A4) 100
Toledo (C4) 499
Tonasket (F2) 958
Toppenish (E4) 5,667
Touchet (G4) 275
Toutle (C4) 800
Tracyton (A2) 600
Trentwood (H3) 1,387
Trinidad (F3) 135
Trout Lake (D5) 500
Tukwila (B2) 1,804
Tulalip (C2) ....
Tumtum (H3) 75
Tumwater (B3) 3,885
Turner (H4) 25
Twisp (E2) 750
Tyler (H3) 59
Underwood (D5) 450
Union (B3) 350
Union Gap (E4) 2,100
Uniontown (H4) 242
Urban (C2) 20
Usk (H2) 200
Vader (B4) 380
Vail (C4) 150
Valley (H2) 225
Valleyford (H3) 213
Van Zandt (C2) 62
Vancouver◉ (C5) 32,464
Vantage (E4) 67
Vashon (A2) 950
Vaughn (C3) 400
Veradale (H3) 2,450
Wahkiacus (D5) 40
Waitsburg (G4) 1,010
Waldron (B2) 50
Walla Walla◉ (G4)....24,536
Wallula (G4) 75
Wapato (E4) 3,137
Warden (F4) 949
Warm Beach (C2) ....
Washougal (C5) 2,672
Washtucna (G4) 331
Waterville◉ (E3) 1,013
Wauconda (F2) 250
Waukon (H3) 45
Wauna (C3) 250
Waverly (H3) 108
Wawawai (H4) 32
Wellpinit (G3) 100
Wenatchee◉ (E3) 16,726
West Richland (F4)......1,347
West Wenatchee (E3)...2,518
Westlake (F3) 298
Westport (A4) 976
Wheeler (F3) 150
White Center (A2)......30,000
White Salmon (D5).......1,590
White Swan (E4) 300
Whites (B3) 60
Wickersham (C2) 160
Wilbur (G3) 1,138
Wiley City (E4) 450
Wilkeson (D3) 412
Willapa (B4) 230
Wilson Creek (F3) 252
Winchester (F3) 125
Winlock (C4) 808
Winona (H4) 100
Winslow (A2) 919
Winthrop (E2) 359
Winton (E3) 25
Wishram (D5) 950
Withrow (F3) 130
Woodinville (B1) 1,500
Woodland (C5) 1,336
Woodway (C3) 713
Yacolt (C5) 375
Yakima◉ (E4) 43,284
Yardley (H3) 200
Yarrow Point (B2) 766
Yelm (C4) 479
Zenith (C3) 710
Zillah (E4) 1,059

OTHER FEATURES

Abercrombie (mt.) ....H 2
Adams (mt.) ....D 4
Admiralty (inlet) ....B 2
Ahtanum (creek) ....D 4
Aix (mt.) ....D 4
Alava (cape) ....A 2
Alder (lake) ....C 4
Asotin (creek) ....H 4
Bainbridge (isl.) ....A 2
Baker (lake) ....D 2
Baker (mt.) ....D 2
Baker (river) ....D 2
Banks (lake) ....F 3
Birch (point) ....C 2
Blue (lake) ....F 3
Blue (mts.) ....H 4
Bonanza (peak) ....E 2
Bonaparte (creek) ....F 2
Bonaparte (mt.) ....F 2
Bonneville (dam) ....D 5
Boundary (bay) ....C 1
Box Canyon (dam)........H 2
Brown (point) ....A 4
Bumping (lake) ....D 4
Camano (isl.) ....C 2
Carlton (pass) ....D 4
Cascade (pass) ....D 2
Cascade (range) ....D 4
Cascade (river) ....D 2
Cavanaugh (lake) ....D 2
Cedar (lake) ....D 3
Celilo (lake) ....E 5
Chehalis (point) ....A 4
Chehalis (river) ....B 4
Chehalis Ind. Res. ....B 4
Chelan (lake) ....E 2
Chelan (range) ....E 2
Chewak (river) ....E 2
Chief Joseph (dam) ......F 3
Chinook (pass) ....D 4
Chiwawa (river) ....E 2
Cispus (pass) ....D 4
Cispus (river) ....D 4
Cle Elum (lake) ....E 3
Coal (creek) ....G 3
Coast (range) ....B 3
Columbia (river) ....B 4
Colville (river) ....H 2
Colville Ind. Res. ....G 2
Constance (mt.) ....B 3
Coulee (dam) ....G 3
Coulee Dam National Recreation Area ....G 2
Cow (creek) ....G 3
Cowlitz (pass) ....D 4
Cowlitz (river) ....C 4
Crab (creek) ....F 3
Crescent (lake) ....B 3
Cushman (lake) ....B 3
Dabob (bay) ....C 3
Dalles, The (dam)...........D 5
Daniel (mt.) ....D 3
Deadman (creek) ....H 4
Deer (lake) ....H 2
Deschutes (river) ....C 4
Destruction (isl.) ....A 3
Diablo (dam) ....D 2
Diablo (lake) ....D 2
Diamond (lake) ....H 2
Disappointment (cape)..A 4
Dry Falls (dam) ....F 3
Ediz Hook (pen.) ....B 2
Elwha (river) ....B 3
Entiat (lake) ....E 3
Entiat (mts.) ....E 2
Entiat (river) ....E 3
Fairchild A.F.B. ....H 3
Fidalgo (isl.) ....C 2
Flattery (cape) ....A 2
Fort Lawton ....A 2
Fort Lewis ....C 3
Fort Vancouver Nat'l Hist. Site ....C 5
Fort Worden ....C 2
Franklin D. Roosevelt (lake) ....G 2
Gardner (mt.) ....E 2
George Wright A.F.B. ..H 3
Georgia (strait) ....B 2
Glacier Peak (mt.) ....D 2
Goat Rocks (mt.) ....D 4
Grand Coulee (canyon) ..F 3
Grand Coulee (dam) ......F 3
Grand Coulee (res.) ....F 3
Grande Ronde (river)....H 5
Grays (harbor) ....A 4
Green (lake) ....A 2
Green (river) ....C 3
Grenville (point) ....A 3
Hanford Atomic Energy Res. ....F 4
Haro (strait) ....B 2
Harts (pass) ....E 2
Hoh (head) ....A 3
Hoh (river) ....A 3
Hoh Ind. Res. ....A 3
Hood (canal) ....B 3
Humptulips (river) ....B 3
Ice Harbor (dam) ....G 4
Icicle (creek) ....E 3
Jack (mt.) ....E 2
John Day (dam) ....E 5
Joseph (creek) ....H 4
Juan de Fuca (strait)....B 2
Kachess (lake) ....D 3
Kalama (river) ....C 4
Kalispel Ind. Res. ....H 2
Keechelus (lake) ....D 3
Kettle (river) ....G 2
Kettle River (range) .....G 2
Klickitat (river) ....D 4
Lake (creek) ....G 3
Larson A.F.B. ....F 3
Latah (creek) ....H 3
Lawton, Fort ....A 2
Leadbetter (point) ......A 4
Lenore (lake) ....F 3
Lewis (river) ....C 5
Lewis, Fort ....C 3
Little Goose (dam) ....H 4
Little Spokane (river) ...H 3
Logan (mt.) ....E 2
Long (isl.) ....A 4
Long (lake) ....F 3
Loon (lake) ....H 2
Lopez (isl.) ....C 2
Lower Crab (creek)........F 4
Lower Granite (dam) .....H 4
Lower Monumental (dam) ....G 4
Lummi (isl.) ....C 2
Lummi Ind. Res. ....C 2
Makah Ind. Res. ....A 2
McChord A.F.B. ....C 3
McNary (dam) ....F 4
Merwin (lake) ....C 5
Methow (river) ....E 2
Moses (lake) ....F 3
Moses Coulee (canyon)...F 3
Mossyrock (res.) ....C 4
Mount Rainier National Park ....D 4
Muckleshoot Ind. Res. ...C 3
Naches (pass) ....D 3
Naches (river) ....E 4
Naselle (river) ....B 4
Newman (lake) ....H 3
Nisqually (river) ....C 4
Nisqually Ind. Res. ....C 4
Nooksack (river) ....C 2
North (river) ....B 4
Okanogan (river) ....F 2
Olympic (mts.) ....B 3
Olympic National Park....B 3
Olympus (mt.) ....B 3
Omak (lake) ....F 2
Orcas (isl.) ....C 2
Osoyoos (lake) ....F 1
O'Sullivan (dam) ....F 4
Ozette (lake) ....A 2
Ozette Ind. Res. ....A 2
Padilla (bay) ....C 2
Palmer (lake) ....F 2
Palouse (river) ....G 4
Pasayten (river) ....E 2
Pataha (creek) ....H 4
Pend Oreille (river).......H 2
Pillar (point) ....A 2
Pine (creek) ....H 3
Port Angeles Ind. Res. B 2
Port Gamble Ind. Res. ..C 3
Port Madison Ind. Res. ..A 1
Potholes (res.) ....F 3
Priest Rapids (dam) ....F 4
Puget (isl.) ....B 4
Puget (sound) ....C 3
Puget Sound Navy Yard..A 2
Puyallup (river) ....C 4
Queets (river) ....A 3
Quillayute Ind. Res. ......A 3
Quinault (lake) ....B 3
Quinault (river) ....A 3
Quinault Ind. Res. ....A 3
Rainier (mt.) ....D 4
Remmel (mt.) ....E 2
Rimrock (lake) ....D 4
Rock (creek) ....H 3
Rock (lake) ....H 3
Rock Island (dam) ....E 3
Rocky Reach (dam) ......E 3
Rosario (strait) ....C 2
Ross (dam) ....D 2
Ross (lake) ....D 2
Rufus Woods (lake) ......F 2
Sacajawea (lake) ....G 4
Sacheen (lake) ....H 2
Saddle (mts.) ....E 4
Saint Helens (mt.) ......C 4
Samish (lake) ....C 2
Sammamish (lake) ....B 2
San Juan (isl.) ....B 2
Sand (isl.) ....A 4
Sanpoil (river) ....G 2
Satus (creek) ....E 4
Sauk (river) ....D 2
Sawtooth Ridge (mt.)....E 2
Seattle Naval Air Sta. ..B 1
Shannon (lake) ....D 2
Shoalwater (cape) ....A 4
Shoalwater Ind. Res. .....B 4
Shuksan (mt.) ....D 2
Silver (lake) ....C 4
Similkameen (river) ......F 1
Skagit (river) ....C 2
Skokomish (mt.) ....B 3
Skokomish Ind. Res. ......B 3
Skykomish (river) ....D 3
Snake (river) ....G 4
Snohomish (river) ....C 3
Snoqualmie (pass) ....D 3
Snoqualmie (river) ....D 3
Snow (peak) ....G 2
Snowfield (peak) ....D 2
Soap (lake) ....F 3
Soleduck (river) ....A 3
Spirit (lake) ....C 4
Spokane (mt.) ....H 3
Spokane (river) ....H 3
Spokane Ind. Res. ....G 3
Sprague (lake) ....G 3
Stevens (pass) ....D 3
Stuart (mt.) ....E 3
Sucia (isl.) ....C 2
Suiattle (river) ....D 2
Sullivan (lake) ....H 2
Sultan (river) ....D 3
Swift Creek (res.)..........C 4
Swinomish Ind. Res. .....C 2
Sylvan (lake) ....G 3
Tatoosh (isl.) ....A 2
Tieton (river) ....D 4
Tiffany (mt.) ....F 2
Toppenish (creek) ....E 4
Touchet (river) ....G 4
Toutle, North Fork (river) ....C 4
Tucannon (river) ....G 4
Tulalip Ind. Res. ....C 2
Twin (lakes) ....G 2
Twin Sisters (mt.)..........D 2
Twisp (pass) ....E 2
Twisp (river) ....E 2
Umatilla (lake) ....E 5
Union (lake) ....B 2
Vancouver (lake) ....C 5
Walla Walla (river)........G 4
Wallula (lake) ....F 4
Walupt (lake) ....D 4
Wanapum (dam) ....E 4
Washington (lake) ....B 2
Wenas (creek) ....E 4
Wenatchee (lake) ....E 3
Wenatchee (mts.) ....E 3
Wenatchee (river) ....E 3
Whatcom (lake) ....C 2
Whidbey (isl.) ....C 2
Whidbey Isl. Naval Air Sta. ....C 2
White (pass) ....D 4
White (river) ....D 3
White Salmon (river).....D 4
Whitman Mission National Hist. Site ....G 4
Willapa (bay) ....A 4
Wilson (creek) ....F 3
Wind (river) ....D 5
Worden, Fort ....C 2
Wynoochee (river) ....B 3
Yakima (ridge) ....E 4
Yakima (river) ....F 4
Yakima Ind. Res. ....E 4
Yale (res.) ....C 4

◉ County Seat.
‡ Name not on map.

West Virginia

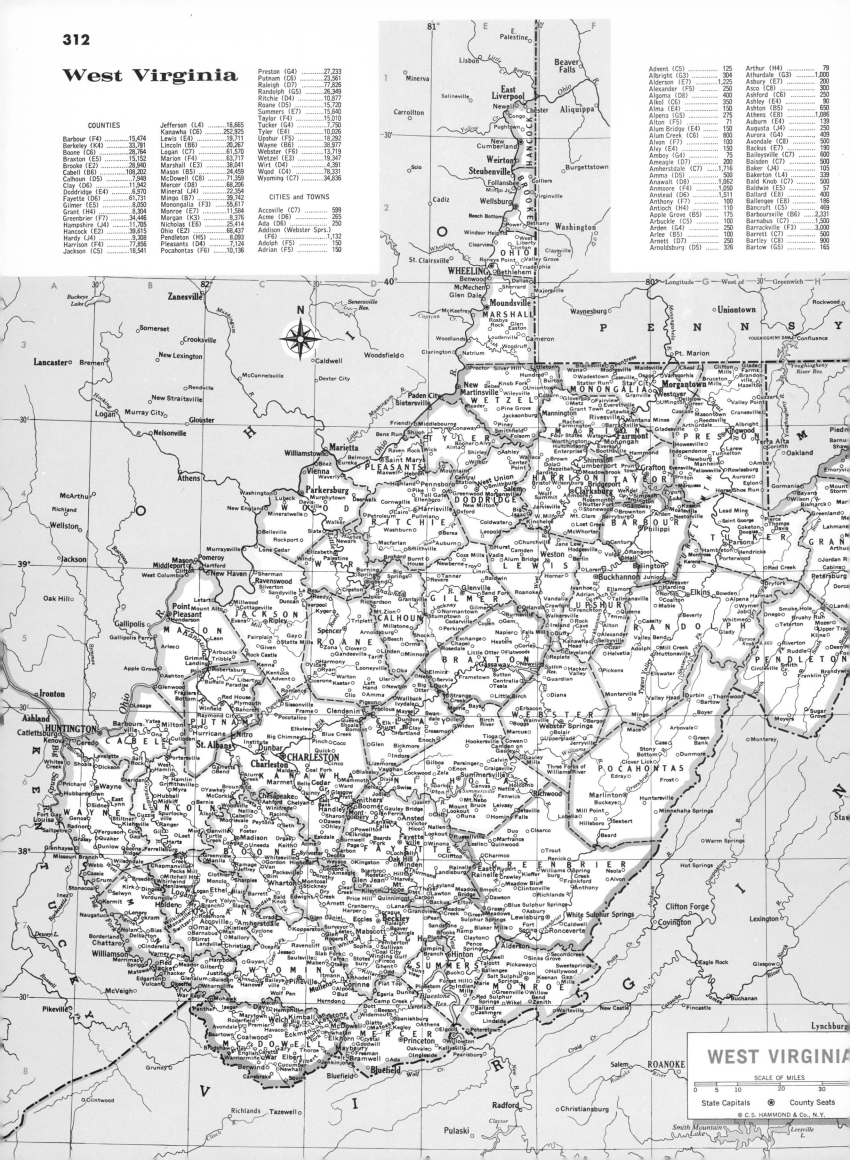

COUNTIES

Barbour (F4)	15,474	Jefferson (L4)	18,665
Berkeley (K4)	33,791	Kanawha (C6)	252,925
Boone (C6)	28,764	Lewis (E4)	19,711
Braxton (E5)	15,152	Lincoln (B6)	20,267
Brooke (E2)	28,940	Logan (C7)	61,570
Cabell (B6)	108,202	Marion (F4)	63,717
Calhoun (D5)	7,948	Marshall (E3)	38,041
Clay (D6)	11,942	Mason (B5)	24,459
Doddridge (D5)	6,970	McDowell (C8)	71,359
Fayette (D6)	61,731	Mercer (D8)	68,206
Gilmer (E5)	8,050	Mineral (J4)	22,354
Grant (H4)	8,304	Mingo (B7)	39,742
Greenbrier (E7)	34,446	Monongalia (F3)	55,617
Hampshire (J4)	11,705	Monroe (E7)	11,584
Hancock (E2)	39,615	Morgan (K3)	8,376
Hardy (J4)	9,308	Nicholas (E6)	25,414
Harrison (F4)	77,856	Ohio (E2)	68,437
Jackson (C5)	18,541	Pendleton (H5)	8,093
		Pleasants (D4)	7,124
		Pocahontas (F6)	10,136

Preston (G4)	27,233
Putnam (C6)	23,561
Raleigh (D7)	77,826
Randolph (G5)	26,349
Ritchie (D4)	10,877
Roane (D5)	15,720
Summers (E7)	15,640
Taylor (F4)	15,010
Tucker (G4)	7,750
Tyler (E4)	10,026
Upshur (F5)	18,292
Wayne (B6)	38,977
Webster (F6)	13,719
Wetzel (E3)	19,347
Wirt (D4)	4,391
Wood (C4)	78,331
Wyoming (C7)	34,836

CITIES and TOWNS

Accoville (C7)	599
Acme (D6)	265
Ada (D6)	250
Addison (Webster Sprs.) (F6)	1,132
Adolph (F5)	150
Adrian (F5)	150

Advent (C5)	125	Arthur (H4)	79
Albright (G3)	304	Athurdale (G3)	1,000
Alderson (E7)	1,225	Asbury (E7)	200
Alexander (F5)	250	Asco (C8)	300
Algoma (D8)	400	Ashford (C6)	250
Alkol (C6)	350	Ashley (E4)	90
Alma (B5)	150	Ashton (B5)	650
Alpena (G5)	275	Athens (E8)	1,086
Alton (F5)	71	Auburn (F4)	139
Alum Bridge (E4)	150	Augusta (J4)	250
Alum Creek (C6)	800	Aurora (J4)	409
Alvon (F7)	100	Avondale (C8)	500
Alvy (E4)	150	Backus (E7)	190
Amboy (G4)	75	Baileysville (C7)	600
Ameagle (D7)	200	Baisden (C7)	500
Amherstdale (C7)	1,716	Baker (J4)	105
Amma (B5)	500	Bakerton (L4)	339
Anawalt (D8)	1,062	Bald Knob (C7)	500
Anmoore (F4)	1,050	Baldwin (E5)	57
Anstead (D6)	1,511	Ballard (F5)	400
Anthony (F7)	100	Ballengee (E8)	186
Antioch (H4)	71	Bancroft (C5)	269
Apple Grove (B5)	175	Barboursville (B6)	2,331
Arbuckle (C5)	100	Barnabus (C7)	1,500
Arden (G4)	250	Barrackville (F3)	3,000
Arlee (B5)	100	Barrett (C7)	500
Arnett (D7)	250	Bartley (C8)	900
Arnoldsburg (D5)	326	Bartow (G5)	165

WEST VIRGINIA

SCALE OF MILES

0 5 10 20 30

★ State Capitals   ⊛ County Seats

© C.S. HAMMOND & Co., N.Y.

WEST VIRGINIA

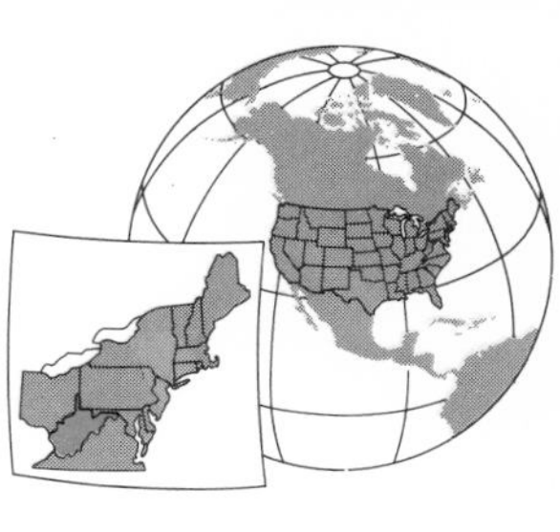

AREA	24,181 sq. mi.
POPULATION	1,812,000
CAPITAL	Charleston
LARGEST CITY	Charleston 85,796
HIGHEST POINT	Spruce Knob 4,860 ft.
SETTLED IN	1774
ADMITTED TO UNION	June 20, 1863
POPULAR NAME	Mountain State
STATE FLOWER	Rhododendron
STATE BIRD	Cardinal

Bath (Berkeley Sprs.) (K3) 1,138
Bayard (H4) 484
Bays (E5) 200
Beards Fork (D6) 500
Beartown (C8) 250
Beaver (D7) 1,230
Bebee (E3) 130
Beckley◉ (D7) 18,642
Bedington (L3) 165
Beech Bottom (E2) 506
Beeson (D8) 150
Belington (F4) 1,528
Belle (C6) 2,000
Belleville (C4) 96
Belmont (D4) 454
Belva (D6) 475
Bens Run (D4) 121
Benwood (E2) 2,850
Bergoo (F6) 490
Berkeley (L4) 500
Berkeley Sprs.◉ (K3) 3,500
Bernie (C6) 294
Berwind (C8) 622
Beryl (H4) 525
Bethany (E2) 992
Bethlehem (E2) 2,308
Beverly (G5) 441
Bias (B7) 100
Bickmore (D6) 500
Big Chimney (C6) 500
Big Creek (B7) 500
Big Four (C8) 225
Big Isaac (E4) 72
Big Otter (D5) 200
Big Springs (D5) 300
Bigbend (D5) 225
Bim (C7) 500
Birch River (E6) 250
Blacksville (F3) 211
Blair (C7) 400
Blakeley (D6) 400
Blaker Mills (E7) 115
Bloomery (K4) 83
Blue Creek (D6) 350
Blue Sulphur Sprs. (E7) 400
Bluefield (D8) 19,256
Boggs (E6) 145
Bolair (F6) 950
Bolivar (L4) 754
Bomont (D6) 79
Booher (E4) 295
Boomer (D6) 1,657
Boothsville (F4) 150
Borderland (B7) 500
Bowden (G5) 130
Bradshaw (C8) 1,200
Bramwell (D8) 1,195
Brandonville (G3) 109
Brandywine (H5) 250
Breeden (B7) 300
Bridgeport (F4) 4,199
Bristol (F4) 800
Brohard (D4) 63
Brooks (E7) 200
Brounland (C6) 1,000
Brown (F4) 200
Brownton (F4) 700
Bruce (E6) 175
Bruceton Mills (G3) 209
Buck (E7) 150
Buckeye (F6) 137
Buckhannon◉ (F5) 6,386
Bud (D7) 500
Buffalo (C5) 396
Bunker Hill (K4) 450
Burlington (J4) 350
Burnsville (E5) 728
Burnwell (D6) 165
Burton (F3) 250
Cabins (H4) 500
Cairo (D4) 418
Caldwell (F7) 450
Calvin (E6) 409

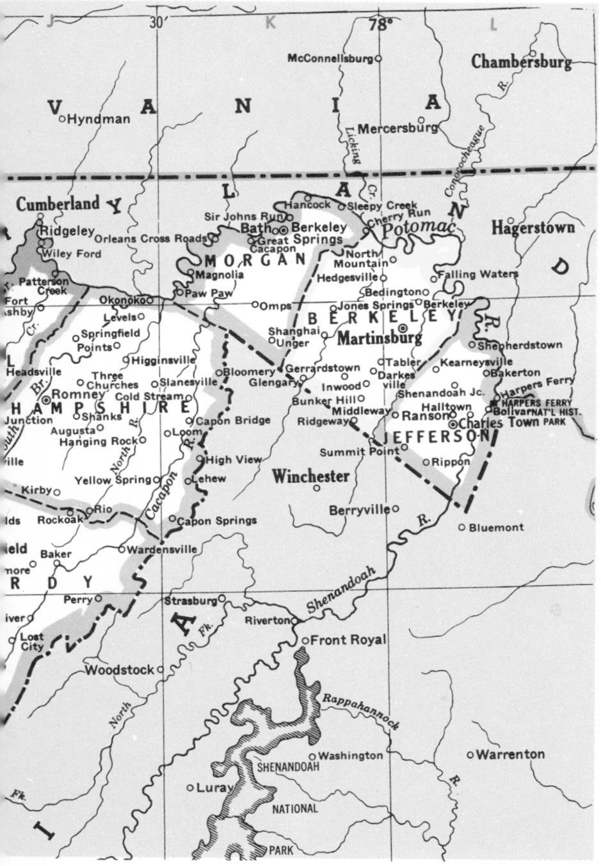
McConnellsburg
Chambersburg
Hyndman
Mercersburg
Cumberland
Hagerstown
Ridgeley
Orleans Cross Roads
Wiley Ford
Sir Johns Run
Hancock
Sleepy Creek
Cherry Run
Bath
Berkeley
Great Springs
Potomac
MORGAN
North Mountain
Falling Waters
Magnolia
Hedgesville
Paw Paw
Bedington
Omps
Jones Springs
BERKELEY
Okonoko
Levels
Springfield
Points
Shanghai
Unger
Martinsburg
Shepherdstown
Higginsville
Tabler
Kearneysville
Three Churches
Slanesville
Bloomery
Gerrardstown
Darkesville
Bakerton
Glengary
Inwood
Harpers Ferry
Romney
Cold Stream
Shenandoah Jc.
Shanks
Bunker Hill
Halltown
Augusta
Capon Bridge
Middleway
Ransom
Charles Town
Hanging Rock
Loom
Ridgeway
JEFFERSON
Summit Point
High View
Rippon
Winchester
Yellow Spring
Lehew
Kirby
Rio
Rockoak
Capon Springs
Berryville
Bluemont
Baker
Wardensville
Perry
Strasburg
Riverton
Lost City
Front Royal
Woodstock
Rappahannock
Washington
Warrenton
Luray
SHENANDOAH
NATIONAL
PARK

Camden (E4) 85
Camden on Gauley (E6) 301
Cameron (E3) 1,652
Camp Creek (D7) 261
Canebrake (C8) 568
Canvas (E6) 500
Capon Bridge (K4) 198
Capon Springs (K4) 200
Carbon (D6) 300
Caretta (C8) 1,092
Cascade (G3) 200
Cashmere (E8) 100
Cass (G6) 327
Cassie (B7) 350
Cassity (F5) 500
Cassville (F3) 750
Catawba (F3) 100
Cedar Grove (D6) 1,569
Cedarville (E5) 200
Center Point (E4) 100
Central Station (E4) 300
Centralia (E5) 133
Century (F4) 600
Ceredo (B6) 1,387
Chapmanville (B7) 1,241
CHARLESTON◉ (D6) 85,796
Charleston (urban area) 169,500
Charles Town◉ (L4) 3,329
Charmco (E6) 900
Chelyan (C6) 950
Cherry Run (L3) 160
Chesapeake (C6) 2,699
Chester (E1) 3,787
Christian (C7) 200
Churchville (E4) 125
Cicerone (D5) 143
Cinco (D6) 650
Cinderella (B7) 150
Circleville (H5) 150
Clarksburg◉ (F4) 28,112
Clay◉ (D6) 486
Clayton (E7) 135
Clearview (E2) 520
Clendenin (D5) 1,510
Cleveland (F5) 150
Clifftop (E6) 350
Clifton (B5) 350
Clifton Mills (G3) 116
Clifty (E6) 200
Clinton (E2) 200
Clintonville (E7) 200
Clio (D5) 250
Clothier (C7) 675
Clover Lick (F6) 324
Coal City (D7) 600
Coal Fork (D6) 1,500
Coalton (G5) 354
Coalwood (C8) 1,199
Coburn (F3) 105
Coco (D6) 150
Coketon (G4) 125
Colcord (D7) 300
Colliers (E2) 1,060
Copen (E5) 280
Corinne (D7) 1,273
Corinth (H4) 225
Costa (C6) 200
Cottageville (C5) 800
Cove Gap (B6) 600
Cowen (E6) 475
Coxs Mills (E4) 100
Craigsville (E6) 350
Cranberry (D7) 270
Crawford (F5) 92
Crawley (E7) 150
Crum (B7) 750
Crystal (D8) 500
Cucumber (C8) 360
Culloden (B6) 1,000
Cuzzart (H3) 125
Cuzzie (B6) 100
Cyclone (C7) 950
Dallas (E2) 124
Daniels (D7) 1,100
Danville (C6) 507
Darkesville (L4) 250
Davis (H4) 898
Davy (C8) 1,331
Dawes (D6) 500
Dawson (E7) 200
Decota (D6) 750
Delbarton (B7) 1,122
Dellslow (G3) 450
Diana (F5) 950
Dickson (B6) 250
Dille (E6) 500
Dingess (B7) 300
Dola (F4) 200
Dorothy (D3) 3,000
Dott (D8) 300
Dry Creek (D7) 362
Duck (E5) 100
Duffy (F5) 200
Dunbar (C6) 11,006
Dundon (D6) 150
Dunlow (B6) 92
Dunmore (G6) 122
Durbin (G5) 431
East Bank (D6) 1,023
East Lynn (B6) 1,750
East Rainelle (E7) 1,244
Eccles (D7) 1,145
Eckman (C8) 1,125
Edgarton (B7) 400
Edray (F6) 100
Edwight (C7) 68
Egeria (D7) 300
Eglon (G4) 95
Elbert (C8) 299
Elgood (E8) 375
Elizabeth◉ (D4) 727
Elk Garden (H4) 329
Elkhorn (D8) 129
Elkins◉ (G5) 8,307
Elkridge (D6) 165
Elkview (C6) 400
Ellamore (F5) 400
Ellenboro (D4) 340
Elmira (E5) 150
Elton (E7) 500
Emoryville (H4) 100
English (C8) 800
Enoch (E6) 282
Enon (E6) 150
Enterprise (F4) 1,400
Erbacon (E5) 300
Eskdale (D6) 1,000
Ethel (C7) 588
Eureka (D4) 86
Evans (C5) 275
Everettville (F3) 375
Everson (F4) 500
Fairmont◉ (F2) 27,477
Fairplain (C5) 175
Fairview (F3) 653
Falling Springs (Renick) (F6) 265
Falling Waters (L3) 150
Farmington (F3) 709
Fayetteville◉ (D6) 1,848
Fellowsville (G4) 130
Fenwick (E6) 500
Ferguson (B6) 250
Ferrellsburg (B6) 150
Filbert (D8) 182
Fireco (D7) 450
Flat Top (D7) 350
Flatwoods (E5) 248
Flemington (F4) 478
Follansbee (E2) 4,052
Folsom (E4) 278
Forest Hill (E7) 800
Fort Ashby (J4) 900
Fort Branch (C7) 300
Fort Gay (A6) 739
Fort Spring (E7) 100
Foster (C6) 600
Four States (F4) 1,000
Frame (C5) 98
Frametown (E5) 500
Frankford (F7) 175
Franklin◉ (H5) 758
Fraziers Bottom (B5) 400
Freeman (D8) 700
French Creek (F5) 250
Frenchton (F5) 250
Friendly (D3) 195
Frost (G6) 100
Gallipolis Ferry (B5) 500
Galloway (F4) 650
Gandeeville (D5) 328
Gap Mills (F7) 140
Garretts Bend (C6) 232
Gary (C8) 1,393
Gassaway (E5) 1,223
Gauley Bridge (D6) 1,800
Gauley Mills (E6) 195
Genoa (A6) 500
Gerrardstown (K4) 250
Ghent (D7) 500
Giatto (G8) 550
Gilbert (C7) 874
Gilboa (E6) 275
Gill (B6) 250
Gilmer (E5) 300
Given (C5) 128
Gladesville (G4) 100
Glady (G5) 300
Glasgow (D6) 914
Glen (D6) 200
Glen Dale (E3) 1,905
Glen Daniel (D7) 390
Glen Easton (E3) 116
Glen Ferris (D6) 300
Glen Hedrick (Beaver) (D7) 1,230
Glen Jean (D7) 1,665
Glen Rogers (D7) 400
Glen White (D7) 600
Glenalum (C7) 175
Glenhayes (A6) 156
Glenville◉ (E5) 1,828
Glenwood (B5) 150
Glovergap (F3) 150
Gordon (C7) 800
Gormania (H4) 326
Grafton◉ (G4) 5,791
Grandview (D7) 155
Grantsville◉ (D5) 866
Grant Town (F3) 1,105
Granville (G3) 806
Grassy Meadows (E7) 150
Great Cacapon (K3) 800
Green Bank (G6) 450
Green Sulphur Springs (E7) 450
Greenville (E7) 125
Greenwood (E4) 289
Griffithsville (B6) 750
Grimms Landing (B5) 300
Guardian (F5) 220
Guyan (C7) 365
Hacker Valley (F5) 250
Halltown (L4) 500
Hambleton (G4) 275
Hamlin◉ (B6) 850
Hampden (C7) 300
Hancock (K3) 125
Handley (D6) 800
Hanging Rock (J4) 100
Hanover (C7) 500
Harding (G5) 220
Harman (G5) 128
Harper (D7) 250
Harpers Ferry (L4) 572
Harrisville◉ (E4) 1,428
Hartford (C4) 376
Hartland (D6) 100
Harts (B6) 160
Harvey (D7) 650
Havaco (C8) 350
Headsville (J4) 350
Heaters (E5) 120
Hedgesville (K3) 342
Helvetia (F5) 160
Hemphill (C8) 1,000
Henderson (B5) 601
Hendricks (G4) 407
Henlawson (B7) 1,670
Hepzibah (F4) 850
Herndon (D7) 300
Hico (D6) 650
Higginsville (J4) 150
Highcoal (C7) 500
Highland (D4) 100
Hillsboro (F6) 210
Hilltop (D7) 575
Hinton◉ (E7) 5,197
Holcomb (E6) 250
Holden (B7) 1,900
Hollywood (F7) 200
Hominy Falls (E6) 240
Hookersville (E6) 452
Horner (F5) 590
Horse Shoe Run (G4) 125
Howesville (G4) 323
Hubball (B6) 2,500
Hubbardstown (A6) 100
Hundred (E3) 475
Huntersville (G6) 100
Huntington◉ (A6) 83,627
Huntington-Ashland (urban area) 165,732
Hurricane (C6) 1,970
Hurst (E4) 115
Hutchinson (F4) 250
Huttonsville (G5) 242
Iaeger (C8) 930
Independence (G4) 250
Indore (D6) 400
Ingleside (E8) 200
Institute (C6) 1,040
Inwood (K7) 450
Itmann (D7) 1,000
Ivanhoe (F5) 100
Ivydale (D5) 400
Jacksonburg (E3) 350
Jane Lew (F4) 426
Jarvisville (F4) 200
Jeffrey (C7) 2,000
Jenkinjones (D8) 800
Jesse (C7) 150
Jetsville (E6) 108
Jodie (D6) 600
Jones Springs (K4) 115
Jumping Branch (E7) 250
Junior (G5) 552
Justice (C7) 600
Kanawha Falls (D6) 188
Kanawha Head (F5) 220
Kasson (G4) 77
Kearneysville (L4) 450
Keenan (F7) 150
Kegley (D8) 500
Keith (C6) 265
Kellysville (E8) 150
Kenna (C5) 106
Kenova (A6) 4,577
Kentuck (C5) 100
Kerens (G4) 76
Kermit (B7) 743
Keyser◉ (J4) 6,192
Keystone (D8) 1,457
Kieffer (E7) 150
Killarney (D7) 200
Kilsyth (D7) 450
Kimball (C8) 1,175
Kingston (D7) 300
Kingwood◉ (G4) 2,530
Kirk (B7) 200
Kistler (C7) 1,084
Kline (H5) 75
Knob Fork (E3) 200
Kopperston (C7) 1,600
Lahmansville (H4) 155
Lanark (D7) 400
Landisburg (E7) 200
Landville (C7) 200
Larew (G4) 200
Lavalette (B6) 600
Lawton (E7) 800
Layland (E7) 500
Layopolis (Sand Fork) (E5) 237
Left Hand (D5) 500
Lehew (K4) 240
Leivasy (E6) 450
Lenore (B7) 350
Leon (C5) 236
Leopold (E4) 64
Lerona (D8) 150
Lesage (B5) 350
Leslie (E6) 250
Lester (D7) 626
Letart (C5) 125
Lewisburg◉ (E7) 2,259
Lindside (E8) 114
Linn (E4) 72
Little Birch (E5) 350
Little Otter (E5) 200
Littleton (F3) 339
Liverpool (C5) 86
Lizemores (D6) 450
Lochgelly (D6) 300
Lockney (E5) 185
Lockwood (D6) 300
Logan◉ (B7) 4,185
Lookout (E6) 600
Looneyville (D5) 79
Lorado (C7) 519
Lorentz (F4) 450
Lost City (J5) 125
Lost Creek (F4) 678
Loudenville (E3) 75
Lowell (E7) 150
Lowgap (C6) 125
Lubeck (C4) 300
Lumberport (F4) 1,031
Lundale (C7) 610
Maben (D7) 300
Mabie (G5) 500
Mabscott (D7) 1,591
Mace (F6) 100
Macfarlan (D4) 200
Madison◉ (C6) 2,215
Maidsville (F3) 500
Malden (C6) 600
Mallory (C7) 1,133
Mammoth (D6) 875
Man (C7) 1,486
Manheim (G4) 198
Manila (C7) 375
Mannington (F3) 2,996
Marfrance (E6) 350
Marie (E7) 150
Marlinton◉ (F6) 1,586
Marmet (C6) 2,500
Martinsburg◉ (K4) 15,179
Marytown (C8) 173
Mason (B4) 1,005
Masontown (G3) 841
Matewan (B5) 896
Mathias (J5) 100
Matoaka (D8) 613
Maxwell (D4) 146
Maybeury (D8) 1,423
Maysel (D5) 550
Maysville (H4) 114
McCorkle (C6) 414
McDowell (D8) 1,109
McKeefrey (E3) 500
McMechen (E3) 2,999
McWhorter (F4) 250
Meador (B7) 500
Meadow Bluff (E7) 150
Meadow Bridge (E7) 426
Meadow Creek (E7) 300
Meadowbrook (F4) 500
Merrimac (B7) 75
Metz (F3) 450
Middlebourne◉ (E3) 711
Middleway (K4) 396
Midkiff (B6) 300
Mill Creek (G5) 817
Millstone (D5) 300
Millwood (C5) 135
Milton (B6) 1,714
Minden (D7) 1,114
Mineralwells (C4) 82
Mingo (F5) 333
Minnora (D5) 240
Missouri Branch (A7) 100
Mitchell Heights (B7) 290
Moatsville (G4) 100
Mohawk (C7) 100
Monaville (B7) 666
Monclo (C7) 117
Monongah (F4) 1,321
Montana Mines (F3) 250
Montcoal (D7) 300
Monterville (F5) 350
Montgomery (D6) 3,000
Montrose (G4) 114
Moorefield◉ (J4) 1,434
Mooresville (F3) 200
Morgantown◉ (G3) 22,487
Moundsville◉ (E3) 15,163
Mount Alto (C5) 100
Mount Carbon (D7) 500
Mount Clare (F4) 1,200
Mount Gay (C7) 3,386
Mount Hope (D7) 2,000
Mount Lookout (E6) 575
Mount Nebo (E6) 125
Mount Storm (H4) 300
Mount Zion (D5) 250
Mountain (E4) 135
Mountview (D7) 230
Moyers (H6) 78
Mozer (H5) 75
Mud (C6) 309
Mullens (D7) 3,544
Murphytown (D4) 250
Myra (B6) 75
Nallen (E6) 200
Napier (E5) 108
Naugatuck (B7) 500
Nebo (D5) 200
Needmore (J4) 450
Nellis (C6) 305
Neola (F7) 100
Nestorville (G4) 65
Nettie (E6) 200
New Creek (J4) 500
New Cumberland◉ (E2) 2,076
New England (C4) 500
New Haven (C5) 1,314
New Martinsville◉ (E3) 5,607
New Milton (E4) 899
Newberne (E4) 75
Newburg (G4) 494
Newell (E1) 1,842
Newhall (C8) 750
Newton (D5) 500
Newville (E5) 250
Nitro (C6) 6,894
Nolan (B7) 759
Normantown (E5) 100
North Mountain (K3) 250
Northfork (D8) 798
Norton (G5) 500
Nutter Fort (F4) 2,440
Oak Hill (D6) 4,711
Oakvale (D8) 267
Oceana (C7) 1,303
Odd (D7) 500
Ohley (D6) 500
Omar (C7) 804
Omps (K4) 100
Ona (B6) 150
Orgas (C6) 175
Orlando (E5) 386
Orleans Cross Roads (J3) 100
Orma (D5) 125
Osage (F3) 614
Otsego (D7) 875
Oxford (E4) 320
Packsville (C7) 200
Paden City (D3) 3,137
Page (D6) 800
Palestine (D4) 106
Panther (C8) 600
Parkersburg◉ (D4) 44,797
Parsons◉ (G4) 1,798
Patterson Creek (J3) 168
Paw Paw (K3) 789
Pax (D7) 408
Pear (E7) 115
Pecks Mill (B7) 500
Pemberton (D7) 500
Pence Springs (E7) 235
Pennsboro (E4) 1,660
Pentress (F3) 300
Perkins (E5) 125
Persinger (E6) 300
Petersburg◉ (H5) 2,079
Peterstown (E8) 616
Petroleum (D4) 110
Peytona (C6) 650
Philippi◉ (G4) 2,228
Pickaway (E7) 125
Pickens (F5) 820
Pie (B7) 250
Piedmont (H4) 2,307
Pike (D4) 150
Pinch (D6) 800
Pine Grove (E3) 760
Pineville◉ (C7) 1,137
Piney (E3) 115
Pipestem (E7) 64
Pliny (B5) 100
Plymouth (C5) 300
Poca (C6) 607
Pocotalico (C6) 100
Point Pleasant◉ (B5) 5,785
Porterwood (G4) 150
Powellton (D6) 1,256
Power (E2) 250
Powhatan (D8) 512
Pratt (D6) 602
Premier (C8) 800
Price Hill (D7) 225
Prichard (A6) 300
Princeton◉ (D8) 8,393
Procious (D5) 900
Proctor (E3) 250
Pruntytown (F4) 250
Pughtown (E1) 250
Pullman (D4) 162
Purgitsville (J4) 200
Quaker (B6) 150
Queen Shoals (D6) 100
Queens (F5) 300
Queens Ridge (B6) 75
Quick (D6) 550
Quincy (C6) 650
Quinnimont (D7) 250
Quinwood (E6) 506
Rachel (F3) 300
Racine (C6) 375
Rainelle (E7) 649
Raleigh (D7) 550
Ramage (C7) 150
Ranger (B6) 275
Rangoon (F4) 100
Ranson (L4) 1,974

(continued on following page)

TOPOGRAPHY

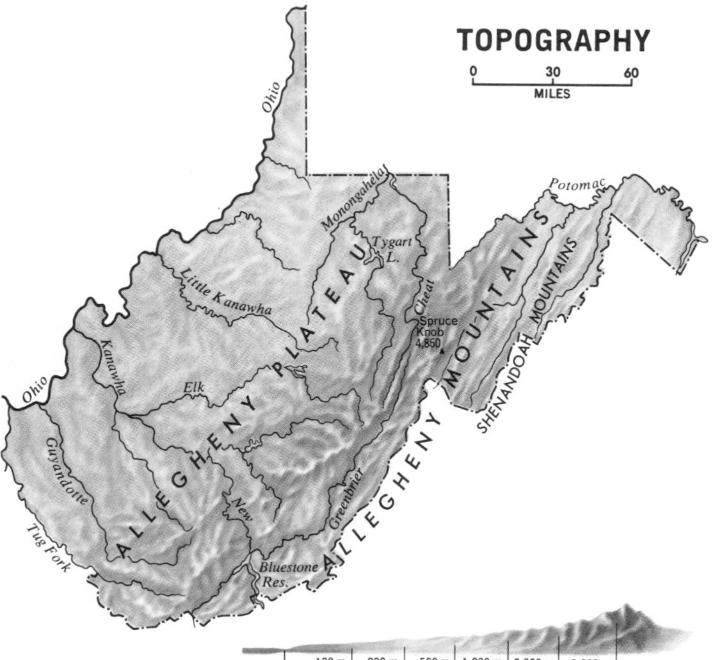
0 30 60
MILES
Ohio
Potomac
Monongahela
Tygart L.
Cheat
Little Kanawha
ALLEGHENY PLATEAU
MOUNTAINS
Spruce Knob 4,860
Elk
Kanawha
Ohio
Guyandotte
Tug Fork
New
Greenbrier
ALLEGHENY
SHENANDOAH MOUNTAINS
Bluestone Res.
Below Sea Level
100 m. 328 ft.
200 m. 656 ft.
500 m. 1,640 ft.
1,000 m. 3,281 ft.
2,000 m. 6,562 ft.
5,000 m. 16,404 ft.

West Virginia
(continued)

AGRICULTURE, INDUSTRY and RESOURCES

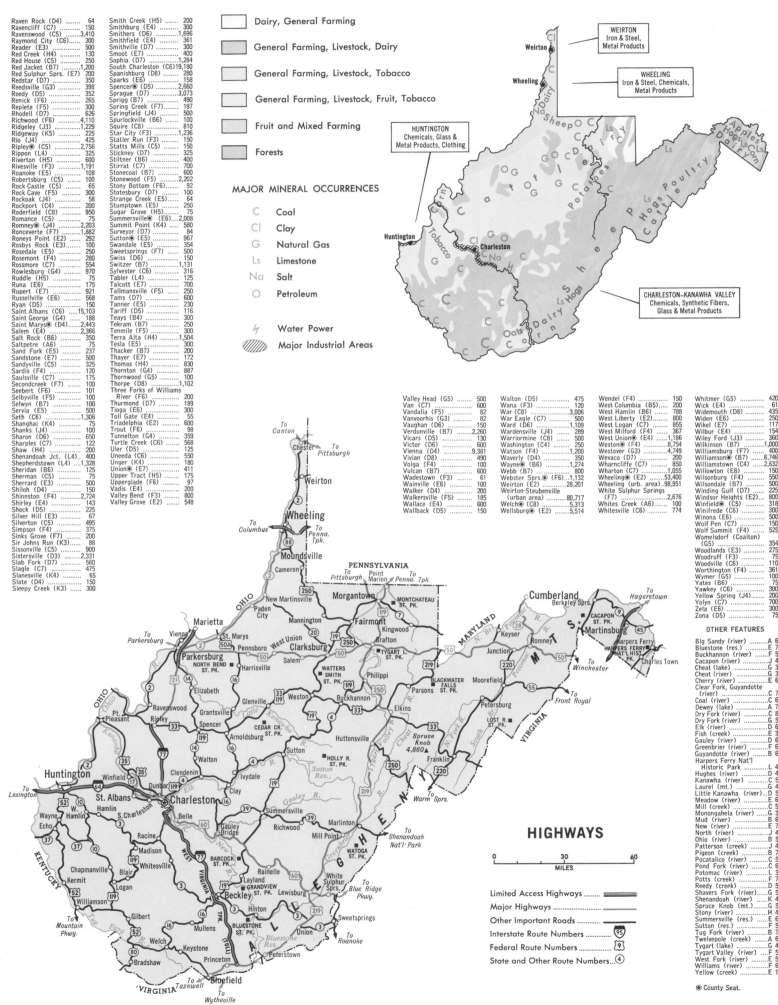

Raven Rock (D4) 64
Ravencliff (C7) 150
Ravenswood (C5) 3,410
Raymond City (C6) 300
Reader (E3) 500
Red Creek (H4) 130
Red House (C5) 250
Red Jacket (B7) 1,200
Red Sulphur Sprs. (E7) 200
Redstar (D7) 350
Reedsville (G3) 398
Reedy (D5) 352
Renick (F6) 265
Replete (F5) 300
Rhodell (D7) 626
Richwood (F6) 4,110
Ridgeley (J3) 1,229
Ridgeway (K5) 225
Rio (J4) 425
Ripley◉ (C5) 2,756
Rippon (L4) 325
Riverton (H5) 600
Rivesville (F3) 1,191
Roanoke (E5) 108
Robertsburg (C5) 100
Rock Castle (C5) 65
Rock Cave (F5) 300
Rockoak (J4) 58
Rockport (C4) 200
Roderfield (C8) 950
Romance (C5) 75
Romney◉ (J4) 2,203
Ronceverte (F6) 1,882
Roneys Point (E2) 292
Rosbys Rock (E3) 100
Rosedale (E5) 250
Rosemont (F4) 280
Rossmore (C7) 554
Rowlesburg (G4) 970
Ruddle (H5) 75
Runa (E6) 175
Rupert (E7) 921
Russellville (E6) 568
Ryan (D5) 150
Saint Albans (C6) 15,103
Saint George (G4) 188
Saint Marys◉ (D4) 2,443
Salem (E4) 2,366
Salt Rock (B6) 350
Saltpetre (A6) 75
Sand Fork (E5) 237
Sandstone (E7) 500
Sandyville (C5) 325
Sardis (F4) 120
Saulsville (C7) 175
Secondcreek (F7) 100
Seebert (F6) 101
Selbyville (F5) 100
Selwyn (B7) 100
Servia (E5) 500
Seth (C6) 1,306
Shanghai (K4) 75
Shanks (J4) 100
Sharon (D6) 650
Sharples (C7) 122
Shaw (H4) 200
Shenandoah Jct. (L4) .. 400
Shepherdstown (L4) ..1,328
Sheridan (B6) 125
Sherman (E3) 75
Sherrard (E3) 500
Shiloh (D4) 150
Shinnston (F4) 2,724
Shirley (H4) 143
Shock (D5) 225
Silver Hill (E3) 67
Silverton (C5) 495
Simpson (F4) 375
Sinks Grove (F7) 200
Sir Johns Run (K3) 88
Sissonville (C5) 900
Sistersville (D3) 2,331
Slab Fork (D7) 560
Slagle (C7) 475
Slanesville (K4) 65
Slate (D4) 150
Sleepy Creek (K3) 300

Smith Creek (H5) 200
Smithburg (E4) 300
Smithers (D6) 1,696
Smithfield (E4) 361
Smithville (D7) 300
Smoot (E7) 400
Sophia (D7) 1,284
South Charleston (C6)19,180
Spanishburg (D8) 280
Sparks (E6) 158
Spencer◉ (D5) 2,660
Sprague (D7) 3,073
Sprigg (B7) 490
Spring Creek (F7) 197
Springfield (J4) 500
Spurlockville (B6) 100
Squire (C8) 810
Star City (F3) 1,236
Statler Run (F3) 150
Statts Mills (C5) 150
Stickney (D7) 325
Stiltner (B6) 400
Stirrat (C7) 700
Stonecoal (B7) 600
Stonewall (F5) 2,202
Stony Bottom (F6) 92
Stotesbury (D7) 100
Strange Creek (E5) 64
Stumptown (E5) 250
Sugar Grove (H5) 75
Summersville◉ (E6) ..2,008
Summit Point (K4) 580
Surveyor (D7) 84
Sutton◉ (E5) 967
Swandale (E4) 354
Sweetsprings (F7) 500
Swiss (D6) 150
Switzer (B7) 1,131
Sylvester (C6) 316
Tabler (L4) 125
Talcott (E7) 700
Tallmansville (F5) 250
Tams (D7) 600
Tanner (E5) 230
Tariff (D5) 116
Teays (B4) 300
Tekram (B7) 250
Tenmile (F5) 300
Terra Alta (H4) 1,504
Tesla (E5) 300
Thacker (B7) 200
Thayer (E7) 172
Thomas (H4) 830
Thornton (G4) 887
Thornwood (G5) 100
Thorpe (D8) 1,102
Three Forks of Williams
  River (F6) 200
Thurmond (D7) 189
Tioga (E6) 300
Toll Gate (E4) 55
Triadelphia (E2) 600
Trout (F6) 98
Tunnelton (G4) 359
Turtle Creek (C6) 568
Uler (D5) 125
Uneeda (C6) 550
Unger (K4) 180
Union◉ (E7) 411
Upper Tract (H5) 175
Upperglade (F6) 97
Vadis (E4) 200
Valley Bend (F3) 800
Valley Grove (E2) 548

Valley Head (G5) 500
Van (C7) 600
Vandalia (F5) 82
Vanvoorhis (G3) 82
Vaughan (D6) 150
Verdunville (B7) 2,260
Vicars (D5) 130
Victor (D6) 600
Vienna (D4) 9,381
Vivian (D8) 490
Volga (F4) 100
Vulcan (B7) 600
Wadestown (F3) 61
Wainville (E6) 100
Walker (D4) 200
Walkersville (F5) 185
Wallace (E4) 600
Wallback (D5) 150

Walton (D5) 475
Wana (F3) 120
War (C8) 3,006
War Eagle (C7) 500
Ward (D6) 1,109
Wardensville (J4) 289
Warriormine (C8) 500
Washington (C4) 250
Watson (F4) 1,200
Waverly (D4) 350
Wayne◉ (B6) 1,274
Webb (B7) 800
Webster Sprs.◉ (F6)..1,132
Weirton (E2) 28,201
Weirton-Steubenville
  (urban area) 80,717
Welch◉ (C8) 5,313
Wellsburg◉ (E2) 5,514

Wendel (F4) 150
West Columbia (B5) 200
West Hamlin (B6) 788
West Liberty (E2) 800
West Logan (C7) 855
West Milford (F4) 367
West Union◉ (E4) 1,186
Weston◉ (F4) 8,754
Westover (G3) 4,749
Wevaco (D7) 200
Wharncliffe (C7) 850
Wharton (C7) 1,055
Wheeler (E2) 53,400
Wheeling (urb. area)..98,951
White Sulphur Springs
  (F7) 2,676
Whites Creek (A6) 100
Whitesville (C6) 774

Whitmer (G5) 420
Wick (E4) 61
Widemouth (D8) 435
Widen (E6) 250
Wikel (E7) 117
Wilbur (E4) 154
Wiley Ford (J3) 360
Wilkinson (B7) 1,000
Williamsburg (F7) 400
Williamson◉ (B7) 6,746
Williamstown (C4) 2,632
Willowton (E8) 150
Wilsonburg (F4) 550
Wilsondale (B7) 500
Winding Gulf (D7) 225
Windsor Heights (E2).. 800
Winfield◉ (C5) 318
Winifrede (C6) 300
Winona (E6) 500
Wolf Pen (C7) 150
Wolf Summit (F4) 525
Womelsdorf (Coalton)
  (G5) 354
Woodlands (E3) 275
Woodruff (F3) 75
Woodville (C6) 110
Worthington (F4) 361
Wymer (G5) 100
Yates (B6) 75
Yawkey (C6) 300
Yellow Spring (J4) 200
Yolyn (C7) 700
Zela (E6) 300
Zona (D5) 75

OTHER FEATURES

Big Sandy (river) ....A 6
Bluestone (res.) ....E 7
Buckhannon (river) ......F 5
Cacapon (river) ....J 4
Cheat (lake) ....G 3
Cheat (river) ....G 3
Cherry (river) ....E 6
Clear Fork, Guyandotte
  (river) ....C 7
Coal (river) ....C 6
Dewey (lake) ....A 7
Dry Fork (river) ....C 8
Dry Fork (river) ....G 5
Elk (river) ....D 6
Fish (creek) ....E 3
Gauley (river) ....D 6
Greenbrier (river) ....F 6
Guyandotte (river) ....B 6
Harpers Ferry Nat'l
  Historic Park ....L 4
Hughes (river) ....D 4
Kanawha (river) ....C 5
Laurel (mt.) ....G 4
Little Kanawha (river)..D 5
Meadow (river) ....E 6
Mill (creek) ....C 5
Monongahela (river) ....G 3
Mud (river) ....B 6
New (river) ....D 7
North (river) ....J 4
Ohio (river) ....B 5
Patterson (creek) ....J 4
Pigeon (creek) ....B 7
Pocatalico (river) ....C 5
Pond Fork (river) ....C 6
Potomac (river) ....L 3
Potts (creek) ....F 7
Reedy (creek) ....D 5
Shavers Fork (river)....G 5
Shenandoah (river) ......K 4
Spruce Knob (mt.) ....G 5
Stony (river) ....H 4
Summersville (res.) ......E 6
Sutton (res.) ....E 5
Tug Fork (river) ....B 7
Twelvepole (creek) ......A 6
Tygart (lake) ....G 4
Tygart Valley (river) ....F 3
West Fork (river) ....E 5
Williams (river) ....E 5
Yellow (creek) ....E 1

DOMINANT LAND USE

Dairy, General Farming

General Farming, Livestock, Dairy

General Farming, Livestock, Tobacco

General Farming, Livestock, Fruit, Tobacco

Fruit and Mixed Farming

Forests

MAJOR MINERAL OCCURRENCES

C — Coal
Cl — Clay
G — Natural Gas
Ls — Limestone
Na — Salt
O — Petroleum

⚡ Water Power
▨ Major Industrial Areas

WEIRTON
Iron & Steel, Metal Products

WHEELING
Iron & Steel, Chemicals, Metal Products

HUNTINGTON
Chemicals, Glass & Metal Products, Clothing

CHARLESTON–KANAWHA VALLEY
Chemicals, Synthetic Fibers, Glass & Metal Products

HIGHWAYS

0   30   60
MILES

Limited Access Highways
Major Highways
Other Important Roads
Interstate Route Numbers
Federal Route Numbers
State and Other Route Numbers

◉ County Seat.

WISCONSIN

AREA	56,154 sq. mi.
POPULATION	4,144,000
CAPITAL	Madison
LARGEST CITY	Milwaukee 741,324
HIGHEST POINT	Timms Hill 1,952 ft.
SETTLED IN	1670
ADMITTED TO UNION	May 29, 1848
POPULAR NAME	Badger State
STATE FLOWER	Wood Violet
STATE BIRD	Robin

COUNTIES

Adams (G8) ...7,566
Ashland (E3) ...17,375
Barron (C5) ...34,270
Bayfield (D3) ...11,910
Brown (L7) ...125,082
Buffalo (C7) ...14,202
Burnett (B4) ...9,214
Calumet (K7) ...22,268
Chippewa (D5) ...45,096
Clark (E6) ...31,527
Columbia (H9) ...36,708
Crawford (E9) ...16,351
Dane (H9) ...222,095
Dodge (J9) ...63,170
Door (M6) ...20,685
Douglas (C3) ...45,008
Dunn (C6) ...26,156
Eau Claire (D6) ...58,300
Florence (K4) ...3,437
Fond du Lac (K8) ...75,085
Forest (J4) ...7,542
Grant (E10) ...44,419
Green (G10) ...25,861
Green Lake (H8) ...15,418
Iowa (F9) ...19,631
Iron (F3) ...7,830
Jackson (E7) ...15,151
Jefferson (J9) ...50,094
Juneau (F8) ...17,490
Kenosha (K10) ...100,615
Kewaunee (L6) ...18,282
La Crosse (D8) ...72,465
Lafayette (F10) ...18,142
Langlade (H5) ...19,916
Lincoln (G5) ...22,338
Manitowoc (L7) ...75,215
Marathon (G6) ...88,874
Marinette (K5) ...34,660
Marquette (H8) ...8,516
Menominee (J5) ...2,626
Milwaukee (L9) ...1,036,047
Monroe (E8) ...31,241
Oconto (K6) ...25,110
Oneida (G4) ...22,112
Outagamie (K7) ...101,794
Ozaukee (L9) ...38,441
Pepin (C6) ...7,332
Pierce (B6) ...22,503
Polk (B5) ...24,968
Portage (G6) ...36,964
Price (F4) ...14,370
Racine (K10) ...141,781
Richland (F9) ...17,684
Rock (H10) ...113,913
Rusk (E5) ...14,794
Saint Croix (B5) ...29,164
Sauk (G8) ...37,167
Sawyer (D4) ...9,475
Shawano (J6) ...34,351
Sheboygan (L8) ...86,484
Taylor (E5) ...17,843
Trempealeau (D7) ...23,377
Vernon (E8) ...25,663
Vilas (G3) ...9,332
Walworth (J10) ...52,368
Washburn (C4) ...10,301
Washington (K9) ...46,119
Waukesha (K9) ...158,249
Waupaca (J6) ...35,340
Waushara (H7) ...13,497
Winnebago (J7) ...107,928
Wood (F7) ...59,105

CITIES and TOWNS

Abbotsford (F6) ...1,171
Abrams (L6) ...275
Adams (G8) ...1,301
Adell (L8) ...398
Afton (H10) ...225
Albany (G10) ...892
Albion (H10) ...200
Algoma (M6) ...3,855
Allenton (K9) ...475
Alma◉ (C7) ...1,008
Alma Center (E7) ...464
Almena (B5) ...398
Almond (G7) ...391
Alto (J8) ...136
Altoona (C6) ...2,114
Amberg (K5) ...275
Amery (B5) ...1,769
Amherst (H7) ...596
Amherst Junction (H7) ...131
Angelo (E8) ...164
Aniwa (H6) ...247
Antigo◉ (H5) ...9,691
Appleton◉ (J7) ...48,411
Arbor Vitae (G4) ...175
Arcadia (D7) ...2,084
Arena (G9) ...309
Argonne (J4) ...350
Argyle (G10) ...786
Arkansaw (B6) ...400
Arlington (H9) ...349
Armstrong Creek (K4) ...680
Arpin (G6) ...325
Ashippun (H1) ...278
Ashland◉ (E2) ...10,132
Athens (G5) ...770
Auburndale (F6) ...396
Augusta (D6) ...1,338
Auroraville (H7) ...250
Avoca (F9) ...363
Babcock (F7) ...320
Bagley (D10) ...275
Baileys Harbor (M5) ...300
Baldwin (B6) ...1,184
Balsam Lake◉ (B5) ...541
Bancroft (G7) ...250
Bangor (E8) ...928
Baraboo◉ (G9) ...7,660
Barneveld (F10) ...420
Barron◉ (C5) ...2,338
Barronett (B4) ...150
Barton (K9) ...1,569
Bay City (B6) ...327
Bayfield (E2) ...969
Bayside (M1) ...3,181
Bear Creek (J6) ...455
Beaver Dam (J9) ...13,118
Beetown (E10) ...175
Belgium (L9) ...643
Bell Center (E9) ...155
Belleville (G10) ...844
Bellevue (L7) ...150
Belmont (F10) ...616
Beloit (J11) ...32,846
Bennett (C3) ...200
Benton (F10) ...837
Berlin (H8) ...4,838
Berryville (M3) ...150
Bethel (F6) ...280
Big Bend (K2) ...797
Big Falls (H6) ...119
Birchwood (C4) ...433
Birnamwood (H6) ...568
Biron (F7) ...726
Black Creek (K7) ...707
Black Earth (F9) ...784
Black River Falls◉ (E7) ...3,195
Blair (D7) ...909
Blanchardville (G10) ...632
Bloomer (D5) ...2,834
Bloomingdale (E8) ...125
Bloomington (E10) ...735
Blue Mounds (G9) ...227
Blue River (E9) ...356
Boaz (E9) ...117
Bonduel (K6) ...876
Boscobel (E9) ...2,608
Boulder Junction (G3) ...150
Bowler (J6) ...274
Boyceville (C5) ...660
Boyd (E6) ...622
Brandon (J8) ...758
Brantwood (F4) ...400
Briggsville (H8) ...210
Brillion (L7) ...1,783
Bristol (K4) ...200
Brodhead (G10) ...2,444
Brokaw (G5) ...319
Brookfield (K1) ...19,812
Brooklyn (H10) ...590
Brooks (G8) ...130
Brothertown (K7) ...124
Brown Deer (L1) ...11,280
Brownsville (J8) ...276
Browntown (G10) ...263
Bruce (E5) ...815
Brussels (L6) ...166
Buffalo (C7) ...484
Burlington (K10) ...5,856
Burnett (J9) ...250
Butler (K1) ...2,274
Butternut (E4) ...499
Cable (D3) ...262
Cadott (D6) ...881
Cambria (H8) ...589
Cambridge (H9) ...605
Cameron (C5) ...982
Camp Douglas (F8) ...489
Campbellsport (K8) ...1,472
Caroline (J6) ...366
Cascade (K8) ...449
Casco (L6) ...460
Cashton (E8) ...828
Cassville (E10) ...1,290
Cataract (E7) ...200
Catawba (E4) ...230
Cavour (J4) ...150
Cazenovia (F8) ...351
Cecil (K6) ...357
Cedar Grove (L8) ...1,175
Cedarburg (L9) ...5,191
Centuria (A5) ...551
Chaseburg (D8) ...242
Chelsea (F5) ...125
Chenequa (J1) ...445
Chetek (C5) ...1,729
Chili (F6) ...200
Chilton◉ (K7) ...2,578
Chippewa Falls◉ (D6) ...11,708
City Point (F7) ...100
Clayton (B5) ...324
Clear Lake (B5) ...724
Clearwater Lake (H4) ...152
Cleghorn (C6) ...200
Cleveland (L8) ...687
Clinton (J10) ...1,274
Clintonville (J6) ...4,778
Clyman (J9) ...259
Cobb (F10) ...387
Cochrane (C7) ...455
Colby (F6) ...1,085
Coleman (L5) ...718
Colfax (C6) ...885
Coloma (H7) ...312
Columbus (H9) ...3,467
Combined Locks (K7) ...1,421
Conover (H3) ...389
Conrath (C5) ...121
Coon Valley (D8) ...536
Cornell (D5) ...1,685
Cornucopia (D2) ...229
Couderay (D4) ...113
Cottage Grove ‡(H9) ...413
Crandon◉ (J4) ...1,679
Cream (C7) ...300
Crivitz (L5) ...700
Cross Plains (G9) ...1,066
Cuba City (F10) ...1,673
Cudahy (M2) ...17,975
Cumberland (C4) ...1,860
Curtiss (F6) ...147
Cushing (A4) ...137
Dale (J7) ...400
Dallas (C5) ...401
Dalton (H8) ...300
Danbury (B3) ...360
Dane (J10) ...805
Darien (J10) ...805
Darlington◉ (F10) ...2,349
De Forest (H9) ...1,223
De Pere (H9) ...10,045
De Soto (D9) ...657
Deer Park (B5) ...221
Deerfield (H9) ...795
Delafield (J11) ...2,334
Delavan (J10) ...4,846
Delavan Lake (J10) ...1,884
Delta (D3) ...175
Denmark (L7) ...1,106
Diamond Bluff (A6) ...220
Dickeyville (E10) ...671
Dodge (D7) ...165
Dodgeville◉ (F10) ...2,911
Dorchester (F5) ...504
Dousman (J1) ...410
Downing (B5) ...241
Downsville (C6) ...300
Doylestown (H9) ...249
Dresser (A5) ...498
Drummond (D3) ...423
Durand◉ (C6) ...2,039
Durham (K2) ...120
Dyckesville (L6) ...300
Eagle (H2) ...620
Eagle River◉ (H4) ...1,367
East Ellsworth (B6) ...400
East Troy (J2) ...1,455
Eastman (D9) ...348
Easton (G8) ...250
Eau Claire◉ (D6) ...37,987
Eau Galle (B6) ...253
Eden (K8) ...312
Edgar (G6) ...803
Edgerton (H10) ...4,000
Egg Harbor (M5) ...192
El Dorado (J8) ...150
Eland (H6) ...213
Elcho (H5) ...500
Elderon (H6) ...177
Eleva (D6) ...548
Elk Creek (C7) ...150
Elk Mound (C6) ...379
Elkhart Lake (L8) ...651
Elkhorn◉ (J10) ...3,586
Ellison Bay (M5) ...160
Ellsworth◉ (A6) ...1,701
Elm Grove (K1) ...4,994
Elmwood (B6) ...776
Elmwood Park ‡(M3) ...412
Elroy (F8) ...1,505
Elton (J5) ...250
Embarrass (J6) ...306
Emerald (B5) ...157
Endeavor (G8) ...280
Ephraim (M5) ...221
Ettrick (D7) ...479
Eureka (J7) ...300
Evansville (H10) ...2,858
Excelsior (E9) ...130
Exeland (D4) ...214
Fair Water (J8) ...330
Fairchild (D6) ...594
Fall Creek (D6) ...710
Fall River (H9) ...584
Falun (B5) ...150
Fence (K4) ...200
Fennimore (E9) ...1,747
Fenwood (F6) ...147
Ferryville (D9) ...194
Fifield (F4) ...375
Fish Creek (M5) ...230
Florence◉ (K4) ...893
Fond du Lac◉ (K8) ...32,719
Fontana (J10) ...1,326
Footville (H10) ...675
Forest Junction (K7) ...275
Forestville (L6) ...324
Fort Atkinson (J10) ...7,908
Fountain City (C7) ...934
Fox Lake (J8) ...1,181
Fox Point (M1) ...7,315
Foxboro (B2) ...700
Francis Creek (L7) ...328
Franklin (L2) ...10,006
Franklin (L1) ...100
Franksville (M3) ...485
Frederic (B4) ...857
Fredonia (L8) ...710
Fremont (J7) ...575
Friendship◉ (G8) ...560
Friesland (H8) ...308
Galesville (D7) ...1,199
Gaslyn (B4) ...200
Gays Mills (E9) ...634
Genesee (J2) ...362
Genesee Depot (J2) ...412
Genoa (D8) ...235
Genoa City (K11) ...1,005
Germantown (K1) ...622
Gibbsville (L8) ...210
Gile (F3) ...600
Gillett (K6) ...1,374
Gilman (E5) ...379
Gilmanton (C7) ...200
Gleason (G5) ...200
Glen Flora (E4) ...75
Glen Haven (E10) ...300
Glenbeulah (L8) ...428
Glendale (M1) ...9,537
Glenwood City (B5) ...835
Glidden (E3) ...920
Goodman (K4) ...800
Gordon (C3) ...300
Gotham (F9) ...280
Grafton (L9) ...3,748
Grand Marsh (G8) ...200
Grandview (D3) ...325
Granton (E6) ...278
Grantsburg◉ (A4) ...900
Granville (L1) ...200
Gratiot (F10) ...294
Green Bay◉ (K6) ...62,888
Green Bay (urb. area) ...97,162
Green Lake◉ (H8) ...1,033
Greendale (L2) ...6,843
Greenfield (L2) ...17,636
Greenleaf (L7) ...250
Greenville (J7) ...250
Greenwood (E6) ...1,041
Gresham (J6) ...458
Gurney (F3) ...100
Hager City (A6) ...185
Hales Corners (K2) ...5,549
Hamburg (G5) ...958
Hammond (A6) ...645
Hancock (G7) ...367
Hanover (H10) ...276
Hartford (K9) ...5,627
Hartland (J1) ...2,088
Hatley (H6) ...306
Haugen (C4) ...265
Hawkins (E4) ...402
Hawthorne (C3) ...500
Hayton (K7) ...125
Hazel Green (F11) ...807
Hazelhurst (G4) ...225
Heafford Junction (G4) ...150
Helenville (J10) ...225
Herbster (D2) ...400
Herrington (D8) ...2,405
Hewitt (F6) ...200
Highland (F9) ...741
Hika (L8) ...200
Hilbert (K7) ...736
Hiles (J4) ...132
Hillsboro (F8) ...1,366
Hillsdale (C5) ...150
Hingham (K8) ...236
Hixton (E7) ...310
Holcombe (D5) ...275
Hollandale (G10) ...275
Holmen (D8) ...635
Honey Creek (J3) ...380
Horicon (J9) ...2,996
Hortonville (J7) ...1,366
Houlton (A5) ...250
Howard (K6) ...3,485
Hubertus (K1) ...285
Hudson◉ (A6) ...4,325
Humbird (E7) ...270
Hurley◉ (F3) ...2,763
Hustisford (J9) ...708
Hustler (F8) ...177
Independence (D7) ...954
Ingram (E5) ...99
Iola (H6) ...831
Iron Belt (F3) ...650
Iron Ridge (K9) ...419
Iron River (D2) ...900
Ironton (F9) ...167
Ixonia (H1) ...200
Jackson (K9) ...458
Jacksonport (M6) ...275
Janesville◉ (J10) ...35,164
Jefferson◉ (J10) ...4,548
Jim Falls (D5) ...289
Johnson Creek (J9) ...686
Juda (H10) ...400
Jump River (E5) ...424
Junction City (G6) ...381
Juneau◉ (J9) ...1,718
Kansasville (L3) ...100
Kaukauna (K7) ...10,096
Kekoskee (J8) ...247
Kellnersville (L7) ...300
Kendall (F8) ...528
Kennan (F5) ...162
Kenosha◉ (M3) ...67,899
Kenosha (urban area) ...72,852
Keshena (J5) ...927
Kewaskum (K8) ...1,572
Kewaunee◉ (M7) ...2,772
Kiel (L8) ...2,524
Kieler (E10) ...177
Kimball (F2) ...600
Kimberly (K7) ...5,322
King (H7) ...950
Kingston (H8) ...343
Knapp (B6) ...374
Kohler (L8) ...1,524
Krakow (K6) ...150
La Crosse◉ (D8) ...47,575
La Farge (E8) ...833
La Pointe (E2) ...186
La Valle (F8) ...417
Lac La Belle (H1) ...276
Ladysmith◉ (D5) ...3,584
Lake Delton (G8) ...714
Lake Geneva (K10) ...4,929
Lake Mills (H9) ...2,951
Lake Nebagamon (C3) ...346
Lake Tomahawk (H4) ...800
Lakewood (K5) ...200
Lancaster◉ (E10) ...3,703
Land O'Lakes (H3) ...600
Lannon (K1) ...1,084
Laona (J4) ...1,430
Leadmine (F10) ...100
Lebanon (H1) ...500
Lena (K6) ...506
Leopolis (J6) ...123
Lewis (B4) ...150
Lily (J5) ...160
Lima Center (J10) ...200

(continued on following page)

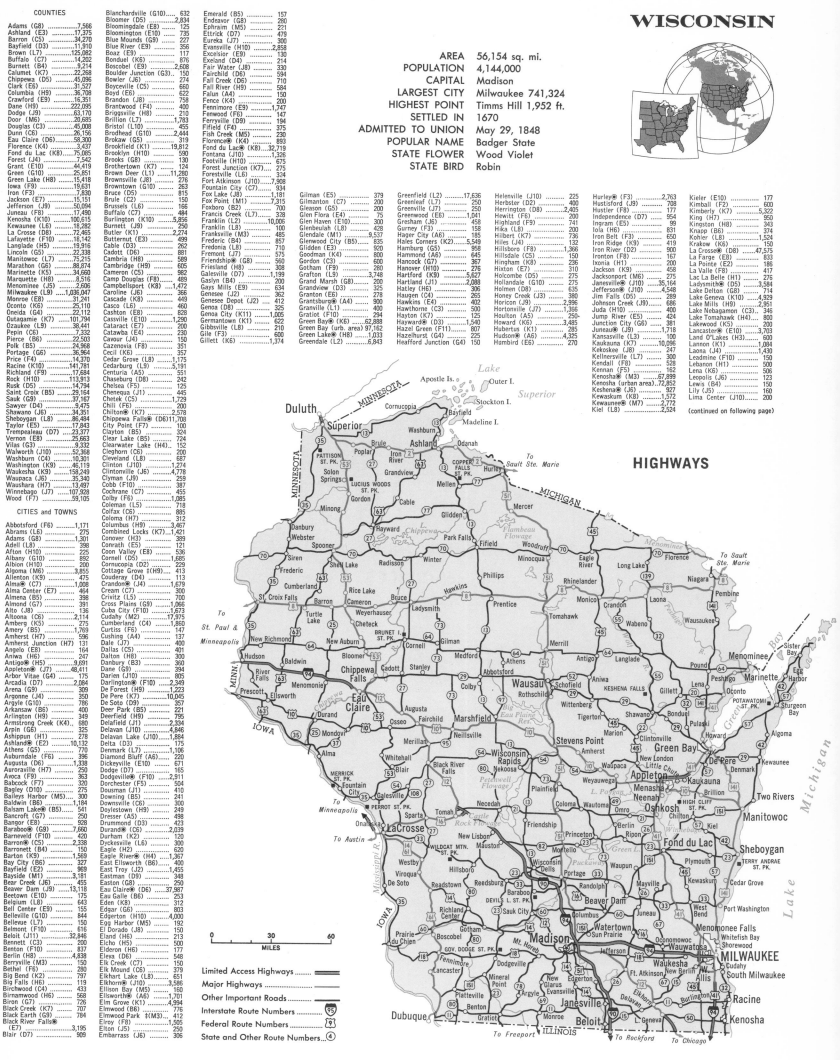

HIGHWAYS

0 30 60 MILES

Limited Access Highways
Major Highways
Other Important Roads
Interstate Route Numbers
Federal Route Numbers
State and Other Route Numbers

Wisconsin

(continued)

TOPOGRAPHY

| Below Sea Level | 100 m. 328 ft. | 200 m. 656 ft. | 500 m. 1,640 ft. | 1,000 m. 3,281 ft. | 2,000 m. 6,562 ft. | 5,000 m. 16,404 ft. |

AGRICULTURE, INDUSTRY and RESOURCES

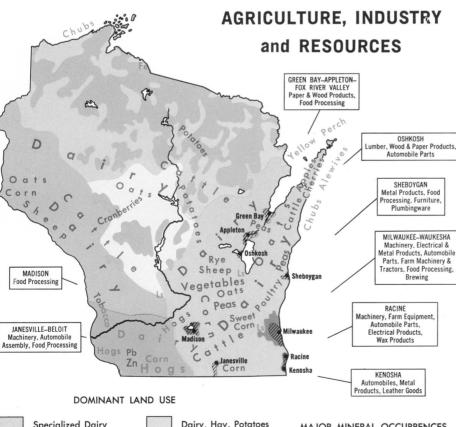

GREEN BAY–APPLETON–FOX RIVER VALLEY
Paper & Wood Products, Food Processing

OSHKOSH
Lumber, Wood & Paper Products, Automobile Parts

SHEBOYGAN
Metal Products, Food Processing, Furniture, Plumbingware

MILWAUKEE–WAUKESHA
Machinery, Electrical & Metal Products, Automobile Parts, Farm Machinery & Tractors, Food Processing, Brewing

RACINE
Machinery, Farm Equipment, Automobile Parts, Electrical Products, Wax Products

KENOSHA
Automobiles, Metal Products, Leather Goods

MADISON
Food Processing

JANESVILLE–BELOIT
Machinery, Automobile Assembly, Food Processing

DOMINANT LAND USE

- Specialized Dairy
- Dairy, General Farming
- Dairy, Livestock
- Dairy, Hay, Potatoes
- Hogs, Dairy
- Forests
- Urban Areas

MAJOR MINERAL OCCURRENCES

Fe Iron Ore
Ls Limestone
Pb Lead
Zn Zinc

Major Industrial Areas

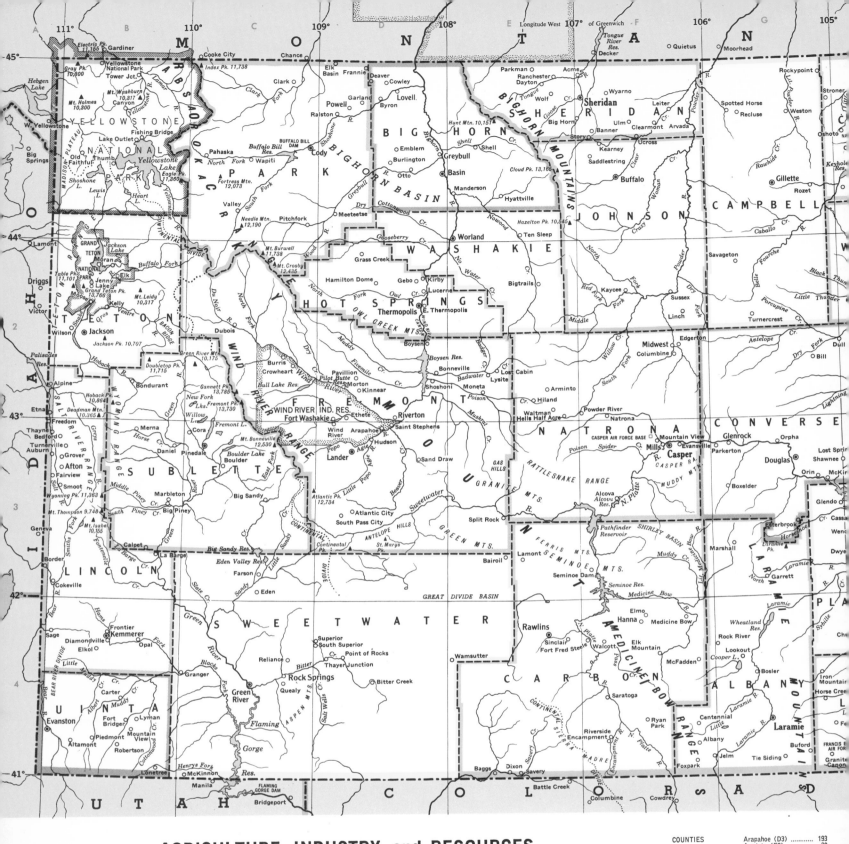

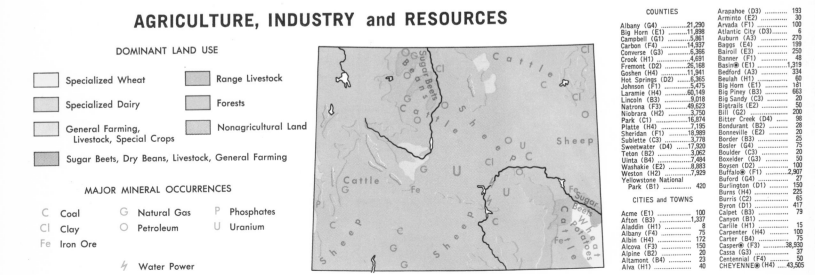

AGRICULTURE, INDUSTRY and RESOURCES

DOMINANT LAND USE

- Specialized Wheat
- Specialized Dairy
- General Farming, Livestock, Special Crops
- Sugar Beets, Dry Beans, Livestock, General Farming
- Range Livestock
- Forests
- Nonagricultural Land

MAJOR MINERAL OCCURRENCES

- C Coal
- Cl Clay
- Fe Iron Ore
- G Natural Gas
- O Petroleum
- P Phosphates
- U Uranium
- ⚡ Water Power

COUNTIES

County	Population
Albany (G4)	21,290
Big Horn (E1)	11,898
Campbell (G1)	5,861
Carbon (F4)	14,937
Converse (G3)	6,366
Crook (H1)	4,691
Fremont (D2)	26,168
Goshen (H4)	11,941
Hot Springs (D2)	6,365
Johnson (F1)	5,475
Laramie (H4)	60,149
Lincoln (B3)	9,018
Natrona (F3)	49,623
Niobrara (H2)	3,750
Park (C1)	16,874
Platte (H4)	7,195
Sheridan (F1)	18,989
Sublette (C3)	3,778
Sweetwater (D4)	17,920
Teton (B2)	3,062
Uinta (B4)	7,484
Washakie (E2)	8,883
Weston (H2)	7,929
Yellowstone National Park (B1)	420

CITIES and TOWNS

Place	Population
Acme (E1)	100
Afton (B3)	1,337
Aladdin (H1)	8
Albany (F4)	75
Albin (H4)	172
Alcova (F3)	150
Alpine (B2)	20
Altamont (B4)	23
Alva (H1)	40
Arapahoe (D3)	193
Arminto (E2)	30
Arvada (F1)	100
Atlantic City (D3)	6
Auburn (A3)	270
Baggs (E4)	199
Bairoil (E3)	250
Banner (F1)	48
Basin⊙ (E1)	1,319
Bedford (A3)	334
Beulah (H1)	60
Big Horn (E1)	181
Big Piney (B3)	663
Big Sandy (C3)	20
Bigtrails (E2)	50
Bill (G2)	200
Bitter Creek (D4)	98
Bondurant (B2)	28
Bonneville (E2)	20
Border (B3)	25
Bosler (G4)	75
Boulder (C3)	20
Boxelder (G3)	50
Boysen (D2)	100
Buffalo⊙ (F1)	2,907
Buford (G4)	27
Burlington (D1)	150
Burns (H4)	225
Burris (C2)	65
Byron (D1)	417
Calpet (B3)	79
Canyon (B1)	
Carlile (H1)	15
Carpenter (H4)	100
Carter (B4)	75
Casper⊙ (F3)	38,930
Cassa (G3)	37
Centennial (F4)	50
CHEYENNE⊙ (H4)	43,505

WYOMING

AREA	97,914 sq. mi.
POPULATION	340,000
CAPITAL	Cheyenne
LARGEST CITY	Cheyenne 43,505
HIGHEST POINT	Gannett Pk. 13,785 ft.
SETTLED IN	1834
ADMITTED TO UNION	July 10, 1890
POPULAR NAME	Equality State
STATE FLOWER	Indian Paintbrush
STATE BIRD	Meadowlark

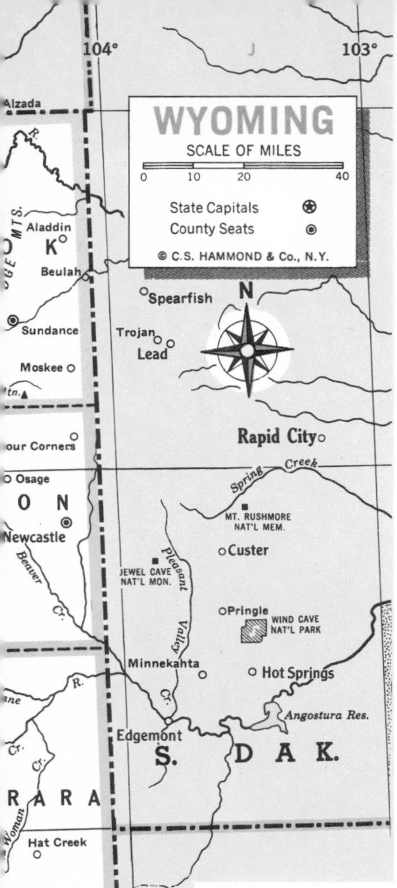

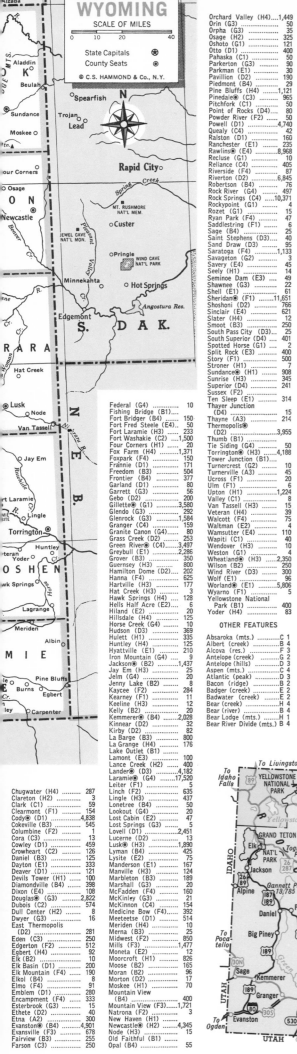

WYOMING
SCALE OF MILES
0 10 20 40
State Capitals
County Seats
© C.S. HAMMOND & Co., N.Y.
104°
103°
Alzada
Aladdin
Beulah
Spearfish
Sundance
Trojan
Lead
Moskee
Rapid City
Four Corners
Osage
Newcastle
MT. RUSHMORE NAT'L MEM.
Custer
JEWEL CAVE NAT'L MON.
Pringle
WIND CAVE NAT'L PARK
Minnekahta
Hot Springs
Angostura Res.
Edgemont
S. DAK.
Hat Creek

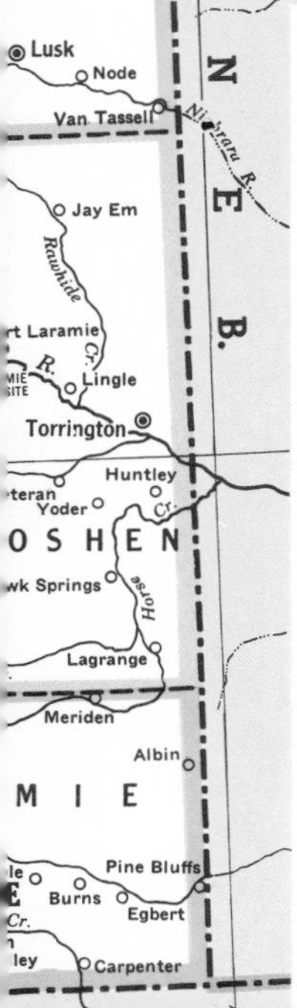

Lusk
Node
Van Tassell
Jay Em
Lingle
Torrington
Huntley
Yoder
Lagrange
Meriden
Albin
Pine Bluffs
Burns
Egbert
Carpenter

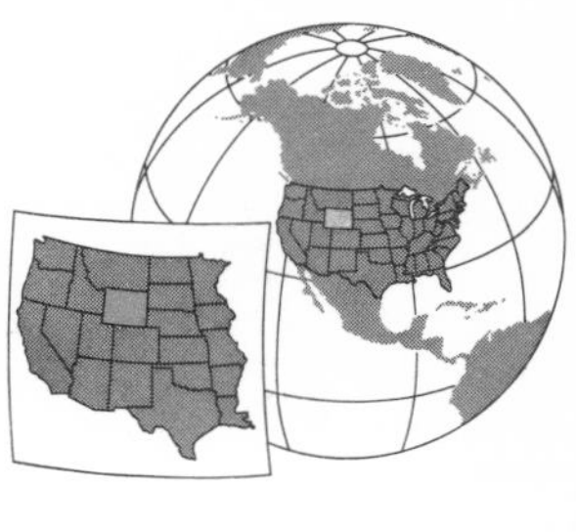

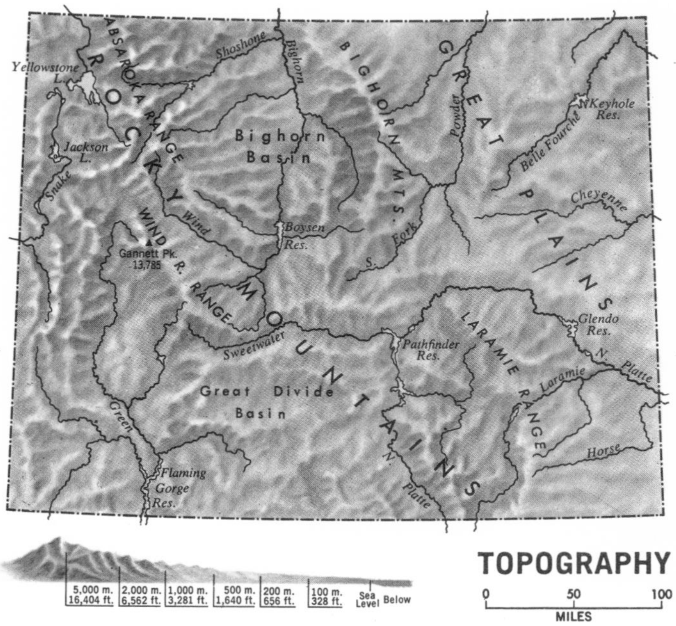

Yellowstone L.
Jackson L.
Shoshone
Bighorn
Bighorn Basin
BIGHORN MTS.
GREAT PLAINS
Keyhole Res.
Belle Fourche
Cheyenne
Boysen Res.
Gannett Pk. 13,785
WIND R. RANGE
ROCKY MOUNTAINS
ABSAROKA RANGE
Sweetwater
Pathfinder Res.
LARAMIE RANGE
Glendo Res.
N. Platte
Laramie
Great Divide Basin
Green
Flaming Gorge Res.
Platte
Horse
5,000 m. 16,404 ft.
2,000 m. 6,562 ft.
1,000 m. 3,281 ft.
500 m. 1,640 ft.
200 m. 656 ft.
100 m. 328 ft.
Sea Level
Below

TOPOGRAPHY

0 50 100
MILES

Chugwater (H4) 287
Clareton (H2) 3
Clark (C1) 59
Clearmont (F1) 154
Cody◉ (D1) 4,838
Cokeville (B3) 545
Columbine (F2) 1
Cora (C3) 13
Cowley (D1) 459
Crowheart (C2) 126
Daniel (B3) 125
Dayton (E1) 333
Deaver (D1) 121
Devils Tower (H1) 100
Diamondville (B4) 398
Dixon (E4) 108
Douglas◉ (G3) 2,822
Dubois (C2) 574
Dull Center (H2) 8
Dwyer (G3) 16
East Thermopolis (D2) 281
Eden (C3) 250
Edgerton (F2) 512
Egbert (H4) 92
Elk (B2) 10
Elk Basin (D1) 200
Elk Mountain (F4) 190
Elkol (B4) 8
Elmo (F4) 91
Emblem (D1) 280
Encampment (F4) 333
Esterbrook (G3) 15
Ethete (D2) 40
Etna (A2) 300
Evanston◉ (B4) 4,901
Evansville (F3) 678
Fairview (B3) 255
Farson (C3) 250
Federal (G4) 10
Fishing Bridge (B1)....
Fort Bridger (B4) 150
Fort Fred Steele (E4).. 50
Fort Laramie (H3) 233
Fort Washakie (C2) 1,500
Four Corners (H1) 20
Fox Farm (H4) 1,371
Foxpark (F4) 150
Frannie (D1) 171
Freedom (B3) 504
Frontier (B4) 377
Garland (D1) 80
Garrett (G3) 56
Gebo (D2) 200
Gillette◉ (G1) 3,580
Glendo (G3) 292
Glenrock (G3) 1,584
Granger (C4) 159
Granite Canon (G4)...... 80
Grass Creek (D2) 253
Green River◉ (C4)..........3,497
Greybull (E1) 2,286
Grover (B3) 350
Guernsey (H3) 800
Hamilton Dome (D2).... 202
Hanna (F4) 625
Hartville (H3) 177
Hat Creek (H3) 3
Hawk Springs (H4) 128
Hells Half Acre (E2).... 6
Hiland (E2) 20
Hillsdale (H4) 125
Horse Creek (G4) 10
Hudson (D3) 369
Hulett (H1) 335
Huntley (H4) 125
Hyattville (E1) 210
Iron Mountain (G4) 9
Jackson◉ (B2) 1,437
Jay Em (H3) 25
Jelm (G4) 20
Jenny Lake (B2) 8
Kaycee (F2) 284
Kearney (F1) 11
Keeline (H3) 12
Kelly (B2) 20
Kemmerer◉ (B4) 2,028
Kinnear (D2) 32
Kirby (D2) 82
La Barge (B3) 800
La Grange (H4) 176
Lake Outlet (B1) ....
Lamont (E3) 100
Lance Creek (H2) 400
Lander◉ (D3) 4,182
Laramie◉ (G4) 17,520
Leiter (F1) 5
Linch (F2) 635
Lingle (H3) 437
Lonetree (B4) 50
Lookout (G4) 20
Lost Cabin (E2) 47
Lost Springs (G3) 5
Lovell (D1) 2,451
Lucerne (D2) 13
Lusk◉ (H3) 1,890
Lyman (B4) 425
Lysite (E2) 75
Manderson (E1) 167
Manville (H3) 124
Marbleton (B3) 189
Marshall (G3) 20
McFadden (F4) 160
McKinley (G3) 21
McKinnon (C4) 154
Medicine Bow (F4).......... 392
Meeteetse (D1) 514
Meriden (H4) 10
Merna (B3) 25
Midwest (F2) 850
Mills (F3) 1,477
Moneta (E2) 12
Moorcroft (H1) 826
Moose (B2) 165
Moran (B2) 96
Morton (D2) 17
Moskee (H1) 70
Mountain View (B4) 400
Mountain View (F3)..........1,721
Natrona (F2) 3
New Haven (H1) ....
Newcastle◉ (H2) 4,345
Node (H3) 15
Old Faithful (B1) ....
Opal (B4) 55
Orchard Valley (H4)....1,449
Orin (G3) 50
Orpha (G3) 35
Osage (H2) 325
Oshoto (G1) 121
Otto (D1) 400
Pahaska (C1) 50
Parkerton (G3) 90
Parkman (E1) 30
Pavillion (D2) 190
Piedmont (B4) 29
Pine Bluffs (H4) 1,121
Pinedale◉ (C3) 965
Pitchfork (C1) 50
Point of Rocks (D4).... 80
Powder River (F2) 50
Powell (D1) 4,740
Quealy (C4) 42
Ralston (D1) 160
Ranchester (E1) 235
Rawlins◉ (E4) 8,968
Recluse (G1) 10
Reliance (C4) 405
Riverside (F4) 87
Riverton (D2) 6,845
Robertson (B4) 76
Rock River (G4) 497
Rock Springs (C4) 10,371
Rockypoint (G1) 4
Rozet (G1) 15
Ryan Park (F4) 47
Saddlestring (F1) 6
Sage (B4) 25
Saint Stephens (D3).... 40
Sand Draw (D3) 95
Saratoga (F4) 1,133
Savageton (G2) 3
Savery (E4) 45
Seely (H1) 14
Seminoe Dam (E3) 49
Shawnee (G3) 22
Shell (E1) 61
Sheridan◉ (F1) 11,651
Shoshoni (D2) 766
Sinclair (E4) 621
Slater (H4) 12
Smoot (B3) 250
South Pass City (D3)... 25
South Superior (D4) 401
Spotted Horse (G1) 2
Split Rock (E3) 400
Story (F1) 500
Stroner (H1) 7
Sundance◉ (H1) 908
Sunrise (H3) 345
Superior (D4) 241
Sussex (F2) ....
Ten Sleep (E1) 314
Thayer Junction (D4) 15
Thayne (A3) 214
Thermopolis◉ (D2) 3,955
Thumb (B1) ....
Tie Siding (G4) 50
Torrington◉ (H3) 4,188
Tower Junction (B1)....
Turnercrest (G2) 10
Turnerville (A3) 45
Ucross (F1) 20
Ulm (F1) 6
Upton (H1) 1,224
Valley (C1) 8
Van Tassell (H3) 15
Veteran (H4) 39
Walcott (F4) 75
Waltman (E2) 4
Wamsutter (E4) 110
Wapiti (C1) 40
Wendover (H3) 10
Weston (G1) 4
Wheatland◉ (H3) 2,350
Wilson (B2) 250
Wind River (D3) 300
Wolf (E1) 96
Worland◉ (E1) 5,806
Wyarno (F1) 5
Yellowstone National Park (B1) 400
Yoder (H4) 83

OTHER FEATURES

Absaroka (mts.) ....C 1
Albert (creek) ....B 4
Alcova (res.) ....F 3
Antelope (creek) ....G 2
Antelope (hills) ....D 3
Aspen (mts.) ....C 4
Atlantic (peak) ....D 3
Bacon (ridge) ....B 2
Badger (creek) ....E 2
Badwater (creek) ....E 2
Bear (creek) ....H 4
Bear (river) ....B 4
Bear Lodge (mts.) ....H 1
Bear River Divide (mts.) B 4
Beaver (creek) ....D 3
Beaver (creek) ....H 2
Belle Fourche (river) ....H 1
Big Sandy (res.) ....C 3
Bighorn (basin) ....D 1
Bighorn (mts.) ....E 1
Bighorn (river) ....D 1
Bitter (creek) ....C 4
Black Thunder (creek) ..G 2
Blacks Fork, Green (river) ....C 4
Bonneville (mt.) ....C 3
Boulder (lake) ....C 3
Boysen (res.) ....D 2
Buffalo Bill (dam) ....C 1
Buffalo Bill (res.) ....C 1
Buffalo Fork (river) ......B 2
Bull Lake (res.) ....C 2
Burwell (mt.) ....C 2
Caballo (creek) ....G 1
Casper (range) ....F 3
Casper A.F.B. ....F 3
Cheyenne (river) ....H 2
Chugwater (creek) ......H 4
Clark Fork (river) ....C 1
Clear (creek) ....F 1
Cloud (peak) ....E 1
Continental (peak) ....D 3
Cooper (lake) ....G 4
Cottonwood (creek) ......B 4
Crazy Woman (creek)....F 1
Crosby (mt.) ....C 2
Crow (creek) ....H 4
Deadman (mt.) ....B 2
Devils Tower National Mon. ....H 1
Doubletop (peak) ....B 2
Dry (creek) ....C 2
Dry Cottonwood (creek)..D 1
Dry Fork, Cheyenne (river) ....G 2
Dry Fork, Powder (river) ....F 2
Du Noir (river) ....C 2
Eagle (peak) ....B 1
Eden Valley (res.) ....C 3
Encampment (river) ......F 4
Ferris (mts.) ....E 3
Fivemile (creek) ....D 2
Flaming Gorge (res.) ....C 4
Fontenelle (creek) ....B 3
Fort Laramie National Historic Site ....H 3
Fortress (mt.) ....C 1
Francis E. Warren A.F.B. ....G 4
Fremont (lake) ....C 3
Fremont (peak) ....C 2
Gannett (peak) ....C 2
Gas (hills) ....E 3
Glendo (res.) ....G 3
Goose (creek) ....E 1
Gooseberry (creek) ......D 1
Grand Teton (peak) ....B 2
Grand Teton National Park ....B 2
Granite (mts.) ....E 3
Gray (peak) ....B 1
Great Divide (basin) ......E 3
Green (mts.) ....E 3
Green (river) ....C 4
Green River (mt.) ....C 2
Greybull (river) ....D 1
Greys (river) ....B 3
Gros Ventre (river) ......B 2
Guernsey (res.) ....H 3
Hams Fork (river)..........B 4
Hazelton (peak) ....E 1
Heart (lake) ....B 1
Henrys Fork, Green (river) ....G 4
Hoback (peak) ....B 2
Hoback (river) ....B 2
Holmes (mt.) ....B 1
Horse (creek) ....B 3
Horse (creek) ....H 4
Horseshoe (creek) ....G 3
Hunt (mt.) ....E 1
Index (peak) ....C 1
Inyan Kara (creek) ....H 1
Inyan Kara (mt.) ....H 1
Isabel (mt.) ....B 3
Jackson (lake) ....B 2
Jackson (peak) ....B 2
Keyhole (res.) ....H 1
La Barge (creek) ....B 3
Lamar (river) ....B 1
Lance (creek) ....H 2
Laramie (mts.) ....G 3
Laramie (peak) ....G 3
Laramie (river) ....G 4
Leidy (mt.) ....B 2
Lewis (lake) ....B 1
Lightning (creek) ....G 2
Little Laramie (river).....G 4
Little Medicine Bow (river) ....F 3
Little Missouri (river)....H 1
Little Muddy (creek) .....B 4
Little Popo Agie (river)..D 3
Little Powder (river) ....G 1
Little Sandy (creek) ......C 3
Little Thunder (creek) ..G 2
Lodgepole (creek) ....H 2
Lodgepole (creek) ....H 4
Madison (plateau) ....B 1
Medicine Bow (range).....F 4
Medicine Bow (river) .....F 3
Middle Piney (creek) ....B 3
Muddy (creek) ....D 2
Muddy (creek) ....F 3
Muddy (mt.) ....F 3
Muskrat (creek) ....E 2
Needle (mt.) ....C 1
New Fork (lakes) ....C 2
Niobrara (river) ....J 3
No Water (creek) ....E 2
North Laramie (river)....G 3
North Platte (river) ......H 4
Nowood (creek) ....E 1
Old Woman (creek) ......H 3
Owl, North Fork (creek) ....D 2
Owl Creek (mts.) ....D 2
Palisades (res.) ....A 2
Pass (creek) ....F 4
Pathfinder (res.) ....F 3
Pilot Butte (res.) ....D 2
Poison (creek) ....E 2
Poison Spider (creek).....F 3
Popo Agie (river) ....D 3
Porcupine (creek) ....G 2
Powder (river) ....F 2
Rattlesnake (range) ......E 3
Rawhide (creek) ....G 1
Rawhide (creek) ....H 3
Red Fork, Powder (river) ....F 2
Rocky (mts.) ....C 1
Saint Marys (peak)..........D 3
Salt (river) ....B 3
Salt River (range) ....B 3
Salt Wells (creek)..........D 4
Sandy (creek) ....C 3
Savery (creek) ....E 4
Seminoe (mts.) ....E 3
Seminoe (res.) ....F 3
Shell (creek) ....E 1
Shirley (basin) ....F 3
Shoshone (lake) ....B 1
Shoshone (river) ....D 1
Sierra Madre (mts.) ....E 4
Slate (creek) ....C 3
Smiths Fork (river)......B 3
Snake (river) ....B 2
South Piney (creek) ......B 3
Sweetwater (river) ......D 3
Sybille (creek) ....G 4
Table (peak) ....B 2
Teton (range) ....B 2
Thompson (mt.) ....B 3
Tongue (river) ....E 1
Washburn (mt.) ....B 1
Wheatland (res.) ....G 4
Willow (creek) ....F 2
Willow (lake) ....C 2
Wind (river) ....C 2
Wind River (canyon) ......C 2
Wind River (range) ....C 2
Wind River Ind. Res. ......C 2
Wood (river) ....C 2
Wyoming (peak) ....B 3
Wyoming (range) ....B 2
Yellowstone (lake) ....B 1
Yellowstone (river) ......B 1
Yellowstone National Park ....B 1

◉ County Seat.

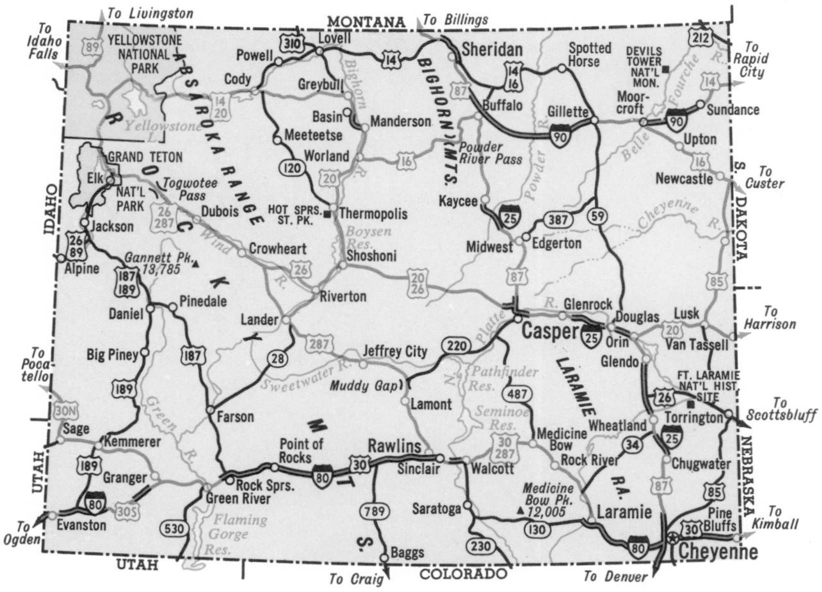

To Livingston
MONTANA
To Billings
To Idaho Falls
YELLOWSTONE NATIONAL PARK
Powell
Lovell
Sheridan
Spotted Horse
DEVILS TOWER NAT'L MON.
To Rapid City
Cody
Greybull
BIGHORN MTS.
Buffalo
Gillette
Moorcroft
Sundance
ABSAROKA RANGE
Basin
Manderson
Meeteetse
Worland
Powder River Pass
Upton
GRAND TETON
Elk
NAT'L PARK
Togwotee Pass
Dubois
HOT SPRS. ST. PK.
Thermopolis
Kaycee
Newcastle
To Custer
IDAHO
Jackson
Boysen Res.
Shoshoni
Midwest
Edgerton
S. DAKOTA
Alpine
Gannett Pk. 13,785
Crowheart
Pinedale
Riverton
Glenrock
Lusk
To Harrison
Daniel
Lander
Casper
Douglas
Orin
Van Tassell
To Pocatello
Big Piney
Jeffrey City
Glendo
Muddy Gap
Pathfinder Res.
FT. LARAMIE NAT'L HIST. SITE
Lamont
Seminoe Res.
Torrington
To Scottsbluff
Farson
LARAMIE RA.
Wheatland
Sage
Kemmerer
Point of Rocks
Rawlins
Medicine Bow
Rock River
Chugwater
Granger
Sinclair
Walcott
NEBRASKA
UTAH
Rock Sprs.
Green River
Saratoga
Medicine Bow Pk. 12,005
Laramie
Pine Bluffs
To Kimball
To Ogden
Evanston
Flaming Gorge Res.
Baggs
Cheyenne
UTAH
To Craig
COLORADO
To Denver

HIGHWAYS

0 60 120
MILES

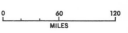

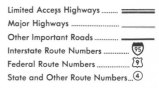

Limited Access Highways ....
Major Highways ....
Other Important Roads ....
Interstate Route Numbers 95
Federal Route Numbers 9
State and Other Route Numbers.... 4

THE FIFTY STATES

ACQUISITIONS OF TERRITORY

The United States in 1783 comprised the thirteen original states and included lands acquired by conquest during the Revolution and by the Treaty of 1783.

RANK BY AREA

RANK BY POPULATION

YEAR OF ADMISSION TO THE UNION

DELAWARE☆	1787
PENNSYLVANIA☆	
NEW JERSEY☆	
GEORGIA☆	1788
CONNECTICUT☆	
MASSACHUSETTS☆	
MARYLAND☆	
SOUTH CAROLINA☆	
NEW HAMPSHIRE☆	
VIRGINIA☆	
NEW YORK☆	
NORTH CAROLINA☆	1789
RHODE ISLAND☆	1790
VERMONT☆	1791
KENTUCKY☆	1792
TENNESSEE☆	1796
OHIO☆	1803
LOUISIANA☆	1812
INDIANA☆	1816
MISSISSIPPI☆	1817
ILLINOIS☆	1818
ALABAMA☆	1819
MAINE☆	1820
MISSOURI☆	1821

1959 ☆ HAWAII ☆ ALASKA
1912 ☆ ARIZONA ☆ NEW MEXICO
1907 ☆ OKLAHOMA

☆ UTAH   IDAHO ☆ ☆ NORTH DAKOTA   ☆ SOUTH DAKOTA
☆ WYOMING ☆ WASHINGTON ☆ MONTANA COLORADO   NEBRASKA   NEVADA ☆ KANSAS ☆ MINNESOTA   OREGON ☆ CALIFORNIA   WISCONSIN   IOWA ☆ ☆ FLORIDA   ARKANSAS
WEST VIRGINIA ☆   MICHIGAN ☆

1896   1889   1876   1867 1864 1861 1858   1848 1845   1836
1890   1863   1859   1850   1846   1837

© Copyright
HAMMOND INCORPORATED

INDEX OF THE WORLD

Introduction

This index is a directory to the atlas as a whole. It contains an alphabetical listing of the major political divisions (countries and administrative subdivisions, i.e., states, provinces, departments), principal cities and towns, and geographical features, such as mountains, rivers, bays, islands, shown on the maps contained in this atlas.

Entries are generally indexed to the map or inset having the largest scale, but in some cases, where the entry has equal coverage or is important to its surroundings on more than one map, more than one reference is given.

Each entry gives the political division in which it is located, or in the case of certain geographical features the appropriate continent or regional name, and the page number of the map on which the name will be found. The user who is unfamiliar with a place name will thus be able to identify the political division to which it belongs and to locate quickly the appropriate map or maps.

Once having found the map listed in this index, the user will easily find the place name on the map by first locating it in the accompanying map index. Here the user will find the necessary index key reference. When there is more than one place of the same name on the same map, only one reference is given. The individual map index will give the multiple listings of names and key references. A glance at adjacent pages will show whether there are additional maps on which the place name may be found, by referring to the accompanying index or by looking in the same relative location on the map.

The abbreviations for the political division names and geographical terms are explained on page XII of the atlas. In some cases place names have been shortened in this index. The full name will be found in the individual index accompanying the map itself.

A

Aa (river), Switz., 39
Aabenraa, Den., 21
Aachen, W. Ger., 22
Aalborg, Den., 21
Aalen, W. Ger., 22
Aalst, Belg., 27
Äänekoski, Fin., 18
Aarau, Switz., 39
Aare (river), Switz., 39
Aargau (canton), Switz., 39
Aarhus, Den., 21
Aba, Nigeria, 106
Abacaxis (riv.), Braz., 132
Abadan, Iran, 66
Abadeh, Iran, 66
Abadla, Alg., 106
Abaetetuba, Braz., 132
Abaiang (atoll), Gilb. & Ell. Is., 87
Abajo (mts.), Utah, 304
Abakan, U.S.S.R., 48
Abancay, Peru, 128
Abarquh, Iran, 66
Abashiri, Japan, 81
Abau, Papua, 85
Abaya (lake), Eth., 111
Abbai (riv.), Eth., 111
Abbe (lake), Africa, 111
Abbeville, Ala., 194
Abbeville, France, 28
Abbeville, La., 238
Abbeville, S.C., 296
Abbeyfeale, Ire., 17
Abbottabad, Pak., 68
Abdulino, U.S.S.R., 52
Abéché, Chad, 111
Abemama (atoll), Gilb. & Ell. Is., 87
Abengourou, Ivory Coast, 106
Abeokuta, Nigeria, 106
Aberayron, Wales, 13
Abercorn, Zambia, 115
Aberdare, Wales, 13
Aberdeen, Md., 245
Aberdeen, Miss., 256
Aberdeen (lake), N.W.T., 187
Aberdeen (county), Scot., 15
Aberdeen, Scot., 15
Aberdeen, S. Dak., 298
Aberdeen, Wash., 310
Aberfeldy, Scot., 15
Abergavenny, Wales, 13
Abertillery, Wales, 13
Aberystwyth, Wales, 13
Abha, Saudi Ar., 59
Ab-i-Diz (river), Iran, 66
Abidjan (cap.), Ivory Coast, 106
Abilene, Kans., 232
Abilene, Tex., 302
Abingdon, Eng., 13
Abingdon, Ill., 222
Abingdon, Va., 307
Abington, Pa., 294
Abitibi (lake), Ont., 177
Abitibi (riv.), Ont., 177
Abkhaz A.S.S.R., U.S.S.R., 52
Abnub, U.A.R., 111
Åbo (Turku), Fin., 18
Abomey, Dahomey, 106
Abony, Hung., 41
Abor (hills), India, 68
Abqaiq, Saudi Ar., 59
Abra (prov.), Phil. Is., 82
Abraham Lincoln Nat'l Hist. Pk., Ky., 237
Abruzzi e Molise (reg.), Italy, 34
Absecon, N. J., 273
Abu, India, 68
Abu 'Arish, Saudi Ar., 59
Abu Dara, Ras (cape), Sudan, 111
Abu Dhabi, Tr. Oman, 59
Abu Hadriya, Saudi Ar., 59
Abu Hamed, Sudan, 111
Abu Kemal, Syria, 63
Abu-mad (cape), Saudi Ar., 59
Abu Road, India, 68
Abunã (riv.), S. Amer., 120
Abu Shagara, Ras (cape), Sudan, 111
Abu Simbil, U.A.R., 111
Abu Zabad, Sudan, 111
Abydos (ruins), U.A.R., 111
Acadia Nat'l Park, Maine, 242
Acadia Valley, Alta., 182
Acajutla, El Sal., 154
Acámbaro, Mex., 150
Acaponeta, Mex., 150
Acapulco, Mex., 150
Acarigua, Venez., 124
Acatlán, Mex., 150
Acatzingo, Mex., 150
Acayucan, Mex., 150
Accra (cap.), Ghana, 106
Accrington, Eng., 10
Achacachi, Bol., 136
Achalpur, India, 68
Achill (head), Ire., 17
Achill (isl.), Ire., 17
Achnasheen, Scot., 15
Acireale, Italy, 34
Acklins (isl.), Bah. Is., 156
Aconcagua (prov.), Chile, 138
Aconcagua (mt.), Arg., 143
Aconchi, Mex., 150
Acoyapa, Nic., 154
Acqui, Italy, 34
Acre (state), Braz., 132
Acre (riv.), Braz., 132
Acre, Israel, 65
Acri, Italy, 34
Actopan, Mex., 150
Ada, Minn., 254
Ada, Ohio, 284
Ada, Okla., 288
Adaja (riv.), Spain, 33
Adalia (gulf), Turkey, 63
Adam, Muscat and Oman, 59
Adamawa (reg.), Africa, 115
Adams (peak), Ceylon, 68
Adams, Mass., 249
Adams (mt.), Wash., 310
Adam's Bridge (shoals), Asia, 68
Adams Nat'l Hist. Site, Mass., 249
Adamstown (cap.), Pitcairn Is., 87
Adana, Turkey, 63
Adapazarı, Turkey, 63
Adare (cape), Ant., 5
Adda (riv.), Italy, 34
Addis Ababa (cap.), Eth., 111
Addis Alam, Eth., 111
Addison, Ill., 222
Ad Diwaniya, Iraq, 66
Adel, Ga., 216
Adelaide (isl.), Ant., 5
Adelaide (cap.), S. Austral., 94
Adelaide (pen.), N.W.T., 187
Adelaide River, Austral., 93
Adelanto, Calif., 204
Adélie Land (reg.), Ant., 5
Aden (gulf), 54
Aden (cap.), So. Arabia, 59
Adige (riv.), Italy, 34
Adilabad, India, 68
Adimi, U.S.S.R., 48
Adirondack (mts.), N.Y., 276
Adjuntas, P. Rico, 161
Adlavik (isls.), Newf., 166
Admiralty (gulf), W. Austral., 92
Admiralty (isls.), Terr. N.G., 87
Ado, Nigeria, 106
Adoni, India, 68
Adour (riv.), France, 28
Adra, Spain, 33
Adrano, Italy, 34
Adrar, Alg., 106
Adrar (reg.), Mauritania, 106
Adrar des Iforas (plat.), Africa, 106
Adria, Italy, 34
Adrian, Mich., 250
Adriatic (sea), Europe, 7
Adwa, Eth., 111
Adygey Aut. Obl., U.S.S.R., 52
Adzhar A.S.S.R., U.S.S.R., 52
Aegean (sea), 45
Aegean Islands (div.), Greece, 45
Afghanistan, 68
Åfjord, Norway, 18
Afmadu, Somali Rep., 115
Africa, 102
Afton, Wyo., 319
Afyon, Turkey, 63
Agadès, Niger, 106
Agadir, Mor., 106
Agaña (cap.), Guam, 87
Agartala, India, 68
Agate Fossil Beds Nat'l Mon., Nebr., 264
Agats, W. Irian, 85
Agatti (isl.), India, 68
Agboville, Ivory Coast, 106
Agdam, U.S.S.R., 52
Agde, France, 28
Agen, France, 28
Aginsk Nat'l Okrug, U.S.S.R., 48
Aginskoye, U.S.S.R., 48
Agiobampo (bay), Mex., 150
Agira, Italy, 34
Agordat, Eth., 111
Agra, India, 68
Agraciada, Urug., 145
Agrigento (prov.), Italy, 34
Agrigento, Italy, 34
Agrihan (isl.), Pac. Is., 87
Agrínion, Greece, 45
Agryz, U.S.S.R., 52
Aguada, P. Rico, 161
Aguadas, Col., 126
Aguadilla (dist.), P. Rico, 161
Aguadilla, P. Rico, 161
Agua Dulce, Mex., 150
Aguadulce, Pan., 154
Agualeguas, Mex., 150
Aguán (riv.), Hond., 154
Aguanaval (riv.), Mex., 150
Aguanus (riv.), Canada,174
Agua Prieta, Mex., 150
Aguarico (riv.), S. Amer., 128
Aguas Buenas, P. Rico, 161
Aguascalientes (state), Mex., 150
Aguascalientes, Mex., 150
Águeda, Port., 33
Aguilar, Colo., 208
Aguilar, Spain, 33
Aguilas, Spain, 33
Aguililla, Mex., 150
Aguja (pt.), Peru, 128
Agulhas (cape), S. Afr., 118
Agusan (prov.), Phil. Is., 82
Ahaggar (range), Alg., 106
Ahau, Fiji, 87
Ahlen, W. Ger., 22
Ahmadabad, India, 68
Ahmadnagar, India, 68
Ahmadpur East, Pak., 68
Ahoskie, N.C., 281
Ahrensburg, W. Ger., 22
Ahuacatlán, Mex., 150
Ahuachapán, El Sal., 154
Ahuás, Hond., 154
Ahurei, Fr. Poly., 87
Åhus, Sweden, 18
Ahvenanmaa (dept.), Fin., 18
Ahvenanmaa (isls.), Fin., 18
Ahwar, So. Arabia, 59
Ahwaz, Iran, 66
Aibonito, P. Rico, 161
Aiea, Hawaii, 218
Aiguá, Urug., 145
Aichi (prefecture), Japan, 81
Aijal, India, 68
Aiken, S.C., 296
Ailinglapalap (atoll), Pac. Is., 87
Ailuk (atoll), Pac. Is., 87
Ain (dept.), France, 28
Ain (riv.), France, 28
Aina Haina, Hawaii, 218
'Ain al Mubarrak, Saudi Ar., 59
Aïn-Béïda, Alg., 106
Aïn-Salah, Alg., 106
Aïn-Sefra, Alg., 106
Ainsworth, Nebr., 264
Aïn-Témouchent, Alg., 106
Aïoun el Atrous, Mauritania, 106
Air (mts.), Niger, 106
Airdrie, Scot., 15
Aire (riv.), Eng., 13
Air Force (isl.), N.W.T., 187
Air Force Acad., Colo., 208
Aisén (prov.), Chile, 138
Aishihik, Yukon, 187
Aisne (dept.), France, 28
Aisne (riv.), France, 28
Aitape, Terr. N.G., 85
Aitkin, Minn., 254
Aitutaki (atoll), Cook Is., 87
Aiud, Rum., 45
Aix-en-Provence, France, 28
Aix-les-Bains, France, 28
Aíyina, Greece, 45
Aíyion, Greece, 45
Aizuwakamatsu, Japan, 81
Ajaccio, France, 28
Ajaccio (gulf), France, 28
Ajalpan, Mex., 150
Ajanta, India, 68
Ajax, Ont., 175
Ajedabia, Libya, 111
Ajka, Hung., 41
'Ajlun (dist.), Jordan, 65
'Ajman, Tr. Oman, 59
Ajmer, India, 68
Ajo, Ariz., 198
Ak (range), Turkey, 63
Akabiri, Japan, 81
Akarai (mts.), Guyana, 131
Akashi, Japan, 81
Aken, E. Ger., 22
Akershus (county), Norway, 18
Aketi, Dem. Rep. of the Congo, 115
Akhaltsikhe, U.S.S.R., 52
Akhdar, Jebel (mts.), Libya, 111
Akhdar, Jebel (range), Muscat and Oman, 59
Akhisar, Turkey, 63
Akhtopol, Bulg., 45
Akhtubinsk, U.S.S.R., 52
Akhtyrka, U.S.S.R., 52
Akimiski (isl.), N.W.T., 187
Akim Oda, Ghana, 106
Akita (prefecture), Japan, 81
Akita, Japan, 81
Akjoujt, Mauritania, 106
Akkerman (Belgorod-Dnestrovskiy), U.S.S.R., 52
Aklan (prov.), Phil. Is., 82
Aklavik, N.W.T., 187
Akmolinsk (Tselinograd), U.S.S.R., 48
Akobo (riv.), Africa, 111
Akola, India, 68
Akpatok (isl.), N.W.T., 187
Akrítas (cape), Greece, 45
Akron, N.Y., 276
Akron, Ohio, 284
Akşehir, Turkey, 63
Aksha, U.S.S.R., 48
Aksum, Eth., 111
Aktí (pen.), Greece, 45
Aktyubinsk, U.S.S.R., 48
Akureyri, Ice., 21
Akyab, Burma, 72
Al, Norway, 18
Alabama (riv.), Ala., 194
Alabama (state), U.S., 194
Alabat (isl.), Phil. Is., 82
Alagir, U.S.S.R., 52
Alagoas (state), Braz., 132
Alagoinhas, Braz., 132
Alagón, Spain, 33
Alagón (riv.), Spain, 33
Al Ahqaf (Bahr es Safi) (des.), Arabia, 59
Alajuela, C. Rica, 154
Alakol' (lake), U.S.S.R., 48
Alameda, Calif., 204
Alamicamba, Nic., 154
Alamo, Mex., 150
Alamo, Tex., 302
Alamogordo, N. Mex., 274
Alamo Hts., Tex., 302
Alamos, Mex., 150
Alamosa, Colo., 208
Åland (isls.), Fin., 18
Alanje, Pan., 154
Alanya, Turkey, 63
Alaotra (lake), Malag. Rep., 118
Alaşehir, Turkey, 63
Alashan (des.), China, 77
Alaska (gulf), Alaska, 196
Alaska (pen.), Alaska, 196
Alaska (range), Alaska, 196
Alaska (state), U.S., 196
Alassio, Italy, 34
Alatri, Italy, 34
Alatyr', U.S.S.R., 52
Alausí, Ecua., 128
Álava (prov.), Spain, 33
Alavus, Fin., 18
Alayor, Spain, 33
Al 'Aziziya, Iraq, 66
Alba, Italy, 34
Alba Iulia, Rum., 45
Albacete (prov.), Spain, 33
Albacete, Spain, 33
Albanel (lake), Que., 174
Albania, 45
Albano (lake), Italy, 34
Albano Laziale, Italy, 34
Albany, Calif., 204
Albany, Ga., 216
Albany, Jam., 158
Albany (cap.), N.Y., 276
Albany, N.Z., 101
Albany (riv.), Ont., 177
Albany, Oreg., 291
Albany, P.E.I., 169
Albany, W. Austral., 92
Albay (prov.), Phil. Is., 82
Albemarle (pt.), Ecuador, 128
Albemarle, N.C., 281
Alberni, Br. Col., 184
Albert (lake), Africa, 115
Albert, France, 28
Alberta (mt.), Alta., 182
Alberta (prov.), Canada, 182
Albert Lea, Minn., 254
Alberton, P.E.I., 169
Alberton, S. Afr., 118
Albertville, Ala., 194
Albertville, France, 28
Albertville, Dem. Rep. of the Congo, 115
Albi, France, 28
Albia, Iowa, 229
Albina, Surinam, 131
Albino, Italy, 34
Albion, Mich., 250
Albion, Nebr., 264
Albion, N.Y., 276
Alborán (isl.), Spain, 33
Albox, Spain, 33
Albuquerque, N. Mex., 274
Alburquerque, Spain, 33
Albury, N.S.W., 97
Albury, N.Z., 101
Alcácer do Sal, Port., 33
Alcalá de Chivert, Spain, 33
Alcalá de Guadaira, Spain, 33
Alcalá de Henares, Spain, 33
Alcalá de los Gazules, Spain, 33
Alcalá la Real, Spain, 33
Alcamo, Italy, 34
Alcanar, Spain, 33
Alcañiz, Spain, 33
Alcántara, Port., 33
Alcántara, Spain, 33
Alcantarilla, Spain, 33
Alcaraz (range), Spain, 33
Alcaudete, Spain, 33
Alcázar de San Juan, Spain, 33
Alcira, Spain, 33
Alcoa, Tenn., 237
Alcobaça, Port., 33
Alcoy, Spain, 33
Alcudia (bay), Spain, 33
Aldabra (isls.), 118
Aldama, Mex., 150
Aldan, Pa., 294
Aldan, U.S.S.R., 48
Aldan (plat.), U.S.S.R., 48
Aldeia Nova, Port., 33
Alderney (isl.), Chan. Is., 13
Aldershot, Eng.,13
Aldridge, Eng., 10
Aledo, Ill., 222
Aleg, Mauritania, 106
Alegrete, Braz., 132
'Aleih, Leb., 63
Aleksandriya, U.S.S.R., 52
Aleksandrov, U.S.S.R., 52
Aleksandrovsk-Sakhalinskiy, U.S.S.R., 48
Alekseyevka, U.S.S.R., 52
Aleksin, U.S.S.R., 52
Aleksinac, Yugo., 45
Alemania, Arg., 143
Além Paraíba, Braz., 135
Alençon, France, 28
Aleppo (prov.), Syria, 63
Aleppo, Syria, 63
Alert, N.W.T., 187
Alert Bay, Br. Col., 184
Alès, France, 28
Alessandria (prov.), Italy, 34
Alessandria, Italy, 34
Ålesund, Norway, 18
Aleutian (isls.), Alaska, 196
Alexander (arch.), Alaska, 196
Alexander (isl.), Ant., 5
Alexander, Minn., 254
Alexander City, Ala., 194
Alexandra, N.Z., 101
Alexandra (falls), N.W.T., 187
Alexandra Land (isl.), U.S.S.R., 48
Alexandretta (gulf), Turkey, 63
Alexandria, Ind., 227
Alexandria, La., 238
Alexandria, Minn., 254
Alexandria, Rum., 45
Alexandria, Scot., 15
Alexandria, S. Afr., 118
Alexandria, U.A.R., 111
Alexandria, Va., 307
Alexandroúpolis, Greece, 45
Aleysk, U.S.S.R., 48
Al Falluja, Iraq, 66
Alfaro, Spain, 33
Alfatar, Bulg., 45
Alfeld, W. Ger., 22
Alfenas, Braz., 135
Alford, Scot., 15
Alfred, N.Y., 276
Alga, U.S.S.R., 48
Algarve (prov.), Port., 33
Algeciras, Spain, 33
Algemesí, Spain, 33
Algeria, 106
Algés, Port., 33
Alghero, Italy, 34
Algiers (cap.), Alg., 106
Algoa (bay), S. Afr., 118
Algoma, Wis., 317
Algona, Iowa, 229
Algonac, Mich., 250
Algonquin Prov. Park, Ont., 175
Alhama de Granada, Spain, 33
Alhama de Murcia, Spain, 33
Alhambra, Calif., 204
Alhaurín el Grande, Spain, 33
Al Hoceima, Mor., 106
Alhos Vedros, Port., 33
'Aliabad (mt.), Iran, 66
Ali-Bayramly, U.S.S.R., 52
Alicante (prov.), Spain, 33
Alicante, Spain, 33
Alice, Tex., 302
Alice Arm, Br. Col., 184
Alice Springs, N. Terr., 93
Aliceville, Ala., 194
Alicudi (isl.), Italy, 34
Aligarh, India, 68
'Alijug (mt.), Iran, 66
Alingsås, Sweden, 18
Aliquippa, Pa., 294
Alisal, Calif., 204
Al Ittihad, So. Arabia, 59
Alivérion, Greece, 45
Aliwal North, S. Afr., 118
Aljezur, Port., 33
Aljojuca, Mex., 150
Aljustrel, Port., 33
Alkmaar, Neth., 27
Al Kufa, Iraq, 66
Al Kuwait (cap.), Kuwait, 66
Allahabad, India, 68
Allakh-Yun', U.S.S.R., 48
Allanmyo, Burma, 72
Allan Water, Ont., 177
Allaykha, U.S.S.R., 48
Allegan, Mich., 250
Allen (lake), Ire., 17
Allendale, N. J., 273
Allendale, S.C., 296
Allende, Mex., 150
Allen Park, Mich., 250
Allentown, Pa., 294
Alleppey, India, 68
Aller (riv.), W. Ger., 22
Allgäu Alps (mts.), Europe, 22
Alliance, Nebr., 264
Alliance, Ohio, 284
Allier (dept.), France, 28
Allier (riv.), France, 28
Allinge-Sandvig, Den., 21
Allingtown, Conn., 210
Allison Pk., Pa., 294
Al Lith, Saudi Ar., 59
Alloa, Scot., 15
All Saints, Antigua, 161
Alma, Ga., 216
Alma, Mich., 250
Alma, Nebr., 264
Alma, Que., 172
Alma-Ata, U.S.S.R., 48
Almada, Port., 33
Almadén, Spain, 33
Almagro, Spain, 33
Almansa, Spain, 33
Almanzor (mt.), Spain, 33
Almanzora (riv.), Spain, 33
Almeirim, Port., 33
Almelo, Neth., 27
Almendralejo, Spain, 33
Almería (prov.), Spain, 33
Almería, Spain, 33
Almería (gulf), Spain, 33
Al'met'yevsk, U.S.S.R., 52
Älmhult, Sweden, 18
Almirante, Pan., 154
Almirós, Greece, 45
Almodóvar del Campo, Spain, 33
Almoloya, Mex., 150
Almonte, Spain, 33
Almora, India, 68
Almuñécar, Spain, 33
Alofi (cap.), Niue, 87
Álora, Spain, 33
Alor Star, Malaysia, 72
Alorton, Ill., 222
Alpena, Mich., 250
Alpes-Maritimes (dept.), France, 28
Alpiarça, Port., 33
Alpine, Tex., 302
Alps (mts.), Europe, 7
Al Qaiyara, Iraq, 66
Al Qatn, So. Arabia, 59
Alsask, Sask., 181
Alsdorf, W. Ger., 22
Alsek (riv.), Yukon, 187
Alsip, Ill., 222
Alst (fjord), Norway, 18
Alsten (isl.), Norway, 18
Alta (riv.), Norway, 18
Altadena, Calif., 204
Alta Gracia, Arg., 143
Altagracia, Venez., 124
Altamira, Mex., 150
Altamont, Oreg., 291
Altar, Mex., 150
Altavista, Va., 307
Altay (mts.), Asia, 54
Alte (lake), Norway, 18
Altena, W. Ger., 22
Altenburg, E. Ger., 22
Altmark (reg.), E. Ger., 22
Altmühl (riv.), W. Ger., 22
Alto Alentejo (prov.), Port., 33
Alto Araguaia, Braz., 132
Alto de las Plumas, Arg., 143
Alton, Ill., 222
Altona, Man., 179
Altona, Victoria, 97
Altoona, Pa., 294
Alto Paraná (dept.), Par., 144
Alto Park, Ga., 216
Alto Ritacuva (mt.), Col.,126
Altotonga, Mex., 150
Alto Velo (chan.), Dom. Rep., 158
Altrincham, Eng., 10
Alturas, Calif., 204
Altus, Okla., 288
Altyn Tagh (mts.), China, 77
Alula, Somali Rep., 115
Alum Rock, Calif., 204
Alushta, U.S.S.R., 52
Alva, Okla., 288
Alva, Scot., 15
Alvarado, Mex., 150
Alvesta, Sweden, 18
Alvin, Tex., 302
Älvsborg (county), Sweden, 18
Älvsbyn, Sweden, 18
Alwar, India, 68
Alyth, Scot., 15
Alytus, U.S.S.R., 53
Alz (riv.), W. Ger., 22
Alzey, W. Ger., 22
Amadeus (lake), N. Terr., 93
'Amadiya, Iraq, 66
Amadora, Port., 33
Amagasaki, Japan, 81
Amakusa (isl.), Japan, 81
Åmål, Sweden, 18
Amaliás, Greece, 45
Amalner, India, 68
Amambaí, Braz., 132
Amambay (dept.), Par., 144
Amami (isls.), Japan, 81
Amami-O-Shima (isl.), Japan, 81
Amapá (terr.), Braz., 132
Amapala, Hond., 154
Amaparí (riv.), Braz., 132
'Amara (prov.), Iraq, 66
'Amara, Iraq, 66
Amarante, Braz., 132
Amarapura, Burma, 72
Amareleja, Port.. 33
Amarillo, Tex., 302
Amasya, Turkey, 63
Amatitlán, Guat., 154
Amatlán, Mex., 150
Amazon (riv.), S. Amer., 120
Amazonas (state), Braz., 132
Amazonas (commissary), Col., 126
Amazonas (dept.), Peru, 128
Amazonas (terr.), Venez., 124
Ambala, India, 68
Ambarawa, Indon., 85
Ambarchik, U.S.S.R., 48
Ambato, Ecuador, 128
Ambatondrazaka, Malag. Rep., 118
Amber (cape), Malag. Rep., 118
Amberg, W. Ger., 22
Ambergris (cay), Br. Hond., 154
Ambergris (cay), Turks & Caicos Is., 156
Ambérieu, France, 28
Amberley, Ohio, 284
Ambert, France, 28
Ambikapur, India, 68
Ambler, Pa., 294
Amboina, Indon., 85
Amboise, France, 28
Ambon (Amboina), Indon., 85
Ambositra, Malag. Rep., 118
Ambridge, Pa., 294
Ambriz, Angola, 115
Ambrizete, Angola, 115
Ambrym (isl.), New Hebr., 87
Ambunti, Terr. N.G., 85
Amchitka (isl.), Alaska, 196
Amealco, Mex., 150
Ameca, Mex., 150
Amecameca, Mex., 150
Americana, Braz., 135
American Highland, Ant., 5
American Falls, Idaho, 220
American Falls (res.), Idaho, 220
American Fork, Utah, 304
American Samoa, 87
Americus, Ga., 216
Amersfoort, Neth., 27
Amery Ice Shelf, Ant., 5
Ames, Iowa, 229
Amesbury, Mass., 249
Amfilokhía, Greece, 45
Ámfissa, Greece, 45
Amhara (reg.), Eth., 111
Amherst, Burma, 72
Amherst, Mass., 249
Amherst, N.S., 169
Amherst, Ohio, 284
Amherstburg, Ont., 175
Amiens, France, 28
Amindivi (isls.), India, 68
Amini (isl.), India, 68
Amisk (lake), Sask., 181
Amite, La., 238
Amityville, N.Y., 276
Amlwch, Wales, 13
Amman (dist.), Jordan, 65
Amman (cap.), Jordan, 65
Ammersee (lake), W. Ger., 22
Amnat, Thai., 72
Amne Machin (mts.), China, 77
Amorgós (isl.), Greece, 45
Amory, Miss., 256
Amos, Que., 174
Amoy, China, 77
Amozoc de Mota, Mex., 150
Amposta, Spain, 33
Amqui, Que., 172
Amravati, India, 68
Amreli, India, 68
Amritsar, India, 68
Amsterdam (isl.), 3
Amsterdam (cap.), Neth., 27
Amsterdam, N.Y., 276
Amstetten, Austria, 41
Am-Timan, Chad, 111
Amuay, Venez., 124
Amu-Dar'ya (riv.), Asia, 48
Amuku (mts.), Guyana, 131
Amul, Iran, 66
Amund Ringnes (isl.), N.W.T., 187
Amundsen (bay), Ant., 5
Amundsen (sea), Ant., 5
Amundsen (gulf), N.W.T., 187
Amur (riv.), Asia, 48
Amya (pass), Asia, 72
'Ana, Iraq, 66
Anaa (atoll), Fr. Poly., 87
Anaco, Venez., 124
Anaconda, Mont., 262
Anacortes, Wash., 310
Anadarko, Okla., 288
Anadyr', U.S.S.R., 48
Anadyr' (gulf), U.S.S.R., 48
Anadyr' (range), U.S.S.R., 48
Anadyr' (riv.), U.S.S.R., 48
Anáfi (isl.), Greece, 45
Anaheim, Calif., 204
Anai Mudi (mt.), India, 68
'Anaiza, Saudi Ar., 59
Anakapalle, India, 68
Anambas (isls.), Indon., 85
Anamosa, Iowa, 229
Anamur (cape),Turkey, 63
Anan, Japan, 81
Anandale, La., 238
Anantapur, India, 68
Anantnag, India, 68
Anapa, U.S.S.R., 52
Anápolis, Braz., 132
Anardarra, Afghan., 68
Añasco, P. Rico, 161
Añatuya, Arg., 143
Anauá (riv.), Braz., 132
Ancash (dept.), Peru, 128
Anchorage, Alaska, 196
Ancohuma (mt.), Bol., 136
Ancona (prov.), Italy, 34
Ancona, Italy, 34
Ancón de Sardinas (bay), Ecuador, 128
Ancud, Chile, 138
Andalgalá, Arg., 143
Åndalsnes, Norway, 18
Andalusia, Ala., 194
Andalusia (reg.), Spain, 33
Andaman (sea), Asia, 54
Andaman (isls.), India, 68
Andaman and Nicobar Islands (terr.), India, 68
Anderlecht, Belg., 27
Andernach, W. Ger., 22
Anderson, Calif., 204
Anderson, Ind., 227
Anderson (riv.), N.W.T., 187
Anderson, S.C., 296
Andes (range), S. Amer., 120
Andheri, India, 68
Andhra Pradesh (state), India, 68
Andikíthira (isl.), Greece, 45
Andizhan, U.S.S.R., 48
Andkhui, Afghan., 68
Ándissa, Greece, 45
Andong, S. Korea, 81
Andorra, 33
Andorra la Vella (cap.), And., 33
Andover, Eng., 13
Andover, N.B., 170
Andravídha, Greece, 45
Andreas (cape), Cyprus, 63
Andrés, Nic., 154
Andrew Johnson Nat'l Mon., Tenn., 237
Andrews, S.C., 296
Andrews, Tex., 302
Andros (isl.), Bah. Is., 156
Ándros, Greece, 45
Ándros (isl.), Greece, 45
Androth (isl.), India, 68
Ands (fjord), Norway, 18
Andújar, Spain, 33
Anécho, Togo, 106
Anegada (isl.), Virgin Is. (Br.), 156
Anegada (passage), W. Indies, 156
Aneityum (isl.), New Hebr., 87
'Aneiza, Jebel (mt.), Asia, 59
Aneto (mt.), Spain, 33
Angara (riv.), U.S.S.R., 48
Angarsk, U.S.S.R., 48
Angaur (isl.), Pac. Is., 87
Ånge, Sweden, 18
Angel (fall), Venez., 124
Ángel de la Guarda (isl.), Mex., 150
Ängelholm, Sweden, 18
Angerman (riv.), Sweden, 18
Angermünde, E. Ger., 22
Angers, France, 28
Angikuni (lake), N.W.T., 187
Angkor Wat (ruins), Cambodia, 72
Anglesey (county), Wales, 13
Angleton, Tex., 302
Angliers, Que., 174
Angmagssalik, Greenl., 4
Ango, Dem. Rep. of the Congo, 115
Angoche (isl.), Mozamb., 118
Angol, Chile, 138
Angola, 115
Angola, Ind., 227
Angoram, Terr. N.G., 85
Angostura, Mex., 150
Angoulême, France, 28
Angra do Heroísmo, Port., 32
Anguilla (isl.), St. Chr.-N.-A., 161
Angul, India, 68
Angus (county), Scot., 15
Anholt (isl.), Den., 21
Anhwei (prov.), China, 77
Aniene (riv.), Italy, 34
Anima, Rum., 45
Anjo, Japan, 81
Anjouan (isl.), Comoro Is., 118
Ankara (cap.), Turkey, 63
Ankeny, Iowa, 229
Anker (riv.), Eng., 10
Anking, China, 77
Anklam, E. Ger., 22
Ankober, Eth., 111
An Loc, S. Vietnam, 72
Ann (cape), Mass., 249
Anna, Ill., 222
Annaba, Alg., 106
Annaberg-Buchholz, E. Ger., 22
An Najaf, Iraq, 66
Annan, Scot., 15
Annapolis (cap.), Md., 245
Annapolis (basin), N.S., 169
Annapolis Royal, N.S., 169
Annapurna (mt.), Nepal, 68
Ann Arbor, Mich., 250
An Nasiriya, Iraq, 66
Annecy, France, 28
Annieopsquotch (mts.), Newf., 166
Anniston, Ala., 194
Annobón (isl.), Eq. Guin., 102
Annonay, France, 28
Annotto Bay, Jam., 158
Annville, Pa., 294
Anoka, Minn., 254
Anóyia, Greece, 45
Áno Viánnos, Greece, 45
Ansbach, W. Ger., 22
Anse la Raye, St. Lucia, 161
Anshan, China, 77
Anshun, China, 77
Ansŏng, S. Korea, 81
Ansonia, Conn., 210
Antâkya, Turkey, 63
Antalaha, Malag. Rep., 118
Antalya, Turkey, 63
Antarctic (pen.), Ant., 5
Antarctica, 5
Antarctic Circle, 5
Antequera, Spain, 33
Anthony, Kans., 232
Anthony, N. Mex., 274
Anti-Atlas (ranges), Mor., 106
Antibes, France, 28
Anticosti (isl.), Que., 174
Antietam Nat'l Battlef. Site, Md., 245
Antigo, Wis., 317
Antigonish, N.S., 169
Antigua, 161
Antigua, Guat., 154
Antigua (riv.), Mex., 150
Antilla, Cuba, 158
Antilles, Greater (isls.), W. Indies, 156,158
Antilles, Lesser (isls.), W. Indies, 156,161
Antioch, Calif., 204
Antioch, Ill., 222
Antioquia (dept.), Col., 126
Antipodes (isls.), N.Z., 3
Antique (prov.), Phil. Is., 82
Anti-Taurus (mts.), Turkey, 63
Antlers, Okla., 288
Antofagasta (prov.), Chile, 138
Antofagasta, Chile, 138
Antofagasta de la Sierra, Arg., 143
Antón, Pan., 154
Antongil (bay), Malag. Rep., 118
Antônio Enes, Mozamb., 118
Antrim (county), N. Ire., 17
Antrim, N. Ire., 17
Antsirabe, Malag. Rep., 118
Antung, China, 77
Antwerp (prov.), Belg., 27
Antwerp, Belg., 27
An Uaimh, Ire., 17
Anuradhapura, Ceylon, 68
Anyang, China, 77
Anyox, Br. Col., 184
Anzhero-Sudzhensk, U.S.S.R., 48
Anzoátegui (state), Venez., 124
Aomori (prefecture), Japan, 81
Aomori, Japan, 81
Aoulef, Alg., 106
Apa (riv.), S. Amer., 144
Apache Jct., Ariz., 198
Apalachee (bay), Fla., 212
Apalachicola, Fla., 212
Apan, Mex., 150
Apaporis (riv.), Col., 126
Aparri, Phil. Is., 82
Apatin, Yugo., 45
Apatity, U.S.S.R., 52
Apatzingán de la Constitución, Mex., 150
Apeldoorn, Neth., 27
Apennines (range), Italy, 34
Apennines, Central (range), Italy, 34
Apennines, Northern (range), Italy, 34
Apennines, Southern (range), Italy, 34
Apia (cap.), W. Samoa, 87
Apizaco, Mex., 150
Apo (vol.), Phil. Is., 82
Apolda, E. Ger., 22
Apollo, Pa., 294
Apopka, Fla., 212
Aporé (riv.), Braz., 132
Appalachian (mts.), U.S., 188
Appenzell, Ausser Rhoden (canton), Switz., 39
Appenzell, Inner Rhoden (canton), Switz., 39
Appleton, Wis., 317
Appleton City, Mo., 261
Apple Valley, Calif., 204
Appomattox C.H. Nat'l Hist. Pk., Va., 307
Apponaug, R.I., 249
Approuague (riv.), Fr. Guiana, 131
Apsheron (pen.), U.S.S.R., 52
Apsheronsk, U.S.S.R., 52
Apt, France, 28
Apulia (reg.), Italy, 34
Apure (state), Venez., 124
Apure (riv.), Venez., 124
Apurímac (dept.), Peru, 128
Apurímac (riv.), Peru, 128
'Aqaba (gulf), Asia, 59
'Aqaba, Jordan, 65
Aqsu, China, 77
Aquidauana, Braz., 132
Aquiles Serdán, Mex., 150
Aquin, Haiti, 158
Arab, Ala., 194
'Arab, Shatt-al- (riv.), Iraq, 66
'Araba, Wadi (dry river), Asia, 65
Arabia (pen.), Asia, 59
Arabian (sea), Asia, 54
Arabian (des.), U.A.R., 111
Aracaju, Braz., 132
Aracati, Braz., 132
Araçatuba, Braz., 135
Aracena, Spain, 33
Arad, Rum., 45
'Arafat, Jebel (mt.), Saudi Ar., 59
Arafura (sea), 85
Aragón (reg.), Spain, 33
Aragón (riv.), Spain, 33
Aragua (state), Venez., 124
Aragua de Barcelona, Venez., 124
Araguaia (riv.), Braz., 132
Araguari, Braz., 132
Araguari (riv.), Braz., 132
Arak, Iran, 66
Arakan (div.), Burma, 72
Arakan Yoma (mts.), Burma, 72
Araks (riv.), 59
Aral (sea), U.S.S.R., 48
Aral'sk, U.S.S.R., 48
Aramberri, Mex., 150
Aran (isl.), Ire., 17
Aran (isls.), Ire., 17
Aranda de Duero, Spain, 33
Arandas, Mex., 150
Aranjuez, Spain, 33
Aransas Pass, Tex., 302
Arapey Grande (riv.), Urug., 145
Arapkir, Turkey, 63
Araranguá, Braz., 132
Araraquara, Braz., 135
Araras, Braz., 135
Ararat (mt.), Turkey, 63
Ararat, Vic., 97
Arauca (intendency), Col., 126
Arauca, Col., 126
Arauca (riv.), S. Amer., 120
Arauco (prov.), Chile, 138
Arauco, Chile, 138
Araxá, Braz., 132
Araxes (Araks)(riv.), Asia, 59
Arbai Khere, Mong., 77
Arbela (Erbil), Iraq, 66
Arboga, Sweden, 18
Arborfield, Sask., 181
Arborg, Man., 179
Arbroath, Scot., 15
Arcachon, France, 28
Arcachon (bay), France, 28
Arcadia, Calif., 204
Arcadia, Fla., 212
Arcadia, La., 238
Arcata, Calif., 204
Arcelia, Mex., 150
Archangel, U.S.S.R., 52
Archbald, Pa., 294
Archena, Spain, 33
Arches Nat'l Mon., Utah, 304
Archidona, Spain, 33
Arco, Idaho, 220
Arcola, Sask., 181
Arcos de la Frontera, Spain, 33
Arcot, India, 68
Arcoverde, Braz., 132
Arctic, R.I., 249
Arctic Circle, 4
Arctic Ocean, 4
Arctic Red (riv.), N.W.T., 187
Arctic Red River, N.W.T., 187
Arda (riv.), Europe, 45
Ardahan, Turkey, 63
Ardal, Norway, 18
Ardebil, Iran, 66
Ardèche (dept.), France, 28
Ardee, Ire., 17
Ardennes (plat.), Belg., 27
Ardennes (dept.), France, 28
Ardhéa, Greece, 45
Ardino, Bulg., 45
Ardistan, Iran, 66
Ardita (pt.), Pan., 154
Ardmore, Ind., 227
Ardmore, Okla., 288
Ardmore, Pa., 294
Ardrossan, Scot., 15
Ardsley, N.Y., 276
Arecibo (dist.), P. Rico, 161
Arecibo, P. Rico, 161
Areia Branca, Braz., 132
Arena (pt.), Mex., 150
Arenas (cay), Mex., 150
Arenas de San Pedro, Spain, 33
Arendal, Norway, 18
Arenys de Mar, Spain, 33
Areópolis, Greece, 45
Arequipa (dept.), Peru, 128
Arequipa, Peru, 128
Arezzo (prov.), Italy, 34
Arezzo, Italy, 34
Argalastí, Greece, 45
Argamasilla de Alba, Spain, 33
Arganda, Spain, 33
Argentan, France, 28
Argenteuil, France, 2[illegible]
Argentia, Newf., 166
Argentina, 143

B

C

Gresham, Oreg., 291
Gresik, Indon., 85
Gretna, La., 238
Gretna Green, Scot., 15
Grevenbroich, W. Ger., 22
Grevenmacher, Lux., 27
Grey (riv.), N.Z., 101
Greybull, Wyo., 319
Greymouth, N.Z., 101
Greystone Park, N. J., 273
Greystones–Delgany, Ire., 17
Greytown (San Juan del Norte), Nic., 154
Gridley, Calif., 204
Griffin, Ga., 216
Griffith, Ind., 227
Griffith, N.S.W., 97
Grijalva (riv.), Mex., 150
Grimsby, Eng., 13
Grimsby, Ont., 175
Grimsel (pass), Switz., 39
Grimshaw, Alta., 182
Grindelwald, Switz., 39
Grinnell, Iowa, 229
Griqualand West (reg.), S. Africa, 118
Gris–Nez (cape), France, 28
Groais (isl.), Newf., 166
Grodno, U.S.S.R., 52
Groix (isl.), France, 28
Gronau, W. Ger., 22
Grondal, Greenl., 4
Groningen (prov.), Neth., 27
Groningen, Neth., 27
Groningen, Sur., 131
Groote Eylandt (isl.), N. Terr., 93
Grootfontein, S.W. Afr., 118
Gros Islet, St. Lucia, 161
Grosse Ile, Mich., 250
Grosse Pte., Mich., 250
Grosse Pte. Farms, Mich., 250
Grosse Pte. Park, Mich., 250
Grosse Pte. Woods, Mich., 250
Grosseto (prov.), Italy, 34
Grosseto, Italy, 34
Grossglockner (mt.), Austria, 41
Groton, Conn., 210
Grottaglie, Italy, 34
Grove City, Ohio, 284
Grove City, Pa., 294
Grover City, Calif., 204
Groves, Tex., 302
Groznyy, U.S.S.R., 52
Grudziądz, Poland, 47
Gryazi, U.S.S.R., 52
Guacanayabo (gulf), Cuba, 158
Guacara, Venez., 124
Guácimo, C. Rica, 154
Guadalajara, Mex., 150
Guadalajara (prov.), Spain, 33
Guadalajara, Spain, 33
Guadalcanal (isl.), Br. Sol. Is., 87
Guadalimar (riv.), Spain, 33
Guadalquivir (riv.), Spain, 33
Guadalupe, Calif., 204
Guadalupe, Mex., 150
Guadalupe (mts.), Spain, 33
Guadalupe (mts.), Tex., 302
Guadalupe (peak), Tex., 302
Guadalupe–Bravos, Mex., 150
Guadalupe Victoria, Mex., 150
Guadarrama (mts.), Spain, 33
Guadarrama (riv.), Spain, 33
Guadeloupe, 161
Guadiana (riv.), Europe, 33
Guadix, Spain, 33
Guainía (intendency), Col., 126
Guainía (riv.), S. Amer., 126
Guairá (dept.), Par., 144
Guairá (falls), S. Amer., 144
Guajira, La (intendency), Col., 126
Guajira (pen.), S. Amer., 120
Gualán, Guat., 154
Gualeguay, Arg., 143
Gualeguaychú, Arg., 143
Guam (isl.), U.S., 87
Guamúchil, Mex., 150
Guanabacoa, Cuba, 158
Guanabara (state), Braz., 132
Guanabara (bay), Braz., 135
Guanaja (isl.), Hond., 154
Guanajay, Cuba, 158
Guanajuato (state), Mex., 150
Guanajuato, Mex., 150
Guanare, Venez., 124
Guanare (riv.), Venez., 124
Guánica, P. Rico, 161
Guano, Ecua., 128
Guantánamo, Cuba, 158
Guantánamo (bay), Cuba, 158
Guaporé (terr.), Braz., 132
Guaporé (riv.), S. Amer., 136
Guaqui, Bol., 136
Guarambaré, Par., 144
Guaranda, Ecua., 128
Guaratinguetá, Braz., 135
Guarda, Port., 33
Guardafui (cape), Somali Rep., 115
Guárico (state), Venez., 124
Guárico (riv.), Venez., 124
Guarulhos, Braz., 135
Guarus, Braz., 135
Guasave, Mex., 150
Guastalla, Italy, 34
Guatemala, 154
Guatemala (cap.), Guat., 154
Guaviare (riv.), Col., 126
Guayabal, Cuba, 158
Guayama (dist.), P. Rico, 161
Guayama, P. Rico, 161
Guayanilla, P. Rico, 161
Guayaquil, Ecua., 128
Guayaquil (gulf), Ecua., 128
Guayas (prov.), Ecua., 128
Guayas (riv.), Ecua., 128
Guaymallén, Arg., 143
Guaymas, Mex., 150
Gubakha, U.S.S.R., 52
Guban (reg.), Somali Rep., 115
Guben (Wilhelm–Pieck–Stadt), E. Ger., 22
Gudenaa (riv.), Den., 21
Guebwiller, France, 28
Guelma, Alg., 106
Guelph, Ont., 175
Güera, Sp. Sahara, 106
Guéret, France, 28
Guernica y Luno, Spain, 33
Guernsey (isl.), Chan. Is., 13
Guerrara, Alg., 106
Guerrero (state), Mex., 150
Guichón, Urug., 145
Güija (lake), Cent. Amer., 154
Guildford, Eng., 13
Guilford Coll., N.C., 281
Guilford C.H. Nat'l Mil. Park, N.C., 281
Guimarães, Port., 33
Guimaras (isl.), Phil. Is., 82
Guinea, 106
Guinea (gulf), Africa, 106
Güines, Cuba, 158
Guipúzcoa (prov.), Spain, 33
Güira, Cuba, 158
Güiria, Venez., 124
Guise, France, 28
Gujarat (state), India, 68
Gujranwala, Pak., 68
Gujrat, Pak., 68
Gukovo, U.S.S.R., 52
Gulbarga, India, 68
Gulf Breeze, Fla., 212
Gulfport, Fla., 212
Gulfport, Miss., 256
Gull Lake, Sask., 181
Gulpaigan, Iran, 66
Gulu, Uganda, 115
Gumma (pref.), Japan, 81
Gummersbach, W. Ger., 22
Gümüşhane, Turkey, 63
Gungu, Dem. Rep. of the Congo, 115
Gunnbjörn (mt.), Greenl., 4
Gunnedah, N.S.W., 97
Gunningsville, N. Br., 170
Gunnison, Colo., 208
Guntakal, India, 68
Guntersville, Ala., 194
Guntur, India, 68
Gurgan, Iran, 66
Gurgueia (riv.), Braz., 132
Gurla Mandhata (mt.), China, 77
Gurupi (range), Braz., 132
Gur'yev, U.S.S.R., 48
Gusau, Nigeria, 106
Gus–Khrustal'nyy, U.S.S.R., 52
Güstrow, E. Ger., 22
Gütersloh, W. Ger., 22
Guthrie, Okla., 288
Gutiérrez Zamora, Mex., 150
Guttenberg, N. J., 273
Guyana, 131
Guymon, Okla., 288
Guysborough, N.S., 169
Guzmán (lake), Mex., 150
Gwalior, India, 68
Gwelo, Rhod., 118
Gyangtse, China, 77
Gyda (pen.), U.S.S.R., 48
Gydan (Kolyma) (range), U.S.S.R., 48
Gympie, Queensland, 95
Gyobingauk, Burma, 72
Gyöngyös, Hung., 41
Győr (county), Hung., 41
Győr, Hung., 41
Gyula, Hung., 41

H

Ha'apai Group (isls.), Tonga, 87
Haarlem, Neth., 27
Haarlemmermeer (polder), Neth., 27
Haasts Bluff, N. Terr., 93
Habbaniya, Iraq, 66
Habomai (isls.), Japan, 81
Hachinohe, Japan, 81
Hachioji, Japan, 81
Hackensack, N. J., 273
Hackettstown, N. J., 273
Hackney, Eng., 10
Hadama, Eth., 111
Hadarba, Ras (cape), Sudan, 111
Hadd, Ras al (cape), Muscat & Oman, 59
Haddington, Scot., 15
Haddonfield, N. J., 273
Haddon Hts., N. J., 273
Hadera, Israel, 65
Haderslev, Den., 21
Hadhar, Iraq, 66
Hadhramaut (dist.), So. Arabia, 59
Hadhramaut, Wadi (dry river), So. Arabia, 59
Haditha, Iraq, 66
Haedo (range), Urug., 145
Haeju, N. Korea, 81
Hafnarfjördhur, Ice., 21
Hafun, Ras (cape), Somali Rep., 115
Hagen, W. Ger., 22
Hagerstown, Md., 245
Hagersville, Ont., 175
Ha Giang, N. Vietnam, 72
Hague (cape), France, 28
Hague, The (cap.,) Neth., 27
Haguenau, France, 28
Hai, Iraq, 66
Haibak, Afghan., 68
Haifa (dist.), Israel, 65
Haifa, Israel, 65
Hail, Saudi Ar., 59
Hailar, China, 77
Haileybury, Ont., 175
Hailung, China, 77
Hainan (isl.), China, 77
Hainault (prov.), Belg., 27
Haines City, Fla., 212
Haiphong, N. Vietnam, 72
Haiti, 158
Haiya Jct., Sudan, 111
Hajdu–Bihar (county), Hung., 41
Hajdubőszőrmény, Hung., 41
Haji Ibrahim (mt.), Iraq, 66
Hakodate, Japan, 81
Halabja, Iraq, 66
Halachó, Mex., 150
Halberstadt, E. Ger., 22
Halden, Norway, 18
Haldensleben, E. Ger., 22
Haleakala Nat'l Park, Hawaii, 218
Haleb (Aleppo) (prov.), Syria, 63
Haleb (Aleppo), Syria, 63
Haledon, N. J., 273
Haleiwa, Hawaii, 218
Hales Corners, Wis., 317
Halesowen, Eng., 10
Halethorpe, Md., 245
Haleyville, Ala., 194
Halfway, Md., 245
Halifax, Eng., 10
Halifax (cap.), N.S., 169
Halkirk, Scot., 15
Hall (isls.), Pac. Is., 87
Halla (mt.), S. Korea, 81
Halland (county), Sweden, 18
Hallandale, Fla., 212
Halle (dist.), E. Ger., 22
Halle, E. Ger., 22
Hallein, Austria, 41
Hallettsville, Tex., 302
Hallowell, Maine, 242
Halls Creek, W. Austral., 92
Hallstahammar, Sweden, 18
Hallstatt, Austria, 41
Halmahera (isl.), Indon., 95
Halmstad, Sweden, 18
Hälsingborg, Sweden, 18
Haltemprice, Eng., 13
Haltia (mt.), Europe, 18
Haltom City, Tex., 302
Hama (prov.), Syria, 63
Hama, Syria, 63
Hamadan (governorate), Iran, 66
Hamadan, Iran, 66
Hamamatsu, Japan, 81
Hamar, Norway, 18
Hamber Prov. Park, Br. Col., 184
Hamburg, Ark., 203
Hamburg, N.Y., 276
Hamburg, Pa., 294
Hamburg (state), W. Ger., 22
Hamburg, W. Ger., 22
Hamden, Conn., 210
Häme (dept.), Fin., 18
Hämeenlinna, Fin., 18
Hameln, W. Ger., 22
Hamersley (range), W. Austral., 92
Hamhŭng, N. Korea, 81
Hami, China, 77
Hamilton (cap.), Berm., 156
Hamilton, Mass., 249
Hamilton, Mont., 262
Hamilton (inlet), Newf., 166
Hamilton, N.Y., 276
Hamilton, N.Z., 101
Hamilton, Ohio, 284
Hamilton, Ont., 175
Hamilton, Scot., 15
Hamilton, Tex., 302
Hamilton, Vic., 97
Hamilton Square, N. J., 273
Hamina, Fin., 18
Hamlet, N.C., 281
Hamlin, Tex., 302
Hamm, W. Ger., 22
Hammamet (gulf), Tun., 106
Hammerfest, Norway, 18
Hammersmith, Eng., 10
Hammond, Ind., 227
Hammond, La., 238
Hammonton, N. J., 273
Hampshire (Hants)(county), Eng., 13
Hampton, Iowa, 229
Hampton, N.H., 268
Hampton, Va., 307
Ham Tan, S. Vietnam, 72
Hamtramck, Mich., 250
Han (riv.), S. Korea, 81
Hanau, W. Ger., 22
Hanchung, China, 77
Hancock, Mich., 250
Haney, Br. Col. 184
Hanford, Calif., 204
Hanford Atomic Energy Res., Wash., 310
Hangchow, China, 77
Hangö, Fin., 18
Han Kiang (riv.), China, 77
Hanko (Hangö), Fin., 18
Hankow, China, 77
Hanku, China, 77
Hanley Hills, Mo., 261
Hanna, Alta., 182
Hannibal, Mo., 261
Hannover, W. Ger., 22
Hanoi (cap.), N. Vietnam, 72
Hanover (isl.), Chile, 138
Hanover, Mass., 249
Hanover, N.H., 268
Hanover, Ont., 175
Hanover, Pa., 294
Hanson, Mass., 249
Hantan, China, 77
Hantsport, N.S., 169
Hao (atoll), Fr. Poly., 87
Hapeville, Ga., 216
Harahan, La., 238
Harar (prov.), Eth., 111
Harar, Eth., 111
Harbin, China, 77
Harbor City, Calif., 204
Harbour (isl.), Bah. Is., 156
Hardanger (fjord), Norway, 18
Hardanger (mts.), Norway, 18
Hardin, Mont., 262
Hardoi, India, 68
Hardt (mts.), W. Ger., 22
Hardwar, India, 68
Hardwick, Ga., 216
Harfleur, France, 28
Harghessa, Somali Rep., 115
Harib, Yemen, 59
Harima (sea), Japan, 81
Haringey, Eng., 10
Harlan, Iowa, 229
Harlan, Ky., 237
Harlingen, Tex., 302
Harlow, Eng., 13
Harmarville, Pa., 294
Harney (lake), Oreg., 291
Harney (peak), S. Dak., 296
Härnösand, Sweden, 18
Harper, Liberia, 106
Harpers Ferry Nat'l Hist. Site, W. Va., 313
Harper Woods, Mich., 250
Harricanaw (riv.), Que., 174
Harriman, Tenn., 237
Harrington (sound), Berm., 156
Harrington Harbour, Que., 174
Harrington Park, N. J., 273
Harris (dist.), Scot., 15
Harrisburg, Ill., 222
Harrisburg (cap.), Pa., 294
Harris Hill, N.Y., 276
Harrismith, S. Africa, 118
Harrison, Ark., 203
Harrison (cape), Newf., 166
Harrison, N. J., 273
Harrison, N.Y., 276
Harrison, Ohio, 284
Harrisonburg, Va., 307
Harrisonville, Mo., 261
Harrodsburg, Ky., 237
Harrow, Eng., 10
Harstad, Norway, 18
Hartebees (riv.), S. Africa, 118
Hartford (cap.), Conn., 210
Hartford, Wis., 317
Hartford City, Ind., 227
Hartland (pt.), Eng., 13
Hartland, N. Br., 170
Hartlepool, Eng., 13
Hartley, Rhod., 118
Hartselle, Ala., 194
Harts Range, N. Terr., 93
Hartsville, S.C., 296
Hartwell, Ga., 216
Harvard, Ill., 222
Harvey, Ill., 222
Harvey, La., 238
Harwich, Eng., 13
Harwich Port, Mass., 249
Harwood Hts., Ill., 222
Harz (mts.), Ger., 22
Hasa (prov.), Saudi Ar., 59
Hasbrouck Hts., N. J., 273
Haskell, N. J., 273
Haskell, Tex., 302
Haslemere, Eng., 13
Hassan, India, 68
Hasselt, Belg., 27
Hassi–Messaoud, Alg., 106
Hässleholm, Sweden, 18
Hastings, Eng., 13
Hastings, Mich., 250
Hastings, Minn., 254
Hastings, Nebr., 264
Hastings, N.Z., 101
Hastings on Hudson, N.Y., 276
Hatboro, Pa., 294
Hathras, India, 68
Hatiba, Ras (cape), Saudi Ar., 59
Ha Tien, S. Vietnam, 72
Hato Rey, P. Rico, 161
Hatteras (cape), N.C., 281
Hattiesburg, Miss., 256
Hatvan, Hung., 41
Haud (plat.), Africa, 115
Haugesund, Norway, 18
Haura, So. Arabia, 59
Hauraki (gulf), N.Z., 101
Hauran (Der'a)(prov.), Syria, 63
Hauta, Saudi Ar., 59
Haut–Congo (prov.), Dem. Rep. of the Congo, 115
Haute–Garonne (dept.), France, 28
Haute–Loire (dept.), France, 28
Haute–Marne (dept.), France, 28
Hauterive, Que., 174
Hautes–Alpes (dept.), France, 28
Haute–Saône (dept.), France, 28
Haute–Savoie (dept.), France, 28
Hautes–Pyrénées (dept.), France, 28
Haute–Vienne (dept.), France, 28
Hautmont, France, 28
Haut–Rhin (dept.), France, 28
Havana (prov.), Cuba, 158
Havana (cap.), Cuba, 158
Havana, Ill., 222
Havasu (lake), U.S., 198
Havel (riv.), E. Ger., 22
Havelock North, N.Z., 101
Haverford, Pa., 294
Haverfordwest, Wales, 13
Haverhill, Mass., 249
Havering, Eng,, 10
Haverstraw, N.Y., 276
Havertown, Pa., 294
Havířov, Czech., 41
Havre, Mont., 262
Havre de Grace, Md., 245
Havre–Saint–Pierre, Que., 174
Hawaii (isl.), Hawaii, 218
Hawaii (state), U.S., 218
Hawaiian (isls.), 218
Hawaii Volcanoes Nat'l Park, Hawaii, 218
Hawarden, Iowa, 229
Hawera, N.Z., 101
Hawick, Scot., 15
Hawke's Bay (prov. dist.), N.Z., 101
Hawkesbury, Ont., 175
Hawkinsville, Ga., 216
Haworth, N. J., 273
Hawthorn, Vic., 97
Hawthorne, Calif., 204
Hawthorne, Nev., 266
Hawthorne, N. J., 273
Hawthorne, N.Y., 276
Hayesville, Oreg., 291
Haynesville, La., 238
Hay River, N.W.T., 187
Hays, Kans., 232
Haysville, Kans., 232
Hayti, Mo., 261
Hayward, Calif., 204
Hazard, Ky., 237
Hazardville, Conn., 210
Hazaribagh, India, 68
Hazel Crest, Ill., 222
Hazel Park, Mich., 250
Hazelwood, Mo., 261
Hazlehurst, Ga., 216
Hazlehurst, Miss., 256
Hazlet, N. J., 273
Hazleton, Pa., 294
Headland, Ala., 194
Healdsburg, Calif., 204
Healdton, Okla., 288
Heanor, Eng., 13
Heard (isl.), Austral., 3
Hearne, Tex., 302
Hearst, Ont., 175
Hebardville, Ga., 216
Hebbronville, Tex., 302
Hebden Royd, Eng., 10
Heber City, Utah, 304
Hébertville, Que., 172
Hebrides (isls.), Scot., 15
Hebrides (sea), Scot., 15
Hebron, Jordan, 65
Hebron, Newf., 166
Hecate (strait), Br. Col., 184
Hecelchakán, Mex., 150
Hedmark (county), Norway, 18
Heemstede, Neth., 27
Hegau (reg.), W. Ger., 22
Heidelberg, Vic., 97
Heidelberg, W. Ger., 22
Heidenheim, W. Ger., 22
Heilbronn, W. Ger., 22
Heiligenblut, Austria, 41
Heilungkiang (prov.), China, 77
Heinola, Fin., 18
Hejaz (prov.), Saudi Ar., 59
Hekla (volcano), Ice., 21
Hel (pen.), Poland, 47
Helena, Ark., 203
Helena (cap.), Mont., 262
Helensburgh, Scot., 15
Helgoland (bay), W. Ger., 22
Helgoland (isl.), W. Ger., 22
Heliopolis, U.A.R., 111
Hellertown, Pa., 294
Hell–Ville, Malag. Rep., 118
Helmand (riv.), Afghan., 68
Helmond, Neth., 27
Helmstedt, W. Ger., 22
Helper, Utah, 304
Helsingør, Den., 21
Helsinki (cap.), Fin., 18
Helwân, U.A.R., 111
Hemel Hempstead, Eng., 13
Hemet, Calif., 204
Hempstead, N.Y., 276
Henares (riv.), Spain, 33
Hendaye, France, 28
Henderson, Ky., 237
Henderson, Nev., 266
Henderson, N.C., 281
Henderson, Tenn., 237
Henderson, Tex., 302
Hendersonville, N.C., 281
Hengelo, Neth., 27
Hénin–Liétard, France, 28
Henrietta, Tex., 302
Henrietta Maria (cape), Ont., 177
Henrique de Carvalho, Angola, 115
Henryetta, Okla., 288
Henyang, China, 77
Henzada, Burma, 72
Herat, Afghan., 68
Hérault (dept.), France, 28
Hérault (riv.), France, 28
Herbert, Sask., 181
Herbert Hoover Nat'l Hist. Site, Iowa, 229
Hercegnovi, Yugo., 45
Heredia, C. Rica, 154
Hereford, Eng., 13
Hereford, Tex., 302
Herefordshire (county), Eng., 13
Herford, W. Ger., 22
Herington, Kans., 232
Herisau, Switz., 39
Herkimer, N.Y., 276
Herm (isl.), Channel Is., 13
Hermann, Mo., 261
Hermannsburg Mission, N. Terr., 93
Hermiston, Oreg., 291
Hermitage (bay), Newf., 166
Hermon (mt.), Asia, 63
Hermosa Beach, Calif., 204
Hermosillo, Mex., 150
Hernád (river), Hung., 41
Hernandarias, Par., 144
Herne, W. Ger., 22
Herne Bay, Eng., 13
Herning, Den., 21
Heroica, Mex., 150
Herrin, Ill., 222
Hershey, Pa., 294
Herstal, Belg., 27
Hertford, Eng., 13
Hertfordshire (county), Eng., 13
Hervey (bay), Queensland, 95
Herzeliyya, Israel, 65
Hespeler, Ont., 175
Hesperia, Calif., 204
Hesse (state), W. Ger., 22
Heves (county), Hung., 41
Hewlett, N.Y., 276
Hialeah, Fla., 212
Hiawatha, Kans., 232
Hibbing, Minn., 254
Hickory, N.C., 281
Hickory Hills, Ill., 222
Hicksville, N.Y., 276
Hicksville, Ohio, 284
Hidalgo (state), Mex., 150
Hierro (isl.), Spain, 33
Higginsville, Mo., 261
High Atlas (ranges), Mor., 106
Highgate, Jam., 158
Highland, Calif., 204
Highland, Ill., 222
Highland, Ind., 227
Highland, N.Y., 276
Highland Creek, Ont., 175
Highland Falls, N.Y., 276
Highland Hts., Ky., 237
Highland Hts., Ohio, 284
Highland Park, Ill., 222
Highland Park, Mich., 250
Highland Park, N. J., 273
Highland Park, Tex., 302
Highlands, N. J., 273
Highlands, Tex., 302
Highland Sprs., Va., 307
High Point, N.C., 281
High Prairie, Alta., 182
High Ridge, Mo., 261
High River, Alta., 182
High Spire, Pa., 294
High Tatra (mts.), Europe, 47
Hightstown, N. J., 273
Highwood, Ill., 222
High Wycombe, Eng., 13
Higüey, Dom. Rep., 158
Hiiumaa (isl.), U.S.S.R., 53
Hikueru (atoll), Fr. Poly., 87
Hikurangi (mt.), N.Z., 101
Hildesheim, W. Ger., 22
Hilla (prov.), Iraq, 66
Hilla, Iraq, 66
Hillcrest Hts., Md., 245
Hillerød, Den., 21
Hilliards, Ohio, 284
Hillingdon, Eng., 10
Hillsboro, Ill., 222
Hillsboro, Ohio, 284
Hillsboro, Oreg., 291
Hillsboro, Tex., 302
Hillsborough, Calif., 204
Hillsdale, Mich., 250
Hillsdale, N. J., 273
Hillside, Ill., 222
Hillside, Md., 245
Hillside, N. J., 273
Hilo, Hawaii, 218
Hilton Inlet (bay), Ant., 5
Hilversum, Neth., 27
Himachal Pradesh (terr.), India, 68
Himalaya (mts.), Asia, 68
Himeji, Japan, 81
Hinche, Haiti, 158
Hinchinbrook (isl.), Queensland, 95
Hinckley, Eng., 13
Hindmarsh, S. Austral., 94
Hindu Kush (range), Asia, 68
Hindupur, India, 68
Hinesville, Ga., 216
Hinganghat, India, 68
Hingham, Mass., 249
Hinlopen (strait), Norway, 18
Hinnøy (isl.), Norway, 18
Hinsdale, Ill., 222
Hinterrhein (riv.), Switz., 39
Hinton, Alta., 182
Hinton, W. Va., 313
Hirakata, Japan, 81
Hiran (prov.), Somali Rep., 115
Hirara, Ryukyu Is., 81
Hiratsuka, Japan, 81
Hirosaki, Japan, 81
Hiroshima (pref.), Japan, 81
Hiroshima, Japan, 81
Hispaniola (isl.), W. Indies, 156, 158
Hissar, India, 68
Hit, Iraq, 66
Hitachi, Japan, 81
Hitchcock, Tex., 302
Hitchin, Eng., 13
Hivaoa (isl.), Fr. Poly., 87
Hjørring, Den., 21
Hkakabo Razi (mt.), Burma, 72
Ho, Ghana, 106
Hoa Binh, N. Vietnam, 77
Hobart, Ind., 227
Hobart, Okla., 288
Hobart (cap.), Tas., 99
Hobbs, N. Mex., 274
Hobbs Coast (reg.), Ant., 5
Hoboken, Belg., 27
Hoboken, N. J., 273
Hobro, Den., 21
Höbsögöl (Khubsugul) (lake), Mong., 77
Hochwan, China, 77
Hockanum, Conn., 210
Hodeida, Yemen, 59
Hodh (reg.), Mauritania, 106
Hódmezővásárhely, Hung., 41
Hodonín, Czech., 41
Hodur, Somali Rep., 115
Hof, W. Ger., 22
Hofei, China, 77
Hofu, Japan, 81
Hofuf, Saudi Ar., 59
Höganäs, Sweden, 18
Hogansville, Ga., 216
Hohe Tauern (range), Austria, 41
Hohe Venn (plat.), Belg., 27
Ho–Ho–Kus, N. J., 273
Hoi An, S. Vietnam, 72
Hoihow, China, 77
Hoisington, Kans., 232
Hokang, China, 77
Hokkaido (pref.), Japan, 81
Hokkaido (isl.), Japan, 81
Holbæk, Den., 21
Holbrook, Ariz., 198
Holbrook, Mass., 249
Holdenville, Okla., 288
Holdrege, Nebr., 264
Holguín, Cuba, 158
Holladay, Utah, 304
Holland, Mich., 250
Hollandale, Miss., 256
Hollandia (Sukarnapura) (cap.), W. Irian, 85
Holland Park, Queensland, 95
Hollick–Kenyon (plat.), Ant., 5
Hollidaysburg, Pa., 294
Hollis, Okla., 288
Hollister, Calif., 204
Holly, Mich., 250
Holly Hill, Fla., 212
Holly Springs, Miss., 256
Hollywood, Calif., 204
Hollywood, Fla., 212
Hollywood, Md., 245
Holmestrand, Norway, 18
Holmsund, Sweden, 18
Holon, Israel, 65
Holstebro, Den., 21
Holsteinsborg, Greenl., 4
Holt, Mich., 250
Holton, Kans., 232
Holtville, Calif., 204
Holy (isl.), Eng., 13
Holy (isl.), Scot., 15
Holyhead, Wales, 13
Holyhead (Holy)(isl.), Wales, 13
Holy Loch (inlet), Scot., 15
Holyoke, Mass., 249
Holywood, N. Ire., 17
Holzminden, W. Ger., 22
Hombori (mts.), Mali, 106
Homburg, W. Ger., 22
Home (bay), N.W.T., 187
Home Corner, Ind., 227
Homer, La., 238
Homer, N.Y., 276
Homerville, Ga., 216
Homestead, Fla., 212
Homestead, Pa., 294
Homestead Nat'l Mon., Nebr., 264
Hometown, Ill., 222
Homewood, Ala., 194
Homewood, Ill., 222
Hominy, Okla., 288
Homs (prov.), Libya, 111
Homs, Libya, 111
Homs (prov.), Syria, 63
Homs, Syria, 63
Hon, Libya, 111
Honan (prov.), China, 77
Honda, Col., 126
Hondo (riv.), Cent. Amer., 154
Hondo, Tex., 302
Honduras, 154
Honduras (gulf), Cent. Amer., 154
Honduras (cape), Hond., 154
Honea Path, S.C., 296
Hønefoss, Norway, 18
Honesdale, Pa., 294
Honfleur, France, 28
Hon Gay, N. Vietnam, 72
Hong Kong, 77
Honiara (cap.), Br. Sol. Is., 87
Honningsvåg, Norway, 18
Honolulu (cap.), Hawaii, 218
Honsdrug (hills), Neth., 27
Honshu (isl.), Japan, 81
Hood (riv.), N.W.T., 187
Hood (mt.), Oreg., 291
Hood River, Oreg., 291
Hooghly (riv.), India, 68
Hooghly–Chinsura, India, 68
Hook of Holland, Neth., 27
Hoopeston, Ill., 222
Hoorn (isls.), Wallis & Futuna, 87
Hoosick Falls, N.Y., 276
Hoover (dam), U.S., 198
Hopatcong, N. J., 273
Hope (bay), Ant., 5
Hope, Ark., 203
Hope, Br. Col., 184
Hopedale, Mass., 249
Hopei (prov.), China, 77
Hopes Advance (cape), Que., 174
Hopewell, Va., 307
Hopkins, Minn., 254
Hopkinsville, Ky., 237
Hopkinton, Mass., 249
Hopkinton, R.I., 249
Hoppo, China, 77
Hoquiam, Wash., 310
Hordaland (county), Norway, 18
Hordio, Somali Rep., 115
Horgen, Switz., 39
Horicon, Wis., 317
Horn (cape), Chile, 138
Hornád (river), Czech., 41
Hornby, N.Z., 101
Hornell, N.Y., 276
Hornepayne, Ont., 175
Hörnli (mt.), Switz., 39
Hornsby, N.S.W., 97
Hornslandet (pen.), Sweden, 18
Horqueta, Par., 144
Horseheads, N.Y., 276
Horsens, Den., 21
Horseshoe Bend Nat'l Mil. Park, Ala., 194
Horsham, Eng., 13
Horsham, Vic., 97
Hørsholm, Den., 21
Horta (dist.), Port., 32
Horta, Port., 32
Horten, Norway, 18
Horton (riv.), N.W.T., 187
Hospet, India, 68
Hospitalet, Spain, 33
Hosseina, Eth., 111
Hoste (isl.), Chile, 138
Hotien (Khotan), China, 77
Hot Springs, S. Dak., 298
Hot Springs Nat'l Park, Ark., 203
Hottah (lake), N.W.T., 187
Houghton, Mich., 250
Houlton, Maine, 242
Houma, La., 238
Hounslow, Eng., 10
Houston, Miss., 256
Houston, Tex., 302
Houtman Abrolhos (isls.), W. Austral., 92
Hove, Eng., 13
Hovenweep Nat'l Mon., U.S., 208, 304
Howard, R.I., 249
Howard, Wis., 317
Howe (cape), N.S.W., 97
Howell, Mich., 250
Howrah, India, 68
Howth, Ire., 17
Hoy (isl.), Scot., 15
Hoyerswerda, E. Ger., 22
Hoylake, Eng., 10
Hoyt Lakes, Minn., 254
Hradec Králové, Czech., 41
Hron (river), Czech., 41
Hsüchang, China, 77
Huachipato, Chile, 138
Huacho, Peru, 128
Hua Hin, Thai., 72
Huahine (isl.), Fr. Poly., 87
Huahua (riv.), Nic., 154
Huajuapán, Mex., 150
Huamantla, Mex., 150
Huambo (dist.), Angola, 115
Huancavelica (prov.), Peru, 128
Huancavelica, Peru, 128
Huancayo, Peru, 128
Huanchaca (mts.), Bol., 136
Huánuco (prov.), Peru, 128
Huánuco, Peru, 128
Huanuni, Bol., 136
Huapí (mts.), Nic., 154
Huaral, Peru, 128
Huarás, Peru, 128
Huascarán (mt.), Peru, 128
Huasco (river), Chile, 138
Huaspuc (riv.), Nic., 154
Huatabampo, Mex., 150
Huatusco de Chicuellar, Mex., 150
Huauchinango, Mex., 150
Huautlá, Mex., 150
Hubbard, Ohio, 284
Hubbell Trading Post Nat'l Hist. Site, Ariz., 198
Hubli, India, 68
Huchow, China, 77
Hucknall, Eng., 13
Huddersfield, Eng., 10
Hudiksvall, Sweden, 18
Hudson (bay), Canada, 187
Hudson (str.), Canada, 187
Hudson, Mass., 249
Hudson, Mich., 250
Hudson, N.H., 268
Hudson, N.Y., 276
Hudson, Que., 172
Hudson (riv.), U.S., 276
Hudson, Wis., 317
Hudson Bay, Sask., 181
Hudson Falls, N.Y., 276
Hudsonville, Mich., 250
Hue, S. Vietnam, 72
Huehuetenango, Guat., 154
Huejotzingo, Mex., 150
Huejutla, Mex., 150
Huelva (prov.), Spain, 33
Huelva, Spain, 33
Huesca (prov.), Spain, 33
Huesca, Spain, 33
Huetamo, Mex., 150
Hueytown, Ala., 194
Hugo, Okla., 288
Hugoton, Kans., 232
Huhehot, China, 77
Huila (dist.), Angola, 115
Huila (dept.), Col., 126
Huila (mt.), Col., 126
Huimanguillo, Mex., 150
Huitzuco, Mex., 150
Huixtla, Mex., 150
Hull (isl.), 87
Hull, Eng., 13
Hull, Mass., 249
Hull, Que., 172
Humacao (dist.), P. Rico, 161
Humacao, P. Rico, 161
Humber (riv.), Eng., 13
Humboldt, Iowa, 229
Humboldt (riv.), Nev., 266
Humboldt, Sask., 181
Humboldt, Tenn., 237
Hume (res.), Austral., 97
Hummelstown, Pa., 294
Humphreys (peak), Ariz., 198
Húnaflói (bay), Ice., 21
Hunan (prov.), China, 77
Hunchun, China, 77
Hunedoara (reg.), Rum., 45
Hunedoara, Rum., 45
Hungary, 41
Hungkiang, China, 77
Hŭngnam, N. Korea, 81
Hungshui Ho (riv.), China, 77
Hungtow (isl.), China, 77
Hungtse (lake), China, 77
Hunsrück (mts.), W. Ger., 22
Hunter (mts.), N.Z., 101
Hunter (isls.), Tas., 99
Hunters Hill, N.S.W., 97
Huntingburg, Ind., 227
Huntingdon, Eng., 13
Huntingdon, Pa., 294
Huntingdon, Que., 172
Huntingdon and Peterborough (county), Eng., 13
Huntington, Ind., 227
Huntington, N.Y., 276
Huntington, W. Va., 313
Huntington Beach, Calif., 204
Huntington Park, Calif., 204
Huntington Sta., N.Y., 276
Huntly, Scot., 15
Huntsville, Ala., 194
Huntsville, Ont., 175
Huntsville, Tex., 302
Hunucmá, Mex., 150
Hunza (Baltit), India, 68
Huon (isls.), New Cal., 87
Huon (gulf), Terr. N.G., 85
Huonville–Ranelagh, Tas., 99
Hupei (prov.), China, 77
Hurd (cape), Ont., 175
Hureidha, So. Arabia, 59
Hurghada, U.A.R., 111
Hurley, Wis., 317
Huron (lake), N. Amer., 188
Huron, Ohio, 284
Huron, S. Dak., 298
Hurstville, N.S.W., 97
Hürth, W. Ger., 22
Húsavík, Ice., 21
Huşi, Rum., 45
Huskvarna, Sweden, 18
Husum, W. Ger., 22
Hutchinson, Kans., 232
Hutchinson, Minn., 254
Huth, Yemen, 59
Hutt (Upper and Lower), N.Z., 101
Hvar (isl.), Yugo., 45
Hvitá (river), Ice., 21
Hwainan, China, 77
Hwang Ho (riv.), China, 77
Hwangshih, China, 77
Hyannis, Mass., 249
Hyattsville, Md., 245
Hyde, Eng., 10
Hyderabad, India, 68
Hyderabad, Pak., 68
Hyères, France, 28
Hyères (isls.), France, 28
Hyogo (pref.), Japan, 81
Hythe, Eng., 13
Hyvinkää, Fin., 18

I

Ia Drang (riv.), Asia, 72
Ialomiţa (riv.), Rum., 45
Iaşi (reg.), Rum., 45
Iaşi, Rum., 45
Ibadan, Nigeria, 106
Ibagué, Col., 126
Ibar (riv.), Yugo., 45
Ibaraki (pref.), Japan, 81
Ibarra, Ecua., 128
Ibb, Yemen, 59
Iberville, Que., 172
Iberville (lake), Que., 174
Ibiza, Spain, 33
Ibiza (Iviza) (isl.), Spain, 33
'Ibri, Muscat and Oman, 59
Içá (riv.), Braz., 132
Ica (dept.), Peru, 128
Ica, Peru, 128
Iceland, 21
Ichang, China, 77
Ichikawa, Japan, 81
Ichinomiya, Japan, 81
Ichinoseki, Japan, 81
Ichun, China, 77
Idabel, Okla., 288
Idaho (state), U.S., 220
Idaho Falls, Idaho, 220
Idar–Oberstein, W. Ger., 22
Idehan (des.), Africa, 111
Idenburg (riv.), W. Irian, 85
Ider (riv.), Mong., 77
Idfu, U.A.R., 111
Idiofa, Dem. Rep. of the Congo, 115
Idjil, Mauritania, 106
Idlib (prov.), Syria, 63
Idlib, Syria, 63
Iesi, Italy, 34
Ifalik (atoll), Pac. Is., 87
Ife, Nigeria, 106
Iférouane, Niger, 106
Ifni (prov.), Spain, 106
Igarka, U.S.S.R., 48
Ighil Izane, Alg., 106
Iglesias, Italy, 34
Igloolik, N.W.T., 187
Iguala, Mex., 150
Igualada, Spain, 33
Iguassú (falls), S. Amer., 132
Iguidi Erg (des.), Africa, 106
Ihosy, Malag. Rep., 118
Ii (riv.), Fin., 18
Iida, Japan, 81

J

K

L

Man (isl.), 13
Man, Ivory Coast, 106
Mana, Fr. Gui., 131
Manabí (prov.), Ecua., 128
Manacor, Spain, 33
Manado, Indon., 85
Managua (cap.), Nic., 154
Managua (lake), Nic., 154
Manakara, Malag. Rep., 118
Manalapan, N. J., 273
Manama (cap.), Bahrein, 59
Mananjary, Malag Rep., 118
Manapouri (lake), N.Z., 101
Manar, Jebel (mt.), Yemen, 59
Manasarowar (lake), China, 77
Manasquan, N. J., 273
Manass (riv.), China, 77
Manassas, Va., 307
Manassas Nat'l Battlef. Park, Va., 307
Manassas Park, Va., 307
Manatí, P. Rico, 161
Manaus, Braz., 132
Mancha, La (reg.), Spain, 33
Manche (dept.), France, 28
Manchester, Conn., 210
Manchester, Eng., 10
Manchester, Ga., 216
Manchester, Iowa, 229
Manchester, N.H., 268
Manchester, Tenn., 237
Manchouli, China, 77
Manchuria (reg.), China, 77
Máncora, Peru, 128
Mandal, Norway, 18
Mandalay (div.), Burma, 72
Mandalay, Burma, 72
Mandal Gobi, Mong., 77
Mandali, Iraq, 66
Mandalya (gulf), Turkey, 63
Mandan, N. Dak., 283
Mandeb, Bab el (str.), 111
Mandeville, Jam., 158
Mand Rud (riv.), Iran, 66
Mandsaur, India, 68
Mandurah, W. Austral., 92
Mandvi, India, 68
Manfalût, U.A.R., 111
Manfredonia, Italy, 34
Mangaia (isl.), Cook Is., 87
Mangalia, Rum., 45
Mangalore, India, 68
Mangareva (isl.), Fr. Poly., 87
Mangere East, N.Z., 101
Mangoky (riv.), Malag. Rep., 118
Mangotsfield, Eng., 13
Mangrol, India, 68
Mangueira (lag.), Braz., 132
Mangum, Okla., 288
Mangyshlak (pen.), U.S.S.R., 48
Manhasset, N.Y., 276
Manhattan, Kans., 232
Manhattan (isl.), N.Y., 276
Manhattan Beach, Calif., 204
Manheim, Pa., 294
Manhiça, Mozamb., 118
Maniamba, Mozamb., 118
Manica e Sofala (dist.), Mozamb., 118
Manicouagan (riv.) Que., 174
Maniema (prov.), Dem. Rep. of the Congo, 115
Manifold (cape), Queensland, 95
Manihiki (atoll), Cook Is., 87
Manila, Phil. Is., 82
Manila (bay), Phil. Is., 82
Manipur (riv.), Asia, 72
Manipur (terr.), India, 68
Manisa, Turkey, 63
Manisht (mt.), Iran, 66
Manistee, Mich., 250
Manistique, Mich., 250
Manitoba (prov.), Canada, 179
Manitoba (lake), Man., 179
Manitoulin (isl.), Ont., 175
Manitou Springs, Colo., 208
Manitouwadge, Ont.,175
Manitowoc, Wis., 317
Maniwaki, Que., 172
Manizales, Col., 126
Manjimup, W. Austral., 92
Mankato, Minn., 254
Mankoya, Zambia, 115
Manly, N.S.W., 97
Manmad, India, 68
Mannar (gulf), Asia, 68
Mannargudi, India, 68
Mannheim, W. Ger., 22
Manning, S.C., 296
Manning, E.C., Prov. Park, Br. Col., 184
Mannington, W. Va., 313
Mannum, S. Austral., 94
Manokwari, W. Irian, 85
Manono, Dem. Rep. of the Congo, 115
Manori (creek), India, 68
Manra (Sydney) (isl.), Gilb. & Ell. Is., 87
Manresa, Spain, 33
Mansel (isl.), N.W.T., 187
Mansfield, Conn., 210
Mansfield, Eng., 13
Mansfield, La., 238
Mansfield, Mass., 249
Mansfield, Ohio, 284
Mansfield, Pa., 294
Mansfield (mt.), Vt., 268
Manta, Ecua., 128
Manteca, Calif., 204
Mantiqueira (range), Braz., 135
Mänttä, Fin., 18
Mantua (prov.), Italy, 34
Mantua, Italy, 34
Manú (riv.), Peru, 128
Manua (isls.), Amer. Samoa, 87
Manuae (atoll), Cook Is., 87
Manurewa, N.Z., 101
Manus (isl.), Terr. N.G., 87
Manville, N. J., 273
Manville, R.I., 249
Many, La., 238
Manych-Gudilo (lake), U.S.S.R., 52
Manyoni, Tanz., 115
Manzanares, Spain, 33
Manzanillo, Cuba, 158
Manzanillo, Mex., 150
Mao, Chad, 111
Mapimí (depr.), Mex., 150
Maple Creek, Sask., 181
Maple Hts., Ohio, 284
Maple Shade, N. J., 273
Maplewood, La., 238
Maplewood, Minn., 254
Maplewood, Mo., 261
Maplewood, N. J., 273
Mapuera (riv.), Braz., 132
Ma'qil, Iraq, 66
Maquoketa, Iowa, 229
Mar (range), Braz., 132
Mar (dist.), Scot., 15
Marabella, Trin. & Tob., 161
Maracá (isl.), Braz., 132
Maracaibo, Venez., 124
Maracaibo (lake), Venez., 124
Maracay, Venez., 124
Maragheh, Iran, 66
Maragogipe, Braz., 132
Marajó (isl.), Braz., 132
Maralinga, S. Austral., 94
Maramba, Zambia, 115
Maramureş (reg.), Rum., 45
Marand, Iran, 66
Marandellas, Rhod., 118
Maranhão (state), Braz., 132
Marañón (riv.), Peru, 128
Maraş, Turkey, 63
Marathón, Greece, 45
Marathon, Ont., 175
Marblehead, Mass., 249
Marburg, W. Ger., 22
Marceline, Mo., 261
March (riv.), Austria, 41
March, Eng., 13
Marche (reg.), Italy, 34
Marchena (isl.), Ecua., 128
Marchena, Spain, 33
Mar Chiquita (lake), Arg., 143
Marcona, Peru, 128
Marcos Juárez, Arg., 143
Marcos Paz, Arg., 143
Marcus (isl.), Pacific, 87
Marcus Hook, Pa., 294
Mardan, Pak., 68
Mar del Plata, Arg., 143
Mardin, Turkey, 63
Maré (isl.), New Cal., 87
Maree (lake), Scot., 15
Mareeba, Queensland, 95
Marengo, Ill., 222
Marettimo (isl.), Italy, 34
Marfa, Tex., 302
Marganets, U.S.S.R., 52
Margarita (isl.), Venez., 124
Margate, Eng., 13
Margate City, N. J., 273
Margherita (mt.), Africa, 115
Margherita, Somali Rep., 115
Margo, Dasht-i- (des.), Afghan., 68
Mari A.S.S.R., U.S.S.R., 52
Maria (isl.), Fr. Poly., 87
María Elena, Chile, 138
Mariager (fjord), Den., 21
Mariana (isls.), Pac. Is., 87
Marianao, Cuba, 158
Mariana Trench, Pacific, 87
Marianna, Ark., 203
Marianna, Fla., 212
Maria Trinidad Sánchez (prov.), Dom. Rep., 158
Maria van Diemen (cape), N.Z., 101
Marib, Yemen, 59
Maribo, Den., 21
Maribor, Yugo., 45
Maridi, Sudan, 111
Marie Byrd Land (reg.), Ant., 5
Marie-Galante (isl.), Guad., 161
Mariehamn, Fin., 18
Mariemont, Ohio, 284
Marienburg, Sur., 131
Mariental, S.W. Afr., 118
Mariestad, Sweden, 18
Marietta, Ga., 216
Marietta, Ohio, 284
Marieville, Que., 172
Marigot, Dominica, 161
Marília, Braz., 135
Marin, Mart., 161
Marinduque (prov.), Phil. Is., 82
Marinduque (isl.), Phil. Is., 82
Marine City, Mich., 250
Marinette, Wis., 317
Marinha Grande, Port., 33
Marino, Italy, 34
Marion, Ala., 194
Marion, Ill., 222
Marion, Ind., 227
Marion, Iowa, 229
Marion, N.C., 281
Marion, Ohio, 284
Marion, S. Austral., 94
Marion, S.C., 296
Marion, Va., 307
Mariscala, Urug., 145
Mariscal Estigarribia, Par., 144
Marismas, Las (marsh), Spain, 33
Maritime Alps (range), Europe, 28
Maritsa, Bulg., 45
Maritsa (riv.), Bulg., 45
Mariupol' (Zhdanov), U.S.S.R., 52
Marked Tree, Ark., 203
Marken (isl.), Neth., 27
Markha (riv.), U.S.S.R., 48
Markham (mt.), Ant., 5
Markham, Ill., 222
Markham, Ont., 175
Markham Dzong, China, 77
Marks, Miss., 256
Marksville, La., 238
Marl, W. Ger., 22
Marlborough, Mass., 249
Marlborough (prov. dist.), N.Z., 101
Marlin, Tex., 302
Marlow, Okla., 288
Marmara (sea), Turkey, 63
Marmolada (mt.), Italy, 34
Marne (dept.), France, 28
Marne (riv.), France, 28
Maroantsetra, Malag. Rep., 118
Maroni (riv.), S. Amer., 131
Maros (riv.), Hung., 41
Maroua, Cameroon, 115
Marovoay, Malag. Rep., 118
Marowijne (dist.), Sur., 131
Marowijne (riv.), Sur., 131
Marple, Eng., 10
Marquesas (isls.), Fr. Poly., 87
Marquês de Valença, Braz., 135
Marquette, Mich., 250
Marquette Hts., Ill., 222
Marra, Jebel (mt.), Sudan, 111
Marrakech, Mor., 106
Marrero, La., 238
Marrickville, N.S.W., 97
Marromeu, Mozamb., 118
Marsabit, Kenya, 115
Marsa el Awegia, Libya, 111
Marsa el Brega, Libya, 111
Marsala, Italy, 34
Marsa Susa, Libya, 111
Marseille, France, 28
Marseilles, Ill., 222
Marshall, Ill., 222
Marshall, Liberia, 106
Marshall, Mich., 250
Marshall, Minn., 254
Marshall, Mo., 261
Marshall (isls.), Pac. Is., 87
Marshall, Tex., 302
Marshalltown, Iowa, 229
Marshfield, Mass., 249
Marshfield, Wis., 317
Martaban (gulf), Burma, 72
Martapura, Indon., 85
Martha's Vineyard (isl.), Mass., 249
Martí, Cuba, 158
Martigny, Switz., 39
Martigues, France, 39
Martin, Czech., 41
Martin, Tenn., 237
Martina Franca, Italy, 34
Martinez, Calif., 204
Martínez de la Torre, Mex., 150
Martín García (isl.), Arg., 143
Martinique, 161
Martinique (passage), W. Indies, 161
Martinsburg, W. Va., 313
Martins Ferry, Ohio, 284
Martinsville, Ind., 227
Martinsville, N. J., 273
Martinsville, Va., 307
Marton, N.Z., 101
Martos, Spain, 33
Marudi (mts.), Guyana, 131
Marudi, Malaysia, 85
Marugame, Japan, 81
Marutea (atoll), Fr. Poly., 87
Mary, U.S.S.R., 48
Maryborough (Port Laoighise), Ire., 17
Maryborough, Queensland, 95
Maryborough, Vic., 97
Mary Kathleen, Queensland, 95
Maryland (state), U.S., 245
Maryport, Eng., 13
Marysville, Br. Col., 184
Marysville, Calif., 204
Marysville, Kans., 232
Marysville, Mich., 250
Marysville, N.B., 170
Marysville, Ohio, 284
Marysville, Pa., 294
Marysville, Wash., 310
Maryville, Mo., 261
Maryville, Tenn., 237
Masagua, Guat., 154
Masai (steppe), Tanz., 115
Masaka, Uganda, 115
Masan, S. Korea, 81
Masatepe, Nic., 154
Masaya, Nic., 154
Masbate (prov.), Phil. Is., 82
Masbate (isl.), Phil. Is., 82
Mascara, Alg., 106
Mascarene (isls.), Africa, 118
Mascota, Mex., 150
Mascoutah, Ill., 222
Maseru (cap.), Basutoland, 118
Mashkel (riv.), Asia, 68
Mashonaland (reg.), Rhod., 118
Masi-Manimba, Dem. Rep. of the Congo, 115
Masindi, Uganda, 115
Masira (isl.), Muscat and Oman, 59
Masjid-i-Sulaiman, Iran, 66
Mask (lake), Ire., 17
Masoala (pen.), Malag. Rep., 118
Mason, Mich., 250
Mason, Ohio, 284
Mason City, Iowa, 229
Masontown, Pa., 294
Massa, Italy, 34
Massa-Carrara (prov.), Italy, 34
Massachusetts (state), U.S., 249
Massakori, Chad, 111
Massapequa, N.Y., 276
Massawa, Eth., 111
Massena, N.Y., 276
Massénya, Chad, 111
Massey, N.Z., 101
Massillon, Ohio, 284
Massinga, Mozamb., 118
Masterton, N.Z., 101
Mastic Beach, N.Y., 276
Masuda, Japan, 81
Masulipatnam, India, 68
Masury, Ohio, 284
Matabeleland (reg.), Rhod., 118
Matadi, Dem. Rep. of the Congo, 115
Matagalpa, Nic., 154
Matagorda (isl.), Tex., 302
Matam, Sen., 106
Matamoros, Mex., 150
Matane, Que., 172
Matanzas (prov.), Cuba, 158
Matanzas, Cuba, 158
Mata Palacio, Dom. Rep., 158
Matapan (Taínaron)(cape), Greece, 45
Matara, Ceylon, 68
Matarani, Peru, 128
Mataró, Spain, 33
Matautu (cap.), Wallis and Futuna, 87
Matawan, N. J., 273
Matehuala, Mex., 150
Matera (prov.), Italy, 34
Matera, Italy, 34
Mateur, Tun., 106
Mathis, Tex., 302
Mathura, India, 68
Matías de Gálvez, Guat., 154
Matías Romero, Mex., 150
Matlock, Eng., 13
Mato Grosso (state), Braz., 132
Mato Grosso (plat.), Braz., 132
Matopos, Rhod., 118
Matosinhos, Port., 33
Matra (mts.), Hung., 41
Matrah, Muscat and Oman, 59
Matrei, Austria, 41
Matrûh, U.A.R., 111
Matsu (isl.), China, 77
Matsudo, Japan, 81
Matsue, Japan, 81
Matsumoto, Japan, 81
Matsusaka, Japan, 81
Matsuyama, Japan, 81
Mattagami (riv.), Ont., 175
Mattancheri, India, 68
Mattapan, Mass., 249
Mattawa, Ont., 175
Matteson, Ill., 222
Mattoon, Ill., 222
Matun, Afghan., 68
Maturín, Venez., 124
Mau, India, 68
Maubeuge, France, 28
Ma-ubin, Burma, 72
Maui (isl.), Hawaii, 218
Mauke (isl.), Cook Is., 87
Maule (prov.), Chile, 138
Maule (river), Chile, 138
Maullín, Chile, 138
Maumee, Ohio, 284
Maun, Bech., 118
Mauna Kea (mt.), Hawaii, 218
Mauna Loa (mt.), Hawaii, 218
Mauritania, 106
Mauritius, 118
Mauston, Wis., 317
Mauvoisin (dam), Switz., 39
Mawson, Ant., 5
Maxcanú, Mex., 150
May (cape), N. J., 273
Mayaguana (isl.), Bah. Is., 156
Mayaguana (passage), Bah. Is., 156
Mayagüez (dist.), P. Rico, 161
Mayagüez, P. Rico, 161
Mayarí (river), Cuba, 158
Mayaro, Trin. and Tob., 161
Maybole, Scot., 15
Mayenne (dept.), France, 28
Mayenne (riv.), France, 28
Mayfield, Ky., 237
Mayfield Hts., Ohio, 284
Maykop, U.S.S.R., 52
Maymyo, Burma, 72
Maynard, Mass., 249
Mayo (county), Ire., 17
Mayo, Yukon, 187
Mayon (vol.), Phil. Is., 82
Mayor (cape), Spain, 33
Mayotte (isl.), Comoro Is., 118
May Pen, Jam., 158
Maysville, Ky., 237
Mayumba, Gabon, 115
Mayuram, India, 68
Mayville, N. Dak., 283
Mayville, Wis., 317
Maywood, Calif., 204
Maywood, Ill., 222
Maywood, N. J., 273
Mazabuka, Zambia, 115
Mazagan (El Jadida), Mor., 106
Mazanderan (prov.), Iran, 66
Mazar-i-Sharif, Afghan., 68
Mazaruni (riv.), Guyana, 131
Mazatenango, Guat., 154
Mazatlán, Mex., 150
Mbabane (cap.), Swaz., 118
M'Baiki, Centr. Afr. Rep., 115
Mbale, Uganda, 115
M'Balmayo, Cameroon, 115
Mbarara, Uganda, 115
Mbeya, Tanz., 115
M'Bigou, Gabon, 115
M'Bour, Senegal, 106
M'Bout, Mauritania, 106
M'Bres, Centr. Afr. Rep., 115
Mbuyapey, Par., 144
McAdam, N.B., 170
McAdoo, Pa., 294
McAlester, Okla., 288
McAllen, Tex., 302
McCamey, Tex., 302
McComb, Miss., 256
McCook, Nebr., 264
McDonald (isls.), Austral., 3
McDonald, Ohio, 284
McDonald, Pa., 294
McFarland, Calif., 204
McFarlane (riv.), Sask., 181
McGehee, Ark., 203
McGill, Nev., 266
McGregor, Tex., 302
McHenry, Ill., 222
Mchinga, Tanz., 115
McKeesport, Pa., 294
McKees Rocks, Pa., 294
McKenzie, Tenn., 237
McKinley (mt.), Alaska, 196
McKinney, Tex., 302
McLeansboro, Ill., 222
McLennan, Alta., 182
M'Clintock (chan.), N.W.T., 187
M'Clure (strait), N.W.T., 187
McMechen, W. Va., 313
McMinnville, Oreg., 291
McMinnville, Tenn., 237
McMurdo (sound), Ant., 5
McPherson, Kans., 232
McRae, Ga., 216
McSherrystown, Pa., 294
Mead (lake), U.S., 198
Meadow Lake, Sask., 181
Meadville, Pa., 294
Meaford, Ont., 175
Mealy (mts.), Newf., 166
Mearim (riv.), Braz., 132
Meath (county), Ire., 17
Meaux, France, 28
Mecatina (river), Que., 174
Mecca (cap.), Saudi Ar., 59
Mechanicsburg, Pa., 294
Mechanicville, N.Y., 276
Mechelen, Belg., 27
Méchéria, Alg., 106
Mecklenburg (reg.), E. Ger., 22
Mecklenburg (bay), Ger., 22
Meconta, Mozamb., 118
Mecsek (mts.), Hung., 41
Medan, Indon., 85
Médéa, Alg., 106
Medellín, Col., 126
Médenine, Tun., 106
Méderdra, Mauritania, 106
Medford, Mass., 249
Medford, Oreg., 291
Medford, Wis., 317
Medford Lakes, N. J., 273
Medgidia, Rum., 45
Media, Pa., 294
Mediaş, Rum., 45
Medical Lake, Wash., 310
Medicine Bow (range), U.S., 208, 319
Medicine Hat, Alta., 182
Medicine Lodge, Kans., 232
Medina, N.Y., 276
Medina, Ohio, 284
Medina, Saudi Ar., 59
Medina del Campo, Spain, 33
Medina-Sidonia, Spain, 33
Mediterranean (sea), 36
Medjerda (riv.), Africa, 106
Mednogorsk, U.S.S.R., 52
Médoc (reg.), France, 28
Medveditsa (riv.), U.S.S.R., 52
Medvezh'yegorsk, U.S.S.R., 52
Meerane, E. Ger., 22
Meerut, India, 68
Megalópolis, Greece, 45
Mégantic (Lac-Mégantic), Que., 172
Mégara, Greece, 45
Megiddo, Israel, 65
Mehetia (isl.), Fr. Poly., 87
Mehrabad, Iran, 66
Mehran (riv.), Iran, 66
Mehsana, India, 68
Meighen (isl.), N.W.T., 187
Meiktila, Burma, 72
Meiners Oaks, Calif., 204
Meiningen, E. Ger., 22
Meiringen, Switz., 39
Meiron (mt.), Israel, 65
Meissen, E. Ger., 22
Mejillones, Chile, 138
Mekambo, Gabon, 115
Meknès, Mor., 106
Mekong (riv.), Asia, 72, 77
Mekong, Mouths of the (delta), S. Vietnam, 72
Melanesia (reg.), Pacific, 87
Melbourne, Fla., 212
Melbourne (cap.), Vic., 97
Melchor Múzquiz, Mex., 150
Melekess, U.S.S.R., 52
Melfi, Chad, 111
Melfi, Italy, 34
Melfort, Sask., 181
Melilla, Spain, 33
Melipilla, Chile, 138
Melita, Man., 179
Melitopol', U.S.S.R., 52
Melo, Urug., 145
Melrhir, Shott (salt lake), Alg., 106
Melrose, Mass., 249
Melrose, Scot., 15
Melrose Park, Ill., 222
Melton Mowbray, Eng., 13
Melun, France, 28
Melville (bay), Greenl., 4
Melville (lake), Newf., 166
Melville (bay), N. Terr., 93
Melville (isl.), N. Terr., 93
Melville (isl.), N.W.T., 187
Melville (pen.), N.W.T., 187
Melville, Sask., 181
Melvin (lake), Ire., 17
Melvindale, Mich., 250
Memba, Mozamb., 118
Membij, Syria, 63
Memel (Klaipėda), U.S.S.R., 53
Memmingen, W. Ger., 22
Memphis, Fla., 212
Memphis, Tenn., 237
Memphis, Tex., 302
Memphis (ruins), U.A.R., 111
Memphremagog (lake), N. Amer., 172
Mena, Ark., 203
Menai (str.), Wales, 13
Ménaka, Mali, 106
Menasha, Wis., 317
Menderes (riv.), Turkey, 63
Mendi, Papua, 85
Mendip (hills), Eng., 13
Mendocino (cape), Calif., 204
Mendota, Ill., 222
Mendota Hts., Minn., 254
Mendoza (prov.), Arg., 143
Mendoza, Arg., 143
Mene Grande, Venez., 124
Menemen, Turkey, 63
Menen, Belg., 27
Menggala, Indon., 85
Mengtsz, China, 77
Menihek (lakes), Newf., 166
Menindee (lake), N.S.W., 97
Menlo Park, Calif., 204
Menlo Park, N. J., 273
Menominee, Mich., 250
Menomonee Falls, Wis., 317
Menomonie, Wis., 317
Menor, Mar (lag.), Spain, 33
Menorca (Minorca) (isl.), Spain, 33
Mentakab, Malaysia, 72
Mentawai (isls.), Indon., 85
Menton, France, 28
Mentone, Calif., 204
Mentor, Ohio, 284
Menzel Bourguiba, Tun., 106
Menzel-Temime, Tun., 106
Meoqui, Mex., 150
Mequon, Wis., 317
Merabéllou (gulf), Greece, 45
Merak, Indon., 85
Merano, Italy, 34
Merauke, W. Irian, 85
Merced, Calif., 204
Mercedario (mt.), Arg., 143
Mercedes, Arg., 143
Mercedes, Tex., 302
Mercedes, Urug., 145
Mercer, Pa., 294
Mercer I., Wash., 310
Mercerville, N. J., 273
Merchantville, N. J., 273
Mercury, Nev., 266
Mercury (bay), N.Z., 101
Mergui, Burma, 72
Mergui (arch.), Burma, 72
Meriç (riv.), Turkey, 63
Mérida, Mex., 150
Mérida, Spain, 33
Mérida (state), Venez., 124
Mérida, Venez., 124
Mérida (mts.), Venez., 124
Meriden, Conn., 210
Meridian, Miss., 256
Merino Vill., Mass., 249
Merionethshire (county), Wales, 13
Merion Sta., Pa., 294
Merir (isl.), Pac. Is., 87
Meriwether Unit, Natchez Trace Pkwy., Tenn., 237
Merj 'Uyun, Leb., 63
Merka, Somali Rep., 115
Merksem, Belg., 27
Merlo, Arg., 143
Meroe (ruins), Sudan, 111
Merowe, Sudan, 111
Merredin, W. Austral., 92
Merriam, Kans., 232
Merrick, N.Y., 276
Merrill, Wis., 317
Merritt, Br. Col., 184
Merritt I., Fla., 212
Mersch, Lux., 27
Mersea (isl.), Eng., 13
Merseburg, E. Ger., 22
Mersey (riv.), Eng., 10
Mersey (riv.), Tas., 99
Mersin, Turkey, 63
Merthyr Tydfil, Wales, 13
Merton, Eng., 10
Meru (mt.), Tanz., 115
Merzifon, Turkey, 63
Mesa, Ariz., 198
Mesagne, Italy, 34
Mesará (gulf), Greece, 45
Mesa Verde Nat'l Park, Colo., 208
Meshed, Iran, 66
Mesilla Park, N. Mex., 274
Mesolóngion, Greece, 45
Mesopotamia (reg.), Iraq, 66
Mesquite, Tex., 302
Messina (prov.), Italy, 34
Messina, Italy, 34
Messina (strait), Italy, 34
Messina, S. Afr., 118
Messíni, Greece, 45
Mesta (riv.), Bulg., 45
Mestre, Italy, 34
Meta (dept.), Col., 126
Meta (riv.), S. Amer., 126
Metairie, La., 238
Metán, Arg., 143
Metapán, El Sal., 154
Metauro (riv.), Italy, 34
Metepec, Mex., 150
Methuen, Mass., 249
Metropolis, Ill., 222
Metuchen, N. J., 273
Metz, France, 28
Meudon, France, 28
Meurthe-et-Moselle (dept.), France, 28
Meuse (riv.), Europe, 28
Meuse (dept.), France, 28
Mexia, Tex., 302
Mexiana (isl.), Braz., 132
Mexicali, Mex., 150
Mexico, 150
Mexico, Maine, 242
Mexico (state), Mex., 150
Mexico, Mo., 261
Mexico (gulf), N. Amer., 146
Mexico City (cap.), Mex., 150
Meyadin, Syria, 63
Meyersdale, Pa., 294
Mezen' (bay), U.S.S.R., 52
Mezen' (riv.), U.S.S.R., 52
Mezőtúr, Hung., 41
Mezquital (riv.), Mex., 150
Mhow, India, 68
Miahuatlán, Mex., 150
Miami, Ariz., 198
Miami, Fla., 212
Miami (riv.), Ohio, 284
Miami, Okla., 288
Miami Beach, Fla., 212
Miamisburg, Ohio, 284
Miami Shores, Fla., 212
Miami Sprs., Fla., 212
Mianeh, Iran, 66
Mianwali, Pak., 68
Michigan (state), U.S., 250
Michigan (lake), U.S., 188
Michigan Ctr., Mich., 250
Michigan City, Ind., 227
Michikamau (lake), Newf., 166
Michipicoten (isl.), Ont., 175
Michoacan (state), Mex., 150
Michurinsk, U.S.S.R., 52
Micoud, St. Lucia, 161
Micronesia (reg.), Pacific, 87
Middelburg, Neth., 27
Middelburg, S. Africa, 118
Middelfart, Den., 21
Middle Atlas (ranges), Mor., 160
Middleboro, Mass., 249
Middleburg Hts., Ohio, 284
Middle Gobi (prov.), Mong., 77
Middleport, Ohio, 284
Middle River, Md., 245
Middlesboro, Ky., 237
Middlesbrough, Eng., 13
Middlesex (county), Jam., 158
Middlesex, N. J., 273
Middleton, Eng., 10
Middleton, N.S., 169
Middleton, Wis., 317
Middletown, Conn., 210
Middletown, Ky., 237
Middletown, N. J., 273
Middletown, N.Y., 276
Middletown, Ohio, 284
Middletown, Pa., 294
Middletown, R.I., 249
Midfield, Ala., 194
Midian (dist.), Saudi Ar., 59
Midland, Mich., 250
Midland, Ont., 175
Midland, Pa., 294
Midland, Tex., 302
Midland, W. Austral., 92
Midland Park, N. J., 273
Midleton, Ire., 17
Midlothian, Ill., 222
Midlothian (county), Scot., 15
Midnapore, India, 68
Midvale, Utah, 304
Midway (isls.), Pacific, 87
Midway City, Calif., 204
Midway Park, N.C., 281
Mid-West (reg.), Nigeria, 106
Midwest City, Okla., 288
Mie (pref.), Japan, 81
Mielec, Poland, 45
Mienning, China, 77
Miercurea Ciuc, Rum., 45
Mieres, Spain, 33
Miesso, Eth., 111
Miguel Azua, Mex., 150
Mihara, Japan, 81
Mihrabi (mt.), Iran, 66
Mijirtein (prov.), Somali Rep., 115
Mikhaylovgrad, Bulg., 45
Mikhaylovka, U.S.S.R., 52
Mikínai, Greece, 45
Mikindani, Tanz., 115
Mikkeli (dept.), Fin., 18
Mikkeli, Fin., 18
Míkonos (isl.), Greece, 45
Milagro, Ecua., 128
Milan, Ill., 222
Milan (prov.), Italy, 34
Milan, Italy, 34
Milan, Mich., 250
Milan, N. Mex., 274
Milan, Tenn., 237
Milâs, Turkey, 63
Milazzo, Italy, 34
Milbank, S. Dak., 298
Mildura, Vic., 97
Miles City, Mont., 262
Milford, Conn., 210
Milford, Del., 245
Milford, Mass., 249
Milford, Mich., 250
Milford, N.H., 268
Milford (sound), N.Z., 101
Milford, Ohio, 284
Milford Haven, Wales, 13
Mili (atoll), Pac. Is., 87
Milk (riv.), N. Amer., 182
Milk, Wadi el (dry riv.), Sudan, 111
Millbrae, Calif., 204
Millbury, Mass., 249
Millburn, N. J., 273
Milledgeville, Ga., 216
Mille Lacs (lake), Minn., 254
Mille Lacs (lake), Ont., 175
Miller, Ga., 216
Miller, S. Dak., 298
Millerovo, U.S.S.R., 52
Millersburg, Ohio, 284
Millersburg, Pa., 294
Millersville, Pa., 294
Millicent, S. Austral., 94
Millington, Tenn., 237
Millinocket, Maine, 242
Millmerran, Queensland, 95
Millport, Scot., 15
Mills, Wyo., 319
Milltown, N. B., 170
Milltown, N. J., 273
Millvale, Pa., 294
Mill Valley, Calif., 204
Millville, N. J., 273
Milne (bay), Papua, 85
Milngavie, Scot., 15
Mílos (isl.), Greece, 45
Milpitas, Calif., 204
Milton, Fla., 212
Milton, Mass., 249
Milton, N.Z., 101
Milton, N.S., 169
Milton, Ont., 175
Milton, Pa., 294
Milton-Freewater, Oreg., 291
Milwaukee, Wis., 317
Milwaukie, Oreg., 291
Mimico, Ont., 175
Mina al Ahmadi, Kuwait, 59
Minami Iwo (isl.), Bonin and Volcano Is., 87
Minas (mts.), Guat., 154
Minas (basin), N.S., 169
Minas, Urug., 145
Mina Sa'ud, Saudi Ar., 59
Minas Gerais (state), Braz., 132
Minatitlán, Mex., 150
Mincio (riv.), Italy, 34
Mindanao (isl.), Phil. Is., 82
Mindanao (sea), Phil. Is., 82
Mindelo, Cape Verde Is., 106
Minden, La., 238
Minden, W. Ger., 22
Mindoro (isl.), Phil. Is., 82
Mindoro (strait), Phil. Is., 82
Mindouli, Rep. of Congo, 115
Mineola, N.Y., 276
Mineola, Tex., 302
Mineral del Monte, Mex., 150
Mineral'nye Vody, U.S.S.R., 52
Mineral Wells, Tex., 302
Minersville, Pa., 294
Minerva, Ohio, 284
Mingan (Jacques-Cartier) (passage), Que., 174
Mingechaur, U.S.S.R., 52
Minginish (dist.), Scot., 15
Mingo Jct., Ohio, 284
Minho (prov.), Port., 33
Minho (riv.), Port., 33
Minhsien, China, 77
Minicoy (isl.), India, 68
Min Kiang (riv.), China, 77
Minna, Nigeria, 106
Minneapolis, Minn., 254
Minnedosa, Man., 179
Minnesota (state), U.S., 254
Minnesota (riv.), Minn., 254
Minnetonka, Minn., 254
Minnetonka (lake), Minn., 254
Miño (riv.), Spain, 33
Minorca (isl.), Spain, 33
Minot, N. Dak., 283
Min Shan (range), China, 77
Minsk, U.S.S.R., 52
Minto, N.B., 170
Minto (lake), Que., 174
Minturno, Italy, 34
Minûf, U.A.R., 111
Minusinsk, U.S.S.R., 48
Minya Konka (mt.), China, 77
Mira (riv.), Port., 33
Miraflores, Peru, 128
Miragoâne, Haiti, 158
Miraj, India, 68
Mira Loma, Calif., 204
Miramar, Fla., 212
Miramichi (bay), N.B., 170
Mira Nacional (mt.), Urug., 145
Miranda (riv.), Braz., 132
Miranda (state), Venez., 124
Miranda de Ebro, Spain, 33
Mira Por Vos (cays), Bah. Is., 156
Mirassol, Braz., 135
Mirebalais, Haiti, 158
Mirgorod, U.S.S.R., 52
Miri (hills), India, 68
Miri, Malaysia, 85
Mirim (lag.), S. Amer., 132
Mirnyy, Ant., 5
Mirpur Khas, Pak., 68
Mirtóön (sea), Greece, 45
Mirzapur, India, 68
Misamis Occidental (prov.), Phil. Is., 82
Misamis Oriental (prov.), Phil. Is., 82
Misantla, Mex., 150
Miscou (isl.), N. B., 170
Misha'ab, Ras (cape), Saudi Ar., 59
Mishawaka, Ind., 227
Mishima, Japan, 81
Mishmi (hills), India, 68
Misima (isl.), Papua, 85
Misiones (prov.), Arg., 143
Misiones (dept.), Par., 144
Miskito (cays), Nic., 154
Miskolc, Hung., 41
Misoöl (isl.), W. Irian, 85
Misquah (hills), Minn., 254
Missinaibi (riv.), Ont., 175
Mission, Kans., 232
Mission, Tex., 302
Mission City, Br. Col., 184
Mississippi (delta), La., 238
Mississippi (state), U.S., 256
Mississippi (riv.), U.S., 188
Mississippi City, Miss., 256
Missolonghi (Mesolóngion), Greece, 45
Missoula, Mont., 262
Missouri (state), U.S., 261
Missouri (riv.), U.S., 188
Missouri Valley, Iowa, 229
Mistassibi (riv.), Que., 174
Mistassini, Que., 174
Mistassini (lake), Que., 174
Mistastin (lake), Newf., 166
Místek-Frýdek, Czech., 41
Misti, El (mt.), Peru, 128
Misurata (prov.), Libya, 111
Misurata, Libya, 111
Mitaka, Japan, 81
Mitcham, S. Austral., 94
Mitchell, Ind., 227
Mitchell (mt.), N.C., 281
Mitchell, Queensland, 95
Mitchell (riv.), Queensland, 95
Mitchell, S. Dak., 298
Mitchelstown, Ire., 17
Mitchelton, Queensland, 95
Mitiaro (isl.), Cook Is., 87
Mitilíni, Greece, 45
Mitla (ruins), Mex., 150
Mito, Japan, 81
Mitsamiouli, Comoro Is., 118
Mittagong, N.S.W., 97
Mittenwald, W. Ger., 22
Mittersill, Austria, 41
Mitú, Col., 126
Mitumba (range), Dem. Rep. of the Congo, 115
Mitwaba, Dem. Rep. of the Congo, 115
Mitzic, Gabon, 115
Miyagi (pref.), Japan, 81
Miyako, Japan, 81
Miyako (isl.), Ryukyu Is., 81
Miyako (isls.), Ryukyu Is., 81
Miyakonojo, Japan, 81
Miyanduab, Iran, 66
Miyazaki (pref.), Japan, 81
Miyazaki, Japan, 81
Mizda, Libya, 111
Mizen (head), Ire., 17
Mjölby, Sweden, 18
Mladá Boleslav, Czech., 41
Mladenovac, Yugo., 45
Mlanje (mt.), Malawi, 115
Mljet (isl.), Yugo., 45
Mo, Norway, 18
Moab, Utah, 304
Moamba, Mozamb., 118
Moanda, Gabon, 115
Moberly, Mo., 261
Mobile, Ala., 194
Mobridge, S. Dak., 298
Moca, Dom. Rep., 158
Moçambique (dist.), Mozamb., 118
Moçambique, Mozamb., 118
Moçâmedes (dist.), Angola, 115
Moçâmedes, Angola, 115
Mocha (isl.), Chile, 138
Mocha, Yemen, 59
Moc Hoa, S. Vietnam, 72
Mochudi, Bech., 118
Mocímboa da Praia, Mozamb., 118
Mocoa, Col., 126
Mococa, Braz., 135
Moctezuma, Mex., 150
Moctezuma (riv.), Mex., 150
Mocuba, Mozamb., 118
Modderfontein, S. Afr., 118
Modena (prov.), Italy, 34
Modena, Italy, 34
Modesto, Calif., 204
Modica, Italy, 34
Modjokerto, Indon., 85
Mödling, Austria, 41
Moe, Vic., 97
Møen (isl.), Den., 21
Moen (isl.), Pac. Is., 87
Moerai, Fr. Poly., 87
Moësa (riv.), Switz., 39
Moffat, Scot., 15
Mogadishu (cap.), Somali Rep., 115
Mogador (Essaouira), Mor., 106
Mogadore, Ohio, 284
Mogi das Cruzes, Braz., 135
Mogilev, U.S.S.R., 52
Mogilev-Podol'skiy, U.S.S.R., 52
Mogi Mirim, Braz., 135
Mohács, Hung., 41
Mohaleshoek, Basutoland, 118
Mohammadia, Alg., 106
Mohammedia, Mor., 106
Mohawk, N.Y., 276
Mohéli (isl.), Comoro Is., 118
Mohenjo Daro (ruins), Pak., 68
Moidart (dist.), Scot., 15
Moineşti, Rum., 45
Moisie, Que., 174
Moisie (riv.), Que., 174

Q

R

Vila Péry, Mozamb., 118
Vila Real, Port., 33
Vila Real de Sto. António, Port., 33
Vila Roçadas, Angola, 115
Vila Salazar, Port. Timor, 85
Vila Serpa Pinto, Angola, 115
Vila Teixeira de Sousa, Angola, 115
Vilcanota (mt.), Peru, 128
Viljandi, U.S.S.R., 53
Villa Alemana, Chile, 138
Villa Altagracia, Dom. Rep., 158
Villa Ángela, Arg., 143
Villa Bruzual, Venez., 124
Villabruzzi, Somali Rep., 115
Villacañas, Spain, 33
Villacarrillo, Spain, 33
Villach, Austria, 41
Villa Cisneros, Sp. Sahara, 106
Villa de Cura, Venez., 124
Villa de San Antonio, Hond., 154
Villa de Seris, Mex., 150
Villa Dolores, Arg., 143
Villa Florida, Par., 144
Villafranca, Spain, 33
Villa Frontera, Mex., 150
Villaguay, Arg., 143
Villa Hayes, Par., 144
Villahermosa, Mex., 150
Villa María, Arg., 143
Villa Montes, Bol., 136
Villanova, Pa., 294
Villanueva, Col., 126
Villanueva, Mex., 150
Villanueva, Spain, 33
Villanueva y Geltrú, Spain, 33
Villa Park, Ill., 222
Villa Rica, Ga., 216
Villarreal de los Infantes, Spain, 33
Villarrica, Chile, 138
Villarrica, Par., 144
Villarrobledo, Spain, 33
Villarrubia de los Ojos, Spain, 33
Villa Serrano, Bol., 136
Villa Unión, Mex., 150
Villavicencio, Col., 126
Villazón, Bol., 136
Villefranche, France, 28
Villejuif, France, 28
Ville-Marie, Que., 174
Villemomble, France, 28
Villena, Spain, 33
Villeneuve, France, 28
Ville Platte, La., 238
Ville-Saint-Georges, Que., 172
Villeta, Par., 144
Villeurbanne, France, 28
Villingen, W. Ger., 22
Villupuram, India, 68
Vilna (Vilnius), U.S.S.R., 53
Vilvoorde, Belg., 27
Vilyuy (range), U.S.S.R., 48
Vilyuy (riv.), U.S.S.R., 48
Viña del Mar, Chile, 138
Vinalhaven (isl.), Maine, 242
Vinaroz, Spain, 33
Vincennes (bay), Ant., 5
Vincennes, France, 28
Vincennes, Ind., 227
Vinces, Ecua., 128
Vindel (riv.), Sweden, 18
Vindhya (range), India, 68
Vineland, N. J., 273
Vineyard (sound), Mass., 249
Vinh, N. Vietnam, 72
Vinh Loi, S. Vietnam, 72
Vinh Long, S. Vietnam, 72
Vinita, Okla., 288
Vinkovci, Yugo., 45
Vinnitsa, U.S.S.R., 52
Vinton, Iowa, 229
Vinton, La., 238
Vinton, Va., 307
Viqueque, Port. Timor, 85
Virac, Phil. Is., 82
Viramgam, India, 68
Virden, Ill., 222
Virden, Man., 179
Virgin (riv.), U.S., 266, 304
Virgin Gorda (isl.), Virgin Is. (Br.), 161
Virginia, Minn., 254
Virginia (state), U.S., 307
Virginia Beach, Va., 307
Virginia City, Mont., 262
Virginia City, Nev., 266
Virgin Islands (Br.), 156, 161
Virgin Islands (U.S.), 161
Virgin Islands Nat'l Hist. Site, Virgin Is. (U.S.), 161
Virgin Islands Nat'l Park, Virgin Is. (U.S.), 161
Viroqua, Wis., 317
Virovitica, Yugo., 45
Virunga (range), Africa, 115
Vis (isl.), Yugo., 45
Visakhapatnam, India, 68
Visalia, Calif., 204
Visayan (sea), Phil. Is., 82
Visby, Sweden, 18
Visconde do Rio Branco, Braz., 135
Viscount Melville (sound), N.W.T., 187
Viseu, Port., 33
Vişeu de Sus, Rum., 45
Vishoek, S. Afr., 118
Visnagar, India, 68
Visp, Switz., 39
Vista, Calif., 204
Vistula (riv.), Poland, 47
Vit (riv.), Bulg., 45
Vitebsk, U.S.S.R., 52
Viterbo (prov.), Italy, 34
Viterbo, Italy, 34
Viti Levu (isl.), Fiji, 87
Vitim (riv.), U.S.S.R., 48
Vitória, Braz., 132
Vitoria, Spain, 33
Vitória da Conquista, Braz., 132
Vitória de Santo Antão, Braz., 132
Vitry, France, 28
Vittoria, Italy, 34
Vittorio Veneto, Italy, 34
Vivian, La., 238
Vizagapatam (Visakhapatnam), India, 68
Vizcaya (prov.), Spain, 33
Vizianagaram, India, 68
Vlaardingen, Neth., 27
Vladimir, U.S.S.R., 52
Vladivostok, U.S.S.R., 48
Vlissingen (Flushing), Neth., 27
Vlonë, Alb., 45
Vltava (riv.), Czech., 41
Vöcklabruck, Austria, 41
Vo Dat, S. Vietnam, 72
Voeune Sai, Cambodia, 72
Vogel (peak), Nigeria, 106
Vogelkop (pen.), W. Irian, 85
Vogelsberg (mt.), W. Ger., 22
Voghera, Italy, 34
Vohémar, Malag. Rep., 118
Vohipeno, Malag. Rep., 118
Voi, Kenya, 115
Voiron, France, 28
Vojens, Den., 21
Vojmsjön (lake), Sweden, 18
Volendam, Neth., 27
Volga (riv.), U.S.S.R., 52
Volga-Don (canal), U.S.S.R., 52
Volgograd, U.S.S.R., 52
Volkhov, U.S.S.R., 52
Volkhov (riv.), U.S.S.R., 52
Völklingen, W. Ger., 22
Volksrust, S. Africa, 118
Vologda, U.S.S.R., 52
Vólos, Greece, 45
Vol'sk, U.S.S.R., 52
Volta (lake), Ghana, 106
Volta (riv.), Ghana, 106
Volta Redonda, Braz., 135
Volturno (riv.), Italy, 34
Vólvi (lake), Greece, 45
Volyn Oblast, U.S.S.R., 52
Volzhsk, U.S.S.R., 52
Volzhskiy, U.S.S.R., 52
Voorne (isl.), Neth., 27
Vopnafjörd (fjord), Iceland, 21
Vorarlberg (prov.), Austria, 41
Vorderrhein (river), Switz., 39
Vordingborg, Den., 21
Vorgod (riv.), Den., 21
Vorkuta, U.S.S.R., 52
Voronezh, U.S.S.R., 52
Voroshilovgrad (Lugansk), U.S.S.R., 52
Vorskla (riv.), U.S.S.R., 52
Vorst (forest), Belg., 27
Võru, U.S.S.R., 53
Vosges (dept.), France, 28
Vosges (mts.), France, 28
Vostok (isl.), Pacific, 87
Votkinsk, U.S.S.R., 52
Votuporanga, Braz., 135
Voyvodina (aut. prov.), Yugo., 45
Voyvozh, U.S.S.R., 52
Voznesensk, U.S.S.R., 52
Vranje, Yugo., 45
Vratsa, Bulg., 45
Vrbas, Yugo., 45
Vrbas (riv.), Yugo., 45
Vrede, S. Africa, 118
Vreed-en-Hoop, Guyana, 131
Vršac, Yugo., 45
Vryburg, S. Afr., 118
Vryheid, S. Afr., 118
Vsetín, Czech., 41
Vught, Neth., 27
Vukovar, Yugo., 45
Vulcan, Alta., 182
Vulcano (isl.), Italy, 34
Vung Tau, S. Vietnam, 72
Vyatka (riv.), U.S.S.R., 52
Vyaz'ma, U.S.S.R., 52
Vyborg, U.S.S.R., 52
Vychegda (riv.), U.S.S.R., 52
Východočeský (reg.), Czech., 41
Východoslovenský (reg.), Czech., 41
Vyksa, U.S.S.R., 52
Vym' (riv.), U.S.S.R., 52
Vyshniy Volochek, U.S.S.R., 52
Vyškov, Czech., 41
Vysoké Tatry, Czech., 41

W

Wa, Ghana, 106
Waal (riv.), Neth., 27
Waalwijk, Neth., 27
Waban, Mass., 249
Wabana (Bell Island), Newf., 166
Wabash, Ind., 227
Wabash (riv.), U.S., 227
Wabasha, Minn., 254
Wabi (riv.), Eth., 111
Wabi Shebelle (riv.), Somali Rep., 115
Wabiskaw (riv.), Alta., 182
Wąbrzeźno, Poland, 47
Wabush Lake, Newf., 166
Waccamaw (lake), N.C., 281
Waco, Tex., 302
Wadai (reg.), Chad, 111
Waddan, Libya, 111
Waddenzee (sound), Neth., 27
Waddington (mt.), Br. Col., 184
Wadena, Minn., 254
Wadena, Sask., 181
Wädenswil, Switz., 39
Wadesboro, N.C., 281
Wadi es Sir, Jordan, 65
Wadi Halfa, Sudan, 111
Wadi Musa, Jordan, 65
Wadmalaw Island, S.C., 296
Wad Medani, Sudan, 111
Wadowice, Poland, 47
Wadsworth, Ohio, 284
Wageningen, Neth., 27
Wager (bay), N.W.T., 187
Wagga Wagga, N.S.W., 97
Wagin, W. Austral., 92
Wagoner, Okla., 288
Wagrowiec, Poland, 47
Wahiawa, Hawaii, 218
Wahoo, Nebr., 264
Wahpeton, N. Dak., 283
Waialua, Hawaii, 218
Waianae-Makaha, Hawaii, 218
Waiau (riv.), N.Z., 101
Waidhofen, Austria, 41
Waigeo (isl.), W. Irian, 85
Waihi, N.Z., 101
Waikanae, N.Z., 101
Waikato (riv.), N.Z., 101
Waikiki, Hawaii, 218
Waikiki (beach), Hawaii, 218
Waikiwi, N.Z., 101
Wailuku, Hawaii, 218
Waimanalo, Hawaii, 218
Waimate, N.Z., 101
Waimea (bay), Hawaii, 218
Wainuiomata, N.Z., 101
Wainwright, Alaska, 196
Waipawa, N.Z., 101
Waipio (pen.), Hawaii, 218
Wairau (riv.), N.Z., 101
Wairoa, N.Z., 101
Wairoa (riv.), N.Z., 101
Waitaki (riv.), N.Z., 101
Waitara, N.Z., 101
Wajir, Kenya, 115
Wakasa (bay), Japan, 81
Wakatipu (lake), N.Z., 101
Wakaw, Sask., 181
Wakayama (prefecture), Japan, 81
Wakayama, Japan, 81
Wake (isl.), Pacific, 87
WaKeeney, Kans., 232
Wakefield, Eng., 13
Wakefield, Mass., 249
Wakefield, Mich., 250
Wakefield, R.I., 249
Wake Forest, N.C., 281
Wakema, Burma, 72
Wakenaam (isl.), Guyana, 131
Wakkanai, Japan, 81
Wala, Kuh-i- (mt.), Afghan., 68
Wałbrzych, Poland, 47
Walcha, N.S.W., 97
Walchensee (lake), W. Ger., 22
Walcheren (isl.), Neth., 27
Wałcz, Poland, 47
Wald, Switz., 39
Walden, N.Y., 276
Waldheim, E. Ger., 22
Waldwick, N. J., 273
Wales, U.K., 13
Walgett, N.S.W., 97
Walgreen Coast (reg.), Ant., 5
Walhalla, S.C., 296
Walker (lake), Nev., 266
Walker A.F.B., N. Mex., 274
Walkerton, Ont., 175
Walkerville, Mont., 262
Wallace, Idaho, 220
Wallaceburg, Ont., 175
Wallaga (prov.), Eth., 111
Wallaroo, S. Austral., 94
Wallasey, Eng., 10
Walla Walla, Wash., 310
Walled Lake, Mich., 250
Wallenstadt (lake), Switz., 39
Wallerawang, N.S.W., 97
Wallingford, Conn., 210
Wallington, N. J., 273
Wallis (isls.), Wallis & Futuna, 87
Wallis and Futuna, 87
Wallo (prov.), Eth., 111
Wallowa (mts.), Oreg., 291
Wallsend, Eng., 13
Wallula (lake), U.S., 291, 310
Walney (isl.), Eng., 13
Walnut Canyon Nat'l Mon., Ariz., 198
Walnut Creek, Calif., 204
Walnut Ridge, Ark., 203
Walsall, Eng., 10
Walsenburg, Colo., 208
Walsrode, W. Ger., 22
Walterboro, S.C., 296
Walter F. George (lake), U.S., 194, 216
Walter Reed Army Med. Ctr., D.C., 245
Walters, Okla., 288
Waltershausen, E. Ger., 22
Waltham, Mass., 249
Waltham Forest, Eng., 10
Waltham Holy Cross, Eng., 10
Walton, N.Y., 276
Walton and Weybridge, Eng., 10
Walvis Bay, S. Africa, 118
Wamba, Dem. Rep. of the Congo, 115
Wanaka (lake), N.Z., 101
Wanamassa, N. J., 273
Wanaque, N. J., 273
Wanaque (res.), N. J., 273
Wandel (sea), Greenl., 4
Wandsworth, Eng., 10
Wang, Mae Nam (riv.), Thai., 72
Wanganui, N.Z., 101
Wangaratta, Vic., 97
Wangen, W. Ger., 22
Wangiwangi (isl.), Indon., 85
Wanhsien, China, 77
Wankie, Rhod., 118
Wanks (Coco)(riv.), Cent. Amer., 154
Wanne-Eickel, W. Ger., 22
Wanneroo, W. Austral., 92
Wantagh, N.Y., 276
Wapakoneta, Ohio, 284
Wapato, Wash., 310
Wapawekka (hills), Sask., 181
Wappingers Falls, N.Y., 276
War, W. Va., 313
Waramaug (lake), Conn., 210
Waranga (res.), Vic., 97
Warangal, India, 68
Waratah (bay), Vic., 97
Warburton, The (riv.), S. Austral., 94
Warburton, Vic., 97
Wardere, Eth., 111
Wardha, India, 68
Ware, Eng., 13
Ware, Mass., 249
Wareham, Mass., 249
Waren, E. Ger., 22
Warendorf, W. Ger., 22
Ware Shoals, S.C., 296
Warfield, Br. Col., 184
Warialda, N.S.W., 97
Warin Chamrap, Thai., 72
Warmbad, S. Afr., 118
Warmbad, S.W. Afr., 118
Warner Robins, Ga., 216
Warnes, Bol., 136
Waroona, W. Austral., 92
Warracknabeal, Vic., 97
Warr Acres, Okla., 288
Warragamba, N.S.W., 97
Warragul, Vic., 97
Warrego (riv.), Austral., 95, 97
Warren, Ark., 203
Warren, Mich., 250
Warren, N.S.W., 97
Warren, Ohio, 284
Warren, Pa., 294
Warren, R.I., 249
Warrenpoint, N. Ire., 17
Warrensburg, Mo., 261
Warrensville Hts., Ohio, 284
Warrenton, S. Afr., 118
Warrenton, Va., 307
Warri, Nigeria, 106
Warrington, Eng., 10
Warrington, Fla., 212
Warrnambool, Vic., 97
Warroad, Minn., 254
Warsaw, Ind., 227
Warsaw, N.Y., 276
Warsaw (prov.), Poland, 47
Warsaw (cap.), Poland, 47
Warta (riv.), Poland, 47
Warwick, Eng., 13
Warwick, N.Y., 276
Warwick, Queensland, 95
Warwick, R.I., 249
Warwickshire (county), Eng., 13
Wasatch (range), U.S., 220, 304
Wasco, Calif., 204
Wash, The (bay), Eng., 13
Washburn (mt.), Wyo., 319
Waseca, Minn., 254
Washington, Ga., 216
Washington, Ill., 222
Washington, Ind., 227
Washington, Iowa, 229
Washington, Mo., 261
Washington (mt.), N.H., 268
Washington, N. J., 273
Washington, N.C., 281
Washington (isl.), Pacific, 87
Washington, Pa., 294
Washington (state), U.S., 310
Washington, D.C. (cap.), U.S., 245
Washington (lake), Wash., 310
Washington (isl.), Wis., 317
Washington C.H., Ohio, 284
Washington Park, Ill., 222
Washington Terr., Utah, 304
Washita (riv.), Tex., 302
Washoe (lake), Nev., 266
Washougal, Wash., 310
Wasmes, Belg., 27
Waspán, Nic., 154
Wasserbillig, Lux., 27
Wassuk (range), Nev., 266
Watauga (lake), Tenn., 237
Watch Hill (pt.), R.I., 249
Watchung, N. J., 273
Waterberg, S.W. Afr., 118
Waterbury, Conn., 210
Waterbury, Vt., 268
Wateree (riv.), S.C., 296
Waterford, Conn., 210
Waterford (county), Ire., 17
Waterford, Ire., 17
Waterford, N.Y., 276
Waterhen (lake), Man., 179
Waterloo, Belg., 27
Waterloo, Ill., 222
Waterloo, Iowa, 229
Waterloo, N.Y., 276
Waterloo, Ont., 175
Waterloo, Que., 172
Watermael-Boitsfort, Belg., 27
Waterton-Glacier Internat'l Peace Park, N. Amer., 182, 262
Waterton Lakes Nat'l Park, Alta., 182
Watertown, Conn., 210
Watertown, Mass., 249
Watertown, N.Y., 276
Watertown, S. Dak., 298
Watertown, Wis., 317
Waterval-Bo, S. Afr., 118
Water Valley, Miss., 256
Waterville, Conn., 210
Waterville, Maine, 242
Watervliet, N.Y., 276
Waterways, Alta., 182
Wates, Indon., 85
Watford, Eng., 10
Watford City, N. Dak., 283
Watkins Glen, N.Y., 276
Watling (San Salvador) (isl.), Bah. Is., 156
Watonga, Okla., 288
Watrous, Sask., 181
Watsa, Dem. Rep. of the Congo, 115
Watseka, Ill., 222
Watson, Sask., 181
Watson Lake, Yukon, 187
Watsonville, Calif., 204
Watts Bar (lake), Tenn., 237
Wattwil, Switz., 39
Watzmann (mt.), W. Ger., 22
Wau, Terr. N.G., 85
Wau, Sudan, 111
Wauchope, N.S.W., 97
Wauchula, Fla., 212
Wauconda, Ill., 222
Waukegan, Ill., 222
Waukesha, Wis., 317
Waukon, Iowa, 229
Waupaca, Wis., 317
Waupun, Wis., 317
Wausau, Wis., 317
Wauseon, Ohio, 284
Wauwatosa, Wis., 317
Waverley, Mass., 249
Waverley, N.S.W., 97
Waverley, Vic., 97
Waverly, Iowa, 229
Waverly, N.Y., 276
Waverly, Ohio, 284
Waverly, Tenn., 237
Wawa, Ont., 175
Waxahachie, Tex., 302
Way, Poulo (isls.), S. Vietnam, 72
Wayatinah, Tas., 99
Waycross, Ga., 216
Wayne, Mich., 250
Wayne, Nebr., 264
Wayne, N. J., 273
Wayne, Pa., 294
Waynesboro, Ga., 216
Waynesboro, Miss., 256
Waynesboro, Pa., 294
Waynesboro, Va., 307
Waynesburg, Pa., 294
Waynesville, N.C., 281
Wayzata, Minn., 254
We (isl.), Indon., 85
Wear (riv.), Eng., 13
Weatherford, Okla., 288
Weatherford, Tex., 302
Weatherly, Pa., 294
Webb A.F.B., Tex., 302
Webb City, Mo., 261
Webster, Maine, 242
Webster, Mass., 249
Webster, N.Y., 276
Webster, S. Dak., 298
Webster City, Iowa, 229
Webster Groves, Mo., 261
Weddell (sea), Ant., 5
Wedel, W. Ger., 22
Wednesbury, Eng., 10
Wednesfield, Eng., 10
Weed, Calif., 204
Weehawken, N. J., 273
Weert, Neth., 27
Weesp, Neth., 27
Wee Waa, N.S.W., 97
Weida, E. Ger., 22
Weiden, W. Ger., 22
Weidenau, W. Ger., 22
Weifang, China, 77
Weihai, China, 77
Wei Ho (riv.), China, 77
Weilheim, W. Ger., 22
Weimar, E. Ger., 22
Weinfelden, Switz., 39
Weingarten, W. Ger., 22
Weinheim, W. Ger., 22
Weipa, Queensland, 95
Weirton, W. Va., 313
Weiser, Idaho, 220
Weissenburg, W. Ger., 22
Weissenfels, E. Ger., 22
Weissensee, E. Ger., 22
Weissenstein (mts.), Switz., 39
Weisshorn (mt.), Switz., 39
Weisswaser, E. Ger., 22
Weiyüan, China, 77
Weiz, Austria, 41
Wejh, Saudi Ar., 59
Wejherowo, Poland, 47
Welch, W. Va., 313
Welkom, S. Afr., 118
Welland, Ont., 175
Wellesley, Mass., 249
Wellesley (isls.), Queensland, 95
Wellesley Hills, Mass., 249
Wellingborough, Eng., 13
Wellington (isl.), Chile, 138
Wellington, Eng., 13
Wellington, Kans., 232
Wellington, N.S.W., 97
Wellington (prov. dist.), N.Z., 101
Wellington (cap.), N.Z., 101
Wellington, Ohio, 284
Wellington, S. Afr., 118
Wellington, Tex., 302
Wells, Minn., 254
Wells, Nev., 266
Wells (lake), W. Austral., 92
Wellsboro, Pa., 294
Wellsburg, W. Va., 313
Wellsford, N.Z., 101
Wellston, Mo., 261
Wellston, Ohio, 284
Wellsville, N.Y., 276
Wellsville, Ohio, 284
Wels, Austria, 41
Welsh, La., 238
Welshpool, Wales, 13
Welwyn (Welwyn Garden City), Eng., 13
Wemmel, Belg., 27
Wenatchee, Wash., 310
Wenatchee (riv.), Wash., 310
Wenchi, Ghana, 106
Wenchow, China, 77
Wendover A.F.B., Utah, 304
Wenhsien, China, 77
Wenlock, Eng., 13
Wentworth, N.S.W., 97
Wentzville, Mo., 261
Werdau, E. Ger., 22
Wernigerode, E. Ger., 22
Werra (riv.), Ger., 22
Werribee, Vic., 97
Werribee South, Vic., 97
Werris Creek, N.S.W., 97
Wertheim, W. Ger., 22
Wervik, Belg., 27
Wesel, W. Ger., 22
Weser (riv.), W. Ger., 22
Weslaco, Tex., 302
Wesley, Dominica, 161
Wesleyville, Newf., 166
Wesleyville, Pa., 294
Wessel (cape), N. Terr., 93
Wessel (isls.), N. Terr., 93
Wessington Springs, S. Dak., 298
West (cape), N.Z., 101
West Allis, Wis., 317
West Azerbaijan (prov.), Iran, 66
West Barrington, R.I., 249
West Belmar, N. J., 273
West Bend, Wis., 317
West Bengal (state), India, 68
West Berlin, N. J., 273
Westboro, Mass., 249
West Bridgewater, Mass., 249
West Bromwich, Eng., 10
Westbrook, Maine, 242
West Burlington, Iowa, 229
Westbury, N.Y., 276
Westbury, Tas., 99
West Caldwell, N. J., 273
West Carrollton, Ohio, 284
Westchester, Ill., 222
West Chester, Pa., 294
West Chicago, Ill., 222
West Columbia, S.C., 296
West Columbia, Tex., 302
West Covina, Calif., 204
West Derry, N.H., 268
West Des Moines, Iowa, 229
West Elmira, N.Y., 276
West End, Virgin Is. (Br.), 161
West Englewood, N. J., 273
Westerly, R.I., 249
Western (prov.), Kenya, 115
Western (reg.), Nigeria, 106
Western (prov.), Somali Rep., 115
Western (prov.), Tanzania, 115
Western (prov.), Uganda, 115
Western Australia (state), Austral., 92
Western Dvina (riv.), U.S.S.R., 52
Western Ghats (mts.), India, 68
Westernport, Md., 245
Western Port (inlet), Vic., 97
Western Samoa, 87
Western Sprs., Ill., 222
Westerstede, W. Ger., 22
Westerville, Ohio, 284
Westerwald (for.), W. Ger., 22
Westfield, Mass., 249
Westfield, N. J., 273
Westfield, N.Y., 276
West Flanders (prov.), Belg., 27
West Frankfort, Ill., 222
West Frisian (isls.), Neth., 27
West Glens Falls, N.Y., 276
West Harbour, N.Z., 101
West Hartford, Conn., 210
West Hartlepool, Eng., 13
West Hartsville, S.C., 296
West Haven, Conn., 210
West Hazleton, Pa., 294
West Helena, Ark., 203
West Hollywood, Calif., 204
West Homestead, Pa., 294
West Indies, 156
West Irian, 85
West Jefferson, Ohio, 284
West Jordan, Utah, 304
West Kilbride, Scot., 15
West Kildonan, Man., 179
West Korea (bay), Asia, 81
West Lafayette, Ind., 227
Westlake, La., 238
Westlake, Ohio, 284
West Lake (prov.), Tanz., 115
Westland (prov. dist.), N.Z., 101
West Lebanon, N.H., 268
West Ledge Flats, Berm., 156
West Linn, Oreg., 291
Westlock, Alta., 182
West Long Branch, N. J., 273
West Los Angeles, Calif., 204
West Lothian (county), Scot., 15
Westmeath (county), Ire., 17
West Memphis, Ark., 203
West Miami, Fla., 212
West Mifflin, Pa., 294
West Milton, Ohio, 284
West Milwaukee, Wis., 317
Westminster, Calif., 204
Westminster, Colo., 208
Westminster, Eng., 10
Westminster, Md., 245
West Monroe, La., 238
Westmont, Ill., 222
Westmont, Pa., 294
Westmorland (county), Eng., 13
Westmount, Que., 172
West Mystic, Conn., 210
West Newton, Mass., 249
West Newton, Pa., 294
West New York, N. J., 273
West Nicholson, Rhod., 118
Weston, Ont., 175
Weston, W. Va., 313
Westonaria, S. Afr., 118
Weston-super-Mare, Eng., 13
West Orange, N. J., 273
West Orange, Tex., 302
Westover, W. Va., 313
Westover A.F.B., Mass., 249
West Pakistan (prov.), Pak., 68
West Palm Beach, Fla., 212
West Paterson, N. J., 273
West Pittsburg, Calif., 204
West Plains, Mo., 261
West Point, Ga., 216
West Point, Miss., 256
West Point, Nebr., 264
West Point, N. Y., 276
Westport, Conn., 210
Westport, Ire., 17
Westport, Mass., 249
Westport, N.Z., 101
West Portsmouth, Ohio, 284
West Quoddy (head), Maine, 242
Westray (isl.), Scot., 15
West Sacramento, Calif., 204
West Saint Paul, Minn., 254
West Seneca, N.Y., 276
West Springfield, Mass., 249
West Swanzey, N.H., 268
West Tapinac, Phil. Is., 82
West Terre Haute, Ind., 227
West Torrens, S. Austral., 94
West Trenton, N. J., 273
West Union, Iowa, 229
West University Place, Tex., 302
West View, Pa., 294
Westville, Ill., 222
Westville, N. J., 273
Westville, N.S., 169
West Virginia (state), U.S., 313
West Warwick, R.I., 249
Westwego, La., 238
West Wenatchee, Wash., 310
Westwood, Calif., 204
Westwood, Ky., 237
Westwood, N. J., 273
Westwood Lakes, Fla., 212
Westworth, Tex., 302
West Wyalong, N.S.W., 97
West York, Pa., 294
Wetar (isl.), Indon., 85
Wetaskiwin, Alta., 182
Wete, Tanz., 115
Wethersfield, Conn., 210
Wetteren, Belg., 27
Wetterhorn (mt.), Switz., 39
Wettingen, Switz., 39
Wetumpka, Ala., 194
Wetzikon, Switz., 39
Wetzlar, W. Ger., 22
Wewak, Terr. N.G., 85
Wewoka, Okla., 288
Wexford (county), Ire., 17
Wexford, Ire., 17
Weyburn, Sask., 181
Weymouth, Mass., 249
Weymouth and Melcombe Regis, Eng., 13
Whaley Bridge, Eng., 10
Whalsay (isl.), Scot., 15
Whangarei, N.Z., 101
Wharfe (riv.), Eng., 13
Wharton, N. J., 273
Wharton, Tex., 302
Wheatland, Wyo., 319
Wheaton, Ill., 222
Wheaton, Md., 245
Wheaton, Minn., 254
Wheat Ridge, Colo., 208
Wheeler (dam), Ala., 194
Wheeler (peak), Nev., 266
Wheeler (peak), N. Mex., 274
Wheeler A.F.B., Hawaii, 218
Wheelersburg, Ohio, 284
Wheeling, Ill., 222
Wheeling, W. Va., 313
Whidbey Isl. N.A.S., Wash., 310
Whippany, N. J., 273
Whitburn, Scot., 15
Whitby, Eng., 13
Whitby, Ont., 175
Whitcombe (mt.), N.Z., 101
White (riv.), Ind., 227
White (lake), La., 238
White (bay), Newf., 166
White (mts.), N.H., 268
White (isl.), N.Z., 101
White (sea), U.S.S.R., 52
White (riv.), U.S., 203, 261
White (riv.), Vt., 268
White Bear Lake, Minn., 254
White Carpathians (mts.), Czech., 41
White Center, Wash., 310
Whitecourt, Alta., 182
White Elster (riv.), E. Ger., 22
Whitefish (bay), Mich., 250
Whitefish, Mont., 262
Whitefish (lake), Mont., 262
Whitefish Bay, Wis., 317
Whitegull (lake), Que., 174
White Hall, Ill., 222
Whitehall, Mich., 250
Whitehall, N.Y., 276
Whitehall, Ohio, 284
Whitehall, Pa., 294
Whitehaven, Eng., 13
Whitehaven, Tenn., 237
Whitehead, N. Ire., 17
Whitehorse (cap.), Yukon, 187
Whiteman A.F.B., Mo., 261
White Nile (riv.), Africa, 111
White Oak, Pa., 294
White Plains, N.Y., 276
White River Jct., Vt., 268
White Rock, Br. Col., 184
White Russian S.S.R., U.S.S.R., 52
White Sands Nat'l Mon., N. Mex., 274
White Sands Proving Grounds, N. Mex., 274
Whitesboro, N.Y., 276
White Settlement, Tex., 302
White Sulphur Springs, Mont., 262
White Sulphur Springs, W. Va., 313
Whiteville, N.C., 281
White Volta (riv.), Africa, 106
Whitewater (lake), Man., 179
Whitewater, Wis., 317
Whiting, Ind., 227
Whitinsville, Mass., 249
Whitley Bay, Eng., 13
Whitman, Mass., 249
Whitman Mission Nat'l Hist. Site, Wash., 310
Whitmire, S.C., 296
Whitney (mt.), Calif., 204
Whitney, S.C., 296
Whitneyville, Conn., 210
Whitstable, Eng., 13
Whitsunday (isl.), Queensland, 95
Whittier, Alaska, 196
Whittier, Calif., 204
Wholdaia (lake), N.W.T., 187
Whonock, Br. Col., 184
Whyalla, S. Austral., 94
Wichita, Kans., 232
Wichita (mts.), Okla., 288
Wichita Falls, Tex., 302
Wick, Scot., 15
Wickenburg, Ariz., 198
Wickham (cape), Tas., 99
Wickiup (res.), Oreg., 291
Wickliffe, Ohio, 284
Wicklow (county), Ire., 17
Wicklow, Ire., 17
Wicklow (mts.), Ire., 17
Wicomico (riv.), Md., 245
Widnes, Eng., 10
Wiedenbrück, W. Ger., 22
Wieliczka, Poland, 47
Wieluń, Poland, 47
Wiener Neustadt, Austria, 41
Wieringermeer Polder, Neth., 27
Wiesbaden, W. Ger., 22
Wigan, Eng., 10
Wight (isl.), Eng., 13
Wight, Isle of (county), Eng., 13
Wigston, Eng., 13
Wigtown (county), Scot., 15
Wigtown (bay), Scot., 15
Wil, Switz., 39
Wilcannia, N.S.W., 97
Wildhorn (mt.), Switz., 39
Wildspitze (mt.), Austria, 41
Wildwood, N. J., 273
Wildwood Crest, N. J., 273
Wilhelm II Coast (reg.), Ant., 5
Wilhelmina (canal), Neth., 27
Wilhelmina (mts.), Sur., 131
Wilhelm-Pieck-Stadt, E. Ger., 22
Wilhelmshaven, W. Ger., 22
Wilkes-Barre, Pa., 294
Wilkes Land (reg.), Ant., 5
Wilkie, Sask., 181
Wilkinsburg, Pa., 294
Willamette (riv.), Oreg., 291
Willard, Ohio, 284
Willcox, Ariz., 198
Willebroek, Belg., 27
Willems (canal), Neth., 27
Willemstad (cap.), Neth. Ant., 161
Willenhall, Eng., 10
William (riv.), Sask., 181
Williams, Ariz., 198
Williams A.F.B., Ariz., 198
Williamsburg, Ky., 237
Williamsburg, Va., 307
Williams Lake, Br. Col., 184
Williamson, W. Va., 313
Williamsport, Pa., 294
Williamston, N.C., 281
Williamston, S.C., 296
Williamstown, Mass., 249
Williamstown, N. J., 273
Williamstown, Vic., 97
Williamstown, W. Va., 313
Williamsville, N.Y., 276
Willimansett, Mass., 249
Willimantic, Conn., 210
Willingboro, N. J., 273
Williston, N. Dak., 283
Williston, S.C., 296
Williston Park, N.Y., 276
Willits, Calif., 204
Willkies Village, Antigua, 161
Willmar, Minn., 254
Willoughby, N.S.W., 97
Willoughby, Ohio, 284
Willoughby (lake), Vt., 268
Willoughby Hills, Ohio, 284
Willow Bunch, Sask., 181
Willow Grove, Pa., 294
Willowick, Ohio, 284
Willows, Calif., 204
Wilmerding, Pa., 294
Wilmette, Ill., 222
Wilmington, Calif., 204
Wilmington, Del., 245
Wilmington, Ill., 222
Wilmington, N.C., 281
Wilmington, Ohio, 284
Wilmore, Ky., 237
Wilmslow, Eng., 10
Wilson (mt.), Calif., 204
Wilson, Conn., 210
Wilson, N.C., 281
Wilson, Pa., 294
Wilsons (prom.), Vic., 97
Wilton, Conn., 210
Wilton Manor, Fla., 212
Wiltshire (county), Eng., 13
Wiltz, Lux., 27
Wimbledon, Eng., 10
Wimmera (riv.), Vic., 97
Winchelsea, Vic., 97
Winchendon, Mass., 249
Winchester, Eng., 13
Winchester, Ind., 227
Winchester, Ky., 237
Winchester, Mass., 249
Winchester, Tenn., 237
Winchester, Va., 307
Windber, Pa., 294
Wind Cave Nat'l Park, S. Dak., 298
Winder, Ga., 216
Windham, Conn., 210
Windham, Ohio, 284
Windhoek (cap.), S.W. Afr., 118
Windisch, Switz., 39
Windom, Minn., 254
Window Rock, Ariz., 198
Wind River (range), Wyo., 319
Windsor, Conn., 210
Windsor (New Windsor), Eng., 13
Windsor, Mo., 261
Windsor, Newf., 166
Windsor, N.S.W., 97
Windsor, N.S., 169
Windsor, Ont., 175
Windsor, Que., 172
Windsor, Queensland, 95
Windsor, Vt., 268
Windsor Hts., Iowa, 229
Windward (isls.), W. Indies, 156
Windward (passage), W. Indies, 156
Winefred (lake), Alta., 182
Winfield, Ala., 194
Winfield, Kans., 232
Winfield, N. J., 273
Wingham, N.S.W., 97
Wingham, Ont., 175
Winisk (lake), Ont., 177
Winisk (riv.), Ont., 177
Winkelman, Ariz., 198
Winkler, Man., 179
Winneba, Ghana, 106
Winnebago (lake), Wis., 317
Winnemucca, Nev., 266
Winnemucca (lake), Nev., 266
Winner, S. Dak., 298
Winnetka, Ill., 222
Winnfield, La., 238
Winnibigoshish (lake), Minn., 254
Winnipeg (cap.), Man., 179
Winnipeg (lake), Man., 179
Winnipegosis, Man., 179
Winnipegosis (lake), Man., 179
Winnipesaukee (lake), N.H., 268
Winnsboro, La., 238
Winnsboro, S.C., 296
Winnsboro, Tex., 302
Winona, Minn., 254
Winona, Miss., 256
Winooski, Vt., 268
Winooski (riv.), Vt., 268
Winschoten, Neth., 27
Winsford, Eng., 10
Winslow, Ariz., 198
Winslow, Maine, 242
Winsted, Conn., 210
Winston-Salem, N.C., 281
Winter Garden, Fla., 212
Winter Haven, Fla., 212
Winter Isl. C.G. Air Sta., Mass., 249
Winter Park, Fla., 212
Winters, Tex., 302
Winterset, Iowa, 229
Wintersville, Ohio, 284
Winterswijk, Neth., 27
Winterthur, Switz., 39
Winthrop, Mass., 249
Winthrop Harbour, Ill., 222
Winton, N.Z., 101
Winton, Pa., 294
Winton, Queensland, 95
Winyah (bay), S.C., 296
Wirral, Eng., 10
Wisbech, Eng., 13
Wisconsin (state), U.S., 317
Wisconsin (riv.), Wis., 317
Wisconsin Dells, Wis., 317
Wisconsin Rapids, Wis., 317
Wise, Va., 307
Wisła (Vistula)(riv.), Poland, 47
Wismar, E. Ger., 22
Wismar, Guyana, 131
Witbank, S. Afr., 118
Witham (riv.), Eng., 13
Withamsville, Ohio, 284

GEOGRAPHICAL TERMS

A. = Arabic   Camb. = Cambodian   Ch. = Chinese   Czech. = Czechoslovakian   Dan. = Danish   Du. = Dutch   Finn. = Finnish   Fr. = French   Ger. = German   Ice. = Icelandic
It. = Italian   Jap. = Japanese   Mong. = Mongol   Nor. = Norwegian   Per. = Persian   Port. = Portuguese   Russ. = Russian   Sp. = Spanish   Sw. = Swedish   Turk. = Turkish

---

Å	Nor., Sw.	Stream
Aas	Dan., Nor.	Hills
Abajo	Sp.	Lower
Ada, Adasi	Turk.	Island
Altipiano	It.	Plateau
Altiplano	Sp.	Plateau
Alv, Alf, Elf	Sw.	River
Arrecife	Sp.	Reef
Asa	Nor., Sw.	Hill
Asaga	Turk.	Lower
Austral	Sp.	Southern
Baai	Du.	Bay
Bab	Arabic	Gate or Strait
Bahia	Sp.	Bay
Bahr	Arabic	Marsh, Lake, Sea, River
Baia	Port.	Bay
Baie	Fr.	Bay, Gulf
Baizo	Port.	Low
Bakke	Dan.	Hill
Bana	Jap.	Cape
Bañados	Sp.	Marshes
Band	Per.	Mt. Range
Barra	Sp.	Reef
Bel	Turk.	Pass
Belt	Ger.	Strait
Ben	Gaelic	Mountain
Bera	Du.	Mountain
Berg	Ger., Du.	Mountain
Bir	Arabic	Well
Birket	Arabic	Pond
Boca	Sp.	Gulf, Inlet
Boğhaz	Turk.	Strait
Bolshoi, Bolshaya	Russ.	Big
Bolson	Sp.	Depression
Bong	Korean	Mountain
Boreal	Sp.	Northern
Breen	Nor.	Glacier
Bro	Dan., Nor., Sw.	Bridge
Bucht	Ger.	Bay
Bugt	Dan.	Bay
Bukhta	Russ.	Bay
Bukit	Malay	Hill, Mountain
Bukt	Nor., Sw.	Bay, Gulf
Burnu, Burun	Turk.	Cape, Point
By	Dan., Nor., Sw.	Town
Cabo	Port., Sp.	Cape
Campos	Port.	Plains
Canal	Port., Sp.	Channel
Cap, Capo	Fr., It.	Cape
Cataratas	Sp.	Falls
Catena	It.	Mt. Range
Catingas	Port.	Open Woodlands
Central, Centrale	Fr., It.	Middle
Cerrito, Cerro	Sp.	Hill
Cerros	Sp.	Hills, Mountains
Chai	Turk.	River
Chow	Ch.	Town of the second rank
Ciénaga	Sp.	Swamp
Ciudad	Sp.	City
Col	Fr.	Pass
Cordillera	Sp.	Mt. Range, Mts.
Côte	Fr.	Coast
Csatoria	Magyar	Canal
Cuchilla	Sp.	Mt. Range
Curiche	Sp.	Swamp
Dag, Dagh	Turk.	Mountain
Dağlari	Turk.	Mt. Range
Dal	Nor., Sw.	Valley
Dar	Arabic	Land
Darya	Per.	Salt Lake
Dasht	Per.	Desert, Plain
Deniz, Denizi	Turk.	Sea, Lake
Desierto	Sp.	Desert
Détroit	Fr.	Strait
Djeziret	Arabic, Turk.	Island
Do	Korean	Island
Doi	Thai	Mountain
Eiland	Du.	Island
Elv	Dan., Nor.	River
Embalse	Sp.	Reservoir
Emi	Berber	Mountain
Erg	Arabic	Dune, Desert
Eski	Turk.	Old
Est, Este	Fr., Port., Sp.	East
Estero	Sp.	Estuary, Creek
Estrecho, Estreito	Sp., Port.	Strait
Etang	Fr.	Pond, Lagoon, Lake
Fedja, Feij	Arabic	Pass
Fiume	It.	River
Fjäll	Sw.	Mountain
Fjeld, Fjell	Nor.	Hills, Mountain
Fjord	Dan., Nor., Sw.	Fiord
Fleuve	Fr.	River
Fljót	Icelandic	Stream
Fluss	Ger.	River
Fokani, Fukani	Arabic	Upper
Fors	Sw.	Waterfall
Fos, Foss	Dan., Nor.	Waterfall
Fu	Ch.	Town of importance
Gamla	Nor.	Old
Gamle	Dan.	Old
Gata	Jap.	Lake
Gawa	Jap.	River
Gebel	Arabic	Mountain
Gebergte	Du.	Mt. Range
Gebirge	Ger.	Mt. Range
Ghubbet	Arabic	Bay
Gobi	Mongol	Desert
Goe	Jap.	Pass
Gol	Mongol, Turk.	Lake, Stream
Golf	Ger., Du.	Gulf
Golfe	Fr.	Gulf
Golfo	Sp., It., Port.	Gulf
Gölü	Turk.	Lake
Gora	Russ.	Mountain
Grand, Grande	Fr., Sp.	Big
Groot	Du.	Big
Gross	Ger.	Big
Grosso	It., Port.	Big
Guba	Russ.	Bay, Gulf
Gunto	Jap.	Archipelago
Gunung	Malay	Mountain
Hai	Ch.	Sea
Halbinsel	Ger.	Peninsula
Hamáda, Hammada	Arabic	Rocky Plateau
Hamn	Sw.	Harbor
Hamún	Per.	Marsh
Hanto	Jap.	Peninsula
Has, Hassi	Arabic	Well
Hav	Dan., Nor., Sw.	Sea, Ocean
Havet	Nor.	Bay
Havn	Dan., Nor.	Harbor
Havre	Fr.	Harbor
Higashi, Higasi	Jap.	East
Ho	Ch.	River
Hochebene	Ger.	Plateau
Hoek	Du.	Cape
Hoku	Jap.	North
Holm	Dan., Nor., Sw.	Island
Hory	Czech.	Mountains
Hoved	Dan., Nor.	Cape, Promontory
Hsien	Ch.	Town of the third class
Hu	Ch.	Lake
Huk	Dan., Nor., Sw.	Point
Hus, Huus	Dan., Nor., Sw.	House
Hwang	Ch.	Yellow
Ile	Fr.	Island
Ilet	Fr.	Islet
Ilot	Fr.	Islet
Indre	Dan., Nor.	Inner
Inferieur, Inferiore	Fr., It.	Lower
Inner, Inre	Sw.	Inner
Insel	Ger.	Island
Irmak	Turk.	River
Isla	Sp.	Island
Isola	It.	Island
Jabal, Jebel	Arabic	Mountains
Järvi	Finn.	Lake
Jaure	Sw.	Lake
Jezira	Arabic	Island
Jima	Jap.	Island
Joki	Finn.	River
Kaap	Du.	Cape
Kabir, Kebir	Arabic	Big
Kai	Jap.	Sea
Kaikyo	Jap.	Strait
Kami	Turk.	Upper
Kanaal	Du.	Canal
Kanal	Russ., Ger.	Canal, Channel
Kao	Thai	Mountain
Kap, Kapp	Nor., Sw., Ice.	Cape
Kaupunki	Finn.	Town
Kawa	Jap.	River
Khao	Thai	Mountain
Khrebet	Russ.	Mt. Range
Kiang	Ch.	River
Kiao	Ch.	Point
Kita	Jap.	North
Klein	Du., Ger.	Small
Klint	Dan.	Promontory
Kô	Jap.	Lake
Ko	Thai	Island
Koh	Camb., Khmer	Island
Kong	Ch.	River
Kop	Du.	Peak, Head
Köping	Sw.	Market, Borough
Körfez, Körfezi	Turk.	Gulf
Kosa	Russ.	Spit
Kosui	Jap.	Lake
Kraal	Du.	Native Village
Kuchuk	Turk.	Small
Kuh	Per.	Mountain
Kul	Sinkiang Turki	Lake
Kum	Turk.	Desert
Kuro	Jap.	Black
Laag	Du.	Low
Lac	Fr.	Lake
Lago	Port., Sp., It.	Lake
Lagoa	Port.	Lagoon
Laguna	Sp.	Lagoon
Lagune	Fr.	Lagoon
Lahti	Finn.	Bay, Bight
Län	Sw.	County
Lilla	Sw.	Small
Lille	Dan., Nor.	Small
Ling	Ch.	Mountain
Llanos	Sp.	Plains
Mae Nam	Thai	River
Mali, Malaya	Russ.	Small
Man	Korean	Bay
Mar	Sp., Port.	Sea
Mare	It.	Sea
Medio	Sp.	Middle
Meer	Du.	Lake
Meer	Ger.	Sea
Mer	Fr.	Sea
Meridionale	It.	Southern
Meseta	Sp.	Plateau
Middelst, Midden	Du.	Middle
Minami	Jap.	Southern
Mir	Per.	Mountain
Mis	Russ.	Cape
Misaki	Jap.	Cape
Mittel	Ger.	Middle
Mont	Fr.	Mountain
Montagne	Fr.	Mountain
Montaña	Sp.	Mountains
Monte	Sp., It., Port.	Mountain
More	Russ.	Sea
Morro	Port., Sp.	Mountain, Promontory
Morue	Fr.	Hill
Moyen	Fr.	Middle
Muong	Siamese	Town
Mys	Russ.	Cape
Nada	Jap.	Sea
Naka	Jap.	Middle
Nam	Burm., Lao	River
Nan	Ch., Jap.	South
Nes	Nor.	Cape, Point
Nevado	Sp.	Snow covered peak
Nieder	Ger.	Lower
Nishi, Nisi	Jap.	West
Nizhni, Nizhnyaya	Russ.	Lower
Njarga	Finn.	Peninsula, Promontory
Nong	Thai	Lake
Noord	Du.	North
Nor	Mong.	Lake
Nord	Fr., Ger.	North
Norte	Sp., It., Port.	North
Nos	Russ.	Cape
Novi, Novaya	Russ.	New
Nusa	Malay	Island
Ny, Nya	Nor., Sw.	New
O	Jap.	Big
ö	Nor., Sw.	Island
Ober	Ger.	Upper
Occidental, Occidentale	Sp., It.	Western
Odde	Dan.	Point
Oeste	Port.	West
Ola	Mong.	Mountains
Ooster	Du.	Eastern
Opper, Over	Du.	Upper
Oriental	Sp., Fr.	Eastern
Orientale	It.	Eastern
Orta	Turk.	Middle
Ost	Ger.	East
Ostrov	Russ.	Island
Ouest	Fr.	West
öy	Nor.	Island
Ozero	Russ.	Lake
Pampa	Sp.	Plain
Pas	Fr.	Channel, Strait
Paso	Sp.	Pass
Passo	It., Port.	Pass
Peh, Pei	Ch.	North
Peña	Sp.	Rock, Mountain
Penisola	It.	Peninsula
Pequeño	Sp.	Small
Pereval	Russ.	Pass
Peski	Russ.	Desert
Petit	Fr.	Small
Phu	Lao, Annamese	Mtn.
Pic	Fr.	Mountain
Piccolo	It.	Small
Pico	Port., Sp.	Mountain, Peak
Pik	Russ.	Mountain, Peak
Piton	Fr.	Mountain, Peak
Planalto	Port.	Plateau
Plato	Russ.	Plateau
Pointe	Fr.	Point
Poluostrov	Russ.	Peninsula
Ponta	Port.	Point
Presa	Sp.	Reservoir
Presqu'île	Fr.	Peninsula
Proliv	Russ.	Strait
Pulou, Pulo	Malay	Island
Punt	Du.	Point
Punta	Sp., It., Port.	Point
Qum	Turk.	Desert
Rada	Sp.	Inlet
Rade	Fr.	Bay, Inlet
Ras	Arabic	Cape
Reka	Russ.	River
Retto	Jap.	Archipelago
Ria	Sp.	Estuary
Río	Sp.	River
Rivier, Rivière	Du., Fr.	River
Rud	Per.	River
Saghir	Arabic	Small
Sai	Jap.	West
Saki	Jap.	Cape
Salar, Salina	Sp.	Salt Deposit
Salto	Sp., Port.	Falls
San	Ch., Jap., Korean	Hill
Sanmaek	Korean	Mt. Range
Schiereiland	Du.	Peninsula
Se	Camb., Khmer	River
See	Ger.	Sea, Lake
Selvas	Sp., Port.	Woods, Forest
Seno	Sp.	Bay, Gulf
Serra	Port.	Mts.
Serranía	Sp.	Mts.
Seto	Jap.	Strait
Settentrionale	It.	Northern
Severni, Severnaya	Russ.	North
Shan	Ch., Jap.	Hill, Mts.
Shang	Ch.	Upper
Shatt	Arabic	River
Shima	Jap.	Island
Shimo	Jap.	Lower
Shin	Jap.	Land
Shiro	Jap.	White
Shoto	Jap.	Islands
Si	Ch.	West
Siao	Ch.	Small
Sierra	Sp.	Mt. Range, Mts.
Sjö	Nor., Sw.	Lake, Sea
Sok, Suk, Souk	Arabic, Ar. Fr.	Market
Song	Annamese	River
Sopka	Russ.	Volcano
Spitze	Ger.	Mt. Peak
Sredni, Srednyaya	Russ.	Middle
Stad	Dan., Nor., Sw.	City
Stari, Staraya	Russ.	Old
Step	Russ.	Treeless Plain
Straat	Du.	Strait
Strasse	Ger.	Strait
Stretto	It.	Strait
Ström	Dan., Nor., Sw.	Sound
Stung	Camb., Khmer	River
Su	Turk.	River
Sud, Süd	Sp., Fr., Ger.	South
Suido	Jap.	Strait, Channel
Sul	Port.	South
Sund	Dan., Nor., Sw.	Sound
Sungei	Malay	River
Supérieur	Fr.	Upper
Superior, Superiore	Sp., It.	Upper
Sur	Sp.	South
Suyu	Turk.	River
Ta	Ch.	Big
Tafelland	Du.	Plateau
Tagh	Turk.	Mt. Range
Take	Jap.	Peak, Ridge
Takht	Arabic	Lower
Tal	Ger.	Valley
Tandjong, Tanjung	Malay	Cape, Point
Tao	Ch.	Island
Tell	Arabic	Hill
Thale	Thai	Sea, Lake
Tind	Nor.	Peak
Tö	Jap.	East
To	Jap.	Island
Toge	Jap.	Pass
Trask	Finn.	Lake
Tso	Tibetan	Lake
Tugh	Somali	Dry River
Tung	Ch.	Eastern
Udjung	Malay	Point
Umi	Jap.	Bay
Unter	Ger.	Lower
Ura	Jap.	Inlet
Val	Fr.	Valley
Vatn	Nor.	Lake
Vecchio	It.	Old
Veld	Du.	Plain, Field
Velho	Port.	Old
Verkhni	Russ.	Upper
Vesi	Finn.	Lake
Vieho	Sp.	Old
Vik	Nor., Sw.	Bay
Vishni, Vishnyaya	Russ.	High
Vodokhranilishche	Russ.	Reservoir
Volcán	Sp.	Volcano
Vostochni, Vostochnaya	Russ.	East, Eastern
Wadi	Arabic	Dry River
Wald	Ger.	Forest
Wan	Jap.	Bay
Westersch	Du.	Western
Wüste	Ger.	Desert
Yama	Jap.	Mountain
Yarim Ada	Turk.	Peninsula
Yokara	Turk.	Upper
Yug, Yuzhni, Yuzhnaya	Russ.	South, Southern
Zaki	Jap.	Cape
Zaliv	Russ.	Bay, Gulf
Zapadni, Zapadnaya	Russ.	Western
Zee	Du.	Sea
Zemlya	Russ.	Land
Zuid	Du.	South

Between Principal Cities in the United States

FROM/TO	Albuquerque, N. Mex.	Atlanta, Ga.	Baltimore, Md.	Boise, Idaho	Boston, Mass.	Brownsville, Tex.	Buffalo, N. Y.	Chicago, Ill.	Cincinnati, Ohio	Cleveland, Ohio	Denver, Colo.	Des Moines, Iowa	Detroit, Mich.	El Paso, Tex.	Fargo, N. Dak.	Fort Worth, Tex.	Galveston, Tex.	Hastings, Nebr.	Hot Springs, Ark.	Houghton, Mich.	Jacksonville, Fla.	Kansas City, Mo.	Los Angeles, Calif.	Louisville, Ky.	Memphis, Tenn.	Miami, Fla.	Minneapolis, Minn.	Missoula, Mont.	Nashville, Tenn.	New Orleans, La.	New York, N. Y.	Norfolk, Va.	Oklahoma, Okla.	Omaha, Nebr.	Philadelphia, Pa.	Phoenix, Ariz.	Pittsburgh, P
Albuquerque, N. Mex.	....	1273	1670	774	1967	838	1577	1126	1248	1417	332	833	1360	228	968	561	803	588	773	1252	1492	717	663	1174	938	1710	980	895	1117	1030	1810	1696	518	718	1748	330	14
Atlanta, Ga.	1273	....	575	1830	933	960	695	583	368	550	1208	738	595	1293	1112	750	688	901	498	947	286	675	1935	317	335	610	905	1790	218	427	747	507	753	815	663	1592	5
Baltimore, Md.	1670	575	....	2055	358	1525	273	603	423	305	1505	913	398	1750	1143	1239	1245	1154	964	808	682	962	2313	498	792	958	948	1947	597	1001	170	167	1173	1026	90	2002	1
Boise, Idaho	774	1830	2055	....	2266	1610	1872	1453	1663	1754	637	1155	1671	969	975	1263	1538	934	1384	1367	2098	1158	663	1623	1506	2368	1140	252	1631	1713	2153	2137	1138	1044	2113	733	18
Boston, Mass.	1967	933	358	2266	....	1881	398	849	737	550	1766	1159	613	2067	1304	1574	1598	1415	1302	922	1015	1250	2590	823	1133	1258	1125	2124	941	1359	188	467	1490	1280	268	2295	4
Brownsville, Tex.	838	960	1525	1610	1881	....	1575	1234	1184	1402	1047	1102	1398	682	1445	471	287	1013	650	1543	1025	923	1370	1093	777	1100	1335	1706	952	536	1695	1465	659	1061	1614	1023	14
Buffalo, N. Y.	1577	695	273	1872	398	1575	....	454	392	175	1368	762	218	1690	923	1221	1289	1019	956	560	880	862	2195	483	802	1184	733	1740	626	1087	291	435	1117	883	278	1904	1
Chicago, Ill.	1126	583	603	1453	849	1234	454	....	249	307	918	310	236	1249	571	820	954	566	585	367	861	413	1741	268	481	1190	356	1348	394	831	711	696	689	432	664	1451	4
Cincinnati, Ohio	1248	368	423	1663	737	1184	392	249	....	218	1090	509	234	1333	818	839	897	742	569	589	628	541	1892	92	410	957	603	1578	239	708	568	474	755	620	501	1578	2
Cleveland, Ohio	1417	550	305	1754	550	1402	175	307	218	....	1223	617	94	1521	838	1046	1116	871	787	518	768	700	2044	309	627	1088	632	1640	456	922	404	429	946	738	343	1745	1
Denver, Colo.	332	1208	1505	637	1766	1047	1368	918	1090	1223	....	607	1153	554	642	643	925	353	749	970	1468	555	828	1035	878	1732	699	670	1018	1079	1628	1562	503	485	1575	585	13
Des Moines, Iowa	833	738	913	1155	1159	1102	762	310	509	617	607	....	545	980	397	640	851	256	488	458	1024	180	1433	477	485	1338	235	1074	523	825	1023	983	469	122	972	1154	7
Detroit, Mich.	1360	595	398	1671	613	1398	218	236	234	94	1153	545	....	1475	745	1018	1111	800	761	427	832	643	1976	315	621	1156	542	1552	468	938	483	522	905	666	444	1685	2
El Paso, Tex.	228	1293	1750	969	2067	682	1690	1249	1333	1521	554	980	1475	....	1161	543	723	757	802	1422	1481	836	702	1253	978	1662	1156	1115	1169	986	1902	1755	578	875	1834	347	15
Fargo, N. Dak.	968	1112	1143	975	1304	1445	923	571	818	838	642	397	745	1161	....	973	1218	440	875	393	1400	548	1426	818	882	1721	219	819	900	1221	1213	1258	786	390	1186	1225	9
Fort Worth, Tex.	561	750	1239	1263	1574	471	1221	820	839	1046	643	640	1018	543	973	....	283	544	273	1093	943	460	1212	751	448	1150	870	1312	643	470	1398	1226	188	590	1324	858	10
Galveston, Tex.	803	688	1245	1538	1598	287	1289	954	897	1116	925	851	1111	723	1218	283	....	808	375	1277	799	677	1423	807	492	941	1087	1595	666	288	1415	1195	456	828	1336	1065	11
Hastings, Nebr.	588	901	1154	934	1415	1013	1019	566	742	871	353	256	800	757	440	544	808	....	513	666	1178	226	1177	693	591	1468	399	891	697	870	1275	1216	357	135	1222	901	9
Hot Springs, Ark.	773	498	964	1384	1302	650	956	585	569	787	749	488	761	802	875	273	375	513	....	901	728	326	1437	480	176	983	722	1385	370	358	1125	955	260	490	1051	1094	8
Houghton, Mich.	1252	947	808	1367	922	1543	560	367	589	518	970	458	427	1422	393	1093	1277	666	901	....	1216	633	1787	636	830	1545	272	1208	760	1187	849	946	926	547	827	1550	6
Jacksonville, Fla.	1492	286	682	2098	1015	1025	880	861	628	768	1468	1024	832	1481	1400	943	799	1178	728	1216	....	952	2153	595	591	328	1192	2070	502	511	838	548	988	1098	758	1800	7
Kansas City, Mo.	717	675	962	1158	1250	923	862	413	541	700	555	180	643	836	548	460	677	226	326	633	952	....	1352	480	370	1247	413	1117	472	678	1097	1009	293	165	1037	1045	7
Los Angeles, Calif.	663	1935	2313	663	2590	1370	2195	1741	1892	2044	828	1433	1976	702	1426	1212	1423	1177	1437	1787	2153	1352	....	1825	1602	2355	1522	910	1777	1675	2446	2352	1182	1312	2388	357	21
Louisville, Ky.	1174	317	498	1623	823	1093	483	268	92	309	1035	477	315	1253	818	751	807	693	480	636	595	480	1825	....	319	923	605	1550	153	623	650	528	675	579	580	1512	3
Memphis, Tenn.	938	335	792	1506	1133	777	802	481	410	627	878	485	621	978	882	448	492	591	176	830	591	370	1602	319	....	878	700	1483	195	358	953	778	422	529	873	1264	6
Miami, Fla.	1710	610	958	2368	1258	1100	1184	1190	957	1088	1732	1338	1156	1662	1721	1150	941	1468	983	1545	328	1247	2355	923	878	....	1516	2359	821	681	1095	802	1233	1402	1023	1998	10
Minneapolis, Minn.	980	905	948	1140	1125	1335	733	356	603	632	699	235	542	1156	219	870	1087	399	722	272	1192	413	1522	605	700	1516	....	1010	695	1050	1019	1047	692	291	985	1279	7
Missoula, Mont.	895	1790	1947	252	2124	1706	1740	1348	1578	1640	670	1074	1552	1115	819	1312	1595	891	1385	1208	2070	1117	910	1550	1483	2359	1010	....	1582	1733	2030	2045	1162	978	1997	932	17
Nashville, Tenn.	1117	218	597	1631	941	952	626	394	239	456	1018	523	468	1169	900	643	666	697	370	760	502	472	1777	153	195	821	695	1582	....	470	758	586	602	604	683	1445	4
New Orleans, La.	1030	427	1001	1713	1359	536	1087	831	708	922	1079	825	938	986	1221	470	288	870	358	1187	511	678	1675	623	358	681	1050	1733	470	....	1173	932	575	845	1090	1318	9
New York, N. Y.	1810	747	170	2153	188	1695	291	711	568	404	1628	1023	483	1902	1213	1398	1415	1275	1125	849	838	1097	2446	650	953	1095	1019	2030	758	1173	....	293	1324	1144	83	2142	3
Norfolk, Va.	1696	507	167	2137	467	1465	435	696	474	429	1562	983	522	1755	1258	1226	1195	1216	955	946	548	1009	2352	528	778	802	1047	2045	586	932	293	....	1186	1095	220	2027	3
Oklahoma, Okla.	518	753	1173	1138	1490	659	1117	689	755	946	503	469	905	578	786	188	456	357	260	926	988	293	1182	675	422	1233	692	1162	602	575	1324	1186	....	405	1256	843	10
Omaha, Nebr.	718	815	1026	1044	1280	1061	883	432	620	738	485	122	666	875	390	590	828	135	490	547	1098	165	1312	579	529	1402	291	978	604	845	1144	1095	405	....	1094	1032	8
Philadelphia, Pa.	1748	663	90	2113	268	1614	278	664	501	343	1575	972	444	1834	1186	1324	1335	1222	1051	827	758	1037	2388	580	878	1023	985	1997	683	1090	83	220	1256	1094	....	2079	2
Phoenix, Ariz.	330	1592	2002	733	2295	1023	1904	1451	1578	1745	585	1154	1685	347	1225	858	1065	901	1094	1550	1800	1045	357	1512	1264	1998	1279	932	1445	1318	2142	2027	843	1032	2079	....	18
Pittsburgh, Pa.	1498	520	194	1863	478	1424	178	411	258	115	1320	718	208	1592	952	1097	1140	967	825	530	703	784	2135	345	660	1014	745	1754	472	923	313	316	1013	837	254	1829	....
Portland, Me.	2015	1022	446	2282	100	1961	438	892	802	603	1803	1197	657	2126	1313	1642	1678	1454	1371	924	1113	1300	2631	892	1205	1357	1145	2133	1015	1445	277	565	1550	1318	360	2345	5
Portland, Oreg.	1107	2172	2367	349	2553	1944	2167	1765	1987	2063	985	1479	1975	1286	1248	1612	1885	1271	1733	1638	2442	1397	825	1953	1852	2740	1445	430	1970	2063	2455	2458	1488	1373	2419	1007	21
Richmond, Va.	1628	470	128	2060	471	1428	375	618	399	353	1488	905	445	1695	1180	1170	1154	1142	897	870	953	937	2283	457	722	831	968	1967	526	899	287	79	1122	1020	205	1960	2
St. Louis, Mo.	938	467	731	1389	1036	975	662	259	308	490	793	270	452	1033	658	568	697	455	325	591	755	238	1585	242	242	1067	464	1331	253	599	873	771	456	352	808	1270	5
Salt Lake City, Utah	483	1580	1858	292	2099	1317	1701	1260	1450	1567	372	952	1490	689	865	977	1249	708	1116	1242	1840	922	577	1400	1250	2098	988	435	1390	1433	1972	1925	862	833	1923	504	16
San Francisco, Calif.	893	2133	2451	516	2696	1675	2298	1855	2037	2163	946	1547	2087	993	1447	1454	1693	1297	1648	1833	2375	1500	345	1983	1800	2603	1585	762	1958	1923	2568	2510	1386	1425	2518	652	22
Schenectady, N. Y.	1823	840	278	2120	150	1770	249	702	605	408	1618	1012	467	1930	1157	1445	1487	1267	1175	776	960	1107	2445	695	1010	1229	975	1978	820	1259	142	426	1354	1133	205	2152	3
Seattle, Wash.	1178	2180	2341	405	2508	2015	2130	1743	1974	2035	1020	1470	1945	1373	1206	1658	1938	1288	1759	1588	2450	1505	956	1945	1867	2740	1403	395	1973	2098	2419	2440	1523	1372	2388	115	21
Shreveport, La.	764	548	1064	1433	1410	510	1080	725	688	904	799	624	891	752	1002	209	233	615	142	1043	733	326	1420	598	279	950	859	1457	470	280	1230	1037	297	617	1153	1067	9
Spokane, Wash.	1028	1960	2110	290	2279	1852	1900	1514	1746	1804	827	1243	1715	1238	976	1470	1753	1061	1552	1360	2239	1286	939	1720	1652	2528	1173	170	1752	1898	2190	2211	1324	1149	2159	1020	19
Springfield, Mass.	1889	863	282	2196	79	1805	325	774	659	473	1692	1085	540	1990	1240	1495	1524	1340	1224	860	957	1173	2515	745	1055	1210	1056	2060	863	1287	120	411	1412	1205	201	2220	4
Vermillion, S. Dak.	742	917	1083	973	1314	1161	916	479	694	785	468	187	705	920	284	689	928	167	605	510	1203	280	1291	663	642	1510	238	887	704	960	1189	1166	502	115	1143	1043	8
Washington, D. C.	1648	542	33	2045	392	1493	290	594	403	303	1490	895	397	1726	1141	1210	1214	1139	936	813	647	943	2295	473	763	927	936	1940	567	968	204	145	1150	1012	122	1980	1

Between Principal Cities of Europe

	Amsterdam	Athens	Baku	Barcelona	Belgrade	Berlin	Brussels	Bucharest	Budapest	Cologne	Copenhagen	Istanbul	Dresden	Dublin	Frankfort	Hamburg	Leningrad	Lisbon	London	Lyon	Madrid	Marseilles	Milan	Moscow	Munich	Oslo	Paris	Riga	Rome	Sofia	Stockholm	Toulouse	Warsaw	Vienna	Zurich
Amsterdam	....	1340	2218	770	875	365	105	1100	710	128	381	1360	385	468	228	232	1090	1140	220	458	912	627	517	1325	415	568	257	820	808	1073	695	625	673	580	375
Athens	1340	....	1395	1160	500	1112	1292	460	698	1200	1320	350	1022	1765	1113	1250	1535	1770	1476	1100	1463	1025	900	1388	925	1610	1300	1310	650	335	1495	1215	990	795	1000
Baku	2218	1395	....	2427	1487	1867	2240	1220	1562	2127	1980	1070	1837	2490	2055	2020	1570	3050	2435	2238	2742	2238	2028	1175	1912	2118	2335	1590	1900	1360	1862	2425	1555	1700	2050
Barcelona	770	1160	2427	....	998	925	658	1210	924	692	1085	1380	860	919	665	910	1740	610	707	327	316	211	450	1852	648	1330	518	1440	530	1072	1410	156	1150	830	513
Belgrade	875	500	1487	998	....	618	850	295	205	750	840	502	530	1327	652	760	1165	1555	1040	752	1235	750	540	1160	475	1112	890	855	440	231	1005	930	510	300	590
Berlin	365	1112	1867	925	618	....	401	798	425	300	225	1068	95	815	268	165	815	1410	575	601	1149	730	570	995	310	520	540	520	730	810	503	815	320	322	410
Brussels	105	1292	2240	658	850	401	....	1110	700	110	475	1345	407	480	192	301	1175	998	202	352	807	521	435	1392	372	672	170	900	730	945	793	515	720	568	312
Bucharest	1100	460	1220	1210	295	798	1110	....	295	982	970	272	725	1560	890	950	1080	1842	1285	1025	1518	1020	819	920	725	1245	1152	870	700	194	1080	1210	580	520	855
Budapest	710	698	1562	924	205	425	700	295	....	590	629	650	345	1176	504	572	965	1515	900	680	1214	718	476	965	350	920	770	685	500	395	820	883	342	128	498
Cologne	128	1200	2127	692	750	300	110	982	590	....	400	1240	292	585	93	228	1090	1126	308	370	875	528	390	1285	282	635	250	805	675	945	722	875	602	460	259
Copenhagen	381	1320	1960	1085	840	225	475	970	629	400	....	1240	315	768	412	180	708	1520	590	760	1272	906	720	970	520	303	634	453	948	1010	330	962	415	538	595
Istanbul	1360	350	1070	1380	502	1068	1345	272	650	1240	1240	....	995	1830	1150	1222	1292	2005	1540	1238	1690	1205	1030	1180	975	1505	1390	1115	840	315	1340	1400	852	790	1090
Dresden	385	1022	1837	860	530	95	407	725	345	292	315	995	....	852	236	238	885	1380	592	540	1100	655	435	1200	227	620	523	585	630	730	598	762	325	235	342
Dublin	468	1765	2490	919	1327	815	480	1560	1176	585	768	1830	852	....	671	668	1440	1015	300	720	902	875	880	1728	855	786	480	1210	1175	1525	1010	761	1130	1040	768
Frankfort	228	1113	2055	665	652	268	198	890	504	93	412	1150	236	671	....	250	1075	1160	392	350	888	492	323	1240	193	675	295	780	698	860	730	560	550	370	193
Hamburg	232	1250	2020	910	760	165	301	950	572	228	180	1222	238	668	250	....	880	1301	448	580	1098	730	570	1100	378	445	459	600	810	954	502	780	462	460	432
Leningrad	1090	1535	1570	1740	1165	815	1175	1080	965	1090	708	1292	885	1440	1075	880	....	2235	1300	1420	1980	1540	1315	391	1100	670	1335	300	1440	1218	435	1635	640	975	1225
Lisbon	1140	1770	3050	610	1555	1410	998	1842	1515	1126	1520	2005	1380	1015	1160	1301	2235	....	975	850	313	810	1350	430	1208	1690	890	1940	1150	1685	1848	640	1700	1415	1058
London	220	1476	2435	707	1040	575	202	1285	900	308	590	1540	592	300	392	448	1300	975	....	455	777	620	595	1540	526	720	210	1035	890	1235	885	550	890	762	480
Lyon	458	1100	2238	327	752	601	352	1025	680	370	760	1238	540	720	350	580	1420	850	455	....	577	170	210	1560	352	1005	248	1122	462	928	1080	228	850	562	206
Madrid	912	1463	2742	316	1235	1149	807	1518	1214	875	1272	1690	1100	902	888	1098	1980	313	777	557	....	394	728	2120	910	1474	645	1670	840	1385	1598	344	1410	1110	765
Marseilles	627	1025	2238	211	750	730	521	1020	718	528	906	1205	655	875	492	730	1540	810	620	170	394	....	238	1642	445	1165	410	1238	372	895	1225	196	950	620	318
Milan	517	900	2028	450	540	570	435	819	476	390	720	1030	435	880	323	570	1315	1350	595	210	728	238	....	1408	215	1020	400	1010	295	775	1020	400	705	385	137
Moscow	1325	1388	1175	1852	1160	995	1392	920	965	1285	970	1180	1200	1728	1240	1100	391	430	1540	1560	2120	1642	1408	....	1220	1030	1538	520	1462	1100	770	1770	710	1028	1350
Munich	415	925	1912	648	475	310	372	725	350	282	520	975	227	855	193	378	1100	1208	526	352	910	445	215	1220	....	810	425	800	430	672	811	570	500	222	158
Oslo	568	1610	2118	1330	1112	520	672	1245	920	635	303	1505	620	786	675	445	670	1690	720	1005	1474	1165	1000	1030	810	....	830	531	1242	1295	267	1140	653	835	869
Paris	257	1300	2335	518	890	540	170	1152	770	250	634	1390	523	480	295	459	1335	890	210	248	645	410	400	1538	425	830	....	1050	690	1080	950	431	845	770	295
Riga	820	1310	1590	1440	855	520	900	870	685	805	453	1115	585	1210	780	600	300	1940	1035	1122	1670	1238	1010	520	800	531	1050	....	1155	985	276	1335	350	685	930
Rome	808	650	1900	530	440	730	730	700	500	675	948	840	630	1175	698	810	1440	1150	890	462	840	372	295	1462	430	1242	690	1155	....	545	1220	569	810	470	421
Sofia	1073	335	1360	1072	231	810	945	194	395	945	1010	315	730	1525	860	954	1218	1685	1235	928	1385	895	715	1100	672	1295	1080	985	545	....	1170	1080	662	500	780
Stockholm	695	1495	1862	1410	1005	503	793	1080	820	722	330	1340	598	1010	730	502	435	1848	885	1080	1598	1225	1020	770	811	267	950	276	1220	1170	....	1281	500	770	908
Toulouse	625	1215	2425	156	930	815	515	1210	883	875	962	1400	762	761	560	780	1635	640	550	228	344	196	400	1770	570	1140	431	1335	569	1080	1281	....	1062	725	425
Warsaw	673	990	1555	1150	510	320	720	580	342	602	415	852	325	1130	550	462	640	1700	890	850	1410	950	705	710	500	653	845	350	810	662	500	1062	....	345	640
Vienna	580	795	1700	830	300	322	568	520	128	460	538	790	235	1040	370	460	975	1415	762	562	1110	620	385	1028	222	835	770	685	470	500	770	725	345	....	365
Zurich	375	1000	2050	513	590	410	312	855	498	259	595	1090	342	768	193	432	1225	1058	480	206	765	318	137	1350	158	869	295	930	421	780	908	425	640	365	....

Richmond, Va.	St. Louis, Mo.	Salt Lake City, Utah	San Francisco, Calif.	Schenectady, N. Y.	Seattle, Wash.	Shreveport, La.	Spokane, Wash.	Springfield, Mass.	Vermillion, S. Dak.	Washington, D.
628	938	483	893	1823	1178	764	1028	1889	742	1648
470	467	1580	2133	840	2180	548	1960	863	917	542
128	731	1858	2451	278	2341	1064	2110	282	1083	33
060	1389	292	516	2120	405	1433	290	2196	973	2045
471	1036	2099	2696	150	2508	1410	2279	79	1314	392
428	975	1317	1675	1770	2015	510	1852	1805	1161	1493
375	662	1701	2298	249	2130	1080	1900	325	916	290
618	259	1260	1855	702	1743	725	1514	774	479	594
399	308	1450	2037	605	1974	688	1746	659	694	403
353	490	1567	2163	408	2035	904	1804	478	785	303
488	793	372	946	1618	1020	799	827	1692	468	1490
905	270	952	1547	1012	1470	624	1243	1085	187	895
445	452	1490	2087	467	1945	891	1715	540	705	397
695	1033	689	993	1930	1373	752	1238	1990	920	1726
180	658	865	1447	1157	1206	1002	976	1240	284	1141
170	568	977	1454	1445	1658	209	1470	1495	689	1210
154	697	1249	1693	1487	1938	233	1753	1524	938	1214
142	455	708	1297	1267	1288	615	1061	1340	167	1139
897	325	1116	1648	1175	1759	142	1552	1224	605	936
870	591	1242	1833	776	1588	1043	1360	860	510	813
953	755	1840	2375	960	2450	733	2239	957	1203	647
937	238	922	1500	1107	1505	326	1286	1173	280	943
283	1585	577	345	2445	956	1420	939	2515	1291	2295
457	242	1400	1983	695	1945	598	1720	745	663	473
722	242	1250	1800	1010	1867	279	1652	1055	642	763
831	1067	2098	2603	1229	2740	950	2528	1210	1510	927
968	464	988	1585	975	1403	859	1173	1056	238	936
967	1331	435	762	1978	395	1457	170	2060	887	1940
526	253	1390	1958	820	1973	470	1752	863	704	567
899	599	1433	1923	1259	2098	280	1898	1287	960	968
287	873	1972	2568	142	2419	1230	2190	120	1189	204
79	771	1925	2510	426	2440	1037	2211	411	1166	145
122	456	862	1386	1354	1523	297	1324	1412	502	1150
020	352	833	1425	1133	1372	617	1149	1205	115	1012
205	808	1923	2518	205	2388	1153	2159	201	1143	122
960	1270	504	652	2152	1112	1067	1020	2220	1043	1980
242	561	1670	2264	350	2145	939	1918	400	891	188
565	1094	2127	2725	197	2513	1484	2285	159	1345	480
381	1723	636	536	2405	143	1783	295	2488	1293	2360
...	699	1850	2436	406	2362	985	2133	407	1089	96
699	....	1158	1738	898	1722	466	1500	958	450	710
850	1158	....	592	1950	697	1155	548	2027	785	1845
436	1738	592	....	2548	680	1655	730	2625	1383	2437
406	898	1950	2548	....	2363	1290	2139	86	1165	313
362	1722	697	680	2363	....	1820	229	2445	1282	2335
985	466	1155	1655	1290	1820	....	1621	1333	726	1035
133	1500	548	730	2139	229	1621	....	2216	1055	2105
407	958	2027	2625	86	2445	1333	2216	....	1242	321
089	450	785	1383	1165	1282	726	1055	1242	....	1073
96	710	1845	2437	313	2335	1035	2105	321	1073	....

New York to	Miles	San Francisco to	Miles	Seattle to	Miles	Washington to	Miles
Buenos Aires	5,295	Buenos Aires	6,487	Buenos Aires	6,956	Buenos Aires	5,205
Bogota	2,474	Bogota	3,863	Bogota	4,166	Bogota	2,344
Caracas	2,100	Caracas	3,900	Caracas	4,100	Caracas	2,040
Guatemala City	2,060	Guatemala City	2,525	Guatemala City	2,930	Guatemala City	1,835
Havana	1,302	Havana	2,600	Havana	2,805	Havana	1,110
La Paz	3,905	La Paz	5,080	La Paz	5,110	La Paz	3,780
Panama	2,211	Panama	3,349	Panama	3,680	Panama	2,020
Para	3,281	Para	5,430	Para	5,550	Para	3,270
Managua	2,100	Managua	2,860	Managua	3,240	Managua	1,920
Rio de Janeiro	4,810	Rio de Janeiro	6,655	Rio de Janeiro	6,945	Rio de Janeiro	4,710
San Jose	2,200	San Jose	3,070	San Jose	3,430	San Jose	2,030
Santiago	5,134	Santiago	5,960	Santiago	6,466	Santiago	4,965
Tampico	1,880	Tampico	1,790	Tampico	2,200	Tampico	1,665

Between Representative Cities of the United States and Latin America

Chicago to	Miles	Denver to	Miles	Los Angeles to	Miles	New Orleans to	Miles
Buenos Aires	5,598	Buenos Aires	5,935	Buenos Aires	6,148	Buenos Aires	4,902
Bogota	2,691	Bogota	3,100	Bogota	3,515	Bogota	1,996
Caracas	2,480	Caracas	3,105	Caracas	3,610	Caracas	1,990
Guatemala City	1,870	Guatemala City	1,935	Guatemala City	2,190	Guatemala City	1,050
Havana	1,315	Havana	1,760	Havana	2,320	Havana	672
La Paz	4,130	La Paz	4,445	La Paz	4,805	La Paz	3,480
Panama	2,320	Panama	2,620	Panama	3,025	Panama	1,600
Para	3,820	Para	4,580	Para	5,110	Para	3,470
Managua	2,060	Managua	2,230	Managua	2,540	Managua	1,250
Rio de Janeiro	5,320	Rio de Janeiro	5,900	Rio de Janeiro	6,330	Rio de Janeiro	4,798
San Jose	2,100	San Jose	2,420	San Jose	2,725	San Jose	1,425
Santiago	5,320	Santiago	5,495	Santiago	5,595	Santiago	4,553
Tampico	1,460	Tampico	1,240	Tampico	1,470	Tampico	720

TABLES OF AIRLINE DISTANCES

All Distances in Statute Miles

Between Principal Cities of the World

FROM/TO	Azores	Bagdad	Berlin	Bombay	Buenos Aires	Callao	Cairo	Cape Town	Chicago	Istanbul	Guam	Honolulu	Juneau	London	Los Angeles	Melbourne	Mexico City	Montreal	New Orleans	New York	Panama	Paris	Rio de Janeiro	San Francisco	Santiago	Seattle	Shanghai	Singapore	Tokyo	Wellington
Azores	....	3906	2148	5930	5385	4825	3325	5670	3305	2880	8985	7421	4715	1562	5034	12190	4584	2548	3718	2604	3918	1617	4312	5114	5718	4720	7324	8338	7370	11475
Bagdad	3906	....	2040	2022	8215	8618	785	4923	6490	1085	6380	8445	6180	2568	7695	8150	8155	5814	7212	6066	7807	2385	7012	7521	8876	6848	4468	4443	5242	9782
Berlin	2148	2040	....	3947	7411	6937	1823	5949	4458	1068	7158	7384	4638	575	5849	9992	6119	3776	5182	4026	5902	540	6246	5744	7842	5121	5323	6226	5623	11384
Bombay	5930	2022	3947	....	9380	10530	2698	5133	8144	3043	4831	8172	6992	4526	8810	6140	9818	7582	8952	7875	9832	4391	8438	8523	10127	7830	3219	2425	4247	7752
Buenos Aires	5385	8215	7411	9380	....	1982	7428	4332	5598	7638	10516	7653	7964	6919	6148	7336	4609	5619	4902	5295	3319	6891	1230	6487	731	6956	12295	9940	11601	6341
Callao	4825	8618	6937	10530	1982	....	7870	6195	3765	7666	9760	5993	5806	6376	4155	8196	2619	3954	2990	3633	1450	6455	2400	4500	1548	4964	10760	11700	9740	6696
Cairo	3325	785	1823	2698	7428	7870	....	4476	6231	780	7175	8925	6352	2218	7675	8720	7807	5502	6862	5701	7230	2020	6242	7554	8100	6915	5290	5152	6005	10360
Cape Town	5670	4923	5949	5133	4332	6195	4476	....	8551	5210	8918	11655	10382	5975	10165	6510	8620	7975	8390	7845	7090	5732	3850	10340	5080	10305	8179	6025	9234	7149
Chicago	3305	6490	4458	8144	5598	3765	6231	8551	....	5530	7510	4315	2310	4015	1741	9837	1690	750	827	727	2320	4219	5320	1875	5325	1753	7155	9475	6410	8465
Istanbul	2880	1085	1068	3043	7638	7666	780	5210	5530	....	7015	8200	5665	1540	6895	9189	7160	4825	6220	5060	6797	1390	6420	6770	8230	6124	5084	5440	5649	10790
Guam	8985	6380	7158	4831	10516	9760	7175	8918	7510	7015	....	3896	5225	7605	6255	3497	7690	7840	7895	8115	9220	7675	11710	5952	9946	5785	1945	2990	1596	4206
Honolulu	7421	8445	7384	8172	7653	5993	8925	11655	4315	8200	3896	....	2825	7320	2620	5581	3846	4992	4305	5051	5347	7525	8400	2407	6935	2707	5009	6874	3940	4676
Juneau	4715	6180	4638	6992	7964	5806	6352	10382	2310	5665	5225	2825	....	4496	1835	8162	3210	2647	2860	2874	4456	4700	7611	1530	7320	870	4968	7375	4117	7501
London	1562	2568	575	4526	6919	6376	2218	5975	4015	1540	7605	7320	4496	....	5496	10590	5605	3370	4656	3500	5310	210	5747	5440	7275	4850	5841	6818	6050	11790
Los Angeles	5034	7695	5849	8810	6148	4155	7675	10165	1741	6895	6255	2620	1835	5496	....	8098	1445	2468	1695	2466	3025	5711	6330	345	5595	961	6598	8955	5600	6806
Melbourne	12190	8150	9992	6140	7336	8196	8720	6510	9837	9189	3497	5581	8162	10590	8098	....	8599	10553	9455	10541	9211	10500	8340	7970	7130	8330	4967	3768	5172	1655
Mexico City	4584	8155	6119	9818	4609	2619	7807	8620	1690	7160	7690	3846	3210	5605	1445	8599	....	2247	940	2110	1532	5800	4810	1870	4122	2339	8120	10495	7190	7003
Montreal	2548	5814	3776	7582	5619	3954	5502	7975	750	4825	7840	4992	2647	3370	2468	10553	2247	....	1390	340	2545	3490	5110	2557	5461	2309	7141	9280	6546	9206
New Orleans	3718	7212	5182	8952	4902	2990	6862	8390	827	6220	7895	4305	2860	4656	1695	9455	940	1390	....	1161	1600	4846	4798	1960	4553	2137	7830	10255	6993	7950
New York	2604	6066	4026	7875	5295	3633	5701	7845	727	5060	8115	5051	2874	3500	2466	10541	2110	340	1161	....	2211	3600	4810	2606	5134	2440	7460	9617	6846	9067
Panama	3918	7807	5902	9832	3319	1450	7230	7090	2320	6797	9220	5347	4456	5310	3025	9211	1532	2545	1600	2211	....	5440	3311	3349	3000	3680	9430	11800	8560	7580
Paris	1617	2385	540	4391	6891	6455	2020	5762	4219	1390	7675	7525	4700	210	5711	10500	5800	3490	4846	3600	5440	....	5710	5680	7300	5080	5855	6730	6132	11865
Rio de Janeiro	4312	7012	6246	8438	1230	2400	6242	3850	5320	6420	11710	8400	7611	5747	6330	8340	4810	5110	4798	4810	3311	5710	....	6655	1852	6945	11510	9875	11600	7510
San Francisco	5114	7521	5744	8523	6487	4500	7554	10340	1875	6770	5952	2407	1530	5440	345	7970	1870	2557	1960	2606	3349	5680	6655	....	5960	692	6245	8440	5250	6800
Santiago	5718	8876	7842	10127	731	1548	8100	5080	5325	8230	9946	6935	7320	7275	5595	7130	4122	5461	4553	5134	3000	7300	1852	5960	....	6466	11850	10270	10850	5925
Seattle	4720	6848	5121	7830	6956	4964	6915	10305	1753	6124	5785	2707	870	4850	961	8330	2339	2309	2137	2440	3680	5080	6945	692	6466	....	5780	8200	4863	7310
Shanghai	7324	4468	5323	3219	12295	10760	5290	8179	7155	5084	1945	5009	4968	5841	6598	4967	8120	7141	7830	7460	9430	5855	11510	6245	11850	5780	....	2395	1095	6080
Singapore	8338	4443	6226	2425	9940	11700	5152	6025	9475	5440	2990	6874	7375	6818	8955	3768	10495	9280	10255	9617	11800	6730	9875	8440	10270	8200	2395	....	3350	5360
Tokyo	7370	5242	5623	4247	11601	9740	6005	9234	6410	5649	1596	3940	4117	6050	5600	5172	7190	6546	6993	6846	8560	6132	11600	5250	10850	4863	1095	3350	....	5730
Wellington	11475	9782	11384	7752	6341	6696	10360	7149	8465	10790	4206	4676	7501	11790	6806	1655	7003	9206	7950	9067	7580	11865	7510	6800	5925	7310	6080	5360	5730	......

WORLD STATISTICAL TABLES

Earth and Solar System

Principal Lakes and Inland Seas

Elements of the Solar System

	Mean Distance From Sun in Miles	Period of Revolution Around Sun	Period of Rotation on Axis	Equatorial Diameter in Miles	Surface Gravity (Earth=1)	Mean Density (Water=1)	Number of Satellites
SUN	....	....	25.4 days	864,000	27.95	1.4	....
MERCURY	36,001,000	87.97 days	59.3 days (?)	3,100	0.30 (?)	4.2 (?)	0
VENUS	67,272,000	224.70 days	225 days (?)	7,700	0.91	4.9	0
EARTH	93,003,000	365.26 days	23h 56m	7,927	1.00	5.5	1
MARS	141,708,000	687 days	24h 37m	4,200	0.38	4.0	2
JUPITER	483,880,000	11.86 years	9h 50m	88,698	2.68	1.3	12
SATURN	887,141,000	29.46 years	10h 14m	75,060	1.15	0.7	9
URANUS	1,782,000,000	84.02 years	10h 45m	29,200	0.99	1.3	5
NEPTUNE	2,792,000,000	164.79 years	15h 48m	27,700	1.28	1.6	2
PLUTO	3,664,000,000	247.7 years	6.4 days (?)	8,700 (?)	0.7	?	0

Dimensions of the Earth

Superficial area	196,950,000	sq. miles
Land surface	57,510,000	" "
North America	8,500,000	" "
South America	6,814,000	" "
Europe	3,872,000	" "
Asia	16,990,000	" "
Africa	11,500,000	" "
Australia	2,974,581	" "
Water surface	139,440,000	" "
Atlantic Ocean	31,830,000	" "
Pacific Ocean	63,801,000	" "
Indian Ocean	28,356,000	" "
Arctic Ocean	5,440,000	" "
Equatorial circumference	24,902	miles
Meridional circumference	24,860	"
Equatorial diameter	7,926.677	"
Polar diameter	7,899.988	"
Equatorial radius	3,963.34	"
Polar radius	3,949.99	"
Volume of the Earth	260,000,000,000	cubic miles
Mass, or weight	6,592,000,000,000,000,000,000	tons
Mean distance from the Sun	92,897,416	miles

The Moon is the Earth's natural satellite. The mean distance which separates the Earth from the Moon is 238,857 miles. The Moon's true period of revolution (sidereal month) is 27⅓ days. The Moon rotates on its own axis once during this time. The phase period or time between new moons (synodic month) is 29½ days. The Moon's diameter is 2,160 miles, its density is 3.3 and its surface gravity is 0.2.

	AREA IN SQ. MILES
Caspian Sea	163,800
Lake Superior	31,820
Lake Victoria	26,828
Lake Aral	24,900
Lake Huron	23,010
Lake Michigan	22,400
Lake Tanganyika	12,700
Lake Baikal	12,150
Great Bear Lake	12,000
Great Slave Lake	11,170
Lake Nyasa	11,000
Lake Erie	9,940
Lake Winnipeg	9,398
Lake Ontario	7,540
Lake Ladoga	7,100
Lake Balkhash	6,700
Lake Chad	6,500
Lake Onega	3,765
Lake Titicaca	3,200
Lake Nicaragua	3,100
Lake Athabasca	3,058
Reindeer Lake	2,444
Issyk-Kul	2,276
Vanern	2,149
Lake Urmia	1,795
Great Salt Lake	1,700
Lake Albert	1,640
Lake Van	1,453
Lake Peipus	1,400
Lake Tana	1,219
Lake Bangweulu	Approx. 1,000
Vattern	733
Dead Sea	405
Lake Balaton	266
Lake Geneva	225
Lake of Constance	208
Lough Neagh	153
Lake Garda	143
Lake Neuchatel	83
Lake Maggiore	82
Lough Corrib	71
Lake Como	56
Lake of Lucerne	44.5
Lake of Zurich	34

Oceans and Seas of the World

	AREA IN SQ. MILES	GREATEST DEPTH IN FEET	VOLUME IN CUBIC MILES
Pacific Ocean	63,801,000	35,400	162,870,600
Atlantic Ocean	31,830,000	30,246	75,533,900
Indian Ocean	28,356,000	22,968	69,225,200
Arctic Ocean	5,440,000	17,850	4,029,400
Mediterranean Sea	1,145,000	15,197	1,019,400
Bering Sea	876,000	13,422	788,500
Caribbean Sea	750,000	23,748	2,298,400
Sea of Okhotsk	590,000	11,070	454,700
East China Sea	482,000	10,500	52,700
Hudson Bay	475,000	1,500	37,590
Japan Sea	389,000	13,242	383,200
North Sea	222,000	2,654	12,890
Red Sea	169,000	7,254	53,700
Black Sea	165,000	7,200	....
Baltic Sea	163,000	1,506	5,360

Great Ship Canals

	LENGTH IN MILES	DEPTH IN FEET
Baltic-White Sea, U.S.S.R.	141	....
Suez, Egypt	100.76	34
Albert, Belgium	81	16.5
Moscow-Volga, U.S.S.R.	80	18
Kiel, Germany	61	37
Gota, Sweden	54	10
Panama, Canal Zone, U.S.A.	50.72	41
Houston, U.S.A.	50	36
Amsterdam-Rhine, Netherlands	45	41
Beaumont-Port Arthur, U.S.A.	40	32
Manchester, England	35.5	28
Chicago Sanitary and Ship, U.S.A.	30	22
Welland, Canada	27.6	25
Juliana, Netherlands	21	11.8
Chesapeake-Delaware, U.S.A.	19	27
Cape Cod, U.S.A.	13	25
Lake Washington, U.S.A.	8	30
Corinth, Greece	4	26.25
Sault Ste. Marie, U.S.A.	1.6	24.5
Sault Ste. Marie, Canada	1.4	18.25

Principal Islands of the World

	AREA IN SQ. MILES
Greenland	839,999
New Guinea	345,054
Borneo	289,859
Madagascar	241,094
Baffin	183,810
Sumatra	164,148
Philippines	115,600
New Zealand: North and South Islands	103,934
England-Scotland-Wales	88,745
Honshu	87,426
Ellesmere	82,119
Victoria	81,930
Celebes	72,986
Java	48,842
Cuba	42,857
Newfoundland	42,734
Luzon	40,420
Iceland	39,709
Mindanao	36,537
Sakhalin	35,400
Novaya Zemlya	35,000
Ireland	32,060
Molucca Islands	30,168
Hispaniola	29,843
Hokkaido	29,600
Tasmania	26,215
Ceylon	25,332
Timor	24,450
Svalbard (Spitsbergen)	24,294
Banks	23,230
Devon	20,861
Bismarck Arch.	19,660
Solomon Islands	18,670
Tierra del Fuego	18,500
Melville	16,369
Southampton	15,700
New Britain	14,600
Taiwan (Formosa)	13,885
Kyushu	13,770
Hainan	13,000
Prince of Wales	12,830
Vancouver	12,408
Sicily	9,926
Somerset	9,370
Sardinia	9,301
New Caledonia	7,201
Fiji Islands	7,015
New Hebrides	5,700
Kuril Islands	5,700
Falkland Islands	4,618
Jamaica	4,411
Bahama Islands	4,404
Hawaii	4,021
Cape Breton	3,970
New Ireland	3,800
Cyprus	3,572
Puerto Rico	3,421
Corsica	3,367
Crete	3,232
Galapagos Islands	3,042
Hebrides	3,000
Canary Islands	2,894
Wrangel	2,819
Kerguelen	2,700
Prince Edward	2,184
Balearic Islands	1,936
Trinidad and Tobago	1,864
Madura	1,752
South Georgia	1,600
Cape Verde Islands	1,557
Long I., New York	1,401
Socotra	1,400
Gotland	1,225
Samoa	1,209
Isle of Pines	1,180
Reunion	970
Azores	890
Fernando Po	785
Tenerife	785
Maui	728
Mauritius	720
Zanzibar	640
Tahiti	600
Oahu	589
Guadeloupe	583
Ahvenanmaa (Aland Is.)	564
Kauai	551
Shetland Islands	550
Rhodes	542
Caroline Islands	525
Martinique	425
Pemba	380
Orkney Islands	376
Madeira Islands	308
Dominica	290
Tonga or Friendly Islands	269
Molokai	261
St. Lucia	238
Corfu	229
Bornholm	227
Isle of Man	227
Singapore	225
Guam	212
Isle Royale	209
Virgin Islands	190
Curacao	173
Barbados	166
Seychelles	155
St. Vincent	150
Isle of Wight	147
Lanai	141
Grenada	133
Malta	122
Tobago	116
Martha's Vineyard	106
Channel Islands	75
Nantucket	60
St. Helena	47
Ascension	34
Hong Kong	29
Manhattan, New York	22
Bermudas	21

Principal Mountains of the World

	FEET
Mt. Everest, Nepal-Tibet	29,028
Mt. Godwin Austen (K2), India	28,250
Kanchenjunga, Nepal-India	28,208
Dhaulagiri, Nepal	26,810
Nanga Parbat, India	26,660
Annapurna, Nepal	26,504
Nanda Devi, India	25,645
Mt. Kamet, India	25,447
Gurla Mandhata, Tibet	25,355
Tirich Mir, Pakistan	25,263
Minya Konka, China	24,900
Mt. Communism, U.S.S.R.	24,590
Pobeda Peak, U.S.S.R.	24,406
Muztagh Ata, China	24,388
Chomo Lhari, India-Tibet	23,997
Muztagh, China	23,890
Aconcagua, Argentina	22,834
Ojos del Salado, Argentina-Chile	22,539
Cerro Mercedario, Argentina	22,211
Huascaran, Peru	22,205
Llullaillaco Volcano, Chile	22,057
Tupungato, Chile-Argentina	21,489
Sajama Volcano, Bolivia	21,391
Illampu, Bolivia	21,276
Vilcanota, Peru	20,664
Chimborazo, Ecuador	20,561
Mt. McKinley, Alaska	20,320
Mt. Logan, Yukon	19,850
Kilimanjaro, Tanzania	19,565
Cotopaxi, Ecuador	19,347
El Misti, Peru	19,199
Mt. Demavend, Iran	18,934
Citlaltepetl, Mexico	18,700
Mt. Elbrus, U.S.S.R.	18,481
Mt. St. Elias, Alaska-Yukon	18,008
Popocatepetl, Mexico	17,887
Dykh-Tau, U.S.S.R.	17,085
Mt. Kenya, Kenya	17,058
Mt. Ararat, Turkey	16,945
Margherita, Africa	16,795
Cartensz, W. Irian	16,400
Vinson Massif, Antarctica	15,970
Klyuchevskaya Sopka, U.S.S.R.	15,912
Mont Blanc, France	15,781
Kazbek, U.S.S.R.	15,558
Monte Rosa, Italy-Switzerland	15,217
Ras Dashan, Ethiopia	15,157
Mt. Markham, Antarctica	15,100
Matterhorn, Switzerland	14,780
Mt. Whitney, California	14,495
Mt. Elbert, Colorado	14,431
Mt. Rainier, Washington	14,410
Mt. Shasta, California	14,162
Pikes Peak, Colorado	14,110
Finsteraarhorn, Switzerland	14,026
Mauna Kea, Hawaii	13,796
Mauna Loa, Hawaii	13,680
Jungfrau, Switzerland	13,667
Toubkal, Morocco	13,665
Cameroon, Cameroon	13,350
Gran Paradiso, Italy	13,323
Mt. Robson, British Columbia	12,972
Grossglockner, Austria	12,461
Fuji, Japan	12,389
Mt. Cook, New Zealand	12,349
Pico de Teyde, Canary Is.	12,192
Mt. Semeru, Java	12,060
Mulhacen, Spain	11,417
Mt. Etna, Italy	10,741
Irazu, Costa Rica	10,525
Lassen Peak, California	10,466
Mt. Kosciusko, Australia	7,316
Mt. Mitchell, No. Carolina	6,684

Longest Rivers of the World

	LENGTH IN MILES
Nile, Africa	4,149
Amazon, S.A.	3,900
Mississippi-Missouri, U.S.A.	3,710
Yangtze, China	3,400
Ob-Irtysh, U.S.S.R.	3,200
Congo, Africa	2,900
Amur, Asia	2,704
Hwang (Yellow), China	2,700
Lena, U.S.S.R.	2,648
Mackenzie, Canada	2,635
Mekong, Asia	2,600
Niger, Africa	2,600
Parana, S.A.	2,450
Yenisey, U.S.S.R.	2,364
Murray-Darling, Australia	2,310
Volga, U.S.S.R.	2,290
Madeira, S.A.	2,000
Yukon, Alaska-Canada	1,979
St. Lawrence, Canada-U.S.A.	1,900
Rio Grande, U.S.A.-Mexico	1,885
Purus, S.A.	1,850
Sao Francisco, S.A.	1,800
Salween, Asia	1,750
Danube, Europe	1,725
Euphrates, Asia	1,700
Indus, Asia	1,700
Tocantins, S.A.	1,700
Brahmaputra, Asia	1,680
Syr-Dar'ya, U.S.S.R.	1,680
Si, China	1,650
Ganges, India	1,650
Orinoco, S.A.	1,600
Nelson, Canada	1,600
Zambezi, Africa	1,600
Ural, U.S.S.R.	1,574
Amu-Dar'ya, U.S.S.R.	1,550
Olenek, U.S.S.R.	1,500
Paraguay, S.A.	1,500
Japura, S.A.	1,500
Arkansas, U.S.A.	1,450
Colorado, U.S.A.-Mexico	1,450
Dnieper, U.S.S.R.	1,418
Rio Negro, S.A.	1,400
Orange, Africa	1,350
Kolyma, U.S.S.R.	1,335
Irrawaddy, Burma	1,325
Ohio, U.S.A.	1,306
Kama, U.S.S.R.	1,262
Don, U.S.S.R.	1,222
Columbia, U.S.A.-Canada	1,214
Saskatchewan, Canada	1,205
Peace, Canada	1,195
Darling, Australia	1,160
Angara, U.S.S.R.	1,151
Tigris, Asia	1,150
Sungari, Asia	1,130
Pechora, U.S.S.R.	1,111
Snake, U.S.A.	1,038
Red, Texas, U.S.A.	1,018
Churchill, Canada	1,000
Pilcomayo, S.A.	1,000
Uruguay, S.A.	1,000
Magdalena, Colombia	1,000
Platte-N. Platte, U.S.A.	990
Oka, U.S.S.R.	918
Canadian, U.S.A.	906
Brazos, U.S.A.	870
South Saskatchewan, Canada	865
Tennessee, U.S.A.	862
Dniester, U.S.S.R.	852
Fraser, Canada	850
Colorado, Texas, U.S.A.	840
Northern Dvina, U.S.S.R.	803
Tisza, Europe	800
Athabasca, Canada	765
North Canadian, U.S.A.	760

MAP PROJECTIONS

by Erwin Raisz

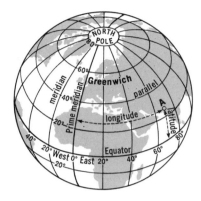

Our earth is rotating around its *axis* once a day. The two end points of its axis are the *poles*; the line circling the earth midway between the poles is the *equator*. The arc from either of the poles to the equator is divided into 90 *degrees*. The distance, expressed in degrees, from the equator to any point is its *latitude* and circles of equal latitude are the *parallels*. On maps it is customary to show parallels of evenly-spaced degrees such as every fifth or every tenth.

The equator is divided into 360 degrees. Lines circling from pole to pole through the degree points on the equator are called *meridians*. They are all equal in length but by international agreement the meridian passing through the Greenwich Observatory in London has been chosen as *prime meridian*. The distance, expressed in degrees, from the prime meridian to any point is its *longitude*. While meridians are all equal in length, parallels become shorter and shorter as they approach the poles. Whereas one degree of latitude represents everywhere approximately 69 miles, one degree of longitude varies from 69 miles at the equator to nothing at the poles.

Each degree is divided into 60 minutes and each minute into 60 seconds. One minute of latitude equals a nautical mile.

The map is flat but the earth is nearly spherical. Neither a rubber ball nor any part of a rubber ball may be flattened without stretching or tearing unless the part is very small. To present the curved surface of the earth on a flat map is not difficult as long as the areas under consideration are small, but the mapping of countries, continents, or the whole earth requires some kind of *projection*. Any regular set of parallels and meridians upon which a map can be drawn makes a map projection. Many systems are used.

In any projection only the parallels or the meridians or some other set of lines can be *true* (the same length as on the globe of corresponding scale); all other lines are too long or too short. Only on a globe is it possible to have both the parallels and the meridians true. The scale given on a flat map cannot be true everywhere. The construction of the various projections begins usually with laying out the parallels or meridians which have true lengths.

RECTANGULAR PROJECTION — This is a set of evenly-placed meridians and horizontal parallels. The central or *standard parallel* and all meridians are true. All other parallels are either too long or too short. The projection is used for simple maps of small areas, as city plans, etc.

MERCATOR PROJECTION — In this projection the meridians are evenly-spaced vertical lines. The parallels are horizontal, spaced so that their length has the same relation to the meridians as on a globe. As the meridians converge at higher latitudes on the globe, while on the map they do not, the parallels have to be drawn also farther and farther apart to maintain the correct relationship. When every very small area has the same shape as on a globe we call the projection *conformal*. The most interesting quality of this projection is that all *compass directions* appear as straight lines. For this reason it is generally used for marine charts. It is also frequently used for world maps in spite of the fact that the high latitudes are very much exaggerated in size. Only the equator is true to scale; all other parallels and meridians are too long. The Mercator projection did *not* derive from projecting a globe upon a cylinder.

SINUSOIDAL PROJECTION — The parallels are truly-spaced horizontal lines. They are divided truly and the connecting curves make the meridians. It does not make a good world map because the outer regions are distorted, but the

Rectangular Projection

Mercator Projection

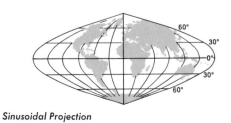

Sinusoidal Projection

central portion is good and this part is often used for maps of Africa and South America. Every part of the map has the same area as the corresponding area on the globe. It is an *equal-area* projection.

MOLLWEIDE PROJECTION — The meridians are equally-spaced ellipses; the parallels are horizontal lines spaced so that every belt of latitude should have the same area as on a globe. This projection is popular for world maps, especially in European atlases.

GOODE'S INTERRUPTED PROJECTIONS—Only the good central part of the Mollweide or sinusoidal (or both) projection is used and the oceans are cut. This makes an equal-area map with little distortion of shape. It is commonly used for world maps.

ECKERT PROJECTIONS — These are similar to the sinusoidal or the Mollweide projections, but the poles are shown as lines half the length of the equator. There are several variants; the meridians are either sine curves or ellipses; the parallels are horizontal and spaced either evenly or so as to make the projection equal area. Their use for world maps is increasing. The figure shows the elliptical equal-area variant.

CONIC PROJECTION — The original idea of the conic projection is that of capping the globe by a cone upon which both the parallels and meridians are projected from the center of the globe. The cone is then cut open and laid flat. A cone can be made tangent to any chosen *standard parallel.*

The actually-used conic projection is a modification of this idea. The radius of the standard parallel is obtained as above. The meridians are straight radiating lines spaced truly on the standard parallel. The parallels are concentric circles spaced at true distances. All parallels except the standard are too long. The projection is used for maps of countries in middle latitudes, as it presents good shapes with small scale error.

There are several variants: The use of *two standard parallels,* one near the top, the other near the bottom of the map, reduces the scale error. In the *Albers projection* the parallels are spaced unevenly, to make the projection equal-area. This is a good projection for the United States. In the *Lambert conformal conic projection* the parallels are spaced so that any small quadrangle of the grid should have the same shape as on the globe. This is the best projection for air-navigation charts as it has relatively straight azimuths.

An *azimuth* is a great-circle direction reckoned clockwise from north. A *great-circle direction* points to a place along the shortest line on the earth's surface. This is not the same as compass direction. The center of a great circle is the center of the globe.

BONNE PROJECTION — The parallels are laid out exactly as in the conic projection. All parallels are divided truly and the connecting curves make the meridians. It is an equal-area projection. It is used for maps of the northern continents, as Asia, Europe, and North America.

POLYCONIC PROJECTION — The central meridian is divided truly. The parallels are non-concentric circles, the radii of which are obtained by drawing tangents to the globe as though the globe were covered by several cones rather than by only one. Each parallel is divided truly and the connecting curves make the meridians. All meridians except the central one are too long. This projection is used for large-scale topographic sheets — less often for countries or continents.

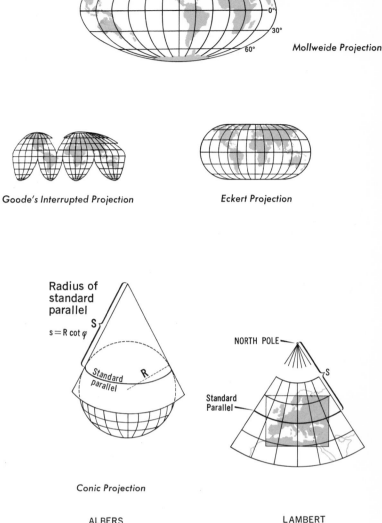

Mollweide Projection

Goode's Interrupted Projection

Eckert Projection

Radius of standard parallel

$s = R \cot \varphi$

Conic Projection

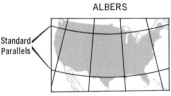

Albers Projection

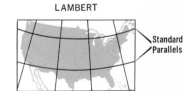

Lambert Conformal Conic Projection

Bonne Projection

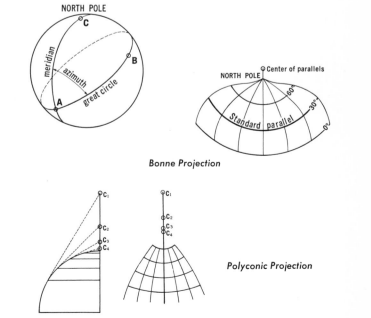

Polyconic Projection

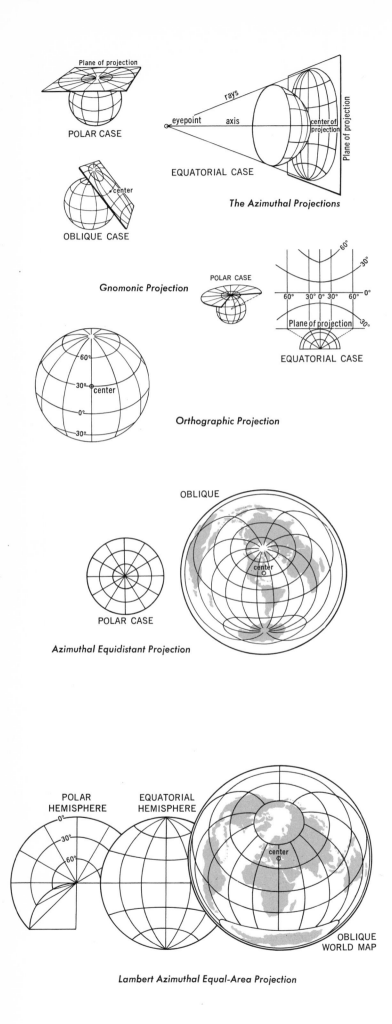

POLAR CASE

OBLIQUE CASE

EQUATORIAL CASE

The Azimuthal Projections

Gnomonic Projection

POLAR CASE

EQUATORIAL CASE

Orthographic Projection

OBLIQUE

POLAR CASE

Azimuthal Equidistant Projection

POLAR HEMISPHERE

EQUATORIAL HEMISPHERE

OBLIQUE WORLD MAP

Lambert Azimuthal Equal-Area Projection

THE AZIMUTHAL PROJECTIONS — In this group a part of the globe is projected from an eyepoint onto a plane. The eyepoint can be at different distances, making different projections. The plane of projection can be tangent at the equator, at a pole, or at any other point on which we want to focus attention. The most important quality of all azimuthal projections is that they show every point at its true direction (azimuth) from the center point, and all points equally distant from the center point will be equally distant on the map also.

GNOMONIC PROJECTION — This projection has the eyepoint at the center of the globe Only the central part is good; the outer regions are badly distorted. Yet the projection has one important quality, all great circles being shown as straight lines. For this reason it is used for laying out the routes for long range flying or trans-oceanic navigation.

ORTHOGRAPHIC PROJECTION — This projection has the eyepoint at infinite distance and the projecting rays are parallel. The polar or equatorial varieties are rare but the oblique case became very popular on account of its visual quality. It looks like a picture of a globe. Although the distortion on the peripheries is extreme, we see it correctly because the eye perceives it not as a map but as a picture of a three-dimensional globe. Obviously only a hemisphere (half globe) can be shown.

Some azimuthal projections do not derive from the actual process of projecting from an eyepoint, but are arrived at by other means:

AZIMUTHAL EQUIDISTANT PROJECTION — This is the only projection in which every point is shown both at true great-circle direction and at true distance from the center point, but all other directions and distances are distorted. The principle of the projection can best be understood from the polar case. Most polar maps are in this projection. The oblique case is used for radio direction finding, for earthquake research, and in long-distance flying. A separate map has to be constructed for each central point selected.

LAMBERT AZIMUTHAL EQUAL-AREA PROJECTION — The construction of this projection can best be understood from the polar case. All three cases are widely used. It makes a good polar map and it is often extended to include the southern continents. It is the most common projection used for maps of the Eastern and Western Hemispheres, and it is a good projection for continents as it shows correct areas with relatively little distortion of shape. Most of the continent maps in this atlas are in this projection.

IN THIS ATLAS, on almost all maps, parallels and meridians have been marked because they are useful for the following:

(a) They show the north-south and east-west directions which appear on many maps at oblique angles especially near the margins.

(b) With the help of parallels and meridians every place can be exactly located; for instance, New York City is at 41° N and 74° W on any map.

(c) They help to measure distances even in the distorted parts of the map. The scale given on each map is true only along certain lines which are specified in the foregoing discussion for each projection. One degree of latitude equals nearly 69 statute miles or 60 nautical miles. The length of one degree of longitude varies (1° long. = 1° lat. × cos lat.).